The V.C. and D.S.O.

VOL. II.

THE DISTINGUISHED SERVICE ORDER

A COMPLETE RECORD OF THOSE WHO WERE AWARDED
THIS DECORATION FROM THE TIME OF ITS INSTITUTION
IN 1886 TO THE 31st DECEMBER, 1915, WITH DESCRIPTIONS
OF THE SERVICES WHICH WON THE DISTINCTION AND
WITH MANY BIOGRAPHICAL AND OTHER DETAILS

With 713 Portrait Illustrations

SOVEREIGNS OF THE ORDER

H.M. QUEEN VICTORIA
H.M. KING EDWARD VII
H.M. KING GEORGE V

CONTENTS

ERRATA

The portrait placed with the record of Brigadier-General John Thorold Evatt on page 94 is that of Brigadier-General James Reginald Maitland Dalrymple Hay, whose record is on page 99, and the portrait placed with the last-mentioned record is that of Brigadier-General John Thorold Evatt.

The portrait placed with the record of Major John Chaplyn Burnett on page 190 is that of Major John Curteis Burnett, whose record is on page 327, and the portrait placed with the last-mentioned record is that of Major John Chaplyn Burnett.

The portrait placed with the record of Major Harold Brown on page 410 is that of Major Hugh Barrington Brown, whose record is on page 415, and should be transferred to that record.

The portraits given as those of Colonel Rowland James Percy Anderson, on page 140 ; of Lieut. J. E. Steel, on page 310 ; of Capt. John Macready, on page 365, and of Major Gerald Burrard, on page 424, are cancelled, as they are not the portraits of these officers. The portrait on page 367 given as that of Major Baptist Johnston Barton is also cancelled, as it is believed not to be a portrait of that officer.

On page 367 in the record of Capt. Harry Kirwan Umfreville it is stated that " he was killed in action 15 June, 1915." This is incorrect : he is still alive. These words were accidentally repeated from the concluding words of the immediately preceding record.

On page 311 in line 3 of the record of Brigadier-General Charles Henry Davies, read " United Service College " for " United Service Club."

THE STATUTES OF THE DISTINGUISHED SERVICE ORDER

VICTORIA R. & I.

VICTORIA, by the Grace of God, of the United Kingdom of Great Britain and Ireland, Queen, Defender of the Faith, Empress of India, to all to whom these presents shall come, greeting ;

Whereas We have taken into Our Royal consideration that the means of adequately rewarding the distinguished services of Officers in Our Naval and Military Services who have been honourably mentioned in despatches are limited ; now for the purpose of attaining an end so desirable as that of rewarding individual instances of meritorious or distinguished service in war, We have instituted and created and by these presents, for Us, Our Heirs and Successors, do institute and create a new Naval and Military Order of Distinction—to be designated as hereinafter described—which We are desirous should be highly prized by the Officers of Our Naval and Military Services, and We are graciously pleased to make, ordain, and establish the following rules and ordinances for the government of the same, which shall henceforth be inviolably observed and kept ;

Firstly : It is ordained that this Order shall henceforth be styled and designated the " Distinguished Service Order."

Secondly : It is ordained that the Order shall consist of the Sovereign, and of such Members or Companions as We, Our Heirs or Successors, shall appoint.

Thirdly : It is ordained that We, Our Heirs and Successors, Kings and Queens, Regnant of the United Kingdom of Great Britain and Ireland, Emperors and Empresses of India, are and for ever shall be Sovereigns of this Order.

Fourthly : It is ordained that no person shall be eligible for this distinction who doth not actually hold, at the time of his nomination, a Commission in Our Navy, in Our Land Forces, or Marines, or in Our Indian or Colonial Naval or Military Forces, or a Commission in one of the Departments of Our Navy or Army, the holder of which is entitled to Honorary or relative Navy or Army rank, nor shall any person be nominated unless his services shall have been marked by the especial mention of his name, by the Admiral or Senior Naval Officer Commanding a Squadron or detached Naval Force, or by the Commander-in-Chief of the Forces in the Field, in despatches for meritorious or distinguished service in the Field, or before the enemy.

Fifthly : It is ordained that Foreign Officers who have been associated in Naval and Military operations with our Forces shall be eligible to be Honorary Members of this Order.

Sixthly : It is ordained that when We, Our Heirs, and Successors, shall be pleased to appoint any person to be a Member of this Order, such appointment shall be made by Warrant under Our Sign Manual, and counter-signed by one of Our Principal Secretaries of State.

Seventhly : It is ordained that the decoration of the Order shall be and shall be worn as hereinafter set forth.

Eighthly : It is ordained that an Officer shall be appointed to this Order, that is to say, a Secretary and Registrar.

Ninthly : It is ordained that the Secretary and Registrar of this Order shall be appointed by Us, Our Heirs and Successors, and shall have the custody of the archives of the Order. He shall attend to the service of the Order and shall execute such directions as he may receive from Our Principal Secretary of State for War.

Tenthly : It is ordained that this Order shall rank next to and immediately after Our Order of the Indian Empire, and that the Companions thereof shall in all places and assemblies whatsoever have place and precedence next to and immediately after the Companions of Our said Order of the Indian Empire and shall rank among themselves according to the dates of their respective nominations.

Eleventhly : It is ordained that the Badge of the Order, which shall consist of a gold cross, enamelled white, edged gold, having on one side thereof in the centre, within a wreath of laurel enamelled green, the Imperial Crown in gold upon a red enamelled ground, and on the reverse, within a similar wreath and on a similar red ground, Our Imperial and Royal cypher V.R.I., shall be suspended from the left breast by a red riband, edged blue, of one inch in width.

Twelfthly : It is ordained that the names of those upon whom We may be pleased to confer the decoration shall be published in the London Gazette, and a registry thereof kept in the office of Our Secretary of State for War.

Lastly : We reserve to Ourself, Our Heirs, and Successors, full power of annulling, altering, abrogating, augmenting, interpreting or dispensing with these Regulations or any part thereof by a notification under the Sign Manual of the Sovereign of the Order.

Given at Our Court at Balmoral this sixth day of September, in the fiftieth year of Our Reign, and in the year of our Lord one thousand eight hundred and eighty-six.

By Her Majesty's Command,
W. H. SMITH.

EDWARD R. & I.

EDWARD, by the Grace of God, of the United Kingdom of Great Britain and Ireland, and of the British Dominions beyond the Seas, King, Defender of the Faith, Emperor of India, Sovereign of the Distinguished Service Order, to all to whom these presents shall come, greeting :

Whereas Her late Majesty, Our Beloved Mother Queen Victoria, by a Warrant under Her Royal Sign Manual, countersigned by one of Her Principal Secretaries of State, and bearing date at Her Court at Balmoral the sixth day of September, one thousand eight hundred and eighty-six, in the fiftieth year of her reign, did institute and create a new Naval and Military Order of Distinction, to be styled and designated the " Distinguished Service Order " ;

And whereas, by the said Royal Warrant it was, among other things, ordained that the said Order should rank next to, and immediately after, Our Order of the Indian Empire, and that the Badge of the Order should have on the reverse Her late Majesty's Imperial and Royal Cypher, V.R.I. ;

And whereas We have thought fit to signify Our Royal Will and Pleasure that the said Order shall rank next to, and immediately after, Our Royal Victorian Order, and that the Badge shall have on the reverse Our Imperial and Royal Cypher, E.R.I. ;

Now, therefore, We do by these presents for Us, Our Heirs and Successors, ordain and appoint :

Firstly, that the Distinguished Service Order shall rank next to, and immediately after, Our Royal Victorian Order, and that the Companions thereof shall, in all places and assemblies whatsoever, have place and precedence next to, and immediately after, the Members of the Fourth Class of Our said Royal Victorian Order, and shall rank among themselves according to the dates of their respective nominations.

Secondly, that the Badge of the Order, which shall consist of a gold cross, enamelled white, edged gold, having on one side thereof in the centre, within a wreath of laurel, enamelled green, the Imperial Crown in gold, upon a red enamelled ground, and on the reverse, within a similar wreath, and on a similar red ground, Our Imperial and Royal Cypher, E.R.I., shall be suspended from the left breast by a red riband, edged blue, of one inch in width.

The Warrant given under Our Sign Manual on the 24th July, 1902, is accordingly hereby cancelled.

Given at Our Court of Saint James's, this second day of July, in the third year of Our Reign, and in the year of Our Lord one thousand nine hundred and three.

By His Majesty's Command,
ST. JOHN BRODRICK.

EDWARD R. & I.

EDWARD, by the Grace of God, of the United Kingdom of Great Britain and Ireland, and of the British Dominions beyond the Seas, King, Defender of the Faith, Emperor of India, Sovereign of the Distinguished Service Order, to all to whom these presents shall come, greeting ;

Whereas Her late Majesty, Our Beloved Mother, Queen Victoria, by a Warrant under Her Royal Sign Manual, countersigned by one of Her Principal Secretaries of State, and bearing date at Her Court at Balmoral the sixth day of September, one thousand eight hundred and eighty-six, in the fiftieth year of her reign, did institute and create a new Naval and Military Order of Distinction, to be styled and designated the " Distinguished Service Order " ;

And whereas, by the said Royal Warrant it was, among other things, ordained that the said Order should rank next to, and immediately after, Our Order of the Indian Empire, and that the Badge of the Order should have on the reverse Her late Majesty's Imperial and Royal Cypher, V.R.I.

And whereas, We have thought fit to signify Our Royal Will and Pleasure that the said Order shall rank next to, and immediately after, Our Royal Victorian Order, and that the Badge shall have on the reverse Our Royal Cypher, E.R. VII.

Now, therefore, We do by these presents for Us, Our Heirs and Successors, ordain and appoint : Firstly, that the Distinguished Service Order shall rank next to, and immediately after, Our Royal Victorian Order, and that the Companions thereof shall, in all places and assemblies whatsoever, have place and precedence next to, and immediately after, the Members of the Fourth Class of Our said Royal Victorian Order, and shall rank among themselves according to the dates of their respective nominations. Secondly, that the Badge of the Order, which shall consist of a gold cross, enamelled white, edged gold, having on one side thereof in the centre, within a wreath of laurel, enamelled green, the Imperial Crown in gold, upon a red enamelled ground, and on the reverse, within a similar wreath, and on a similar red ground, Our Royal Cypher, E.R. VII., shall be suspended from the left breast by a red riband, edged blue, of one inch in width.

The Warrants given under Our Sign Manual on the 24th July, 1902, and 2nd July, 1903, are accordingly hereby cancelled.

Given at Our Court of Saint James's, this fifteenth day of October, in the third year of Our Reign, and in the year of our Lord one thousand nine hundred and three.

By His Majesty's Command,
H. O. ARNOLD-FORSTER.

GEORGE R. & I.

WHEREAS We are desirous of providing for the recognition of further distinguished services in the case of Officers who have been awarded the " Distinguished Service Order."

It is Our will and pleasure and We do hereby ordain that anyone who, after having performed services for which the Distinguished Service Order is awarded, subsequently performs an approved act of gallantry which, if he had not received the Order, would have entitled him to it, shall be awarded a Bar to be attached to the riband by which the Order is suspended, and for every additional such act an additional Bar may be added.

Given at Our Court of St. James's this twenty-third day of August, 1916, in the seventh year of Our Reign.

By His Majesty's Command,
D. LLOYD GEORGE.

The Distinguished Service Order

THE STATUTES

OF THE

DISTINGUISHED SERVICE ORDER

The Order instituted 6th September, 1886.
The Bar instituted 23rd August, 1916.

GEORGE R. I.

GEORGE THE FIFTH, by the Grace of God, of the United Kingdom of Great Britain and Ireland, and of the British Dominions beyond the Seas, King, Defender of the Faith, Emperor of India, to all to whom these presents shall come, greeting;

Whereas Her late Majesty Our Beloved Grandmother Queen Victoria by a Warrant dated the 6th day of September, 1886, did institute and create a new Naval and Military Order of Distinction designated the Distinguished Service Order for the purpose of rewarding individual instances of meritorious or distinguished service in war;

And Whereas the said Royal Warrant was subsequently amended by Royal Warrants dated 24th July, 1902, 2nd July, 1903, 15th October, 1903, and 23rd August, 1916;

And Whereas it is Our Royal Will and Pleasure that the Officers of Our recently constituted Air Force shall be eligible for appointment to Our said Distinguished Service Order;

And Whereas We deem it expedient that all amendments to the Statutes of Our said Order heretofore promulgated, or now to be promulgated, shall be incorporated in a Royal Warrant under Our Sign Manual;

Now Therefore We do hereby declare that the rules and ordinances heretofore in force for the government of Our said Order shall be abrogated, cancelled and annulled, and We are graciously pleased to make, ordain and establish the following rules and ordinances in substitution for the same, which shall henceforth be inviolably observed and kept;

Firstly : It is ordained that this Order shall henceforth be styled and designated the " Distinguished Service Order."

Secondly : It is ordained that the Order shall consist of the Sovereign and of such Members or Companions as We, Our Heirs or Successors, shall appoint.

Thirdly : It is ordained that We, Our Heirs and Successors, Kings and Queens, Regnant of the United Kingdom of Great Britain and Ireland, Emperors and Empresses of India, are and for ever shall be Sovereigns of this Order.

Fourthly : It is ordained that no person shall be eligible for this distinction who doth not actually hold, at the time of his nomination, a Commission in Our Navy, in Our Land Forces or Marines, in Our Air Force or in Our Indian or Colonial Naval or Military Forces, or a Commission in one of the Departments of Our Navy, Army or Air Force, the holder of which is entitled to Honorary or relative Navy, Army or Air Force rank, nor shall any person be nominated unless his services shall have been marked by the especial mention of his name, by the Admiral or Senior Naval Officer Commanding a Squadron or detached Naval Force, or by the Commander-in-Chief of the Forces in the Field, in despatches for meritorious or distinguished service in the Field, or before the enemy.

Fifthly : It is ordained that Foreign Officers who have been associated in Naval, Military or Aerial operations with Our Forces shall be eligible to be Honorary Members of this Order.

Sixthly : It is ordained that when We, Our Heirs and Successors, shall be pleased to appoint any person to be a Member of this Order, such appointment shall be made by Warrant under Our Sign Manual, and countersigned by one of Our Principal Secretaries of State.

Seventhly : It is ordained that anyone who, after having performed services for which this Order is awarded, subsequently performs an approved act of gallantry which, if he had not received the Order, would have entitled him to it, shall be awarded a Bar to be attached to the riband by which the Badge is suspended, and for every additional such act an additional Bar may be added.

Eighthly : It is ordained that an Officer shall be appointed to this Order, that is to say, a Secretary and Registrar.

Ninthly : It is ordained that the Secretary and Registrar of this Order shall be appointed by Us, Our Heirs and Successors, and shall have the custody of the archives of the Order. He shall attend to the service of the Order and shall execute such directions as he may receive from our Principal Secretary of State for War.

Tenthly : It is ordained that this Order shall rank next to and immediately after Our Order of the British Empire, and that the Companions thereof shall in all places and assemblies whatsoever have place and precedency next to and immediately after the Commanders of Our said Order of the British Empire and shall rank among themselves according to the date of their respective nominations.

Eleventhly : It is ordained that the Badge of the Order shall consist of a gold cross, enamelled white, edged gold, having on one side thereof in the centre, within a wreath of laurel enamelled green, the Imperial Crown in gold upon a red enamelled ground and on the reverse, within a similar wreath and on a similar red ground, the Royal Cypher, and shall be suspended from the left breast by a red riband, edged blue, of one inch in width.

Twelfthly : It is ordained that the names of those whom We may be pleased to admit to Membership of this Order shall be published in the London Gazette, and a registry thereof kept in the Office of Our Secretary of State for War.

Thirteenthly : In order to make such additional provision as sha effectively preserve pure this honourable distinction, it is ordained that if any person admitted to Membership of this Order shall be convicted of treason, cowardice, felony, or of any infamous crime, or if he be accused of any such offence and doth not after a reasonable time surrender himself to be tried for the same, his name shall be erased, by an Order under the Royal Sign Manual, from the register of Members of the said Order. And it is hereby declared that We, Our Heirs and Successors, shall be the sole judge of the conduct which may require the erasure from the register of the name of the offending person, and that it shall at all times be competent for Us, Our Heirs and Successors, to restore the name if such restoration should be justified by the circumstances of the case.

Lastly : We reserve to Ourselves, Our Heirs and Successors, full power of annulling, altering, abrogating, augmenting, interpreting or dispensing with these Regulations or any part thereof by a notification under the Sign Manual of the Sovereign of the Order.

Given at Our Court at St. James's this first day of April, in the eighth year of Our Reign, and in the year of our Lord one thousand nine hundred and eighteen.

By His Majesty's Command,
MILNER.

A

The Queen was created a Companion of the Distinguished Service Order [London Gazette, 26 Nov. 1886]. The Insignia were presented to Her Majesty by the Secretary of State.

London Gazette, 26 Nov. 1886.—" War Office, 25 Nov. 1886. The Queen has been further pleased to confer upon the undermentioned Officers the distinction of Companion of the Distinguished Service Order, for Action at Ginnis."

LITHGOW, STEWART AARON, Deputy Surgeon-General, was born in 1833, at Dundee, son of Aaron Lithgow, Esq., and Lydia Stewart, and was educated at Dundee Academy, and Edinburgh University (L.R.C.S.

Stewart Aaron Lithgow.

Edin. 1875 ; M.D., and B.Sc. Edin. 1876) ; joined the Army Medical Department in 1855. Served through the Indian Mutiny 1857–9, attached to the 75th Regt. (Gordon Highlanders). He was present at the Battle of Budlekeserai (wounded) ; at the siege, assault and capture of Delhi, the battles of Bulandshahr and Agra, the affairs of Allygur, Akrabad and Kanoj ; in the Oudh Campaign, at the actions of Alambagh and Dilkusa ; at the Relief of Lucknow and occupation of Alambagh ; at the affair of Suilee and the pursuit of Tanta Topi (Mutiny Medal with two clasps). In 1866, on the 3rd of Sept., at Blackheath, London, S.E., he married Elizabeth Charlotte, daughter of the Rev. John Davis (Oxon.), Ordinary of Newgate, and of his wife, M. J. Cooks. Their children are : Stewart James Douglas (died in infancy) ; Edwin Malcolm (served in the Kent Artillery, Cameron Highlanders, resigned ; became M.B., Ch.M., and F.R.C.S., Edinburgh, and served in the European War as Captain, R.A.M.C.) ; and a daughter, Ethel. Assistant Surgeon S. A. Lithgow became Surgeon in 1867, and Surgeon-Major in 1873. In 1878 he organized a large European Base Hospital at Karachi, during the Kandahar Campaign, being a P.M.O. to the British troops at the base of operations while the Bombay Column advanced to Kandahar in 1880. He was attached respectively to the 17th Lancers, Gordon Highlanders, Carbineers and Cameron Highlanders, and was promoted to Brigade Surgeon in 1880. In 1884 and 1885 he served with the Nile Expeditionary Force as P.M.O., Line of Communication ; was specially mentioned in Despatches [London Gazette, 25 Aug. 1885] ; received the Bronze Star, Medal and Clasp, and was created a C.B., having been promoted to Deputy Surgeon-General in 1884. He served in 1885 as P.M.O. during the operations on the Upper Nile, and was again mentioned in Despatches [London Gazette, 9 Feb. 1886], and created a Companion of the Distinguished Service Order [London Gazette, 26 Nov. 1886] : " Stewart Aaron Lithgow, C.B., M.D , Deputy Surgeon-General, Medical Staff. For action at Ginnis." General Lithgow was the first officer to be gazetted after the institution of the Distinguished Service Order.

An extract from Sir Reginald Wingate's " History of the Sudan " (page 272 and following pages) gives the following account of the action at Ginnis :

" The Frontier Force was busily preparing for the impending attack. On the 27th of November the fighting strength was disposed as follows :

	British.	Egyptian.
Kosheh	600	300
Mograkeh	—	266
Sarkamatto and Dal	—	200
Akasheh	600	350
Halfa	500	350

Besides small detachments at Tanjur Road, Ambigol Wells, Murat Wells, and Sarras.

" On the 29th of November the first sight of the advancing enemy was obtained by Capt. Hunter, Intelligence Officer to the Force, who telegraphed that the Arab Infantry were visible in large numbers on hill-tops east of Amara. On the following day the armed stern-wheeler Lotus exchanged shots with them. The first attempt on the line of communications took place at Ambigol Wells, a station in the desert on the railway line some twenty miles north of Akasheh. A party of Arabs under the Emir Ez Zein, mounted on camels and horses, with a few men on foot and one gun, had left Amara on the 29th Nov., having previously destroyed the line for about a mile. They attacked on the 2nd Dec. the Ambigol post of thirty men, under Capt. Ferrier, R.E., consisting of detachments of the Berkshire and West Kent Regts. under Lieuts. Fitton and Annesley. They were driven off with some loss. The next day they again attacked the fort, and destroyed a portion of the line to the north. The attack was renewed once more on the 4th. During the intervals of these attacks a redan was constructed to cover the entrance of the redoubt, and several sorties were made under fire to bring in telegraph instruments, ammunition, blankets, etc., while a patrol of the Egyptian Camel Corps, under Lieut. Said Radwan, and Mounted Infantry, under Lieut. de Lisle, succeeded in reaching the fort. This reinforcement, the timely arrival of a train from Halfa with troops, and the advance of a strong force under General Butler, caused the besiegers to withdraw—a great relief to this small garrison, which had held its own for three days with gallantry against overwhelming numbers.

" In the meantime the Lotus was doing good work, and in co-operation with the mounted troops, harassed the enemy, who had by this time occupied in force the villages of Ginnis and Kosheh. In the early morning of the 12th, a party of Arabs, under the Kordofan Emir, Siwari ed Dahab, turned Kosheh Fort and attacked Mograkeh Fort from the north. Here Capt.

Besant, in command of a force of some 200 men of the 3rd Battn. of the Egyptian Army, held his own, making repeated attacks on the Arabs, getting within forty yards of their position, and inflicting some loss on them. During this attack the Emir Ez Zein raided the village of Ferkeh, and secured a number of cattle and some money. The enemy drew off during the night. While the line of communication was thus being harassed, the main position of the enemy in front of Kosheh was being steadily reinforced, and the fort of Kosheh was now completely invested on the south side. To understand the situation a slight description of the surrounding country is necessary. From the village of Ginnis to within a short distance of the fort of Kosheh a narrow stretch of cultivation extends along the east bank of the Nile, planted with numerous palm trees. Along this narrow strip and close to the river is a continuous row of strongly built mud houses, for the most part detached. Sometimes they are clustered thickly together, and then perhaps there is a considerable gap, but the whole presents the appearance of a long, straggling village. The village of Kosheh was now strongly held by the enemy, and though the ground to the immediate south of the fort had been cleared to a distance of some 500 yards, this did not prevent the enemy occupying a large black rock which jutted out on the foreshore, from which a very harassing fire was continually kept up on the fort ; and had it not been for the excellent construction of this earthwork and the innumerable traverses which it had been found necessary to erect, the loss during the month of investment would have been very much heavier. Close to the rock a palm grove also gave good cover to the enemy's sharp-shooters ; casualties daily occurred within the fort, and on the 15th Dec. the fire from the black rock and the palm grove became so unusually harassing that a sortie was made by a party of Cameron Highlanders, under the command of Lieut.-Colonel Everett, who succeeded in surprising and bayoneting fourteen of the enemy, but with the severe loss of Lieut. Cameron mortally wounded, Capt. Hunter severely, and Major Chalmers slightly wounded, one man killed, and three men wounded.

" In the meantime all the posts were being rapidly reinforced. General Grenfell had arrived at Wady Halfa on the 4th Dec., being followed on the 19th Dec. by General Sir F. Stephenson, commanding in Egypt, whc assumed supreme command, while General Grenfell became Chief of the Staff. The fire from the enemy's guns was now getting very accurate, and on 20 Dec. a shell passed through an embrasure of Kosheh Fort, dismounting a Gardner gun and severely wounding Major Hassan Radwan, as well as an armourer-sergeant and a private of the Cameron Highlanders. On the 22nd Dec. General Butler, with the mounted infantry, Egyptian Camel Corps, and a troop of the 20th Hussars, reconnoitred from Mograkeh towards Ginnis to ascertain the enemy's strength and position. Before, however, they could reach the high ground, the enemy advanced from Ginnis in force, and the reconnaissance fell back fighting. General Butler's casualties were very slight, but the enemy lost five killed, amongst whom was an important Kordofan Emir named Bedawi el Azrak, who, it was subsequently ascertained, was held in great respect by the Arabs on account of his personal bravery. He alone, considerably in advance of the mounted party he was leading, charged and succeeded in getting close to the mounted infantry before he was shot dead, his horse being captured. All arrangements were now made to inflict a blow on the Arabs, who, elated by the ease with which they had advanced hitherto, boldly pushed their advanced parties north from the village of Ginnis, which was the headquarters of their main body.

" At the same time some 1,000 men with one gun threatened the zariba on the west bank, held by portions of the 9th Sudanese and the 3rd Egyptian battalions. The Arabs appeared entirely ignorant of the impending attack, and indeed their Emirs assured them that the quantities of transport which daily arrived in the Government lines were but preparations for a retreat. On the 29th Dec. Lieut.-General Sir F. Stephenson, Major-General Grenfell, and their staffs marched from Ferkeh to Kosheh, and bivouacked on the east bank below the fort of Kosheh, where the whole of the fighting force was concentrated for the day, viz. :

Mounted Troops.

Lieut.-Colonel Blake, 20th Hussars, commanding.
Capt. E. R. Courtenay, 20th Hussars, Staff Officer.

British Mounted Infantry—Lieut.-Colonel C. Barrow, commanding.
British Camel Corps—Capt. Maunsell, West Kents, commanding.
Egyptian Cavalry—Major Bakir Kamil, commanding.
Egyptian Camel Corps—Lieut. Marriott, commanding.

Artillery

Lieut.-Colonel Herbert, R.A., commanding.
Lieut. Warre, R.A., Adjutant.

No. 2 Battery, 1st Brigade, South Irish Division, Royal Artillery—Major Whateley, Royal Artillery.
Egyptian Camel Battery—Major Wodehouse.
Gardner Guns—Lieut. Nercer, Yorkshire Regt.

Engineers

Major A. J. Hepper, commanding Royal Engineers, Frontier Field Force Section.
11th Company, R.E., Capt. Blackburn, R.E.

1st Infantry Brigade

Brigadier-General W. F. Butler, C.B., A.D.C., commanding.
Lieut.-Colonel Crofton, South Staffordshire Regt., Brigade-Major.
Lieut. Daubeney, South Staffordshire Regt., Aide-de-Camp.

Berkshire Battn.—Major Temple.
West Kent Battn.—Lieut.-Colonel Tweedie.
Durham Battn.—Colonel Coker.

2nd Infantry Brigade

Colonel Huyshe, C.B., Berkshire Regt., commanding.
Major Dixon, Berkshire Regt., Brigade-Major.
Lieut. Feetham, Berkshire Regt., Aide-de-Camp.

Cameron Highlanders—Lieut.-Colonel Everett, in Kosheh Fort.
Yorkshire Battn.—Lieut.-Colonel Bennett.
Detachment, 1st Battn., Egyptian Army.
Detachment, 9th Battn., Egyptian Army.
English Bearer Company—Surgeon-Major Barrow.

Egyptian Troops

Major Wodehouse, commanding.
Capt. Smith-Dorrien, Staff Officer.

Egyptian Bearer Company—Surgeon Keating.
Kosheh Fort—Colonel St. Leger, Cameron Highlanders.
Mograkeh Fort—Capt. Tapp, E.A.
Ferkeh Fort—Lieut. Or, Yorkshire Regt.
Barrow's Zariba—Lieut. Gibb, E.A.
Lotus Stern-wheeler—Major Lloyd, E.A.

" On the 28th and 29th artillery fire was kept up on the enemy's position, and at 5 a.m. on the morning of the 30th the whole force began to move off, . . . The general plan of attack was briefly as follows :

" The 2nd Brigade to crown the heights above Ginnis, and by artillery and rifle fire to prepare for the attack on the north end of the village of Ginnis by the Cameron Highlanders and the 9th Sudanese.

" The 1st Brigade to sweep round to the south end of the village and attack the enemy's camp.

" The cavalry and mounted troops to protect the left flank of the two brigades and pursue south when the village and camp were taken.

" The detailed movements of the troops were to be as follows : The mounted infantry troops, consisting of the 20th Hussars, Mounted Infantry, and the Egyptian Cavalry and Egyptian Camel Corps, to march in rear of the 1st Infantry Brigade, eventually diverging to the east and scouting on the left flank during the advance.

" The English Camel Corps to support and keep in touch with the 2nd Brigade.

" The attack on Ginnis to be carried out by the 1st Brigade with the Egyptian battery and the Egyptian Camel Corps.

" The 2nd Infantry Brigade, with the English Battery, to attack, in the first instance, the enemy's position between Kosheh Fort and Ginnis.

" The Yorkshire Battn. and the 1st Battn. Egyptian Army to conform to the movements of the screw-gun battery, while six companies of the Cameron Highlanders and two companies of the 9th Battn. Sudanese were to advance along the river bank and capture the village of Kosheh, which would be previously shelled by the screw-gun battery. The armed stern-wheeler Lotus was to steam slowly in advance of the Camerons and fire on the beach and foreshore. The 2nd Brigade had, by daylight, taken up a strong position 1,200 yards from and directly opposite to the village of Kosheh : at 6.10 a.m. the English battery began to shell the village. A quarter of an hour later the Cameron Highlanders and two batteries of the 9th Sudanese rushed the houses in the most gallant manner. This village was captured at 6.50 a.m., and one brass gun taken. The Lotus co-operated in this movement, and inflicted considerable loss on the retreating Arabs. In the meantime the 1st Brigade, under General Butler, who knew the ground thoroughly, marched over the broken and hilly desert, selecting first a prominent mountain top on the horizon as a line for the advance. When the day broke the brigade had gained a position in the hills about a mile south of the river and a mile and a half south-east of the western end of the village of Ginnis, which was the headquarters of the enemy. Up to this time the advance along the enemy's flank had not been observed, but as the eastern horizon became brighter behind the advance, the Arabs, seeing that they had been surprised, came streaming in long lines and groups from the villages and low ground along the river towards the front. Soon the brigades were lined with their riflemen, who opened and maintained an irregular fire for about forty minutes.

" In the meantime the Egyptian Battery had been brought into action on the right, while the Berkshire, deployed to the left, about 200 yards in advance of the guns ; the Durham Light Infantry prolonging the line farther to the left, while the West Kents were eventually moved to the left flank of the Durham Light Infantry, and the cavalry conformed to the general movement some distance from the left flank of the infantry.

" Unchecked by the strength of the fire, a large body of the enemy's spearmen crept up unobserved through a deep khor (or valley) into a nullah where the dismounted camels of the Egyptian Camel Corps had been placed ; so rapidly did the spearmen advance that the Camel Corps were unable to mount, and were forced to retire slowly before the Arabs, who pressed them heavily, and several hand-to-hand encounters took place. Numbers of the enemy were, however, quickly shot down by the right troops of the Camel Corps and the left company of the West Kents, and the remainder of their column fell back and dispersed amongst the hills. The brigade then swinging round to the left, was directed towards the village of Ginnis ; crest after crest was abandoned before the steady advance, and though several attempts at a stand were made, all were eventually dispersed. In the meantime the Arabs were streaming out of the village in a southerly direction towards Atab, and at 9.15 a.m. Ginnis was occupied,

while the mounted troops followed the enemy's line of retreat towards the river. The 2nd Brigade, continuing its advance towards Ginnis, arrived there a quarter of an hour after the 1st Brigade had entered. The pursuit was continued till 10 a.m., and by that time the Arab army was a disorganized mass of fugitives. Their camp was occupied, their treasury, four guns, and twenty standards falling into the hands of the British and Egyptian troops. The Arab force on the west bank made a show of attacking the fort, but when they perceived the retreat along the east bank, they, too, retreated, followed by the garrison of the fort, who destroyed their batteries and trenches.

" General Grenfell, in his Despatch to Sir F. Stephenson, characterizes ' the behaviour of all ranks during the action as steady and the conduct of the whole force of Egyptian troops very creditable.'

" It may not be here out of place to remark that a camaraderie sprang up between the Cameron Highlanders and the 9th Sudanese Battn. which has been perpetuated by the former presenting to the latter a banner inscribed ' Ginnis,' which is always carried on parade alongside the Khedivial colour. On the same day the 1st Brigade advanced to Atab, while the cavalry continued the pursuit to Abri, and on the following day Abri was occupied by General Butler's brigade. From here the Lotus, with the British and Egyptian cavalry under Capt. Smith-Dorrien, continued the pursuit south as far as Absaret, capturing nine large boats, two standards, and a miscellaneous assortment of Arab stores. The total British and Egyptian losses were seven killed, amongst whom was a promising young officer, Lieut. Soltau, and thirty-four wounded. Shortly after the fight it was found that a small party of the enemy still occupied a house in the village of Kosheh, in the capture of which an Egyptian officer was killed. Though frequently summoned, the inmates refused to surrender until guns were brought up, the house shelled, and every man killed. It is estimated that the Arab force engaged on the 30th amounted to some 6,000 men, of whom 500 were killed and 300 wounded.

" Abd el Mejid, the Emir in command, was wounded, while his second, Abd el Mejid el Khalik, was killed, as well as eighteen minor chiefs. The remnant of the scattered forces were collected at Kermeh, where Mohammed el Kheir awaited reinforcements from Berber, which Nejumi could not or would not send him. Abdallah Taashi was said to be furious with Mejid for bringing on an action instead of leisurely besieging the Government troops as he had ordered. The action at Ginnis was a severe blow to the Khalifa."

In 1890 General Lithgow served with the Zhob Field Force as P.M.O., and was again mentioned in Despatches, and in the following year he was promoted to Surgeon-Major-General. He was for some time P.M.O., Southern District, and was appointed Honorary Physician to Queen Victoria. In 1893 Surgeon-Major-General Lithgow retired from the Army, and was appointed Superintendent of the Royal Infirmary, Edinburgh, where he was a highly respected and most popular official. He was much interested in genealogical and antiquarian matters, and also wrote and was consulted by writers as an authority on genealogical subjects. General Lithgow belonged to the family of Lithgows of Drygrange, Roxburghshire, and could trace three royal descents. The property of Drygrange was a grant from the Abbey and Convent of Melrose to John Lithgow, also of Weltown, Linlithgowshire " for services rendered to the Abbey in resisting robbers and depredators." This property was sold during the lifetime of General Lithgow's grandfather, the Rev. John Lithgow, of Etal, Northumberland. A small piece of the same land is included in the property of Fanhope, Roxburghshire, now held by the family. Surgeon-Major-General Lithgow died on 20 Sept. 1899, at his residence, Fanhope, Melrose.

ST. LEGER, HENRY HUNGERFORD, Lieut.-Colonel, was born 26 April, 1833, and entered the Army, 18 Aug. 1851. He served in the Indian Mutiny campaign in 1858, being present with the Flying Column at the engagement on the banks of the Jumna, and with the Camel Corps at the Battle of Gowlowlee, and at the capture of Calpee, and received the Medal and clasp. In 1860 he was promoted to Captain, and in the same year he married Florence Stuart (who died in 1892), daughter of the late John Moore, Esq. Capt. St. Leger became Major in 1873, and from 1875 to 1880 he was an Adjutant of Auxiliary Forces. In Feb. 1881, he joined the Cameron Highlanders as Major, from the 71st Highlanders, and he became Lieutenant-Colonel, Cameron Highlanders, 1 July, 1881. In the Egyptian Campaign of 1882 he was present at the Battle of Tel-el-Kebir (Medal with clasp, and Khedive's Bronze Star). He served throughout the Nile Expedition of 1884-5 (clasp). On 18 Aug. 1884, he became Lieutenant-Colonel Commanding. " On the 31st March, 1885, to the great regret of all ranks, Colonel J. M. Leith, C.B., left the regiment to take up the appointment of Assistant Adjutant-General to the Suakim Field Force, and he was succeeded in the Command by Lieut.-Colonel H. H. St. Leger, who became Colonel in 1885," and commanded the advanced posts and the Cameron Highlanders in the operations in the Eastern Sudan in 1885-86. Colonel St. Leger was present, as Commandant, at the defence of Fort Kosheh, during its investment, and at the action of Ginniss. " The Records of the Cameron Highlanders " gives the following account of the preparations for the Defence of Kosheh : " On the 19th of November, 1885, the headquarters and right half battalion, under Colonel St. Leger, moved to Akasheh, being joined at Sarras by D Company. They bivouacked for the night at Akasheh, and proceeded the following day by whale-boats to the Dal Cataract, and from thence to Firket, eight miles further on. On the 21st, in pursuance of orders, the headquarters and right half battalion moved from Firket to Mograkeh, an old Arab Fort in total ruins, which Colonel St. Leger had been directed to place in a state of defence with a view to keeping open the communications between Akasheh and Kosheh. Work was at once commenced, the old towers were loop-holed, the walls cut down and rendered defensible, and a zeriba was made around the most exposed sides. In the meantime Lieut.-Colonel Everett and the left half battalion were working hard at the defences of Kosheh, where the trees were felled, the ground cleared, and a large zeriba constructed on the west bank of the Nile. . . . On the 29th of Dec. 1885, Lieut.-General Sir Frederick Stephenson attacked and dispersed the Dervishes at Ginniss. . . . It was known that the Soudanese Army was approaching rapidly, and might be expected before Kosheh in a few days. . . . The garrison of Kosheh now consisted of one troop of the 20th Hussars, one troop of Mounted Infantry, a few British and Egyptian artillerymen, the Cameron Highlanders, and 100 men of the 9th Soudan Battn., under Major Archibald Hunter; 150 blacks from the same battalion, under Major Borrow, occupied the zeriba on the west bank. Mograkeh was held by the 3rd Battn. of the Egyptian Army, under Major Besant, and some of the Egyptian Camel Corps. The armed steamers Lotus and Shaban patrolled the river." For his services in this campaign Colonel St. Leger was mentioned in Despatches by Sir Frederick Stephenson [London Gazette, 9 Feb. 1886], and was created a Companion of the Distinguished Service Order [London Gazette, 26 Nov. 1886]: "For action at Ginniss, Henry Hungerford St. Leger, Lieut.-Colonel, Cameron Highlanders." He also received the Medal with clasp, and the Khedive's Bronze Star. Colonel St. Leger retired on 2 April, 1883.

COKER, EDMUND ROGERS, Colonel, was born 4 Jan. 1844, at St. Croix, West Indies, son of the late William Worthington Coker, Ash-in-Stourpaine, Dorset, and of Matilda Augusta, daughter of W. Dewhurst, of Santa Cruz, West Indies. He was educated at a private school and at Addiscombe, and entered the Madras Army in 1861; was transferred to the 106th Light Infantry in 1863; appointed Adjutant in 1874; promoted Major and Lieutenant-Colonel in 1881, and Colonel in 1885. He served with the Frontier Field Force in the Sudan in 1885 and 1886, in command of the 2nd Battn. Durham Light Infantry; was mentioned in Despatches, received the Medal and the Khedive's Bronze Star, and was created a Companion of the Distinguished Service Order [London Gazette, 26 Nov. 1886]: "For services at the action at Ginniss, 30 Dec. 1885, Edmund Rogers Coker, Lieut.-Colonel and Colonel, Durham Light Infantry." Soon after the battle of Ginniss "most of the troops" (says Colonel A. Haggard, in "Under Crescent and Star," page 391) "were in a few days' time marched back northwards to Akasheh, and gradually to Wady Halfa, only a very small force being left at Ginniss to form the extreme frontier guard. This force consisted of the 2nd Battn. of the Durham Light Infantry, under Lieut.-Colonel Coker, which regiment was encamped near the old fort at Kosheh; of my battalion of Egyptians, 300 men of whom took possession of Fort Mograkeh, the remainder being either with Hartayne at Akasheh, or on detachment under Frith at Sarkametto; of the Black Battalion, now under Gibb, and a few details of British Mounted Infantry, under a smart young officer named Tudway." He married, in 1889, Agnes Gertrude, daughter of the late Charles Meade-King, of Taunton. Colonel Coker's favourite recreations were shooting and riding. He died on 11 March, 1914.

MURRAY, KENELM DIGBY, Lieut.-Colonel, was born at Dover 6 Feb. 1879, third son of Lieut.-Colonel Sir J. Digby Murray, 10th Bart., of Black Barony, Peeblesshire, N.B., and of Frances, his wife, daughter of the late Peter Pattern Bold. He was educated at Trinity College, Glenalmond, and at private schools, and joined the 9th Regt. in 1860, exchanging into the 89th in 1869. He married in 1870, Caroline, daughter of the late Colonel George Thompson, C.B., and their children were: Archibald Digby, born in 1878; Kenelm Digby Bold, born in 1879; Frances Anna, and Constance Digby. He passed through the Staff College in 1876, and was D.A.A. and Q.M.G., 2nd Division, being present at the Battle of Tel-el-Kebir. He was mentioned in Despatches [London Gazette, 2 Nov. 1882], received the Medal and clasp and the Bronze Star, the Brevet of Lieutenant-Colonel, and the 4th Class Osmanieh. He was D.A.A. and Q.M.G. at Alexandria, 1882–85, and A.A.G., Frontier Force, Egypt, from 1885 to 1886. For his services in the Sudan Campaign, and especially at the action at Ginniss, he was mentioned in Despatches [London Gazette, 9 Feb. 1886], and was created a Companion of the Distinguished Service Order [London Gazette, 26 Nov. 1886]: "Kenelm Digby Murray, Lieut.-Colonel, Royal Irish Fusiliers. For the Action at Ginniss." In 1888 Lieut.-Colonel Murray succeeded to the command of the 1st Battn. Princess Victoria's Regt., the Royal Irish Fusiliers, and he became Colonel 9 Jan. 1889. From 1889 to 1894 he was A.A.G., Headquarters, India. He was placed on half-pay, late Staff, 6 Jan. 1894. Colonel Murray's favourite recreations were shooting, riding, golf, etc. Colonel Murray died 19 Feb. 1915.

TWEEDIE, JOHN LANNOY, Colonel, was born 6 May, 1842, fifth son of the late Capt. Michael Tweedie, R.A., of Quarter, Peeblesshire, N.B., J.P. for Kent, and of his wife, Frances, daughter of the late Richard Walter Forbes, of Watertown, County Aberdeen, N.B. Educated privately, he passed for a direct commission, and joined the 97th (Earl of Ulster's) Regt. 3 July, 1860. He became Captain in 1869 and Major in 1879. In 1881 Major Tweedie served in South Africa with the Natal Field Force, with the Royal West Kent Regt. He became Lieutenant-Colonel in 1884, and commanded the 1st Battn. (Queen's Own) Royal West Kent Regt. from 29 Dec. 1884, to 29 Dec. 1889, taking part in the Sudan Expedition in 1884 and 1885, and receiving the Nile Medal with clasp, and the Khedive's Bronze Star. In 1885 and 1886 he served with the Sudan Field Force, was present at the Action of Ginniss, was mentioned in Despatches and created a Companion of the Distinguished Service Order [London Gazette, 26 Nov. 1886]: "John Lannoy Tweedie, Lieut.-Colonel, Royal West Kent Regt. For Action at Ginniss, in command of the 1st Battn. Royal West Kent Regt." He became Colonel 11 June, 1888, and from that date until 1 April, 1897, when he went on half-pay, Colonel Tweedie commanded the 39th Regimental District. He retired on 6 May, 1899. He married on 15 Sept. 1891, Emma Constance, third daughter of William Craig Murray, Esq., of Avonmore, Ballybrack, County Dublin, and they have two daughters: Kathleen Hay Lannoy and Olive Murray Lannoy.

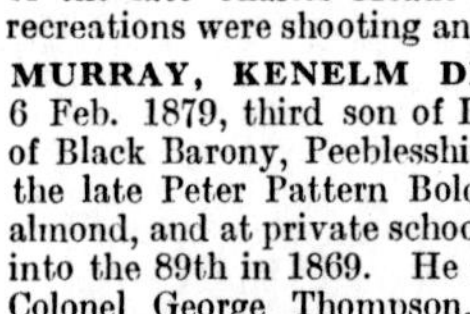

John Lannoy Tweedie.

BENNETT, WILLIAM, Colonel, was born 15 Nov. 1835, at Athlone, Ireland, eldest son of Capt. Thomas Bennett, 14th Hussars, and of Winifred Bennett, daughter of the late N. Keatinge. He was educated at private schools, and joined the 1st Battn. 19th Foot in India, as Ensign, in 1858, the battalion in which he afterwards served for 32 years. Shortly afterwards he passed in Hindustani, and was appointed Regimental Interpreter. In 1862 he obtained a first-class certificate at the School of Musketry, Hythe, and held the appointment of Instructor of Musketry to the 3rd Depôt Battn. at Chatham, and afterwards to his regiment. He took part in the Hazara Campaign, North-West Frontier of India, including the expedition against the Black Mountain Tribes, 1868 (Medal with clasp). He married, in 1869, Belinda, daughter of the late William Rosher, of Woodfield, Northfleet, Kent. He was promoted Captain in 1871, and in July, 1877, returned to Hythe as Captain Instructor at the school, and was appointed D.A.A.G. for Musketry at Aldershot 1 March, 1878, remaining in that position until, on getting his majority in 1881, he rejoined the Yorkshire Regt. at Halifax, Nova Scotia. When on the Staff at Aldershot, he founded in 1878 the Annual Aldershot Rifle Meeting. Colonel Bennett always took a keen interest in shooting, being himself one of the best shots in the Army, and the winner of many important trophies in the matches of the Northern Indian Rifle Association, as well as a successful big game shot in Kashmir. An instance of his fine marksmanship in target-shooting was witnessed one day on the rifle range when, as Regimental Musketry Instructor, he was endeavouring to train a batch of third-class shots to make the best of the very inferior Lee-Enfield rifles which were at that time issued to the battalions in India. One of the men, after several tries, failed altogether to get a single shot on the target. "How is it, Private Atkins, that you are shooting so badly?" inquired the instructor. "Well, sir," said the man, "I think this 'ere rifle is a very bad one; I can't make nothing of it." Capt. Bennett took the rifle from the man with his right hand only, put it to his shoulder, and without touching it at all with his other hand, aimed at the target, and immediately made a bull's-eye. "I do not think there is much fault to be found with that rifle," he remarked to the greatly surprised Mr. Atkins. After much "testing," those rifles were ultimately changed for a superior make, with the result that the shooting of the regiment was so good the next year (1871) as to draw forth the following favourable remarks from the Commander-in-Chief in India: "The shooting is excellent, and evinces a degree of care in the performance of the annual course of musketry which is very creditable to the battalion. The exertions of the Officer Instructors, Capt. Bennett and Lieut. Emerson, have been reported to His Excellency as being worthy of special commendation, an expression of which Lord Napier of Magdala accordingly desires may be communicated to those officers." As Major he served in the Nile Expedition of 1884–5 (Medal and clasp; Bronze Star); was promoted Lieutenant-Colonel in 1885; served in the Sudan, 1885–6. He commanded the 1st Battn. Yorkshire Regt. in the action of Ginniss; was created a Companion of the Distinguished Service Order [London Gazette, 26 Nov. 1886]: "For action at Ginniss, William Bennett, Colonel, Yorkshire Regt." Mentioned in Despatches. He retired as full Colonel in 1890. After 22 years on the retired list, during which time, being very fond of travelling, Colonel Bennett visited the Holy Land and many parts of Europe and North Africa, he died of pneumonia and heart failure on 2 Aug. 1912, at Whitby, Yorkshire, aged 76.

William Bennett.

SKINNER, JAMES TIERNAY, Lieut.-Colonel, was born in Bengal, 26 July, 1845, son of R. M. Skinner, Esq., of the Indian Civil Service. He was educated at Wimbledon (Brackenbury and Wynne), and at the Royal Military College, Sandhurst, and entered the Royal Irish Regt. in 1864, joining the C. and T. Staff in 1866, and being appointed D.A.Q.M.G. in Dec. In 1872 he married Jessie Rose, daughter of George Walpole Leake, Esq., of Perth, Western Australia. He became Assistant Commissary-General in April, 1880. In 1884–85 he served in the Sudan Expedition (Medal and clasp and Despatches). In 1885 he was promoted Honorary Lieutenant-Colonel, and in that year and 1886 he served in the Nile Expedition, was mentioned in Despatches and created a Companion of the Distinguished Service Order [London Gazette, 26 Nov. 1886]: "James Tiernay Skinner, Assistant Commissary-General and Honorary Lieut.-Colonel, Commissariat and Transport Staff. For the Action at Ginniss." Colonel Andrew Haggard, on page 390 of "Under Crescent and Star," says that the transport service was "admirably organized by Colonel Skinner, of the Army Service Corps." In 1888 he was a Colonel in the Army Service Corps; he was A.A.G at Aldershot, 1889–93, and was afterwards A.Q.M.G. at Headquarters. In 1894 he was created a C.B. Colonel Skinner died 11 Nov. 1902.

EVERETT, EDWARD, Lieut.-Colonel, was born 4 June, 1837. He was educated at Marlborough, and joined the 79th Regt. as Ensign 1 March, 1855; served in the Crimea after the fall of Sebastopol; served in the Indian Mutiny Campaign, 1858–59, including the Siege and Capture of Lucknow; attack on the Fort of Rooyah, actions at Allygunge, Bareilly and Shahjehanpore; capture of Forts Bammiar and Mahomdie; passage of the Gagra at Fyzabad ; capture of Rampore Kussia, and subsequent operations in Oudh, across the Gagra and Raptee Rivers (Despatches [London Gazette, 25 May, 1858], Medal, clasp). He served throughout the Nile Expedition of 1884–85 (mentioned in Despatches [London Gazette, 25 Aug. 1885], Brevet of Lieutenant-Colonel, Medal and clasp, and Khedive's Star) ; he served throughout the operations of the Indian Frontier Field Force, 1885–86, being present at Kosheh during the investment ; commanded the reconnaissance of the 16th Dec., and the night attack, carried out by the Cameron Highlanders and the 9th Soudanese, on the village of Kosheh at the engagement of Ginniss. Colonel Andrew Haggard, in "Under Crescent and Star" (page 372), says that "the force advancing on the village of Ginniss consisted of two very strong companies of the Egyptian Black Battn., who were on

Edward Everett.

the right of six companies of the Cameron Highlanders under that gallant soldier Lieut.-Colonel Everett, then the second in command of this fine regiment. Colonel Everett was especially selected to command the regiment in action that day." On the 16th Dec. 1885, F and H Companies, under Lieut.-Colonel Everett, were sent out at 6 a.m. to make a demonstration against the enemy occupying the village of Absari. As the companies approached the Dervishes opened a heavy fire from the loop-holed houses, which was vigorously replied to (page 263, "Records of the Cameron Highlanders"). Having advanced close to the village, the companies retired again under cover of the guns in the fort. In this reconnaissance the Cameron Highlanders had Major Chalmers (severely), and Lieut. W. G. Cameron (mortally), and four rank and file wounded. Major Archibald Hunter, 9th Battn. Egyptian Army, was also very dangerously wounded. On the 29th of Dec. 1885, Lieut.-General Sir Frederick Stephenson arrived at Mograkeh with 4,000 Egyptian and British troops, and the investment of Kosheh, which had lasted 31 days, terminated. The following morning the Anglo-Egyptian force, under Lieut.-General Stephenson, attacked and dispersed the Dervishes at Ginniss. The Cameron Highlanders and the 9th Soudan Battn. of the Egyptian Army, under the command of Lieut.-Colonel Everett, took the village of Absari at the point of the bayonet, and afterwards occupied and burnt the village of Ginniss. All the enemy's standards, five guns and his ammunition and nuggars fell into the hands of the British and Egyptians. In this engagement the Cameron Highlanders had eight rank and file wounded. The regiment bivouacked for the night at Ginniss, and on the morning of the 31st D and E companies, under Captains Hackett-Thompson and Urquhart, were sent to dislodge some Dervishes who were still holding out in some houses near Kosheh ; this they accomplished without further loss, returning the same evening to Ginniss. Colonel St. Leger, Lieut.-Colonel Everett and Major Money were mentioned in Sir Frederick Stephenson's Despatches [London Gazette, 9 Feb. 1886], and received the D.S.O. (page 267, "Records of the Cameron Highlanders"). Lieut.-Colonel Everett was created a Companion of the Distinguished Service Order [London Gazette, 26 Nov. 1886] : "For action at Ginniss. Edward Everett, Lieut.-Colonel, Cameron Highlanders." Before the departure of the regiment His Highness the Khedive conferred the 3rd class of the Order of the Medjidie upon Lieut.-Colonel Everett, D.S.O., in recognition of his services at the engagement of Ginniss. On the 16th July, 1887, Colonel St. Leger retired from the command of the regiment, being succeeded by Lieut.-Colonel Everett, D.S.O. He was promoted Colonel on 15 June, 1889. "On the 20th of May Colonel E. Everett, D.S.O., who had greatly endeared himself to all ranks, retired from command of the regiment." He was created a C.B. in 1897.

The late G. W. Steevens wrote in "With Kitchener to Khartum" (pages 5–7) : "Little by little, Egypt—British Egypt now—gained strength and new resolution. Four battles mark the stages from weakness and abandonment to confidence and the resolution to reconquer. At Ginnis, on the last day but one of 1885, came the first Anglo-Egyptian strategical victory. The Mahdists had been tactically beaten before—well beaten ; but the result had always been that we fell back and they came on. After Ginnis, fought by the British Army of occupation, aided by a small number of the new Egyptian Army, we stood firm, and the Dervishes were washed back. There were men of the Cameron Highlanders on the Atbara who had fought in that battle ; it was not perhaps a very great one, but it was the first time the enemy had been brought to a standstill. He retired behind the Third Cataract. Then followed three years of raid and counter-raid. Chermside cut up their advance-guard at Sarras ; they captured the fort of Khor-Musa, the 13th Sudanese drove them out within twelve hours. On the Suakin side the present Sirdar made head against Osman Digna with what irregulars and friendlies he could get together. Then in 1888 Osman waxed insolent and threw up trenches against Suakin. It became a regular siege, and Dervish shells fell into the town. But on 20 Dec. Sir Francis Grenfell, the Sirdar, came down and attacked the trenches at the Battle of Gemaizeh, and Osman fell back shattered : never again did he come so near his soul's ambition. Meanwhile, Wad-en-Nejumi—the great Emir, the conqueror of Hicks and the captor of Khartum—had hung on the southern frontier, gathering strength for his attack on Egypt. He came in 1889, skirting Halfa in the Western desert, striking for a point in Egypt proper above Assuan. His Emirs got out of hand and tried to get up the Nile ; in a hard day's tussle at Argin, Colonel Wodehouse and the Halfa garrison threw him back into the desert again. Nejumi pushed on southward, certain of death, certain of Paradise. At Toski Grenfell brought him to battle with the flower of the Egyptian Army. At the end of the day Nejumi was dead, and his army was beginning to die of thirst in the desert. Egypt has never been attacked since. Finally, in 1891, Colonel Holled-Smith marched against Osman Digna's base outside Suakin, the oasis of Tokat. The Dervishes sprang upon him at Afafit, but the days of surprise and panic were over. They were rolled back and shattered to pieces ; their base was occupied, and Suakin as well as Halfa had peace."

SCOTT, DOUGLAS ALEXANDER, Capt., Brevet Lieut.-Colonel, was born 14 Dec. 1848, at Boulogne, France ; son of the late John Scott, M.D. (Edinburgh, London and Paris), and Alicia Lucy Murray, granddaughter of the late Admiral Sir George Murray, K.C.B. He was educated at Milton Abbas Grammar School, Blandford, and at the Royal Military Academy, Woolwich, and was gazetted to the Royal Engineers as Lieutenant on 8 Jan. 1870. After a period of home training he was ordered to India, when he entered the Railway Department, Public Works Department, and was selected to have charge of the Royal Train on Government Railways on the occasion of the visit of the Prince of Wales (subsequently King Edward VII.) to India in the cold weather of 1875, for which Lieut. Scott received the thanks of the Government of India.

Douglas Alexander Scott.

He was later appointed Consulting Engineer to the Government of India, for Guaranteed Railways, which post he retained until 1877. He was then appointed an Assistant Director of the State Railways, and in 1872 joined the Khyber Column in the Afghan War of 1878–79 (Medal). He returned to England in 1880 ; was promoted Captain 8 Jan. 1882 ; was ordered to join the Egyptian Expedition in 1882, and was employed on the Railway Works ; was mentioned in Despatches 2 Nov. 1882 ; received the Brevet of Major 18 Nov. 1882, the British Medal and the Khedive's Star. For some months previous to proceeding to Egypt he was employed on the Ordnance Survey of England. Towards the end of 1884, when the Nile Expedition was decided upon, Major Scott was ordered to Egypt. Shortly after his arrival he was appointed a D.A.A.G. and D.Q.M.G., and as Director of Military Railways he was responsible for laying the desert line of railway from Sarras to Ginniss, when the action against the Arabs was subsequently fought. In these operations he was mentioned in Despatches, and received the brevet rank of Lieutenant-Colonel. Later on he was employed with the Frontier Field Force, being again mentioned in Despatches 25 Aug. 1885, and created a Companion of the Distinguished Service Order [London Gazette, 26 Nov. 1886] : "For action at Ginniss, Douglas Alexander Scott, Capt. and Brevet Lieut.-Colonel, Royal Engineers." In July, 1888, he got his regimental majority and was a full Colonel in 1889. In June, 1894, he was appointed A.A.G., Royal Engineers at Headquarters, which appointment he held till June, 1899. On leaving the War Office he was appointed Colonel on the Staff, C.R.E., Southern District, and commanded the Southern District during the absence of Lieut.-General Sir Baker Russell, G.C.B., at the time of the death of Her Majesty Queen Victoria. For his services during this period he was appointed C.V.O. in March, 1901. In Sept. 1902, he was promoted a Major-General, and made C.R.E., 2nd Army Corps, subsequently being made Chief Engineer, Southern Command. In Dec. 1906, he received the appointment of Commander, Thames and Medway Defences, and retired from the Service in 1909. He was made a C.B. in 1897, on the occasion of Queen Victoria's Diamond Jubilee. He is an F.G.S., and Hon. Colonel, Engineer and Railway Staff Corps. He married in 1894, Mary, daughter of the late Capt. Cardew, of the Highland Light Infantry, and of the late Hon. Mrs. Cardew, daughter of the late 1st Baron Westbury, for some time Lord Chancellor of England. He had one son and two daughters. His favourite recreations were cycling, music and golf. Major-General Scott died on 29 June, 1918.

BARROW, CHARLES THESIGER, Brevet Lieut.-Colonel, joined the Scottish Rifles as Lieutenant 3 July, 1872, and became Captain 12 Feb. 1881, serving with the first Egyptian Expedition in 1882 as Commandant of the Auxiliary Transport (Medal and Khedive's Star). He became Major 23 May, 1883, and served with the Nile Expedition in 1884–85, with the Mounted Infantry, and was present at the action of Abu Klea (mentioned in Despatches, Brevet of Lieutenant-Colonel 15 June, 1885, two clasps). He served with the Sudan Frontier Field Force in 1885–86, in command of Mounted Infantry, and was present in the engagement at Ginniss ; was mentioned in Despatches and created a Companion of the Distinguished Service Order [London Gazette, 26 Nov. 1886] : "Frederick Thesiger Barrow, Major and Brevet Lieut.-Colonel, Scottish Rifles. For the action at Ginniss." He also served in the operations at Suakin in Dec. 1888, including the engagement at Gemaizah (Despatches, Brevet of Colonel, clasp). He served with the Mounted Infantry from 1884 continuously till the close of the Egyptian operations, and was present at most of the engagements which occurred. He became Colonel 28 Dec. 1888, and was second in command of the Cameronians at the time of his death, which occurred at Brindisi on 28 April, 1892. He was buried at Saltwood Castle, Sandling.

Morgan Samuel Crofton.

CROFTON, MORGAN SAMUEL, Brevet Lieut.-Colonel, was born 2 Jan. 1850, son of the late Rev. Morgan Crofton. He was educated at Cheltenham

College, and joined the Army in 1868, as Ensign, South Staffordshire Regt. From 1879 to 1880 he served on the Staff in South Africa, and in the Zulu War. In June, 1879, he was on special service, and as Staff Officer and D.A.Q.M.G. from Oct. 1879, to April, 1880 (Medal with clasp). From 1881 he was A.D.C. to the General Commanding, Scotland; and in 1884–86 he served in the Nile Expedition; was mentioned in Despatches; received the Medal with clasp and Bronze Star, and was given the Brevet of Lieutenant-Colonel. He was also created a Companion of the Distinguished Service Order [London Gazette, 26 Nov. 1886]: "Morgan Samuel Crofton, Major and Brevet Lieut.-Colonel, South Staffordshire Regt. For Action of Ginniss." From 1894 to 1899 he was Chief Staff Officer in South Africa, and he was created a C.B. in 1899; was promoted to Colonel and was Chief Staff Officer, Eastern District, Commanding the Eastern Counties Militia Brigade. In 1894 Colonel Crofton married Ruperta, daughter of the late Colonel Charles Edward Gostling Murray, and widow of W. H. Willats, of Denton Court, Kent. Colonel Crofton died on 9 Jan. 1916.

TEMPLE, CHARLES PILCHER, Lieut.-Colonel, was born 13 March, 1843, son of the late James Temple, Esq., of St. Margaret's, near Dover. He was educated at a private school, and entered the 49th Regt. in 1862, being promoted to Captain in 1874. In 1875 Capt. Temple married Rosabell Charlotte Campbell (who died in 1893), only daughter of Admiral Charles Wright Bonham. In 1881 he was promoted Major, and from 1885 to 1886, served with the Egyptian Frontier Field Force, being present at the action of Ginniss, in command of the 1st Battn. Royal Berkshire Regt. He was mentioned in Despatches; received the Medal and the Khedive's Bronze Star, and was created a Companion of the Distinguished Service Order [London Gazette, 26 Nov. 1886]: "Charles Pilcher Temple, Lieut.-Colonel, Royal Berkshire Regt. For Action at Ginniss." He had become Lieutenant-Colonel in July 1886, and from 1887 to 1891 commanded the 1st Battn. Princess Charlotte of Wales's (Royal Berkshire) Regt. From 1892 to 1895 he commanded Regimental District No. 29, and he was Assistant Adjutant-General, Cork District, from 1895 to 1902, in which latter year he retired, having been promoted to Colonel in 1890.

Charles Pilcher Temple.

HEPPER, ALBERT JAMES, Major, was born at Gibraltar 24 Oct. 1839, 2nd son of the late Richard Lawless Hepper, of Gibraltar. He was educated at a private school; at King's College, London, and the Royal Military Academy, Woolwich, and entered the Royal Engineers in 1859. In 1867 he married Sophia Henrietta (died in 1907), youngest daughter of the late Richard Lees, of Oaken, Staffs, and they had five sons and two daughters: Sir H. A. Lawless Hepper, late Major R.E. (retired), born 30 Jan. 1870, Agent G.I.P. Railway, Bombay; Lieut.-Colonel L. L. Hepper, D.S.O., R.A., born 4 April, 1871; Florence Sophie (married H. Cradock-Watson, M.A.); Lieut.-Colonel E. C. Hepper, I.M.S., born 6 Oct. 1876; Major A. W. Hepper, R.E., born 5 Dec. 1878; Margaret; Captain J. E. Hepper, R.A.M.C., born 19 March, 1889. He became Captain in 1872, and Major in 1881; was Adjutant of Auxiliary Forces, 1877–84; commanded the Royal Engineers on lines of communication in Egypt 1884–85, with the Nile Expedition. He was in command of the Royal Engineers with the Nile Frontier Field Force, 1885–86, being present at the action of Ginniss (Despatches, 3rd Class Medjidie, and the Khedive's Bronze Star, Egyptian Medal, and created a Companion of the Distinguished Service Order) [London Gazette, 26 Nov. 1886]: "For action at Ginniss. Albert James Hepper, Major, Royal Engineers." In 1887 he was promoted Lieutenant-Colonel. From 1888 to 1890 Colonel Hepper was the Commandant of the Royal Engineers in Guernsey, and from 1890 to 1892 he was Assistant Commandant of the School of Military Engineering at Chatham. From 1892 to 1896, when he retired from the Army, he was a Member of the Ordnance Committee, and from 1897 to 1906 Engineering Inspector, Local Government Board. The "Times" of 26 April, 1915, says: "On 23 April, at 4, Durham Terrace, Westbourne Gardens, Colonel A. J. Hepper, D.S.O., R.E., retired, aged 75."

MONEY, GORDON LORN CAMPBELL, Major, was born 14 Sept. 1848, 3rd son of the late William J. H. Money, Bengal Civil Service, and Elizabeth, daughter of the late William Moffat, of Eden Hall, Roxburghshire. He was educated at a private school, and at the Royal Military College, Sandhurst, and joined the 79th Highlanders 8 Feb. 1868. He was promoted Lieut. in 1871; Captain in 1880, and Major in 1884. He served with the Nile Expedition, 1884–85, and for his services received the Medal and clasp and the Khedive's Bronze Star. On the 11th May, 1885, Major G. L. C. Money was appointed Assistant Military Secretary to Lieut.-General Sir Frederick Stephenson, commanding in Lower Egypt, and in that capacity took part in the operations in the Sudan in 1883 and 1886. He held the appointment until 1887; was mentioned in Sir F. Stephenson's Despatches 9 Feb. 1886, and created a Companion of the Distinguished Service Order [London Gazette, 26 Nov. 1886]: "For action at Ginniss. Gordon Lorn Campbell Money, Major, Cameron Highlanders." The fourth class of the Order of the Osmanieh was conferred upon Major Money by His Highness the Khedive. In 1888 he became Brevet Lieutenant-Colonel. In 1893 he married Ellin, 3rd daughter of the late Major-General Ross, I.S.C., and they have one son and two daughters. On the 21st May, 1894, Lieut.-Colonel G. L. C. Money, D.S.O., took over command of the regiment from Lieut.-Colonel A. Y. Leslie, who, owing to ill-health, had not been with the battalion since Aug. 1893, and Lieut.-Colonel Money had been acting in temporary command during his absence. On the 21st Jan. 1895, Lieut.-Colonel Money was appointed A.D.C. to the Queen with the brevet rank of Colonel. As he was the first A.D.C. to Queen Victoria selected from the Cameron Highlanders, his appointment was received in the regiment with the greatest pride and satisfaction. He arrived at Alexandria with the 1st Battn. Cameron Highlanders on 4 Oct. 1897; went up the Nile on 14 Jan. 1898, and on 8 April, 1898, "the troops were formed for the assault, the Cameron Highlanders, under Colonel G. L. C. Money, D.S.O., A.D.C., being deployed into line in front of the British Brigade." For its conduct during the battle the regiment received Royal permission for "Atbara" to be inscribed upon its colours and appointments. Colonel Money was mentioned in the Sirdar's Despatch of 24 May, 1898, and the Queen, in her congratulatory telegram to Sir H. Kitchener, said: "Am proud of the gallantry of my soldiers; so glad my Cameron Highlanders should have been amongst them." Lieut.-Colonel Money became Colonel 6 June, 1903. He commanded the Cameron Highlanders in the Battle of Omdurman (when his horse was shot under him), and was present at the Memorial Service for General Gordon at Khartum. He was mentioned in Sir H. Kitchener's Despatches of the 30th Sept. and 8th Dec. 1898, and created a C.B. [London Gazette, 15 Nov. 1898]. On the 15th Oct. 1898, Colonel Money was presented with an address of welcome in the Town Hall of Inverness. He received the Khedive's Medal with clasps for Atbara and Khartum, and the English Medal. Colonel Money commanded the 1st Battn. Cameron Highlanders till the 21st May, 1899. In 1901 he was appointed A.D.C. to Kind Edward VII.; was Brigadier-General on the Staff in Ceylon, and retired 14 Sept. 1905. He holds the Jubilee and Coronation Medals. He is a D.L. and a J.P. for Berwickshire. Brigadier-General Money's favourite recreations are shooting and fishing.

QUIRK, JOHN OWEN, Major, was born 13 Aug. 1847, 3rd son of the late Philip Quirk, of Knockaloe House, Bromborough, Cheshire, and of Annie Eliza, daughter of Edmund Brown Wilton, of Limerick. He was educated at a private school, and at Trinity College, Dublin (B.A.), and joined the 41st (The Welsh) Regt. on 1 Dec. 1869. He became Captain in 1880; and served in the Boer War of 1881, in the Transvaal Campaign, with the Natal Field Force. Colonel Andrew Haggard tells how Colonel Valentine Baker, late of the 10th Hussars, relinquished a high command in the Turkish Army to come to Egypt and reorganize the Egyptian Army. "Baker Pasha did his part of the business excessively well; but when all was ready, and the recruits for the new regiments were actually being raised by conscription among the young men in the provinces—when his lists of officers, both English and Egyptian, were all ready—there occurred a contretemps which was to rob him of all the fruits of his toil, and to prevent his becoming the Sirdar or Commander-in-Chief. Her Majesty the Queen intimated to her Ministers that she would not allow Baker Pasha to be in any position in which he would have English full-pay officers under his command. The whole thing was at a deadlock at once. What was to be done? Baker behaved splendidly. Although between two stools he had fallen to the ground—for he could not go back to Turkey, and could not command the new Egyptian Army—he handed over all his arrangements unconditionally to the British authorities, and told them to place them in the hands of any other man whom they might select. Another man was chosen in the person of Sir Evelyn Wood, V.C., and he became the Sirdar of the new Egyptian Army at a salary of £5,000 a year, while Baker . . . was relegated to the command of the gendarmerie, both horse and foot, all worthless troops, as they proved afterwards at the first battle of El Teb. . . . In addition to myself, Stuart Wortley, Slade and Pigott . . . I will give below the names of the others who joined the force of the Egyptians under Major-General Sir Evelyn Wood, V.C., G.C.M.G., K.C.B., himself an officer well deserving all the letters of the alphabet which a grateful War Office has tacked on to his name. The remainder of the little band under his orders from the first start off were as follows: Lieut.-Colonel Grenfell and Major C. Holled Smith, both of the 60th Royal Rifles; Lieut.-Colonel Fraser, C.M.G., Major Watson, Capt. and Brevet Major Chermside, Capt. Kitchener and Lieut. Mantell, all Sappers; Lieut.-Colonel Duncan, Capt. Wodehouse, Lieuts. Parsons, Rundle and Carter, Gunners; Lieut.-Colonel Taylor, 19th Hussars; Lieut. Sinclair, Indian Cavalry (the only Indian); Capt. and Brevet Major Parr, 13th Light Infantry, who, like Pigott, had been wounded in the leg while serving in the Mounted Infantry in the 1882 Campaign; Capt. Shakespear and Lieut. Marriott, Royal Marine Artillery; Capt. Owen Quirk, 41st Welsh Regt.; Major A. Singleton Wynne, 51st Regt.; Lieut. Chamley Turner, 53rd Shropshire Regt., and Lieut. Davidson, 79th Highlanders." Major Quirk served in the Egyptian Expedition of 1884 in the Sudan, being employed on transport duties, and was present at the Battles of El Teb and Tamai, and in the advance on Tamanieb. He was mentioned in Despatches, and received the Medal with clasp and the Bronze Star. He took part in the Sudan Expedition of 1884–85 (Nile), and was employed on the lines of communication, as A.A.G. to the Egyptian Army. He was present at the action of Ginniss (horse shot); was mentioned in Despatches; received a clasp to his Egyptian Medal, and was created a Companion of the Distinguished Service Order [London Gazette, 26 Nov. 1886]: "John Owen Quirk, Major, Welsh Regt. For action at Ginniss." He again saw active service in the Sudan with the Nile Field Force in 1889, as Commandant of Korosko, and for his services received the 3rd Class Osmanieh. Major Quirk became Lieutenant-Colonel in 1893; was created a C.B. in 1897; promoted Colonel 26 Jan. 1899, and commanded the 41st Regimental District until Jan. 1904. He married in 1875, Eugenie Marie, daughter of the late Octavius O'Brien, of Kildare Street, Dublin.

HUNTER, ARCHIBALD, Capt. and Brevet Major, was born 6 Sept. 1856. He was educated at Glasgow Academy, and Sandhurst; joined the Army as Sub-Lieutenant (unattached) 13 June, 1874; was gazetted to the 4th The King's Own Regt., afterwards Royal Lancaster Regt., 13 June, 1874; Lieutenant, Instructor of Musketry, 4th Foot, 25 Jan. 1879, to 19 April, 1880. He was Adjutant Royal Lancaster Regt. 20 April, 1880, to 11 Nov. 1882, and became Captain, Royal Lancaster Regt., 3 Aug. 1882. He was employed with the Egyptian Army 28 Feb. 1884, to 19 Jan. 1887; and 11 March, 1888, to April, 1899; served in the Sudan Expedition, 1884–85 (Nile), with the Egyptian Army. Colonel Andrew Haggard says, in "Under Crescent and Star" (page 331): "The black regiment . . . was the 9th Battn. of the Egyptian Army, commanded by Archibald Hunter, a splendid fellow, and . . . raised during the past year entirely from Sudanese negroes, many of them being those who had been sent back from Suakin, whilst others had come from Khartoum." He was mentioned in Despatches; received the Medal with clasp, and the Bronze Star; was given the Brevet of Major 15 June, 1885, and 4th Class Osmanieh. He again served in the Sudan 1885–86–89; was present at the action of Ginniss; was severely wounded; mentioned in Despatches; received the 3rd Class Medjidie, and was created a Companion of the Distinguished Service Order [London Gazette, 26 Nov. 1886]: "Archibald Hunter, Capt. and Brevet Major, R. Lanc. R. For action at Ginniss." Present at action of Arguin; at the action of Toski (wounded); in command of a Brigade of the Egyptian Army. He was mentioned in Despatches [London Gazette, 6 Sept. 1889]; received a clasp and the Brevet of Lieutenant-Colonel 17 Aug. 1889. He was promoted to Major 15 June, 1892; and was Governor of the Red Sea Littoral, and Commandant, Suakin, 11 Aug. 1892, to 28 July, 1894. He was Governor of the Frontier, and Commandant, Field Force, Egypt, 29 July, 1894, to 30 Nov. 1896. In the Expedition to Dongola in 1896, he commanded the Egyptian Infantry Division, taking part in the operations of the 7th June and 19th Sept. He was mentioned in Despatches [London Gazette, 3 Nov. 1896]; received the Medal and the Egyptian Medal with two clasps, and was promoted to Major-General for distinguished service 18 Nov. 1896. From 1 Dec. 1896, to 6 April, 1899, Major-General Hunter was Governor of Dongola Province, and Commandant, Field Force, Egypt. In the Nile Expedition of 1897 he was in command of columns, and took part in the action at Abu Hamed, in the occupation of Berber and the Flying Column to the Atbara. He was mentioned in Despatches [London Gazette, 25 Jan. 1898]; received the 2nd Class Osmanieh and two clasps to the Egyptian Medal. In the Nile Expedition of 1898 he commanded the four Infantry Divisions of the Egyptian Army, also the Cavalry Reconnaissances of the 30th March and 4th April, and was present at the Battles of Atbara and Khartoum. He was mentioned in Despatches [London Gazette, 24 May and 30 Sept. 1898]; was created a K.C.B.; thanked by both Houses of Parliament, and received two clasps to the Egyptian Medal. Sir Archibald Hunter was Major-General, in India, 14 May, 1899, to 5 May, 1901. He was Major-General (Chief of Staff), Natal, from 21 Sept. 1899, to 8 Oct. 1899; Chief of Staff, South Africa, from 9 Oct. 1899, to 9 Jan. 1900; Chief of Staff, Natal, from 10 Jan. 1900, to 5 March, 1900; and Lieutenant-General Infantry Division 6 March, 1900, to 5 May, 1901 (promoted to Lieutenant-General 6 March, 1900). His services in the South African War from 1899 to 1901 were as follows: Chief of Staff, South Africa, afterwards Chief of Staff, Natal. Operations in Natal, 1899, including operations at Rietfontein and Lombard's Kop. Defence of Ladysmith, including sortie of 7 Dec. 1899. In command of the 10th Division. Operations in Cape Colony, North of Orange River, April and May, 1900, including action at Ruidam. Operations in the Transvaal in May and June, 1900. In command of operations in Orange River Colony, July to Nov. 1900, including action at Wittebergen (29 July), and Witpoort. Commanded in Orange River Colony 9 Nov. 1900, to 24 Jan. 1901. Despatches [London Gazette, 8 Feb. 1901] (Sir G. S. White, 2 Dec. 1899, and 23 March, 1900, and Lord Roberts, 25 Sept. 1900), and Despatches [London Gazette, 16 April, 1901. Queen's Medal with six clasps. Promoted Lieutenant-General for distinguished service. In his "History of the Great Boer War," Sir A. Conan Doyle describes Sir A. Hunter as the "youngest and most dashing of British Generals," and says that in the operations when he occupied Heidelberg, "Ian Hamilton broke his collar-bone, and for a time the command of his division passed to Hunter—the one man, perhaps, whom the Army would regard as an adequate successor." From 6 May, 1901, to 30 Sept. 1903, Sir A. Hunter was Lieutenant-General, Scottish District, and he was G.O.C., Southern Army, India, from 30 Oct. 1903, to 29 Oct. 1908. He became General on 8 Dec. 1905. From 30 Sept. 1910, to 1 July, 1913, he was Governor and Commander-in-Chief at Gibraltar. He was created a G.C.B. in 1911, and a G.C.V.O. in 1912. General Hunter commanded the Aldershot Training Centre from 23 Aug. 1914, and the 4th Army in 1914. He is Colonel of the King's Own Lancaster Regt. In 1910 Sir A. Hunter married Mary, daughter of Hickson Fergusson and widow of the 2nd Lord Inverclyde. He was elected M.P. for Lancaster Division at the General Election in 1918 as a Coalition Unionist. There is a graphic account of the Sortie from Ladysmith on 7 Dec. 1899 (described by Sir Ian Hamilton as "a brilliant stroke of arms"), in General Sir Frederick Maurice's official "History of the War in South Africa, 1899–1902," published by Messrs. Hurst and Blackett. We cannot resist the temptation to quote it here: "The practice of the 94-pr. gun and a 4.7-in. Howitzer on Gun Hill had for some time been so harassing that Brevet Major D. Henderson, Argyll and Sutherland Highlanders, D.A.A.G. for Intelligence on Sir G. White's Staff, asked leave to make an attempt with 50 men to destroy them at night. Permission was at first refused; subsequently, however, it was decided to carry through the enterprise with a stronger body. A force of 650 men was therefore placed under the command of Major-General Sir A. Hunter, the Chief of the Staff. It consisted of 500 Natal Carbineers, under Colonel Royston; 100 Imperial Light Horse, under Lieut.-Colonel A. H. M. Edwards, 5th Dragoon Guards; 18 of the Corps of Guides, under Brevet Major D. Henderson; a detachment Royal Engineers, under Capt. G. H. Fowke, R.E., and a detachment of No. 10 Mountain Battery. The venture was perfectly successful. As a preliminary, the 1st Devon Regt., moving out after dark, entrenched in a covering position north of the Helpmakaar Ridge. Skilfully led by Major Henderson and his guides, the column, marching in sections, then covered the two miles of rough scrub-grown country between the Helpmakaar Ridge and Gun Hill without incident or confusion, despite the black darkness, and by 2 a.m. reached the base of the flat-topped under-feature whereon stood the Boer guns. Shortly before this the force had divided. The main body of the Natal Carbineers branched out to right and left to cover the flanks, and now, between these wings, 200 men, taken equally from the Imperial Light Horse and the rest of the Natal Carbineers, lined up for assault. The surprise was complete. Sweeping aside the piquet, which confronted them with a hurried fire, the troopers of the Imperial Light Horse broke into the work containing the 94-pr., the Natal Carbineers soon afterwards discovering that of the 4.7-in. Howitzer. Charges of cotton were fixed on the breeches and muzzles of both guns and successfully fired with fuses ignited by burning cigars. Sir A. Hunter then called for three cheers for H.M. the Queen, and collecting his force, of which Major Henderson and seven men were wounded, withdrew in safety, taking with him a Maxim captured on the hill. By 7 a.m. all were back in Ladysmith."

Archibald Hunter.

There is an appreciation of Sir Archibald Hunter written by the late G. W. Steevens in "With Kitchener to Khartum": "If the Sirdar is the brain of the Egyptian Army, General Hunter is its sword-arm. First and above everything he is a fighter. For fourteen years he has been in the front of all the fighting on the Southern border. He was Intelligence Officer during the anxious days before Ginnis, when the Camerons and 9th Sudanese were beset by triumphant Dervishes in Kosheh fort, and reinforcements were far to the northward. Going out on a sortie one day, he lingered behind the retiring force to pick off Dervishes with a rifle he was wont to carry on such occasions: there he received a wound in the shoulder which he is not quit of to-day. When Nejumi came down in '89, Hunter was in the front of everything: he fought all day at the head of the blacks at Argin, and commanded a brigade of them at Toski. Here he was again wounded—a spear-thrust in the arm while he was charging the thickest of the dervishes at the head of the 13th. Thereafter he was Governor of the frontier at Halfa, Governor of the frontier at Dongola, Governor of the frontier at Berber—always on the frontier. When there was fighting he always led the way to it with his blacks, whom he loves like children, and who love him like a father. Fourteen years of bugle and bullet by night and day, in summer and winter, fighting dervishes, dervishes, year in and year out—till fighting dervishes has come to be a holy mission pursued with zeal and fanaticism. Hunter Pasha is the crusader of the nineteenth century. In all he is and does he is the true knight-errant—a paladin drifted into his wrong century. He is one of those happy men whom nature has made all in one piece—consistent, simple, unvarying; everything he does is just like him. He is short and thick-set; but that, instead of making him unromantic, only draws your eye to his long sword. From the feather in his helmet to the spurs on his heels, he is all energy and dancing triumph; every movement is vivacious, and he walks with his keen, conquering hazel eye looking out and upwards, like an eagle's. Sometimes you will see on his face a look of strain and tension, which tells of the wound he always carries with him. Then you will see him lolling under a palm tree, while his staff are sitting on chairs, light brown hair rumpled over his bare head, like a happy schoolboy. When I first saw him thus, being blind, I conceived him a subaltern, and offered opinions with indecorous freedom. He left the error to rebuke itself. Reconnoitring almost alone up to the muzzles of the enemy's rifles, charging bare-headed and cheering on his blacks, going without his rest to watch over the comfort of the wounded, he is always the same—always the same impossible hero of a book of chivalry. He is renowned as a brave man even among British officers: you know what that means. But he is much more than a tilting knight-errant: he is one of the finest leaders of troops in the Army. Report has it that the Sirdar, knowing his worth, leaves the handling of the actual fighting largely to Hunter, and he never fails to plan and execute a masterly victory. A sound and brilliant general, you would say that his one fault was his reckless daring; but that too, in an army of semi-savages, is a necessary quality of generalship. Furthermore, they say he is as good in an office as he is in action. Above all, he can stir and captivate and lead men. 'General Archie' is the wonder and the darling of all the Egyptian Army."

George Evan Lloyd.

LLOYD, GEORGE EVAN, Capt., was born in 1855, son of the Rev. Rhys Thomas Lloyd (brother of the 1st Baronet, of Bronwydd, Cardiganshire), and of Anna, daughter of Lewis Lloyd, Esq., of Nantgwilt, co. Radnor. He served in the Afghan War, 1878–79 (Medal and clasp). For his services in the Sudan

Campaign in 1885–86, he was created a Companion of the Distinguished Service Order [London Gazette, 26 Nov. 1886]: "George Evan Lloyd, Capt. and Brevet Major, South Yorkshire Regt. For action at Ginniss." The Insignia of the Order were presented to him by Queen Victoria. He became Major, South Staffordshire Regt., and was attached to the Egyptian Army, with the temporary rank of Lieutenant-Colonel. He held the 3rd Class Medjidie. Lieut.-Colonel G. E. Lloyd died on 29 Nov. 1900.

MARRIOTT, REGINALD ADAMS, Capt. and Brevet Major, was born in Nov. 1857; joined the Royal Marine Artillery in Oct. 1875. He served on H.M.S. Monarch, and during the French operations at Tunis was employed as Secretary to the Sfax Commission. On the Institution of the Distinguished Service Order, Capt. Marriott was selected specially for services rendered before the bombardment of Alexandria, when he inspected the Mex Forts in the guise of an Italian ship's stoker; for work in the Consulate at Alexandria before and during the massacre; and generally for the excellence of the training and special equipment of the Egyptian Camel Corps, which acted as Mounted Infantry for the River Column in the Gordon Relief Expedition. Capt. Marriott was of the first landing party directly after the bombardment, and his Order was given him partly for work done before that, so he could certainly claim to be one of the very first Companions of the Distinguished Service Order. He afterwards served with the Royal Marine Battn. at Kassassin and Tel-el-Kebir, being mentioned in Despatches. He joined the Egyptian Army from the day of its formation, and was first Drill and Musketry Instructor to the native recruits, and subsequently organized and commanded the Egyptian Camel Corps in the Nile Expedition, 1885–86. Colonel Andrew Haggard describes on page 388 of "Under Crescent and Star" how, "although Marriott and Smith-Dorrien, both Egyptians, pushed on with both the Egyptian and British Camel Corps and Mounted Infantry, and captured nine of the enemy's barges laden with arms and food, Abri was as far as the remainder of the troops went up the Nile. In fact, the advance on Abri ended the campaign." He was given the Brevet of Major 23 March, 1886; was mentioned in Despatches, and created a Companion of the Distinguished Service Order [London Gazette, 26 Nov. 1886]: "Reginald Adams Marriott, Capt. and Brevet Major, Royal Marine Artillery. For the action at Ginniss." The Insignia of the Order were presented to him by Queen Victoria on the first occasion of the Investiture of the Order 17 Dec. 1886. He was afterwards invited with others to breakfast at Osborne, where they signed their names in the Queen's birthday-book. Capt. Marriott, for his services in Egypt, also received the Medal with four clasps, the 4th Class Osmanieh and the 5th Class Medjidie. He was in the Naval Intelligence Department for five years, from its formation in 1887. After Major Marriott's retirement from the Royal Marine Artillery on 2 Aug. 1891, he joined H.M. Prison Service, and has been Governor of Lincoln, Chelmsford and Lewes Prisons. He was ent to the Intelligence Department of the Admiralty during the war. He s an acknowledged linguist, and has written on natural science, championng General Drayson's discovery in astronomy, in "The Change of Climate and its Cause," "The Glacial Epoch Explained," and other pamphlets on geology and kindred subjects.

Reginald Adams Marriott.

SMITH-DORRIEN, HORACE LOCKWOOD, Capt., was born 26 May, 1858, son of Colonel R. A. Smith-Dorrien and Mrs. Smith-Dorrien, of Haresfoot, Berkhampstead. He was educated at Harrow, and entered the Sherwood Foresters (Derby Regt.) on 26 Feb. 1876. He served in the Zulu War of 1879; was one of the few survivors of Isandhlwana, and was recommended for a V.C.; was at the Battle of Ulundi; was mentioned in Despatches [London Gazette, 15 and 21 March, 1879], and received the Medal and clasp. He took part in the Egyptian Expedition of 1882; raised and commanded a corps of Mounted Infantry; received a Medal and clasp, and the Bronze Star. Sir Evelyn Wood wrote: "Horace Smith-Dorrien has done brilliant work in North and South Africa and in India. It is needless to repeat what the Commander-in-Chief wrote of his conduct in the Retreat from Mons, which must have made his wife and all his friends proud. In 1882 I was left twelve miles outside Alexandria with six battalions to cover a frontage of over five miles, which in the previous weeks, before the departure of another brigade, had been penetrated by small parties of the enemy, sixteen of whom had been killed in one garden. I sent an order into Alexandria for a smart subaltern, who was to go to the Khedive's stable and all the saddlers' shops and produce in one day some mounted infantry. Smith-Dorrien received the order at 1.30 p.m., and at 6.30., with twenty-one horses, three mules and a donkey, carrying Derbyshire men, the Sherwood Foresters—few of whom had ridden before—he passed me at Ramleh, and went out into the desert, engaged an Egyptian outpost, killed its commander, and never let the enemy inside our line of outposts again." Lieut. Smith-Dorrien became Captain 22 Aug. 1882. He served with the Egyptian Army in the Nile Expedition (1884), and with Mounted Infantry in the Sudan Expedition (1885) (clasp). He again saw active service in the Sudan in 1885–86, with the Frontier Field Force. For his services in this last campaign Capt. Smith-Dorrien was mentioned in Despatches, awarded the 4th Class Medjidie and created a Companion of the Distinguished Service Order [London Gazette, 26 Nov. 1886]: "Horace Lockwood Smith-Dorrien, Capt., Derbyshire Regt. For action at Ginniss." The Insignia were presented to him by the Queen. At the Battle of Ginniss, when the Dervishes were retreating, the cavalry posted to cut them off had failed to do so. Capt. Smith-Dorrien, at that time a Lieutenant-Colonel on the Staff of the Egyptian Army, was thereupon ordered to take a mixed mounted force of cavalry and mounted infantry, and to pursue—with strict orders not to go beyond—to Koheymatto, 19 miles distant. He, however, took on himself to go 60 miles, cutting across the desert to cut the Dervishes off at Absarat, accomplishing this in 23 hours, cutting off and capturing all the enemy's river transport, many prisoners and booty. Being successful, his disobedience was rewarded with the D.S.O., as above recorded. It was one of the first ever given. In 1887 he received the 4th Class of the Osmanieh, and the same year joined the Staff College, where he gained the *p.s.c.* He became Major 11 May, 1892; was D.A.A.G., Bengal, 1893–94; A.A.G., Bengal, 1894–96. He was D.A.A.G. of a brigade in the Chitral Relief Force in 1895. In 1897–98 he served in the Sherwood Foresters in the Tirah Campaign, on the North-West Frontier of India; was mentioned in Despatches [London Gazette, 30 Sept. 1898]; was given the Brevet of Lieutenant-Colonel 20 May, 1898; received the Medal and two clasps. He served with the Nile Expedition of 1898, and in the pursuit after the Battle of Omdurman was the first to break into the Mahdi's house. He commanded the troops which accompanied Lord Kitchener to Fashoda. He was mentioned in Despatches [London Gazette, 30 Sept. 1898]; received the Brevet of Colonel 16 Nov. 1898, and the Medal. He served in the South African War, 1899–1900, first in command of the 1st Battn. Sherwood Foresters, and then as a Major-General commanding a brigade and a division. At Paardeberg, Sir Conan Doyle writes in his "Great Boer War" (page 253), "Smith-Dorrien's Brigade, who were winning in the western army something of the reputation which Hart's Irishmen had won in Natal, were placed astride of the river to the west, with orders to push gradually up, as occasion served, using trenches for their approach." Sir Conan Doyle goes on to describe the battle, and later says: "The two brigades at either end of the Boer lines had lost no chance of pushing in, and now they had come within striking distance. On the night of 26 Feb. it was determined that Smith-Dorrien's men should try their luck. The front trenches of the British were at that time seven hundred yards from the Boer lines. They were held by the Gordons and by the Canadians, the latter being the nearer to the river. It is worth while entering into details as to the arrangement of the attack, as the success of the campaign was at least accelerated by it. The orders were that the Canadians were to advance, the Gordons to support, and the Shropshires to take such a position on the left as would outflank any counter-attack upon the part of the Boers. The Canadians advanced in the darkness of the early morning before the rise of the moon. The front rank held their rifles in the left hand and each extended right hand grasped the sleeve of the man next it. The rear rank had their rifles slung and carried spades. Nearest the river bank were two companies (G and H), who were followed by the 7th Company of Royal Engineers carrying picks and empty sand-bags. The long line stole through a pitchy darkness, knowing that at any instant a blaze of fire such as flamed before the Highlanders at Magersfontein might crash out in front of them. A hundred, two, three, four, five hundred paces were taken. They knew that they must be close upon the trenches. If they could only creep silently enough, they might spring upon the defenders unannounced. On and on they stole, step by step, praying for silence. Would the gentle shuffle of feet be heard by the men who lay within stone-throw of them? Their hopes had begun to rise when there broke upon the silence of the night a resonant metallic rattle, the thud of a falling man, an empty clatter! They had walked into a line of meat-cans slung upon a wire. By measurement it was only ninety yards from the trench. At that instant a single rifle sounded, and the Canadians hurled themselves down upon the ground. Their bodies had hardly touched it when from a line six hundred yards long there came one furious glare of rifle fire, with a hiss like water on a red-hot plate, of speeding bullets. In that terrible red light the men as they lay and scraped desperately for cover could see the heads of the Boers pop up and down, and the fringe of rifle barrels quiver and gleam. How the regiment, lying helpless under this fire, escaped destruction is extraordinary. To rush the trench in the face of such a continuous blast of lead seemed impossible, and it was equally impossible to remain where they were. In a short time the moon would be up, and they would be picked off to a man. The outer companies upon the plain were ordered to retire. Breaking up into loose order, they made their way back with surprisingly little loss; but a strange contretemps occurred, for, leaping suddenly into a trench held by the Gordons, they transfixed themselves upon the bayonets of the men. A subaltern and twelve men received bayonet thrusts—none of them fortunately of a very serious nature." He was promoted to Major-General 11 Feb. 1900, for distinguished service at the Battle of Paardeberg; was mentioned in Despatches [London Gazette, 8 Feb. and 16 April, 1901, and 29 July, 1902], and received the Queen's Medal with four clasps. He was Adjutant-General in India, 1901–3; commanded the 4th (Quetta) Division in India, 1903–7; was created a K.C.B. in 1904; promoted to Lieutenant-General on 9 April, 1906, and became Commander-in-Chief, Aldershot, 1907. He was promoted to General 10 Aug. 1912; held the Southern command, 1912–14; and was created a G.C.B. in 1913. General Sir Horace Smith-Dorrien commanded first the 2nd Army Corps, and then the 2nd Army, British Expeditionary Force, 1914–15. The Commander-in-Chief said in his Despatches regarding the Battle of Le Cateau: "I cannot close the brief account of this glorious stand without

Horace L. Smith-Dorrien.

putting on record my deep appreciation of the services of Sir Horace Smith-Dorrien. I say without hesitation that the saving of the left wing of the Army under my command on the morning of 26th Aug. could never have been accomplished unless a Commander of rare and unusual coolness, intrepidity and determination had been present to personally conduct the operation." Major A. Corbett Smith says in his "Retreat from Mons": "If the Commander-in-Chief owed much to General Smith-Dorrien, I can only say that the Second Corps would have stormed the gates of Hell for their leader, and would have trusted in him implicitly to bring them through." When Lord French wrote his book, "1914," he had changed his mind about General Smith-Dorrien. The Hon. John Fortescue reviewed the Field-Marshal's book in the "Quarterly Review" of Oct. 1919. Mr. Fortescue gives Lord French credit for his own part in the war. He says: "On 19 Oct. the 1st Corps came in from the Aisne, and Lord French had to make up his mind whether he should use it to reinforce his sorely-tried troops from Menin southward to La Bassée, or to meet, by a counter-offensive, the enemy's threats against Ypres and the Yser. On the one hand, if the Germans succeeded in driving a wedge through the British at some point south of Menin—and the place of junction with the French about La Bassée was likely to be chosen for the purpose—then they would either force the British Army to surrender or drive it into the sea. On the other hand, if they broke through the line about Ypres or to the north of it, they would reach the seaboard and master the Channel Ports. Lord French, as he puts it, had to choose between the certain disaster of losing the Channel Ports and the less certain though, if it should overtake him, more overwhelming disaster of being driven into the sea. He decided to avert the certain disaster, thereby taking terrible risks, and the event showed that his judgment was correct. This, in our opinion, is the one great thing that Lord French did during his period of command on the Western Front, and too gladly admit that it was really and truly great. He had every right to select for himself the title of Lord French of Ypres." Mr. Fortescue also says: "No man, it has been well said, was ever written down except by himself, and we wish that Lord French had pondered this aphorism before he sat down to write his book. The Field-Marshal, at the opening of the war, enjoyed a military reputation which was second only to Lord Kitchener's in this country, and he had worthily earned it. The memories of South Africa are swamped in those of the past five terrible years, yet there are some who have not yet forgotten the name of Colesberg, and the excellent and audacious service of General French, which is associated with that name. At the close of the Boer War no one was surprised to see him rise successively to the command of the 1st Army Corps at Aldershot, to the Inspectorship-General of the Forces, and to the supreme post of Chief of the General Staff. Lord Haldane has testified to the valuable assistance which he received from Sir John French in preparing the forces of the Empire for the great struggle which has been so recently brought to a successful end: and this is a thing which we must never forget. The time will come when the country will set aside old political prejudices and acknowledge the vast debt which it owes to Lord Haldane: and then the names of the officers who were associated with him in his reorganization of the forces of the Empire will likewise be remembered with honour. The country, therefore, heard with confidence and satisfaction of the appointment of Sir John French to command the British Expeditionary Force in Aug. 1914. People hardly realized that his army was, though small in numbers, incomparably the best trained, the best equipped, the best organized and the best disciplined that Britain had ever put into the field." A good part of Mr. Fortescue's review of Lord French's book, however, is given up to a criticism of Lord French's change of front about General Smith-Dorrien, whom he had previously so highly praised in his Despatches. Major-General Sir F. Maurice, K.C.M.G., wrote an article in the "National Review" for Nov. 1919, on "The 'Unnecessary' Battle of Le Cateau." General Maurice was at that time on the Staff of Sir Hubert Hamilton, Commanding the 3rd Division of the 2nd Corps. He tells us how the 7th Brigade had been marching and fighting since 3 a.m. on the 25th: moreover, a good part of the men had not reached their billets at Caudry. "General Hamilton," he says, "then made up his mind that the 3rd Division was not in condition to carry out Sir Horace's orders for retreat, and at once went off to the 2nd Corps Headquarters, which were close by. Hamilton took me with him in case he wished to send me back with fresh orders. Almost simultaneously, Allenby arrived with Vaughan, his Senior General Staff Officer, and a conference with Sir Horace took place between 1 and 2 a.m. I was not present at the conference, but immediately it was over Hamilton came out and said to me: 'Smith-Dorrien is a man. He has decided to stand and fight.' On the way back to our headquarters he told me that he had informed Sir Horace that he did not think he could get the 3rd Division formed for retreat before 9 a.m., that Allenby had said that, in his opinion, it would be necessary to retire before daylight if we were to avoid a battle, and that owing to his division being so scattered, he would be unable to cover the retreat the next morning. Sir Horace, thereupon determined to take command of the cavalry, of the 19th Brigade, and of the 4th Division, in addition to his own corps, and to fight. This version of Allenby's conversation with Sir Horace is, I may point out, very different to that given by Lord French." At the conclusion of his article Sir F. Maurice says: "As to the strength and position of the German troops, we know that Sir Horace was right, and that Lord French was wrong. Personally, I believed at the time that Sir Horace's decision to fight on the 26th saved us from disaster, and everything that I have learnt since has confirmed me in that opinion. It required great courage to make such a decision, contrary to the orders of the Commander-in-Chief, and it was a decision which, I believe, history will not only justify but commend. A commander-in-chief is entitled to form his own opinion of a subordinate, and to act on that opinion, but when, after praising him publicly, he condemns him publicly, and for his change of opinion gives reasons which are wrong in almost every particular, his opinion ceases to carry weight." Mr. Fortescue, in his article

in the "Quarterly Review," goes fully into Lord French's somewhat belated criticisms of General Smith-Dorrien's action at Le Cateau, which he had previously praised. He describes the events leading up to the Battle of Le Cateau from the time when Sir James Grierson died suddenly and Lord French asked that Sir Herbert Plumer might take General Grierson's place in command of the 2nd Corps. Lord Kitchener preferred to send Sir Horace Smith-Dorrien, who had risen to fame in the Derbyshire regiment, which he commanded when the Transvaal War began. He held important staff appointments, and was specially selected to attend His Majesty the King during his visit to India in 1910-11. All soldiers had the highest opinion of his capacity in the field, which he had proved as a junior officer in Egypt and in high command in South Africa. Lord Kitchener's selection of this gallant officer was highly appreciated in the Army. Mr. Fortescue says: "The Field-Marshal's orders were for the retreat to be continued on the 26th, and General Smith-Dorrien had issued his commands accordingly to the 2nd Corps. It was past midnight, however, before he could ascertain the whereabouts of all his troops; and then he discovered that the 4th Division, which had joined the army on the 25th, was in isolation in advance of his line, that his troops were greatly exhausted, and that the cavalry was so weary and so much dispersed, that it could not be counted on longer to cover the retreat. He therefore took his memorable decision to stand and fight, in spite of the Field-Marshal's orders. Lord French condemns this resolution, omitting, however, to say anything about the situation of the 4th Division. . . . In his Despatch of 7 Sept. 1914, the Field-Marshal gave General Smith-Dorrien full credit for the cool courage he had shown in accepting battle at Le Cateau. Further, he by implication blamed the French General Sordet, for failing to help Smith-Dorrien. In the volume before us he takes back his praise, alleging that when he wrote his despatch, he was unaware of the service rendered by General Sordet: and he now contends that but for General Sordet, Sir Horace would have been pinned to his ground and surrounded. Now it is an indisputable fact, established by documentary evidence, that General Smith-Dorrien, in addition to writing his own thanks to General Sordet and recounting his obligations to him in a special order to his troops, reported within three days to Lord French himself the good help that he had received from General Sordet, and begged that thanks might be sent to him through General Joffre. . . . Lord French contends that without General Sordet, General Smith-Dorrien would never have escaped. Yet the safe retreat of the 2nd Corps was assured long before General Sordet came into action." Not long since, when the shooting began at Phœnix Park, a Roman Catholic priest, whose family has the proud distinction of having in old days killed the heir to the throne of England, the Earl of March, was speaking of the alarming outlook. This priest's sympathies are with the so-called ideals of the Sinn Feiners, though not altogether with the means they use to attain their objects in life. He said: "No, I don't think they'll shoot Lord French. After all, he is Irish and a famous soldier, and belongs to a good old Irish family. But they don't *altogether* approve of him." One gathers from "1914" that Lord French shares to the full the gallantry, the prejudice, the glorious inconsistency of the fellow-countrymen he has tried to govern. This Irish priest's family has been almost wiped out fighting for England in the Great War. Yet he resents the "meddlesomeness" of the English as much as any Sinn Feiner of them all. "Oh! that mine enemy had written a book!" said the wise man of old, and perhaps Lord French has in this case been his own worst enemy. But if he has by any means helped to bring peace to his torn and distracted country his literary indiscretions will surely be forgotten, or at least forgiven. In 1915, Sir Horace Smith-Dorrien was created a G.C.M.G. In 1915 and 1916 he commanded the East African Forces, which command a dangerous attack of pleuro-pneumonia compelled him to relinquish. He was made Grand Officier, Légion d'Honneur, by the French. In July, 1918, Sir Horace Smith-Dorrien was appointed Governor of Gibraltar. He married on 3 Sept. 1902, at St. Peter's, Eaton Square, Olive Crofton, eldest daughter of Colonel and Mrs. Schneider, of Oak Lea, Furness Abbey, and their children are: Grenfell Horace, Peter Lockwood and David Bromley. Sir Ian Hamilton said: "Smith-Dorrien was one of my two brigadiers in the great march up from Bloemfontein to Pretoria: the other being Bruce Hamilton. He always proved himself a commander of judgment and mettle." Sir Conan Doyle, in describing the northern operations from Jan. to April, 1901, in his "Great Boer War," says on page 436: "The town of Belfast was strongly held by Smith-Dorrien with 1,750 men, of which 1,300 were infantry belonging to the Royal Irish, the Shropshires and the Gordons. The perimeter of defence, however, was fifteen miles, and each little fort too far from its neighbour for mutual support, though connected with headquarters by telephone. It is probable that the leaders and burghers engaged in this very gallant attack were in part the same as those concerned in the successful attempt at Helvetia upon 29 Dec., for the assault was delivered in the same way, at the same hour, and apparently with the same primary object. This was to gain possession of the big 5-inch gun, which is as helpless by night as it is formidable by day. At Helvetia they attained their object, and even succeeded not merely in destroying, but in removing their gigantic trophy. At Belfast they would have performed the same feat had it not been for the foresight of General Smith-Dorrien, who had the heavy gun trundled back into the town every night." Sir Conan Doyle says on pages 446-448 of the "Great Boer War": "In the month of Jan. 1901 there had been a considerable concentration of the Transvaal Boers into that large triangle which is bounded by the Delagoa railway line upon the north, the Natal railway line upon the south, and the Swazi and Zulu frontiers upon the east. . . . Their concentration had not escaped the notice of the British military authorities, who welcomed any movement which might bring to a focus that resistance which had been so nebulous and elusive. Lord Kitchener having once seen the enemy fairly gathered into this huge cover, undertook the difficult task of driving it from end to end. For this enterprise General French was given the chief command, and had under his orders no fewer than seven columns, which started from different points of the Delagoa and of the Natal railway lines, keeping in touch with each other, and all trending south and east." . . . Smith-Dorrien's was the most easterly of the three columns that started from the Delagoa line, and his went from Wonderfontein and later moved on Carolina, and thence on Bothwell, near Lake Chrissie. "The arduous duty of passing supplies down from the line fell mainly upon him, and his force was in consequence larger than the others, consisting of 3,500 men with thirteen guns." Sir Conan Doyle tells us how the seven columns, like a huge drag-net, closed in upon the Boers. "Cavalry and mounted infantry were all hot upon the scent. Botha, however, was a leader of spirit, not to be hustled with impunity. Having several thousand burghers with him, it was evident that if he threw himself suddenly upon any part of the British line he might hope for a time to make an equal fight, and possibly to overwhelm it. Were Smith-Dorrien out of the way there would be a clear road of escape for his whole convoy to the north, while a defeat of any of the other columns would not help him much. It was on Smith-Dorrien, therefore, that he threw himself with great impetuosity. That general's force was, however, formidable, consisting of the Suffolks, West Yorks, and Camerons, 5th Lancers, 2nd Imperial Light Horse, and 3rd Mounted Infantry, with eight field guns and three heavy pieces. Such a force could hardly be defeated in the open, but no one can foresee the effect of a night surprise well pushed home, and such was the attack delivered by Botha at 3 a.m. upon 6 Feb., when his opponent was encamped at Bothwell Farm. The night was favourable to the attempt, as it was dark and misty. Fortunately, however, the British commander had fortified himself and was ready for an assault. The Boer forlorn hope came on with a gallant dash, driving a troop of loose horses in upon the outposts, and charging forward into the camp. The West Yorkshires, however, who bore the brunt of the attack, were veterans of the Tugela, who were no more to be flurried at three in the morning than at three in the afternoon. The attack was blown backwards, and twenty dead Boers, with their brave leader Spruyt, were left within the British lines. The main body of the Boers contented themselves with a heavy fusillade out of the darkness, which was answered and crushed by the return fire of the infantry. In the morning no trace save their dead was to be seen of the enemy, but twenty killed and fifty wounded in Smith-Dorrien's column showed how heavy had been the fire which had swept through the sleeping camp. The Carolina attack, which was to have co-operated with that of the Heidelbergers, was never delivered, through difficulties of the ground, and considerable recriminations ensued among the Boers in consequence. Beyond a series of skirmishes and rearguard actions this attack of Botha's was the one effort made to stay the course of French's columns. It did not succeed, however, in arresting them for an hour. From that day began a record of captures of men, herds, guns, and wagons, as the fugitives were rounded up from the north, the west and the south."

HAGGARD, ANDREW CHARLES PARKER, Lieut.-Colonel, was born at Bradenham Hall, Norfolk, 7 Feb. 1854, 5th son of the late William Meybohm Rider Haggard, and Ella, daughter and co-heiress of the late Bazett Doveton, E.I.C.S. He was educated at Westminster School; joined The King's Own Borderers, afterwards The King's Own Scottish Borderers, in 1873; served in India and at Aden; also on the Staff in Egypt, 1882; was Adjutant, 1st Reserve Depôt, Ismailia, 1882, until the close of the operations against Arabi Pasha. He was one of the 25 officers who, under Sir Evelyn Wood, V.C., in the year 1883, raised the new Egyptian Army, and owing to his knowledge of Arabic was sent to the different Provinces of Egypt to curb the injustices and cruelties of the Mudirs in their methods of raising recruits. He became Major and Second-in-Command of the 4th Battn. Egyptian Army, and subsequently Lieutenant-Colonel Commanding the 1st Battn. Being applied for by Admiral Sir William Hewett, V.C., Governor General of the Red Sea Littoral, he was attached to the Royal Navy and went on Special Service to Suakin in Feb. 1884, where he was instrumental in organizing the defences and in quelling a mutiny of two Black Regiments (one of which had previously served under General Gordon), which had deserted their posts to the danger of the capture of the town by the enemy, under Osman Digna. After assisting the landing of the Expeditionary Force under Sir Gerald Graham, V.C., he was attached to it, and was present at the Battle of Tamai and advance on Tamanieb (Medal with clasp, Khedive's Bronze Star; mentioned in Special Naval Despatches in April, 1884, and also in Army Despatches). He proceeded on H.M.S. Sphinx to Massowah; became Governor, and organized defences of that place in 1884; went subsequently to meet the Abyssinian brigand outlaw, Bal Ambaras Yasus Kefla, in the passes of the mountains of Bogos, and then on to Senheit and Keren; rescued a Swedish missionary from him, and induced him to open up the road to permit the egress of an Egyptian regiment cut off there under Khusru Bey, one of General Gordon's old officers. He surveyed part, and wrote itinerary of route to Khartoum, via Kassala, adopted by the Intelligence Department, War Office. He was in command of the 1st Battn. Egyptian Army at Suakin for a year, while the place was invested and constantly attacked by Osman Digna, 1884–85. He was present at the reconnaissance to Hasheen and operations of the British Army at Suakin, 1885 (4th Class Osmanieh); awarded "for distinguished services before the enemy" [London Gazette, 1885]. He was on a special recruiting commission with Brigadier General Yusuf Pasha Schudi, which reformed the abuses of the conscription in Upper Egypt. He commanded the 1st Battn. Egyptian Army in operations on the Nile, under General Sir Frederick Stephenson, including the Battle of Ginniss 1885–87, and subsequently commanded all the Egyptian troops on the Frontier. For his services in this campaign Lieut.-Colonel Haggard was mentioned in Despatches, and for those at the Battle of Ginniss he was awarded the, then new, distinction of the Companionship of the Distinguished Service Order, in the first Gazette of which Order his appointment was announced, 26 Nov. 1886: "For action at Ginniss, Andrew Charles Parker Haggard, Capt., King's Own Scottish Borderers." Lieut.-Colonel Andrew Haggard was awarded the 3rd Class of the Order of the Medjidieh for subsequent services in Egypt. In 1906 he married Ethel Fowler, of Whitestock Hall, Lancashire. He is a well-known sporting writer and novelist, and has published many French historical biographies. His favourite recreations are fishing, shooting and exploring, especially in connection with little-known rivers and districts in Canada. Since the outbreak of the Great War he has been instrumental in the formation of Veterans' Associations for men of both Services in British Columbia. A great many quotations have been made in this work from Colonel Haggard's valuable and charming book, "Under Crescent and Star."

Andrew C. P. Haggard.

RHODES, ELMHIRST, Capt., was born 28 April, 1858, son of the Rev. F. W. Rhodes, Rector of Bishop's Stortford. He was gazetted to the Royal Berkshire Regt. 25 May, 1878, and served in the Egyptian War of 1882, being present at the Surrender of Kafr Dowar (Medal and Bronze Star). He again saw active service in the Sudan Expedition of 1885 (Suakin); and was employed in the Signalling Department; reconnaissance to Hasheen; actions at Hasheen and Tofrek; operations at and destruction of Tamai. Despatches [London Gazette, 25 Aug. 1885]; two clasps. He served in the Sudan, 1885–86; with the Frontier Field Force, and was employed in the Signalling Department at Kosheh, and in the action at Ginniss; was mentioned in Despatches, and created a Companion of the Distinguished Service Order [London Gazette, 26 Nov. 1886]: "Elmhirst Rhodes, Capt., Royal Berkshire Regt. For action of Ginniss." The Insignia of the Order were presented to Capt. Rhodes by Queen Victoria. He became Major 30 Aug. 1893. Major Rhodes served from 1899 to 1900 as Director of Signalling to the South African Field Force. Afterwards as Station Commandant. He was present in the advance on Kimberley, including the actions at Belmont, Enslin, Modder River and Magersfontein. Operations in the Orange Free State, Feb. to May, 1900, including operations at Paardeberg (17 to 26 Feb.); actions at Poplar Grove and Dreifontein. Operations in the Transvaal, east of Pretoria, July to Nov. 1900. Operations in the Transvaal, west of Pretoria, July and Aug. 1900, including actions at Zilikat's Nek (slightly wounded). Operations in Orange River Colony, May to July, 1900. Operations in the Transvaal, Nov. 1900, to July, 1901. Operations in Capt Colony, July, 1901, to 31 May, 1902. He was mentioned in Despatches [London Gazette, 26 Jan. 1900, and 7 May and 10 Sept. 1901], and received the Queen's Medal with five clasps, and the King's Medal with two clasps. He retired 3 Oct. 1903.

FERRIER, JAMES ARCHIBALD, Capt., was born 25 March, 1854, at Malacca, Straits Settlements, son of Major Ilay Ferrier, of Belsyde, Linlithgowshire, and of Catherine Maria, daughter of E. de Wind, Esq. He was educated at St. James's Collegiate School, Jersey, and at the Royal Military Academy, Woolwich; was gazetted to the Royal Engineers on 9 Jan. 1873, and joined the Royal Engineers 15 Sept. 1873, as Lieutenant. He served in the Afghan War, 1878–80 (Medal). In 1884–85 he served in the Sudan Expedition (Nile), and received the Sudan Medal with Nile clasp, and the Khedive's Bronze Star. He was promoted to Captain 8 Jan. 1885, and again saw active service in the Sudan in 1885–86, with the Frontier Field Force. He was specially mentioned, War Office letter, Royal Engineers, No. 7700/4106, dated H.Q., W.O., 2 April, 1886, for his services when commanding the defence of Ambigole Wells, in Dec. 1885, against an incursion of Dervishes, who destroyed two and a half miles of the railway between Wady Halfa and the advanced base at Akasheh. He was created a Companion of the Distinguished Service Order [London Gazette, 26 Nov. 1886]: "James Archibald Ferrier, Capt., Royal Engineers. For the action at Ginniss." The Insignia were presented to him by Her Majesty Queen Victoria. He was mentioned in Despatches for the action of Ginniss. From 1888 to 1892 Capt. Ferrier was Adjutant, Royal Engineers. He was promoted to Major 3 May, 1892. Major Ferrier served in the Tirah Campaign, 1897–98, as Field Engineer, 1st Division, and afterwards on the Staff as Brigade Major. He was present at the capture of the Sampagha and Arhanga Passes, and in the operations against the Khani Khel Chamkanis, and in the operations in the Bazar Valley 25 to 30 Dec. 1897. He was mentioned in Despatches [London Gazette, 5 April, 1898]; was given the Brevet of Lieutenant-Colonel 20 May, 1898, and received the Medal with two clasps. From 1899 to 1903, he commanded the Training Battn. Royal Engineers; and from 1903 to 1904, was C.R.E., Natal, and in charge of Intelligence. He commanded troops in Natal, April to Aug. 1904. From 1905 to 1908 he was Chief Engineer, Eastern Coast Defences; and he was created a C.B. in 1907. He was Commandant, S.M.E., Chatham, 1908 to 1910, and was promoted to Major-General 5 June, 1910. From 1911 to 1914, he commanded the troops on the West Coast of Africa. In the European War General Ferrier was Garrison Commander (Coast Defences) 5 May, 1915, to 16 Feb. 1917. His services were acknowledged in the London Gazette of 24 Feb. 1917.

James Archibald Ferrier.

He retired 17 Feb. 1918. On 1 Nov. 1887, at Watford, Herts, General Ferrier married Louisa Emily, second daughter of J. F. Watkins, J.P. for Herts, and of Annie McMaster Shaw (Watkins), and their children are: Hay Ferrier, born 28 April, 1889, Captain, Indian Army; Tyrrell Ferrier, born 2 May, 1890, Captain, A.O.D., Inspector of Ordnance Machinery, and Alan Ferrier, M.C., born 26 May, 1894, Captain, Royal Engineers.

DAUBENEY, EDWARD KAYE, Capt., was born 3 May, 1858, son of the Rev. T. Daubeney, of Eastington, Cirencester. He was educated at Wellington, joined the Army 11 May, 1878, and served in the 80th Foot through the Sekukuni Campaign of 1878 and the Zulu War of 1879, being present at Ulundi (South African Medal and clasp for 1878–79). He became Lieutenant, South Staffordshire Regt., 1 Dec. 1880. In 1884–85 he served in the Nile Expedition, with the Egyptian Army (Egyptian Medal with clasp for the Nile and Khedive's Bronze Star). He was promoted to Captain 7 Aug. 1886, and again saw active service in the Sudan in 1886, as A.D.C. to the Brigadier-General commanding the Nile Frontier Force, Egypt, and was present at the action of Ginniss. He was mentioned in Despatches and created a Companion of the Distinguished Service Order [London Gazette, 26 Nov. 1886]: "Edward Kaye Daubeney, Capt., South Staffordshire Regt. For Action at Ginniss." Capt. Daubeney had been employed with the Egyptian Army from 28 Feb. 1884, to 30 Oct. 1885. He was promoted to Major, 18 Nov. 1896, and was Adjutant, Militia, 21 Jan. 1896, to 20 Jan. 1901. He became Lieutenant-Colonel 16 Oct. 1903, and was given the Brevet of Colonel 16 Oct. 1906, becoming substantive Colonel 4 July, 1908. Colonel Daubeney served in the European War from 1914, as temporary Brigadier-General commanding the Gloucestershire and Worcestershire Brigade. From 1915 he commanded the Warwickshire (Infantry) Brigade, and from 1916 the Reserve Highland Brigade. He retired with the rank of Brigadier-General in 1918. He was awarded the C.B.E. in 1919. He married Eileen Gertrude, daughter of Sir P. Fitzgerald, Bart., 19th Knight of Kerry, and they have one son.

BORROW, FREDERICK RONALD, Capt., joined the 81st Foot 8 Dec. 1877; served with his regiment in the Afghan War of 1878–79, and was present at the capture of Ali Masjid (Medal and clasp). He became Lieutenant 6 March, 1880, and again saw active service in the Nile Expedition of 1884–85, in the Egyptian Army (Medal with clasp and Khedive's Star). Also served in the operations of the Sudan Frontier Force in 1885–87, including the investment of Kosheh and the engagements at Ginniss and Sarras. He was mentioned in Despatches, received the 4th Class of the Osmanieh, and was created a Companion of the Distinguished Service Order [London Gazette, 26 Nov. 1886]: "Frederick Ronald Borrow, Capt., North Lancashire Regt. For the Action at Ginniss." He had been promoted to Captain 28 March, 1886. He was mentioned again in Despatches for the action at Sarras, and received the 3rd Class of the Medjidie. A further account of Capt. Borrow's services is given in this book in the account of Sir Leslie Rundle. Capt. Borrow died at Winchester 11 Dec. 1892.

ROMILLY, FREDERICK WILLIAM, Lieut., was born at Edinburgh, 22 July, 1854, second son of the late Lieut.-Colonel Romilly (who died in 1887; he was a brother of the 1st Baron Romilly) and of Lady Elizabeth, daughter of the 2nd Earl of Minto (she died in 1892). He was educated privately, and at the Royal Military Academy, Woolwich, and passed first in the examination for a direct commission in the Army, 1892, entering the Scots Fusilier Guards, 30 April, 1873, as Lieutenant. He served in the Egyptian Expedition of 1882–84, and was present at the action at Mahuta and at the Battle of Tel-el-Kebir, receiving the Medal with clasp and the Bronze Star. He was A.D.C. to the General Commanding in Egypt, 18 May, 1883, to 31 Dec. 1887, and, as A.D.C. to the General Commanding, was present at the battles of El Teb and Tamai. He was mentioned in Despatches [London Gazette, 6 May, 1884], and received two clasps. He served in the Guards' Camel Regt. in the Nile Expedition of 1884–85, and was present at the battles of Abu Klea and Gubat, and at the action near Metammeh (two clasps). In the Sudan in 1885–86 he served in the Egyptian Frontier Campaign, as A.D.C. to the General Officer Commanding, and was present at the action of Ginniss, and was mentioned in the Despatch of General Sir F. Stephenson, G.C.B., dated 2 Jan. 1886 [London Gazette, 9 Feb. 1886]: "As regards my own personal Staff, I venture to bring to your notice Major Gordon Money and Lieut. Romilly, Scots Guards. The latter, by his intelligence, professional acquirements and intimate knowledge of Soudanese warfare (this being his third campaign against the Soudanese), proved himself an excellent A.D.C. To both these officers I am indebted for much valuable assistance during the time they have been on my staff, and especially since I have taken the field." Lieut. Romilly received the 4th Class Medjidie, and was created a Companion of the Distinguished Service Order [London Gazette, 26 Nov. 1886]: "Frederick William Romilly, Lieut., Scots Guards. For Action at Ginniss.' He became Captain 1 April, 1887; was given the Brevet of Major 1 Jan. 1888, and was D.A.A.G., Malta, 23 Oct. 1890, to 22 Oct. 1893; was promoted to Major 12 Dec. 1894, and was Military Secretary to the Governor of Madras 18 March, 1896, to 23 Nov. 1898. He became Lieutenant-Colonel, Scots Guards, 1 April, 1900. Lieut.-Colonel Romilly served in the South African War from 1900 to 1902. He obtained command of the 2nd Battalion on arrival in South Africa, was wounded at Biddulphsberg 29 May, 1900, and commanded several mobile columns. He was selected by Sir A. Hunter to make the night assault on the "Slaapkranz" position, with his battalion, which successfully achieved the biggest surrender of the war, viz., that of Prinsloo and 5,000 Boers (1901). He was selected with his battalion to safeguard their present Majesties during their visit to Natal, just before Louis Botha's raid south. In Sept. 1901, he ran a blockhouse line from Potchefstroom across the Vaal River. In Oct. 1901, he ran a blockhouse line by Piet Retief to the Swazi border, and occupied same till the end of the war. He was wounded, mentioned in Despatches [London Gazette, 16 April, 1901], received the Queen's Medal with three clasps, the King's Medal with two clasps, and was created a C.B. He was given the Brevet of Colonel 10 Feb. 1904, and commanded the Scots Guards and Regimental District from 23 Sept. 1905, on which date he became substantive Colonel, until 9 Oct. 1909. In 1908 he was created a C.V.O., and on 22 July, 1911, he retired under the age limit. On mobilization in 1914, he became A.Q.M.G., 2nd Army, Central Force, which appointment he held until 12 March, 1916, and he was A.Q.M.G., Southern Army, Home Defence, up to 31 Aug. 1917, and was then appointed a Munition Area Inspector under the Ministry of Munitions, and so acted till March, 1919. Colonel Romilly married, on 27 Oct. 1891, at the Guards' Chapel, Wellington Barracks, Gwendoline Powys, daughter of the late Arthur Pratt Barlow and widow of Charles Russell Hole, Esq. He studied at the Slade School of Art, under Sir Edward Poynter. For nearly all its first five years he was Honorary Secretary and Treasurer of the Sporting Club in Cairo, and initiated nearly all its present attractions, and while in India he was President of the Ootacamund Hunt.

Frederick W. Romilly.

MAXWELL, JOHN GRENFELL, Lieut., was born 12 July, 1859, son of Robert Maxwell; was educated at Cheltenham College; gazetted to the 42nd Highlanders on 22 March, 1879; and became Lieutenant, Royal Highlanders, 1 July, 1881. He served in the Egyptian War of 1882, with the 1st Battn. Black Watch, and was present at the Battle of Tel-el-Kebir (Medal with clasp, Khedive's Bronze Star). He was Staff Captain, Military Police, Egypt, from 18 June, 1883, to July, 1883. Lieut. Maxwell served in the Sudan Expedition, 1884–85 (Nile), as Headquarters Commandant and Provost-Marshal, and employed in the Intelligence Department; was mentioned in Despatches [London Gazette, 25 Aug. 1885] (clasp). He served in the Sudan Expedition of 1885–86, as A.D.C. to General Grenfell, was present at the action of Ginniss, was mentioned in Despatches, and was created a Companion of the Distinguished Service Order [London Gazette, 26 Nov. 1886]: "John Grenfell Maxwell, Lieut., Royal Highlanders. For Action at Ginniss." He was present at the action of Gemaizah, also as A.D.C. to the General Officer Commanding, was mentioned in Despatches [London Gazette, 11 Jan. 1889], received the 4th Class Osmanieh, and a clasp. He was present at the Action of Toski, was mentioned in Despatches [London Gazette, 6 Sept. 1889] (Brevet of Major and clasp). He had been employed with the Egyptian Army 7 Sept. 1886, to 14 Sept. 1887, as A.D.C. to the Sirdar. He was promoted to Captain, 28 Sept. 1887. In 1896 he took part in the expedition to Dongola, commanding the 3rd Egyptian Brigade, and was present at the operations of 7 June and 19 Sept. He was mentioned in Despatches [London Gazette, 3 Nov. 1896], and was appointed Brevet Lieutenant-Colonel on 18 Nov. 1896, and received the Egyptian Medal with two clasps. For his services in the Nile Expedition of 1897 he was mentioned in Despatches [London Gazette, 25 Jan. 1898], and received a clasp to the Egyptian Medal. He was again employed with the Egyptian Army, 15 Sept. 1897, to 12 Feb. 1900, as A.D.C. and A.M.S. to the Sirdar. In the Nile Expedition of 1898 he commanded the 2nd Sudanese Brigade in the battles of the Atbara and Khartoum. He was mentioned in Despatches [London Gazette, 24 May, 1898, and 30 Sept. 1898], appointed Brevet Colonel 16 Nov. 1898, thanked by both Houses of Parliament, received a Medal and two clasps to the Egyptian Medal. He was on special service in South Africa from 10 April, 1900, to 25 Sept. 1902, as Major-General Commanding the 14th Brigade, 7th Division (1901); Military Governor of Pretoria, 1901–02; G.O.C., North-West Transvaal, 1902. He took part in the operations in the Orange Free State, Feb. to May, 1900, including operations at Vet River (5th and 6th May) and Zand River. Operations in the Transvaal in May and June, 1900, including actions near Johannesburg and Pretoria. He was mentioned in Despatches [London Gazette, 16 April, 1901, and 29 July, 1902], received the Queen's Medal with three clasps, the King's Medal with two clasps, was created a K.C.B. and a C.M.G. Sir John Maxwell was Chief Staff Officer (Brigadier-General on Staff), 3rd Army Corps, Ireland, 7 Nov. 1902, to 15 May, 1904; and was created a C.V.O.; and was Staff Officer to the Inspector-General of the Forces, 16 May, 1904, to 20 Dec. 1907. Major-General 1 Dec. 1906; General 3 June, 1919; was Chief Staff Officer, General Staff, Mediterranean, 21 Dec. 1907, to 3 Sept. 1908. From 4 Sept. 1908, to 19 Nov. 1912, he was G.O.C., Egypt; and he was promoted to Lieutenant-General 4 Sept. 1912. Sir John Maxwell was on Special Service in the European War, as Chief Liaison Officer with the French Army, 4 Aug. 1914, to Sept. 1914, and was G.O.C. in Egypt, Sept. 1914, to March, 1916. He was G.O.C.-in-C., Ireland, April, 1916, to Nov. 1916, when he was appointed G.O.C.-in-C. Northern Command, until 31 May, 1919. Sir John Maxwell has the Grand Cross of the Order of the Legion of Honour (France); 1st Class Order of the Nile (Egypt); White Eagle (Russia); Crown of Italy; Charles III. (Spain). He was created a G.C.B., 1917; and a K.C.M.G., 1916. He married in 1892, Louise Selina, only daughter of the late C. W. Bonynge, of 42, Prince's Gate, London, S.W., and they have one daughter, married 1 July, 1919, to Lieut. Clifford Carver, of Locust Valley, Long Island, U.S.A.

Mr. W. T. Massey, in "The Desert Campaigns" (published by Messrs. Constable in 1918), gives some account of General Maxwell's work in Egypt: "I arrived in Egypt when the concern of officials had been greatly lessened by the improvement in the outlook. I saw the first 30,000 Australian and New Zealand troops to take part in the war set foot in Egypt, and their physique and 'stand-no-nonsense' attitude greatly impressed the people with the fact that we were determined to go through with the war, and that the Mother-country had a mighty reserve in Britons overseas. Though there were undercurrents, more or less strong, when the Turks got to the Canal early in the following year, and when the Grand Sheikh of the Senussi became an open enemy, the Egyptian people from an uncertain quantity became well in hand. For this the Empire had to thank the officials of the Residency, and perhaps more particularly General Maxwell, commanding the forces in Egypt, whose policy, firm and just, was based on a deep knowledge of the Egyptian character, and was framed to serve our highest interests at a point which, at the time, was not an over strong link in the Imperial chain. Sir John Maxwell's initial success had an important bearing on future events, and his work, sterling as it was held to be at the time, will be even more highly appraised as the years roll on. We have not always been so fortunate in the choice of our administrators in Egypt. On the Young Turk Party arriving at a decision which spelt ruin for Turkey, it became vitally necessary to prepare for the defence of the Suez Canal. At all costs that highway connecting the seas and countries of East and West must be kept open, and it was just as much the concern of neutrals as of the Allies that no enemy hand should grasp it. . . We took the Canal defences in hand in Nov., although a strong military element believed no serious attempt to get to the Canal would ever be made. I confess their arguments at the time convinced me of the impossibility of an advance to the Canal by any substantial body, but subsequent events proved that given resources and men the desert of Sinai can be crossed by armies just as it was by Napoleon, by Mohammed Ali and by the warriors of the ancient kings. General Maxwell accepted a scheme prepared by Sir Murdoch Macdonald, Under-Secretary for Public Works in Egypt, an engineer who has planned nearly all the improvements effected in the country since the Assouan Dam was opened, in the building of which he had taken a very responsible part. East of the northern end of the Canal to beyond Pelusium the desert is below the level of the sea. It was decided to flood this area, but, instead of opening a channel through the low sand dunes on the shore, Sir Murdoch proposed that the Canal bank should be cut in a few places to flood many miles of the desert, so as to make a water defence to the Canal for some eighteen or twenty miles of its length. This was a comparatively simple matter in expert hands, and, at the cost of a few thousand sandbags and some cheap labour, many troops were spared for other sections which could not be so readily defended. This reduced the line of front to between sixty or seventy miles, and of this length the Bitter Lakes should be omitted, because naval patrol launches took over the duty of guarding them. A few defence posts were built and entrenched on the east bank to cover certain ferries, but the main defences in the early days were on the west bank, and consisted of trenches from which attempts to cross the water could be repelled. The railway and the Sweet Water Canal, which brought Nile water to the labourers who excavated the Suez Canal, and was now utilized to supply the drinking water for our troops, were protected, and armoured and other trains were kept at strategic points for the movements of troops. . . . General Maxwell had to find new troops for the Canal zone. There were plenty available. On the Canal were battalions of Indian regulars and regiments of Imperial Service troops. They were very good, and it went hard with anyone who met a patrol and did not know the password."

We quote some passages from G. W. Steevens's account of the battles of the Atbara and of Omdurman ("With Kitchener to Khartum," page 58 and following pages): "The Second Brigade consisted of three Sudanese battalions and one Egyptian, the 12th, 13th and 14th Sudanese (Townshend, Collinson and Shekleton Beys), and the 8th Egyptian under Kiloussi Bey, a soldierly old Turk who went through the Russo-Turkish War. Lieut.-Colonel Maxwell commanded it—an officer who has served in the Egyptian Army through all its successes; big, masterful, keen and reputed an especially able administrator, he is but just entering middle age, and ought to have a brilliant career before him. This brigade was quartered at Assillem, about half-way between Berber and the Atbara." Mr. Steevens says that in the Battle of the Atbara only the generals were allowed to ride or the casualties would have been greater. "Generals Hunter, Macdonald and Maxwell all rode over the trenches at the head of their men. The Second Brigade condescended to a mere four miles an hour, and 'By George! you know,' said the Bey, 'they're lovely; they're rippers. I've seen Sikhs and I've seen Gurkhas, and these are good enough for me. This has been the happiest day of my life. I wasn't happier the day I got the D.S.O. than I've been to-day.'" In describing the Battle of Omdurman Mr. Steevens wrote: "Our camp for the night of 1 Sept. was in the village of Agaiga, a mile south of Herreri Hill. On our left front was another hill, higher but single-peaked and rounder—Gebel Surgham. In front the ground was open for five miles or so—sand and grass broken only by a few folds—with a group of hills beyond. The force had formed up in position in the afternoon, when the Dervishes had followed the cavalry home, and had remained under arms all night. At half-past five in the morning, when the first howitzer shell from opposite Omdurman opened the day's work, every man was in his place. The line formed an obtuse angle; the order of brigades and battalions, counting from the left, was the following: Lyttelton's 2nd British (Rifle Brigade, Lancashire Fusiliers, Northumberland Fusiliers, Grenadier Guards), Wauchope's 1st British (Warwicks, Seaforths, Camerons, Lincolns); Maxwell's 2nd Egyptian (14th, 12th, 13th Sudanese, and 8th Egyptian) in support. Here came the point of the angle; to the right of it were Macdonald's 1st Egyptian (11th, 10th, 9th Sudanese, 2nd Egyptian supporting); Lewis's 3rd Egyptian (4th, 15th and 3rd and 7th Egyptian, in column on the right flank). Collinson's 4th Egyptian Brigade (1st, 5th, 17th and 18th Egyptian) was in reserve in the village. All the Egyptian battalions in the front were in their usual formation, with four companies in line and two in support. The British had six in line and two in support. On the extreme left were the 32nd Field Battery; the Maxims and Egyptian field-guns were mounted at intervals in the infantry line. The cavalry had gone out at the first streak of grey, British on the left, as usual, Egyptians with camel corps and horse battery from the right, moving across our front. The gunboats lay with steam up off the village. Light stole quietly into the sky behind us. There was no sound from the plain or the hills before us; there was hardly a sound from our own line. Everybody was very silent but very curious. Would they be so mad as to come out and run their heads into our fire? It seemed beyond hoping for; yet certainly they had been full of war the day before. But most of us were expecting instantly the order to advance on Omdurman. A trooper rose out of the dimness from behind the shoulder of Gebel Surgham, grew larger and plainer, spurred violently up to the line and inside. A couple more were silhouetted across our front. Then the electric whisper came racing down the line; they were coming. The Lancers came in on the left; the Egyptian mounted troops drew like a curtain across us from left to right. As they passed a flicker of white flags began to extend and fill up the front in their place. The noise of something began to creep in upon us; it cleared and divided into the tap of drums and the far-away surf of raucous war-cries. A shiver of expectancy thrilled along our army, and then a sigh of content. They were coming on, Allah help them! They were coming on. It was now half-past six. The flags seemed still very distant, the roar very faint, and the thud of our first guns was almost startling. It may have startled them too, but it startled them into life. The line of flags swung forward, and a mass of flying white linen swung forward with it too. They came very fast, and they came very straight; and then presently they came no further. With a crash the bullets leaped out of the British rifles. It began with the Guards and Warwicks—section volleys at 2,000 yards, then, as the Dervishes edged rightward, it ran along to the Highlanders, the Lincolns and to Maxwell's Brigade. The British stood up in double rank behind their zariba; the blacks lay down in their shelter-trench. Both poured out death as fast as they could load and press trigger. Shrapnel whistled and Maxims growled savagely. From all the line came perpetual fire, fire, fire, and shrieked forth in great gusts of destruction. And the enemy? No white troops would have faced that torrent of death for five minutes, but the Baggara and the blacks came on. The torrent swept into them and hurled them down in whole companies. You saw a rigid line gather itself up and rush on evenly; then, before a shrapnel shell or a Maxim, the line suddenly quivered and stopped. The line was yet unbroken, but it was quite still. But other lines gathered up, again, again and yet again; they went down, and yet others rushed on. . . . It was the last day of Mahdism and the greatest. They could never get near and yet they refused to hold back. . . . It was not a battle but an execution. . . . Only by now—small wonder—they were not coming on. They were not driven back; they were all killed in coming on. . . . We waited half an hour or so and then the sudden bugle called us to our feet. 'Advance,' it cried—'to Omdurman,' added we. Slowly the force broke up and expanded. The evident intention was to march in echelon of brigades—the Second British leading along the river, the First British on their right rear, then Maxwell's, Lewis's and Macdonald's, with Collinson's still supporting. . . . Movement was slow . . . We passed over a corner of the field of fire and saw for certain what awful slaughter we had done. It was now twenty minutes to ten. The British had crested a low ridge between Gebel Surgham and the Nile. Maxwell's brigade was just ascending it, Lewis's just coming up under the hill. . . . Suddenly from rearward broke out a heavy crackle of fire. . . . The crackle became a crashing, and the crashing waxed to a roar. Dervishes were firing at us from the top of Gebel Surgham, Dervishes were firing behind and to the right of it. . . . What was it? Had they come to life again? No time to ask; reinforcements or ghosts, they were on us, and the battle was begun again." Mr. Steevens next describes the doings of Broadwood's force, and the charge of the 21st Lancers: "When the Sirdar moved his brigades southward," he continues, "he knew what he was doing. He was giving his right to an unbeaten enemy; with his usual daring he made it so. His game now was to get between the Dervishes and Omdurman. . . . The blacks of the 13th Battn. were storming Gebel Surgham; Lewis and Macdonald, facing west and south, had formed a right angle. They were receiving the fire of the Khalifa's division and the charge of the Khalifa's horsemen; behind them the Khalifa's huge black standard flapped ravenlike. The Baggara horsemen were few and ill-mounted—perhaps 200 altogether—but they rode to get home or die. They died. . . . A second time the attack guttered and flickered out. It was just past ten. Once more to Omdurman! Two minutes' silence. Then once more the howling storm rushed down upon us; once more crashed forth the answering tempest." Then Steevens describes the battle as only he could describe it. "Hunter sent for Wauchope's first British Brigade to fill the gap between Macdonald and Lewis. The order went to General Gatacre first, instead of to the Sirdar. With the soldier's instinct he set the brigade moving on the instant. . . . The cockpit of the fighting was Macdonald's." And after the Battle was won, Steevens says: "And the Dervishes? The honour of the fight must still go with the men who died. Our men were perfect, but the Dervishes were superb—beyond perfection. It was their largest, best and bravest army that ever fought against us for Mahdism, and it died worthy of the huge empire that Mahdism kept so long."

Henry de B. de Lisle.

DE LISLE, HENRY DE BEAUVOIR, Lieut., was born 27 July, 1864 son of the late Richard V. de Lisle, Esq., of Guernsey, and of his wife, C. E. de Lisle. He was educated in Jersey, and joined the Durham Light Infantry at Gibraltar, as Lieutenant, 10 March, 1883. He served in the Sudan in 1885 and 1886, with the Frontier Field Force, being employed with the Mounted

Infantry. He was mentioned in Despatches and awarded the D.S.O. for his services at the Battle of Ginniss, and for special service connected with the attack on the fort at Ambigole Wells by Arabs. He carried Despatches unto the beleaguered fort at Ambigole Wells, south of Wady Halfa, Egypt, and broke out with two men with news that—for want of ammunition and water—the fort could not hold out for more than 24 hours. It was relieved the next morning. His D.S.O. was gazetted 26 Nov. 1886: "Henry de Beauvoir de Lisle, Lieut., Durham Light Infantry. For Action at Ginniss." He became Captain 1 Oct. 1891, and was Adjutant, Durham Light Infantry, 1 July, 1892, to 30 June, 1896. For ten years he was Captain of the Durham Light Infantry Polo team. Captain de Lisle passed the Staff College in 1899. He served in South Africa from the beginning of the war in 1899 to the end, on the Staff (including command of a Mounted Infantry Battalion, of 2nd Mounted Infantry Corps, of mobile column, of Cavalry Brigade (temporary), and of Australian Commonwealth Brigade). He raised and commanded the 6th Mounted Infantry, and an independent column of Mounted Infantry, from 1 June, 1900, to 14 Aug. 1902. He was present at the Relief of Kimberley. Operations in the Orange Free State, Feb. to May, 1900, including operations at Paardeberg (17 to 26 Feb.); actions at Poplar Grove, Karee Siding, Houtnek (Thoba Mountain), Vet River (5 and 6 May), and Zand River. Operations in the Transvaal, actions near Johannesburg, Pretoria and Diamond Hill; operations west of Pretoria (Venterskroon), severely wounded (14 Aug.). Operations in Orange River Colony (May to Aug., and Sept. to Nov. 1900), including actions at Wittebergen (1 to 29 July), and Bothaville. Operations in Cape Colony, south of Orange River, 1899–1900, including actions at Colesberg (1 Jan. to 12 Feb.). Operations in the Transvaal, Orange River Colony, and Cape Colony, 30 Nov. 1900, to 31 May, 1902. He was mentioned in Despatches [London Gazette, 4 May, 1900, 8 Feb. and 16 April, 1901, and 29 July, 1902]; was given the Brevet of Lieutenant-Colonel 2 Jan. 1902; received the Queen's Medal with five clasps, and the King's Medal with two clasps, and was created a C.B. He had become Major, Durham Light Infantry, 1 Jan. 1902; 5th Dragoon Guards, 22 Oct. 1902, and 1st Royal Dragoons, 19 Dec. 1903; and Lieutenant-Colonel 2 Feb. 1906. He was given the Brevet of Colonel 22 Aug. 1906, and commanded the 1st Royal Dragoons from 1906 to 1910. He was promoted to Colonel 2 Feb. 1910. From 1 March, 1910, to 4 Aug. 1911, he was G.S.O., 1st Grade, 2nd Division, Aldershot Command; and he was Brigade Commander, 2nd Cavalry Brigade, from 5 Aug. 1911, to 9 Oct. 1914. He served in the European War from 1914, as temporary Major-General from 10 Oct. 1914, to 17 Feb. 1915; and became Major-General on 18 Feb. 1915. He commanded the 2nd Cavalry Brigade, 1st Cavalry Division, from 10 Oct. 1914; the 29th Division from 4 June, 1915; the 13th Corps from 12 March, 1918; and the 15th Corps from 10 April to the end of the war. He was promoted Major-General for services in the field, and created a K.C.B. 1 Jan. 1917; promoted Lieutenant-General 1 Jan. 1919, and created K.C.M.G. June, 1919; was created Commander of the Legion of Honour, 1918; Grand Officer, Order of Leopold, 1919, and Grand Cross, White Eagle of Serbia, 1919. Sir Beauvoir de Lisle married in 1902, Leila, daughter of the late Wilberforce Bryant, of Stoke Park, Stoke Poges, Bucks, and they have one son.

From time to time in the histories of the South African War we get glimpses of De Lisle and his wild horsemen scaling impossible places, achieving wonderful feats of arms. One cannot tell all the tale of them, but these short extracts may form a fitting end to this all too brief notice of De Lisle: There is a fascinating description of the operations at Houtnek (Thoba Mountain) in the official "History of the War in South Africa" (pages 328–332), compiled by General Sir F. Maurice, K.C.B., and published by Messrs. Hurst and Blackett, which may not be out of place at the close of this brief account of the career of Sir Beauvoir de Lisle: "At daybreak on 30 April Ian Hamilton set his troops in motion towards Winburg, where the Commander-in-Chief desired him to arrive on the 5th of May. His column consisted of Smith-Dorrien's infantry brigade (19th), Ridley's brigade of three mounted infantry corps, and two batteries of artillery. For some hours the enemy made no sign, but at 8.30 a.m. the mounted infantry, which formed the right flank guard, came under the distant fire of guns and pom-poms posted on a range of hills four or five miles in length, which crosses the Winburg road from west to east and then turns sharply to the south. The right of the Boer position rested on the most western hill, a high flat-topped kopje, named Thoba Mountain; the centre occupied a series of sharp rocky knolls which stretch about three miles eastwards from Thoba; the left held the kopjes which run from north to south. In front of the centre of the position is a bare shallow valley, about two thousand yards in width. The Winburg road crosses Houtnek between Thoba Mountain and the sharp, rocky knolls; it is dominated in every direction by these heights. The officers commanding the advanced troops at once took measures for the safety of the column. Bainbridge, with the 7th Mounted Infantry, kept the enemy on the right flank and right rear. De Lisle led the 6th Mounted Infantry and the New Zealanders at a gallop to the southern edge of the broad valley and occupied it. Major N. Legge, 20th Hussars, who with Kitchener's Horse was on the left front, noticed that Thoba Mountain was but lightly held, and instantly directed his corps against it. These various movements, made on the initiative of the officers commanding units, exactly anticipated the orders issued by Major-General Hamilton. After reconnoitring the ground, Hamilton realized that a frontal attack on such a position, especially as it was strengthened with well-placed stone breastworks, was impossible. Equally impossible did it seem to turn it by the east. He therefore determined to seize Thoba Mountain, and then, passing his mounted troops round its western flank, to assail the enemy from the rear. During the time occupied in the reconnaissance, Smith-Dorrien, dropping the Duke of Cornwall's Light Infantry as rear and baggage guard, had reinforced de Lisle. As soon as Hamilton was satisfied that Kitchener's Horse had made good their footing on Thoba Mountain, he ordered the 19th Brigade to support them. Smith-Dorrien, leaving himself only six companies of the Shropshire Light Infantry to hold the southern edge of the valley, sent the remainder of the Shropshire, the Gordon Highlanders, and the Royal Canadian regiment against Thoba Mountain. As they marched in the open across the enemy's front these troops came under heavy artillery fire; but it was remarkable that though the shells fell fast among their ranks, only one man was killed, though many were knocked down by the explosions, stunned, or slightly injured. As soon as the Boers saw that Thoba was threatened, they began to reinforce the burghers on the mountain, and before long they had become so strong there that the 19th Brigade could gain no further ground. About 2 p.m. the enemy began to take the offensive, and advanced in several lines from the northern end of the mountain to thrust back those of the British who had reached the southern crest. So regular were the formations, so soldierly the bearing of these men—European adventurers who had served in the armies of their own countries—that it was hard to believe they were not British troops. Until the General through a telescope saw that each time they raised their rifles to their shoulder they pointed them to the south, he refused to allow his artillery to play upon them. Though the shells seemed to burst accurately over them, about 150 of the enemy pushed steadily forward towards a knoll, to which Capt. E. B. Towse, Gordon Highlanders, was leading a dozen of his men and a handful of Kitchener's Horse. Owing to the lie of the ground neither side could see the movements of the other until they were little more than fifty yards apart. Then Towse caught sight of the foe, dashed forward, and opened a very rapid fire. The surprise was complete, and the enemy recoiled before him, just as he fell to the earth, struck by a bullet which totally destroyed his sight. The success of this unexpected stroke was great, for it enabled Ian Hamilton to keep his hold upon the southern crest of the mountain, though he was unable to make headway across the plateau on the summit. For his gallantry and initiative on this occasion Capt. Towse was awarded the Victoria Cross. To prevent further Boer reinforcements reaching Thoba, Smith-Dorrien and de Lisle kept up a hot fusillade against the centre of the enemy's position. In this they were successful, but the burghers, seeing that their comrades had not been driven from the mountain, took heart and gathered in threatening masses upon the right flank and right rear of Smith-Dorrien, and from the kopjes running north and south hotly engaged the mounted infantry and shelled the transport and the rearguard which escorted it. Until darkness put an end to the combat the situation remained unchanged. Then the General ordered that every man should stay during the night on the ground he had occupied by the day, in readiness to resume the battle at earliest dawn; and as his mounted infantry were so fully employed in holding back the enemy that none were available for the turning of Thoba Mountain, which was essential to the success of his plan, he called upon Lieut.-General French at Thabanchu for assistance. At daylight on 1 May firing began all along the line, and Smith-Dorrien renewed his efforts to possess himself of Thoba Mountain. Fortunately the enemy was slow in reinforcing its defenders, and the knolls on its western crest were gradually overrun by detachments of Gordon Highlanders, Canadians and Shropshire Light Infantry. A half-company of the latter, well handled by their colour-sergeant, Scowse, worked their way across part of the plateau and maintained their position under a heavy cross-fire, which killed or wounded twenty-five per cent. of their numbers. Lower down the western slopes the Victorian Mounted Infantry, under Major K. E. Lean, did useful work in co-operation with these movements. In the course of the morning Lieut.-Colonel P. L. Clowes, 8th Hussars, arrived from Thabanchu with reinforcements consisting of his own regiment, a composite Lancer regiment, the East Yorkshire and a field battery. The guns and the infantry were sent off to strengthen the right rear, which at the time was very hard pressed, while Clowes, with his mounted men and Hamilton's Horse battery, was directed to move eastward, if possible circle right round Thoba, and threaten the enemy from the rear. At about 10 a.m. some of the Boer guns, after shelling the summit of Thoba with great vigour for nearly an hour, began to retire; but this movement by no means heralded a general retreat, for the fire on the right rear between Bainbridge's Mounted Infantry and the Boers continued to be heavy, and the burghers on Thoba held its northern crest with great tenacity. About noon the 21st Infantry Brigade (Bruce Hamilton) and the 2nd Cavalry Brigade (Broadwood) could be seen about five miles away on the plain to the north and west of Thoba. Smith-Dorrien, who, since early morning had watched the combat from the southern crest, saw that the time had come to sweep the enemy off the top of Thoba, and thus, by securing the nek, enable the troops and baggage to cross it in broad daylight. He therefore arranged for a general advance across the plateau, so as to drive the Boers from it, and then to rake with musketry the centre of their position. A line of the Shropshire Light Infantry and the Gordon Highlanders dashed forward by rushes under a heavy fusillade from the northern edge, and when the troops charged, the Boers broke into headlong flight. The pressure of Broadwood's and Bruce Hamilton's advance in the north-west and of Clowes' turning movement round the mountain had already made themselves felt, and when Thoba was lost, the Boers abandoned the whole of their position, and retired towards Clocolan. By 3.30 all the transport was safely through the nek, at the northern end of which Colonel Clowes, having completely circled Thoba Mountain after a sharp encounter, had halted. Ian Hamilton marched on that afternoon to Jacobsrust, where he was joined by Broadwood's and Bruce Hamilton's brigades." Sir Conan Doyle tells us in "The Great Boer War," when describing the Colesberg operations, how "De Lisle with his mounted infantry carried the position which they had originally held. In this successful and well-managed action the Boer loss was ninety, and we took, in addition, twenty-one prisoners." Again, "at Diamond Hill the temptation to an assault was great, but even now it might mean heavy loss of life, and Hamilton shrank from the sacrifice. In the morning his judgment was justified, for Botha had abandoned the position, and his army was in full retreat. The mounted men followed as far as Elands River Station, which is twenty-five miles from Pretoria ; but the enemy were not overtaken, save by a small body of De Lisle's Australians and Regular Mounted Infantry. This force, less than a hundred in number, gained a kopje which overlooked a portion of the Boer Army. Had they been more numerous the effect would have been incalculable. As it was, the Australians fired every cartridge which they possessed into the throng, and killed many horses and men." In an engagement on 27 Oct., during the pursuit of De Wet, "the Boers were . . . outflanked by the extension of the British line, and were forced to fall back. At half-past eight De Lisle, whose force had trotted and galloped for twelve miles, arrived with several companies of Australians, and the success of the day was assured." In the second invasion of Cape Colony : "On 6 Feb., after a fine march, De Lisle and his men took possession of Calvinia, which had been abandoned by the Boers. . . . De Lisle hardly halted at Calvinia, but pushed on towards Williston, covering seventy-two miles of broken country in forty-eight hours, one of the most amazing performances of the war." And a little later : "De Lisle, who had passed over five hundred miles of barren country since he advanced from Piquetburg, made for the railway at Victoria West, and was dispatched from that place on 22 Feb. to the scene of action in the north." In the skirmish near the hamlet of Reitz on 6 June : "For four hours the battle raged, until at last the parched and powder-stained survivors breathed a prayer of thanks as they saw upon the southern horizon the vanguard of De Lisle riding furiously to the rescue." And then at the end of the march to Pretoria one reads in the "Official History" that : "Hamilton, who had early ridden to the front, had at once perceived the weakness of the Boer right, and the possibility of outflanking it. Broadwood, with the cavalry, carrying out the original plan, were by this time circling widely toward the west. But the mounted infantry under Colonel de Lisle were at hand, and with them Hamilton decided to effect his purpose. To the left front, a narrow nek, cut like a nick in the ridge, seemed to promise access to the easy ground which bordered on the enemy's position. Towards this De Lisle led his men, about 350 strong. The nek was incredibly steep, especially on the northern side, down which the mounted infantrymen, leading their ponies, scrambled with great difficulty. Once at the bottom, and all again in the saddle, De Lisle began to gallop clear round the hostile position, capturing on the way a Maxim gun and two wagon loads of ammunition. The Boers, fearing to be cut off, and already much shaken by the bombardment, fled at full speed, and the 14th and 15th Brigades pressed forward at once to occupy the abandoned ground. Reaching a height overlooking Pretoria, De Lisle, at 4.45 p.m., summoned the city in the name of Lord Roberts to surrender."

ANNESLEY, WILLIAM RICHARD NORTON, Lieut., was born at Colchester 12 June, 1863, eldest son of the late Major-General W. R. Annesley and Isabel, daughter of the late Hon. and Rev. James Norton, of Anningsly Park, Ottershaw. He was educated at Cheltenham College, and at the Royal Military College, Sandhurst, and joined the Yorkshire Regt. 6 Feb. 1884, as Lieutenant, and was transferred to the Royal West Kent Regt. 27 Feb. 1884. He was employed in the Egyptian Army 27 Nov. 1888, to 6 Oct. 1890, and served in the Sudan in 1885 and 1886 with the Frontier Field Force, and was present at the attack on Ambigole Wells and the action at Ginniss. He was mentioned in Despatches, received the Medal, the Bronze Star, and was created a Companion of the Distinguished Service Order [London Gazette, 26 Nov. 1886]: "William Richard Norton Annesley, Lieut., Royal West Kent Regt. For the action at Ginniss." He was Staff Officer at Assouan for the operations at Toski. He became Captain 15 July, 1891, and Major 16 July, 1902, and retired 15 Dec. 1905, joining the Reserve of Officers. He died 29 Nov. 1914.

RADWAN HASSAN BEY, Major, was born in Egypt in 1853, 3rd son of the late Right Hon. Sheikh Ahmed Fayed, Judge (who died in 1874). His mother is a descendant of the Prophet. Radwan Hassan Bey is married. He was educated at Polytechnic Artillery Colleges ; was first in school, especially mathematics. He joined the 1st Regt. Artillery in 1871 ; was Professor for the Artillery Officers in 1873 ; in 1881 he was Commandant, Field Artillery Battery ; and in 1882 was in the Battle of Tel-el-Kebir ; was severely wounded and taken prisoner. In 1884 and 1885, he was a Captain, and commanded a Field Battery in the Sudan Expedition, under General Earle, taking part in the battle of Keerbakaan. He was promoted Major-Commandant, Artillery, was present at the battles of Kosheh and Ginniss. Colonel Andrew Haggard says, in "Under Crescent and Star" (page 354) : "Major Hassan Radwan, a very plucky fellow, of the Egyptian Artillery, was wounded very severely. This officer had distinguished himself a few days previously, when a small party of English were surrounded by a large party of the enemy, who had a gun with them, at a small sand-bag post at Ambigol Wells on the railway. Major Hassan Radwan, having with him Lieut. de Lisle, a young officer in the Durham Light Infantry, and a few men mounted on camels, had broken through the enemy's lines and ridden in to assist in the defence. I believe that both the Egyptian and the English officer were afterwards the recipients of the Distinguished Service Order for this smart little affair." He received the Medjidie, 4th and 3rd Classes ; also the Osmanieh (4th Class) ; the Egyptian Star and the English Medal ; and was created a Companion of the Distinguished Service Order [London Gazette, 26 Nov. 1886]: "Radwan Hassan, Major, Egyptian Artillery. For Action at Ginniss." He was present at the battles of Toski and Argeen ; was promoted to Lieutenant-Colonel ; Inspector of Artillery and Ammunition Stores. In 1902 he was appointed Sub-Governor of the Frontier ; he was promoted to Colonel and appointed Mudir of Beni Souef, 1895 ; Prefect of Ghizeh, 1898 ; Mudir of Mimeh, 1901–4. He has the Osmanieh, 3rd Class ; is a Pasha ; Mir Miran Mondir of Menonjah Province, 1903 ; Mudir (Prefect) of Ghorbich since 1904. He has written "A Pamphlet on the Art of Artillery." Colonel Radwan Hassan Bey's favourite recreation is shooting.

RADWAN SAID, Lieut., served in the Sudan in 1885 and 1886, and was created a Companion of the Distinguished Service Order [London Gazette, 26 Nov. 1886] : "Radwan Said, Lieut., Egyptian Camel Corps."

The following refers to Colonel Hassan Radwan, D.S.O., and to Major Said Radwan, D.S.O. :

"H.Q., Egyptian Army,
"War Office, Cairo.
"24 Dec. 1894.

"From the Sirdar, Egyptian Army.
"To H.B. Majesty's Agent and Consul-General in Egypt.

"MY LORD,
"I have the honour to inform you that Major, now Lieut.-Colonel, Hassan Radwan, D.S.O., Egyptian Army, is still alive, and is now holding the appointment of Sub-Governor, Frontier. With reference to Lieut., since promoted Adjutant, Major Said Radwan, D.S.O., this officer left Cairo on or about July, 1892, for Tripoli, with the intention of returning overland to Cairo. He has not been heard of since, and, as when he left Cairo he was in an advanced stage of consumption, there is no doubt that he is dead. He was struck off the strength of the Egyptian Army on the 1st Jan. 1893.
"I have the honour to be, My Lord,
"Your most obedient servant,
"HERBERT KITCHENER,
"Sirdar."

London Gazette, 26 Nov. 1886.—"The late Honorary Major-General Alfred George Huyshe, C.B., would have been recommended for this distinction had he survived."

London Gazette, 26 Nov. 1886.—"The Queen has been graciously pleased to give orders for the appointment of the undermentioned Officer to be a Companion of the Distinguished Service Order. For operations in Burma."

CHANNER, BERNARD, Colonel, was born at Allahabad 20 Sept. 1846, son of George Birdwood Channer, Colonel, Bengal Artillery, and Susan, daughter of the Rev. Nicholas Kendall, M.A., Vicar of Lanlivery, Cornwall, cousin of Nicholas Kendall, J.P., D.L., M.P. He was a brother of the late Colonel G. N. Channer, V.C., C.B. He was educated at Cheltenham College, and joined the 3rd West India Regt. as Ensign 13 Feb. 1867 ; became Lieutenant, 14th Foot, 14 March, 1868, and Lieutenant, 2nd Native Infantry Regt., 18 Feb. 1871. He served in the Afghan Campaign of 1878–79–80 (Medal) ; became Captain, B.S.C. (now I.S.C.), 1879 ; Colonel Channer married, 5 Jan. 1881, at Sydenham, Kent, Alice Bovell Cramp, daughter of Francis Cramp, Esq., and their children are : (1) Bernard Gordon, born 7 Oct. 1881, Major, 54th Sikhs, General Staff, Simla ; (2) Guy, born, 12 Nov. 1884, Major, 14th Sikhs, General Staff, Simla, (wounded at the Dardanelles, May, 1915 ; proceeded to Mesopotamia in 1917 ;

Bernard Channer.

wounded Oct. 1918, and on the same day was awarded the D.S.O. for gallantry while commanding his regiment in action) ; (3) Keith Francis, born 18 Feb. 1892, Captain, 36th Jacob's Horse, Indian Army. He served in the Burma Campaign of 1885–7, and was present at the taking of Minhla and at the action of Napeh ; received the Medal with clasp, and was created a Companion of the Distinguished Service Order [London Gazette, 26 Nov. 1886]: "For operations in Burma, Bernard Channer, Capt., Bengal Staff Corps." The decoration is thought to have been awarded for services in connection with the raising of Mounted Infantry in Burma, and for services with them on active service. It is believed that Capt. Channer suggested the raising of the Mounted Infantry ; and this is supported by letters, extracts from which are given below.

The first is from General F. B. Norman :

"MY DEAR CHANNER,
"I sent your report, and also your note about raising a Corps of Mounted Infantry, to the A.A.G. for submission to the General, and I supported your proposal.
"Yours truly,
"F. B. NORMAN."

The next letter was also from General Norman :

"I have received your scheme for a small Corps of M.I., and at once sent it on to General Prendergast."

This was dated 21 Dec. 1885. The final letter from General Prendergast, dated 4 Dec. 1885 (Mandalay), says :

"I have read your interesting letter to General Norman, and am glad to hear you are going on so well. I have sanctioned your Light Horse. . . ."

Capt. Channer was senior of the first batch of officers ordered to attend at Windsor Castle for the first Investiture of the Distinguished Service Order. He was very ill at the time, or he would have been the first officer personally decorated with the D.S.O. by Queen Victoria. As it is, he was the first on the list of three summoned to the Investiture. The

Warrant for the D.S.O., signed by Queen Victoria, is dated 25 Nov. 1886. He became Major in 1887; served on the North-West Frontier of India, Lushai, 1889 (Despatches, G.G.O., 292 of '89. Clasp); became Lieutenant-Colonel 13 Feb. 1893; served on the North-West Frontier of India, 1897–8, Tochi; Colonel on the Staff, and commanded the Base of Edwardabad (Medal with clasp). He was given the Brevet of Colonel 1 July, 1898, and retired from the 2nd Q.V.O. Rajput Light Infantry 20 Sept. 1903. In 1903 Colonel Channer settled down at High Bickington, North Devon. He occupied himself in all country sports, especially shooting and fishing; took a great interest in politics and all local affairs, and never lost his keenness for his profession, which he loved so well. Colonel Channer died at High Bickington 4 Dec. 1918.

ALDWORTH, WILLIAM, Capt., was born at Harmony Lodge, Carrigtwohill, co. Cork, on 3 Oct. 1855, eldest surviving son of Colonel Robert Aldworth, North Cork Rifles, J.P. co. Cork, formerly Captain, 94th Regt., and Olivia Catherine, daughter of the Rev. James Morton, Rector, Newmarket, co. Cork. He was educated at Rossall and Clifton. His first commission was antedated 13 June, 1874. He joined the 16th Regt. 20 July, 1876; was Adjutant, Bedfordshire Regt. 1877–81; became Captain 30 March, 1881; was A.D.C. to Lieut.-General Sir H. Prendergast, V.C., K.C.B., in Madras and in the Burma Expedition, 1885–7, and was mentioned in Despatches. He was A.D.C. to the General Officer Commanding in Burma, and was mentioned again in Despatches by Major-General L. B. Gordon: The Burma Campaign, from London Gazette, 3 Dec. 1887: "Capt. William Aldworth, 2nd Bedfordshire Regt., formerly my acting A.D.C., deserves special notice for the dashing manner in which he relieved Thabyabin. He started at a two-hours' notice, and rode 55 miles through a very disturbed country to Taindak, where he took command of the small body of men who relieved the beleaguered garrison." Capt. Aldworth received the Medal and clasp, and was created a Companion of the Distinguished Service Order [London Gazette, 26 Nov. 1886]: "William Aldworth, Capt., of Bedfordshire Regt. For operations in Burma." He passed in French, German, Hindu and Urdu, and qualified in 1889 as interpreter in Russian. In 1894 he passed the Staff College. He served in the Isazai Expedition, 1895 (clasp); with the Chitral Relief Force; was present at the storming of the Malakand, and at the action near Khar (Medal, clasp for Relief of Chitral); officiated as A.A.G., Pindi, 1st Sept. to 30 Nov. 1895; was D.A.A.G., 2nd Brigade, Tirah Field Force, 5 Oct. 1897, to 6 April, 1898; promoted Major 1 Feb. 1898; was present at the action at the Sampagha Pass and at the action of the Arhanga Pass (Despatches). He took part in the operations against the Khani Khel Chamkanis, and in the operations in the Bazar Valley (Despatches, Brevet of Lieutenant-Colonel). He was D.A.A.G., 2nd Brigade, Kyber Force, 7 April to 11 June, 1898. Lieut.-Colonel Aldworth was specially selected to command the 2nd Battn. of the Duke of Cornwall's Light Infantry in Sept. 1898, and took them to South Africa in 1899. He was killed in action 18 Feb. 1900, when leading a forlorn hope at Paardeberg. Lieut. W. H. Fife, 2nd Duke of Cornwall's Light Infantry (who was himself killed soon afterwards by a spent bullet), wrote of Lieut.-Colonel Aldworth: "I can only say that he was the most gallant soldier I shall ever see, or wish to see, and it was owing to his splendid example that we advanced so steadily when others refused to budge. I would willingly have been killed instead of him, as I could have easily been replaced, and he cannot. I can only add that those who saw the advance said it was magnificent, and, though it has been called the Cornwalls' and the Canadians' charge, it was the Cornwalls' charge only, and Colonel Aldworth's charge in particular. His loss is quite irretrievable. He was hit in the forehead just as he had said: 'Come on, Dukes! Come on, Cornwalls!' He fell, but, raising himself on his elbow, added: 'Go on men, and finish it!'" In a long list of recommendations in 1901, Lord Roberts added Lieut.-Colonel Aldworth, D.S.O., Commanding the 2nd Battn. Duke of Cornwall's Light Infantry, as one whom he would specially have selected for reward, and he wrote in a private letter to Miss Aldworth, dated 17 March, 1901: "When I submitted to Her Majesty's Government a list of names of officers who had rendered 'conspicuously valuable services' before their death, I felt that the list would be incomplete unless it included that of your brother, the late Lieut.-Colonel Aldworth. At Paardeberg he led his men under a withering fire with a courage and devotion which elicited admiration of all who witnessed it, and he died with his face to the foe, like a gallant Irish gentleman. . . ." A writer in an Indian paper said: "Lieut.-Colonel Aldworth, D.S.O., was one of the finest horsemen and most successful jockeys that India has ever seen. He could train a horse as well as ride one." In May, 1877, he and a brother officer walked from Hyde Park Corner to Portsmouth, 76 miles, and several miles more by mistake—started at 6 p.m. and arrived between 7 and 8 p.m. (25 hours). They did the 50th mile at 5 miles an hour.

DORWARD, ARTHUR ROBERT FORD, Capt., was born 13 July, 1848, at Ootacamund, son of James Dorward, Inspector-General of Hospitals, Madras, and Charlotte Ford. He was educated at Cheltenham and at the Royal Military Academy, Woolwich, and joined the Royal Engineers on 15 July, 1868. In 1879–80, he served in the Afghan War, being present at the action of Kam Dakka, and in the operations in the Kama District (Despatches, Medal). He was promoted to Captain 1 May, 1881. He served in the Burmese Expedition of 1885–88; for three months commanded the Queen's Own Sappers and Miners, and

then Commanding Royal Engineers. He was mentioned in Despatches [London Gazette, 22 June, 1886, and 2 Sept. 1887], received a clasp, was thanked by the Government of India, and created a Companion of the Distinguished Service Order, for mention in Despatches as having proved capability of leading men. The Brevet of Major was given in the same campaign (1 July, 1887), for mention in Despatches as one whose promotion would be of advantage to the Army. His D.S.O. was gazetted 26 Nov. 1886: "Arthur Robert Ford Dorward, Capt., Royal Engineers. For operations in Burma." He became Major, 1 Oct. 1887, and Lieutenant-Colonel 21 June, 1894, and commanded the Royal Engineers in Jamaica in 1897–99. He was promoted to Colonel 10 Aug. 1899, and was Colonel on the Staff, Wei-hai-Wei, 10 Aug. 1899, to 20 June, 1900; in the Chinese Expedition of 1900 was Brigadier-General commanding the British troops until the arrival of the Indian Contingent. He commanded British, American and Russian troops in the action near Tientsin, 9 July, and British, American and Austrian troops at the capture of Tientsin city, July, 1900 (Despatches [London Gazette, 14 May, 1901], Medal with clasp, K.C.B.). He commanded Allied troops in the defeat of the Boxers, near Tientsin, in August, and subsequently in the Expedition to Tu Liu. From the date of his arrival in Tientsin he collected junks for the advance of the British, Austrian and Italian troops from Tientsin to Peking, and he commanded troops at Shanghai till 25 June, 1902, when he was ordered home. He commanded troops in the Straits Settlements 1903–5; was promoted to Major-General 15 July, 1905; was on the Staff in Charge of Administration, South Africa, from 15 July, 1905, till Nov. 1909. Sir Arthur Dorward retired on 13 July, 1910. Shortly after the outbreak of the European War he was asked by Lord Kitchener to undertake the hutting of Colonial troops on Salisbury Plain. On completion of that job he was appointed Inspector of Hutting at the War Office, having supervision of all military camps and roads in Great Britain and Ireland. He was mentioned in Despatches.

Arthur R. F. Dorward.

WACE, ERNEST CHARLES, Capt., was born 19 March, 1850, at Goring, Oxfordshire, son of the Rev. Richard Henry Wace, of Wadhurst, Sussex, and of Eulelia Wace. He was educated at Marlborough College, and was gazetted to the Royal Artillery 15 Dec. 1871, serving in the Jowaki Expedition, 1877–78, on the North-West Frontier of India (Medal with clasp for Jowaki). He served in the Afghan War, 1878–80, with No. 4 Hazara Mountain Battery, throughout the war, being in temporary command of it from 18 July to 23 Sept. 1879, and from 29 Oct. to 7 Nov. 1879, and taking part in the capture of Ali Masjid and in the operations in the Lughman Valley (Despatches), and in the advance to the relief of Sherpur (Medal and two clasps, for Ali Masjid and Kabul). He served in the Burmese Expedition, 1885–86, commanding the Hazara Mountain Battery until April, 1886 (slightly wounded). He was present at the capture of Mandalay and the subsequent advance to Bhamo. At Bhamo he commanded the expedition by river to Moogoung, and also that against the Kachin tribes on the Chinese Border. He was mentioned in Despatches [London Gazette, 2 Sept. 1887], and, for the part he took in the Burmese War, as the Officer Commanding No. 4 Hazara Mountain Battery, was created a Companion of the Distinguished Service Order [London Gazette, 26 Nov. 1886]: "Ernest Charles Wace, Capt., Royal Artillery. For operations in Burma." He became Lieutenant-Colonel, 18 May, 1898, and was given the Brevet of Colonel 18 May, 1902, and retired on 18 May, 1903, as Colonel, Royal Artillery. Colonel Wace married, in Aug. 1891, in Bombay, India, Gertrude Mary Hay, daughter of Charles Nathan, Esq., F.R.C.S., of Sydney, New South Wales, and they have one son and two daughters.

Ernest Charles Wace.

SMYTH, OWEN STUART, Capt., was born, 14 Aug. 1853, and was gazetted to the Royal Garrison Artillery 9 Jan. 1873. He served in the Afghan War in 1878 and 1880, taking part in the capture of Ali Masjid and in the operations in the Bazar Valley, in the action at Jugdullack, in the march from Kabul to the Relief of Kandahar, and in the battle of the 1st Sept. He was mentioned in Despatches [London Gazette, 7 Nov. 1879], received the Medal with two clasps, and the Bronze Star. He again saw active service in the Burmese War, 1885–6–7 and 1891, was mentioned in Despatches and created a Companion of the Distinguished Service Order [London Gazette, 26 Nov. 1886]: "Owen Stuart Smyth, Capt., Royal Artillery. For operations in Burma." (The Insignia were presented to him by the Queen.) He served in the Wuntho Expedition of 1891, commanding the Southern Column; received a clasp, and was mentioned in Despatches [London Gazette, 9 Feb. 1892]. He took part also in the Manipur Expedition, 1891, was mentioned in Despatches 14 Aug. 1891, and received a clasp, and he commanded mountain batteries at Intogh. He became Lieutenant-Colonel 31 Dec. 1898, and was given the Brevet of Colonel 31 Dec. 1892, retiring as Colonel, Royal Artillery, 11 June, 1904.

CATHER, THOMAS PLUNKET, Capt., became Lieutenant, Royal Engineers, 15 Dec. 1871, and Captain 15 Dec. 1883. He served in the

William Aldworth.

Burmese War, and was created a Companion of the Distinguished Service Order [London Gazette, 26 Nov. 1886]: "Thomas Plunket Cather, Capt., Royal Engineers. For services in Burma." He was given the Brevet of Major 1 July, 1887. Major Cather died in 1889.

DUNDAS, LAURENCE CHARLES, Capt., was born in Ireland in 1857·

Laurence Charles Dundas.

He joined the King's (Liverpool) Regt. in 1878; served in the Afghan War of 1878–80; was present at the action of 28 Nov. 1878, in the Kurram Valley; at the battle and capture of Paiwar Kotal (Medal with clasp), and in the Zaimukt Expedition, 1879. He was acting Adjutant of his battalion from 1878 to 1880; Adjutant 1883–87. He served in the Burmese Expedition, 1885–87; was mentioned in Despatches, recommended for the V.C., received the Medal and clasp, and was created a Companion of the Distinguished Service Order [London Gazette, 26 Nov. 1886]: "For operations in Burma. Laurence Charles Dundas, Capt., Liverpool Regt." Queen Victoria presented the Insignia of the Order to Capt. Dundas on 26 Nov. 1886, and he was the first officer to be personally decorated by Her Majesty with the new Decoration. He was Political Officer in Upper Burma in 1886; was Brigade-Major 1887–88; Staff Officer, 1st Class, 1888–90; D.A.A.G. 1890–93; officiating A.A.G. 1893–95. He served for four years in the Quartermaster-General's Department. He retired from the Army, and was Deputy Governor of Liverpool Prison 1887–89; of Portland Prison 1889–1900, and Governor of Maidstone Prison 1900–02. Major Dundas married Lady Mary Bertie, daughter of the 11th Earl of Lindsey. He died 9 June, 1909. Colonel Grogan (late commanding the King's Regt.) said of Major Dundas that he was a "good and zealous officer." He was appointed D.A.A.G. in India in 1886, in consequence of the very favourable reports which reached the Commander-in-Chief in India of the services rendered by him in Upper Burma. Colonel Le Mesurier (late commanding the 2nd King's Liverpool Regt.) wrote of Major Dundas's "distinguished conduct throughout the campaign." His "brilliant soldier-like qualities" were mentioned in Regimental Orders, dated 10 Oct. 1887; and Colonel St. John Mitchell said that Major Dundas was one of the quickest and most business-like workers he had ever known, if not the best of all the officers who had ever worked under him, and had he—Lieut.-Colonel St. John Mitchell—a big job to do, such as the sudden preparation and despatch of a large expedition, Major L. C. Dundas was the first man he would ask for—a man who could conduct the great business operation of the trooping at Calcutta without a hitch is not found every day or every year.

MILNE, RICHARD LEWIS, Capt., was born 10 April, 1852, son of the late Lieut.-General R. Milne, of the Bengal Army. He was gazetted to the 72nd Foot 31 Aug. 1872, and became Lieutenant, Seaforth Highlanders, 31 Aug. 1873. He served with his regiment, the 72nd (1st Battn. Seaforth Highlanders), throughout the Afghan War of 1878–80, with the Kurram Field Force, and took part in the Khost Valley Expedition, action of Matun and minor affairs. He was with the Kabul Field Force in the night attack at Zahidabad, action at Charasiab and subsequent occupation of Kabul, operations in and around Kabul and Sherpur, attack on Bala Hissar Hill, Takt-I-Shah, passage of Deh Mazung Gorge, and final repulse of the enemy. Also in the march from Kabul to the relief of Kandahar and the battle of the 1st Sept. He was mentioned in Despatches [London Gazette, 4 May and 3 Dec. 1880], received the Medal awith three clasps, and the Bronze Star. He became Captain, Liverpool Regt., 18 March, 1885. He again served with his regiment, still as a subaltern, in the Egyptian War of 1882, including the Battle of Tel-el-Kebir (Medal with clasp, Khedive's Star). He again saw active service on the Staff of the 2nd Brigade of the Burma Expedition, as D.A.A. and Q.M.G., in 1885 and 1886, when he was mentioned in Despatches [London Gazette, 22 June, 1886, and 2 Sept. 1887], received the Medal with clasp, and was created a Companion of the Distinguished Service Order [London Gazette, 26 Nov. 1886]: "Richard Lewis Milne, Capt., Liverpool Regt. For operations in Burma." He was Adjutant, Rangoon Volunteer R.C., 25 Nov. 1888, to 24 Nov. 1893. He was promoted Major into the Leicestershire Regt. (2nd Battn.) 18 Nov. 1891, at Chatham, and was with the battalion at Aldershot, Cork and the Curragh. He became Lieutenant-Colonel 18 Jan. 1899, and was Commandant, Niger Coast Constabulary 18 Jan. 1899, to 30 June, 1899. He served on the Staff, and as Assistant Press Censor, in South Africa in 1900, receiving the Queen's Medal with three clasps and the King's Medal with two clasps. The "Times" of Friday, 2 Feb. 1906, says: "Lieut.-Colonel Richard Lewis Milne, D.S.O., late of the 72nd (1st Battn. Seaforth Highlanders) and the Leicestershire Regt., died yesterday in London, at the age of 54. . . . The funeral will take place to-morrow at the Kensal Green Cemetery, at 11.30 o'clock."

PAYNE, RICHARD LLOYD, Capt., was born 24 May, 1854, second son of the late John Selwyn Payne. He was gazetted to the Somerset Light Infantry 19 Jan. 1876, as Lieutenant, and served in the South African War in 1878–79, in the Kaffir Campaign. Expedition against Sekukuni. Zulu Campaign: engagement of Zungen Nek, action of Kambula and Battle of Ulundi. (Medal with clasp.) He became Captain 8 May, 1885. Capt. Payne served in the Burmese Expedition, 1885–86, was mentioned in Despatches, and created a Companion of the Distinguished Service Order [London Gazette, 26 Nov. 1886]: "Richard Lloyd Payne, Capt., Liverpool Regt. For services in Burma." He was Adjutant, Volunteers, 15 Sept. 1887, to 14 Sept. 1892; and became Major 8 Nov. 1894. Capt. Payne

served in the South African War, 1899 to 1902, taking part in operations in Natal, March to June, 1900. Operations in the Transvaal, east of Pretoria, July to 29 Nov. 1900, including actions at Belfast (26 and 27 Aug.), and Lydenburg (5 to 8 Sept.). He was in command of 1st Battn. Royal Inniskilling Fusiliers from 22 April, 1900, to 22 April, 1901, and from March 9, 1902, to 31 May, 1902. Operations in the Transvaal, 30 Nov. 1900, to April, 1901, and Dec. 1901. Operations in Orange River Colony, March to 31 May, 1902. He was mentioned in Despatches by Sir Redvers Buller 13 Sept. ℩n1 9 Nov. 1900 [London Gazette, 8 Feb. 1901]. He was given the Brevet of Colonel 29 Nov. 1900, and received the Queen's Medal with three clasps and the King's Medal with two clasps. He had been promoted to Lieutenant-Colonel 27 Jan. 1900; was created a C.B. in 1905, and became Colonel 18 July, 1905, from which date until 6 Feb. 1908, he was Brigadier-General, 16th Brigade, Irish Command. He was promoted to Major-General 14 Nov. 1907; and commanded a brigade in India, 14 April, 1909, to 29 Oct. 1912; and a division in India from 30 Oct. 1912. He retired 23 June, 1917. Major-General R. L. Payne married, in 1884, Clara Fripp Agnes, only daughter of the late Brigadier-General Henry Bethune Patton, and they have one son.

PRESTON, JENICO EDWARD, Capt., was born at St. Servan, France, 30 Nov. 1855, eldest son of the late Hon.

Jenico Edward Preston.

Charles Preston, of County Meath, and of A. M. North, of County Galway. He was educated at Beaumont College, and joined the 51st Foot, as Sub-Lieutenant, 21 Sept. 1874. He took part in the Jowaki Expedition in 1877 (India Medal with clasp); and in the Afghan War, 1880, with the Khyber Line Force (Medal). On 20 Sept. 1880, he was transferred as Lieutenant to the Madras Staff Corps, and served in the 41st Bengal Infantry, the 36th and the 13th Madras Infantry. He became Captain 21 Sept. 1885. Capt. Preston served in the Burma War, 1885–89, when he was severely wounded in a night attack by Shans on Lamaing Post, near Mandalay, lately occupied by two companies of the 12th Madras Infantry. He was twice mentioned in Despatches [London Gazette, 22 June, 1886, and 2 Sept. 1887], received the Medal with two clasps, and was created a Companion of the Distinguished Service Order [London Gazette, 26 Nov. 1886]: "Jenico Edward Preston, Capt., Madras Staff Corps. For services in Burma." From 1891 to 1898 he commanded the 3rd Burma Infantry. He became Lieutenant-Colonel 21 Sept. 1900; was created a C.B. in 1909; and placed on the Unemployed Supernumerary List 30 Nov. 1916.

DOWNES, WILLIAM KNOX, Lieut., was born 15 June, 1855, at Pagrave, Suffolk, son of William Edward

William Knox Downes.

Downes, Rector of Baylham, Suffolk, and Sophia Judith Downes (née Bonner). He was educated at Eton, and entered the Army as Sub-Lieutenant, Unattached, 10 Sept. 1875, being gazetted to the 18th Foot 10 Sept. 1876. He was transferred to the Bengal Staff Corps 7 May, 1877; and served in the Afghan War, 1879–80 (Medal). He again saw active service in the Burmese Expedition of 1885–87. At the time the war broke out he was a Lieutenant in the 11th Rajputs. He proceeded with his regiment up the river Irrawaddy, and was engaged in the chief action of the war, viz., the attack on the Mindla Forts. On this occasion he was the first man to enter the fort, and it was for this action that he was awarded the Distinguished Service Order, being the first Lieutenant to receive it. He was mentioned in Despatches [London Gazette, 22 June, 1886]; received the Medal with clasp, and was created a Companion of the Distinguished Service Order, as related above [London Gazette, 26 Nov. 1886]: "William Knox Downes, Lieut., Bengal Staff Corps. For services in Burma." He became Captain, Indian Staff Corps, 10 Sept. 1887, and served on the North-West Frontier of India, in Waziristan, 1901–2 (Medal with clasp). Capt. Downes commanded the 11th Bengal Infantry, with the temporary rank of Major, and was promoted to Major 10 Sept. 1896. Major Downes died on 22 March, 1912, at Batheaston, of which place his brother, the Rev. A. M. Downes, is the Vicar.

London Gazette, 8 Dec. 1886.—"War Office, 8 Dec. 1886. The Queen has been graciously pleased to give orders for the appointment of the following Officer to be a Companion of the Distinguished Service Order. For operations in Burma."

MACKINNON, HENRY WILLIAM ALEXANDER, Brigade Surgeon-Lieut.-Colonel, was born in 1842, son of the late Inspector-General Charles Mackinnon, H.E.I.C.S., of Millbrook, near Southampton. He was educated at King's College, London (M.R.C.S. and L.S.A., London), and entered the Army Medical Service as Assistant Surgeon 2 Oct. 1865; became Surgeon 1 March, 1873, and Surgeon-Major 2 Oct. 1877; served in the Egyptian War of 1882, and was present at the Battle of Tel-el-Kebir, when he was slightly wounded. For his services was mentioned in Despatches; he received the Medal with clasp and the Khedive's Star. In the Burmese

Expedition in 1885–86, he saw service with the Upper Burma Field Force, under Sir George White, and was part of the time Principal Medical Officer. He was mentioned in Despatches [London Gazette, 2 Sept. 1887]; received the Medal and clasp, and was created a Companion of the Distinguished Service Order [London Gazette, 8 Dec. 1886]: "Henry William Alexander Mackinnon, Surgeon-Lieut.-Colonel, Royal Army Medical Corps. For operations in Burma." Brigade Surgeon-Lieut.-Colonel Mackinnon became Medical Officer for Recruiting, London. He retired in Oct. 1895, and died at Weybridge, Surrey, on 24 March, 1905, aged 63. He was twice married—in 1881, to Dora Jessie (who died in 1891), daughter of Surgeon-General William Munro, C.B., M.D., and in 1893, to Mabel, daughter of the late Thomas Keown, Esq.

London Gazette, 13 Jan. 1887.—"War Office, 13 Jan. 1887. The Queen has been graciously pleased to give orders for the appointment of the following Officers to be Companions of the Distinguished Service Order. For operations in Burma."

DURNFORD, JOHN, Commander, Royal Navy, was born on the 6th Feb. 1849, son of the Rev. Francis E. Durnford, Fellow of Eton, and Rector of Greeting St. Mary, Suffolk, and of Mrs. Durnford, daughter of Admiral John Thompson, of Longparish, Hants. He was educated at Eton, and entered the Royal Navy in 1862. In 1881 he married Mary, daughter of the Rev. John Henry Kirwan, Rector of St. John's, Cornwall, and they had one son, Frederick John, Lieutenant, Royal Navy; and three daughters. He became Commander in 1882; served in the Upper Burma Expedition of 1885–86, on the Staff of Sir H. Prendergast, V.C., K.C.B., and with the Naval Brigade, being present at the engagement at Minhla. He was mentioned in Despatches, and created a Companion of the Distinguished Service Order [London Gazette, 13 Jan. 1887]: "For operations in Burma. John Durnford, Commander, Royal Navy." Commander Durnford commanded the Naval Brigade for manning armed steam launches in Upper Burma in 1887; was mentioned in Despatches and thanked by the Governor-General of India. He was promoted to Captain in 1888; was created a C.B. in 1897; became Junior Naval Lord in 1901; Commander-in-Chief, Cape of Good Hope, 1904–7; was created a K.C.B. in 1906, and was Admiral President, Royal Naval College, Greenwich, from 1908 to 1911. In 1913 he was created a G.C.B. Admiral Sir John Durnford, G.C.B., D.S.O., died on 13 June, 1914.

The "Times" of Monday, 15 June, 1914, has the following notice: "We regret to announce the death, which took place suddenly on Saturday, at his residence, Elmshurst, Catisham, Fareham, in his 66th year, of Admiral Sir John Durnford, G.C.B., D.S.O., a former Sea Lord, who saw active service in Burma. Sir John Durnford was a son of the late Rev. Francis E. Durnford, a Fellow of Eton and Rector of Creeting St. Mary, Suffolk. He was born 6 Feb. 1849, and, after preliminary education at Eton, entered the Royal Navy as a Cadet from the Britannia in Sept. 1862. He became Sub-Lieutenant in 1868, and a Lieutenant in 1872, receiving honorary certificates at the Royal Naval College on passing his examination for the latter grade. Ten years later he was promoted a Commander, and when in charge of the Mariner, on the East Indies station, took part in the Burmese War of 1885–86. He served with the field force on the staff of General Sir H. Prendergast, V.C., and also with the Naval Brigade, being present at the engagement at Minhla. For his services he was specially mentioned in Naval and Military Despatches, and was granted the Distinguished Service Order. In the following year he was placed in command of a naval brigade and a flotilla of armed launches, engaged in the suppression of dacoity in Upper Burma, when he was again mentioned in Despatches, his services receiving the approbation of the Admiralty, and being specially acknowledged by the Viceroy and by the Secretary of State for India. At the conclusion of the operations he received the India Medal with clasp for Burma, 1885–87. On 30 June, 1888, he was promoted a Captain, and among other posts held while in this rank he commanded the Vernon, the torpedo school of the Navy, from 1895 to 1899. On the occasion of Queen Victoria's Diamond Jubilee, in 1897, he was made a C.B., and attained flag rank in 1902. In the meanwhile he had gone to the Admiralty as Junior Sea Lord, and continued a member of the board after his promotion until Dec. 1903. His next appointment was as Commander-in-Chief on the Cape of Good Hope Station from 11 Feb. 1904, to March, 1907, and while there he became, in Oct. 1906, a Vice-Admiral. Although he held no further commands afloat his wide experience, ripe judgment and talent for organization continued to be drawn upon and utilized for the benefit and advancement of the Service, particularly as a member of various committees. He was president of the committee appointed to inquire into the Naval Medical Service, and from March, 1908, to March, 1911, was President of the Royal Naval College at Greenwich. He was actually serving on a committee in connection with the rehousing of the Museum at Greenwich at the time of his death. He became an Admiral in 1910, and retired from active service in May of last year, when, on the King's birthday, he received the G.C.B. Admiral Durnford married, in 1881, Mary Louisa Eleanor, daughter of the late Rev. J. H. Kirwan, Rector of St. John's, Cornwall, and he has a son and three daughters. Sincere, warm-hearted, and a staunch comrade, his sudden death will arouse feelings of keen regret and sorrow in a very wide circle of friends and brother officers." The "Times" of 17 June, 1914, says: "The funeral of Admiral John Durnford took place at Longparish yesterday, with naval honours. The pall-bearers were Admiral of the Fleet Lord Walter Kerr, Admiral of the Fleet Sir Gerard Noel, Admiral of the Fleet Sir Arthur Fanshawe, Admiral Lord Charles Beresford, Admiral Sir Arthur Moore, Admiral Barlow, Admiral Robinson, Surgeon-General Sir James Porter, Rear-Admiral De Chair and Rear-Admiral Napier, and Mr. C. H. Stansfield, C.B., Director of Greenwich Hospital. The King was represented by Admiral the Hon. Sir Hedworth Meux, Commander-in-Chief, Portsmouth, and Admiral Archibald Moore represented the Admiralty."

Alfred Carpenter.

CARPENTER, ALFRED, Commander, Royal Navy, was born at Brighton on 2 Aug. 1847, son of Commander Charles Carpenter, R.N., J.P. for Sussex (died in 1883), and of Sophia Wilson (died in 1882), daughter of Thomas Wilson, of Walthamstow. He was educated at Brighton College, and entered the Royal Navy in 1861, becoming Lieutenant in 1870. In 1879 he married (1) Henrietta, daughter of G. A. F. Shadwell, and they had one son and one daughter. He was promoted to Commander in 1883; served in the Challenger Expedition (Albert Medal, 2nd Class, for saving life), and in the Sudan Expedition, 1884, in command of Myrmidon (Medal and thanks of the Admiralty). Whilst in charge of the Marine Survey of India, he piloted the War Flotilla under fire to Mandalay and Bhamo in 1885; was specially mentioned in Despatches; received the Medal, and was created a Companion of the Distinguished Service Order [London Gazette, 13 Jan. 1887]: "For operations in Burma, Alfred Carpenter, Commander, Royal Navy." Captain Carpenter was for nine years in charge of surveying vessels, and his last service H.M. Coastguard, Cowes. He married secondly, in 1891, Aetheldreda, daughter of Judge Homershan Cox, formerly a Judge of County Courts, of Marlfield House, Tonbridge, Kent. He retired from the Royal Navy in 1895, with the rank of Captain. Capt. Carpenter is the author of "Nature Notes for Ocean Voyagers." His favourite recreations are billiards and golf, and he is interested in collections of corals, in meteorology and astronomy. His son, Capt. Carpenter, R.N., of the Vindictive, won the V.C. in the European War.

BARLOW, CHARLES JAMES, Commander, Royal Navy, was born on 11 Aug. 1848. He entered the Royal Navy in 1862; served in Egypt as First Lieutenant, H.M.S. Inflexible, in the bombardment of Alexandria and ashore, 1882 (Medal); Alexandria Clasp; Khedive's Star; 4th Class Osmanieh). He became Commander in 1884; served in Burma as Second-in-Command, Naval Brigade, during Annexation War, 1885–86; was mentioned in Naval and Military Despatches, and created a Companion of the Distinguished Service Order [London Gazette, 13 Jan. 1887]: "For operations in Burma, Charles James Barlow, Commander, Royal Navy." He became Captain in 1888, and married, in 1892, Elizabeth Hume Dight, daughter of Arthur Dight, of Queensland and New South Wales, Australia. He was Second-in-Command of the Home Fleet in 1905, and was Admiral Superintendent of Devonport Dockyard, 1905–8. Admiral Barlow retired from the Service in 1911.

LAMBERT, WALTER MILLER, Major, was born 8 May, 1843, youngest son of Richard Lambert, of Lyston Hall, Essex, and of Charlotte, daughter of John Campbell. He was educated at Cheltenham College, and entered the Royal Marine Artillery 26 June, 1860, becoming Captain in 1875 and Major in 1885. He served in Burma, 1885–86, in command of the Royal Marines attached to the Naval Brigade; was mentioned in Despatches [London Gazette, 22 June, 1886], and created a Companion of the Distinguished Service Order [London Gazette, 13 Jan. 1887]: "Walter Miller Lambert, Major, Royal Marine Artillery. For the operations in Burma." The Insignia were presented to him by the Queen 14 Feb. 1887. He had been promoted to Major 6 Aug. 1885. He retired on 1 Aug. 1886. Lieut.-Colonel Lambert's favourite recreations are shooting, fishing and riding. In 1878 he married Frances, only child of F. B. Courtenay, and they have one son and two daughters.

London Gazette, 1 Feb. 1887.—"War Office, 29 Jan. 1887. The Queen has been graciously pleased to give orders for the appointment of the following Officer to be a Companion of the Distinguished Service Order. For Operations in the Soudan."

ROGERS, JOHN GODFREY, M.B., Surgeon-Major, was born 11 April, 1850, and educated at Trinity College, Dublin (B.A., 1870; M.B., M.Ch., 1871). He entered the Army Medical Department 30 Sept. 1871, and became Surgeon in 1873. He served in the Afghan War 1878–79–80; with the Kandahar Column and Ghazni Field Force from Oct. 1878, to Feb. 1880, and with the Column under Major-General Sir R. Phayre, from Aug. 1880, to June, 1881 (Medal). He took part in the Egyptian Expedition of 1882—attached to the 19th Hussars—and was present at the action of Kassassin and Battle of Tel-el-Kebir (Despatches; Medal with clasp; Bronze Star; promoted Surgeon-Major). He again saw active service in the Sudan Expedition of 1884–85, on the Nile, being employed with the Egyptian Army as Principal Medical Officer. He was mentioned in Despatches, and received a clasp. He had temporarily held the post of P.M.O., Egyptian Army, during the cholera epidemic of 1883, and he was appointed P.M.O. in 1883, and held the appointment until 1890. He again served in the Sudan in 1885–86–88, with the Frontier Field Force as Principal Medical Officer, Egyptian Army. He was present at the Action of Ginniss; was mentioned in Despatches, and created a Companion of the Distinguished Service Order [London Gazette, 29 Jan. 1887]: "John Godfrey Rogers, M.B., Surgeon-Major, Medical Staff. For operations in the Soudan." He served at Suakin as Principal Medical Officer, and was present at the Action of Gamaizah. He was mentioned in Despatches [London Gazette, 11 Jan. 1889]; received a clasp and the 2nd Class Medjidie. In 1891 he became Surgeon-Lieutenant-Colonel, and from 1892 to 1899 he was Director-General, Sanitary Department (2nd Class Osmanieh, Grand Cordon Medjidie). He retired 3 Feb. 1892. In 1896 he was created a C.M.G., and in 1898 he became K.C.M.G. He was Commissioner, British

Red Cross and Order of St. John, at Cairo, Egypt, 1916–17–18. He is a Knight of St. John. Lieut.-Colonel Sir J. G. Rogers has published "Sport in Vancouver and Newfoundland" (1912). His favourite recreations are fishing and shooting. He married in 1883, Edith Louisa Julie, daughter of the late Major Sykes, Bombay Cavalry.

London Gazette, 20 May, 1887.—"War Office, 16 May, 1887. The Queen has been graciously pleased to give orders for the appointment of the undermentioned Officer to be a Companion of the Distinguished Service Order. For Operations in Burma."

CAMPBELL, ALEXANDER, Capt., was born at Ballyalton, County Down, in 1839, son of the late William Campbell; educated at Belfast; entered the Bombay Marine in 1865. He served in the Abyssinian Expeditions, 1885–86, and in Burma; was mentioned in Despatches and created a Companion of the Distinguished Service Order [London Gazette, 20 May, 1887]: "Alexander Campbell, Capt., R.I.M. For operations in Burma." He was also created a Comp. of the Indian Empire. Capt. Campbell married, in 1872, Jane (she died in 1893), daughter of Weston Grimshaw, and they had three sons: Capt. E. P. Campbell, R.E.; Commander C. R. Campbell, R.I.M., D.S.O., and Major W. Campbell, I.A., D.S.O., and two daughters: Alexandra and Constance. He married again in 1908, Ellinore, daughter of Richard Pardon,

Alexander Campbell.

M.D., and they had two sons and one daughter. Capt. Campbell died on the 26th Sept. 1914.

London Gazette, 21 June, 1887.—"The Queen has been graciously pleased to give orders for the appointment of the undermentioned Officers to be Companions of the Distinguished Service Order. For Operations in Burma."

BROMLOW, THOMAS D'ARCY, M.D., Fleet Surgeon R.N., served in Burma, and was created a Companion of the Distinguished Service Order [London Gazette, 21 June, 1887]: "Thomas D'Arcy Bromlow, M.D., Fleet Surgeon R.N. For operations in Burma." He died 2 Feb. 1892.

NICKLIN, WILLIAM, Staff Engineer, Royal Navy; entered the Royal Navy in 1864, and became Engineer in 1871. He served in the Zulu War in 1879 (Medal); in Egypt in 1882, including the bombardment of Alexandria (Medal with clasp, Bronze Star, promoted). He became Chief Engineer in 1882, and served as Chief Engineer in the Turquoise, being present in the Eastern Sudan at the defence of Suakin in 1884; in Burma, as Chief Engineer of the Naval Brigade, at the bombardment of Minhla, the occupation of Mandalay, and at the expedition to Bhamo, 1885–86, when he was twice mentioned in Despatches, received the Medal with clasp, and was created a Companion of the Distinguished Service Order [London Gazette, 21 June, 1887]: "William Nicklin, Staff Engineer, Royal Navy. For Operations in Burma." He became Inspector of Machinery, retiring in 1896, and lived at 20, Lion Terrace, Portsmouth. He died on 19th April, 1902.

London Gazette, 12 Aug. 1887.—"War Office, 9 Aug. 1887. The Queen has been graciously pleased to give orders for the appointment of the undermentioned Officers to be Companions of the Distinguished Service Order." For Action at Sarras, in the Soudan."

RUNDLE, HENRY MACLEOD LESLIE, Bt. Major, was born at Newton Abbot, Devon, 6 Jan. 1856, second son of the late Joseph Sparkhall Rundle, Captain, Royal Navy, and of Remira Catherine, daughter of the late W. W.

Leslie, Commander, Royal Navy. He was educated at the Royal Military Academy, Woolwich, and entered the Royal Artillery 14 Aug. 1876. He first saw active service in the South African War of 1879–81, taking part in the Zulu War; he was present at the Battle of Ulundi; horse shot; mentioned in Despatches [London Gazette, 21 Aug. 1879], and received the Medal and clasp. In the Transvaal War he was present at the defence of Potchefstroom; was wounded and mentioned in Despatches. In 1882 he served in the Egyptian Campaign, and was present at the Battle of Tel-el-Kebir (Medal with clasp and Bronze Star). In the Sudan Expedition of 1884–85 (Nile) he was doing duty with the Egyptian Army, being employed on

Henry M. Leslie Rundle.

Lines of Communication in charge of Bedouin tribes. He was mentioned in Despatches [London Gazette, 25 Aug. 1885]; received a clasp, and was given the Brevet of Major 15 June, 1885. He was promoted to Captain 13 March, 1885. He served in the Sudan 1885–86–87–89–91. He took part in the operations of the Frontier Field Force (3rd Class Medjidie), and in the action of Sarras. He commanded a mounted corps and served as A.A.G. He was mentioned in Despatches [London Gazette, 21 June, 1887]; received the 3rd Class Osmanieh, and was created a Companion of the Distinguished Service Order [London Gazette, 12 Aug. 1887]: "Henry Macleod Leslie Rundle, Bt. Major, Royal Artillery. For Action at Sarras in

the Soudan." At the action of Toski he was in command of Artillery, and was mentioned in Despatches [London Gazette, 6 Sept. 1889] (Clasp, Brevet of Lieutenant-Colonel 17 Aug. 1889). For the action of Tokar (serving as A.A.G.), he was given a clasp to the Bronze Star. In the Dongola Expeditionary Force, in 1896, as Chief of the Staff (2 June to 7 Oct.), he took part in the operations of 7 June and 19 Sept.; was mentioned in Despatches [London Gazette, 3 Nov. 1896]; was promoted Major-General for Distinguished Service 19 Nov. 1896, and received the Egyptian Medal with two clasps. For his services in the Nile Expedition of 1897, as Chief of the Staff and G.O.C. Merowi Force, he was mentioned in Despatches [London Gazette, 25 Jan. 1898], and received a clasp to the Egyptian Medal. He was General of Communications in the Nile Expedition of 1898, during the operations on Atbara, and he was afterwards Chief of Staff, being present at the Battle of Khartoum; horse shot. He was mentioned in Despatches [London Gazette, 24 May and 30 Sept. 1898]; was created a K.C.B.; received a Medal and a clasp to the Egyptian Medal, and was thanked by both Houses of Parliament. He was Major-General, South-Eastern District 29 Dec. 1898, to 8 Oct. 1899; D.A.G. to the Forces, Headquarters of Army, 9 Oct. 1899, to 18 Jan. 1900; and he commanded a Division at Aldershot 19 Jan. 1900, to 9 March, 1900. Sir Leslie Rundle was Lieutenant-General on the Staff, commanding the 8th Division, South African Field Force, 10 March, 1900, to 13 May, 1902; afterwards commanding Harrismith District. He was slightly wounded; took part in operations in the Orange Free State, Feb. to May, 1900. Operations in Orange River Colony (May to 29 Nov. 1900), including actions at Biddulphsberg and Wittebergen (1 to 29 July); two horses shot. Operations in Orange River Colony 30 Nov. 1900, to May, 1902. He was mentioned in Despatches [London Gazette, 16 April, 1901, and 29 July, 1902]; received the Queen's Medal with three clasps, the King's Medal with two clasps, and was created a K.C.M.G.; Major-General, 5th Division, 2nd Army Corps, 14 May, 1902, to 9 Nov. 1903. He was G.O.C., Northern Command, 10 Nov. 1903, to 2 April, 1906, and was promoted Lieutenant-General 3 April, 1905. He was G.O.C. in Chief (2nd Class), Northern Command, 3 April, 1905, to 9 Nov. 1907; Colonel Commandant, R.A., 1907; General 10 Sept. 1909. Sir Leslie Rundle was Governor and Commander-in-Chief, Malta, 21 Sept. 1909, to 19 Feb. 1915; G.O.C in Chief, Central Force, 1915–1916. He was created a G.C.B. in 1911, and created a G.C.M.G. in 1915; G.O.C. in Chief, 1915–16. He is a Knight of Grace of St. John of Jerusalem in England, and a Pasha in Egypt, and a J.P. for Herts. Sir Leslie Rundle married in 1887, Eleanor Georgina, daughter of the late Capt. H. J. Montgomery Campbell, R.A., who has the King George V. Coronation Medal and is a Lady of Grace of St. John of Jerusalem in England. The following extract is from Sir Reginald Wingate's "Mahdiism and the Egyptian Sudan" (pages 315–318): "News reached Colonel Chermside, commanding at Halfa, at noon, on the 27th April, that Nur el Kauzi with his force had occupied Sarras and pushed on an outpost to Gemai. With the recollection of the last Arab advance fresh in his mind, Colonel Chermside at once decided to oust the intruders from their position. Mindful of the fact that his every movement would be reported to the enemy, and well knowing that he must strike at once before the rebels were further reinforced, he decided on a secret and sudden coup de main. Four hours after he received news of the enemy's arrival he had already despatched as advanced guard, under Major Rundle, R.A., the second cavalry squadron, 100 men, under Major Hilmi Effendi; the 2nd Camel Corps, 40 men, under Lieut. Dunning; the Irregulars, 60 men, under Lieut. Rycroft; two guns of the 1st Camel Battery, under Major Bakir Effendi. These troops were ordered to march by night as rapidly and as secretly as possible to Sarras, and to prevent en route any natives from giving warning to the enemy that troops were approaching. A small patrol also marched parallel with this force on the west bank with similar orders. The 9th Sudanese Battn., under Capt. Borrow, which formed the main body of the advance guard, was concentrated at Abka—twelve miles from Sarras—by 7 p.m., and thence continued their way to Sarras—twenty miles distant by route march. A second column, under the command of Major Lloyd, and consisting of the 1st Egyptian Battn. and Supply and Transport Columns, moved out by rail and route march, and were all concentrated at Abka in the early morning, where they were to await orders for a further advance. Major Rundle had orders to halt within three miles of Sarras and await the dawn; he was then to push on, get touch of the enemy, and engage him until the arrival of the infantry and guns. Accordingly, at dawn a dismounted picket occupied a block-house on the hills overlooking Sarras, while Lieut. Rycroft's Irregulars, supporting the Camel Corps, pushed rapidly into Sarras and seized the old railway station and the block of buildings close to it. This movement was executed under fire from a block-house in the hills to the east, some 340 yards distant, held by the enemy's riflemen. The Irregulars then seized a spur some eighty yards distant from the block-house, and held this position, which was partially defiladed from the enemy's fire, whilst the Camel Corps opened fire on the block-house from some hilly ground in front of the station. At 5.15 a.m. a strong cavalry patrol was pushed along the destroyed railway line, but before it had covered 400 yards the Arab main body, to the number of some 300, showed behind some rising ground 600 yards in front, while groups of spearmen were seen in the hills in the rear. The cavalry patrol, having accomplished its object, fell back behind the station, from which a heavy fire was now opened on the enemy's position. Messages were also sent back to Colonel Chermside, who (with Capt. Kempster, Chief Staff Officer, and Lieut. Palmer, Junior Staff Officer) was advancing rapidly with the remainder of the column. At 6.30 the two guns of the Camel Battery arrived, having marched the whole distance from Halfa—thirty-four and a half miles—in little over twelve hours, and taking up a position close to the station, opened fire with common shell on the block-house, which, unless silenced, must have inflicted considerable loss on the infantry attacking the enemy's main position. Fortunately, after firing twenty-one rounds, the gun succeeded in breaching the block-house, which was then stormed and carried by the Irregulars. The guns were then turned on the enemy's main position, which was shelled with some effect. In the meantime the infantry had arrived, and by 7 a.m., when the block-house had fallen, they were advancing to the attack. The ground now traversed by the infantry requires some description. At this time of the year the river was low. The banks here are high and unusually steep, while a sandy foreshore dotted with rugged boulders intervenes between bank and river. The left of the Arabs' position rested on the scarped bank, but the enemy when exposed to artillery fire had evacuated the open ground on which their camp stood, and had retired into a narrow valley or khor about 200 yards distant from the river. Two companies of the battalion were therefore detached, under cover of the steep bank along the foreshore, to turn the left of the enemy's position. The remainder of the battalion was left as support south of the railway station on the level ground above, while the regulars and the Camel Corps conformed to the advance on the extreme left. Previous to this the cavalry had been sent to turn the enemy's position. This they succeeded in doing simultaneously with the delivery of the front attack, driving in with considerable loss a detached party of some fifty Arabs. The second line of the enemy, consisting chiefly of ill-armed Danagla, seeing the cavalry in their rear, made no attempt to join the first line, but making straight for the river, swam across and succeeded in escaping. In the meantime, as the right flank company had neared the left of the position, the Arab spearmen, with wild yells, rose up from the khor, and, headed by their three mounted leaders, dashed down the bank. The full shock of their charge fell on the slender Egyptian fighting line, which had slowly to fall back on their supports, fighting hand to hand with their assailants. Capt. Borrow, seeing this, at once reinforced the two companies, and the heavily-pressed left company, as they felt the impetus of reinforcement, immediately began slowly to advance; the enemy, contesting every foot, fought with desperate bravery, and fell almost to a man. Many were actually killed in the water, while others, attempting to turn the left flank of the infantry, had scaled the high bank, and fell from the fire of the Irregulars, the Camel Corps, and reserve of the fighting line; it was here Nur el Kauzi was killed. By 7.45 the position, with ten standards and a considerable quantity of arms and ammunition, was captured. Almost the entire Arab fighting force of 200 men had been annihilated, while the Egyptian loss was 21 killed and 30 wounded, including two officers who had been severely wounded in the hand-to-hand fighting." The Official "History of the War in South Africa, 1899–1902" (compiled by Major-General Sir Frederick Maurice, K.C.B.; published by Messrs. Hurst and Blackett), says, in the chapter on "The Defence of Wepener," that "the 8th Division, which had been destined originally for Kimberley, was now, as fast as its units landed from England, to concentrate at Edenburg, under Lieut.-General Sir Leslie Rundle, who was then to march to Dewetsdorp, get in touch with Brabant, and when the burghers besieging Wepener had been driven north, endeavour to cut them off." On the 18th April Rundle had concentrated his division at Rosendal, and next day moved to Ooorlog's Post, and on the 20th his scouts were met by Boer patrols. "The enemy's advanced posts were found near Wakkerstroom, on the edge of a high plateau, from which rises a long ridge that proved to be the main position. Attempts on the 20th and the 21st to turn the flanks of this ridge were unsuccessful, but on the information obtained during the engagement, Rundle based a scheme for an attack on the 22nd, which he submitted by telegraph to the Commander-in-Chief. In his answer Lord Roberts told him that French was advancing via Leeuwkop on Dewetsdorp with the 3rd and 4th Cavalry Brigades and the 11th division (Pole-Carew), and desired that he should not commit himself to a definite assault until he was in touch with them. . . . Rundle accordingly halted for the next three days; he pushed mounted reconnaissances round the enemy's right flank, and kept up a desultory shell and rifle fire against the front of the Boers' main position until the 24th, when he established connection with Pole-Carew." Sir Conan Doyle says, in his "Great Boer War" (page 297): "It is probable that the deliberation with which the operations were conducted was due to Rundle's instructions to wait until the other forces were in position. His subsequent movements showed that he was not a general who feared to strike. . . . On the Wednesday morning Rundle, with the addition of Pole-Carew's division, was strong enough for any attack, while French was in a position on the flank. Every requisite for a great victory was there except the presence of an enemy. The Wepener siege had been raised, and the force in front of Rundle had disappeared as only Boer armies can disappear. . . . Lord Roberts failed in his plan of cutting off De Wet's army, but, at the expense of many marches and skirmishes, the south-east of the state was cleared of the enemy." With an army, Conan Doyle tells us later, between forty and fifty thousand strong, "Lord Roberts advanced upon the Transvaal. . . . Rundle, with the 8th Division and Brabant's Colonial Division, remained in rear of the right flank to confront any force which might turn it. . . . When Lord Roberts had occupied Pretoria, he had left his long line of communications very imperfectly guarded behind him. On the flank of this line of communications were President Steyn and his Free Staters. This army was held in check by Rundle's Division and the Colonial Division on the south, while Colvile, and afterwards Methuen, endeavoured to pen them in on the west. The task was a hard one, however, and though Rundle succeeded in holding his line intact, it appeared to be impossible in that wide country to coop up an enemy so mobile. A strange game of hide-and-seek ensued, in which De Wet, who led the Boer raids, was able again and again to strike our line of rails and to get back without serious loss." Conan Doyle describes the Battle of Diamond Hill, and then describes the general military situation in the Free State: "When Lord Roberts had swept past to the north he had brushed aside the flower of the Orange Free State army, who occupied the considerable quadrilateral which is formed by the north-east of that State. The function of Rundle's 8th Division and of Brabant's Colonial Division was to separate the sheep from the goats by preventing the fighting burghers from coming south and disturbing those districts which had been settled. For this purpose Rundle formed a long line which should serve as a cordon. Moving up through Trommel and Clocolan, Ficksburg was occupied on 25 May by the Colonial Division, while Rundle seized Senekal, forty miles to the north-west. The Boers were in full retreat, but now, as always, they were dangerous. One cannot take them for granted, for the very moment of defeat is that at which they are capable of some surprising effort. Rundle, following them up from Senekal, found them in strong possession of the kopjes at Biddulphsberg, and received a check in his endeavour to drive them off. It was an action fought amid great grass fires, where the possible fate of the wounded was horrible to contemplate. The 2nd Grenadiers, the Scots Guards, the East Yorkshires, and the West Kents were all engaged, with the 2nd and 79th Field Batteries and a force of Yeomanry. Our losses incurred in the open from unseen rifles were thirty killed and 130 wounded, including Colonel Lloyd of the Grenadiers. Two days later Rundle, from Senekal, joined hands with Brabant from Ficksburg, and a defensive line was formed between those two places, which was held unbroken for two months, when the operations ended in the capture of the greater part of the force opposed to him. Clements's Brigade, consisting of the 1st Royal Irish, the 2nd Bedfords, the 2nd Worcesters, and the 2nd Wiltshires, had come to strengthen Rundle, and altogether he may have had as many as twelve thousand men under his orders. It was not a large force with which to hold a mobile adversary at least eight thousand strong, who might attack him at any point of his extended line. So well, however, did he select his positions that every attempt of the enemy, and there were many, ended in failure. Badly supplied with food, he and his half-starved men held bravely to their task, and no soldiers in all that great host deserve better of their country. At the end of May, then, the Colonial Division, Rundle's Division, and Clements's Brigade held the Boers from Ficksburg on the Basuto border to Senekal. This prevented them from coming south. But what was there to prevent them from coming west and falling upon the railway line? There was the weak point of the British position." Conan Doyle goes on to describe the campaign against De Wet, and says that in Oct. and Nov. Hunter, Rundle, Brabant and Bruce Hamilton were in the Orange River Colony. Their forces with others were engaged in breaking up small bodies of the enemy, hunting for arms, bringing in refugees, collecting supplies and rounding up cattle. Later on General Rundle commanded Harrismith District, where "he was kept busy in exploring the rough country in his district, the same district which had been the scene of the operations against Prinsloo and the Fouriesburg surrender."

KEMPSTER, FRANCIS JAMES, Capt., was born on the 12th March, 1855. He entered the Army in 1875; served in the Afghan War in 1880, with the Khyber Line Force, Hissarak Expedition (Medal); in Bechuanaland, 1884–85, commanding the Corps of Guides (honourably mentioned); with the Sudan Frontier Field Force, 1887–88–89. Action of Sarras—Senior Staff Officer to the Column. For his services in the last-mentioned campaign he was mentioned in Despatches (17 June, 1887); received the Medal, the 3rd Class Medjidie, the Khedive's Star, and was created a Companion of the Distinguished Service Order [London Gazette, 12 Aug. 1887]: "For the Action at Sarras, in the Sudan, Francis James Kempster, Capt., Prince of Wales's Leinster Regt. (Royal Canadians)." He was present at the action of Gemaizah, and was mentioned in Despatches [London Gazette, 11 Jan. 1889]; Medal with clasp; Bronze Star. Action of Arguin. Action of Toski. He was mentioned in Despatches [London Gazette, 6 Sept. 1889], and received the Brevet of Lieutenant-Colonel, and a clasp. He became Colonel in 1896. For Ashanti in 1896, as Second in Command, he was mentioned in Despatches, appointed an A.D.C. to the Queen, and received a Star; and for the North-West Frontier in 1897, with the Tirah Expedition, in command of the 3rd Brigade, and was present at the action of Dargai, he was mentioned in Despatches 1 March 1898, and received the Medal with two clasps. He became A.A.G., Madras, and retired in 1902.

London Gazette, 25 Nov. 1887.—"The Queen has been graciously pleased to give orders for the appointment of the undermentioned Officers to be Companions of the Distinguished Service Order. The Queen has also been pleased to direct that these distinctions shall take effect from 1 July, 1887."

CUBITT, WILLIAM GEORGE, V.C., Lieut.-Colonel, was created a Companion of the Distinguished Service Order [London Gazette, 25 Nov. 1887]: "William George Cubitt, V.C., Lieut.-Colonel and Colonel, Bengal Staff Corps, Commanding at the Ruby Mines, Burma." He died 23 Jan. 1903. [See V.C. Volume.]

DICKEN, WILLIAM POPHAM, Colonel, was born 19 March, 1834, eldest son of the late William Stephens Dicken, M.D., I.M.S., Deputy Inspector-General of Hospitals, Bengal, and of Catherine Lamb, youngest daughter of Capt. Joseph Lamb Popham, R.N., and niece of Admiral Sir Home Popham. He was educated at Blundell's School, Tiverton, at Charterhouse, and at Addiscombe, and entered the Madras Army on 9 Dec. 1853. He became Captain in 1865; Major, Madras Staff Corps (now Indian Army) in 1873; Lieutenant-Colonel in 1879; Brevet Colonel in 1883; Colonel 9 Dec. 1883; Colonel Commandant, 3rd Madras Light Infantry (now 63rd Palamcottah Light Infantry) in 1884. He was mentioned in Despatches [London Gazette, 22 June, 1886, and 2 Sept. 1887]; received the Medal and clasp, and was created a Companion of the Distinguished Service Order [London Gazette, 25 Nov. 1887]: "William Popham Dicken, Lieut.-

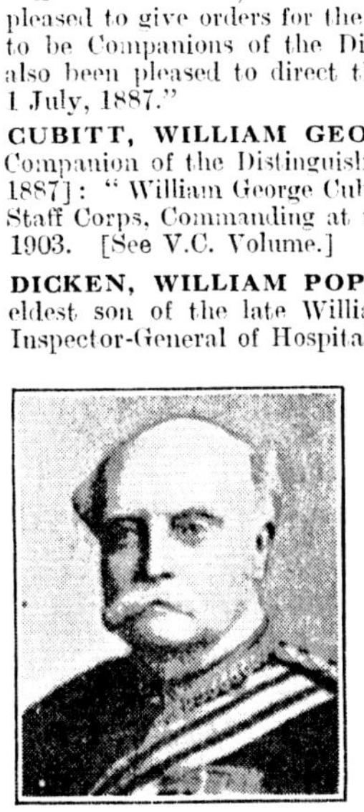

William Popham Dicken.

Colonel and Colonel, Madras Staff Corps. For services in Burma." He was awarded a Distinguished Service Pension in 1890; created a C.B. in 1891, and placed upon the Unemployed Supernumerary List 9 Dec. 1891. Col. Dicken died 4 May, 1912.

MIDDLETON, FRANCIS BECKFORD, Colonel, was born in 1838, and entered the 21st Madras Native Infantry in 1856; became Captain, Madras Staff Corps, in 1868; Major in 1876; served in the Afghan War, 1878–80 (Medal); became Lieutenant-Colonel in 1882, and Colonel in 1886; served in the Burma Campaign of 1885–87, being created a Companion of the Distinguished Service Order [London Gazette, 25 Nov. 1887]: "Francis Beckford Middleton, Lieut.-Colonel and Colonel, Madras Staff Corps. For services in Burma." He retired in 1888, and died in the summer of 1895.

UPCHER, RUSSELL, Lieut.-Colonel, was born 3 Feb. 1844, son of the late R. W. Upcher, of Sheringham Hall, Norfolk. He was educated at Harrow (West Acre), and entered the 67th Foot, as Ensign, 21 Nov. 1862, and the 24th Regt. 9 Jan. 1863, becoming Lieutenant 29 Oct. 1866, and Captain 31 Oct. 1871. He served in the South African War of 1877–78–79. In the Kaffir Campaign he commanded the Left Column, and he commanded the troops at the Battle of Quintana, and was present at the action of Kei River. In the Zulu Campaign he commanded the 1st Battn. 24th Foot after the Battle of Isandhlwana. He was mentioned in Despatches [London Gazette, 26 Feb. and 26 March, 1878, and 15 March and 21 Aug. 1879. He received the Medal with clasp, and was given the Brevet of Major 11 Nov. 1878. He was promoted to Major 4 Sept. 1880; to Lieutenant-Colonel 9 June, 1882, and to Colonel 9 June, 1886. He served in the Burmese War of 1885–89; was mentioned in Despatches, G.G.O. 864 of '87; received the Medal with two clasps, and was created a Companion of the Distinguished Service Order [London Gazette, 25 Nov. 1887]: "Russell Upcher, Lieut.-Colonel and Colonel, South Wales Borderers. For services in Burma." He commanded the 5th and 68th Regimental Districts; was created a C.B. in 1897; became Major-General 6 July, 1898. Major-General R. Upcher retired on 3 Sept. 1902. He has been Colonel, The Durham Light Infantry, since 1908. In 1877 he married Marian Elizabeth, daughter of John Rogers, of Holt Hall, Norfolk, and they have one son and one daughter.

DEEDES, WILLIAM HENRY, Colonel, was born 23 Feb. 1839, at Cadogan Place, London, S.W., son of William Henry Deedes (Civil Service, India Office), and Harriet M. Deedes, daughter of the Rev. John Jeffreys. He was educated at Rugby, and was gazetted to the Rifle Brigade as Ensign on 1 May, 1855. He became Lieutenant-Colonel 9 Aug. 1882, and Brevet Colonel in Dec. 1886. He served in the Burmese Expedition in 1886–87, commanding the 1st Battn. Rifle Brigade. The following is an extract from the Records at Simla: "History of the Burmese War, 1885–86–87: Diary of Events. Colonel Deedes, Rifle Brigade, with a small party of riflemen and sappers, whilst reconnoitring, came upon an obstruction in a nullah. The party consisted of Lieut. Radclyffe, seven riflemen, nine sappers (natives), and a few Burmese Police. The latter bolted, and the sappers did not join in the charge up the hill. The party lined the bank, and the sappers were sent down to clear it. Fire was opened on them from an ambush, and two sappers were killed. Colonel Deedes, while endeavouring to drag one of the sappers (mortally wounded) out of the fire, was himself severely wounded. The party then charged, and the enemy fled. A corporal was also severely wounded when charging." "From the Commander-in-Chief, Mandalay, 1 Dec. 1886: In action near Mimba, on 30th ult., Colonel W. H. Deedes and Corpl. C. Deadman, both of the 1st Battn. Rifle Brigade, severely wounded. They are doing well." "Dec. 15th, 1886: Colonel Deedes was wounded while carrying a wounded soldier out of fire; a Havildar of Sappers being killed at the same time." He was severely wounded; mentioned in Despatches [London Gazette, 2 Sept. 1887]; received the Medal with clasp, and was created a Companion of the Distinguished Service Order [London Gazette, 25 Nov. 1887]: "William Henry Deedes, Lieut.-Colonel and Colonel, Rifle Brigade. For Operations in Burma." He retired with the rank of Major-General 7 Dec. 1887, and died at Cimiez 20 Oct. 1915.

BUDGEN, WILLIAM THOMAS, Colonel, was born on 11 June, 1839, believed at the Bahama Islands, son of Major-General Budgen, Royal Engineers, and Mrs. Budgen (née F. C. Maule). He joined the Royal Artillery about 1856; served in the Burma Campaign of 1885–87, commanding R.A. through most of it, and was created a Companion of the Distinguished Service Order [London Gazette, 25 Nov. 1887]: "William Thomas Budgeon, Lieut.-Colonel and Colonel, Royal Artillery. For services in Burma." He commanded Royal Artillery, Karachi, Sind, India, 1887–89; Brigadier-General commanding Bombay District, India, 1889–94. He died 28 Feb. 1894, at Mentone, France, on his way home from India, of pneumonia, after influenza. He married Olivia G. M. Jervois, daughter of Major-General John Gordon Jervois, R.E., of Bath, and had two sons: Temple Gordon de Courcy, Cape Civil Service, served as a private during the South African War (wounded), and also in the European War (two Medals); William Napier, Brevet Lieut.-Colonel, R.A., D.S.O., and one daughter: Florence Clara, married, in 1908, Lieut.-Colonel Lewis Stratford Tolemache Halliday, V.C., C.B., R.M.L.I.

GORDON, JAMES HENRY, Colonel, was born 25 Jan. 1839, at Blackheath, Kent, son of Adam and Susan Gordon. He joined the Indian Army on 20 April, 1857. He married 29 Jan. 1869, Arabella Hewit Sams, daughter of the late Charles Hewit Sams, of Lee, Kent, and their children were: Lucy; Charles Cecil (deceased), born 29 Sept. 1871; Margaret Julia Arabella, and George Hamilton, born 29 March, 1875. He served in Burma 1885–86, commanding the 23rd Madras Light Infantry; was present at the taking of Mandalay, and at the later operations; was twice mentioned in Despatches for general efficiency in Camp and Field, and received the Medal; was created a C.B. [London Gazette, 3 June, 1893]

and a Companion of the Distinguished Service Order [London Gazette, 25 Nov. 1887]: "James Henry Gordon, Lieut.-Colonel and Colonel, Madras Staff Corps." He became Colonel 20 April, 1887, and was placed on the Unemployed Supernumerary List 15 Jan. 1895.

PATTERSON, THOMAS WILLIAM, Surgeon-Major, was born in 1844, son of the late Thomas Patterson, of Gortlee, Letterkenny. He joined the Army Medical Staff 31 March, 1866; served in Afghanistan 1879–80 (Medal); the Expedition against the Mahsud Waziris in 1881; the Expedition to Suakin in 1885 (Medal and Khedive's Bronze Star); with the Upper Burma Field Force in 1886–88, as Senior Medical Officer 4th Brigade. For his services in this campaign he received the Frontier Medal, was mentioned in Despatches [London Gazette, 2 Sept. 1887], and was created a Companion of the Distinguished Service Order [London Gazette, 25 Nov. 1887]: "Thomas William Patterson, Surgeon-Major, Medical Staff. For operations in Burma." The Insignia were presented to him by the Queen. Lieut.-Colonel Patterson retired on 5 June, 1889, and died on 2 Sept. 1903.

SKENE, CHARLES McDOWALL, Lieut.-Colonel, was born about 1844, son of W. A. Skene, Lethenty, Aberdeenshire, and a kinsman of the Duke of Fife; was educated at Addiscombe, and joined the 43rd Gurkha Rifles (then the 43rd Assam Light Infantry), Indian Army. He served in the North-West Frontier Campaign in 1863. He married, 24 June, 1870, at Ryde, Isle of Wight, Rosalie Purnell George, eldest daughter of the late Mr. James Thorne-George, and had four children: Charles George; Madeleine; Alice Beatrice, and John Gordon (now Major, 2/8th Gurkha Rifles, Indian Army). He was present at the Forcing of the Ambala Pass in the Duffla Expedition in 1874; the Akka Expedition, 1873–74; the Burmese Expedition, 1886–89, when he took the Ruby Mines; was

Charles McDowall Skene.

mentioned in Despatches, and created a Companion of the Distinguished Service Order [London Gazette, 25 Nov. 1887]: "Charles McDowall Skene, Lieut.-Colonel, Bengal Infantry. For operations in Burma." He commanded the Northern Column in the Chin-Lushai Expedition, and was repeatedly mentioned in Despatches from the Government of India. Colonel Skene was killed in action at Manipur in March, 1891, aged 47, having been transferred to 42nd Gurkh Rifles as Commanding Officer just previously.

CAMPBELL, COLIN CHARLES, Colonel, was born on 18 June, 1842, in India, and entered the Madras Army in 1860; became Captain, M.S.C. (now I.A.) in 1872; Major, 1880; served in the Burmese Expedition, 1885–86–87, commanding expedition to Kandat. He was mentioned in Despatches [London Gazette, 22 June, 1886], and created a Companion of the Distinguished Service Order [London Gazette, 25 Nov. 1887]: "Colin Charles Campbell, Lieut.-Colonel, Madras Infantry. For operations in Burma." He became Lieut.-Colonel 22 Dec. 1886, and Colonel 22 Dec. 1890. Colonel Campbell retired from the service in 1893.

Colin Charles Campbell.

CUMMINS, JAMES TURNER, Lieut.-Colonel, was born in 1843, son of the late Nicholas Cummins, Esq., J.P., of Ashley House, and Myrtleville House, County Cork. He was educated at Cheltenham College, and at Addiscombe, and entered the Madras Army in 1861. He married, in 1869, Louie, daughter of the late T. Dunman, Esq. (Commissioner of Police, Straits Settlements), of Clovelly, Bournemouth. He became Captain in 1873, was transferred to the Madras Staff Corps (now Indian Staff Corps) in 1875; became Major in 1883; Lieutenant-Colonel in 1887, and Colonel in 1894. He served in the Afghan Campaign, 1878–80, and in both Bazar Valley Expeditions, as Staff Officer, Kurram Valley Transport (Medal, Brevet of Major). He served in the Egyptian Expedition of 1882, as Second-in-Command of the Punjab Mule Corps; with the Sudan Expedition of 1885, taking part in the operations at and burning of Tamai (Medal with clasp and Bronze Star). For his services in the Burma Campaign of 1886–89, he received special mention in Despatches [London Gazette, 2 Sept. 1887]; received the Medal with two clasps, and was created a Companion of the Distinguished Service Order [London Gazette, 25 Nov. 1887]: "James Turner Cummins, Lieut.-General, Madras Staff Corps. For services in Burma." He was A.A.G., Madras Forces, in 1895, since when he was Q.M.G. He served in China 14 May, 1901; was created a C.B., and received a Medal. Major-General J. T. Cummins died 14 Oct. 1912, at 8, King's Avenue, Ealing.

M'LEOD, DONALD JAMES SIM, Lieut.-Colonel, was born in India, 22 Feb. 1845, second son of Lieut.-General W. C. M'Leod. He was educated at Kensington Proprietary School, and joined the Madras Cavalry as Cornet 20 July, 1861, becoming Lieutenant 20 July, 1862. He was given the Brevet of Captain 20 July, 1873, and became Captain, Madras Cavalry, 4 Nov. 1874. From 1877 to 1888 he served on the Army Staff in India. He became Major 20 July, 1881, and Lieutenant-Colonel 20 July, 1887. He served in the Burmese Expedition of 1886–87, as D.Q.M.G., Madras

Cavalry ; was mentioned in Despatches [London Gazette, 2 Sept. 1887] ; received the Medal and clasp, and was created a Companion of the Distinguished Service Order [London Gazette, 25 Nov. 1887] : " Donald James Sim M'Leod, Deputy Quartermaster-General, Madras. For services in Burma." From 1890 to 1893 he commanded the Madras Lancers. He became Colonel 12 Aug. 1893 ; was A.A.G., District, 1893–95 ; Brigadier-General, India, 3 July, 1895 ; created a C.B. in 1898 ; promoted to Major-General 11 Feb. 1899 ; Major-General Commanding a First Class District, 1901–3 ; Lieutenant-General, commanding the Burma Division, 1903–1908 ; promoted to General 7 May, 1906 ; retired 8 May, 1906. In that year he was created a K.C.I.E., and a K.C.B. in 1913. Sir Donald M'Leod's favourite recreations are riding, fishing and shooting. He married in 1877, Camilla, daughter of Major J. Nicholas, and they have one son and one daughter.

HENNELL, REGINALD, Lieut.-Colonel, entered the Bombay Army (Infantry) in 1861 ; became Lieutenant in 1863 ; served in the Abyssinian Expedition in 1867–68 (Medal) ; was promoted Captain in 1871 ; served in the Afghan War in 1879–80 (services acknowledged by Government ; Medal) ; was promoted Major in 1871 ; served in the Burma Campaign in 1886 ; was mentioned in Despatches 2 Sept. 1887 ; received Medal and clasp, and was created a Companion of the Distinguished Service Order [London Gazette, 25 Nov. 1887] : " Reginald Hennell, Lieut.-Colonel, Bombay Infantry." He was Colonel Commanding the 1st Volunteer Battn. Middlesex Regt. in 1891, and retired in 1901, being knighted in 1902. In 1892 he was appointed to the Honourable Corps of Gentlemen-at-Arms ; in 1894 became Exon of H.M.'s Royal Body Guard of the Yeomen of the Guard ; Clerk of the Cheque and Adjutant of this Guard in 1895, and Lieutenant Senior Permanent Officer in 1901. In 1910 he was created a C.V.O., and in 1915 was appointed Honorary Colonel 3rd Cadet Battn. Middlesex Regt. Colonel Sir Reginald Hennell has written the " History of the Yeomen of the Guard, 1485–1904," " Our Birthright," " Looking Ahead," and other military essays dealing with the Volunteer, Territorial and Cadet Training. His D.S.O. was awarded for operations in Burma.

CORBETT, ROBERT DE LA COUR, Surgeon-Major, was born at Innishannon, County Cork, Ireland, on 1 July, 1844, fourth son of the late Richard Corbett, M.D., and Mary de la Cour, eldest daughter of the late Capt. W. H. Herrick, Royal Navy. He was educated privately, and at Queen's College, Cork, and Trinity College, Dublin (M.D., F.R.C.S.I.), and became Assistant Surgeon, Army Medical Department, in 1867. In 1879 he became Surgeon-Major. He served during the Burmese War, 1885–87, in charge of No. 5 Field Hospital ; was Senior Medical Officer with the Bhamo Expeditionary Force, and Acting Principal Medical Officer, Upper Burma Field Force. For his services during the Burmese War he was mentioned in Despatches [London Gazette, 2 Sept. 1887] He was created a Companion of the Distinguished Service Order [London Gazette, 25 Nov. 1887] : " Robert de la Cour Corbett, Surg.-Maj., M.S. For operations in Burma." In 1887 he became Surgeon-Lieut.-Colonel ; in 1893 Brigade Surgeon-Lieutenant-Colonel, and in 1898, Colonel, Royal Army Medical Corps. He was P.M.O., Oudh and Rohilkhand District, North-Western Provinces, India. Colonel Corbett married Harriet Lucie, eldest daughter of Robert Gregg, of Cork. He died 24 March, 1904.

STEAD, ALFRED JAMES, Major, served on the Indian Frontier, 1864–66 (Medal) ; in Afghanistan, 1878–80 (Medal) ; in Burma, 1885–87. In the Burmese War he commanded a detachment at Pagan ; was mentioned in Despatches (22 June, 1886, and 2 Sept. 1887) ; received a clasp, and was created a Companion of the Distinguished Service Order [London Gazette, 25 Nov. 1887] : " Alfred James Stead, Major, Bengal Infantry. For operations in Burma." In 1891 he served in the Hazara Campaign. He was promoted to Lieutenant-Colonel 4 Oct. 1887, and retired. He died on the 20th of March, 1909.

WRIGHT, FREDERICK WILLIAM, Surgeon-Major, Indian Medical Service, Bengal, was born in 1850, son of the late Robert John Wright, of Norwich ; is C.M. and M.C., Edinburgh ; entered the Indian Medical Service in 1873 ; served in the Afghan War, 1878–80, being present in the affair of Jugdulluk, action of Charasiah, march from Kabul to the relief of Kandahar and battle of 1 Sept. Operations against the Maris. He received the Medal with clasp for Kandahar, and the Bronze Decoration. Served in Burma, 1886–87 (Despatches [London Gazette, 2 Sept. 1887] ; Medal with clasp) ; created a Companion of the Distinguished Service Order [London Gazette, 25 Nov. 1887] : " Frederick William Wright, Surgeon-Major, Indian Medical Service. For operations in Burma." He served with the British Contingent, China Expeditionary Force, 1900–1 (Medal) ; in Waziristan, 1901–2 (Medal and clasp). He was promoted to Lieutenant-Colonel 1 April, 1893, and has retired. Lieut.-Colonel Wright married in 1914, Edith Bella Freeman, of Dover.

ROSE, HENRY METCALFE, Major, was born at Sangor, East Indies, 30 July, 1848, eldest son of General Hugh Rose, of Kilravock, Silverdale Road, Eastbourne ; was educated at a private school, and at the Royal Military College, Sandhurst ; joined the 107th Regt. 8 March, 1867, and entered the Indian Staff Corps in Sept. 1869. He married in 1870, Georgina Julie, third daughter of Sir Norman Robert Leslie, 6th Baronet. He served in the Afghanistan Campaign, 1879–80 ; with the Khyber Field Force (Medal) ; served on North-West Frontier of India, Hazara, in 1891 (clasp) ; also in the Second Miranzai Expedition in 1891 (clasp) ; served in the Burma Campaign, 1886–87 ; operations of 3rd and 4th Brigades, Southern Shan Column ; was mentioned in Despatches ; received the Medal with two clasps ; was created a Companion of the Distinguished Service Order [London Gazette, 25 Nov. 1887] : " Henry Metcalfe Rose, Major, Bengal Staff Corps. For operations in Burma." He was Colonel on the Staff, India, and Malakand Force. He became Colonel 26 Sept. 1897, and was placed on the Supernumerary List 30 July, 1905.

DENING, LEWIS, Major, was born in 1848, son of John Dening, Esq., of Pitt House, Ottery St. Mary. He was educated in Devonshire, and entered the 75th Regt. 11 May, 1867, as Ensign ; was transferred to the 39th Regt. 11 June, 1868, and to the B.S.C. (now I.S.C.) 20 April, 1871. He married firstly, at Plymouth, in 1872, Eliza Janet (died in 1876), daughter of the late W. Eales, Esq., and secondly, in 1877, Beatrice Catherine, daughter of the late E. J. Scott, Esq., of Portland Lodge, Southsea. His sons are : Major Lewis Eales Dening ; Major Harold Dening ; Capt. Roland Dening, and Lieut. John Pitt Dening. His daughters are Honoria, wife of Colonel A. J. Macnab, I.M.S. ; Irene, wife of Major L. Gascoigne, R.F.A. ; Gladys Violet, and Eva Joan. He served in the Afghan War, 1878–79 (Medal) ; was Brigade-Major, Bengal, 1880–81, and D.A.A.G., Bengal, 1885 ; became Captain 11 May, 1879.

Lewis Dening.

He served with the Burma Field Force, 1886–87 ; was mentioned in Despatches ; Medal with clasp, and was created a Companion of the Distinguished Service Order [London Gazette, 25 Nov. 1887] : " Lewis Dening, Major, Bengal Staff Corps." Personally thanked by the Commander-in-Chief ; was promoted Major 11 May, 1887, and Lieutenant-Colonel 11 May, 1893 ; served with the Expedition to Dongola in 1896 (British and Egyptian Medals) ; with the Mohmand Field Force, 1897–98 ; mentioned in Despatches [London Gazette, 11 Jan. 1898] ; Brevet of Colonel 11 May, 1897 ; Colonel 1 Sept. 1900. Medal with clasp. He served with the Waziristan Expedition, 1901–2 ; mentioned in Despatches [London Gazette, 8 Aug. 1902] ; Clasp ; created a C.B. ; became Lieutenant-General, 1 Jan. 1904 ; commanded Burma Division, India, 7 Feb. 1907 ; Lieutenant-General 11 Dec. 1907 ; K.C.B. in 1909. Sir Lewis Dening died 16 Feb. 1911, at Jubbulpore, India, when en route for England. His D.S.O. was awarded for operations in Burma.

RAWLINSON, SPENCER RICHARD, Major, was born in 1848, son of the late Rev. George Rawlinson. He entered the 45th Regt. in 1867 ; was transferred to the M.S.C. (now I.S.C.), 1871. He married, in 1877, Mary (who died in 1882), daughter of H. Mann, Esq., of Hedenham Hall, Norfolk. He became Captain in 1879 ; served with the Burma Field Force in 1885–87 (Medal with clasp) ; mentioned in Despatches 2 Sept. 1887 ; created a Companion of the Distinguished Service Order [London Gazette, 25 Nov. 1887] : " Spencer Richard Rawlinson, Major, Madras Staff Corps." He became Major in 1887 ; Lieut.-Colonel 20 July, 1893. Colonel Rawlinson died on 15 April, 1903. His D.S.O. was awarded for operations in Burma.

STREET, ALFRED WILLIAM FREDERICK, Surgeon, Indian Medical Service, Bombay, was born 22 Oct. 1852, son of the late Rev. Benjamin Street, Vicar of Barnetby, Lincolnshire ; became M.R.C.S. England, in 1874 ; L.R.C.P. London, in 1876 ; joined the Bombay Medical Service as Surgeon 1 Oct. 1877. Served in the Afghan War 1878–80 ; action on the Helmund 14 July, 1880 ; cavalry affair 23 July, 1880 ; battle of Maiwand, defence of Kandahar, and battle of 1 Sept. (mentioned in Despatches, Medal with clasp). He married, in 1884, Helen, daughter of the Rev. Edward Mitford Moongall, Vicar of Frodingham, Lincolnshire. He served with the Burma Field Force (Despatches, London Gazette, 2 Sept. 1887) ; Medal with two clasps ; and was created a Companion of the Distinguished Service Order [London Gazette, 25 Nov. 1887] : " Alfred William Frederick Street, Surgeon, Indian Medical Service, Bombay. For operations in Burma." Surg.-Maj. 1 Oct. 1897 ; Deputy Sanitary Commissioner, Bombay. Lieut.-Colonel A. W. F. Street died 30 Jan. 1911.

ELLIOT, EDWARD LOCKE, Capt., was born 28 Jan. 1850, son of the late Colonel Edward King Elliot. He was educated at Harrow, and at the R.M.C., Sandhurst ; entered the 108th Regt. 22 Jan. 1868 ; served in the Afghan War in 1879 (Medal) ; became Captain, Bombay Staff Corps (now I.S.C.), 22 Jan. 1880 ; served in the Burma Campaign in 1887–89 (Despatches 2 Sept. 1887) ; medal with two clasps ; created a Companion of the Distinguished Service Order [London Gazette, 25 Nov. 1887] : " Edward Locke Elliot, Capt., Bombay Staff Corps. For services in Burma." He became Major 22 Jan. 1888 He married, in 1893, Eva Sybil, daughter of Colonel Percy Smith, and they have one daughter. He became Lieutenant-Colonel 22 Jan. 1894. Lieut.-Colonel Elliot served with the Dongola Expeditionary Force in 1896 (C.B., Medal, Khedive's Medal, and mentioned in Despatches) ; in South Africa in 1901–2, on Staff (as Special Service Officer, graded as Major-General on Staff in command of Mobile Cavalry Division, from 26 March, 1901) ; operations in Orange River Colony March, 1901, to 31 May, 1902. He was mentioned in Despatches [London Gazette, 17 June and 29 July, 1902] ; received Queen's Medal with four clasps, and was created a K.C.B. Sir Edward Elliot was Inspector-General of Cavalry in India, 1898–1901 ; became Major-General 1 April, 1902 ; Lieutenant-General 30 June, 1906 ; commanded 8th Division, Indian Army, 1905–10 ; retired 3 Oct. 1911. He is Honorary Colonel, 31st Lancers ; Commander of the Legion of Honour. He served during the European War in France from 28 Sept. 1914, as Military Adviser, Indian Army.

ADAMS, ALEXANDER PEERS, Surgeon, joined the Indian Medical Service, and served in Burma in 1886–87. He was created a Companion of the Distinguished Service Order [London Gazette, 25 Nov. 1887] : " Alexander Peers Adams, Surgeon, Indian Medical Service, Madras. For services in Burma." He died 12 Sept. 1887, in Madras.

SHEPHARD, CHARLES SINCLAIR, Capt., was born at Mount Clare, Roehampton, 9 March, 1848 ; youngest son of John Shephard, Proctor, Doctors' Commons, and Harriet Strachey Harper. He was educated at Eton ; Brasenose College, Oxford ; Sandhurst, and Dresden. He entered the 4th King's Own Regt. 11 Sept. 1872. He married (1st), in 1875, Ada Katharine (died in 1909), daughter of Bransby William Powys, of the Vandreys, Cheshire ; and (2ndly) Bertha Joan, daughter of the late Reginald Bosworth Smith. He served in the South African Expedition, Zulu Campaign, 1886–87 (Despatches and Medal) ; A.D.C. to Sir James Fergusson, Governor of Bombay, and to Sir Arthur Hardinge, Commander-in-Chief, Bombay, 1880–86 ; served as Brigade-Major in Burma, 1886–87 ; was mentioned in Despatches [London Gazette, 2 Sept. 1887] ; Military Secretary to Governor at Gibraltar, 1887 ; served as Brigade-Major, Burma, 1886–87 ; and was created a Companion of the Distinguished Service Order [London Gazette, 25 Nov. 1887] : " Charles Sinclair Shephard, Capt., King's Own (Royal Lancaster) Regt. ; Assistant Military Secretary and A.D.C. to the Governor and C.-in-C., Gibraltar." He was mentioned in Despatches [London Gazette, 2 Sept. 1887]. He became Major, 7th Fusiliers, 9 July, 1890 ; retired 8 July, 1891. Is Lieutenant-Colonel, 4th Somerset Light Infantry, and was Brigade-Major to the Western Counties Volunteer Brigade. He joined the 6th Wiltshire Regt. Nov. 1914 ; served in France July to Dec. 1915 ; commanded 7th Royal Lancaster Regt. 21 Sept. to 19 Dec. 1915, in France ; commanded No. 2 Group, Machine Gun Corps, Grantham, Feb. to May, 1916 ; commanded 13th Devons Works Battn. June, 1916. His D.S.O. was awarded for operations in Burma.

SPRAGGE, BASIL EDWARD, Capt., was born 9 Oct. 1851, son of the late F. H. Spragge, J.P., of Paignton, Devon ; was educated at Cheltenham College, and Trinity College, Cambridge, and joined the 51st Light Infantry 19 Oct. 1872 ; served in the Jowaki Expedition in 1877, as Orderly Officer to Brigadier-General Doran (Medal with clasp). He served in the First Campaign in First Afghan War in 1878–79, as Superintendent, Army Signalling (Despatches) ; in Second Afghan War in 1879–80, as Adjutant to regiment ; assault and capture of Ali Masjid ; operations in the Shiliman Valley and in the Bazar Valley (Despatches 7 Nov. 1879 ; Medal and clasp). He served in Burma, 1885–89, as D.A.A.G. and Q.M.G. ; was created a Companion of the Distinguished Service Order [London Gazette, 25 Nov. 1887] : " Basil Edward Spragge, Capt., King's Own (Yorkshire) Light Infantry, D.A.Q.M.G., Bengal. For services in Burma." He retired 12 Feb. 1890, with the rank of Major, and died at Cimiez 20 Oct. 1915.

SYKES, WILLIAM AINLEY, M.B. London, Surgeon, was born 19 July, 1859, at Golcar, Yorkshire, son of the late James Sykes, of Golcar. He was educated at Huddersfield College, and St. Bartholomew's Hospital ; became Surgeon, Bengal Medical Service, in 1882 ; served with the Sudan Expedition in 1885 (Medal with two clasps ; Bronze Star), and during the Burmese War, 1886–89 (Despatches 2 Sept. 1887) ; created a Companion of the Distinguished Service Order [London Gazette, 25 Nov. 1887] : " William Ainley Sykes, Surgeon, Indian Medical Service. For services in Burma." He also received the Medal with two clasps ; became Major 1 April, 1894 ; served in Waziri Expedition in 1894 (clasp) ; Malakand in 1897 (Medal with two clasps) ; operations in Bajaur, and in the Mamund country, Buner ; attack and capture of the Tanga Pass. He was mentioned in Despatches [London Gazette, 22 April, 1898], and received the Medal and clasp ; China Expedition (Medal). He became Lieutenant-Colonel 1 April, 1902 ; retired 20 July, 1912.

SHONE, WILLIAM TERENCE, Capt., was born in 1850, son of John Allen Shone, Esq., Barrister-at-Law, of 30, Pembroke Gardens, Kensington, and Eleanor, daughter of Terence Fitzgerald, Lieut., 33rd Regt., subsequently Sheriff of Madras. He was educated at the R.M.A., Woolwich ; entered the Royal Engineers 4 Jan. 1871 ; served in the Afghan War, 1878–80 (Medal) ; with the Mahsud Waziri Expedition in 1881, as Adjutant, R.E. ; was mentioned in Despatches ; in Burma Campaign, 1885–87 ; mentioned in Despatches 2 Sept. 1887 ; received the Medal with two clasps, and was created a Companion of the Distinguished Service Order [London Gazette, 25 Nov. 1887] : " William Terence Shone, Capt., Royal Engineers." He was promoted to Major in 1889 ; served in the two Miranzai Expeditions in 1891, as Commanding Royal Engineer (Despatches 15 Sept. 1891 ; clasp ; Brevet of Lieutenant-Colonel) Lieut.-Colonel Shone married, in 1893, Janet, daughter of the late Right Honourable Gerald Fitzgibbon, Lord Justice of Appeal, Ireland, and they have one son and one daughter. He served in 1895 with the Chitral Relief Force, as Commanding Royal Engineer Lines of Communication 28 March to Aug. 1895 (Despatches [London Gazette, 15 Nov. 1895] ; Medal with clasp ; created a C.B.). He was promoted Brevet Colonel in 1895 ; served with the China Field Force, 1900–1, as Chief Engineer and Brigadier-General (Despatches [London Gazette, 13 Sept. 1901] ; Medal). He was Director-General of Military Works in India, 1901–3 ; became Major-General in 1902, and Lieutenant-General 19 Dec. 1903 ; was Inspector-General of Fortifications, Army Headquarters, 1903–4 ; was created a K.C.B. in 1906. Sir W. T. Shone became Col. Commandant, R.E., in 1918. His D.S.O. was awarded for operations in Burma.

EARLE, HENRY, Capt., was born at Brook Farm, in the parish of West Derby, Lancashire, 15 Aug. 1854, eldest son of the 2nd Baronet, of Allerton Tower, Woolton, Lancashire, and Emily, daughter of William Fletcher, Esq. He was educated

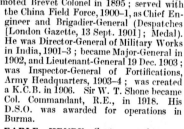
Henry Earle.

at Eton, and at Trinity College, Oxford (Honorary M.A., Cambridge), and joined the Army 11 Sept. 1876 ; served in the Jowaki Campaign with the 51st Light Infantry, in 1877 (Medal and clasp) ; in the Afghan War, 1878–80 (Medal), as Orderly Officer during the Second Campaign to Sir R. Bright ; operations in the Lughman and Hissarak Valleys (Medal) ; in the Egyptian Expedition of 1882, as A.D.C. to Major-General Earle, being present at El Magfar, Tel-el-Mahuta, Kassassin and Tel-el-Kebir, in 1882 (Medal and clasp ; Fifth Class Medjidie ; Khedive's Star) ; in the Burmese Expedition, 1886–87 ; Ruby Mine Column in 1886. For his services in the Mainloung Expedition he was mentioned in Despatches [London Gazette, 2 Sept. 1887] ; received two clasps, and was created a Companion of the Distinguished Service Order [London Gazette, 25 Nov. 1887] : " Henry Earle, Capt., King's Own Yorkshire Light Infantry." He was with the King's Own Yorkshire Light Infantry in the Frontier Campaign in Tirah, 1897–98 (severely wounded at Shinkamar 29 Jan. 1898), and received the Medal and two clasps. Also in the South African War, 1899–1900, as Second-in-Command of Yorkshire Light Infantry, being present in the advance on Kimberley, including actions at Belmont, Enslin and Modder River 28 Nov. 1899 (severely wounded). Operations in the Orange River Colony, July, 1900, and in the Transvaal north and west of Pretoria, Oct. 1900. Mentioned in Despatches [London Gazette, 26 Jan. 1900] ; was promoted to Lieutenant-Colonel on half-pay 29 Nov. 1900, and received the Queen's Medal and two clasps. In 1900 Lieut.-Colonel H. Earle succeeded his father as 3rd Baronet (created 1869). He retired from the Army on 9 Aug. 1902, ceasing to belong to the Reserve 15 Aug. 1909. He served as an Intelligence Officer in the European War from 1914 to 1916. Sir Henry Earle married, in 1891, Evelyn Grace, daughter of Major Boileau, 61st Regt., and they have one daughter. His D.S.O. was awarded for operations in Burma.

KEENE, ALFRED, Capt., was born 17 April, 1855, son of the late H. G. Keene, C.I.E., and Mrs. Keene, daughter of Brigadier-General Moore, Indian Army ; entered the Army 12 Feb. 1874 ; served in the Afghan War of 1878–80, taking part in the march from Quetta to the relief of Kandahar. He was mentioned in Despatches [London Gazette, 25 Jan. 1881], receiving the Medal. He served in Burma, 1885–86, when he was mentioned in Despatches [London Gazette, 2 Sept. 1887], received the Medal and clasp, and was created a Companion of the Distinguished Service Order [London Gazette, 25 Nov. 1886] : " Alfred Keene, Capt., Royal Artillery." He was promoted to Lieutenant-Colonel 5 April, 1900, and was given the Brevet of Colonel 10 Feb. 1894, becoming Colonel in 1904, and was put on half-pay, late R.A., 5 April, 1905. He married, in 1894, Janet Frances, widow of Colonel Ayrton Pullan, at the War Office from Dec. 1914 ; later as a Staff Captain. In Jan. 1918, Colonel Keene was made a C.M.G. He died on 21 April, 1918. His D.S.O. was awarded for operations in Burma.

SHERSTON, JOHN, Lieut.-Colonel, was born in 1857, son of J. Davis Sherston, Esq., of Evercreech House, Somerset, and of Innes Eliza Maxwell. He was educated at Marlborough and Sandhurst, and entered the Rifle Brigade in 1877 ; served in the Afghan War, 1879–80, as A.D.C. to General Sir Frederick Roberts, G.C.B., and was twice mentioned in Despatches, gaining the Medal with three clasps, and the Bronze Star. He took part in the Waziri Expedition in 1881, and was promoted Captain in 1884. In 1882 he married Alice, daughter of General A. H. Bamfield. He served with the Upper Burma Field Force, 1886–87, as D.A.A. and Q.G. at Headquarters, and was mentioned in Despatches, gaining the Medal with clasp, and was awarded the Distinguished Service Order [London Gazette, 25 Nov. 1887] : " John Sherston, Lieut.-Colonel, Rifle Brigade. For services in Burma." He was appointed D.A.A.G. for Bengal, 1886–91, and D.A.A.G. for Instruction, Punjab, in 1893. He was killed at Talana Hill, South Africa, 20 Oct. 1899.

WILLCOCKS, JAMES, Capt., was born 1 April, 1857, fourth son of the late Capt. W. Willcocks, R.E., I.C.S., and Mrs. Willcocks. He was educated at Easton, Somersetshire, and at the Royal Military College, Sand-

James Willcocks.

hurst, and joined the 101st Foot (Leinster Regt.) as Second Lieutenant 30 Jan. 1878, becoming Lieutenant 20 Oct. 1879. He served in the Afghan War in 1878–80 (Medal), and in the Mahsud Waziri Expedition in 1881 (mentioned in Despatches). On 21 Aug. 1884, he became Captain, Leinster Regt. Capt. Willcocks served in the Sudan Expedition in 1885 (Suakin) ; was mentioned in Despatches, received the Bronze Star, and the Medal and clasp. From 1885 to 1889 he accompanied the Burmese Expedition as Transport Officer, and in charge of Field Commissariat ; also acted as Road Commandant. He was mentioned in Despatches [London Gazette, 2 Sept. 1887] ; received the Medal with two clasps, and was created a Companion of the Distinguished Service Order [London Gazette, 25 Nov. 1887] : " James Willcocks, Capt., Leinster Regt. For services in Burma." He was Adjutant, Leinster Regt., from 27 Dec. 1887, to 8 July, 1889. In 1889 and 1890 he served with the Chin Lushai Expedition (clasp). He was Station Staff Officer, First Class, Bengal, 7 July, 1890, to 15 June, 1893. In 1891 he served with the Manipur Expedition as Chief Transport Officer ; was mentioned in Despatches [London Gazette, 14 Aug. 1891], and received the Medal and clasp. He was promoted to Major 29 Sept. 1893 ; was D.A.A.G., Bombay, 1 Aug. 1894, to 26 Nov. 1897. He was A.A.G. Tochi Field Force, N.W. Frontier of India, 1897–98 ; was mentioned in Despatches [London Gazette, 11 Feb. 1898] ; received the Brevet of Lieutenant-Colonel 20 May, 1898, and the

Medal with clasp. He was employed as Second in Command with the West African Frontier Force 27 Nov. 1897, to 9 July, 1899; took part in the operations on the Niger; was in command of the Forces in Borgu (Medal and clasp); Kaduna in 1898 (clasp); was mentioned in Despatches [London Gazette, 7 March, 1899]; received the special thanks of H.M.'s Government; was created a C.M.G.; was promoted to Lieutenant-Colonel 8 July, 1899; received the Medal and clasp. Lieut.-Colonel Willcocks was specially employed on the Gold Coast, Commanding the Ashanti Field Force 26 May, 1900, to 3 Jan. 1901, with which he relieved Kumassi, and was given the Brevet of Colonel 15 July, 1900; received the Medal and clasp, and was created a K.C.M.G. For these services he also was granted the freedom of the City of London; was presented with a sword of honour by the Corporation, and was mentioned in the King's Speech at the opening of his first Parliament. He became Colonel 29 March, 1902. He was on Special Service on the Staff in South Africa, with the Frontier Field Force, 23 Jan. 1902, to 7 March, 1904, and received the Queen's Medal with clasp. He commanded the Nowshera Brigade in India 29 March, 1902, to 28 March, 1907; became Major-General 1 Dec. 1906; commanded the Peshawar Division from 9 Jan. 1908. In that year he was in command of the operations in the Zakka Khel country, and he was mentioned in Despatches [London Gazette, 22 May, 1908]; received the thanks of the Governor-General of India in Council. He commanded the Mohmand Expedition in 1908; was mentioned in Despatches [London Gazette, 22 May, 1908]; was promoted to Lieutenant-General 16 July, 1908, for Distinguished Service in the Field, and received the thanks of the Governor-General of India (Medal with clasp). Sir James Willcocks served in the European War in 1914 and 1915, in command of the Indian Army Corps. Lieut.-Colonel J. W. B. Merewether, C.I.E., and the Right Hon. Sir Frederick Smith say of General Willcocks in "The Indian Corps in France" (pages 17, 18, 19): "On the 30th Sept. Lieut.-General Sir James Willcocks arrived with his Staff by the S.S. Malwa. His appointment as Corps Commander of the Indian troops in France had been announced on the 27th Sept., and was received with the greatest enthusiasm by all ranks. Nor was his great reputation undeserved. His name stood high in the Army as that of a very stout, skilful and efficient soldier, who had carved out a career for himself without the aid of patronage, and in complete indifference to social and political influences." Having described his military services, the authors of this most interesting and delightful book go on to say: "Such was the remarkable record of the General who led the Army of India to their great adventure in Flanders. No man in the British Army wore more decorations on his breast for active service than James Willcocks, and none bore his honours more modestly and more gallantly. He was now to be tested in surroundings which were novel even to his vast military experience. He was to be placed in situations more difficult, it may be boldly claimed, than any other Corps Commander had to face. His task demanded a subtle and intuitive insight into the mentality of the East; much sympathy, much allowance, and yet on occasion an unpitying severity. He had at once to hold, with two small, untried Indian divisions, a line which had tested the endurance of the two divisions of English veterans under General Smith-Dorrien, whom he relieved, and through all his difficulties, which were far greater than even at this time it is possible to explain, he never faltered in his courage and never lost the devotion of the troops whom he understood so well. One of the writers will never forget his conversation, after the battle of Neuve Chapelle, with an Indian officer of a shattered but heroic battalion. 'There are very few of you left, Subadar Sahib,' said the General, with deep emotion. 'There are twice as many as there were until the General Sahib visited us,' replied the officer, bleeding as he spoke from two severe wounds. General Willcocks has preserved a complete documentary record of the whole period during which he commanded the Indian Corps. His advice as to the demands which it was possible to make upon the troops for which he was responsible was not always accepted by superior authority; perhaps imperious necessity sometimes prescribed a different course. But he was seldom wrong in his estimate, and a close study of his confidential papers establishes more and more clearly his sagacity, his prescience and his courage." The Indian troops were received in France with the greatest enthusiasm. The story of their gallantry in France is admirably told in the book from which we have quoted. For his services in the European War Sir James Willcocks was twice mentioned in Despatches, and created a G.C.M.G. He is a Grand Officier of the Legion of Honour; was created a K.C.B. in 1913; a K.C.S.I. in 1914; was promoted to General in 1915. He is Colonel, Loyal North Lancashire Regt., and was appointed Governor and Commander-in-Chief, Bermuda, in 1917. He is fond of polo, shooting and riding. Sir James Willcocks married, in 1889, Winifred, second daughter of Colonel G. A. Way, C.B., B.S.C., and they have one son, Capt. James L. Willcocks, M.C.

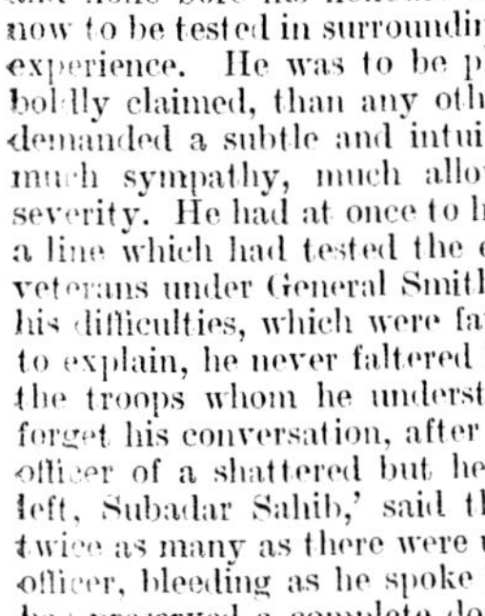
Samuel A. E. Hickson.

HICKSON, SAMUEL ARTHUR EINEM, Deputy Assistant Adjutant and Quartermaster-General, was born at Highgate 6 Sept. 1858, son of James Hickson and Wilhelmina von Einem, of Hanover. He was educated at Highgate School, and obtained a commission in the Royal Engineers 29 April, 1873; served in the Afghan War in 1878–80; took part in the relief of Kandahar as Field Engineer; employed on Quetta Railway and Bolan Pass high level road. He served also in the Suakin Campaign of 1885; in the Gordon Relief Expedition (Medal with clasp; Bronze Star). He became Captain 8 Jan. 1885, and again saw active service in the Burma Campaign of 1885–87, being present at the capture of Mandalay. Became D.A.A.G. and Q.M.G. on the Staff of Sir George White; was mentioned in Despatches 2 Sept. 1887, and was created a Companion of the Distinguished Service Order [London Gazette, 25 Nov. 1887]: "Samuel Arthur Einem Hickson, Royal Engineers, Deputy Assistant Adjutant and Quartermaster-General, Bengal. For services in Burma." He became Major 7 Oct. 1892, and P.S.C. as well as Q.S., and Lieutenant-Colonel 29 March, 1900; was given the Brevet of Colonel 10 Feb. 1904; became Colonel 8 Sept. 1905, when he became Chief Engineer, Plymouth Coast Defences. He retired from the Army as a Colonel in 1909. He married (1st) in 1892, Margaret Emmeline (who died in 1895), daughter of the Rev. Vernon Blake, of Stoke Poges; (2ndly) Annette Laura, daughter of Colonel Cuming, late Queen's Own Cameron Highlanders, of Crover, County Cavan, Ireland. He served in the European War in 1914–17, as Chief Engineer Headquarters Staff, Salisbury Command, and late C.R.E. Hounslow, and was promoted to Honorary Brigadier-General, and awarded the C.B. for his services in supervising the construction of hutments in Salisbury Command, including Salisbury Plain and in all the construction of hutments for 230,000 men, besides horses and guns.

BELEY, CHARLES HAROLD HEPWORTH, Capt., served in the Burma Campaign of 1885–86. He was created a Companion of the Distinguished Service Order [London Gazette, 25 Nov. 1887]: "Charles Harold Hepworth Beley, Capt., Bengal Staff Corps; Deputy Assistant Quartermaster-General, Bengal. For services in Burma."

HASTINGS, EDWARD SPENCE, Capt., was born 17 Jan. 1856, and entered the Army 28 Feb. 1874; the 109th Foot, and the Madras Staff Corps 17 Aug. 1876. He served in the Afghan War in 1880 (Medal); as General Transport Officer, Kama Expedition (Medal); and in the Boer War of 1881; in the Basuto War of 1881 (Cape G.S. Medal with two clasps). He became Captain, I.S.C., 28 Feb. 1885, and served in the Burma Campaign of 1885–88, when he was mentioned in Despatches 2 Sept. 1887; received the Medal with two clasps, and was created a Companion of the Distinguished Service Order [London Gazette, 25 Nov. 1887]: "Edward Spence Hastings, Capt., Madras Staff Corps. For services in Burma." He took part in the Chin Lushai Expedition in 1899–90 (Clasp), and in the Manipur Expedition of 1891 (Clasp); was promoted to Major 28 Feb. 1894, and Lieutenant-Colonel 28 Feb. 1900; was given the Brevet of Colonel 10 Feb. 1904; created a C.B. in 1906; became Colonel 1 June, 1907; commanded a brigade in India 1 June, 1907, to 11 April, 1912. He was promoted to Major-General 15 Nov. 1907. He was appointed to the command of the 92nd Punjabis.

DUN, EDWARD WILLIAM, Capt., served in Burma in 1885–86, and was created a Companion of the Distinguished Service Order [London Gazette, 25 Nov. 1887]: "Edward William Dun, Capt., Madras Staff Corps. For services in Burma." He died on 4 June, 1895.

BAYLY, ALFRED WILLIAM LAMBERT, Capt., was born at Paisley, 18 Feb. 1856, youngest son of the late Major George Bayly, and Eliza, daughter of Lieut.-General Savage, R.E. He was educated at Wellington College, and joined the 104th Regt. 13 June, 1874, and the Bombay Staff Corps 8 March, 1879. He served in the Afghan War of 1880–81, taking part in the defence and battle of Kandahar in 1880 (Medal and clasp). He was promoted to Captain 18 June, 1885, and in the same year served in the Sudan, with the Suakin Expedition, taking part in various attacks on convoys and in the operations at Tamai. In 1885 and 1886 he was officiating D.A.Q.M.G. Bombay. In 1885–87 he served in the Burma War as D.A.Q.M.G.; was mentioned in Despatches [London Gazette, 2 Sept. 1887]; received the Medal and five clasps, and was created a Companion of the Distinguished Service Order [London Gazette, 25 Nov. 1887]: "Alfred William Lambert Bayly, Capt., Bombay Staff Corps. Deputy Assistant Quartermaster-General, Bengal. For services in Burma." From the 25th Nov. 1887, to 1892, he served in Mhow District as D.A.Q.M.G. In 1893 Capt. Bayly passed through the Staff College, and he became Major 13 June, 1894. In 1896 he assumed command of the 126th Bombay Infantry (Baluchistan Regt.). He served in the South African War in 1899–1900, on the Staff, and was present at the relief of Ladysmith, including the action at Colenso; operations of 17 to 24 Jan. 1900, and action at Spion Kop (slightly wounded); operations of 5 to 7 Feb. 1900, and action at Vaal Kranz; operations on Tugela Heights 14 to 27 Feb. 1900, and action at Pieter's Hill; operations in Natal, March to June, 1900, including action at Laing's Nek (6 to 9 June); operations in the Transvaal east of Pretoria, Aug. to Oct. 1900, including actions at Lydenburg (5 to 8 Sept.). He was mentioned in Despatches (Sir R. H. Buller, 30 March and 9 Nov. 1900) [London Gazette, 8 Feb. 1900]; received the Queen's Medal with five clasps, and was created a C.B. He was A.D.C. to the King in 1902–6; A.A.G. India, 1903–4; D.A.G., Commandant, Indian Staff College, 1905–6; Secretary to the Government of India, Army Department, 1906–9; created a C.S.I. in 1909; Colonel, 126th Baluchistan Light Infantry; created a K.C.B. in 1911; promoted to Major-General 19 March, 1906; retired 19 March, 1912. Sir Alfred Bayly married (1st) Ada Margaret (who died in 1880), daughter of the late Major-General S. Thacker, Bombay; and (2ndly) Eva, daughter of the late John Naylor, of Leighton Hall, Montgomeryshire, and they have one son.

LUGARD, FREDERICK JOHN DEALTRY, Capt., was born 22 Jan. 1858; son of the Rev. F. G. Lugard, M.A., and Mary, daughter of the Rev. Garton Howard. He was educated at Rossall and Sandhurst, and entered the Army 11 May, 1878; served in the Afghan War, 1879–80, being present at the affairs of Saidabad (Medal); in the Sudan Campaign, 1885 (Suakin), employed with Indian Transport (Despatches; Medal and clasp; Bronze Star); was promoted Captain, 2nd Battn. Norfolk Regt. 1885. Capt. Lugard served with the Burma Field Force in 1886–87, in charge of Transport of Ruby Mines Column and Woonthoo Column, and as Staff Officer to the Director of Transport. He was mentioned in Despatches

[London Gazette, 2 Sept. 1887], and on two other occasions, received Medal with two clasps for Burma, and was created a Companion of the Distinguished Service Order [London Gazette, 25 Nov. 1887]: "Frederick John Dealtry Lugard, Capt., Norfolk Regt." He commanded an expedition against Arab slave traders on Lake Nyassa in 1888 (severely wounded); concluded treaties which secured Uganda against the rival efforts of Emin Pasha and Karl Peters, and administered the country in 1889–1902 (Medal of I.B.E.A. Chartered Company). Commanded an expedition to Borgu and made treaties for the inclusion of that country in the British territory of Nigeria, acting on behalf of the Royal Niger Company in 1894–95 (Medal of Royal Niger Chartered Company); created a C.B. in 1895). He became Lieutenant-Colonel 8 July, 1899, and full Colonel in July; was appointed H.M.'s Commissioner and Commandant of all forces in the Hinterland of Lagos in 1897; raised and commanded 6th A.F.F., with rank of Brigadier-General; appointed first High Commissioner of Northern Nigeria 1 Jan. 1900, until Sept. 1905; created K.C.M.G. on 1 Jan. 1901. Sir Frederick Lugard took part in the Kano-Sokoto Expedition in 1903 and various operations (two Medals with clasps), and retired with the rank of Colonel 22 July, 1905. He was Governor and Commander-in-Chief of Hong-Kong in 1907–1912; was created a G.C.M.G. in 1911; was Governor and Commander-in-Chief of Northern Nigeria and Southern Nigeria (simultaneously) in 1912–13; became Governor-General of Nigeria in 1914; retired 15 July, 1919. In 1902 he married Flora Louise, daughter of the late General Shaw, C.B. Sir F. J. D. Lugard is Honorary D.C.L. (Oxon.); Honorary D.C.L. (Durham), and Honorary LL.D. of Hong-Kong University, of which he was the first Chancellor. He was made a Commander of the Legion of Honour in 1918.

Frederick J. D. Lugard.

The "Daily Telegraph" for 29 Jan. 1920, says in an article on "Modern Nigeria: "Six years ago, when on the great plain at Kano 30,000 African horsemen charged at the gallop, brandishing their weapons, to give the Salute of the Desert to British sovereignty, modern Nigeria was founded. It ranks as the largest of all the Crown Colonies and Protectorates of the Empire, with an area about one-third the extent of British India, and a population nearly half that of England. Already it is to European civilization one of the most important divisions of the tropical zone, and in the near future it must become far more valuable. The account, therefore, which Sir Frederick Lugard, its first Governor-General, has just given of his stewardship deserves wide publicity. The existing 'Colony and Protectorate' was formed, we may recall, by the amalgamation of Northern and Southern Nigeria, two areas divided by an arbitrary line, and for their administration, organization and development interdependent, but presenting diverse conditions. The North is, in general, prairie country, high and dry; had been for long under the influence of Islam, and in the last half of the nineteenth century was devastated by intertribal warfare and slave-hunting Emirs. The South receives the equatorial rainfall, is a land of dense forests and dense population, yam fields and mangrove swamps, with a religion of fetish worship, witchcraft and human sacrifice. The worst evils of this dispensation—we need only recall the suppression of the blood-stained tyranny of Benin—as well as the ravages of the Northern Emirs, one of whom boasted that he would 'die with a slave in his mouth,' had been abolished by British arms before the amalgamation. The task which Sir Frederick Lugard set himself was not merely to achieve political and financial unity, but to raise 'each part of Nigeria to the level of the highest plane attained by any particular part.' The North needed material development; the South a better native administration and judicial system. The first duty of the Government is that of a protector and trustee of the welfare of the native races. Without the social chaos of sudden abolition slavery is being brought to an end. An elaborate system of Courts has been established, by which petty chiefs, natives learned in their own law, and paramount chiefs and their officials, dispense justice. The sale of imported spirits to the natives, a traffic which Mr. Chamberlain pronounced discreditable to the British name, is now only permitted in one-fifth and strictly controlled in the rest of the Protectorate, and Sir Frederick Lugard claims to have proved that the Government does not need the revenue nor commerce the profits derived from the trade. The importance of Nigeria to our own industries consists primarily in the fact that it is many thousands of miles nearer the United Kingdom than the other countries of the Empire from which tropical produce is exported. Lagos is about a fortnight's voyage from Liverpool, and Lagos and the other ports of that coast can provide us with an inexhaustible supply of vegetable oils. Before the war the greater part of this store, nearly 400,000 tons of oil and oilseeds, to a value of more than £5,300,000 in a year, was shipped to Germany. Sir Frederick Lugard supports the levying in Nigeria of an export duty on produce consigned to foreign countries, thus enabling the Empire to supply its needs at bed-rock price, with possible discrimination between Allies, neutrals, and enemies, and suggests that the duty should be used for the development of Nigeria and the payment of the charges on the £6,000,000 of the Imperial War Debt which the Colony has taken over." His D.S.O. was awarded for operations in Burma.

SINCLAIR, ALFRED LAW, Capt., was born 30 April, 1853, at Lifford, near Strabane, son of W. Sinclair, Esq., J.P. and D.L., of Holy Hill, Strabane, County Tyrone, and Sarah Strode. He was educated at Kingstown School (Stackpoole's), and at Wimbledon School (Brackenbury's); and was Lieutenant, P.W.O., Donegal Militia, 1872–74; A.D.C. to the Viceroy of Ireland, 1874; Lieutenant, King's Own Borderers, 1874–76; Lieutenant, Bombay Staff Corps (1st Baluch Battn.), 18 Jan. 1877; Captain, Bombay Staff Corps, 2 Dec. 1885. He served in the Burmese Expedition in 1886–88; was mentioned in Despatches 2 Sept. 1887; received the Medal with clasp, and was created a Companion of the Distinguished Service Order [London Gazette, 25 Nov. 1887]: "Alfred Law Sinclair, Capt., Bombay Staff Corps. For services in Burma." He became Major, Indian Staff Corps, 2 Dec. 1894; was Commandant, 129th D.C.O. Baluch Infantry, 1896–1903; Lieutenant-Colonel, Indian Staff Corps, 1900. Lieut.-Colonel Sinclair retired 30 April, 1908, and died 14 Oct. 1911. He married Kate Adele Jane, daughter of H. P. Rushton, of Calcutta, and they have one son, Malcolm Cecil.

LYLE, HUGH THOMAS, Capt., was born at Wilsborough, Eglinton, Londonderry, 24 April, 1858, eldest son of the Rev. John Lyle of Knocktarna, and Mrs. Lyle (*née* Scott, of Wilsborough, Eglinton). He was educated at Uppingham, and Sandhurst, entering the Army 22 Jan. 1879, and becoming Lieutenant 13 April, 1881, and Captain 6 Dec. 1885. He served in the Burma Campaign of 1885–86, and was dangerously wounded 22 April, 1886, north of Bhamo, in the Kachin Hills, when in command of a raiding party. He was mentioned in Despatches [London Gazette, 2 Sept. 1887]; received the Medal and clasp, and was created a Companion of the Distinguished Service Order [London Gazette, 25 Nov. 1887]: "Hugh Thomas Lyle, Capt., Royal Welch Fusiliers. For services in Burma." Capt. Lyle served in the Hazara Expedition in 1891, as Orderly Officer to Brigadier-General Williamson, C.B., and was mentioned in Despatches [London Gazette, 20 Oct. 1891]. He was promoted to Major 9 Sept. 1896, and from 1899 to 1902 served in the South African War, as Second in Command of the 1st Battn Royal Welch Fusiliers. He took part in operations in the Transvaal, west of Pretoria, including actions at Frederickstad (17 to 25 Oct. 1900). Operations in Orange River Colony (May to Nov. 1900), including actions at Wittebergen (1 to 29 July). Operations in the Transvaal 30 Nov. 1900, to Sept. 1901. Operations in Orange River Colony, Sept. 1901, to 31 May, 1902. He was mentioned in Despatches [London Gazette, 9 July and 10 Sept. 1901]; was given the Brevet of Lieutenant-Colonel, and received the Queen's Medal with three clasps, and the King's Medal with two clasps. He became Lieutenant-Colonel 26 Aug. 1902; commanded the 2nd Royal Welch Fusiliers 21 Aug. 1903, to Aug. 1907; was given the Brevet of Colonel 19 April, 1905. He was placed on retired pay with the rank of Colonel 2 Nov. 1907. He commanded the 8th Battn. Royal Irish Rifles, Sept. 1914, to July, 1915, and was appointed to command the 17th Reserve Battn. Royal Irish Rifles in Nov. 1915, which appointment he held to 9 May, 1918, when the Ulster Division was disbanded. He received the C.B.E. for services during the war. Colonel Lyle married, in 1886, Alice Fanny, second daughter of Sir Warren Hastings D'Oyly, 10th Baronet, and they have one son, Lieut. Hugh D'Oyly, Royal Welch Fusiliers.

Hugh Thomas Lyle.

GOLIGHTLY, ROBERT EDMUND, Colonel, was born 16 Sept. 1856, son of the late Rev. Canon Golightly, Shipton Moyne, Tetbury. He was educated at Eton and Sandhurst; became Sub-Lieutenant in 1875; Sub-Lieutenant, King's Royal Rifles, in 1876. He served in the Afghan War, 1878–80, being present at the action of Takt-i-Pul, advance and occupation of Kandahar and Khelat-i-Ghilzai; marched from Kandahar to Kabul with the force under Sir Donald Stewart; was present at the Battle of Ahmed Kheyl and action of Urzoo (Despatches); marched from Kabul to Kandahar with the force under Sir F. Roberts, and was present at the Battle of Kandahar on 1 Sept. He was mentioned in Despatches [London Gazette, 30 July, 1880]; received the Medal with two clasps, and the Bronze Star. He was Superintendent of Army Signalling in the Mari Expedition; Acting Quartermaster to the 2nd Battn. K.R.R. during the Boer Campaign of 1881; Adjutant to the 2nd Battn. 1881–85; Captain, 1886. He commanded the Mounted Infantry, 6th Brigade, Upper Burma Field Force, 1886–87; was twice mentioned in Despatches, and created a Companion of the Distinguished Service Order [London Gazette, 25 Nov. 1887]: "Robert Edmund Golightly, Capt., King's Royal Rifle Corps, Mounted Infantry, Burma Expeditionary Force. For services in Burma." He was acting A.A.G., Meerut Division, in 1889; Adjutant, 1st Volunteer Battn. Durham Light Infantry, in 1890; commanded 1st Battn. Imperial Yeomanry, in South Africa, 1900 to 25 April, 1901 (Despatches [London Gazette, 10 Sept. 1901]; promoted Colonel in the Reserve of Officers; Queen's Medal, four clasps); commanded 8th Provisional Battn. 1902–8; appointed Section Commandant No. 1, Lines of Communication, 14 Nov. 1914; appointed Defence Commander No. 1, Lines of Communication, Dec. 1916; appointed Assistant Director Territorial and Volunteer Forces, April, 1918. He was created a C.B.E. in 1918. Colonel Golightly married, in 1886, Agnes Frances, daughter of the late W. M'Dowell Aiken. His favourite recreations are shooting, hunting, motoring, cricket and golf.

GOODWYN, HENRY EDWARD, Capt., was born 11 Oct. 1855, and joined the Royal Engineers on 28 Jan. 1875, serving in the Afghan War of 1878–80 (Medal); in the Egyptian Expedition of 1882—Battle of Tel-el-Kebir (Medal with clasp and Bronze Star). He again saw active service in the Burma Campaign of 1885–86; was mentioned in Despatches [London Gazette, 2 Sept. 1887]; received the Bronze Star, and was created a Companion of the Distinguished Service Order [London Gazette, 25 Nov. 1887]: "Henry Edward Goodwyn, Capt., Royal Engineers. For services in

Burma." He had been promoted to Captain 28 Jan. 1886, and became Major, Royal Engineers, 12 Dec. 1894, and retired 1 Feb. 1907.

BARRETT, ALFRED LLOYD, Capt., was born in 1855, son of the late Rev. A. Barrett, D.D., of Carshalton House, Surrey. He joined the Army in 1875 ; became Captain, B.S.C. (now I.S.C.) in 1876, and Major in 1895 ; served with Naga Hills Expedition, 1879–80 (Medal with clasp) ; with Akha Expedition, 1883–4 ; with Burma Expedition, 1886–88 (wounded) ; two clasps, created a Companion of the Distinguished Service Order [London Gazette, 25 Nov. 1887] : " Alfred Lloyd Barrett, Capt., Bombay Staff Corps. For services in Burma." He was with the Manipur Expedition in 1891 (clasp) ; was Commandant, 43rd Bengal Infantry, with temporary rank of Lieutenant-Colonel, Bengal. He died 7 March, 1900.

COUCHMAN, GEORGE HENRY HOLBECHE, Capt., was born 7 Dec. 1859, son of the late Colonel E. H. Couchman, R.A., and the late Mrs. Couchman (née Whitlock), daughter of Sir George Cornish Whitlock, K.C.B.). He was educated at Haileybury College, and joined the 13th Foot 11 May, 1878, and became Lieutenant, Somerset Light Infantry, 20 March, 1880, and Captain 1 Aug. 1886. He served in Burma, 1885–6–7 ; was mentioned in Despatches [London Gazette, 22 June, 1886, and 2 Sept. 1887] ; received the Medal with clasp, and was created a Companion of the Distinguished Service Order [London Gazette, 25 Nov. 1887] : " George Henry Holbeche Couchman, Capt., Somersetshire Light Infantry. For services in Burma." He served again in Burma, 1891–92, taking part in the operations of the North-Eastern Column. He became Major 9 March, 1898, and was given the Brevet of Lieutenant-Colonel 5 Oct. 1898. He commanded the 2nd Battn. Somersetshire Light Infantry, 1906–10. He was D.A.Q.M.G. for Intelligence, Burma, 1892–98, and A.A.G., India, 1900–1902 ; was given the Brevet of Colonel 10 Feb. 1904. He commanded the South-Western Infantry Brigade from 1910 to 1914. He retired in Jan. 1914 ; commanded 107th Infantry Brigade, Sept. 1914, to Oct. 1915, and was Area Commandant, British Expeditionary Force, 1917–18–19. He married, in 1899, Helen Mary, daughter of Richard S. Chattock, of Newbury. He was also awarded R.H.S. Bronze Medal for saving life in 1897.

George H. H. Couchman.

TEVERSHAM, RICHARD KINLOCK, Capt., was born 6 Sept. 1856, son of Mark Teversham (late Major, 2nd Battn. 16th Foot), and of Mrs. Teversham. He entered the Army 10 Sept. 1875, and joined the M.S.C. 3 July, 1877 ; was Adjutant, 3rd Palamcottah Light Infantry, 1878–87 ; became Captain 10 Sept. 1886 ; Staff Officer to Toungoo-Nymguan Column, 1886–87. On 26 July, 1886, at Coimbatore, India, he married Ethel Mary, eldest daughter of W. A. Symonds, Esq., Superintendent of the Central Gaol, Coimbatore, and their children are : " Lieut. Mark S. Teversham, I.A. ; Esmé (married to Lieut. E. Ballard, R.F.A.), and Frances Teversham. He served in Burma, 1886–87, received the Medal with clasp ; was mentioned in Despatches [London Gazette, 2 Sept. 1887] : " Brigadier-General Lockhart recommends the following for special recognition : Capt. Teversham, 3rd Madras Light Infantry, has been engaged in very numerous affairs against the enemy in the Nyingyan Command, and has proved himself a good soldier and a promising Staff Officer." He was created a Companion of the Distinguished Service Order [London Gazette, 25 Nov. 1887] : " Richard Kinlock Teversham, Capt., Madras Staff Corps. For services in Burma." He became Major 10 Sept. 1895 ; Lieutenant-Colonel 10 Sept. 1901, commanded the 2nd Madras Infantry ; late officiating A.A.G., Poona District ; was given the Brevet of Colonel 10 Sept. 1901 ; was A.A.G., Headquarters, Southern Command, 1904 to 1905, and was placed on the unemployed Supernumerary List 26 Feb. 1910. Colonel Teversham has been on the General Staff, War Office, during the European War, and was mentioned in Despatches for valuable services [London Gazette, 24 Feb. 1917].

WILKINSON, HENRY THOMAS DIEDRICH, Capt., was born on 19 June, 1860, eldest son of Colonel H. J. Wilkinson, and of Mrs. L. C. Wilkinson. He was educated at St. Columba's College, Ireland, and Sandhurst, and entered the Army 22 Jan. 1881 ; became Captain 13 April, 1887 ; served in Burma, 1885–86, being present at the storming of the Minhla Redoubt, when attached to the 12th Madras N.I. ; was wounded ; mentioned in Despatches 22 June, 1886 ; received the Medal and clasp, and was created a Companion of the Distinguished Service Order [London Gazette, 25 Nov. 1887] : " Henry Thomas Diedrich Wilkinson, Capt., Essex Regt. For services in Burma." He became Captain, Reserve of Officers, in April, 1893 ; Temporary Major 25 April, 1915, 5th Battn. Duke of Wellington's West Riding Regt. ; Attached Depot, Durham Light Infantry, till demobilized 15 Sept. 1919.

HUGGINS, PONSONBY GLENN, Capt., was born 21 Jan. 1857, fourth son of the late J. J. Huggins, Chief Justice, Sierra Leone, and Letitia, daughter of the late William Laborde. He was educated at private schools in Würtemberg and in Switzerland ; at the Royal Naval School, New Cross, and at the Royal Military College, Sandhurst. He joined the Army 19 April, 1876 ; became Lieutenant 19 April, 1876 ; Madras S.C., 5 Nov. 1877, and served in the Afghan War, 1878–79 (Medal). In 1883 he married (1st) Elizabeth Sophia (who died in 1893), only daughter of Commander W. Grierson, R.N., and they had one son and three daughters. He served in Burma, 1885–89 ; received the Medal with two clasps ; was mentioned in Despatches 2 Sept. 1887, and created a Companion of the Distinguished Service Order [London Gazette, 25 Nov. 1887] : " Ponsonby Glenn Huggins,

Capt., Madras Staff Corps. For services in Burma." N. Chin Hills, 1892–93 (clasp) ; Tirah, 1897–98 ; actions of Chagru Kotal and Dargai ; operations in the Bazar Valley 25 to 30 Dec. 1897 (Despatches, Medal with two clasps). He was created a C.B. in 1909 ; became Lieutenant-Colonel in 1902, and retired from the 81st Pioneers, Indian Army. In 1912 he married (2ndly) Margaret Rose, daughter of the late J. E. M. Wylie, and widow of G. F. W. Grierson.

FENDALL, CHARLES PEARS, Lieut., born 19 Nov. 1860, at Hatton Hall, Windlesham, eldest son of the Rev. Charles Bathurst Fendall and Frances Cecilia, daughter of the Rev. James Robert Pears, of Woodcote House, Windlesham. He was educated at Woodcote House, Windlesham ; Sherborne School, and Royal Military Academy, Woolwich. Commissioned Lieutenant, R.A., 30 July, 1879 ; Captain 1887, Major 1897, Lieutenant-Colonel 1905, Brevet Colonel 1908, Substantive Colonel 1910, retired 1911. Served in Burma 1885–86 ; commanded section 3/1 Mountain Battery, South Irish Division, R.A., with Eastern Frontier Column, and was Staff Officer of column and at Taungdwingyi. Commanded independent columns on several occasions. Despatches thrice. Created a Companion of the Distinguished Service Order [London Gazette, 25 Nov. 1887] : " Charles Pears Fendall, Lieut., Royal Artillery. For operations in Burma." Medal with clasp, " Burma, 1885–87." Served with the Chitral Relief Force, Additional Adjutant, R.A., and Staff Captain, R.A. Medal with clasp, " Relief of Chitral 1895." Served in the European War, A.A. and Q.M.G., Dover, 5 Aug. 1914, to 2 Dec. 1916 ; A.A.G., East Africa Force, 3 Dec. 1916, to 3 March, 1918 ; D.A. and Q.M.G. (Temporary Brigadier-General) East Africa Force, 4 March, 1918, to 10 March, 1919 ; Created C.M.G. 1 Jan. 1917 ; C.B. 1 Jan. 1919 ; St. Maurice and St. Lazarus (Officer), Italy, in 1917. He married, 15 Sept. 1888, at Dalhousie, Punjab, India, Rose Emly Ryan, daughter of the late James Ryan, Public Works Department, and has had issue one daughter, Frances Mary, born in 1891, and three sons : Charles Magrath, born in 1892, Lieutenant, Royal Artillery (killed in action, 1915) ; Patrick George, born in 1898 (died 1900), and William Pears, born in 1901 (Cadet, R.M.A.).

Charles Pears Fendall.

TANNER, JOHN ARTHUR, Lieut., was born 27 Feb. 1858, at Tidcombe Manor, Wilts, eldest son of the late John and Marian Tanner, of Poulton, Marlborough. He was educated at Cheltenham College, which he entered in April, 1868, as a boarder at Teighmore, and he went on to Hazelwell, becoming head of his House during his last year at College. At school he had a distinguished career, being Junior Mathematic Scholar, 1870–71 ; Senior Mathematic Scholar in 1873 ; Dobson Scholar in 1874 ; Jex-Blake Scholar in 1875, winning the Cheltenham Society Prize in 1874, and being Silver (Mathematical) Medallist in 1874 and 1875. He was noted for his quiet force of character, and in athletics, without being specially prominent, he was a vigorous member of several house teams, and obtained his XXII. at cricket. Two of Brigadier-General Tanner's brothers are the Rev. Maurice Tanner, formerly of Cheltenham College, Rector of Eversley, Hants, and the Rev. G. F. Tanner, Rector of Collingbourne Ducis. John Arthur Tanner passed fourth into Woolwich in July, 1875, and while there obtained prizes for Fortification, Geometrical Drawing, Drills and Exercises, and entered the Royal Engineers on 19 June, 1877. He served in the Mahsud Wazuree Expedition in 1881 ; in the Sudan Expedition in 1885 ; Suakin, Medal and clasp, and Bronze Star. He served in the Burmese Expedition, 1885–88, as Adjutant, Royal Engineers ; was twice mentioned in Despatches [London Gazettes, 22 June, 1886, and 2 Sept. 1887] ; received the Medal and clasp, and was created a Companion of the Distinguished Service Order [London Gazette, 25 Nov. 1887] : " John Arthur Tanner, Lieut., and Adjt. R.E. For services in Burma." He became Captain 1 April, 1888, and Major 1 Oct. 1895 ; served during the operations in Chitral in 1895, with the Relief Force, as Adjutant, R.E., 27 March to Aug. 1895 ; was present at the storming of the Malakand Pass, and the actions at Swat River and Panjkora River ; was mentioned in Despatches [London Gazette, 15 Nov. 1895], and received the Medal with clasp. He served on the North-West Frontier of India, 1897–98 (clasp) ; became Lieutenant-Colonel in 1903 ; served on the Staff in India, as D.A.A.G., R.E., 1900–3 ; A.A.G., R.E., 1903–6 ; General Staff Officer, 1st Grade, Headquarters, 1910 to 1913. He became Colonel 1 July, 1906 ; was created a C.B. in 1911, and retired 1 April, 1914. On the outbreak of the European War, Colonel Tanner volunteered his services as a retired officer. In Oct. 1914, he was given the work of a Lieutenant-Colonel, as C.R.E., 22nd Division, and helped to train the R.E.'s for the New Army, with whom he went to France in Sept. 1915. In Oct. 1915, he was made C.E. of the 7th Corps, with the rank of Brigadier-General. He was three times mentioned in Despatches, and created a C.M.G. He married on 24 Feb. 1916, Gladys Helen, daughter of the late C. T. Murdoch, M.P., of Buckhurst, Wokingham. Brigadier-General Tanner was killed in action, almost instantaneously, by a piece of shrapnel which struck him behind the ear 23 July, 1917. In

John Arthur Tanner.

announcing the news of his death, the "Times" (26 July, 1917) said: " A correspondent writes: ' General Tanner had retired from the Service before the war broke out, and was close on 60 years of age, but there was no officer of his grade at the front more vigorous in the performance of his duties, and more worthy of imitation in this respect. In the saddle all day, for he did not allow himself a midday meal, no single detail of his many responsibilities was ever neglected. In the days before civilian authorities took over responsibilities for the roads, his corps' roads were an example for all, while yet, before recent offensives, we remained immobilized in face of the old German line, the base line of defences, for which he was answerable, was a pattern worthy of imitation by all other corps. He had an extraordinary power of getting good work from his subordinates. "Thorough," was his watchword. There was never a soldier more conscientious of his duty.'" An obituary notice in the " Cheltonian " (Oct. 1917), closes thus: " The following are a few extracts from some of the letters received about him: From the Regimental Sergeant-Major, 22nd Division: 'I knew him so very well. We have shared food together, travelled together, slept together. I came to look upon him as a father, and my men would have done anything for him.' From various officers: 'His dogged determination to do his duty in all matters and under all circumstances, quietly and conscientiously, were the most notable features of his character.' 'The nation has lost a valuable servant, and his brother officers a highly respected and valued friend.' ' Everyone who met the General liked and admired him, and it is no exaggeration to say that those, like myself, who were fortunate enough to serve directly under him absolutely loved him.' ' A gallant and modest gentleman, who was at the same time one of the best Generals in all the British Armies.' We add some lines from a well-known epitaph of other days, which he admired, and which, in fact, describes the spirit of his own life:

> " '. . . Friend to truth! Of soul sincere,
> In action faithful, and in honour clear;
> Who broke no promise, served no private end,
> Who gained no title, and who lost no friend !'"

WESTLAKE, ALMOND PAUL, Lieut., was born 2 March, 1858; was educated at King's College School, London; entered the Army as a Sub-Lieutenant (unattached) 29 Nov. 1876; 3rd Dragoon Guards 29 Nov. 1876; 70th Foot, 15 Aug. 1877; Lieut. Army, 29 Nov. 1877; Madras Staff Corps 2 Sept. 1878. He served in the Afghan War of 1879-80 (Medal). He married, in 1884, Alice Agnes, eldest surviving daughter of General W. D'Oyly Kerrich, late R.H.A., and they have one daughter. He served in the Burmese War of 1886-89; was mentioned in Despatches [London Gazette, 2 Sept. 1887], received the Medal with two clasps, and was created a Companion of the Distinguished Service Order [London Gazette, 25 Nov. 1887]: " Almond Paul Westlake,

Almond Paul Westlake.

Lieut., Madras Staff Corps. For services in Burma." He became Captain, Indian Staff Corps, 29 Nov. 1888; Major, Indian Army, 29 Nov. 1897. He was Superintendent of an Army Remount Rearing Depot, Hapur, India, 1892-99; Lieutenant-Colonel, Indian Army, 28 Nov. 1903; Brevet Colonel 29 Nov. 1906; commanded and reconstituted the 26th (K.G.O.) Light Infantry, Indian Army, 1899-1909; was Commanding Hounslow Horse Depot 5 Aug. 1914, to 14 Sept. 1914; was Superintendent, Remount Depot, Ormskirk, Lancashire, 28 Sept. 1914, to 31 March, 1915; Commandant, Remount Depot, Ormskirk, Lancashire, 1 April, 1915, to 23 June, 1916; was Commandant, Remount Base Depot British Expeditionary Force, 23 June, 1916.

McSWINEY, EDWARD FREDERICK HENRY, Lieut., was born at Cronstadt, Russia, 28 Feb. 1857, son of the Rev. John Herbert McSwiney, M.A., British Chaplain at Cronstadt, and of Mrs. Emily Sarah McSwiney, daughter of the late Admiral Hills, R.N., and second cousin of the late Sir Harry Verney. He was educated at Cronstadt; Victoria College, Jersey; Oxford Military College, and the Royal Military College, Sandhurst; was gazetted Second-Lieutenant to the 40th Foot 22 Jan. 1879, arriving in India 3 April, 1879. He served with the Kurram Valley Field Force during the Second Afghan War, 1880, as Sub-Assistant Commissary-General (Medal); transferred to the 3rd Cavalry H.C. in May, 1884. He married, 13 Dec. 1885, in Bombay Cathedral, Ida F. Knaggs, daughter of Colonel Henry Knaggs, A.M.S., and their children were: Herbert Frederick Cyril, born 8 Nov. 1886 (Captain, Temporary Major, 2/3rd Q.A.O. Gurkha Rifles; mentioned in Despatches, 1918 and 1919, for services

Edward F. H. McSwiney.

rendered as D.A.Q.M.G., 75th Division, under General Allenby, Egyptian Expeditionary Force; awarded M.C., 1917); Hugh Norman Claude, born 3 April, 1891 (died in Sept. 1902), and Ida Kathleen. He commanded a Squadron in the Burma Campaign, 1886-87; defeated large bands of Dacoits at Pindin on the 3rd Dec., and at Chounghwa on 11 Dec. 1886 (congratulated by Brigadier-General R. C. Stewart); completed the subjugation of Nazasin District by utterly routing the Dacoits at Theo, June,

1887 (acknowledgments of Major-General Sir G. S. White, V.C.; Despatches; Medal with two clasps, and created a Companion of the Distinguished Service Order [London Gazette, 25 Nov. 1889]: " Edward Frederick Henry McSwiney, Lieut., Bengal Staff Corps. For services in Burma.") He was transferred to 4th Lancers, H.C., in Aug. 1888; qualified as Russian Interpreter, 1889; appointed Adjutant, 4th Lancers, H.C., May, 1889; promoted Captain, 22 Jan. 1890; Attaché, Intelligence Branch, Quartermaster-General's Department, Army H.Q., 1891; Brigade Major of Cavalry during cavalry manœuvres in the Meerut District; D.A.Q.M.G., Intelligence Branch, Army H.Q., Simla, 5 June, 1894; served in Waziristan, 1895 (clasp); appointed Second in Command, 1st Lancers, H.C., but remained seconded Camp Commandant and Intelligence Officer, Pamir Boundary Commission, 1895 (thanks of the Government of India, 1896, and Brevet of Major, 1897); Officiating Commandant, 1st Lancers, H.C., 1 July, 1897; D.A.A.G., Kurram-Kohat Force, under Major-General Yeatman-Biggs, C.B. 1897; present at the action of the Uhlan Pass, 27 Aug. 1897; operations on the Samana and in the Kurram Valley, Aug. and Sept. 1897; Defence of the Samana Forts, Relief of Gulistan (Despatches [London Gazette, 11 Feb. 1898], Medal and two clasps, recommended for promotion to A.A.G.). When the Kurram-Kohat Field Force was merged into the Tirah Expeditionary Force, Major McSwiney was appointed D.A.A.G. to the Kurram Movable Column; was present at the reconnaissance of the Khurmana Defile and action of 7 Nov.; operations against the Khami Khel Chamkanis, 1st and 2nd Dec. (Despatches [London Gazette, 1 March, 1898]; clasp; Brevet of Lieutenant-Colonel, 21 May, 1898). Colonel W. Hill, in his Despatches, dated 12 and 24 Dec. 1897, said that Major McSwiney's services were " invaluable " and that he had " great ability, zeal, and tact." In 1898 he was Staff Captain at the Intelligence Division, War Office, and in 1899 was appointed Commandant, 1st Lancers, Hyderabad Contingent, in March; in 1900 was Special Service Officer, China Expeditionary Force; created a C.B., 1905; appointed Brigadier, Ambala Cavalry Brigade, 1906. Colonel E. F. McSwiney died at Ambala 21 Jan. 1907.

WILKINSON, THOMAS HENRY DES VOEUX, Lieut., was born on 11 June, 1858, eldest son of the Right Rev. the Bishop of St. Andrews, and Caroline, daughter of Lieut.-Colonel Benfield Des Voeux, late Scots Guards. He was educated at the Royal Military College, Sandhurst, and was gazetted to the Rifle Brigade in 1879; served in the Mahsud-Waziri Expedition, 1881; in the Burmese Expedition, 1886-88; was mentioned in Despatches [London Gazette, 2 Sept. 1887]; received the India Medal and two clasps, and was created a Companion of the Distinguished Service Order [London Gazette, 25 Nov. 1887]: " Thomas Henry Des Voeux Wilkinson, Lieut. and Adjutant, Rifle Brigade. For services in Burma." Capt. Wilkinson received the Jubilee Decoration of 22 June, 1897; was promoted to Major 5 Sept. 1897. He has retired.

STANTON, HENRY ERNEST, Lieut., was born at Yanworth, Gloucestershire, 10 Nov. 1861, youngest son of the late Rev. Canon W. H. Stanton, Hasleton, Gloucestershire. He was educated at Marlborough, and at the Royal Military Academy, Woolwich (and at the Staff College); joined the Royal Artillery 26 July, 1881; served with the Upper Burma Field Force 1885-87, and 1887-88, in Mountain Artillery, and later on as Special Duty Officer; was mentioned in Despatches [London Gazette, 2 Sept. 1887]; received the Medal and two clasps, and was created a Companion of the Distinguished Service Order [London Gazette, 25 Nov. 1887]: " Henry Ernest Stanton, Lieut., Royal Artillery. For services in Burma." He was Attaché to the Intelligence Branch, India, 1887-88; Cadet Officer, Royal Military Academy, Woolwich, 1888-89; became Captain, 1 Jan. 1890; Officiating D.A.A.G., Bengal, 1894-95; Brigade-Major, 1st Brigade, Chitral Relief Force, 1895; was present at the storming of the Malakand Pass, and action near Khar (Despatches [London Gazette, 15 Nov. 1896]; Medal and clasp). He was Staff Captain, Intelligence Branch, India, 1897; D.A.Q.M.G., I.B., Malakand and Buner Field Forces, 1897-98; was present at the action of Landakai, Bajaur and at the Tanga Pass; in operations against the Mohmands, Utmankhels, and with the Buner Field Force at the action at the Tanga Pass; mentioned in Despatches, 5 Nov. 1897; 11 Jan. 1898, and 22 May, 1898; received the Brevet of Major 20 May, 1898, and a clasp. He was D.A.A.G., Khyber Brigade, 1898; promoted to Major, 9 Oct. 1899; was Assistant Military Secretary, Bombay, 1899-1902. In 1899 he married Olive Talbot, daughter of General Sir R. Low, G.C.B., and they had one son and two daughters. He was A.A.G., India, in 1902; Chief Staff Officer, Somaliland Field Force, 1903-4, being present at the action of Jidballi (Despatches [London Gazette, 2 Sept. 1904]; Brevet of Lieutenant-Colonel, 7 Sept. 1904; Medal and two clasps). He was appointed A.D.C. to the King in 1906, and given the Brevet of Colonel 1 Dec. 1906; was General Staff Officer, 2nd Grade, 1908-9; 1st Grade (India), 1911; created a C.B. in 1911; was D.Q.M.G., India, 1912-14. From Aug. 1914, he served in the European War as officiating Q.M.G., India; Brigadier-General, i/c Administration, Egypt; D.A. and Q.M.G., Force in Egypt, and Coast Defence Commander. He was mentioned in Despatches; promoted Major-General for distinguished service; was created K.C.M.G. in 1919, and received the 1914-15 Star.

GLANVILLE, FRANCIS, Lieut., was born 16 May, 1862, son of the late Major-General F. R. Glanville, R.A., of Catchpench, Cornwall. He entered the Royal Engineers 26 July, 1881; served in Burma, 1886-88; was severely wounded; received the Medal and clasp; was mentioned in Despatches, 2 Sept. 1887, and created a Companion of the Distinguished Service Order [London Gazette, 25 Nov. 1887]: " Francis Glanville, Lieut., Royal Engineers. For services in Burma." He married, in 1888, Frances Gwenevere, daughter of the late E. H. J. Crawford, and they have two daughters. He was promoted to Captain 19 May, 1890; Major 21 June,1899, and Lieutenant-Colonel 1 April, 1906, and was given the Brevet of Colonel 1 May, 1909, becoming Colonel 1 May, 1911. He became temporary Brigadier-General 4 Feb.1916, commanding the Bareilly Brigade, Indian Army.

CAULFEILD, ALGERNON MONTGOMERIE, Lieut., was born 28 Aug. 1860, 4th son of the late Lieut.-Colonel Montgomerie Caulfeild, Weston Park, Lucan, County Dublin. He was educated at the Royal Academy, Gosport, and Heidelberg College, and joined the 66th Berkshire Regt. 17 Dec. 1881; served in Afghanistan; was present at the engagement at Girishk with the Walli's mutinous troops at the Battle of Maiwand (wounded) as a Corporal, and subsequent defence of Kandahar (Medal for distinguished conduct in the field, and Medal with clasp). He, though wounded at Maiwand, saw to Capt. Melliss, who was also wounded, being placed on a camel. He afterwards got a mule, and rode with Lieut. Lynd, who was wounded, taking him to Kandahar. The late Sir John Slade, then in command of E Battery, B Brigade, recommended him for the V.C. He was made a Sergeant, and asked, when the Distinguished Conduct Medal was given him by Her late Majesty Queen Victoria, to change his name from Sergt. Williams to Sergeant Caulfeild, and soon after was given a commission in the 5th Fusiliers. He served in Burma, 1886-88, as Brigade Transport Officer to Major-General Sir Robert Low, K.C.B.; was mentioned in Despatches, 2 Sept. 1887, and created a Companion of the Distinguished Service Order [London Gazette, 25 Nov. 1887]: "Algernon Montgomerie Caulfeild, Lieut., Northumberland Fusiliers. For services in Burma." He was made a Captain in the 2nd Border Regt. In 1889 he was serving with mounted infantry in the Chin Lushai country (Medal with three clasps). He was promoted to Major, 23 Feb. 1898, and retired 27 Aug. 1902. He served in the European War, as Second in Command of the Border Regt., and was killed in action on 9 Aug. 1915, at Gallipoli.

The following are some details sent by relatives:

The first is a letter written by the only surviving officer of the 6th Border Regt., 29th Division, who was wounded at Suvla in the attack on Hill 70, Gallipoli Peninsula, 10 Aug. 1915:

"Mayfield,
"Freshfield, near Liverpool.

"DEAR MISS CAULFEILD,
"I am sorry to say I can hold out no hope of Major Caulfeild being alive; in fact, when I made up the return I felt I ought to have shown him as killed, but I could find no man that ever saw him again after he went off towards the fire on Burnt Hill—he went walking off towards the Turkish trenches as if he were walking down Piccadilly. Capt. Gilbanks, who went off in that direction with his Platoon, was killed, and his Platoon practically wiped out. Any men of it that I have seen did not see him. It is possible that his body will never be found. I feel I have lost a great friend, and one of the bravest comrades it was possible to serve with; he did not know what fear was. I saw him down the front of the two supporting companies under a hail of bullets in a way no living man could forget. There is another point that may go to prove that he is killed; as far as I know he was the only man that wore leggings. Well, during the attack on Burnt Hill an officer called Blake, attached to the South Wales Borderers, who was next me in Hospital, said that on the 21st he saw as he passed a smartly dressed Major lying near the top dressed in leggings; of course he had no time to look, and afterwards we were driven off the Hill again. If I hear any more I will let you know. I am glad to feel I have been privileged to serve under Major Caulfeild. Colonel Broadrick I know had the highest opinion of him, and we all know that if he had chosen he could have obtained a comparatively soft job; but he preferred to go into action leading men. Please accept my deepest sympathy.

"Yours very truly,
"G. DARWELL."

"NOTE—
"My brother having been seen by General Maxwell from Chocolate Hill on 9th August advancing towards enemy, but no other news has been heard of him since. He was known to have been badly wounded. This makes me think that the Major seen on top of hill is he, and not being able to get along he would lie still. So his little daughter and I, knowing he has been in many a tight corner, 'hope on,' and think he is in Constantinople, a prisoner of war. He is well acquainted with Eastern customs, having served for 20 years in India, two years in Egyptian Army, and can talk French, Hindustani, a little German, and Turkish. So will be cared well for by the Turk.

"JAMES M. CAULFEILD,
"Capt. R.N.

"General Lord Byng got this information for me from General Maxwell.—M. CAULFEILD."

WYNYARD, EDWARD GEORGE, Lieut., was born at Saharanpur, North-West Provinces, India, 1 April, 1861, son of the late William Wynyard, J.P., of Hursley, Hants, Judge of the High Court, Allahabad, Bengal Civil Service. He was educated at Woodcote House, Windlesham, and at Charterhouse, and joined the Army 12 May, 1883. He served in the King's Regt. from 1883 to 1890; took part in the Burma Expedition of 1885-87 (Despatches twice; Medal with clasp, and created a Companion of the Distinguished Service Order [London Gazette, 25 Nov. 1887]: "Edward George Wynyard, Lieut., Liverpool Regt. For services during the recent operations in Burma.") The decoration was awarded for the following services: "On 12 June, 1885, in Upper Burma, a large force of rebels under Oo Tenah were beaten off after attacking a

Edward George Wynyard.

small force of the 8th King's Liverpool Regt. and 2nd Bengal Infantry. They were followed and found entrenched strongly in a walled pagoda, which was carried by assault." General Sir Robert Low, K.C.B., etc., etc., in his Despatch, stated that "owing to the bold leading of a handful of tired men by Lieut. Wynyard, after the death of Capt. Dunsford (2nd Bengal Infantry), a position of considerable danger was averted, and as a result of this success order was restored in the surrounding district." General Sir G. S. White, V.C., emphasized the above in his Despatch, and Lieut. Wynyard was specially promoted to a company into the 41st Welsh Regt. He was awarded the Humane Society's Medal in 1895 for rescuing a Swiss peasant from under the ice on the lake of Davos. He became Captain in 1890 in the Welsh Regt. From 1897-1899 he was captain of the Hampshire County Cricket Eleven. Capt. Wynyard was asked by Stoddart to join the All England Eleven v. Australia, but declined on account of Army duties. He was Adjutant, Oxford University Volunteers, 1899-1900; Instructor in Military Engineering at the Royal Military College, 1900; retired in 1903. He was Captain, M.C.C. New Zealand Team, 1906; was invited to Captain M.C.C. Australian Team in 1907, but was obliged to decline for family reasons. He twice accompanied representative M.C.C. teams to South Africa in 1905 and 1909, and the M.C.C. team to America, 1907; was appointed representative of the South African Cricket Association in England, 1908. In 1914, Capt. Wynyard married Sarah Louise, daughter of the late James G. Worts, of Toronto, and they have one son, born 23 May, 1918. He became Major, King's Liverpool Regt. in Sept. 1914; was attached for duty with the Army Ordnance Corps, May, 1915; appointed to the Middlesex Regt. Nov. 1916. Major Wynyard's favourite recreations, besides cricket, are football (Old Carthusians and Corinthians); golf (Camberley Heath); tobogganing (Champion Tobogganer of Europe, 1894).

MORSE, FRANK ALEXANDER, Lieut., became Lieutenant, South Staffordshire Regt., 4 May, 1884; served in Burma in 1885-87, part of the time with the Mounted Infantry; was several times mentioned in Despatches; received the Medal and clasp, and was created a Companion of the Distinguished Service Order [London Gazette, 25 Nov. 1887]: "Frank Alexander Morse, Lieut., Somerset Light Infantry. For services in Burma." He became Captain 4 Jan. 1890, and he resigned from the Army 11 Feb. 1891.

COXHEAD, THOMAS LANGHORNE, Lieut., was born at Petersham, Surrey, 8 Oct. 1864, 2nd son of Henry George Coxhead, Merchant, formerly of Hardwick House, and Susan Amelia, daughter of the Rev. Cornelius Thompson. He was educated at Bute House, Petersham, Surrey, and the Royal Military Academy, Woolwich; entered the Royal Artillery 5 July, 1884; served with the Burmese Expedition, with an elephant battery 10 Oct. 1886 (severely wounded); Despatches, and created a Companion of the Distinguished Service Order [London Gazette, 25 Nov. 1887]: "Thomas Langhorne Coxhead, Lieut., Royal Artillery." The D.S.O. was awarded (probably not for any particular act) for services generally during the 1886 Burma Campaign, on being mentioned by Lord Roberts in Despatches. Lord Roberts, in a private letter to Lieut.-Colonel Coxhead, says: "It gives me great pleasure to express my opinion of your services as an officer of the Royal Artillery,

Thomas L. Coxhead.

especially during the Burma Campaign in 1886, when I was Commander-in-Chief in that country. Your conduct was brought to my notice at the time, and was such as to enable me to recommend you for the Distinguished Service Order." The Lieutenant-Colonel Commanding Royal Artillery, Burma Field Force, remarked on the reports of Lieuts. Pullen and Coxhead "on the recent operations near Yermethin and Ningyan." He said: "The reports of these officers do them much credit, the more so as the notes and sketches from which they were framed must have been made in the face of somewhat adverse circumstances." Major Sorell, R.A., wrote, 28 Feb. 1887, of Lieut. Coxhead: "This officer has served with the battery under my command from 20 April, 1886. He has been many times in action, both with me and in command of a half-battery of artillery, and on every occasion showed self-reliance, courage and knowledge of his duties rare in so young an officer. He was on one occasion placed in command of a column, by his senior officer being killed, and brought it back from a difficult position with skill and tact. He was very severely wounded on 10 Oct. 1886, and had to be invalided home. Brigadier-General Lockhart, C.B., C.S.I., asked for him as orderly officer, but his services at that time could not be spared. I consider him about the best subaltern officer I have met during my service." Lieut. Coxhead's services were also specially mentioned in a report of Major-General Sir G. S. White, K.C.B., V.C., commanding the Upper Burma Field Force, published in the London Gazette of 2 Sept. 1887. He was again specially mentioned in a Despatch by Lieut.-General Gaselee, commanding the British Contingent, China Field Force [London Gazette, 13 Sept. 1901] (Despatches, Medal). He became Captain in July, 1893. Capt. Coxhead married, in 1900, Eliza Lort Winter, daughter of the Rev. D. Winter Morris, Vicar of St. Ishmael's, Milford Haven, and their children are: John Ralph Winter Coxhead, born 19 May, 1903, and Caroline May Coxhead, born 8 May, 1907. From Aug. 1900, to Aug. 1901 Capt. Coxhead served as Brigade-Major with the China Expeditionary Force. He received the China Medal, and was specially mentioned in a Despatch of Lieut.-General A. Gaselee, commanding the British Contingent, China Field Force [London Gazette, 13 Sept. 1901]. He was promoted Major May, 1903; Lieutenant-Colonel 21 May, 1912, and retired 13 July, 1912. Lieut.-Colonel Coxhead was appointed a Military Knight of Windsor, 1914. He was in the R.M.A. Cricket Eleven, 1883 and 1884, and played three times for the R.A. in the R.A. and R.E. matches later, and played golf for the R.A. He was appointed Lieutenant-Colonel R.G.A. on outbreak of war on 10 Sept. 1914.

LAMPORT, WILLIAM, Lieut., joined the Royal Artillery; became Lieutenant 5 July, 1884; served in Burma 1886-87, as Orderly Officer to Brigadier-General Lockhart; was mentioned in Despatches, received the Medal and clasp, and was created a Companion of the Distinguished Service Order [London Gazette, 25 Nov. 1887]: "William Lamport, Lieut., Royal Artillery. For services in Burma." He died 1 June, 1890.

London Gazette, 3 Jan. 1888.—"War Office, 3 Jan. 1888. The Queen has been graciously pleased to give orders for the appointment of the undermentioned officer to be Companion of the Distinguished Service Order, viz. :—For operations in Burma."

AIREY, HENRY PARKE, Capt., was born at Kingthorpe Hall, Yorkshire, 3 Aug. 1844, 2nd son of Capt. H. C. Airey. He was educated at Marlborough, and at the Royal Military College, Addiscombe; was gazetted to the 101st R.M. Fusiliers as Ensign in 1859; served in India six years, on the North-Western Frontier, and retired in 1866; also in the same year went to Australia, joining the New South Wales Artillery in 1878. He served as Lieutenant with the New South Wales Contingent in Egypt, 1885; A.D.C. to General Fremantle at advance and capture of Tamai (Egyptian Medal; clasp, and Khedive's Star), 1885. Capt. Airey volunteered for service in Burma, 1886-7, attached to Sir G. White's Staff; commanded Gardner Gun Battery at attack on Hwai-Hwaing; was severely wounded, losing an arm, and was mentioned in Despatches, and thanked by the Governor-General of India. He received the Brevet of Major for distinguished services; was made Honorary A.D.C. to the Governor of New South Wales, received the Burma Medal and clasp, and was created a Companion of the Distinguished Service Order [London Gazette, 3 Jan. 1888]: "Henry Parke Airey, Capt., New South Wales Artillery." The D.S.O. was awarded for distinguished service, coolness under fire, and marked gallantry (His Excellency the Commander-in-Chief, Burma, letter to the Viceroy of India). He was created a C.M.G. in 1900, and became Lieutenant-Colonel, commanding the Brigade, Divisional Field Artillery, New South Wales. He served in South Africa in 1900, and was mentioned in Despatches. He was promoted to Colonel. He married Florence Ada, youngest daughter of A. H. M'Culloch, of Sydney, New South Wales. Colonel Airey died on the 12th Oct. 1911, at Panplaats, Transvaal, and an obituary notice of him appeared in the "Times." His favourite recreations were cricket (1st Eleven, Marlborough College; Captain, Addiscombe College Eleven, and Regimental, 1885-6; Captain, New South Wales Artillery Eleven); hunting and driving; Master of Sydney Hunt Club.

London Gazette, 9 March, 1888.—"War Office, 9 March, 1888. The Queen has further been graciously pleased to give orders for the appointment of the undermentioned officers to be Companions of the Distinguished Service Order."

PIGOTT, CHARLES BERKELEY, Capt., was born 13 Jan. 1859, son of Sir Charles Robert Pigott, 3rd Baronet, and Mary Louisa (who died in 1873), daughter of the late Capt. C. Hallowell Carew, R.N., of Beddington Park, Surrey. He joined the 60th King's Royal Rifles; served in the Zulu War, 1879 (Medal with clasp); in the Boer War, 1881, with Mounted Infantry; in the Egyptian Campaign of 1882, in which he was dangerously wounded. He received the Medal, Bronze Star, the 5th Class Medjidie, and was promoted Captain, and given a troop in the 21st Lancers. He served in the Eastern Sudan Campaign in 1884 (two clasps); with the Nile Expedition, 1884-5 (two clasps). He was given the Brevet of Major in 1886, and in the same year married Fanny Ada, daughter of the Rev. Wellesley Pole Pigott, and Fanny, daughter of the late Bernard Granville, Esq., of Wellesbourne Hall, Warwickshire, and they had two children : Berkeley (the present Baronet), and

Charles Berkeley Pigott.

Florence Ada Cecile. He served on the West Coast of Africa, 1887-8; and was created a Companion of the Distinguished Service Order [London Gazette, 9 March, 1888]: "Charles Berkeley Pigott, Major, 21st Lancers." For services in Burma. He was promoted Lieutenant-Colonel in 1896, and created a C.B. Lieut.-Colonel Pigott took part in the Ashanti Expedition of 1895-96, and was made Commandant of Kurnasi. All his promotions were Brevet, for services, and he was mentioned many times in Despatches. Lieut.-Colonel C. B. Pigott died 12 Sept. 1897. Colonel Andrew Haggard says that when Sir Evelyn Wood took over the formation of the new Egyptian Army from Baker Pasha he himself had the good fortune to be one of the officers whom the General selected as his Staff in the new force. "Accordingly, the end of January, 1883, found me on my way back to Cairo. I travelled out with Berkeley Pigott, a young officer who in those days had only four years' seniority, during which time he had been constantly on active service, and had gained four decorations for war service. Pigott had been serving in the Mounted Infantry in the late Egyptian Campaign, and had the bad luck to get a bullet through his leg at Kassassin. However, he was none the worse for that, and was, like myself, one of the selected officers for the Egyptian Army. . . . When Pigott and I arrived at Cairo on the evening of the last day of January, 1883, we descended at

that jolly old caravanserai, Shepheard's Hotel." Later on Colonel Haggard describes Pigott's splendid services at the time of the cholera outbreak of 1883. He says he and some of the other officers broke into the Abbasiyeh Lunatic Asylum, and the stench and awful sights in it were "so terrible that they made even Berkeley Pigott too ill to accompany us on our rounds. Now, when it is considered that he was a brave soldier, accustomed to face war in all its most terrible aspects without flinching, it must, I think, be conceded that the lunatic asylum . . . was something awful indeed." Colonel Huggard says that "after El Teb, Pigott still remained attached to the Egyptian Cavalry. . . . Long before I reached the troops" (at the Battle of Tamai) "I noticed among them all the only three officers of the Egyptian Army who were not distinctly serving with the English Army as Englishmen. These were Chamley Turner, Hallam Parr and Pigott. They all wore, as I did myself, a bright red puggaree round their white helmets, for we had on active service discarded the fez and taken to the helmet. Very pretty, too, I thought it looked, as I saw Pigott sitting on his horse in front of a cavalry regiment, his one spot of colour relieving the whole tedium of a regiment in sad-coloured khaki."

VALENTINE, FRANCIS ALFRID, Lieut., was born in 1858, son of the Rev. William Valentine, Vicar of Whixley, Yorkshire. He entered the Royal Navy in 1871; became a Lieutenant in 1882; served in the Boadicea in the Zulu War in 1879, gaining the Medals, and was in command of the Osprey's boats when on detached service for the suppression of the slave traffic in the Red Sea; Zanzibar, Mafic Chan Common Islands, and East Coast of Arabia in 1883. In 1887-88 he took part in the Yonnie Expedition, being in command of the Naval Brigade assisting in the capture of Rohari, Rorrietto, and other towns, gaining the Distinguished Service Order [London Gazette, 9 March, 1888]: "Francis Alfrid Valentine, Lieut., Royal Navy." He also received the Medal with clasp. Lieut. Valentine died on the 22nd Aug. 1897.

BROWNE, GEORGE FITZHERBERT, Capt., was born on the 29th Jan. 1851. He entered the 48th Regt. 6 July, 1870; became Captain, Northamptonshire Regt. in 1882. He was D.A.A.G. and Q.M.G., and Q.M.G. Dublin District, 1884-85, and D.A.A.G. at Headquarters, Ireland, 1885-89; went on Special Service to the West Coast of Africa, serving in the expedition against the Yonnies, 1887-88; was mentioned in Despatches, received the Medal and clasp, and was created a Companion of the Distinguished Service Order [London Gazette, 9 March, 1888]: "George Fitzherbert Browne, Capt., Northamptonshire Regt." For operations in Burma. He also served on the West Coast of Africa in 1892, taking part in the attack on Tambi; was wounded, and received an additional clasp. From 1896 to 1903 he was Military Attaché at Pekin (Medal). He was created a C.B. in 1905, and became Major-General 10 Oct. 1906, retiring from the Service on 15 Feb. 1913. Major-General G. F. Browne holds the Jubilee and Coronation Medals. He married in 1911, Harriet, widow of Capt. Bankes Tomlin.

London Gazette, 3 Aug. 1888.—"War Office, 2 Aug. 1888. The Queen has further been pleased to give orders for the following appointments to the Distinguished Service Order, and for promotions in the Army by Brevet, in recognition of the services of the undermentioned officers during the operations in Burma, 1887-88. To be Companions of the Distinguished Service Order."

GROVE, ALEXANDER SINCLAIR, Colonel, was born at Dumfries in 1840, son of Henry Jones Grove, K.H., and Major, 80th Foot (who died in March, 1847), and Mary Anne Sinclair, daughter of Capt. Sinclair, R.N. He entered the Madras Army in 1858; became Captain, Madras Staff Corps (now Indian Staff Corps), 12 June, 1870. Capt. Grove married, in 1873, Catherine, daughter of the late Major-General Ezekiel Gage, Indian Army. On 12 June, 1878, he was promoted to Major. He served in the Afghan War in 1880 (Medal); became Lieut.-Colonel in 1884; served in the Burma Campaign, 1887-88 (Medal and two clasps; created a Companion of the Distinguished Service Order [London Gazette, 3 Aug. 1888]: "For services during the operations in Burma. Alexander Sinclair Grove, Colonel, Madras

Alexander S. Grove.

Staff Corps"). He was A.A.G., Madras and Burma, 1892-95, and Colonel on the Staff in 1895. Colonel Grove died on the 13th Sept. 1897.

ILDERTON, CHARLES EDWARD, Major, was born 1 March, 1841, eldest son of the Rev. Canon Ilderton, of Ilderton, Northumberland. He was educated at Harrow; entered the 68th Regt. 5 Sept. 1862; served in the New Zealand War, 1864-66, being present at the attack on Gate Pah, and at other minor operations (Medal); became Captain, 1871; Major, Queen's (Royal West Surrey) Regt., 1881; served with Burma Expedition, 1886-88 (Despatches; Brevet of Lieut.-Colonel; Medal with two clasps; created a Companion of the Distinguished Service Order [London Gazette, 3 Aug. 1888]: "For services during the operations in Burma. Charles Edward Ilderton, Major, Royal West Surrey Regt."). He became Lieut.-Colonel 29 Sept. 1890, and was given the Brevet of Colonel 29 Sept. 1894; was appointed to command the 2nd Battn. The Queen's (Royal West Surrey) Regt., 1890; became Colonel, 1894, and was put on half-pay, 1894. Colonel Ilderton retired 25 March, 1886, and died 25 Jan. 1905.

FRERE, SIR BARTLE COMPTON ARTHUR, Major, Bart., was born on 24 Oct. 1854, only son of the Right Honourable Sir H. Bartle E. Frere, G.C.B., G.C.S.I. (1st Bart.), and Catherine, daughter of Lieut.-General the

Right Honourable Sir George Arthur (1st Bart.). He was educated at Eton and Trinity College, Cambridge, taking his B.A. degree, and was gazetted to the Rifle Brigade; served in the Zulu War in 1879 (Medal with clasp); in the Bechuanaland Expedition in 1884–85 (Brevet of Major). For his services in the Burma Campaign of 1886–88 he received the Medal and clasp, and was created a Companion of the Distinguished Service Order [London Gazette, 3 Aug. 1888]: "For services during the operations in Burma, Sir Bartle Compton Arthur Frere, Bart., Capt. and Brevet Major, The Rifle Brigade." The Decoration was awarded for services in command of the mounted infantry of his regiment, the 1st Rifle Brigade, in the operations against the Dacoits in Upper Burma, including the pursuit and capture of Boh-Toke-Ji, a noted Dacoit chief. He succeeded his father as 2nd Baronet in 1884, and retired from the Army 6 Dec. 1893.

TRISCOTT, CHARLES PRIDEAUX, Capt., was born 2 Sept. 1857, son of the late Joseph Blake Triscott, Esq., of Plymouth and Helston. He was educated at the Royal Military Academy, and became a Lieutenant in the Royal Artillery 14 Aug. 1876. He served in Afghanistan, including the action at Charasai and the march from Kabul to Relief of Kandahar, and battle of 1 Sept. (Medal with clasp, and Bronze Star). He was promoted to Captain 15 April, 1885, and served in the Burma Campaign, 1885–88. He commanded the expedition against the Salay Hill Kachins, and also that to Lake Endawgyee and the Jade Mines; was mentioned in Despatches; received the Medal with two clasps, and created a Companion of the Distinguished Service Order [London Gazette, 3 Aug. 1888]: "Charles Prideaux Triscott, Capt., Royal Artillery. For services during the operations in Burma, 1887–88." From 30 July, 1891, to 22 Aug. 1894, he was Instructor at the Royal Military Academy, and was promoted to Major on 27 June, 1894. He was D.A.A.G., India, from 10 Jan. 1897, to 21 April, 1898: served as A.Q.M.G. with the Tirah Expeditionary Force from 1 Oct. 1897, to 8 April, 1898 (Despatches: Medal with two clasps), and as A.A.G., India, from April, 1898, to March, 1902. He became Lieut.-Colonel in July, 1903; Brevet-Colonel, 15 July, 1906, and Colonel, 15 July, 1908. In 1910 he was created a Companion of the Bath, and he was Colonel-in-Charge, Royal Garrison Artillery Records, Dover, 1 April, 1911, to 6 Aug. 1912; Temporary Brigadier-General, 7 Aug. 1912, and Officer Commanding Western Coast Defences until 27 April, 1916, when he was placed on retired pay. He was created a C.M.G. in 1917.

CAPEL CURE, HERBERT, Capt., was born 23 Oct. 1859, at Eaton Place, London, son of the late Robert Capel Cure, Esq., of Blake Hall, Ongar, Essex, by his first wife, who was a daughter of the Right Rev. George

Herbert Capel Cure.

Murray, Bishop of Rochester. He was educated for the Navy, but was too ill at the time of the examination, and entered the 61st (Gloucestershire) Regt. 11 May, 1878; served in the Afghan War, 1879–80 (Medal). He was considered in the first ranks of polo players in India between 1883 and 1894. He captained the 2nd (Gloucestershire (old 61st) Regimental Polo Team in India, when the regiment won the Inter-Regimental Cup; played at Lucknow in 1892, and again in 1893. He was also captain of the Gloucester team which played in the Final and lost by one point (a disputed one), and again in the Baroda Tournament—probably in the same year—which was won by the regiment. He was secretary of the Karachi Races, 1883–84, and was a winner on several occasions in these races. He also managed the Karachi and Hyderabad (Scinde) Pig-Sticking Club during the same time. He won the Guzerat Pig-Sticking Cup in 1885, was a very fine revolver shot. He became Major 4 Sept. 1895; served during the Burma Campaign, 1886–88, and for his services as Transport Officer with the Ruby Mines Column, Burma, was created a Companion of the Distinguished Service Order [London Gazette, 3 Aug. 1888]: "For services during operations in Burma. Herbert Capel Cure, Capt., Gloucestershire Regt." He also received the Medal with clasp, and was mentioned in Despatches for services during the operations in Burma. He served in the Boer War, 1899–1902, and was taken prisoner. He took part in the operations in Natal in 1899, including the actions at Reitfontein and Lombard's Kop, and received the Queen's Medal and clasp. He became Lieut.-Colonel 25 Oct. 1903, and was given Brevet of Colonel 25 Oct. 1906, becoming Colonel 25 Oct. 1907. He afterwards commanded his regiment. The "Times" of 21 March, 1909, says: "On 19 March, at Srinagar, Kashmir, Lieut.-Colonel H. Capel Cure, D.S.O., lately commanding 1st Battn. The Gloucestershire Regt., aged 49." Colonel Capel Cure married, in India, Mary, daughter of W. J. Angerstein, of Weeting Hall, Norfolk.

WOOD, HASTINGS ST. LEGER, Capt., was born 8 May, 1856, son of the late General Sir H. H. Wood. He entered the Army (15th Regt. of Foot) 31 Oct. 1877; became Lieutenant, East Yorkshire Regt., 30 Nov. 1878. He served in the Afghan War, 1879–80, as Brigade Transport Officer, Kandahar Field Force, taking part in the defence of Kandahar, as Orderly Officer, in the sortie of 16 Aug., and attack on the village of Deh Khoja (severely wounded, and horse killed); received Medal. He took part in the Nile Expedition, 1884–85 (Despatches [London Gazette, 25 Aug. 1885]; Medal with clasp; Khedive's Star). He served in the Burma Campaign of 1887–89 as Brigade Transport Officer, and as D.A.A. and Q.M.G., 2nd Brigade. He was mentioned in Despatches [London Gazette, 3 Aug. 1888]; received the Medal and two clasps, and was created a Companion of the Distinguished Service Order [London Gazette, 3 Aug. 1888]: "For services during the operations in Burma. Hastings St. Leger Wood, Capt., East Yorkshire Regt." He became Captain 6 May, 1886,

and Major 24 July, 1895. He served in the Tirah Expeditionary Force, on the Staff, 1897–98 (Despatches [London Gazette, 5 April, 1898]; Medal with two clasps). He became Lieut.-Colonel 14 Nov. 1906, and Colonel 7 Nov. 1908; was A.A.G., Royal Guernsey Militia, 1911–14; A.A. and Q.M.G., Guernsey District, 1914. Colonel Wood married, in 1891, Mary Judith V., daughter of the Rev. J. Parker.

SCALLON, ROBERT IRVIN, Capt., was born at Long Ditton, Surbiton, 3 April, 1857, third son of the late T. N. Scallon (died in 1879; eldest son of the late Capt. Robert Scallon, R.N.), and of Sarah Jane Grey (died in 1911), eldest daughter of

Robert Irvin Scallon.

the late Rev. Thomas Irvin, Vicar of Ormesby, Yorkshire. He was educated in London, and at the Royal Military College, Sandhurst, and entered the Army as a Sub-Lieutenant, unattached, 12 Feb. 1876; 72nd Highlanders, 12 Jan. 1877; became Lieutenant, Bombay Staff Corps, 3 Sept. 1877. He served in the Afghan War, 1879–80, taking part in the engagements of Khelat-i-Ghilzai, and Sir-i-asp; in the march from Khelat-i-Ghilzai to the Relief of Kandahar, and battle of 1 Sept. (Despatches; Medal and clasp, and Bronze Star). He was Adjutant, 23rd Bombay Light Infantry, 1881; Extra A.D.C. to Commander-in-Chief, Bombay Army, 1884; First Class Station Staff Officer, 1884–86. He served in the Burma Campaign as (1) Staff Officer, Kanlé Column (Medal and clasp), 1886–87; (2) commanded Myaing Column (Despatches; clasp); created a Companion of the Distinguished Service Order [London Gazette, 3 Aug. 1888]: "For services during operations in Burma. Robert Irvin Scallon, Capt., Bombay Staff Corps." He became Captain, I.S.C., 12 Feb. 1887, and Major, 1896; Officiating Deputy-Assistant-Adjutant-General, 1891–92; Inspecting Officer, 1894–95; Punjab Imperial Service Sappers and Infantry, 1895–99; officiated as Inspector-General, Imperial Service Troops, 1897. He served on the N.W. Frontier of India, 1897–98, taking part in the operations on the Samana, and in the Kurram Valley, during Aug. and Sept. 1897 (Medal with two clasps), and in the Tirah Expedition, 1897–98. He took part in the charge of the Imperial Service Sappers and Infantry; action of Chagru Kotal, and capture of the Sampagha Pass. He was mentioned in Despatches [London Gazette, 5 April, 1898] (Clasp). He commanded 23rd Bombay Rifles, 1898–1904; created a C.I.E., 1898; became Lieut.-Colonel, 12 Feb. 1902; Brevet-Colonel, 1902; commanded Zhob Section, Mahsud-Waziri Blockading Force, 1900–2 (Commendation of the Government of India twice; Clasp; Brevet of Colonel, 7 June, 1902), and troops in Zhob district during disturbances in Sheranni country, 1902 (Commended by Government); commanded the Aden Column during operations in the Aden Hinterland, 1903 (Despatches, 11 Feb. 1905). Colonel Scallon married, in 1904, Jeannette, daughter of the late John Gordon, Master of the Supreme Court. He commanded the Infantry Brigade, Bangalore, 1904; became Colonel on the Staff, 14 Dec. 1904; created a C.B.; was Officiating Political Resident and Commanding at Aden, 1905; Commanded Bangalore Brigade, 1906; Major-General, 1 Dec. 1906; Adjutant-General in India, 1908; was Secretary to the Government of India, Army Department, 1909; created a K.C.I.E., 1910; Lieut.-General, 23 June, 1911; in command of Burma Division, 1911; A.D.C.-General to the King, 1911–15; Lucknow Division, 1913; created a K.C.B., 1913, and G.C.B. in 1918; Northern Army, 1914–15; invalided, 1915; General, 1917; Staff-Lieutenant at the War Office, 1918; member of the Territorial Force Association (1917) and a Justice of the Peace for the county of Worcester (1918).

SCUDAMORE, CHARLES PHILIP, Lieut., was born 27 Sept. 1861, son of the late Major-General A. Scudamore, C.B., 11th and 7th Hussars, and of Mrs. Scudamore. He was educated at Wellington College, and at the Royal Military College, Sandhurst; entered the Royal Scots Fusiliers 22 Oct. 1881. He served in the Burmese Expedition, 1885–86–87, as Transport Officer to a column, as a Brigade Transport Officer, and as Staff Officer to the Director of Transport. He was mentioned in Despatches, 2 Sept. 1887; received the Medal with two clasps, and was created a Companion of the Distinguished Service Order [London Gazette, 3 Aug. 1888]: "Charles Philip Scudamore, Lieut., Royal Scots Fusiliers. For services during operations in Burma." He was Adjutant, Royal Scots Fusiliers, 1890–94. He married, in 1890, Gertrude Caroline, daughter of Samuel Bircham, of Beech House, Mayford, and The Moor House, Reepham, Norfolk. He served in the Hazara Expedition, 1888, as Assistant to the Divisional Transport Officer; was mentioned in Despatches, and received a clasp. Lieut. Scudamore was promoted to Captain 15 Nov. 1902. He again saw active service on the N.W. Frontier of India, 1897–98, serving as D.A.Q.M.G. He was present at the action of the Ublan Pass, 27 Aug. 1897. Operations on the Samana, and in the Kurram Valley during Aug. and Sept. 1897; defences of the Samana Forts; Relief of Gulistan. Operations of the Flying Column in the Kurram Valley, under Colonel Richardson, 20 Aug. to 7 Oct. 1897 (Despatches [London Gazette, 11 Feb. 1898]; Medal with two clasps). He took part in the Tirah Campaign, 1897–98, on the Staff. Reconnaissance of the Kharmana Defile, and action of 7 Nov. 1897. Operations against the Khani Khel Chamkanis (Despatches [London Gazette, 5 April, 1898]; Brevet of Major, 20 May, 1898; Clasp). He was Inspector of Army Signalling, Punjab, 1898–1904. He served in the South African War, 1899–1900. Operations in the Transvaal in May and June, 1900; operations in Natal (March and April); operations in Cape Colony, north of Orange River, including action at Ruidam (Queen's Medal with two clasps). He became Major

25 Aug. 1902; was Commandant, School of Signalling, Aldershot, 1906–9. Major Scudamore retired on 18 May, 1910, and in that year became Secretary of the Surrey Territorial Force Association. He served in the European War, became Temporary Lieut.-Colonel, and was D.A.A.G., Mediterranean Expeditionary Force, 1915, and A.A.G., Egyptian Expeditionary Force (C.M.G., 1916; Despatches twice).

JENNER, ALBERT VICTOR, Lieut., was born on 19 Dec. 1862, son of Sir William Jenner, 1st Baronet, Physician, and Adela, daughter of Stephen Adey; and brother of Sir Walter Jenner. He was educated at Winchester; entered the Rifle Brigade 9 Sept. 1882; served in the Burmese Expedition, 1886–88; was mentioned in Despatches; received the Medal with two clasps, and was created a Companion of the Distinguished Service Order [London Gazette, 3 Aug. 1888]: "Albert Victor Jenner, Lieut., Rifle Brigade. For services during operations in Burma." Insignia were presented to him by Queen Victoria. He became Captain 2 Dec. 1891; served in South Africa in 1896; commanded Mounted Infantry in North Mashonaland; Despatches [London Gazette, 9 March, 1897], and given the Brevet of Major, and received the Medal. He became Major 2 Aug. 1899; served in South Africa, 1900–2, on the Staff; commanded Mounted Infantry Corps (graded A.A.G.) from 28 Dec. 1900. Operations in the Transvaal, east of Pretoria, July to 29 Nov. 1900; operations in the Transvaal, 30 Nov. 1900, to 31 May, 1902; operations in Orange River Colony, July to Aug. 1901; operations on the Zululand Frontier of Natal, Sept. and Oct. 1901 (Despatches [London Gazette, 10 Sept. 1901]; Brevet of Lieut.-Colonel, 26 June, 1902; Queen's Medal with four clasps; King's Medal with two clasps). He retired 23 Jan. 1904, with the rank of Lieut.-Colonel. He served as a General Staff Officer at the War Office, 1915–19, and was created C.M.G. in 1918. Lieut.-Colonel A. V. Jenner is a J.P. and F.R.G.S.

London Gazette, 12 April, 1889.—"War Office, 9 April, 1889. The Queen has been graciously pleased to give orders for the following appointments in recognition of the services of the undermentioned Officers during the operations at Sikkim, bearing date 2 Nov. 1888. To be Companions of the Distinguished Service Order."

CAREW, RICHARD HUGH, Surgeon-Major, adopted the medical profession, and became L.R.C.P. and L.R.C.S.I. He joined the Medical Staff, and served in the Abyssinian Expedition, 1868; Capture of Magdala (Medal). He took part in the Sikkim Expedition, 1888, as Senior Medical Officer; was mentioned in Despatches; received the Medal with clasp, and was created a Companion of the Distinguished Service Order [London Gazette, 12 April 1889]: "Richard Hugh Carew, Surgeon-Major, Medical Staff. In recognition of services during operations in Sikkim." He became Lieut.-Colonel, Royal Army Medical Corps, 7 Dec. 1891, and Colonel, 11 Dec. 1895; took part in the operations on the North-West Frontier of India, 1897–98, serving as Senior Medical Officer with the Tochi Field Force. He was mentioned in Despatches [London Gazette, 11 Feb. 1898], and received the Medal and clasp. He became Colonel 7 Dec. 1895. Colonel Carew died 24 Sept. 1902.

ROGERS, GEORGE WILLIAM, Lieut.-Colonel, was born 11 Sept. 1843. He became Lieutenant, R.A., 1 Sept. 1862; Lieutenant, Bengal Staff Corps, 22 Dec. 1868. He served in the Lushai Expedition, 1871–72 (Medal with clasp). He again saw active service in the Afghan War, 1879–80, taking part in the action of Ali Khel; operations around Kabul and Sherpur, March from Kabul to the Relief of Kandahar, and battle of 1 Sept. (Despatches [London Gazette, 4 May and 3 Dec. 1880]; Medal with two clasps; Bronze Star; Brevet of Major, 1 Sept. 1882). He was D.A.A.G. (Musketry), Bengal, 24 July, 1884, to 17 Feb. 1886. He served in the Sikkim Expedition, 1888, and was created a Companion of the Distinguished Service Order [London Gazette, 12 April 1889]: "In recognition of services during the operations at Sikkim. George William Rogers, Lieut.-Colonel, Bengal Staff Corps." He became Lieut.-Colonel 1 Sept. 1888; Brevet Colonel, 19 Sept. 1902, and retired on 19 Sept. 1902, with the rank of Colonel. Colonel Rogers married in 1892, Jane Isabella, daughter of Major-General J. S. Rawlins. He died 27 April, 1917.

London Gazette, 12 April, 1889.—"War Office, 12 April, 1889. The Queen has further been pleased to give orders for the following appointments to the Distinguished Service Order, in recognition of the services of the undermentioned Officers during the operations of Hazara, bearing date the 7th Dec. 1888. To be Companions of the Distinguished Service Order."

GATACRE, WILLIAM FORBES, Colonel, was born 3 Dec. 1843, at Herbertshire Castle, Stirlingshire, the residence of his grandmother. He was the third son of Edward Lloyd Gatacre, J.P., of Gatacre in Shropshire, and of Jessie, daughter of William Forbes, Esq., of Callendar, Stirlingshire. It is shown in Doomsday Book that the family were King's Tenants of lands of this name before the Conquest; John de Gatacre was High Sheriff in 1409, and Sir William's father held the same office in 1856. Young Gatacre entered the Royal Military College, Sandhurst, in Aug. 1860, and in Feb. 1862, was gazetted an Ensign in the 77th Foot (now the 2nd Battn. Middlesex Regt.), which he joined in India. In 1873 he passed into the Staff College, and from 1875 to 1879 was Instructor in Surveying at the Royal Military College. Later he officiated for a year as D.A.A. and Q.M.G. at Aldershot. In 1880 he returned to India with his regiment, succeeding to the command in 1884 at Secunderabad. In 1885 he was appointed D.Q.M.G. at Headquarters by Sir Frederick Roberts, Commander-in-Chief in India. It was while holding this post in 1888 that he had his first taste of active service, being appointed Chief Staff Officer to Sir John McQueen, commanding a small punitive force sent against the tribes of the Black Mountain. The little force of 8,000 men was divided into three columns; one day, in order to get in touch with Galbraith's Column in the Indus Valley, Gatacre volunteered to make his way across the mountains on foot. The mission was successfully accomplished in twenty-four hours, and as Gatacre was the only man to complete the double journey, the feat attracted considerable notice at the time. He was mentioned in Despatches, awarded the Frontier Medal with Hazara clasp, and created a Companion of the Distinguished Service Order [London Gazette, 12 April, 1889]: "For services during the operations of Hazara. William Forbes Gatacre, Lieut.-Colonel and Colonel, Half-Pay." In 1889 Gatacre was sent to Mandalay as Brigadier-General Acting for Sir George Wolseley, and there earned another bar to his Frontier Medal. In 1890 he was given the substantive appointment of Adjutant-General, Bombay Army, with the rank of Brigadier-General, a post which he held for nearly four years under three successive Commanders-in-Chief. In Jan. 1894, he was appointed to the command of the Bombay District. The following year we find him commanding the 3rd Brigade of the Chitral Relief Force under Sir Robert Low. The object of this expedition was the relief of Surgeon-Major Robertson, who, with a small garrison, was reported to be shut up in the Fort at Chitral. Gatacre's Brigade was in reserve during the first action at the Malakand Pass; but after crossing the Panjkora River the 3rd Brigade was pushed forward, encountering some opposition at Mamugai. Shortly after this Gatacre got permission to advance rapidly up the valley with a lightly-equipped force of 500 men. The Lowari Pass was under snow, but good progress had been made when the news came through that the siege had been raised on 22 April on the approach of Colonel Kelly's Force moving southward from Gilgit. Sir R. Low's troops made their way on to the Fort, establishing such good lines of communication, as they traversed passes and valleys hitherto unknown to Englishmen, that the route then cut has become the roadway for the annual reliefs. For his part in this campaign, Gatacre received the C.B., the thanks of the Government of India, and the new Frontier Medal with clasp. Gatacre's last few months in his substantive post at Bombay were marked by a severe outbreak of bubonic plague. He presided over the commission set up to provide hospitals and to carry out precautionary measures, and before the hot weather of 1897 the situation was well in hand for that season. In August that year Gatacre came home to take up the command of an Infantry Brigade at Aldershot, but had only held the post five months when he was sent to Egypt to take command of the British Brigade which was to form part of Sir Herbert Kitchener's Expedition for the recovery of Khartoum. Soon after his arrival at Railhead, Gatacre was summoned by the Sirdar to bring his troops by forced marches to Berber. On Good Friday, 8 April, 1898, a fierce and effective action took place with the Dervish Army on the banks of the Atbara, in which the British Brigade took a prominent part. The advance on Omdurman was planned for the early autumn, but before the move began, the arrival of another brigade of British troops had raised Gatacre's command to a division, and he was given the permanent rank of Major-General. The Battle of Omdurman was fought on 1 Sept., and Khartoum was occupied next day. In recognition of his services Gatacre was gazetted K.C.B., and received from the Khedive the Order of the Medjidie, Second Class. His name appears next to Lord Kitchener's in the Vote of Thanks in both Houses of Parliament. A new British Medal for Egypt was issued for all ranks, and an Egyptian one was received from the Khedive. In Oct. 1899, the British Government dispatched a force under Sir Redvers Buller, V.C., as a reply to the invasion of Natal and Cape Colony by the Boers from the Transvaal and Orange River Free State. Gatacre was gazetted to the 3rd Division, with the temporary rank of Lieut.-General. The three Divisional Commanders sailed in the same ship, but at Cape Town a new distribution of the troops was made, in order to meet pressure at certain points, by which Gatacre's command was reduced to two battalions, with Headquarters at Queenstown. To this half-brigade were added certain hastily raised volunteers, but it must be remembered that Gatacre's force, while in theory a complete division, never at any time reached a fully-equipped brigade of infantry, and that he never had any regular artillery or cavalry. All three columns were unfortunate in their first contact with the enemy. At Magersfontein, on 11 Dec., the casualties were 948 out of 14,964 troops engaged; at Colenso the casualties were 1,139 out of a force of 19,378; at Stormberg, the loss in killed and wounded was 135 with 571 missing, out of a total of 3,035 engaged. In none of these engagements were the recently landed British troops able to gain their objective, but in no case was ground lost. The Official History of the War says: "Sir William Gatacre's decision to advance on Stormberg was fully justified by the strategical position. General Buller's telegram, although it left him a free hand in time and opportunity, had suggested that operation. The plan, though bold, was sound in its design, and would have succeeded had not exceptional misfortune attended its execution" (Vol. I., page 301). After the arrival of Lord Roberts in Bloemfontein in March, 1900, with large reinforcements, Gatacre's troops were employed to distribute Peace Proclamations behind the front line of defence at the express command of the Commander-in-Chief. As a consequence of the unfortunate affair at Sanna's Post, in which the Boers got possession of the Bloemfontein Waterworks, Gatacre's peace patrols were exposed to attack. One little group of colonials held on finely at Wepener until relieved; but in the process of withdrawal a small British force, about 190 rifles, was overtaken at Reddersburg, and surrendered an hour before assistance reached them. After this incident Sir William Gatacre returned to England, but was reinstated in his command of the Eastern District. Extraordinary demonstrations of affection greeted his return, notably at Colchester and Norwich. His noble bearing, silence,

William Forbes Gatacre

and high sense of duty impressed those who came in contact with him, and his influence among all ranks was always for good. In 1905 Sir William's love of adventure and of the East led him to join an expedition to report on the rubber fields of Abyssinia. He died of fever near Gambela, 18 Jan. 1906, aged 62. Sir William Gatacre was twice married; two sons survived him, Major W. E. Gatacre, K.O.Y.L.I., and Capt. J. K. Gatacre, 11th Bengal Lancers, killed in action in France 12 Oct. 1914.

Sir Ian Hamilton wrote: "General Gatacre was one of the hardest working men I ever struck, whether at his desk as D.Q.M.G. in India, or on horseback, or on his own legs. In the Chitral Campaign and in Egypt, he well justified the name which the soldiers affectionately bestowed upon him of General Backacher. As to Stormberg, I think it was very largely the case of that fickle jade called the Fortune of War. Without entering into controversy or detail, I think it will be generally admitted by those who have studied the matter, that General Gatacre's luck was dead out on that occasion."

Colonel Ronald Brooke, D.S.O., writes of Sir William Gatacre: "I was with him in Chitral, 1895, and in the Sudan, 1898, also at Colchester, 1899, for a short period. His boundless energy and determination to succeed in whatever he took up were the dominant features in his character. He was an extremely brave man, and once, at some hill station in India (I am not sure which), a native sepoy had run amok with his rifle, shooting several people. He took up his stand in the centre of an open space and threatened to kill anyone who approached him. General Gatacre, who was then, I think, a Colonel, arrived on the scene, and immediately walked straight up to the man, ordering him to hand over his rifle. The man had only one cartridge left, and, instead of killing Gatacre, he blew his own brains out. Had he still been in possession of two cartridges he would undoubtedly have killed Gatacre first of all. At the Atbara, General Gatacre accompanied the attacking force, and when the leading line hesitated to face the heavy fire and make a break in the zareba which surrounded the dervish entrenchments and stockade, General Gatacre, to my horror, stepped in front of the leading men, who continued firing vigorously at the enemy round his body, and pulled the first thorn-branch out. This gave the men the lead they required; they rushed forward, tore away the brush fence, and we were shortly inside the entrenchments. General Gatacre, after setting this example, at once retired behind his leading men, and went to our left flank, which he considered might be attacked by Osman's cavalry, which we had seen withdrawing out of the enemy's entrenchments just before we attacked and heading up the River Atbara beyond our left. The General was criticized unfavourably afterwards for unnecessarily endangering his own life, but in my opinion a leader should be where he is most required, and at the Battle of the Atbara, General Gatacre carried out the axiom. He unceasingly exerted himself to ensure the comfort of his officers and men in the Sudan Campaign of 1898, and, owing to his efforts during several months, he at last succeeded in obtaining a daily jam ration for everyone. This had never been given before, and it was solely owing to his exertions that this excellent custom was instituted, and the fact that rations have ever since included jam proves how right he was. He was clever at sketching and drawing, and took an immense interest in everything he undertook. During the Chitral Campaign he brought an official photographer with him (a Sergeant-Major in the Royal Engineers), who took excellent photos of the country. He also collected specimens of every flower we saw, and thus, although he knew nothing about botany, he succeeded in obtaining some rare and valuable plants, and adding to the knowledge of plant life on the frontier."

The author of an article, "Campaigning with Kitchener," in "Blackwood," for Dec. 1902, says, when describing the Battle of the Atbara: "When the fighting folk had had their say, the looters had a merry time, and many a battle relic that now hangs in hall and cottage was garnered by those anxious for a memento of the day. K. was dictating his despatch to the Queen when there passed in front of us a pony led by a syce, and laden with spoils selected from that field of plenty with the praiseworthy discrimination of an art connoisseur. K. hailed the man, and, selecting the finest coat of mail and the most beautifully finished spear, bade me take it to General Gatacre with his warmest thanks for the splendid gallantry and good judgment with which he had led his fine brigade. I seem to see now the pleasant light that shone in that brave soldier's eyes as I gave him the message word for word. Gatacre! What a splendid fellow, and how willingly any of us, whom he worked to death in the Sudan, would have given our right hands to save him from the fate that befell him—at the hands of his own chiefs—in South Africa. He taught us, in Chitral, the Sudan and South Africa, two great lessons: first, never to make difficulties; secondly, never to complain of any hard knocks of fate, and to take the rough and the smooth things of life as they came. Oh, you poor deluded British public, will you never distinguish between the real men and the dummies?"

The following is contributed: "No bare record of the posts which Gatacre held can give any idea of his personality. There can be no question of the influence for good on his generation; all those who were closely associated with him felt his power and his charm: his modesty was almost as surprising as his capacity for work, and his gentleness as arresting as his stern sense of duty. It was said of Gatacre that he was born out of due time, that he ought to have been one of Cromwell's Ironsides; indeed, he was an enthusiast, a man of clear vision and exalted ideals, and a physique that never failed his will. But he was also an artist, and loved mountains and storms, and the desert and the night with a poet's affection for nature unspoilt by man. Though deeply beloved by his friends, he did not shine in general society, and when an adverse fate drove him into retirement, he regretted leaving the Army because the Army had been his field of activity, but it cost him little to leave ' the world.' He became one of ' the great silent men.' I suppose that very few men now know whether there is a sound explanation of his return from South Africa;

most of the actors in that mystery-play are now underground. But retirement did not quench Gatacre's ' will to work '; he sought a new field for his activities: he returned to the desert which he loved, to the Egypt that had given him his great day at the Atbara. He sought solace there and found it. His death, while on a shooting expedition, was in the spirit of the Viking warriors of old, whose instinct led them to sail away alone in a ship when they knew that their hour was come. Gatacre was a solitary figure in life and in death."

O'GRADY-HALY, RICHARD HEBDEN, Lieut.-Colonel, was born 22 Feb. 1841, at Tunbridge Wells, eldest son of the late General Sir William O'Grady-Haly, K.C.B., and of Harriette, daughter of H. Hebden, Esq.,

Richard O'Grady-Haly.

of Ely Grange, Tunbridge Wells. He was educated at the Royal Military College, Sandhurst, and joined the Army 6 Nov. 1858. He married in 1865, Geraldine Mary, youngest daughter of Major-General Gostling, R.A., and Mary, daughter of John Easpard Le Marchant, Major-General (founder of Sandhurst College). Their children are: Ethel Mary Gertrude, Mabel Violet (married, 1899, Robert Balmain Low, eldest son of Sir Robert Low, G.C.B.), and Hilda Fanshawe. General O'Grady-Haly was A.D.C. to General Atherley in Malta, 1863; became Captain, 1866; was A.D.C. to Sir Hastings Doyle in Canada, 1870; was A.D.C. to his father, Sir William O'Grady-Haly, in Canada, 1874–78; became Major, 1879; entered the Staff College, 1880; served with the Egyptian Expedition, 1882; Action of El Maffar; both actions at Kassassin, and Battle of Tel-el-Kebir (Despatches; Medal with clasp; Bronze Star, and Brevet of Lieut.-Colonel, 1882); with the Hazara Field Force, 1888, in command of the Second Column; was mentioned in Despatches, G.G.O., 978 of 88; received the Medal and clasp, and was created a Companion of the Distinguished Service Order [London Gazette, 12 April 1889]: " For services during the operations of Hazara. Richard O'Grady-Haly, Lieut.-Colonel and Colonel, The Suffolk Regt." The Insignia were presented to him by Queen Victoria. He commanded the 1st Battn. 12th Suffolk Regt. in India; was A.A.G. in Belfast from 1891 to 1896; he was in command of Canadian Militia, 1900 to 1902, and was in command while H.R.H. The Duke of York made his visit to Canada. He held the appointment of Inspector of Warlike Stores for Canada from 1904 to 1911. Major-General O'Grady-Haly died 8 July, 1911. He was a beautiful draughtsman, and wrote several official books while at the Intelligence Department, London. He was a good horseman and a first-class fisherman.

MURRAY, ANDREW, Colonel, was born 6 June, 1837, in Edinburgh, son of Andrew Murray, Esq., Junior Advocate, Edinburgh, and Mary Stewart. He joined the Edinburgh County Militia in 1855; became

Andrew Murray.

Ensign, 60th Foot, 7 Feb. 1858, and was transferred to the 78th Highlanders 19 Feb. 1858; became Lieutenant, 16 Aug. 1861; Captain, 2 Oct., 1866, and Brevet Major, 16 Jan. 1880. He served with the 78th Highlanders in the Afghan War in 1880 (Medal); in the Egyptian War, 1882, in command of the detachments, 2nd Seaforth Highlanders, and was present at the Battle of Tel-el-Kebir (Medal and clasp; Fourth Class Osmanieh, and Khedive's Star). He became Major, 1 July, 1881; Lieut.-Colonel, 27 March, 1883, and Colonel, 27 March, 1887. In the Hazara Campaign in 1888, he was in command of a Reserve Column. He later commanded the Second Advance Column until the conclusion of the campaign. He received a Medal, was twice mentioned in Despatches, once by General G. N. Channer, Commanding the 1st Brigade, Hazara Field Force; received the Medal with clasp, and in recognition of his distinguished service when in command of the Advance Column, was created a Companion of the Distinguished Service Order [London Gazette, 12 April, 1889]: " For services during the operations in Hazara. Andrew Murray, Lieut.-Colonel and Colonel, Half-Pay." Colonel Murray commanded the 72nd and 79th Regimental Districts from 6 June, 1890, to Dec. 1894. He retired on retired pay 6 June, 1904 (having retired on half-pay in March, 1899), and died on the 4th May, 1915. An obituary notice appeared in the " Times " of 6 May, 1915.

HAWES, ALEXANDER JAMES DONNELLY, Colonel, was born in 1840. He entered the Bengal Army in 1859; was on active service abroad in 1866, and against the Bezotis, 1869; with the Jowaki Expedition, 1877–78 (Despatches; Medal with clasp); during the Afghan War, 1878–79 (Despatches and Medal); in the Zhob Valley Expeditionary Force, 1884 (Despatches); with Hazara Field Force, 1888. He was created a Companion of the Distinguished Service Order [London Gazette, 12 April, 1889]: " For services during the operations of Hazara. Alexander James Donnelly Hawes, Lieut.-Colonel and Colonel, Bengal Staff Corps." Colonel Hawes died 2 March, 1899.

SUNDERLAND, MARSDEN SAMUEL JAMES, Lieut.-Colonel, entered the Army in 1861; became Captain in 1876, and Major in 1881. He served in the Nile Expedition, 1884–85, and actions of Abu Klea and

Gubat (Despatches twice; Brevet of Lieut.-Colonel; Medal with two clasps; Khedive's Star); became Lieut.-Colonel in 1885, and Colonel in 1892. He took part in the Hazara Campaign, 1888 (Despatches; Medal with clasp), and was created a Companion of the Distinguished Service Order [London Gazette, 12 April, 1889]: " For services during the operations of Hazara. Marsden Samuel James Sunderland, Lieut.-Colonel, Royal Sussex Regt." He commanded 91st Regimental District, 1892–97. His favourite recreation was farming Prince of Wales's pheasants, which he introduced into England in 1903. Colonel Sunderland died 25 March, 1914.

DESHON, CHARLES JOHN, Lieut.-Colonel, was born 18 Dec. 1840, son of the late Lieut.-Colonel C. J. Deshon, 17th Regt. He entered the Army 22 Dec. 1859. He became Lieut.-Colonel 21 Dec. 1886, and served in the Burma Campaign, 1886–87; was mentioned in Despatches [London Gazette, 2 Sept. 1887]. In 1888 he took part in the Hazara Expedition, commanding Royal Artillery; was mentioned in Despatches, and created a Companion of the Distinguished Service Order [London Gazette, 12 April, 1889]: " For services during the operations of Hazara. Charles John Deshon, Lieut.-Colonel, Royal Artillery." He became Colonel 21 Dec. 1890; was put on half-pay 21 Dec. 1891, and on retired pay 9 March, 1892. He married in 1864, Mary Henrietta (who died in 1911), eldest daughter of the late Major Loftus Cassidy.

HAMMOND, ARTHUR GEORGE, V.C., Lieut.-Colonel, was created a Companion of the Distinguished Service Order [London Gazette, 12 April, 1889]: " Arthur George Hammond, V.C., Lieut.-Colonel, Bengal Staff Corps. For services during the operations of Hazara." (See " Victoria Cross " Volume.)

KEIGHLEY, CHARLES MARSH, Major, was born in 1847. He entered the Army in 1867; served in the Afghan War, 1878–79, taking part in both Bazar Valley Expeditions, and in the advance to Kabul of 1878–79 (Despatches; Medal). He became Captain, B.S.C. (now I.S.C.), 1879; served with the Mahsud-Wuzeeree Expedition in 1881, as Chief Commissariat Officer (Despatches). He became Major in 1887; served with the Hazara Field Force in 1888; was mentioned in Despatches; received the Medal with clasp, and was created a Companion of the Distinguished Service Order [London Gazette, 12 April, 1889]: " For services during the operations of Hazara. Charles Marsh Keighley, Major, Bengal Staff Corps." He served on the North-West Frontier in 1897 and 1898; was mentioned in Despatches, and received the Medal with two clasps. He served in Tirah, 1897–98, as Chief Commissariat Officer, Lines of Communication (11 Oct. 1897, to 21 Jan. 1898), and subsequently on the Staff. He was mentioned in Despatches [London Gazette, 5 April, 1898]; received the Clasp, and was created a C.B. He served in the South African War as District Commissioner, Queen's Medal with two clasps. Colonel Keighley died 10 July, 1911.

London Gazette, 12 April, 1889.—" War Office, 12 April, 1889. The Queen has been graciously pleased to give orders for the following appointment to the Distinguished Service Order, in recognition of the services of the undermentioned Officer during the operations in the Suly-mah District."

MACKAY, HUNTLEY BRODIE, Lieut., became Lieutenant, Royal Engineers, 25 June, 1881, and Captain 20 Dec. 1889. He served with the Bechuanaland Expedition under Sir C. Warren in 1884–85 on special service. Served in the expedition against the Younies, on the West Coast of Africa, in 1887–88; was mentioned in Despatches, and created a Companion of the Distinguished Service Order [London Gazette, 12 April, 1889]: " Huntley Brodie MacKay, Lieut., Royal Engineers, having local rank of Captain whilst commanding Royal Engineers on the West Coast of Africa. For services during the operations in the Suly-mah District." He was promoted to Captain, and died in 1891.

London Gazette, 10 Oct. 1889.—" War Office, 8 Oct. 1889. The Queen has been graciously pleased to give orders for the appointment of the undermentioned Officer to be a Companion of the Distinguished Service Order. For operations against the Awunahs."

GRAHAM, HERMAN WITSIUS GORE, Lieut., was born 28 Oct. 1859, second son of Robert Gore Graham, J.P., of Southmead, Westbury-on-Trym, Gloucestershire, He was educated privately, and at the Royal Military College, Sandhurst; was gazetted to the 1st West India Regt. 5 March, 1884, being transferred to the 5th Lancers in 1887. He served on the West Coast of Africa in 1889, taking part in the operations against the Awunhas; was mentioned in Despatches, and created a Companion of the Distinguished Service Order [London Gazette, 10 Oct. 1889]: " For operations against the Awunhas. Herman Witsius Gore Graham, Lieut., 5th Lancers." The insignia were presented to him by the Queen. Lieut. Graham served with the Egyptian Cavalry, 1891–93; became Captain in 1892. He has passed the Staff College. He served in Ashanti, 1895 (Honourably Mentioned; Star); on the North-West Frontier in the Tirah Expedition, 1897, on the Staff; was D.A.A.G., 3rd Brigade (Clasp). He was promoted to Major in 1899, and served in the South African War of 1899–1902, as Brigade-Major of the 1st Cavalry Brigade, taking part in the operations in Natal, 1899; in the relief of Ladysmith, including action at Colenso; operations of 17 to 24 Jan. 1900, and 5 to 7 Feb. 1900, and action at Vaal Krantz; operations on the Tugela Heights (14 to 27 Feb. 1900), and action at Pieter's Hill; operations in Natal, March to June, 1900. Afterwards Provisional District Commissioner, Utrecht (from 12 Sept. 1900), and as District Commandant; Administrator, Martial Law Area, Cape Colony District, and as Administrator of General Districts. In command " Marshall's Horse," 1 to 31 May, 1902. Operations in the Transvaal, Cape Colony, 30 Nov. 1900, to 31 May, 1902 (Despatches [London Gazette, 8 Feb. 1901]; Queen's Medal with four clasps). He was

District Commissioner, Transvaal, 1900–1; employed under the Government of Cape Colony, 1902–3; became Lieut.-Colonel 19 Oct. 1905; was in command of the 5th Lancers, 1905–9; was given the Brevet of Colonel 19 Oct. 1908; was Commandant, West African Regt., 1909–13. He retired with the rank of Colonel from the West African Regt. 2 Jan. 1913. Colonel Graham was re-employed on the General Staff of the New Armies in 1914.

London Gazette, 8 Nov. 1889.—" The Queen has been graciously pleased to give orders for the following appointments to the Distinguished Service Order, in recognition of the services of the undermentioned Officers during the action at Toski, bearing date the 17th Aug. 1889. To be Companions of the Distinguished Service Order."

WINGATE, SIR FRANCIS REGINALD, General, G.C.B., G.C.V.O., G.B.E., K.C.M.G., D.S.O., D.C.L. (Oxon), LL.D. (Edinburgh), was born at Broadfield, Renfrewshire, 25 June, 1861, seventh son of the late Andrew

Sir Francis R. Wingate.

Wingate, Glasgow, and Bessie, daughter of Richard Turner, of Dublin. He was educated at St. James's Collegiate School, Jersey, and at the R.M.A., Woolwich, and became Lieutenant, Royal Artillery, 27 July, 1880; served in India and Aden, 1881–83; was employed with Egyptian Army, 4 June, 1883, to 4 June, 1885; was Commandant, Cholera Hospital, 1883 (Fourth Class Osmanieh); acted as A.D.C. and Military Secretary to General Sir Evelyn Wood during the Nile Expedition, and in the Bayuda Desert, 1884–85 (Medal with clasp; Bronze Star; Fourth Class Medjidie; Despatches, 25 Aug. 1885); was A.D.C. to G.O.C., Eastern District, 1 April, 1886, to 30 April, 1886; rejoined the Egyptian Army, May, 1886. He was present at the Battle of Toski as A.A.G. Intelligence, 1889; was mentioned in Despatches [London Gazette, 1889], and created a Companion of the Distinguished Service Order [London Gazette, 8 Nov. 1889]: " Francis Reginald Wingate, Capt. and Brevet Major, Royal Artillery. In recognition of services during the action at Toski." The insignia were presented to him in Egypt by the Sirdar, 1 Aug. 1890. He was promoted Captain 14 Jan. 1889, and Brevet Major 15 Jan. 1889. In 1888 he married Catherine Leslie, daughter of the late Capt. Joseph Sparkhall Rundle, R.N. (she is a Lady of Grace of the Order of St. John of Jerusalem, and has the Grand Cordon of the Order of Kemal of Egypt); they had two sons (one of whom was the late Capt. and Brevet Major Malcolm Roy Wingate, D.S.O., M.C., Croix de Guerre avec Palmes, who was killed near Lagnicourt, France, on the 21st March, 1918, whilst in command of the 459th Field Company, Royal Engineers. His elder son, Ronald E. L. Wingate, of the Indian Civil Service, is Political Agent and Consul at Muscat), and one daughter, Victoria Alexandrina Catharine, god-daughter of Her Majesty Queen Victoria. He was present at the action of Afafit and recapture of Tokar, 1891 (Clasp to Bronze Star, and Third Class Medjidie); was A.M.S. 31 May, to 31 Dec. 1893; Director of Military Intelligence 1 Jan. 1894, to 31 Dec. 1898; acted as Governor, Red Sea Littoral, and O.C. troops, Suakin, 1894; created a C.B. (civil) 1895. He took part in the Dongola Campaign as Director of Military Intelligence, being present at the operations of 7 June and 19 Sept. 1896 (Despatches [London Gazette, 3 Nov. 1896]; Brevet Lieut.-Colonel, 18 Nov. 1896; Medal with two clasps); Member of Special Mission to King Menelik of Abyssinia, 1897 (Second Class Star of Ethiopia). For his services in the Nile Expedition, 1897, A.D.C. to the Sovereign, 17 June, 1897, to 26 June, 1908; Colonel, 17 Dec. 1897 (Clasp). In the Nile Expedition of 1898, as Director of Military Intelligence, he was present at the Battle of the Atbara (Despatches; Clasp); Battle of Khartoum and Expedition to Fashoda (Despatches, 24 May and 30 Sept. 1898; K.C.M.G.; Clasp; thanked by both Houses of Parliament); was Adjutant-General, 1 Jan. 1899, to 21 Dec. 1899, and was Sirdar of the Egyptian Army and Governor-General of the Sudan from 22 Dec. 1899, till 31 Dec. 1916. In the Nile Expedition of 1899 he was in command of operations resulting in the death of the Khalifa, near Gedid (Despatches, 30 Jan. 1900; K.C.B. (Mil.); Second Class Osmanieh; two clasps to Egyptian Medal); in charge of special mission to Somaliland, 1909. During the tenure of his appointment in the Sudan he organized a large number of expeditions for the pacification of that country, including the reconquest of Darfur in 1916 (Sudan Medal and clasp). Since the inception of the Arab Revolt in Arabia (1916), he has been General Officer Commanding Hedjaz operations. During the War 1914–19 he was frequently mentioned in Despatches in connection with operations in the Sudan, Palestine, and Arabia (" Overseas " and " Victory " Medals). He was appointed High Commissioner for Egypt on 1 Jan. 1917, in which appointment he was succeeded by Field-Marshal Viscount Allenby on 15 Oct. 1919. He became Major-General, 27 June, 1903; Lieut.-General, 26 June, 1908; General, Nov. 1913; G.C.V.O., 1912; G.C.B. (Mil.), 1914; G.B.E., 1918; Pasha of Egypt; has Grand Cordon of Osmanieh, 1905; Medjidie, 1900; the Nile, 1915; and Mohammed Ali, 1916; Coronation Medals, 1902 and 1911; is a Knight of Grace of the Order of St. John of Jerusalem; D.C.L. Oxford, 1905; LL.D. Edinburgh, 1919; Hon. Member, Zoological Society of London; F.R.G.S.; Freedom, Royal Borough of Dunbar, 1900; Colonel Commandant of the Royal Regiment of Artillery, and Hon. Colonel of the 7th Battn. (T.F.) The Manchester Regt.; District Grand Master of Egypt and the Sudan since 1900, and of North Africa (Mark Master Masons). He has written " Mahdiism and the Egyptian Sudan," 1889; " Ten Years' Captivity in the Mahdi's Camp," 1891; translated and edited Slatin Pasha's " Fire and Sword in the Sudan," 1895.

HAYES, AYLMER ELLIS, Surgeon-Major, was born in 1850; joined the Army Medical Staff, 1877, and became Surgeon-Major, 1889; served during the Afghan War of 1878–80 (Medal). He again saw active service in the Sudan Campaign of 1888–89, being present at the actions of Gemaizah and of Toski (as P.M.O. of Egyptian Army). He was mentioned in Despatches [London Gazette, 11 Jan. and 6 Sept. 1889; received the Medal with two clasps, the Bronze Star, the Third Class Medjidie, and was created a Companion of the Distinguished Service Order [London Gazette, 8 Nov. 1889]: "In recognition of services during the action of Toski. Aylmer Ellis Hayes, Surgeon-Major, Army Medical Staff." Insignia presented by the Queen 19 Aug. 1890. Lieut.-Colonel A. E. Hayes, D.S.O., died 19 May, 1900.

COLES, ARTHUR HORSMAN, Capt., was born 7 Sept. 1856, son of the late T. Horsman Coles, Esq., of 76, Westbourne Terrace, London, W. He was educated at Winchester; entered the 3rd Foot (The Buffs, East Kent Regt.) 11 Sept. 1876, and became Captain in 1885. He served with the Nile Expedition, 1884–85 (Medal with clasp; Bronze Star), and in the Sudan, 1887–89, being present at the actions of Sarras, 1887, and of Toski, 1889. For his services in this campaign he received a Clasp; the Fourth Class Osmanieh; the Fourth Class Medjidie, and was created a Companion of the Distinguished Service Order [London Gazette, 8 Nov. 1889]: "Arthur Horsman Coles, Capt., The Buffs (East Kent Regt.). In recognition of services during the action at Toski." The Insignia were presented by the G.O.C. in Egypt, 29 Aug. 1890. He was also mentioned in Despatches [London Gazette, 6 Sept. 1889]. He commanded the Expeditionary Force, Uganda, 1893 (Medal and clasp); became Major, Warwickshire Regt., 1895; Lieut.-Colonel, 24 Oct. 1900; Brevet Colonel, 10 Feb. 1904. He commanded troops in the Uganda Protectorate; was created a C.M.G. in 1904, and retired with the rank of Colonel 25 Sept. 1907. He served in the European War, commanding the 5th Battn. Northumberland Fusiliers (Despatches).

HICKMAN, THOMAS EDGECUMBE, Capt., was born 25 July, 1859, son of the late Sir A. Hickman, first Baronet, M.P. for West Wolverhampton, and Lucy Owen Smith, of Portsea, Hants. He was educated at Cheltenham College, and entered the Army 19 Feb. 1881, serving in the Egyptian Camel Corps in 1884–85, and accompanying the River Column (Medal with two clasps; Bronze Star; Fourth Class Medjidie). He took part in the operations at Suakin in 1887; action of Handoub; operations at Suakin, 1888; action of Gemaizah, as D.A.A.G. to General Grenfell (Despatches [London Gazette, 11 Jan. 1889]; Fourth Class Osmanieh; Clasp); operations on the Egyptian Frontier, 1889; as D.A.A.G. to Colonel Wodehouse's Column; action at Arguin; action of Toski, as Brigade-Major to Colonel Kitchener, Commanding Mounted Troops. For his services in this last-mentioned campaign he was mentioned in Despatches [London Gazette, 6 Sept. 1889]; received a clasp, and was created a Companion of the Distinguished Service Order [London Gazette, 8 Nov. 1889]: "Thomas Edgecumbe Hickman, Capt., The Worcestershire Regt. In recognition of services during the action at Toski." He became Brevet Major in 1896. He took part in the operations in the Sudan, 1896–99; Dongola Expedition in 1896, as A.A.G., Infantry Division, to General Hunter, until invalided (Despatches [London Gazette, 3 Nov. 1896]; Medal; Brevet of Major; Clasp); in the operations in the Sudan, 1898; commanded the 15th Battn. Egyptian Infantry; commanded troops at the capture of Shendy and destruction of Mahmud's Depôt; Battle of the Atbara (Despatches; Clasp); Battle of Omdurman; Despatches; Clasp; Khartoum Medal; Brevet of Lieut.-Colonel); operations round Gedarif in command of the 12th Sudanese Regt. (Clasp); final operations round Gedid as Chief Staff Officer to General Wingate; defeat and death of the Khalifa (Despatches and Brevet of Colonel, March, 1900). In 1899 and 1900 he commanded troops in the Dongola District, and in 1899 was appointed Governor of the Dongola Province. He was on special service in South Africa, 1900–1 (Despatches; created a C.B. 1900); commanded a column of mounted troops in the Transvaal, Orange River Colony and Cape Colony in 1900; was Inspector-General, Cape Colonial Forces, in 1901; commanded the Western District, Cape Colony, 1902; commanded columns under General French in the Southern District, Cape Colony, 1901–2 (Queen's Medal with three clasps; King's Medal with two clasps); commanded Middelburg District, Cape Colony, as Brigadier-General, 1902–8. He became Colonel 19 Dec. 1903, and was on half-pay (late Staff) from 29 Feb. 1908, and on retired pay 4 April, 1914. He became Temporary Brigadier-General 14 Sept. 1914. Brigadier-General Hickman has been Unionist M.P. for Wolverhampton since 1910, and is D.L. for the county of Staffordshire. He married, in 1908, Elizabeth Maud Mackenzie, daughter of the late Surgeon-General D. A. Smith, of Kimberley, and they have one son and one daughter. His favourite recreations are hunting, shooting, fishing and stalking.

TERNAN, TREVOR PATRICK BREFFNEY, Capt., was born at Bath, 1 April, 1860, fifth son of the late General A. H. Ternan, I.S.C. He was educated at Bromsgrove School and Sandhurst, and was gazetted to the 63rd Foot 13 Aug. 1879, serving in the Afghan War, 1879–80 (Medal), and in the Egyptian War, 1882 (Medal and Khedive's Star). He joined the Egyptian Army in 1884, and was with the 9th Sudanese in the Nile Expedition in 1884 (Clasp). He was present at the action of Ginniss in 1885; D.A.A.G., with the Nile Frontier Force, 1886–87, 1888–89 (Fourth Class Osmanieh). He was present at the Battle of Toski as Brigade-Major of Infantry; his horse was shot; he received a clasp, was mentioned in Despatches, and created a Companion of the Distinguished Service Order [London Gazette, 8 Nov. 1889]: "In recognition of services during the action at Toski. Trevor Patrick Ternan, Capt., Manchester Regt." The Insignia were presented by the G.O.C. in Egypt, on the 29th Aug. 1890. He was A.A.G., War Office, Cairo, from 1890 to 1891; commanded the 1st Battn. Egyptian Army, 1892–93; joined the Uganda Rifles, 1894; served in the Expedition in Unyoro, 1895 (Despatches; Medal); was Commandant, Uganda Rifles, 1896; served in various expeditions in 1896–97; acted as Commissioner and Consul-General, Uganda Protectorate, in 1897; commanded the operations against King Mwanga, 1897, including the action of Kabawoko and defeat of Mwanga (slightly wounded; promoted Major in the Royal Warwickshire Regt. and Brevet Lieut.-Colonel). He commanded troops in Uganda against mutineers and rebels, Oct. 1898, to end of operations, 1899 (Medal and clasp). He was given the Brevet of Colonel; acted as Commissioner and Consul-General, British East Africa, 1900; commanded punitive expeditions against the Ogaden Somalis, 1900–1 (Medal and clasp, and created a C.M.G.); served in the South African War, 1901–2 (Medal and four clasps); as A.A.G., Southern District, 1903; commanded a column in the Orange River Colony; was A.A.G., South Africa, 1903–5; became Colonel, 20 May, 1903; Brigadier-General, Commanding Standerton District, Transvaal, 1906–7; retired, Staff, 9 Nov. 1907. Colonel Ternan married, in 1906, Dorothy, daughter of the late G. Alsop, of Teignmouth, and they have one son and two daughters. He rejoined on the outbreak of the European War on 4 Aug. 1914, as A.A.G. and Quartermaster-General, Northumbrian Division (T.F.); Brigadier-General, 102nd Tyneside Scottish Brigade (20th, 21st, 22nd and 23rd Northumberland Fusiliers), 28 Dec. 1914. He was created a C.B. in 1917.

DUNNING, HARRY GORDON, Capt., joined the Royal Fusiliers 22 Jan. 1881; became Lieutenant 1 July, 1881, and Captain 28 Nov. 1888; served in the operations of the Sudan Frontier Field Force in 1887, including the engagement at Sarras; was mentioned in Despatches; received the Medal, Fourth Class Osmanieh and Khedive's Star; and also in the operations on the Sudan Frontier in 1889, including the engagement at Toski; was mentioned in Despatches; received the Medal and clasp, and was created a Companion of the Distinguished Service Order [London Gazette, 8 Nov. 1889]: "Harry Gordon Dunning, Capt., Royal Fusiliers (City of London Regt.). In recognition of services during the action at Toski." Insignia were presented by the Sirdar at Halfa, 2 Feb. 1891. He died 9 March, 1895.

McMURDO, ARTHUR MONTAGU, Capt., was born at Fulham 15 March, 1861, youngest son of the late General Sir M. McMurdo, G.C.B., etc., and Susan, daughter to the late Sir Charles Napier; was educated at Haileybury and Sandhurst, and joined 71st Highland Light Infantry in 1882; was attached Egyptian Army, 1886–1894; operations in Sudan, 1888–89; action at Handoub, wounded, camel shot (Fourth Class Medjidie); attack on Fort Khor Mousa; action at Gemaizah (Medal with clasp; Bronze Star); action of Toski (Despatches; Clasp; created a Companion of the Distinguished Service Order [London Gazette, 8 Nov. 1889]: "Arthur Montagu McMurdo, Lieut., H.L.I. "For services during action at Toski." Presented by the Sirdar at Halfa, 2 Feb. 1891); was on Headquarters, Egyptian Army, 1894. He married Helen Estcourt, daughter of the late B. Cotton, Afton, Isle of Wight. Became Director, Slavery Department, Cairo, 1898; retired from the Army 8 Nov. 1900; Reserve of Officers. Major McMurdo was also Secretary of the Egyptian Agricultural Society. He died 15 April, 1914. An obituary notice of McMurdo Pasha appeared in the "Times" of 16 April, 1914.

JUDGE, SPENCER FRANCIS, Lieut., was born 21 Jan. 1861, son of T. E. B. Judge, and Maria, daughter of Major H. Bellew, D.A.Q.M.G. He was educated at Repton; joined the Shropshire Light Infantry 12 May, 1883, as Lieutenant, from the Militia; was employed with the Egyptian Army 8 April, 1886, to 6 June, 1887, and 13 April, 1888, to 27 Oct. 1896. He served in the Sudan, 1888 to 1889, being present at the action of Gemaizah; action of Arguin; action of Toski; was mentioned in Despatches; received the Medal with two clasps, the Bronze Star, the Fourth Class Osmanieh, the Fourth Class Medjidie, and was created a Companion of the Distinguished Service Order [London Gazette, 8 Nov. 1889]: "For services during the action of Toski. Spencer Francis Judge, Lieut., The King's (Shropshire) Light Infantry." Insignia presented by the Sirdar, 1 Aug. 1890. He became Captain 30 March, 1891, and took part in the Expedition to Dongola, 1896, as Brigade-Major, 4th Brigade; was present at the action of Hafir and at the occupation of Dongola; was mentioned in Despatches, and received a Medal and clasp. He became Adjutant, Militia, 19 Sept. 1898. He married Florence, sixth daughter of E. M. Clifton. Captain S. F. Judge, D.S.O., died 19 Nov. 1911.

"London Gazette, 12 Nov. 1889.—The Queen has further been pleased to give orders for the following appointments to the Distinguished Service Order, and promotions in the Army, in recognition of the services of the undermentioned Officers during the late operations in Burma, bearing date 23 Aug. 1889. To be Companions of the Distinguished Service Order."

MACGREGOR, CHARLES REGINALD, Major, was born in 1847, son of Rev. Sir Charles Macgregor (3rd Baronet); entered the 96th Regt in 1868; was transferred to the B.S.C. (now I.S.C.) in 1872; Duffla Ex. 1874–5; Naga, 1875 and 1879 (twice mentioned in Despatches; Medal with clasp; Brevet of Major); in Afghan Campaign in 1880, including March from Kabul to Kandahar (Despatches; Medal with clasp; Bronze Star); in Mari Expedition in 1880 (Despatches); in Burma Expedition, 1897–8–9 (twice mentioned in Despatches; Brevet Lieutenant-Colonel; clasp); created a Companion of the Distinguished Service Order [London Gazette, 12 Nov. 1889]: "In recognition of services during the late operations in Burma. Charles Reginald Macgregor, Major and Brevet Lieut.-Colonel, Bengal Staff Corps;" and with Wuntho Expedition in 1891 (Despatches); became Lieutenant-Colonel in 1888. In 1893 Lieut.-Colonel Macgregor married Maud, daughter of A. des Moustiers Campbell, Esq., of Oakley House, Abingdon, Berks, and their surviving daughter is Helen Maud. He became Colonel in 1895. Served N.W.F. 1897–8. Colonel C. R. Macgregor, C.B., D.S.O., died 20 June, 1902.

HARVEY, JOHN JAMES, Major and Brevet Lieut-Colonel, joined the 24th Regt., South Wales Borderers, 21 March, 1865 ; became Lieutenant 30 Sept. 1868 ; Captain 24 July, 1878 ; Major 9 June, 1882 ; Brevet Lieutenant-Colonel 2 Aug. 1888. He served in the Kaffir War in 1877–78, and was present during the operations against the Galekas and Gaikas, including the engagement at the Perie Bush ; also served in the Zulu War in 1879 (Medal and clasp). He served in Burma, and was created a Companion of the Distinguished Service Order [London Gazette, 12 Nov. 1889] : " John James Harvey, Major and Brevet Lieutenant-Colonel, South Wales Borderers. For services in Burma." Lieut.-Colonel Harvey died in 1890.

SHEPHERD, CHARLES HERBERT, Major, was born 4 April, 1846, second son of the late Thomas Shepherd, of Beverley, Yorkshire ; was educated at Rugby ; gazetted Ensign, 9th Foot, 2 May, 1865 ; Lieutenant 15 Feb. 1871 ; served in the Afghan War, 1879–80 : as Transport Officer, Khyber Line, at Bosawal and Jellalabad (Medal) ; Captain, 1 Sept. 1880 ; Adjutant, Auxiliary Forces, 28 Nov. 1881 ; Major, 10 Jan 1883 ; served in Burmese Expedition, 1887–89 ; operations in the Chin Hills ; officiated as Deputy Judge Advocate (Despatches, 22 June, 1886, and 2 Sept. 1887 ; Medal with two clasps) ; created a Companion of the Distinguished Service Order [London Gazette, 12 Nov. 1889] : " In recognition of services during the late operations in Burma. Charles Herbert Shepherd, Major, The Norfolk Regt." Insignia presented by the Queen 1 Aug. 1890. He served in Chin-Lushai Expedition, 1889–90 (clasp) ; became Colonel 28 Oct. 1898 ; retired 4 April, 1903. Colonel Shepherd is married.

MACDONALD, REGINALD PERCY, Capt., was born 10 June, 1856, eldest son of Major-General J. C. Macdonald. He was educated at Clifton College ; served in the Royal Pembroke Artillery Militia, 1875 and 1876 ; joined the 67th Hampshire Regt. as Mounted Captain in 1884 (Medal) ; served in Burma Expedition, 1885–87, with the 2nd Battn. Hampshire Regt., including the expedition to Moganney (Despatches, clasp ; created a Companion of the Distinguished Service Order [London Gazette, 12 Nov. 1889] : " In recognition of services during the late operations in Burma. Reginald Percy Macdonald, Capt., The Hampshire Regt. Decorated for Distinguished Service when on active service in the field." Insignia presented by the Queen 1 Aug. 1890). Lieut.-Colonel Macdonald married, in 1890, the daughter of Thomas Chard, of Ramsgate, and widow of Alexander Murray, of Polmaire, Stirling. He retired from the Army 19 May, 1892. He is fond of all sports.

DOYLE, IGNATIUS PURCELL, Surgeon, I.M.S., was born 1 June, 1863, in India, son of the late Surgeon-Major William Doyle and the late Jane Doyle (*née* Corbett). He was educated at the French College, Blackrock, County Dublin, and School of Physic, Trinity College Dublin. He joined the Army 30 Sept. 1886 ; served in Burma, 1888–89 (twice wounded ; Despatches 15 Nov. 1889 ; Medal and clasp) ; created a Companion of the Distinguished Service Order [London Gazette, 12 Nov. 1889] : " In recognition of services during the late operations in Burma. Ignatius Purcell Doyle, Surgeon, Indian Medical Service." He served in the Chin-Lushai Expedition, 1889–90 (clasp) ; in the Chin Hills, 1891–93 (clasp) ; in the Lushai Expedition in 1892 (clasp) ; the Somaliland Field Force in 1903 (Medal and clasp). He commanded No. 1 Native General Hospital, Upper Shaikh ; promoted Major 30 Sept. 1898. Major Doyle retired 31 Dec. 1903.

PINK, FRANCIS JOHN, C.B., C.M.G., D.S.O., Colonel (Temporary Brigadier-General), was born 19 Nov. 1857, son of the late Charles Pink, of Woodend House, Hants, and Hester Goldsmith, daughter of John Cousins Stares, Esq., of the Manor House, Upham. He entered the Queen's Regt. as Second Lieutenant 10 Feb. 1878, from the Royal Wiltshire Militia ; served in the Afghan War, 1879–80 ; as Officiating Sub-Assistant Commissary - General, Khyber Line (Medal) ; became Lieutenant 9 March, 1881 ; Captain 31 March, 1888 ; served with the Burmese Expedition, with 2nd Battn. The Queen's, and as Orderly and Intelligence Officer to Brigadier-General Lockhart, 1886–87 (Despatches), and D.A.A. and Q.M.G., 3rd Brigade, 21 Sept. 1887, to 31 March, 1889 ; and later as Staff Officer to the Karen Field Force. He was mentioned in Despatches [London Gazette, 2 Sept. 1887, and 15 Nov. 1889, and on a later occasion], and received the Medal with two clasps ; was created a Companion of the Distinguished Service Order [London Gazette, 12 Nov. 1889] : " In recognition of services during the late operations in Burma. Francis John Pink, Capt., The Queen's (Royal West Surrey) Regt." (Insignia presented by the Queen 1 Aug. 1890). He was attached to the Egyptian Army in 1895, and served in the Expedition to Dongola in 1896, taking part in the operations of 7 June and 19 Sept. ; was mentioned in Despatches [London Gazette, 3 Nov. 1896] (Egyptian Medal and two clasps). Colonel Pink was employed with the Egyptian Army from 10 May, 1895, to 29 April, 1899, and again from 28 Sept. 1909, to 20 May, 1910, in command of troops at Khartoum. In the Nile Expedition of 1897 (Despatches [London Gazette, 25 Jan. 1898] ; clasp to Egyptian Medal) ; and subsequent operations till the fall of Khartoum (commanded 2nd Battn. Egyptian Army in Macdonald's Brigade at battles of Atbara and Khartoum) ; Despatches 24 May and 30 Sept. 1898 ; Brevet of Lieutenant-Colonel, British Medal, Khedive's Medal, and two clasps to Egyptian Medal. He became Major 30 Dec. 1896 ; Brevet Lieutenant-Colonel 16 Nov. 1898 ; Brevet Colonel 16 Nov. 1904 ; Lieutenant-Colonel 2 March, 1905, and Colonel 2 March, 1909. He served in the South African War, 1899–1902, and commanded the 2nd Battn. The Queen's Regt., 1900–1902, in the field ; was present at the actions of Colenso and all subsequent actions up to and including Relief of Ladysmith, Allamand's Nek and subsequent operations in Transvaal and Orange River Colony up to signing of Peace (Despatches, C.M.G., Queen's Medal, five clasps, King's Medal, two clasps). He commanded 1st Battn. The Queen's Regt, 1905–9 ; was Colonel commanding No. 10 District (Hounslow), 1911–1914 ; also I.C. Records on outbreak of war with Germany ; commanded S.R. Brigades, 1914–16, as Temporary Brigadier-General in the Southern and Northern commands. He married, in 1909, Alice Evelyn (died 1916), daughter of the Rev. John Fleming, M.A., of Edinburgh. He voluntarily retired on retired pay 17 Sept. 1916 (Despatches, Honorary Brigadier-General). He was granted a Distinguished Service Pension.

Francis John Pink.

O'DONNELL, HUGH, Capt., was born 9 Feb. 1858, at Jubbulpore, Central Provinces, India, son of John Walter O'Donnell, C.E., P.W.D., and Rosabella O'Donnell. He was educated privately in Germany ; at Streatham School, and at the Royal Military College, Sandhurst, and began his military career 30 Jan. 1878, as an Ensign in the 1st Battn. 8th King's Regt. In the following year he volunteered for active service in the Zulu War, and joined the 24th Regt. He received the South African Medal and clasp, and received a letter of thanks from the War Office through the Quartermaster-General from H.R.H. Commanding-in-Chief : " For a sketch made by order of O.C. detachment of 24th Regt. of the track taken by the fugitives from Isandlwhana, 1879, from which information was gained." In July, 1880, he entered the Bengal Staff Corps, and was posted to the 44th Gurkha Rifles, and was successively Quartermaster and Adjutant of that regiment. In Aug. 1886, he received orders to raise a Police Levy for service in Burma, and in Jan. 1887, was appointed Commandant of Military Police for Upper Burma, and held this appointment from then to 1891. He was with the Mogoung Field Force, 1887–88, and commanded it (under Brigadier-General G. B. Wolseley, C.B.), 1888–89, for which he received mention in Despatches and the thanks of the Government of India ; and was in the Tonhon Expedition of 1889–90, and with the Wuntho Field Force, 1891. He was mentioned in Despatches by Sir George White, K.C.B., V.C. : " For his conduct while in command of the Column operating against the rebellious Kachin tribes round and beyond Mogoung ; " received the Burmese Medal with three clasps, and was created a Companion of the Distinguished Service Order [London Gazette, 12 Nov. 1889] : " Hugh O'Donnell, Capt., Bengal Staff Corps. In recognition of services during the late operations in Burma." In 1892 he rejoined his old regiment, the 44th Gurkha Rifles, as Major and Second in Command. In 1899 he was transferred, as Commandant of the 42nd Gurkha Rifles. In 1904 he returned to his old regiment, the 44th Gurkha Rifles, now renamed the 6th Gurkha Rifles, as Commandant, and was granted a year's extension and appointed A.A.G., 1st Peshawar Division, then A.A.G. for musketry to the Northern Army from 1907 to 1910. At the end of that period he again got another extension for a year, and was appointed Colonel on the Staff ; and later Brigadier-General Commanding Bannu Brigade, North-West Frontier, Jan. 1911, receiving in the same year the commendation of the Commander-in-Chief on his successful operations against the Britiani Khels, and later against the Hathi Khels. He was Brigade Commander, Jan. 1912, Major-General, Bannu Brigade, April, 1912. He received a letter signifying the full approval from the Commander-in-Chief of the operations of the Bannu Movable Column in the Tochi Valley in April, 1913. At the Coronation Durbar at Delhi he commanded the 20th Brigade, and was invested with the C.B. at the Durbar by the King in person. In 1913 he was made Colonel, 6th Gurkha Rifles. In the Great War he commanded the Bannu Movable Column in the field in successful operations against Khostwal tribesmen, and at Spina Khaisora the enemy was driven over the frontier. After these operations the Viceroy and Commander-in-Chief commended the able manner in which they were carried out by General O'Donnell. Three weeks later, in Feb. 1915, General O'Donnell was suddenly taken ill, from exposure in very inclement weather while with the Column. He was put on sick leave, arriving in England in April, 1916. Although he greatly improved in health, he never became fit for active service, and failed to be accepted when he offered to work in any capacity during the late War. His death occurred unexpectedly in Dec. 1917, while on a visit to friends at Cromhall, Gloucestershire. He was buried at Halton, Lancashire. He had a strong and commanding personality, and his profession was his supreme interest in life. He was an enthusiast at cricket, a fine tennis and billiard player, also a photographer in his spare time. He married, in 1894, Susan, daughter of T. G. Garnett, J.P., of Shefferlands, Halton, Lancashire. She and their only son died in 1908.

Hugh O'Donnell.

JACKSON, SYDNEY CHARLES FISHBURN, Lieut., was born at Dedham Grove, near Colchester, 21 April, 1863, son of the late Commander W. T. F. Jackson, R.N. He was educated at Wellington, and at the Royal Military College, Sandhurst, and was gazetted to the Royal Irish Rifles 9 Sept. 1882 ; transferred to the Hampshire Regt. 11 Oct. 1882. He served throughout the Burma Campaign, 1885–89, and was A.D.C. to the G.O.C., Upper Burma Field Force, 4 Sept. 1886, to 31 March, 1889 ; was mentioned in Despatches [London Gazette, 2 Sept. 1887, and 15 Nov. 1889] ; received the Medal with two clasps, and was created a Companion of the Distinguished Service Order [London Gazette, 12 Nov. 1889] : " Sydney Charles Fishburn Jackson, Lieut., The Hampshire Regt., Aide-de-Camp to Major-General, Bengal. In recognition of services during the late operations in Burma." He was A.D.C. to Major-General, Bengal, 1 April, 1889, to 7 April, 1893 ; was promoted to Captain 1 July, 1890. In 1890 he took part in the operations of the Zhob Valley Field Force, as A.D.C. to the G.O.C. He was A.D.C. to the Commander-in-Chief, East Indies, 8 April, 1893, to 12 April, 1894 ; was Station Staff Officer, 1st Class, India, 21 April, 1897, to 9 July, 1897 ; D.A.A.G., Headquarters, Bombay, 10 July, 1897, to 2) April, 1902 ; D.A.A. and Q.M.G., 6th Division, 1906–10 ; A.Q.M.G., Eastern Command Headquarters, 1 Dec. 1917, to 27 April, 1918 ; A.A. and Q.M.G., Gibraltar, 3 June, 1918 to date. He served with the Zhob Field Force; and also with the Somaliland Field Force, 1903–4, in command of detachment, Hampshire Regt. (Despatches [London Gazette, 2 Sept. 1904]. Medal with two clasps, Brevet of Lieutenant-Colonel). Colonel Jackson served in the European War in 1914 and 1915, commanding the 1st Battn. Hampshire Regt., and was severely wounded. He was mentioned in Despatches 19 Oct. 1914 ; decorated with C.M.G. 1 Jan. 1919 ; Mons Star with clasp " 1914 " ; British War Medal and Victory Medal. His favourite recreations are hunting, golf and rowing. In 1898 Colonel Jackson married Lucy Beatrice, second daughter of the late Sir W. H. Drake K.C.B., and they have two sons.

FOWLER, FRANCIS JOHN, Lieut., was born 31 July, 1864, at Mian Mir, India, son of Deputy Surgeon-General Henry Day Fowler (deceased), Army Medical Staff, and of Caroline Mary Fowler (née Oliver) (who died 3 Jan. 1919).

Francis John Fowler.

He was educated at King William's College, Isle of Man ; at Bedford Modern School, and at Sandhurst ; became Lieutenant, North Lancashire Regt., 25 Aug. 1883 ; served in the Zhob Valley Expedition in 1884, and was transferred to the Indian Staff Corps 13 Nov. 1885. He served in the Burmese Expedition, 1887–8–9 ; was mentioned in Despatches [London Gazette (G.G.O. 613, of 29 Nov. 1889)], for services in Upper Burma ; received the Frontier Medal and clasp for Burma, and was created a Companion of the Distinguished Service Order [London Gazette, 12 Nov. 1889] : " Francis John Fowler, Lieut., Bombay Staff Corps. In recognition of services in the late Expedition to Burma."

The St. James's Gazette of 5 July, 1888, says :

" The recapture of Moné from the rebel leader, Twek-nga-lu, in the beginning of May is a good example of what rapid and determined action will do with a semi-civilized enemy. The relieving party, under Colonel Sartorius, of the 1st Beloochees, started at daybreak, in a downpour of rain, from a village in the hills to the west of Moné. About two miles from the town, Mr. Scott, the Assistant-Superintendent of the Shan States, with Lieut. Fowler, of the Beloochees, and six men of the Rifle Brigade, mounted on officers' ponies, went off from the main column to make a dash on the palace. Mr Scott had been in Moné several times before, and was able to take the party by a jungle path round the south of the town. From there they galloped straight on the palace, disregarding the armed men in the streets. The eastern gate was fortunately ajar, so that it was not necessary to dismount. The clatter of the hoofs brought Twek-nga-lu to a window. Mr. Scott knew him by sight, and, with the assistance of a soldier, had the rebel tied to his own bedpost within two minutes of entering the palace enclosure, which is over a hundred yards square and full of detached houses. Twek-nga-lu had a repeating rifle loaded with sixteen cartridges lying by his bedside, but had not time to seize it. The four gates were then closed and guarded by one man each, and another guarded Twek-nga-lu. Mr. Scott and Mr. Fowler, with the corporal of the party, then went to meet the bodyguard of twenty men, all armed with guns. Mr. Scott demanded the name of the leader, who proved to be Twek-nga-lu's chief fighting-man. He then announced who he was, and called on them in Shan to sit down, advancing all the time. Kun-sang, the leader, refused ; whereupon Mr. Scott promptly knocked him down, seized the gun of the man behind him, and shouted out that he would shoot anyone who did not sit down immediately. The corporal and Mr. Fowler each covered his man as he came on. Before the Shans could realize the situation five had been disarmed and the rest then gave in. Messrs. Scott and Fowler collected all the guns and swords, the corporal kneeling in the Hythe position, ready to fire. In five minutes the palace was completely in their hands, and the main column was heard firing to the north of the town. A quarter of an hour later they marched into the palace and found everything settled, Twek-nga-lu bound and his chief leaders under guard. When it is considered that the town was held by 400 men and that the force inside the palace outnumbered the capturing party by nearly ten to one, the affair may be considered as successful an example of prompt daring as is to be found out of a lady's romance. The capture of Twek-nga-lu is likely to have the most satisfactory results. The disturbances which broke out in the Southern Shan States during April were mainly due to his advance and his intrigues, and now that he and his chief leaders have been captured the complete establishment of peace may be anticipated. The interest of our readers in this story will not be diminished when we add that Mr. Scott was the writer of the amusing and informing articles about Burma which appeared over the signature, ' Shway Yoe,' in the ' St. James's Budget,' some time ago."

The above was also published in the " St. James's Budget," 7 July, 1888.

An extract from another paper runs as follows:

" The Baluchis have come out with their full share of honours for the campaign, and richly, from all accounts, they deserve what they have got. Besides the V.C. given to Dr. Crimmim, and the Distinguished Service Order to Capt. Sinclair for his services in the Nyingyan district, the decoration of C.B. has been bestowed upon Colonel George Sartorius, the commandant, the Distinguished Service Order going to Lieut. Fowler and Lieut. Tighe. Thus the 1st Baluchis gained five decorations during the two and a half years which they spent in Burmah. Work such as that which Colonel Sartorius had to do for the greater part of two years would test the ingenuity, the fertility of resource, and the patience of any commander. Lieut. Fowler distinguished himself by a very smart night surprise of the free-booter Twet Nga Sa, whom, with the help of half a dozen men of the Rifle Brigade, he seized in bed. His other exploit was an attack upon a stockade south of Mankine, in which the enemy were beaten by a small force of eighty men, leaving behind them one hundred and fifty killed and wounded. Lieut. Tighe did equally meritorious service in the advance on Saulou, the Karen capital. The Bombay Army has shown by its services in Burmah how cruel and unjustifiable are the aspersions sometimes cast upon it."

A Bedford paper says :

" Lieut. Fowler, the officer referred to in the following extract from a Kurachi paper of 7 Oct. last, is a son of Dr. Fowler, of Waldeck Avenue, and was educated in the Bedford Modern School : ' The troops in garrison paraded this morning at seven o'clock on the general parade ground, behind the Native Infantry lines, under the command of Brigadier-General Boyce-Combe, for the purpose of conferring the Distinguished Service Order on Lieut. Fowler, 1st Belooch Battn. Light Infantry. After the General had been received with the usual salute, the troops formed three sides of a square, and Lieut. Fowler was called to the front. The General then made a speech, in which he described how this gallant young officer, in the winter of 1888, being in command of a detachment of eighty of the 1st Baluchis, marched all night through a pouring rain, and having traversed twenty-five miles, surprised at daybreak a party of Shans 500 strong occupying seven stockades. Lieut. Fowler, after pouring in a well-directed volley, led the rush of his men on the enemy's position. In a few minutes the Shans had fled, leaving eighty of their number killed. The General extolled the prompt gallantry of Lieut. Fowler, and expressed his belief that all the subaltern officers present would behave as well under similar circumstances. He then handed the Cross of the Order to Lieut. Fowler, and the proceedings terminated with the usual march past.' "

He became Captain 25 Aug. 1894, and again saw active service in Uganda in 1897–98, being present at the action at Jeruba. He was mentioned in Despatches ; received the Brevet of Major 4 Oct. 1899, and the East and Central Africa Medal with two clasps. He served in China, 1900–1 (Medal). On 22 Jan. 1901, he was promoted to Major ; on 28 Jan. 1907, to Lieutenant-Colonel, and on 6 May, 1911, to Colonel. From 1908 to 1910 he commanded troops in Somaliland (Medal and clasp). Colonel Fowler was A.Q.M.G., India, 19 Dec. 1913, to 18 Nov. 1914. He was Temporary Brigadier-General 19 Nov. 1914, to 11 Feb. 1916 ; commanded the Derajat Brigade from 19 Nov. 1914, to 13 Feb. 1916. He was created C.B., [London Gazette, 1 Jan. 1916]. Joined the Mesopotamia Expeditionary Force in Feb. 1916, in command of a brigade ; was wounded on 8 March, 1916, and invalided in Sept. 1916 ; commanded the Poona Divisional Area from 1 Dec. 1916 ; commanded at Kurachi. Major-General F. J. Fowler married, on 8 June, 1896, at Godalming, Surrey, Rita Mary, daughter of the late Colonel G. Sartorius, C.B., Indian Army. He retired 1 Jan. 1921.

TIGHE, MICHAEL JOSEPH, Lieut., was born 21 May, 1864, at Trincomalee, Ceylon, eldest son of Major Michael Joseph Tighe, 70th Regt. (deceased). He was educated at a private school, and at Sandhurst, and joined the 1st Battn. The Leinster Regt.

Michael Joseph Tighe.

25 Aug. 1883, and the Indian Staff Corps 27 June, 1885. He served in the Burmese War, 1886–89, with the Mounted Infantry (Medal with clasp) ; with the Red Karen Expedition in 1889 ; served with the Mounted Infantry ; was mentioned in Despatches 15 Nov. 1889, and received a clasp, and was created a Companion of the Distinguished Service Order [London Gazette, 12 Nov. 1889] : " In recognition of services during the late operations in Burma. Michael Joseph Tighe, Lieut., Bombay Staff Corps." The D.S.O was awarded for personal gallantry at the action of Niza Kaing 1 June, 1899, when in command of the M.I. of the A.G. to Sir N. Collet's Force (Field operations, Burma, General Orders, No. 17, 6 May, 1889) : " In this action the M.I., under Lieut. Tighe, attacked and destroyed the Karen Force at Niza Kaing ; this officer himself killed eight of the enemy in the hand-to-hand fighting." He served with the Chin-Lushai Expedition in 1890 (clasp) ; Chin Hills Expedition, 1890–92, as Political Officer (two clasps). He became Captain 25 Aug. 1894. He served in East Africa, 1895–96 ; operations against the Mazrin Arabs, also with the Naval Brigade in operation on the coast (Medal and Brilliant Star of Zanzibar awarded for distinguished service before the enemy) ; Ufunda, 1897–99 ; operations against the Wa Zeita ; operations against the Soudanese Mutineers (Despatches, Medal and clasp, Brevet Major, 4 Oct. 1899) ; Mikron Expedition and operations in East Persia in 1901 ; storm and capture of Wadisfort, in command ; Brevet of Lieutenant-Colonel. In

1902 he accompanied the Indian Contingent at King Edward's Coronation (Medal); in 1911 commanded Indian Contingent at Coronation of King George V. (C.I.S. and Medal); in 1911 awarded C.B.; in European War, 1914, commanded Composite Brigade, British East Africa; commanded Expeditionary Force, B.E.F., in operations against the Germans up to 1 April, 1918. He was promoted Major-General for Distinguished Service in the Field 3 June, 1915; awarded K.C.M.G. 28 March, 1916. He married in London, 14 June, 1900, Katherine Helen Mackay, daughter of the late Mackay Hugh Bailie Scott, and they have one son, Valentine Michael Vincent, born 14 Feb. 1904.

London Gazette, 22 Feb. 1890.—" War Office, 22 Feb. 1890. The Queen has been graciously pleased to give orders for the appointment of the undermentioned Officer to be a Companion of the Distinguished Service Order. For the operations against the slave traders at Foulah Town and its vicinity on the West Coast of Africa."

LENDY, EDWARD AUGUSTUS ARMSTRONG, Lieut., was gazetted to the West India Regt. 21 Dec. 1887. He was created a Companion of the Distinguished Service Order [London Gazette, 22 Feb. 1890]: " Edward Augustus William Lendy, Lieut., West India Regt. For the operations against the slave traders at Foulah Town and its vicinity on the West Coast of Africa." He was promoted to Captain, and died 23 Dec. 1893.

London Gazette, 25 Feb. 1890.—" War Office, 25 Feb. 1890. The Queen has been graciously pleased to give orders for the appointment of the undermentioned Officer to be a Companion of the Distinguished Service Order. For the action at Toski."

MACDONALD, HECTOR ARCHIBALD, Capt., was born at Rootfield in the parish of Urquhart, in Ross-shire, the youngest of five sons of William Macdonald, a Crofter and Stonemason. At the age of fifteen Hector Macdonald was apprenticed to a Draper at Dingwall. Here he joined the Inverness-shire Highland Rifle Volunteers, and acquired that passion for soldiering which was destined to determine his future career. In June, 1870, he left his employer without giving notice, and enlisted in the 92nd Regt., now the 2nd Battn. Gordon Highlanders, and soon afterwards he sailed for India. Within three years he was Colour-Sergeant of his company, and in 1879 the 92nd Highlanders formed part of General Roberts's small force which marched to Kabul to avenge the massacre of Cavagnari and the rest of the British Mission. On the 27th Sept. Macdonald showed skill and energy in driving the enemy from Hazardaraki Pass, near Karatiga, thus enabling Sir F. Roberts to continue his march to Kushi. Together with Jemadar Sher Mahomed—3rd Sikhs—he again distinguished himself at the action at Charasiah on the 6th Oct. following, when he dislodged a picquet which was causing much annoyance by its fire. On both occasions Macdonald was mentioned in Despatches. After the occupation of Kabul, he took part in the Maidan Expedition; the operations round Kabul in Dec. 1879, including the affair at Shapur Cantonments, the attack on Takt-i-Shah, the engagement of Childukran, and the second action at Charasiah, and accompanied Lord Roberts on the march from Kabul to Kandahar in Aug. 1880. He was present at the reconnaissance of 31 Aug., and at the battle of 1 Sept., and distinguished himself at the capture of Ayub Khan's Camp at Babawati. " His dash and prowess in the field, which won him the sobriquet of ' Fighting Mac,' led General Roberts to promote him at Kabul to the rank of Second Lieutenant in the Gordon Highlanders." His commission was ratified on 7 Jan. 1880, when his claymore was presented to him by his brother officers. For his services in this campaign Macdonald received the Afghan Medal with three clasps, the Bronze Decoration, and was mentioned in Despatches [London Gazette, 16 Jan. 1880]. The 92nd Highlanders returned home, but Macdonald was landed with two companies in Natal to join in Sir G. Colley's ill-fated attempt to relieve the garrison in the Transvaal. Macdonald was taken prisoner at Majuba (1881), but his gallantry so impressed Joubert that he gave him back his sword. He was again mentioned in Despatches. The year 1883 saw a new phase in Macdonald's career, when he served in the Egyptian Constabulary under Sir Valentine Baker in 1883; took part in the Nile Expedition in 1885; was Garrison Adjutant at Assiout from 22 Jan. to 5 June, 1885. After the failure of the British Expedition and the British retreat, Macdonald was transferred to the Egyptian Army, and helped with its reorganization. He was promoted Captain in 1888, and made the 9th Sudanese as much like Highlanders as he possibly could, and the Sudan Campaign of 1888–91 tested the Highlanders-Sudanese, and they stood the test triumphantly. Capt. Macdonald was engaged in the operations round Suakin, the action at Gemaizah, at Toski on 3 Aug. 1889, and at the capture of Tokar 19 Feb. 1891. He was mentioned in Despatches 11 Jan. 1888; received the Medal and clasp, the Third Class Medjidie and the Khedive's Star for Suakin, 1888, and was mentioned in Despatches 6 Sept. 1889, for Suakin (1889), received a clasp, and for his services at Toski was created a Companion of the Distinguished Service Order [London Gazette, 25 Feb. 1890]: " For the action at Toski. Hector Archibald Macdonald, Capt., Gordon Highlanders." For the capture of Tokar he received the Third Class Osmanieh and a Clasp to the Khedive's Star. He was promoted Major 17 July, 1891, and attached to the 7th Royal Fusiliers whilst remaining in Egypt. In 1896 Lord Kitchener began his reconquest of the Sudan, and Macdonald was given command of the 2nd Infantry Brigade in the Expedition to Dongola. He was conspicuous in the actions of Farket (7 June) and Hafir (19 Sept.), and was given the Brevet of Lieut.-Colonel 18 Nov. 1896, and received the Egyptian Medal with two clasps. He took part in the Nile Expedition of 1897–98, and commanded the Egyptian Brigade at the action of Abu Hamed (Despatches [London Gazette, 25 Jan. 1898], and two clasps), and at Atbara, 8 April, 1898 (Despatches [London Gazette, 24 May, 1898]). At the Battle of Omdurman, 2 Sept. 1898, Macdonald reached the zenith of his career when he wheeled his brigade round in a complete half-circle, half-battalion by half-battalion, to meet a sudden and unexpected attack by dervishes. He was mentioned in Despatches, 20 Sept. 1898; created a C.B. 22 June, 1897; appointed A.D.C. to the Queen; given the Brevet of Colonel 16 Nov. 1898; received two clasps, and was thanked by both Houses of Parliament. From 24 Oct. 1899, to 3 Jan. 1900, he was Brigadier-General in India, commanding the Sirhind District, with Headquarters at Umballa. On relinquishing this command he was promoted Major-General. On the death of General Wauchope, 10 Dec. 1899, at Magersfontein, Major-General Macdonald was summoned to South Africa to take command of the Highland Brigade. He arrived at Modder River in the end of Jan. 1900; seized Koodoosberg Drift, 5–8 Feb. 1900, and thus prepared the way for the relief of Kimberley. A few days later he led the brigade in the historic march to Bloemfontein. He was present at the operations at Paardeberg (16–27 Feb. 1900), which led to the surrender of Cronje, and was wounded in the ankle; twice mentioned in Despatches and created a K.C.B. He recovered from his wound sufficiently to rejoin his brigade a month later, and took part in General Colville's march to Lindley and Heilbron, with several severely contested actions on the way. For the next two months he was engaged in the operations which ended in Prinsloo's surrender. The Highland Brigade was then broken up, and Sir Hector Macdonald directed various bodies of troops, first in the south-east of Orange River Colony, and from the beginning of 1901 in Aliwal North. A few months later he was given command of the Belgaum district of Southern India. After a visit to Australia, he was transferred to the command of the forces in Ceylon. Rumours got about that he would have to face a court-martial, and Sir Hector Macdonald was given leave of absence and came home—it was believed—to prepare his defence. He shot himself in Paris 25 March, 1903, having served thirty-three years in the Army, nine of them in the ranks.

London Gazette, 14 Nov. 1890.—" The Queen has been pleased to give orders for the following appointments to the Distinguished Service Order, in recognition of the services of the undermentioned Officers during the late Chin-Lushai Expedition, bearing date the 28th July, 1890. To be Companions of the Distinguished Service Order."

WESTMACOTT, RICHARD, Colonel, was born 16 March, 1841, at Chastleton Rectory, Moreton-in-Marsh, Oxfordshire, second son of the Rev. Horatio Westmacott; was educated at Rossall, and entered the Bombay Army 19 March, 1859. He served in the Mutiny in 1859, and was present at the Siege of Beyt and at Dworka (Medal), and in 1860 in the operations against rebel Bheels in Gujerat. In 1868 he took part in the operations against the rebel Naikras; was present at the action of Warak, and received the commendation of the Government (G.P.O. 161 of 1868); in the Afghan Campaign of 1878–80 he was Road Commandant, commanding troops on the Lines of Communication, Quetta to Kandahar; took part in the engagements in the Khozak Pass; was present at the Relief of Kandahar (Despatches; G.P.O. 645 and 975 of 1880; Medal and two clasps). He served in the Sudan in 1885, taking part in the operations at Suakin, Hasheem and Tofrick; in various attacks on convoys and in the advance on Tamai (Medal with two clasps; Despatches [London Gazette, 25 Aug. 1885]). He became Lieut.-Colonel in 1885, and Colonel in 1889. On 22 Jan. 1889, Colonel Westmacott married, at Kirkee, India, Margaret Rose, elder daughter of Major-General Caldecott, R.A., C.B., and their surviving son is Capt. Guy Roudolph Westmacott, D.S.O., Capt., Grenadier Guards, born 16 July, 1891. Lieut.-Colonel Westmacott served with the Chin-Lushai Expedition, North-West Frontier of India, in command of an advance column on Haka (mentioned in Despatches, 990, 430, 1890), and was created a Companion of the Distinguished Service Order [London Gazette, 14 Nov. 1890]: " Richard Westmacott, Lieut.-Colonel, and Colonel, Indian Staff Corps. For services in the Chin-Lushai Expedition." (Insignia presented 22 Jan. 1891.) He was created a C.B. (Military) in 1891; commanded the 28th Bombay Pioneers, 1889–95; commanded the 1st Brigade, Mohmand Field Force, N.W. Frontier, in the action of Bedmanai and others (Despatches 990, 1318, 1897). He served in the Tirah Campaign, 1897–98; commanded the 4th Brigade in the actions of Dargai twice, at the Sampagha and Arhanga Passes; reconnaissance of Saran Sar; action of 9 Nov. 1897; operations at and around Dwatoi, action 24 Nov.; operations in Dera Valley, 7 to 14 Dec.; rear-guard actions, 13 and 14 Dec.; commanded at Shin Wara on 29 Jan. 1898 (Despatches, G.G.O., 58 and 244, 1898; clasp; created a K.C.B.). He became Major-General 22 June, 1899; commanded a First Class District at Mhow, 1900–3; has been on the Unemployed List since 16 March, 1906. Sir R. Westmacott's favourite recreations are hunting, shooting and fishing. His D.S.O. was awarded " In recognition of services during the late Chin-Lushai Expedition."

Richard Westmacott.

SKINNER, GEORGE JOHN, Colonel, was born 16 June, 1841, son of James Skinner, Esq., J.P., and of Mrs. Skinner. He was educated at the Scottish Naval and Military Academy, Edinburgh; entered the 100th Regt. 16 Sept. 1859; 38th Regt., 1860, and B.S.C. (now Indian Army), 1865; became Captain, 1871; Major, 1879, and Lieut.-Colonel, 1885. He served during the Afghan Campaign of 1879–80 with 3rd Bengal Infantry (mentioned in Despatches; Medal). He became Colonel 16 Sept. 1889. For his services in the Chin-Lushai Expedition, 1889 and 1890, he received the thanks of the Government of India; the Medal with clasp; and was created a Companion of the Distinguished Service Order [London Gazette, 14 Nov. 1890]: "George John Skinner, Lieut.-Colonel, and Colonel, Indian Army." Colonel Skinner was placed on the Unemployed List 16 June, 1908. He married (1) Robina Agnes (who died in 1876), daughter of Rev. W. Asher, D.D., and (2) Katherine Fox, daughter of the late Lieut.-Colonel A. Baird. His D.S.O. was awarded "In recognition of services during the late Chin-Lushai Expedition."

MURPHY, WILLIAM REED, Major, was born 23 Oct. 1849, son of

William Reed Murphy.

John Doyle Murphy and Rebecca Reed; educated at Clongowes Wood College, County Kildare; Trinity College, Dublin, and Royal College of Surgeons, Ireland. Took all prizes there during student course, and all at Meath Hospital. Took first place and First Herbert Prize at Netley on entering Indian Medical Service on 30 March, 1872; served with the Indian Contingent, Malta and Cyprus 1878; in the Afghanistan Campaign of 1878-80 (Despatches; Medal and clasp; received the "Special thanks of the Brigadier-General Commanding the Cavalry Brigade," when with his regiment, 19th Bengal Lancers at the cavalry action of Pat Kao Shana, for conduct in action "at great personal risk" [London Gazette, 22 Oct. 1880]); Hazara Campaign of 1888 (Despatches; Indian Medal and clasp); Lushai Campaign of 1888-89 (clasp). P.M.O. Lushai Column, Chin-Lushai Field Force, 1889-90 (Despatches; Mentioned by the Government of India; clasp). Created Companion of the Distinguished Service Order [London Gazette, 14 Nov. 1890]: "William Reed Murphy, Surgeon-Major, Indian Medical Service, Bengal." Chitral Relief Force, 1895 (Medal and clasp). P.M.O. Kurram Kohat Force, 1897 (Despatches and two clasps). P.M.O. Kurram Movable Column, Tirah Field Force, 1897-98 (Despatches and clasp). Is a Member of the Royal Institution of Great Britain. Promoted Surgeon-Major in 1884, and Lieut.-Colonel in 1892. Retired in 1899. His D.S.O. was awarded "In recognition of services during the late Chin-Lushai Expedition."

BROWNE, ARTHUR GEORGE FREDERIC, Capt., was born 21

Arthur G. F. Browne.

June, 1851, son of the late Colonel St. John Thomas Browne, R.A., and grandson of the late Lieut.-Colonel Arthur Browne, Lieut.-Governor of Kinsale and Charles Fort (present as Lieutenant Fireworker of Artillery when Wolfe was fatally wounded at the heights of Abraham, 1759); was educated at Wellington College; entered the 44th Regt. in 1871 as Ensign; Bengal Staff Corps (now Indian Staff Corps), 1876; served during Afghan War of 1878-79 (Medal). He married, 1882, Kate Fisher, daughter of the late Rev. J. S. Budden, and they have one son and four daughters. He became Captain in 1883; served in Burma War of 1886 (Medal with clasp); with Lushai Expedition, 1889 (was mentioned in Despatches; received clasp, and was created a Companion of the Distinguished Service Order, 14 Nov. 1890: "Arthur George Frederic Browne, Capt., Bengal Staff Corps"). He served in the Chin Hills operations, 1892; was in command of Tlantlang Column (clasp); was promoted Major, 1894; served with the Chitral Relief Force, 1895 (Medal and clasp); with the Tirah Expedition, 1897-99; was present at the actions of Sampagha, Arhanga and Saransar; operations against Khani Kheyl Cham-Kannis; operations Bazar Valley, 25 to 30 Dec. 1897, and with the Khyber Field Force, 1898 (Despatches; two clasps; Brevet of Colonel); promoted Colonel in 1902, and appointed in 1902 to command a Second Class District in India; created a C.B., 1903; became Major-General, 1904, and commanded Garhwal Brigade, 1904; Colonel, 4th Gurkha Rifles, 1906; 5th (Mhow) Division, 1907; 3rd (Lahore) Division, 1907-8; became Lieut.-General 21 March, 1908; created a K.C.B., 1909; retired 15 Feb. 1909. His D.S.O. was awarded "In recognition of services during the late Chin-Lushai Expedition."

ROGERS, FREDERICK ARTHUR, Surgeon, was born 7 Sept. 1861, son of the late Moses Rogers, Esq., Deputy Inspector-General of Hospitals, Madras, and Caroline Rogers. He entered the Indian Medical Service, and served in the Burmese War of 1885-89 (twice mentioned in Despatches), and received the Medal with two clasps), and with the Chin-Lushai Expedition, 1890 (Despatches, and created a Companion of the Distinguished Service Order [London Gazette, 14 Nov. 1890]: "Frederick Arthur Rogers, Surgeon, Indian Medical Service." The Letter and Insignia were handed to Mr. Rogers by Mr. Hobart, Secretary and Registrar, 3 March, 1891). He married, 1892, Janet Felicia, daughter of the late

Frederick A. Rogers.

John Churchill, Esq., of Wimbledon. Lieut.-Colonel Rogers retired in 1905, and died 2 Nov. 1912. His D.S.O. was awarded "In recognition of services during the late Chin Lushai Expedition."

SHAKESPEAR, JOHN, Capt., was born at Indore 1 Sept. 1861, youngest son of the late Colonel Sir Richmond C. Shakespear, C.B., Bengal Artillery, and Marion Sophia Thompson. He was educated at Wellington College, and the R.M.C., Sandhurst, and gazetted to the 100th Regt. 22 Jan. 1881; became Adjutant, 1886; served as Intelligence Officer with the Lushai Expeditionary Force, 1888, and with the Chin-Lushai Expedition, 1889 (Medal), and created a Companion of the Distinguished Service Order [London Gazette, 14 Nov. 1890]: "John Shakespear, Capt., The Prince of Wales's Leinster Regt." He was Assistant Police Officer, 1890; Superintendent, South Lushai Hills, 1891-96. He married, in 1892, Charlotte F. B., daughter of Arthur Disney Dunne. He became Major, 1895; admitted to I.S.C., 1896; Assistant Commissioner, Assam Commission, 1896; Deputy Commissioner, 1897; Police Officer, North Lushai Hills, 1897; First Superintendent, Lushai Hills, 1898; was transferred to Supernumerary List, 1 May, 1900, after ten years' permanent civil employment; became Lieut.-Colonel 22 Jan. 1907; became Deputy Commissioner, Assam, and Political Agent in Manipur in 1905. Lieut.-Colonel Shakespear has written "The Lushais and the Land they live in" (Silver Medal of the Society of Arts), 1894, and "The Lushai Kuki Clans," 1912. Lieut.-Colonel Shakespear says his recreations are outdoor sports generally, but that he is a "duffer" at them all. He commanded the 18th Battn. Northumberland Fusiliers at the time of the European War, and was created a C.M.G. in 1917. His D.S.O. was awarded "In recognition of services during the late Chin-Lushai Expedition."

MORRIS, ARTHUR HENRY, Lieut., was born 3 Jan. 1861, at Ryde, Isle of Wight, eldest son of the late Rev. Henry Morris and Eliza Jemima Morris (née Broughton). He was educated at Canterbury, and joined the

Arthur Henry Morris.

Royal Irish Regt. 27 Jan. 1883, from the Yorkshire Artillery Militia; took part in the Soudan Expedition, 1884-85 (Medal with clasp, and Bronze Star); served in the Burma Campaign and Expedition against the Red Karens, 1885-87 (Despatches; Medal with two clasps); was Chief Transport Officer to Chin-Lushai Expedition (Despatches; clasp; thanked by the Government of India, and created a Companion of the Distinguished Service Order [London Gazette, 14 Nov. 1890]: "Arthur Henry Morris, Lieut., The Royal Irish Regt. In recognition of services during the Chin-Lushai Expedition." He became Captain in 1891, commanded two expeditions against tribes in the Northern Territories of the Gold Coast, 1900; (Despatches twice); West Africa, 1900; operations in Ashanti, commanded column which forced its way into Kumasi from the north (severely wounded); defence of Kumasi, commanded garrison, and later on commanded the column which cut its way out of Kumasi (Medal with clasp; Brevet of Lieutenant-Colonel; Despatches); commanded Expedition against the Tiansis, 1902 (Despatches); Chief Commissioner, Northern Territories, Gold Coast, 1899-1904; created a C.M.G., 1904. Lieut.-Colonel Morris married, in 1902, Dorothy Mary Wilkie, niece and adopted daughter of Walter Laverton, of Manchester, and they have one son, John Henry Morris (born 4 Oct. 1908). He commanded the Duke of York's Royal Military School, 1908-13; became Colonel, 23 Nov. 1908, and retired in July, 1913. He was Commandant of an internment camp from 1915. His favourite recreations are hunting and shooting.

LUGARD, EDWARD JAMES, Lieut., was born at Worcester, 23 March, 1865, youngest son of the Rev. F. G. Lugard, M.A., and Mary Jane, daughter of the Rev. Garton Howard. He passed first in the military competitive examination from the Militia into

Edward James Lugard.

the Line; was farming in Manitoba and N.W.T., Canada, 1883-84; joined the 3rd Worcestershire Regt., 1885; joined Northumberland Fusiliers 10 Nov. 1886; was transferred to the Bengal Staff Corps (now Indian Army), 1888; served in Burmese Expedition, 1888-89, under Brigadier-General Faunce (Medal with clasp); Chin-Lushai Expedition, 1889-90, with the 42nd Gurkha Light Infantry (Despatches; clasp, and created a Companion of the Distinguished Service Order [London Gazette, 14 Nov. 1890]: "Edward James Lugard, Lieut., Bengal Staff Corps"). Extract from Despatch of Brigadier-General W. P. Symons, dated 1 May, 1890: "I beg to submit the names of the following officers, who have rendered specially valuable services: Lieut. E. J. Lugard served with distinction in the Chin Expedition of 1888-89, and has displayed conspicuous gallantry and intelligence in leading his men on several occasions during the operations of this season" [London Gazette, 12 Sept. 1890]. He served in the Manipur Expedition, 1891 (slightly wounded; clasp). He married, 1893, Charlotte Eleanor, elder daughter of the Rev. G. B. Howard, B.A., and has one son. He served as Second-in-Command with the British West Chartered Company's Expedition to Ngamiland, South Central Africa, and in command of the Expedition, 1897-99; served as a Special Service Officer in South African War, 1899-1900 (Medal with three clasps).

Promoted Major 10 Nov. 1904; retired from the Army 10 Nov. 1906; was Political Assistant to the High Commissioner of Northern Nigeria, 1903–6; Secretary to Imperial Institute, 1908–12; Political Secretary to the Governor of Northern and Southern Nigeria, 1912–13, and to the Governor-General of Nigeria, 1914–15; served with Machine Gun Corps, 1915–16, and in Naval Intelligence Department, 1916–18; created O.B.E., 1918. Major Lugard's favourite recreations are shooting and travel. His D.S.O. was awarded " In recognition of services during the late Chin-Lushai Expedition."

HOLLAND, GERALD EDWARD, First Grade Officer, Royal Indian Marine, was born in Dublin in 1860; went to sea, 1876; entered Royal Indian Marine, 1880; served with the Burma Expeditionary Force, 1887–89, and in the Chin-Lushai Expedition, and for his services was created a Companion of the Distinguished Service Order [London Gazette, 14 Nov. 1890]: " Gerald Edward Holland, First Grade Officer, Royal Indian Marine." He commanded the Warren Hastings when that ship was lost off Reunion Island in 1897; was court-martialled, and the result was a simple reprimand; received an exemplary order from the Governor of India for his fine conduct and saving of life. Later he served on the Naval Transport Staff, Durban, and as Divisional Officer, 1900–1, being thrice mentioned in Despatches and receiving the C.I.E. For three years he was principal Port Officer at Rangoon; retired from the R.I.M. in 1905; held the post of Marine Superintendent (L. & N. W. Rly. and L. &. Y. Rly.), Fleetwood, in 1907, and from 1907 onwards held the post of Marine Superintendent, L. & N. W. Rly., Holyhead. In Dec. 1914, shortly after the outbreak of the European War, became Lieut.-Colonel, R.E., and Assistant Director of Inland Water Transport in France. It was largely owing to his efforts that this corps was created. Became Colonel and Deputy Director in 1915; became Director in 1916, and Brigadier-General in 1917, but was head of the Department in France since its creation in 1914. For his services he was three times mentioned in Despatches; received the C.B. and C.M.G.; was decorated by the King of the Belgians with the Order of Leopold of Belgium, and also by the King of Italy with the Order of St. Maurice and St. Lazarus. Died, whilst on sick leave, at St. Leonards-on-Sea, 26 June, 1917, from illness contracted on active service in France. His D.S.O. was awarded " In recognition of services during the late Chin-Lushai Expedition."

London Gazette, 12 Dec. 1890.—" War Office, 12 Dec. 1890. The Queen has been graciously pleased to give orders for the following appointment to the Distinguished Service Order, in recognition of the services of the undermentioned Officer during the late Chin-Lushai Expedition."

NUNN, JOSHUA ARTHUR, 1st Class Veterinary Surgeon, A.V.D., was born 10 May, 1853, eldest son of the late Edward W. Nunn, J.P., D.L., of Hill Castle, County Wicklow, Ireland. He was educated at Wimbledon School, and at the Royal Veterinary College, London, and became a Barrister-at-Law, Lincoln's Inn, and Advocate, Supreme Court, Transvaal. He was a Fellow of the Royal College of Veterinary Surgeons; an F.R.G.S., F.R.S. Edinburgh; passed through the Royal College of Veterinary Surgeons with Honours; received the Royal Agricultural Society's Prize in 1876; was Lieutenant, Royal Monmouthshire Engineer Militia, from 1871–77; Veterinary Surgeon, R.A., 1877. He served with the R.A. in the Afghan War, 1878–80 (Medal); was Veterinary Surgeon to the Punjab Government, 1880–85; on special duty with the Natal and Cape Governments, investigating South African horse sickness, 1886–88. He served in the Chin-Lushai Expedition, as Principal Veterinary Officer, 1889–90, on the Indian Frontier (Medal and clasp; Despatches); served in the Zulu Rebellion in 1888; was present at the surrender of the chief Somkeli at St. Lucia Lagoon; was Principal, Punjab Veterinary College, 1890–96; Deputy Inspector-General, A.V.D., 1901–4; P.V.O., Eastern Command, 1904–5; P.V.O., South Africa, 1905–6; Examiner in Hygiene, Royal College of Veterinary Surgeons; and in Toxicology at Liverpool University. He was created a Companion of the Distinguished Service Order [London Gazette, 12 Dec. 1890]: " Joshua Arthur Nunn, Army Veterinary Department. In recognition of services in the Chin-Lushai Expedition." He was created a C.I.E. for services in Lahore Veterinary College. Colonel Nunn married, in 1907, Gertrude Anne, widow of the late W. Chamberlain, and widow of the late E. Kellner, C.I.E. He wrote " Stable Management in India; " " Lectures on Saddlery and Harness; " a " Report on the South African Horse Sickness; " a " Report on South African Horses; " " Diseases of the Mammary Gland in Domestic Animals; " " Veterinary Toxicology; " and many articles in the various professional publications on veterinary medicine and surgery. He was Editor of the " Veterinary Journal." This distinguished officer died 23 Feb. 1908.

London Gazette, 2 Jan. 1891.—" War Office, 1 Jan. 1891. The Queen has been graciously pleased to give orders for the following appointment, in recognition of the services of the undermentioned Officer during the late operations against the Sultanate of Witu."

MARTIN, JAMES HAMILTON, Fleet Surgeon, Royal Navy, was born on 8 Aug. 1841, at Truro, son of Hamilton Duckworth Martin and of Louisa Martin. He was educated at Grammar School, Truro, and University College, London. His record of services is as follows: Surgeon of H.M.S. Nassau during encounters with Sulu pirates and present at destruction of Carang, 1872; Staff Surgeon in charge of Transports during Zulu War, 1879 (mentioned in Despatches; Zulu Medal and clasp); Staff Surgeon of Thalia, Egyptian War, 1882; Senior Medical Officer in charge of Transports (received thanks of the Admiralty; Egyptian Medal; Khedive's Bronze Star); Principal Medical Officer of Royal Marine Battn. in Eastern Soudan, 1884; present at Battles of El Teb and Tamaai (mentioned in Despatches; wounded; promoted to Fleet Surgeon for these services; Suakin and El Teb-Tamaai clasps); served in H.M.S. Boadicea, Flag as P.M.O., in Naval Brigade under the command of Vice-Admiral Hon. Sir E. R. Fremantle, K.C.B., C.M.G., Commander-in-Chief on East Indies Station, for the punitive expedition against the Sultan of Witu in East Africa, Oct. 1890 (mentioned in Despatches; D.S.O. for this service; General Africa Medal; Witu 1890 clasp). His appointment to the Distinguished Service Order was gazetted 2 Jan. 1891: " In recognition of services during the late operations against the Sultanate of Witu. James Hamilton Martin, Fleet Surgeon, Royal Navy." He was promoted to Inspector-General, 1 Jan. 1900.

London Gazette, 30 May, 1891.—" The Queen has been graciously pleased to give orders for the following appointments to the Distinguished Service Order."

BENBOW, HENRY, Chief Engineer, R.N., was born in London 5 Sept. 1838, son of James Benbow, of Thornton Heath, Surrey, and his wife, Caroline (*née* Parrey); educated at a private school; entered the Royal Navy as Assistant Engineer, 1861; became Chief Engineer, 1879; served in Nile Expedition for relief of General Gordon, 1884–85, being attached as Chief Engineer to the Naval Brigade, under the command of Lord Charles Beresford, in connection with river steam-boat flotilla. The Naval Brigade did not accompany General Stewart, but crossed the desert later, and was not at the Battle of Abu Klea. A desperate effort, in which Colonel Fred Burnaby was killed, was made to save General Gordon before the fall of Khartoum. The Expedition reached the Nile at Gubat. Here it was met by four little steamers sent down by General Gordon from Khartoum. Sir Charles Wilson, with a score of British soldiers and 260 Soudanese troops, started off at once for Khartoum in two of the steamers. On 1 Feb. 1885, Lieut. Stuart Wortley brought down word that General Gordon was dead, that Khartoum had fallen, and that Sir Charles Wilson's two steamers had been wrecked thirty miles up river. Lord Charles Beresford started to the rescue on the Safia, which had originally been a " penny steamboat " on the Thames, with Benbow and a crew of bluejackets, a few picked soldier marksmen, two Gardner guns, and two brass four-pounder Egyptian mountain guns on board. The Safia was old, and could only make two and a half knots per hour against the stream. The following morning they had to pass the fort of Wad-el-Habeshi, where three heavy Krupp guns were mounted, with 5,000 dervishes well entrenched, while a quarter of a mile further on could be seen the wreck of one of Sir Charles Wilson's steamers and the island on which he and his men had taken refuge. By concentrating machine-gun fire on the embrasures, they ran the gauntlet, and had passed some two hundred yards up stream, when a shot from the fort pierced the crazy vessel's boiler, killing or scalding all the engine-room hands except one leading stoker, Royal Navy. The way on the boat enabled it to be headed across and anchored on the opposite shore. Although the dash across the desert had been carried out in the lightest possible order, Chief Engineer Benbow had brought with him the necessary plates, bolts, nuts, tools, etc., for dealing with such an emergency. With his own hands he cut out and bent a new plate sixteen inches by fourteen inches, drilled the holes, cut the threads of the screws on bolts and nuts, and after some ten hours' work standing in water, he was able to report that the job was done. During all this time bullets pattered continually on the hull, some of them piercing it and striking the wounded who lay below, and any moment a shell might have burst into the engine-room. At 5 a.m. the fires were lit with the utmost caution and steam got up. The guns of the fort were safely eluded, Sir Charles Wilson's party picked up, and the whole expedition brought back to Gubat. The plate is now in the Museum of the Royal Naval College, Greenwich, having been cut out and sent home some fifteen years later by Lord Kitchener. In his official report, Lord Charles Beresford stated: " Too much credit cannot be given to this officer." Lord Charles Beresford, in his Memoirs, writes: " He ought to have received the V.C., but owing to the fact that I did not know that the decoration could be granted for a service of that nature, I did not, to my great regret, recommend him for that honour." On the return to Korti, Mr. Benbow was specially complimented on parade for his skill and bravery by Lord Wolseley, who presented him with his cigarette-case. Sent to England shortly after to prepare special light-draft steamers. Specially mentioned by Lord Wolseley in Despatches; received the Medal and clasp, and Khedive's Bronze Star. On the discussion of the Naval Estimates in the House of Commons in 1885, Lord (then Sir Thomas) Brassey, Secretary to the Admiralty, stated: " I particularly desire to place on record the services rendered by the Naval Engineer, Mr. Benbow." Promoted to be Inspector of Machinery, " for gallantry in action during the late operations in Egypt " [Gazette, 13 June, 1886]; Chief Inspector of Machinery, 1888. He was created a Companion of the Distinguished Service Order [London Gazette, 30 May, 1891]: " Henry Benbow, Chief Inspector of Machinery, Royal Navy." Insignia presented by the Queen, 17 Aug. 1891. Sir Henry Benbow married, 1892, Elizabeth Jean, only daughter of the late Henry Bird, of Uxbridge, and their only child is a daughter, Muriel Caroline. He was created a K.C.B. (Military), 26 June, 1902. Sir Henry Benbow, K.C.B., D.S.O., died 20 Oct. 1916.

Henry Benbow.

BEGBIE, ELPHINSTONE WATERS, Colonel, was born at Cheltenham, 15 June, 1842, fifth son of the late Major-General P. J. Begbie, Madras Artillery. He was educated at Crewkerne Grammar School; by private tuition, and at Bonn and Cannstatt, Germany, and was gazetted an Ensign in the Madras Infantry in 1859, becoming Lieutenant in 1861; Captain in 1871; Major, 1879; Lieutenant-Colonel, 1885; Colonel, 1889, and Major-General, 1898. He served with the Abyssian Expedition, 1867–68; served as Sub-Assistant Commissioner-General (Despatches [London Gazette, 30 June, 1868]; Medal). He accompanied the Duffla Expedition, 1874–75; served as Superintendent of Army Signalling (mentioned in Despatches). Joined the Burmese Expedition, 1885–86; served as Superintendent of Army Signalling (Despatches [London Gazette, 22 June, 1886]; Medal with clasp). He was created a Companion of the Distinguished Service Order [London Gazette, 30 May, 1891]: "Elphinstone Waters Begbie, Colonel, Indian Staff Corps. Assistant Adjutant General." He was admitted to a Good Service Pension in 1897; attached to the Queen's Own Madras Sappers and Miners, 1871–88; Instructor in Army Signalling for Madras Presidency, 1872–88; Commandant, Bangalore Rifle Volunteers, 1880–90; A.A.G., Headquarters, Madras Army, 1891–94; Officiating A.G., Madras Army, 1894–95; D.A.G., Madras Command, with rank of Brigadier-General, 1895. He was transferred to the Unemployed Supernumerary List in 1902. He was created a C.B. in 1896. Major-General Begbie died 11 Feb. 1915.

RHODES, FRANCIS WILLIAM, Colonel, was born in 1851, son of the Rev. F. W. Rhodes; was educated at Eton, and became Lieutenant, 1st Dragoons, 23 April, 1873, becoming Captain, 15 Oct. 1884, and Major, 19 Sept. 1885. He served with the Egyptian Expedition, 1884, and also in the Soudan Expedition under Sir Gerald Graham in 1884, as A.D.C. to Major-General Sir Herbert Stewart, Commanding the Cavalry Brigade. Was present at the Battles of Teb and Tamai (Despatches; Medal with clasp; Bronze Star). He was promoted to Captain in 1885. Capt. Rhodes was also present at the battles of Abu Klea and Gubat; afterwards A.D.C. to Major-General Hon. J. C. Horner (horse shot; Despatches); Action of Gemaizah, near Suakin, in Dec. 1888 (Despatches; two clasps; Brevet of Lieut.-Colonel, and created a Companion of the Distinguished Service Order [London Gazette, 30 May, 1891]: "Francis William Rhodes, Major and Colonel, 1st Dragoons, Military Secretary to the Governor of Bombay." The Insignia, etc., were sent out to the Commander-in-Chief in India, and presented 31 Aug. 1891; Third Class Medjidie). Colonel Rhodes was Military Secretary to the Governor of Bombay, 1890–93; served with the British South African Company; administered the Government of Marhmaland and Matabeleland, 1894. He retired in 1896, and died 21 Sept. 1905. An obituary notice of him appeared in the "Times" of 22 Sept. 1905.

HAMILTON, IAN STANDISH MONTEITH, General, was born at Corfu, 16 Jan. 1853, son of Capt. Christian Monteith Hamilton, who later commanded the Gordon Highlanders, and was himself the son of John George Hamilton and of Christina Cameron Monteith, daughter of Henry Monteith, of Carstairs, some time Member of Parliament for Lanarkshire. Ian Hamilton's mother was the Honourable Maria Corinna Vereker, daughter of John, third Viscount Gort, by Maria O'Grady, daughter of Viscount Guillamore. The family is one of the elder branches of the Scottish Hamiltons, and Sir Ian represents the male line of the Hamiltons of Westport.

Ian Standish M. Hamilton.

He was educated first at Cheam, and later at Wellington College; studied in Germany, and then went to Sandhurst; was gazetted to the 12th Foot as Second Lieutenant 24 April, 1872, and was transferred to his father's old regiment, the 92nd, 24 April, 1873, becoming Lieutenant 24 Sept. 1873. In the Afghan War of 1878–80, Ian Hamilton was first brought to the notice of Sir Frederick Roberts, on account of his having made his way with one brother subaltern into a signalling post which had been rushed by the Afghans. The two subalterns recovered the arms and accoutrements left therein, and held the post until a relief party arrived upon the scene. They then organized a pursuit and killed the leader of the Afghan raiders, whose body they brought back into camp. As a result of this adventure, Ian Hamilton was made Aide-de-Camp to the Commander of the British Cavalry Brigade, and was present at the engagement of Charasieh, 6 Oct. 1879, including the subsequent pursuit of the Afghans (mentioned in Despatches). He also took part in the operations round Kabul in Dec. 1879 (mentioned in Despatches; Medal with two clasps).

Lieut. Hamilton served in the Boer War in 1881, and was severely wounded at the action of Majuba Hill, where he was subaltern in charge of a weak picket of Gordon Highlanders. He was wounded in the wrist, knee and hand, and taken prisoner; but the Boer commander (probably Joubert) let him keep his sword, which had been his father's before him. Hamilton thanked the Boer General, and remarked: "This has been a bad day for us." "What can you expect," retorted the Boer, "from fighting on a Sunday?" A Dutch hospital assistant inspected the prisoners, and thought Hamilton was too badly wounded to take. He was dismissed with the remark: "You will probably die. You may go." All night he lay in a marsh at the foot of the mountain, and next morning he was found lying there by his own little dog, which had come out with a search party from camp. He was mentioned in Despatches; became Captain, Gordon Highlanders, 25 Feb. 1882.

In 1884 and 1885 he saw service in the Nile Expedition, for he was on his way home from India on leave, and when the steamer reached Suez he ran across the sands to a train just leaving for Cairo, caught it by the skin of his teeth, and again, by a margin of only a few hours, caught the headquarters of his own regiment as it was leaving Cairo for the front.

At Wady Halfa, with great difficulty, he got himself definitely posted to a vacancy in the Gordon Highlanders, in the River Column. Toiling up the river, Hamilton's company gradually pulled away from the rest of the regiment, until at last they came up with the fighting front in the middle of the only action fought by the River Column.

He and his company alone of the Gordon Highlanders fought in the action of Kirbeekan and wear the clasp for that engagement. For his services in this campaign he was mentioned in Despatches; given the Brevet of Major 7 Nov. 1885; received the Medal with two clasps and the Khedive's Star.

On his return to India he became an Aide-de-Camp on the Staff of Lord Roberts, then commanding the Madras Army. Lord Roberts was doing his best to improve the shooting of the Army, and he and his Staff formed themselves into teams, and had rifle matches with the regiments in the Madras Command. "In these competitions Hamilton's skill with the rifle and his keen interest in musketry stood him in good stead." He was A.D.C. and afterwards Persian Interpreter to Lord Roberts, Commander-in-Chief in India, from 9 March, 1886, to 30 June, 1890, and in 1886 and 1887 he took part in the Burma Campaign (Despatches; Brevet of Lieut.-Colonel, 1 July, 1887; Medal with clasp).

About this time he wrote a book inculcating the supreme importance of musketry in the Army, and insisting on the necessity for a more practical course than bull's-eye shooting. Moving targets and celerity and precision practices were therein advocated for the first time as a part of a regular military curriculum. The book was called "The Fighting of the Future." During the same period was published, "A Jaunt in a Junk"; a volume of verses, "The Ballad of Hadji and the Boar," and one or two other things. Andrew Lang dedicated a book of poems to him in the following lines:

"TO COLONEL IAN HAMILTON.

"To you who know the face of war,
You that from England wander far,
You that have seen the Ghazis fly
From English lads not sworn to die,
You that have lain where, deadly chill,
The mist creeps o'er the Shameful Hill,
You that have conquered, mile by mile,
The currents of unfriendly Nile,
And cheered the march and eased the strain
When politics made valour vain,
Ian, to you, from banks of Ken,
We send you lays of Englishmen."

After the Burma Expedition, Lord Roberts, who, it is said, was greatly taken with Ian Hamilton's book on musketry, "The Fighting of the Future," made him Assistant Adjutant-General for Musketry at Army Headquarters in India. As A.A.G. for Musketry Ian Hamilton was strongly backed by Lord Roberts in his assiduous work for the improvement of musketry in the Indian Army. The Army at home was still tied to the pure bull's-eye system, but Lord Roberts encouraged his A.A.G. to break away from the old tradition with the shooting course of the native army, which until then had followed closely on the lines of the British Musketry Regulations. So encouraged, Ian Hamilton wrote out the native musketry regulations afresh on original principles, the British Army Regulations being similarly remodelled some years later. He was created a Companion of the Distinguished Service Order [London Gazette, 30 May, 1891]. He was Military Secretary to General Sir George White, Commander-in-Chief in India, 8 April, 1893, to 10 Oct. 1895, and then became Deputy Quartermaster-General for India; but from this appointment he was sent to take part in the operations of the Chitral Relief Force, with which he served under Sir Robert Low in 1895 as A.A.G. and Q.M.G., Lines of Communication (Despatches; created a C.B.; Medal and clasp). In 1896 he was given command of a brigade in the Tirah Expedition. After marching through the Kohat Pass, his horse fell with him and broke his leg, so that he was obliged to resign his command. When his leg had mended after a fashion, Sir William Lockhart again gave Hamilton command of a brigade (the 3rd Brigade), but the fighting was practically over, though for his services in holding the advanced posts in the Bara Valley General Lockhart mentioned him in Despatches, and he received the Medal with clasp. Whilst holding the outlet of the Bara Valley with his brigade, he received a letter from General Sir William Lockhart offering him the officiating appointment of Quartermaster-General in India, and a cable from Sir Evelyn Wood, Adjutant-General to the Home Forces, offering him the Commandantship of the School of Musketry, Hythe, "in consideration of good services rendered in that branch of military instruction." The Indian post was the more important and much the more highly paid; but Ian Hamilton was a musketry fanatic, and he accepted the Home appointment, thus from 11 May, 1898, to 15 Sept. 1899, being Commandant, School of Musketry, Hythe. When Sir George White was sent to Natal in Sept. 1899, he selected Ian Hamilton as his Assistant Adjutant-General (16 Sept. 1899, to 11 Oct. 1899). He became Major-General (supernumerary) commanding an infantry brigade 12 Oct. 1899, and thus had command of a brigade practically from the beginning of the fighting in the South African War. He took part in the operations in Natal in 1899, including the action of Elandslaagte, where he commanded the infantry, and was recommended by Sir John French—who was himself eye-witness to the personal action of Ian Hamilton—for the Victoria Cross. It was, however, held that a Brigadier-General was too senior to be eligible for that distinction, as it was undesirable that officers of that rank should be encouraged to run too many personal risks. The following letter was given to Sir Ian Hamilton by Lord Roberts. It is interesting both with reference to General Hamilton and to the other officers and men mentioned in it:

"[Copy, C.-in-C., 290.]

"War Office, London, S.W.,

"7 July, 1900.

"SIR,—I am directed by the Secretary of State for War to acknowledge the receipt of your letter of the 5th April last, recommending that the Victoria Cross should be conferred upon four officers, four non-commissioned officers and one trooper, named in the margin" (*i.e.*, Ian Hamilton and eight others), "for conspicuous bravery displayed by them on 21 Oct. (at Elandslaagte), 30 Oct. and 4 Nov. 1899, respectively.

"In reply, I am to acquaint you that the Commander-in-Chief will submit to the Queen that the decoration in question be granted to Capt. Meiklejohn, Second Lieut. Norwood and Sergt.-Major Robertson, and that the medal for distinguished conduct in the field be awarded to Sergt. Drummer Lawrence, Corpl. Piper McLeod, L.-Corpl. Dryden and Trooper Evans, whose conduct, though gallant, was not, in his opinion, of such a nature as to merit the high distinction of the Victoria Cross. With regard to Colonel (local Major-General) Ian Hamilton, I am to observe that the act for which he was recommended was performed when he was commanding a brigade—i.e., in the position of a General Officer. The Victoria Cross has never been conferred upon an officer so high in rank. The Commander-in-Chief thinks this limitation a wise one, and that it would not be desirable to establish a precedent opposed to it. He is unable, therefore, to submit Major-General Hamilton's name to the Queen.

"I am to add that while Colonel Wools-Sampson evidently led his men with much gallantry, Lord Wolseley does not feel that his conduct was sufficiently exceptional to call for the bestowal of the great favour of the Victoria Cross.

"I have the honour to be, Sir,

"Your obedient Servant,

(Sd.) "COLERIDGE GROVE,

"M.S."

Ian Hamilton fought in command of his brigade at Rietfontein and Lombard's Kop, and in the defence of Ladysmith, including the action of the 6th Jan. 1900, when he commanded on Waggon Hill and Cæsar's Camp. He took part in the operations in the Orange Free State from Feb to May, 1900, including the actions at Houtnek, Vet River and the Zand River, during which time he was nominally Lieut.-General commanding a Mounted Infantry Division, but actually in command of two brigades of infantry under Generals Smith-Dorrien and Bruce Hamilton, as well as a large force of cavalry, artillery and mounted infantry. With this force he fought successfully at Welkom Farm, Winburg, Zand River, Lindley, Heilbron, Florida, near Johannesburg and at Pretoria. At Diamond Hill he commanded the right attack which eventually broke through the enemy's line. Shortly afterwards he broke his collar-bone by a fall from his horse, but after a brief delay he was fitted out with another column, and took part in the operations in the Transvaal, east of Pretoria, July to 29 Nov. 1900, including the action at Zilikat's Nek. He was Military Secretary at the War Office 11 Dec. 1900, to 9 Nov. 1901, when he returned to South Africa as Chief of the Staff to Lord Kitchener, until 8 April, 1902, when he took command and directed operations in the Western Transvaal. During this period he fought the last serious battle of the war at Roodewal, completely defeating De la Rey's lieutenant, Kemp, who had collected large Boer forces in the Western Transvaal to oppose him, and recapturing Lord Methuen's guns, captured by De la Rey at Tweebosch. The news of this defeat reached the Boer delegates at Pretoria, where the question of peace was being discussed, and was a factor in inducing them to come to terms (vide "Times History of the War in South Africa," Vol. V., pages 525–527).

In his "Great Boer War" (pages 299–300) Sir A. Conan Doyle gives his impressions of Ian Hamilton at this time: "A thin, aquiline man, of soft voice and gentle manners, he had already proved more than once during his adventurous career that he not only possessed in a high degree the courage of the soldier, but also the equanimity and decision of the born leader. A languid elegance in his bearing covered a shrewd brain and a soul of fire. A distorted and half-paralysed hand reminded the observer that Hamilton, as a young lieutenant, had known at Majuba what it was to face the Boer rifles. Now, in his forty-seventh year, he had returned, matured and formidable, to reverse the results of that first deplorable campaign. This was the man to whom Lord Roberts entrusted the command of that powerful flanking column which eventually formed the right wing of his main advance." (Three times mentioned in Despatches, and promoted Major-General and subsequently Lieut.-General for distinguished services in the field; created a K.C.B.; Queen's Medal with six clasps, King's Medal with two clasps). He was reappointed Military Secretary at the War Office, holding this appointment from 12 Sept. 1902, to 26 April, 1903; was Quartermaster-General to the Forces, Headquarters of Army, 17 April, 1903, to 1 Feb. 1904; was appointed Colonel, Queen's Own Cameron Highlanders, 1904; served as Military Representative of India with the Japanese Army in the Field, in Manchuria, 22 March, 1904, to 22 April, 1905, being present at most of the principal battles and engagements during the campaign, including the repulse of Count Keller's attack in the Pass of Montienling, at Yanseling, at Liao-Yang, the Shaho and Heikotai, and received the Japanese War Medal and the Order of the Sacred Treasure. He was also created a G.C.B. He was G.O.C. in Chief, Southern Command, 1 June, 1905, to 31 May, 1909; Adjutant-General to the Forces, 1 June, 1909, to 31 July, 1910; General Officer Commanding in Chief, Mediterranean, and Inspector-General, Overseas Force, 1 Aug. 1910, to 1 Aug. 1914; General Commanding-in-Chief, Central Striking Force, Horse Guards, London, 10 Aug. 1914, to 13 March, 1915. He commanded the Mediterranean Expeditionary Force in 1915, of which the "Observer" of 26 Dec. 1915, says: "It was from beginning to end a fighting adventure surpassing the Homeric Legend of Troy over the Straits. It marks an epoch in human estimate of the courage and fibre of modern men among the English-speaking peoples. It will live for ever in the history of our race, and thrill posterity as long as Britain and her sea-bred breed endure." An Australian General, and one of the island continent's most distinguished sons, gave it as his opinion to the present writer that no other general could have done better than Sir Ian Hamilton under the circumstances. Like the Charge of the Light Brigade, the Dardanelles Campaign may or may not have been war, but it was magnificent. There the sons of the island continent went to their deaths as to a picnic, and made for their country a history and for themselves a fame that shall live for ever. And their lives are no more wasted than was the water from the well of Bethlehem which King David poured out before the Lord because it was too precious to drink. And not the Australians only—seasoned soldiers, Territorials, barristers and farmers, clerks and country gentlemen from the Cotswold country and from the Ever Faithful City, Gurkhas and Connaught Rangers—there they lived or died as Fate would have it. There on the heights of Chunak Bair they beheld, like Moses, the promised land which they should not themselves possess. Crusaders of a later day, they weakened the power of the infidel and his devilish allies, and prepared the way for others more fortunate but not more glorious than themselves. They died, but their names shall live for ever. But to return to Sir Ian Hamilton personally. Bled white for Salonika, and only half-heartedly supported by the politicians at home and by some of its military leaders, the expedition seemed doomed to failure from the first. Not the enthusiasm of Ian Hamilton himself, or the whole-hearted support of his friends, could make of the Mediterranean Expedition anything but the glorious failure, which appeals to some of us more than ninety-and-nine successful campaigns. Major the Marquess of Ailesbury, D.S.O., writes: "You ask me what I can tell you of Sir Ian Hamilton. But why ask such a question? You place me in a difficulty. It has been my privilege to have had his acquaintance, to have served several months under his command, to have seen him in action. He is the beau-ideal of an English gentleman: educated, polite, good-hearted, charming. In short, he is a Sahib. But I am not myself a soldier, and though I have had the good fortune to wear uniform in two wars, I am none the less an amateur, and was only called in with many thousand others when the 'Regulars' found they had bitten off more than they could chew. Therefore, on military subjects my opinion must be worthless. I can only say that I believe Sir Ian is never so happy, so entirely self-contained, as when under fire. I believe he experiences a real pleasure in the face of danger. With regard to the work he did for the improvement of the soldier's ability in shooting—this is historical, and it is enough to say that Sir Ian practised, before 1882, what Lord Roberts advocated twenty years later. As to the tragedy of Gallipoli, British commanders seldom have the opportunity to dictate the strategy of a campaign, and Hamilton cannot be blamed for the policy which planted an insufficient force at the far end of what is really a vast defile. Believing, as I always have, that no occupation of Constantinople is possible until the defending field army is crushed, accepting the axiom that 'numbers alone can annihilate,' it appears certain to me that the Cabinet erred grievously both in their choice of ground and in the resources they employed. Possibly history will decide that any movement against the Turk, with the exception of the occupation of Basra, was entirely unsound. We should have struck at the heart—the heart was in Berlin; our nearest base to the heart was on the Marne." Mr. Henry Nevinson, in his great book on the Dardanelles (pages 64–67), says of Sir Ian Hamilton: "The appointment to command the military forces had come to him unexpectedly but five days earlier, and on 13 March he started from London. He had received only slight and vague instructions from Lord Kitchener, but on certain limitations the Secretary for War insisted, and all of them strongly influenced Sir Ian's subsequent action. If possible, a landing was to be avoided; none was to be attempted until the Fleet had made every effort to penetrate the Straits and had failed; if a landing became unavoidable, none should be made until the full force available had assembled, and no adventurous operations were to be undertaken on the Asiatic side. All these instructions were followed. But they revealed the hesitating reluctance with which the Dardanelles campaign was regarded, not only by Lord Kitchener himself, but by his subordinate generals at home and in France. The 'Westerners' were naturally in the ascendant. The danger to the Allied cause lay close at hand. It had only recently been averted from the Channel and from Paris. The British Staff, equally with the French, represented that not a man could be spared from France, and that the only assured road to victory lay straight through the German lines. The opposition to any 'side-show,' especially if it diverted a Regular division such as the 29th, was expressed with the emphasis of jealous alarm. Even the appointment of Sir Ian Hamilton to the distant enterprise was likely to be received with mingled sentiments. He counted forty-two years of service in the Army. Since the days of the Afghan War and Majuba Hill (where his left hand was shattered), he had risen step by step to all but the highest commands. The Nile, Burma, Chitral and Tirah had known him. He commanded the infantry in the rapid but vital engagement at Elandslaagte, and during the siege of Ladysmith had charge of the extensive and dangerous sector known as Cæsar's Camp and Waggon Hill. In the final months of the Boer War he was Lord Kitchener's Chief of Staff, and commanded mobile columns in the Western Transvaal, greatly contributing to the conclusion of the war. Since then he had served at home as Quartermaster-General, as G.O.C.-in-Chief of the Southern Command, and as Adjutant-General. Abroad he had served as Military Representative of India with the Japanese Army in Manchuria (1904–5), when, in 'A Staff Officer's Scrap-Book,' he foretold the disappearance of cavalry and the prevalence of the trench in future warfare; as General Officer Commanding-in-Chief in the Mediterranean, and Inspector-General of the Overseas Forces (1910–15). Except that he had never yet held supreme command in any considerable campaign, his experience in military affairs and in almost every phase of our Army's activity was hardly to be surpassed. On the other hand, he was sixty-two; and though he was a year younger than Lord French, and retained a slim and active figure such as enabled Lord Roberts to take command in South Africa at seventy, sixty-two was regarded as a full age for any officer in so difficult a campaign upon a desert promontory. From a mingled Highland and Irish descent he had inherited the so-called Celtic qualities which are regarded by thorough Englishmen with varying admiration and dislike. His blood gave him so conspicuous a physical courage that after the battles of Cæsar's Camp and Diamond Hill, the present writer, who knew him there, regarded him as an example of the rare type which not merely conceals fear with success, but does not feel it. Undoubtedly he was deeply tinged with the Celtic 'charm'—that glamour of mind and courtesy of behaviour which create suspicion among people endowed with neither. Through his nature ran a strain of the idealistic spirit which some despise as quixotic, and others salute as chivalrous, while, with cautious solicitude, they avoid it in themselves. It was known also that Sir Ian was susceptible to the influence of beauty in other forms than those usually conceded to military men. He was an acknowledged master of English prose, and though our people read more in quantity than any other nation, the literary gift is regarded among us as a sign of incapacity, and is not, as in France and ancient Greece, accepted as assurance of far-reaching powers. What was worse, he was known to have written poetry. Before the war his opposition to the introduction of conscription in the United Kingdom had roused the animosity of all who aimed at establishing militarism as a permanent system in this country. Thus political animosity was added to the official prejudice against a buoyant and liberal temperament conjoined with a politeness and an open-hearted manner startlingly at variance with official usage. One must acknowledge that, in choosing the man for command, Lord Kitchener hardly took sufficient account of qualities likely to arouse antipathy among certain influential classes and the newspapers which represent their opinions. But careless of such prudent considerations, as his manner was, he allowed his decision to be guided by the General's long experience in warfare, and designedly selected an eager temperament liable to incautious impetuosity, but suited, as might be supposed, to an undertaking which demanded impetuous action. It was, however, probably in fear lest natural impulse should be given too loose a rein that the instructions mentioned above impressed only caution upon the appointed commander. In view of the strong opposition to the whole enterprise, it was also assumed that no reinforcements could be promised, and none should be asked for. Even the allotted divisions were not allowed the ten per cent. extra men usually granted to fill up the gaps of immediate loss. After that conference in the Queen Elizabeth on 22 March (when Sir Ian left the final decision to the Naval authorities), it was evident that a military landing could not be avoided unless the whole expedition were abandoned. It is easy now for belated prudence to maintain that Sir Ian should then have abandoned it, secured (if he could) the acquiescence of the Navy in defeat, counter-ordered the assembling troops and returned to London." Mrs. Stuart Menzies says, in "Sir Stanley Maude and Other Memories" (pages 8–10): "There are various stories told of General Maude at this time, one being that when orders were given to evacuate Cape Helles, and it became known that the Gallipoli Campaign was a thing to be wiped off the slate, and, if possible, forgotten, General Maude could not at first believe it, the idea of evacuation being most painful to him, and there were some, who did not know his stern sense of duty and his love of strict soldierly discipline, who feared he might 'queer the whole evacuation at the last moment by starting an attack on the Turks all on his own,' for they knew how firmly he believed—in fact, never doubted for a moment—that with proper reinforcements and munitions they could have taken Constantinople. . . . General Maude said: 'It (speaking of the evacuation) came as a bombshell to us all. In Sept. we were told we were to have the reinforcements that were needed, consisting of four French divisions, under ——, and two divisions of fresh British troops, which, in the opinion of every officer who carried any weight was ample to enable us to push through; but that miserable Loos spoilt everything.'" In this connection it is interesting to recall a remark made by Gunner Lodge, V.C., whose plain soldier's tale of his experiences in South Africa is, General Creagh says, "the best thing in this book." He said: "When I hear people saying that Lord French and Sir Ian Hamilton didn't do things in this war, I say to myself, *They didn't do things because they hadn't got the men.* No general, however good he is, can do anything without men. Not but what General French, in South Africa, could do a job and mop it up with about three hundred men, where another leader would want twice the number." General Maude wrote to his wife on 26 Dec. 1915: "It was a pity that we could not go on at Suvla and get through, and if they had given us the means to, I am sure we should have been successful. But without the necessary men, guns and munitions and transport, it was of course no use trying, and the next best thing was to get out as we have done. My only regret is that they did not get out of Helles at the same time, and this is indeed, in my opinion, a blunder. Everything seems very stationary everywhere, and I suppose the frost and snow are mainly responsible." Maybe the Dardanelles was a forlorn hope. Maybe Andrew Lang was gifted with second-sight when he wrote to Ian Hamilton of times "when politics made valour vain." Andrew Lang wrote a poem in the same book about Melvill and Coghill—Melvill hampered in mid-stream by the Queen's Colour; Coghill, who could have saved himself, but returned to throw away his life too. And all for a flag. Sir Ian Hamilton was created Lieutenant of the Tower of London. In the final "War Honours" Gazette, dated 3 June, 1919, General Sir Ian Hamilton, G.C.B., D.S.O. (Colonel, Gordon Highlanders, Lieutenant of the Tower), to be Knight Grand Cross of the Order of St. Michael and St. George. In Feb. 1887, Sir Ian Hamilton married Jean, eldest daughter of Sir John Muir, First Baronet, of Deanston Perthshire.

General Maude wrote on 24 Oct. 1915:

"Things are still very unsettled here. General Munro has not arrived yet, and Birdwood is temporarily in command, but both he and Byng are more or less on the sick-list. It is difficult with the scanty news we get to make out the position in the Balkans, but Servia seems to be faced by the Germans and Austrians on the north, and by the Bulgarians on the east, whilst the Turks are said to be rushing troops there too. If that is correctly the situation it seems essential that there should be a big blow somewhere, either in the West or in Russia or here. I only hope things are not going to 'drift' again, but our conduct of this war has been so bad throughout and our strategy so farcical that we cannot help having misgivings. We talk and threaten too much, and say what we are going to do after the war, instead of getting down to business, selecting our point and striking hard at it and effectively, like the Germans do. For instance, this business here should be well within our compass if taken in hand resolutely and with adequate means. But it is no use trying to do it by halves. It is all the more necessary that we should strike early here as, if the Germans are successful against Servia, things will be very much more difficult for us here. I do hope that we shall drop our 'wait and see' attitude, and get on and at least try to do something."

In "In the Side Shows," Capt. Wedgwood Benn, D.S.O., D.F.C., M.P., gives us some sidelights on the Dardanelles Campaign, and on the feelings of the troops. Here is one of them: "The news received . . . of the recall of Sir Ian Hamilton did nothing, needless to say, to raise our spirits. We regretted the loss of a chief who had, on all occasions, loyally and generously appreciated the efforts made by the forces under his command."

Sir George Arthur, after describing Kitchener's relief at the successful evacuation of Gallipoli, says in Volume III. of his "Life of Lord Kitchener" (page 210): "Nor—now that all was over—did he forget that the adventure to the Dardanelles, politically well conceived, would be far from barren of eventual effect. He saw from the first that a blow at Turkey's heart—even if not immediately fatal—must weaken and might paralyse her activities in the East. He did not live to gauge how far Gallipoli cleared the road to Jerusalem, but he could realize the real worth of Ian Hamilton's work, and knew that the heroes of the Dardanelles Expedition, thwarted in their main object, had still, like an iron rod, broken the spine of Turkish military power."

CLEMENTS, RALPH ARTHUR PENRHYN, Brevet Lieut.-Colonel, was born 9 Feb. 1855, youngest son of the Rev. Jacob Clements, Sub-Dean and Canon Residentiary of Lincoln. He was educated at Rossall, and joined the 24th Regt. 2 Dec. 1874; served in the Galeka and Zulu Wars, 1877–79 (Despatches; Medal with clasp); became Captain, South Wales Borderers, 4 Dec. 1880, and Major 24 Feb. 1886. He served with the Burma Expedition, 1885–89, as Brigade-Major (thrice wounded; mentioned in Despatches; Medal with two clasps; Brevet of Lieut.-Colonel; created a Companion of the Distinguished Service Order [London Gazette, 30 May, 1891]: "Ralph Arthur Penrhyn Clements, Major and Brevet Lieut.-Colonel, South Wales Borderers." Insignia, etc., sent to Commander-in-Chief in India; presentation 4 Nov. 1891). He became Lieut.-Colonel 1 July, 1887, and Colonel 4 Dec. 1896; served in South Africa, commanding the 12th Brigade, and as Major-General on the Staff (Despatches; Queen's Medal and three clasps; King's Medal and two clasps); was created a C.B. 1904; commanded a First Class District in India, 1904; became Lieut.-General. He died at Quetta 2 April, 1909. The "Times" of 3 April, 1909, says, in an obituary notice of him: "His first active service was as a Lieutenant in the 24th Foot, during the South African War of 1877–79. In the Kaffir Campaign he was present at the Battle of Newmarks, and in the Zulu Campaign at the Battle of Ulundi. He was mentioned in Despatches [London Gazette, 26 Feb. 1878], and received the Medal with clasp. Promoted to Captain in the South Wales Borderers in Dec. 1880, and to Major in Feb. 1886, he served on the Staff during this period as Brigade Major in the Burmese Expedition, and as A.P.M. He was twice wounded in action, and was mentioned in Despatches [London Gazette, 22 June, 1886]; received the Medal with clasps, and the Brevet of Lieutenant-Colonel in July, 1887. During the war in South Africa he served as Major-General on the Staff, and also in command of the districts of Pretoria and Standerton-Heidelburg. He was mentioned in Despatches [London Gazette, 29 July, 1902]; received the Queen's Medal with three clasps, and the King's Medal with two clasps. Lieut.-General Clements was A.D.C. to Queen Victoria from 1896, and to King Edward VII. from 1901. He received the D.S.O. in 1891, and a C.B. in 1904. From Feb. 1900, he served in India, where from 1907 he commanded the 4th Division at Quetta. He died 2 April, 1909, after an operation for appendicitis." All through the "Official History of the War in South Africa" we get accounts of the services of this distinguished officer. On page 404 of Vol. I. we read that "while the affair at Slingersfontein was in progress a welcome reinforcement arrived. Major-General R. A. P. Clements brought with him the 1st Royal Irish and the remainder of the 2nd Worcestershire men of his brigade (12th), in all an addition of 18 officers and 874 men. Clements was immediately placed in command of the Slingersfontein area."

On 29 Jan. 1900, Colonel J. Watkins Yardley tells us in "With the Inniskilling Dragoons in South Africa" (page 20), "General French left for

Cape Town to meet Lord Roberts and arrange for the famous Relief of Kimberley. He handed over the command of the forces before Colesberg to Major-General Clements. These now consisted of the 18th Royal Irish, Worcesters, Berks, Wilts and Essex Regiments, J Battery R.H.A., four 15-pounders, 4th R.F.A., two howitzers, Victorian Mounted Rifles, South and West Australian Mounted Infantry, etc., but early in February they were much weakened by the departure of all the Regular Cavalry, except B and C Squadrons, Inniskilling Dragoons, for Orange River, *en route* to Kimberley. A Squadron, Inniskilling Dragoons, was attached to the Scots Greys, and left with them for Modder River. The Boers at this time were in great strength at Colesberg, nearly 10,000 strong, with many guns, and were most aggressive. They were daily being increased, whereas our forces were being lessened for the Kimberley relief. So General Clements was left in a most trying position, but he proved himself equal to the task." Colonel Yardley goes on to describe the fighting. throughout February, which culminated in the capture of Colesberg on 28 Feb. On 7 March the Inniskillings in advance seized Norval's Pont. On 20 March " General Clements started to march to Bloemfontein, via Philippolis, Jagersfontein and Fauresmith. . . . The columns marched to Bloemfontein without opposition, the inhabitants coming in and surrendering their arms. The march occupied sixteen days, the forces arriving at Bloemfontein on 5 April."

Later on in his book (pages 222-3) Colonel Yardley tells us how, on 13 Dec., news was received of General Clements's disaster in the Magaliesburg, so headquarters, with the remainder of the Inniskillings, under Major Allenby, marched the same day in great haste with the 1st Cavalry Brigade to his assistance. Having reached Vlakfontein Farm, near Houtkop, a lamp message was received to move on at 3 a.m. and join Colonel Gordon at Jaroosfontein. This having been done, the brigade moved on by Van Wyk's Rust to the Roodepoort mines, and by another night march to Krugersdorp. Being Dingaan's Day, it was expected that the Boers would attack Krugersdorp. The 14th Hussars joined by rail from Heidelberg, and the brigade marched at 3 a.m., with the 14th Hussars, Scots Guards and Dublins in support, to co-operate with General Clements to the north-west. " We heard his guns firing heavily all the morning. Near Zeekoehoek we came on the flank of some 2,000 to 3,000 Boers, under De la Rey, falling back west before Clements. Unfortunately we were too late, and they got away with some casualties. Bivouacking at Vaalbank, we started again at 4 a.m., but only succeeded in slightly engaging the Boer rearguard, which was retiring south-west. Colonel Gordon was now appointed to command the whole force, Colonel Hamilton, 14th Hussars, taking command of the Brigade next day. General Clements, supported by Alderson's Mounted Infantry, attacked Naauwpoort Hill, to the west of us."

On 9 Jan. 1901, Colonel Yardley tells us that " the Inniskillings, 14th Hussars, two guns and a pom-pom, all under Major Allenby, reconnoitred towards Breedt's Nek, and got into communication with General Clements."

Apropos of Lord Allenby it is said that many publishers approached him with the object of getting him to write a book on the Palestine Campaign. He was made an offer by at least one publisher which ran into thousands of pounds, but did not agree to write the book. At last an American came, who said, " Whatever any of the others have offered, I'll pay you double. And, what's more, *I'll write the book myself.*" Even this sporting offer did not tempt Lord Allenby.

SETTLE, HENRY HAMILTON, Major and Brevet Lieut.-Colonel, son of Capt. H. T. Settle, of Southover, Lewes; born 27 Jan. 1847; was educated at Heidelberg and Cheltenham; entered the R.E. 10 July, 1867; became Captain 1879; passed Staff College 1883; Major 1886; Lieutenant-Colonel 1893; Colonel 1893; Major-General 1902; Lieutenant-General 1908; retired 1911. Served in Nile Expedition, 1884-5, as D.A.A.G. and D.A.Q.M.G. (Despatches, Medal with clasp, Bronze Star, Brevet Major); in Anglo-Egyptian Expeditions as Chief Staff Officer at action of Gemaizah, Suakin, 1888 (Despatches, clasp, Brevet of Lieutenant-Colonel), and at action of Toski, 1889 (Despatches, clasp, 2nd Class Medjidie); Chief Staff Officer in expedition to retake Tokar Delta at action of Afafit, 1891 (Despatches, clasp); created a Companion of the Distinguished Service Order [London Gazette, 30 May, 1891]: " Henry Hamilton Settle, Major and Brevet Lieut.-Colonel, R.E., attached Egyptian Army." Served in the South African War, 1899-1902, as Brigadier-General on the Staff, Inspector-General, Lines of Communication, also commanded Columns (Despatches twice, two Medals with clasps; K.C.B. (Military); promoted Major-General for distinguished service in the field); Surveyor-General and Q.M.G. Egyptian Army, 1886-92; Inspector-General, Egyptian Police, 1892-4; Assistant Inspector-General of Fortifications, War Office, 1895-9; Commanding R.E. Malta, 1899; G.O.C. Cape Colony District, S. of Orange River, 1901-2, and Cape Colony, 1903; G.O.C. Portsmouth Defences, 1905-8; has rank of Pasha, 2nd Class Osmanieh and Grand Cordon Medjidie; created D.S.O. 1891; C.B. (Military) 1898; K.C.B. (Military) 1900. He married, in 1875, Edith, only daughter of the late Jonathan Rigg, of Wrotham Hill Park, Kent.

In the " Official History of the Boer War " (Vol. I., page 182), we read how " Lord Kitchener, leaving Naauwpoort, had spent a day at De Aar, and there arranged with Brigadier-General H. H. Settle, commanding the section of the line of communications to the south of the Orange River, for the despatch westward of three small flying columns . . . to deal

Henry Hamilton Settle.

with the hostile bands assembling n the direction of Prieska and Van Wyk's Vlei."

On page 212 Sir F. Maurice says that except for these three columns under Settle, Adye and Parsons, and the immobile troops guarding the railway, the whole of Cape Colony, west of a line drawn from Cape Town to Kimberley, was for a time without military protection.

In Vol. III., pages 11–16 is given an account of the suppression of the rebellion in the North-West of Cape Colony, in which he took part. When the western area of the Transvaal (see Vol. III., page 228) was divided into military districts, in order to carry out the pacification, the command of the south-west area, with Headquarters at Vryburg, was given to Sir H. H. Settle.

He took part in the operations in the Western Transvaal. He fought through the operations in the Orange River Colony, and on page 496 of Vol. III. we are told how Settle, who had been skirmishing and foraging for some time in the south-west of the Colony, . . . arrived at Edenburg laden with booty of every description."

On page 513: " Since the middle of October, Major-General Settle, with a force of 600 mounted men, ten guns and 1,350 infantry, had been operating between Christiana and Bothaville."

When De Wet invaded Cape Colony, sixteen bodies of troops were within the border and organized for the field (Vol. IV., page 65). All these were placed under the general command of Major-General Sir H. H. Settle, and in the ensuing pages we read about the movements of these troops.

For a time Lieut.-General Sir N. G. Lyttelton took command, and Sir H. H. Settle resumed command after his departure. The record of services given above shows how for the South African War Sir H. Settle received two Medals with clasps; was twice mentioned in Despatches; received a K.C.B., and was promoted Major-General for distinguished service in the field.

WINTLE, FRANK GRAHAM, Lieut.-Colonel, was born at Jullundur, India, 2 Dec. 1852, 3rd son of the late Major-General Alfred Wintle, Royal (Bengal) Horse Artillery. He was educated at a private school, and at Merchant Taylors' School, and joined the Control Department in 1872. He was posted, on its breaking up, to the Ordnance Store (now Army Ordnance) Department, becoming D.A. Commissary-General of Ordnance 31 Jan. 1880. He served in the Sudan Expedition, 1884-85; on the Nile (Despatches [London Gazette, 25 Aug. 1885]; Medal with clasp; Bronze Star; promoted Assistant Commissary-General of Ordnance 15 June, 1885). He again served in the Sudan, 1884-85, on the Nile; was present at the action of Ginniss and was mentioned in Despatches [London Gazette, 6 Feb. 1886]. He was created a Companion of the Distinguished Service Order [London Gazette, 30 May, 1891]: " Frank Graham Wintle, Honorary Lieut.-Colonel, Assistant Commissary-General of Ordnance, Ordnance Store Department." The Insignia were presented to him by the Queen, 17 Aug. 1891. He became Deputy Commissary-General of Ordnance 24 April, 1895, and Colonel and Ordnance Officer, 1st Class, 1 April, 1896. Colonel Wintle retired. He died, unmarried, 24 Feb. 1907.

LEACH, HAROLD PEMBERTON, Major and Brevet Lieut.-Colonel, late R.E., 4th son of the late Lieut.-Colonel Sir George Archibald Leach, K.C.B., R.E.; born 1851; first commission 1871; promoted Colonel by Brevet in 1894; retired in 1908 and became Honorary Brigadier-General in 1912. He joined the 1st Division Khyber Field Force in command of Company, Bengal Sappers and Miners, 1878-79; was present at capture of Ali Musjid, action at Deh Savak and the operation in the Bazar Valley (Despatches). Subsequently in the Kurram Valley, 1879-80, when he took part in Zaimuckt Expedition, including the taking of Zowa (Despatches, thanks of Government of India, Medal with clasp). Lent to Home Government for service with Camel Transport during the Nile Expedition, 1884-85; present at the actions of Abu Klea and Gubat; Senior Transport Officer on withdrawal of Force from Metemneh (Medal with two clasps;

Harold Pemberton Leach.

Bronze Star; Brevet of Major). Senior R.E. with Lushai Expedition 1888-89 (honourably mentioned; Medal with clasp). C.R.E. with Chin-Lushai Expedition, 1889-90 (Despatches, clasp, Brevet of Lieutenant-Colonel); C.R.E. (Colonel on the Staff) with Chitral Relief Force, 1895. Present at taking of Malakand and action on Panjkora River (Despatches, Medal with clasp; C.B.). Commandant Bombay Sappers, 1890-91. Military Secretary to C.-in-C. Bombay, 1891-93. Commandant Bengal Sappers, 1893-1900; Brigadier-General commanding Presidency District, 1900-05 (thanks of Government of India for despatch of China Expedition from Calcutta); also officiated in command of Peshawar District in 1896, and again in 1898; Lahore District in 1901 and as D.Q.M.G. Army Headquarters, India, in 1898. During the Great War commanded the 89th Brigade, 4th Army (subsequently turned into 1st Training Reserve Brigade), 1914-1917 (Secretary of State's List, C.B.E.). Subsequently served as Group Commander, Surrey Volunteers. Created a Companion of the Distinguished Service Order [London Gazette, 30 May, 1891]: " Harold Pemberton Leach, Major and Brevet Lieut.-Colonel, Royal Engineers."

WILKINS, JAMES SUTHERLAND, Surgeon-Major, was born 18 May, 1851, and was educated for the medical profession, attaining the degrees of L.R.C.P. and M.R.C.S. He entered the Indian Medical Service as Surgeon 31 March, 1874, and served in the Afghan War of 1880, taking part in the march from Quetta to the relief of Kandahar, and receiving the Medal.

He became Surgeon-Major 31 March, 1886, and again saw active service in the Burmese Expedition of 1886–87. He was mentioned in Despatches [London Gazette, 2 Sept. 1887], and received the Medal and two clasps. He was created a Companion of the Distinguished Service Order [London Gazette, 30 May, 1891]: "James Sutherland Wilkins, Surgeon-Major, Indian Medical Service." The Insignia were sent to the Commander-in-Chief in India and the presentation took place on 7 Dec. 1891. He was promoted to Brigade Surgeon-Major, ranking as Lieutenant-Colonel, 31 March, 1894, and later became Colonel. He married, in 1905, Dora Sophia Lee (who died in 1906), second daughter of the Rev. F. French, of Worlingworth Rectory, Suffolk, and they had one son. Colonel Wilkins died 27 Oct. 1916.

EGERTON, CHARLES COMYN, Major, was born 10 Nov. 1848, at Parsonstown, King's County, Ireland, son of the late Major-General C. R. Egerton (Colonel, 89th P.V.O. Regt.); educated at Rossall and Sandhurst; entered the Army in 1867 as Ensign, 76th Foot. He married, in 1877, Anna Wellwood (died 1890), daughter of the late J. L. Hill, Esq., W.S., of Edinburgh, and their children were: Wion de Malpas, born in 1879 (is Captain, R.N., and D.S.O.); James Boswell, born in 1880 (killed in action 1918), and Charles Caledon, born in 1886 (killed in action 1915). He served during the Afghan War, 1879; was with General Sir F. Roberts, Bart., V.C., G.C.B., in his march from Kabul to Kandahar; Battle of Kandahar (Despatches, 3 Dec. 1880; Medal with clasp, Bronze Decoration); Mari Expedition, 1880; Black Mountain Expedition, 1888 (Despatches, Medal); 1st and 2nd Miranzai Expeditions; was severely wounded, mentioned in Despatches, and given the Brevet of Colonel, clasp, and created a Companion of the Distinguished Service Order [London Gazette, 30 May, 1891]: "Charles Comyn Egerton, Major, Indian Staff Corps, Assistant Adjutant-General, Punjab Frontier Force." (Insignia sent to Commander-in-Chief in India, and presented in India.) He served in the Waziristan Field Force, 1894–5, in command of a column (Despatches [London Gazette, 2 July, 1895], created a C.B. 1895, clasp); with the Dongola Expedition, commanded Indian Contingent (Despatches, British and Khedive's Medals, A.D.C. to H.M. Queen Victoria); commanded 1st Brigade, Tochi Force, 1897–8 (Despatches, 11 Feb. 1898, Medal with clasp); commanded Expeditions against Mahsud Waziris, 1900–2, and Darwesh Khel Waziris, 1902–3; commanded Somaliland Field Force, 1903–4; action of Jidballi (Medal, two clasps, created a K.C.B. 1903); and created a G.C.B. 1904; commanding troops in Madras, 1904–7; General 28 Oct. 1906; retired 5 Feb. 1907; is Colonel, Cavalry Frontier Force, India; Member of Council of India, 1907–17; Field-Marshal, March, 1917. Field-Marshal Sir C. C. Egerton has the Afghan Medal and clasp for Kandahar; the Indian Frontier Medal and three clasps; the Indian General Service Medal and two clasps; the Dongola Medal and Khedive's Medal; the Somaliland Medal and two clasps. He was four times mentioned in Despatches; awarded the D.S.O.; holds the Coronation Medal and the Jubilee Medal.

Charles Comyn Egerton.

The London Gazette of 2 Sept. 1904, published a series of Despatches relating to the operations in Somaliland, from 18 Jan. 1902, to 31 May, 1904. These give a full and exhaustive account of the fighting against the Mullah till the cessation of the operations in April, 1904. The reasons for bringing them to a close were set forth in a telegram from Major-General Egerton to the Secretary of State for War, dated 12 Aug. 1904. In part of this telegram General Egerton said: "Reports from both Fasken and Manning, as to the state of both troops and transport, confirm me in my opinion that further operations at this season are impossible. If the rain sets in in the Najal the withdrawal of the troops there will become an impossibility on account of the deep nature of the soil, as will also be the supplying of them in the present advanced position." After giving other reasons for the withdrawal, General Egerton goes on to describe how the power of the Mullah has been broken: "The Mullah has been outmanœuvred, and forced north. His military power was broken by the decisive defeat at Jidballi. Subsequent operations on the Najal have completed his rout, driven him out of the Protectorate and dispersed his followers. Large numbers in an indigent and demoralized condition have fled from the Protectorate to their own country. The Dolbahantas are scattered, and are at present without proper or tribal organization, and are to a large extent disorganized refugees among the Protectorate tribes. These have received a lesson that should teach them to avoid collision with us in future. The Mullah, with practically only his Aligheri following, is a discredited refugee in the Mijjarten territory, at the mercy of Osman Mahmud. His actual capture by the Field Force is under present conditions, in my opinion, impracticable. There is now no enemy in arms against us in the Protectorate. It is under these conditions that I advocate the cessation of operations, the reduction of the Field Force, and the early relief of the units required for the support of the civil administration, to enable it to take advantage of this present favourable state of affairs."

We give extracts from the obituary notices of those two out of Sir Charles Egerton's three gallant sons, who were killed in action in the Great War. The eldest and surviving son received a Letter of Commendation from the Admiralty on 30 June, 1915, and was subsequently awarded the D.S.O.

The "Times" of 23 April, 1915, says: "Lieut. Charles Caledon Egerton, Duke of Wellington's Regt., who fell on 18 April, aged 28 years, was the third and youngest son of General Sir Charles Egerton, G.C.B., D.S.O. He entered the Army in Aug. 1905; was promoted Lieutenant in 1908, and from Jan. 1911, to 1913, served as Adjutant of his regiment."

The "Times" of 15 Nov. 1918, says: "Major J. B. Egerton, Indian Cavalry, who was killed in action on 27 Oct., was the second son of Field-Marshal Sir Charles Egerton, and was born on 4 Nov. 1880. He was educated at Rossall and at the Royal Military College, Sandhurst, and received his first commission on 17 Jan. 1900, on the unattached list of the Indian Army. On arrival in India he was attached to the Somerset Light Infantry, and in 1901 he was posted to a regiment of Punjab Cavalry in the Indian Frontier Force. He served on the North-West Frontier of India in the Waziristan operations in 1901 and 1902, and in the operations against the Darwesh Khel Waziris of 1902 (Medal and clasp), and in East Africa in 1903–4, in operations in Somaliland, including the action of Jidballi; he was mentioned in Despatches and received the Medal and two clasps. He served in France during the autumn and winter of 1914–15, with a regiment of Hussars. In the summer of that year his own regiment, being ordered on service, he rejoined, and had served continuously with them up to the date of his death. He was mentioned in Despatches and received the Croix de Guerre. His younger brother, Lieut. C. C. Egerton, Duke of Wellington's Regt., was one of the original Expeditionary Force, and was killed in action at Hill 60 in April, 1915.

MANSEL, ALFRED, Capt., was born 5 Feb. 1852, son of the late Capt. W. H. Mansel; entered R.A. 12 Sept. 1872; served in Naga Expeditionary Force, 1879–80, in command of R.A.; was present at the storming of Khonoma (Despatches, Medal with clasp); Mahsud-Wuzeree Expedition, 1881, with Tank Column, and with Burma Expedition, 1886–7, in command of R.A., and was present at the advance on Nyaungwe (Despatches, two clasps); created a Companion of the Distinguished Service Order [London Gazette, 30 May 1891]: "Alfred Mansel, Capt., Royal Artillery." Insignia presented in India; became Lieutenant-Colonel, 15 July, 1898; Brevet Colonel 15 July, 1902; late commanding Northern Section, R.A., Plymouth; retired, with the rank of Colonel, 15 July, 1903. He died 7 July, 1918.

YEILDING, WILLIAM RICHARD, Capt., was born 13 Jan. 1856, at Carrig Kerry, Co. Limerick, son of the late Hugh Eldon and Margaret Yeilding, of Woodlands, Tarbert, Co. Kerry. He was educated at Rathmines School, Dublin; Ennis College, Co. Clare, and Mr. Mulcaster's, Woodwich, and joined the 54th Regt. 29 Nov. 1876, and was transferred to the B.S.C. (now Indian Army), 1879; served in the Afghan War, 1879–80, with the 1st Sikhs, and the 5th Gurkhas, at Jellalabad and Kabul; took part in the March from Kabul to Kandahar, and at the Battle of Kandahar (Medal with clasp and Bronze Star); with Mari Expedition, 1880; with Mahsud-Waziri Expedition 1881, and Hazara Campaign, 1888 (Black Mountain). He was mentioned in Despatches; G.G.O. 978 of 1888, states: "Capt. W. R. Yeilding, A.C.G., Divisional Transport Officer, who, under the orders of the Chief Commissariat Officer, ably superintended the transport arrangements of the Force. His powers of organization have been shown in the manner in which the large amount of Government and hired transport has been worked with complete success. I consider him a most excellent officer." Capt. Yeilding, who was several times in action during the Hazara Campaign, also received the Medal with clasp, and was created a Companion of the Distinguished Service Order [London Gazette, 30 May, 1891]: "William Richard Yeilding, Capt., Indian Staff Corps." He served in the Tirah Campaign and Bazar Valley Expedition, 1897–98 (India Medal with two clasps); Tirah, 1897–98, and Punjab Frontier, 1897–98 (mentioned in Despatches); with the Somaliland Field Force, 1903–4, on the Staff. In Tirah he was present at the storming of the Sampagha and Arhanga Passes and in the fighting round Bagh, and on the return march of the 1st Division to India via the Mastura Valley. The London Gazette of 3 Sept. 1904, publishes Lieut.-General Sir C. Egerton's Despatches for Somaliland, 1903–4 (extract): "One most satisfactory feature of the campaign has been the smooth and efficient working of the Staff and of all departments. The Supply and Transport Department has, doubtless, been the most severely taxed, but owing to the admirable organization of the transport, and the foresight and resource of the Director, it has proved equal to all emergencies. . . . Lieut.-Colonel W. R. Yeilding, C.I.E., D.S.O., is an officer of great force of character whom no difficulty dismays, or sudden change of plans can disconcert. His powers of organization are immense, and it is due to him that this Field Force has been able to maintain itself in the field so long." He received the African Medal with clasp, Somaliland, 1903–4, and was given the Brevet of Colonel. He was employed on special duty in Kashmir, 1892–97 (thanked by the Government of India, and by the Home Government, and created a C.I.E. 1895); held various administrative appointments in the Supply and Transport Corps; became a substantive Colonel in 1905; was created a C.B., 1908, and retired 1910. Is in receipt of a wound pension for an injury received on active service during the Somaliland Campaign, 1903–4. He married, 9 Dec. 1881, at Calcutta, Theresa, daughter of Richard Magrath Fitzgerald, of Limerick, and they had one daughter, Eileen Geraldine, who died in 1913.

William R. Yeilding.

BEECH, JOHN ROBERT, Capt., was born 2 July, 1860, 2nd son of the late James Dixon Beech, Esq., of Ballintemple, Co. Cork, and Susan, daughter of John Malone, of Co. Wexford. He was educated at Newton School, Waterford. When the Egyptian War broke out he was about 18 years old, and studying at the Edinburgh Veterinary College. He was expecting to become a land agent, and was making a study of animals and their diseases. He passed out top of all the students, gaining the Medal. Being eager to get to the front, he joined the Army as a Veterinary Surgeon, the only means of entrance available to him. He did much valuable work, buying horses and camels for the Government, and served through the Egyptian War and the Gordon Relief Expedition, and the Sudan, receiving the only seven-clasp Medal of that campaign, the clasps being: Toski, 1889; Gemaizah, 1888; Abu Klea, The Nile, 1884–85; El Teb, Tamaai, Suakin, 1884; Tel-el-Kebir. After the Gordon Relief Expedition he went with Sir Gerald Portal on a mission from Queen Victoria to King John of Abyssinia, and carried the Queen's letter alone to King John through a most difficult and hostile country, and was given the C.M.G. His D.S.O. he got after the Battle of Toski, instead of the V.C., for

John Robert Beech.

which he was recommended by two Generals. His Companionship of the Distinguished Service Order was gazetted 30 May, 1891: "John Robert Beech, Capt. (C.M.G.), 20th Hussars (attached to Egyptian Army)." The Insignia, Warrant, etc., were sent to the Governor of Egypt, and presented by him 7 Dec. 1891. For his services after the Gordon Relief Expedition, King Edward (then Prince of Wales) recommended him for a combatant commission, and he was gazetted as Lieutenant to the 21st Lancers, and almost immediately got seven years' promotion in one day, and was appointed to the 20th Hussars as Captain (1901). He served in the Egyptian Cavalry for many years, and on two occasions, when only 25 years of age, commanded them in most successful engagements against the Dervishes. At 28 he married, left the Egyptian Cavalry, and rejoined the 20th Hussars. The then Inspector-General of Cavalry, Sir Keith Fraser, singled him out for special mention when on manœuvres, saying before the whole Cavalry Division that it was a picture to see Capt. Beech at his work. Shortly after this (1894), he sent in his papers and entered the Reserve of Officers, but rejoined for the Boer War, serving on General French's Staff, and got the Queen's Medal with five clasps. In the Great War he was in command of a Regiment of Scottish Horse. In addition to the Egyptian and South African Medals, he had the Osmanieh, Medjidie and the Khedive's Star and clasp. On 1 Dec. 1894, he married Alexandria Marion, daughter of the late Kenneth Mackenzie, Esq., of Stornaway, and widow of John Bullough, of Meggerie Castle, Glen Lynn, Perthshire. Their sons are: Clyde, born 13 April, 1896 (Capt. Rifle Brigade, killed 18 Oct. 1916, aged 20); George, born 3 Feb. 1900; Alexander Frederic Charles, born 13 April, 1902, died 25 Oct. 1905; Graham, born 25 Dec. 1905, and Gerald, born 25 July, 1908. Lieut.-Colonel J. R. Beech, C.M.G., D.S.O., died a short time ago at Louth, Lincolnshire, from a chill caught in camp, whilst commanding the 2/1st Scottish Horse.

London Gazette, 19 Nov. 1891.—"War Office, 19 Nov. 1891. The Queen has further been pleased to give orders for the following appointments to the Distinguished Service Order, and Promotions in the Army, in recognition of the Services of the undermentioned Officers during the late Zhob, Hazara, Miranzai and Chin Hills Expeditions. To be Companions of the Distinguished Service Order."

HARVEY, ROBERT, Surgeon-Major, was born in 1842, son of the late Alexander Harvey, Esq., M.D., of Broomhill, Aberdeen. He entered the Bengal Medical Service, 1865; served with the Bhootan Expedition, 1865 (Medal with clasp); with the Lushai Expedition, 1871–2 (Despatches, clasp, etc.). He married, 1875, Ermine Josephine, daughter of Theodore Grimké-Drayton, Esq., of Ashley Grange and Charleton, South Carolina. He became Surgeon-Major, 1877; was promoted Brigade-Surgeon, 1888; served as P.M.O. with both Miranzai Expeditions (twice mentioned in Despatches, clasp); and created a Companion of the Distinguished Service Order [London Gazette, 19 Nov. 1891]: "In recognition of services during the late Miranzai Expedition. Robert Harvey, M.B., Indian Medical Service." Insignia sent to Commander-in-Chief in India; presentation in India 22 July, 1892. He became Deputy Surgeon-General, 1891; served with the Hazara Field Force, 1891 (clasp), and with Isazai Expedition, 1892, as P.M.O. (Despatches); formerly Inspector-General of Hospitals, Bengal; appointed P.M.O. to Punjab Forces, 1895; became Surgeon-Major-General, 1895; was a Fellow of the Calcutta University and of the Obstetrical Society. He was created a C.B. Surgeon-General R. Harvey died on 1 Dec. 1901, and an obituary notice of him appeared in the "Times" of the following day.

KEITH, JAMES, Lieut.-Colonel, was born 5 Nov. 1842, son of William Keith, M.D.; entered the R.A. 15 Dec. 1861; became Captain, 1875; served in Afghanistan, 1878–9 (Medal); became Major, 1881; was D.A.A.G., R.A., Bengal, 1882–87; served with Sikkim Expedition, 1888 (Despatches, Medal with clasp); became Lieutenant-Colonel 1 Sept. 1890; served with Hazara Expedition, 1891 (Despatches, clasp); created a Companion of the Distinguished Service Order [London Gazette, 19 Nov. 1891]: "In recognition of services during the late Hazara Expedition. James Keith, Lieut.-Colonel, Royal Artillery." Insignia, etc., sent to Commander-in-Chief in India; presented in India 22 July, 1892. Lieut.-Colonel Keith served with the Isazai Expedition in 1892; was put on retired pay 1 Sept. 1895.

RUNDALL, FRANK MONTAGU, Capt., was born 18 May, 1851, son of the late General F. H. Rundall, R.E., C.S.I. He was educated at Marlborough, and was gazetted to the 49th Foot, as Sub-Lieutenant, 9 March, 1872, becoming Lieutenant, 26 Nov. 1874, and Captain, Indian Staff Corps,

9 March, 1884. He served in the 49th (Royal Berkshire Regt.), 4th Bengal Infantry, 9th Bengal Infantry, 3rd Gurkha Rifles, and 4th Gurkha Rifles. Capt. Rundall was on the Staff of General Sir William Lockhart, in the Upper Burma Campaign, 28 Sept. 1886, to 2 Feb. 1887, and received the Medal and clasp. In 1889–90 he served in the Chin-Lushai Expedition, receiving a clasp. He became Officer Commanding the Chin Hills, and Political Officer, Fort White, and conducted operations against Kanbow, China, in 1891; received a clasp, and was created a Companion of the Distinguished Service Order [London Gazette, 19 Nov. 1891]: "Frank Montagu Rundall, Capt., Indian Staff Corps. For services in the Chin Hills." The Insignia were presented by the Queen at Osborne 10 Jan. 1893. He was promoted to Major 9 March, 1892. In 1891 he served in the Manipur Expedition, commanding in the action of Bapam. He was mentioned in Despatches [London Gazette, 14 Aug. 1891], and received a clasp. He again saw active service in the Waziristan Expedition, 1894–95, and received a clasp. Capt. Rundall was promoted to Lieutenant-Colonel 9 March, 1898. He served with the China Field Force, 1900–01 (Medal). He was created a C.B. 1901; became Colonel, and was put on the Supernumerary Employed List, Indian Army. He commands Group A, City of London Volunteer Regt. Colonel Rundall has published a Manual of the Chin Language. He married, in 1876, Emily Rosa, daughter of the Right Rev. E. H. Bickersteith and they have two sons and two daughters.

MASON, ALEXANDER HERBERT, Capt., was born in 1856, son of the late Martin Mason; entered the R.E. 1874; served during Afghan War, 1878–9–80 (Medal); with Nile Expedition, 1884–85, and in the operations on the Upper Nile in 1885–86 (Medal and Khedive's Star); with Hazara Expedition, 1888, as D.A.Q.M.G. for Intelligence (Despatches, Medal with clasp); with Zhob Field Force, 1890, under Sir George White, as D.A.Q.M.G. for Intelligence (Despatches, clasp). He served with the second Miranzai Expedition in 1891; was mentioned in Despatches and received a clasp, and was created a Companion of the Distinguished Service Order [London Gazette, 19 Nov. 1891]: "In recognition of services during the late Zhob and Hazara Expeditions. Alexander Herbert Mason, Capt., Royal Engineers." Insignia presented at Chatham by Lieut.-General Grant, 18 May, 1892. Capt. Mason served with the Isazai Expedition, 1892, as D.A.Q.M.G. (Intelligence); was present at the action at Wana, 1894 (Despatches, created a C.B. 1895, clasp). Capt. Mason married, 1893, Eva, daughter of General Sir Robert Biddulph, C.B., G.C.M.G. Lieut.-Colonel Mason died 8 May, 1896.

MACONCHY, ERNEST WILLIAM STUART KING, Lieut., was born 18 June, 1860, son of the late George Maconchy, of Rathmore, Co. Longford, and Louisa, daughter of Solomon Richards, of Ardamine, Co. Wexford;

E. W. S. K. Maconchy.

entered the Army, 1882; served with the Hazara Expedition, 1888 (Medal with clasp); He served in Hazara, 1891 (wounded, Despatches, clasp, D.S.O.). The following is an entry from the Despatches on the Hazara Expedition, 1891: Despatch by Major-General W. K. Elles, C.B.: "I now beg to bring to the notice of His Excellency the good service of Lieut. Maconchy, who arrived on the scene at a critical moment and was himself wounded." (G.G.O. No. 816, paragraph 6; dated 28 Aug. 1891.) This is part of the account of the action at Ghazikot, when Lieut. Maconchy's detachment of 60 men was charged at night by 400 fanatics. Lieut. Maconchy was created a Companion of the Distinguished Service Order [London Gazette, 19 Nov. 1891]: "In recognition of services during the late Hazara Expedition. Ernest William Stuart King Maconchy, Lieut., Indian Staff Corps." Insignia sent to the C.-in-C. in India; presented 6 May, 1892. Served Isazai Exp. 1892: Chitral Relief Force, 1895 (Medal with clasp). Capt. Maconchy married, 1895, Caroline Agnes, daughter of Alexander H. Campbell, J.P., D.L., of 8, Cornwall Gardens, S.W., and they have one son and one daughter. He served on the North-West Frontier of India, 1897–98 (Despatches, Brevet of Major, 1898, three clasps). He served in Waziristan in 1901 (clasp). In the Waziristan Expedition, 1901, the following telegram was received by the G.O.C.: Telegram from Adjutant-General in India, No. 528.9A of 31 Dec. 1901: "The C.-in-C. has heard with much satisfaction of the gallant behaviour of Major Maconchy, D.S.O. and ——, who, by their promptness at a trying moment probably saved much loss of life." Major, 1901; A.Q.M.G., Intelligence, India, 1903; Lieutenant-Colonel, 1904; commanding 51st Sikhs, Frontier Force, 1904; Secretary, Government of India, Department of Military Supply, 1906–9; Colonel, 11 June, 1907; Deputy Secretary, Army Department, Government of India, 1909–12; created a C.I.E. 1909; created a C.B. 1911; retired 28 Jan. 1914; commanding 178th Brigade, Sherwood Foresters, 1915. Brigadier-General E. W. S. K. Maconchy was created a C.M.G. in 1917.

HARMAN, RICHARD, Lieut., was born 22 Sept. 1864, 3rd son of the late Rev. Edward Harman, Rector of Pickwell, Oakham, and Louisa, his wife. He was educated at Uppingham School, and at Emmanuel College, Cambridge; entered the Oxfordshire Light Infantry in 1886; became Lieutenant in 4th (afterwards 54th)

Richard Harman.

Sikhs (Frontier Force) in 1888 ; served with Hazara Field Force, 1891 (wounded, mentioned in Despatches) ; created a Companion of the Distinguished Service Order [London Gazette, 19 Nov. 1891] : " In recognition of services during the recent Hazara Expeditions. Richard Harman, Lieut., Indian Staff Corps." Insignia sent to Commander-in-Chief in India ; presentation in India 7 Dec. 1892. Present with the Chitral Relief Force in 1895 at the action of the Malakand Pass (wounded and mentioned in Despatches). Captain and Brevet Major. N. W. F. 1897-8 : action of Landakai, 1897. Appointed Commandant of the South Waziristan Militia, May, 1900. Brevet Lieutenant-Colonel, 1902. While holding this command he was killed at Wana by a fanatical Mahsud Sepoy on 12 Feb. 1905.

London Gazette, 18 March, 1892.—" War Office, 18 March, 1892. The Queen has been graciously pleased to give orders for the following appointments to the Distinguished Service Order, in recognition of the services of the undermentioned Officers during the operations against the Lun Saing Tonhon Kachins, and in the Wuntho District, Upper Burma. To be a Companion of the Distinguished Service Order."

HALE, GEORGE ERNEST, Surgeon, was born 13 June, 1861, at Eastbourne, son of George Wills Hale (M.A. Cambridge), of Glenwood, Paignton, and Elizabeth Jane Hale, daughter of —— Edwards, Esq., of

George Ernest Hale.

Cambridge. He was educated at Cheltenham College ; is M.R.C.S. England and L.R.C.P. Edinburgh. He joined the Army on 31 Jan. 1885. He served with the Sudan Frontier Force, 1885–86, and was present at the action of Ginnis (Medal and Khedive's Star) ; in Burma, 1889–91 ; received the Medal and two clasps, and was mentioned in Despatches, for the Pounkham Expedition, 1889 ; for the Tonhon Expedition was recommended for a V.C., but received the thanks of the Government instead. No military rewards were given for this expedition. In the Wuntho Expedition, the following winter, 1891, he was mentioned in Despatches for special gallantry on the Field, received two clasps, and was created a Companion of the Distinguished Service Order [London Gazette, 18 March, 1892] : " In recognition of services against the Lun Saing Tonhon Kachins, and in the Wuntho District, Upper Burma. George Ernest Hale, Surgeon, Medical Staff." The Insignia, Warrant and Statutes were sent to the Commander-in-Chief in India, and presented by him 26 Oct. 1892. Promoted to Surgeon-Major in 1897, he served in South Africa, 1900–02, as O.C., Imperial Yeomanry Bearer Company, and Senior Medical Officer, General Mahon's Column (mentioned in Lord Roberts's Despatches) ; later as O.C., 23rd Bearer Company, and S.M.O., Colonel Sitwell's Column (Queen's Medal with three clasps, King's Medal with two clasps). On 17 Dec. 1902, he married, firstly, Kathleen (died 1904), youngest daughter of Dr. Wadd, of Richmond. In 1908 he was appointed Honorary Surgeon to the Viceroy of India. The Gazette was worded : " For special gallantry in the field in South Africa." He married, secondly, in 1908, Lucy Fead, youngest daughter of the late Capt. W. Scott, R.A., granddaughter of the late Lieut.-Colonel G. Fead, C.B., Grenadier Guards. Lieut.-Colonel G. E. Hale retired from the Royal Army Medical Corps in 1912. He was re-employed 7 June, 1915, and joined the British Expeditionary Field Force as O.C., 45th Brigade, 15th Scottish Division, and was present at the Battle of Loos. Lieut.-Colonel G. E. Hale is fond of big game shooting, which was his special sport in India ; nine tigers fell to his rifle ; also buffalo, bear, leopard, samber, etc. He also shot small game. He holds many cups for bicycle-racing, fencing, putting the shot, rowing and shooting. He still continues fly-fishing and boating, also shooting.

KEARY, HENRY D'URBAN, Capt., was born 28 April, 1857, at Holkham, Norfolk, son of the late Hall William Keary, of Bridgenorth, Shropshire, and Helen D'Urban Keary, daughter of the late Lionel Rodwell, of Staithe

Henry D'Urban Keary.

House, Brancaster, Norfolk. He was educated at Marlborough, and joined the Army as Sub-Lieutenant (unattached), 10 Sept. 1875 ; became Second Lieutenant, 12th Foot, 29 Aug. 1876 ; Lieutenant, Army, 10 Sept. 1877 ; was appointed to the Madras Staff Corps 7 May, 1877, and proceeded to India. He served with the 1st Madras Infantry, 1876–77, and with it took part in the Afghan War, 1879–80 (Afghan Medal) ; served with the Madras Pioneers, 1883–85 ; through the Burma Campaign, and subsequent annexation, to the end of the operations, 1885–7 and 1887–89 (Despatches, Frontier Medal with four clasps) : raised and commanded a Military Police Battalion, 1887–92 (clasp) ; became Captain, Indian Staff Corps, 10 Sept. 1888 ; commanded a Company of Mounted Infantry during the rebellion of the Wuntho State, 1891–92–93 ; received a clasp, and was mentioned in Despatches for the action near Kawbei. Sir G. Wolseley writes : " I desire to bring prominently to notice the brilliant services of Capt. H. d'U. Keary. I consider that the advancement of this Officer would be of benefit to the Service. The spirit of dash and confidence

inspired by his presence at Kawbei and the prompt manner in which he grappled with the situation and turned the hitherto needlessly cautious state of defence into one of vigorous and determined attack, is worthy of special acknowledgment." Sir James Downes writes : " Capt. Keary of the Military Police seems to be an officer of great intrepidity and decision for at a critical moment he assumed—with a position of his Mounted Infantry—the rôle of Cavalry, and dispersed the enemy, who were attacking Kawbei on three sides." (G.G.O. No. 985, dated 16 Oct. 1891.) Capt. Keary was created a Companion of the Distinguished Service Order [London Gazette, 18 March, 1892] : " In recognition of services during the operations in the Wuntho District, Upper Burma. Henry D'Urban Keary, Capt., Indian Staff Corps." Insignia, Warrant, etc., sent to the Commander-in-Chief in India 7 July, 1892, and presented by him 26 Oct. 1892. Sir Henry Keary commanded the 91st Punjabs from 1892 to 1909, and is Colonel of the Regiment. He served in the Rebellion of the Northern Chin Hills, 1892–93, and was given the Brevet of Major 29 Dec. 1893, and mentioned in Despatches. He became Major, Indian Army, 10 Sept. 1897. Major Keary served in China, 1900–1902 (China Medal, Despatches, [London Gazette, 14 May, 1901]). He became Lieutenant-Colonel 10 Sept. 1903. He was given the Brevet of Colonel 10 Sept. 1906 ; was A.D.C. to H.M. the King 2 Sept. 1907, to 30 Nov. 1911 ; became Colonel 20 Jan. 1910, and commanded the 2nd Infantry Brigade, Secunderabad, 1909–10 ; was Brigade Commander (Colonel on Staff, India), 20 Jan. 1910, to 13 Nov. 1911 ; was promoted Major-General 1 Dec. 1911 ; was Brigade Commander, India, 14 Nov. 1911, to 12 Oct. 1914 ; Brigade Commander, Garhwal Brigade, B.E.F., 13 Oct. 1914, to 7 Jan. 1915 ; promoted Lieutenant-General 1 Aug. 1917 ; was Divisional Commander, Lahore Division, B.E.F. ; Mesopotamian Expeditionary Force, 8 Jan. 1915, to 1917 ; Divisional Commander, India, 16 Oct. 1917, to 12 Aug. 1918 ; Divisional Commander, India, 13 Aug. 1918. He was created a K.C.I.E. in 1917, and is Colonel, 91st Punjabs.

The Garhwal Brigade consisted of the 2nd Battn. Leicestershire Regt., the 2nd Battn. 3rd Queen Alexandra's Own Gurkha Rifles, the 1st Battn. 39th Garhwal Rifles, and the 2nd Battn. 39th Garhwal Rifles.

After the Battle of Givenchy the Corps Commander showed his appreciation of the work done by the following message to the Division : " I congratulate you on the good work done last night, which shows what can be done by enterprise and care. Please send my hearty congratulations to Major-General Keary, the Leicesters, and the 2/3rd Gurkhas, for their gallant behaviour."

On the 7th May, 1915, a letter was received from General Smith-Dorrien, from which we give an extract : " Having read the very complete and excellent report on the work of the Lahore Division in the heavy fighting near Ypres, on the 26th and 27th April, 1915, the Commander of the 2nd Army is confirmed in the views he formed at the time, that the Division had been handled with great skill and determination by Major-General Keary."

From the 28th April till its departure on the 3rd May, the Division was under the orders of Lieut.-General Sir Herbert Plumer, commanding Plumer's Force.

On the 2nd May, Sir Herbert Plumer wrote as under to General Keary : " Will you please convey to the Brigadiers, Commanding Officers, and all Officers, Non-commissioned Officers and men of your Division, my thanks for the assistance they have rendered in the recent severe fighting, and my appreciation of the way in which they have carried out the very arduous duties entrusted to them while under my command. I deeply regret the very heavy casualties they have suffered."

General Sir James Willcocks sent the following message to General Keary : " Please convey to all ranks of Division my own and all their other comrades' best congratulations on having taken part in the battle near Ypres. We are proud of you all. Well done."

We are told in " The Indian Corps in France " (page 288) that during the Second Battle of Ypres, " When General Keary moved up to his advanced headquarters near St. Jean, he found the road strewn with corpses and dead animals. He himself had a narrow escape, for a shell, bursting in close proximity to his car, blew his kit off the roof, but luckily did no more serious damage."

On the 31st July, 1906, at St. James's Church, Piccadilly, London, W., he married Mabel Louisa Lloyd, daughter of the late Colonel Malcolm Lloyd, Deputy Commissioner, Burma.

London Gazette, 12 July, 1892.—" War Office, 12 July, 1892. The Queen has further been pleased to give orders for the following appointment to the Distinguished Service Order, and promotion in the Army, in recognition of the services of the undermentioned Officer during the recent operations in Hunza and Nagar. To be Companion of the Distinguished Service Order."

BADCOCK, FRANCIS FREDERICK, Lieut., was born 13 Sept. 1867, son of General Sir A. R. Badcock ; educated at Wellington College ; entered the Wiltshire Regt. 25 Aug. 1886, and became Lieutenant, I.S.C., 1887 ; served with Hazara Expedition, 1891 (clasp, Despatches) ; Miranzai Expedition 1891 (clasp) ; Hunza and Nagar Expedition, 1891 (severely wounded ; mentioned in Despatches ; created a Companion of the Distinguished Service Order [London Gazette, 12 July, 1892] : " In recognition of his gallant conduct at the capture of the Nilt Fort. Francis Frederick Badcock, Lieut., I.S.C." ; received by Lieut. Badcock through the India Office). He served with Waziristan Expedition, 1894–5 (clasp) ; Tirah Expeditionary Force (severely wounded, Medal with three clasps) ; North-West Frontier of India, Zakka Khel Expedition (Medal with clasp). He married, in 1896, Eleanor Sara Austen, daughter of the late Rev. G. F. de Gex, and has one son and one daughter. He was promoted Captain 25 Aug. 1897 ; Major 25 Aug. 1904 ; Lieutenant-Colonel 11 July, 1912. Lieut.-Colonel Badcock became Commandant of the 2nd Battn. 6th Gurkha Rifles.

London Gazette, 9 Aug. 1892.—" The Queen has been graciously pleased to give orders for the following appointments to the Distinguished Service Order, in recognition of the services of the undermentioned Officers during the recent operations on the West Coast of Africa resulting in the capture of Tambi and Toniataba."

NORRIS, RICHARD JOSEPH, Capt., was born 27 Feb. 1854, youngest son of the late Edward Norris, who was a grandson of Jeremiah Norris, Colney Hall, Norwich, descended from a branch of the Norris family of Speke, Lancashire. He was educated at Mount St. Mary's, Derbyshire ; Beaumont College, Old Windsor, and at Sandhurst, and joined the 1st West India Regt. 19 Feb. 1879, as Second Lieutenant, becoming Lieutenant 1 Dec. 1880, and Captain 29 Jan. 1888. He served in the operations in the Tambaku country, West Africa, 1892, being present at the capture of Tambi ; was mentioned in Despatches, and created a Companion of the Distinguished Service Order [London Gazette, 9 Aug. 1892] : " Richard Joseph Norris, Capt., West India Regt. For services in West Africa." He became

Richard Joseph Norris.

Major 1 April, 1894, and commanded the Karene Expedition (first phase), 1898, and Lieutenant-Colonel 27 March, 1902, and retired 5 July, 1905. During the European War Lieut.-Colonel Norris served as Draft Conducting Officer, 1915–1916. He married, in 1894, Beatrice Marion, daughter of His Excellency the late Arthur van de Velde, Belgian Minister Resident, and Mme. Van de Velde, of 109, Lancaster Gate, W., and they have one daughter, Marion Beatrice Catharine.

MERRIMAN, REGINALD GORDON, Lieut. was born 10 Nov. 1866, at Aden, son of General Charles James Merriman, C.S.I., Royal Engineers (late Bombay Engineers), and Eugenia Sybilla, daughter of Colonel Richard Bulkeley, Indian Army. He was educated at the United Services College, Westward Ho ! North Devon, and at the Royal Military Academy, Woolwich (Tombs Memorial Scholar, 1884). He joined the Royal Artillery 9 Dec. 1884, and served in the Expedition to the Tambaku Country, West Africa, 1892, and was decorated for his services in this Expedition, particularly in the capture of Tambi. He received the West African Medal with clasp, and was created a Companion of the Distinguished Service Order [London Gazette, 9 Aug. 1892] : " In recognition of his services during the recent operations on the West Coast of Africa, resulting in the capture of Tambi and Toniataba. Reginald Gordon Merriman, Lieut., Royal Artillery." The Insignia were presented by the Queen at Osborne 10 Jan. 1893. He was promoted Captain 31 Dec. 1893, and Major 9 Dec. 1903. On 13 Nov. 1894, at Ickham, near Canterbury, Kent, he married Mary Gertrude Rose, 2nd daughter of the late S. Gregson Fell, Esq., J.P., of Ickham Hall, Ickham, Kent. Capt. Merriman was Adjutant of the Kent Artillery, E.D.R.A., 1895–99 ; Recruiting Staff Officer, London (temporary), 1899–1900 ; D.A.A.G. for Auxiliary Forces, H.Q., 1900–02 ; D.A.A.G. Woolwich District, 1902–3 ; became Lieutenant-Colonel 29 Jan. 1913. Lieut.-Colonel Merriman served in France from Aug. 1916, to Jan. 1917, with the Siege Artillery.

London Gazette, 30 Sept. 1892.—" War Office, 30 Sept. 1892. The Queen has been graciously pleased to give orders for the following appointment to the Distinguished Service Order, and promotion in the Army, in recognition of the services of the undermentioned Officer during the recent expedition against the Jebus. To be a Companion of the Distinguished Service Order."

MADDEN, GEORGE COLQUHOUN, Major, was born 9 Feb. 1856, at Brighton, son of Henry Riderwood Madden, M.P., and Helen Madden (*née* Cowan). He won the Dux Medal while a boy at school in Edinburgh. Entered the Army in 1875 ; was promoted Captain in 1877 ; served against the Jebus and Sofas, West Coast of Africa, 1892. " During the attack on the town of Toniataba, Major G. C. Madden, West India Regt., who was in command of the troops, was superintending a party of twelve men who were endeavouring with a heavy beam to break down the south gate of the town, when suddenly a number of musket muzzles were projected through a double row of loopholes which had been masked. Some of these were within two or three yards of that officer's back, and before he realized what had happened, L.-Corpl. Gordon threw himself between Major Madden and the muskets, pushing that officer out of the way, and exclaiming, ' Look out, sir ! ' At the same moment L.-Corpl. Gordon was shot through the lungs. By his bravery and self-devotion on this occasion, the L.-Corpl. probably saved the life of his commanding officer." The above is the description (taken from the London Gazette of 9 Dec. 1892) of how L.-Corpl. W. J. Gordon (the first coloured man to be given the Victoria Cross) won his decoration. In the same year Major Madden accompanied the Expedition against the Jebus, Lagos, when he was mentioned in Despatches, received the Medal and clasp, and was created a Companion of the Distinguished Service Order [London Gazette 30 Sept. 1892] : " For his services during the recent operations against the Jebus. George Colquhoun Madden, Major, West India Regt." Presentation by the Governor of Sierra Leone 2 Jan. 1903. Two years later there was another expedition to the Gambia, against Fodey Silah, when Major Madden was again mentioned in Despatches, received a clasp, and was created a C.B. Lieut.-Colonel Madden was placed on half-pay in 1895, and three years later retired from the Army. He was an athlete and won several cups for running and jumping. He died at 51, Gunterstone Road, West Kensington, W., on 20 April, 1912.

London Gazette, 1 Nov. 1892.—" War Office, 1 Nov. 1892. The Queen has been graciously pleased to give orders for the following appointments to the Distinguished Service Order, in recognition of the services of the undermentioned Officers during the recent operations in connection with the defence of Sadon. To be Companions of the Distinguished Service Order."

HARRISON-TOPHAM, THOMAS, Capt., was born at Old Charlton, Kent, 21 May, 1864, second son of the late Capt. T. A. J. Harrison, R.A. He was educated at Wellington College, and at the Royal Military Academy, Woolwich, and joined the Royal Engineers 15 Feb. 1884. He married, in 1888, Muriel, eldest daughter of the Ven. A. F. Clarke, Archdeacon of Lancaster. He served in the Expedition to Northern Chin Hills, Burma, 1890–91, and with the Irrawaddy Column, Upper Burma, 1891–92. He received the Medal and clasp and was created a Companion of the Distinguished Service Order [London Gazette, 1 Nov. 1892] : " Thomas Harrison (now Harrison-Topham), Capt., Royal Engineers. For services in the defence of Sadon." Insignia presented in India by G.O.C., Burma, on 27 Jan. 1893. He was decorated for the defence of Sadon, Kachin Hills. He became Major 2 Aug. 1900, and retired 18 Oct. 1905. He became temporary Lieut.-Colonel in 1915. Lieut.-Colonel Harrison-Topham's favourite recreations are shooting and boating.

MACMUNN, GEORGE FLETCHER, Lieut., was born 14 Aug. 1869, eldest son of J. A. MacMunn, M.D., late Surgeon, R.A., and P.M.O., Chelsea Hospital, and Charlotte Edith, daughter of the Rev. George Mathias, Chaplain Royal. He was educated at Kensington Grammar School ; is Gold Medallist, R.A. Institution ; Gold Medallist, U.S. Institution, India, 1904 ; passed the Staff College, 1903. He entered the Royal Artillery 27 July, 1888 ; became Lieutenant 27 July, 1891, and Capt. 5 Dec. 1898 ; Major 1 April, 1904 ; was Temporary Brigadier-General 23 Nov. 1915, to 27 March, 1916 ; Temporary Major-General 16 April to 31 Dec. 1916 ; was promoted to Major-General 1 Jan. 1917. He was Station Staff officer, South Africa, 1 April to 2 May, 1900 ; A.P.M., South Africa, 27 May to 12 Sept. 1900 ; D.A.A.G., South

George F. MacMunn.

Africa, 11 April to 24 Sept. 1902 ; D.A.A.G., India, 1 Nov. 1904 to 22 April, 1908 ; D.A.Q.M.G., Headquarters, India, 23 April to 31 Oct. 1908 ; D.A.D. of Remounts, War Office, 20 June, 1914, to 6 July, 1915 ; A.Q.M.G., Lines of Communication, Mediterranean Expeditionary Force, 7 July to 22 Nov. 1915 ; D.A. and Q.M.G., Dardanelles Army, Mediterranean Expeditionary Force, 29 Nov. 1915, to 17 Jan. 1916 ; D.A. and Q.M.G., 15th Army Corps, Mediterranean Expeditionary Force, 18 Jan. to 27 March, 1916 ; Inspector-General of Communications, Indian Expeditionary Force " D," Mesopotamian Expeditionary Force, 16 April, 1916. He served in Burma, 1892, during the operations of Irrawaddy Column ; at the defence of Sadon (slightly wounded ; horse wounded ; mentioned in Despatches ; Medal with clasp). He was created a Companion of the Distinguished Service Order [London Gazette, 1 Nov. 1892] : " George Fletcher MacMunn, Lieut., Royal Artillery. For services during the recent operations in connection with the defence of Sadon." He served in Burma, 1893, during the operations in Kachin Hills (clasp) ; took part in the operations on North-West Frontier of India, 1897–98, during the operations on the Samana and in the Kurram Valley, with Jaypur Transport Corps as Staff Officer ; also with Tirah Expeditionary Force, in command of a mountain battery (Medal with three clasps) ; served in the South African War, 1899–1902, on Staff ; took part in the advance on Kimberley ; took part in the operations in the Orange Free State, Feb. to May, 1900 ; in the Transvaal in May and June, 1900 ; in the Transvaal, west of Pretoria, July to 29 Nov. 1900 ; in Orange River Colony, May to 29 Nov. 1900 ; also in Cape Colony, north of Orange River ; again in the Transvaal, March to April, 1901,and April to 31 May, 1902 ; in Orange River Colony, Dec. 1900, and April, 1901, to April, 1902 ; also during the operations in Cape Colony, Dec. 1900, to March. 1901 (Despatches [London Gazette, 7 May and 10 Sept. 1901] ; Brevet of Major 29 Nov. 1900 ; Queen's Medal with three clasps, and King's Medal with two clasps) ; placed on the list of Officers considered qualified for Staff employment, in consequence of services on the Staff in the field. He was given the Brevet of Lieutenant-Colonel 10 May, 1913. For his services in the European War at the Dardanelles and in Mesopotamia, 1914–18, he was 12 times mentioned in Despatches ; was given the Brevet of Colonel 1 April, 1915 ; promoted to Major-General ; created a C.B. in 1916 ; a C.S.I. in 1918 ; a K.C.B. in 1917, and a K.C.S.I. in 1919 ; was made Officier, Legion of Honour.

In " The Life of Sir Stanley Maude " (page 238), Sir C. E. Callwell says : " The important post of Inspector-General of Communications was in the hands of Major-General G. F. MacMunn, with whom Maude had had frequent dealings while in the Gallipoli Peninsula and while in Egypt, as he had then held a high position on the line of communications in the Eastern campaign." Again on page 251 : " The Army Commander felt sure that, with General MacMunn as Inspector-General of Communications, and with ample reserves of everything actually in the country, the flow of personnel and material from the base up to the front, as required, was assured." On page 268, in the chapter on the Campaign of Baghdad, General Callwell says : " The Army Commander was intent upon giving the enemy no rest, but . . . he had been compelled to stay the forward movement for fear of entirely outrunning his supplies. The Staff had found some difficulty in persuading him of the need for this pause, but the arrival of General MacMunn with a flotilla of vessels crammed with food and stores as soon as navigation was safe, and his representations as to the imperative need of getting these forward before a fresh rush to the front was undertaken, decided the matter. The Inspector-General of Communications went aboard the steamer on which Maude, with Army Headquarters, was on the point of moving upstream. The Staff feared that further advance was for the moment premature, and they urged General MacMunn to make representations. ' I was literally pushed into his curtained-off space,' is General MacMunn's account of what followed. ' He said, " How are supplies ? " I said, " Coming on well, but it is two miles of river for every one mile by land, and I can't feed you and supply ammunition if you move another yard yet." He looked at me quizzically, and asked, " When may they start ? " So I said, " Not before the 5th," when all he remarked was ' Right.' By that time we had the show in hand. You see, I had received no warning of his proposed push for Baghdad.' " On page 302 Sir Charles Callwell says : " Sir George MacMunn, who had played so important a part in rendering possible the brilliant campaign carried out by the Army Commander, and who assumed command on the return home of Sir W. Marshall, sends the following account, dated the 17th July, 1919, of the relations that existed between them, and of what Maude accomplished during his period of service in Mesopotamia : ' I write this note on our late chief from his quarters in Baghdad (where died also Von der Goltz), and from the room in which he died, in which I work in some hope that his hand may rest on my shoulder. I first met Maude at the War Office in those strenuous years of preparation before the war. We next met in Gallipoli, where I had official dealings with him as Commander of the 13th Division. But we first came really together when, one of the last to leave Suvla Bay, he landed on peaceful Imbros, to find his tired men drawing hot Maconochie rations as they stepped off their lighters. That gift of the old officer, care and thought for his men, lay very deep within him. In Egypt I helped to equip his division for Mesopotamia, following him thither shortly afterwards as Inspector-General of Communications. In May, 1916, just after the fall of Kut, I found him at Sheikh Saad on the Tigris, once again re-forming that division that had been so often battle-swept, and we talked far into the night of how to maintain the army in health and efficiency in an undeveloped land of great extremes. It was not, however, until Sept. 1916, when he had succeeded to the command of the army, and I was constantly thrown with him, that I came to appreciate and to understand the determination, the vision, and the knowledge of principle and detail that animated him. Few knew how anxious were his days from the advance beyond Kut to the last days in 1917. The army hung by a thread, and the enemy attempts to expel us were considerable ; but maintenance was his chief anxiety in my interviews with him during and after the advance, and at times he would wire to me twice or thrice a day. It was this strain on mind and body, continued through a long and abnormally hot summer, that left him little strength when the trial came. Efficiency and thoroughness had been his watchword, and he died at the height of his achievement.' "

Sir G. F. MacMunn has published " The Armies of India," in 1911 ; " Pike and Carronade," in 1912 ; " A Free Lance in Kashmir : A Tale of the Great Anarchy," in 1914. He married, in 1893, Alice Emily, eldest daughter of Colonel J. R. Watson, I.S.C., and they have one son and one daughter.

London Gazette, 10 Jan. 1893.—" The Queen has been graciously pleased to give orders for the following appointments to the Distinguished Service Order, in recognition of the services of the undermentioned Officers during the recent operations on the West Coast of Africa, resulting in the capture of Tambi and Toniataba. To be Companions of the Distinguished Service Order."

ROYLE, HENRY LUCIUS FANSHAWE, Capt., R.N., was born 26 March, 1849, son of the late Peter Royle, M.P., of Vernon Lodge, Brooklands, near Manchester. He was educated privately, and entered the Royal Navy in 1862, and became Lieutenant 1872. He married, in 1879, Anna Mary, daughter of the late Capt. Joseph Hind, 104th Bengal Fusiliers, of Greatwood, Mylor, Cornwall, and they had one son and one daughter. He served during the Egyptian War of 1882 (Medal and Bronze Star) ; became Commander, 1887, and Captain, 1892. He was in command of a punitive Expedition on the River Gambia, West Coast of Africa, 1892 (Medal). He was created a Companion of the Distinguished Service Order [London Gazette, 10 Jan. 1893] : " For services on the West Coast of Africa, resulting in the capture of Tambi and Toniataba, 1891 and 1892. Henry Lucius Fanshawe Royle, Capt., Royal Navy." Decoration, Warrant and Statutes sent to the Admiralty for presentation. Presentation reported by the Admiralty 27 June, 1893. He commanded H.M. Fleet Reserve at Portsmouth, and retired as Rear-Admiral in 1905, and died on 13 June, 1906.

FRASER, IAN MACKENZIE, Capt., Royal Navy, was born 15 Nov. 1854, at Dundee, eldest son of the late Capt. Ian Fraser, 93rd Sutherland Highlanders, of Whitehill, County of Fife, and Charlotte, daughter of the late John Mackenzie, of Ness House, Inverness. He was educated at a private school, and joined the Royal Navy on 25 Aug. 1868 ; became Lieutenant, 1879. He married, 7 Dec. 1887, Effie, daughter of William P. Edwards, J.P., of 17, Belgrave Crescent, Edinburgh, and Broadwell, Perth. He served in command of H.M.S. Sparrow, and was Second in Command of Naval Brigade at night attack on Fodey Kabba, at Marigé, Gambia, 1891 (highly mentioned in Despatches), received the thanks of the Governor of Gambia, specially commended by him to the Secretary of State for the Colonies) ;

Ian Mackenzie Fraser.

was in command of H.M.S. Sparrow with Gambia Expedition, 1892, resulting in the capture of Tambi and Toniataba (Medal with clasp ; created a Companion of the Distinguished Service Order [London Gazette, 10 Jan. 1893] : " In recognition of his services in the recent operations on the West Coast of Africa. Ian Mackenzie Fraser, Lieut., Royal Navy." Decoration, Warrant and Statutes sent to Admiralty for presentation ; presentation reported by the Admiralty 27 June, 1893). He became Commander in 1893 ; Captain (retired). Appointed Divisional Coast Watch Officer and Competent Naval Authority for Coastal Area, Llanrhystyd (Wales) to Solway Firth, 21 July, 1915.

WILKIN, HENRY DOUGLAS, Lieut., Royal Navy, was born at Umbala, India, 27 March, 1862, only son of the late Major H. J. Wilkin, 11th and 7th Hussars. He was educated at Eastman's Preparatory School, and on H.M.S. Britannia ; was Midshipman on

Henry Douglas Wilkin.

H.M.S. Superb at bombardment of Alexandria, 1882, and during Egyptian War : landed with Naval Brigade during operations of Alexandria and Ramleh (Egyptian Medal, Alexandria clasp and Khedive's Star) ; Lieutenant-Commander of Widgeon during Gambia River Expedition, Vintang Creek, 1891–2 ; landed with Naval Brigade : First Lieutenant of Racer during second Gambia River Expedition, 1892 ; landed in command of Naval Brigade from H.M. Ships Racer, Sparrow and Alecto, in conjunction with 1st Battn. West India Regt., resulting in the storming and capture of Fort Toniataba (Despatches, West African Medal ; clasp ; created a Companion of the Distinguished Service Order [London Gazette, 10 Jan. 1893] : " In recognition of his services in the recent operations on the West Coast of Africa, resulting in the capture of Tambi and Toniataba. Henry Douglas Wilkin, Royal Navy." Decoration, Warrant and Statutes sent to Admiralty ; presentation reported by Admiralty 27 June, 1893). He commanded H.M.S. Sparrow during the South African War ; when in command of H.M.S. Otter, rescued crew of H.M.S. Sandpiper in a typhoon at Hong-Kong (promoted Commander) ; received Bronze Medal, Royal Humane Society, for jumping overboard and assisting to save a marine, the place being infested with sharks, 1885 ; while in command of H.M.S. Clio, received the thanks of the Admiralty and Colonial Office for work done in connection with Tongan Islands, 1904-5 ; landed with British Naval Brigade at Shanghai, Dec. 1905, for suppression of riots at Shanghai. He married, in 1913, Elfrida, younger daughter of the late Egbert Iveson, of Charters, Ascot, and they had one son, Henry Egbert Peter, born 9 March, 1914, and two daughters, Maureen Winifred, born 22 July, 1915, and Barbara Marguerite, born 8 Nov. 1916. Capt. Wilkin, who had retired, was appointed Senior Naval Officer at Belfast for the War. He was promoted Rear-Admiral 1 Oct. 1918. His favourite recreations are shooting, hunting, polo and boat-sailing.

London Gazette, 31 Jan. 1893.—" The Queen has been graciously pleased to give orders for the following appointment to the Distinguished Service Order, in recognition of the services of the following Officer during the operations in Burma and the Chin Hills."

DAVIES, THOMAS ARTHUR HARKNESS, Capt., was born in Calcutta, 29 Nov. 1857, third son of the late Major-General Horatio Nelson Davies, Bengal Staff Corps, and Helena Adelaide, daughter of the late John Anderson, Esq., H.E.I.C., of Straquhan, Dumfries, N.B. He was educated at Wellington ; joined the Devonshire Regt. 11 Sept. 1876 ; served in the Afghan War (Medal), and was Adjutant, 2nd Battn. from 1889 to 1892. He was S.S.O. Madras Command, from 1892–1891 ; served in the Wuntho Expedition, Burma, 1892 ; commanded the N.E. Column in the Kachen Hills, Burma, in 1892 ; received the Medal and clasp, and was created a Companion of the Distinguished Service Order [London Gazette, 31 Jan. 1893] : " In recognition of services during the recent operations in Burma and the Chin Hills. Thomas Arthur Harkness Davies, Capt., Devonshire Regt." (The Decoration was sent out to the Commander-in-Chief in India, and was presented in Burma 31 May, 1893.) He commanded the Sima Column in the Kachin Hills, Burma, in 1893 ; served in the Tirah Expedition, 1897 (Medal and two clasps) ; in South Africa, 1899–1902, including operations on the Tugela Heights, the Relief of Ladysmith and Belfast (Despatches, Brevet of Lieutenant-Colonel, Medals and five clasps). He became Colonel 23 Feb. 1907 ; was created a C.B. in 1909 ; retired 14 Dec. 1910 ; served in the European War from 1914, commanded 9th Devon Regt. (Kitchener's Army) from Sept. 1914, to Sept. 1915. The following is part of the Despatch of General Sir R. Stewart, K.C.B. Commanding Burma Division on operations of Columns in Burma, 1902-3 : " All the officers commanding columns have acted with energy and spirit, and I particularly wish to bring to notice the services of Capt. Davies and Major Yule ; the former officer, although a comparatively young officer, has commanded his column with judgment, and I consider his services worthy of notice. . . . I consider Capt. Davies has conducted the operations of the column entrusted to his command with skill and discretion."

London Gazette, 15 Aug. 1893.—" War Office, 15 Aug. 1893. The Queen has been graciously pleased to give orders for the following appointment to the Distinguished Service Order, in recognition of the services of the undermentioned Officer during the recent action at Chilas, on the North-West Frontier of India, on 5 March, 1893. To be Companion of the Distinguished Service Order."

MOBERLY, FREDERICK JAMES, Lieutenant, was born in Madras 15 Sept. 1867, second son of the late Colonel C. M. Moberly, I.S.C., and Mrs.

Moberly. He was educated at Cheltenham, Edinburgh Academy, the Royal Military College, Sandhurst, and the Staff College, Camberley, and was gazetted to the Oxford Light Infantry on 22 Aug. 1888, and served in India, becoming Lieutenant, Indian Staff Corps, 4 Oct. 1891 ; in which year he took part with the 37th Dogras in the Expedition to Manipur, 1891, receiving the Medal with clasp. In 1891 he also served with the Wuntho Field Force, and received a clasp. He served in Gilgit, 1892 to 1896, on special duty under the Foreign Office, was slightly wounded in the action at Chilas, mentioned in Despatches [London Gazette, 14 July, 1893], and created a Companion of the Distinguished Service Order [London Gazette, 15 Aug. 1893] ; " Frederick James Moberly, Lieut., Indian Staff Corps. For services during the recent action at Chilas on the North-West Frontier." The Insignia were sent to the Commander-in-Chief in India for transmission, and presented 14 Nov. 1893. He took part in the operations in Chitral in 1895, commanded at Mastuj during its investment, and took part in Colonel Kelly's march. He was mentioned in Despatches [London Gazette, 16 July, 1895], was specially promoted to Captain, 10 July, 1895, and received the Medal with clasp. He served on the North-West Frontier in 1898 (clasp) ; in South Africa in 1900 (Despatches, Medal with six clasps, Brevet of Major). In 1899 he was on plague duty under the Government of Bombay, and was thanked for his services by the Government of Bombay. He was Assistant Secretary to the Government of India, Military Department, 1902–06 ; in 1903 he was transferred to the 25th Punjabis ; D.A.A.G., Presidency Brigade, 1908–10. He took part in the operations in the Zakka Khel country (Medal with clasp), and was specially promoted Major 13 Feb. 1905. Major Moberly was on the General Staff, Hong-Kong, 1914 ; in 1915 and 1916 he was on the General Staff, England ; and he was A.A. and Q.M.G., England, 1917 ; and on the General Staff, A.H.Q., India, 1917. Lieut.-Colonel F. J. Moberly is Commandant 25th Punjabis. He married, in 1901, May, daughter of the Rev. Thomas Johns, of Manor Owen, Co. Pembroke, and they have one son and one daughter.

London Gazette, 12 Dec. 1893.—" War Office, 12 Dec. 1893. The Queen has been graciously pleased to give orders for the following appointment to the Distinguished Service Order, in recognition of the services of the undermentioned Officer during the recent operations in aid of the British East Africa Company against the Somalis, etc., on the Juba. To be Companion of the Distinguished Service Order."

LEWES, PRICE VAUGHAN, Lieut., Royal Navy, was born in 1865, son of Colonel John Lewes, formerly of The Buffs, of Llanlear, Talsarn, South Wales. He was educated at Reading, on H.M.S. Britannia, and at the Royal Military College, Greenwich ; entered the Royal Navy in 1878 ; became Lieutenant, 1888 ; served in the operations against the Somalis on the Juba River in British East Africa, 1893 ; received the General African Medal with clasp, and was created a Companion of the Distinguished Service Order [London Gazette, 12 Dec. 1893] : " In recognition of services during the recent operations in aid of the British East Africa Company, against the Somalis, on the Juba. Price Vaughan Lewes, Lieut., Royal Navy." Insignia sent to Admiralty for presentation ; presented 26 Jan. 1894. Capt. Lewes married, in 1894, Anne Josephine, daughter of the late Lieut.-Colonel J. G. M. G. Tulloch, 21st Regt. He died 9 Nov. 1914.

London Gazette, 2 Jan. 1894.—" The Queen has also been graciously pleased to give orders for the following appointments to the Distinguished Service Order, in recognition of the services of the undermentioned Officers during the operations in Burma and the Northern Chin Hills in 1892–93. To be Companions of the Distinguished Service Order."

CAULFIELD, GORDON NAPIER, Captain, was born 27 Jan. 1862, son of the late Colonel Robert Caulfield and Anne Lovell Bury. He entered the Army on 22 Jan. 1881, as Second Lieutenant, 50th Foot ; was transferred to the 24th Foot 1 July, 1881 ; became Lieutenant, South Wales Borderers 1 July, 1881, and Indian Staff Corps 23 April, 1883. He served with the Burma Expedition, 1885–87, and 1887–89, and received the Medal and two clasps ; in the Wuntho Expedition in 1891 (clasp), and in the operations in the Northern Chin Hills, 1892–93 ; received a clasp ; was mentioned in Despatches, G.G.O. 733 of '93, and was created a Companion of the Distinguished Service Order [London Gazette, 2 Jan. 1894] : " Gordon Napier Caulfield, Capt., Indian Staff Corps. In recognition of services during the operations in Burma and in the Northern Chin Hills." The Insignia, etc., were sent to India and presented 13 Nov. 1894. He had been promoted to Captain, Indian Army, 22 Jan. 1892, and became Major 22 April, 1901 ; Lieutenant-Colonel 1 June, 1904 ; Brevet Colonel 11 May, 1907, and retired as Colonel, Indian Army, 18 Feb. 1913. Colonel Caulfield commanded the 17th (Reserve) Battn. Durham Light Infantry from 1914. He married, in 1902, Mildred, youngest daughter of Philip O'Reilly, D.L., and they have two daughters.

TAYLOR, HUGH NEUFVILLE, Capt., was born 20 Dec. 1859, at Blackheath, Kent, son of the late Capt. J. H. Taylor, Master Attendant, Madras Presidency, and of Mrs. J. H. Taylor. He was educated at Carshalton House, Carshalton, Surrey, and joined the 1st Bedfordshire Regt. 29 Feb. 1882 ; became Lieutenant, Indian Staff Corps, 2 May, 1883, and Capt. 28 Jan. 1893. He served in Burma, 1887–89, and 1889–92 (Medal with two clasps ; Despatches) ; in Burma, 1892–93. Operations in the Northern Chin Hills, in command of a detachment of the 90th Punjabis. He was mentioned in Despatches, G.G.O. 733 of '93 ; received a clasp, and was created a Companion of the Distinguished Service Order [London Gazette, 2 Jan. 1894] : " Hugh Neufville Taylor, Capt., Indian Staff Corps. In recognition of services during the operations in Burma and the Northern Chin Hills." He became Major 10 July, 1901, and Lieutenant-Colonel 1 June, 1904, and commanded the 20th Punjabis from 1897 to 1905. He was Deputy Inspector-General, Military Police, Burma, and retired 1 Feb. 1914. He has the Delhi Durbar Medal. He married, 17

Dec. 1907, at Colombo, Cicely May, daughter of W. R. Arbuthnot, Esq., of Plaw Hatch, East Grinstead.

HENEGAN, JOHN, Lieutenant, was born 29 Jan. 1865, and entered the South Wales Borderers 6 Feb. 1884 ; became Captain, Indian Staff Corps, 30 Dec. 1885 ; served in Burma, 1886–89 (Medal with clasp), and in the Chin-Lushai Expedition in 1892 (clasp). He served in the Northern Chin Hills, 1892–93, when he was mentioned in Despatches, G.G.O. 733 of '93 ; received a clasp, and was created a Companion of the Distinguished Service Order [London Gazette, 2 Jan. 1894] : " John Henegan, Lieut., Indian Staff Corps. In recognition of services during the operations in Burma and the Northern Chin Hills." He again served in Burma in 1895–96. He became Major, Indian Army, 6 Feb. 1902 ; Lieutenant-Colonel, Indian Army, 3 Jan. 1909, and is Commandant, 10th Gurkha Rifles.

London Gazette, 26 May, 1894.—" War Office, 26 May, 1894. The Queen has been graciously pleased to give orders for the following appointments to the Distinguished Service Order, in recognition of the services of the undermentioned Officers in the recent operations against Fodey Silah, in Combo, on the Gambia. To be Companions of the Distinguished Service Order."

HALL, HERBERT GOODENOUGH KING-, Lieut.-Commander, Royal Navy, was born 15 March, 1862, youngest son of the late Admiral Sir William King-Hall and Louisa, daughter of James Forman. He was educated at a private school and in H.M.S. Britannia, and joined the Royal Navy in 1875, becoming Lieutenant in 1882. He served in H.M.S. Sultan in the bombardment of Alexandria and the Egyptian War of 1882 (Egyptian War Medal, clasp and Bronze Star). He served in command of H.M.S. Magpie in the Expedition against the Mandingoes in the Gambia in 1894 ; acted as Chief of Staff to Admiral Bedford, Commander-in-Chief ; received the Medal and clasp, and was created a Companion of the Distinguished Service Order [London Gazette, 26 May, 1894] : " Herbert Goodenough King-Hall, Lieut.-Commander, Royal Navy. In recognition of services in the recent operations against Fodey Silah, in Combo, on the Gambia." The Warrants, Statutes and Insignia were sent to the Admiralty, and presented 6 July, 1894. He was promoted to Commander in 1895 ; was a member of the Naval Intelligence Department, 1895–96 ; served as Naval Transport Officer in Natal during the South African War (Medal and clasp). He was promoted to Captain in 1900 ; created a C.B. in 1907, and a C.V.O. in 1908 ; appointed A.D.C. to the King, 1908–9 ; Director of Naval Intelligence. As Commodore in H.M.S. Indomitable he took His Royal Highness the Prince of Wales to Canada in 1908 ; he became Rear-Admiral in 1909 ; was Director of Naval Mobilization at the Admiralty, 1909–11 ; Rear-Admiral, Second Division, Home Fleet, 1911–12. He was Commander-in-Chief at the Cape of Good Hope, 1913–16, and directed the operations resulting in the destruction of the German cruiser, Königsberg. He was created a K.C.B. in 1916, and became Vice-Admiral in 1915. He married Lady Mabel Murray, sister to the 5th Earl of Mansfield. The record of his services is as follows : Sub-Lieutenant, H.M.S. Sultan at bombardment of Alexandria, July, 1882 ; Gambia, 1894 ; mentioned in Despatches by Rear-Admiral Sir Fred Bedford for service as his Chief of Staff ; South Africa as Captain ; mentioned in Despatches by Lord Kitchener for service as Naval Transport Officer, South African War, 1901–2 ; Commander-in-Chief, Cape of Good Hope Station, Jan. 1913, to Feb. 1916 ; conducted Naval portion of South-West Africa campaign ; blockade of East Coast of Africa, and in command at destruction of German cruiser Könisberg, July, 1915.

BOWDEN, WALTER, Surgeon, Royal Navy, was born in London, 10 June, 1859, son of the late William Bowden, of 45, Hilldrop Crescent, Camden Road, N. He was educated at University College Hospital, London (M.R.C.S., England, and L.R.C.P., London, 1886) ; entered the Royal Naval Medical Service in 1887 ; became Staff Surgeon in 1899 ; served during operations against Fodey Silah on the Gambia in 1894, in medical charge ; was present at the destruction of Busimballa, action of Sabages, and with the Naval Brigade at the bombardment of Gunpur in 1894. He was created a Companion of the Distinguished Service Order [London Gazette, 26 May, 1894] : " Walter Bowden, Surgeon, Royal Navy. In recognition of services against Fodey Silah, in Combo, on the Gambia." The Insignia were

Walter Bowden.

sent to the Admiralty, and presented 6 July, 1894 ; he also received the General African Medal and Gambia Clasp, the South African Medal, 1901–2, and the Somaliland Medal. He married Alithea M., daughter of J. Ogilvie, J.P., of Queenstown, Ireland, and they have two sons and two daughters. He became Staff Surgeon in 1900, and retired in 1908 as Deputy Inspector-General. The following are fuller details of his war services : Whilst Surgeon of H.M.S. Raleigh he served in the Naval Brigade at Bathurst, on the River Gambia, West Coast of Africa, in Feb. 1894, in co-operation with two companies of the 1st West India Regt., for the punishment of Fodey Silah, a rebellious slave-raiding chief ; was in medical charge of the Royal Marines ; volunteered to take charge of the ammunition ; especially recommended and mentioned in Despatches ; was present in medical charge at the bombardment and occupation of Gunjur in 1894 ; he was appointed to the Distinguished Service Order, and granted a Medal with clasp. He was the first Naval Medical Officer to receive the distinction of Companionship of the D.S.O. He served in H.M.S. Naiad during the Boer War and Somaliland Expedition, 1901 to 1904.

London Gazette, 8 June, 1894.—"The Queen has further been pleased to give orders for the following appointments to the Distinguished Service Order, and promotions in the Army, in recognition of the services of the undermentioned Officers during the recent operations on the West Coast of Africa. To be Companions of the Distinguished Service Order."

MORGAN, ANTHONY HICKMAN, Surgeon-Major, was born in 1858, son of the late Capt. Anthony Morgan, of Skibbereen, County Cork (late Captain, 95th Regt.), and Eliza Tymons, of Riverstown, County Clare. He entered the Army Medical Service 5 Feb. 1881; served in the Egyptian Campaign in 1882 (Medal and Khedive's Star. He served in the Expedition against the native chief, Fodey Kabba, 1891–92 (Medal and clasp); on the West Coast of Africa, 1893–94, and in the operations against the Sofas (Despatches [London Gazette, 28 Feb. 1894]). In 1894 he was again on active service in Gambia in the expedition against the native chief, Fodey Silah; was mentioned in Despatches [London Gazette, 4 May, 1894]; received a clasp, and was created a Companion of the Distinguished Service Order [London Gazette, 8 June, 1894]: "Anthony Hickman Morgan, Surgeon-Major, Army Medical Staff. In recognition of services during the operations on the West Coast of Africa." He served on board the hospital ship Princess of Wales, in South Africa, 1889–90, as Officer Commanding troops and P.M.O. (Despatches; Medal and clasp). Lieut.-Colonel Hickman Morgan retired 7 July, 1897, and in the same year married Mary, daughter of the late C. E. Bagnall, of Clonkennan, Limerick. He became High Sheriff, County of Cork, and a J.P. in 1904, and Deputy Lieutenant; is a Knight of the Order of St. John of Jerusalem, a Fellow of the Royal Geographical Society, and a Fellow of the Zoological Society. He contested the Isle of Wight in the Conservative interest in 1906. Lieut.-Colonel Hickman Morgan is a member of the Iron and Steel Institute. His favourite recreations are yachting, shooting and motoring.

STEELE, FREDERICK WILLIAM, Capt., was born 24 Jan. 1858, and entered the 46th Regt. on 11 Nov. 1876. He served with the Egyptian Expedition in 1882; was present at the reconnaissance in force on Kafr Dowar, action at El Magfar and Tel-el-Mahuta, both actions at Kassassin, the Battle of Tel-el-Kebir (Medal with clasp, Bronze Star), and with the Sudan Expedition, 1884–85, as Transport Officer (clasp). He had become Captain, Duke of Cornwall's Light Infantry, in 1886, and he transferred to the Army Service Corps in 1889. He served on the West Coast of Africa in 1893–94, taking part in the operations against the Sofas, 1893–94 (Despatches [London Gazette, 28 Feb. 1894]), and in the expedition to the Gambia against Fodey Silah. For this he was mentioned in Despatches 4 May, 1894; was given the Brevet of Lieutenant-Colonel 2 April, 1895, and was created a Companion of the Distinguished Service Order [London Gazette, 8 June, 1894]: "Frederick William Steele, Capt., Royal Army Medical Corps. In recognition of services during the recent operations on the West Coast of Africa." He became Major in 1895. The Insignia were sent to Capt. Steele at Liscard, Cheshire. He retired as Lieutenant-Colonel from the Army Service Corps 2 Feb. 1898. Lieut.-Colonel F. W. Steele, D.S.O., died in Jan. 1909, and an obituary notice of him appeared in the "Times" of 5 Jan. 1909.

BOURKE, HENRY BERESFORD, Capt., was born 12 June, 1855, son of the Rev. John Bourke and Louisa Maria, daughter of James Potts, Esq.; and is a grandson of the 3rd Earl of Mayo. He was educated at Sherbourne School, and entered the 1st West India Regt. on 30 Nov. 1876. He was Acting Fort Adjutant, Cape Coast Castle, 28 April, 1892, to 30 May, 1892, and became Captain 5 Oct. 1887. He served in the Tambaka Expedition in 1892, and was present at the capture of Tambi (Medal and clasp). He took part in the operations against the Sofas, West Coast of Africa, in 1893–94; was mentioned in Despatches [London Gazette, 28 Feb. 1894], and created a Companion of the Distinguished Service Order [London Gazette, 8 June, 1894]: "Henry Beresford Bourke, Capt., West India Regt. In recognition of services during the recent operations on the West Coast of Africa." The Insignia, etc., were sent to Capt. Bourke 28 June, 1894. He became Major 1 April, 1894, and Lieutenant-Colonel 28 March, 1898; operations Sierra Leone; Karene Expedition, 1898–99 (clasp). Retired 9 May, 1903. Lieut.-Colonel H. B. Bourke served during the European War as Draft Conducting Officer.

WAY, ALFRED COTTON, Capt., was born 16 Dec. 1860, at Santa Warrea, India, son of the late Major Cotton Way, B.S.C., and Elizabeth Charlotte, daughter of the late Capt. Eager, 90th Regt. He was educated at private schools, and joined the 31st East Surrey Regt. 29 July, 1882; was transferred to the 24th Regt. in 1883, and to the Indian Staff Corps in 1886. He served with the Burma Expedition, 1885–89; was mentioned in Despatches, and received the special thanks of the Commander-in-Chief for the capture of the Dacoit Chief, Bo Shway, also Medal with two clasps. In 1886 Lieut. Way rejoined the 24th Regt., the South Wales Borderers. He was seconded in 1890, and joined the Houssa Force, West Africa, and commanded the expedition against the ex-King Quasi Mensah, of Ashanti. He rejoined the 24th Regt. in 1892; became Captain 9 June, 1892, and exchanged to the 1st West India Regt. in 1893. Capt. Way was Staff Officer, Sierra Leone; Staff Officer in operations against Sofas in 1894 (Despatches [London Gazette, 28 Feb. 1894]). He served in the expedition to Gambia against Fodey Silah in 1894 as Staff Captain, and was created a Companion of the Distinguished Service Order [London Gazette, 8 June, 1894]: "Alfred Cotton Way, Capt., West India Regt. In recognition of services during the recent operations on the West Coast of Africa." He was appointed Garrison Adjutant at St. Lucia, 1895–98, and retired from the West India Regt. 23 Oct. 1897. Capt. Way died on 11 Dec. 1911, at Bannenoby, Islay, N.B.

GWYNN, CHARLES WILLIAM, Lieut., was born 4 Feb. 1870, at Ramelton, Co. Donegal, Ireland, 3rd son of the Rev. John Gwynn, D.D., Regius Professor of Divinity, Trinity College, Dublin, and Lucy Josephine, daughter of William Smith O'Brien, Cahirmoyle, Co. Limerick. He was educated at St. Columba's College, Rathfarnham, Dublin, and at the Royal Military Academy, Woolwich, and at the Staff College, Camberley; became Second Lieutenant, Royal Engineers, 15 Feb. 1889, and Lieutenant 15 Feb. 1892. Lieut. Gwynn served on the West Coast of Africa, 1893–94, taking part in the operations against the Sofas, when he was three times wounded, mentioned in Despatches [London Gazette, 28 Feb. 1894], was given the Brevet of Major 16 Feb. 1900, and created a Companion of the Distinguished Service Order [London Gazette, 8 June, 1894]: "Charles William Gwynn, Lieut., Royal Engineers. In recognition of services in the recent operations in West Africa." He was Staff Captain (Intelligence), Headquarters of Army, 1 Sept. 1897, to 26 June, 1901; was employed on Survey Duty, Egypt, 4 Oct. 1899, to 6 June, 1901; was promoted to Captain 15 Feb. 1900; employed on Survey Duty, Egypt, 27 June, 1901, to 9 Oct. 1901; employed with the Egyptian Army 10 Oct. 1901, to 12 Aug. 1904; Commissioner, Abyssinia and East African Protectorate Boundary Commission, 18 June, 1908, to 1 Oct. 1909; created a C.M.G. 1903; became Major 1 Oct. 1908. From 20 Jan. 1911, to 25 Sept. 1914, Major Gwynn was employed with the Australian Commonwealth Military Forces as Director of Military Art, Royal Military College, Duntroon. He served in the European War from 1914; was G.S.O.1, 57th Division, Central Force, Home Defence, 24 Jan. 1915, to 2 July, 1915; held a special appointment (graded G.S.O.2) with the Mediterranean Expeditionary Force 3 July, 1915, to 20 July, 1915; and as G.S.O.1, 2nd Australian Division, Mediterranean Expeditionary Force, 21 July, 1915, to 9 Dec. 1915. From 10 Dec. 1915, to 28 Feb. 1916, he commanded a brigade, 6th Australian Division, Mediterranean Expeditionary Force; and from 29 Feb. 1916, was Brigadier-General, General Staff, 2nd Australian and New Zealand Army Corps (afterwards XXII. Corps), with the Mediterranean Expeditionary Force, and afterwards with the British Armies in France; commanded 1st Midland Brigade, British Army of the Rhine, 3 March to 20 Sept. 1919; appointed G.S.O. 1st Division, Aldershot, 18 Nov. 1919. He was given the Brevet of Lieutenant-Colonel 3 June, 1916; became Lieutenant-Colonel 1 Oct. 1916, and was given the Brevet of Colonel 1 Jan. 1917. He was created a C.B. in 1918; was given the Belgian Croix de Guerre, 1918, and the Legion of Honour, 1919. Colonel (temporary Brigadier-General) C. W. Gwynn is a Fellow of the Royal Geographical Society, and was awarded the R.G.S. Peake Fund Medal in 1909. He married on 1 Nov. 1904, at All Saints' Church, Raheny, Co. Dublin, Mary, widow of Lieut. Lowry Armstrong, R.N. His brothers are Capt. Stephen Gwynn, M.P.; Edward Gwynn, Fellow of Trinity College, Dublin; the Rev. Robert Gwynn, B.D., Fellow, Tutor and Chaplain of Trinity College, Dublin, and J. T. Gwynn, I.C.S.

London Gazette, 21 Dec. 1894.—"The Queen has been graciously pleased to give orders for the following appointments to the Distinguished Service Order, in recognition of the services of the undermentioned Officers in the recent operations against the Chief Nana of the Brohemie in the Benin River."

HEUGH, JOHN GEORGE, Lieut. and Commander, Royal Navy, entered the Royal Navy in 1870; served with the Naval Brigade in Zululand, 1879, being one of the garrison of Ekone (Despatches; promoted Lieutenant; Zulu Medal and clasp); during the Egyptian War of 1882 he was present at the seizure of the canal and at the destruction of Aboukir Bay Forts (Medal and Bronze Star). He was thanked by the Admiralty for manœuvring H.M.S. Rattler during a severe gale in the Japanese Sea, and thereby saving a man's life. He served in the operations against the Chief Nana in the Benin River in 1894. He was slightly wounded, mentioned in Despatches, promoted Commander and was created a Companion of the Distinguished Service Order [London Gazette, 21 Dec. 1894]: "John George Heugh, Lieut. and Commander, Royal Navy, in recognition of services against the Chief Nana of Brohemie, in the Benin River." The Warrant, Statutes and Insignia were sent to the Admiralty for presentation; presented 18 April, 1895. In 1899 he married Helene, daughter of Richard Sherman, of Düsseldorf. He died 19 March, 1915.

HICKLEY, JOHN DENNIS, Lieut., Royal Navy, was born 13 Jan. 1862, at Anglesea, Hants, son of Admiral Henry Dennis Hickley and Mary, his wife (née Rundle). He was educated at Mannamead School, Plymouth, and Foster's, Hants, and joined the Royal Navy about 1874. He served with distinction in the Benin Expedition as First Lieutenant, H.M.S. Phœbe (commanded by Capt. F. Powell, now Admiral Powell), and won much esteem, and for his services at this time was created a Companion of the Distinguished Service Order [London Gazette, 21 Dec. 1894]: "John Dennis Hickley, Lieut., Royal Navy." He also received the Medal for the Benin Expedition. Lieut. Hickley wrote a graphic account of the Expedition, which came out in the "United Service Magazine." He

John Dennis Hickley.

was a very keen sportsman, and kept an interesting account of his sporting expeditions also. Lieut. Hickley was drowned on 17 Feb. 1895, at Lourenço Marques, no one knew how, when out shooting with a native. He was 33 years of age. His death was deeply lamented as a great loss to the Service. His D.S.O. was awarded for services against the Chief Nana of the Brohemie.

D

GORE-BROWNE, GODFREY, Lieut. Royal Navy, was born in Hobart, Tasmania, 30 March, 1862, son of Sir Thomas Gore-Browne, K.C.M.G., C.B. (some time Governor of St. Helena, New Zealand, Tasmania and Bermuda), and of Harriett, daughter of James Campbell, of Craigie House, Ayr, N.B. He was educated at Mr. Allen's School, and H.M.S. Britannia, and joined the Royal Navy. He was Midshipman of the Euryalus during the Egyptian War of 1882 (Egyptian Medal and Khedive's Bronze Star). He was mentioned by Rear-Admiral Sir W. N. W. Henett, K.C.B. in his Despatch [London Gazette, 8 Sept. 1882]: "I beg to bring to favourable notice services of Mr. Gore-Browne, Midshipman, my A.D.C., who was most useful to me" (page 4172 of Gazette).

Godfrey Gore-Browne.

He became First Lieutenant of Philomel, on the West Coast of Africa in 1894, and was created a Companion of the Distinguished Service Order [London Gazette, 21 Dec. 1894]: "Godfrey Gore-Browne, Lieut., Royal Navy. In recognition of his services against the Chief Nana of Brohemie on the Benin River." Lieut. Gore-Browne was mentioned in Rear-Admiral Bedford's Report [London Gazette, 21 Dec. 1894]: "I desire especially to mention the executive officers of Philomel and Phœbe, Lieuts. Gore-Browne and Hickley. It would be difficult to find two more able and zealous officers." Awarded General African Medal, Benin River, and 1894 clasp. On one occasion Lieut. Gore-Browne was watching from a ship's boat other naval officers bathing. Sharks were sighted and the bathers hastened to climb the boat. As one was drawing himself into the boat a shark was seen rising and turning over to seize his legs. Lieut. Gore-Browne jumped from the thwart of the boat (with his boots on) on to the shark, which made off hastily, and Lieut. Gore-Browne returned to the boat none the worse. Commander Gore-Browne died at Mentone 5 April, 1900.

London Gazette, 4 Jan. 1895.—"The Queen has been graciously pleased to give orders for the following appointment to the Distinguished Service Order, in recognition of the services of the undermentioned Officer in the expedition against the Zebus in 1892, and during the recent operations in Central Africa."

OWEN, EDWARD RODERIC, Major, was born on 4 May, 1856, at The Hewletts, Prestbury, Gloucestershire, where his father then resided, son of Hugh Darby Owen, Esq., of Bettws Hall, Montgomeryshire, North Wales, and of Mrs. Hugh Owen. "Roddy" Owen was educated at a private school at Malvern, and at Eton (1869-73), and for a year with a tutor, during which time he began his riding career by winning the Duke of Beaufort's Blue Coat Race at Dauntsey on the late Mr. E. Chaplin's Holland. He entered the Army through the Militia, receiving on the 3rd March, 1875, a commission in the 2nd Battn. South Devon Infantry Militia (11th Foot). On the 11th Sept. 1876, he was transferred to the 1st Battn. of the 20th (East Devonshire) Regt., which, in 1881, became known as the Lancashire Fusiliers. He joined his new regiment at Halifax, Nova Scotia. He shot in the Rocky Mountains; came home on leave in 1878; kept a few horses

Edward Roderic Owen.

(which were trained by his elder brother Hugh at Cirencester), and rode some races. In 1879 his regiment was stationed at Malta, and in 1881 Roddy hunted to his heart's content, and won many important races. In 1883 he was stationed at Mhow in India, and in March, 1884, was attached to the Staff of the Viceroy, Lord Ripon, as Extra A.D.C. He became well known on all the race-courses in Bengal. In Aug. 1884, at the age of 28, he was promoted to Captain, and returned to Ireland, where he migrated from the staff of Lord Ripon to that of Lord Spencer, Lord Lieutenant of Ireland. He won the great Sandown Steeplechase in 1884, and in two successive years he rode the winning mount in the Sandown Grand Prize. Twice he won the great Sandown Steeple-chase on the same horse, Kilworth. In 1889 he had the highest average of wins among gentlemen riders for the year. In 1889 and 1900 he was A.D.C. to General Sir Evelyn Wood at Aldershot. In 1891 he was selected for the Mounted Infantry Regt. at Aldershot, which had been raised and was then commanded by Colonel Hutton. In 1892 he steered Father O'Flynn to victory in the Grand National, and directly after the race he took the train to London, applied at the War Office for active service, and served as Chief of the Staff to General Sir Francis Scott, Inspector-General of the Gold Coast Constabulary; commanded the expedition against Zebus in West Africa, and left England for Lagos. In 1892 he served with Sir Gerald Portal's Mission in Uganda. He was chosen as Commandant of the Equatorial Provinces of Torn and Unyoro, 1893-94, during which time he quelled single-handed a Moslem revolt of a critical nature. He was then entrusted with the important mission of planting the British flag under circumstances of extreme difficulty at Wadelai, thus safeguarding the upper reaches of the Nile for Great Britain. He received the African Medal, 1892, the Brilliant Star of Zanzibar, and was created a Companion of the Distinguished Service Order [London Gazette, 4 Jan. 1895]: "In recognition of services against the Zebus in 1892, and during the recent operations in Central Africa, Edward Roderic Owen, Captain and Brevet Major, The Lancashire Fusiliers." The

Insignia were presented 3 Sept. 1895. In the summer of 1894 he was home on leave, and in Jan. 1905, sailed for India to join his regiment at Quetta. He became Official Correspondent of the "Westminster Gazette" during the North-West Frontier Campaign, and being attached to the King's Own Scottish Borderers, took part in their well-known charge. He and Colonel Sir Younghusband were the first to enter the Fort of Chitral, after a forty-mile ride in a hostile country, in advance of the Relief Force. Major Owen travelled in the Pamirs; joined the Sudan Expedition, receiving the Medal and the Firket Medal. In the endeavour to stamp out cholera at Ambigol Wells, where he was Commandant, he contracted illness and died there. The Arabs, who loved him, placed circles of white stones round his grave. A Memoir of him has been written by his sister, Lady Owen-Mackenzie.

London Gazette, 12 Feb. 1895.—"The Queen has been graciously pleased to give orders for the following appointments to the Distinguished Service Order, in recognition of the services of the undermentioned Officers during the operations carried out in the Chin Hills in 1892-3 and 1893-4."

PRESGRAVE, EDWARD ROBERT JOHN, Capt. and Brevet Major, was born in London, 29 June, 1855, only son of the late Lieut. Edward Presgrave, H.E.I.C.S. (retired), and of Margaret Crane. He was educated at Wellington College, and was gazetted to the 21st Regt., the Royal Scots Fusiliers 11 Feb. 1875, becoming Lieutenant 11 Feb. 1875. On 19 Dec. 1878, he was admitted to the Madras Staff Corps. He was employed in the Rumpa Rebellion in 1879; served in the Afghan Campaign, 1879-80 (Medal); was Adjutant, 15th Madras Infantry, 1882-86; became Captain 11 Feb. 1886; served in the Burma Campaign, 1886-7-9 (Medal and two clasps). He was Second-in-Command, 12th Regt. 2nd Burma Battn. Mounted Infantry, 1890-93. He served in the Expedition to Manipur, 1891 (Despatches [London Gazette, 14 Aug. 1891], clasp). He again saw active service in Burma, 1892-93-94, with the Tashon Column and in the operations in the Northern Chin Hills. He was mentioned in Despatches, G.G.O. 733 of '93; was given the Brevet of Major 29 Dec. 1893, received a clasp, and was created a Companion of the Distinguished Service Order [London Gazette, 12 Feb. 1895]: "Edward Robert John Presgrave, Capt. and Brevet Major, Indian Staff Corps. In recognition of services during the operations carried on in Burma and the Northern Chin Hills in 1892-93 and 1893-94." The Warrant, Statutes and Insignia were sent to India 25 April, 1895. He was Commandant, 10th Gurkha Rifles, 1893-1902; became Major and temporary Lieutenant-Colonel 11 Feb. 1895. He was A.A.G. India 20 July, 1900, to 24 July, 1901, and 3 Jan. 1902, to 31 Aug. 1906; was given the Brevet of Colonel in 1904, and became Colonel 11 Feb. 1904. Colonel Presgrave was put on the Unemployed Supernumerary List 29 June, 1912. He was given a special appointment, Military Intelligence, in 1914; became G.S.O., 2nd Grade, in 1917, and was mentioned for services rendered [London Gazette, 13 March, 1918].

Edward R. J. Presgrave.

EAST, LIONEL WILLIAM PELLEW, Lieut., was born 27 July, 1866, son of Rear-Admiral J. W. East, R.N., and of Ruth East (née Cunningham). He was educated at the Royal Military Academy, Woolwich; entered the Royal Artillery 16 Sept. 1885; became Captain 18 Dec. 1895; served in the Hazara Expedition, 1891, and in the Second Miranzai Expedition, 1891; was mentioned in Despatches [London Gazette, 15 Sept. 1891], and was created a Companion of the Distinguished Service Order [London Gazette, 12 Feb. 1895]: "Lionel William Pellew East, Lieut., Royal Artillery. In recognition of services during the operations carried out in the Northern Chin Hills in 1892-3 and 1893-4." The Insignia were presented on 2 March, 1895. He served on the North-West Frontier of Assam, 1894, and in the Abor Expedition, and was severely wounded. He became Major 18 May, 1904. He was D.A.A.G., India, 12 Sept. 1904, to 11 Sept. 1908, and G.S.O.2, Welsh Division, Western Command, 29 Sept. 1909, to 28 Sept. 1913, and was promoted to Lieutenant-Colonel 15 April, 1914. Lieut.-Colonel East served in the European War, and was four times mentioned in Despatches; was given temporary rank as Brigadier-General, 1916, and given the Brevet of Colonel, 1917, and created a C.M.G. 1916. He was killed in action in France in Sept. 1918. He was a member of the Russian Order of St. Stanislas. He married, in 1897, Margaret, daughter of Colonel A. Stephen, I.M.S. (retired), and they have one son, James Arthur Cumming, born on 21 Oct. 1915, and three daughters, Ruth, Margaret and Elizabeth.

London Gazette, 16 July, 1895.—"The Queen has been graciously pleased to give orders for the following appointments to the Distinguished Service Order, in recognition of the services of the undermentioned Officers during the recent operations in Chitral."

BORRADAILE, HARRY BENN, Capt. and Brevet-Major, was born 4 Oct. 1860, son of Harry Borradaile, Bombay Civil Service, and of Mrs. Harry Borradaile. He was educated at Charterhouse, and was gazetted to the 25th Foot as Lieutenant 15 Jan. 1880, becoming Lieutenant, King's Own Scottish Borderers, 26 April, 1881. He served in the Burmese Expedition of 1885-89 (Medal and two clasps), and in the Sikkim Expedition, 1889; promoted to Capt. Jan. 1891, and given the Brevet of Major 10 July, 1895. In 1895 he took part in the operations in Chitral, serving with the relief force from Gilgit. He was mentioned in Despatches [London Gazette, 16 July, 1895]; was given the Brevet of Major 10 July, 1895; received the Medal and clasp, and was created a Companion of the Distinguished Service Order [London Gazette, 16 July, 1895]: "Harry Benn

Borradaile, Capt. and Brevet Major, Indian Staff Corps. In recognition of services during the operations in Chitral." The Insignia were presented 9 Nov. 1895. He became Major, Indian Army 14 Jan. 1900; commanded the 34th Sikh Pioneers, 1902–09; was promoted to Lieutenant-Colonel 1 June, 1904, and given the Brevet of Colonel 8 June, 1907; he became Colonel 1 Jan. 1911; retired 30 Dec. 1912. He served in the European War; was wounded and given the honorary rank of Brigadier-General 12 June, 1919. Brigadier-General H. B. Borradaile married, in 1890, Florence, only child of H. Soden, and they have one son and three daughters.

JONES, HERBERT JOHN, Lieut., was born 23 Dec. 1865, and became Lieutenant, Royal Irish Regt., 23 Aug. 1884; served with the Nile Expedition, 1884–85, with the Desert Column, and was present at the actions at Abu Klea (Medal with clasp, Bronze Star); Hazara Expedition, 1888 (Medal with clasp); in operations against the Kachins in Upper Burma, 1891–92 (received the thanks of the Government); with the Chitral Relief Expedition, 1895, with the Relief Force. He was wounded; took part in the Defence of Mastuj (wounded); was mentioned in Despatches [London Gazette, 16 July, 1895]; received the Medal with clasp, and was created a Companion of the Distinguished Service Order [London Gazette, 16 July, 1895]: "In recognition of services during the recent operations in Chitral. Herbert John Jones, Lieut., Indian Staff Corps." The Insignia were presented by the Queen at Osborne on Monday, 12 Aug. 1895. He became Captain 23 Aug. 1895; served with the Tochi Expedition, 1897 (clasp); China Expedition, 1900–01 (Medal); promoted Major 23 Aug. 1902, and Lieutenant-Colonel 25 Aug. 1908. He commanded the 14th (K.G.O.) Sikhs, 1908–13, and received the Durbar Medal in 1911. On the 19th Sept. 1914, Lieut.-Colonel H. J. Jones was given command of the 13th Battn. the Manchester Regt. He retired on 18 March, 1919.

Herbert John Jones.

EDWARDES, STANLEY MALCOLM, Lieut., was born 18 Nov. 1863, son of the late General Sir Stanley Edwardes, and Adelaide Jane, daughter of General George Alexander Leckie, I.S.C. He became Lieutenant, North Lancashire Regt., 23 Aug. 1884, and transferred to the Indian Staff Corps 24 Jan. 1886, becoming Captain, Indian Staff Corps, 23 Aug. 1895. Capt. Edwardes took part in the operations in Chitral, 1895, being present at the defence of the post of Reshan. He was mentioned in Despatches [London Gazette, 16 July, 1895], received the Medal and clasp, and was created a Companion of the Distinguished Service Order [London Gazette, 16 July, 1895]: "Stanley Malcolm Edwardes, Lieut., Indian Staff Corps. In recognition of services during the recent operations in Chitral." He was commandant, Base Depot, Native Troops, Tirah Expeditionary Force, 12 Oct. 1897, to 21 Jan. 1898 (clasp), and on the Punjab Frontier, 1898 (clasp); became Major 23 Oct. 1902; served in Aden, 1903–04. Operations in the interior; was Brigade Major, India, 1 June, 1904, to 1908; was promoted to Lieutenant-Colonel 17 Sept. 1909, and to Colonel 5 Feb. 1914. He commanded a Brigade in India 5 March, 1916, to 4 March, 1916, and from 5 March, 1916, to 9 March, 1916, commanded the 9th Infantry Brigade in the Indian Expeditionary Force "D." From 10 March, 1916, to 31 March, 1916, he commanded the 37th Infantry Brigade in the Indian Expeditionary Force "D," and from 1 April, 1916, he commanded an Infantry Brigade in the Indian Expeditionary Force "D" and the Mesopotamian Expeditionary Force. He was created a C.M.G. in 1917. He married, in 1909, Emma, daughter of the late Colonel C. F. James and widow of Capt. C. R. Stevens, and they have one son.

FOWLER, JOHN SHARMAN, Lieut., was born 29 July, 1864, son of R. Fowler, Esq., J.P., D.L., of Rahinstown, Co. Meath, and Mrs. Fowler. He was educated at Cheltenham College, and was commissioned in the Royal Engineers, as Lieutenant, 6 Jan. 1886, serving in the Isazai Expedition in 1892. In 1895 he took part in the operations in Chitral, and served with the Gilgit Force during the fighting near and defence of the post of Reshan (wounded). He was afterwards with the Relief Force and was present at the action at Mamagai. Lieut. Fowler was mentioned in Despatches [London Gazette, 16 July, 1895], received the Medal and clasp, and was created a Companion of the Distinguished Service Order [London Gazette, 16 July, 1895]: "John Sharman Fowler, Lieut., Royal Engineers. In recognition of services during the recent operations in Chitral." He became Captain 24 Sept. 1895. In 1897 and 1898 he served on the North-West Frontier of India, taking part in the Mohmand Expedition; was mentioned in Despatches [London Gazette, 11 Jan. 1898], and received a clasp. He also received a clasp for the Tirah Expedition in 1897–98. Capt. Fowler served in South Africa on special service from 1899 to 1902. He was present at the operations in the Orange Free State, Feb. to May, 1900. Operations in Orange River Colony, May to 29 Nov. 1900; Director of Telegraphs, Orange River Colony, 1 June, 1900, to 1 Sept. 1902. He was mentioned in Despatches [London Gazette, 17 June, 1902]; was given the Brevet of Major 26 June, 1902; received the Queen's Medal with three clasps, and the King's Medal with two clasps. He became Major 21 Dec. 1903. Major Fowler was D.A.A.G., 2nd Division, Aldershot Army Corps, 13 March, 1905, to 11 May, 1905, and from 1 June, 1905, to 7 March, 1909; was given the Brevet of Lieutenant-Colonel 18 Jan. 1911; was G.S.O.2, Staff College, 1 Jan. 1911, to 31 March, 1913, and was promoted to Lieutenant-Colonel 31 Dec. 1911. From 5 Aug. 1914, to 15 May, 1918, he was Director of Army Signals, B.E.F., and from 16 May, 1918, to 21 May, 1919, Director of British Signals, British Armies in France. He was given the Brevet of Colonel 1 Jan. 1916; was temporary Brigadier-General from 26 Oct. 1914, to 31 Dec. 1916; and was promoted to Major-General 1 Jan. 1917. He was created a C.B. in 1915, and a K.C.M.G. in 1918. Sir John Fowler married, in 1904, Mary Henrietta Olivia, daughter of the late John M. Brooke, and they have two daughters.

GURDON, BERTRAND EVELYN MELLISH, Lieut., was born 2 Sept. 1867, third son of Major-General Evelyn Pulteney Gurdon, late I.S.C., and Mary, daughter of the late General Sandeman. He was educated at Haileybury and Sandhurst; was gazetted Lieutenant in the Manchester Regt. 25 Aug. 1886, and entered the Indian Army in 1887. He was transferred to the Indian Political Department in 1889, and became Assistant to the British Agent at Gilgit in 1892. In Dec. 1894, he was appointed Assistant British Agent in Chitral, and served as one of the Garrison of Chitral Fort during the siege, March and April, 1895. He was mentioned in Despatches, and was created a Companion of the Distinguished Service Order [London Gazette, 16 July, 1895]: "In recognition of services during the recent operations in Chitral, Bertrand Evelyn Mellish Gurdon, Lieut., Indian Staff Corps." The Insignia were presented by the Queen at Osborne on Monday, 12 Aug. 1895. He was created a Companion of the Order of the Indian Empire in 1900. He became Lieutenant-Colonel in 1912, and retired in 1918. He held the following appointments during his period of service in the Indian Political Department: Boundary Settlement Officer in Central India; Assistant British Agent, Gilgit; Assistant Political Agent, Chitral; Political Agent, Gilgit; Political Agent, Khyber; Political Agent, Southern States, Rajputana; Political Agent, Eastern States, Rajputana; Political Agent, Bhopawar; Political Agent, Phulkian States. In 1916 he was selected for the appointment of Agent to the Governor-General in Rajputana, but owing to ill-health was unable to continue to serve in India, and took leave pending retirement. He married, in 1907, Evelyn Agnes, daughter of the late Frederick Clarke and widow of Capt. Frank Duncan, Indian Army, and they have two daughters.

Bertrand E. M. Gurdon.

BEYNON, WILLIAM GEORGE LAURENCE, Lieut., was born at Agra, India, 5 Nov. 1866, son of General W. H. Beynon, of 25, Ashburn Place, London, S.W., and Charlotte, daughter of Lieut.-General Sir G. St. Patrick Laurence, K.C.S.I., C.B. He was educated at Marlborough, and Sandhurst Royal Military College; joined the 2nd Battn. Royal Sussex Regt. as Second Lieutenant 5 Feb. 1887. He served in the Black Mountain Expedition, 1888 (Medal and clasp); became Lieutenant, Indian Staff Corps, 11 Dec. 1889. He served as Staff Officer to Colonel Kelly in the Gilgit Field Force; in the Siege of Chitral 1895; was mentioned in Despatches [London Gazette, 16 July, 1895], received the Medal and clasp, and was created a Companion of the Distinguished Service Order [London Gazette, 16 July, 1895]: "In recognition of services during the recent operations in Chitral, William George Laurence Beynon, Lieut., Indian Staff Corps." The Insignia were presented 7 Nov. 1895. He served in the Hazara Campaign, North-West Frontier of India, 1897–98. Operations in Samana and in the Kurram Valley during Aug. and Sept. 1897. Relief of Gulistan (two clasps). He again saw active service in the Tirah Campaign, 1897–98, being present at the actions of Chagra Kotal and Dargai, and capture of the Sampagha and Arhanga Passes. Reconnaissance of the Saran Sar and action of 2 Nov. 1897. Operations in and around Dwatoi and action of 24 Nov. 1897. Operations in the Bara Valley 7–14 Dec. 1897. Affair at Shinkamar on 29 Jan. 1898. He was mentioned in Despatches [London Gazette, 1 March, 1898]; was given the Brevet of Major 20 May, 1898, and received a clasp. He served in the Somaliland Expedition in 1901 in command of the Mounted troops; was mentioned in Despatches [London Gazette, 18 April, 1902], received the Medal and clasp, and the Brevet of Lieutenant-Colonel on attaining substantive Majority. He served in Tibet in 1904 as D.A.Q.M.G.; was present at the action of Niani, and at the operations in and around Gyantse. He was mentioned in Despatches [London Gazette, 13 Dec. 1904]; received the Medal and clasp, and the Brevet of Lieutenant-Colonel 10 Nov. 1904. He became Major 5 Feb. 1905; was given the Brevet of Colonel 10 Nov. 1910; became Colonel, 1 Jan. 1911; served in the Abor Expedition, 1911–12. He served in the European War from 1915; was Brigade Commander (Colonel on Staff), India, 2 Nov. 1914, to 6 May, 1917; Brigade Commander, India, 1 Sept. 1917, to 14 June, 1918; Divisional Commander, India, 15 June, 1918; was promoted to Major-General 1 Jan. 1917. He was created a C.B. in 1915; a C.I.E. in 1916, and a K.C.I.E. in 1917, and mentioned in Despatches in 1916. Sir William Beynon married, in 1898, Edith Norah, youngest daughter of George Petrie, of 1, De Vere Gardens, W., and they have three daughters. He wrote "With Kelly to Chitral."

STEWART, COSMO GORDON, Lieut., was born 21 Nov. 1869, 8th son of Sir J. M. Stewart, 3rd Bart., and Lady Stewart, and was gazetted to the Royal Artillery 27 July, 1888, becoming Lieutenant 27 July, 1891. He served in the Chitral Campaign, 1895, with the Relief Force from Gilgit; was mentioned in Despatches [London Gazette, 16 July, 1895], and was created a Companion of the Distinguished Service Order [London Gazette, 16 July, 1895]: "Cosmo Gordon Stewart, Lieut., Royal Artillery. In recognition of services during the recent operations in Chitral." The Insignia were presented to him 7 Nov. 1895. He was employed with the Egyptian Army 6 May, 1897, to 25 Dec. 1900. In 1897 he served in the Nile Expedition (Egyptian Medal and clasp). In the Nile Expedition of 1898 he was present in the Battle of Khartoum, was mentioned in Despatches [London Gazette, 30 Sept. 1898], received the 4th Class of the Medjidie, the Medal and the clasp to the Egyptian Medal. He served in the Nile Expedition of 1890, in the first advance against the Khalifa (clasp to the Egyptian Medal). He had become Captain on 19 Nov. 1898. Capt. Stewart served in the South African War, 1901–02, on the Staff; took part in the operations in the Transvaal, May to Dec. 1901; and in the operations in Orange River Colony, Dec. 1901, to Feb. 1902, and received the Queen's Medal with four clasps. He became Major 1 April, 1904; was D.A.Q.M.G., Headquarters, India, 9 June, 1906, to 5 Dec. 1907; was D.A.A.G. India 6 Dec. 1907, to 27 Jan. 1909; G.S.O.2, Staff College, 28 Jan. 1909, to 21 Dec. 1913. Major Stewart was given the Brevet of Lieutenant-Colonel 5 Aug. 1914; became Lieutenant-Colonel 30 Oct. 1914, and served in the European War from 1914. He was G.S.O.1, 24th Division, New Armies, B.E.F., 16 May, 1915, to 22 Feb. 1916; temporary Brigadier-General 1 April, 1916; Brigade Commander, Home Forces, and commanding 183rd Infantry Brigade, B.E.F., 3 May, 1916, to 29 July, 1916; Brigadier-General, R.A., 33rd Division, B.E.F., 26 March, 1917, to 28 July, 1918; Brigade Commander, South Midland Reserve Brigade, Forces in Great Britain, 9 Sept. 1918. He was given the Brevet of Colonel 3 June, 1917; was mentioned in Despatches and created a C.M.G. He married, in 1911, Gladys Berry, daughter of the late Dr. J. H. Honeyman, of Auckland, and of Mrs. Bruce-Porter, 6, Grosvenor Street, W.

HARLEY, HENRY KELLETT, Lieut., was born 2 Dec. 1868, and was gazetted to the Royal Dublin Fusiliers, as Second Lieutenant, 14 July, 1890, being transferred to the Indian Staff Corps 13 June, 1892. He served in the Chitral Expedition in 1895; took part in the defence of the Fort of Chitral. He commanded the British Agents' Escort. Lieut. Harley was mentioned in Despatches [London Gazette, 16 July, 1895], received the Medal and clasp; was promoted to Captain 16 July, 1898; given the Brevet of Major 17 July, 1898, and was created a Companion of the Distinguished Service Order [London Gazette, 16 July, 1895]: "Henry Kellett Harley, Lieut., Indian Staff Corps. In recognition of services during the recent operations in Chitral." The Insignia were presented to him 11 Nov. 1895. He was employed with the Egyptian Army 18 Jan. 1897, to 30 June, 1898, and served in the Nile Expedition of 1897 (Medal with clasp). In the Nile Expedition of 1898 he was present at the Battle of the Atbara; was severely wounded, mentioned in Despatches [London Gazette, 24 May, 1898], and received the Medal. He became Captain, Dorsetshire Regt. 24 June, 1900, and 7th Hussars 24 June, 1900; and served in the South African War in 1901 and 1902, taking part in the operations in the Transvaal, March to 31 May, 1902; operations in Orange River Colony, January 10 to May, 1902; operations in Cape Colony, Dec. 1901, to Jan. 1902. He received the Queen's Medal with five clasps. He was Adjutant, Imperial Yeomanry, 18 Jan. 1905, to 31 March, 1908; and Adjutant, Territorial Force, 1 April, 1908; and retired from the 7th Hussars 3 July, 1909. Major Harley served in the European War in France, with the R.F.A. and R.G.A., 1916–17; was mentioned in Despatches; received the Croix de Guerre and the Bronze Military Medal for Valour, and was promoted to Lieutenant-Colonel 3 June, 1919. He served on the Staff of the British Mission, G.H.Q., Italy. Lieut.-Colonel Harley married, in 1899, the Hon. Margaret Holland, daughter of the 1st Lord Rotherham, and they had one son and one daughter. He married (2ndly) Thella, daughter of Henri Bluston, of Kovno, Russian Poland, and they had three sons. Colonel Harley died 9 Jan. 1921. An obituary notice ("Times" of 12 Jan.) said that the death had occurred, "in his fifty-third year, of Lieut.-Colonel H. K. Harley, who served with distinction in the Chitral Expedition of 1895, and gained the D.S.O. in the defence of Chitral Fort. . . . He was a descendant of Robert Harley, Earl of Oxford."

London Gazette, 27 Aug. 1895.—"The Queen has been graciously pleased to give orders for the following appointment to the Distinguished Service Order, in recognition of the services of the undermentioned Officer during the recent operations in Chitral."

PETERSON, FREDERICK HOPEWELL, Lieut., was born 5 Sept. 1864, son of F. V. W. Peterson and Mrs. F. V. W. Peterson. He entered the Yorkshire Light Infantry 25 Nov. 1885, and joined the Indian Staff Corps 4 Sept. 1887. He served in the Sikkim Expedition, 1888 (Medal and clasp); in the Hazara Expedition, 1891 (clasp). He served in the operations in Chitral, 1895, with the Relief Force from Gilgit; was mentioned in Despatches [London Gazette, 23 Aug. 1895], received the Medal and clasp, and was created a Companion of the Distinguished Service Order [London Gazette, 27 Aug. 1895]: "Frederick Hopewell Peterson, Lieut., Indian Staff Corps. In recognition of services during the recent operations in Chitral." The Insignia were presented 20 Nov. 1895. He became Captain, Indian Army, 25 Nov. 1896, and Major 25 Nov. 1903. He served in Tibet, 1903–04; was present at the action of Niarri, and in the operations at and around Gyantsi and in the march to Lhassa. Major Peterson was mentioned in Despatches [London Gazette, 13 Dec. 1904], and received the Medal and clasp. He became Lieutenant-Colonel 31 Dec. 1909; served in the Abor Expedition, 1911–12; was mentioned in Despatches; received the Medal and clasp, and was given the Brevet of Colonel 6 June, 1912. He became Colonel 20 March, 1914; temporary Brigade Commander (Colonel on the Staff), India, Jhelum Brigade, 9 Aug. 1915. He was created a C.B. in 1916. He married, in 1896, Mary Elizabeth, daughter of H. Howard.

London Gazette, 27 Aug. 1895.—"The Queen has been graciously pleased to give orders for the following appointments to the Distinguished Service Order, and promotions in the Army, in recognition of the services of the undermentioned Officers during the recent operations in Waziristan. To be Companions of the Distinguished Service Order."

THOMPSON, WILLIAM OLIVER, Lieut.-Colonel, was born on 14 Nov. 1844, in Birmingham, son of Major George Thompson, 21st Fusiliers, and Elizabeth Thompson (*née* Masterman). He entered the Army 18 March, 1863, as Ensign, 82nd Foot; became Lieutenant, Bengal Staff Corps, 12 Oct. 1866, and Captain 18 March, 1875; served in the Afghan War, 1878–79 (Medal); in the Mahsud-Waziri Expedition, 1881. He was promoted Major 18 March, 1883; served in the Hazara Expedition, 1888 (Medal with clasp); in the 1st and 2nd Miranzai Expeditions in 1891 (Despatches; G.G.O. 632 of 1891; clasp); became Lieutenant-Colonel 18 March, 1889; commanded the 3rd Sikhs, Frontier Force (now 53rd Sikhs), from 3 July, 1891. The following is a report on the regiment made by Lord Roberts: "Inspected the 3rd Sikhs at Kohat last November, and was very pleased to find it in the admirable condition for which it has been noted for some years past. It is composed of a fine, serviceable body of men, who are well-drilled, smart and well set-up. A grand spirit pervades all ranks, and the regiment is fit for any services. The Assistant Adjutant-General for Musketry reports that 'this is the best battalion I have seen on the Frontier. There is a finish and smartness about the drill that is seldom seen. The men are satisfactory as shots and brilliant as regards fire discipline. The native officers and non-commissioned officers are very good all round—especially as Section Commanders. The present efficient state of the 3rd Sikhs is no doubt due to its having an exceptionally good set of British officers, and to the general wise and careful supervision exercised by the Commandant, Lieut.-Colonel Thompson, to whom the greatest credit is due.' Capt. Codrington is particularly noticed for zeal and energy. (Sgd.) Roberts, General, C.-in-C., India. Dated 19 July, 1892, Adjutant-General's Office, Simla." "Capt. Fasken desires to congratulate, on behalf of Colonel Thompson and himself, the British and native officers and non-commissioned officers and men on the report on the regiment by His Excellency the Commander-in-Chief, which has just been received, and he is sure he is expressing the opinion of Colonel Thompson that the splendid report is entirely due to the excellent spirit which pervades all ranks, and the constant endeavour of all to maintain its reputation for smartness and general efficiency. The regiment is therefore, as the Commander-in-Chief remarks, 'fit for any service.'" Lieut.-Colonel W. O. Thompson served in the Waziristan Expedition of 1894–95, in command of the 3rd Sikh Infantry, and was given the Brevet of Colonel, received clasp, mentioned in Despatches twice, G.S.O. 268 and 473 of 1895, and created a Companion of the Distinguished Service Order [London Gazette, 27 Aug. 1895]: "In recognition of services during the recent operations in Waziristan, William Oliver Thompson, Lieut.-Colonel, Indian Staff Corps." The Insignia, Warrant and Statutes of the D.S.O. were sent to Colonel Thompson on 4 Dec. 1895. He retired with the rank of Colonel 1 April, 1901, and died 10 Sept. 1917.

DAVIS, GEORGE McBRIDE, Lieut.-Colonel, was born at Newry, Ireland, 29 March, 1846, third son of the late Dr. W. A. Davis and of Mrs. W. A. Davis. He was educated at a private school; Queen's College, Belfast, and the Royal (late Queen's) University of Ireland (M.B., M.Ch.); entered the Bengal Medical Service as Assistant Surgeon 1 April, 1869, becoming Surgeon 1 July, 1873, and Surgeon-Major 1 April, 1881. He served on the N.W.F. of India, Mahsud-Waziri, 1881; Miranzai (1st) 1891; Hazara, 1891 (Medal with clasp); became Brigade Surgeon Lieut.-Colonel 17 Jan. 1894; served in Waziristan as P.M.O., Delimitation Escort, 1894. He was present at the action at Wano, 1894; was mentioned in Despatches [London Gazette, 14 June, 1895], received a clasp, and was created a Companion of the Distinguished Service Order [London Gazette, 27 Aug. 1895]: "George McBride Davis, Brigade Surgeon Lieut.-Colonel, Indian Medical Service. In recognition of services during the recent operations in Waziristan." The Insignia were presented 11 Sept. 1895. He served in the operations on the N.W. Frontier of India, 1897–98, with the Tirah Expeditionary Force as Principal Medical Officer, 2nd Division; was present at the actions of Dargai, Sampagha, etc., and in the march down the Bara (Despatches [London Gazette, 5 April, 1898]; Medal and two clasps, and created a C.B., 1898). He became Surgeon Colonel 2 April, 1898 Colonel Davis took part in the China Campaign of 1901 as P.M.O. Expeditionary Force (Despatches [London Gazette, 13 Sept. 1901]; Medal). He served on the N.W. Frontier of India, in Waziristan, 1901–2, as P.M.O.; received a clasp, and was mentioned in Despatches [London Gazette, 8 Aug. 1902]. He was later Principal Medical Officer at Peshawar. Colonel G. McBride Davis, who had retired 24 Oct. 1907, was granted the Good Service pension in 1900. He died 4 Oct. 1909.

WHARRY, HERBERT, Capt., was born in 1857, son of Charles Wharry, Esq., Charlton Lodge, Thornton Heath, Surrey, and of Mrs. Charles Wharry. He entered the Army in 1876; became Captain, I.S.C., in 1887; served with the First and Second Miranzai Expeditions (Despatches; Medal and clasp). He again saw active service in Waziristan, 1894–95, and was present at the action of Wano. He was mentioned in Despatches; received a clasp, and was created a Companion of the Distinguished Service Order [London Gazette, 27 Aug. 1895]: "Herbert Wharry, Capt., Indian Staff Corps. In recognition of services during the recent operations in Waziristan." The Insignia were presented 8 Dec. 1895. He died 23 Sept. 1898.

EWART, RICHARD HENRY, Capt., was born 26 Dec. 1864, son of the late Colonel C. H. Ewart, I.S.C., of Clifton, Bristol. He entered the Royal Dublin Fusiliers as Lieutenant 25 Aug. 1883; became Lieutenant, Hampshire Regt., 20 Oct. 1883; Indian Staff Corps, 27 March, 1886. He served with the Hazara Expedition, 1891 (Medal and clasp); Isazai Expedition, 1892; became Captain, I.S.C., 25 Aug. 1894. He served with the Waziristan Field Force, 1894–95 (Despatches, 2 July, 1895); created a Companion of the Distinguished Service Order [London Gazette, 27 Aug. 1895]: "Richard Henry Ewart, Capt., Indian Staff Corps. In recognition of services during the recent operations in Waziristan." He became Major, Indian Army, 25 Aug. 1901; was A.Q.M.G. for Supply, India, and Assistant Director of Farms, India, 1 May, 1905, to 21 March, 1912; became Lieut.-Colonel 1 May, 1906; was given the Brevet of Colonel 1 May, 1910; was promoted to Colonel 3 May, 1911; A.D.C. to the King 3 Oct. 1911; C.I.E., 1912; Deputy Director of Supplies and

Transport 30 Sept. 1914, to 3 Dec. 1915; European War, 1914–15 (Despatches). He was D.A.Q.M.G., graded Brigadier-General, East African Force, 4 Dec. 1915 (Despatches); created a C.B. 1915; was promoted to Major-General 1 Jan. 1917. He was created a K.C.M.G. in 1919. He married (1st), in 1889, Charlotte Frewen Laurie. He married (2ndly), in 1899, Marion Annie, daughter of Lieut.-Colonel Morris Baker, Redholme, Folkestone, and widow of J. R. Thomas, and they have one son and three daughters.

HERBERT, CLAUDE, Lieut., was born at Alipore, 20 Oct. 1862, fourth son of the late Major-General Charles Herbert, and of Sophy Geraldine, his wife. He was educated at Florence, and served in the Militia (3rd Battn. Lincolnshire Regt.), 1881–84. He entered the Army 12 Nov. 1884, and was commissioned 12 Nov. 1884, into the East Yorkshire Regt.; served in Burma, 1886–87 and 1888–89 (Medal and two clasps); Sikkim Expedition, 1891 (clasp); Waziristan, 1894 (mentioned in Despatches; received a clasp, and was created a Companion of the Distinguished Service Order [London Gazette, 27 Aug. 1895]: "Claude Herbert, Lieut., Indian Staff Corps. In recognition of services during the recent operations in Waziristan." The Insignia were presented by the Queen 5 Dec. 1895). Decoration awarded for gallantry at a night attack on Camp Wano, Waziristan, when his post was attacked in front and rear. In the same year (1895) he married Amy Elizabeth, eldest daughter of the late William Handford, Director of Education, Oudh. Promoted Captain 12 Nov. 1895; Major 12 Nov. 1902. Lieut.-Colonel Herbert was promoted to Lieut.-Colonel, 1st Gurkha Rifles, 12 Nov. 1919; became Cantonment Magistrate at Ranikhet, India. Retired on 2 June, 1919.

HORNBY, MONTAGUE LEYLAND, Lieut., was born 23 July, 1870, son of Major R. M. Hornby and Lucy Turner. He was educated at Shrewsbury School, and was gazetted to the East Lancashire Regt. as Second Lieutenant 30 Jan. 1889, becoming Lieutenant, East Lancashire Regt. 18 March, 1891, and Indian Staff Corps 27 March, 1892. He served in the Waziristan Expedition of 1894–95, as Orderly Officer to the G.O.C., Waziristan Delimitation Escort in 1894; was present at the action at Wano, and was severely wounded. He was afterwards Orderly Officer to the G.O.C., 1st Brigade. Lieut. Hornby was mentioned in Despatches [London Gazette, 14 June, 1895]; received the Medal with clasp, and was created a Companion of the Distinguished Service Order [London Gazette, 27 Aug. 1895]: "Montague Leyland Hornby, Lieut., Indian Staff Corps. In recognition of services in the recent operations in Waziristan." The Insignia, Warrant and Statutes were sent to Lieut. Hornby in Russia. He served in the Tirah Campaign in 1897–98, taking part in the operations in the Bara Valley 7–14 Dec. 1897 (Medal with two clasps). Lieut. Hornby was employed with the King's African Rifles 10 March, 1898, to 21 June, 1904, serving as Adjutant and Quarter Master, Uganda Rifles, and taking part in the operations against the Ogaden Somalis (Medal with clasp). In Uganda in 1898–99 he served as Adjutant and Quarter Master, Uganda Rifles, and was present in the operations in Unyoro against Kabarega, acting as Transport and Signalling Officer to the Column (clasp). He became Captain, Indian Army, 30 Jan. 1900, and local Major in 1901. In 1900 he served in Uganda in the Nandi Expedition, in command of a column; was mentioned in Despatches [London Gazette, 10 Sept. 1901], and received the Medal and clasp. From 16 July, 1903, to 2 Aug. 1903, he was Base Commandant, Somaliland Field Force; from 22 June, 1904, to 31 March, 1907, was Staff Officer to His Majesty's Commander-in-Chief in Somaliland, 1904–06, with rank of Lieutenant-Colonel, and commanded the troops in Somaliland, 1906–7. From 1 April, 1907, to 20 Nov. 1907, was employed as Chief Transport Officer in the Somaliland Expedition; mentioned in Despatches [London Gazette, 2 Sept. 1904; received a clasp, and was given the Brevet of Major 7 Sept. 1904, becoming Major 30 Jan. 1907. Major Hornby served in the European War from 1914; as Brigade Major, 70th Infantry Brigade, New Armies, 23 Sept. 1914, to 25 May, 1915; as Brigade Commander, 116th Infantry Brigade, British Expeditionary Force and British Armies in France, 14 April, 1916, to 13 April, 1918, and 21 Oct. 1918, to 10 Nov. 1918, and as Brigade Commander, 137th Infantry Brigade, British Armies in France, from 11 Nov. 1918. He became Lieutenant-Colonel 24 Nov. 1917, and was given the Brevet of Colonel 3 June, 1918. He was created a C.M.G. in 1918, and was six times mentioned in Despatches during the war. He has published "How to March" (1914); "The Platoon Roll-Book" (1915); "How to buy Land in Canada" (1913). He married, in 1902, Harriet Millicent, daughter of Major Corbett Winder, of Vaynor Park, and they have four daughters.

London Gazette, 21 Jan. 1896.—"The Queen has also been graciously pleased to give orders for the following appointments to the Distinguished Service Order, and promotions in the Army, in recognition of the services of the undermentioned Officers during the operations of the Chitral Relief Force. To be Companions of the Distinguished Service Order."

GORDON, STANNUS VERNER, Lieut.-Colonel, was born 20 Aug. 1846, and was gazetted to the 36th Foot as Ensign 9 Aug. 1864, becoming Lieutenant, 36th Foot, 22 May, 1868, and Lieutenant, Bengal Staff Corps, 1 Aug. 1868. He served in the Afghan War, 1878–80, including the passage of the Mungiar Defile Expedition into the Khost Valley; action of Charasiah, and subsequent pursuit; defence of Camp Latabund; affair at Saidabad; march from Kabul to the relief of Kandahar, and battle of 1 Sept. He received the Medal and three clasps, and the Bronze Star; was given the Brevet of Major 2 March, 1881, and was mentioned in Despatches [London Gazette, 4 May, 1880, and 3 Dec. 1880]. He served in the First Miranzai Expedition in 1891. In the Chitral Campaign he was Commandant, 23rd Bengal Infantry, serving with the Relief Force. He was mentioned in Despatches 15 Nov. 1895; received the Medal with clasp, and was created a Companion of the Distinguished Service Order [London Gazette, 21 Jan. 1896]: "Stannus Verner Gordon, Lieut.-Colonel, Indian Staff Corps. In

recognition of services during the operations of the Chitral Relief Force." The Insignia were presented to him 11 April, 1896. He was given the Brevet of Colonel 23 June, 1897, and retired with the rank of Colonel 2 March, 1904.

YALDWIN, ALFRED GEORGE, Lieut.-Colonel, entered the Army in 1896; served in the Afghan War, 1879 and 1889 (Medal); in the Chitral Campaign, 1895. He was mentioned in Despatches; received the Medal and clasp, and was created a Companion of the Distinguished Service Order [London Gazette, 21 Jan. 1896]: Alfred George Yaldwin, Lieut.-Colonel, Indian Staff Corps. In recognition of services during operations of the Chitral Field Force." The Insignia were presented 28 June, 1896. He became Lieut.-Colonel 14 Sept. 1892. Lieut.-Colonel A. G. Yaldwin became Assistant Commissary-General, First Class, and retired 17 Nov. 1898. He died 7 Feb. 1905.

POYSER, RICHARD, Colonel, was born 7 April, 1842, at Ashover, Derbyshire, son of Joseph Poyser, of Wirksworth, Derbyshire, and his wife, Anne Poyser (née Frost). He was educated at Wirksworth Grammar

Richard Poyser.

School, and at the Royal Veterinary College, London, and joined the Army 12 Sept. 1865; gazetted to 7th Dragoon Guards Jan. 1867; exchanged into the Royal Horse Artillery, and in 1876 was transferred to the 6th Dragoon Guards (Carabiniers), and served with that regiment through the Afghan War of 1879–80, under General Sir R. O. Bright, K.C.B., being present in the expeditions to the Lughman Valley and against the Wuzeeri Kugianis (Medal); joined the A.V.D. in 1883. Colonel Poyser was Principal Veterinary Officer, Chitral Relief Force, under Sir Robert Lowe, K.C.B., 1895. He was mentioned in Despatches [London Gazette, 15 Nov. 1895]; received the Medal and clasp, and was created a Companion of the Distinguished Service Order [London Gazette, 21 Jan. 1896]: "Richard Poyser, Veterinary Lieut.-Colonel, Army Veterinary Department. In recognition of services during the operations of the Chitral Relief Force." Insignia presented 28 June, 1896. Till his retirement on 7 April, 1897, he was P.V.O., Punjab Army, India, and was promoted to Colonel in 1902 for services during the South African War, and received the thanks of Earl Roberts, Commander-in-Chief. Colonel Poyser was a good polo player in the rougher game of the earlier seventies in India, and played with the Carabiniers later in England, for which, and other mounted sports, he had numerous trophies. He also went in for pig-sticking in various parts, and racing. He was a collector of war and memorial medals, and of old Chinese, English and other pottery and porcelain; old Persian and Indian swords, and Hindu Temple and other bronzes, etc. He married 11 Jan. 1870, at Peshawar, India, Annie Maria, daughter of John Cruikshank, of Ecclefechan, Dumfries, and they have a son, Richard Cruikshank, M.R.C.S. and L.R.C.P. Capt., R.A.M.C., and two daughters, Annie (married to Colonel H. G. H. Kennard, C.B.E., 5th Dragoon Guards), and Ida Evelyne (married to Major O. E. M. Saunders, 5th Dragoon Guards). He died 4 June, 1919.

BARROW, ARTHUR FREDERICK, Lieut.-Colonel, was born at Bangalore 18 Oct. 1850, eldest son of Major-General de S. Barrow. He was educated at Cheltenham College, and was gazetted to the 101st Regiment as Ensign 18 Aug. 1869. He joined the 105th Light Infantry 21 Aug. 1869, and the Indian Staff Corps 3 Dec. 1872. He served in the Afghan War, 1878–80 (Medal); became Captain 18 Feb. 1881; passed through the Staff College in 1883; was in the Afghan Boundary Commission, 1884–85 (Despatches; Brevet of Major 16 Feb. 1887, and C.M.G.). He served as Base Commandant at Nowshera, Chitral Relief Force (was mentioned in Despatches [London Gazette, 15 Nov. 1895]; received the Medal and clasp), and was created a Companion of the Distinguished Service Order [London Gazette, 21 Jan. 1896]: "Arthur Frederick Barrow, C.M.G., Lieut.-Colonel, Indian Staff Corps. In recognition of services during the recent operations in Chitral." Insignia presented on 17 Nov. 1896. He was D.A.Q.M.G., Peshawar, 1875; D.A.Q.M.G., Gwalior, 1881; in the Intelligence Division, War Office, 1886–91; Personal Assistant, Military Member of Indian Council, 1891; officiating A.Q.M.G., Intelligence Branch, India. He was promoted to Colonel. Colonel A. F. Barrow, C.M.G., D.S.O., died on 5 Jan. 1903.

HUGHES-HALLETT, JAMES WYNDHAM, Major, was born at Petham, near Canterbury, Kent, 15 Sept. 1852, third surviving son of the late Rev. James Hughes-Hallett, of Higham, Canterbury, and Dunmow, Essex, and of Mary Frances, eldest daughter of the late General Sir Thomas Gage Montresor, K.C.K.H. He was educated at Haileybury and Sandhurst, and was gazetted to the 53rd Foot as Sub-Lieutenant 26 June, 1872, and transferred to the 72nd Foot 15 Nov. 1872, becoming Lieutenant, 27th Foot, 26 June, 1873. He served during the Afghan War, 1878–79, with the Kurram Field Force, and was present in the reconnaissance in force and assault and capture of Peiwar Kotal, and at the passage of Chappri defile. He was mentioned in Despatches, and received the Medal and clasp. He became Captain,

J. W. Hughes-Hallett.

Seaforth Highlanders, 2 Sept. 1880, and served in the Egyptian Expedition of 1882, being present at the engagement of Chalouf; at the seizure of the Suez Canal, east of Ismailia; at the Battle of Tel-el-Kebir, occupation of Zagazig and of Cairo. He was mentioned in Despatches [London Gazette, 8 Sept. 1882]; received the Medal with clasp, and the Khedive's Bronze Star. He became Major 27 March, 1890, and in 1895 served with the Chitral Relief Force, in command of the 2nd Battn. of his regiment. He was mentioned in Despatches [London Gazette, 15 Nov. 1895], and created a Companion of the Distinguished Service Order [London Gazette, 21 Jan. 1896]: "James Wyndham Hughes-Hallett, Major, Seaforth Highlanders. In recognition of services during the operations of the Chitral Relief Force." He was promoted to Lieut.-Colonel 22 Dec. 1897. Lieut.-Colonel Hughes-Hallett served in South Africa, 1899–1902, in command of his regiment and temporarily in command of the Highland Brigade. He took part in the advance on Kimberley, including the action at Magersfontein. Operations in the Orange Free State, Feb. to May, 1900 (including operations at Paardeberg, 17–26 Feb.); actions at Poplar Grove and Dreifontein. Operations in Orange River Colony, May to 29 Nov. 1900 (slightly wounded), including actions at Wittebergen (1 to 29 July). He was mentioned in Despatches [London Gazette, 8 Feb. 1901]; was given the Brevet of Colonel; received the Queen's Medal with five clasps, the King's Medal with two clasps, and was created a C.B. He was promoted to Colonel 5 Aug. 1902; commanded the 72nd and 79th Regimental Districts, 1902; was created a C.V.O. in 1905. On 5 Aug. 1906, half-pay, late Regimental District, and on 20 Oct. 1906, on retired pay. He commanded the Gordon Volunteer Infantry Brigade, 1906; commanded the Gordon Territorial Brigade, 1906–11. His favourite recreations are shooting and cricket. Colonel Hughes-Hallett married, on 26 Oct. 1893, Alice, daughter of the late Capt. Harry William Sanders. Colonel Hughes-Hallett distinguished himself in the South African War. After the death of General Wauchope he took command of the Highland Brigade at Magersfontein. We read also, in the "Official History of the War in South Africa," how he relieved the garrison at Jagersfontein, and of his services under General Macdonald and under Sir Bindon Blood.

HADOW, REGINALD CAMPBELL, Major, was born 6 July, 1851, son of the late Patrick Douglas Hadow, J.P. (chairman of the P. & O. Steam Navigation Company), of The Priory, Sudbury, Middlesex, and Mrs. P. D. Hadow. He was educated at Cheltenham, and was gazetted to the 55th Foot as Ensign 27 April, 1870, becoming Lieutenant, 55th Foot, 28 Oct. 1871, and Bengal Staff Corps, 26 July, 1876. He served in the Afghan War, 1878–80, taking part in the advance on Ghuznee, actions of Ahmed Khel and Urzoo, march from Kabul to the relief of Kandahar, and battle of 1 Sept. (Medal with two clasps; Bronze Star). He became Captain 27 April, 1882, and in 1885 again saw active service in the Sudan Expedition, Suakin; action of Tofrek and operations at Tamai (Medal with two clasps; Bronze Star). He was promoted to Major 27 April, 1890, and in the following year served in the Second Miranzai Expedition (Medal with clasp). In 1895 he served in the Chitral Expedition, with the Relief Force, and was present at the storming of the Malakand Pass and the forcing of the passage of the Swat River. Was mentioned in Despatches [London Gazette, 15 Nov. 1895]; received the Medal and clasp, and was created a Companion of the Distinguished Service Order [London Gazette, 21 Jan. 1896]: "Reginald Campbell Hadow, Major, Indian Staff Corps. In recognition of services during the recent operations in Chitral." The Insignia were presented to him 11 April, 1896. He was promoted to Lieut.-Colonel 27 April, 1896. In 1897–98 Lieut.-Colonel Hadow served on the N.W. Frontier of India, being present at the operations on the Samana and in the Kurram Valley during Aug. and Sept. 1897. Operations of the Flying Column in the Kurram Valley, under Colonel Richardson, 20 Aug. to 1 Oct. 1897 (two clasps). He served in Tirah, 1897–98; actions of Chagru Kotal and Dargai, and operations in the Khauki Valley. He was very severely wounded (clasp). He commanded the 15th Sikhs. On 15 Feb. 1902, he was given the Brevet of Colonel, and on 27 April, 1902, retired with the rank of Colonel. Colonel Hadow's favourite recreations are cricket, golf and shooting. He married, in 1876, Annie Sophia Erskine (she died in 1912), daughter of the late General David Pott, C.B., of Borthwickshiel, Hawick, N.B.

SHIRRES, JOHN CHIVAS, Major, became Lieutenant, Royal Artillery, 11 Sept. 1873; Captain 4 Oct. 1882, and Major 23 May, 1890. He was created a Companion of the Distinguished Service Order [London Gazette, 21 Jan. 1896]: "John Chivas Shirres, Major, Royal Artillery. In recognition of services during the recent operations in Chitral." Major Shirres was personally decorated by Her Majesty 7 Sept. 1896. He was given the Brevet of Lieutenant-Colonel 20 May, 1898, and died 31 March, 1899.

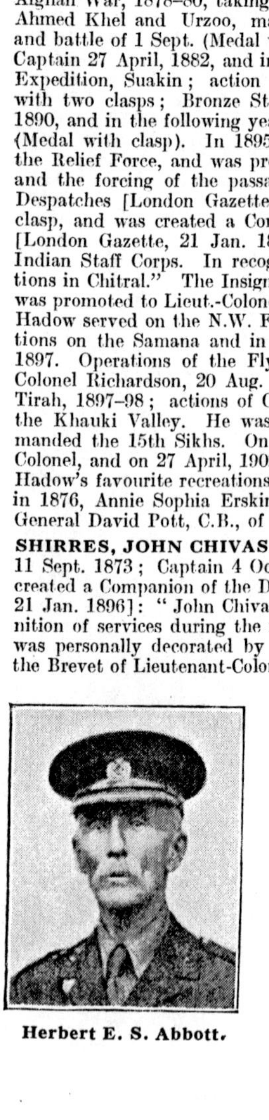

Herbert E. S. Abbott.

ABBOTT, HERBERT EDWARD STACY, Major, was born at Alipore, India, 6 April, 1855, son of the late General Herbert Edward Stacy Abbott, Bengal Infantry. He was educated at Elizabeth College, Guernsey, and at the R.M.A., Woolwich; was commissioned in the Royal Engineers 17 Aug. 1874; went to India, 1877; served in the Afghan War as Assistant Engineer, Khyber Line Force and Khyber Brigade, 1878–79–80 (Medal). He was employed in Public Works Department, Punjab; became Captain 17 Aug. 1885; served with the Hazara Expedition, 1888 (Medal with clasp); Hazara Expedition, 1892 (clasp and Despatches [London Gazette, 20 Oct. 1891]). He became Major 6 Aug. 1894. He served with the Chitral Relief Force, 1895 (Despatches; Medal with clasp, and created a Companion of the Distinguished Service Order [London Gazette, 21 Jan. 1896]: "Herbert Edward Stacy Abbott, Major, Royal Engineers. In recognition of services during the operations of the Chitral Relief Force." Presentation in June, 1896). He was invalided to England in 1897; returned to India, 1898; Lieut.-Colonel, 1901; officiating Chief Engineer, Punjab, P.W.D., 1903–4; returned to England, 1904; Brevet Colonel 1 Oct. 1904; Colonel, retired, 1 Oct. 1906; re-employed, 1909, as War Office Inspector of Territorial Buildings, and in charge of building operations, Duke of York's Headquarters, Chelsea; special duty, London District, 1915–19. Colonel Abbott was awarded a C.B.E. in the War Honours List, Jan. 1919. He married, 8 March, 1881, at Bangalore, India, Mary, daughter of Thomas Aveling, of Rochester, Kent, and their children were: Thomas Aveling Abbott, born 13 Oct. 1882 (Captain, R.A., killed in action), and Ida Daisy Abbott.

HAMILTON, WILLIAM GEORGE, Major, was born 2 Jan. 1900. He was gazetted to the 30th Foot 11 May, 1878, and became Lieutenant, East Lancashire Regt., 23 June, 1880. He was Adjutant, East Lancashire Regt., 10 Nov. 1880, to 9 Nov. 1885; became Captain 18 April, 1885; was Station Staff Officer, First Class, Bengal, 27 June, 1889, to 27 July, 1890. He served in the Isazai Expedition, 1892, as Brigade Major, and became Major, East Lancashire Regt., 17 Sept. 1895. In 1895 he served in the Chitral Campaign with the Relief Force. On the Staff, taking part in the storming of the Malakand Pass, the passage of the Swat River, and action at the Panjkora River. He was mentioned in Despatches [London Gazette, 15 Nov. 1895]; received the Medal with clasp, and was created a Companion of the Distinguished Service Order [London Gazette, 21 Jan. 1896]: "William George Hamilton, Major, The East Lancashire Regt. In recognition of services during the recent operations in Chitral." Major Hamilton was personally decorated by Her Majesty 15 May, 1896. He was D.A.Q.M.G., Headquarters, Bengal, 15 Aug. 1900, to 27 Sept. 1900; was transferred to the Norfolk Regt. 20 Feb. 1901; was promoted to Lieut.-Colonel 12 March, 1904; was A.A.G., India, 1 Sept. 1904, to 19 June, 1908; was given the Brevet of Colonel 12 March, 1907; was A.A.G., Musketry, Headquarters, India, 20 June, 1908; became Colonel 10 Feb. 1909. He commanded the Southern Brigade, India, 1913–15; served in the European War from 1914; in Mesopotamia (Despatches); as D.A.Q.M.G., 1915–16; was created a C.B. in 1915, and retired from the Staff, with the rank of Brigadier-General, 27 Jan. 1919. He was created a C.S.I. in 1918.

EDWARDS, JOHN BURNARD, Capt., was born at Saharanpore 6 May, 1857, son of the late R. M. Edwards, B.C.S. He was educated at Haileybury and Sandhurst, and joined the 13th Foot 30 Jan. 1878, and the 8th Foot 24 July, 1878. He served in the Afghan War, 1875–80, and was present at the action of 28 Nov. 1878, in Kurram Valley, and in the battle and capture of Peiwar Kotal (Medal with clasp). He became Lieutenant, Liverpool Regt., 11 March, 1880, and Bengal Staff Corps 27 Nov. 1881. He became Captain, Indian Staff Corps, 30 Jan. 1889; was Inspecting Officer, Imperial Service Cavalry, in Central India, 1891–96. Capt. Edwards served in the Chitral Campaign in 1895, with the Relief Force, in charge of the Imperial Service Gwalior Transport Corps; was mentioned in Despatches [London Gazette, 15 Nov. 1895]; received the Medal with clasp, and was created a Companion of the Distinguished Service Order [London Gazette, 21 Jan. 1896]: "John Burnard Edwards, Capt., Indian Staff Corps. In recognition of his services during the recent operations in Chitral." The Insignia were presented 2 May, 1896. He acted as Staff Officer from the Indian Army to the late Duke of Clarence during the Duke's Indian tour. He became Major, Indian Army, 30 Jan. 1898; Lieut.-Colonel, Indian Army, 30 Jan. 1904; was given the Brevet of Colonel 12 Feb. 1907, and became Colonel 1 March, 1908; was Inspecting Officer of Imperial Service Cavalry in Central India, 1908–13, retiring 31 Jan. 1913. Colonel Edwards served in the European War from 1914, as a Mounted Brigade Commander, and was appointed Honorary Brigadier-General. He joined the B.E.F., France, in July, 1916, in command of the 19th Labour Battn. Scottish Rifles, and was transferred to the Labour Corps; was mentioned in Despatches and created a C.B. Brigadier-General J. B. Edwards married, in 1896, Mildred Amy Lilian, daughter of the late P. J. White, I.C.S.

NUGENT, OLIVER STEWART WOOD, Capt., was born 9 Nov. 1860, son of the late Major-General St. George M. Nugent, and Emily, daughter of the Right Hon. Edward Litton. He was educated at Harrow, and gazetted to the Royal Munster Fusiliers 29 July, 1882, becoming Lieutenant, K.R.R.C., 14 April, 1883, and Captain, 15 Oct. 1890. He served in the Hazara Expedition in 1891 (Medal with clasp), and in the Miranzai Expedition, 1891, as extra Orderly Officer to the G.O.C.; was mentioned in Despatches [London Gazette, 15 Sept. 1891], and received a clasp. In 1892 he served in the Isazai Expedition. He took part in the operations in Chitral in 1895, with the Relief Force, including the storming of the Malakand Pass (slightly wounded) and the engagement at Khar. He was mentioned in Despatches, slightly wounded; received the Medal and clasp, and was created a Companion of the Distinguished Service Order [London Gazette, 21 Jan. 1896]: "Oliver Stewart Wood Nugent, Capt., King's Royal Rifle Corps. In recognition of services during the recent operations in Chitral. Capt. Nugent was personally decorated by Her Majesty 3 July, 1896. He was promoted to Major 21 Oct. 1899, and from 1899 to 1900 served in the South African War, taking part in the operations in Natal, 1899, including the action at Talana (dangerously wounded). He was mentioned in Despatches [London Gazette, 10 Sept. 1901], and received the Queen's Medal with two clasps. He was D.A.A.G., H.Q., Ireland, 1 Jan. 1901, to 3 Oct. 1902; was D.A.Q.M.G., 3rd Army Corps, 19 Oct. 1902, to 10 Dec. 1903; was promoted to Lieut.-Colonel 15 Oct. 1906; Brevet Colonel 23 June, 1909; A.D.C. to the King 23 June, 1909, to 31 Dec. 1915; Colonel 15 Oct. 1910; Brigade Commander, Hampshire

Infantry Brigade, Southern Command, 1 Jan. 1911, to 13 Feb. 1914. He served in the European War from 1914; was Commander, Humber Defences, 5 Aug. 1914, to 5 May, 1915; Brigade Commander, 41st Infantry Brigade, B.E.F., 6 May, 1915, to 16 Sept. 1915; Divisional Commander, 36th Division, B.E.F., and British Armies in France, 17 Sept. 1915, to 1918; promoted to Major-General 1 Jan. 1916; Divisional Commander, India, 3 Aug. 1918. He was created a C.B. in 1917. Major-General O. S. W. Nugent married, in 1899, Catharine Percy, daughter of the late T. Evans Lees and of Mrs. Lees, of Beaucroft, Wimborne, Dorset, and they have one son and two daughters.

BRETHERTON, GEORGE HOWARD, Capt., was born at Gloucester 6 March, 1860, son of the late Edward Bretherton, of Clifton, Bristol, and S. Georgiana, daughter of the late W. Barton Price. He was educated privately, and joined the Royal Irish Regt. 29 July, 1882, from the Militia, and the I.S.C. 18 Sept. 1883; served in the Queen's Own Corps of Guides, 1884–87, becoming Lieutenant 15 Feb. 1884; served with the First and Second Miranzai Expeditions, 1891; was mentioned in Despatches [London Gazette, 15 Sept. 1891], and received the Medal and clasp; was on special duty at Gilgit, 1893–97 (services acknowledged by Government). He became Captain 29 July, 1893. Capt. Bretherton served in the Chitral Campaign in 1895, being present at the investment of the Fort at Mastuj. He was mentioned in Despatches; received Medal with clasp, and was created a Companion of the Distinguished Service Order [London Gazette, 21 Jan. 1896]: "George Howard Bretherton, Capt., Indian Staff Corps. In recognition of services during the operations of the Chitral Relief Force." The Insignia were presented 14 April, 1886. The Decoration was awarded for his services during the investment of Mastuj Fort by Chitralis. He took part in the operations on the North-West Frontier of India, 1897–98, with the Tirah Expeditionary Force as Brigade Commissariat Officer, Peshawar Column (Despatches [London Gazette, 5 April, 1898]; two clasps). From 1897 Major Bretherton was on special duty with the Supply Transport Corps in Kashmir. He married Katherine Murray, eldest daughter of Major-General R. P. Campbell, I.S.C. He was a Fellow of the Royal Geographical Society, and his favourite recreations were shooting, riding and fishing. Major Bretherton was drowned 25 July, 1904.

ROBERTSON, WILLIAM ROBERT, Capt., was born at Welbourne, Lincolnshire, 14 Sept. 1859, son of Thomas C. Robertson and Mrs. T. C. Robertson. He was educated at a private school, and was commissioned in the 3rd Dragoon Guards 27 June, 1888, becoming Lieutenant 1 March, 1891, and Captain 3 April, 1895. He was Staff Lieutenant, Intelligence Branch, Q.M.G. Department, India, 5 June, 1892, to 2 April, 1895, and Staff Captain (Intelligence Branch) 1 April, 1899, to 8 Oct. 1899. He served in the Chitral Campaign in 1895, with the Relief Force, as Field Intelligence Officer (22 March to 17 July, 1895); was mentioned in Despatches [London Gazette, 15 Nov. 1895]; received the Medal with clasp, and was created a Companion of the Distinguished Service Order [London Gazette, 21 Jan. 1896]: "William Robert Robertson, Capt., 3rd Dragoon Guards. In recognition of services during the recent operations in Chitral." The Warrant, Statutes and Insignia were sent to the Commander-in-Chief in India, and presented 9 April, 1896. He was D.A.A.G., Intelligence, Head Quarters of Army, 9 Oct. 1899, to 14 Feb. 1900; D.A.A.G., South Africa, 15 Feb. 1900, to 28 Oct. 1900; Staff Captain (Intelligence), Head Quarters Army, 29 Oct. 1900, to 30 Sept. 1901. In the South African War, in 1899 and 1900, he took part in the operations in the Orange Free State, Feb. to May, 1900, including operations at Paardeberg (17 to 26 Feb.); actions at Poplar Grove, Dreifontein, Vet River (5 and 6 May) and Zand River. Operations in the Transvaal in May and June, 1900, including actions near Johannesburg and Pretoria. Operations in the Transvaal, east of Pretoria, July to Oct. 1900 (Despatches, [London Gazette, 16 April, 1901]; Brevet of Lieutenant-Colonel 29 Nov. 1900; Queen's Medal with four clasps). He was promoted to Major, 10 March, 1900, and was A.Q.M.G. (Intelligence) Headquarters of Army 1 Oct. 1901, to 31 Jan. 1907; promoted to Colonel 29 Nov. 1903; created a C.B. in 1905; A.Q.M.G., Aldershot Army Corps, 14 May, 1907, to 28 Nov. 1907; Brigadier-General, General Staff, Aldershot Command, 29 Nov. 1907, to 31 July, 1910; Commandant, Staff College, 1 Aug. 1910, to 25 Dec. 1910, and 26 Dec. 1910, to 8 Oct. 1913; promoted to Major-General 26 Dec. 1910; Director of Military Training, War Office, 9 Oct. 1913, to 4 Aug. 1914; created a K.C.V.O. in 1913. He served in the European War from 1914. As Quartermaster-General, B.E.F., 5 Aug. 1914, to 24 Jan. 1915; Chief of General Staff, B.E.F., 25 Jan. 1915, to 22 Dec. 1915; promoted Lieutenant-General 28 Oct. 1915; Chief of Imperial General Staff, War Office, 23 Dec. 1915, to 18 Feb. 1918; created a K.C.B. in 1915; promoted to General 3 June, 1916; appointed A.D.C. to the King 15 Jan. 1917; created a G.C.B. in 1917; General Officer Commanding-in-Chief (temporary), Eastern Command, 19 Feb. to 29 May, 1918; General Officer Commanding-in-Chief, Great Britain, 30 May, 1918, to 21 April, 1919; General Officer Commanding-in-Chief, British Army of the Rhine, 22 April, 1919. Sir William Robertson was created a Baronet in 1919, and a G.C.M.G. in 1919. He married, in 1894, Mildred Adelaide, second daughter of the late Lieut.-General T. C. Palin, Bombay Staff Corps, and they have two sons and two daughters.

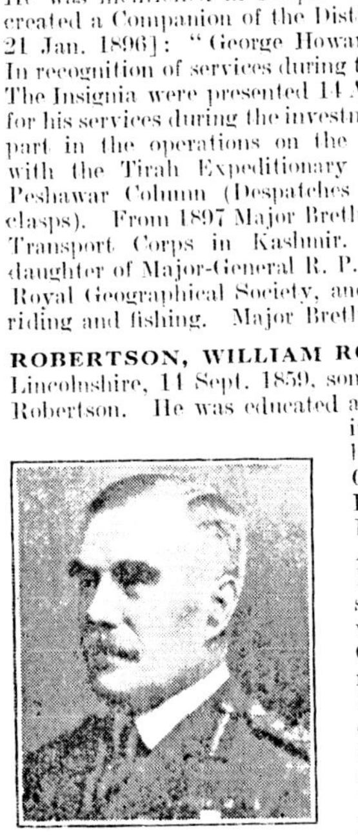

William R. Robertson.

We have given the bare outlines of the career of that distinguished soldier who has been called "our most silent general," and is known as "Wullie" to the Army.

Of Sir W. Robertson as Quartermaster-General, B.E.F., a writer in the "Sketch" of 2 Dec. 1914, says: "His is the case of a man prepared. His line of business ever since he looked after the railway transport during the Miranzai and Black Mountain Expeditions twenty-three years ago has had to do with the care of soldier men. Born some fifty odd years ago, Sir William comes of old Lincolnshire stock. From Welbourne, the place of his nativity, he went to a private school, where he is said to have been the matron's right-hand boy, and to have taken supreme command of the tuck-shop. His first regiment was the 3rd Dragoon Guards, which he entered in 1888; after doing useful transport work in the Black Mountains he was promoted to Staff Captain and D.A.Q.M.G. of the Intelligence Branch at Simla. For four years he worked hard at the provisioning and quartering of men in India. It will be seen that he has worked at the same subjects in several parts of the world. In the meantime, in 1895, he acted as Intelligence Officer to the Headquarters Staff of the Chitral Relief Force. Mentioned in Despatches and severely wounded, he got his D.S.O. at the end of the campaign, and was pounced upon by the War Office for its particular service. With his wife, whom he had met in India, and who was the daughter of another distinguished soldier (the late Lieut.-General T. C. Palin), he settled down for a short time to town life, but to a town life that was never for a moment oblivious to the interests of the camp and the field. With the outbreak of hostilities in South Africa he was very soon called upon to take up his duties as an active overseer of the discipline of the British forces on active service. There is no need to dwell on the connection between the work of a D.A.A.G. and the work of a Quartermaster-General. Discipline and supply, behaviour and the cook-pot, are inseparable. General Buller won the devotion and confidence of his men largely on account of his extreme thoughtfulness for their necessities and comforts, and . . . the efficiency and good discipline of our troops is increased by the excellence of the British commissariat. Pluck, dry powder and Providence are the three P's on which one noted leader sets his faith; provender making a good fourth. After South Africa, Sir William was booked for seven years by a War Office very desirous of reform. Afterwards he went to Aldershot as Assistant Quartermaster-General. Aldershot, of all places, was the right school for one who had to prepare for European complications."

How well Sir W. Robertson did his work when war broke out is seen in Sir John French's Despatch in Sept. 1914: "The Quartermaster-General, Sir William Robertson, has met what appeared to be almost insuperable difficulties with his characteristic energy, skill and despatch."

We get a glimpse in Sir Aylmer Haldane's book, "A Brigade of the Old Army" (pages 67–68), of the way in which Sir W. Robertson prepared the officers at the Staff College for the Great War. General Haldane says: "Though our training in peace-time had largely consisted of practice in offensive operations, the question of retreats, from that of Xenophon onwards, had always interested me. And from the time that I was appointed to command the troops at Shorncliffe I had realized more strongly than before the possibility that if ever our Army were to take part in a European War, the opening operation which it might be called upon to execute would not improbably take the form of a retreat. In this opinion I had been fortified by reading in the 'Army Journal,' I think in 1912, an address by Sir William Robertson to the students at the Staff College; and a part of what he then stated has, through the events that followed, gained such additional interest that I venture to quote it. 'Our regulations,' he said, 'justly lay stress on the value of the offensive; but think what may be the effect of this teaching upon the troops if it alone is given, when they are ordered to retire instead of go forward—that is, to abandon that method of war by which alone, according to the training they have previously received, decisive victory can be achieved! Think, too, of the disintegration and demoralization which nearly always accompany retrograde movements, even when an army has not been previously defeated! It seems to me that there is practically no chance of successfully carrying out this operation in war unless we thoroughly study and practise it beforehand during peace. If we have this previous practice, the operation will not then come as a surprise to the troops in war; they will understand better what they are expected to do, and they will recognize it as being a form of war which may have to be adopted by any army, and can be adopted, not only without failure, but with a certain measure, ultimately, of success.' As, prior to the events at Mons, nothing was further from the minds of most British officers than the possibility of a retreat, the words quoted above seem to me to be all the more striking."

Sir George Arthur says in his "Life of Lord Kitchener" (Vol. III., page 297): "The multiplication of theatres of war had vastly increased the ever-present need of a highly-trained General Staff, and Kitchener had long determined on the man who should be at the head. The officer of his desire was Sir William Robertson, then Chief of the General Staff in France; a strong, shrewd, honest and exceptionally able soldier, to whose marked powers of administration the War Secretary wanted to give full play in his office. He had waited for Robertson about as many weary months as Jacob waited years for Rachel; he would not deprive Sir John of so important a subordinate, but he knew that this self-denying ordinance would not be perpetual. After the Battle of Loos it was understood that a change in the command in France was more than a likelihood, but Kitchener set his face sternly—and spoke his mind in high quarters—against any word or hint which might tend to impair the prestige or undermine the authority of the Commander-in-Chief. But so soon as a term was set to Sir John's command he seized the opportunity offered by changes at the front, and by the revelation of new talent, to bring new blood into the War Office without crippling the armies in the field. With the Prime Minister's willing consent he paid one of his many visits to General Headquarters early in December, and there discussed the future with Robertson, and asked him to put on paper the suggestions he had to make. In a document which was really a covering ground for both men, Robertson postulated as conditions normally essential to the successful conduct of military operations: 'There must be a supreme directing authority to promulgate policy, to determine the theatres of war and their relative importance, to choose the men to execute its plans; its power must be absolute; it must be an executive, and not merely an advisory body.' The War Council should be capable of performing the functions of the supreme authority, provided it is relieved of responsibility to the Cabinet as a whole as regards the conduct of military operations; advice regarding military operations emanating from members of the Cabinet, or of the War Council in their individual capacity, or from any other individual, should be examined and presented, if necessary with reasoned conclusions, to the War Council by the Chief of the Imperial General Staff before it is accepted by the War Council. The Chief of the Staff elect also said that if all communications with the Commander-in-Chief in the field regarding military operations were issued and received by him, it would greatly expedite the despatch of business, and make for greater secrecy than had prevailed. Finally, he proposed some changes which would fortify the Imperial General Staff. A long conversation between Kitchener and Robertson took place in Paris early in December; some modifications of Robertson's proposals were adopted, and arrangements for future war-work wholly agreeable to both were decided upon."

A newspaper said of Sir W. Robertson: "He has a large mind and wide vision, and he has risen to the high position he now occupies by sheer force of ability. If he has not acquired the reputation which Lord Kitchener has as an organizer, this is not from want of capacity, but because the opportunity has never come in his way. As a student of Imperial Strategy, he can walk round Lord Kitchener or any other living soldier."

An interview with Sir W. Robertson is described in the "New York Times":

"'From the soldier's point of view?' I asked him, 'how goes the war?' If he had said, 'It goes well,' I should have thought I had stumbled by accident on Marshal Hindenburg. If he had protested an overwhelming faith in the future, I should have thought a politician had stolen the khaki of England's Man of Iron.

"He said, 'That's so big a question that I should like it in detail.'

"This he said with a portentousness, but with as whimsical a smile as you could wish, waiting for me to speak. The man is characteristically English. You would never think of setting up his wooden effigy in Trafalgar Square for the tin-tacks of emotional patriots. The dark eyes under their thick eyebrows, which are as black as night, have the flashing good-humour of a schoolboy. There's no scowl on his face. He stands with feet wide apart, firm planted, a middle-sized, thick-set, stubborn and tenacious person, husky of voice, hard as nails, with a bright eye, a chin of iron, and a forehead that has the look of a rock. He has those minor flourishes of manner which are second nature to every cavalryman; but his instincts are so sound, his soldiership is so entirely intellectual, and his wit is so quick and human and good-tempered that he escapes swagger as completely as he escapes a deportment of gravity. He gives you the feeling of a man who could never be knocked off his feet by a sudden blow.

"Here's the English Moltke, the organizer of victory, the director of five or six enormous campaigns scattered all over the world, the man who has taken Kitchener's place, the man who fed the British Army on the historic retreat from Mons, the man in whom Britain places its supreme military confidence—a man who never strikes an attitude, never indulges in rhetoric, never gets into a fuss, never asks to be placed anywhere near the limelight, but who gets things quietly and thoroughly done. Kitchener was too prodigious a hero to be characteristic English. He was a legend in his lifetime, a thing almost unknown in English history; for the English like their heroes to be a hundred years dead. More perfectly does this stubborn and good-natured man, firm as a rock, true as steel, and entirely unaffected, passing himself off as an average man, admirably personate the nation. He is its energy, its doggedness, its good-humour, its quiet confidence and its common sense.

"You say of him at the first glance, 'Here is a robust, good-tempered and agreeable Englishman,' and that would leave it. But presently you look harder at him, and say, 'Here is a man of action, with fire ready to spring out of him, cautious in reflection, audacious in act, and like a bull-dog until he gets his way.' His personality makes itself felt in this way, gradually. He has no theatrical effects. He is the country itself, which seems only a pretty garden full of charming people till you stir it up with a walking-stick and discover it's a beehive. No Englishman likes to be thought a hero. He resents it, counts any such tendency a sign of bad breeding; what he likes is to be average." Later on in this interview is the following: "We spoke of Lord Kitchener's prophecy about the duration of the war.

"'Kitchener,' he said, 'had a most extraordinary instinct in military matters. He never thought things out; he seemed to know them. This faculty of his amounted to genius. People who criticize him for mistakes forget that he was seldom wrong in the big things. Some infallible instinct guided him in matters of life and death. His services to the freedom of the world at the outset of this terrible encounter can never be exaggerated. He was a genius. And this must be said of him too. He knew that he could trust his countrymen—trust in their grit, their loyalty, their good, sound, wholesome British stuff. How could he have faced the crisis of three years ago without that faith in the stuff of British character? Kitchener believed in the British nation, believed in British character. That was his strength.'

"'America's entry into the war would have heartened him, wouldn't it?'

"'Well,' said Sir William, with a twinkle, 'he wouldn't have said that it was an advantage to the other side.'"

Lord Milner said after he became a Minister (1916): "The men we look to in these days are men of the stamp of Sir William Robertson; and the next best thing that men like myself and others in a similar position can do is to put our backs into the work that lies before us and give them all the help we possibly can. We must look to their wisdom, experience and judgment to show us the right way, and we must put our shoulders to the wheel and drive the coach as hard as we can on the road they mark out for us."

A writer in the "Globe" of 2 Oct. 1917, says: "Sir William Robertson's main work—though we must not forget that it has been carried on side by side with other labours . . . has been the organization of victory across the Channel, with the result that in the summer of 1916 Sir Douglas Haig for the first time found himself at the head of an army which was able to take the offensive on a wide front, and which has ever since been asserting its ascendancy over the most formidable military power in the world. . . . It would be impossible to exaggerate the debt which the Army and the Empire owe to this great, because devoted, public servant, Sir William Robertson."

An article in the "Saturday Review" on "The Chiefs of the War Office, by One Who Knows Them," says: "The Chief of the Staff, General Sir William Robertson, is the strongest and most interesting personality in the Empire at the present time. He is head and shoulders above most men, and is one who was bound by great ability and sheer force of character to rise to the top of any profession which he adopted. He has risen to the head of the Army, and there is not a dissentient voice which would suggest another better qualified for such a post. . . . Lord Kitchener reposed perfect confidence in him, as does the whole Army, which is the only good judge of those who are set in authority over it."

Elsewhere Sir W. Robertson is described as "a great organizer and a great strategist." "During Lord Kitchener's tenure of office Sir William Robertson, by Order in Council, was entrusted with the organization of the Army and with its strategical dispositions. As it is essential that the man who is responsible for the work to be done should choose his own instruments, so to Sir William Robertson is confided the task of making appointments."

In an appreciation of Sir Stanley Maude, written for and inserted in the Life of that General, by Sir C. E. Callwell, Sir William Robertson says: "When it became necessary to appoint a new commander to our forces in Mesopotamia, I had not a moment's hesitation in recommending Maude for the place.

"It was very important that no mistake should be made in the selection, for the campaign had hitherto been a series of dismal failures and disappointments, and had entailed great hardships and suffering upon the troops." How well Sir William's choice of Maude, "then practically an unknown man to the War Cabinet," was justified, history relates.

Of Sir William Robertson, Clemenceau said that he was "One of the greatest military minds of the war." General Pershing eulogized him. When France mourned "La mort tragique de Lord Kitchener," she spoke in the same breath of "Le successeur du Maréchal Kitchener: Sir William Robertson." Other French writers describe Robertson as "un linguiste d'un talent exceptionnel, qui a passé brillamment des examens dans les différents dialects indiens." This last writer goes on to say that as C.I.G.S. Sir W. Robertson controlled "les dispositions et les opérations des armées britanniques sur tous les champs de bataille de la Guerre. C'est lui qui a été chargé de l'état-major de l'armée. C'est un homme qui n'est jamais prompt à se faire une opinion, bien que sur le terrain il puisse se décider en deux minutes. Mais une fois qu'il a pris un parti, comme on le dit communément dans l'armée, aucun art humain ne peut l'en faire changer par la parole. Il est de race de ceux qui ne pensent jamais à eux-mêmes, mais à leur devoir et à l'honneur de leur pays, et c'est peut-être la raison pour laquelle il a avancé si vite et si haut."

On 19 April, 1916, the "Evening Standard" said: "Sir William Robertson is the most persistent enemy of self-advertisement we have, and he himself would be surprised probably if he were told how strong is the belief of the nation in his capacity as a war winner. He has no axe to grind; he stands solely for efficiency and the job he has in hand."

After the Government and Sir William Robertson came to the parting of the ways, James Douglas said in "London Opinion" of 2 March, 1918: "The Germans stick to their Hindenburg and their Ludendorff, but the British do not stick to their great soldiers and sailors. If Lord Kitchener had lived he would have been shelved or shunted like Lord Fisher, Sir John Jellicoe and Sir William Robertson. It is very strange that three great men like Fisher, Jellicoe and Robertson have all been shelved or shunted. If there were three men left of equal ability, it would still be a tragedy to lose their services, for in this great struggle we need all the genius for war available. If they had all been drowned, like Kitchener, how we should have felt the loss. . . . Fisher—Jellicoe—Robertson! What a triumvirate! There are more brains in those three skulls than in any other three. But by a triple calamity they are all out of it at the supreme moment of the War!"

LOW, ROBERT BALMAIN, Lieut., was born 7 Oct. 1864, son of General Sir Robert Cunliffe Low, G.C.B., and Constance (who died in 1900), daughter of the late Capt. Taylor, H.E.I.C.S.; became Lieutenant, Royal Irish Regt., 7 Feb. 1885; joined the Indian Staff Corps 12 Oct. 1885; served in the Lushai Expedition, 1889 (clasp); in the Hazara Expedition, 1891 (Medal and clasp). He was A.D.C. to Major-General, Bengal, 1 April, 1892, to 2 Nov. 1895; was A.D.C. to the G.O.C., Chitral Relief Expedition, 24 March, 1895, to 28 Aug. 1895. For his services in this campaign he was mentioned in Despatches 15 Nov. 1895; received the Medal with clasp, and was created a Companion of the Distinguished Service Order [London Gazette, 21 Jan. 1896]: "Robert Balmain Low, Lieut., Indian Staff Corps, A.D.C. to Major-General Sir K. C. Low, K.C.B., Commanding a First-Class District in India. In recognition of services during the operations of the Chitral Relief Force." The Insignia were presented by Her Majesty 24 Feb. 1896. He became Captain 19 Feb. 1896; served in the Tirah Expedition, 1897–98, taking part in the operations in the Bara Valley 7–14 Dec. 1897 (two clasps); was A.D.C. to Lieut.-General, India, 29 Oct. 1898, to 28 June, 1905 Commandant, Headquarters Camp, and Provost Marshal, China Expedition, 31 July, 1900, to 30 June, 1902, and was present at the relief of Pekin and at the action of Peitsang and Yangtsun (Despatches [London Gazette, 14 May, 1901]; Medal with clasp; Brevet Majority, 29 Nov. 1900). He became Major, Indian Army, 7 Feb. 1903; was D.A.A.G., India, 17 Sept. 1905, to 16 Sept. 1909; was promoted to Lieut.-Colonel, Hodson's Horse, Indian Army, 7 Feb. 1911. On 18 May, 1915, Lieut.-Colonel R. B. Low was given a special appointment (graded D.A.A.G.). He married, in 1899, Mabel Violet, daughter of Major-General O'Grady Haly, C.B.

BALDWIN, GUY MELFORT, Lieut., was born at Penang 22 March, 1865, second son of the late Colonel A. T. Baldwin and the late Margaret, daughter of the late Colonel J. Johnston, K.T.S. He was educated at the Royal High School, Edinburgh, and Wimbledon College; joined the 1st Battn. Loyal North Lancashire Regt. as Second Lieutenant on 30 Jan. 1886, becoming Lieutenant 10 March, 1886. He was transferred to the Indian Staff Corps on 22 March, 1888, and appointed to the 4th Punjab Infantry; served in this regiment as Wing Officer in the Hazara Expedition, 1888, and was present at the action of Kotkai, receiving the Medal and clasp. In 1890 he was appointed to the Q.O. Corps of Guides (Cavalry); served with the above regiment as Squadron Commander during the operations in Chitral, 1895, and was present with the Relief Force in the action near Khar on the descent into the Swat Valley; was slightly wounded; mentioned in Despatches [London Gazette, 15 Nov. 1895], and received the Medal with clasp, and was created a Companion of the Distinguished Service Order [London Gazette, 21 Jan. 1896]: "Guy Melfort Baldwin, Lieut., Indian Staff Corps. In recognition of services during the operations of the Chitral Relief Force." The Insignia were presented by Her Majesty 24 Feb. 1896. He became Captain, Indian Army, 30 Jan. 1897, and in 1897 and 1898 served on the North-West Frontier of India, taking part in the defence of Malakand, the Relief of Chakdara (severely wounded). Malakand. Operations in Bajaur and in the Mamund country and Buner. He was mentioned in Despatches [London Gazette, 5 Nov. 1897]; received two clasps, and was given the Brevet of Major 20 May, 1898. He was D.A.A.G., India, 1 April, 1905, to 31 March, 1908. In 1915 he took part in the operations on the North-West Frontier; was mentioned in Despatches, and given the Brevet of Colonel 3 June, 1915, and became Temporary Brigadier-General 15 Feb. 1916, commanding the Derajat Brigade, N.W.F.P., 10 May, 1917. In 1898 he married Margaret, daughter of the late Christopher Sparrow, of Urmston Lodge, Urmston, and they have two sons. His favourite recreations are polo and shooting.

KERR, FREDERIC WALTER, Lieut., was born 20 May, 1867, third son of the late Admiral Lord Frederic H. Kerr, and Emily, daughter of the late General Sir Peregrine Maitland, G.C.B. He was educated at Charterhouse; was Page of Honour to H.M. the Queen, 1879–83, and became Lieutenant, Gordon Highlanders, 25 Aug. 1886; Adjutant, Gordon Highlanders, 31 Jan. 1892, to 30 Jan. 1896; took part in the operations in Chitral, 1895, serving with the Relief Force, and was present at the storming of the Malakand Pass. He was mentioned in Despatches [London Gazette, 15 Nov. 1895]; received the Medal with clasp, and was created a Companion of the Distinguished Service Order [London Gazette, 21 Jan. 1896]: "Frederic Walter Kerr, Lieut., Gordon Highlanders. For services during the operations of the Chitral Relief Force." He served at Tirah and in the South African War. He was D.A.Q.M.G., 1st Division, 1st Army Corps, 1904 to 1905; became Major 21 Dec. 1904; D.A.A. and Q.M.G., 1st Division, Aldershot Army Corps, 1905 to 1908; was promoted to Lieut.-Colonel 4 July, 1908; was Deputy Assistant Director of Movements, Headquarters of Army, 6 Oct. 1908; was promoted to Colonel. He was killed in action on 31 Oct. 1914. He married, in 1902, Lady Helen Kerr, daughter of the 9th Marquess of Lothian, and they had two sons.

Colonel Kerr's later services are below given in more detail. He served in 1897–98 on the North West Frontier of India, with the Tirah Expeditionary Force, and took part in the action of Dargai, receiving two additional clasps to his Medal. After serving for some time with his battalion in the South African War, he was appointed a Brigade-Major in April, 1900, holding that appointment till Dec. 1901. He took part in the advance on Kimberley, including the action at Magersfontein; was present at operations in the Orange Free State, at Paardeberg, and the actions at Poplar Grove and Dreifontein; in Cape Colony, 1899–1900, and at operations in the Orange River Colony in 1900–1. He was mentioned in Despatches [London Gazette, 16 April, 1901]; was given the Brevet of Major 29 Nov. 1900, and received the Queen's Medal with four clasps. As D.A.D. of Movements, War Office, from Oct. 1908, he did valuable service in connection with the new mobilization scheme, which has stood successfully the test imposed on it by the war. In the spring of 1913 he became G.S.O 1, Scottish Command, and in the Great War he went out as G.S.O.1 on the Line of Communication, his appointment dating from 5 Aug. 1914. On the 21 Sept. he was appointed G.S.O.1 with the 1st Division. He was killed by a bursting shell at the headquarters of the 1st and 2nd Divisions at Château Hooge, near Ypres, on 31 Oct. 1914. For his services in the Great War he was mentioned in Sir J. French's Despatch of 8 Oct. 1914.

London Gazette, 10 April, 1896.—"War Office, 10 April, 1896. The Queen has been graciously pleased to give orders for the following appointments to the Distinguished Service Order, in recognition of the services of the undermentioned Officers on the West Coast of Africa. For services in the operations against the Chief Nanna of Benin during the period Aug. to Oct. 1894. To be Companions of the Distinguished Service Order."

COPLAND-CRAWFORD, PETER WADE GRANT, Major, served in West Africa, and was created a Companion of the Distinguished Service Order [London Gazette, 10 April, 1896]: "Peter Wade Grant Copland-Crawford, Major, 7th Battn. K.R.R.C. In recognition of services on the West Coast of Africa . . . in the operations against the Chief Nanna of Benin during the period Aug. to Oct. 1894."

CAMPBELL, KENNETH JEFFERY RANKIN, Capt., was employed with the forces of the Niger Coast Protectorate in the operations against the Chief Nanna in Benin River in 1894; was mentioned in Despatches [London Gazette, 21 Dec. 1894], received the Medal and clasp, and was created a Companion of the Distinguished Service Order [London Gazette, 10 April, 1896]: "Kenneth Jeffery Rankin Campbell, Capt., The Suffolk Regt. In recognition of services during the recent operations on the Benin River." Lieut.-Colonel K. J. R. Campbell served in the European War.

SCAIFE, GEORGE SPENCER GARLAND, Capt., served in the operations on the Benin River in 1894, and was created a Companion of the Distinguished Service Order [London Gazette, 10 April, 1896]: "George Spencer Garland Scaife, Capt., West Yorkshire Regt. In recognition of services during the recent operations on the Benin River."

GALWAY, HENRY LIONEL, Capt., was born 25 Sept. 1859, son of the late Lieut.-Colonel Sir Thomas Lionel Gallway, K.C.M.G., Colonel Commandant, Royal Engineers, and Alicia Dorinda Lefanu (who died in 1905), daughter of Major Macdougall, late K. O. Scottish Borderers. He was educated at Cheltenham College, and Sandhurst, and was gazetted Second Lieutenant in the 58th Foot 11 May, 1878, and transferred to the 30th Foot 19 Oct. 1878. He became Lieutenant, East Lancashire Regt. 30 March, 1881, and was A.D.C. to the Commander-in-Chief and Governor, Bermuda, 22 Dec. 1882, to 22 Aug. 1888, and 13 Oct. 1888, to 26 May 1889; was promoted to Captain 1 Oct. 1887, and was Deputy Commissioner and Vice-Consul, Niger Coast Protectorate, 4 July, 1891, to 28 Jan. 1897; was present in several minor operations against natives in the Protectorate, 1891–1902, and concluded a treaty with the King of Benin at Benin City, 1892. In 1895 he commanded the Hausa Force under Sir Frederick Bedford at attack and capture of Nirube, and further operations against Brass villages. In command of the forces of the Niger Coast Protectorate. He was mentioned in Despatches, received the Medal and clasp, and was created a Companion of the Distinguished Service Order [London Gazette, 10 April, 1896]: "Henry Lionel Gallway, Capt., East Lancashire Regt. In recognition of services in the recent operations against Nirube and Brass villages." (His name was changed to Galway by Deed Poll, dated 3 Nov. 1911.) He was Acting Consul-General, Niger Coast Protectorate, etc., 1896–1898, and was appointed Deputy Commissioner and Consul, Niger Coast Protectorate, 29 Jan. 1897. He was attached to Sir H. Rawlinson's Intelligence Staff, and also in command of a Hausa Company during the operations in the Benin country, including the capture of Benin City, 1897; was mentioned in Despatches [London Gazette, 7 May, 1897]; was given Brevet of Major 25 May, 1897. He was promoted to Major 18 March, 1899; received a clasp, and was created a C.M.G., 1899. He was Acting High Commissioner, Southern Nigeria, 1900; Chief Political Officer, Aro Expedition, 1901–02; was mentioned in Despatches [London Gazette, 12 Sept. 1902], and received the Medal and clasp. He retired from the Army 24 Feb. 1902. He was Divisional Commissioner, Southern Nigeria; Governor of St. Helena, 1902–11; was created a K.C.M.G., 1910; was Governor of the Gambia, 1911–14; Governor of South Australia, 1914; Lieut.-Colonel Sir H. L. Galway married, in 1913, Baroness Marie Carola, daughter of the late Right Hon. Sir Rowland Blennerhasset, 4th Bart., and widow of Baron Raphael d'Erlanger.

Henry Lionel Galway.

London Gazette, 3 Nov. 1896.—"The Queen has been graciously pleased to give orders for the following appointments to the Distinguished Service Order, in recognition of the services of the undermentioned Officers during the recent operations against slave-trading Arabs in the Uganda Protectorate."

CUNNINGHAM, GEORGE GLENCAIRN, Capt. and Brevet Major, was born 24 July, 1862, second son of the late Major William Cunningham, M.S.C., and of Mrs. William Cunningham. He was educated at Wellington and Sandhurst, and was gazetted to the Duke of Cornwall's Light Infantry 22 Oct. 1881; served in the Egyptian War of 1882, including El Magfar, Tel-el-Mahuta, Kassassin (twice wounded; Despatches [London Gazette, 19 Sept. and 2 Nov. 1882]; Medal; Brevet of Major 15 Aug. 1889; 4th Class Medjidie and Khedive's Star). He took part in the Nile Expedition, 1884–85, with the River Column (clasp); served with the Egyptian Army with the Sudan Frontier Field Force, 1887–89, including Sarras, Arguin (wounded) and Toski (Despatches [London Gazette, 6 Sept. 1889]; 4th Class Osmanieh; clasp). He commanded the Unyoro Expedition, 1895 (wounded; Despatches and Medal). In 1895 and 1896 he commanded the Nandi Expedition. He was mentioned in Despatches and was created a Companion of the Distinguished Service Order [London Gazette, 3 Nov. 1896]: "George Glencairn Cunningham, Capt. and Brevet Major, The Derbyshire Regt. In recognition of services during the recent operations against the slave-trading Arabs in the Uganda Protectorate." Personally decorated by Her Majesty the Queen at Windsor on the 24th Nov. 1896. He was Assistant Commissioner and Commandant of Troops, Uganda, 1895–96; served in the Niger-Sudan Campaign, 1897, as Second-in-Command; Expeditions to Egbon, Bida and Ilorin (Despatches, 11 June, 1897; Brevet of Lieutenant-Colonel 16 June, 1897; Clasp). In the Sierra Leone Rising, 1898–99; in command and as O.C. Mendiland and Karene Columns and Protectorate Expedition (Despatches 29 Dec. 1899; Brevet of Colonel 10 Jan. 1900; clasp). He commanded the West African Regt. in 1899.

He served in the South African War 1899–1902, on the Staff, and in command of a portion of the Lines of Communication. Operations in Natal, 1899. Operations in the Orange Free State Feb. to May, 1900, including actions at Vet River (5 and 6 May), and Zand River. Operations in the Transvaal in May and June, 1900, including actions near Johannesburg, Pretoria and Diamond Hill (11 and 12 June) (horse wounded). Operations in the Transvaal, east of Pretoria, July to Sept. 1900. Operations in the Transvaal, west of Pretoria, July to 29 Nov. 1900, including actions at Zilikat's Nek. Operations in the Orange River Colony May to July, 1900. Operations in Cape Colony May to July, 1900. Operations in Cape Colony, south of Orange River, 1899–1900. Operations in the Transvaal 30 Nov. 1900, to Feb. 1902. Operations in Cape Colony Feb. to March, 1902. He was mentioned in Despatches [London Gazette, 16 April, 1901]; created a C.B.; received the Queen's Medal with four clasps and the King's Medal with two clasps. He became temporary Brigadier-General, Plymouth Garrison Brigade, 5 Aug. 1914, and retired with the honorary rank of Brigadier-General 24 Dec. 1916. He was created a C.B.E., 1919. Brigadier-General G. G. Cunningham married, in 1902, Dorothy L., daughter of the late R. Yeo, and they have one son and one daughter.

PULTENEY, WILLIAM PULTENEY, Capt., was born on 18 May, 1861, youngest son of the late Rev. R. T. Pulteney, of Ashley, Market Harborough, and Emma, third daughter of Maximilian Hammond Dalison, of Hamptons, Tonbridge. He was educated at Eton; joined the Scots Guards as Second Lieutenant from the Militia 23 April, 1881; became Lieutenant, Scots Guards, 1 July, 1881; served in Egypt in 1882, being present at the action of Mahuta and Battle of Tel-el-Kebir; became Captain 4 May, 1892; was employed under the Foreign Office in Uganda 15 Feb. 1895, to 22 Sept. 1897. He served in the Unyoro Expedition, 1895 (Medal). For the Nandi Expedition, 1895–96, he was mentioned in Despatches, created a Companion of the Distinguished Service Order [London Gazette, 3 Nov. 1896]: "William Pulteney Pulteney, Capt., The Scots Guards. In recognition of services in the recent operations against slave-trading Arabs in the Uganda Protectorate." (Insignia presented by the Queen at Windsor 9 July, 1897.) He became Major 1 May, 1897; Vice-Consul, Congo Free State, 31 Dec. 1898, to 17 Jan. 1899. He served in the South African War from 1899 to 1902. Advance on Kimberley, including actions at Belmont, Enslin, Modder River and Magersfontein. In command 1st Battn. Scots Guards (9 April, 1900, to 17 Jan. 1901). Operations in the Orange Free State, Feb. to May, 1900, including actions at Poplar Grove, Dreifontein, Vet River (5 and 6 May) and Zand River. Operations in the Transvaal in May and June, 1900, including actions near Johannesburg, Pretoria and Diamond Hill (11 and 12 June). Op. in the Transvaal, east and west of Pretoria, July to 29 Nov. 1900. Operations in the Orange River Colony May to 29 Nov. 1900. Operations in the Transvaal Dec. 1900, to April, 1902. Operations in Cape Colony Dec. 1900. In command of a column 17 Jan. 1901, to April, 1902. He was mentioned in Despatches [London Gazette, 26 Jan. 1900; 10 Sept. 1901, and 29 July, 1902]; was given the Brevet of Lt.-Col. 11 Nov. 1899, and received the Queen's Medal with six clasps and the King's Medal with two clasps. He was promoted to Lieutenant-Colonel 1 April, 1904; was created a C.B. in 1905; became Colonel 1 Jan. 1908; was Brigadier-General, Irish Command, 7 Feb. 1908, to 13 March, 1909; was promoted to Major-General 1 Jan. 1909; was G.O.C., 6th Division, Irish Command, 16 July, 1910, to 15 July, 1914. He served in the European War from 1914; was temporary Lieutenant-General from 5 Aug. 1914, to 3 May, 1915, promoted to Lieutenant-General 4 May, 1915; commanded the 3rd Army Corps from 5 Aug. 1914, to 19 Feb. 1918; and the 23rd Army Corps 20 Feb. 1918, to 15 April, 1919; was specially employed, British Military Mission to Japan, 18 May, 1918, to 9 Sept. 1918. He was created a K.C.B., 1915; a K.C.M.G., 1917, and a K.C.V.O., 1918. Sir William Pulteney married, in 1917, Jessie, daughter of the late Sir John Arnott, Bart.

William P. Pulteney.

We read of the doings of the 3rd Army Corps in 1914 in Lord Ernest Hamilton's book, "The First Seven Divisions." In the chapter called "Manœuvring Westward" (page 142), he says: "On 12 Oct. the 3rd A.C., under General Pulteney, arrived at St. Omer, and moved forward to Hazebrouck. The moment this Army Corps was in position, Sir Horace made the first move in the contemplated sweep by pushing forward the 3rd Division, which was on the left of the 2nd A.C., with orders to cross the Lawe Canal, which the enemy was reported to be holding in force." On page 157 Lord Ernest says: "In the Armentières district, the 3rd A.C. was making great efforts to play up to its allotted part in the wheel to the south, the 4th Division being north of Armentières, the 6th Division south of it." On page 160: "The 9th Brigade, which had throughout these operations been on the left of the 3rd Division, was now temporarily transferred to the 3rd A.C. . . . With the additional assistance which had been lent him, General Pulteney was everywhere successful in holding his ground." In the chapter on "The Birth of the Ypres Salient," Lord E. Hamilton says: "The British force in Flanders now consisted of two distinct and separate armies, which we may call the North and South Army. The South Army was made up of the 2nd A.C., the 3rd A.C., and the 19th Brigade, and was supported by Conneau's Cavalry, which operated between these two army corps, and by the Lahore Indians in rear. The line of this army extended as far north as Le Gheir, or rather, let us say, Ploegsteert, to which place the left of the 3rd A.C. shortly withdrew." "The terrific fighting of the end of October and beginning of November may be considered as taking place," Lord Ernest says, "in three distinct sections, viz., the South Army, the Cavalry Corps, and the North Army."

In "The Indian Corps in France" (page 42), we are told that during the First Battle of Ypres "the line east of Messines and Armentières to a front west of Radhinghem was held by General Allenby's Cavalry Corps and General Pulteney's 3rd Corps, with General Conneau's French Cavalry on its right." The writers of this book then go on to describe the relief of the French Cavalry under General Conneau by the Jullundur Brigade. At the beginning of March the same writers tell us that in the Battle of Neuve Chapelle, "the 3rd Corps, under General Pulteney, occupied its old position opposite Armentières, whence the line was continuing southwards from Estaires to the west of Neuve Chapelle by the 4th Corps, under General Rawlinson." In the Battle of Loos General Pulteney's 3rd Corps was near Bois Grenier. Of the later operations of the 3rd Army Corps up to 1918 we have no particulars at hand, but these quotations will show to some extent where General Pulteney was in the early part of the Great War.

VANDELEUR, CECIL FOSTER SEYMOUR, Lieut., was born 11 July, 1869, and was gazetted to the Scots Guards as Second Lieutenant 6 Feb. 1889, becoming Lieutenant 23 May, 1892. He was employed in the Uganda Protectorate 11 Aug. 1894, to 26 Aug. 1896, and served in the Unyoro Expedition, 1895 (Despatches and Medal). For the Nandi Expedition, 1895–96, he was mentioned in Despatches and created a Companion of the Distinguished Service Order [London Gazette, 3 Nov. 1896]: "Cecil Foster Seymour Vandeleur, Lieut., Scots Guards. In recognition of services during the recent operations against slave-trading Arabs in the Uganda Protectorate." He was personally decorated by the Queen at Windsor 24 Nov. 1896. He was on Special Extra Regimental Employment 28 Nov. 1896, to 5 April, 1897, and took part in the operations on the Niger in 1897; in the Expeditions to Egbon, Bida and Ilorin. He was mentioned in Despatches [London Gazette, 11 June, 1897]; was given the Brevet of Major 25 June, 1899, and received the Medal with clasp. He was employed with the Egyptian Army 24 Dec. 1897, to 8 Dec. 1899; served in the Nile Expedition of 1898, and was present at the battles of the Atbara and Khartum (slightly wounded). He was mentioned in Despatches [London Gazette, 30 Sept. 1898]; received the 4th Class Medjidie, and two clasps to the Egyptian Medal. He became Captain 24 June, 1899, and was on Special Service, South Africa, from 17 Oct. 1899. He was promoted to Lieutenant-Colonel, and was killed 31 Aug. 1901. Sir Arthur Conan Doyle says, in his "Great Boer War" (page 467), when describing train-wreckings by the Boers: "Another train disaster of an even more tragic character occurred near Waterval, fifteen miles north of Pretoria, upon the last day of August. The explosion of a mine wrecked the train, and a hundred Boers who lined the banks of the cutting opened fire upon the derailed carriages. Colonel Vandeleur, an officer of great promise, was killed, and twenty men, chiefly of the West Riding Regt., were shot. Nurse Page was also among the wounded. It was after this fatal affair that the regulation of carrying Boer hostages upon the trains was at last carried out."

Lieut.-General Sir Ivor Maxse wrote a biography, "Seymour Vandeleur," in the concluding pages of which he says: "Men of Seymour Vandeleur's stamp do not die in their beds, and it is in accordance with the life they have chosen that they should meet death in the discharge of duty and in the service of their country. But in Vandeleur's case it is bitter to think that when the end came he did not fall in the fair field of battle, where his life had been risked on so many occasions. To be the victim of a pitiful highway robbery, murdered in cold blood without the chance of reprisal by a dastardly scoundrel who wrecked trains for loot—such is not the kind of death which his friends can contemplate without a feeling of vengeance in their hearts. Yet, after all, it is a man's life not his death that matters, and the memory of Seymour Vandeleur as he was—a bright, ambitious, happy companion—still lingers with those who follow his calling and sympathize with his spirit. To them he will ever remain an example of straight, young manhood, and of a life spent in the pursuit of that which is best and highest in the profession he loved, heedless of any notoriety it might happen to bring him. To those who have read this memoir of his short career it will be obvious that he possessed a tenacious purpose through life, that he was rapidly developing along the natural lines of his character, and that he had emerged, a distinct personality, from the junior ranks of the Army. But by those who worked with him for years in different places and had the best opportunities of judging his strength, Vandeleur's death is recognized as a distinct loss to his country. Viewed in this light it was a public calamity, though this was known to few outside his profession. . . . One purpose of this book is to afford to Vandeleur's countrymen a glimpse of what is being done by hundreds of picked officers, who are the real builders of the Dependencies and Crown Colonies of our Empire. They long ago laid the foundations upon which our Indian Dominion was reared; they are now toiling ceaselessly and successfully in such places as Somaliland, Uganda, East Africa, Nigeria, the Egyptian Sudan—in fact wherever the Union Jack flies. Sometimes recognized but more often snubbed by official England, their names are unknown to the British public, and rightly so, because men should not acquire notoriety for merely doing their duty well. Their reward is in the knowledge that they are sowing seed which will ripen into an abundant harvest whose true value will be appreciated by future generations of Britons. When, however, one of their number is cut off in the prime of his manhood and with his promise unfulfilled, it is meet that the story of his life should be recorded, as an instance of the toll exacted by Empire and a reminder to us who sit at home that there still are men whose pride it is to render service to the State." On pages 56 and 57 of "Seymour Vandeleur" there is an account of the death of Capt. Dunning, D.S.O., who was mortally wounded during the expedition against Kabarega.

London Gazette, 17 Nov. 1896.—"War Office, 17 Nov. 1896. The Queen has been graciously pleased to give orders for the following appointments to the Distinguished Service Order, in recognition of the services of the undermentioned Officers during the recent operations in the Sudan."

MARTYR, CYRIL GODFREY, Major, was born 5 Aug. 1860, son of Joseph Martyr, of Stoke Fleming, Devon, and Mrs. Joseph Martyr. He was gazetted to the Duke of Cornwall's Light Infantry, 23 Oct. 1880, and became Lieutenant 1 July, 1881. He was employed with the Egyptian Army 24 Feb. 1886, to 23 Feb. 1896, and served in the Egyptian War of 1882, including the reconnaissance in force on Kafr Dowar, actions at El Magfar and Tel-el-Mahuta, both actions at Kassassin, battle of Tel-el-Kebir (Medal with clasp and Khedive's Star). He again saw active service in the Sudan Expedition of 1884–85, on the Nile, with Mounted Infantry, and was present at both actions at Abu Klea, actions at Gubat and Metammeh, attack on convoy 14 Feb. (two clasps). He became Captain 14 Aug. 1889. In the Sudan in 1888–91 he was present at the action of Gemaizah (clasp ; 4th Class Medjidie) ; and at the

Cyril Godfrey Martyr.

action of Toski (clasp). For his services at the capture of Tokar in Feb. 1891, he received the 4th Class Osmanieh and the clasp to the Bronze Star. He was promoted to Major 26 Feb. 1896. He served in the Expedition to Dongola in 1896, as A.A.G., Headquarters Staff, and took part in the operations of 7 June and 19 Sept. He was mentioned in Despatches [London Gazette, 3 Nov. 1896], received the Egyptian Medal with two clasps, and was created a Companion of the Distinguished Service Order [London Gazette, 17 Nov. 1896] : "Cyril Godfrey Martyr, Major, The Duke of Cornwall's Light Infantry. In recognition of services in the recent operations in the Sudan." The Insignia were presented to him by Her Majesty the Queen 20 Feb. 1897. He commanded the Expedition which resulted in the capture of the Sudanese Forts near Mruli and in action at Jeruba. He was mentioned in Despatches, was given the Brevet of Lieutenant-Colonel 25 Jan. 1899, and received the Medal and clasp. In Uganda in 1899 he took part in the operations against the Kabarega (clasp). He served in the South African War from 1899 to 1900, as Special Service Officer, also Commanding a Corps of Mounted Infantry. He took part in the operations in Natal in 1899 for the Relief of Ladysmith. Relief of Kimberley. Operations in the Orange Free State Feb. to May, 1900, including operations at Paardeberg 17 to 26 Feb. ; actions at Poplar Grove and Dreifontein, Vet River (5 and 6 May) and Zand River. Operations in the Transvaal in May and June, 1900, including actions near Johannesburg, Pretoria and Diamond Hill (11 and 12 June). Operations in the Transvaal, east of Pretoria, July to Sept. 1900, including actions at Reit Vlei and Belfast (27 Aug.). Operations in Cape Colony, south of Orange River, 1900. He was mentioned in Despatches [London Gazette, 8 Feb. 1901], and received the Queen's Medal and seven clasps. During the European War Lieut.-Colonel Martyr was employed as General Staff Officer from 3 Aug. 1914, to 3 Aug. 1916. He married, in 1901, Emma Maud, daughter of the late W. J. Bellville and Mrs. Bellville, of 22, Berkeley Square, London, W., and they have two sons : Alan Godfrey Martyr and Peter Denys Martyr, and a daughter, Marjorie Bellville Martyr.

HUNTER, GEORGE DOUGLAS, Surgeon-Major, was born 28 Aug. 1860, second son of the late Brigade-Surgeon George Yeates Hunter, Indian Army. He entered the Royal Army Medical Corps in 1884 ; served in the Nile Expedition in 1884 and 1885 (Medal with clasp, and Khedive's Star) ; served with the Sudan Frontier Field Force in 1885–1886 ; in the Sudan 1888–89 (action of Gemaizah) (clasp) ; became Surgeon-Major in 1896, and in that year served with the Dongola Expeditionary Force, taking part in the operations of 7 June and 19 Sept. He was mentioned in Despatches [London Gazette, 3 Nov. 1896], received the British Medal and the Egyptian Medal with two clasps, and was created a Companion of the Distinguished Service Order [London Gazette, 17 Nov. 1896] : "George Douglas Hunter, Surgeon-Major, Army Medical Staff. In recognition of services in the recent operations in the Sudan." (Insignia presented by Her Majesty 20 Feb. 1897). He took part in the operations of 1898, including the Battle of Khartum (Despatches [London Gazette, 9 Dec. 1898], clasp to Khedive's Medal, 4th Class Osmanieh). He was promoted to Lieutenant-Colonel in 1904 ; was Principal Medical Officer, Egyptian Army, 1905–8 (2nd Class Mejidie). He became Colonel 15 Sept. 1913 ; served in the European War from 1914 ; was Surgeon-General, British East Africa Expeditionary Forces from Dec. 1915 ; was created a C.M.G. in 1916, and a C.B. in 1917, and was appointed Director of Medical Services : retired 26 Dec. 1917 and was given the honorary rank of Major-General 12 May, 1918. Major-General Hunter married, in 1895, Eliza Hannah, daughter of the late T. W. V. Robinson, of Houghton-le-Spring, Durham, and they have one son and one daughter.

HEYGATE, ROBERT HENRY GAGE, Major, was born in London, 26 July, 1859, second son of Sir Frederick W. Heygate, 2nd Bart., of Bellarena, and of Lady Heygate. He was educated at Eton and Sandhurst ; was gazetted to the 34th Foot 1 May, 1878, becoming Lieutenant 19 Sept. 1880, and Captain 28 March, 1886. He became Major 26 Aug. 1896. He was employed on the Staff, Egyptian Army, 10 March, 1893, to 20 Oct. 1898, and served in the Dongola Expedition of 1896, including the engagement of Firket. He was mentioned in Despatches [London Gazette, 3 Nov. 1896] ; received the Khedive's Medal with two clasps, and was created a Companion of the Distinguished Service Order [London Gazette, 17 Nov. 1896] : "Robert Henry Gage Heygate, Major, The Border Regt. In recognition of services during the recent operations in Egypt and the Sudan." He was present at the operations in 1897–98 (British Medal, 4th Class Osmanieh,

clasp). He served in South Africa, 1899–1900 ; was present at the Relief of Ladysmith, including action at Colenso (severely wounded). Operations in Natal, 1899. Operations in Cape Colony, south of Orange River, 1899. He was mentioned in Despatches [London Gazette, 8 Feb. 1901], and received the Queen's Medal with two clasps. He became Lieutenant-Colonel 1 July, 1904, commanding the 1st Border Regt ; was given the Brevet of Colonel 1 July, 1907, and retired 21 July, 1909. Colonel Heygate was employed under the War Office during the Great War 2 Oct. 1914, to 17 Dec. 1916.

PENTON, RICHARD HUGH, Capt., was born at Wroxham, Norfolk 25 April, 1863, son of General John Penton and Rosa Alexandra Penton. He was educated at Norwich ; joined the Army 7 Feb. 1887, and was employed with the Egyptian Army 12 Feb. 1892, to 28 Feb. 1905 (Principal Medical Officer, 1898 to 1905), and became Captain, R.A.M.C., in 1896. He served in the Expedition to Dongola, 1896, taking part in the operations of 7 June and 19 Sept. ; was mentioned in Despatches [London Gazette, 3 Nov. 1896], received the Egyptian Medal with clasps, and was created a Companion of the Distinguished Service Order [London Gazette, 17 Nov. 1896] : "Richard Hugh Penton, Surgeon-Capt., Army Medical Staff. In recognition of his services in the recent operations in the Sudan." The Insignia, Warrant and Statutes were sent to the G.O.C., Cairo, and presented 25 Jan. 1897. He served in the Nile Expedition in 1898, being present at the battles of the Atbara and Khartum (as Senior Medical Officer, Infantry Division, Egyptian Army, at the latter) ; was mentioned in Despatches [London Gazette, 24 May and 30 Sept. 1898] ; promoted to Major 16 Nov. 1898 ; received the 4th Class Osmanieh, the Medal and two clasps to the Egyptian Medal. In the Nile Expedition of 1899 he served as P.M.O., Egyptian Army, in the first advance against the Khalifa, received a clasp to the Egyptian Medal and the 3rd Class Medjidie. He was altogether four times mentioned in Despatches by Kitchener for services in the Sudan. He was promoted to Lieutenant-Colonel 28 July, 1906. He served in the European War, as A.D.M.S., 1st Indian Cavalry Division, during 1915, and subsequently as A.D.M.S., Dunkerque ; became Colonel 1 March, 1915, and retired 22 May, 1919. He was twice mentioned in Despatches during the European War, was created Commander of the Order of Avir (confirmed by the President of the Portuguese Republic, 1919), for service in France. He married, 7 Aug. 1892, at Langham, Colchester, Kathleen Rosa, second daughter of the late Lieut.-Colonel Richard Spurgeon Green, and they have one son, John Hugh Barrow Penton.

LEGGE, NORTON, Capt., served in the Sudan, and was created a Companion of the Distinguished Service Order [London Gazette, 17 Nov. 1896] : "Norton Legge, Capt., 20th Hussars. In recognition of services during the recent operations in Egypt and the Sudan." The Decoration was presented to Capt. Norton Legge by the Queen at Windsor 3 Dec. 1896. He died 18 Dec. 1900.

MAHON, BRYAN THOMAS, Capt., was born 2 April, 1862, son of the late Henry Blake Mahon, of Belleville, County Galway, and Matilda, daughter of Colonel Seymour, of Ballymore Castle, County Galway. He

Bryan Thomas Mahon.

was educated privately, and gazetted to the 21st Hussars 27 Jan. 1883, and transferred to the 8th Hussars 14 Feb. 1883, serving continuously in this regiment until he joined the Egyptian Army. He served in India until 1889 ; became Captain 19 April, 1888, and was Adjutant, 8th Hussars, 31 May, 1890, to 19 Jan. 1893. He was employed with the Egyptian Army 20 Jan. 1893, to 24 Jan. 1900 ; served in the Expedition to Dongola in 1896, as Staff Officer, Cavalry Brigade, taking part in the operations of 7 June and 19 Sept. He was mentioned in Despatches 3 Nov. 1896 ; received the Egyptian Medal with two clasps, and was created a Companion of the Distinguished Service Order [London Gazette, 17 Nov. 1896] : "Bryan Thomas Mahon, Capt., 8th Hussars. In recognition of services in the recent operations in Egypt and the Sudan." (Insignia presented 25 Jan. 1897.) He served in the Nile Expedition in 1897 (clasp to Egyptian Medal, 4th Class Osmanieh), and in the Nile Expedition in 1898, being present at the battles of the Atbara and Khartum ; was mentioned in Despatches [London Gazette, 30 Sept. 1898] ; received the Brevet of Lieutenant-Colonel 14 Nov. 1898 ; two clasps to the Egyptian Medal ; Medal Relief of Gedaref ; clasp to the Egyptian Medal ; served in the Nile Expedition, 1899 ; operations resulting in the final defeat of the Khalifa. As A.A.G., Flying Column, and in charge of the Intelligence Department ; actions at Abu Aadel and Om Dubreikat (Despatches [London Gazette, 30 Jan. 1900] ; Brevet of Colonel 14 March, 1900 ; two clasps to Egyptian Medal). He served in the South African War 1899–1900, as Special Service Officer, afterwards on the Staff (including services as Brigadier-General, Cavalry Brigade). He commanded the Mafeking Relief Force in May, 1900. After describing the state of affairs in Mafeking, Sir A. Conan Doyle says, on pages 315–317 of "The Great Boer War" :

"So in a small blaze of glory ended the historic siege of Mafeking, for Eloff's attack was the last, though by no means the worst, of the trials which the garrison had to face. Six killed and ten wounded were the British losses in this admirably managed affair. On 17 May, five days after the fight, the relieving force arrived, the besiegers were scattered, and the long-imprisoned garrison were free men once more. Many who had looked at their maps and saw this post isolated in the very heart of Africa had despaired of ever reaching their heroic fellow-countrymen ; and now one universal outbreak of joybells and bonfires from Toronto to Melbourne proclaimed that there is no spot so inaccessible that the long arm of the Empire cannot reach it when her children are in peril. Colonel Mahon, a young Irish officer who had made his reputation as a cavalry leader in Egypt, had started early in May from Kimberley with a small but mobile force consisting of the Imperial Light Horse (brought round from Natal for the purpose), the Kimberley Mounted Corps, the Diamond Fields Horse, some Imperial Yeomanry, a detachment of the Cape Police, and 100 volunteers from the Fusilier Brigade, with M Battery, R.H.A., and pom-poms —twelve hundred men in all. Whilst Hunter was fighting his action at Rooidam on 4 May, Mahon with his men struck round the western flank of the Boers and moved rapidly to the northward. On 11 May they had left Vryburg, the halfway house, behind them, having done one hundred and twenty miles in five days. They pushed on, encountering no opposition save that of nature, though they knew that they were being closely watched by the enemy. At Koodoosrand it was found that a Boer force was in position in front, but Mahon avoided them by turning somewhat to the westward. His detour took him, however, into a bushy country, and here the enemy headed him off, opening fire at short range upon the ubiquitous Imperial Light Horse, who led the column. A short engagement ensued, in which the casualties amounted to thirty killed and wounded, but which ended in the defeat and dispersal of the Boers, whose force was certainly very much weaker than the British. On 15 May, the relieving column arrived without further opposition at Masibi Stadt, twenty miles to the west of Mafeking. In the meantime Plumer's force upon the north had been strengthened by the addition of C Battery of four 12-pounder guns of the Canadian Artillery under Major Eudon and a body of Queenslanders. These forces had been part of the small army which had come with General Carrington through Beira, and after a detour of thousands of miles, through their own wonderful energy they had arrived in time to form portion of the relieving column. Foreign military critics, whose experience of warfare is to move troops across a frontier, should think of what the Empire has to do before her men go into battle. These contingents had been assembled by long railway journeys, conveyed across thousands of miles of ocean to Cape Town, brought round another two thousand or so to Beira, transferred by a narrow-gauge railway to Bamboo Creek, changed to a broader gauge to Marandellas, sent on in coaches for hundreds of miles to Bulawayo, transferred to trains for another four or five hundred miles to Ootsi, and had finally a forced march of a hundred miles, which brought them up a few hours before their presence was urgently needed upon the field. Their advance, which averaged twenty-five miles a day on foot for four consecutive days over deplorable roads, was one of the finest performances of the war. With these high-spirited reinforcements and with his own hardy Rhodesians Plumer pushed on, and the two columns reached the hamlet of Masibi Stadt within an hour of each other. Their united strength was far superior to anything which Snyman's force could place against them. But the gallant and tenacious Boers would not abandon their prey without a last effort. As the little army advanced upon Mafeking they found the enemy waiting in a strong position. For some hours the Boers gallantly held their ground, and their artillery fire was, as usual, most accurate. But our own guns were more numerous and equally well served, and the position was soon made untenable. The Boers retired past Mafeking and took refuge in the trenches upon the eastern side; but Baden-Powell with his war-hardened garrison sallied out, and, supported by the artillery fire of the relieving column, drove them from their shelter. With their usual admirable tactics their larger guns had been removed, but one small cannon was secured as a souvenir by the townsfolk, together with a number of wagons and a considerable quantity of supplies. A long rolling trail of dust upon the eastern horizon told that the famous siege of Mafeking had at last come to an end."

Col. Mahon was mentioned in Despatches [London Gazette, 9 Feb. and 16 April, 1901], received the Queen's Medal with three clasps, and was created a C.B. He was Military Governor, Kordofan from 1901 to 1904; became Colonel 12 April, 1904; commanded a 2nd Class District in India 12 April, 1904, to 11 April, 1908; became Major-General 1 Dec. 1908, commanded a Division in India 16 Aug. 1909, to 15 Aug. 1913; was created a K.C.V.O. in 1911, and promoted to Lieutenant-General 4 Sept. 1912. He served in the European War from 1914; was G.O.C., 10th (Irish) Division, New Armies, and 10th Division, Mediterranean Expeditionary Force, 24 Aug. 1914, to 27 Oct. 1915. He was Commander-in-Chief, Salonika Army, 28 Oct. 1915, to 9 May, 1916, and Commander-in-Chief in Ireland 15 Nov. 1916, to June, 1918. Sir Bryan Mahon served in the B.E.F., France, from Sept. 1918, to April, 1919. He was appointed Colonel, 8th Hussars, 7 March, 1910; is a K.C.B., and was made a Privy Councillor, Ireland, in 1917. His favourite recreations are shooting, hunting, polo and pig-sticking and steeple-chase riding.

MORGAN, HILL GODFREY, Capt., was born 20 June, 1862, son of the late Capt. Hill Faulconer Morgan, 28th Foot. He joined the 1st Gloucestershire Regt. (28th) from the Militia in 1883, and transferred to the Army Service Corps in 1888, as Captain. Capt. Morgan served in the Dongola Expeditionary Force in 1896–8, being present at the operations of 19 Sept.; was mentioned in Despatches [London Gazette, 3 Nov. 1896], and created a Companion of the Distinguished Service Order [London Gazette, 17 Nov. 1896]: "Hill Godfrey Morgan, Capt., Army Service Corps. In recognition of services during the recent operations in Egypt and the Sudan." For his services in this campaign he also received the 4th Class Medjidie, the British Medal and the Khedive's Medal with two clasps. He served in the Nile Expedition, including Khartum (Despatches, 30 Sept. 1898, 4th Class Osmanieh, clasp). He served in the South African War, 1899–1902, as Director of Supplies; operations in Natal, 1899; Relief of Ladysmith, including action at Colenso; operations of 17–24 Jan. 1900, and action at Spion Kop; operations of 5–7 Feb. 1900, and action at Vaal Kranz; operations at the Tugela Heights 14–27 Feb. 1900, and action at Pieters Hill; operations in Natal (March to June, 1900); operations in the Transvaal, east of Pretoria, 1900, including action at Belfast; operations in the Transvaal, Orange River Colony and Cape Colony, 30 Nov. 1900, to 31 May, 1902. He was mentioned in Despatches (Sir G. S. White, 2 Dec. 1899; Sir R. H. Buller, 30 March and 9 Nov. 1900) [London Gazette, 8 Feb. 1901] and 29 July, 1902; was given the Brevet of Lieutenant-Colonel, Queen's Medal with six clasps, King's Medal with two clasps, created a C.B. He was promoted to Lieutenant-Colonel on 3 Feb. 1905; was given the Brevet of Colonel, and retired 7 Nov. 1906. During the European War Colonel Morgan served from Aug. 1914, as Assistant Director of Supplies, Central Force, and from Jan. 1915, as Administrative Member, Forage Committee. He was mentioned three times for services, promoted Brigadier-General 1919; created a C.M.G. in 1918 and a Knight of the British Empire in 1919 (War Medal). Sir H. G. Morgan married in 1886, Fanny, daughter of the late J. Bousfield, of Grassmere, Craneswater Park, Southsea.

GRIFFITH, GEORGE RICHARD, Capt., was born 5 July, 1857; joined the Army Veterinary Department 26 May, 1880, and served in the Egyptian Expedition of 1882, being present at the actions of El Magfar, Masameh and Kassassin, Battle of Tel-el-Kebir and forced march to Cairo (Medal with clasp; Bronze Star). He served in the Sudan Expedition of 1884–85, Nile, and received a clasp; and again in the Sudan in 1888–91, Suakin, as Principal Veterinary Surgeon. Action at Gemaizah; mentioned in Despatches, clasp. Action of Toski (clasp). Capture of Tokar, Feb. 1891 (4th Class Osmanieh; clasp to Bronze Star). He served in the Expedition to Dongola, 1896, as Principal Veterinary Officer; operations of 7 June and 19 Sept.; was mentioned in Despatches [London Gazette, 3 Nov. 1896]; received the Egyptian Medal with two clasps; was created a Companion of the Distinguished Service Order [London Gazette, 17 Nov. 1896]: "George Richard Griffith, Veterinary Capt., Army Veterinary Department. In recognition of services during the recent operations in Egypt and the Sudan." For the Nile Expedition of 1898 he was mentioned in Despatches [London Gazette, 30 Sept. 1898], received the 3rd Class of the Medjidie, was granted the next higher rate of pay of rank; the Medal and a clasp to the Egyptian Medal. He served also in the Nile Expedition of 1899 (clasp to Egyptian Medal). He became Lieutenant-Colonel 12 Dec. 1903; was Principal Veterinary Officer, Egyptian Army, and retired 20 Nov. 1908, entering the Reserve of Officers. Lieut.-Colonel Griffith married, in 1909, Alice Maud, eldest daughter of the Rev. G. D. Redpath, of Harbledown.

George Richard Griffith.

BEATTY, DAVID, Lieut., Royal Navy, was born in 1871, son of Capt. D. L. Beatty, of Borodale, County Wexford. He entered the Royal Navy in 1884; was employed on the Nile, in the Sudan, in co-operation with the Egyptian Army under the Sirdar, Sir H. Kitchener, K.C.B., and rendered excellent service in getting the gunboats over the cataract. He was second in command of the flotilla at the forcing of the Dervishes' batteries at Hafir, and exposed to a heavy fire. He took command of the flotilla on Commander Colvin being wounded, and fought the gunboats in front of the enemy's batteries most persistently and successfully, eventually bombarding their position at Dongola and dismounting their guns. For this service he was mentioned in Despatches and created a Companion of the Distinguished Service Order [London Gazette, 17 Nov. 1896]: "David Beatty, Lieut., Royal Navy. In recognition of services during the recent operations in the Sudan." He was mentioned in Despatches by the Sirdar for services with the gunboats employed on the Nile during the operations of 1898 in the Sudan, including the battles of Atbara and Khartum (Medal; promoted to Commander, and awarded the 4th Class of the Order of the Medjidie, 1898). As Commander of the Barfleur he showed exceptional tenacity in endeavouring, with 200 bluejackets, to capture the Chinese guns that caused considerable trouble to the forces and inhabitants at Tien-tsin, June, 1900. He managed to get close to the guns, but a heavy fire therefrom necessitated withdrawing his force. Although twice wounded, he still led his men in the attack. He was promoted to Captain in Nov. 1900, for these services. On 28 April, 1905, he was created an M.V.O., and on 5 Nov. 1908, was appointed Aide-de-Camp to the King. He became Rear-Admiral 1 Jan. 1910; was created a C.B. on the Coronation of King George V. 19 June, 1911. From 8 Jan. 1912, to Feb. 1913, he was Naval Secretary to the First Lord of the Admiralty. During the Naval Manœuvres in July, 1912, he was Rear-Admiral commanding the Sixth Cruiser Squadron, with his flag in H.M.S. Aboukir. He was Rear-Admiral commanding the First Cruiser Squadron from 1 March, 1913, and on 22 June, 1913, was created a K.C.B. On 3 Aug. 1914, he was promoted to Acting Vice-Admiral. Vice-Admiral Sir David Beatty, in H.M.S. Lion, commanded the force engaged with the German Squadron in Heligoland Bight on 28 Aug. 1914, which resulted in the destruction of the German cruisers Mainz, Ariadne and Köln, and several destroyers. Some extracts from the London Gazette of 28 Aug. 1914, read as follows:

"THE BATTLE OF THE 'BIGHT.'

"Submarines:—Commodore Roger Keyes, in the destroyer Lurcher, in company with the destroyer Firedrake, and submarines D2, D8, E4, E5, E6, E7, E8, E9, of the 8th Submarine Flotilla, proceeded at midnight on 26 Aug. to take part in the operations in the Bight of Heligoland arranged for on the morning of 28 Aug. At daybreak on 28 Aug. the Lurcher and Firedrake searched the area through which the battle-cruisers were to advance for hostile submarines, and then proceeded towards Heligoland in the wake of submarines E6, E7, E8, which were exposing themselves with the object of enticing the enemy to chase them to the westward. The other submarines were allotted in favourable positions to attack enemy's forces where the opportunity presented itself.

"Destroyers:—The Arethusa, with 1st and 3rd Flotillas, under the command of Commodore Reginald Tyrwhitt, left harbour at 5 a.m. on 27 Aug. H.M.S. Fearless joined the flotilla at sea on the same afternoon. At daybreak on 28 Aug. the operations commenced. At 6.52 a.m. enemy's destroyers were sighted and chased by the 4th Division of the 3rd Flotilla. From 7.20 to 7.57 the Arethusa and 3rd Flotilla were engaged with numerous enemy T.B.D.'s and T.B.'s, which were making for Heligoland; course was altered to cut them off from their base. At 7.57 two cruisers, with four and two funnels respectively, were sighted, the nearest of which was engaged. The Arethusa received a heavy fire from both these cruisers and several destroyers until 8.15 a.m., when the four-funneller transferred her fire to the Fearless. Close action continued with the two-funnelled cruiser until 8.25 a.m., when a 6-in. projectile from the Arethusa landed on the fore bridge of the enemy's ship, who turned away at once in the direction of Heligoland, which now hove in sight on the starboard bow. Commodore Tyrwhitt then ordered all his force to turn to the westward, and speed was reduced to 20 knots. During this action Arethusa was hit many times and considerably damaged; one 6-in. gun only remained in action; all other guns and tubes were temporarily disabled. Fearless reported the 3rd and 5th Divisions of 1st Flotilla had sunk the German destroyer V187, which carried the Commodore of the German Flotilla. At 10.55 a four-funnelled German cruiser was sighted, who opened a heavy fire on Arethusa. The Fearless and 1st Flotilla were ordered to attack her; this was carried out with great spirit, and the cruiser turned away and disappeared in the haze. At 11.10 the same cruiser reappeared on the starboard quarter of the British force, and was heavily engaged by Arethusa and Fearless, the former's guns being now in working order. Simultaneously one division of destroyers attacked her with torpedoes, but without success. Apparently she was feeling the effect of this concentrated fire from Arethusa and Fearless, for she turned away in the direction of Heligoland. Commodore Tyrwhitt continued leading his force to the westward, and, four minutes later, sighted S.M.S. Mainz, a light cruiser of the Köln class, who endured a heavy fire from Arethusa, Fearless, and many destroyers; after an action lasting twenty-five minutes she was seen sinking by the head with engines stopped, and besides being on fire. At this moment our light-cruiser squadron appeared, and very speedily reduced the Mainz to an indescribable condition. The Fearless and destroyers were then recalled, and orders to cease fire were given. The battle-cruisers now joined up, sank a four-funnelled cruiser, and set another on fire.

"Battle-Cruisers:—We will now follow the vicissitudes of the battle-cruisers from the time they put to sea on the morning of the 27th. At 5 a.m., 27 Aug., the 1st Battle-Cruiser Squadron and 1st Light-Cruiser Squadron left harbour and steered for the rendezvous to meet the Invincible and New Zealand. Nothing of interest occurred until the following morning. At 4 a.m., 28 Aug., the destroyers under Commodore Tyrwhitt commenced operations as described above, with the battle-cruisers and light-cruisers in support. The Invincible and New Zealand joined up at the prearranged rendezvous at 11 a.m. The battle-cruisers were unsuccessfully attacked by three enemy submarines shortly after 11 a.m. Commodore Tyrwhitt and Commodore Keyes signalled to Admiral Beatty that they were in need of assistance. Admiral Beatty then sent the Light-Cruiser Force to support Arethusa and the destroyers. At 11.30 a.m. Admiral Beatty, anxious as to the welfare of Commodore Tyrwhitt and his force, left his rendezvous and proceeded at full speed E.S.E. to render assistance. He felt himself justified in risking attack from enemy submarines, thanks to his speed, and he calculated that he was powerful enough to take on any force which might come out. Enemy's battleships need not be taken into account, as they would take time to get steam up, locate him, and bring him to action; there again he had the legs of them. 12.15 p.m.—He sighted the Fearless and 1st Flotilla retiring west, and observed his Light-Cruiser Squadron engaging an enemy's cruiser (the Mainz) ahead. He then altered course to the N.E., and at 12.30 sighted the Arethusa and 3rd Flotilla retiring to the westward, engaging a cruiser of the Kolberg class (Köln). Course was shaped to cut her off from Heligoland. At 12.37 opened fire on her; she steered N.E., and Admiral Beatty chased at 27 knots. 12.56 p.m.—Sighted and engaged a two-funnelled cruiser ahead. The Lion fired two salvoes at her which took effect; she disappeared into the mist, burning furiously and in a sinking condition. Admiral Beatty considered it inadvisable to pursue her further, owing to floating mines having been reported by our destroyers to the eastward. He then turned his battle-cruiser north, and circled to port to finish off the previously engaged Köln. She was sighted once more at 1.25 p.m., steering south with colours flying. The Lion opened fire with two turrets, and at 1.35 she was sunk. Four destroyers were sent to pick up the survivors, but none could be found, although the area was thoroughly searched. At 1.40 p.m. the battle-cruisers turned north and covered the retirement of our light forces. At 6 p.m., the retirement having been well executed and all our destroyers accounted for, a sweep was carried out to the northward. The force was then dispersed to their respective bases."

Sir David Beatty was mentioned in Despatches [London Gazette, 21 Oct. 1914].

Mr. A. H. Bullen says in "The Navy in Battle" (pages 84–85): "In . . . the affair off Heligoland the torpedo figures largely, because visibility was limited to about 6,000 yards. The affair off Heligoland cannot be described as an engagement. It was primarily a reconnaissance in force developed into a series of skirmishes and single ship actions, which began at seven in the morning and ended at mid-day. Submarines, destroyers, cruisers of several types, and, finally, battle-cruisers were employed on the British side. There were sharp artillery engagements between destroyers, there were torpedo attacks made by destroyers on light cruisers and by submarines on battle-cruisers. But they were not massed attacks on ships in formation, but isolated attempts at marksmanship, and they were all of them successful. This failure of the torpedo as a weapon of precision is of considerable technical interest. The light thrown on gunnery problems by the events of the day is less easy to define. The chief interest of this raid into the Bight lies in the strategical idea which prompted it and its moral effects on the British and German naval forces. That Sir David Beatty, in command of four battle-cruisers, should coolly have challenged the German fleet to fight, and that this challenge was not accepted, was extremely significant. It was of special value to our side, for it showed the British Navy to possess a naval leader who knew how to combine dash and caution and marked by a talent for leadership as conspicuous as the personal bravery which had won him his early promotions. These qualities were still better displayed in the engagement of the Dogger Bank." Sir David Beatty also commanded the force engaged with the German battle and armoured cruisers, light cruisers and destroyers, off the Dogger Bank, 24 Jan. 1915, when the Blucher was sunk and other vessels severely injured [London Gazette, 3 March, 1915]. Mr. A. H. Bullen says in "The Navy in Battle" (pages 84 and 85): "This action (the engagement of the Dogger Bank) is remarkable in several respects. For the first time destroyers were here employed to make massed torpedo attacks on a squadron of capital ships. The particular defensive functions of such torpedo attacks will be discussed in the proper place. Suffice it to say here that no torpedo hit, but that the British were robbed of victory by a chance shot which disabled Sir David Beatty's flagship, and deprived the squadron of its leader at a time when bold leadership was most needed."

Commander the Hon. Barry Bingham, V.C., R.N., says in "Falklands, Jutland and The Bight" (pages 133–134): "Things seemed as peaceful as could be on the afternoon of Tuesday, 30 May, when Maurice Bethell and I went ashore for a round of golf at Bruntsfield, near Edinburgh. After a thoroughly enjoyable game over this course, whose delightful inland surroundings reflected all the charm of early summer, we adjourned for tea to 'Rospletha'—the little house I had rented on the side of the links—and then found our way down to Queensferry Pier at the regulation hour of 6 p.m., in order to catch the routine boat. While we stood waiting on the pier amid a throng of fellow-officers, all eyes were suddenly drawn in the direction of the Lion, from whose masthead there floated a string of flags with this message to all ships: 'Raise steam for 22 knots and bank fires at half an hour's notice.' Next, observing the significance of the fact that this signal was being made to the seaplane-carrier ships, we not unnaturally concluded that a Pemberton-Billing benefit or air-raid picnic was about to develop. In this state of mind we reached our various ships. Before another half an hour had elapsed the bustling activity and constant changes of signals on board the flagship produced throughout the other ships that atmosphere of suppressed excitement which is the herald of great events. Clearly some further change of plans was in the air. Another half-hour, and then up went those flags for the last time that evening, bearing the message: 'Raise steam for full speed with all despatch.' There was now not a shadow of doubt that something considerably more than an air-picnic was impending. . . . Steaming at high speed eastwards in the direction of the Skagerrack, the force found itself at noon on the following day (May 31st) in a position approximately 120 miles west of the north coast of Jutland. . . . It was a glorious sunny day, the sea almost a dead calm, the atmosphere clear and conducive to good visibility." There is a stirring account of the battle and of the crippling of the Nestor and preparations to leave the doomed ship. "These orders were rapidly executed, and there was still time on our hands, for nothing had as yet happened. By a brilliant inspiration, Bethell then suggested to me that the cables might be ranged on deck—ostensibly for use in case of a friendly tow, but in reality to keep the men busy to the last. This suggestion I readily accepted, and the hands were still thus employed when the end came. . . . It was clear that the doomed Nestor was sinking rapidly, and at that moment I gave my last order as her commander, 'Abandon ship.' The motor-boat and Carley floats were quickly filled; and as the dinghy was badly broken up by shell fire, there seemed to remain for me only the possibility of a place in the whaler. Bethell was standing beside me, and I turned to him with the question: 'Now where shall *we* go?' His answer was only characteristic of that gallant spirit: 'To Heaven, I trust, sir!' As she sank, her sharp stern and stockless anchors alone visible, we gave our gallant but cruelly short-lived Nestor three rousing cheers and sang 'God save the King.' A reverential pause followed, broken almost immediately by the voice of a typical A.B.: 'Are we down-'earted? No!' Then: 'Wot abart Tipperary?' His words and spirit were infectious, and all joined lustily in the chorus of that hackneyed but inspiring modern war song." Such were the officers and such the men who won for us the Battle of Jutland.

Mr. A. H. Bullen says in "The Navy in Battle" (pages 85–86): "The Battle of Jutland eclipses in interest all the other engagements put together. It presents, of course on a far larger scale, all the problems hitherto met separately. We are still far too imperfectly informed as to many of the incidents of this battle for it to be possible to attempt any complete analysis of its tactics, or to indicate the line on which judgment will ultimately declare itself. We are, for example, entirely without information either about the method of deployment prescribed by the Commander-in-Chief of the Grand Fleet at six o'clock, or of the theory on which the night attack by the destroyers on the retreating German Fleet was ordered. We do not know how it was that a misunderstanding arose between the battle-cruiser fleet and the battle fleet as to the time and place of junction, nor the arrangements which resulted in contact with the German Fleet being lost after the action was over."

For his services in the Battle of Jutland Bank, 31 May, 1916, Admiral Beatty was created a K.C.V.O. and was mentioned by Sir John Jellicoe in his Despatch (dated 6 July, 1916): "Sir David Beatty once again showed his fine qualities of gallant leadership, firm determination, and correct strategic insight. He appreciated the situations at once on sighting first the enemy's lighter forces, then his battle cruisers, and finally his battle fleet. I can fully sympathize with his feelings when the evening mist and fading light robbed the Fleet of that complete victory for which he had manœuvred and for which the vessels in company with him had striven so hard. The services rendered by him, not only on this, but on two previous occasions, have been of the very greatest value."

Admiral David Beatty wrote to Admiral Sir Hedworth Meux after the action: "We drew the enemy into the jaws of our Fleet. I have no regrets, except for the gallant comrades, all pals, that have gone, who died gloriously. It would have warmed your heart to see the gallant Hood bring his squadron into action. . . . We are ready for the next time. Please God it will come soon. The Battle Cruiser Fleet is alive, and has got a very big kick in her."

The "Times" Naval Correspondent says in the "Times" of Friday, 7 July, 1916, in commenting on Admiral Jellicoe's Despatch: "This candid relation of the great event, with its accompanying sketch-plan, supplies convincing testimony to the judgment and skill displayed by those in high command, the courage and competency of the ships' companies, and the high standard of efficiency of the Fleet as a whole. Tried in the stern ordeal of battle, British seamen proved themselves to be inspired by the dauntless spirit of their forefathers, and showed how, under the new conditions and with the new material of warfare, they were superior in technical proficiency to their German opponents, and knew their business better. . . . It is revealed that we used for the first time a seaplane in a fleet action, and Sir David Beatty refers to the possibility of Zeppelins being used by the enemy for scouting. Although the importance of a sea battle is not to be assessed solely by the material damage done on either side, it is shown in the list of enemy ships lost or seriously disabled which Sir John Jellicoe supplies that, even when measured by this standard, our position is stronger than it ever was before. We can much better afford to lose capital ships than the Germans, and yet absolutely as well as relatively, their losses were greater than ours. It is the human interest to be found in these narratives which must strongly appeal to everyone. There were many glorious and inspiring incidents during both the day and night fighting—incidents which had no exact counterpart in the old wars. The explanation is to be found in the large number of small vessels engaged, and the anecdotes of gallantry and heroism, of cool leading and hard fighting, both in the small craft and in the bigger units, make conspicuous features in the story of the battle. Among the more striking of the larger movements there are three which stand out prominently and which will be famous for ever. Splendid as was the manner in which Sir David Beatty took the offensive, and pressed it in the face of overwhelming force, the way in which he utilized his speed to turn the van of the enemy at six o'clock affords a shining example of technical insight and masterly resolution. By this manœuvre he obtained more favourable conditions of visibility than the enemy, enabling us to punish them very severely and establish a definite superiority over them. The head of their line was crumpled up under the fire of the battle-cruisers, admirably supported by the Fifth Battle Squadron, commanded by Rear-Admiral Hugh Evan-Thomas. The handling of the Third Battle-Cruiser Squadron by the intrepid and lamented Hood was another fine feat. It is thus described by Sir David Beatty: 'I ordered them to take station ahead, which was carried out magnificently, Rear-Admiral Hood bringing his squadron into action ahead in a most inspiring manner, worthy of his great ancestors.' Finally, there is the movement of which the Commander-in-Chief writes: 'I formed the Battle Fleet in line of battle on receipt of Sir David Beatty's report, and during deployment the fleets became engaged.' Imagine the situation! The reports of guns were audible and flashes of fire were visible from right ahead to the starboard beam, but in the mist no ship could be distinguished. The positions both of friends and enemies were known only by signal, and there were other circumstances which added to the uncertainty. Yet with unerring judgment and magnificent courage, Sir John Jellicoe swung his huge battle fleet across the bows of the advancing enemy, enabling him to bring a concentrated fire upon the leading ships of Von Scheer's fleet. This turn in the battle—the climax, as it proved—is shown on the sketch-plan to have occurred about seven o'clock. No wonder that after this the enemy's tactics were all of a nature generally to avoid further action. Although the engagement between the battle fleets lasted intermittently for two hours, the enemy constantly turned away and obscured the range by smoke-screens. His vessels were seen to be constantly hit; some were observed to fall out of line, and one at least to sink, while the damage done to our own ships was insignificant. It must have been with a feeling of relief that the Germans learnt next morning that on the first occasion in which they had been unable to avoid a conflict with our main fleet they had escaped complete annihilation. Thus were the traditions of the Senior Service worthily upheld, and if the cloud of witnesses are as near to us as St. Paul thought, the spirits of Nelson and Drake and Blake and the Hoods must have looked on well pleased at their successors and descendants; at the Admirals that are—and were—and the Admirals 'yet to be.' Nelson—some of whose mantle has surely fallen on Lord Beatty—with his swiftness of decision, his power of calculating chances, and taking risks which were hardly risks at all, he knew the game so well. This war seems to have brought the dead nearer to us, so many young and splendid souls have passed unfaltering through fire and space and deep waters to the other side. And if Drake and Nelson are as near us as Sir Henry Newbolt and Admiral Fisher think, why then, they must have been well pleased at that day's work. And they must have welcomed on the farther shore those who died so gloriously for their King and country and their fellow-men. Great Britain shall not perish while these her sons remain to her—while, rent asunder by dissensions, Nationalists, Ulstermen, Scotsmen, Welsh and English make common cause against a common enemy. These great seamen—some of them—have died, but their names shall live for ever—the youngest midshipman who went down in the Queen Mary—the Boy, Jack Cornwell—Arbuthnot and Hood. Seamen and Admirals, they gave all they had to give—their lives. Surely the cloud of witnesses rejoiced that day! There are no tears on that farther shore, nor any pain. There was nothing but rejoicing. Greater love hath no man than this; and the souls of the righteous are in the hand of God.

"'Admirals all, they said their say,
And its echoes are ringing still.
Admirals all, they went their way
To the haven under the hill.'"

Sir David Beatty was created a G.C.B. in 1916, and a G.C.V.O. in 1917. He commanded the Grand Fleet from 1916. He was created an Earl in 1919. Earl Beatty is a Grand Officer of the Legion of Honour; and he holds the Order of St. George of Russia (4th Class). He married in 1901, Ethel, only daughter of Marshall Field, senior, of Chicago, and they have two sons.

FITTON, HUGH GREGORY, Capt., was born 15 Nov. 1863, at Gloucester Crescent, Hyde Park, London, W., son of Edward Brown Fitton, Barrister and Inspector of Factories, and Harriet Margaret Fitton. He was educated at Eton (elected K.S., Eton College, 1877); entered Sandhurst (was first on the list), 1883; joined the 1st Berkshire Regt. 5 Feb. 1884. He served in the Royal Warwickshire and Royal West Kent Regts., Eastern Sudan, 1885 (Medal with clasp and Khedive's Star). He served in the Sudan, 1885–86, with the Frontier Field Force. Action at Ginniss and attack on Ambigole Wells. He again saw active service in the Expedition to Dongola, 1896. As D.A.A.G., Infantry Division (wounded). Operations of 7 June (horse killed). He received the Egyptian Medal with two clasps, was mentioned in Despatches [London Gazette, 3 Nov. 1896], and was created a Companion of the Distinguished Service Order [London Gazette, 17 Nov. 1896]: "Hugh Gregory Fitton, Capt., Berkshire Regt. In recognition of services during recent operations in the Sudan." In the Nile Expedition of 1897, he served as Staff Officer to the G.O.C., Flying Columns, for the occupation of Berber, and the Atbara River. He was mentioned in Despatches [London Gazette, 26 Jan. 1898], received the 4th Class Medjidie, and a clasp to the Egyptian Medal. He served in the Sudan Campaign of 1898, as D.A.A.G.; was present at the battles of Atbara and Khartum, and was mentioned in Lord Kitchener's Despatch of April, 1898, as having "directed the line of advance with the greatest accuracy," and was mentioned in the Despatch of Sept. 1898, for "good service." He received the Medal and two clasps to the Egyptian Medal, and was given the Brevet of Major 16 Nov. 1898. In the South African War 1899–1902, he was D.A.Q.M.G., 7th Division, 3rd Army Corps, and took part in the operations in the Orange Free State, Feb. to May, 1900, including operations at Paardeberg, actions at Poplar Grove, Karee Siding, Vet River (5 and 6 May) and Zand River. Operations in the Transvaal in May and June, 1900, including actions near Johannesburg and Pretoria. Operations in the Transvaal 30 Nov. 1900, to 31 May, 1902. He was mentioned in Despatches [London Gazette, 10 Sept. 1901, and 29 July, 1902]; was given the Brevet of Lieutenant-Colonel 22 Aug. 1902, and received the Queen's Medal with three clasps and the King's Medal with two clasps. From 1905–07 he commanded the West Kent Regt. in Hong-Kong and Singapore. In 1907 he was appointed A.D.C. to King Edward VII., and in that year he was given the Brevet of Colonel 12 Feb. 1907. In 1910, A.D.C. to King George V. He married, 5 Oct. 1910, at St. Mary Abbot's, Kensington, W., May, sixth daughter of Sir Alfred Hickman, Bart., of Wightwick, Wolverhampton. In 1910 he was A.A.G., Eastern Command; in 1911 was created a C.B., and in 1913 became Director of Recruiting and Organization at the War Office. In 1914 he was given the command of the 101st Brigade, and went with it to France in Jan. 1916. He was shot by a sniper while visiting the trenches, and died of his wounds 20 Jan. 1916.

Hugh Gregory Fitton.

WATSON, JAMES KIERO, Capt., was born 19 June, 1855, son of the late Major-General James Watson (late 60th Rifles) and Mrs. James Watson. He was educated at Clifton College and Sandhurst, and was gazetted to the King's Royal Rifle Corps 25 April, 1885. In 1891 and 1892 he served in Burma, taking part in the operations in the Chin Hills. He was attached to the Egyptian Army, 1894–99, and served in the Expedition to Dongola in 1896 as A.D.C. to the Sirdar, being present at the operations of 7 June and 19 Sept. He was mentioned in Despatches [London Gazette, 3 Nov. 1896], received the Egyptian Medal with clasp, and was created a Companion of the Distinguished Service Order [London Gazette, 17 Nov. 1896]: "James Kiero Watson, Capt., King's Royal Rifle Corps. In recognition of services during the recent operations in the Sudan." He served in the Nile Expedition, 1897, as A.D.C. to the G.O.C., was awarded the 4th Class Medjidie, and received a clasp to the Egyptian Medal. He was again A.D.C. to the G.O.C. in the Nile Expedition of 1898, and was present at the battles of the Atbara and Khartum. He was mentioned in Despatches [London Gazette, 24 May and 30 Sept. 1898], received the Medal and two clasps to the Egyptian Medal, and was given the Brevet of Major 16 Nov. 1898. He served in the Nile Expedition of 1899, taking part in the operations which resulted in the final defeat of the Khalifa, as D.A.A.G., Flying Column. He was mentioned in Despatches [London Gazette, 30 Jan. 1900], received the 4th Class Osmanieh and two clasps to the Egyptian Medal. He served in the South African War as A.D.C. to Lord Kitchener, 1899–1901, and was present at the Relief of Kimberley. Also in the operations in the Orange Free State, Feb. to May, 1900, including operations at Paardeberg (17 to 26 Feb.). Operations in the Transvaal in May and June, 1900, including actions near Johannesburg and Pretoria. Operations in the Transvaal, east and west of Pretoria, July to 29 Nov. 1900. Operations in Orange River Colony (May to 29 Nov. 1900). Operations in Cape Colony, south of Orange River, 1899–1900. Operations in the Transvaal and Cape Colony, Dec. 1900, to April, 1901. Operations in Orange River Colony 30 Nov. to Dec. 1900. He was mentioned in Despatches [London Gazette, 16 April, 1901], received the Queen's Medal and three clasps, and was created a C.M.G. In 1901 Capt. Watson returned to the Egyptian Army, and he became Major 19 Oct. 1902, retired 3 May, 1905, and was 1st A.D.C. to H.H. The Khedive of Egypt from 1905 to 1914. He was created a C.V.O. in 1912. Lieut.-Colonel J. K. Watson served in the European War from 1914; was Military Attaché, Egypt, from 1916; was mentioned in Despatches, given the Legion of Honour, and created a C.B.E. in 1919. He married, in 1902, Katherine Emelia, daughter of H. C. Nisbet, of The Old House, Wimbledon, and they have one son.

GORRINGE, GEORGE FREDERICK, Lieut., was born at Southwick, Sussex, 10 Feb. 1868, second son of Hugh Gorringe, J.P., Kingston-by-Sea, Sussex, and of Mrs. Hugh Gorringe. He was educated at Lee's School, Brighton, and at Wellington College, and joined the Royal Engineers at Chatham 17 Feb. 1888, becoming Lieutenant 17 Feb. 1891. He was employed with the Egyptian Army 14 Jan. 1893, to 21 Dec. 1899, and was employed as D.A.A.G., Headquarters Staff, in the Expedition to Dongola in 1898, taking part in the operations of 7 June and 19 Sept. He was mentioned in Despatches [London Gazette, 3 Nov. 1896], received the Egyptian Medal with two clasps (Firket and Hafir), and was created a Companion of the Distinguished Service Order [London Gazette, 17 Nov. 1896]: "George Frederick Gorringe, Lieut., Royal Engineers. In recognition of services during the recent operations in the Sudan." He served in the Nile Expedition of 1897, on the Staff of the G.O.C. (Despatches [London Gazette, 25 Jan. 1898]; Brevet of Major 18 Feb. 1899; clasps to the Egyptian Medal [Abu Hamed]). In the Nile Expedition of 1898 he served as Staff Officer, Headquarters Staff, and was present at the battle of the Atbara as D.A.A.G., Headquarters Staff; at the battle of Khartum and subsequent operations at Gedarif. He was mentioned in Despatches [London Gazette, 24 May and 30 Sept. 1898], received the 4th Class of the Medjidie, the Medal, and two clasps to the Egyptian Medal (Atbara, Abu Hamed and Gedarif). He became Captain 17 Feb. 1899, and in that year served in the Nile Expedition and was present in the operations resulting in the final defeat of the Khalifa, commanding irregulars at actions of Abu Adel and Om Devrikat (Despatches [London Gazette, 30 Jan. 1900]; Brevet of Lieutenant-Colonel 14 March, 1900; two clasps to Egyptian Medal). He was specially employed in charge of the reconstruction of Khartum. He served in the South African War 23 Dec. 1899, to 1 Nov. 1901, as A.D.C. to Lord Kitchener; as D.A.A.G., Headquarters Staff, and in command of a flying column and of the Loyal Farmers' Light Horse (1 Jan. to 12 Oct. 1901). He was present at the operations in Cape Colony, Jan. to March, 1900, and April, 1900. Operations in Orange Free State, Feb. 1900, and March to May, 1900. Operations in Orange River Colony, May and June, 1900. Operations in the Transvaal, May to 29 Nov. 1900. Operations in the Transvaal 30 Nov. to Dec. 1899. Operations in Orange River Colony, Dec. 1900, and Aug. 1901. Operations in Cape Colony, Dec. 1900, to Oct. 1901. (Despatches [London Gazette, 16 April and 9 July, 1901]; Queen's Medal and four clasps; created a C.M.G.). Sir A. Conan Doyle tells us, in Chapter XXXV. of "The Great Boer War," how in the spring of 1901 in Cape Colony "Kritzinger's original force broke into many bands. . . . The total number of Boers who were wandering over the eastern and midland districts may have been about two thousand, who were divided into bands which varied from fifty to three hundred. The chief leaders of separate commandos were Kritzinger, Scheepers, Malan, Myburgh, Fouché, Lotter, Smuts, Van Reenen, Lategan, Maritz and Conroy, the two latter operating on the western side of the country. To hunt down these numerous and active bodies the British were compelled to put many similar detachments into the field, known as the columns of Gorringe, Crabbe, Henniker, Scobell, Doran Kavanagh, Alexander, and others. These two sets of miniature armies performed an intricate devil's dance over the Colony. . . . At the beginning of August the connected systematic work of French's columns began to tell. In a huge semicircle the British were pushing north, driving the guerillas in front of them. Scheepers, in his usual wayward fashion, had broken away to the south; but the others had been unable to penetrate the cordon, and were herded over the Stormberg–Naauwport line. The main body of the Boers was hustled swiftly along from August 7 to August 10, from Graaf Reinet to Thebus, and thrust over the railway line at that point with some loss of men and a great shedding of horses. It was hoped that the blockhouses on the railroad would have held the enemy, but they slipped across by night, and got into the Steynsburg district, where Gorringe's Colonials took up the running. On August 13 he followed the commandos from Steynsburg to Venterstad, killing twenty of them and taking several prisoners." The rest of the chapter, describing the work done by the British flying columns, makes very interesting reading. Major Gorringe was mentioned in Despatches [London Gazette, 16 April and 9 July, 1901], received the Queen's Medal with four clasps; was created a C.M.G., and given the Brevet of Lieutenant-Colonel 14 March, 1900. In 1904 he was in command of the operations at Jebel Jerok in Southern Sennar, receiving a clasp (Jerok) to the Egyptian Medal, and the Brevet of Colonel 10 Feb. 1904; 3rd Class Osmanieh, 1904. He was promoted to Colonel 23 June, 1906, and was Director of Movements and Quartering at the War Office 23 June, 1906, to 31 March, 1909. Brigade Commander, 18th Brigade, Northern Command, 1 April, 1909, to 5 Dec. 1911; promoted to Major-General 6 Sept. 1911; commanding Bombay Brigade, India, 1 May, 1912, to 31 March, 1915. From 1 April, 1915, to 10 March, 1916, he commanded the 12th Division, Indian Expeditionary Force, Mesopotamia, in the operations in Southern Arabistan and the Euphrates Valley, terminating with the capture of Nasiriyeh. He was mentioned in Despatches and created a K.C.B.; was temporary Lieutenant-General from 11 March, 1916, to 22 Sept. 1916; was Chief of Staff, Tigris Force, Jan. 1916, to March, 1916; commanding the 3rd Indian Army Corps, Kut Relief Force, 11 March, 1916, to 10 July, 1916. From 20 Sept. 1916, to 1919, Sir G. F. Gorringe commanded the 47th Division, British Armies in France. He was created a K.C.M.G. in 1918. His favourite recreations are hunting, polo and shooting.

General Townshend remarks on page 39 of "My Campaign in Mesopotamia": "The new 12th Division, under the command of General Gorringe, could not be called complete, as it had no artillery." On page 87 he says: "Gorringe had taken Nasiriyeh on 24th July, after a stubborn resistance of a week or so on the part of the Turks, the bulk of whom retreated north along the Hai, and were said to have united with Nureddin's force at Kut-el-Amara." In the entry in his diary for October 3rd Sir Charles Townshend writes: "We are now some 380 miles from the sea, and we have only two weak divisions, including my own, in the country! There is my division to do the fighting, and Gorringe's to hold the line of communications from Kut to the sea. Thus there is no possible support to give me if I receive a check." On page 256 Sir Charles says: "It was plain that Aylmer could do nothing to aid me until reinforcements reached him. Sir Percy Lake, the Commander-in-Chief in Mesopotamia, who was at Basra, evidently took the same view." Sir Percy suggested that General Aylmer should establish himself on the best position he could, holding both banks of the river, with the bridge connecting them behind him, and there unload all his river-craft and send them back empty. "Gorringe had been sent to Amarah to organize the reinforcements as they arrived there from Basra, and send them on to Aylmer. The date on which these reinforcements would arrive depended on the rapidity with which Aylmer could free his river-craft." On the 12th March Major-General Gorringe succeeded to the command of the Tigris Corps, that gallant soldier, Sir Fenton Aylmer, V.C., having been superseded by the War Office. But really a General's only chance of not being superseded in that inhospitable country was to go out of existence. It is only the strategist—amateur or otherwise—in the War Office who can sit unmoved and limpet-like while unfriendly waves and billows of criticism wash over his official rock. Many pages of General Townshend's book are devoted to General Gorringe's magnificent efforts to win through to his relief. In Lord Kitchener's speech after the fall of Kut and very shortly before his death, he said: "No praise would seem extravagant for the troops under Sir Percy Lake and Sir George Gorringe, and that they did not reap the fruit of their courage and devotion is solely due to the circumstances which fought against them."

GIROUARD, EDOUARD PERCY CRANWILL, Lieut., was born at Montreal 26 Jan. 1867, son of the late Hon. Desiré Girouard. He was educated at the Royal Military College, Kingston, and was gazetted to the Royal Engineers as Second Lieutenant 28 July, 1888; becoming Lieutenant 28 July, 1891. He was Railway Traffic Manager, Royal Arsenal, 1 July, 1890, to 14 Aug. 1895, and was employed with the Egyptian Army as Director of Sudan Railways 10 April, 1896, to 11 Sept. 1898. He served with the Dongola Expeditionary Force, 1896, as Director of Railways, taking part in the operations of 19 Sept. He was mentioned in Despatches [London Gazette, 8 Nov. 1896], received the Egyptian Medal with clasp, and was created a Companion of the Distinguished Service Order [London Gazette, 17 Nov. 1896]: "Edouard Percy Cranwill Girouard, Lieut., Royal Engineers. In recognition of services during the recent operations in the Sudan." The Insignia, Warrant and Statutes were sent to the G.O.C., Cairo, and presented 25 Jan. 1897. He served in the Nile Expedition of 1897, was mentioned in Despatches [London Gazette, 25 Jan. 1898], received the clasp to the Egyptian Medal, and was given the Brevet of Major 29 July, 1899, being promoted to Captain 28 July, 1899. For the Nile Expedition of 1898 he received a Medal. He was President of the Egyptian Railway Board, 1898 and 1899 (2nd Class Medjidie). In the South African War he served on the Staff from 1899 to 1902, as Director of Railways. Operations in Natal, 1899. Advance on Kimberley. Operations in the Orange Free State Feb. to May, 1900. Operations in the Transvaal in May and June, 1900. Operations in Orange River Colony May to 29 Nov. 1900. Operations in Cape Colony, south of Orange River, 1899-1900. Operations in Cape Colony, north of Orange River. Operations in the Transvaal, Orange River Colony and Cape Colony. One comes across him in Sir A. Conan Doyle's "Great Boer War": "Roberts's main column kept on the railroad, which was mended with extraordinary speed by the Railway Pioneer Regt. and the Engineers, under Girouard and the ill-fated Seymour. It was amazing to note the shattered culverts as one passed, and yet to be overtaken by trains within a day." In describing Methuen's search for De Wet, Sir A. Conan Doyle says on pages 348–349: "That wily and indefatigable man was not long out of our ken. On June 14 he appeared once more at Rhenoster, where the construction trains, under the famous Girouard, were working furiously at the repair of the damage which he had already done. This time the guard was sufficient to beat him off, and he vanished again to the eastward. He succeeded, however, in doing some harm, and very nearly captured Lord Kitchener himself. A permanent post had been established at Rhenoster under the charge of Colonel Spens of the Shropshires, with his own regiment and several guns. Smith-Dorrien, one of the youngest and most energetic of the divisional commanders, had at the same time undertaken the supervision and patrolling of the line. An attack had at this period been made by a commando of some hundred Boers at the Sand River to the south of Kroonstad, where there is a most important bridge. The attempt was frustrated by the Royal Lancaster Regt. and the Railway Pioneer Regt., helped by some mounted infantry and yeomanry. The fight was for a time a brisk one, and the Pioneers, upon whom the brunt of it fell, behaved with great steadiness. The skirmish is principally remarkable for the death of Major Seymour of the Pioneers, a noble American who gave his services and at last his life for what, in the face of all slander and misrepresentation, he knew to be the cause of justice and liberty." For his services in the South African War Brevet Major Girouard was mentioned in Despatches [London Gazette, 8 Feb. and 19 April, 1901, and 29 July, 1902]. He received the Queen's Medal with three clasps, the King's Medal with two clasps, and was created a K.C.M.G. He was Commissioner of Railways, Transvaal and Orange River Colony, 1 July, 1902, to 21 Dec. 1904; was given the Brevet of Lieutenant-Colonel 7 Nov. 1904; was A.Q.M.G., Western Command, 6 Sept. 1906, to 2 Feb. 1907; High Commissioner and Commander-in-Chief, Northern Nigeria, 3 Feb. 1907, to 6 May, 1908; Major, Royal Engineers, 26 May, 1908; Governor and Commander-in-Chief, Northern Nigeria, 7 May, 1908, to 1909; Brevet Colonel 13 Sept. 1908; Governor and Commander-in-Chief of the East Africa Protectorate, 1909–12; retired from the Royal Engineers 13 July, 1912; has been on the Board, Elswick Works, Newcastle, since 1912. He has published a "History of the Railways during the War in South Africa." Sir Percy Girouard married, in 1903, Mary Gwendoline (who divorced him in 1914), only daughter of the late Hon. Sir Richard Solomon, and they had one son.

Colonel Repington says, in "Vestiagia" (pages 105 and 106), that at the time of the decision to send an Expedition to Dongola, "Sarras was the terminus of the railway southward from Wadi Halfa, and as the navigation of the river was impeded by rapids, it was determined to push on the railway, which would eventually to terminate at Kerma, close to Dongola, as a temporary measure. After combats at Firket and Hafir, and after the overcoming of serious difficulties owing to cholera and storms, Dongola was occupied on 23 Sept., and a few days later the historic town of Merowi, at the foot of the Fourth Cataract, was taken. Then came the important decision to construct a railway across the desert from Wadi Halfa to Abu Hamed, an enterprise which made the fame of Percy Girouard and his able young assistants, and when this railway was about two-thirds of the way across the desert Kitchener determined to occupy Abu Hamed from Merowi, and after a sharp fight General Hunter carried out the plan with entire success. Berber, having been evacuated by the dervishes, was occupied by the Egyptian Army at the end of Aug. 1897, and the continuation of the railway from Abu Hamed to Berber was at once taken in hand. In Dec. Kassala was occupied by an Egyptian force under Colonel Parsons, and the chess-board was now set out for the decisive operations."

FATHY BEY, Miralei, served in the Sudan, and was created a Companion of the Distinguished Service Order (honorary) [London Gazette, 17 Nov. 1896]: "Fathy Bey, Miralei, Egyptian Army. In recognition of services during the recent operations in the Sudan." The Insignia, Warrant and Statutes were sent to the G.O.C., Cairo, and presented on 25 Jan. 1897.

London Gazette, 7 May, 1897.—"War Office, 7 May, 1897. The Queen has been graciously pleased to give orders for the following appointments to the Distinguished Service Order . . . in recognition of the services of the undermentioned Officers during the operations in South Africa, 1896."

HALE, CHARLES HENRY, Surgeon-Capt., was born at Eastbourne, Sussex, 9 March, 1863, second son of G. W. Hale, M.A., Trinity College, Cambridge, and Mrs. Hale (deceased). He was educated at Plymouth Grammar School, and became Captain, R.A.M.C., 5 Feb. 1887. Capt. Hale served in South Africa, 1890–7, was mentioned in Despatches [London Gazette, March, 1897], and created a Companion of the Distinguished Service Order [London Gazette, 7 May, 1897]: "Charles Henry Hale, Surgeon-Capt., Royal Army Medical Corps. In recognition of services during the recent operations in South Africa, 1896." The Insignia were presented to him by the Queen at Windsor 19 May, 1897. He became Major, 5 Feb. 1899; served in the South African War, 1901–1902, taking part in the operations in Orange River Colony, March, 1901, to 31 May, 1902. Operations in Cape Colony, Feb. to March, 1901–02 (Queen's Medal with 4 clasps). He became Lieutenant-Colonel 7 June, 1911. Lieut.-Colonel Hale served in the European War from 1914; became Colonel 1 March, 1915; Assistant Director of Medical Services 28 April, 1915, to 28 Dec. 1915, and D.A.M.S., 9th Corps, to the evacuation of Suvla Bay, and then D.D.M.S., 8th Corps, to the evacuation of Cape Helles; created a C.M.G. 1916, for services in Gallipoli. Colonel Hale retired on retired pay 23 May, 1917. He is a widower, and has one daughter, Eva Willes Hale, married to Lieut-. Colonel E. Kerans, The Worcester Regt.

EVELEIGH-DE-MOLEYNS, FREDERICK ROSSMORE WAUCHOPE, Capt. The Hon. (Lord Ventry), was born 11 Dec. 1861, eldest son of the 4th Baron Ventry and Harriet (who died in 1906), daughter of Andrew Wauchope, Niddrie Marischal, Midlothian. He was educated at Harrow, and was gazetted to the 4th Hussars 9 Sept. 1882; was A.D.C. to the Governor and Commander-in-Chief, Victoria, 1889–90; became Captain 1 May, 1890, and was Adjutant, 4th Hussars, 10 May, 1893, to 19 May, 1896. He served in South Africa in 1896–97, acting as extra Staff Officer, and was mentioned in Despatches [London Gazette, 9 March, 1897]. He was in general

Charles Henry Hale.

command of the troops in 1897, was mentioned in Despatches [London Gazette, 18 Feb. 1898], was given the Brevet of Lieutenant-Colonel 20 May, 1898, and created a Companion of the Distinguished Service Order [London Gazette, 7 May, 1897]: "The Hon. Frederick Rossmore Wauchope Eveleigh-de-Moleyns, Capt., 4th Hussars. In recognition of services during the recent operations in South Africa, 1896." The Insignia were presented by the Deputy Commissioner at Salisbury, South Africa, 14 Aug. 1897, at a parade of the Forces at Salisbury. He became Major 2 March, 1898, and retired in 1901 as Lieutenant-Colonel. He became Commissioner of Police in Mashonaland. He succeeded his father as 5th Baron Ventry in 1914.

NICHOLSON, JOHN SANCTUARY, Capt., was born in London 19 May, 1863, second son of W. Nicholson, of Basing Park, Alton, Hampshire, and of Mrs. W. Nicholson. He was educated at Harrow, was gazetted to the 7th Hussars as Lieutenant 6 Feb. 1884, and became Captain 23 Jan. 1891. He was on special service in South Africa, and acted as Staff Officer in the operations in Matabeleland in 1896, under General Carrington. He was mentioned in Despatches [London Gazette, 9 March, 1897], received the Medal, and was created a Companion of the Distinguished Service Order [London Gazette, 7 May, 1897]: "John Sanctuary Nicholson, Capt., 7th Hussars. In recognition of services during the recent operations in South Africa, 1896." He was Commandant-General of the British South African Police (which he raised), 25 Nov. 1898, to 22 Oct. 1900; became Major 27 May, 1899, and served in the South African War, 1899–1902, first in command of the B.S.A. Police, and afterwards in command of the 1st Brigade, Rhodesia Field Force. Colonel Nicholson served in the European War from 1914, holding a special appointment (graded A.A.G., B.E.F.), 15 Sept. 1914, to 23 April, 1915; was Base Commandant, B.E.F., 24 April, 1915, to 1 Dec. 1916; was Temporary Brigadier-General 2 Dec. 1916, to 31 Dec. 1918, and Base Commandant, British Armies in France, 2 Dec. 1916, to 31 Dec. 1918. He was created a C.B.E. in 1919. He was mentioned in Despatches [London Gazette, 16 April, 1901]; was given the Brevet of Lieut.-Colonel 29 Nov. 1900; received the Queen's Medal with four clasps and the King's Medal with two clasps, and was created a C.B. He was employed with the South African Constabulary 23 Oct. 1902, to 7 July, 1903; and 8 July, 1903, to 20 Aug. 1905, as Inspector-General. He became Lieut.-Colonel 8 July, 1903; was given the Brevet of Colonel 16 Feb. 1905, and became Colonel 23 Feb. 1907. He was created a C.M.G. in 1905.

M'MAHON, SIR HORACE WESTROPP, Bart., Capt., was born 28 Oct. 1863, second son of the third baronet, and Frances Mary, daughter of John Holford. He joined the Royal Warwickshire Regt. 25 Nov. 1885, and the Royal Welsh Fusiliers 16 Dec 1885, becoming Captain 2 April, 1895. He took part in the operations in South Africa in 1896, with Mounted Infantry; was severely wounded, and mentioned in Despatches [London Gazette, 9 March, 1897], and created a Companion of the Distinguished Service Order [London Gazette, 7 May, 1897]: "Sir Horace Westropp M'Mahon, Bart., Capt., The Royal Welsh Fusiliers. In recognition of services during the recent operations in South Africa, 1896." For his services in Crete in 1898 he received the Brevet of Major 8 March, 1899. He served in the South African War, 1899–1900, as Special Service Officer (employed with Mounted Infantry), and was present at the operations in the Transvaal in May and June, 1900, including actions near Johannesburg, Pretoria and Diamond Hill (11 and 12 June). Operations in Orange River Colony, May to Aug. 1900, including actions at Wittebergen (1–29 July). He received the Queen's Medal with four clasps. Sir Horace M'Mahon was promoted to Major 15 July, 1905; retired 28 Sept. 1907, and joined the Reserve of Officers. He was created O.B.E. in 1919. He married, in 1911, Ellie Maude, daughter of the Hon. L. Moses, M.L.C., Sydney, and widow of Capt. C. E. Bancroft, Royal Welsh Fusiliers.

VERNON, HUBERT EDWARD, Capt., was born 7 May, 1867, at Hanbury Hall, Worcestershire, son of Sir Harry Foley Vernon, Bart., and Lady Georgina Sophia Baillie Hamilton, daughter of the tenth Earl of Haddington and Georgina, daughter of Archdeacon Robert Markham. He was educated at Eton and Sandhurst; was gazetted on 20 June, 1888, to the 1st Battn. The Rifle Brigade, which he joined in India, and served with it till 30 March. 1892, when he was transferred to the 4th Battn. Capt. Vernon served in Mashonaland in 1896, with Mounted Infantry, as Temporary Staff Officer. He was mentioned in Despatches [London Gazette, 9 March, 1897, and created a Companion of the Distinguished Service Order [London Gazette, 7 May, 1897]: "Hubert Edward Vernon, Capt., The Rifle Brigade. In recognition of services during the recent operations in South Africa, 1896." The Insignia were presented by F.M. Lord Roberts, Commander-in-Chief in Ireland,

Hubert Edward Vernon.

at a manœuvre review parade 17 Aug. 1897. He was awarded the D.S.O. for his services in Mashonaland, and particularly for the leading part he took in the storming of Makoni's Kraal, Aug. 1896. Sir F. Carrington wrote of him in a Despatch, dated 3 Dec. 1896, "that he was cool and dashing, an ideal Mounted Infantry officer." He was transferred, 7 March, 1897, to the 4th Battn. Rifle Brigade, of which he was appointed Adjutant in Oct. 1897, a post which he held till Oct. 1899, where, on the South African War breaking out, he was seconded for service on General Sir Francis Howard's Staff, and under him took part in the Siege of Ladysmith. After the siege was raised he was in Sir Redvers Buller's advance to Lydenburg (forming part of the division commanded by General the

Hon. Sir Neville Lyttelton), including the action of Bergendal. Subsequently he served successively as Staff Officer to a Mounted Infantry Column, and as D.A.A.G. to the Inspector-General of Mounted Infantry, and saw much service in the Transvaal and Orange River Colony. He was Staff Officer to Capt. Jenner's Column under Colonel Alderson. Brevet Major H. E. Vernon, D.S.O., died on 21 Sept. 1902. General the Hon. Sir Neville Lyttelton, Commander-in-Chief in South Africa, wrote: "He was one of the finest officers I have ever known in the regiment, both in peace and war." And again: "It was a sight to see him in action—a leader whom men would follow anywhere." Lord Roberts wrote: "He was an exceptionally promising officer." General Alderson, Inspector-General of Mounted Infantry in South Africa, wrote from Pretoria, Sept. 1902: "I have known him since 1894. He was with me in Rhodesia in 1896. I then saw what an exceptionally fine and dashing officer he was. For the last few months he has been one of my Staff officers, and I had got to appreciate his charming and upright personality and to realize his ability." He was a splendid horseman, equally at home in the hunting field or at polo. In 1898 and 1899 he played in several prominent polo matches. He was a keen sportsman all round, both after big game in India and Africa and small game at home. For the South African Campaign he received both South African Medals and seven clasps, and was several times mentioned in Despatches.

McCULLOCH, ROBERT HENRY FREDERICK, Lieut., was born at Bath 21 Oct. 1869, eldest surviving son of the late Robert McCulloch, of Hymenstown House, Cahir, County Tipperary. He was educated at Eastman's Royal Naval Academy; at Bath College, and at the Royal Military Academy, Woolwich, and joined the Royal Artillery 27 July, 1888, becoming Lieutenant 27 July, 1891. He served in Matabeleland in 1896, in command of a section of the 10th Mountain Battery, R.A.; was slightly wounded, mentioned in Despatches, and created a Companion of the Distinguished Service Order [London Gazette, 7 May, 1897]: "Robert Henry Frederick McCulloch, Lieut., Royal Artillery. In recognition of services during the recent operations in South Africa, 1896." He became Captain 23 Jan. 1899, and served in the South African War as D.A.A.G., Lines of Communication, 1900–1, taking part in the operations in Cape Colony, 1900–1 (Queen's Medal with two clasps). He was Divisional Adjutant, Royal Artillery, 10 Oct. 1901, to 31 March, 1903, and Adjutant, Royal Artillery, 1 April, 1903, to 11 Dec. 1903; Adjutant, Militia, 12 Dec. 1903, to 11 Dec. 1906. He was promoted to Major 8 March, 1909. He served in the European War, 1914–18; was Temporary Lieut.-Colonel, Royal Artillery, 9 Jan. 1916, to 10 March, 1916; Lieut.-Colonel 11 March, 1916; Temporary Brigadier-General 4 Feb. 1917, to 7 Sept. 1918; Brigadier-General, Royal Artillery, Heavy Artillery, 19th Army Corps, British Armies in France, 4 Feb. 1917, to 1 Oct. 1917; Brigadier-General, Royal Artillery, Heavy Artillery, 11th Army Corps, British Armies in France, 15 Nov. 1917, to 7 Sept. 1918. He was created a C.M.G. in 1916; is an Officer of the Legion of Honour; has the French Croix de Guerre and the 1914 Star.

FRASER, NORMAN WARDEN, Lieut., served in South Africa, and was created a Companion of the Distinguished Service Order [London Gazette, 7 May, 1897]: "Norman Warden Fraser, Lieut., West Riding Regt. In recognition of his services during the recent operations in South Africa, 1898." The Insignia were presented to him by the Queen at Windsor 19 May, 1897.

London Gazette, 25 May, 1897.—"The Queen has been graciously pleased to give orders for the following appointments to the Distinguished Service Order . . . in recognition of the services of the undermentioned Officers during the recent operations in Benin. To be Companions of the Distinguished Service Order."

CAMPBELL, CHARLES, Capt., Royal Navy, was born at St. Andrews 26 March, 1847, eldest son of John Campbell, of Saddell. He was educated at Brenchley Vicarage, Staplehurst; at the Royal Naval Academy, Gosport, and entered the Britannia in 1860. He gained the diving prize for longest under water—one minute, 53 seconds (then a record). He joined H.M.S. Magicienne under Prince Leiningen; served in the Marlborough, Mediterranean Flagship, and after seeing service in the Amphion, Royal Oak and Racer, he joined, in 1868, Galatea, under H.R.H. the Duke of Edinburgh, and made a trip round the world. He was Flag-Lieutenant to Admirals Campbell and Lord John Hay. He was present at the insurrection in Crete; at the taking of Cyprus; was Transport Officer during Lord Wolseley's Campaign against Arabi Pasha (Egyptian Medal and Khedive's Star); appointed to command H.M.S. Lily; then in the Philomel in command of the East Coast of Africa. He suppressed the uprisings at Lamu and Witu; seized the Palace at Zanzibar; commanded the road-cutting party to Nana's stronghold, four days under fire, and led the centre attack; was created a C.B., and received the African Medal. In the Theseus he went to Benin, and was Second in Command of the Expedition against the King. He saved 27 wounded from the fire that swept the city, and was created a Companion of the Distinguished Service Order [London Gazette, 25 May, 1897]: "Charles Campbell, C.B., Capt., Royal Navy. In recognition of services during the recent Expedition to Benin." He was Second in Command to Admirals Harris and Noel during the operations in Crete, 1897–99; commanded Medway Gunnery School, 1899–1902; was A.D.C. to Queen Victoria and to King Edward 1899 to Jan. 1902. Rear-Admiral C. Campbell married (1st), Esther Constance, daughter of Colonel J. O. Fairlie, of Coodham, Ayrshire, and (2ndly), Florence Geraldine, daughter of Colonel A. E. Ross. He died 8 Feb. 1911, and an obituary notice of him appeared in the "Times" of 10 Feb. 1911.

BACON, REGINALD HUGH SPENCER, Commander, was born in 1863, son of the Rev. T. Bacon and Emma, daughter of George Shaw. He was educated in H.M.S. Britannia; entered the Britannia, 1877; received a silver medal from the Italian Government for saving life at the wreck of the Utopia in 1891; Commander H.M.S. Theseus; Chief of the Intelligence Department, Benin Expedition, 1897; received the Medal and Clasp; was mentioned in Despatches, and created a Companion of the Distinguished Service Order [London Gazette, 25 May, 1897]: "Reginald Hugh Spencer Bacon, Commander, Royal Navy. In recognition of services during the recent Expedition to Benin." Commander Bacon started the submarine boat service in the Royal Navy; was Naval Assistant to the First Sea Lord of the Admiralty, 1905; created a C.V.O., 1907; Captain of H.M.S. Dreadnought during her first commission; A.D.C., 1909; Director of Naval Ordnance and Torpedoes, 1907–9. He retired in Nov. 1909, to take the post of managing director of the Coventry Ordnance Works, 1910–14; resigned the appointment, and was gazetted Colonel, Second Commandant, R.M.A., 1915; commanded Heavy Howitzer Brigade, R.M.A., with Expeditionary Force in France; appointed to command the Dover Patrol, 1915, to 31 Dec. 1917; promoted Vice-Admiral; created a K.C.B. and a K.C.V.O., 1916; promoted Admiral, 1918. From Feb. 1918, to March, 1919, he was Controller of the Inventions Department of the Ministry of Munitions. Sir Reginald Bacon is the author of "Benin, the City of Blood," and of "The Dover Patrol, 1915–1917." His favourite recreation is shooting. He is a Deputy-Lieutenant for Hampshire. He married, in 1894, Cicely, daughter of Henry Surtees, of Redworth, and they have one daughter.

Sir Reginald Bacon wrote a book called "The Dover Patrol" (published by Messrs. Hutchinson). The chapter headed "Matters of Strategy" begins thus:

"'Well, Bill, all I knows about strategy is what I 'eard the old man (the Admiral) say, 'ow that the strategy of these 'yer Straits was so to dispose 'is destroyers as to prevent the enemy knowing as 'ow 'e 'adn't got none.'"

At the beginning of another chapter is:

"THE NAVY AND THE GUNS.

"The Navy, through the 'istory of Britain's bloody wars,
'As always helped the Army with 'er blooming Ordnance Stores.
They've landed guns to help them, and I'd 'ave you know, m'lad,
They were always one size larger than what the Army 'ad.

"During the Indian Mutiny the Army cheered us when
Peel landed 'is ole broadside to be lugged by sailor-men.
The Boer War saw us up-to-date when Percy Scott, by 'eavens,
'E made extempore mountings for the naval four-point-sevens.

"The Army's got a 'Mother,' and they've got a 'Grannie,' too,
So we 'ave got our work cut out to do as we should do.
It must be a reg'lar whopper, so bear a hand, my men,
For we'll land our largest twelve-inch, the fifty-ton mark ten."

In the preface Admiral Bacon says: "It is interesting to speculate how the historical verdict of years to come will differ from current opinions on the conduct of the late war at sea. Full credit will certainly be given to those who were responsible for the existence of the Grand Fleet, for the superior armament of its ships over those of the enemy, and for its concentration in the North Sea. Three names are indissolubly associated with this foresight. First and foremost, the historian will remember Lord Fisher, to whose genius and almost uncanny prevision we owe the all-big gun ship of high speed. . . . He prepared for the birth and sturdy growth of the Grand Fleet, which in the grim end the Germans found facing them on the day of battle. Mr. Reginald McKenna was closely associated with this development; in fact, it was generally credited at the time that for three days he was practically outside the Cabinet while fighting the Navy's battle at what, in reality, was the most critical period of our history. Then Mr. Churchill carried on the work, and, in our day of peril, with his characteristic courage, authorized without hesitation the mobilization of the Fleet at a moment when hesitation might have appeared to be excusable, but would have been fatal. For these reasons these three names in particular will be indissolubly associated in history with our battle-fleet supremacy during the war—with that Grand Fleet appropriately so-called. There it lay at Scapa, in the North Sea, with every muscle strained and nerve vibrating. It was like a spear poised in the hand of a giant, ready to be hurled at the wild beast offending against humanity should he venture from his den. Once he crawled out, and Lord Jellicoe's far-reaching victory of Jutland dealt him a blow which sent him snarling back with many wounds which, eventually festering from inactivity and broken hopes and lowered pride, led to his dishonourable and inglorious end. And what of Dover? That is the story with which this book is concerned. The Grand Fleet was in the far North; Commodore Tyrwhitt had a force based on Harwich, and then, farther south, was the Dover Patrol, which held the southern exit from the North Sea, as the Grand Fleet may be said to have held the northern exit."

In describing "The Drifters and their Tasks and their Appliances," in Vol. II., page 419, Sir Reginald Bacon says: "Many minor improvements of the gear were made and employed, but without doubt the most successful adjunct to the nets was 'the net-mine,' invented by Admiral of the Fleet Sir A. K. Wilson, V.C. This electrically-fired mine proved of immense value, and completely revolutionized the method of employing the nets. It was really the combination of two instruments of destruction deadly to submarines—the net and the mine."

Admiral Bacon says that the Dover drifters "were manned by ordinary everyday fishermen, who in war-time had been suddenly called upon to face the enemy and work new nets on new methods under fire, their divisions being commanded by gallant officers of the Royal Naval Reserve

E

They worked as thoroughly, steadily and pluckily as if fighting was their trade. After the raid of 26-27 Oct. 1916, they went on with their duty of watching the nets as steadily as before. They had fought the sea all their lives, and they fought the enemy with equal confidence. They continued to patrol with the thinnest of support, since the waters in the forefront of the patrol, with their varied vital interests, were too extensive to admit of real support being given to them; no larger vessels could be spared, so the bulk of the vidette work fell on the gallant little drifters. This work they cheerfully did, and earned a reputation of which they may always be proud. May good luck attend them! No officer of the Dover Patrol will ever pass a 'Dover' drifter without going on board, and wishing her skipper and crew good luck in remembrance of their old association in the Great War."

"One of the chief events at Dover was the inspection of the patrol by H.M. the King. It may be difficult for some persons, perhaps, in these extremely democratic days to realize how much good this visit did to the patrol. Hitherto officers and men of the patrol had looked on their work as prosaic. True, they were at war, and were doing their bit; but the fact of the King thinking it worth while to come to Dover and inspect the various activities at once brought home to them the national importance of their services in a way that nothing else could have done, and their morale was greatly strengthened. The trawler and drifter crews valued immensely the fact that the King boarded one of each of these craft, and examined the details of their accommodation and their war appliances. I was glad to have the opportunity of presenting Lieut.-Commander Gartside Tipping to His Majesty, as the oldest officer serving afloat. Next day he was killed in action with the King's congratulations still fresh in his mind."

"We won the war, not of ourselves, but by virtue of that vast procession of seamen and sea-fighters, from the forerunners of Hubert de Burgh down to our own fathers—men of the Royal Navy, the merchant traders, the fishermen, whose sea-blood has been transmitted to us through male and female forbears. It is the bestowal of sea instinct by heredity from our sea-folk of the past centuries that is the sure shield of our Empire against all assailants on the sea."

ROCHE, THOMAS HORATIO DE MONTMORENCY, Capt., was born 31 Aug. 1854, son of Colonel C. B. Roche, 45th and 34th Regiments. He was educated at King's School, Rochester, and joined the Royal Marines as Lieutenant 1 July, 1874. He served in the Egyptian Expedition in 1882, being present at the actions at Malaha, Tel-el-Mahuta, both actions at Kassassin, Battle of Tel-el-Kebir, occupation of Cairo (Medal with clasp, Bronze Star). He was promoted to Captain 28 May, 1884. In 1887 he served in the Benin Expedition, in command of Royal Marines, and was mentioned in Despatches [London Gazette, 7 May, 1897]: "Thomas Horatio de Montmorency Roche, Capt., Royal Marines. In recognition of services during the recent Expedition to Benin." He was also given the Brevet of Lieut.-Colonel 25 May, 1897, and became Lieut.-Colonel 22 June, 1898; retired 2 Oct. 1908, as Colonel; was given the honorary rank of Major-General 2 Oct. 1908. He married in 1886, Emily Jane, daughter of J. W. Owen Richards, D.L., J.P., of Barnagh, County Mayo, and Tempo, County Fermanagh.

MARTIN, JAMES McCARDIE, Surgeon, Royal Navy, was born in 1859, at Camus House, Coleraine, third son of the Rev. John F. Martin and Mrs. Martin. He was educated at the Academical Institution, Coleraine, and at Edinburgh University, and entered the Royal Navy in 1882. He served with the Royal Marine Battn. in the Benin Expedition as Senior Medical Officer of the Flying Column to Benin City. He was mentioned in Despatches, received the Medal and clasp, and was created a Companion of the Distinguished Service Order [London Gazette, 25 May, 1897]: "James McCardie Martin, Staff Surgeon, Royal Navy. In recognition of services during the recent Expedition to Benin." He was Senior Medical Officer, H.M.S. Barfleur, Flagship of Sir James Bruce, K.C.M.G., at Yaku, during the Pekin Relief Expedition, 1900. He became Deputy Inspector-General, R.N., and has retired. His favourite recreations are hunting, shooting and golf. He married, in 1899, Edith Lambert, daughter of the late Henry Matier, of Dunlambert, Belfast.

James McCardie Martin.

DIMSEY, EDGAR RALPH, Staff Surgeon, was born in 1861, son of D. G. Dimsey, late of the Admiralty, and Mrs. Dimsey. He became Surgeon, Royal Navy, in 1883, and Staff Surgeon in 1895. He served in the Benin Expedition in 1897; was mentioned in Despatches; received the General African Medal with a clasp for Benin, and was created a Companion of the Distinguished Service Order [London Gazette, 25 May, 1897]: "Edgar Ralph Dimsey, Staff Surgeon, Royal Navy. In recognition of services during the recent Expedition to Benin." He was promoted to Fleet Surgeon. In 1900 he married Edith Elizabeth, eldest daughter of the Rev. W. H. Whitting, Rector of Stower Provost, Dorset, and they have two sons and a daughter.

London Gazette, 15 June, 1897.—"The Queen has been graciously pleased to give orders for the following appointment to the Distinguished Service Order, in recognition of the services of the undermentioned Officer during the Niger Sudan Campaign. To be a Companion of the Distinguished Service Order."

ARNOLD, ALFRED JAMES, Lieut., was born in Manchester 10 April, 1866, third son of Alfred R. Arnold, and Durnvilia, daughter of W. J. Taaffe, County Dublin. He was educated at a private school, and at Corpus Christi College, Cambridge. He enlisted in the 5th Dragoon Guards, 1886; was gazetted Second Lieutenant, 3rd Hussars, 1893; joined the Royal Niger Constabulary in 1894; commanded the same from 1895 to 1899; commanded troops throughout the Niger Sudan Campaign operations of 1895-96; battles of Egbon, Bida and Ilorin, 1897; was mentioned in Despatches [London Gazette, 11 June, 1897]; promoted to Captain and Brevet-Major; received the Medal and clasp, and was created a Companion of the Distinguished Service Order [London Gazette, 15 June, 1897]: "Alfred James Arnold, Lieut., 3rd Hussars, commanding the Forces of the Royal Niger Company, In recognition of services during the Sudan Campaign." He became Captain, 3rd Dragoon Guards, 3 March, 1898. He served on the Niger, 1899; Expedition to Siama; promoted to Major, and given the Brevet of Lieut.-Colonel, 8 July, 1899. For his services in the Transvaal War of 1901 he was mentioned in Despatches 7 March, 1899, and received the Medal with clasp. He was given the Brevet of Colonel 8 July, 1905. Colonel A. J. Arnold retired 14 Nov. 1906. He was Inspecteur-Général d'Exploitation, Mozambique Company, East Africa, 1899-1913. Commanded 20th Battn. Manchester Regt. 1914-15, and 1st V.B. Royal Welsh Fusiliers, 1915-19. Mentioned for services in Great War, 1918; created Commander of the Order of the British Empire 1 Jan. 1919. Colonel Arnold is an F.R.G.S. His favourite recreations are cricket, tennis and golf.

London Gazette, 21 Sept. 1897.—"War Office, 21 Sept. 1897. The Queen has been graciously pleased to give orders for the following appointment to the Distinguished Service Order, in recognition of the services of the undermentioned Officer on the occasion of the attack on the Political Officer's Escort at Maizar, in the Tochi Valley, on 10 June, 1897. To be a Companion of the Distinguished Service Order."

SETON-BROWNE, CLEMENT LAWRENCE SETON, Lieut., was born 9 March, 1869. He joined the Wiltshire Regt. as Second Lieutenant, from the Militia, 10 Oct. 1891; became Lieutenant, Wiltshire Regt., 6 March, 1893; Lieutenant, Indian Staff Corps, 7 March, 1894. He served on the North-West Frontier of India, 1897-98, being present at the action of Maizar 10 June, 1897 (severely wounded), and at Tochi. He was mentioned in Despatches [London Gazette, 7 Sept. 1897]; received the Medal and clasp, and was created a Companion of the Distinguished Service Order [London Gazette, 21 Sept. 1897]: "Clement Lawrence Seton Seton-Browne, Lieut., Indian Staff Corps. In recognition of services on the occasion of an attack on the Political Officer's Escort at Maizar in the Tochi Valley 10 June, 1897." The Insignia were presented by the Queen at Windsor 20 Nov. 1897. He became Captain, Indian Army, 10 July, 1901; served on the N.W. Frontier of India in Waziristan, 1901-2 (Clasp); became Major 10 Oct. 1909. Major Seton-Browne became Second-in-Command, 55th Coke's Rifles, F.F.; he was promoted to Lieut.-Colonel 1 Jan. 1917. He married, in 1896, F. G., daughter of J. E. Bates.

London Gazette, 11 Oct. 1897.—"War Office, 11 Oct. 1897. The Queen has been graciously pleased to give orders for the following appointments to the Distinguished Service Order. In recognition of their services with the Indian Contingent during the operations in Mombasa, 1895-6.

BARRATT, WILLIAM CROSS, Capt., was born 2 June, 1862, second son of the late James Barratt, of Hanslope, Buckinghamshire. He was educated at Bedford Grammar School, and entered the Militia, from which he joined the Royal Berkshire Regt. 5 Dec. 1883. He served in the Sudan Expedition in 1885; Suakin, Reconnaissance to Hasheen, actions at Hasheen and Tofrek, operations at and destruction of Tamai (Medal with two clasps; Bronze Star). He became Lieutenant, Indian Staff Corps, 11 Nov. 1886; served in the Zhob Valley Expedition, 1890; in the Waziristan Expedition; became Captain 5 Dec. 1894; served in the operations against the Mazrui rebels; was Commandant, Indian Contingent. He was mentioned in Despatches; received the 1st Grade, 3rd Class, Brilliant Star of Zanzibar, and the Medal, and was created a Companion of the Distinguished Service Order [London Gazette, 11 Oct. 1897]: "William Cross Barratt, Capt., Indian Staff Corps. In recognition of his services during the operations in Mombasa." Capt. Barratt's Insignia were sent out to East Africa, where the presentation had to be deferred until his return from the interior, where he then was, in connection with the troubles in Uganda. It was finally presented to him in England by the Queen on 11 May, 1899. He served in Uganda, 1897-98, in command of the Indian Contingent; was present in the attack at Kijembo, capture of Kabagambi, engagement near Mruli, actions of Kakrugura, Jass Camp and Mruli. He was mentioned in Despatches; was given the Brevet of Major 25 Jan. 1899, and received the Medal with two clasps. In China, in 1900, he was present at the relief of Pekin; actions at Peitsang and Yangtsun. He was mentioned in Despatches [London Gazette, 14 May, 1901], and received the Medal with clasp. He served on the N.W. Frontier of India in 1902; operations against the Darwesh Khel Waziris; was promoted to Major 5 Dec. 1901; was given the Brevet of Lieut.-Colonel 25 July, 1905; the Brevet of Colonel 25 July, 1909; became Colonel 1 Jan. 1911, and was created a C.B. in 1911. He was Divisional Area Commander, India, 13 Sept. 1914, to 4 Dec. 1919; promoted Major-General 1 Jan. 1917. Major-General W. C. Barratt married, in 1907, Katherine Mathilde Goldsmith, formerly of Betton Hall, Market Drayton.

SCOTT, THOMAS EDWIN, Lieut., was born 6 March, 1867, at Bagnalstown, Co. Carlow, Ireland, son of the Rev. James Richard Scott (deceased), Clerk in Holy Orders, Ireland, and of Mrs. J. R. Scott. He joined the Royal Irish Fusiliers as Second Lieutenant from the Militia 9 May, 1888; became Lieutenant 18 Dec. 1889; Lieutenant, Indian Staff Corps, 17 April, 1890; served on the North-West Frontier of India First Miranzai Expedition, 1891; Waziristan Field Force, 1894-95 (Medal and clasp). He was specially employed with the Indian Contingent, East Africa 6 Nov. 1895, to 16 Nov. 1898; Second-in-Command, operations against the Mazrui rebels; was mentioned in Despatches, received the 1st Grade, 2nd Class, Brilliant Star of Zanzibar and the Medal; and was created a Companion of the Distinguished Service Order [London Gazette, 11 Oct. 1897]: "Thomas Edwin Scott, Lieut., Indian Staff Corps. In recognition of services with the Indian Contingent during the operations in Mombasa, 1895–96." The Insignia were presented by the Queen 26 Feb. 1899. He served in Uganda, 1897–98; Second-in-Command, Indian Contingent, and commanded the Flying Column for the disarmament of the mutinous Indian garrisons in Unyoro (Despatches; Medal with two clasps; Brevet of Major). He became Captain 9 May, 1899; served in China, 1900; actions of Peitsang, Yangtsun and Relief of Pekin; Road Commandant, Lines of Communication (Despatches twice [London Gazette, 16 May and 24 Nov. 1901]; Medal with clasp; created a C.I.E.). He was D.A.A.G., Headquarters, Northern Command, India, 12 Nov. 1904, to 16 May, 1906 (clasp twice). He became Major, Indian Army, 13 Feb. 1905; was a D.A.A.G., Headquarters, India, 17 May, 1906, to 11 Nov. 1908; Assistant Secretary, Committee of Imperial Defence (G.S.O., 2nd Grade), 26 Aug. 1909, to 26 April, 1912; Lieutenant-Colonel, Indian Army, 19 May, 1912; temporary Colonel, 8 March, 1914, to 28 Nov. 1915; is Commandant, 57th Rifles, Frontier Force. Brigadier-General T. E. Scott was Military Secretary to His Excellency the Commander-in-Chief, India, 8 March, 1914, to 30 Sept. 1916 He was given the Brevet of Colonel 29 Nov. 1915; was specially employed in East Africa 30 Sept. 1917, to 7 Jan. 1918; was created a C.B. in 1917 and promoted to Major-General 3 June, 1918. He married on the 12th Sept. 1904, Demira Josephine Anna, youngest daughter of the late Rev. Morland Chaplin, at St. Mary Abbot's Church, Kensington, W., and they have one son, Thomas Patrick David, born 1 March, 1905.

FAIRTLOUGH, EDWARD CHARLES D'HEILLEMAR, Capt. joined the 4th Royal Dublin Fusiliers, and became Captain. He commanded the Sierra Leone Frontier Force, 1894; commanded Expedition against the Bawarume; was mentioned in Despatches, and created a Companion of the Distinguished Service Order [London Gazette, 11 Oct. 1897]: "Edward Charles d'Heillemar Fairtlough, Capt., 4th Battn. The Royal Dublin Fusiliers. In recognition of services against Bawarume, a marauding native chief, on the frontier between Sierra Leone and Liberia, 1896." He was appointed District Commissioner, Ronietta, Sierra Leone, 1898; in Military Charge of operations in Ronietta and Pangoma during Sierra Leone Rebellion, 1898–99; commanded Expedition for Relief of Pangoma Fort June and July, 1898; successful after 29 days' bush-fighting. He was created a C.M.G., 1900. He became Official Member, Legislative Council, Sierra Leone. Major Fairtlough married, in 1901, Gertrude, daughter of Thomas Murray, of Milmount House, Westmeath, and they have two daughters.

London Gazette, 7 Jan. 1898.—"War Office, 7 Jan. 1898. The Queen has been graciously pleased to give orders for the following appointment to the Distinguished Service Order, in recognition of the services of the undermentioned Officer on the occasion of his advancing with reinforcements to the relief of the Political Officer's escort, when attacked at Maizar, in the Tochi Valley, on the 10th June, 1897. To be a Companion of the Distinguished Service Order."

DE BRETT, HARRY SIMONDS, Lieut., was born 20 Sept. 1870, was educated at Clifton, and joined the Royal Artillery 15 Feb. 1889, becoming Lieutenant 15 Feb. 1892. He served on the North-West Frontier of India, 1897–98, taking part in the action at Maizar, Tochi. He was mentioned in Despatches [London Gazette, 7 Dec. 1897], received the Medal with clasp and was created a Companion of the Distinguished Service Order [London Gazette, 7 Jan. 1898]: "Harry Simonds de Brett, Lieut., Royal Artillery. In recognition of services at Maizar, in the Tochi Valley, 10 June, 1897." The Warrant, Insignia and Statutes were sent to the Commander-in-Chief in India, and the Insignia presented on 22 March, 1898, by the G.O.C., Tochi Brigade, at a Brigade Parade. He became Captain 1 Sept. 1899, and was Adjutant, Royal Artillery, 7 July, 1900, to 2 Jan. 1901, serving in the South African War from 1899 to 1900, and taking part in the operations in the Orange Free State Feb. to May, 1900, including operations at Paardeberg (26 Feb.); actions at Poplar Grove and Dreifontein (Queen's Medal and three clasps). He served in China in 1900 (Medal). He was Brigade Major, India, 31 Oct. 1904, to 31 Oct. 1908; became Major 15 Sept. 1909; was specially employed in Somaliland 11 Nov. 1909, to 21 May, 1910 (Medal with clasp); G.S.O.2, War Office, 30 Sept. 1910, to 17 Dec. 1914. He served in the European War from 1914, as G.S.O.2, 28th Division, New Armies, British Expeditionary Force, 18 Dec. 1914, to 11 Aug. 1915; G.S.O.1, 3rd Division, British Expeditionary Force, British Armies in France, 12 Aug. 1915, to 16 Nov. 1916; was given the Brevet of Lieutenant-Colonel 1 Jan. 1916; became Lieutenant-Colonel 18 June, 1916; was Brigadier-General, Royal Artillery, Heavy Artillery, 3rd Army Corps, Mesopotamia Expeditionary Force, 4 March, 1918, to 14 July, 1918; A.A.G., War Office (temporary), 1 Sept. 1918. He was created a C.M.G. in 1917, and given the Brevet of Colonel 1 Jan. 1919. He married, in 1901, Alice Maud, second daughter of the late Arthur Davies, and they have one son and one daughter.

London Gazette, 8 March, 1898.—"War Office, 8 March, 1898. The Queen has been graciously pleased to give orders for the following appointment to the Distinguished Service Order, in recognition of the services of the undermentioned Officer in the conduct of certain military operations against the Sofas in West Africa in April last, while holding the appointment of Travelling Commissioner under the Governor of the Gold Coast Colony. To be a Companion of the Distinguished Service Order."

HENDERSON, FRANCIS BERKLEY, Lieut., Royal Navy, was born in Ely in 1859, fourth son of the late Rev. J. H. Henderson and Anne, daughter of Rear-Admiral H. G. Morris. He was educated in H.M.S. Britannia, Dartmouth; won the Goodenough Medal for gunnery, and entered the Royal Navy in 1872, becoming Midshipman in 1874; Sub-Lieutenant, 1878, and Lieutenant, 1882. He was invalided in 1884. In 1895 and 1896 he was Private Secretary and Aide-de-Camp to Sir W. E. Maxwell, K.C.M.G., Governor of the Gold Coast Colony, 1895–96, and went with him to Kumasi (awarded Ashanti Star). From 1896 to 1902 he was Travelling Commissioner, Gold Coast Colony; and he was Acting Chief Commissioner of Ashanti, 1902–1904, being invalided in 1904. He was created a Companion of the Distinguished Service Order [London Gazette, 8 March, 1898]: "Francis Berkley Henderson, Lieut. (retired list), Royal Navy. In recognition of services in conducting the operations against the Sofas in 1897." He received the West African Medal, with a special clasp for Dawkita. In 1902 he was created a C.M.G.; he is a J.P., and an F.R.G.S. His favourite recreations are shooting and lawn tennis. Lieut.-Commander F. B. Henderson married, in 1890, Editha Devereux, eldest daughter of the late T. N. Fonnereau, of Christ Church Park, Ipswich.

London Gazette.—"War Office, 11 March, 1898. The Queen has been pleased to give orders for the following appointments to the Distinguished Service Order, and promotions in the Army, in recognition of the services of the undermentioned Officers while attached to the Egyptian Army during the recent operations in the Sudan, resulting in the capture of Abu Hamed and the subsequent occupation of Berber. To be Companions of the Distinguished Service Order."

KEPPEL, COLIN RICHARD, Commander, Royal Navy, was born 3 Dec. 1862, in London, son of the late Admiral of the Fleet the Hon. Sir Henry Keppel and Lady Keppel, daughter of Martin West, Esq., Barrister-at-Law, and Lady Maria West. He joined H.M.S. Britannia in 1875; was Midshipman of Inconstant during the Egyptian War of 1882 (Egyptian Medal; Khedive's Bronze Star); Sub-Lieutenant of Invincible; served with the Naval Brigade landed for service in the Sudan; with the Nile Expedition for the relief of General Gordon at Khartum 1884–85; present in the S.S. Sophis with Lord C. Beresford at the relief of Sir C. Wilson. He most highly distinguished himself. Lord Charles Beresford thus speaks of him in his Despatch: "I consider that we owe our safety on the steamer, as well as the safety of Sir C. Wilson and his party, who undoubtedly would have been killed if the steamer had been destroyed, to the untiring energy of Sub-Lieut. Keppel." The correspondent of the "Army and Navy Gazette" says: "Then came a characteristic piece of calculated audacity. Lord Charles noticed that a nuggar in which Sir Charles Wilson had escaped from the wreck of his steamer, had drifted down with some of Gordon's men on board, and had stranded close to the fort. The hero of the Condor sent Keppel with a small boat and half a dozen blue-jackets to the rescue. They cut her out under the very guns and brought her safely off, Keppel being hit in the groin, but luckily only by a spent, or more probably a ricochet, bullet." He was wounded, promoted to Lieutenant for this service (Nile, 1884; five clasps). Appointed to be Equerry to H.R.H. Admiral the Duke of Edinburgh 28 Dec. 1886. He was appointed Extra Equerry Jan. 1896. Flag-Lieutenant to His Royal Highness the Duke of Edinburgh when Commander-in-Chief in the Mediterranean, 1886–89, and at Plymouth Aug. 1899 to June, 1893; lent to Egyptian Government for service on the Nile, 1897–98; commanded the Flotilla on the Nile. Queen Victoria was pleased to give orders for the following appointment to the Distinguished Service Order "in recognition of the services of the undermentioned Officer, while attached to the Egyptian Army during the recent operations in the Sudan, resulting in the capture of Abu Hamed and the subsequent occupation of Berber. To be a Companion of the Distinguished Service Order, viz.: Commander Colin Richard Keppel, R.N., 11 March, 1898;" services in command of the gun-boats with the Nile Expedition, 1898, and was thus mentioned in Despatches by the Sirdar: "The exceptional services performed by Commander Keppel and his subordinate officers of the Royal Navy is deserving of special mention. These gun-boats have been for a long time past almost constantly under fire; they have made bold reconnaissances past the enemy's forts and rifle pits, and on the 1st and 2nd of Sept. aided in the capture of all the forts on both banks of the Nile, and in making the fortifications of Omdurman untenable. In bringing to notice the readiness of resource, daring and ability of Commander Keppel and his officers, I wish also to add my appreciation of the services rendered by Engineer E. Boyd, R.N., and the engineering staff, as well as of the detachment of the Royal Marine Artillery and the gun crews, who have gained the hearty praise of their commanders." Commander Keppel was again mentioned in Despatches after the fall of Khartum, and received the C.B. for his services on this occasion (1898). He was noted for promotion on having the requisite sea service (Medal and two clasps); promoted to the rank of Captain 30 May, 1899, and received the thanks of both Houses of Parliament, 1899, for services in the Sudan (1899); C.V.O. 3 April, 1906; Cross of the Order of Naval and Military Merit from the King of Spain; Rear-Admiral in Command of Atlantic Fleet, 1909–10. Admiral Keppel retired in 1913. He was created a K.C.V.O. in 1908 and a K.C.I.E. in 1911, and was appointed Serjeant-at-Arms, House of Commons, in 1915. Sir Colin Keppel is Extra Equerry to His Majesty, and was Equerry in Ordinary. He is a Director of Hawthorn, Leslie and Co., Engineers. Admiral Keppel married, in 1889, Henrietta Mary, daughter of Major-General R. Blundell, and they have two sons.

DRAGE, WILLIAM HENRY, Major, was born 3 Nov. 1852, son of the late John Drage. He was educated at a private school; was commissioned in the Commissariat and Supply Department 15 June, 1885; A.S.C. 11 Dec. 1888. He served in the Sudan Expedition of 1884–85 (Nile); was promoted, received the Medal and clasp, and the Bronze Star. In 1885–86–89 he again served in the Sudan; action of Toski; Commissariat Officer of Force (Despatches [London Gazette 6 Sept. 1889]; clasp; promoted to rank of Captain 13 Sept. 1889; 4th Class Medjidie). He served in the Expedition to Dongola in 1896 as D.A.A.G., Headquarters Staff; was mentioned in Despatches [London Gazette, 3 Nov. 1896]; promoted to rank of Major; received the Egyptian Medal. He served in the Nile Expedition of 1897, as D.A.A.G., Headquarters Staff; was present at the capture of Abu Hamed and subsequent occupation of Berber. He was mentioned in Despatches [London Gazette 25 Jan. 1898], received a clasp to the Egyptian Medal, and was created a Companion of the Distinguished Service Order [London Gazette, 11 March, 1898]: "William Henry Drage, Major, Army Service Corps. In recognition of services during the recent operations in the Sudan." In the Nile Expedition in 1898 he was present at the Battle of Khartum (Despatches [London Gazette, 30 Sept. 1898]; granted the honorary rank of Lieutenant-Colonel 16 Nov. 1898; clasp to the Egyptian Medal and Medal); and for the Nile Expedition of 1899 he received a clasp to the Egyptian Medal and the 3rd Class Osmanieh. Lieut.-Colonel W. H. Drage retired from the Army Service Corps on the 22 Oct. 1904, and died 3 Nov. 1915.

London Gazette, 20 May, 1898.—"War Office, 20 May, 1898. The Queen has been graciously pleased to give orders for the following appointment to the Distinguished Service Order and promotion in the Army, in recognition of the services of the undermentioned Officer during the operations in Mashonaland in 1897. To be a Companion of the Distinguished Service Order."

CAREW, GEORGE ALBERT LADE, Major, was born 10 March, 1862, son of the late Robert R. Carew and Mrs. Robert R. Carew. He was commissioned in the Hampshire Militia in 1879, and was gazetted to the 7th Hussars as Lieutenant (from the Militia) 31 Oct. 1883, becoming Captain 19 Dec. 1889, and Major 2 April, 1898. He took part in the operations in South Africa in 1896–97; was mentioned in Despatches [London Gazette, 9 March, 1897]; commanded a column in the campaign of 1897; was again mentioned in Despatches [London Gazette, 18 Feb. 1898]; received the Medals and clasps, and was created a Companion of the Distinguished Service Order [London Gazette, 20 May, 1898]: "George Albert Lade Carew, Major, 7th Hussars. In recognition of services during the operations in Mashonaland in 1897." Insignia sent to G.O.C., Cape; forwarded by O.C., 7th Hussars, Natal, 24 July, 1898. He served with the Rhodesian Field Force, 1900, as Special Service Officer, and with the 7th Hussars, 1901–2, in the South African War. He took part in the operations in Rhodesia, March to May, 1900, and in the operations in the Transvaal, March to Aug. 1900; operations in the Transvaal, March to 31 May, 1902; operations in Cape Colony, Dec. 1901, to March, 1902. Major Carew retired in 1902.

London Gazette, 20 May, 1898.—"War Office, 20 May, 1898. The Queen has been graciously pleased to give orders for the following appointments to the Distinguished Service Order and promotions in the Army, in recognition of the services of the undermentioned Officers during the recent operations in Uganda."

KIRKPATRICK, RICHARD TRENCH, Capt., was created a Companion of the Distinguished Service Order [London Gazette, 20 May, 1898]: "Richard Trench Kirkpatrick, Capt., Leinster Regt. In recognition of services during the recent operations in Uganda." Capt. Kirkpatrick died 26 Nov. 1898.

HOBART, CLAUD VERE CAVENDISH, Lieut., was born 12 March, 1870, only son of Sir Robert Henry Hobart, Bart., K.C.V.O., C.B., Official Verderer of the New Forest, of Langdown, Hants, and of the Hon. Julia Trollope, eldest daughter of the first Baron Kesteven. He was educated at Eton and Sandhurst, and entered the Grenadier Guards 16 July, 1890. Lieut. Hobart, after serving nearly seven years in the Grenadier Guards, was in 1897 seconded for service in the Uganda Protectorate, at that time under the administration of the Foreign Office, and joined the Protectorate Forces, consisting chiefly of Sudanese, who had previously served under Emin Pasha at Wadelai, whilst on a punitive expedition in the Nandi country. Order having been restored, he was detailed to march two companies of Sudanese back to Headquarters at Kampala. On the way he received news of the disaffection of Mwanga, the native King of Uganda, who had raised the standard of revolt in Buddu, one of the southern provinces of his kingdom. He hastened on to the capital, and was thence despatched with his men in a fleet of canoes down the west coast of Victoria Nyanza to occupy and hold the crossing over the Katonga River, separating Buddu from the rest of Uganda, whilst the main forces of the Protectorate under Colonel T. P. B. Ternan, D.S.O., moved down overland. He successfully carried out his instructions, and the rebels were subsequently defeated in two engagements, at which he was present, which resulted in King Mwanga fleeing into German territory and the bulk of his followers dispersing into the wilds of Ankole. Lieut. Hobart was left in charge of the reconquered province with two and a half companies of Sudanese. These remained loyal during the subsequent mutiny of portion of the same force in the eastern part of the Protectorate, and though hard pressed at one time, he succeeded in holding his own against the Baganda rebels, who collected again on the news of the mutiny, being joined by the ex-King Mwanga, who contrived to escape from German custody. After several expeditions had been organized against them, in all of which he took part, he was fortunately enabled, whilst in command of an advanced guard composed

Claud Vere C. Hobart.

of Baganda levies, to come up to and inflict a decisive blow on King Mwanga's main forces at Kisalera. Mwanga's ally, the rebel King of Koki, was killed, and Mwanga himself barely escaped, only to be captured a few months later in the north of the Protectorate with the remnants of the Sudanese mutineers, who were finally defeated with the assistance of a native regiment from India. For his services during the above operations he was mentioned in Despatches, and also in Parliament, and received the Uganda Medal and clasp. He was also created a Companion of the Distinguished Service Order [London Gazette, 20 May, 1898]: "Claud Vere Cavendish Hobart, Lieut., Grenadier Guards. In recognition of the services during the recent operations in Uganda" (the first award of this Order to an officer of this regiment). On the outbreak of the South African War in 1899, Capt. Hobart had just returned to England, and was sent out with the first contingent of troops to the Cape to act as Staff Officer on the Midland Line of Communications. In this capacity he assisted in raising several corps of local volunteers, by whom the Midland Line of railway from Port Elizabeth to Naauwpoort was seized and garrisoned; but falling a victim to a severe attack of enteric fever, he was invalided home in the summer of 1900, subsequently receiving the Queen's South African Medal with clasp for Cape Colony. In 1902 Capt. Hobart officiated as a Gold Staff Officer at the Coronation of T.M. King Edward VII. and Queen Alexandra, and was also in charge of Apolo Kagwa, the native Prime Minister and Regent of Uganda, who came over to attend the ceremony, and for whom he interpreted on the occasion of his being granted an audience by King Edward. In Dec. 1906, Major Hobart retired from the Regular Army, and was placed on the Reserve of Officers; but in 1908, on the inauguration of the Territorial Force, he was appointed Lieut.-Colonel Commanding Princess Beatrice's Isle of Wight Rifles (8th Battn. The Hampshire Regt.), which he raised and reorganized from a small volunteer nucleus and commanded till 1913, when he retired. He again acted as Gold Staff Officer at a Coronation—that of T.M. King George V. and Queen Mary, in 1911. On the European War breaking out in 1914, Lieut.-Colonel Hobart, after serving for short periods on the Embarkation Staff at Southampton and the Military Landing Staff at Havre, was sent to the front in Flanders as a Railhead Commandant, being subsequently appointed Administrative Commandant of the railheads of an army. He was mentioned in Despatches in 1916 and 1918, and received the "1914" Star. Lieut.-Colonel C. V. C. Hobart married, on 10 Dec. 1900, at St. Peter's, Eaton Square, S.W., Violet Verve, second daughter of the late John Wylie, Esq., of West Cliff Hall, Hants, owner of the celebrated racing cutter Oimara, and they have one son, Robert Hampden, born 7 May, 1915.

London Gazette, 20 May, 1898.—"War Office, Pall Mall, 20 May, 1898. The Queen has been graciously pleased to give orders for the following appointments to the Distinguished Service Order, in recognition of the services of the undermentioned Officers during the recent operations on the North-West Frontier of India. To be Companions of the Distinguished Service Order."

SWAYNE, CHARLES HENRY, Lieut.-Colonel, was born at Carrick-on-Shannon, Ireland, 18 Sept. 1848, second son of the late Abraham Crawford Swayne, M.D., J.P., of Carrick-on-Shannon, and Anne, daughter of D. Brown. He was educated at a private school, and at the Ledwich School of Medicine, Dublin (Prizeman in Medicine, Surgery and Midwifery). He entered the Army as Staff Assistant Surgeon, 1872; served with distinction during the yellow fever outbreak in Trinidad, West Indies, 1881; in the Nile campaign, 1884–85, in charge of Dongola Field Hospital (thanked for services; Medal and clasp; Khedive's Star). He became Surgeon-Major, 1886; served in Burmese Campaign, 1886–89 (specially thanked for services; Medal and two clasps). He became Brigade Surgeon Lieut.-Colonel, 1897; was in charge of No. 6 B.F.H., and Senior Medical Officer, 1st Brigade, Tirah Expeditionary Force, N.W.P., 1897–98. He received the Medal and two clasps; was

Charles Henry Swayne.

mentioned in Despatches [London Gazette, 3 April, 1898], and was created a Companion of the Distinguished Service Order [London Gazette, 20 May, 1898]: "Charles Henry Swayne, Brigade Surgeon Lieut.-Colonel, Army Medical Service. In recognition of services during the recent operations on the North-West Frontier of India." The Insignia were sent to the Commander-in-Chief, India, and were presented by Sir B. Blood at Meerut 4 Nov. 1898. Lieut.-Colonel Swayne had been on leave until the 15th Oct., and the presentation was therefore delayed. Colonel Swayne says: "I have no record of the official account as to why I was granted the D.S.O. I was Senior Medical Officer, 1st Brigade, 1st Division, throughout the campaign, and presumed it was for good service as such that I was granted it. During the yellow fever epidemic, Trinidad, British West Indies, 1881, I was recommended for award for distinguished services by my P.M.O. and G.O.C. and the Governor of Trinidad, Sir Sandford Freeling, K.C.M.G. For the Nile Campaign, my P.M.O., Surgeon-General J. O'Nial, put my name forward to Lord Wolseley; but General Buller wrote to say that 'though Lord Wolseley knew I did good service, he could not recommend me for promotion, as he would have to do the same for others.' For the Burmese Campaign both the P.M.O.'s under whom I served for two and a half years also sent in my name, but no result. For the Tirah I did get mentioned in Despatches, and got the D.S.O." He became Lieut.-Colonel, Royal Army Medical Corps; Colonel, 5 Nov.

1892, and retired 18 Sept. 1905. His favourite recreations are golfing and fishing. He married, on 1 Feb. 1896, Margaret Blakeney, daughter of the late David Gillies, and they had three daughters, Dorothy Marguerite (deceased), Doris Margaret and Muriel Florence Constance.

EVANS, CHARLES WILLIAM HENRY, Major, was born 19 Aug. 1851, and entered the Army 28 Feb. 1874 ; served in the Egyptian Expedition of 1882 (Medal and Bronze Star) ; in the Sudan Expedition of 1884–85 (clasp) ; in the Sudan, 1885–86, Frontier Field Force, action of Ginnis. He took part in the operations on the North-West Frontier of India, 1897–98, with the Malakand Field Force ; action of Landakai ; expedition into Mohmand country ; attack on the villages of Agrah and Gat ; in command of battalion (Despatches [London Gazette, 18 March, 1898]) with Buner Field Force ; attack and capture of the Tanga Pass. He was mentioned in Despatches [London Gazette, 22 April, 1890] ; received the Medal with clasp, and was created a Companion of the Distinguished Service Order [London Gazette, 20 May, 1898] : " Charles William Henry Evans, Major, Royal West Kent Regt. In recognition of services during the recent operations on the North-West Frontier of India. The Insignia were presented by the Queen at Windsor 25 June, 1898. He became Lieut.-Colonel 28 Dec. 1898 ; commanded the Royal West Kent Regt., and retired 21 March, 1900. Lieut.-Colonel Evans died on 2 Nov. 1909, at Bognor. An obituary notice of him appeared in the " Times." He was twice married ; 1st, to Annie Thomasina, fourth daughter of the late T. B. Herrick, and he married 2ndly, in 1902, Rose, only daughter of J. Hadlow.

SHEARER, JOHNSTON, Major, was born at Aberdeen 22 Oct. 1852, son of J. Shearer, Esq., and of Mrs. J. Shearer. He was educated at the Grammar School, and University, Aberdeen ; M.A., Honours in Natural Science, 1873 ; M.B., C.M., Honours, 1877 ; Maclaine Prizeman in Military Surgery, Army Medical School, Netley, 1881 ; D.P.H., Aberdeen, 1897. He joined the I.M.S. 2 Oct. 1880 ; served in the Egyptian Expedition, 1882 (Medal and Bronze Star) ; Burmese Expedition, 1887–88 (Medal and two clasps) ; Miranzai Ex., 1891 ; Hazara Expedition, 1891 (clasp) ; Waziristan Expedition, 1894–95 (clasp, and Despatches [London Gazette, 2 July, 1895]) ; Tirah Expeditionary Force, 1897–98. He received the Medal and two clasps ; was mentioned in Despatches [London Gazette, April, 1898], and was created a Companion of the Distinguished Service Order [London Gazette, 20 May, 1898] : " Johnston Shearer, Surgeon-Major, Indian Medical Service. In recognition of services during the recent operations on the North-West Frontier of India." Colonel Shearer retired 11 Nov. 1910. His favourite recreations were reading and shooting. He married, in 1890, Elizabeth, daughter of the late J. Kinghorn, J.P., Aberdeen, and they have two sons. He died 6 Feb. 1916.

CAMPBELL, FREDERICK, Brevet Major, was born 25 Feb. 1860, youngest son of the late Capt. Leveson Granville Alexander Campbell, of Fairfield, Ayrshire, and Annie, daughter of the late David Cowan, Lieut., 93rd Highlanders. He was educated at Wellington College, and became Lieutenant Royal Ayr and Wigton Militia, 1877–78 ; under-officer, Royal Military College, 1878, and joined H.M. 40th Foot as Second Lieutenant 13 Aug. 1879. He became Lieutenant, South Lancashire Regt., 15 March, 1880, and Lieutenant, Bengal Staff Corps, 18 Sept. 1882 ; Queen's Own Corps of Guides, 1882–89. He served in the Hazara Expedition, 1888 ; Assistant Superintendent, Signalling (Medal with clasp) ; became Captain, I.S.C., 13 Aug. 1890 ; was D.A.A.G. (Musketry), Bengal, from 22 Aug. 1891, to 2 March, 1895. He served in the Chitral Relief Force, 1895 ; was present at the storming of the Malakand Pass and at the action at the Panjkora River. He was mentioned in

Frederick Campbell.

Despatches [London Gazette, 15 Nov. 1895] ; was given the Brevet of Major 22 Jan. 1896, and received the Medal and clasp ; North-West Frontier, India, 1897–98 ; Malakand, operations in Bajaur and the Mamund country, Utmankheyl (Despatches, 11 Jan. 1898) ; in Buner, and was mentioned in Despatches 18 March and 22 April, 1898 ; received a clasp, and was created a Companion of the Distinguished Service Order [London Gazette, 20 May, 1898] : " Frederick Campbell, Capt. and Brevet Major, Indian Staff Corps. In recognition of services during the recent operations on the North-West Frontier of India." The Insignia, etc., were sent to the Commander-in-Chief in India, and presented by Lieut.-General Sir William Lockhart. Capt. Campbell became Major, I.A., 13 Aug. 1899 ; was Commandant, 40th Pathans, 1899–1906 ; Tibet, 1903–4 ; operations at and around Gyantse ; took part in the march to Lhassa (Medal with clasp ; Despatches, 13 Dec. 1904 ; Brevet Colonel, 10 Nov. 1904) ; was A.A.G. (Musketry), Headquarters, India, 4 June, 1906, to 19 June, 1908 ; Colonel, 4 June, 1907 ; Brigade Commander (Colonel on the Staff), India, 20 June, 1908, to 17 March, 1911 ; Major-General 19 June, 1911 ; created a C.B. ; Colonel, 40th Pathans, 1911 ; Brigade Commander, India, 18 March, 1911, to 25 June, 1915 ; Divisional Commander, India, 26 June, 1915, to 25 June, 1919. He served in the war, 1914–16 (Despatches ; created a K.C.B., and was promoted General. Lieut.-General 1919. He married, in 1886, Eleanor Martha, daughter of the late J. Cannon, and they have a son, Frederick Charles Gunning, M.C., Capt., 40th Pathans, born on 11 Aug. 1887, and a daughter, Eleanor May Alexandra, married, in 1916, to Capt. G. E. D. Learoyd, Adjutant, 21st (E. of I.) Lancers.

Henry Vero Biggs.

BIGGS, HENRY VERO, Capt., was born at Belgaum 9 May, 1860, third son of the late Colonel Thomas Biggs, R.A. (previously of the Bombay Artillery, who died in 1905), and Mary, daughter of the late Rev. W. Beynon. He was educated first at a private school at Clifton, and passed into the R.M.A., Woolwich, 1877 ; joined the R.E. 30 July, 1879 ; embarked for India, 1882, and was posted to the Bombay S. and M. ; spent nearly three years on the Afghan Frontier (including the 1884 Zhob Expedition) ; served in the third Burmese War, 1885–87 (Medal with clasp) ; joined the Military Works from the S. and M., 1887. He became Captain, 1889 ; Adjutant, R.E., Tirah Expeditionary Force, 1897–98 ; operations on the N.W. Frontier, 1897 ; operations in the Kurram and on the Samana, the Chagru Kotal, capture of the Sampagha Pass and operations in the Khyber. He was mentioned in Despatches, received the Medal with three clasps, and was created a Companion of the Distinguished Service Order [London Gazette, 20 May, 1898] : " Henry Vero Biggs, Capt., Royal Engineers, in recognition of services on the North-West Frontier of India." He became Major, 1898 ; Lieut.-Colonel, 1905 ; officiated A.A.G., R.E., India, 1906 ; Brevet Colonel, 1908 ; commanded R.E., 5th (Mhow) Division, 1906–7, 6th (Poona) and 2nd (Rawalpindi) Division, 1909–12 ; became Colonel 27 May, 1912 ; retired, Military Works, India (Royal Engineers), 29 Nov. 1912 ; re-employed on account of war, 1914 (Despatches [London Gazette, 24 Feb. 1917]). Colonel Bigg's favourite recreations are fishing and shooting, especially the big game of India. He married, Oct. 1887, at Kasauli, India, Frances Kate, eldest daughter of the late Colonel C. H. Ewart, B.S.C., and they have one son, Henry Ewart Biggs (born 28 June, 1893, at Secunderabad, India, now Captain, R.E. (permanent).

MILLER-WALLNUTT, CLAUDE CHARLES, Major, was born 30 March, 1861, and was gazetted to the 75th Foot 23 April, 1881, becoming Lieutenant, Gordon Highlanders, 1 July, 1881. He served in the Egyptian Expedition, 1882–84, and was present at the Battle of Tel-el-Kebir (Medal with clasp ; Bronze Star) ; in the Sudan in 1884 he was present at the Battles of Teb and Tamai (two clasps). He served in the Sudan Expedition of 1884–85 (Nile), and received a clasp ; became Captain 14 Jan. 1888. Chitral, 1895. In the Tirah Campaign he took part in the operations on the North-West Frontier of India in 1897–98, being present at the action of Dargai. He was mentioned in Despatches [London Gazette, 1 March, 1898] ; received two clasps, and was created a Companion of the Distinguished Service Order [London Gazette, 20 May, 1898] : " Claude Charles Miller-Wallnutt, Major, Gordon Highlanders. In recognition of services during the recent operations on the North-West Frontier of India." He was promoted to Major 18 May, 1898. Major Miller-Wallnutt served in the South African War, and was killed in action 6 Jan. 1900. Sir A. Conan Doyle says, in " The Great Boer War " (pages 175–177) :

" At the same time as—or rather earlier than—the onslaught upon Cæsar's Camp a similar attack had been made with secrecy and determination upon the western end of the position called Waggon Hill. The barefooted Boers burst suddenly with a roll of rifle fire into the little garrison of Imperial Light Horse and Sappers who held the position. Mathias of the former, Digby-Jones and Dennis of the latter, showed that ' two in the morning ' courage which Napoleon rated as the highest of military virtues. They and their men were surprised but not disconcerted, and stood desperately in a slogging match at the closest quarters. Seventeen Sappers were down out of thirty, and more than half the little body of irregulars. This end of the position was feebly fortified, and it is surprising that so experienced and sound a soldier as Ian Hamilton should have left it so. The defence had no marked advantage as compared with the attack—neither trench, sangar, nor wire entanglement—and in numbers they were immensely inferior. Two companies of the 60th Rifles and a small body of the ubiquitous Gordons happened to be upon the hill and threw themselves into the fray, but they were unable to turn the tide. Of thirty-three Gordons under Lieut. MacNaughten thirty were wounded. [The Gordons and the Sappers were there that morning to re-escort one of Lambton's 4.7 guns, which was to be mounted there. Ten seamen were with the gun, and lost three of their number in the defence.] As our men retired under the shelter of the northern slope they were reinforced by another hundred and fifty Gordons under the stalwart Miller-Wallnutt, a man cast in the mould of a Berserk Viking. To their aid also came two hundred of the Imperial Light Horse, burning to assist their comrades. Another half-battalion of Rifles came with them. At each end of the long ridge the situation at the dawn of day was almost identical. In each the stormers had seized one side, but were brought to a stand by the defenders upon the other, while the British guns fired over the heads of their own infantry to rake the farther slope.

" It was on the Waggon Hill side, however, that the Boer exertions were most continuous and strenuous and our own resistance most desperate. There fought the gallant De Villiers, while Ian Hamilton rallied the defenders and led them in repeated rushes against the enemy's line. Continually reinforced from below, the Boers fought with extraordinary resolution. Never will any one who witnessed that Homeric contest question the valour of our foes. It was a murderous business on both sides. Edwardes of the Light Horse was struck down. In a gun emplacement a strange encounter took place at point-blank range between a group of Boers and of Britons. De Villiers of the Free State shot Miller-Wallnutt dead, Ian Hamilton fired at De Villiers with his revolver and missed him.

Young Albrecht of the Light Horse shot De Villiers. A Boer named De Jaeger shot Albrecht. Digby-Jones of the Sappers shot De Jaeger. Only a few minutes later the gallant lad, who had already won fame enough for a veteran, was himself mortally wounded, and Dennis, his comrade in arms and in glory, fell by his side.

"There has been no better fighting in our time than that upon Waggon Hill on that January morning, and no better fighters than the Imperial Light Horsemen who formed the centre of the defence. Here, as at Elandslaagte, they proved themselves worthy to stand in line with the crack regiments of the British army.

"Through the long day the fight maintained its equilibrium along the summit of the ridge, swaying a little that way or this, but never amounting to a repulse of the stormers or to a rout of the defenders. So intermixed were the combatants that a wounded man more than once found himself a rest for the rifles of his enemies. One unfortunate soldier in this position received six more bullets from his own comrades in their efforts to reach the deadly rifleman behind him. At four o'clock a huge bank of clouds which had towered upwards unheeded by the struggling men burst suddenly into a terrific thunderstorm with vivid lightnings and lashing rain. It is curious that the British victory at Elandslaagte was heralded by just such another storm. Up on the bullet-swept hill the long fringes of fighting men took no more heed of the elements than would two bulldogs who have each other by the throat. Up the greasy hillside, foul with mud and with blood, came the Boer reserves, and up the northern slope came our own reserve, the Devon Regt., fit representatives of that virile county. Admirably led by Park, their gallant colonel, the Devons swept the Boers before them, and the Rifles, Gordons, and Light Horse joined in the wild charge which finally cleared the ridge.

"But the end was not yet. The Boer had taken a risk over this venture, and now he had to pay the stakes. Down the hill he passed, crouching, darting, but the spruits behind him were turned into swirling streams, and as he hesitated for an instant upon the brink the relentless sleet of bullets came from behind. Many were swept away down the gorges and into the Klip River, never again to be accounted for in the lists of their field-cornet. The majority splashed through, found their horses in their shelter, and galloped off across the great Bulwana Plain, as fairly beaten in as fair a fight as ever brave men were yet.

"The cheers of victory as the Devons swept the ridge had heartened the weary men upon Cæsar's Camp to a similar effort. Manchesters, Gordons, and Rifles, aided by the fire of two batteries, cleared the long-debated position. Wet, cold, weary, and without food for twenty-six hours, the bedraggled Tommies stood yelling and waving, amid the litter of dead and of dying.

"It was a near thing. Had the ridge fallen the town must have followed, and history perhaps have been changed. In the old stiff-rank Majuba days we should have been swept in an hour from the position. But the wily man behind the rock was now to find an equally wily man in front of him. The soldier had at last learned something of the craft of the hunter. He clung to his shelter, he dwelled on his aim, he ignored his dressings, he laid aside the eighteenth-century traditions of his pigtailed ancestor, and he hit the Boers harder than they had been hit yet. No return may ever come to us of their losses on that occasion; 80 dead bodies were returned to them from the ridge alone, while the slopes, the dongas, and the river each had its own separate tale. No possible estimate can make it less than 300 killed and wounded, while many place it at a much higher figure. Our own casualties were very serious, and the proportion of dead to wounded unusually high owing to the fact that the greater part of the wounds were necessarily of the head. In killed we lost 13 officers, 135 men; in wounded, 28 officers, 244 men—a total of 420. Lord Ava, the honoured son of an honoured father, the fiery Dick-Cunyngham, stalwart Miller-Wallnutt, the brave boy sappers Digby-Jones and Dennis, Adams and Packman of the Light Horse, the chivalrous Lafone—we had to mourn quality as well as numbers. The grim test of the casualty returns shows that it was to the Imperial Light Horse (ten officers down, and the regiment commanded by a junior captain), the Manchesters, the Gordons, the Devons, and the 2nd Rifle Brigade that the honours of the day are due."

THACKWELL, COLQUHOUN GRANT ROCHE, Capt., was born 8 Dec. 1857, and was gazetted to the 37th Foot 1 May, 1878, and transferred to the 51st Foot 12 June, 1878, becoming Lieutenant, South Yorkshire Regt., 29 Jan. 1879, and Bengal Staff Corps, 23 Feb. 1881. He served in the Mahsud–Wuzeeree Expedition, 1881, and in the Egyptian Expedition, 1882, Battle of Tel-el-Kebir (Medal and clasp); was promoted to Captain, Indian Staff Corps, 1 May, 1889. He served in the Chitral Campaign in 1895, with the Relief Force as Commissariat Officer, 2nd Brigade (1 April to Aug. 1895), and was present at the storming of the Malakand Pass (Medal and clasp). He served on the N.W. Frontier of India, 1897–98, Malakand, as Divisional Transport Officer (July to Oct. 1897); operations in Bajaur and in the Mamund country, Mohmand, Utman Khel and Buner, as Chief Transport Officer. He was present at the attack and capture of the Tanga Pass; was mentioned in Despatches [London Gazette, 11 Jan. and 22 April, 1898]; received a clasp, and was created a Companion of the Distinguished Service Order [London Gazette, 20 May, 1898]: "Colquhoun Grant Roche Thackwell, Capt., Indian Staff Corps. In recognition of services during the recent operations on the North-West Frontier of India." The D.S.O. was presented to Major Thackwell, 11 Nov. 1898, by the G.O.C., Lahore District. He had been promoted to Major 1 May, 1898; became Lieut.-Colonel 1 May, 1904, and was given the Brevet of Colonel 1 May, 1907, and was promoted to Colonel 1 Dec. 1908. He was created a C.B. in 1912. Colonel Thackwell married Lilian, daughter of Robert Spencer.

ALRIGHT, HEDLEY, Capt., was created a Companion of the Distinguished Service Order [London Gazette, 20 May, 1898]: "Hedley Alright, Capt., Indian Staff Corps. In recognition of services during the recent operations on the North-West Frontier of India." The Insignia were presented by the Queen at Windsor 17 Nov. 1898. Capt. Alright died in March, 1903.

HALDANE, JAMES AYLMER LOWTHORPE, Capt., was born 17 Nov. 1862, only son of the late D. Rutherford Haldane, M.D., and Mrs. Haldane. He was educated at Edinburgh Academy and Wimbledon School, and passed with Honours, Royal Military College, Sandhurst, joining the Gordon Highlanders 9 Sept. 1882, as Lieutenant. He was Adjutant, Gordon Highlanders, 1 Sept. 1888, to 31 Jan. 1892, and became Captain 8 April, 1892. Capt. Haldane served in the Waziristan Expedition, 1894–95 (Medal with clasp), and in the operations in Chitral in 1895, with the Relief Force (Medal with clasp). He was A.D.C. to General Sir William Lockhart, 1896–99. In 1897–98 he served in the Tirah Expedition as D.A.A.G., Headquarters Staff, and was present at the actions of Chagra Kotal and Dargai, and at the capture of the Sampagha and Arhanga Passes. Reconnaissance at and around Dwatoi and action of 24 Nov. 1897. Operations against the Khani Khel Chamkanis. Operations in the Bara Valley 7 to 14 Dec. 1897. Operations in the Bazar Valley 25 to 30 Dec. 1897. He was mentioned in Despatches [London Gazette, 5 April, 1898]; received two clasps, and was created a Companion of the Distinguished Service Order [London Gazette, 20 May, 1898]: "James Aylmer Lowthorpe Haldane, Capt., Gordon Highlanders. In recognition of services during the recent operations on the North-West Frontier of India." The Insignia were presented to him by the Queen at Windsor 25 June, 1898. He served in South Africa, 1899–1902, with the 2nd Gordon Highlanders, taking part in the operations in Natal in 1899, including the action at Elandslaagte, where he was severely wounded. He was in command of the Chieveley Armoured Train. Sir A. Conan Doyle says, in "The Great Boer War" (page 166): "The Boers suddenly took the initiative, and in dramatic fashion. North of Estcourt, where General Hildyard was being daily reinforced from the sea, there are two small townlets, or at least geographical (and railway) points. Frere is about ten miles north of Estcourt, and Chieveley is five miles north of that, and about as far to the south of Colenso. On 15 Nov. an armoured train was despatched from Estcourt to see what was going on up the line. Already one disaster had befallen us in this campaign on account of these clumsy contrivances, and a heavier one was now to confirm the opinion that, acting alone, they are totally inadmissible. As a means of carrying artillery for a force operating upon either flank of them, with an assured retreat behind, there may be a place for them in modern war, but as a method of scouting they appear to be the most inefficient and also the most expensive that has ever been invented. An intelligent horseman would gather more information, be less visible, and retain some freedom as to route. After our experience the armoured train may steam out of military history. The train contained 90 Dublin Fusiliers, 80 Durban Volunteers, and 10 sailors, with a naval 7-pounder gun. Capt. Haldane, of the Gordons, Lieut. Frankland (Dublin Fusiliers) and Winston Churchill, the well-known correspondent, accompanied the expedition. What might have been foreseen occurred. The train steamed into the advancing Boer army, was fired upon, tried to escape, found the rails blocked behind it, and upset. Dublins and Durbans were shot helplessly out of their trucks, under a heavy fire. A railway accident is a nervous thing, and so is an ambuscade, but the combination of the two must be appalling. Yet there were brave hearts which rose to the occasion. Haldane and Frankland rallied the troops, and Churchill the engine-driver. The engine was disentangled and sent on with its cab full of wounded. Churchill, who had escaped upon it, came gallantly back to share the fate of his comrades. The dazed, shaken soldiers continued a futile resistance for some time, but there was neither help nor escape and nothing for them but surrender. The most Spartan military critic cannot blame them. A few slipped away besides those who escaped upon the engine. Our losses were two killed, 20 wounded, and about 80 taken. It is remarkable that of the three leaders both Haldane and Churchill succeeded in escaping from Pretoria." Capt. Haldane was slightly wounded on this occasion. Operations in Natal, March to June, 1900, including action at Laing's Nek (6 to 9 June). Operations in the Transvaal, east of Pretoria, July to 20 Nov. 1900, including actions at Belfast (26 and 27 Aug.) and Lydenberg (5 to 8 Sept.). He was mentioned in Despatches [London Gazette, 8 Feb. 1901]; received the Queen's Medal with four clasps, and the Brevet of Lieutenant-Colonel 24 July, 1902. He was promoted to Major 23 July, 1902. In 1904 and 1905 he was attached to the Japanese Army in Manchuria, during the Russo-Japanese War. He was present at the Battles of Liao-Yang, Sha-ho and Mukden, and received the Japanese War Medal and clasp, the Order of the Sacred Treasure (3rd Class), and was created a C.B. (1906). He was given the Brevet of Colonel 11 Jan. 1906, and became Colonel 29 Oct. 1906; was Assistant Director of Military Operations, Headquarters of Army, 29 Oct. 1906, to 30 Sept. 1909; was Brigadier-General, General Staff, Eastern Command, 1 Oct. 1909, to 27 April, 1912; Brigade Commander, 10th Brigade, Eastern Command, 28 April, 1912, to 4 Aug. 1912. He served in the European War from 5 Aug. 1914, as Brigade Commander, 10th Infantry Brigade, British Expeditionary Force, up to 20 Nov. 1914; as General Officer Commanding 3rd Division, British Expeditionary Force and British Armies in France, 21 Nov. 1914, to 7 Aug. 1916, and as Army Corps Commander, 6th Army Corps, British Armies in France, 8 Aug. 1916. He was promoted to Major-General 26 Oct. 1914;

James A. L. Haldane.

to Lieutenant-General 1 Jan. 1919; was eight times mentioned in Despatches; created a K.C.B. in 1918; Grand Officier de l'Ordre de la Couronne; Commander, Legion of Honour, in 1918; Croix de Guerre (French and Belgian). He was made a Knight of Grace of St. John of Jerusalem in 1912. Sir Aylmer Haldane has published "How we escaped from Pretoria." His favourite recreations are shooting and travelling.

The "Daily Sketch," of 26 Feb. 1920, says: "Because it is so full of human touches, Mr. Philip Gibbs's book, 'Realities of War,' published to-day by Heinemann, hard on the heels of his brother's much criticized volume, provides the best account yet written of the fighting on the Western Front."

Mr. Gibbs tells the following story of a General's promise to the children: "General Haldane, when things were at their worst in April, 1918, was surrounded by a group of children who were asking anxiously whether Arras would be taken. He drew a map for them in the dust of the roadway, and showed them where the enemy was attacking and the general strategy. He spoke simply and gravely, as though to a group of Staff officers, and the children followed his diagram in the dust and understood him perfectly. 'They will not take Arras if I can help it,' he said. 'You will be all right here.' They did not take Arras."

Sir Aylmer Haldane wrote at the front in the spring of 1915, "A Brigade of the Old Army, 1914," which was published by Edward Arnold in 1920. It is "Dedicated to the 10th Infantry Brigade, 1st Battn. The Royal Warwickshire Regt., 2nd Battn. The Seaforth Highlanders, 1st Battn. The Royal Irish Fusiliers, 2nd Battn. The Royal Dublin Fusiliers." General Haldane says of his book that it "was intended originally for the officers, non-commissioned officers and men who served under my command during those eventful months" (Aug. to Nov. 1914). "Many of those gallant fellows—indeed, it is to be feared the majority—have fallen in the service of their country." He tells us how, on the 7th Aug. 1914, the 10th Brigade was ordered to York. Some hours were spent hunting for quarters for the troops, which were eventually found "in the grand stand on the Knavesmire Racecourse, in the Exhibition Hall, and in certain store sheds which Mr. Eric Geddes, of the North-Eastern Railway Company, speedily caused to be cleared and placed at my disposal. I was struck by the promptitude with which he appreciated my difficulties, and the speed with which he helped to eliminate them, but at that time I had no idea that he was destined soon to rise to heights of far greater national usefulness."

When the brigade went to France, General Haldane was struck by the remarkably tranquil appearance of the docks at Southampton: "Here were we, a part of the greatest force which had ever been assembled to leave the shores of England in the space of so few days, about to embark on a venture from which few would return alive or uninjured, and yet, but for the season of the year, we might have been sharing in the annual trooping movement to the East."

Arrived in France, the troops "were pestered all day by the inhabitants to hand over as souvenirs their metal cap or shoulder badges. . . . This passion for souvenirs followed us everywhere, and in spite of strict orders against parting with any portion of their uniform, I should say that a large percentage of the population of Northern France, more particularly of the seaports where our troops landed, managed to secure a metal memento of the British soldier. Later on, when we were retreating before the Germans, and passing through a village, I was told that one of the Dublin Fusiliers in my brigade, who was wearily dragging himself along in the ranks of his company, hearing the too-familiar cry of 'Souvenir,' turned an angry glance over his shoulder and growled, 'Here, you can have my blooming pack for a souvenir!'"

He describes the destruction of the footbridge and of the steel bridge over the northern arm of the river at Pont l'Evêque, and says that the bridge over the southern arm of the river was not so easily destroyed. "The bridge had been made unsafe for vehicles, but there was no gap in it when a party of German Lancers came in sight. The engineer officer at the bridge, whose situation was a critical one, hurriedly withdrew his men, and ordered the village to be evacuated. Bullets were now falling thickly, and, crashing through the windows of the houses, caused the horses of the engineer tool-cart to stampede with that vehicle. But the engineer officer, Lieut. Gourlay, had not effected all that was required, and was not to be diverted from his duty; so, snatching up the electrical leads, he fixed them into the exploder and pressed the handle down. The charge exploded instantaneously, blowing a huge gap in the bridge and causing several houses in the village to collapse. Not a moment too soon was the work completed, for dismounted Uhlans were working up the side streets of the village, and the retreat of the demolition party was in imminent danger of being cut off. Indeed, so little time was left that Gourlay and several of his men only escaped capture by springing up behind the troopers of their escort, who speedily galloped off with them to safety, only three men being lost in the whole incident."

Sir Alymer tells us of an imaginative Celt among a particularly fine draft of his old regiment, the Gordon Highlanders. This soldier wrote a postcard to his sweetheart. "In this he stated . . . that on his march up country he had passed thousands of dead Germans, and that it was only with difficulty that he and his comrades could move along the road, so great was the crowd of prisoners who were being conducted to the rear!"

Of the letters from soldiers published in newspapers General Haldane says: "The value of such communications as true representations of occurrences in the field will be apparent if it is remembered that in many cases the further the writer happened to be from the danger zone the more lurid did his descriptions become, for by flights of imagination he was forced to supply deficiencies of fact."

In the chapter "On the Aisne," Sir Aylmer Haldane tells us how "a message came from the Seaforth Highlanders to say that their commanding officer, Lieut.-Colonel Sir Evelyn Bradford, had been killed. I at once went to the battalion, and found that a single shell, which had been fired at the flank of its position, had killed him instantaneously, while he was engaged in examining the ground in front in view of a possible advance. His death was a great loss to the brigade and to myself personally, making the fourth and last of my battalion commanders who had become non-effective since we landed in France, though he alone fell in action."

EDWARDS, FITZJAMES MAINE, Capt., was born 21 May, 1861, son of James Edwards, of Benarth, Conway. He entered the Royal West Surrey Regt. as Lieutenant 22 Oct. 1881, and the Indian Staff Corps 8 Nov. 1883, becoming Captain, Indian Staff Corps, 22 Oct. 1892. He served on the North-West Frontier of India, 1897–98; in Mohmand Expedition, on the Staff. He was mentioned in Despatches [London Gazette, 11 Jan. 1898, and received the Medal and clasp. He served in the Tirah Campaign, 1897–98, on the Staff, and was present at the actions of Dargai, and of the Sampagha and Arhanga Passes; at the reconnaissance of Saran Sar, and the action of 9 Nov. 1897. Operations in and around Dwatoi, and actions of 24 Nov. 1897. Operations in the Bara Valley 7 to 14 Dec. 1897. He received a clasp, and was created a Companion of the Distinguished Service Order [London Gazette, 20 May, 1898]: "Fitzjames Maine Edwards, Capt., Indian Staff Corps. In recognition of services during the recent operations on the North-West Frontier of India. The Insignia, etc., were presented on 12 Aug. 1898, at Mhow. China, 1900 (Medal). He became Major 10 July, 1901, and Lieutenant-Colonel 22 Oct. 1907; was G.S.O., 1st Grade, India, 3 June, 1911, to 28 Sept. 1913; became Colonel 14 Jan. 1912; was Brigade Commander, India, 20 Sept. 1913, to 13 Dec. 1914. He was Brigade Commander, Meerut Cavalry Brigade, British Expeditionary Force, 14 Dec. 1914, to 26 May, 1916; Brigade Commander, 71st Infantry Brigade, British Armies in France, 27 May, 1916, to 4 Oct. 1916; Brigade Commander, 179th Infantry Brigade, British Armies in France, British Salonika Force, Egyptian Expeditionary Force, from 10 Nov. 1916, to 16 Feb. 1918; appointed A.D.C. to the King 1 Jan. 1917; Brigade Commander, 19th Infantry Brigade, Egyptian Expeditionary Force, 17 Feb. 1918, to 1 March, 1918. He served in the European War from 1915; was present at the capture of Jerusalem; was created a C.M.G. in 1917, and a C.B. in 1918. He married, in 1896, Eva Lilian, only daughter of the late Theodore Henry Stewart, B.C.S.

GOODWIN, THOMAS HERBERT JOHN CHAPMAN, Capt., was born at Kandy, Ceylon, 24 May, 1871, eldest son of Surgeon-Major John Goodwin, Army Medical Staff, and Marion Agnes Power. He was educated at Newton College, Devon, and St. Mary's Hospital, London; joined the Army 29 July, 1893, and became Captain 29 July, 1896. He served on the North-West Frontier of India, 1897–98; was present at the Battle of Shabkadr; was mentioned in Despatches 4 Jan. 1898; received the Medal and clasp, and was created a Companion of the Distinguished Service Order [London Gazette, 20 May, 1898]: "Thomas Herbert John Chapman Goodwin, Surgeon-Captain, Army Medical Staff. In recognition of services in the recent operations on the North-West Frontier of India." (Insignia presented by Major-General Moorsom at Murree 20 Feb. 1898.) He became Major 30 Jan. 1905. Major Goodwin served in the European War from 1914, being present at Mons and the retreat to the Marne, the First and Second Ypres Battles, the fighting on the Somme, etc. Commanded No. 4 Cavalry Field Ambulance, No. 14 General Hospital, and was Assistant Director of Medical Services, 2nd Cavalry Division, British Expeditionary Force, 22 Sept. 1914, to 21 June, 1915; became Lieutenant-Colonel 1 March, 1915; was Assistant Director of Medical Services, Guards Division, British Armies in France, 21 Jan. 1917, to 16 April, 1917. In April, 1917, he was appointed A.D.M.S. with Mr. Balfour's Mission to America (with acting rank as Colonel). Promoted Colonel 26 Dec. 1917; appointed Honorary Surgeon to the King 26 Dec. 1917; became Major-General 18 Jan. 1918; was Deputy Director-General, Army Medical Service, 24 March, 1918, to 28 Feb. 1918; Director-General, Army Medical Service (temporary), 1 March, 1918, to 31 March, 1918; Director-General 1 June, 1918, with the rank of Lieutenant-General.

T. H. J. C. Goodwin.

A newspaper correspondent wrote:

"The choice of Colonel Goodwin as the new Acting Director-General of Army Medical Services is appropriate on more than professional grounds. For the entry of the United States into the war has brought this country an increasingly large number of American medical men, who, with great devotion, offered their help at the first call made upon them, and it is fitting that the soldier who, as Assistant Director of Medical Services to the British Mission which went to America under Mr. Balfour and later Lord Northcliffe, was foremost in voicing the call for help, and who, from the beginning of his work in the United States, endeared himself to the whole of a great and very critical medical profession, should become the new Director-General. Colonel Goodwin was one of those who served through the heroic days of Mons, and the Marne and Ypres, and has placed British Medicine deeply in his debt by the manner in which he has fostered and strengthened the bond between our doctors in this country and the American doctors who are coming to work side by side with them. The fruits of his labours are manifest already, for a strong spirit of comradeship has sprung up. An American physician of high standing, who has recently come to this country says of Colonel Goodwin: 'He is a splendid man. We took to him from the first minute. He was so sound in the advice he gave to us, so "live" and so thorough . . . and over all so tactful. It would be a joy to serve under him.' That impression was certainly no isolated one. When the degree of Master of Arts was conferred on Colonel Goodwin by the University of Michigan on 12 Oct. last, the Journal of the American Medical Association commented thus: 'Distinguished scholar and soldier, possessor of the Order of St. Michael and St. George, one of the few survivors of the first British Force in France, gentle in word and in manner, resolute in action.' Colonel Goodwin, therefore, almost more than any living man, will be in a position to understand the respective points of view of the British and American Medical Services, and to encourage the close co-operation between them upon which so much depends. Moreover, his own splendid record of service—North-West Frontier, 1897–1898, Battle of Shabkadr, Despatches, D.S.O., Medal and clasp, three times mentioned in the present war—proves that the welfare of the fighting men will be safe in his hands. He has learnt his war medicine in the field; he knows, above all, the practical necessities of the situation."

He became Lieutenant-General 1 June, 1919, and was created a C.M.G. in 1915; a C.B. in 1918; a K.C.B. in 1919; F.R.C.S., England, in 1919; and is a Knight of Grace of St. John of Jerusalem; Commander, Belgian Order of Leopold; Commander of the Italian Order of the Crown; was awarded the American Distinguished Service Medal. In 1917 he was made Honorary Fellow of the American College of Surgeons, and Master of Arts of the University of Michigan. He is the author of "Notes for Medical Officers on Field Service in India," "Field Service Notes for R.A.M.C.," "Prevention of Disease when on Active Service," "Notes for Army Medical Officers," etc. On 29 Dec. 1897, at Simla, Sir J. Goodwin married Lilian Isabel Ronaldson, youngest daughter of the late James Torrance Ronaldson.

FISHER, JOHN, Capt., was born at Preston 8 Jan. 1867, son of the late William Fisher, of Lancaster Bank, Preston. He was educated at Downing College, Cambridge (M.B., B.S. and B.A.), and at St. Thomas's Hospital, London, and entered the Indian Medical Service in 1894, and became Captain 29 Jan. 1897. He served on the North-West Frontier o India in 1897, with the Malakand Field Force, in the Expedition into the Mamund country, and was present at the attack of 16 Sept. He was mentioned in Despatches [London Gazette, 11 Jan. and 18 March, 1898, and was created a Companion of the Distinguished Service Order [London Gazette, 20 May, 1898]: "John Fisher, Capt., Indian Medical Service. In recognition of services during the recent operations in the Mamund Valley." The Insignia, Warrant and Statutes were sent to the Commander-in-Chief in India, and the Insignia presented at Almora on 22 Aug. 1898, by the Officer Commanding at Almora. He served with the Buner Field Force in 1898. He received the Medal and clasp. He was Vice-Consul. Meshed, 1903–4; and became Lieutenant-Colonel 29 Jan. 1906. Lieut.-Colonel Fisher became Medical Officer, 2nd Central India Horse.

SLADEN, DAVID RAMSAY, Capt., was born 7 Feb. 1869, son of the late Lieut.-Colonel John Ramsay Sladen. He was gazetted to the King's Own Scottish Borderers 13 June, 1888, and served in the Sudan in 1888, being present at the action of Gamaizah (Medal with clasp; Bronze Star). He took part in the operations on the Nile in 1889, and was promoted to Captain 21 July, 1897. In 1897 and 1898 he served in the Tirah Expedition; was slightly wounded; received the Medal and two clasps, and was mentioned in Despatches 1 March, and 5 April, 1898, and was created a Companion of the Distinguished Service Order [London Gazette, 20 May, 1898]: "David Ramsay Sladen, Capt., King's Own Scottish Borderers. In recognition of his services during the recent operations on the North-West Frontier of India." Insignia presented by the Queen at Windsor 25 June, 1898. He served in the South African War, 1900–2. Operations in the Orange Free State Feb. to May, 1900, including operations at Paardeberg (17 to 26 Feb.); actions at Poplar Grove, Karee Siding and Vet River (5 and 6 May). Operations in the Transvaal in May and June, 1900, including actions near Johannesburg and Pretoria. Operations in the Transvaal, east of Pretoria, in 1900. Operations in the Transvaal, west of Pretoria, in 1900, including actions at Zilikat's Nek. Operations in Cape Colony in 1900. Operations in the Transvaal 30 Nov. 1900, to March, 1901. Operations in Orange River Colony in March, 1901, to 31 May, 1902. He was mentioned in Despatches [London Gazette, 10 Sept. 1901]; received the Queen's Medal with three clasps, and the King's Medal with two clasps. He was Adjutant, Volunteers, 1 Sept. 1904, to 31 July, 1908, and was promoted to Major 18 Oct. 1907. He served in the European War from 1914; became Lieutenant-Colonel 3 Dec. 1914, and Colonel 3 Dec. 1918; commanded the 46th Infantry Brigade, British Armies in France, 2 Aug. 1917, to 11 Feb. 1918; Brigade Commander, Welsh Reserve Infantry Brigade, Home Forces, 13 April, 1918, to 24 June, 1918. He was wounded, and was created a C.M.G. in 1915. He married, in 1911, Isabel, eldest daughter of John Blakiston Houston, of Orangefield, County Down, and they have one son and one daughter.

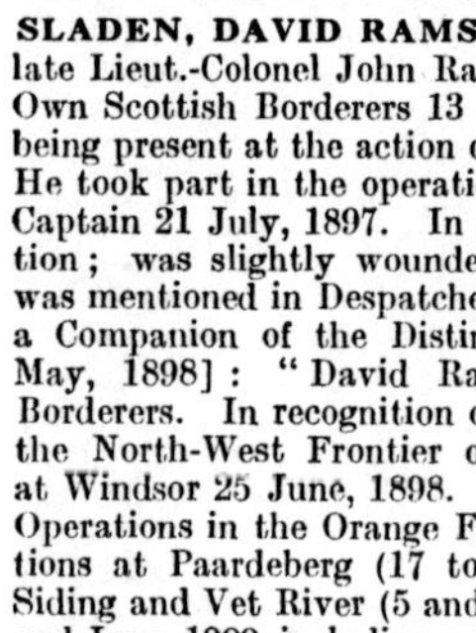

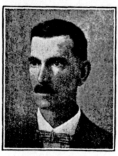

William Selby.

SELBY, WILLIAM, Surgeon-Capt., was born at Dunedin, New Zealand, 16 June, 1869, youngest son of the late Prideaux Selby, Koroit, Park Hill, Croydon, and Rose Anne, daughter of the late John Wise. He was educated at Whitgift Grammar School, and St. Bartholomew's Hospital (M.R.C.S., England; L.R.C.P., London, 1890; F.R.C.S., England, 1905). He joined the Indian Medical Service in 1894, and in the following year served with the Chitral Relief Force, received the Medal and clasp, and in 1897–98, on the North-West Frontier of India, taking part in the operations on the Samana, during August and Sept. 1897, and in the relief of Gulistan (two clasps); actions of Chagru Kotal, Dargai, and capture of the Sampagha and Arhanga Passes; operations in the Waran Valley, and action of 16 Nov. 1897; operations at and around Dwatoi and action of 24 Nov. 1897; operations against the Khani Khel Chamkanis; operations in the Bara Valley 7 to 14 Dec. 1897. He was mentioned in Despatches [London Gazette, 5 April, 1898], received a clasp, and was created a Companion of the Distinguished Service Order [London Gazette, 20 May, 1898]: "William Selby, Surgeon-Captain, Indian Medical Service. In recognition of services during the recent operations on the North-West Frontier of India." The Insignia were sent to the Commander-in-Chief in India, and the Presentation delayed until the furlough men returned to Dehra Dun. The Distinguished Service Order was presented at Dehra Dun on the 14th Sept. 1898, by the Officer Commanding the troops there. He had become Captain 28 July, 1897, and was promoted to Major 29 Jan. 1906. Lieut.-Colonel Selby was Honorary Surgeon to the Viceroy and Principal of King George's Medical College, Lucknow. He died on the 8th of Sept. 1916, and an obituary notice of him appeared in the "Times" of 11 Sept. 1916. He married Eliza Kinsman, daughter of the late Frederick Benjamin, Wood Lane, Falmouth, in 1896.

LUCAS, FREDERIC GEORGE, Capt., was born at Falmouth 20 Oct. 1866, eldest son of the late Frederic Lucas, Paymaster, Royal Navy, and Mrs. Lucas. He was educated at the Royal Naval School, New Cross; at the Royal Academy, Gosport (Burney's), and t the Royal Military College, Sandhurst, and was gazetted to the East Lancashire Regt. 25 Aug. 1886, and to the Indian Staff Corps 1 Aug. 1888, becoming Captain, Indian Army, 25 Aug. 1897. Capt. Lucas served in the Hazara Expedition, 1891 (Medal with clasp), and in the Isazai Expedition, 1892. He served in the Tirah Campaign, 1897–98, in command of the Gurkha Scouts. Action of Chagru Kotal and capture of the Sampagha and Arhanga Passes. Reconnaissance of the Saran Sar. Operations in and around Dwatoi, and action of 24 Nov. 1897. Operations against the Khani Khel Chamkanis. Operations in the Bara Valley 7 to 14 Dec. 1897. Operations in the Bazar Valley 25 to 30 Dec. 1897. He was mentioned in Despatches [London Gazette, 1 March and 5 April, 1898], received the Medal with two clasps, was given the Brevet of Major 20 May, 1898, and was created a Companion of the Distinguished Service Order [London Gazette, 20 May, 1898]: "Frederic George Lucas, Capt., Indian Staff Corps. In recognition of services during the recent operations on the North-West Frontier of India." The D.S.O. was presented to him 28 Oct. 1898. He served on the North-West Frontier of India, in Waziristan, 1901–02; was mentioned in Despatches [London Gazette, 22 May, 1908], and received a clasp. He became Major 25 Aug. 1904. In 1908 he again saw active service on the North-West Frontier of India, taking part in the operations in the Zakka Khel country, and was mentioned in Despatches [London Gazette, 22 May, 1908]. He was promoted to Lieutenant-Colonel 22 Oct. 1911; became Commandant, 2nd Battn. 5th Gurkha Rifles. Lieut.-Colonel Lucas served in the European War, including Mesopotamia, from 1914, and was given the Brevet of Colonel 3 June, 1917. He was Brigade Commander, 42nd Brigade, Indian Army, Indian Expeditionary Force "D," Mesopotamia Expeditionary Force, from 1 April, 1916, to 14 March, 1919.

MACQUOID, CHARLES EDWARD EVERY FRANCIS KIRWAN, Lieut., was born 2 Aug. 1869, eldest son of Colonel R. K. Macquoid and Frances Every, daughter of General Alfred Cooper. He was educated at Dover College; joined the King's (Liverpool) Regt. 11 Feb. 1888; became Lieutenant, Indian Staff Cor,s, 26 Aug. 1888, and Lieutenant, 3rd Infantry, H.C., and exchanged into the 20th Deccan Horse in 1891. Employed on Special Service, North-East Frontier of Burma, 1895–96, for which he received the thanks of the Commander-in-Chief in India and the local Government of Burma. He served on the North-West Frontier of India, 1897–98, in the Mohmand Expedition, as Field Intelligence Officer (Sept. to Oct. 1897); was mentioned in Despatches [London Gazette, 11 Jan. 1898]. He took part in the operations on the Samana and in the Kurram Valley during Aug. and Sept. 1897, and received the Medal and one clasp. He served in the Tirah Campaign of 1897–98 as Field Intelligence Officer, 1st Division (10 Oct. 1897, to April, 1898). He was present at the capture of the Arhanga and Sampagha Passes. Reconnaissance of the Saran Sar and action of 9 Nov. 1897. Operations against the Khani Khel Chamkanis. Operations in the Bazar Valley 25 to 30 Dec. 1897. He received a clasp, was mentioned in Despatches [London Gazette, 5 April, 1898], and was created a Companion of the Distinguished Service Order [London Gazette, 20 May, 1898]: "Charles Edward Every Francis Kirwan Macquoid, Lieut., Indian Staff Corps. In recognition of services during the recent operations on the North-West Frontier of India." The Insignia were sent to the Commander-in-Chief in India, and presented on 31 Aug. 1898, at Rangoon, by the Brigadier-General Commanding the Rangoon District. He became Captain, Indian Army, 11 Feb. 1899. In 1900 and 1901 he served in South Africa, and received the Queen's Medal and clasp. On 11 Feb. 1906, he was promoted to Major, and in 1912 he was transferred from the 20th Deccan Horse into the 4th Cavalry, Indian Army, as Second-in-Command. He became Lieutenant-Colonel 11 Feb. 1914. He served in the European War, in France and Mesopotamia from Oct. 1914 to 1916 (Mons Star). A.A.G, G.H.Q., Mesopotamia (mentioned in Despatches). Promoted Brigadier-General, 1918. G.O.C. Kuki punitive measures, Sept. 1918, to May, 1919. G.O.C. 46th Brigade, Afghan War, May, 1919. Brigadier-General Macquoid's favourite recreations are shooting, polo, etc. He is the author of "Strategy illustrated by British Campaigns," with preface by Field-Marshal Lord Roberts.

CLIMO, SKIPTON HILL, Lieut., was born at Longford 24 Dec. 1868, second son of Colonel W. Hill Climo, A.M.S., and Mrs. Hill Climo, Yateley, Hampshire. He was educated at Shrewsbury and Sandhurst, and was gazetted to the 2nd Border Regt. as Second Lieutenant 11 Feb. 1888; served with the 1st Battn. Border Regt. in ndia in 1889; became Lieutenant, Border Regt., 11 July, 1889, and Indian Staff Corps, 14 Sept. 1889 (24th Punjab Infantry). He served on the North-West Frontier of India

1897–98, taking part in the defence of Malakand, and in the relief of Chakdara. He was present also at the operations in Bajaur and in the Mamund country, was mentioned in Despatches [London Gazette, 5 Nov. 1897], was given the Brevet of Major 12 Feb. 1899, and created a Companion of the Distinguished Service Order [London Gazette, 20 May, 1897]: "Skipton Hill Climo, Lieut., Indian Staff Corps. In recognition of services during the recent operations on the North-West Frontier of India." The Insignia were presented to him by the Queen at Windsor 17 Nov. 1898. He became Captain 11 Feb. 1899, and served in China in 1900, when he was present at the relief of Pekin and at the actions of Peitsang and Yangtsun; was mentioned in Despatches [London Gazette, 14 May, 1901], and received the Medal and clasp. He served in Tibet in 1904, and received the Medal, and he was promoted to Major 13 Feb. 1905. In 1908 Major Climo again saw active service on the North-West Frontier of India, taking part in the operations in the Mamund country. He was mentioned in Despatches [London Gazette, 14 Aug. 1908], and received the Medal with clasp. He became Lieutenant-Colonel 13 Feb. 1912. Lieut.-Colonel Climo served in the European War from 1914, serving in 1914 and 1915 in Egypt and the Suez Canal (Despatches). He served in Mesopotamia in 1915 and 1916, was mentioned in Despatches, given the Brevet of Colonel 29 Oct. 1915, and created a C.B. 1916. He was wounded four times. He was promoted to Brigadier-General 15 Jan. 1916. Brigadier-General Climo commanded the 24th Punjabis, 1912–1916. He holds the Order of the Nile, 3rd Class. Promoted Major-General for Special War Services 3 June, 1918. His favourite recreations are polo, fishing, shooting and golf.

Skipton Hill Climo.

When Brigadier-General Dobbie had to go home on sick leave, Sir Charles Townshend asked that Colonel Climo, of the 24th Punjabis, should be made temporary Brigadier-General in command of his brigade, and this was done. At the Battle of Kurna General Townshend signalled to Colonel Climo his congratulations on the brilliant dash of the Oxfordshire and Buckinghamshire Light Infantry. In his account of the Battle of Ctesiphon Sir C. Townshend speaks of "the 30th Brigade under the gallant Climo," and of "the gallant 30th Brigade under Climo," and tells us how, later on in the conflict, Colonel Climo was carried past him "severely wounded in three places, but quite cheery. This gallant soldier would have been a great loss to me at any time, but at such a critical moment it was a disaster." Sir Charles Townshend complains in his book that the 6th Division was neglected in the way of rewards and promotions: "None of my lieutenant-colonels had been promoted to higher commands, except Colonel Climo, whom I had strongly recommended twice for promotion, giving him temporary command of a brigade in the actions of Kurna, Kut-al-Amara and Ctesiphon, in which last battle he had been severely wounded."

EDLMANN, ERNEST ELLIOTT, Lieut., was born 24 Nov., 1868, son of the late Major Joseph Ernest Edlmann, King's Dragoon Guards, and Caroline, daughter of the late W. Elliott, Madras Civil Service. He was educated at Leamington College, and at the Royal Military Academy, and commissioned 17 Feb. 1888, in the Royal Artillery, becoming Lieutenant 17 Feb. 1891, and serving in Burma, in the Chin Hills, 1892–93 (Medal and clasp). He served in the Expedition to Dongola, 1896 (Egyptian Medal and Medal). In 1898 Lieut. Edlmann served on the North-West Frontier of India, with the Mohmand Field Force; also with the Tirah Expeditionary Force. He was present at the actions of Dargai and Saran Sar; was mentioned in Despatches [London Gazette, 5 April, 1898], received the Medal with two clasps, and was created a Companion of the Distinguished Service Order [London Gazette, 20 May, 1898]: "Ernest Elliott Edlmann, Lieut., Royal Artillery. In recognition of services during the recent operations on the North-West Frontier of India." The Insignia were presented by the Queen at Windsor 17 Nov. 1898. He became Captain 24 Oct. 1898. In 1903–04 he served in Aden and took part in operations in the interior. He was promoted to Major 15 Dec. 1908. Major Edlmann served in the European War. The "Times" of 22 April, 1915 contains the following notice: "Edlmann.—On the 17th inst. at Shaiba, Persian Gulf, from wounds received on the 14th, Major Ernest Elliott Edlmann, D.S.O., R.A., 23rd Peshawar Mountain Battery, aged 46, fifth son of the late Major Joseph Ernest Edlmann, Kent House, Leamington." Major Edlmann had married, in 1908, Evelyn, daughter of the late Major-General L. R. H. D. Campbell, and they had one son and two daughters.

WINSLOE, ALFRED RAYNAUD, Lieut., was born in 1868, second son of Colonel Richard William Charles Winsloe, C.B., and Constance Edwards, second daughter of the late F. M. Cromartie, Superintendent of Stores, Ordnance Department. He entered the Royal Engineers as Second Lieutenant 17 Feb. 1888; became Lieutenant, Royal Engineers, 17 Feb. 1891; served with the Chitral Relief Force 1895 (Medal and clasp). Also with the Malakand and Buner Field Forces, North-West Frontier of India, 1897–98; present at the defence of Malakand and relief of Chakdara, Malakand. Action at Landakai, Utman Khel and Buner. Attack and capture of the Tanga Pass. He was mentioned in Despatches [London Gazette, 5 Nov. 1897], received the Medal and clasp, and was created a Companion of the Distinguished Service Order [London Gazette, 20 May, 1898]: "Alfred Raynaud Winsloe, Lieut., Royal Engineers. In recognition of services during the recent operations on the North-West Frontier of India." (Insignia presented by the Queen at Windsor 7 Nov. 1898.) He became Captain 8 Nov. 1898; Major 13 Aug. 1906, and was promoted to Lieutenant-Colonel 30 Oct. 1914. He was created a C.M.G. for services during the European War. Lieut.-Colonel Winsloe married, in 1903, Dorothy Crellin, second daughter of Dr. Tellet, J.P., of Ramsey, Isle of Man. His favourite recreations are polo, racquets and the study of theology.

FERGUSON-DAVIE, ARTHUR FRANCIS, Lieut., was born 11 July, 1867, third son of Sir William Augustus Ferguson-Davie, 3rd Baronet, and Frances Harriet, fifth daughter of Sir William Miles, 1st Baronet. He was educated at Marlborough; entered the Army in 1888; Lieut. I.S.C. 12 Oct. 1891; served with the Waziristan Delimitation Escort; was present at the action at Wana, 1894; with the Waziristan Expedition, 1894–95 (Medal with clasp); Chitral Relief Expedition, 1895 (Medal and clasp). He served in the Tirah Campaign, 1897–98; was present at the capture of the Sampagha and Arhanga Passes; reconnaissance of the Saran Sar and action of 9 Nov. 1897. Operations in and around Dwatoi, and action of 24 Nov. 1899. Operations against the Khani Khel Chamkanis. Operations in the Bara Valley 7 to 14 Dec. 1897. Operations in the Bazar Valley 25 to 30 Dec. 1897. He was mentioned in Despatches [London Gazette, 5 April, 1898], received two clasps, and was created a Companion of the Distinguished Service Order [London Gazette, 20 May, 1898]: "Arthur Francis Ferguson-Davie, Lieut., Indian Staff Corps. In recognition of services during the recent operations on the North-West Frontier of India." The Insignia were presented on the 29th Aug. 1898, by the Officer Commanding at Kohat. He was promoted to Captain 22 Aug. 1899. In 1901 and 1902 served on the North-West Frontier of India, in Waziristan; was mentioned in Despatches [London Gazette, 8 Aug. 1902], and received a clasp. In 1902 he took part in the operations against the Darwesh Khel Waziris. He was promoted to Major 22 Aug. 1906, and in the same year was created a C.I.E. He served with the Bazar Valley Field Force in 1908 (Medal and clasp). He was Staff Captain, India, 6 April, 1908, to 27 Dec. 1908; served in the Mohmand Field Force, taking part in the operations in the Bazar Valley as D.A.Q.M.G. 28 April, 1908, to 16 May, 1908; was D.A.A.G., India, 28 Dec. 1908, to 12 May, 1911. He served in the European War; became Lieutenant-Colonel, Indian Army, 22 Aug. 1914; held a special appointment (graded D.A.A.G.) from 13 Oct. 1914. He died of wounds in April, 1916. Lieut.-Colonel Ferguson-Davie married, in 1906, Eleanor Blanche Daphne, eldest daughter of C. T. Naylor, of Dean House, Kilmeston, Hants, and they had two sons: William Antony and Arthur Patrick.

RAWLINS, ARTHUR KENNEDY, Lieut., was born 15 May, 1868, at Dharmsala, Punjab, son of the late Major-General J. S. Rawlins, Indian Army. He was educated at Haileybury, and gazetted to the East Surrey Regt. as Second Lieutenant 21 Dec. 1889, becoming Lieutenant, Indian Staff Corps, 19 May, 1892. He served on the North-West Frontier of India, 1897–98, and was present at the defence of Malakand, relief of Chakdara, Malakand, and the action at Landakai. Operations in Bajaur and in the Mamund country. He was mentioned in Despatches [London Gazette, 5 Nov. 1897], received the Medal with two clasps, and was created a Companion of the Distinguished Service Order [London Gazette, 20 May, 1898]: "Arthur Kennedy Rawlins, Lieut., Indian Staff Corps. In recognition of services during the recent operations on the North-West Frontier of India." The Insignia were presented at Peshawar on 17 Aug. 1898. He served in China in 1900, and in the same year was promoted to Captain, Indian Army, on 21 Dec. In 1903–04 he served in Somaliland, and was present at the action of Jidballi. He was mentioned in Despatches [London Gazette, 2 Sept. 1904], and received the Medal and clasp. He became Major 21 Dec. 1907. Major Rawlins served in the European War as Special Service Officer from 17 Aug. 1914, in charge of the Bikanir Camel Corps. He became Lieutenant-Colonel, 24th Punjab Infantry, 21 Dec. 1915; was created a C.I.E. in 1916; and a C.B.E.

TILLARD, ARTHUR BASIL, Lieut., was born at Lowestoft 10 June, 1870, youngest son of Major-General John Arthur Tillard and Eliza Scott (who died 1895), daughter of General G. P. Whish, B.S.C.; was educated at Dover and Sandhurst, and gazetted to the Hampshire Regt. as Second Lieutenant 24 Dec. 1890; became Lieutenant, Indian Staff Corps, 30 Jan. 1892; 3rd Gurkhas, 1892. He served in South Lushai, 1892–93; on the North-West Frontier of India, 1897–98; operations on the Samana and in the Kurram Valley during Aug. and Sept. 1897; relief of Gulistan (Medal with two clasps). He served in Tirah with Sir William Lockhart in 1897–98, in command of the 3rd Gurkha Scouts, and was present at the actions of Chagru Kotal, Dargai, and of the Sampagha and Arhanga Passes; at the reconnaissance of the Saran Sar and the action of 11 Nov. 1897; at the operations in the Waran Valley and the action of 16 Nov. 1897; the operations at and around Dwatoi, and the action of the 24th Nov. 1897. He was mentioned in Despatches twice, viz.: G.G.O.'s Nos. 68 and 244 of 1898 [London Gazette, 1 March and 5 April, 1898]; received a clasp, and was created a Companion of the Distinguished Service Order [London Gazette, 20 May, 1898]: "Arthur Basil Tillard, Lieut., Indian Staff Corps. In recognition of services during the recent operations on the North-West Frontier of India." Insignia, etc., sent to the Commander-in-Chief in India, and presented at Almora on 6 Aug. 1898, by Officer Commanding at Almora. The decoration was awarded for work done with the Scouts of the 1/3rd Gurkhas during the Tirah Campaign, and in the actions at Dargai 18 and 20 Oct. 1891; Sampagha Pass, Arhanga Pass, Saran Sar, and in the Waran Valley. He became Captain 10 July, 1901, and served on the North-West Frontier of India, in Waziristan, 1901–2 (clasp), and in Tibet, 1903–4 (Medal) was promoted to Major 24 Dec. 1908. He served

Arthur Basil Tillard.

in France in 1915, and was present at the action of Neuve Chapelle, and actions of the 9th and 16th May (Despatches). Major Tillard served in Gallipoli from 15 Sept. to the evacuation (Despatches), and in Egypt, 1916. Served in Mesopotamia, 1916–17; action at Abdul Hassan, Jan. 1917 (Despatches); promoted Lieutenant-Colonel 24 Dec. 1916, Commanding 1/4th Gurkhas.

RATTRAY, HALDANE BURNEY, Lieut., was born 27 May, 1870, son of the late Colonel Thomas Rattray, C.B., C.S.I. He entered the Derbyshire Regt. as Second Lieutenant 29 March, 1890; became Lieutenant, Indian Staff Corps, 1 March, 1892. He served on the North-West Frontier of India, 1897–98, taking part in the defence of Chakdara (severely wounded); Malakand; action at Landakai; operations in Bajaur. He was mentioned in Despatches [London Gazette, 5 Nov. 1897], was given the Brevet of Major 30 March, 1901, and was created a Companion of the Distinguished Service Order [London Gazette, 20 May, 1898]: " Haldane Burney Rattray, Lieut., Indian Staff Corps. In recognition of services during the recent operations on the North-West Frontier of India." The Insignia were presented at Youti, Jubaland, by H.M. Consul for British East Africa. He served in the Tirah Campaign, 1897–98 (clasp); and in British East Africa, 1898, taking part in the operations against the Ogaden Somalis (Medal with clasp). In 1898 and 1899 he served in Uganda. On 20 March, 1901, he was promoted to Captain, Indian Army. He became Wing Commander, 45th Bengal Infantry, and was promoted to Lieutenant-Colonel. In 1905 he married Ethel Marguerite, daughter of the late W. Piper, of Ackleton Hall, Shropshire, and they had one son. Lieut.-Colonel Rattray was killed in action 1 Feb. 1917.

WYNTER, FRANCIS ARTHUR, Lieut., was born 19 July, 1870, son of Lieut.-Colonel A. L. Wynter (late K.O.S.B.), and Mrs. Wynter, daughter of the late Charles Moore, Temperley, Cheshire. He became Second Lieutenant, Royal Artillery, 14 Feb. 1890; Lieutenant 14 Feb. 1893; served on the North-West Frontier of India in 1897, and commanded the 8th Bengal Mountain Battery throughout the defence of the Malakand (severely wounded); was mentioned in Despatches [London Gazette, 5 Nov. 1897]. He served with the Malakand Field Force in the Expedition into the Mamund country, and was present in the attack of 16 Sept. (severely wounded). He was mentioned in Despatches [London Gazette, 18 March, 1898], received the Medal with two clasps, and was created a Companion of the Distinguished Service Order [London Gazette, 20 May, 1898]: " Francis Arthur Wynter, Lieut., Royal Artillery. In recognition of services during the recent operations on the North-West Frontier of India." (Insignia presented by the Queen at Windsor 25 June, 1898.) He became Captain in Dec. 1899. Capt. Wynter served in the Mahsud Blockade, and in Waziristan in 1901 and 1902 (clasp); became Major in Dec. 1910. Major Wynter served in the European War in the Dardanelles in 1915 (Brevet of Lieutenant-Colonel 8 Nov. 1915); in Egypt, 1916; was promoted to Lieutenant-Colonel in Sept. 1916; in France, 1916–17–18, and was created a C.M.G. 1 Jan. 1918; was made temporary Brigadier-General 21 April, 1918, to 3 Feb. 1919, Royal Artillery, Heavy Artillery, British Armies in France; promoted to Colonel 3 June, 1919; Commandant, Clyde Garrison, 14 Feb. 1919.

CHANCELLOR, JOHN ROBERT, Lieut., was born in Edinburgh 20 Oct. 1870, second son of E. Chancellor, of Woodhall, Juniper Green, Midlothian. He was educated at a private school, and at the Royal Military Academy, Woolwich; joined the Royal Engineers as Second Lieutenant 25 July, 1890; served in the Dongola Expedition in 1896, with the Indian Contingent at Suakin (Khedive's Medal and English Medal); in the Tirah Expedition 1897–98, he was in charge of the Sirmur Imperial Service Sappers; was present at the capture of Dargai Heights, of Sampagha Pass and Arhanga Pass; operations in Bara Valley 7 to 14 Dec. 1897. For his services in this campaign he was mentioned in Despatches 5 April, 1898, received the Medal and three clasps, and was created a Companion of the Distinguished Service Order [London Gazette, 20 May, 1898]: " John Robert Chancellor, Lieut., Royal Engineers. In recognition of services during the recent operations on the North-West Frontier of India." (Insignia presented by the Queen at Windsor 25 June, 1898.) He became Captain 20 May, 1901; passed the Staff College in 1902; was Staff Captain (Intelligence), H.Q. of Army, 7 Oct. 1903, to 17 July, 1904, and Assistant Secretary (Military), Committee of Imperial Defence, 18 July, 1904, to 10 July, 1906; Secretary (G.S.O., 2nd Grade), Overseas Defence Committee, 27 Oct. 1906, to 29 Sept. 1911; created a C.M.G. in 1909; was promoted to Major 25 July, 1910. He was Governor and Commander-in-Chief of Mauritius 13 Nov. 1911, to 7 March, 1915; was created a K.C.M.G., 1913; was appointed Governor and Commander-in-Chief of Trinidad and Tobago in 1916; promoted to Lieutenant-Colonel 24 Sept. 1918. Sir R. Chancellor married, in 1903, Elsie, third daughter of G. Rodie Thompson, of Lynwood, Ascot.

TOMKINS, HARRY LEITH, Lieut., was born 25 Jan. 1870, son of the late Samuel Leith Tomkins and Annie Bella Newry Tomkins. He joined the 4th King's Own (Royal Lancaster) Regt. as Second Lieutenant 29 Oct. 1890; became Lieutenant 28 July, 1893, and Lieutenant, Indian Staff Corps, 14 Oct. 1894; served on the North-West Frontier of India, 1894–95; Waziristan, 1897–98, as Railway Staff Officer, Lines of Communication (Medal and clasp; Despatches; created a Companion of the Distinguished Service Order [London Gazette, 20 May, 1898]: " Harry Leith Tomkins, Lieut., Indian Staff Corps. In recognition of services in the recent operations on the North-West Frontier of India.") Insignia presented by the Queen at Windsor 17 Nov. 1898. He became Captain 10 July, 1901; served on the North-West Frontier of India, 1901–2; served in Somaliland, 1903–4 (Medal and clasp); operations in the Zakka Khel country, 1908 (Medal and clasp); became Major, Indian Army, 29 Oct. 1908; A.M.S. and A.D.C. to G.O.C., Northern Army, India, 19 Oct. 1909, to 5 Oct. 1910, and 6 Oct. 1910, to 29 Sept. 1914; A.M.S. 30 Sept. 1914, to 16 Oct. 1915. He served in the European War from 1914 (Despatches twice, Brevet of Lieutenant-Colonel, 28th Punjabis, Indian Army, 3 June, 1915); Lieutenant-Colonel 29 Oct. 1918; became D.A.A. and Q.M.G. to Expeditionary Force' 3rd Division, Indian Expeditionary Force " D," 17 Oct. 1915, to 5 Feb. 1916. Was severely wounded in 1916. He was created a C.M.G. in 1917.

MAXWELL, FRANCIS AYLMER, Lieut., Indian Staff Corps, was created a Companion of the Distinguished Service Order [London Gazette, 20 May, 1898]: " Francis Aylmer Maxwell, Lieut., Indian Staff Corps. In recognition of services on the North-West Frontier of India." The Insignia were presented to him by the Queen at Windsor 25 June, 1898. (See Victoria Cross volume of this book.)

MACKENZIE, GEORGE DOUGLAS, Lieut., was created a Companion of the Distinguished Service Order [London Gazette, 20 May, 1898]: " George Douglas Mackenzie, Lieut., Gordon Highlanders. In recognition of services during the recent operations on the North-West Frontier of India." He died 9 March, 1899.

SHOUBRIDGE, THOMAS HERBERT, Lieut., was born 15 June, 1871, and was gazetted to the Dorsetshire Regt. 15 March, 1893, becoming Lieutenant 18 June, 1896. He served in the Tirah Campaign in 1897–98, taking part in the actions of Chagru Kotal and Dargai; the capture of the Sampagha and Arhanga Passes, reconnaissance of the Saran Sar and action of 9 Nov. 1897. Operations in the Waran Valley and action of 16 Nov. 1897. Operations in the Bara Valley. He received the Medal with two clasps, and was created a Companion of the Distinguished Service Order [London Gazette, 20 May, 1898]: " Thomas Shoubridge, Lieut., Dorsetshire Regt. In recognition of services during the recent operations on the North-West Frontier of India." (The Insignia, etc., sent to the Commander-in-Chief in India. Presented at Cherat 17 Aug. 1898.) He served in the South African War, 1899–1902, on the Staff. Operations in Natal, 1899. Relief of Ladysmith, including operations on the Tugela Heights (14 to 27 Feb. 1900). Operations in Natal, March to June, 1900. Operations in the Transvaal and Orange River Colony 30 Nov. 1900, to 31 May, 1902. Operations on the Zululand Frontier of Natal in Sept. and Oct. 1901. He was mentioned in Despatches [London Gazette, 8 Feb. 1901, and 29 July, 1902]; received the Brevet of Major 29 Nov. 1900; the Queen's Medal with four clasps, and the King's Medal with two clasps. He became Captain, Northumberland Fusiliers, 9 May, 1900; was D.A.Q.M.G., Headquarters, South Africa, up to 23 June, 1905, and Brigade Major, Irish Command, from 1 Nov. 1906. He was G.S.O.2, West Lancashire Division, 5 Sept. 1912, to 18 Feb. 1914; was G.S.O.2, Southern Command, 18 Feb. 1914, to 4 Aug. 1914; was given the Brevet of Lieutenant-Colonel 21 Feb. 1914. He served in the European War from 1914; was promoted to Major 14 Sept. 1914; was given the Brevet of Colonel 1 Jan. 1917, and became Major-General 1 Jan. 1919. He was G.S.O.2, 2nd Army Corps, British Expeditionary Force, 5 Aug. 1914, to 3 Oct. 1914; A.A. and Q.M.G., 4th Army Corps, B.E.F., 12 Jan. 1915, to 27 Feb. 1915; G.S.O.1, 18th Division, New Armies, B.E.F., 3 March, 1915, to 14 Dec. 1915; Brigade Commander, 54th Infantry Brigade, B.E.F., and British Armies in France, 15 Dec. 1915, to 28 March, 1917; Divisional Commander, British Armies in France, and British Force in Italy, 29 March, 1917; temporary Commander, Shorncliffe, 8 Feb. 1919, to 5 June, 1919. He was created a C.M.G. in 1916, and a C.B. Major-General Shoubridge married, in 1910, Gladys Constance, eldest daughter of the late Major Dugdale, 16th Lancers, and they have two daughters.

HUGO, JAMES HENRY, Lieut., was born 16 July, 1870, and educated at Foyle College, Londonderry, and St. Bartholomew's Hospital, where he was interim House Physician and Clinical Assistant, Orthopædic Department. House Surgeon, General Hospital, Nottingham; Assistant Medical Superintendent, Dulwich Infirmary; is M.R.C.S. (England); L.R.C.P. (London); D.P.H. He entered Netley in the Indian Medical Service in 1896; became Lieutenant 28 Jan. 1897; was attached to the Punjab Infantry in 1897. He served on the North-West Frontier of India, 1897–98, being present at the defence of Malakand; action at Landakai; operations in Bajaur and in the Mamund country. He was mentioned in Despatches [London Gazette, 5 Nov. 1897], received the Medal with two clasps and for the action during the siege of Malakand was created a Companion of the Distinguished Service Order [London Gazette, 20 May, 1898]: " James Henry Hugo, Lieut., Indian Medical Service. In recognition of services during the recent operations on the North-West Frontier of India." (The Insignia, etc., sent to the Commander-in-Chief in India, and presented at Murree on 7 Oct. 1898.) He became Captain 28 Jan. 1900; Major 29 July, 1908, and Lieutenant-Colonel 29 July, 1816. He was appointed Major Residency Surgeon in Kashmir, and Superintending Surgeon, Jammu and Kashmir States, Lieut.-Colonel Hugo married, in 1902, Minnie Alice Muriel, daughter of Colonel C. Dempster, Indian Army.

PRATT, HENRY ROGER EVELYN, Lieut., was born 8 Dec. 1875, son of William Dering Pratt and Louisa Constance Steel. He was educated at Clifton College, and entered the Army 14 Aug. 1895, as Second Lieutenant (unattached), joining the Indian Staff Corps 13 Dec. 1896, and becoming Lieutenant, Indian Army, 14 Nov. 1897. He served on the North-West Frontier of India, 1897–98, attached to the 36th Sikhs, taking part in the operations in Samana and in the Kurram Valley during Aug. and Sept. 1897; the defence of Gulistan. He was mentioned in Despatches [London Gazette, 11 Feb. 1898, and received the Medal and two clasps. He served in the Tirah Campaign in 1897–98, being present at the capture of the Sampagha and Arhanga Passes. Reconnaissance of the Saran Sar Valley and action of 16 Nov. 1897. Operations in the Bara Valley 7–14 Dec. 1897. He received a clasp, and was created a Companion of the Distinguished Service Order [London Gazette, 20 May, 1898]: " Henry Roger Evelyn Pratt, Lieut., Indian Staff Corps. In recognition of services during the recent operations on the North-West Frontier of India." (The Insignia, etc., sent to the Commander-in-Chief in India. Presented by Colonel Coats at Rawal Pindi.) He was promoted to Captain 14 Aug 1904, and to Major 14 Aug 1913; was transferred to the 35th Sikhs in 1916. During the European War he was with the Army Signal Service from 11 Sept. 1914;

was Second-in-Command, 5th Northamptonshire Regt., March, 1915; with the B.E.F. in France and Flanders from June, 1915; commanding 6th Battn. East Kent Regt. as temporary Lieutenant-Colonel from 5 Nov. 1915, to 10 March, 1916; acting Lieutenant-Colonel, Indian Army, 29 March, 1918. He married, in 1909, Yolande Beatrix Tower, and they have one son.

WHEATLEY, LEONARD LANE, Second Lieut., was born at Newbridge, County Kildare, 18 June, 1876, eldest son of the late Lieut.-Colonel Charles R. E. Wheatley, Royal Artillery, and of Mrs. R. E. Wheatley. He was educated at Wellington College, and at the Royal Military College, Sandhurst, and entered the Army 22 Jan. 1896, as Second-Lieutenant (unattached), joining the Indian Staff Corps 1 April, 1897. He served on the North-West Frontier of India, 1897–98, taking part in the defence of Chakdara, Malakand, and the action at Landakai; and in the operations in Bajaur and in the Mamund country. He was mentioned in Despatches [London Gazette, 5 Nov. 1897], received the Medal with two clasps, and was created a Companion of the Distinguished Service Order [London Gazette, 20 May, 1898]: "Leonard Lane Wheatley, Second Lieut., Indian Staff Corps. In recognition of services during the recent operations on the North-West Frontier of India." The Insignia were presented to him by the Queen at Windsor 25 June, 1898. He was promoted to Lieutenant 22 April, 1898. He served in Waziristan in 1901–02; was mentioned in Despatches [London Gazette, 8 Aug. 1902], and received a clasp. He became Captain, Indian Army, 22 Jan. 1905, and Argyll and Sutherland Highlanders, 22 July, 1908; was Adjutant, Territorial Force, 25 Aug. 1909; A.D.C. to the Governor of Victoria 14 April, 1911, to 30 June, 1913; Officer, Company of Gentlemen Cadets, Royal Military College, 4 Sept. 1913, to 26 Nov. 1914; was promoted to Major 1 Sept. 1915; G.S.O., Royal Military College, 27 Nov. 1914, to 7 Dec. 1915; Staff Captain, 168th Infantry Brigade, B.E.F., 5 Feb. 1916, to 6 April, 1916; Brigade Commander, 197th Infantry Brigade, British Armies in France, 3 April, 1918, to 21 Sept. 1918; Brigade Commander, 1st Infantry Brigade, British Armies in France, 22 Sept. 1918, to 6 March, 1919. For his services during the European War from 1914 he was given the Brevet of Lieutenant-Colonel 1 Jan. 1917; and created a C.M.G. 1918. He married, in 1917, Esther, eldest daughter of Charles Fairbairn, of Banogill, Australia.

VAN SOMEREN, WILLIAM WEYMOUTH, Lieut., was born 17 Sept. 1876, at Madras, son of the late Godlies George Bennett Van Someren, Barrister-at-Law, and Mrs. G. B. Van Someren. He was educated at Clifton College and Sandhurst, and entered the Army 5 Aug. 1896, as Second Lieutenant (unattached); joined I.S.C. 8 Oct. 1897. He served in the Tirah Campaign and was present at the actions of Chagru Kotal, Arhanga and Sampagha Passes; at the reconnaissance of Saran Sar, and the action of 9 Nov. 1897; at the operations in the Waran Valley, and the action of 16 Nov. 1897. Also at the operations at and around Dwatoi and at the action of 24 Nov. 1897, and at the operations in the Bara Valley 7 to 14 Dec. 1897. Affair at Shinkamar 29 Jan. 1898. For his services in this campaign he was mentioned in Despatches (G.G.O. No. 244 of 1898), received the Medal with two clasps, and—for drawing the regiment (36th Sikhs) out of action at the affair of Shinkamar 29 Jan. 1898—was created a Companion of the Distinguished Service Order [London Gazette, 20 May, 1898]: "William Weymouth Van Someren, Lieut., Indian Staff Corps." Insignia presented by the Queen at Windsor, 25 June, 1898. He became Lieutenant, Indian Army, 5 Nov. 1898; Captain 5 Aug. 1905. Capt. Van Someren married, 30 June, 1906, at Madras, Kathleen Beatrice Grahame, daughter of W. F. Grahame, late I.C.S., and they have a daughter, Clare Kathleen Mary. He became Major 5 Aug. 1914, and is Double-Company Commander, 45th Rattray's Sikhs. In the Great War he arrived in France 26 Nov. 1914, and was wounded at Festubert on 21 Dec. 1914. Was G.S.O.3, War Office, 1 March, 1918, to 4 June, 1918; G.S.O.3, North Russian Expeditionary Force, 5 June, 1918.

London Gazette, 4 Oct. 1898.—"The Queen has been graciously pleased to give orders for the following appointments to the Distinguished Service Order, and promotions in the Army, in recognition of the services of the undermentioned Officers during the recent operations in Mekran."

JACOB, ARTHUR LE GRAND, Capt., was born at Bhuj, India, 19 Feb. 1867, son of Major-General W. Jacob, Indian Army. He was educated at Sherborne School, and at the Royal Military College, Sandhurst; was gazetted to the 1st North Lancashire Regt. as Lieutenant on 30 Jan. 1886; transferred to the Indian Staff Corps 11 June, 1887, and served in the Zhob Valley Expedition, 1890. He was promoted to Captain, Indian Army, 30 Jan. 1897; and in the following year served in the operations at Mekran, being present at the action of Gok Parosh. He was mentioned in Despatches [London Gazette, 15 July, 1898], and was created a Companion of the Distinguished Service Order [London Gazette, 4 Oct. 1898]: "Arthur Le Grand Jacob, Captain, Indian Staff Corps. In recognition of services during the recent operations in Mekran." The Insignia were presented to him by the Queen at Windsor 17 Nov. 1898. In 1901 and 1902 he again saw active service on the North-West Frontier of India, in Waziristan (Medal with clasp). He was promoted to Major 31 Jan. 1904, and to Lieutenant-Colonel 1 Oct. 1911; and was created a C.M.G. in 1907. Lieut.-Colonel Jacob served in the European War from 1914, as A.A. and Q.M.G., Indian Expeditionary Force "D," Mesopotamia Expeditionary Force, 21 March, 1917, to 26 March, 1919; and as Base Commandant, Mesopotamia Expeditionary Force, 27 March, 1919. He was appointed A.D.C. to the King 3 June, 1918; was given the Brevet of Colonel 3 June, 1918, and created a C.M.G. in 1918. Colonel Jacob married, in 1895, Mary Hilston, daughter of the late Fleet-Paymaster J. T. Sueter, R.N.

PAINE, JAMES HENRY, Lieut., was born 8 Sept. 1870; educated at Marlborough; entered the Royal Artillery as Second Lieutenant 14 Feb. 1890; became Lieutenant 14 Feb. 1893; served during the operations in Mekran, 1898. He was present at the action of Gok Parosh, was mentioned in Despatches [London Gazette, 15 July, 1898], and was created a Companion of the Distinguished Service Order [London Gazette, 4 Oct. 1898]: "James Henry Paine, Lieut., Royal Artillery. In recognition of services during the recent operations in Mekran." He became Captain 1 Oct. 1899, and Major 1 Dec. 1910, serving during the European War with the 26th Battery, Native Mountain Artillery, in India. He died 25 July, 1918. Major Paine had married, in 1896, Caroline Mary, daughter of Deputy Inspector-General Henry Piers, R.N.

London Gazette, 15 Nov. 1898.—"War Office, 15 Nov. 1898. The Queen has been graciously pleased to give orders for the following appointments to the Distinguished Service Order, and promotions in the Army, in recognition of the services of the undermentioned Officers in Egypt and the Sudan, including the battles of Atbara and Khartoum."

BRINDLE, ROBERT, The Rev., was born in Liverpool 4 Nov. 1837. He studied for twelve years at the English College at Lisbon; was ordained Deacon, and became Priest in 1862. He worked on the Missions at Plymouth for some twelve years, and became Military Chaplain in 1874, his first experience being at Woolwich. Thence he passed to Halifax, Nova Scotia, for five years, and on his return served for a short time at Aldershot. In 1882 came the campaign against Arabi Pasha, and for four years he saw constant active service in Egypt. Of the landing of the troops the Bishop was wont to give a very lively description. The scene of hopeless confusion in the unloading of the transports at Ishmailia, the horses swimming from the ships on to the shore, the men encumbered with all manner of military stores and equipments, he would relate in an amusing manner—adding the remark of one of the British Tars who said that he had hitherto considered himself as one of Her Majesty's seamen, but had now been turned into a commissariat mule! He was continually with the fighting line. He was present at a great many battles, in which he shared the risks of the combatants. Speaking to the students at Lisbon College in 1909, His Lordship frankly admitted that in the first engagement with the enemy, when the English lost about a hundred men, he felt anything but comfortable, and called himself a fool for having left congenial work in England to go out to a desert place where he thought he would certainly be shot. Such, however, was not to be, and in future, when under fire, he experienced no such fear, although he had some narrow escapes. He was not present at the Battle of Tel-el-Kebir, being stricken down with cholera just previously. While he was in Cairo he worked among the numerous cases of enteric fever. One who was with him says that he cheered all by his companionship, and was never downhearted. He was always in the best of spirits, and was always most popular with the soldiers. In the Nile Expedition of 1884, he captained one of the boats of the Royal Irish Regt.—the regiment which won the prize of £100 offered by Lord Wolseley to the first boat to reach the end of the river journey. Field-Marshal Sir Evelyn Wood says: "I was riding up the banks of the Nile on a camel, and he was pulling in a boat of the Royal Irish Regt. About sundown on Christmas Day I saw a little flotilla of boats flying the Royal Irish flag toiling up the river. Father Brindle got out when he had pulled up to us, hot, tired and irritable, with his hands blistered and the perspiration running down his face. Said I: 'Father, what have you been doing?' 'Pulling stroke in order to encourage them.' 'Any result?' I asked. What he really said was 'Devil a bit.' But I interpreted it to the clerics, 'No, none at all.' The Father was, however, unduly pessimistic, for the Royal Irish won Lord Wolseley's prize, given to the battalion which made the best time for the three or four hundred miles up the river, and also which brought up in good order the largest amount of public stores intact." This incident occurred on Christmas Day, 1884, during the Gordon Relief Expedition, and is related by Field-Marshal Sir E. Wood, V.C., in "Winnowed Memories." A Protestant friend of Dr. Brindle's, a doctor attached to the Expedition, relates how, after the Battle of Metemmeh, "the Royal Irish were ordered across the desert to assist in the return of the force. Lord Wolseley was aware that to send the regiment without Father Brindle was out of the question, and so he accompanied the regiment, and was provided with a camel for the hundreds of miles of the march. But Father Brindle did not use the camel, and did the whole desert journey to Metemmeh and back on foot. I went out a few miles, from Korti, to meet the returning force, and found the Father marching with the regiment, but the soles of his boots were gone, and rags rolled about his feet had replaced them. According to my experience, everyone that met him appreciated him. He was a wonderful man for making friends, and Lord Wolseley had a very high opinion of him." After being present at the Battle of Ginniss, he returned to England, and for the next ten years served as Chaplain at Colchester and Aldershot. During this period of his life, says his friend, the Very Rev. Canon Vere, "I saw him from time to time, and was his guest at Aldershot. In the thirty-fifth year of his priesthood, and nearing the fifty-ninth year of his age, Father Brindle again set sail for Egypt, and, in 1896, was attached to Lord Kitchener's Expedition to Dongola. During the long and trying period of inaction at Sarras, the soldier-Chaplain distinguished himself by his devotion to the sick. He was, when cholera invaded the camp, tireless in his ministration to the troops, who were always cheered by his undaunted spirit." Mr. R. Caton Woodville, in his "Random Recollections," speaks of Father Brindle thus: "All the Tommies loved him when he was Army Chaplain. It was he who carried the Tommies out of their quarters in his arms, placed them in the ambulance to convey them to the hospital when nobody else would come near them, as the cholera

Robert Brindle.

was raging and the men were dying like flies, and even many of the doctors themselves had died. When I asked him how it was that he never caught it himself, he replied that he never ate anything that was not freshly cooked. It was during the halt at Atbara that Father Brindle performed a very heroic deed. It was a Saturday night, and word came from another camp some nine miles away that a Catholic soldier was dying. Unarmed, he set out at once, and walked across the El Teb, which was infested by the enemy. He administered the last rites to the dying man, and stayed with him to the end. He then tramped back without rest or food, and reached the camp in time to say Mass for his men on Sunday morning." On Good Friday, the 8th of April, Father Brindle was present at the Battle of the Atbara, which wiped out the finest Dervish Army that had opposed the British. In the three great attacks of the Battle of Omdurman, the heroic priest was in the fighting line. At the Memorial Service for General Gordon, held in Khartoum, Father Brindle was one of the officiating Chaplains, and composed a prayer which he recited on that occasion, and which by Lord Kitchener's orders was printed for distribution. G. W. Steevens says, on page 314 of his book "With Kitchener to Khartoum": "Next fell a deeper hush than ever, except for the solemn minute guns that had followed the fierce salute. Four Chaplains—Catholic, Anglican, Presbyterian and Methodist—came slowly forward and ranged themselves with their backs to the palace, just before the Sirdar. The Presbyterian read the fifteenth Psalm, the Anglican led the rustling whisper of the Lord's Prayer. Snow-haired Father Brindle, best beloved of Priests, laid his helmet at his feet and read a memorial prayer bareheaded in the sun." Father Brindle was five times mentioned in Despatches, and received rapid promotion. For the Nile Expedition of 1884, he received the British War Medal with four clasps, and for the Khartoum Expedition the Medal with three clasps. He was given a Good Service Pension, and received the Turkish Orders of the Medjidie with three clasps, the Osmanieh with four clasps, and the Khedive's Bronze Star. He was created a Companion of the Distinguished Service Order [London Gazette, 15 Nov. 1898]: "Rev. Robert Brindle, Chaplain to the Forces, 1st Class, in recognition of services in Egypt and the Sudan, including the battles of Atbara and Khartoum." The Insignia were sent to the General O.C. in Egypt, and presented by him 20 Dec. 1898, at a full dress parade at the Cairo Garrison. Father Brindle had his decoration stolen from him in Rome, and obtained another at his own expense, and this was presented to him by Queen Victoria on 11 May, 1899. He retired from the Army in 1899; journeyed from Egypt to Rome, and on 12 March, 1899, was consecrated Titular Bishop of Hermopolis by Cardinal Satolli. After the death of Monsignor Barry, Bishop Brindle became Provost of the Westminster Chapter, and for nearly three years he worked as Auxiliary in the Archdiocese. On Thursday, 20 Sept. 1900, he consecrated St. Patrick's Church in Soho Square. Most of the information given in this account of the Bishop is supplied by his friend, the Very Rev. Canon Vere, of St. Patrick's Presbytery. In the 65th year of his age Bishop Brindle was translated to the See of Nottingham, 6 Dec. 1901. In the Advent of 1911 the soldier Bishop uttered these solemn words of warning: "There is a strange feeling of unrest everywhere; vast armies stand ready for the bugle-call as though an enemy were at their gates; huge navies armed with the most powerful engines of destruction the world has ever known keep watch and ward upon the seas; while mistrust of each other sits like a ghost at every council board; and this is reacting in the daily life of the people; we are growing less and less inclined to fulfil our duties for duty's sake; pleasure takes the place of duty wherever it can be obtained; regard for law has no influence for its own sake, if only we can escape detection, and the obligations of our state of life are seldom sweetened by the thought of 'something attempted, something done.'" Bishop Brindle resigned the See of Nottingham, and died on 26 June, 1916, at Mount St. Mary's College, near Sheffield, where he had been on a visit since March. He was given a soldier's funeral at Nottingham Cathedral on Wednesday, 5 July, 1916. Lord Kitchener's death had just taken place. A letter from Lord Kitchener to Bishop Brindle is given below:

"Honiton, 2 October.

"MY DEAR FATHER,

"I like this form of address better than your exalted title of Bishop. I wonder you did not excommunicate the War Office and all its contents, including the Staff that now rule there; perhaps you had not a bell, book and candle with you, and only murmured the formula. As an Irishman I much wish I could come and see your Irish friends, but it is a far cry to Liverpool. Next time I stay at Knowsley, which I do sometimes, I will see what can be done. I often look back in memory to the old Soudan days when you used to lead the troops across the desert, and wish those days back again. I am shortly going back to Khartoum for the winter, and to shoot up the White Nile. I was delighted to get your letter, and to feel that you still have a kindly remembrance for your old friend,

"KITCHENER."

Bishop Brindle's photograph stood on the mantelpiece of Lord Wolseley's office in London. A stranger happened to notice the portrait, and asked the Field-Marshal who it was. He replied: "That is one of the finest soldiers in the British Army, Father Brindle."

TOWNSHEND, CHARLES VERE FERRERS, Capt. and Brevet Lieutenant-Colonel, was born 21 Feb. 1861. He is a cousin of the 6th Marquess Townshend. He became Lieutenant, Royal Marines, 1 Feb. 1881, and served in the Sudan Expedition of 1884–85. Suakin and the Nile. Operations round Suakin in 1884 (mentioned in Despatches). Nile Expedition. With the Royal Marines, attached to Guards' Camel Regt. Actions at Abu Klea and El Gubat, and reconnaissance on Metemmeh (Medal with two clasps; Bronze Star). He was transferred to the Indian Staff Corps 15 Jan. 1886. In 1891–92 he served in the Hunza Nagar Expedition. Taking of Nilt (Despatches [London Gazette, 21 June, 1892]; Medal with clasp). He was promoted to Captain 1 Feb. 1892. In 1895 he served in the Chitral Expedition, and commanded the Garrison of Chitral during the siege of the fort. He was thanked by the Government of India; mentioned in Despatches [London Gazette, 16 July, 1895]; received the Medal and clasp; was created a C.B., and was given the Brevet of Major 10 July, 1895. He was employed with the Egyptian Army 11 Feb. 1896, to 1 Dec. 1898, and in 1896 served in the Expedition to Dongola, taking part in the operations of 7 June and 19 Sept. He was mentioned in Despatches [London Gazette, 3 Nov. 1896]; received the Egyptian Medal with two clasps, and was given the Brevet of Lieutenant-Colonel 18 Nov. 1896. He served in the Nile Expedition of 1898, and was present at the battles of the Atbara and Khartoum; was mentioned in Despatches [London Gazette, 24 May and 30 Sept. 1898]; received the Medal, and two clasps to the Egyptian Medal, and was created a Companion of the Distinguished Service Order [London Gazette, 15 Nov. 1898]: "Charles Vere Ferrers Townshend, Capt. and Brevet Lieutenant-Colonel, Indian Staff Corps. In recognition of services during the recent operations in the Sudan." The Insignia were presented to him by the Queen at Windsor 1 Dec. 1898. He served in the South African War, 1899–1900, as Special Service Officer, and afterwards on the Staff of the Military Governor of Bloemfontein. He was present at the operations in the Orange Free State, Feb. to May, 1900. Operations in Orange River Colony, May to Sept. 1900. Operations in Cape Colony in 1900 (Queen's Medal with two clasps). He was given the Brevet of Colonel 10 Feb. 1904; became Major, Royal Fusiliers, 28 July, 1900; Acting Military Attaché, Paris, in 1903, and Major, Shropshire Light Infantry, 7 March, 1906; became Colonel 2 Aug. 1907; Assistant Adjutant-General, 9th Division, Army in India, 2 Aug. 1907, to 8 April, 1909; Officer Commanding District, South Africa, 9 April, 1909, to 20 Sept. 1911; promoted to Major-General 18 June, 1911; G.O.C., Home Counties Division, Eastern Command, 1 April, 1912, to 5 June, 1913; Brigade Commander, India, 30 June, 1913, to 17 April, 1915. He commanded the 6th Division, Indian Expeditionary Force "D", 18 April, 1915; was created a K.C.B.; was besieged in Kut, and eventually taken prisoner by the Turks, and released after the Armistice.

C. V. F. Townshend.

A very interesting book was written by Major E. W. C. Sandes, M.C., R.E., called "In Kut and Captivity." The story "mainly follows the fortunes of the 6th Indian Division and its attached troops in prosperity and adversity, in victory and disaster, during their struggle against the Ottoman troops in Mesopotamia, and it describes the adventures of a small portion of the garrison of Kut when in captivity in Turkey." Major Sandes says, in Chapter XI.: "Why did the 6th Indian Division and the 30th Brigade halt at Kut-el-Amarah in the retreat from Ctesiphon instead of continuing their retirement towards Amarah? This is a question which has been asked many times and around which much heated discussion has raged; for the fate of the unfortunate force under the command of General Townshend was due to the fact that it remained in Kut, when it was overtaken and surrounded by the Turks, and lacked sufficient food supplies to enable it to hold out till relieved by an army which was hampered and delayed by atrocious weather conditions. As in the case of the vexed question of the advance on Baghdad in 1915, I will leave the reader to draw his own conclusions and make his own criticisms; yet some aspects of the problem which confronted General Townshend on his arrival at Kut-el-Amarah present an interesting study. Before enumerating the pros and cons of the question, let me quote an extract from General Townshend's communiqué to his troops in Kut, dated 26 Jan. 1916. . . . The communiqué runs as follows: 'I desire all ranks to know why I decided to make a stand at Kut during the retirement from Ctesiphon. It was because as long as we hold Kut, the Turks cannot get their ships, barges, stores and munitions past this, and so cannot move down to attack Amarah; and thus we are holding up the whole of the Turkish advance. It also gives time for our reinforcements to come up from Busrah, and so restore success to our arms. It gives time to our allies the Russians, who are now over-running Persia, to move towards Baghdad. . . . By standing at Kut I maintain the territory won in the past year—and thus we maintain the campaign as a glorious one instead of letting disaster pursue its course to Amarah and perhaps beyond.' This statement enumerates most of the points in favour of the halt of our retiring force at Kut, but I may perhaps add one or two others for the consideration of my readers. Our troops had come through some very strenuous fighting, consequently were much fatigued and in need of rest in order to recuperate and refit. In addition, the strategical importance of Kut with regard to the Shatt-al-Hai Channel to Nasariyeh should not be overlooked. The evacuation of Kut would have left the Shatt-al-Hai Channel—which would shortly be filled with flood water—open to the boat traffic of the enemy down to Nasariyeh, thus enabling the Turk to mass troops and stores with ease for a flank attack on Amarah, or for an attack on Nasariyeh itself, and also to make use of the great supplies of grain available in the area around the Shatt-al-Hai Channel. Again, with the shipping available, it would not have been possible to remove from Kut all the stores and ammunition accumulated at that place, and enormous quantities of both would consequently have had to be destroyed to prevent them falling into the hands of the enemy. A further consideration was the fact that the town of Kut was known to contain a very great quantity of provisions of all sorts, seemingly ample for a force of 13,000 men besieged for what would probably be a short period. Lastly, the unfortunate loss of prestige caused by our unavoidable retirement from Ctesiphon would be partially redeemed if our force remained in Kut and retired no farther. Recapitulating the advantages gained by a halt at Kut, we find the following: (*a*) It held up the river transport of any large Turkish force advancing on Amarah by the Tigris. (*b*) It gave time for our reinforcements to arrive from Busrah and beyond, and to concentrate for action. (*c*) It assisted the Russian move on Baghdad from Persia by diverting many of the enemy's troops to Kut. (*d*) It enabled our fatigued troops to rest and refit. (*e*) It closed the Shatt-al-Hai Channel to the river-transport of the enemy. (*f*) It obviated the necessity of destroying a great quantity of valuable stores. (*g*) It took advantage of the mass of provisions available in Kut which would otherwise have been lost. (*h*) It saved a further and more serious loss of prestige, such as would have been entailed by a continued retreat downstream. Any reasonable person will admit that some or all of these considerations would carry weight when placed before a commander in the field; yet, as there are two sides to every question, it will be well to examine the case for the opposition. The main objection to holding Kut lay in the fact that by remaining in Kut, the 6th Division, which had outdistanced the Turkish pursuit from Ctesiphon, allowed the enemy to regain touch with it before it had reached reinforcements sufficient to defeat that enemy. Another objection to the holding of Kut was that, in nine cases out of ten, the correct place for a fighting force is in the open field, where its liberty of action will not be restricted and it can still retain the initiative. In most cases a force besieged is a force wasted, for it deliberately adopts the defensive attitude, which tends to develop into a passive defence late in a siege; and a passive defence is liable to cause loss of moral among the besieged. Again, the approaching flood season of the River Tigris was a matter of the gravest importance. At high flood the river can be made to swamp most of the country below Kut, and this was likely to render the advance of a relieving force, faced by determined opposition, a matter of extreme difficulty, probably involving great loss of life. Lastly, if the 6th Division had retired towards Amarah and joined hands with the force collecting there under General Aylmer, the concentration thus effected would have created a large field force, unhampered by any necessity for an urgent advance under unfavourable conditions; and all our troops would have been comparatively close to their depôts of supplies and ammunition, and the enemy more distant from his own. Summing up the case against the holding of Kut, the leading points are as follows: (*a*) It caused the halt of a retreating force, which had succeeded in eluding pursuit, but had not been adequately reinforced. (*b*) It imprisoned in a restricted and unfavourably situated area a force designed for fighting in the field. (*c*) It incurred the danger of the capture of that force, owing to the difficulty of a relief force reaching Kut across flooded country. (*d*) It entailed strategical dispersion of force by having a portion of our army in Kut and the remainder near Amarah. The decision to halt in Kut was not reached hastily, nor without very lengthy discussion of the problem from every point of view. Of this we may be sure. No one unacquainted with the whole of the information at the disposal of our generals is qualified to give an opinion on the subject, or to criticize the decision reached about 8 Dec. 1915—viz., that the 6th Division and the 30th Brigade should remain in Kut, and keep the Union Jack flying far up the Tigris till relief arrived from below. That this decision should have led to the disastrous termination of the siege of Kut was the result of a combination of misfortunes and delays which none foresaw in Dec. 1915." The book is certainly very well worth reading. It tells us the story of the hopes and fears and sufferings of the garrison throughout the siege; and after the fall of Kut we are enabled in some degree to realize the gross ill-treatment meted out to many of their prisoners by the Turks, which in somes cases did not stop short of actual and very deliberate murder. The "Morning Post" of 14 Jan. 1920, publishes a letter from a correspondent, from which we give an extract: "The announcement that Major-General Sir Charles Townshend has tendered his resignation is a serious blow to the prospects of the future British Army. Those who, like the present writer, had had the advantage of talking over the military position with Sir Charles Townshend before the Great War must have felt what a cruel chance of Fate it was that sent this brilliant officer to be sacrificed to other people's stupidity in Mesopotamia. For he was a man who saw, with an insight that was so clear as to be super-intellectual, not only that the Germans had prepared for a war in 1914 or thereabouts, but also the main lines of their plan of campaign. The Western Front had been a subject for his close study long before 1914; and if it had been his lot to serve there, without a shadow of doubt his value to the Allies' cause would have been of vital significance. But it was ruled otherwise. The field assigned to him was Mesopotamia. There the strategical judgment of a leader who was of the intellectual school of Marshal Foch was nullified by higher authority; he was driven to a task which he knew to be impossible, and his services to the country as a soldier were lost with the fall of Kut, though as a captive in Constantinople he was able at a later stage to do brilliant diplomatic service to the Empire. Not that the first Mesopotamian campaign, which ended with the fall of Kut, was without glory. General Townshend had estimated with exactness what forces he would require to take Baghdad; he was given about one-third of the necessary forces. Even so, he conducted a vigorous campaign until the Turkish Empire, finding its great Asian capital threatened, rallied its forces, obtained help from the Germans, and massed an overwhelming army against the British forlorn hope. General Townshend, after his great victories against heavy odds at Kut, at Karna, and at Ctesiphon, was forced, on the arrival of a new Turkish Army Corps, to fall back on Kut and stand a siege there. He was left without relief until forced by starvation to surrender. It is not difficult to understand that the authorities who put this General into an impossible position would be inclined to withhold from him the recognition to give which would involve grave censure on their own competency. But it is to the last degree regrettable that the services of this splendid soldier should be lost to the country for this reason."

We give some extracts from Sir Charles Townshend's book, "My Campaign in Mesopotamia":

"The exploits of my soldiers were great in themselves and great in their consequences, for we conquered over three hundred miles of territory by our three victories, all of which were battles of manœuvre. The victories of Kut-al-Amara and Ctesiphon—second to none in the glorious records of the Indian Army—are signal examples of heroic conduct and devoted zeal on the part of the troops I commanded."

General Townshend remarks in the Preface on the inadequacy of the means placed at his disposal for the campaign:

"Such a task with a handful of troops was one at which Bonaparte or Hannibal might have despaired. And its magnitude will be the better appreciated when it is considered that General Maude, to effect the same task, was given 113,000 to 120,000 troops, as against my 13,000, with a full proportion of guns, supplies, steamers, railways, etc."

"The resolution I took—to stand at Kut—saved us from being simply kicked out of Mesopotamia. All Mesopotamia would have risen behind us had I continued my retreat past this point, which is at the bifurcation of the Tigris and Hai Rivers, whence Feld-Marschall Von der Goltz, then commanding the 6th Turkish Army, could have directed a strategic turning movement viâ the Hai to Nasiriyeh, which was only some three or four days' march from Basra. To stand at Kut was the only way to enable Government to bring reinforcements from overseas and to repair the disaster. But I bargained to be relieved in two months; or else, as I wired to Sir John Nixon, it would be impossible to relieve us."

These extracts are from the Preface, and when the book is drawing to a close General Townshend writes:

"It seems to me that I cannot better end the story of the defence of Kut than by quoting the speech of Lord Kitchener, then Minister for War, in the House of Lords, on May 4th, 1916—perhaps the last occasion that he spoke in public. He quoted my last message before hoisting the white flag over Kut and burning the tattered Union Jack, which we had kept flying for just on five months, with my own hands, so that it might not fall into those of the enemy:

"'Lord Beresford asked the Secretary of State for War how many British prisoners were taken at the surrender of Kut, and whether it was a fact that the Turkish Commander-in-Chief was so impressed by the heroic defence made by General Townshend that he granted him the full honours of war by allowing him to retain his sword.'

"'Earl Kitchener: I am glad that the noble and gallant lord has offered me this opportunity of paying a tribute to General Townshend and his troops, whose dogged determination and splendid courage have earned for them so honourable a record. It is well known how, after a series of brilliantly-fought engagements, General Townshend decided to hold the strategically important position at Kut-al-Amara, and it will not be forgotten that his dispositions for the defence of the place were so excellent and so complete that the enemy, notwithstanding large numerical superiority, was wholly unable to penetrate his lines. Noble lords will not fail to realize how tense was the strain borne by those troops who, for more than twenty weeks, held to their posts under conditions of abnormal climatic difficulty, and on rations calculated for protraction to the furthest possible period, until, as it was proved, imminent starvation itself compelled the capitulation of this gallant garrison, which consisted of 2,970 British and some 6,000 Indian troops, including followers. General Townshend and his troops, in their honourable captivity, will have the satisfaction of knowing that, in the opinion of their comrades, which I think I may say that the country and this House fully share, they did all that was humanly possible to resist to the last, and that their surrender reflects no discredit on themselves or on the record of the British and Indian Armies. Every effort was, of course, made to relieve the beleaguered force, and I am not travelling beyond the actual facts in saying that to the adverse elements alone was due the denial of success; the constant rain and consequent floods not only impeding the advance, but compelling—in lieu of turning movements—direct attacks on an almost impossibly narrow front. No praise would seem extravagant for the troops under Sir Percy Lake and Sir George Gorringe, and that they did not reap the fruit of their courage and devotion is solely due to the circumstances which fought against them. The last message sent by General Townshend from Kut was addressed in these terms: "We are pleased to know that we have done our duty, and recognize that our situation is one of the fortunes of war. We thank you and General Gorringe and all ranks of the Tigris force for the great efforts you have made to save us." I think the House, no less than the country at large, will endorse these words, and I am sure that those who held and those who strained every nerve to relieve Kut have alike earned our admiration and our gratitude. I am glad to endorse what the noble lord has said in regard to the conduct of the Turkish Commander.'

"'Lord Grenfell said the eulogy of General Townshend which had been pronounced would be very satisfactory to the House and to the Army, including the force which remained in Mesopotamia. In spite of the difficulties of various kinds, sickness, want of food, and lack of medical stores, General Townshend and the Anglo-Indian force held Kut in the most admirable manner until, the food supplies being exhausted, to save the lives of his men, General Townshend consented to capitulate. The defence of Kut by General Townshend and the determination of his troops would long be remembered with great admiration by the Army and the country.'" (From the "Times," 5 May, 1916.)

In this most interesting book General Townshend claims to have shortened the war by some months by his negotiations which brought about the premature surrender of Turkey. He pleads that the Turkish Empire in Europe should not be dismembered, and says that the best of the Turks have, and always have had, friendly sentiments towards Great Britain.

HUGHES, GEORGE ARTHUR, Lieut.-Colonel, was born 18 May, 1851, fifth son of the late James Hughes, of Curragh Priven, Rathcormac, County Cork. He was educated at Trinity College, Dublin (Bachelor of Arts; Bachelor of Medicine; Master of Surgery), and joined the R.A.M.C. 4 Feb. 1877; served in the Afghan War, 1878–80 (Medal); in the Bechuanaland Expedition, 1884–85, and in the Ashanti Expedition, 1895–96 (Honourably mentioned; Star). He served in the Nile Expedition in 1898, and was present at the Battle of Khartoum; received the Egyptian Medal with clasp; was mentioned in Despatches [London Gazette, 30 Sept. 1898], and created a Companion of the Distinguished Service Order [London Gazette, 15 Nov. 1898]: "George Arthur Hughes, Lieut.-Colonel, Royal Army Medical Corps. In recognition of services during the recent operations in the Sudan." (The Insignia, etc., were sent to the G.O.C., Malta, 21 Dec. 1898, and presented by General Sir L. Fremantle 15 Feb. 1898.) He became Colonel 25 March, 1904, and retired 26 Aug. 1905.

BLOMFIELD, CHARLES JAMES, Colonel, was born at Bow, Devonshire, 26 May, 1855, second son of the Rev. George J. Blomfield, Rector of Aldington, Kent, and Isabel, daughter of the late Right Rev. Charles James Blomfield, Lord Bishop of London. He was educated at Haileybury, and the Royal Military College, Sandhurst; entered the Army as Sub-Lieutenant (unattached) 11 Feb. 1875; 20th Foot 11 Feb. 1875; for 1st Class at Royal Military College, became Lieutenant, 20th Foot, 11 Feb. 1875; was Adjutant, Lancashire Fusiliers, 27 Aug. 1880, to 20 Nov. 1883; Captain, Lancashire Fusiliers, 1 July, 1881. He married, 18 Aug. 1881, in Dublin, Henriette Elizabeth Briscoe, daughter of Major E. Briscoe (The Lancashire Fusiliers), and their sons are: Myles Aldington Blomfield, Commander, Royal Navy (born in 1885), and Patrick Valentine Blomfield, Lieutenant, 2nd Lancers, Indian Army (born 1893). He was Adjutant, Auxiliary Forces, 18 Jan. 1884, to 17 Jan. 1889; became Major 31 July, 1890; was Acting Military Secretary to His Excellency the Commander-in-Chief, Bombay Army, in 1891; D.A.A.G., Bombay, 27 Oct. 1892, to 9 Jan. 1897; A.A.G., India, 10 Jan. 1897, to 31 Dec. 1897. He became Lieutenant-Colonel 15 Oct. 1898; served in the Sudan Expedition in 1898; was present at the Battle of Khartoum; was mentioned in Despatches [London Gazette, 30 Sept. 1898]; received the Egyptian Medal with clasp, and the Queen's Medal, and was created a Companion of the Distinguished Service Order [London Gazette, 15 Nov. 1898]: "Charles James Blomfield, Colonel, The Lancashire Fusiliers. In recognition of services during the recent operations in the Sudan." The Insignia, Warrant and Statutes were sent to the G.O.C., Gibraltar and presented by him 15 Dec. 1898. He was in command of the 2nd Lancashire Fusiliers from Dec. 1899, to 27 Oct. 1900; commanded 2nd Lancashire Fusiliers in the South African War, 1899–1902; was with the Ladysmith Relief Force in the operations of 17 to 24 Jan. 1900, and was severely wounded at Spion Kop.

Charles J. Blomfield.

Sir A. Conan Doyle says, on pages 196 and 197 of "The Great Boer War": "By the morning of Jan. 22 the regiments were clustering thickly all round the edges of the Boer main position, and the day was spent in resting the weary men and in determining at what point the final assault should be delivered. On the right front, commanding the Boer lines on either side, towered the stark eminence of Spion Kop, so called because from its summit the Boer voortrekkers had first in 1835 gazed down upon the promised land of Natal. If that could only be seized and held! Buller and Warren swept its bald summit with their field-glasses. It was a venture. But all war is a venture; and the brave man is he who ventures most. One fiery rush and the master-key of all these locked doors might be in our keeping. That evening there came a telegram to London which left the whole empire in a hush of anticipation. Spion Kop was to be attacked that night. The troops which were selected for the task were eight companies of the 2nd Lancashire Fusiliers, six of the 2nd Royal Lancasters, two of the 1st South Lancashires, 180 of Thorneycroft's, and half a company of Sappers. It was to be a North of England job. Under the friendly cover of a starless night the men, in Indian file, like a party of Iroquois braves upon the war-trail, stole up the winding and ill-defined path which led to the summit. Woodgate, the Lancashire brigadier, and Blomfield of the Fusiliers, led the way. It was a severe climb of 2,000 feet, coming after arduous work over broken ground, but the affair was well timed, and it was at that blackest hour which precedes the dawn that the last steep ascent was reached. The Fusiliers crouched down among the rocks to recover their breath, and saw far down in the plain beneath them the placid lights which showed where their comrades were resting. A fine rain was falling, and rolling clouds hung low over their heads. The men with unloaded rifles and fixed bayonets stole on once more, their bodies bent, their eyes peering through the mirk for the first sign of the enemy—that enemy whose first sign has usually been a shattering volley. Thorneycroft's men with their gallant leader had threaded their way up into the advance. Then the leading files found that they were walking on the level. The crest had been gained. With slow steps and bated breath the open line of skirmishers stole across it. Was it possible that it had been entirely abandoned? Suddenly a raucous shout of 'Wie da?' came out of the darkness, then a shot, then a splutter of musketry and a yell, as the Fusiliers sprang onwards with their bayonets. The Boer post of Vryheid burghers clattered and scrambled away into the darkness, and a cheer that roused both the sleeping armies told that the surprise had been complete and the position won. In the grey light of the breaking day the men advanced along the narrow, undulating ridge, the prominent end of which they had captured. Another trench faced them, but it was weakly held and abandoned. Then the men, uncertain what remained beyond, halted and waited for full light to see where they were, and what the work was which lay before them—a fatal halt, as the result proved, and yet one so natural that it is hard to blame the officer who ordered it. Indeed, he might have seemed more culpable had he pushed blindly on, and so lost the advantage which had been already gained."

Sir A. Conan Doyle goes on to describe the action at Spion Kop, and says that "the losses in the action were very heavy, not fewer than fifteen hundred being killed, wounded or missing, the proportion of killed, being, on account of the shell fire, abnormally high. The Lancashire Fusiliers were the heaviest sufferers, and their Colonel, Blomfield, was wounded, and fell into the hands of the enemy."

Colonel Blomfield took part in the operations in the Transvaal, east of Pretoria, 30 Nov. 1900, to 31 May, 1902 (was Colonel on the Staff to command District in 1900, and in command of columns); operations on the Zululand Frontier of Natal in Sept. 1901; was mentioned in Despatches [London Gazette, 8 Feb. 1901, and 29 July, 1902], and received the Brevet of Colonel 29 Nov. 1900, the Queen's Medal with four clasps, and the King's Medal with two clasps. He became Colonel 24 June, 1902; was Colonel on the Staff, commanding Harrismith and Natal Sub-District, South Africa, from 24 June, 1902, to 29 June, 1906; was created a C.B. in 1906; became Major-General 12 Feb. 1907; was G.O.C., Wessex Division, Southern Command, from 1 Jan. 1909, to 9 Feb. 1911; commanded Mhow Division, India, from 3 March, 1911, to Nov. 1912; commanded the Peshawar Division from 1913 to 25 June, 1915, and a Division, Territorial Force, from Nov. 1915, to July, 1917. Major-General C. J. Bomfield, C.B., D.S.O., was placed on the retired list on account of having attained the age limit 18 July, 1917.

LLOYD, FRANCIS, Lieut.-Colonel, was born 12 Aug. 1853, son of Colonel R. T. Lloyd and the Lady Frances, daughter of Thomas Robert, 10th Earl of Kinnoull. He was educated at Harrow, and was gazetted to the 32nd Duke of Wellington's Regt. 18 March, 1874; was transferred to the Grenadier Guards 29 Aug. 1874; became Lieutenant 18 March, 1875, and Captain 1 April, 1885. Capt. Lloyd served in the Sudan Expedition in 1885 (Suakin), and was employed as Signalling Officer, Guards Brigade; was present at the Battle of Hasheen; was mentioned in Despatches [London Gazette, 25 Aug. 1885]; received the Medal with clasp, and the Bronze Star. He was Regimental Adjutant, Grenadier Guards, 7 May, 1889, to 6 May, 1893; was promoted to Major 10 Aug. 1892. He was Commandant, School of Instruction for Militia and Volunteers, London, 1 Jan. 1894, to 24 Aug. 1896, and commanded the Guards' Depôt 25 Aug. 1896, to 18 May, 1897; was promoted to Lieutenant-Colonel 23 Oct. 1898. He served in the Nile Expedition of 1898, and was present at the Battle of Khartoum; was mentioned in Despatches [London Gazette, 30 Sept. 1898]; received the Egyptian Medal with clasp; the Medal, and was created a Companion of the Distinguished Service Order [London Gazette, 15 Nov. 1898]: "Francis Lloyd, Lieut.-Colonel, Grenadier Guards. In recognition of services during the recent operations in the Sudan." Lieut.-Colonel Francis Lloyd served in the South African War from 1900–2, in command of the 2nd Battn. Grenadier Guards. He took part in operations in the Orange Free State, April to May, 1900; operations in Orange River Colony, May to 29 Nov. 1900, including operations at Biddulphsberg (severely wounded). Sir A. Conan Doyle says, in "The Great Boer War" (page 341): "The Boers were in full retreat, but now, as always, they were dangerous. One cannot take them for granted, for the very moment of defeat is that at which they are capable of some surprising effort. Rundle, following them up from Senekal, found them in strong possession of the kopjes at Biddulphsberg, and received a check in his endeavour to drive them off. It was an action fought amid great grass fires, where the possible fate of the wounded was horrible to contemplate. The 2nd Grenadiers, the Scots Guards, the East Yorkshires and the West Kents were all engaged, with the 2nd and 79th Field Batteries and a force of Yeomanry. Our losses incurred in the open from unseen rifles were thirty killed and 130 wounded, including Colonel Lloyd of the Grenadiers." Operations in the Transvaal, Feb. to March, 1901; operations in Orange River Colony, Dec. 1900, to Feb. 1901, and March, 1901, to 31 May, 1902. He was mentioned in Despatches [London Gazette, 10 Sept. 1901, and 29 July, 1902]; received the Queen's Medal with three clasps; the King's Medal with two clasps, and was created a C.B. He was given the Brevet of Colonel 23 Oct. 1902; became Colonel 2 May, 1904; was Brigadier-General, 1st Brigade, 1st Army Corps, 27 April, 1904, to 1 May, 1908; created a C.V.O. in 1909; was G.O.C., Welsh Division, Western Command, 26 Jan. 1909, to 2 Sept. 1913; promoted to Major-General 7 Dec. 1909; created a K.C.B. in 1911; was G.O.C., London District, 3 Sept. 1913, to 30 Sept. 1918; was promoted to Lieutenant-General, 1 Jan. 1917; created a G.C.V.O. in Sept. 1918; was placed on half-pay 30 Sept. 1918; placed on retired pay 12 Aug. 1920. He was appointed Colonel, Royal Welch Fusiliers, 2 Feb. 1915. Sir Francis Lloyd has the Grand Cross of St. Sava (Serbia); is Grand Officer, Crown of Belgium; has the White Eagle of Russia, 2nd Class of the Danebrog, and is a Knight of Grace of St. John of Jerusalem (1916). He married, in 1881, Mary, daughter of George Gunnis Leckie, of Stirling, N.B.

STUART-WORTLEY, THE HON. EDWARD JAMES MONTAGU, Major, was born 31 July, 1857, second son of the Hon. F. D. Montagu Stuart-Wortley and the eldest daughter of William Bennet Martin, of Worsborough Hall, Yorkshire. He was educated at Eton; was gazetted to the 60th Foot 13 Oct. 1877, and served in the Afghan War in 1879–80, as Assistant Superintendent of Signalling with the Kurram Field Force, and was present at the assault of Zawa, and mentioned in Despatches.

He became Lieutenant, King's Royal Rifle Corps, 13 March, 1880, and in the following year again saw active service in the South African War, Transvaal Campaign, with the Natal Field Force. He was employed with the Egyptian Army 21 Dec. 1882; was Military Secretary to General Valentine Baker in Egypt in 1882; A.D.C. to General Sir Evelyn Wood in Egypt, 1883–84, and was present at Tel-el-Kebir (Medal with clasp, Bronze Star). He served throughout the Nile Expedition of 1884–85; was present at the Battles of Abu Klea and Gubat, and in the reconnaissance under Sir Charles Wilson to Khartoum (Despatches [London Gazette, 10 March, 10 April, and 25 Aug. 1885]; two clasps). He was Military Attaché to Sir H. Drummond-Wolff's special mission to Turkey in 1885. In 1885 and 1886 he was D.A.A.G to Sir F. Grenfell, with the Sudan Frontier Field Force; was present at the action of Ginniss in 1886, and was given the Brevet of Major (2 March, 1886). He was created a C.M.G. in 1886. He was promoted to Captain 1 March, 1886; to Major 4 April, 1897, and was Second-in-Command of the Gunboat Flotilla in the Nile Expedition of 1897, being present at the occupation of Berber and at the actions of Metemneh. In the Nile Expedition of 1898 he commanded friendly Arabs at the capture of Omdurman. He received the Medal; was mentioned in Despatches [London Gazette, 30 Sept. 1898], and was created a Companion of the Distinguished Service Order [London Gazette, 15 Nov. 1898]: "Edward James Montagu Stuart-Wortley, C.M.G., Major, King's Royal Rifle Corps. In recognition of services during the recent operations in the Sudan." The Insignia were presented to him by the Queen, at Windsor 1 Dec. 1898. Major Stuart-Wortley was Brigade Major, Malta, 18 Aug. 1893, to 17 Aug. 1896; was on Special Service, Egypt, 24 July, 1897, to 2 Dec. 1897; passed the Staff College. He served in the South African War 9 Dec. 1899, to 13 March, 1900, on the Staff; raised and commanded a Volunteer Corps of Stretcher-bearers, and commanded a battalion of Rifle Reservists. From 2 March to 20 June, 1900, he was in command of the 2nd Battn. King's Royal Rifle Corps at the relief of Ladysmith, including actions at Colenso, operations of 17 to 24 Jan. 1900, 5 to 7 Feb. 1900, and action at Vaal Krantz; operations on Tugela Heights (14–27 Feb. 1900), and also action at Laing's Nek (6 to 9 June). Operations in Orange River Colony, May to Oct. 1900. He was mentioned in Despatches (Sir R. H. Buller, 30 March and 9 Nov. 1900) [London Gazette, 8 Feb. 1901]; was given the Brevet of Lieutenant-Colonel 29 Nov. 1900, and received the Queen's Medal with six clasps. From 13 July, 1901, to 12 July, 1904, he was Military Attaché at Paris and Berne; was created an M.V.O. in 1903. He was given the Brevet of Colonel 21 March, 1904; created a C.B. in 1906, and became Colonel 23 Feb. 1907; was Brigadier-General, commanding the 10th Infantry Brigade, Shorncliffe, 8 April, 1908, to 27 April, 1912; was promoted to Major-General 8 March, 1913; commanded the North Midland Division from 1 June, 1914, to 5 July, 1916, in France, Belgium and Egypt, and the 65th Division, Home Forces, from 23 Dec. 1916, to 18 March, 1918. He holds the 2nd Class Red Eagle and Star; is an Officer of the Legion of Honour and a Knight of the Medjidie. General Stuart-Wortley married, in 1891, Violet, C.B.E., daughter of the late James Alexander Guthrie, of Craigie, N.B., and they have one son and two daughters.

WILSON, EDMOND MUNKHOUSE, Major, was born 4 Oct. 1855, at Oundle, Northamptonshire, youngest son of the late C. T. Wilson. He was educated at Sherborne and St. George's Hospital (M.R.C.S., England, L.R.C.P., London; D.P.H., Cambridge). He served as a Civil Surgeon in the Zulu War, receiving the Medal and clasp, and joined the Army 30 July, 1881, serving in the Sudan Expedition, 1884–85 (Nile Medal and clasp; Bronze Star). In the Sudan in 1885–86, he served with the Frontier Field Force. He served in the expedition up the Gambia against the Native Chief, Fodey Kabba, 1891–92. He became Major 30 July, 1893. In the Ashanti Expedition, Major Wilson was in command of a base hospital; was honourably mentioned; created a C.M.G., and received the Star. He served in the Nile Expedition of 1898, and was present at the Battle of Khartoum; was mentioned in Despatches [London Gazette, 30 Sept. 1898]; received the Egyptian Medal with clasp, and was created a Companion of the Distinguished Service Order [London Gazette, 15 Nov. 1898]: "Edmond Munkhouse Wilson, C.M.G., Major, Royal Army Medical Corps. In recognition of services during the recent operations in the Sudan." The Insignia were presented by the Queen at Windsor 1 Dec. 1898. Lieut.-Colonel Wilson was Director-General of A.M.S. at Headquarters, 1899 to 23 Sept. 1904, when he retired from the R.A.M.C. He was created a C.B. in 1902. He was at the R.A.M.C. Record Office, 1905 to 1913, and 1914 to 1916. He has written "Notes on Malarial Fever in connection with Meteorological Conditions at Sierra Leone, 1896–98."

COCKBURN, GEORGE MURRAY, Major, was born 9 Jan. 1856, son of Admiral J. H. Cockburn. He was educated at Eton, and joined the 80th Foot, as Lieutenant, 11 Nov. 1876, and the Rifle Brigade 30 Dec. 1876; was Instructor of Musketry, Rifle Brigade, 7 Aug. 1880, to 31 March, 1883; Captain 28 Aug. 1884; Adjutant, Rifle Brigade, 1 April, 1884, to 31 March, 1889, and Major 14 Nov. 1894. He served in the Nile Expedition in 1898, being present at the Battle of Khartoum; was mentioned in Despatches 30 Sept. 1898; received the Medal and the Egyptian Medal with clasp, and was created a Companion of the Distinguished Service Order [London Gazette, 15 Nov. 1898]: "George Murray Cockburn, Major, The Rifle Brigade, The Prince Consort's Own. In recognition of

George M. Cockburn.

services during the recent operations in the Sudan." The Insignia were sent to the Officer Commanding, Malta. The Presentation was deferred, and the decoration was presented at Kandia, Crete, by Sir H. Chermside, on 3 April, 1899. Major Cockburn was District Inspector of Musketry, Eastern District, 14 July, 1896, to 21 Jan. 1898. He served in the South African War, 1899 to 1901, being present at the operations in Natal in 1899, including the action at Lombard's Kop. Defence of Ladysmith, including action of 6 Jan. 1900. Operations in Natal, March to June, 1900, including action at Laing's Nek (6 to 9 June). Operations in the Transvaal 10 Nov. 1900, to Nov. 1901. He was in command of the 2nd Battn. Rifle Brigade, from 28 Aug. 1900, to 13 Oct. 1901; was mentioned in Despatches (Sir R. H. Buller, 13 Sept. and 9 Nov. 1900) [London Gazette, 8 Feb. 1901]; was given the Brevet of Lieutenant-Colonel, and received the Queen's Medal with three clasps. He became Lieutenant-Colonel 15 Oct. 1901; was given the Brevet of Colonel 8 May, 1904, and retired with the rank of Colonel 15 Oct. 1905. Colonel Cockburn married, in 1905, Alice Lindsay, daughter of Hasell Rodwell, of Tower House, Ipswich, and widow of Charles Reginald Orde, Rifle Brigade.

LAMBTON, THE HON. CHARLES, Major, was born 3 Nov. 1857, fourth son of the 2nd Earl of Durham and Beatrix, daughter of the 1st Duke of Abercorn. He was educated at Eton, and was gazetted to the 5th Foot 31 May, 1876, becoming Lieutenant 31 May, 1877; Adjutant, Northumberland Fusiliers, 2 Feb. 1881, to 8 March, 1882; Captain 25 July, 1883. He was A.D.C. to the Viceroy of Ireland 12 March, 1886, to 4 Aug. 1886, and 13 Sept. 1886, to 5 Oct. 1889, and became Major 21 Jan. 1895. He served in the Nile Expedition in 1898, being present at the Battle of Khartoum; was mentioned in Despatches [London Gazette, 30 Sept. 1898]; received the Egyptian Medal with clasp, and was created a Companion of the Distinguished Service Order [London Gazette, 15 Nov. 1898]: "The Hon. Charles Lambton, Major, The Northumberland Fusiliers. In recognition of services during the recent operations in the Sudan." The Insignia were presented

The Hon. C. Lambton.

by the Queen at Windsor 1 Dec. 1898. He served in the South African War from 1899 to 1902, in command of the 2nd Battn. Northumberland Fusiliers from 9 April, 1900, to 31 May, 1902. He was present in the advance on Kimberley, including actions at Belmont, Enslin, Modder River and Magersfontein. Operations in the Orange Free State, Feb. to May, 1900. Operations in the Transvaal, west of Pretoria, July to 29 Nov. 1900. Operations in Orange River Colony, May to June, 1900. Operations in Cape Colony, south of Orange River, 1899–1900. Operations in Cape Colony, north of Orange River. Commandant, Dewetsdorp. Operations in the Transvaal 30 Nov. 1900, to Aug. 1901. Operations in Orange River Colony, Aug. 1901, to 31 May, 1902. He was mentioned in Despatches [London Gazette, 26 Jan. 1900]; received the Queen's Medal with four clasps; the King's Medal with two clasps, and was given the Brevet of Colonel 29 Nov. 1900. He commanded the 2nd Batta. 5th Fusiliers, 1900–4, and retired with the rank of Colonel 17 Feb. 1904. Colonel Lambton married Marion, daughter of H. Garforth, and they have one daughter.

YOUNG, NORMAN EDWARD, Capt. and Brevet Major, was born 26 Oct. 1862. He was gazetted to the Royal Artillery 25 July, 1882, as Lieutenant, becoming Captain 20 May, 1891. From 14 July, 1892, to 23 Nov. 1898, Capt. Young was employed with the Egyptian Army. He took part in the expedition to Dongola in 1896, and was present at the operations of 7 June and 19 Sept. He was mentioned in Despatches [London Gazette, 3 Nov. 1896]; received the Brevet of Major 18 Nov. 1896, and the Egyptian Medal with two clasps. In the Nile Expedition of 1897 he was present at the action of Abu Hamed. He was mentioned in Despatches [London Gazette, 25 Jan. 1898], and received two clasps to his Egyptian Medal. He again saw service in the Nile Expedition of 1898, taking part in the Cavalry reconnaissance of 30 March, and in the Battles of Atbara and Khartoum. He was mentioned in Despatches [London Gazette, 30 Sept. 1898]; received the 4th Class Osmanieh; the Medal, and two clasps to the Egyptian Medal, and was created a Companion of the Distinguished Service Order [London Gazette, 15 Nov. 1898]: "Norman Edward Young, Capt. and Brevet Major, Royal Artillery. In recognition of services during the recent operations in the Sudan." The Insignia were presented by the Queen at Windsor 1 Dec. 1898.

LAWRIE, CHARLES EDWARD, Capt. and Brevet Major, was born in London 7 Dec. 1864, youngest son of the late Andrew Lawrie, of Mount Maseal, Bexley, Kent, and 1, Chesham Place, London, S.W., and of Eleanor, daughter of the late Rev. E. Johnson. He was educated at Cheam; Eton, and the Royal Military Academy, Woolwich, and joined the Royal Artillery 15 Feb. 1884. He was employed with the Bechuanaland Border Police Force 1 Jan. 1889, to 3 Jan. 1892; was on special service with the Lagos Jebu Expedition 30 March, 1892, to 30 July, 1892 (Medal and clasp; Despatches [London Gazette, 1 July, 1892]; slightly wounded). He became Captain 4 March, 1893; was employed with the Egyptian Army 13 Oct. 1893, to 29 Nov. 1898; served in the Expedition to Dongola. Operations of 7 June and 19 Sept. (Despatches [London Gazette, 3 Nov. 1896]; Brevet of Major 18 Nov. 1896; Khedive's Medal with two clasps). Nile Expedition in 1897 (clasp). Nile Expedition in 1898. Cavalry reconnaissance of 30 March. Battle of the Atbara (clasp; 4th Class Osmanieh); Battle of Omdurman. He was mentioned in Despatches 30 Nov. 1898; two clasps; Sudan Medal, and created a Companion of the Distinguished Service Order [London Gazette, 15 Nov. 1898]: "Charles

Edward Lawrie, Capt. and Brevet Major, Royal Artillery. In recognition of services in Egypt and the Sudan, including the Battles of Atbara and Khartoum." The Insignia were sent to the G.O.C., Egypt, and presented by the Duke of Connaught at Omdurman. He served in South Africa, 1899–1900, taking part in operations in the Orange Free State, Feb. to May, 1900. Operations in Orange River Colony, May to 29 Nov. 1900, including action at Wittebergen 1 to 29 July. Operations in Cape Colony, south of Orange River, 1899–1900. He was mentioned in Despatches [London Gazette, 10 Sept. 1901], and received the Queen's Medal with three clasps. He was promoted to Major 15 March, 1900; Lieutenant-Colonel 23 April, 1910, and Colonel 14 Dec. 1913. Colonel Lawrie served in the European War from 1914, as Temporary Brigadier-General, Royal Artillery, 19th Division, New Armies, British Expeditionary Force, 3 June, 1915, to 25 Dec. 1915; Brigadier-General, Royal Artillery, 2nd Army Corps, British Armies in France, 26 Dec. 1915, to 18 Feb. 1917; Temporary Major-General Commanding 63rd Division, British Armies in France, 19 Feb. 1917, to 1 Sept. 1918. He was mentioned in Despatches, and created a C.B. in 1915. He married, in 1898, Constance, only daughter of F. B. Salomans.

MAXSE, FREDERICK IVOR, Major, was born 22 Dec. 1862, eldest son of the late Admiral Maxse. He was educated at Rugby and Sandhurst, and gazetted to the Royal Fusiliers, as Lieutenant, 9 Sept. 1882; becoming Captain, Royal Fusiliers, 25 Oct. 1889, and Coldstream Guards 23 May, 1891. He was A.D.C. to the G.O.C., Scottish District, 23 Feb. 1893, to 4 Jan. 1894, and A.D.C. to the Governor and Commander-in-Chief, Malta, 5 Jan. 1894, to 12 Sept. 1894. He was employed with the Egyptian Army 12 Jan. 1897, to 8 Dec. 1899; served in the Nile Expedition in 1897, on the Staff of the G.O.C., and was present at the action of Abu Hamed. In the Nile Expedition of 1898 he served as Brigade Major, and was present at the Battles of the Atbara and Khartoum. He was mentioned in Despatches [London Gazette, 24 May and 30 Sept. 1898]; received two clasps to the Egyptian Medal, and was created a Companion of the Distinguished Service Order [London Gazette, 15 Nov. 1898]: "Frederick Ivor Maxse, Major, Coldstream Guards. In recognition of services during the recent operations in the Sudan." The Insignia were sent to the G.O.C., Egypt, and presented by the Duke of Connaught 19 Feb. 1899. He had been promoted to Major 1 Dec. 1897. Major Maxse was for a time Chief Staff Officer to the Military Governor of Khartoum. In the Nile Expedition of 1899 he was in command of the Sudanese Battn. in the Battle of El Gedid and the operations resulting in the final defeat of the Khalifa. He was mentioned in Despatches [London Gazette, 30 Jan. 1900]; was given the Brevet of Lieutenant-Colonel 14 March, 1900, and received the Medal and two clasps to the Egyptian Medal. He served in the South African War from 30 Dec. 1899; was employed with Transport 20 Jan. 1900, to 6 June, 1900, being A.A.G. for all transport columns of Mounted Infantry and Colonial Corps during the advance to Bloemfontein; commanded the transport of Ian Hamilton's force (12,000 men) during the march from Bloemfontein to Pretoria, and was Commissioner of Police 7 June, 1900, to 8 Oct. 1900, and commanded the Transvaal Constabulary after the entry of Lord Roberts into Pretoria in June, 1900. He was present at the Relief of Kimberley; at the operations in the Orange Free State, Feb. to May, 1900, including the operations at Paardeberg (17 to 26 Feb.); actions at Poplar Grove; Vet River (5 and 6 May) and Zand River. Operations in the Transvaal in May and June, 1900, including actions near Johannesburg and Pretoria. He was mentioned in Despatches [London Gazette, 8 Feb. 1901]: was created a C.B. (1900), and received the Queen's Medal with three clasps. He became Lieutenant-Colonel 29 Nov. 1903, and was given the Brevet of Colonel 20 Jan. 1905; commanded the 2nd Battn. Coldstream Guards, 1903–7; the Coldstream Regt. of Foot Guards, 1907–10; commanded the 1st Brigade, Aldershot Command, 1 Aug. 1910, to 4 Aug. 1914. He proceeded with the 1st Guards Brigade to France 12 Aug. 1914, and was promoted to Major-General 18 Aug. 1914; was present at the Retreat from Mons to Paris, and in the Battles of the Marne and the Aisne. In Oct. 1914, he was appointed to the command of the 18th Division at Colchester, and was on active service with this Division in 1915 and 1916, being present in the Battles of the Somme and the Ancre (Despatches five times). On 15 Jan. 1917, he assumed command of the 18th Army Corps, and in June, 1918, became Inspector-General of Training, British Armies in France. He was promoted to Lieutenant-General 1 Jan. 1919, and created a K.C.B. in 1917. Sir Ivor Maxse has the Grand Cross of the Crown of Belgium; is Commander of the Legion of Honour; has the Military Medal (France) and the Military Medal (Belgium). He published a book called "Seymour Vandeleur," in 1906. General Maxse married, in 1899, the Hon. Mary Caroline Wyndham, eldest daughter of the 2nd Baron Leconfield, and they have two sons and one daughter.

Frederick Ivor Maxse.

One of the most interesting chapters in "Seymour Vandeleur" describes "Omdurman, Sept. 1898," and we give an extract from the part of it which describes the second phase of the battle. "It had," says General Maxse, "lasted over four hours without many pauses, and was being more hotly contested than ever, when MacDonald was suddenly called upon to face another crisis. This time it menaced his right rear from the direction of the Kerreri hills. The Green Flags of Ali Wad Helu and Sheik-el-Din—the latter only just returned from his exhausting and abortive pursuit of Broadwood—were descending upon the rear of the 9th Sudanese whilst the battalion still confronted the Black Flags. It was a question of minutes and drill, and the minutes were at the disposal of one man—MacDonald. If he misused them his brigade would be swept away, Lewis's would follow a few minutes later, Collinson's too must be wiped out—together with hospitals, transport and reserve ammunition. Wauchope was moving to the scene of action at the double, but could scarcely have saved the situation if MacDonald's brigade had been overwhelmed. Thus Mahdism's last and only remaining chance depended on MacDonald's making a mistake, and he made none. He saw what was coming, knew exactly what to do, and did it. It was a matter of drill under high pressure, and he had been drilling his brigade under all circumstances during several years. He had risen from private soldier to the command of a brigade, and was now to justify his promotion. With calm precision he issued his orders, and in a few minutes all his battalions, batteries and Maxims were extricating themselves from their engagement with the Black Flags and threading their way at the double by the shortest route into a new alignment facing the Green Flags. The change of front had barely been executed when the Baggara Horse came charging home, followed by solid masses of riflemen and spearmen, just as the Black Flags had done before. Only this time there was only the cavalry and camel corps to come in on their flank. Vandeleur, writing home within a week of the event, said: 'The 9th, which was the first battalion to form up on the new front, had just got into position when down came another charge of horse, almost a better one than the last, followed by the attack of the footmen. Laurie's battery, on our left, soon exhausted its ammunition, but there were Maxims on our right, and the noise was tremendous. If the Green Flags had co-operated with the former attack and caught us in rear when we were engaged in front, it would have been extremely unpleasant. But the earlier attack had exhausted itself before the second came on, so we beat them in detail. The 1st British (Wauchope's) could be seen hurrying to support us, but the Dervish attack was done for before they came up. The thing was over and the cease fire sounded.'"

In "Seymour Vandeleur," in the chapter on "England on the Nile" (pages 135–136), Sir Ivor Maxse describes the state of the Egyptian Army before "one of the best days for Egypt occurred, when the Khedive signed the laconic decree, 'The Army is hereby disbanded.' That was in 1882. The young British officers who subsequently undertook to organize and command the squadrons, batteries and battalions of the new army, started the machine with a totally different conception of duty and military service to any which had hitherto prevailed. Indeed, the change was so bewildering to the native officers and men that at first the task seemed hopeless. However, with stubborn insular determination, they persevered on their own lines, without compromise, and without appearing to see any difficulty. Exact pay was handed out to the men on fixed dates; good barracks, solid food and clean clothing were provided; the discipline was strict and carefully enforced; promotion went solely by merit, and no intrigue could avail to alter a selection; furloughs were granted each year, and men went home to their squalid villages smart in appearance and with plenty of money in their pockets. They were no longer ashamed of themselves or their calling. When their term of six years' service expired, they left the colours to become local policemen. Then came years of active service, first on the lines of communication of Lord Wolseley's Nile Expedition, then on the frontier, continuously in touch with Dervishes, unsupported by other troops—with eyes always turned towards the desert and the enemy beyond. At intervals the Dervishes would attack patrols, or raid villages, and a skirmish would take place, a more or less serious affair, but always a useful experience to an army in training. Two pitched battles, at Ginniss in 1885 and Toski in 1889, attested the progress of the force. The fellaheen soldier began to feel he was a man, in fact became one. He at last understood his British officers, those curious foreigners who insisted on everyone doing his duty without shirking, and who did it themselves! In action, there they were always to the front, never excited; in cholera camp, still they were present working like slaves to stamp out the pestilence: always cheerful and approachable, yet maintaining their position as officers and the respect due to their rank."

Sir I. Maxse says elsewhere that Vandeleur "held that, though the Sudanese might be considered the flower of the army, the fellaheen cavalry, artillery and infantry were absolutely trustworthy troops."

This is a very fascinating book, and it grows upon the reader who takes it up a second time.

BUNBURY, VESEY THOMAS, Capt., was born 25 Sept. 1859, second son of the late Right Rev. Thomas Bunbury, D.D., Lord Bishop of Limerick. He was educated at St. Columba's College, County Dublin, and was commissioned in the 35th Foot 22 Jan. 1879, and transferred to the 3rd Foot 15 March, 1879; becoming Lieutenant, East Kent Regt., 20 Oct. 1880; Captain 1 July, 1887, and Captain, Leicestershire Regt., 19 Nov. 1887. He served in the Burmese War of 1889 (Medal and clasp); was Adjutant, Leicestershire Regt., 14 Jan. 1891, to 13 Jan. 1895, and was employed with the Egyptian Army 29 Nov. 1895, to 27 Aug. 1901; he served in the expedition to Dongola in 1896, taking part in the operations of 7 June and 19 Sept.; was mentioned in Despatches [London Gazette, 3 Nov. 1896]; Egyptian Medal with two clasps. In 1897 he served in the Nile Expedition, and was present at the capture of Abu Hamed. He was mentioned in Despatches [London Gazette, 4 Nov. 1898]; received the Medal; the clasp to the Egyptian Medal; the 3rd Class Medjidie, and was given the Brevet of Major 11 Dec. 1897. He served in the Nile Expedition of 1898, being present at the Battle of Khartoum; was mentioned in Despatches [London Gazette, 4 Nov. 1898]; received the Medal; a clasp to the Egyptian Medal, and was created a Companion of the Distinguished Service Order [London Gazette, 15 Nov. 1898]: "Vesey Thomas Bunbury, Capt. and Brevet Major, The Leicestershire Regt. In recognition of services during the recent operations in the Sudan." The Insignia were sent to the Office Commanding, Egypt, 2 Nov. 1898, and presented by the Duke of Connaught at Omdurman 29 Feb. 1899. He served in the Nile Expedition of 1899, and received a clasp to the Egyptian Medal. He became Major 27 Feb. 1900, and Lieutenant-Colonel 11 Nov. 1906. He became Colonel 11 Nov. 1910; was created a C.B. in 1911, and retired 21 May, 1913, with the rank of Brigadier-General. He served in the European War as Provost-Marshal to the British Expeditionary Force from Aug. 1914, to Dec. 1915; was mentioned in Despatches; created a C.M.G.; received the 1914 Star, the Croix de Guerre of Belgium, and was made Commander of the Crown of Belgium. He was retired from the Army 25 Sept. 1916, having reached the age limit for his rank, and was re-employed as Permanent President of an Area Quartering Committee, April, 1917, to May, 1918. General Bunbury has the Coronation Medal of 1902. He married, in 1904, the Hon. Daisy Carleton, daughter of Baroness Dorchester.

FERGUSSON, CHARLES, Capt. and Brevet Major, was born in Edinburgh 17 Jan. 1865, eldest son of the 6th Baronet of Kilkerran, Ayrshire, and Edith (who died in 1871), daughter of the Marquis of Dalhousie (extinct). He was educated at Eton and Sandhurst; became Lieutenant, Grenadier Guards, 7 Nov. 1883; was Adjutant, Grenadier Guards, 11 April, 1890, to 10 April, 1894, and was promoted Captain 1 Oct. 1895. He was employed with the Egyptian Army from 23 Jan. 1896, to 15 Oct. 1903; served with the expedition to Dongola in 1896, during operations of 7 June and 19 Sept. He was mentioned in Despatches [London Gazette, 3 Nov. 1896], and received the Egyptian Medal with two clasps. He served with the Nile Expedition in 1897; was present at the capture of Abu Hamed and subsequent occupation of Berber. He was mentioned in Despatches [London Gazette, 25 Jan. 1898], and received the Brevet of Major 17 Dec. 1897, and two clasps to Egyptian Medal. He took part in the Nile Expedition of 1898; was present at the Battle of the Atbara and Khartoum; defeat of Ahmed Fedil's Army (severely wounded). He was mentioned in Despatches [London Gazette, 24 May and 30 Sept. 1898, and 5 May, 1899]; received the Brevet of Lieutenant-Colonel 26 Dec. 1898, and three clasps to Egyptian Medal, and was also created a Companion of the Distinguished Service Order [London Gazette, 15 Nov. 1898]: "Charles Fergusson, Capt. and Brevet Major, Grenadier Guards. In recognition of services in Egypt and the Sudan, including the Battles of Atbara and Khartoum." He served with the Nile Expedition in 1899; took part in the first advance against the Khalifa; received clasp to Egyptian Medal and 3rd Class Medjidie; received Brevet of Colonel 29 Dec. 1900. He was promoted Major 23 Nov. 1898; Lieutenant-Colonel 8 Nov. 1904. He was Adjutant-General, Egyptian Army, 24 May, 1901, to 15 Oct. 1903; was created an M.V.O. in 1906; commanded the 3rd Battn. Grenadier Guards, from 1904 to 1907; promoted Colonel 1 Oct. 1907; was Brigadier-General, General Staff, Irish Command, from 1 Oct. 1907, to 16 Oct. 1908; created a C.B. in 1911; was Inspector of Infantry 1 April, 1909, to 8 Dec. 1912; commanded 5th Division, Feb. 1913, and served with it in the European War from Aug. 1914, to 18 Oct. 1914. He became Lieutenant-General on 18 Aug. 1914; commanded 9th Division, New Armies, British Expeditionary Force, 25 Oct. 1914, to 30 Dec. 1914; commanded 2nd Army Corps, British Expeditionary Force, 31 Dec. 1914, to 24 May, 1916; commanded 17th Army Corps, British Armies in France, from 25 May, 1916, to 31 March, 1919; was Military Governor of British Occupied German Territory from beginning of occupation until 15 Aug. 1919. He was seven times mentioned in Despatches, and created a K.C.B. in 1915, and K.C.M.G. in 1918. His foreign decorations are: France: Legion of Honour (Grand Officer) and Croix de Guerre avec Palme. Belgium: Order of the Crown (Grand Officer) and Croix de Guerre. Egypt: Medjidieh, 2nd Class. He had succeeded his father in 1907 as 7th Baronet of Kilkerran. In 1901 he married Lady Alice Mary Boyle, second daughter of the 7th Earl of Glasgow and Dorothea, daughter of Sir Edward Hunter-Blair, 4th Baronet, and they have three sons living: James, born 18 Sept. 1904; Simon Charles David, born 5 June, 1907, and Bernard Edward, born 6 May, 1911; and one daughter, Helen Dorothea.

CECIL, LORD EDWARD HERBERT, Brevet Major, was born on 12 July, 1867, and was the fourth son of the 3rd Marquess of Salisbury and of Georgina, daughter of the Hon. Sir Edward Hall Alderson, a Baron of the Exchequer. He was educated at Eton, and was gazetted to the Grenadier Guards 30 April, 1887, and was for some time on the Staff of Lord Wolseley, Commander-in-Chief in Ireland. He became Lieutenant 16 March, 1892. On 18 June, 1894, he married Violet Georgina, daughter of the late Admiral Maxse, and they had one daughter, Helen, and a son, George Edward, who was killed in action in France in Sept. 1914. As A.D.C. to the G.O. Commanding, he served with the Dongola Expeditionary Force in 1896, being present at the operations of 7 June and 19 Sept. 1896; was mentioned in Despatches 3 Nov. 1896; was given the Brevet of Major, and received the 4th Class Medjidie, the British Medal, and the Khedive's Medal with two clasps. He accompanied Sir Rennell Rodd in the special mission to King Menelik of Abyssinia in 1897, receiving the Star of Ethiopia and the Abyssinian Order. In 1898 he served in the Egyptian Campaign, which culminated in the fall of Khartoum and the conquest of the Sudan, being present at the action of Atbara and the Battle of Omdurman. Lord Edward Cecil was mentioned in Despatches 24 May and 30 Sept. 1898; received two clasps, and was created a Companion of the Distinguished Service Order [London Gazette, 15 Nov. 1898]: "Lord Edward Herbert Cecil, Capt. and Brevet Major, Grenadier Guards. In recognition of services in Egypt and the Sudan, including the Battles of Atbara and Khartoum." The Insignia were presented by the Queen at Windsor 1 Dec. 1898. He served throughout the South African War, in which he took a prominent part as Chief of the Staff, and afterwards as A.A.G. for the defence of Mafeking. Sir A. Conan Doyle tells us, in "The Great Boer War" (page 305), how, before the siege, "Baden-Powell, with the aid of an excellent group of special officers, who included Colonel Gould Adams, Lord Edward Cecil, the soldier son of England's Premier, and Colonel Hore, had done all that was possible to put the place in a state of defence." Lord Edward was subsequently Administrator of Marico and Rustenburg Districts (Queen's Medal with two clasps; Despatches, 8 Feb. 1901; Brevet of Lieutenant-Colonel 29 Nov. 1900). He returned to Egypt at the close of the South African War, and was subsequently for a time Sudan Secretary in Cairo. He was promoted to Major on 19 Aug. 1903, and Brevet Colonel 29 Nov. 1906, and retired 3 Aug. 1907, with the rank of Colonel. In 1904 Lord Edward became Agent-General of the Sudan and Director of Intelligence to the Egyptian Army at Cairo, where his conspicuous abilities soon came under the notice of Lord Cromer. In 1906 he was appointed Under Secretary of War to the Egyptian Government, and in the same year became Under Secretary of State for Finance, jointly with Mr. Mitchell-Innes, and in 1907, on the retirement of Mr. Mitchell-Innes, he became sole Under Secretary for Finance, and in 1912 was appointed, in succession to Sir Paul Harvey, Financial Adviser to the Egyptian Government, a post which he held up to the time of his death. He had become Colonel, and had retired from the Grenadier Guards on 3 Aug. 1907. The "Times" says of Lord Edward Cecil that "it fell to his lot, in a country where, perhaps more than in any other, all questions tend to resolve themselves into questions of finance, to take a prominent part in nearly every question of importance which arose in Egypt during a period of upwards of ten years. As Financial Adviser he had to deal with the new and unexpected situation created on the outbreak of the war and the consequent establishment of a protectorate in Egypt; and it is in no small measure due to the tact and firmness with which the financial aspects of the situation were handled that the Egyptian masses have remained quiet and contented throughout the war. Lord Edward Cecil possessed in a high degree that aptitude for public affairs which is a tradition of his great family. Imbued with the highest ideals and always unsparing of himself, he was ever most considerate and loyal both to superiors and subordinates, regardless of possible prejudice to his own interests or advancement. To all with whom he came in contact his manner was always most cordial and utterly devoid of condescension. In him the British Empire loses a servant who worked for it with a single-minded devotion to duty and without a thought of self-advancement. To his friends in Egypt and elsewhere (and they were many) Lord Edward's charm of manner, ability to talk well and interestingly on almost any subject, and readiness to help and advise when asked, will always be a grateful memory." He died at midnight on Saturday, 14 Dec. 1919, at Leysin, Switzerland, after a long illness contracted in serving his country.

Lord Edward Cecil.

HAMILTON, HUBERT ION WETHERALL, Major, was born 27 June, 1861; entered the Queen's Regt. in 1880; was Adjutant, 1886–90; served in the Burmese Expedition, 1886–88; received Medal with two clasps. He served in the Nile Expedition of 1897, and received Egyptian Medal with clasp; in the Expedition of 1898, and was present at the Battles of the Atbara and Khartoum; mentioned in Despatches [London Gazette, 24 May and 30 Sept. 1898]; received two clasps to Egyptian Medal, and also Medal; was created a Companion of the Distinguished Service Order [London Gazette, 15 Nov. 1898]: "Hubert Ion Wetherall Hamilton, Major, Royal West Surrey Regt. In recognition of services in Egypt and the Sudan, including the Battles of Atbara and Khartoum." The Insignia were sent to G.O.C., Egypt, 9 Dec. 1898, and presented by the Duke of Connaught at Omdurman 19 Feb. 1899). Capt. Hamilton was promoted Major in 1898; served in the Nile Expedition, 1899, as D.A.G.; in operations in first advance against Khalifa, and received a clasp to the Egyptian Medal. He served in South Africa, 1899–1902, as D.A.A.G., during operations in the Orange Free State, Feb. to May, 1900, including operations at Paardeberg (17 to 26 Feb.); during operations in the Transvaal in May and June, 1900, including actions near Johannesburg and Pretoria; during operations in the Transvaal, east of Pretoria, July to 29 Nov. 1900; during operations in the Transvaal, west of Pretoria, July to 29 Nov. 1900; in the operations in Orange River Colony, May to 29 Nov. 1900; during operations in Cape Colony, south of Orange River, 1899–1900; operations in the Transvaal, Orange River Colony; on the Zululand Frontier of Natal and in Cape Colony 30 Nov 1900, to 31 May, 1902; mentioned in Despatches [London Gazette, 8 Feb. and 16 April, 1901, and 29 July, 1902]. Promoted Lieutenant-Colonel (half-pay); A.D.C. to the King with Brevet of Colonel. He received the Queen's Medal with four clasps, and the King's Medal with two clasps; A.A.G., Army Headquarters, South Africa, in 1900. From 1900 to 1902 he was Military Secretary to General Lord Kitchener, Commander-in-Chief, South Africa. He was Military Secretary to General Lord Kitchener, Commander-in-Chief, India, 1902–5; was created a C.B. in 1906; commanded the 7th Brigade, 1906–8; became Major-General, General Staff, Mediterranean Command, 1908–9; was created a C.V.O. in 1909, and a K.C.B. in 1914. Sir Hubert Hamilton was killed in action 14 Oct. 1914, at La Coûture, France.

Lord Ernest Hamilton, in "The First Seven Divisions" (page 146), says: "Sir Hubert Hamilton, the Divisional General, . . . came along on foot to inspect the trenches, disregarding warnings as to the great danger he was running. He proceeded on foot down the Richebourg Road, which was swept by shell fire, in company with Capt. Strutt, commanding the Royal Scots, and was almost immediately killed by a shell, Capt. Strutt, being at the same time rendered unconscious. The General's A.D.C. Capt. Thorp, ran forward and knelt by Sir Hubert's body, trying to screen it from the shells which were now falling thickly on the road. Capt. Strutt shortly afterwards recovered consciousness, but was almost immediately wounded by another shell, and the command of the Royal Scots devolved upon Lieut. Cazenove."

An obituary notice of General Hamilton appeared in the "Times" of 19 Oct. 1914.

MATHIAS, HUGH BRODRICK, Major, was born at Tenby, Carmarthenshire, 9 March, 1863, second surviving son of the late George Mathias, of Tenby, and Caroline, daughter of the late Edward Law, of Staplegrove, Somerset; and brother of the late Colonel Mathias, C.B., A.D.C. He was educated at Allhallows Grammar School, Honiton, Devon, and St. Bartholomew's Hospital, London. He entered the Army as Surgeon in 1886; served in the Sudan Expedition in 1898, in medical charge of the 79th Queen's Own Cameron Highlanders. He was present at the Battles of Atbara and Khartoum; was mentioned in Despatches [London Gazette, 24 May and 30 Sept. 1898]; received the Egyptian Medal with two clasps, and Medal, and was created a Companion of the Distinguished Service Order [London Gazette, 15 Nov. 1898]: "Hugh Brodrick Mathias, Major, Royal Army Medical Corps. In recognition of services in Egypt and the Sudan, including the Battles of Atbara and Khartoum." The Insignia were presented by the Queen at Osborne 6 Jan. 1899. He served in the South African War, in medical charge of the Princess Christian Hospital (Despatches [London Gazette, 10 Sept. 1901]; received South African Medal with two clasps, and the King's Medal with two clasps). He was promoted to Lieutenant-Colonel 28 July, 1906, and was appointed P.M.O., Egyptian Army, 23 July, 1908. The late Lieut.-Colonel Mathias married, in 1893, Margaret Mary, only daughter of Paul Swain, F.R.C.S., of The Crescent, Plymouth, and they had one daughter.

SPONG, CHARLES STUART, Capt., was born at Faversham, Kent, 12 June, 1859, son of W. Nash Spong, F.R.C.S., and of Mrs. Spong. He was educated at Epsom College, and Guy's Hospital; is F.R.C.S., England, and joined the Army as Surgeon in 1887; was seconded to the Egyptian Army in 1890; served through the Sudan Campaign as S.M.O. to the 1st Egyptian Brigade. For his services in the Expedition to Dongola in 1896 he was mentioned in Despatches [London Gazette, 3 Nov. 1896], and received the 4th Class Medjidie. He served in the Nile Expedition of 1887, and was mentioned in Despatches [London Gazette, 25 Jan. 1898]. He again served in the Nile Expedition of 1898; was mentioned in Despatches [London Gazette, 24 May and 30 Sept. 1898]; received the English Sudan Medal, the Egyptian Sudan Medal wlth six clasps, and was created a Companion of the Distinguished Service Order [London Gazette, 15 Nov. 1898]: "Charles Stuart Spong, Capt., Royal Army Medical Corps. In recognition of services during the recent operations in the Sudan, including the Battle of Khartoum." The Insignia were sent to the G.O.C., Egypt, and presented by him at a full dress parade of the Cairo Garrison 20 Dec. 1899. He was promoted to Major 27 July, 1899, and has retired from the Royal Army Medical Corps. He was appointed Medical Officer to the Egyptian State Railways. He married, in 1890, Mary Barnsley, daughter of the late Henry Y. Pickering, of Titusville, Pennsylvania, and they have one daughter.

GODDEN, HENRY TUFTON, Major, was born 6 Dec. 1858, in London, son of Frederick Mares and Sarah Mary Godden. He was educated at the Royal Naval School, New Cross, and at private schools and the Royal Military College, Sandhurst; entered the Bedfordshire Regt. 13 Aug. 1879; was Adjutant, Bedfordshire Regt., 1 Jan. 1888, to 3 Dec. 1891, and became Captain 7 March, 1888. He served in the Dongola Expeditionary Force in 1896, as Brigade Major, 3rd Brigade; operations of 8 Sept. to 5 Oct. 1896; was mentioned in Despatches [London Gazette, 3 Nov. 1896], and received the Egyptian Medal with clasps for Firket and Hafir. He served in the Nile Expedition of 1897 (clasp to Medal); in the Nile Expedition of 1898, and was present at the Battle of Atbara; was mentioned in Despatches [London Gazette, 24 May, 1898]; received a clasp to Medal; the English Medal, and in recognition of his services in Egypt and the Sudan, including the Battle of Atbara, was created a Companion of the Distinguished Service Order [London Gazette, 15 Nov. 1898]: "Henry Tufton Godden, Capt., The Bedfordshire Regt." The Insignia were sent to the G.O.C., Egypt, and presented to the Commandant of Suakin at Suakin. He became Major 10 July, 1899. He served in the Nile Expedition of 1899; in the first advance against the Khalifa (clasp to Medal). He was Acting Governor of the Red Sea Littoral and Commandant at Suakin 29 April, 1898, to 6 March, 1899, and Administrator and Commandant at Suakin 7 March, 1899, to 25 March, 1902; received the 3rd Class Medjidie [London Gazette, 19 April, 1901], and the 3rd Class Osmanieh [London Gazette, 26 Sept. 1902]. He retired from the Army in 1906. On 11 Jan. 1911, at Fremantle, Western Australia, Major Godden married Amelia Marguerite Axell (English), second daughter of A. Axell, of Sittingbourne, Kent, and they have one son, Philip Axell Godden, born 16 Nov. 1911. Major Godden returned to England 29 Nov. 1914; was posted to the 9th Battn. The Bedfordshire Regt. 15 Jan. 1915, as Major; appointed Second-in-Command of the 9th Battn. The Bedfordshire Regt. 21 Jan. 1915, and appointed to command the 9th Battn. The Bedfordshire Regt. 7 Feb. 1915, and was replaced on retired pay 14 June, 1916.

FORD-HUTCHINSON, GEORGE HIGGINSON, Capt., was born 21 Oct. 1863, at Stranocum, County Antrim, Ireland, son of William Ford-Hutchinson, Esq., J.P., of Stranocum House, County Antrim, and Alice, daughter of the Rev. Leslie Creery, Archdeacon of Connor. He was educated at Monaghan Diocesan School; at Foyle College, Londonderry; at Trinity College, Dublin, and at the R.M. College, Sandhurst; and was gazetted to the Connaught Rangers as Lieutenant 9 May, 1885, becoming Captain 2 Nov 1891. He was on Special Service, Egypt, 21 March, 1896, to 18 Feb. 1897, and served in the Expedition to Dongola, 1896 (Egyptian Medal). From 19 Feb. 1897, to 26 March, 1899, he was employed with the Egyptian Army, and in 1897 he served in the Nile Expedition (clasp to Egyptian Medal). In the Nile Expedition of 1898 he was present at the Battles of Atbara and Khartoum; was mentioned in Despatches [London Gazette, 24 May and 30 Sept. 1898]; received the Medal and two clasps to the Egyptian Medal, and was created a Companion of the Distinguished Service Order [London Gazette, 15 Nov. 1898]: "George Ford-Hutchinson, Capt., The Connaught Rangers. In recognition of services during the recent operations in Egypt and the Sudan, including the Battles of the Atbara and Khartoum." The Insignia were presented by the Queen at Windsor 1 Dec. 1898. He served in the South African War from 8 June, 1900, to 8 July, 1902; as Railway Staff Officer (graded Staff Captain), South Africa, 8 June, 1900, to 21 May, 1901; as Railway Staff Officer 22 May, 1901, to 18 July, 1902. He was present at the Relief of Ladysmith, including the action at Colenso. Operations in the Transvaal, east of Pretoria, Aug. to Oct. 1900, including action at Belfast (26 and 27 Aug.). Operations in the Transvaal, west of Pretoria, Nov. 1900. Operations in Orange River Colony, Nov. 1900, on the Staff. He received the Queen's Medal with four clasps, and the King's Medal with two clasps. He was Adjutant, Militia, 10 Oct. 1902, to 15 Nov. 1904; became Major 16 Nov. 1904; became Lieut.-Colonel 16 July, 1910; commanded the 1st Battn. Connaught Rangers, 1910–14; retired 16 July, 1914. During the European War he commanded the 15th Service Battn. Connaught Rangers in 1914 and 1915, and served on the French front in command of this battalion in 1915. He married, 3 Sept. 1902, at Banagher Church, County Londonderry, Mary Stewart Moore, daughter of the late Rev. Canon Creery.

G. H. Ford-Hutchinson.

BOND, EDMUND EDWARD, Engineer-Capt., Royal Navy, was born on 19 Oct. 1865, son of Edmund and Sarah Bond. He was educated at the Royal Naval Engineering College, Devonport, and entered the Royal Navy 1 July, 1887; served in the Nile Campaign, 1898–99; from 1900 to 1914 was Director of Steamers Department, Sudan Government, in charge of gunboats, transport steamers, and other Government craft in the Upper Nile, from the Sixth Cataract (Assuan) to the Lakes (Uganda). Attached to Egyptian Army with successive ranks of Bimbashi, Kaimakam, Miralai and Lewa. He received the British and Egyptian Medals and one clasp; the Medjidie, Fourth Class; and was created a Companion of the Distinguished Service Order [London Gazette, 15 Nov. 1898]: "Edmund Edward Bond, Engineer-Capt., Royal Navy. In recognition of services in Egypt and the Sudan, including the Battle of Khartoum." Supervised reconstruction of three twin-screw gunboats sent out from England in parts, at Abodieh, near Berber, April to July, 1898. Acted as Supervising Engineer of flotilla in the operations up to Battle of Omdurman and subsequent defeat of the Khalifa, 1899. The Insignia were sent to the G.O.C., Egypt, and presented by the Duke of Connaught at Omdurman 19 Feb. 1899. He was specially promoted Chief Engineer 2 March, 1900; became Engineer-Commander 2 March, 1904, and retired Aug. 1907. He received other decorations for his services, these being the Third Class Osmanieh in 1907; a Companionship of St. Michael and St. George in 1913, and the Order of the Medjidie (Second Class) in 1914. He was appointed Engineer-Commander, H.M.S. Brilliant, Aug. 1914; present in operations on Belgian coast in Oct. 1914; from April, 1915, to July, 1919, on special service in connection with construction of light-draught gunboats, and as Engineer-Overseer, Manchester; Acting Engineer-Captain, Jan. 1917; retired with rank of Engineer-Captain, July, 1919.

COWAN, WALTER HENRY, Lieut., Royal Navy, was born on 11 June, 1871, at Alveston, son of Capt. W. F. Cowan, Royal Welsh Fusiliers, of Alveston, Warwickshire. He was educated on H.M.S. Britannia, Dartmouth, and joined the Royal Navy in 1886. He served in the Brass River Expedition, 1895; Mwele Expedition, Aug. 1895, H.M.S. Barrosa. Received the Royal Humane Society's Medal for, with two Able Seamen of that ship, saving the life of a Sepoy of the 24th Baluchistan Regt. in the Pungwe River, East Africa, whilst on a punitive expedition. He served in the Expedition to Benin, 1897. Mentioned in Despatches for Benin; General African Medal with two clasps. In 1898 he served in the Nile Expediton; in the Khartoum Campaign and at Fashoda, and in 1899 at the final defeat and death of the Khalifa. Twice mentioned in Despatches; Sudan Medal and three clasps; Medjidie, Fourth Class; British Sudan Medal, and created a Companion of the Distinguished Service Order [London Gazette, 15 Nov. 1898]: "Walter Henry Cowan, Lieut., Royal Navy. In recognition of services in Egypt and the Sudan." A.D.C. to Lord Kitchener in the South African War, 1900, and subsequently Naval A.D.C. to Lord Roberts (South African Medal and three clasps; mentioned in Despatches); M.V.O., 1904, and was promoted Captain, 1906. From 1910 to 1912 he was Captain, H.M.S. Gloucester. He served in the European War; took part in the Battle of Jutland, in command of H.M.S. Princess Royal, 31 May, 1916, and greatly distinguished himself. He was mentioned in Despatches, created a C.B., and a K.C.B. 1 Jan. 1919. He was afterwards in command of the 1st Light Cruiser Squadron, and served in the Baltic, 1919. He became Captain, H.M.S. Princess Royal, in 1916, and was Rear-Admiral 2 Sept. 1918. Sir W. Cowan married, in 1901, Catherine, daughter of Digby Cayley.

BLENKINSOP, LAYTON JOHN, Capt., was born 27 June, 1862, third son of Lieut.-Colonel William Blenkinsop and Elizabeth, daughter of William Sandford. He was educated at King's School, Canterbury, and at the Royal Veterinary College, London, and was Coleman Medallist, 1883. He entered the Army Veterinary Department, 1883; was Advising Veterinary Surgeon to the Punjab Government, and Professor at Lahore Veterinary College, 1891–93; was S.V.O. for British troops, Sudan Expedition, 1898 (Despatches; Egyptian Medal with clasp; English Medal; created a Companion of the Distinguished Service Order [London Gazette, 15 Nov. 1898]: "Layton John Blenkinsop, Capt., Army Veterinary Department. In recognition of services during the recent operations in Egypt and the Sudan, including the Battle of Khartoum." Insignia sent to G.O.C., Egypt, and presented by him, 20 Dec. 1898, at a full-dress parade of the Cairo Garrison). He was Senior Veterinary Officer in Egypt, 1896–99; served in South Africa, 1899–1902, as S.V.O., Cavalry Division, under Lieut.-General Sir J. D. F. French, until Sept. 1901, and S.V.O. Remounts in South Africa to Dec. 1902 (Despatches; South African Medal with six clasps; King's Medal with two clasps; promoted Major); became Lieut.-Colonel, A.V.C., 15 March, 1903; Principal Veterinary Officer, 3rd Army Corps, and P.V.O., Irish Command, 19 April, 1904, to 3 Aug. 1906. He was Principal Veterinary Officer, South Africa, 2 Sept. 1906, to 24 Nov. 1909; became Colonel 15 March, 1908; was Principal Veterinary Officer, Northern Command, 22 Feb. 1910, to 20 April, 1910; Principal Veterinary Officer, Southern Command, 20 April, 1910, to 31 Dec, 1912, and Assistant Director of Veterinary Services, Aldershot Command, 1 Jan. 1913, to 1 Jan. 1914. Colonel Blenkinsop became Inspecting Veterinary Officer, India, 8 Feb. 1914, and Director, Veterinary Service in India, with rank of Brigadier-General, on 24 July, 1916, and on the 1st Dec. 1918, was appointed Director-General, Army Veterinary Service, War Office, with rank of Major-General. He was made a Fellow of the Royal Geographical Society in 1905. He married, 1905, Ethel Alice, daughter of John Wells, Esq., J.P., Booth Ferry House, Goole, Yorkshire.

MATHEW, CHARLES MASSY, Capt., was born at Wexford 16 May, 1866, eldest son of the late Surgeon-Major C. B. Mathew and Mary, daughter of the late Capt. J. M'Call, 4th Dragoon Guards. He was educated at a private school, and at Portsmouth Grammar School, and joined the 2nd Durham Light Infantry 23 Aug. 1884. He served in the Sudan, 1885–86, with the Frontier Field Force, being present at the action of Ginniss (Medal and Bronze Star). He became Captain, Durham Light Infantry, 11 April, 1894; was transferred to the Army Ordnance Corps, and was Adjutant, A.O. Corps, 3 July, 1899, to 7 Sept. 1903. He served in the Ashanti Expedition, 1895–96 (Star). In 1896 he served in the Expedition to Dongola, being present at the action of Hafir; was mentioned in Despatches 3 Nov. 1896, and received the Egyptian Medal with clasp. He served in the Nile Expedition of 1898, and was present at the Battle of Khartum. He was mentioned in Despatches 30 Sept. 1898; received the Medal and clasp, and was created a Companion of the Distinguished Service Order [London Gazette, 15 Nov. 1898]: "Charles Massy Mathew, Capt., The Durham Light Infantry. In recognition of services during the recent operations in the Sudan, including the Battle of Khartoum." The Insignia were sent to the G.O.C., Egypt, and presented at a full-dress parade of the Cairo Garrison. He served in the South African War, 1899–1901, and was present at the operations in Orange River Colony, Feb. to July, 1901; operations in Cape Colony, Feb., July and Aug. 1901. He received the Queen's Medal and three clasps. He became Major 1 Feb. 1904; Lieut.-Colonel 19 Jan. 1905, and Colonel 26 Nov. 1910. In 1910 he became Chief Ordnance Officer, Southern Command, and he was created a C.B. in 1911. He was Assistant Director of Ordance Stores, Southern Command. He served in the European War from 1914; was mentioned in Despatches twice, and created a C.M.G. On 17 Aug. 1917, Colonel Mathew was appointed Principal Ordnance Officer (temporary), and he was promoted to Major-General 17 Aug. 1917, and created a K.C.M.G. Sir Charles Mathew married, in 1911, Janet, second daughter of Sir James Knox, and they have two daughters. His favourite recreations are shooting, golf and lawn tennis.

TECK, HIS SERENE HIGHNESS PRINCE FRANCIS JOSEPH LEOPOLD FREDERICK OF, Capt., was born at Kensington Palace 9 Jan. 1870, second son of the late Duke of Teck and of Her Royal Highness late Princess Mary Adelaide. He was educated at Wellington College; Cheltenham, and at the Royal Military College, Sandhurst, and was gazetted to the 9th Lancers 30 Jan. 1889; to the K.R.R.C. 17 April, 1889, and to the 1st Dragoons 8 Oct. 1890. He became Lieutenant 26 Aug. 1891, and Captain 25 July, 1894. He was A.D.C. to the General Officer Commanding at Quetta 25 Nov. 1896, to 2 Aug. 1897; was on Special Service, Egypt, 6 Aug. to 6 Dec. 1897; was employed with the Egyptian Army 7 Dec. 1897, to 15 Sept. 1898, and served in the Nile Expedition in 1897 (Medal). He again saw active service in the Nile Expedition of 1898; Battles of the Atbara and Khartoum. He was mentioned in Despatches [London Gazette, 24 May and 30 Sept. 1898]; received two clasps, and was created a Companion of the Distinguished Service Order [London Gazette, 15 Nov. 1898]: "His Serene Highness Prince Francis Joseph Leopold Frederick of Teck, Capt., 1st Dragoons. In recognition of services during the recent operations in Egypt and the Sudan, including the Battles of the Atbara and Khartoum." The Insignia were presented by the Queen at Windsor 1 Dec. 1896. He was A.D.C. to the G.O.C., South-Eastern District, 11 Jan. to 23 July, 1899, and was Staff Captain, Remount Establishment, 24 July, 1899. He served in the South African War on the Staff from 1899–1902; employed with the Remount Department (graded D.A.A.G.), 29 May to 9 Dec. 1900. He was present at the operations in the Transvaal in May, 1902; was mentioned in Despatches [London Gazette, 1 April, 1901]; was given the Brevet of Major, and received the Queen's Medal with three clasps. He became Major 29 Nov. 1900, and retired from the Army in 1902. Prince Francis was created a K.C.V.O., and was a Knight of Justice of St. John of Jerusalem. He died 22 Oct. 1910.

The following is an extract from an appreciation of Prince Francis which appeared in the "Times" of 24 Oct. 1910:

"The death of Prince Francis will be mourned by a singularly large circle of friends. A man of frank and genial personality, an interesting companion, a keen sportsman, and a staunch friend, he was extremely popular in society. 'He had great charm,' a gentleman who had known the Prince for many years remarked on hearing of his serious illness, 'and everybody who knew him liked him enormously.' In his outlook upon life and in temperament generally, Prince Francis was essentially English. Like his brothers and sister, he was devoted to his mother, and proud of his descent from George III. The Duchess of Teck, for her part, was devoted to her sons. The Bishop of Peterborough once remarked—as recorded in Sir C. Kinlock-Cooke's Memoir of the Princess: 'The Duchess of Teck often talked to me about her boys, sometimes with tears in her eyes.' On one occasion she said to Mrs. Dalrymple, speaking with much earnestness, "I pray they may each of them in turn grow up a credit to us all, and be thorough English boys; they are so as yet, thank God."'

"The happy childhood of the Queen and her brothers at the White Lodge had a lasting effect upon their characters. The words of a correspondent who contributed to the 'Times' an appreciation of Queen Mary soon after the death of the late King, may fittingly be recalled: 'A singularly united family, and one, moreover, taught from the earliest days that a man's life does not consist in the abundance of his possessions, sister and brothers grew up to enjoy simple, wholesome pleasures, to make their own amusements, enter into each other's games and sports, and share each other's childish joys and sorrows. . . . The Duke and Duchess of Teck, believing as they did most thoroughly in the value of home life, were careful never to omit those little family observances which mean so much to the young. Every birthday, as it came round, was duly remarked by some special concession to the honoured child. . . . The remembrance of these days and of many joyous Christmases spent in the family circle is still among their happiest recollections.'

"In the published correspondence of the Duchess of Teck and in her diary there are frequent references to Prince Francis and the other children. One interesting passage may be quoted. Writing to the Hon. Lucy Kerr, in Sept. 1872, the Duchess says: 'I am thankful to say that May is once more a strong child, though a tall, wiry one by the side of her sturdy brothers, the younger of whom is a perfect little giant and a great pet. Dolly and Frank are splendid specimens of boyhood, the one brown-haired, the other chestnut-brown, and fully answer to their sister's appellation of "Beauty Boys."'

"Prince Francis grew up with a passion for the English open-air life, for English sports and for the British Army. Like his brothers, he was destined for a military career. It was the wish of the Duchess of Teck that her sons should be soldiers, and one after another they gratified this desire of their mother's heart by entering the Army.

"Sir C. Kinlock-Cooke relates that one day the Princess was making some purchases at a well-known shop in the West End of London. Ascertaining from one of the partners in the firm that he had boys at school, she began talking about her own sons, remarking, 'No one knows what we parents have to go through with all these examinations.' Each of the sons was sent to a public school—Prince Francis to Wellington, and afterwards to Cheltenham. . . .

"Prince Francis was an expert horseman and an enthusiastic fox hunter. Horses, indeed, may be said to have been a hobby with him. His work in the Remount Department, therefore, was a labour of love. In Ireland, when quartered in Dublin, he won the sympathy of the humbler classes, his courteous and genial manners, his kindness of heart and his cheerfulness being still recollected by those whom he visited in hospital there. Some years ago he paid a visit to India, while his friend, Lord Sandhurst, was the Governor of Bombay, and, with characteristic eagerness to acquire knowledge of any subject in which he was interested, took the opportunity to study some phases of the problem of Indian administration. The Prince was 'thorough' in everything he undertook. He was deeply interested in his military work, and was known in the Army as a keen and capable soldier. His devoted labours in the cause of the medical charities of London—and more particularly on behalf of the Middlesex Hospital—are well known. The Prince was an enthusiastic theatre-goer, and was generally to be seen in the audience on the occasion of a 'first-night.' His was a familiar figure at the gatherings of the Beefsteak Club. . . .

"Keenly interested in every aspect of motoring, Prince Francis—with the approval of King Edward, Patron of the Royal Automobile Club—accepted the unanimous invitation of the club, in June, 1908, to succeed Mr. (now Sir) C. D. Rose, M.P., as its chairman. In taking the chair, on the proposition of the Hon. Arthur Stanley, seconded by Sir Boverton Redwood, Prince Francis said: 'I will do my best to promote the welfare of the Royal Automobile Club in every possible way. I will leave no stone unturned to see that the interests of the automobile world of Great Britain and Ireland receive careful attention.' He was as good as his word, and again gave the amplest proofs of his administrative ability and his absolute mastery of details, while he spared no pains to encourage the vigorous growth of local associations. As chairman of the R.A.C. he was closely concerned in the erection of the new club house in Pall Mall, and devoted much thought and care to the decoration of the building. The scheme also by which the R.A.C. admitted associate members was largely due to him. Motoring may be said to have lost in him a very valuable friend, whose great influence and thoughtful advice were ever at its service."

PEYTON, WILLIAM ELIOT, Capt., was born 7 May, 1866, third son of the late Colonel J. Peyton, late Commanding 7th Dragoon Guards. He was educated at Brighton College, and enlisted in the 7th Dragoon Guards in 1885; was commissioned 7th Dragoon Guards 18 June, 1887; became

Lieutenant 20 June, 1892, and was Adjutant 20 June, 1892, to 26 March, 1896. He was employed with the Egyptian Army 27 March, 1896, to 24 Nov. 1898; became Captain 8 April, 1896. He served in the Expedition to Dongola, 1896, taking part in the operations of 7 June and 19 Sept. He was mentioned in Despatches [London Gazette, 3 Nov. 1896], and received the Egyptian Medal with two clasps. He served in the Nile Expedition of 1897; was dangerously wounded, and had his horse speared in the cavalry engagement at Salamat (Fourth Class Medjidie and clasp to Egyptian Medal). In the Nile Expedition of 1898 he was present at the Reconnaissance of 4 April, Battles of the Atbara and Khartum. He was mentioned in Despatches [London Gazette, 30 Sept. 1898]; received the Medal, two clasps to the Egyptian Medal, and was created a Companion of the Distinguished Service Order [London Gazette, 15 Nov. 1898]: "William Eliot Peyton, Capt., 15th Hussars. In recognition of services during the recent operations in the Sudan, including the Battles of Atbara and Khartum." The Insignia were presented to him by the Queen at Windsor 1 Dec. 1898. He was promoted to Major 15 Oct. 1899. He served in the South African War from 19 May, 1900, to 25 Oct. 1900, as Special Service Officer. He served with Thorneycroft's Mounted Infantry. He took part in the operations in Natal, May to June, 1900, including the action at Laing's Nek. Operations in the Transvaal, June to Aug. 1900; operations in the Orange River Colony, Sept. 1900. He was mentioned in Despatches [London Gazette, 8 Feb. 1901; was given the Brevet of Lieut.-Colonel 29 Nov. 1900, and received the Queen's Medal with three clasps. He became Lieut.-Colonel 10 Jan. 1907, and commanded the 15th Hussars from 1903 to 1907; was given the Brevet of Colonel 5 May, 1905, and promoted to Colonel 10 Oct. 1907; was A.Q.M.G., H.Q., India, 18 Oct. 1907, to 2 July, 1908; commanded Meerut Cavalry Brigade 3 July, 1908, to 30 June, 1912; was Military Secretary to H.E. the Commander-in-Chief in India 1 July, 1912, to 7 March, 1914, and Delhi Herald of Arms Extraordinary for the occasion of the Coronation Durbar 12 Dec. 1911. On the outbreak of the European War he became G.S.O.1, 1st Mounted Division, Central Force, Home Defence, and he commanded the 2nd Mounted Division on Gallipoli Peninsula; action of 21 Aug. 1915, and final evacuation 19 Dec. 1915 (Despatches twice). On 26 Oct. 1914, he was promoted to Major-General. He commanded the Western Frontier Force, Egypt (20 Jan. 1916, to 7 May, 1916) in the expedition against the Senussi, including the reoccupation of Barani and Sollum, and the rescue of the shipwrecked British prisoners of H.M.S. Tara (received special thanks of the Admiralty; Despatches). General Peyton was Military Secretary, British Armies in France, 8 May, 1916, to 6 April, 1918; Army Commander, Reserve Army, British Armies in France, 7 April, 1918, to 3 July, 1918; commanded the 40th Division during the operations in France and Flanders 4 July, 1918, to March, 1919; commanded the cavalry of the British Army on the Rhine. He was created a K.C.B. (1917); Commandeur, Légion d'Honneur; was given the Order of the Nile, Second Class, 1916. He was appointed Colonel of the 15th Hussars, 1916. Sir William Peyton married (1st) Mabel Maria (who died in 1901), daughter of the late Lieut.-General the Hon. E. T. Gage, C.B., third son of the 4th Viscount Gage, and they had one daughter. He married (2ndly) in 1903, Gertrude (who died in 1916), daughter of Major-General A. R. Lemprière and widow of Capt. Stuart Robertson, 14th Hussars, and they had one son.

In Sir John Maxwell's Despatch, dated 9 April, 1916, he described the operations under General Peyton and the distinguished services of Brigadier-General H. T. Lukin, C.M.G., D.S.O., Colonel Soutar, the Duke of Westminster and other officers.

He concludes his Despatch with these words: "I think it may be fairly claimed that seldom has a small campaign been so completely successful or had such far-reaching results. The effect of this success has been to remove the anxiety which was at once felt as to the possibility of hostile outbreaks in Egypt itself, where agitation was known to be rife. The attitude of the people in Alexandria, and more especially of the very large Bedouin population of the Behera province, has completely changed, and any prestige which we have lost through the evacuation of Sollum has been more than recovered. Moreover, through his failure as a temporal leader, Sayed Ahmed has lost much of the influence which was attached to him as a spiritual head."

MACBEAN, JOHN ALBERT EMMANUEL, Capt., was born 6 June, 1865, and joined the Royal Dublin Fusiliers 4 May, 1887, becoming Lieutenant 6 March, 1889, and Captain 6 May, 1896. He served in the Nile Expedition in 1897, being present at the action of Abu Hamed. He was mentioned in Despatches [London Gazette, 25 Jan. 1898], and received two clasps to the Egyptian Medal. In the Nile Expedition of 1898 he was present at the Battles of the Atbara and Khartum; was mentioned in Despatches [London Gazette, 24 May and 30 Sept. 1898]; received two clasps to the Egyptian Medal, and was created a Companion of the Distinguished Service Order [London Gazette, 15 Nov. 1898]: "John Albert Emmanuel MacBean, Capt., The Royal Dublin Fusiliers. In recognition of services during the recent operations in Egypt and the Sudan, including the Battles of the Atbara and Khartum." The Insignia, etc., sent to the G.O.C., Egypt, 2 Dec. 1898, and presented by the Adjutant-General, Egyptian Army, Cairo. Capt. MacBean died 13 Dec. 1900.

BROOKE, RONALD GEORGE, Capt., was born 25 Sept. 1866, second son of Sir Victor Brooke, 3rd Baronet, and Alice, daughter of Sir Alan Bellingham, 3rd Baronet. He was educated at Marlborough,

Ronald George Brooke.

and Sandhurst; passed the Staff College; was gazetted to the 7th Hussars, 1886; was extra A.D.C. to the Governor of Bombay; Orderly Officer to General Gatacre, commanding 3rd Brigade, Chitral Relief Force (mentioned in Despatches [London Gazette, 15 Nov. 1895]; Medal with clasp); Orderly Officer to General Yeatman Biggs, commanding 2nd Division, Tirah Expeditionary Force, 1897 (two clasps); was A.D.C. to General Gatacre during the Atbara and Khartum Campaigns, 1898; received the Medal with two clasps, was mentioned in Despatches [London Gazette, 24 May and 30 Sept. 1898], and was created a Companion of the Distinguished Service Order [London Gazette, 15 Nov. 1898]: "Ronald George Brooke, Capt., 7th Hussars. In recognition of services in Egypt and the Sudan, including the Battles of Atbara and Khartum." Insignia presented by the Queen at Windsor 1 Dec. 1898. He was also A.D.C. to General Gatacre when the latter was commanding the Eastern District. He served in the South African War, 1899–1902, as A.D.C. on the Staff to Lieut.-General Sir George White, and D.A.A.G. to Elliot's Division from Feb. 1902, and employed with the South African Light Horse. He served in the operations in Natal, 1899, including the action at Elandslaagte (severely wounded), and at the Defence of Ladysmith; operations in Orange River Colony, Jan. to 31 May, 1902; operations in Cape Colony, Dec. 1901, to Jan. 1902. He was mentioned in Despatches by Sir George White 2 Dec. 1899; by Sir Redvers Buller 19 June and 9 Nov. 1900 [London Gazette, 8 Feb. 1901]; received the Queen's Medal with seven clasps, the King's Medal with two clasps, and was given the Brevet of Major. He served in East Africa from 1902 to 1904, in Somaliland, on the Staff, as D.A.A.G., Lines of Communication, Obbia Force, from 16 Jan. 1903. He was mentioned in Despatches by Brigadier-General Manning 17 Aug. 1903, and Sir C. Egerton 30 May, 1904 [London Gazette, 2 Sept. 1904]; received the Medal with two clasps, and was given the Brevet of Lieut.-Colonel 1 July, 1904. He retired 13 June, 1908, with the rank of Colonel. In the European War Colonel Brooke commanded the 12th Reserve Cavalry Regt. He was given a C.B.E. in 1919. He married in 1908, Haller, daughter of the late Orville Horwitz, of Baltimore, Maryland, formerly wife of C. A. C. Ponsonby, whom she divorced in 1907.

PIRIE, ARTHUR MURRAY, Lieut., was born 3 May, 1869, third son of Gordon Pirie, of Waterton. He entered the 21st Lancers 30 Jan. 1889; served in the Sudan, 1898, including Khartum (slightly wounded). He was mentioned in Despatches [London Gazette, 30 Sept. 1898]; received the British Medal, Khedive's Medal with clasp, and the Fourth Class Medjidie, and was created a Companion of the Distinguished Service Order [London Gazette, 15 Nov. 1898]: "Arthur Murray Pirie, Lieut. 21st Lancers. In recognition of services in Egypt and the Sudan, including the Battles of Atbara and Khartum." Insignia, etc., sent to G.O.C., Egypt, and presented by the Duke of Connaught 19 Feb. 1899. He became Captain, 1899;

Arthur Murray Pirie.

Major 23 Dec. 1903, and retired 17 Sept. 1904. Major Pirie went out to France with the B.E.F. in 1914, and served with the Irish Life Guards as Second-in-Command, commanding a brigade of machine guns; was mentioned in Despatches Jan. 1917. In 1917 he went to Palestine, commanding the Berkshire Yeomanry, and was killed in action 21 Nov. 1917, at Beylunia, about 20 miles north of Jerusalem, a hill which he held for two days against tremendous odds, and where he is buried. The following notices appeared in the newspapers: "Killed in action on the 21st Nov., Lieut.-Colonel Arthur Murray Pirie, D.S.O., Lancers, Commanding Yeomanry, of St. Mary's, Medmenham Abbey, Marlow, and Heliopolis, Egypt." "A memorial service for Lieut.-Colonel Arthur Murray Pirie, D.S.O., Lancers, Commanding Yeomanry, killed in action on 21 Nov., will take place in St. Peter's Church, Medmenham, Marlow, to-morrow at 3."

TULLIBARDINE, THE MARQUIS OF (DUKE OF ATHOLL), Lieut., was born 15 Dec. 1871, son of the 7th Duke of Atholl (who died in 1917) and Louisa (who died in 1902), daughter of Sir Thomas Moncrieffe, 7th Baronet. He was educated at Eton; was Lieutenant, 3rd Battn. Black Watch, 1890–91; joined the Royal Horse Guards 28 Dec. 1892, as Second Lieutenant, from the Militia, and became Lieutenant 30 Dec. 1893; was specially employed with the Egyptian Army 18 Jan. 1898, to 26 Sept. 1898. He served with the Egyptian Cavalry as Staff Captain to Colonel Birdwood; was present at the reconnaissance of Atbara, and at the Battles of Atbara and Khartum; received the Medal and two clasps; was mentioned in Despatches twice (24 May and 30 Sept. 1898), and was created a Companion of the Distinguished Service Order [London Gazette, 15 Nov. 1898]: "John George, Marquis of Tullibardine, Lieut., Royal Horse Guards. In recognition of services in Egypt and the Sudan, including the Battles of Atbara and Khartum." The Insignia were presented to him by the Queen at Windsor 1 Dec. 1898. Lord Tullibardine became Captain 20 Nov. 1899. He served in the South African War, 1899–1902, on the Staff, attached to the Royal Dragoons, and was present at the Relief of Ladysmith, including operations at Colenso; operations of 17 to 24 Jan. 1900, and action at Spion Kop; operations of 5–7 Feb. 1900, and action at Vaal Kranz; operations on Tugela Heights 14 to 27 Feb. 1900, and action at Pieter's Hill; operations in Natal, March to June, 1900; afterwards as Lieut.-Colonel, commanding the 1st and 2nd Scottish Horse. He was mentioned in Despatches [London Gazette, 8 Feb. and 10 Sept. 1901, and 29 July, 1902]; was given the Brevet of Major 20 Nov. 1900, and received the Queen's Medal with three clasps. In the European

War Lord Tullibardine commanded the Scottish Horse Mounted Brigade, Home Defence; 1st Dismounted Brigade, Gallipoli and Egypt, 15 Aug. 1914, to 26 Oct. 1916, and was Brigade-Commander, 10th Cyclist Brigade, Home Forces, from 12 June, 1917. He was mentioned in Despatches for Gallipoli and Egypt; created a C.B.; received the Serbian Order of the White Eagle of Serbia, with crossed swords, Third Class. His brother, Lord George Stewart Murray, Major, Black Watch, was killed in action in 1914. His other brother, Lord James Thomas Stewart Murray, was a prisoner of war in Germany. In a letter to the "Morning Post," appealing for more recruits, Lord Tullibardine said: "With regard to the district of Atholl—the district I know best—there may still be a few men left, but I think not many. I can only say that if there are any on my estate they can trust that their dependents will be looked after while they are away, that their places will be kept open for them." He succeeded his father in 1917 as 8th Duke of Atholl. From 1910 to 1917 he was M.P. (U.) for West Perthshire; he is D.L., and has been created an M.V.O. "The Duke of Atholl has been described as a Highlander of the Highlanders, and he is a true Scotsman in his amusements—shoots, fishes and plays the national game of curling." The Duke of Atholl married, in 1899, Katharine Marjory, O.B.E., daughter of Sir James Ramsay, 10th Baronet, of Banff.

STEVENSON, ALEXANDER GAVIN, Lieut., was born 15 Oct. 1871, son of the late Archibald Stevenson, South Garth, South Shields. He was educated at Woolwich; entered the Royal Engineers 13 Feb. 1891; became Lieutenant 12 Feb. 1894, and was employed with the Egyptian Army 13 Sept. 1895, to 12 Nov. 1899. He served in the Dongola Expeditionary Force, 1896 (Despatches [London Gazette, 3 Nov. 1896]; Fourth Class Medjidie). For the Nile Expedition of 1898 he received a clasp, and a clasp to the Egyptian Medal. He served in the Nile Expedition of 1898; was present at the Battle of Khartum; was mentioned in Despatches [London Gazette, 30 Sept. 1898]; received the Medal, and a clasp to the Egyptian Medal, and was created a Companion of the Distinguished Service Order [London Gazette, 15 Nov. 1898]: "Alexander Gavin Stevenson, Lieut., Royal Engineers. In recognition of services in Egypt and the Sudan, including the Battle of Khartum." The Insignia were presented to him by the High Commissioner of Cyprus, at Nigeria, 29 Dec. 1898. He served as Railway Staff Officer, South Africa, 15 Jan. to 2 Dec. 1900, and Locomotive Superintendent, South Africa, 5 July, 1900, to 4 July, 1901, and was promoted to Captain 1 Oct. 1901. He was present in the advance on Kimberley; operations in the Orange Free State, Feb. to May, 1900; operations in the Transvaal, Orange River Colony and Cape Colony, Nov. 1900, to March, 1901. Capt. Stevenson was mentioned in Despatches [London Gazette, 10 Sept. 1901], and received the Queen's Medal with three clasps. He was employed on the South African Railways up to 30 June, 1904; was employed on Central South African Railways (Special Extra-Regimental Employment), 1 July, 1904, to 30 March, 1905; employed on Railway Survey, Uganda and East African Protectorates, 24 May, 1907, to 7 May, 1909; Inspector of Iron Structures, H.Q. of Army, 1 Oct. 1909, to 30 Sept. 1913, and Inspector of Iron Structures, War Office. He became Major 31 Dec. 1910. Major Stevenson served in the European War; became Temp. Lieut.-Colonel 15 Aug. 1915; was mentioned in Despatches, and given the Brevet of Lieut.-Colonel 1 Jan. 1915. He was promoted to Colonel; is O.C. 20th Company, R.E.; was created a C.M.G. in 1917, and a C.B. in 1918. Colonel Stevenson married, in 1909, Elizabeth Nicoll, eldest daughter of the late Surgeon-Major W. Jobson, A.M.D., and they have two sons and one daughter.

PRITCHARD, HARRY LIONEL, Lieut., was born 16 Nov. 1871, son of the late Lieut.-Colonel Burlock Pritchard. He was educated at Charterhouse, and entered the Royal Engineers 13 Feb. 1891, becoming Lieutenant 13 Feb. 1894. He was on Special Service in the Ashanti Expedition, 1895–96 (honourably mentioned; Star). He served with the Expedition to Dongola, 1896, being present at the operations of 19 Sept. (Despatches [London Gazette, 3 Nov. 1896]; Fourth Class Medjidie; Egyptian Medal with clasp). For the Nile Expedition of 1897 he received a clasp to the Egyptian Medal. He served in the Nile Expedition of 1898, and was present at the Battle of Khartum. He was mentioned in Despatches [London Gazette, 30 Sept. 1898], received a clasp to the Egyptian Medal, and was created a Companion of the Distinguished Service Order [London Gazette, 15 Nov. 1898]: "Harry Lionel Pritchard, Lieut., Royal Engineers. In recognition of services during the recent operations in Egypt and the Sudan, including the Battle of Khartum." The Insignia were presented by the High Commissioner of Cyprus, in Nigeria, 21 Dec. 1898. He was specially employed in Cyprus 4 Dec. 1898, to 16 April, 1899. From 1 Jan. 1900, to 23 June, 1902, he served in the South African War, on the Staff, being present at the advance on Kimberley, including actions at Belmont, Enslin, Modder River and Magersfontein; operations in the Orange Free State, Feb. to May, 1900; operations in the Transvaal in May and June, 1900; operations in the Transvaal, east of Pretoria, July and Aug. 1900; operations in Orange River Colony, May to Nov. 1900; operations in Cape Colony, south of Orange River, 1899–1900; operations in the Transvaal, 30 Nov. to Dec. 1900, and March, 1901, to 31 May, 1902; operations in Orange River Colony; operations in Cape Colony, Dec. 1900, to March, 1901. He was mentioned in Despatches [London Gazette, 29 July, 1902]; received the Queen's Medal with four clasps and the King's Medal with two clasps. Capt. Pritchard was employed on the Central South African Railway 1 July, to 6 Nov. 1904; was Deputy Assistant Director, Headquarters of Army, 7 Nov. 1904, to 14 Feb. 1907; D.A.Q.M.G., India, 13 March to 8 July, 1907; was promoted Major 13 Feb. 1911. He served in the European War from 18 Feb. 1916, to 9 Jan. 1919, as Chief Engineer, 16th Army Corps, Mediterranean Expeditionary Force, and Salonika Expeditionary Force, and was severely wounded, and mentioned in Despatches. He was given the Brevet of Lieut.-Colonel 18 Feb. 1915; became Lieut.-Colonel 24 Sept. 1918, and was given the Brevet of Colonel 1 Jan. 1919. He was Temporary Brigadier-General 16 Feb. 1916, to 9 Jan. 1919. Colonel Pritchard was created a C.M.G. in 1917. He has written and published "The Sudan Campaign" and "Army Organization and Administration." He married, in 1902, Elizabeth Gilbert, daughter of E. Furse, of Alphington, Frimley, and they have two daughters.

BLAKENEY, ROBERT BYRON DRURY, Lieut., was born 18 April, 1872, at Mitcham, Surrey, son of William Blakeney, Paymaster-in-Chief, R.N., of Hillsborough, Westward Ho! He entered the Royal Engineers 24 July, 1891; became Lieutenant 24 July, 1894; was specially employed with the Egyptian Army 13 April, 1896, to 9 Oct. 1896, and employed with the Egyptian Army 10 Oct. 1896, to 22 April, 1899. He served in the Expedition to Dongola in 1896, taking part in the operations of 19 Sept. He was mentioned in Despatches [London Gazette, 3 Nov. 1896], and received the Egyptian Medal with clasp. He served in the Nile Expedition of 1897 (clasp to Egyptian Medal), and in the Nile Expedition of 1898, when he was present at the Battle of Khartum; was mentioned in Despatches [London Gazette, 30 Sept. 1898]; received the Medal and a clasp to the Egyptian Medal, and was created a Companion of the Distinguished Service Order [London Gazette, 15 Nov. 1898]: "Robert Byron Drury Blakeney, Lieut., Royal Engineers. In recognition of services during the recent operations in Egypt and the Sudan, including the Battle of Khartum." (The Insignia presented by the Queen at Windsor 12 Jan. 1899.) He was on special extra-regimental employment 23 April, 1899, to 24 Jan. 1900, in command of the 3rd Balloon Section, South African War, 1900–1; was D.A.D. Railways, South Africa, 1 July, 1900, to 17 June, 1901; took part in the operations in Orange River Colony and Cape Colony, 1900. He was on extra-regimental employment, 18 June, 1901. He was given the Third Class Osmanieh, 1905; was Deputy General Manager, Egyptian State Railways, 1906–13; became Major 24 July, 1911; received the Second Class Medjidie, 1912; retired from the Army 4 Feb. 1914. Major Blakeney served in the operations on the Suez Canal, 1914–15; was present at the action of 2 Feb., and mentioned in Despatches [London Gazette, 21 June, 1916]. He served in the Dardanelles Expedition as A.D., Railway Transport, and Temp. Lieut.-Colonel, and served in the Egyptian Expeditionary Force, 1915, 1916, 1917 and 1918, as Deputy Director of Railway Traffic. He received the Order of the Nile, Second Class, 1916; was present at preliminary operations round Gaza 29 and 30 Oct. 1917. Four times mentioned in Despatches; C.M.G., 3 June, 1918; Director of Railway Traffic, E.E.F., 8 April, 1919, with temporary rank of Brigadier-General; General Manager, Egyptian State Railways, 1 April, 1919. Major Blakeney married, 6 May, 1903, Dorothy, daughter of the late Major Nelson Ellis, 101st Royal Munster Fusiliers, and they have two sons and one surviving daughter.

MICKLEM, HENRY ANDREW, Lieut., was born at Farnborough 29 June, 1872, eldest son of Major-General Edward Micklem and Eva, daughter of T. M. Weguelin, Esq., M.P. He was educated at Winchester College, and joined the Royal Engineers 1 Aug. 1891, becoming Lieutenant 1 Aug. 1894. He was employed with the Egyptian Army 25 June, 1897, to 3 Oct. 1899, and served in the Nile Expedition of 1897 (Egyptian Medal with clasp). In the Nile Expedition of 1898 he was present at the Battle of Khartum (slightly wounded); was mentioned in Despatches [London Gazette, 30 Sept. 1898]; received the Fourth Class Medjidie, the Medal, and a clasp to the Egyptian Medal. He was also created a Companion of the Distinguished Service Order [London Gazette, 15 Nov. 1898]: "Henry Andrew Micklem, Lieut., Royal Engineers. In recognition of services during the recent operations in Egypt and the Sudan, including the Battle of Khartum." (The Insignia presented by the Duke of Connaught at Atbara 24 Feb. 1899.) He served in the South African War 1 Jan. 1900, to 30 June, 1902, as Superintendent of Works, and on the Staff, and took part in the operations in the Orange Free State, Feb. to May, 1900; operations in the Transvaal, east of Pretoria, July to 29 Nov. 1900; operations in Orange River Colony, June, 1900; operations in Cape Colony, south of Orange River, 1899–1900; operations in Cape Colony, north of Orange River; operations in the Transvaal, 30 Nov. 1900, to 31 May, 1902. He was severely wounded; was mentioned in Despatches [London Gazette, 10 Sept. 1901]; was given the Brevet of Major, 2 Aug. 1902; received the Queen's Medal with three clasps, and the King's Medal with two clasps. He was employed on the Central South African Railways 1 July, to 1902, to 18 April, 1903, and employed under the Chinese Mining and Engineering Company 16 June, 1904. He retired from the Royal Engineers 2 June, 1909. He served in the European War from 1914 to 1918; was Major, Reserve of Officers, 27 Aug. 1918; was given the Brevet of Lieut.-Colonel; created a C.M.G., 1918, and a C.B.E., 1919.

PIGOTT, GRENVILLE EDMUND, Lieut., was born 18 Feb. 1870; educated at Harrow (Church Hill), and at Corpus Christi College, Cambridge, and was gazetted to the Royal Welsh Fusiliers 18 June, 1892, becoming Lieutenant, Army Service Corps, 30 March, 1895. He served in the Nile Expedition of 1898, as Staff Officer, British Brigade, Battles of the Atbara and Khartum; was mentioned in Despatches [London Gazette, 24 May and 30 Sept. 1898]; received the Medal, and the Egyptian Medal with two clasps, and was created a Companion of the Distinguished Service Order [London Gazette, 15 Nov. 1898]: "Grenville Edmund Pigott, Lieut., Army Service Corps. In recognition of services during the recent operations in Egypt and in the Sudan, including the Battles of Atbara and Khartum." (The Insignia presented by the Queen at Windsor 1 Dec. 1898.) He became Captain 20 July, 1899; served in the South African War, 1899 to 1902, on the Staff, taking part in the advance on Kimberley, including actions at Modder River and Magersfontein; operations in the Orange Free State, Feb. to May, 1900, including operations at Paardeberg (17 to 26 Feb.); operations at Poplar Grove and Dreifontein; operations in Orange River Colony, May to 29 Nov. 1900, including actions at Wittebergen (1 to 29 July); operations in Orange River Colony 30 Nov. 1900, to April, 1902. He received the Queen's Medal with five clasps, and the King's Medal with two clasps. He was promoted to Major 2 Oct. 1906.

Major Pigott was Adjutant, A.S.C., 25 Oct. 1908, to 31 March, 1909. He served in the Somaliland Expedition, 21 Jan. 1909, to 21 Jan. 1910, as Director of Supplies and Transport (Despatches; thanks of Colonial Office; Medal and clasp). He was D.A.D. of Supplies and Transport, Aldershot Command, 24 Feb. 1912, to 11 Nov. 1912. He served in the European War from 1914; became Lieut.-Colonel, 30 Oct. 1914; was A.A. and Q.M.G., British Armies in France, 27 June, 1915, to 12 Dec. 1916; was mentioned in Despatches, and created a C.M.G. in 1916. Lieut.-Colonel Pigott married, in 1902, Alice Molesworth (who died in 1919), only daughter of Lieut.-Colonel A. J. Ogilvie.

Edward C. Midwinter.

MIDWINTER, EDWARD COLPOYS, Lieut., was born 1 Nov. 1872, son of the late Rev. E. A. Midwinter. He was gazetted to the Royal Engineers 22 July, 1892; became Lieutenant 22 July, 1895; was employed with the Egyptian Army from 13 Jan. 1897, and served in the Nile Expedition of 1897 (Egyptian Medal with clasp; Fourth Class Medjidie). He served in the Nile Expedition in 1898; was present at the Battle of Khartum; was mentioned in Despatches 30 Sept. 1898; received the Medal, and was created a Companion of the Distinguished Service Order [London Gazette, 15 Nov. 1898]: "Edward Colpoys Midwinter, Lieut., Royal Engineers. In recognition of services during the recent operations in Egypt and the Sudan, including the Battle of Khartum." The Insignia were presented to him by the Duke of Connaught at Atbara 27 Feb. 1899. Capt. Midwinter resigned from the Royal Engineers in 1907. He was appointed Manager of the Egyptian State Railways in 1907; was created a C.M.G. in 1911, and a C.B. in 1912.

GASCOIGNE, ERNEST FREDERICK ORBY, Lieut., was born 19 April, 1873, son of the late Lieut.-Colonel Gascoigne, formerly of the Grenadier Guards. He entered the Grenadier Guards 23 March, 1892; became Adjutant, 1st Battn. Grenadier Guards, 1898; served in the Sudan, in the Nile Expedition of 1898, and was present at the Battle of Khartum. He was mentioned in Despatches [London Gazette, 30 Sept. 1898]; received the Egyptian Medal with clasp, the Medal, and was created a Companion of the Distinguished Service Order [London Gazette, 15 Nov. 1898]: "Ernest Frederick Orby Gascoigne, Lieut., Grenadier Guards. In recognition of services in Egypt and the Sudan, including the Battle of Khartum." (The Insignia presented by Queen Victoria at Windsor 1 Dec. 1898.) He became Captain 28 Oct. 1899; served in the South African War, 1900-2, on the Staff (as Brigade-Major, 16th Infantry Brigade), from 13 March, 1900; during operations in the Orange Free State, April to May, 1902; during operations in the Orange River Colony (May to 29 Nov. 1900), including actions at Biddulphsberg and Wittebergen (1 to 29 July). Operations in the Orange River Colony 30 Nov. 1900, to Feb. 1901, and March, 1901, to 31 May, 1902. Operations in the Transvaal, Feb. to March, 1901, and was mentioned in Despatches [London Gazette, 16 April, 1901]; received Brevet of Major 26 June, 1902; Queen's Medal with three clasps, and King's Medal with two clasps. He was placed on the list of officers considered qualified for Staff employment, in consequence of service on the Staff in the Field. Major Gascoigne married, in 1902, Cicely, third daughter of the late General Edward Clive, Grenadier Guards, and they have four sons and one daughter. He retired from the Army 24 July, 1907; entered the Reserve of Officers, and was appointed to the Royal Bodyguard (Hon. Corps of Gentlemen-at-Arms) in Oct. 1912. He served on the Staff in the European War; was in the Dardanelles, 1915 (Despatches; Brevet Lieut.-Colonel; St. Anne, Second Class, with Swords). He served in Europe in 1916, with the temporary rank of Brigadier-General, and was mentioned in Despatches. For his services in Palestine in 1917 he was mentioned in Despatches, created a C.M.G., and given the honorary rank of Brigadier-General, 1918.

LOCH, EDWARD DOUGLAS (LORD LOCH), Lieut. The Hon., was born 4 April, 1873, only son of the 1st Baron Loch and Elizabeth, daughter of the Hon. E. E. Villiers and niece of the 4th Earl of Clarendon. He entered the Grenadier Guards as 2nd Lieut. 3 May, 1893, from the local Militia Forces, Cape of Good Hope, and became Lieutenant 12 May, 1897; served in the Sudan, 1898, including Khartum (Despatches, 30 Sept. 1898; British Medal; Khedive's Medal with clasp, and created a Companion of the Distinguished Service Order [London Gazette, 15 Nov. 1898]: "The Honourable Edward Douglas Loch, Lieut., Grenadier Guards. In recognition of services during the recent operations in Egypt and the Sudan, including the Battle of Khartum.") The Insignia were presented by the Queen at Windsor, Dec. 1898). He became Captain 30 Nov. 1899; served as Divisional Signalling Officer (graded Staff Captain) in South Africa 9 Oct. 1899, to 28 Sept. 1900. He was present in the advance on Kimberley, including the actions at Belmont, Enslin, Modder River and Magersfontein; operations in the Orange Free State, Feb. to May, 1900; operations in the Transvaal, west of Pretoria, Aug. to Nov. 1900, including the action at Venterskroon; operations in Orange River Colony, May to July, 1900, including actions at Lindley and Rhenoster River; operations in Cape Colony, north of Orange River, March, 1900. He was on the Staff, and was also employed under the Censor. He was severely wounded; was mentioned in Despatches [London Gazette, 16 April, 1901]; received the Queen's Medal and four clasps, and was given the Brevet of Major 29 Nov. 1900. He succeeded his father as 2nd Baron Loch, 1900; was Adjutant, Grenadier Guards, from 26 Jan. 1903, to 30 June, 1905. Lord Loch became Major 15 Aug. 1908; was Brigade-Major, 3rd Brigade, Aldershot Command, 12 April, 1910, to 15 Aug. 1911;

was G.S.O., Second Grade, War Office, 16 Aug. 1911, to 11 April, 1914; Brevet Lieut.-Colonel 10 May, 1913; Lieut.-Colonel 13 March, 1915; held a special appointment with the B.E.F. 5 Aug. 1914, to 28 Aug. 1914; served in the European War, 1914-18; was given the Brevet of G.S.O., Second Grade, 16 Dec. 1914, to 26 May, 1915; Brigadier-General, General Staff, B.E.F., British Armies in France, 27 May, 1915, to 21 July, 1917; Brigade Commander, 110th Infantry Brigade, B.E.F., 22 July, 1917, to 8 Jan. 1918; Brigadier-General, General Staff, Irish Command, 16 May, 1918. He was five times mentioned in Despatches, and was created a C.M.G., 1915; given the Brevet of Colonel 1 Jan. 1916; created a C.B., 1918, and promoted to Major-General 1 Jan. 1919. Lord Loch is an M.V.O., Fourth Class. He was Gentleman-in-Waiting to the King, 1913-14. He married, in 1905, Lady Margaret Compton, only daughter of the 5th Marquis of Northampton, and they have one son, The Hon. George Henry Compton Loch, born 3 Feb. 1916, and two daughters.

London Gazette, 2 Dec. 1898.—"War Office, 2 Dec. 1898. The Queen has been graciously pleased to give orders for the following appointment to the Distinguished Service Order, in recognition of the services of the undermentioned Officer during the outbreak at Candia on the 6th Sept. 1898. To be a Companion of the Distinguished Service Order."

Edward H. M. Nicholson.

NICHOLSON, EDWARD HUGH MEREDITH, Lieut., R.N. was born 3 Sept. 1876, eldest son of Colonel E. H. Nicholson (4th Nottinghamshire Regt.), Newark-on-Trent, Nottinghamshire, and Sarah, daughter of J. Prior, late of Shipton Manor, Shipton-on-Cherwell. He was educated at Eastman's, and at Stubbington, Fareham, and joined the Britannia in 1890. He served in the Royal Sovereign, 1892-93; as Midshipman in the Raleigh, 1893-94; in the Naval Brigade, with Admiral Bedford, at Bathurst, River Gambia, West Coast of Africa, Feb. 1894, for the punishment of the Fodi Silah, a slave-raiding chief (African Medal, Gambia, 1894; clasp); as Midshipman in the St. George (1894-96), he served with the punitive expedition against King Koko of Nimbi, Brass River, West Coast of Africa, Feb. 1896 (Brass River, 1895; clasp). He was at the R.N. College, 1896-97; in the Haughty, 1897. He served with the Naval Brigade under Admiral Rawson, C.B., at Mombasa, for the punishment of Mbaruk, an Arab chief; at the capture of Mwele, 17 Aug. 1895 (Mwele, 1895, engraved on General African Medal). As Sub-Lieutenant in the Hazard (1897-99), in command of a company of bluejackets and marines, he landed at Candia, 6 Sept. 1898, for the protection of the Dime Office and the quelling of disturbances. For these services he was created a Companion of the Distinguished Service Order [London Gazette, 2 Dec. 1898]: "Edward Hugh Meredith Nicholson, Lieut., Royal Navy. In recognition of services during the outbreak in Candia on the 6th Sept. 1898." (The Insignia presented by the Queen 15 Dec. 1898.) In the Excellent, 1900-1, for a gunnery course; Cambridge, 1902; Australia, 1902; Venus, 1903; Bulwark, 1904. Commander Nicholson was invalided from the Service in 1906. He is a Director of Hadfields, Limited, Sheffield. Commander Nicholson married, in 1904, Ethel, only daughter of R. L. Lambert, and they have one daughter.

London Gazette, 16 Dec. 1898.—"War Office, 16 Dec. 1898. The Queen has been graciously pleased to give orders for the following appointments to the Distinguished Service Order, in recognition of the services of the following Officers during the recent operations in the Sudan. To be Companions of the Distinguished Service Order."

FLEMING, CHARLES CHRISTIE, Capt., was born 6 Nov. 1864, second son of the late Deputy-Surgeon-General A. Fleming and Catherine, daughter of Capt. Joseph Henry Garner. He was educated at Edinburgh University (M.B., C.M.); entered the Army Medical Service in 1892, and became Surgeon-Captain (now Royal Army Medical Corps) 30 Jan. 1895. He served as Senior Medical Officer in the operations on the Upper Atbara, and in the action of Gedaref, defence of Gedaref, and subsequent operations in the neighbourhood. He was mentioned in Despatches 9 Dec. 1898; received the Medal, the Egyptian Medal and clasp, and was created a Companion of the Distinguished Service Order [London Gazette, 16 Dec. 1898]: "Charles Christie Fleming, M.B., Capt., Royal Army Medical Corps. In recognition of services during the recent operations in the Sudan." (The Insignia, etc., sent to the G.O.C., Egypt. The Insignia presented by the Commandant, Karsala District, at Gedaref.) Capt.

Charles Christie Fleming.

Fleming served in the South African War, 1899 to 1902, as M.O. in charge of No. 2 Ambulance Train, taking part in the advance on Kimberley, including the actions at Belmont and Magersfontein, and Relief of Kimberley; operations in the Orange Free State, Feb. to May, 1900; operations in Cape Colony, south of Orange River, 1899-1900. He received the Queen's Medal with three clasps and the King's Medal with two clasps. He became Major 30 Jan. 1904. From 3 Sept. 1902, to 13 Oct. 1905, he was Adjutant, R.A.M.C. (Volunteers). From 1915 he was Assistant Director of Medical Services, Highland District, with the rank of Colonel ; he was formerly Secretary (Scottish Branch), British Red Cross Society, Headquarters, Glasgow. Major Fleming died 24 Dec. 1917.

HALL, GEORGE CLIFFORD MILLER, Lieut., was born 26 Jan. 1872, son of the late Capt. W. H. Hall, R.N. He entered the Royal Engineers 12 Feb. 1892 ; became Lieutenant 12 Feb. 1895 ; Major 19 Dec. 1902, and Temporary Lieutenant-Colonel. He served with the Nile Expedition, 1897 (Egyptian Medal with clasp ; 4th Class Medjidie) ; again with the Nile Expedition, 1898 (Despatches [London Gazette, 9 Dec. 1898] ; Medal). He was created a Companion of the Distinguished Service Order [London Gazette, 16 Dec. 1898] : "George Clifford Miller Hall, Lieut., Royal Engineers. In recognition of services during the recent operations in the Sudan." He has the Order of the Nile, 2nd Class, and the 3rd Class Osmanieh. He was formerly Traffic Manager, Egyptian State Railways. He married (1st), in 1901, Genevieve (who died in 1902), daughter of J. B. Stickney, of St. Augustine, Florida, and in 1906 he married (2ndly) Annie E. M., daughter of the late Fitzroy Kelly, M.A., of Lincoln's Inn, and they have two sons and two daughters.

KENNARD, FRANK, Lieut., was created a Companion of the Distinguished Service Order [London Gazette, 16 Dec. 1898] : "Frank Kennard, Lieut., Army Service Corps. In recognition of services during the recent operations in the Sudan." He died 13 June, 1900.

London Gazette, 24 Jan. 1899.—"War Office, 24 Jan. 1899. The Queen has been graciously pleased to give orders for the following appointments to the Distinguished Service Order, in recognition of the services of the undermentioned Officers during the recent operations in Uganda."

SITWELL, CLAUDE GEORGE HENRY, Major, was born 18 Oct. 1858. He joined the 85th Foot as Second Lieutenant from the Militia 14 Sept. 1878, and served in the Afghan War, 1879–80, with the Kuram Division, Yarmusht Expedition (Medal). He became Lieutenant, Shropshire Light Infantry, 1 July, 1881, and in 1882 served with the Egyptian Expedition, being present at the defence of Alexandria, occupation of Kafr Dowar and surrender of Damietta. He was promoted to Captain 13 July, 1886. From 11 May, 1895, to 10 Oct. 1899, he was employed in the Uganda Protectorate. He commanded the expeditions against the Kitosh, Kabras and Kikelwa tribes, 1895. For the Nandi Expedition, 1895–96, he was mentioned in Despatches. In Uganda, in 1897–98 ; in Feb. and March, 1898, he commanded the operations against the Mwanga, and fought an action near Katonga River, and other engagements. He was mentioned in Despatches ; was given the Brevet of Lieut.-Colonel 4 Oct. 1899 (he had been promoted to Major 13 Oct. 1898), and was created a Companion of the Distinguished Service Order [London Gazette, 24 Jan. 1899] : "Claude George Henry Sitwell, Major, Royal Dublin Fusiliers. In recognition of services during the recent operations in Uganda." The Insignia were sent to the Foreign Office, and sent by the Foreign Office to H.M. Commissioner in Uganda. Lieut.-Colonel C. G. H. Sitwell's Insignia, etc., were returned by Sir R. Buller, Lieut.-Colonel C. G. H. Sitwell having been killed at Tugela. The D.S.O., Warrant and Statutes were sent to Miss Blanche Sitwell for Colonel Sitwell's daughter, Miss C. D. C. Sitwell. Colonel Sitwell was killed in action 24 Feb. 1900. Sir A. Conan Doyle says, on pages 216 to 219 of " The Great Boer War " :

" Brigadier Fitzroy Hart, to whom the assault was entrusted, is in some ways as singular and picturesque a type as has been evolved in the war. A dandy soldier, always the picture of neatness from the top of his helmet to the heels of his well-polished brown boots, he brings to military matters the same precision which he affects in dress. Pedantic in his accuracy, he actually at the battle of Colenso drilled the Irish Brigade for half an hour before leading them into action, and threw out markers under a deadly fire in order that his change from close to extended formation might be academically correct. The heavy loss of the brigade at this action was to some extent ascribed to him, and affected his popularity ; but as his men came to know him better—his romantic bravery, his whimsical soldierly humour—their dislike changed into admiration. His personal disregard for danger was notorious and reprehensible. ' Where is General Hart ? ' asked someone in action. ' I have not seen him, but I know where you will find him. Go ahead of the skirmish line, and you will see him standing on a rock,' was the answer. He bore a charmed life. It was a danger to be near him. ' Whom are you going to ? ' ' General Hart,' said the aide-de-camp. ' Then good-bye ! ' cried his fellows. A grim humour ran through his nature. It is gravely recorded and widely believed that he lined up a regiment on a hill-top in order to teach them not to shrink from fire. Amid the laughter of his Irishmen, he walked through the open files of his firing line holding a laggard by the ear. This was the man who had put such a spirit into the Irish Brigade that amid that army of valiant men there were none who held such a record. ' Their rushes were the quickest, their rushes were the longest, and they stayed the shortest time under cover,' said a shrewd military observer. To Hart and his brigade was given the task of clearing the way to Ladysmith.

" The regiments which he took with him on his perilous enterprise were the 1st Inniskilling Fusiliers, the 2nd Dublin Fusiliers, the 1st Connaught Rangers, and the Imperial Light Infantry, the whole forming the famous 5th Brigade. They were already in the extreme British advance, and now, as they moved forwards, the Durham Light Infantry and the 1st Rifle Brigade from Lyttelton's Brigade came up to take their place. The hill to be taken lay on the right, and the soldiers were compelled to pass in single file under a heavy fire for more than a mile until they reached the spot which seemed best for their enterprise. There, short already of sixty of their comrades, they assembled and began a cautious advance upon the lines of trenches and sangars which seamed the brown slope above them.

" For a time they were able to keep some cover, and the casualties were comparatively few. But now at last, as the evening sun threw a long shadow from the hills, the leading regiment, the Inniskillings, found themselves at the utmost fringe of boulders with a clear slope between them and the main trench of the enemy. Up there where the shrapnel was spurting and the great lyddite shells crashing they could dimly see a line of bearded faces and the black dots of the slouch hats. With a yell the Inniskillings sprang out, carried with a rush the first trench, and charged desperately onwards for the second one. It was a supremely dashing attack against supremely steady resistance, for among all their gallant deeds the Boers have never fought better than on that February evening. Amid such a smashing shell fire as living mortals have never yet endured they stood doggedly, these hardy men of the veldt, and fired fast and true into the fiery ranks of the Irishmen. The yell of the stormers was answered by the remorseless roar of the Mausers and the deep-chested shouts of the farmers. Up and up surged the infantry, falling, rising, dashing bull-headed at the crackling line of the trench. But still the bearded faces glared at them over the edge, and still the sheet of lead pelted through their ranks. The regiment staggered, came on, staggered again, was overtaken by supporting companies of the Dublins and the Connaughts, came on, staggered once more, and finally dissolved into shreds, who ran swiftly back for cover, threading their way among their stricken comrades. Never on this earth was there a retreat of which the survivors had less reason to be ashamed. They had held on to the utmost capacity of human endurance. Their colonel, ten officers, and more than half the regiment were lying on the fatal hill. Honour to them, and honour also to the gallant Dutchmen who, rooted in the trenches, had faced the rush and fury of such an onslaught ! To-day to them, to-morrow to us ; but it is for a soldier to thank the God of battles for worthy foes.

" It is one thing, however, to repulse the British soldier, and it is another to rout him. Within a few hundred yards of their horrible ordeal at Magersfontein, the Highlanders re-formed into a military body. So now the Irishmen fell back no farther than the nearest cover, and there held grimly on to the ground which they had won. If you would know the advantage which the defence has over the attack, then do you come and assault this line of tenacious men, now in your hour of victory and exultation, friend Boer ! Friend Boer did attempt it, and skilfully too, moving a flanking party to sweep the position with their fire. But the brigade, though sorely hurt, held them off without difficulty, and was found on the morning of the 24th to be still lying upon the ground which they had won.

" Our losses had been very heavy—Colonel Thackeray of the Inniskillings, Colonel Sitwell of the Dublins, three majors, twenty officers, and a total of about 600 out of 1,200 actually engaged. To take such punishment and to remain undemoralized is the supreme test to which troops can be put. Could the loss have been avoided ? By following the original line of advance from Monte Christo, perhaps, when we should have turned the enemy's left. But otherwise no. The hill was in the way, and had to be taken. In the war game you cannot play without a stake. You lose and you pay forfeit, and where the game is fair the best player is he who pays with the best grace. The attack was well prepared, well delivered, and only miscarried on account of the excellence of the defence. We proved once more, what we had proved so often before, that all valour and all discipline will not avail in a frontal attack against brave, cool-headed men armed with quick-firing rifles.

" While the Irish Brigade assaulted Railway Hill an attack had been made upon the left, which was probably meant as a demonstration to keep the Boers from reinforcing their comrades rather than as an actual attempt upon their lines. Such as it was, however, it cost the life of at least one brave soldier, for Colonel Thorold of the Welsh Fusiliers was among the fallen. Thorold, Thackeray and Sitwell in one evening. Who can say that British colonels have not given their men a lead ? "

M'LOUGHLIN, GEORGE SOMERS, Capt., was born 13 May, 1867, second son of the late Lieut.-Colonel J. M'Loughlin. He became Captain, R.A.M.C., 29 July, 1890, and served in Uganda, 1897–98, as Senior Medical Officer. He was present in several engagements, was mentioned in Despatches, received the 3rd Class Brilliant Star of Zanzibar, the Medal with two clasps, and was created a Companion of the Distinguished Service Order [London Gazette, 24 Jan. 1899] : "George Somers M'Loughlin, M.B., Capt., Royal Army Medical Corps. In recognition of services during the recent operations in Uganda." The D.S.O. was presented to Capt. M'Loughlin by the Queen at Windsor 30 Nov. 1899. He served in the South African War, 1899 to 1901, taking part in the operations in the Transvaal, east of Pretoria, July to 29 Nov. 1900. Operations in Orange River Colony, May to 29 Nov. 1900. Operations in the Transvaal 30 Nov. 1900, to Feb. 1901. He received the Queen's Medal with four clasps. He was promoted to Major 29 July, 1902, and to Lieutenant-Colonel 11 Sept. 1912. Colonel M'Loughlin served in the European War from 1914, as Assistant Director of Medical Services, 3rd Division, B.E.F., 26 Oct. 1914, to 4 Jan. 1915 ; was Assistant Director of Medical Services, 47th Division, B.E.F., 18 July, 1915, to 17 Aug. 1915 ; Assistant Director of Medical Services, Guards Division, B.E.F., British Armies in France, 18 Aug. 1915, to 18 Sept. 1916 ; was promoted to Colonel 28 Dec. 1917. He was mentioned in Despatches and was created a C.M.G. in 1915. Colonel M'Loughlin married, in 1901, Katharine, daughter of the Rev. A. H. Harrison.

FERGUSON, JOHN DAVID, Capt., was born 24 Oct. 1866. He became Captain, R.A.M.C., 29 July, 1890. From 18 Jan. 1897, to 30 Nov. 1899, Capt. Ferguson was employed in the East African Protectorate, and he served in Uganda in 1897–98, and was present in the attack on Kijembo and several skirmishes. He was mentioned in Despatches, received the 3rd Class Brilliant Star of Zanzibar, the Medal with two clasps, and was created a Companion of the Distinguished Service Order [London Gazette, 24 Jan. 1899] : "John David Ferguson, Capt., Royal Army Medical Corps. In recognition of services during the recent operations in Uganda." The Insignia were presented by the Queen at Windsor 30 Nov. 1899. Capt. Ferguson served in the South African War, 1899–1902, and was present at the relief of Kimberley. Operations in the Orange Free State, Feb. to May,

1900, including operations at Paardeberg (17 to 26 Feb.) ; actions at Poplar Grove and Dreifontein. Operations in Orange River Colony, May to 29 Nov. 1900. Operations in Cape Colony, north of Orange River. He received the Queen's Medal with three clasps, and the King's Medal with two clasps. He was promoted to Major 29 July, 1902, and in 1903 and 1904 served in East Africa, taking part in the operations in Somaliland, and receiving the Medal with clasp. He was Instructor, R.A.M.C. School of Instruction, 13 Aug. 1905, to 12 June, 1909. He became Lieutenant-Colonel 31 Dec. 1912. He served in the European War from 1915, as Assistant Director of Medical Services, 47th Division, British Expeditionary Force, British Armies in France, 19 Aug. 1915, to 31 May, 1917. He was promoted to Colonel 30 May, 1917.

HARRISON, EDGAR GARSTON, Capt., was born 11 May, 1863, son of Daniel Harrison, of The Abbey, Staveley, Kendal. He was educated at Haileybury, and joined the Dorsetshire Militia in 1881, and was gazetted to the West Riding Regt. as Lieutenant from the Militia 23 May, 1885, becoming Capt. 1 Feb. 1892. He was on Special Extra Regimental Employment 11 Sept. 1895, to Oct. 1895 ; was employed in British East Africa Protectorate from Oct. 1895, and commanded H.H. the Sultan of Zanzibar's Forces in the operations against the Mazrui rebels, receiving the Medal, 2nd Class Brilliant Star of Zanzibar, and the Zanzibar War Medal. Capt. Harrison again saw active service in Uganda in 1897–98, was in command at the capture of Kabagambi, and took part in several other engagements, leading the final counter-attack at Kijembo and conducting various operations in Unyoro. He was mentioned in Despatches, was given the Brevet of Major 25 Jan. 1899, received the Medal with two clasps, and was created a Companion of the Distinguished Service Order [London Gazette, 24 Jan. 1899] : " Edgar Garston Harrison, Capt., West Riding Regt. In recognition of services during the recent operations in Uganda." The Insignia were presented to him by the Queen at Osborne 1 Feb. 1899. He was in command of the operations in Nandi in 1905–06, received the Medal and clasp, and was created a C.B. He served with the King's African Rifles, 1903–7. Bt. Major Harrison retired from the W. Riding Regt. 1905. He served in the European War from 1914 (2nd Battn. Duke of Wellington's Regt.), in France, from Oct. to Dec. 1914 ; (12th Service Battn. Manchester Regt.) in France, 1914–17. He was twice wounded, mentioned in Despatches, and given the Brevet of Lieutenant-Colonel 1 Jan. 1917

TICKELL, EDWARD JAMES, Capt., was born 9 Feb. 1861, eldest son of the late T. Tickell, Commander, R.N., of The Lypiatts, Cheltenham. He was educated at Trinity College, Cambridge, and entered the West India Regt. as Lieutenant 7 Feb. 1885, becoming Lieutenant, 14th Hussars, 8 Feb. 1888. He was employed in the Uganda Protectorate 6 Jan. 1898, to 13 Feb. 1900, and during the operations of 1898 he took part in several engagements ; was mentioned in Despatches, received the Medal and clasp, and was created a Companion of the Distinguished Service Order [London Gazette, 24 Jan. 1899] : " Edward James Tickell, Capt., 14th Hussars. In recognition of services during the recent operations in Uganda." He became Major 22 Feb. 1899 ; served in the South African War, 1899 to 1901, being on Special Service with the Rhodesian Field Force 14 Feb. 1900, to 24 Dec. 1900, and was mentioned in Despatches [London Gazette, 10 Sept. 1901], and received the Queen's Medal with four clasps. He was promoted to Lieutenant-Colonel 9 Feb. 1909, and retired 9 Feb. 1914. Lieut.-Colonel Tickell commanded the 13th Cavalry Reserve from 1915. He is a J.P., County Kildare.

MALCOLM, NEILL, Lieut., was born 8 Oct. 1869, second son of Colonel Edward Douglas Malcolm, of Poltallock, C.B., R.E., J.P., Deputy Lieutenant for the County of Argyll, and of Isabella Wyld, daughter of the late John Brown. He was educated at Eton, and entered Princess Louise's Argyll and Sutherland Highlanders 20 Feb. 1889, becoming Lieutenant 23 Aug. 1893. He served on the North-West Frontier of India, 1897–98 (Medal and clasp). He was employed in the Uganda Protectorate 5 Oct. 1897, to 25 Oct. 1899, and conducted operations in the Shuli country, taking part in several engagements ; was mentioned in Despatches, received the Medal with two clasps, and was created a Companion of the Distinguished Service Order [London Gazette, 24 Jan. 1899] : " Neill Malcolm, Lieut., Argyll and Sutherland Highlanders. In recognition of services during the recent operations in Uganda." He was promoted to Captain 21 Dec. 1898, and from 1899 to 1900 served in the South African War as Special Service Officer, and was present in operations in the Orange Free State, Feb. to May, 1900, including operations at Paardeberg 17 to 26 Feb. (severely wounded 18 Feb.). He received the Queen's Medal with two clasps. Capt. Malcolm was on Special Service with the Somaliland Field Force 25 Sept. 1903, to 18 June, 1904 ; took part in the operations in Somaliland ; was present at the action of Jidballi and received the Medal with two clasps. He was Staff Captain, Headquarters of Army, 22 Aug. 1904, to 31 Dec. 1905 ; accompanied the British Mission to Fez, 1905 ; was D.A.Q.M.G., Headquarters of Army, 1 Jan. 1906, to 31 March, 1908 ; Secretary, Historical Section, Committee of Imperial Defence, 1 April, 1908, to 30 Sept. 1910 ; was given the Brevet of Major 18 Dec. 1909, and became Major 20 Aug. 1910 ; was G.S.O.2, Staff College, 22 Jan. 1912, to 4 Aug. 1914. Major Malcolm served in the European War from 1914 ; as G.S.O.2, 1st Army, B.E.F., 5 Aug. 1914, to 31 Oct. 1914 ; as G.S.O.1, 11th Division, Mediterranean Expeditionary Force, 1 Nov. 1914, to 28 Sept. 1915 ; was given the Brevet of Lieutenant-Colonel 18 Feb. 1915. He was G.S.O.1, Salonika Army, Mediterranean Expeditionary Force, 29 Sept. 1915, to 17 Nov. 1915 ; was Brigadier-General, General Staff, Mediterranean Expeditionary Force ; Egyptian Expeditionary Force 18 Nov. 1915, to 4 April, 1916. He was given the Brevet of Colonel 1 Jan. 1916. He was Brigadier-General, General Staff, Reserve Corps, British Armies in France, 14 April to 6 July, 1916 ; was promoted to Lieutenant-Colonel 13 May, 1916 ; Major-General, General Staff, Reserve Army, 5th Army, British Armies in France, 7 July, 1916, to 21 Dec. 1917 ; promoted to Major-General 1 Jan. 1917 ; commanded 66th Division, British Armies in France, Dec. 1917, till wounded 29 March,

1918 ; and 59th Division 8 Sept. to 26 Dec. 1918 ; commanded 30th Division 27 Dec. 1918, to 5 Feb. 1919. Major-General N. Malcolm was mentioned in Despatches, created a C.B., promoted to Brevet Lieutenant-Colonel, Brevet Colonel and Major-General ; received the Order of the Nile, 3rd Class, 1916, and was made a Commander of the Legion of Honour. He is F.R.G.S. ; is Editor of " The Science of War." He married, in 1907, Angela, only daughter of W. R. Malcolm, and they have two sons and one daughter.

OSBORN, PHILIP BARLOW, Lieut., was born 16 Oct. 1870, and joined the Oxfordshire Light Infantry as Second Lieutenant from the Militia 28 Sept. 1892, becoming Lieutenant 9 Nov. 1894. He was employed in the Uganda Protectorate 18 June, 1897, to 8 Feb. 1899, and took part in the operations in Uganda in 1897–98, being present at the capture of Kabagambi (severely wounded) ; at the attack of Kijembo, and several other engagements. He was mentioned in Despatches, received the Medal with two clasps, and was created a Companion of the Distinguished Service Order [London Gazette, 24 Jan. 1899] : " Philip Barlow Osborn, Lieut., Oxfordshire Light Infantry. In recognition of services during the recent operations in Uganda." The Insignia were presented by the Queen at Osborne 1 Feb. 1899. He was employed in the British East African Protectorate 9 Feb. 1899, to 17 June, 1907 ; and served with the King's African Rifles, taking part in the operations against the Ogaden Somalis in Jubaland (Medal with clasp). He was promoted to Captain 27 Feb. 1900. In East Africa, in 1902–04, he served as Base Staff Officer to 21 Dec. 1902, took part in the operations in Somaliland and was present at the action at Jidballi. He was mentioned in Despatches (by Lieut.-Colonel Swayne 20 Feb. 1903 ; Brigadier-General Manning 17 Aug. 1903, and Sir C. C. Egerton 20 May, 1904) [London Gazette, 2 Sept. 1904] : was given the Brevet of Major 7 Sept. 1904, and received two clasps. He died 12 Feb. 1909, and an obituary notice of him appeared in the " Times."

DUGMORE, WILLIAM FRANCIS BROUGHAM RADCLYFFE, Lieut., was born 1 Oct. 1868, eldest son of the late Capt. Francis Dugmore, 64th Regt., and the Hon. Evelyn Mary, daughter of the 2nd Baron Brougham and Vaux. He was educated at the Oratory, Egdbaston, and at St. Mary's College, Oscott, and was commissioned in the Prince of Wales's North Staffordshire Regt. 20 June, 1894, as Second Lieutenant. He was employed in the Uganda Protectorate 27 Dec. 1899, to 23 Jan. 1902, serving with the King's African Rifles in the East African Arab War, taking part in the operations against the Mazrui rebels (Medal) ; in Unyoro, 1896–97 (Medal), and in the Uganda Mutiny in 1897–98, when he averted the threatened insurrection of 500 Sudanese. He was mentioned in Despatches, received the Medal and clasp, and was created a Companion of the Distinguished Service Order [London Gazette, 24 Jan. 1899] : " William Francis Brougham Radclyffe Dugmore, Lieut., North Staffordshire Regt. In recognition of services during the recent operations in Uganda." The Insignia were presented by the Queen at Osborne 1 Feb. 1899. He had been promoted to Lieutenant 12 Oct. 1897. He served in the South African War from 1899 to 1902, on Special Service from 6 May, 1901, to 31 Aug. 1901 ; and was promoted to Captain 12 Jan. 1901. He was employed with Kitchener's Fighting Scouts, took part in the operations in the Tranvsaal to 31 May, 1902, and received the Queen's Medal with five clasps. He was on Special Service with the Somaliland Field Force 7 Nov. 1902, to 27 May, 1904, taking part in the operations in Somaliland (Medal with clasp). He was employed under the Liberian Development Company 27 March, 1906, to 17 Sept. 1907 ; and retired in 1909. In 1914 he was Second-in-Command, 72nd Highlanders, Canada. He served in the European War from 1914, and the London Gazette of 25 Aug. 1916, announced the appointment of Capt. W. F. B. R. Dugmore, D.S.O., Reserve of Officers, to be temporary Major (24 March, 1916). He was Second-in-Command, 72nd Highlanders, Canada. He was killed in action 12 June, 1917. He had married, in 1910, Phyllis, daughter of J. Wilson Usher.

London Gazette, 7 March, 1899.—" War Office, 7 March, 1899. The Queen has been graciously pleased to give orders for the following appointments to the Distinguished Service Order, in recognition of the services of the undermentioned Officers during the outbreak at Kandia on the 6th Sept. 1898."

COWAN, JAMES WILLIAM ALSTON, Capt., was created a Companion of the Distinguished Service Order [London Gazette, 7 March, 1899] : " James William Alston Cowan, Capt., Highland Light Infantry. In recognition of services during the outbreak at Kandia on the 6th Sept. 1898." The Insignia were presented by the Queen on 11 May, 1899.

KENNEDY, MACDOUGALL RALSTON, Lieut., was born 20 Dec. 1873, son of the Rev. A. Kennedy. He was educated at Edinburgh Academy, and at the Royal Military Academy, Woolwich, and entered the Royal Engineers 25 July, 1893, becoming Lieutenant 25 July, 1896. He served in Kandia in the affair of 6th Sept., was mentioned in Despatches [London Gazette, 24 Jan. 1899], and created a Companion of the Distinguished Service Order [London Gazette, 7 March, 1899] : " Macdougall Ralston Kennedy, Lieut., Royal Engineers. In recognition of services during the recent outbreak in Kandia, Crete, including the affair of the 6th Sept. 1898." The Insignia were presented by H.R.H. The Princess of Wales on board the Royal yacht Osborne, at Canea, Crete, on 28 April, 1899. He was employed with the Egyptian Army from 21 July, 1899, and served in the Nile Expedition of 1899, receiving the Egyptian Medal and clasp. He was promoted to Captain 21 July, 1899, and was appointed Director of Public Works, Sudan, on 1 April, 1904. He retired from the Royal Engineers 21 July, 1909, and was created a C.M.G. in 1912 ; became Major, Reserve of Officers, 2 Nov. 1916. In 1904 Capt. Kennedy married a daughter of Major-General William Henry Ralston and Christina Jane, second daughter of the late Alexander Mitchell, of Sanchrie.

CLARKE, THOMAS HENRY MATTHEWS, Lieut., was born 15 June, 1869, only son of the late Staff Surgeon Thomas Matthews Clarke, B.A., M.B., Trinity College, Dublin, Army Medical Department. He was educated at Trinity College, Dublin (B.A., M.B., B.Ch., B.A.O.), and entered the Army Medical Service 28 Jan. 1897, and served in Kandia, Crete, in 1898, during the massacre of Christians by Moslems, taking part in the affair of 6 Sept., in which he was wounded in leading a sortie to the rescue of a wounded man, half the sortie party being killed or wounded. He was mentioned in Despatches [London Gazette, 24 Jan. 1899], and was created a Companion of the Distinguished Service Order [London Gazette, 7 March, 1899]: "Thomas Henry Matthews Clarke, Lieut., Royal Army Medical Corps. In recognition of services during the outbreak in Kandia, Crete, including the affair of the 6th Sept. 1898." He became Captain 28 Jan. 1900; was "seconded" under the Foreign Office; was Personal Physician to Prince George of Greece, 1900–03; received the thanks of the Cretan Chamber of Deputies, 1903; created a C.M.G. in 1903; is a Knight of the Order of St. Saviour of Greece. He became Major 28 Jan. 1909; was appointed Physician and Surgeon, Royal Hospital, Kilmainham, 1 Oct. 1912; became Lieutenant-Colonel 1 March, 1915, and Colonel 27 Jan. 1918; created a C.B.E., 1919. He has published "Sanitary Work in Crete;" "Blue Book, Turkey, No. 1;" "Prehistoric Sanitation in Crete (Knossus)" ("British Medical Journal," Sept. 1903). Colonel Clarke married Susan Morrell, daughter of P. E. Chaplin, of Washington and Paris, and granddaughter of the Hon. D. J. Morrell, of Pennsylvania, U.S.A., and they have one daughter.

SEGRAVE, WILLIAM HENRY ERIK, Second Lieut., was born 26 Nov. 1875, son of the late Capt. W. F. Segrave, Highland Light Infantry. He entered the Highland Light Infantry as Second Lieutenant from the Militia 7 May, 1898; served in Kandia, 1898, being present in the affair of 6 Sept.; was slightly wounded, mentioned in Despatches [London Gazette, 24 Jan. 1899], and created a Companion of the Distinguished Service Order [London Gazette, 7 March, 1899]: "William Henry Erik Segrave, Second Lieut., Highland Light Infantry. In recognition of services during the outbreak in Kandia, Crete, including the affair of the 6th Sept. 1898." (The Insignia sent to the G.O.C., Ceylon, and the D.S.O. presented on the Queen's birthday, before all the troops in Garrison, Colombo.) He was promoted to Lieutenant on 12 Feb. 1900. Lieut. Segrave served in the South African War from 1901 to 1902; employed with the Mounted Infantry. Operations in the Transvaal, March, 1901, to 31 May, 1902 (Queen's Medal with clasp). He was promoted Captain 23 Jan. 1907; was Adjutant, Volunteers 15 Dec. 1903, to 31 March, 1908; Adjutant, Territorial Force, 1 April, 1908, to 14 Dec. 1908; Staff Captain, War Office, 1 Jan. 1914, to 4 Aug. 1914; D.A.A.G. 5 Aug. 1914, to 26 Sept. 1914; Brigade-Major 27 Sept. 1914, to 11 Aug. 1915; Major 1 Sept. 1915; G.S.O., 2nd Grade, War Office (temporary), 26 Aug. 1915, to 7 Jan. 1916; G.S.O., 2nd Grade, 8 Jan. 1916, to 3 Feb. 1916; G.S.O.2, G.H.Q., B.E.F., 4 Feb. 1916, to 12 May, 1916; G.S.O.2, 48th Division, British Armies in France, 13 May, 1916, to 27 Dec. 1916; G.S.O.1, 4th Division, British Armies in France, 28 Dec. 1916, to 12 March, 1917; Military Assistant to the Chief Port Construction Engineer, British Armies in France, 23 April, 1917, to 27 Aug. 1917; Brigade Commander, 152nd Brigade, British Armies in France, 8 Aug. 1918. For his services in the European War from 1914, he was six times mentioned in Despatches; was given the Brevet of Major 3 June, 1915, and the Brevet of Lieutenant-Colonel 3 June, 1919; was given the Legion of Honour, and awarded two Bars to the Distinguished Service Order. He married, in 1904, Nellie Borlase, daughter of the late Vice-Admiral J. J. Kennedy, C.B., and they have one daughter.

London Gazette, 16 May, 1899.—"War Office, 16 May, 1899. The Queen has been graciously pleased to give orders for the following appointments to the Distinguished Service Order, in recognition of the services of the undermentioned Officers during the recent operations on the North-West Frontier of India."

MORE-MOLYNEUX, GEORGE HAND, Colonel, was born at Littleton, near Guildford, Surrey, 6 May, 1851, son of Lieut.-Colonel A. More-Molyneux, H.E.I.C., grandson of J. More-Molyneux, Losely Park, Surrey. He was educated at Guildford Grammar School, and at Bedford Grammar School, and was gazetted Ensign in the 87th Foot 5 Jan. 1870, and transferred to the 37th Foot 1 April, 1870. He became Lieutenant, 37th Foot, 27 Oct. 1871, and Bengal Staff Corps, 21 July, 1874; served in the Afghan War, 1878-80 (Medal); and was promoted to Captain 5 Jan. 1882. He was on Special Service, Expeditionary Force, Suakin, 20 Feb. 1885, to 5 March, 1885; attached to the Intelligence Department; was present at the actions of Hasheen and Thakool, and operations at Tamai (Medal with clasp; Bronze Star). He was D.A.A. and Q.M.G., Egypt, 6 March, 1885, to June, 1885. From 1885 to 1889 he served in the Burmese Expedition as D.A.A. General; was mentioned in Despatches 15 Nov. 1889; received the Medal with two clasps, and was given the Brevet of Lieutenant-Colonel 6 Jan. 1890. He had been promoted to Major, I.S.C., 5 Jan. 1890. From 8 Dec. 1890, to 5 Feb. 1892, he was Military Attaché at St. Petersburg; and from 30 Nov. 1893 to 5 Jan. 1894, he was A.Q.M.G. (Intelligence), Headquarters, India. He became Colonel 5 Jan. 1896. In 1897–98 he took part in the operations on the North-West Frontier of India, serving with the Tirah Expeditionary Force as A.Q.M.G. for Intelligence, and being present at the action of Saran Sar. He was mentioned in Despatches 5 April, 1898, received the Medal with two clasps, and was created a Companion of the Distinguished Service Order [London Gazette, 16 May, 1899]: "George Hand More-Molyneux, Colonel, Indian Staff Corps. In recognition of services during the recent operations on the North-West Frontier of India." The Insignia were sent to the Commander-in-Chief in India and sent to Colonel More-Molyneux. Owing to her presence at Balmoral the Queen regretted that she was unable personally to decorate Colonel More-Molyneux previous to his departure for India 8 Sept. 1899. He was Colonel on the Staff, India, 29 July, 1898; was created a C.B. in 1900; commanded Rohilkand District, India, from 1901. He had married, in 1889, Alice Julia, daughter of C. P. Matthews, of Havering-atte-Bower, Essex. Colonel More-Molyneux died 21 Nov. 1903.

BARTON, MAURICE CHARLES, Lieut.-Colonel, was born 13 April, 1852, son of Charles Barton, of Holbrook, Wincanton, Somerset. He entered the Royal Engineers 2 May, 1872, as Lieutenant; served in the Afghan War, 1878–79 (Despatches, Medal); in the Akha Expedition, 1883–84 (Despatches); became Captain 2 May, 1884. From 1885 to 1887 he served in the Burmese Expedition; was mentioned in Despatches [London Gazette, 22 June, 1886, and 2 Sept. 1887], and received the Medal with clasp. He became Major 8 Sept. 1891, and in the following year again saw active service in the Isazai Expedition, as Commanding Officer, Royal Engineers. In 1895 he took part in the operations in Chitral, serving with the Relief Force, in charge of Field Park, Royal Engineers. He was mentioned in Despatches [London Gazette, 15 Nov. 1895], and received the Medal and clasp. He was present in the operations on the North-West Frontier of India, 1897–98, with the Malakand Field Force and with the Buner Field Force as Field Engineer, and took part in the attack and capture of the Tanga Pass. He was mentioned in Despatches [London Gazette, 22 April, 1898], received a clasp, and was created a Companion of the Distinguished Service Order [London Gazette, 16 May, 1899]: "Maurice Charles Barton, Lieut.-Colonel, Royal Engineers. In recognition of services during the recent operations on the North-West Frontier of India." The Insignia were presented to him by the Queen at Windsor 1 July, 1899. He had been promoted to Lieutenant-Colonel 14 March, 1899. He was given the Brevet of Colonel 14 March, 1903, and retired as Colonel 14 Jan. 1905. Colonel Barton married, in 1887, Harriet, daughter of Colonel Brandreth, Royal Engineers.

ROWCROFT, GEORGE FRANCIS, Capt., was born in London 4 May, 1861, eldest son of Major-General George Cleland Rowcroft, of Buckden, Huntingdon, and of Oriana Rachel Rowcroft, daughter of the late Hon. P. D. Souper, Registrar-General of Mauritius. He was educated at Bradfield College, at Cheltenham College, and at the Royal Military College, Sandhurst, and was gazetted to the 54th Foot (designated in 1881 the 2nd Battn. Dorsetshire Regt.) on 12 Aug. 1879, joining his regiment in Nov. 1879, in India, and becoming Lieutenant 26 July, 1881. He was transferred on 16 Nov. 1881, to the 15th Ludhiana Sikhs, Bengal Staff Corps, and served in the Sudan Campaign of 1885, as Adjutant of that Regiment, being present at the action of Hasheen and operations of Tamai (Medal with clasp, Bronze Star). He became Captain 13 Aug. 1890, and served in 1895 in the Chitral Campaign (Medal and clasp). Capt. Rowcroft served on the North-West Frontier of India in the Tirah Campaign, 1897–98. He was mentioned in Despatches [London Gazette, 5 April, 1898], and was created a Companion of the Distinguished Service Order [London Gazette, 16 May, 1899]: "George Francis Rowcroft, Capt., Indian Staff Corps. In recognition of services during the recent operations on the North-West Frontier of India." (Insignia sent to the Commander-in-Chief in India, and presented by the Officer Commanding at Ferozepore at a Review Order Parade on 5 Aug. 1899.) The D.S.O. was given to Capt. Rowcroft two years after the Tirah Campaign, but no official account was published, nor any intimation given as to the particular act for which it was awarded. In the Tirah Campaign Capt. Rowcroft carried in two or three wounded men under fire, and went back alone, looking for a wounded man who had been left behind, and he also got a badly wounded officer on to a mule, when three men who helped him were in turn shot down, one after the other. He was mentioned in Despatches on two other occasions in this campaign. He was a temporary Major from 15 Feb. 1898; was promoted to Major 13 Aug. 1899; was temporary Lieutenant-Colonel 27 April, 1902, received the Delhi Durbar Medal, 1902, and promoted to Lieutenant-Colonel 1 June, 1904, and given the Brevet of Colonel 8 June, 1907. He commanded the 15th Sikhs (Bengal Infantry), and retired with the rank of Colonel 20 Nov. 1907. Colonel Rowcroft is M.R.C.S. and L.R.C.P., London (St. Bartholomew's Hospital). In Jan. 1915, he became a temporary Major, Indian Medical Service. He married 24 Oct. 1884, Florence Marion Eva, daughter of the late Major-General Henessy, and they have two sons, Maurice George, Capt., 8th Lincolnshire Regt., and Eric Bertram, Capt., Army Service Corps, and a daughter, Ruby Frances.

George Francis Rowcroft.

WELLS-COLE, HENRY, Capt., was born 9 May, 1864, son of the late William Wells-Cole, of Fenton, Lincolnshire. He was educated at the Royal Military College, Sandhurst, and became Lieutenant, Yorkshire Light Infantry, 23 Aug. 1884, and Captain 17 May, 1892; was Adjutant, Yorkshire Light Infantry, 23 July, 1897, to 25 Jan. 1901. He served on the North-West Frontier of India in the Tirah Expedition, 1897–98, was mentioned in Despatches [London Gazette, 7 June, 1898], received the Medal with two clasps, and was created a Companion of the Distinguished Service Order [London Gazette, 16 May, 1899]: "Henry Wells-Cole, Capt., Yorkshire Light Infantry. In recognition of services during the recent operations on the North-West Frontier of India." (The Insignia, etc., sent to the G.O.C., Mauritius. D.S.O. presented by the G.O.C. Mauritius at a parade of the half battalion in Port Louis, previous to embarkation for South Africa, on the morning of the 6th Oct. 1899.) Capt. Wells-Cole served in the South African War, 1899–1902. He was in command of the 2nd Battn. Yorkshire Light Infantry 2 June to 6 Aug. 1900; served as Adjutant, 2nd Battn. Yorkshire Light Infantry, 30 Nov. 1900, to 25 Jan. 1901; was Assistant Provost-Marshal 26 Jan. 1901, to 27 April, 1901; was D.A.A.G. 28 April, 1901, to 13 Sept. 1902. He took part in the advance on Kimberley, including the actions at Belmont, Enslin, Modder River and Magersfontein. Operations in the Transvaal, west of Pretoria, Aug. to Nov. 1900. Operations in Orange River Colony, May to Aug. 1900, including actions at Lindley (28 June), Bethlehem (6 and 7 July) and Wittebergen (1 to 29 July). He was mentioned in Despatches [London Gazette, 10 Sept. 1901), was given the Brevet of Major 29 Nov. 1900; received the Queen's Medal with four clasps, the King's Medal with two clasps, and was placed on the list of officers considered qualified for Staff employment in consequence of service in the Field. He was promoted to Major 10 May, 1902; was Officer, Company of Gentlemen Cadets, Royal Military College, 28 Jan. 1903, to 28 Aug. 1903; Commander, Company of Gentlemen Cadets, Royal Military College, 29 Aug. 1903, to 22 Jan. 1904; G.S.O.2, Royal Military College, 1 March, 1903, to 27 Jan. 1908. He was given the Brevet of Lieutenant-Colonel in 1911; was G.S.O.2, South Africa. Lieut.-Colonel Wells-Cole died 30 April, 1914.

HILL, JOHN, Capt., was born at Bangalore 14 Jan. 1866, eldest son of Major-General W. Hill and Charlotte Miller, daughter of Beauchamp Colclough Urquhart, of Meldrum and Blyth, N.B. He was educated at Bedford, and Sandhurst, and was gazetted to the 52nd Light Infantry 5 Feb. 1887, and transferred to the 15th Sikhs 11 Feb. 1888. Lushai Expedition, 1889 (Medal with clasp); Miranzai Exped. 1891 (clasp), Chitral, 1895 (Medal and clasp). In 1897–98 he served on the North-West Frontier of India, taking part in the operations on the Samana and in the Kurram Valley, during Aug. and Sept. 1897. Operations of the Flying Column in the Kurram Valley, under Colonel Richardson, 20 Aug. to 1 Oct. 1897 (two clasps). In the Tirah Campaign in 1897–98 he was present at the actions of Chagru Kotal and Dargai, and the capture of the Sampagha and Arhanga Passes. Operations in the Waran Valley, and actions of 16 Nov. 1897. He was mentioned in Despatches [London Gazette, 7 June, 1898], received a clasp, and was created a Companion of the Distinguished Service Order [London Gazette, 16 May, 1899]: "John Hill, Capt., Indian Staff Corps. In recognition of services during the recent operations on the North-West Frontier of India." The Insignia were sent to the Commander-in-Chief in India and the D.S.O. presented by the Officer Commanding at Ferozepore, at a Review Order Parade on 5 Aug. 1899. He became Captain 5 Feb. 1898; Major 5 Feb. 1905; Lieutenant-Colonel 5 Feb. 1913; was Commandant, 15th Sikhs, till 1 Jan. 1918. Lieut.-Colonel Hill served in the European War from 1914; was given the Brevet of Colonel 3 June, 1915; was Brigade Commander, 34th Infantry Brigade, Mediterranean Expeditionary Force; and British Armies in France 2 Oct. 1915, to 9 Feb. 1917; Brigade Commander, 180th Infantry Brigade, Egyptian Expeditionary Force, 30 Aug. 1917, to 10 Sept. 1917; Divisional Commander, 52nd Division, Egyptian Expeditionary Force; and British Armies in France 11 Sept. 1917, to 24 Sept. 1918; promoted to Major-General 3 June, 1918. For his services in the European War General Hill was mentioned in Despatches six times; received the 1914 Star; was given the Brevet of Colonel; appointed A.D.C. to the King 3 June, 1916; received the 3rd Class Order of the White Eagle of Serbia and the 2nd Class Order of the Nile; created a C.B. 13 April, 1918, and promoted to Major-General.

ELIOTT-LOCKHART, PERCY CLARE, Capt., was born at Kamptee, India, 21 Sept. 1867, son of Colonel William Eliott-Lockhart, late Royal Artillery, and Ada, daughter of the late Henry Cardew. He was educated at Somerset College, Bath, and gazetted to the 1st West Indian Regt. 23 Nov. 1887; became Lieutenant, West Indian Regt., 5 June, 1889, and I.S.C. 14 Nov. 1890. He served in the Waziristan Expedition, 1894–95, as Brigade Transport Officer (Medal with clasp). In 1895 he took part in the operations in Chitral, serving with the Relief Force and was present at the storming of the Malakand Pass (Medal with clasp). In 1897–98, on the North-West Frontier of India, he was present at the Defence and Relief of Malakand, and at the Relief of Chakdara; at the operations in Bajaur and in the Mamund country; Utman Khel; Buner. He was mentioned in Despatches [London Gazette, 5 Nov. 1897], received two clasps, and was created a Companion of the Distinguished Service Order [London Gazette, 16 May, 1899]: "Percy Clare Eliott-Lockhart, Capt., Indian Staff Corps. In recognition of services during the recent operations on the North-West Frontier of India." The Insignia were sent to the Commander-in-Chief in India, and presented by the O.C. at Mardan, in presence of the Cavalry and Infantry of the Corps of Guides, 18 July, 1899. He had been promoted to Captain 23 Nov. 1898. Capt. Eliott-Lockhart served in China in 1900 (Medal). He was on Special Service, Somaliland Field Force, 14 March, 1903, to 15 July, 1903; and was D.A.A. and Q.M.G., 2nd Brigade, Somaliland Field Force, 16 July, 1903, to June, 1904. During the operations in Somaliland he was present at the action of Jidballi, was mentioned in Despatches [London Gazette, 2 Sept. 1904], and received the Medal and two clasps. He was promoted to Major, Queen's Own Corps of Guides, 23 Nov. 1905. In the European War Lieut.-Colonel P. C. Eliott-Lockhart commanded the 50th Scinde Rifles in France, and died on 13 March, 1915, of wounds received at Neuve Chapelle. He was mentioned in Despatches for "Distinguished conduct in the field." He had married, in 1905, Katharine Mary, daughter of James Worrall, and they had one son.

London Gazette, 30 June, 1899.—"War Office, 30 June, 1899. The Queen has been pleased to give orders for the following appointments to the Distinguished Service Order, in recognition of the services of the following Officers during the recent operations in the Sudan."

NASON, FORTESCUE JOHN, Major, was born 14 Sept. 1859, son of the late Major-General John Nason. He was educated at Harrow, and was gazetted to the 26th Foot as Second Lieutenant 11 Aug. 1880, becoming Lieutenant, Scottish Rifles, 1 July, 1881, and Captain 17 May, 1886; and was employed with the Egyptian Army 30 July, 1888, to 5 March, 1890; and again from 18 April, 1896. He served in the Sudan in 1889; was present at the action of Arguin, and was wounded (4th Class Medjidie; Medal and Bronze Star). He was Adjutant, Scottish Rifles, 29 Oct. 1890, to 28 Oct. 1894. He served in the Expedition to Dongola, 1896, as Brigade Major, 1st Brigade, taking part in the operations of 7 June and 19 Sept.; was mentioned in Despatches [London Gazette, 3 Nov. 1896], and received the Egyptian Medal and two clasps. He served in the Nile Expedition of 1897 (clasp to Egyptian Medal). On 22 Dec. 1897, he was promoted to Major. In 1898 he served in the Nile Expedition, was present at the battles of the Atbara and Khartum, and at the defeat of Ahmed Fedil's Army. He was mentioned in Despatches [London Gazette, 30 Sept. 1898, and 5 May, 1899]; was given the Brevet of Lieutenant-Colonel 16 Nov. 1898; received the Medal, and three clasps to the Egyptian Medal, and was created a Companion of the Distinguished Service Order [London Gazette, 30 June, 1899]: "Fortescue John Nason, Major and Brevet Lieut.-Colonel, Indian Staff Corps. In recognition of services during the recent operations in the Sudan, including the battles of the Atbara and Khartum." The Insignia were presented to him by the Queen at Osborne 5 Aug. 1899. He served in the Nile Expedition of 1899, taking part in the first advance against the Khalifa, and received the 3rd Class Osmanieh, and a clasp to the Egyptian Medal. He retired with the rank of Colonel 27 May, 1905. Colonel Nason served in the European War from 1914 to 1918; was three times mentioned in Despatches; received the Bronze Star (1914); was created a C.M.G., 1915, and a C.B., 1918.

JENNINGS, JAMES WILLES, Capt., was born 25 Feb. 1866, son of the late Robert Jennings, of Woodlawn, Cork. He was educated at Monmouth; was 1st Senior Medallist, Surgery, R.C.S., Ireland, 1886–87; 1st Prizeman, Surgery, Adelaide Hospital, Dublin, 1886; L.R.C.S., L.M., Ireland; L.M., Rotunda; F.Z.S., F.R.G.S.; Member Royal Institute of Public Health. He became Captain, Army Medical Department, 31 Jan. 1891; served in the Dongola Expedition, 1896 (Egyptian Medal). He was selected for service in the Egyptian Army in Jan. 1897; served in the Nile Expedition of 1897 (clasp to Egyptian Medal). He served in the Nile Expedition of 1898, was present at the Battle of Khartum, and in the defeat of Ahmed Fedil's Army at Rosaires 26 Dec. 1898. He was mentioned in Despatches [London Gazette, 30 Sept. 1898, and 5 May, 1899]; received a clasp to the Egyptian Medal, the Medal, the 4th Class Medjidie, and was created a Companion of the Distinguished Service Order [London Gazette, 30 June, 1899]: "James Willes Jennings, Capt., Royal Army Medical Corps. In recognition of services during the recent operations in Egypt and the Sudan, including the Battle of Khartum." The Insignia were presented to him by the Queen at Osborne 5 Aug. 1899. Capt. Jennings was Senior Medical Officer, Blue Nile District, Sudan, 1898–99. He served in South Africa, 1899–1902, and was present at the Relief of Ladysmith; operations on Tugela Heights 14 to 27 Feb. 1900 (in Medical Charge of the 2nd West Yorkshire Regt.). Operations in Natal, March to June, 1900, including action of Laing's Nek. Operations in the Transvaal, east of Pretoria, July to 29 Nov. 1900. Operations in the Transvaal and Orange River Colony 30 Nov. 1900, to 31 May, 1902 (Despatches [London Gazette, 8 Feb. 1901]; Queen's Medal with five clasps; King's Medal with two clasps). He became Major 31 Jan. 1903, and was specially selected for service with the Abyssinian Army against the Mullah, 1903–04 (Despatches, London Gazette, 2 Sept. 1904; Medal and clasp). He served on the Army Headquarters Staff, India, 1905–07. Major Jennings retired 31 Jan. 1911. He served in the European War as Lieutenant-Colonel, Commanding 56th Field Ambulance, B.E.F., France, 1915–16; commanding St. Andrew's Military Hospital, Malta, 1917–18, and No. 5 Stationary Hospital, B.E.F., France, 1919. Lieut.-Colonel Jennings published "Cordite Eating" (1903), and "With the Abyssinians in Somaliland" (1906). He married, in 1899, Katie (who died in 1900), daughter of the late Archibald Grey, of 37, Holland Park, W.

STRICKLAND, EDWARD PETER, Lieut., was born at Snitterfield, Warwickshire, 3 Aug. 1869, third son of the late Major F. W. Strickland. He was educated at Warwick School, and was gazetted to the Norfolk Regt. 10 Nov. 1888, becoming Lieutenant 29 April, 1891. He was employed with the Egyptian Army 1 April, 1896, to 31 March, 1903. He served in the Expedition to Dongola, 1896. Operations of 7 June and 19 Sept. He was mentioned in Despatches [London Gazette, 3 Nov. 1896], and received the Egyptian Medal with two clasps. For the Nile Expedition of 1897 he was mentioned in Despatches [London Gazette, 25 Jan. 1898], and received a clasp to the Egyptian Medal. In the Nile Expedition of 1898 he was present in the battles of the Atbara and Khartum, was mentioned in Despatches [London Gazette, 24 May and 30 Sept. 1898], was given the Brevet of Major 22 Oct. 1899, and two clasps to the Egyptian Medal. He served in the Nile Expedition of 1899, taking part in the operations on the White Nile against Ahmed Fedil's Army. He was created a Companion of the Distinguished Service Order [London Gazette, 30 June, 1899]: "Edward Peter Strickland, Lieut., The Norfolk Regt. In recognition of services during the recent operations in Egypt and the Sudan." (Insignia presented by the Queen at Osborne 5 Aug. 1899.) He was present also in the first advance against the Khalifa, and received a clasp to the Egyptian Medal. He became Captain 21 Oct. 1899. From 3 Feb. 1906, to 2 Aug. 1913, he was employed with the West African Frontier Force. He was promoted to Major 1 Sept. 1908: became temporary Colonel, North Nigerian Regt., 1909; was created a C.M.G., 1913; became Lieutenant-Colonel, The Manchester Regt., 1 June, 1914. He served in the European War from 1914 to 1918; was given the Brevet of Colonel 18 Feb. 1915; was Brigade Commander, Jullundur Brigade, B.E.F., Indian Expeditionary Force "D," 4 Jan. 1915, to 15 Nov. 1915; Brigade Commander, 95th Infantry Brigade, B.E.F., British Armies in France, 16 Nov. 1915, to 11 June, 1916; Divisional Commander, 1st Division British Armies in France, 12 June, 1916; promoted to Major-General 1 Jan. 1918; appointed Colonel, Norfolk Regt., 24 Dec. 1917. For his services in the European War he was mentioned in Despatches, created a C.B. 1917, and a K.C.B. in 1919; promoted to Lieutenant-Colonel, Manchester Regt., 1914; was given the Brevet of Colonel; promoted to Brigadier-General, 1915, and to Major-General, 1918. Sir Edward Strickland married, in 1918, Barbara, daughter of the late Martin W. W. ffolkes and widow of Capt. F. J. Cresswell, Norfolk Regt.

London Gazette, 30 June, 1899.—" War Office, 30 June, 1899. The Queen has been pleased to give orders for the following appointments to the Distinguished Service Order, in recognition of the services of the under-mentioned Officers with the Royal Niger Constabulary, during the recent operations in the Benin Hinterland, Siama, etc. To be Companions of the Distinguished Service Order."

WILLIAMS, WEIR DE LANCEY, Capt., was born 2 March, 1872, son of Sir W. J. Williams, K.C.B., of Pembroke, Wales. He was educated at the United Services College, Westward Ho! and entered the Hampshire Regt. 17 June, 1891, becoming Lieutenant 17 Sept. 1892. He took part in the operations on the North-West Frontier of India, 1897–98, with the Tirah Expeditionary Force, and was severely wounded (Medal and two clasps). He became Captain 17 April, 1898, and was on Special Extra-Regimental Employment 23 June, 1898, to 30 Sept. 1899, and served in West Africa in 1898, in the operations in the Niger Territories, including the Illah (wounded) and Siama Expeditions. He was mentioned in Despatches [London Gazette, 30 May, 1899, and was created a Companion of the Distinguished Service Order [London Gazette, 30 June, 1899]: "Weir de Lancey Williams, Capt., Hampshire Regt. In recognition of services during the recent operations in West Africa." The Insignia were presented to him by the Queen at Windsor 30 Nov. 1899. Capt. Williams served in the South African War in 1900, and was severely wounded. Operations in the Orange Free State, Feb. to May, 1900, including operations at Paardeberg (17 to 26 Feb.); actions at Poplar Frove and Karee Siding. He was mentioned in Despatches [London Gazette, 10 Sept. 1901], and received the Queen's Medal with two clasps. He was Station Staff Officer, 1st Class, India, 3 Sept. 1903, to 31 May, 1904; Brigade-Major, India, 1 June, 1904, to 30 June, 1906; D.A.A.G., India, 10 Feb. 1908, to 15 Feb. 1912. He was promoted to Major 3 Jan. 1909, and was G.S.O.2, Welsh Division, Western Command, 29 Sept. 1913, to 4 Aug. 1914. He served in the European War, 1914–18, as G.S.O.1, 1/1st Welsh Division, Central Force, Home Defence, 5 Aug. 1914, to 2 March, 1915; as G.S.O.1, Headquarters, Mediterranean Expeditionary Force, 3 March, 1915, to 25 April, 1915; became Lieutenant-Colonel, Hampshire Regt., 28 Aug. 1915; commanded the 88th Infantry Brigade, Mediterranean Expeditionary Force, 28 April, 1915, to 26 May, 1915; was given the Brevet of Colonel 3 June, 1915; commanded the 86th Infantry Brigade, Mediterranean Expeditionary Force, and British Armies in France, 21 Dec. 1915, to 29 April, 1917; was Divisional Commander, 30th Division, British Armies in France, 30 April, 1917, to 6 Jan. 1919; was promoted to Major-General 1 Jan. 1919; was Inspector of Infantry 7 Jan. 1919, to 20 Jan. 1919; Temporary Commander, Southern District, Irish Command, 21 Jan. 1919. For his services in the European War he was mentioned in Despatches; created a C.M.G. in 1917; given the Brevet of Colonel, and promoted to Major-General. General Williams married, in 1899, Nina Henrietta, daughter of Colonel Field, late 6th Foot, and they have one daughter.

DIGAN, AUGUSTIN J., Captain, was born in 1878, and entered the Mid-Ulster Artillery in 1897, becoming Captain 29 April, 1899. He served in West Africa in 1898, taking part in the operations in the Niger Territory, including Benin Hinterland and Siama Expeditions; was mentioned in Despatches 30 May, 1899, and created a Companion of the Distinguished Service Order [London Gazette, 30 June, 1899]: "Augustin J. Digan, Capt., Mid-Ulster Artillery. In recognition of services during the recent operations in West Africa." The Insignia, Warrant and Statutes were sent to the Foreign Office, and thence forwarded to the Royal Niger Company. The D.S.O. was presented at Lokija, 27 Sept. 1899. He later joined the 3rd Battn. (Reserve) Connaught Rangers. In 1914 Major Digan married Helen, daughter of Angus Macgregor.

BOWKER, WILLIAM JAMES, Lieut., was born 8 June, 1869, son of the late Frederick Bowker, of Lankhills, Barrister, of Lincoln's Inn; Livery Skinners' Company. He entered Prince Albert's Somerset Light Infantry 21 Dec. 1889, and became Lieutenant 14 June, 1892. He served in West Africa in 1898, taking part in the operations in the Niger Territories, including the Illah and Siama Expeditions. He was mentioned in Despatches, and was created a Companion of the Distinguished Service Order [London Gazette, 30 June, 1899]: "William James Bowker, Lieut., Somerset Light Infantry. In recognition of services during the recent operations in West Africa." The Insignia were kept by the Foreign Office until Capt. Bowker's return from East Africa. The D.S.O. was presented to him by the King 24 Oct. 1902. (This is the first entry of a presentation by King Edward VII.) Lieut. Bowker was promoted to Captain 2 Aug. 1899, and served in South Africa from 1899 to 1902, taking part in the operations in Natal in 1899. Relief of Ladysmith, including operations of 17 to 24 Jan. 1900, and action at Spion Kop; operations of 5 to 7 Feb. 1900, and action at Vaal Kranz; operations on Tugela Heights (14 to 27 Feb. 1900). Operations in the Orange Free State, April to May, 1900. Operations in the Transvaal, in June, 1900. Operations in Natal, March to April, 1900. Operations in the Transvaal, west of Pretoria, July to 29 Nov. 1900. Operations in Cape Colony, north of Orange River, in 1900. Operations in the Transvaal, April, 1901, to May, 1902. Operations in Orange River Colony, June and July, 1901 (Queen's Medal with five clasps; King's Medal with two clasps). He became Major 26 June, 1909. Major Bowker served in the European War from 1914. From Oct. 1915, to May, 1917, he was Temporary Lieutenant-Colonel, and from 5 May, 1917, to 31 Aug. 1917, he was Brigade-Commander, 231st Infantry Brigade, Egyptian Expeditionary Force. From 12 Feb. 1918, to 30 June, 1918, he commanded the 230th Infantry Brigade, Egyptian Expeditionary Force, and later, British Armies in France. He became Lieutenant-Colonel 21 April, 1918; was mentioned in Despatches, and created a C.M.G. in 1916, for services in the war.

WORSHIP, VERELST TURNER, Lieut., was born at Great Yarmouth 21 Feb. 1871, son of the late William Worship and Rebecca Branford, daughter of the late Capt. R. Glasspoole, H.E.I.C. He was educated at Rugby, and joined the 101st Regt. 9 Jan. 1892, becoming Lieutenant 8 July, 1893. He was on Special Extra Regimental Employment 10 Sept. 1898, to 1 Dec. 1899, and saw active service in West Africa in 1898, taking part in the operations under the Royal Niger Company, Benin Hinterland Expedition, Niger Territories, including the Illah and Siama Expeditions. He was mentioned in Despatches [London Gazette, 30 May, 1899]; received the Medal with clasp, and was created a Companion of the Distinguished Service Order [London Gazette, 30 June, 1899]: "Verelst Turner Worship, Lieut., Royal Munster Fusiliers. In recognition of services during the recent operations in West Africa." From 1 Sept. 1907, to 31 March, 1908, he was Adjutant, Volunteers, and from 1 April, 1908, to 15 Sept. 1909, was Adjutant, Territorial Force. During the European War he was in command of the 6th Battn. Royal Munster Fusiliers, 19 Aug. 1914, to 15 Dec. 1916; he was Temporary Lieutenant-Colonel 19 Aug. 1914, to 22 May, 1915. He became Lieutenant-Colonel 23 May, 1915; commanded a Special Reserve Battn. Dorsetshire Regt. from 16 Dec. 1916, to 10 Dec. 1918.

WAKE, WILLIAM ST. AUBYN, Lieut., was born 26 Oct. 1871, and was gazetted to the Middlesex Regt. 18 June, 1892, becoming Lieutenant 17 Aug. 1894. He was on Special Extra Regimental Employment 27 Aug. 1898, serving under the Royal Niger Company, and taking part in the operations in the Niger Territories, including Benin Hinterland and Siama Expeditions. He was wounded; was mentioned in Despatches [London Gazette, 30 May, 1899], and created a Companion of the Distinguished Service Order [London Gazette, 30 June, 1899]: "William St. Aubyn Wake, Lieut., Middlesex Regt. In recognition of services during the recent operations on the West Coast of Africa. Lieut. Wake died 4 Feb. 1900, and the Insignia, Warrant and Statutes of the D.S.O. were returned through the Foreign Office, and sent to the mother of Lieut. Wake, Mrs. Wake, 43, Brompton Square, S.W.

WILLIAMS, WILLIAM ARTHUR GLANMOR, Lieut., was born 18 Sept. 1873. He was gazetted to the South Wales Borderers 20 May, 1893, and became Lieutenant 9 Oct. 1895. From 10 Sept. 1898, to 17 Nov. 1899, he was on Special Extra Regimental Employment, and served under the Royal Niger Company in the operations in the Niger Territories, including the Benin Hinterland and Siama Expeditions. He was wounded; mentioned in Despatches [London Gazette, 30 May, 1899], and was created a Companion of the Distinguished Service Order [London Gazette, 30 June, 1899]: "William Arthur Glanmor Williams, Lieut., South Wales Borderers. In recognition of services during the recent operations in West Africa." The Insignia, Warrant and Statutes were forwarded to the Royal Niger Company, and the D.S.O. was presented at Likoja 20 Oct. 1899. Lieut. Williams died 6 Nov. 1900.

LAWRENCE, FREELING ROSS, Lieut., was born 21 Sept. 1872; was educated at Wellington College, and became Second Lieutenant, 14th Hussars, 7 March, 1894, and was promoted to Lieutenant 13 Nov. 1895. He was on Special Extra Regimental Employment 27 Aug. 1898, to 17 Nov. 1899, serving in West Africa in 1898, under the Royal Niger Company, in the operations in the Niger Territories, including the Illah and Siama Expeditions. He was mentioned in Despatches, and created a Companion of the Distinguished Service Order [London Gazette, 30 June, 1899]: "Freeling Ross Lawrence, Lieut., 14th Hussars. In recognition of services during the recent operations in West Africa." The Insignia, etc., were forwarded to the Royal Niger Company, and presented to Lieut. Lawrence at Likoja 20 Oct. 1899. He served in the South African War, 1899–1902, as Adjutant, 14th Hussars, 18 Nov. 1899, to 11 Aug. 1901. He became Captain 11 July, 1900. He was present at the Relief of Ladysmith, including operations of 5 to 7 Feb. 1900, and action at Vaal Kranz; operations on Tugela Heights (14 to 27 Feb. 1900), and action at Pieter's Hill. Operations in the Orange Free State, Feb. to May, 1900, including actions at Houtnek (Thoba Mountain) and Zand River. Operations in the Transvaal in May and June, 1900, including actions near Johannesburg, Pretoria and Diamond Hill (11 and 12 June). Operations in the Transvaal, east of Pretoria, July to 29 Nov. 1900, including actions at Belfast (26 and 27 Aug.). Operations in the Transvaal 30 Nov. 1900, to April, 1901, and Aug. to Dec. 1901. He was mentioned in Despatches [London Gazette, 8 Feb. and 10 Sept. 1901]; received the Queen's Medal with nine clasps, and was given the Brevet of Major 29 Nov. 1900. He was Brigade Major, 2nd Cavalry Brigade, 24 May, 1905, to 30 June, 1907; became Major 22 Feb. 1907; was G.S.O., 3rd Grade, Headquarters of Army, from 1 July, 1907. Major Lawrence was in 1913 General Staff Officer, 9th Division, Secunderabad. He died on 9 March, 1914, at Netley Hospital.

FORBES, ARCHIBALD JONES, Lieut., was born 15 Jan. 1873. He was gazetted to the South Wales Borderers 20 May, 1893, and became Lieutenant 18 Nov. 1895. From 10 Sept. 1898, he was on Special Extra Regimental Employment, under the Royal Niger Company, and he took part in 1898 in the operations in the Niger Territories, including the Benin Hinterland and Siama Expeditions. He was mentioned in Despatches [London Gazette, 30 May, 1899], and was created a Companion of the Distinguished Service Order [London Gazette, 30 June, 1899]: "Archibald Jones Forbes, Lieut., South Wales Borderers. In recognition of services during the recent operations in West Africa." The Insignia, Warrant and Statutes were sent to the Foreign Office, and forwarded to the Royal Niger Company. The D.S.O. was presented at Likoja 27 Sept. 1899. Lieut. Forbes died 13 May, 1901.

TIGHE, VINCENT AUGUSTINE, Lieut., was born 13 Aug. 1863, son of the late Major M. J. Tighe (70th East Surrey Regt.). Gazetted to West Riding Regt. as Second Lieutenant 7 Feb. 1894; was on Special Extra Regimental Employment 24 Oct. 1896, to 19 Sept. 1899, serving under the Royal Niger Company in the expeditions to Egbon, Bida and Ilorin (Medal with clasp). He was transferred to the West India Regt. as Lieutenant 12 Jan. 1898; and took part in the operations in the Niger

Territories, including Benin Hinterland and Siama Expeditions (wounded). He was mentioned in Despatches [London Gazette, 30 May, 1899], and was created a Companion of the Distinguished Service Order [London Gazette, 30 June, 1899]: "Vincent John Tighe, Lieut., West India Regt. In recognition of services during the recent operations in West Africa." The Insignia were presented by the Queen. The London Gazette of 30 June, 1899, gave Lieut. Tighe's name incorrectly, and it was later announced that his second name was "Augustine, according to his baptismal certificate." He became Captain 22 Sept. 1900. Capt. Tighe again saw active service in West Africa in 1900, taking part in the operations in Ashanti, and being present at the Relief of Kumasi. He was slightly wounded. He retired on 13 Aug. 1908 (late West India Regt. and Manchester Regt.). He married, in 1906, Angela Lucy, fourth daughter of Osmond Seager, and they had four daughters. Major Tighe died 7 June, 1919.

London Gazette, 7 July, 1899.—"The Queen has been graciously pleased to give orders for the following appointment to the Distinguished Service Order, in recognition of the services of the undermentioned Officer during the recent operations in Uganda. To be a Companion of the Distinguished Service Order."

PRICE, CHARLES HENRY UVEDALE, Capt. and Brevet Major, was born 16 June, 1862, third son of General G. Uvedale Price and Harriette Anne Wilhelmina, daughter of the Rev. C. R. Gayer. He became Lieutenant, Welsh Regt., 22 Oct. 1881, and Indian Staff Corps, 16 June, 1883. From 1886–88 he served in the Burmese Expedition; was severely wounded, and received the Medal with two clasps. He became Captain 22 Oct. 1892. In 1898 and 1899 he served in Uganda, in command of the Singe Field Force, of operations in Ankole, and, for some time, of troops in Unyoro. He commanded a column against the Sudanese Mutineers, including the action at Jeruba, and several other engagements. He was mentioned in Despatches; was given the Brevet of Major 25 Jan. 1899; received the Medal and two clasps, and was created a Companion of the Distinguished Service Order [London Gazette, 7 July, 1899]: "Charles Henry Uvedale Price, Capt. and Brevet Major, Indian Staff Corps. In recognition of services during the recent operations in Uganda." The Insignia, Warrant and Statutes were sent to the Commander-in-Chief in India, and the Insignia presented by the G.O.C., Tirah District, on 13 Sept. 1899, at a full-dress parade of the troops at Karachi. He was D.A.A.G., India, from 26 April, 1900; became Major, Indian Army, 10 July, 1901; Lieutenant-Colonel 1 March, 1905, and was given the Brevet of Colonel 1 March, 1908, becoming Colonel 1 Jan. 1911. He was Brigade Commander (Colonel on the Staff), India, 16 Nov. 1914, to 22 July, 1915; was created a C.B. in 1914; was Brigade Commander, India, 22 July, 1915, to 20 May, 1916; President, Area Quartering Committee, Cardiff Area, 29 May, 1917. He married, in 1889, Ada Mary, daughter of J. O. H. N. Oliver, C.S.I.

London Gazette, 7 July, 1899.—"War Office, 7 July, 1899. The Queen has been graciously pleased to give orders for the following appointment to the Distinguished Service Order, in recognition of the services of the undermentioned Officer whilst employed in the protected territories adjacent to the Gold Coast and Lagos, and on the Niger. To be a Companion of the Distinguished Service Order."

FESTING, ARTHUR HOSKYNS, Capt. and Brevet Major, was born on 9 Feb. 1869, son of Henry Blaythwayt Festing, of Bois Hall, Addlestone, and Mary Eliza, eldest child of Richard James Todd, of Great Eppleton Hall, Durham (Count of the Holy Roman Empire, created 1704; title not assumed in England). He was educated privately; on the Continent, and at Sandhurst; was gazetted to the Royal Irish Rifles on 11 Feb. 1888, and served with his regiment in the Nile Campaign of 1889, becoming Lieutenant 3 July, 1889. He was seconded for service with the Royal Niger Company in 1895, and served as Adjutant to the Force in the Niger-Sudan Campaign of 1896–97, taking part in the expeditions to Egbon, Bida and Ilorin. He was mentioned in Despatches [London Gazette, 11 June, 1897], and received the West African Medal with Clasp (Niger, 1897), and was given the Brevet of Major (16 Jan. 1898) on promotion to Captain 15 Jan. 1898. He also received the Jubilee Medal. He served with the combined Imperial Troops (West African Frontier Force), and with the Royal Niger Company's troops in 1898 and 1899, being present in the operations on the Niger. He served in Borgu, and took part in the expeditions to Lapia, Argeyah, Ibouza (in command) and Anam (in command). He was mentioned in Despatches [London Gazette, 7 March, 1899]; received a clasp, and was created a Companion of the Distinguished Service Order [London Gazette, 7 July, 1899]: "Arthur Hoskyns Festing, Capt. and Brevet Major, Royal Irish Rifles. In recognition of services whilst employed in the protected territories adjacent to the Gold Coast and Lagos, and on the Niger." The Insignia were presented to him at Likoja. He served in the South African War, 1899–1900, in command of the 11th Mounted Infantry, and on the Staff of the Rhodesian Field Force, taking part in the operations in the Orange Free State, Feb. to May, 1900; in the operations in Cape Colony, south of the Orange River, in 1900; in the operations in Rhodesia in May, 1900; operations in the Transvaal, west of Pretoria, July to Nov. 1900. He received the Queen's Medal with five clasps. He served in West Africa (Southern Nigeria), 1901–2, and in the Aro Expedition, commanding various columns. He was mentioned in Despatches (London Gazette, 12 Sept. 1902]; received the Medal with clasp, and was created a C.M.G. in 1902. In 1903 he served as Base Commandant in West Africa (Northern Nigeria), with the Kano-Sokoto Expeditionary Force. He was mentioned in Despatches [London Gazette, 31 July, 1903], and received a clasp. Major Festing retired from the Army in 1905, on receiving a civil appointment under the Colonial Office. He served in the European War, and was killed in action on 9 May, 1915. Major Festing had married Victoria Eugenie Valentine, Comtesse de Valette, who died in 1913. His favourite recreations were hunting, big game shooting and polo.

London Gazette, 3 Oct. 1899.—"War Office, 3 Oct. 1899. The Queen has been graciously pleased to give orders for the following appointments to the Distinguished Service Order, in recognition of the services of the undermentioned Officers during the recent operations in Uganda and British Central Africa. To be Companions of the Distinguished Service Order."

AUSTIN, HERBERT HENRY, Capt. and Brevet Major, was born at Thayetmyo, Burma, 1 June, 1868, son of Colonel Edmund Austin (deceased), late 76th Regt. and Indian Army, and of Ellen Mary Austin (deceased). He was educated at Clifton College; entered the Army 16 Feb. 1887, as Second Lieutenant in the Royal Engineers; became Lieutenant 16 Feb. 1890; was employed in India on trans-frontier surveys on Kabul River and Zhob Valley Railway surveys, 1890–91; created a Fellow of the Royal Geographical Society in 1893; assisted in preliminary survey for Uganda Railway, 1891–92. He served in the Waziristan Expedition, 1894–95 (Medal with clasp); was promoted to Captain 1 Oct. 1897. He served in Uganda in 1897–98, and commanded during the skirmish at Lubwas; repelled the attack at Kijembo; captured Kabagambi; was afterwards in command at Mruli. He was mentioned in Despatches by Lieut.-Colonel J. R. L. Macdonald; received the Brevet of Major 25 Jan. 1899; 3rd Class Order Brilliant Star of Zanzibar; the Medal with two clasps, and was created a Companion of the Distinguished Service Order [London Gazette, 3 Oct. 1899]: "Herbert Henry Austin, Capt. and Brevet Major, Royal Engineers. In recognition of services during the recent operations in Uganda and British Central Africa. The Insignia were presented by the Queen at Osborne 20 Aug. 1900. He was engaged in operations in East African Protectorate, in direction of Lake Rudolf, 1898–99 (mentioned in Despatches). He conducted two survey expeditions, Western Borders of Abyssinia 4 Oct. 1899, to 28 Nov. 1900 (awarded C.M.G.); and 29 Nov. 1900, to 30 June, 1902; passed through the Staff College, Camberley, 1903–4; awarded the Cuthbert Peck Grant by the Royal Geographical Society in 1906. He was D.A.Q.M.G., Headquarters, India; G.S.O., 2nd Grade, Headquarters, India, from 10 June, 1907, to 11 Nov. 1911; operations in the Persian Gulf in connection with gun-running, 1909–10; Brevet Lieutenant-Colonel in Jan. 1911. He was G.S.O., 2nd Grade, Headquarters, India, 17 April, 1913, to 20 Jan. 1914; G.S.O., 2nd Grade, Staff College, Quetta, 21 Jan. 1914, to 15 Sept. 1914; G.S.O., 1st Grade, Headquarters, India (Temporary), 21 Jan. 1914, to 31 March, 1915; was Brigadier-General, General Staff, Indian Expeditionary Force "D," 19 Dec. 1915, to 27 Jan. 1916; Brigade Commander, Lines of Communication, Indian Expeditionary Force "D," 28 Jan. 1916, to 30 Sept. 1918; was Commandant (Class S) from 1 Oct. 1918. For his services in the Indian Expeditionary Force "D" (Mesopotamia) he was mentioned in Despatches in 1916 by Sir Percy Lake, and given the Brevet of Colonel 3 June, 1917. He was created a C.B. in 1918. He also received the Serbian Decoration, 3rd Class White Eagle. He has published: "Among Swamps and Giants in Equatorial Africa," 1902; "With Macdonald in Uganda," 1903; and "A Scamper through the Far East," 1909. He married, at Bournemouth, 13 Nov. 1912, Winifred, elder daughter of Lieut.-Colonel and Mrs. W. H. McCausland, of Bournemouth, and they have two sons: Rudolf Edmund Austin, born 11 March, 1914, and Antony Herbert Austin, born 25 July, 1916.

Herbert Henry Austin.

BRAKE, HERBERT EDWARD JOHN, Capt., was born at Melksham, Wilts, 9 Feb. 1866, only son of Surgeon-General Brake, I.M.S. He was educated at Westward Ho! and joined the Royal Artillery as Lieutenant 18 Feb. 1886. He served on the Punjab Frontier of India, 1887 to 1896, and was promoted to Captain 1 Nov. 1896. Capt. Brake was employed in the British Central African Protectorate 24 July, 1897, to 1 Dec. 1898, taking part in the expedition against the Mpezeni. He was mentioned in Despatches; received the Medal with clasp, and was created a Companion of the Distinguished Service Order [London Gazette, 3 Oct. 1899]: "Herbert Edward John Brake, Capt., Royal Artillery. In recognition of services during the recent operations in Uganda and Dutch Central Africa." The Insignia, etc., were sent to the Officer Commanding, Mauritius, who transferred the D.S.O. to the G.O.C., Aden. Temporary Lieut.-Colonel H. E. J. Brake acknowledged receipt of the Insignia, etc., 6 May, 1900, forwarded to him by Officer Commanding the Troops, Mauritius. No official presentation was possible. Colonel Brake served in West Africa 1 Jan. 1899, to 2 Aug. 1902, with the King's African Rifles, taking part in the operations in Ashanti. He was slightly wounded; was mentioned in Despatches [London Gazette, 8 March, 1901], and was given the Brevet of Major 29 Nov. 1900. He was specially employed in West Africa in 1900, commanding the Field Force up the Gambia, and the operations against Fodi Kabba 29 Dec. 1900, to 4 June, 1901. He was mentioned in Despatches [London Gazette, 10 Sept. 1901]; received the Medal with clasp and was created a C.B. in 1901. He raised the 2nd Battn. King's African Rifles, and commanded it 1 Jan. 1899, to 2 Aug. 1902. He was Commandant of the Local Forces, and Inspector-General of Police, Trinidad, 17 Sept. 1902, to 16 Sept. 1907. He was promoted Major 6 Jan. 1905. He served in the European War from 1914; was promoted Lieutenant-Colonel 30 Oct. 1914, and given the Brevet of Colonel 1 Jan. 1916; was Brigadier-General, Royal Artillery, Heavy Artillery, 18th Army Corps,

British Armies in France, 15 Jan. 1917, to 2 April, 1918; Commandant, Heavy Artillery, Training Centre, Forces in Great Britain, from 1 June, 1918. He was created a C.M.G. in 1918.

London Gazette, 9 Jan. 1900.—" War Office, 9 Jan. 1900. The Queen has been graciously pleased to give orders for the following appointments to the Distinguished Service Order, in recognition of the services of the undermentioned Officers, while employed in Sierra Leone, the Niger Territories and Uganda."

THOMAS, ARTHUR HAVILLAND, Major, was born in India, 31 July, 1860, third son of the late Henry Sullivan Thomas Indian Civil Service (retired), and Julia Ellen, daughter of the Rev. Nicholas Walters, of Stamford. He was educated at Cheltenham College and at the Royal Military College, Sandhurst, and joined the 31st Regt. 11 Aug. 1880, and became Lieutenant, East Surrey Regt., 28 Feb. 1881; was D.A.C.G., Commissariat and Transport Staff, 19 Nov. 1886, to 10 Dec. 1888; was promoted to Captain, East Surrey Regt., 14 Dec. 1887, and attached to the Army Service Corps 11 Dec. 1888, being transferred to the Army Service Corps 1 April, 1889. He was D.A.A.G., China and Hong-Kong 14 June, 1893, to 26 May, 1896, and became Major 31 July, 1895. He was in charge of the Supply and Transport, Sierra Leone Rebellion, 1898–99, taking part in the Karene Expedition and in the Protectorate Expedition, in command of the Army Service Corps; was mentioned in Despatches [London Gazette, 29 Dec. 1899]; received the Medal and clasp, and was created a Companion of the Distinguished Service Order [London Gazette, 9 Jan. 1900]: " Arthur Havilland Thomas, Major, Army Service Corps. In recognition of services whilst employed in Sierra Leone." Major Thomas served in the South African War, as D.A.A.G., Field Army, 9 Oct. 1899, to 11 Nov. 1900; and A.A.G. and Director of Supplies, Cape Colony District, 5 July, 1901, to 29 May, 1902. He was present at the operations in Orange River Colony, May to Sept. 1900, including the action at Wittebergen. He took part also in the operations in Cape Colony 30 Nov. 1900, to 31 May, 1902; was mentioned in Despatches [London Gazette, 10 Sept. 1901]; received the Queen's Medal with three clasps; the King's Medal with two clasps, and was created a C.B. in 1902. He became a Lieutenant-Colonel 12 Nov. 1900; was given the Brevet of Colonel 10 Feb. 1904, and became Colonel 15 Oct. 1905, on which date he was appointed Assistant Director of Supplies and Transport, Southern Command. He retired 16 April, 1910. Colonel Thomas served in the European War as Assistant Director of Supplies and Transport. He married, in Feb. 1903, Louie Marion, daughter of Edward Druce, of Dover.

CROFTS, RICHARD, Major, was born 11 Aug. 1859. He joined the Royal Army Medical Corps 31 Jan. 1885. He took part in the expedition against the Jebus, Lagos, in 1892; was mentioned in Despatches [London Gazette, 1 July, 1892], and received the Medal and clasp. He became Major 31 Jan. 1897, and in 1898 served in Sierra Leone, taking part in the Karene Expedition. He was mentioned in Despatches [London Gazette, 29 Dec. 1899], and received a clasp, and was created a Companion of the Distinguished Service Order [London Gazette, 9 Jan. 1900]: " Richard Crofts, Major, Royal Army Medical Corps. In recognition of services whilst employed in Sierra Leone." The Insignia, Warrant and Statutes were sent to the Officer Commanding Troops, Sierra Leone. The D.S.O. was presented to him by Lady Cardew, wife of the Governor of Sierra Leone, at a parade of all the troops in garrison in review order 19 May, 1900. The D.S.O. was presented at the same time to Major Morgan. Major Crofts was Senior Medical Officer, Sierra Leone. He retired from the Royal Army Medical Corps 31 Jan. 1905.

MORGAN, CECIL BUCKLEY, Major, was born 18 Nov. 1860, at Streatham, London, S.W., son of the late Thomas Morgan, Esq., F.S.A. He was educated at Dulwich College, and at Sandhurst; entered the West India Regt. 23 Aug. 1884. He served in West Africa, 1892–93–95; took part in the operations on the Niger Territories, and was twice wounded. He married, on 13 June, 1895, Maud Mary, daughter of Richard Keeling, and their children are: Hermione; Phyllis; Basil Morgan, Second Lieutenant, Hampshire Regt., born in 1898; Evadne, and Donald, born in 1900. Major Morgan served in West Africa, 1897–98, taking part in the operations in Sierra Leone and in the Mendiland Expedition (severely wounded); commanded an Expedition up the Jong River. He was mentioned in Despatches [London Gazette, 29 Dec. 1899], and was created a Companion of the Distinguished Service Order [London Gazette, 9 Jan. 1900]: " Cecil Buckley Morgan, Major, West India Regt. In recognition of services in Sierra Leone." The Insignia were presented by Lady Cardew, wife of the Governor of Sierra Leone, at a parade of all the troops in garrison in review order 19 May, 1900. He had been promoted Major 20 Jan. 1898. Major Morgan served in the South African War, 1901–2, on the Staff, and as District Commandant, afterwards Administrator, No. 9 Area. He took part in the operations in Cape Colony, 1901–2, and received the Queen's Medal with three clasps. He retired and joined the Reserve of Officers. Major Morgan served in the European War; became Temporary Lieutenant-Colonel, and commanded the 22nd (Service) Battn. of the Durham Light Infantry, British Expeditionary Force, France. Lieut.-Colonel C. B. Morgan died on 29 March, 1918, of a gunshot wound received in action.

A paragraph in the " Times " said:

" Second Lieut. Basil Algernon Cecil Morgan, Hampshire Regt., officially reported missing on 28 March, since unofficially reported killed, aged 19, obtained his commission in Oct. 1916, from Sandhurst, and last Feb. joined his regiment at the front, where he remained until the day of his death. He was the elder son of Lieut.-Colonel Cecil B. Morgan, D.S.O., Durham Light Infantry, who was killed in the same battle. Lieut. Morgan's Commanding Officer wrote: ' I shall regret his loss very deeply. During the short time he had been with the Hampshire Regt. he had made himself very popular both amongst the officers and men, and was a very promising officer.' "

GOODWYN, NORTON JAMES, Capt., was born on 7 Oct. 1861, second son of General J. E. Goodwyn, C.B. He became Lieutenant, Devonshire Regt., 9 Sept. 1882; Captain 1 April, 1891; served in Burma, 1891–92, with the Irrawaddy Column (received the Medal and clasp). He was Adjutant, Devonshire Regt., 17 Oct. 1892, to 5 April, 1894; was employed with the Egyptian Army 6 April, 1894, to 29 Feb. 1896. He was attached to the West African Regt. 9 April, 1898, to 24 June, 1899; was present at the operations in Sierra Leone, 1898–99, taking part in the Mendiland Expedition, including Songo Town–Kwalu Expedition. He served afterwards with the Karene and Protectorate Expeditions. He was mentioned in Despatches [London Gazette, 29 Dec. 1899], and was created a Companion of the Distinguished Service Order [London Gazette, 9 Jan. 1900]: " Norton James Goodwyn, Capt., Devonshire Regt. In recognition of services in the recent operations in Sierra Leone." The Insignia were sent to Capt. Goodwyn at home. He was promoted to Major. He served in the South African War, 1899–1900: as Second-in-Command of Thorneycroft's Mounted Infantry from 1900 (was severely wounded in the Battle of Colenso, and mentioned in Despatches). He was given the Brevet of Lieutenant-Colonel in 1902, and was appointed Inspector of Gymnasia in India in 1904. He died 6 May, 1906, in Australia, on his way home on leave from India.

CARLETON, FREDERICK MONTGOMERIE, Capt., was born 21 July, 1867, youngest son of the late General Henry Carleton, C.B., Royal Artillery. He was educated at the Military College, Oxford; joined the King's Own Regt. 3 Oct. 1888; became Lieutenant 1 April, 1890; was Adjutant, Royal Lancaster Regt., 12 July, 1891, to 11 July, 1895; was employed with the Egyptian Army 21 March, 1896, to 16 Oct. 1897; served with the Expedition to Dongola in 1896, and was mentioned in Despatches [London Gazette, 3 Nov. 1896]. He also served in the Nile Expedition in 1897 (Medal); was promoted to Captain, King's Own Regt., 11 May, 1898, and was attached to the West African Regt. 9 April, 1898, to 24 June, 1899. He was Acting Staff Officer, Mendiland Expedition (including Songo Town–Kwalu Expedition), afterwards with the Karene and Protectorate Expeditions. He was mentioned in Despatches [London Gazette, 29 Dec. 1899]; received the Medal and Clasp, and was created a Companion of the Distinguished Service Order [London Gazette, 9 Jan. 1900]: " Frederick Montgomerie Carleton, Capt., Royal Lancaster Regt. For services whilst employed in Sierra Leone." The Insignia, etc., were sent to the Commander-in-Chief, South Africa, and the D.S.O. presented by Lieut.-General Hildyard, Commanding 5th Division, 22 April, 1900, in Tonono Valley Camp, near Elandslaagte. He became A.D.C. to the Major-General Commanding the 5th Infantry Brigade, South Africa, 13 Nov. 1899, to 11 Dec. 1901. He was present at the Relief of Ladysmith, including the operations of the 17th to the 24th Jan. 1900, and the action at Spion Kop (slightly wounded). He was mentioned in Despatches by Sir R. Buller 30 March; 19 June and 9 Nov. 1900 [London Gazette, 8 Feb. 1901]: received the Brevet of Major; Queen's Medal with six clasps, and the King's Medal with two clasps. He passed the Staff College in 1902; became Major 26 June, 1906, and retired 22 Feb. 1908. He served in the European War and retired with the rank of Brigadier-General 20 Oct. 1917. In 1890, he married Gwendolen, eldest daughter of the late S. Lloyd, of The Priory, Warwick, and of Dolobran, Montgomeryshire, and they have two sons and one daughter. His favourite recreations are hunting, shooting and polo.

RUSSELL, HORATIO DOUGLAS, Lieut., was born 11 July, 1874, son of the late Colonel Horatio Albert Russell, C.B., and of Elizabeth D. Young, daughter of D. D. Young, of Quebec. He entered the West India Regt. 20 Sept. 1895, as Second Lieutenant; became Lieutenant 23 Oct. 1897; took part in the operations in Sierra Leone, 1898–99; was present in the Karene and Mendiland Expeditions. He was twice wounded; was mentioned in Despatches [London Gazette, 29 Dec. 1899]; received the Medal and clasp, and was created a Companion of the Distinguished Service Order [London Gazette, 9 Jan. 1900]: " Horatio Douglas Russell, Lieut., West India Regt. In recognition of services whilst employed in Sierra Leone." The Insignia, etc., were sent to the G.O.C., Egypt, and forwarded to the Sirdar for presentation. The D.S.O. was presented by the Sirdar 14 April, 1900. He was employed with the Egyptian Army from 17 Feb. 1900, to 23 June, 1910; became Captain 27 June, 1900, and was transferred to the Army Service Corps 1 Feb. 1902. In 1907 Capt. Russell married Eileen, daughter of H. R. Mullock Emerson, of Dublin. He was promoted Major 15 Dec. 1913. He served in the European War from 1914 to 1918, and was promoted to Lieutenant-Colonel 13 June, 1918.

FERGUSON, HENRY GASPARD DE LAVALETTE, Capt., is the son of the late Major-General C. Johnston-Ferguson. He joined the 4th (Militia) Battn. Norfolk Regt., and served in Sierra Leone, 1898–99, taking part in the Mendiland and Protectorate Expeditions. He was slightly wounded; mentioned in Despatches [London Gazette, 29 Dec. 1899], and created a Companion of the Distinguished Service Order [London Gazette, 9 Jan. 1900]: " Henry Gaspard de Lavalette Ferguson, Capt., 4th (Militia) Battn. Norfolk Regt. In recognition of services whilst employed in Sierra Leone." The Insignia, Warrant and Statutes were sent to Capt. Ferguson at home. He served in South Africa, 1900–2, as Assistant Provost-Marshal, Lines of Communication (received the Queen's Medal with three clasps, and the King's Medal with two clasps. Major Ferguson retired 13 July, 1901, and joined the Reserve of Officers. He served in the European War from 1914 to 1918; was given the Brevet of Lieutenant-Colonel; became Lieutenant-Colonel, and was awarded a Bar to the Distinguished Service Order. His favourite recreations are racing, polo, hunting and big game shooting.

HOWELL, WILFRED RUSSELL, Lieut., was born at Outreaux, France, 13 May, 1864, son of Russell Howell, M.A., Chamberlain to the Pope. He was educated at Feldkirch College, Austria and at Fort Augustus

College, Scotland. He raised a volunteer corps, and, in command of a composite body of gunners and the West Indian Regt., served through the Mendi Rising in Sierra Leone in 1898–99. He was mentioned in Despatches; received the thanks of the Government, and was created a Companion of the Distinguished Service Order [London Gazette, 9 Jan. 1900]: "Wilfred Russell Howell, Lieut., 1st Glamorgan Volunteer Artillery. In recognition of services whilst employed in Sierra Leone." Lieut. Howell was the first Volunteer Officer to receive the D.S.O. He served through the South African War with the West Somerset Imperial Yeomanry, the Transvaal Constabulary, and the South African Constabulary; was severely wounded; received the Queen's Medal and six clasps, and the King's Medal and two clasps. He raised and commanded the Engineer Company, Rhodesian Volunteers, and Sierra Leone Volunteers; became Captain in the South African Constabulary, West Somerset Yeomanry, and Glamorgan Volunteer Artillery. He resigned his commission in 1910. He was Resident Engineer of the Rhodesian and Mashonaland Railways; was General Manager of the Western Railway of Havana, Southern Longitudinal and Transandian of Chili. He served in the European War as Major on the General Staff, 1st Canadian Contingent; in the Secret Service with the Home Office, Admiralty and Foreign Office; Lieutenant-Colonel Commanding the 1st G.B. Battn. Royal Welsh Fusiliers; Colonel and Controller-in-Chief of the Bagdad Railway. Colonel Howell was twice mentioned in Despatches. He married, in 1901, Elsie, youngest daughter of the late Colonel Lucius Cary, of Torr Abbey, Torquay, and they have four daughters.

KER, CHARLES ARTHUR, Lieut., was born 18 April, 1875, at Clifton, Gloucestershire, son of Charles Buchanan Ker, of Clifton, Gloucestershire. He joined the Royal Artillery 15 June, 1895. He became Lieutenant 15 June, 1898; was employed with the West African Frontier Force 16 Feb. 1898, to 9 April, 1899; took part in the operations on the Niger, including the Illah Expedition, and was present at four engagements, including that of Iseli Nipatima. He was mentioned in Despatches [London Gazette, 23 May, 1899]; received the Medal and Clasp, and was created a Companion of the Distinguished Service Order [London Gazette, 9 Jan. 1900]: "Charles Arthur Ker, Lieut., Royal Artillery. In recognition of services in the recent operations in the Niger Territories." The Insignia, Warrant and Statutes were sent to the Commander-in-Chief, South Africa, and the D.S.O. presented by the Colonel on the Staff, Commanding Royal Artillery, 22 April, 1900, at Ladysmith (Vide Sir R. Buller, 22 April, 1900). He served in the South African War, 1897–98, and was present at the Relief of Ladysmith, including the operations of 17 to 24 Jan. 1900, and action at Spion Kop; operations of 5–7 Feb. 1900, and action at Vaal Kranz; operations on Tugela Heights (14–27 Feb. 1900). Operations in Orange River Colony, Nov. 1900, to April, 1901 (Despatches [London Gazette, 10 Sept. 1901]; Queen's Medal with six clasps). Lieut. Ker was promoted to Captain 1 March, 1901; was Divisional Adjutant, Plymouth, Royal Artillery, 6 Oct. 1902, to 31 March, 1903; Adjutant, Royal Artillery, 1 April, 1903, to 5 Oct. 1905. He was Officer, Company of Gentlemen Cadets, Royal Military College, Camberley, 1 Sept. 1906, to 21 Jan. 1910; Student at the Staff College, Camberley, 1910 to 1911; D.A.A. and Q.M.G., South-West Coast Defences, Southern Command, 6 June, 1912, to 21 April, 1914; G.S.O., 2nd Grade, Royal Military College, Kingston, Canada, 22 April, 1914, to 30 Nov. 1914; was awarded the Brevet rank of Major 5 Aug. 1914. He served in the European War. Was Brigade-Major, Royal Artillery, 1 Dec. 1914, to 30 April, 1915; G.S.O., 2nd Grade, Royal Artillery, France, 1 May, 1915, to 1 Feb. 1916; G.S.O., 1st Grade, France, 5 Feb. 1916, to 23 May, 1916; G.S.O.1, Royal Naval Division, British Armies in France, 24 May, 1916, to 28 July, 1916; G.S.O.1., Lines of Communication, British Armies in France, 29 July, 1916, to 22 Dec. 1916; G.S.O.1, attached Portuguese Division, British Armies in France, 23 Dec. 1916, to 6 Jan. 1918; Brigadier-General, General Staff (British Mission, attached to Portuguese Expeditionary Force, British Armies in France), 7 Jan. 1918. He was twice mentioned in Despatches; was given the Brevet of Lieutenant-Colonel 1 Jan. 1917, and of Colonel 1 Jan. 1918, and created a C.M.G.. On 18 July, 1898, at Yealmpton, Devonshire, he married Blanche, second daughter of Charles Bewes, of Gnaton Hall, Devon, and their children are: Alan Charles Bewes Ker and Mary Blanche Ker.

EVATT, JOHN THOROLD, Capt., was born 1 Aug. 1861, son of the late Henry Ashmore, 90th Light Infantry, and Public Works Department, Ceylon, and Mary Frances, daughter of the Rev. John Hinde. He was educated at Whitgift School, Croydon, and entered the 54th Foot 23 April, 1881, as Second Lieutenant, from the 4th or Royal South Middlesex Militia; became Lieutenant, Dorset Regt., 1 July, 1881, and Indian Staff Corps 14 July, 1883, becoming Captain, Indian Staff Corps, 23 April, 1892. He served in Burma, 1891–92, with the Tlang-Tlang and Tashon Columns (Medal with two clasps); took part in the operations on the North-West Frontier of India, 1897–98, serving in the Mohmand and Malakand operations in Bajaur; also with the Tirah Expeditionary Force (Medal with two clasps). He served in British East Africa in 1898, taking part in the expedition against the Ogaden Somalis (Medal and clasp). Capt. Evatt served in Uganda, 1898–99, and was in command at the capture of Kabarega and Mwanga, Kings of Unyoro and Uganda. He was mentioned in Despatches [London Gazette, 2 Jan. 1900]; received a clasp, and was created a Companion of

John Thorold Evatt.

J.R.M Dalrymple Hay.

the Distinguished Service Order [London Gazette, 9 Jan. 1900]: "John Thorold Evatt, Capt., Indian Staff Corps. In recognition of services in Uganda." The D.S.O. was presented by Her Majesty's Commissioner and Consul-General in Uganda. Capt. Evatt was again in command in the Nandi Expedition in Uganda in 1900 (was mentioned in Despatches [London Gazette, 10 Sept. 1901]; was given the Brevet of Lieutenant-Colonel 24 April, 1901, and the Medal with clasp). He was promoted to Major 23 April, 1901. He raised and commanded the first Indian Contingent for Uganda; commanded the Uganda Military Force; raised and commanded the 2nd Battn. 39th Garhwal Rifles; became Lieutenant-Colonel 1 June, 1904; was given the Brevet of Colonel 30 April, 1904; became Substantive Colonel 23 Nov. 1907, and Temporary Brigadier-General, Commanding the Madras Brigade until 1910. He retired from the Army 23 April, 1913, with the rank of Brigadier-General, and was appointed Colonel of the 39th Garhwal Rifles in 1914. Brigadier-General J. T. Evatt was re-employed in 1914, and appointed Brigade-Commander (mentioned in Secretary of State's Despatch [London Gazette, 25 Jan. 1917). He subsequently served as Deputy Assistant Censor, 1916–17, and as Area Commandant in France in 1917.

London Gazette, 6 Nov. 1900.— "War Office, 6 Nov. 1900. The Queen has been graciously pleased to give orders for the following appointments to the Distinguished Service Order, in recognition of the services of the undermentioned Officers during the war in South Africa. To be Companions of the Distinguished Service Order."

HUNT, GEORGE PERCY EDWARD, Lieut., Royal Navy, was born 15 April, 1863, at Shooling, Southampton, son of George Jenkins Hunt and Mary Hooper. He was educated in the Conway, and left the Mercantile Marine to join the Royal Navy as a Supplementary Lieutenant in Oct. 1895. As a Lieutenant in the Forte he served with distinction with the Naval Brigade in South Africa in 1900, with the two 4.7 guns which did such excellent work. Capt. Jones (H.M.S. Forte), in his report, said: "Lieut. Hunt has acted as Brigade-Major, Quartermaster, Chief of my Staff, all rolled into one, as well as commanding a 4.7 gun after being up the greater part of the night with paper work, after long fatiguing days. His services have been invaluable to me." Lieut. Hunt was mentioned three times in Despatches, and was created a Companion of the Distinguished Service Order [London Gazette, 6 Nov. 1900]: "George Percy Edward Hunt, Lieut., Royal Navy. In recognition of services during the war in South Africa." The Insignia, Warrant and Statutes were sent to the Admiralty, and presented by the Governor of the Gambia on board H.M.S. Forte (Admiralty, 23 July, 1901). In 1901 Lieut. Hunt took command of a Naval Brigade landed at Attwaboe, West Africa, for the purpose of capturing 150 mutineers of the West African Regt. He was promoted to Commander in Jan. 1902, and in the same year served in the Gambia Expedition. On 28 March, 1905, at Wheathampstead, Herts, Commander Hunt married Cecilia Teresa Clementi, third daughter of the late Right Honourable Sir Cecil Clementi Smith, P.C., G.C.M.G. He became Captain in June, 1907. In Feb. 1908, Capt. Hunt received a letter of commendation from the Lords of the Admiralty for the good result obtained by H.M.S. Prince George in the Annual Test of Gun-layers for 1907. He retired from the Service in July, 1913, at the age of fifty, but returned to serve again in Aug. 1914. He was in charge of fitting out merchant cruisers on the Thames, Aug. and Sept. 1914, and their Lordships expressed their appreciation of his services. He was Assistant Captain of H.M. Dockyard at Devonport at the time of his death, which took place on the 22nd Aug. 1917. He was buried at Almeley on the 25th Aug. 1917. During three years of service in Devonport Dockyard, their Lordships expressed their appreciation of his work in salving vessels on several occasions.

George Percy E. Hunt.

JONES, WALTER THOMAS CRESSWELL, Lieut., was born on 31 Jan. 1874, son of the Rev. George Jones and Rosamond Alice Jones, daughter of Capt. Ward, late Devon Regt. He was educated at Bradfield College, Berkshire, and by the Rev. J. Scott Ramsay, Army Tutor; entered the Royal Marine Light Infantry 1 Sept. 1893, becoming Lieutenant 1 July, 1894. He served in the South African War with the Naval Brigade; was present in the advance on Kimberley, including actions at Belmont and Enslin (Graspan) (wounded); was mentioned in Despatches [London Gazette, 26 Jan. and 30 March, 1900, and 10 Sept. 1901], and created a Companion of the Distinguished Service Order [London Gazette, 6 Nov. 1900]: "Walter Thomas Cresswell Jones, Lieut., Royal Marine Light Infantry. In recognition of services during the war in South Africa." "Admiralty, 9 Nov. 1900.—With reference to the notice in the London Gazette of 6 Nov. 1900, the rank of Walter Thomas Cresswell Jones, R.M.L.I., upon whom His Majesty has conferred the D.S.O., is Captain, and not Lieutenant, as therein stated." He became Captain on 16 March, 1900. Capt. Jones was decorated by Her Majesty the Queen at Windsor 15 Dec. 1900. He served on the China Station, 1901–8. In 1911 he married Hildred, eldest daughter of A. St. Clair Buxton, and they have one son, Peter Cresswell, born on 8 June, 1913, and two daughters: Mary Hildred and Rachel Elizabeth. He became Major 23 April, 1911; was employed in the Naval Intelligence Department, Admiralty, 17 July, 1911, to 2 April, 1915. He served in the European War in 1915 (Dardanelles), and was mentioned in Despatches. He became Assistant Director Operations Division, Admiralty War Staff (Staff Officer, 1st Grade); Temporary

Lieutenant-Colonel 17 Sept. 1915, and was given the Brevet of Lieutenant-Colonel 23 April, 1918.

MACMILLAN, CHARLES CLARKE, Surgeon, Royal Navy, was born in Australia in April, 1873, son of the Rev. J. K. Macmillan and Janet M. Clarke. He was educated at Edinburgh University (M.B., Ch.M., Edinburgh); graduated in 1897. He entered the Royal Navy. He served in South Africa in 1900, with 12-pounder Naval Guns with General Buller in Natal. For his services with the Naval Brigade at the Relief of Ladysmith he was created a Companion of the Distinguished Service Order [London Gazette, 6 Nov. 1900]: "Charles Clarke Macmillan, Surgeon, Royal Navy. In recognition of services during the war in South Africa." The Insignia were presented at Hong-Kong by the Rear-Admiral, Second-in-Command on the China Station. He again saw active service as Surgeon in H.M.S. Terrible, in the China War of 1900. He served in H.M.S. London in the Mediterranean, at landing in Gallipoli in April, 1915, at Anzac Cove. Fleet-Surgeon C. C. Macmillan married, in Sept. 1903, Katherine Marie Campbell, youngest daughter of the Rev. J. Conway Walter, of Langton, Lincolnshire.

COLQUHOUN, WILLIAM JARVIE, Lieut., Victorian Navy, was born in Dumbartonshire 19 Feb. 1859. He served in the South African War, with the Naval Brigade, 1899–1900, and was present at Paardeberg. He was created a Companion of the Distinguished Service Order [London Gazette, 6 Nov. 1900]: "William Jarvie Colquhoun, Lieut., Victorian Navy. In recognition of services during the war in South Africa." The Insignia were sent to the Admiralty, and were presented on 31 Jan. 1901, at Hong-Kong, by the Rear-Admiral, Second-in-Command on the China Station. He also received the Queen's Medal and five clasps, and was mentioned in Despatches. He was Naval A.D.C. to the Governor-General of Australia. In the Russo-Japanese War of 1904, he acted as Special Naval Correspondent for the "Times." He died at Sydney, New South Wales, 17 Aug. 1908. Commander Colquhoun married, in 1887, Emmie, daughter of William Kelly, of Blackheath, and they had two sons and one daughter.

CHIAZZARI, NICHOLAS WILLIAM, Lieut., Natal Naval Volunteers, was born in 1868, son of Joseph Chiazzari. He served in South Africa. He was created a Companion of the Distinguished Service Order [London Gazette, 6 Nov. 1900]: "Nicholas William Chiazzari, Lieut., Natal Naval Volunteers. In recognition of services during the war in South Africa." The Insignia were presented by the Governor of Natal, 31 Jan. 1901, at a Parade of the Natal Naval Volunteers at Durban (Admiralty, 11 March, 1901). He was promoted Commander. Commander Chiazzari married, in 1890, Elizabeth Kavanagh.

London Gazette, 9 Nov. 1900.—"War Office, 9 Nov. 1900. The Queen has been graciously pleased to give orders for the following appointments to the Distinguished Service Order, in recognition of services rendered during the recent disturbances in China."

LOWTHER-CROFTON, EDWARD GEORGE, Lieut., Royal Navy, was born 9 Aug. 1873, son of Major Lowther-Crofton. He entered the Royal Navy in 1888; served in China, 1900. He was created a Companion of the Distinguished Service Order [London Gazette, 9 Nov. 1900]: "Edward George Lowther-Crofton, Lieut., Royal Navy. In recognition of services during the recent disturbances in China." The Insignia, etc., were sent to the Admiralty, and presented 31 Jan. 1901, at Hong-Kong, by the Rear-Admiral, Second-in-Command on the China Station. He served in the European War, commanding the 9th Destroyer Flotilla, and as Assistant to the Admiral of Patrols. Capt. Lowther-Crofton married, in 1911, Magdalen, daughter of Charles Anderson, and they have one son.

CHARRINGTON, ERIC, Lieut., Royal Navy, was born 30 Aug. 1873, youngest son of the late Spencer Charrington, Esq., M.P. He was educated at Brighton and Portsmouth; obtained four first-classes at College as Sub-Lieutenant, and entered the Navy in 1885. He served in Zanzibar in 1896; in Benin, 1897 (Medal). He served in China (1900), with the storming party at the attack and capture of the Taku Forts, relief of and operations round Tientsin. He received the China Medal, and for services at the attack and capture of the Taku Forts was created a Companion of the Distinguished Service Order [London Gazette, 9 Nov. 1900]: "Eric Charrington, Lieut., Royal Navy. In recognition of services in China." The Insignia, etc., were sent to the Admiralty, and presented on 31 Jan. 1901, at Hong-Kong, by the Rear-Admiral, Second-in-Command on the China Station. He has retired from the Navy. Capt. Charrington married, in 1905, Rose Evelyn, youngest daughter of Lieut.-Colonel St. J. Daubeney, and they have one son.

MACKENZIE, COLIN, Lieut., Royal Navy, was born in 1872, son of the late Donald Mackenzie, of Gairloch, Perth. He entered the Royal Navy in 1885, and became Lieutenant in 1894. He served in China, 1900. He was created a Companion of the Distinguished Service Order [London Gazette, 9 Nov. 1900]: "Colin Mackenzie, Lieut., Royal Navy. In recognition of services in China." The Insignia, etc., were sent to the Admiralty, and presented on 31 Jan. 1901, at Hong-Kong, by Rear-Admiral Sir J. A. T. Bruce, Second-in-Command on the China Station. Lieut. Mackenzie was promoted to Commander in 1906. He served in the European War on the Tigris River, and took part in the operations north of Qurna, and in the occupation of Amara, 1915. He was mentioned in Despatches, and promoted to Captain. He later was in H.M.S. Warrior, in the Home Fleet, at Devonport. In 1890 he married Clare, eldest daughter of Franklin Homan, and widow of Henry Stamford Harris.

PHILLIMORE, VALENTINE EGERTON BAGOT, Lieut., Royal Navy, was born 14 Feb. 1875, son of the late Admiral Sir A. Phillimore, K.C.B. He was educated in H.M.S. Britannia; entered the Royal Navy in 1883, and served in China in 1900. He was mentioned in Despatches, Naval and Military; received a letter of thanks from the Senior American Officer, for services during the attack on Tientsin Native City, and was created a Companion of the Distinguished Service Order [London Gazette, 9 Nov. 1900]: "Valentine Egerton Bagot Phillimore, Lieut., Royal Navy. In recognition of services in China." The Insignia were sent to the Admiralty, and presented on 31 Jan. 1901, by Rear-Admiral Sir J. A. T. Bruce, Second-in-Command on the China Station. Capt. Phillimore married (1st), in 1908, Mary Kathleen (who died in 1909), daughter of George Robinson, of Overdale, Yorkshire; and (2ndly) the Noble Ines Sceberras D'Amico, daughter of the 16th Baron of Castel Cicciano.

BROMWICH, GEORGE HERBERT, Engineer, Royal Navy, was born on 27 Nov. 1871, at Frome, Somerset, son of Edmund Cockey, Esq., M.D., Surgeon. He was educated at Bloxham, Banbury, Oxford, and entered the Royal Navy in July, 1887. In 1893 he assisted in the salvage operations at Ferrol, on board H.M.S. Home, and he served on the Australian Station in H.M.S. Karrakatta, 1894–7; at the Royal Naval College at Osborne; in the Goliath, the Good Hope, etc. In 1900 he served in China, and was present at the Relief of Pekin, and Lean's Navy List says of his services in the campaign: "Promoted D.S.O. for services in China, 1900. Mentioned in Despatches; landed with the Naval Brigade for the defence of Tientsin, and accompanied brigade during Admiral Seymour's attempted relief of Legations; employed in repairing and constructing temporary armoured trucks; did Company Officer's work with Royal Marines after Capt. Beyts, R.M.A., was killed, and was left behind in the Tse-ku Arsenal, with Marines under Major Johnstone, as guard to the party left to destroy Arsenal. Employed mounting 4-inch guns of Algerine in Tientsin and near Pai Yang Arsenal; present at the taking of Native City of Tientsin." He received the Medal and was created a Companion of the Distinguished Service Order [London Gazette, 9 Nov. 1900]: "George Herbert Cockey, Engineer, Royal Navy. In recognition of services during the recent operations in China." (An additional entry says: "Name changed to Bromwich. Letter from the Admiralty dated 15 June, 1912.") He was decorated for his services with the Royal Marines during Admiral Seymour's retreat to Tientsin, and for mounting 4-inch guns at Tientsin afterwards. The Insignia, Warrant and Statutes of the D.S.O. were sent to the Admiralty, and the Insignia presented on 31 Jan. 1901, by Rear-Admiral Sir J. A. T. Bruce, Second-in-Command on the China Station. Engineer-Commander Cockey changed his name to Bromwich by deed-poll in 1912. Capt. Bromwich married, on 19 July, 1909, at Portsmouth, Evelyn Mary Newton, daughter of Richard Newton, Esq., of Brisbane, Queensland, and their children are Frank Bromwich (born 9 July, 1911), and Elizabeth Bromwich. Acting-Capt. Bromwich became General Manager, Naval Yard, Garden Island, Sydney, in 1913.

London Gazette, 15 Jan. 1901.—"The Queen has been graciously pleased to give orders for the appointment of the following Officers to the Distinguished Service Order, in recognition of services during the recent operations in Ashanti."

HOLFORD, JAMES HENRY EDWARD, Capt., was born 22 Dec. 1873. He was gazetted to the 7th Hussars 7 March, 1894, and took part in operations in South Africa in 1896, becoming Lieutenant 11 May, 1898. He served in Ashanti in 1900, and was created a Companion of the Distinguished Service Order [London Gazette, 15 Jan. 1901]: "James Henry Edward Holford, Capt., 7th Hussars. In recognition of services during the recent operations in Ashanti." The Insignia were presented by the King at St. James's Palace 12 March, 1901. Capt. Holford married, in 1901, the Hon. Blanche Grosvenor, the daughter of the 1st Baron Stalbridge and of Eleanor, daughter of the late Robert Hamilton Stubber, of Moyne, Queen's County.

COCHRANE, JOHN ERNEST CHARLES JAMES, Capt., was born 15 April, 1870, eldest son of the late John Cochrane, of Edenmore, Stranorlar, County Donegal, and of Combermore, Lifford. He was educated at Sherborne School, and Trinity College, Dublin (B.A., 1893; F.R.G.S.). Member of the Institute of Automobile Engineers; M.I.Mech.E. He joined the Donegal Artillery 16 Nov. 1895. He was selected for service with the Lagos Hausa Force in 1895, and served with the Expedition to the Gold Coast Hinterland, 1895–96 (Medal and clasp). He served in West Africa in 1900; took part in the operations in Ashanti, and was present at the defence of Kumassi. He was severely wounded, mentioned in Despatches [London Gazette, 4 Nov. 1900], received the Medal and clasp, and was created a Companion of the Distinguished Service Order [London Gazette, 15 Jan. 1901]: "John Ernest Charles Cochrane, Capt., Donegal Artillery. In recognition of services in Ashanti." The Insignia were presented by the King at Marlborough House 16 April, 1901. He retired on 7 Nov. 1900, and joined the Reserve of Officers. In 1902 he served as Adjutant, Imperial Yeomanry, in South Africa. He was with the Mechanical Transport, Army Service Corps, in 1903. Major Cochrane married Eileen Mary, daughter of Sir George Fottrell, K.C.B., Ballybrack, County Dublin, Ireland, and they have one son. He served in the European War, and as Temporary Lieutenant-Colonel on the Staff, he commanded a Brigade of Artillery from 1915 at the Dardanelles; was in France, commanding the same Brigade, from 15 Feb. 1916. He is a J.P., Hants. His favourite recreations are hunting and shooting.

NEAL, HENRY VINCENT McCANN, Capt., joined the 3rd Battn. Scottish Rifles 29 Sept. 1894; served in West Africa, 1897–98, in Lagos, and was employed in the Hinterland; was present at the attack by the Baribas in the Borgu country, and was mentioned in Despatches [London Gazette, 7 March, 1899] (Medal and clasp). He served in West Africa in 1899, taking part in the Expedition into the Central Division of the Niger Coast Protectorate (clasp). In West Africa in 1900 he served in the operations in Ashanti, was mentioned in Despatches [London Gazette, 4 Dec. 1900], received the Medal with clasp, and was created a Companion of the Distinguished Service Order [London Gazette, 15 Jan. 1901]: "Henry

Vincent McCann Neal, Capt., 3rd Battn. Scottish Rifles. In recognition of services in the recent operations in West Africa." The Insignia were presented by the King 25 July, 1901. Capt. Neal retired from the Army 16 July, 1902, and joined the Special Reserve, from which he retired on 15 March, 1913. He was appointed a 1st Class District Commissioner in Southern Nigeria in 1905, and was Assistant Colonial Secretary, Lagos. He married Mary, daughter of Frank Lane, and they have one daughter.

BISHOP, FREDERICK EDWARD, Capt., was born at Secunderabad, Deccan, 23 March, 1872, son of the late Lieut.-Colonel F. F. R. Bishop, Indian Staff Corps, and of Ellen, daughter of the late Rev. E. Symms, of Ringmer, Sussex. He was educated privately, and was gazetted to the 3rd Battn. Bedfordshire Regt. in 1891, and was seconded for service under the Colonial Office, as Assistant Inspector, Gold Coast Constabulary, 29 May, 1896. He became Captain, 1st Battn. Gold Coast Regt., West African Frontier Force, 1900; served in Ashanti, 1900; was left in command of the Fort of Kumasi when it was evacuated by the Garrison on the 23rd of June, 1900, until it was relieved by Colonel Sir James Willcocks, K.C.M.G., D.S.O. on the 15th July. Capt. Bishop was slightly wounded, mentioned in Despatches 4 Dec. 1900, and received the Medal and clasp. He was created a Companion of the Distinguished Service Order [London Gazette, 15 Jan. 1901]: "Frederick Bishop, Capt., 3rd Battn. Bedfordshire Regt. In recognition of services during the recent operations in Ashanti." The Insignia were presented by the King 25 July, 1901. He was appointed Travelling Commissioner, Northern Territories, Gold Coast, 1906, and invalided from the Colonial Service in 1908. He served in the late European War from Aug. 1914, till May, 1917, with the 3rd and 9th Battns. Bedfordshire Regt., and at the Depôt, Middlesex Regt. Capt. Bishop married, in 1909, Julia Ethel, daughter of Bromley Symons.

ARMITAGE, CECIL HAMILTON, Capt., was born 8 Oct. 1869, son of S. H. D. Armitage, Esq., M.D. He joined the 3rd Battn. South Wales Borderers 23 Oct. 1895; served in West Africa, in the Ashanti Expedition, 1895–96 (Star); in the Northern Territories (Central Zone), 1897 (Medal and clasp). He served in West Africa, 1900, during the operations in Ashanti, as Acting Resident during the Defence of Kumasi; was twice wounded (once severely), mentioned in Despatches [London Gazette, 4 Dec. 1900, and was created a Companion of the Distinguished Service Order [London Gazette, 15 Jan. 1901]: "Cecil Hamilton Armitage, Capt., 3rd Battn. South Wales Borderers. In recognition of services during the recent operations in Ashanti." The Insignia were presented by the King 3 June, 1901. Major Armitage was appointed Chief Commissioner, Northern Territories, 1910. He was created a C.M.G., 1911. He wrote a book on "The Ashanti Campaign of 1910."

ROUPELL, ERNEST PERCY STUART, Capt., Fisheries Division, Board of Agriculture and Fisheries, was born on 18 Nov. 1870, son of John Stuart Roupell, LL.D., D.L., of Brightlands, Richmond Hill, S.W. He was educated at Marlborough; was gazetted to the 4th Battn. Royal Welsh Fusiliers in 1888, and was transferred to the Milford Haven Division (Militia), Royal Engineers, in 1891. He served on the West Coast of Africa in 1894, and took part in the operations against the Chief Nanna, on the Benin River, and in the Benin City Expedition, where he was appointed British Resident. He was employed with the Forces of the Niger Coast Protectorate (Medal with clasp; Despatches); and was in command of several minor operations; was repeatedly mentioned in Despatches. On 22 Nov. 1898, he had become Divisional Commissioner, Niger Coast Protectorate, and in 1896 he served as Assistant Commissioner, Anglo-German Boundary Commission, Niger Coast Protectorate. In 1897 and 1898 he was Political Officer, prior to which he held the appointments of Forestry and also of Commercial Intelligence Officer. He served in the Ashanti Expedition, 1900. He was very severely wounded, mentioned in Despatches, and created a Companion of the Distinguished Service Order [London Gazette, 15 Jan. 1901]: "Ernest Percy Stuart Roupell, Capt., Milford Haven Division, Royal Engineers (Militia), Submarine Miners. In recognition of services during the recent operations in Ashanti." In 1902 he was promoted to the command of the Milford Haven Division, Submarine Miners, which he held until their disbandment in 1905. He was temporary clerk, Colonial Office, 1902–06; retired from the Army 22 April, 1905; was specially promoted Lieutenant-Colonel for "gallantry in action, and in view of long period spent on active service," in 1907; Assistant Secretary to the Government of Malta, 1905, and for a time Acting Lieutenant-Governor; Postmaster-General, Malta, 1911; Member of the Legislative and Executive Councils, 1912. Since 1 Jan. 1918, employed as Assistant Inspector, Fisheries Division, Board of Agriculture and Fisheries. Lieut.-Colonel Roupell married, in 1913, Rosellen Elwyn, daughter of the Rev. G. Smith, and they have two sons.

O'MALLEY, CHARLES EDWARD JOSEPH GLYNN, Capt., was born on 23 Sept. 1882, son of Inspector-General J. W. J. O'Malley, R.N. He was gazetted to the 6th Battn. Middlesex Regt., and served in Burma, 1893–96. He served in West Africa, 1897–98, with Sir F. Lugard, taking part in the operations on the Niger, Lagos, and employed in the Hinterland; He was mentioned in Despatches [London Gazette, 23 May, 1899], and received the Medal with clasp. He helped to raise the West African Force. He served in West Africa, 1900, in the operations in Ashanti, being present at the relief of Kumassi. He was severely wounded; mentioned in Despatches [London Gazette, 4 Nov. 1900], and was created a Companion of the Distinguished Service Order [London Gazette, 15 Jan. 1901]: "Charles Edward Joseph Glynn O'Malley, Capt., 6th Battn., Middlesex Regt. In recognition of his services during the recent operations in Ashanti." He was invested by the King 24 Oct. 1901. He served in the South African War, 1902, taking part in the operations in Cape Colony, April to 31 May, 1902 (he received the Queen's Medal with two clasps). He was present at the relief of Ookiep, with Colonel Cowper, C.M.G. He served with the Namaqua Field Force. Capt. O'Malley, who had retired and joined the Special Reserve of Officers, died at Southsea 9 April, 1910.

PHILLIPS, EDWARD HAWTIN, Lieut., was born 22 Feb. 1876, son of John Hawtin Phillips, of Hurstcroft, Ascot, Berkshire, and of 101, Cromwell Road, London, S.W. He was educated at Wellington College (Benson, 1890–93), and entered the Royal Artillery 16 Jan. 1897, as Second Lieutenant, from the Militia; served in the operations in Sierra Leone in 1898–99, in the Protectorate Expedition (Medal and clasp), and became Lieutenant, 1900. In 1900 he served in West Africa, took part in the operations in Ashanti, and was present at the relief of Kumassi, when he was severely wounded. He was mentioned in Despatches [London Gazette, 4 Dec. 1900], received the Medal with clasp, and was created a Companion of the Distinguished Service Order [London Gazette, 15 Jan. 1901]: "Edward Hawtin Phillips, Lieut., Royal Artillery. In recognition of services during the recent operations in Ashanti." The Insignia were presented by the King, about June, 1901. He had been employed with the West African Frontier Force from 22 April, 1899, to 28 Oct. 1900. He served in the South African War, 1901–02; was severely wounded; took part in the operations in the Orange River Colony, Jan. to March, 1902, and in the operations in Cape Colony and the Transvaal, March to May, 1902. He was mentioned in Despatches [London Gazette, 18 July, 1902], and received the Queen's Medal with five clasps. He became Captain 11 March, 1902, and was again employed with the West African Frontier Force 23 Jan. 1904, to 16 Nov. 1905, in Northern Nigeria, where he served in the operations against the people of Semolika, receiving the Medal with clasp. He was Adjutant, Royal Horse Artillery, 4 Dec. 1908, to March, 1914, when he was promoted to Major, into the Royal Field Artillery, and was appointed to command the 28th Battery. Capt. Phillips came from India with the Meerut Division of the Indian Army Corps, to take part in the European War, and had only been three days at the Front when he was wounded, near La Bassée, on the 5th of Nov. 1914, and died the next day. An obituary notice of him appeared in the "Times" of 2 Dec. 1914, and his death is recorded in the Army List for Dec. 1914. The Inspector-General of Artillery wrote of Major Phillips: "There was no man in all the Artillery under my control, belonging to this force, whom I would have selected before him for any duty which called for all the highest personal qualifications of a soldier. It was the same in India. If I wanted anything done or tried, I always knew it could never be in better hands than his. As a most gallant soldier and gentleman, a thorough sportsman and a true friend, he will be very deeply regretted by the regiment" ("Wellington Year Book," 1914). His younger brother, Capt. R. N. Phillips, Royal Welsh Fusiliers, died on the 27th of Dec. 1914, of wounds received in action. Major Phillips was a keen sportsman, and very fond of hunting, pig-sticking and big game shooting. He was badly mauled by a tiger in India, and had a stiff arm and hand, which did not prevent him from taking his pilot's certificate at Brooklands in May, 1914. He was the hero of the rescue at a dangerous fire explosion (see "Royal Artillery Institution Leaflet," Dec. 1914). He was a man of unlimited vigour, cheerfulness and courage.

SHORTLAND, HENRY VINCENT, Lieut., was the third son of Colonel Daniel Vincent Shortland, R.A. He was gazetted to the Royal Irish Regt., becoming Lieutenant 26 May, 1894. He served in West Africa, 1897–98 (Medal with clasp), and in Ashanti, 1900. He was mentioned in Despatches and created a Companion of the Distinguished Service Order [London Gazette, 15 Jan. 1901]: "Henry Vincent Shortland, Lieut., 3rd Battn. Royal Irish Regt. In recognition of services during the recent operations in Ashanti." The Insignia were presented by the King 25 July, 1901. He was promoted Captain. Capt. Shortland married, in 1901, Violet Theresa, youngest daughter of the late Colonel John Willoughby Osborne, Madras Staff Corps. He resigned in 1904, and died, 23 April, 1913.

EDWARDS, WILLIAM FREDERICK SAVERY, Lieut., was born on 27 July, 1872, at East Budleigh, son of the late Rev. N. W. Edwards, of Dowland Vicarage, North Devon, and of Martha Ellen Allan. He was educated at Christ's Hospital, and was gazetted to the 4th Battn. Devon Regt. in Jan. 1897. He was employed with the Sierra Leone Frontier Police from 1899 to 1901, serving with the Ashanti Field Force in 1900. He was slightly wounded; was twice mentioned in Despatches; received the Medal with clasp, and was created a Companion of the Distinguished Service Order [London Gazette, 15 Jan. 1901]: "William Frederick Savery Edwards, Lieut., 4th Battn. Devonshire Regt. In recognition of services during the recent operations in Ashanti." The Insignia were presented by Colonel C. Ridley. The D.S.O. was awarded for the taking of Kumassi, for commanding the advance forward of the Relief Column. Lieut. Edwards was then seriously wounded. He retired from the Army on 17 July, 1901, and joined the Reserve of Officers; was employed with the South African Constabulary from 1901 until 1906, serving with them in the South African War in 1902. He was present in the operations in the Transvaal, Orange River Colony and Cape Colony in 1902 (Queen's Medal with two clasps). Capt. Edwards was appointed Inspector-General of Police in Uganda, 1906, and Inspector-General of Police of the East Africa and Uganda Protectorates, 1908. He received the Police Medal in 1911, for services in connection with the organization of the Police and Prisons Departments of the East Africa and Uganda Protectorates, and for services rendered while in command of the Police Punitive Force against Wamiro in 1907. On the outbreak of war, Capt. Edwards was on leave, returning to East Africa on the 8th Aug. 1914. He served with the East African Expeditionary Force from 1914 until 1918, being Inspector-General of Communications, 1915–17, with rank of Brigadier-General, and a Brigade Commander, 1917–18. He was mentioned in Despatches five times, being awarded the Brevet of Major, C.M.G., C.B. and 2nd Class Order of St. Anne (with swords), while he received the 1914–15 Star, and the General Service and Victory Medals. He took the surrender of General Von Lettow Vorbeck and the German Forces at Abercorn, in Northern Rhodesia, on the 25th Nov. 1918. Commanded Turkana Expedition, East Africa, 1915 (mentioned in Despatches and awarded the Brevet of Lieutenant-Colonel and the African General

Service Medal with clasp). Granted honorary rank of Brigadier-General, 1919. Promoted Lieutenant-Colonel, Reserve of Officers, Nov. 1919. Is an F.R.G.S. and F.R.A.I. He married on 8 Aug. 1902, at St. Minver, Cornwall, Evelyn G. M. Bingham, daughter of the late Major Denis Bingham, 60th King's Royal Rifle Corps, and they have a daughter, Eleanor Bingham, and a son, Denis Savery Bingham, born on 5 June, 1905, and died 6 Dec. 1905. His favourite recreations are polo, shooting and cricket.

London Gazette, 26 April, 1901.—" The King has been graciously pleased to give orders for the following appointments to the Distinguished Service Order, in recognition of the services of the undermentioned Officers during operations in West Africa, 1900. For operations in Ashanti. To be Companions of the Distinguished Service Order."

GORDON, ALISTER FRASER, Capt., was born 1 Feb. 1872, third son, of William Grant Gordon, of Drumdevan, Inverness-shire, and Louisa, daughter of John Fraser, of Achnagairn, Inverness-shire. He was educated at The College, Inverness, and at the Royal Military College, Sandhurst, and was gazetted to the Royal Highlanders 8 Oct. 1890; was transferred to the Gordon Highlanders 12 Nov. 1890, becoming Lieutenant 1 Sept. 1893. He served in Chitral, 1895, with the Relief Force (Medal and clasp); and on the North-West Frontier of India, 1897–98, including the actions of Chagru Kotal and Dargai, where, as Lieutenant, he commanded a company and led it across the zone of fire and was the first across it; was present at the capture of the Sampagha and Arhanga Passes; operations in the Waran Valley, and at the action of 16 Nov. 1897, and at the operations in the Bara Valley, 7 to 14 Dec. 1897. He was mentioned in Despatches [London Gazette, 5 April, 1898], and received two clasps. He was promoted to Captain 28 May, 1899; was employed with the Central African Rifles, and with the King's African Rifles, 12 April, 1899, to 11 April, 1902, and served with the 2nd British Central African Regt. in the Ashanti Campaign of 1900. He was mentioned in Despatches [London Gazette, 8 March, 1901], and created a Companion of the Distinguished Service Order [London Gazette, 26 April, 1901]: " Alister Fraser Gordon, Capt., Gordon Highlanders. In recognition of services during the recent operations in Ashanti." Invested by the King 24 Oct. 1902. He served in the South African War, 1901–02, as Railway Staff Officer and Station Staff Officer, taking part in the operations in the Transvaal, Sept. 1901, to 31 May, 1902 (Queen's Medal with three clasps). He was G.S.O., 3rd Grade, Coast Defences, Northern Command, 18 Feb. 1908, to 17 Feb. 1912; was promoted to Major 4 July, 1908; was D.A.A. and Q.M.G., Highland Division, Scottish Command, 6 June, 1913, to 20 Jan. 1914. He served in the European War from 1914, as D.A.A. and Q.M.G. 5 Aug. 1914, to 17 Sept. 1914; was promoted Lieutenant-Colonel, Gordon Highlanders, in April, 1915, and was severely wounded in the leg at the Battle of Festubert 16 May, 1915; A.A. and Q.M.G. 18 Sept. 1914, to 9 April, 1915; G.S.O., 2nd Grade, War Office (temporary), 1 Dec. 1915, to 12 Feb. 1916; Brigade Commander 13 Feb. 1916. For his services in the European War he was six times mentioned in Despatches, and created a C.M.G. in 1915, and Brevet Colonel in 1917. Temporary Brigadier-General A. F. Gordon died on the 31st of July, 1917, of wounds received in action, aged 45. He was a highly scientific and brilliant officer—a loss to the Army and the nation. The following is an account of General Gordon's death: " On the Sunday morning, 29 July, 1917, General Gordon was visiting the front-line trenches, as was his custom, when the trench that he was in was hit by a direct German shell, which killed his Brigade Major and two Gordon Highland N.C.O.'s on the spot, and mortally wounded him. He died two days later in the Casualty Clearing Station to which he had been carried, and was buried in the Cemetery at Esporinghe. By the King's Special Order, a printed copy of his six Mentions in the European War was sent from the War Office to Mrs. Alister Gordon, 18 Dec. 1917, with a kind message of ' high appreciation of these services,' by His Majesty." He had married, in Jan. 1908, Pilar Mary, daughter of the late C. E. H. Edmondstoune Cranstoun, of Corehouse, and they had one son, Alastair Joseph Edgar, and two daughters, Margaret Colette Mary and Elizabeth Pilar Mary.

Alister Fraser Gordon.

WRIGHT, BACHE ALLEN, Capt., was born 12 Dec. 1874, son of the late Colonel William Frederick Wright, C.B. He was educated at Dover College and Sandhurst, and joined the Manchester Regt. as Second Lieutenant 28 Sept. 1895; became Lieutenant 13 Jan. 1897; served on the North-West Frontier of India, 1897–98, with the Tochi Field Force (Medal and clasp). He was employed with the West African Frontier Field Force 6 May, 1899, to 26 June, 1901, and became Captain 27 Dec. 1899. He was Staff Officer, Lines of Communication, Ashanti Field Force, 8 July, 1900, to 31 Dec. 1900; took part in the operations in Ashanti, and was present at the relief of Kumassi. He was mentioned in Despatches [London Gazette, 8 March, 1901]; received the Medal with clasp, and was created a Companion of the Distinguished Service Order [London Gazette, 26 April, 1901]: " Bache Allen Wright, Capt., Manchester Regt. In recognition of services during the recent operations in Ashanti." The Insignia were presented by the King 3 Jan. 1901. Capt. Wright was Adjutant, Manchester Regt., 6 May, 1905, to 15 July, 1907; Adjutant, Volunteers, 4 Nov. 1907, to 31 March, 1908; Adjutant, Territorial Force, 1 April, 1908, to 3 Nov. 1911; was promoted to Major, 24 Feb. 1912. He served in the European War from 1914, in command of the 11th Battn. Manchester Regt. from 19 Aug. 1914. He served in the Dardanelles in 1915; Egypt and France, 1916. He was mentioned in Despatches three times; Serbian Eagle, 4th Class; promoted Lieutenant-Colonel, to command 2nd Battn. The Manchester Regt. 22 Aug. 1919.

COBBE, ALEXANDER STANHOPE, Capt., served in the Ashanti Campaign, was severely wounded, mentioned in Despatches [London Gazette, 4 Dec. 1900, and 8 March, 1901], and created a Companion of the Distinguished Service Order [London Gazette, 26 April, 1901]: " Alexander Stanhope Cobbe, Capt., Indian Staff Corps. In recognition of services during the operations in Ashanti." (See Victoria Cross Volume.)

LUARD, CHARLES ELMHIRST, Lieut., was born 5 Aug. 1876, eldest surviving son of the late General C. E. Luard, R.E., and Mrs. Luard, of Igtham Knoll, Sevenoaks, Kent. He was educated at Harrow, and the Royal Military College, Sandhurst; was gazetted to the Norfolk Regt. 18 Nov. 1896; became Lieutenant 10 Feb. 1898. He served in British Central Africa, 1899; took part in the Expedition against Thwamba, and received the Medal and clasp. He served in West Africa in 1900; took part in the operations in Ashanti. He was severely wounded; mentioned in Despatches [London Gazette, 8 March, 1901]; received the Medal, and was created a Companion of the Distinguished Service Order [London Gazette, 26 April, 1901]: " Charles Elmhirst Luard, Lieut., Norfolk Regt. In recognition of services during the recent operations in Ashanti." The Insignia were sent to his father, Major-General C. E. Luard, 21 May, 1901. He served in East Africa, 1903, taking part in the operations in Somaliland (clasp). He was promoted to Captain 4 Feb. 1905. Major Luard served in the European War from 1914. The " Times " of 8 March, 1916, says: " Previously reported missing, now reported killed in action on 15 Sept. 1914, at Chivers Hill, near Massy-sur-Aisne, Major Charles Elmhirst Luard, D.S.O., 1st Battn. The Norfolk Regt., only surviving son of the late Major-General C. E. Luard, R.E., and husband of Dorothy Luard, aged 38. Prospice."

LELAND, HERBERT JOHN COLLETT, Lieut., was born 27 Feb. 1873. He served in the Gold Coast Constabulary, and West African Frontier Force, for three years and three hundred and nineteen days, in West Africa, 1897–98, Northern Territories, Gold Coast (Medal with clasp); received a direct commission in the 5th Battn. Royal Munster Fusiliers 24 Nov. 1900. He served in West Africa in 1906, taking part in the operations in Ashanti, being present at the relief of Kumassi and the action at Obassa, as A.D.C. to the O.C., Field Force. He was mentioned in Despatches [London Gazette, 8 March, 1901]; received the Medal with clasps, and was created a Companion of the Distinguished Service Order [London Gazette, 26 April, 1901]: " Herbert John Collett Leland, Second Lieut., Royal Munster Fusiliers. In recognition of services during the recent operations in Ashanti." The Insignia were handed to him by Mrs. C. W. Hill 22 July, 1901. He was Adjutant, Militia, and Adjutant, Special Reserve (5th Battn. Royal Munster Fusiliers), 10 Nov. 1904, to 9 Nov. 1909; was promoted Captain, into the 1st Battn. South Staffordshire Regt. 7 Aug. 1915; employed with the West African Frontier Force 4 Dec. 1912, to 6 Aug. 1914. He was later employed with the Colonial Office. Capt. Leland married, in 1902, Lena, daughter of the late Alexander Duncan, of Glencairn, Stirlingshire, and they have one son and two daughters.

London Gazette, 19 April, 1901.—" War Office, 19 April, 1901. The King has been graciously pleased to give orders for the following appointments to the Distinguished Service Order, in recognition of the services of the undermentioned Officers during the operations in South Africa. The rewards given are for services in South Africa up to the 29th Nov. 1900, the day on which Field-Marshal Lord Roberts handed over the command, and which date (except where otherwise stated) they bear. Owing to the multitude of recommendations forwarded to the Commander-in-Chief it has not yet been possible to fully examine those for regimental service, or those relating to the Militia, Yeomanry, Volunteers, and certain other Services. Further distinctions will be notified later. These will bear the same date as these now given, viz., the 29th Nov. 1900, except where otherwise stated."

COLLINS, REGINALD FRANCIS, The Rev., was born in Paris 1 April, 1851, son of Michael Collins, of Carrignavar, Co. Cork. He was educated at St. Charles's College, and was for many years a member of the congregation of the Oblates of St. Charles, under Cardinal Manning. He joined the Army in 1879, and gained the Government grant for Arabic in Egypt. In 1890 he was appointed a Member of the Senate of the University of Malta. He served in Egypt in 1882, with the 1st Battn. Royal Irish Fusiliers, and was present at the Battle of Tel-el-Kebir (Medal with clasp; Khedive's Bronze Star). He served in the Sudan Expedition (Suakin) in 1884–85, and was present at the actions of Hasheen and Tofrek, Tamai and McNeill's Zareba. He was mentioned in Despatches [London Gazette, 25 Aug. 1885]; received two clasps, and was promoted to Chaplain, 3rd Class. He became Senior Chaplain, 5th Division. Father Collins served in the South African War, 1899–1900, and was present at Spion Kop and at the engagements at Pieter's Hill, and at the Relief of Ladysmith. He was mentioned in Despatches [London Gazette, 8 Feb. 1901], and received the Queen's Medal with five clasps (for Cape Colony, Tugela Heights, Relief of Ladysmith, Laing's Nek and Belfast); and was created a Companion of the Distinguished Service Order [London Gazette, 19 April, 1901]: " The Rev. Reginald Collins, Chaplain to the Forces, 1st Class. In recognition of services during the operations in South Africa." The Insignia, Warrant and Statutes were sent to the Commander-in-Chief in South Africa. Lord Kitchener was asked to return the Insignia, Warrant, etc., and they were sent to the Governor and Commander-in-Chief, Gibraltar, and presented to Father Collins by Sir George White, 3 Feb. 1902, at the Convent, Gibraltar. He became Chaplain to the Forces, 1st Class, and was Senior Military Chaplain in the Army, 1904–11.

FALKNER, THOMAS FELTON, The Rev., was born 17 July, 1847, son of Thomas Falkner, of Bath, and of Caroline Elizabeth, daughter of William Stratton Large, of that city. He was educated at Christ's College, Cambridge (B.A., 1870 ; M.A., 1875).

Thomas F. Falkner.

He was Sub-Warden of St. Thomas's College, Colombo, 1872–79 ; Chaplain to the Bishop of Colombo 1873 ; Chaplain to the Forces, Colombo, 1874–75. He was Priest in Charge of Woolland, Dorset, 1879–81 ; became Chaplain to the Forces 15 Sept. 1881 ; served at Aldershot, Bermuda, Guards' Depôt, Chatham, Aldershot, Portsmouth, and with the South African Field Forces, 1899–1900, having been promoted to Chaplain to the Forces, Third Class, on 15 Sept. 1891, and to Second Class on 15 Sept. 1896. During the South African War he was present in the advance on Kimberley, including the actions at Belmont, Enslin, Modder River and Magersfontein. Operations in the Orange Free State, Feb. to May, 1900, including actions at Poplar Grove, Dreifontien, Vet River (5 and 6 May) and Zand River. Operations in the Transvaal in May and June, 1900, including actions near Johannesburg and Pretoria. He was mentioned in Despatches [London Gazette, 16 April, 1901] ; was promoted to Chaplain, First Class ; received the Queen's Medal with four clasps, and was created a Companion of the Distinguished Service Order [London Gazette, 19 April, 1901], for services with Lord Methuen's Division and the Brigade of Guards : " The Rev. Thomas Felton Falkner, M.A., Chaplain to the Forces, First Class. In recognition of services during the recent operations in South Africa." He was the first Church of England Chaplain to receive this distinction. The Insignia were presented to him by the King 25 July, 1901. Mr. Falkner became Rector of Burnham Westgate with Burnham Norton, King's Lynn, on the presentation of the Master and Fellows of Christ's College, Cambridge, in Nov. 1903. Mr. Falkner married, in 1877, Maria Louisa, eldest daughter of the Rev. James Bacon, B.D., and they have two sons : Eric Felton (q.v.), Lieut.-Colonel, C.M.G., D.S.O., born 30 March, 1880, and Harold Arthur, born 6 Feb. 1882 ; and two daughters : Mabel Irene, born 26 July, 1883, and Dorothy Mary, born 7 Feb. 1885.

MITFORD, BERTRAM REVELEY, Capt., was born 6 Feb. 1863, son of Major Henry Reveley Mitford, 51st King's Own Yorkshire Light Infantry, and Dora, third daughter of Capt. William Broughton, R.N. He joined " The Buffs " as Lieutenant 9 Sept. 1882 ; served in the Sudan, 1887–89, taking part in the action of Sarras. He was mentioned in Despatches [London Gazette, 17 June, 1887], and received the Fourth Class Medjidie ; and he was also present at the action of Gemaizah, and received the Medal with clasp and the Bronze Star. He was present at the action of Arguin and at the action of Toski ; was again mentioned in Despatches [London Gazette, 6 Sept. 1889] ; received a clasp and the Fourth Class Osmanieh. He took part in the Expedition to Dongola, 1896, as Brigade-Major, 2nd (Sudanese) Brigade ; was mentioned in Despatches for the operations of the 7th June and 19th Sept. [London Gazette, 3 Nov. 1896] ; received the Brevet of Major 18 Nov. 1896 (he had been promoted Captain 24 June, 1891), and the Egyptian Medal with two clasps. He took part in the Nile Expedition of 1898, employed on the Headquarters Staff, and was present at the Battle of Khartum ; was mentioned in Despatches [London Gazette, 30 Sept. 1898] ; was given the Brevet of Lieut.-Colonel 16 Nov. 1898, the British Medal, and a clasp to the Egyptian Medal. He was present at the relief of Gedaref ; at the operations on the Blue Nile, as Chief Staff Officer, and with the Kordofan Field Force, as Chief Staff Officer. He served in the Nile Expedition of 1899, employed on the Headquarters Staff, in the operations in the first advance against the Khalifa, and received a clasp to the Egyptian Medal. He had been employed with the Egyptian Army from 2 Sept. 1886, to 6 Oct. 1891, and on special service in Egypt 15 April, 1896, to 25 Jan. 1897. He was D.A.A.G., Guernsey, 28 Sept. 1897, to 22 July, 1898 ; specially employed with the Egyptian Army 22 July, 1898, to 10 Nov. 1899. He was on Special Service in South Africa 26 Nov. 1899, to 24 Jan. 1901 ; was Staff Officer to a column, South Africa, 25 Jan. 1901, to 31 March, 1901 ; A.A.G., South Africa, 1 April, 1901, to 23 June, 1902. He was present at the relief of Kimberley ; operations in the Orange Free State, Feb. to May, 1900, including Battle of Paardeberg (17 to 26 Feb.) ; action at Poplar Grove ; operations in the Transvaal in May and June, 1900, including actions near Johannesburg, Pretoria and Diamond Hill (11 and 13 June) ; operations in the Transvaal, east of Pretoria, July to 29 Nov. 1900, including action at Rhenoster Kop ; operations in the Transvaal, west of Pretoria, July to 29 Nov. 1900, including action at Zilikat's Nek ; operations in Cape Colony, south of Orange River, 1899 to 1900 ; operations in the Transvaal 30 Nov. 1900, to 31 May, 1902 ; operations on the Zululand Frontier of Natal in Sept. and Oct. 1901. He was mentioned in Despatches [London Gazette, 16 April, 1901] ; received the Queen's Medal with four clasps, and was created a Companion of the Distinguished Service Order [London Gazette, 19 April, 1901] : " Bertram Reveley Mitford, Capt. and Brevet Lieut.-Colonel, East Surrey Regt. In recognition of services during the recent operations in South Africa." He became Colonel 24 June, 1902 ; was A.A.G., Transvaal District, South Africa, 24 June, 1902, to 28 July, 1905. Colonel Mitford was Temporary Brigadier-General 4 Dec. 1906, to 20 April, 1910, commanding the 9th Infantry Brigade at Portsmouth. He retired on 20 April, 1910, with the rank of Brigadier-General. He had been created a C.B. in 1907. In 1912 he was appointed Gentleman-at-Arms. He served in the European War from 1914, being appointed to the command of the

72nd Infantry Brigade on 19 Sept. 1914, taking part in the Battle of Loos, Sept. 1915, and Battle of the Somme, Aug. and Sept. 1916. Appointed Temporary Major-General to command 42nd Division, 11 March, 1917, being present at Passchendaele, Aug. and Sept. 1917. Promoted Major-General 1 Feb. 1918. He was three times mentioned in Despatches, and created a C.M.G. June, 1917. He married, in 1890, the Honourable Etheldreda Mary Manners, youngest daughter of the 2nd Baron Manners, and they have three daughters, Josceline Etheldreda, Enid Constance and Stella Gladys.

SANDBACH, ARTHUR EDMUND, Major and Brevet Lieut.-Colonel, was born 30 July, 1859, at Hafodunos, Llangerniew, Denbighshire, son of Henry Robertson Sandbach, Esq., J.P., D.L., and Elizabeth Charlotte, daughter and co-heiress of Martin Williams, Esq., of Bryn Gwyn, Montgomeryshire.

Arthur E. Sandbach.

He was educated at Eton and at the R.M.A., Woolwich, and joined the Royal Engineers as Lieutenant 6 April, 1879 ; Egypt, 1882 ; the Sudan Expedition (Suakin) in 1885, being present at the affair at Thakool (clasp). In 1886–87 he served in the Burmese Expedition (horse shot ; Medal with clasp), and in 1888 in the Sikkim Expedition. He became Captain 1 April, 1889, and was A.D.C. to Major-General, Bengal, 27 Dec. 1890, to 25 Sept. 1892. In 1891 he served in the Hazara Expedition as A.D.C. to the G.O.C. ; received a clasp, and was mentioned in Despatches [London Gazette, 20 Oct. 1891]. He was promoted to Major 23 Nov. 1897, and was employed with the Egyptian Army 31 Dec. 1897, to 30 Nov. 1898. In the Nile Expedition of 1898 he served as Commandant, Wady Halfa, and A.A.G. of Communications ; afterwards as A.A.G., Headquarters Staff, Battle of Khartum. He was mentioned in Despatches [London Gazette, 30 Sept. 1898] ; received the Egyptian Medal with clasp, the Medal, and was given the Brevet of Lieut.-Colonel 16 Nov. 1898 ; was Military Secretary to Lord Curzon of Kedleston, Governor-General of India, 1898 to 1899. He served in the South African War, 1899–1900 ; was Special Service Officer, afterwards on the Staff (A.A.G. for Intelligence). He was present at the relief of Ladysmith, including operations of 17 to 24 Jan. 1900, and action at Spion Kop ; operations of 5 to 7 Feb. 1900, and action at Vaal Kranz ; operations on the Tugela Heights 14 to 27 Feb. 1900, and action at Pieter's Hill ; operations in Natal, March to June, 1900, including action at Laing's Nek (6 to 9 June) ; operations in the Transvaal, east of Pretoria, July to Oct. 1900, including actions at Belfast (26 and 27 Aug.) and Lydenburg (5 to 8 Sept.). He was mentioned in Despatches (by Sir R. H. Buller, 30 March, 19 June and 9 Nov. 1900 [London Gazette, 8 Feb. 1901]) ; received the Queen's Medal with six clasps, and was created a Companion of the Distinguished Service Order [London Gazette, 19 April, 1901] : " Arthur Edmund Sandbach, Major and Brevet Lieut.-Colonel, Royal Engineers. In recognition of services during the operations in South Africa." The D.S.O. was awarded for services in Natal, during the South African War, and specially for reconnaissance duty in finding a crossing over the River Tugela at Pieter's Hill, where the pontoon bridge and approaches were entirely protected from hostile fire. The Insignia were presented to him by the King. He was specially employed (Mobilization), Headquarters of Army, 1 April, 1901, to 25 Sept. 1902 ; was given the Brevet of Colonel 10 Feb. 1904 ; became Colonel 9 April, 1910 ; was created a C.B. in 1910 ; was Chief Engineer, Irish Command, 7 Oct. 1910, to 4 Aug. 1914, and 5 Aug. to 5 Oct. 1914, and was promoted to Major-General 26 Oct. 1914. He served in the European War from 1914, as Chief Engineer, 2nd Army, B.E.F., 26 Feb. 1915, to 11 May, 1915 ; Inspector of Royal Engineers 18 May to 14 Nov. 1915 ; Divisional Commander, 68th Division, 15 Nov. 1915, to 12 Feb. 1916 ; Home Forces ; Divisional Commander, British Armies in France, 15 Feb. 1916, to 10 April, 1917. He was three times mentioned in Despatches ; was wounded, and promoted to Major-General for distinguished service in the field. He is D.L. and J.P. for Montgomeryshire ; High Sheriff, 1919 ; Chairman of the County Territorial Force since 1908. Major-General Sandbach married, 15 Jan. 1902, at St. Paul's, Knightsbridge, the Honourable Ina Douglas-Pennant, daughter of the 2nd Baron Penrhyn, and they have one daughter, Geraldine Pamela Violet.

SITWELL, WILLIAM HENRY, Major and Brevet Lieut.-Colonel, was born at Benares 20 Nov. 1860, eldest son of the late Major Francis Henry Massey Sitwell, of Barmoor Castle, Northumberland, formerly of the Bengal Army, and Elizabeth Maria, only daughter of Ogle D'Olier, Esq., of Ely Place, Dublin. He was educated at Harrow, and the Royal Military College, Sandhurst, and gazetted to the 16th Foot as Second Lieutenant, 14 Jan. 1880 ; became Second Lieutenant, 5th Foot, 31 Jan. 1880. He served in the Afghan Campaign of 1880 (Medal) ; was promoted to Captain 10 April, 1889 ; was employed as Adjutant to the Bechuanaland Border Police 20 March, 1891, to 9 May, 1893 ; was D.A.A.G., Guernsey, 15 May, 1895, to 29 Aug. 1897. He was on Special Service, Ashanti, 7 Dec. 1895, to 24 Feb. 1896, and took part in the Ashanti Expedition, 1895–96 (Star). From 9 Sept. 1897, to Dec. 1899, he was employed with the Egyptian Army, and

William Henry Sitwell

served in the Nile Expedition of 1898 ; was severely wounded at Shebalia ; took part in the capture of Shendy, and in the Battles of the Atbara and Khartum. He was mentioned in Despatches [London Gazette, 30 Sept. 1898] ; was given the Brevet of Lieut.-Colonel 16 Nov. 1898 ; received the Medal, and three clasps to the Egyptian Medal. He served also in the Nile Expedition of 1899, commanded the 14th Sudanese in the first pursuit of the Khalifa, and received a clasp to the Egyptian Medal. In South Africa, Jan. to 31 Aug. 1900, he commanded the 9th and 10th Mounted Infantry, 3rd Division, and afterwards raised the 22nd Mounted Infantry and commanded a Column of All Arms to the end of the war (March, 1901, to 31 May, 1902). He was present in the operations in the Orange Free State, Feb. to May, 1900 ; operations in Orange River Colony, May to 29 Nov. 1900 ; operations in Cape Colony, south of Orange River, 1899–1900 ; operations in the Transvaal, Orange River Colony and Cape Colony, 30 Nov. 1900, to 31 May, 1902. He was mentioned in Despatches [London Gazette, 16 April, 1901, and 29 July, 1902] ; received the Queen's Medal with three clasps, the King's Medal with two clasps, and created a Companion of the Distinguished Service Order [London Gazette, 19 April, 1901] : "William Henry Sitwell, Major and Brevet Lieut.-Colonel, Northumberland Fusiliers. In recognition of services during the recent operations in South Africa." There is no official account of his D.S.O., but it is understood to have been awarded for capturing a hill in the attack on Dewetsdorp in April, 1900, two Victoria Crosses being awarded to Colonel Sitwell's command on the same occasion. Lieut.-Colonel Sitwell was given the Brevet of Colonel 2 July, 1904. He commanded the 4th Northumberland Fusiliers, and on its disbandment commanded the 2nd East Lancashire Regt. from 1906 to 1908. He was promoted to Colonel 17 Feb. 1908, and was created a C.B. on King Edward VII.'s birthday, 1908. Colonel Sitwell was A.A.G. and G.S.O.1, 3rd Lahore Division, 14 March, 1909, to 14 March, 1913, and received the Delhi Durbar Medal, 1910. He commanded the Quetta 1st Infantry Brigade, 1913–14, and became Temporary Brigadier-General, Nov. 1913. He served in the European War, and commanded the 34th Infantry Brigade at the landing in Suvla Bay, 6 Aug. 1915. He commanded the 17th Reserve Training Brigade and Prees Heath Reserve Centre, 1915 to 1917. Brigadier-General W. H. Sitwell is F.R.G.S. and J.P. for the county and city of Dublin. He married (1st), in London, in Aug. 1902, Constance Selina (who died in 1908), daughter of the Honourable Sydney Meade. He married (2ndly), in Aug. 1912, Constance Evelyn Mary, daughter of Gustavus Talbot, of Marchmont House, Hemel Hempstead, and their children are Constance Ann, and William Reresby (born 2 July, 1915).

DALRYMPLE-HAY, JAMES REGINALD MAITLAND, Major and Brevet Lieut.-Colonel, was born 30 July, 1858, son of Colonel G. J. Dalrymple-Hay, B.S.C., and of Amelia Emily, daughter of Colonel H. D. Maitland. He was educated at Edinburgh Academy and University, and joined the 21st Royal Scots Fusiliers as Second Lieutenant, from the Militia, 1 Nov. 1879. He served in the South African War, 1880–81 ; took part in the Transvaal campaign at the siege of Potchefstroom (wounded ; mentioned in Despatches). He became Lieutenant, Royal Scots Fusiliers, 1 July, 1881 ; transferred to the West India Regt. 21 April, 1886 ; promoted to Captain 5 Feb. 1890 ; was Adjutant, 4th (V.B.) Argyll and Sutherland Highlanders, 1892–96 ; became Major 7 May, 1895. He served in West Africa, 1897–98 ; Lagos—employed in Hinterland (Despatches [London Gazette, 7 March, 1899]) ; Brevet of Lieut.-Colonel 8 July, 1899 ; Medal with clasp). He took part in the operations in Sierra Leone, 1898–99 (clasp). He served in the South African War, 1899–1901, as Special Service Officer ; afterwards on Staff (A.A.G.), and subsequently District Commissioner and District Commandant. He served during the operations in Cape Colony, March to April, 1900 ; in Natal, April to June, 1900 ; in the Transvaal, June, 1900, to June, 1901 ; also in Cape Colony, June to Nov. 1901. He was mentioned in Despatches [London Gazette, 8 Feb., 1901] ; received the Queen's Medal with four clasps, and was created a Companion of the Distinguished Service Order [London Gazette, 19 April, 1901] : "James Reginald Maitland Dalrymple-Hay, Major and Brevet Lieut.-Colonel, West India Regt. In recognition of services during the recent operations in South Africa." He became Lieut.-Colonel 4 Sept. 1901. He commanded troops in St. Lucia, Feb. to Dec. 1902, and was Acting Administrator of the island, May–Nov. 1902 ; commanded 2nd West India Regt. 1904–7 ; was given the Brevet of Colonel [London Gazette, 25 Oct. 1904]. Colonel Dalrymple-Hay was wounded in the Jamaica earthquake, 1907. He was created a C.B. 24 June, 1910, and was Brigadier-General, Inspector of West Indian Local Forces and Officer Commanding the troops in Jamaica 27 Aug. 1910, to 16 Sept. 1914. In the European War he commanded Infantry Brigades (Home ; East Coast), 28 Nov. 1914, to 27 Feb. 1917. He was mentioned in Despatches 26 Feb. 1916, and retired 27 Feb. 1917, as Hon. Brigadier-General. His service overseas in the European War was : Special Appointment, Commandant 6th Corps Troops, B.E.F., which he held up to 13 Feb. 1917. He vacated this appointment owing to disability. General Dalrymple-Hay married, in 1892, Catherine Margaret, daughter of Henry Billinghurst, late of Stedham Hall, Sussex.

J. R. M. Dalrymple-Hay.
John Thorold Evatt

FORTESCUE, THE HONOURABLE CHARLES GRANVILLE, Major and Brevet Lieut.-Colonel, was born 30 Oct. 1861, sixth son of the 3rd Earl Fortescue, and Georgina (who died in 1866), daughter of the

Right Hon. George Dawson-Damer. He was gazetted to the Rifle Brigade 22 Jan. 1881 ; became Lieutenant 1 July, 1881, and served in the Burmese Expedition, 1888–89 (Medal with two clasps). He was promoted to Captain 14 Dec. 1890, and was Adjutant, Rifle Brigade, 27 June, 1895, to 15 Oct. 1897. He served in West Africa, 1897–99, in the Northern Territories, Gold Coast, and took part in the expeditions to Karega. He was mentioned in Despatches [London Gazette, 7 March, 1899] ; received the Medal and clasp ; was created a C.M.G., and given the Brevet of Lieut.-Colonel 8 July, 1899. He was Private Secretary to the Secretary of State for War 5 Aug. to 6 Oct. 1899. He served in the South African War, 1899–1902 (Brigade-Major, Natal, 7 Oct. 1899, to 3 Feb. 1901 ; D.A.A.G., South Africa, 4 Feb. 1901, to 1 April, 1902 ; Military Secretary to Lieut.-General, Transvaal and Orange River Colony, 24 June to 16 Sept. 1902). He commanded a Mobile Column, Oct. 1901, to 31 May, 1902 ; took part in the defence of Ladysmith, and in the operations in Natal, March to June, 1900, including the action at Laing's Nek (6 to 9 June). Operations in the Transvaal, July to 29 Nov. 1900, including actions at Belfast (26 and 27 Aug.) and Lydenberg (5 to 8 Sept.). Operations in the Transvaal and Orange River Colony 30 Nov. 1900, to 31 May, 1902. He was mentioned in Despatches (Sir G. S. White, 23 March, 1900 ; Sir R. H. Buller, 9 Nov. 1900) [London Gazette, 8 Feb. 1901, and 29 July, 1902] ; received the Queen's Medal with five clasps, and the King's Medal with two clasps, and the D.S.O. He was given the Brevet of Colonel 8 July, 1905 ; became Colonel 16 Dec. 1909 ; was promoted to Brigadier-General 28 April, 1912 ; Brigadier-General, General Staff, Eastern Command, 28 April, 1912, to 4 Aug. 1914. He was Brigadier-General, General Staff, 3rd Army, Central Force, Home Defence ; New Armies, B.E.F., 22 Nov. 1914, to 25 March, 1915 ; Brigadier-General, General Staff, 1st Army, Central Force, Home Defence, Home Forces, 19 April, 1915, to 22 Feb. 1916 ; Brigade Commander, 6th Provincial Brigade, 212th Brigade, Home Forces, 20 July, 1916, to 20 Nov. 1917 ; Brigade Commander, 226th Infantry Brigade, Home Forces, 21 Nov. 1917, to 10 March, 1918 ; Special Appointment, Serbian Mission, 11 March, 1918. He married, in 1906, Mrs. Ernest Campbell, widow of Capt. Ernest G. Campbell, Rifle Brigade, and eldest daughter of General Sir Charles Mansfield Clarke, G.C.B., G.C.V.O., and Gemma Cecilia, daughter of William Pitt Adams, and they have two daughters.

His Distinguished Service Order was gazetted 19 April, 1901 : "The Hon. Charles Granville Fortescue, Major and Brevet Lieut.-Colonel, Rifle Brigade. In recognition of services during the recent operations in South Africa."

GIFFARD, WILLIAM CARTER, Major and Brevet Lieut.-Colonel, was born 25 June, 1859, son of the late Major E. C. Giffard, 60th Rifles, and L. Gillies Lowndes. He was educated at Winchester College, and Sandhurst, and entered the Army 11 May, 1878 ; became Lieutenant, Welsh Regt., 13 March, 1880. He served in the South African War, 1881 ; became Captain 17 Aug. 1886 ; served in the Sudan in 1888 (Suakin) ; was present at the action at Gemaizah. He was mentioned in Despatches [London Gazette, 11 Jan. 1889] ; received the Medal with clasp, and the Fourth Class Medjidie and Khedive's Star. He was employed on the Gold Coast 16 Oct. 1897, to June, 1899, and served in West Africa, 1897–99, in the Northern Territories, Gold Coast ; was present in the Expedition to Karaga (slightly wounded) ; was mentioned in Despatches [London Gazette, 7 March, 1899] ; received the Medal with clasp, and was given the Brevet of Lieut.-Colonel

William Carter Giffard.

8 July, 1899. He had been promoted to Major 14 June, 1899. Major Giffard served in the South African War from 1899 to 1902, on the Staff (as Station Commandant) 15 Dec. 1899, to 27 Feb. 1900 ; in command of the 1st Battn. Welsh Regt., 4 March to 23 April, 1900. He took part in the operations in Orange Free State, March to May, 1900, including actions at Poplar Grove and Dreifontein (wounded) ; Vet River (5 and 6 May) and Zand River. Operations in the Transvaal, May and June, 1900, including actions near Johannesburg, Pretoria and Diamond Hill (11 and 12 June) ; operations in the Transvaal, east of Pretoria, 1900, including action at Belfast (26 and 27 Aug.) ; operations in Cape Colony, south of Orange River, 1899 to 1900. He was mentioned in Despatches [London Gazette, 8 Feb. 1901] ; received the Queen's Medal with five clasps ; King's Medal with two clasps, and was created a Companion of the Distinguished Service Order [London Gazette, 19 April, 1901] : "William Carter Giffard, Major and Brevet Lieut.-Colonel, Welsh Regt. In recognition of services during the recent operations in South Africa." Towards the end of the Boer War he was Commandant at Barberton. He retired with the rank of Lieut.-Colonel 7 Jan. 1903. He served in the European War ; commanded 13th (S.) Battn. Welsh Regt., April, 1915, to March, 1916, at home and in France, and was employed in command of other battalions at home till Feb. 1918 (Despatches ; 1914–15 Star, and Brevet of Colonel 3 June, 1918). Colonel W. C. Giffard married, in 1906, Cecil Margaret Stewart, daughter of Mrs. Schwabe.

BUSTON, PHILIP THOMAS, Lieut.-Colonel, was born 16 Feb. 1853. He was educated at Cheltenham College, and was gazetted to the Royal Engineers 12 Sept. 1872, and served in the Afghan War, 1878–79–80, being present at the action of Charasiah and operations in the neighbourhood of Kabul in Dec. 1879 (Despatches [London Gazette, 4 May, 1880] ; Medal with two clasps). He became Captain 12 Sept. 1884. Capt. Buston served in the Hazara Expedition in 1888 ; was mentioned in Despatches ; received the Medal with clasp, and was given the Brevet of Major 7 Dec. 1888. For his services in the Hazara Expedition of 1891, he was mentioned in Despatches [London Gazette, 20 Oct. 1891], and received a clasp. He was promoted to Major 16 March, 1892, and to Lieut.-Colonel 20 Sept. 1899, and from 1899 to 1902 he served in the South African War as C.R.E., Infantry Division, afterwards C.R.E., Bloemfontein. He was present at the relief of Kimberley; operations in the Orange Free State, including operations at Paardeberg and action at Dreifontein. He was mentioned in Despatches [London Gazette, 10 April, 1901]; received the Queen's Medal with four clasps, the King's Medal with two clasps, and was created a Companion of the Distinguished Service Order [London Gazette, 19 April, 1901]: " Philip Thomas Buston, Lieut.-Colonel, Royal Engineers. In recognition of services during the operations in South Africa." The Insignia were presented to him by Lieut.-General Sir C. Tucker, K.C.B., 9 Nov. 1901. He was given the Brevet of Colonel 20 Sept. 1903: became Colonel 21 Aug. 1905, and was created a C.B. in 1906. Colonel Buston was appointed Chief Engineer, Aldershot Command, 21 Aug. 1905. He retired 16 Feb. 1910, and was given the honorary rank of Brigadier-General 24 Aug. 1912. General Buston served in the European War from 1914 to 1918, and was created a C.M.G. in 1918.

BETHELL, EDWARD HUGH, Lieut.-Colonel, was born 27 Jan. 1854, son of the late W. F. Bethell, of Rise, Yorkshire, and of Mrs. Bethell (née Elizabeth Denison). He was educated at Rugby School, and for a short time at Wimbledon. He was gazetted to the Royal Engineers on 9 Jan. 1873. He served in the Afghan War, 1878–80; was mentioned in Despatches, and received the Medal. He became Captain 8 Jan. 1885; passed the Staff College, 1888–90; was Brigade-Major, Royal Engineers, Headquarters, Ireland, Aug. 1890, to Aug. 1895; promoted Major 1 Oct. 1892, and Lieut.-Colonel in Nov. 1899. He served in the South African War from 1899 to 1902; on the Staff as Staff Officer, R.E., at Headquarters, to Nov. 1901, and then as Inspector of Blockhouse Lines. He was twice mentioned in Despatches; received the Queen's Medal with five clasps, and the King's Medal with two clasps; created a Companion of the Distinguished Service Order [London Gazette, 19 April, 1901]: " Edward Hugh Bethell, Lieut.-Colonel, Royal Engineers. In recognition of services during the recent operations in South Africa; " and was given a Brevet Colonelcy for distinguished service in the field 28 June, 1902. Colonel Bethell was promoted to substantive Colonel in 1905, and appointed Chief Engineer, Southern Command, in Aug. of that year; he retired in Aug. 1906. He served as a Chief Engineer, and in equivalent positions from June, 1915, to Nov. 1917, and was awarded the C.M.G. in 1917. Colonel Bethell married (1st), in 1881, Gertrude (who died in 1888), daughter of Colonel Eustace Hill, and they had two sons: (1) Hugh Keppel, who joined the R.A. in 1903, transferred to the Indian Army, and served in the 7th Gurkhas, passed the Indian Staff College, transferred to the 7th Hussars, was Staff Captain of Mixed Cavalry Brigade in 1914 in France, then Brigade-Major of 6th Cavalry Brigade, then commanding 1st Northamptons, then commanding a brigade, and finally as Major-General Commanding the 66th Division. He received his Brevet Majority, Brevet Lieut.-Colonel and Brevet Colonel, also the D.S.O. and C.M.G. and C.B. (2) Christopher, who enlisted as a Private in the Foot Guards in Sept. 1914, was given a commission in the 10th K.O.Y.L.I., promoted to Captain in 1915, and was killed in action at Armentières in Feb. 1916. Colonel Bethell married (2ndly), in 1890, Annie, daughter of the Rev. J. G. Lonsdale, Canon of Lichfield, and they have one son, David Jardine, who served as Lieutenant and Acting Captain, first in the 9th K.O.Y.L.I., and then for three years in the 2nd Scots Guards. He was awarded the Military Cross and a Bar to the same.

MABERLY, CHARLES EVAN, Lieut.-Colonel, was born 5 April, 1854, son of the late Major-General Evan Maberly, C.B., of Avonmouth House, Christchurch. He was educated at the Royal Military Academy, Woolwich; was gazetted to the Royal Artillery 12 Feb. 1884, and served in the Nile Campaign of 1884–85, being employed on transport duty (Medal and clasp; Bronze Star). He served in the South African War, 1899–1900; was present at the advance on Kimberley, including the action at Magersfontein (severely wounded). He was mentioned in Despatches [London Gazette, 16 March, 1900]; received the Queen's Medal with clasp, and was created a Companion of the Distinguished Service Order [London Gazette, 19 April, 1901]: " Charles Evan Maberly, Lieut.-Colonel, Royal Artillery. In recognition of services during the recent operations in South Africa." The Insignia were presented by the King 3 June, 1901. He had become Lieut.-Colonel 14 Feb. 1900, and was given the Brevet of Colonel 10 Feb. 1904, when he retired from the Royal Horse Artillery with the rank of Colonel.

INGLEFIELD, FRANCIS SEYMOUR, Lieut.-Colonel, was born 6 Dec· 1855, at Devonport, son of Rear-Admiral Valentine Otway Inglefield, and Mrs. Inglefield, daughter of Baron Tiebault. He was educated at private schools; was gazetted to the 15th Foot, as Sub-Lieutenant, 13 June, 1874; became Lieutenant, East Yorkshire Regt., 13 June, 1874; Captain 30 June, 1884. He passed the Staff College in 1885; was Brigade Major at Gibraltar 21 Sept. 1888, to 4 Jan. 1892; was promoted to Major 2 July, 1892; was Instructor, Royal Military College, 1 Sept. 1892, to 25 June, 1896. Major Inglefield was on Special Service in South Africa 3 Nov. 1899, to 10 Feb. 1900; was Brigade Major and A.A.G. to General Smith-Dorrien 11 Feb. 1900, to 25 Dec. 1900. He was present at the operations

Francis S. Inglefield.

in the Orange Free State, Feb. to May, 1900, including operations at Paardeberg (17 to 26 Feb.), actions at Poplar Grove, Dreifontein, Houtnek and Zand River. Operations in the Transvaal in May and June, 1900, including actions near Johannesburg and Pretoria; operations in the Transvaal, east of Pretoria, including actions at Lydenberg (5–8 Sept.); operations in the Transvaal, west of Pretoria, July and Aug. 1900 (two horses shot); operations in Orange River Colony, March, 1901, to 31 May, 1902. He was mentioned twice in Despatches; received the Queen's Medal with four clasps, and King's Medal with two clasps, and was created a Companion of the Distinguished Service Order [London Gazette, 19 April, 1901]: " Francis Seymour Inglefield, Lieut.-Colonel, East Yorkshire Regt. In recognition of services during the recent operations in South Africa." The Insignia, Warrant and Statutes were sent to the Commander-in-Chief in South Africa, and presented there. He was given the Brevet of Colonel 10 Feb. 1904; became Colonel 1 Nov. 1905; was A.A.G., 7th Division, and G.S.O., First Grade, 5th Division, 1 Nov. 1905, to 21 July, 1909; was created a C.B. in 1908. He commanded the 12th Infantry Brigade 22 July, 1909, to 6 June, 1912; became Major-General 7 March, 1912; commanded the 54th East Anglian Division (T.F.), and the 72nd Division from 1913 and during the European War in England, Gallipoli and Egypt. He was mentioned in Despatches [London Gazette, 28 Jan. 1916]; brought to the notice of the Secretary of State for War on the 24th Feb. 1917, for valuable services rendered in connection with the War ; 1914–15 Star; British War Medal and Victory Medal. Major-General F. S. Inglefield married, on 18 July, 1885, at St. Andrew's Church, Wells Street, London, W., Zoe Sophia Barbara, second daughter of the late Henry Linwood Strong, Esq., and they have one son, Valentine Erskine, born on 6 May, 1886.

KENNEY, ARTHUR HERBERT, Lieut.-Colonel, was born at Plymouth, 4 Jan. 1855, son of the late Capt. E. H. Kenney, R.N., and Charlotte Mary, daughter of the late Capt. Bignell, R.N. He was educated by private tuition, and at the R.M.A., Woolwich, and was gazetted to the Royal Engineers as Lieutenant 29 April, 1873. He served in the Afghan War, 1878–80, being present at the capture of the Peiwar Kotal (Medal with clasp). He served in the Sudan Expedition in 1884–85 (Nile); was present at the action of Kirbekan; was in charge of the boat-repairing party, River Column; was mentioned in Despatches, and received the Medal with two clasps. He became Captain 8 Jan. 1885; was British Commissioner of the Anglo-French Commissions for delimiting the frontiers of the Colonies of the Gambia and of Sierra Leone of, 1890–92, and was promoted to Major 23 Nov. 1892; was created a C.M.G. in 1893. He served in the South African War, 1899–1900, as O.C. Advance Depôt, R.E.; as C.R.E., 10th Division, and C.R.E., General Ian Hamilton's Force, and was present at the operations in the Transvaal, east of Pretoria, July to Nov. 1900, including the action at Lydenberg (5 Sept.); operations in the Transvaal, west of Pretoria, July to Nov. 1900, including action at Zilikat's Nek; operations in Cape Colony, south of Orange River, 1899 to 1900; operations in Cape Colony, north of Orange River, including action at Ruidam. He was mentioned in Despatches [London Gazette, 16 April, 1901]; received the Queen's Medal with three clasps, and was created a Companion of the Distinguished Service Order [London Gazette, 19 April, 1901]: " Arthur Herbert Kenney, C.M.G., Lieut.-Colonel, Royal Engineers. In recognition of services during the operations in South Africa." The Insignia were presented to him by the King 3 June, 1901. He was promoted to Lieut.-Colonel 6 May, 1900, and was given the Brevet of Colonel 10 Feb. 1904. He commanded the Royal Engineers, Devon Sub-District. Colonel Kenney retired 6 May, 1905, and was re-employed from the Retired List, 1 Sept. 1914, as C.R.E. of a division till 31 July, 1915, and as Commandant of a Training Centre till 30 May, 1916 (Despatches).

TALBOT, LORD EDMUND BERNARD, Lieut.-Colonel, was born 1 June, 1855, son of the 17th Duke of Norfolk and Augusta Mary Hinna Catherine, second daughter of Edmund, 1st Lord Lyons. He was educated

Lord Edmund Talbot.

at the Oratory School, Edgbaston, and joined the 11th Hussars, as Second Lieutenant, from the Militia 20 Nov. 1875. In 1876 he took the name of Talbot, in lieu of Howard, by Royal License on inheriting under the will of Bertram, Earl of Shrewsbury. Lord Edmund was Adjutant, 11th Hussars, from 24 Aug. 1881, to 14 Aug. 1883; became Captain 14 Sept. 1881; was Adjutant, Auxiliary Forces, 15 Aug. 1883, to 31 Aug. 1888; became Major, 11th Hussars, 19 Nov. 1891. He served in the South African War, on Special Service, from 21 Oct. 1899, to 19 Feb. 1900. On the Staff (as D.A.A.G.) 20 Feb. to 28 Sept. 1900. He took part in the Relief of Kimberley, and in the operations in the Orange Free State, including operations at Paardeberg, actions at Poplar Grove and Dreifontein. Operations in the Transvaal, May and June, 1900, including actions near Johannesburg, Pretoria and Diamond Hill. Operations in Cape Colony, south of Orange River, 1899–1900, including actions at Colesberg. He was mentioned in Despatches [London Gazette, 16 April, 1901]; received the Queen's Medal with five clasps, and was created a Companion of the Distinguished Service Order [London Gazette, 19 April, 1901]: " Lord Edmund Bernard Talbot, Lieut.-Colonel (half-pay). In recognition of services during the recent operations in South Africa." The Insignia were presented to him by the King 3 June, 1901. He was created an M.V.O. in 1902, and had become Lieutenant-Colonel 17 June, 1900; retired 29 Sept. 1905. He had contested Burnley as a Conservative in 1880, and a Division of Sheffield in

1883 and 1886. He has been M.P. for Chichester since 1894. Lord Edmund Talbot was Private Secretary to Mr. Brodrick when the latter was Secretary of State for War; also when he was Secretary of State for India. He was Junior Lord of the Treasury and Whip, 1905–6, and has been Unionist Chief Whip since 1913. He became a Director of the London, Brighton and South Coast Railway in 1913; was Joint Parliamentary Secretary at the Treasury, 1915–16, and has been Deputy Earl Marshal of England since 1917, and a Privy Councillor since 16 Jan. 1918. Lord Edmund Talbot married, in 1879, Lady Mary Caroline Bertie, daughter of the 7th Earl of Abingdon and of Caroline Theresa, daughter of Charles Towneley, of Towneley, and they have one son, Henry, and one daughter, Magdalen. Lady Edmund Talbot is the founder of the Catholic Social Union Clubs for Girls, in London and Sheffield, and has been associated with the Ladies of Charity since 1900. In 1911 she served on the Government Departmental Committee to inquire into Reformatory and Industrial Schools. She has opened, at the Settlement in East London, a Domestic Economy Centre for children and girls, which is under the Board of Education and the London County Council, likewise a School Clinic for children under those bodies. She has written on Settlement work.

BELL-IRVING, ANDREW, Lieut.-Colonel, was born on 9 July, 1855, fourth son of the late John Bell-Irving, of Whitehill, Dumfriesshire. He was educated at Merchiston Castle School, Edinburgh, and was gazetted to the Royal Artillery 28 Jan. 1875, as Lieutenant. He served in the Afghan War, 1878–80; was present at the defence of Kandahar and the battle of 1 Sept. He was mentioned in Despatches [London Gazette, 3 Dec. 1880], and received the Medal with clasp. He was promoted to Captain on the 1st Dec. 1883, and to Major. Major Bell-Irving served throughout the South African War, in command of the 11th Brigade, Divisional Royal Field Artillery, to 31 May, 1902. He took part in the operations in the Orange Free State, Feb. to May, 1900, including actions at Poplar Grove, Dreifontein, Vet River (5 and 6 May) and Zand River. Operations in the Transvaal in May and June, 1900, including actions near Johannesburg, Pretoria and Diamond Hill (11 and 12 June). Operations in the Transvaal, east of Pretoria, in 1900, including action at Belfast 26 and 27 of Aug. Operations in the Transvaal 30 Nov. 1900, to 31 May, 1902. He was mentioned in Despatches [London Gazette, 16 April, 1901, and 29 July, 1902]; was created a Companion of the Distinguished Service Order [London Gazette, 19 April, 1901]: "Andrew Bell-Irving, Lieut.-Colonel, Royal Artillery. In recognition of services during the recent operations in South Africa." The Insignia were presented by the Duke of Cornwall and York 14 Aug. 1901. He received the Queen's Medal with five clasps, and the King's Medal with two clasps. Major Bell-Irving had become Lieutenant-Colonel on 30 June, 1900, and retired on 4 July, 1903.

ALEXANDER, HARVEY, Lieut.-Colonel, was born 3 June, 1859, son of Caledon Dufre Alexander, of 30, Belgrave Square, S.W. He joined the 10th Hussars, as Second Lieutenant, 24 Jan. 1880; became Lieutenant 1 July, 1881; Captain 16 March, 1889; was Adjutant, Yeomanry Cavalry, 1 Feb. 1890, to 31 Jan. 1895. He was promoted to Major 2 Jan. 1897. He served throughout the South African War of 1899–1902. He was twice wounded; was mentioned in Despatches [London Gazette, 16 April, 1901]; received the Queen's Medal with five clasps; King's Medal with two clasps, and was created a Companion of the Distinguished Service Order [London Gazette, 19 April, 1901]: "Harvey Alexander, Lieut.-Colonel, 10th Hussars. In recognition of services during the recent operations in South Africa." He had been promoted Lieutenant-Colonel 3 Aug. 1900. On 17 Sept. 1904, he was given the Brevet of Colonel, and on 3 Nov. 1906, he retired from the Staff. Colonel Alexander married, in 1890, Mildred, youngest daughter of the late C. G. Prideaux-Brune, of Prideaux Place, Padstow.

MURRAY, ARCHIBALD JAMES, Lieut.-Colonel, was born 21 April, 1860, son of the late Charles Murray, Esq., of Woodhouse, near Kingsclere, Hants, and of Anna, daughter of John Baker Graves, Puisne Judge of Ceylon. He was educated at Cheltenham College and Sandhurst, and was gazetted to the 27th Foot, as Second Lieutenant, 13 Aug. 1879, becoming Lieutenant, Royal Inniskilling Fusiliers, 1 July, 1881. He was Adjutant, Royal Inniskilling Fusiliers, 12 Feb. 1886, to 14 Dec. 1890, and was promoted to Captain 1 July, 1887. Capt. Murray served in the Zululand Expedition of 1888. He was Adjutant, Militia, 15 Dec. 1890, to 14 Dec. 1895, and became Major 1 June, 1898; graduated at the Staff College in 1898. He served in South Africa, as D.A.A.G., 9 Oct. 1899, to 5 March, 1900; as A.A.G. 6 March, 1900, to 5 March, 1901, taking part in the operations in Natal in 1899, including actions at Talana and Lombard's Kop, and in the Defence of Ladysmith, including the action of 6 Jan. 1900. In the operations in the Transvaal, east of Pretoria, July to 29 Nov. 1900, including the action at Lydenberg (5 to 8 Sept.). Operations in the Transvaal, west of Pretoria, July to 29 Nov. 1900, including actions at Zilikat's Nek. Operations in Cape Colony, north of Orange River, including action at Ruidam. Operations in the Transvaal and Orange River Colony in 1902. In command of 2nd Battn. Royal Inniskilling Fusiliers (7 Feb. to 31 May). Dangerously wounded (8 April, 1902). He was mentioned in Despatches by Sir G. S. White 2 Dec. 1899, and 23 March, 1900 [London Gazette, 8 Feb. 1901, and 29 July, 1902]; received the Queen's Medal with five clasps; the King's Medal with two clasps, and was created a Companion of the Distinguished Service Order [London Gazette, 19 April, 1901]: "Archibald James Murray, Lieut.-Colonel, Royal Inniskilling Fusiliers. In recognition of services during the recent operations in South Africa." The Insignia, Warrant and Statutes were sent to the Commander-in-Chief in India, and the Insignia were presented by the Lieutenant-Governor of the Punjab 1 Jan. 1902. He had been promoted to Lieutenant-Colonel, Royal Inniskilling Fusiliers, 29 Oct 1900 (Lieutenant-Colonel, Staff Employment, 1902). He was A.A.G., Aldershot Army Corps, 3 Nov. 1902, to 21 Nov. 1905; became Colonel 29 Oct. 1903; was created a C.B. in 1904; was Brigadier-General, General Staff, Aldershot Army Corps, 22 Nov. 1905, to 8 Nov. 1907; was created a C.V.O. in 1907; Director of Military Training, Headquarters of Army, 9 Nov. 1907, to 30 June, 1912; was created a K.C.B. in 1911; became Major-General 13 July, 1910. Sir A. Murray was specially employed at the War Office from 1 July to 6 Nov. 1912; was Inspector of Infantry 9 Dec. 1912, to 31 Jan. 1914; G.O.C., 2nd Division, Aldershot Command, 1 Feb. to 4 Aug. 1914. On the outbreak of the European War he became Temporary Lieutenant-General and Chief of General Staff, British Expeditionary Force, 5 Aug. 1914; was Deputy Chief of the Imperial General Staff (Temporary) 10 Feb. to 26 Sept. 1915; Chief of the Imperial General Staff 26 Sept. to 22 Dec. 1915; was promoted to Lieutenant-General 28 Oct. 1915; Temporary General 23 Dec. 1915; General Officer Commanding, 1st Class, in 1916; Commander-in-Chief in Egypt 10 Jan. 1916, to 28 June, 1917.

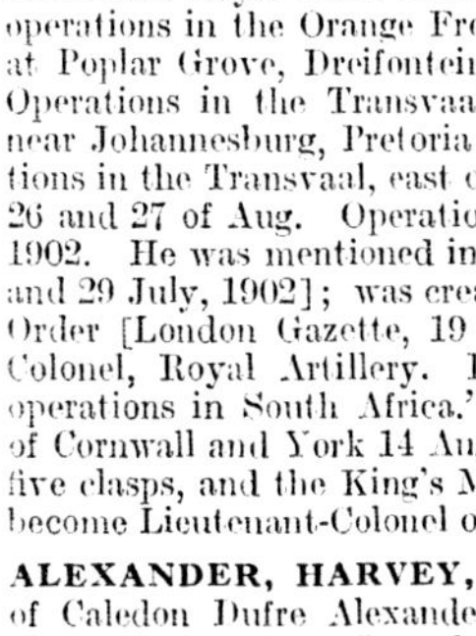

Archibald J. Murray.

Field-Marshal Lord Allenby said, in his Despatch dated 28 June, 1919 [London Gazette, 11 Aug. 1919]:

"The campaigns in Sinai, Palestine and Syria formed an important part of the general Allied effort against the Central Powers, and I propose to give here a brief summary of their relation to the operations in the main theatre on the Western Front, of their general features and results. The forces employed in this theatre may be regarded in the nature of a detachment from the main forces on the Western Front; but engaged in the same great battle, changing its rôle and action according to the sway of events in the main theatre and the other minor theatres. In the first instance, the object of this detachment was the protection of Egypt and the Suez Canal, a vital link in the communications of the Allies. By the summer of 1917, when I assumed command of the Egyptian Expeditionary Force, Lieut.-General Sir A. Murray's brilliant campaign in Sinai had removed the danger to Egypt, and had forced the enemy back across his own frontiers. The original purpose of the detachment had been accomplished. But events elsewhere had given a fresh importance and another rôle to the operations in this theatre. The collapse of Russia had given a new lease of life to the Central Powers' weakest member, and had freed the main Turkish forces for action elsewhere. It was believed that they would be used in an offensive, planned and organized by the Germans, for the recapture of Bagdad. It was therefore important to keep up the pressure on Turkey, and to anticipate the threatened attack on Bagdad by striking hard elsewhere. The operations which commenced with the Gaza–Beersheba Battle, and led to the capture of Jerusalem and the freeing of all Southern Palestine, were therefore planned. These operations had far-reaching results. The danger to Mesopotamia was removed, and it became possible to reduce the forces in that theatre. Instead of drawing fresh strength from the reserve of Turkish troops released by Russia's collapse, the Central Alliance found themselves compelled to send further support to their Eastern Ally; while a fresh impetus was given to the Arab struggle for freedom. The moral results were even greater. Germany, hard put to it to hold her own in the close-locked struggle in the West, saw a great blow struck at her Eastern ambitions; while the capture of Jerusalem stirred the imagination of the Christian world. I desire to express my indebtedness to my predecessor, Lieut.-General Sir A. J. Murray, who, by his bridging of the desert between Egypt and Palestine, laid the foundations for the subsequent advances of the Egyptian Expeditionary Force. I reaped the fruits of his foresight and strategical imagination, which brought the waters of the Nile to the borders of Palestine, planned the skilful military operations by which the Turks were driven from strong positions in the desert over the frontier of Egypt, and carried a standard gauge railway to the gates of Gaza. The organization he created, both in Sinai and in Egypt, stood all tests and formed the cornerstone of my successes."

Mr. W. T. Massey says, in Chapter IV. of "The Desert Campaigns": "After Lord Kitchener had paid his memorable visit to Gallipoli, he came to Egypt, which, from long associations, was bound to hold a firm place in his war anxieties. At that time it was believed the Germans were sending four or six divisions to Constantinople to form the backbone of a Turkish Army to March across the Sinai desert and try to cut the Suez Canal, that artery of traffic between East and West described by the Kaiser as the 'jugular vein of the British Empire.' Lord Kitchener went to the Canal, saw the defences, and is credited with the remark made to a distinguished General: 'Are you defending the Canal, or is the Canal defending you?' That brief question so admirably sums up the situation as it was in Egypt at the time of the evacuation of Gallipoli that it deserves to be true. I know there is one school of military thought which strongly supports the view that our best policy was to allow the Turk to encounter the difficulties of the desert and to meet him on the Canal or within a few miles of it. General Sir John Maxwell said to me at the end of 1914: 'The desert is our great ally, and it will beat the Turk in the end.' There is much force in that, I agree, but the attack of Feb. 1915, proved that the Turk could bring a substantial body of troops over the desert and hold up shipping in the Canal, and if, as the Turk claimed, that expedition was in the nature of a reconnaissance, when six-inch guns were hauled into action and hit one of the ships of the Indian Marine in the waterway, the knowledge gained during the march was of great value for any future attack. And we ascertained a year and a half later at the Battle of Romani (which is not much more than twenty-five miles from Port Said), that the knowledge was brought into such practical use that eight-inch as well as six-inch guns were transported over the desert a hundred miles from any

Turkish railway. It is claimed by the critics of the scheme which Sir Archibald Murray lost no time in putting into operation, that if the Turks' big guns got within range of the Canal they could not damage it, that no long-range fire would breach its banks, and that the stoppage of shipping for a week, a fortnight, or a month, till such time as want of water and supplies compelled the Turk to retire, was of no consequence. To this I reply that there is no certainty that if the Turks once stopped traffic on the Canal they would ever lack supplies, for if they scored such a success they would concentrate all their energies on holding the advantage. Further, no military censorship would prevent the news reaching the people in Egypt, that home of exaggerations based on a substratum of fact. Egyptian opinion strongly leans on the winning side, and the regard in which we are held in Egypt is because of our strength, and not for the lasting good we have done the people. An undercurrent of disaffection would have been inconvenient; open rebellion would have compelled the retention of the whole of the troops in the country in the spring of 1916. The Australians and New Zealanders and some of the divisions of tried troops were urgently needed on the Western front. And then what would have been the consequences in India, in Afghanistan, in Persia, if the fact was established that the Turks had got the British Empire by its Suez Canal throat? How could we supply our Army in Mesopotamia, which was then, as we afterwards had the pain of learning, in sore straits from lack of munitions, rations, transport, medical supplies and comforts? . . . General Murray, taking the wide view that his responsibilities were for the whole Empire and not for Egypt alone, tackled the strategic problem by ' thinking Imperially,' and, looking at the nature of subsequent operations, few will say he was wrong. To my mind the most eloquent proof that he was absolutely right is to be found in the events of July and Aug., when the Turks, with an enterprise which all military men must admire, brought some 20,000 men and heavy guns up to Romani across an exceedingly difficult piece of desert, and strongly attacked our defences. And he kept up a fight for ten days, although harassed by some of the finest irregular cavalry in the world. The new strategic plan meant vast expenditure in money and labour, but it secured the safety of the Canal at least during the war, and perhaps for all time. The vast work of preparation could not be more strikingly illustrated than by realizing what was done in making railways and roads, laying down pipe lines for water supply, and the quantities of material used on the eastern defences of Egypt. The good work has gone on at an ever accelerated pace; the railway, then some miles short of El Arish, has been thrust out to Rafa, on the Turco-Egyptian frontier, to Khan Yunus, and to Deir el Belar, just short of Gaza, another seventy miles. Pipes have gone forward, too, and the amount of sandbags and barbed wire needed and supplied has grown enormously. A glance at the map shows the extent of ground covered. The engineering work which had to be undertaken shows how the Sinai Desert has been throbbing with life and industry. It is due to the troops engaged in Egypt that people at home should know the extent of the labour which fell upon them during a very trying period. It was not all honey for a man in the Egyptian Expeditionary Force." Mr Massey says, in Chapter VIII.: " The Battle of Romani was the most important battle fought on Egyptian territory during the campaign. It proved beyond doubt the wisdom of General Murray's policy in going out to meet the enemy and denying him all the ground which was necessary for him if he were to attack the Canal with even temporary success. . . . Our victory there once and for all settled the attempts of the Turks to get to the Canal, for once Romani was won, nothing could prevent us from compelling an advancing enemy to meet us on ground of our choice, getting farther east every day, with the best sites always entrenched. Romani will stand out as the big decisive battle fought on Egyptian soil in this war, and it put an end to the dream of the Kaiser of bleeding the British Empire to death by severing what he had well termed its most vital artery." Mr. Massey goes on to describe the Battle of Maghdaba and the Rafa victory; the campaign against the Senussi; the march on Sollum and the dash on Siwa. He gives accounts of the doings of Generals Chetwode and Chauvel, and later on in the book of General Peyton, and extols the fighting qualities of the Australians and New Zealanders.

Sir Archibald Murray was created a K.C.M.G. in 1915, and a G.C.M.G. in 1917; is Grand Officier, Legion of Honour; Grand Cordon, White Eagle of Serbia; Grand Cordon of the Nile; Grand Officer, St. Maurice and St. Lazarus, Italy; Grand Cordon of the Sacred Treasure, Japan; G.O.C., Commanding Aldershot Division, 1 Oct. 1917, to 14 Nov. 1919. He married (1st), in 1890, Caroline Helen (who died in 1910), eldest daughter of the late Lieut.-Colonel Henry Baker Sweet, of Hillersdon, Tiverton, and they had one son, Capt. Louis Gerald Murray, Gordon Highlanders. He married (2ndly), Mildred Georgina, daughter of Colonel William Toke Dooner, of Ditton Place, near Maidstone, and of his wife, Augusta, fifth daughter of W. P. Metchim, of Petersham Lodge, Surrey.

London Gazette, 6 Sept. 1919.—" War Office, 6 Sept. 1919. The King has been graciously pleased to approve of the undermentioned reward for distinguished service in connection with military operations in the Field. Dated 25 Aug. 1919. To be General."

LINDSAY, WALTER FULLERTON LODOVIC, Lieut.-Colonel, was born 15 May, 1855, son of the late Capt. Alexander Lindsay, 8th Hussars, and of Jane Christian, daughter of M. Lindsay Carnegie, Esq., of Spynie and Boysack. He was educated at St. Andrews, and Wimbledon School, and was gazetted to the Royal Artillery as Lieutenant 28 Jan. 1875; served in the Egyptian Expedition of 1882, being present at the action of Kassassin and at the Battle of Tel-el-Kebir (Medal with clasp, and Bronze Star). He was promoted to Captain 1 Jan. 1884, and Major 27 Jan. 1892. Major Lindsay served in the South African War from 1899 to 1900, and took part in the advance on Kimberley, including actions at Belmont, Enslin, Modder River (severely wounded) and Magersfontein; in the operations in the Orange Free State, Feb. to May, 1900, including the operations at

Paardeberg (17 to 26 Feb.); actions at Poplar Grove, Karee Siding, Vet River (5 and 6 May) and Zand River. Operations in the Transvaal, May and June, 1900, including actions near Johannesburg and Pretoria. He was mentioned in Despatches [London Gazette, 26 Jan. 1900]; received the Queen's Medal with four clasps, and was created a Companion of the Distinguished Service Order [London Gazette, 19 April, 1901]: " Walter Fullerton Lodovic Lindsay, Lieut.-Colonel, Royal Artillery. In recognition of services during the recent operations in South Africa." The Insignia were presented by the King 3 June, 1901. He had become Lieutenant-Colonel 14 Nov. 1900, and he was given the Brevet of Colonel 10 Feb. 1904, becoming Colonel 29 Nov. 1905. He was Staff Officer for Horse and Field Artillery, Southern Command, 29 Nov. 1905, to 20 July, 1906. Commander of Horse and Field Artillery, Southern Command, 20 Aug. 1906, to 19 Aug. 1907; Temporary Brigadier-General, Commanding Artillery, 3rd Division, Southern Command, 20 Aug. 1907, to 30 Sept. 1908; Inspector of Royal Field Artillery 1 Oct. 1908, to 30 April, 1912; promoted to Major-General 7 Feb. 1912; G.O.C., West Lancashire Division, Western Command, 3 June, 1912, to 4 Aug. 1914. He served in the European War, 1914–15, as Major-General Commanding Royal Artillery from 5 Aug. 1914, and Inspector of Royal Horse and Royal Field Artillery from 1 March, 1915, to 8 April, 1915. For his services in the European War he was mentioned in Despatches, and created a K.C.B. (1916). Sir Walter Lindsay retired in Oct. 1917.

THOMAS, SIR GODFREY VIGNOLES, Lieut.-Colonel, Bart., was born 21 March, 1856, at Hafod, Cardiganshire, son of Sir Godfrey John Thomas, 8th Bart., and Emily, daughter of W. Chambers. He succeeded his father as 9th Baronet in 1861; was educated at Brighton College, and at the Royal Military Academy, Woolwich, and was gazetted to the Royal Artillery 28 Jan. 1875. He served in the Afghan War, 1878–79, being present at the occupation of Kandahar and Khelat-i-Ghilzai (Medal). He served in the Egyptian Expedition, 1882–84, and was present at the action at Kassassin of 9 Sept.; at the Battle of Tel-el-Kebir, and the forced march to Cairo (Medal with clasp, and Bronze Star). He was promoted to Captain 1 Jan. 1884, and in that year served in the Sudan, being present at the Battle of Teb (horse killed), Relief of Tokar, Battle of Tamai, and affair at Tamanieh (two clasps, 4th Class Medjidie). He was Adjutant, Royal Artillery, 2 April, 1890, to 2 March, 1892, and became Major 3 March, 1892. He served in the South African War, 1899–1901, being present in the advance on Kimberley and at the Relief of Kimberley. Operations in the Orange Free State, Feb. to May, 1900, including operations at Paardeberg; actions at Poplar Grove, Dreifontein, Karee Siding, Houtnek (Thoba Mountain), Zand River and Vet River (5 and 6 May). Operations in the Transvaal in May and June, 1900, including actions near Johannesburg, Pretoria and Diamond Hill. Operations in the Transvaal, west of Pretoria. Operations in Orange River Colony, including actions at Bethlehem and Wittebergen. C.R.A., Johannesburg District. He was mentioned in Despatches [London Gazette, 16 April and 7 May, 1901]; received the Queen's Medal with seven clasps, and was created a Companion of the Distinguished Service Order [London Gazette, 19 April, 1901]: " Godfrey Vignoles Thomas, Bart., Lieut.-Colonel, Royal Artillery. In recognition of services during the recent operations in South Africa." He was invested by the King 17 Feb. 1901. Sir Godfrey Thomas became Lieutenant-Colonel 14 Nov. 1900, and was given the Brevet of Colonel 10 Feb. 1904, becoming Colonel 6 Aug. 1906. He was created a C.B. in 1904; was Staff Officer for Horse and Field Artillery, Southern Command, 6 Aug. 1906, to 21 Dec. 1907 and retired 18 Jan. 1911. He served in the European War as Brigadier-General, 3rd Division, Royal Artillery, 1914–17. Sir Godfrey Thomas died in 1919. He had married, 30 April, 1887, in London, Mary F. Isabella, daughter of the late C. Oppenheim, Esq., of 40, Great Cumberland Place, W., and they had one son, Godfrey John Vignoles Thomas, born 14 April, 1889, who has now succeeded his father as 10th Baronet.

HUNTER-WESTON, AYLMER, Brevet-Major, was born 23 Sept. 1864, eldest son of Lieut.-Colonel Gould Hunter-Weston and Mrs. Jane Hunter-Weston, of Hunterston, Ayrshire, Scotland. He was educated at Wellington College; at the Royal Military Academy, Woolwich, and at the Staff College. He joined the Royal Engineers in 1884, and became Captain in 1892. Lieut. Hunter-Weston took part in the Miranzai Expedition in 1891, as a Company Officer in the Bengal Sappers and Miners. In 1894 he served as a Captain Commanding a company of Bengal Sappers and Miners in the Waziristan Delimitation Escort, and was present at the night action of Wana (Despatches). He commanded two companies of Bengal Sappers and Miners, and was Acting C.R.E. on Sir William Lockhart's Staff with the Waziristan Field Force, 1894–95 (Despatches; Brevet of Major, and Medal with clasp). He served with the Dongola Expeditionary Force in 1896, as a Special Service Officer on Sir Herbert Kitchener's Staff, and was present at the

Godfrey V. Thomas.

Aylmer Hunter-Weston.

Battle of Firket (Despatches; 4th Class Medjidie; Queen's Medal; Khedive's Medal with clasp). Brevet-Major Aylmer Hunter-Weston served in the South African War from 1899 to 1901. He was successively in command of Mounted Engineers; Commanding Royal Engineers with Lieut.-General French's Cavalry Division; D.A.A.G., Cavalry Division; Chief Staff Officer to Lieut.-General French, and finally in independent command of a Mounted Column. He was present at the operations round Colesberg; actions at Dekiel's Drift and Klip Drift; Relief of Kimberley; operations at Paardeberg, and actions near Poplar Grove, Dreifontein, Thaba Nchu, Karee Siding, Zand River, Johannesburg, Diamond Hill, Belfast, Carolina, Barberton, Ermelo, Pietretief, etc, etc. During the advance to Pretoria he commanded the cavalry raids described below. Lieut.-General Sir Aylmer Hunter-Weston, Royal Engineers, gained the D.S.O. while holding the rank of Brevet-Major, for distinguished service in the South African War (1899–1901), and especially for his success in breaking through the Boer positions and cutting the railway behind them. He commanded five such raids, the parties in each case being composed of Mounted Royal Engineers and Cavalry. His principal raids were made with the object of cutting the railway (1) north of Bloemfontein, at Rustfontein, 13 March; (2) north of Kronstadt, near Amerika Siding, 11 and 12 May; (3) north of Bloemhof, at Grootvlei, 22 and 23 May; (4) east of Pretoria (Delagoa Bay Railway), 1 and 2 June; and (5) north of Pretoria 5 June, 1900.

Referring to Major Aylmer Hunter-Weston, and the raids carried out by him in the South African War, Sir Arthur Conan Doyle, in his historic work, "The Great Boer War," writes as under:

"There is a Victoria Cross gallantry which leads to nothing save personal decoration, and there is another and far higher gallantry of calculation, which springs from a cool brain as well as a hot heart, and it is from the men who possess this rare quality that great warriors arise. Such feats as those performed by Major Hunter-Weston are of more service to the country than any degree of mere valour untempered by judgment."

A War Correspondent of the "Times," during the South African War, wrote the following account, in June, 1900, of Major Hunter-Weston's successful enterprise north of Bloemfontein, the first of the above-mentioned raids:

"Brevet-Major Aylmer Hunter-Weston's successful raid on the enemy's railway communications north of Bloemfontein furnishes a brilliant episode in the Campaign. It was an operation which led to far-reaching results, and admirably illustrates the advantage of having efficiently trained Mounted Engineers with the Cavalry. This officer had already distinguished himself by deeds of gallantry in General French's operations near Colesberg, at Riet Drift on the Modder River, during the advance of the Cavalry to relieve Kimberley, and at Paardeberg. In the late afternoon of the 12th March, 1900, the advanced troops of the Cavalry Division, under Lieut.-General French, following up the victory of Abraham's Kraal, were held up by a strong Boer force on the low hills south of Bloemfontein and north of Ferreira Spruit. The action was pressed vigorously till after nightfall, but without success. A feature of this action was the use made of pom-poms, or automatic guns, firing one-inch shells. These pom-poms are a new development of the artillery art. They did not have any great material effect, but the moral effect of this stream of little shells was considerable on those near the line of fire. To a Correspondent, like myself, well removed from their sphere of influence, the principal impression created was admiration for this novel form of fireworks in the growing darkness. The position held by the Boers was one of considerable strength, and the Cavalry were unable to drive them in or to reach Bloemfontein, which it was of importance to attain, not only for the moral effect of its capture, but from the fact that unless the locomotives and rolling stock at that railway centre could be captured it would be difficult for Lord Roberts to feed his force. With great boldness and true strategic conception, Lord Roberts had cut himself adrift from the Kimberley Railway, and had effected his movement north-east towards Bloemfontein, trusting to be able to establish a good line of communication, with his Base at Cape Town, by the Orange River-Bloemfontein Railway. As, however, our troops in that part of Cape Colony had been unsuccessful in preventing the Boers from blowing up the big railway bridge over the Orange River, it was impossible to get trucks or locomotives from Cape Colony into the Orange Free State until such time as the lengthy business of making a diversion and a new bridge had been completed. In the meanwhile the British Forces at Bloemfontein were dependent for their supplies on such locomotives and trucks as they could capture in the Free State, the bullock transport available being insufficient to feed so large a force at such a distance from the railhead at the other side of the Orange River. Brevet-Major Aylmer Hunter-Weston, who was on General French's Staff as Commander of the Mounted Engineers, recognizing the importance of the capture of this rolling stock, begged General French to allow him to make an attempt to break through the Boer line and to blow up the railway line north of Bloemfontein. This the Cavalry Commander at first refused, for he considered that the enterprise was an impossible one, and could only lead to the death of the Officer Commanding the Mounted Engineers, without any corresponding advantages. After nightfall, however, Major Hunter-Weston again reiterated his request, pointing out that the enterprise was a possible one under cover of darkness, if led by a man, who, like himself, had had experience of scouting and of deer-stalking. Having found it impossible to break the Boer line with the force he had immediately available, and knowing well the great importance of the object to be attained, General French, at 8.30 p.m., gave permission for an attempt to be made. Brevet-Major Aylmer Hunter-Weston, having received the desired authority, proceeded forthwith from the Cavalry Divisional Headquarters to the Royal Engineer Field Troops' Lines, to select from the men and horses of the Mounted Engineers and attached Cavalry Pioneers one officer and seven N.C.O.'s and men to accompany him in the operation. Two local men who could talk the 'Taal' fluently were also selected to accompany the expedition. The eleven forming this forlorn hope were mounted on the best horses that could be obtained from the whole of the Cavalry and Royal Engineers' horses in or near the Field Troop camp. Each man had the general plan and his particular rôle carefully explained to him, so that each might be able to carry on independently if his superiors became casualties. The party consisted of Brevet Major Aylmer Hunter-Weston, R.E.; Lieut. J. R. E. Charles, R.E.; Sergt Engleheart, Pioneer-Sergt., 10th Hussars; Corpl. Kirby, Royal Engineers, three other specially selected Royal Engineers; two other specially selected Cavalry Pioneers, and two local guides. The expedition was carefully equipped with the necessary tools and gun-cotton, and took with them two spare horses to allow for casualties among their mounts. Starting at 1 a.m. (midnight), on the 13th of March, led by Major Aylmer Hunter-Weston, the party moved off in a north-north-easterly direction, keeping well to the east of Bloemfontein, the lights of which could from time to time be discerned away to their left. The night was dark, and the ground traversed was rough and broken. Great care had to be taken by the leader to move along valleys where there was no chance of his party showing against the sky-line. The task of getting through the Boer outpost line was no easy one, for the Boers are well-trained veldt men, whose sight and hearing are keen. The local knowledge of the guides was found not to stand the test of night work, and as guides they proved of but little use under conditions so different to those to which they were accustomed. Their knowledge of the language, however, was invaluable, for the leader had arranged that, in case his party came across any of the enemy, the guides should immediately challenge them, and should pretend that the Raiders were a party of 'Zarps,' as the 'Zuid Afrikanshes Republiks Polizei' (South African Republic Police) are generally called. The Zarps are disciplined, are clothed in drab uniforms, and are therefore something like our men. By careful guiding, the enemy's outpost line and support line were successfully passed, though on one occasion the Raiders were very nearly discovered by a patrol. When, however, they had got safely through the outpost line, and were well east of Bloemfontein, north of the Thaba Nchu Road and the partially constructed Ladybrand–Wepener Railway, a small Boer party ran into the group, and the value of the arrangement above described was proved. The guide immediately challenged them in Dutch, and, pretending that the party was a Zarp Patrol, he ordered the burghers back to their commando, threatening them with severe penalties for their irregularity in being away from their commando at night! The distance traversed in order to avoid the vicinity of Bloemfontein and the main body of the enemy was in truth considerable, but in the darkness, and with the many perpendicular-sided river beds to cross, the journey seemed to the devoted band of Raiders to be interminable, and they could not but feel anxious as to whether it would be possible to reach the railway line before the kindly cloak of darkness, which hid them from their enemy's eyes, was dispersed by daylight. However, the longest journey has its end, and the railway line was reached north-east of Rustfontein at 4.20 a.m. One of the horses had broken down from fatigue, but the rest of the little party had successfully reached their goal. On arrival at the railway line, each man proceeded to the duty that had been allotted to him; the leader and Lieut. Charles proceeding outwards along the railway to seek for a culvert, the destruction of which would put the railway out of action for some time; some men prepared the charges; some cut the telegraph line, and yet others went out as scouts, while the two guides held the horses of the party. The leader was successful in discovering a big culvert, spanned by iron girders. These girders were soon prepared for demolition by placing gun-cotton round them at each end. When all was ready the party was sent away, and the two officers remained to light the fuses. As soon as the duplicate fuses for each charge had been lit, the officers got away as quickly as possible. It need hardly be said, however, that to get away quickly in the dark over such rough ground was not easy, and both officers had heavy falls while getting back to their horses. To fall at such a time is far from pleasant, when it is remembered that the fuse was burning all the time, and that at any moment the charge might go off. However, they reached their horses safely, and just before daybreak the charges exploded, sending pieces of iron hurling over great distances through the air. Two of these pieces went through the hut of some Kaffirs nearly one hundred yards from the scene of the explosion. These Kaffirs, who had heard and seen nothing of the Raiders, were suddenly awakened by this, to them, terrible explosion, followed immediately by the whizz of iron fragments through the hut. Thinking that the end of the world had come, the Kaffirs *en bloc* took to their heels and ran away to the mountains, where it was afterwards discovered they remained for some three days in a state of great terror. The explosions, which were completely successful in demolishing the railway bridge, had more important results than frightening the Kaffirs. They were heard by General French, who, knowing his man, immediately reported by field telegraph to Lord Roberts that the raid had been successful and that the line was cut. The Boers in Bloemfontein, hearing these loud explosions far behind and to the north of them, thought they were surrounded and were severely shaken in moral. The railway officials, who were getting away the locomotives and rolling stock as rapidly as they could from Bloemfontein to the north, to prevent them falling into our hands, were prevented from getting any more stuff away, and thus the great object of the raid was accomplished. As far as regards the immediate fortunes of the Raiders, the explosions had an effect that was far from pleasant, for they gave the alarm to the Boer troops in these parts, and as day broke the fate of the little party, trying to get back to the British forces from a situation so many miles away behind the Boer lines, became more and more precarious. Both they and their horses were very tired, and the country to be traversed was badly cut up with perpendicular-sided nullahs, or water-courses, up and down which it was difficult to get a path to lead horses. As the little party rode off to the east to circumvent the main body of the enemy lying to the south, the leader espied a strong Boer piquet in one of these nullahs right in front of them. The situation was a desperate one. To avoid the piquet by moving to either flank was impossible, for during their movement to a flank they would have afforded easy targets to the Boer rifles at that short range. The Boers on the far side of the nullah were perfectly safe from any mounted attack if only they kept their heads; but the leader, knowing the value of decided action, and the great moral effect of a mounted charge, gave to his men the stirring command, 'Charge.' Cheering as they did so, the party galloped after him. On arrival at the nullah, the leader, Major Hunter-Weston, cheering, jumped straight into it. As is almost always the case in war, boldness succeeded, and the Boers, quitting the security of their positions on the other side of the nullah, ran away down the bottom of the nullah at their very best speed, without leaving anyone behind to fire on the raiders, or to take advantage of the easy target that they and their horses presented. Elated by this success, the little party pressed forward on its way home; but soon Boers appeared on either flank behind them, and fire was opened on them both by long range rifle fire and later by field guns. In descending into the last of the nullahs one horse got shot, and one man, Sapper Webb, got wounded. In order to save this man and to safeguard the retreat of the party, Major Hunter-Weston, retaining Sergt. Engleheart with him, sent on the remainder of the party, under Lieut. Charles, to take up a position on the line of low kopjes about a mile further on, while he himself, with Sergt. Engleheart, got the wounded man on to a horse, which was led on by Sergt. Engleheart while the other acted as a rearguard, and, firing from time to time, checked the advancing Boers. The fire brought to bear upon this little party was fortunately erratic, and neither the men of Lieut. Charles' party, nor the detachment with the wounded man, were hit either by rifle or shell fire, though the latter detachment, encumbered as they were by the wounded man, had many narrow escapes. As soon as the Boers came under the fire of the party established on the line of kopjes, and the rear detachment had passed through the line behind the hills, the Boers gave up the pursuit, and the Raiders, covered by a small rearguard, were able to make their way back by a very wide detour to the east and then south and south-west to the British lines, where they were received by the advanced scouts of the 2nd Cavalry Brigade, which was then advancing north to sweep round the east of Bloemfontein. The Raiders reached Cavalry Division Head-quarters shortly before midday, and were in time to take part in the historic ceremony of the surrender of Bloemfontein that afternoon. The result of this excellently executed and most successful raid was that 25 locomotives and 108 trucks, 50 of which were loaded with coal, fell into our hands. It transpired that the Boers had been getting their accumulation of rolling stock away from Bloemfontein as quickly as time would allow, and that if the line had not been cut all would have been cleared by the morning. The smashing of the line not only prevented this rolling stock from being evacuated, but the news of it, telegraphed north, prevented Joubert from bringing to Bloemfontein the trains of reinforcements that were on their way. It had, furthermore, a great effect on the Boer troops holding Bloemfontein, for the noise of the explosion in their rear, and the absurdly exaggerated reports as to the strength of the raiders, made them believe that a strong cavalry force with artillery was across their line of retreat. The effect of this news was to convert the previous orderly retirement of our enemy into a rout, and to cause such a panic that no further defence of the hills south of Bloemfontein was attempted. Immediately after the surrender of Bloemfontein, the Mounted Engineers, under Major Aylmer Hunter-Weston, went forward to the railway station, and, taking over control of the railways, were able, with the aid of those of the railway staff who were of British sympathies and had remained, to organize, with the captured rolling stock, that same night a train service from Bloemfontein to the south. The Mounted Engineers continued to work this line until the arrival of the regular British Railway Staff some days later. It was due to this captured rolling stock that we were able to send troops down south to clear the railway line, and to get the much needed supplies up from the Orange River to our troops near Bloemfonteim. For their services in this raid, Sergt. Engleheart was given the Victoria Cross; Lieut. Charles was given the Distinguished Service Order, and every man of the party was given the D.C.M.; Major Hunter-Weston himself receiving the special thanks of Lord Roberts."

Of Brevet-Major Aylmer Hunter-Weston's second exploit the "Times" Correspondent gave the following description under his account dated 13 May, 1900, of the "Occupation of Kronstadt":

"When the Cavalry Division, under General French, arrived at the farm of Boshof, west-south-west of Kronstadt, on the night of 11 May, Major Hunter-Weston, commanding the Royal Engineers with the Cavalry Division, volunteered to attempt a raid on the railway communication north of Kronstadt, similar to the enterprise which he carried out so successfully on the night previous to the occupation of Bloemfontein. General French gave his sanction. Volunteers were called for, and again it had to be a matter of selection. Taking Mr. Burnham, the American scout, and Lieut. Charles, R.E., Major Hunter-Weston chose the following eight sappers: Corpls. C. Hyde and F. Kirby; Sappers J. Austin, C. Collins, T. Costin, J. Crisp, B. Fearnley and T. Pearce. As it was anticipated that it might be necessary to employ force to pass the raiding party through the enemy's outposts, General French placed under Major Hunter-Weston's command a composite squadron picked from the 1st Cavalry Brigade and officered by Capt. Yardley, Inniskilling Dragoons, and Lieut. Harrison, Scots Greys. Crossing the Bospoortspruit, the little column of desperate men moved north, parallel with the Valsch River. Major Hunter-Weston led the column, steering by the stars, and Burnham brought his extraordinary faculties of sight and hearing into use to prevent the party from running into any outlying patrol or piquet. About a mile north of the Modderspruit, Burnham discovered a patrol of four men moving across the front. As it was impossible for the column to avoid detection, Major Hunter-Weston determined to capture the group. The Cavalry divided and charged in upon both flanks. It was a wonderful scene. The thud of the galloping horses in the deep silence of night, the sabres flashing bare in the strong moonlight, the intense excitement of the moment. The party was captured and proved to be a Kaffir patrol, which had been sent out by a Boer piquet lying about a mile to the east. Having located this Boer piquet to the left, and having passed a strong Boer piquet on the right, Major Hunter-Weston judged that the outpost cordon was pierced. He, therefore, left Capt. Yardley, with the Cavalry, in observation of the Boers, with orders to return to camp as soon as the raiding party was clear. The little raiding party itself, now 11 strong, with two led horses, moved off north-east, taking advantage of the ground to avoid being seen. On a ridge near Fairfield, Burnham descried an enemy piquet. It was located at a junction of two long wire fences, as was so often the custom of the Boers on outpost. The situation is an excellent one, for wherever in their length the fences be climbed or cut the wire transmits the sound and the piquet at once becomes aware of the fact. To avoid the patrol, Major Hunter-Weston made a detour, but the patrol had seen the party, and the Boers were moving parallel with them and were collecting the vedettes along the line. To discover the Boers' movements, Burnham scouted out to them, while the remainder of the party lay quiet. He discovered that four men were going rapidly forward, evidently to lie in ambush at a small nek which lay in the line of the raiders' advance, while the others were trying to follow. To shake off this following, the party dived into the deep and wooded Dornspruit, giving the nek and the Boers a wide berth. On reconnoitring the ridge after arrival at the Dornspruit dam, they found that they had shaken off the Boers and that they were clear of the enemy. They then crossed the Damfontein Hills, from which position they could see the Boer camp fires extending in an almost unbroken line from Kronstadt to Honingspruit. The retreating force was encamped all along the railway line, and was interposed between the raiders and their objective. As it was impossible to get right round behind the enemy, Major Hunter-Weston decided to try to slip through the Boer camps to the railway. But to do this the horses had to be concealed. Burnham went forward and found a spruit in which it would have been possible to have hidden the horses. But just as the party arrived at the edge of the depression a Boer camp fire flared up and showed them a number of Boers camped in the spruit. Time was now getting short; there was only half an hour of moonlight and an hour of darkness left before dawn. Retiring west from the spruit, they passed by a farm full of Boers, and moving through their hobbled horses, finally got within sight of the low railway embankment. Between them and the railway, however, ran the main road from Kronstadt to Pretoria, and along this road the Boer commandos were retiring all night. As the raiders approached the road the head of a large commando of mounted Boers turned up over a fold in the veldt. Thanks to Burnham, the Boers were seen before they made the British out. Major Hunter-Weston at once gave the preconcerted signal for everyone to lie flat upon their horses' necks. As the commando passed, the leading file challenged. For a moment it seemed that they must be discovered, and that it would be necessary to give the other preconcerted signal for the little party to break up, and, as individuals, make a bid for safety by galloping off in different directions. But as no movement was seen and no sound heard, the Boers apparently mistook the group for a bunch of loose horses, and passed on. It was a moment of extreme suspense; a moment when you hear each beat of your heart, and the relief was intense when the serried ranks of burghers passed on, laughing and joking, into the darkness. When the commando had passed the raiders moved on again to a place further away from the line, where the horses and the majority of the party were left concealed under Lieut. Charles, while Major Hunter-Weston, accompanied by Burnham, went forward to blow up the railway line at a point that proved to be near Amerika Siding. The leader had just left the rest of the party, and was giving Lieut. Charles some last instructions, when three Boers, who were sleeping in the field, suddenly sprang up out of the grass. Hunter-West and Burnham each immediately 'covered' a man with their revolvers, and Lieut. Charles with great promptitude seized the carbine of the third. They proved to be three scouts of the Afrikander Horse. They were left with Lieut. Charles and the sappers, while Major Hunter-Weston and Burnham went forward alone on foot to attempt the demolition. Almost at once they met a piquet in search of the prisoners. Avoiding these by lying flat on the ground, they waited until they heard the men move on before again going forward. The Boers disappeared, accusing the patrol of deserting its post. Boers were all round, but the two desperate men crawled to the road. Here they lay in the grass, and waited while another long commando passed. Then came some wagons, and then a break in the column. In this gap behind the last wagon, and under cover of the dust and noise, both crossed the road in safety, crawled through the wire fence between the road and the railway, and, choosing their time during the intervals between bodies of troops, they were able to crawl to the top of the embankment and lay themselves flat in the angle between the top of the earthwork of the embankment and the side of the ballast of the permanent way. Burnham, being one of the greatest scouts in the world, and Hunter-Weston a practised stalker, they were able, with the ballast as a background, to lie unnoticed within ten yards of the Boer commandos passing along the road, while Hunter-Weston attached the charges to the rail and made them ready for lighting. When the charges were fixed and the detonators in position, they waited until Burnham's practised ear told him that an interval in the continuous stream of troops and wagons was approaching. Hunter-Weston then, under cover of Burnham's broad-brimmed hat, lit the fuses, and they both slipped off down the little embankment, through the fence and across the road, behind the last of one lot of wagons and before the head of the next commando of Burghers arrived. Then at 4.15 a.m. came the explosion. It was followed by a babel of noise from the waking men, scared cattle, and a rush 'to horse.' It was a regular swarming of bees. Under cover of this tumult Major Hunter-Weston and Burnham reached the horses, and, mounting the prisoners on the led horses, the whole party moved off north-west in the grey light of approaching daybreak. As soon as the leader considered that they were clear of the surrounding Boers, he increased the pace, and they trotted steadily on for three miles up and over the low range they had crossed further north on their outward journey. At sunrise they were clear of the main body, but they had yet to get through the outposts. And as they dropped down into the valley, shortly after sunrise, they made out a piquet of some twenty Boers directly in their path. Fortunately these Boers were dismounted and engaged in catching their horses. One man only remained by the fire as a sentry over the arms. Immediate attack was the only possible salvation, and the leader, ordering a charge, headed the best attempt that the horses could do towards a gallop. The sentry levelled his rifle at the leader, but the sight of the charging horse and man made his courage fail, his hand shook, and the shot went wide. He then threw up his hands to save his own life. The leader, flinging himself from his horse, seized the man's rifle, and, to render it and the six other rifles lying there useless, he broke their stocks. There was no time to wait, for the Boers far outnumbered the raiders, and the raiders were encumbered by the three prisoners they had taken, two of whom were mounted on one horse. The order, therefore, was at once given to press on, and to get over the next ridge before the Boers could collect themselves and their horses, and, in turn, attack. For some little time the Burghers were dumbfounded, and were intent only on saving themselves and on catching their horses, which had as usual been allowed to graze during the night. These minutes of confusion were the saving of our party, for it enabled them to make good progress towards the ridge, and before the Boers had collected, had mounted and had begun to follow, the raiders were cresting the rise. By their fire they wounded one of the raiders, Sapper Collins, and, seeing that it would be necessary to check this Boer piquet (now left with some twelve rifles) Major Hunter-Weston ordered everyone to move on under the command of Lieut. Charles, while he himself remained behind to cover the retreat. Dismounting behind the ridge, he took up a concealed position, and opened rapid fire on the advancing Boers with one of the Mauser carbines captured from the prisoners taken near the railway. Providence aided him, for his first shot killed the leading man, and the rest of the piquet immediately threw themselves from their horses and began firing at the unseen enemy on the ridge. Seeing that the pursuit was checked, the Major, after discharging some more rounds from different positions, so as to give the impression that the ridge was held in strength, mounted his horse and rode on to rejoin his party. Rearguards were dropped on each vantage ground to secure themselves against pursuit, but nothing was seen of that piquet. The journey back with tired men leading tired horses, and with three prisoners to guard, was long and wearisome, and the vigilance of the leaders could never be relaxed, for they were still within the territory covered by the Boer patrols. At length they got back to country where they judged they should be clear of the Boers, but what was their discomfiture to espy in the distance in front of them a mounted force of Boers. The raiders tried to avoid being seen by this force, but it was evident that the advanced scouts had discovered them, and a pretty little bit of manœuvring ensued, neither party knowing the strength nor disposition of the other, and each keeping hidden from his opponent. By good fortune, before fire was opened, the raiders got a view of some of their opponents and discovered that they were British! But danger was not yet over, for the raiders had either slouch hats or bare heads, and it was difficult to make it clear that the returning raiders were in sooth British. As soon, however, as junction was effected with this Cavalry Squadron, the difficulties and dangers of the raiders were over, and, after watering and feeding and resting for a short time at a farmhouse, the gallant little cortège, with its three prisoners, returned quietly, reaching Cavalry Division Headquarters Camp, three miles north of Kronstadt, at 3 p.m., having accomplished an expedition which, in its sequence of miraculous escapes, reads more like a fairy tale than a stern episode of war, and which presents one of the most stirring, gallant and self-sacrificing side-histories of this war."

Colonel Watkins Yardley, D.S.O., in his delightful book, "With the Inniskilling Dragoons in South Africa," gives an account of his adventures when he went out to escort Major Hunter-Weston, as described at the beginning of this account. He ends his narrative by saying:

"One of our squadrons was detailed to reconnoitre at daylight for the enemy in the direction of our previous night's expedition. They espied Major Hunter-Weston's small party attempting to return, and pursued them, thinking that they were Boers. Major Hunter-Weston similarly mistook them for Boers, and tried to avoid them; so much delay arose before each discovered the error. My squadron was first detailed for this duty, and it would have been strange if, after escorting them out, I had been hunting them when returning. But in this vast country, where the air is so clear, figures can be seen at great distances, and you are within range of rifle fire ere it can be decided whether it is that of friend or foe."

The following extract gives an account of Brevet-Major Aylmer Hunter-Weston's third raid:

"On the 17th May, 1900, while still at Kronstadt, Brevet-Major Aylmer Hunter-Weston, realizing the importance of interrupting the Boers' railway communications, and seeing the futility, under the existing conditions, of trying to cut the railway line close behind the Boers, where its effect could be but slight, begged to be allowed to go right forward over the Vaal River and to break the line, many days' march ahead, near the big railway depôt at Johannesburg. If he had been successful in blowing up the line near this great centre of the Boer railway system, and, lying up for some days in the neighbourhood, had been able to continue to keep it cut, he would have upset the whole of the Boer railway communications. Lord Roberts, to whom the matter was referred, decided that the chance of success of so distant an enterprise was not worth the almost certain death of so valuable an officer, for even if the raid were successful the chance of the raider being able to return was very slight. On 22 May, however, when the Cavalry had done two days' march forward to Welgelegen, near the junction of the Rhenoster River and Honingspruit, Lord Roberts decided to allow Hunter-Weston to try and cut the line at some point within a night's ride, though he still refused to allow him to attempt the forlorn hope of trying to cut the line north of Johannesburg. He therefore sent a telegram to General French to say that if Major Hunter-Weston were to cut the line so as to prevent the Boers getting away their guns he would be performing a signal service to the State. Armed with this permission, Brevet-Major Aylmer Hunter-Weston set about selecting the best hundred men and 120 horses from the 1st Cavalry Brigade. Escorted by this squadron, under the command of Major Scobell, of the Scots Greys, Hunter-Weston, accompanied by Lieut. Earle, R.E., by two scouts and a black shepherd, left the Cavalry Division at Engelschekuil, and proceeded with the squadron to Bloemhof, which place they reached at sunset. From Bloemhof the squadron returned to rejoin the Cavalry Division, while Major Hunter-Weston, with his little party of four, went on through the night to try and blow up the big railway bridge at Grootvlei. After a long and very difficult journey, steered by Hunter-Weston by the aid of the stars, the raiders hit off the bridge exactly, but found that the enemy were camped in strength around the bridge. Major Hunter-Weston and one man, leaving the remainder with the horses, crept through the Boer camps and got up to the bridge, but only to find that the Boers themselves had already destroyed it. With great difficulty they got back, through the Boers to the rest of their party, and with them, at 2 a.m., slipped away through the darkness. By careful leading they were able to avoid the Boer piquets on the return, as on the outward journey, and, passing Shepstone at 8 a.m., they reported their arrival to General French at Essenbosch at 9.30 a.m., after a very long and difficult journey, practically all of which had to be carried out on foot, so as to save the horses for carrying the explosives and for an emergency."

With the exception of cutting the railway at Roodepoort on the 30th May—a small and comparatively easy affair—the next important raid carried out by Brevet-Major Hunter-Weston was that described below by a war correspondent:

"At the beginning of June the British Army was in and about Johannesburg, the Boers at that time holding the hills south of Pretoria, with outposts pushed well out towards Johannesburg. It was known that the Boers had at Pretoria a large amount of coal and of railway rolling stock, including engines and trucks, all of which were badly needed. Furthermore, in and about Pretoria there were known to be some 4,000 British prisoners, whom the enemy intended to move east, down the Delagoa Bay Railway into the low and unhealthy country near Barberton and Koomatipoort. To prevent this great danger to the health and lives of our prisoners, and to capture the much-needed coal and rolling stock, the Commander-in-Chief decided to entrust to Brevet-Major Aylmer Hunter-Weston the task of cutting some big bridge on the railway from Pretoria to Delagoa Bay. The difficulties of such an enterprise, in view of the distance from Johannesburg to this railway, and in view of the large numbers of Boers now collected in the vicinity of Pretoria and Johannesburg, were obvious, but Hunter-Weston had overcome even greater difficulties in his former raids, and the value to the prisoners was such as to justify the taking of big risks. On 1 June, therefore, Lord Roberts sent for Major Hunter-Weston to come to his Army Headquarters at Orange Grove Hotel, near Johannesburg, where Lord Kitchener, his Chief of the Staff, explained the situation, placed the famous scout Burnham at his disposal, and gave him authority to take with him the best two hundred men and horses that the 3rd Cavalry Brigade could produce, to help him on his way to the big bridge at Bronkerspruit, or such other railway bridge on the Delagoa Bay Railway as he could get in at. These orders were given to him at about 4.30 p.m., and by 8.30 p.m. Major Hunter-Weston had started from the Dynamite Works with Burnham, Corpl. Kirby, and three other selected Sappers, escorted by 200 men and 220 horses of the 9th, 16th and 17th Lancers. The Boers had many outposts out, and it needed both skill and good fortune to elude them. Fortunately the skill in leading was provided both by Major Hunter-Weston, who had done so much raiding, and to whom night work and guiding by the stars apparently presented no difficulties, and by Burnham, the great American scout. Fred Burnham, who was afterwards both made a Major in the British Service and created a Companion of the Distinguished Service Order, is a man of whalebone and iron, with a very alert and intelligent brain, and with highly trained senses of sight, hearing and smell—senses which he had cultivated in his early days as a scout in the Red Indian Wars in North America. He is, perhaps, the most wonderful scout in the history of the world. Major Hunter-Weston could see in the dark much further than any ordinary man, but Burnham's powers of sight were out of all comparison better than his, and in the matter of hearing and smell all other white men were immeasurably his inferior. Even the natives could not compete with him in this respect. Twice in this night's ride he was able to make out the presence of a farm by his sense of smell, long before anyone else could either see or hear anything of them. At daybreak on June 2nd, some time before the sun rose, Burnham, who was then leading, descried a Boer scout ahead of him. He scouted up close to him with the intention of capturing him. In so doing he discovered that there were many other Boers close by him still wrapped in their blankets sleeping, and with their horses knee-haltered and grazing in a little depression beyond. He immediately returned to report this to the leader, and the latter at once sent a troop round to cut them off before they could get back and give the alarm to their main body. Unfortunately the Boers were able to elude this troop, and the enemy made good their escape. By this time, in the growing light, the smoke of many fires could be seen over the crest of a neighbouring rise. These extended for about half a mile, and about another half-mile beyond them again, near Bapfontein, the bivouac of another and much larger commando could be made out through glasses. The fires of this latter commando extended to a considerable distance, and it was evident that the party were in the presence of a strong assembly of Boers amounting to several thousand. In these circumstances, further advance was out of the question, and it only remained for the raiders to retire as rapidly and as gracefully as they could, for their chance of being able to avoid envelopment and capture by so large a body of the enemy with fresh horses was but small, having regard to the open nature of the country, and the fact that our men's mounts, which had started tired, had now been marching all night. However, the troops were drawn from three of the best of the British Cavalry Regiments, under good officers, and there ensued what an eye-witness of considerable military experience described as 'the prettiest rearguard action that it was possible to imagine.' The British, under Major Hunter-Weston, retired successively under cover of the fire of small rearguards and small flank guards, who pushed out wide on each flank to prevent the Boers from getting round and heading them off. This the Boers were constantly attempting to do, but the accurate long-range shooting of the flanking parties took such toll of the Boers that they never gained their object. When this running fight had continued successfully for some miles, and the leader saw that there was a good chance of the party being able to get back within range of our own troops, he despatched Burnham, who was mounted on a splendid little colonial pony, to take a message to the nearest British Cavalry Brigade to report the situation, and to request that some Cavalry and Horse Artillery might be sent out to a Kaffir kraal, west of Six-Mile Spruit, near which the ground afforded an excellent position for the raiders to hold. On arrival at this Kaffir kraal the raiders took up, with great skill, an extended and concealed position among the rocks, where they themselves and their horses were well hidden, and whence they could annihilate with fire any Boers that approached over the surrounding open country. The Boers, finding that their attempts to cut the British off had been unsuccessful, and disliking the appearance of the British position, and especially disliking the bullets that came with such frequency and accuracy from that position, gave up the game, and the little British force had the satisfaction of watching their enemies retire crestfallen to their distant camp, from rest in which they had been so unceremoniously disturbed before sunrise. As soon as our scouts, who had been sent out immediately the Boers were seen to retire, reported that the enemy had indeed disappeared, the party of raiders continued their journey back towards Johannesburg, and met, at about four miles from their camp, the force of cavalry and guns that General Dickson had sent out to extricate them from what would have been a very awkward predicament if it had not been for the skill in leading, and the courage, high training and good shooting of the troops. Thus ended, with only 16 casualties, an episode which, in less skilful hands, might have resulted in a gain to the Boers of over 200 good horses and good rifles, and of captivity, and its attendant discomforts, to some of the very flower of our troops." For his exceptional gallantry among this goodly company of gallant men, Corpl. Kirby, Royal Engineers, was awarded the much coveted distinction of the Victoria Cross, the second V.C. awarded to men who had taken part in raids with Brevet-Major Aylmer Hunter-Weston. For his services in command of these raids he was created a Companion of the Distinguished Service Order [London Gazette, 19 April, 1901]: "Aylmer Hunter-Weston, Brevet-Major, Royal Engineers. In recognition of services during the operations in South Africa." For his further services in the South African War, Brevet-Major Aylmer Hunter-Weston was mentioned in Despatches; received the Queen's Medal with seven clasps, and was given the Brevet of Lieutenant-Colonel. After the South African War, Brevet Lieut.-Colonel Aylmer Hunter-Weston commanded a Field Company, Royal Engineers, at Shorncliffe till 1904, when he was made D.A.A.G., 4th Army Corps in London. He was transferred to the General Staff on its inception, and served on the General Staff in the Eastern Command from 1904–1908; in the Scottish Command, 1908–11; and as Assistant Director of Military Training, General Staff, War Office, 1911–14. In Feb. 1914, he was promoted to Brigadier-General, and given the command of the 11th Infantry Brigade at Colchester. On the outbreak of War, Aug. 1914, he took the 11th Infantry Brigade of the 4th Division to France and took part in the Great Retreat, and in all the battles in France and Flanders up till Feb. 1915, when he was sent home to command the 29th Division (Despatches four times; promoted Major-General for distinguished service in the field). Major-General Aylmer Hunter-Weston left England with the 29th Division in March, 1915, and commanded it at the landing at Cape Helles, Dardanelles, on 25 April, and in the subsequent operations on the Gallipoli Peninsula. He was promoted temporary Lieutenant-General on 24 May, 1915, and commanded the 8th Army Corps at the Dardanelles, and subsequently in France till the conclusion of hostilities, when he was promoted Lieutenant-General "for distinguished service in the field." He was created a K.C.B. on 11 Aug. 1915. Sir Aylmer Hunter-Weston of Hunterston was elected M.P. for his county (North Ayrshire) as Coalition candidate in Oct. 1916, on the nomination of all parties, Unionist, Liberal and Labour, while he was at the front in command of his Army Corps. He was re-elected with an enormous majority in Dec. 1918. On the 24th Jan. 1918, in support of the Military Service Bill, Lieut.-General Sir Aylmer Hunter-Weston, in a maiden speech, said: "It is with great diffidence that I rise to make my first speech in this House. I am a plain, blunt soldier, more accustomed to the ways of war than the eloquence of Parliament. But from the fullness of the heart the mouth speaketh, and the question of man-power, with which this Bill is concerned, is of such vital importance to us, who are fighting your battles at the front, that, as a serving soldier at present commanding an Army Corps in Flanders, I cannot refrain from giving you the thoughts and feelings of my comrades of all ranks at the front. I speak not as a General only. Among the many true friends and trusty comrades I have among those who are risking their lives, and more than their lives, none are truer or more valued by me than my friends and comrades in the ranks. And it is as one who has had the privilege of sharing with his men danger, sickness and privation that I venture to speak haltingly and feebly, but from a full heart, in their name to-night. Our Army, your Army, the flower of the manhood of these islands, and of the great self-governing Dominions across the seas, is in magnificent fettle, full of courage and confidence and unconquerable cheeriness, imbued with a magnificent spirit of self-sacrifice and devotion to duty, determined to 'stick it out' doggedly when it is a question of defence, and ready to strike, and strike hard, when the time comes for attack or counter-attack. But we need men, and, above all, we need the confidence and co-operation of the nation. We need that every man and woman at home, and everyone in the army abroad, should have confidence in each other, and that each and all should exert all their strength, physical, mental and moral, to help to win the war. Let there be no mistake. We are fighting for our national existence; we are fighting for our lives, and for the lives and honour of our women and children. If we do not now beat Germany and make her people feel that militarism does not pay, she will attack us again when we have not so many Allies, and if she does, and if she wins, she will do to us all and more than all that she has done to Serbia, to Belgium, and to Northern France—she will destroy us utterly. She has chastised the small nations with whips. If she were to succeed in a second campaign against us she would chastise us with scorpions. Germany is waging war not for military supremacy only, but also for commercial supremacy, and to attain this commercial supremacy she undoubtedly desires to destroy the productivity of the working classes of the United Kingdom. I am no believer in distinction of classes. We as a nation stand or fall together, and what affects one part of the nation affects all; but undoubtedly those who would suffer most by a German victory would be the workers, the producers in this country. See how Germany has removed all machinery from Belgium and Northern France. See how she has forced the workmen of Belgium to work as quasi-slaves for German taskmasters. See how she has torn the young women of Northern France from their homes, and sent them to a fate their parents know not what. It is the working men and women of the conquered territories that have suffered most at German hands. I hope that Hon. Members will make this great fact known to the people of this country. If she got the chance she would do the same by us. She would destroy our factories and ship-building yards, remove our machinery, injure our wharves and harbours, and, by thus destroying our means of production, would leave our people to starve. To realize what a fate you would lay up for your children and for your old age, if you leave Germany free to attack us at her pleasure, come and see the reconquered territory; that land of desolation, of destruction, and of death. Of German atrocities you have incontrovertible evidence in the Report of Lord Bryce's Commission, but as the spoken word is worth a wilderness of paper, I will ask you to pardon me if I give you an example from my own experience. My advanced troops had entered a certain town in Northern France, from which they had driven the Germans. The women of the town came to us scattering flowers and greeting us with cries of 'Nous sommes sauvées!' A sturdy peasant woman of France cried to me, as commander of the advanced guard, to press on my already quick-moving troops to 'Kill, kill, kill!' the retreating fiends who had raped her daughter publicly before her very eyes. Can you wonder, then, that I appeal, through you, to the men and women of Great Britain and Ireland to support the Government in their determination to give the Army the young men it needs to carry this war through to victory? Objection has been taken that there are still many men capable of being combed out in France. If steps were not being taken to comb out in France at the same time as in England, I think this would be a fair and valid criticism. From my own experience and knowledge, however, and I speak, I may say, from the standpoint of one who is sufficiently high in the scale to be able to get a general view, while not so high up that I am in any way responsible either for policy or for strategy, I know that within recent times the harrow has been passed over the men behind the line in France, and with very considerable success. Now again the process of combing out is being gone through, not with a harrow, but with a small tooth comb. The exceeding bitter cry of the so-called indispensable is going up from works and offices in France, as at home. But it is being ruthlessly disregarded out there in the case of the really young men who cannot truly be called indispensable anywhere but in the front line. There young men are indispensable. But when every man has been combed out in France, and when as many as possible have been replaced by women of the Women's Army Auxiliary Corps—and in this connection I may say that the Women's Army Auxiliary Corps are doing a most admirable work, and we soldiers owe and pay a great tribute of admiration and gratitude to these women for what they are doing—I say that when every man has been combed out, and when every man has been replaced by a woman, there will still be need, and urgent need, for young men from this country. Objection has furthermore been made that sufficient use has not been made of the best brains, and that there is a prejudice against the Territorials and the New Army men. Nothing could be further from the truth. When men are fighting for their lives and honour, as we are out there, they do their utmost to get hold of the men who will help them best. They do not ask whether an officer was a Territorial, a Regular, or a New Army man in the past when choosing an assistant for the present. They ask who is the best man to be got now. We want to get the best assistance to help us to win the war. A man at the front is taken for what he is, and not for what he was. The Army does not resent criticism, It welcomes it. It welcomes constructive and well-informed criticism, but destructive and ill-informed criticism is good for no portion of the nation at any time. It is especially bad in war, for it tends to reduce the moral and confidence not only of the Army but of the nation. There are many points which may justly be criticised. There are faults. But I may say, from what I have seen out there, that every man in authority is honestly, constantly, and earnestly doing his best to minimize those faults and to overcome them. Let us have co-operation and mutual confidence—soldiers and politicians, civilians and military, trusting each other and working hand-in-hand. Both are needed. We at the front feel that the Army is but the point of the spear, of which the shaft is ship-building and the many other industries necessary for the successful prosecution of the war; the driving-power being the determination of the nation as a whole to co-operate with us, to stick it out, and to drive the spear home to victory. What most strikes an observant but at the present time a somewhat infrequent visitor to England and Scotland is the immense amount of courage, resolution and self-sacrifice of the majority of the nation. But there is a minority whose selfishness, ignorance and self-complacency are but too apparent. And there are a noisy and vociferous few—some of whom are honest, though mistaken—who do infinite harm to our cause. May I, as a representative of those at the front, appeal to those who are selfish from ignorance of the facts of the situation, and to the honest though vociferous few, to do what they can to help us—by helping the cause of Victory by every means in their power? Amongst the soldiers serving at the front there is a very strong feeling of resentment against the young, able-bodied men who are staying at home in comfort and safety and drawing large pay, while better men than they are doing not only their own share in the mud, discomfort and danger of the trenches, but also the share that should be borne by these young 'stay-at-homes,' who claim privileges denied to the rest of the nation. This feeling of resentment is so strong that it will, I fear, last beyond the war. It may also—and this, I think, is an important point—cause a line of cleavage in the nation which will be very deplorable. But I defy any man with ordinary human feelings not to feel in sympathy with a gallant soldier when, speaking of these young 'stay-at-homes,' he says, with ill-concealed resentment and heat in his tone, that he and his mates who have 'done their bit' 'will take good care to get even with those blessed skulkers,' as he calls them, using another adjective! Those of us who have had the privilege of serving with Irishmen and Irish Regiments know the charm of that most lovable race, so unaccountable and difficult if badly led, so glorious in their heroism, so easily led to almost unbelievable flights of heroism, loyalty and devotion to duty, if only they are led by a strong, just, fearless man, who has courage—courage not only physical but moral, and who adds to that courage human sympathy allied with well-balanced judgment and iron inflexibility of will. Are we men of action at the front guilty of too great idealism, too great optimism, if we still hope that among the great men of Ireland there will arise such a leader, be he known or unknown now, who will cause Ireland to join America, France, and the great Dominions across the seas in fighting this great fight for liberty, justice and right? Through the poor agency, therefore, of the voice of one who has borne the burden of the war from the beginning, fighting alongside Irishmen and Irish Regiments, may I say that your brother Irishmen and their true comrades in the Allied Armies, who are fighting with them on the other side of the water, appeal to their comrades in Ireland who are young and who are still in Ireland, both North and South, to be true to the glorious traditions and history of Ireland, and to come in full strength to take their rightful place alongside us. The future of these islands, of the Empire, and of the world lies in the hands of the men who have fought and who are fighting. It is they who will undoubtedly mould and shape the world. The great majority out there have given up all voluntarily at the call of duty and have been fighting with the greatest devotion, gallantry and self-sacrifice. It is those qualities, that self-sacrifice, devotion and resolution which, applied hereafter, will have the effect, as I believe, in making these islands better and brighter places than ever they have been before. May I, through this House, appeal to every man who is under twenty-five, and who is, therefore, more indispensable in the front line than anywhere else, to come willingly to join the men in whose hands the future of this country lies, and with them safeguard the noble heritage which our forefathers have bequeathed to us. Above all, let the men of England realize that they are directly and personally responsible for the lives of their fellow-countrymen at the front if by any action of theirs or of their friends they restrict or retard in any way the necessary output of munitions of war, ships, aeroplanes, guns, ammunition—munitions of every kind. These are the necessities of the situation out there. Guns, aeroplanes, munitions are our life-savers. Without them our men suffer heavy casualties. With them, we can so deal with the enemy that our losses are reduced to a minimum. Therefore, I would beg them to remember that any interruption or cessation of work means wounds and death to the brave lads who are fighting for you. A local defeat by the enemy has often much less serious military consequences than the stoppage of work by our fellow-workers at home. It is only by the whole-hearted co-operation of the men and women at home with us who are fighting at the front that we can carry our cause to victory. In this, as in everything else, we require solidarity in the nation—between the nation, which is the Army at home, and the Army, which is the nation at the front. We need men. We specially need young men. We need men to hold and work and fight on our front line. We need men to continue working on our many defensive lines. We need men to continue to improve the communications, on which so enormous an amount of work has been done during this past year. Above all, we need men to train for offensive and counter-attack action, so that we may have strong, well-trained divisions with which to meet and defeat the enemy. In this connection it is necessary for us all to face the facts and to preserve our sense of perspective and proportion. From a review of the general military situation, we know that whatever the available force the enemy may bring against us on the Western Front there is no cause for despondency. The military situation is good, and when America comes in it will be overwhelming. But until America is able to make her full strength felt we must expect heavy fighting if the enemy choose to attack. We hope they will attack, for if they do attack we shall undoubtedly defeat them, and they will suffer very heavy losses. In the sway of battle, however, we are sure to suffer local and temporary reverses, and it would be well for the British public to face this fact. I say, therefore, to all: Have Courage, Confidence and Resolution! Do not fear to face facts. We are sure to have difficulties, both at home and at the front, but the difficulties of the future are as nothing to the difficulties we have surmounted in the past. Our position and resources are such that, if only the nation will stick it out, we are certain to win through. Germany is hard pressed. Her men are hungry and in distress. Her allies are in even a worse plight. We are in every respect better off than she is. But her Army is still intact. Her leaders understand the merit and necessity of resolution. It is on our resolution, our determination, and our grit that the immense issues of the future now depend. A great flood of liberty and justice has been surging against the great dam formed by the Prussian desire to attain a world domination based on might and long-prepared military force. To the superficial observer that dam still seems to stand fast. But under the dam a steady, if unseen, process of disintegration has been going on, and some day the dam of might will burst, and the great flood of right will carry all before it. If only the Empire will but to herself be true; if all individuals and classes in the nation, which is the Army at home, will co-operate loyally with each other and with the Army, which is the nation at the front, standing resolutely shoulder to shoulder, calmly, confidently, and courageously, we are certain of ultimate victory, and of the only peace which would be a lasting peace—the only peace which would not be treason to the heroes, your sons and brothers, who have passed before us over the Great Divide to safeguard our honour and the prosperity of our people, and to ensure the triumph of right, liberty and justice."—Mr. Herbert Samuel: "The House in every quarter will desire to express to the hon. and gallant Member its cordial congratulations upon the admirable speech which he has just delivered, and its thanks for the observations he has made. Forcible, eloquent, and vivid, the hon. and gallant Gentleman has admirably fulfilled the function which I may describe as liaison officer between the Army and Parliament. We can assure him that the same spirit of resolute determination which he breathed throughout his speech animates this House."

Lieut.-General Hunter-Weston married Grace (Lady of Grace of the Order of St. John of Jerusalem, only daughter of the late William Strang Steel, of Philiphaugh, Selkirkshire, on 5 Dec. 1905.

He is 27th Laird of Hunterston and head of the ancient families both of Weston of Weston-under-Lizar, and of Hunter of Hunterston. He is J.P. and D.L. of Ayrshire; Knight of Justice of St. John of Jerusalem, of the English Priory of which Order his collateral ancestor Sir William Weston was Grand Prior on its suppression in England in the time of Henry VIII. He is Commandeur Légion d'Honneur, Grand Officer of the Belgian Crown, Member of the Medjidieh, D.S.O. and K.C.B.

ROBERTSON, JAMES, The Rev., was born 19 Aug. 1855, son of the late Robert Robertson, of Grantown-on-Spey. He was educated at Aberdeen and Edinburgh Universities, and joined the Army 18 April, 1884, as Chaplain to the Forces, 4th Class. He served during the operations of the Sudan Frontier Field Force in 1885, being present at the action of Kosheh during its investment, at the reconnaissance on the 16th Dec., and at the engagement of Giniss. He was mentioned in Despatches and received the Medal and the Khedive's Bronze Star. Mr. Robertson married, in 1887, Nellie (who died in 1911), daughter of the late Hugh Allan, J.P., of Glassaugh, County Banff. He became Chaplain to the Forces, 3rd Class, 21 Dec. 1896. He served in the South African War, 1899–1902, as Chaplain to the Highland Brigade, and took part in the advance on Kimberley, including the actions at Modder River and Magersfontein. Operations in the Orange Free State, Feb. to May, 1900, including operations at Paardeberg (17 to 29 Feb.); actions at Koodoosburg, Poplar Grove and Dreifontein; operations in Orange River Colony, May to 29 Nov. 1900, including occupation of Bloemfontein, actions at Waterval, Vet River, Blaauberg, Roodepoort, and in the Wittebergen (1 to 29 July) and Witpoort. He was Senior Presbyterian Chaplain to the South African Field Force from Oct. 1901. He was mentioned in Despatches [London Gazette, 8 Feb. 1901, and 29 July, 1902]; received the Queen's Medal with five clasps; King's Medal with two clasps; was promoted Chaplain to the Forces, 2nd Class, and created a Companion of the Distinguished Service Order [London Gazette, 19 April, 1901]: "The Rev. James Robertson, Chaplain to the Forces, 3rd Class (now promoted Chaplain to the Forces, 2nd Class). In recognition of services during the recent operations in South Africa." The Insignia were presented to him by the Duke of Cornwall and York 14 Aug. 1901. He retired from the Army 3 Sept. 1904, and became Minister of the Parish of Methven, Perthshire. Mr. Robertson was given the honorary degree of D.D. of Aberdeen University.

DOUGLAS, WILLIAM, Major, was born at Cranborne Lodge, Dorset, 13 Aug. 1858, son of William Douglas, late East India Civil Service, and of his wife, Caroline (*née* Hare). He was educated at Bath; was gazetted to the 1st Battn. The Royal Scots 30 Jan. 1878, and was promoted to Lieutenant 25 Nov. 1878, serving as Adjutant, 1st Battn. The Royal Scots, 24 March, 1880, to 23 March, 1887. He served in the Bechuanaland Expedition, 1884–85; became Captain 24 June, 1885; was Adjutant, 3rd Royal Scots (Militia), Feb. 1888, to Feb. 1893; and Adjutant, 1st Royal Scots, 20 Feb. 1893, to 20 Aug. 1894. He was promoted to Major 24 July, 1895; was at the Staff College, 1896–97. He served in South Africa, 1900–02, and took part in the operations in the Orange Free State, Feb. to May, 1900. Operations in the Transvaal, east of Pretoria, July to 29 Nov. 1900, including the actions at Belfast (26 and 27 Aug.) and Lydenberg (5 to 8 Sept.). He was in command of 1st Battn. Royal Scots from 24 Aug. 1900, and in command of a column, and took part in the operations in the Transvaal, Nov. 1900, to Nov. 1901. He was mentioned in Despatches [London Gazette, 16 April, 1901], received the Queen's Medal with three clasps, the King' Medal with two clasps, and was created a Companion of the Distinguished Service Order [London Gazette, 19 April, 1901]: "William Douglas, Major (now Lieut.-Colonel), Royal Scots, Lothian Regt. In recognition of services during the recent operations in South Africa." The Insignia were presented to him in South Africa. Major Douglas had been promoted to Lieutenant-Colonel 5 Dec. 1900. He was given the Brevet of Colonel 10 Feb. 1904; became Colonel 1 March, 1906; was Colonel, General Staff, 6th Division, and subsequently became (when the name of the appointment was changed) G.S.O., 1st Grade, 8th Division (the 6th Division becoming the 8th Division), Irish Command, 1 March, 1906, to 31 Oct. 1909. He was created a C.B. in 1908; was Brigade Commander, 14th Infantry Brigade, 1 Nov. 1909, to

9 Nov. 1912 ; became Major-General 10 Aug. 1912 ; commanded the 42nd (East Lancashire) Division from May, 1913, to 11 March, 1917. He served in the European War from 1914 ; in Egypt, 10 Sept. 1914, to 4 May, 1915 ; the Dardanelles, 5 May, 1915, to 2 Jan. 1916 (Despatches twice [London Gazette, 21 Sept. 1915 and Nov. 1915] ; created a K.C.M.G. Nov. 1915] ; Sinai, 1916-17, including the Battle of Romani and taking of El Arish ; commanded the Desert Column from 23 Oct. 1916, to 8 Dec. 1916 (Despatches twice, Dec. 1916 and 6 July, 1917 ; Croix de Guerre with Palm [London Gazette, 21 May, 1917]) ; commanded the Western Reserve Centre in 1917 and 1918. He married, in Dec. 1885, Ellen Lytcott (a Lady of Grace of St. John of Jerusalem), daughter of the late S. Taylor, Crown Solicitor, Barbados.

MATTHEWS, FRANK BROADWOOD, Major, was born at Romford, Essex, 7 Sept. 1857, son of Charles Peter Matthews, of The Bower, Havering-atte-Bower, Essex, and 23, Hertford Street, Mayfair, W., and of Frances, Capper Matthews. He was educated at Harrow (Rendall's) ; was gazetted Sub-Lieutenant, unattached, 15 July, 1876, and joined the 4th King's Own Royal Regt. 15 July, 1876. He served in the South African War of 1879, i n the Zulu Campaign, and received the Medal and clasp. He was Adjutant, King's Own Regt., 14 Oct. 1879, to 22 Dec. 1885, and became Captain 14 April, 1885 ; was Adjutant, Militia, 13 Jan. 1891, to 14 Jan. 1896, and became Major 12 July, 1893. Major Matthews served in the South African War, 1899-1902, being in command 2nd Battn. Royal Lancaster Regt. 23 Feb. to 27 May, 1900, and from 2 Feb. 1901, to 31 May, 1902. He was present at the Relief of Ladysmith, including the operations of 17 to 24 Jan. 1900, and action at Spion Kop ; operations of 5 to 7 Feb. 1900, and action at Vaal Kranz ; operations on Tugela Heights (14 to 27 Feb. 1900), and action at Pieter's Hill. Operations in Natal, March to May, 1900 ; operations in the Transvaal, Feb. to April, 1901, and Sept. to Oct. 1901 ; operations in Orange River Colony, July, 1901. He was mentioned in Despatches by Sir R. H. Buller 30 March and Nov. 1900 [London Gazette, 8 Feb. 1901] ; was given the Brevet of Lieutenant-Colonel 8 Dec. 1900 ; received the Queen's Medal with five clasps, the King's Medal with two clasps, and was created a Companion of the Distinguished Service Order [London Gazette, 19 April, 1901] : " Frank Broadwood Matthews, Major (now Lieut.-Colonel), the King's Own (Royal Lancaster) Regt. In recognition of services during the recent operations in South Africa." (Insignia, etc., sent to Commander-in-Chief, South Africa, and presented by the Duke of Cornwall and York 14 Aug. 1901.) He became Lieutenant-Colonel 13 Dec. 1900 ; commanded the 2nd Battn. King's Own (Royal Lancaster) Regt., and was given the Brevet of Colonel 10 Feb. 1904. He retired with the rank of Colonel 13 Dec. 1904. Colonel Matthews served in the European War ; became a temporary Brigadier-General 11 March, 1915 ; was created a C.B., 1916, and on 18 March, 1919, was given the honorary rank of Brigadier-General. He married, in 1889, Edith Mabel Warner, daughter of R. G. Price, of 26, Hyde Park Gardens, London, W., and they have one son and one daughter.

FORD, RICHARD WILLIAM, Major, was born 26 Sept. 1857. He joined the Army 5 Feb. 1881, and served in the Egyptian Expedition of 1882 (Medal and Bronze Star) ; became Major, Royal Army Medical Corps 5 Feb. 1893. He served in the South African War, 1899-1900, in charge of a Stationary Hospital, Pretoria. He took part in the Relief of Kimberley, and was present in the operations in Orange Free State, Feb. to May, 1900, including operations at Paardeberg (17 to 26 Feb.) ; actions at Poplar Grove and Dreifontein ; operations in Orange River Colony, including actions at Vet River (5 and 6 May) and Zand River. Operations in the Transvaal, June, 1900 ; operations in the Transvaal, east of Pretoria, July, 1900. He was mentioned in Despatches [London Gazette, 16 April, 1904] ; received the Queen's Medal with four clasps, and was created a Companion of the Distinguished Service Order [London Gazette, 19 April, 1901] : " Richard William Ford, Major (now Lieut.-Colonel), Royal Army Medical Corps. In recognition of services during the recent operations in South Africa." The Insignia were presented by the King 3 June, 1901. He had become Lieutenant-Colonel 5 Feb. 1901. From 17 Aug. 1901, to 16 Aug. 1906, he was Deputy Surgeon, Royal Hospital, Chelsea, and from 4 May, 1911, to 25 Jan. 1913, he was Assistant Director of Medical Services, Eastern Command. He became Major-General 1 June, 1914 ; Deputy Director of Medical Services, Northern Command, 14 July, 1914. He served in the European War from 1914 to 1917 ; was created a C.B. in 1916 ; was Administrative Medical Officer, Woolwich ; created a K.C.M.G. 1917 ; retired 26 Dec. 1917. Sir W. Ford married, in 1884, Mary Augusta, daughter of the late Rear-Admiral Wainwright, R.N.

O'DONNELL, THOMAS JOSEPH, Major, was born 18 Jan. 1858, third son of the late P. O'Donnell, High Constable of the Barony of Glenquin, of Killeedy, Ashford, County Limerick. He was educated at Stanislas' College, Tullabeg, King's County, and is a Fellow of the Institute of Public Health. He served with the Field Artillery, Egypt, 1881-82 (Medal and Bronze Star). Under Sir C. Warren, with the Kimberley Light Horse, in the Bechuanaland Expedition, 1885 ; with the Inniskilling Dragoons, in the operations in Zululand, 1888. After twelve years' service, he became Major, Royal Army Medical Corps, 5 Feb. 1893. Major O'Donnell served in the Tirah Campaign, with the 3rd Battn. The Rifle Brigade, 1897-98 (Medal with clasp). He served in the South African War, 1899-1902, and was present at the advance on Kimberley, including the action at Magersfontein ; Relief of Kimberley ; operations in the Orange Free State, Feb. to May, 1900, including operations at Paardeberg (17 to 26 Feb.) ; actions at Poplar Grove, Dreifontein, Karee Siding, Houtnek (Thoba Mountain), Vet River (5 and 6 May) and Zand River. Operations in the Transvaal in May and June, including actions near Johannesburg, Pretoria and Diamond Hill (11 and 12 June). Operations in Orange River Colony, May to 29 Nov. 1900, including actions at Bethlehem (6 and 7 July) and Wittebergen (1 to 29 July) ; operations in the Transvaal, July, 1901, to 31 May, 1902. He was mentioned in Despatches [London Gazette, 16 March, 1900, and 16 April, 1901] ; received the Queen's Medal with six clasps ;

King's Medal with two clasps ; and was created a Companion of the Distinguished Service Order [London Gazette, 19 April, 1901] : " Thomas Joseph O'Donnell, Major (now Lieut.-Colonel), Royal Army Medical Corps. In recognition of services during the recent operations in South Africa." The Insignia were presented by the King 3 June, 1901. He had become Lieutenant-Colonel 5 Feb. 1901 ; was promoted to Colonel 7 July, 1910 ; was P.M.O., India, 7 July, 1910 ; Administrative Medical Officer, Southern Command, up to the 6th July, 1914. He served in the European War from 1914 ; was Assistant Director of Medical Services 5 Aug. 1914, to 31 Dec. 1914 ; Deputy Director-General of Medical Services 1 Jan. 1915 ; became Surgeon-General 13 Feb. 1915 ; was Administrative Medical Officer at Tidworth. Surgeon-General T. J. O'Donnell was mentioned twice in Despatches (1914 and 1916) for his services in the European War, and was created a C.B. in 1916 and a K.C.I.E. in 1919. He retired 18 Jan. 1918. Sir T. J. O'Donnell is fond of hunting, shooting and racing, and rode many winners in South Africa and India.

KELLY, RICHARD MAKDOUGALL BRISBANE FRANCIS, Major, was born 24 Sept. 1857, youngest son of General Sir R. D. Kelly, K.C.B., Colonel, 34th Regt. (The O'Kelly), and Ellen, daughter of Sir William Dillon 4th Bart., of Lismullen, County Meath. He was educated at Marlborough, and the Royal Military Academy, Woolwich, and entered the Royal Artillery, as Lieutenant, 14 Aug. 1876, becoming Captain 13 March, 1885. He served in the second Miranzai Expedition, 1891, in No. 3 Mountain Battery, Royal Artillery (Medal with clasp) ; was promoted to Major 31 Jan. 1894 ; was Instructor, School of Gunnery, 10 April, 1895, to 12 Nov. 1899. He served in the South African War, as A.D.C. to Lieutenant-General, 5th Infantry Division, South Africa, 13 Nov. 1899, to 19 April, 1900 ; was severely wounded. He took part in the Relief of Ladysmith ; was present at Spion Kop, Vaal Kranz, Tugela Heights, Pieter's Hill ; was twice wounded (once severely), and had his horse shot under him twice. He was District Commandant in South Africa 15 Feb. 1901, to 13 Feb. 1903. He was mentioned in Despatches (Sir R. H. Buller), 30 March, 1900 ; also by Sir C. Warren 29 June, 1900 [London Gazette, 3 Feb. 1901] : received the Queen's Medal with three clasps, and the King's Medal with two clasps ; and was created a Companion of the Distinguished Service Order [London Gazette, 19 April, 1901] : " Richard Makdougall Brisbane Francis Kelly, Major, Royal Artillery. In recognition of services during the recent operations in South Africa." He became Lieutenant-Colonel 1 May, 1903 ; Chief Instructor, School of Gunnery, 22 April, 1904, to 21 April, 1908 ; was given the Brevet of Colonel 1 May, 1906 ; and promoted Colonel 1 May, 1908. He was Commandant, Royal Artillery, East Lancashire Division (T.F.), 1909 to 1910 ; commanded Royal Artillery, Southern Coast Defences, Portsmouth, from 1910, with the temporary rank of Brigadier-General. He was created a C.B. in 1911. He died, 20 Feb. 1915, and an obituary notice of him appeared in the " Times " of 22 Feb. 1915. He married, in 1887, Mary Piercy, daughter of Major-General P. Bedingfield, and they had two daughters.

FAYLE, ROBERT JAMES LEACH, Major, was born 1 April, 1857, son of the late B. W. Fayle, Esq., of Moor Park, Parsonstown. He joined the Army 4 Feb. 1882 ; became Major, Royal Army Medical Corps, 4 Feb. 1894 (previous service, 12 years). He served in the South African War, 1899-1902 ; took part in the Relief of Kimberley ; operations in the Orange Free State, 1900 ; operations in Orange River Colony, 1900. He was mentioned in Despatches [London Gazette, 16 April, 1901] ; received the Queen's Medal with three clasps ; King's Medal with two clasps, and was created a Companion of the Distinguished Service Order [London Gazette, 19 April, 1901] : " Robert James Leach Fayle, Major, Royal Army Medical Corps. In recognition of services during the recent operations in South Africa." The Insignia were sent to Major Fayle through Colonel Byng. He became Lieutenant-Colonel 4 Feb. 1902, and retired 29 Oct. 1902. Lieut.-Colonel Fayle married, in 1887, Mary, daughter of Joseph Leach, of Burwalls-Leigh Woods, near Bristol.

PIKE, WILLIAM WATSON, Major, was born 10 March, 1860, son of the late William Pike, J.P., of Glendaray. He entered the Army in 1882, and became Major, Royal Army Medical Corps, 4 Feb. 1894 (12 years' service). He served in the South African War, 1899 to 1902 ; was present at the Relief of Kimberley ; took part in the operations in the Orange Free State, Feb. to May, 1900, including operations at Paardeberg (17 to 24 Feb.) ; actions at Poplar Grove and Dreifontein ; operations in the Transvaal, east of Pretoria, July to 29 Nov. 1900 ; operations in Cape Colony, south of Orange River, 1899-1900 ; operations in Cape Colony, 1901. He was mentioned in Despatches [London Gazette, 8 Feb. and 16 April, 1901] ; received the Queen's Medal with five clasps ; King's Medal with two clasps ; and was created a Companion of the Distinguished Service Order [London Gazette, 19 April, 1901] : " William Watson Pike, Major, Royal Army Medical Corps." In recognition of services during the recent operations in South Africa." The Insignia were presented by the King 3 June, 1901. He became Lieutenant-Colonel 4 Feb. 1903 ; Colonel, 9 Nov. 1911. Colonel Pike served in the European War from 1914 ; was appointed Deputy Director of Medical Services 31 Oct. 1915 : Director of Medical Services, 1st Army, B.E.F., 1 Nov. 1915, to 20 July, 1917 ; was promoted to Temporary Surgeon-General 1 Nov. 1915, and to Major-General 3 March, 1917. He was mentioned in Despatches ; created a C.M.G., 1916, and a K.C.M.G., 1919. Sir W. W. Pike was a Rugby International, Ireland, 1879-83, and a Hockey Inter-Provincial, Ireland, 1898. He is an F.R.C.S.I.

O'NEILL, WILLIAM HENRY SLINGSBY, Major, was born 28 May, 1854, son of the Rev. John O'Neill, of Clonmore, County Carlow. He was educated at Caius College, Cambridge, and joined the Army as Sub-Lieutenant, unattached, 10 Sept. 1875, and the 103rd Foot (The Royal Dublin Fusiliers), 10 Sept. 1875. He became Captain 20 Jan. 1884 ; Adjutant, Auxiliary Forces, 9 Feb. 1886, to 8 Feb. 1891 ; was promoted Major 16 May, 1894. Major O'Neill served in the South African War from 1899 to 1902, in command 1st Battn. Royal Dublin Fusiliers (12 June to 16

Aug. 1900). He was present at the Relief of Ladysmith; operations in the Transvaal, June, 1900; operations in Natal (March to June, 1900), including the action at Laing's Nek (6 to 9 June); operations in the Transvaal, east of Pretoria, July, 1900. Operations in the Orange River Colony, June, 1900. He took part in the operations in the Transvaal, Dec. 1900; was Commandant at Durban from 20 Dec. 1900. He was mentioned in Despatches [London Gazette, 7 Feb. 1901]: received the Queen's Medal with five clasps; King's Medal with two clasps, and was created a Companion of the Distinguished Service Order [London Gazette, 19 April, 1901]: "William Henry Slingsby O'Neill, Major, Royal Dublin Fusiliers. In recognition of services during the recent operations in South Africa." The Insignia were presented by Colonel Lyttleton, at Lyttleton, South Africa. He retired 28 May, 1902. He served in the European War as Lieutenant-Colonel Commanding the 3rd Royal Dublin Fusilisers. Colonel O'Neill married, in 1889, Selina, daughter of Hugh Henry, of Firment, County Kildare, and they have one daughter.

SAVILE, WALTER CLARE, Major, was born 4 July, 1857, son of Colonel H. B. Savile. He was educated at Clifton College, and was gazetted to the Royal Artillery, as Lieutenant, 25 Jan. 1877; was Inspector of Warlike Stores, Bermuda, 21 March, 1881, to 21 July, 1882; became Captain 6 May, 1885; was Assistant to the Director of Artillery, Headquarters of Army, 19 May, 1888, to 31 March, 1902; was 2nd Class Assistant Inspector of Warlike Stores, Devonport, 7 April, 1892, to 14 May, 1892; became Major 29 Sept. 1894.; was Ordnance Officer, 3rd Class, 6 Aug. 1896, to 5 Aug. 1901. He served in the South African War, 1899–1901; took part in operations in Natal and in the defence of Ladysmith. Operations in Natal, March to June, 1900. He was mentioned in Despatches (by Sir George White, 2 Dec. 1899, and 23 March, 1900; by Sir R. H. Buller, 9 Nov. 1900 [London Gazette, 8 Feb. 1901]; received the Queen's Medal with three clasps, and was created a Companion of the Distinguished Service Order [London Gazette, 19 April, 1901]: "Walter Clare Savile, Major, Royal Artillery, Ordnance Officer, 3rd Class, Army Ordnance Department. In recognition of services during the recent operations in South Africa." The Insignia were presented by the Duke of Cornwall and York 4 Aug. 1901. He was given the Brevet of Colonel 30 Jan. 1907, and became Colonel 28 Jan. 1909, retiring from the Staff with the honorary rank of Brigadier-General 4 July, 1914. General Savile was re-employed at the War Office, 1914–15, and at the Ministry of Munitions, 1917, and was created a C.B. in 1917. He married, in 1881, Helen, fourth daughter of William Ruxton, Ardee House, County Louth, and they have one son and one daughter.

BENSON, HENRY WIGHTMAN, Major, was born 22 July, 1855, at the Manor House, Teddington, Middlesex, son of the late General Henry Roxby Benson, C.B., Colonel, 17th Lancers, and Mary Henrietta, daughter of the late Hon. Sir William Wightman, Judge of Queen's Bench. He was educated at Eton, and at Brasenose College, Oxford. He rowed in Eton Eight, 1873; Oxford Eight, 1874; Leander Eight, 1875. At Eton he won the ¼-mile, also sculling and pairs twice. He joined the 1st West India Regt., as Sub-Lieutenant, from the Militia, 15 July, 1876; became Lieutenant, West India Regt., 15 July, 1876; East Surrey Regt. 18 Sept. 1879; Captain, 10 Aug. 1884; was Adjutant, Militia, 1 Jan. 1892, to 31 Dec. 1897; became Major 8 Feb. 1895. He served in the South African War, 1899–1902. He was in command 2nd Battn. East Surrey Regt. 2 May, to 30 June, 1900, and 17 Dec. 1901, to 16 Jan. 1902. He took part in the operations in Natal, March to June, 1900, including action at Laing's Nek. Operations in the Transvaal 30 Nov. 1900, to 31 May, 1902. He was twice mentioned in Despatches by Sir Redvers Buller, 19 June and 9 Nov. 1900 [London Gazette, 8 Feb. 1901], and by Lord Kitchener, 29 July, 1902; received the Queen's Medal with three clasps, the King's Medal with two clasps, and was created a Companion of the Distinguished Service Order [London Gazette, 19 April, 1901]: "Henry Wightman Benson, Major, East Surrey Regt. In recognition of services during the recent operations in South Africa." (The Insignia, etc., were sent to the Commander-in-Chief in South Africa, and presented there.) He retired as Major, for age, 22 July, 1903, and was made Honorary Lieutenant-Colonel for Home Service in raising a Battalion. Became Temporary Lieutenant-Colonel 1 Oct. 1914; Honorary Lieutenant-Colonel 6 March, 1917.

Henry Wightman Benson.

WRIGHT, HARRY, Major, was born 5 Dec. 1856. He joined the Gordon Highlanders, as Lieutenant, 29 Nov. 1876; served in the Afghan War, 1879–80; was present at the action of Charasiah and subsequent pursuit; final occupation of Kabul; expedition to Maidan; operations between 10 and 25 Dec. 1879; actions of 23 Dec. and Childukteau; march from Kabul to Relief of Kandahar; reconnaissance of 31 Aug. and battle of 1 Sept. He received the Medal with clasp; Bronze Star. He served in the South African War of 1881, taking part in the Transvaal Campaign and the battle of Amajuba Mountain. He was mentioned in Despatches [London Gazette, 3 May and 10 June, 1881]. On 9 March, 1886, he was promoted to Captain. He was Adjutant, Volunteers, from 1 Feb. 1889, to 31 Jan. 1894, and was promoted Major 14 Feb. 1895. Major Wright served in the South African War of 1899–1902, and took part in the operations in Natal in 1899, including the action at Elandslaagte (severely wounded); in the Relief of Ladysmith, including action at Colenso; the operations of 17 to 24 Jan. 1900, and action at Spion Kop; operations of 5 to 7 Feb. 1900, and action at Vaal Kranz; operations on Tugela Heights (14 to 27 Feb. 1900) and action at Pieter's Hill; operations in Orange River Colony, May to 29 Nov. 1900; employed with the Corps of Volunteer Stretcher-bearers. Was present in the operations in the Transvaal in Dec. 1901, and was afterwards a District Commissioner. He was mentioned in Despatches [London Gazette, 8 Feb. 1901]; received the Queen's Medal with five clasps, and was created a Companion of the Distinguished Service Order [London Gazette, 19 April, 1901]: "Harry Wright, Major, Gordon Highlanders. In recognition of services during the recent operations in South Africa." The Insignia were presented by the King 29 Oct. 1901. Major Wright became Lieutenant-Colonel 14 Dec. 1903; Brevet Colonel 14 Dec. 1906, and retired 14 Dec. 1907. He served in the European War from 1914, commanding the 8th Battn. The Gordon Highlanders. He was created a C.M.G., 1916; was mentioned in Despatches, and severely wounded. He served in Palestine in 1917–18, and was again mentioned in Despatches.

SMITH, HENRY LOCKHART, Major, was born 24 April, 1859, eldest son of the late Henry Smith, J.P., D.L., Barrister-at-Law, of Ellingham Hall, Norfolk, Lord of the Manor of Ellingham Nevells (who died 18 May, 1910), and of Amelia Harriet, daughter of Colonel Greene, C.B., of Kirby Cane Hall, Norfolk. He was educated at Marlborough College, and at Sandhurst; was gazetted to the 70th Foot 11 May, 1878. He served in the Afghan War, 1878–80 (Medal). He became Lieutenant, East Surrey Regt., 15 March, 1880, and Captain 25 Oct. 1884. He served in the Sudan Expedition, 1885; Suakin (Medal with clasp; Bronze Star). Capt. Smith was Adjutant of Volunteers 15 Jan. 1894, to 14 Jan. 1899; became Major 16 Oct. 1895. He served in the South African War from Oct. 1899, to the end of the war, and was present at the Relief of Ladysmith, including the action at Colenso; operations of 17 to 24 Jan. 1900, and action at Spion Kop; operations of 5 to 7 Feb. 1900, and action at Vaal Kranz; operations on Tugela Heights (14 to 27 Feb. 1900). He was severely wounded on the 22nd of Feb., and again later. He took part in the operations in the Transvaal, Dec. 1900, to 31 May, 1902; operations in Cape Colony, Dec. 1900. He was mentioned in Despatches by Sir R. H. Buller, 30 March and 9 Nov. 1900 [London Gazette, 8 Feb. 1901]; received the Queen's Medal with four clasps, and was created a Companion of the Distinguished Service Order [London Gazette, 19 April, 1901], for his services at Pieter's Hill and the Relief of Ladysmith: "Henry Lockhart Smith, Major, East Surrey Regt. In recognition of services during the recent operations in South Africa." The Insignia were presented in South Africa. He was promoted to Lieutenant-Colonel 21 June, 1907; commanded the 1st Battn. East Surrey Regt., Jan. 1907, to June, 1911; and retired 21 June, 1911. Lieut.-Colonel H. L. Smith rejoined on the outbreak of the European War, and commanded the 8th (Service) Battn. East Surrey Regt. 11 Sept. 1914, to Feb. 1915; was invalided out and awarded a Silver Badge. He is Lord of the Manor of Ellingham Nevells, and is a J.P. He married, 24 March, 1908, at Chester Cathedral, Edith Claribel Tomlin, daughter of John Read Tomlin, of Stoke Field, Notts (deceased).

Henry Lockhart Smith.

GARLAND, ERNEST ALFRED CROWDER, Major, was born 5 Feb. 1857, eldest son of the late Rev. J. Garland, late Rector of Mordiford, Herefordshire, and Vicar of Ombersley, Worcestershire. He entered the Army 11 Nov. 1876, as Sub-Lieutenant, unattached, and joined the 71st Foot 11 Nov. 1876; Lieutenant, Highland Light Infantry, 11 Nov. 1878. He served in the Egyptian Expedition, 1882, and was present at the Battle of Tel-el-Kebir (Medal with clasp, and Bronze Star). He was promoted Captain 24 Jan. 1888. In 1897–98 he took part in the operations on the North-West Frontier of India, with the Malakand and Buner Field Forces, and was present at the attack and capture of the Tanga Pass (Medal with clasp). Capt. Garland became Major 13 Nov. 1895. He served in the South African War from 1899 to 1902; was in command of the 1st Battn. Highland Light Infantry 14 Aug. to 4 Oct. 1900, taking part in the advance on Kimberley, including action at Magersfontein, and the operations in the Orange Free State, from Feb. to May, 1900. In the operations in Orange River Colony (May to 29 Nov. 1900), including actions at Wittebergen and Witpoort. Afterwards he was (1) Commandant at Smithfield; (2) in command of troops at Dordrecht, and (3) in command of troops, Orange River, Aliwal, Herschel District. He was present at the operations in Orange River Colony 30 Nov. 1900, to Feb. 1901. Operations in Cape Colony, Feb. 1901, to Jan. 1902, and May, 1902. He was mentioned in Despatches [London Gazette, 16 March, 1900]; received the Queen's Medal with two clasps; King's Medal with two clasps, and was created a Companion of the Distinguished Service Order [London Gazette, 19 April, 1901]: "Ernest Alfred Crowder Garland, Major, Highland Light Infantry. In recognition of services during the recent operations in South Africa." The Insignia were presented by Major-General Fitzroy Hart, C.B., C.M.G., at Aliwal North, 18 Nov. 1901. He became Lieutenant-Colonel 4 Nov. 1903; was given the Brevet of Colonel 4 Nov. 1906; retired with the rank of Colonel 4 Nov. 1907, and joined the Reserve of Officers. He married the youngest daughter of the late A. C. Hooper, Claines Grange, Worcestershire.

CURTIS, REGINALD SALMOND, Major, was born 21 Nov. 1863, eldest son of Major-General Reginald Curtis, R.A. He was educated at Cheltenham College, and at the Royal Military Academy, Woolwich; was commissioned in the Royal Engineers, as Lieutenant, 28 July, 1883; was employed in the Egyptian Army 11 Feb. 1891, to 19 Feb. 1893; became Captain 31 Dec. 1891. He served in the Eastern Sudan in 1891, including the capture of Tokar (Bronze Star with clasp; 4th Class Medjidie). He served in the Ashanti Expedition, 1895–96, as Director of Telegraphs (Star; Brevet of Major 25 March, 1896; mentioned in Despatches); was specially employed at Headquarters of Army 1 April, 1897, to 29 Jan. 1899; in the Falkland Islands, under the Admiralty, 30 Jan. 1899, to 13 Aug. 1899, and at H.Q. of Army 14 Aug. 1899, to 8 Oct. 1899; was A.D.C. to Major-General R.E., South Africa, 9 Oct. 1899, to 1 Aug. 1900; became Major 12 Aug. 1900; was Assistant Director of Telegraphs, and also employed as Chief Staff Officer with the South African Constabulary 27 Nov. 1900, to 20 Aug. 1905. He was present at the operations in the Orange Free State, Feb. to May, 1900, including the operations at Paardeberg (19 to 26 Feb.), Vet River (5 and 6 May) and Zand River. Operations in the Transvaal in May and June, 1900, including actions near Johannesburg and Pretoria. Operations in the Transvaal, east of Pretoria, July to Oct. 1900, including action at Belfast (26 and 27 Aug.) Operations in Cape Colony, south of Orange River, 1899–1900. Operations in Cape Colony, north of Orange River. Operations in the Transvaal and Orange River Colony 30 Nov. 1900, to 31 May, 1902. He was mentioned in Despatches [London Gazette, 16 April, 1901, and 29 July, 1902]; received the Queen's Medal with five clasps; King's Medal with two clasps, and was given the Brevet of Lieutenant-Colonel. He was created a Companion of the Distinguished Service Order [London Gazette, 19 April, 1901]: "Reginald Salmond Curtis, Major and Local Lieut.-Colonel, Royal Engineers. In recognition of services during the recent operations in South Africa." The Insignia were presented by the Duke of Cornwall and York in South Africa 14 Aug. 1901. He was a Member of the International Council of the Transvaal, O.R.C., 1904–08; was Inspector-General, S.A. Constabulary, 21 Aug. 1905, to 31 Dec. 1908; became Lieutenant-Colonel 26 May, 1908; was Commandant, Army Signal School, 12 Aug. 1912, to 31 March, 1913; became Colonel 1 April, 1913; created a C.M.G. 1913; was A.A.G. for the Royal Engineers, War Office, from 1 April, 1913, to 23 Feb. 1917; created a C.B., 1915; promoted Major-General 1 Jan. 1916, for valuable services rendered in connection with the European War, from 1914, and created a K.C.M.G. in 1917. He commanded Cromarty Garrison 18 July, 1917, to 4 Oct. 1917; Major-General, Aldershot Command, 5 Oct. 1917. Sir Reginald Curtis married, in 1894, the Hon. Hilda Margaret, youngest daughter of the 9th Viscount Barrington, and Mary Isabella (who died in 1903), daughter of the Rev. Richard Bogue, and they have three daughters.

LECKY, FREDERIC BEAUCHAMP, Major, was born 11 Oct. 1858, son of John Frederic Lecky, D.L., of Ballykealey, Tullow, County Carlow. He was educated at Uppingham School, and at the R.M.A., Woolwich, and entered the Royal Artillery 31 Jan. 1878. He took part in the Egyptian Expedition, 1882, and was present at the Battle of Tel-el-Kebir (Medal and clasp, and Bronze Star). He became Captain 24 March, 1886, and Major 1 April, 1896. He served in the South African War, 1899–1902; was present at the Relief of Kimberley; at the operations in the Orange Free State, Feb. to May, 1900, including operations at Paardeberg (17 to 26 Feb.); actions at Poplar Grove, Dreifontein, Vet River (5 and 6 May) and Zand River; operations in the Transvaal in May and June, 1900, including actions near Johannesburg, Pretoria and Diamond Hill (11 and 12 June); operations in the Transvaal, east of Pretoria, July to 29 Nov. 1900, including actions at Reitvlei and Belfast (26 and 27 Aug.); operations in the Transvaal, 30 Nov. 1900, to Jan. 1902, and March to 31 May, 1902; operations in Orange River Colony, Jan. to March, 1902. He was mentioned in Despatches [London Gazette, 16 April, 1901]; received the Queen's Medal with six clasps, the King's Medal with two clasps, and was created a Companion of the Distinguished Service Order [London Gazette, 19 April, 1901]: "Frederic Beauchamp Lecky, Major, Royal Artillery. In recognition of services during the recent operations in South Africa." The Insignia were presented by the Duke of Cornwall and York 14 Aug. 1901. He became Lieut.-Colonel 17 Aug. 1903; was given the Brevet of Colonel 17 Aug. 1908, and retired with the rank of Colonel 17 Aug. 1908.

McLEOD, REGINALD GEORGE McQUEEN, Major, was born 25 June, 1859. He was gazetted to the Royal Artillery 31 Jan. 1878, as Lieutenant, becoming Captain 3 July, 1886, and Major 30 July, 1896. He served in the South African War, 1899–1902, as Commandant at Elandsfontein; took part in the operations in the Orange Free State, Feb. to May, 1900, including actions at Houtnek (Thoba Mountain), Vet River (5 and 6 May) and Zand River; operations in the Transvaal, May and June, 1900, including actions near Johannesburg and Pretoria; operations in Cape Colony, south of Orange River, 1899–1900; operations in the Transvaal 30 Nov. 1900, to June, 1901; Aug. 1901, to May, 1902; operations in Orange River Colony, June to Aug. 1901; operations in Cape Colony, April to May, 1902. He was mentioned in Despatches [London Gazette, 16 April, 1901]; received the Queen's Medal with three clasps; King's Medal with two clasps, and was created a Companion of the Distinguished Service Order [London Gazette, 19 April, 1901]: "Reginald George McQueen McLeod, Major, Royal Artillery. In recognition of services during the recent operations in South Africa." The Warrant, Insignia and Statutes were sent to the Commander-in-Chief in South Africa, and Insignia presented by the Duke of Cornwall and York 14 Aug. 1901. He became Lieut.-Colonel, 19 Oct. 1903; was given the Brevet of Colonel, 19 Oct. 1906, and retired 19 Oct. 1908, with the rank of Colonel. Colonel McLeod died 21 Sept. 1910. He had married, in 1902, Cicely Knightley, daughter of W. Boyd, of North House, Long Benton, Newcastle.

JACKSON, HERBERT KENDALL, Major, was born 17 March, 1859, son of the late Thomas Jackson, of Springfield Place, Chelmsford. He was educated at Wellington College, and at the Royal Military Academy, Woolwich, and joined the Royal Artillery, as Lieutenant, 18 Dec. 1878; became Captain 29 Oct. 1886; Major 1 Nov. 1896. He served in the South African War, 1900–1901; was present at the Relief of Mafeking. He received the Queen's Medal with four clasps; Despatches, 16 April, 1901, and was created a Companion of the Distinguished Service Order [London Gazette, 19 April, 1901]: "Herbert Kendall Jackson, Major, Royal Artillery. In recognition of services during the recent operations in South Africa." The Insignia were presented in South Africa, 14 Aug. 1901, by the Duke of Cornwall and York. He became Lieut.-Colonel 5 Aug. 1904; Brevet Colonel 5 Aug. 1907; Colonel 5 Aug. 1909; Temporary Brigadier-General 1 April, 1910, to 31 March, 1914; Commanding R.A., 2nd Division, Aldershot Command; Temporary Brigadier-General 5 Aug. 1914; Brigadier-General H. K. Jackson served in the European War, 1914–15. He was twice mentioned in Despatches, and created a C.B. in 1915. He retired from the Staff 27 Dec. 1917, with the rank of Brigadier-General. Major Jackson married, in 1904, Winifred Gladys, daughter of the late G. W. Llewhellin, of Brookfield, Blandford, and they have one son and two daughters.

CURRY, MONTAGU CREIGHTON, Major, was born 18 Feb. 1856. He entered the 11th Foot as Second Lieutenant, from the Militia, 13 Oct. 1877; became Lieutenant, Devonshire Regt., 25 July, 1878; was Adjutant, Devonshire Regt., 18 July, 1885, to 28 July, 1890; Second Class Inspector of Warlike Stores 29 July, 1890, to 9 April, 1894; was promoted to Captain 24 March, 1897. He served on the North-West Frontier of India, 1897–98, with the Tirah Expeditionary Force, and was present at the capture of the Arhanga and Sampagha Passes (Medal and two clasps). Capt. Curry served in the South African War from 1899 to 1901, taking part in the operations in Natal, 1899, including actions at Elandslaagte, Rietfontein and Lombard's Kop. He was present at the defence of Ladysmith, including the action of 6 Jan. 1900; acted as Station Commandant. He took part in the operations in the Transvaal, June to July, 1900. He was in command of Imperial Light Infantry 19 June, 1900, to 30 July, 1901, taking part in the operations in the Orange River Colony, May, 1901. He was mentioned in Despatches by Sir G. White, 2 Dec. 1899, and 23 March, 1900, and by Sir R. H. Buller, 9 Nov. 1900 [London Gazette, 8 Feb. 1901]; received the Queen's Medal with four clasps, and was created a Companion of the Distinguished Service Order [London Gazette, 19 April, 1901]: "Montagu Creighton Curry, Major (Local Lieut.-Colonel), Devonshire Regt. In recognition of services during the recent operations in South Africa." The Insignia were presented by the King 29 Oct. 1901. He became Lieut.-Colonel, Lincolnshire Regt., 11 March, 1902; was given the Brevet of Colonel 11 March, 1905; became Colonel 23 Feb. 1907; commanded No. 4 District, and was in charge of Records, 1909 to 1913; was created a C.B. in 1911, and retired on 18 Feb. 1913. Colonel Curry became Temporary Brigadier-General 7 Sept. 1914. He was given the honorary rank of Brigadier-General 11 April, 1917, and created a C.B.E. in 1919.

MALCOLM, HENRY HUNTLY LEITH, C.B., C.M.G., D.S.O., Brigadier-General, was born 10 Dec. 1860, son of the late William Malcolm, of Glenmorag, Argyllshire, and of the late Amelia Jane, daughter of the late Rev. H. H. Holdsworth, of Fishtoft, Lincolnshire. He joined the 42nd Foot, as Second Lieutenant, 22 Jan. 1879; became Lieutenant, Cameron Highlanders, 29 Sept. 1880; was on special service in Egypt from 27 Nov. 1884, to 14 June, 1885; served with the Cameron Highlanders, 1882, including Tel-el-Kebir (twice wounded; Medal with clasp; Khedive's Star); served in the Nile Expedition, 1884–85, as Staff Captain with whaler boats (clasp); became Captain 24 Aug. 1885, and Major 3 April, 1897. He served in the South African War, 1900–1902, in command 1st Battn. Cameron Highlanders (from Dec. 1900, to 25 Oct. 1901, excepting periods from 2 to 9 June and 12 to 17 Oct. 1901); operations in the Orange Free State, Feb. to May, 1900, including actions at Vet River (5 and 6 May) and Zand River; operations in the Transvaal in May and June, 1900, including actions near Johannesburg, Pretoria and Diamond Hill (11 and 12 June); operations in Orange River Colony, May to 29 Nov. 1900, including action at Wittebergen (1 to 29 July) and Ladybrand (2 to 5 Sept.); operations in the Transvaal, Jan. to Sept. 1901, and Oct. 1901, to 31 May, 1902; operations in Orange River Colony, 30 Nov. 1900, to Jan. 1901; operations on the Zululand Frontier of Natal in Sept. and Oct. 1901. He was mentioned in Despatches [London Gazette, 6 April, 1901, and 29 July, 1902]; received the Queen's Medal with four clasps, the King's Medal with two clasps, and was created a Companion of the Distinguished Service Order [London Gazette, 19 April, 1901]: "Henry Huntly Leith Malcolm, Major, Cameron Highlanders. In recognition of services during the recent operations in South Africa." Insignia presented in South Africa. He became Lieut.-Colonel 3 April, 1902; Brevet Colonel 3 April, 1905; commanded the Seaforth and Cameron Brigade, Scottish Command, 1 April, 1906, to 8 May, 1911. He became Colonel 5 Nov. 1910; was Temporary Brigadier-General 28 Oct. 1911, to 29 Dec. 1915; was created a C.B., 1911; commanded O.R.C. District in South Africa 28 Oct. 1911, to 7 May, 1913; was O.C. in Ceylon 8 May, 1913, to 18 Sept. 1915, including the suppression of the Rising there in 1915 under martial law; Brigade Commander 27 Sept. 1915, to 29 Dec. 1915; Brigade Major, France, 1917; retired (for age) 10 Dec. 1917. For his services in the European War he was created a C.M.G. in 1916, and awarded a special pension as a reward for distinguished and meritorious service, 1919, with a Capital R in the Army List. Colonel Malcolm married, in 1908, Edith, only child of the late Ernest E. Sabel, and they have one daughter, E. Betty E. A. Malcolm, born 22 Oct. 1913.

Henry H. L. Malcolm.

GARRATT, FRANCIS SUDLOW, Major, was born 18 June, 1859, eldest son of the late Rev. Sudlow Garratt, of Merifield, Devonport. He was educated at Winchester and Sandhurst, and was gazetted to the 6th Dragoon Guards 1 May, 1878; served in the Afghan War, 1879–80, with the Khyber Division, Kabul Field Force; became Lieutenant 1 July, 1881, and Captain 3 Oct. 1887. He was Adjutant, Yeomanry Cavalry, 1 June, 1888, to 31 May, 1893; was promoted to Major 3 April, 1897. He served in the South African War, 1899–1902, in command of the 6th Dragoons. Also in command of a column (afterwards of a group of columns), 21 June, 1901, to 31 May, 1902; operations in the Orange River Colony and Transvaal, June, 1901, to 31 May, 1902; operations on the Zululand Frontier of Natal, Sept. and Oct. 1901. He was mentioned in Despatches [London Gazette, 4 May, 1900]; received the Queen's Medal with six clasps, the King's Medal with two clasps, was created a C.B., and created a Companion of the Distinguished Service Order [London Gazette, 19 April, 1901]: "Francis Sudlow Garratt, Major, 6th Dragoons. In recognition of services during the operations in South Africa." The Insignia, Warrant and Statutes were sent to the Commander-in-Chief in South Africa, and the Insignia presented to him by Brigadier-General E. V. F. Hamilton. He became Lieut.-Colonel, 3rd Dragoon Guards, 14 Jan. 1903, and 6th Dragoon Guards, 3 July, 1904; was Colonel on the Staff, India; Brigade Commander, India, from 1 May, 1905; became Colonel 14 Jan. 1906; retired 5 July, 1911; was given the honorary rank of Brigadier-General 10 Feb. 1912. He served in the European War; was twice mentioned in Despatches; created a C.M.G., 1915, and a K.C.M.G., 1918. Sir Francis Garratt married, in 1897, Frances Lucy, eldest daughter of Colonel Troyte, of Huntsham Court, Devon, and they have three daughters.

HUME, CHARLES VERNON, Major, was born 12 July, 1860. He was educated at Marlborough, and entered the Royal Field Artillery on 6 April, 1879, as Lieutenant; was A.D.C. to the Commander-in-Chief, West Indies, 28 Nov. 1885, to 20 Sept. 1892. He served in Burma, 1886–87, as Intelligence Officer, 5th Brigade, and A.D.C. to the General in Command; was mentioned in Despatches [London Gazette, 2 Sept. 1887], and received the Medal with clasp. He was promoted to Captain 21 Sept. 1887. From 31 Oct. 1895, to 31 Oct. 1896, he was Staff Captain, R.E., North-Eastern District; he was on Special Extra Regimental Employment 1 Nov. 1896, to 20 Dec. 1899, and became Major 8 April, 1897. Major Hume was on special service, South Africa, 23 Dec. 1899, to 9 Jan. 1900; was D.A.A.G., South Africa, 10 Jan. 1900, to 30 May, 1900; Director of Military Intelligence (graded A.A.G.), South Africa, 31 May, 1900, to 1 Feb. 1901. He was mentioned in Despatches [London Gazette, 8 Feb. and 16 April, 1901]; received the Queen's Medal with five clasps, and was created a Companion of the Distinguished Service Order [London Gazette, 19 April, 1901]: "Charles Vernon Hume, Major, Royal Artillery. In recognition of services during the recent operations in South Africa." The Insignia were presented to him by the King 3 June, 1901. He was specially employed (Mobilization), Headquarters of Army, 28 May, 1901, to 16 July, 1903; was Military Attaché, Tokio and Corea, 17 July, 1903, to 22 Dec. 1904, and 23 Dec. 1904, to 16 July, 1907; was promoted Lieut.-Colonel 23 Dec. 1904; attached to the Japanese Army in Manchuria 17 May, 1905; was given the Brevet of Colonel 17 March, 1906, and created an M.V.O. in 1906, and was employed under the Siamese Government from 1911. Colonel Hume married, in 1897, Ursula Wilhelmina, daughter of Reginald Dykes Marshall, D.L., J.P., of Castlerigg Manor, Cumberland, and they had one son and two daughters. He died on 2 Feb. 1915, at Arundel, and a notice of his death appeared in the "Times" of 4 Feb. 1915.

Charles Vernon Hume.

GOULBURN, CUTHBERT EDWARD, Major, was born 6 Feb. 1860, son of Colonel Goulburn, of Betchworth House, Betchworth, Surrey. He was educated at Cheltenham College, and at the R.M.A., Woolwich, and entered the Royal Artillery 6 April, 1879, becoming Captain 21 Sept. 1887, and Major 8 April, 1897. He served in India and Africa, commanding the 42nd Battery, R.F.A. He also served in the South African War, 1899–1901, from the commencement till 1 May, 1901, taking part in the operations in Natal, 1899, including actions at Elandslaagte, Rietfontein and Lombard's Kop, and Defence of Ladysmith; operations in the Transvaal 30 Nov. 1900, to May, 1901. He was mentioned in Despatches (Sir George White, 2 Dec. 1899, and 23 March, 1900; Sir R. H. Buller, 9 Nov. 1900) [London Gazette, 8 Feb. 1901]; received the Queen's Medal with four clasps, and was created a Companion of the Distinguished Service Order [London Gazette, 19 April, 1901]: "Cuthbert Edward Goulburn, Major, Royal Artillery. In recognition of services during the operations in South Africa." The Insignia were presented to him by the King 25 July, 1901. He became Lieut.-Colonel 23 Dec. 1904, and retired 29 March, 1905; commanded R.A. (Territorial), North Midland Division, from 1909 to 1914, and became Colonel (Reserve of Officers), 1 Oct. 1912, and for his services during the European War was given the honorary rank of Brigadier-General 26 Feb. 1916. From 1905 to 1910 Brigadier-General Goulburn was Master of the Albrighton Hounds. He married, in 1902, Grace Ethel, eldest daughter of W. E. Foster, of Apley Park, Bridgnorth, and they have two sons and one daughter.

SHUTE, HENRY GWYNN DEANE, Major, was born 4 Dec. 1860, son of General Sir Charles Cameron Shute, K.C.B., Colonel, 6th Inniskilling Dragoons (late M.P. for Brighton), and Rhoda, daughter of the late Henry Turnour Dowler, and granddaughter of Lady Broughton, of Posen Court, Herefordshire, and of Capt. Nason Dickinson, Coldstream Guards, 1862. He was gazetted to the Coldstream Guards 30 Sept. 1880, becoming Lieutenant 1 July, 1881. He took part in the Egyptian Expedition in 1882, being present at the action of Mahuta and the Battle of Tel-el-Kebir (Medal with clasp; Bronze Star). He served in the Sudan Expedition of 1885 (Suakin); was present at the action of Haseen, and at the attack on the convoy, 24 March, and the action at Tamai (clasp). He became Captain 27 Jan. 1891, and was Regimental Adjutant, Coldstream Guards, 29 July, 1891, to 31 Dec. 1893; Brigade Major, Home District, 1 Jan. 1894, to 31 Dec. 1896; was promoted to Major 19 May, 1897. Major Shute served in the South African War, 1899–1902; was present in the advance on Kimberley, including actions at Belmont, Enslin, Modder River and Magersfontein; operations in the Orange Free State, Feb. to May, 1900, including actions at Poplar Grove, Dreifontein, Vet River and Zand River; operations in the Transvaal in May and June, 1900, including actions near Johannesburg, Pretoria and Diamond Hill; operations in the Transvaal, east of Pretoria, July to Oct. 1900, including action at Belfast; operations in the Transvaal, west of Pretoria, Nov. 1900; operations in Cape Colony, south of Orange River, 1900; operations in Cape Colony, Nov. 1900, to 31 May, 1902; operations in the Transvaal, 1900; in command of a mobile column (17 Dec. 1900, to 5 Jan. 1901). Commandant, Graaff Reinet (5 Jan. to 30 Nov. 1901); afterwards as Administrator, No. 8 Martial Law Area, Cape Colony District (1 Dec. 1901, to end of operations). He was mentioned in Despatches [London Gazette, 26 Jan. 1900, and 29 July, 1902]; was given the Brevet of Lieut.-Colonel 22 Aug. 1902; received the Queen's Medal with six clasps, and the King's Medal with two clasps, and was created a Companion of the Distinguished Service Order [London Gazette, 19 April, 1901]: "Henry Gwynn Deane Shute, Major, Coldstream Guards. In recognition of services during the recent operations in South Africa." He was Principal Private Secretary to the Right Honourable H. O. Arnold-Forster, Secretary of State for War, 12 Oct. 1903, to 31 Dec. 1904; became Lieut.-Colonel, Coldstream Guards, 29 Nov. 1903; Staff employment 1 Jan. 1905; was A.A.G., Home District, 1 Jan. to 31 May, 1905, and 1 June, 1905, to 31 Dec. 1908; became Colonel 22 Aug. 1905. Colonel Shute died on 8 Oct. 1909.

BIRD, WILKINSON DENT, Capt. and Brevet Major, was born 4 May, 1869, son of the late Capt. J. D. Bird, of the 20th Hussars, and Kathleen Shortt. He was educated at Wellington College, and at the Royal Military College, Sandhurst, and joined the Queen's (West Surrey) Regt. 22 Aug. 1888; became Lieutenant 1 Dec. 1890. He served under the Niger Company in the Niger Expedition, 1897, taking part in the expeditions to Egbon, Bida and Ilorin. He was mentioned in Despatches [London Gazette, 11 June, 1897]; was given the Brevet of Major 16 June, 1897, and received the Medal and clasp. He took part with the 1st Battn. of the Queen's in the operations on the North-West Frontier of India, 1897–98, serving with the Mohmand Field and Tirah Expeditionary Forces (Medal and two clasps). He was on Special Service in South Africa, 15 July, 1899, to 16 Aug. 1900, with the Rhodesian Regt. He was severely wounded; mentioned in Despatches [London Gazette, 19 April, 1901]; received the Queen's Medal with three clasps, and was created a Companion of the Distinguished Service Order [London Gazette, 19 April, 1901]: "Wilkinson Dent Bird, Capt. and Brevet Major, Royal West Surrey Regt. In recognition of services during the recent operations in South Africa." The Insignia were presented by the King 29 Oct. 1901. Capt. and Brevet Major Bird passed the Staff College in 1901. He was specially employed at the War Office from 1 Jan. 1902, to 26 April, 1903; was Chief Instructor and Staff Officer, School of Musketry, Hythe, 27 April, 1903, to 8 June, 1905; was Professor, Staff College, India, 24 June, 1905, to 13 Jan. 1909; was given the Brevet of Lieut.-Colonel 18 Dec. 1909; was G.S.O., Second Grade, War Office, 23 Jan. 1910, to 23 Sept. 1913; was promoted to Major 29 Sept. 1910; Lieut.-Colonel, Royal Irish Rifles, 24 Sept. 1913, to 7 June, 1915; Colonel 2 June, 1913 (by antedate). He served in the European War, with the 2nd Battn. Royal Irish Rifles, in 1914, and was severely wounded; was mentioned in Despatches; was appointed A.D.C. to the King, with the Brevet rank of Colonel, 18 Feb. 1915. He was specially employed at the War Office, 16 April, 1915, to 7 June, 1915; was G.S.O., First Grade (temporary), War Office, 8 June, 1915, to 3 Feb. 1916; Director of Staff Duties, War Office (temporary), and Temporary Brigadier-General, 4 Feb. 1916, to 31 Dec. 1917. Lieut.-Governor and Secretary, Royal Hospital, Chelsea, 19 May, 1918, and Temporary Major-General. He was created a C.B. in 1916, and C.M.G. in 1918. Is an officer of the Legion of Honour and has the French Croix de Guerre. He has the Royal Geographical Society's Diploma, and has published lectures on the strategy of the Franco-German and Russo-Japanese Wars; also a Précis of Strategy. He married, in 1902, Winifred Editha, daughter of Major J. B. Barker, and they have two daughters.

Wilkinson Dent Bird.

STOKES, ALFRED, Major, was born 14 Oct. 1860, son of the late Lieut.-General Sir John Stokes, K.C.B., of Ewell, Surrey, and Henrietta Georgina de Villiers (who died in 1893), second daughter of Charles Maynard, of Grahamstown, Cape of Good Hope. He was educated at Cheltenham, and joined the Royal Artillery, as a Lieutenant, 18 Feb. 1880, serving in South Africa in 1881; in the Bechuanaland Expedition 23 Dec. 1884, to 12 March, 1885, and was honourably mentioned in Despatches. He became Captain 25 April, 1888, and Major 25 Dec. 1897. Major Stokes served in the South African War from 1899 to 1900; was present at the Relief of Ladysmith, including the operations of 17 to 24 Jan. 1900, and action of Spion Kop; operations of 5 to 7 Feb. 1900, and action at Vaal Kranz; operations on Tugela Heights 14 to 27 Feb. 1900, and action at Pieter's Hill; operations in the Transvaal, May and June, 1900; operations in the Transvaal, west of Pretoria, July to 29 Nov. 1900; operations in Cape Colony, north of Orange River, including action at Ruidam. He was mentioned in Despatches [London Gazette, 8 Feb. 1901]; received the Queen's Medal with five clasps, and was created a Companion of the Distinguished Service Order [London Gazette, 19 April, 1901]: "Alfred Stokes, Major, Royal Artillery. In recognition of services during the recent operations in South Africa." The Insignia were presented by the King 3 June, 1901. He became Lieut.-Colonel 14 Nov. 1905; was given the Brevet of Colonel 14 Nov. 1908, and was promoted to Colonel 14 Nov. 1910. Colonel Stokes was Temporary Brigadier-General, commanding Royal Artillery in India, from 22 Dec. 1911, and served in the European War from 1914; was mentioned in Despatches, and created a C.B. in 1915, and a C.M.G. in 1916. He retired from the Staff 2 Sept. 1918, with the rank of Brigadier-General. Brigadier-General Stokes married, in 1891, Margaret Dunbar, daughter of the late Sir James Laing, of Etal Manor, Northumberland.

HILL, FELIX FREDERIC, Major, was born 8 July, 1860, son of the late Rev. Joseph Hill, Rector of Wimblingdon, Cambridgeshire. He was educated at Cheltenham College, and became Second Lieutenant, 89th Foot, 14 Jan. 1880, and Lieutenant in the Royal Irish Fusiliers 13 April, 1881. He served in the Eastern Sudan Campaign in 1884, and was present at the Battles of El Teb and Tamai; relief of Tokar and affair at Tasmanieb (Egyptian Medal and clasp, and Khedive's Star). He was promoted to Captain 25 Jan. 1888, and Major, 1898. Major Hill served in the South African War, 1899–1902, with the Royal Irish Fusiliers; was present at the Relief of Ladysmith, including the action at Colenso 15 Dec. 1899, the operations on Tugela Heights 14 to 27 Feb. 1900, and Battle of Pieter's Hill (severely wounded); operations in the Transvaal, May and June, 1900; operations in the Transvaal, east of Pretoria, July to 29 Nov. 1900, including action at Reit Vlei; operations in Cape Colony, north of Orange River, including action at Ruidam; operations in the Transvaal, April, 1901, to Jan. 1902; operations in Orange River Colony, Jan. to 31 May, 1902. He was mentioned in Despatches [London Gazette, 8 Feb. 1901]; received the Queen's Medal with five clasps, and the King's Medal with two clasps, and was created a Companion of the Distinguished Service Order [London Gazette, 19 April, 1901]: "Felix Frederic Hill, Major, Royal Irish Fusiliers. In recognition of services during the operations in South Africa." The Insignia were presented to him in South Africa by the Duke of Cornwall and York 13 July, 1901. He was promoted to Lieut.-Colonel, commanding the 87th Royal Irish Fusiliers, 14 Sept. 1902; was given the Brevet of Colonel 14 Sept. 1905; became Colonel 13 July, 1907, and O.C., No. 11 District, Irish Command, 25 June, 1910, to 24 June, 1914; was created a C.B. in 1912. Colonel Hill served in the European War from 1914; became Temporary Brigadier-General 26 Aug. 1914, commanding the 31st Brigade, 10th Division, with which he served in Gallipoli (Suvla Bay Landing). He was mentioned in Despatches, and created a C.M.G. (1916). He subsequently served in France in command of the 186th Infantry Brigade, 62nd Division, until 11 Nov. 1917, when, having reached the age limit, he was placed on retired pay, and granted the honorary rank of Brigadier-General (Despatches, Dec. 1917). He married, in 1895, Edith Leonie, daughter of H. H. Askew, and they have a son, Reginald Askew Hill, and a daughter, Mary Emily Hill.

PERCEVAL, EDWARD MAXWELL, Major, was born 13 Aug. 1861, at Bellewstown, County Meath, Ireland, son of the late General John Maxwell Perceval, C.B., J.P., Colonel of the Suffolk Regt., and of Isabel Catherine, daughter of the Rev. The Honourable R. Maude, Dean of Clogher. He was educated at the Royal Academy, Gosport, and at the Royal Military Academy (has passed the Staff College, and holds the Diploma of the Royal Geographical Society), and was gazetted to the Royal Artillery as Lieutenant, 19 May, 1880. He became Captain 4 Aug. 1888, and Major 23 Feb. 1898, serving in India and Burma. He served in the South African War, 1899 to 1902; in command of a battalion of the Imperial Yeomanry from 5 Jan. 1902, to 31 May, 1902, and was severely wounded. He took part in the operations in the Orange Free State, Feb. to May, 1900; operations in the Transvaal, east of Pretoria, July to 29 Nov. 1900, including action at Wittebergen (1 to 29 July); operations in Cape Colony, south of Orange River, 1899–1900; operations in the Transvaal and Orange River Colony 30 Nov. 1900, to 31 May, 1902. He received the Queen's Medal with three clasps; the King's Medal with two clasps. He was mentioned in Despatches 16 March, 1900. General Gatacre, in his Despatch on the Battle of Stormberg, mentioned that Major Perceval was severely wounded at the beginning of that action, and that he remained in command of his battery until the fighting was finished. He was given the D.S.O. in the next Gazette. Major Perceval received the Queen's Medal with three clasps, the King's Medal with two clasps, and was created a Companion of the Distinguished Service Order [London Gazette, 19 April, 1901]: "Edward Maxwell Perceval, Major, Royal Artillery. In recognition of services during the recent operations in South Africa." The Insignia were presented to him in South Africa. From 15 Jan. 1903, to 8 March, 1904, Major Perceval was Instructor at the Royal Military College. He was Chief Instructor there from 9 March to 24 March, 1904; D.A.A.G., Headquarters of Army, 25 March, 1904, to 13 Nov. 1905; D.A.A.G. (G.S.O., Second Grade, Staff College) and G.S.O., Second Grade, Staff College, 15 May, 1908, to 20 March, 1909; was given the Brevet of Colonel 22 Aug. 1908; G.S.O., First Grade, Staff College, 21 March, 1909, to 14 May, 1912. He was promoted to Colonel 7 Dec. 1909; was Assistant Director of Movements, War Office, 6 Oct. 1912, to 31 March, 1914; commanding R.A, 2nd Division, Aldershot Command, 1 April to 4 Aug. 1914. He served in the European War from 1914; as Brigadier-General, Royal Artillery, 5 Aug. 1914, to 26 Jan. 1915; awarded C.B., Jan. 1915; Sub-Chief of the Staff to General Sir William Robertson at G.H.Q., France, 26 Jan. to 16 July, 1915; promoted to Major-General 3 June, 1915. In July, 1915, he was given command of the 49th West Riding Division in France. He was five times mentioned in Despatches. Major-General Perceval's favourite recreations are small and big game shooting, hunting, golf, tennis, etc. He married (1st), 11 Jan. 1894, Marian, daughter of R. L. Bowles, Esq., M.D., and their son, Lieut. (and Temporary Major) Robert Rawnsley Maxwell Perceval, M.C., R.F.A., was born 8 Jan. 1895. He married (2ndly), Norah Sabine Mayne, daughter of Admiral R. E. Mayne, C.B., M.P., and their children are Diana, and John Richard, born 13 April, 1909.

Edward M. Perceval.

POORE, ROBERT MONTAGU, Capt., was born at Carysfort House, near Dublin, 20 March, 1866, eldest son of Major Robert Poore, late 8th Hussars, and of Juliana Benita, daughter of Rear-Admiral Sir Armar Lowry Corry, K.C.B. He joined the Wiltshire Regt., as Lieutenant, from the Militia, 28 April, 1886; was transferred to the 7th Hussars, as Lieutenant, 13 Oct. 1886. He served in India from 1886 to 1895; was A.D.C. to H.E. the Governor of Bombay 24 Oct. 1892, to 17 Feb. 1895. He served in South Africa, 1895 to 1905, including the Matabele (1896) and Mashonaland (1897) Campaigns. He was mentioned in Despatches [London Gazette, 18 Feb. 1898], and was given the Brevet of Major 20 May, 1898, having been promoted to Captain 1 July, 1896. He served in the South African War, 1899–1902, with the Military Mounted Police 9 Oct. to 12 Nov. 1899; as Provost-Marshal 13 Nov. 1899, to 7 July, 1902, being present at the operations in the Orange Free State, Feb. to May, 1900, including operations at Paardeberg (17 to 26 Feb.); actions at Poplar Grove, Dreifontein, Vet River (5 and 6 May) and Zand River; operations in the Transvaal in May and June, 1900, including actions near Johannesburg, Pretoria and Diamond Hill (11 and 12 June); operations in the Transvaal, east of Pretoria, July to 29 Nov. 1900, including action at Belfast (26 and 27 Aug.); operations in the Transvaal 30 Nov. 1900, to 31 May, 1902. He was mentioned in Despatches [London Gazette, 8 Feb. and 16 April, 1901]; received the Queen's Medal with six clasps; the King's Medal with two clasps, and was created a Companion of the Distinguished Service Order [London Gazette, 19 April, 1901]: "Robert Montagu Poore, Capt. and Brevet Major, 7th Hussars. In recognition of services during the recent operations in South Africa." The Insignia were presented by the Duke of Cornwall and York 14 Aug. 1901. He became Major 17 July, 1901, and Lieutenant-Colonel 26 June, 1911. He commanded the 7th Hussars, 1911–15. He served in the European War from 1914; was promoted to Colonel 15 Dec. 1914, and Temporary Brigadier-General 14 Oct. 1915; commanded the Jhansi Brigade (India), 1915–19; was mentioned in Despatches, and created a C.I.E. in the Birthday Honours, 1918. He played cricket for the Bombay Presidency (India), 1892–95 and 1912–13, and for South Africa against Lord Hawke's English team during the winter of 1897–98, scoring two centuries. He was kept out of English first-class cricket till he was in his thirty-third year, owing to his regiment being on foreign service in India and South Africa. 1899 was his best year. He headed the season's batting in first-class matches, scoring 1,551 runs for 21 innings, his average working out to 91.23, which has never been equalled in first-class cricket for so large a number of runs. For Hampshire his average was 116.58. He scored seven centuries this season, three being successive ones, which included double centuries against Somerset, and his highest score was 304. A partnership with Capt. E. G. Wynyard produced 411 runs before they were parted. He played for the Gentlemen *v.* Players in 1899. He did not limit his activities to the game of cricket. He was one of the finest swordsmen in the Army, being Best Man-at-Arms (Mounted events) for four consecutive years in which he competed at the Royal Naval and Military Tournament (1898, 1899, 1906, 1907). He was a first-class polo player, and played "back" for his regimental team, taking part in several successful Inter-Regimental tournaments in India and finally in 1899 at Hurlingham. In 1899 he had a phenomenal fortnight, in which he played in the winning team (7th Hussars) in the Inter-Regimental Polo Tournament, when he hit the winning goal; was Best Man-at-Arms at the Royal Naval and Military Tournament, and scored three successive centuries for his county in first-class cricket. He has won several racquet, squash racquet and lawn tennis tournaments, and is a good shot both with the rifle and gun. He married, in 1898, Lady Flora Douglas-Hamilton, sister of the 13th Duke of Hamilton.

Robert Montagu Poore.

HOLLAND, ARTHUR EDWARD AVELING, Major, was born 13 April 1862, youngest son of Major-General A. Butcher. He entered the Royal Artillery on 19 May, 1880, as Lieutenant; served in the Burmese Expedition, 1885–87 and 1887–89 (Medal and two clasps), becoming Captain 29 Nov. 1888; was D.A.A.G., R.A., India, 11 Dec. 1895, to 4 Aug. 1898; was promoted to Major 1 July, 1898. Major Butcher served in the South

African War, 1899–1901; operations in the Transvaal, west of Pretoria, July to 29 Nov. 1900, including actions at Venterskroon (7 and 9 Aug.); operations in Orange River Colony, May to 17 July, 1900, including action at Lindley (1 June); operations in Cape Colony, south of Orange River, 1899–1900, including actions at Colesberg (1 Jan. to 12 Feb.); operations in Cape Colony, north of Orange River, including action at Ruidam; operations in the Transvaal 30 Nov. 1900, to Feb. 1901; operations in Orange River Colony, Feb. to May, 1901; operations in Cape Colony, Feb. 1901. He received the Queen's Medal with four clasps, and was created a Companion of the Distinguished Service Order [London Gazette, 19 April, 1901]: "Arthur Edward Aveling Butcher, Major, Royal Artillery. In recognition of services during the operations in South Africa." The Insignia were presented to him by the King 25 July, 1905. He was A.M.S. to the Governor and Commander-in-Chief, Malta, 26 March, 1903, to 13 Nov. 1905; was created an M.V.O. in 1903; was promoted to Lieut.-Colonel 14 Nov. 1905, and given the Brevet of Colonel 14 Nov. 1908. Colonel Butcher changed his name to Holland in 1910. He was Assistant Military Secretary, War Office, 1 Jan. 1910, to 10 Sept. 1912; Commandant, R.M. Academy, 11 Sept. 1912, to 29 Sept. 1914. He served in the European War from 1914; as Brigadier-General, R.A., 8th Division, B.E.F., 30 Sept. 1914, to 18 July, 1915; Brigadier-General, R.A., 7th Army Corps, B.E.F., 19 July to 4 Sept. 1915; Divisional Commander, 1st Division, B.E.F., 5 Sept. 1915, to 11 June, 1916; Major-General, R.A., 3rd Army, British Armies in France, 12 June, 1916, to 18 Feb. 1917; Army Corps Commander, British Armies in France, 19 Feb. 1917. He was promoted to Major-General 1 Jan. 1916, and to Lieut.-General 1 Jan. 1919; created a C.B., 1915; a K.C.B., 1918, and a K.C.M.G., 1919. Sir Arthur Holland married Mary Kate Duval, only daughter of Lewis Duval Hall, J.P., D.L., and they have one daughter.

LAMBTON, THE HONOURABLE WILLIAM, Major, was born 4 Dec. 1863, son of the 2nd Earl of Durham and of Lady Beatrix, daughter of the 1st Duke of Abercorn, and is a brother of the 3rd Earl of Durham. He was educated at Eton and Sandhurst, and joined the 2nd Battn. Coldstream Guards 6 Feb. 1884, as Lieutenant; was Adjutant, Coldstream Guards, 29 Dec. 1888, to 28 Dec. 1892, and became Captain 18 May, 1892. He was employed with the Egyptian Army 31 Dec. 1897, to 14 Oct. 1898, and served in the Nile Campaign of 1898; was present at the Battles of Atbara and Omdurman. He was mentioned in Despatches [London Gazette, 30 Sept. 1898]; received the British Medal, and the Egyptian Medal with two clasps. He was promoted to Major 29 Sept. 1898; was Military Secretary to Lord Milner, the High Commissioner, South Africa, Governor and Commander-in-Chief, Transvaal and Orange River Colony, 8 Dec. 1900, to 29 April, 1904. He served in the South African War, 1899–1902, and took part in the advance on Kimberley, including the actions at Belmont, Enslin, Modder River and Magersfontein (wounded), and was afterwards on the Staff of Lord Milner. He was mentioned in Despatches [London Gazette, 16 March, 1900, and 29 July, 1902]; received the Queen's Medal with four clasps, the King's Medal with two clasps, and was created a Companion of the Distinguished Service Order [London Gazette, 19 April, 1901]: "The Honourable William Lambton, Major, Coldstream Guards. In recognition of services during the recent operations in South Africa." The Insignia were presented by the Duke of Cornwall and York 14 Aug. 1901. He passed the Staff College, 1898. In 1904 he was created a C.M.G., and in 1907 an M.V.O. On 28 Oct. 1906, he became Lieut.-Colonel, and on 28 Oct. 1909, was given the Brevet of Colonel, being promoted to Colonel 1 Aug. 1910. He commanded the 1st Battn. Coldstream Guards in 1906, and the Coldstream Regt. in 1910, and was A.A. and Q.M.G., London District, 1 Jan. 1913, to 4 Aug. 1914, and was created a C.V.O. in 1914. He was Assistant Military Secretary to the Field-Marshal, Commanding-in-Chief in France, 5 Aug. to 1 Sept. 1914; was Temporary Brigadier-General 2 Sept. 1914, to 2 June, 1915; Military Secretary 2 Sept. 1914, to 5 Sept. 1915; Major-General 3 June, 1915. He was created a C.B., 1915; is a Commander of the Legion of Honour, and was created a K.C.B. in 1918, and commanded the 4th Division, Sept. 1915, to Sept. 1917; Battles of the Somme, July and Oct. 1916, and Arras, 1917.

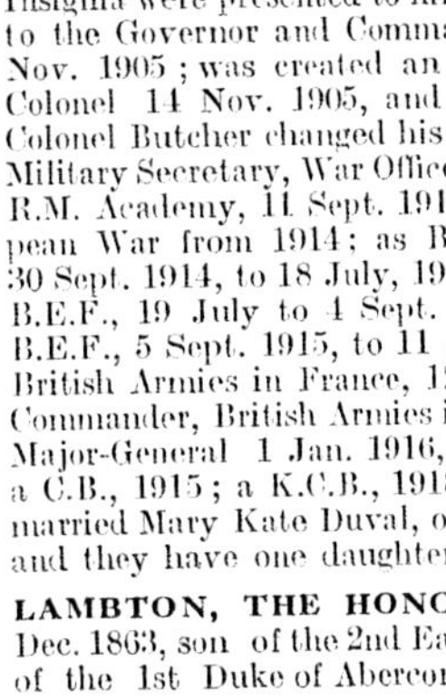

The Hon. W. Lambton.

GLEICHEN, COUNT (later **Lord Albert Edward Wilfred**), Major-General, was born in London 15 Jan. 1863, son of Admiral Prince (and Princess) Victor of Hohenlohe-Langenburg. He was educated at Cheam, Charterhouse, and Sandhurst, and joined the Grenadier Guards, 1881. He served in the Guards' Camel Regt. in the Nile Expedition, 1884. Count Gleichen published "With the Camel Corps up the Nile": "One day in September, 1884, on coming off one of those numerous guards in Dublin that make the subaltern's life a burden to him, I found the joyful news awaiting me that I was to go out to the Sudan at once with the Camel Corps detachment of my battalion. As everybody knows, this sudden despatch of troops to the Nile was due to the Government having suddenly taken into its head the idea that it was necessary to rescue General Gordon from his perilous position at Khartoum, which he had held since the previous February. Better late than never! Accordingly an expedition was equipped to proceed up the river in pursuance of a determination which ought to have been carried out at least three months earlier. The idea had only recently been started that, in order to allow of troops acting with any success up the Nile, it was absolutely necessary that a certain proportion of them should be mounted on camels, both for facility of transport across the desert (if necessary) to Khartoum, and for rapidity of action. Accordingly a Camel Corps was organized, drawn half from the Cavalry and half from the Infantry. The Cavalry part was to be composed of detachments from all the Cavalry regiments in Great Britain—at the time subdivided into 'Heavies' and 'Lights'; the Infantry part of the detachments from the Brigade of Guards, and from the regiments already out in Egypt, these last to go by the name of (Camel) Mounted Infantry. They were as good men as could be got anywhere, and a finer ship-load than those on board the Deccan never left England. Mounting a frisky camel is exciting work for a beginner and nearly always results in a cropper. The mode of procedure should be thus: Having made your camel to kneel by clearing your throat loudly at him and tugging at his rope, shorten your rein till you bring his head round to his shoulder, put your foot in the stirrup to throw your leg over. With his head jammed like that, he cannot rise, and must wait until you give him his head. Unless you do as directed, he will get up before your leg is over; if this happens, stand up in the stirrup till he is up, and then throw your leg over, otherwise you will infallibly meet with a hideous catastrophe. A camel's leg will reach anywhere—over his head, round his chest, and on to his hump. He will chew the root of his tail, nip you in the calf, or lay the top of his head on his hump. To the uninitiated a camel going for one with his mouth open and gurgling horribly is a terrifying spectacle, but do not mind him, it is only his way. A camel is not intended by nature to be groomed, so do not groom him. You might as well groom an Irish pig. With infinite pains you beat the dust out of his skin, remove as many as possible of the ticks and maggots that infest him, wipe his nose (if he has a cold), and finish up by washing off any mud, and drying him with a wisp of dhurra stalk. What is the result? The moment your back is turned over he goes, and enjoys a delicious roll in the dust and dirt again, making himself filthier than before. The natives understand all this, and instead of cleaning him, and making him more susceptible to the heat of the sun, plaster him all over with mud during the hot months, which keeps the sun and flies off during the day, and maybe protects him from the cold at night." Count Gleichen lost his camel: "I made every inquiry afterwards about a big white camel with a blue and white nose-band, a vile temper, and a hole in his head big enough to put your helmet in. I never heard any more of him. Peace to his bones! Beyond Dongola, the G.C.R. had long ceased to be a camel regiment, and we were once more to be genuine infantry. It was very sad to compare our present state with what we were seven months before, going up country. Then each man had a camel of his own, real breeches and putties, and a respectable grey tunic. Now every man was reduced to his own legs as a transport, khaki trousers much too short for him, and a badly-fitting khaki tunic. Then the G.C.R. was over 400 strong, with every hope for the future; now the object for which we came was gone, and there were 90 of us gone also." He was promoted to Captain 21 Sept. 1892; was Equerry to the Prince of Wales, 12 Jan. to 11 Feb. 1892; Extra Equerry to the Queen 12 Feb. 1892, to 22 Jan. 1901; Staff Captain and D.A.A.G. (Intelligence), Headquarters of Army, 5 May, 1895, to 14 July, 1899. He served in the Expedition to Dongola, 1896, receiving the Medal and Egyptian Medal; accompanied the Rodd Mission to Abyssinia in 1897, and became Major 28 Oct. 1898. Count Gleichen served in the South African War from 1899 to 1900, first with the 3rd Battn. Grenadier Guards, in the Guards Brigade, and then as D.A.A.G., Transport, 20 Jan. to 22 Feb. 1900, taking part in the advance on Kimberley, including the actions at Belmont, Enslin and Modder River (severely wounded). He was with the 9th Division as Intelligence Officer 23 Feb. to 29 June, 1900, and was present in the operations in the Orange Free State, including those at Paardeberg, and the actions at Poplar Grove, Blaauweberg and Heilbron, and was Provost-Marshal under the Military Governor, Pretoria, 30 June to 19 Aug. 1900. Then he was I.O. to Eastern Line of Communications to 30 Nov. 1900. He was mentioned twice in Despatches [London Gazette, 26 Jan. 1900 and 8 Feb. 1901]; received the Queen's Medal with five clasps, and was created a Companion of the Distinguished Service Order [London Gazette, 19 April, 1901]: "Albert Edward Wilfred, Count Gleichen, C.V.O., C.M.G., Major Grenadier Guards. In recognition of services during the recent operations in South Africa." The Insignia were presented by the Sirdar 6 Nov. 1901. He was appointed an Extra Equerry to King Edward 23 July, 1901, and was employed with the Egyptian Army 7 Feb. 1901, to 14 Oct. 1903, as Director of Intelligence and Sudan Agent (Second Class Medjidie); was promoted to Lieut.-Colonel 14 Oct. 1903; was Military Attaché, Berlin, 15 Oct. 1903, to 27 Jan. 1906, and Military Attaché, Washington and Mexico, 28 Jan. 1906, to 29 Jan. 1907; was given the Brevet of Colonel 15 Oct. 1906; Assistant Director of Military Operations, War Office, 1 Feb. 1907, to 31 July, 1911; Extra Equerry to King George 10 June, 1910. He was Temporary Brigadier-General 1 Aug. 1911, to 1 March, 1915; commanded the 15th Brigade, Irish Command, and was in charge at Belfast during the Churchill meeting and other troubles. Count Gleichen served in the European War (as Brigade Commander 5 Aug. 1914, to 1 March, 1915), and took the brigade to France 14 Aug. 1914. He was present at the Battles of Mons and Le Cateau, at the Retreat from Mons, and the Battles of the Marne, Aisne, Festubert and Ypres. He was promoted to Major-General, "for distinguished service," 18 Feb. 1915, and appointed to train and command the 37th Division 6 April, 1915, taking it to France on 30 July, 1915. He assisted in the Great Push of 1 July, 1916. In 1917 he organized and directed the Intelligence Bureau, Department of Information, 1917–18, and was afterwards employed in the Ministry of Information. He was

Lord Edward Gleichen.

twice mentioned in Despatches. Lord Edward Gleichen has written several interesting and amusing books: "With the Camel Corps up the Nile" (1888); "Armies of Europe" (translation, 1890); "With the Mission to Menelik, 1897"; "The Doings of the 15th Brigade" (1917), etc., etc., and has compiled and edited the "Chronology of the War" (in three volumes). His favourite recreations are shooting and travelling. He married, in 1910, the Honourable Sylvia Edwardes (a Maid of Honour to Queen Alexandra), daughter of the Honourable Mrs. Henry Edwardes; and in 1917 he dropped his foreign title and became Lord Edward Gleichen. We give some extracts from "The Doings of the Fifteenth Infantry Brigade, Aug. 1914, to March, 1915, by its Commander": "In the neighbourhood of Pradelle we put up at a nice, bright, ugly little château belonging to an elderly lady, who was most civil, and told us stories of what the Germans had done when they passed through a week or two ago on their retreat eastwards. Amongst other abominations, they had, on arrival, demanded of the old curé the key of the church tower, on which they wished to put a Maxim. The old man, not having the key, had hobbled off to get it from the garde-champêtre, who happened to be in possession of it for the time being. He could not, however, find him, and the officer in command, being in a diabolical temper, put the poor old priest up against a wall and shot him dead on the spot. This was recounted by the curé's sister, and there was not a shadow of doubt on the matter, for it was confirmed by all. . . . These belonged to the Frankfort-am-Main Corps (VII.). I examined one prisoner, a regular 'Schwabe' from Heilbronn, a jolly man with a red beard, who told me that his company was commanded by a cavalry captain, who considered it beneath his dignity to charge with infantry, and remained snugly ensconced behind a wall whilst he shouted encouragement to his men." . . . At the Château of Beukenhorst (Ypres): "There were some late roses in the garden, or rather in the scattered flower-beds near the house, which lasted out even when the snow was on them; but about the only live beings who took any interest in them were three or four goats, who haunted the precincts of the Château and were everlastingly trying to get inside. Indeed, when Moulton-Barrett first came to take possession there were two goats in the best bedroom upstairs, who peered out of the windows at the undesired visitors, and had to be evicted after a display of considerable force. . . . During the chief hours of the day, when not (or whilst) being shelled, we were pretty busy with telegrams and reports and queries and excursions and alarums. We were comfortable enough in the housekeeper's room, and got our meals 'reg'lar,' and we even had two or three arm-chairs, and got our newspapers and mails fairly well, which used to arrive with our rations at 9 p.m. or thereabouts. But a minor trial was the fact that two out of our five panes of glass had been blown in by shell, and let in an icy draught on most days. So we got some partially oiled paper, and made some paste and stuck up the panes. The first shell explosion made the paper sag, the second made it shiver, and the third blew it out. The paste would not stick—it was the wrong sort of flour, or something. Then we used jam—that glutinous saccharine mess known as 'best plum jam'—and blue sugar paper, and it stuck quite fairly well. But it wouldn't dry, and tears of jam used to trickle down the paper panes and mingle with the tintacks and the breadcrumbs on the sill. The room was even then fairly dark, but the shell-bursts again shivered the jam paper and burst it, and we had to take to cardboard and drawing-boards. This made it still darker, and was not even then successful, for the explosions still shook the boards down and eventually broke another pane; it was most trying. On the last day but one four panes had been broken, and on the last day, as will be recounted, all were broken and the whole window blown in. Then we left. But what was of much vaster interest, of course, than these trifles, was the desperate fighting which was being waged along our front, not 1,000 yards from the Château. Our two battalions being entrenched in the wood, did not receive such a severe hammering as the brigades on either side—the 7th and 9th, respectively on our right and left—who were more in the open, and the shelling and attacks on them were incessant, as well as on troops still further off on the other side of them. The 11th November was a typically unpleasant day. It started with a touch of comedy, Weatherby arriving stark naked in my room at 6.30 a.m., just when I was shaving, saying, 'I say, Sir, may I finish my dressing in here? They're shelling the bath-room!' He had a towel and a few clothes on his arm, *et praeterea nihil*. . . . The shelling continued till 10. It was on this morning that Brown was damaged and lots of windows blown in." August 20, 1914 (pages 9–10): "We had arrived on the Tuesday (18th), and on the Thursday Sir C. Fergusson (commanding 5th Division) paraded the Brigade by battalions and made them a short speech, telling us we were to move on the morrow, and giving us a few technical tips about the Germans and how to meet their various wiles, largely about machine guns and their methods of attack in large numbers. The Bedfords were the most interested audience, and interrupted him every now and then with ''Ear, 'ear,' and a little hand-clapping at important points. I think the General was a little nonplussed at this attention: I know I was. Whether it was due or not to the audience being accustomed to attending political meetings at home, or to the air of Bedfordshire being extremely vitalizing, I don't know; but once or twice afterwards, when the battalion was addressed by General Smith-Dorrien, and even by Sir J. French, they showed their approbation in the manner above set forth—somewhat to my confusion." Later on Lord Edward writes: "We were inspected both by Sir Horace and, half an hour later, by Sir John French, who were both pleased to say complimentary things of the brigade. It did us good. The Bedfords again put me to confusion by calling out ''Ear, 'ear!' at telling points of the speeches—curious folk—the only battalion I ever heard do so: 587 men and two officers on parade, not one of the latter of whom, except the Quartermaster, had come out with the battalion. Griffith was on leave, his place being taken by Major Mackenzie, V.C., who had just joined. All the other officers who had left Ireland with me in Aug. were either killed, wounded, or sick. We were under orders to go into the trenches again shortly, taking over from Maude (the victor of Bagdad), now commanding the 14th Brigade; he also had the Dorsets and Norfolks, scraped up from various places, attached to him. His line was in front of Dranoutre. On the 29th Nov. we took over there, a most complicated arrangement which only evolved itself clearly during the next week. I had the East Surreys and Manchesters under me for a time, and then the K.O.S.B.'s, all interchanging and intershuffling with my battalions, the main reason being that I had not got the Cheshires, so had to shift as best I could without them, picking up a battalion of the 13th or 14th Brigade when one was available. The line was not exactly nice. We had, it is true, got rid of the worst bit, Hill 73, on to the 3rd Division, which was next door on the left; but it extended all the same for an unpleasant length on our right, which was south of the Wulverghem-Messines road, the right of the brigade on our right being on the Douve. At the longest—the length that the brigade had to defend varied according to circumstances—the line was just over 2,500 yards; at its shortest it was about 2,200. Considering that the normal frontage (defensive) of the Brigade at full strength was 900 to 1,300 yards, this was a bit 'thin' in more senses than one. As we were here for three months off and on—from the beginning of Dec. till the end of Feb.—it may be worth while trying to describe it, if I can. Imagine a bit of rolling country—rather like parts of Leicestershire—fair-sized fields, separated mostly by straggling fences interspersed with wire (largely barbed), and punctuated by tall trees. Patches of wood in places, spinney size for the most part. Low hills here and there—Kemmel, Scherpenberg, Ploegsteert Wood—but all outside our area. For villages, Danoutre, Neuve Eglise, Wulverghem and Lindenhoek, of which the two last-named were already more than half shot to pieces and almost deserted. Opposite our right was Messines—a mile and a half in front of our line—its big, square, old church tower still standing; it may have had a spire on the top, but, if so, it had disappeared before we came. Nearly opposite our extreme left, but out of our jurisdiction and in the sphere of the division on our left, was Wytschaete (pronounce Wich Khâte), one and a half miles off. The cavalry had held both Messines (locally pronounced Mersé) and Wytschaete at the end of Oct., but had been overwhelmingly attacked here and driven out of them, so that the two villages formed a hostile bulge into our line. We had been in hopes of driving attacks into the base of the bulge and thus forcing a retirement. But the Germans reinforced the bulge and entrenched it heavily, and instead of our cutting off the bulge, it became flatter and flatter, without giving way at the point, so that we had to retire slightly on either side, and not they. Farms, nearly all of them roofless and half ruined, were dotted about over the country; small ones for the most part they were, and of the usual type—a liquid and stinking manure-heap, surrounded on three sides by a living house and barns. Of the roads, those from Danoutre to Neuve Eglise, via Wulverghem to Messines, were pavé—i.e., cobblestones down the centre and mud on both sides. Those joining Lindenhoek to Neuve Eglise and Wulverghem were also mostly pavé. The remainder were mere field tracks for the most part, rarely metalled, and in wet weather almost impassable for mud. Oh, that mud! We have heard lots about Flanders mud, but the reality transcends imagination, especially in winter. Greasy, slippery, holding clay, over your toes in most places and over your ankles in all the rest—where it is not over your knees—it is the most horrible 'going' I know anywhere. Whether you are moving across ploughed or grass fields or along lanes, you are perpetually skating about and slipping up on the firmer bits and held fast by the ankles in the softer ones. There is no stone in the district, nothing but rich loamy clay, *alias* mud. However much you dig, you never come across stone, nothing but sticky mud which clings to your shovel and refuses to be parted from it—mud that has to be scraped off at almost every stroke, mud that absorbs water like a sponge, yet refuses to give it up again. Every little puddle and rut, every hoof depression full of rain, remains like that for weeks. Even when the weather is fine, the water does not seem to evaporate, but remains on the surface. And when it rains, as it did all that winter (except when it snowed), the state of the trenches is indescribable. Some were, frankly, so full of water that they had to be abandoned, and a breastwork erected behind. But a breastwork is slow work, especially if you are less than 100 yards from the enemy. For weeks, indeed, the garrison of one particular trench had to lie out on the mud or on what waterproofs they could get, behind a shelter two to three feet high—always growing a little yet never to be made to a real six-feet height by reason of conspicuousness and consequent clusters of Black Marias. Other trenches varied from five inches to five feet deep in mud; in one a Dorset man was literally almost drowned and drawn forth with great difficulty. Many cases occurred of semi-submersion, and as for moving up the communication trenches during the winter, it was generally an impossibility, for they were either knee-deep in water or in mud, and simply refused to be drained. So men preferred the risk of a stray bullet to the certainty of liquid mud to the knees and consequent icy discomfort for twenty-four hours and more. And as for the unfortunate ration-parties and men bringing up heavy trench stores, their task was really one of frightful labour, for, for two men to cross a large and slippery muddy series of fields, carrying a 100-lb. box between them, was no joke. First, one would slide up and skate off in one direction, whilst the other did his best to hold on, generally resulting in dropping his end of the box or finding himself on the flat of his back. Then the parts would be reversed, but they always slid up in opposite directions—the mud saw to that—and they would arrive in the trenches, after their stroll of a mile or less, absolutely exhausted and dripping with sweat. It was difficult enough, over much of the ground, to avoid slipping up even when burdened by nothing more than a walking-stick—that I know from personal experience. Yet for many weeks the men had to do this and suffer, for fascines and bricks, besides sandbags, were only just beginning to make their appearance in Dec., and floor-boards and gratings and gravel and trench stores and wire-netting and revetments and planks and iron sheeting and trestles and hurdles of all sorts, did not really materialize in anything like sufficient numbers till March. The drainage of the trenches was heart-breaking. After a heavy day or two of rain the parapets would fall down in hunks into the foot of water or so in the trenches, and would churn up into liquid mud, only to be removed by large spoons, of which we had none, or buckets, of which we had but very few. It was too thick to drain off down the very, very gradual slopes which were the best we could do, and too liquid to be shovelled away; so there it would remain, and our strenuous efforts in rebuilding the parapets (for at this period we had no revetting material) would only result, a night or two later, in still further collapse. The R.E. companies, both 17th and 59th, worked like heroes, and so particularly did the Norfolks and Bedfords; but it was most disheartening work. No sooner was one parapet fairly complete than another fell in; and when this was mended, the first one would collapse again under the incessant downpour. And all this time wire entanglements had to be put up in front under hostile fire, trenches connected up and drained, support trenches dug, communication trenches improved, loopholes made, defences thickened and strengthened, saps pushed out, all under the fire of an enemy anything from 60 to 200 yards off, and always on rather higher ground than ourselves, worse luck, so that he had the whip-hand. Soon came the period of hand grenades, in which he had six to one the best of us in numbers; and then in rifle grenades ditto, ditto; and then in trench mortars, flare-lights, searchlights and rockets—wherein we followed him feebly and at a great distance; for where he sent up 100 (say) light balls at night, we could only afford five or six, and other things in proportion. Later on came the Minenwerfer, an expanded type of trench mortar, and its bomb; but up to the end of Feb. his efforts in this direction were not very serious, though I allow that he did us more harm thereby than we him. For our trench mortars were in an experimental stage, made locally by the R.E., and constructed of thin gas-pipe iron, and home-made jam-pot bombs, whose behaviour was always erratic, and sometimes, I regret to say, fatal to the mortarist. (Poor Rogers, R.E., a capital subaltern, was killed thus, besides others, I fear.)" Later Lord Edward Gleichen writes: "As regards myself . . . my days of connection with the brigade were numbered. I had heard, with mixed but pleasant feelings, that I had been promoted Major-General, 'for distinguished service' on the 18th Feb. (Weatherby got a Brevet Majority in the same Gazette), and I was now ordered to go home and report myself in London."

NASH, WILLIAM FLEETWOOD, Major, was born 27 Sept. 1861, son of the late Henry Fleetwood Nash, Esq., of Upton Lea, Slough, Buckinghamshire. His mother was Maria, daughter of Charles Wilkinson, Esq., of Hornsea, Yorkshire. He was educated at Rugby and Sandhurst, and obtained his commission 22 Jan. 1881, and joined the 34th Regt. of Infantry (afterwards called the Border Regt.) at Carlisle. He was Adjutant of the Militia. In 1889 he was promoted Captain, and in 1894 was selected as Adjutant of the 1st Border Regt. He served in the Burmese Expedition of 1889–90, when he was entrusted with the care of the battalion treasure chest. He received the Medal and clasp inscribed "Burmah, 1889–1892." On 31 Oct. 1898, he was promoted to the rank of Major. He proceeded with the 1st Battn. to South Africa on the outbreak of war there in 1899, and in Nov. of the same year was specially selected to raise and command a battalion, afterwards called the Imperial Light Infantry, and took part in many engagements in Natal, notably Spion Kop, in which action, on the retirement being ordered, he was one of the last to leave the top of the hill which he and his battalion had held with much tenacity. The record of his services in South Africa as given in the Army List is as follows: "South African War, 1899–1902. In command Imperial Light Infantry from Dec. 1899; operations in Natal, 1899; Relief of Ladysmith, including operations of 17 to 24 Jan. 1900, and action at Spion Kop; operations of 5–7 Feb. 1900, and action at Vaal Kranz; operations on Tugela Heights (14 to 27 Feb. 1900), and action at Pieter's Hill; operations in Natal (March to June, 1900), including action at Laing's Nek (6 to 9 June); operations in Cape Colony, south of Orange River, 1899; operations in the Transvaal from 30 Nov. 1900. Despatches [London Gazette, 8 Feb. 1901]; created a Companion of the Distinguished Service Order [London Gazette, 19 April, 1901]: William Fleetwood Nash, Major, Border Regt. In recognition of services during the recent operations in South Africa." Lieut.-Colonel Nash was mentioned in Despatches by Sir R. Buller, *re* the Relief of Ladysmith, in which he reported: "Major (Local Lieut.-Colonel) W. F. Nash, Border Regt., commanded the Imperial Light Infantry. The extremely good work done by this battalion is due to the excellent manner in which it was commanded by Lieut.-Colonel Nash." He received the Queen's Medal with five clasps, inscribed, "Laing's Nek," "Transvaal," "Tugela Heights" and "Cape Colony," and King's Medal with two clasps. He retired from the Army in Nov. 1905, and was placed on the List of Reserve of Officers. On the outbreak of war in Aug. 1914, he was appointed to the command of the Border Depôt and 34th Regimental District at Carlisle, with the temporary rank of Lieut.-Colonel. He died at Carlisle on the 28th Dec. 1915, after a short illness following a severe operation for an internal complaint, at the age of 54. He was a fine soldier, being a man of great coolness and resource, and very keen on his profession.

William Fleetwood Nash.

KING, ALEXANDER JAMES, Lieut.-Colonel, was born 15 July, 1863, eldest son of the late Rev. Edward King, B.A., F.R.H.S., F.S.A. Scotland. He was educated at Radley College, and joined the King's Own Regt. as Lieutenant, from the Militia, 12 Nov. 1884, and became Captain 27 July, 1892. He took part in the Expedition to Dongola, 1896; in the operations of 7 June and 19 Sept.; in the Camel Corps, and was present at the actions of Firket, Hafir and Dongola. He was mentioned in Despatches [London Gazette, 3 Nov. 1896]; received the Medal; 4th Class Medjidie, and the Egyptian Medal with two clasps. He served in the Nile Expedition of 1897, including the Flying Column up the River Atbara. He received a clasp to the Egyptian Medal; in the Nile Expedition of 1898, when he was present at the Battles of Atbara and Khartum. He was mentioned in Despatches [London Gazette, 24 May and 30 Sept. 1898]; was given the Brevet of Major 16 Nov. 1898, and two clasps to the Egyptian Medal. He had been employed with the Egyptian Army from 19 Oct. 1894, to 28 Nov. 1898. He was appointed A.D.C. to Lieut.-General Sir Archibald Hunter, K.C.B., D.S.O., in India (14 May to 20 Sept. 1890), and in the South African Campaign of 1899–1902; in Natal, 21 Sept. to 8 Oct. 1899, and in South Africa 24 June, 1899, and commanded the Kimberley Mounted Corps during the Relief of Kimberley. Served during operations in Natal, 1899, including actions at Rietfontein and Lombard's Kop; Defence of Ladysmith, including sortie of 7 Dec. 1899, and action of 6 Jan. 1900; Relief of Mafeking; operations in the Transvaal and Orange River Colony, July to Nov. 1900, including action at Wittebergen. He was mentioned in Despatches by Sir G. S. White, 2 Dec. 1899, and 23 March, 1900 [London Gazette, 8 Feb. 1901]; received the Queen's Medal with five clasps, and was created a Companion of the Distinguished Service Order [London Gazette, 19 April, 1901]: "Alexander James King, Captain and Brevet Major (Local Lieut.-Colonel), King's Own Royal Lancaster Regt. In recognition of services during the recent operations in South Africa." He became Captain, and Major 22 Jan. 1904. He retired 8 Sept. 1906. He is honorary Lieut.-Colonel, Fife and Forfar Yeomanry, and is a J.P. for Aberdeenshire. He served in the European War, in the Remount Department, in France, Egypt and Palestine, and was mentioned in Sir A. J. Murray's Despatch of 26 Sept. 1916, and created a C.M.G. in 1918.

INGOUVILLE-WILLIAMS, EDWARD CHARLES, Major (Local Lieut.-Colonel), was born 13 Dec. 1861, son of the late General Sir J. W. C. Williams, K.C.B., and of Isabella Georgiana, daughter of John Ingouville, Esq., of La Frégonière, Jersey. He was gazetted to the 3rd Foot, as Second Lieutenant, from the Militia, 23 April, 1881, and became Lieutenant, The Buffs, 1 July, 1881. He served in the Sudan Expedition, 1884–85 (Nile), as Special Officer for Boats (Staff Captain), and received the Medal with clasp, and Khedive's Star. He was promoted to Captain 1 Nov. 1892; was Adjutant, The Buffs, 20 May, 1894, to 21 Jan. 1898. From 22 Jan. 1898, to 10 April, 1899, he was specially employed with the Egyptian Army, as Special Service Officer, and served in the Nile Expedition of 1898, taking part in the battles of Atbara and Khartum. He was mentioned in Despatches [London Gazette, 24 May, and 30 Sept. 1898]; was given the Brevet of Major 16 Nov. 1898; received the Medal and the Egyptian Medal with two clasps. In the Nile Expedition of 1899 he served as D.A.A.G. to the Kordofan Field Force, and received a clasp to the Egyptian Medal. He served in the South African War, 1899 to 1902, on Sir Charles Warren's Staff; as Provost-Marshal, Nov. 1899, to 19 May, 1900; Brigade-Major from May to 31 Dec. 1900; Commanding Mounted Infantry Corps, and Commanding a Mobile Column 1 Jan. 1901, to 25 Sept. 1902; was present at the Relief of Ladysmith, including operations of 17 to 24 Jan. 1900; action at Spion Kop; operations of 5 to 7 Jan. 1900, and action at Vaal Kranz; operations on Tugela Heights 14 to 27 Feb. 1900, and action at Pieter's Hill. Operations in Natal, March to June, 1890, including actions at Laing's Nek (6 to 9 June). Operations in Orange Free State and Transvaal. Operations in Orange River Colony, Jan. to May, 1901. Operations in the Transvaal, May, 1901, to 31 May, 1902. He was mentioned in Despatches [London Gazette, 8 Feb. 1900 (Sir R. H. Buller); 30 March, 17 June, and 9 Nov. 1900, and London Gazette, 9 July to 11 Oct. 1901]; was given the Brevet of Lieutenant-Colonel 12 Oct. 1901; received the Queen's Medal with six clasps; King's Medal with two clasps, and was created a Companion of the Distinguished Service Order [London Gazette, 19 April, 1901]: "Edward Charles Ingouville-Williams, Major (now Local Lieutenant-Colonel), The Buffs (East Kent Regt.). In recognition of services during the recent operations in South Africa." The Insignia were presented in South Africa. He was transferred to the Worcestershire Regt. 4 April, 1903; commanded the 2nd Battn. Worcestershire Regt., 1904 to 1908, and became Lieutenant-Colonel 10 March, 1904. He was created a C.B. in 1910; was Commandant, School of Mounted Infantry, Longmoor Camp 1 March, 1910, to 17 June, 1912; was given the Brevet of Colonel 25 Dec. 1905; became Colonel 10 March, 1908; Temporary Brigadier-General 18 June, 1912, to 2 June, 1915; Commanding 16th Infantry Brigade, Irish Command, 16 June, 1912, to 4 Aug. 1914. On the outbreak of war with Germany he took his Brigade to France, commanding it until he was promoted to Major-General, in June, 1915, for distinguished service in the field, and given command of the 34th Division, which he trained and took to the front in Jan. 1916, being in the front line till 4 July, when the division was withdrawn to refit, but was again put into the line, with two fresh brigades to replace the 102nd and the 103rd, which had lost heavily. The Division was in the fighting line till the 19th July, when it was again withdrawn to rest and to refit. On the 22nd July, Major-General Ingouville-Williams went with his A.D.C. to the Bois-de-Mametz

E. C. Ingouville-Williams.

to make a personal reconnaissance of the ground where he was to take his Division into action the following week; was caught in a barrage of fire, hit by a piece of shell and killed instantly. He had been mentioned in Despatches four times for his services in the European War.

TWYFORD, ERNEST HENRY SAMUEL, Major, was born 28 Oct. 1863. He joined the Scottish Rifles 5 Dec. 1883, as Lieutenant, from the Militia, and was Adjutant, Scottish Rifles, 20 Nov. 1887, to 19 Nov. 1891. He served in the Chin-Lushai Expedition in 1889, as Transport Officer. He became Captain, Scottish Rifles, 7 March, 1894, and Major 3 April, 1899. Major Twyford served in the South African War, and was created a Companion of the Distinguished Service Order, 29 Nov. 1900, and the decoration was gazetted on 19 April, 1901: "Ernest Henry Samuel Twyford, Major, Scottish Rifles. In recognition of services during the recent operations in South Africa." Major Twyford was killed 13 April, 1901, in the Badfontein Valley, on his way to join the Royal Scots, into which regiment he had been promoted to Second-in-Command for good service in Natal.

BONUS WILLIAM JOHN, Major, was born 9 July, 1862, son of Major-General Joseph Bonus, K.P. He was educated at Harrow and Sandhurst; was gazetted to the Dorsetshire Regt., as Lieutenant, 9 Sept. 1882. He served in India and Egypt. He became Captain 21 June, 1890; was A.D.C. in 1890; D.A.A.G., Scottish District, 23 July, 1895, to 23 Nov. 1899, and was promoted Major 30 April, 1899. He served in the South African War, from 1899 to 1902, with the Dorsetshire Regt. in Natal until the Relief of Ladysmith, being present at the operations to 24 Jan. 1900, and at the action of Spion Kop; operations of 5 to 7 Feb. 1900, and action at Vaal Kranz; operations on Tugela Heights (14 to 27 Feb. 1900), and action at Pieter's Hill. He was D.A.A.G., 4th Division, 22 March, 1900, to 11 Dec. 1902, and took part in the operations in Natal (March to June, 1900), taking part in the operations in Laing's Nek (6 to 9 June); operations in the Transvaal, east of Pretoria, July to 29 Nov. 1900, including actions at Reit Vlei, Belfast (26 and 27 Aug.); Lydenberg (6 to 8 Sept.) and Rhenoster Kop. He was mentioned in Despatches [London Gazette, 8 Feb. 1901]; received the Queen's Medal and five clasps; King's Medal and two clasps. At the Battle of Spion Kop, when acting as Brigade-Major, Major Bonus "found it necessary to go up and remain in the firing line. He took a party round the Boer flank and enfiladed it, all the other members of the party—officers and men—being killed." It was especially for his services on this occasion that he was created a Companion of the Distinguished Service Order [London Gazette, 19 April, 1901]: "William John Bonus, Major, Dorsetshire Regt. In recognition of services during the recent operations in South Africa." The Insignia were presented to him by the Duke of Cornwall and York, in South Africa, 14 Aug. 1901. He was D.A.A.G., Belfast District, 29 Jan. 1903, to 7 March, 1904; became Lieutenant-Colonel 25 Oct. 1900; commanded the Dorsetshire Regt. from 1906 to 1910; was given the Brevet of Colonel 25 Oct. 1909, and retired with the rank of Colonel 16 Dec. 1911. He served as A.Q.M.G., Scottish District, 4 Aug. 1914, to July, 1916, and subsequently in other capacities (he was Cable Censor from Jan. 1917) until Peace was proclaimed in 1919.

William John Bonus.

MANSEL, GEORGE CLAVELL, Major, was born 9 Feb. 1861, youngest son of the late Lieut.-Colonel George Pleydell Mansel, of Smedmore, Dorset, and of Jemina Henrietta, daughter of the late William Gambier, Esq., and Henrietta, Countess of Athlone. He was educated at Eton and Sandhurst, and was gazetted to the 68th Foot, as Second Lieutenant, 11 Aug. 1880, and became Lieutenant 1 July, 1881, and Captain 1 April, 1889. He was promoted Major on 9 Aug. 1899. He served in the South African War, 1899–1902; was present at the Relief of Ladysmith, including the action at Colenso, and in the operations of 17 to 24 Jan. 1900; operations of 5 to 7 Feb. 1900, and action at Vaal Kranz; operations on Tugela Heights (14 to 27 Feb. 1900); actions at Pieter's Hill; operations in Natal, March to June, 1900, including action at Laing's Nek (6 to 9 June). Operations in the Transvaal 30 Nov. 1900, to 31 May, 1902. He was mentioned in Despatches by Sir R. H. Buller, 30 March and 9 Nov. 1900 (London Gazette, 3 Feb. 1901]; received the Queen's Medal with four clasps; King's Medal with two clasps, and was created a Companion of the Distinguished Service Order [London Gazette, 19 April, 1901]: "George Clavell Mansel, Major, Durham Light Infantry. In recognition of services during the recent operations in South Africa." He became Lieutenant-Colonel 29 Feb. 1904; was given the Brevet of Colonel 1 March, 1907; retired 13 June, 1908, with the rank of Colonel, having served the whole of his service (28 years) in one battalion of the Durham Light Infantry. He died 12 July, 1910, and an obituary notice of him appeared in the "Times."

HEATH, GERARD MOORE, Major, was born 7 June, 1863, youngest son of the late Admiral Sir Leopold George Heath, K.C.B., and of Mary Marsh, his wife. He was educated at Wimbledon and the Royal Military Academy, Woolwich, and joined the Royal Engineers, as Lieutenant, 22 Feb. 1882. He served in the Bechuanaland Expedition, 1884–85, with the Telegraph Battn., and became Captain 3 Aug. 1890. He served in Chitral, with the Relief Force, in 1895. He received the Medal and clasp. Capt. Heath was promoted Major 4 Oct. 1899. He served in the South African War, 1899–1902, taking part in the operations in Natal in 1899, including the action at Lombard's Kop. He served during the defence of Ladysmith, when he was in charge of a balloon section, and afterwards in command of a Field Troop, R.E. He took part in the operations in Natal in 1900, including the action at Laing's Nek, and in the operations in the Transvaal in 1900, including the actions at Belfast and Lydenberg. He was present in the operations in the Transvaal and Orange River Colony from 1900 to 1902, serving as D.A.A.G. 11 Dec. 1901, to 18 March, 1902. He was mentioned in Despatches by Sir G. S. White, 23 March, 1900, and by Sir R. H. Buller, 9 Nov. 1900 [London Gazette, 8 Feb. 1901]; was given the Brevet of Lieutenant-Colonel 22 Aug. 1902; received the Queen's Medal with five clasps; King's Medal with two clasps, and was created a Companion of the Distinguished Service Order [London Gazette, 19 April, 1901]: "Gerard Moore Heath, Major, Royal Engineers. In recognition of services during the recent operations in South Africa." The Insignia were presented to him 3 June, 1901. He was Instructor, School of Military Engineering, 11 June, 1902, to 10 June, 1906; Lieutenant-Colonel 18 Aug. 1903; G.S.O., 1st Grade, 3 June, 1910, to 8 Dec. 1911; Temporary Brigadier-General, General Staff, South Africa, 16 March, 1912, to the outbreak of the Great War. He served in the European War from 1914; as Inspector of Royal Engineers 21 Sept. 1914, to 6 May, 1915; Chief Engineer 7 May, 1915; Temporary Major-General 6 Nov. 1915, on appointment as Chief Engineer, First Army; was promoted Major-General for distinguished service in the field, and became Engineer-in-Chief to the British Armies in France in Nov. 1917, which post he held until the end of the war. He was six times mentioned in Despatches. He was created a C.B. and K.C.M.G. Major-General C. M. Heath married, in 1885, Mary, youngest daughter of the late Philip Henry Egerton, B.C.S.

GORDON, FREDERICK, Major The Honourable, was born 9 Oct. 1861, son of Edward Strathearn, Baron Gordon of Drumearn, and of his wife, Agnes Joanna, Baroness Gordon of Drumearn (both parents are dead). He was educated at Edinburgh Academy, and the Royal Military College, Sandhurst; joined the Army 22 Jan. 1881, serving in the 49th Regt. from Jan. to Oct. 1881, as Subaltern; became Lieutenant 1 July, 1881. He served in the Gordon Highlanders from 14 Sept. 1881, to Aug. 1911. He took part in the Egyptian Campaign of 1882–84, being present at the Battle of Tel-el-Kebir (Medal with clasp; Bronze Star). In the Sudan in 1884 he was present at the battles of El Teb and Tamai (two clasps). He again served in the Sudan in 1889; was present at the action of Toski, and received a clasp, having been employed with the Egyptian Army from 1 July, 1889, to 17 Aug. 1889. He was promoted to Captain 1 Nov. 1890; was Brigade-Major, Malta, 12 Aug. 1896, to 8 Oct. 1899; became Major 22 Oct. 1899. He served in the South African War, 1899–1902, as D.A.A.G. (Intelligence), 9 Oct. 1899, to 6 Nov. 1899, and D.A.A.G. 7 Nov. 1899, to 11 Sept. 1902. From Oct. 1899 to Oct. 1900, he was with Sir Redvers Buller's Force, and from Oct. 1900, to June, 1902, he was D.A.A.G., Headquarters, South Africa. He was present at the Relief of Ladysmith, including the operations of 17 to 24 Jan. 1900; operations of 5 to 7 Feb. 1900, and action at Vaal Kranz; operations on Tugela Heights (14 to 27 Feb. 1900), and action at Pieter's Hill. Operations in Natal (March to June, 1900), including action at Laing's Nek (6 to 9 June). Operations in the Transvaal, east of Pretoria, July to 29 Nov. 1900, including actions at Belfast (26 and 27 Aug.) and Lydenberg (5 to 8 Sept.). Operations in the Transvaal 30 Nov. 1900, to 31 May, 1902. He was mentioned in Despatches by Sir R. H. Buller, 30 March, 19 June and 9 Nov. 1900 [London Gazette 8 Feb. 1901, and 29 July, 1902]; was given the Brevet of Lieut.-Col. 22 Aug. 1902. He was promoted to Lieutenant-Colonel 9 Jan. 1903, and commanded the 1st Battn. Gordon Highlanders from Jan. 1908, to Aug. 1911. He became Colonel 30 Aug. 1911; was G.S.O., 1st Grade, to the 2nd Division, Aldershot Command, 10 Aug. 1911, to 4 Aug. 1914. On the outbreak of the European War he accompanied the Division to France (G.S.O., 1st Grade, 5 Aug. 1914, to 4 Sept. 1914). On 5 Sept. 1914, he was appointed Temporary Brigadier-General, and to command the 18th Infantry Brigade in the field. He was promoted Major-General 3 June, 1915, for distinguished service in the field, and was appointed to command a division of New Armies 17 June, 1915, and in the same year was created a C.B. In 1917 he was created a K.C.B., having been mentioned in Despatches five times from 1914 to 1917. Sir Frederick Gordon received the Serbian Order of the White Eagle, 2nd Class, with Swords, in 1917. He married Mabel Rose, daughter of the late James Douglas Robinson (late Madras Civil Service) and Mrs. Robinson, and they have one son and one daughter. He was created a Companion of the Distinguished Service Order [London Gazette, 19 April, 1901]: "Frederick Gordon, Major, Gordon Highlanders. For services during the recent operations in South Africa."

KING, ALGERNON D'AGUILAR, Major, was born 28 May, 1862, son of the late Major-General A. H. King, C.B., R.A. He was educated at Cheltenham, and at the Royal Military Academy, Woolwich; was gazetted to the Royal Artillery 25 June, 1882, as Lieutenant; became Captain 23 Sept. 1891. Capt. King served in the South African War from 1899 to 1902; was promoted Major 3 Feb. 1900. He was present at the operations in the Transvaal, Dec. 1900, to June, 1901; in the operations in the Orange River Colony, Dec. 1901, to 31 May, 1902. He was mentioned in Despatches [London Gazette, 4 May, 1900]; received the Queen's Medal with four clasps; the King's Medal with two clasps, and was created a Companion of the Distinguished Service Order [London Gazette, 19 April, 1901]: "Algernon D'Aguilar King, Major, Royal Artillery. In recognition of services during the recent operations in South Africa." The Insignia were presented to him by General Lyttleton, at Newcastle, Natal, 4 Nov. 1901. He became Colonel 30 Oct. 1912, and retired on the 20th June, 1914. On 5 Aug. 1914, he became a Temporary Brigadier-General, and he served in the European War in 1914 in Egypt; in 1915 in the Dardanelles, and in 1916, 1917 and 1918 in Egypt and Palestine, as G.O.C., R.A., Desert Mounted Corps. Colonel King was six times mentioned in Despatches. He was created a C.B. in 1916, and a C.M.G. in 1918. He married, in 1894, Lilian, daughter of Mrs. Hargreaves, of Arborfield Hall, Berks, and they have one daughter, Lilian Cecily.

HEADLAM, JOHN EMERSON WHARTON, Major, was born at Whorlton, County Durham, 16 April, 1864, son of the late Morley Headlam, of Gilmonny Hall, Yorkshire, and Whorlton Grange, Durham, and of Mrs. Headlam, daughter of the late Caulfield Heamish, Esq., of County Cork, Ireland. He was educated at King's College School, and the Royal Military Academy, and joined the Royal Artillery, as Lieutenant, 28 July, 1883; became Captain 22 March, 1892; was Instructor, School of Gunnery, 1 July, 1892, to 30 June, 1897, and was promoted Major 13 Feb. 1900. Major Headlam served in the South African War from 1900 to 1902, as D.A.A.G., for Royal Artillery, Headquarters Staff, in South Africa, 13 Feb. 1900, to 23 June, 1902. He was present in the operations in the Orange Free State from Feb. to May, 1900, including operations at Paardeberg (17 to 26 Feb.); action at Poplar Grove; operations in the Transvaal, May and June, 1900, including actions near Johannesburg, Pretoria and Diamond Hill (11 and 12 June); operations in the Transvaal, east of Pretoria, July to Nov. 1900; operations in Cape Colony, south of Orange River. He was mentioned in Despatches [London Gazette, 16 April, 1901, and 20 July, 1902]; was given the Brevet of Lieutenant-Colonel 22 Aug. 1902; received the Queen's Medal with four clasps; the King's Medal with two clasps, and was created a Companion of the Distinguished Service Order [London Gazette, 19 April, 1901]: "John Emerson Wharton Headlam, Major, Royal Artillery. In recognition of services during the recent operations in South Africa." The Insignia were presented to him by the Duke of Cornwall and York 14 Aug. 1901, at Pieter Maritzburg, Natal. He was D.A.A.G., South Africa, 24 June, 1902, to 3 June, 1903; Assistant Director of Artillery, Headquarters of Army, 1 April, 1904, to 19 July, 1906; was given the Brevet of Colonel 22 Aug. 1905; A.Q.M.G., Headquarters, India, 3 July, 1908, to 4 Dec. 1908; was promoted to Colonel 25 Nov. 1908; Director of Staff Duties and Military Training, General Staff, India, 5 Dec. 1908, to 2 April, 1913; Temporary Brigadier-General 7 Jan. 1911, to 2 April, 1913; was created a C.B. in 1913; Brigadier-General, Commanding Royal Artillery, 5th Division, 1 Oct. 1913. He served during the European War from the beginning, still commanding the 5th Divisional Artillery until 18 Feb. 1915, when he was promoted to Major-General for distinguished services in the field. He was Major-General, Royal Artillery, Headquarters, Second Army, from Feb. to Dec. 1915; Major-General, Royal Artillery, General Headquarters, Dec. 1915, to May, 1916; on Special Duty from May, 1916, including the Allied Mission to Russia in 1917, and the Artillery Mission to the United States in 1918. He was wounded at Le Cateau on 26 Aug. 1914, and was twice mentioned in Despatches. He was created a K.B.E. in 1919. Sir J. E. W. Headlam holds the 1st Class of the Order of St. Anne, with Swords (Russia), the Legion of Honour (Croix de Commandeur), and the American Distinguished Service Medal. He is a Deputy Lieutenant for County Durham. On 26 Dec. 1890, he married Mary, daughter of Perceval Wilkinson, of Mount Oswald, County Durham, and they have two daughters: Margaret Ellen and Mary Phyllis.

John E. W. Headlam.

GORDON, LAURENCE GEORGE FRANK, Major, was born 21 May, 1864, son of the late Colonel G. G. Gordon, C.B., C.V.O. He was gazetted to the Royal Artillery 1 Aug. 1883; was extra A.D.C. to the Viceroy of India 30 Sept. 1886, to 13 April, 1908; became Captain 10 Jan. 1893, and Major 13 Feb. 1900; served in South Africa, 1899–1900; was present at the Relief of Ladysmith, including operations on Tugela Heights (22 to 27 Feb. 1900), and action at Pieter's Hill; during operations in Natal, March to June, 1900, including actions at Laing's Nek 6 to 9 June; during operations in the Transvaal, east of Pretoria, Aug. to 29 Nov. 1900, including actions at Belfast (26 and 27 Aug.), and Lydenberg (5 to 8 Sept.). Took part in the operations in the Transvaal 30 Nov. 1900, to June, 1901; Dec. 1901, to May, 1902; during operations in Orange River Colony in May, 1902. He was mentioned in Despatches [London Gazette, 8 Feb. 1901], and received the Queen's Medal with four clasps, and the King's Medal with two clasps. He was created a Companion of the Distinguished Service Order [London Gazette, 19 April, 1901]: "Laurence George Frank Gordon, Major, Royal Artillery. In recognition of services during the operations in South Africa." (Insignia, etc., sent to the Commander-in-Chief, South Africa. Presented by the Duke of Cornwall and York 14 Aug. 1901.) He was promoted Lieutenant-Colonel 13 Feb. 1910. Lieutenant-Colonel Gordon served in the European War from 1914; became Colonel 17 May, 1915; was mentioned in Despatches, and created a C.B. in 1915. He was Colonel, Royal Artillery, graded A.A.G., 11 Feb. 1916; Temporary Brigadier-General 21 June, 1917. Colonel Gordon married, in 1895, Florence Juliette, daughter of C. A. Walters, and widow of Alexander M'Hinch, C.I.E., and they have one daughter.

SCHOFIELD, HARRY NORTON, Major, served in the Boer War, and was created a Companion of the Distinguished Service Order [London Gazette, 19 April, 1901]: "Harry Norton Schofield, Major, Royal Artillery. In recognition of services during the operations in South Africa." He was granted the Victoria Cross [London Gazette, 30 Aug. 1901], and the award of the Distinguished Service Order was cancelled.

SAVILE, GEORGE WALTER WREY, Major, was born on 14 March, 1860, at Torquay, Devon, son of Lieut.-Colonel John Walter Savile, J.P., and Sarah Emma Savile. He was educated at Marlborough College, and joined the Army on 6 Aug. 1879, as Second Lieutenant; was promoted Lieutenant in 1880; Captain in 1887, and Major in 1900. He served in the South African War from 1899 to 1902, and was present at the Relief of Ladysmith, including the operations of 17 to 24 Jan. 1900, and action at Spion Kop (severely wounded); operations on Tugela Heights (14 to 27 Feb. 1900), and action at Pieter's Hill. Operations in the Transvaal in June, 1900. Operations in Natal, March to June, 1900, including action at Laing's Nek (6 to 9 June). Operations in the Transvaal, east of Pretoria, July to 29 Nov. 1900. Operations in Orange River Colony, June, 1900. Operations in Cape Colony, south of Orange River, in 1899. Mentioned in Despatches [London Gazette, 8 Feb. 1901], received the Queen's Medal with five clasps; the King's Medal with two clasps, and was created a Companion of the Distinguished Service Order [London Gazette, 19 April, 1901]: "George Walter Wrey Savile, Major, Middlesex Regt. In recognition of services during the operations in South Africa." The Insignia were sent to South Africa, and presented there to Major Savile by the Duke of Cornwall and York 14 Aug. 1901. He commanded the 2nd Middlesex Regt. from 1905 to 1909; served in the Great War from 1914 to 1919, as A.A. and Q.M.G., 49th (West Riding) Division, 1914–1915; Officer Commanding Troops, Town and Port, Rouen, 1915–1919; was three times mentioned in Despatches, and created a C.B.E. in 1919. He married Ellen Louisa Parsons, daughter of Colonel A. D. Parsons, 2nd Madras Lancers, in 1891.

FURSE, WILLIAM THOMAS, Major, son of the Venerable the late Archdeacon of Westminster, and Diana Monsell, was born 21 April, 1865. He was educated at Eton, becoming Lieutenant in the Royal Artillery 5 July, 1884. From 1890 to 1893 Lieut. Furse was A.D.C. to Lord Roberts when Commander-in-Chief in India, getting his Captaincy 30 May, 1893. In 1897 he graduated at the Staff College. He served with distinction throughout the South African Campaign, from the 14th Nov. 1899, to the 10th Jan. 1900; he was D.A.A.G., Headquarters of Army. He was then employed in South Africa on Special Service; became D.A.A.G., South Africa, for a short period, and was appointed 15 March, 1900, A.A.G. for Transport, taking part in the operations in the Orange Free State, Feb. to May, 1900, including operations at Paardeberg (19 to 26 Feb.); actions at Poplar Grove, Dreifontein, Vet River (5 and 6 May) and Zand River; during the operations in the Transvaal in May and June, 1900, including actions near Johannesburg, Pretoria, and Diamond Hill (11 and 12 June). He was mentioned in Despatches [London Gazette, 8 Feb. 1901], and in recognition of his services in the Boer War was created a Companion of the Distinguished Service Order [London Gazette, 19 April, 1901]: "William Thomas Furse, Major, Royal Artillery. In recognition of services during the recent operations in South Africa." From the 22nd Jan. 1901, to 14 Oct. 1904, he was employed at Army Headquarters as D.A.A.G. (Mobilization), and D.A.Q.M.G. (Mobilization), and was at Headquarters, acting as D.A.Q.M.G. (Intelligence), and G.S.O., 2nd Grade, from the 1st Oct. 1905, to the 2nd Aug. 1907, and was promoted Brevet Lieutenant-Colonel on 1 Jan. 1908, attaining substantive rank on the 24th Sept. 1910. From 1908 to 1911 he served at the Staff College as D.A.A.G. (G.S.O., 2nd Grade), and G.S.O., 2nd Grade. He became Colonel in Oct. 1911. Colonel Furse served with distinction in the European War from 1914, and was appointed Temporary Brigadier-General on the General Staff 1 Jan. 1915, and created a C.B. He was promoted Temporary Major-General 27th of the following Sept., and Major-General 1 Jan. 1916. He commanded the 9th (Scottish) Division from 27 Sept. 1915, to 4 Dec. 1916, when he was appointed Master-General of the Ordnance. He was created a K.C.B. in Jan. 1917, and promoted to Lieutenant-General 1 Jan. 1919. Lieut.-General Furse married, in 1899, Jean Adelaide, second daughter of the late H. Evans-Gordon, of Prestons, Ightham, and they have two sons and one daughter.

LONGDEN, ARTHUR EDMUND, Major, was born 27 March, 1861. He was gazetted to the Lincolnshire Regt. 7 Feb. 1885, as Lieutenant; transferred to the North Staffordshire Regt. on 23 March, 1887; took part in the operations in Zululand in 1888; was transferred to the Army Service Corps 15 Sept. 1890. He became Captain 3 April, 1892, and subsequently Major. He served in the South African War, and was created a Companion of the Distinguished Service Order [London Gazette, 19 April, 1901]: "Arthur Edmund Longden, Major, Army Service Corps. In recognition of services in the recent operations in South Africa." Major Longden died 20 April, 1901.

ROGERS, JOHN MIDDLETON, Major, was born 24 Aug. 1864, eldest son of the late Capt. John Thornton Rogers, of Riverhill. He was gazetted to the 1st Dragoons, as Lieutenant, 7 Feb. 1885; became Captain 25 Nov. 1891; was on Special Extra-Regimental Employment 7 Dec. 1898. He served in the South African War, 1899–1901; was present at the Relief of Ladysmith, including the action at Colenso; operations of 17 to 24 Jan. 1900, and action at Spion Kop; operations of 5 to 7 Feb. 1900, and action at Vaal Kranz; operations on Tugela Heights 14 to 27 Feb. 1900, and action at Pieter's Hill. Operations in Natal, March to June, 1900. Operations in Orange River Colony, May to 29 Nov. 1900. He was in command of the 1st Dragoons from 15 July to 12 Dec. 1901. Operations in the Transvaal, April to Aug. 1901. Operations in Orange River Colony 30 Nov. 1900, to April, 1901, and Aug. to Dec. 1901. He was mentioned in Despatches (by Sir R. H. Buller, 30 March and 9 Nov. 1900) [London Gazette, 8 Feb. 1901]: received the Queen's Medal with five clasps, and was created a Companion of the Distinguished Service Order [London Gazette, 19 April, 1901]: "John Middleton Rogers, Major, 1st Dragoons. In recognition of services during the operations in South Africa." The Insignia were sent to the Commander-in-Chief in South Africa, and presented by Major-General C. Knox, at Bethulie, 6 Dec. 1901. He had been promoted to Major 23 April, 1900. Lieutenant-Colonel Rogers retired. He is Lieutenant-Colonel, 2nd County of London Yeomanry, and J.P. for Kent. He married, in 1899, Muriel Blanche Gwendoline, daughter of Sir Charles Morrison-Bell, 1st Bart., of Otterburn Hall, Otterburn, and they have three sons and two daughters.

WHITE-THOMSON, HUGH DAVIE, Major, was born 6 Sept. 1866, youngest son of Colonel Sir Robert Thomas White-Thomson, K.C.B., and Fanny Julia, daughter of General Sir H. Ferguson Davie, 1st Baronet. He was educated at Eton, and was gazetted to the Royal Artillery 9 Dec. 1884. In 1895 he became Captain, and was Divisional Adjutant, Royal Artillery, 9 Oct. 1899, to 8 Feb. 1900, being promoted to Major 28 May, 1900. He served in the South African War of 1899–1902; was present at the Relief of Ladysmith, including action at Colenso (slightly wounded) during the operations of 17 to 24 Jan. 1900; operations of 5 to 7 Feb. 1900, and action at Vaal Kranz; taking part in the operations on Tugela Heights (14 to 27 Feb. 1900), and action at Pieter's Hill; during operations in Natal, March to June, 1900, including action at Laing's Nek (6 to 9 June); in the operations in the Transvaal, east of Pretoria, July to 29 Nov. 1900, including actions at Belfast (26 and 27 Aug.) and Lydenburg (5 to 8 Sept.). He was mentioned in Despatches (Sir R. H. Buller, 30 March and 9 Nov. 1900) [London Gazette, 8 Feb. 1901]; received the Queen's Medal with five clasps, and was created a Companion of the Distinguished Service Order [London Gazette, 19 April, 1901]: "Hugh Davie White-Thomson, Major, R.A. In recognition of services during the operations in South Africa." (Insignia presented by Major-General A. Wynne, C.B., 1 Nov. 1901.) In 1910 he was created a K.B.E. He was promoted to Lieutenant-Colonel 29 Nov. 1911, and Colonel 29 Nov. 1915. He served during the European War, and became Temporary Brigadier-General 12 Feb. 1915, and served as Brigadier-General, Royal Artillery, Cavalry Corps, British Expeditionary Force, 12 Feb. 1915, to 9 Sept. 1915; Brigadier-General, Royal Artillery, 27th Division, British Expeditionary Force, 10 Sept. 1915; Brigadier-General, Royal Artillery, 27th Division, Mediterranean Expeditionary Force, Egyptian Expeditionary Force, 21 Jan. 1916, to 19 Sept. 1916; Brigadier-General, Royal Artillery, 12th Army Corps, Egyptian Expeditionary Force, 20 Sept. 1916, to 18 Jan. 1919; Brigadier-General, Royal Artillery, 23 March, 1919. He was three times mentioned in Despatches; created a C.B., 1915, and a C.M.G. in 1917. Sir Hugh White-Thomson married, in 1893, Ella Louisa Agatha (who died in 1894), daughter of the late Rev. J. S. Ruddach.

LONG, ARTHUR, Major, was born 26 Feb. 1866, son of James and Elizabeth Long, of Henlow, Bedfordshire. He was educated at the Modern School, Bedford, joining the 1st Battn. Leinster Regt., from the Militia, 16 Nov. 1887, and being transferred to the Army Service Corps 10 Feb. 1890. He became Lieutenant 16 Nov. 1890, and Captain 1 Jan. 1893; served in the South African War, as D.A.A.G. (Special Service), 9 Oct. 1899, to 25 March, 1900, including actions at Elandslaagte, Rietfontein and Lombard's Kop. He served in the defence of Ladysmith, Dec. 1899, to 25 March, 1900, including action of 6 Jan. 1900; became Major, Army Service Corps, 1 Aug. 1900; was D.A.A.G., Assistant Director of Supplies, South Africa, 27 March, 1900, to 5 March, 1902; on the Staff, General Hunter's Division, under General Sir Ian Hamilton. He took part in the operations in the Transvaal, east of Pretoria, July to 29 Nov. 1900, including action at Lydenburg 5 to 8 Sept. Operations in the Transvaal, west of Pretoria, July to 29 Nov. 1900, including action at Zilikat's Nek. Operations in Cape Colony, north of Orange River, including action at Ruidam. Operations in Cape Colony, Dec. 1900, to 31 May, 1902. He was slightly wounded; was mentioned in Despatches (Sir G. S. White, 2 Dec. 1899, and 23 March, 1900) [London Gazette, 8 Feb. 1901]; received the Queen's Medal with four clasps; the King's Medal with two clasps, and was created a Companion of the Distinguished Service Order [London Gazette, 19 April, 1901]: "Arthur Long, Major, A.S.C. In recognition of services during the operations in South Africa." The Insignia were presented by Major-General A. Wynne, C.B., 19 Nov. 1901. He was Assistant Director of Transport, South Africa, 25 June, 1904, to 31 March, 1905; was promoted to Lieutenant-Colonel, Army Service Corps, Feb. 1908; and to Colonel, Army Service Corps, 4 Oct. 1911; District Barrack Officer, Southern Command, 14 July, 1913, to 15 Oct. 1913; Assistant Director of Supplies and Transport, Southern Command, 16 Oct. 1913, to 4 Aug. 1914. He served in the European War from 1914; was Deputy Director of Supplies 5 Aug. 1914, to 31 Jan. 1915; Deputy Director of Supplies and Transport 1 Feb. 1915, to 15 Jan. 1916; Temporary Brigadier-General from 7 Jan. 1916; Director of Supplies and Transport in Macedonia and the Black Sea from Jan. 1916. He was mentioned in Despatches by Sir A. Murray 1 June, 1916. He served with the Salonika Forces, Greece, 26 Sept. 1916. He was created a C.M.G. in 1916; a C.B. in 1917, and a K.B.E. in 1919. Sir Arthur Long was mentioned in Despatches eight times during the war. He married Maud Eleanor, second daughter of the Rev. Canon S. Davenport Kelly, of Manchester.

FANSHAWE, ROBERT, Major, was born 5 Nov. 1863, son of the Rev. H. L. Fanshawe. He was educated at Marlborough, and was commissioned in the Oxfordshire Light Infantry 25 Aug. 1883; was Adjutant, Oxfordshire Light Infantry, 1 July, 1887, to 31 Oct. 1891, serving with this regiment, principally in India, up to the outbreak of the South African War. He was promoted to Captain 15 April, 1892, and served on the North-West Frontier, 1897–98 (Indian Frontier Medal and two clasps). He was on Special Service, Natal, 4 Nov. 1899, to 22 Dec. 1899; was Staff Officer to the Assistant Inspector-General, Lines of Communication, South Africa, 28 Dec. 1899, to 6 April, 1900; Staff Officer, Mounted Infantry Corps, 7 April, 1900, to 26 Jan. 1902. He was wounded at Paardeberg. From 1901 to the end of the war he commanded a Mobile Column. He was present at the Relief of Kimberley. Operations in the Orange Free State, Feb. to May, 1900, including operations at Paardeberg (17 to 26 Feb.; wounded 18 Feb.); actions at Poplar Grove, Karee Siding, Houtnek (Thoba Mountain), Vet River (5 and 6 May) and Zand River. Operations in the Transvaal in May and June, 1900, including actions near Johannesburg, Pretoria and Diamond Hill (11 and 12 June). Operations in the Transvaal, west of Pretoria, July to 29 Nov. 1900, including actions at Venterskroon (7 and 9 Aug.). Operations in Orange River Colony (May to 29 Nov. 1900), including actions at Wittebergen (1 to 29 July) and Bothaville. Operations in Cape Colony, south of Orange River, 1899–1900. Operations in the Transvaal, Orange River Colony and Cape Colony, 30 Nov. 1900, to 31 May, 1902. He was twice mentioned in Despatches; given the Brevet of Lieutenant-Colonel 22 Aug. 1902; received the Queen's Medal with five clasps; the King's Medal with two clasps, and was created a Companion of the Distinguished Service Order [London Gazette, 19 April, 1901]: "Robert Fanshawe, Major, Oxford Light Infantry. In recognition of services during the operations in South Africa." The Insignia, etc., were sent to the Commander-in-Chief, South Africa, and presented in South Africa. He was D.A.A.G., 4th Division, 2nd Army Corps, 11 Sept. 1902, to 11 Dec. 1903; became Lieutenant-Colonel 18 Sept. 1907; commanded the Oxfordshire and Buckinghamshire Light Infantry from 1907 to 1911; was given the Brevet of Colonel 5 March, 1908; became Colonel 18 Sept. 1911; was G.S.O., 1st Grade, 1st Division, Aldershot Command, 25 Oct. 1911, to 4 Aug. 1914. He served in the European War from 1914; was Temporary Brigadier-General from 20 Sept. 1914, to 29 May, 1915, commanding 6th Infantry Brigade; became Major-General 3 June, 1915. He commanded 48th South Midland Division, British Expeditionary Force, and British Armies in France, 30 May, 1915, to 24 June, 1918, and commanded the 69th Division, 1918–19. He was created a C.B. in 1915, and a K.C.B. in 1917, and was eight times mentioned in Despatches; is G.S.O.1. His favourite recreations are polo and pig-sticking.

TAGART, HAROLD ARTHUR LEWIS, Major, was born 20 June, 1870, at Old Sneyd Park, Gloucestershire, son of Francis Tagart, Esq., J.P., D.L., of Old Sneyd Park, Gloucestershire, and 199, Queen's Gate, S.W., and of Isabella Ongley Hopson, daughter of Capt. Ongley Hopson, 23rd Light Dragoons. He was educated at Eton, and at Trinity College, Cambridge; was gazetted to the 15th Hussars, as Second Lieutenant, 3 Dec. 1890; became Lieutenant 25 May, 1892, and Capt. 13 June, 1896; was A.D.C. to H.R.H. the Duke of Connaught, G.O.C. at Aldershot, 1897. He served in the South African War, as Brigade-Major, Cavalry Brigade, 19 Feb. 1900, to 30 Aug. 1901; was promoted to Major 17 Sept. 1900. He was present at the operations in the Orange Free State, May, 1900, including actions at Houtnek (Thoba Mountain), Vet River (5 and 6 May) and Zand River. Operations in the Transvaal, May and June, 1900, including action near Johannesburg. Operations in Cape Colony, south of Orange River, 1900. He was invalided home with enteric fever. For his services in this campaign he was mentioned in Despatches [London Gazette, 16 April, 1901]; received the Queen's Medal with three clasps, and was created a Companion of the Distinguished Service Order [London Gazette, 19 April, 1901]: "Harold Arthur Lewis Tagart, Major, 15th Hussars. In recognition of services during the operations in South Africa." The Insignia were presented by the King 3 June, 1901. He was Brigade-Major, Cavalry Brigade, Aldershot, 21 Dec. 1901, to 30 Sept. 1902; was D.A.A.G., Presidency District, Calcutta, 2 July, 1904; Brigade-Major, Meerut Cavalry Brigade, 20 Feb. 1905, to 1 Nov. 1906. Major Tagart was promoted to Lieutenant-Colonel 10 Oct. 1911. From 1914 he served in the European War; as D.A. and Q.M.G., Cavalry Corps, from 10 Oct. 1914; Temporary Brigadier-General from 10 Oct. 1914, to 24 Oct. 1915, commanding a brigade on the Aisne, and became Major-General 25 Oct. 1915. He was made a Commander of the Legion of Honour, and was created a C.B. in 1915; was D.A. and Q.M.G., 3rd Army, 1915 and 1916, and was invalided home in 1916; D.A.G., Home Forces, 1916 to 1918, when he was again invalided. He retired 18 March, 1919. Major-General Tagart was created a K.C.M.G. in 1918; mentioned in Despatches five times. Sir H. A. L. Tagart's favourite recreations are farming, hunting and shooting. He married (1st), in 1900, Lady Mary Stuart Keppel (who died in 1903), sixth daughter of the 7th Earl of Albemarle, and (2ndly), in 1908, Josephine Mary Charlotte, daughter of the late Hubert Washington Hibbert, Esq.

HARRISON, ESMÉ STUART ERSKINE, Major, was born 21 Sept. 1864, son of Lieut.-General Broadley Harrison, late 11th Hussars. He was educated at Wellington College, and was gazetted to the 11th Hussars 9 May, 1885. He became Captain 4 Jan. 1892, and took part in the operations on the North-West Frontier of India, 1897–98 (Medal with clasp). He was Adjutant, 11th Hussars, 8 March, 1898, to 27 Nov. 1898. He was promoted to Major, and served in the South African War, 1899 to 1900; was mentioned in Despatches twice; received the Queen's Medal with five clasps, and was created a Companion of the Distinguished Service Order [London Gazette, 19 April, 1901]: "Esmé Stuart Erskine Harrison, Major, 11th Hussars. In recognition of services during the operations in South Africa." The Insignia were presented to him by the G.O.C., Egypt. Major Harrison's favourite recreations were hunting, shooting, fishing and polo. He died 1 Nov. 1902.

BOYCE, WILLIAM GEORGE BERTRAM, Major, was born 27 May, 1868, second son of the late Rev. W. G. Boyce, of Ballinoulart, County Wexford. He was gazetted to the Royal Berkshire Regt., as Second Lieutenant, 14 Sept. 1887, becoming Lieutenant, Royal Berkshire Regt., 2 April, 1891; Army Service Corps 1 April, 1892, and Captain, Army Service Corps, 7 July, 1893. He was Staff Captain, Cork District, 1 July, 1899, to 8 Oct. 1899. From 9 Oct. 1899, to 10 Jan. 1901, he was D.A.A.G., 2nd Division, South African Field Force. He was present at the Relief of Ladysmith, including the action at Colenso; operations of 17 to 24 Jan. 1900, and action at Spion Kop; operations of 5 to 7 Feb. 1900, and action at Vaal Kranz; operations on Tugela Heights (14 to 27 Feb. 1900), and action at Pieter's Hill. Operations in the Transvaal, in June, 1900. Operations in Natal (March to June, 1900), including action at Laing's Nek (6 to 9 June). Operations in Cape Colony, south of Orange River, 1899–1900. He was mentioned in Despatches (Sir R. H. Buller, 30 March and 9 Nov. 1900) [London Gazette, 8 Feb. 1901]; received the Queen's Medal with five clasps, and was created a Companion of the Distinguished

Service Order [London Gazette, 19 April, 1901]: "William George Bertram Boyce, A.S.C. In recognition of services in the recent operations in South Africa." He was promoted to Major 1 Jan. 1901, and Lieutenant-Colonel 12 Jan. 1909. From 4 July, 1909, to 14 Aug. 1913, Lieut.-Colonel Boyce was Commandant, Army Service Corps Training Establishment; became Colonel 30 Oct. 1912; from 15 Aug. 1913, to 14 Dec. 1913, he was Assistant Director of Supplies and Transport, Aldershot Command, and from 15 Dec. 1913, to 4 Aug. 1914, he was Assistant Director of Supplies and Transport, Eastern Command. He served in the European War from 1914; was Deputy Director of Transport 5 Aug. 1914, to 29 Nov. 1914; became Temporary Brigadier-General 30 Nov. 1914, and was Director of Transport, British Expeditionary Force, 30 Nov. 1914, to 13 May, 1918, and Director of Transport, British Armies in France, from 16 May, 1918. He was seven times mentioned in Despatches; promoted Major-General 3 June, 1917; created a C.B., 1915; a C.M.G., Jan. 1919, and a K.C.M.G. in 1919. He was awarded the Order of St. Stanislaus, 2nd Class, with Swords, and Legion of Honour (Officier). In 1895 Sir William Boyce married Maud, eldest daughter of the late Capt. J. C. Boyce, King's Own Regt., of Wentworth, Merrion Road, Dublin.

RYAN, CHARLES MONTGOMERIE, Major, was born 12 Aug. 1867, son of the late Lieut.-Colonel E. M. Ryan, Bengal Staff Corps. He was gazetted to the Royal Dublin Fusiliers 22 Aug. 1888, and transferred to the Devonshire Regt. 10 April, 1889, and to the A.S.C. 15 Sept. 1890; became Captain 1 Dec. 1894, and Major 1 Jan. 1901. He served in the South African War, 1899 to 1902, as D.A.A.G., 6 Sept. 1899, to 7 May, 1902, and was present at the defence of Mafeking, including the action of 26 Dec. 1899, and 12 May, 1900. Operations in the Transvaal, July to 29 Nov. 1900. Operations in Cape Colony 30 Nov. 1900, to 31 May, 1902. He was mentioned in Despatches [London Gazette, 8 Feb. 1901], received the Queen's Medal with two clasps; the King's Medal with two clasps, and was created a Companion of the Distinguished Service Order [London Gazette, 19 April, 1901]: "Charles Montgomerie Ryan, Major, Army Service Corps. In recognition of services during the operations in South Africa." Insignia, etc., sent to Commander-in-Chief, South Africa, and presented by G.O.C., Cape Colony, 19 Nov. 1901 From 1 Nov. 1903, to 31 Oct. 1906, he was Assistant Director of Supplies, Woolwich Dockyard; Deputy Assistant Director of Quartering, Headquarters of Army, 20 April, 1908, to 19 April, 1911; was promoted to Lieutenant-Colonel 15 Oct. 1910. He served in the European War from 1914; as A.A. and Q.M.G., 7th Division, B.E.F., 28 Oct. 1914, to 9 Nov. 1914; as Assistant Director of Supplies, B.E.F., 21 March, 1915, to 13 July, 1915; became Colonel 15 Oct. 1915; was Deputy Director of Supplies, B.E.F., 14 July, 1915, to 13 Sept. 1918; Deputy Director of Supplies, B.E.F., 14 Sept. 1918; became Temporary Brigadier-General 14 Sept. 1918. He was created a C.M.G. in 1916, and a C.B.E. in 1919. He married, in 1891, Ethel, daughter of Capt. Hyde Pearson.

OUSELEY, RALPH GLYNN, Major, was born 5 May, 1866; joined the Royal Artillery, as Lieutenant, 17 Feb. 1886; was promoted Captain 7 April, 1896; was made Major 16 Jan. 1901; served in South Africa, 1899–1902; during operations in Natal, 1899, including actions at Rietfontein and Lombard's Kop; was present at the defence of Ladysmith, including action of 6 Jan. 1900; during operations in Natal, March to June, 1900, including action at Laing's Nek (6 to 9 June); during operations in the Transvaal, east of Pretoria, July to 29 Nov. 1900, including action at Belfast (26 to 27 Aug.) and Lydenberg (5 to 8 Sept.). He was mentioned in Despatches [London Gazette, 8 Feb. 1901], and received the Queen's and King's Medals with four clasps; was created a Companion of the Distinguished Service Order [London Gazette, 19 April, 1901]: "Ralph Glynn Ouseley, Major, Royal Artillery. In recognition of services in the recent operations in South Africa." He acted as Magistrate in Pretoria (Transvaal), 19 July, 1902, to 15 Sept. 1902; was employed on Special Extra-Regimental Duties under the Civil Government, Transvaal, from 16 Sept. 1902, to 30 Sept. 1904. He became Lieutenant-Colonel 5 May, 1913. He served in the European War from 1914; was wounded, mentioned in Despatches, created a C.M.G. in 1915, and a C.B. in 1916; was Temporary Brigadier-General, R.A., 17th Division, British Expeditionary Force, British Armies in France, 3 Jan. to 8 Aug. 1916; Brigadier-General, R.A., 59th Division, Home Forces; British Armies in France, 7 Nov. 1916, to 21 April, 1917; Brigadier-General, R.A., 61st Division, British Armies in France, 22 April, 1917. He married, in 1899, Peggy Harriet O'Donnell.

BOOTH, WILLIAM HENRY, Major, was born 6 July, 1862, son of Major-General W. Booth, late Royal Artillery; was educated at Wellington College, and the Royal Military College, Sandhurst; entered The Buffs, as Lieutenant, 10 May, 1882; became Captain, 1893; Major 16 Feb. 1901; served in the South African War, 1899–1900, on the Staff (as A.D.C. to Lieutenant-General, Infantry Division, 4 Dec. 1899, to 4 March, 1901); was present at the Relief of Kimberley; during operations in the Orange Free State, Feb. to May, 1900, including operations at Paardeberg (17 to 26 Feb.), and actions at Poplar Grove and Dreifontein; during operations in the Transvaal, east of Pretoria; during operations in Orange River Colony (May to 29 Nov. 1900); in the operations in Cape Colony, south of Orange River, 1899–1900; during operations in Cape Colony, north of Orange River, 1900. He was mentioned in Despatches [London Gazette, 8 Feb. 1901], and created a Companion of the Distinguished Service Order [London Gazette, 19 April, 1901]: "William Henry Booth, Major, East Kent Regt. In recognition of services during the operations in South Africa." (Insignia presented by the King, 3 June, 1901.) He retired from the East Kent Regt. 23 June, 1906, and was made J.P., Herefordshire. Major Booth was created an O.B.E. in 1918.

SLOMAN, HENRY STANHOPE, Capt., was born 29 Aug. 1861, son of the late Major J. Sloman. He was educated at Sherborne, and entered the East Surrey Regt. 10 May, 1882, as Lieutenant; served in the Sudan in 1885, with Mounted Infantry; was present at Hasheen and Tamai (Medal with clasp, Khedive's Star); was made Captain 20 Nov. 1888, and Adjutant, East Surrey Regt., 11 Dec. 1890 to 10 Dec. 1894. He served in the Sudan, 1897–98, including the expedition to Shendy and the battles of the Atbara and Khartum (Despatches twice [London Gazette, 25 Jan. 1898, and 30 Sept. 1898], British Medal, 4th Class Medjidie, Khedive's Medal and three clasps). He was employed on Special Service in South Africa 4 March, 1900, to 8 April, 1900, and as Assistant Provost-Marshal (graded D.A.A.G.), 29 April, 1900, to 7 Dec. 1900. He was promoted to Major 11 Dec. 1901. He was present at the operations in the Orange Free State, March to May, 1900, including action at Vet River (3 and 6 May) and Zand River. Operations in the Transvaal in May and June, 1900, including actions near Johannesburg, Pretoria and Diamond Hill (11 and 12 June). Operations in Orange River Colony (July to 29 Nov. 1900), including actions at Wittebergen (1 to 29 July). Operations in Orange River Colony 30 Nov. 1900, to Jan. 1901. Operations in Cape Colony, Jan. 1901, to 31 May, 1902. He was mentioned in Despatches [London Gazette, 16 April, 1901], received the Queen's Medal with four clasps, the King's Medal with two clasps, and was created a Companion of the Distinguished Service Order [London Gazette, 19 April, 1901]: "Henry Stanhope Sloman, Capt., East Surrey Regt. In recognition of services in the recent operations in South Africa." (Insignia presented 13 July, 1901.) He was D.A.A.G. (Intelligence), 8 Nov. 1900, to 9 Aug. 1902; D.A.A. and Q.M.G., Bermuda, from 1 Nov. 1905, to 11 Dec. 1906; was promoted to Lieutenant-Colonel 14 Jan. 1909, and Colonel 21 Sept. 1912; became G.S.O., 2nd Grade, War Office, 3 May, 1911, to 20 Sept. 1912; G.S.O., 1st Grade, War Office, 21 Sept. 1912, to 1 Nov. 1914; G.S.O., 1st Grade, 2 Nov. 1914, to 7 Jan. 1915. He was A.A.G., Scottish Command, 8 Jan. 1915, to 16 April, 1915, and G.S.O., 1st Grade, 17 April, 1915, to 17 Jan. 1916; Brigade-Commander (graded A.A.G.), 19 Feb. 1916. He was created a C.M.G. in 1918, and retired, with the rank of Brigadier-General, 2 Sept. 1918. General Sloman married, in 1903, Mary Charlotte, daughter of the late Admiral Sir A. L. Douglas.

CODDINGTON, HERBERT ADOLPHE, Capt., was born at Masuri, India, on the 19th Sept. 1864, eldest son of the late Colonel Fitzherbert Coddington, Bengal Staff Corps, and Julia Richard de Valmency (French). Lieut. South Yorks Regt. 6 Feb. 1884; Lieut. Royal Irish Fusiliers 2 April, 1884; promoted Captain, 1890; served as Adjutant, 1890–94, and as Volunteer Adjutant, 1894–99, and received Queen Victoria's Jubilee Medal in 1899; promoted Major, 1902; served throughout South African War, 1899–1902; operations in Natal and Orange Free State (mentioned in Despatches twice; received the Brevet of Lieutenant-Colonel in 1902; Queen's Medal and three clasps, King's Medal and two clasps); was created a Companion of the Distinguished Service Order [London Gazette, 19 April, 1901]: "Herbert Adolphe Coddington, Capt., Royal Irish Fusiliers. In recognition of services during the operations in South Africa." (Insignia, etc., sent to Natal, and presented at Pietermaritzburg by the Duke of Cornwall and York 14 Aug. 1901.) Was Staff Captain on Natal Lines of Communication, 1900–1; D.A.A.G. on Headquarters, Natal Command, 1901–3, and Chief Staff Officer, Natal, 1903–4. Retired from Royal Irish Fusiliers, March, 1904. He was employed under the Chilworth Gunpowder Company in the manufacture of high explosives for the Army and Navy, 1908–12. Recalled to military duty, to a special appointment under the Intelligence Branch of the War Office, and graded as a G.S.O.2, dated 3 Aug. 1914 (mentioned in London Gazette, Feb. 1917). He married, in Feb. 1903, Bertha Violet Mary, the only child of the late Mr. G. C. Kempthorne Bennett, of Maldivia, Wynberg, Cape Colony; no issue.

VALLANCEY, HENRY D'ESTAMPES, Capt., was born 16 Dec. 1861. He entered the Army, being gazetted as Second Lieutenant to the 29th Foot 22 Jan. 1881, and to the Argyll and Sutherland Highlanders, and subsequently to the 91st Regt. of Foot, becoming Lieutenant, Argyll and Sutherland Highlanders 1 July, 1881. He was D.A.C.G., Commissariat and Transport Staff, 12 July, 1886, to 10 Dec. 1888; took part in the operations in Zululand, 1888; became Captain 26 Feb. 1890; was attached Army Service Corps for a period ending in 1891; was Commandant, Base Depôt, British Troops, 8 Aug. 1897, to 15 Feb. 1898, serving on the N.W. Frontier of India (Malakand); Medal and clasp. Capt. Vallancey served in the South African War of 1899–1902, as Assistant Provost-Marshal, Natal, 9 Oct. 1899, to 23 March, 1900; as Brigade-Major, South Africa, 29 March, 1900, to 14 Feb. 1901; as D.A.A.G., South Africa, 15 Feb. 1901, to 30 Nov. 1901; from 1 Dec. 1901, he was in command of the Pietersburg Light Horse. He was present at the operations in Natal, including the actions at Talana and Lombard's Kop; defence of Ladysmith; operations in Natal, March to June, 1900, including action at Laing's Nek; operations in the Transvaal, east of Pretoria, July to Nov. 1900, including actions at Belfast (26 and 27 Aug.) and Lydenberg (5 to 8 Sept.); operations in the Transvaal, Nov. 1900, to May, 1902. He was mentioned in Despatches (Sir R. H. Buller, 13 Sept. and 9 Nov. 1900 [London Gazette, 8 Feb. 1901]); received the Queen's Medal with four clasps, the King's Medal with two clasps, and was created a Companion of the Distinguished Service Order [London Gazette, 19 April, 1901]: "Henry d'Estampes Vallancey, Capt., Argyll and Sutherland Highlanders. In recognition of services during the operations in South Africa." The Insignia, Warrant and Statutes were sent to the Commander-in-Chief in South Africa, and presented by Colonel S. H. Harrison at Pietersburg. He was Staff Officer, Transvaal and Orange River Colony, 10 Aug. 1902, to 11 March, 1903; was promoted to Major, 27 June, 1903; was D.A.A.G., India, 16 Nov. 1905.

GODLEY, HARRY CREWE, Capt., was born at Fermoy, County Cork, Ireland, 30 Oct. 1861, son of Major H. R. C. Godley, 28th Regt., and Mrs. Frances Godley. He was educated at the Grammar School, Chard, Somerset, and was gazetted to a Regular Commission from the Militia 30 Jan. 1884; was Adjutant, 3rd Volunteer Battn. Norfolk Regt., from 15 Sept. 1892, to 14 Sept. 1897. He served in the South African War of 1899 to

1902, and was in South Africa from Oct. 1899, to Jan. 1900, during which time he was mentioned in Despatches [London Gazette, 16 April, 1901], and was created a Companion of the Distinguished Service Order [London Gazette, 19 April, 1901]: "Harry Crewe Godley, Capt., Northumberland Fusiliers. In recognition of services during the operations in South Africa." The D.S.O. was awarded for the excellent services he rendered during the campaign, when he was left in command of a post with two companies of the Northampton Regt., to command Enslin Railway Station, on the (2nd or) 8th Sept. 1899, and defended it for nine hours against a force of from 900 to 1,000 mounted Boers with two guns, under Commandant Prinsloo, who made a surprise attack in order to destroy the line and capture the stores which were being guarded; and, notwithstanding the very superior force of the burghers, the two companies of the Northampton Regt. successfully resisted the attack until relieved by reinforcements from Lord Methuen, when the enemy retreated. He returned to England Jan. 1900, was granted sick leave, and appointed Deputy Assistant Adjutant-General, Jersey, during 1902, and died at Ryde, Isle of Wight, 19 Feb. 1907, after a service of 23 years and 21 days. He always took a great interest in the regimental sports, and his company was first for the "Evelyn Wood" Competition, 1898, and second the year following. He was very sociable and popular with all ranks, very active, a good rider, fond of horses, and very keen on hunting. Major Godley married, at Monkstown, Dublin, 23 April, 1892, Elizabeth Mary Annesley; they had three sons: Francis William Crewe, born 25 Jan. 1893; Gerald Annesley George, born 15 April, 1897; Richard Harry Fetherston, born 31 May, 1902; and a daughter, Elizabeth Adeline Faith.

WOLLEY-DOD, OWEN CADOGAN, Capt., was born 2 May, 1863, sixth son of Rev. Charles Wolley-Dod, of Edge Hall, Malpas, Cheshire, by his wife, Frances Lucy (*née* Parker). He was educated at Eton and Sandhurst; graduate of the Staff College, 1899; he joined the Lancashire Fusiliers as Lieutenant 25 Aug. 1883; promoted Captain 20 Nov. 1892, and Major 4 Sept. 1901; transferred to the Sherwood Foresters as Second-in-Command 24 Aug. 1904; promoted Lieut.-Colonel 11 Feb. 1908, and Colonel 4 Oct. 1911; was Adjutant of 2nd Lancashire Fusiliers from 15 March, 1892, to 14 March, 1896; Brigade-Major, Aldershot, 24 May, 1902, to 26 Sept. 1904; Second-in-Command, R.M.C., Sandhurst, 3 May, 1912, to 31 Jan. 1914; G.S.O., First Grade, 5th Division, Curragh, Ireland, 1 Feb. 1914. He served in the Sudan Campaign, 1898, with the 2nd Lancashire Fusiliers (Despatches); in the occupation of Crete, 1898; in the South African War, 1899 to 1901, with 2nd Lancashire Fusiliers, and as A.P.M., 5th Division (wounded; Despatches). In his Despatch after the Spion Kop action, Sir Charles Warren said, referring to the fight at Venter's Spruit on 20–21 Jan. 1900: "Lancashire Fusiliers . . . Capt. O. C. Wolley-Dod, though severely wounded, remained in action, and led his company into action the next day." He was made a Companion of the Distinguished Service Order [London Gazette, 19 April, 1901]: "Owen Cadogan Wolley-Dod, Capt., Lancashire Fusiliers. In recognition of services during the operations in South Africa." The Insignia were presented by King Edward VII. 3 June, 1901. During the war, 1914 *et seq.*, he officiated as A.Q.M.G., Irish Command, from 5 Aug. 1914; was G.S.O., First Grade, War Office, from 16 Sept. 1914, to 19 Jan. 1915; G.S.O., First Grade, 29th Division, from 20 Jan. 1915, to 4 June, 1915, and commanded the 86th Brigade, 29th Division, from 5 June, 1915, to 17 Aug. 1915, when he was invalided home (wounded; Despatches twice). Of the landing in Gallipoli on 25 April, 1915, Sir Ian Hamilton said, in his Despatch of 20 May, 1915: "'W' Beach.—Brigadier-General Hare had been wounded earlier in the day, and Colonel Wolley-Dod, General Staff, 29th Division, was sent on shore to take command at 'W' Beach and organize a further advance." He was made a Companion of the Order of the Bath [London Gazette, 2 June, 1915]; appointed an Inspector of Territorial Forces 27 Dec. 1915, and a Brigade Commander 25 Nov. 1917.

Owen C. Wolley-Dod.

RENNIE, JOHN GEORGE, Capt., was born 25 Feb. 1865. He was educated at Cheltenham, and entered the Black Watch 30 Jan. 1886, as Lieutenant, becoming Captain 22 March, 1893. Capt. Rennie was Adjutant, Royal Highlanders, 29 May, 1893, to 28 May, 1897. He served as A.D.C. to the Brigadier-General commanding the 1st Brigade, British Division, Sudan Expeditionary Force, 13 July, 1898, to 29 Sept. 1898, and was present at the Battle of Khartum. He was mentioned in Despatches [London Gazette, 30 Sept. 1898]: awarded the 4th Class Medjidie, the Medal, the Egyptian Medal and clasp. He served in the South African War, 1899–1902, as A.D.C. to Major-General, Infantry Brigade, South Africa, 9 Oct. to 11 Dec. 1899, and took part in the advance on Kimberley, including the action at Magersfontein; operations in the Orange Free State, Feb. to May, 1900, including operations at Paardeberg; actions at Poplar Grove, Dreifontein and Vet River; operations in Orange River Colony, including actions at Rhenoster River, Wittebergen and Witpoort; operations in Cape Colony, south of Orange River, 1899; operations in the Transvaal in Nov. 1901; operations in Orange River Colony, Nov. 1900, to Sept. 1901, and Dec. 1901, to May, 1902; operations on the Zululand Frontier of Natal in Oct. 1901. He was mentioned in Despatches [London Gazette, 16 April, 1901]; received the Queen's Medal with five clasps, the King's Medal with two clasps, and was created a Companion of the Distinguished Service Order [London Gazette, 19 April, 1901]: "John George Rennie, Capt., Black Watch. In recognition of services during the operations in South Africa." The Insignia were sent to the Commander-in-Chief in South Africa, and presented by General Lyttelton at Newcastle, Natal, 4 Nov. 1901. Major Rennie, who retired 3 June, 1905, was Adjutant, 5th (V.B.) Highland Light Infantry, from 1902. He is married, and has one son and one daughter.

THOMPSON, ROLAND WYCLIFFE, Capt., was born 4 Nov. 1864, fourth son of the late General C. W. Thompson. He joined the Loyal North Lancashire Regt. 7 Feb. 1885; was promoted to Captain; served in South Africa, 1899–1902, on the Staff, and was present at the Relief of Kimberley; operations in Orange Free State Feb. to May, 1900, including operations at Paardeberg; actions at Poplar Grove and Dreifontein; operations in the Transvaal, Oct. 1900; operations in the Orange River Colony, May to 29 Nov. 1900, including actions at Bothaville and Caledon River (27 to 29 Nov.); operations in Cape Colony, Jan. to Feb. 1900; operations in Orange River Colony 30 Nov. 1900, to Feb. 1901, and March, 1901, to April, 1902; operations in Cape Colony, Feb. to March, 1901, and April to 31 May, 1902. He was mentioned in Despatches [London Gazette, 16 April, 1901]; received the Queen's Medal with four clasps, the King's Medal with two clasps, and was created a Companion of the Distinguished Service Order [London Gazette, 19 April, 1901]: "Roland Wycliffe Thompson, Capt., Loyal North Lancashire Regt. In recognition of services during the recent operations in South Africa." (Insignia sent to the Commander-in-Chief, South Africa, and presented by Major-General C. Knox, at Bethulie, 6 Dec. 1901.) He became Lieut.-Colonel 1 June, 1910, and retired 4 June, 1910. Lieut.-Colonel Thompson married, in 1911, the widow of Commander Hill-Lowe, R.N.

MINCHIN, CHARLES FREDERICK, Capt., was born 22 Sept. 1862, eldest son of Charles Nicholls Minchin and Mary J. Minchin, *née* Lugard. He was educated at Cheltenham College; the United Services College, Westward Ho! and the Royal Military College, Sandhurst, and was gazetted to the Bedfordshire Regt. as Lieutenant 10 May, 1882, and transferred to the Indian Staff Corps 3 Feb. 1885. He joined the 1st (Prince Albert Victor's Own) Punjab Cavalry in 1886; served in the Hazara Campaign in 1888, and received the Medal and clasp. He was selected for the Indian Political Service in 1891; became Captain 10 May, 1893; served in the Chitral Campaign in 1895, with the Relief Force (Medal with clasp): was employed in the Indian Political Service as Attaché, Calcutta; was Assistant Political Officer, Khyber; Political Agent, Zhob, 1897. In 1897 he was Second-in-Command of an expedition sent by the British West Charterland Company, London, to Lake Ngami country in South Africa. He served with the South African Field Force 23 Dec. 1899, to 5 Feb. 1902, first with Thorneycroft's Mounted Infantry, and later as Lieut.-Colonel, 18th Battn. Imperial Yeomanry, 1 May, 1901, to 6 Feb. 1902, and of a mobile column 17 July to 22 Dec. 1901, and was present at the Relief of Ladysmith, including operations of 5 to 7 Feb. 1900, and action at Vaal Kranz; operations on Tugela Heights (14 to 27 Feb.) and action at Pieter's Hill; operations in Natal, March to June, 1900, including actions at Laing's Nek (6 to 9 June); operations in the Transvaal, east of Pretoria, July to 29 Nov. 1900; operations in the Transvaal 30 Nov. to Dec. 1900; operations in Cape Colony, Dec. 1900, to March, 1901, also during the operations in the Orange River Colony from Dec. 1900, to March, 1901, to Feb. 1902. He was mentioned in Despatches [London Gazette, 8 Feb. 1901 (Sir R. H. Buller, 19 June and 9 Nov. 1900) and London Gazette, 3 Dec. 1901]; received the Queen's and King's Medals with eight clasps, and was created a Companion of the Distinguished Service Order [London Gazette, 19 April, 1901]: "Charles Frederick Minchin, Capt., Indian Staff Corps. In recognition of services during the operations in South Africa." The Insignia were sent to the Commander-in-Chief in South Africa, and presented by Colonel Ternan at Spitzkop 8 Jan. 1902. He acted as Political Agent in Bikanir in 1902, and as Consul-General, Khorassan and Seistan, 1904. He was transferred to the Supernumerary List after two years in permanent civil employment 30 March, 1904, and in 1906 was made Superintendent of Gazetteer Revision, Baluchistan, and acted as Political Agent, Dir Swat, Chitral, Bagnelkhand and N.W. Frontier Province, 1907–8. He became Lieutenant-Colonel 10 May, 1908; was Deputy Commissioner, Bannu, 1908–11, and in 1911 became Divisional and Sessions Judge, Derajat. He holds the Coronation Medal and the Hessian Order of Philip. Lieut.-Colonel Minchin married, in 1905, Violet Winifred, daughter of Henry Ellis, of Charters House, Branksome Park, Bournemouth, and they have one daughter, Mary Violet Ellis Minchin.

Charles F. Minchin.

JERVIS, THE HON. ST. LEGER HENRY, Capt., was born 7 Sept. 1863, at Godmersham Park, Canterbury, Kent, fifth son of the 3rd Viscount St. Vincent and Lucy, daughter of Baskervyle Glegg, of Withington Hall, Chester. He was commissioned in the King's Royal Rifle Corps 6 May, 1885, and became Captain in 1893; served in South Africa, 1899–1902, on the Staff (as A.D.C. to Major-General, Infantry Brigade, to 15 Dec. 1899, and 9 July to 17 Nov. 1900; Brigade-Major 18 Nov. 1900, to 7 Nov. 1901; D.A.A.G. from 8 Nov. 1901); was present at Relief of Ladysmith, including action at Colenso (severely wounded). He was twice mentioned in Despatches, 8 Feb. 1901, and 29 July, 1902; received the Queen's Medal with four clasps, the King's Medal with two clasps, and was created a Companion of the Distinguished Service Order [London Gazette, 19 April, 1901]: "The Hon. Henry St. Leger Jervis, Capt., King's Royal Rifle Corps. In recognition of services during the operations in South Africa." The

Insignia were sent to the Commander-in-Chief in South Africa and presented there. He was promoted to Major 21 Feb. 1903; was made D.A.A.G., South Africa, 1901–4; retired from the King's Royal Rifle Corps, 12 Oct. 1904. On the outbreak of the war he became Temporary Lieut.-Colonel, 3rd Battn. Norfolk Regt. He married, in 1905, Hilda Maud, daughter of Thomas Collin, and they have two daughters.

YARDE-BULLER, THE HON. HENRY, Capt., was born 2 Nov. 1862, fourth son of the 1st Baron Churston and Charlotte Chandos-Pole, of Radbourne Hall, Derbyshire. He was educated at Radley, and was gazetted to the Rifle Brigade as Lieutenant 12 Nov. 1884; was A.D.C. (extra) to the Governor of Bombay 19 May, 1887, to April, 1888, and extra A.D.C. to G.O.C., Aldershot, 26 Nov. 1896, to 31 Dec. 1897. He was promoted Captain 15 Oct. 1893; served in the Waziristan Expedition, 1894–95 (Medal and clasp); in the Sudan Expedition, 1898, including the Battle of Khartum (Medal and clasp; Queen's Medal). After the Sudan Campaign he served with the Rifle Brigade in Crete, in the troublous times there in 1898–99, where he was appointed Governor of the district of Temenos. He served in the South African War of 1899–1902; was present at the Relief of Ladysmith, including action at Colenso; during operations of 17 to 24 Jan. 1900, and action at Spion Kop; during operations of 5 to 7 Feb. 1900, and action at Vaal Kranz; in the operations on Tugela Heights (14 to 27 Feb. 1900), and action at Pieter's Hill; during operations in Natal, March to June, 1900, including action at Laing's Nek (6 to 9 June); during operations in the Transvaal, east of Pretoria, July to 29 Nov. 1900, including actions at Belfast (26 and 27 Aug.) and Lydenberg (5 to 8 Sept.). He was mentioned in Sir R. H. Buller's Despatches, 30 March and 9 Nov. 1900 [London Gazette, 8 Feb. 1901], and received the Queen's Medal with five clasps, and the King's Medal with two clasps; was D.A.A.G., Intelligence, 27 June, 1900, to 2 Sept. 1902, and was created a Companion of the Distinguished Service Order [London Gazette, 19 April, 1901]: "The Honourable Henry Yarde-Buller, Capt., Rifle Brigade. In recognition of services during the operations in South Africa." The Insignia were sent to the Commander-in-Chief in South Africa, and presented by the Duke of Cornwall and York 14 Aug. 1901. The Hon. H. Yarde-Buller was specially employed (Intelligence), Headquarters of Army, 8 Oct. 1903, to 31 March, 1904; as Staff Captain, Headquarters of Army, 1 April, 1904, to 1 Feb. 1905; was Military Attaché, Copenhagen, Stockholm and Christiania, 12 March, to 16 May, 1906, and Military Attaché, Brussels, The Hague, Copenhagen, Stockholm and Christiania, 17 May, 1906, to 25 June, 1907. He was created Commander, Second Class, Dannebrog, 1906; Commander, Second Class, Epee; Commander, Second Class, St. Olaf, and Commander, Second Class, Leopold. On 25 June, 1907, he was promoted to Lieut.-Colonel, and in 1908 was created an M.V.O. He was Assistant Military Secretary to the G.O. Commanding-in-Chief the Forces in Ireland, 13 March, 1910, to 9th May, 1912, and he was promoted to Colonel 19 July, 1911. From 10 May, to 28 June, 1912, he was specially employed at the War Office, and he was Military Attaché (G.S.O.) at Paris, Madrid and Lisbon, 29 June, 1912, to 30 Dec. 1915. Shortly after the outbreak of the European War, in Sept. 1914, he was appointed Chief of the Military Mission to the French Army, which appointment he held from Sept. 1914, till Dec. 1916. He was Temporary Brigadier-General from Sept. 1914, and was created Commander of the Légion d'Honneur, 1916. From 28 Dec. 1916, he was Military Attaché (General Staff Officer), Christiania and Stockholm. He was created a C.B. in 1917, and a K.B.E. in 1919. Sir H. Yarde-Buller married, in 1902, Adelaide Maude Sophia, daughter of the late Colonel Charles Meeking, of Richings Park, Colnbrook.

Hon. H. Yarde-Buller.

WILSON, HENRY HUGHES, Capt., was born 5 May, 1864, son of James Wilson, D.L., J.P., of Currygrane, Edgeworthstown, Ireland. He was educated at Marlborough College, and is a Graduate of the Staff College. On 12 Nov. 1884, he was gazetted to the Royal Irish Regt. from the Militia, and he was transferred to the Rifle Brigade 26 Nov. 1884. He served in the Burma Campaign, 1885–87; was wounded, and served again in Burma, 1887–89 (Medal with two clasps). He was promoted Captain 6 Dec. 1893; was at the Staff College, 1892–94; was Staff Captain (Intelligence Division), Headquarters of Army, 24 June, 1895, to 31 Aug. 1897. From 1 Sept. 1897, to 8 Oct. 1899, he was Brigade-Major, 2nd Brigade, Aldershot. He served in the South African War, as Brigade-Major, Light Brigade, 9 Oct. 1899, to 31 Aug. 1900; as D.A.A.G., Army Headquarters, 1900 to 1901. He was present at the Relief of Ladysmith, including action at Colenso; during the operations of 17 to 24 Jan. 1900, and action at Spion Kop; during actions of 5 to 7 Feb. 1900, and action at Vaal Kranz; in the operations on Tugela Heights 14 to 27 Feb. 1900, and action at Pieter's Hill; during operations in Natal (March to June, 1900), including actions at Laing's Nek (6 to 9 June); during the operations in the Transvaal, east of Pretoria, July to 29 Nov. 1900, including operations in Cape Colony, south of Orange River, 1900; during the operations in the Transvaal, Dec. 1900, to May, 1901. For his services in this campaign he was four times mentioned in Despatches (Sir R. H. Buller's, 9 March and 9 Nov. 1900) [London Gazette, 8 Feb. and 16 April, 1901]; received the Queen's Medal with five clasps; was given the Brevet of Lieutenant-Colonel 2 Dec. 1901, on promotion to Major, and was created a Companion of the Distinguished Service Order [London Gazette, 19 April, 1901]: "Henry Hughes Wilson, Capt., Rifle Brigade. In recognition of services during the operations in South Africa." He was specially employed, Headquarters of Army, 3 Jan. 1901, to 23 Feb. 1902; was promoted to Lieutenant-Colonel 24 Feb. 1902; commanded the 9th Provisional Battn., 1902–3; was D.A.A.G. for Military Education and Training, Army Headquarters, 1 April to 31 May, 1903; A.A.G. Military Education and Training, Headquarters of Army, 1 June, 1903, to 31 Dec. 1906, and from 1 June, 1903, to 31 Dec. 1906, he was Assistant Director of Staff Duties, War Office. On the 2nd Dec. 1904, he was given the Brevet of Colonel. He became Colonel 1 Jan. 1907, and was created a C.B. in 1908; was Commandant (Brigadier-General, General Staff), Staff College, 1 Jan. 1907, to 31 July, 1910; Director of Military Operations, War Office, 1 Aug. 1910, to 4 Aug. 1914; promoted to Major-General 1 Jan. 1913. He was Sub-Chief of Staff, B.E.F., 1914; Chief Liaison Officer with French G.H.Q.; commanded IVth Army Corps, 1915–18; was created a K.C.B., 1915; promoted to Lieutenant-General 16 March, 1917; was appointed Military Representative, Supreme War Council at Versailles; Chief of the Imperial General Staff and a member of the War Cabinet, Feb. 1918; promoted to General 3 June, 1918, and to Field-Marshal, 1919. Sir Henry Wilson was created a Baronet in 1919; appointed Colonel, Royal Irish Rifles, 11 Nov. 1915.

Henry Hughes Wilson.

As the above record shows, Sir Henry Wilson is an Irishman. "An impression exists that Sir Henry's talents were not recognized earlier owing to his attitude towards the Ulster trouble before the war. Whether this is really so perhaps only Mr. Asquith can really tell. As an Irishman born, Sir Henry rather justifiably regarded the suppression of the Ulster 'rebellion' by force as a terrible mistake. It was probably owing to his hesitancy that the whole thing fizzled, and also that the British Army was saved the loss of dozens of good officers. It is not generally known that every day he received letters from officers who preferred to resign their commissions rather than kill their fellow-countrymen. Instead of sending their resignations in, he kept them in his pocket until Ulster had simmered down, and then quietly tore them up."

Educated at Marlborough, he years afterwards thus addressed the O.T.C. of his old school: "We belong to the finest empire the world has ever seen, and you young fellows have the future of that Empire in your hands. There is an old saying which I am fond of quoting. It is the soldier's creed, and it is my advice to you: Be kindly to children, be courteous to women, be loyal and true to your comrades."

Some of his speeches make interesting reading. At Australia House he said: "I have been a soldier for 39 years, and I have always understood that we in the Army were soldiers because we could not pass exams or make money. We weave education into the life of the soldier, so that when the men of the Army, the Navy and the Air Force go back into civil life they will not only be good soldiers, sailors and airmen, but good citizens."

The O.T.C., he said, had produced a number of great gentlemen and great soldiers. He himself, the Field-Marshal remarked, was a man of no knowledge, and very little experience for a great number of years. He told his audience that in Germany they were "trying to get a bigger outlook, but having let go the handle of the parish pump, they appear to have fallen into the horse-pond. . . . There never was such a story as the story of the British Empire. As an Irishman, I tell you English people that if you are wise you will continue to paint the salt-water red, and subject everybody who bathes in it to a fine of 2s. 6d. for trespass."

We are told that when the Prince of Wales was made a Freeman of the Mercers' Company, and Sir Henry Wilson made a speech, the latter said he felt like an old West Country parson who had to hold two services, one in his own church and one in a church over the moor. On arriving at the church over the moor, he said he had forgotten to bring a most admirable sermon he had written. "Luckily," he said, "as I came across the moor I remembered a beautiful story, which I will tell you in place of the sermon." Then he said, "Damn. I have forgotten that too."

Henry Wilson joined the Militia Battalion of the Royal Irish Rifles, of which regiment he subsequently became honorary Colonel, and was gazetted first to the Royal Irish Regt., and later to the Rifle Brigade, serving with his regiment in the Burmese Expedition of 1886–88. In June, 1887, he was wounded, but making a quick recovery, saw the campaign through to a finish. He took a course at the Staff College, Camberley, from 1892 to 1894, and on passing out (with honours) served with the Intelligence Division as a Staff Captain for three years, until, in Sept. 1897, he went down to Aldershot as Brigade-Major of the 2nd Infantry Brigade. There he remained until the outbreak of the Boer War, when he went out as Brigade-Major of the Light Brigade in General Buller's Corps. The Brigade perpetually harassed the Boers, and Wilson's good work as Brigade-Major, allied to his "inimitable quality of seeing things for himself," attracted the notice of Lord Roberts, who appointed him D.A.A.G. on his Staff. Wilson remained with his new Chief until the latter left South Africa to take over the post of Commander-in-Chief in London. As soon as Lord Roberts was installed as Commander-in-Chief, he brought Lieut.-Colonel Wilson, as he then was, up to the War Office to assist him in winding up the business of the South African Campaign. This occupied his time for nearly a year, when, anxious to have a turn of regimental duty, he was given command of a provisional battalion for a year, after which he went back to the War Office, and was A.A.G. under the late General Sir Henry Hildyard, who was Director-General of Military Education and Training. After holding this post for three years, he had, in 1917, "the great honour of becoming the Commandant of the Staff College he had entered 25 years previously. Of the many officers who passed through his hands during the three years he was there, few will ever forget Sir Henry's perpetual admonition to 'see everything you are about to undertake.' . . . For thirty years he has pursued the policy of seeing things for himself." He tried to prepare these officers for the war he knew would come.

After the war had broken out he was thus described: "Tall and spare of figure, with calculation and determination written all over his face, he has few illusions as to the best way to win the war. As far back as 1911, in addressing Eton College O.T.C., he told them that the foreign nations were drilling and preparing for an early war. In 1913 he told the students of the London University that a huge empire such as ours could not be maintained without a big army as well as a navy. It has been left to the present war to prove the truth of his statement. A man who harbours no illusions is most likely to serve his country in a critical hour best."

During his tenure of office at Camberley he was created a C.B., and in 1910 he came back to the War Office as Director of Military Operations, a post in which he did some of his best work and which he held up to the outbreak of war. As at Camberley, he tried to have everything prepared for the European War, which, in common with Lord Roberts and many other soldiers, he had foreseen, and for which, so far as in him lay, he was determined to be forearmed. In Lord Roberts's book about National Service, that great soldier foretold, not only that war would come, but that the Germans would attack France by breaking through Belgium. Many turned a deaf ear to the Field-Marshal's warnings, but not so Sir Henry Wilson, and it was largely owing to his long-sightedness that the Expeditionary Force was ready when the hour struck. A newspaper says of Wilson's work as Director of Military Operations: "It was while he was at the head of this directorate that he made his mark as an administrator, rendering valuable service to Lord Haldane when he was organizing the Expeditionary Force. After the Agadir incident he went, at Lord Haldane's request, with Lord French to Paris, and carried on the 'conversations,' of which we have heard so much, with the French General Staff, and which prepared the way for the share taken by our Expeditionary Force in the campaign of 1914. Sir Henry speaks French as easily as English, and while in France was very helpful to Lord French, who has a very slight acquaintance with the French language."

It has been truly said that the British Army contains no more unassuming soldier than Sir Henry Wilson. His name came before the public but little up to about the beginning of 1918. In the early days of the war he crossed the Channel as understudy to Sir Archibald Murray, who was Chief of the General Staff in France during the first year of the campaign. Early in 1915 Wilson handed over his duties as Deputy Chief of the Staff to General Maurice, and took up the duties of Chief Liaison Officer at French G.H.Q. In this capacity he was a great success, as he got on so well with the French. Indeed, he became a great favourite, and we are told that he won the complete confidence of General Joffre and his Staff. He was created a K.C.B. in 1915.

From 1915 to 1917 he commanded the IVth Army Corps, opposite Vimy Ridge, where he gained a great reputation, and from 17 March to 13 July, 1917, he was Chief of the British Mission to the French Army.

Sir Henry Wilson and General De Castelnau went as military members of the diplomatic mission to Petrograd. Then Lord Milner and Lord Revelstoke and their companions saw only too plainly the crisis which was coming, and the mission ended abortively owing to the outbreak of the Russian Revolution. On his return from Petrograd Wilson resumed his duties at French Army Headquarters, and there remained until he was appointed, in Sept. 1917, to succeed General Wolfe Murray as General Officer Commanding-in-Chief, Eastern District. This appointment surprised many people at the time, as, after his conspicuous Staff services during the war, it was generally supposed that he would be given a high command at the front. His new appointment lasted from 1 Sept. to 1 Nov. 1917, and then his presence in London at the crisis in the Italian campaign enabled Sir Henry Wilson to take up his new duties as British Military Representative at the Supreme War Council at Versailles (2 Nov. 1917, to 18 Feb. 1918).

A newspaper said of him at this time: "This distinguished soldier, whose activities have been chiefly diverted into Staff channels, none the less possesses all those qualities of leadership which eminently fit him for the position to which he has been called. The functions of the new Committee and its relations to the unified War Council, which has been created at the same time, have not been publicly defined; but its rôle will naturally be consultative and advisory rather than executive. Without interfering with the conduct of military operations, the Committee, working collectively and harmoniously, will examine the situations as they occur, and co-ordinate strategy as between the four Commanders-in-Chief who have charge of the operations in the Western theatres of war. By this means will the Allied belligerent Powers secure that unity of direction which has been so marked a feature of the enemy's strategical combinations. With his recent experience of liaison work, and with his extensive knowledge of the strategical side of war, Sir Henry Wilson will prove to be a tower of strength on the Committee."

In airing his views on the composition of the War Council, a journalist remarks: "The men chosen are all true and tried, even though, with the exception of Irish Wilson, they are not precisely of an age at which one looks for brilliant offensive strategy. Wilson is 53, and one of our brightest and best, with plenty of actual fighting experience, as well as the highest reputation for Staff work."

Another writer says: "Modesty is proverbially a trait in the character of great British soldiers. From Wellington down to Haig all our military chiefs have been men to whom advertisement of any kind was loathsome. But probably this effacement of self never had a more rigorous exponent than the soldier who is to represent Great Britain at the Allied War Council, with its headquarters in Paris. Lieut.-General Sir Henry Hughes Wilson is the name of the British representative, and it is safe to say that few people outside the Army have ever heard of him. How this comparatively unknown Irishman comes to be appointed to such an enormously important post will probably mystify many civilians. But there is no mystery to the men who have soldiered with him. Wilson is a soldier born and bred, a man, who, after 33 years' struggle and study in his profession, is about to gain his reward. It is rarely, indeed, in the military history of Great Britain that an infantryman succeeds in reaching high strategical office. Kitchener was a Royal Engineer; French and Haig are both cavalrymen. Wilson is the product of a line regiment, for on being commissioned in 1884 he was posted to the Royal Irish Rifles. He did not stay with them long, however, for a few months after he was transferred to the Rifle Brigade. . . . Exactly what effect the appointment of an infantry officer to a position of strategical control will have, only the future can tell The enormously important factor which the line regiments represent in all battles makes Sir Henry's presence at the Council all the more valuable. The Prime Minister, it is said, possesses the greatest confidence in Sir Henry Wilson's grip of the war situation. . . . The chance of his lifetime came with dramatic suddenness during the height of the Austro-German advance on Italy, when he was notified that he was relieved of his command and was to proceed to Italy with Mr. Lloyd George, Sir William Robertson and General Smuts. . . . Perhaps Wilson's most outstanding quality is his determination to see things for himself. This is a virtue which commends him enormously to the officers and men who do the actual fighting. How greatly Sir Henry believes in this policy and how he has devoted himself to his profession is proved by the fact that for 25 years prior to the war he spent practically all his holidays cycling up and down what is now the Western front. Perhaps the reason was to be found in that uncanny instinct for war which most Irishmen possess; perhaps it was an intelligent premonition of the fact that Flanders—for centuries the cockpit of Europe—would not belie its past history. Certain it is that Sir Henry, often accompanied by his wife, spent all his leisure time pedalling round and about the roads which are now given over to the tramp of armed men and never-ending transport. French officers even now are amazed at the wonderful knowledge which Sir Henry possesses. Passchendaele, the centre of some of the most fierce fighting, is as well known to him as his native village of Currygrane, in Ireland."

Another extract is from an appreciation with the doubtfully complimentary title, "Sir Henry Wilson (By One Who Knows Him)":

"The selection of Lieut.-General Sir Henry Wilson to be the British member of the Central Military Committee which has been appointed to secure unity of strategical direction in the Western theatre of war, will meet with general approval, for there is no one quite so well qualified as he is by his antecedent career to fill a position which will require the exercise of great tact, in addition to the knowledge of war which Sir Henry Wilson possesses in so high a degree. An Irishman, fifty-three years of age, of fine physique and soldierly bearing, he has had a distinguished military career, during which he has acquired an accumulated experience of war in all its branches."

On 19 Feb. 1918, Sir Henry became Chief of the Imperial General Staff and a member of the War Cabinet, in succession to Sir William Robertson. The "Times" of 18 Feb. 1918, gives a sketch of Sir Henry's services up to that date. "To this brief record of a remarkable career," continues the writer, "it may be added that the new Chief of the Imperial General Staff is before everything else an enthusiast for his profession. A devoted friend and admirer of Lord Roberts, he shared to the full the conviction that the German War was coming, and that its result would depend on the 'preparedness' of the British people. As Director of Military Training and Commandant of the Staff College he played a large part in creating the new school of Staff Officers, who have created in turn the organization of the great armies now in the field. As Director of Military Operations he was mainly responsible for the perfection of the arrangements which brought the B.E.F. into action. With the French he has always been an immensely popular figure. With General Foch, in particular, he has always worked on terms of special intimacy. The Versailles Council seemed to provide him with exactly the scope for which he was fitted, and it is a matter of real regret that he should be lost at so early a stage to that new and promising body. Only the vital importance of supporting it thoroughly in London compensates for the transfer of his services. He of all men can be trusted to see that it has every chance of development. For the rest, Sir Henry Wilson is a tall, loose-limbed Irishman, with a keen sense of humour and a broad outlook on life, a thinker and teacher rather than a leader of men, recognized everywhere as one of the shrewdest brains in the Army. . . . He . . . has still to be proved in one of the highest places which the Army has to offer."

Another writer speaks of "the charm with which he enmeshes you in less than ten-minutes' talk. Subtle and genial, with an armour-piercing sense of humour—a blend of Leo XIII. and Bernard Shaw—no man was ever less of a dour Ulsterman."

He married, in 1891, Cecil Mary, daughter of the late George Cecil Gore Wray, J.P., of Ardnamona, Donegal.

ROSS, CHARLES, Capt., was born 10 March, 1864, third son of the late General Sir C. C. Ross, K.C.B.; was educated at Stubbington, and gazetted to the Norfolk Regt. 12 Nov. 1884; was promoted to Captain. He was attached to the Egyptian Army, 1893–1904, and was at the Staff College, 1897–99. Capt. Ross served in the South African War, 1900–02, on the Staff, and was present at the Relief of Kimberley. Operations in the Orange River Colony, Feb. to May, 1900, including operations at Paardeberg (17 to 26 Feb.), actions at Poplar Grove, Houtnek (Thoba Mountain) and Zand River. Operations in the Transvaal, in May and June, 1900, including actions near Johannesburg, Pretoria, and Diamond Hill (11 and 12 June). Operations in the Orange River Colony, May to 29 Nov. 1900, including actions at Wittebergen (1 to 26 July, 1900) and Witpoort. Operations in the Orange River Colony, 30 Nov. 1900, to June, 1901. Operations in

Cape Colony, June, 1901, to Jan. 1902. Operations in the Transvaal, Jan. to May, 1902. He was mentioned in Despatches [London Gazette, 16 April, 1901], received the Queen's Medal with five clasps, the King's Medal with two clasps, and was created a Companion of the Distinguished Service Order [London Gazette, 19 April, 1901]: "Charles Ross, Capt., Norfolk Regt. In recognition of services during the operations in South Africa." The Insignia were sent to the Commander-in-Chief in South Africa, and presented by Major-General A. Wynne, C.B., 19 Nov. 1901. He was an Instructor at Woolwich, then three years an Instructor at Sandhurst, and was Instructor at the Staff College; became Colonel 4 Oct. 1911. Colonel Ross served in the European War from 1914; was mentioned in Despatches, created a C.B., and became Temporary Major-General 15 Nov. 1915; commanded 6th Division, B.E.F., from Nov. 1915, to Sept. 1917; was transferred to the 69th Division, which he commanded until reverted to unemployment, Nov. 1918. He has written "Representative Government and War," 1903; "The Problem of National Defence," 1907; and "An Outline of the Russo-Japanese War, 1904 and 1905," 1912. Colonel Ross married, in 1905, Clara Marion, daughter of the late Rev. J. E. L. Schreiber and widow of Capt. S. Horton, R.A.

RADCLYFFE, CHARLES EDWARD, Capt., was born 24 Dec. 1864, son of C. E. Radclyffe, J.P., Little Park, Wickham, Hants, and Constance, daughter of Colonel and the Lady Maria Saunderson. He was educated at Eton; entered the Rifle Brigade as Lieutenant (from Militia), 25 Nov. 1885; served in Burmese War, 1885–87 (Burmese Medal, two clasps); was severely wounded; served again, 1887–89; became Captain, 12 Dec. 1894. He married, in 1898, Theresa, daughter of John S. Mott, Esq., of Barningham Hall, Norfolk, and they have one son, Charles Edward, born in 1911. He served in the South African War, 1899–1902; was on the Staff; was present at the Relief of Ladysmith, including action at Colenso; during operations of 17 to 24 Jan. 1900; during operations of 5 to 7 Feb. 1900, and action of Vaal Kranz; in the operations on Tugela Heights (14 to 27 Feb. 1900) and action of Pieter's Hill; during operations in Natal (March to June, 1900), including action at Laing's Nek (6 to 9 June); during operations in the Transvaal, east of Pretoria, July to 29 Nov. 1900; during operations in the Transvaal 30 Nov. 1900, to July, 1901 (wounded, mentioned in Despatches twice [London Gazette, 8 Feb. and 10 May, 1900]: Queen's Medal, six clasps; King's Medal, two clasps, and created a Companion of the Distinguished Service Order [London Gazette, 19 April, 1901]: "Charles Edward Radclyffe, Capt., Rifle Brigade. In recognition of services during the operations in South Africa." The Insignia were presented by the Duke of Cornwall and York 14 Aug. 1901. He was Assistant Provost-Marshal 1 July, 1901, to 5 March, 1902; became Major, Rifle Brigade, 16 April, 1903; Lieutenant-Colonel 1 Dec. 1909, when he took command of the 4th Battn. Rifle Brigade in Egypt, Khartum and India. On the outbreak of the European War he was appointed to the command of the 11th Battn. Essex Regt., 18 Sept. 1914, and took them to France. He was twice wounded at the Battle of Loos, the second time very severely, and was reported "wounded and missing" that day (26 Sept. 1915), and is now presumed killed.

ANDERSON, ERNEST CHESTER, Capt., was born 26 Nov. 1863. He became Captain, Royal Army Medical Corps, 30 Jan. 1895. He married 1899, Aimée, daughter of the late Capt. Harris. Capt. Anderson served in the South African War in 1901, being present at the Relief of Kimberley; during operations in the Orange Free State, Feb. to May, 1900, including operations at Paardeberg 17 to 26 Feb., taking part in the actions at Poplar Grove and Dreifontein. He was mentioned in Despatches [London Gazette, 8 Feb. 1901], and received the Queen's Medal with four clasps, the King's Medal with two clasps, and created a Companion of the Distinguished Service Order [London Gazette, 19 April, 1901]: "Ernest Chester Anderson, Capt., Royal Army Medical Corps. In recognition of services during the operations in South Africa. He became Major 30 Jan. 1904, and died on 22 Dec. 1913, at Golden Hill, Isle of Wight.

HUTTON, GILBERT MONTGOMERIE, Capt., was born 13 June, 1865, son of Capt. F. W. Hutton, F.R.S., late 23rd Royal Welsh Fusiliers. He was educated at Christchurch College, and Canterbury College, New Zealand (B.A.); became Lieutenant, Royal Engineers, 3 Feb. 1886, and Captain 22 Oct. 1895. He served in the Chin Lushai Expedition (Medal and clasp); in South Africa, 1899–1901; was present at the Relief of Ladysmith, including action at Colenso; during operations of 17 to 24 Jan. 1900, and action at Spion Kop; during operations of 5 to 7 Feb. 1900, and action at Vaal Kranz; during operations on Tugela Heights (14 to 27 Feb. 1900), and action at Pieter's Hill; during operations in Natal (March to June, 1900), including action at Laing's Nek (6 to 9 June); during operations in the Transvaal, east of Pretoria, including actions at Belfast (26 and 27 Aug.) and Lydenberg (5 to 8 Sept.). During operations in the Transvaal, Nov. 1900, to May, 1901, and Oct. 1901, to Feb. 1902; during operations in Cape Colony, July to Oct. 1901. He was mentioned in Sir R. H. Buller's Despatches (30 March and 9 Nov. 1900) [London Gazette, 8 Feb. 1901], and received the Queen's Medal with six clasps, and the King's Medal with two clasps, and was created a Companion of the Distinguished Service Order [London Gazette, 19 April, 1901]: "Gilbert Montgomerie Hutton, Capt., Royal Engineers. In recognition of services during the operations in South Africa." He was decorated for services in Natal and the Transvaal as Staff Officer, Royal Engineers. Capt. Hutton's recreations were "anything that's going." He died 19 Oct. 1911.

HIGGINSON, CECIL PICKFORD, Capt., was born 8 April, 1866, son of the late James Pickford Higginson, of Fir Vale, Wavertree, near Liverpool; was educated at Repton, and is a Graduate of the Staff College. He joined the Shropshire Light Infantry 10 Nov. 1886; became Capt. 27 Nov. 1895; was Adjutant, Shropshire Light Infantry, 19 Sept. 1897, to 21 Jan. 1901; was promoted to Major 2 Aug. 1897. Major Higginson served in the South African War, as Brigade-Major 22 Jan. 1901, to 31 May, 1901, and as D.A.A.G. 1 June, 1901, to 10 July, 1901 (slightly wounded). He was present during operations in the Orange Free State, Feb. to May, 1900, including operations at Paardeberg (17 to 26 Feb. 1900); during actions at Poplar Grove, Dreifontein, Houtnek (Thoba Mountain), Vet River (5 and 6 May) and Zand River; during operations in the Transvaal in May and June, 1900, including actions near Johannesburg and Pretoria; in the operations in the Transvaal, east of Pretoria, July to 29 Nov.; during operations in the Transvaal, west of Pretoria, July to 29 Nov. 1900, including actions at Elands River (4 to 16 Aug.); also during operations in Orange River Colony, May to 29 Nov. 1900, including action at Rhenoster River; during operations in Cape Colony, south of Orange River, 1899–1900. He took part in the operations in the Transvaal 30 Nov. 1900, to 31 May, 1902. He was mentioned in Despatches [London Gazette, 8 Feb. 1901, and 29 July, 1902], received the Queen's Medal with four clasps, the King's Medal with two clasps, and was created a Companion of the Distinguished Service Order [London Gazette, 14 April, 1901]: "Cecil Pickford Higginson, Capt., Shropshire Light Infantry. In recognition of services during the operations in South Africa." (Insignia presented by the Duke of Cornwall and York 14 Aug. 1901.) He was placed on the list of officers considered qualified for Staff employment in consequence of service on the Staff in the Field. He was employed with the Rand Rifles from 1 April, 1902, to 9 Feb. 1903; was Brigade-Major, 2nd Brigade, 1st Army Corps, Aldershot, 10 Feb. 1903, to 21 Jan. 1906; D.A.A.G. and Q.M.G., China, 9 Feb. 1909, to 3 April, 1913; was promoted to Lieutenant-Colonel 19 Aug. 1913. He served in the European War, as Lieutenant-Colonel Commanding the 1st Battn. King's Shropshire Light Infantry, from 1914; became G.S.O., 2nd Grade, 3 June, 1915, to 2 Sept. 1915, and G.S.O., 1st Grade, 3 Sept. 1915; was wounded, mentioned in Despatches, and created a C.M.G., 1915. He married, in 1904, Maud, second daughter of the late Lieut.-Colonel Goslin, of Rathvilly, County Carlow, and they have two sons and one daughter.

ASTELL, SOMERSET CHARLES GODFREY FAIRFAX, Capt., was born on the 15th July, 1866, son of the late General C. E. Astell (and grandson of W. Astell, M.P.), and of H. D., daughter of F. Spaight, of Derry Castle, Tipperary. He was educated at St. Columba College, Dublin, and joined the service 4 May, 1887, becoming Capt. 17 Dec. 1895. He served in the Sudan (Dongola), 1896, and received two medals, the Queen's and the Khedive's. He served in the South African War in 1900; was Intelligence Officer, Wakkerstroom, April, 1901; in charge of the Johannesburg Criminal Investigation Department 6 June, 1900, to 25 Feb. 1901; was present at the Relief of Kimberley, during operations in the Orange Free State, Feb. to May, 1900; during actions at Karee Siding, Vet River (5 and 6 May) and Zand River; during operations in the Transvaal in May, 1900, including actions near Johannesburg. He was mentioned in Despatches [London Gazette, 16 April, 1901], and received the Queen's Medal with three clasps, and the King's Medal with two clasps, and was created a Companion of the Distinguished Service Order [London Gazette, 19 April, 1901]: "Somerset Charles Godfrey Fairfax Astell, Capt., North Staffordshire Regt. In recognition of services during the operations in South Africa. (Insignia, etc., sent to the Commander-in-Chief, South Africa, and presented by the Duke of Cornwall and York 14 Aug. 1901). Capt. Astell was Adjutant, 4th North Staffordshire Quarters, Lichfield, 1902–3. He married, in 1903, Frederica Beatrice, only child of James Frederick Roberts, Esq., C.M.G., F.R.G.S., and Mary Beatrice, second daughter of Sankey Gardner, Esq., J.P., of Eaglesbush, Neath. Capt. Astell's favourite recreations were hunting, shooting and fishing. He died 24 March, 1917.

Somerset C. G. F. Astell.

M'MAHON, NORMAN REGINALD, Capt., was born in London 24 Jan. 1866, youngest son of the late General Sir Thomas M'Mahon, Bart., C.B., and Lady M'Mahon. He was educated at Eton and gazetted to the Royal Fusiliers as Lieutenant, May, 1885. He accompanied the Burmese Expedition of 1886–87 (Medal with clasp); was Adjutant of his battalion from Feb. 1890, to Feb. 1894, and became Captain in Nov. 1896. Capt. M'Mahon served in the South African War, 1899–1901, during which time he was on the Staff as A.D.C. to a Major-General; commanded an infantry brigade from Oct. 1899, to April, 1900, and was Brigade-Major from April to Aug. 1900; and as D.A.A.G. from Feb. to June, 1902, and was present at the Relief of Ladysmith, including the action at Colenso, at the operations on the Tugela Heights, in Natal, Cape Colony (severely wounded), Transvaal and Orange River Colony, and at the action at Pieter's Hill. He was mentioned in Despatches [London Gazette, 8 Feb. 1901]; received the Queen's Medal with five clasps, the King's Medal with two clasps, and was created a Companion of the Distinguished Service Order [London Gazette, 19 April, 1901]: "Norman Reginald M'Mahon, Capt., Royal Fusiliers. In recognition of services during the recent operations in South Africa." The Insignia, Warrant, etc., were sent to the Commander-in-Chief in South Africa, and presented in South Africa. He was promoted to Major in Nov. 1901. From June, 1905, to June, 1909,

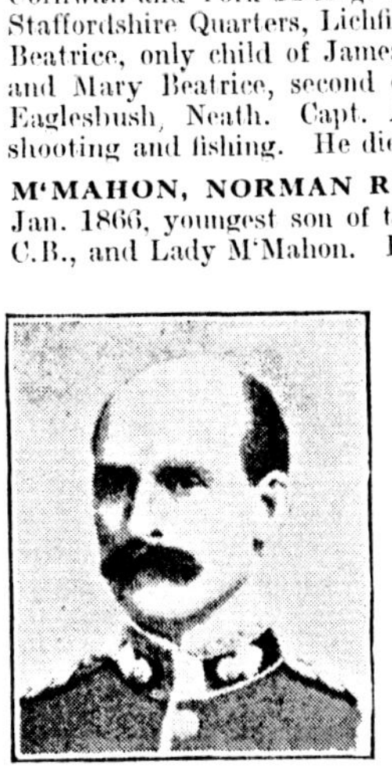

Norman R. M'Mahon.

he was Chief Instructor and Staff Officer at the School of Musketry, and from June, 1909, to Jan. 1910, was specially employed at the Headquarters of the Army. He passed the final examination of the Staff College in Dec. 1910, and was promoted to Lieut.-Colonel in May, 1911. Lieut.-Colonel M'Mahon served in the European War, and was mentioned in Sir John French's Despatches of the 8th Oct. 1914, and 14th Jan. 1915. He was appointed to the command of a brigade, with the temporary rank of Brigadier-General, which command he was to have taken up on the 12th Nov. 1914 ; but on the 11th Nov., at the First Battle of Ypres, he was killed in action.

EUSTACE, CHARLES LEGGE-EUSTACE, Capt., was born in

C. Legge-Eustace Eustace.

1867, son of Colonel R. J. E. Eustace, late Lieut.-Colonel, 60th Rifles, and Lady Katharine Eustace, daughter of the 4th Earl of Dartmouth. He was educated at Eton, and joined the King's Royal Rifles in 1889. He served in the Manipur Expedition, 1891 (Medal and clasp) ; in the Chin-Lushai Expedition, 1891–92 (clasp) ; in Mashonaland, 1896 (very severely wounded ; Medal). He served also in the South African War, 1899–1901, and was created a Companion of the Distinguished Service Order [London Gazette, 19 April, 1901] : "Charles Legge-Eustace Eustace, Capt., King's Royal Rifle Corps. In recognition of services during the operations in South Africa."

BENNETT, CHARLES HUGH, Capt., was born 13 Oct. 1867, son of Thomas Millord Bennett and Elizabeth Bennett (née Long) ; was educated at Hereford Cathedral School, and was gazetted to the Worcestershire

Charles Hugh Bennett.

Regt. 9 May, 1888, becoming Capt. 11 Aug. 1897. He served in the South African War, 1899–1902, on the Staff ; during operations in the Orange Free State, April and May, 1900 ; during operations in Orange River Colony, May to 29 Nov. 1900, including actions at Biddulphsberg and Wittebergen (1 to 29 July) ; during operations in Cape Colony, south of Orange River, March and April, 1900 ; in the operations in the Transvaal, July, 1901 ; during operations in the Orange River Colony, Dec. 1900, to 31 May, 1902. He was mentioned in Despatches [London Gazette, 16 April, 1901], and received the Queen's Medal with three clasps, and the King's Medal with two clasps, and was created a Companion of the Distinguished Service Order [London Gazette, 19 April, 1901] : "Charles Hugh Bennett, Capt., Worcestershire Regt. In recognition of services during the operations in South Africa." The Insignia of the D.S.O. were sent to South Africa and presented there. Capt. Bennett was promoted to Major 17 Feb. 1904, and retired from the Worcestershire Regt. 27 Jan. 1912. He served in the European War from 1914 as Temporary Lieut.-Colonel, and commanded the 20th Battn. Royal Fusiliers 7 Oct. 1914, to Feb. 1917. He went to France in command, Nov. 1915 ; was wounded in the Battle of the Somme, July, 1916, mentioned in Despatches, and placed on Reserve Feb. 1917. In 1912 he married Frederica, daughter of the late James Turle, M.D., and they have two sons, Peter and Thomas, and two daughters, Joan and Margery.

MACANDREW, HENRY JOHN MILNES, Capt., was born 7 Aug. 1866, son of the late Sir Henry Macandrew, Aisthorp, Inverness. He was educated at the Inverness College ; joined the 2nd Battn. Cameron Highlanders, 1884 ; transferred to the Lincolnshire Regt. 10 Nov. 1886, and to the Indian Staff Corps 20 March, 1888, joining the Bengal Cavalry in 1889. He served as Brigade Transport Officer, 2nd Brigade, Tirah Expeditionary Force, 1898 (Indian Frontier Medal with two clasps ; Despatches) ; served during the South African War, in Kitchener's Horse, Feb. to June, 1900 ; was appointed Intelligence Officer, Delagoa Line, from July to Sept. 1900, and D.A.A.G., Intelligence, to Feb. 1901 ; to General the Hon. Neville Lyttelton's Column from Feb. to May, 1901, and to General Bruce Hamilton from May, 1901, to June, 1902. He was later employed as D.A.A.G., Intelligence, Army Headquarters Staff, South Africa ; also served with Kitchener's Horse ; during operations in the Orange Free State, Feb. to May, 1900, including operations at Paardeberg (17 to 26 Feb.) ; actions at Poplar Grove, Dreifontein, Karee Siding and Houtnek (Thoba Mountain) ; during operations in the Transvaal in May and June, 1900, including actions near Johannesburg and Pretoria ; during operations in the Transvaal, east of Pretoria, July to Sept. 1900 ; in the operations west of Pretoria, Sept. to 29 Nov. 1900. He was present during the operations in the Transvaal, Orange River Colony and Cape Colony 30 Nov. 1900, to 31 May, 1902. He was mentioned in Despatches [London Gazette, 8 Feb. and 7 May, 1901]. He received the Queen's Medal and four clasps, the King's Medal and two clasps, and was created a Companion of the Distinguished Service Order [London Gazette, 19 April, 1901] : "Henry John Milnes Macandrew, Capt., Indian Staff Corps. In recognition of services during the operations in South Africa." The Insignia were sent to South Africa, but were returned and presented by H.M. the King 24 Oct. 1902. He was Brigade-Major to the Inspector-General of Cavalry in India 16 Nov. 1903, to 5 Jan. 1906 ; was promoted to Major, Indian Army, 10 Nov. 1904 ; was D.A.Q.M.G., Headquarters, India, 6 Jan. 1906, and 10 April, 1907 ; became Lieut.-Colonel 10 Nov. 1912. He served in the European

War from 1914 ; as Temporary Brigadier-General, General Staff, 18 Dec. 1914, to 7 Oct. 1915 ; commanded a brigade from 16 Nov. 1915. On 3 June, 1915, he was given the Brevet of Colonel, and he was mentioned in Despatches and promoted to Major-General, and created a C.B. 1918. Major-General Macandrew was a gentleman rider, across country and on the flat. He married, in 1892, Esther, youngest daughter of Henry Ritchie Cooper, J.P., of Ballindalloch, Stirlingshire, and they have one son and one daughter. He died 16 July, 1919.

BRIDGFORD, ROBERT JAMES, Capt., was born 10 March, 1869, son of the late Sir Robert Bridgford, K.C.B. He joined the Manchester Regt., from the Militia, 21 Dec. 1889 ; became Lieutenant 3 Dec. 1891, and Captain 24 Jan. 1898. He served in South Africa, 1898–1902 ; during the operations in Natal, 1899, including action at Lombard's Kop ; taking part in the defence of Ladysmith, including action of 6 Jan. 1900 ; during operations in Natal, March to June, 1900, including action at Laing's Nek (6 to 9 June) ; during operations in the Transvaal, east of Pretoria, July to 29 Nov. 1900, including action at Belfast (26 and 27 Aug.) and Lydenberg (5 to 8 Sept.). He was present during the operations in the Transvaal, Dec. 1900, to July, 1901, and Nov. 1901, to April, 1902 ; during operations in Orange River Colony, March, 1901, July to Sept. 1901, and Nov. 1901 ; in the operations in Cape Colony, March, 1901. He was employed with 1st Johannesburg Mounted Rifles, and in command of Mounted Infantry Battn. (from 24 April, 1901). He was mentioned in Despatches [London Gazette, 8 Feb. 1901], and received the Queen's Medal with three clasps and the King's Medal with two clasps, and was created a Companion of the Distinguished Service Order [London Gazette, 19 April, 1901] : "Robert James Bridgford, Capt., Manchester Regt. In recognition of services during operations in South Africa." The Insignia were sent to the Commander-in-Chief in South Africa, and presented there. He was promoted to Major 24 Feb. 1904, and was transferred to the Shropshire Light Infantry 16 Sept. 1905. From 8 Jan. 1908, to 15 Aug. 1908, he served as Commandant, Mounted Infantry, in Egypt. Major Bridgford was promoted to Lieut.-Colonel 11 Feb. 1914. He served in the European War from 1914 ; as Temporary Brigadier-General, 18th Infantry Brigade, B.E.F., 14 Aug. 1915, to 2 May, 1916 ; Brigade Commander, 141st Infantry Brigade, British Armies in France, 8 July, to 18 Aug. 1916 ; Brigade Commander, 18th Infantry Brigade, British Armies in France, 19 Aug. 1916, to 29 Aug. 1917 ; Brigade Commander, 2nd Reserve Infantry Brigade, Home Forces, 14 Oct. 1917, to 18 March, 1918 ; Divisional Commander, British Armies in France, 9 April, to 26 April, 1918 ; Temporary Major-General 9 April, to 30 May, 1918 ; Divisional Commander, 32nd Division, British Armies in France, 27 April to 30 May, 1918 ; Brigade Commander, 222nd Division, Infantry Brigade, Forces in Great Britain, 6 Aug. 1918. He was created a C.B. Colonel Bridgford married, in 1898, Mary Constance, daughter of the Ven. Frederick Charles Hamilton.

BANKS, HENRY JOHN ARCHIBALD, Capt., was born 4 Jan. 1869 ; educated at Wellington and at the Royal Military College, Sandhurst ; gazetted Second Lieutenant to the Hampshire Regt. 9 Nov. 1889, and promoted to Lieutenant 22 July, 1891. He was promoted to Captain 26 Jan. 1898. Capt. Banks served in the South African War as Brigade Signalling Officer (graded Staff Captain) 31 Jan. to 3 March, 1900, and as Divisional Signalling Officer 24 March, 1900, to 9 Feb. 1901. He took part during operations in the Orange Free State, Feb. to May, 1900, including operations at Paardeberg (17 to 26 Feb.) ; actions at Poplar Grove, Karee Siding, Vet River (5 and 6 May) and Zand River ; during operations in the Transvaal in May and June, 1900, including actions near Johannesburg and Pretoria ; during operations in the Transvaal, July to 29 Nov. 1900 ; taking part during the operations in the Transvaal 30 Nov. 1900, to April, 1901. He was mentioned in Despatches [London Gazette, 16 April, 1901], and created a Companion of the Distinguished Service Order [London Gazette, 19 April, 1901] : "Henry John Archibald Banks, Capt., Hampshire Regt. In recognition of services during operations in South Africa." The Insignia, etc., were sent to South Africa, to the Commander-in-Chief, and presented by the Duke of Cornwall and York 14 Aug. 1901. He was appointed Assistant Inspector, Army Ordnance Department, 14 Feb. 1903, and filled this post until 4 April, 1904, becoming Inspector, A.O.D., 5 April, 1904, and continuing in the appointment until 31 Dec. 1906. He was promoted to Major, Hampshire Regt., 24 March, 1907 ; was Ordnance Officer, 4th Class, from Jan. 1907, to 16 Dec. 1909, and Ordnance Officer, 3rd Class, 17 Dec. 1909 ; transferred to the Army Ordnance Department, 1910. He was Deputy Assistant Director, War Office, 23 Dec. 1911 ; became D.A.G., Artillery. During the European War he served in the Dardanelles and Salonika as Assistant Director of Ordnance, and from Sept. 1915, he was employed at the War Office, and was given the Brevet rank of Lieut.-Colonel. His favourite recreations

Edward M. J. Molyneux.

are music, fishing and shooting. Major Banks married (1st), in 1897, Eleanor Eva, daughter of the late Colonel S. G. Huskisson, late commanding 57th D.C.O. Middlesex Regt., and they had two daughters. He married (2ndly), in 1911, Ethel Winifred, daughter of Frampton Day, of Elvaston Place, Queen's Gate, S.W., and they have one son and one daughter.

MOLYNEUX, EDWARD MARY JOSEPH, Capt., was born 13 March, 1866 ; was educated at Stonyhurst College and Sandhurst, and entered the 3rd Dragoon Guards in 1887, being transferred in 1891 to the Indian Staff Corps. He served on the N.W. Frontier of India, taking part in the operations in 1897 and 1898 (Medal and clasp). He took part in the South African War in 1899–1902 (was severely wounded), as Squadron Commander of Thorneycroft's Mounted Infantry. He was decorated for conspicuous gallantry at Colenso on 20 Feb. 1900, in swimming the River Tugela under heavy fire from Boers, whilst covering a party of Thorneycroft's Mounted Infantry, in the attack of General Hart's Brigade; he took part in the operations in Natal and in the Relief of Ladysmith, including operations of 5 to 7 Feb. 1900, and action at Vaal Kranz; during operations on Tugela Heights (14 to 27 Feb.), and action at Pieter's Hill; during operations in Natal, March to June, 1900, including action at Laing's Nek (6 to 9 June, 1900); during operations in the Transvaal, east of Pretoria, July to 29 Nov. 1900. He was mentioned in Despatches (Sir R. H. Buller, 30 March and 9 Nov. 1900 [London Gazette, 8 Feb. 1901]), received the Queen's Medal with four clasps, and was created a Companion of the Distinguished Service Order [London Gazette, 19 April, 1901]: "Edward Mary Joseph Molyneux, Capt., Indian Staff Corps. In recognition of services during the operations in South Africa." The Insignia, Warrant and Statutes were sent to the Commander-in-Chief in India, and presented by the Lieut.-Governor of the N.W. Provinces and Oudh 1 Jan. 1902. Capt. Molyneux married, in 1902, Mary Alison, youngest daughter of Thomas H. W. Knolles, of Oatlands, County Cork. He subsequently served with the Punjab Cavalry, and as Inspecting Officer of the Imperial Service Troops. He was created C.I.E. Major Molyneux won considerable success as a painter. He had large pictures hung in the Royal Academy in 1899, 1900 and 1901, and three times won the gold medal given by the Viceroy of India for the best picture painted in India. His favourite recreations were painting, polo, mountaineering and swimming. He was Squadron-Commander, 12th Bengal Cavalry. Major Molyneux died at Umballa, India, on 29 Jan. 1913, and an obituary notice of him appeared in the "Times" of 29 Feb. 1913.

LYON, FRANCIS, Capt., was born 10 July, 1867, son of the late Colonel Francis Lyon, R.H.A., and the Honourable Mrs. Lyon, sister of the 11th Viscount Valentia. He joined the Royal Artillery as Second Lieutenant 23 July, 1887; was A.D.C. to the Commander-in-Chief, East Indies, from 21 March, 1895, to 7 Oct. 1897; served on the North-West Frontier of India with Malakand Field Force, including Utman Khel Column; also with Buner Field Force; was present at the attack and capture of the Tanga Pass, and received Medal with clasp. He became Captain 18 May, 1898. He served in South Africa, 1899–1900, on the Staff; during operations in Natal, including actions at Elandslaagte, Rietfontein and Lombard's Kop; took part in the defence of Ladysmith, including action of 6 Jan. He was mentioned in Despatches (Sir G. S. White, 2 Dec. 1899, and 23 March, 1900 [London Gazette, 8 Feb. 1901]), received the Queen's Medal with three clasps, and was created a Companion of the Distinguished Service Order [London Gazette, 19 April, 1901]: "Francis Lyon, Capt., Royal Artillery. In recognition of services during the operations in South Africa." The Insignia were presented by the King 3 June, 1901. He became A.D.C. to Lieut.-General, Natal, 16 Sept. 1899, to 28 March, 1900; was specially employed on the Gold Coast 22 Aug. 1900, to 21 Jan. 1901, during the Ashanti operations (Despatches [London Gazette, 8 March, 1901]; Medal); became Major, Royal Artillery, 21 Oct. 1903; was employed with the West African Frontier Force, Northern Nigeria, 15 Oct. 1902, to 14 Oct. 1905, in the Kano-Sokoto Campaign (Despatches [London Gazette, 31 July, 1902]; Medal with clasp); was appointed Assistant Secretary (Military), G.S.O., 2nd Grade, Committee of Imperial Defence, 11 July, 1906, to 30 Sept. 1910. He was specially employed at the War Office 4 July to 14 Aug. 1911; was Military Attaché (G.S.O.), Bucharest, Sofia, Belgrade and Athens, from 15 Aug. 1911, to 14 Aug. 1913. He was promoted to Lieut.-Colonel 30 Dec. 1914. He served in the European War; was G.S.O., 2nd Grade, from 5 Aug. 1914, to 5 March, 1915, and Brigadier-General, General Staff, from 11 July, 1915. He was five times mentioned in Despatches, and created a C.M.G. and given the rank of Brevet Colonel. In 1910 he married Jane, eldest daughter of Joseph C. Borwick, and their children are: Ann; Paul, born in 1915, and Joan, born in 1915.

CAMPBELL, JOHN HAY, Capt., was born in Edinburgh 31 Dec. 1871, son of the late Major-General Thomas Hay Campbell, R.A. He was educated at Linton House School, and at St. Mary's Hospital, London; matriculated at the London University, 1888; became M.R.C.S. (England) and L.R.C.P. (London), 1894, and was gazetted to the Royal Army Medical Corps as Lieutenant 29 July, 1895; was promoted to Captain 29 July, 1898. In the South African War he served with the 3rd King's Royal Rifle Corps from Dec. 1899, to Oct. 1900, during operations in Natal, 1899; was present at the Relief of Ladysmith, including operations of 17 to 24 Jan. 1900, and action at Spion Kop; during operations of 5 to 7 Feb. 1900, and action at Vaal Kranz; operations on Tugela Heights 14 to 27 Feb. 1900 (severely wounded 24 Feb.); during operations in the Transvaal, July to Oct. 1900. He was mentioned in Despatches (Sir R. H. Buller, 30 March and 9 Nov. 1900 [London Gazette, 8 Feb. 1901]); received the Queen's Medal with three clasps, and was created a Companion of the Distinguished Service Order [London Gazette, 19 April, 1901]: "John Hay Campbell, Capt., Royal Army Medical Corps. In recognition of services during the operations in South Africa." The decoration was awarded for meritorious services whilst in medical charge of 3rd King's Royal Rifles. The Insignia were sent to the Commander-in-Chief, South Africa, and were presented by the O.C., Secunderabad District, 7 March, 1902. Capt. Campbell was promoted to Major, A.M.C., 29 April, 1907; became Lieut.-Colonel 1 March, 1915, and a Medical Officer, London Recruiting Area. He married, in 1895, Clara Edith, daughter of the late James Hedley, Richmond, Yorkshire.

McHARDY, ALEXANDER ANDERSON, Capt., was born 9 Nov. 1868, only son of the late Lieut.-Colonel Sir Alexander McHardy, K.C.B., and Elise, daughter of the late Sir John and Lady Anderson; educated at Westminster School; joined the Royal Artillery 17 Feb. 1888; Lieutenant 17 Feb. 1891; served in Mauritius, South Africa, England, and the N.W. Frontier of India with Sir Bindon Blood's Division, 1897–98, as Lieutenant in No. 7 Mountain Battery, R.A.; Captain 17 Aug. 1898; took part in the South African War as Divisional Signalling Officer 13 Nov. 1899, to 14 Dec. 1900 (Despatches; Queen's Medal, six clasps; King's Medal, two clasps). Created a Companion of the Distinguished Service Order [London Gazette, 19 April, 1901]: "Alexander McHardy, Capt., Royal Artillery. In recognition of services during the operations in South Africa." D.A.A.G., Intelligence, Natal, Dec. 1900, to July, 1902; D.A.A.G., Prisoners of War, 1902 to 1903; in Somaliland with the Boer Contingent and as Staff Officer, Mounted Troops, 1903 (Despatches; Medal with clasps); Staff Captain, R.A., Western Command, 1904–5; G.S.O.3, North-Western Coast Defences, 1905–8; was D.A.A. and Q.M.G., 2nd Division, Aldershot Command, 1909–11. From there he went to the Staff College; was appointed G.S.O., 2nd Grade, South China, 1913. During the European War he served as D.A.Q.M.G. from 14 Dec. 1914, to 5 June, 1915, and as A.A. and Q.M.G. from 6 June, 1915, to 30 Aug. 1916, and as D.A. and Q.M.G. from 30 Aug. 1916, to present time (with temporary rank of Brigadier-General). Mentioned in Despatches; Brevet Lieut.-Colonel 23 June, 1915; C.M.G. 3 June, 1916; Brevet Colonel, 1 Jan. 1917; C.B. 1 Jan. 1918; Commandeur de l'Ordre du Mérite Agricole 28 Sept. 1917; Croix de Guerre avec Palme 19 Nov. 1918. He married, in 1904, Lilian Amy Byde, daughter of Coghlan McHardy, 1 Grenville Place, London, S.W., and they have one son.

Alexander A. McHardy.

RUCK KEENE, HARRY LANCELOT, Capt., was born 5 May, 1868, son of the late Colonel Ruck Keene, Queen's Bays and 15th Hussars, and Mrs. Ruck Keene (*née* Elmhirst), of Ashby, Lincolnshire (who died in 1875); was educated at Winchester College, and gazetted to the Oxfordshire Light Infantry 24 April, 1889, becoming Lieutenant 16 March, 1892, and Captain 28 Oct. 1898. He served as Adjutant of a Mounted Infantry battalion during the South African War, from 1899 to 1900; was employed with the Mounted Infantry during operations in Cape Colony, south of Orange River, 1899–1900, including actions at Colesberg (1 Jan. to 12 Feb. 1900). He was mentioned in Despatches [London Gazette, 4 May, 1900], and received the Queen's Medal with two clasps, and was created a Companion of the Distinguished Service Order [London Gazette, 19 April, 1901]: "Harry Lancelot Ruck Keene, Capt., Oxfordshire Light Infantry. In recognition of services during the operations in South Africa. Capt. Ruck Keene was promoted to Major 14 Sept. 1907. He held a special appointment, Lines of Communication, British Armies in France, 27 June to 15 Nov. 1917, and became Temporary Lieut.-Colonel 16 Nov. 1917, and Acting Lieut.-Colonel 27 June, 1918. He was created an O.B.E. Major Ruck Keene has the degree of Honorary Master of Arts, Oxon. His favourite recreations are hunting, shooting, fishing and cricket.

HARVEY, ROBERT NAPIER, Capt., was born 17 May, 1868, son of John Harvey, of Messrs. John Harvey and Sons, Bristol, and of Mary Russell, daughter of George Prentice, Esq., of Fifeshire, N.B. He was educated at Marlborough College; Redcliffe House, Clifton, and the R.M.A., Woolwich; joined the Royal Engineers as Second Lieutenant 17 Feb. 1888; was promoted Captain 12 Jan. 1899; employed as Regimental Officer, Royal Engineers. He served in the South African War as A.D.C. to Major-General, Royal Engineers, 2nd Aug. 1900, to 11 Nov. 1901, and was present in the operations in the Orange Free State Feb. to May, 1900; operations in the Transvaal, east of Pretoria, July to 29 Nov. 1900, including action at Belfast; operations in the Transvaal, west of Pretoria, July to 29 Nov. 1900, including action at Zilikat's Nek; operations in Orange River Colony May to 29 Nov. 1900; operations in Cape Colony, south of Orange River, 1899–1900; operations in Cape Colony, north of Orange River; operations in the Transvaal, 30 Nov. 1900, to 31 May, 1902. He was mentioned in Despatches [London Gazette, 16 April, 1901]; received the Queen's Medal with three clasps, the King's Medal with two clasps, and was created a Companion of the Distinguished Service Order [London Gazette, 19 April, 1901]: "Robert Napier Harvey, Capt., Royal Engineers. In recognition of services during the operations in South Africa." The Insignia were presented in South Africa 13 July, 1901. He was Staff Officer, Royal Engineers, in South Africa, 12 Nov. 1901, to 5 April, 1903, and was employed under the Civil Government, Transvaal, from 6 April, 1903, to 13 Dec. 1905, and was promoted to Major 25 Sept. 1906. He was Chief Instructor in Fortification, School of Military Engineering, and obtained the Brevet of Lieut.-Colonel 26 Nov. 1913. On the outbreak of the European War he became Assistant (with the rank of Lieut.-Colonel) to the Engineer-in-Chief, British Expeditionary Force, from 15 Jan. 1915. He was appointed Inspector of Mines, and promoted to Temporary Brigadier-General 2 Jan. 1916, and Chief Engineer of 6th Army Corps, Jan. 1918, to 1919; was mentioned in Despatches five times; created a C.M.G. Jan. 1916; was given the Brevet of Colonel 3 June, 1916. In Aug. 1917, he was awarded the C.B. for valuable services rendered in the field. In 1909 he married Mabel, daughter of Bourchier Hawksley, of 14, Hyde Park Gardens, W., and they have two sons.

PROBYN, PERCY JOHN, Capt., is the eldest son of the late Frederick Probyn, J.P., Cambridge House, Trevethen, Monmouthshire; was educated privately at Weston-super-Mare; at the University Colleges, Cardiff, and Aberystwith; Charing Cross Medical School and Hospital (entrance

Science Scholar, Pereira Prizeman, three silver medals, several Honours Certificates); Member Royal College of Surgeons (England); Licentiate Royal College of Physicians, London; entered the Army Medical Corps in 1896; served in the Lagos Expeditionary Force (Medal and clasp), 1897 to 1898; in the Sierra Leone Expedition, 1898–99 (clasp). He served in the South African War, taking part in the advance on Kimberley, including the action at Magersfontein; Relief of Kimberley; operations in the Orange Free State, Feb. to May, 1900, including operations at Paardeberg (17 to 26 Feb.), actions at Poplar Grove, Dreifontein, Vet River (5 and 6 May) and Zand River; operations in the Transvaal in May and June, 1900, including actions near Johannesburg, Pretoria and Diamond Hill (11 and 12 June); operations in Orange River Colony May, 1901; operations on the Zululand Frontier of Natal, Sept and Oct. 1901; operations in the Transvaal, May, 1901, to Feb. 1902. He was mentioned in Despatches [London Gazette, 8 Feb. 1901]; received the Queen's Medal with four clasps, the King's Medal with two clasps, and was created a Companion of the Distinguished Service Order [London Gazette, 19 April, 1901]: "Percy John Probyn, Capt., Royal Army Medical Corps. In recognition of services during the operations in South Africa." The Insignia, etc., were sent to South Africa, and presented there. He became Major 29 Oct. 1907, and Lieut.-Colonel 1 March, 1915. In 1906 he took his degree of M.B. and B.S. (Intermediate, 1905), London University; D.P.H. (Royal College of Physicians and Surgeons), 1907; became Barrister-at-Law, 1908; Fellow of the Hon. Society of Lincoln's Inn; became an F.R.I.P.H.; Member of the Royal Sanitary Institute, and Member of the Hardwicke Society; was Assistant Demonstrator Pathology, Charing Cross Hospital Medical School; obtained Hon. Mention in Medicine, Army Medical School, Netley; was appointed Prosector Royal College of Surgeons, and Sanitary Specialist Officer, South China Command. His favourite recreations are cycling, shooting, riding and fishing. He married Sara Marie, daughter of the late Eugène Colhoun, and they have two daughters.

HOOPER, ARTHUR WINSMORE, Capt., was born 22 Feb. 1869, son of John Harward Hooper, M.D., F.R.C.S., and Annie Hooper, *née* Dyer. He joined the Royal Army Medical Corps as Lieutenant 29 Jan. 1896; became Captain 29 Jan. 1899; served in South Africa, 1899–1902; took part in the advance on Kimberley, including actions at Belmont, Enslin, Modder River and Magersfontein; during operations in the Orange Free State, Feb. to May, 1900, including actions at Poplar Grove, Dreifontein, Vet River (5 and 6 May) and Zand River; in the operations in the Transvaal in May and June, 1900, including actions near Johannesburg, Pretoria and Diamond Hill (11 and 12 June); during operations in the Transvaal, east of Pretoria, July to 29 Nov. 1900, including actions at Belfast (26 and 27 Aug.); also during operations in the Orange River Colony, Nov. 1900; served during operations in Cape Colony 30 Nov. 1900, to 31 May, 1902. He was mentioned in Despatches [London Gazette, 16 April, 1901]; received the Queen's Medal with six clasps, the King's Medal with two clasps, and was created a Companion of the Distinguished Service Order [London Gazette, 19 April, 1901]: "Arthur Winsmore Hooper, Capt., Royal Army Medical Corps. In recognition of services during the operations in South Africa." The Insignia were sent to the Commander-in-Chief in South Africa, and presented by the Officer Commanding. He was promoted to Major, R.A.M.C., 29 Oct. 1907. For his services in the European War he has been mentioned in Despatches, received the Brevet of Lieut.-Colonel, and created a C.M.G. On 24 March, 1916, he was promoted Temporary Colonel, and appointed Assistant Director of Medical Service. He married, in 1910, Amy Harriet, daughter of Sir B. T. Brandreth Gibbs.

MAYNARD, CHARLES CLARKSON MARTIN, Capt., was born 15 Sept. 1870, youngest son of the late Forster Fowler Martin Maynard L.R.C.P., M.R.C.S.; was educated at St. Paul's School (Junior and Senior Foundation Scholar), and at the R.M.C., Sandhurst (Honours and Prize winner); joined the Devonshire Regt. as Second Lieutenant 8 Oct. 1890; served in the Burma Campaign (Medal and clasp), 1889–92; was appointed Superintendent of Gymnasia, Malta, 1894; served in the Tirah Campaign, 1897 (Medal and two clasps); was promoted to Captain 17 Feb. 1899; held the appointments of Railway Transport Officer, Punjab, and Station Staff Officer, Mian Mir, 1898–99. He served in the South African War, 1899–1902, as Press Censor, from 11 Sept. 1901, to 31 Aug. 1902; was employed with the Imperial Light Infantry; was present at the Relief of Ladysmith, including action at Colenso during operations of 17 to 24 Jan. 1900, and action at Spion Kop; operations of 5 to 7 Feb. 1900, and action at Vaal Kranz; during operations on Tugela Heights (14 to 27 Feb. 1900), also action of Pieter's Hill; during operations in Natal, March to June, 1900, including action at Laing's Nek (6 to 9 June); afterwards on the Staff. He was mentioned in Despatches (Sir R. H. Buller, 30 March and 9 Nov. 1900 [London Gazette, 8 Feb. 1901]); received the Queen's Medal with six clasps, the King's Medal with two clasps, and was created a Companion of the Distinguished Service Order [London Gazette, 19 April, 1901]: "Charles Clarkson Martin Maynard, Capt., Devonshire Regt. In recognition of services in the operations in South Africa." The Insignia, etc., were sent to the Commander-in-Chief in South Africa, and presented by the Officer Commanding. In 1902 he became Staff Officer, Zululand; graduated from the Staff College, 1903–4; was Brigade-Major, 7th Brigade, Southern Command, 27 March, 1905, and 30 June, 1907; was G.S.O., 3rd Grade, Headquarters of Army, 1 July, 1907, to 26 March, 1909; was given the Brevet of Major 23 July, 1910; was G.S.O., 3rd Grade, War Office, 17 March, 1910, to 31 March, 1911, and G.S.O., 2nd Grade, War Office, 1 April, 1911, to 16 March, 1914. He served during the European War, 1914 to 1920, as D.A.A. and Q.M.G., 3rd Division, British Expeditionary Force, 30 Sept. 1914, to 5 Feb. 1915; A.Q.M.G., 2nd Army Corps, 3rd Army, British Expeditionary Force, 6 Feb. 1915, to 12 July, 1915; A.Q.M.G., 3rd Army, British Expeditionary Force, 13 July to 19 Aug. 1915. He was made Brigade Commander, 13th Infantry Brigade, British Expeditionary Force, 20 Aug. 1915, to Nov. 1915, and General Staff Officer, 1st Grade (Liaison Officer), British Salonika Force, 5 Aug. to 5 Dec. 1916; Brigade Commander, 82nd Infantry Brigade, British Salonika Force, 12 Jan. 1917, to 12 Jan. 1918; General Officer, Commanding-in-Chief, Allied Forces at Murmansk. He was given the Brevet of Lieut.-Colonel 18 Feb. 1915, and Brevet of Colonel 1 Jan. 1917. He was created C.B. 1918, C.M.G. 1918, and K.C.B. 1919, and received the 1914 Star, and was five times mentioned in Despatches. He is fond of outdoor sports of all kinds. Colonel Maynard married, in 1909, Dorothy Agnes, eldest daughter of Arthur Davidson, Kenilworth Avenue, Wimbledon Park, and they have one son and one daughter.

TAYLOR, ARTHUR HENRY MENDLE, Capt., was born in India 11 Jan. 1870, and was educated at Clifton College; was commissioned into the 21st Hussars, from the Militia, 1890. He served in the 21st (Empress of India's) Lancers, 1890, at Omdurman; became Lieutenant, 21st Lancers, 25 Jan. 1893; was promoted into the 13th Hussars 22 Feb. 1899. He served in South Africa, 1899–1902; was present at the Relief of Ladysmith, including action at Colenso during the operations of 17 to 24 Jan. 1900; action at Spion Kop; during the operations of 5 to 7 Feb. 1900, and took part in the action at Vaal Kranz; operations on Tugela Heights 14 to 27 Feb. 1900, and action at Pieter's Hill; was afterwards on the Staff. He took part in the operations in the Transvaal, and in the Orange River Colony, 30 Nov. 1900, to 31 May, 1902, and was mentioned in Despatches (Sir R. H. Buller, 30 March and 9 Nov. 1900 [London Gazette, 8 Feb. 1901]); received the Queen's Medal with four clasps, the King's Medal with two clasps, and was created a Companion of the Distinguished Service Order [London Gazette, 19 April, 1901]: "Arthur Henry Mendle Taylor, Capt., 13th Hussars. In recognition of services during the operations in South Africa." The Insignia were sent to the Commander-in-Chief in South Africa, and presented by the Duke of Cornwall and York 14 Aug. 1901. Capt. Taylor was promoted to Major in the 13th Hussars 3 Nov. 1903, and Lieut.-Colonel 1 July, 1909; became Colonel 2 Jan. 1913, and Temporary Brigadier-General 3 Aug. 1914. In the European War he served at the Dardanelles, Salonika, Egypt, Palestine, and was twice mentioned in Despatches. He retired with the rank of Brigadier-General in 1919. He married, in 1903, Margaret Coutts, second daughter of W. M. Strachan, of Strood Park, Horsham.

MANNERS, LORD ROBERT WILLIAM ORLANDO, Capt., was born 4 Feb. 1870, fourth son of the 7th Duke of Rutland and of the Duchess of Rutland, and half-brother of the 8th Duke. He was educated at Wellington College, and gazetted to the King's Royal Rifles 4 Feb. 1891, serving in the Isazai Expedition in 1892. During the South African War, 1899–1902, he took part in the Relief of Ladysmith, including the action at Colenso; was present at the actions of Spion Kop and Vaal Kranz, in the operations on Tugela Heights, and in the action at Pieter's Hill. During the Natal operations he was in the action of Laing's Nek, 1900, and in the Transvaal he fought in the actions of Belfast and Lydenberg. For these services he was mentioned in Despatches; received the Queen's Medal with six clasps, the King's Medal with two clasps, and for his services with the Natal Bearer Company he was created a Companion of the Distinguished Service Order [London Gazette, 19 April, 1901]: "Lord Robert William Orlando Manners, Capt., King's Royal Rifles. In recognition of services during the War in South Africa." The Insignia, Warrant, etc., were sent to the Commander-in-Chief, South Africa, and presented by Colonel T. E. Hickman, C.B., D.S.O. He attained to the substantive rank of Major in 1908, and retired to the Reserve of Officers in 1910, having previously served for some years as Adjutant of the 22nd R.V.C. (Central London Rangers), 1903–9. A keen sportsman and a good rider to hounds, he accepted the joint mastership of the Belvoir Hounds, his partner in the mastership being Major T. Bourke, and they hunted the country successfully until the outbreak of the European War, when both returned to active service. An officer of great experience in South African fighting, Lord Robert Manners was gazetted a Brigade-Major in Oct. 1914, and in July, 1916, was given the command of a service battalion of the Northumberland Fusiliers. For his services on the Somme, Aug.–Sept. 1916, he was created a C.M.G., 1916. The Northumberland troops had been actively engaged with the enemy at Villeret, north-east of St. Quentin, and had succeeded in pushing them back about three-quarters of a mile, when Lord Robert fell in action, 11 Sept. 1917, a week after Sir Douglas Haig's communiqué specially mentioning the splendid services rendered by the Northumberland Fusiliers. Lord Robert married, in 1902, Mildred Mary, daughter of the Rev. Charles Buckworth and widow of Major H. E. Buchanan Riddell, and there is one daughter, Elizabeth.

HART-SYNNOT, ARTHUR HENRY SETON, Capt., was born 19 July, 1870, eldest son of the late Major-General Arthur Fitzroy Hart Synnot, C.B., C.M.G., of Ballymoyer, County Armagh, and of May Hart Synnot; was educated at Clifton College; King William's College; the R.M.C., Sandhurst, and subsequently entered and graduated in the Staff College, Camberley. He is a Fellow of the Royal Geographical Society. He joined the East Surrey Regt. 8 Oct. 1890; became Lieutenant 7 June, 1892, and was Adjutant 1 Jan. 1894, to 31 Dec. 1897. He served in the Relief of Chitral, 1895, in command of the Maxim Gun Section (Medal and clasp); in the Tirah Expedition, 1897–98, as A.D.C. to G.O.C., 1st Brigade (two clasps). In the South African War, 1899–1902, he served first with the Mounted Infantry and subsequently as D.A.A.G

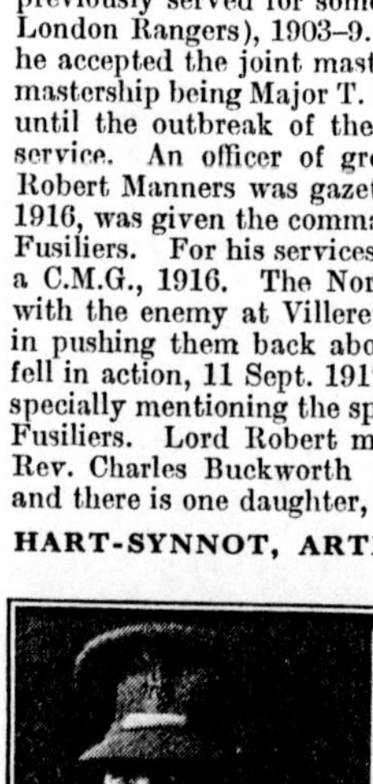

A. H. S. Hart-Synnot.

He was twice wounded, mentioned in Despatches, received the Queen's Medal with seven clasps, the King's Medal with two clasps, and was created a Companion of the Distinguished Service Order [London Gazette, 19 April, 1900]: "Arthur Henry Seton Hart-Synnot, Capt., East Surrey Regt. In recognition of services during the operations in South Africa." The Insignia were sent to the Commander-in-Chief, South Africa, and presented by the Duke of Cornwall and York 14 Aug. 1901. He was promoted Captain 21 June, 1899. Capt. Hart-Synot was appointed British Military Attaché with the Japanese Army in Manchuria, 1904–5, and received from H.M. the Mikado the 4th Class of the Order of the Sacred Treasure and the Japanese War Medal. He was G.S.O., 2nd Grade, South China, 20 March, 1907, to 9 June, 1911, and was promoted Major 17 March, 1908, and appointed to the General Staff, India, Oct. 1913. He was transferred to the General Staff in France in Oct. 1916; on the General Staff, 17th Division, and on the General Staff, 40th Division; commanded the 1/4th East Lancashire Regt.; commanded the 1st Battn. Lancashire Fusiliers, including the period of the Third Battle of Ypres (Passchendaele); commanded temporarily the 86th Brigade and the 25th Brigade; was given the Brevet of Lieut.-Colonel 1 Jan. 1917, and promoted substantive Lieut.-Colonel 16 Jan. 1917, and Brigadier-General April, 1917. He commanded the 6th Brigade. He was dangerously wounded May, 1918 (loss of both legs), was awarded a bar to the Distinguished Service Order and was made a Chevalier of the Legion of Honour. He received the French Croix de Guerre, and was created a C.M.G. in 1919. General Hart-Synnot married, in July, 1919, Violette, only daughter of J. E. Drower, Esq., C.B.E.

FREETH, GEORGE HENRY BASIL, Capt., was born in London 31 Dec. 1872, son of Colonel William Freeth, M.V.O., Chief Constable, Isle of Man (1888–1911), and Helen Macpherson, daughter of General Macpherson, of Inverness. He was educated at Merchant Taylors' School, London; King William's College, Isle of Man, and the R.M.C., Sandhurst, 1891, and joined the Lancashire Fusiliers as Second Lieutenant 19 Nov. 1892, becoming Lieutenant 23 May, 1894. He served in India and Egypt, and in the Nile Expedition of 1898 he was present at the Battle of Khartum, and received the Medal and the Egyptian Medal with clasp. He was promoted to Captain 27 Sept. 1899. He served during the occupation of Crete. From 1899 to 1902 he served in South Africa, and took part in the Relief of Ladysmith, including the operations of 17 to 24 Jan. 1900, and the action at Spion Kop; operations in the Transvaal in May and June, 1900; operations in the Transvaal, east of Pretoria, July to 29 Nov. 1900. He performed the duties of Commandant and Railway Staff Officer. He took part in the operations in the Transvaal, May, 1901, to 31 May, 1902; operations in Orange River Colony, Nov. 1900, to May, 1901. He was mentioned in Despatches [London Gazette, 8 Feb. 1901]; received the Queen's Medal with three clasps, the King's Medal with two clasps, and was created a Companion of the Distinguished Service Order [London Gazette, 19 April, 1901]: "George Henry Basil Freeth, Capt., Lancashire Fusiliers. In recognition of services during the operations in South Africa." The Insignia were sent to the Commander-in-Chief in South Africa, and presented by the Duke of Cornwall and York 14 Aug. 1901. He was Adjutant, Militia, 20 Sept. 1902, to 19 Sept. 1905; Major 24 June, 1910; was at the Staff College, 1909–10; D.A.A.G., Northern Command, 31 Oct. 1911, to 4 Aug. 1914. He was given the Brevet of Lieut.-Colonel 21 Feb. 1912. He served in the European War from 1914 to 1918; as D.A.A.G., G.H.Q., B.E.F., 5 Aug. 1914, to 16 March, 1915; as A.A.G., G.H.Q., B.E.F., 17 March to 7 Dec. 1915; as Brigade Commander, 2nd Lancashire Brigade, British Armies in France, until 27 June, 1916; Brigade Commander, 167th Infantry Brigade, 27 July, 1916. He was promoted to Lieut.-Colonel 3 June, 1916; was given the Brevet of Colonel 3 June, 1917. Colonel Freeth was four times mentioned in Despatches, was created a C.M.G. 1916, and a C.B. 1919. He married, in 1903, Ruth Elaine, daughter of James W. Scott, of Westlands, Queenstown, and they have two daughters, Barbara and Felicity.

SCRATCHLEY, VICTOR HENRY SYLVESTER, Capt., was born 6 July, 1870. He entered the Army 25 March, 1891; served in the Isazai Expedition, 1892, and in the Chitral Campaign, 1895 (Medal with clasp); became Captain 22 Oct. 1899. He served in the South African War from 1899 to 1900; during operations in Natal, 1899; also in the operations in Natal, March to June, 1900, including action at Laing's Nek (6 to 9 June); during operations in the Transvaal, east of Pretoria, July to 29 Nov. 1900, including actions at Belfast (26 and 27 Aug.) and Lydenberg (5 to 8 Sept.). He was mentioned in Despatches [London Gazette, 8 Feb. 1901]; and received the Queen's Medal with four clasps, and created a Companion of the Distinguished Service Order [London Gazette, 19 April, 1901]: "Victor Henry Sylvester Scratchley, Capt., King's Royal Rifle Corps. In recognition of services in the operations in South Africa." The Insignia were presented by the King 17 Dec. 1901. Capt. Scratchley was Superintendent of Gymnasia, 1901 to 1904; retired from the K.R.R.C. 20 June, 1906, and joined the Reserve of Officers. He served during the European War as Temporary Lieut.-Colonel, and was created O.B.E. In 1901 he married Anna Clementine, daughter of John Harvey, of Mayfield, Shooter's Hill, Kent.

TROTTER, ALGERNON RICHARD, Capt., was born in London 20 June, 1870, son of the late Major-General Sir H. Trotter, G.C.V.O., and the Hon. Lady Trotter (*née* Hon. Eva Gifford), daughter of the 2nd Baron Gifford. He joined the 2nd Life Guards as Second Lieutenant 10 Feb. 1892; became Lieutenant 5 April, 1893; was Adjutant, 2nd Life Guards, 22 May, 1895, to 8 Oct. 1898; passed the Staff College; was A.D.C. (extra) to G.O.C., Aldershot, 9 Oct. 1898, to 8 Oct. 1899; became Captain 16 Nov. 1899; served in South African Campaign, 1899–1900; was A.D.C. to General Commanding-in-Chief, Sir R. Buller, V.C.; was present at the Relief of Ladysmith, including operations on Tugela Heights; during operations in Natal, 1900, including action at Laing's Nek; was mentioned in Despatches (Sir R. H. Buller, 30 March and 9 Nov. 1900); received the Queen's Medal and six clasps, and was created a Companion of the Distinguished Service Order [London Gazette, 19 April, 1901]: "Algernon Richard Trotter, Capt., 2nd Life Guards. In recognition of services during the operations in South Africa. The Insignia were presented by the King 3 June, 1901. He was appointed A.D.C. to G.O.C., Natal, 10 Jan. 1900, to 9 Jan. 1901. On his return to England he was appointed A.D.C. (extra) to G.O.C., Aldershot, 10 Jan. 1901, to 30 Sept. 1901; was created an M.V.O. (4th Class), 1902. He was promoted Major 12 Jan. 1907, and was Brigade-Major, Lowland Mounted Brigade, Scottish Command (Special Extra-Regimental Employment), 29 April, 1910, to 9 April, 1911. He received the Brevet of Lieut.-Colonel 18 Jan. 1911. He served during the European War, 1914–18; was Temporary Lieut.-Colonel, Commanding Reserve Regt. of 2nd Life Guards, 11 Aug. 1916, to 22 April, 1918, and Machine Gun Guards and Regimental District 23 April to 31 Dec. 1918; became Temporary Colonel 23 April to Dec. 1918; Machine Gun Guards and Regimental District 10 May, 1918. He received the Brevet of Colonel 1 Jan. 1919. In 1901, he married Lady Edith Mary Montgomery, youngest daughter of 15th Earl of Eglinton and Winton, and they have four sons and one daughter.

BARNES, REGINALD WALTER RALPH, Capt., was born 13 April, 1871, son of Prebendary R. H. Barnes, of Stoke Canon, near Exeter. He was educated at Westminster; entered the 4th Hussars, from the Militia, as Second Lieutenant, 31 Dec. 1890; became Lieutenant 10 May, 1893; served with the Spanish Army in the Cuban Insurrection, 1895; was Adjutant, 4th Hussars, 20 May, 1896, to 19 May, 1900; became Captain, 4th Hussars, 31 Dec. 1899. He served in South Africa as Adjutant, Imperial Light Horse, 1899–1900, and as Lieut.-Colonel, 2nd Imperial Yeomanry, 18 May, 1901, to 11 March, 1902; was present during operations in Natal, 1899, including action at Elandslaagte; took part in the Relief of Ladysmith, including operations on Tugela Heights (14 to 27 Feb.); was present at the Relief of Mafeking; during operations in the Transvaal in May and June, 1900; in operations in the Transvaal, east and west of Pretoria, July to 29 Nov. 1900, including action at Belfast (26 and 27 Aug.); during operations in Cape Colony, north of Orange River, 1899–1900. Took part in the operations in the Transvaal and Orange River Colony, and was severely wounded. He was created a Companion of the Distinguished Service Order [London Gazette, 19 April, 1901]: "Reginald Walter Ralph Barnes, Capt., 4th Hussars. In recognition of services in the operations in South Africa." The Insignia were sent to South Africa, to the Commander-in-Chief, and were presented by Lieut.-Colonel the Hon. J. H. G. Byng. Major-General Barnes was A.D.C. to the Commander-in-Chief, East Indies, 1 May, 1904, to 6 Jan. 1906; was Instructor, Cavalry School, 5 Feb. 1906, to 3 Sept. 1907; became Major, 17th Lancers, 17 July, 1907; was employed as Assistant Military Secretary to the Governor and Commander-in-Chief, Malta, 6 Oct. 1909, to 3 Feb. 1911; was promoted to Lieut.-Colonel, 10th Hussars, 4 Feb. 1911, and Colonel 15 June, 1914. He served continuously throughout the European War, first as O.C., 10th Royal Hussars, then promoted Temporary Brigadier-General 9 April, 1915, to command 111th Infantry Brigade; Temporary Major-General 21 Nov. 1916, and Major-General 3 June, 1918. He commanded the 32nd and 57th Divisions as Major-General 1 July, 1917, to 26 March, 1919, and commanded the West London Division 29 May, 1919. He was created C.B., June, 1916, and awarded the Croix de Guerre, Dec. 1918; created K.C.B. in 1919. Sir Reginald Barnes married, in 1919, Gunhilla, widow of C. J. Wijk.

HERIOT-MAITLAND, JAMES DALGLEISH, Capt., was born 21 Jan. 1874, eldest son of the late Sir James Makgill Heriot-Maitland, K.C.B., and Frances Lorna Campbell, and a descendant of the 6th Earl of Lauderdale. He became Second Lieutenant, The Rifle Brigade, 5 Oct. 1892; Lieutenant 24 June, 1895, and Captain 3 Feb. 1900. Captain Heriot-Maitland served in the South African War, 1899–1902; was severely wounded, received the Queen's Medal with four clasps, the King's Medal with two clasps, and was created a Companion of the Distinguished Service Order [London Gazette, 19 April, 1901]: "James Dalgleish Heriot-Maitland, Capt., The Rifle Brigade." In recognition of services during the operations in South Africa." The Insignia were presented in South Africa by the G.O.C., Transvaal and Orange River Colony, 2 Sept. 1902. He became Adjutant, Rifle Brigade, 21 Nov. 1900, to 2 Sept. 1904; was Adjutant, Rifle Depôt, 16 May, 1906, to 15 May, 1909. He was promoted to Major 1 Dec. 1909. After the outbreak of the European War he was appointed to command the 7th Battn. The Rifle Brigade, 19 Aug. 1914, to 31 Aug. 1916, when he became Temporary Brigadier-General. He had meantime been promoted to Lieut.-Colonel 15 June, 1915. From 1 Sept. 1916, to 9 Nov. 1918, he commanded the 98th Infantry Brigade in France. He was commanding troops at Bordon from 14 Jan. 1919. He was promoted Colonel 15 June, 1919. For his services in the Great War he was mentioned in Despatches, given the Brevet of Colonel 3 June, 1917, and created a C.M.G. in 1916. He married, in Aug. 1903, Mary Turner, daughter of H. S. Wedderburn, of Wedderburn, and they have a son, Richard Ogilvy Heriot-Maitland, and two daughters, Katharine Lorna and Margaret Heriot-Maitland.

Prince Alexander of Teck.

TECK, HIS SERENE HIGHNESS PRINCE ALEXANDER AUGUSTUS FREDERICK WILLIAM ALFRED GEORGE OF, Capt. (now Earl of Athlone), was born 14 April, 1874, in

Kensington Palace, third son of His Serene Highness the late Duke of Teck, Honorary Major-General, and of Her Royal Highness the late Princess Mary Adelaide. He was educated at Eton, and the Royal Military College, Sandhurst; became Second Lieutenant, 7th Hussars, 24 Oct. 1894, and served in Matabeleland as Officer (Staff), 1896 (mentioned in Despatches [London Gazette, 9 March, 1897]; Medal); became Lieutenant 26 July, 1899, and Captain 20 Feb. 1900. He served in the South African War, 1899–1900, on the Staff; was present at the Relief of Kimberley; during operations in the Orange Free State (Feb. to March, 1900), including operations at Paardeberg (17 to 28 Feb.); actions at Poplar Grove, Dreifontein and Karee Siding; was present at the Relief of Mafeking; during operations in the Transvaal, west of Pretoria, Aug. 1900, including action at Zilikat's Nek; during operations in Cape Colony, south of Orange River, 1899–1900, including action at Colesberg (1 Jan. to 12 Feb.). He was mentioned in Despatches [London Gazette, 16 April, 1901], and received the Queen's Medal with five clasps, and was created a Companion of the Distinguished Service Order [London Gazette, 19 April, 1901]: "His Serene Highness Prince Alexander Augustus Frederick William Alfred George of Teck, Capt., 7th Hussars. In recognition of services during the recent operations in South Africa." The Insignia, etc., were sent to Adelaide for presentation by H.R.H. the Duke of Cornwall and York, and were presented by His Royal Highness 10 July, 1901, at Adelaide. Prince Alexander was transferred to the Royal Horse Guards 3 Sept. 1904; became Major, 2nd Life Guards, 12 Jan. 1911, and was created a G.C.B. in 1911. Soon after the outbreak of the European War he became G.S.O., 2nd Grade (28 Oct. 1914, to 30 June, 1915), and was gazetted G.S.O., 1st Grade, 13 Dec. 1915. He was G.S.O.2, British Mission to Belgian Headquarters, 28 Oct. 1914, to 30 June, 1915; Assistant Military Secretary 1 July to 12 Dec. 1915; G.S.O.1 (Chief of British Mission to Belgian Headquarters), 13 Dec. 1915, to 6 Jan. 1918; Brigadier-General, General Staff, British Mission to Belgian Headquarters, 1 Jan. 1918; Personal A.D.C. to the King 1 Jan. 1919. For his services in the European War from 1914 he was twice mentioned in Despatches, and given the Brevet of Lieut.-Colonel 12 Jan. 1915, and of Colonel 3 June, 1919. He was been created a G.C.V.O.; is Grand Officier of the Legion of Honour; holds the Belgian Grand Cordon Order of Leopold, and the Croix de Guerre, and is a Knight of St. John of Jerusalem. Prince Alexander of Teck became Earl of Athlone in 1917. He married, in Windsor Castle, 10 Feb. 1904, Her Royal Highness Princess Alice of Albany, daughter of His late Royal Highness Prince Leopold of Albany, and of the Duchess of Albany, and they have two children: Lady Mary Helen Emma, born 23 Jan. 1906, and Viscount Trematon (Rupert Alexander George Augustus), born 4 Aug. 1907.

SPRY, LEIGHTON HUME, Capt., was born 14 Jan. 1871, eldest son of the late Arthur Hume Spry, Indian Civil Service. He was gazetted to the West Yorkshire Regt. as Second Lieutenant, from the Militia, 12 March, 1892; became Lieutenant 22 Nov. 1893; served in the Ashanti Expedition, 1895–96, for which he received the Ashanti Star, and was promoted to Captain 24 Feb. 1900. He served in the South African War, 1899–1902, as A.D.C. to Major-General, Infantry Brigade, 10 April to 23 Aug. 1900, and as Staff Officer to Mobile Column 24 Aug. 1900, to 19 June, 1902, taking part in the operations in Natal, 1899; was present at the Relief of Ladysmith, including action at Colenso; during operations of 17 to 24 Jan. 1900, and action at Spion Kop; in the operations on Tugela Heights (14 to 27 Feb. 1900) and action at Pieter's Hill (slightly wounded). He took part during operations in Natal (March to June, 1900), including action at Laing's Nek (6 to 9 June); during operations in the Transvaal, east of Pretoria, July to Oct. 1900, including actions at Belfast (26 and 27 Aug.) and Lydenberg (5 to 8 Sept.); served during operations in the Transvaal 30 Nov. 1900, to 31 May, 1902; was again severely wounded 19 Dec. 1901. He was mentioned in Despatches [London Gazette, 8 Feb. 1901 (Sir R. H. Buller, 30 March, 13 Sept. and 9 Nov. 1900), and London Gazette, 29 July, 1902]; received the Queen's Medal with six clasps, the King's Medal with two clasps, and was created a Companion of the Distinguished Service Order [London Gazette, 19 April, 1901]: "Leighton Hume Spry, Capt., West Yorkshire Regt. In recognition of services during the operations in South Africa." He was Brigade-Major, India, 6 June, 1907, to 26 Oct. 1909; was D.A.A.G., India, 27 Oct. 1909, to 5 June, 1911; promoted to Major 23 Feb. 1912; G.S.O., 2nd Grade, Northumbrian Division, Northern Command, 16 March, 1912, to 4 Aug. 1914. On the outbreak of the European War he was G.S.O., 1st Grade, 5 Aug. 1914, to 9 May, 1915, and A.A. and Q.M.G., 30th Division, B.E.F., 13 Sept. 1915, to 9 April, 1916, and Temporary Lieut.-Colonel, West Yorkshire Regt., 10 May, 1916. He married, in 1894, Emily, youngest daughter of W. Peacock-Edwards.

Viscount Crichton.

CRICHTON (VISCOUNT), HENRY WILLIAM, Capt., was born 30 Sept. 1872, son of the 4th Earl of Erne (deceased), and Lady Florence Cole, daughter of the 3rd Earl of Enniskillen. He was educated at Eton, and the R.M.C., Sandhurst; joined the Royal Horse Guards 5 May, 1894; became Lieutenant 6 Feb. 1895; was Adjutant, R.H.G., 8 Dec. 1896, to 6 Oct. 1899. He served in the South African War as A.D.C. to Major-General Brocklehurst, Cavalry Brigade, Natal, 7 Oct. 1899, to 24 Jan. 1901; was present at the Defence of Ladysmith; operations in Natal, March to June, 1900; operations in the Transvaal, east of Pretoria, July to Nov. 1900. He was mentioned in Despatches [London Gazette, 8 Feb. 1901]; received the Queen's Medal with five clasps, and was created a Companion of the Distinguished Service Order [London Gazette, 19 April, 1901]: "Henry William, Viscount Crichton, Capt., Royal Horse Guards. In recognition of services during the operations in South Africa." He had become Captain 24 Feb. 1900; was Equerry to His Royal Highness the Duke of Cornwall and York during his colonial tour. The Insignia of the D.S.O. were sent to Adelaide, South Australia, and presented there by H.R.H. the Duke of Cornwall and York. He was appointed Equerry-in-Ordinary to H.R.H. the Prince of Wales from 21 Feb. 1903, to 12 May, 1908; was created an M.V.O. in 1906, and Extra Equerry to H.M. King George V. in 1910. During the European War Lord Crichton served as Major, Royal Horse Guards, with the British Expeditionary Force; was mentioned in Despatches, and created an Officer of the Legion of Honour. He was reported missing at Wytschaete 1 Nov. 1914, and reported dead June, 1916. Lord Crichton married, in 1903, Lady Mary Grosvenor, daughter of the 1st Duke of Westminster, and they had one son, John Henry George, Earl of Erne, and one daughter, Mary Kathleen.

SOLLY-FLOOD, ARTHUR, Capt., was born 28 Jan. 1871, son of the late Major-General Sir F. R. Solly-Flood, K.C.B. (of Slaney Lodge, Wexford, and of Porthmawr, Crickhowell, South Wales), and of Constance Eliza, eldest daughter of W. E. Frere. He joined the South Lancashire Regt. as Second Lieutenant 25 March, 1891; became Lieutenant 12 Jan. 1894; was Adjutant, South Lancashire Regt., 24 April, 1895, to 23 April, 1899; was promoted Captain 28 Feb. 1900; served in South Africa during the Boer War on Special Service from 20 Oct. 1899, to 18 Jan. 1902; as Adjutant, South African Light Horse, Dec. 1899, to Jan. 1901; was present at the Relief of Ladysmith, including operations of 17 to 24 Jan. 1900, and action at Spion Kop; during operations of 5 to 7 Feb. 1900; action at Vaal Kranz; during operations on Tugela Heights (14 to 27 Feb. 1900) and action at Pieter's Hill; during operations in Natal, March to June, 1900, including action at Laing's Nek (6 to 9 June); during operations in the Transvaal in June, 1900, also during operations in the Transvaal, east of Pretoria, July to 29 Nov. 1900, including actions at Belfast (26 and 27 Aug.) and Lydenberg (5 to 8 Sept.); operations in Orange River Colony, June, 1900. He also served during the operations in the Transvaal 30 Nov. to Dec. 1900; during operations in Orange River Colony, Dec. 1900, and Feb. 1901, to Jan. 1902; during operations in Cape Colony, Dec. 1900, to Feb. 1901; was mentioned in Despatches [London Gazette, 8 Feb. 1901]; received the Queen's Medal with six clasps, and the King's Medal with two clasps. He was created a Companion of the Distinguished Service Order [London Gazette, 19 April, 1901]: "Arthur Solly-Flood, Capt., South Lancashire Regt. In recognition of services during the operations in South Africa. The Insignia were sent to South Africa, and presented there. He was appointed Staff Captain, H.Q. of Army, 3 Aug. 1904, to 14 Oct. 1906; was D.A.Q.M.G., H.Q. of Army, and G.S.O., 2nd Grade, H.Q. of Army, 15 Oct. 1906, to 2 Aug. 1908; Major, 4th Dragoon Guards, 19 Aug. 1908; G.S.O., 2nd Grade, Egypt, 26 Feb. 1910, to 30 Oct. 1912. He served in the European War, 1914–18; as Temporary Lieut.-Colonel, 4th Dragoon Guards, 10 Nov. 1914, to 2 Nov. 1915; Temporary Brigadier-General 2 Nov. 1915; served in France on the General Staff of Sir Douglas Haig, as Director of Training in France, 28 Jan. 1917, to 6 Oct. 1918 (Despatches; created a C.M.G. 1915); promoted Temporary Major-General to command 42nd East Lancashire Division, Oct. 1917. For his services in the European War he was mentioned in Despatches [London Gazette, 17 Feb. 1915, 15 June, 1916, 4 Jan. and 11 Dec. 1917, 20 May and 20 Dec. 1918]; was given the Brevets of Lieut.-Colonel 18 Feb. 1915, and Colonel 1 Jan. 1917; promoted to Major-General 3 June, 1919; created a C.B. [London Gazette, 1 Jan. 1919]; a C.M.G. [London Gazette, 3 June, 1916], and awarded the Ordre de la Couronne Commandeur 26 July, 1917, and the Belgian Croix de Guerre 11 March, 1918. Major-General Solly-Flood married, in 1916, Elise Martin, only daughter of Ferdinand Hanbury, J.P., of Nantoer, Abergavenny, Monmouthshire.

Arthur Solly-Flood.

HARINGTON, CHARLES HARINGTON, Capt., was born in Chichester 31 May, 1872, son of the late E. J. Harington, of 11, Inverness Terrace, Hyde Park, W., and of Mrs. Harington, Friston Lodge, Eastbourne. He was educated at Cheltenham College, and the R.M.C., Sandhurst; joined the King's Liverpool Regt. as Second Lieutenant 9 Jan. 1892; became Lieutenant 4 Feb. 1895; was Adjutant, King's Liverpool Regt., 17 Nov. 1897, to 1 Nov. 1899. He was employed on Special Service in the South African War 2 Nov. 1899, to 22 Nov. 1901. He was present at the Relief of Ladysmith; operations in Natal, March to June, 1900, including action at Laing's Nek; operations in the Transvaal, east of Pretoria, July to Nov. 1900; operations in Cape Colony, south of Orange River, 1899. He was mentioned in Despatches (Sir R. H. Buller, 30 March and 9 Nov. 1900 [London Gazette, 8 Feb. 1901]); received the Queen's Medal with three clasps, and was created a Companion of the Distinguished Service Order [London Gazette, 19 April, 1901]: "Charles Harington Harington, Capt., The Liverpool Regt. In recognition of services during the operations in South Africa." The Insignia, etc., were presented by H.M. the King 3 June, 1901. He became Captain 21 March, 1900; was appointed Officer, Company of Gentlemen Cadets, R.M. College, 18 Feb. 1903. Capt. Harington was specially employed, H.Q. of Army, 15 April to 30 Nov. 1909; appointed G.S.O., 3rd Grade, H.Q. of Army, 1 Dec. 1909, to 30 Sept. 1911;

became Brevet Major 21 Feb. 1912, and Brigade-Major, 6th Brigade, Aldershot Command, 27 Sept. 1911, to 30 Sept. 1913; was specially employed in the War Office 20 March to 4 Aug. 1914; became Major 15 April, 1914; appointed G.S.O., 2nd Grade, 5 Aug. 1914, to 20 April, 1915, and G.S.O., 1st Grade, 21 April to 12 Sept. 1915. He served in the European War from 1914 (Despatches; Brevet Lieut.-Colonel 18 Feb. 1915; Brevet Colonel 3 June, 1916; appointed B.G.G.S.; Temporary Brigadier-General, General Staff, 13 Sept. 1915; appointed M.G.G.S.; Temporary Major-General, General Staff, 5 June, 1916). He received the C.B. 1 Jan. 1917; was promoted Major-General 1 Jan. 1918; appointed Deputy Chief of the Imperial General Staff 29 April, 1918, and Member of Army Council. He was created a K.C.B. in 1919. Sir Charles Harington married, in 1904, Gladys Norah, eldest daughter of Colonel O'D. C. Grattan, D.S.O.

EWART, FRANK ROWLAND, Capt., was born 31 Jan. 1874; joined the King's Liverpool Regt. as Second Lieutenant 7 March, 1894, and became Captain 8 July, 1898. Capt. Ewart served in the South African War of 1899–1902, and was created a Companion of the Distinguished Service Order [London Gazette, 19 April, 1901]: "Frank Rowland Ewart, Capt., King's Liverpool Regt. In recognition of services during the operations in South Africa." He died 13 June, 1906.

STIRLING, SIR GEORGE MURRAY HOME, Capt., Bart., of Glorat, was born at 16, Bryanston Square, London, W., 4 Sept. 1869, son of Sir Charles Elphinstone Fleming Stirling, 8th Bart., of Glorat (Nova Scotia Baronetcy, 1666), formerly Highland Borderers Militia, J.P. and D.L. for Stirlingshire, and of Anne Georgina, eldest daughter of James Murray. He was educated at Eton College, and the R.M.C., Sandhurst; joined the 2nd Essex Regt. (56th Foot, The Pompadours) as Second Lieutenant 9 Nov. 1889; became Lieutenant 7 Oct. 1892; served in the Chitral Campaign, 1895 (Medal and clasp); in the Tirah Campaign, 1897–98 (as Transport Officer); operations against the Khani Khel Chamkanis; operations in the Bazar Valley 25–30 Dec. 1897 (two clasps). He became Capt. 29 Jan. 1900. He served in the South African Campaign, 1899–1902; from Jan. to June, 1900, as Adjutant, Burma Mounted Infantry. He took part in the operations in the Orange Free State, March to May, 1900, including the actions of Poplar Grove, Dreifontein, Houtnek (Thoba Mountain,) Vet River (5 and 6 May) and Zand River. Also in the operations in the Transvaal in May and June, 1900, including actions near Johannesburg, Pretoria and Diamond Hill (11 and 12 June); operations in the Transvaal, west of Pretoria, 1 Aug. to Oct. 1900; operations in Orange River Colony, June to 31 July, 1900; operations in Transvaal till wounded in Sept. 1900; operations in the Transvaal, Jan. to April, 1901. He served as Staff Captain, Mounted Infantry Brigade, from 18 Oct. 1900, to 18 Feb. 1902, and was afterwards attached to the Army Service Corps as Officer Commanding Transport, Bloemfontein District, till June, 1902, when he returned to England. The following is an extract from C. S. Goldmann's "With General French and the Cavalry in South Africa," which gives a good account of the engagement at Sanna's Post, for which Sir George Stirling afterwards received the D.S.O.: "Reduced to ten men (seven gunners, one sergeant, one corporal and a bombardier), and himself the sole officer left with the battery, Major Hornby had to call volunteers to rescue the guns. The appeal was responded to by Capt. Humphreys, who was close by, by Lieut. Stirling (2nd Essex), Burma Mounted Infantry, by Lieut. Maxwell (18th Bengal Lancers), attached to Roberts's Horse, and a number of privates showed equal alacrity in lending help. Five of the men by themselves working with a will arranged to drag the two guns on the left a distance of 50 yards to a point behind the Station buildings, and the two on the outside were hauled by ten non-commissioned officers and gunners 100 yards to the shelter of a camp close up the line; the limbers also had to be brought up by manual effort. Singling out the middle gun, the Boers poured on it an unmeasured fire till it seemed as if nothing could live under such a fury of shell and bullet. The five dauntless men resumed the attempt at rescue by hand, but their strength was exhausted, and they had to turn to the horses that were standing in poor shelter behind a tin shed at the station. Four of the animals were brought forward in pairs only to be shot down. Another pair met the same fate. A gunner went out with each pair to hook in, while the driver held the horses. It was observed that when the men emerged from the shelter of the buildings, they bent their heads towards the direction from which the bullets were coming, as if they were withstanding a storm of hail. There had been 87 horses under the shelter of the shed; 85 were killed or disabled, and upon the remaining two animals depended the fate of the guns. Several bullets dropped hard by these two animals, throwing up dust to their middles, but the whizzing of the lead scarcely seemed to frighten them. They were with the utmost haste hitched up to the limber, and Lieut. Stirling proceeded to back them to the gun. The short space of a single yard separated the trail from the limber hook; one instant more and they would have plunged forward bearing the gun away into safety, but it was not to be. A few Boer muzzles, with unerring aim, snatched away the success that seemed so nearly assured and so richly deserved. Both horses were shot through the eyes and dropped dead. Driver Glasock was wounded at the same moment, and the last gun stood hopelessly derelict. All means of rescue had been exhausted and the gun must be abandoned." Sir George Stirling was wounded at Zandfontein. For his services in the South African War he was mentioned in Despatches [London Gazette, 8 Feb. 1901]; received the Queen's South African Medal with four clasps, the King's Medal with two clasps, and was created a Companion of the Distinguished Service Order [London Gazette, 19 April, 1901]: "Sir George Murray Home Stirling, Capt., Essex Regt. In recognition of services during the operations in South Africa." Served Somaliland F.F. 1903-4, and commanded the 7th Somali Camel Corps from 12 Nov. 1903, to June, 1904, taking part in operations in Somaliland and receiving the Medal and clasp. He succeeded to the Baronetcy 10 Sept. 1910; was appointed D.A.A.G., Mhow Division, India, 13 Jan. 1911, which appointment he vacated in Nov. 1914, in order to join his regiment in France. He had become Major on 12 Feb. 1912. After the outbreak of the European War he was appointed Provost-Marshal to the 5th Army Corps 29 Dec. 1914, to 15 Nov. 1915, and Temporary Lieut.-Colonel 16 Nov. 1915, on getting command of the 2nd Essex Regt. He was Commandant, Lines of Communication, British Armies in France, from 3 Oct. 1918, and Temporary Colonel from 1 Oct. 1918. He was wounded, and thrice mentioned in Despatches in 1915, 1917, and again in 1918, besides receiving a Brevet Lieut.-Colonelcy 1 Jan. 1918. Sir George Stirling is a member of the King's Bodyguard of Scotland, and a J.P. and D.L. for Stirlingshire. Sir George Stirling married, 4 Nov. 1904, at St. Andrews, Fife, N.B., Mabel Elizabeth, second daughter of Colonel Sir Alexander Sprot, Bart., C.M.G., of Garnkirk and Stravithie, late of the Carabiniers (served in Afghan, South African and European Wars). They have two sons: Charles Alexander Sprot Home, born 3 April, 1910; George Archibald Mungo, born 10 March, 1915, and two daughters, Elizabeth Gloriana and Jean Margaret.

BARRY, STANLEY LEONARD, Capt., was born 31 Dec. 1873, youngest son of Sir F. T. Barry, 1st Baronet, and of Sarah Herron. He was educated at Harrow; became Second Lieutenant, R. Berks Regt. (Militia), 1891, and Lieutenant, 10th Royal Hussars, in 1894. He served in South Africa, 1899–1902, on the Staff (as Divisional Officer, graded Staff Captain), 1 Jan. to 2 Nov. 1900; D.A.A.G. (Intelligence) 24 Nov. 1900, to 31 May, 1902; was present at the Relief of Kimberley; during operations in the Orange Free State, Feb. to May, 1900, including operations at Paardeberg 17 to 26 Feb.; and actions at Poplar Grove, Dreifontein and Karee Siding; in the operations in the Transvaal in May and June, 1900, including actions near Johannesburg, Pretoria and Diamond Hill (11 and 12 June); during operations in the Transvaal, east of Pretoria, July to 29 Nov. 1900, including actions at Belfast (26 and 27 Aug.); during the operations in the Transvaal, west of Pretoria, July to 29 Nov. 1900; in the operations in Cape Colony, south of Orange River, 1899 to 1900, including actions at Colesberg (1 Jan. to 12 Feb.). Also during the operations in the Transvaal and Cape Colony 30 Nov. 1900, to 31 May, 1902. He was mentioned in Despatches [London Gazette, 4 May, 1902]; received the Queen's Medal with six clasps, and the King's Medal with two clasps, and given the Brevet of Major, and created a Companion of the Distinguished Service Order [London Gazette, 19 April, 1901]: "Stanley Leonard Barry, Capt., 10th Hussars. In recognition of services during the operations in South Africa." The Insignia, etc., were sent to South Africa, and presented there. He served as Signalling Officer, D.A.A.G. (Intelligence) and A.M.S. to General Sir John French from 1909 to 1906, and as Brigade-Major, London Mounted Brigade, from 1908–11. Lieut.-Colonel S. L. Barry served in the European War as A.D.C. to Field-Marshal Sir John French, Commander-in-Chief, B.E.F., France, and in attendance on H.R.H. the Prince of Wales, 1914–15. From 1916 he was Assistant Military Secretary, Home Forces, Horse Guards. He was mentioned in Despatches; created an M.V.O. (1915); a C.M.G., 1915; was given an O.B.E. in 1919, and a Brevet Colonelcy. Colonel Barry married, in 1906, Hannah Mary, eldest daughter of James Hainsworth, and they have one daughter, Jeanne Irene.

Stanley Leonard Barry.

KENRICK, GEORGE EDMUND REGINALD, Capt., was born 16 Jan. 1871, second son of the late W. M. Kenrick, of Broome Fleet, Hants. He was educated at Charterhouse; joined the Royal West Surrey Regt. as Second Lieutenant (from the Militia) 18 Nov. 1891; became Lieutenant 10 May, 1895; served on the North-West Frontier, India, 1897–98, taking part in the operations in Bajaur and the Malakand country (Medal with clasp). He served with the Tirah Expeditionary Forces as Brigade Signalling Officer, 2nd Brigade, 1st Division (12 Oct. 1897, to April, 1898); was present at the capture of the Sampagha and Arhanga Passes; during the reconnaissance of the Saran Sar, and action of 9 Nov. 1897; during operations against the Khani Khel Chamkanis; during operations in the Bazar Valley 25 to 30 Dec. 1897. He received clasp. He was made Captain 7 May, 1900; served in South Africa as Divisional Signalling Officer (graded as Staff Captain), 1899–1901; during operations in Natal, 1899, including actions at Talana and Lombard's Kop; took part in the Defence of Ladysmith, including action of 6 Jan. 1900; during the operations in the Transvaal, east and west of Pretoria, July to 29 Nov. 1900, including actions at Zilikat's Nek and Lydenberg (5 to 8 Sept.); during operations in Cape Colony, north of Orange River, including action at Ruidam; operations in the Transvaal 30 Nov. 1900, to 1901, and May, 1902. He was mentioned in Despatches [London Gazette, 16 April, 1900]; received the Queen's Medal and five clasps, the King's Medal and two clasps, and was created a Companion of the Distinguished Service Order [London Gazette, 19 April, 1901]: "George Edmund Reginald Kenrick, Capt., Royal West Surrey Regt. In recognition of services during the operations in South Africa." The Insignia were sent to South Africa, and presented by the Duke of Cornwall and York in Aug. 1901. He was Staff Captain 27 Oct. 1900, to 23 June, 1902; was Temporary Assistant Military Secretary to the Lieut.-General Commanding the Forces in South Africa from 24 June, 1902, to 11 Feb. 1904. He served as Brigade-Major, Hampshire Infantry Brigade, Southern Command, 25 Aug. 1913, to 4 Aug. 1914. He became Lieut.-Colonel 4 Feb. 1914, and served as Brigade-Major, Hampshire Infantry Brigade, Central Force, Home Defence, 5 Aug. 1914, to 2 March,

1915; as D.A.Q.M.G., 5th Division, B.E.F., 3 March to 13 July, 1915; as D.A.Q.M.G., 3rd Army, B.E.F., 14 July to 11 Oct. 1915; as A.Q.M.G., 2nd Army Corps, B.E.F., and British Armies in France, 12 Oct. 1915. He was given the Brevet of Colonel 3 June, 1917; was created a C.M.G. in 1916; a C.B. in 1919, and was mentioned in Despatches. In 1904 he married Amy Marion, daughter of G. O'Flaherty, J.P., of The Lodge, Ballyconneely, and Ardnasella, Outherard, and they have one son.

TOOGOOD, CECIL, Capt., was born 31 March, 1870, son of the late Capt. A. D. Toogood, Bengal Fusiliers, and later Queen's Bodyguard. He was gazetted, 29 Oct. 1890, Second Lieutenant, Border Regt. He became Lieutenant 21 Dec. 1892. He served during the Waziristan Expedition, 1894–95; became Captain, Manchester Regt., 26 May, 1900. He served in the South African War, 1899–1900, on the Staff, afterwards employed with the Mounted Infantry; was present at the Relief of Ladysmith; during the operations in the Transvaal Oct. to Dec. 1901, and Feb. to April 1902; in the operations in Orange River Colony, Dec. 1901, to Feb. 1902; during operations in Cape Colony in Sept. to Oct. 1901. He was mentioned in Despatches (Sir R. H. Buller, 30 March and Nov. 1900 [London Gazette, 8 Feb. 1901, and 25 April, 1902]). He received the Queen's Medal with three clasps, and the King's Medal with two clasps, and was created a Companion of the Distinguished Service Order [London Gazette, 19 April, 1901]: "Cecil Toogood, Capt., Manchester Regt. In recognition of services during the operations in South Africa." The Insignia were sent to South Africa, and presented there by the Duke of Cornwall and York 14 Aug. 1901. He was Adjutant, Volunteers, 3 Jan. 1904, to 31 Oct. 1907, and Regimental Staff Officer 13 Dec. 1907; was promoted to Captain, Lincolnshire Regt., 18 Jan. 1908; Recruiting Staff Officer, Sheffield Recruiting Area, 3 Dec. 1907, to 4 May, 1911; Recruiting Staff Officer, Belfast Recruiting Area, 5 May, 1911, to 31 March, 1912; promoted to Major 15 May, 1914; Adjutant, Officers' Training Corps, 23 May to 4 Aug. 1914. He served in the European War from 1914, commanding the 2nd Battn. Lincolnshire Regt.; was mentioned in Despatches, and promoted to Lieut.-Colonel 11 March, 1918. He married, in 1899, Mary Elizabeth, eldest daughter of General Henry Pipon, C.B., and Louisa Anne, daughter of Admiral Sir William Edmonstone, 4th Bart., C.B., of Duntreath, Stirlingshire, Scotland.

EDEN, WILLIAM RUSHBROOKE, Capt., was born at Bath 11 Oct. 1873, son of the late Lieut.-Colonel A. D. Eden (late The Cameronians), of Beaufort House, Bournemouth, and of Louisa, daughter of Capt. John Jarvis, 52nd Light Infantry. He was educated at Haileybury College, and at the R.M.A., Woolwich, and joined the Royal Artillery as Second Lieutenant 4 March, 1893; became Lieutenant 4 May, 1896; Captain 28 May, 1900; served in the South African Campaign, 1900; was present at the Relief of Ladysmith, including the operations of 5 to 7 Feb. 1900, and action at Vaal Kranz; operations on Tugela Heights (14 to 27 Feb. 1900), and action at Pieter's Hill. Operations in Natal, March to June, 1900, including action at Laing's Nek 6 to 9 June; operations in the Transvaal, east of Pretoria, July to 29 Nov. 1900 (including actions at Belfast (26 and 27 Aug.) and Lydenberg (5 to 8 Sept.). He was mentioned in Despatches [London Gazette, 8 Feb. 1901]; received the Queen's Medal with six clasps, and was created a Companion of the Distinguished Service Order [London Gazette, 19 April, 1901]: "William Rushbrooke Eden, Capt., Royal Artillery. In recognition of services during the operations in South Africa." He was Adjutant, Royal Artillery, 1 April, 1901, to 23 Nov. 1904, and Major 26 Feb. 1910. He was promoted Lieut.-Colonel 10 Nov. 1915; was Brigadier-General, Royal Artillery, 27th Division, Salonika Army, 21 Sept. 1916; created a C.M.G. 14 June, 1917, and Officier Légion d'Honneur, 1917. He was mentioned in Despatches 7 Jan. 1916, and 8 Oct. 1916, 18 July, 1917, and 11 June, 1918. He married, in 1911, Marjorie, daughter of the late Major Lyon Campbell, 74th Highlanders, and they have one son, Robert Archibald, born 1 Aug. 1912, and a daughter, Joan Agnes, born 27 Aug. 1913.

BLAIR, ARTHUR, Captain, was born 2 Sept. 1869, in India, son of the late Capt. James Jenkins Blair, Central Indian Horse, and Mrs. E. C. C. Blair. He was educated at Cheltenham College, and Sandhurst; was gazetted to the King's Own Scottish Borderers as Second Lieutenant 1 March, 1890; promoted Lieutenant 13 Feb. 1893; served in the Nile Expedition, 1898, including the Battle of the Atbara (Egyptian Medal with clasp; Atbara Medal); acted as A.D.C. to Major-General, Infantry Brigade, at Aldershot, 10 Aug. to 8 Oct. 1899; served in South African War on Staff; was present at the Relief of Ladysmith, including action at Colenso; participated in the operations of 17 to 24 Jan. 1900, and in the action at Spion Kop; took part in the operations of 5 to 7 Feb. 1900, and in the action at Vaal Kranz; in the operations on the Tugela Heights (14 to 27 Feb. 1900), and in the action at Pieter's Hill. He served in the operations in Natal, March to June, 1900, including action at Laing's Nek (6 to 9 June); was severely wounded. He commanded a regiment of Scottish Horse from 17 Dec. 1900; took part in the operations in Orange River Colony, Dec. 1900, and in operations in Cape Colony, Dec. 1900, to Jan. 1901. During the South African War he was mentioned in Despatches six times [London Gazette, 26 Jan. 1900, 8 Feb. 1901, and 18 July, 1902 (Sir R. Buller), 30 March, 19 June and 9 Nov. 1900]. He received the Queen's Medal with six clasps and the King's Medal with two clasps, and for gallantry at Spion Kop, in 1899, he was created a Companion of the Distinguished Service Order [London Gazette, 19 April, 1901]: "Arthur Blair, Captain, King's Own Scottish Borderers. In recognition of services during the operations in South Africa. The Insignia were sent to the Commander-in-Chief, South Africa, and presented by H.R.H. the Duke of Cornwall and York 14 Aug. 1901. He served in the Transvaal, Feb. 1901, to 31 May, 1902; was appointed D.A.A.G., Cape Colony District, 10 Sept. 1902, to 22 March, 1904, and D.A.Q.M.G., Cape Colony District, 23 March, 1904, to 9 Sept. 1905; became Staff Captain and G.S.O., 3rd Grade, H.Q. of Army, 26 Jan. 1907, to 25 Oct. 1908; became Major 4 July, 1908; was appointed Brigade-Major, 10th Brigade, Eastern Command, 26 Oct. 1908, to 25 Jan. 1911; was G.S.O., 2nd Grade, South Africa, 9 March, to 26 Sept. 1912; held the same appointment in Egypt 27 Sept. 1912, to 6 Aug. 1914. He served in the European War from 1914, and was temporarily in the War Office 6 Nov. to 6 Dec. 1914; became Lieutenant-Colonel 28 April, 1915; was D.A.A. and Q.M.G., New Armies, B.E.F., 7 Dec. 1914, to 23 March, 1915; G.S.O.2, 54th Division, B.E.F., 24 March to 3 May, 1915; G.S.O.1, New Armies, B.E.F., 24 June, 1915, to 12 Feb. 1916; Brigadier-General, General Staff, 5th Army Corps, B.E.F., 13 Feb. to 19 June 1916; Brigade Commander, 21st Infantry Brigade, Home Forces, 27 Oct. 1916, to 26 Feb. 1917; Brigade Commander, South Midland Reserve Brigade, Home Forces, 14 May to 18 July, 1917; Commander, No. 3 Section, Tyne Garrison, 19 July, 1917, to 8 Sept. 1918; Commander, Tees Garrison, 9 Sept. 1918; promoted to Colonel, April, 1919. For his services in the European War he was twice mentioned in Despatches, and given the Brevet of Colonel 1 Jan. 1916, for distinguished service in the field. He married (1st), Mary Beryl, daughter of the late General Buchanan, C.B. She died in 1912. He married (2ndly), in London, 11 June, 1914, Elizabeth Mary, daughter of Sir Charles Chandos Hoskyns, Bart., and they have three children: Jean Aileen Chandos; David, born 13 Feb. 1916, and Chandos, born in 1919.

COWIE, HUGH NORMAN RAMSAY, Capt., was born at Arrochar, N.B., 17 Sept. 1872, son of Hugh Cowie, Q.C., J.P. He was educated at Charterhouse and Sandhurst, and joined the Dorsetshire Regt. 18 May, 1892, becoming Lieutenant 28 Aug. 1894. He served in the Tirah Expedition in 1897–98, being present at the actions of Chagra Kotal and Dargai, and the capture of Sampagha and Arhanga Passes. Reconnaissance of the Saran Sar and action of 16 Nov. 1897. Operations in the Waran Valley and action of 16 Nov. 1897. Operations in the Bara Valley 7 to 14 Dec. 1897 (Medal with two clasps). He served in the South African War, 1899–1900; operations in Natal, 1899, including operations at Elandslaagte, Rietfontein and Lombard's Kop. In the Defence of Ladysmith, including the sortie of 7 Dec. 1899, and action of 6 Jan. 1900; operations in the Transvaal, east of Pretoria, July to 29 Nov. 1900, including actions of Belfast (26 and 27 Aug.) and Lydenberg 5 to 8 Sept. He was mentioned in Despatches (Sir R. H. Buller, 13 Sept. and 9 Nov. 1900 [London Gazette, 8 Feb. 1901]): received the Queen's Medal with three clasps, and was created a Companion of the Distinguished Service Order [London Gazette, 19 April, 1901]: "Hugh Norman Ramsay Cowie, Capt., Dorsetshire Regt. In recognition of services during the operations in South Africa." The Insignia, etc., were sent to the Commander-in-Chief in South Africa, and presented by the Duke of Cornwall and York 14 Aug. 1901. He had become Captain 13 June, 1900. From 5 June, 1901, to 17 Feb. 1904, he was Adjutant, Volunteers, and he was Adjutant, Dorsetshire Regt. from 9 Sept. 1904, to 22 Jan. 1905, when he went to the Staff College. He was D.A.Q.M.G., Headquarters, South Africa, 20 April, 1907, to 1909; from 1909 to 1911 a Staff Captain at the War Office, and from 1912–14 Commander of a Company of Gentlemen Cadets at Sandhurst. In 1914 he was appointed Commandant of the 1st School of Instruction in France. He was created a C.M.G. Major Cowie died on 20 May, 1915, of wounds received whilst in command of the 1st Battn. of his regiment. He had married, in 1898, Victoria Alexandrina, eldest daughter of the late Sir Howard Elphinstone, V.C., K.C.B., C.M.G.

Hugh N. R. Cowie.

GREEN, ARTHUR DOWSON, Capt., was born 13 April, 1874, at Belvedere, Kent, son of the late Henry Green, Esq., of Blacknall, Old Charlton. He was educated at Haileybury College, where he had a reputation as an athlete, and joined the 1st Essex Regt. as Second Lieutenant on 2 June, 1894, becoming Lieutenant on 14 Aug. 1897. He served with the West African Regt. in the Sierra Leone Hinterland Expedition, under the late General Sir E. R. P. Woodgate, from April, 1898, to June, 1899, taking part in the Karene, Mendiland and Protectorate Expeditions. For these services he received the West African Medal and two clasps. He passed the Staff College. From 1899 to 1902 he served in the Boer War with Thorneycroft's Mounted Infantry, and was present at the Relief of Ladysmith; operations on the Tugela Heights, and also in Natal, including the action at Laing's Nek. He also took part in the operations at Cape Colony, Orange River Colony and the Transvaal, and was mentioned in Despatches by General Sir Redvers Buller, 19 June and 9 Nov. 1900 [London Gazette, 29 July, 1902]. He received the Queen's Medal with six clasps, the King's Medal with two clasps, and was created a Companion of the Distinguished Service Order [London Gazette, 19 April, 1901]: "Arthur Dowson Green, Capt., Worcestershire Regt. In recognition of services during the operations in South Africa." The Insignia, etc., were sent to the Commander-in-Chief in South Africa, and presented by Colonel Ternan 8 Jan. 1902. He was promoted Captain into the Worcestershire Regt. on the 20th June, 1900. From Jan. 1903, to Feb. 1907, he was employed with the West African Frontier Force. He was mentioned in Despatches (by Major Goodwin on the 15th March, 1906, and by Colonel Cole on the 20th May, 1906, recorded in the London Gazette, 2 July, 1907), and received the Medal and clasp. He was appointed Brigade-Major, 17th Infantry Brigade, in the Irish Command, in June, 1911. He served in the European War, and when he met his death on 28 Sept. 1914, he was reconnoitring with his General in the trenches at Soupir, and was shot through the heart by a sniper. He was fond of hunting, and was Master of the Staff College Drag Hounds in 1909 and 1910. Major A. D. Green married Isabella Margaret, second daughter of the late William Lindsay Stewart, Esq., of Stanmore, Lanarkshire, N.B., and their son is Henry James Lindsay Green, born 24 Sept. 1911.

REYNOLDS, PHILIP GUY, Major, was born 19 Jan. 1871, at Raddon Court, Cheshire, third son of Sylvanus Reynolds, of Raddon Court, Cheshire. He was educated at Malvern College, Worcestershire; gazetted to 17th Lancers 28 June, 1893; transferred to 5th Dragoon Guards 12 Nov. 1893. He served in the South African War, 1899–1902, employed with S.A. Constabulary 9 Dec. 1900, to 19 Feb. 1907; operations in Natal, 1899, including action at Elandslaagte; Defence of Ladysmith, including sortie of 7 Dec. 1899, and 6 Jan. 1900; operations in Natal, including action at Laing's Nek; operations in the Transvaal and Orange River Colony, May to 29 Nov. 1900; operations in the Transvaal and Orange River Colony 30 Nov. 1900, to 31 May, 1902 (slightly wounded). He was mentioned in Despatches [London Gazette, 8 Feb. 1901, and 29 July, 1902]; was given the Brevet of Major 22 Aug. 1902; received the Queen's Medal with six clasps, and the King's Medal with two clasps, and was created a Companion of the Distinguished Service Order [London Gazette, 19 April 1901]: "Philip Guy Reynolds, Major, 3rd Dragoon Guards. In recognition of services during the recent operations in South Africa." The Insignia were sent to the Commander-in-Chief, South Africa, and were presented by H.R.H. the Duke of Cornwall and York 14 Aug. 1901. He had been promoted to Captain, 3rd Dragoon Guards, 27 June, 1900; was Adjutant, Imperial Yeomanry, 20 Feb. 1903, to 19 Feb. 1907; became Major 2 July, 1908, and retired 2 March, 1912. He married, 15 July, 1905, in Cheshire, Daisy, second daughter of Charlie Holly (American); they have one daughter, Leila Joan, born 4 Oct. 1906.

ANNESLEY, JAMES HOWARD ADOLPHUS, Capt., was born 3 March, 1868, son of Capt. F. G. Annesley, 28th Regt., and cousin of the 5th Earl Annesley. He was educated at Eastman's Royal Naval Academy; joined the 18th Hussars, and served five years and thirty days in the ranks; became Second Lieutenant 15 Feb. 1893, and was promoted to Lieutenant 6 April, 1898; served as A.D.C. to G.O.C., Tirah Field Force, throughout the Expedition, 1897–98, being present at the actions of Chagra Kotal and Dargai; capture of the Arhanga and Sampagha Passes; reconnaissance of the Saran Sar and action of 9 Nov. 1897; operations at and around Dwatoi and action of 24 Nov. 1897; operations against the Khani Khel Chamkanis; operations in the Bara Valley 7 to 14 Dec. 1897; operations in the Bazar Valley 25 to 30 Dec. 1897 (Despatches [London Gazette, 5 April, 1898]; Medal with two clasps). He was A.D.C. to the Lieut.-Governor, Punjab, 5 March, 1897, to 3 Oct. 1899; became Captain 4 July, 1900. He served in the South African War as Adjutant, Bethune's Mounted Infantry, 20 Nov. 1899, to Nov. 1900, and was afterwards employed with the Imperial Yeomanry. He was present at the Relief of Ladysmith, including the action at Colenso; operations of 17 to 24 Jan. 1900, and action at Spion Kop; operations of 5 to 7 Feb. 1900, and action at Vaal Kranz; operations on Tugela Heights 14 to 27 Feb. 1900; operations in Natal, March to June, 1900, including action at Laing's Nek; operations in Orange River Colony, May to 29 Nov. 1900; operations in the Transvaal, May and July, 1901; operations in Orange River Colony, Feb. 1901, to 31 May, 1902; operations on the Zululand Frontier of Natal in Sept. and Oct. 1901; operations in Cape Colony, Feb. 1901. He was mentioned in Despatches [London Gazette, 8 Feb. 1901]; received the Queen's Medal with six clasps, the King's Medal with two clasps, and was created a Companion of the Distinguished Service Order [London Gazette, 19 April, 1901]: "James Howard Adolphus Annesley, Capt., 3rd Dragoon Guards. In recognition of services during the operations in South Africa." The Insignia were presented by His Royal Highness the Duke of Cornwall and York 14 Aug. 1901. He served as Captain, Imperial Yeomanry, from 27 July, 1901, to 13 March, 1902. Captain Annesley was promoted Major into the 6th Dragoon Guards 11 Oct. 1905, being at that time Staff Captain, Pretoria Sub-District, South Africa, 16 May, 1904, to 10 Feb. 1906. Major Annesley was Brigade-Major, India, 13 Aug. 1906, to 16 Feb. 1909; D.A.A.G., India, 17 Feb. to 3 Sept. 1909, and was promoted to Lieut.-Colonel, 6th Dragoon Guards, 1 May, 1913. He served in the European War as Camp Commandant (graded as A.A.G.) from 29 Nov. 1914; special appointment 17 Feb. to 13 June, 1915; A.A. and Q.M.G. from 14 June, 1915. For his services in this war he was created a Companion of the Order of St. Michael and St. George. He was wounded. Lieut.-Colonel J. H. A. Annesley married Hélène Marie, daughter of the late C. E. Johnston, Esq. He died 22 April, 1919.

KERRY, EARL OF, HENRY WILLIAM EDMUND PETTY-FITZMAURICE, Capt., was born 14 Jan. 1872, eldest son of the 5th Marquess of Lansdowne and Lady Maud Evelyn, daughter of the 1st Duke of Abercorn, K.G. He took his degree (M.A.) at Oxford; served in South Africa, 1899–1900; took part in the advance on Kimberley, including actions at Belmont, Enslin, Modder River and Magersfontein; afterwards served on the Staff (as A.D.C. extra to Field-Marshal Commanding-in-Chief the Forces, 1 Feb. 1900, to 2 Jan. 1901); during operations in the Orange Free State, Feb. to May, 1900, including operations at Paardeberg 17 to 26 Feb. 1900, and actions at Poplar Grove and Dreifontein; was mentioned in Despatches [London Gazette, 16 April, 1901]; received the Queen's Medal with seven clasps, and was created a Companion of the Distinguished Service Order [London Gazette, 19 April, 1901]: "Henry William Edmund, Earl of Kerry, Capt., Irish Guards. In recognition of services during the operations in South Africa." The Insignia were presented by His Majesty the King 3 June, 1901. He retired as Major from the Irish Guards, previously Grenadier Guards; was made a Member of the Victorian Order, 1905; became a Member of the London County Council (West Marylebone), 1907, and M.P. (Unionist) for West Derby, 1908 to 1918, and commanded the 3rd (Reserve) Battn. Irish Guards from 1914 to 1916. Lord Kerry became a Member of the Wiltshire County Council in 1919. He married, in 1904, Elsie, daughter of Sir E. S. Hope, K.C.B., and they have two sons and one daughter.

SHERSTON, WILLIAM MAXWELL, Capt., was born 14 April, 1859, son of the late J. D. Sherston, J.P., Somerset, of Evercreech, near Bath. He was educated at Marlborough, and Pembroke College, Cambridge; enlisted in the 7th Dragoon Guards, 1877; was promoted Lieutenant in the Rifle Brigade, 1882; made Captain, 18th Hussars, 1888, and retired from the 18th Hussars 8 Aug. 1898; served in the South African War, 1881, Transvaal Campaign; served in Egypt, 1884–85 (Medal and two clasps); in Burma, 1887 (Medal and one clasp; mentioned in Despatches [London Gazette, 2 Sept. 1887]). He served in South Africa, 1900–1, with the Imperial Yeomanry, during operations in the Orange Free State, May, 1900, including actions at Vet River (5 and 6 May) and Zand River; during operations in the Transvaal in May and June, 1900, including actions near Johannesburg, Pretoria and Diamond Hill (11 and 12 June); during operations in the Transvaal, east of Pretoria, July to 29 Nov. 1900, including action at Belfast (26 and 27 Aug.). He was mentioned in Despatches [London Gazette, 16 April, 1901], and received the Queen's Medal with five clasps, and was created a Companion of the Distinguished Service Order [London Gazette, 19 April, 1901]: "William Maxwell Sherston, Capt., Imperial Yeomanry. In recognition of services during the operations in South Africa." He was appointed A.D.C. to Commander-in-Chief, 1901 to 1904; commanded North Somerset Yeomanry, 1904–9; Sub-Lieutenant, R.N.V.R., from Aug. 1914; was subsequently Lieut.-Commander, Squadron of Naval Armoured Cars, Yeomanry Base Depôt, Egypt. Lieut.-Colonel, and Honorary Colonel from 1904; appointed to the command of the Yeomanry at "B" Divisional Base Depôt in Egypt, and in April, 1917, was posted to the command of the 22nd Infantry Base Depôt, France, and was Camp Commandant, 17th Corps, France, 1918. Colonel Sherston is a J.P. for Somerset. He married, in 1894, Evelyn Maude Maitland, eldest daughter of the late J. Maitland Spencer, of Oakhill, near Bath.

FITZWILLIAM, EARL (WILLIAM CHARLES DE MEURON WENTWORTH-FITZWILLIAM), Capt. Born 1872, son of Viscount Milton, J.P., and Laura, daughter of the late Lord Charles Beauclerk. He is the 7th Earl Fitzwilliam. The first Earl served five times as Queen Elizabeth's Lord Deputy in Ireland, being created Baron Fitzwilliam in 1620. He was educated at Eton and at Trinity College, Cambridge; was A.D.C. to the Marquess of Lansdowne in India, 1892–93; Major, 4th Battn. Oxfordshire Light Infantry. He was M.P. (Liberal Unionist) for Wakefield, 1895 to 1902. Lord Fitzwilliam served in South Africa, 1900, being employed under the Director of Supplies, Army Headquarters (graded as a Staff Captain), and taking part in the operations in Cape Colony and Orange River Colony, 1900. He was mentioned in Despatches [London Gazette, 16 April, 1901]; received the Queen's Medal with four clasps, and was created a Companion of the Distinguished Service Order [London Gazette, 19 April, 1901]: "William Charles De Meuron, Earl Wentworth-Fitzwilliam, Capt., 4th Battn. Oxfordshire Light Infantry. In recognition of services during the operations in South Africa." The Insignia were presented by the King 25 July, 1901. He succeeded his grandfather in 1902; became a Member of the County Council, Wicklow, and J.P., County Wicklow and West Yorkshire, also D.L., County Wicklow. Earl Fitzwilliam has travelled much in India, Europe and America, and is much interested in engineering, especially mining engineering. His favourite recreations are hunting, riding, shooting, cycling and polo. He was created K.C.V.O. in 1911. He became a Major, 4th Battn. Oxfordshire Light Infantry, and Major, West Riding Royal Horse Artillery, 1908, and was promoted to Brevet Lieut.-Colonel in 1913. He served in the European War from 1914; was mentioned in Despatches, and created a C.B.E. in 1919. In 1896 he married Lady Maud Frederica Elizabeth Dundas, daughter of the 1st Marquess of Zetland, and they have one son, Viscount Milton, born 31 Dec. 1910, and four daughters.

MACINNES, DUNCAN SAYRE, Lieut., was born at Hamilton, Ontario, Canada, 19 July, 1870, younger son of the late Honourable Donald MacInnes, of Hamilton, who, moving to Canada from Scotland in early life, became a Member of the Senate, and Mary MacInnes, daughter of the late Sir John Beverley Robinson, Bart., C.B., Chief Justice of Upper Canada (now the Province of Quebec). He was educated for some time for the Navy, in the Britannia, but his father ultimately determining on a military career for him, he entered the Royal Military College, Kingston, Canada, from which he passed out at the head of his year with Sword of Honour and Gold Medal, obtaining a commission as Second Lieutenant in the Corps of Royal Engineers on 16 July, 1891. He became Lieutenant 16 July, 1894. He saw much active service in the expedition to Ashanti; he was honourably mentioned, and awarded the Star issued for that campaign. Later he was employed on the erection of the fort at Coomassie, the capital of Ashanti, for the defence of the garrison of that place, and that its plan and execution reflected great credit on him and others concerned on its design and constitution is evidenced by the fact that it was for some time besieged by fifteen thousand Ashantis in 1900, and held out until relieved by Colonel (now General) Sir James Willcocks, who described it in "From Kabul to Kumassi" as the best defensive post he saw in West Africa." Lieut. MacInnes acted for a time

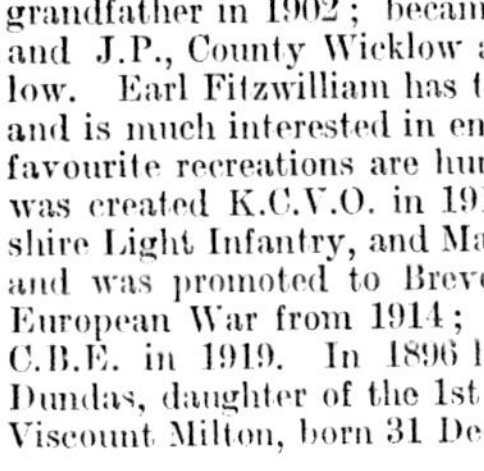

Duncan Sayre MacInnes.

as Resident at Coomassie. During the South African War he performed specially valuable services between Feb. and May, 1900, in the Orange Free State, and particularly in the defence of Kimberley. Here he was employed on Corps duties, and in addition as Staff Officer to Colonel Kekewich, by whom he was mentioned in Despatches [London Gazette, 8 May, 1900], for most valuable services in both the above capacities. A distinguished officer wrote to his father, whom he had known in Canada : " His praises are in everyone's mouth, and I am told that the success was in a large measure, for so young an officer, due to him." Between May and Nov. 1900, he was further engaged in operations in the Orange River Colony. He was again mentioned in Despatches [London Gazette, 29 July, 1902], and was created a Companion of the Distinguished Service Order for his valuable services during the war [London Gazette, 19 April, 1901]: " Duncan Sayres MacInnes, Lieut., Royal Engineers. In recognition of services during the operations in South Africa." The Insignia were sent to the Commander-in-Chief in South Africa, and presented there. He was Captain on 1 April, 1902, and had the Queen's Medal with three clasps, and the King's Medal with two clasps. He was married, on 22 Oct. 1902, at Montreal, Canada, to Millicent Wolfeston Thomas, daughter of F. Wolfeston Thomas and Harriet Goodhue Thomas, and their children are: Duncan Wolfeston, born 5 April, 1904 (now at Eton), and Elizabeth Robinson. He was employed with the South African Constabulary from Nov. 1902, to Dec. 1904. From 1905 to 1908 he was employed on the Staff in Canada, first as Deputy Assistant Quartermaster-General, at Halifax, Nova Scotia, and afterwards as Deputy Assistant Adjutant-General with the Canadian Dominion Forces. His work in connection with the taking over of the defences of Halifax by the Dominion from the Imperial Government was very valuable, and a General Officer under whom he worked said that he was not surprised when, a year or two later, an officer holding a very high position in England spoke of him as one of the best Staff Officers he knew. From Halifax he went to Shorncliffe as Major, Royal Engineers, in charge of works which included the building of the Women's Hospital at that place, and from thence to the Staff College. He was General Staff Officer, 3rd Grade, from 1 April, 1910, to 10 Oct. 1912, and in 1912 was employed as Secretary to the Royal Flying Corps Committee, the result of whose deliberations was the formation of the Royal Flying Corps, which has since developed into the Royal Air Force. He was Major on 16 July, 1911. He passed the Staff College, and was General Staff Officer, 2nd Grade, from 1 April, 1913, to 4 Aug. 1914, on the Staff of the Staff College. He served in the European War, taking part in the Retreat from Mons, for which he had the Star. He was wounded in Nov. 1914. He was Deputy Assistant Director, War Office (temporary), from 19 Feb. 1915, to 8 March, 1915; Assistant Director from 9 March, 1915, to 30 Oct. 1915; Deputy Director 31 Oct. 1915; Director 27 March, 1916. He was Brevet Lieutenant-Colonel in 1915, and Brevet Colonel 29 Nov. 1915. In 1916 and 1917 he was Director of Aeronautical Equipment, with the rank of Brigadier-General, and did much good work. He resigned to go to the Front again, although it involved his relinquishing the rank of Brigadier-General. He was created a Companion of the Order of St. Michael and St. George. He went to France in March, 1917, to perform the duties of Commanding Royal Engineer to the 42nd Division, and from thence after nine months was appointed Inspector of Mines at Headquarters, with the rank of Brigadier-General. On 23 May, 1918, he was killed while engaged in this duty, and was buried in the Military Cemetery at Etaples, close to the sea, 25 May, 1918. During the war he had been twice mentioned in Despatches, and had the Russian Order of St. Stanislaus, with the French Legion of Honour (Croix d'Officier), in 1917. The following are a few quotations from letters written after his death: (From a Field Officer): " He was one of the very bravest and most chivalrous characters I have ever known, and he was universally beloved by all who met him, from the highest in command to our car drivers, servants and orderlies. Everybody felt strangely drawn to him." (From another Field Officer): " He quickly won the admiration of all of us by his gallantry, unbounded energy and kind consideration of others, no matter what rank they held." (From a General Officer, under whom he immediately served): " He was so tremendously brave at Nieuwpoort and other nasty places, a well-known figure in his Division, and perfectly splendid in his work." The Service, his family, and his numerous friends have suffered a very great loss in his death.

BROOKE, VICTOR REGINALD, Lieut., was born at 53, Eaton Square, London, S.W., 22 Jan. 1873, son of Sir Victor Alexander Brooke, Bart., and Alice Sophia, daughter of Sir Alan Bellingham, Bart. He joined the 9th Lancers 12 Dec. 1894; became Lieutenant 29 April, 1896, and went to South Africa at the beginning of the Boer War (1899–1902). He took part in the Advance on Kimberley, including the actions at Belmont, Enslin, Modder River and Magersfontein; in the Relief of Kimberley; the operations in the Orange Free State, Feb. to May, 1900, including operations at Paardeberg; actions at Poplar Grove and Karee Siding. He was one of the first of our men to be wounded, and in a diary picked up off a wounded Boer was set down the enemy's regret that so good a friend and fighter had been, as they thought, killed. He returned to England to recover from his wounds, and had to have a finger removed. He passed the Staff College in the autumn; became Captain 6 May, 1901; returned to South Africa in Oct. 1901, as A.D.C. to Lieut.-General Sir Ian Hamilton, Chief of the Staff (9 Nov. 1901, to 11 Sept. 1902). He was mentioned in Despatches [London Gazette, 19 April, 1901, and 29 July, 1902]; received the Queen's Medal with three clasps; the King's Medal with two clasps, and was created a Companion of the Distinguished Service Order [London Gazette, 19 April, 1901: " Victor Reginald Brooke, Lieut., 9th Lancers. In recognition of services during the operations in South Africa." Capt. Brooke became A.D.C. to Lord Kitchener, and served with him in that capacity in India (28 Nov. 1902, to 21 Dec. 1905); and as Assistant Military Secretary from 22 Dec. 1905, to 31 May, 1907. He was sent to Kabul with Sir Louis Dane's Mission at the end of 1904, when the Amir of Afghanistan bestowed an Afghan decoration on him. Capt. Brooke was given the Brevet of Major 7 June, 1905; accompanied the Amir of Afghanistan on his visit to India, Jan. and Feb. 1907, and was presented with the Afghan Order of " Harmat." He was promoted to Major, 9th Lancers, 6 Feb. 1907, and became Temporary Lieutenant-Colonel 1 June, 1907, and was Military Secretary to Lord Minto from 1 June, 1907, until Lord Minto left India at the end of 1910, when he rejoined his regiment. In Aug. 1914, he proceeded to France, forming part of General Headquarters Staff, as Liaison Officer, with General Sardet's Cavalry Corps, during the retreat from Belgium. The following is an extract from an appreciation of Major Brooke in the " Daily Telegraph," written by " A Friend ": " As to the manner of his death and burial, there is something to be recorded. He died on the night of 29 Aug., and was buried early next morning at Château d'Annel, near Compiègne. The house had been turned into a hospital by Mrs. Depew, who left at eleven on the same day, owing to the approach of the German forces. The estate carpenter made his coffin, and one of the old men of the estate dug his grave. After the burial the old man said to Mrs. Depew: ' Regardez, Madame.' He pointed out a gravestone to the north of the grave, which had the inscription underneath the date, 1879, ' Chevalier de la Légion d'Honneur.' It belonged to one of the family which owned the Château d'Annel in those days, all of whom were buried there. Beside them the old gravedigger thought it right to lay Victor Brooke—Chevalier de la Légion d'Honneur indeed." Lord Kitchener said of him: " Victor Brooke is one of the best Staff Officers I have ever had, and quite one of the best all-round men to be found." When Lord Hardinge came home, he said to a friend: " Victor Brooke was loved by tens of thousands in India." Lady Minto wrote: " He was an ideal Military Secretary. An indefatigable worker himself, he had that rare gift of getting the best out of others. His example was such a stimulus to everyone to try and live up to his own high standard. Victor was beloved by the Viceroy and every member of his household, and no one was ever in his presence without feeling the better for the magnetic influence of his manly, straightforward character."

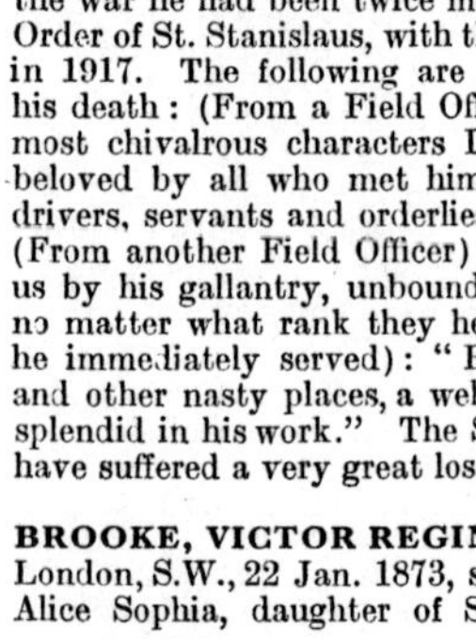

Victor Reginald Brooke.

AINSWORTH, WILLIAM JOHN, Lieut., was born in Jhansi, India, 11 Aug. 1873, the eldest son of the late Capt. Ainsworth, late 106th Light Infantry, of Spotland, Rochdale, Lancashire, and Trentham House, Twickenham Park, S.W. He was educated at St. Paul's School; entered the Royal Military College, Sandhurst, in 1892; joined the Durham Light Infantry, as Second Lieutenant, 19 July, 1893; became Lieutenant 23 July, 1896. He served in the South African War, 1899–1900, and took part in the operations in the Orange Free State, Feb. to May, 1900, including actions at Poplar Grove, Dreifontein, Houtnek (Thoba Mountain), Vet River (5 and 6 May) and Zand River. Operations in the Transvaal, in May and June, 1900, including actions near Johannesburg, Pretoria and Diamond Hill (11 and 12 June). Operations in Orange River Colony, June to Aug. 1900. He was mentioned in Despatches [London Gazette, 8 Feb. 1901]; received the Queen's Medal with four clasps, and was created a Companion of the Distinguished Service Order [London Gazette, 19 April, 1901]: " William John Ainsworth, Lieut., Durham Light Infantry. In recognition of services during the recent operations in South Africa." The decoration was especially awarded for conspicuous gallantry in the affair at Sanna's Post 31 March, 1901. Lieut. Ainsworth was Adjutant, Durham Light Infantry, 15 March, 1901, to 31 Jan. 1905; was promoted to Captain 2 July, 1901; was attached General Staff, War Office, 1 Feb. 1905, to 30 Nov. 1906; was Garrison Adjutant, Eastern Command, 1 June, 1907, to 31 May, 1909; Staff Captain, No. 5 District, Northern Command, 6 June, 1911, to 4 Aug. 1914. He was promoted to Major 21 July, 1914. Major Ainsworth served during the European War; as D.A.A.G., Northern Command, 5 Aug. 1914, to 21 Feb. 1915; D.A.A.G., Base, Mediterranean Expeditionary Force, 22 Feb. to 30 Nov. 1915; A.A.G., Force in Egypt, 1 Dec. 1915, to 21 March, 1916; A.A.G., General Headquarters, Egyptian Expeditionary Force, from 1 April, 1916. He was mentioned in Despatches; given the Brevet of Lieutenant-Colonel 3 June, 1917, and created a C.B.E. in 1919.

McCLINTOCK, ROBERT LYLE, Lieut., was born 26 March, 1874, son of the late Colonel W. McClintock, R.A., of Dunmore, County Donegal. He was educated at Wellington College; entered the Army, as Second Lieutenant, Royal Engineers, 25 July, 1893; became Lieutenant, Royal Engineers, 25 July, 1896; served with the Niger Expeditionary Force, 1897–1898, including the Illah Expedition. He was mentioned in Despatches [London Gazette, 2 Jan. 1900], and received the Medal with clasp. He served in the South African War, 1899–1902, on the Staff, and was present at the Defence of Kimberley (slightly wounded). Operations in the Orange Free State, Feb. to May, 1900, including actions at Poplar Grove and Dreifontein. Operations in Orange River Colony, May to Nov. 1900, including action at Wittebergen. Operations in Orange River Colony and Cape Colony, 1900–02. He was mentioned in Despatches [London Gazette, 8 May, 1900]; received the Queen's Medal with three clasps, " Kimberley Siege," " Dreifontein," and " Wittebergen," the King's Medal with two clasps, and was created a Companion of the Distinguished Service Order [London Gazette, 19 April, 1901]: " Robert Lyle McClintock, Lieut., Royal Engineers. In recognition of services during the operations in South Africa." The Insignia were presented by Lieut.-General Sir C.

Tucker, K.C.B., 9 Nov. 1901. He became Captain 1 April, 1904, and was given the Brevet of Major 2 April, 1904. He served in the European War, in East Africa, 1914–18; was given the Brevet of Lieutenant-Colonel 1 Jan. 1917, and created a C.M.G., 1916. He was married, in 1908, to Jeanie, daughter of Sir G. Casson Walker, K.C.S.I., Assistant Minister of Finance to His Highness the Nizam of Hyderabad's Government.

SMITH, HUGH WILLIAM, Lieut., was born 30 May, 1873, son of Horace Smith, Metropolitan Magistrate of Westminster, and Susan, daughter of the Rev. C. Watkins. He was educated at Uppingham, and gazetted to the Royal West Surrey Regt. 17 Dec. 1892, as Second Lieutenant, becoming Lieutenant 29 Sept. 1896. He served with the expedition to South Borgu and Lagos Hinterland, 1897–99 (Medal with clasp). In the South African War he served from 1899 to 1902, with the 2nd Queen's Regt. and Damant's Horse; was present at the Relief of Ladysmith, including action at Colenso, and at the operations of 17 to 24 Jan. 1900 (wounded 21 Jan.), and action at Spion Kop); operations of 5 to 7 Feb. 1900, and action at Vaal Kranz; operations on Tugela Heights (14 to 27 Feb. 1900), and action at Pieter's Hill. Operations in Natal, March to June, 1900, including action at Laing's Nek (6 to 9 Jan.). Operations in the Transvaal 30 Nov. 1900, to Sept. 1901, and Oct. to Nov. 1901. Operations in Orange River Colony, Sept. to Oct. 1901, and Nov. 1901, to 31 May, 1902. He was mentioned in Despatches (Sir R. Buller, 3 Feb., 30 March and 9 Nov. 1900 [London Gazette, 8 Feb. 1901]); received the Queen's Medal with six clasps, the King's Medal with two clasps, and was created a Companion of the Distinguished Service Order [London Gazette, 19 April, 1901]: "Hugh William Smith, Lieut., Royal West Surrey Regt. In recognition of services during the operations in South Africa." The Insignia were sent to the Commander-in-Chief, South Africa, and presented by H.R.H. the Duke of Cornwall and York 14 Aug. 1901. He was promoted to Captain 24 Aug. 1901, and was Adjutant, Royal West Surrey Regt., 27 June, 1902, to 27 May, 1904; was Assistant Resident in Northern Nigeria 26 May, 1904, to 11 Sept. 1905, and appointed Officer, Company of Gentlemen Cadets, Royal Military College, 30 Jan. 1906, to 29 Jan. 1910; was Adjutant (attached General Staff), Officers' Training Corps, 22 Jan. 1911, to 16 Jan. 1913, and was employed under the Australian Government 17 Jan. 1913, to 8 Sept. 1915. He served in the European War from 1914 to 4 Oct. 1915; was promoted to Major 5 Nov. 1914, and became Temporary Lieutenant-Colonel 10 Oct. 1915. He commanded the 2nd Battn. The Queen's Regt., Oct. 1915, to March, 1916; was Commandant, General Headquarters Cadet School, B.E.F., Aug. 1916 to May, 1917; Commandant Officer, Cadet Battn., Oct. 1917, to Oct. 1918; Officer Commanding, No. 3 Young Soldiers' Battn., B.E.F., Nov. 1918, to Dec. 1918; Officer Commanding, IX. Corps Schools, B.E.F., Jan. 1919. He was given the Brevet of Lieutenant-Colonel in June, 1917.

NORTHEY, WILLIAM, Lieut., was born 29 Jan. 1876, son of the Rev. Edward William Northey, M.A., J.P., of Woodcote House, Epsom. He served in South Africa, as Lieutenant, Durham Light Infantry, on the Staff, 1899 to 1902; was present at the Relief of Ladysmith, including the action at Colenso; operations of 17 to 24 Jan. 1900, and 5 to 7 Feb. 1900, and action at Vaal Kranz; operations on Tugela Heights 14 to 27 Feb. 1900, and action at Pieter's Hill; operations in Natal, March to June, 1900, including action at Laing's Nek (6 to 9 June); operations in the Transvaal, east of Pretoria, July to 29 Nov. 1900. He served as Adjutant, 13th Battn. Mounted Infantry, 30 Nov. 1900, to March, 1902; operations in the Transvaal and Orange River Colony 30 Nov. 1900, to April, 1902; operations on the Zululand Frontier of Natal, Sept. and Oct. 1901. He received the Queen's Medal with five clasps, the King's Medal with two clasps, and was mentioned in Despatches [London Gazette, 8 Feb. 1901, and 29 July, 1902], and created a Companion of the Distinguished Service Order [London Gazette, 19 April, 1901]: "William Northey, Lieut., Durham Light Infantry. In recognition of services during the operations in South Africa." The Insignia were sent to the Commander-in-Chief in South Africa, and presented there. He became Captain 26 Nov. 1901; was Paymaster, A.P. Department, 12 May, 1903, and 2nd Class Assistant, Army Accounts Department, 1 May, 1905. He married, in 1905, Violet, daughter of the late Thomas James Ferguson, of Calicut, India, and there are two sons: William Edward, born in 1909, and Denys Vernon, born in 1910. Capt. Northey served in the European War in 1914, and died of wounds 22 Oct. 1914, at the Base Hospital, Boulogne. An obituary notice of him appeared in the "Times" of 27 Oct. 1914.

DAUNT, RICHARD ALGERNON CRAIGIE, Lieut., was born 1 Oct. 1872, at Dawlish, Devon, son of the late Lieut.-Colonel Richard Daunt, of County Cork, and of Charlotte Isabella Craigie. He was educated at Haileybury College; joined the Royal Irish Rifles, as Second Lieutenant, 7 March, 1894; became Lieutenant 1 Feb. 1897; served with the Royal Irish Rifles in Malta, India, Ireland and South Africa. In the South African War he served from 1899 to 1902, on the Staff, as Divisional Signalling Officer, 3rd Division, South African Field Force, 1900. He took part in the operations in the Orange Free State, Feb. to May, 1900. Operations in the Orange River Colony, May to Nov. 1900. Operations in Cape Colony, south of Orange River, 1899, to 1900; Transvaal, 1900 to 1902. He was mentioned in Despatches [London Gazette, 16 April, 1901]; received the Queen's Medal with eight clasps, the King's Medal with two clasps, and was created a Companion of the Distinguished Service Order [London Gazette, 19 April, 1901]: "Richard Algernon Craigie Daunt, Lieut., Royal Irish Rifles. For services during operations in South Africa." The Insignia were presented there. He became Captain 11 Oct. 1902. He was Adjutant of Militia and Special Reserve 2 Jan. 1904, to 1 Jan. 1909, and was promoted to Major 5 Sept. 1912. He served in the European War from 1914; commanded, as Major, the 2nd Royal Irish Rifles, from 18 Sept. 1914; became Temporary Lieutenant-Colonel 19 Oct. 1914, and Lieutenant-Colonel 27 May, 1915. He was present at Mons, Le Cateau, the Marne and the Aisne, and the First Battle of Ypres; was invalided with shell-shock 4 Oct. 1914; served in Flanders, June, 1915, to 28 Feb. 1916; was invalided to England, March, 1916; returned to France, April, 1917, and commanded the 1st Royal Irish Rifles till 27 June, 1917. He returned to England on account of ill health 30 Aug. 1917. Lieut.-Colonel Daunt is a Fellow of the Royal Astronomical Society. He married, 4 Feb. 1903, at Tarporley, Cheshire, Ellen Georgina Ferozepore, daughter of the late Capt. Cooper, Suffolk Regt., and they have two children: Richard Hubert, born 31 Dec. 1903, and Moira Bridget.

Richard A. C. Daunt.

BURNETT-STUART, JOHN THEODOSIUS, Lieut., was born 14 March, 1875, eldest son of E. R. Burnett-Stuart, J.P., D.L., of Dens and Crichie, Aberdeenshire, N.B. He was educated at Repton and Sandhurst, and joined the Rifle Brigade, as Second Lieutenant, 6 March, 1895; became Lieutenant 26 July, 1897; served in the North-West Frontier Expedition, 1897–98 (Medal with clasp); in the South African War, as Divisional Signalling Officer (graded Staff Captain), 4 Dec. 1899, to 7 Dec. 1901, and as Signalling Officer, 8 Dec. 1901, to 30 June, 1902. He took part in the operations in Cape Colony, south of the Orange River, Jan. to Feb. 1900; in the Relief of Kimberley; operations in Orange Free State, Feb. to May, 1900, including operations at Paardeberg (17 to 26 Feb.), and actions at Poplar Grove and Dreifontein; operations in Orange River Colony and the Transvaal, May, 1900, to 31 May, 1902. He was mentioned in Despatches [London Gazette, 16 April, 1901]; received the Queen's Medal with four clasps, the King's Medal with two clasps, and was created a Companion of the Distinguished Service Order [London Gazette, 19 April, 1901]: "John Theodosius Burnett-Stuart, Lieut., Rifle Brigade. In recognition of services during the operations in South Africa." He was promoted to Captain 20 Feb. 1901. He was Staff Captain and G.S.O., 3rd Grade, Headquarters of Army, from 13 Feb. to 23 June, 1908; G.S.O., 2nd Grade, 24 June, 1908, to 12 Feb. 1915. He served in the European War from 1914, as G.S.O., 2nd Grade, 5 Aug. 1914, to 16 Feb. 1915; G.S.O., 1st Grade, 27 Feb. 1915, to 1 Feb. 1916; was Brigadier-General, General Staff, General Headquarters, British Expeditionary Force, and British Armies in France 2 Feb. 1916, to 3 Feb. 1917; Brigadier-General, General Staff, 19th Army Corps, British Armies in France, 9 Feb. to 25 Dec. 1917; Deputy Adjutant-General, General Headquarters, British Armies in France, 26 Dec. 1917. He was mentioned in Despatches; created a C.M.G., 1916; a C.B., 1917; given the Brevet of Colonel, June, 1916, and promoted to Major-General 3 June, 1919. In 1904 he married Nina, daughter of Major Nelson, late 5th Dragoon Guards, and they have one son, Iain Robert, and two daughters: Elizabeth and Kathron Lilias.

WILLIAMS, ARTHUR FREDERICK CARLISLE, Lieut., was born 19 June, 1876, son of the late G. R. C. Williams, I.C.S., of The Ivy Gates, Guernsey, and of the late Mrs. G. R. C. Williams. He joined the 4th Queen's Own Hussars, as Second Lieutenant, 5 Aug. 1896; became Lieutenant 4 Aug. 1897; was transferred to the Indian Staff Corps 20 Dec. 1897. He served in South Africa, 1899–1900, as Adjutant, 2nd Brabant's Horse, and was dangerously wounded 3 July, 1900. He took part in the operations in Cape Colony, south of the Orange River, Dec. 1899, to March, 1900; in the operations in Orange River Colony, May to July, 1900, including actions near Wepener, Lindley and Bethlehem. He was mentioned in Despatches [London Gazette, 16 April, 1901]; received the Queen's Medal with three clasps, and was created a Companion of the Distinguished Service Order [London Gazette, 19 April, 1901]: "Arthur Frederick Carlisle Williams, Lieut., Indian Staff Corps, Adjutant, Brabant's Horse. In recognition of services during the recent operations in South Africa." The Insignia were presented by His Majesty King Edward 20 July, 1901. He became Captain, 31st (D.C.O.) Lancers, 5 Aug. 1905, and was employed with the Canadian Military Forces from 6 Aug. 1910. He was promoted to Major, Indian Army, 5 Aug. 1914. Major Williams served in the European War from 1914, as Brigade Major, G.S.O., 2nd and G.S.O. 1st. From 1914 to 1917 he served in Belgium and France, and from 1918 in Italy. From 28 Jan. 1916, to 13 Feb. 1917, he was G.S.O.2, 2nd Indian Cavalry Division; 5th Cavalry Division, British Expeditionary Force, 28 Jan. 1916, to 13 Feb. 1917; G.S.O.2, 5th Division, British Armies in France, 14 Feb. 1917, to 5 July, 1917; G.S.O.2, 14th Army Corps, British Army in France, 6 July to 30 July, 1917; Temporary Lieutenant-Colonel 1 July, 1917; G.S.O.1, 4th Division, British Armies in France, 31 July to 17 Sept. 1917; G.S.O.1 (Liaison Officer with the British Force in Italy 11 March, 1918). In Aug. 1916, he was awarded the Order of St. Stanislas, 3rd Class. In 1907 he married Mabel, youngest daughter of Edward Franks, of The Priory, Bishop's Cleeve, Gloucestershire, and they have one daughter, and one son, born in 1914.

FITZGERALD, PERCY DESMOND, Lieut., was born 18 April, 1873, son of the Hon. N. Fitzgerald, of County Galway, Ireland, and of Moira, St. Kilda, Australia, and of Marian, daughter of Sir John O'Shanassy. He was educated at Oscott Roman Catholic College; joined the Royal Kent Regt. as Second Lieutenant, from Local Military Forces, Victoria, 23 Dec. 1893, and the 11th Hussars 24 Jan. 1894; was made Lieutenant, 11th Hussars, 20 Nov. 1897; served in South Africa, 1899–1900, as Intelligence Officer, graded D.A.A.G.; as Adjutant, Imperial Light Horse, from 22 Oct. 1899, to 15 March, 1900; during operations in Natal, 1899, including actions at Rietfontein and Lombard's Kop; took part in the Defence of Ladysmith, including sortie of 7 Dec. 1899, and action of 6 Jan. 1900, afterwards on the Staff; during operations in Natal, March to June, 1900, including action at Laing's Nek (6 to 9 June); during operations in the Transvaal, east of Pretoria, July to 29 Nov. 1900, including actions at Belfast (26 and 27 Aug.) and Lydenberg (5 to 8 Sept.); during operations in Orange River Colony, May to 29 Nov. 1900; was mentioned in Despatches (Sir G. S. White, 2 Dec. 1899, and 23 March, 1900; Sir R. H. Buller, 9 Nov. 1900 [London Gazette, 8 Feb. 1901]). He received the Queen's Medal and four clasps, and was created a Companion of the Distinguished Service Order [London Gazette, 19 April, 1901]: "Percy Desmond Fitzgerald, Lieut. 11th Hussars. In recognition of services during the operations in South Africa." The Insignia was sent to South Africa, forwarded to Egypt, and presented in Egypt 29 Nov. 1901. He was appointed Adjutant, 11 Hussars, 6 May, 1902, to 10 Dec. 1903; became Captain, 11th Hussars, 12 Nov. 1904; Major, 23 Dec. 1908; promoted Brigade-Major, 1st Cavalry Brigade, Aldershot Command, 16 April, 1909, to 15 April, 1913; G.S.O.3, War Office, 1 April, 1914, to 13 Sept. 1914; G.S.O.2, 2nd Mounted Division, Central Force, Home Defence, 14 Sept. 1914, to 1 Feb. 1915; G.S.O.2, 1st Cavalry Division, British Expeditionary Force, 8 Feb. 1915, to 3 May, 1915; G.S.O.1, 2nd Cavalry Division, British Armies in France, 4 May, 1915, to 8 Aug. 1916; Inspector of Mounted Troops, Egypt (Temporary Brigadier-General) 19 Aug. 1916, to 9 April, 1917; Brigade-Commander, 5th Mounted Brigade, Egyptian Expeditionary Force, 10 April, 1917, to 3 Dec. 1917; Brigade-Commander, 22nd Mounted Brigade, Egyptian Expeditionary Force, 4 Dec. 1917, to 7 April, 1918. He was mentioned in Despatches; made an Officer of the Legion of Honour; given the Brevet of Lieutenant-Colonel 1 Jan. 1917. He married, in 1917, Millicent, Duchess of Sutherland.

CAVENDISH, LORD JOHN SPENCER, Lieut., was born 25 March, 1875, third son of the late Lord Edward Cavendish and Lady Edward Cavendish, and grandson of the 7th Duke of Devonshire. He joined the 1st Life Guards, from the Militia, in Feb. 1897; becoming Lieutenant in April, 1898. Lord John Spencer Cavendish served in the South African War of 1899–1902, as Divisional and Brigade Signalling Officer, from Oct. 1899, to 31 Oct. 1900, and was present at the Relief of Ladysmith, including the action at Colenso; at the actions of Spion Kop and Vaal Kranz; operations on the Tugela Heights and action at Pieter's Hill; in the Orange Free State, and action at Zand River; in the Transvaal, and near Johannesburg, Pretoria and Diamond Hill; also in the Transvaal, west of Pretoria, including actions at Elands River; in the Orange River Colony, including actions at Bethlehem and Wittebergen. He was mentioned in Despatches [London Gazette, 1 Feb. 1901]; received the Queen's Medal with six clasps, and was created a Companion of the Distinguished Service Order [London Gazette, 19 April, 1901]: "Lord John Spencer Cavendish, Lieut., 1st Life Guards. For services during operations in South Africa." He was promoted to Captain in Aug. 1902, and from June, 1907, to Sept. 1910, was employed with the West African Frontier Force, being promoted to Major in April, 1911. He served in the European War, and was killed in action on the 20th Oct. 1914.

Lord John S. Cavendish.

CUTHBERT, JAMES HAROLD, Lieut., was born 21 July, 1876, at Melster, Pietermaritzburg, Natal, son of Sidney Cuthbert, of Melster, Pietermaritzburg (second son of William Cuthbert, of Beaufront Castle, Hexham, Northumberland), and Frances Yates Griffin, daughter of J. Griffin, of Pietermaritzburg, Natal; was educated at Sandroyd, Eton and Sandhurst; joined the Scots Guards 12 Aug. 1896; served as Lieutenant in South Africa, 1899–1902; was extra A.D.C. to the G.O.C., 1st Division, in the advance on Kimberley, and was present at the actions of Belmont, Enslin, Modder River and Magersfontein (Despatches); took part in operations in the Orange Free State, Feb. to May, 1900, including actions at Poplar Grove, Dreifontein, Vet River and Zand River; participated in operations in the Transvaal in May and June, 1900, including actions at Johannesburg, Pretoria and Diamond Hill; in operations in the Transvaal, east of Pretoria, July to Nov., including action at Belfast; operations, west of Pretoria, and in the Orange River Colony. He was mentioned in Despatches [London Gazette, 16 March, 1900]: ". . . . Having shown considerable coolness in taking a message from Lord Methuen to the Gordon Highlanders;" was created a Companion of the Distinguished Service Order [London Gazette, 19 April, 1901]: "James Harold Cuthbert, Lieut., Scots Guards. In recognition of services during operations in South Africa." The Insignia were sent to the Commander-in-Chief, South Africa, and presented 14 Aug. 1901. He was appointed High Sheriff of Northumberland in 1911. On the outbreak of the European War he rejoined the 1st Battn. Scots Guards (from the Reserve of Officers), in France, 15 April, 1915. He was reported as wounded and missing 27 Sept. 1915, and finally, on 7 May, 1917, was reported as having been killed on 27 Sept. 1915. He was mentioned in Despatches [London Gazette, 1 Jan. 1916]. He won the Army Revolver Championship in 1904, and published "The 1st Battalion Scots Guards in South Africa, 1899–1902." He married (1st) Anne Dorothy Frederica Byng, third daughter of the 5th Earl of Strafford, at Wrotham Park Private Chapel, 24 Sept. 1903. She died in Jan. 1907. (2ndly), Kathleen Alice Straker, elder daughter of John Straker, of Stagshaw Corbridge, Northumberland, at Hexham Abbey, 12 Oct. 1908, and there are three sons: Harold David, born 11 Sept. 1909; Gerald Ivo, born 25 Jan. 1912; Sidney John, born 13 Jan. 1914, and one daughter, Vida, born 24 Dec. 1910.

INNES, JAMES ARCHIBALD, Lieut., was born 30 July, 1875, son of the late James Innes, of Roffey Park, Horsham. He joined the Rifle Brigade, and served in South Africa, 1899–1902; was present at the Relief of Ladysmith, including action at Colenso; during operations of 17 to 24 Jan. 1900; operations of 5 to 7 Feb. 1900, and action at Vaal Kranz; during operations on Tugela Heights 14 to 27 Feb. and action at Pieter's Hill; during operations in Natal, March to June, 1900, including action at Laing's Nek (6 to 9 June); during operations in the Transvaal, east of Pretoria, July to 29 Nov. 1900. Also during operations in the Transvaal 30 Nov. 1900, to Sept. 1901; in the operations in Orange River Colony, Sept. to Dec. 1901. He was mentioned in Despatches (Sir R. H. Buller, 30 March and 9 Nov. 1900 [London Gazette, 8 Feb. 1901]); received the Queen's Medal with six clasps, and King's Medal with two clasps, and was created a Companion of the Distinguished Service Order [London Gazette, 19 April, 1901]: "James Archibald Innes, Lieut., Rifle Brigade. In recognition of services during the operations in South Africa." He was Captain, Rifle Brigade, 1901 to 1909, and became a Major in the Sussex Yeomanry. Lieut.-Colonel J. A. Innes married (1st), Marjorie (who died in 1912), third daughter of the late Abraham John Roberts; and (2ndly), in 1914, Barbara, eldest daughter of the Hon. E. L. Lowther, and they have a son and a daughter.

WALKER, JOHN DOUGLAS GLEN, Lieut., was born 18 Dec. 1873, son of Colonel John S. Walker, late of Shotts, Hamilton, County Lanark, and of Louisa M. Walker. He was educated at Wellington College, and the Royal Military College, Sandhurst, and gazetted to the Royal Highlanders 10 Oct. 1894, becoming Lieutenant 1 Aug. 1898. He served in the South African War from 1899 to 1902, as Divisional Signalling Officer, 24 Oct. 1899, to 17 Oct. 1900, taking part in operations in Natal, 1899, and in the Defence of Ladysmith. He was present in the operations in the Transvaal in Dec. 1901; in the operations in Orange River Colony, Dec. 1901, to Feb. 1902. Operations in the Transvaal and Orange River Colony, March, 1902, to 31 May, 1902. He was mentioned in Despatches [London Gazette, 8 Feb. 1901]; received the Queen's Medal with seven clasps, the King's Medal with two clasps, and was created a Companion of the Distinguished Service Order [London Gazette, 19 April, 1901]: "John Douglas Glen Walker, Lieut., Black Watch. In recognition of services during the operations in South Africa." The Insignia were presented to him by the King. He became Captain 25 Oct. 1901; was Divisional Signalling Officer, South Africa, 24 Oct. 1899, to 17 Oct. 1900; Adjutant, Volunteers, 18 March, 1907, to 31 March, 1908; Adjutant, Territorial Force, 1 June, 1908. He retired 23 April, 1910. He served in the European War, 1914; was mentioned in Despatches, given the Brevet of Major, 8 May, 1916, and awarded the Croix de Guerre, and created an O.B.E. in 1919. He married, in 1912, Florence Selina, daughter of the late Thomas Hodson Ellis, of Liverpool, and they have one son.

WAUCHOPE, ARTHUR GRENFELL, Lieut., was born 1 March, 1874, son of David Baird Wauchope, Edinburgh; was educated at St. Ninian's, Moffat; Repton, Derbyshire; appointed Second Lieutenant, 4th Argyll and Sutherland Highlanders, in 1893, and Second Lieutenant, 2nd Battn. The Black Watch (Royal Highlanders), 1896; was promoted Lieutenant 3 Aug. 1898; served on the Staff of the late Major-General Wauchope, commanding Highland Brigade in South Africa; was severely wounded at Magersfontein. He took part in the operations in Cape Colony, south of the Orange River, 1899; received the Queen's Medal with clasp; King's Medal with two clasps; was mentioned in Despatches, 16 April, 1901, and created a Companion of the Distinguished Service Order [London Gazette, 19 April, 1901]: "Arthur Grenfell Wauchope, Lieut., Black Watch. In recognition of services during the recent operations in South Africa." The Insignia were presented by H.M. the King 3 June, 1901. He was appointed A.D.C. (Extra) to the Governor and Commander-in-Chief, Cape of Good Hope, from 17 April, 1902, to 1 March, 1903. On the outbreak of the European War he became Major, 26 Sept. 1914, and temporary Lieutenant-Colonel, 6 Sept. 1915; was wounded, mentioned in Despatches, and created Officer of the Legion of Honour. Commanded 2nd Battn. The Black Watch in France and in Mesopotamia; Brevet Lieutenant-Colonel, 1916; wounded, Jan. 1916; Brevet Colonel, 1917; was created a C.M.G., 1917, and Temporary Brigadier-General, and given command of the 24th Infantry Brigade, Indian Expeditionary Force "D," Mesopotamia Expeditionary Force, 11 May, 1917. He was created a C.I.E. in 1919.

DAVIDSON, JOHN HUMPHREY, Lieut., was born 24 July, 1876, son of George Walter Davidson, of 167, Queen's Gate, South Kensington, London, S.W. He was educated at Harrow and Sandhurst; entered King's Royal Rifle Corps, as Second Lieutenant, 28 March, 1896; became Lieutenant 15 Oct. 1898; Captain 25 Oct. 1901; served in the South African War, as Regimental Officer and subsequently as Divisional Signalling Officer (graded Staff Captain), 1899–1902; as Adjutant, Damant's Horse (from Dec. 1901, to 31 May, 1902); during operations in Natal, 1899, including action at Talana; was present at the Relief of Ladysmith, including operations at Colenso, also of 17 to 24 Jan. 1900, and action at Spion Kop, and of 5 to 7 Feb. 1900; on Tugela Heights (14 to 27 Feb. 1900), and action at Pieter's Hill; during operations in Natal, March to June, 1900, including action at Laing's Nek (6 to 9 June); during operations in the Transvaal, east of Pretoria, July to 29 Nov. 1900, including actions at Belfast, 26 and 27 Aug. and Lydenberg (5 to 8 Sept.). During operations in the Transvaal, 30 Nov. 1901; in the operations in Orange River Colony, Dec. 1901, to March, 1902; during operations in the Zululand Frontier of Natal, Sept. and Oct. 1901; during operations in Cape Colony, 1902. He was mentioned in Despatches [London Gazette, 8 Feb. 1901]; received the Queen's Medal and seven clasps, the King's Medal with two clasps, and was created a Companion of the Distinguished Service Order [London Gazette, 19 April, 1901]: "John Humphrey Davidson, Lieut., King's Royal Rifle Corps. In recognition of services during the operations in South Africa." The Insignia, etc., were sent to the Commander-in-Chief in South Africa, and presented by the G.O.C., Natal. He was Adjutant, 1st Battn. King's Royal Rifle Corps, 3 Sept. 1902, to 2 Sept. 1905. After passing through the Staff College, 1906–07, he was appointed G.S.O., 3rd Grade, H.Q. of Army, and G.S.O., 3rd Grade, War Office, 1 April, 1908, to 31 March, 1910;

promoted Brigade-Major, 5th Brigade, Aldershot Command, 1 April, 1910, to 31 March, 1912; received the Brevet of Major 10 May, 1913; became Major, King's Royal Rifle Corps, 1 April, 1914; appointed G.S.O., 2nd Grade, Staff College, 16 April, 1912, to 15 May, 1914, when he rejoined his regiment at Aldershot. He served in the European War from Aug. 1914; was G.S.O., 2nd Grade, 5 Aug. 1914, to 14 July, 1915; Brevet of Colonel; Temporary Brigadier-General 18 Feb. 1915; G.S.O., 1st Grade, 15 July, 1915, to 21 Dec. 1915.; Brigadier-General, G.S., B.E.F., British Armies in France, 22 Dec. 1915, to 13 March, 1918; Major-General, G.S., G.H.Q., British Armies in France, 14 March, 1918. He was promoted to Major-General, 1 Jan. 1918; created a C.B. in 1917, and a K.C.M.G. in 1917. For his services in the European War he also received the Legion of Honour (Croix d'Officier), in 1915; promoted to Commandeur, 1916; Croix de Guerre, 1917; Belgian Croix de Couronne, Commandeur, 1916; Croix de Guerre, (Belgian), 1916; Croix de Guerre (French), second citation, 1919; American Distinguished Service Medal, 1919. Sir John Davidson has been M.P. for the Fareham division of Hants since 1918. He married, in 1905, Margaret, youngest daughter of the late J. P. Grant, of Rothiemurchus, and they have one daughter, Diana.

WAKE, HEREWARD, Lieut., was born 11 Feb. 1876, eldest son and heir of Sir H. Wake, 12th Bart., of Courteenhall, Northampton, and Catherine, daughter of Sir Edward St. Aubyn, 1st Bart., St. Michael's Mount, Cornwall, and sister of the 1st Lord St. Levan; was educated at Eton, and at the Royal Military College, Sandhurst, and Staff College, and joined the King's Royal Rifle Corps, as Second Lieutenant, 17 March, 1897; served in the South African War, with 3rd Battn. King's Royal Rifle Corps, in Natal till Relief of Ladysmith; as A.D.C. to Field-Marshal Lord Roberts, from March, 1900, to Dec. 1900; also with Mounted Infantry Battn. King's Royal Rifle Corps, 1901 and 1902. During the campaign he was wounded once, mentioned in Despatches four times, Queen's Medal and five clasps, King's Medal and two clasps, and was created a Companion of the Distinguished Service Order [London Gazette, 19 April, 1901]: "Hereward Wake, Lieut., King's Royal Rifle Corps. In recognition of services during the operations in South Africa." He was promoted Captain, King's Royal Rifle Corps, 7 Jan. 1902; became Adjutant 27 June, 1905, to 26 June, 1916; was Brigade Major, 2nd Infantry Brigade, 1911–13, and held various Staff appointments. He served in France, 1914–19; with the 61st Division in France from 1 March, 1916, to 11 Dec. 1917; appointed Brigadier-General, General Staff, to the Supreme War Council at Versailles, 12 Dec. 1917; Brevet Lieutenant-Colonel 1 Jan. 1917; C.M.G. 1 Jan. 1918; Bronze Star for 1914. He holds the Bronze Medal of the Royal Humane Society. He owns about 3,000 acres. He married, in 1912, Daisy, eldest daughter of R. H. Benson, of Buckhurst, Sussex, senior partner of Robert Benson and Co., Merchant Bankers, London, and a Trustee of the National Gallery since 1912. They have two sons and two daughters.

Hereward Wake.

CLIFFORD, WIGRAM, Lieut., was born 20 Feb. 1876, son of Major-General R. M. Clifford; was educated at U.S. College, Westward Ho! and the Royal Military College, Sandhurst; joined the Loyal North Lancashire Regt., as Second Lieutenant, 25 March, 1896; became Lieutenant 16 April, 1899; served in South Africa, 1899–1901; was present at the Defence of Kimberley (slightly wounded; Despatches, 8 May, 1900; created a Companion of the Distinguished Service Order [London Gazette, 19 April, 1901]: "Wigram Clifford, Lieut., North Lancashire Regt. In recognition of services during the operations in South Africa." The Insignia were sent to the Commander-in-Chief in South Africa, and Lord Kitchener was asked to return it. It was presented by H.M. the King 25 July, 1901). He was promoted Captain, Northumberland Fusiliers, 12 Oct. 1901. He served on the North-West Frontier of India, 1908; took part in the Mohmand Expedition (Medal with clasp); became Adjutant, Indian Volunteers, 17 Aug. 1912, to 1915. He served in the European War, 1914 to 1918, and was promoted Major, Northumberland Fusiliers, 1 Sept. 1915. He married Eva, youngest daughter of the late Major T. C. Miles.

PRESCOTT, JOHN JOSEPH WHITWORTH, Lieut., was born 5 Sept. 1875, son of G. Prescott, The Hermitage, Merrion, Dublin. Was educated at R.C.S.I., Meath Hospital, Dublin; Charing Cross Hospital, and Royal London Ophthalmic Hospital; entered the Army as Lieutenant, Royal Army Medical Corps, on 27 July, 1899; served in the South African War, 1899–1902, and was present in the operations in Natal, 1899. Relief of Ladysmith, including action at Colenso; operations of 17 to 24 Jan. 1900, and action at Spion Kop; operations 5 to 7 Feb. 1900, and action at Vaal Kranz; operations on Tugela Heights (14 to 27 Feb. 1900), and action at Pieter's Hill; operations in Natal, March to June, 1900, including action at Laing's Nek (6 to 9 June); operations in the Transvaal, July to 29 Nov. 1900; operations in the Transvaal 30 Nov. to 31 May, 1902. Was mentioned in Despatches [London Gazette, 8 and 22 Feb. 1900], received the Queen's Medal with five clasps, King's Medal with two clasps, and was created a Companion of the Distinguished Service Order [London Gazette, 19 April, 1901]: "John Joseph Whitworth Prescott, Lieut., Royal Army Medical Corps. In recognition of services during the operations in South Africa." The Insignia were sent to South Africa, and presented by H.R.H. the Duke of Cornwall and York 14 Aug. 1901. He was promoted Captain 27 July, 1902; became Adjutant, Territorial Force, 27 Nov. 1908. Qualified as Specialist in Ophthalmology, and obtained accelerated promotion to Major on 27 April, 1911; became Lieutenant-Colonel 1 March, 1915. He served in the European War from Aug. 1914, and was mentioned in Despatches by Field-Marshal Sir John French. He organized the Northumberland War Hospital, and commanded it to 25 Sept. 1915, when he proceeded to Gallipoli, as O.C., 17th Stationary Hospital, until the evacuation of the Peninsula; subsequently commanded the same hospital in Egypt, Taj Mahal War Hospital, Alexandra War Hospital, and Cumballa War Hospital, Bombay, and later was O.C., 34th General Hospital, Deolali. Lieut.-Colonel Prescott was brought to the notice of the Government of India [Indian Gazette of Sept. 1918]. Appointed Honorary Surgeon to the Viceroy from 5 Nov. 1918.

DOUGLAS, HENRY EDWARD MANNING, V.C., Lieut., served in the South African War; was mentioned in Despatches [London Gazette, 16 March, 1900], awarded the Victoria Cross, and created a Companion of the Distinguished Service Order [London Gazette, 19 April, 1901]: "Henry Edward Manning Douglas, V.C., Lieut., Royal Army Medical Corps. In recognition of services during the operations in South Africa." The Insignia were sent to the Commander-in-Chief, South Africa, and presented by Major-General Stephenson, at Friedrichstad, 4 April, 1904. (See Victoria Cross volume.)

CHARLTON, LIONEL EVELYN OSWALD, Lieut., was born 7 July, 1879, son of the late William O. Charlton, of Hesleyside, Northumberland. He was educated at Brighton College; passed the Staff College; joined the Lancashire Fusiliers, as Second Lieutenant, 28 Sept. 1898; became Lieutenant, Lancashire Fusiliers, 1 Sept. 1899. He served in the South African War, 1899–1902. Relief of Ladysmith, including operations of 17 to 24 Jan. 1900, and action at Spion Kop (slightly wounded). Operations in the Transvaal in May and June, 1900, including action at Laing's Nek (6 to 9 June). Operations in the Transvaal, east of Pretoria, July to 29 Nov. 1900. Operations in Orange River Colony, May to 29 Nov. 1900. Employed with Imperial Yeomanry. Again slightly wounded (Feb. 1902). He was mentioned in Despatches [London Gazette, 8 Feb. 1901]; received the Queen's Medal with five clasps, the King's Medal with two clasps, and was created a Companion of the Distinguished Service Order [London Gazette, 19 April, 1901]: "Lionel Evelyn Oswald Charlton, Lieut., Lancashire Fusiliers. In recognition of services during the operations in South Africa." The Insignia, etc., were sent to South Africa, but returned, and presented by H.M. the King to Capt. Charlton. He was promoted Captain, Lancashire Fusiliers, 5 Oct. 1901; became Lieutenant, Imperial Yeomanry, 17 April, 1901, to 23 Sept. 1902; became A.D.C. to Governor and Commander-in-Chief, Leeward Islands, 29 April, 1908, to 18 April, 1909; became Captain, Royal Flying Corps, 28 April, 1914; was Temporary Lieutenant-Colonel, Lancashire Fusiliers, 18 Aug. 1915, to 31 Dec. 1916, and Major, Lancashire Fusiliers, 1 Sept. 1915. During the European War he has been created a C.M.G.; was G.S.O.1, War Office, 19 March, 1916, to 27 Feb. 1917; was given the Brevet of Lieutenant-Colonel 1 Jan. 1917; was temporary Brigadier-General 28 Feb. 1917, to 31 March, 1918; and Director of Military Aeronautics, War Office, 28 Feb. 1917, to 17 Oct. 1917; Brigade-Commander, 5th Brigade, Royal Flying Corps, British Armies in France, 18 Oct. 1917, to 31 March, 1918; employed under the Air Ministry, 1 April, 1918. For his services in the European War he was given the Brevet of Lieutenant-Colonel, created a C.M.G., 1916, and a C.B., 1919. In 1919 he was appointed Air Attaché, British Embassy, Washington. He has written a book for the use of students in Hausa.

CAMPBELL, DUNCAN FREDERICK, Lieut., was born 28 April, 1876. He was gazetted to the Lancashire Fusiliers, 23 Nov. 1898; became Lieutenant 27 Sept. 1899. He served in the South African War, 1899–1901, and was present at the Relief of Ladysmith, including operations of 17 to 24 Jan. 1900 (wounded, 20 Jan.), and action at Spion Kop; operations of 5 to 7 Feb. 1900, and action at Vaal Kranz. Operations in the Transvaal in May and June, 1900. Operations in Natal, March to June, 1900, including action at Laing's Nek (6 to 9 June). Operations in the Transvaal, east of Pretoria, July to 29 Nov. 1900. Operations in Orange River Colony, May to 29 Nov. 1900. Operations in the Transvaal 30 Nov. 1900, to Jan. 1901. Served as Adjutant, 2nd Battn. Lancashire Fusiliers. He was mentioned in Despatches (Sir R. H. Buller, 30 March, 19 June and 19 Nov. 1900 [London Gazette, 8 Feb. 1901]); received the Queen's Medal with six clasps, and was created a Companion of the Distinguished Service Order [London Gazette, 19 April, 1901]: "Duncan Frederick Campbell, Lieut., Lancashire Fusiliers. In recognition of services during the operations in South Africa." He was promoted to Captain 5 Oct. 1901; transferred to the Royal Highlanders 13 June, 1908. He was Adjutant, Volunteers, 6 May, 1904, to 31 March, 1908, and Adjutant, Territorial Force, 1 April, 1908. He retired 13 July, 1910. Capt. Campbell served during the European War, as Lieutenant-Colonel, Territorial Force Battn. West Riding Regt. He died 4 Sept. 1916, and was buried at Kilmarnock, several prominent Unionists attending his funeral. An obituary notice said: "We regret to announce the death, after a few days' illness, of Colonel Duncan F. Campbell, who had represented North Ayrshire in the Unionist interest since 1911. He entered the House of Commons in that year, at a by-election, defeating Mr. A. M. Anderson (now Lord Anderson), who sought re-election on being appointed Solicitor-General. Colonel Campbell, who was born in 1876, entered the Black Watch in 1908, and fought through the South African War from 1899 to 1901. He was in the operations for the relief of Ladysmith, and afterwards took part in many other famous actions. He did not escape scathless. He recovered, however, from his wounds, won the D.S.O., and had also the Queen's Medal with six clasps. He was thrice mentioned in the Despatches of Sir Redvers Buller. Colonel Campbell, who had retired in 1910, rejoined his old regiment for the war with Germany, and saw much service. For a time he was attached to the Gordon Highlanders, and afterwards received the rank of Lieutenant-Colonel for service with the Duke of Wellington's Regt.—the West Ridings. His death recalls an interesting incident in the House of Commons in January last, when the gallant officer entered an indignant protest against what he termed 'the voluminous verbiage' of a group of members below the Ministerial gangway. 'Get on with the war,' he demanded, 'and finish everything that interferes with the progress of the war.' 'If I had had the member for Hanley (Mr. Outhwaite) in my battalion,' he added, 'he would have been strung up by the thumbs before he had been there half an hour.' Mr. Outhwaite inquired: 'How many of your battalion would it take to do it?' Colonel Campbell replied: 'I would leave that task to myself, even though I have only one arm, having lost the use of the other in a task which the member for Hanley would not think of attempting or daring to risk,' a statement which naturally evoked loud cheers."

PRICE-DAVIES, LLEWELLYN ALBERIC EMILIUS, Lieut., served in the South African War; was mentioned in Despatches [London Gazette, 26 Jan. 1900, and 8 Feb. 1901]; received the Queen's Medal with five clasps, the King's Medal with two clasps, and was created a Companion of the Distinguished Service Order [London Gazette, 19 April, 1901]: "Llewellyn Alberic Emilius Price-Davies, Lieut., King's Royal Rifle Corps. In recognition of services during the operations in South Africa." He was afterwards awarded the Victoria Cross. (See Victoria Cross volume.)

HOOPER, RICHARD GRENSIDE, Lieut., was born at Plymouth 8 Nov. 1873, son of the late Richard Brinsley Hooper and Annie Katrine (*née* Thorold); was educated at Clifton College, and at Pembroke College, Cambridge; was gazetted to the 5th Lancers 7 Dec. 1895, and served in India till 1898. He served in the South African War, 1899–1900, being present at the Defence of Ladysmith; was mentioned in Despatches [London Gazette, 8 Feb. 1901]; received the Queen's Medal with clasp, and was created a Companion of the Distinguished Service Order [London Gazette, 19 April, 1901]: "Richard Grenside Hooper, Lieut., 5th Lancers (now Capt., 21st Lancers). In recognition of services during the operations in South Africa." The Insignia were presented by H.M. the King 29 Oct. 1901. He was A.D.C. to Field-Marshal Sir George White at Gibraltar 6 July, 1900, to 15 Aug. 1902; was promoted to Captain into the 21st Lancers 29 May, 1901; was Instructor, Cavalry School, 9 Jan. to 11 Nov. 1906. He was promoted to Major 25 Aug. 1909, and retired from the 21st Lancers 10 Dec. 1913. He commanded a squadron in the 7th Reserve Calvary Regt., Aug. 1914, at Tidworth, and was Second-in-Command, 1st Reserve Cavalry Regt., Feb. 1917, at the Curragh. In 1906 he married Ellen Dorothea, daughter of the late Sir E. Frankland, K.C.B., F.R.S., and they have one son, Richard George Frankland Ironside.

Richard G. Hooper.

THEOBALD, HENRY CHARLES, WEBB, Lieut., was born 26 June, 1876, son of Colonel Percy Theobald, late R.A. He was educated at Cheltenham College, and joined the 1st Battn. Gloucestershire Regt. 4 May, 1898, becoming Lieutenant 24 Feb. 1900. He served in the South African Campaign, 1899–1900, and was present in the engagements at Rietfontein and Lombard's Kop; at the Siege of Ladysmith, including the night sortie on Gun Hill. He took part in the operations of the Drakensburg Defence Force, including the seizure of Van Reenen's Pass; also served with Mounted Infantry, 1901–2; operations in Orange River Colony (dangerously wounded). He was mentioned in Despatches [London Gazette, 8 Feb. 1901]; was recommended for extra-regimental promotion to the rank of Captain; received the Queen's Medal with four clasps, the King's Medal with two clasps, and for the night sortie at Ladysmith was created a Companion of the Distinguished Service Order [London Gazette, 19 April, 1901]: "Henry Charles Webb Theobald, Lieut., Gloucestershire Regt. In recognition of services during the operations in South Africa." The Insignia were presented to him by H.M. The King 24 Oct. 1902. He became Captain, Manchester Regt., 30 July, 1901. Capt. Theobald served in the European War as Temporary Major, Manchester Regt., 29 April to 31 Aug. 1915; was promoted to Major 1 Sept. 1915; was Brigade-Major, 26th Reserve Infantry Brigade, New Armies, 2 May, 1916, to 15 June, 1917. He was Temporary Lieut.-Colonel Dec. 1917, to 2 May, 1918, commanding 13th Battn. Manchester Regt., and Acting Lieut.-Colonel 3 May to 18 May, 1918; Commandant, School of Musketry, Eastern Command, 6 Aug. 1918.

STANSFELD, JOHN RAYMOND EVELYN, Lieut., was born 20 April, 1880, the only son of John Birbeck Evelyn Stansfeld, M.A. He was educated at Uppingham and Sandhurst; gained the Sword of Honour in 1897, and was gazetted to the Gordon Highlanders 18 April, 1899; served in the South African War from 1899–1902, first as Railway Staff Officer, being promoted to Lieutenant 25 Feb. 1900. He took part in the operations in Natal in 1899; Relief of Ladysmith, including the action at Colenso; in the operations of 17 to 24 Jan. 1900, and the action at Spion Kop; the operations of 5 to 7 Feb. 1900, and action at Vaal Kranz; Tugela Heights 14–27 Feb. 1900, and Pieter's Hill; was in the fighting in Natal, March to June, 1900, including the action at Laing's Nek 6–9 June; in the Transvaal operations, east of Pretoria, July to 29 Nov. 1900; Belfast 26 and 27 Aug. and Lydenberg 5 to 8 Sept.; in the Transvaal, west of Pretoria, July to Nov. 1900; in the Transvaal operations, Nov. 1900, to Sept. 1901, and Nov.–Dec. 1901, and in the operations in Orange River Colony, Sept. to Nov. 1901. He was mentioned in Despatches by Sir R. H. Buller, 3 Feb. and 30 March, 1901; received the Queen's Medal with six clasps, the King's Medal with two clasps, and for his conduct in attending the wounded under fire at Spion Kop was created a Companion of the Distinguished Service Order [London Gazette, 19 April, 1901]: "John Raymond Evelyn Stansfeld, Lieut., Gordon Highlanders. In recognition of services during the operations in South Africa." The Insignia were sent to the Commander-in-Chief in South Africa, and presented by the Duke of Cornwall and York 14 Aug. 1901. He was heavy-weight boxing champion in the Army Boxing in 1903, at Aldershot; became Captain 30 May, 1904; was Adjutant to the 5th Gordon Highlanders (Territorial Force) from 26 Aug. 1904, to 1909. He served with the 2nd Gordon Highlanders in India and Egypt, 1910–14; was at the Delhi Durbar, 1911, where he organized the Boxing Tournament. He received the Durbar Medal. He served in the Great War, leaving England with the 2nd Gordon Highlanders on 4 Oct. 1914, and landed in Belgium with the 7th Division; was wounded in the First Battle of Ypres, Nov. 1914, and at Neuve Chapelle on 13 March, 1915. He was promoted Brevet Major, Jan. 1915; was appointed to command his battalion, May, 1915; was gazetted Lieut.-Colonel 23 June, 1915; was thrice mentioned in Despatches. He was mortally wounded at Loos 25 Sept. 1915, while leading his battalion into action. He continued to command and direct after he was wounded, until he was taken to the dressing station some hours later. In April, 1904, Capt. Stansfeld married Constance Yolande, eldest daughter of the late Major-General Le Marquis de Bourbel de Montpinçon, R.E., and has one son, John de Bourbel Stansfeld, born 22 Feb. 1905. He died on 28 Sept. at Choques, and his body is buried in the Military Cemetery at that place. He was awarded the "1914 Star."

John R. E. Stansfeld.

READE, ROBERT ERNEST, Lieut., was born 18 April, 1879, son of R. H. S. Reade, Esq., J.P. He was gazetted to the King's Royal Rifle Corps 2 Aug. 1899; was promoted to Lieutenant, and served in the South African War. For his services in this campaign he was created a Companion of the Distinguished Service Order [London Gazette, 19 April, 1901]: "Robert Ernest Reade, Lieut., King's Royal Rifle Corps. In recognition of services during the operations in South Africa." The Insignia, Warrant and Statutes were sent to his father, R. H. S. Reade, Esq.

MARSH, CUNLIFFE HEBBERT, Lieut., was born 30 Oct. 1878, son of Colonel Hippisley Cunliffe Marsh, late Indian Staff Corps, and of Emma Brett, second daughter of Colonel W. G. Hebbert, R.E. He was educated at Repton; joined the 1st South Lancashire Regt. (from the Militia), as Second Lieutenant, 20 May, 1899; became Lieutenant 8 Aug. 1900; served in South Africa, 1899–1901; was present at the Relief of Ladysmith, including operations of 17 to 24 Jan. 1900, and action at Spion Kop; during operations of 5 to 7 Feb. 1900, and action at Vaal Kranz; taking part during operations on Tugela Heights 14 to 27 Feb. 1900 (he was wounded 23 Feb.), and action at Pieter's Hill; during operations in Natal, March to June, 1900, including action at Laing's Nek (6 to 9 June); during operations in Orange River Colony, June, 1900; taking part in the operations in the Transvaal, July to 29 Nov. 1900. He served during operations in the Transvaal 30 Nov. 1900, to Aug. 1901; in the operations in Cape Colony, Aug. to Sept. 1901. He was mentioned in Despatches [London Gazette, 8 Feb. 1901], and received the Queen's Medal with seven clasps; was recommended for the Victoria Cross for services at Pieter's Hill, and created a Companion of the Distinguished Service Order [London Gazette, 19 April, 1901]: "Cunliffe Hebbert Marsh, Lieut., South Lancashire Regt. In recognition of services during the operations in South Africa." The Insignia, etc., were sent to South Africa, and presented at Nowgong, 28 Oct. 1903. He was transferred to the Indian Army, as Lieutenant in the 18th King George's Own Lancers 6 Sept. 1902; became Captain in the Indian Army 20 May, 1908. Capt. Marsh proceeded to France with the Indian Cavalry in Nov. 1914. He was promoted Major 1 Sept. 1915. In Nov. 1915, he was appointed Second-in-Command of a Service Battn. King's Own Scottish Borderers, and shortly afterwards Lieutenant-Colonel (temporary), commanding the 7th Battn. of Cameron Highlanders (mentioned in Despatches, Jan. 1917). He was recalled to India 9 June, 1918, to command a battalion, Indian Infantry, and was appointed to the 2/10th Jats. He married, in 1909, Nina Helen, eldest daughter of George James Smith, of Row, Dumbartonshire, and they have two daughters: Helen Barbara, born 15 Aug. 1910, and Sylvia Mary, born 25 Feb. 1913.

SETTRINGTON, LORD (CHARLES HENRY GORDON-LENNOX) (now Earl of March), was born 30 Dec. 1870, eldest son of the 7th Duke of Richmond, K.G., and Amy, daughter of Percy Ricardo. He joined the Militia, and served as A.D.C. to Field-Marshal Lord Roberts, Commander-in-Chief the Forces, South Africa, 23 Dec. 1899, to 2 Jan. 1901. Lord Settrington was gazetted to the 1st Irish Guards 15 Aug. 1900; became Lieutenant 6 Oct. 1900, and Captain 19 Feb. 1901. He took part in the operations in the Orange Free State, Feb. to May, 1900, including operations at Paardeberg 17 to 26 Feb. and the actions of Poplar Grove and Dreifontein; was mentioned in Despatches [London Gazette, 16 April, 1901]; received the Queen's Medal with five clasps, and was created a Companion of the Distinguished Service Order [London Gazette, 19 April, 1901]: "Charles Henry, Lord Settrington, Lieut., Irish Guards. In recognition of services during the operations in South Africa." The Insignia were presented to him by the King 3 June, 1901. He became Major, Irish Guards; was A.D.C. to General Sir C. Douglas, Inspector-General, Home Forces; and Colonel, Sussex Yeomanry and Reserve of Officers; was created an M.V.O., 1905. Lord March has written "Records of the Old Charlton Hunt" (1910) and "A Duke and His Friends" (1911). He married, in 1893, Hilda, daughter of the late Henry Arthur Brassey, of Preston Hall, Kent, and has two sons and two daughters.

MONTAGU-DOUGLAS-SCOTT, LORD HERBERT ANDREW, Lieut., was born 30 Nov. 1872, fifth son of the late Duke of Buccleuch and Queensberry. He was educated at Eton College, and Trinity Hall, Cambridge; he held a commission in the 3rd Battn. The Royal Scots (Militia), from 1890 to 1900, when he was gazetted Second Lieutenant, Irish Guards, and served in that Regiment up to 1907, and retired from the Army to take up a business appointment, and was transferred to the Reserve of Officers (Irish Guards). He was gazetted to the 23rd London Regt. (T.F.), 1910, and commanded the same from 1910 to 1916, when he was transferred to the Territorial Reserve. During his service Lord Herbert Scott has held Staff appointments abroad, both in India and Malta. In the South African War he served as A.D.C. to Field-Marshal Earl Roberts, Commander-in-Chief, South Africa, from 1899 to 1900, and with the Guards Mounted Infantry from 1901 to Aug. 1902. He was present at the Relief of Kimberley; in the operations in the Orange Free State, Feb. to May, 1900, including operations at Paardeberg 17 to 26 Feb. 1900, actions at Poplar Grove and Dreifontein; operations in the Transvaal in May and June, 1900, including actions near Johannesburg, Pretoria and Diamond Hill 11 and 12 June, 1900. Operations in the Transvaal, east of Pretoria, including the action of Belfast (26 and 27 Aug. 1900); and subsequently took part in operations in Cape Colony, Dec. 1901, to 31 May, 1902. For services rendered during 1900 he was created a Companion of the Distinguished Service Order [London Gazette, 19 April, 1901]: "Lord Herbert Andrew Montagu-Douglas-Scott, Lieut., Guards Mounted Infantry. In recognition of services during the operations in South Africa." The Insignia were presented by His Majesty King Edward 3 June, 1901. He was also mentioned in Despatches [London Gazette, 16 April, 1901]. Lord Herbert Scott served in the European War from Aug. 1914, to Jan. 1919, both as a Regimental and Staff Officer. He commanded the 23rd Battn. London Regt. in France during 1915, and also saw service in the Dardanelles, returning again to France until invalided to England, when he was appointed Deputy Assistant Military Secretary at the War Office. He was mentioned in Despatches [London Gazette, 1 Jan. 1916, and 1 Jan. 1917], and was created a C.M.G. 2 Feb. 1916, for services rendered during 1915. He was further awarded the Croix d'Officier, Légion d'Honneur (France), 8 Feb. 1917, for services in France, and Brevet Lieutenant-Colonel in the Reserve of Officers, Irish Guards, 3 June, 1918. He has the King's South African Medal with eight clasps; the 1914–15 Star; King George V. Coronation Medal; is a Knight of Justice of St. John of Jerusalem, and a Member of the King's Bodyguard of Scotland. He is a Director of the Sun Life and Fire Office, and of Rolls-Royce Limited.

Lord Herbert Scott.

BAKER, ARTHUR BRANDER, Capt., was born 4 Aug. 1868, at Calcutta, India, son of the late Capt. Arthur Baker, R.N. He was educated at the Royal Academy (Burney's), Gosport, and the Royal Military College, Sandhurst; joined the 1st Battn. The Royal Sussex Regt. 14 Sept. 1887; served on the Indian Frontier in the Hazara Expedition, 1888 (Medal and clasp); raised and commanded the Colonial Light Horse Regt. for the Cape Colony Government, and the Composite Regt. of Australian Bushmen in the South African War, 1899–1902; was present at Elands River, and at Witkop (between Mafeking and Rustenberg). He was mentioned in Despatches; received the Queen's Medal and five clasps; King's Medal and two clasps, and created a Companion of the Distinguished Service Order [London Gazette, 19 April, 1901]: "Arthur Brander Baker, Capt., New South Wales Bushmen. In recognition of services during the operations in South Africa." The Insignia, etc., were sent to the Commander-in-Chief in South Africa 13 July, 1901. During the European War he served as Brigade-Major, Australian Light Horse; served at Gallipoli in 1915, and was wounded. He was unmarried, and was Secretary to the Vancouver Club, British Columbia. He died 28 Oct. 1918.

BENNETT, ALFRED JOSHUA, Capt., was born at Brucedale Park, Wagga Wagga, New South Wales, 10 Jan. 1865, son of B. B. Bennett, J.P. He was educated at Wagga Wagga, New South Wales, and at Fort Street College, Sydney; served with the New South Wales Contingent in Egypt, 1885; took part in the advance on Tarrai (Medal with clasp for Suakin, and Khedive's Star); served for 15 years with the New South Wales Military Forces. He served in the South African War as Captain, 1900–02, commanding a squadron of the 2nd New South Wales Contingent, 1900; took part in the operations in the Orange Free State, Feb. to May, 1900, including the actions at Poplar Grove, Dreifontein (where he was severely wounded) and Karee Siding. He was also present at the operations in the Orange River Colony (May to Nov. 1900); at all the engagements under Colonel de Lisle, including Bothaville. He was promoted to Major in 1901, and was in command of the 2nd Contingent, New South Wales Mounted Infantry (Dec. 26 1900, to March 29, 1901). Operations in the Transvaal, Orange River Colony and Cape Colony, Nov. 1900, to May, 1902; was with Colonel Rimington's Column. For general service throughout the war, and especially for courage and resource at Bothaville, he was created a Companion of the Distinguished Service Order [London Gazette, 19 April, 1901]: "Alfred Joshua Bennett, Capt., New South Wales Mounted Infantry. In recognition of services during the operations in South Africa." The Insignia, etc., were presented by H.R.H. the Prince of Wales, on Horse Guards' Parade, 1 July, 1902. He became Major, Reserve of Officers, 8 July, 1905. During the European War he was created a C.M.G., 1915, and was promoted to Lieutenant-Colonel.

HOLMES, WILLIAM, Capt., was born in Sydney, Australia, 12 Sept. 1862, son of William Holmes, Capt., Staff, New South Wales Military Forces, and Jane Holmes. He was educated at Public Schools in New South Wales, and by private tuition, and joined the Australian Military Forces, as Second Lieutenant, in 1885. Capt. Holmes served in the South African War, as a Squadron Commander, 1899–1900; was present at the Relief of Kimberley; the operations in the Orange Free State, Feb. to May, 1900 (including operations at Paardeberg, 17 to 26 Feb.); actions at Poplar Grove, Dreifontein, Vet River (5 to 6 May) and Zand River. Operations in the Transvaal in May and June, 1900, including actions near Johannesburg, Pretoria and Diamond Hill (11 and 12 June). Operations in the Transvaal, east and west of Pretoria, July to 29 Nov. 1900, including actions at Riet Vlei and Zilikat's Nek. Operations in Cape Colony, north of Orange River. Operations in Cape Colony 30 Nov. to Dec. 1900. After being wounded at Diamond Hill, Capt. Holmes was invalided home. He was mentioned in Despatches [London Gazette, 8 Feb. and 16 April, 1901]; received the Queen's Medal with five clasps, and was created a Companion of the Distinguished Service Order [London Gazette, 19 April, 1901]: "William Holmes, Capt., New South Wales Infantry. In recognition of services during the operations in South Africa." On the outbreak of the European War, Colonel Holmes—then commanding the 6th Australian Infantry Brigade—was selected to command the Australian Naval and Military Expeditionary Force which successfully occupied all the possessions of Germany in the Pacific, south of the Equator, with the exception of Samoa. He was then appointed Administrator of this occupied German territory, which position he held for six months. On returning to Sydney, he was appointed to command the 5th Australian Infantry Brigade, Australian Imperial Force, and commanded this Brigade in Egypt, Gallipoli and France, and commanded the 2nd Australian Division during the evacuation of Gallipoli. He was created a C.M.G.; promoted Major-General, and was appointed to the command of the 4th Division, Australian Imperial Force, on 1 Jan. 1917. He was killed in action by shell-fire in France on 2 July, 1917. He had received the Volunteer Decoration in 1905, and in 1916 the 2nd Class Order of St. Anne of Russia. Major-General, Holmes was a keen sportsman, and all his exercise was taken on horseback, He married, 24 Aug. 1887, at St. Matthias's Church, Paddington, New South Wales, Australia, Susan Ellen, daughter of Henry Green, Lieut. Reserve of Officers, New South Wales, and there are two children: Dorothy Mabel, and Basil (born, 11 Sept. 1892; at the time of his father's death a Major in the 17th Battn. Australian Imperial Force, and, like his father, a Companion of the Distinguished Service Order).

William Holmes.

HILLIARD, MAURICE ALFRED, Capt., was born at Gladstone, Queensland, 19 March, 1863, third son of Capt. W. E. Hilliard, of Kensington, near Sydney. His grandfathers were Dr. Hilliard (a well-known figure with the Warwickshire Hounds) and the Rev. Frederick Deacon, of Leicester. He was educated at Sydney Grammar School and at Sydney University, and was gazetted Second Lieutenant in the Artillery (Bulli Battery), 1886; and Lieutenant, Illawarra Light Horse, 1887. He was Adjutant, Senior Cadet Battn., 1891–92. In India, from 1892 to 1894, he was attached 2nd Dragoon Guards (Queen's Bays), and 1st Battn. Devonshire Regt. In 1894 he was appointed to the General Staff; and in 1895 was gazetted Captain. From April, 1894, to June, 1895, he was Adjutant, 3rd Infantry Regt., and from 1895 to 1900, Adjutant, 4th Infantry Regt. Capt. Hilliard left for South Africa with the 2nd Contingent, New South Wales Mounted Infantry, in 1900. For leading the attack at Vet River, 1900 (Despatches), and for leading the assault at Diamond Hill, 1900 (Despatches), he was created a Companion of the Distinguished Service Order [London Gazette, 19 April, 1901]: "Maurice Alfred Hilliard, Capt., New South Wales Mounted Infantry. In recognition of services during the operations in South Africa." The Insignia were presented to him by the Lieutenant-Governor of New South Wales. Capt. Hilliard was on the General Staff, New South Wales Military Forces, and was Adjutant, 1st Infantry Regt. He died at Sydney, New South Wales, 11 April, 1907. Capt. Hilliard had married the second daughter of T. A. Reddall, Esq., of Bowral, New South Wales. She died in 1900.

ROTH, REUTER EMERICH, Capt., was born 20 March, 1858, at Brighton, son of Mathias Roth (Hungarian Patriot, Surgeon on General Kossuth's Staff, exiled, settled in England), and Anna Maria Collins. He was educated at University College School; University College and Hospital, London; took his degree as Member of the Royal College of Surgeons in England; joined the "Artists" in 1874 as Private. He obtained his first commission in 1894; served in the South African War, as Captain, Queensland Contingent, New South Wales No. 1 Bearer Company, attached to Ridley's Brigade in Ian Hamilton's Division, 1899–1900; took part in operations in the Orange Free State, Feb. to May, 1900, including operations at Paardeberg (17 to 26 Feb.); actions at Poplar Grove, Dreifontein, Karee Siding, Vet River (5 and 6 May) and Zand River. Operations in the Transvaal in May and June, 1900, including actions near Johannesburg, Pretoria, and Diamond Hill (11 and 12 June). Operations in the Transvaal, west of Pretoria, July to Nov. 1900. Operations in Orange River Colony (May to Nov. 1900), including actions at Bethlehem (6 and 7 July). He was mentioned in Despatches [London Gazette, 16 April, 1901]; received the Queen's Medal with six clasps, and was created a Companion of the Distinguished Service Order [London Gazette, 19 April, 1901]: "Reuter Emerich Roth, Capt., New South Wales Bearer Company. In recognition of services during the operations in South Africa." The Insignia, etc., were forwarded to the Governor of New South Wales by Lord Kitchener, and presented by the Lieutenant-Governor of New South Wales 4 Dec. 1901. He received the Brevet rank of Lieutenant-Colonel 1 July, 1903; became Lieutenant-Colonel 20 Sept. 1909; became Colonel, P.M.O., Commonwealth Military Forces, New South Wales (vacated this position 30 Sept. 1911); appointed Physician Royal Prince Alfred Hospital; Medical Adviser and Medical Inspector, Department of Public Instruction; created Knight of Grace, Order of St. John of Jerusalem; Officier d'Instruction Publique; awarded the Colonial Auxiliary Forces Long Service Decoration. During the European War he has served in Gallipoli, Egypt and France, as Lieutenant-Colonel, C.O., 5th Field Ambulance, Australian Imperial Force; appointed D.D.M.S., 1st Anzac, in March; transferred with same position to 2nd Anzac; invalided back to Australia unfit for further service. He was created a C.M.G. in 1917. He married, in 1883, Lily May Hart, of Christchurch, New Zealand, and they have three daughters: Mattea, Daphne and Olga.

GREEN, TERENCE ALBERT, Capt., was born 11 April, 1871, son of S. S. Green, of Sydney. He served in the South African War, 1899–1902; was mentioned in Despatches twice; received the Queen's Medal and four clasps; the King's Medal and two clasps, and was created a Companion of the Distinguished Service Order [London Gazette, 19 April, 1901]: "Terence Albert Green, Capt., New South Wales Bearer Company. In recognition of services during the operations in South Africa." The Insignia, etc., were sent to the Commander-in-Chief in South Africa, forwarded by Lord Kitchener to New South Wales, and presented by the Lieutenant-Governor of that Colony. He was promoted to Major. He married, in 1893, Ada Beatrice, daughter of Thomas Dee.

PERKINS, ALFRED EDWARD, Captain, was born 21 Feb. 1863, at Mount Capicuri, Eastern Creek, New South Wales, son of the late Lewis Perkins, J.P., and the late Sarah Madeleine Perkins. He served in the South African War, in 1900, as Captain, New South Wales Bearer Company, Australian Army Medical Corps, taking part in the operations in the Orange Free State, Feb. to May, 1900, including operations at Paardeberg (17 to 26 Feb.); actions at Poplar Grove, Dreifontein, Vet River (5 and 6 May) and Zand River. Operations in the Transvaal in May and June, 1900, including actions near Johannesburg, Thabanchu, Pretoria and Diamond Hill (11 and 12 June). Operations in the Transvaal, west of Pretoria, July to Nov. 1900. Operations in Orange River Colony (May to Nov. 1900), including operations at Bethlehem (6 and 7 July). He was mentioned in Despatches [London Gazette, 19 April, 1901], awarded the Queen's Medal and six clasps, and created a Companion of the Distinguished Service Order [London Gazette, 19 April, 1901]: "Alfred Edward Perkins, Capt., New South Wales Bearer Company. In recognition of services during the operations in South Africa." The Insignia, etc., were forwarded by Lord Kitchener to New South Wales, and presented by the Lieutenant-Governor of that Colony 4 Dec. 1901. He was promoted Lieutenant-Colonel, Australian Army Medical Corps, 20 Sept. 1909; appointed Lieutenant-Colonel to the Pyrmont Training Area 1 July, 1912; became P.M.O., 2nd Military District, April to Nov. 1915; created Honorary Serving Brother of St. John, and awarded the Volunteer Officers' Decoration. He married, in 1884, Elizabeth, daughter of the late Richard Shortlands, of Sydney.

CHRISTIE, HERBERT BERTRAM, Lieut., was born in 1863, son of the late Marshall Christie. He served in the South African War as Lieutenant, New South Wales Imperial Bushmen Contingent, 1900. He was mentioned in Despatches; received the Queen's Medal with four clasps, and was created a Companion of the Distinguished Service Order [London Gazette, 19 April, 1901]: "Herbert Bertram Christie, Lieut., New South Wales Imperial Bushmen. In recognition of services during the operations in South Africa." The Insignia, etc., were sent to the Colonial Office, forwarded, as requested by Brigadier-General Finn, from Sydney, and sent to Lieut. Christie by the Governor of New South Wales 7 June, 1902. He died 9 Dec. 1916.

DOVE, FREDERICK ALLAN, Lieut., was born 20 Dec. 1867. He joined the Australian Military Forces, and served in the South African War, 1899–1902, and was slightly wounded. He was present in the advance on Kimberley. Operations in the Orange Free State, Feb. to May, 1900, including actions at Houtnek (Thoba Mountain), Vet River (5 and 6 May) and Zand River. Operations in the Transvaal in May and June, 1900, including actions near Johannesburg, Pretoria and Diamond Hill (11 and 12 June). Operations in Cape Colony, south of Orange River, 1900, including actions at Colesberg, Feb. 1900. He served as Adjutant, 3rd Battn. Australian Commonwealth Horse, 27 March, 1902, to 31 May, 1902,; was mentioned in Despatches [London Gazette, 16 April, 1901]; received the Queen's Medal with five clasps, and was created a Companion of the Distinguished Service Order [London Gazette, 19 April, 1901]: "Frederick Allan Dove, Lieut., New South Wales Mounted Infantry. For services during the operations in South Africa." The Insignia were presented by the Lieut.-Governor of N.S.W. 4 Dec. 1901. He was promoted to Major. Major Dove served in the European War, and died of wounds 9 Dec. 1916.

DOYLE, RICHARD DINES, Lieut., served in the South African War, 1902, as Lieutenant in the New South Wales Imperial Bushmen; was mentioned in Despatches [London Gazette, 29 July, 1902], received the Queen's Medal with four clasps, the King's Medal with two clasps, and was created a Companion of the Distinguished Service Order [London Gazette, 19 April, 1901]: "Richard Dines Doyle, Lieut., New South Wales Bushmen. In recognition of services during the operations in South Africa." The Insignia, etc., were sent to the Commander-in-Chief, South Africa; forwarded on by Lord Kitchener, and presented by the Lieutenant-Governor of New South Wales 13 July, 1901. He was promoted to Captain.

MOORE, THOMAS MITCHELL, Lieut., was born in 1875. He served in the South African War, 1900, as Lieutenant in the New South Wales Imperial Bushmen; was awarded the Queen's Medal with four clasps, and created a Companion of the Distinguished Service Order [London Gazette, 19 April, 1901]: "Thomas Mitchell Moore, Lieut., New South Wales Imperial Bushmen. In recognition of services during the operations in South Africa." The Insignia were sent to the Commander-in-Chief in South Africa, forwarded on by Lord Kitchener, and presented by the Lieutenant-Governor of New South Wales.

CAPE, CHARLES SCARVELL, Lieut., was born 3 July, 1866, son of William Frederick Cape, of Sydney. He was educated in Sydney; joined the Australian Military Forces, and served in the South African War, 1899–1901; was mentioned in Despatches, and created a Companion of the Distinguished Service Order [London Gazette, 19 April, 1901]: "Charles Scarvell Cape, Lieut., New South Wales Mounted Infantry. In recognition of services during the operations in South Africa." The Insignia were presented to him by the King 25 July, 1901. He was promoted to Captain. Capt. Cape married, in 1906, Maude, daughter of the late George Frederick Want.

LIVINGSTONE-LEARMONTH, FREDERICK VALIANT COTTON, Lieut., was born at Ercildoune, Victoria, 6 June, 1862, third son of Thomas Livingstone-Learmonth, of Park Hall, Stirlingshire, N.B., and of Louisa, youngest daughter of General Sir Thomas Valiant, K.C.B. He was educated at Westminster; obtained his degree, M.A., at Pembroke College, Cambridge. At the early age of 21 went out to Australia, and took up squatting pursuits; went to South Africa, to help in the Boer War, with the 2nd Contingent, New South Wales Mounted Rifles, in Jan. 1900; took part in engagements at Osfontein and Dreifontein; in the march to Pretoria, under Lieut.-Colonel de Lisle, in General Ian Hamilton's Column; served under de Lisle at Diamond Hill; was in the Transvaal for two months, under Lieut.-Colonel Hickman, and subsequently up to April, 1901, served continuously with Lieut.-Colonel de Lisle in his operations in the Orange River Colony and Cape Colony; was twice mentioned in Despatches. He was created a Companion of the Distinguished Service Order for his services in the field [London Gazette, 19 April, 1901]: "Frederick Valiant Cotton Livingstone-Learmonth, Lieut., New South Wales Mounted Rifles. In recognition of services during the operations in South Africa." The Insignia, etc., were sent to the Commander-in-Chief in South Africa, forwarded by Lord Kitchener, and presented by the Governor of New South Wales 4 Nov. 1901. During the European War he took up organizing work with the Volunteer Training Corps for Home Defence. He married, in Oct. 1901, Rin, only daughter of the Rev. Canon Carlisle, of Melbourne, and has one son and two daughters.

F. V. C. Livingstone-Learmonth.

FIASCHI, THOMAS HENRY, Major, was born in Florence 3 May, 1853, son of the late Professor L. Fiaschi, of Florence, and Clarissa Fisher. He was educated at the Pisa and Florence Universities (M.D., Ch.D., Pisa and Florence); went to Australia in 1875; practised in Windsor, New South Wales, and settled in Sydney in 1883; he is Honorary Consulting Surgeon, Sydney Hospital. He was attached as Medical Officer to the New South Wales Lancers; obtained leave of absence for six months, and joined the Italian Army in Abyssinia in 1896; marched with them to Kassala; was awarded the Cross of Cavaliere dei S.S. Maurizio e Lazzaro from the late King Humbert, for special merits during the Italo-Abyssinian Campaign. He took part in the South African War, 1899–1900, in command of the New South Wales No. 1 Field Hospital; specially mentioned by Lord Roberts for services rendered at Paardeberg; was S.M.O. to General Hutton's Brigade, and was created a Companion of the Distinguished Service Order [London Gazette, 19 April, 1901]: "Thomas Henry Fiaschi, Major, New South Wales Medical Corps. In recognition of services during the operations in South Africa." The Insignia, etc., were sent to the Commander-in-Chief in South Africa; forwarded by Lord Kitchener, and presented by the Lieutenant-Governor of New South Wales 4 Dec. 1901. He was promoted Colonel, Army Medical Corps, 8 June, 1911; appointed P.M.O. of the Militia (Australian Commonwealth) in conjunction with Colonel Stokes; practised as Surgeon in Sydney Hospital; appointed P.M.O. for New South Wales. In the European War he served with the Australian Imperial Force, at Lemnos, as Officer Commanding the 3rd Australian General Hospital; was invalided to England; went to Italy, and served as Surgeon with the Italian Red Cross, 73 Ospedale de Guerra, at Schio. He has published "Da Cheren a Cassala" (1896). Colonel Fiaschi married, in 1886, Katherine Anna, daughter of James W. Reynolds.

MAJOR, THOMAS CHARLES, Capt., was born 11 Dec. 1869. He joined the New Zealand Military Forces, and served in South Africa, 1899–1901; was mentioned in Despatches [London Gazette, 16 April, 1901]; received the Queen's Medal with four clasps, and was created a Companion of the Distinguished Service Order [London Gazette, 19 April, 1901]: "Thomas Charles Major, Capt., New Zealand Mounted Rifles. In recognition of services during the operations in South Africa." He subsequently attained the rank of Colonel.

POLSON, DONALD, Capt., was born in New Zealand, 10 Oct. 1871, son of George M'Leod Polson, of Helmsdale, Scotland. He was educated at Christchurch, New Zealand; served for six years in the New Zealand Volunteer Force; took part in the South African War, as Captain in the 5th New Zealand Contingent in South Africa, 1900. He was mentioned in Despatches, and created a Companion of the Distinguished Service Order [London Gazette, 19 April, 1901]: "Donald Polson, Capt., New

Zealand Mounted Rifles. In recognition of services during the operations in South Africa." The Insignia, etc., were sent to the Colonial Office, and presented by the Earl of Ranfurly 29 Jan. 1902, at Wellington, New Zealand. The decoration was especially awarded for services in the North-Western Transvaal. He retired with the rank of Major, 31 July, 1912, from the New Zealand Mounted Rifles.

HUGHES, JOHN GETHIN, Lieut., was born 12 March, 1866. He served in the South African War, 1899 to 1902, and was present at the Relief of Kimberley. Operations in the Orange Free State, Feb. to May, 1900, including actions at Poplar Grove, Dreifontein, Houtnek (Thoba Mountain), Vet River (5 and 6 May) and Zand River. Operations in the Transvaal in May and June, 1900, including actions near Johannesburg, Pretoria and Diamond Hill (11 and 12 June). Operations in the Transvaal, east and west of Pretoria, July to Oct. 1900, including actions at Reit Vlei and Zilikat's Nek. Operations in Cape Colony, south of Orange River, Nov. 1899, to Feb. 1900, including actions at Colesberg (1 Jan. to 7 Feb.). He served as Adjutant, 1st Regt., New Zealand Contingent, April and May, 1902; was mentioned in Despatches [London Gazette, 16 April, 1901]; received the Queen's Medal with five clasps, and was created a Companion of the Distinguished Service Order [London Gazette, 19 April, 1901]: "John Gethin Hughes, Lieut., New Zealand Mounted Rifles. In recognition of services during the operations in South Africa." The Insignia were presented to him in South Africa. Lieut.-Colonel Hughes served in the European War from 1914 to 1916; and was created a C.M.G. He married, in 1909, Marion de Vere, daughter of Robert de Vere O'Connor, of Carrigfoyle, County Kerry.

TODD, THOMAS JOHN MARR, Lieut., was born in Christchurch, New Zealand, 2 March, 1873, son of James Todd, of Auckland, New Zealand. He was educated at Christchurch and Auckland; received a commission in the New Zealand Volunteer Force, 1898; joined the 2nd New Zealand Contingent for South Africa, 1899; was Adjutant from 1900, and Captain; served under Colonel Robin, C.B., commanding the New Zealand Mounted Forces serving in South Africa. He was created a Companion of the Distinguished Service Order [London Gazette, 19 April, 1901]: "Thomas John Marr Todd, Lieut., New Zealand Mounted Rifles. In recognition of services during the operations in South Africa." The Insignia, etc., were sent to the Commander-in-Chief in South Africa, and presented there 23 March, 1903.

DUKA, ALBERT THEOPHILUS, Capt., was born 18 April, 1866, youngest son of the late Theodore Duka, M.D., F.R.C.S., H.M. Indian Medical Service (retired), ranking as Lieutenant-Colonel. He was educated at Cheltenham College and at Cambridge University (M.A.), and joined the Queensland Military Forces, serving in the South African War, 1900–1. He took part in the operations in Rhodesia (26 April to 25 May, 1900). Operations in the Transvaal, west of Pretoria, July to 29 Nov. 1900, including actions at Elands River (4 to 16 Aug.). He was mentioned in Despatches [London Gazette, 16 April, 1901]; received the Queen's Medal with two clasps, and was created a Companion of the Distinguished Service Order [London Gazette, 19 April, 1901]: "Albert Theophilus Duka, Capt., Queensland Mounted Infantry. In recognition of services during the operations in South Africa." The Insignia were presented in South Africa. The decoration was awarded particularly for medical services during the Elands River Siege, 1900. He served in the European War in 1914–15 (Despatches). Capt. Duka is Medical Officer, Queensland Mounted Infantry. He married (1st), in 1893, Amy Maud, daughter of W. Fitch Storey, and (2ndly), in 1903, Isabella Jean, daughter of Major Walter S. Helpman, of Melbourne.

REID, DAVID ELDER, Capt., was born 4 Nov. 1864. He served in the South African War, 1899–1900. He took part in the Relief of Kimberley. Operations in the Orange Free State, Feb. to May, 1900, including operations at Paardeberg (17 to 26 Feb.); actions at Poplar Grove, Dreifontein, Vet River (5 and 6 May) and Zand River. Operations in the Transvaal in May and June, 1900, including actions near Johannesburg, Pretoria and Diamond Hill (11 and 12 June). Operations in the Transvaal, east and west of Pretoria, July to 29 Nov. 1900, including actions at Reit Vlei and Zilikat's Nek. Operations in Cape Colony, north of Orange River. Operations in Cape Colony 30 Nov. to Dec. 1900. He was mentioned in Despatches [London Gazette, 8 Feb. and 16 April, 1901]; received the Queen's Medal with five clasps, and was created a Companion of the Distinguished Service Order [London Gazette, 19 April, 1901]: David Elder Reid, Capt., Queensland Mounted Infantry. In recognition of services during the operations in South Africa." The Insignia were presented by the King 29 Oct. 1901. Capt. Reid was given the Brevet of Major, and became Major, 5th Light Horse Brigade. He holds the Volunteer Decoration.

GORDON, ROBERT, Capt., was born 22 Dec. 1866, son of the late James Gordon, of Nunbank, Dumfries, N.B., and later of Townsville, Queensland, Australia, for many years Magistrate and Mining Commissioner at Townsville, Queensland. He was educated at the Brisbane Grammar School, and at the High School, Hobart, Tasmania; joined the Queensland Mounted Infantry, 1891; served in the Tirah Campaign, attached to the 1st Gordon Highlanders, 1897–98 (Despatches; Medal and two clasps); went to South Africa with 1st Queensland Contingent, and was transferred to the 1st Gordon Highlanders, 1900; given command of the Gordon Highlanders Mounted Infantry Company; in command till wounded 30 Jan. 1901. He took part in the operations in Cape Colony, Nov. 1899, to Feb. 1900. Operations in Orange Free State, Feb. to May, 1900, including operations at Paardeberg (17 to 26 Feb.), actions at Poplar Grove, Vet River (5 and 6 May) and Zand River. Operations in the Transvaal in May and June, 1900, including actions at Johannesburg, Pretoria and Diamond Hill (11 and 12 June). Operations in Orange River Colony, July to 29 Nov. 1900, including action at Wittebergen. Operations in the Transvaal and Orange River Colony 30 Nov. 1900, to Jan. 1901 (severely wounded). He was mentioned in Despatches; received the Queen's Medal with six clasps, and was created a Companion of the Distinguished Service Order [London Gazette, 19 April, 1901]: "Robert Gordon, Capt., Queensland Mounted Infantry. In recognition of services during the operations in South Africa." The Insignia, etc., were presented by the King 3 June, 1901. He retired from the 1st Contingent, Queensland Mounted Infantry, 5 Oct. 1902; was transferred as Major from the Reserve of Officers to the Queensland Mounted Infantry, 10 Dec. 1904; became Hon. Captain in the Army. At the outbreak of the European War he was sent to German East Africa on Special Service, resigning for this purpose from the command of the North Rhodesian Rifles. During the European War, 1914–18, he was appointed Intelligence Officer, in command of the North Rhodesian Scouts in German South-West Angolaland and on the borders of North Rhodesia. He pursued and captured a party of Germans who were endeavouring to break through German South-West to German East Africa. These Germans belonged to the Camel Corps in German South-West Africa, were mounted on camels, and had penetrated far into Angola. Lieut.-General Smuts, Minister of Defence in the South African Union, sent his congratulations through the Rhodesian Commandant-General on this capture. He went to British East Africa in Feb. 1916, and commanded the Remount Landing Depôt at Mombasa, and later No. 1 Base Remount Depôt, Maktau; commanded Remount Depôt at Daressalaam, Kilwa, and Linde. Lieut.-Colonel Gordon was twice mentioned in Despatches; was given the O.B.E. in 1918, and created a C.M.G. in 1919.

GLASGOW, THOMAS WILLIAM, Lieut., was born in 1876. He served in the South African War, 1899–1900, as Lieutenant, Queensland Mounted Infantry, taking part in the operations in the Orange Free State, Feb. to May, 1900, including operations at Paardeberg (17 to 26 Feb.); actions at Poplar Grove, Dreifontein, Vet River (5 and 6 May) and Zand River. Operations in the Transvaal in May and June, 1900, including actions near Johannesburg, Pretoria and Diamond Hill. Operations in the Transvaal, east and west of Pretoria, July to 29 Nov. 1900, including actions at Reit Vlei and Zilikat's Nek. Operations in Cape Colony, north of Orange River, 1900. Operations in Cape Colony, 30 Nov. to Dec. 1900. He was mentioned in Despatches [London Gazette, 16 April, 1901]; received the Queen's Medal with five clasps, and was created a Companion of the Distinguished Service Order [London Gazette, 19 April, 1901]: "Thomas William Glasgow, Lieut., Queensland Mounted Infantry. In recognition of services during the operations in South Africa." The Insignia, etc., were sent to the Commander-in-Chief in South Africa, and presented there. He became Major, 1st Light Horse, 1 July, 1914; served in the European War from 1914 to 1918; was mentioned in Despatches; promoted to Lieutenant-Colonel; created a C.M.G., 1916; a C.B., 1918, and a K.C.B., 1919.

COLLINS, ANGUS EDWARD, Capt., was born in London, 13 May, 1870, son of William S. Collins, of Wood Hall, Pinner, and Frances Anne Collins, daughter of William Perry. He was educated at Wellington College; served in the South African War as Captain, Australian Light Horse, taking part in operations in the Transvaal. Operations in Orange River Colony. Operations in Rhodesia. He was mentioned in Despatches [London Gazette, 16 April, 1901]; received the Queen's Medal with six clasps; the King's Medal with two clasps, and was created a Companion of the Distinguished Service Order [London Gazette, 19 April, 1901]: "Angus Edward Collins, Capt., South Australian Mounted Infantry. In recognition of services during the operations in South Africa." The Insignia were presented by His Majesty the King 25 July, 1901. Lieut.-Colonel Collins retired after the South African War, but returned on commencement of the European War, 1914; commanded the 11th Battn. Durham Light Infantry from Nov. 1915, to 1918, chiefly in France. He was mentioned in Despatches.

STAPLETON, JOHN HENRY, Lieut., was born in 1866. He served in the South African War, as Lieutenant in the South Australian Mounted Infantry, 1899–1900, and was present at operations in the Transvaal, 1900, including actions at Diamond Hill. Operations in the Transvaal, east of Pretoria, including action at Belfast. Operations in Orange River Colony and Cape Colony. He was mentioned in Despatches [London Gazette, 16 April, 1901]; received the Queen's Medal with four clasps, and was created a Companion of the Distinguished Service Order [London Gazette, 19 April, 1901]: "John Henry Stapleton, Lieut., South Australian Mounted Infantry. For services in the operations in South Africa." The Insignia, etc., were forwarded to Australia, and presented in Adelaide. He was placed on the Reserve of Officers 21 Aug. 1911; awarded the Volunteers' Decoration.

HUMPHRIS, JOSEPH FRANCIS, Lieut., was born 6 May, 1868, second son of Edmund Humphris. He joined the South Australian Military Forces in 1888, and was a member of the contingent proceeding to England to take part in the Queen's Diamond Jubilee. He joined the 2nd South Australian Contingent, as Second-in-Command, for service in South Africa, and took part in the march from Bloemfontein to Komati Poort. The Army List says of his services in South Africa that he took part in "operations in the Transvaal in May and June, 1900, including actions near Johannesburg, Pretoria and Diamond Hill. Operations in Orange River Colony. Operations in Cape Colony, south of Orange River, 1900, including actions at Colesberg." He was mentioned in Despatches [London Gazette, 16 April, 1901]; received the Queen's Medal with five clasps, and was created a Companion of the Distinguished Service Order [London Gazette, 19 April, 1901]: "J. F. Humphris, Lieut., South Australian Mounted Infantry. In recognition of services during the operations in South Africa." The decoration was particularly awarded for distinguished conduct while acting as gun escort at Brandfort. Lieut.-

Colonel Humphris was placed on the unattached list, Commonwealth Military Forces, and he has the Volunteer Decoration. He became Mayor of Jamestown. He married Frances Emily Chanter, stepdaughter of the Hon. Alfred and Mrs. Catt.

IVES, CHARLES MARSH, Lieut., was born at Bradfield Hall, Norfolk, 10 Sept. 1872, son of George Ives, of Bradfield Hall, Norwich. He was educated at Queen Elizabeth's School, Ipswich; was a Pastoralist in the interior of Australia; volunteered for active service at the outbreak of the Boer War, South Africa, and was given a commission, and served as Acting Lieutenant of the South Australian Mounted Infantry, taking part in the operations in the Transvaal and Rhodesia. He was mentioned in Despatches; received the Queen's Medal and five clasps, and was created a Companion of the Distinguished Service Order [London Gazette, 19 April, 1901]: "Charles Marsh Ives, Lieut., South Australian Mounted Infantry. In recognition of services during the operations in South Africa." The Insignia were presented by the King 25 July, 1901.

Charles Marsh Ives.

The following is an account of the particular deed for which he was created a Companion of the Distinguished Service Order: "The British troops were surrounded by Boers, but in touch (by telegraph) with General Lord Methuen's Column. Information was received that the Boers were expecting reinforcements with artillery on a certain date. Lieut. C. M. Ives volunteered to locate Boer laager, and ascertain the strength of Boers and artillery. He got through the Boer lines at night, located enemy laager ten miles from British camp, and returned with the necessary information, which enabled General Lord Methuen to surround and capture the laager." He was offered a commission in the British Army, but was unable to accept; volunteered for service in the European War, but failed in eyesight test. He married, 23 June, 1909, at Adelaide, South Australia, Beatrice, daughter of William and Jane Dobbie, and they have two children: Barbara, and Philip, born in 1913.

LEWIS, RICHARD CHARLES, Capt., served in the South African War, 1900-1, in command of 1st Tasmanian Imperial Bushmen, and was present at the operations in the Transvaal, east of Pretoria, May to 29 Nov. 1900, including actions at Rhenoster Kop. Operations in Orange River Colony, 1900, including actions at Lindley, Bethlehem and Wittebergen. Operations in the Transvaal 30 Nov. 1900, to Feb. 1901; April and June, 1901. Operations in Cape Colony, Feb. to March, 1901. He was mentioned in Despatches [London Gazette, 16 April, 1901]; received the Queen's Medal and four clasps, and was created a Companion of the Distinguished Service Order [London Gazette, 19 April, 1901]: "Richard Charles Lewis, Capt., Tasmanian Imperial Yeomanry. In recognition of services during the operations in South Africa." The Insignia, etc., were sent to the Commander-in-Chief in South Africa, and presented there. He was awarded the Volunteer Decoration in 1906. Lieut.-Colonel Lewis was the Officer Commanding the Australian Garrison Artillery, Tasmania.

RIGGALL, ARTHUR HORTON, Capt., was born 8 May, 1867, son of Thomas Riggall. He served in the South African War, as Captain, Tasmanian Imperial Bushmen, 1901-2, and was present at operations in Rhodesia, the Transvaal, Orange River Colony and Cape Colony. He received the Queen's Medal with four clasps, and was created a Companion of the Distinguished Service Order [London Gazette, 19 April, 1901]: "Arthur Horton Riggall, Capt., Tasmanian Imperial Bushmen. In recognition of services during the operations in South Africa." The Insignia were sent to the Commander-in-Chief in South Africa, and presented there. He was awarded the Volunteer Decoration.

ANDERSON, ROWLAND JAMES PERCY, Major, was born in London 12 July, 1873, son of the late Sir Percy Anderson, K.C.B., K.C.M.G., Foreign Office, and Fanny Isabella Cuthbert, of Beaufront Castle, Northumberland. He was educated at Winchester; joined the 11th Hussars, as Second Lieutenant, 13 March, 1893; became Lieutenant, 13 Sept. 1895; served on the North-West Frontier, 1897-98 (Medal with clasp); in Uganda, 1898 (Medal with clasp). He served in the South African War, 1900-2, as Special Service Officer, with the Rhodesian Field Force, and afterwards on the Staff. He took part in the operations in the Transvaal, west of Pretoria, July to 29 Nov. 1900, including the action at Rhenoster Kop. Operations in the Transvaal, west of Pretoria, July to 29 Nov. 1900. Operations in the Transvaal,

Rowland J. P. Anderson.

Orange River Colony and Cape Colony. He was mentioned in Despatches [London Gazette, 16 April and 7 May, 1901]; received the Queen's Medal with four clasps; the King's Medal with two clasps, and was created a Companion of the Distinguished Service Order [London Gazette, 19 April, 1901]: "Rowland James Percy Anderson, Major, 11th Hussars. In recognition of services during the operations in South Africa." He was promoted Captain 22 Nov. 1902, and Major 13 June, 1908. He was Adjutant, Imperial Yeomanry, 27 Nov. 1903, to 26 Nov. 1906; Instructor,

Cavalry School, 22 Feb. 1909, to 3 April, 1910. He has served in the European War; went out with the Expeditionary Force; was present at Mons, the Marne, and the Aisne; wounded at Messines 31 Oct. 1914; was present at the first and second battles of Ypres; commanded the 11th Hussars from May, 1915; was promoted Lieutenant-Colonel 29 Sept. 1916. He was mentioned in Despatches twice, and created a C.M.G., Jan. 1918. His favourite sports are hunting, polo and racing. He married, at Aldershot, 11 Aug. 1914, Phyllis, only daughter of T. Stanley Chappell, of Chadshunt, Warwick.

PERKINS, RAYMOND, Lieut., was born 27 April, 1869, son of the late John Perkins, of Hobart. He served in the South African War; was mentioned in Despatches; received the Queen's Medal with three clasps, and was created a Companion of the Distinguished Service Order [London Gazette, 19 April, 1901]: "Raymond Perkins, Lieut., Tasmanian Imperial Bushmen. In recognition of services during the operations in South Africa." Lieut. Perkins married, in 1893, Louisa Caroline Howells, daughter of N. P. Alison, of Hunterston, Bothwell, Tasmania.

STAUGHTON, S. T., Lieut., was born at Eynesbury, Melton, Victoria, Australia, 30 Dec. 1876, son of S. T. Staughton, M.L.A., of Victoria. He was educated at the Church of England Grammar School, Melbourne, and was a member of the Victorian Contingent to England at the late Queen's Diamond Jubilee. He was commissioned in 1898 in the Victorian Mounted Rifles, and proceeded to South Africa as Lieutenant in the 1st Victorian Contingent in 1899. He was three times mentioned in Despatches, and was created a Companion of the Distinguished Service Order [London Gazette, 19 April, 1901]: "S. T. Staughton, Lieut., Victorian Mounted Rifles. In recognition of services during the operations in South Africa." The Insignia were sent to South Africa, forwarded to Australia; returned to South Africa again, and presented there 3 Sept. 1903. He was promoted to Captain, 1900, and in that year returned with the 1st Contingent to Victoria. Capt. Staughton commanded the Victorian returned South African troops in Sydney during the Commonwealth celebrations. Capt. Staughton was a Grazier; his favourite recreations were polo, hunting, rowing, cricket and shooting. He married, in 1902, Tassie Mary, daughter of the Hon. Howard Spensley.

LILLEY, JAMES LINDSAY, Lieut., was born in 1871. He joined the Victorian Military Forces; served in the South African War, 1900-1, and took part in operations in the Orange Free State. He was dangerously wounded. Lieut. Lilley was also present at the operations in Cape Colony. He served as Adjutant, Victorian Contingent, from 13 Jan. to 30 April, 1900; was mentioned in Despatches [London Gazette, 16 April, 1901]; received the Queen's Medal with two clasps, and was created a Companion of the Distinguished Service Order [London Gazette, 19 April, 1901]: "James Lindsay Lilley, Lieut., Victorian Mounted Rifles. In recognition of services during the operations in South Africa." The Insignia was sent to South Africa; forwarded to the Colonial Office for transmission to Australia; sent to the Governor of Victoria, and presented by the Commanding Officer 27 Dec. 1901. He retired from the Victorian Mounted Infantry in 1901. Capt. Lilley married, in 1913, Olive Agatha Hope, youngest daughter of the late Rev. C. E. Cummings and Mrs. Geoffrey Ffolkes, of Smytham, Little Torrington, Devon.

KIRBY, MARK THOMAS ANTHONY, Lieut., was born at Knightsbridge, London, S.W., 4 Feb. 1874, son of Mark Dalton Kirby, late of Windsor. He was educated at Windsor, and joined when he was 18 years of age the Victorian Horse Artillery (Rupertswood Battery; Sir William J. Clarke, Bart.). At 23 years of age he joined the Victorian Field Artillery Brigade, and he was selected 28 Dec. 1899, as one of the officers for the 2nd Victorian Contingent for service in South Africa. He served in the South African War, 1900-2; took part in the main advance under Earl Roberts, through Colesberg, Orange Free State and the Transvaal, and was promoted to Captain on the field; received his discharge from the 2nd Victorian Contingent on 9 May, 1901, and rejoined the Field Artillery Brigade. Capt. Kirby returned to South Africa in command of a squadron of Commonwealth Horse. He was present at the operations in the Orange Free State, including actions at Houtnek (Thoba Mountain), Vet River and Zand River. Operations in the Transvaal in May and June, 1900, including actions near Johannesburg, Pretoria and Diamond Hill. Operations in the Transvaal, east of Pretoria, including action at Belfast. Operations in Cape Colony. He was mentioned in Despatches [London Gazette, 16 April, 1901]; received the Queen's Medal with six clasps, and was created a Companion of the Distinguished Service Order [London Gazette, 19 April, 1901]: Mark Thomas Anthony Kirby, Lieut., Victorian Mounted Rifles. In recognition of services during the operations in South Africa." The Insignia were sent to the Commander-in-Chief in South Africa, and presented there. Capt. Kirby served as A.D.C. to Major-General Sir E. T. Hutton.

PARKER, FRANCIS MAITLAND WYBORN, Capt., was born 18 Sept. 1876, eldest son of Chief Justice Parker (now Sir Stephen Henry Parker, K.C.M.G.) and Amy Katherine, daughter of G. W. Leake, Q.C. He was educated at Perth High School, Western Australia; admitted a Barrister and Solicitor of the Supreme Court of West Australia in 1899. He served in the South African Campaign, 1899-1902, with the West Australian Mounted Infantry; was Embarkation Staff Officer, Staff of the Base, Cape Town, 1901-2, and was present at the actions at Vet River; operations in the Transvaal in May and June, 1900, including actions near Johannesburg, Pretoria and Diamond Hill (11 and 12 June); operations in Cape Colony, south of Orange River, 1899-1900, including the actions at Colesberg. He was mentioned in Despatches [London Gazette, 16 April, 1901]; received the Queen's Medal with four clasps, the King's Medal with two clasps, and was created a Companion of the Distinguished Service Order [London Gazette, 19 April, 1901]: "Francis Maitland Wyborn Parker, Capt., West

Australian Mounted Infantry. In recognition of services during the operations in South Africa." (Insignia, etc., sent to Commander-in-Chief in South Africa, and presented in South Africa by Major-General A. Wynne, C.B., 19 Nov. 1901.) He was given the Brevet of Major in 1902. He served in the European War, and an obituary notice in the "Times" said : "On the 17th March, 1915, at Mena Camp, Cairo, after a short illness, Capt. and Brevet Major Francis Maitland Wyborn Parker, D.S.O., Imperial Force, Egypt, elder son of the Hon. Sir Stephen Parker, K.C.M.G." He had married, in 1901, Jessie Dorothy, daughter of J. Stenhouse, of Melbourne, Victoria.

DARLING, HERBERT FERGUSON, Lieut., was born 24 April, 1879, son of Robert Darling, of Gerardton, West Australia. He joined the West Australian Military Forces ; served in the South African War, 1899–1902 ; was slightly wounded, and was present at the operations in the Orange Free State, including the actions at Vet River and Zand River ; operations in the Transvaal in May and June, 1900, including actions near Johannesburg, Pretoria and Diamond Hill ; operations in Natal ; operations in the Transvaal, east of Pretoria, including actions at Belfast and Rhenoster Kop ; operations in Orange River Colony. He was mentioned in Despatches [London Gazette, 16 April, 1901, and 29 Aug. 1902] ; received the Queen's Medal with two clasps, and was created a Companion of the Distinguished Service Order [London Gazette, 19 April, 1901] : "H. F. Darling, Lieut., West Australian Mounted Infantry. In recognition of services during the operations in South Africa." The Insignia, etc., were sent to South Africa and presented there. He was appointed Hon. Captain, West Australian Infantry Regt., 30 June, 1912.

DE CASTILLA, JOHN STEPHEN RAMOS, Lieut., was born in Scotland 22 Dec. 1866, son of Henry de Castilla. He was educated at Aberdeen ; joined the Western Australian Field Force Artillery in March, 1899 ; proceeded to South Africa as Lieutenant in the West Australian Mounted Infantry (2nd Contingent), and served in the South African War, 1899–1902. He took part in the operations in the Orange Free State, including actions at Vet River and Zand River ; operations in the Transvaal in May and June, 1900, including actions near Johannesburg, Pretoria and Diamond Hill ; operations in Cape Colony. He was mentioned in Despatches [London Gazette, 16 April, 1901] ; received the Queen's Medal with five clasps, the King's Medal with two clasps, and was created a Companion of the Distinguished Service Order [London Gazette, 19 April, 1901] : "John Stephen Ramos de Castilla, Lieut., West Australian Mounted Infantry. In recognition of services during the operations in South Africa." The Insignia were sent to Western Australia and presented there. He was promoted to Captain in 1901. He became Major, South African Constabulary, in Dec. 1901. Major de Castilla was placed on the Reserve of Officers, Union Defence Force, from Oct. 1904. When the European War broke out he helped to suppress the rebellion in South Africa, 1914–15. He afterwards served in the German East African Campaign, 1916–17, as Major, Imperial Service Contingent, and was promoted Lieut.-Colonel in Sept. 1918 ; he was Commandant, British Troops, Beira, Portuguese East Africa. He was appointed Resident Magistrate, Wolmaransstad, Transvaal. Lieut.-Colonel de Castilla married, on 10 March, 1904, at Winburg, Orange River Colony, Maude Lilian, eldest daughter of Benjamin Bremner, of Charlottetown, P.E.I., Canada.

VERNON, RUPERT ROBERT, Lieut., was born 31 Dec. 1872, son of the Hon. Greville Richard Vernon, J.P., D.L., of Orchard Portman (fourth son of the 1st Baron Lyveden and Emma Mary Fitzpatrick, daughter of the 2nd and last Earl of Upper Ossory), and Susan Caroline, daughter of the late Richard Howe Cockerell, Commander, R.N. He was educated in Somerset, and served in the South African War ; was mentioned in Despatches, and created a Companion of the Distinguished Service Order [London Gazette, 19 April, 1901] : "Rupert Robert Vernon, Lieut., West Australian Mounted Infantry. In recognition of services during the operations in South Africa." The Insignia, etc., were sent to South Africa, returned by the General Commanding Officer, Cape Colony, and presented by H.M. the King 29 Oct. 1901. He married, in 1906, Dorothy Inez Elinor, daughter of Mr. Thorneycroft, of Dunston, Staffs, and they have two sons and one daughter : Greville Archibald Fitzpatrick, born 2 July, 1908 ; Mervyn Sydney Bobus, born 8 April, 1912, and Susan Diana Mary.

OLLIVER, SPENCER ALWYNNE, Lieut., was born in May, 1859, at Kingston Manor, near Worthing, son of George Olliver, D.L., of Kingston Manor, Sussex, and Fanny, daughter of John King, of Southampton. He was educated for the Navy at a preparatory school, and after that at the Naval School, Portsmouth ; passed into the Britannia, and joined the Royal Navy in 1872, retiring as Lieutenant in 1882. He served in South Africa, 1900 and 1901, with the West Australian Mounted Rifles ; resigned his commission in 1901, and joined Baden-Powell's South African Constabulary as Captain (commission dated 3 March, 1900). For his services in the South African War he received the two Medals and seven clasps, and was created a Companion of the Distinguished Service Order [London Gazette, 19 April, 1901] : "S. A. Olliver, Lieut., West Australian Mounted Infantry. In recognition of services during the operations in South Africa." The Insignia were presented by H.R.H. the Duke of Cornwall and York on his visit to Natal 14 Aug. 1901. Capt. Olliver died at Pretoria on 28 April, 1902, and an obituary notice describes the action for which he had been awarded the D.S.O. : "Capt. Spencer Alwynne Olliver, D.S.O., South African Constabulary, who died on 28 April, at Pretoria, of enteric, as has been announced, was the youngest son of the late George Olliver, D.L., of Kingston (Sussex). He was born in 1859, entered the Royal Navy, 1872, and retired as Lieutenant in 1882. Shortly after the outbreak of the war he joined the West Australian Mounted Rifles, in which he did gallant service ; was mentioned in Despatches, and received the D.S.O. He was afterwards transferred to the S.A.C., in which he was serving at the time of his death, which occurred after he was pronounced out of danger and shortly expected home. The last fight with which Capt. Olliver was prominently connected was described by Reuter's correspondent as a smart engagement, which took place on 6 Feb., between a force of West Australians, Dragoon Guards and Cape Police, and Kruitsinger's Commando, in Cape Colony, about 15 miles from Klipplaat. The British force, numbering only 27 men all told, was under the command of Capt. Olliver, and was carrying Despatches. On drawing close to Featherstonehaugh's Farm, they sighted a small body of Boers. To the rear of the Boers was a fairly high kopje, and on this they fell back. Hot firing ensued, and the Boers, after being reinforced, executed a wide detour, and surrounded Capt. Olliver's little band. Just before sunset a body of Boers, estimated at 300, opened a terrific fire upon the two kopjes held by the British, and about 200 of their horsemen were seen to be charging the British position. Not one of the gallant band so heavily outnumbered thought of surrendering, but eventually they were all overpowered and captured. The Boers admitted five killed, one of whom was shot by Capt. Olliver at five yards distance. After being marched three miles under escort, and stripped of their arms and ammunition, the prisoners were released. The death of the gallant captain, at the end of the war, and after much laborious and distinguished service, is naturally a great blow to his relatives and friends." An obelisk was erected, inscribed as follows : "In memory of Sergt. John Jacobs, age 30 years, Private Samuel Chance, age 22 years, Private James Peck, age 22 years, 7th Dragoon Guards, who with 28 others under Capt. Olliver for seven hours kept at bay a force of over 400 of the King's enemies, and thus nobly died at Featherstonehaugh 6 Feb. 1901. This stone was erected by the residents of Klipplaat and vicinity." Capt. Olliver had married Sophy, daughter of Henry Duncan, Esq.

Spencer Alwynne Olliver.

CAMERON, GEORGE W., Capt., was born at Thurso, Quebec, Canada, son of John Archibald Cameron. He was educated at Woodstock College, Ontario, and began his military career in the 5th Royal Scots, the Highland Regt. of Montreal, in 1887, which he eventually commanded. He became Captain in 1891, and Major in 1897. He saw active service in the South African War as a Lieutenant in Lord Strathcona's Corps, taking part in the operations in Natal in May and June, 1900, and serving in the Orange River Colony and Transvaal till May, 1902. He was promoted to Captain in March, 1900, and received the Medal with clasps ; was promoted Major in Dec. 1901, and Honorary Major in the Army in Sept. 1901, and was created a Companion of the Distinguished Service Order [London Gazette, 19 April, 1901] : "George W. Cameron, Capt., Lord Strathcona's Corps. In recognition of services during the operations in South Africa." The Insignia, Warrant, etc., were sent to the Colonial Office for transmission to Canada 1 Nov. 1901, and presented by Lieut.-Colonel A. Roy 27 Nov. 1901. Lieut.-Colonel Cameron, who had latterly been on the permanent staff of the Canadian Mounted Artillery, was an enthusiastic rifleman, a keen supporter of cross-country riding, and fond of most outdoor sports. He died 28 Aug. 1907, in Winnipeg. In an obituary notice in the "Times" of 12 Sept. 1907, his name is given as George H. Cameron.

CARTWRIGHT, FRANCIS LENNOX, Captain, was born 27 March, 1874, fifth son of the late Right Hon. Sir R. J. Cartwright, G.C.M.G., P.C. He was educated at Bishop Ridley College ; St. Catherine's, Canada, and Queen's University, Kingston, Canada ; became Captain 14th Battn. Princess of Wales's Own Rifles, Canadian Militia, in 1896 ; joined the North-West Mounted Police in 1897 ; served in Yukon and N.W. Territories. He served in the South African War, 1899–1902, in Lord Strathcona's Horse, taking part in operations in the Transvaal, east of Pretoria, 10 July to 29 Nov. 1900, including actions at Belfast (26 and 27 Aug.) and Lydenberg (5 to 8 Sept.) ; operations in the Transvaal, west of Pretoria, July to 29 Nov. 1900, including actions at Frederickstad (17 to 25 Oct.) ; operations in Orange River Colony 30 Nov. 1900, to 31 May, 1902. He received the Queen's Medal with four clasps, and was created a Companion of the Distinguished Service Order [London Gazette, 19 April, 1901] : "Francis Lennox Cartwright, Capt., Lord Strathcona's Horse. In recognition of services during the operations in South Africa." The Insignia, Warrant, etc., were sent to the Commander-in-Chief in South Africa ; returned by Lord Kitchener to be forwarded to the Governor-General, Canada ; sent to Colonial Office for transmission to Canada, and presented by the Lieut.-Governor of the North-West Territories 29 Nov. 1901. He returned to N.W. Mounted Police, 1901 ; retired in 1904 ; became Captain, 5th Field Battery, Canadian Artillery, 1906 ; Captain, Strathcona's Horse (Royal Canadians), 1910 ; appointed Inspector N.W. Mounted Police, Canada. He served in the European War, 1914–16 and was given the Brevet of Major 1 July, 1915. He married, in 1901, Ada Maria Carlos, eldest daughter of Augustus F. Perkins, of Oak Dene, Holmwood, Surrey.

Archibald C. Macdonell.

MACDONELL, ARCHIBALD CAMERON, Capt., was born 6 Oct. 1864, at Windsor, Ontario, Canada. His father was the late Samuel Smith Macdonell, Q.C., LL.D., D.C.L., for many years

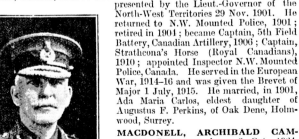

Lieutenant-Colonel Commanding the 2nd Essex Battn., Windsor, Ontario, youngest son of Colonel the Honourable Alexander Macdonell, of Collachie, Inverness-shire, Scotland, who belonged to a cadet family of Glengarry; was a United Empire Loyalist, and fought through the Revolutionary War of 1776 to 1783, and was Colonel and Assistant Paymaster-General during the war of 1812–14. He belonged to the 84th, "the Royal Highland Emigrant Regt.," in which his father was a Captain, and later to Butler's Rangers. The mother of Major-General Macdonell was Ellen Guillot Macdonell, eldest daughter of the late Colonel D. D. Brodhead, grandniece of Brigadier-General Daniel Brodhead, one of Washington's Brigadiers, and niece of Brigadier-General Thornton Brodhead, who was mortally wounded at the Second Battle of Bull's Run, whilst in command of the Michigan Cavalry Brigade. Major-General Macdonell was educated at Trinity College School, Port Hope, Canada, and at the Royal Military College of Canada, Kingston, Ontario, and on graduating from the last-named institution received a commission in the Royal Artillery. This, for family reasons, he resigned without actually joining. He became a Lieutenant in the Canadian Militia on 26 June, 1886, and joined the Regular Canadian Army as a Lieutenant in the Canadian Mounted Infantry, Permanent Corps of Canada, on 6 April, 1888. He exchanged into the Royal North-West Mounted Police in Sept. 1889, and was Adjutant of the whole force, and later was in command of C Division and the Battleford District. He volunteered into the 2nd Battn. Canadian Mounted Rifles for service in South Africa in Jan. 1900, as Captain, and was promoted Major in May, 1900. He went through the Boer lines on the night of 5–6 May, 1900, after the Battle of Vet River, in command of a composite squadron of four troops from C and D Squadrons of his battalion, and blew up the culvert behind the Boer lines, near Smaldeel, and cut the telegraph wires. He was dangerously wounded at Diamond Hill on 12 June, 1900, and was invalided home to Canada in July, 1901. He was created a Companion of the Distinguished Service Order [London Gazette, 19 April, 1901]: "Archibald Cameron Macdonell, Capt., Canadian Mounted Rifles. In recognition of services during the operations in South Africa." He returned to South Africa in 1902, in command of the 5th or Western Regt., Canadian Mounted Rifles, and arrived at Durban just after the declaration of peace. He was mentioned in Despatches 16 April, 1901, and received the Queen's Medal with four clasps. He served in the Royal North-West Mounted Police until 5 March, 1907, when he was appointed Major, Second-in-Command of the Royal Canadian Mounted Rifles, now Lord Strathcona's Horse. He became Lieutenant-Colonel of his regiment on 1 April, 1912, and held the command until 22 Dec. 1915. He served throughout the European War, arriving in England with the First Canadian Contingents in Oct. 1914. He was present at Festubert, and at all the big battle, afterwards. He was promoted Colonel, Canadian Permanent Corps Service in May, 1916, and was Brigadier-General of the 7th Canadian Infantry Brigade from 23 Dec. 1915, to 8 June, 1917. On 17 Feb. 1917, he had his left arm broken by a bullet near the shoulder, and had another through the top of the shoulder, when caught in the open by a sniper. He resumed command of his brigade two months later, and was promoted Major-General on 9 June, 1917. He was created a Companion of St. Michael and St. George in the Honours Gazette of 29 Jan. 1916; a Companion of the Bath in the Honours Gazette of June, 1917, and a Knight Commander of the Bath in Jan. 1919. He was created an Officer of the Legion of Honour (France) in Nov. 1918, and awarded the Croix de Guerre of France in July, 1919. He was mentioned in Despatches no fewer than seven times, viz.: Jan. 1916; Jan. 1917; June, 1917; Jan. 1918; June, 1918; Jan. 1919, and July, 1919. He was formerly Captain of many Rugby and cricket teams, and played twice for Canada in the Western International Cricket Match against the United States. He has gone in a great deal for wolf-hunting with Long-dogs, Highland deer-hounds and Borzois in the North-West District. He is now Commandant of the Royal Military College of Canada, Kingston, Ontario. He was married at Winnipeg on 14 April, 1890, to Mary Maud Flora, third daughter of the late Lieut.-Colonel J. T. Campbell, sometime 72nd Highlanders and Royal Canadian Rifles, a Crimean Veteran (*vide* Campbells of Possil and Glendarnel). They had five children, of whom three, Jean, Maud and Alastair, died in infancy; one, Ian Cameron, born 11 March, 1895, Lieutenant, Lord Strathcona's Horse (Royal Canadians); Flying Officer, Royal Flying Corps, was killed in action on the Somme 2 July, 1916, and one, Alison Cameron, is still living.

MACKIE, ERNEST F., Capt., served in the South African War, 1900–1, as Adjutant, Lord Strathcona's Corps. He was mentioned in Despatches [London Gazette, 8 Feb. and 16 April, 1901]; was awarded the Queen's Medal with four clasps, and created a Companion of the Distinguished Service Order [London Gazette, 19 April, 1901]: "Ernest F. Mackie, Capt., Lord Strathcona's Horse. In recognition of services during the operations in South Africa." The Insignia were sent to the Commander-in-Chief in South Africa; returned by Lord Kitchener, to be forwarded to the Governor-General of Canada 1 Nov. 1901; sent to Colonial Office for transmission to Canada, and presented by the Lieut.-Governor of Manitoba. He was promoted Captain 16 March, 1901; Major 1 April, 1912; has served in the European War, 1914–16, and was given the Brevet of Lieut.-Colonel 1 July, 1915.

KEENAN, CAMPBELL B., Surgeon-Lieut., was born in 1871, son of D. D. Keenan, of Ottawa. He served in the South African War, 1899–1901; was mentioned in Despatches, and created a Companion of the Distinguished Service Order [London Gazette, 19 April, 1901]: "Campbell B. Keenan, Surgeon-Lieut., Lord Strathcona's Horse. In recognition of services during the operations in South Africa." The Insignia, etc., were sent to the Commander-in-Chief, South Africa; returned to Lord Kitchener to be forwarded to the Governor-General of Canada, and sent to the Colonial Office for transmission to Canada. Presented by Lieut.-Colonel A. Roy. He was promoted Surgeon-Captain, Strathcona's Horse, 16 March, 1901. Lieut.-Colonel Keenan served in the European War from 1914.

PANET, HENRI ALEXANDRE, Capt., was born 24 July, 1869, son of the late Colonel Charles Eugene Panet. He graduated at the Royal Military College of Canada, and served in the South African War, 1899–1900, and was present at the Relief of Mafeking. He was mentioned in Despatches [London Gazette, 16 April, 1901]; was given the Brevet of Major, and was created a Companion of the Distinguished Service Order [London Gazette, 19 April, 1901]: "Henri Alexandre Panet, Captain, Royal Canadians. In recognition of services during the operations in South Africa." The Insignia were presented to him by the Commandant, Royal Military College, Canada. He was Staff Adjutant, Royal Military College of Canada, 1901–5; A.A.G., 1905–7; D.A.G., 1907–9. He was promoted to Colonel, Royal Canadian Horse Artillery; served in the European War; was wounded and mentioned in Despatches; became Brigadier-General; was created a C.M.G., 1916, and a C.B. in 1919. He married, in 1902, Mary A., youngest daughter of the late James Bermingham, of Kingston, Ontario, Canada.

CHRISTIE, ALBERT EDWARD, Lieut., was born 3 Dec. 1860, son of the late Charles Robertson Christie, of Toronto. He served in the North-West Rebellion in 1885. He again saw active service in South Africa in 1900, and was created a Companion of the Distinguished Service Order [London Gazette, 19 April, 1901]: Albert Edward Christie, Lieut., Lord Strathcona's Corps. In recognition of services during the operations in South Africa." The Insignia, etc., "were sent to Canada, and presented to him by Miss Wetmore, daughter of Judge Wetmore." He became Major, 16th Light Horse, and served in the European War with the Canadian Expeditionary Force. Major Christie married Mary Ludlow, daughter of Chief Justice Wetmore, and they have three sons and one daughter.

IRVING, LEWIS ERSKINE WENTWORTH, Lieut., was born in Hamilton, Canada, 16 Aug. 1868, fifth son of Sir Aemilius Irving, K.C., Treasurer of the Law Society of Upper Canada, who had fought at Waterloo (Medal), and of Augusta Louisa, daughter of Colonel Gugy, Quebec. He was educated at the Upper Canada College, Toronto, the McGill College, Montreal, and Trinity University, Toronto (M.D., C.M.); became Captain, Canadian Artillery, in 1891; Lieutenant, Royal Canadian Artillery, in 1899; served in the South African War in 1899, and took part in the advance from Beira to Mafeking, in the Rhodesian Field Force. He was mentioned in Despatches 16 April, 1901; received the Brevet of Major, 1901; Queen's Medal and four clasps, and created a Companion of the Distinguished Service Order [London Gazette, 19 April, 1901]: "Lewis Erskine Wentworth Irving, Lieut., Royal Canadian Artillery. In recognition of services during the operations in South Africa." The Insignia, etc., were sent to the Commander-in-Chief in South Africa; returned by Lord Kitchener to be forwarded to the Governor-General of Canada, and sent to Colonial Office for transmission to Canada. He was placed on the Reserve of Officers 17 May, 1901. Major Irving served in the European War, 1914–18.

LECKIE, JOHN EDWARDS, Lieut., was born in Canada 19 Feb. 1872, son of Major R. G. Leckie, Sudbury, Ontario. He was educated at Lennoxville; graduated from the Royal Military College after four years' course; postgraduate course at King's College (B.Sc.); served in the South African War as Lieutenant (16 March, 1901), Lord Strathcona's Horse, and Captain, 2nd Canadian Mounted Rifles. He was mentioned in Despatches; received the Queen's Medal with five clasps, and was created a Companion of the Distinguished Service Order [London Gazette, 19 April, 1901]: "John Edwards Leckie, Lieut., Lord Strathcona's Corps. In recognition of services during the operations in South Africa." The Insignia, etc., were sent to the Commander-in-Chief in South Africa, and presented by Major-General Stephenson at Friedrichstad 4 April, 1904. He became Captain, 72nd Seaforth Highlanders of Canada, and was promoted Major in the same regiment 30 Sept. 1913. He served throughout the European War from 1914, and commanded the 16th Battn. Canadian Scottish from 1915. He became Colonel, and was created a C.M.G. in 1917. Colonel Leckie is a mining engineer, and is a member of the Canadian Mining Institute and American Institute of Mining Engineers.

OGILVY, JOHN HERBERT CECIL, Lieut., served in the South African War with the Canadian Military Forces, and was transferred to the Gordon Highlanders. He was created a Companion of the Distinguished Service Order [London Gazette, 19 April, 1901]: "John Herbert Cecil Ogilvy, Lieut., Royal Canadian Regt. (now Capt., Gordon Highlanders). In recognition of services during the operations in South Africa." The Insignia were sent to the Commander-in-Chief in South Africa, and thence to the G.O.C., Transvaal, and presented 25 July, 1901. Capt. Ogilvy died 19 Dec. 1901.

TURNER, R. E. W., Lieut., was created a Companion of the Distinguished Service Order [London Gazette, 19 April, 1901]: "R. E. W. Turner, Lieut., Royal Canadian Dragoons. In recognition of services during the operations in South Africa." Sir R. E. W. Turner was awarded the Victoria Cross (see V.C. Volume). The "Canadian Gazette" of 5 July, 1917, says: "The high place which that gallant war veteran, Major-General Sir Richard Turner, V.C., D.S.O., now holds in the Canadian Military organization was made evident to all at the Jubilee Service in Westminster Abbey. He and Sir George Perley, walking side by side, were the only Canadians in the royal procession as it made its way through the nave to the sanctuary. What Sir William Robertson is to the whole British forces, General

R. E. W. Turner

Turner is, in a sense, to the Canadian forces overseas. He holds the senior military appointment, and is chief military adviser to the Overseas Minister of Militia, Sir George Perley, who is, so to speak, the Lord Derby of the Canadian organization; while the post of Major-General Sir Arthur Currie, in command of the Canadian Army Corps, may be said to resemble in its lesser degree that of General Haig in command of the whole British Empire forces on the Western front." The "Canadian Gazette" account of Sir R. E. W. Turner says also that: "He went to the front early in the present war, and was in command of the Canadian Highland Brigade during the fighting at Langemarck, where 75 per cent. of the men engaged were killed, wounded, or taken prisoners. In the terrible fighting the Germans would have been able to break through at Langemarck had it not been for the courage and resourcefulness shown by the Canadian forces, including those led by General Turner and the officers and men under him."

CAPELL, ALGERNON ESSEX, Capt., was born at Tettenhall, near Wolverhampton, 1 Nov. 1869 (a member of the Essex family of Capell, direct line), and was educated at Felsted School. He joined the Cape Mounted Rifles as a trooper in 1889, and remained in the corps till 1899, when he joined Bethune's Mounted Infantry as Lieutenant, having served through Pondoland at the annexation. He served in the South African War, 1899–1902, and was promoted to Captain in 1900 " for gallantry in the field " at Scheeper's Nek. He joined the S.A.C. in 1900, and was promoted to Major in 1902; was mentioned in Despatches (twice by General Buller and once each by Lord Roberts and Lord Kitchener), and created a Companion of the Distinguished Service Order [London Gazette, 19 April, 1901]: " Algernon Essex Capel, Capt., Bethune's Mounted Infantry." In recognition of services during the operations in South Africa." The Insignia, etc., were sent to the Commander-in-Chief in South Africa, and presented by the Duke of Cornwall and York 14 Aug. 1901. Major Capell was " ejected from the S.A.C. by the Boer Government of 1908." He was appointed Assistant District Commissioner, Dagoretti, British East Africa; Chief of Police, Grenada, 1910–12 (awarded King's Police Medal), and Assistant Commissioner, British South African Police, in Southern Rhodesia, since 1913. He served in the European War from 1914; commanded a column to German South-West Africa; captured Shuckmansburg, the capital of Caprivi Zippel strip of German territory; given command in Dec. 1914, of the 2nd Rhodesian Regt., with the rank of Lieut.-Colonel; was mentioned in Despatches by General Smuts, and received the Croix de Guerre. Major Capell has " devoted most of his life to big game and other shooting when on leave." He married, in 1903, Lois Ethel, daughter of W. Slatter, of Stratton, Cirencester, and they have one son and one daughter.

COLLOPY, C. J., Capt., served in the South African War, was mentioned in Despatches, and was created a Companion of the Distinguished Service Order [London Gazette, 19 April, 1901]: " C. J. Collopy, Capt., Bethune's Mounted Infantry. In recognition of services during the operations in South Africa." The Insignia were sent to South Africa, and presented by Colonel Monro, commanding Bethune's Mounted Infantry, on full-dress parade.

MINSHULL-FORD, F. J., Capt., served in the South African War, and was created a Companion of the Distinguished Service Order [London Gazette, 19 April, 1901]: " F. C. Minshull-Ford, Capt., Bethune's Mounted Infantry. In recognition of services during the operations in South Africa." The Insignia, Warrant and Statutes were sent to Mrs. Minshull-Ford. Capt. Minshull-Ford had been killed in action 17 Oct. 1901.

PRIOR, MONTAGU, Lieut., served in the South African War, was slightly wounded, and created a Companion of the Distinguished Service Order [London Gazette, 19 April, 1901]: " Montagu Prior, Lieut., Bethune's Mounted Infantry. In recognition of services during the operations in South Africa." The Insignia, etc., were sent to the Commander-in-Chief in South Africa, and presented by Major-General Stephenson at Friedrichstad 4 April, 1904.

CHOLMONDELEY, HENRY REGINALD, Capt., was born 11 June, 1861, fourth son of the late Rev. the Hon. H. P. Cholmondeley. He served in South Africa in 1900, was mentioned in Despatches, and created a Companion of the Distinguished Service Order [London Gazette, 19 April, 1901]: " H. R. Cholmondeley, Capt., Brabant's Horse. In recognition of services during the operations in South Africa. The Insignia, Warrant and Statutes were sent to the Commander-in-Chief, South Africa; sent to the G.O.C., Transvaal, and presented 1 Jan. 1902. Major Cholmondeley served in the European War in the 10th Battn. Devonshire Regt. He married, in 1903, Cordelia Mercy, daughter of the late James Cross Ormrod, of Wyrsdale Park, Garstang.

DOUGLAS, JAMES SHOLTO GORDON, Capt., was born at Walmer, Kent, 2 May, 1872, son of the late Admiral and Mrs. R. Gordon Douglas, of Seafield. He was educated at Ascham School, Bournemouth, and at the Royal Academy, Gosport, and joined the Cape Royal Riflemen in 1893. When the South African War began, he joined 1st Brabant's Horse in 1899, and was transferred to the South African Constabulary. He served in the South African War, 1899–1902; was mentioned in Despatches [London Gazette, 16 April, 1901]; received the Queen's Medal with four clasps, the King's Medal with two clasps, and was created a Companion of the Distinguished Service Order [London Gazette, 19 April, 1901]: " James Sholto Gordon Douglas, Capt., South African Constabulary. In recognition of services during the operations in South Africa." He was promoted to Major in 1902. He served with the South African Constabulary, with the Transvaal Police and the South African Police. He was appointed Deputy Commissioner in command of the South African Police, Johannesburg, from 1908, and became, during the European War, Lieut.-Colonel Commanding No. 8 Military District, Union of South Africa, 1915. Major Douglas married, in 1902, Mabel Kate, eldest daughter of Capt. J. O'Donnell, late 16th Lancers, and they have one son.

OGILVY, THE HONOURABLE LYULPH GILCHRIST STANLEY, Capt., was born at Airlie Lodge, Campden Hill, London, 25 June, 1861, son of David, 7th Earl of Airlie. He was educated at Winton House, Winchester, and Eton; was a subaltern, 2nd Lanark Militia; joined Brabant's Horse, 1899; promoted to Captain. He says: " I do not remember when I joined the Army. My rank at the time when I won the D.S.O. was Captain, I think, but I do not know exactly what it was. My last service was in 1914–15, Lieutenant, A.S.C., Scottish Horse. I do not know why I was given the D.S.O.; the reasons were not stated in any communication when the British Consul at Denver handed me the D.S.O. I was a Corporal in the 2nd U.S. Cavalry (Torrey's Rough Riders), in the Spanish-American War of 1898. I think I was mentioned in Despatches twice. Once, I know, as foreman on a mule ship, Hurona, in charge of mules, New Orleans to Cape Town. Joined Brabant's Horse at Queenstown, South Africa, after delivering mules at Cape Town. First engagement, Dordrecht, others Labuscagne, Aliwal North. Went on relief to Wepener, surrounding movement, and surrender of Fouriesberg; thence to Kroonstad and Pretoria. At Belfast with Lord Roberts, to Machaderdorp, Davel's Kantoor; with General Stephenson (Essex) at Nicto Spruit. Back to Machaderdorp, where we were compelled to turn our horses over to General French, and back to Pretoria for new horses. Resigned and came home on account of my brother Lord Airlie's death at Diamond Hill, where he commanded the 12th Lancers. This was about Dec. 1900. Applied for another (commission) about Feb. 1901; after waiting a couple of months in London, and not receiving it, notified them that as they did not need me I would return to U.S. This was by no means a solitary case; it occurred to several people as strongly recommended as I was. I mention this for your information, as I was afterwards gazetted. Lord Roberts inquired about the matter, and on my explaining it, said I had done quite right in the matter. In every case I have found it only with difficulty one could press one's services on the War Office, even when they claim most bitterly that men are scarce. I repeat, however, that this is merely for your information, in case there should be any confusion in regard to that commission which, as I did no service, did not count. Please excuse this ill-typed letter; machines are strange to me, but my writing is even worse." He received the Queen's Medal with three clasps, and was created a Companion of the Distinguished Service Order [London Gazette, 19 April, 1901]: " The Hon. Lyulph Gilchrist Stanley Ogilvy, Capt., Brabant's Horse. In recognition of services during the operations in South Africa." He married, on 27 Aug. 1902, at Waterdale, Loneland, Colorado, U.S.A., Gertrude Edith Boothroyd, daughter of Philip Henry and Edith Boothroyd, and they had two children: Jack David Angus Ogilvy, born at La Lalle, Colorado, 18 June, 1903 (the boy is having a military training), and Blanche Edith Maude Ogilvy, who was born at La Lalle, Colorado, U.S.A., 27 Sept. 1905, and died 26 March, 1915.

Hon. L. G. S. Ogilvy.

PERKINS, ROBERT CLARK, Surgeon-Capt., was born on 8 May, 1864, son of Thomas Cooper Perkins and Jane Clark. He was educated at Wesley College, Dublin; is a Member of the Royal College of Surgeons and a Licentiate of the Royal College of Physicians. He served in the South African War, and became Surgeon-Captain in 1899. He was twice mentioned in Despatches, and was created a Companion of the Distinguished Service Order [London Gazette, 19 April, 1901]: " Robert Clark Perkins, Surgeon-Capt., Brabant's Horse. For services during the operations in South Africa." The Insignia were presented to Capt. Perkins in South Africa; a public presentation being impracticable, they were handed to him at Heidelberg. He was appointed Medical Officer to the Swaziland Administration. He married Alice Eva Knox, on 22 Aug. 1894, and they had two children: Norah Kathleen Knox, and Arthur Desmond Knox, born 25 April, 1897. Capt. Perkins died 7 May, 1916, at Bremersdorp, Swaziland, South Africa. A newspaper cutting says: " We take the following obituary notice of the late Capt. Perkins, eldest son of the late Mr. T. C. Perkins, Farra, Killala, whose death we announced with deep regret some time ago, from the columns of the ' Lake Chrissie Chronicle ' of 12 May: ' We deeply regret to announce the death on Sunday last of Capt. R. Clark Perkins, D.S.O., Resident Justice of the Peace for Bremersdorp, and formerly Principal Medical Officer for Swaziland. He was ill for a few days. He leaves a widow, son and daughter to whom we tender our most sincere sympathies. The funeral took place at Bremersdorp on Monday. About sixty persons were present to pay the last tribute of respect, including the acting Resident Commissioner, Major Gibson, D.S.O., Mr. Marwick, Mr. Warner and many other officials. The coffin was covered with the Union Jack and many wreaths. The Rev. C. C. Watts read the Burial Service. Capt. Perkins was one of the oldest officials in Swaziland, and came to the country with the S.A.C. in 1902 immediately after the Boer War, and has been officially connected with the Administration ever since. About three years ago his health broke down, and he was ordered to England for rest.

Robert Clark Perkins.

His health became sufficiently restored for him to resume active work, and Capt. Perkins returned to Swaziland, where he relinquished the post of Principal Medical Officer in Swaziland on his appointment as Resident Justice of the Peace at Bremersdorp. He gained his D.S.O. during the Boer War whilst serving with the C.M.R. at Wepener for attending wounded under fire. He took an energetic part in the organization of the Swaziland Contingent for service in South-West Africa, and his son, Desmond Perkins, went through the campaign with the corps, and is now in training at Sandhurst.' "

STEPHENSON, ERIC SEYMOUR, Lieut., was born 21 April, 1879, son of Ernest Percy Stephenson. He was educated at Eton, and served in South Africa with the Mounted Infantry, Brabant's Horse and the Gloucestershire Regt., 1899–1902, taking part in operations in the Orange Free State, Feb. to May, 1900, including the defence of Wepener. Operations in the Transvaal, west of Pretoria, July, to 29 Nov. 1900. Operations in Orange River Colony, May, to 29 Nov. 1900, including actions at Wittebergen (1 to 29 July). Operations in Cape Colony, south of Orange River, 1899–1900. Operations in Cape Colony, north of Orange River. Operations in the Transvaal 30 Nov. 1900, to Feb. 1901. Operations in the Transvaal, April to Aug. 1901, and Nov. to Dec. 1901. Operations in Orange River Colony, Aug. to Sept. 1901, and Dec. 1901, to 31 May, 1902. Operations on the Zululand Frontier of Natal in Sept. and Oct. 1901. He was mentioned in Despatches [London Gazette, 16 April and 10 Sept. 1901]; received the Queen's Medal with four clasps, the King's Medal with two clasps, and was created a Companion of the Distinguished Service Order [London Gazette, 19 April, 1901]: "Eric Seymour Stephenson, Lieut., Brabant's Horse. In recognition of services during the operations in South Africa." He was gazetted 30 May, 1900, to the Gloucestershire Regt., from Brabant's Horse; he was promoted Lieutenant 14 Feb. 1905, and employed on the Staff 12 April, 1906, with the Egyptian Army. He served during the European War, and died of wounds received in action 6 March, 1915, in the Dardanelles.

WALFORD, J. A. H., Colonel, served in the South African War, and was created a Companion of the Distinguished Service Order [London Gazette, 19 April, 1901]: "J. A. H. Walford, Colonel, British South African Police. In recognition of services during the operations in South Africa." The Insignia were presented to him in South Africa. Colonel Walford died on his way home from South Africa in June, 1903.

WHITE, H., Lieut.-Colonel, served during the South African War in the British South African Police, and was created a Companion of the Distinguished Service Order [London Gazette, 19 April, 1901]: "H. White, Lieut.-Colonel, British South African Police. In recognition of services during the operations in South Africa." He died on the 17th Aug. 1903, at Pieterburg, Transvaal. An obituary notice appeared in "The Times."

WILLIAMS, ASHLEY PAGET WILMOT, Capt., was born 7 Jan. 1867, second son of Edward Wilmot Williams, of Herrington, Dorset. He served in the South African War; was mentioned in Despatches, received the Queen's Medal with three clasps, and was created a Companion of the Distinguished Service Order [London Gazette, 19 April, 1901]: "Ashley Paget Wilmot Williams, Capt., British South African Police. In recognition of services during the operations in South Africa." He died on 30 Oct. 1912, aged 45 ("Times").

GREENER, HERBERT, Capt., was born 10 Nov. 1862, son of Thomas Greener, of Tulse Hill, London, S.E.; was educated at a private school (Rev. J. C. C. Pepon, Chester); entered the Civil Service, Cape Colony, 1884; was appointed on the Staff of the Administration, British Bechuanaland, 1888; promoted Receiver of Revenue and Acting Postmaster-General, British Bechuanaland, 1889; became Accountant High Commissioner, Cape Town, 1890; Paymaster, British Bechuanaland Police, 1891. He was appointed Paymaster and Chief Customs Officer for the Bechuanaland Protectorate, which office he retained during the war, till 1900. For valuable war service in connection with the Siege of Mafeking he was created a Companion of the Distinguished Service Order [London Gazette, 19 April, 1901]: "Herbert Greener, Capt., British South African Police. In recognition of services during the operations in South Africa." The Insignia were sent to the Commander-in-Chief in South Africa, and presented in South Africa. He was appointed Financial Assistant to the Military Governor, Bloemfontein, 1901; became Chief Paymaster and Accountant-General of the South African Constabulary; retired from the Constabulary with the local rank of Lieutenant-Colonel. He was appointed Registrar, Rhodes University College, Grahamstown, in 1912. His favourite recreations are shooting, tennis, riding and outdoor exercise. He married, in 1898, Helen Olive, daughter of C. Bennett, late of Isle of Wight; they have one son.

BOWDEN, FRANK LAKE, Capt., was the son of John Thomas Bowden, City Carlton Club, St. Swithin's Lane, and was educated at Dulwich College. He served throughout the Matabele War (Medal); took part in the Jameson Raid in charge of Maxims; served in the Matabele Rebellion in 1896 (clasp). He served in the South African War of 1899–1900, with Brigadier-General Plumer; was present at the Relief of Mafeking. He received the Medal with four clasps and was created a Companion of the Distinguished Service Order [London Gazette, 19 April, 1901]: "Frank Lake Bowden, Capt., British South African Police. In recognition of services during the operations in South Africa." He died 26 June, 1906, at Gwelo, Rhodesia, South Africa, of blackwater fever, aged 42 years.

LLEWELLYN, HOEL, Capt., was born 24 Nov. 1871, son of the late Colonel Evan Henry Llewellyn, M.P. He was educated for the Royal Navy, and as a Midshipman saw active service on the East Coast of Africa, 1888–90 (Despatches). He served as Artillery Officer in the Matabele War, 1893–94 (Despatches); commanding artillery for the Matabele War, 1896–97 (recommended for the V.C. by the General Commanding). He became Captain, British South African Police, and J.P., Matabeleland, 1896; served throughout the South African War; commanded armoured trains north of Mafeking, and the artillery of General Plumer; was transferred to the South African Constabulary, 1901; was Commandant, Lichtenburg District, and J.P., Transvaal Colony, 1902. He was created a Companion of the Distinguished Service Order [London Gazette, 19 April, 1901]: "Hoel Llewellyn, Capt., British South African Police. In recognition of services during the operations in South Africa." (The Insignia, etc., sent to the Commander-in-Chief in South Africa, 13 July, 1901. Presented in South Africa.) He served with the Mediterranean Expeditionary Forces, 1914–15 (wounded); was promoted to the rank of Colonel, graded as A.A.G. on the General Headquarters Staff, and appointed Provost-Marshal of Egypt and the British Mediterranean Expeditionary Force. He has been Chief Constable, Wiltshire, since 1908. Colonel Llewellyn married, in 1902, Winifred, youngest daughter of A. Berens.

HOLMDEN, FRANK ALFRED AMPHLETT, Major, was born 9 April, 1861, son of the late Frank Holmden (who died, 22 April, 1910), of Marlpit House, Kent, and Lay Rector of Edenbridge, Kent, and the late Sarah Ann Holmden (who died 24 Sept. 1910). He was educated at the Edinburgh University; the Middle Temple, London, and Jesus College, Cambridge, taking his degree of M.B. in 1889. He joined the Army, 18 Oct. 1893, as Surgeon-Captain, Bechuanaland Border Police; served as Surgeon-Captain with the Mounted Infantry (Bechuanaland Border Police), in the Matabele War, 1893; he received the Medal. He served with the Bechuanaland Protectorate Division of the British South African Police, 1st Battn. Loyal North Lancashire Regt., and 3rd Battn. King's Own Scottish Borderers, in the South African Campaign (including the Siege of Mafeking), 1899–1902. He received the Queen's Medal with two clasps, and the King's Medal with two clasps; was mentioned twice in Despatches, and created a Companion of the Distinguished Service Order [London Gazette, 19 April, 1901]: "Frank Alfred Amphlett Holmden, Surgeon-Major, British South African Police. In recognition of services during the operations in South Africa." The Insignia were sent to the Commander-in-Chief in South Africa, and presented there. Major Holmden served in the British North Borneo Protectorate, and resigned 8 May, 1913. On the outbreak of the European War he was re-employed by the War Office as Captain, Royal Army Medical Corps, 3 May, 1915; and was promoted Major 16 Feb. 1916. He was formerly attached to the 78th Infantry Brigade, and as one of the Senior Recruiting Officers for Birmingham, was President of the Recruiting Board for the counties of Oxford and Bucks, in the 43rd Regimental District, and now Senior Medical Officer, British Troops, Bulford, and Major, Colonial Office Forces. Major Holmden married, 5 June, 1906, Elsie Mary, eldest daughter of R. A. Foster, formerly of Tutshill House, Tidenham, Chepstow, now of 29, Hans Mansions, London, S.W. They have one son, Richard Frank Douglas, born 15 May, 1908, and one daughter, Eileen Mary, born 15 April, 1907, died 22 April, 1908. His favourite recreations are hunting, polo, and big game shooting; he has had much sport in the latter in South Central Africa, India and British North Borneo.

Frank A. A. Holmden.

GRANT, RONALD CHARLES, Capt., was born 22 Nov. 1864, the eldest son of Lieut.-Colonel James Murray Grant, late Cape Mounted Rifles. He was educated at the Public Schools, Cape Colony; joined the Cape Mounted Rifles in 1880, and served in the Basutoland Campaign, 1880 to 1901, taking part in the Relief of Mohali's Hoed, action of Kalibani, relief of Mafeking, first and second affairs of Lerothodi's Village. He received the Medal with clasp. He again saw active service in South Africa, 1899–1902, as Camp Adjutant, Colonial Division (March to Sept. 1900); during operations in the Orange Free State, March to May, 1900, including defence of Wepener; during operations in the Transvaal, west of Pretoria, Aug. to Nov. 1900; in the operations in the Orange River Colony (May to Aug. 1900), including actions at Wittebergen (1 to 29 July); during operations in Cape Colony, south of Orange River, 1899–1900; taking part in the operations in Cape Colony, Nov. 1900, to May, 1902. He was mentioned in Despatches [London Gazette, 8 Feb. 1901, and 16 April, 1901]; he received the Queen's Medal with four clasps; the King's Medal with two clasps, and was created a Companion of the Distinguished Service Order [London Gazette, 19 April, 1901]: "Ronald Charles Grant, Capt., Cape Mounted Rifles. In recognition of services during the operations in South Africa." The Insignia were sent to South Africa, and presented by Colonel Lukin at Queenstown 7 Dec. 1901. He was promoted Major (became Second-in-Command) 1 Jan. 1903, and received the Brevet of Lieutenant-Colonel 6 June, 1902. For services during the European War he was given the O.B.E. Lieut.-Colonel Grant married, in 1898, Nina, eldest daughter of the Rev. James Stewart, M.D., D.D., of Lovedale, South Africa.

LUKIN, HENRY TIMSON, Capt., was born 24 May, 1860, son of R. H. Lukin, Barrister-at-Law. He was educated at Merchant Taylors' School; served in the South African War, 1879; in the Zulu Campaign; was attached to the Cavalry Brigade in advance on Ulundi, and was present at the battle (severely wounded; Medal with clasp); took part in the operations in Basutoland, 1881 (Medal and clasp). He acted as Field Adjutant, Bechuanaland Field Force, Langeberg Campaign, 1896–97 (Despatches several times); was promoted to Lieutenant-Colonel in 1900. served in the South African War, 1899–1902. Operations in the Orange Free State, March to May, 1900, including the defence of Wepener (in command of Artillery). Operations in the Transvaal, west of Pretoria, Aug. to Nov. 1900. Operations in Orange River Colony, May to Aug.

1900, including actions at Wittebergen (1 to 28 July). Operations in Cape Colony, south of Orange River, 1899–1900. Operations in the Orange River Colony, Nov. 1900, to April, 1901. Operations in Cape Colony, 1901–2. Commanded a column, 1901–2. He was mentioned in Despatches [London Gazette, 8 Feb., 16 April and 20 Aug. 1901], and was granted the honorary rank of Lieutenant-Colonel; the Queen's Medal with four clasps; the King's Medal with two clasps; was created a C.M.G., and created a Companion of the Distinguished Service Order [London Gazette, 19 April, 1901]: "Henry Timson Lukin, Capt., Cape Mounted Rifles. In recognition of services during the operations in South Africa." The Insignia were sent to South Africa, and presented at Umtata by Major Waring, Cape Mounted Rifles, 26 Nov. 1901. He became Commandant, General Defence Department, Cape of Good Hope, 1 June, 1904. He became Honorary Lieutenant-Colonel in the Army 1 Jan. 1903, and Colonel, in command of the Cape Mounted Riflemen, 1905–12, and Inspector-General of the Permanent Force, Union of South Africa, in 1912. He subsequently became Temporary Brigadier-General. Brigadier-General Lukin served in the European War; was created a C.B. in 1916, and was awarded the Order of the Nile, 3rd Class. He was created a K.C.B. in 1918; became Temporary Major-General. His favourite recreations are golf, polo and tennis.

ROY, JOSEPH EDENSOR GASCOIGNE, Lieut., was born 15 April, 1872, son of the late Rev. Richard Clark Roy. He was educated at Rossall, and joined the Cape Mounted Rifles 29 Nov. 1891, and served in the First Matabele War, 1893–94 (Medal), and in Bechuanaland, 1897 (Medal and clasp). He served in the South African War, 1899–1902, as Lieutenant and Captain, taking part in operations in the Orange Free State, March to May, 1900, including the defence of Wepener. Operations in the Transvaal, west of Pretoria, Aug. to Nov. 1900. Operations in Orange River Colony, May to Aug. 1900, including actions at Wittebergen (1 to 29 July). Operations in Cape Colony, south of Orange River, 1899–1900. Operations in the Transvaal, Dec. 1900. Operations in the Orange River Colony, Dec. 1900, to Feb. 1901. Operations in Cape Colony, 1901–2. He was Adjutant, Cape Mounted Riflemen, Dec. 1901, to April, 1902; was mentioned in Despatches [London Gazette, 16 April, 1901]; received the Queen's Medal with four clasps; the King's Medal with two clasps, and was created a Companion of the Distinguished Service Order [London Gazette, 19 April, 1901]: "Joseph Edensor Gascoigne Roy, Lieut., Cape Mounted Rifles. In recognition of services during the operations in South Africa. The Insignia were sent to South Africa, and presented to him at Umtata by Major Waring, Cape Mounted Rifles, 26 Nov. 1901. He was appointed Gunnery Instructor, Cape Mounted Rifles, 1 Jan. 1903, and was promoted to Major. In 1910 Major Roy was appointed to command the Cape Mounted Rifles at the opening of the Union Parliament at Cape Town, for which services he was awarded a Medal, and created an M.V.O., 1911. He subsequently held the rank of Lieutenant-Colonel in the South African Mounted Riflemen.

MITCHELL, WILLIAM EDWARD CLIFTON Capt., was born 29 March, 1875, at Lincoln, in England, son of Henry Mitchell, Stockbroker. He went to South Africa in 1882, and was educated at the South African College, and joined the Railway Pioneer Regt., as Lieutenant, 28 Dec. 1889, becoming Captain 24 March, 1900. He served in the South African War, 1899–1902; received the Queen's and King's Medals, and was created a Companion of the Distinguished Service Order [London Gazette, 19 April, 1901]: "William Edward Clifton Mitchell, Capt., Cape Pioneer Regt. In recognition of services during operations in South Africa." The Insignia were sent to South Africa, and presented to him by Lady Milner at Johannesburg 9 Aug. 1902. In the European War Capt. Mitchell served in France, as Lieutenant, Royal Engineers (Tunnelling Section). His wife is Mrs. Sybil Dorothy Mitchell, whom he married at Cape Town 12 Oct. 1910.

WILSON, NATHANIEL, Major, served in the Cape Pioneer Regt. in the South African War, 1899–1900. He was mentioned in Despatches; received the Queen's Medal with three clasps, and was created a Companion of the Distinguished Service Order [London Gazette, 19 April, 1901]: "Nathaniel Wilson, Major, Cape Pioneer Regt. In recognition of services during the operations in South Africa." The Insignia were presented to him by His Majesty the King 15 July, 1901. He was subsequently promoted to Lieutenant-Colonel, and in 1917 was created a C.M.G. Lieut.-Colonel Wilson is married, and has two daughters.

WATERMEYER, JOUBERT HENRY HUTTON, Capt., was born at Forest Cottage, Plumstead, South Africa, 7 March, 1867, son of C. F. J. Watermeyer and Julia, daughter of the Rev. H. Hutton, of Filleagh, Devonshire. He was educated at the South African College, Cape Town, South Africa; matriculated at the University of the Cape of Good Hope, 1884; passed the Theoretical examination in land-surveying, 1886; was admitted as a Government Land Surveyor, Cape Colony, 1889. He joined the Cape Town Highlanders in 1893; was promoted to Captain, 1895; passed the Military Examination in Tactics and Topography, 1896; took part in the Bechuanaland Campaign, 1897 (Medal with clasp). Capt. Watermeyer served in the South African War, 1899–1902, and was A.D.C. to Field-Marshal Lord Roberts, Commanding-in-Chief. He took part in operations in the Orange Free State, Feb. to May, 1900, including operations at Paardeberg and action at Dreifontein. Operations in the Transvaal, including action near Johannesburg. Operations in the Transvaal, east of Pretoria, including action at Belfast. Operations in Cape Colony. He was mentioned in Despatches [London Gazette, 8 Feb. and 16 April, 1901]; received the Queen's Medal with five clasps; the King's Medal with two clasps, and was created a Companion of the Distinguished Service Order [London Gazette, 19 April, 1901]: "J. H. H. Watermeyer, Capt., Cape Town Highlanders. In recognition of services during the operations in South Africa." The Insignia, Warrant and Statutes were sent to the Commander-in-Chief in South Africa, and presented in South Africa by Major-General A. Wynne 19 Nov. 1901. The decoration was especially awarded for Capt. Watermeyer's services whilst A.D.C. to the Commander-in-Chief, in charge of transport and baggage. He is connected with almost every form of sport, and is President of the National Sporting Club of South Africa.

POPE-HENNESSEY, G., Capt., served in the South African War of 1899–1902, and was created a Companion of the Distinguished Service Order [London Gazette, 19 April, 1901]: "G. Pope-Hennessey, Capt., Cape Police. In recognition of services during the operations in South Africa." The Insignia were sent to the Commander-in-Chief in South Africa, and presented there.

BROWNLEE, JOHN INNES, Capt., was born 20 April, 1860, son of the late Hon. Charles P. Brownlee, C.M.G. He served in the South African War, 1899–1900, taking part in operations in the Orange Free State, Feb. to May, 1900, including operations at Paardeberg and actions at Poplar Grove and Dreifontein. He was mentioned in Despatches [London Gazette, 8 Feb. 1901]; received the Queen's Medal with three clasps, and was created a Companion of the Distinguished Service Order [London Gazette, 19 April, 1901]: "John Innes Brownlee, Capt., Cape Medical Corps. In recognition of services during the operations in South Africa." The Insignia were sent to the Commander-in-Chief in South Africa, and presented by Colonel Hutchinson 21 Dec. 1901, at King William's Town. Major Brownlee served during the European War from Aug. 1914, as Lieutenant-Colonel, South African Medical Corps; as A.D.M.S., No. 3 Military District, Cape Province; served in the operations in German South-West Africa, in command of the 1st M.B.F.A. from Sept. 1914, to June, 1915. He has the Volunteer Decoration. Lieut.-Colonel Brownlee married, in 1888, Blanche Augusta Stevens.

RODGER, THOMAS HENDERSON, Major, was born at Wynberg, near Cape Town, 10 March, 1860. He served in the D.E.O.V.R. in the Gaika–Galeka War of 1877–78, and in the D.F. Horse in the Langberg Rebellion, Bechuanaland, 1896–97 (Medal and clasp). He was promoted Captain, 1894; Major, 1899, and again saw active service in the South African War, 1899–1902, taking part in the defence of Kimberley. Operations in Orange Free State, Feb. to May, 1900. Relief of Mafeking. Operations in the Transvaal, May and June, 1900. Operations in Orange River Colony, May to 29 Nov. 1900. Operations in Cape Colony, north of Orange River. Operations in the Transvaal, Orange River Colony and Cape Colony 30 Nov. 1900, to 31 May, 1902. He was mentioned in Despatches [London Gazette, 8 May, 1900, and 16 April, 1901]; received the Queen's Medal with four clasps; the King's Medal with two clasps, and was created a Companion of the Distinguished Service Order [London Gazette, 19 April, 1901]: "Thomas Henderson Rodger, Major, Diamond Fields Horse. In recognition of services during the operations in South Africa." The Insignia were sent to the Commander-in-Chief in South Africa, and presented there. In 1902 he became Officer Commanding the Kimberley Horse, with the rank of Lieutenant-Colonel. Lieut.-Colonel Rodger married, in 1885, Elizabeth Johanna, daughter of W. J. Merrington, of Claremont, Cape Colony.

TURNER, HENRY GORDON, Capt., was born in 1862, son of the Rev. J. Turner, of Mansfield-Woodhouse, Nottinghamshire. He served in the South African War, 1902, and was created a Companion of the Distinguished Service Order [London Gazette, 19 April, 1901]: "Henry Gordon Turner, Capt., De Montmorency's Scouts. In recognition of services during the operations in South Africa." The Insignia were sent to the Commander-in-Chief in South Africa, and presented by Colonel Long at Dordrecht 25 Dec. 1901. Capt. Turner married, in 1890, Mabel Eugene, daughter of Myles L. Formby. De Montmorency's Scouts were raised by Capt. the Hon. R. H. L. J. de Montmorency, V.C. Sir A. Conan Doyle, on page 158 of his "Great Boer War," says of him, when describing the doings of General Gatacre's small force while holding the district from Sterkstroom to East London unflinchingly: "Scouting and raiding expeditions, chiefly organized by Capt. de Montmonrency—whose early death cut short the career of one who possessed every quality of a partisan leader—broke the monotony of inaction. On 23 Feb. 1900, General Gatacre sent out a force to reconnoitre the enemy's position at Stormberg. The incident is memorable as having been the cause of the death of Capt. de Montmorency, one of the most promising of the younger officers of the British Army. He had formed a corps of scouts, consisting originally of four men, but soon expanding to seventy or eighty. At the head of these men he confirmed the reputation for desperate valour which he had won in the Soudan, and added to it proofs of the energy and judgment which go to make a leader of light cavalry. In the course of the reconnaissance he ascended a small kopje, accompanied by three companions—Colonel Hoskier, a London Volunteer soldier; Vice, a civilian, and Sergt. Howe. 'They are right on the top of us,' he cried to his comrades as he reached the summit, and dropped next instant with a bullet through his heart. Hoskier was shot in five places, and Vice was mortally wounded, only Howe escaping. The rest of the scouts, being farther back, were able to get under cover and to keep up a fight until they were extricated by the remainder of the force. . . . De Montmorency had established a remarkable influence over his rough followers. To the end of the war they could not speak of him without tears in their eyes. When I asked Sergt. Howe why his Captain went almost alone up the hill, his answer was, 'Because the Captain knew no fear.' Byrne, his soldier servant (an Omdurman V.C., like his master) galloped madly off next morning with a saddled horse to bring back his Captain alive or dead, and had to be forcibly seized and restrained by our cavalry."

DRISCOLL, DANIEL PATRICK, Capt., was born in Burma 11 May, 1862, son of John Driscoll. He received instruction at school in Burma, but at an early age turned to Service in the Mercantile Marine. He subsequently served in the Burma Campaign, 1886–88 (Medal and clasp). Capt. Driscoll served in South Africa throughout the war, 1899–1902, first as Captain of Scouting Party, attached to the "Colonial Division," and later as Commander of Driscoll's Scouts, and, in 1901, as Column Commander (promoted to Lieutenant-Colonel). He was mentioned in Despatches twice; received the Queen's Medal with two clasps, and was created a Companion of the Distinguished Service Order [London Gazette, 19 April, 1901]: "Daniel Patrick Driscoll, Capt., Driscoll's Scouts. In recognition of services during the operations in South Africa." The Insignia, Warrant and Statutes were sent to the Commander-in-Chief in South Africa, and presented there. Driscoll's Scouts are often mentioned in the official "History of the War in South Africa" (compiled by General Sir F. Maurice, G.C.B., and published by Messrs. Hurst and Blackett). In Volume II. (pages 315–316) we are told that the Scouts (with three officers, 53 other ranks and 56 horses) were engaged in the defence of Wepener. On page 122 of Volume III. we read that "Sir L. Rundle took the Bethlehem Road with the following force: 4th Battn. and one company of the 11th Battn. Imperial Yeomanry, the 2nd and 79th Batteries, Royal Field Artillery, Driscoll's Scouts, 2nd Grenadier Guards, 2nd Scots Guards, 2nd East Yorkshire Regt., and, to complete the brigade, the 2nd Royal West Kent Regt. from Boye's (17th) Brigade." On 29 May, Sir L. Rundle fought the action at Biddulphs Berg. On 12 and 13 July, 1900, Driscoll's Scouts were still with Sir L. Rundle, and engaged in the chase after de Wet, and (after the escape of de Wet) in the attack on Slabbert's Nek. On the 25th Sir L. Rundle occupied Commando Nek; on the 26th, Fouriesburg, and on the 27th he engaged the enemy at Slaap Kranz. In the middle of Aug. 1901, Driscoll's Scouts formed part of the garrison at Harrismith. Lieut.-Colonel Driscoll was appointed Chief Executive Officer, Legion of Frontiersmen. He served in the European War from 1915, in command of the 25th Battn. Royal Fusiliers, with great distinction, and his genius of resource greatly contributed to victory achieved against heavy odds on more than one momentous occasion. Lieut.-Colonel Driscoll was mentioned in Despatches four times by General Smuts; was awarded the Croix de Guerre (May, 1917), and created a C.M.G. in 1919. Having been offered a grant of Government land in British East Africa, Colonel Driscoll decided to accept it, and resigning the command of the Legion of Frontiersmen, with which World-Force he had been associated for about twelve years, he sailed for East Africa early in Dec. 1919. Before his departure Colonel Driscoll was the recipient of many marks of esteem from the Legion as a whole, and also from separate units and individuals. Entertained at a farewell banquet a few days before his departure, Colonel Driscoll eulogized the high spirit distinguishing the Legion of Frontiersmen as a whole, and, in particular, the wonderful pluck, power of endurance, dash and bravery of those who had served throughout the campaign in East Africa, and he called upon all present to stick to the Legion as one of the finest organizations on earth.

Daniel Patrick Driscoll.

MILFORD, A., Lieut., served in the South African War of 1899–1902; was mentioned in Despatches, and created a Companion of the Distinguished Service Order [London Gazette, 19 April, 1901]: "A. Milford, Lieut., Frontier Mounted Rifles. In recognition of services during the operations in South Africa." The Insignia were sent to the Commander-in-Chief in South Africa, and presented in South Africa."

DAVIES, WILLIAM THOMAS FREDERICK, Major, was born 13 Aug. 1860, at Swansea, South Wales, son of the late Dr. Ebenezer Davies, of Swansea, and of Mrs. E. J. C. Davies (*née* Bluett). He is M.D., B.S., London, and M.R.C.S., England. He served in the South African War, 1899–1900, as Surgeon-Major, South African Light Horse, which force he had helped to raise. He took part in operations in Natal in 1899, including actions at Elandslaagte, Rietfontein and Lombard's Kop. He was in Medical Charge of the Regiment during the Siege of Ladysmith, when he was present at the sortie of 7 Dec. 1899, and action of 6 Jan. 1900. He was in Medical Charge of the Relief Column under Colonel Bryan Mahon, on the march to Mafeking, and was present at the Relief of Mafeking. He was invalided owing to an injury to the knee. He took part also in the operations in the Transvaal, east and west of Pretoria, July to Nov. 1900. He received the Queen's Medal with five clasps, and was created a Companion of the Distinguished Service Order [London Gazette, 19 April, 1901]: "William Thomas Frederick Davies, Surgeon-Major, Imperial Light Horse. In recognition of services during the operations in South Africa." The Insignia were presented by the King 3 June, 1901. The receipt of the Warrant and Statutes was acknowledged by the officer's father, as Major Davies had left for South Africa. He was promoted to the rank of Lieutenant-Colonel, Imperial Light Horse Volunteers; was appointed President of the Transvaal Medical Council, and Surgeon to the Johannesburg Hospital. When the European War broke out in 1914 he raised the 2nd Imperial Light Horse, and was given command of it, serving throughout the German South-West African Campaign. He was in the action of Gibeon, and was wounded. He served in the Royal Army Medical Corps as Major, June, 1917, to April, 1919, and was appointed Surgeon Specialist to the General Military Hospital, Colchester. He married, in 1886, Florence, daughter of T. Dixon.

FOWLER, CHARLES HENRY, Capt., was born 13 July, 1869, son of Charles Henry Fowler, M.D. He was educated at Cheltenham College; and served in the South African War in 1900; was mentioned in Despatches, received the Queen's Medal with seven clasps, the King's Medal with two clasps, and was created a Companion of the Distinguished Service Order [London Gazette, 19 April, 1901]: "Charles Henry Fowler, Capt., Imperial Light Horse. In recognition of services during the operations in South Africa." The Insignia were sent to the Commander-in-Chief in South Africa, and presented there. The decoration was awarded for Ladysmith. He became Captain, South African Constabulary.

NORMAND, PATRICK HILL, Lieut., was born 20 Feb. 1876, son of Patrick Hill Normand. He was educated at Fettes College, Edinburgh; joined the Imperial Light Horse, as Lieutenant, in 1899, at Maritzburg, Natal, and helped to form the regiment. He was present at the battle of Elandslaagte (wounded); in the Siege of Ladysmith; was wounded at Waggon Hill on 6 Jan.; went with General Mahon's Column to the Relief of Mafeking; took part in the advance on Barberton, with General French's Column. He became Deputy Governor, Transvaal Prisons Department, in 1903, and Governor in 1908. From May, 1917, to March, 1919, he served with the Expeditionary Force in France as Deputy Assistant Provost-Marshal. He was mentioned in Despatches, and created a Companion of the Distinguished Service Order [London Gazette, 19 April, 1901]: "Patrick Hill Normand, Lieut., Imperial Light Horse. In recognition of services during the operations in South Africa." Capt. Normand married, in 1907, Matilda M. Marsh, and they have three sons.

FARRAR, GEORGE HERBERT, Capt., was born at Chatteris, Cambridgeshire, 17 June, 1859, son of the late Charles Farrar, M.D., and his wife, Helen (The Crescent Lodge, Bedford), daughter of John Howard. He was educated at the Modern School, Bedford, and on leaving school entered the engineering business of his uncle, Sir Frederick Howard, going in 1879 to South Africa, to the Port Elizabeth and East London Branches. Eight years later he and his brothers settled in Johannesburg, where, in a few years, he became one of the leading men in the mining industry of the Witwatersrand. His chief enterprise was the formation of the East Rand Proprietary Mines, of which he was Chairman from the inception of the undertaking until the day of his death. He was for some time a Member of the Legislative Assembly of the Transvaal and Leader of the Opposition. He was tried for treason and sentenced to death for his share in the Jameson Raid, but the sentence was remitted on payment of a fine of £25,000. When the South African War broke out, he raised two regiments of South African Horse, and was appointed Major, Kaffrarian Rifles, 1 Dec. 1900, and served in this campaign as Captain, and afterwards Major, Kaffrarian Rifles, and as Major on the Staff of the Colonial Division. He took part in the operations in the Orange Free State, including the Defence of Wepener; operations in the Transvaal, west of Pretoria, Aug. to Sept. 1900; operations in Orange River Colony, 1900, including actions at Wittebergen (1 to 29 July), and in Cape Colony, south of the Orange River. He was mentioned in Despatches, 16 April, 1901; received the Queen's Medal with four clasps, and created a Companion of the Distinguished Service Order [London Gazette, 19 April, 1901]: "George Herbert Farrar, Capt., Kaffrarian Rifles. In recognition of services during the operations in South Africa." (The Insignia presented by the King.) He was knighted in 1902. After the conclusion of peace, in 1902, he took an active part in the work of reorganization, and when Responsible Government was granted to the Transvaal he was unanimously elected leader of the Progressive Party in the House of Assembly, in opposition to the Ministry of General Botha. In 1903 Sir George Farrar was elected President of the Witwatersrand Chamber of Mines, and he took a leading part in the negotiations which led up to the formation of the Union of South Africa. For his services in this matter he was created a Baronet 2 Feb. 1911, and he became M.P. for Georgetown, in the first Parliament of the Union of South Africa, 1910–11, but in Dec. 1911, the claims of business in connection with the East Rand Company compelled him to retire from political affairs in order to devote his whole time for the reorganization of that enterprise. When the European War broke out he was on a visit to England, and was about to join General Sir Hubert Hamilton's Staff with the Army in Belgium, but he was ordered by the authorities to South Africa on the day before he was to have left. He was appointed to General McKenzie's Force, with the rank of Colonel, and was despatched to German South-West Africa as Acting Assistant Quartermaster-General. He went to Luderitz Bay in advance of the main force, and was engaged in the organization of the base camp, and later had charge of the restoration of the railway and of providing the water supply to the force, an operation of the first importance in that country. On the 19th of May, 1915, he was returning from a tour of inspection when the motor trolley on which he was travelling collided with a construction train at Knibis, near Gibeon, in German South-West Africa. Sir George was fatally injured, and only lingered until the next morning. He was one of the best-known men in South Africa, and had contributed to the progress of that country by legislative work, and by attention to mining and agricultural enterprise. He married, on 3 June, 1893, at Johannesburg, Ella Mabel, daughter of the late Dr. Charles Waylen, I.M.S., and had six daughters: Helen Mabel; Muriel Frances; Gwendoline; Georgina Marjorie; Kathleen Elizabeth and Ella Marguerite. Lady Farrar lives at Chicheley Hall, Newport Pagnall, Bucks, and has a residence in South Africa, Bedford Farm, near Johannesburg, Transvaal.

FARRAR, JOHN PERCY, Capt., was born in 1857, son of the late Charles Farrar, M.D., and brother of the late Sir George Farrar. He served in the South African War of 1899–1902; received the Queen's Medal with four clasps, and was created a Companion of the Distinguished Service Order [London Gazette, 19 April, 1901]: "John Percy Farrar, Capt., Kaffrarian Rifles. In recognition of services during the operations in South Africa." The Insignia were sent to South Africa, returned to England, and presented by the King. Capt. Farrar married, in 1886, Mary, daughter of F. Beswick, of Queenstown.

RICKMAN, WILLIAM EDWARD, Capt., was born in 1855. He served in the South African War, 1900–02; was mentioned in Despatches, awarded the Queen's Medal with three clasps, and the King's Medal with two clasps, and created a Companion of the Distinguished Service Order [London Gazette, 19 April, 1901]: "William Edward Rickman, Capt., Kimberley Light Horse. In recognition of services during the operations in South Africa." The Insignia were presented by the King 29 Oct. 1901. Capt. Rickman married, in 1895, Margaret Menzies Haliburton.

HEBERDEN, GEORGE ALFRED, Capt., was born 27 April, 1860, son of the late Rev. George Heberden. He was educated at Malvern College; at Jesus College, Cambridge (B.A., Cantab., 1882), and at St. George's Hospital, London (M.R.C.S., England; L.R.C.P., London, 1888). He was District Commissioner of Predasdorp, 1888–89; Surgeon, Cape Government Railway, 1890–92; District Surgeon, Kenhardt, 1893–94; Barkly West, 1895. He served in the South African War, as Medical Officer to Mounted Forces during the Siege of Kimberley; was mentioned in Despatches, and created a Companion of the Distinguished Service Order [London Gazette 19 April, 1901]: "George Alfred Heberden, Surgeon-Captain (Medical Officer), Kimberley Light Horse. In recognition of services during the operations in South Africa." The Insignia were sent to the Commander-in-Chief in South Africa, and presented by Colonel Garstin. Capt. Heberden married, in 1895, Winifred, daughter of the late Rev. Henry Cottam.

ANGEL, THOMAS LOMBARD, Capt., was born 10 Jan. 1867, son of John Angel, of Torquay, Devon. He was educated at St. Luke's, Torquay, and became a Mechanical Engineer. He served with the Kimberley Regt. in Bechuanaland (Medal and clasp). He again saw active service in the South African War, 1900–01, as Captain, Kimberley Cycle Corps, during the siege of that place. He was mentioned in Despatches, and created a Companion of the Distinguished Service Order [London Gazette, 19 April, 1901]: "Thomas Lombard Angel, Capt., Kimberley Town Guard. In recognition of services during the operations in South Africa." The Insignia were sent to the Commander-in-Chief in South Africa, and presented there. He served in the European War, 1914–15, as Captain in the Imperial Army, and was later invalided home, and became Assistant to the Colonel in Charge of Records, No. 6 District, Lichfield, and No. 10 District, Hounslow. Capt. Angel married (1st), Mabel, daughter of Charles Abbey, Sculptor, of Richmond, Surrey; and (2ndly), Agnes Dunlop, daughter of J. Carbery, M.D.

O'MEARA, BULKELEY ERNEST ADOLPHUS, Capt., was born at Umballa, India, 1 Feb. 1867, son of the late Alfred O'Meara, of St. Mark's, Simla, India. He was educated at Dulwich College, and at King's College School, Somerset House, London. He served as a trooper in the original Pioneer Force which annexed Rhodesia to the British Empire, 1889–91; was Surveyor in the De Beers Consolidated Mines, Limited, Kimberley. He served in the South African War, 1899–1901, in the Kimberley Town Guard; was transferred to the Intelligence Department in 1900, and was Intelligence Officer for Griqualand West, as far as Mafeking; was S.O.1 to Vryberg and Carnarvon Columns; Press Censor and Interpreter and Intelligence Officer at Oudtshoorn, under Acting Inspector-General Western. He was four times mentioned in Despatches, and was created a Companion of the Distinguished Service Order [London Gazette, 19 April, 1901]: "Bulkeley Ernest Adolphus O'Meara, Capt., Kimberley Town Guard. In recognition of services during the operations in South Africa." The Insignia were sent to South Africa, and presented to him there. He was subsequently appointed Government Surveyor for the Cape and Transvaal Colonies, practising at Johannesburg. He was a keen sportsman, taking part in all kinds of South African sport, including big game shooting in the north. Capt. O'Meara died 31 Aug. 1916.

RICHARDS, SIDNEY, Capt., was educated at Cheltenham College. He served throughout the Siege of Kimberley, in the Kimberley Town Guard, during the South African War, 1899–1900, and for his services was mentioned in Despatches, and created a Companion of the Distinguished Service Order [London Gazette, 19 April, 1901]: "Sidney Richards, Capt., Kimberley Town Guard. In recognition of services during the operations in South Africa." The Insignia, etc., were sent to South Africa, and presented there. He was also promoted to Major. He joined the Victoria Rifles, late Duke of Edinburgh's Own Volunteer Rifles.

RAYNHAM, EUSTACE FREDERICK, Lieut., served in the South African War, 1900, and for his services received the Queen's Medal with clasp, and was created a Companion of the Distinguished Service Order [London Gazette, 19 April, 1901]: "Eustace Frederick Raynham, Lieut., Kimberley Town Guard. In recognition of services during the operations in South Africa." The Insignia, etc., were sent to the Commander-in-Chief in South Africa, and presented there. He became Secretary of the De Beers Consolidated Mines in 1917.

SMITH, JAMES ALEXANDER JONES, Major, served during the South African War, 1899–1901, in the Kimberley Regt., and for his services was mentioned in Despatches and created a Companion of the Distinguished Service Order [London Gazette, 19 April, 1901]: "James Alexander Jones Smith, Surgeon-Major, Kimberley Regt. In recognition of services during the operations in South Africa." The Insignia were sent to the Commander-in-Chief in South Africa, and presented there.

George H. Mills Richey.

RICHEY, GEORGE HENRY MILLS, Capt., was born at Woolwich 18 May, 1867, son of the late Capt. E. Mills Richey, R.A., City Marshal of London, and Eliza Louise, daughter of Alexander Luke, of Carsluke, Scotland. He served as a volunteer in Methuen's Horse, in the Bechuanaland Expedition, 1884–85; was in the 12th Royal Lancers in 1886, and the 2nd

Dragoon Guards. He entered the Colonial Service in 1895, and went through the Matabele War of 1896, and the Mashona Campaign of 1897–98, and received the General Service South African Medal and clasp. He served in the South African War, 1899–1902, part of the time as Adjutant of Kitchener's Horse. During part of the South African War he was Chief of Police, Krugersdorp District, in 1900, and later on Staff Officer to Dean's Column, operating in the Cape Colony towards the end of the war. He served under Ian Hamilton in his march to Johannesburg and Pretoria. The Army List says that he took part in "the Relief of Kimberley. Operations in the Orange Free State, Feb., including operations at Paardeberg, and action at Dreifontein. Operations in the Transvaal, including action near Johannesburg." He was wounded at Waterval Drift in 1900, and at Houtnek in 1900. He was mentioned three times in Despatches; recommended for the Victoria Cross, and created a Companion of the Distinguished Service Order [London Gazette, 19 April, 1901]: "George Henry Mills Richey, Capt., Kitchener's Horse. In recognition of services during the operations in South Africa." The decoration was awarded "For gallantry in the field, and devotion to duty and good work."

The following is an extract from a letter written by Lieut.-Colonel Norton Legge, 20th Hussars, Commanding Kitchener's Horse, dated Pretoria, 10 Aug. 1900:

"Capt. George Richey served in the regiment under my command—first as a subaltern and afterwards as my Adjutant, for which position I selected him on the promotion of Major Congreve, V.C., and I have had many opportunities of noticing his exceptional ability. He was promoted Captain by request of General Broadwood, C.B., Commanding 2nd Cavalry Brigade, for a clever reconnaissance of the Boer position at Poplar Grove. He got by himself to within 800 yards of their main position, and succeeded in sketching it and locating their guns. For this service (which had important results) Lord Roberts personally complimented him. As my Adjutant he was ever ready for work, and he carried out his arduous duties to my entire satisfaction."

Major George Cookson, 16th Lancers, Commanding Kitchener's Horse, wrote:

"Capt. G. H. M. Richey was Adjutant of Kitchener's Horse, and was all through the fighting under General Ian Hamilton, and his Winburg Column; on three different occasions his name was sent in for gallant conduct in the field; on one occasion, when with an officer's patrol, he gave up his horse to a trooper who had had a fall and lost his own horse, and walked back under fire on foot."

From Major-General H. J. M. MacAndrew, C.B., D.S.O.:

"Capt. G. H. M. Richey served under me as a troop leader in D Squadron, Kitchener's Horse, for about one month, and until he was promoted to the appointment of Adjutant of the regiment. During the time Capt. Richey served under me I had the pleasure of bringing his gallant conduct in action to the notice of the Commanding Officer on three separate occasions, and I believe his services have been brought to the notice of His Excellency the Commander-in-Chief."

He was subsequently promoted to Major. During the early part of the European War he was Second-in-Command of the 23rd Royal Fusiliers (1st Sportsman's), under Viscount Maitland. Lieut.-Colonel G. H. M. Richey later commanded the 4th East Lancashire Regt., British Expeditionary Force. He won many prizes in India for skill at arms. At Rawal Pindi in 1892 he won five first prizes, and two second at the Punjab Assault-at-Arms. He won the tent-pegging after 14 runs, four of which were at the peg sideways. All the pegs were "taken."

JACKSON, JOHN EDWARD, Lieut., was born at Ormskirk, Lancashire, in 1872, the youngest son of Thomas Jackson. He was educated at the Grammar School, Ormskirk. He joined Kitchener's Horse in 1900, and fought right through the South African War, 1899–1901; was present at the Relief of Mafeking, at Paardeberg; took part in the marches to Bloemfontein and to Pretoria, under Ian Hamilton; was at the Diamond Hill action; took part in the Wittebergen operations and subsequent pursuit of De Wet, and served for six months in Cape Colony. He received the South African War Medal with seven clasps, and for the conspicuous gallantry displayed by him in the field at Osfontein, Orange River Colony, in 1900, he was created a Companion of the Distinguished Service Order [London Gazette, 19 April, 1901]: "John Edward Jackson, Lieut., Kitchener's Horse. In recognition of services during the operations in South Africa." The Insignia, etc., were sent to South Africa, and presented to him by the Officer Commanding, Cape Town District. He was promoted to Captain. Capt. Jackson married, in 1902, Winifred Mabel, youngest daughter of B. Dennis, St. James, Cape Town.

CRAIG, S. E., Lieut., served in the South African War, and was created a Companion of the Distinguished Service Order [London Gazette, 19 April, 1901]: "S. E. Craig, Lieut., Loch's Horse. In recognition of services during the operations in South Africa." The Insignia were presented by the King 25 July, 1901.

RUTHERFORD, JOHN BROWNLEY, Capt., was born 11 Oct. 1864, son of John Rutherford. He served in the South African War, and was created a Companion of the Distinguished Service Order [London Gazette, 19 April, 1901]: "J. B. Rutherford, Capt., Lumsden's Horse. In recognition of services during the operations in South Africa." The Insignia were forwarded to the Commander-in-Chief in India, and presented to Capt. Rutherford by the Lieutenant-Governor of Bengal 20 Jan. 1902. He became Captain in the Behar Light Horse, and Honorary Captain in the Army. He died in India.

PUGH, HERBERT OWAIN, Major, was born 9 July, 1874, son of the late L. P. Pugh, Esq., M.P., D.L., of Abermaed, Cardiganshire, and of Mrs. V. H. Pugh, of Cynmerau, Cardiganshire. He was educated at Sherborne and Rugby, and became a Merchant in India (1891–1900). He proceeded to South Africa with Lumsden's Horse in 1900, and was appointed Assistant District Commissioner, Heilbron, in 1900. He joined the South African Constabulary in 1901. For his services in the South African War he received the Queen's Medal with three clasps ; the King's Medal with two clasps, and was created a Companion of the Distinguished Service Order [London Gazette, 19 April, 1901]: " Herbert Owain Pugh, Lieut., Lumsden's Horse. In recognition of services during the operations in South Africa." In 1908 he was appointed Secretary to the Territorial Force Association of the Counties of Carmarthen, Cardigan and Pembroke. In 1914 he assisted in raising the Welsh Horse, and was gazetted a Major 30 Aug. 1914. He served in Gallipoli, Egypt and Palestine, and was appointed Second-in-Command of the Berkshire Yeomanry in March, 1917. He was severely wounded at Gaza 19 April, 1917, and invalided on account of wounds 7 May, 1918. Major Pugh is married and has one son and one daughter.

NESBITT, CHARLES WARREN, Capt., was born in 1866, son of the late Lieut.-Colonel R. A. Nesbitt. He served in the South African War, 1900–1, in command of Nesbitt's Horse. The Official " History of the War in South Africa " (compiled by Major-General Sir F. Maurice, K.C.B., and published by Messrs. Hurst and Blackett), says on page 415 of Volume 1. : " Immediately on his arrival the Field-Marshal (Lord Roberts) strove to systematize and support the efforts of the many South African Colonists who were pressing to be allowed to take up arms in self-defence. Their embodiment had already been sanctioned by Sir R. Buller, and approved by the Home Government. Colonel Brabant's Corps was expanded into two regiments, and their leader appointed a Brigadier-General to command a Colonial division composed of his own two regiments (Brabant's Horse), the Cape Mounted Rifles, Kaffrarian Rifles, Border Horse and Queenstown Rifle Volunteers. Two new mounted corps, entitled Roberts's Horse and Kitchener's Horse, were raised, besides numerous local defence corps, such as Nesbitt's and Bayley's from the Eastern province, and Orpen's from the Hopetown district. Colonel C. P. Ridley, in charge of the Western line of communications, commanded the 2nd Mounted Infantry Brigade, made up by the 2nd, 4th, 6th and 8th Mounted Infantry Regiments, the City Imperial Volunteers, Queensland Mounted Infantry and Nesbitt's Horse." For his services in this campaign Capt. Nesbitt was mentioned in Despatches, and created a Companion of the Distinguished Service Order [London Gazette, 19 April, 1901]: " Charles Warren Nesbitt, Capt., Nesbitt's Horse. In recognition of services during the operations in South Africa." The Insignia were presented to him by the King 25 July, 1901.

BRIDGES, GEORGE, Lieut., was born 20 Feb. 1876, only son of Capt. Edward Bridges, of Zeals, Bath. He served in the Malay Peninsula from 1893 to 1895, and in South Africa from 1899 to 1900, including the Siege of Mafeking. He was wounded in this campaign, mentioned in Despatches, and created a Companion of the Distinguished Service Order [London Gazette, 19 April, 1901]: " George Bridges, Lieut., Protectorate Regt. In recognition of services during the operations in South Africa." The Insignia were presented by the King 29 Oct. 1901. Lieut.-Colonel Bridges served in the French Remount Commission in the Argentine Republic Aug. 1914, to May, 1915. He served in the European War from 1915 to 1918 ; was three times mentioned in Despatches, and created a C.M.G., 1917. He was C.R.A., Kent Force, Aug. 1917, to April, 1919, and was formerly in the Derbyshire Imperial Yeomanry. He married Gwendoline Elizabeth, daughter of R. Pegau, M.D., and widow of Capt. George Farrar, Lancashire Fusiliers.

FELTHAM, JOHN ALRIC PERCY, Lieut., was born at Bridport, Dorset, 12 May, 1862, son of Henry John Feltham, and Louisa du Rieu, of Stellenberg, Kenilworth, Cape Town. He gained his degree B.A. at Cambridge University. He served in the Matabeleland Campaign in 1896 (thrice wounded ; Despatches ; Medal with clasp, " Mashonaland, 1897 ") as Captain, Rhodesian Horse Artillery. He took part in the South African War as Lieutenant, afterwards Captain, in the Protectorate Regt., 1899–1902, being present at operations in the Transvaal and Orange River Colony 30 Nov. 1900, to 31 May, 1902 ; was thrice wounded ; mentioned in Despatches ; Queen's Medal with three clasps (" Siege of Mafeking," " Transvaal " and " Free State "), and the King's Medal. He was created a Companion of the Distinguished Service Order [London Gazette, 19 April, 1901]: " John Alric Percy Feltham, Lieut., Protectorate Regt. In recognition of services during the operations in South Africa." The Insignia, etc., were sent to South Africa and presented by Colonel Crewe at Morriesburg. He is Captain, Reserve of Officers, South African Defence Force. Capt. Feltham is an Attorney, Supreme Court, Transvaal. He married, in 1903, Beatrice Jane, daughter of Frederick W. Good, of Alington, Wickford, Essex, and widow of A. Pinsent Scott, of Adelaide.

GLYN, GEOFFREY CARR, Capt., was born 19 April, 1864, eldest son of the late Hon. Pascoe Glyn and Caroline Henrietta, daughter of Capt. W. Amherst Hale. He served in the South African War, in the Rhodesian Regt., 1900–2 ; was mentioned in Despatches ; received the Queen's Medal and four clasps, and was created a Companion of the Distinguished Service Order [London Gazette, 19 April, 1901]: " Geoffrey Carr Glyn, Capt., Rhodesia Regt. In recognition of services during the operations in South Africa." The Insignia were presented by H.M. the King 19 July, 1901. He was Private Secretary to the Lieut.-Governor, Transvaal, 1903–5, and Military Secretary to the Governor of Madras, 1905–8. He became Lieut.-Colonel Commanding the North Somerset Yeomanry. Lieut.-Colonel G. Carr Glyn served in the European War, 1914–15 ; was mentioned in Despatches, wounded, and created a C.M.G. in 1916. He married, in 1889, the Hon. Winifred Harbord, sixth daughter of the 5th Baron Suffield, and they have one daughter.

HOOK, GODFREY BLAIR, Capt., was born at Grahamstown, South Africa, in 1872, the son of Major David Blair Hook. He was educated at St. Andrew's College, Grahamstown ; served in the British Bechuanaland Police during the Matabele War of 1893, and took part in the occupation of Matabeleland. He was Lieutenant in the Bulawayo Field Force during the Matabele Rebellion, 1896 ; was severely wounded at Maqusa 22 April. In Oct. 1899, he became Lieutenant in the Southern Rhodesia Volunteers. He served in the South African War with General Plumer's Force ; was promoted Captain, and became D.A.A.G. on General Plumer's Staff in March, 1900. He was present at the Relief of Mafeking, and served with General Plumer until the Rhodesian Brigade was disbanded in Nov. 1900. For his services while acting as D.A.A.G. on General Plumer's Staff he was created a Companion of the Distinguished Service Order [London Gazette, 19 April, 1901]: " Godfrey Blair Hook, Capt., Southern Rhodesia Volunteers. In recognition of services during the operations in South Africa." The Insignia, etc., were sent to South Africa, and presented in South Africa. He was appointed Military Commandant at Bedford, Cape Colony, in Jan. 1901. He married, in 1899, Annye, daughter of C. Cornwallis de Smidt, of Beaufort West, South Africa.

SMITHEMAN, FRANK JAMES, Capt., was born at Witney, Oxon, 16 June, 1872. He was educated at Witney ; became a hunter and explorer, and served in the South African War, 1900–2, as Captain in the Rhodesian Horse ; took Despatches through the Boer lines into Mafeking ; was mentioned in Despatches three times ; received the Queen's Medal and four clasps, the King's Medal and two clasps, and was created a Companion of the Distinguished Service Order [London Gazette, 19 April, 1901]: " Frank James Smitheman, Capt., Rhodesian Horse. In recognition of services during the operations in South Africa." The Insignia, etc., were sent to the Commander-in-Chief in South Africa, and presented to him there. He became Lieutenant of the B.F.F., and was attached to the Scouts, M.R.F., during the Matabele Rebellion, 1906 (Medal). Capt. Smitheman became D.A.A.G., Army Headquarters, South Africa. He is fond of polo and big game shooting.

MURRAY, WILLIAM FLOOD, Lieut., served in the South African War, and was created a Companion of the Distinguished Service Order [London Gazette, 19 April, 1901]: " William Flood Murray, Lieut., Rimington's Guides (Capt., 5th Connaught Rangers). In recognition of services during the operations in South Africa." He died about 1903 or 1904.

KING, EDWARD REX, Capt., was born 13 Nov. 1869, son of W. King, J.P. Somerset, and Elizabeth, daughter of Dr. Mules, of Ilminster, Somerset. He was educated at Winchester, and was gazetted to the 3rd Battn. Royal Scots (1887–91). He went to America, engaged in the lumber business and in ranching in Minnesota, and returned to England in 1898. He sailed for South Africa 1 Jan. 1900 ; enlisted in Roberts's Horse ; was given a commission 2 Feb. 1900 ; promoted to Captain 24 June, 1900 ; wounded 28 June, 1900. He was created a Companion of the Distinguished Service Order [London Gazette, 19 April, 1901]: " Edward Rex King, Capt., Roberts's Horse. In recognition of services during the recent operations in South Africa." Capt. King joined the South African Constabulary in 1901. In 1903 he was appointed Assistant Chief Secretary for Permits, Transvaal, and in the same year he became A.D.C. to the Lieut.-Governor, Transvaal.

ROSS, CHARLES, Lieut., was born at Orange, New South Wales, the son of Scotch parents. He was educated at Santa Clara College, California, and became a Scout in the U.S.A. Service (Ness Percy, Indian War, 1877 ; Bannock, Indian War, 1878 ; Ute, Indian War, 1879). He was Chief of Scouts for Colonel Otter's Column in the North-Western Rebellion, Canada, in 1885, and was several times mentioned in Despatches. He had eight years' service in the North-West Mounted Police, Canada. In the South African War he served in Roberts's Horse as Lieutenant from Jan. to April, 1900, and was three times mentioned in Despatches. He served under General Hulton in command of the 1st M.I. Scouts from May to Nov. 1900. Sir A. Conan Doyle describes (page 529) in " The Great Boer War " the campaign of Jan.–April, 1902. He tells us of a drive, sweeping backwards towards the Heilbron–Wolvehoek line, which " ended in the total capture of 147 of the enemy, who were picked out of holes, retrieved from amid the reeds of the river, called down out of trees, or otherwise collected. So thorough was the operation, that it is recorded that the angle which formed the apex of the drive was one drove of game upon the last day, all the many types of antelope which form one of the characteristics and charms of the country having been herded into it. More important even than the results of the drive was the discovery of one of De Wet's arsenals in a cave in the Vrede district. Half-way down a precipitous krantz, with its mouth covered by creepers, no writer of romance could have imagined a more fitting headquarters for a guerrilla chief. The find was made by Ross's Canadian Scouts, who celebrated Dominion Day by this most useful achievement. Forty wagon-loads of ammunition and supplies were taken out of the cave." He was mentioned in Despatches, and for his services at Sanna's Post was created a Companion of the Distinguished Service Order [London Gazette, 19 April, 1901]: " Charles Ross, Lieut., Roberts's Horse. In recognition of services during the operations in South Africa," The Insignia were presented to him by the Duke of Cornwall and York 14 Aug. 1901. He was subsequently promoted to Major. Major Ross married, in 1889, Nellie Buchanan, a Canadian lady of Scotch descent.

TUCKER, S. N., Capt., was born at Kimberley, South Africa, 22 June, 1876, son of Henry Tucker, of Canterbury, England, and of Annie Cawood Cradock, Cape Colony. He was educated at Bedford, Cape Colony ; was a Private in the Kimberley Rifles, 1891–95, and the same in the D.E.O.U.R., 1895–97. He was a Trooper (promoted to Corporal) in Plumer's Matabeleland Relief Force, 1896 ; Major, Watt's Column to Mashonaland, 1896 ;

Trooper, Mounted Company, D.E.O.V.R., Mashonaland Campaign, 1897; Clerk in the C.G. Railways and C.T. Harbour Board, 1897–99; Lieutenant, South African Light Horse, 1899; Captain, S.A.L. Horse, 1900; Captain, S.A. Constabulary, 1900. He served in the South African War, 1899–1900, and for services rendered in the S.A.L. Horse in Natal and the Eastern Transvaal was created a Companion of the Distinguished Service Order [London Gazette, 19 April, 1901]: "S. N. Tucker, Capt., South African Light Horse. In recognition of services during the operations in South Africa." Capt. Tucker was unmarried. He was killed 4 Feb. 1902.

BARKER, WILLIAM FRANK, Lieut., served in the South African War, in command of the South African Light Horse, 1900–1. He was present at the Relief of Ladysmith, including the operations on the Tugela Heights (14 to 27 Feb.); operations in Natal (March to June, 1900), including action at Belfast (26 and 27 Aug.). We get some interesting glimpses of the South African Light Horse in the Official "History of the War in South Africa," compiled by Major-General Sir Frederick Maurice, K.C.B., published by Messrs. Hurst and Blackett): "The calling out of colonial mounted corps, both in Cape Colony and Natal, is mentioned in Chapter I. and Chapter II. Mounted men were urgently needed by all the columns in process of preparation, but, adhering to his opinion that success in the relief of Ladysmith was a most crucial matter, Sir Redvers decided to despatch to Natal the first unit enlisted at Cape Town—the South African Light Horse. The first party of 'Light Horse' embarked at Cape Town for Natal on the 22nd Nov. In Natal itself two mounted corps, under the command of Major (local Lieut.-Colonel) A. W. Thorneycroft, Royal Scots Fusiliers, and Major (local Lieut.-Colonel) E. C. Bethune, 16th Lancers, were already being formed." On page 332 Sir F. Maurice says: "Sir Redvers Buller reached Durham on 25 Nov. . . . He spent a few days at Maritzburg in inspecting this advanced base of the Natal Army, and in directing preparations for the reception of a large number of wounded. He then pushed on to Frere, reaching that place on 6 Dec. The enemy's raiding columns had now retired across the Tugela, and by the 9th a well-equipped British force of all three arms was concentrated at Frere. The mounted brigade, commanded by Colonel the Earl of Dundonald, consisted of the Royal Dragoons, 13th Hussars, Thorneycroft's and Bethune's newly-raised regiments of mounted infantry, the South African Light Horse, also only just enlisted and brought round from Cape Town, a squadron of the Imperial Light Horse, detachments of the Natal Carbineers and Natal Police, and one company of British Mounted Infantry." At Colenso Lord Dundonald despatched the South African Light Horse, under Lieut.-Colonel the Hon. Julian Byng, to demonstrate against the southern slope of the Hlangwhane Mountain, which the mounted brigade was endeavouring to occupy, in order to assist the main attack on Colenso by a flank fire. The Boers, however, were found to be in full possession of the mountain, and the advance of the South African Light Horse against its southern slope was checked. The attack was eventually abandoned, as General Buller decided that "the occupation of Hlangwhane would be useless unless he had first forced the passage of the Tugela at Colenso, and of this he had already relinquished hope." He watched Capt. Reed's gallant attempt to save Long's guns, and, after its failure, rode through the extended battalions of the 2nd Brigade and decided that the men were exhausted. He decided to abandon the guns, and to withdraw the whole of his force to camp. Major-General Lyttelton and Lieut.-Colonel Parsons successfully covered the retreat of Hart's Brigade. Most of Hildyard's Brigade reached camp at 3.30 p.m. The Naval guns withdrew from Naval Gun Hill. "The order to retreat reached the officer commanding the mounted troops about noon. The brigade was still hotly engaged with the enemy, and its gradual disentanglement took nearly three hours. Colonel Thorneycroft was told by Lord Dundonald to fall back slowly along the Gomba Spruit, protecting the flank of the South African Light Horse. His retreat, which was covered by the 13th Hussars and three companies of the Royal Fusiliers, was a good deal harassed by the enemy, who crept up through the bush on the east and on the north. The well-directed fire of the 7th Battery checked this attempt at pursuit. Eventually Lord Dundonald succeeded in extricating his whole force safely, except a small section of two officers and sixteen men of the South African Light Horse, who were taken prisoners." Sir F. Maurice says that it was decided to recruit from the loyal population of South Africa, and he goes on to say: "Considerable use had been made of the patriotic spirit. Practically the whole of the Volunteer forces of the colony had been called out in the first phase of the war, and were still under arms. The good services of the South African Light Horse and of Brabant's Horse, raised respectively in the western and eastern province, showed that the time had now come to make fuller use of the admirable recruiting material that was available." In Jan. 1900, Lord Dundonald was ordered to occupy Springfield. "He improved his command of Potgieter's Drift by the capture of the ferry boat from under the very eyes of the enemy. The boat had been moored to the northern bank of the river, and though parties of Boers were to be seen riding down to it, some troopers of the South African Light Horse volunteered to swim across and capture it. The enemy detected the attempt, but the adventurous swimmers safely reached the boat, cut it adrift, and brought it rapidly back amid a shower of bullets." In the Spion Kop Campaign a patrol, under Major H. W. G. Graham, skilfully guided by the commander of the Natal Carbineers (Major D. McKenzie), surprised 300 Boers. He "sent back for his supports, the mounted infantry of the King's Royal Rifles and a squadron of the South African Light Horse, and these, hurrying into the firing line, soon assisted to overcome the resistance amongst the rocks of the outnumbered Boers, who rose to their feet and surrendered." On 20 Jan. Dundonald "set about the capture of Bastion Hill. This was easily effected at 2.50 p.m. by a dismounted squadron of the South African Light Horse, supported by Thorneycroft's Mounted Infantry." The South African Light Horse took part in the capture of Cingolo and in the other operations before the relief of Ladysmith. Sir F. Maurice describes the part they took in the clearing of Northern Natal. "On 27 May Sir R. Buller sent two columns across the Buffalo. One consisting of the 11th (Wynne) Brigade, with two 4.7-in. and four 12-pr. Naval guns, and the South African Light Horse, under Hildyard, crossing by Wools Drift, marched on Utrecht on the 29th, and two days later received the surrender of the town." "General Buller . . . on 6 June . . . flung the South African Light Horse at Van Wyk's Hill, ousted the Boer piquets which held it, and despatched Major-General Talbot Coke with three battalions of the 10th Brigade and a battery to occupy it under Botha's direction, thus possessing himself of the command of the southern side of the mouth of Botha's Pass." "At 10 a.m., on 8 June, whilst all the artillery opened fire, the South African Light Horse moved from their bivouac at Yellowboom Farm straight upon Spitz Kop, which they occupied without fighting." Botha's Pass was next captured by Sir R. Buller, and "thus, with little loss, was effected the capture of Botha's Pass, and the road into the Orange Free State was opened. . . . On the 10th Sir R. Buller resumed the general advance, the South African Light Horse and 10th Brigade leading; the objective was a prominent hill situated near the junction of the Klip River and the Gansvlei Spruit. This was found to be occupied by the Boer rearguard, which was speedily driven off by the South African Light Horse and artillery. The former, pushing on into high ground beyond the Spruit, found another detachment of the enemy somewhat strongly posted, and a sharp engagement, in which a squadron of the 18th Hussars lent valuable assistance, was necessary to dislodge him." At the action at Alleman's Nek on 11 June, "to the South African Light Horse was entrusted the guardianship of the rear, by no means the least vulnerable portion of the force at this period." During the advance towards Komati Poort, at the occupation of Ermelo, "a fourteen-mile march on the 13th brought the column to the source of the Vaal river with no more opposition than an affair of patrols on the right, which cost the enemy four men and the South African Light Horse one man wounded." On 23 Aug. 1900, was fought the action at Geluk. A rocky ridge was first occupied, and "the South African Light Horse, who were working through rough ground beneath the southern end of the ridge, came upon a party who fired hotly with rifles and three guns, killing an officer and wounding another officer and two men." On 10 May, 1901, in the Orange River Colony, Lieut.-Colonel W. H. Williams had started from Springfontein and had been engaged in "a sharp affair fifteen miles south-west of Fauresmith, where two squadrons of the South African Light Horse killed and wounded three and captured fourteen burghers, including a noted Field-Cornet, Van der Merwe." About 16 Sept. Byng was moving up the Valsch towards Kronstadt. He had taken 81 prisoners, and the enemy had suffered a good deal, while his own losses had been small, "the heaviest in one day having been one killed and ten taken prisoners in an attack made by a commando under Liebenberg upon a party of South African Light Horse which was returning from a patrol to Klerksdorp." On the night of 2 Feb. 1902, Byng made a raid, and came on a party under Commandants Mears and Wessels. Byng at once attacked, and "after a close combat in which his South African Light Horse and Garratt's New Zealanders and Queensland Bushmen much distinguished themselves, recaptured the three guns lost at Tweefontein, taking, in addition, twenty-seven prisoners, including three officers, and six carts. Besides these, the Boers suffered the loss of some dozen killed and wounded, amongst the former being Wessels. Byng's casualties, in spite of, or perhaps because of, the determined nature of his attack, numbered but three." For his services in this campaign in command of the South African Light Horse, Lieut. Barker was mentioned in Despatches [London Gazette, 8 Feb. 1901 (Sir R. H. Buller, 30 March and 9 Nov. 1900), and London Gazette, 16 April, 1901, and 25 April, 1902]. He received the Queen's Medal with six clasps, the King's Medal with two clasps, and was created a Companion of the Distinguished Service Order [London Gazette, 19 April, 1901]: "William Frank Barker, Lieut., South African Light Horse. In recognition of services during the operations in South Africa." The Insignia were sent to the Commander-in-Chief in South Africa and presented there. He again saw active service during the Natal Native Rebellion of 1906 in command of the Transvaal Mounted Rifles; was mentioned in Despatches [London Gazette, 25 June, 1907], and created a C.M.G., 1907. He served in the European War from 1914 to 1918, and was given the honorary rank of Colonel.

TURNER, REGINALD, Lieut., was born in 1870, son of Frederick Turner, Surgeon, Buxton. He was educated at St. John's College, Cambridge, and served in the South African War, 1899–1901. He was mentioned three times in Despatches; awarded the Medal with six clasps, and was created a Companion of the Distinguished Service Order [London Gazette, 19 April, 1901]: "Reginald Turner, Lieut., South African Light Horse. In recognition of services during the operations in South Africa." The Insignia were presented by the King 3 June, 1901. He served in the European War; became Captain, Nottinghamshire and Derbyshire Regt., 6th Battn; Major, Royal Fusiliers, 9 Sept. 1914; went out to France as Second-in-Command; was wounded; mentioned three times in Despatches. As a mining engineer he has had experience of most goldfields of the world.

MARSDEN, GEORGE, Lieut., was born 9 Feb. 1874, son of the late Capt. Richard Marsden, R.N.R., J.P. He was educated at St. Paul's School, and joined the 3rd West Yorkshire Regt.; passed the School of Instruction, Chelsea; resigned his commission. He joined the Perth (Western Australian) Artillery; was employed on a special mission to inquire into the condition of the aborigines of Western Australia, 1896–97. He was appointed A.D.C. to the Governor of Western Australia (Sir Gerard Smith, K.C.M.G.); resigned in 1899, and in the same year joined the South African Light Horse. He served in the South African War of 1899–1902; was mentioned in Despatches three times, and created a Companion of the Distinguished Service Order [London Gazette, 19 April, 1901]:

"George Marsden, Lieut., South African Light Horse. In recognition of services during the operations in South Africa." The Insignia were sent to the Commander-in-Chief in South Africa and presented in South Africa. He later joined the 4th Battn. The Cheshire Regt. Capt. Marsden married, in 1904, Julia, daughter of the late George Booker, and they had one daughter.

WICKHAM, THOMAS STRANGE, Lieut., was born 2 June, 1878, eldest son of R. W. Wickham, of Ebley Court, Stroud. He was educated at Marlborough, and served as a Trooper during the operations in South Africa. He served in the South African War as Lieutenant in the South African Light Horse, 1899–1902, being present at the Relief of Ladysmith, including operations on Tugela Heights (14 to 27 Feb.); operations in Natal, March to June 1900, including the action at Laing's Nek (6 to 9 June); operations in the Transvaal, east of Pretoria, July to 29 Nov. 1900, including the action at Belfast (26 and 27 Aug.); operations in Orange River Colony, June, 1900; operations in the Transvaal 30 Nov. to 10 Dec. 1900; operations in Orange River Colony, Dec. 1900, to Feb. 1901. He was mentioned in Despatches [London Gazette, 8 Feb., 16 April and 20 Aug. 1901, and 29 July, 1902]; received the Queen's Medal with six clasps, the King's Medal with two clasps, and was created a Companion of the Distinguished Service Order [London Gazette, 19 April, 1901]: "Thomas Strange Wickham, Lieut., South African Light Horse. In recognition of services during the operations in South Africa." The Insignia were sent to South Africa and presented by H.R.H. the Prince of Wales on the Horse Guards' Parade 1 July, 1902. He was gazetted to the Manchester Regt. as Second Lieutenant 14 Sept. 1901; became Lieutenant 12 Nov. 1902; was employed with the West African Field Force in Northern Nigeria in 1904 (Medal and clasp). He became Captain. He married, in 1905, Bertha, daughter of John Grieveson. Capt. Wickham served in the European War, and was killed in action in the Cameroons. His death was announced in a War Office Communiqué 10 Sept. 1914.

FARQUHAR, MOUBRAY GORE, Capt., was born in 1862, son of the late Admiral Sir Arthur Farquhar, K.C.B., and Ellen (who died in 1898), daughter of S. P. Rickman. He served with the B.S.A. Company's Forces in Matabeleland, 1893 (Medal) and in 1896 (clasp). He again saw active service in the South African War of 1899–1901; was mentioned in Despatches; received the Medal with seven clasps, and was created a Companion of the Distinguished Service Order [London Gazette, 19 April, 1901]: "Moubray Gore Farquhar, Capt., Thorneycroft's Mounted Infantry. In recognition of services during the operations in South Africa." The Insignia were sent to the Commander-in-Chief in South Africa, and presented at Bulawayo. He became Lieut.-Colonel. Of Thorneycroft's Mounted Infantry we are told, in the Official "History of the War in South Africa" (compiled by Major-General Sir F. Maurice, K.C.B., and published by Messrs. Hurst and Blackett) (page 206): "In Natal itself two mounted corps, under the command of Major (local Lieut.-Colonel) A. W. Thorneycroft, Royal Scots Fusiliers, and Major (local Lieut.-Colonel) E. C. Bethune, 16th Lancers, were already being formed." Elsewhere we read that the corps was raised at Maritzburg, and on page 332 that it formed part of the mounted brigade commanded by Colonel the Earl of Dundonald. Thorneycroft and his men were engaged in the attempt to capture Hlangwhane Mountain at the Battle of Colenso. In the retreat after Colenso, "Colonel Thorneycroft was told by Lord Dundonald to fall back slowly along the Gomba Spruit, protecting the flank of the South African Light Horse. His retreat, which was covered by the 13th Hussars and three companies of the Royal Fusiliers, was a good deal harassed by the enemy." In the Spion Kop Campaign a dismounted squadron of the South African Light Horse, supported by Thorneycroft's Mounted Infantry, captured Bastion Hill. In the chapter on the capture and evacuation of Spion Kop, Sir F. Maurice says that when Woodgate attacked Spion Kop on 24 Jan. 1900, Thorneycroft offered his services as guide, and he was desired by Woodgate to take his men to the front and lead the column. Having climbed the hill and arrived at the edge of an open plateau, "Thorneycroft's men, who had been climbing in double files, halted, and having formed line, stole forward again over the crest with fixed bayonets, expectant of a volley which they had been previously ordered to receive by flinging themselves to the ground. Behind them, the Lancashire Fusiliers followed closely in column of double companies, single rank, about one hundred yards intervening between the companies. Suddenly a loud challenge, twice repeated in Dutch, rang out from the depths of the mist, followed by a burst of fire from a surprised Boer piquet, whose position was revealed by a line of dancing flashes from a dozen rifles. Flat upon the grass dropped the soldiers, and lay motionless in accordance with their orders, suffering few casualties, whilst the bullets whistled close above them for two or three minutes. Then when the magazines of the Mausers were nearly exhausted, and the fire slackened, the word was given, and the men, leaping to their feet, charged down upon the piquet, which disappeared into the protecting fog escaping with the loss of one man only. The rest of the Boer outposts upon the mountain, numbering some seventy men, vanished without offering opposition and undiscovered. Thus, at 4 a.m., by skill and good fortune, the summit of Spion Kop was almost bloodlessly delivered into our hands." Woodgate gave orders to entrench, which was done in the fog, and on very difficult ground, and when the mist lifted a little it was discovered that the entrenchments were wrongly placed. The Boers rallied and returned, and the fog began to disperse and disclosed Woodgate's position to the Boers. The troops, almost without cover, were almost surrounded by fire, and the Boer reinforcements arrived and began an enveloping movement. Woodgate was mortally wounded. The fight went on, watched by Buller through a telescope from Mount Alice. "Even at that distance, the energetic and courageous movements of a single officer—Thorneycroft—a man of great stature, were to be singled out from the swaying knots of figures," and General Buller suggested to Sir C. Warren that Thorneycroft should be put in command. The situation had, however, become very critical. The official and other histories of the war tell the story of the fighting, and of the final evacuation of the hill. "Never since Inkerman," says Sir A. Conan Doyle, in his "Great Boer War" (page 199), "had we so grim a soldiers' battle. The company officers were superb. . . . Grenfell, of Thorneycroft's, was shot, and exclaimed, 'That's all right. It's not much.' A second wound made him remark, 'I can get on all right.' The third killed him." And in the end (page 202, "Great Boer War"): "Thorneycroft saw the frightful havoc of one day, and he shrank from the thought of such another. 'Better six battalions safely down the hill than a mop up in the morning,' said he, and he gave the word to retire. One who had met the troops as they staggered down has told me how far they were from being routed. In mixed array, but steadily and in order, the long thin line trudged through the darkness. Their parched lips would not articulate, but they whispered 'Water! where is water?' as they toiled upon their way. At the bottom of the hill they formed into regiments once more, and marched back to the camp. In the morning the blood-spattered hill-top, with its piles of dead and of wounded, was in the hands of Botha and his men, whose valour and perseverance deserved the victory which they had won. There is no doubt now that at 3 a.m. of that morning Botha, knowing that the Rifles had carried Burger's position, regarded the affair as hopeless, and that no one was more astonished than he when he found, on the report of two scouts, that it was a victory and not a defeat which had come to him. How shall we sum up such an action save that it was a gallant attempt, gallantly carried out, and as gallantly met? On both sides the results of artillery fire during the war have been disappointing, but at Spion Kop beyond all question it was the Boer guns which won the action for them. So keen was the disappointment at home that there was a tendency to criticize the battle with some harshness, but it is difficult now, with the evidence at our command, to say what was left undone which could have altered the result. Had Thorneycroft known all that we know, he would have kept his grip upon the hill. On the face of it one finds it difficult to understand why so momentous a decision, upon which the whole operations depended, should have been left entirely to the judgment of one who in the morning had been a simple lieutenant-colonel. 'Where are the bosses?' cried a Fusilier, and the historian can only repeat the question." Thorneycroft's Mounted Infantry took a prominent part in the Relief of Ladysmith. When Northern Natal was being cleared, Thorneycroft's men were once more to the fore, on 13 May, 1900, in the action at Helpmakaar, at Alleman's Nek and Laing's Nek. They took part also in the advance towards Komati Poort, and in the operations on the Johannesburg–Durban line. In the operations in the Orange River Colony they were engaged in the forcing of Springhaan Nek on 14 Dec. 1900, and thereafter we read a great deal of the doings of Thorneycroft, now in command of a column. On 20 Sept. 1901, Thorneycroft discovered, attacked and defeated the Boer leader, Kritzinger. Some of Thorneycroft's men were with Ternan when, in the course of his clearance of the vicinity of Bultfontein, he met with a reverse near Bultfontein 8 April, 1900. After this affair, which crippled Ternan for a time, he was ordered to Eensgevonden to refit. "This was effected," says Sir F. Maurice, in Volume IV. (page 489) of the Official History, "by 15 April, when, after escorting a convoy to Hoopstad, Ternan marched to Bothaville on the 23rd. Thence he despatched Thorneycroft's M.I. to rejoin the officer from whom this veteran corps took its name. Thorneycroft being now at Klerksdorp in command of a new column of Australians and New Zealanders. Three days later Thorneycroft took his force into Kroonstad, where it was broken up." For his services in the campaign Capt. Farquhar was mentioned in Despatches; received the Queen's Medal with seven clasps, and was created a Companion of the Distinguished Service Order [London Gazette, 19 April, 1901]: "M. G. Farquhar, Capt., Thorneycroft's Mounted Infantry. In recognition of services during the operations in South Africa." The Insignia were sent to the Commander-in-Chief in South Africa and presented at Bulawayo.

HAMILTON, C., Capt., served in the South African War. He was created a Companion of the Distinguished Service Order [London Gazette, 19 April, 1901]: "C. Hamilton, Capt., Thorneycroft's Mounted Infantry. In recognition of services during the operations in South Africa." The Insignia were sent to the Commander-in-Chief in South Africa, and presented to Capt. Hamilton at Bulawayo.

VILLIERS, REGINALD HYDE, Lieut., was born 4 Aug. 1876, son of Frederick E. Villiers and Jane Isabella, eldest daughter of the late Douglas Baird, of Closeburn, Dumfries. He served in South Africa, 1899–1902; was twice mentioned in Despatches; received the Queen's Medal with six clasps, the King's Medal with two clasps, and was created a Companion of the Distinguished Service Order [London Gazette, 19 April, 1901]: "Reginald Hyde Villiers, Lieut., Thorneycroft's Mounted Infantry (now Second Lieut., 12th Lancers). In recognition of services during the operations in South Africa." The Insignia were sent to the Commander-in-Chief in South Africa, and presented there. He became Lieutenant, 12th Lancers. He married Marianne Stockwell, and they have two sons and one daughter.

FORBES, GORDON STEWART DRUMMOND, Lieut., was born in 1868, son of the late General Sir J. Forbes, G.C.B., of Inverness. He was mining in South Africa (Johannesburg) in 1889–93; in Rhodesia as Managing Director of Companies, 1893–1900. He served through the Matabele War of 1896 on Colonel Plumer's Staff, and then on Colonel Spreckley's Staff at the Battle of Umyussa (Medal). In 1891 he visited the West Coast of Africa, and was for a time engaged in mining there. He served in the South African War, and, for gallantry at Spion Kop, was created a Companion of the Distinguished Service Order [London Gazette, 19 April, 1901]: "Gordon Stewart Drummond Forbes, Lieut., Thorneycroft's Mounted Infantry. In recognition of services during the operations in South Africa." The Insignia were presented to him by the King 3 June,

1901. He lived in Rhodesia, and was Managing Director of Companies there, his favourite recreations being steeplechasing and hunting. He was a member of the Legislative Council, Rhodesia, and was created a C.M.G. in 1910. He served in the European War and died of wounds in France 21 May, 1915.

HOWARD, THOMAS WALTER JOHN WRIGHT, Lieut., was born at Sheen, Surrey, in 1865. He was educated at Winchester (and Middle Temple), and served in the Bechuanaland Border Police, and took part in the Matabele War in 1893. He volunteered to ascertain the fate of Alan Wilson's party, Shanghani River. In 1896 he served during the Matabele Rebellion (Despatches; Medal with clasp), and he joined Thorneycroft's Mounted Infantry at the beginning of the Boer War, being dangerously wounded at Spion Kop, and, for gallantry in the field, was created a Companion of the Distinguished Service Order [London Gazette, 19 April, 1901]: "T. W. Howard, Lieut., Thorneycroft's Mounted Infantry. In recognition of services during the operations in South Africa." The Insignia, Warrant and Statutes were sent to the Commander-in-Chief in South Africa and presented there." His Christian name was afterwards given correctly in the official records. He served in the Zululand Rebellion (Natal Decoration) in 1906. Capt. Howard is a Justice of the Peace. He married, in 1886, Lizzie Amelia (who died in 1905), daughter of G. Huddy.

PONSONBY, WILLIAM RANDALL, Lieut., was born in Aug. 1874, eldest surviving son of Colonel Justinian Gordon Ponsonby. He served in the South African War in Thorneycroft's Mounted Infantry, and in the South African Constabulary, and was created a Companion of the Distinguished Service Order [London Gazette, 19 April, 1901]: "W. R. Ponsonby, Lieut., Thorneycroft's Mounted Infantry. In recognition of services during the operations in South Africa." The Insignia were presented by the King 29 Oct. 1901. He was gazetted to the 3rd Dragoon Guards and retired. Capt. Ponsonby married, in 1902, Lilian Patteson, daughter of the late Sir Patteson Nickalls and Florence, daughter of T. S. Womersley. He died 18 Jan. 1919.

William R. Ponsonby.

HYSLOP, J., Major, was born 3 March, 1856, son of Thomas Hyslop, Wood Park, Kirkcudbrightshire. He was educated at Hutton Hall, Edinburgh University, Berlin, Vienna and Munich (M.B., C.M., Edinburgh University). He was formerly Assistant Medical Officer, Border Counties Asylum, Melrose, and Assistant Physician, Royal Edinburgh Asylum, Morningside. He was delegate from the Natal Government to the Conference of South African States and Colonies on Plague, held at Pretoria in 1899. He served in the South African War, and took part in operations in Natal, 1899, including actions at Rietfontein and Lombard's Kop; defence of Ladysmith, including action of 6 Jan. 1900; operations in Natal, March to June, 1900, including action at Laing's Nek. In command, Natal Volunteer Medical Corps. Operations on the Zululand Frontier of Natal, Sept. and Oct. 1901. He was mentioned in Despatches [London Gazette, 8 Feb. and 16 April, 1901]; received the Queen's Medal with two clasps, and was created a Companion of the Distinguished Service Order [London Gazette, 19 April, 1901]: "James Hyslop, Major (P.M.O.), Natal Volunteers. In recognition of services during the operations in South Africa." The Insignia were presented to him by the King 29 Oct. 1901. He served in the Natal Native Rebellion, 1906; was mentioned in Despatches [London Gazette, 25 June, 1907], and received the Medal and clasp. Lieut.-Colonel J. Hyslop was Medical Superintendent of the Natal Government Asylum and President of the Natal Medical Council. He published "Investigation Anatomy of the Central Nervous System." His favourite recreations were cricket, golf, tennis and photography. He married, in 1882, Christina Flemming Cullen Elphinstone Brown. Lieut.-Colonel Hyslop died 5 Oct. 1917.

THOMPSON, THOMAS, Lieut., is the son of Thomas Thompson, of Hillside, Pakenham, Victoria, Australia. He was educated at a private school in Victoria, Australia, and served a year with the Victorian Rangers, two years with the Victorian Mounted Rifles, and twenty months with Thorneycroft's Mounted Infantry. He served in the South African War of 1899–1902; was mentioned in Despatches; received the King's Medal with two clasps, and was created a Companion of the Distinguished Service Order [London Gazette, 19 April, 1901]: "Thomas Thompson, Lieut., Thorneycroft's Mounted Infantry. In recognition of services during the operations in South Africa." The Insignia were sent to the Commander-in-Chief in South Africa, and presented by Colonel Ternan at Spitzkop 8 Jan. 1902. Mr. Pakenham's favourite recreations are cricket and racing.

WARWICK, JOHN ABRAHAM, Capt., was born at Durban, 14 Aug. 1871, son of Mark Warwick and Esther Linnell, both of Warwickshire. He was educated at St. Cyprian's, Kimberley, and in Cape Colony, and served two years with the Bechuanaland Border Police, seeing active service in the Matabele War of 1893 and in the Matabele Rebellion of 1896. He served in the South African War, 1900–2, in Lieut. Gifford's Horse and as Captain commanding a troop of Matabeleland Mounted Police, raised by himself for the duration of the war. He was mentioned in Despatches; received the King's Medal with two clasps, and was created a Companion of the Distinguished Service Order [London Gazette, 19 April, 1901]: "John Abraham Warwick, Capt., Warwick's Scouts. In recognition of services during the operations in South Africa." The Insignia were sent to the Commander-in-Chief in South Africa, and presented there. Capt. Warwick has been Managing Gold Mining Commis-

sioner in Rhodesia. He is a member of the firm of Macandrew and Warwick, Engineers and Contractors, Bulawayo, and is also Intelligence Officer, 1st Division, Western District. His sister married Mr. R. H. Henderson, C.M.G., who was the Chief Citizen of Kimberley when it was besieged by the Boers.

MACANDREW, HAROLD, Lieut., was born 17 July, 1868, son of Major-General I. F. Macandrew. He served in South Africa in Warwick's Scouts and with the 5th Battn. Imperial Yeomanry in 1901; was mentioned in Despatches, and created a Companion of the Distinguished Service Order [London Gazette, 19 April, 1901]: "Harold Macandrew, Lieut., Warwick's Scouts. In recognition of services during the operations in South Africa." Capt. Macandrew has been a Captain in the 7th Reserve Regt. of Cavalry since 1914.

London Gazette, 25 March, 1901.—"War Office, 25 March, 1901. The King has been pleased to give orders for the following appointments to the Distinguished Service Order. In recognition of the services of the under-mentioned Officers during the operations in South Africa."

TIVEY, EDWIN, Capt., was born in 1866. He served in the South African War, 1900–2, taking part in operations in Rhodesia, Transvaal and Orange River Colony. He was mentioned in Despatches [London Gazette (Supplement), 22 March, and London Gazette, 7 May, 1901]. He received the Queen's Medal with four clasps, and was created a Companion of the Distinguished Service Order [London Gazette, 25 March, 1901]: "E. Tivey, Capt., Victorian Imperial Bushmen. For prompt action and brave defence, which prevented occupation of Phillipstown, Cape Colony. Dated 12 Feb. 1901." The Insignia were presented by the King 29 Oct. 1901. Colonel Tivey served in the European War, 1914–18, with the Australian Imperial Force, and was created a C.B. in 1917 and a C.M.G. in 1918.

THACKWELL, CHARLES JOSEPH, Lieut., was born 17 Oct. 1870, son of the Rev. W. H. Thackwell. He was educated at Marlborough, and was gazetted to the 18th Hussars 28 June, 1893, becoming Lieutenant 9 April, 1898. He served in the South African War, 1899 to 1901, and was twice severely wounded. He took part in operations in Natal in 1899, including actions at Talana and Lombard's Kop. Defence of Ladysmith, including sorties of 7 Dec. 1899, and action of 6 Jan. 1900. Operations in Natal, March to June, 1900, including action at Laing's Nek (6 to 9 June). Operations in the Transvaal, east of Pretoria, July to 29 Nov. 1900, including actions at Belfast (26 and 27 Aug.) and Lydenburg (5 to 8 Sept.). Operations in the Transvaal 30 Nov. 1900, to April, 1901. He was mentioned in Despatches [London Gazette, 8 Feb. and 7 May, 1901, and London Gazette (Supplement), 22 March, 1901]; received the Queen's Medal with six clasps, and was created a Companion of the Distinguished Service Order [London Gazette, 25 March, 1901]: "Charles Joseph Thackwell, Lieut., 18th Hussars. For management of patrol at Vitkyk, near Middelburg, in addition to other good service during the campaign. Dated 24 Dec. 1900." He became Captain 27 Aug. 1904; Major 14 May, 1915; G.S.O.2, 1915, and retired 27 March, 1919.

London Gazette, 23 April, 1901.—"War Office, 23 April, 1901. The King has been graciously pleased to give orders for the following appointments to the Distinguished Service Order in recognition of the services of the undermentioned Officers during the operations in South Africa. To be Companions of the Distinguished Service Order."

MARKER, RAYMOND JOHN, Capt., was the son of Richard Marker, Esq., J.P., of Combe, Honiton, and the Hon. Venetia Alexandrina (née Digby), eldest daughter of Edward, 9th Baron Digby. He was born at Upcerne Manor, Dorchester, 18 April, 1867; was educated at Evelyn's Preparatory School, Eton, and the Royal Military College, Sandhurst, and was gazetted Second Lieutenant, Coldstream Guards, 15 Nov. 1888, becoming Lieutenant 29 Sept. 1890. From 1892 to 1896 he was Adjutant of the 1st Battn. Coldstream Guards, and from 1896 to 1897 A.D.C. to Sir J. West Ridgeway, Governor and Commander-in-Chief in Ceylon, and from 1899 to 1900 A.D.C. to Lord Curzon, Viceroy of India. He was on Special Service in South Africa 7 April, 1900, to 8 March, 1901, and A.D.C. to Lord Kitchener, Commander-in-Chief of the Forces in South Africa, 9 March, 1901, to Sept. 1902. He served throughout the campaign, taking part in the operations in the Orange Free State, April to May, 1900, including actions at Vet River and Zand River; operations in the Transvaal, May to June, 1900, including actions near Johannesburg, Pretoria and Diamond Hill. Operations in the Transvaal, east of Pretoria, July to Aug. 1900, including the action at Belfast; operations in Orange River Colony, Sept. to 29 Nov. 1900, and 30 Nov. to Dec. 1900. Operations in Cape Colony, Dec. 1900, to March, 1901, and operations in the Transvaal, March, 1901, to 31 May, 1902. He was three times mentioned in Despatches [London Gazette, 23 April, 7 May and 10 Sept. 1901]; was given the Brevet of Major 26 June, 1902; received the Queen's Medal with five clasps; the King's Medal with two clasps; was placed on the list of officers considered qualified for Staff employment in consequence of services on the Staff in the Field, and was created a Companion of the Distinguished Service Order [London Gazette, 23 April, 1901]: "Raymond John Marker, Capt., Coldstream Guards. For the capture of De Wet's gun and pom-pom in Cape Colony.

Raymond John Marker.

Dated 23 April, 1901." The Insignia were presented to him by the Duke of Cornwall and York 14 Aug. 1901. Capt. Marker and the then Colonel Hubert Hamilton brought home Peace Despatches to the King at Windsor in June, 1902. He accompanied Lord Kitchener to India as A.D.C. (28 Nov. 1902, to 30 April, 1904]; became Major 29 Nov. 1903, and in 1904 proceeded to the Staff College, qualifying in the following year. For part of 1905 he was Private Secretary to Mr. Arnold Forster, Secretary of State for War, and he was later appointed A.D.C. to the Commander-in-Chief in India (5 Nov. 1905, to 27 Oct. 1906). From 1 April, 1908, to 12 June, 1910, he was G.S.O.2, Home Counties Division, Eastern Command; became Lieutenant-Colonel 11 March, 1911, and from March, 1912, to Nov. 1913, was in command of the 1st Battn. Coldstream Guards. He was A.Q.M.G., Aldershot Command, 29 Nov. 1913, to Aug. 1914; was promoted to Colonel 5 Aug. 1914, and accompanied the British Expeditionary Force to France as A.A. and Q.M.G., 1st Army Corps; served through the Retreat from Mons, the battles of the Aisne and the Marne; was twice mentioned in Sir John French's Despatches [London Gazette, 19 Oct. 1914, and 17 Feb. 1915], and was made an Officer of the Legion of Honour for his services during the retirement from Mons. Colonel Marker was hit by a shell on the 4th Nov. 1914, outside the reporting centre of the 1st Army Corps at Ypres, and died of his wounds at Boulogne on the 13th of the same month. He was buried at Gittisham, Honiton. He had married, on 21 Nov. 1906, at the Guards' Chapel, Wellington Barracks, Beatrice Minnie Shrieve, third daughter of Sir Thomas Jackson, Bart., and Amelia Lydia Dare, and they had one son, Richard Raymond Kitchener, born 18 June, 1908.

WILSON, HERBERT HAYDON, Capt., was born 14 Feb. 1875, youngest son of the late Sir Samuel Wilson, of Ercildoune, Victoria. He served in the South African War, 1900–1, with the Imperial Yeomanry, taking part in operations in the Orange Free State, April and May, 1900. Operations in the Transvaal, west of Pretoria, July to 29 Nov. 1900, including actions at Venterskroom (7 to 9 Aug.). Operations in Orange River Colony, May to July, 1900, including actions at Lindley (1 June) and Rhenoster River. He was mentioned in Despatches [London Gazette, 23 April and 10 Sept. 1901]; received the Queen's Medal with four clasps, and was created a Companion of the Distinguished Service Order [London Gazette, 23 April, 1901]: Herbert Haydon Wilson, Capt., 3rd Battn. The Imperial Yeomanry. For gallantry in defence of posts in the Boer attack on Lichtenburg. Dated 6 March, 1901." The Insignia were presented to Capt. Wilson by the King 25 July, 1901. He became Honorary Captain in the Army in 1901. He served in the European War, and was killed in action on 11 April, 1917. An obituary notice says: "Capt. Herbert Wilson, D.S.O., late a Major in the Nottinghamshire Yeomanry, and attached to the Household Cavalry, is reported killed in action on 11 April. Capt. Wilson was the youngest son of the late Sir Samuel Wilson and Lady Wilson. He served with the Yeomanry during the Boer War, and his services were rewarded with the D.S.O. and the rank of a Captain in the Army. He was well known with the Quorn, Cottesmore and Belvoir Hounds in Leicestershire, where he resided for many years at Ashby Folville. In polo he was a prominent figure, and, indeed, was a member of the Hurlingham Committee, the governing body of the game in this country. He played for England against America in 1909, when we lost the Cup, and was one of the members of Capt. Hardress Lloyd's team which attempted to regain the trophy in America two years later. He was one of the famous Roehampton team which won the Champion Cup at Hurlingham in 1905 and 1906, and the Open Cup at Ranelagh in four successive seasons (1904–1907), while he assisted England on three occasions (1908, 1909 and 1911) to gain victories over Ireland in the annual international match. Of late years his summer residence was Lower Grove, Roehampton, adjacent to the polo ground. His eldest brother was Lieut.-Colonel Gordon Wilson, M.V.O., Royal Horse Guards, who was killed in action during the First Battle of Ypres; his second brother, Wilfred (of the Northumberland Yeomanry), lost his life during the South African War, in which campaign another brother, Clarence, attached to the 8th Hussars, was severely wounded." A memorial service for Capt. Wilson was held at Christ Church, Down Street, Piccadilly.

MAGNIAC, HUBERT, Capt., was the son of the late Charles Magniac, of Colworth, Bedfordshire, M.P. for Bedfordshire, and of the Hon. Augusta, daughter of the 1st Baron Castletown, of Upper Ossory. He was educated at Eton and Cambridge (1st Class History and Political Economy), and served in the South African War, 1899–1902; was twice mentioned in Despatches, received the Queen's Medal with three clasps, and was created a Companion of the Distinguished Service Order [London Gazette, 23 April, 1901]: "Hubert Magniac, Capt., 15th Battn. the Imperial Yeomanry. For gallantry in defence of posts in the Boer attack on Modderfontein. Dated 31 Jan. 1901." The Insignia were presented to Major Magniac by the King 2 June, 1902. He died 24 March, 1909, and an obituary notice of him appeared in the "Times."

FRANKLAND, ARTHUR PELHAM, Lieut., was born at Dover 23 Dec. 1874, youngest son of Lieut.-Colonel Sir William Frankland, R.E., 9th Bart., of Thirkleby, and Lucy Ducarel, eldest daughter of Francis Adams, of Clifton. He was educated at Oxford Military College, and the Royal Military College, Sandhurst. He joined the Suffolk Regt. 21 Sept. 1895, as Second Lieutenant. He served in the South African War, 1899–1901, with the Suffolk Regt., on the Staff, attached General Hutton's and General Bethune's Columns (graded Staff Captain), 15 Aug. 1900, to 7 Aug. 1901; took part in operations in the Orange Free State, April to May, 1900. Operations in the Transvaal, including action at Pretoria. Operations in the Transvaal, east of Pretoria, July to 29 Nov. 1900. Operations in Cape Colony, south of Orange River, 1899–1900. Operations in the Transvaal, 30 Nov. 1900, to Feb. 1901. Operations in Orange River Colony, March to May, 1901. Operations in Cape Colony, Feb. to March, 1901. He was mentioned in Despatches [London Gazette, 23 April, 1901], received the Queen's Medal with five clasps, and was created a Companion of the Distinguished Service Order [London Gazette, 23 April, 1901]: "Arthur Pelham Frankland, Lieut., the Suffolk Regt. For conduct of a convoy near Petrusberg. Dated 23 April, 1901." "His good disposition, pluck and coolness saved the convoy." (*vide* London Gazette, 23 April, 1901). The Insignia were presented to him by the King 25 July, 1901. He was specially promoted Captain, Lancashire Fusiliers, 5 Oct. 1901; appointed Captain, Reserve of Officers, Lancashire Fusiliers, on retirement, 21 July, 1906, and Temporary Major 19 Sept. 1914. During the European War he was employed in the Railway Transport Establishment, British Expeditionary Force, France, Sept. 1914, to Sept. 1916; became D.A.Q.M.G. 1 Nov. 1916; promoted Major, Reserve of Officers, 18 Jan. 1917. Is Chief Organizer for the West of England of its Agricultural Organization Society. He married, at Clungunford Church, Shropshire, 12 Oct. 1898, Margaret Annie Phœbe, daughter of C. C. Seton, and they have two children: Marion Annie Margaret and Rosalind Lucy Seton.

CLARKE, LANCELOT FOX, Major, was born 15 June, 1858. He served in the South African War, 1900–02, with the Victorian Imperial Regt., Rhodesian Field Force. O.C.N., Western Districts; and as Administrator, No. 13 Martial Law Area, Cape Colony District. He served in Command of 4th Victorian Mounted Rifles 23 Feb. to 23 June, 1901, and took part in operations in the Transvaal. He was mentioned in Despatches [London Gazette, 23 April, 1901], received the King's Medal with two clasps, and was created a Companion of the Distinguished Service Order [London Gazette, 23 April, 1901]: "Lancelot Fox Clarke, Major, Victorian Bushmen. For able command in operations against De Wet. Dated 23 April, 1901." The Insignia were presented to him in South Africa. He became Colonel, commanding the 91st Infantry (Tasmanian Rangers), Commonwealth Military Forces. Colonel Clarke married, in 1889, Marion (who died in 1906), daughter of John Young and widow of Arthur Gilbert.

WALKER, GEORGE HENRY, Capt., was born at Taranaki, New Zealand, in 1875. He served in South Africa, with the 4th New Zealand Rough Riders and the Colonial Light Horse, 1899–1901. On 6 March, 1901, "De La Rey" (says the official "History of the War in South Africa," Vol. IV., pages 134–135), "beset one of Babington's patrols at Geduld, within twenty miles of his Headquarters. The patrol, which was composed of men of the 1st Imperial Light Horse, was less than half the strength of the enemy, and had but one Vickers-Maxim, but it was well handled by Major C. J. Briggs (King's Dragoon Guards), and defended itself so resolutely that once more De La Rey had the mortification of seeing his men retire beaten from a field where all the odds had been in their favour. The Boers lost some two dozen killed and wounded; the British party two officers and five men killed, three officers and thirteen men wounded. Babington, coming up next day, drove the Boers still further northward, and on the 24th completed their rout by overtaking and capturing the whole of their guns, nine in number, including two 15-pounders, a Vickers-Maxim and six Maxims, all with ammunition complete; transport to the number of seventy-seven wagons and carts, and all the camp stuff, together with the escort of 140 men, on the banks of the Taaibosch Spruit. The action which brought this about was a model of pursuing tactics. The enemy continually took up strong rearguard positions, out of which Babington as constantly manœuvred them by vigorous threats at the flanks, withholding a powerful and menacing front until the defence had begun to dissolve under the lateral pressure. The result was a series of hasty retreats on the part of De La Rey's rearguard, soon degenerating into a rout which infected the whole force and hurried it in disorder from the field. This was a heavy blow to De La Rey." Capt. Walker was mentioned in Despatches, received the Queen's Medal with three clasps, the King's Medal with three clasps, and was created a Companion of the Distinguished Service Order [London Gazette, 23 April, 1901]: "George Henry Walker, Capt., 4th New Zealand Rough Riders. For good service on the occasion of the capture of Boer guns by Major-General Babington's Column. Dated 23 April, 1901." The Insignia were presented to him by the Governor of New Zealand, 6 Sept. 1901. Capt. Walker became Commissioner of Police, Nigeria, and was given the King's Police Medal for good service in punishing and bringing to justice the murderers of Mr. James, Assistant Commissioner at Forcados, Nigeria.

LOGAN, EDWARD TOWNSHEND, Capt., was born at Valparaiso 6 Nov. 1865, son of Edward Logan, of West Kirby (latterly of Chester), and was educated at Westminster. He joined the Army 27 June, 1888, and served in the South African War, 1900–2, being present at operations in the Orange Free State, Feb. to May, 1900, including actions at Karee Siding, Vet River (5 to 6 May) and Zand River. Operations in the Transvaal in May and June, 1900, including actions near Johannesburg. He was employed with Mounted Infantry. On one occasion Capt. Logan conducted a very successful night march, which resulted in the capture of several Boer laagers near Kaffirs' Kraal, and at another time, while his company was acting as escort to an empty convoy, it was heavily attacked by the enemy a few miles out of Klerksdorp, on both flanks and in the rear, but the convoy and men were brought into Klerksdorp in safety with a loss of two men wounded. At another period during the operations (in Jan. 1901) towards Potchefstroom, Capt. Logan guarded the bridge at Nauenpoort, and he was commanding the company when in the following month they started out from Elands-

Edward T. Logan

fontein with the Scottish Horse to clear the country. He was mentioned in Despatches [London Gazette, 23 April and 10 Sept. 1901]; received the Queen's Medal with three clasps, the King's Medal with two clasps, and was created a Companion of the Distinguished Service Order [London Gazette, 23 April, 1901]: "Edward T. Logan, Capt., 3rd Battn. the Cheshire Regt. For gallant leading of the advanced guard on the occasion of the capture of Boer guns by Major-General Babington's Column. Dated 24 March, 1901." The Insignia were sent to the Commander-in-Chief in South Africa, and were presented by Colonel Sir H. S. Rawlinson, Bart. (now Lord Rawlinson). After peace was restored in the Colony, Capt. Logan joined the South African Constabulary. He was a strenuous advocate of universal military training, and was for some years Secretary to the National Service League in Cheshire and North Wales. He was a warm supporter of the Boy Scout movement, and in politics was a staunch Unionist. He married, 22 Jan. 1906, at Rossett, Denbighshire, Hilda Emma Frances, daughter of Charles Carruthers Johnstone, of Chorlton Hall, Cheshire, and widow of Walter Duckworth. Lieut.-Colonel E. T. Logan served in the European War, and was killed in action in France 25-27 Sept. 1915.

HUNT, FREDERICK ECKSTEIN, Second Lieut., was born 15 Dec.

Frederick Eckstein Hunt.

1879, son of A. W. Hunt. He was gazetted to the King's Own Royal Lancaster Regt. 26 June, 1901, and served in the South African War in 1901, taking part in operations in Cape Colony, Jan. to July, 1901. He was mentioned in Despatches [London Gazette, 23 April, 1901]; received the Queen's Medal with two clasps, and was created a Companion of the Distinguished Service Order [London Gazette, 23 April, 1901]: "Frederick Eckstein Hunt, Second Lieut., 4th Battn. Royal Lancaster Regt. In recognition of services at the defence of Fish River Station." The Insignia were presented by the King 29 Sept. 1901. He became Lieutenant, 125th Napier's Rifles, Indian Army, 15 Dec. 1905, and the 29th Lancers, Deccan Horse, in 1906, being promoted to Captain 18 Oct. 1911, and to Major 18 Oct. 1917. He married, in 1908, Helen Ornis (Hebe), youngest daughter of Dr. M. Cassidy, and they have one son and one daughter.

London Gazette, 26 April, 1901.—"War Office, 26 April, 1901. The King has been graciously pleased to give orders for the following appointment to the Distinguished Service Order, in recognition of services rendered during the operations in South Africa."

WILLIAMS, HUGH BRUCE, Capt. and Brevet Major, was born at Simla 24 July, 1865, son of the late General Sir Edward Williams, K.C.I.E., Colonel Commandant, Royal Engineers, and Clementina Bruce, eldest daughter of Thomas Bruce, Esq., of Arnot, N.B. He was educated at Cargilfield, Edinburgh (1877–78); at Winchester College, 1879–82, and entered the Royal Engineers 29 April, 1885, from the R.M.A., Woolwich, becoming Lieutenant 19 March, 1894. He was Adjutant, R.E. Troops, 16 Jan. 1896, to 22 Jan. 1899. From 1899 to 1902 he served in the South African War, as D.A.A.G., Intelligence, 5 June, 1900, to 24 Sept. 1902, taking part in the advance on Kimberley; operations in the Orange Free State, Feb to May, 1900; operations in the Transvaal, May and June, 1900. On the Staff from 5 June. Operations in the Transvaal, east of Pretoria, Aug. to 29 Nov. 1900, including action at Rhenoster Kop; operations in Orange River Colony, June and July, 1900, including actions at Lindley, (26 June) and Wittebergen; operations in the Transvaal 30 Nov. 1900, to July, 1901, and Nov. 1901, to 31 May, 1902; operations in Orange River Colony, March to Oct. 1901, and March, 1902; operations on the Zululand Frontier of Natal, Oct. 1901; operations in Cape Colony, Feb. and March, 1901. He was mentioned in Despatches [London Gazette, 16 and 26 April, 7 May and 9 July, 1901; was given the Brevet of Major 20 Nov. 1900; received the Queen's Medal with three clasps, the King's Medal with two clasps, and was created a Companion of the Distinguished Service Order [London Gazette, 26 April, 1901]: "Hugh Bruce Williams, Capt. and Brevet Major, Royal Engineers. In recognition of his Intelligence work with Brigadier-General Plumer. Dated 24 April, 1901." The Insignia were sent to the Commander-in-Chief in South Africa and presented there. He became Major 1 Oct. 1902; specially promoted to a Half-pay Lieut.-Colonelcy 4 July, 1908; became Colonel 7 March, 1912, and Major-General 3 June, 1917. His Staff appointments from the South African War have been as follows: Staff Captain (Intelligence), H.Q. of Army 1 Jan. 1903, to 31 March, 1904; D.A.Q.M.G., H.Q. of Army, 1 April, 1904, to 31 Dec. 1905; G.S.O., 2nd Grade, S. Command, 1 Jan. to 31 Dec. 1906; Brigade-Major and Secretary, School of Military Engineering, 15 Oct. 1907, to 17 June, 1908; G.S.O.2, E. Command, 18 June to 3 July, 1908; G.S.O.2, Irish Command, 3 Jan. 1912, to 23 March, 1914; G.S.O.2, Irish Command, 15 April to 27 Aug. 1914; Commandant, L. of C. (graded Brigadier-General), B.E.F., 23 Nov. 1914, to 14 July, 1915; Major-General, General Staff, B.E.F., British Armies in France, 15 July, 1915, to 4 June, 1916; Brigade Commander, 137th Infantry Brigade, British Armies in France, 5 June, 1916, to 8 Nov. 1918; Divisional Commander, 37th Division, British Armies in France, 9 Nov. 1916; G.S.O.1, Irish Command. He served in the European War in France and Flanders from 1914 to 1918; was mentioned in Despatches; created a C.B. in 1915 and a K.C.B. in 1919. Colonel Sir Hugh Bruce Williams married, in 1889, Mabel, only daughter of the late Stephen Howard, of Toronto, and they have one son and one daughter.

London Gazette, 10 May, 1901.—"War Office, 10 May, 1901. The King has been graciously pleased to give orders for the following appointment to the Distinguished Service Order, in recognition of services rendered during the operations in South Africa. To be a Companion of the Distinguished Service Order."

REID, HERBERT AMBROSE, Lieut., was born 4 May, 1877, at Darlington, Yorkshire, son of Alfred Reid; was educated at Carlton College, Victoria, Australia, and served with the Australian Bushmen and the Australian Commonwealth Horse in the South African War, 1900–2, taking part in operations in Cape Colony, Orange River Colony and the Transvaal, and receiving the Queen's Medal with three clasps. He was also mentioned in Despatches, and was created a Companion of the Distinguished Service Order [London Gazette, 10 May, 1901]: "Herbert Ambrose Reid, Lieut., Imperial Bushmen, who, with 20 men of his corps, on the 25th April, 1901, surprised a party of Boers, and dispersed them, capturing their Commandant, 41 men, a Maxim gun and many stores." Sir A. Conan Doyle says, in "The Great Boer War" (page 457): "Forty-one of the formidable Zarps, with Schroeder their leader, were captured in the north by the gallantry and wit of a young Australian named Reid." He became Honorary Captain and Major, Australian Remount Service. Major Reid served in the European War in Egypt. He married, in 1906, Annie Chaulk, second daughter of the late Walter Chaulk Baudinet, of Lake Victoria, Gippsland, Victoria, and they have one son and one daughter.

London Gazette, 19 April, 1901.—"The King has been graciously pleased to give orders for the following promotions in, and appointments to, the Distinguished Service Order, in recognition of the services of the undermentioned Officers during the operations in South Africa. The rewards given below are for services in South Africa up to the 29th Nov. 1900, the day on which Field-Marshal Lord Roberts handed over the command, and which date (except where otherwise stated) they bear. To be Companions of the Distinguished Service Order."

LOMAS, ERNEST COURTNEY. Staff Surgeon, was born 24 Dec. 1864, son of George Lomas, Esq., Mus. Bac. Oxon., of Didsbury, Lancs. He was educated at Owens College, Manchester: M.B., Ch.B., Victoria

Ernest Courtney Lomas.

(M.R.C.S., England, 1888). He became a Surgeon in the Royal Navy 11 Feb. 1891. During the South African War, 1899–1900, he accompanied the Naval Brigade, attached to the Ladysmith Relief Column (Despatches; Medal, two clasps, and was created a Companion of the Distinguished Service Order [London Gazette, 19 April, 1901]: "Ernest Courtney Lomas, M.B., Staff Surgeon R.N. In recognition of services during the operations in South Africa." The Insignia were sent to the Admiralty 12 July, 1901, and presented by the King 25 July, 1901. Dr. Lomas was specially promoted Staff Surgeon 21 Oct. 1900; Fleet Surgeon 21 Oct. 1904; Surgeon-Captain 13 Sept. 1918; retired 28 July, 1919. He married, in 1901, Eleanor Mary Ruthven, daughter of Robert Howden, of East Lothian. He became a Fellow of the Royal College of Surgeons (Edinburgh), 1907. Dr. Lomas was the Senior Medical Officer in charge of the Hospital Ships Maine and Rohilla when the vessels were totally wrecked in 1914; S.M.O. of the Hospital Ship Garth Castle, 1915, and was created a C.B. in 1916 for his services during the war; Senior Medical Officer in charge of Royal Naval Hospital, Granton, Edinburgh, 1916–18.

WILSON, LESLIE ORME, Lieut., was born in London 1 Aug. 1876, eldest son of the late Henry Wilson, of 3, Stanhope Street, Hyde Park, London, W., and of Ada Alexandrina Wilson (née Orme), of Orme Square, Bayswater, W. He was educated at St. Michael's, Westgate-on-Sea, and at St. Paul's School. He joined the Army as Second Lieutenant, Royal Marine Light Infantry, 1 Jan. 1895; promoted Lieutenant 1 Jan. 1896; served in the South African War, 1899–1900, as Adjutant, Naval Brigade; took part in the advance on Kimberley; including action at Magersfontein; operations in the Orange Free State, including operations at Zand River; operations in the Transvaal, including actions near Pretoria and Diamond Hill; operations in the Transvaal, including actions at Belfast: was seriously wounded on 26 Aug. 1900, at the action of Monument Hill; received pension for wounds. He was mentioned in Despatches; awarded the Queen's Medal and five clasps, and created a Companion of the Distinguished Service Order [London Gazette, 19 April, 1901]: "Leslie Orme Wilson, Lieut., Royal Marine Light Infantry. In recognition of services during the operations in South Africa." The Insignia were presented by H.M. King Edward VII. He was A.D.C. to the Governor of New South Wales, 1903–9. He became Captain, Berkshire Royal Horse Artillery (Territorials); promoted Lieut.-Colonel, Royal Marines, and appointed to command Hawke Battn. 63rd Division, R.N.D. He served through operations in Gallipoli, 1914–15; was mentioned in Sir Ian Hamilton's Despatches, and created a C.M.G. Severely

Leslie Orme Wilson.

wounded at the action at Beaumont Hamel, on the Ancre, on 13 Nov. 1916, and invalided home. Passed unfit for further service, he held an appointment at the Admiralty from March, 1917, to Feb. 1916, when he as made Parliamentary Secretary to the War Cabinet. On re-election to Parliament at the General Election in Dec. 1918, he was included in the Coalition Government as Parliamentary Secretary to the Ministry of Shipping, and has been Chairman of the National Maritime Board since 1919. He contested Poplar Division of Tower Hamlets as a Unionist in 1910, and was elected Member of Parliament for Reading, Berks, 13 Nov. 1913. He married, in London, 10 June, 1909, Winifred May, eldest daughter of Capt. Charles Smith, of Goderich, Sydney, New South Wales, and they have three children: Peter Leslie Orme, born 4 June, 1910; David Orme, born 18 March, 1913, and Majorie Leila, born 22 April, 1914.

SAUNDERS, FREDERICK JOHN, Lieut., was born at Peckham 18 Sept. 1876, fifth and youngest son of William Saunders, of Clevedon, Sydenham. He was educated at the Mercers' School, London. He was appointed to his first commission in the Royal Marine Light Infantry 1 Feb. 1895, and promoted Lieutenant in Jan. 1896. He was sent to China, where he joined the Powerful, and served with the Royal Marine Guard at Wei-hai-Wei in July, 1898. In 1899, on the outbreak of the Boer War, the Powerful was ordered to the Cape, and on 20 Oct. 1899, the first Naval Brigade was landed to defend Stormberg, Lieut. Saunders commanding a detachment. He fought in every action in which the brigade took part, including the Battles of Belmont, Graspan and Modder River (preceding the Relief of Kimberley), and at Paardeberg, where Lord Roberts defeated Cronje and decided the fate of Bloemfontein. He took part in Lord Roberts's march into Bloemfontein, acting as Adjutant, Naval Brigade. He advanced to Kronstad, was seized with enteric and invalided home. He was mentioned in Despatches 30 March, 1900; received the Queen's Medal with four clasps, and was created a Companion of the Distinguished Service Order [London Gazette, 19 April, 1901]: "Frederick John Saunders, Lieut., Royal Marine Light Infantry. In recognition of services during the operations in South Africa." An official despatch says that the decoration was awarded "for his gallant work at the Battle of Graspan, where he climbed to the top of a hill, gallantly leading his men all the time under a heavy fire" (Official Despatch). The Insignia were sent to the Commander-in-Chief in South Africa, 29 Nov. 1900, and presented in South Africa 11 June, 1901. Being the tallest man in the Naval Brigade, he had some very narrow escapes; one bullet passed through his pocket-book, another through the magazine of the rifle he was firing (without exploding four live cartridges still remaining in the magazine); one went through his sleeve, another through his helmet, and yet another through his water-bottle. Before the close of the campaign, he was awarded the Queen's Medal, with clasps for Belmont, Modder River, Paardeberg and Bloemfontein, and also the King's Medal. He was promoted Captain in 1901. Lieut.-Colonel Saunders was appointed Naval Intelligence Officer at Singapore, 1909–12, and served on the Staff of the Royal Marine Light Infantry at Chatham, 1913–14. He was promoted Major, July, 1914. During the European War he served in Gallipoli as Brigade-Major of the 3rd Royal Marine Division, and was mentioned in General Monro's Despatches for distinguished service during the evacuation. On the transference of the Royal Naval Division to France in May, 1916, he was promoted Temporary Lieut.-Colonel in command of the 1st Anson Battn. He was killed in action from shell fire 12 Nov. 1916, after commanding his battalion with the utmost valour and distinction. His death occurred only the day before the date of Sir Douglas Haig's Despatches in which the gallantry of Lieut.-Colonel Saunders receives conspicuous mention. He married, 31 July, 1902, Muriel, only daughter of A. Maxwell Tod, of Walmer, Kent, and they had one son, Maxwell Pomeroy, born 29 Oct. 1903.

London Gazette, 11 June, 1901.—"War Office, 11 June, 1901. The King has been graciously pleased to give orders for the following appointment to the Distinguished Service Order. In recognition of the services of the undermentioned Officer during the recent operations in Ashanti."

FLETCHER, WILLIAM, Surgeon-Capt., was born 20 Feb. 1863. He served in West Africa, 1899, in the Expedition in the Central Division of the Niger Coast Protectorate (Medal with clasp); took part in the operations in West Africa, 1900; was slightly wounded, and mentioned in Despatches [London Gazette, 4 Dec. 1900], and was created a Companion of the Distinguished Service Order [London Gazette, 11 June, 1901]: "William Fletcher, Surgeon-Capt., Militia Medical Staff Corps. In recognition of services during the operations in Ashanti." The Insignia were presented by the King 25 July, 1901. He served in South Nigeria, 1901–2, in the Aro Expedition (Despatches [London Gazette, 12 Sept. 1902]; Medal with clasp). Surgeon-Major W. Fletcher has retired. He married, in 1893, Evie Lawson, daughter of the Rev. A. Rodger.

O. B. B. Smith-Bingham.

London Gazette, 2 July, 1901.—"War Office, 2 July, 1901. The King has been graciously pleased to give orders for the following appointments to the Distinguished Service Order, in recognition of the services of the undermentioned Officers during the operations in South Africa."

SMITH-BINGHAM, OSWALD BUCKLEY BINGHAM, Capt., was born 7 Oct. 1868, second son of the late O. Smith-Bingham and of Mrs. Smith-Bingham. He was educated at Winchester, and joined the 3rd Prince of Wales's Dragoon Guards as Second Lieutenant 8 June, 1889; served in India, 1889–92; in South Africa, 1892–95; became Captain 30 Jan. 1898; served in the South African War, 1900–2; took part in operations in the Transvaal, May and July, 1901; Orange River Colony, Feb. 1901, to 31 May, 1902; Zululand Frontier of Natal, Sept. and Oct. 1901; Cape Colony, Feb. 1901. He was mentioned in Despatches [London Gazette, 2 July, 1901]; received the Queen's Medal with five clasps, and was created a Companion of the Distinguished Service Order [London Gazette, 2 July, 1901]: "Oswald Buckley Bingham Smith-Bingham, Capt., 3rd Dragoon Guards. For marked gallantry in the rearguard action on the 3rd June, 1901, near Vrede." The Insignia were sent to the Commander-in-Chief in South Africa, and presented there. He was promoted Major, Dragoon Guards, 1 April, 1903; Lieut.-Colonel 2 July, 1912. He took part in the European War, 1914–17; was twice severely wounded, on 13 May, 1915, at Ypres, and on 27 Sept. 1915, at Loos; promoted Colonel 2 July, 1916, and created a C.M.G., 1916. Brigadier-General 28 Sept. 1917, and Inspector-General of Cavalry. He married, in 1903, Edythe Mary, second daughter of the late R. Turnstall Moore, of Stodalt, County Meath, Ireland, and they have three sons: Oswald Cyril, born 29 Jan. 1904; Arthur Turberville, born 28 March, 1906, and Denis Robert.

WHITE, JAMES ROBERT, Lieut., was born 22 May, 1879, son of the late Field-Marshal Sir George White and of Lady White, *née* Amy Baly. He was educated at Winchester. He served in the South African War, 1899–1902, as Lieutenant, Gordon Highlanders. He was present at Kimberley, including action at Magersfontein; took part in operations in the Orange Free State, including operations at Paardeberg; fought in actions at Poplar Grove; Dreifontein; Vet River; was present in the Transvaal, May and June, 1900, including actions near Johannesburg and Pretoria, July to 29 Nov. 1900; took part in operations in Cape Colony, March, 1901, and in the Orange River Colony, April to June, 1901; in operations in the Transvaal. He was mentioned in Despatches [London Gazette, 2 July, 1901]; awarded the Queen's Medal and five clasps; King's Medal and two clasps, and was created a Companion of the Distinguished Service Order [London Gazette, 2 July, 1901]: "James Robert White, Lieut., The Gordon Highlanders. For having, when taken prisoner, owing to mistaking advancing Boers for British troops, and stripped, escaped from custody and run six miles, warning Colonel de Lisle, and advancing with him to relief of Major Sladen's force." The Insignia were sent to the Commander-in-Chief in South Africa, and presented by Major Sladen, Officer Commanding 6th Regt. Mounted Infantry, about March, 1902. Details from letter from Capt. J. R. White: "Awarded Distinguished Service Order for bringing up relief to a detached force attacked by Boers, having found his way to main column after being taken prisoner and released by Boers." He resigned his commission in 1908, impressed with the truth of the Tolstoyan position. He says he has since been "identified with the Irish and Socialist Revolutionary movements, and is a convinced believer in Communist principles." Capt. White married, 24 April, 1907, Mercedes (Dolly), daughter of Alexander Mosley, partner in the banking firm of Thomas Mosley & Co., Gibraltar.

LANGLEY, EDGAR JOHN FLYNN, Lieut., was born 4 March, 1878, son of the late P. R. Langley. He served in the South African War, 1900–2, taking part in operations in the Transvaal in May and June, 1900, including actions near Johannesburg, Pretoria and Diamond Hill; operations in Orange River Colony; operations in Cape Colony, south of Orange River, 1900, including action at Colesberg. He was mentioned in Despatches [London Gazette, 2 July, 1901]; received the Queen's Medal with five clasps, the King's Medal with two clasps, and was created a Companion of the Distinguished Service Order [London Gazette, 2 July, 1901]: "Edgar John Flynn Langley, South Australian Mounted Infantry. For gallantry during the action with Major Sladen's force." In the same Gazette [2 July, 1901] it is announced that the Brevet of Lieut.-Colonel has been given to "Major J. R. F. Sladen, the East Yorkshire Regt., for seizing a large convoy with 200 men and gallantly defending the same, though attacked by superior numbers of the enemy for two hours." Sir A. Conan Doyle, in "The Great Boer War" (page 469), says that "Elliot's column had trekked during the month of May from Kroonstad to Harrismith, and then turning north, found itself upon that date near the hamlet of Reitz. Major Sladen, with 200 Mounted Infantry, when detached from the main body, came upon the track of a Boer convoy and ran it down. Over a hundred vehicles with forty-five prisoners were the fruits of their enterprise. Well satisfied with his morning's work, the British leader despatched a party of his men to convey the news to De Lisle, who was behind, while he established himself with his loot and his prisoners in a convenient kraal. Thence they had an excellent view of a large body of horsemen approaching them with scouts, flankers, and all military precautions. One warm-hearted officer seems actually to have sallied out to meet his comrades, and it was not till his greeting of them took the extreme form of handing over his rifle that the suspicion of danger entered the heads of his companions. But if there was some lack of wit, there was none of heart in Sladen and his men. With forty-five Boers to hold down, and 500 under Fourie, De Wet, and Delarey around them, the little band made rapid preparation for a desperate resistance; the prisoners were laid upon their faces, the men knocked loopholes in the mud walls of the kraal, and a blunt soldierly answer was returned to the demand for surrender. But it was a desperate business. The attackers were five to one, and the five were soldiers of De Wet, the hard-bitten veterans of a hundred encounters. The captured wagons in a long double row stretched out over the plain, and under this cover the Dutchmen swarmed up to the kraal. But the men who faced them were veterans also, and the defence made up for the disparity of numbers. With fine courage the Boers made their way up to the village and established themselves in the outlying huts; but the Mounted Infantry clung desperately to their position. Out of the few officers present Findlay was shot through the head, Moir and Cameron through the heart, and

Strong through the stomach. It was a Waggon Hill upon a small scale, two dour lines of skirmishers emptying their rifles into each other at point-blank range. Once more, as at Bothaville, the British Mounted Infantry proved that when it came to a dogged pelting match they could stand punishment longer than their enemy. They suffered terribly. Fifty-one out of the little force were on the ground, and the survivors were not much more numerous than their prisoners. To the 1st Gordons, the 2nd Bedfords, the South Australians, and the New South Welshmen belongs the honour of this magnificent defence. For four hours the fierce battle raged, until at last the parched and powder-stained survivors breathed a prayer of thanks as they saw on the southern horizon the vanguard of De Lisle riding furiously to the rescue. For the last hour, since they had despaired of carrying the kraal, the Boers had busied themselves in removing their convoy; but now, for the second time in one day, the drivers found British rifles pointed at their heads, and the oxen were turned once more and brought back to those who had fought so hard to hold them. Twenty-eight killed and twenty-six wounded were the losses in this desperate affair. Of the Boers seventeen were left dead in front of the kraal, and the forty-five had not escaped from the bulldog grip which held them. There seems for some reason to have been no effective pursuit of the Boers, and the British column held on its way to Kroonstad." Major E. J. F. Langley became Second-in-Command, 13th Regt. Australian (Victoria) Cavalry. He served in the European War, 1914–17.

London Gazette, 5 July, 1901.—" War Office, 5 July, 1901. The King has been graciously pleased to give orders for the following appointment to the Distinguished Service Order, in recognition of the services of the undermentioned Officer during the operations in South Africa. To be a Companion of the Distinguished Service Order."

CAMPBELL, DUNCAN LORN, Second Lieut., was born 12 June, 1881, son of the late Major-General Lorn Campbell, C.B. He was educated at the United Services College, Westward Ho! and was gazetted to the Welsh Regt., serving in South Africa, 1900–1. He was mentioned in Despatches, and was created a Companion of the Distinguished Service Order [London Gazette, 5 July, 1901]: " Duncan Lorn Campbell, the Welsh Regt. For the defence of a train near Alkmaar, on the 20th May, 1901, with four men against 50 Boers at close quarters. Dated 20 May, 1901." Capt. D. L. Campbell served in the European War, 1914–17.

London Gazette, 19 April, 1901.—" War Office, 19 April, 1901. Memorandum.—The death of Capt. and Brevet Major His Highness Prince Christian Victor Albert Ludwig Ernst Anton of Schleswig-Holstein, G.C.B., G.C.V.O., occurred before the Commander-in-Chief in South Africa had forwarded the recommendation for the Distinguished Service Order, which, had he survived, would have been awarded to him by His Majesty, in recognition of his services during the campaign in South Africa, 1899–1900."

SCHLESWIG - HOLSTEIN, HIS HIGHNESS CHRISTIAN VICTOR, PRINCE OF, Capt. and Brevet Major, was born on 14 April, 1867, at Windsor Castle, son of Prince Christian of Schleswig-Holstein, K.G., G.C.V.O., General in the British Army, and grandson of Queen Victoria. He was educated at Wellington College; at Magdalen College, Oxford, and at the Royal Military College, Sandhurst. He joined the Army in Aug. 1888, as a Second Lieutenant in the King's Royal Rifles (60th Foot). He saw a great deal of active service. He was on General Elles's Staff, as his Orderly Officer, in the Black Mountain Expedition in Jan. 1891, and was mentioned in Despatches. In April of the same year he served in the Miranzai Expedition, under General Sir William Lockhart, with his battalion, the 1st King's Royal Rifles. He also took part in the second Black Mountain Expedition (Hazara), and served under Sir Francis Scott, in the Ashanti Expedition, being present at Koomassi when King Prempeh and the Queen-Mother made submission to the English Governor, Mr. Maxwell. He was promoted, and received the Brevet Majority in recognition of his services in India and Ashanti on 11 Dec. 1896. He took part in the South African War; and for his services in that campaign was created a Companion of the Distinguished Service Order [London Gazette, 19 April, 1901]: " His Highness Prince Christian Victor of Schleswig-Holstein, Capt. and Brevet Major, King's Royal Rifles." He was a Knight Grand Cross of the Order of the Bath and of the Royal Victorian Order, and had the Indian Frontier Medal, the Ashanti Expeditionary Medal, the Egyptian and Khedival Medal, the South African Medal, and two Jubilee Medals, and belonged to the Order of St. John of Jerusalem, as well as several foreign Orders. He was an excellent cricketer, and just failed to get his " Blue " at Oxford.

Prince Christian Victor.

A Memoir of Prince Christian Victor was written by T. Herbert Warren, M.A., President of Magdalen College, Oxford, entitled, " Christian Victor, The Story of a Young Soldier." The book brings clearly before us the picture of the clever yet painstaking and absolutely dependable boy who was Captain of the Wellington Eleven, and just missed his place in the Oxford Eleven by the skin of the teeth. He played cricket in every sense of the word, and his biographer says of him:

" The Prince did not want naturally for steadiness and solid qualities. Possibly some of his love of fair play, his cheery tolerance of all sorts and conditions of men, and good-tempered patience when luck was against him, may have been enhanced by the discipline of his favourite game. He certainly drew his own metaphors from it, as when he wrote from Natal, in the letter already quoted, 'The Boers played up awfully well in the first innings, but since then our own game has been improving.' "

A noticeable and delightful trait in Prince Christian Victor's character, was his objection to having anything given to him which he felt he had not fairly earned on his own merits. At school, at Oxford, at Sandhurst, and in the Army, he never wanted any favours or promotions which might come his way because he was Queen Victoria's grandson. He seems to have possessed much of the charm of manner, shrewdness, business capacity and sound common sense which distinguished his uncle King Edward VII.

A strong sense of religion, which was none the less real because he did not wear it on his sleeve, was with him throughout his life until his death in South Africa, when he died fortified indeed by the rites of the Church of England and the presence of many friends, but far away from the parents and sisters he loved so tenderly. He faced death with uncomplaining courage, as he had several times previously faced it on the battlefield, even amid the storm of shrapnel and hail of bullets at Colenso. For he would not be taken care of because he was a prince. As a boy at school he did not love reading, indeed, his father once wrote to his son's House Master, the Rev. C. W. Penny: " It is my constant complaint during the holidays that I never see him open a book. I trust, however, that he will try to do better when the great question is settled and regain the lost ground." " The great question " being whether Prince Christian Victor would attain his heart's desire, a place in the Wellington Eleven.

The Prince got his colours. The Eleven that year was made up as follows: M. H. Milner (Captain), C. E. F. Bunbury, P. N. Salmond, D. N. Pollock, E. P. Simpson, W. G. Raphael, A. C. M. Croome, F. A. Browning, G. N. Spiller, H.H. Prince Christian Victor and Hon. W. Cairns.

On 27 Aug. of the same year, he sent the following telegram to his father: " Balmoral, 1883, 27, 8. 9 p.m.—To-day shot fine stag with ten points, at one hundred and forty-three yards. The ball hit the right spot.—Christian Victor." By the end of the month he had shot thirty-one stags in thirteen days and two half-days' shooting.

He wrote about the same time to his old tutor, Mr. Bourdillon: " I never told you that I got into the XI. Second choice, or 8th in the entire order. I was deer-stalking at Balmoral for five weeks last holidays, and did very well. By the by, my cricket average was 18½ for 11 innings, twice not out, 168 runs highest score; 46 *v.* Marlborough. I hope very soon to be Head of the House, which means being made a prefect or monitor, and being in the VI.—With much love, believe me ever, your affectionate friend and pupil, Christian Victor."

And again, to his father: " I have not yet answered your letter, but this term I have so little time to write. I send you the 'Wellingtonian,' and you will see that I am 'in great form.' In the first match here (only a pick-up amongst ourselves) I made 50; for my house I have made 82, and got a new bat for it; for the school against C.C.C. I made 50 again, and got another new bat for that. Yesterday, against Kensington Park, I made 13 and 22 not out. . . . Charterhouse came here on 5 July, and another good match on 28 June. I have no more time, and so remain, etc."

On 1 and 2 July, 1885, he thus records one of the great school matches of the year, namely, that against Haileybury College: " Haileybury Match, at Wellington College; first day. We scored 173 first innings, myself 65; they, 115 for 7 wickets. Papa and Mr. Fisher came over." " Haileybury Match; second day. They made 131, and we 139; myself 21; they then made 116; we won by 60."

The Eleven of this year consisted of: H.H. Prince Christian Victor (Captain), A. Parker, E. W. Markham, B. M. N. Perkins, H. D. Hanbury, W. R. Collins, R. H. Pitcairn, A. L. Wood, R. W. Fox, C. Philcox and J. W. Watson.

Despite his disappointment when he narrowly missed getting his Cricket Blue, Prince Christian had a very happy time at Oxford, where he worked and played cricket as hard as ever.

His biographer says: " If the Prince did not find a place in the Oxford team, he was very successful in his cricket elsewhere. On 18 June (1887) he played for the Oxford Harlequins against Harrow School. The School Eleven then contained some players of great promise, since fulfilled, such as Mr. A. C. M'Laren and Mr. (now the Hon.) F. S. Jackson, but the Harlequins were too strong for them; Mr. E. F. S. Tylecote, as the Prince says, was in splendid form behind the sticks, and the Prince himself made 103, a long way the best score achieved in the match. In his next matches he made 46, 52, 83 not out; 68, 43, 32, 86, 46, 2, 13, 22 not out; 4, 13, 35; a remarkable series, giving an average of 45$\frac{7}{14}$ for fourteen innings. He was also very successful at the wickets and in bowling."

While a cadet at Sandhurst, Prince Christian came of age, and on his birthday was presented with the Freedom of the Borough of Windsor, in which he had been born. It was decided that he should join the 60th King's Royal Rifles. " He made their acquaintance by becoming their guest at Aldershot for a cricket match. They were, he says, very friendly, and welcomed him, 'because they say they want a wicket-keeper in the regiment.' "

On the 10th Oct. 1888, he joined his regiment at Aldershot, and in 1891 he was in India, and served in the Black Mountain Expedition as Orderly Officer to the G.O.C., General Elles, and was mentioned in Despatches 20 Oct. 1891: " Prince Christian Victor of Schleswig-Holstein was most zealous in the performance of all duties that fell to him, and takes great interest in his profession. On the battalion being ordered for service in the field elsewhere, he requested and obtained permission to rejoin it." He received the Medal and clasp. He was next to see active service in the Miranzai Expedition, under Sir William Lockhart. During this time he wrote to the Queen on a bit of paper, for which he apologized, and said he was limited to forty pounds of kit. The same day he sent his father instructions for a cricket match between Cumberland Lodge and the

Household Brigade, which was to take place on the occasion of Prince and Princess Christian's silver wedding. The Prince specially impressed it on his father to find out if any of the 2nd Battn. of the 60th were at Aldershot, and to invite them, and also to have their band to play, as well as the Guards. "They play splendidly, and people are apt to forget that there are other bands and other regiments besides the Guards. The arrangements about the band had better be made with Lord Tewkesbury." Having disposed of the silver wedding, he remarks: "Here we have had a good fight and have shot a frightful lot of the enemy. . . . My Colour Sergeant was shot in the leg as I was talking to him. The enemy shot very well, and we lost a pretty good lot for a frontier war."

In another letter he says: "We have been pushing the enemy about all over the place. . . . The native troops are splendid. I think that the German officers would say that there are no troops in the world to touch our troops in India. I have never seen anything to touch them anywhere. Soldiering out here spoils one for soldiering in England. . . . I got a very kind letter and telegram from Grandmamma on my birthday. Will you explain that I shall not be able to write to her for her birthday till I can get some paper next week?" He received a clasp to his Medal for this expedition.

He arrived in London on 29 May, 1891, and at Buckingham Palace evidently found some note-paper, on which he wrote to the Queen: "I ought to have written and thanked you for your very kind letter of congratulation after our two actions of 17 and 20 April. We were indeed fortunate, and Sir William Lockhart has done wonders."

General Lockhart had written to the Governor-General, on 28 April, of Prince Christian: "His Highness is a very keen, promising soldier, much liked in his battalion. He has been engaged in every action hitherto."

From 16 June to 11 July, he played and watched cricket every available moment, could not go to a State concert because his uniform had not arrived, wrote some particulars in his diary about his parents' silver wedding, his sister's wedding, a garden-party, at which the German Emperor and Empress were present, and last, but not least, the cricket match which he had thought out during the Miranzai Expedition.

On 10 July he went to the Eton and Harrow Match, and on 11 July: "Wimbledon Review. I was galloping for Uncle Arthur. It was a great success. We all went to the Crystal Palace for dinner, where there were the most splendid fireworks."

Cricket took up most of his time till 15 Aug., and on 17 Aug. he went to Germany and brought back some music for his band. On the 18th he sailed for India. He had more cricket; was concerned in a match, "Ghazial *v.* The World," and had hopes of getting a leopard that was prowling round his hut. "He gave at this time a great deal of attention to shooting. Musketry appears in the diary every day for many days together."

He later wrote home a description of how he got his first bear, and in another letter of more bear and ibex shooting, of his successes among the natives as an amateur doctor. "His remedies were nervine for toothache, and Cockle's pills for everything. The latter he found had a moral as well as a medical effect on the Kashmiris." About this time he remarked with great pride that he calculated that he was living at the rate of three and sixpence a day!

In 1892 he accompanied the Isazai Expedition, under Sir William Lockhart.

In Nov. 1892, he wrote to the Queen: "I go down to Meerut on the 12th of next month for the Rifle Meeting, at which I am competing for the championship of India, and also am shooting in my regimental team for the Inter-Regimental Prize."

In 1893 he wrote home: "My score of 242 points in the musketry course has not been beaten, and so I believe I am the best in the regiment."

28 Feb.: "I have just bought a beautiful carpet from Amritsar; it was very cheap, about £13 in English money; you would pay about £35 in London for the same thing, and then could not be sure it was genuine."

On 14 Feb. he had written: "Four of us went out shooting here on Saturday, and got sixteen hares, thirteen partridges, two jackals, and one wild cat, which I was lucky enough to shoot." And on 13 March he stayed with a Mr. Armstrong, at Markham Grant, Dehra Dun, and gives an account of the shoot: There were five guns: Armstrong, two officers of the Gurkhas from Dehra, Maclachlan of his own regiment, and himself: "So far we have shot a sambur, thirteen cheetah, two pigs, a porcupine, and some twenty jungle fowl." He himself got the sambur and seven of the cheetah. "No easy matter shooting from an elephant in high grass. We tried to eat the porcupine; it ought to have tasted very good, but this one was horrid."

"5 March: My latest purchase has been two camels, which will be of the greatest use when we move to the hills, since it will cost me hardly anything to move my things, as you have to give the camels no food, and they only graze by the roadside."

On 24 June he comments on the loss of the Victoria. "People always say, why do these things happen to us? I always say the other nations don't dare to do the things we do, and run no risks. Sir George Tryon was, I believe, one of the best admirals we had."

"In this country," he remarks later, "musketry is looked upon as more important than drill, and I am sure it is, but, unfortunately, in England it is not of so much importance."

On 21 Aug.: "You'll be glad to hear that in a cricket match between my regiment and the Devonshire Regt. we made 531, out of which I made 205 myself."

22 Oct.: "We have played our last match, and I made 114 and 20, so that I have finished up the season as well as I began. I have made 1,362 runs in 24 innings."

He writes to the Queen, 22 Oct.: "The greater portion of our time is spent in musketry. . . . I am now responsible to the Colonel for the shooting, he having made it my special department. . . . I am also managing the band, and that gives me great enjoyment."

In the beginning of the year 1894, Prince Christian Victor, who had left the 1st Battn. at Peshawar, often wrote to the officers, but his chief correspondent was a non-commissioned officer, Mr. J. W. Dwane, a very remarkable man, who, about the time of the Prince's death, had risen to the rank of Major.

For a great part of this year he was in the Citadel at Dover, going to Hythe for some weeks in the spring for a course of musketry.

In 1895 he served in the Ashanti War, as extra A.D.C. to Sir Francis Scott. Prince Henry of Battenberg later obtained leave to go. "No two gentlemen," said Mr. Bennet Burleigh, "ever more quickly won golden opinions by their gentle manners than Prince Henry and Prince Christian Victor. They stuck to their duty, which they performed without the slightest fuss or grumbling." On 30 Jan. 1896, Prince Christian wrote home that he had just heard of Prince Henry's death. "I am so awfully sorry for poor Aunt Beatrice and those little children. It is very sad."

Sir Evelyn Wood wrote to the Queen: "Your Majesty would be much gratified by hearing the accounts given by the officers returning from Ashanti of your grandson, who is also a great favourite with them all."

For his services in the Ashanti Expedition he was honourably mentioned; received the Star, and later the Queen telegraphed to his mother that she had just signed his promotion and brevet Majority. The Prince explains his new position in a letter to his father: "I get two shillings a day more than a Captain. I wear the uniform of a Major. It can never happen to me now that I should be turned out on account of the age clause."

Of this provision for old age, Prince Christian Victor wrote to his old friend Dwane: "You will have seen by the time that this arrives that I have been promoted and also have been given a brevet Majority. I suppose it is a great job, but still I flatter myself that I am quite as much entitled to one as many others who have been given brevets before."

In 1897 he was at Aldershot, and saw a good deal of perhaps his greatest friend, a young lieutenant in the battalion, Mr. Dermot Blundell. He was in the Jubilee Procession in London; rode with the Queen at the Naval Review at Spithead, and was with his company in the great Military Review on Laffan's Plain on 1 July.

Prince Christian Victor served in the Nile Expedition in 1898. He went on the gunboats with Sir Colin Keppel. On 25 Aug. the Zaphir sank, and though all were safely landed, Prince Christian lost most of his personal possessions.

He wrote to the Queen on the 5th from Omdurman: "I lost all I possess except my sword and a change of underclothing and my blankets. . . . The battle on the 2nd was very exciting; my ship protected the right side of the Zariba, and we fired shell after shell into dense masses of Dervishes, and must have done fearful execution."

On 9 Dec. 1898, he was invested with the G.C.V.O. by the Queen at Windsor. For the Nile Expedition he had been mentioned in Despatches 30 Sept. 1898; received the Medal and the 4th Class Osmanieh. The University of Oxford gave him an honorary degree, an honour which he valued very much. From Dec. 1898, he was stationed in Ireland, where he made many friends. In 1899 he passed the Staff College. On 6 Oct. 1899, he started for South Africa, for what proved to be his last campaign.

On arrival at Cape Town he could not get through to join the 1st Battn. King's Royal Rifles at Ladysmith, so he went on Capt. Percy Scott's Staff. at Durban. Sir Percy Scott wrote of him after his death: "I wish now that I had kept his letters, as he was one of the few that believed in heavy long-range guns before the Boers taught us their value. He went to more than one General about heavy artillery, and wrote to me, 'They cannot see that Rail Head is practically our fighting position, and that we might bring up guns of any calibre we like.' Events afterwards showed how very true this was. At the final attack on Colenso we had one six-inch gun; at the first attack we might have had a dozen, which would very likely have changed it from defeat to victory. Prince Christian's strong point was to employ *heavy* artillery—'not a fire engine,' as he said to me—to attack men in an entrenched position. Events have demonstrated that he was quite correct."

In one of Prince Christian's letters, written from South Africa, he says: "One of the West York Reservists, a small baker in London, was shot through the leg. He got a friend to turn him over, and then fired 25 more shots, till he was hit again; he is doing well in hospital."

General Hildyard got Prince Christian appointed Assistant Staff Officer to the Brigade. His friend Mr. Dermot Blundell had arrived in Africa, came up to Frere with the 4th or Light Brigade, and found the Prince there on 6 Dec.

A week later, 13 Dec., both Brigades moved together to Chieveley, where everything was preparing for the grand movement and attack upon Colenso. The next day, the 14th, the Prince watched the naval guns bombarding the centre of the Boer position. His Brigade, the 2nd, was entrusted with the central portion of the attack, and made their way for the big road bridge crossing the Tugela, going, in fact, straight for Colenso village. In doing so they came under a very hot fire. The Prince, who was Staff Officer to General Hildyard, was employed in carrying messages both for him and for General Clery. Some attempt had been made, without his knowledge, to keep him from any special exposure, but, as a matter of fact, he was for a considerable time very much in the thick of the fight, but was never touched. His own account in one of his letters was as follows:

"I was with Clery and Buller, and got into an awfully hot corner near the guns; most people were killed or hit, but somehow, although the bullets were ploughing the ground up all round, neither I nor my pony was touched; a bit of shell grazed my pony's neck and a bullet passed over my wallets, but these were the nearest. Their shells did not burst properly. One officer remarked to me that it was a ' confoundedly hot corner,' and that ' pheasant shooting was not in it.' Tommy Atkins was splendid all day and did not mind the bullets one bit. Blundell was not under fire, but poor young Roberts was terribly shot, and died the next day, and was buried on Sunday."

General Hildyard, speaking of the Battle of Colenso, said of Prince Christian : " I had endeavoured to avoid placing him in any position of unnecessary exposure. But when next I saw the Prince he was right forward in an exposed position, to which Clery had accompanied Buller, who had ridden forward to try and get the remnants of his batteries, which had moved right up into effective fire, extricated. Happily, he was not hit, and was only quite pleased at his experience."

Later the 2nd Brigade made its way first to Pretorius' Farm, and later, under General Warren, to Trichardt's Drift. " In Warren's attack the Prince was on the left part of the line. The 1st Brigade also went by Trichardt's Drift, and were engaged in the action leading up to the assault on Spion Kop, in which the Light Brigade played what was an important, and might have been a still more important part, capturing one of the side spurs and endeavouring to draw off some of the fire which fell with such awful severity on the main plateaux ; the Prince took no part, the force with which he was being held in reserve. After the abandonment of Spion Kop and the failure of the flanking movement, the whole force withdrew once more to the south of the Tugela, the Prince's Brigade going on to Spearman's Camp Farm, which they reached on 29 Jan."

About this time Prince Christian wrote : " The country is dreadfully difficult, unfordable rivers and high mountains. . . . I think this will do the Army no end of good, and will be an excellent preparation if ever we have a European War."

And again : " You really can't have any idea of the country. It's really impossible, like Switzerland, and with all the mountains made into fortresses."

After the failure of the attack on Vaalkrantz, Sir Redvers Buller ordered a retirement, via Springfield, to Chieveley. On Vaalkrantz the brigade had been under fire from three sides. The Prince wrote home : " We had a bad day at Vaalkrantz, under a cross shell-fire for fourteen hours : some came very close."

He was in the affairs at Cingolo and Monte Cristo, which paved the way for the capture of the Middleburg laager. Two days later Sir Charles Warren took Hlangwavé, and on the 22nd, at two in the morning, Sir Redvers Buller threw his troops across the Tugela, the 2nd Brigade taking part in the operation. That night Mr. Blundell was slightly wounded near the left eye with the splash of a bullet. He did not want to report himself wounded, but Prince Christian insisted that he should ; saying : " Your eye may go wrong, and if you're not reported you won't get your doctor's bill paid, or any compensation." " Advice," said Mr. Blundell, " which turned out afterwards to be very sound."

Prince Christian said, when writing to King George (then Duke of York) : " What we shall have to have in the Army are batteries of heavy ordnance shooting 10,000 yards : these will, of course, not be able to move rapidly ; the Field Artillery will do this, as at present, but these heavy guns will come up later with the infantry : this is a point which this war has shown us to be necessary."

He spent his last birthday at Elandslaagte, his thirty-third, 14 April, 1900. On 19 April, Major-General Hildyard took over the 5th Division from Sir Charles Warren, and Prince Christian acted for some time as D.A.A.G. to the Division. General Hildyard followed the railway by Wessel's Nek and Waschbank.

He entered the Transvaal Territory on the 28th, at Buffalo River, spent a few days about Utrecht and Ingogo River ; after that went back and was with Buller at the forcing of Botha's Pass, and with him marched round the Boer right to Allman's Nek. The capture of this position opened the gate into the Transvaal ; Laing's Nek was secured, and the 5th Division occupied Volksrust, being the first Division of the Natal Army to enter and occupy a Transvaal town.

In Aug. Prince Christian was appointed an extra A.D.C. to Lord Roberts.

He was at Pretoria on 8 Oct., when he began his last letter home, which he ended up on the 10th : " I played cricket two days ago, and made 31 and 69. Unfortunately, the unaccustomed exertion has given me fever ; but it is not bad, only about 100°. But I have had it two days, which is a bore." It turned out to be enteric.

On the 29th he was very weak, and the Rev. George H. Colbeck, Army chaplain, gave him by his own desire the Holy Communion just before he lost consciousness, Lord Roberts, Prince Francis of Teck, Lord Stanley, and his doctors and nurses being present. On the 29th he died. The Prince had always told his mother he did not want to be brought home if he died on active service, and he was buried on All Saints' Day at Pretoria. His great friend, Mr. Blundell, only arrived in time to attend his funeral. Lords Roberts and Kitchener were present, and so was Prince Francis of Teck, and eight Generals were the pall-bearers : Kelly, Brabazon, Wood, Marshall, Maxwell, Inigo Jones, Baden-Powell and Surgeon-General Wilson, while Colonel Campbell and the officers of the 1st Battn. King's Royal Rifles headed the mourners.

One of the most touching accounts of the funeral was written in Germany by the war correspondent of the Austrian " Neue Freie Presse."

The news of Prince Christian Victor's death was a crushing blow to his family. Queen Victoria had been optimistic to the last—and she heard of his death at Balmoral on the afternoon of the 29th. London was at the moment celebrating the return of the City Imperial Volunteers. The Queen kept back the mournful news until the evening, when, in a message to the Lord Mayor congratulating the city and its brave sons on their return and speaking of those who had fallen, Her Majesty announced to them her own bereavement in the words : " I, alas, have to grieve for the loss of a dear and most gallant grandson, who, like so many of your companions, has served and died for his Queen and country."

London Gazette, 26 July, 1901.—" War Office, 26 July, 1901. The King has been graciously pleased to give orders for the following appointments to the Distinguished Service Order, in recognition of the services of the undermentioned Officers during the recent operations in South Africa."

SHAW, CECIL ARTHUR, Lieut., was born 10 June, 1870. He entered the 7th Dragoon Guards 28 March, 1900. He served in the South African War, 1899–1902. He was present at operations east of Pretoria, Sept. to Nov. 1900 ; in the Orange River Colony, Aug. to Sept. 1900 ; in the Transvaal, Dec. 1900 ; in the Orange River Colony, Feb. 1901, to May, 1902 ; on the Zululand Frontier of Natal in Oct. 1901. Operations in Cape Colony, Dec. 1900, to Feb. 1901. He was mentioned in Despatches [London Gazette, 26 July, 1901] ; awarded the Queen's Medal and two clasps ; the King's Medal and two clasps, and was created a Companion of the Distinguished Service Order [London Gazette, 26 July, 1901] : " Cecil Arthur Shaw, Lieut., 7th Dragoon Guards. For good service in the capture of Steyn's following at Reitz." On this occasion Broadwood, with a small British column, surprised the Boers in the town of Reitz on 11 July, 1901, and captured nearly every member of the late Government of the Free State except Steyn, whom, of course, they most wanted. The column was made up of 200 Yeomen, 200 of the 7th Dragoon Guards and two guns. The raiders started at 11 at night ; rode hard all night, and raced into the sleeping village at dawn, seizing the startled Boers as they rushed from their houses. Steyn, however, mounted his horse and escaped half-clad out of the town. Two Boer Generals, two commandants, Steyn's brother, his secretary and several other officials were, however, captured, and the Boer Treasury was also secured. The Insignia of the Distinguished Service Order were sent to the Commander-in-Chief in South Africa, and there presented to Lieut. Shaw. He had been promoted to Lieutenant 22 Jan. 1901, and became Captain, 9th Lancers, 10 Jan. 1906. He was employed with the South Rhodesian Volunteers from 30 Oct. 1907. Capt. Shaw was appointed Brigade-Major, 1st Reserve Cavalry Brigade, and served in the European War. He married, in 1915, Sylvia, only daughter of the late Mr. de Grasse Fox.

EDWARDS, HUBERT DE BURGH, Second Lieut., was born 24 June, 1880. He served in the South African War ; was mentioned in Despatches ; received the Queen's Medal with four clasps, and was created a Companion of the Distinguished Service Order [London Gazette, 26 July, 1901] : " Hubert de Burgh Edwards, Second Lieut., Royal Welsh Fusiliers. For surrounding and attacking at night a party of Boers with fourteen men, killing four and taking four prisoners." The Insignia were presented to him by the King 17 Dec. 1901. He was promoted to Lieutenant, and retired from the Army.

London Gazette, 25 July, 1901.—" War Office, 24 July, 1901. The King has been graciously pleased to give orders for the following appointments to the Distinguished Service Order, in recognition of the services of the undermentioned Officers during the recent operations in China. Except where otherwise stated, their rewards will bear date of 29 Nov. 1900. To be Companions of the Distinguished Service Order."

ELDERTON, FERDINAND HALFORD, Commander, was born 25 Jan. 1865, son of the late Capt. E. H. P. Elderton, 26th Cameronians. He was educated at Leamington College, and served at Suakin, 1885 (Medal and clasp ; Khedive's Star). As Lieutenant he commanded the R.I.M. river gunboat Pagan in the Upper Burma Expedition of 1892–93 (Medal and clasp for Chin Hills). He served in China, 1900–1, as Senior Marine and Principal Transport Officer ; was twice mentioned in Despatches ; received the Medal with clasp (Peking), and was created a Companion of the Distinguished Service Order [London Gazette, 25 July, 1901] : " Ferdinand Halford Elderton, Commander, Indian Marine. In recognition of services during the recent operations in China." The Insignia were sent to the India Office 28 Sept. 1901, and were presented by Major-General Creagh, at Tientsin, China, 7 Nov. 1901. He was gazetted Commander, R.N., 1 Sept. 1914 ; was sent on Special Duties to Antwerp, on the Antwerp Mission, 2 Sept. 1914 ; was appointed Naval Transport Officer, Marseilles, 8 Sept. 1914 ; Naval Transport Officer, 15 June, 1915 ; promoted to Captain, R.N., and Divisional Naval Transport Officer, Rouen, May, 1916 (Despatches) ; Senior Naval Transport Officer, Rouen, April, 1917. Capt. Elderton married, in 1901, Ada Alice, eldest daughter of A. M. Eckford, of Chifoo, China, and they have one son and one daughter.

JOHNSON, FRANK ERNEST, Major, was born 29 Jan. 1861. He joined the Royal Artillery, as Lieutenant, 27 July, 1880, and was promoted Captain 15 Feb. 1889, and Major 30 Sept. 1898. He served on the North-West Frontier, 1897–98 ; with the Mohmand Field and Tirah Expeditionary Forces, and received Medal with two clasps. He again saw active service in China, 1900 ; was present at the Relief of Peking, taking part in the actions of Peitsang and Yangtsun ; he was mentioned in Despatches [London Gazette, 14 May, 1901] ; he received Medal with clasp, and was created a Companion of the Distinguished Service Order [London Gazette, 25 July, 1901] : " Frank Ernest Johnson, Major, Royal Artillery. In recognition of services during the recent operations in China." The Insignia were sent to the G.O.C., Hong-Kong, 26 Sept. 1901 ; forwarded by him to the G.O.C., British Contingent, China Field Force, for presentation ; sent on to the G.O.C., Madras, and finally presented by the G.O.C., Bangalore District, 1 Jan. 1902. He was promoted Lieutenant-Colonel 20 Dec. 1905 ; received the Brevet of Colonel 20 Dec. 1908, and became Colonel 20 Dec. 1910. He held the temporary rank of Brigadier-General 13 Oct. 1911, commanding R.A. India ; became A.Q.M.G., India 17 May, 1911. He served during the European War ; was mentioned in Despatches [London Gazette, 17 Feb. 1915, and 1 Jan. 1916], and created C.M.G., 1915, and C.S.I., 1919. He became Temporary Major-General 9 Oct. 1915, to 12 June, 1916, and was Temporary Inspector to the Royal Horse and Royal Field Artillery. Colonel Johnson married, in 1903, Alexa, eldest daughter of Sir W. Macpherson, Judge of the High Court, Calcutta, India.

PEREIRA, GEORGE EDWARD, Major, was born 26 Jan. 1865, son of Edward and the Hon. Margaret Pereira. He was educated at the Oratory School, Edgbaston, Birmingham, and was gazetted Second Lieutenant, Grenadier Guards, 10 May, 1882. He was employed on Home Service, 1884 to 1899; attached to Chinese Regt. till 1900. He was promoted Captain 4 Nov. 1896, and Major 2 May, 1900. He served in China in 1900 (was slightly wounded); mentioned in Despatches [London Gazette, 6 Nov. 1900]. He received Medal with clasp, and was created a Companion of the Distinguished Service Order [London Gazette, 25 July, 1901]: "George Edward Pereira, Major, Grenadier Guards. In recognition of services during the recent operations in China." The Insignia were sent direct to Major Pereira 25 Feb. 1902. He again saw active service in South Africa, 1902; served during operations in the Transvaal and Cape Colony, May, 1902, and received Queen's Medal with three clasps. During the Russo-Japanese War, 1905, was attached to the Japanese Army in Manchuria; received the Japanese War Medal and Order of the Rising Sun (4th Class), and was created C.M.G., being Military Attaché, Peking, from 1905 to 1910. He retired from the Grenadier Guards 17 July, 1909, and was placed in the Reserve of Officers 17 Sept. 1913. He served during the European War, and was mentioned in Despatches [London Gazette, 1 Jan. 1916; 15 June, 1916, and 4 Jan. 1917]. Major Pereira received the Brevet of Colonel in the Reserve of Officers, June, 1916, and was created C.B., 1917, and was given the honorary rank of Brigadier-General 21 March, 1919.

PHILIPPS, IVOR, Capt., was born 9 Sept. 1861, second son of the late Canon Sir J. Erasmus Philipps, 12th Bart., of Picton, and the Hon. Mary Margaret, daughter of the Hon. Samuel Best and sister of the 4th Lord Wynford. He was educated at Felsted School, Essex; served in the Royal Wilts Militia, 1881–83; became Lieutenant in Manchester Regt. 12 May, 1883; transferred to 5th Gurkha Rifles, Indian Army, Oct. 1884; served in the Burma Campaign, 1887–89 (Medal and two clasps); as Commandant of Military Police Battn., and in Chin-Lushai Expedition, 1889. He passed the Staff College, 1894–95; was promoted Captain 12 May, 1894. He served in the Miranzai Expedition, 1891 (Clasp); Isazai Expedition, 1892; on the North-West Frontier of India, 1897–98 (Medal and two clasps). Operations on the Samana and in the Kurram Valley during Aug. and Sept. 1897 (Medal with two clasps), and in the Tirah Expedition, 1897–98, as D.A.A. and Q.M.G. on the Lines of Communication; was present at the action of Chagru Kotal (mentioned in Despatches [London Gazette, 1 March and 5 April, 1898]; clasp); served in China (Relief of Peking) as D.A.A. and Q.M.G., Headquarters Staff (mentioned in Despatches [London Gazette, 14 May, 1901]; Medal with clasp), and was created a Companion of the Distinguished Service Order [London Gazette, 25 July, 1901]: "Ivor Philipps, Capt., Indian Staff Corps. In recognition of services during the operations in China." He was promoted Major, 5th Gurkha Rifles, 10 July, 1901; retired from Regular Army 20 July, 1903. He joined Pembroke Yeomanry in 1903, as Second-in-Command, Major and Hon. Lieutenant-Colonel. Sir Ivor Philipps was elected M.P. (Liberal) for Southampton, Jan. 1906, Jan. 1910, Dec. 1910, and Jan. 1919; commanded the Pembroke Yeomanry, 1908–12. On the outbreak of the European War he joined the War Office, G.S.O.2; became Brigadier-General, 115th Brigade, Nov. 1914; Major-General Commanding 38th Welsh Division, Jan. 1915, which division he raised and took to France in Dec. 1915. He was present in command of the division at the Battle of the Somme in July, 1916. He was created a K.C.B. in 1917. In July, 1915, he was appointed Parliamentary Secretary to the Ministry of Munitions of War, which appointment he vacated to rejoin his division on its departure for France. He has taken active interest in local government as Alderman, Pembrokeshire County Council; as Chairman, Main Roads Committee, and as Chairman of the County Council. He is a Knight of Grace of Order of St. John of Jerusalem. Is a J.P. for the county of Pembroke, and for the town and county of Haverfordwest. Is a Deputy Lieutenant and Vice-Lieutenant for the county of Pembroke. Sir I. Philipps wrote "The Issue of Orders in the Field." He married, in 1891, Marian Isobel, daughter of the late James Buchanan Mirrlees, of Redlands, Glasgow, and they have one daughter.

GRIFFIN, CECIL PENDER GRIFFITH, Capt., was born at Parkhurst 22 Jan. 1864, son of the late Colonel C. Griffin, who commanded the Sherwood Foresters. He was educated at Wellington College, and at the Royal Military College, Sandhurst, and joined the Royal Dublin Fusiliers 7 Feb. 1885, becoming Lieutenant, Worcestershire Regt., 5 Aug. 1885, and Indian Staff Corps, 14 July, 1886. He became Captain 7 Feb. 1896. He served on the North-West Frontier of India, 1898 (Medal and clasps). In China in 1900 he was present at the Relief of Peking and at the actions of Peitsang and Yangtsun; was mentioned in Despatches [London Gazette, 14 May, 1901], received the Medal and clasp, and was created a Companion of the Distinguished Service Order [London Gazette, 25 July, 1901]: "Cecil Pender Griffith Griffin, Capt., Indian Staff Corps. In recognition of services during the recent operations in China." The Insignia were presented to him by the King 29 Oct. 1901. He was promoted to Major 7 Feb. 1903, and to Lieutenant-Colonel 7 Feb. 1911; and retired 1 March, 1912. On the outbreak of the European War in 1914 he rejoined the 1st Lancers, and was wounded. Lieut.-Colonel Griffin holds the Silver Medal of the Royal Humane Society (1893). He married, at Plymouth, Annie, only daughter of E. James, and they have a son, C. S. J. Griffin (Captain, Gordon Highlanders), and a daughter, Evelyn Griffin.

PELL, BEAUCHAMP TYNDALL, Capt., was born 6 July, 1866, youngest son of the late Rev. Beauchamp Pell, Rector of Ickenham, Middlesex, and was educated at Wellington College, where his deeds of daring and love of natural history made him conspicuous; and at the Royal Military College, Sandhurst, where he gained distinction as an athlete. He was gazetted

Second Lieutenant in the Queen's Regt. 14 Sept. 1887, becoming Lieutenant 7 May, 1890. From Dec. 1890, to Nov. 1894, he was Adjutant, Queen's Regt. He served on the North-West Frontier of India, 1897–98, with the Malakand Field, Mohmand Field and Tirah Expeditionary Forces. He was mentioned in Despatches [London Gazette, 18 March, 1898], and received the Medal and two clasps. He served in China in 1900, as A.D.C. to Sir A. Gaselee, 26 June, 1900, to 20 July, 1901; was present at the Relief of Peking, actions of Peitsang and Yangtsun. He was mentioned in Despatches [London Gazette, 14 May, 1901], received the Medal with clasp, and was created a Companion of the Distinguished Service Order [London Gazette, 25 July, 1901]: "Beauchamp Tyndall Pell, Capt., Royal West Surrey Regt. In recognition of services during the operations in Pekin." The Insignia were sent to the Commander-in-Chief in South Africa 18 Jan. 1902, and privately presented at Pretoria. He served in South Africa, 1901–2, on the Staff, and as Assistant Provost-Marshal in the early part of 1902, receiving the Queen's Medal with five clasps. From Nov. 1902, to April, 1905, he was A.D.C. to different General Officers in India, and from April, 1905, to June, 1908, he was D.A.A.G. of one of the brigades of the Meerut Division and Assistant Military Secretary to the General Officer commanding the Northern Army there. He was promoted to Major in Sept. 1906. In 1912 he became G.S.O.3, at the War Office, being advanced to the 2nd Grade in April, 1913. In Sept. 1914, he succeeded to the command of the 1st Battn. the Queen's. Lieut.-Colonel Pell had only held the command a month when he was reported wounded and missing. It was subsequently ascertained that he was badly wounded at Gheluvelt, in the First Battle of Ypres, on the morning of 31 Oct. 1914; that, owing to heavy shell fire, it was impossible to move him while it was daylight, and that in the afternoon he, with other wounded, was captured by the Germans. Some weeks afterwards news was received that he had been taken to the Field Hospital of the 15th Army Corps at Werwick, Belgium, and that an operation had had to be performed, which, unhappily, did not save his life. He died on 14 Nov. 1914. In "The First Seven Divisions" (published by Messrs. Hutchinson), Lord Ernest Hamilton says, in his account of the action at Gheluvelt, on page 258: "The shell fire had been mainly focused on the 3rd and 22nd Brigades in the neighbourhood of Gheluvelt. By the association of these two Brigades, the 1st and 2nd Battns. of the Queen's (Royal West Surrey Regt.) for the first time in history found themselves fighting side by side. The occasion was an historic one, but not without a strong note of tragedy, both battalions being in the direct track of the bombardment and suffering very severely. Each battalion, too, lost its C.O. during the morning, Colonel Pell of the 1st Battn. being killed and Colonel Coles of the 2nd Battn. wounded." This, of course, is not quite correct, as Colonel Pell did not die of his wounds until later.

ROWCROFT, ERNEST CAVE, Capt., was born 6 Oct. 1866, son of Major-General G. C. Rowcroft. He was educated at Eastbourne and Sandhurst. He joined the Indian Service Corps, and was promoted Captain 5 Feb. 1898. He served in China, 1900; was present at the taking of Tientsin and advance from Tientsin on Peking, and at the Relief of the Legations; was mentioned in Despatches [London Gazette, 14 May, 1901], and received the Medal with clasp, and was created a Companion of the Distinguished Service Order [London Gazette, 25 July, 1901]: "Ernest Cave Rowcroft, Capt., Indian Service Corps. In recognition of services during the recent operations in China." The Insignia were presented by the King 29 Oct. 1901. He was promoted Major and retired in 1907. Major Rowcroft died 27 July, 1916.

POOLE, FRANCIS GARDEN, Lieut., was born at St. Paul's Cray, Kent, 24 June, 1870, youngest child of the late Rev. G. W. Poole, M.D. He was educated at Cambridge, and at the Royal Military College, and was gazetted to the East Yorkshire Regt. as Second Lieutenant 20 Feb. 1892, and became Lieutenant 1 March, 1896. He served in the Lake Shirwa Expedition, Central Africa, 1897; in the operations against the Angoni-Zulus in Northern Rhodesia in 1898 (Medal with clasp). He became Captain in 1899, and served in China in 1900, taking part in the defence of the Legations. He was attached to the Royal Marine Guard; was in command of International Volunteers, and acted as Adjutant of the defence (slightly wounded; Despatches). He served with the China Field Force, as Transport Officer; as British Member of the International Commission, Paoting Fu, to inquire into the massacre of Europeans there and to punish the perpetrators; and as Railway Staff Officer, 1900–01. He was mentioned in Despatches [London Gazette, 11 Dec. 1900], received the Medal with clasp, and was created a Companion of the Distinguished Service Order [London Gazette, 25 July, 1901]: "Francis Garden Poole, Lieut., East Yorkshire Regt. In recognition of services during the recent operations in China." The Insignia were sent to the G.O.C., Hong-Kong, and sent by him to the G.O.C., British Contingent, China Field Force, for presentation. Sent to Peking and presented by O.C. Troops, Peking, 15 Nov. 1901. He also was awarded the Order of the Dragon. He passed as Interpreter in the Chinese language. Capt. Poole was employed with the Egyptian Army, 20 Jan. 1903, to 1910, and served in Bahr-el-Ghazai, Sudan, 1903–04 (Despatches); was in the Intelligence Department, Egyptian Army, 1906–8. He became Captain 30 Dec. 1905, and Major 18 Dec. 1912. Major Poole has travelled in North and South America, India, Korea, Japan, Mongolia, Manchuria, Siberia, Tunisia, Tripoli of Barbary, Algeria, Morocco, Asia Minor, Syria and Caucasia. He was with the 15th Sudanese as Senior Inspector, Berber Province, Sudan. He has the 4th Class Osmanieh. He has published various articles and reports on China, Africa and elsewhere. During the European War Major Poole held a Special appointment 25 March, 1915, to 27 March, 1916; was Brigade-Major, 8th Reserve Infantry Brigade, New Armies, 28 March, 1916, to 18 April, 1916; G.S.O. 2nd Grade, Forth Garrison, 19 April, 1916, to 3 July, 1918; G.S.O. 2nd Grade, 2nd Army, British Armies in France, 1 Dec. 1918, to 31 March, 1919; G.S.O. 2nd Grade, War Office (Temporary), 1 April, 1919. He was created an O.B.E. in 1919.

GAUSSEN, JAMES ROBERT, Lieut., was born 20 March, 1871, son of David Gaussen, of Broughton Hall, Lechlade. He was educated at Uppingham and Sandhurst, and joined the Army 20 Feb. 1892, becoming Lieutenant, Indian Staff Corps, 21 June, 1894. He served in China, 1900–1, and was present at the Relief of Peking; was wounded, mentioned in Despatches [London Gazette, 14 May, 1901], received the Medal and clasp, and was created a Companion of the Distinguished Service Order [London Gazette, 25 July, 1901]: "James Robert Gaussen, Lieut., Indian Staff Corps. In recognition of services during the recent operations in China." The Insignia were sent to the India Office, and were presented by Major-General D. I. MacLeod, at Meerut, 1 Jan. 1902. He was promoted to Captain, Indian Army, 10 July, 1901. Capt. Gaussen was given the American Order of the Dragon. He became Major 20 Feb. 1910, and Lieutenant-Colonel 20 Feb. 1918, commanding 3rd Skinner's Horse. For the Relief of Pekin he was mentioned in American, as well as English, Despatches. He served in the Great War; commanded the 11th S.W.B., 1913–17, as Lieutenant-Colonel; was created a C.M.G.; was twice mentioned in Despatches; received the 1914 Star, War and Victory Medal, and the Indian Frontier Medal, 1918; was wounded and created a C.I.E. He raised the 40th Indian Cavalry in 1918; served in the Afghan Campaign in 1919; was promoted to Brigadier-General, 1919, to command forces in East Persia. He married, in 1896, Hilda, daughter of Colonel Hennessy, I.S.C., and they have one son and two daughters.

BAINBRIDGE, WILLIAM FRANK, Lieut., was born 15 Jan. 1873, eldest son of the late Major-General F. T. Bainbridge. He was educated at Cheltenham College, and was gazetted to the Scottish Rifles 7 Nov. 1891, becoming Lieutenant, Scottish Rifles, 13 June, 1894, and Indian Staff Corps, 21 May, 1895, serving on the North-West Frontier of India, 1897–98, with the Tochi Expedition (Medal with clasp). He served in China in 1900, and was present at the Relief of Peking and the actions at Peitsang and Yangtsun. He was mentioned in Despatches [London Gazette, 6 Nov. 1900, and 14 May, 1901], received the Medal with clasp, and was created a Companion of the Distinguished Service Order [London Gazette, 25 July, 1901: "William Frank Bainbridge, Lieut., Indian Staff Corps. In recognition of services during the recent operations in China." The Insignia were sent to the India Office and presented by Colonel H. Hervey at Kohat, Kurrum, 4 Dec. 1901. He became Captain, Indian Army, 10 July, 1901; Major 7 Nov. 1909; was D.A.A.G., India, 20 March, 1909, to 31 Dec. 1911. He passed the Staff College, and became G.S.O.2, Headquarters, India, 1 Jan. 1912, to 19 March, 1914. He was given the Brevet of Lieutenant-Colonel 7 Jan. 1914, and was G.S.O.1, Indian Expeditionary Force, 24 Dec. 1914, to 9 April, 1916; G.S.O.1, India, 23 March, 1916, to 4 May, 1916; was promoted to Lieutenant-Colonel 24 May, 1916; was G.S.O.1 5 May, 1916, to 26 March, 1917; Temporary Brigadier-General 27 March, 1917. He was created a C.M.G. in 1915, and has the Order of the Nile, 4th Class. Lieut.-Colonel Bainbridge married, in 1902, Violet Maud, eldest daughter of Capt. J. Henderson, of Rylstone, Yorkshire, and Rylstone House, Cheltenham, and they have one son.

WALWYN, FULKE JAMES, Lieut., was born 9 Nov. 1875, son of Colonel Walwyn, late Royal Welsh Fusiliers, of Croftybula, Monmouth. He was educated at Winchester and Sandhurst, and was gazetted to the Royal Welsh Fusiliers 8 April, 1896, and became Lieutenant 23 March, 1898, serving in China, 1900, when he was present at the Relief of Peking; was mentioned in Despatches [London Gazette, 6 Nov. 1900], received the Medal with clasp, and was created a Companion of the Distinguished Service Order [London Gazette, 25 July, 1901]: "Fulke James Walwyn, Lieut., Royal Welsh Fusiliers. In recognition of services during the recent operations in China." He was A.D.C. to the O.C., Shorncliffe, 7 Sept. 1901, to 14 May, 1902; A.D.C. to the O.C., North-West District, 5 May, 1902, to 13 Nov. 1902; was promoted to Captain 12 May, 1904; was Temporary Major, Royal Welsh Fusiliers, 31 Oct. 1914, to 30 Jan. 1915; became Major 31 Jan. 1915; was Brigade Major, 114th Infantry Brigade, New Armies, 14 Oct. 1915, to 8 Nov. 1915; Adjutant, Special Reserve, 9 Nov. 1915, to 28 May, 1916; Brigade Major, 21st Reserve Infantry Brigade, Home Forces, 29 May, 1916, to 31 Dec. 1916; G.S.O.2, Headquarters, Australian Imperial Force Depôts in the United Kingdom, 1 Jan. 1917, to 9 Dec. 1917; G.S.O.2, Plymouth Garrison, 10 Dec. 1917, to 2 April, 1919. Major Walwyn served in the European War, and was wounded with the Royal Welsh Fusiliers. He married, in 1904, Louise Norah, eldest daughter of Robert L. Greenshields.

London Gazette, 10 Sept. 1901.—"War Office, 10 Sept. 1901. The King has been graciously pleased to give orders for the following appointments to the Distinguished Service Order, in recognition of the services of the following Officers during recent operations in South Africa."

DAMANT, FREDERICK HUGH, Major, was born in the District of King William's Town, South Africa, in 1864, youngest son of Hugh Atherstone Damant. He served in South Africa, 1899–1904, in the famous corps commanded by Major M. F. Rimington (now Major-General Rimington, C.B., C.V.O.), known as Rimington's Guides, and later as Damant's Horse. In any history of the South African War the doings of Rimington's Guides are related at considerable length, and the official record of General Rimington's services as given in the Army List gives some faint idea of the extent of his services and of the services of his Guides: "South African War, 1899–1902. Special Service Officer, and in command Rimington's Guides. Advance on Kimberley, including action at Enslin. Afterwards in command of a column from 6 May, 1901. Despatches [London Gazette, 4 May, 1900; 8 Feb. 1901 (Lord Roberts, 31 March, 1900; Sir A. Hunter, 4 Aug. 1900)], and Despatches [London Gazette, 16 April, 1901; 17 Jan. and 29 July, 1902]; Brevet of Colonel; Queen's Medal with eight clasps, King's Medal with two clasps; created a C.B." Major Damant served during the Siege of Kimberley, in command of a mounted section of the Town Guard Station at Otto's Kopje. After the Relief of Kimberley he served with Rimington's Guides, and in 1901 was appointed to command them. In the same year the name of the Guides was changed to Damant's Horse. Shortly afterwards Major Damant commanded a column in the Orange Free State, and was promoted to Lieutenant-Colonel. In a desperate struggle with 800 Boers he received five bullet wounds, but succeeded in saving the guns entrusted to his charge; later he took part in operations in the Western Transvaal until the cessation of hostilities. Sir A. Conan Doyle tells us at length ("The Great Boer War," pages 511–512) about Damant's desperate encounter with 800 Boers. A portion of De Wet's force had been harassing the block-house builders, and three bodies, under Damant, Rimington and Wilson, were at once despatched to clear away the enemy. The British line had become extended over many miles, and was dangerously weak in the centre, where "Colonel Damant and his small staff were alone with the two guns and the Maxim, save for a handful of Imperial Yeomanry (91st), who acted as escort to the guns. Across the face of this small force there rode a body of men in khaki uniforms, keeping British formation, and actually firing bogus volleys from time to time in the direction of some distant Boers." Damant and his staff seem to have mistaken these Boers for some of Rimington's men. In a few minutes the enemy were over the kopje where the guns stood, and had ridden among the gunners, supported in their attack by a flank fire from a number of dismounted riflemen. As soon as Damant, his Staff and the escort of forty Yeomen realized the danger, they dashed for the crest of the kopje, but the Boers had already overwhelmed the gunners. In the ensuing conflict Damant was hit in five places, "all of his Staff were wounded, and hardly a man of the small body of Yeomanry was left standing. Nothing could exceed their gallantry. Gaussen, their Captain, fell at their head. On the ridge the men about the guns were nearly all killed or wounded. Of the gun detachment only two men remained, both of them hit, and Jeffcoat, their dying Captain, bequeathed them fifty pounds each in a will drawn up on the spot. In half an hour the centre of the British line had been absolutely annihilated." However, the wide spread British wings had begun to realize that something was wrong An officer on the far right brought up his squadron and Scott's squadron of Damant's Horse to the rescue. Rimington's men came up, on the other side, and the Boers rode off, leaving the guns behind them. The Boers were dressed in British uniforms, and wore the tiger-skin, the badge of Damant's Horse, round their hats. Sir A. Conan Doyle says that in the last three months of 1901, as the block-house system developed, the small bands of Boers found it increasingly difficult to escape from the British columns, who were for ever at their heels. "Of the column commanders, Williams, Damant, Du Moulin, Lowry Cole and Wilson were the most successful. In their operations they were much aided by the South African Constabulary." For his services in this campaign Major Damant was created a C.B. in 1902, and was created a Companion of the Distinguished Service Order [London Gazette, 10 Sept. 1901]: "Frederick Hugh (first gazetted as J.H.) Damant, Major, Rimington's Guides. For excellent work in the command of a column in Orange River Colony." The Warrant and Insignia were sent out to South Africa, and presented to Lieut.-Colonel Damant by Brigadier-General E. O. F. Hamilton, at Heilbron, 12 March, 1902. Lieut.-Colonel Damant afterwards became Resident Magistrate for the District of Lydenberg, Transvaal.

SHEA, JOHN STUART MACKENZIE, Capt., was born 17 Jan. 1869, son of Colonel H. J. F. Shea, R.A. He was educated at Sedbergh and Sandhurst, and was gazetted to the Royal Irish Rifles 11 Feb. 1888, becoming Lieutenant, Royal Irish Rifles, 18 Feb. 1890, and Indian Staff Corps, 24 Nov. 1891. He served in the Chitral Campaign, 1895, with the Relief Force, receiving the Medal with clasp, and was promoted to Captain 11 Feb. 1899. He served in the South African War, 1900–2, being employed with Thorneycroft's Mounted Infantry, and afterwards in command of the 5th and 6th Australian Contingents, from March, 1901, to March, 1902 Operations in Natal in June, 1900, including the action at Laing's Nek (6 to 9 June). Operations in the Transvaal, east of Pretoria, July to 29 Nov. 1900. Operations in the Transvaal, March to 31 May, 1902. Operations in Orange River Colony, Dec. 1900, and March, 1901, to March, 1902. Operations in Cape Colony, Dec. 1900, to March, 1901. He was mentioned in Despatches [London Gazette, 10 Sept. and 15 Nov. 1901]; was given the Brevet of Major 22 Aug. 1902; received the Queen's Medal with four clasps, the King's Medal with two clasps; was placed on the list of Officers considered qualified for Staff employment, in consequence of service on the Staff in the Field, and was created a Companion of the Distinguished Service Order [London Gazette, 10 Sept. 1901]: "John Stuart Mackenzie Shea, Capt., 15th Bengal Lancers, commanding South Australian Mounted Infantry. For gallant leading of a night attack on Smit's Laager, 1 Aug., against a superior force of the enemy." The Insignia and Warrant were sent to the Commander-in-Chief in South Africa, and presented by Major-General Elliott in South Africa. He became Major 11 Feb. 1906, and was a Professor at the Staff College, India, 26 June, 1906, to 20 Jan. 1910; and was given the Brevet of Lieutenant-Colonel 10 July, 1912, and promoted to Lieutenant-Colonel 11 Feb. 1914. Lieut.-Colonel Shea served throughout the European War, holding a special appointment from 5 Aug. 1914, to 28 Aug. 1914, as G.S.O.1, B.E.F.; as G.S.O.2, B.E.F., 29 Aug. 1914, to 28 Dec. 1914; as G.S.O.1, 6th Division, B.E.F., 29 Dec. 1914, to 3 July, 1915; as Brigade Commander, 151st Infantry Brigade, B.E.F., British Armies in France, 4 July, 1915, to 16 May, 1916. He was given the Brevet of Colonel 1 Jan. 1916; was Divisional Commander, 30th Division, British Armies in France, 17 May, 1916, to 31 March, 1917; became Major-General 1 Jan. 1917, and was appointed Divisional Commander, 60th Division, Egyptian Expeditionary Force, 2 Aug. 1917. He was mentioned in Despatches, created a C.B. (1915); given the Brevet of Colonel; created a C.M.G. (1918), and a K.C.M.G. (1919). Sir John Shea married, in 1902, Winifred Mary, daughter of the late William Congreve, of Burton and Congreve, and they have three daughters.

SHEPPARD, PONSONBY, Lieut., was born 10 Jan. 1879, son of Major-General Ponsonby Sheppard. He entered the Royal Field Artillery 23 June, 1898, becoming Lieutenant 16 Feb. 1901. He served in the South African War, 1899–1901, taking part in operations in Natal, April to June, 1900, including action at Laing's Nek (6 to 9 June). Operations in the Transvaal, 30 Nov. 1900, to Sept. 1901. Operations on the Zululand Frontier of Natal, Sept. and Oct. 1901. He was mentioned in Despatches [London Gazette, 10 Sept. 1901 (Lord Roberts and Lord Kitchener)], and [London Gazette, 15 Nov. 1901]; received the Queen's Medal with two clasps and was created a Companion of the Distinguished Service Order [London Gazette, 10 Sept. 1901]: "Ponsonby Sheppard, Lieut., Royal Field Artillery. For conspicuous service in action, Nondweni, 28 July." He became Captain 11 Feb. 1906; was Staff Captain, South Africa, 10 Sept. 1909, to 21 Oct. 1913. Capt. Sheppard served in the European War from 1914; as Brigade Major, R.A., 33rd Division, New Armies, B.E.F., 8 Oct. 1915, to 24 April, 1916; was promoted to Major 30 Oct. 1914; was Major-Instructor in Gunnery, School of Instruction, for R.H. and R.F.A., 5 Oct. 1916, to 28 Feb. 1917; Brigade Major, R.A., 73rd Division, Home Forces, 3 Dec. 1917, to 4 Feb. 1918; Brigade Major, R.A., 64th Division, Home Forces, 5 Feb. 1918, to 19 April, 1918; Brigade Major, R.A., 27th Division, British Salonika Force, 7 April, 1918, to 23 June, 1918. He was promoted to Lieutenant-Colonel 2 Oct. 1918. Lieut.-Colonel Sheppard married, in 1906, Nellie Marion, eldest daughter of Henry Adler, of Avondale, Dornfontein, Johannesburg.

London Gazette, 27 Sept. 1901.—"War Office, 27 Sept. 1901. The King has been graciously pleased to give orders for the following appointments to the Distinguished Service Order to the undermentioned Officers, in recognition of services during the operations in South Africa. To bear date 29 Nov. 1900. To be Companions of the Distinguished Service Order."

PAGET, HAROLD, Brevet Colonel, was born 9 Sept. 1849, son of Leopold G. Paget (son of the Hon. Berkeley Paget) and Georgina, daughter of the Rev. J. F. Moore Halsey, of Gaddesden Park, Hertfordshire. He was educated at Wellington, and was gazetted to the 10th Foot as Ensign 23 Jan. 1869, becoming Cornet, 18th Hussars, on the same date, and Cornet, 7th Hussars, 27 Feb. 1869; Lieutenant 22 Feb. 1871. He was A.D.C. to the G.O.C., Eastern District, 1873–77; promoted to Captain 23 July, 1879; extra A.D.C. to the Viceroy of Ireland, 1879–81. Capt. Paget served in the Sudan, 1884–85, in the Nile Expedition, as Adjutant, Light Camel Regt., and was present at the affair at Abu Klea on 17 Feb. (slightly wounded). He was mentioned in Despatches [London Gazette, 25 Aug. 1885]; was given the Brevet of Major 15 June, 1885; received the Medal with clasp and the Bronze Star. He became Major 5 May, 1886, and in the same year passed the Staff College; was Brigade Major, Cavalry, Aldershot, 1888–91; Military Secretary to the Provincial Commander-in-Chief, Bombay, 1893; promoted to Lieut.-Colonel 26 Jan. 1895, commanding the 7th Hussars from 1895 to 1899. In 1896–97 he served in the Matabeleland Campaign; was mentioned in Despatches 9 March, 1897, and created a C.B., and on 26 June, 1899, was given the Brevet of Colonel. He served in South Africa in command of a battalion of Imperial Yeomanry (Paget's Horse) in 1900. Some of Paget's Horse were present at the action at Faber's Put, by which Sir C. Warren crushed the rebellion in Griqualand. When the Boers attacked Lichtenburg on 3 March, 1901, the defenders were 600 in number, consisting of Paget's Horse and three companies of the 1st Battn. Northumberland Fusiliers. The attack was made by Delarey, Smuts and Celliers, with 1,500 men. Sir A. Conan Doyle says, in "The Great Boer War" (page 440), that a garrison made up of "less sturdy material might have been overborne by the vigour of the attack. As it was, the garrison were driven to their last trench, but held out under very heavy fire all day, and next morning the Boers abandoned the attack. Their losses appear to have been over fifty in number, and included Commandant Celliers, who was badly wounded and afterwards taken prisoner at Warm Baths. The brave garrison lost fourteen killed, including two officers of the Northumberlands, and twenty wounded." Colonel Paget also performed the duties of Commandant at Ottoshoop. He was mentioned in Despatches [London Gazette, 27 Sept. 1901], and created a Companion of the Distinguished Service Order [London Gazette, 27 Sept. 1901]: "Harold Paget, C.B., Lieut.-Colonel and Brevet Colonel, Commanding the 19th Battn. Imperial Yeomanry, in recognition of services during the operations in South Africa." The Insignia were sent to the Commander-in-Chief in India, and presented there 15 May, 1902. Colonel Paget retired 26 June, 1904.

FENWICK HENRY THOMAS, Brevet Lieut.-Colonel, was born 20 Dec. 1863, second son of the late Henry Fenwick and Jane Sutwidge, daughter of John Cookson, of Meldon Park, Northumberland. He joined the Royal Horse Guards 11 March, 1885, as Lieutenant, becoming Captain 15 April, 1891, and Major 19 Sept. 1896. He was given the Brevet of Lieut.-Colonel 7 Oct. 1899, and became Second-in-Command, and served in the South African War, 1899–1900, taking part in the Relief of Kimberley; operations in the Orange Free State, Feb. to May, 1900, including operations at Paardeberg (17 to 26 Feb.), actions at Poplar Grove, Dreifontein, Houtnek (Thoba Mountain), Vet River (5 and 6 May) and Zand River; operations in the Transvaal in May and June, 1900, including actions near Johannesburg, Pretoria and Diamond Hill (11 and 12 June); operations in the Transvaal, west of Pretoria, 1900, including action at Elands River (4 to 16 Aug.); operations in Orange River Colony, May to November, 1900, including actions at Bethlehem (6 and 7 July) and Wittebergen (1 to 29 July); operations in Cape Colony, south of Orange River, 1899–1900, including actions at Colesberg (5 Jan. to 2 Feb.). He was mentioned in Despatches [London Gazette, 27 Sept. 1901]; received the Queen's Medal with six clasps, and was created a Companion of the Distinguished Service Order [London Gazette, 27 Sept. 1901]: "Henry Thomas Fenwick, M.V.O., Major and Brevet Lieut.-Colonel, Royal Horse Guards. In recognition of services during the operations in South Africa." The Insignia were presented to him by the King 29 Oct. 1901. He had been created an M.V.O. in 1901. He became Lieut.-Colonel 7 Oct. 1903, and Colonel 27 Oct. 1909, and commanded the Royal Horse Guards, retiring 14 Oct. 1911. Colonel Fenwick was created a C.M.G. in 1917. He was M.P. for Houghton-le-Spring, Durham, 1892–95.

GRATTAN, O'DONNEL COLLEY, Lieut.-Colonel, was born 13 June, 1855, at Crawley, Sussex, son of Henry Colley Grattan and Lucy Nugent Grattan. He was privately educated, and at the Royal Military College, Sandhurst. He was commissioned as Second Lieutenant in the King's Liverpool Regt. in 1876, becoming Lieutenant 10 March, 1877. Lieut. Grattan served in the Afghan War, 1878–80, with the Kurram Valley Force, under Sir F. Roberts (Field-Marshal Lord Roberts); was present at the action of 28 Nov. 1878, in the Kurram Valley, and battle and capture of Peiwar Kotal; affair at Ali Khel (Medal with clasp); was promoted Capt. 20 Sept. 1882; Major 26 Oct. 1892; Lieutenant-Colonel 17 Feb. 1900. He served in the South African War, 1899–1900; operations in Natal in 1899, including actions at Rietfontein and Lombard's Kop; Defence of Ladysmith. He was mentioned in Despatches [London Gazette, 10 Sept. 1901]; received the Queen's Medal with clasp, and for services rendered at Ladysmith was created a Companion of the Distinguished Service Order [London Gazette, 27 Sept. 1901]: "O'Donnel Colley Grattan, Lieut.-Colonel, Liverpool Regt. In recognition of services during the operations in South Africa." The Insignia were presented by the King 29 Oct. 1901. He was given the Brevet of Colonel 10 Feb. 1904. He was Brigade Commander, 1st West Riding Infantry Brigade, 1909–13. He was called up in 1914, and raised and trained 61st Brigade, 20th Light Division, and commanded same till the departure of the division to France, 1915; put in command 3rd Line West Lancashire Division, 1915 to 1916, when it was formed into "groups"; Commandant, Prisoner of War Camp, to Oct. 1919. He was twice mentioned in Despatches. He married, at Aldershot, 4 Jan. 1877, Helen Randall, second daughter of Major-General H. Le Poer Trench. They have two daughters: Gladys Norah, born in 1885, married Major-General Sir C. H. Harington, K.C.B., D.S.O., and Aileen Nugent, born in 1887, married Temporary Capt. F. C. Bedwell, West Yorkshire Regt.

HALL-DEMPSTER, REGINALD HAWKINS, Lt.-Col. was born 14 March, 1854, son of the late Capt. Henry Hall. He was educated at Wellington College, and was gazetted to the South Lancashire Regt. 12 Nov. 1873, as Lieutenant; was Adjutant, South Lancashire Regt., 10 Jan. 1883, to 9 Jan. 1888; Captain 15 July, 1883; Major 27 March, 1893. He served in the South African War, 1899–1902; was present at the Relief of Ladysmith, including the operations of 17 to 24 Jan. 1900, and action at Spion Kop; operations of 5 to 7 Feb. 1900, and action at Vaal Kranz; operations on Tugela Heights (14 to 27 Feb. 1900). In command of 1st Battn. South Lancashire Regt. during operations in the Transvaal, 30 Nov. 1900, to March, 1901, and Nov. 1901, to 31 May, 1902. He was mentioned in Despatches [London Gazette, 8 Feb. 1901, and 29 July, 1902]; received the Queen's Medal with five clasps, the King's Medal with two clasps, and was created a Companion of the Distinguished Service Order [London Gazette, 27 Sept. 1901]: "Reginald Hawkins Hall, Lieut.-Colonel, South Lancashire Regt. In recognition of services during the operations in South Africa." The Insignia were sent to Lord Roberts in South Africa, and presented by Lieut.-General Lyttelton at Newcastle 28 April, 1902. He as given the Brevet of Colonel 10 Feb. 1904, and retired with the rank of Colonel 3 Aug. 1904. Colonel Hall married, in 1894, Edith Gertrude Dickson, eldest daughter of the late Rev. Francis Horne Atkinson, of Morland Hall, Westmorland, and they have one daughter. His name was changed by deed-poll to R. H. Hall-Dempster.

SURTEES, HERBERT CONYERS, Lieut.-Colonel, was born 13 Jan. 1858, only son of the late Colonel C. F. Surtees, D.L., J.P., late 10th Hussars, of Nainsforth Hall, Ferryhill, and M.P. for South Durham, 1865–68, and of Bertha, daughter of N. S. Chauncy, Esq., of Green End, Hertfordshire. He was educated at Sandhurst; entered the 49th Foot 11 Sept. 1876; became Second Lieutenant, Coldstream Guards, 31 Oct. 1877; Lieutenant, Army, 11 Sept. 1876; Coldstream Guards, 31 Oct. 1877; Instructor of Musketry, Coldstream Guards, 1 Feb. 1882, to 31 March, 1883. He was employed with the Egyptian Army 23 Feb. 1884, to 12 June, 1887, and served in the Nile Expedition, 1884–85, in command of the Turkish Mounted Infantry of the Egyptian Army, and afterwards of a boat convoy, receiving the Medal with clasp, the Bronze Star, and the 4th Class Medjidie. In 1885–86 he again saw active service in the Sudan with the Frontier Field Force, taking part in the action of Giniss, in command of the 3rd Camel Corps, Egyptian Army. He was promoted to Captain 7 May, 1887; to Major 5 Feb. 1895. He passed the Staff College. Major Surtees was D.A.A.G., Southern District, 1 July, 1897, to 30 Jan. 1899. He served in the South African War, 1899–1900, in command of the 1st Battn. Coldstream Guards (23 March to 14 Dec. 1900), taking part in the advance on Kimberley, including actions at Belmont, Enslin, Modder River and Magersfontein; operations in the Orange Free State, Feb. to May, 1900, including actions at Dreifontein, Vet River (5 and 6 May) and Zand River. Operations in the Transvaal in May and June, 1900, including actions near Johannesburg, Pretoria and Diamond Hill (11 and 12 June); operations in the Transvaal, east of Pretoria, July to 29 Nov. 1900, including actions at Belfast (26 and 27 Aug.). He was mentioned in Despatches [London Gazette, 10 Sept. 1901]; received the Queen's Medal with six clasps, and was created a Companion of the Distinguished Service Order [London Gazette, 27 Sept. 1901]: "Herbert Conyers Surtees, Lieut.-Colonel, Coldstream Guards. In recognition of services during the operations in South Africa." The Insignia were presented to him by the King 29 Oct. 1901. He became Lieut.-Colonel 3 Oct. 1900; was given the Brevet of Colonel 10 Feb. 1904; was Military Attaché, Constantinople and Athens, 15 Aug. 1905, to 1909 (Cross of the Grand Commander of St. Saviour of Greece); was created a C.B. in 1906 and a M.V.O. in the same year, and retired 14 Aug.

1912. During the European War General Surtees commanded the 52nd Infantry Brigade in France and Belgium (1915–16), and was an Inspector of Infantry in 1916; was twice mentioned in Despatches; given the honorary rank of Brigadier-General 12 April, 1917, and created a C.M.G. in 1919. He is an F.S.A. and an F.R.G.S., and is Lord of the Manor of Mainsforth; is County Commissioner for Boy Scouts, County Durham, Deputy Lieutenant and a Justice of the Peace. General Surtees has been M.P. for Gateshead since 1918. He married, in 1887, Madeline Augusta (Mrs. Surtees has the Turkish Order of the Chefaket), daughter of Edward Crabbe, and they have two daughters.

PEARSE, HUGH WODEHOUSE, Brevet Lieut.-Colonel, was born 13 Aug. 1855, son of the late Rev. Robert W. Pearse and Mrs. Robert Pearse. He joined the 70th Foot 11 Feb. 1875, as Sub-Lieutenant, becoming Lieutenant, East Surrey Regt., 11 Feb. 1875; served in the Afghan War, 1879–80 (Medal); was D.A.C.G., Commissariat and Transport Staff, from 13 Aug. 1881; was promoted to Captain 30 June, 1883; was Adjutant, Volunteers, 15 Jan. 1889, to 13 Jan. 1894; became Major, 12 July, 1892. He served in the South African War from 1899 to 1902, being present at the Relief of Ladysmith, including the action at Colenso; operations of 17 to 24 Jan. 1900, and action at Spion Kop; operations of 5 to 7 Feb. 1900, and action at Vaal Kranz; operations on Tugela Heights, and action at Pieter's Hill. He was in command of the 2nd Battn. East Surrey Regt. 23 Feb. to 1 May, 1900, and 1 July, 1900, to 31 May, 1902; operations in the Transvaal 30 Nov. 1900, to 31 May, 1902; operations in Orange River Colony, May, 1901. Major Pearse was mentioned in Despatches [London Gazette, 8 Feb. and 29 July, 1902]; was given the Brevet of Lieut.-Colonel 29 Nov. 1900; received the Queen's Medal with four clasps, the King's Medal with two clasps, and was created a Companion of the Distinguished Service Order [London Gazette, 27 Sept. 1901]: "Hugh Wodehouse Pearse, Major and Brevet Lieut.-Colonel, East Surrey Regt. In recognition of services during the operations in South Africa." The Insignia were sent to Lord Kitchener in South Africa, and presented by Major-General Clements at Standerton 13 April, 1902. He became Lieut.-Colonel 14 Jan. 1901; Brevet Colonel 10 Feb. 1904, and Colonel 25 Feb. 1907; was Assistant Director of Dress and Clothing, H.Q. of Army, from 25 Feb. 1907. Colonel Pearse retired from the Staff 25 Feb. 1911. He has written several books: "The Memoirs of Colonel Alexander Gardner;" "The Crimean Diary of Lieut.-General Sir Charles Windham;" "The Hearseys" (1905); "The Life of General Viscount Lake" (1908) and "The History of the East Surrey Regiment" (1916). Colonel Pearse married, in 1899, Ada Gordon, daughter of the late Walter Scott, of Goldielea, Kirkcudbrightshire, N.B., and they have one son and one daughter.

GERARD (LORD), SIR WILLIAM CANSFIELD, Colonel, was born in London, 21 June, 1851, son of Sir Tolver Gerard, Bart., 1st Lord Gerard, of the Carabiniers, Colonel of Lancashire Hussars, Yeomanry Cavalry, Aide-de-Camp to Queen Victoria, and of Harriet, daughter of Edward Clifton. He was educated at Oscott College, and at Stonyhurst College, Lancashire. He was gazetted to the 2nd Life Guards about 1870, and retired as Lieutenant. In 1876 he joined the Lancashire Hussars, and served with them in the South African Campaign, 1899–1901, when Lord Gerard acted as Staff Officer to General Sir Redvers Buller. He was present at the Battle of Colenso, where he was with the guns when Lord Roberts's son was killed; he had his horse shot under him. He was mentioned in Sir Redvers Buller's Despatches, and was created a Companion of the Distinguished Service Order [London Gazette, 27 Sept. 1901]: "William Cansfield, Lord Gerard, Lieut.-Colonel and Honorary Colonel, Lancashire Hussars. In recognition of services during the operations in South Africa." The Insignia were presented to Lord Gerard by the King 29 Oct. 1901. He died at his residence, Eastwell Park, Ashford, Kent, in 1902. He had married, 7 Aug. 1877, in King Henry VIII.'s Chapel, Westminster Abbey, May Laura, daughter of Henry Beilby Milner, of West Retford House, Nottinghamshire, granddaughter of Sir William Milner and of Archbishop Beresford, Primate of Ireland, and they had one son, Frederick John, born 10 Nov. 1883, Captain, Royal Horse Guards (who served in the European War, 1914–17, and was severely wounded)—the present (3rd) Lord Gerard; and one daughter, Ethel Catharine Hannah, born in 1881, married in Feb. 1904, to Baron de Forest.

GASCOIGNE, FREDERIC RICHARD TRENCH, Lieut.-Colonel, was born 4 July, 1851, only son of the late Frederic Charles Trench Gascoigne, Esq., and of Mrs. Gascoigne, eldest daughter and co-heir of the late R. Oliver Gascoigne, of Parlington, Yorkshire, and Castle Oliver, County Limerick. He was gazetted to the Royal Horse Guards, and served in the Sudan Expedition of 1884–85 (Nile), with the Intelligence Department, as Staff Captain. He was present at the actions of Abu Klea and near Metemmeh, and with the force in the advance up the Nile towards Khartum. He was afterwards attached to the Heavy Camel Corps; received the Medal with two clasps and the Bronze Star. Capt. Gascoigne retired from the Royal Horse Guards, and when the South African War broke out he commanded the 10th Squadron Yorkshire Hussars (Imperial Yeomanry), when they went out to South Africa, Jan. 1900; he was afterwards promoted Major and Lieutenant-Colonel commanding the 3rd Imperial Yeomanry Battn. 10 Aug. 1900, to 12 April, 1901. He was present in operations in the Transvaal, west of Pretoria, July to 29 Nov. 1900, including actions at Venterskroon (7 and 9 Aug.); operations in the Orange River Colony, May to Nov. 1900, including actions at Lindley (1 June) and Rhenoster River; operations in the Transvaal 30 Nov. to April, 1901. He was mentioned in Despatches [London Gazette, 10 Sept. 1901]; received the Queen's Medal with four clasps, and was created a Companion of the Distinguished Service Order [London Gazette, 27 Sept. 1901]: "Frederic Richard Thomas Trench Gascoigne, Lieut.-Colonel, 3rd Battn. Imperial Yeomanry. In recognition of services during the operations in South Africa." The Insignia were presented by the King 17 Dec. 1901. He was also placed on the list of officers considered qualified for Staff Employment, in consequence of service in the field. He was appointed Colonel and Honorary Colonel commanding the Yorkshire Hussars (Imperial Yeomanry), 1904–8, and Honorary Colonel in the Army, 1904. He possesses King Edward's Coronation Medal. Colonel Gascoigne is very fond of big game sport—has killed buffalo on the prairie in Colorado in 1873; shot in the Rocky Mountains (1876), and in the Abyssinian Sudan (1879). He is a keen yachtsman; member of the Royal Yacht Society, and fond of travelling. He is a Justice of the Peace for the West Riding, Yorkshire. Colonel Gascoigne took out two motor-cars to France in 1914, working with them for Dr. Garrett-Anderson's Hospital, at Wimereux, all that winter; worked for the Y.M.C.A. all the summer of 1915, in the Boulogne District, and was an Inspector of Church Army Huts and Canteens in France in 1916. Colonel Gascoigne maintained a V.A.D. Hospital in Lotherton Hall (35–40 beds) for four and a half years (Nov. 1914, to March, 1919). He married, 16 Feb. 1892, at St. Peter's, Eaton Square, London, S.W., Laura Gwendolen, C.B.E., Lady of Grace of the Order of St. John of Jerusalem, daughter of Sir Douglas and Lady Galton, of Himbleton Manor, Droitwich, and they have one son, Alvary Douglas Frederick (Coldstream Guards), born 6 Aug. 1893; and one daughter, Cynthia Mary, born 6 Feb. 1898.

BROMLEY-DAVENPORT, WILLIAM, Lieut.-Colonel, was born 21 Jan. 1863, eldest son of the late Lieut.-Colonel W. Bromley-Davenport, M.P. He was educated at Eton, and at Balliol College, Oxford; joined the Staffordshire Yeomanry, serving in the South African War in command of the 4th Imperial Yeomanry Battn. He was mentioned in Despatches [London Gazette, 10 Sept. 1901]; received the Queen's Medal with four clasps, and was created a Companion of the Distinguished Service Order [London Gazette, 27 Sept. 1901]: "William Bromley-Davenport, Lieut.-Colonel, 4th Battn. Imperial Yeomanry. In recognition of services during the recent operations in South Africa." The Insignia were presented to him by the King 29 Oct. 1901. Colonel Bromley-Davenport is a Justice of the Peace and Deputy Lieutenant. He was Member of Parliament (Conservative) for the Macclesfield Division of Cheshire, 1886–1906, and contested the same Division in 1910. He was Financial Secretary, War Office, 1903–5. Colonel Bromley-Davenport commanded the 1st Staffordshire Yeomanry from the outbreak of the War, and went with them to Egypt in Nov. 1915. He was Brigadier-General commanding the 1/1st North Midland Brigade, Egyptian Expeditionary Force; Brigadier-General in Command of the 22nd Mounted Brigade, Egypt, 1916; Assistant Director of Labour, France, from 1917 (created a C.M.G., 1918); Assistant Director of Labour, 2nd Army, Italian Expeditionary Force, from Nov. 1917, to April, 1918. Commandant of Labour, France. Colonel Bromley-Davenport was created a C.B.E. in 1919.

FIRMAN, ROBERT BERTRAM, Lieut.-Colonel, was born 13 Sept. 1859, son of H. B. Firman, of Brayton, Yorkshire. He was gazetted to the Middlesex Regt., and served in the Nile Expedition of 1884–85, employed on Transport duties; and was present at the action of Kirbekan (Medal with two clasps, and Khedive's Star). He served in the Burmese Expedition of 1886–87 (Medal with clasp). He became Captain 21 April, 1886; retired from the Middlesex Regt., and joined the Reserve of Officers. He served in the South African War, 1899–1900, in command of the 11th Imperial Yeomanry Battn., and took part in operations in the Orange Free State, Feb. to May, 1900. Operations in Orange River Colony, May to 28 Nov. 1900, including actions at Biddulphsberg, Bethlehem, Wittebergen, Witpoort and Caledon River. Operations in the Transvaal and Orange River Colony 30 Nov. 1900, to 31 May, 1902. He was mentioned in Despatches [London Gazette, 10 Sept. 1901]; received the Queen's Medal with three clasps, and was created a Companion of the Distinguished Service Order [London Gazette, 27 Sept. 1901]: "Robert Bertram Firman, Lieut.-Colonel, Imperial Yeomanry. In recognition of services during the operations in South Africa." The Insignia were sent to Lord Roberts in South Africa, and were presented by Lieut.-General Lyttelton at Newcastle 28 April, 1902. Lieut.-Colonel R. B. Firman married, in 1896, N. Eveline, daughter of the late Anthony Hordern, of Sydney.

WILSON, RICHARD HENRY FRANCIS WHARTON, Lieut.-Colonel, was born 18 Aug. 1855, son of Sir M. W. Wilson, 2nd Bart. He served in the Royal Navy, 1869 to 1874; and in the 10th Royal Hussars, 1876–96. He served in the Ashanti War in 1873 (Medal). He entered the Army 26 July, 1876, and served in the Afghan War in 1878–79–80, being present at the assault of Ali Musjid and action of Futtehabad, affairs around Kabul and Sherpur, and march from Kabul to the relief of Kandahar and battle of 1 Sept. He was mentioned in Despatches [London Gazette, 4 May and 3 Dec. 1880], received the Medal with three clasps, and the Bronze Star. He again saw active service in the Egyptian Expedition of 1884, and was present at the battles of Teb and Tamai (Medal with clasp and Bronze Star). He served in the Sudan Expedition of 1885 (Suakin), attached to the Cavalry Brigade; was mentioned in Despatches, received the clasp, and was given the Brevet of Major. He retired and joined the Reserve of Officers. He served in the South African War, 1900–01, in command of the 12th Battn. Imperial Yeomanry, Feb. 1900, to June, 1901. He commanded Mounted Troops, Potchefstroom Column, 26 Aug. 1900, to 30 Jan. 1901. He was present at the operations in Cape Colony, south of Orange River, March, to May, 1900. Operations in Orange River Colony, May to Aug. 1900, including actions at Rhenoster River and Wittebergen (1 to 29 July). Operations in the Transvaal, west of Pretoria, Aug. to 29 Nov. 1900. Operations in the Transvaal 30 Nov. 1900, to March, 1901. Operations in Orange River Colony, March to April, 1901. He was mentioned in Despatches [London Gazette, 10 Sept. 1901]; received the Queen's Medal with four clasps; was promoted to Major, Reserve of Officers, and created a Companion of the Distinguished Service Order [London Gazette, 27 Sept. 1901]: "Richard Henry Francis Wharton Wilson, Lieut.-Colonel, Imperial Yeomanry. In recognition of services during the operations in South Africa." The Insignia were presented to him by the King 29 Oct. 1901. During the

European War he was Assistant Military Secretary, Irish Command, Dec. 1914, to July, 1916. Lieut.-Colonel Wilson married, in 1889, Annabella Margaret, daughter of John Forbes Drummond, of Ednam House, Kelso.

DUNCOMBE, THE HONOURABLE HUBERT VALENTINE, Lieut.-Colonel, was born 14 Feb. 1862, son of the 1st Earl of Feversham and the Countess of Feversham. He was educated at Harrow; at the Royal Military Academy, Woolwich, and at Magdalene College, Cambridge, and joined the 2nd Volunteer Battn. Princess of Wales's Own Yorkshire Regt., becoming Major 13 May, 1896, and Honorary Lieutenant-Colonel 14 May, 1901. He served in the South African War from 1900 to 1902, in command of a battalion of the Imperial Yeomanry; was mentioned in Despatches [London Gazette, 10 Sept. 1901]; received the Queen's Medal with three clasps, and was created a Companion of the Distinguished Service Order [London Gazette, 27 Sept. 1901]: "The Honourable Hubert Valentine Duncombe, Lieut.-Colonel, Imperial Yeomanry. In recognition of services during the operations in South Africa." The Insignia were presented to him by the King 27 Oct. 1901. He was M.P. (Conservative) for the Egremont Division of Cumberland, 1895–1900. Lieut.-Colonel the Hon. H. V. Duncombe died 21 Oct. 1918.

LE ROY-LEWIS, HERMAN Lieut.-Colonel, was born 27 June, 1860, second son of General Robert Le Roy and Amelia, cousin of J. Delaware Lewis, M.P. He was educated at Eton, and at Trinity College, Cambridge (M.A.), and became a Member of the Inner Temple; is an F.R.G.S. and F.S.S., and is D.L. and J.P. for Hampshire, and assumed the additional name of Lewis in 1884. He became Major, Hampshire Yeomanry Cavalry (Carabiniers) 3 July, 1895, and Lieutenant-Colonel 20 April, 1901, and served in the South African War, 1899–1901, as Commandant of a Battalion of Yeomanry (3 Oct. to 31 Dec. 1900), and afterwards as Commandant, Imperial Yeomanry, Cape Town (graded as an A.A.G.). Operations in the Orange Free State, Feb. to May, 1900. Operations in the Transvaal in May and June, 1900. Operations in the Transvaal, east of Pretoria, August, 1900. Operations in the Transvaal, west of Pretoria, July and Sept. to Nov. 1900. Operations in Orange River Colony, including actions at Lindley (1 June) and Rhenoster River. Operations in the Transvaal 30 Nov. to Dec. 1900. Operations in Orange River Colony, Dec. 1900, to Jan. 1901. Operations in Cape Colony, Jan. to Feb. 1901. He was mentioned in Despatches [London Gazette, 10 Sept. 1901], received the Queen's Medal with four clasps, and was created a Companion of the Distinguished Service Order [London Gazette, 27 Sept. 1901]: "Herman Le Roy-Lewis, Lieut.-Colonel, Imperial Yeomanry. In recognition of services during the operations in South Africa." The Insignia were presented by the King 17 Dec. 1901. He was a D.A.A.G., Headquarters of Army, from 1901; a Member of the Auxiliary Force Advisory Board from 1902; Brigade Commander, 1st South-West Mounted Brigade, from 1908 to 1912. He became Colonel. He was Military Attaché in Paris, 1915 to 1919. He received the Territorial Decoration in 1909; was created a C.B. in 1912, and a C.M.G. in 1918; is a Commander of the Legion of Honour and has been awarded the Croix de Guerre avec Palme; the Belgian Croix de Guerre; the Order of Danilo, 2nd Class (in 1917), and the Crown of Roumania. He has written articles for the "National Review," the "United Service Magazine," "The National Defence Magazine," "Baily's," "The Army Review," etc. Colonel Lewis married, in 1888, Kathleen Teresa Turner, eldest daughter of the late A. H. Turner Newcomen, of Kirkleatham Hall, Yorkshire, and they have one son, Henry, born 28 Feb. 1895, and four daughters.

BLAKE, NAPOLEON JOSEPH RODOLPH, Major, was born at Portsmouth, 20 July, 1853, son of the late Capt. Maurice Lynch Blake and the late Margaret Louisa Blake. He joined the 57th Foot 12 Nov. 1873, as Lieutenant; served in the Zulu War (Medal); became Captain, Middlesex Regt., 14 March, 1881, and Major 19 March, 1890. He served in the South African War, 1899 to 1901, taking part in the Relief of Ladysmith, including the operations of 17 to 24 Jan. 1900, and action at Spion Kop; operations of 5 to 7 Feb. 1900, and action at Vaal Kranz; operations on Tugela Heights (14 to 27 Feb. 1900), and action at Pieter's Hill. Operations in the Transvaal in June, 1900. Operations in Natal, March to June, 1900, including action at Laing's Nek (6 to 9 June). Operations in the Transvaal, east of Pretoria, July to 29 Nov. 1900. Operations in Orange River Colony, June, 1900. Operations in Cape Colony, south of Orange River, 1899. Operations in the Transvaal, 30 Nov. 1900, to May, 1901. He was mentioned in Despatches [London Gazette, 10 Sept. 1901]; received the Queen's Medal with seven clasps, and was created a Companion of the Distinguished Service Order [London Gazette, 27 Sept. 1901]: "Napoleon Joseph Rodolph Blake, Major, Middlesex Regt. In recognition of services during the operations in South Africa." He retired 20 July 1901. Major Blake married, in 1888, Alice, daughter of the late R. H. Page-Henderson, of Oswaldkirk, Yorkshire, and they have one daughter.

HATCHELL, HENRY MELVILLE, Major, was born 31 May, 1852, son of the late G. W. Hatchell, M.D., of Dublin. He was gazetted to the 18th Foot 28 Feb. 1874; served in the Afghan War, 1879–80, serving as Orderly Officer to Major-General Roberts, who commanded a Brigade at Kabul (Medal). He was promoted Captain 1 July, 1881; took part in the Egyptian War, 1882 (Medal with Tel-el-Kebir clasp; Khedive's Star). He became Major 29 April, 1891. He served in the South African War, 1899–1900, as Major, Royal Irish Regt., and commanded 5th Battn. Mounted Infantry, and was slightly wounded. He was

Henry Melville Hatchell.

present at operations in Cape Colony in 1900. Operations in Orange Free State, Feb. to May, 1900, including action at Poplar Grove. Operations in Orange River Colony, May to July, 1900, including action at Bethlehem Operations in the Transvaal, east of Pretoria, July to Nov. 1900, including actions at Belfast and Lydenburg. He was mentioned in Despatches [London Gazette, 10 Sept. 1901]; received the Queen's Medal and three clasps, and was created a Companion of the Distinguished Service Order [London Gazette, 27 Sept. 1901]: "Henry Melville Hatchell, Major, Royal Irish Regt. In recognition of services during operations in South Africa." The Insignia were presented by the King 29 Oct. 1901. In 1902 he was promoted to Lieutenant-Colonel, to command the 5th Battn. Royal Garrison Regt. (Aldershot and Halifax, Nova Scotia), and he became Substantive Lieutenant-Colonel 26 Feb. 1902, being given the Brevet of Colonel 26 Feb. 1905, and retiring from the Royal Garrison Regt. 26 Feb. 1906, with the rank of Colonel. During the European War, Colonel Hatchell commanded the 25th Service Battn. Northumberland Fusiliers (Tyneside Irish) in England, and also commanded the 30th Reserve Battn. Northumberland Fusiliers. Colonel Hatchell married, in 1901, Frances Mary Elizabeth, eldest daughter of the late Rev. H. S. Rush, of Haywards Heath, Sussex.

BIRD, SPENCER GODFREY, Major, was born 5 Jan. 1854, son of the Rev. Godfrey Bird (Rector of Great Wigborough, Colchester, Essex) and of Sarah Jane, his wife. He was educated at Haileybury, and joined the Militia (West Essex) 28 Feb. 1871, being commissioned in the 102nd Regt. 28 Feb. 1874, as Lieutenant; was Adjutant, 102nd Foot, 7 Aug. 1875, to 11 March, 1881, and became Captain, Royal Dublin Fusiliers, 15 Aug. 1883. He was Adjutant, Auxiliary Forces, 1 Oct. 1886, to 24 Oct. 1889, and became Major 21 May, 1892. Major Bird served in the South African War, with the 2nd Battn. Royal Dublin Fusiliers, 1899 to 1902; was present in operations in Natal, 1899, including actions at Talana and Lombard's Kop. He was in command of the battalion at Talana Hill and the retirement on Ladysmith, and was Second-in-Command during the remainder of the campaign, taking part in the operations in the Orange Free State, Feb. to May, 1900. Operations in the Transvaal, west of Pretoria, July to 29 Nov. 1900. He was afterwards Commandant at Krugersdorp. He was mentioned in Despatches [London Gazette, 8 Feb. 1901 (Sir G. S. White, 2 Dec. 1899; Sir R. H. Buller, 9 Nov. 1900), and London Gazette, 10 Sept. 1901]; received the Queen's Medal with four clasps; the King's Medal with two clasps, and was created a Companion of the Distinguished Service Order [London Gazette, 27 Sept. 1901]: "Spencer Godfrey Bird, Major, Royal Irish Regt. In recognition of services during the operations in South Africa." The Insignia were presented by the King 24 Oct. 1902. He became Lieutenant-Colonel 7 June, 1902; was given the Brevet of Colonel 7 June, 1905, and retired 7 July, 1906. Colonel Bird volunteered for service in the European War, and was called up in Oct. 1914. He commanded the 15th Battn. Royal Fusiliers (Kitchener's Army), at Dover and Shoreham, and again at Dover. He proceeded to France in Dec. 1915, to visit the trenches and see special requirements for training men before going out. He is Secretary to the Oriental Club. Colonel Bird is a keen cricketer. He married, in 1880, Mary, daughter of the late W. C. Macready, Ceylon Civil Service, and they have one son and one daughter.

Spencer Godfrey Bird.

PALMES, GEORGE CHAMPNEY, Major, was born 9 Feb. 1857, third son of the late Venerable James Palmes, D.D. He entered the Army 10 Sept. 1875, as Sub-Lieutenant, unattached, and the 24th Foot 10 Sept. 1875; becoming Lieutenant, South Wales Borderers, 10 Sept. 1877, and serving in the South African War of 1877–78–79, taking part in the Kaffir Campaign. Operations against the Galekas, Battle of Quintana (Medal and clasp). He was promoted to Captain 9 June, 1882; was Adjutant, Volunteers, 1 Oct. 1891, to 30 Sept. 1896, and became Major 9 June, 1892. He served in the South African War, 1899–1902; was Commandant at Klerksdorp, and took part in operations in the Orange Free State, Feb. to May, 1900, including actions at Karee Siding, Vet River (5 and 6 May) and Zand River. Operations in the Transvaal in May and June, 1900, including the action near Johannesburg. Operations in the Transvaal, west of Pretoria, Aug. to 29 Nov. 1900. Operations in Orange River Colony, June to Aug. 1900. Operations in the Transvaal, 30 Nov. 1900 to May, 1902. He was mentioned in Despatches [London Gazette, 10 Sept. 1901]; received the Queen's Medal with two clasps, and was created a Companion of the Distinguished Service Order [London Gazette, 27 Sept. 1901]: "George Champney Palmes, Major, South Wales Borderers. In recognition of services during the operations in South Africa." The Insignia were sent to Lord Kitchener in South Africa, and were presented by Brigadier-General Barber at Klerksdorp 16 March, 1902. Major Palmes retired 23 July, 1902. He married Mary Lowndes, widow of C. Faber.

Frederick John Tobin.

TOBIN, FREDERICK JOHN, Colonel, was born at Withycombe Raleigh, Devon, 29 Aug. 1856, son of the late George Edward Alexander Tobin, Capt., 2nd

Queen's Royal Regt., 2nd of Exmouth, Devon, and of Louisa, daughter of the late Thomas Williams, Esq., of Lowdon House, Devon. He was educated at King Alfred's School, Wantage, Berks, and at the Hermitage School, Bath. He joined the Army 12 May, 1875, becoming Lieutenant 12 May, 1877, and served in the Afghan War, 1879–80, where he was severely wounded at the skirmish at Sinari. He was mentioned in Despatches for services rendered when in charge of retirement of detachments holding Spintange and Koochalie, etc., and received the commendation of the Government and the Commander-in-Chief (Medal). He became Captain 1 April, 1883; was Adjutant, Auxiliary Forces, 15 April, 1885, to 14 April, 1890, and became Major 10 Jan. 1893. In 1895 he rendered valuable service when in command of the troops stationed there, in suppressing the riots in Ahmadabad, and was specially thanked by the Bombay Government. During the South African War he commanded the 2nd Battn. Royal Irish Rifles, 1899–1901, acting as Commandant at Smithfield, and taking part in operations in the Orange Free State, Feb. to May, 1900. Operations in Orange River Colony, May to 29 Nov. 1900. Operations in Cape Colony, south of Orange River, 1899–1900. He was mentioned in Despatches [London Gazette, 10 Sept. 1901]; received the Queen's Medal with three clasps, and was created a Companion of the Distinguished Service Order [London Gazette, 27 Sept. 1901]: "Frederick John Tobin, Major, Royal Irish Rifles. In recognition of services during the operations in South Africa." The Insignia and Warrant were sent to the Commander-in-Chief in India 30 Jan. 1902, and presented by the Lieutenant-General Commanding the Forces, Oudh, India, 14 March, 1902. He became Lieutenant-Colonel 21 July, 1904, and retired 10 Aug. 1907, with the rank of Colonel. He married, in Feb. 1884, at St. George's, Hanover Square, London, W., Clare Edith Georgina, daughter of the late Thomas Waters, of Birr, King's County, Ireland.

BULMAN, PHILIP, Major, was born 3 Nov. 1857, son of John Bulman, of Clifton. He was gazetted to the 85th Foot 11 Sept. 1876, becoming Lieutenant, Shropshire Light Infantry on the same date, and serving in the Afghan War, 1879–80, with the Kurram Division in the Yarmusht Expedition (Medal). He became Captain 4 Feb. 1885; Major 11 Feb. 1894, and was Vice-Consul, Asia Minor, 27 Nov. 1895, to 16 Oct. 1897. Major Bulman served in the South African War, 1899–1901, and in command of the 2nd Battn. Shropshire Light Infantry from 1 May to 5 June, 1900, also from 22 Jan. to 13 March, and from 16 May to 4 Sept. 1901. Operations in the Orange Free State, Feb. to May, 1900, including operations at Paardeberg (17 to 26 Feb.); actions at Poplar Grove, Dreifontein, Houtnek (Thoba Mountain), Vet River (5 and 6 May) and Zand River. Operations in the Transvaal in May and June, 1900, including actions near Johannesburg and Pretoria. Operations in the Transvaal, east of Pretoria, July to 29 Nov. 1900, including operations at Elands River (4 to 16 Aug.). Operations in Orange River Colony, May to 28 Nov. 1900, including action at Rhenoster River. Operations in Cape Colony, south of Orange River, 1899–1900. Operations in the Transvaal 30 Nov. 1900, to Sept. 1901. He was mentioned in Despatches [London Gazette, 10 Sept. 1901]; received the Queen's Medal with five clasps, and was created a Companion of the Distinguished Service Order [London Gazette, 27 Sept. 1901]: "Philip Bulman, Major, Shropshire Light Infantry. In recognition of services during the operations in South Africa." He was promoted to Lieutenant-Colonel 19 Aug. 1901; was given the Brevet of Colonel 19 Aug. 1904, and retired 24 Oct. 1906, entering the Reserve of Officers.

HARVEY, WILLIAM LUEG, Major, was born 17 July, 1858, son of the late Nicholas Oliver Harvey, of Hayle, Cornwall. He was commissioned in the 46th Foot 30 Jan. 1878; became Lieutenant, Duke of Cornwall's Light Infantry, 18 June, 1881, serving in the Egyptian Expedition, 1882, and being present at the battle of Tel-el-Kebir (Medal with clasp and Bronze Star). He was promoted to Captain 24 Sept. 1884, and served in the Sudan in 1884–85, in the Nile Expedition, with the River Column (clasp). He became Captain 24 Sept. 1884, and Major 31 Aug. 1894. Major Harvey served in the South African War, 1899 to 1902. He was Commandant at Kaspminden, and he took part in the operations in the Orange Free State, Feb. to May, 1900, including the operations at Paardeberg (17 to 26 Feb.); actions at Poplar Grove, Dreifontein, Houtnek (Thoba Mountain), Vet River (5 and 6 May) and Zand River. Operations in the Transvaal in May and June, 1900, including actions near Johannesburg and Pretoria. Operations in the Transvaal 30 Nov. 1900, to 31 May, 1902. He was mentioned in Despatches [London Gazette, 10 Sept. 1901, and 29 July, 1902; received the Queen's Medal with four clasps, and was created a Companion of the Distinguished Service Order [London Gazette, 27 Sept. 1901]: "Robert Lueg Harvey, Major, Duke of Cornwall's Light Infantry. In recognition of services during the operations in South Africa." The Insignia were sent to Lord Kitchener in South Africa, and presented by Brigadier-General Dixon, at Barberton, 7 March, 1902. He retired 5 Nov. 1902, with the rank of Lieutenant-Colonel. During the European War he became Lieutenant-Colonel (temporary), commanding the Duke of Cornwall's Light Infantry Depôt at Bodmin, 1914–17. Lieut.-Colonel Harvey is a Justice of the Peace. He married, in 1893, Florence, daughter of the late Capt. F. C. Hooper, 18th Hussars, and they have one son and one daughter.

PORTER, REGINALD WHITWORTH, Major, was born 18 May, 1856. He entered the Oxford Light Infantry 6 Sept. 1876, as Second Lieutenant from the Militia, becoming Captain 11 Jan. 1886, and Major 9 Nov. 1894. Major Porter served on the North-West Frontier of India, 1897–98, with the Mohmand Field and Tirah Expeditionary Forces (Medal with two clasps). He served in the South African War, 1899–1902, and was created a Companion of the Distinguished Service Order [London Gazette, 27 Sept. 1901]: "Reginald Whitworth Porter, Major, Oxford Light Infantry. In recognition of services during the operations in South Africa." The Insignia were sent to Lord Roberts, and were presented by Major-General Knox at Kroonstad 21 March, 1902. Major Porter died 10 May, 1902.

MAXWELL, THE HONOURABLE HENRY EDWARD, Major, was born 27 Nov. 1857, son of the late Honourable Richard Maxwell, and brother of the 10th Baron Farnham. He entered the Army 11 Sept. 1876, as Sub-Lieutenant, unattached; was gazetted to the 107th Foot 11 Sept. 1876, and transferred to the 73rd Foot 31 Oct. 1877, becoming Lieutenant, Royal Highlanders, 11 Sept. 1878. He was Adjutant, Royal Highlanders, 24 Dec. 1884, to 31 Oct. 1888; was promoted to Captain 15 May, 1885; was Adjutant, Militia, 1 Nov. 1888, to 31 Oct. 1893; became Major, Royal Highlanders, 3 Jan. 1895. He served in the South African War, 1899–1902. In command 2nd Battn. Royal Highlanders (from 11 Dec. 1899, to 25 Jan. 1900). Afterwards in command of section, Harrismith-Bethlehem Line. Advance on Kimberley, including action at Magersfontein. Operations in the Orange Free State, Feb. to May, 1900, including operations at Paardeberg 17 to 26 Feb. (slightly wounded); action at Vet River. Operations in Orange River Colony, including actions at Rhenoster River, Wittebergen, and Witpoort. Operations in Cape Colony, south of Orange River, 1899. Operations in the Transvaal, Nov. 1901, to March, 1902. Operations in Orange River Colony, Nov. 1900, to Sept. 1901, and April to May, 1902. Operations on the Zululand Frontier of Natal in Oct. 1901. He was mentioned in Despatches [London Gazette, 10 Sept. 1901], received the Queen's Medal with four clasps, the King's Medal with two clasps, and was created a Companion of the Distinguished Service Order [London Gazette, 27 Sept. 1901]: "The Honourable Henry Edward Maxwell, Major, Royal Highlanders. In recognition of services during the operations in South Africa." The Insignia were sent to Lord Kitchener 18 Jan. 1902, and were presented by Major-General E. S. Brook, C.B., at Tredonw, 4 June, 1902. He became Lieutenant-Colonel 12 Dec. 1903; was given the Brevet of Colonel 12 Dec. 1906, and retired with the rank of Colonel 12 Dec. 1907. He is a J.P. and D.L., and was High Sheriff, County Cavan, 1910. He married Edith, daughter of Colonel R. A. G. Cosby, of Stradbally Hall, Queen's County, and they have one son and one daughter.

The Hon. H. E. Maxwell.

ANSTRUTHER-THOMSON, CHARLES FREDERICK ST. CLAIR, Major, was born 6 May, 1855, eldest surviving son of John Anstruther-Thomson, of Charleton, Fife. He entered the Army as Sub-Lieutenant, unattached, 13 June, 1874; was gazetted to the 2nd Dragoons 13 June, 1874; to the 17th Lancers 28 Aug. 1875, becoming Lieutenant, 2nd Life Guards, Sept. 1876; Captain 12 Jan. 1885, and Major 12 Jan. 1895. He served in the South African War, 1899–1900, taking part in the Relief of Kimberley; operations in the Orange Free State, Feb. to May, 1900, including operations at Paardeberg (17 to 26 Feb.); actions at Poplar Grove and Dreifontein. Operations in the Transvaal in May and June, 1900, including actions near Johannesburg and Diamond Hill (11 and 12 June). He was mentioned in Despatches [London Gazette, 10 Sept. 1901]; received the Queen's Medal with six clasps, and was created a Companion of the Distinguished Service Order [London Gazette, 27 Sept. 1901]: "Charles Frederick St. Clair Anstruther-Thomson, Major, 2nd Life Guards. In recognition of services during the operations in South Africa." The Insignia were presented by the King 17 Dec. 1901. He was promoted to Lieutenant-Colonel 12 Jan. 1903; commanded the 2nd Life Guards; was given the Brevet of Colonel 13 July, 1905, and retired with the rank of Colonel 12 Jan. 1907. Colonel Anstruther-Thomson married, in 1882, Agnes, third daughter of the late James A. Guthrie, of Craigie, and they have one daughter.

LEWIS, BRIDGES GEORGE, Major, was born 3 March, 1857, son of the Rev. G. B. Lewis. He was educated at Uppingham and Sandhurst, and was gazetted to the 30th Foot 27 March, 1878, becoming Lieutenant, East Lancashire Regt., 31 July, 1879. He was Instructor of Musketry, East Lancashire Regt., 6 April, 1881, to 1 Nov. 1889; Captain 18 March, 1885; Adjutant, 2nd Battn. East Lancashire Regt., 1 April, 1888, to 31 March, 1892; Adjutant, Militia, 18 Feb. 1893, to 17 Feb. 1898; Major 14 March, 1895. He served in the South African War, 1900–01; operations in the Orange Free State, Feb. to May, 1900, including actions at Vet River (5 and 6 May) and Zand River; operations in the Transvaal in May, 1900, including actions near Johannesburg; operations in the Transvaal to 29 Nov. 1900; operations in Cape Colony, Feb. 1900; operations in the Transvaal 30 Nov. 1900, to July, 1901, and Aug. to Oct. 1901; operations in Orange River Colony, July to Aug. 1901. He was mentioned in Despatches [London Gazette, 10 Sept. 1901], received the Queen's Medal with four clasps, and was created a Companion of the Distinguished Service Order [London Gazette, 27 Sept. 1901]: "Bridges George Lewis, Major, East Lancashire Regt. In recognition of services during the operations in South Africa." The Insignia were sent to South Africa, and he was invested by the Commander-in-Chief 30 Dec. 1901. He became Lieutenant-Colonel 23 Sept. 1901; was given the Brevet of Colonel 23 Sept. 1904; commanded the 1st Battn. East Lancashire Regt.; became Colonel 25 Feb. 1907; retired 23 March, 1910. Colonel Lewis served in the European War, 1914–18, as Temporary Brigadier-General, commanding 56th Infantry Brigade, 2nd New Army, from Sept. 1914. He was given the honorary rank of Brigadier-General 13 Nov. 1917, and was created a C.B., 1918. He is a J.P., County Carlow. Brigadier-General Bridges married (1st), in 1879, Mary (who died in 1917), daughter of the Rev. Canon Burn-Murdoch; and they had one son and one daughter. He married (2ndly), Laura Montgomery, daughter of the Rev. W. Glenn, and they have one son.

HERAPATH, EDGAR, Major, was born 3 May, 1853, son of the late Spencer Herapath, F.G.S., F.S.A., F.S.S., of Westwood, St. Peter's, Thanet, and 18, Upper Phillimore Gardens, Kensington, W. He was educated at the Grammar School, Kensington, W., and on the Continent, and entered the West India Regt., as Sub-Lieutenant, 11 Feb. 1875, becoming Lieutenant, West India Regt., 11 Feb. 1877, and Lincolnshire Regt. 13 March, 1878 ; Captain 1 July, 1884 ; was Adjutant, Auxiliary Forces, 1 Jan. 1886, to 7 Sept. 1886, and was promoted to Major 29 May, 1895. He served in the South African War in 1900, taking part in operations in the Orange Free State, Feb. to May, 1900, including operations at Paardeberg, Karee Siding, Vet River and Zand River ; operations in the Transvaal in May and June, 1900, including actions near Johannesburg and Pretoria ; operations in the Transvaal, July, 1900 (severely wounded). He was mentioned in Despatches [London Gazette, 10 Sept. 1901] ; received the Queen's Medal with three clasps, and was created a Companion of the Distinguished Service Order [London Gazette, 27 Sept. 1901] : " Edgar Herapath, Major, Lincolnshire Regt. In recognition of services during the operations in South Africa." The Insignia were presented by the King 29 Oct. 1901. Major Herapath retired 3 May, 1901. He is F.R.G.S., and his favourite recreations are hunting, fishing, shooting and travelling. He married, in 1885, Sophia, youngest daughter of the late G. H. Fletcher, J.P., of Barrow Hedges, Carshalton.

PELLY, JOHN STANNUS, Major, was born 13 Jan. 1859, son of the late C. R. Pelly, Johnstown House, Cabinteely, Dublin, and of Jane (née Hamilton), of Vesington, County Meath. He was educated at Rugby School. He entered the Army 14 Jan. 1880 ; served in the Bechuanaland Expedition under Sir Charles Warren, 1884–85 ; was promoted Captain 1 July, 1885 ; Major, July, 1895 ; took part in operations in the last rising in Crete, 1898 ; served in the South African War, 1899–1901 ; in command of the 1st Battn. Border Regt., from Jan. to 4 Sept. 1900, and March, 1901, to Aug. 1901 ; operations in Natal, 1899 ; Relief of Ladysmith, including action at Colenso ; operations on Tugela Heights (14 to 27 Feb. 1900), and action at Pieter's Hill ; operations in the Orange Free State, April and May, 1900 ; operations in the Transvaal in June, 1900 ; operations in the Transvaal, east of Pretoria, in July ; operations in the Transvaal, west of Pretoria, July to Nov. 1900 ; operations in Orange River Colony, May, 1900 ; operations in Cape Colony, south of Orange River, 1899 ; operations in Cape Colony, north of Orange River, May, 1900 ; operations in the Transvaal 30 Nov. 1900, to Nov. 1901 He was mentioned in Despatches [London Gazette, 8 Feb. and 10 Sept. 1901] ; received the Queen's Medal with six clasps, and was created a Companion of the Distinguished Service Order [London Gazette, 27 Sept. 1901] : " John Stannus Pelly, Major, Border Regt. In recognition of services during the operations in South Africa." He was invested by the King 17 Feb. 1901. He became Lieutenant-Colonel 20 Oct. 1901 ; was given the Brevet of Colonel 20 Oct. 1904, and retired from the Border Regt. 20 Oct. 1905, with the rank of Colonel. He served during the European War ; commanded 7th Border Regt. (Kitchener's Army), Sept. 1914, to March, 1915 ; commanded a Junior Officers' Company, May, 1915, to Jan. 1916 ; employed on recruiting duties, North-West District, March, 1916, to Jan. 1918. Colonel Pelly married, in 1900, Lilian Louisa, daughter of the late W. B. Page, and they have one daughter.

GLUBB, FREDERIC MANLEY, Major, was born 19 Aug. 1857, son of the late Orlando Manley Glubb, 37th B.N.I. (descended from an old Cornish family), and of the late Frances Letitia Kelly. He entered the Royal Engineers 25 Jan. 1877, as Lieutenant ; was promoted Captain 25 Jan. 1888, and Major 12 Aug. 1895. Major Glubb served in the South African War, 1899–1901, taking part in operations in Natal, March to June, 1900, including action at Laing's Nek 6 to 9 June ; operations in the Transvaal, June, 1900 ; operations in the Transvaal, east of Pretoria, July to 29 Nov. 1900. He was mentioned in Despatches [London Gazette, 10 Sept. 1901] ; received the Queen's Medal with five clasps, and was created a Companion of the Distinguished Service Order [London Gazette, 27 Sept. 1901] : " Frederic Manley Glubb, Major, Royal Engineers. In recognition of services during the operations in South Africa." He was promoted to Lieutenant-Colonel 16 April, 1903 ; was given the Brevet of Colonel 16 April, 1906 ; became Colonel 16 Aug. 1908, and was appointed Chief Engineer, Northern Command, 1909–12, and was Chief Engineer, Southern Command, Salisbury, 1912–14. When the European War broke out he was appointed Chief Engineer, 3rd Corps, British Expeditionary Force, France, and in May, 1915, Chief Engineer, 2nd Army, British Expeditionary Force, in which capacity he served till the end of the war in France, Belgium, Italy and Germany. He has been mentioned several times in Despatches ; created a C.B., 1914 ; promoted Major-General for Distinguished Service in the Field in 1915 ; created a K.C.M.G. on 1 Jan. 1918 ; created Commandeur of the Légion d'Honneur, and of the Order of Leopold of Belgium in 1917, and of the Corona d' Italia in 1918. He married, in 1889, Frances Letitia, daughter of the late B. W. Bagot, J.P., of Carranure, County Roscommon.

Henry Hyde W. Nason.

NASON, HENRY HYDE WILLIAMSON, Major, was born 8 March, 1857, son of the late Major-General John Nason, 49th Regt., and of Abigal Mary Williamson. He was educated at Harrow, and entered Cambridgeshire Militia 1 May, 1875 ; entered the 44th Regt. 8 Dec. 1878 ; became Captain in the Essex Regt. on 10 Dec. 1884, and was promoted Major 7 Oct. 1895. Major Nason served in the South African War, 1899–1902,

and was present at the Relief of Kimberley ; operations in the Orange Free State, including operations at Paardeberg (17 to 26 Feb.) ; actions at Poplar Grove, Dreifontein, Vet River (5 and 6 May) and Zand River ; operations in the Transvaal in May and June, 1900, including actions near Johannesburg, Pretoria and Diamond Hill (1 to 12 June) ; operations in the Transvaal, east of Pretoria, including action at Belfast (26 and 27 Aug.) ; operations in Cape Colony, south of Orange River, 1899–1900, including actions at Colesberg (1 to 29 Jan.) ; operations in the Transvaal, April to 31 May, 1902. He was mentioned in Despatches [London Gazette, 8 Feb. and 10 Sept. 1901] ; received the Queen's Medal with six clasps ; the King's Medal with one clasp, and was created a Companion of the Distinguished Service Order [London Gazette, 27 Sept. 1901] : " Henry Hyde Williamson Nason, Major, Essex Regt. In recognition of services during the operations in South Africa." The decoration was awarded for services in the field at the actions of Paardeberg, Dreifontein, etc. The Insignia were presented by the King 29 Oct. 1901. He retired from the Essex Regt. 8 March, 1905, and became Lieutenant-Colonel commanding 2nd Reserve Battn. Royal Guernsey Light Infantry, 1913. Major Nason served in the European War, at Albert and Aveluy Wood, Feb. 1916, on Senior Officers' Instructional Course. In 1916 he was appointed to command the 2nd Reserve Battn. Royal Guernsey Light Infantry. He was mentioned in Despatches 2 March, 1917. He married, in 1899, Florence, daughter of the late Colonel E. A. Hannay, and they have two sons : Second Lieut. Robert Fortescue Nason, Seaforth Highlanders, born on 13 Feb. 1900, and Claude Fortescue Nason, born on 23 Feb. 1904.

GEDDES, ROBERT JAMES, Major, M.B., was born 13 Aug. 1858, son of the late James Geddes, Solicitor, Dumfries. He entered the Army in 1884 ; served in the Burmese Expedition, 1886–89 (Medal with two clasps) ; in the Chin-Lushai Expedition, 1889–90 (clasp). He became Major, R.A.M.C., 2 Feb. 1896, and took part in the operations in Mekran, 1898. Major Geddes served in the South African War, 1899–1902 ; Relief of Kimberley ; operations in Orange Free State, Feb. to May, 1900, including operations at Paardeberg 17 to 26 Feb. ; action at Dreifontein ; operations in the Transvaal in June, 1900 ; operations in the Transvaal, east of Pretoria, July to 29 Nov. 1900 ; operations in Orange River Colony, May to 29 Nov. 1900 ; operations in Cape Colony, south of Orange River, 1899–1900 ; operations in the Transvaal 30 Nov. 1900, to 31 May, 1902. He was mentioned in Despatches [London Gazette, 10 Sept. 1901] ; received the Queen's Medal with four clasps ; the King's Medal with two clasps, and was created a Companion of the Distinguished Service Order [London Gazette, 27 Sept. 1901] : " Robert James Geddes, Major, Royal Army Medical Corps. In recognition of services during the operations in South Africa." The Insignia were sent to Lord Roberts in South Africa, and presented by Major-General G. Barton in South Africa. He became Lieutenant-Colonel 2 Feb. 1904, and Colonel 5 Feb. 1913. Colonel Geddes served in the European War, 1914–17, as D.D.M.S. ; was twice mentioned in Despatches, and created a C.B. He retired 26 Dec. 1917. Colonel Geddes married, in 1907, Christina Gowans, daughter of the late J. G. Whyte, of Helensburgh.

RICHARDSON-GRIFFITHS, CHARLES DU PLAT, Major, was born 2 June, 1855. He joined the 13th Foot 20 Nov. 1875 ; became Lieutenant, Bedfordshire Regt., 5 Jan. 1876 ; served in the Afghan War, 1879–80 (Medal) ; was Adjutant 5 Oct. 1883, to 31 Dec. 1887 ; was promoted Captain 4 Oct. 1885 ; was Adjutant, Militia, 14 July, 1888, to 19 Aug. 1893 ; became Major, Gloucestershire Regt., 19 Feb. 1896. Major Richardson-Griffiths served in the South African War, 1900–2. In command 2nd Battn. Gloucestershire Regt. from May to Oct. 1900. He was present at the Relief of Kimberley ; operations in the Orange Free State, Feb. to May, 1900, including operations at Paardeberg (17 to 26 Feb.) ; actions at Poplar Grove and Dreifontein ; operations in Orange River Colony, May to 29 Nov. 1900 ; operations in Cape Colony, south of Orange River, 1900 ; operations in Cape Colony, north of Orange River ; operations in Orange River Colony 30 Nov. 1900, to 31 May, 1902. He was mentioned in Despatches [London Gazette, 10 Sept. 1901] ; received the Queen's Medal with three clasps ; the King's Medal with two clasps, and was created a Companion of the Distinguished Service Order [London Gazette, 27 Sept. 1901] : " Charles du Plat Richardson-Griffiths, Major, Gloucestershire Regt. In recognition of services during the operations in South Africa." The Insignia and Warrant were sent to Lord Kitchener, and presented to Major Richardson-Griffiths by Major-General G. Barton in South Africa. Major Richardson-Griffiths retired 2 June, 1903. He married, in 1894, Florence, daughter of the late H. Schwabe.

TREEBY, HENRY PAUL, Major, was born 30 Aug. 1858, son of the late T. W. G. Treeby, of Marmion House, Southsea, and Georgina Mary Anne, daughter of the late Rev. E. A. Gibson, Rector of Holybourne, Hants. He was educated at the Naval and Military College, Southsea, and privately, and entered the Army 6 Aug. 1879 ; became Captain 5 Aug. 1885. He was Adjutant, Volunteers, from 1 Aug. 1893, and was promoted to Major 24 March, 1896. Major Treeby served in the South African War, 1899–1900, and was present at the Relief of Ladysmith, including the action at Colenso ; operations of 17 to 24 Jan. 1900, and action at Spion Kop ; operations of 5 to 7 Feb. 1900 ; action at Vaal Kranz, and operations on Tugela Heights (severely wounded 23 Feb. 1900). He was mentioned in Despatches [London

Henry Paul Treeby.

Gazette, 10 Sept. 1901]; received the Queen's Medal with two clasps, and was created a Companion of the Distinguished Service Order [London Gazette, 27 Sept. 1901]: "Henry Paul Treeby, Major, East Surrey Regt. In recognition of services during operations in South Africa." The Insignia were presented by the King 29 Oct. 1901; the Warrant sent 24 Jan. 1902. Major Treeby retired 11 Dec. 1901. He was Brigade Major, Wilts and Dorset Volunteer Brigade, 30 Jan. 1903; Brigade Major, East Surrey Regt., 1 June, 1906. He was appointed to command East Surrey Regimental Depôt and 31st Regimental District Recruiting Area, 3 Aug. 1914, with rank of Lieutenant-Colonel. He is a J.P. for Surrey. He married Eliza, daughter of the Rev. F. Paynter, of Stoke Hill, Guildford, and they have one son and two daughters. Lieut.-Colonel Treeby was Joint Hon. Sec. Surrey County Prisoners of War Fund.

NEVILLE, WILLIAM CANDLER, Major, was born 22 Jan. 1859, at Fermoy, Ireland, son of Major Robert Neville, late 51st King's Own Light Infantry, of Rockfield, Ballybrack, and Ahanure, County Kilkenny, and Emma Helsham Candler, daughter of William Helsham Candler Brown, of St. Mary's Hall, King's Lynn. He was educated at Cheltenham College; joined the Army (22nd Regt.) 5 Oct. 1878; was promoted Lieutenant, Cheshire Regt., 7 April, 1880; was Adjutant, Cheshire Regt., 21 April, 1889, to 20 April, 1893; served in the Burmese Expedition, 1887–88 (Medal with clasp); became Captain 6 Sept. 1885, and Major 21 April, 1896. Major Neville served in South Africa, 1900–2, and was present at operations in the Orange Free State, Feb. to May, 1900, including actions at Karee Siding, Vet River (5 and 6 May) and Zand River; operations in the Transvaal 30 Nov. 1900, to June, 1901; operations in Orange River Colony, June to Sept. 1901; operations in Cape Colony, Sept. 1901. He was mentioned in Despatches 10 Sept. 1901; received the Queen's Medal with four clasps, and was created a Companion of the Distinguished Service Order [London Gazette, 27 Sept. 1901]: "William Candler Neville, Major, Cheshire Regt. In recognition of services during operations in South Africa." The Insignia were presented by the King 17 Dec. 1901. He became Lieutenant-Colonel 21 April, 1904; commanded the 2nd Battn. Cheshire Regt. 1904–8; became Brevet Colonel 21 April, 1907, and retired 6 March, 1908, with the rank of Colonel. Colonel Neville commanded the Depôt and 22nd Area, 1914–16. He married, 5 Jan. 1892, at Newcastle Cathedral, Amy, youngest daughter of Colin G. Ross, of Gruinards, Ross-shire, and Christine Henderson, and they have one son and one daughter.

William Candler Neville.

SMITHSON, WALTER CHARLES, Major, was born at Heighington, Darlington, 26 Jan. 1860, son of Samuel Smithson, Esq., J.P., of Lentran, Inverness, and of Mrs. Samuel Smithson. He was educated at Faithfull's, Storrington, and joined the Militia in 1877, and the 13th Hussars 7 Jan. 1880, becoming Lieutenant 1 July, 1881, and Captain 21 Sept. 1885. He was Adjutant, 13th Hussars, 23 Nov. 1887, to 22 Nov. 1891; was A.D.C. to the late Field-Marshal Viscount Wolseley, K.P., 2 Dec. 1891, to 30 Sept. 1895. He was promoted to Major 1 July, 1896. Major Smithson served in the South African War, 1899 to 1902, and was severely wounded. He was in command of the 13th Hussars 21 July, 1901, to 31 May, 1902, and was present at the Relief of Ladysmith, including the action at Colenso; operations of 17 to 24 Jan. 1900, and action at Spion Kop; operations of 5 to 7 Feb. 1900, and action at Vaal Kranz; operations on Tugela Heights (14 to 27 Feb. 1900) and action at Pieter's Hill; operations in the Transvaal, Aug. to Sept. 1901; Oct. 1901, to April, 1902, and May, 1902; operations in Orange River Colony, April to May, 1902; operations on the Zululand Frontier of Natal in Sept. and Oct. 1901; operations in Cape Colony, Aug. 1901. He was mentioned in Despatches [London Gazette, 8 Feb. 1901 (Sir R. H. Buller, 30 March and 9 Nov. 1900), and London Gazette, 10 Sept. 1901 (Field-Marshal Lord Roberts) and 29 July, 1902 (Field-Marshal Lord Kitchener)]; received the Queen's Medal with five clasps; the King's Medal with two clasps, and was created a Companion of the Distinguished Service Order [London Gazette, 27 Sept. 1901]: "Walter Charles Smithson, Major, 13th Hussars. In recognition of services during the operations in South Africa." The Insignia were sent to Lord Kitchener in South Africa, and presented there. He became Lieutenant-Colonel 1 July, 1901; was given the Brevet of Colonel 1 July, 1904, and retired with the rank of Colonel 2 Feb. 1907. During the European War he commanded the 2/6th Gordon Highlanders, Oct. 1914; was Officer Commanding, Northern Cavalry Depôt, Scarborough, Nov. 1914, to Feb. 1915; was appointed to command 2/1st Yorkshire Mounted Brigade, Feb. 1915, to Nov. 1916. Colonel Smithson was mentioned in the Secretary of State's List [Supplement to the London Gazette, 24 Feb. 1917]. He was given the honorary rank of Brigadier-General 14 Aug. 1917, and was created a C.B.E. in 1919. His favourite pursuits were pig-sticking, polo, stalking and shooting. Brigadier-General W. C. Smithson married, in Feb. 1901, Anne Charlotte Legendre Starkie, daughter of the late John Piers Chamberlain Starkie, of Ashton Hall, Lancaster.

Walter Charles Smithson.

CHUTE, PIERCE THOMAS, Major, was born at Ballyheigul, County Kerry, 21 Jan. 1856, eldest son of Capt. Thomas Chute (late Captain, 22nd Regt.), of Glenfield, Tralee, County Kerry, and Mrs. Thomas Chute. He was educated privately, and joined the 4th Foot 29 Nov. 1876, becoming Lieutenant 13 Oct. 1877, and Captain 7 Dec. 1885. Capt. Chute served in the Burmese Expedition, 1885–89, and received the Indian Medal of 1854, with two clasps (Burmah, 1885–87). He became Major 29 July, 1896. From 1899 to 1902 he served in the South African War. He was Commandant, Nilge River; operations in the Transvaal, east of Pretoria, July to 29 Nov. 1900, including action at Rhenoster Kop; operations in the Transvaal, west of Pretoria, July to 29 Nov. 1900; operations in Orange River Colony (May to 29 Nov. 1900), including actions at Lindley (26 June), Bethlehem (6 and 7 July), Wittebergen (1 to 29 July); operations in Cape Colony, July, 1901, to Feb. 1902; March, 1902; April to 31 May, 1902. He was mentioned in Despatches [London Gazette, 7 May and 10 Sept. 1901]; received the Queen's Medal with two clasps (for Cape Colony, Transvaal and Wittebergen); the King's Medal with two clasps, and was created a Companion of the Distinguished Service Order [London Gazette, 27 Sept. 1901]: "Pierce Thomas Chute, Major, Royal Munster Fusiliers. In recognition of services during the operations in South Africa." The Insignia, Warrant and Statutes were sent to South Africa to Lord Kitchener, and presented by Major-General E. S. Brook at Bethlehem 3 May, 1902. Major Chute retired 21 Jan. 1904. He served in the European War from Oct. 1915, to Jan. 1916, in France, and was Commanding Officer (Temporary Lieutenant-Colonel) at the Depôt, Royal Munster Fusiliers, July, 1916, to Sept. 1918. He was given the rank of Lieutenant-Colonel in the Army 6 June, 1916. Lieut.-Colonel Chute married, 3 July, 1903, at Murree, Punjab, India, Caroline Rosia Langton, daughter of the late Charles Langton, J.P., D.L., of Barkhill, Aigburth, Liverpool.

Pierce Thomas Chute.

GORDON-GILMOUR, ROBERT, Major, of Liberton and Craigmillar, was born 27 Feb. 1857, son of Colonel Wolrige Gordon and Anne, daughter of Robert Gordon, of Hallhead and Esslemont. He was educated at Eton and at Christ Church, Oxford, and joined the 94th Foot 23 Jan. 1878, becoming Second Lieutenant, Grenadier Guards, 17 May, 1879. He served in the South African War of 1879, in the Zulu Campaign, being present at the Battle of Ulundi (Medal with clasp). He became Lieutenant 1 July, 1881, and served in the Sudan Expedition, 1884–85 (Nile), with the Guards' Camel Corps, actions of Abu Klea and Abou Krou, and operations against Metemmeh, Jan. 1885 (Medal with two clasps; Bronze Star). He was promoted to Captain 23 July, 1890. He was Assistant Private Secretary to the Secretary of State for War 27 Jan. 1891, to Aug. 1892, and was promoted to Major 25 Aug. 1896. Major Gordon-Gilmour served in the South African War, 1900–2. He was in command of the 2nd Battn. Grenadier Guards from 30 May to 11 Oct. 1900, and from 28 March to 21 June, 1901, and 8 Aug. to 3 Nov. 1901; operations in the Orange Free State, April to May, 1900; operations in Orange River Colony, May to 29 Nov. 1900, including actions of Biddulphsberg and Wittebergen (1 to 29 July); operations in the Transvaal, Feb. to March, 1901; operations in Orange River Colony, Dec. 1900, to Feb. 1901, and March, 1901 to 31 May, 1902. He was mentioned in Despatches [London Gazette, 10 Sept. 1901, and 29 July, 1902]; received the Queen's Medal with three clasps; the King's Medal with two clasps; was created a C.B., and created a Companion of the Distinguished Service Order [London Gazette, 27 Sept. 1901]: "Robert Gordon-Gilmour, Major, Grenadier Guards. In recognition of services during the operations in South Africa." The Insignia were sent out to South Africa to Lord Kitchener, and presented by General E. S. Brook at Bethlehem 3 May, 1902. He was promoted to Lieutenant-Colonel 28 Oct. 1902; was given the Brevet of Colonel 28 Oct. 1905; was created an M.V.O. in 1905, and became Colonel 13 July, 1907. He commanded the Grenadier Guards, 1908–10; was created a C.V.O. in 1910, and retired 16 July, 1910. He has the Jubilee Medal and King George's Coronation Medal. He commanded the Grenadier Guards in Aug. and Sept. 1914; the 98th Infantry Brigade in Sept. and Nov., and took it to France. He was given the honorary rank of Brigadier-General 3 April, 1917, and was Area Commandant, June to Oct. 1917; Commandant, Cape Troops, XIXth Corps, Nov. to Feb. 1919 (Despatches). He assumed the name of Gilmour in 1887, on succeeding to the estates of his great-uncle, W. L. Gilmour, of Craigmillar. Brigadier-General Gordon-Gilmour is Brigadier and Adjutant, Royal Company of Archers (King's Bodyguard for Scotland); Gentleman Usher of the Green Rod (Order of the Thistle); Grand Master Mason of Scotland. He is a J.P. and D.L. He married, on 19 Oct. 1889, at Madresfield Church, Worcestershire, the Lady Susan Lygon, second daughter of Frederick, 6th Earl Beauchamp, and they have three daughters: Mary, Margaret and Grizel, and a son, John, born 5 June, 1899.

Robert Gordon-Gilmour.

POWELL, ATHERTON FFOLLIOT, Major, was born 6 Jan. 1858, son of the late Capt. Thomas Ffolliot Powell, formerly of the 16th Lancers, and H.M.'s Commissioner of Prisons for Scotland. He was educated at Cheltenham, and joined the Royal Artillery as Lieutenant 31 Jan. 1878, and served in the Sudan, 1885–86, with the Frontier Field Force (Despatches, Medal and clasp, Bronze Star). He became Captain 21 July, 1886, and Major 29 Aug. 1896. In 1897–98 he took part in the operations on the North-West Frontier of India, with the Tirah Expeditionary Force, taking part in the action of Dargai. Operations on the Samana Range and in the Kurram Valley (Medal with three clasps). Major Powell served in the South African War, 1899–1902 (on Special Service with the Rhodesian Field Force, 6 April, 1900, to 30 Sept. 1901); and was present at operations in the Transvaal and Cape Colony 30 Nov. 1900, to 31 May, 1902; operations in Orange River Colony, May and June, 1901. He was mentioned in Despatches [London Gazette, 10 Sept. 1901]; received the Queen's Medal with four clasps, the King's Medal with two clasps, and was created a Companion of the Distinguished Service Order [London Gazette, 27 Sept. 1901]: "Atherton Ffolliot Powell, Major, Royal Garrison Artillery. In recognition of services during the operations in South Africa." The Insignia were sent to Lord Kitchener, and presented by Lieut.-Colonel Vyvyan at Vryberg. He was promoted to Lieutenant-Colonel 2 Nov. 1904; commanded the Heavy Brigade at Plymouth, 1906–10; was given the Brevet of Colonel 2 Nov. 1907, and retired with the rank of Colonel 4 Dec. 1909. Colonel Powell rejoined the Army for temporary service 7 Oct. 1914, and became Commandant, Siege Training Centre, Deepcut. He married, in 1909, Alice, daughter of Major S. H. Powell, of Park Hill, King's Lynn, and they have one son and one daughter.

WHITE, FREDERICK, Major, was born 14 Oct. 1861, son of the late Major George White, R.M.L.I. He joined the Royal Marine Light Infantry 1 Feb. 1879, and served in the Egyptian Expedition of 1882–84, taking part in the bombardment of Alexandria, occupation of the Lines of the town, occupation of Port Said (Medal with clasp; Bronze Star). He again saw active service in the Sudan in 1884, was present at the battles of El Teb and Tamai, and the relief of Tokar (two clasps; 5th Class Medjidie). He was promoted to Captain 26 Aug. 1888; to Major 6 Sept. 1896; was on the Staff, Royal Marines, 29 June, 1896, to 12 Feb. 1899. Major White served in the South African War 3 Feb. 1900, to 13 April, 1902, as Special Service Officer, including service as D.A.A.G., Headquarters, Cape Town; Railway Staff Officer, Sterkstroom; Commandant, Bethulie Bridges, and District command under the Military Governor, Orange River Colony. He was present at operations in Orange River Colony, including the action at Wittebergen; was mentioned in Despatches [London Gazette, 10 Sept. 1901]; received the Queen's Medal with two clasps, the King's Medal with two clasps, and for the defence of Ladybrand was created a Companion of the Distinguished Service Order [London Gazette, 27 Sept. 1901]: "Frederick White, Major, Royal Marine Light Infantry. In recognition of services during the operations in South Africa." Major White's defence of Ladybrand is described by Sir A. Conan Doyle in his "Great Boer War" (pages 377 and 378): "On September 2 another commando of Free State Boers under Fourie emerged from the mountain country on the Basuto border, and fell upon Ladybrand, which was held by a feeble garrison consisting of one company of the Worcester regiment and forty-three men of the Wiltshire Yeomanry. The Boers, who had several guns with them, appear to have been the same force which had been repulsed at Winburg. Major White, a gallant marine, whose fighting qualities do not seem to have deteriorated with his distance from salt water, had arranged his defences upon a hill, after the Wepener model, and held his own most stoutly. So great was the disparity of the forces that for days acute anxiety was felt lest another of those humiliating surrenders should interrupt the record of victories, and encourage the Boers to further resistance. The point was distant, and it was some time before relief could reach them. But the dusky chiefs, who from their native mountains looked down on the military drama which was played so close to their frontier, were again, as on the Jammersberg, to see the Boer attack beaten back by the constancy of the British defence. The thin line of soldiers, 150 of them covering a mile and a half of ground, endured a heavy shell and rifle fire with unshaken resolution, repulsed every attempt of the burghers, and held the flag flying until relieved by the forces under White and Bruce Hamilton." He became Lieutenant-Colonel 11 April, 1903; was given the Brevet of Colonel 11 April, 1906, and retired with the rank of Colonel 11 April, 1909. Colonel White was Draft Conducting Officer from 1915 to 1919 (three Medals).

SCOTT-KERR, ROBERT, Major, was born 8 Nov. 1859, eldest son of the late William Scott-Kerr, of Sunlaws and Chatto, and of his second wife, Frances Louisa, daughter of Robert Fennessy. He was gazetted to the 24th Foot 26 March, 1879, and became Second Lieutenant, Grenadier Guards, 26 Nov. 1879; served in the Zulu Campaign of 1879, and was present at the Battle of Ulundi (Medal with clasp). He became Lieutenant 1 July, 1881, and served in the Sudan Expedition of 1885 (Suakin), receiving the Medal with clasp and the Bronze Star. He was promoted to Captain 16 Dec. 1890, and to Major 19 Sept. 1896. Major Scott-Kerr served in the South African War, 1900–2, and was present in operations in the Orange River Colony, April to May, 1900; operations in Orange River Colony, May to 29 Nov. 1900, including actions at Biddulphsberg and Wittebergen (1 to 29 July); operations in the Transvaal, Feb. to March, 1901. operations in Orange River Colony, Dec. 1900, to Feb. 1901, and March, 1901, to 31 May, 1902. He was mentioned in Despatches [London Gazette, 10 Sept. 1901], received the Queen's Medal with three clasps, the King's Medal with two clasps, and was created a Companion of the Distinguished Service Order [London Gazette, 27 Sept. 1901]: "Robert Scott-Kerr, Major, Grenadier Guards. In recognition of services during the operations in South Africa." The Insignia were sent to Lord Kitchener in South Africa, and were presented by Brigadier-General E. O. F. Hamilton at Heilbron 12 March, 1902. He became Lieutenant-Colonel 14 Feb. 1904; was given the Brevet of Colonel 14 Feb. 1907; became Colonel 7 Nov. 1908. Colonel Scott-Kerr commanded the Grenadier Guards and Regimental District 30 July, 1910, to 29 July, 1914. At the beginning of the war (from 5 Aug. 1914), he commanded the 4th (Guards') Brigade, B.E.F., and he was severely wounded during the Retreat from Mons. Lord Ernest Hamilton, in "The First Seven Divisions" (published by Messrs. Hutchinson), says on pages 76 and 77 that at Villers-Cotterêts "we were again forced into a rearguard action. At nine o'clock the 4th (Guards') Brigade, which was acting rearguard, was overtaken at Soucy, where—in accordance with orders—it had faced about while the 2nd Division was having a two hours' halt for rest and dinner. It was no case of surprise, the brigade being thoroughly prepared, and, indeed, expecting to have to hold the enemy in check. Dispositions were therefore made accordingly. The 2nd Granadiers and 3rd Coldstream held the ground from Montgobert to Soucy, with the Coldstream lining the long grass ride that runs through the woods at Haramont. They were supported by two batteries of the 41st Brigade, R.F.A. The 2nd Coldstream and Irish Guards were posted in rear of the first line along the northern edge of the Forêt de Villers-Cotterêts, at the base of the ridge known as the Rond de la Reine. The enemy commenced by shelling the front line, and shelling it with such accuracy that General Scott-Kerr ordered the Grenadiers and 3rd Coldstream to fall back through the second line, and take up a position in rear. This was done, but subsequently these two battalions were brought up into line with the Irish Guards along the northern edge of the wood, whilst the 2nd Coldstream were sent back to take up a covering position in rear of the wood, along the railway east and west of Villers-Cotterêts Halte. Such was the position without much change up to midday, when the enemy's attack began to slacken, and shortly afterwards they appeared to have had enough of it, and drew off. The 4th Brigade thereupon resumed its march as far as Thury, which was reached about 10.30 p.m. Their casualties in this action amounted to over 300. The Irish Guards in this action had Colonel the Honourable G. Morris and Lieut. Tisdall killed; Major Crichton and Lord Castlerosse wounded. In the Grenadiers the Hon. J. Manners and Lieut. McDougall were killed, and in the Coldstream, Lieut. G. Lambton was killed and Capt. Burton and Capt. Tritton wounded. The Brigadier-General Scott-Kerr was himself badly wounded in the thigh, and the command of the brigade was taken over by Colonel Corry." Brigadier-General Scott-Kerr commanded a brigade, Central Force, Home Defence, from 2 Jan. 1915, to 26 March, 1915; he was commander (graded A.A.G.), 10th and 11th Divisions, New Armies, 15 Oct. 1915, to 7 Dec. 1915; and Brigade Commander, 191st Infantry Brigade, Home Forces, 8 Dec. 1915, to 14 Jan. 1918. He was created a C.B. in 1914, and a C.M.G. in 1919; was mentioned in Despatches twice, and has the Mons Star.

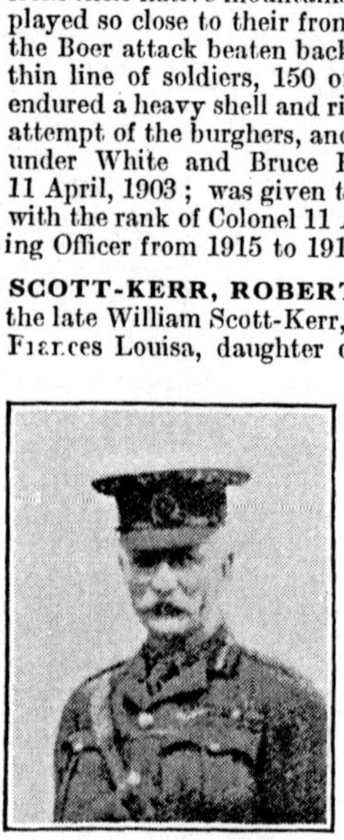

Robert Scott-Kerr.

GIBB, JOHN HASSARD STEWART, Major, was born 13 Feb. 1859, son of Alexander James Gibb, and of Marguerite Vance Balbirnie-Vans. He was educated on the Continent, and at Sandhurst, and was gazetted to the 29th Regt. 13 Aug. 1879; promoted into the 36th Regt. in 1880. He served in the Nile Expedition, 1884 to 1885, and received the Medal with clasp and Khedive's Star, taking part in the operations with the Sudan Frontier Field Force, 1885 to 1886, taking part in the action at Giniss; received the 4th Class Osmanieh; was promoted Captain, Worcestershire Regt., 1 Sept. 1886. He served in Uganda, under Sir Gerald Portal, in the Unyoro Campaign, 1894; was appointed in command of the Expedition to Mruli; received 3rd Class Brilliant Star of Zanzibar. He was promoted Major, 1896. He again saw active service in South Africa, from 1900, to 1902, taking part during the operations in the Orange Free State, Feb. to May, 1900; in the operations in Orange River Colony, May to Nov. 1900; during the operations in Orange River Colony, 30 Nov. 1900, to 31 May, 1902. He was mentioned in Despatches [London Gazette, 10 Sept. 1901]; received the Queen's Medal with three clasps and the King's Medal with two clasps, and was created a Companion of the Distinguished Service Order [London Gazette, 27 Sept. 1901]: "John Hassard Stewart Gibb, Major, Worcestershire Regt. In recognition of services during the operations in South Africa." The Insignia were sent to Lord Roberts 18 Jan. 1902, and presented by Major-General E. O. F. Hamilton at Heilbron 12 March, 1902. He was promoted Lieutenant-Colonel 2 March, 1903, and received the Brevet of Colonel, 1906, and retired 2 March, 1907. He was awarded the Medal of the Royal Humane Society, 1884. He served during the European War, 1914 to 1916, in France; was appointed Commandant, Base Depôt, 25th Division, Sept. 1915. Colonel Gibb married, in 1887, Annie Isabella (who died in 1892), eldest daughter of Major George N. Saunders, Bengal Staff Corps; they have one daughter.

WRIGHT, GEORGE, Major, Royal Artillery, was born on the 18th July, 1860. He entered the Army as Lieutenant, Royal Artillery, 6 April, 1879; became Captain 15 Aug. 1887, and Major 15 Feb. 1897. He served during the South African War, 1899–1902, as Special Service Officer (commanding Rhodesian Field Force Artillery), afterwards on the Staff; during operations in the Transvaal, Dec. to March, 1901, and May, 1901, to March, 1902; taking part in the operations in Orange River Colony, April, 1901; during operations in Cape Colony, Jan. 1901. He was mentioned in Despatches [London Gazette, 10 Sept. 1901], and received the Queen's Medal with four clasps and the King's Medal with two clasps. He was created a Companion of the Distinguished Service Order [London Gazette, 27 Sept. 1901]: "George Wright, Major, Royal Garrison Artillery. In recognition of services during the operations in South Africa." The Insignia were sent to Lord Roberts 18 Jan. 1902. They were presented by Major-General Maxwell at Vryburg 1 April, 1902. He was promoted Lieutenant-Colonel 13 July, 1904, and received the Brevet of Colonel 13 July, 1907, and attained the substantive rank in 1909, retiring in 1910. He served during the European War, and was created a C.B.E. in 1919.

THOMPSON, CHARLES WILLIAM, Major, was born at Sialkote, 24 Nov. 1859, son of General C. W. Thompson; was educated at Felsted School, Essex; joined the 7th Dragoon Guards as Lieutenant 28 Jan. 1882; served in Egypt, 1882, and was present at the actions at Kassassin, Tel-el-Kebir, and the capture of Cairo (Medal with clasp for Tel-el-Kebir, and the Khedive's Star). He was appointed Adjutant, 7th Dragoon Guards, 1886–88; Adjutant to the Dorset Queen's Own Yeomanry, 1888–93. He was promoted Major, 1897, and became Second-in-Command, 1899; passed the Staff College; took part in the South African War, 1900–02, on duty under Military Governor, Pretoria, from 26 June, 1900; was in command of 7th Dragoon Guards, 19 Dec. 1900, to 31 May, 1902, taking part in the operations in the Orange Free State, May, 1900; during operations in the Transvaal in May and June, 1900, including actions near Johannesburg, Pretoria and Diamond Hill (11 and 12 June); operations in the Transvaal, east of Pretoria, July to 29 Nov. 1900; serving during operations in the Transvaal, Dec. 1900; in the operations in Orange River Colony, Feb. 1901, to 31 May, 1902; taking part in the operations on the Zululand Frontier of Natal in Oct. 1901, and in the operations in Cape Colony, Dec. 1900, to Feb. 1901.; was mentioned twice in Despatches [London Gazette, 10 Sept. 1901, and 29 July, 1902]; received the Brevet of Lieutenant-Colonel; awarded the Queen's Medal with four clasps, the King's Medal with two clasps, and created a Companion of the Distinguished Service Order [London Gazette, 27 Sept. 1901]: "Charles William Thompson, Major, 7th Dragoon Guards. In recognition of services during operations in South Africa." The Insignia were sent to Lord Roberts, 18 Jan. 1902, and presented by Major-General Elliott. He was appointed in command of the Dorset Yeomanry from Christmas, 1901, to June, 1902, and again from 1903 to 1907; promoted Lieutenant-Colonel, 1903; Colonel, 1907; G.S.O., 1st Grade, Western Command, 1908–11; created a C.B. in 1911; appointed A.A.G., War Office, 1911–13, and Brigadier-General, commanding Cape of Good Hope District, 1913–14. After the outbreak of the European War he was promoted Major-General, commanding in South Africa, 1914–16, and in command of the troops, West Africa, 1917. He possesses great literary ability; has published "Records of the Dorset Yeomanry" (1893) and "The Story of the Regiment" (1913). His favourite recreations are hunting, shooting, fishing and falconry. He married, 1 Jan. 1889, at Christ Church, Folkestone, Rose Offley Ada, only child of the late Henry Offley Harvey; they have three sons: John Wycliffe, born 2 Dec. 1889; Offley Charles Wycliffe, late Lieutenant, West Yorkshire Regt., born 21 Jan. 1891, killed in action 20 Sept. 1914, and John Rodolf Perronet, Lieutenant, Royal Navy, born in Aug. 1892; and one daughter, Marcella Wycliffe, born 6 March, 1907.

PILSON, ARTHUR FORDE, Major, was born 17 May, 1865, at Downpatrick, County Down, son of the late Conway Pilson, J.P., of Rathvilla, Downpatrick, and of Sarah Overend. He was educated at the Royal School, Armagh, and entered the Royal Dublin Fusiliers 9 May, 1888; was Adjutant, 1st Battn. Royal Dublin Fusiliers, 1890–94. He was promoted Captain, 20 Dec. 1896; took part in operations in Matabeleland, 1896, and acted as Adjutant to the Mounted Infantry (Despatches [London Gazette, 9 March, 1897]; Brevet of Major, and Medal); served in South Africa, 1899–1903, on special service, including service with the Rhodesian Protectorate Regt. and the South African Constabulary; was appointed Assistant District Commissioner, subsequently District Commandant, and afterwards Administrator, No. 4 Martial Law Area, Cape Colony; was mentioned in Despatches [London Gazette, 16 April, 1901], awarded the South African Medal with four clasps; the King's Medal with two clasps, and created a Companion of the Distinguished Service Order [London Gazette, 27 Sept. 1901]: "Arthur Forde Pilson, Capt. and Brevet Major, Royal Dublin Fusiliers. In recognition of services during the operations in South Africa." The Insignia were sent to Lord Roberts 18 Jan. 1902, and presented privately 24 March, 1902. He retired in 1908, and joined the Reserve of Officers. On mobilization at the outbreak of the European War he was appointed Second-in-Command, Depôt, The Royal Irish Regt., and subsequently Adjutant. The following extract appeared in the "Irish Times" of 28 March, 1919: "Mentions for service.—The names of the undermentioned, with others, have been brought to the notice of the Secretary of State for War for valuable services rendered in connection with the war, etc.—Pilson, Brevet Major A. F., D.S.O., R.P., Royal Irish Regt." Major Pilson was demobilized 12 Feb. 1919. He married, 14 Jan. 1907, Aida Constance, second daughter of the late Robert St. John Mayne, of Mount Sedborough, County Fermanagh, and of Mrs. A. C. Ormsby, of Elm Park, County Dublin.

Arthur Forde Pilson.

STEWART, BRYCE, Major, was born 18 June, 1857, son of the late Bryce Stewart, of Rothesay, N.B. He joined the Royal Munster Fusiliers as Second Lieutenant 8 Aug. 1879. He served in the Burmese Expedition, 1885–1888, and received the Medal with two clasps. He next saw active service in South Africa, 1899–1902, and served on the Staff (as Brigade Major, Infantry Brigade, 23 March, 1900, to 26 Jan. 1901); he was afterwards Commandant at Bronkhurst Spruit from 29 June, 1901, and at Orange River from 30 Oct. 1901; he took part in the advance on Kimberley, including action at Belmont; during operations in the Transvaal, east and west of Pretoria, July to 29 Nov. 1900; during operations in Orange River Colony, May to 29 Nov. 1900, including actions at Lindley (26 June), Bethlehem (6 and 7 July), Wittebergen (1 to 29 July); during operations in Cape Colony, south of Orange River, 1899–1900; in the operations in Cape Colony, north of Orange River. Taking part in the operations in the Transvaal 30 Nov. 1900, to July, 1901; operations in Cape Colony, July, 1901, to 31 May, 1902. He was mentioned in Despatches [London Gazette, 10 Sept. 1901], and received the Queen's Medal with three clasps, the King's Medal with two clasps, and created a Companion of the Distinguished Service Order [London Gazette, 27 Sept. 1901]: "Bryce Stewart, Major, Royal Munster Fusiliers. In recognition of services during the recent operations in South Africa." The Insignia were sent to Lord Kitchener, and presented by Colonel Garston at Kimberley 16 May, 1902. He was promoted Lieutenant-Colonel 23 July, 1905, and received the Brevet of Colonel 23 July, 1908, and retired 23 July, 1909. Colonel Stewart married, in 1891, Georgie Gholson, daughter of Norman S. Walter, of Stanten Island, New Zealand.

SUTTON, ALEXANDER ARTHUR, Major, was born 30 Nov. 1861. He took his degree, L.R.C.P., at Edinburgh, and entered the Army (Royal Army Medical Corps) in 1885, and became Major 1 Aug. 1897. He served during operations in Sierra Leone, 1898 to 1899, in the Protectorate Expedition, and was severely wounded; received Medal with clasp. He again saw active service in South Africa, 1899–1902, taking part in the operations in the Orange Free State, Feb. to May, 1903, including operations at Paardeberg 17 to 26 Feb. (slightly wounded); actions at Poplar Grove, Karee Siding, Vet River (5 and 6 May) and Zand River; during operations in the Transvaal in May and June, 1900, including actions near Johannesburg, Pretoria and Diamond Hill (11 and 12 June), and in the Transvaal operations of Aug. to 29 Nov. 1900. Taking part in the operations in the Transvaal 30 Nov. 1900, to May, 1902. He was mentioned in Despatches [London Gazette, 16 April, 1901], and received the Queen's Medal with four clasps, the King's Medal with three clasps, and was created a Companion of the Distinguished Service Order [London Gazette, 27 Sept. 1901]: "Alexander Arthur Sutton, Major, Royal Army Medical Corps. In recognition of services during the operations in South Africa." The Insignia were sent to Lord Roberts 18 Jan. 1902, and were presented by Major-General G. Barton, C.B., in South Africa. He was promoted Lieutenant-Colonel 1 Aug. 1905. He served during the European War; became Colonel 1 March, 1915, and Temporary Surgeon-General 3 Aug. 1916, to 25 Dec. 1917, and was promoted Major-General 26 Dec. 1917. He was commandant, Royal Army Medical Corps, School of Instruction, and O.C., Depôt, 20 Sept. 1913, to 3 Oct. 1915; Deputy Director of Medical Services, Lines of Communication, Salonika Army, Mediterranean Expeditionary Force; British Salonika Force, 11 Nov. 1915, to 14 May, 1917. He was created a C.B. in 1917. Major-General Sutton married (1st), in 1887, Annie, eldest daughter of the late General H. F. Dunsford, C.B.; they had two sons and two daughters. He married (2ndly), 1917, Mary Wilson, R.R.C.

COOPER, EDWARD JOSHUA, Major, was born 21 April, 1858, eldest son of the late Colonel J. H. Cooper, Royal Fusiliers, of Dunboden, Westmeath. He was educated at Marlborough, and at the Royal Military College, Sandhurst; joined the Royal Fusiliers 11 Sept. 1876; was promoted Captain 13 Feb. 1885. He served in the Sudan Expedition, 1886–87, taking part in the operations of the Frontier Field Force, as A.D.C. to the G.O.C. He became Major 28 Nov. 1897. He took part in the South African War, 1899 to 1902. In command of the 2nd Battn. Royal Fusiliers from 25 Dec. 1899, to 13 Feb. 1900; was present at the Relief of Ladysmith, including action at Colenso; operations on Tugela Heights 14 to 27 Feb. 1900, and action at Pieter's Hill; taking part in the Transvaal in May and June, 1900; during operations in Natal, March to June, 1900; taking part in the Transvaal, east of Pretoria, July to 29 Nov. 1900; in the operations in Cape Colony, north of Orange River, including action at Ruidam District from 20 June, 1901, and Stattin from 17 Jan. 1902. Took part in the operations in the Transvaal, Orange River Colony and Cape Colony. He was mentioned in Despatches [London Gazette, 10 Sept. 1901]; received the Queen's Medal with five clasps; the King's Medal with two clasps, and was created a Companion of the Distinguished Service Order [London Gazette, 27 Sept. 1901]: "Edward Joshua Cooper, Major, Royal Fusiliers. In recognition of services during the operations in South Africa." The Insignia were sent to the Commander-in-Chief in India 30 Jan. 1902, and presented by Brigadier-General A. G. F. Browne, commanding Mandalay District 30 May, 1902. He was promoted Lieutenant-Colonel 28 Nov. 1901; Colonel 28 Nov. 1904; served in Tibet 1904, including the march to Lhassa; was mentioned in Despatches, and created a C.B. and a Member of the Victorian Order, 1906; commanded the troops in North China, 1910–14. He took part in the European War, 1914–15, in command of 13th Brigade. Commanded 58th London Division, 1915–16; was mentioned in Despatches, and retired 5 Jan. 1918, with the honorary rank of Major-General. He is a Deputy Lieutenant for Westmeath. He married, 15 Nov. 1894, Effie, eldest daughter of J. F. Balmain, of Dalvrek, Perthshire; they have no children.

Edward Joshua Cooper.

HENEAGE, ALFRED RENÉ, Major, was born 10 June, 1858, son of the late Edward Heneage, M.P. He was educated at Cheltenham College, and entered the Army 11 Sept. 1876. He served with the 2nd Battn. Highland Light Infantry in the Egyptian Expedition, taking part in the Battle of Tel-el-Kebir (wounded), and received Medal with clasp, and Bronze Star. He became Major 22 June, 1898, and took part in the South African Campaign, 1899–1902; during operations in Natal, 1899, including action at Lombard's Kop; taking part in the defence of Ladysmith, including sortie of 7 Dec. 1899, and action of 6 Jan. 1900; during operations in the Transvaal, east of Pretoria, 1900; in the operations in Natal, 1900; during operations in the Transvaal, east of Pretoria, 1900, and operations in Orange River Colony, 1900. Taking part in the Transvaal 30 Nov. 1900, to Aug. 1901, and Nov. to Dec. 1901; in the operations in Orange River Colony, May, 1901. He was mentioned in Despatches [London Gazette, 10 Sept. 1901]; received the Queen's Medal with three clasps; the King's Medal with two clasps, and was created a Companion of the Distinguished Service Order [London Gazette, 27 Sept. 1901]: "Alfred René Heneage, Major, 5th Dragoon Guards. In recognition of services during the operations in South Africa." The Insignia were presented by the King 12 May, 1902. Major Heneage retired from the 5th Dragoon Guards 11 Nov. 1903.

BODE, LOUIS WILLIAM, Major, was born 10 June, 1860. He entered the Army 11 May, 1878; passed the Staff College; served in the Zulu War, 1879, taking part in the action at Ginginhlovo (received Medal with clasp); was promoted Captain 18 Sept. 1887; Major 27 April, 1898; served in the South African War, 1899–1900, taking part in the operations in the Orange Free State, Feb. to May, 1900; during operations in the Transvaal, east of Pretoria, July to 29 Nov. 1900, including actions at Belfast (26 and 27 Aug.) and Lydenberg 5 to 8 Sept.; during operations in Orange River Colony, May to 29 Nov. 1900; during operations in Cape Colony, south of Orange River, 1899–1900. He was mentioned in Despatches [London Gazette, 10 Sept. 1901], and created a Companion of the Distinguished Service Order [London Gazette, 27 Sept. 1901]: "Louis William Bode, Major, Royal Scots. In recognition of services during operations in South Africa." The Insignia were presented by the King 29 Oct. 1901, and the Warrant sent 24 Jan. 1902. He retired from the Royal Scots with the rank of Major. Major Bode married, in 1911, Ethel van Someren, daughter of the late Andrew Taylor, Bombay Civil Service.

MACFARLANE, DUNCAN ALWYN, Major, was born 19 Nov. 1857, son of the late Rev. J. D. Macfarlane, M.A. He entered the Army as Lieutenant in 1st West India Regt., 6 May, 1882; 2nd West India Regt. 20 May, 1882; became Captain, 2nd West India Regt., 11 Jan. 1888, and Captain, King's Own Scottish Borderers, 16 May, 1888. He served on the West Coast of Africa, 1883, in the expedition to Sherbro; took part in the action of Gamaizah in the Sudan Expedition of 1888; received Medal with clasp, and Bronze Star. Took part in the operations on the Nile, 1889; during the operations in Chitral, 1895, with the relief force; was present at the storming of the Malakand Pass (was dangerously wounded); received Medal with clasp. Served during operations on the North-West Frontier of India, 1897–98, with the Tirah Expeditionary Force; was mentioned in Despatches [London Gazette, 5 April, 1898], and received Brevet of Major 20 May, 1898, and two clasps; he became Major 5 Jan. 1900. He took part in the South African Campaign, 1899–1902; during operations in the Orange Free State, 1900, including action at Vet River (5 and 6 May) and Zand River; during operations in the Transvaal in May and June, 1900, including actions near Johannesburg and Pretoria; operations in the Transvaal, east of Pretoria, 1900; operations in the Transvaal, west of Pretoria, 1900, including action at Zilikat's Nek; operations in the Transvaal 30 Nov. 1900 to 31 May, 1902: he was Commandant at Bronkhurst Spruit 11 to 17 April, 1901, afterwards at Eareste Fabreiken 18 April to 3 May, 1901; he was mentioned in Despatches [London Gazette 10 Sept. 1901, and 29 July, 1902]; received the Brevet of Lieutenant-Colonel 22 Aug. 1902; the Queen's Medal with three clasps; the King's Medal with two clasps, and was created a Companion of the Distinguished Service Order [London Gazette, 27 Sept. 1901]: "Duncan Alwyn Macfarlane, Major, King's Own Scottish Borderers. In recognition of services during the operations in South Africa." The Insignia were sent to the Commander-in-Chief in South Africa 2 Aug. 1902, and forwarded to Major Macfarlane's private address. He became Lieutenant-Colonel 10 Nov. 1905; received the Brevet of Colonel 1 April, 1907, and promoted Colonel, 1909. He was Brigade-Commander, Seaforth and Cameron Infantry Brigade, Scottish Command, May, 1911. He served during the European War, and became Brigadier-General, and was employed as Inspector of Infantry from 1915. He was created a C.B., 1915. He retired 10 July, 1918. He married, in 1913, Edith Lavinia, daughter of Rear-Admiral the Hon. Richard Bingham.

KING-KING, JAMES GURWOOD, Major, was born 2 Sept. 1863, son of Capt. Francis J. King-King (late 13th Hussars) and of Zumala, daughter of Colonel Gurwood, C.B. He was educated at Rugby, and entered the Army 10 March, 1883. He was promoted Captain, May, 1891. He served in the North-West Frontier of India, 1897–98, as Adjutant, 1st Battn. Royal West Surrey Regt., Mohmand-Malakand; during the operations in Bajaur and in the Mamund Country; received Medal with clasp. He accompanied the Tirah Expeditionary Force in 1897–98; was present at the capture of the Sampagha and Arhanga Passes; during the reconnaissance of the Saran Sar and action of 9 Nov. 1897, taking part in the operations against the Khani Khel Chamkanis; during operations in the Bazar Valley 25 to 30 Dec. 1897; was mentioned in Despatches [London Gazette, 18 March and 5 April, 1898]; received the Brevet of Major and clasp. He served in South Africa, 1899–1902, as Special Service Officer, afterwards on the Staff; during operations in the Orange Free State, Feb. to May, 1900; in the operations in the Transvaal, west of Pretoria, July to 29 Nov. 1900; taking part in the operations in Orange River Colony (May to 29 Nov. 1900), including actions at Wittebergen (1 to 29 July, 1900); in the operations in Cape Colony, south of Orange River, 1899–1900; he was employed with Mounted Infantry. He was mentioned in Despatches [London Gazette, 10 Sept. 1901, and 29 July, 1902]; awarded the Queen's Medal and three clasps; the King's Medal and two clasps, and was created a Companion of the Distinguished Service Order [London Gazette, 27 Sept. 1901]: "James Gurwood King-King, Major, Royal West Surrey Regt. In recognition of services during the operations in South Africa." The Insignia were sent to the Commander-in-Chief in South Africa 2 Aug. 1902, and forwarded with the Warrant to Major King-King's private address. He was promoted Lieutenant-Colonel, Sept. 1910; commanded 2nd Battn. Queen's Regt., and retired in 1912. On the outbreak of the European War he was appointed in Aug. 1914, to be G.S.O., 10th Division; served as Brigadier-General, 10th Division; mentioned in Despatches, and received the Brevet of Colonel; and afterwards Brigadier-General, General Staff, Southern Command; was C.B. 1 Jan. 1919; appointed Honorary Brigadier-General on retirement, March, 1919. He is a Justice of the Peace, County Hereford. He married (1st), in 1887, Annie, daughter of Major Kiggell, J.P., of Limerick (died 1889), and they had one son; and (2ndly) in 1892, Dina May, eldest daughter of Frederick Sillem, of The Green, Esher, and they had a daughter.

SHORE, OFFLEY BOHUM STOVIN FAIRLESS, Major, was born 9 Aug. 1863, the only son of Offley Bohum Shore and Anna Maria Shore, *née* Leishman. He was educated privately and abroad; he entered the Army as Second Lieutenant, the West Yorkshire Regt., 19 May, 1882, and was transferred to the Bengal Cavalry 27 April, 1884; was promoted Captain 10 May, 1893; appointed D.A.A.G., India, 1895–1900, and passed the Staff College. He served on the North-West Frontier of India, 1897–98; in Malakand, as Section Commandant, Lines of Column, 5 Aug. to 30 Sept. 1897; took part in the action at Landakai, and during operations in Bajaur; received Medal and clasp. He took part in the Tirah Expedition, 1897–98, as Section Commandant, Lines of Column (5 Oct. 1897, to 10 Feb. 1898), afterwards on Staff; served during the action of Chagru Kotal; he was mentioned in Despatches [London Gazette, 5 April, 1898]; received the Brevet of Major 20 May, 1898, and clasp. He became Major 10 July, 1901. He next saw active service in South Africa, 1900–2; served as Special Staff Officer, afterwards on Staff; as Commandant, Matjesfontein, and as Deputy Administrator at Ceres; in the Transvaal, July, 1900, to 29 Nov. 1900, taking part in the operations in Orange Free State from March to May, 1900; in the operations in Cape Colony, Feb. to March and May to June; taking part in the operations in the Transvaal 30 Nov. 1900, to Feb. 1901, and April to 31 May, 1902; in the operations in Orange River Colony, May, 1902; operations in Cape Colony, Feb. to March, 1902. He was mentioned in Despatches [London Gazette, 10 Sept. 1901]; received the Queen's Medal with three clasps; the King's Medal with two clasps, and was created a Companion of the Distinguished Service Order [London Gazette, 27 Sept. 1901]: "Offley Bohum Stovin Fairless Shore, Major, Indian Army. In recognition of services during operations in South Africa." The Insignia were sent to the Commander-in-Chief in India 31 Oct. 1903, and presented at Delhi 27 Dec. 1903. He was promoted Lieutenant-Colonel 1 June, 1906. He received the Brevet of Colonel 30 July, 1910, and became Colonel 1 Jan. 1911, and Temporary Brigadier-General 3 April, 1913, to 29 April, 1918. He was General Staff Officer, 1st Grade, Headquarters, India, 11 April, 1909, to 2 April, 1913. He was Director of Staff Duties and Military Training, India, 3 April, 1913, to 12 Jan. 1916. He served in the European War in the Indian Expeditionary Force "D," 13 Jan. to 11 Oct. 1916; as Deputy Inspector-General of Commissions, Indian Expeditionary Force "D," Mesopotamian Expeditionary Force, 12 Oct. 1916, to 9 July, 1917; he was appointed General Staff Officer, 1st Grade, Mesopotamian Expeditionary Force, 10 July, 1917, to 29 April, 1918. He was created C.B., 1914, and C.I.E., 1916. Colonel Shore married, in 1908, Caroline Perry, daughter of Charles P. Sinnickson, of Philadelphia, U.S.A.

CAMPBELL, WALTER Capt. and Brevet Major, was born 30 July, 1864, son of the late John Campbell, of Rathfern, County Antrim. He was educated at Wellington, and at Trinity College, Cambridge; graduated B.A. 1885; joining the Gordon Highlanders as Second Lieutenant, 5 Feb. 1887. He was promoted Lieutenant, Dec. 1890, and served with the Waziristan Field Force from 1894 to 1895 (Medal with clasp). He took part in the operations of the Chitral Relief Force in 1895, and was in the storming of the Malakand Pass (Medal with clasp). From 31 Jan. 1896, to 20 Jan. 1899, he was Adjutant to the Gordon Highlanders; was promoted Captain 11 Jan. 1897; Major 28 April, 1906; Lieutenant-Colonel 1 Jan. 1907, and Colonel 19 July, 1911. He accompanied the Tirah Expeditionary Force (1897–98); was present at the actions at Dargai and Sampagha and Arhanga; he was mentioned in Despatches [London Gazette, 1 March and 5 April, 1898], received Brevet of Major, with two clasps. Major Campbell served with great distinction throughout the South African War (1899–1902), with the 1st Battn. Gordon Highlanders. He was subsequently transferred to the Highland Brigade as Brigade Major, and finally appointed D.A.A.G. Army Headquarters, taking part in the advance on Kimberley, including action at Magersfontein; during operations in the Orange Free State, Feb. to May, 1900, including operations at Paardeberg (17 to 26 Feb.); actions at Poplar Grove, Dreifontein and Vet River (5 and 6 May); during operations in the Transvaal, east and west of Pretoria, July to 29 Nov. 1900; during operations in Orange River Colony, May to 29 Nov. 1900, including actions at Wittebergen (1 to 29 July); in the operations in Cape Colony, south of Orange River, 1899–1900; in the operations in Cape Colony, north of Orange River. Taking part in the operations in the Transvaal 30 Nov. 1900, to 31 May, 1902; he was mentioned in Despatches [London Gazette, 16 April, 10 Sept. 1901, and 29 July, 1902], and awarded the Queen's Medal with five clasps, the King's Medal with two clasps, and was created a Companion of the Distinguished Service Order [London Gazette, 27 Sept. 1901]: "Walter Campbell, Capt. and Brevet Major, Gordon Highlanders. In recognition of services during operations in South Africa." The Insignia were presented by King Edward VII. 24 Oct. 1902; the Warrant sent 4 Nov. 1902. From 19 Oct. 1902, to 17 May, 1903, Major Campbell was D.A.A.G. to the 3rd Army Corps, when he was posted as D.A.Q.M.G. at the War Office. He was appointed in 1904 Deputy Assistant Director of Movements at the War Office, remaining in the post until 5 Oct. 1908. General Staff Officer, 2nd Grade, Aldershot Command, 1908 to 1911; A.Q.M.G., Scottish Command, 1911 to 1914. During the European War Colonel Campbell rendered valuable service to the nation. In the opening months he acted as A.A. and Q.M.G., becoming D.A. and Q.M.G., Temporary Brigadier-General, 1 Oct. 1914, and Temporary Major-General, 13 July, 1915. In Oct. 1915, he was appointed D.Q.M.G. He was mentioned eleven times in Despatches, created a C.B. in 1915, K.C.M.G. in 1917, and K.C.B. in 1919, and became Major-General 1 Jan. 1916. In 1904 he married Gladys Isabella, eldest daughter of Major Lutley Jordan, late 34th Regt. They have two daughters.

LAMING, HENRY THORNTON, Major, was born 28 July, 1863, son of the late James Laming. He was educated at Eton and Sandhurst; entered the Army 10 March, 1883; became Captain, 1888, and Major 8 July, 1898. He served in South Africa, 1899–1902, during operations in Natal, 1899, including actions at Talana and Lombard's Kop; taking part in the defence of Ladysmith, including sortie of 7 Dec. 1899, and action of 6 Jan. 1900; taking part in the operations in Natal, March to June, 1900, including action at Laing's Nek (6 to 9 June); during operations in the Transvaal, east of Pretoria, July to 29 Nov. 1900, including actions at Belfast (26 and 27 Aug.) and Lydenberg (5 to 8 Sept.). He was in command of the 18th Hussars 19 Dec. 1900, to 9 April, 1901; afterwards in command of the 24th Battn. Imperial Yeomanry 16 Sept. 1901, to 31 May, 1902; during operations in the Transvaal 30 Nov. to Sept. 1901; during operations in the Orange River Colony, Sept. 1901, to 31 May, 1902; he was mentioned in Despatches [London Gazette, 8 Feb. 1901 (Sir G. S. White, 23 March, 1900; Sir R. H. Buller, 9 Nov. 1900), and [London Gazette, 10 Sept. 1901]. He received the Queen's Medal with six clasps, and the King's Medal with two clasps; and was created a Companion of the Distinguished Service Order [London Gazette, 27 Sept. 1901]: "Henry Thornton Laming, Major, 18th Hussars. In recognition of services during the operations in South Africa." The Insignia were presented by the King 24 Oct. 1902; the Warrant was sent 4 Nov. 1902, to Major Laming. He retired from the 18th Hussars 7 Oct. 1903. He served during the European War as Second-in-Command, 11th Reserve (now 5th Reserve) Cavalry, since 1914. He was given the O.B.E., 1919. Major Laming married, in 1898, Ella Lœtitia, daughter of the late Robert Cunliffe, D.L. They have two sons and one daughter.

DE ROUGEMONT, CECIL HENRY, Major, was born 17 Dec. 1865, son of Irving Frederick de Rougemont and of Mary Rugge de Rougemont (*née* Rugge-Price). He was educated at Harrow, and the Royal Military Academy, Woolwich, and entered the Royal Artillery 29 April, 1885; was promoted Captain 1 April, 1895; took part in the Expeditionary Force sent out to Dongola, when he was given command of a gunboat (Despatches [London Gazette, 13 Nov. 1896]; 4th Class Medjidie; British Medal; Khedive's Medal with two clasps); took part in the operations on the Nile, 1897 (clasp); received the Brevet of Major 16 Nov. 1898, and became Major 30 June, 1900; was present at Atbara (Despatches [London Gazette, 24 May and 28 Sept. 1898]; clasp); and was wounded at Khartum (Brevet of Major; British Medal, and clasp to Khedive's Medal). He served in the South African War, 1899–1901; in command of 12th Battn. Imperial Yeomanry 7 May to 30 Nov. 1901; taking part in the advance on Kimberley and the Relief of Kimberley; during operations in the Orange Free State, Feb. to May, 1900, including operations at Paardeberg, actions at Poplar Grove, Dreifontein, Houtnek (Thoba Mountain), Vet River (5 and 6 May) and Zand River; during the operations in the Transvaal, May and June, 1900, including actions near Johannesburg, Pretoria and Diamond Hill; during operations in the Transvaal, west of Pretoria; during operations in the Orange River Colony, including actions at Bethlehem and Wittebergen; taking part during the operations in the Transvaal and Orange River Colony, Nov. 1900, to Dec. 1901. He was mentioned in Despatches [London Gazette, 10 Sept. 1901]; received the Queen's Medal with seven clasps, and was created a Companion of the Distinguished Service Order [London Gazette, 27 Sept. 1901]: "Cecil Henry de Rougemont, Major, Royal Horse Artillery. In recognition of services during the operations in South Africa." The Insignia were presented by the King 24 Oct. 1902; the Warrant sent 4 Nov. 1902. He was Brigade Major, Woolwich District, 12 Feb. to 31 March, 1903; Brigade Major, IVth Army Corps, 1 April to 30 Sept. 1903; D.A.A.G., Woolwich District, 1 Oct. 1903, to 31 May, 1905; D.A.A. and Q.M.G., Second-in-Command, 1 June, 1905, to 30 Sept. 1907; General Staff Officer, 2nd Grade, East Anglian Division, Eastern Command, 30 Sept. 1911, to 7 March, 1913. Colonel 18 May, 1916, and retired as Brigadier-General, 1920. He served in the European War, 1914–19, as General Staff Officer, 1st Grade, 19th Division, British Expeditionary Force, 7 Jan. to 23 July, 1915; became Temporary Brigadier-General, Royal Artillery, 8th and 9th Army Corps, Mediterranean Expeditionary Force, 2 Aug. 1915, to 17 May, 1916; was Brigadier-General, 63rd (R.N.) Division, England; British Armies in France, 20 June, 1916, to 8 Jan. 1919; was Brigadier-General, Royal Artillery, B.E.F., in France, 9 Jan. to 24 June, 1919. He was mentioned in Despatches and created a C.B. in 1916; C.M.G., 1918, and received the Légion d'Honneur. He is a member of the Victorian Order. Colonel de Rougemont married, in 1914, Muriel Evelyn, only daughter of Evelyn Heseltine, of The Goldings, Great Warley, Essex. They have one son.

CAMPBELL, JOHN, Capt. and Brevet Major, was born 7 March, 1871, son of Capt. W. H. Campbell, Madras Staff Corps, and of Ellen Magdalena, eldest daughter of Major-General J. D. Mein, Madras Royal Horse Artillery. He was educated at Haileybury, and entered the Army from Sandhurst 7 Jan. 1892; posted to the 79th Cameron Highlanders; was promoted Captain, April, 1898; served in the Sudan, 1898; was present at the actions of Atbara and Omdurman; was mentioned twice in Despatches [London Gazette, 24 May and 30 Sept. 1898]; was promoted Brevet Major, and awarded the British Medal, and Khedive's Medal with two clasps; was Adjutant, 1st Cameron Highlanders, 1 Feb. 1898, to 4 Dec. 1900; Staff College, 1901–3; Staff Captain, War Office, April, 1904, to Dec. 1905; Brigade Major, Aldershot, Dec. 1905, to April, 1908; Chief Instructor, School of Musketry, Hythe, June, 1909, to June 1913. He served in South Africa, 1900–1, as Adjutant, 1st Battn. Cameron Highlanders, March to Sept. 1900, and 1 June to 5 Dec. 1901; during operations in the Orange Free State, Feb. to May, 1900, including actions at Vet River (5 and 6 May) and Zand River; taking part in the operations in the Transvaal in May and June, 1900, including actions near Johannesburg, Pretoria and Diamond Hill (11 and 12 June); during operations in Orange River Colony, May to Sept. 1900, including actions at Wittebergen (1 to 29 July), and Ladybrand (2 to 7 Sept.); during operations in the Transvaal, June to Dec. 1901. He was mentioned in Despatches [London Gazette, 10 Sept. 1901]; awarded the Queen's Medal with five clasps, and created a Companion of the Distinguished Service Order [London Gazette, 27 Sept. 1901]: "John Campbell, Capt. and Brevet Major, Cameron Highlanders. In recognition of services during the operations in South Africa." The Insignia were presented by the King 12 March, 1902; the Warrant sent 19 March, 1902. He was promoted Major 9 March, 1905, and Brevet Lieutenant-Colonel 21 Feb. 1914. He commanded the 2nd Cameron Highlanders May, 1914, to May, 1915; wounded at Hooge 10 May, 1915; appointed Temporary Brigadier-General commanding 121st Brigade 7 Oct. 1915, to April, 1918, and attained the substantive rank of Lieutenant-Colonel, 1916. He was created a C.M.G., 1915; awarded the Order of St. Stanislaus, 3rd Class, with Swords, Aug. 1915; promoted Brevet Colonel, Jan. 1917; created a C.B. Jan., 1918; appointed Temporary Major-General commanding 32nd Division, April, 1918; transferred to command 31st Division, May, 1918, to March, 1919. Mentioned in Despatches seven times; Commandeur de l'Ordre de la Couronne and Croix de Guerre (Belgian), March, 1919; appointed Temporary Brigadier-General commanding 1st Highland Brigade in Germany, March, 1919, to 31 Oct. 1919; appointed Brigadier-General commanding 11th Infantry Brigade 1 Nov. 1919; promoted Colonel, June, 1919; Commandeur de la Légion d'Honneur, Oct. 1919. Colonel Campbell married, in 1901, Amy Leighton, third daughter of the Rev. Canon Hopkins.

HAYDEN, FREDERICK ARTHUR, Major, was born at Helmdon, Northamptonshire, on 10 Aug. 1861, son of the Rev. C. F. Hayden, late Scholar and Fellow of Corpus Christi College, Oxford. He was educated at Winchester College, and entered the Army 22 Jan. 1881. He was promoted Captain, 1888, and Major, 1898. Major Hayden took part in the South African War, 1900–1902; as Acting Commandant, Simon's Town, 25 Aug. to 9 Oct. 1900; during operations in Cape Colony, south of Orange River, 1900. He served as Adjutant, 3rd Battn. West Riding Regt. 1 Jan. to 10 May, 1902; during operations in Cape Colony 30 Nov. 1900, to May, 1902. He was mentioned in Despatches [London Gazette, 10 Sept. 1901], awarded the Queen's Medal with clasp, King's Medal with two clasps, and created a Companion of the Distinguished Service Order [London Gazette, 27 Sept. 1901]: "Frederick Arthur Hayden, Major, West Riding Regt. In recognition of services during the operations in South Africa." The Insignia were presented by the King 18 Dec. 1902; the Warrant sent 14 Jan. 1903. He was promoted Lieutenant-Colonel, Duke of Wellington's Regt., 2 Feb. 1908, and retired on full pay, 1912. When the European War broke out he was called out for service and was employed with the New Armies; served in France, 1915–19, in command of the 9th Battn. Duke of Wellington's Regt., and has been mentioned twice in Despatches, and given the O.B.E. He married, at Murree, India, 17 Sept. 1885, Henrietta Grace Lambert, daughter of Colonel Anthony Stewart (Bengal Staff Corps), of Ardvorlich.

MAUDE, FREDERICK STANLEY, Major, was born 24 June, 1864, youngest son of General Sir Frederick Francis Maude, V.C., G.C.B., and Lady Maude. He was educated at Eton and Sandhurst, and was gazetted to the Coldstream Guards in Feb. 1884. He served in the Sudan; was present at the actions of Hasheen and Tamai (1885), receiving the Medal and clasp and the Khedive's Star. Lieut. Maude was appointed Adjutant, 1st Battn. The Coldstream Guards, in 1888, and held this appointment until 1892. He was promoted to Captain in 1891; passed the Staff College in 1896; became Major in 1899. The following notes are supplied by Colonel Sir James Magill, K.C.B.: "At the outbreak of the South African War, Major Maude was Brigade Major, Brigade of Guards, in the Home District, so he was unable to accompany the troops first sent out. Resigning his post in London, he speedily followed, and on the 12th of Feb. 1900, joined the Staff of Major-General Pole-Carew, as Brigade Major, Guards Brigade, then encamped at Modder River. A few days subsequently, as he was observing the Boer position at Magersfontein, he came to the conclusion that the enemy had retired, and this proved to be correct. Marching from Modder River, the Guards Brigade arrived at Klip Drift on 19 Feb. The possession of the Drift was a most important item in the scheme of attack which Lord Roberts was planning against the Boer forces under General Cronje, who had taken up a position at Paardeberg, some 20 miles distant. After an obstinate defence General Cronje surrendered on the 27th Feb. and next day some 4,000 prisoners passed through the lines of the Guards Brigade, *en route* for Cape Town. On the 7th of March the action of Poplar Grove was

Frederick Stanley Maude.

fought, and on the 10th that of Dreifontein, this latter by the 6th Division. To complete the success of the day, an advance of the Guards was ordered (but eventually countermanded). While making the necessary dispositions Major Maude met with a severe accident. His horse fell and crushed him badly, injuring his right shoulder. Though he was only a few days absent from duty the injury proved very grave, and lasting in its effects, and he never fully recovered the use of his right arm. Bloemfontein, the capital of the Free State, was occupied on 13 March, and two days later a flying column under Major-General Pole-Carew left to open up the railway communications to the south. During the halt at Bloemfontein the 11th Division was formed. It was composed of the Guards and the 18th Brigade, and was under the command of Major-General Pole-Carew, while Major Maude continued as Brigade Major to the Guards Brigade, under Major-General Inigo Jones. It was not until 1 May that the march on Pretoria was resumed. Kroonstad was reached on 5 May, Johannesburg was occupied on the 31st, and on 5 June the troops entered Pretoria, and Major Maude, with one company of the 2nd Battn. Coldstream Guards, took formal possession of various official buildings. The Union Jack was hoisted in the Market Square, and that afternoon the troops were marched past Lord Roberts, the Guards Brigade leading. A week later, negotiations for peace having broken down, Lord Roberts attacked the Boers at Diamond Hill. Continuing the advance, Belfast was reached on 25 Aug. Here Lord Roberts's force met that under Sir Redvers Buller coming up from Natal, and both were heavily engaged that day and the succeeding. From Belfast the 11th Division marched, and reached Nooitgedacht on the 31st inst. This was the principal camp of the British prisoners of war. The enemy still retiring, the Guards Brigade pushed on, and eventually arrived at Koomati Poort, the extreme limit of the Transvaal Territory, on 24 Sept. After a brief stay the Guards entrained for Pretoria, and the 11th Division having been broken up, Major-General Inigo Jones's Brigade proceeded to Bloemfontein, and thence to guard the Drifts on the Orange River, a movement rendered necessary by the enemy having sent sundry raiding parties into Cape Town. The headquarters of the Guards was established at Naaupoort Junction on 24 Dec., and here Major Maude remained until his departure from South Africa on the 9th March, 1901, to take up another appointment. While at Naaupoort, his work was mainly concerned with Staff duties connected with the various mobile columns and small garrisons which the changed features of the campaign had rendered necessary. From his arrival in South Africa till his departure, he carried out the lesson of his favourite motto, ' with both hands earnestly.' " The official record of his service is: "South African War, 1899–1901, including advance on Kimberley, operations in the Orange Free State, actions at Poplar Grove, Dreifontein, Karee Siding, Vet River and Zand River; and operations in the Transvaal, actions near Johannesburg, Pretoria, Diamond Hill and Belfast; operations in Cape Colony." Major Maude was mentioned in Despatches, received the Queen's Medal with six clasps and—for general gallantry during the campaign, when acting as Brigade Major—was created a Companion of the Distinguished Service Order [London Gazette, 27 Sept. 1901]: "Frederick Stanley Maude, Major, Coldstream Guards. For services in South Africa." The Insignia were presented in Canada by the Earl of Minto. In May, 1901, Major Maude had gone out to Canada as Lord Minto's Military Secretary, and he held this appointment until 1904. He made all the arrangements for the Royal Tour in Canada in Sept. and Oct. 1901, and was awarded a Companionship of St. Michael and St. George. The Insignia of the Order were presented to him by the Duke of York at Ottawa in Sept. 1901. He became Private Secretary to the Secretary of State for War in 1905; was Chief Staff Officer, Coast Defences, Plymouth, from 1906 to 1908, and D.A.A. and Q.M.G., General Staff, 2nd London Division, Territorial Force, under Sir Henry Mackinnon, from 1908 to 1909; Assistant Director, Territorial Force, 1909–12. His work in the Military Training Directorate in connection with the Territorial Force was most valuable. He became Lieutenant-Colonel in 1907; Colonel in 1911, and was Chief Staff Officer, 5th Division, at the Curragh, from 1912 to 1914. He was at the War Office, in the Military Training Branch, under Sir William Robertson, from Jan. 1914, until the outbreak of the European War, when he was appointed to the Staff of the 3rd Corps, under General Pulteney, and proceeded to France. Colonel Maude was promoted to Brigadier-General in Oct. 1914, and was given command of the 14th Infantry Brigade. He took an active part in the fighting in Flanders, under General Sir Charles Fergusson, and was present at Hill 60. He was created C.B. in Feb. 1915. In April, 1915, he was severely wounded, spending three weeks in Lady Ridley's Hospital in London, when he returned to his Brigade in France. He became Major-General in June, and assumed command of the 33rd Infantry Division in England, but had hardly settled down to his new duties when, in Aug. 1915, he was sent at a few hours' notice to the Dardanelles. Maude arrived at the Dardanelles on the 23rd Aug.; interviewed Sir Ian Hamilton on that date, and was given command of the 13th Division, which had seen some very hard fighting. In Dec. a few days after the evacuation at Suvla Bay had been successfully accomplished, Maude was sent with his Division to assist at the evacuation of the Helles area, and he had to carry out the disembarkation from Gully Beach. A sudden storm made Gully Beach impracticable, the sea was rising fast, and Maude had to trek down to " W " Beach, to see if he and his men could not manage to get away from there. The situation was intensely critical. At any moment the Turks might have awakened to the fact that the British Army was stealing away, and that the rearguard were at their mercy. Here Maude was at his best; all ranks testify to his conduct and to the nerve and example by which he kept everyone cool and steady. Nothing would induce him to part with a huge valise he was carrying; he was about the last man to embark, and the higher command became very anxious about him. After the event an amusing parody was written, beginning " Come into the lighter, Maude," and went the rounds of the Expeditionary Force, amongst whom Maude's reluctance to leave enemy soil was well known. For he had always held that an allowance of drafts and munitions on the Western scale would have given

us the Peninsula, thereby enabling our fleet to get through the Straits to Constantinople. The 13th Division went to Egypt from the Dardanelles, and subsequently to Mesopotamia. In June, 1916, Major-General Maude was created a K.C.B., and the award was gazetted on the 23rd Dec. 1916. In July, 1916, he was given command of the Tigris Corps, with the rank of Temporary Lieutenant-General, and in Aug. he was appointed Commander-in-Chief to the whole Expeditionary Force. He at once recognized that his first task was to reorganize his Army and improve his line of communications, which he proceeded to do, and did it so thoroughly and well that it was possible to resume operations in Dec. The following is a typical letter from Sir Stanley Maude to an old Army colleague, showing the simple, straightforward nature of the General, and his ingrained modesty:

" General Headquarters,
" Mesopotamian Expeditionary Force,
" January 22nd, 1917.
" My dear ——,
" Many thanks for your letter, dated the 8th July, and for all the good wishes that it contains. I can assure you that I appreciate them very greatly, more especially so, coming as they do from one whom I have had the honour of serving under in the field. I cannot help feeling, however, that you rate any service that I may have rendered too highly, for I think that any measure of success I may have gained during the war has been due almost entirely to those men I have had the good fortune to command. . . . We have had a very strenuous time out here. Our long line of communications by water with, at first, inadequate river craft, the absence of roads and railways, the lack of water, except at the rivers, the great shortage of local supplies, and the long time which it necessarily takes for our stores and supplies to reach us, all make it an intensely complicated problem. But it is, at the same time, an absorbingly interesting one, and I live every minute of it. When I first took over command I devoted three months to organization and developing our resources, and, that done, I moved my headquarters up to the front. In the middle of December, having accumulated a sufficiency of supplies, we were well forward to warrant a movement. Everyone is cheery and in good spirits, and the men get good food and plenty of it. The transport and supply arrangements are working magnificently, and with everyone pulling together like one man, we are bound to make progress. In fact, it is indeed a privilege to command forces full of such willing, obedient, and gallant soldiers. Will you please forgive these hurried lines, but I am very busy ? My kind regards, and with every good wish for 1917 to you both,
" Yours sincerely,
" F. S. Maude."

Sir Stanley Maude was promoted to Lieutenant-General after the recapture of Kut in Feb. 1917. He was seven times mentioned in Despatches during the European War. It is unnecessary to describe here his victorious campaign in Mesopotamia, as extracts are given below from the writings of his friends and from the speeches of Mr. Lloyd George, Lord Curzon and Mr. McKenna. In the hour of his triumph General Maude was smitten down by a sudden illness, and died on 18 Nov. 1917, to the grief and consternation of the whole Empire. His Majesty the King at once sent a message to the General Officer commanding the forces in Mesopotamia, expressing his sorrow and sympathy. Sir Stanley Maude was buried at Baghdad on 19 Nov.

It was written at the time:

" Sometimes by a soldier's grave the near presence of Death is brought home to the mourners by the thud of bullets and the sound of bursting shell; sometimes it is possible for the burial to be accompanied and its impressiveness enhanced by such music and ceremony as befit the occasion. To-day we stood beyond the sound of the enemy guns; but though no drum beat and no funeral note sounded, though no gun-carriage bore the coffin, though the mind was not stirred by that most touching of all symbols, the charger carrying the empty saddle, yet the greatness of the man and the honour in which all held him lent more dignity and weight to the ceremony than could any outside suggestion have given. And this scene by the bare desert, engraved on the mind of every mourner—and none were present but those who had served and loved him—an impression so deep and lasting as can never be effaced nor ever put into words. Officers from nearly every brigade in Mesopotamia were present, and all his Staff, and among the khaki soldiers stood a group of seamen; yet the figures who seemed most in keeping with the ceremony and most in touch with the General's spirit were the few private soldiers of his old division, who stood as the procession slowly passed, silent and motionless, each leaning over his rifle with bowed head. . . .

" Lieut.-General S. Maude was a typical example of the corps of officers of the Old Army. Tall, courteous, firm and thoroughly acquainted with the profession of arms, he was always popular and always successful. His bright spirit could never brook pessimism of any kind, and his invincible cheerfulness and fine character were worth a King's ransom on service. He never thought of himself, but only of his troops and the cause, and his letters were full of admiration for the men he commanded. They breathe a noble spirit, while the record of his deeds upon the great rivers speaks for itself."

A brother General says of General Maude : " His successes were among the most brilliant of the war, and in Mesopotamia he reaped the laurels that will go down the ages. The modern type of General, planning campaigns to scale, says, ' On the 20th of next month, at 3.3 a.m.,' a certain thing will happen—and it possibly may. Maude was a real General, a fighting General in the old Napoleonic sense. He was always ready for the unexpected, and could always grapple with the unforeseen. I have never known him in a difficulty he could not get out of by sheer resource and audacity. This is not saying he was irresponsible and reckless. If necessary he could bide his time; but he always believed in giving the enemy no rest, and his almost invariable plan—it worked, too—was to force the fighting. Like all leaders, he was a good judge of men, and had a quick, keen eye for favourable position in the terrain of campaign. As a personality he was a simple, kindly man, straight as a die and honest as the day. His men were always devoted to him, and they had good reason, for the welfare of those who fought under him was always a guiding thought with him. He could not be happy and comfortable if his soldiers were miserable and uncomfortable. He himself has earned the title of the good soldier in this world and the next."

Mr. Lloyd George moved in the House of Commons that a sum not exceeding £25,000 should be granted to Lady Maude, in recognition of the eminent services rendered by the late Lieut.-General Sir Frederick Stanley Maude, K.C.B., C.M.G., D.S.O., while commanding His Majesty's Forces during the late campaign in Mesopotamia. He said: "The services which Sir Stanley Maude rendered to the Empire, notably in Mesopotamia, were distinguished, far-reaching and permanent in their effects. He found British prestige at a very low ebb in a quarter of the globe where prestige counts for much. The British Army in the East had suffered a series of severe reverses. One great enterprise on which a good deal of the strength of the Empire had been concentrated had to be abandoned. One British Army had surrendered to the Turkish forces, after another British Army had been defeated in an attempt to relieve it. In Egypt we had a large force sheltering behind the desert and the canal from an inferior Turkish Army. This tale of discomfiture and humiliation spread throughout every bazaar in the East, and, like a tree, grew as it spread. Before it ran into irreparable mischief for the Empire, the genius of Sir Stanley Maude had changed and restored the position. I know well how much of this success was due to the reorganization of the transport service by Sir John Cowans and his able Staff, the reorganization of the Medical Service by Sir Alfred Keogh and his assistants, and the reinforcements brought in by Sir William Robertson and Sir Charles Munro. But the enemy also had time to reinforce and to strengthen his forces. The ground lent itself to entrenchments. These entrenchments were constructed under the advice and direction of German engineers. The Turk was fighting his best in a climate which suited him and did not suit us. But against all these obstacles the leadership of Sir Stanley Maude and the valour of his Army triumphed. The highest proof of generalship is not so much in the winning of a victory as in its exploitation. No General ever made better or wiser use of his victory than did Sir Stanley Maude. The relentless pursuit of the defeated Army, which ultimately destroyed it, and ended in the dramatic capture of Baghdad, sounded throughout the East. These were amongst the finest feats in military history, and they had a magical effect on the fame and position of Britain throughout the whole of the East. The Germans realized it. Sir Stanley Maude's achievements had destroyed their cherished dream. They sent one of their ablest Generals there to effect a reconquest, and I do not think that it is too much to say that their abandonment of that enterprise was due very largely to their appreciation of the fact, when they came there, that they were confronted by a leader of exceptional resource and power. But Sir Stanley Maude's real greatness was displayed in the use which he made of the victory after it had been obtained. He showed as much wisdom as an administrator as he displayed skill as a General. Every great General has a strain of statesmanship, and Sir Stanley Maude exhibited great gifts of statesmanship in his administration of that difficult country. Whilst ruling with a firm hand, he won the esteem and affection of that gifted but suspicious race, not merely by the equity of his rule, but by the intelligent sympathy which he displayed. He possessed that rare tact which is a blend of gentleness and understanding, and the article that appeared in an Arab paper after his death, and which was, I think, reproduced in the British Press last week, is the highest tribute that could have been paid to his great qualities as a Governor and a man. He died a victim of the inbred courtesy of his fine character. I heard a story from a member of his Staff the other day. Sir Stanley Maude visited a plague-stricken area at the invitation of the inhabitants. They were anxious to extend him a welcome for the many kindnesses which he had displayed. They gave him a great one, and they offered him a small hospitality. Though he so well knew the peril that he had actually forbidden any soldier in his escort to eat or drink while on that visit, he himself ran the risk rather than hurt the susceptibilities of a people anxious to give him a welcome. There was poison in the cup, and he died within a few days. Sir Stanley Maude will always be remembered as one of the great figures of this war, not merely for what he achieved, but for what he was. I know not what destiny may have in store for the famed land which he conquered, but of two things I am certain. The first is that the whole course of its history will be changed for the better as a result of the victory and the rule of Sir Stanley Maude; and the second is that his name will always be cherished by the inhabitants of that land as that of the gentlest conqueror who ever entered the Gates of Baghdad."

Mr. McKenna said, in seconding the motion moved by the Prime Minister: "Sir Stanley Maude's great services are so recent that they live fresh in the memory of each of us. He found a situation full of anxiety and even of peril, and he converted it into a triumph of organization and of military achievement. He died in the full tide of victory and glory."

Lord Curzon said in the House of Lords: "The late General Maude was a man who was destined, not merely by birth but by natural inspiration, to a soldier's career. The son of an eminent General, who himself won the Victoria Cross, an Eton boy, a Guardsman, he had served in many capacities in this country and abroad, in Canada, in South Africa, in Egypt, and at the War Office, before his opportunity came. War is a great leveller of distinction, but it is also a supreme discoverer of merit; and it is not too much to say that General Maude was one of the discoveries, although to none of his friends was he one of the surprises, of the present war. At the beginning of the war he was only a Lieutenant-Colonel. In 1914 he was given a brigade and went to France. He took part in the Battle of Mons, and was wounded in the retreat upon Paris. In 1915 he was sent in command of a division to the Dardanelles, and there, in command of his force—known locally, I believe, as the 'Iron Legion'—he shared, not merely in the perils and privations, but also in the glories of that momentous and fateful campaign. He was indeed almost the last British officer to leave the Peninsula when evacuation took place. And I have also been told that had the Turkish forces shown anything like the alertness which might have been expected, they might have materially altered the course of future events and themselves captured on the beaches the future conqueror of Baghdad. In 1916 General Maude was sent with his division to Mesopotamia, and there he took part in the arduous operations that were then in course of being carried out for the relief of the beleaguered garrison of Kut. As your Lordships will remember, that place fell after an heroic defence by General Townshend and his brave men; and in August of that year General Maude succeeded Sir Percy Lake as Commander-in-Chief of the British Expeditionary Force in Mesopotamia. It was a dark moment in the history of the war; it was a critical moment in the fortunes of Great Britain in the East. The issues of the conflict themselves trembled in the balance, and the prestige of the British Empire may be described not unfairly as having been at stake. General Maude had to deal with an enemy flushed with victory, entrenched in a position of exceptional strength, provided with all the scientific military resources which he had received from his European ally. The advance upon Baghdad in the month of December, 1916, the dramatic crossing of the Tigris, the forced evacuation of Kut by the Turks, the disorderly retreat of the flying enemy upon Baghdad, the rapid pursuit by General Maude and his men, constituted a military achievement of no mean order. But General Maude was by no means content with his initial victory; he was not the kind of man to rest upon his laurels. Following the Turks with great speed up the Dialah River in one direction, up the Tigris in another, and, at a later date, up the waters of the Euphrates, he inflicted upon them a series of crushing defeats, which rendered them incapable of any further sustained military effort. He lifted the danger which overhung the Persian border, and which might, unless arrested, have reacted through Persia upon Afghanistan, and upon India itself, and he occupied the whole of the Baghdad villayet. And be it remembered that he carried out the series of operations which I have described, labouring under a sense of bitter disappointment at the failure of our Russian Allies, who were at that time in the north-western part of Persia, to extend to him the support which he had reason to expect. The last few months of General Maude's life were devoted to the task of organizing and administering the territories which he had won; and there, in November, 1917, in an act of unthinking courtesy, he contracted that fatal pestilence which always broods behind the atmosphere of the East, and in a few hours passed away. Thus, in a few months of time, it was given to General Maude to achieve what many military commanders do not attain in a lifetime. He retrieved a great disaster; he won a resounding victory; he recovered a province—almost a country—once one of the gardens of the East, which had mouldered for centuries under the blight of Turkish misrule. Nay, more. By a single stroke or series of strokes, he may be said to have altered the history of the world. It is surely inconceivable that the inhabitants of those fair regions can ever be thrust back into the servitude from which General Maude and his forces succeeded in emancipating them. And then, in the hour of his triumph, the General was stricken down, not indeed on the battlefield, but, as I have pointed out, by a death not less honourable and infinitely more pathetic. My Lords, if we turn from the contemplation of the soldier to that of the man, there is a consensus of opinion among those who knew General Maude well—of whom, unfortunately, I was not one—that not merely did he possess the genius of a military commander, but that he had many of those qualities of personal character which endeared him to all those with whom he was associated. The soul of chivalry, he was not less strict in the discipline that he applied to himself than he was in that which he applied to others. A non-smoker, almost a total abstainer, he set an example of conscientious abnegation and self-control which profoundly affected the conduct of those who served under him. At the same time, he was kind and thoughtful to a degree of his soldiers, and, as abundant testimony confirms, he was exceptionally considerate to the native inhabitants of the countries that had passed under his sway. Thus I think we may say of the departed General that in manifold respects he fulfilled the ideal of the Happy Warrior which was drawn for us in such moving terms by one of the greatest of our poets more than a century ago."

In 1893, Sir Stanley Maude married Cecil Cornelia Marianne St. Leger, daughter of the late Colonel the Right Honourable Thomas Edward Taylor, M.P., of Ardgillan Castle, County Dublin, and their children are: Edward Frederick (Lieutenant, Royal Horse Artillery); Stella Cecil and Beryl Mary.

YALE, JAMES CORBET, Major, was born 1 March, 1859, eldest surviving son of the late W. C. Corbet Yale Jones-Parry. He was educated at Marlborough; entered the Army 13 Aug. 1879; was promoted Captain, 1888. He was promoted Major, 1899, and served in the South African War, 1899–1902, as Commandant, Frederikstad, from 13 Sept. 1901, taking part in the operations in Natal, 1899; was present at the Relief of Ladysmith, including action at Colenso; during operations of 17 to 24 Jan. 1900, and action at Spion Kop; operations of 5 to 7 Feb. 1900, and action at Vaal Kranz; took part in the operations on Tugela Heights 14 to 27 Feb. 1900, and actions at Pieter's Hill; during operations in Natal, March and April, 1900; serving during operations in the Transvaal, April, 1901, to May, 1902. He was mentioned in Despatches [London Gazette, 10 Sept. 1901]; awarded the Queen's and King's Medals and five clasps, and was created a Companion of the Distinguished Service Order [London Gazette, 27 Sept. 1901]: "James Corbet Yale, Major, West Yorkshire Regt. In recognition of services during the operations in South Africa." The Insignia, Warrant, etc., were sent to Major Yale's private address

1 Aug. 1902. At the end of the South African War, Major Yale was appointed in command 1st Battn. P.W.O. West Yorkshire Regt., 1902–6. He retired from the Army with the rank of Colonel. He married, in 1896, Violette, second daughter of C. L. Halbot, of Bradford, and they have four sons and two daughters.

DOBELL, CHARLES MACPHERSON, Capt. and Brevet Major, was born 22 June, 1869, son of Richard R. Dobell, of Beauvoir Manor, Quebec. He entered the Army 20 Aug. 1890; served in the Hazara Expedition, 1891 (Medal with clasp); became Lieu-

Charles M. Dobell.

tenant 13 July, 1892; was Adjutant, Royal Welsh Fusiliers, 7 July, 1896, to 6 Nov. 1900; took part in operations in Crete, 1897–98 (Brevet of Major 8 March, 1899); became Captain 22 Feb. 1899. He served in the South African War, 1899–1900, in command of a regiment of Mounted Infantry (22 Feb. to 13 July, 1900); Relief of Kimberley; operations in the Orange Free State, Feb. to May, 1900, including operations at Paardeberg (17 to 26 Feb.), actions at Poplar Grove, Dreifontein, Houtnek (Thoba Mountain), Vet River (3 and 4 May) and Zand River; operations in the Transvaal in May and June, 1900, including actions near Johannesburg, Pretoria and Diamond Hill (11 and 12 June); operations in Orange River Colony, May to 15 July, 1900, including actions at Wittebergen (1 to 13 July). He was mentioned in Despatches [London Gazette, 10 Sept., 1901]; received the Queen's Medal with six clasps, and was created a Companion of the Distinguished Service Order [London Gazette, 27 Sept. 1901]: "Charles Macpherson Dobell, Capt. and Brevet Major, Royal Welsh Fusiliers. In recognition of services during the operations in South Africa." The Insignia, Warrant and Statutes were sent to the G.O.C. troops in Hong-Kong, and presented by him on 17 March, 1902. He served in China in 1900 (Medal), and West Africa (Northern Nigeria) in 1906; was mentioned in Despatches [London Gazette, 18 Sept. 1906, and 2 July, 1907]; was given the Brevet of Lieut.-Colonel (29 Sept. 1907), and received the Medal and clasp. He was promoted to Major 28 Sept. 1907. He was G.S.O.3, H.Q. of Army, 1 April, 1907, to 1 Feb. 1909; was promoted to Lieut.-Colonel, Bedfordshire Regt., 4 May, 1912; was G.S.O.2, H.Q. of Army, 2 Feb. 1909, to 31 March, 1911; was Military A.D.C. to the King 4 Nov. 1910, to 2 June, 1915; was given the Brevet of Colonel 4 Nov. 1910; became Colonel 1 Sept. 1913; was Temporary Brigadier-General and Inspector-General, West African Frontier Force, 1 Sept. 1913, to 22 April, 1916, during which time he commanded the Allied Forces in the Cameroons, having been promoted to Major-General 3 June, 1915. General Dobell commanded the Western Frontier Force, Egyptian Expeditionary Force, 9 June to 18 Sept. 1916; was Temporary Lieut.-General 19 Sept. 1916, to 21 April, 1917, commanding No. 3 Section, Canal Defences, Egyptian Expeditionary Force (19 Sept. to 22 Oct. 1916), and commanding Eastern Frontier Force, Egyptian Expeditionary Force, 23 Oct. 1916, to 1 May, 1917. He was Divisional Commander, India, from 6 Aug. 1917. He was created a C.M.G. in 1914, and a K.C.B. in 1916. He is a Fellow of the Royal Geographical Society.

The following is an extract from General Dobell's Despatch, dated

"War Office, 31st May, 1916.

"The following Despatch has been received by the Secretary of State for War from Major-General Sir Charles M. Dobell, K.C.B., Commanding the Allied Forces in the Cameroons :—

"General Headquarters,
"Cameroons, 1st March, 1916.

"My Lord,

"I have the honour to forward herewith a summary of the operations carried out by the Allied force under my command, covering the period between the capitulation of Duala, 27th September, 1914, and the termination of active operations.

"I have, in this despatch, endeavoured to maintain a correct perspective, remembering that our operations in this theatre of war are incomparable in magnitude to those taking place elsewhere. For purposes of comparison I may, however, add that the number of troops of both nations at my immediate disposal at the commencement of the campaign amounted to 4,300 West African native soldiers; on the 21st November, 1915, this number had been increased to 9,700, including Indian troops. In these numbers the British and French forces were approximately equal.

"As Your Lordship is aware, I have kept the proper authorities informed in some detail as to the proceedings and progress of the troops under my command. These despatches I have endeavoured to forward at intervals of about a fortnight; I do not, therefore, propose to enlarge on such questions as the organization and preparation of the force placed at my disposal, nor the naval measures that were taken in a campaign to which the adjective 'amphibious' may be applied in its widest sense. It is perhaps sufficient to state I fully realized, that the conquest of a country which is some 306,000 square miles in area, or roughly one and a half times the size of the German Empire, defended by a well-led and well-trained native force, plentifully supplied with machine guns, was no light task.

"2. On my passage from the United Kingdom early in September, 1914, I learnt at various ports of call that the operations which had taken place on the Nigerian frontier had not been as successful as had been anticipated,

thus confirming my opinion that Duala, the capital and chief port of the Cameroons, must be made my immediate objective. I entertained no doubts as to the ability of the Royal Navy to overcome the difficulties and make a landing at Duala feasible, and my best hopes were realized when I was informed that H.M.S. Challenger could force a passage through the sunken wrecks and other obstructions in the Cameroon River, and reach a point 7,000 yards from the town. This was made possible owing to the mine sweeping and other preparatory work which had been carried out by the Royal Navy and Nigeria Marine, under the direction of Captain Fuller, R.N., H.M.S. Cumberland.

"On my summons for the surrender of the Colony being refused, and after duly notifying the German Commandant of my intention, I ordered a bombardment of the town to commence early on 26th September; this in combination with a land demonstration, made by way of one of the neighbouring creeks, was sufficient to induce the Commandant, on 27th September, to surrender the towns of Duala and Bonaberi, with a small strip of land in their environs. The surrender of Duala secured us a safe and convenient base for the future absorption of German territory; further, the capture of stores, supplies, field guns, and the removal of over 400 German Europeans was a great loss to the German Field Force, whilst the seizure of the large amount of shipping and numerous small craft in the harbour was an inestimable advantage to us.

"3. My first object was to consolidate the position already won, and with this object in view an Allied force was allotted the task of clearing the country up to and including the Japoma Bridge, Midland Railway, whilst a British force commenced to make headway towards Maka on the Northern Railway line. Reconnaissances by land and water were carried out with uniformly successful results. I may remark incidentally that neither the climate nor the character of the country favoured the offensive: officers and men were exposed to the most trying conditions; incessant tropical rains, absence of roads or even paths, a country covered with the densest African forest—all contributed to the difficulties with which the troops were faced. Had it not been for the existing railways, which formed a line of advance as well as supply, it is difficult to see how progress could have been made.

"The country in the immediate vicinity of Duala is perhaps typical of the greater portion of the Cameroons in which my troops have operated, excepting beyond Northern railhead where the country becomes open and, on account of its greater altitude, healthier; but all the coast line, and for some 150 miles inland, one meets the same monotonous impenetrable African forest fringed, on the coast line, by an area of mangrove swamp in varying depth. The zone is well watered by numerous rivers, of which the Wuri, Sanaga and Njong present serious military obstacles. Once outside this belt conditions change at once, supplies and live stock are obtainable, and open grass lands are reached; the one unusual geographical feature is the Cameroon Mountain, some 13,000 feet high, which rises abruptly from the sea, its slopes clothed with valuable plantations, and on which the hill station of Buea, the former administrative capital of the Protectorate, is perched.

"4. By the first week in October we had made good the country as far as Maka and the left bank of the Dibamba creek. The Japoma railway bridge, 900 yards in length, was broken in two places, but a fine feat was performed by the French tirailleurs in forcing this passage under a galling rifle and machine-gun fire. The Royal Navy and Royal Marine Light Infantry also materially contributed to this success.

"I now judged that I could move a force by the Wuri River on Jabassi, so as to secure Duala from any attack from the north-east; a mixed Naval and Military force, supported by armed craft, was organized and an attack was delivered on 8th October. It is regrettable that this operation was not at first successful, difficult country, novel conditions and the fact that our native troops encountered machine-gun fire for the first time are contributory causes to failure; nevertheless it became necessary completely to reorganize the force and repeat the operation, with the result that Jabassi was taken on 14th October. From this place a force was pushed out to Njamtan, and the country around Jabassi was cleared of the enemy.

"My next objective was Edea, on which place I determined an advance should be made from three directions, two by land and one by river. Strong forces were moved from Japoma and by the Njong River to Dehane, thence by a track towards Edea. The third force proceeded by the Sanaga River; the navigation of this river is most difficult, dangerous bars hinder entrance into its mouth and sand banks obstruct the passage up to Edea. The feat performed by Commander L. W. Braithwaite, R.N., in navigating an armed flotilla on the Sanaga was a remarkable one. Thus the combined movement, outlined above, was entirely successful and Edea was occupied on the morning of 26th October. This result had not been achieved without hard fighting, particularly on the part of the force operating by the line of the railway. It was during the preliminary operations in this undertaking that Lieutenant Child, Director of Nigeria Marine, Commander Gray, and Captain Franqueville, of the French Army, lost their lives through the capsizing of their boat in the surf at the mouth of the Njong River—valuable lives whose losses it was difficult to replace.

"5. During the latter half of October the small force under Lieut.-Colonel Hayward was continuously engaged with the enemy on the line of the Northern Railway, but had made such good progress that I was in a position to arrange for an attack on Victoria, Soppo, and Buea. As in previous operations I divided my force, part of which was moved by water to Tiko, part from Susa by Mpundu on the Mungo River, and the third portion supplied by the Royal Navy and Royal Marine Light Infantry moved by sea to Victoria. The opposition met with cannot be described as serious, but the country was very trying to troops; the energy with which our advantage was pushed appeared to demoralize the Germans, and by the 15th November we had secured Buea, with Soppo and Victoria. We inflicted considerable casualties on the enemy whilst escaping very lightly ourselves.

"With the double object of striking an effective blow at the enemy and at the same time relieving the pressure on the southern frontier of Nigeria I decided to clear the whole of the Northern Railway of the enemy, and for this purpose concentrated a force at Mujuka, under command of Colonel Gorges, on 30th November. This force gradually fought its way to the North and reached Nkongsamba (railhead), which was surrendered to us on 10th December. It is worthy of remark that we took two aeroplanes at this place—the first machines that had ever arrived in West Africa. The advance was continued to Dschang, which was occupied on 3rd January, and the fort destroyed; most of the hostile resistance was met with at the Nkam River, but our columns rarely remained unmolested and experienced difficulties in operating in a class of country totally different to that to which they had by then become accustomed. I decided, as soon as the fort at Dschang had been destroyed, that the place should be evacuated and Nkongsamba, with its outpost at Bare, should be our most advanced position. It was unfortunate that we could not continue to hold Dschang, as our withdrawal gave a false impression to the natives and emboldened the enemy. However, with the troops at my disposal I did not feel strong enough to maintain and supply a post 55 miles north of railhead, in a difficult and mountainous country.

"6. Early in 1915 the situation was as follows:—

"British troops holding Duala, the Northern Railway with Bare, Victoria, and Dibombe (a defended post south-west of Jabassi).

"French troops on the line of the Midland Railway up to and including Edea, which place was partially isolated as one span of the first of the two bridges had been destroyed. A detachment at Kribi was protecting that seaport from land attack.

"Ships and armed craft of the Allied Navies had visited the whole of the Cameroons seaboard, and had established bases for small craft to patrol the rivers where navigable.

"By this time approximately 1,000 male Europeans, only 32 of whom were incapable of bearing arms, had been deported for internment in Europe.

"Towards the end of 1914 the French, under General Aymerich, and Belgian troops based on French Equatorial Africa, commenced to make their presence felt in the South and South-East, but my force was separated from them by a distance of approximately 400 miles.

"In the North an Allied force was fully occupied in observing Mora and Garua.

"At and near Ossidinge a small British force from Nigeria and German forces were in contact.

"Notwithstanding the number of troops—British, French, and Belgian—in the country it was impossible at this period to co-ordinate their movements, owing to the vastness of the area over which they were scattered and the impossibility of establishing any means of intercommunication between the various Commanders. Furthermore, it was difficult for me to pursue a very active policy, as it was necessary to maintain comparatively strong garrisons in the places already occupied. Posts on our lines of communications were also absorbing troops from my somewhat depleted force, amongst which sickness was beginning to play its part.

"7. It was on the 5th January that the German Commander endeavoured to deliver a serious blow to the French force commanded by Colonel Mayer. Two practically simultaneous attacks were made against his force; the first at Kopongo, on the railway, the second at Edea. I had obtained some knowledge of the German Commander's intention, and the post at Kopongo had been slightly augmented, with the happy result that the attack on this point was easily repulsed, but not until the railway and telegraph lines had both been cut and all communication with Edea severed. The troops at Edea had, however, to bear the brunt of a more serious movement. The locality of Edea is by no means easy to defend owing to the proximity of the forest, the scattered nature of the buildings, and inequality of the ground; but so skilfully were the defences devised, and so good was the French marksmanship, that at the termination of the combat the Germans left on the field 23 Europeans dead and 190 native soldiers killed and wounded. The French loss consisted of 1 European sergeant and 3 tirailleurs killed and 11 tirailleurs wounded. A machine gun, number of rifles, ammunition and equipment fell into the French hands. It is significant that this was the first and last occasion on which the Germans attempted an operation of this nature on a comparatively large scale.

"Towards the end of January, Lieut.-Colonel (now Brigadier-General) Cunliffe arrived at Duala on a mission from Lagos, and as a result of a conference it was agreed that a more active prosecution of the campaign in the Northern Cameroons should be undertaken. I detached Major (now Lieut.-Colonel) W. D. Wright, V.C., a most able officer, from the staff of the British Contingent under my command and placed his services at the disposal of the Officer Commanding the Allied Forces at Garua. I also arranged with Captain Fuller, R.N., for the despatch of a naval field gun to Yola, via the Niger and Benue Rivers, for eventual use against the forts at Garua.

"The early days of February were marked by great hostile activity in the neighbourhood of Northern Railhead. Lieut.-Colonel Cockburn, commanding a battalion of the Nigeria Regiment, had a serious encounter with the enemy at Mbureku on the morning of the 3rd February, resulting in the capture of the hostile camp, a large quantity of small-arm ammunition, and equipment. We were, however, unable to reap the full advantage of our success, as Lieut.-Colonel Cockburn was obliged to transfer his force to the neighbourhood of Harmann's Farm, where the Sierra Leone Battalion was engaged with the enemy. During these two incidents we lost nearly 120 native soldiers killed, wounded, or missing; but, after we had consolidated our position at Bare, the enemy did not follow up the slight advantage he had gained.

"Constant activity during February had failed to gain for us any material advantage to the north of the railway, and there were a series of small incidents which culminated in the second attack by our troops on the points known as Stoebel's and Harmann's Farms on 4th March. I regret that this attack was not successful and we lost some valuable lives, including Major (Lieut.-Colonel) G. P. Newstead, commanding the Sierra Leone Battalion, and Captain C. H. Dinnen, Staff Captain, an officer of great promise. The enemy must, however, have suffered in a similar degree, as it was later found that he had evacuated his defensive position and retired further north.

"During February I received valuable reinforcements from French and British West African Colonies, and I was enabled to reconstitute my force and place a more homogeneous unit at the disposal of Lieut.-Colonel R. A. de B. Rose, commanding the Gold Coast Regiment.

"8. On the 12th March a mission from French Equatorial Africa, at the head of which was Monsieur Fourneau, Lieutenant-Gouverneur du Moyen Congo, reached Duala. Its object was to invite my co-operation in an immediate advance, in conjunction with the troops under General Aymerich from south-east and east, against Jaunde. Since the occupation of Duala, Jaunde had been transformed into the temporary seat of the Colonial Administration. I fully realized the political and strategic importance of Jaunde, but demurred embarking on such an operation at that moment. It was late in the season and the rains were already beginning, besides which the troops I was able to employ were insufficient to ensure success in the absence of effective co-operation, in the immediate vicinity of Jaunde, by the troops under General Aymerich. Owing to the difficulty of communication it was quite unsafe to count on this. However, in view of the great advantage which would follow an early occupation of Jaunde, I consented to co-operate with all my available strength, and the 20th April was fixed as the date on which an advance should be made from the line Ngwe-So Dibanga, on the Kele River. I consequently entrained a British force, commanded by Lieut.-Colonel Haywood, on 7th April, which was to commence a methodical advance in co-operation with the French troops under Colonel Mayer. The forcing of the line of the Kele River and the position at Ngwe, both of which places were obstinately defended, occasioned my troops some losses. I further found it necessary to despatch a force to Sakbajeme to deny the crossing of the Sanaga River at that place to the enemy. It soon became evident that the enemy was withdrawing troops from other and more distant parts of the Colony to resist our further advance.

"At midnight 23rd/24th April the blockade of the Cameroons was declared, and every artifice was used to deceive the enemy, and incessant and unremitting activity was maintained by the Royal Navy on the coast line, so as to induce the enemy to believe that disembarkation would be made at a point from which a force could be marched on Jaunde. Campo had been occupied by a Naval detachment, and boat patrol of the river as far as Dipikar was maintained.

"The advance from the line already mentioned was subsequently postponed till 1st May, on which date the French and British columns moved forward to make good Eseka and Wum Biagas respectively.

"The French advance on Eseka was conducted with some difficulty, as broken bridges denied them the use of the railway line for supply trains. Commandant Mechet, who conducted the advance, successfully overcame all difficulties, and after being seriously opposed at Sende, reached Eseka on 11th May.

"Turning to the British advance, on 1st May Lieut.-Colonel Haywood recommenced his march eastwards from Ngwe, and driving in the hostile outposts at Ndupe, on the 3rd May his force was facing the formidable position which the enemy had established on the left bank of the Mbila River at Wum Biagas. We captured the position on 4th May, but not without serious losses in European officers. A warm tribute is due to the bravery and steadiness displayed by our Native troops, and to the pluck and endurance of the European ranks in face of such stubborn resistance.

"As previously arranged, the French force at Eseka now moved north and joined the British at Wum Biagas, and Colonel Mayer left Edea to assume command of the Allied expedition. Stores and supplies were pushed forward by road, and a naval 12-pounder gun was despatched to reinforce our artillery.

"Owing to the heavy casualties which had occurred in the ranks of the two battalions of the Nigeria Regiment and the inability of Nigeria, owing to the many calls made by General Cunliffe's troops, to supply me with trained soldiers, I decided towards the end of May to establish a training depot at Duala. The recruits were enlisted in Nigeria, and transferred to Duala for training. This proved a great success, and by its means 536 soldiers were trained and passed into the ranks.

"9. On 11th May I received a message from the Governor-General of French Equatorial Africa, which informed me that the progress of the troops under General Aymerich had not been as rapid as expected, and that as neither Dume nor Lomie had been captured, no definite date could be given for the advance from those places. As I realized that the advance on Jaunde, if delayed for any length of time, would be seriously interfered with by the rains, and the sickness among both Europeans and natives, which was already causing me some anxiety, would rapidly increase, I instructed Colonel Mayer to push on with all vigour, in consequence of which he left Wum Biagas on 25th May.

"I regret that supply difficulties soon made themselves evident; the country was barren, and with all available carriers and the few motor vehicles at my disposal, at that time only three, I was unable to transport food for Europeans and natives with sufficient rapidity. Handicapped by the almost impenetrable bush and a terrain which afforded many defensive positions, the advance became exceedingly slow. At every turn of the road the advance was met by machine-gun fire, so that during the 25th and 26th May only 5 miles was made good. It took two days to force the enemy from Njok. The enemy evidently had received reinforcements and commenced to interfere with our line of communication, which was peculiarly susceptible to attack, while the long convoys of carriers were singularly prone to panic. I received an appeal from Colonel Mayer for reinforcements, as in addition to other disabilities dysentery had broken out in his force. I sent forward such troops as were available and took measures to obtain more carriers from the West African Colonies.

"From 31st May till 4th June Colonel Mayer was held up at a position at Matem which presented more than usual difficulties owing to the swamps, which rendered a turning movement impossible. By the 5th June only 12 miles from Wum Biagas had been made good. About this date Colonel Mayer informed me that owing to sickness, especially amongst Europeans, and to the stubborn resistance of the enemy, he was of opinion that the further advance of his column on Jaunde was impracticable, and he proposed, pending further instructions, to establish himself on the Puge River, where he could await the approach of General Aymerich's troops. I immediately informed the Governor-General of Equatorial Africa of the situation, adding that unless he had recent news of General Aymerich's advance I should be obliged to withdraw Colonel Mayer's force to the line of the Kele River. On 7th June Governor-General Merlin informed me by telegraph that he had received no further news from the Southern Cameroons. I thereupon decided to withdraw our force to the Ndupe River preparatory to holding a line So Dibanga–Ngwe. A serious attack on one of our convoys of 500 carriers, and the consequent loss of food supplies, decided Colonel Mayer to retire without further delay. During the 16th and 17th June our rearguards were harassed, but never broken, and the enemy suffered considerably in his attacks. I deemed it advisable to send forward a reinforcement of the last troops at my disposal so that the pressure on our withdrawal could be relieved; these troops, after leaving Duala on the morning of the 15th June, bivouacked the following day at Ngui, 35 miles beyond Edea, having completed much of the distance in heavy tropical rains. On the following morning, after resuming their march, they reached Colonel Mayer's column at a most opportune moment during a heavy attack on the rearguard. Not till 28th June did the hostile activity cease, when our posts were firmly established at Ngwe and on the Kele River at So Dibanga. In comparison to the size of our force the casulaties were serious, 25 per cent. being either killed or wounded. I regret that this operation was not more fruitful in results, and I fully recognize the fact that Colonel Mayer was not in a position to undertake, single-handed, an advance on Jaunde, but I had hoped that the pressure that was being brought on the hostile forces in the Southern Cameroons would have had the effect of preventing a concentration against us.

"During this period our troops near Northern Railhead were not in a position to undertake any serious offensive action.

"10. There was now an unavoidable lull in the operations caused by the rains. I seized this opportunity to send as many British officers and non-commissioned officers as possible to the United Kingdom for a few weeks' rest, and I arranged that most of the native troops from Nigeria and the Gold Coast should, in turn, visit their own Colonies. I managed, however, to send detachments to operate near the Njong and Campo Rivers respectively. A French detachment from Ngwe also carried out a successful reconnaissance in July.

"It was on 25th and 26th August, 1915, at a conference which took place at Duala between Governor-General Merlin, General Aymerich, and myself, that the plan was decided on by which the Cameroons was eventually conquered.

"The fall of Garua, in the north, early in June enabled a British and French force to be set free which could move through the highlands of the Cameroons to the south.

"General Aymerich, whose troops were now established at Bertua and Dume, promised definite co-operation, with Jaunde, as before, the objective, whilst a force under Lieut.-Colonel le Meillour moved parallel to the eastern frontier of Muni, and was to cross the Campo River and move in the direction of Ebolowa. It was also arranged that I should show such activity as was possible from Northern Railhead so as to assist the British force at Ossidinge in its attempt to link up with other troops from Nigeria, and further that a force should land at Campo and move parallel to the northern frontier of Spanish Guinea.

"It was unfortunate that Brigadier-General Cunliffe was unable to attend this conference, but all details were communicated to him, and he was asked to exercise all possible pressure from the north. His rôle was most admirably carried out.

"The arrival of the 5th Light Infantry of the Indian Army strengthened my command, and further reinforcements from French West Africa were promised. The General Officer Commanding at Freetown and the Governors of Nigeria and the Gold Coast agreed to send me the carriers I required and to maintain them by monthly drafts. It was thanks to these officers that, in spite of a rather heavy sick roll among carriers, an efficient transport service was maintained throughout. My requirements in motor transport were also met; this service proved invaluable and far exceeded my expectations. Thus by 22nd September preparations were sufficiently far advanced for a move to be made in an easterly direction. Many of the earlier operations were a repetition of those which had taken place in May and June, but the general plan differed in so much that I arranged for the British and French lines of supply to be kept distinct, whilst I also determined that Eseka should be made the French advanced base from which operations could be carried forward to the Jaunde–Kribi road, and that our general advance should be carried out by means of parallel columns by road and railway. Our communications needed much repair, including the total reconstruction of a heavy railway bridge and a deviation necessitating considerable labour on earthwork. Many other smaller bridges were broken or destroyed; those on the road were made fit for heavy traffic, those on the railway were practically rebuilt.

"The British force, as previously, experienced stiff resistance at Wum Biagas, but on 9th October that place was captured after a lively action, in which the Nigerian and Gold Coast troops once more distinguished themselves. From here we were enabled to send out flanking columns and render some assistance to the French troops who were fighting their way to Eseka. The Kele River, in flood, proved a formidable obstacle and its crossing somewhat delayed the British flanking columns sent out from Wum Biagas. Sende was occupied by the French on 25th October and the enemy was driven from Eseka on 30th October. Considerable rolling stock, left behind after our previous advance, was retaken, and proved a valuable addition to our exiguous supply of engines and wagons. By 23rd November, both British and French forces were ready for the final advance, the bush track from Edea to Wum Biagas had been converted into a good motor road, and through railway communication, Duala-Eseka, was nearing completion. There were also over 7,000 carriers employed on such sections of the communications as were still unfit for motor or rail traffic. Dschang Mangas was selected as the primary objective of the British force, whilst the French were directed to make good the line of the Jaunde-Kribi road. Both forces slightly modified their tactics, and the advance was generally carried out by a main body, with two wings moving on as wide a front as the nature of the country permitted. The method of our advance appears to have entirely disconcerted the enemy and, although he still continued strenuously to resist our advance, it became apparent that his strength was gradually becoming exhausted. Towards the end of November the fighting in and around Lesogs by the troops under Lieut.-Colonel Cockburn was of a very severe nature, but the troops from the Northern Provinces of Nigeria gallantly rose to the occasion and, despite all difficulties of the country, were not to be denied in their endeavour to dislodge the enemy. Much credit is due to these troops and their leaders for the admirable conduct of this operation. Ngung was reached on the 30th November, and, up to this place, every defensive position was disputed by the enemy. On 7th December the advance on Dschang Mangas was continued and both main and flank columns were subject to opposition. A well executed move by a small force of the Gold Coast Regiment, under Captain Butler, V.C., considerably disturbed the enemy; the capture of one of his machine guns and several thousand rounds of ammunition, in addition to important documents, produced considerable effect. On 17th December the more open and cultivated country was reached and we took Dschang Mangas.

"From 26th November onwards the French were fighting their way through very broken country to Mangeles; they had to face determined opposition and lost a considerable number of European and native soldiers, but their tenacity of purpose was rewarded by the capture of Mangeles on 21st December, after intermittent fighting covering a period of five days. The column halted at this place for rest and to establish a supply depot.

"11. I must now indicate the turn that events had taken beyond Northern Railhead. I was informed from Nigeria that the British force at Ossidinge, under Major Crookenden, would be prepared to move on Bamenda on 12th October. I therefore ordered a force consisting of portions of the West African Regiment, 5th Light Infantry, and some artillery, under Lieut.-Colonel Cotton, 5th Light Infantry, to move on Dschang from Bare, also starting on 12th October. Hostile opposition was experienced at Mwu and Nkam Rivers and from an entrenched position at Sanschu. On 6th November Dschang was occupied. On receipt of information that Major Crookenden's force had reached Bamenda on 22nd October I ordered Lieut.-Colonel Cotton to leave a garrison in Dschang and move a force to Bagam to co-operate with Major Crookenden in an attack on that place. The enemy had, however, forestalled us and withdrawn to Fumban, whither we pursued him after experiencing some difficulty in effecting the crossing of the Nun River. On 2nd December the important centre of Fumban was occupied and an abortive effort of the enemy to retake it was frustrated. Brigadier-General Cunliffe, foreseeing the possibility of obstinate resistance at Fumban, had directed two other small columns to co-operate in our movement on that place. These columns arrived almost simultaneously with that under Lieut.-Colonel Cotton. Major Crookenden's troops then continued their advance under Brigadier-General Cunliffe's direction, whilst I placed garrisons in Fumban, Bana, and Bagam, and the bulk of Lieut.-Colonel Cotton's troops returned to railhead. I was thus enabled to withdraw a small force to move from Nkongsamba to Jabassi and penetrate the Bafia country, where I still believed there were small hostile parties. I also was enabled to detach a force to assist the French column operating from Campo. I think I may consider our operations in the Northern area were entirely satisfactory, and the simultaneous advance of our columns took the heart out of the remnants of the enemy forces in that district. Furthermore, we had established touch with Brigadier-General Cunliffe's columns, which were now converging on the Sanaga River, at a point known as the Nachtigal Rapids. Our losses were slight and the health of all ranks was considerably better than that of the troops fighting in the lower altitudes.

"12. Reverting to the operations of the main forces. On receiving information that the British force had arrived at Dschang Mangas, I decided that it would be more advantageous to move on Jaunde direct, rather than await the French advance to the Jaunde–Kribi road. In arriving at this decision I was influenced by the fact that the mind of the native does not understand the meaning nor necessity of delay, and from a political point of view the early occupation of Jaunde appeared to be all important. From 22nd December, the hostile resistance gradually weakened, strongly entrenched positions were abandoned, and on the morning of the 1st January Colonel Gorges entered Jaunde with his force. The enemy appeared to have completely broken under the pressure which he was now experiencing from all sides. Allied troops from the north, troops from French Equatorial Africa and the Belgian Congo commenced to arrive in Jaunde during the first week in January. It is, I think, a remarkable feat that troops that had fought and marched for a period of seventeen months should have converged on their objective within a few days of one another.

"The direct effect of the occupation of Jaunde was to relieve all pressure in front of the French force advancing from Mangeles, the Jaunde–Kribi road being reached early in January. British and French forces were moved during the first week in January to Widemenge and in the direction of Ebolowa via Olama and Onana Besa crossings of the Njong River. At Kol Maka, Lieut.-Colonel Haywood succeeded in securing the release of officers, non-commissioned officers, civilian and native non-combatants who had been taken prisoners by the Germans at various times during the war; his force, supported by a strong French column, continued its advance on Ebolowa, on which place a second Allied column was also advancing. A French force under Lieut.-Colonel Faucon occupied Ebolowa on 19th January, after experiencing some slight resistance. The definite move of the remnants of the German forces towards Spanish territory now became apparent, and Lieut.-Colonel Haywood proceeded with all despatch to follow them up as far as Nkan, from which place I diverted him via Efulen on Kribi, in order to clear the western area of stragglers. A British force was also moved to Lolodorf.

"Colonel Morisson took command of a strong French force, and, moving towards the Spanish frontier, succeeded in driving the German force in front of him across the Campo River into neutral territory. A similar operation was conducted by the French force which had operated from Campo, so that by the middle of February no Germans were left in the Cameroons, and the conquest of the country had been completed. . . .

"C. M. Dobell,
"Major-General,
"Commanding the Allied Forces."

MONTGOMERY, ROBERT ARUNDEL KERR, Major, was born 21 Jan. 1862. He entered the Army 23 Feb. 1881, becoming Captain 1 July, 1889; was Staff Captain, R.A., Northern District, 16 Nov. 1895, to 15 Nov. 1898, and was promoted to Major 1 March, 1899. He passed the Staff College. Major Montgomery served in the South African War, 1899–1902; as Brigade Major, South Africa, 1 Sept. 1901, to 18 Feb. 1902; as D.A.A.G., Intelligence, 19 Feb. to 24 Sept. 1902, taking part in the advance on Kimberley; operations in the Orange Free State, Feb. to May, 1900; operations in the Transvaal, west of Pretoria, July to 29 Nov. 1900; operations in Cape Colony, north of Orange River; operations in the Transvaal, Orange River Colony, and Cape Colony, 30 Nov. 1900, to 31 May, 1902; operations on the Zululand Frontier of Natal in Oct. 1901. He was mentioned in Despatches [London Gazette, 10 Sept. 1901, and 29 July, 1902]; was given the Brevet of Lieut.-Colonel 22 Aug. 1902; received the Queen's Medal with three clasps, the King's Medal with two clasps, and was created a Companion of the Distinguished Service Order [London Gazette, 27 Sept. 1901]: "Robert Arundel Kerr Montgomery, Major, Royal Artillery. In recognition of services during the operations in South Africa." The Insignia were presented to him by the King 24 Oct. 1902. He was D.A.Q.M.G., 1st Army Corps, 25 Sept. 1902, to 13 July 1905; was given the Brevet of Colonel 22 Aug. 1905; was a Professor at the Staff College, India, from 29 July, 1905, to 13 Jan. 1909; was promoted to Lieut.-Colonel 11 Feb. 1906, and to Colonel 17 Dec. 1909; was G.S.O.1, 1st Division, Aldershot Command, 17 Dec. 1909, to 15 Oct. 1911; created a C.B. in 1911; Brigadier-General, General Staff, Southern Command, 16 Oct. 1911, to 4 Aug. 1914. On the outbreak of the European War, he became Brigadier-General, General Staff, 2nd Army, Central Force, Home Defence, 5 Aug. to 4 Oct. 1914. He was Brigadier-General, General Staff, 4th Army Corps, British Expeditionary Force, 5 Oct. to 31 Dec. 1914; Brigadier-General, Royal Artillery, 1st Army Corps, British Expeditionary Force, 1 Jan. to 18 July, 1915. He was promoted to Major-General 3 June, 1915; was Major-General, Royal Artillery, 3rd Army, B.E.F., 19 July to 6 Sept. 1915; Commander, Tyne Garrison, from 15 Sept. 1915. For his services in the European War he was twice mentioned in Despatches, and was created a K.C.M.G. in 1919. Sir Robert Montgomery married, in 1887, Annie Rosalie, eldest daughter of John Lecky Phelps, of Waterpark, Clare, and they have one son and one daughter.

BEGBIE, GEORGE EDWARD, Brevet Major, was born 9 Sept. 1868, son of the late James W. Begbie, LL.D. He joined the Highland Light Infantry 10 April, 1889, becoming Lieutenant on 3 Feb. 1892, and was Adjutant, Highland Light Infantry, 14 Jan. 1894, to 13 Jan. 1898, being promoted to Captain 15 April, 1897. In Kandia, in 1898, he took part in the affair of 6 Sept.; was mentioned in Despatches [London Gazette, 24 Jan. 1899], and given the Brevet of Major 8 March, 1899. He served in the South African War, 1899–1902; was mentioned in Despatches; received both Medals with clasps, and was created a Companion of the Distinguished Service Order [London Gazette, 27 Sept. 1901]: "George Edward Begbie, Captain and Brevet Major, Highland Light Infantry. In recognition of services during the operations in South Africa." The Insignia were sent to the Commander-in-Chief in India 30 Jan. 1902, and presented by the G.O.C., Peshawar District, India, 19 March, 1902. He was promoted to Major. Major Begbie died at Netley Hospital 15 Jan. 1907.

ELLIS, CONYNGHAM RICHARD CECIL, Major, was born 28 March, 1863, only son of the late Rev. Conygham Ellis. He was educated at Marlborough, and entered the Army 5 Dec. 1883; was promoted Captain 5 April, 1893; became Major 29 March, 1899. He served in the South African War, 1899–1900, and was present at the Relief of Ladysmith, including the action at Colenso; operations of 17 to 24 Jan. 1900, and action at Spion Kop (very severely wounded). He was mentioned in Despatches [London Gazette, 10 Sept. 1901]; received the Queen's Medal with clasp, and was created a Companion of the Distinguished Service Order [London Gazette, 27 Sept. 1901]: "Conyngham Richard Cecil Ellis, Major, Scottish Rifles. In recognition of services during the operations in South Africa." The Insignia were sent to the Commander-in-Chief in India 30 Jan. 1902, and presented by the G.O.C., Peshawar District, India, 19 March, 1902. Major Ellis retired from the Cameronians 9 March, 1903.

COLERIDGE, HUGH FORTESCUE, Major, was born 11 Jan. 1859, son of the Rev. F. J. Coleridge, of Cadbury, Thorverton. He was gazetted to the 47th Foot 22 Jan. 1879; was promoted Captain, North Lancashire Regt., 1 July, 1887; was Adjutant, Volunteers, 1 May, 1893, to 1 Nov. 1898. Major Coleridge served in the South African War, 1899–1902, as Provost-Marshal, and he also performed the duties of Intelligence Officer to a column. He took part in the advance on Kimberley, including actions at Belmont, Enslin, Modder River and Magersfontein; operations in Orange Free State, April to May, 1900; operations in the Transvaal, west of Pretoria, July to 29 Nov. 1900, including actions at Lindley (1 June) and Rhenoster River; operations in Cape Colony, north and south of Orange River, 1899 to 1900; operations in the Transvaal 30 Nov. 1900, to 31 May, 1902. He was mentioned in Despatches [London Gazette, 10 Sept. 1901]; received the Queen's Medal with four clasps, the King's Medal with two clasps, and was created a Companion of the Distinguished Service Order [London Gazette, 27 Sept. 1901]: "Hugh Fortescue Coleridge, Major, Loyal North Lancashire Regt. In recognition of services during the operations in South Africa." Major Coleridge was invested by the King 24 Oct. 1902. He was promoted to Lieut.-Colonel 1 June, 1906; commanded the 1st Battn. Loyal North Lancashire Regt.; was given the Brevet of Colonel 1 June, 1909, and retired 1 June, 1910, with the rank of Colonel. Colonel Coleridge served in the European War, 1914–18, and was created a C.B.E. in 1919. He married, in 1906, Kathleen, eldest daughter of the late Rear-Admiral J. H. Bainbridge and of Mrs. Bainbridge, of Elfordleigh, Plympton, and they have five sons.

DAVIDSON, CHARLES JOHN LLOYD, Major, was born 6 Oct. 1858, eldest son of the late James (Brebner) Davidson, of Eglinton, County Derry, and of Murlingden, Brechin, N.B., and Margaret Jane Lloyd, of Summerhill, Londonderry, daughter of Minchin Lloyd, of Summerhill, Londonderry. He was educated privately, and at the Royal Military College, Sandhurst; entered the 27th Inniskilling Regt. 13 Aug. 1879; was promoted Capt. 1 Feb. 1888. He was promoted Major 24 Oct. 1899, and took part in the South African War, 1899–1902, when he was severely wounded at Inniskilling Hill (Pieter's Hill) on 23 Feb. 1900. Major Davidson was present at the operations during the Relief of Ladysmith, including the action at Colenso; operations of 17 to 24 Jan. 1900, and action at Spion Kop; operations of 5 to 7 Feb. 1900, and action at Vaal Kranz. He was also present during the operations in the Transvaal, to the east of Pretoria, from July to 29 Nov. 1900, including actions at Belfast (26 and 27 Aug.) and Lydenberg (5 to 8 Sept.). He was afterwards Commandant at Lindley; operations in the Transvaal 30 Nov. 1900, to Feb. 1901, and May to Dec. 1901; operations in Orange River Colony, Dec. 1901, to 31 May, 1902. He was mentioned in Despatches [London Gazette, 8 Feb. and 10 Sept. 1901]; received the Queen's Medal with five clasps; the King's Medal with two clasps, and was created a Companion of the Distinguished Service Order [London Gazette, 27 Sept. 1901]: "Charles John Lloyd Davidson, Major, Royal Inniskilling Fusiliers. In recognition of services during the operations in South Africa." The Insignia were presented by the King 18 Dec. 1902; the Warrant sent 8 Jan. 1903. He was promoted Lieutenant-Colonel 3 Nov. 1906. He was given the Brevet of Colonel 3 Nov. 1909, and retired from the Royal Inniskilling Fusiliers with the rank of Colonel 3 Nov. 1910. He married (1st), in 1890, Sophia Mary (died 1897), the daughter of Major Burleigh Stuart, of Dergmony, Omagh. He married (2ndly), in 1906, Mary Nathalie (who died in 1916), daughter of the late Colonel A. B. Cumberlege, of Kingsfield, Southwick, Sussex, and they had two sons: Claude John Lloyd and Kenneth Bulstrode Lloyd, born on 30 Sept. 1907, and 7 Dec. 1908, and one daughter, Christine Rosemary.

Charles J. L. Davidson.

JOHNSTONE, FRANCIS BUCHANAN, Major, was born 2 Feb. 1863, son of the late David Johnstone, of Croy Row, Dumbarton. He was commissioned in the Royal Artillery 22 Feb. 1882; became Captain 23 May, 1890; was Divisional Adjutant, R.A., 9 Oct. to 17 Dec. 1899; was promoted Major 18 Dec. 1899. He served in the South African War, 1899–1900, taking part in the advance on Kimberley, including actions at Belmont, Enslin, Modder River and Magersfontein. He was present at the Relief of Kimberley; operations in the Orange Free State, Feb. to May, 1900, including operations at Paardeberg (17 to 26 Feb.); actions at Poplar Grove, Karee Siding, Vet River (5 and 6 May) and Zand River; operations in the Transvaal in May and June, 1900, including actions near Johannesburg and Pretoria. He was mentioned in Despatches [London Gazette, 10 Sept. 1901], and created a Companion of the Distinguished Service Order [London Gazette, 27 Sept. 1901]: "Francis Buchanan Johnstone, Major, Royal Artillery. In recognition of services during the operations in South Africa." The Insignia were presented by the King 29 Oct. 1901; the Warrant sent 24 Jan. 1902. He was promoted Lieut.-Colonel 19 Jan. 1908, and Colonel 4 Oct. 1911. From 1 April, 1913, to 19 Dec. 1915, he commanded Royal Artillery, Lowland Division, Scottish Command, and 52nd Division, Mediterranean Expeditionary Force; from 20 Dec. 1915, to Feb. 1916, he was Brigadier-General, R.A., 12th Army Corps, Mediterranean Expeditionary Force, and from 2 Nov. 1916, to 9 March, 1918, Brigadier-General, R.A., 72nd Division, Home Defences. During the European War he was wounded in the Balkan Expedition. He married, in 1887, Edith Arethusa, daughter of the late Frederick Padwick, of West Thorney, Sussex, and they have one daughter.

MORRICE, LEWIS EDWARD, Major, was born 20 Dec. 1862, youngest son of the late J. W. Morrice, of Catthorpe Towers, county Leicester, and of Mary Selby Donaldson-Selby. He was educated at Eton, and Caius College, Cambridge. He entered the Royal Warwickshire Regt. 14 May,

1884; was promoted Captain 1 Dec. 1890; served as Brigade Major, Queensland Forces, 13 Nov. 1890, to 30 Sept. 1893; was Adjutant, Warwickshire Militia, 28 Aug. 1894, to 27 Aug. 1899; was promoted to Major 3 Feb. 1900. Lieut.-Colonel Morrice served in the South African War, 1899–1901; as a Major with the 2nd Battn., commanding for six months. He also acted at Commandant at Komati Poort. Major Morrice took part in operations in the Orange Free State, Feb. to May, 1900, including actions at Vet River (5 and 6 May) and Zand River; operations in the Transvaal in May and June, 1900, including actions near Johannesburg, Pretoria and Diamond Hill (11 and 12 June); operations in the Transvaal, east of Pretoria, July to 28 Nov. 1900, including action at Belfast (26 and 27 Aug.); operations in the Transvaal 30 Nov. 1900, to June, 1901. He was mentioned in Despatches [London Gazette, 10 Sept. 1901]; received the Queen's Medal and six clasps, and was created a Companion of the Distinguished Service Order [London Gazette, 27 Sept. 1901]: "Lewis Edward Morrice, Major, Royal Warwickshire Regt. In recognition of services during the operations in South Africa." He became Second-in-Command, 1st Royal Warwickshire Regt., in 1902, and retired 3 Sept. 1904. Lieut.-Colonel Morrice was employed as a General Staff Officer at the War Office during the European War. Mentioned and awarded Brevet of Lieut.-Colonel 1 Jan. 1918. He is a J.P. for the county of Wilts, and a member of the Wilts County Council. He married, in 1897, Eleanor Constance, daughter of the late Rev. G. Murray, of Shrivenham, Berks, and they have one daughter, Mary Constance, surviving. His son, Midshipman John Walter Morrice, R.N., was lost in H.M.S. Formidable.

GAY, ARTHUR WILLIAM, Major, was born in London 22 March, 1863, son of the late John Gay, F.R.C.S., and Elizabeth Gay. He entered the Royal Field Artillery 1 Oct. 1882; served in Burma, 1885–87 (Medal with clasp); was appointed to the Royal Horse Artillery in 1886; was promoted Captain 1 Oct. 1891. He was Adjutant, Royal Artillery, 17 July, 1893, to 17 May, 1896; Staff Captain, R.A., Cork District, 18 May, 1896, to 21 Jan. 1898; Staff Captain, Headquarters of Army, 27 Nov. to 19 Dec. 1899; passed the Staff College, 1899; was promoted to Major 3 Feb. 1900. He served in the South African War, 1899–1901, and was present at operations in the Orange Free State, Feb. to May, 1900, including actions at Poplar Grove, Dreifontein, Vet River (5 and 6 May) and Zand River; operations in the Transvaal, May and June, 1900, including actions near Johannesburg, Pretoria and Diamond Hill (11 and 12 June); operations in the Transvaal, east of Pretoria, July to Aug. 1900. He was mentioned in Despatches [London Gazette, 10 Sept. 1901]; received the Queen's Medal with four clasps, and was created a Companion of the Distinguished Service Order [London Gazette, 27 Sept. 1901]: "Arthur William Gay, Major, Royal Artillery. In recognition of services during the operations in South Africa." The Insignia were presented by the King 29 Oct. 1901. He was Brigade Major, R.A., 3rd Army Corps, 24 Oct. 1902, to 23 Oct. 1905; G.S.O., 2nd Grade, Wessex Division, Southern Command, 1 April, 1908, to 30 Nov. 1910; promoted to Lieut.-Colonel 5 March, 1909, and to Colonel, 30 Oct. 1912; commanding Royal Artillery, West Lancashire Division, Central Force, Home Defence, 1 April to 31 Dec. 1914. Colonel Gay was Temporary Brigadier-General 5 Aug. 1914, to 9 March, 1917; Brigadier-General, R.A., 28th Division, New Armies, B.E.F., 1 Jan. to 8 March, 1915; Brigadier-General, R.A., 22nd Division, New Armies, Mediterranean Expeditionary Force, 29 June to 17 Dec. 1915; Brigadier-General, R.A., 16th Army Corps, Mediterranean Expeditionary Force; British Salonika Expeditionary Force 18 Dec. 1915, to 9 March, 1917; Temporary Major-General 10 March, 1917, to 30 May, 1919; Divisional Commander, 26th Division, British Salonika Force. He was mentioned in Despatches, and was created a C.B. in 1916, and a C.M.G. in 1917 He married, 3 Oct. 1893, Maud, eldest daughter of Colonel R. C. Evanson, and they have one son.

FOX, ROBERT FANSHAWE, Major, was born 29 Nov. 1862, son of the late William Fox, of Adbury, Berkshire. He was gazetted to the Royal Artillery 1 Oct. 1882; was promoted Captain 4 Nov. 1891, and Major 3 Feb. 1900. Major Fox served in the South African War, 1899–1900, and was present at the Relief of Ladysmith, including operations of 17 to 24 Jan. 1900, and action at Spion Kop; operations of 5 to 7 Feb. 1900, and action at Vaal Kranz; operations on Tugela Heights (14 to 27 Feb.), and action at Pieter's Hill; operations in Natal, March to June, 1900, including action at Laing's Nek (6 to 9 June). He was mentioned in Despatches [London Gazette, 8 Feb. 1901 (Sir R. H. Buller, 30 March and 9 Nov. 1900), and London Gazette, 10 Sept. 1901]; received the Queen's Medal with five clasps, and was created a Companion of the Distinguished Service Order [London Gazette, 27 Sept. 1901]: "Robert Fanshawe Fox, Major, Royal Artillery. In recognition of services during the operations in South Africa." The Insignia were presented by the King 29 Oct. 1901; the Warrant sent 24 Jan. 1902. He became Lieut.-Colonel 5 Aug. 1909, and Colonel 6 March, 1913. During the European War he served as Brigadier-General, R.A., 4th Division, B.E.F., 8 Sept. 1915, to 16 June, 1916; Brigadier-General, R.A., 7th Army Corps, B.E.F., 8 Sept. 1915, to 16 June, 1916; Inspector of Royal Horse and Royal Field Artillery (temporary) 20 July, 1916, to 31 Oct. 1917; as Brigadier-General, R.A., 67th Division, Home Forces, 7 Nov. 1917, to 15 June, 1918. He was mentioned in Despatches, and created a C.B. in 1915.

KNOX, ARTHUR RICE, Major, was born 8 March, 1863, son of the late Major-General T. Knox, R.A. He was educated at Cheltenham College, and entered the Royal Artillery 21 March, 1883; was promoted Captain 19 March, 1892; became Major 13 Feb. 1900. He served in the South African War, 1899–1900; was present at the Relief of Ladysmith, including the action at Colenso; operations of 17 to 24 Jan. 1900, and action at Spion Kop; operations of 5 to 7 Feb. 1900, and action at Vaal Kranz; operations on Tugela Heights (14 to 27 Feb. 1900), and action at Pieter's Hill; operations in Natal, March to June, 1900, including action at Laing's Nek (6 to 9 June); operations in the Transvaal, west of Pretoria, July to Oct. 1900. He was mentioned in Despatches [London Gazette, 10 Sept. 1901]; received the Queen's Medal with five clasps, and was created a Companion of the Distinguished Service Order [London Gazette, 27 Sept. 1901]: "Arthur Rice Knox, Major, Royal Artillery. In recognition of services during the operations in South Africa." The Insignia were presented by the King 29 Oct. 1901; the Warrant sent 24 Jan. 1902. Major Knox retired 15 April, 1908. He died 22 April, 1917, of wounds received in action.

KIRKWOOD, CARLETON HOOPER MORRISON, Major, was born 4 Feb. 1860, son of the late J. Townsend Kirkwood, of Yeo Vale, North Devon. He was educated at Cheltenham College, and entered the 2nd West India Regt. 14 June, 1882; was Garrison Adjutant, Jamaica, 1 Dec. 1885, to 4 Aug. 1886; was promoted Captain 18 Jan. 1888; became Major 22 Feb. 1900. Major Kirkwood served in the South African War, 1900–2, as Commandant, Waterval North, and afterwards Pietpotgietersrust. Operations in Orange River Colony, 1900, including actions at Bethlehem (6 and 7 July) and Wittebergen (1 to 29 July); operations in the Transvaal 30 Nov. 1900, to Jan. 1901, and April, 1901, to 31 May, 1902; operations in Cape Colony, Jan. to April, 1901. He was in command of the 2nd Battn. Wiltshire Regt., from 20 July, 1900, to 9 Feb. 1901; was mentioned in Despatches [London Gazette, 10 Sept. 1901]; received the Queen's Medal with three clasps, the King's Medal with two clasps, and was created a Companion of the Distinguished Service Order [London Gazette, 27 Sept. 1901]: "Carleton Hooper Morrison Kirkwood, Major, Wiltshire Regt. In recognition of services during the operations in South Africa." Major Kirkwood was invested by the King 24 Oct. 1902. He was promoted Lieut.-Colonel 6 Jan. 1906; was given the Brevet of Colonel 6 Jan. 1909; retired with the rank of Colonel 18 June, 1910. During the European War he was employed in France as Commandant on the Lines of Communication from Aug. 1914; was mentioned in Despatches twice, and created a C.M.G. in 1918. His favourite recreations are shooting, golf and fishing.

BARTON, CHARLES GERARD, Major, was born 26 April, 1860, son of the Rev. J. Barton. He was educated at Tonbridge School, and at Sherborne. He entered the 46th Foot 22 Jan. 1881; transferred to the 75th Foot 26 Feb. 1881, and to the 4th Foot 8 June, 1881; became Lieutenant 1 July, 1881; was promoted Captain in 1899, and became Major 23 Feb. 1900. Major Barton served in the South African War, 1899–1902; was present at the Relief of Ladysmith, including operations of 17 to 24 Jan. 1900, and action at Spion Kop; operations of 5 to 7 Feb. 1900, and action at Vaal Kranz; operations on Tugela Heights (14 to 27 Feb. 1900), and action at Pieter's Hill; operations in the Transvaal 30 Nov. 1900, to 31 May, 1902. He was mentioned in Despatches [London Gazette, 10 Sept. 1901]; received the Queen's Medal with three clasps, the King's Medal with two clasps, and was created a Companion of the Distinguished Service Order [London Gazette, 27 Sept. 1901]: "Charles Gerard Barton, Major, Royal Lancashire Regt. In recognition of services during the operations in South Africa." The Insignia were sent to the G.O.C. Natal District 15 Nov. 1902, for presentation to Major Barton. He retired 21 June, 1905. Major Barton has played cricket for Hampshire. He married Mabel Eleanor, widow of Capt. Maurice W. Kirk.

HIBBERT, GODFREY LEICESTER, Major, was born 31 Jan. 1864, son of Leicester Hibbert, of Crofton Grange, Orpington, and of Mrs. Hibbert. He was educated at Cheltenham College; joined the Northamptonshire Regt. 6 Feb. 1884, and was transferred to the Royal Lancaster Regt. 27 Feb. 1884; was promoted Captain, Aug. 1891; became Major, Feb. 1900. Major Hibbert served in the South African War, 1900–1; as Adjutant, 4th Battn. Royal Lancaster Regt., 27 March, 1900, to 11 July, 1901. Operations in Cape Colony, south of Orange River, March to 29 Nov. 1900; operations in Orange River Colony, May to July, 1901; operations in Cape Colony 30 Nov. 1900, to May, 1901. He was mentioned in Despatches [London Gazette, 10 Sept. 1901]; received the Queen's Medal with three clasps, and was created a Companion of the Distinguished Service Order [London Gazette, 27 Sept. 1901]: "Godfrey Leicester Hibbert, Major, Royal Lancaster Regt. In recognition of services during the operations in South Africa." The Insignia were presented to him by the King 29 Oct. 1901. He was appointed Brigade Commander, North Lancashire Territorial Brigade, in Feb. 1913, and on the outbreak of war was appointed Brigadier-General. Colonel Hibbert served overseas in command of the 154th Infantry Brigade in France, and the 77th Infantry Brigade in Salonika (mentioned twice in Despatches). During 1917–18 commanded brigade at home until demobilization. He was created a C.B. in 1917, and a C.M.G. in 1919. Colonel Hibbert married, in 1902, Mabel, youngest daughter of the late General E. Faunce.

Frederic J. Heyworth.

HEYWORTH, FREDERIC JAMES, Major, was born 25 March, 1863. He entered the Scots Guards 5 Dec. 1883; served in the Sudan, 1885 (Medal with clasp, and Khedive's Star); was A.D.C. to Brigadier-General, Curragh, 1 April, 1890, to 30 April, 1891; A.D.C. to Major-General, Dublin District, 1 May, 1891, to 31 March, 1895; was promoted Captain 29 July, 1896; became Major 7 March, 1900. Major Heyworth served in the South African War, 1899–1902, taking part in the advance on Kimberley, including the actions at Belmont, Enslin, Modder River and Magersfontein; operations in the Orange Free State, Feb. to May, 1900, including actions at Poplar Grove, Dreifontein, Vet River (5 and 6

May) and Zand River; operations in the Transvaal in May and June, 1900, including actions near Johannesburg, Pretoria and Diamond Hill (11 and 12 June); operations in the Transvaal, east of Pretoria, July to 29 Nov. 1900, including action at Belfast (26 and 27 Aug.); operations in the Transvaal, west of Pretoria, July to 29 Nov. 1900; operations in Orange River Colony, May to 29 Nov. 1900. He was mentioned in Despatches [London Gazette, 10 Sept. 1901]; received the Queen's Medal with two clasps, and was created a Companion of the Distinguished Service Order [London Gazette, 27 Oct. 1901]: "Frederic James Heyworth, Major, Scots Guards. In recognition of services during the operations in South Africa." The Insignia were presented by the King 24 Oct. 1902. He was promoted Lieut.-Colonel 1 April, 1908, and Colonel 6 Dec. 1911. He was Colonel, Scots Guards and Regimental District, 9 Oct. 1913. In 1913 he married Mrs. Hatfeild-Harter. Colonel Heyworth served in the European War from 1914; was Temporary Brigadier-General from 13 Nov. 1914, and was killed in action, and an obituary notice of him appeared in the "Times" of 17 May, 1916.

BRUNKER, CAPEL MOLYNEUX, Major, was born 15 Oct. 1858, in Ceylon, son of Major-General James Robert Brunker and Marianne (*née* Molyneux). He was educated at Cheltenham College, and joined the 43rd Foot 23 Oct. 1880; the 81st Foot 8 Dec. 1880; became Lieutenant, North Lancashire Regt., 1 July, 1881; was Adjutant, North Lancashire Regt., 6 Aug. 1884, to 5 Aug. 1889; became Captain 17 Feb. 1888; exchanged into the Lancashire Fusiliers 18 Feb. 1891. He served in the Nile Expedition of 1898; was present at the Battle of Khartum; received the Medal and the Egyptian Medal with clasp. In the same year he also served in Crete. He was promoted to Major 7 March, 1900. Major Brunker served in the South African War, 1899–1900, being present at the Relief of Ladysmith, including the operations of 17 to 24 Jan. 1900, and action at Spion Kop; operations of 5 to 7 Feb. 1900, and action at Vaal Kranz; operations on Tugela Heights (14 to 27 Feb. 1900); operations in Natal, April and May, 1900. He was in command of the 2nd Battn. Lancashire Fusiliers, from 25 Jan. to 29 March, 1900. He was mentioned in Despatches [London Gazette, 8 Feb. and 10 Sept. 1901]; received the Queen's Medal with two clasps, and for services at Spion Kop was created a Companion of the Distinguished Service Order [London Gazette, 27 Sept. 1901]: "Charles Molyneux Brunker, Major, Lancashire Fusiliers. In recognition of services during the operations in South Africa." The Insignia were presented to him by the King 29 Oct. 1901. He became Lieut.-Colonel 24 June, 1906; was given the Brevet of Colonel 14 June, 1909; became Colonel 24 June, 1910. He served in the European War, 1914–17; on the Western Front in 1914; at Gallipoli in 1915; was mentioned in Despatches for valuable services in connection with the war [London Gazette, 27 July, 1917], and created a C.M.G. in 1917. He retired from the Staff with the honorary rank of Brigadier-General 3 Jan. 1918. General Brunker married (1st), in 1902, Marcia Caroline (who died in 1913), daughter of the Rev. Joseph Barker. He married (2ndly), in 1914, Dorothy Manners, daughter of A. Leland Noel.

HOWELL, HUGH DE BERDT, Major, served in the South African War of 1899–1902. He was created a Companion of the Distinguished Service Order [London Gazette, 27 Sept. 1901]: "Hugh de Berdt Howell, Major, Worcestershire Regt. In recognition of services during the operations in South Africa." The Insignia were sent to the G.O.C. Transvaal 15 Nov. 1902, and were presented at Bloemfontein 16 March, 1903.

HUMPHREYS, GARDINER, Major, was born 2 March, 1865. He was commissioned in the Royal Artillery 8 July, 1884; was promoted Captain 14 Oct. 1893, and became Major 5 April, 1900. Major Humphreys served in the South African War, 1899–1901; took part in the advance on Kimberley, and was twice slightly wounded. Operations in the Transvaal 30 Nov. 1900, to July, 1901; operations in Orange River Colony, July, 1901; operations in Cape Colony, July to Dec. 1901. He was mentioned in Despatches [London Gazette, 10 Sept. 1901]; received the Queen's Medal with six clasps, and was created a Companion of the Distinguished Service Order [London Gazette, 27 Sept. 1901]: "Gardiner Humphreys, Major, Royal Artillery. In recognition of services during the operations in South Africa." The Insignia were presented by the King 12 March, 1902. He became Lieut.-Colonel 14 Nov. 1910, and Colonel 15 June, 1914. Colonel Humphreys was Brigadier-General, R.A., 6th Division, B.E.F., 27 May, 1915, to 21 June, 1916, and Brigadier-General, R.A., 9th Army Corps, British Armies in France, from 22 June, 1916. He was mentioned in Despatches, and created a C.B. in 1915, and a C.M.G. in 1918. He married, in 1906, Lady Emily Nugent, daughter of the 10th Earl of Westmeath.

DU PLAT-TAYLOR, ST. J. LOUIS HYDE, Major, was born 22 Jan. 1865, son of the late Colonel J. L. du Plat-Taylor, C.B. He was commissioned in the Royal Artillery 9 Dec. 1884; was promoted Captain 22 March, 1894, and Major 18 April, 1900. Major du Plat-Taylor served in the South African War, 1899–1900, taking part in operations in the Orange Free State in April, 1900. He was present at the Relief of Mafeking. Operations in the Transvaal in May and June, 1900; operations in the Transvaal, east of Pretoria, in July, 1900; operations in the Transvaal, west of Pretoria, including action at Zilikat's Nek. He was mentioned in Despatches [London Gazette, 16 April, 1901]; received the Queen's Medal with three clasps, and was created a Companion of the Distinguished Service Order [London Gazette, 27 Sept. 1901]: "St. John Louis Hyde du Plat-Taylor, Major, Royal Artillery. In recognition of services during the operations in South Africa." The Insignia were presented to him by the King 28 Oct. 1901. Major Taylor retired 16 May, 1906. He served in the European War, 1914–18, and was mentioned in Despatches. Major du Plat-Taylor married, in 1904, Alice, sister of Sir John Purves-Hume Campbell, 8th Bart., and they have one daughter.

ORR, ALEXANDER STEWART, Major, was born 10 May, 1861, son of the late William Orr, of Hougomont, Ballymena. He was gazetted to the Royal Irish Regt. 22 Oct. 1881; served in the Egyptian Expedition, 1882, being present at the action at Kassassin and at the Battle of Tel-el-Kebir (Medal with clasp, and Khedive's Star); was promoted Captain 30 Oct. 1888; took part in the Hazara Expedition, 1888 (Medal with clasp); participated in operations on the North-West Frontier of India, 1897–98, being present at the operations on the Samana (Medal with two clasps); was promoted Major 31 May, 1900. Major Orr served in the South African War, 1899–1902, taking part in operations in the Orange Free State, March to May, 1900; operations in the Transvaal, east of Pretoria, in Nov. 1900; operations in Orange River Colony, May to Nov. 1900; operations in Cape Colony, south of Orange River, 1900, including actions at Colesberg (24 Jan. to 12 Feb.). He was afterwards Station Staff Officer. Operations in the Transvaal 30 Nov. 1900, to 31 May, 1902. He was mentioned in Despatches [London Gazette, 10 Sept. 1901, and 25 April, 1902]; received the Queen's Medal with three clasps, the King's Medal with two clasps, and was created a Companion of the Distinguished Service Order [London Gazette, 27 Sept. 1901]: "Alexander Stewart Orr, Major, Royal Irish Regt. In recognition of services during the operations in South Africa." The Insignia were presented by the King 24 Oct. 1902; the Warrant, etc., sent 4 Nov. 1902. He was promoted Lieut.-Colonel 19 Feb. 1905, given the Brevet of Colonel 19 Feb. 1908, and retired with the rank of Colonel in 1909. Colonel Orr died 10 Jan. 1914.

ARMSTRONG, GERALD DENNE, Major, was born 26 Nov. 1865, son of Lieut.-General J. W. Armstrong, C.B., Inspector-General of Auxiliary Forces. He entered the Royal Warwickshire Regt. 7 Feb. 1885; was promoted Capt. 3 March, 1892; was Adjutant, Royal Warwickshire Regt., 9 Dec. 1896, to 8 June, 1900. Capt. Armstrong served in the South African War, 1899–1901, as Adjutant, 2nd Battn. Royal Warwickshire Regt., from 16 Dec. 1899, to 13 Oct. 1900, and was promoted to Major 9 June, 1900. He was present at operations in the Orange Free State, Feb. to May, 1900, including actions at Vet River (5 and 6 May) and Zand River; operations in the Transvaal in May and June, 1900, including actions near Johannesburg, Pretoria and Diamond Hill (11 and 12 June); operations in the Transvaal, east of Pretoria, July to 29 Nov. 1900, including action at Belfast (26 and 27 Aug.); operations in the Transvaal 30 Nov. 1900, to May, 1901. He was mentioned in Despatches [London Gazette, 10 Sept. 1901]; received the Queen's Medal with six clasps, and was created a Companion of the Distinguished Service Order [London Gazette, 27 Sept. 1901]: "Gerald Denne Armstrong, Major, Royal Warwickshire Regt. In recognition of services during the operations in South Africa." The Insignia were sent to the G.O.C., Bermuda, 12 Feb. 1902, and presented by General Geary 11 March, 1902. He was promoted to Lieut.-Colonel 6 April, 1906; was given the Brevet of Colonel 6 April, 1909, and retired with the rank of Colonel 6 April, 1910. Colonel Armstrong married Annie Augusta, daughter of the late E. Vahland, of Plymouth.

GOUGH, ALAN PERCY GEORGE, Major, was born 13 Sept. 1863, son of the late General Sir John B. Gough, G.C.B. He was educated at Wellington College, and at the R.M.C., Sandhurst, and was gazetted to the Royal Welsh Fusiliers as Lieutenant 9 Sept. 1882; served in the Burmese Expedition, 1885–87; was slightly wounded; mentioned in Despatches [London Gazette, 22 June, 1886, and 2 Sept. 1887]; Medal with clasp). He was A.D.C. to Major-General, Bengal, 16 July, 1887, to 31 March, 1890; became Captain 15 June, 1892; was Adjutant, Volunteers, 15 Sept. 1892, to 15 March, 1898; was promoted to Major 25 July, 1900. Major Gough served in the South African War, 1899–1902, on the Staff (as D.A.A.G.) 27 Dec. 1899, to 26 Feb. 1900; Station Staff Officer (graded D.A.A.G.) from 9 July, 1900; D.A.A.G. from 26 Aug. 1900. In command of 1st Battn. Royal Welsh Fusiliers from 26 Feb. to 24 June, 1900, excepting period 2 to 11 May. Relief of Ladysmith, including action at Colenso; operations of 17 to 24 Jan. 1900, and action at Spion Kop; operations of 5 to 7 Feb. 1900, and action at Vaal Kranz; operations on Tugela Heights (14 to 27 Feb. 1900) and action at Pieter's Hill; operations in the Transvaal, west of Pretoria, July and Aug. 1900, including actions at Venterskroon (7 Aug.; slightly wounded); operations in Orange River Colony 30 Nov. 1900, to May, 1902. He was mentioned in Despatches [London Gazette, 8 Feb. and 10 Sept. 1901]; received the Queen's Medal with five clasps, the King's Medal with two clasps, and was created a Companion of the Distinguished Service Order [London Gazette, 27 Oct. 1901]: "Alan Percy George Gough, Major, Royal Welsh Fusiliers. In recognition of services during the operations in South Africa." Major Gough retired 25 Oct. 1902. He joined the Denbighshire Hussars, Imperial Yeomanry, as Major and Honorary Lieut.-Colonel, 1904, and resigned in 1905. In 1914 he was recalled for service, and served with the B.E.F. in France, 1914–16; was three times mentioned in Despatches; created a C.M.G. in 1918, and a C.B.E. in 1919, and promoted to Lieut.-Colonel, Reserve of Officers, 18 Feb. 1917. He was employed at the War Office, 1917–19. Lieut.-Colonel Gough is J.P. and D.L., Carnarvonshire. In 1895 he married Mary Georgina, daughter of the late F. W. Lloyd Edwards, of Nanhoron, J.P., D.L., Chairman of Quarter Sessions, Carnarvonshire.

TIDSWELL, EDWARD CECIL, Major, was born 13 Sept. 1862, son of the late B. K. Tidswell, of Birkdale, Lancashire. He was educated at Harrow, and entered the Lancashire Fusiliers 10 May, 1882, as Lieutenant, becoming Captain 26 Nov. 1891; served in the Nile Expedition, 1898, being present at the Battle of Khartum (Medal and Egyptian Medal with clasp). He was promoted to Major 31 July, 1900, while serving in the South African War, 1899 to 1902; was Commandant at Pan; was present at the Relief of Ladysmith, including operations of 17 to 24 Jan. 1900, and action at Spion Kop; operations of 5 to 7 Feb. 1900, and action at Vaal Kranz; operations on Tugela Heights (14 to 27 Feb. 1900); operations in the Transvaal in May and June, 1900; operations in Natal, March to June, 1900, including action at Laing's Nek (6 to 9 June); operations in the Transvaal, east of Pretoria, July to 29 Nov. 1900; operations in Orange River Colony, May to 29 Nov. 1900. He was in command of the 2nd Battn. Lancashire Fusiliers 5 Nov. to 26 Dec. 1901; operations in the Transvaal, Jan. 1901, to 31 May, 1902. He was mentioned in Despatches [London Gazette, 8 Feb. and 10 Sept. 1901, and 29 July, 1902]; received the Queen's Medal with five clasps, the King's Medal with two clasps, and was created a Companion of the Distinguished Service Order [London Gazette, 27 Sept. 1901]: "Edward Cecil Tidswell, Major, Royal Lancashire Fusiliers. In recognition of services during the operations in South Africa." The Insignia were presented by the King 18 Dec. 1902. He was employed with the West African Frontier Force 11 April, 1903, to 28 Dec. 1905; became Lieut.-Colonel 21 Nov. 1907, and Colonel 30 Aug. 1911; was A.Q.M.G., India, 1 Sept. 1913, to 27 Dec. 1914. He served in the European War as Temporary Brigadier-General from 30 Nov. 1914, to 11 May, 1919; commanding the 34th Infantry Brigade, Indian Expeditionary Force "D," Mesopotamia Expeditionary Force, 2 Dec. 1915, to 3 Sept. 1917; as Commander, Euphrates Front; Nasiriyeh Front, Mesopotamia, E.F., 4 Sept. 1917, to 8 March, 1918; as Brigade Commander, 56th Infantry Brigade, Mesopotamia Expeditionary Force, 10 March, 1918, to 11 May, 1919. He was mentioned in Despatches three times; was created a C.B. in 1917, and received the Serbian Order of the White Eagle with Swords. In 1902 he married Ella, daughter of the late T. W. Pilcher, of Harrow.

WINGFIELD, JOHN MAURICE, Major, was born 1 Feb. 1863, son of the late J. H. L. Wingfield, of Tickencote and Market Overton, Rutland, and of Elizabeth Anne, eldest daughter of Maurice Johnson, Esq., of

Ascoughfee Hall, Spalding. He was educated at Harrow, and Trinity College, Cambridge; was Lieutenant in Northamptonshire and Rutland Militia, 1880–85; was gazetted to the Coldstream Guards as Lieutenant 16 June, 1885, and promoted Captain 3 April, 1897, and Major 3 Sept. 1900. He served in South Africa, being present at the advance on Kimberley, including actions at Belmont, Enslin, Modder River and Magersfontein; operations in the Orange Free State, Feb. to May, 1900, including actions at Poplar Grove and Dreifontein; operations in the Transvaal in May and June, 1900, including actions near Johannesburg, Pretoria and Diamond Hill (11 and 12 June); operations in the Transvaal, east of Pretoria, July to 20 Nov. 1900, including action at Belfast (26 and 27 Aug.). He was mentioned in Despatches [London Gazette, 10 Sept. 1901]; received the Queen's Medal with six clasps, and was created a Companion of the Distinguished Service Order [London Gazette, 27 Sept. 1901]: "John Maurice Wingfield, Major, Coldstream Guards. In recognition of services during the operations in South Africa." The Insignia were presented by the King 17 Dec. 1901. Major Wingfield retired 4 March, 1903. Lieut.-Colonel Wingfield served as Railway Staff Officer from 5 Aug. 1914, to 1 May, 1919. He served as High Sheriff of Rutland, 1911. He is a Justice of the Peace, Fellow of the Royal Geographical Society, and a Fellow of the Zoological Society.

John Maurice Wingfield.

MANTELL, PATRICK RINERS, Major, was born 28 Dec. 1862, son of Lieut.-Colonel Mantell, late I.M.S. He was gazetted to the Leinster Regt. as Lieutenant 30 Aug. 1883; became Lieutenant, Royal Welsh Fusiliers, 20 Oct. 1883; served in the Burmese Expedition, 1885–87 (Medal with clasp), and in the Hazara Expedition, 1891. He was promoted to Captain 13 July, 1892, and to Major, 6 Oct. 1900. From 1899 to 1902 Major Mantell served in the South African War, being present at the Relief of Ladysmith, including the action at Colenso; operations on Tugela Heights (14 to 27 Feb. 1900) and action at Pieter's Hill; operations in the Transvaal in May and June, 1900; operations in the Transvaal, west of Pretoria, including actions at Frederickstad (17 to 25 Oct.); operations in Cape Colony, north of Orange River, including action at Ruidam; operations in the Transvaal 30 Nov. 1900, to Sept. 1901; operations in Orange River Colony, Sept. 1901, to May, 1902. He was Garrison Adjutant at Potchefstroom and Commandant at Frederickstad, and was slightly wounded; was mentioned in Despatches [London Gazette, 8 Feb. and 10 Sept. 1901]; received the Queen's Medal with five clasps, the King's Medal with two clasps, and was created a Companion of the Distinguished Service Order [London Gazette, 27 Sept. 1901]: "Patrick Riners Mantell, Major, Royal Welsh Fusiliers. In recognition of services during the operations in South Africa." The Insignia were presented by the King 28 March, 1903. He became Lieut.-Colonel 21 Aug. 1907, and Colonel 30 Aug. 1911, and retired 5 June, 1912. Colonel Mantell married, in 1904, Helen Campbell, daughter of Colonel G. Campbell Ross.

GAMBLE, RICHARD NARRIEN, Major, was born at Edinburgh 10 March, 1860, son of the late Lieut.-General D. J. Gamble, C.B., and the late Mrs. M. E. Gamble. He was educated at Blair Lodge, and R.M.C., Sandhurst, and was commissioned in the 10th Lincolnshire Regt. 13 Aug. 1879; was Adjutant in the same regiment 30 Nov. 1881, to 20 Nov. 1884. He served in the Bechuanaland Expedition, 1884–85; became Captain 3 Aug. 1887; passed the Staff College, 1890–91; was A.D.C. to G.O.C., Scottish District, 16 Jan. 1894, to 30 Sept. 1895, and D.A.A.G., Cork District, 2 Oct. 1895, to 6 Jan. 1898. He took part in the Egyptian Campaign, 1898–99; was present at the operations at Atbara and Khartum; was mentioned in Despatches [London Gazette, 30 Sept. 1898, and on another occasion]; awarded the Medjidie, 3rd Class, and the British Medal and Egyptian Medal with three clasps. He was promoted Major, Royal Berkshire Regt., 3 Nov. 1900, and served in the South African War,

1900–1, as D.A.A.G., Mounted Infantry, 7 April to 2 Nov. 1900, and on the General Staff; during operations in the Orange Free State, including action at Houtnek (Thoba Mountain); taking part in the operations in the Transvaal in May and June, 1900, including actions near Johannesburg and Diamond Hill; during operations in Orange River Colony, including action at Wittebergen. He was mentioned in Despatches [London Gazette, 10 Sept. 1901]; received the Queen's Medal with four clasps, and was created a Companion of the Distinguished Service Order [London Gazette, 27 Sept. 1901]: "Richard Narrien Gamble, Major, Royal Berkshire Regt. In recognition of services during the operations in South Africa." The Insignia were presented by the King 29 Oct. 1901; the Warrant sent 18 Jan. 1902. He was D.A.Q.M.G., 6th Division, 2nd Army Corps, 1 Jan. to 12 May, 1903, and was Major, Second-in-Command, 2nd Royal Berkshire Regt., 1905–8; promoted Lieut.-Colonel 30 April, 1907, commanding the same regiment, 1908–11; was promoted Colonel 19 July, 1911; was G.S.O., 1st Grade, 6th (Poona) Division, 1912–14. At the outbreak of the European War, 1914, he was sent to Mesopotamia as G.S.O., 6th Division, and was promoted Brigadier-General commanding 17th Brigade in Mesopotamia, 1915, where he was thrice mentioned in Despatches for valuable service, and created C.B. in 1915. He was transferred to India in 1916, where he served as Deputy-Adjutant-General at Army Headquarters, Simla, and subsequently as Inspector of Volunteers in India and Burma. Brigadier-General Gamble retired 13 Oct. 1918. He married, in 1901, Audrey Nona, daughter of the late Francis A. Bevan, D.L., J.P., late Chairman of Barclay and Company.

CLARK, ROBERT LEAVER, Major, was born 20 Feb. 1862. He entered the Army as Inspector of Ordnance Machinery; became 2nd Class Inspector 1 April, 1896; (attached) 1st Class 24 Jan. 1900. He served in the South African War, 1899–1902, taking part in the advance on Kimberley; during operations in the Transvaal, west of Pretoria, July to 29 Nov. 1900; during operations in Orange River Colony, May to Nov. 1900; in the operations in Cape Colony, south of Orange River, 1899–1900; during operations in the Transvaal 30 Nov. 1900, to Sept. 1901, and Oct. 1901, to 31 May, 1902; in the operations in Cape Colony, Sept. and Oct. 1901. He was mentioned in Despatches [London Gazette, 10 Sept. 1901, and 29 July, 1902]; awarded the Queen's Medal with three clasps, the King's Medal with two clasps, and was created a Companion of the Distinguished Service Order [London Gazette, 27 Sept. 1901]: "Robert Leaver Clark, Inspector of Ordnance Machinery, 1st Class, and Honorary Major A.O.D. In recognition of services in the operations in South Africa." The Insignia were presented by the King 18 Dec. 1902. He was promoted to Chief Inspector 1 Aug. 1907. He served during the European War; became Lieut.-Colonel 27 Aug. 1918, and received the O.B.E. Major Clark married, in 1914, Dorothy, eldest daughter of J. E. Moulton, King's Heath, Worcestershire.

LUARD, ARTHUR JOHN HAMILTON, Major, was born 3 Sept. 1861, at Waltair, India, son of the late Colonel George Francis Luard, Indian Staff Corps, and Jane, daughter of Lieut.-Colonel Johnstone Hamilton, Indian Staff Corps. He was educated at Cheltenham College, and at the Royal Military College, Sandhurst. He joined the Army 10 May, 1882; took part in the Burmese Expedition, 1886–87 (Medal with clasp); served in Upper Burma, 1888–89, during operations in the Chin Hills (clasp). He was promoted Captain, 2nd Battn. Norfolk Regt., 1889. He was Superintendent of Gymnasia 12 April, 1897, to 14 Dec. 1899; was promoted Major 9 Sept. 1900. Major Luard served in South Africa, 1900–2 (was slightly wounded), as Assistant to Military Governor, Johannesburg; afterwards Assistant to Commissioner of Police, Johannesburg, 6 June, 1900, to 19 Nov. 1901, taking part in the operations in the Orange Free State, Feb. to May, 1900, including operations at Paardeberg (17 to 27 Feb.); actions at Poplar Grove and Karee Siding; taking part in the operations in the Transvaal in May and June, 1900, including actions near Johannesburg. He was mentioned in Despatches 10 Sept. 1901; awarded two Medals and five clasps, and created a Companion of the Distinguished Service Order [London Gazette, 27 Sept. 1901]: "Arthur John Hamilton Luard, Major, Norfolk Regt. In recognition of services during the operations in South Africa." The Insignia were sent to the G.O.C., Transvaal, 3 Feb. 1903, and presented by the G.O.C. the Forces in South Africa, at Pretoria, 25 March, 1903. He was promoted to Lieut.-Colonel 1 Sept. 1908, and Colonel 6 April, 1912, and retired 1 Sept. 1912. Colonel Luard played five years for Gloucestershire C.C., 1892–96, and two years for Hants County C.C., 1897–98. He is a member of the M.C.C., Free Foresters, Incogniti and Hampshire Hogs. Capt. Luard married, 15 Oct. 1890, at Cheltenham, Rosa, daughter of the late Edmund Yates Peel, of Cheltenham, and they have one son, Edmund Arthur Peel Luard, born 31 July, 1891, now Major, R.G.A.

BAILEY, THE HON. JOSEPH HENRY RUSSELL (LORD GLANUSK), Major, was born at Glanusk Park, Crickhowell, 26 Oct. 1864, eldest son of the 1st Baron Glanusk, and Mary, daughter of Henry Lucas, M.D. He was educated at Eton, and the Royal Military College, Sandhurst, and was gazetted to the Grenadier Guards 7 Feb. 1885; became Capt. 11 Nov. 1896; was A.D.C. to Major-General, Home District, from 16 July, 1897. He became Major 29 Nov. 1900, and served in the South African War in 1900 as Adjutant, C.I.V. (Infantry); was mentioned in Despatches [London Gazette, 10 Sept. 1901]; received the Queen's Medal with four clasps, and was created a Companion of the Distinguished Service Order [London Gazette,

Lord Glanusk.

27 Sept. 1901]: "The Hon. Joseph Henry Russell Bailey, Major, Grenadier Guards. In recognition of services during operations in South Africa." The Insignia were presented by the King 29 Oct. 1901; the Warrant sent 24 Jan. 1902. He commanded the Guards' Depôt, Caterham, 1901–3; resigned his commission in 1903, and became Lieut.-Colonel, 3rd Battn. South Wales Borderers, 1904–10; succeeded to peerage as 2nd Baron Glanusk in 1906. He was Lieut.-Colonel, Brecknock Battn. South Wales Borderers, 1911–16, and was created a C.B., 1911, and a C.B.E., 1919. Lord Glanusk became Lord-Lieutenant of Brecknock in 1905; Chairman of the County Association; Commissioner of Boy Scouts for Wales; Honorary Colonel, Brecknock Battn., and Chairman of the County Council. His favourite recreations were cricket and football (captain Eton Football, 1883), and are now shooting, fishing, hunting, etc. He married, in 1890, Editha Alma, daughter of the late Major Warden Sergison, of Cuckfield Park, Sussex, and they have one son, Lieut.-Colonel the Hon. Wilfred Russell Bailey, D.S.O., born 27 June, 1891, and one daughter.

PARSONS, FREDERICK GEORGE, Major, was born in 1856, son of the late Robert Parsons, and entered the Royal West Surrey Regt. as Lieutenant, becoming Captain 18 April, 1896. He served in South Africa, 1900–2, as Major, 3rd Battn. Royal West Surrey Regt.; as District Commandant, Lines of Communication, from 24 June, 1901, to 5 April, 1902; during operations in Cape Colony, south of Orange River, 1900; taking part in the operations in Cape Colony, Nov. 1900, to April, 1902. He was mentioned in Despatches [London Gazette, 10 Sept. 1901]: awarded the Queen's Medal and King's Medal with two clasps, and was created a Companion of the Distinguished Service Order [London Gazette, 27 Sept. 1901]: "Frederick George Parsons, Major, 3rd Battn. Royal West Surrey Regt. In recognition of services during the operations in South Africa." The Insignia were presented by the King 29 Oct. 1902; the Warrant sent 24 Jan. 1903. Lieut.-Colonel Parsons commanded the Royal West Surrey Regt., and retired from the Army on 23 Oct. 1905. He married (1st), in 1892, Maria Eliza Mary (died in 1903), daughter of the late Colonel Henry Penton, of Pentonville, Middlesex, and widow of J. L. M. Parkinson, Ludford Park, Ludlow; and (2ndly), in 1904, Rosalie, youngest daughter of the late J. G. O'Dwyer, Entre Rios, Argentina.

TYLDEN-PATTENSON, ARTHUR HENRY, Major, was born 30 Sept. 1856, second son of Capt. Tylden-Pattenson, J.P., D.L., of Dashmonden and Ibornden, Kent. He was privately educated, and at Brasenose College, Oxford, and entered the Army 14 Sept. 1878; served in the Zulu War, 1879; was present at the Battle of Ginginhlovo (Medal with clasp); was promoted Captain in 1886; retired 3 Nov. 1897. He served in the South African War, 1900–1, as Major, 3rd Battn. The Buffs; during operations in Orange River Colony 30 Nov. 1900, to March, 1901; during operations in Cape Colony, Dec. 1900. He was mentioned in Despatches [London Gazette, 10 Sept. 1901]; awarded the Queen's Medal with three clasps, and created a Companion of the Distinguished Service Order [London Gazette, 27 Sept. 1901]: "Arthur Henry Tylden-Pattenson, Major, 3rd Battn. East Kent Regt. In recognition of services during the operations in South Africa." The Insignia were presented by the King 29 Oct. 1901; the Warrant sent 18 Jan. 1902. He became Major, Reserve of Officers, 18 Oct. 1902. He married, in 1893, Alice Maude Mary, daughter of the late Cyrus Andrews, of Alverton Grange, Nottinghamshire, and they have one daughter.

FITZHERBERT, THE RIGHT HON. FRANCIS EDWARD (LORD STAFFORD), Major and Hon. Lieut.-Colonel, was born at Swynnerton Park 28 Aug. 1859, son of Basil Thomas Fitzherbert, D.L., J.P., of Swynnerton Park, Stone, Staffordshire, and Emily Charlotte, daughter of the late Hon. Edward Stafford Jerningham, second son of the 8th Baron. He was educated at Beaumont College, Windsor, and joined the Lancashire Militia in 1877. He served with the Staffordshire Yeomanry from 1882 to 1898; in the South African War, 1900–2; was Commandant, Staffordshire Volunteer Regt. during the war. He was mentioned in Despatches; awarded the Queen's Medal with three clasps, the King's Medal with two clasps, and was created a Companion of the Distinguished Service Order [London Gazette, 27 Sept. 1901]: "The Right Hon. Francis Edward Fitzherbert, Major and Hon. Lieut.-Colonel, 3rd Battn. Royal Lancashire Regt., and Lieut.-Colonel Commandant, Staffordshire Volunteer Regt. In recognition of services during the operations in South Africa." The Insignia were presented by the King 12 March, 1902; the Warrant sent 24 Jan. 1902. He succeeded to the peerage in 1913, and is the 12th Baron (created 1640, confirmed 1825). His brother, Basil John, born 28 Oct. 1861, is his heir. Lord Stafford holds King Edward's and King George's Coronation Medals · he is Deputy Lieutenant and Justice of the Peace for Staffordshire. He married, in London, in the Brompton Oratory, 20 April, 1903, Dorothy Hilda, third daughter of Albert O. Worthington, D.L., J.P., of Maple Hayes, Lichfield.

Lord Stafford.

CAMPBELL, JOHN EDWARD ROBERT, Major and Hon. Lieut.-Colonel, was born 20 July, 1855, the eldest son of the late George Campbell, of Duntroon, New South Wales, and Marrianne Collinson, only daughter of the late E. C. Close, formerly Lieutenant, 48th Regt. of Foot. He was educated privately, and at Jesus College, Cambridge, and entered the Militia, becoming Lieutenant 6 Dec. 1876. He was promoted Captain 19 Jan. 1881, and Major 8 May, 1895. He served in the South African

John E. R. Campbell.

War, 1900–1; was appointed Commandant, Prisoners of War, on board the City of Cambridge, at Simon's Town; but on the prisoners being sent to St. Helena, he rejoined his battalion, and proceeded with it to the scene of operations in the Orange Free State. He was appointed Commandant at Sanna's Post, and continued to hold that appointment until ordered to bring his battalion back to England. He was mentioned in Despatches; awarded the Queen's Medal with three clasps, and was created a Companion of the Distinguished Service Order [London Gazette, 27 Sept. 1901]: "John Edward Robert Campbell, Major and Hon. Lieut.-Colonel, 6th Battn. Royal Warwickshire Regt. In recognition of services during the operations in South Africa." The Insignia were presented by the King 29 Oct. 1901. He was promoted Lieut.-Colonel 11 Dec. 1902; retired with honorary rank of Colonel in 1903. Colonel Campbell is a Deputy Lieutenant and Justice of the Peace for Herefordshire. He was appointed Military Representative, and subsequently National Service Representative, for the Leominster Rural District of Herefordshire, during the Great War, 1914–18, and received the thanks of the respective authorities for his services. He married, in 1881, Helen, youngest daughter of the late Richard Spooner, H.E.I.C.S.; they have two sons: Donald Neil (Lieutenant, R.A.S.C., M.T.), and George Cecil (Captain, Royal Engineers), and one daughter, Winifred Helen.

MAHON, SIR WILLIAM HENRY, Baronet, Major, was born 31 Dec. 1856. He succeeded his father, 1893, and is the 5th Baronet. He served in the South African War, 1899–1902; was District Commandant, in command of the 4th Battn. West Yorkshire Regt., 21 Oct. 1900, to 31 Jan. 1901; operations in the Transvaal, Oct. 1900; operations in Orange River Colony, Sept. 1900; operations in Cape Colony, March to Aug. 1900, and Oct. to 29 Nov. 1900; operations in Cape Colony 30 Nov. 1900, to March, 1900. He was mentioned in Despatches [London Gazette, 10 Sept. 1901]; received the Queen's Medal with three clasps, the King's Medal with two clasps, and was created a Companion of the Distinguished Service Order [London Gazette, 27 Sept. 1901]: "Sir William Henry Mahon, Bart., Major, 4th Battn. West Yorkshire Regt. In recognition of services during the operations in South Africa." The Insignia were presented by the King 29 Oct. 1901. He is a Justice of the Peace and Deputy Lieutenant. Sir William Mahon married, in 1905, the Hon. Edith Dillon, second daughter of the 4th Lord Clonbrock, and they have one son, George Edward John, born 22 June, 1911, and one daughter.

LAURIE, CLAUDE VILLIERS EMILIUS (now **Sir C. V. E. Laurie, Bart.**), Major, was born 25 Nov. 1855, the eldest son of Sir Emilius Laurie, 3rd Baronet, and Maranne Sophia (who died in 1909), daughter of the late Edward R. Rice, M.P., of Dane Court, Kent. He was educated at Eton, and Trinity College, Cambridge, and served in South Africa, 1900–2, as Commandant at Modder River, and afterwards at Jacobsdal; operations in the Transvaal, west of Pretoria, Sept. to Oct. and Nov. 1900; operations in Orange River Colony, Oct. to Nov. 1900; operations in Cape Colony, Orange River, March to Sept. and Nov. 1900; operations in the Transvaal 30 Nov. to Jan. 1901; operations in Orange River Colony, Feb. to May, 1902; operations in Cape Colony. He was mentioned in Despatches [London Gazette, 10 Sept. 1901]; received the Queen's Medal with three clasps, the King's Medal with two clasps, and was created a Companion of the Distinguished Service Order [London Gazette, 27 Sept. 1901]: "Claude Villiers Emilius Laurie, Major, 3rd Battn. King's Own Scottish Borderers. In recognition of services during the operations in South Africa." He was created a C.B. in 1909. He was Lieut.-Colonel, 2/5th King's Own Scottish Borderers, 1914–16. Sir C. V. E. Laurie is a Barrister.

MACKIE, JOHN, Major, was born 9 May, 1857, eldest son of the late James Mackie, of Bargaly, Kirkcudbright. He served in the South African War. He was mentioned in Despatches; awarded the Queen's Medal with three clasps, the King's Medal with two clasps, and was created a Companion of the Distinguished Service Order [London Gazette, 27 Sept. 1901]: "John Mackie, Major, 3rd Battn. King's Own Scottish Borderers. In recognition of services during the operations in South Africa." The Insignia were presented by the King 24 Oct. 1902; the Warrant sent 4 Nov. 1902. Major Mackie married, in 1910, Violet, eldest daughter of Sir Oswald Mosley, 1st Bart.

Montague G. Johnstone.

JOHNSTONE, MONTAGUE GEORGE, Lieut.-Colonel, was born 21 March, 1848, second son of the late General Montague Cholmeley Johnstone and Louisa, daughter of the late Lieut.-General Sir Henry Somerset, K.C.B., K.H., and granddaughter of Lord Charles Somerset. He was educated at Cheltenham College; joined the Royal Scots Greys on 22 June, 1870, and was appointed an extra A.D.C. to the Duke of Marlborough, the Lord-Lieutenant of Ireland, 1880. In 1883 he assisted in raising the 2nd Mounted Rifles (Carrington's Horse); took part in the Bechuanaland Expedition, on the Headquarters Staff; served in the South African Campaign, 1900–1, when he commanded a wing of the 4th Scottish Rifles in the operations with Lord Methuen's 1st Division in the Orange River Colony, which led to the surrender of Prinsloo at Slabert's Nek. He was for some time in command of his regiment, and was also Commandant of Boshof. He afterwards was promoted to the command of the 3rd King's Own Yorkshire Light Infantry during its embodiment in the Mediterranean, and for the remainder of the war, which regiment he commanded for six years, until promoted to be its Hon. Colonel. He was mentioned in Despatches; awarded the Medal with four clasps; given a Lieut.-Colonelcy, and was created a Companion of the Distinguished Service Order [London Gazette, 27 Sept. 1901]: "Montague George Johnstone, Major and Honorary Lieut.-Colonel, 4th Battn. Scottish Rifles. In recognition of services during the operations in South Africa." The Insignia were presented by the King 29 Oct. 1901; the Warrant sent 24 Jan. 1902. Colonel Johnstone has held several military appointments; has been employed by the Master of the Horse, and by the Colonial Office; was Commandant of Lambeth Palace Camp during the Coronation of King Edward VII.; belongs to the King's Bodyguard for Scotland; commands 1st Westminster Battn. National Reserve; holds the 1911 Coronation Medal; is a Justice of the Peace for Fife, and has been a Lieut.-Colonel, Reserve of Officers. He married, in 1880, Agnes, widow of Capt. Johnston Stansfeld, and daughter of the late Joseph Harrison, J.P., D.L., of Galligreaves Hall, and of Samlesbury Hall, Lancashire, and Lord of the Manor of Hadley, Essex; they had two sons: Montague Joseph Charles Somerset and Reginald FitzRoy Lewis, born on 16 June, 1882, and 3 June, 1884, and one daughter, Violet Agnes Charlotte Mary. His younger son, in the Cameron Highlanders (1st Battn.), was killed in action during the Great War, 8 Sept. 1914. His elder son served in the Scots Greys, on the Western Front, during the Great War.

SECKHAM, BASSETT THORNE, Major, was born 22 Nov. 1863, eldest son of the late Samuel Lipscomb Seckham, J.P., D.L., and of the late Kinbarra Swene Seckham. He was educated at Charterhouse, and joined the 4th Royal Welsh Fusiliers 18 Jan. 1882, becoming Captain, 4th South Staffordshire Regt., 31 May, 1886, and Major 4 Feb. 1899. He served in the South African Campaign, 1900–1; was present at actions of Lindley, Bethlehem and Winburg; O.C. Infantry, with a column under Lord Methuen, at Kimberley, Barkly West, Likatleng and Dronfield, March, 1900. He took part in the operations which ended in the surrender of Prinsloo and 4,000 men. He was mentioned in Despatches; awarded the Queen's Medal with three clasps, and created a Companion of the Distinguished Service Order [London Gazette, 27 Sept. 1901]: "Bassett Thorne Seckham, Major, 4th Battn. South Staffordshire Regt. In recognition of services during the operations in South Africa." The Insignia were presented by the King 29 Oct. 1901; the warrant sent 24 Jan. 1902. He was Lieut.-Colonel commanding 13 Dec. 1905, to 1910; was given the honorary rank of Colonel 2 Aug. 1908; retired 31 Dec. 1910. On the outbreak of the European War he offered his services as Major, and was attached for duty to the 4th South Staffordshire Regt. Sept. 1914, and served with them and other battalions of the regiment until 8 March, 1919; coast defences and recruit training. Colonel Seckham is Justice of the Peace, Staffordshire. He married, in 1888, Alice Dorothy, daughter of W. F. Moore, of Cronkbourne, Douglas, and they have one son, Lionel Bassett Lipscomb, born on 17 June, 1891, and two daughters.

HALL, MONTAGU HEATH, Major, was born 26 Dec. 1856, son of the late Isaac Hall, of Upton Bank, Macclesfield, and Castleton, Derbyshire. He was educated at Repton, and Trinity Hall, Cambridge, and joined the 4th Royal Lancashire Militia in 1876, serving in South Africa, 1900–1. He was Assistant Press Censor, and Commandant at Springfontein. In command 3rd Battn. South Lancashire Regt. 26 April to 22 Nov. 1900. Operations in Cape Colony, south of Orange River, Feb. to April, 1900; operations in Orange River Colony 30 Nov. 1900, to July, 1901. He was mentioned in Despatches [London Gazette, 10 Sept. 1901 and 29 July, 1902], received the Queen's Medal and three clasps, and was created a Companion of the Distinguished Service Order [London Gazette, 27 Sept. 1901]: "Montagu Heath Hall, Major, 3rd Battn. South Lancashire Regt. In recognition of services during the operations in South Africa." The Insignia were presented to him by the King 27 Oct. 1901. He became Lieutenant-Colonel commanding the 3rd Battn. South Lancashire Regt., and has retired. Lieut.-Colonel M. H. Hall is a Solicitor, practising in Manchester.

TARBET, ALEXANDER FRANCIS, Major, was born 29 Dec. 1860, son of the late William Tarbet, of 4, Park Avenue, Bedford. He was educated at Wellington College; joined the 4th Royal Lancashire Militia in 1881; served in Methuen's Horse, with the Bechuanaland Field Force in 1885; took part in operations with the Lagos Hausa Force, 1887–94. He was appointed Private Secretary to Sir Gilbert Carter, K.C.M.G., 1892–94; commanded Lagos Hausas in the Jebu Expedition, 1892 (Despatches, 1 July, 1892; Medal with clasp); was appointed Inspector-General to the Sierra Leone Frontier Force, 1894 (Despatches, Special). He helped to quell the disturbances in Sierra Leone, 1897–99, when he commanded the Frontier Police, and was mentioned in Despatches [London Gazette, 29 Dec. 1899], received a clasp and was created a C.M.G. (1898). He served in the South African War, 1900–1 as Railway Staff Officer (graded as a D.A.A.G.), Lines of Communication; afterwards as Commandant, Jagersfontein Road. Operations in Orange River Colony, May to 29 Nov. 1900; operations in Cape Colony, south of Orange River, Feb. to April, 1900; operations in Orange River Colony 30 Nov. 1900, to July, 1901. He was mentioned in Despatches [London Gazette, 10 Sept. 1901], received the Queen's Medal and three clasps, and was created a Companion of the Distinguished Service Order [London Gazette, 27 Sept. 1901]: "Alexander Francis Tarbet, C.M.G., Major, 3rd Battn. South Lancashire Regt. In recognition of services during the operations in South Africa." He became Honorary Lieutenant-Colonel; resigned his commission in 1907, and rejoined the 3rd Battn. South Lancashire Regt. in Oct. 1914, till retiring in

June, 1919. He married, in 1890, Elsie Maud, daughter of the late Edmund Hooper, of Weston Lodge, Albury, Surrey, and they had one son (deceased).

FORREST, WILLIAM, Major, was born 30 Sept. 1868, son of Colonel Peter Forrest, of The Hirst, Edinburgh. He was educated at Ayr and Edinburgh University, and was commissioned in the 3rd Battn. Welsh Regt., as Second Lieutenant (22 June to 19 July, 1889), becoming Lieutenant (20 July, 1889, to 12 July, 1891); Captain (13 July, 1891, to 5 June, 1900), and Major (6 June, 1900, to 4 Feb. 1910). Major Forrest served in the South African War, 1900–2. He was Commandant, Prieska District, and employed under the Assistant Provost-Marshal, Kimberley District. He took part in operations in Cape Colony 30 Nov. 1900, to Feb. 1902; was mentioned in Despatches [London Gazette, 10 Sept. 1901], received the Queen's Medal with one clasp, the King's Medal with two clasps, and was created a Companion of the Distinguished Service Order [London Gazette, 27 Sept. 1901]: "William Forrest, Major, 3rd Battn. Welsh Regt. In recognition of services during the operations in South Africa." The Insignia were presented by the King 2 June, 1902; the Warrant sent 4 June, 1902. He became Honorary Lieutenant-Colonel 4 Oct. 1905. On 11 Aug. 1908 he was gazetted Major and Honorary Lieutenant-Colonel in the Special Reserve, and Lieutenant-Colonel (5 Feb. 1910, to 2 April, 1913), resigning his commission on 2 April, 1913. Lieut.-Colonel Forrest was in command of a Territorial Reserve Battn. from Jan. 1916, till April, 1917, at Kinmel Park, North Wales. He married, in 1898, the Hon. Marie Spencer Lewis, daughter of the 1st Baron Merthyr, and they have one son, born on 16 Aug. 1899.

WILKINSON, GEORGE ALEXANDER EASON, Lieut.-Colonel, was born 25 Feb. 1860, eldest son of the late Mathew Eason-Wilkinson, of Middlethorpe, and Greenheyes, Manchester, by his second wife, Louisa, only child of George Henry Walker, of Longford, Philadelphia, U.S.A. He was educated at Charterhouse; joined the Royal Sherwood Foresters (Militia) in 1880. He served in South Africa, 1899–1900, as Major and Honorary Lieutenant-Colonel, 4th Battn. Derbyshire Regt. He was created a Companion of the Distinguished Service Order [London Gazette, 27 Sept. 1901]: "George Alexander Eason Wilkinson, Major and Honorary Lieutenant-Colonel, 4th Battn. Derbyshire Regt. In recognition of services during the operations in South Africa." The Insignia were presented by the King 29 Oct. 1901. He afterwards commanded the Regiment, and retired in 1907, with the rank of Honorary Lieutenant-Colonel. He served in the European War from Sept. 1914, to April, 1919, in command of supernumerary companies, and as Supervising Officer, Royal Defence Corps, Northern Command, with rank of Lieutenant-Colonel. He was awarded the C.B.E. (Military) in Jan. 1919, and was given the rank of Colonel. Colonel Wilkinson is a Justice of the Peace for both East and West Ridings of Yorkshire. He married, in 1886, the Hon. Caroline Catherine, eldest daughter of the 3rd Baron Decies.

TWEMLOW, FRANCIS RANDLE, Lieut.-Colonel, was born at Smallwood, Cheshire, 20 Dec. 1852, son of Francis Cradock Twemlow, of Peatswood, Staffordshire, Clerk in Holy Orders. He was educated at Winchester, and at Christ Church, Oxford (M.A., 1st Class Honours in Modern History, 1875), and the Inner Temple, and joined the Militia 8 Aug. 1874 Lieut.-Colonel Twemlow served in South Africa, March, 1900, to May, 1902; was Commandant, Fraserburg District, Dec. 1900, to Aug. 1901; O.C., 4th North Staffordshire Regt., Aug. 1901, to Feb. 1902 (in the absence of Colonel Mirehouse, C.M.G., on sick leave). He took part in operations in Cape Colony, south of Orange River, 1900; operations in the Transvaal and Orange River Colony, March, 1902; operations in Cape Colony, 30 Nov. 1900, to May, 1902. For his services in South Africa he was mentioned in Despatches [London Gazette, 10 Sept. 1901]; received the Queen's Medal and three clasps; King's

Francis R. Twemlow.

Medal and two clasps, and was created a Companion of the Distinguished Service Order [London Gazette, 27 Sept. 1901]: "Francis Randle Twemlow, Major and Honorary Lieutenant-Colonel, 4th Battn. North Staffordshire Regt. In recognition of services during the operations in South Africa." The Insignia were presented by the King 24 Oct. 1902. He commanded the 4th North Staffordshire Regt. from 13 Dec. 1905, to 29 Aug. 1908; was promoted Honorary Colonel 14 Dec. 1906, and retired under the age clause, 29 Aug. 1908. After the outbreak of the European War he was commissioned to raise a new Territorial Battalion (3/6th North Staffordshire Regt.), 4 April, 1915. He was gazetted to the Territorial Force Reserve from 14 Dec. 1915. He married (1st), at Topsham, Devon, 17 Dec. 1878, Evelyn Harriet (who died in 1880), daughter of Sir J. T. B. Duckworth, 2nd Bart.; and (2ndly), 11 July, 1882, at St. George's, Hanover Square, Annie Mary Gertrude, daughter of the Rev. Edward Lewis, and they have one daughter, Evelyn Dorothy.

CAMPBELL, MONTAGU DOUGLAS, Major and Honorary Lieut.-Colonel, was born 16 Oct. 1852, youngest son of Archibald Campbell, of Mains and Blythswood. He served in the South African War, 1899–1900, as Commandant, America

Montagu D. Campbell.

Siding. Operations in Cape Colony and Orange Free State, Feb. to May, 1900; operations in Orange River Colony, May to 29 Nov. 1900; operations in Orange River Colony 30 Nov. 1900, to July, 1901; operations in Cape Colony, July, 1901. He was mentioned in Despatches [London Gazette, 10 Sept. 1901]; received the Queen's Medal and four clasps, and was created a Companion of the Distinguished Service Order [London Gazette, 27 Sept. 1901]: "Montagu Douglas Campbell, Major and Honorary Lieut.-Colonel, 4th Battn. Argyll and Sutherland Highlanders. In recognition of services during the operations in South Africa." The Insignia were presented by the King 29 Oct. 1901. Lieut.-Colonel Campbell was a Justice of the Peace, County Renfrew. He died on the 12th of Feb. 1916.

LUTTMAN-JOHNSON, FREDERIC, Major, was born at Benderton House, Chichester, 22 Jan. 1845, son of the Rev. Henry W. R. Luttman-Johnson, and Sarah Elizabeth Fooks. He was educated abroad; at Brighton College, and at the Royal Military College, Sandhurst; became Ensign 10 Oct. 1865; Lieutenant 7 Nov. 1868; Lieutenant, 65th Foot, 17 April, 1869; Captain 19 April, 1876; Major, York and Lancaster Regt., 1 July, 1881; Brigade Major, Cyprus, 21 Sept. 1879, to 21 Sept. 1884; passed the Staff College, 1889; promoted Lieutenant-Colonel on full pay 14 Dec. 1894, and retired with the rank of Lieutenant-Colonel, 1899. He served in the South African War, 1900–2, as Major in the Militia, with the idea of assisting Colonel Holroyd Smyth, commanding 3rd Leinsters. He was at the time Staff Officer to the Inspector-General, Lines of Communication, Eastern District.

F. Luttman-Johnson.

He assisted Colonel Smyth to collect horses in the Molteno District, for which services Colonel Smyth recommended him for the Distinguished Service Order. He assisted in operations in Kimberley; was transferred to the Western Section, where he helped construct about fifty blockhouses of rubble stone, from the debris heaps at Kimberley, delivering same in sandbags; was appointed Commandant at Modder River, where there was a garrison of four regiments; was Commandant at Queenstown, and at Stormberg. He took part in operations in Cape Colony, April to 29 Nov. 1900; operations in the Orange River Colony, Jan to April, 1901; operations in Cape Colony 30 Nov. 1900, to Jan. 1901, and April, 1901, to May, 1902. He was mentioned in Despatches [London Gazette, 10 Sept. 1901]; received the Queen's Medal with three clasps; King's Medal with two clasps, and was created a Companion of the Distinguished Service Order [London Gazette, 27 Sept. 1901]: "Frederic Luttman-Johnson, Major, 3rd Battn. Royal Canadians (Leinster Regt.). In recognition of services during the operations in South Africa." The Insignia were presented by the King 18 Dec. 1902. He retired with the rank of Lieutenant-Colonel, and Honorary Colonel of the 3rd Leinster Regt. Colonel Luttman-Johnson was a Justice of the Peace, West Sussex. He died on the 11th Aug. 1917.

WELDON, SIR ANTHONY ARTHUR, Major, was born in London 1 March, 1863, eldest son of the 5th Baronet and Elizabeth, daughter of the late Colonel Arthur Kennedy. He was educated at Charterhouse, and at Trinity College, Cambridge, where he took his B.A. in 1884; joined the 4th Battn. Leinster Regt. in 1885, and became Major 13 Oct. 1898; was A.D.C. to F.M. Lord Wolseley, Commander-in-Chief, 1895–1900; served in the South African Campaign, 1899–1900, as Special Service Officer, with the Natal Field Force, under Sir Redvers Buller; as Railway Staff Officer, Lines of Communication, afterwards attached to the Army Service Corps. Operations in Natal, 1899; Relief of Ladysmith, including actions at Colenso, Spion Kop, Vaal Kranz; operations on Tugela Heights (14 to 27 Feb. 1900), and action at Pieter's Hill; operations in Natal, March to June, 1900. He was mentioned in Despatches [London Gazette, 8 Feb. and 10 Sept. 1901], received the Queen's Medal with two clasps, and was created a Companion of the Distinguished Service Order [London Gazette, 27 Sept. 1901]: "Sir Anthony Arthur Weldon, Bart., Major, 4th Battn. Royal Canadians (Leinster Regt.). In recognition of services during the operations in South Africa." The Insignia were presented by the King 17 Dec. 1901; the Warrant sent 24 Jan. 1902. He was created a C.V.O., 1911. He was Deputy-Lieutenant, Queen's County; Justice of the Peace, Queen's County and County Kildare; State Steward and Chamberlain to the Lord-Lieutenant of Ireland. He married, in 1902, Winifred, daughter of the late Colonel Varty Rogers, of Broxmore Park, Romsey, late of the Royal Dublin Fusiliers and His Majesty's Bodyguard of Gentlemen-at-Arms; and they had three sons. Sir A. A. Weldon died 29 June, 1917, and was succeeded in the baronetcy by his eldest son, Anthony Edward Wolseley Weldon, born 1 Dec. 1902.

SHAW, SIR FREDERICK WILLIAM, Bart., Major, was born in Dublin, 15 March, 1858, eldest son of the late Lieut.-Colonel Sir Robert Shaw, D.L., 4th Bart., and Kate, daughter of William Barton, of Grove, County Tipperary. He was educated at Harrow, Oriel College, Oxford, and at Sandhurst. He received his first commission as Lieutenant, Royal Dragoons, 13 Aug. 1879; resigned in Aug. 1885; joined the 5th Royal Dublin Fusiliers as Captain, 1887. He succeeded to the baronetcy in 1895. He served in the South African War, 1900–2; as Station Commandant, afterwards Commandant, Barkly West; Station Staff Officer and Commandant, Warrenton. He was in command of the 5th Battn. Royal Dublin Fusiliers, May and June, 1901. Operations in the Transvaal and Orange River Colony, Jan. to 31 May, 1902; operations in Cape Colony, 30 Nov. 1900, to Jan. 1902. He was mentioned in Despatches [London Gazette, 10 Sept. 1901]; received the Queen's and the King's Medals with five clasps, and

was created a Companion of the Distinguished Service Order [London Gazette, 27 Sept. 1901]: "Sir Frederick William Shaw, Bart., Major, 5th Battn. Royal Dublin Fusiliers. In recognition of services during operations in South Africa." The Insignia were presented by the King 12 March, 1902. He commanded the 5th Battn. Royal Dublin Fusiliers from 1907 to 1913. Sir F. W. Shaw served in the European War in command of the 8th Battn. Royal Dublin Fusiliers (14 Oct. 1914). He raised this Corps, and took it to France, Dec. 1915, and from 16 March, 1916, he commanded the 2nd (Home Service) Garrison Battn. Royal Irish Regt. He is a Deputy-Lieutenant and a Justice of the Peace. He married, on 9 July, 1885, Eleanor Hester, daughter of Major Horace de Vere, R.E., of Curragh Chase, at Bookcer Church, County Galway, and they have two sons: Capt. Robert de Vere Shaw, M.C., R.F.A., born 24 Feb. 1890 (who served in the European War, 1914–18, and was mentioned in Despatches), and Lieut. F. C. Shaw, 5th King's African Rifles, born 17 Jan. 1895; and four daughters: Annie Kate, born in 1886, wife of Lieut.-Colonel C. de Putron, Lancashire Fusiliers; Mary, born in 1887; Grace Eleanor, born in 1889, wife of Major C. Goodlife, Royal Fusiliers; and Eile de Vere, born in 1892.

BAGOT, THE HONOURABLE WALTER LEWIS, Major, was born at Blithfield, Rugeley, 22 April, 1864, son of William, 3rd Baron Bagot, and Lucia, his wife, daughter of Lord and Lady Dover. He was educated at Eton, and the Royal Military College, Sandhurst; joined the Grenadier Guards 23 Aug. 1884; was A.D.C. to the Governor of South Australia, 1891. He was Regimental Adjutant, Grenadier Guards, 1893–97; served in the Sudan Expedition, 1898; was slightly wounded at the Battle of Omdurman; was awarded the Queen's Medal and Khedive's Medal with clasp. He retired from the Grenadier Guards in Dec. 1898. When the South African War broke out Major Bagot returned to active service, first as D.A.A.G., Imperial Yeomanry, Jan. 1900; subsequently as Administrator of Postal Services, Transvaal (8 July, 1900, to 1 April, 1901), and later on he became Staff Officer to Sir Henry Rawlinson's Columns, March, 1901, to termination of war. He was present at operations in the Orange Free State, April and May, 1900; operations in the Transvaal in June, 1900, including actions near Pretoria and Diamond Hill (11 and 12 June); operations in the Transvaal and Orange River Colony, April, 1901, to 31 May, 1902. He was mentioned in Despatches [London Gazette, 10 Sept. 1901, and on another occasion]; promoted to Major, Reserve of Officers; received the Queen's Medal and four clasps, the King's Medal and two clasps, and, for general good service, was created a Companion of the Distinguished Service Order [London Gazette, 27 Sept. 1901]: "Honourable Walter Lewis Bagot, Major, D.A.A.G. for Imperial Yeomanry. In recognition of services during the operations in South Africa." The Insignia, Warrant, etc., were sent to the G.O.C., Transvaal, 3 Feb. 1902, and privately presented in South Africa 26 June, 1903. He was appointed A.D.C. to Lieut.-General Sir Henry Rawlinson, 4th Army Corps, in France, 5 Nov. 1914, to June, 1915, subsequently he became Director in the Ministry of Munitions of War, June, 1915, to Jan. 1916. Major Bagot is General Manager, The Victoria Falls and Transvaal Power Company, Ltd., and Chairman of Rand Mines Power Supply Co., Ltd., registered at Johannesburg. He has the Jubilee Medal, 1897. He married, in 1892, Margaret Jane Caroline, daughter of the Hon. Frederick and Lady Adelaide Cadogan, and they have one daughter.

WYNDHAM-QUIN, WINDHAM HENRY, Major, was born in London 7 July, 1857, son of the late Capt. the Hon. W. H. Wyndham-Quin, and cousin and heir to the Earl of Dunraven. He was educated at Eton, and at the Royal Military College, Sandhurst. He served with the Inniskilling Dragoons in the Transvaal Campaign of 1881, and he raised and commanded the Glamorganshire Yeomanry. Major Wyndham-Quin served in the South African War in 1900, in command of a battalion of Imperial Yeomanry 13 April to 1 June, 1900. Operations in Orange River Colony, including actions at Wittebergen. He was mentioned in Despatches [London Gazette, 10 Sept. 1901]; received the Queen's Medal with three clasps, and for capable commanding of the Glamorgan Yeomanry was created

W. H. Wyndham-Quin.

a Companion of the Distinguished Service Order [London Gazette, 27 Sept. 1901]: "Windham Henry Wyndham-Quin, Major, 1st Battn. Imperial Yeomanry. In recognition of services during the operations in South Africa." The Insignia were presented by the King 17 Dec. 1901; the Warrant sent 24 Jan. 1902. Colonel Wyndham-Quin was created a C.B., 1903. He was elected M.P. (C.) for South Glamorganshire, 1895–1906. During the European War he was in command of the 22nd Division Base Depot. He has published a book entitled "Sir Charles Tyler, G.C.B., Admiral of the White" (1912), also "The Yeomanry Cavalry of Gloucester and Monmouth" (1897), and "The Foxhound in County Limerick" (1918). He was High Sheriff of County Kilkenny in 1914. He married, in 1885, Lady Eva Constance Aline Bourke, daughter of the 6th Earl of Mayo, and they have two sons and one daughter.

BERESFORD-PEIRSE, HENRY BERNARD DE LA POER, Major, was born in London 9 Jan. 1875, eldest son of Sir Henry Beresford-Peirse, 3rd Bart., and Lady Adelaide Bernard, daughter of the 3rd Earl of Bandon. He was educated at Eton, and Magdalen College, Oxford (B.A.). He served for fifteen months in South Africa, 1900–1, with the 3rd Imperial Yeomanry. He left England, as Lieutenant; was gazetted Captain on landing; was promoted to Major and Second-in-Command 1 June, 1900; in command of the 3rd Imperial Yeomanry in 1901; brought the regiment home, and retired from the Army in 1901, with the honorary rank of Major.

He was awarded the South African Medal with three bars; mentioned in Despatches; became a Companion of the Distinguished Service Order, at the recommendation of Colonel (now Major-General) Sir G. J. Younghusband [London Gazette, 27 Sept. 1901]: "Henry Bernard de la Poer Beresford-Peirse, Major, 3rd Battn. Imperial Yeomanry. In recognition of services during the operations in South Africa." He was appointed Under Treasurer, Middle Temple, E.C. Major Beresford-Peirse married, in 1904, Lady Mabel M. Campbell, daughter of the 3rd Earl Cawdor, and they have two sons.

HARRISON, THOMAS ELLIOT, Major, was born 14 June, 1862, son of T. E. Harrison, of Whitburn, Sunderland-on-Wear. He was educated at Eton, and Trinity College, Cambridge, and served in the 1st Dragoons. From 1900 to 1902 he served in the South African Campaign, in command of the 4th Battn. Imperial Yeomanry; was mentioned in Despatches [London Gazette, 10 Sept. 1901]; received the King's and Queen's Medals, and was created a Companion of the Distinguished Service Order [London Gazette, 27 Sept. 1901]: "Thomas Elliot Harrison, Major, 4th Battn. Imperial Yeomanry. In recognition of services during the operations in South Africa." The Insignia were presented by the King 29 Oct. 1901; the Warrant was sent 24 Jan. 1902 He became Lieutenant-Colonel. In 1898 and 1899 he was Master of the East Galway Hounds. He married, in 1890, Daisy, youngest daughter of William Wright, of Sazelbye Park, Melton Mowbray.

ANDERSON, WILLIAM CAMPBELL, Major, was born 14 Dec. 1868. He was educated at Harrow, and was gazetted to the 15th Hussars 29 March, 1890; became Captain 13 June, 1896. He served in West Africa, 1897–98, in the Northern Territories, Gold Coast, received the Medal with clasp. Capt. Anderson retired 30 Dec. 1899. He served in South Africa, 1900–2, as Commandant of an Imperial Yeomanry Battalion; was mentioned in Despatches [London Gazette, 7 May and 10 Sept. 1901]; received the Queen's and the King's Medals with five clasps, and was created a Companion of the Distinguished Service Order [London Gazette, 27 Sept. 1901]: "William Campbell Anderson, Major, 5th Battn. Imperial Yeomanry. In recognition of services during the operations in South Africa." The Insignia were presented to him by the King 29 Oct. 1901. He was given the honorary rank of Lieutenant-Colonel 9 Oct. 1902, and is a Honorary Colonel, 3rd Battn. Scottish Rifles. Colonel Anderson is a Fellow of the Royal Geographical Society. He married, in 1894, Elizabeth, daughter of the late Edward Barnes. Sir A. Conan Doyle, in "The Great Boer War" (pages 533–535), describes the gallant fight against overwhelming odds put up by Colonel Anderson when attacked by Delarey on 25 Feb. 1902. Von Donop had sent in an empty convoy from Wolmannstad to Klerksdorp, and the journey was nearly over and the detachment of Paget's Horse had ridden on into the town, when Delarey made his appearance. "The escort of the convoy consisted of the 5th Imperial Yeomanry, sixty of Paget's Horse, two companies of the ubiquitous Northumberland Fusiliers, two guns of the 4th R.F.A., and a pom-pom, amounting in all to 630 men. Colonel Anderson was in command." Nothing could have averted disaster, and it was well that some of the escort had ridden on, and were not there to share it. When the first turmoil of the attack was over, the wagons had been re-marshalled and rearranged. "It was Colonel Anderson's hope that he might be able to send them on into safety while he with the escort covered their retreat. His plan was certainly the best one, and if it did not succeed it was due to nothing which he could avert, but to the nature of the ground and the gallantry of the enemy. . . . A small force sallied out from Klerksdorp in the hope of helping Anderson, but on reaching the Jagd Drift it was found that the fighting was over and that the field was in possession of the Boers."

BOLITHO, WILLIAM EDWARD THOMAS, Major, was born at Penzance 2 July, 1862, son of the late William Bolitho, of Polwithen, He was educated at Harrow, and Trinity College, Oxford. He played for Harrow and Oxford at Lord's Cricket Ground (two years for Harrow, and two years for Oxford). He joined, as Second Lieutenant, the 1st Royal Devon Yeomanry in May, 1889; served with the 7th Battn. 27th Imperial Yeomanry in the South African War, 1900–1; was wounded at Noitgedacht, Transvaal, Nov. 1900; took part in advance to Pretoria, Battle of Diamond Hill, and holding the Mahaliesburg range of hills. He was mentioned twice in Despatches, and created a Companion of the Distinguished Service Order [London Gazette, 27 Sept. 1901]: "William Edward Thomas Bolitho, Major, 7th Battn. Imperial Yeomanry. In recognition of services during the operations in South Africa." The Insignia were presented by the King 29 Oct. 1901. He won the D.S.O. at Noitgedacht, Transvaal, when he led a forlorn hope up the kloof in the early morning, from General Clement's Camp, to relieve the Northumberland Fusiliers on top of the hill. He was wounded in the thigh, and lay out with his men for two days before being fetched in to an ambulance. He became Captain, 1st Royal Devon Yeomanry, 7 Aug. 1914. He became Acting Lieutenant-Colonel, 2/1st Royal Devon Yeomanry 15 Sept. 1914, and commanded the Regt. until 11 Nov. 1918, when he resigned on account of bad health, and went to Bath for treatment, where he died on 21 Feb. 1919. Lieut.-Colonel Bolitho was joint Master of the Foxhounds (Western), and hunted the hounds himself. Hunting was his great passion; he was also a good cricketer and fisherman. He had married, at Iverness, 21 June, 1888, Ethel Grace Macleod, daughter of R. B. Æneas Macleod, of Cadboll, and they have two sons: William Torquill Macleod (late 19th Hussars; killed in action 24 May, 1915), and Simon Bruce (who died in 1910); and one daughter, Brenda Grace.

LAWSON, THE HONOURABLE WILLIAM ARNOLD WEBSTER, Major, was born 10 March, 1864, youngest son of the 1st Baron Burnham and of Ethel Georgiana, only daughter of B. N. Webster. His elder brother is the 2nd Baron Burnham, now created a Viscount. The Hon. W. A. W. Lawson was educated at Eton and Sandhurst, and entered the Scots Guards in 1884; was promoted to Captain in 1897, and retired

Hon. W. A. W. Lawson.

to the Reserve of Officers in 1899. He raised the 38th Company, Imperial Yeomanry, in 1899, and commanded the 10th Battn. Imperial Yeomanry in South Africa, 1900–1. He was present at operations in the Orange Free State, March to May, 1900; operations in the Orange River Colony, May and June, 1900; operations in Cape Colony, March, 1900; operations in the Transvaal, Orange River Colony and Cape Colony, 30 Nov. 1900, to May, 1901. He was mentioned in Despatches [London Gazette, 7 May and 10 Sept. 1901], received the Queen's Medal with four clasps, was promoted to Major, Reserve of Officers, and created a Companion of the Distinguished Service Order [London Gazette, 27 Sept. 1901]: "The Honourable William Arnold Webster Lawson, Major, 10th Battn. Imperial Yeomanry. In recognition of services during the operations in South Africa." The Insignia were presented to him by the King 29 Oct. 1901. In Aug. 1903, he was promoted to Lieutenant-Colonel. On the outbreak of war in 1914, he was called up as R.S.O. at Paddington. In Sept. 1914, he raised the 2/1st Royal Buckinghamshire Hussars. He was mentioned in Despatches in 1916; was given the Brevet of Colonel 1 Jan. 1918, and received the War Medal. Colonel Lawson married, in 1887, Sybil Mary (whom he divorced in 1912), eldest daughter of the late Sir Frederick Marshall; they had two sons and two daughters: Edward Frederick, D.S.O., M.C., Captain, Royal Bucks Hussars, Temporary Acting Lieutenant-Colonel, 1/1st Middlesex Hussars (twice mentioned in Despatches), born 1890; William Bernard Webster, Lieutenant, Scots Guards (who was killed in action 22 Oct. 1914, at Steenstraate), born 1893; Margery, married Capt. J. F. Harrison, Royal Horse Guards, and Olive, married Major Jack Murray Smith, Royal Horse Guards.

JENKINSON, GEORGE SEYMOUR CHARLES, Major, was born 18 Feb. 1858, son of J. H. Jenkinson, of Ocklye, Crowborough, Sussex. He entered the Army in May, 1878; was promoted Captain in Dec. 1884; served in the Burmese Expedition, 1885–87, where he was severely wounded (Medal and clasp). He became Major, June, 1896; saw active service on the West Coast of Africa in the Northern Territories of the Gold Coast, 1897–98 (Medal with clasp). He retired in Oct. 1899, to the Reserve of Officers, from the Derbyshire Regt., and served with the 15th Battn. Imperial Yeomanry during the War in South Africa, 1900–1. He was mentioned in Despatches, received the Queen's Medal with clasp, and was created a Companion of the Distinguished Service Order [London Gazette, 27 Sept. 1901]: "George Seymour Charles Jenkinson, Major, Imperial Yeomanry. In recognition of services during the operations in South Africa." The Insignia were presented by the King 29 Oct. 1901. He became Lieutenant-Colonel, Northamptonshire Yeomanry, 29 Nov. 1903. Lieut.-Colonel Jenkinson died 27 Sept. 1907, at Lamport Grange, Northampton. He had married, in 1899, Ada, daughter of Cæsar Czarnikow, of Effingham Hill and Eaton Square.

LOVAT, LORD (SIMON JOSEPH), Major, was born 25 Nov. 1871, son of the 5th Baron, and Alice, daughter of T. Weld Blundell, of Ince Blundell Hall, near Liverpool. He was educated at Fort Augustus Abbey, and at Oxford; succeeded his father in 1887; became Lieutenant, 1st Life Guards, and Captain, 1st Volunteer Battn. Queen's Own Cameron Highlanders, being promoted to Major 13 Dec. 1899; became temporary Captain in the Army 21 Feb. 1900; raised and served with Lovat's Scouts in the South African War of 1899–1902; commanded Lovat's Scouts from the 20th Sept, 1901, to the 31st May, 1902; in command mobile force from Nov. 1901, to May, 1902; operations in the Orange Free State, Feb. to May, 1900; operations in the Orange River Colony, May to 29 Nov. 1900, including actions in the Wittebergen (1 to 29 July) and on Caledon River 27 to 29 Nov.; operations in Cape Colony, north and south of Orange River, 1899–1900; operations in Cape Colony, Orange River Colony and the Transvaal 30 Nov. 1900, to 31 May, 1902 (Despatches [London Gazette, 18 Feb. and 10 Sept. 1901, and 29 July, 1902]; Queen's Medal with two clasps; King's Medal with two clasps; created a C.B., and a Companion of the Distinguished Service Order [London Gazette, 27 Sept. 1901]: "Simon Joseph, Lord Lovat, Major, 1st Volunteer Battn. Cameron Highlanders. In recognition of services during the operations in South Africa." He became Lieut.-Colonel, Lovat's Scouts, 30 March, 1903; was created a C.V.O., 1903; became Colonel 9 Nov. 1908; created a K.C.V.O. in 1908. On his return from South Africa Lord Lovat formed two Yeomanry Regiments, which at present form part of the Highland Mounted Brigade. Major-General Lord Lovat was created a Knight of the Thistle in 1914. He commanded the Highland Mounted Brigade in Gallipoli, 1915; IVth Mounted Division on East Coast of England, 1916; Lovat Scouts observers in France, 1916–17; was appointed Director of Forestry, B.E.F., April, 1917. He is a landlord who owns about 181,800 acres. He married, in 1910, the Hon. Laura Lister, second daughter of the 4th Baron Ribblesdale and Charlotte Monckton (who died in 1911), daughter of Sir Charles Tennant, 1st Bart., and they have one son, Simon Christopher, Master of Lovat, born 9 July, 1911, and one daughter.

SCOTT, HARVEY, Major, was born in 1868, son of the late Alderman John Oliver

Harvey Scott.

Scott, a former Sheriff and Mayor of Newcastle. He was an ardent Artillery Volunteer Officer; became Major, 1st Northumberland Volunteer Artillery, 11 Aug. 1897, and commanded the Elswick Battery in the South African War. He was mentioned in Despatches, and created a Companion of the Distinguished Service Order [London Gazette, 27 Sept. 1901]: "Harvey Scott, Major, Elswick Battery, 1st Northumberland Volunteer Artillery. In recognition of services during the operations in South Africa." The Insignia were presented by the King 29 Oct. 1901. Major Scott was a member of the firm of Messrs. John O. Scott and Co., Shipowners and Colliery Owners. He went in for farming in Australia, and died at Sydney, New South Wales, on 25 June, 1912.

LEE, GEORGE LEONARD, Major, was born at West Maitland, New South Wales, 25 June, 1860, son of the late John Leonard Lee, Leeholme, Paterson, New South Wales, and of his wife, Mary Ann Lee. He was educated at the Grammar School, Armidale, New South Wales; entered the Military Forces in 1888, and commanded the New South Wales Lancers in the South African War, 1899–1900. He was present at the Relief of Kimberley; operations in the Orange Free State, Feb. to May, 1900, including operations at Paardeberg (17 to 26 Feb.) and actions at Poplar Grove, Dreifontein and Zand River; operations in the Transvaal, May and June, 1900, including actions near Johannesburg, Pretoria and Diamond Hill; operations in the Transvaal, east of Pretoria, July to 29 Nov. 1900, including actions at Reit Vlei and Belfast; operations in Cape Colony, south of Orange River, 1899–1900, including actions at Colesberg (1 Jan. to 12 Feb.). He was mentioned in Despatches [London Gazette, 10 Sept. 1901]; received the Queen's Medal with six clasps, and was created a Companion of the Distinguished Service Order [London Gazette, 27 Sept. 1901]: "George Leonard Lee, Major, New South Wales Lancers. In recognition of services during the operations in South Africa." The Insignia, Warrant, etc., were presented by Brigadier-General Finn at Sydney 26 April, 1902. He was given the Brevet of Lieutenant-Colonel, and was on the Instructional Staff, New South Wales Military Forces. After the outbreak of the European War he was appointed Brigadier-General, commanding 2nd Military District (Queensland), Military Forces of the Commonwealth. He was created a C.M.G. in 1917, and promoted to Major-General. He married, at Homebush, New South Wales, 2 Jan. 1896, Emma Ormo Town, daughter of the late Andrew Town, of Richmond, New South Wales.

HOWARD, A. L., Major, entered the Canadian Military Forces, and served in the South African War. He was created a Companion of the Distinguished Service Order [London Gazette, 27 Sept. 1901]: "A. L. Howard, Major, Canadian Contingent. In recognition of services during the operations in South Africa." The Insignia, Warrant, etc., were sent to his son, N. G. Howard, Esq., 18 Dec. 1901, as Major Howard had been killed in action not long after the D.S.O. had been awarded to him.

SANDERS, GILBERT EDWARD, Major, was born at Fort Yale, British Columbia, 25 Dec. 1863, eldest son of E. H. Sanders, Judge of County Courts, British Columbia. He was educated at King Alfred's School, Wantage, and at the Royal Military College, Kingston; entered the Royal North-West Mounted Police in 1884, as Inspector, and subsequently was appointed Superintendent. He assisted in quelling the Riel Rebellion, 1885 (Medal); served in the South African War, 1899–1900, in command of a squadron of Canadian Mounted Rifles, and was present at operations in the Orange Free State, Feb. to May, 1900; operations in the Transvaal in May and June, 1900, including actions near Johannesburg, Pretoria and Diamond Hill (11 and 12 June); operations in the Transvaal, east of Pretoria, July to 29 Nov. 1900, including action at Reit Vlei; operations in Cape Colony, south of Orange River, 1899–1900. He was twice wounded; was mentioned in Despatches [London Gazette, 10 Sept. 1901], received the Queen's Medal with four clasps, and—for saving the life of Sergt. Tryon, whom he brought into safety on his own horse, under heavy fire—was created a Companion of the Distinguished Service Order [London Gazette, 27 Sept. 1901]: "Gilbert Edward Sanders, Major, Canadian Contingent. In recognition of services during the operations in South Africa." The Insignia, Warrant, etc., were sent to South Africa, and presented at Regina 6 June, 1902. Lieut.-Colonel Sanders served in the European War, 1915–17, in France; was mentioned in Despatches, and created a C.M.G. in 1917. He is Police Magistrate at Calgary. His favourite recreation is golf. He married Caroline, second daughter of Dr. Jukes, and they have two daughters.

NOLAN-NEYLAN, JOHN, Major, was born 14 May, 1854, in the County Clare, Ireland, the son of D. Neylan and Mary Nolan, his wife; and nephew of Capt. L. E. Nolan. On his mother's side, therefore, he was a member of that famous if turbulent Irish family whose proudest boast it was—if it is not yet—in bygone years that some of its members had killed the Earl of March, heir to the throne of England, in battle. One of the latter-day Nolans is said to have attended King Edward's coronation, "just to show that there was no ill-feeling!" Though one would have thought the ill-feeling might have been on King Edward's side. These typically Irish people, doubtless some of them with doubtful, if not disloyal sentiments on their lips, rushed headlong into the conflict, as troopers or cavalry officers, they cared not which, on the outbreak of the European War, and fought for Great Britain and Ireland until the old soldier's family who attended the coronation was almost wiped out, and is now represented by his infant grandchild. One of the family

John Nolan-Neylan.

went down with Kitchener, a trusted member of his Staff. Soldiers of fortune, the blood of the Nolans has been poured out on almost every battle-field in Europe:

> "For in far foreign lands from . . . to Belgrade
> Lie the captains and chiefs of the Irish Brigade."

The famous Capt. Louis Edmond Nolan, of the 15th Hussars, Colonel Nolan-Neylan's uncle, brought the order for the deathless charge of which it was said: "C'est magnifique, mais ce n'est pas la guerre."

> " ' Forward the Light Brigade!
> Charge for the guns! ' he said.
> Into the Valley of Death
> Rode the Six Hundred."

And for some time afterwards many people mistakenly thought that Nolan was the "someone" described by the poet as having "blundered." It was ultimately proved, however, to the satisfaction of most authorities, that it was not Capt. Nolan who had made a mistake. He is said to have perished in the act of trying to point out where the guns really were which formed the objective of the Charge of the Light Brigade. We are all of us hero-worshippers, and perhaps Capt. Nolan has had countless fervent admirers since his death, and some in his lifetime. Though many of his contemporaries looked on him with suspicion as a crank who studied his profession and wrote books. He died at the age of thirty-four, a recognized authority on cavalry movements, and one who had written one or two standard works. His great idea seems to have been that the steeplechase horse and his rider, and the cavalry officer and his mount, are one and indivisible, and interchangeable. He received his early military training, together with his elder brothers, in the Austrian Army, and the fact that he was born in Canada and the particulars of his early career were made known to an English inquirer by the courtesy of the Austrian Embassy and War Office in pre-war days. It is to be feared that Nolan learned to ride as an Austrian cavalry officer, though his stirring and ambitious old father never rested until he obtained for Louis, or "Ned," Nolan a commission in the British Army. Ned Nolan it was who was Lindsay Gordon's especial hero.

"I remember," says the Australian laureate, who died fretting after the Cotswold Hills:

> "I remember the lowering wintry morn,
> And the mist on the Cotswold Hills,
> Where I once heard the blast of the huntsman's horn,
> Not far from the Seven Rills.
> Jack Esdaile was there, and Hugh St. Clair,
> Bob Chapman and Andrew Kerr,
> And big George Griffiths on Devil-May-Care,
> And black Tom Oliver,
> And one who rode on a dark-brown steed
> Clean-jointed, sinewy, spare,
> With the lean game head of the Blacklock breed,
> And the resolute eye that loves the lead,
> And the quarters massive and square—
> A tower of strength with a promise of speed
> (There was Celtic blood in the pair)."

Captain L. E. Nolan this was, and though Lindsay Gordon admired him above all men he must needs describe his mount first. Nolan and another man were riding to hounds up there by the Seven Springs:

> "And between the pair on a chestnut mare,
> The duffer who writes this lay.
> What business had this child there to ride?
> But little or none at all;
> Yet I held my own for a while ' in the pride
> That goeth before a fall.'
> Though rashness can hope for but one result,
> We are heedless when fate draws nigh us,
> And the maxim holds good:
> ' Quem perdere vult
> Deus dementat prius ! '
> The right-hand man to the left-hand said,
> As down in the vale we went,
> ' Harden your heart as a millstone, Ned,
> And set your face as a flint—
> Solid and tall is the rasping wall
> That stretches before us yonder.
> You must have it or not at all:
> 'Twere better to halt than to ponder,
> For the stream runs wide on the take-off side,
> And washes the clay bank under;
> Here goes for a pull, 'tis a madman's ride
> And a broken neck if you blunder.'

> " No word in reply his comrade spoke,
> Nor waver'd nor once looked round,
> But I saw him shorten his horse's stride
> As we splash'd through the marshy ground.

. . . .

"I remember one thrust he gave to his hat,
    And two to the flanks of the brown,
And still as a statue of old he sat,
    And he shot to the front, hands down ;
I remember the start and the stag-like bound
    Of the steed six lengths to the fore,
And the laugh of the rider; while landing sound,
He turned in his saddle and glanced around ;
    I remember—but little more,
Save a bird's-eye gleam of the dashing stream,
    A jarring thud on the wall,
A shock and the blank of a nightmare's dream—
    I was down with a stunning fall."

Again and again in his poems Gordon goes back to Louis Nolan :

"Where bullets whistle and round shots whiz,
    Hoofs trample and blades flash bare,
God send me an ending as fair as his
    Who died in his stirrups there ! "

And in " Ye Wearie Wayfarer " the Gay Gordon poet has one hope in his saddest mood :

"Vain dreams, again and again retold,
    Must you crowd on the weary brain,
Till the fingers are cold that entwined of old
    Round foil and trigger and rein,
Till stay'd for aye are the roving feet,
    Till the restless hands are quiet,
Till the stubborn heart has forgotten to beat,
    Till the hot blood has ceas'd to riot.

    .   .   .   .   .   .

"But *Nolan's* name will flourish in fame
    When our galloping days are past,
When we go to the place from whence we came,
    Perchance to find rest at last.

    .   .   .   .   .   .

"Though our future lot is a sable blot,
    Though the wise ones of earth will blame us,
Though our saddles will rot and our rides be forgot,
    ' Dum Vivimus, Vivamus ! ' "

Nolan's death was the part of his life Gordon always envied him :

"Oh, the minutes of yonder maddening ride
    Long pleasures of life outvie ! "

The Gordons and the Nolans are in this book—and Ned Griffiths's kith and kin. And the rebel Irish and the English, the Austrians and Count O'Kelly and Eclipse and the Nolans are all mixed up together in that weird pedigree of his family in the possession of the Very Reverend Monsignor Edmond Nolan, cousin of Capt. L. E. Nolan. Ned Nolan's nephew, John Nolan, first saw active service in 1877–78–79, in Gaika, Gaeleka and Moirosi's Mountain (Medal with clasp). He joined the Cape Mounted Riflemen on 1 Nov. 1879, and was present in operations in Basutoland and Transkei, 1880–81 (Medal with clasp). He served with the Cape Mounted Police in Bechuanaland, 1896–97 (General Service Medal with clasp). In the South African War of 1899 to 1902, this Irishman from the County Clare was also present. His deeds are told at length by Sir A. Conan Doyle's " Great Boer War," as are those of another of his name, at Spion Kop, when : " A detached group of the South Lancashires was summoned to surrender. ' When I surrender,' cried Colour-Sergt. Nolan, ' it will be my dead body ! ' " When Bethulie Railway Bridge had been blown to smithereens by the re- treating Boers, the only hope of preserving some means of crossing the Orange River lay in the hope that the British troops might be beforehand with the Boers, who were just going to destroy the old road bridge also. " In this," says Sir A. Conan Doyle, in " The Great Boer War " (pages 270–271), " they were singularly favoured by fortune. On the arrival of a small party of scouts and of the Cape Police under Major Nolan-Neylan at the end of the bridge it was found that all was ready to blow it up, the mine sunk, the detonator fixed, and the wire laid. Only the connection between the wire and the charge had not been made. To make sure, the Boers had also laid several boxes of dynamite under the last span, in case the mine should fail in its effect. The advance guard of the Police, only six in number, with Nolan-Neylan at their head, threw themselves into a building which commanded the approaches of the bridge, and this handful of men opened so spirited and well-aimed a fire that the Boers were unable to approach it. As fresh scouts and policemen came up they were thrown into the firing line, and for a whole long day they kept the destroyers from the bridge. Had the enemy known how weak they were and how far from supports, they could have easily destroyed them ; but the game of bluff was admirably played, and a fire kept up which held the enemy to their rifle pits. The Boers were in a trench commanding the bridge, and their brisk fire made it impossible to cross. On the other hand, our rifle fire commanded the mine and prevented any one from exploding it. But at the approach of darkness it was certain that this would be done. The situation was saved by the gallantry of young Popham of the Derbyshires, who crept across with two men and removed the detonators. There still remained the dynamite under the further span, and this also they removed,

carrying it off across the bridge under a heavy fire. The work was made absolutely complete a little later by the exploit of Capt. Grant, of the Sappers, who drew the charges from the holes in which they had been sunk, and dropped them into the river, thus avoiding the chance that they might be exploded next morning by shell fire. The feat of Popham and of Grant was not only most gallant, but of extraordinary service to the country ; but the highest credit belongs to Nolan-Neylan, of the Police, for the great promptitude and gallantry of his attack, and to M'Neill for his support. On that road bridge and on the pontoon bridge at Norval's Pont Lord Robert's army was for a whole month dependent for their supplies."

This was really a much more useful performance than the Charge of the Light Brigade. Another account says :

" On 2 Jan. 1900, Major Nolan-Neylan, in command of 75 European details at Molteno, the advanced post of the 3rd Division, under General Sir William Gatacre, was attacked at 5 a.m. by a strong force of Boers, with two 15-pounder guns. The enemy started off by firing on a mounted piquet about to take a post on the eastern kopje at dawn. Major Neylan posted one officer and twenty men in fort to watch the west, and with the remainder took up a position behind the rocks and embankment along the Molteno–Cyphergat railway line and immediately opposite the enemy's central position—a kopje behind which they were massing and from whence they charged. Their object was to capture the low-lying hills along the railway parallel to the line taken up by Neylan. A well-directed fire, how- ever, checked and forced them to retire, and they subsequently occupied positions round about, and kept up incessant gun and rifle fire all day long. At one time the enemy occupied Cyphergat, and actually brought up guns into position on the high Looperberg Ridge, and shelled General Gatacre's Relief Column, which did not come into action as the Boer forces retired to Stormberg. In face of overwhelming numbers, the important positions through which the main road runs were held by a small force and the road to the Stormberg stronghold kept open. On 10 March, 1900, the 3rd Division Column, under General Sir William Gatacre, had just halted at Knapdaar, on the Burghersdorp–Bethulie railway line, when a despatch- rider, who had ridden his horse to a standstill, reported that the Boers were recrossing the Orange River from the Free State to the Colony, and that assistance was urgently needed by Scouts sent ahead from the column the day before. The G.O.C. ordered Major Nolan-Neylan to move forward with about 50 details, and to use his own discretion. About 10.30 p.m. this officer came up with the Scouts, five miles from the bridge. Their O.C. reported both railway and road bridges destroyed. Before daylight Major Nolan-Neylan found the railway bridge destroyed, but, on creeping near, discovered the road bridge intact. Boer sentries were marching up and down between the parapets, and the sand dunes, embankments and rough ground between the bridges were held by a strong force of the enemy. He crept back and despatched his orderly for Scouts and Police. Whilst waiting, a native manservant crossed the bridge with a white flag as a protection. This native said the bridge would be destroyed at 10 a.m. It was then about 9 a.m. He also said that Bethulie town was full of Boer soldiers, and they had very big guns. No time was to be lost under these circumstances, so when the forces galloped up and dismounted, leaving their horses under cover behind the hills, the Scouts extended to the left, the Police to the right, while Major Nolan-Neylan moved in the centre in the direction of the bridge. At this moment the enemy horsemen were galloping over the plain between the river and the village, and their artillery coming into action. No time was to be lost, something had to be done quickly, so Major Nolan-Neylan called in the three men on his right, and the three on his left, and they readily volunteered to go with him. The officer and his six men moved rapidly towards the stone boundary walls, near the approaches to the bridge. Firing from all sides opened on the small party, who climbed one stone wall, crossed a garden, over the next stone wall, past Holm's house, and over open ground to a brick wall in rear of the old Police Camp. Removing some bricks from the top of the wall, the men were able to rest their rifles and take steady aim. All being good shots, the range to a bare patch on the Free State side of the bridge was soon found, and all who ventured within range had a very warm reception. Very soon riderless horses were wandering about the veldt. Shells were bursting unpleasantly close, the rain of bullets was incessant, but the six held on. A little later they moved to a toll-house within ninety yards of the bridge ; here one of the six was mortally wounded. He was carried to shelter by Private Blake, who subsequently was decorated (D.C.M.). After some hours, during which the small party held the bridge, the main column arrived and joined in the fight. Major Nolan-Neylan and Capt. Schenk built a wall across the road from behind which rifle fire was kept up directly on to the bridge all night, and from the kraals men were posted, some to fire on the Free State side, some on the centre, and some on the near side of the bridge, to prevent any attempt by the enemy to link up wire from the parapet to an electric battery in the toll-house. Capt. Woon took up a position in the Cemetery, about a mile away, where he was held fast by men from our Column firing on him in mistake, and enemy shrapnel constantly bursting over him. After the enemy retired, the dynamite charges were withdrawn by the Royal Engi- neers. In a short while rails were laid on the saved bridge, and it was used immediately for transporting supplies to Lord Roberts's Army."

Major Neylan was wounded in action 13 Aug. 1901 ; was mentioned three times in Despatches ; received the Queen's Medal with three clasps, King's Medal with two clasps, and was created a Companion of the Distinguished Service Order [London Gazette, 27 Sept. 1901]: " John Nolan-Neylan Major, Cape Police. In recognition of services during the operations in Cape Colony." He was Second-in-Command of General Gorringe's Flying Column, and was Commander of the Orange River Scouts. Lieut.-Colonel Nolan-Neylan has retired from the Cape Mounted Police. He married, 17 Aug. 1881, Minnie, daughter of R. P. Impey, of Aliwal North, Cape Colony ; they have four sons : Lawrence, born 14 Nov. 1886 ; Denis, born 2 May, 1890 ; Richard, born 8 April, 1896, and Vivian, born 14 Oct. 1901 ; and six daughters : Kathleen, Eily, Clare, Marié, Nora and Ita.

SCOTT, ROBERT GEORGE, Major, served in the South African War of 1877–79; in the Gaika and Gaeleka Campaigns, and was present at the attack on Moirosi's Mountain, when he was severely wounded. He received the Medal and clasp, and was awarded the Victoria Cross. In the South African War of 1899–1902, he served in the operations in Cape Colony, the Transvaal and the Orange Free State; received the Queen's Medal with three clasps, the King's Medal with two clasps, and was created a Companion of the Distinguished Service Order [London Gazette, 27 Sept. 1901]: "R. G. Scott, V.C., Major, Kimberley Light Horse. In recognition of services during the operations in South Africa." The story of how he won the Victoria Cross is given in the first volume of this book, but the following extracts have been lately received, and are now given:

"The Cape Times" of 4 Oct. 1918, says:

"DEATH OF COLONEL SCOTT, V.C., D.S.O.

"The death occurred at Mount Curtis, Wynberg, yesterday, of Colonel Robert George Scott, V.C., D.S.O., at the age of 60. Deceased served during the Gaeleka, Gaika and Moirosi Campaigns, 1877–78–79 (V.C.), and between 1899 and 1901 he was Lieutenant-Colonel of the Kimberley Light Horse, and had command of Scott's Railway Guards (which he raised) and the Cape Railway Sharpshooters. He was present during the siege of Kimberley, was mentioned in Despatches, and awarded the D.S.O. in 1900. The funeral will take place at Plumstead Cemetery at 4.45 this afternoon."

"South Africa" for 26 Oct. 1918, says:

"THE LATE LIEUT.-COLONEL SCOTT, V.C., D.S.O.

"Lieut.-Colonel Robert George Scott, V.C., D.S.O., Cape Colonial Forces and late Cape Mounted Rifles, was born in 1857, and was a son of Fleet-Surgeon R. C. Scott, R.N. Colonel Scott served in the Kaffir War of 1877–79, and the South African War of 1900–2, being mentioned in Despatches for meritorious conduct in the latter, receiving the Queen's Medal and three clasps, as well as the King's Medal and two clasps, and the D.S.O. In 1879, when serving as Sergeant, he received the Victoria Cross for conspicuous gallantry and devotion during an attack on Moirosi's Mountain. He volunteered to throw time-fuse shells as hand-grenades, over a line of stone barricades from behind which the enemy were bringing a heavy fire to bear on the Colonial troops, which it was impossible effectually to return. After causing all the men of his party to seek cover lest the shell should burst prematurely—by which precaution many lives were, in all probability, saved—Sergeant Scott advanced under heavy fire, and reaching the wall, made two attempts to throw shells across to the other side. In consequence of some defect in the fuse, which had been ignited before casting, the shell exploded at the second attempt. His right hand was blown to pieces, and he was severely wounded in the left leg, suffering also minor wounds on the body and limbs. His escape from death was miraculous, but he recovered, and lived until 3 Oct. last, when he died at Cape Town."

Major the Marquess of Ailesbury saw the proofs of part of the Victoria Cross Volume, and he wrote the following:

"I well remember a day towards the end of March, 1900. Having ridden out from Kimberley to join a yeomanry battalion to which I had been posted, I chanced, in the course of my wanderings, to bump into the Staff of the G.O.C. A more depressed-looking lot I never saw. With their Chief sitting on a chair reading a book, they stood round conversing in whispers. On asking where I might find my unit, they took council together and then whispered that they didn't know. I felt as if I was intruding on a funeral. At that moment came up an active-looking, wiry, one-armed man in his shirt-sleeves. Addressing me as if he, at least, was not ashamed of the sound of his own voice, he demanded my wants, led me to the top of a small neighbouring kopje, and pointed out the camp of my people about half a mile away. It was long afterwards I learnt that this was Scott, but I knew on the moment that I had met a good soldier, and it was no surprise to me to hear that his services on that Staff were rewarded with the D.S.O."

One of Colonel Scott's sons sent these notes after the account in the Victoria Cross Volume was printed:

Robert George Scott, Lieut.-Colonel, was born 22 April, 1857, son of Fleet-Surgeon R. C. Scott, R.N., and Mary Elizabeth, daughter of the Rev. Richard Sinclair, Vicar of Cashel. He was educated at Epsom College and Burney's. Being of an adventurous spirit, he went to South Africa, and found service after his heart's desire in the now extinct border regiment, the Cape Mounted Rifles. He served in the Kaffir Wars of 1877–79, and was awarded the Victoria Cross for an act of most self-sacrificing devotion. Scott undertook to throw time-fuse shells as hand-grenades over a wall against the Basutos. The exploit was a most perilous one, and Scott knew it; he directed his men to fall back under cover, and then climbed up a steep wall of rock, at the top of which the Basutos were lying in wait behind a barricade of stones. During the whole operation he was under a heavy fire. He then endeavoured to toss the shell over the barricade; the first time he failed; he tried again, and the very thing happened which he had feared when he directed his men to fall back. He had scarcely lighted the fuse when the shell exploded in his hand; one piece entering the left leg, wounding him very severely, and the right hand was shattered to pieces. In addition the explosion of the shell, which was filled with black powder, set alight to his clothing, so that in addition to his wounds he had to suffer the agonies of burning. His men rushed forward to rescue him from this perilous position, but with perfect calm and magnificent self-control he ordered them back again; then, by rolling over, he managed to reach the edge of the wall of rock and dropped over—a vertical drop of about 25 feet. During all that day he refused to let his men carry him back to the main camp, as it would have been a dangerous operation attempting to cross the intervening open country in daylight. He took distinguished part in the South African War, 1900–2, being in command of the Kimberley Light Horse during the siege of Kimberley, after which he raised and commanded Scott's Railway Guards and Cape Railway Sharpshooters, which kept the railway open from De Aar to Mafeking and enabled supplies to come through regularly. He was mentioned in Despatches, awarded the Queen's Medal with three clasps, the King's Medal with two clasps, and was created a Companion of the Distinguished Service Order [London Gazette, 27 Sept. 1901]: "Robert George Scott, Lieut.-Colonel, Kimberley Light Horse. In recognition of services during the operations in South Africa." At the outbreak of the late World War Lieut.-Colonel Scott, though in a precarious state of health, again volunteered his services, which were gladly accepted by the authorities. During the Rebellion he raised and commanded the Kimberley Central Commando, and in spite of the very grave condition of his health, he led this Commando through the region of the Kalahari, and took part in the engagement at Uppington. The hardships entailed by this campaign accentuated his illness, and he died on the 3rd of Oct. 1918. His one great regret was that he was unable to take a larger part in the war. Lieut.-Colonel Scott had married, in 1885, Constance, daughter of Lieut.-Colonel C. A. Daniell; they had three sons: John Daynell Sinclair, Robert Falkiner Sinclair and Guy Sinclair; and one daughter, Dulcie Mary. He was a Lieutenant-Colonel in the Cape Colonial Forces.

BURNHAM, FREDERICK RUSSELL, Major, was born at Tivoli, Minnesota, 11 May, 1861, son of the Rev. Edwin O. Burnham and Rebecca Burnham (*née* Russell). The family removed to Los Angeles in 1870. Fred Burnham was educated at the Clinton High School, and was successively a cowboy, scout, guide, miner, Deputy Sheriff, etc., in the West. In 1884 he married Blanche Blick, of Clinton, Iowa. In 1893 he went to South Africa, and served as a scout in the Matabele War in Rhodesia, which had broken out mainly because the subjects of Lobengula often raided Mashonaland, which the King had ceded to the British. Dr. Jameson, the Administrator of Mashonaland, remonstrated with Lobengula, who expressed regret after one of these raids, saying that the chief Lomaghondi (whose territory was under British Protection) had been killed by mistake. In spite of his apologies several other raids occurred, and on 9 July, 1893, the impi began to slaughter every Mashoni they could lay hands upon. Since the King thus defied the British it became necessary either to break the power of Lobengula or to evacuate the territory. The former course was decided upon, and about 1,000 or 1,200 white men, led by Dr. Jameson, invaded Matabeleland. Lobengula, after being beaten in the battles of the Shangani (25 Oct. 1891) and the Imbembezi (1 Nov. 1891), fled from Bulawayo, and did not surrender himself. A force under Major Patrick Forbes was sent to follow and capture the King. The column could not proceed quickly, owing to bad weather, short rations and the absence of roads, so Major Forbes ordered Major Wilson and 18 men to go forward and reconnoitre. The understanding was that if the party did not return by sundown, it was to be supported by the whole column. This patrol was accompanied by Mr. Burnham, the American Scout, "one of the three men who were eye-witnesses of that eventful night's work which ended so tragically at dawn."

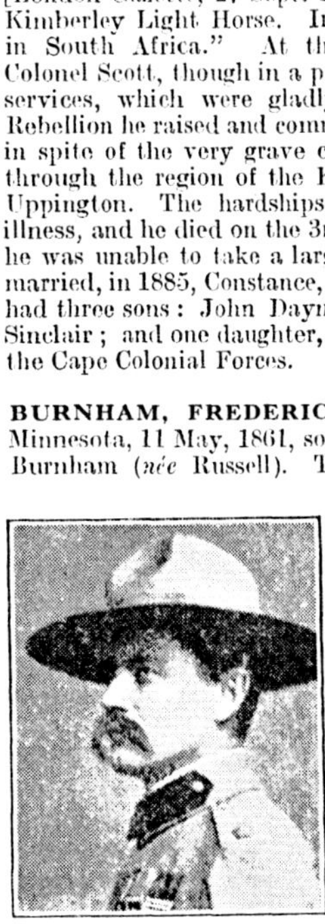

Frederick R. Burnham.

For his services in the Matabele Campaign, the Government presented Mr. Burnham with the Campaign Medal and—jointly with two companions—he was given 300 square miles of land in Rhodesia, in recognition of exceptional service. Mr. Burnham discovered in the granite ruins of an ancient civilization of Rhodesia a buried treasure of gold and gold ornaments, dating from before the Christian era. He led an expedition to explore Barotzeland preparatory to the building of the Cape to Cairo Railroad. In the Second Matabele War, Mr. Burnham took an active part on the Staff of Sir Frederick Carrington, and was commissioned to capture or kill the Matabele "God" Umlimo, and succeeded in entering his cave in the Matopa mountains and killing him.

Lieut.-Colonel Sir Robert Baden-Powell writes as follows: "My first introduction to Burnham was at Bulawayo, in the Matabele Campaign of 1896. I was on the Staff of General Sir F. Carrington. We had only arrived there a few days previously when on the 5th June, just as we were going to bed, Sir Charles Metcalfe called in with Burnham to report that there was an army of the enemy close by, not three miles outside the tent. This seemed to be so improbable that we could not believe it, even though reported by this celebrated American Scout. However, he soon cured any doubts by taking me to the spot, and there they were right enough. During the night we collected a force, and took them with success at dawn. After that Burnham and I had several scouting trips together against the Matabele, and in the course of these I learned a lot from him, especially from his experience of the Red Indians and their methods. Owing to his wonderfully quick eye in taking 'sign,' whether far away or close by, I gave him the nickname of 'Hawk Eye,' and he gave me the name of Sherlock for piecing together the meaning of the sign after he had discovered it. So we worked in close accord with the happiest results. We only differed in one detail, and that was the pace at which to ride one's horse. He maintained that to walk and go slow saved the horse. I held that to loup fairly fast over the open ground and to halt when under cover was the better way. And neither of us convinced the other. His expedition with Armstrong, a native commissioner, into the cave of Mlimo is well known. The Mlimo was a medicine man among the natives with a reputation of being supernatural, and it was owing to his directions that the Matabele kept the field. He inhabited the back part of a cave, which had qualities like the ear of Dionysius of Syracuse, from which he gave out oracular orders and prophecies. They made their way in there, and Burnham shot the man and practically put an end to the rebellion in that part of the country. Though he was thus capable of deliberately killing his man where necessary, Burnham had the warmest heart possible. I know what he suffered when he lost his child at Bulawayo, and I have by me a most pathetic, heartbroken letter from him describing how, later on, he lost his little boy, a boy scout, who was accidentally drowned in the Thames some years after the Boer War. It was that which largely drove him from his peaceful retreat in England to go back to the wild in Mexico."

He operated mines in Klondyke from 1898 to 1900. In Jan. 1900, the following message reached him: "Burnham, P.O. Box 62, Skagway, Alaska. Lord Roberts appoints you to his personal Staff. All expenses paid. If you accept, start shortest way Cape Town, and report yourself to him.—Capt. White, Naval and Military Club, London." On his arrival in South Africa, Mr. Burnham was appointed to Lord Roberts's Staff, and was made Chief of Scouts of the British Armies in the Field in South Africa.

Lieut.-General Sir Aylmer Hunter-Weston, K.C.B., D.S.O., writes: " The address of my friend, Major Fred Burnham, D.S.O., the celebrated Scout, is La Cuesta (The Slope), Three Rivers, California. He is an American who came over to fight for us in the Boer War, and did invaluable work there for England. For his services he was made a Major and given the D.S.O."

Major F. R. Burnham, D.S.O., wrote the following story of the raids in which he accompanied Brevet Major Hunter-Weston : " The cutting of the Delagoa Bay Railway to prevent the 4,000 British prisoners of war being sent into the deadly fever-stricken swamps of the East Coast of Africa.—On 1 June, 1900, it was well known at Headquarters that the Boers could not defend Pretoria, but would retreat along the railway from Pretoria to Delagoa Bay. At Waterval-Onder, sixteen miles north of Pretoria, were 4,000 British prisoners, and it was reported the Boers intended sending them by rail to the low country. This would according to the opinion of medical officers be probably the death of fully 50 per cent., if not more, as they were much reduced by a diet of mealies, with only an occasional small ration of very poor meat—they were also very ragged, and suffered from the biting winds of the high veldt. There was a possibility that a dash by picked men might find a gap in the Boer lines, or fight a way through and destroy the line for a sufficient length of time for the cavalry under General French to recapture the prisoners. If this plan failed there remained only the chance for a solitary scout with charges of gun-cotton to keep the line closed. It was finally ordered that Major Aylmer Hunter-Weston, who had previously been so successful in such raids, select 200 men—these were chosen from the Lancer regiments. It was more difficult to get good mounts than good men, and no officer at this period of the war would have been allowed to weaken our already starving squadrons except for important work. It was also hoped that we could make possible the capture of a quantity of badly needed rolling stock, engines, coal supplies, and some of the Boer Artillery, known to be on sidings in and around Pretoria. At dark the column moved out of Johannesburg ; I was selected by Major Hunter-Weston to lead. The Boers had many Cossack posts and scouts, but by good fortune and care we eluded them. At break of day I saw a Boer scout, and slipped up very near, with the intention of capturing him, but discovered there were several still lying in their blankets with horses knee-haltered about 200 yards away. Reporting at once to the Major, a quick deployment of a troop was ordered to envelop the entire picquet before they could carry the alarm to the main Boer commando. We dashed away on our already tired horses, but the Boers had seen us and eluded us by at most 200 yards. By this time we could see the smoke of early fires along the base of a small ridge ; they extended for about half a mile, then a gap of about half a mile, then with our glasses we could see another and much larger commando. The good fortune of the night had deserted us just when we were within striking distance of our objective. It was impossible to cut through the Boer lines, and considering the condition of our mounts, it looked as if we must within an hour be entirely surrounded by fresh commandos. The order to retire was given, and I again was asked to lead. The most difficult position was now the rear—taken by Major Hunter-Weston. The Boers came on almost at once and opened fire. Fortunately, ever since the disaster at Sanna's Post, I had been mounted on a fine swift Colonial pony—he seemed to be a combination of iron and whalebone. I fed him on soldiers' hard tack, and begged many a ration of sugar for my coffee that was added to the tit-bits in his nose-bag. But this day he paid it all back to me, and enabled me to locate the swift-moving Boers and lead our forlorn handful around their ambushes. The Boers did not enjoy closing in, even when they had four to one, or more. Their plan was to get possession of passes, dongas and kopjes as near safe as possible, yet bringing the enemy under deadly fire. Still, it is a wonder the rear, where were our wounded men and weakest horses, was not entirely demoralized, and it would have been with almost any other men, even when led by such officers as we fortunately had. After nearly four hours of running fight, I saw a commanding slope and some Kaffir huts, that seemed a good place to make a stand—by this time many horses were only capable of walking. I rode back some two miles, and met Major Hunter-Weston on the extreme rear and under fire. I told him the Boers were now outflanking us and there was a likelihood of a complete envelopment. He gave me verbal instructions and written memo. to any British Officer Commanding I could find, and asked me to make the dash through before the Boers closed up. This dash was made without incident, thanks again to the pony, which, after all the hours under saddle, outran several Boer scouts in a hard five-mile gallop. I reached Major-General Dickson's lines. . . . He promptly sent some guns and 200 men ; they met our force only a few

miles out. It seems the check given the Boers at the Kaffir huts had discouraged them, and they withdrew at what was for them just the wrong moment—the failure in a long running fight to surround the small force was rather an unusual occurrence for them. By skilful handling, Major Hunter-Weston brought out the little force with only 16 casualties."

Sir A. Hunter-Weston writes : " The above account of one of our exploits in South Africa has been sent to me by Major Fred Burnham, D.S.O. These last few words refer to a very gallant exploit that Major Burnham did alone."

" It was next decided at Headquarters that Major Hunter-Weston be sent with a force to the west and north ; I had expected to have the good fortune to go with him, but received word that Lord Roberts would permit me to try alone to cut the Delagoa Bay Line. This I finally succeeded in doing, but unfortunately got rather smashed up myself, and my beloved pony shot. But it was my good friend Hunter-Weston that finally brought me in an Indian ambulance to Lord Roberts's Headquarters in Pretoria."

Major Burnham was wounded 2 June, 1901, as has been related, while on scout duty (destroying the enemy's railroad base), and invalided home. For his services there he was promoted a Major in the British Army, presented with a large sum of money, and received a personal letter of thanks from Lord Roberts, which he says is the greatest treasure he possesses. It runs as follows :

" Pretoria,
" 25 June, 1900.

" DEAR MAJOR BURNHAM,

" As I hear you are about to return to Europe, I take this opportunity of thanking you for the valuable services you have performed since you joined my Headquarters at Paardeberg last February. I doubt whether any other man in the force could have successfully carried out the perilous enterprises on which you have from time to time been engaged, demanding, as they did, the training of a lifetime, combined with exceptional courage, caution and powers of endurance. I was very sorry to hear of the serious accident you met with in your last successful attempt on the enemy's line of railway, and I trust soon to hear that you are quite well again.

" Believe me, Yours very truly,
" ROBERTS, F.M."

The following is an extract from Army Orders, South Africa :

" Army Headquarters, Pretoria, 25 June, 1900.
2. Rank.—Capt. F. R. Burnham to have local rank of Major, in recognition of his distinguished service in the Field Intelligence Department. Certified true copy :
" C. V. HUME, Lieutenant-Colonel, D.M.I.
" Pretoria, 26 June, 1900."

Her late Majesty Queen Victoria showed much appreciation of Major Burnham's services to the British Empire, as will be seen from the following letters received by the famous American Scout on his arrival in London :

" Osborne,
" 24 July, 1900.

" DEAR SIR,

" The Queen would much like to see you if you could come here some day. But as it is understood your health has suffered by your hard work in South Africa, Her Majesty desires me first to ascertain whether you are in a condition to travel. Perhaps you might sleep at Portsmouth and come across in the morning. If you are to be in England some time, you might possibly prefer to delay your visit here. But Her Majesty only wishes to consider your convenience in the event of your being able to come.

" Yours very faithfully,
" ARTHUR BIGGE,
" Private Secretary.
" Burnham, Esq."

" Osborne,
" 27 July, 1900.

" DEAR SIR,

" It would give the Queen much pleasure to receive you on Monday, the 6th of August, at about 6 p.m., and the Prince of Wales would be very glad to see you the same day. Will you give my wife and me the pleasure of your company at Albert Cottage, which is within the grounds, for Monday night ? There are boats which run from either Portsmouth or Southampton to Cowes. I will let you know later on about the hour at which the Prince of Wales would receive you.

" Yours very truly,
" ARTHUR BIGGE.
" Capt. F. R. Burnham."

He was created a Companion of the Distinguished Service Order [London Gazette, 27 Sept. 1901]: " Frederick Russell Burnham, Local Major. In recognition of services during operations in South Africa." Major Burnham was invested with the Insignia by the King 17 Dec. 1901.

Major Burnham has the following Memorandum : " Frederick Russell Burnham, Esquire, Local Major in South Africa, was made a Member of the Distinguished Service Order on the 26th day of Sept. 1901.—St. John Brodrick, The Principal Secretary of State having the Department of War for the time being."

Major Burnham also received the South African Medal with five clasps. In 1902 he made surveys of the Volter River in West Africa, exploring parts of the French Nigeria Hinterland of the Gold Coast Colony, and he took an active part in native troubles of that time; commanded an exploration of magnitude from Lake Rudolph to German East Africa, covering a vast region along the Congo basin and head of the Nile, 1903–4. He discovered a lake of 49 square miles, composed almost entirely of carbonate of soda, of unknown depth. Major Burnham has been associated with the Hon. John Hays Hammond in his mining interests since 1905. He was one of the eighteen officers selected by Roosevelt t oraise volunteers for service in France in 1917. The account of the killing of Umlimo by Major Burnham was published in the "Daily Telegraph," 1896 or 1897, by permission of the late Earl Grey, who was then Administrator of Rhodesia, and it is on a copy of Major Burnham's reports to Earl Grey that Sir H. Rider Haggard wrote a description of Wilson's last stand, in Longman's "Real True Story Book," published in 1894. "Sir H. Rider Haggard," says Major Burnham, "might have a copy, but mine was destroyed by Indians in our fighting in Mexico." When the late Richard Harding Davis selected six men as typical real soldiers of fortune, Major Burnham was one of them. He modestly says himself that what he did fell far short of what he might have done, but that Lord Roberts and all the men with whom he worked, whatever his shortcomings, were still his friends, and this is the list of some of them: General Carrington, General Baden-Powell, Colonel the Hon. Maurice Gifford, Colonel Hume, General Hunter-Weston, Cecil Rhodes and the romantic soldier, Major Allan Wilson. "Yet I feel that all our little wars, sieges and combats sink into such insignificance compared with what is being done now, that it seems a little presumptuous to have anything more than a bare mention in such a book as you are preparing."

MACLAREN, KENNETH, Capt., was born 18 Oct. 1860. He was educated at Harrow School, and entered the 13th Hussars 11 Aug. 1880; became Lieutenant 1 July, 1881; was Adjutant, 13th Hussars, 19 May, to 31 Aug. 1886; was promoted to Captain 3 Aug. 1887; was A.D.C. to Major-General, Cavalry Brigade, Aldershot, 1 Jan. 1890, to 4 Oct. 1890; A.D.C. to G.O.C., Forces, Ireland, 5 Oct. 1890, to 1 Dec. 1891; Adjutant, 13th Hussars, 2 Dec. 1891, to 1 May, 1895; A.D.C. to G.O.C., North-Western Districts, 11 April, 1895, to 18 Oct. 1896; A.D.C. to Lieutenant-General, Bengal, 9 Nov. 1896, to 5 Oct. 1898. He served on the North-West Frontier of India, Mohmand, as Orderly Officer to the G.O.C., 1897–98; was mentioned in Despatches [London Gazette, 11 Jan. 1898], and received the Medal and clasp; was A.D.C. to G.O.C., Southern District, 10 Nov. 1898, to 14 July, 1899; on Special Service, South Africa, 15 July, 1899. He served in the South African War, 1899–1900, as Special Service Officer, including service with the Rhodesian Regt.; was severely wounded; was mentioned in Despatches [London Gazette, 19 Oct. 1901]; received the Queen's Medal with three clasps, and was created a Companion of the Distinguished Service Order [London Gazette, 27 Sept. 1901]: "Kenneth MacLaren, Capt., 13th Hussars. In recognition of services during the operations in South Africa." The Insignia were presented by the King 29 Oct. 1901. He married (1st) Leila Evelyn (who died in 1904), and they had one daughter, and (2ndly) Ethel Mary Wilson, in 1910. Major MacLaren retired 8 Nov. 1905.

FOSTER, MONTAGU AMOS, Capt., was born 19 March, 1861, son of William Foster, of Wilbury Road, Brighton. He was gazetted to the Somerset Light Infantry 28 Jan. 1882; was promoted to Captain 23 Sept. 1887; was Adjutant, Militia, 15 May, 1899, to 25 Feb. 1904. Capt. Foster served in the South African War, 1900–2; as Adjutant, 4th Battn. Somerset Light Infantry, April, 1900, to 20 April, 1902; operations in Cape Colony, south of Orange River, April to 29 Nov. 1900; operations in Cape Colony 30 Nov. 1900, to April, 1902. He was mentioned in Despatches [London Gazette, 10 Sept. 1901, and 29 July, 1902]; received the Queen's Medal with clasp; the King's Medal with two clasps, and was created a Companion of the Distinguished Service Order [London Gazette, 27 Sept. 1901]: "Montagu Amos Foster, Capt., Somersetshire Light Infantry. In recognition of services during the operations in South Africa." The Insignia were presented by the King 29 Oct. 1901. He was promoted to Major 21 April, 1902. Major Foster retired from the Somersetshire Light Infantry 19 March, 1909. He married, in 1898, Yda Frances, daughter of the late Colonel G. C. Thompson, I.S.C.

CASS, CHARLES HERBERT DAVIS, Capt., was born 13 Aug. 1858, eldest son of the Rev. Charles William Cass and Elizabeth Frances Cass. He was educated at Winchester; was gazetted to the 69th Foot 13 July, 1878; became Lieutenant, Welsh Regt., 2 Feb. 1881, and Captain 19 Jan. 1888. He served in the South African War, 1899–1902, taking part in operations in the Transvaal in May and June, 1900; operations in the Transvaal, east of Pretoria, July to 20 Nov. 1900, including action at Reit Vlei; operations in Cape Colony, north of Orange River, May, 1900; operations in the Transvaal 30 Nov. to Dec. 1900; operations in Orange River Colony, Dec. 1900, to April, 1901. He was mentioned in Despatches [London Gazette, 10 Sept. 1901]; received the Queen's Medal with three clasps; the King's Medal with two clasps, and was created a Companion of the Distinguished Service Order, for defending Eland's River with about 180 men against some 500 Boers with three guns [London Gazette, 27 Sept. 1901]: "Charles Herbert Davis Cass, Capt., Connaught Rangers. In recognition of services during the operations in South Africa." The Insignia were presented by the King 28 March, 1903. He was promoted to Major 27 Aug. 1902, and retired from the Worcestershire Regt. 6 July, 1904. Major Cass was appointed High Sheriff for Cardiganshire in 1913. He is a Justice of the Peace for Cardiganshire. He served on the Army Recruiting Staff (voluntarily) from 1917 to 1919.

OGILVY, ANGUS HOWARD REGINALD, Capt., was born on 12 Aug. 1860. He entered the 13th Hussars 22 Jan. 1881; became Lieutenant 1 July, 1881, and Captain 1 July, 1888; was Adjutant, Yeomanry Cavalry, 1 Aug. 1890, to 31 July, 1895. He served in the South African War, and was created a Companion of the Distinguished Service Order [London Gazette, 27 Sept. 1901]: "Angus Howard Reginald Ogilvy, Capt., 13th Hussars. In recognition of services during the operations in South Africa." The Insignia were presented by the King 17 Dec. 1901. He was promoted to Major. Major Ogilvy died at Fez 4 July, 1906.

LONGRIDGE, THEODORE, Capt., was born 20 July, 1860, son of the late J. A. Longridge, of Grève d'Azette, Jersey. He was educated at Eton; entered the 16th Foot 14 Jan. 1880; was Adjutant, Bedfordshire Regt., 1 July, 1881, to 30 April, 1892; was promoted Captain 1 Feb. 1889. He served in the Isazai Expedition. Capt. Longridge served with the Chitral Relief Force, 1895, and was present at the storming of the Malakand Pass; at the action near Khar and the descent into the Swat Valley. He received the Medal with clasp. He was Adjutant, Militia, 1 Oct. 1896, to 18 Aug. 1898. He served in the South African War, 1899–1902, as Garrison Adjutant; as Adjutant, 3rd Battn. Royal Munster Fusiliers, during the operations in the Transvaal, west of Pretoria; operations in Orange River Colony; operations in Cape Colony 30 Nov. 1900, to March, 1902. He was mentioned in Despatches [London Gazette, 10 Sept. 1901]; received the Queen's Medal with three clasps; the King's Medal with two clasps, and was created a Companion of the Distinguished Service Order [London Gazette, 27 Sept. 1901]: "Theodore Longridge, Capt., Bedfordshire Regt. In recognition of services during the operations in South Africa." The Insignia, Warrant and Statutes were sent to the G.O.C., Transvaal and Orange River Colony, and were presented at Bloemfontein in Jan. 1903. He became Major 11 Jan. 1902; was Staff Officer, Transvaal and Orange River Colony, 1 Dec. 1902, to 11 March, 1903; became Lieutenant-Colonel 2 May, 1908, and retired from the Bedfordshire Regt. 2 May, 1912, joining the Reserve of Officers; served during the European War from 1914, as Commandant at Headquarters. He married, in 1893, Emma Harriet Elizabeth, daughter of the late T. E. Fowle, of Chute Lodge, Hants, J.P., D.L.

DOWNING, HENRY JOHN, Capt., was born 20 Jan. 1862, son of Samuel Downing, LL.D., Professor of Civil Engineering, Trinity College, Dublin, and of Elizabeth, only daughter of William Plummer, Esq., of Brislington, near Bristol. He was educated at Rugby and Trinity College, Dublin, and was appointed Lieutenant in the Royal Irish Regt. 29 July, 1882. He served with the Hazara Expedition, 1888 (Medal with clasp); was promoted Captain 20 Nov. 1889; was Adjutant, Royal Irish Regt. 31 Oct. 1898, to 2 July, 1901. He served in the South African War, 1899–1902, as Adjutant, 1st Battn. Royal Irish Regt., from 12 Jan. 1900, to 2 July, 1901; operations in the Orange Free State, March to May, 1900; operations in the Transvaal, east of Pretoria, including actions at Belfast (26 and 27 Aug.) and Lydenberg (5 to 8 Sept.); operations in Orange River Colony, May to Aug. 1900, including actions at Bethlehem (6 and 7 July) and Wittebergen (1 to 29 July); operations in Cape Colony, south of Orange River, 1900, including action at Colesberg (15 Jan. to 12 Feb.); operations in the Transvaal 30 Nov. 1900, to March, 1902; Station Staff Officer. He was mentioned in Despatches [London Gazette, 10 Sept. 1901, and 29 July, 1902]; received the Queen's Medal with three clasps; the King's Medal with two clasps, and was created a Companion of the Distinguished Service Order [London Gazette, 27 Sept. 1901]: "Henry John Downing, Capt., Royal Irish Regt. In recognition of services during the operations in South Africa." The Insignia were presented by the King 2 June, 1902. He was promoted to Major 3 July, 1901, and to Lieutenant-Colonel 12 March, 1908. He retired from the Army 12 March, 1912. When the European War commenced he was appointed to command the 8th Service Battn. Royal Inniskilling Fusiliers 1 Oct. 1914, and proceeded to France in command of same, Feb. 1916; invalided; appointed to command the 10th (Training) Battn. East Lancashire Regt., June, 1916; retired Jan. 1918; appointed to command 3rd Volunteer Battn. Devonshire Regt. Oct. 1918; brought to notice of Secretary of State for War for valuable services rendered, Feb. 1917; appointed O.B.E. 3 June, 1919. He married, in 1887, Emily Harriet, daughter of Capt. Arthur French Lloyd, late 52nd Oxfordshire Light Infantry, and they have two sons: Samuel Arthur Lloyd, born 5 Sept. 1890, and Henry Geoffrey Owen, born 3 May, 1896.

Henry John Downing.

AYTOUN, ANDREW, Capt., was born 2 July, 1860, son of the late Robert Aytoun, W.S., of Capeldrae, Fife, and of his wife, Helena Louisa Adelaide Maugham. He joined the Argyll and Sutherland Highlanders 19 Feb. 1881; became Lieutenant 1 July, 1881; was Adjutant, Queensland Volunteer Corps, 6 Dec. 1888, to 31 Jan. 1892; became Captain 26 Feb. 1890; was Adjutant, Militia, 19 Sept. 1892, to 22 Feb. 1898. Capt. Aytoun was employed with Colonial Forces, Queensland, from 18 March, 1898. He served in the South African War, 1900–1, in command of the 4th Queensland Contingent (Imperial Bushmen); operations in the Transvaal, east and west of Pretoria, July to 29 Nov. 1900, including action at Zilikat's Nek; operations in the Orange River Colony, May to 29 Nov. 1900. He was mentioned in Despatches [London Gazette, 10 Sept. 1901]; received the Queen's Medal with three clasps, and was created a Companion of the Distinguished Service Order [London Gazette, 27 Sept. 1901]; "Andrew Aytoun, Capt., Argyll and Sutherland Highlanders. In recognition of services during the operations in South Africa." The Insignia were sent to the Colonial Office 27 Nov. 1902, for presentation by Lord Tennyson; returned and presented by the King 12 June, 1903. He was promoted Major 9 Aug. 1902, and retired 2 July, 1908. During the European War he served as Assistant Embarkation Officer, with the temporary rank of Colonel. He was created a C.M.G. in 1917; a C.B.E.

in 1919; was made Officer of the Crown of Belgium, 1917, and Officer of the Legion of Honour, France, 1918. He married, in 1889, Helen Lilias, fourth daughter of the late Robert Graham, of Fintry, and their son, Robert Merlin Graham, born 19 Jan. 1890, Lieutenant, Argyll and Sutherland Highlanders, died 27 Aug. 1914, of wounds received the previous day at Le Cateau.

SAPTE, FRANCIS, Capt., was born 26 April, 1862, son of the late Capt. William Sapte. He was educated at Haileybury, and at Sandhurst; entered the Army in 1882; was promoted Captain in 1890; became Adjutant, 6th Battn. Middlesex Regt., in 1897, and served in that capacity in South Africa, 1899–1902, and as Staff Officer to Commandant of a Colonial Defence Area; operations in Cape Colony, south of Orange River, 1900; operations in Cape Colony 30 Nov. 1900, to March, 1902. He was mentioned in Despatches [London Gazette, 10 Sept. 1901]; received the Queen's Medal with clasp; the King's Medal with two clasps, and was created a Companion of the Distinguished Service Order [London Gazette, 27 Sept. 1901]: "Francis Sapte, Capt., Middlesex Regt. In recognition of services during the operations in South Africa." The Insignia were presented by the King 2 June, 1902, and the Warrant sent 4 June, 1902. Major Sapte retired in 1902.

SMITH, FREDERICK, Capt., was born in 1858. He was educated for the medical profession (L.R.C.P.I., L.R.C.S.I., D.P.H., Durham), and joined the Army; served in the Zulu War, 1879, receiving the Medal with clasp; on the North-West Frontier of India, 1897–98, and accompanied the Mohmund Expedition (Medal and clasp). He served in Sierra Leone in 1898 and 1899, taking part in the Mendi and Protectorate Expeditions (Medal with clasp). He served in the South African War, 1900–1; attached to the 2nd Wiltshire Regt., and later on as Secretary to P.M.O.; took part in operations in the Orange Free State, Feb. to May, 1900; operations in Orange River Colony and the Transvaal, east of Pretoria, May to 29 Nov. 1900, including actions at Biddulphsberg, Bethlehem (6 and 7 July) and Wittebergen (1 to 29 July); operations in Cape Colony, south of Orange River, 1899–1900; operations in the Transvaal 30 Nov. 1900, to May, 1901. He became a Captain, R.A.M.C., 30 March, 1890. For his services in South Africa he was mentioned in Despatches [London Gazette, 10 Sept. 1901]; received the Queen's Medal and four clasps, and was created a Companion of the Distinguished Service Order [London Gazette, 27 Sept. 1901]: "Frederick Smith, Capt., Royal Army Medical Corps. In recognition of services during the operations in South Africa." The Insignia were presented by the King 2 June, 1902, and the Warrant sent 4 June, 1902. He was promoted to Major 30 March, 1902. He served in the European War; on mobilization he commanded a stationary hospital; afterwards took command of a general hospital in France; was promoted to be A.D.M.S. of a division, and finally D.D.M.S. of a corps. He received the Mons Star; was twice mentioned in Despatches; created a C.M.G. (1916), and a C.B. (1918), and promoted Brevet Colonel. Colonel Smith is the author of "Modern Bullet Wounds" (1903) and "Drainage in Tropical Countries" (1904). He married Jane Violet Laing, and has one daughter and two sons: Violet Overton; Hector, and Helier Laing.

Frederick Smith.

PARRY, HENRY JULES, Capt., was born 5 Feb. 1867. He was educated for the medical profession, and became Captain, Royal Army Medical Corps, 29 July, 1890. Capt. Parry served in the South African War, 1899–1902, taking part in the Relief of Ladysmith, including the action of Colenso; operations of 17 to 24 Jan. 1900, and action at Spion Kop; operations of 5 to 7 Feb. 1900, and action at Vaal Kranz; operations on Tugela Heights (14 to 27 Feb. 1900) and action at Pieter's Hill; operations in the Transvaal in Orange River Colony; operations on the Zululand Frontier of Natal, Sept. 1901. He was mentioned in Despatches [London Gazette, 8 Feb. 1901]; received the Queen's Medal with five clasps; the King's Medal with two clasps, and was created a Companion of the Distinguished Service Order [London Gazette, 27 Sept. 1901]: "Henry Jules Parry, M.B., Capt., Royal Army Medical Corps. In recognition of services during the operations in South Africa." The Insignia were presented by the King 18 Dec. 1902. He became Major 27 July, 1902, and retired 29 July, 1910. He served in the European War, 1914–19; was given the Brevet of Lieutenant-Colonel 1 Jan. 1918, and created a C.B.E. in 1919. Lieut.-Colonel Parry married, in 1899, Helen Dorothea Elizabeth Cockburn, daughter of the late Robert Pitcairn, Barrister-at-Law.

MARRIOTT, JOHN, Capt., was born 3 Nov. 1861, son of the late John Marriott, of Stowmarket, Advocate-General, Bombay. He joined the Norfolk Regt. 5 Dec. 1883; was promoted Capt. 5 Sept. 1890. He was captured by brigands in Asia Minor in Oct. 1896, who demanded a ransom of £16,000, but was released by Turkish troops. He served in the South African War, 1900–2; being present at operations in the Orange Free State, Feb. to May, 1900, including operations at Paardeberg (17 to 26 Feb.); actions at Poplar Grove, Karee Siding, Vet River (5 and 6 May) and Zand River; operations in the Transvaal in May and June, 1900, including actions near Johannesburg and Pretoria; operations in the Transvaal 30 Nov. 1900, to 31 May, 1902. He was mentioned in Despatches [London Gazette, 8 Feb. and 10 Sept. 1901]; received the Queen's Medal with three clasps; the King's Medal with two clasps, and was created a Companion of the Distinguished Service Order [London Gazette, 27 Sept. 1901]: "John Marriott, Capt., Norfolk Regt. In recognition of services during the operations in South Africa." The Insignia, Warrant, etc., were sent to the G.O.C., Transvaal and Orange River Colony, 15 Nov. 1902, and presented by Brigadier-General Munro at Potchefstroom 11 Jan. 1903. He was promoted Major 12 March, 1904, and was specially employed on the Military Survey and Reconnaissance of Manaqualand and Bechuanaland, South Africa, 1907. He became Lieutenant-Colonel 12 Jan. 1909; was created an M.V.O. in 1909, and promoted Colonel 30 Oct. 1912. He was Brigade Commander, Surrey Infantry Brigade, from 1913, and during the European War he commanded the following brigades: The Surrey, 2/1st Surrey, 112th, in France, 200th and 221st Mixed Brigade. He was specially mentioned for valuable services in connection with the War in 1918; was created a C.B.E. in 1919, and retired from the Staff with the honorary rank of Brigadier-General 11 April, 1919. General Marriott is a Fellow of the Royal Geographical Society and of the Royal Zoological Society, and is an authority on big game. He married, in 1902, Cordelia C. Nevers, of St. Johnsburg, Vermont, U.S.A., and they have three daughters.

RICHARDSON, JOHN, Capt., was born at 14, Park Terrace, Glasgow, 3 April, 1859, son of the late John Richardson, of 17, Wilton Crescent, London, S.W. He was educated at Eton; joined the Army 13 Aug. 1879; served in Crete, 1898; was promoted Captain 22 Nov. 1890. He served in South Africa, 1899–1902; was promoted Major, Highland Light Infantry, 4 Dec. 1900; took part in the advance on Kimberley, including the action at Magersfontein, where he was slightly wounded. He took part in operations in the Orange Free State, Feb. to May, 1901; at further operations after the Free State had been annexed to Great Britain under the name of the Orange River Colony, May to 29 Nov. 1900, including actions at Wittebergen (1 to 29 July) and Witpoort; and in the operations of 30 Nov. 1900, to Feb. 1901. He also took part in the operations in Cape Colony, Feb. 1901, to 31 May, 1902. He was mentioned twice in Despatches [London Gazette, 16 March, 1900, and 10 Sept. 1901]; was awarded the Queen's Medal and two clasps; King's Medal and two clasps, and created a Companion of the Distinguished Service Order [London Gazette, 27 Sept. 1901]: "John Richardson, Capt., Highland Light Infantry. In recognition of services during the operations in South Africa." The Insignia were presented by the King 24 Oct. 1902; the Warrant sent 4 Nov. 1902. He retired from the Army in Sept. 1904, on retired pay. He served as a Temporary Lieutenant-Colonel, in command of the Depôt, Highland Light Infantry, from 13 Nov. 1914, to 30 Aug. 1916; promoted Honorary Lieutenant-Colonel [London Gazette, 11 April, 1917]. He is unmarried.

VIGORS, PHILIP URBAN WALTER, Capt, was born 8 Feb. 1863, third son of the late T. M. Vigors, of Burgage, County Carlow, Ireland. He was gazetted to the Devonshire Regt., as Lieutenant, 9 Sept. 1882; was promoted Captain 4 Feb. 1891. He served in Burma in 1891, taking part in operations in the Kachin Hills (Medal with clasp). Capt. Vigors served in the South African War, 1899–1902, being present at the Relief of Ladysmith, including actions at Colenso (slightly wounded); operations of 17 to 24 Jan. 1900, and action at Spion Kop; operations of 5 to 7 Feb. 1900, and action at Vaal Kranz; operations on Tugela Heights 14 to 27 Feb. 1900 (wounded, 23 Feb.), and action at Pieter's Hill; operations in Natal, March to June, 1900, including action at Laing's Nek (6 to 9 June). He performed the duties of Railway Staff Officer. He was mentioned in Despatches [London Gazette, 8 Feb. 1901 (Sir R. H. Buller, 30 March and 9 Nov. 1900), and London Gazette, 10 Sept. 1901]; received the Queen's Medal with five clasps; the King's Medal with two clasps, and was created a Companion of the Distinguished Service Order [London Gazette, 27 Sept. 1901]: "Philip Urban Walter Vigors, Capt., Devonshire Regt. In recognition of services during the operations in South Africa." The Insignia were presented by the King 24 Oct. 1902; the Warrant sent 4 Nov. 1902. He was promoted to Major 9 May, 1902. Major Vigors retired 25 Oct. 1900, and joined the Reserve of Officers. He was appointed Second-in-Command, Depôt, Devonshire Regt., Exeter. He married, in 1891, Anna Louisa Hyacinth D'Arcy, third daughter of the Rev. Hyacinth D'Arcy, of Clifden Castle, County Galway, and they have two daughters.

FEILDEN, CECIL WILLIAM MONTAGU, Capt., was born 13 Jan. 1863, at Quebec, son of Lieut.-General Feilden, C.M.G., of Witton Park, Blackburn, M.P. for North Lancashire. He was educated at Eton and Sandhurst, and was gazetted as Lieutenant to the Royal Scots Greys 2 Aug. 1882; became Captain 14 Feb. 1891; was A.D.C. (extra) to the Lord-Lieutenant, Ireland, 2 Feb. 1891, to 17 Aug. 1892; A.D.C. to the Lord-Lieutenant, Ireland, 3 Oct. 1892 to 8 July, 1895; A.D.C. to the Lord-Lieutenant of Ireland (Lord Cadogan) 30 July, 1895, to 31 Oct. 1895; also Military Secretary to Earl Cadogan. Private Secretary to Viscount Wolseley, Commander-in-Chief, 1 Nov. 1895, to 15 Jan. 1897; A.D.C. (extra) to the Lieutenant-General and Governor-General, Ireland, 26 Jan. 1897, to 15 Nov. 1899. He served in the South African War, and was created a Companion of the Distinguished Service Order [London Gazette, 27 Sept. 1901]: "Cecil William Montagu Feilden, Capt., 2nd Dragoons. In recognition of services during the operations in South Africa." He was a J.P. for Lancashire and Cheshire. Capt. Feilden died 7 Feb. 1902.

CHICHESTER, ARLINGTON AUGUSTUS, Capt., was born 2 July, 1863, son of the late Major-General J. O. Chichester, of Western House, Chudleigh, Devon, and Mrs. Chichester (*née* Preston). He was educated at Cheltenham College, and at the Royal Military College, Sandhurst, 1883, and has passed the Staff College. He entered the Dorsetshire Regt. 23 Aug. 1884, and was promoted to Captain 11 March, 1891. He served in the South African War, 1899–1901, as Assistant Provost-Marshal 13 June, 1900, to 4 March, 1903; was present at the Relief of Ladysmith, and at the action at Spion Kop; took part in operations 5 to 7 Feb. 1900; was present at action at Vaal Kranz; participated in operations on Tugela Heights, and fought in the action at Pieter's Hill; took part in operations in the Transvaal, June, 1900; in operations in Natal, March to June, 1900, including action at Laing's Nek, and in operations in Orange River Colony, June, 1900. He was mentioned in Despatches [London Gazette, 10 Sept. 1901]; received the Queen's Medal, with five clasps; the King's Medal with two clasps, and was created a Companion of the Distinguished Service Order [London Gazette, 27 Sept. 1901]: "Arlington Augustus Chichester, Capt., Dorsetshire Regt. In recognition of services during the operations in South Africa." The Insignia were presented by the King 28 March, 1903. He became Major 26 Feb. 1902; was on the General Staff, Hong-Kong, 19 March, 1903, to 23 Aug. 1904, as D.A.Q.M.G., and was D.A.A.G., South China, 24 Aug. 1904, to 18 May, 1907. He was promoted Lieutenant-Colonel 19 Feb. 1910, and Colonel 2 June, 1913. He served in the European War from 5 Aug. 1914, to 18 Oct. 1914, as A.A. and Q.M.G., 2nd Army Corps. B.E.F.; as Brigade Commander, Reserve Troops, B.E.F., 20 Oct. 1914, to 29 Dec. 1914. He commanded the 5th Infantry Brigade, B.E.F., from 30 Dec. 1914, to 12 July, 1915; and was D.A.Q.M.G., B.E.F., 13 July, 1915, to 8 Nov. 1915; D.A.Q.M.G., B.E.F., and British Armies in France, 9 Nov. 1915, to 11 Nov. 1917; D.Q.M.G., British Armies in Italy, 12 Nov. 1917. He was mentioned in Despatches eleven times; promoted to Major-General for distinguished service 3 June, 1917; created a C.B. in 1915, and a K.C.M.G. in 1919. Sir A. A. Chichester has the 1914 Star, the Belgian Order of the Crown and Croix de Guerre; the Italian Order of St. Maurice and St. Lazarus; the French Legion of Honour and Croix de Guerre. He married, in 1891, Eva Isabella Maude, third daughter of Major-General H. Justice, formerly I.S.C., of Riven Hall, Southsea; they have one son.

WHITE, SAMUEL ROBERT LLEWELLYN, Capt., was born at Black-rock, County Dublin, Ireland, on 4 June, 1863, son of Robert White, of Scotch Rath, Dalkey, County Dublin (eldest son of the late Samuel White, of Ballybrophy, Queen's County), and Adelaide Susan White, daughter of P. Roe, Esq., of Gortnaclea, Queen's County. He was privately educated, and joined the Leinster Regt. 6 May, 1885; becoming Captain 14 July, 1891. He was Adjutant, Militia, 5 Dec. 1894, to 31 Aug. 1896. Capt. White served in the South African War, 1900–2; he took part in operations in Orange River Colony, including action of Wittebergen; surrender of Prinsloo's Commando. The Army List says that Capt. White was present at "operations in the Orange Free State, May, 1900; operations in Orange River Colony, May to 29 Nov. 1900, including action at Wittebergen; operations in the Transvaal,

Samuel R. Ll. White.

Oct. 1900; operations in Cape Colony, May, 1900; operations in the Transvaal, March to April, 1901, and July, 1901; operations in Orange River Colony 30 Nov. 1900, to March, 1901, and April, 1901, to 31 May, 1902." He was mentioned in Despatches by Lord Roberts [London Gazette, 10 Sept. 1901]; received the Queen's Medal with three clasps; the King's Medal with two clasps, and was created a Companion of the Distinguished Service Order [London Gazette, 27 Sept. 1901]: "Samuel Robert Llewellyn White, Capt., Leinster Regt. In recognition of services during the operations in South Africa." The Insignia were presented by the King 18 Dec. 1902. He was promoted Major 6 Jan. 1901. He was promoted Lieutenant-Colonel 6 May, 1911. He commanded the 1st Battn. Leinster Regt. from 1911 to 1915, and took his Battalion to France in Nov. 1914; invalided home in March, 1915; Home service till June, 1918, when he retired owing to ill-health. He was appointed to the command of the 17th Battn. Yorkshire Regt. on its formation in Nov. 1916, and served with it until it was disbanded towards the end of 1917. He holds the Coronation Medal, and has the 1914 Star and War Medals. He married (1st), at Gloucester, in 1895, Dorothy Hey, daughter of the Rev. B. Fearnley Carlyle, Vicar of Cam, Gloucester-shire; they had one son, Robert Carlyle Llewellyn, born 27 Jan. 1898 (a Lieutenant in the Royal Field Artillery). In 1903 Major White lost his first wife; in 1913 he married again, Louisa Mary, daughter of John Charles Hughes, Esq., of Bryndedwydd, Dolgelly, North Wales.

PORTER, FREDERICK JOSEPH WILLIAM, Capt., was born 17 April, 1867, son of Capt. J. Porter, R.A., and Mrs. Porter. He was educated for the medical profession (qualifying as Member of the Royal College of Surgeons and Licentiate Royal College of Physicians. He became Captain, Royal Army Medical Corps, 28 July, 1891. Capt. Porter served in the South African War, 1899–1902; was present at the Relief of Kimberley; operations in the Orange Free State, Feb. to May, 1900, including operations at Paardeberg 17 to 26 Feb., and actions at Poplar Grove, Karee Siding and Zand River; operations in the Transvaal in May and June, 1900, including actions near Johannesburg, Pretoria and Diamond Hill; operations in the Transvaal, west of Pretoria, July to 29 Nov. 1900; operations in the Orange River Colony, May to 26 Nov. 1900, including action at Wittebergen; opera-

Frederick J. W. Porter.

tions in the Transvaal, April, 1901, to 31 May, 1902; operations in Orange River Colony 30 Nov. 1900, to March, 1901, and April, 1901; operations in Cape Colony, March to April, 1901. He was mentioned in Despatches [London Gazette, 16 April, 1901]; received the Queen's Medal with five

clasps; the King's Medal with two clasps, and was created a Companion of the Distinguished Service Order [London Gazette, 27 Sept. 1901]: "Frederick Joseph William Porter, Capt., Royal Army Medical Corps. In recognition of services during the operations in South Africa." He was employed with the South African Constabulary 1 July, 1901, to 28 Feb. 1905, and was promoted to Major 28 July, 1903. Major Porter retired from the Army 22 Nov. 1913. He was Senior Medical Officer, Sierra Leone, and later practised as an operating surgeon in Bombay. He married (1st), in 1891, Margaret, daughter of the late William Goff, and they had one son and two daughters; and (2ndly), in 1915, Katherine Margery, youngest daughter of the late Henry Shaw, and they have a son.

BUIST, HERBERT JOHN MARTIN, Capt., was born 5 May, 1868, son of the late Major-General D. S. Buist. He was educated at George Watson's College, Edinburgh, and Edinburgh University, and became Captain, Royal Army Medical Corps, 28 July, 1891; served on the North-West Frontier, India, 1897, including operations with the Malakand Field Force, 3rd Brigade, and with the Tirah Expeditionary Force. He was mentioned in Despatches 18 March, 1898, and received the Medal with two clasps. Capt. Buist served in the South African War, 1899 to 1902. He acted as Secretary to the Principal Medical Officer, Cavalry Division, and General Sir John French's Columns in Cape Colony from June, 1900, to the termination of the South African War, and was present at the Relief of Kimberley; operations in the Orange Free State, Feb. to May, 1900, including operations at Paardeberg (17 to 26 Feb.); actions at Poplar Grove, Dreifontein, Houtnek (Thoba Mountain) and Zand River; operations in the Transvaal in May and June, 1900, including actions near Johannesburg, Pretoria and Diamond Hill (11 and 12 June); operations in the Transvaal, east of Pretoria, July to Nov. 1900, including actions at Belfast (26 and 27 Aug.); operations in Cape Colony, south of Orange River, 1899–1900, including actions at Colesberg in Jan. 1900; opera-tions in Cape Colony, June to Dec. 1901. He was mentioned in Despatches [London Gazette, 16 April, 1901]; received the Queen's Medal with six clasps; the King's Medal with two clasps, and was created a Companion of the Distinguished Service Order [London Gazette, 27 Sept. 1901]: "Herbert John Martin Buist, Capt., Royal Army Medical Corps. In recognition of services during the operations in South Africa." The Insignia were presented by the King 18 Dec. 1902. He was Staff Officer to the Principal Medical Officer, South Africa, 1903 till 1906, in which year on the 1st May he became Deputy Assistant Director-General, War Office, which appointment he filled till 30 April, 1910. He had been promoted to Major 28 July, 1903, and became Lieutenant-Colonel 22 Aug. 1913. He served in the European War; from Oct. 1914, to Nov. 1915, served as Senior Medical Officer, Cape Town Base, during the German South-West operations. From June, 1916, to May, 1917, served as Officer Commanding, 37th British General Hospital, attached to the Royal Serbian Army with the Salonika Force. Acted as A.D.M.S., British Salonika Army, from 1 June to Dec. 1917; promoted Colonel, A.M.S., 28 Dec. 1917, and appointed D.D.M.S., Lines of Communication, Salonika Army, 1 Nov. 1918. Colonel Buist has the Croix de Guerre; the Order of St. Sava (2nd Class), and was made Officier, Legion of Honour, 1917. He was mentioned in Despatches. He married, in 1912, Gertrude M. K. Logan, daughter of J. D. Logan, J.P., of Matjesfontein, Cape Province, South Africa, and they have one son.

DODGSON, HEATHFIELD BUTLER, Capt., was born 2 Oct. 1863, son of the late W. O. Dodgson, of Sevenoaks, and of Lucy Elizabeth Dodgson. He was educated at Winchester and Royal Military Academy, Woolwich, and entered the Army 14 Feb. 1883. He was promoted Captain, Jan. 1892, and served in South Africa, 1900–2; on Staff, as Remount Officer, during operations in the Transvaal, west of Pretoria, July to 29 Nov. 1900; during operations in Orange River Colony, May to July, 1900, including actions at Lindley (1 June) and Rhenoster River; taking part in the operations in the Transvaal 30 Nov. to Dec. 1900; in the operations in Cape Colony, Jan. 1901, to 31 May, 1902. He was mentioned in Despatches [London Gazette, 10 Sept. 1901]; received the Queen's Medal and three clasps; the King's Medal and two clasps, and was created a Companion of the Distinguished Service Order [London Gazette, 27 Sept. 1901]: "Heathfield Butler Dodgson, Capt., Royal Garrison Artillery. In recognition of services during the operations in South Africa." The Insignia were presented by the King 18 Dec. 1902. He was promoted Major, 1903, subsequently retiring from the Royal Garrison Artillery, 1903. He was medically unfit for Service in 1914. He married, in 1889, Sybil Agnes, eldest daughter of the Hon. John C. W. Vivian, and they have one son and daughters.

BRITTAN, REGINALD, Capt., was born 26 Jan. 1865, son of the late Rev. C. Brittan and of Julia Brittan, daughter of Hartley P. Gisborne. He was educated at Clifton and Malvern Colleges, and entered the Army (The Sherwood Foresters) 29 Aug. 1885; became Captain, Sherwood Foresters, 1892. He was appointed Adjutant, 4th Battn. Sherwood Foresters, 1895; served in the South African War, 1899–1901; as Adjutant, 4th Battn. Derbyshire Regt. (from 11 Jan. 1900, to 10 May, 1901), taking part in the Transvaal, west of Pretoria, July to 29 Nov. 1900; during operations in Cape Colony, south of Orange River, 1899–1900; serving in the operations in Cape Colony 30 Nov. 1900, to April, 1901. He was men-tioned in Despatches [London Gazette, 10 Sept. 1901]; received the Queen's Medal with four clasps, and was created a Companion of the Distinguished Service Order [London Gazette, 27 Sept. 1901]: "Reginald Brittan, Capt., Derbyshire Regt. In recognition of services during opera-tions in South Africa." The Insignia were presented by the King 29 Oct. 1901. He commanded the 4th Battn. Sherwood Foresters from 1908. After the outbreak of the European War he commanded the 14th Sherwood Foresters, Nov. 1914, to Oct. 1916, when the name was changed to the 13th Battn. Training Reserve, and later to the 53rd Sherwood Foresters.

He gave up the Command, and was demobilized in April, 1919, and awarded the O.B.E. He married, in 1893, Alice, daughter of the late William Gisborne, of Allestree Hall, Derbyshire, and they have one son, Jack Reginald, born on 6 May, 1897, and one daughter.

BOUCHER, BENJAMIN HAMILTON, Capt., was born 20 Feb. 1864, son of the late B. Boucher, of The Croft, Wiveliscombe, Somerset. He was educated at Marlborough; entered the Army 25 Nov. 1885; served with the Burmese Expedition, 1887–89 (Medal with clasp); became Captain 29 Aug. 1892; was appointed Station Staff Officer, Bengal, 1893–95; served with the Chitral Relief Force, 1895, and was Adjutant, 1st Battn. Hampshire Regt. 1896–1900. He served in the South African War, 1899–1900, as Captain of the Hampshire Regt., taking part in the operations in the Orange Free State, Feb. to May, 1900, including operations at Paardeberg (17 to 26 Feb.); actions at Poplar Grove, Karee Siding, Vet River (5 and 6 May) and Zand River; during the operations in the Transvaal in May and June, 1900, including actions near Johannesburg and Pretoria. He was mentioned in Despatches 10 Sept. 1901; received the Medal and three clasps, and was created a Companion of the Distinguished Service Order [London Gazette, 27 Sept. 1901]: "Benjamin Hamilton Boucher, Capt., Hampshire Regt. In recognition of services in the operations in South Africa." The Insignia were presented by the King 29 Oct. 1901. Major Boucher was appointed Adjutant, 4th Volunteer Battn., 1900–4. On retiring from the Army he was appointed Governor of H.M.'s Prison, Knutsford. Since 1917 he has commanded 1st Gar. Battn. Oxford and Buckinghamshire Light Infantry. He married, in 1896 (1st), Helen, eldest daughter of the late J. C. Boucher, J.P., of Eaglemont, Kilmington, Devon, and of Lambcroft, Lincolnshire; she died in 1904, leaving three sons. He married (2ndly), in 1907, Dorothy (who died in 1916), daughter of the late Engledene Prideaux, of Leeson, Wellington, Somerset.

HARPER, GEORGE MONTAGUE, Capt., was born 11 Jan. 1865, son of the late Charles Harper. He entered the Army 5 July, 1884; became Captain 1 Oct. 1892. He served in South Africa, 1899–1900, as Captain, Royal Engineers; was present at the Relief of Ladysmith, including operations of 17 to 24 Jan. 1900, and action at Spion Kop; during operations of 5 to 7 Feb. 1900, and action at Vaal Kranz; in the operations on Tugela Heights (14 to 27 Feb. 1900), and action at Pieter's Hill; during operations in Natal, March to June, 1900, and operations in the Transvaal, east of Pretoria, July to Oct. 1900. He was mentioned four times in Despatches; received the Queen's Medal with four clasps, and was created a Companion of the Distinguished Service Order [London Gazette, 27 Sept. 1901]: "George Montague Harper, Capt., Royal Engineers. In recognition of services during operations in South Africa." The Insignia were presented by the King 29 Oct. 1901, and the

George Montague Harper.

Warrant was sent 27 Jan. 1902. He became Major 1 April, 1901. He was promoted Lieutenant-Colonel 1 Jan. 1907; Colonel 19 July, 1911, and was General Staff Officer, War Office, from 1911. During the European War was Temporary Brigadier-General 7 Nov. 1914, to 24 Sept. 1915, and served as General Staff Officer, 1st Grade, B.E.F., from 5 Aug. to 6 Nov. 1914, also on the General Staff, B.E.F., from 7 Nov. 1914, to 10 Feb. 1915; became Temporary Major-General 25 Sept. to 31 Dec. 1915, and served as Division Commander, 51st Division, B.E.F., British Armies in France, 25 Sept. 1915, to 10 March, 1918; promoted Major-General 1 Jan. 1916, and Temporary Lieutenant-General 11 March, 1918, to 31 Dec. 1918; was Army Corps Commander, 4th Army Corps, British Armies in France, 11 March, 1918, to 31 May, 1919; promoted Lieutenant-General 1 Jan. 1919; has been G.O.C., Southern Command, since 1 June, 1919; was mentioned in Despatches; created a C.B. in 1915; Commander of the Legion of Honour, and K.C.B. in 1918. Sir George Harper married, in 1893, the Hon. Ella Constance Jackson, second daughter of the 1st Baron Allerton.

DANIEL, CHARLES JAMES, Capt., was born in York 1 Nov. 1861, son of the late Rev. R. Daniel, B.D., Vicar of Osbaldwick, York, and of Mrs. Daniel, of Jevington Gardens, Eastbourne. He was educated at St. Peter's School, York, and at the Royal Military College, Sandhurst; joined the Army 10 May, 1882. He served in the Zhob Valley Expedition, 1884. He was appointed Adjutant, 3rd Battn. King's Own Royal Lancaster Regt. from 23 Jan. 1900, and served in the South African War, 1899–1902; during operations in Orange River Colony, May to 29 Nov. 1900; taking part in the operations in Cape Colony, south of Orange River, March to May, 1900; serving during operations in Orange River Colony 30 Nov. 1900, to Sept. 1901; in the operations in Cape Colony, Sept. 1901, to Jan. 1902. He was mentioned in Despatches; received the Queen's Medal and two clasps; the King's Medal and two clasps, and was created a Companion of the Distinguished Service Order [London Gazette, 27 Sept. 1901]: "Charles James Daniel, Capt., Loyal North Lancashire Regt. In recognition of services during the operations in South Africa." The Insignia were presented by the King 12 March, 1902, and the Warrant sent 19 March, 1902. He retired with the rank of Major 27 June, 1903. He served during the European War as Temporary Lieutenant-Colonel, in charge of No. 1 Record Office, Preston, and was created Commander of the Order of the British Empire 1 Jan. 1919. He married, 6 April, 1891, in Jersey, Agnes Margaret, elder daughter of the late Admiral T. Saumarez, C.B., and they have one son, Charles, born 23 June, 1894 (now Lieutenant, R.N.), and one daughter, Dorothy.

VENABLES, CHARLES JOHN, Capt., was born 21 Jan. 1865, son of the late Right Reverend Addington R. P. Venables, Bishop of Nassau. He entered the Army 20 Aug. 1885; became Captain, 1892. He served in South Africa as Captain, Gloucestershire Regt., 1899–1901, taking part in the operations in Natal, 1899, including actions at Rietfontein and Lombard's Kop, and in the defence of Ladysmith. He was mentioned in Despatches [London Gazette, 10 Sept 1901]; received the Queen's Medal and two clasps, and was created a Companion of the Distinguished Service Order [London Gazette, 27 Sept. 1901]: "Charles John Venables, Capt., Gloucestershire Regt. In recognition of services during the operations in South Africa." The Insignia were presented by the King 29 Oct. 1901. He was promoted Major 1 Nov 1905, and retired 26 Nov. 1913. He took part in the European War, and was killed in action 8 Aug. 1915, at the Dardanelles. He had married, in 1896, Helen Margaret, daughter of the late Robert Terry.

MOLYNEUX-SEEL, EDWARD HONORE, Capt., was born 24 June, 1862, son of E. R. T. Molyneux-Seel, of Huyton Hey, Lancaster. He entered the Army 19 Dec. 1883; was Adjutant, Royal Scots, 17 Feb. 1891, to 27 Dec. 1892. He became Captain, 16 Jan. 1893; was Adjutant, Volunteers, for a period ending 14 June, 1899; served in the South African War, 1899–1901; during the operations in the Orange Free State, including defence of Wepener; taking part in the operations in Orange River Colony, May to 29 Nov. 1900, including actions at Bethlehem (6 and 7 July) and Wittebergen (1 to 29 July); in the operations in Cape Colony, south of Orange River, 1899 to 1900; during the operations in the Transvaal, June to Sept. 1901; in the operations in Orange River Colony and Cape Colony, 1900–1901; commanded Mounted Infantry, Lines of Communication, Bloemfontein District, from 1 Sept. 1900; afterwards on the Staff, as Staff Officer, graded D.A.A.G., to Assistant-Inspector of Remounts, 24 Dec. 1900, to 3 June, 1901. He was mentioned in Despatches [London Gazette, 10 Sept. 1901]; received the Queen's Medal and five clasps, and was created a Companion of the Distinguished Service Order [London Gazette, 27 Sept. 1901]: "Edward Honoré Molyneux-Seel, Capt., Royal Scots. In recognition of services during the operations in South Africa." The Insignia were presented by the King 18 Dec. 1902. He was promoted Major 13 March, 1901, and retired from the Royal Scots 22 Nov. 1905. He married, in 1892, Margaret, eldest daughter of Matthew Bullock, and they have two daughters.

BURNETT, JOHN CHAPLYN, Capt., was born 24 Dec. 1863, son of the late Charles Mountford Burnett and Emily Jane Chaplyn. He was educated privately. He entered the Army 15 Feb. 1884; became Captain, 1893; served in the South African War, 1900–1902, as Captain, first in the Pompoms, afterwards as Staff Officer, Dynamite Factory, Middelfontein, near Johannesburg; taking part in the operations in the Transvaal in May and June, 1900, including actions near Johannesburg and Pretoria; during operations in the Transvaal, east of Pretoria, July to 29 Nov. 1900, including action at Reit Vlei; during operations in the Transvaal, April to Sept. 1901, and Oct. 1901, to May, 1902; during operations in the Orange River Colony; operations on the Zululand Frontier of Natal. He was mentioned in Despatches [London Gazette, 10 Sept. 1901]; received the Queen's Medal with three clasps;

John Curteis Burnett.

the King's Medal with two clasps, and was created a Companion of the Distinguished Service Order [London Gazette, 27 Sept. 1901]: "John Chaplyn Burnett, Capt., R. Garrison Artillery. In recognition of services during the operations in South Africa." The Insignia were presented by the King 18 Dec. 1902; the Warrant sent 6 Jan. 1903. He became Major 1 Oct. 1902, and retired from the Royal Garrison Artillery 5 May, 1909, and joined the Reserve of Officers. Major Burnett took part in the European War, 1914–1917. Commanded Garrison Artillery Company at Pembroke Dock, 1914–1915; volunteered for Khartum, Sudan, 1915; was invalided home. Served in Ministry of Munitions as Safety Service Officer in No. 1 N.F.F., Leeds.

COATES, HENRY WISE UNETT, Capt., was born 3 Dec. 1865, at Rockhampton, Gloucestershire, son of the Rev. W. U. Coates, of The Cottage, Hill, Falfield, Gloucestershire. He was educated at Marlborough College; received his first commission in the Bedfordshire Regt. 7 Feb. 1885; was promoted Captain 1 Feb. 1893; was Adjutant, 4th Battn., 16 Feb. 1895, to 15 June, 1901. He served in the South African War, 1899–1902; as Staff Officer to Commandant, Fourteen Streams, 29 May, to 25 June, 1900; afterwards Garrison Adjutant, Mafeking, 29 June to 13 Aug. 1900, and 4 Sept. 1900; served as Adjutant, 4th Battn. Bedfordshire Regt.; during operations in the Orange Free State, May, 1900; during operations in the Transvaal, west of Pretoria, Aug. and Sept. 1900; during operations in Cape Colony, north and south of Orange River. He was mentioned in Despatches [London Gazette, 10 Sept. 1901], received the Queen's Medal and three clasps; the King's Medal and two clasps, and was created a Companion of the Distinguished Service Order [London Gazette, 27 Sept. 1901]: "Henry Wise Unett Coates, Capt., Bedfordshire Regt. In recognition of services during the operations in South Africa." The Insignia and Warrant were sent to the G.O.C., Transvaal, 3 Feb. 1903; were presented by the King 12 June, 1903. He was promoted Major 5 April, 1903, subsequently becoming Lieutenant-Colonel. He married, 28 Dec. 1895, Eleanor Alice, daughter of the late D.T. Surgeon-General A. Rudge, of The Town, Compton, Plymouth.

CAVENDISH-BENTINCK, LORD WILLIAM AUGUSTUS, Capt., was born on 31 Jan. 1865, son of the late Lieut.-General Arthur Cavendish-Bentinck (great-grandson of the 3rd Duke), half-brother of the 6th Duke of Portland. He was educated at Eton, and entered the 10th Hussars, from the Militia, 16 Nov. 1887; became Lieutenant 10 Aug. 1889, and Captain 1 Feb. 1893. He was created a Companion of the Distinguished Service Order [London Gazette, 27 Sept. 1901]: "Lord William Augustus Cavendish-Bentinck, Capt., 10th Hussars. In recognition of services during the operations in South Africa." He died 4 Nov. 1903.

Lord W. A. Cavendish-Bentinck.

AMPHLETT, CHARLES GROVE, Capt., was born 8 March, 1862. He entered the Army 12 Nov. 1884; was promoted Captain in 1893. He served in the South African War, 1899–1900, commanding the 1st Mounted Infantry Regt. He was mentioned in Despatches [London Gazette, 10 Sept. 1901]; received the Queen's Medal with four clasps, and was created a Companion of the Distinguished Service Order [London Gazette, 27 Sept. 1901]: "Charles Grove Amphlett, Capt., North Staffordshire Regt. In recognition of services during the operations in South Africa." The Insignia were presented by the King 17 Dec. 1901. He was promoted Major 14 March, 1901; was placed on the Reserve of Officers, North Staffordshire Regt.; and is a Justice of the Peace for Salop and Staffordshire.

BARNETT, WILLIAM ALEXANDER, Capt., was born on 5 Sept. 1866, and entered the Army on 7 Feb. 1885. He served during the operations in Zululand in 1888; was promoted Captain 1 May, 1893, and Major 12 Feb. 1902. Major Barnett served in the South African War, 1900–2, as Assistant to the Military Governor of Johannesburg, from 6 Jan. 1900. Operations in the Orange Free State, Feb. to May, 1900, including actions at Karee Siding, Vet River (5 and 6 May) and Zand River; operations in the Transvaal in May, 1900, including actions near Johannesburg; operations in the Transvaal 30 Nov. 1900, to 31 May, 1902. He was mentioned in Despatches [London Gazette, 10 Sept. 1901]; received the Queen's Medal with three clasps, and was created a Companion of the Distinguished Service Order [London Gazette, 27 Sept. 1901]: "William Alexander Barnett, Capt., North Staffordshire Regt. In recognition of services during the operations in South Africa." The Insignia were presented by the King 17 Dec. 1901. He was employed with the Johannesburg Police 1 May, 1901, to 30 June, 1906. He died 21 Sept. 1910.

SCHREIBER, ACTON LEMUEL, Capt., was born 30 March, 1865, at Barham Rectory, Suffolk, son of the late Rev. J. E. L. Schreiber, M.A., J.P. (son of the late Capt. C. Schreiber, of the 11th Light Dragoons), and Lucy, daughter of the late Capt. C. Phillipps, 13th Light Dragoons, of Barham Hall. He was educated at Tonbridge School, and at the Oxford Military College, and entered the Army 9 Dec. 1884. Lieut. Schreiber was promoted Captain, 1893, and served on the North-West Frontier of India, 1897–98; at Tochi, as Field Engineer (26 June to Nov. 1897) (received Medal with clasp). He again saw active service in the South African Campaign, 1899–1902 (slightly wounded); during operations in the Orange Free State, March to May, 1900, including actions at Vet River (5 and 6 May) and Zand River; taking part during operations in the Transvaal in May and June, 1900, including actions near Johannesburg, Pretoria and Diamond Hill (11 and 12 June); during

Acton L. Schreiber.

operations in the Transvaal, east of Pretoria, including actions at Belfast (26 and 27 Aug.); during operations in Cape Colony, south of Orange River, 1899–1900, including operations in Orange River Colony. He was mentioned in Despatches [London Gazette, 10 Sept. 1901], received the Queen's Medal with five clasps, the King's Medal with two clasps, and was created a Companion of the Distinguished Service Order [London Gazette, 27 Sept. 1901]: "Acton Lemuel Schreiber, Capt., Royal Engineers. In recognition of services during operations in South Africa." The Insignia were presented by the King 24 Oct. 1902; the Warrant, etc., sent 4 Nov. 1902. He was appointed C.R.E., 1st Division, 1910–15; served in the European War, 1914–1915; Chief Engineer, 3rd Corps, July, 1915; Temporary Brigadier-General, July, 1915; was Aide-de-Camp to the King, 1915; he was six times mentioned in Despatches; created a C.B., 1916; C.M.G., 1918. He married, 18 June, 1889, at St. Paul's Church, Onslow Square, S.W., Evelyn Amy, daughter of Lieut.-Colonel Edmund D'Arcy Hunt, late Inniskilling Dragoons; they had two sons: E. A. Schreiber, born 26 April, 1890, now Capt. (Brevet Major), Royal Field Artillery, D.S.O.; and Acting Major O. R. Schreiber, born Oct. 1893, Capt., Royal Field Artillery, M.C. with Bar; killed at Ypres 22 Oct. 1917.

EUSTACE, HENRY MONTAGUE, Capt., was born at Sampford Grange, Great Sampford, Essex, 28 Nov. 1863, eldest surviving son of the late Rev. P. H. Eustace, Rector of Great Sampford, and Emily Henrietta, daughter of the late Sir Thomas P. Bridges. He was educated at Harrow; received his first commission in the Middlesex Regt. 29 Aug. 1885, serving in the 1st and 2nd Battns. of this regiment for twenty-two years. He was promoted Captain. He served in the South African War, 1899–1903; was present

at the Relief of Ladysmith, including operations of 17 to 24 Jan. 1900, and action at Spion Kop; during operations of 5 to 7 Feb. 1900, and action at Vaal Kranz; taking part in the operations on Tugela Heights (14 to 27 Feb. 1900) and action at Pieter's Hill; during operations in Natal, March to June, 1900; in the operations in the Transvaal, east of Pretoria, July to 29 Nov. 1900; during operations in Cape Colony, south of Orange River, 1899; taking part in the operations in the Transvaal, 30 Nov. 1900, to May, 1901, and Nov. 1901 to 31 May, 1902; during operations in Orange River Colony, May to Nov. 1901. He was mentioned in Despatches [London Gazette, 10 Sept. 1901], received the Queen's Medal and six clasps, King's Medal and two clasps, and for continuous and brilliant work, especially at Spion Kop, he was created a Member of the Distinguished Service Order [London Gazette, 27 Sept. 1901]: "Henry Montague Eustace, Capt., Middlesex Regt. In recognition of services during operations in South Africa." The Insignia were presented by the King 28 March, 1903. He was promoted Major 16 Aug. 1902. Major Eustace retired from the Middlesex Regt. in 1905. He was called out on the outbreak of the European War, Aug. 1914, rejoining the Army as Major, 11th Service Battn. Middlesex Regt. Nov. 1914; took command of the 6th Battn. York and Lancaster Regt. April, 1915. Lieut.-Colonel Eustace took part in the landing at Suvla; was very dangerously wounded at the Dardanelles 28 Sept. 1915, and was mentioned in Despatches by Sir Ian Hamilton. He is a Justice of the Peace, County Wexford. He married, in 1903, Monica Alice Eustace, daughter of Colonel J. T. Eustace, of Wynberg, South Africa, and they have two sons and one daughter.

LETHBRIDGE, ERNEST ASTLEY EDMUND, Capt., was born 26 Dec. 1864, second son of Sir Wroth A. Lethbridge, 4th Bart., and of Anne Williams Benyon. He was educated at Eton, and at the Royal Military College, Sandhurst; entered the Army 10 Oct. 1885; promoted Captain 27 Sept. 1893; Major 2 Sept. 1904, and Lieutenant-Colonel 25 Oct. 1913. He served in the South African War, 1899–1902; was present at the Relief of Kimberley; during operations in the Orange Free State, Feb. to May, 1900, including operations at Paardeberg (17 to 26 Feb.), actions at Poplar Grove and Driefontein; during operations in Orange River Colony, May to Nov. 1900; taking part in the operations in Orange River Colony, Dec. 1900, to 31 May, 1902. He was mentioned in Despatches twice [London Gazette, 8 Feb. and 10 Sept. 1901]; received the Queen's Medal and three clasps; King's Medal and two clasps, and was created a Companion of the Distinguished Service

Ernest A. E. Lethbridge.

Order [London Gazette, 27 Sept. 1901]: "Ernest Astley Edmund Lethbridge, Capt., Oxfordshire Light Infantry. In recognition of services during operations in South Africa." The Insignia were presented by the King 24 Oct. 1902. He served during the European War; commanded the 1st Battn. Oxford and Bucks Light Infantry in Mesopotamia from 1914 to April, 1916, to the termination of the Siege of Kut; he was three times mentioned in Despatches, and created a C.M.G., 1916, and received the Brevet of Colonel.

BOWEN, GERARD CHRISTOPHER, Capt., was born 28 July, 1864, son of the late Major-General W. T. Bowen and Rosa Bowen (née Pack). He was educated at Malvern College, and entered the Army 25 Nov. 1885. He was promoted Captain 11 Dec. 1893. He served in South Africa, in the Mounted Infantry, 1899–1902; during operations in Cape Colony, Orange River Colony and the Transvaal, 1899–1900, taking part in the operations in Cape Colony, Orange River Colony and the Transvaal 30 Nov. 1900, to 31 May, 1902. He was mentioned in Despatches [London Gazette, 10 Sept. 1901]; received the Queen's Medal with three clasps, and was created a Companion of the Distinguished Service Order [London Gazette, 27 Sept. 1901]: "Gerard Christopher Bowen, Capt., Royal Munster Fusiliers. In recognition of services during operations in South Africa." The Insignia were presented by the King 18 Dec. 1902. He retired from the Royal Munster Fusiliers 14 Sept. 1904; was re-employed after the outbreak of the hostilities in 1914. He was mentioned in Despatches, and promoted Major, 1916. He married (1st), in 1889, Kathleen Rachel (died 1890), daughter of the Rev. H. V. Russell, and (2ndly), in 1896, Mildred Hilda, daughter of P. Hughes.

GREEN, THOMAS HAROLD MORTIMER, Major, was born 24 April, 1863, eldest son of the late Rev. W. Green, of Pontyrhun, Glamorganshire. He received his commission as Second Lieutenant 16 May, 1888; became Lieutenant 1 May, 1890; was promoted Captain 1 Jan. 1894, and was Adjutant, 2nd Battn. Nottinghamshire and Derbyshire Regt. 2 July, 1895, to 1 Jan. 1899. He took part in the Chitral Relief Force Expedition, 1895, with the Relief Force as Transport Officer (Medal and clasp); in operations on the North-West Frontier of India, 1897–98, taking part in the action of Dargai and capture of the Sampagha and Arhanga Passes; during operations in the Bazar Valley 25 to 30 Dec. 1897, and received two clasps. He served in the South African War, 1899–1902 (was severely wounded); during operations in the Orange Free State, including actions at Houtnek (Thoba Mountain), Vet River and Zand River; operations in the Transvaal, including actions near Johannesburg, Pretoria and Diamond Hill; operations in Cape Colony, south of Orange River, taking part in the operations in the Transvaal, June, 1901, to 31 May, 1902. He was mentioned in Despatches 10 Sept. 1901; received the Queen's Medal and four clasps; the King's Medal and two clasps, and was created a Companion of the Distinguished Service Order [London Gazette, 27 Sept. 1901]: "Thomas Harold Mortimer

Green, Capt., Derbyshire Regt. In recognition of services during operations in South Africa." The Insignia, Warrant and Statutes were sent to the G.O.C., China Station, 23 Oct. 1903, and presented in China 31 May, 1903. He was promoted Major 5 Aug. 1907 ; was Commandant, Detention Barracks, 3 April, 1907, to 23 April, 1913, and Governor of Military Prison 24 April, 1913, to 2 June, 1915 ; 1st Class Governor, Military Prison (Temporary), 3 June, 1918. Major Green married, in 1908, Kathleen, youngest daughter of the late W. J. Steele, of Vanbrugh Park, Blackheath, S.E.

FORBES-SEMPILL, THE HONOURABLE DOUGLAS, Major, was born in 1865, second son of the 17th Lord Sempill and Frances, daughter of Sir Robert Abercromby, Bart. He was educated at Marlborough, and

the Royal Military College, Sandhurst ; joined 2nd Battn. Seaforth Highlanders, 1885 ; served with the 2nd Seaforth Highlanders in Hazara Campaign, 1888 (Medal with clasp), and in the Chitral Campaign ; was present at the late Sir William Gatacre's action at Mamugai (Medal with clasp). In the South African War the 2nd Seaforth Highlanders were in Lord Methuen's Division, and Major the Hon. Douglas Forbes-Sempill was present during the advances to the Relief of Kimberley, including the night attack and Battle of Magersfontein. On the death in action of the Adjutant at Magersfontein, he was appointed Adjutant of the battalion, and was present at the Paardeberg operations. He served through the tedious guerilla fighting to the end of the war. He was

Hon. D. Forbes-Sempill.

three times mentioned in Despatches ; received the Queen's Medal with five clasps ; the King's Medal with two clasps, and was decorated with the Distinguished Service Order [London Gazette, 27 Sept. 1901]: "The Honourable Douglas Forbes-Sempill, Major Seaforth Highlanders. In recognition of services during the operations in South Africa." In 1905 he was appointed Second-in-Command of the 1st Battn. Seaforth Highlanders, and served in the operations against the Zakka Khels, and was killed in action on Friday, 21 Feb. 1908, while commanding the battalion. At morning service on Sunday, 23rd, in St. Columba's (Church of Scotland), Park Street, S.W., the Rev. A. Fleming, D.D., made the following reference to Major Forbes-Sempill's untimely death : " A devoted member of the Scottish Church we love so well, ' a distinguished soldier and so good,' as one who loved him touchingly writes, he leaves behind him a noble and inspiring memory. There will be many a sore heart in the hills of Don to-day, but many a proud and thankful one as well. For the hillsman has died on the hill, and the soldier on the field of battle, and another name has been added to the long roll of Scotsmen who have earned in life the proud title ' without fear ; without reproach.' " Handel's Dead March was played after the service.

LLOYD, ARTHUR ATHELWOLD, Capt., was born 26 May, 1864, son of Pennant Athelwold Lloyd, of Pentre Hobyn, Mold. He was educated at Wimbledon and Sandhurst, and entered the Army 7 Feb. 1885 ; was promoted Captain, Northamptonshire Regt., 1 April, 1894 ; served in South Africa, 1899–1902 (slightly wounded), taking part in the advance on Kimberley, including actions at Belmont, Enslin, Modder River and Magersfontein ; during operations in the Transvaal, west of Pretoria, July to Nov. 1900, including action at Venterskroom (7 and 9 Aug.) ; during operations in Orange River Colony (May and Nov. 1900), including actions at Rhenoster River ; afterwards served as Staff Officer to Officer Commanding, Eastern Districts, 30 Dec. 1901, to 29 July, 1902. He was mentioned twice in Despatches [London Gazette, 10 Sept. 1901] ; received the Queen's Medal and four clasps ; the King's Medal and two clasps, and was created a Companion of the Distinguished Service Order [London Gazette, 27 Sept. 1901]: " Arthur Athelwold Lloyd, Capt., Northamptonshire Regt. In recognition of services during operations in South Africa." The Insignia were presented by the King 24 Oct. 1902. Capt. Lloyd retired from the Northamptonshire Regt. in 1905, and became Secretary to the Sussex Territorial Force Association in 1908. He served during the European War, and was awarded the O.B.E.

ELWES, LINCOLN EDMUND CARY, Capt., was born 10 June, 1865, at Thorganby, Lincolnshire, son of Richard James Cary Elwes, J.P., of Walland Cary, Bideford, Devon, and Selina (née Jephson, his wife). He

was educated at Twyford School, Cheltenham College, and at the Royal Military College, Sandhurst. He joined the Army, Oct. 1885 ; was promoted Captain, Durham Light Infantry, 1894 ; served in South Africa, 1899–1901 ; was present at the Battle of Colenso with 1st Durham Light Infantry, and was then attached to an improvised Balloon Section, Royal Engineers, until after the Relief of Ladysmith, when he rejoined his regiment. He was mentioned in Despatches [London Gazette, 8 Feb. and 10 Sept. 1901]; received the Queen's Medal with seven clasps, and was created a Companion of the Distinguished Service Order [London Gazette, 27 Sept. 1901]: " Lincoln Edmund Cary Elwes, Capt., Durham Light Infantry. In recognition of services during

Lincoln E. C. Elwes.

the operations in South Africa." The Insignia were presented by the King 29 Oct. 1901, and the Warrant sent 25 Jan. 1902. He was promoted Major, Dec. 1903. He was placed on the List of Reserve of Officers, June, 1905. At the outbreak of the European War he was appointed Temporary Lieutenant-Colonel, 12th (Service) Battn. Durham Light Infantry, Sept. 1914. He trained this battalion, and commanded it for two years, including nine months in France on the Western Front. He was invalided home in Aug. 1916 ; was attached for light duty to a reserve battalion from Jan. 1917, to March, 1918, when he was appointed Commandant of the Whitley Bay Musketry Camp, which appointment he held until after the Armistice, when he was finally discharged on account of ill-health. He retired Jan. 1919, with the rank of Lieutenant-Colonel. Capt. Elwes married, 14 Nov. 1903, at Gainford, Darlington, Kathleen, daughter of Charles Hunter, J.P., of Selaby, Gainford, Darlington, and they have two sons : Robert Cary Elwes, born 1904, and James Cary Elwes, born 1909.

MANGLES, WALTER JAMES, Capt., was born 13 Sept. 1862, eldest surviving son of the late Ross Mangles, V.C. He entered the Army 12 Nov. 1884 ; became Major 26 June, 1902. He served during the South African War, 1899–1902 ; was present at the Relief of Ladysmith, including operations of 17 to 24 Jan. 1900, and action at Spion Kop ; during operations 5 Feb. 1900, and action at Vaal Kranz ; during operations on Tugela Heights (14 to 27 Feb. 1900) and action at Pieter's Hill ; taking part in the operations in the Transvaal, May and June, 1900 ; operations in Natal, March to June, 1900, including action at Laing's Nek ; during operations in Orange River Colony, June, 1900, also in the Transvaal 30 Nov. 1900, to 31 May, 1902. He was mentioned in Despatches [London Gazette, 10 Sept. 1901] ; received the Queen's Medal with five clasps ; the King's Medal with two clasps, and was created a Companion of the Distinguished Service Order [London Gazette, 27 Sept. 1901]: " Walter James Mangles, Capt., Royal Lancaster Regt. In recognition of services during the operations in South Africa." He was invested with the Insignia of the Distinguished Service Order by the King 18 Dec. 1902. Major Mangles retired 7 Jan. 1903.

EGERTON, ARTHUR FREDERICK, Capt., was born 15 Jan. 1866, son of the late Lieut.-Colonel A. F. Egerton and Helen, daughter of Martin Tucker Smith, his wife (she married, 2ndly, Sir W. J. Gascoigne). He entered the Army, 1886 ; was promoted Captain, 1894 ; served in the Sudan, 1898 ; was present at the actions at Atbara and Khartum (British Medal ; Khedive's Medal with two clasps). He served in the South African War, 1900–2 ; during operations in the Orange Free State, Feb. to May, 1900, and in the Transvaal in May and June, 1900, including actions at Johannesburg, Pretoria and Diamond Hill (11 and 12 June) ; during operations in Orange River Colony, May to 29 Nov. 1900 including actions at Wittebergen (1 to 29 July) and Ladybrand (2 to 5 Sept.). Capt. Egerton served on the Staff, as Assistant Provost-Marshal, from 24 June, 1900 ; during operations in the Transvaal, Jan. 1901, to 31 May, 1902, and Orange River Colony 30 Nov. 1900, to Jan. 1902. He was mentioned in Despatches [London Gazette, 10 Sept. 1901] ; received the Queen's Medal with four clasps ; the King's Medal with two clasps, and was created a Companion of the Distinguished Service Order [London Gazette, 27 Sept. 1901]: " Arthur Frederick Egerton, Capt., Cameron Highlanders. In recognition of services during the operations in South Africa." The Insignia were presented by the King 24 Oct. 1902. He retired from the Cameron Highlanders, 1902, and is Captain, Reserve of Officers.

BRETT, CHARLES ARTHUR HUGH, Capt., was born at Muttra, India, 28 March, 1865, son of the late Lieut.-Colonel Arthur Brett, A.P.D. (formerly 2nd Dragoon Guards, Queen's Bays), and Georgina, his wife,

daughter of Hugh Hannay, Paymaster, R.N. He entered the Army as Lieutenant in the Suffolk Regt. 9 May, 1885. He served in the Hazara Expedition in 1888, and received the Medal with clasp ; was promoted Captain 15 June, 1894. From Jan. 1895, to Jan. 1899, he was Adjutant of the 1st Battn. of the Suffolk Regt., and Adjutant, 4th Battn., 15 Nov. 1900, to 14 Nov. 1905. He again saw active service in the South African War, taking part in the operations south of the Orange River, 1899–1900, including the action at Colesberg, when he was severely wounded. Later he saw service in the Transvaal, east of Pretoria, and in the Orange River Colony from July to Oct. 1900. He was mentioned in Despatches 10 Sept. 1901, and received the Queen's

Charles Arthur H. Brett.

Medal with three clasps. For his gallantry at Colesberg, in 1900, when, though shot through the lungs, he kept up command of his company actually charging the Boer trenches in this state until he fell exhausted from loss of blood, he was created a Companion of the Distinguished Service Order [London Gazette, 27 Sept. 1901]: " Charles Arthur Hugh Brett, Capt., Suffolk Regt. In recognition of services during the operations in South Africa." The Insignia were presented by the King 29 Oct. 1901, and the Warrant, etc., sent 25 Jan. 1902. He was promoted Major 24 Feb. 1906. When European hostilities commenced he left the Curragh, Aug. 1914, in command of the 2nd Battn., to go to France, and fell in action at Le Cateau 26 Aug. 1914, whilst leading his men. He was mentioned in Sir John French's Despatches, Sept. 1914. Major Brett married, in 1909, Enid Geraldine, daughter of the late Lieutenant-Colonel H. H. St. George, Senior Ordnance Officer, Scottish District, and they had one daughter, Ione Moncrieff St. George, born 10 Oct. 1909.

LAYTON, EDWARD, Capt., was born 21 March, 1857, and joined the Army, 1877; became Lieutenant, Royal Welsh Fusiliers, 2 July, 1890, and was promoted Captain, South Staffordshire Regt., 20 June, 1894. He was Adjutant, South Staffordshire Regt., 1 Feb. 1899, to 1901. Major Layton served in the South African War, 1900–2, as Adjutant of 1st Battn. South Staffordshire Regt., from April, 1900, to 13 Aug. 1901; operations in the Orange Free State, April and May, 1900; operations in Orange River Colony, May to 29 Nov. 1900, including actions at Wittebergen (1 to 29 July); operations in Orange River Colony 30 Nov. 1900, to Sept. 1901; operations in the Transvaal, Oct. 1901, to 31 May, 1902. He was mentioned in Despatches [London Gazette, 10 Sept. 1901]; received the Queen's Medal with two clasps; the King's Medal with two clasps, and was created a Companion of the Distinguished Service Order [London Gazette, 27 Sept. 1901]: "Edward Layton, Capt., South Staffordshire Regt. In recognition of services during the operations in South Africa." The Insignia, Warrant, etc., were sent to the G.O.C., Natal District, 15 Nov. 1902, and were presented by the Governor of Natal at Pietermaritzburg 19 April, 1903. He was promoted Major, West Yorkshire Regt., 14 Aug. 1901; was subsequently appointed D.A.Q.M.G., Natal, and Staff Captain, Middelburg Sub-District, Transvaal. He retired from the Army 21 March, 1905. Major Layton died in the early days of the war. He had married, in 1884, Jane Elizabeth, eldest daughter of the late J. Clexton, of Queen's County, and they had one daughter.

MATCHAM, WILLIAM EYRE, Capt., was born 16 May, 1865, second son of the late William Eyre Eyre-Matcham, of New House. He entered the Army 6 May, 1885; was promoted Captain 11 July, 1894; served in South Africa, 1900–2, with the Prince of Wales's Light Horse; during the operations in the Transvaal, west of Pretoria, Aug. to Nov. 1900; in the operations in Orange River Colony, including actions at Bethlehem and Wittebergen; taking part in the operations in Cape Colony, south of Orange River, 1900, including actions at Colesberg (25 Jan. to 12 Feb.). He was mentioned in Despatches [London Gazette, 10 Sept. 1901]; received the Queen's Medal with three clasps; the King's Medal with two clasps, and was created a Companion of the Distinguished Service Order [London Gazette, 27 Sept. 1901]: "William Eyre Matcham, Capt., Wiltshire Regt. In recognition of services during the operations in South Africa." The Insignia were presented by the King 18 Dec. 1902, and the Warrant sent 14 Jan. 1903. He was appointed Deputy Assistant Director of Remounts, and is Captain of the Reserve of Officers. He retired 10 May, 1905. Major Matcham served during the European War, 1914 to 1917; became Temporary Lieutenant-Colonel, 1916, and received the Brevet of Major 1 Jan. 1917. He married, in 1903, Edith Evelyn, youngest daughter of the late N. J. Betterton.

BOND, REGINALD COPLESTON, Capt., was born 28 April, 1866, son of the late Rev. F. H. Bond, M.A. (Oxon.). He entered the Yorkshire Light Infantry, from the Militia, 10 Nov. 1888; served with the Zhob Field Force, 1890; was promoted Lieutenant 1 April, 1890, and Captain 19 July, 1894; was A.D.C. to G.O.C., Poona District, 7 Sept. 1895, to 28 March, 1896. He served on the North-West Frontier of India, 1897–98, with the Tirah Expeditionary Force; affair at Shinkamar 29 Jan. 1898 (Medal with two clasps). Capt. Bond saw active service in South Africa, 1899–1902. He took part in the advance on Kimberley, including the actions at Belmont, Enslin, Modder River and Magersfontein; operations in the Transvaal, west of Pretoria, Aug. to 29 Nov. 1900; operations in Orange River Colony, May to Aug. 1900, including actions at Lindley (26 June), Bethlehem (6 and 7 July) and Wittebergen (1 to 29 July); operations in the Transvaal 30 Nov. 1900, to 31 May, 1902. He was mentioned in Despatches [London Gazette, 10 Sept. 1901]; received the Queen's Medal with four clasps, the King's Medal with two clasps, and was created a Companion of the Distinguished Service Order [London Gazette, 27 Sept. 1901]: "Reginald Copleston Bond, Capt., Yorkshire Light Infantry. In recognition of services during the operations in South Africa." The Insignia, Warrant, etc., were sent to the G.O.C., Transvaal and Orange River Colony, 15 Nov. 1902, and presented by General Lyttelton at Pretoria 14 Jan. 1903. He became Major 7 Sept. 1902; Lt.-Col. 1 May, 1914. He died 1 Sept. 1914. He had married, in 1897, Isabel Maud, daughter of Major-General T. B. Tyler, Inspector-General, Royal Artillery, India.

Reginald C. Bond.

ELGER, EDWARD GWYN, Capt., was born 3 Aug. 1864, son of the late G. G. Elger, of Bricklehampton Hall, Worcester. He entered the Army 25 Nov. 1885; served in the Burmese Expedition, 1885–87 (Medal and clasp). He was promoted Captain 8 Nov. 1894. Capt. Elger served in the South African War, 1899–1902, taking part in operations in Natal, 1899; Relief of Ladysmith, including operations of 17 to 24 Jan. 1900, and action at Spion Kop; operations on Tugela Heights (14 to 27 Feb. 1900). He was wounded 21 Feb. Operations in the Orange Free State, April to May, 1900; operations in the Transvaal, west of Pretoria, July to Nov. 1900. He was severely wounded 27 Nov. He was present at operations in the Transvaal, May, 1901, to 31 May, 1902; was wounded a third time. He was mentioned in Despatches [London Gazette, 7 May and 10 Sept. 1901]; received the Queen's Medal with five clasps, the King's Medal with two clasps, and was created a Companion of the Distinguished Service Order [London Gazette, 27 Sept. 1901]: "Edward Gwyn Elger, Capt., Somerset Light Infantry. In recognition of services during the operations in South Africa." The Insignia were presented by the King 24 Oct. 1902. He retired from the Somerset Light Infantry. Major Elger served in the European War as Assistant Provost-Marshal, 4th Division, B.E.F., 1915; 19th Army Corps, B.E.F., 1917. He married, in 1891, Hilda Eva, daughter of the late Charles Mayhew, of 6, Chester Terrace, N.W.

COLVILE, GEORGE NORTHCOTE, Capt., was born 9 July, 1867, son of Lieut.-General Sir Fiennes M. Colvile, K.C.B. He was gazetted to the Oxfordshire Light Infantry 5 Feb. 1887; became Lieutenant 3 May, 1889, and Captain 9 Nov. 1894. Capt. Colvile served in the South African War, 1899 to 1901, employed with Mounted Infantry, and was Embarking Staff Officer, Cape Town. He was severely wounded. He was present at operations in the Orange Free State, Feb. to May, 1900, including actions at Vet River (5 and 6 May) and Zand River; operations in the Transvaal in May and June, 1900, including action near Johannesburg; operations in the Transvaal, west of Pretoria, July to 29 Nov. 1900; operations in Orange River Colony (May to Nov. 1900), including actions at Ladybrand (2 to 5 Sept.) and Bothaville; operations in Cape Colony, south of Orange River, 1899–1900; operations in Cape Colony, Dec. 1900, to March, 1901. He was mentioned in Despatches [London Gazette, 10 Sept. 1901]; received the Queen's Medal with four clasps, and was created a Companion of the Distinguished Service Order [London Gazette, 27 Sept. 1901]: "George Northcote Colvile, Capt., Oxfordshire Light Infantry. In recognition of services during the operations in South Africa." He was promoted to Major 25 Aug. 1906, and retired 10 July, 1907. On the outbreak of the European War he served from 1914, first in the 7th Battn. Sherwood Foresters, and later he rejoined the 52nd Oxfordshire and Buckinghamshire Light Infantry; was Colonel in the 7th Duke of Cornwall's Light Infantry, July, 1915; was mentioned twice in Despatches, and he was given the honorary rank of Brigadier-General 28 Oct. 1917. He married, in 1894, Eleanor Harriet, daughter of Sir W. A. Ferguson Davie, Bart.

PEEBLES, EVELYN CHIAPPINI, Capt., was born 17 May, 1865, son of the late Colonel Thomas Peebles. He was educated at Cheltenham College; was gazetted to the Norfolk Regt. 23 Aug. 1884; served in the Burmese Expedition, 1891–92, with the Irrawaddy Column (Medal with clasp); became Captain 1 Nov. 1894; was Adjutant, Norfolk Regt., 28 Aug. 1895, to 19 Aug. 1899. He served in the South African War in 1900; was present at the Relief of Kimberley and at operations in the Orange Free State, Feb. to May, 1900, including operations at Paardeberg (17 to 26 Feb.), actions at Poplar Grove and Karee Siding. He was severely wounded; was mentioned in Despatches [London Gazette, 10 Sept. 1901]; received the Queen's Medal with two clasps, and was created a Companion of the Distinguished Service Order [London Gazette, 27 Sept. 1901]: "Evelyn Chiappini Peebles, Capt., Norfolk Regt. In recognition of services during the operations in South Africa." The Insignia were presented by the King 29 Oct. 1901 He was Adjutant, Volunteers, 24 Jan 1901, to 25 Jan 1902. He was promoted Major 17 Dec. 1904, and Lieut.-Colonel 1 Sept. 1912. He served in the European War from 1914, in command of the 2nd Norfolk Regt.; given the Brevet of Colonel 3 June, 1915; commanded the 19th Infantry Brigade, Indian Expeditionary Force "D," 25 Jan. 1916, to 3 July, 1917; was promoted to Colonel 1 Sept. 1916; commanded a brigade in India 25 July, 1917; was created a C.B. in 1916, and a C.M.G. in 1917. He married, in 1901, Marion (who died in 1910), daughter of Charles Corbett Turnbull, of Cheltenham.

WARRE, HENRY CHARLES, Capt., was born 22 Oct. 1866, eldest son of the Rev. Edmond Warre, D.D., C.B., C.V.O., Honorary Chaplain to the King, and of his wife, Florence Dora, second daughter of Lieut.-Colonel C. Malet, Fontmell Parva, Dorset. He entered the King's Royal Rifle Corps 5 Oct. 1887; became Lieutenant 12 April, 1890; served in the Hazara Expedition, 1891 (Medal with clasp), and in the Miranzai Expedition, 1891 (Clasp); was promoted Captain 23 Jan. 1895. He served with the Chitral Relief Force, 1895 (Medal with clasp). Capt. Warre served in the South African War, 1899–1902, on the Staff. He was present at the Relief of Ladysmith, including action at Colenso; operations of 17 to 24 Jan. 1900, and action at Spion Kop; operations of 5 to 7 Feb. 1900, and action at Vaal Kranz; operations on Tugela Heights (14 to 16 Feb. 1900). He was mentioned in Despatches [London Gazette, 8 Feb. and 10 Sept. 1901, and 18 July, 1902]; received the Queen's Medal with five clasps, the King's Medal with two clasps, and was created a Companion of the Distinguished Service Order [London Gazette, 27 Sept. 1901]: "Henry Charles Warre, Capt., King's Royal Rifle Corps. In recognition of services during the operations in South Africa." The Insignia were presented by the King 18 Dec. 1902. He was Brigade Major, Indian Army, 1 Jan. 1903, to 19 Jan. 1905; became Major 5 Dec. 1906; was G.S.O.2, West Riding Division, N. Command, 24 April, 1908, to 23 April, 1912. He served in the European War with the 2nd Battn. King's Royal Rifle Corps; commanded the 1st Battn. King's Royal Rifles from 4 Nov. 1914, to the end of the First Battle of Ypres, and subsequently served on the General Staff. He was G.S.O.1, Lines of Communication, British Armies in France, from 23 Dec. 1916, to 17 Oct. 1917; was mentioned in Despatches four times, and given the Brevet of Lieut.-Colonel 18 Feb. 1915. Major Warre married, in 1905, Gwenhwyvar, daughter of Newton Apperley, M.V.O., of South End, Durham.

PILCHER, EDGAR MONTAGU, Capt., was born at Meerut, India, 25 April, 1865, son of Colonel J. G. Pilcher, F.R.G.S. He was educated at Clifton College; Clare College, Cambridge, and Guy's Hospital; B.A., M.B. and B.C. (Cantab.) in 1890; F.R.C.S., England, in 1905. He became Captain, R.A.M.C., 30 Jan. 1895, having previously served three years, and was present at the operations on the North-West Frontier of India, 1897–98, with the Tirah Expeditionary Force, receiving the Medal with two clasps. Capt. Pilcher served in the South African War, 1899 to 1902, and took part in the Relief of Ladysmith, including the action at Colenso; operations of 17 to 24 Jan. 1900, and action at Spion Kop; operations of 5 to 7 Feb. 1900, and action at Vaal Kranz; operations on Tugela Heights (14 to 27 Feb.) and action at Pieter's Hill; operations in the Orange River Colony, May to July, 1912; operations in the Transvaal, Nov. 1900, to Jan. 1902,

He was mentioned in Despatches [London Gazette, 8 Feb. and 10 Sept. 1901]; received the Queen's Medal with five clasps, the King's Medal with two clasps, and for services in connection with the Relief of Ladysmith was created a Companion of the Distinguished Service Order [London Gazette, 27 Sept. 1901]: "Edgar Montagu Pilcher, Capt., Royal Army Medical Corps. In recognition of services during the operations in South Africa." The Insignia were presented to him by the King 18 Dec. 1902. He was promoted to Major 30 Jan. 1904; was appointed Professor, Royal Army Medical College, 1 Aug. 1910; was given the Brevet of Lieut.-Colonel 26 Nov. 1913. In the European War he served as Consulting Surgeon to the Forces; was given the Brevet of Colonel 12 Sept. 1916; became Colonel 26 Dec. 1917; was appointed Honorary Surgeon to the King 26 Dec. 1917; was twice mentioned in Despatches, and created a C.B. in June, 1918, and a C.B.E. in 1919. Colonel Pilcher married, in 1899, Lilias Mary, daughter of the late Capt. Henri Campbell, Indian Staff Corps.

TRAVERS, JOSEPH OATES, Capt., was born 19 May, 1867, son of the late Colonel H. F. Travers and grandson of Major-General Sir Robert Travers, K.C.B., K.C.M.G. He was educated at Bradfield College. He entered the Devonshire Regt. 25 Aug. 1886; served in Burma, 1891–92, in the Wuntho Expedition (Medal with clasp); became Captain 20 Feb. 1895. He was present in the operations on the N.W. Frontier of India, 1897–98 (clasp), and in the Tirah Campaign, 1897–98, taking part in the capture of the Sampagha and Arhanga Passes. Capt. Travers next saw active service in South Africa, 1899–1902, when he was present in operations in Natal, 1899, including actions at Elandslaagte, Rietfontein and Lombard's Kop. He took part in the Defence of Ladysmith, including the sortie of 7 Dec. 1899, and action of 6 Jan. 1900; operations in Natal, March to Jan. 1900; operations in the Transvaal, east of Pretoria, July to 29 Nov. 1900, including actions at Belfast (26 and 27 Aug.) and Lydenburg (5 to 8 Sept.). He was employed with the Imperial Yeomanry 1 Aug. to 19 Dec. 1901, and served with the South African Constabulary 30 Dec. 1901, to 31 May, 1902. He was mentioned in Despatches [London Gazette, 10 Sept. 1901]; received the Queen's Medal with five clasps, the King's Medal with two clasps, and was created a Companion of the Distinguished Service Order [London Gazette, 27 Sept. 1901]: "Joseph Oates Travers, Capt., Devonshire Regt. In recognition of services during the operations in South Africa." The Insignia, Warrant, etc., were sent to the G.O.C., Transvaal, 3 Feb. 1903, and presented by the G.O.C., South Africa, at Pretoria, 5 March, 1903. He became Major 22 Nov. 1904, and Lieut.-Colonel 22 Nov. 1912. Lieut.-Colonel Travers served in the European War from 1914. He was twice mentioned in Despatches; created a C.M.G., 1915, and promoted Colonel 22 Nov. 1916; commanded the 199th Infantry Brigade, Home Forces, 20 May to 6 July, 1916; commanded the 199th Brigade, Home Forces; British Armies in France, 7 July, 1916, to 16 March, 1918.

STUART-WORTLEY, THE HON. ALAN RICHARD MONTAGU, Capt., was born 20 Jan. 1868, son of the Hon. F. D. Stuart-Wortley (second son of the 2nd Baron Wharncliffe) and of the eldest daughter of William Bennet Martin, of Worsborough Hall, Yorkshire. He is a brother of the 2nd Earl of Wharncliffe. He was educated at Wellington College, and was gazetted to the King's Royal Rifle Corps as Second Lieutenant 5 Nov. 1887; became Lieutenant 16 April, 1890; was Adjutant, K.R.R.C., 11 March, 1895, to 10 March, 1899. He became Captain 11 March, 1895. He served in the Chitral Campaign in 1895, with the Relief Force, and was present at the storming of the Malakand Pass (Medal with clasp). Capt. Stuart-Wortley served in the South African War, 1899–1900, taking part in operations in Natal, 1899, including the action of Talana (severely wounded) and Lombard's Kop. He took part in the Defence of Ladysmith; was mentioned in Despatches [London Gazette, 10 Sept. 1901]; received the Queen's Medal with three clasps, and for his services in the Battle of Talana was created a Companion of the Distinguished Service Order [London Gazette, 27 Sept. 1901]: "The Honourable Alan Richard Montagu Stuart-Wortley, Capt., King's Royal Rifle Corps. In recognition of services during the operations in South Africa." The Insignia were presented by the King 29 Oct. 1901. He became Major 4 May, 1904; passed the Staff College; was General Staff Officer, 3rd Grade, Headquarters of Army, 8 Aug. 1904, to 14 Oct. 1907; G.S.O., 2nd Grade, Headquarters of Army, 15 Oct. 1907, to 7 Aug. 1908; Lieut.-Colonel 15 Oct. 1910, and Colonel 15 June, 1914; Assistant Director of Movements 1 April, 1914, to 28 Jan. 1915. He served in the European War from 1914; was Director of Movements, War Office, 29 Jan. 1915, to 24 Jan. 1917; was created a C.B., 1915, and commanded the 4th Battn. King's Royal Rifles; commanded the 68th Infantry Brigade, British Armies in France, 27 Feb. to 30 March, 1917; commanded the 19th Division, British Armies in France, 7 April to 24 May, 1917, and the 32nd Division, British Armies in France, 25 May to 19 June, 1917. Major-General Stuart-Wortley was D.Q.M.G. Mesopotamia Expeditionary Force, 18 Aug. 1917, to 3 April, 1919; Major-General in Charge of Administration, Southern Command, from 1 June, 1919. He was created a C.B. in 1915; was specially promoted Major-General 1 Jan. 1917; was created a K.C.M.G. in 1918. Sir Alan Stuart-Wortley is an Officer of the Legion of Honour, and has the Ordre de la Couronne (Belgium). He married, in 1900, the Hon. Maud Julia Mary Winn, daughter of the 1st Baron St. Oswald, and they have one son and one daughter.

GRIFFITH, CHARLES RICHARD JEBB, Capt., was born 4 Oct. 1867, son of Colonel R. Griffith. He was educated at Clifton College, Oundle and Sandhurst; entered the Bedfordshire Regt. 14 Sept. 1887; was promoted Captain 3 June, 1895; was Adjutant, Bedfordshire Regt., 16 Dec. 1895, to 5 Dec. 1902. Capt. Griffith served in the South African War, 1899–1902, taking part in operations in the Orange River Colony, May to 29 Nov. 1900, including action at Wittebergen (1 to 29 July); operations in Cape Colony, south of Orange River, 1899–1900, including actions at Colesberg (1 Jan. to 12 Feb.). He was present at operations in Orange River Colony 30 Nov. 1900, to 31 May, 1902. He was mentioned in Despatches [London Gazette, 10 Sept. 1901]: received the Queen's Medal with two clasps, the King's Medal with two clasps, and was created a Companion of the Distinguished Service Order [London Gazette, 27 Sept. 1901]: "Charles Richard Jebb Griffith, Capt., Bedfordshire Regt. In recognition of services during the operations in South Africa." The Insignia were presented by the King 29 Oct. 1901. He became Major 2 April, 1906, and Lieut.-Colonel 16 Oct. 1913. Lieut.-Colonel Griffith served in the European War from 1914; commanded the 108th Infantry Brigade (Ulster Division), B.E.F., British Armies in France and Flanders, 4 Dec. 1915, to 21 May, 1918; was given the Brevet of Colonel 1 Jan. 1916; became Colonel 16 Oct. 1917; commanded the 20th Training Reserve Brigade, No. 1 Machine Gun Corps, 6 Jan. to 31 Dec. 1918; was Member, Standing Committee of Enquiry, *re* Prisoners of War, War Office, from 1 Jan. 1919. He was seven times mentioned in Despatches; created a C.M.G. in 1915, and a C.B. in 1918; given the Brevet of Colonel, and made an Officer of the Legion of Honour.

JOURDAIN, CHARLES EDWARD ARTHUR, Capt., was born 7 May, 1869, son of the late Rev. F. Jourdain, M.A., R.D., Vicar of Ashbourne and Rector of Mapleton, and of Mrs. E. Jourdain, of 24, St. Margaret's Road, Oxford. He was educated at Sandhurst, and entered the Service on the 22nd Aug. 1888, joining the 1st Battn. Loyal North Lancashire Regt. at Mhow, and serving with them at Mhow, Kamptee, Poona, and in Ceylon, from whence he proceeded to Cape Town, where the battalion was stationed at the outbreak of the South African War. From Aug. to Dec. he served as Adjutant of the half-battalion of that regiment outside Kimberley, and took part in Lord Methuen's advance, including the Battles of Belmont, Enslin, Modder River and Magersfontein. He then was given command of the Mounted Infantry Company of his regiment in the 3rd Mounted Infantry, and took part with it in the Relief of Kimberley, the Battles of Paardeberg, Dreifontein, Zand River, Johannesburg, capture of Pretoria and Diamond Hill, afterwards being present at the operations near Belfast. He served throughout the whole war from start to finish, and was only absent for one short period of ten days through malaria in 1901, and at the conclusion of hostilities was mentioned in Despatches [London Gazette, 4 Sept. 1901]; received the Queen's Medal with six clasps, the King's Medal with two clasps, and was created a Companion of the Distinguished Service Order [London Gazette, 27 Sept. 1901]: "Charles Edward Arthur Jourdain, Capt., Loyal North Lancashire Regt. In recognition of services during the operations in South Africa." The Insignia were presented by the King 24 Oct. 1902; the Warrant sent 4 Nov. 1902. He proceeded home with the battalion in 1902, serving at Devonport and the Curragh, and later serving as Adjutant of his battalion, and also commanding the Depôt at Preston. From there he exchanged to the 2nd Battn. at Mauritius, and with them he served at Poona and Bangalore, being awarded the Delhi Durbar Medal, 1911. He was promoted to command the 2nd Battn. in Dec. 1913, and on the outbreak of war he proceeded in command of the battalion to East Africa, where he performed most arduous and efficient service in command of a large district, as well as commanding his own battalion, and at the action of Tanga he displayed great resource and bravery, and it was mainly through the fine stand made by his battalion, which he commanded most efficiently, that the force was able to re-embark and make good its retirement. Colonel Jourdain remained in East Africa for over three years, and then proceeded to Egypt and Palestine, still in command of his battalion. In 1918 his battalion was brought to France, and took part in the first fighting of the counter-offensive in July, 1918, under the French General Mangin, near Rheims, where he displayed great bravery, and was killed by a shell on the 29th July, 1918, when gallantly leading his battalion in the counter-offensive near Grand Rozoy. He was buried near where he fell on the Grand Rozoy Road. Although his four years' command of the battalion terminated in Dec. 1917, he preferred to remain with his battalion, and he thus met his death after four years' arduous, continuous active service, and seven years' active service, including South Africa. He was awarded by the French General the Croix de Guerre of the 1st Class after his death. He was also awarded the 1914–15 Star and the General Service Medal, and the Victory Medal for the Great War, 1914–18. During the trying campaign in East Africa he was one of the two officers who had never gone sick or been away from duty during the campaign, and in South Africa he was one of the few officers who served right through the campaign. At the time of his death he had nearly completed thirty years' service, the whole of which had been spent in his regiment, to which he was entirely devoted and in which he had served seven years on active service. He married, 9 Oct. 1912, Alexia Grace, younger daughter of Capt. Frederick Papilion, R.N., who survives him.

Charles E. A. Jourdain.

BLACKADER, CHARLES GUINAND, Capt., was born 20 Sept. 1869, son of Charles George Blackader, M.A., and of Charlotte (*née* Guinand). He was educated at Aldin House School, Slough, by the Rev. — Hastings, and abroad. He was gazetted to the Leicestershire Regt. 22 Aug. 1888; became Lieutenant 21 March, 1890, and Captain 6 Dec. 1895. He was employed with the West African Frontier Force 27 Nov. 1897, to 24 June, 1899, taking part in operations on the Niger, including the expedition to Lapia. He was mentioned in Despatches [London Gazette, 23 May, 1899], and received the Medal and clasp. Capt. Blackader served in the South African War, 1899–1902, and was present at operations in Natal, 1899, including actions at Talana and Lombard's Kop. He took part in the Defence of Ladysmith; operations in Natal, March to June, 1900, including action at Laing's Nek (6 to 9 June); operations in the Transvaal, east of Pretoria, including actions at Belfast (26 to 27 Aug.) and Lydenberg (5 to 8 Sept.). He was Commandant at Witbank; afterwards Station Staff Officer; operations in the Transvaal 30 Nov. 1900, to 31 May, 1902. He was mentioned in Despatches [London Gazette, 8 Feb. and 10 Sept. 1901]; received the Queen's Medal with four clasps, the King's Medal with two clasps, and was created a Companion of the Distinguished Service Order [London Gazette, 27 Sept. 1901]: "Charles Guinand Blackader, Capt., Leicestershire Regt. In recognition of services during the operations in South Africa." He was Adjutant, Volunteers, 1 Aug. 1902, to 9 Sept. 1904; was promoted Major 10 Sept. 1904, and Lieut.-Colonel 10 Sept. 1912. He served in the European War from 1914, first commanding 2nd Leicestershire Regt. From 8 Jan. to 30 Nov. 1915 he commanded the Garhwal Brigade, B.E.F.; he was A.D.C. (extra) to the King 1 Jan. 1916, to 31 Dec. 1917; commanded 177th Infantry Brigade, Home Forces, 8 Jan. to 25 June, 1916; became Colonel 10 Sept. 1916; commanded 38th Division, British Armies in France, 12 July, 1916, to 8 June, 1918; promoted Major-General 1 Jan. 1918; commanded the Southern District, Ireland, 21 Nov. 1918. He was twice mentioned in Despatches, and created a C.B. in 1917. He married, in 1888, Marian Ethel, daughter of the late George Melbourne, and they had two daughters.

LE MARCHANT, LOUIS ST. GRATIEN, Capt., was born at Little Rissington, Bourton, Gloucestershire, 2 Dec. 1866, son of the Rev. Robert Le Marchant, Rector of Little Rissington. He joined the East Lancashire Regt. 10 Nov. 1886, from the Gloucester Militia; was promoted Captain 11 Dec. 1895; served in the Chitral Expedition in 1895 (Medal and clasp). He was Adjutant, 1st Battn., from 29 Oct. 1898, to 28 Oct. 1902. Capt. Le Marchant served in the South African War, 1900–2, as Adjutant, 1st Battn. East Lancashire Regt., taking part in operations in the Orange Free State, Feb. to May, 1900, including actions at Karee Siding, Vet River (5 and 6 May) and Zand River; operations in the Transvaal in May, 1900, including action near Johannesburg; operations in the Transvaal 30 Nov. 1900, to Oct. 1901; operations in Orange River Colony, Oct. 1901, to 31 May, 1902. He was mentioned in Despatches [London Gazette, 10 Sept. 1901, and 29 July, 1902]; received the Queen's Medal with three clasps, King's Medal with two clasps, and was created a Companion of the Distinguished Service Order [London Gazette, 27 Sept. 1901]: "Louis St. Gratien Le Marchant, Capt., East Lancashire Regt. In recognition of services during the operations in South Africa." The Insignia were presented by the King 24 Oct. 1901: the Warrant sent, 4 Nov. 1902. He was promoted Major 11 April, 1906; became Brigade Major, 1906; D.A.A.G., 2 March, 1908, and Lieutenant-Colonel, 1913. When the European War commenced, Lieut.-Colonel Le Marchant accompanied the Expeditionary Force to France and Flanders. He was mentioned in Despatches 19 Oct. 1914, and 10 Dec. 1914, and fell at La Ferté-sous-Jouarre, at the Battle of the Marne, 9 Sept. 1914. He was unmarried. One of the Senior Officers of the regiment, in writing to the family, says: "It is with the deepest regret that I have to inform you of the death of our Commanding Officer, Lieut.-Colonel Le Marchant, on Wednesday, 9 Sept., about 10.30 a.m. The battalion was at that time in action in a town, and he went forward to visit and encourage a party of men who were in a loft of one of the houses. As he reached the loft and passed a small window he was struck by a bullet in the neck and expired immediately. He was, as you know, absolutely without personal fear, constantly exposing himself to danger in encouraging others, and cool and collected in action. To us, as you know, his loss is irreparable, and we can only ask you to accept our deepest sympathy in the grief you must feel. He was loved and honoured by all ranks, but by none more than by those who knew him best."

Louis St. G. Le Marchant.

O'BRIEN, THE HONOURABLE MURROUGH, Capt., was born 8 Nov. 1866, son of the 14th Baron Inchiquin. He was gazetted to the Northumberland Fusiliers 26 Feb. 1887; was promoted Lieutenant 27 Jan. 1890, and Captain 20 Dec. 1895. He was A.D.C. to the Lord-Lieutenant of Ireland from 30 July, 1895. Capt. O'Brien served in the South African War, 1899–1901 (employed with Mounted Infantry). He was Commandant at Edenburg; was slightly wounded; took part in operations in the Orange Free State, Feb to May, 1900; operations in Cape Colony, south of Orange River, 1899–1900. He was mentioned in Despatches [London Gazette, 10 Sept. 1901], received the Queen's Medal with two clasps, and was created a Companion of the Distinguished Service Order [London Gazette, 27 Sept. 1901]: "The Honourable Murrough O'Brien, Capt., Northumberland Fusiliers. In recognition of services during the operations in South Africa." The Insignia, Warrant, etc., were sent on the 6th March, 1902. He was promoted to Major 2 Oct. 1901. Major O'Brien was created an M.V.O. in 1903, and retired from the Northumberland Fusiliers 10 Nov. 1906. He was appointed to the post of Military Attaché at Washington. He married, in 1906, Marguerite, daughter of William Lewis, of New York, and they have two sons.

SWETTENHAM, GEORGE KILNER, Capt., was born 7 June, 1866, son of the late George Fletcher Swettenham, of South Lodge, Eastbourne. He was educated at Cheltenham College; entered the Army in Nov. 1886; was promoted Captain in April, 1896. Lieut.-Colonel Swettenham served in South Africa, 1899–1901. He was present at the actions at Colenso, Pieter's Hill, Tugela Heights and Monte Cristo; took part in the Relief of Ladysmith under Sir Redvers Buller; also taking part in the operations in Cape Colony and in Bechuanaland (Relief of Mafeking). He was present at the action at Rooidam, under Sir A. Hunter; took part in the operations in the Eastern Transvaal, subsequent to the occupation of Pretoria; was also present at the actions at Witpoort and Oliphantsfontein. He was mentioned in Despatches [London Gazette, 10 Sept. 1901], received the Medal with six clasps, and was created a Companion of the Distinguished Service Order [London Gazette, 27 Sept. 1901]: "George Kilner Swettenham, Capt., Royal Irish Fusiliers. In recognition of services during the operations in South Africa." The Insignia were presented by the King 29 Oct. 1901. He retired from the Army in Nov. 1906; joined the 3rd Battn. Royal Irish Fusiliers in 1913, as Major, and was appointed to Command the 5th Battn. Royal Irish Rifles (Royal South Down Militia) 1 Dec. 1915, becoming substantive Lieutenant-Colonel in April, 1917. He was twice mentioned in Despatches during the European War, and created a C.B.E. Lieut.-Colonel Swettenham married, in Nov. 1904, Catherine Anne Eleanor, eldest daughter of the late Very Rev. Augustine FitzGerald, Dean of Armagh, and they have one son, Kilner, born 1 Aug. 1910, and one daughter.

DAVIDSON, GEORGE HARRY, Capt., was born 16 Sept. 1866, at Inveresk House, Inveresk, Midlothian, son of Archibald Davidson, Esq., grandson of the late Rev. Dr. Davidson, of Muirhouse and Hatton, Midlothian, late Sheriff of the Lothians and Peebles. He was educated at Wellington College. He was commissioned in the Royal Scots 4 May, 1887, becoming Lieutenant 12 Oct. 1889, and serving in Zululand with Mounted Infantry. From 21 Aug. 1894, to 19 Feb. 1898, he was Adjutant, Royal Scots, and from 21 Feb. 1898, to 20 Feb. 1903, Adjutant, Militia, and he was promoted to Captain 14 March, 1899. Capt. Davidson served in South Africa, 1900–2, as Adjutant, 3rd Battn. Royal Scots, from 28 March, 1900. He was present in operations in the Orange Free State, Feb. to May, 1900; operations in the Transvaal, west of Pretoria, July to 29 Nov. 1900, including the action at Venterskroon (9 Aug.); operations in Orange River Colony May to 29 Nov. 1900; operations in Cape Colony, south of Orange River, 1900; operations in Orange River Colony from 31 Nov. 1900. He was mentioned in Despatches [London Gazette, 10 Sept. 1901], received the Queen's Medal with three clasps, the King's Medal with two clasps, and was created a Companion of the Distinguished Service Order [London Gazette, 27 Sept. 1901]: "George Harry Davidson, Capt., Royal Scots. In recognition of services during the operations in Cape Colony." The Insignia, Warrant, etc., were sent to the O.C., Sc. District, Edinburgh, 16 June, 1902, and presented by Colonel A. Broadwood 19 June, 1902. He was promoted to Major 14 Aug. 1904, and retired from the Royal Scots 8 Oct. 1910, entering the Reserve of Officers. Major Davidson married, 12 Aug. 1891, at Claremont, Cape Colony, Ethel Maud Fairbairn, daughter of the late James Fairbairn, Esq., of Ledgerwood, Claremont, and they have one son, Archibald Randall, and two daughters, Nancy Valentine Enid and Sheila Mary.

George H. Davidson.

CLOWES, ERNEST WILLIAM, Capt., was born 11 Jan. 1869, in London, son of the late Samuel William Clowes, of Norbury, erbyshire, and of Broughton Hall, Lancashire. He was educated at Eton, and joined the 1st Life Guards, 30 July, 1890; was promoted to Lieutenant 2 Sept. 1891, and Captain 14 March, 1896. Capt. Clowes served in the South African War, 1899–1900, and was present at the Relief of Kimberley; operations in the Orange Free State, Feb. to May, 1900, including operations at Paardeberg (17 to 20 Feb.), actions at Poplar Grove, Dreifontein, Houtnek (Thoba Mountain), Vet River (3 and 6 May) and Zand River; operations in the Transvaal in May and June, 1900, including actions near Johannesburg, Pretoria and Diamond Hill (11 and 12 June); operations in the Transvaal, west of Pretoria, including action at Eland's River (4 to 16 Aug.); operations in Orange River Colony in 1900, including actions at Bethlehem and Wittebergen (15 to 29 July); operations in Cape Colony, south of Orange River, 1898 to 1900, including actions at Colesberg (5 Jan. to 2 Feb.). He was mentioned in Despatches [London Gazette, 10 Sept. 1901]; received the Queen's Medal with six clasps, and was created a Companion of the Distinguished Service Order [London Gazette, 27 Nov. 1901]: "Ernest William Clowes, Capt., 1st Life Guards. In recognition of services during the operations in South Africa." The Insignia were presented by the King 17 Dec. 1901. Capt. Clowes resigned his commission in July, 1904. Major Clowes rejoined the Reserve Regt., 1st Life Guards, in Aug. 1914, and served until demobilized in Jan. 1919. He was promoted Major in 1915.—Extract from Regimental Orders: "Hyde Park Barracks, S.W., 2 Sept, 1919. he names of the undermentioned have been brought to the notice of the Secretary of State for War, for valuable services rendered in connection with the war: Major E. W. Clowes, D.S.O." He married, on 1 June, 1909, at St. Peter's, Eaton Square, Blanche, daughter of the late Admiral the Hon. A. Lyttelton and Lady Margaret Lyttelton, and they have two sons: John Ernest, born 7 Nov. 1910, and Henry Nelson, born 21 Oct. 1911.

TALBOT, FREDERICK GILBERT, Capt., was born in 1868, son of the late Colonel the Hon. Sir W. P. M. Chetwynd-Talbot, eighth son of the 2nd Earl Talbot and Lady Emma Charlotte Stanley, daughter of the 14th Earl of Derby. He was educated at Wellington; entered the Army 29 Dec. 1888; was promoted Lieutenant 18 Nov. 1891, and Captain 18 March, 1896. Capt. Talbot served in the South African War, 1899 to 1902, and was present at the Relief of Ladysmith, including action at Colenso; operations of 17 to 24 Jan. 1900 ; operations of 5 to 7 Feb. 1900, and action at Vaal Kranz, where he was wounded ; operations on Tugela Heights 14 to 27 Feb. 1900, and action at Pieter's Hill ; operations in Natal, March to June, 1900, including action at Laing's Nek (6 to 9 June) ; operations in the Transvaal, east of Pretoria, July to 29 Nov. 1900 ; operations in the Transvaal 30 Nov. 1900, to 31 May, 1902. He was mentioned in Despatches [London Gazette, 27 Oct. 1901, and 29 July, 1902]; received the Queen's Medal with t.ve clasps, the King's Medal with two clasps, and was created a Companion of the Distinguished Service Order [London Gazette, 27 Sept. 1901] : " Frederick Gilbert Talbot, Capt., Rifle Brigade. In recognition of services during the operations in South Africa." The Insignia were presented to him by the King 24 Oct. 1902. At the conclusion of the war, Capt. Talbot served on the Compensation Board. He was promoted Major 7 Sept. 1904, and retired 6 May, 1908 ; became Honorary Lieutenant-Colonel in 1908 ; Lieut.-Colonel in 1913. Lieut.-Colonel Talbot was given command of the 5th Battn. Rifle Brigade. He is a Fellow of the Royal Geographical Society, and wrote the " Memoirs of Baber."

PILLEAU, HENRY CHARLES, Capt., was born at Bermuda 17 Feb. 1866, only child of Colonel H. G. Pilleau, R.E., and a great-nephew of the late General Thomas Addison, C.B., Colonel Commanding the Queen's

Regt. He was educated at Wellington College, and the Royal Military College, Sandhurst, where he was Senior Under-Officer, and passed out with honours, taking the prize for military topography. He was gazetted to the Royal West Surrey Regt. in Feb. 1887 ; became Lieutenant in July, 1889, and Capt. in March, 1896. He served in the South African War, 1899–1902, and was present at the Relief of Lady-smith, and actions of Colenso, Spion Kop, Vaal Kranz and Pieter's Hill ; operations on Tugela Heights, also in Natal, including Laing's Nek. He was twice mentioned in Despatches [London Gazette, 8 Feb. and 10 Sept. 1901]; received the Queen's Medal with five clasps ; King's Medal with two clasps, and was created a Companion

Henry Charles Pilleau.

of the Distinguished Service Order [London Gazette, 27 Sept. 1901] : " Henry Charles Pilleau, Capt., Royal West Surrey Regt. In recognition of services during the operations in South Africa." He was invested by the King 24 Oct. 1902. Major Pilleau served in the European War ; was promoted to Lieutenant-Colonel on the 18th of Sept. 1914, and was mortally wounded in the Battle of the Aisne. Notwithstanding his dying condition, Lieut.-Colonel Pilleau continued for four hours to direct his men. It was not known till dark, when retiring, that he had been wounded. He died a week afterwards, on the 21st of Sept. 1914, in the American Ambulance of Neuilly. In July, 1904, he had married Edith Maud, daughter of the late Lieut.-Colonel W. E. Mockler, 4th Battn. West India Regt.

ROBINSON, FREDERICK WILLIAM TEMPLETOWN, Capt., was born 21 April, 1863, eldest son of the late Sir William C. F. Robinson, G.C.M.G., and nephew of the Right Hon. Sir Hercules Robinson, Bart.,

afterwards Lord Rosmead. He was educated at the Rev. T. Hawtrey's, Windsor, and at Foster's, Stubbington, Hants. He joined the Yorkshire Regt., as Lieutenant, from the Militia, 12 Nov. 1884 ; was A.D.C. to the Governor of Western Australia 26 July, 1893, to 11 July, 1894 ; was appointed Commandant of the Fremantle Rifle Volunteers, Western Australia, 1893, receiving the thanks of the Australian Government for successful service ; became Captain, Royal Sussex Regt., 8 April, 1896. He served in the South African War, 1899–1902 ; was Commandant at Bethulie and performed the duties of Commandant at Hoopstad. He took part in operations in the Orange Free State, Feb. to May, 1900,

F. W. T. Robinson.

including the action at Zand River ; operations in Orange River Colony, 30 Nov. 1900, to Feb. 1901, and March, 1901, to 31 May, 1902 ; operations in Cape Colony, Feb. to March, 1901. He was mentioned in Despatches [London Gazette, 10 Sept. 1901], received the Queen's Medal with three clasps, the King's Medal with two clasps, and was created a Companion of the Distinguished Service Order [London Gazette, 27 Sept. 1901] : " Frederick William Templetown Robinson, Capt., Royal Sussex Regt. In recognition of services during the operations in South Africa." The Insignia were presented by the King 24 Oct. 1902 ; the Warrant, etc., sent 4 Nov. 1902. He was promoted Major, Royal Garrison Regt., 17 Dec. 1902, and retired 7 Dec. 1905. He became Brigade Major, Liverpool Infantry Volunteer Brigade, in 1906. He served as Major, Second-in-Command of the 2/16th (County of London) Regt., Queen's Westminsters, 1914–15–16 ; Major Robinson was appointed Recruiting Officer under the Ministry of National Service at Halifax, Yorkshire, 9 May, 1918. He married, in 1888, Gertrude Maria, daughter of the late Sir Alfred Hughes, 9th Bart., of East Bergholt Lodge, Suffolk.

McMICKING, HARRY, Capt., was born 28 Oct. 1867, youngest son. of the late G. McMicking, of Miltonise, Wigtownshire. He was gazetted to the Royal Scots 14 Sept. 1887 ; became Lieutenant, 4 June, 1890, and Captain, 24 June, 1896. He served in the South African War, as Adjutant, Mounted Infantry, 9 Oct. 1899, to 6 Oct. 1900 ; as Staff Officer to Mounted Infantry 7 Oct. 1900, to 17 Oct. 1900 ; as Brigade Major 18 Oct. 1900, to

26 June, 1902. Capt. McMicking was present at the Relief of Kimberley ; operations in the Orange Free State, Feb. to May, 1900, including operations at Paardeberg, 17 to 26 Feb., actions at Poplar Grove, Dreifontein, Vet River (5 and 6 May) and Zand River ; operations in the Transvaal in May and June, 1900, including actions near Johannesburg, Pretoria and Diamond Hill (11 and 12 June) ; operations in the Transvaal, east of Pretoria, July to 29 Nov. 1900, including action at Reit Vlei ; operations in the Transvaal 30 Nov. 1900, to April, 1902 (in command of a column 21 April to 28 July, 1901, and 7 Dec. 1901, to 20 Jan. 1902) ; in command of a column during operations in the Transvaal and Orange River Colony, April to 31 May, 1902. He was mentioned in Despatches [London Gazette, 16 April, 1901, and 29 July, 1902], received the Queen's Medal with six clasps, the King's Medal with two clasps, was placed on the list of officers qualified for Staff employment in consequence of service on the Staff in the Field, and was created a Companion of the Distinguished Service Order [London Gazette, 27 Sept. 1901] : " Harry McMicking, Capt., Royal Scots. In recognition of services during the operations in South Africa." The Insignia were presented by the King 24 Oct. 1902. He was Staff Captain, Infantry Brigade, Malta, 10 Feb. 1903, to 9 Feb. 1906 ; and was promoted to Major 5 Dec. 1904. Major McMicking was G.S.O.2, Lowland Division, Scottish Command, 18 Oct. 1909, to 30 Sept. 1911 ; became Lieutenant-Colonel, 14 Aug. 1912. He served in the European War, 1914–15 ; was mentioned in Despatches ; held a special appointment at Aldershot 1 Oct. 1918, to 12 Jan. 1919 ; was temporarily in command of the 3rd Battn. Royal Scots, from 6 Jan. 1919 ; was given the Brevet of Colonel 3 June, 1919. Colonel McMicking married, in 1907, Gertrude, only daughter of the Duke de Stacpoole and Pauline, only child of Edward MacEvoy, late M.P., County Meath, and they have two sons.

MARRIOTT, RICHARD GEORGE ARMINE, Capt., was born 26 Jan. 1867, son of the late Humphrey R. G. Marriott, of Abbot's Hall, Shalford, Essex, and of the late Edith Alice Smyth, youngest daughter of Thomas

White, J.P., D.L., of Wethersfield, Essex, and of Colchester. He was educated at Harrow ; was gazetted to the Buffs 4 May, 1887 ; was promoted Lieutenant 1 April, 1890 ; and Captain 25 June, 1896. He served in South Africa, 1899–1902 ; was present at the Relief of Kimberley, and at operations in the Orange Free State in Feb. and May, 1900, including operations at Paardeberg (17 to 23 Feb.) (severely wounded) ; operations in the Transvaal, east of Pretoria, July to 29 Nov. 1900. He was Commandant at Pienaar's Poort ; operations in the Transvaal 30 Nov. 1900, to 31 May, 1902. Capt. Marriott was mentioned in Despatches [London Gazette, 10 Sept. 1901], received the Queen's Medal with three clasps, the King's Medal with two clasps, and was created a Companion

Richard G. A. Marriott.

of the Distinguished Service Order [London Gazette, 27 Sept. 1901] : " Richard George Armine Marriott, Capt., East Kent Regt. In recognition of services during the operations in South Africa." The Insignia were presented by the King 18 Dec. 1902 ; the Warrant sent 17 Jan. 1903. He was promoted Major 26 Aug. 1906 ; retired and entered the Reserve of Officers 28 Aug. 1907. He is a J.P. for Essex. Major Marriott married, in 1912, Eileen Anita, eldest daughter of Brigadier-General Robert Albert Hickson, C.B., late of The Buffs, and of Ballytaggart, County Kerry, and of his wife, Annette Emilie, youngest daughter of the late T. W. Young-husband, of Bamburgh, Northumberland, and they have three daughters and one son.

FORD, REGINALD, Capt., was born 7 Dec. 1868, son of the late Rev. C. H. Ford, of Bishopton. He entered the Royal Marines 1 Feb. 1889 ; became Lieutenant, Army Service Corps, 15 Jan. 1893, and Captain 1 July, 1896. He served in the South African War, 1899–1900, in charge of Supply Park 24 March, 1900, to 31 Aug. 1900 ; and was present at operations in the Orange Free State, Feb. to May, 1900, including operations at Paardeberg (17 to 26 Feb.) and action at Dreifontein ; operations in the Transvaal, May to June, 1900, including action near Johannesburg ; operations in the Transvaal, east of Pretoria, July to Nov. 1900, including action at Belfast (26 to 27 Aug.). He was mentioned in Despatches [London Gazette, 8 Feb. and 10 Sept. 1901]; received the Queen's Medal with six clasps, and was created a Companion of the Distinguished Service Order [London Gazette 27 Sept. 1901] : " Reginald Ford, Capt., Army Service Corps. In recognition of services during the operations in South Africa." The Insignia were presented by the King 29 Oct. 1901. He was promoted to Major 1 April, 1903 ; was Assistant Director of Supplies and Transport, 1st Army Corps, 14 Oct. 1903, to 31 May, 1905, and Deputy Director of Supplies and Transport, Aldershot Army Corps, 1 June, 1905, to 13 Oct. 1906 ; was promoted to Lieutenant-Colonel 27 Oct. 1911. He served in the European War, from 5 Aug. 1914, to 1 Nov. 1914, as Assistant Director of Supplies, British Expeditionary Force ; from 2 Nov. 1914, to 28 Aug. 1915, as Deputy Director of Supplies, B.E.F. ; from 29 Aug. 1915, to 3 Nov. 1915, as D.A. and Q.M.G., 11th Army Corps, B.E.F. He became Colonel 27 Oct. 1915 ; was Director of Supplies and Transport, Levant Base, Mediterranean Expeditionary Force, 4 Nov. 1915, to 14 March, 1916 ; D.A.Q.M.G., Egyptian Expeditionary Force, and British Armies in France, 28 March, 1916, to 28 Oct. 1916 ; D.A.Q.M.G., Headquarters, British Armies in France, 30 Oct. 1916. He was promoted to Major-General 3 June, 1918 ; for his services in the Great War was mentioned in Despatches, created a C.M.G. in 1915, a C.B. in 1917, and a K.C.M.G. in 1919. Sir Reginald Ford married, in 1894, Alice Hope, daughter of Major-General Balmain and widow of E. H. Lockley, of The Grange, Chobham, Surrey.

DUNCAN, FRANCIS JOHN, Capt., was born 16 May, 1870. He was educated at Shrewsbury, and was gazetted to the Royal Scots 1 Sept. 1889; became Lieutenant 7 March, 1892; was Adjutant, Royal Scots, 1 Nov. 1895, to 31 Oct. 1899; was promoted to Captain 12 Aug. 1896. He served in the South African War, 1900-2; on Special duty under the Military Governor of Johannesburg; afterwards as Commandant, Edenburg, and in command of a Mounted Infantry Battalion (from 18 Aug. 1901). Operations in the Orange Free State, Feb. to May, 1900; operations in the Orange River Colony, May to 29 Nov. 1900; operations in Cape Colony, south of Orange River, 1899-1900. He was mentioned in Despatches [London Gazette, 10 Sept. 1901, and 17 Jan. 1902]; was given the Brevet of Major 22 Aug. 1902; received the Queen's Medal with two clasps; King's Medal with two clasps, and was created a Companion of the Distinguished Service Order [London Gazette, 27 Sept. 1901]: "Francis John Duncan, Capt., Royal Scots. In recognition of services during the operations in South Africa." The Insignia were presented by the King 29 Nov. 1901; the Warrant sent 24 Jan. 1902. He was promoted to Major 22 May, 1905. He served in the European War, 1914-17, as G.S.O.2, B.E.F., 20 May, 1915, to 3 Aug. 1915; became Lieutenant-Colonel 27 Nov. 1914; was in command of the 165th Infantry Brigade, British Armies in France, 3 Jan. 1916, to 10 April, 1917. He commanded the 214th Infantry Brigade, Home Forces, 14 April, 1917, to 21 Oct. 1917; and the 60th Infantry Brigade, British Armies in France, 24 Oct. 1917, to 13 June, 1918; was Temporary Major-General 14 June, 1918, commanding 61st Division, British Armies in France. He was mentioned twice in Despatches, created a C.M.G. (1915), a C.B. in 1919, and received the Brevet of Colonel 1 Jan. 1917. Colonel Duncan married, in 1905, Lili, daughter of the late Moritz Linder, of Vienna.

STREATFEILD, ERIC, Capt., was born 6 Feb. 1864; he was gazetted Lieutenant in the Gordon Highlanders, from the Militia, 28 April, 1886; was A.D.C. to the G.O.C., Militia, Dominion of Canada, 8 May, 1890, to 30 June, 1890, and 5 Dec. 1890, to 31 Aug. 1895; became Captain, 1 Sept. 1896, and Adjutant, Gordon Highlanders, 18 Nov. 1897. He served in the South African War; was created a Companion of the Distinguished Service Order [London Gazette, 27 Sept. 1901]: "Eric Streatfeild, Capt., Gordon Highlanders. In recognition of services during the operations in South Africa." The Insignia were presented by the King 29 Oct. 1901. Capt. Streatfeild died 26 May, 1902.

WELDON, FRANCIS HARRY, Capt., was born 24 April, 1869, in Madras, son of Colonel Thomas Weldon, C.I.E., Madras Staff Corps, and of Mrs. H. R. L. Weldon, daughter of the late General Simpson, R.A. He was educated at Cheltenham College, and at University College School, and joined the Sherwood Foresters 30 July, 1890, becoming Lieutenant 21 July, 1892, and Captain 28 Nov. 1896. Capt. Weldon served in the South African War, 1899 to 1902, on the Staff (as D.A.A.G. from 11 June, 1900). He was present at operations in the Orange Free State, Feb. to May, 1900, including actions at Houtnek (Thoba Mountain) and Vet River (5 May); operations in the Transvaal in May and June, 1900, including action near Pretoria; operations in the Transvaal, east of Pretoria, July to 29 Nov. 1900, including actions at Lydenburg (5 to 8 Sept.); operations in the Transvaal, west of Pretoria, July to 29 Nov. 1900, including actions at Eland's River (4 to 6 Aug.); operations in Cape Colony, south of Orange River, 1899-1900; operations in the Transvaal, 30 Nov. 1900, to May, 1901; operations in Orange River Colony, May, 1901, to March, 1902. He was mentioned in Despatches [London Gazette, 10 Sept. 1901]; received the Queen's Medal with three clasps; the King's Medal with two clasps; was placed on the list of Officers considered qualified for Staff Employment in consequence of service on the Staff in the Field, and was created a Companion of the Distinguished Service Order [London Gazette, 27 Sept. 1901]: "Francis Harry Weldon, Capt., Derbyshire Regt. In recognition of services during the operations in South Africa." The Insignia were presented by the King 18 Dec. 1902. He retired 14 Feb. 1906, and is Honorary Major, 4th Battn. Sherwood Foresters. Major Weldon married, 16 Sept. 1902, at St. Mary Bolton's, London, Eveleen Campbell, of Rivermount House, Pangbourne, daughter of the late Thomas Fiehlen Campbell, and they have two children, Sybil May, and George Anthony Thomas, born 6 June, 1908.

Francis Harry Weldon.

BOYS, REGINALD HARVEY HENDERSON, Capt., was born 17 Oct. 1867, son of the late Admiral Henry Boys. He entered the Royal Engineers 24 July, 1886. He received the thanks of the community of Hong-Kong and a service of plate for services rendered during the plague in 1894. He became Captain 31 Dec. 1896; served in the South African War, 1899-1902, and took part in operations in Natal, 1899; the defence of Ladysmith; operations in Natal, March to June, 1900; operations in the Transvaal, east of Pretoria, July to 28 Nov. 1900; operations in Cape Colony and Orange River Colony 30 Nov. 1900, to 31 May, 1902; was Assistant Director of Army Telegraphs, Cape Colony. He was mentioned in Despatches [London Gazette, 8 Feb. and 10 Sept. 1901, and 29 July, 1902]; received the Queen's Medal with five clasps; the King's Medal with two clasps, and was created a Companion of the Distinguished Service Order [London Gazette, 27 Sept. 1901]: "Reginald Harvey Henderson Boys, Capt., Royal Engineers. In recognition of the operations in South Africa." He was invested by the King 24 Oct. 1902. He was promoted to Major 9 April, 1905; was Staff Captain, War Office, 1 Sept. 1910, to 24 July, 1913; became Lieutenant-Colonel 1 Aug. 1913. Lieut.-Colonel Boys served in the European War from 1917; as Com-

mandant, Signal Service Training Centre, 6 May, 1915, to 30 Nov. 1915; Deputy Director of Army Signals, Forces in Great Britain, 6 May, 1918, to 21 Nov. 1918. He was twice mentioned in Despatches; wounded; was given the Brevet of Colonel 3 June, 1917, and created a C.B. in 1915. He became Deputy Chief Engineer, Eastern Command, 18 Jan. 1919, with the temporary rank of Brigadier-General. Colonel Boys married (1st), in 1896, Elizabeth Mary (who died in 1908), daughter of the late Kenneth Murray, of Geanies, County Ross. He married (2ndly), in 1912, Dorothy Conyers, daughter of Conyers Baker, and they have two sons and one daughter.

LASCELLES, WALTER CHARLES, Capt., was born 5 July, 1867, third son of the Rev. the Honourable J. W. Lascelles, Canon of Ripon. He was educated at Marlborough, and entered the Army 27 Nov. 1888, becoming Captain 1 Jan. 1897. Capt. Lascelles served in the South African War, 1899 to 1900, and was present at the Relief of Ladysmith, including operations of 5 to 7 Feb. 1900, and action at Vaal Kranz, where he was severely wounded. He was mentioned in Despatches [London Gazette, 10 Sept. 1901];

Walter Charles Lascelles.

received the Queen's Medal with two clasps; the King's Medal with two clasps, and was created a Companion of the Distinguished Service Order [London Gazette, 27 Sept. 1901]: "Walter Charles Lascelles, Capt., Durham Light Infantry. In recognition of services during the operations in South Africa." He was invested by the King 17 Feb. 1901. Capt. Lascelles married, in 1902, Louisa Gertrude, only daughter of Colonel Knox, of Creagh, Ballinrobe, Ireland. He retired 19 Oct. 1904, and died 18 May, 1911.

BOLS, LOUIS JEAN, Capt., was born 23 Nov. 1867, son of L. J. Bols, late Consul-General, Belgian Diplomatic Service, and of Brussels, and Mary Wilhelmina Bols. He was educated at Lancing College, and obtained his first commission in the Devonshire Regt. 5 Feb. 1887, and became Lieutenant 22 Sept. 1889; served in Burma, 1891-92; during operations in Kachin Hills, and received the Medal with clasp. He accompanied the Chitral Relief Force, 1895. He was promoted Captain 18 Jan. 1897; became Adjutant 17 Feb. 1899. He served in the South African War, 1899-1902; was present at the Relief of Ladysmith, including action at Colenso; during operations of 17 to 24 Jan. 1900, and action at Spion Kop; operations of 5 to 7 Feb. 1900, and action at Vaal Kranz; during operations on Tugela Heights 14 to 27 Feb. 1900, and action at Pieter's Hill; during operations in Natal, March to June, 1900, including action at Laing's Nek; taking part in the

Louis Jean Bols.

operations in the Transvaal 30 Nov. 1900, to 31 May, 1902. He was mentioned three times in Despatches [L. G., 8 Feb. 1901 (Sir R. H. Buller, 30 March and 9 Nov. 1900); L. G., 10 Sept. 1901]; awarded the Queen's Medal and five clasps; the King's Medal and two clasps, and was created a Companion of the Distinguished Service Order [London Gazette, 27 Sept. 1901]: "Louis Jean Bols, Capt., Devonshire Regt. In recognition of services during the operations in South Africa." The Insignia were presented by the King 17 Dec. 1901, and the Warrant sent 24 Jan. 1902. He was promoted Major 2 Oct. 1906; was given the Brevet of Lieutenant-Colonel, 1912, and became Lieutenant-Colonel 19 Feb. 1914, and (Temporary) Brigadier-General 24 Feb. 1915; became G.S.O., 2nd Grade, 1912-14. He again saw active service in the European War, as Lieutenant-Colonel, Dorsetshire Regt. (1914); received the Brevet of Colonel 3 June, 1915. He was mentioned three times in Despatches, created a C.B. in 1915, and Commander of the Legion of Honour and St. Vladimir with Swords. He became General Allenby's Chief Staff Officer in 1916, and was given a Division in 1917. He was also promoted Major-General 1 Jan. 1917. General Allenby said in his Despatch [London Gazette, 25 Jan. 1918] that Major-General L. J. Bols had "done brilliant work, and was a General Staff Officer of the first rank." He was created a K.C.M.G. [London Gazette, 1 Jan. 1917]: "For valuable services culminating in the capture of Jerusalem," and was created a K.C.B., 1919. Sir Louis Bols married, in 1897, Augusta Blanche, second daughter of Capt. Walter Cecil Strickland, of The Rise, Dawlish, Devon, and they have two sons.

CHETWODE, PHILIP WALHOUSE, Capt., was born 21 Sept. 1869, eldest son of Lieut.-Colonel Sir George Chetwode, 6th Baronet, and Alice, daughter of the late Michael T. Bass, of Rangemore, Staffordshire. He was educated at Eton, and joined the 19th Hussars (from the Militia), as Second Lieutenant, 20 Nov. 1889, becoming Lieutenant 6 Aug. 1890. He took part in the operations in the Chin Hills, Burma, 1892-93, and for his services

Philip W. Chetwode.

in this campaign was awarded the Medal with clasp. He served in South Africa from 1899 to 1902; during operations in Natal, 1899; including actions at Rietfontein and Lombard's Kop; taking part in the defence of Ladysmith, including sortie of 7 Dec. 1899, and action of 6 Jan. 1900; during operations in Natal, March to June, 1900, including action at Laing's Nek; during operations in the Transvaal, east of Pretoria, July to 29 Nov. 1900, including actions at Belfast and Lydenberg, and operations in the Orange River Colony, May to 29 Nov. 1900; during operations in the Transvaal 30 Nov. 1900, to May, 1901; in Orange River Colony, July, 1901; in Cape Colony, Aug. 1901, to 31 May, 1902. He was mentioned twice in Despatches (Feb. and 10 Sept. 1901); awarded the Queen's Medal with five clasps, and the King's Medal with two clasps. In Sept. 1901, he was created a Companion of the Distinguished Service Order [London Gazette, 27 Sept. 1901]: "Philip Walhouse Chetwode, Capt., 19th Hussars. In recognition of services during operations in South Africa." The Insignia were presented by the King 24 Oct. 1902, and the Warrant sent 4 Nov. 1902, and acknowledged by his mother 6 Nov. 1902. He was promoted Major 21 Dec. 1901, and succeeded his father to the Baronetcy in 1905. From 1906 to 1907 Major Chetwode was employed as A.M.S. to the G.O. Commanding-in-Chief (1st Class), Aldershot Army Corps, and from Dec. 1907, to May, 1908, he acted in the same capacity to the G.O. Commanding-in-Chief, Aldershot Command. He became Lieutenant-Colonel 3 Jan. 1908, and Colonel 4 Oct. 1911. In April, 1912, he was appointed Brigadier Commander of the London Mounted Brigade, London District, and in May, 1914, commanded the 5th Cavalry Brigade, Northern Command. He served during the European War, 1914–18, as Brigade Commander, 5th Cavalry Brigade, B.E.F., 5 Aug. 1914, to 14 July, 1915; was Divisional Commander, 2nd Cavalry Division, B.E.F., British Armies in France, 15 July, 1915, to 15 Nov. 1916. He commanded the Desert Column, No. 3 Section, Canal Defences, Egyptian Expeditionary Force, 3 Dec. 1916, to 21 April, 1917; Commander, Eastern Force, Egypt, 22 April, 1917, to 1 Aug. 1917. He was created a K.C.M.G. in 1917.

General Sir Archibald Murray, G.C.M.G., K.C.B., late General Officer Commanding-in-Chief, Egyptian Expeditionary Force, said in his Despatch, dated 28 June, 1917: "The General Officer Commanding Eastern Force, Lieut.-General Sir P. W. Chetwode, Bart., K.C.M.G., C.B., D.S.O., has united the qualities of brilliant leadership and sure judgment, and has invariably inspired confidence in all ranks."

Sir Philip Chetwode commanded the 20th Army Corps, Egyptian Expeditionary Force, 2 Aug. 1917, to 8 June, 1919, taking part in the operations in Palestine and Syria.

General Sir Edmund Allenby, G.C.M.G., K.C.B., Commanding-in-Chief, Egyptian Expeditionary Force, says in his Despatch, dated 16 Dec. 1917 [London Gazette, 25 Jan. 1918]: "Major-General (Temporary Lieutenant-General) Sir Philip Chetwode, Bart., K.C.M.G., C.B., D.S.O. My plan of operations was based on his appreciation of the situation, and on the scheme which he put forward to me on my arrival in Egypt last summer. To his strategical foresight and tactical skill the success of the campaign is largely due."

General Sir Edmund Allenby said in his Despatch, dated 31 Oct. 1918 [London Gazette, 30 Dec. 1918]: "I ordered Lieut.-General Sir Philip Chetwode, Bart., K.C.B., K.C.M.G., D.S.O., commanding the 20th Corps, to advance his line, east of the Bireh-Nablus road, on the night preceding the main attack, so as to place the 53rd Division on his right flank, which was somewhat drawn back, in a more favourable position to block the exits to the lower valley of the Jordan. I ordered him to be prepared to carry out a further advance, with both the 53rd and 10th Divisions, on the evening of the day on which the attack in the coastal plain took place, or later, as circumstances demanded."

Sir Philip Chetwode was created a K.C.B. [London Gazette, 1 Jan. 1918]: "For valuable services in connection with the military operations culminating in the capture of Jerusalem." He was made a Commandeur, Legion of Honour; he received the Croix de Guerre; is Grand Officier, Order of the Nile, and was promoted to Lieutenant-General 1 Jan. 1919. He became Military Secretary to the Secretary of State for War, and Secretary, Selection Board, 9 June, 1919. Sir Philip Chetwode married, in 1899, Hester Alice Camilla, eldest daughter of Colonel the Honourable Richard Stapleton-Cotton, and they have one son, Roger Charles George, born 18 April, 1906, and one daughter.

GODFREY-FAUSSETT, OWEN GODFREY, Capt., was born 13 May, 1866. He was the eldest surviving son of the late Colonel W. Godfrey-Faussett, of Farley Moor, Binfield. He was gazetted to the Essex Regt. as Lieutenant 30 Jan. 1886, and became Captain 15 Feb. 1897. He served in the South African War, 1899–1902, and was present at the Relief of Kimberley; operations in the Orange Free State, including operations at Paardeberg (17 to 26 Feb.); actions at Poplar Grove, Dreifontein, Vet River (5 and 6 May) and Zand River; operations in the Transvaal in May and June, 1900, including actions near Johannesburg, Pretoria and Diamond Hill (11 and 12 June); operations in the Transvaal, east of Pretoria, including action at Belfast (26 and 27 Aug.); operations in the Transvaal, west of Pretoria, including action at Frederickstad (17 to 25 Oct.); operations in Cape Colony, south of Orange River, 1899–1900, including actions at Colesberg (1 to 29 Jan.); operations in the Transvaal and Cape Colony 30 Nov. 1900, to 31 May, 1902. He was mentioned in Despatches [London Gazette, 8 Feb. and 10 Sept. 1901]; received the Queen's Medal with six clasps, the King's Medal with two clasps, and was created a Companion of the Distinguished Service Order [London Gazette, 27 Sept. 1901]: "Owen Godfrey Godfrey-Faussett, Capt., Essex Regt. In recognition of services during the operations in South Africa." He was invested by the King 24 Jan. 1902. Capt. Godfrey-Faussett was Adjutant, Volunteers, 14 June, 1902, to 31 Oct. 1905, and he was promoted to Major 25 Nov. 1905. He served in the European War, and was killed in action at the Dardanelles on 4 May, 1915. Lieut.-Colonel Godfrey-Faussett married, in 1899, Annette Gertrude, daughter of the late Rev. Alfred du Cane, and they had two daughters.

CRASKE, JOHN, Capt., was born 7 Nov. 1869, son of the late Deputy Inspector-General C. B. Craske, Madras Army, and Mrs. Craske. He was educated at Cheltenham College, and was commissioned in the Leinster Regt. 1 March, 1890, becoming Lieutenant 18 Dec. 1891, and Captain 31 March, 1897. He served in the South African War, 1900–1, taking part in operations in the Orange Free State in May, 1900; operations in Orange River Colony, May to 29 Nov. 1900, including action at Wittebergen; operations in the Transvaal, Oct. 1900; operations in Cape Colony, May, 1900; operations in Orange River Colony 30 Nov. 1900, to Feb. 1901. He was present at the action of Slaap Kranz and General Prinsloo's surrender. He was mentioned in Despatches [London Gazette, 10 Sept. 1901]; received the Queen's Medal with four clasps, and was created a Companion of the Distinguished Service Order [London Gazette, 27 Sept. 1901]: "John Craske, Capt., Leinster Regt. In recognition of services during the operations in South Africa." He was invested by the King 24 Oct. 1902. He was promoted to Major 11 May, 1907. Major Craske served in the European War in 1914 and 1915, in command of the 6th Battn. Leinster Regt. 19 Aug. 1914; was Temporary Lieut.-Colonel 19 Aug. 1914, to 22 May, 1915, and was promoted to Lieut.-Colonel 23 May, 1915. He was wounded, and was created a C.M.G. in 1916. Lieut.-Colonel Craske married, in 1899, Clara Grace, daughter of Surgeon-General W. S. Oliver, R.A.M.C., and granddaughter of Sir Thomas Galt, of Toronto, Canada.

KENNARD, ARTHUR MOLLOY, Capt., was born 7 July, 1867, eldest son of Arthur C. Kennard, of 17, Eaton Place, S.W. He was educated at Eton, and joined the Royal Field Artillery 24 July, 1886; was promoted Captain in 1897. He served in the South African War, 1899–1902; got his D.S.O. as a Captain with Q Battery at Sanna's Post, serving under General Phipps-Hornby, V.C., who was then commanding the battery. He was slightly wounded; mentioned in Despatches [London Gazette, 10 Sept. 1901]; received the Queen's Medal and four clasps, the King's Medal and two clasps, and was created a Companion of the Distinguished Service Order [London Gazette, 27 Sept. 1901]: "Arthur Molloy Kennard, Capt., Royal Horse and Royal Field Artillery. In recognition of services during the operations in South Africa." The Insignia were presented by the King 24 Oct. 1902, and the Warrant sent 4 Nov. 1902. He was promoted Major 16 Nov. 1901, and retired 16 March, 1904. He served in the European War as Second-in-Command, 1/2nd Scottish Horse; went to France in Aug. 1915, as Temporary Lieut.-Colonel in command of the 95th Brigade Artillery, 21st Division. He was wounded at Loos and returned to England. In 1916 he again saw active service in France, commanding the 79th Brigade Artillery, 39th Division, from March, 1916; was invalided home in Aug. 1916, and died 2 Jan. 1917. He had been for some years Justice of the Peace and Deputy-Lieutenant for Stirlingshire, and Managing Director of the Falkirk Iron Company. Major Kennard had married, on 30 Dec. 1911, at St. Barnabas', London, Evelyn Mary, widow of Charles H. Helbert, and only daughter of Lord David and Lady Mary Kennedy. They had one son, David Arthur, born 4 Jan. 1916.

Arthur M. Kennard.

RICHARDSON, FRANCIS JAMES, Capt., was born 8 March, 1866, son of Francis Richardson, of Juniper Hall, Dorking. He was educated at Cheam; Charterhouse, and Jesus College, Cambridge. He was gazetted to the Argyll and Sutherland Highlanders 9 May, 1888; became Lieutenant 26 Feb. 1890, and Captain 1 July, 1897. Capt. Richardson served in the South African War, 1899–1901, as Adjutant, 4th Battn. Argyll and Sutherland Highlanders (1 May to 5 Aug. 1901). He took part in the advance on Kimberley, including the actions at Modder River and Magersfontein; operations in Orange Free State, Feb. to May, 1900, including operations at Paardeberg (17 to 26 Feb.); actions at Poplar Grove, Dreifontein, Vet River (5 and 6 May) and Zand River; operations in the Transvaal in May and June, 1900, including actions near Johannesburg, Pretoria and Diamond Hill (11 and 12 June); operations in the Transvaal, west of Pretoria, July to 29 Nov. 1900, including action at Zilikat's Nek; operations in the Transvaal 30 Nov. 1900, to May, 1901; operations in Orange River Colony, May to July, 1901; operations in Cape Colony, July, 1901. He was mentioned in Despatches [London Gazette, 10 Sept. 1901]; received the Queen's Medal with six clasps, and was created a Companion of the Distinguished Service Order [London Gazette, 27 Sept. 1901]: "Francis James Richardson, Capt., Argyll and Sutherland Highlanders. In recognition of services during the operations in South Africa." The Insigina were presented by the King 29 Oct. 1901. He retired 16 June, 1906, and became Major, Special Reserve Battn. Argyll and Sutherland Highlanders, and in 1912, D.A.D. Remounts, Eastern Command. He married, 19 July, 1899, in Ireland, Rhoda Dagmar Richardson, daughter of Restell R. Bevis, and their children are Francis Desmond, born in 1902, and Elspeth Rhoda. Major Richardson died 11 Dec. 1917, of wounds received in action.

GRIFFIN, HENRY LYSAGHT, Capt., was born in Dublin 26 Feb. 1866, son of E. L. Griffin, Esq., Barrister, of Violet Hill, Ireland (who died 1 April, 1884), and B. F. Griffin (who died 27 Nov. 1916). He was educated at Harrow, and at the R.M.A., Woolwich, and entered the Royal Artillery 24 July, 1886, as Lieutenant, becoming Captain 3 July, 1897. He was A.D.C. to the G.O.C., Southern District, 10 Jan. to 27 Oct. 1899. Capt. Griffin served in the South African War, 1899 to 1902, taking part in operations in the Transvaal in May and June, 1900, including actions near Johannesburg, Pretoria and Diamond Hill (11 and 12 June); operations in the Transvaal, east of Pretoria, July to 29 Nov. 1900, including actions at Reit Vlei and Belfast (26 and 27 Aug.); operations in the Transvaal 30 Nov. 1900, to Oct. 1901; operations in Orange River Colony, Oct. 1901, to 31 May, 1902. He was mentioned in Despatches [London Gazette, 10 Sept. 1901, and 29 July, 1902]; received the Queen's Medal with five clasps, the King's Medal with two clasps, and was created a Companion of the Distinguished Service Order [London Gazette, 27 Sept. 1901]: "Harry Lysaght Griffin, Capt., Royal Garrison Artillery. In recognition of services during the operations in South Africa." He was invested by the King 18 Dec. 1902. Capt. Griffin retired with a gratuity and permission to retain rank and wear uniform 16 May, 1903. He became D.A. Director of Supplies, Ceylon, in 1915. He married, in Ceylon, 7 Feb. 1917, E. K. Graham Stewart, daughter of the Rev. J. Stewart, of Little Stukeley, Huntingdon.

RICARDO, AMBROSE ST. QUINTIN, Capt., was born at Gatcombe, Minchinhampton, Gloucestershire, 21 Nov. 1866, fourth son of Henry David Ricardo, of Gatcombe, Minchinhampton, and Ellen Crawley, daughter of Archdeacon Crawley, of Llandaff. He was educated at Winchester; Cooper's Hill, and Cambridge. He joined the Army 10 Nov. 1888; became Lieutenant 15 Dec. 1890, and Captain 6 Aug. 1897. Capt. Ricardo served in the Tirah Campaign on the North-West Frontier of India, 1897–98, with the Peshawar Column, 5th Brigade (Medal with two clasps). Capt. Ricardo served in South Africa, 1899 to 1902, and was present at operations in Natal, March to June, 1900; operations in the Transvaal, east of Pretoria, July to 29 Nov. 1900, including actions at Belfast (26 and 27 Aug.) and Lydenberg (5 to 8 Sept.). He served as Adjutant, 1st Battn. Royal Inniskilling Fusiliers, from 1 to 31 Dec. 1901, and from 4 Feb. 1901, to 31 May, 1902, and as Station Staff Officer. Operations in the Transvaal 30 Nov. 1900, to Dec. 1901; operations in Orange River Colony, Dec. 1901, to 31 May, 1902. He was mentioned in Despatches [London Gazette, 8 Feb. and 10 Sept. 1901, and 29 July, 1902 (by Sir R. H. Buller, Lord Kitchener, etc.)]; received the Queen's Medal with two clasps, and for the part he played in taking Bergendal Farm was created a Companion of the Distinguished Service Order [London Gazette, 27 Sept. 1901]: "Ambrose St. Quintin Ricardo, Capt., Royal Inniskilling Fusiliers. In recognition of services during the operations in South Africa." The Insignia, Warrant and Statutes were sent to the G.O.C., Cape Colony, and were presented in Cape Town 17 Jan. 1903. He retired 17 Jan. 1903. Capt. Ricardo served in the European War; was given the Brevet of Major 3 June, 1917; the Brevet of Lieut.-Colonel 1 Jan. 1918; was Temporary Brigadier-General; was created a C.M.G. in 1917, and a C.B.E. in 1919. He married, 13 July, 1893, at Thayet Myo, Burma, Elizabeth Alice, second daughter of Emerson Tennent Herdman, of Sion House, County Tyrone.

FITZGERALD, GEORGE ALFRED, Capt., was born 31 Jan. 1868, son of the late Capt. M. G. B. FitzGerald, 16th Lancers, and of Louisa Anna FitzGerald (deceased), daughter of the Rev. J. S. Halifax. He was educated at Clifton College. He entered the Royal Artillery 16 Feb. 1887; became Lieutenant 16 Feb. 1890, and Captain 9 Oct. 1897. Capt. FitzGerald served in the South African War, 1899–1901, and was present in operations in Orange Free State, Feb. to May, 1900; operations in Orange River Colony, May to July, 1900, including the actions at Lindley (1 and 26 June), where he was wounded. He was mentioned in Despatches [London Gazette, 10 Sept. 1901]; received the Queen's Medal with two clasps, and was created a Companion of the Distinguished Service Order [London Gazette, 27 Sept. 1901]: "George Alfred FitzGerald, Capt., Royal Horse and Royal Field Artillery. In recognition of services during the operations in South Africa." The Insignia were presented by the King 29 Oct. 1901; the Warrant sent 25 Jan. 1902. Major FitzGerald rejoined the Army on the outbreak of hostilities in Europe, as Assistant Director of Remounts, British Expeditionary Force; accompanied the British Expeditionary Force to France, 1914–18; appointed Deputy Director of Remounts 22 May, 1916 (Temporary Colonel); promoted Brevet Lieut.-Colonel (Reserve of Officers), New Year's Honours List, 1 Jan. 1917, and created a C.M.G. He was promoted Colonel in the Reserve of Officers on ceasing to be employed in April, 1919.

FOLEY, FRANK WIGRAM, Capt., was born 24 June, 1865, fourth son of the late Capt. Edward Foley, Royal Navy. He was educated at Tonbridge School, and entered the Royal Berkshire Regt. 8 Dec. 1886, as Lieutenant; was promoted Captain 25 Oct. 1897. Capt. Foley served with the Mounted Infantry in the South African War, 1899–1901, taking part in operations in the Orange Free State, March to May, 1900; operations in the Transvaal, west of Pretoria, July to Oct. 1900; operations in Orange River Colony, May to Oct. 1900, including actions at Rhenoster River and Lindley; operations in Cape Colony, Nov. 1900, to April, 1901. He received the Queen's Medal with four clasps, and was created a Companion of the Distinguished Service Order [London Gazette, 27 Sept. 1901]: "Frank Wigram Foley, Capt., Royal Berkshire Regt. In recognition of services during the operations in South Africa." The Insignia were presented by King Edward VII.; the Warrant sent

Frank Wigram Foley.

24 Jan. 1902. He was Instructor in Military Engineering, Royal Military College, Sandhurst, from Sept. 1901, to Sept. 1905. He served in the European War, 1914–16, being promoted Lieut.-Colonel in Aug. 1914;

raised 5th Battn. Royal Berkshire Regt. in Aug. 1914, and went in command with it to France and commanded it there till severely wounded at Givenchy 21 Dec. 1915. He was awarded the C.B.E., May, 1919; promoted full Colonel 10 May, 1919. Capt. Foley married, in 1903, Baroness Berkeley, and they have two daughters, the Hon. Mary Lalle and the Hon. Cynthia Ella.

HOWLEY, JASPER JOSEPH, Capt., was born 5 Aug. 1868, son of the late Lieut.-Colonel John Howley, D.L., of Rich Hill, Lisnagry, County Limerick. He was educated at Oscott College, and at Sandhurst, and

Jasper Joseph Howley.

joined the Lincolnshire Regt. 11 Feb. 1888, being promoted Lieutenant 9 July, 1890, and Captain 19 Nov. 1897. He served in the South African War, taking part in the operations in the Orange Free State, Feb. to May, 1900, including operations at Paardeberg; was present at the actions at Poplar Grove, Karee Siding, Vet River and Zand River; was on active service in the Transvaal in May and June, 1900, including actions near Johannesburg and Pretoria. He was severely wounded: was mentioned in Despatches twice [London Gazette, 8 Feb. and 10 Sept. 1901]; awarded the Queen's Medal with three clasps, and created a Companion of the Distinguished Service Order [London Gazette, 27 Sept. 1901]: "Jasper Joseph Howley, Capt., Lincolnshire Regt. In recognition of services during the operations in South Africa." The Insignia were presented by the King 17 Dec. 1901. Capt. Howley was Adjutant, Volunteers, 19 Jan. 1902, to 10 March, 1906, and was promoted to Major 11 March, 1906. He served in the European War, in the Lincolnshire Regt., accompanying the British Expeditionary Force to France. He fell at Neuve Chapelle 11 March, 1915, being killed instantaneously by a shell in the trench in the early morning while writing orders. His Colonel, Colonel McAndrew, had been killed the day before at almost the same hour, and Major Howley had taken over the command of the regiment. Major Howley was a good cricketer, a member of the M.C.C. and Incogniti, rode well to hounds, and was a good shot. He was unmarried.

LEMPRIÈRE, HENRY ANDERSON, Capt., was born 30 Jan. 1867. He was gazetted to the 7th Dragoon Guards 14 March, 1888, becoming Lieutenant 23 Dec. 1891. He was Adjutant, 7th Dragoon Guards, 1 April, 1900, to 8 Feb. 1903, and was promoted Captain in Jan. 1898. Capt. Lemprière served in the South African War, 1899–1902, on the Staff; as Adjutant, 7th Dragoon Guards, from April, 1900, to 31 May, 1902, and as D.A.A.G. till 26 June, 1902. He was present at operations in the Transvaal in May and June, 1900, including actions near Johannesburg, Pretoria and Diamond Hill (11 and 12 June); operations in the Transvaal, east of Pretoria, including action at Belfast (26 and 27 Aug.); operations in Cape Colony, south of Orange River, March, 1900; operations in the Transvaal, Dec. 1900; operations in Orange River Colony, Feb. 1901, to 31 May, 1902; operations on the Zululand Frontier of Natal in Oct. 1901; operations in Cape Colony, Dec. 1900, to Feb. 1901. He was mentioned in Despatches [London Gazette, 10 Sept. 1901, and 29 July, 1902]; was given the Brevet of Major 22 Aug. 1902; placed on the list of officers considered qualified for Staff employment in consequence of service on the Staff in the Field; received the Queen's Medal with five clasps, the King's Medal with two clasps, and was created a Companion of the Distinguished Service Order [London Gazette, 27 Sept. 1901]: "Henry Anderson Lemprière, Capt., 7th Dragoon Guards. In recognition of services during the operations in South Africa." The Insignia, Warrant and Statutes were sent to the G.O.C., Natal District, 15 Nov. 1902, and the Insignia were presented to Capt. Lemprière by Major-General Fetherstonhaugh at Pietermaritzburg 24 Dec. 1902. He was Adjutant, Cavalry Depot, 9 Feb. to 5 May, 1903; became Major 1 April, 1903; was Brigade Major, 3rd Cavalry Brigade, 3rd Army Corps, 23 May, 1903, to 21 Jan. 1904. He was at the Staff College in 1904; was promoted to Lieut.-Colonel in 1911. Lieut.-Colonel Lemprière served in the European War in 1914, and was killed in action 23 Dec. 1914.

WILSON, CECIL WILLIAM, Capt., was born 5 June, 1870, at Frascati, Blackrock, County Dublin, fourth son of James Wilson, of Currygrane Longford. He was educated at Harrow, and was commissioned in the King's Royal Rifle Corps 23 April, 1890; was promoted Lieutenant 18 May, 1892, and Captain 27 Jan. 1898. He served in the South African War, 1899–1901, as Adjutant, 3rd Battn. King's Royal Rifle Corps, and was present at the Relief of Ladysmith, including the action at Colenso; operations of 17 to 24 Jan. 1900, and action at Spion Kop; operations of 5 to 7 Feb. 1900, and action at Vaal Kranz; operations on Tugela Heights 14 to 27 Feb. 1900, and action at Pieter's Hill; operations in Natal, March to June, 1900, including action at Laing's Nek (6 to 9 June). He was mentioned four times in Despatches [London Gazette, 8 Feb. 1901 (Sir R. H. Buller, 3 Feb. and 9 Nov. 1900), and London Gazette, 10 Sept. 1901]; received the Queen's Medal with five clasps, and was created a Companion of the Distinguished Service Order [London Gazette, 27 Sept. 1901]: "Cecil William Wilson, Capt., King's Royal Rifle Corps. In recognition of services during the operations in South Africa." The Insignia were presented by the King 12 March, 1902; the Warrant, etc., were sent 19 March, 1902. In the European War served from mobilization, Aug. 1914, to Nov. 1916, in France and Egypt. He was promoted to Major 9 Aug. 1905, and retired from the Army 5 Dec. 1906. Capt. Wilson married, in 1903, in London, Winifred Aline, daughter of the late Sir R. Sutton, 4th Baronet.

BYRON, RICHARD, Capt., was born 19 Feb. 1870, at Secunderabad, India, eldest son of the late Major-General John Byron. He was educated at Wellington College and the Royal Military College, Sandhurst, and was gazetted to the King's Royal Rifle Corps 7 May, 1890. He served in the Hazara Expedition, 1891 (Medal with clasp); in the Miranzai Expedition, 1891 (clasp). He became Lieutenant 23 Nov. 1892, and served in the Isazai Expedition, 1892. He served with the Chitral Relief Force, 1895 (Medal with clasp), and was promoted to Captain 27 Jan. 1898. He was Adjutant, Militia, 16 Aug. 1899, to 15 Aug. 1904. Capt. Byron served in the South African War, 1900–1, as Adjutant, 9th Battn. King's Royal Rifle Corps, and was present at the operations in the Orange Free State, April to May, 1900; operations in Orange River Colony, May to 29 Nov. 1900; operations in Cape Colony, south of Orange River, Feb. to April, 1900; operations in the Transvaal, May and June, 1901; operations in Orange River Colony, Nov. 1900, to May, 1901; operations in Cape Colony, June and July, 1901. He was mentioned in Despatches [London Gazette, 10 Sept. 1901]; received the Medal and four clasps, and was created a Companion of the Distinguished Service Order [London Gazette, 27 Sept. 1901]: "Richard Byron, Capt., King's Royal Rifle Corps. In recognition of services during the operations in South Africa." The Insignia were presented by the King 29 Oct. 1901. He was promoted to Major 7 Oct. 1905, and retired 23 Jan. 1909, joining the Reserve of Officers. In 1913 he was appointed to command the 5th Battn. King's Royal Rifle Corps. He served in the European War, 1914 to 1919; was mentioned in Despatches, and given the Brevet of Colonel (1917). He commanded the Medway Reserve Brigade, 1916 to April, 1919. Colonel Byron married, in 1896, Mabel Mackenzie, daughter of C. A. Winter, Esq., of 33, Hyde Park Square, W., and they have one son, Second Lieut. R. G. Byron, 4th Dragoon Guards, born on 3 Nov. 1899, and one daughter, Sheila Margaret.

GODMAN, SHERARD HAUGHTON, Capt., was born 3 Jan. 1865, son of the late Joseph Godman, of Park Hatch, Godalming. He entered the Scots Guards 9 March, 1887; became Lieutenant 15 May, 1889, and Captain 2 Feb. 1898. He served in the South African War, 1900–2, and was present at operations in Orange River Colony, May to 29 Nov. 1900, including actions at Biddulphsberg and Wittebergen (1 to 29 July); operations in the Transvaal and Orange River Colony 30 Nov. 1900, to 31 May, 1902. He was mentioned in Despatches [London Gazette, 10 Sept. 1901]; received the Queen's Medal with three clasps; the King's Medal with two clasps, and was created a Companion of the Distinguished Service Order [London Gazette, 27 Sept. 1901]: "Sherard Haughton Godman, Capt., Scots Guards. In recognition of services during the operations in South Africa." The Insignia were presented by the King 24 Oct. 1902. He was promoted Major 16 March, 1901, and retired from the Scots Guards 15 April, 1908. He served in the European War, 1915–17, in France, and was wounded at Loos, and in 1918 he served in Mesopotamia. He was mentioned in Despatches, and given the Brevet of Lieutenant-Colonel, Reserve of Officers, 1 June, 1916, and promoted Lieutenant-Colonel. Major Godman married, in 1904, Florence (who died in 1912), widow of Sir A. C. Jervoise, 3rd Baronet.

LAINSON, ALEXANDER JOHN, Capt., was born 24 July, 1869, only son of J. A. Lainson, of Horringer House, Bury St. Edmund's. He was educated at Elstree and at Harrow. He entered the King's Royal Rifle Corps 28 June, 1890; saw active service in Burma, 1891–92, and was present at the operations in the Chin Hills; was promoted to Lieutenant 4 Jan. 1893, and to Captain 18 Feb. 1898. He served in South Africa, 1900, and was present at the defence of Ladysmith. He was mentioned in Despatches [London Gazette, 10 Sept. 1901]; received the Queen's Medal with clasp, and was created a Companion of the Distinguished Service Order [London Gazette, 27 Sept. 1901]: "Alexander John Lainson, Capt., King's Royal Rifle Corps. In recognition of services during the operations in South Africa." The Insignia and Warrant were sent to the Commander-in-Chief in India, and were presented by the Lieutenant-General Commanding the Forces in the Punjab 5 March, 1902. He retired 22 Jan. 1904. He was promoted Major, Special Reserve Battn. King's Royal Rifle Corps, in 1908, and served as Major, Labour Corps. Major Lainson married, in 1907, Ethel Mary, second daughter of John Eardley Yerburgh, of Wavendon Lodge, Buckinghamshire.

PALMES, GERALD LINDSAY, Capt., was born 18 Aug. 1864, sixth son of the late Venerable Archdeacon James Palmes, D.D. He was educated at Aysgarth and Uppingham, and was gazetted Second Lieutenant, Royal Lancaster Regt., 12 Sept. 1888; became Lieutenant 22 Dec. 1889; was Adjutant, Royal Lancaster Regt., 5 May, 1897, to 25 Aug. 1897, and Captain 23 March, 1898. Capt. Palmes served in the South African War, 1899 to 1902; was present at the Relief of Ladysmith, including the operations of 17 to 24 Jan. 1900, and action at Spion Kop; operations of 5 to 7 Feb. 1900, and action at Vaal Kranz; operations on Tugela Heights 14 to 27 Feb. 1900 (dangerously wounded 27 Feb.). He was mentioned in Despatches [London Gazette, 10 Sept. 1901]; received the Queen's Medal with two clasps, and was created a Companion of the Distinguished Service Order [London Gazette, 27 Sept. 1901]: "Gerald Lindsay Palmes, Capt., Royal Lancashire Regt. In recognition of services during the operations in South Africa." The Insignia were presented by the King 29 Oct. 1901. Capt. Palmes retired 1 Oct. 1906. He served as Grade 3 Staff Officer, Aug, 1914 to July, 1917; was mentioned in Despatches, 1917, and retired, owing to ill-health, July, 1917. He married, in 1897, Inez Charlotte, daughter of the late Albyn Saunders, 9th Lancers.

GORLE, HARRY VAUGHAN, Capt., was born at Poughill, Cornwall, 3 Sept. 1868, third son of the late Capt. John Taylor Gorle, late of H.M. 28th Regiment of Foot. He was educated privately, and joined the Royal Berkshire Regt. from the 4th (Militia) Battn. Lincolnshire Regt. 28 June, 1890, becoming Lieutenant, Lincolnshire Regt., 29 Sept. 1893; Army Service Corps 1 Oct. 1893, and Captain, Army Service Corps, 1 April, 1898. Capt. Gorle served in the South African War, on the Staff, as D.A.A.G., Oct. 1899, to 15 Feb. 1900, and from 24 March, 1902. He was present at the defence of Kimberley (arranged supplies and transport); operations in Orange River Colony, May to 29 Nov. 1900; operations in Cape Colony, north of Orange River; operations in Orange River Colony, March to 31 May, 1902; operations in Cape Colony 30 Nov. 1900, to March, 1902. He was mentioned in Despatches [London Gazette, 6 May, 1900, and 10 Sept. 1901]; received the Queen's Medal with two clasps; the King's Medal with two clasps, and was created a Companion of the Distinguished Service Order [London Gazette, 27 Sept. 1901]: "Harry Vaughan Gorle, Capt., Army Service Corps. In recognition of services during the operations in South Africa." The Insignia were sent to the Commander-in-Chief in South Africa, and presented by the Officer Commanding Troops, Kronstadt, 14 Sept. 1902. He was promoted to Major 3 Feb. 1905, and retired 6 June, 1908. Major Gorle married (1st), in 1895, Ethel Catharine (who died in 1904), eldest daughter of the Rev. Canon Archdall, Rector of Glanmire, County Cork. Their son is Temporary Lieut. Robert Vaughan Gorle, V.C., A Battery, 50th Brigade, Royal Field Artillery, who was born at Southsea 6 May, 1896. Major Gorle married (2ndly), in 1914, Edith Mary, daughter of the Rev. J. Lovebond Francis, Rector of Bridston, and they have one daughter.

Harry Vaughan Gorle.

UNETT, JOHN ALFRED, Capt., was born 3 Oct. 1868, only son of the late Capt. John Unett, 3rd Hussars. He was educated at the United Services College, Westward Ho! and entered the East Yorkshire Regt. 8 June, 1889; was promoted Lieutenant 15 Dec. 1891, and Captain 2 April, 1898. He served in the South African War, 1900–2, as Station Staff Officer, taking part in operations in the Orange Free State, including action at Houtnek (Thoba Mountain); operations in Orange River Colony, Dec. 1900, to Feb. 1901; March, 1901, to 31 May, 1902. He was mentioned in Despatches [London Gazette, 10 Sept. 1901]; received the Queen's Medal with three clasps; the King's Medal with two clasps, and was created a Companion of the Distinguished Service Order [London Gazette, 27 Sept. 1901]: "John Alfred Unett, Capt., East Yorkshire Regt. In recognition of services during the operations in South Africa." The Insignia were sent to the G.O.C., Transvaal and Orange River Colony, 15 Nov. 1902; were returned to England, and subsequently presented by the King 24 Oct. 1902. He retired 3 Oct. 1908, and entered the Reserve of Officers from the East Yorkshire Regt. He was appointed Chief Constable of Essex in 1915. Capt. Unett married, in 1905, Daisy, youngest daughter of the late S. Slater, J.P., of Farsley, Yorkshire.

FEILDING, GEOFFREY PERCY THYNNE, Capt., was born 21st Sept. 1866, eldest son of the late General the Hon. Sir Percy R. B. Feilding, K.C.B., and Lady Louisa Thynne, only daughter of the 3rd Marquis of Bath. He was educated at Wellington College, and entered the Army 28 April, 1888; was promoted to Lieutenant 27 Nov. 1890, and to Captain 6 April, 1898. He served throughout the South African War, 1899–1901, taking part in the advance on Kimberley, including actions at Belmont, Modder River, Magersfontein and Paardeberg, and in the march into Bloemfontein. He afterwards acted as A.D.C. to Major-General Sir Mildmay Wilson, K.C.B., commanding the Western Transvaal. He was transferred to the 11th Mounted Infantry, and commanded the 14th Mounted Infantry to the end of the war. He was mentioned in Despatches [London Gazette, 26 Jan. 1900, and 10 Sept. 1901]; received the Queen's Medal and four clasps, the King's Medal and three clasps, and was created a Companion of the Distinguished Service Order [London Gazette, 27 Sept. 1901]: "Geoffrey Percy Thynne Feilding, Capt., Coldstream Guards. In recognition of services during the operations in South Africa." The Insignia were presented by the King 24 Oct. 1902. He was promoted Major 29 Nov. 1903; was Commandant, Guards' Depôt, 1 June, 1908, to 31 May, 1911; became Lieutenant-Colonel 3 Sept. 1912. Lieut.-Colonel Feilding saw active service in the European War; went to France in Aug. 1914, with the original Expeditionary Force, in command of the 3rd Battn. Coldstream Guards, serving with the 4th Guards' Brigade. Lord Ernest Hamilton describes the fight at Landrecies in "The First Seven Divisions" (published by Messrs. Hutchinson), pages 43–47. He tells us how the 4th (Guards') Brigade had reached Landrecies at 1 p.m., very tired, and had had about four hours' rest when there came an alarm that the Germans were advancing on the town, "and the brigade got to its feet. The four battalions were split up into companies—one to each of the exits from the town. The Grenadiers were on the western side; the 2nd Coldstream on the south and east; and the 3rd Coldstream to the north and north-west. The Irish Guards saw to the barricading of the streets with transport wagons and such-like obstacles. They also loopholed the end houses of the streets facing the country. As a matter of fact, the attack did not take place till 8.30 p.m., and then it was entirely borne by two companies of the 3rd Battn. Coldstream Guards. At the north-west angle of the town there is a narrow street known as the Faubourg Soyère. Two

Geoffrey P. T. Feilding.

hundred yards from the town this branches out into two roads, each leading into the Forêt de Mormal. Here, at the junction of the roads, the Hon. A. Monck's company had been stationed. The sky was very overcast, and the darkness fell early. Shortly after 8.30 p.m. infantry was heard advancing from the direction of the forest; they were singing French songs, and a flashlight turned upon the head of the column showed up French uniforms. It was not till they were practically at arm's-length that a second flashlight detected the German uniforms in rear of the leading sections. The machine gun had no time to speak before the man in charge was bayoneted and the gun itself captured. A hand-to-hand fight in the dark followed, in which revolvers and bayonets played the principal part, the Coldstream being gradually forced back by weight of numbers towards the entrance to the town. Here Capt. Longueville's company was in reserve in the Faubourg Soyère itself, and through a heavy fire he rushed up his men to the support of Capt. Monck. The arrival of the reserve company made things rather more level as regards numbers, though—as it afterwards transpired—the Germans were throughout in a majority of at least two to one. Colonel Feilding and Major Matheson now arrived on the spot, and took over control. Inspired by their presence and example, the two Coldstream companies now attacked their assailants with great vigour and drove them back with considerable loss into the shadows of the forest. From here the Germans trained a light field-gun on to the mouth of the Faubourg Soyère, and firing shrapnel and star shells at point-blank range, made things very unpleasant for the defenders. Flames began to shoot up from a wooden barn at the end of the street, but were quickly got under with much promptitude and courage by a private of the name of Wyatt." Lord Ernest Hamilton here describes one of the acts for which Wyatt was later awarded the Victoria Cross. "In the meantime, Colonel Feilding had sent off for a howitzer, which duly arrived, and was aimed at the flash of the German gun. By an extraordinary piece of marksmanship, or of luck, as the case may be, the third shot got it full, and the field-gun ceased from troubling. The German infantry thereupon renewed their attack, but failed to make any further headway during the night, and in the end went off in their motor-lorries, taking their wounded with them. It turned out that the attacking force, consisting of a battalion of 1,200 men, with one light field-piece, had been sent on in these lorries, in advance of the general pursuit, with the idea of seizing Landrecies and its important bridge before the British could arrive and link up with the 2nd A.C. The attack *quâ* attack failed conspicuously, inasmuch as the enemy was driven back with very heavy loss; but it is possible that it accomplished its purpose in helping to prevent the junction of the two A.C.'s. This, however, is in a region of speculation, which it is profitless to pursue further. The Landrecies fight lasted six hours and was a very brilliant little victory for the 3rd Coldstream; but it was expensive." Lord Hawarden and the Hon. A. Windsor Clive were killed, while Capt. Whitehead, Lieut. Keppel and Lieut. Rowley were wounded. Among the rank and file the casualties amounted to 170. Sergt. Fox and Private Thomas showed great gallantry—as did many others—and each of them was awarded the D.C.M. The German losses were certainly very much higher than ours. At 3.30 a.m. on the 26th Lord Ernest tells us that "the 4th Brigade left Landrecies and continued its retirement down the beautiful valley of the Sambre." At Zonnebeke, on the 21st Oct., the casualties in the Guards' Brigade were considerable, especially so in the 3rd Coldstream. The Hon. C. Monck and Lieut. Waller were killed, and Colonel Feilding, Lieut. Darrell and Lieut. Leese wounded. For his gallantry on this occasion Lord Feilding won the D.S.O. From 2 Sept. to 26 Sept. Colonel Feilding commanded the 4th Guards' Brigade, owing to the Brigadier being wounded. During this time the Brigade fought at the crossing of Le Petit Morin and the Battle of the Aisne. The brilliant capture of the Cour de Sempir Farm by the Guards' Brigade, when Colonel Feilding was acting Brigadier, is described by Lord Ernest Hamilton in his enthralling book. In this engagement, in the 3rd Coldstream, Capt. Banbury, Lieut. Ives, Lieut. Bingham and Lieut. P. Wyndham were killed, and Capt. Vaughan and Lieut. Fane wounded, while the casualties among the rank and file amounted to 160. The important position then gained was never afterwards lost, but, from 14 Sept. on, was held by the Guards' Brigade for twenty-nine consecutive days, despite a quick succession of the most determined counter-attacks by the Germans. Colonel Feilding commanded the 149th Infantry Brigade from 26 April, 1915, to June, 1915; the 4th Guards' Brigade from June, 1915, to 3 Jan. 1916, and the Guards' Division from 3 Jan. 1916, to 1918 For this distinguished record of services he was mentioned in Despatches, Feb. 1915, was given the Brevet of Colonel 18 Feb. 1915; was mentioned in Despatches in Jan. and June, 1916, and again in Jan. 1917; was Temporary Brigadier-General from 3 Jan. 1916; Major-General 1 Jan. 1918; created a C.B., 1916, and C.M.G, 1917, and a K.C.B. in 1919. Sir Geoffrey Feilding is also a Commander of the Order of St. Maurice and St. Lazarus, and Commander of the Order of St. Leopold, also Commander of the Légion d'Honneur. He was appointed to the command of the London District 1 Oct. 1918.

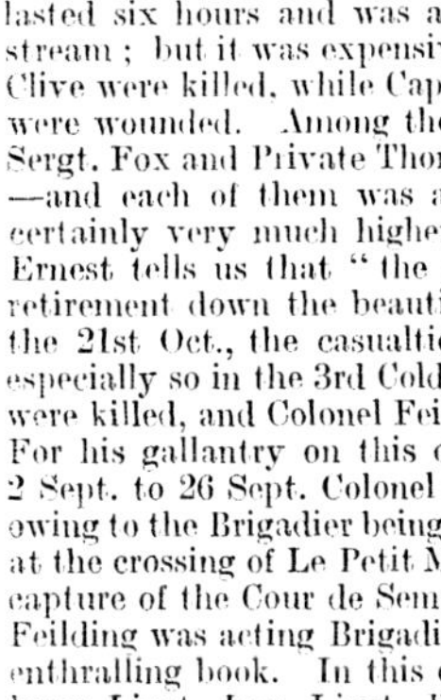

Amherst B. Whatman.

WHATMAN, AMHERST BLUNT, Capt., was born 8 Jan. 1867. He was gazetted to the Somerset Light Infantry 4 May, 1887, and became Lieutenant 4 Jan. 1890. In 1897–98 he was present at operations on the North-West Frontier of India, with the Mohmand Field Force and the Peshawar Column, Tirah Expeditionary Force (Medal and two clasps). He was promoted to Captain 9 April, 1898; and from 1899 to 1901 he served in the South African War, on the Staff, as Brigade Signalling Officer, 11 Sept. 1900, to 11 June, 1901, and was present at the operations in Natal, 1899; at the Relief of Ladysmith, including the operations of 17 to 24 Jan. 1900, and action at Spion Kop; operations of 5 to 7 Feb. 1900, and action at Vaal Kranz; operations on Tugela Heights, 14 to 27 Feb. 1900; operations in the Orange Free State, April to May, 1900; operations in the Transvaal in June, 1900; operations in Natal, March to April, 1900; operations in the Transvaal, west of Pretoria, July to 29 Nov. 1900; operations in the Transvaal, 30 Nov. 1900, to May, 1901; operations in Orange River Colony, June to July, 1901. He was mentioned in Despatches [London Gazette, 10 Sept. 1901]; received the Queen's Medal with five clasps, and was created a Companion of the Distinguished Service Order [London Gazette, 27 Sept. 1901]: "Amherst Blunt Whatman, Capt., Somerset Light Infantry. In recognition of services during the operations in South Africa." The Insignia, Warrant and Statutes were sent to the Commander-in-Chief, South Africa, and the Insignia presented by the Lieutenant-General Commanding the Forces, Punjab. Capt. Whatman was Inspector of Army Signalling, India, 1 April, 1904, to 31 March, 1908. He again saw active service on the North-West Frontier of India in 1908, as Chief Signalling Officer, taking part in operations in the Zakka Khel country. He was mentioned in Despatches [London Gazette, 22 May, 1908], and was given the Brevet of Major 16 July, 1908. He was promoted to Major, and retired in 1910 from the Somerset Light Infantry. Major Whatman married Myrtle Elen, daughter of Colonel H. J. Waller Barrow, and they had one son. Major Whatman died 23 Oct. 1913.

RADCLIFFE, JASPER FITZGERALD, Capt., was born 18 Aug. 1867, son of the late W. C. Radcliffe, of Warleigh. He was educated at Cheltenham, and entered the Devonshire Regt. 22 Aug. 1888, becoming Lieutenant 31 Oct. 1890, and Captain 9 April, 1898. Capt. Radcliffe accompanied his regiment to South Africa, serving in the South African War, 1899–1900, and was present at the Relief of Ladysmith, including the action at Colenso, where he was severely wounded. He was mentioned in Despatches 8 Feb. and 10 Sept. 1901; awarded the Queen's Medal with clasp, and was created a Companion of the Distinguished Service Order [London Gazette, 27 Sept. 1901]: "Jasper Fitzgerald Radcliffe, Capt., Devonshire Regt. In recognition of services during the operations in South Africa." The Insignia were presented by the King 29 Oct. 1901. Capt. Radcliffe was Adjutant, Discharge Depôt, 2 Sept. 1900, to 2 Sept. 1905. He was promoted Major on 7 May, 1907. He served in the European War, and fell in action 2 Feb. 1916. He had married, in 1893, Emily Maude, daughter of the Rev. E. C. Orpen, of Exleigh, Starcross, Devon.

YATMAN, CLEMENT, Capt., was born 1 Feb. 1871. He was gazetted to the Northumberland Fusiliers 29 Oct. 1890; became Lieutenant 18 Sept. 1892; Captain 9 April, 1898; was Adjutant, Northumberland Fusiliers, 13 Feb. to 1 Nov. 1899. Capt. Yatman served in the South African War, 1899–1902, and was present at operations in the Orange Free State, Feb. to May, 1900; operations in the Transvaal, west of Pretoria, May to Nov. 1900; operations in Cape Colony, south of Orange River, 1899–1900; operations in the Transvaal, Nov. 1900, to Aug. 1901; operations in Orange River Colony, Aug. 1901, to 31 May, 1902. He was mentioned in Despatches [London Gazette, 10 Sept. 1901]; received the Queen's Medal with three clasps; the King's Medal with two clasps, and was created a Companion of the Distinguished Service Order [London Gazette, 27 Sept. 1901]: "Clement Yatman, Capt., Northumberland Fusiliers. In recognition of services during the operations in South Africa." He was promoted to Major 17 Feb. 1904. Major Yatman served in the European War from 1914 to 1918; was Temporary Brigadier-General from 28 Aug. 1915; commanded the 96th Brigade, New Armies, B.E.F., 28 Aug. 1915, to 3 Dec. 1916; the 50th Infantry Brigade, British Armies in France, 4 Dec. 1916, to 18 April, 1918; commanded the 1st Dover Special Reserve Brigade, Forces in Great Britain, 8 Aug. 1918. He was twice wounded, twice mentioned in Despatches, given the Brevets of Lieutenant-Colonel (18 Feb. 1915) and Colonel (3 Dec. 1916), and created a C.M.G. in 1918.

DE FALBE, VIGANT WILLIAM, Capt., was born 10 Nov. 1867, son of the late Capt. C. V. M. de Falbe, Danish Royal Navy, and of Emmeline McArthur. He was educated privately, then went through Sandhurst, and entered the Army 22 Aug. 1888; was promoted Lieutenant 15 Oct. 1890; was Adjutant, North Staffordshire Regt., 22 Jan. 1898, to 21 July, 1902; became Captain 18 May, 1898. He served in the South African War, 1900–1902, as Adjutant, 2nd Battn. North Staffordshire Regt., and was present at operations in the Orange Free State, Feb. to May, 1900, including actions at Karee Siding, Vet River (5 and 6 May) and Zand River; operations in the Transvaal in May, 1900, including actions near Johannesburg; operations in the Transvaal, west of Pretoria, Sept. and Oct. 1900; operations in the Transvaal 30 Nov. 1900, to 31 May, 1902. He was mentioned in Despatches [London Gazette, 10 Sept. 1901]; received the Queen's Medal with three clasps, the King's Medal with two clasps, and was created a Companion of the Distinguished Service Order [London Gazette, 27 Sept. 1901]: "Vigant William de Falbe, Capt., North Staffordshire Regt. In recognition of services during the operations in South Africa." He was awarded the D.S.O. for his good services in South Africa for nearly three years, being Adjutant of his battalion all the time. The Insignia were presented by the King 24 Oct. 1902; the Warrant sent 4 Nov. 1902. He was promoted Major 7 April, 1906. He became Lieutenant-Colonel 14 March, 1913, commanding 1s Battn. The Prince of Wales's (North Staffordshire) Regt. Lieut.-Colonel

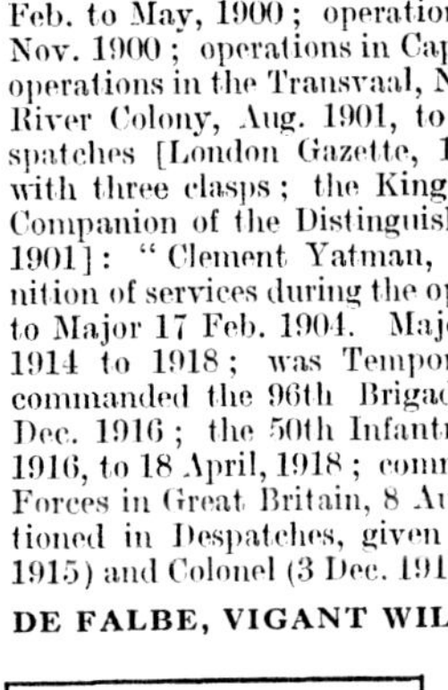

Vigant William de Falb .

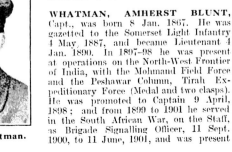

de Falbe again saw active service in the European War, 1914–15, commanding his battalion in France from Sept. 1914, till Dec. 1915, when he was given the 185th Infantry Brigade, West Yorkshire Regt. His health failing, he returned from France in Sept. 1917, and was given the Home Counties Reserve Brigade until demobilized in 1919, when he was given No. 9 Regimental District. He was mentioned in Despatches; created a C.M.G. in 1915, and promoted to Brigadier-General 1 Jan. 1916. He became full Colonel on 14 March, 1917, though at that time holding the rank of Brigadier-General, which continued until 22 Feb., when he went to Warley, commanding No. 9 Regimental District. Brigadier-General de Falbe married, in 1912, Amy Rhona, youngest daughter of Edmund Hanbury, of Poles, Hertfordshire, and they had one son, who was born in 1916 and died in 1917, and three daughters.

SINCLAIR-MACLAGAN, EWEN GEORGE, Capt., was born 24 Dec. 1868, son of Robert Ewen Sinclair-Maclagan, of Glenquiech, Forfarshire, N.B., and Mrs. R. E. Sinclair-Maclagan. He was gazetted to the Border

Regt. 21 Dec. 1889; became Lieutenant 2 March, 1892; served in the Waziristan Expedition 1894–95 (Medal with clasp); became Captain 26 May, 1898. Capt. Sinclair-Maclagan served in the South African War, 1899 to 1901, and was present at the operations in Natal, 1899; at the Relief of Ladysmith, including the action at Colenso; operations of 17 to 24 Jan. 1900 (wounded 22 Jan.); operations in the Orange Free State, April and May, 1900; operations in the Transvaal, June, 1900; operations in the Transvaal, east of Pretoria, July, 1900; operations in the Transvaal, west of Pretoria, July to Nov. 1900; operations in Orange River Colony (May, 1900); operations in Cape Colony, south of Orange River, 1899; operations in Cape Colony north of Orange

E. G. Sinclair-Maclagan.

River, May, 1900. He was mentioned in Despatches [London Gazette, 10 Sept. 1901], received the Queen's Medal with five clasps, and was created a Companion of the Distinguished Service Order [London Gazette, 27 Sept. 1901]: " Ewen George Sinclair-Maclagan, Capt., The Border Regt. In recognition of services during the operations in South Africa." The Insignia were presented to him by the King 24 Oct. 1902. Capt. Sinclair-Maclagan was employed with the New South Wales Military Forces 29 Aug. 1902, to 30 Aug. 1904. He was promoted to Major, Yorkshire Regt., 28 Oct. 1908. Major Sinclair-Maclagan was employed with the Australian Military Forces 20 Jan. 1911, to 19 May, 1919. He served in the European War, at the Dardanelles, 1914–16; in France and Flanders, 1916–19; as Temporary Brigadier-General from 15 Aug. 1914, to 15 July, 1917. He was promoted to Lieutenant-Colonel, Yorkshire Regt., 28 March, 1915; was given the Brevet of Colonel 3 June, 1915; commanded the 4th Australian Division, as Temporary Major-General, 16 July, 1917, to 30 Dec. 1919, and as Major-General 1 Jan. 1919, to 19 May, 1919; commanded the Highland Division, T.F., from 1919. Major-General Sinclair-Maclagan was five times mentioned in Despatches; was given the Brevet of Colonel 3 June, 1915; became Major-General 1 Jan. 1919; was created a C.B. in 1917; a C.M.G. in 1919; received the 3rd Class White Eagle, Serbia; the French Croix de Guerre, and the American Distinguished Service Medal. He married, in 1902, Kathleen, daughter of Major-General Sir George A. French and Janet Clarke (who died in 1917), daughter of Robert Long Innes, formerly of the 37th Regt., and they have one daughter.

PINE-COFFIN, JOHN EDWARD, Capt., was born 24 Dec. 1866, son of the late John Richard Pine-Coffin, J.P., D.L., County of Devon, and Mrs. Pine Coffin (Matilda, youngest daughter of William Speke, of Jordans,

Somerset), of Kenwith Castle, Bideford, Devon. He was educated at Eton (served in the Eton Rifle Corps for three years) and Cambridge, and from 1886 to 1888 was Lieutenant, North Lancashire Militia. He was gazetted to the Loyal North Lancashire Regt. 10 Nov. 1888, and joined the 2nd Battn. in Jersey, as Second Lieutenant, and he became Lieutenant 13 Oct. 1891. In 1896 he was specially selected to go to Aldershot in command of Mounted Infantry, and he became Captain 5 June, 1898. In Jan. 1900, he went on active service to South Africa, commanding Mounted Infantry. Specially selected to join Colonial Division, and commanded the advance guard to Wepener. Later, was selected to command the 9th Battn. Mounted Infantry, and with that

John Edward Pine-Coffin.

battalion was constantly engaged in fighting. Specially mentioned in " War Despatches," by Lord Roberts, in a special despatch for " good work in an independent command," and received a Brevet Majority dated 24 April, 1901 : " He was in an independent command, near Ventersburg, Orange River Colony, and the Boers captured the American Consul and Lord Lennox, who was carrying important despatches to Lord Roberts. Capt. Pine-Coffin, with a patrol of thirty-five men, followed up the enemy for twenty miles, engaged their rear guard, recovered the despatches, and captured many Boer prisoners. The Boer force was over two hundred, and commanded by General Theron, the well-known Boer Scout." Specially selected to command a column of " all arms " to operate in the Orange River Colony. Was continually engaged in fighting, and on more than

one occasion these fights had important results. His command was now increased up to 2,000 men, consisting of Irish Colonials, Boer Scouts, and the 9th Battn. Mounted Infantry, which required considerable tact to manage. They fought several engagements, of which the principal one was an action with General Philip Botha. In this engagement, which lasted from 6 a.m. to 5 p.m., and in which our troops were greatly outnumbered, they captured the Boer laager, and General Philip Botha and his son fell in the engagement. The success of this engagement had very important results in the Orange River Colony. He was mentioned in Special Despatch, and received Commander-in-Chief's nomination for the Staff College, and was created a Companion of the Distinguished Service Order [London Gazette, 27 Sept. 1901]: " John Edward Pine-Coffin, Capt., Loyal North Lancashire Regt. In recognition of services during operations in South Africa." (Invested by the King 12 March, 1902.) After this he was engaged for many months in the country extending from the Vaal River to Bloemfontein, in dispersing any raiding parties of Boers, and generally administering magisterial duties in the district. He served in Egypt, 1903–7, and became Major 26 June, 1907. The following is an extract from the London Gazette : " Brevet Major Pine-Coffin, D.S.O., Loyal North Lancashire Regt., who rendered valuable service in command of a battalion of Mounted Infantry, and afterwards at the head of a column, in South Africa, has been selected for the command of the Mounted Infantry in Egypt." In 1906 a state of great unrest prevailed in Egypt, and his duties consisted of moving about with British troops and Egyptian Police all through the country engaged in Intelligence and Police Duties. During one of these marches they were attacked by a large number of fanatical Mohammedans, and it was with extreme difficulty that they got away with the loss of one officer killed.

The following are extracts from official documents :

" The conduct of our officers and men on this tragic occasion was marked by a remarkable forbearance and humanity in the face of great provocation."

" We should like to express our admiration of the conduct of the British officers, which was worthy of the best traditions of the Army. Major Pine-Coffin, who was in command of the party, did all that was in his power to quiet the villagers. We have lost a gallant and distinguished officer, but the self-restraint and forbearance shown on this tragic occasion adds to the honour of the British Army."—Letter from Judge Perry, Supreme Court, Cairo.

" We are deeply grieved at your sufferings from the dastardly attack made on you and your brother officers, and how proud we feel of the cool and gallant behaviour of our countrymen, and not least of your own, which was worthy of your name and your noble county at home."

The following is an extract from orders, Headquarters, Cairo, 18 May, 1906 :

" A small disturbance in Cairo may have to be suppressed. A half company Mounted Police, half company Mounted Infantry, and two companies K.R.R.C., will be ready to move at short notice under the command of Major Pine-Coffin, D.S.O."

At the termination of Major Pine-Coffin's appointment, he was offered an extension of one year by the War Office, which he accepted. In 1907 he left Egypt and took over command of the 2nd Battn. Loyal North Lancashire Regt. in Mauritius, which he held for one year, and then retired voluntarily in 1909. Major Pine-Coffin married, at Londonderry, Ireland, Louisa Gertrude Douglas, youngest daughter of the late John Barré Beresford, J.P. and D.L., of Learmount and Ashbrooke, County Londonderry, and their children are : Edward Claude, born in 1895 ; Richard Geoffrey, born in 1908 ; Gertrude Beresford, and Gwendolyn May.

MOLONY, TREVOR CHARLES WHELER, Capt., was born 28 July, 1868, son of the late Colonel C. M. Molony, C.B. He was educated at Marlborough and Woolwich, and entered the Royal Artillery 17 Feb. 1888 ; became Lieutenant 17 Feb. 1891, and served on the North-West Frontier of India, 1897–98, taking part in operations on the Samana and the action at the Ublan Pass. He also served with the Tirah Expeditionary Force (Medal with three clasps). He was promoted to Captain 2 July, 1898, and served in the South African War, 1899–1902, taking part in the Relief of Kimberley ; operations in the Orange Free State, Feb. to May, 1900, including operations at Paardeberg (17 to 26 Feb.) ; actions at Poplar Grove, Dreifontein, Vet River and Zand River ; operations in the Transvaal in May and June, 1900, including operations near Johannesburg, Pretoria and Diamond Hill ; operations in Orange River Colony, May to 29 Nov. 1900, including action at Wittebergen ; operations in Orange River Colony, Nov. and Dec. 1900, to April, 1901. He was mentioned in Despatches [London Gazette, 10 Sept. 1901]: received the Queen's Medal with six clasps ; the King's Medal with two clasps, and was created a Companion of the Distinguished Service Order [London

Gazette, 27 Sept. 1901]: " Trevor Charles Wheler Molony, Capt., Royal Artillery. In recognition of services during the operations in South Africa." Capt. Molony was invested by the King 18 Dec. 1902. He was promoted to Major 3 Feb. 1904; passed the Staff College, and held the appointment of D.A.A. and Q.M.G., Malta (9 Feb. 1910, to 28 March, 1914); became Lieutenant-Colonel 30 Oct. 1914. Lieut-Colonel Molony married, in 1899, Beatrice Annie, daughter of the late Major-General W. H. Beynon, and they have two sons and one daughter.

Matthew Perceval Buckle.

BUCKLE, MATTHEW PERCEVAL, Capt., was born 29 Sept. 1869, at Wray Cottage, Ambleside, son of Admiral C. E. and Mrs. Buckle, The Red House,

Raithby, Spilsby, Lincolnshire. He was educated at Summerfield, Oxford, and at Winchester, and was gazetted to the Royal West Kent Regt. in April, 1889, becoming Lieutenant in Dec. 1892. From June, 1897, to Aug. 1901, he was Adjutant of his battalion, and was promoted Captain in July, 1898. He served in the South African War, and was present at the operations in the Orange Free State in 1900 (severely wounded); operations in the Orange River Colony, including action at Wittebergen; operations in Cape Colony and the Transvaal; later operations in the Orange River Colony, and on the Zululand Frontier of Natal in 1901. He was mentioned in Despatches [London Gazette, 10 Sept. 1901]: received the Queen's Medal with four clasps, the King's Medal with two clasps, and was created a Companion of the Distinguished Service Order [London Gazette, 27 Sept. 1901]: "Matthew Perceval Buckle, Capt., Royal West Kent Regt. In recognition of services during the operations in South Africa." In 1903 he passed out of the Staff College with distinction, and from Jan. 1904, to Jan. 1906, he was Staff Captain (Mobilization) at Headquarters, War Office, and from Jan. 1906, to Jan. 1908, Brigade Major at Aldershot. Major Buckle was a qualified Second Class Interpreter in French, and was appointed in March, 1909, Professor at the Staff College, India, with the temporary rank of Lieut.-Colonel. He later became G.S.O., 2nd Grade, Staff College, Quetta, from July, 1909. He became Major in the Army, March, 1907. On the outbreak of the European War, Major Buckle was on the point of departure for Albania, to take up a Staff appointment at Scutari, for which he had been specially chosen. The orders were, however, cancelled, and he rejoined his regiment, as Second-in-Command, at Richmond Barracks, Dublin, whence he sailed for France on the 13th Aug. 1914. Major Buckle was present at the Retreat from Mons and the Battles of the Marne and the Aisne. He was twice mentioned in Despatches (8 Oct. 1914, and 14 Jan. 1915). He was killed in action near Neuve Chapelle on the 27th Oct. 1914, while in command of his battalion. At this time the Royal West Kents held their position for eight days without losing a trench. The "Queen's Own Gazette" published the following appreciation written by Brigadier-General Grove: "The regiment has sustained a grievous loss in the death of Major Buckle. He was quite the finest type of officer that can be met. Thoroughly knowing his duty, and very strict in the performance of it, he was at the same time always gentle and courteous. He was most conscientious, and never spared himself as long as there was work to be done. It may well be said of him that he was *sans peur et sans reproche*." Major Buckle's favourite recreations were cricket, shooting, polo and racquets. He was a member of the Army and Navy Club and a Freemason, belonging to the following lodges: Old Wykehamists (London), Shakespeare (Spilsby), and the Baluchistan (Quetta). In 1909, he married Marjorie Ethel, elder daughter of Colonel C. A. Swan, C.M.G., and they had two children: Margaret Elizabeth and Peter Claude Matthew (born in May, 1914).

CHRISTIAN, GERARD, Capt., was born 2 June, 1867, at Valetta, Malta, son of Alfred Christian, Esq., C.M.G., and Mrs. Alfred Christian (*née* Miss Hall, of Dunglass). He was educated at Cheltenham College, and joined the Yorkshire Regt. as Second Lieutenant 5 Feb. 1887; became Lieutenant 2 May, 1890; was Adjutant, Yorkshire Regt., 16 Jan. 1897, to 15 Jan. 1901; was promoted to Captain 17 Aug. 1898. He served in the South African War, 1899–1902, as Captain and Adjutant, 1st Battn. He was present at the Relief of Kimberley; took part in the operations in the Orange Free State, Feb. and March, 1900, including operations at Paardeberg; actions at Poplar Grove and Dreifontein; operations in the Transvaal, east of Pretoria, including action at Belfast; operations in Cape Colony, south of Orange River, including action at Colesberg. Capt. Christian was Staff Officer of the Town Guards in the Cape Peninsula. He took part in the operations in the Transvaal from 30 Nov. 1900, to 21 May, 1902. He was mentioned in Despatches [London Gazette, 10 Sept. 1901]; received the Queen's Medal with four clasps, the King's Medal with two clasps, and was created a Companion of the Distinguished Service Order [London Gazette, 27 Sept. 1901]: "Gerard Christian, Capt., Yorkshire Regt. In recognition of services during the operations in South Africa." The Insignia were presented by the King 24 Oct. 1902. He became Major 21 Jan. 1906, and was Lieut.-Colonel, Yorkshire Regt., 28 March, 1911, to 13 April, 1913. He became Colonel 15 June, 1914, and Temporary Brigadier-General 14 April, 1915; commanded the 4th Brigade in India during the Mohmand operations Aug. to Dec. 1915. He was mentioned in Despatches. Brigadier-General G. Christian commanded the 36th Brigade, Indian Expeditionary Force "D," in Mesopotamia, Dec. 1915, to 1 Oct. 1916, and was mentioned in Despatches. He was Inspector of Infantry, H.Q., India, 28 Dec. 1916, to 2 Oct. 1918; was created a C.B. (Military), 1916, and received the Serbian Order of the White Eagle with Swords. He became Inspector of Infantry in India. Lieut.-Colonel Christian married, 16 Sept. 1913, in London, S.W., Evelyn Hilliard, daughter of E. B. Hilliard, Esq., of Writtle, Essex.

Gerard Christian.

PONSONBY, JOHN, Capt., was born 25 March, 1866, eldest son of the late General The Right Hon. Sir Henry Ponsonby. He was gazetted to the Royal Irish Rifles 16 Nov. 1887, and to the Coldstream Guards 15 Aug. 1888, becoming Lieutenant 29 June, 1891. He was A.D.C. to the Governor and Commander-in-Chief, South Africa, 10 Aug. 1891, to 30 Jan. 1895; served in operations in Matabeleland (Medal); was promoted to Captain 7 Sept. 1898, and in that year served in Uganda (Medal), and again in 1899, during the operations against Kabarega (clasp). Capt. Ponsonby served in the South African War, 1899–1902, on special service with the Rhodesian Field Force, 19 Feb. 1900, to 7 July, 1901. He was Adjutant, 5th New Zealand Regt., 8 June, 1900, to 1 Jan. 1901; afterwards in command 1 Jan. to 18 Jan. 1901. From Feb. to May, 1900, he was employed with Mounted Infantry, and he took part in operations in the Transvaal, west of Pretoria, from July to 29 Nov. 1900; operations in the Transvaal, Feb. to June, 1901; operations in Cape Colony, Feb. to 31 May, 1902. He was mentioned in Despatches [London Gazette, 10 Sept. 1901]; received the Queen's Medal with four clasps, the King's Medal with two clasps, and was created a Companion of the Distinguished Service Order [London Gazette, 27 Sept. 1901]: "John Ponsonby, Capt., Coldstream Guards. In recognition of services during the operations in South Africa." The Insignia were presented by the King 27 Oct. 1901. He was promoted to Major 23 Jan. 1904, and commanded the Guards' Depôt 1 March, 1905, to 28 Feb. 1907. He became Lieut.-Colonel 28 Oct. 1913. Lieut.-Colonel Ponsonby served in the European War, 1914–18; commanded the 2nd Guards Brigade, B.E.F., 26 Aug. 1915, to 19 Nov. 1916; was given the Brevet of Colonel 1 Jan. 1916; commanded the Special Reserve Infantry Brigade 28 Nov. 1916, to 7 March, 1917; commanded the 21st Infantry Brigade, B.E.F., 8 March to 20 March, 1917; became Colonel 20 March, 1917; commanded the 2nd Guards Brigade, British Armies in France, 21 March to 21 Aug. 1917; commanded the 40th Division, British Armies in France, 22 Aug. 1917, to 3 July, 1918; subsequently commanded the 5th Division, British Armies in France, 4 July, 1918, to 1 April, 1919; was promoted to Major-General 1 Jan. 1919. He was mentioned in Despatches; created a C.M.G. in 1915, a C.B. in 1918, and was given the Brevet of Colonel.

SAUNDERS, GEORGE FREDERICK CULLEN, Capt., was born 16 April, 1869, son of the late Major G. N. Saunders, Bengal Staff Corps. He was gazetted to the Bedfordshire Regt. 9 Nov. 1889, becoming Lieutenant 29 March, 1892. He served in the Isazai Expedition, 1892; in the Chitral Expedition, 1895, with the Relief Force (Medal with clasp); was promoted to Captain 12 Oct. 1898. Capt. Saunders served in the South African War, 1899–1902, taking part in operations in the Orange Free State, Feb. to May, 1900; operations in the Orange River Colony, May to 29 Nov. 1900, including action at Wittebergen (1 to 29 July); operations in Cape Colony, south of Orange River, 1899–1900, including action at Colesberg (1 Jan. to 12 Feb.); operations in the Transvaal, April to May, 1902; operations in Orange River Colony 30 Nov. 1900, to May, 1902. He was mentioned in Despatches [London Gazette, 10 Sept. 1901]; received the Queen's Medal with three clasps, the King's Medal with two clasps, and was created a Companion of the Distinguished Service Order [London Gazette, 27 Sept. 1901]: "George Frederick Cullen Saunders, Capt., Bedfordshire Regt. In recognition of services during the operations in South Africa." The Insignia, Warrant and Statutes were sent to the G.O.C., Cape Colony District, 15 Nov. 1902, and the Insignia were presented by Colonel Pilcher at Naauwpoort 22 Feb. 1903. He was Adjutant, Militia, from 4 Jan. 1908; became Major 1 Sept. 1913, and retired 18 March, 1914. Major Saunders married, in 1907, Mabel Elizabeth Wilgress (who died in 1919), daughter of the late T. Wilgress Mills, of Eltham, Kent.

CORRY, NOEL ARMAR LOWRY, Capt., a great-grandson of the 2nd Earl Belmore, was born 25 Dec. 1867. He was educated at Harrow, Cheltenham and Sandhurst, and entered the Grenadier Guards 15 Feb. 1888, becoming Lieutenant 11 May, 1892, and Captain 23 Nov. 1898. He served in the South African War, 1899–1901, taking part in the advance on Kimberley, including the actions at Belmont, Enslin, Modder River and Magersfontein; operations in the Orange Free State, Feb. to May, 1900, including actions at Poplar Grove, Dreifontein, Vet River (5 and 6 May) and Zand River; operations in the Transvaal in May and June, 1900, including actions near Johannesburg, Pretoria and Diamond Hill (11 and 12 June); operations in the Transvaal, east of Pretoria, July to 29 Nov. 1900, including actions at Belfast (26 and 27 Aug.); operations in Cape Colony, Dec. 1900, to July, 1901. He was Commandant at Achtertang; was mentioned in Despatches [London Gazette, 10 Sept. 1901]; received the Queen's Medal with seven clasps, and was created a Companion of the Distinguished Service Order [London Gazette, 27 Sept. 1901]: "Noel Armar Lowry Corry, Capt., Grenadier Guards. In recognition of services during the operations in South Africa." The Insignia were presented by the King 29 Oct. 1901. He was promoted to Major 29 Jan. 1904; to Lieut.-Colonel 28 Oct. 1910; to Colonel 15 June, 1914, commanding the 2nd Battn. Grenadier Guards. He commanded the London Reserve Brigade, Central Force, Home Defence, 24 Oct. 1914, to 9 Jan. 1916. Colonel Lowry Corry married (1st), Rosalind Gertrude (who died in 1903), daughter of Lieut.-Colonel Anstruther, of Hindlesham Hall, Ipswich, and they had one daughter. He married (2ndly), in 1904, the Hon. Clare O'Brien, daughter of the 14th Baron Inchiquin, and they have one daughter.

DUNCAN, JOHN, Capt., was born 24 Feb. 1872. He was gazetted to the Royal Scots Fusiliers 4 March, 1891; became Lieutenant 8 April, 1893; was A.D.C. to Major-General, India, 7 Oct. 1896, to 5 Sept. 1898. He served on the North-West Frontier of India, 1897–98 (Malakand), as Regimental Transport Officer, 1st Brigade (7 Aug. to Oct. 1897); action at Landakai; expedition into the Bajaur and Mohmand country; in the Buner Expedition, as Regimental Transport Officer, in the attack and capture of the Tanga Pass (Medal with clasp). He was promoted to Captain 22 Dec. 1898. Capt. Duncan served in the South African War, 1899 to 1900, taking part in the Relief of Ladysmith, including the operations of 17 to 24 Jan. 1900; operations of 5 to 7 Feb. 1900, and action at Vaal Kranz; operations on Tugela Heights (14 to 27 Feb. 1900), and action at Pieter's Hill; operations in the Transvaal in May and June, 1900; operations in Natal, March and April, 1900; operations in the Transvaal, west of Pretoria, July to 29 Nov. 1900, including actions at Frederickstad (17 to 25 Oct.); operations in Cape Colony, north of Orange River, including action at Ruidam. He was mentioned in Despatches [London Gazette, 10 Sept. 1901]; received the Queen's Medal with five clasps, and was created a Companion of the Distinguished Service Order [London Gazette, 27 Sept. 1901]: "John Duncan, Capt., Royal Scots Fusiliers. In recognition of services during the operations in South Africa." The Insignia were presented by the King 29 Oct. 1901. He passed the Staff College; was Brigade Major, Infantry Brigade, Malta, 31 Jan. 1902, to 21 Dec. 1903; Staff Captain, H.Q. of Army, 1 April, 1904, to 30 June, 1907; G.S.O.2, H.Q. of Army, 1 July, 1907, to 31 May, 1908; became Major 25 Aug. 1910; was G.S.O.2, Wessex Division, Southern Command, 1 Dec. 1910, to 7 May, 1914. Major Duncan served in the European War as G.S.O.2, 11th Division, New Armies; Mediterranean Expeditionary Force 25 Aug. 1914, to 28 Sept. 1915; was promoted to Lieut.-Colonel 1 July, 1915; was G.S.O.1, to a division, Mediterranean Expeditionary Force; Australian Forces, 4th Australian Division, Egyptian Expeditionary Force, 6 Feb. to 21 April, 1916; commanded the 78th Infantry Brigade, Egyptian Expeditionary Force, Salonika Expeditionary Force, 26 April, 1916, to 16 June, 1917; was given the Brevet of Colonel 1 Jan. 1917; commanded the 22nd Division, British Salonika Force, 17 June, 1917, to 31 March, 1919; Major-General, General Staff, British Salonika Force; British Army of the Black Sea 1 April, 1919; G.S.O., 1st Grade, and was promoted to Major-General 1 April, 1919. He was created a C.M.G. in 1916, and a C.B. in 1918. Major-General J. Duncan married (1st), in 1896, Helen (who died in 1903), daughter of the late William Boyd Buckle, B.C.S., and they had one daughter. He married (2ndly), in 1906, Vivien, daughter of Emile R. Merton, and they have one daughter.

WOOD, EVELYN FITZGERALD MICHELL, Capt., was born 16 Nov. 1869, eldest son of Field-Marshal Sir Evelyn Wood and the Hon. Mary Paulina Southwell (who died in 1891), sister of the 4th Viscount Southwell. He was commissioned in the Devonshire Regt. 9 Nov. 1889; Major, 14 March, 1906; retired, 1st Dragoons, 4 April, 1914; Hon. Colonel, 1 Jan. 1918; served in Ashanti, 1895 (Star); South Africa, 1899–1901, on special service, including Belmont, Graspan, Modder River, Magersfontein (Medal and three clasps; created a Companion of the Distinguished Service Order [London Gazette, 27 Sept. 1901]: "Evelyn Fitzgerald Michell Wood, Capt., Devonshire Regt. In recognition of services during the operations in South Africa); and as A.M.S. and A.D.C. to Sir F. Forestier-Walker; D.A.A.G., Dublin District Staff; London Heavy Brigade, late the Royal Dragoons; G.S.O.2, 1st Division, 1909–14. He served in the European War, 1914–18 (Despatches; O.B.E.). He is Secretary of the City of London Territorial Force Association. He married Lilian (who died in 1910), daughter of the late C. E. Hutton, and they had three daughters. Col. Wood married (2ndly) Alla, widow of Hatherly Wood, and they have two sons.

BRINTON, JOHN CHAYTOR, Capt., was born 5 April, 1867. He was gazetted to the 2nd Life Guards 28 Jan. 1891; became Lieutenant 13 April, 1892, serving in the Nile Expedition of 1898, when he was present at the Battle of Khartum (severely wounded); mentioned in Despatches [London Gazette, 30 Sept. 1898]; received the Egyptian Medal with clasp; became Captain 12 Jan. 1899. He was on Special Service in South Africa 16 Nov. 1899, to 16 Sept. 1900; on Remount Duty, and on the Staff of Lieut.-General Sir J. D. P. French. He was present at the Relief of Kimberley; operations in the Orange Free State, Feb. to May, 1900, including operations at Paardeberg and action at Dreifontein; operations in the Transvaal in May and June, 1900, including actions near Johannesburg and Diamond Hill (11 and 12 June). He was mentioned in Despatches [London Gazette, 10 Sept. 1901]; received the Queen's Medal with five clasps, and was created a Companion of the Distinguished Service Order [London Gazette, 27 Sept. 1901]: "John Chaytor Brinton, Capt., 2nd Life Guards. In recognition of services during the operations in South Africa." The Insignia were presented by the King 27 Oct. 1901. He was A.D.C. (extra) to the Viceroy of Ireland 1 July, 1901, to 10 Aug. 1902; was created an M.V.O., 1905; promoted to Major 20 Oct. 1906, and retired 18 Jan. 1911. He rejoined in 1914, and served in the European War, 1914–16; was mentioned in Despatches twice; was given the Brevet of Lieut.-Colonel 1 Jan. 1919, and was made a Chevalier of the Legion of Honour. Lieut.-Colonel Brinton is Gentleman Usher-in-Ordinary to His Majesty. He married, in 1913, Evelyn Elizabeth, eldest daughter of Sir Charles Forbes, 4th Bart., of Newe, and widow of William D. James, of West Dean, Sussex

MACKENZIE, EDWARD LESLIE, Capt., was born 6 May, 1870, son of the late Major C. G. Mackenzie, 28th Regt. He was gazetted to the Royal Sussex Regt. 29 Oct. 1890, becoming Lieutenant 10 Feb. 1892, and Captain 4 Feb. 1899. Capt. Mackenzie served in the South African War, 1900–2, taking part in operations in Orange River Colony, Jan. to 31 May, 1902. He was severely wounded; was mentioned in Despatches [London Gazette, 10 Sept. 1901]; received the Queen's Medal with four clasps, the King's Medal with two clasps, and was created a Companion of the Distinguished Service Order [London Gazette, 27 Sept. 1901]: "Edward Leslie Mackenzie, Capt., Royal Sussex Regt. In recognition of services during the operations in South Africa." The Insignia were presented to him by the King 29 Oct. 1901. He was employed with the West African Frontier Force 8 Sept. 1906, to 14 July, 1912. Major Mackenzie served in the European War from 1914, and became Lieut.-Colonel 12 Aug. 1915, commanding the 1st Battn. Royal Sussex Regt. He was created a C.I.E. in 1919.

BOWEN, CHARLES OTWAY COLE, Capt., was born 30 Aug. 1867. He entered the Royal Engineers 17 Feb. 1888, becoming Lieutenant 17 Feb. 1891, and Captain 17 Feb. 1899. Capt. Bowen served in the South African War, 1899–1902, being present at the Relief of Kimberley; at the operations in the Orange Free State, including operations at Paardeberg and action at Dreifontein; operations in the Transvaal, including actions near Johannesburg and Diamond Hill; operations in the Transvaal, east of Pretoria, including action at Belfast; operations in Cape Colony, south of Orange River, including action at Colesberg; operations in the Transvaal 30 Nov. 1900, to 31 May, 1902. He was mentioned in Despatches [London Gazette, 4 May, 1900, and 10 Sept. 1901]; received the Queen's Medal with six clasps, the King's Medal with two clasps, and was created a Companion of the Distinguished Service Order [London Gazette, 27 Sept. 1901]: "Charles Otway Cole Bowen, Capt., Royal Engineers. In recognition of services during the operations in South Africa." The Insignia were sent to the Commander-in-Chief in South Africa, and presented by the G.O.C., Transvaal and Orange Free State, 2 Sept. 1902. He was promoted to Major 1 Oct. 1906, and died at King's Hill, near Harrismith, Orange River Colony, 18 March, 1910. An obituary notice of Major Bowen appeared in the "Times" of 24 March, 1910.

SWINTON, ERNEST DUNLOP, Capt., was born 21 Oct. 1868. He was educated at Rugby and Cheltenham, and was gazetted to the Royal Engineers 17 Feb. 1888, becoming Lieutenant 17 Feb. 1891. He was Assistant Inspector, School of Military Engineering, 3 Nov. 1896, to 10 Nov. 1899; became Captain 17 Feb. 1899. Capt. Swinton served in the South African War, 1899–1902, as Adjutant, 1st Battn. Railway Pioneer Regt. (from 22 Dec. 1899); afterwards in command of the 1st Battn. Railway Pioneer Regt. from 15 Nov. 1900; operations in the Orange Free State, April to May, 1900; operations in Orange River Colony, May to Sept. 1900; operations in the Transvaal, Sept. to 29 Nov. 1900; operations in Cape Colony, Nov. 1899, to April, 1900; operations in the Transvaal 30 Nov. 1900, to 31 May, 1902; operations in Orange River Colony, May, 1902. He was mentioned in Despatches [London Gazette, 10 Sept. 1901]; received the Queen's Medal with three clasps, the King's Medal with two clasps, and was created a Companion of the Distinguished Service Order [London Gazette, 27 Sept. 1901]: "Ernest Dunlop Swinton, Capt., Royal Engineers. In recognition of services during the operations in South Africa." He was invested with the Insignia by the King 18 Dec. 1902. He was promoted to Major 31 Dec. 1906; was Chief Instructor, R.M.A., 1 Feb. 1907, to 8 Sept. 1910; Secretary, Historical Section, Committee of Imperial Defence, 30 Sept. 1910, to 30 Sept. 1913; Assistant Secretary, Committee of Imperial Defence, 1 Oct. 1913, to 4 Aug. 1914. He served in the European War from 1914, as Deputy Director of Railway Transport, British Expeditionary Force, 5 Aug. to 8 Sept. 1914; as G.S.O.2, G.H.Q., B.E.F., 9 Sept. 1914, to 18 July, 1915; was promoted to Lieut.-Colonel 6 May, 1915; was G.S.O.1, whilst employed as Assistant Secretary, Committee of Imperial Defence, 19 July, 1915, to 18 March, 1916; Commander, Heavy Section, Machine Gun Corps, 19 March to 8 Nov. 1916. He was given the Brevet of Colonel 1 Jan. 1917; was employed under the Ministry of Munitions 14 Aug. to 17 Nov. 1918; Temporary Major-General 3 Jan. 1918; employed under the Ministry of Labour 18 Nov. 1918; Controller of Inspection Department of Civil Aviation, For his services in the European War he was mentioned three times in Despatches; was created a C.B. in 1917; given the Brevet of Colonel, and made a Chevalier of the Legion of Honour. He had to do with the evolution of the Tank. He journeyed through the United States, speaking about the War, in 1918. Under the pseudonym, "Ole-Luk-Oie," he wrote the famous "Green Curve," in 1909. He wrote "The Defence of Duffer's Drift," in 1904, under the pseudonym of "Backright-Forethought." In 1915 he wrote "The Great Tab Dope," and in 1916, "A Year Ago." He married, in 1897, Grace Louisa, second daughter of Sir Edward G. Clayton, and they have two sons and one daughter.

COOPER-KING, GEORGE COURTENAY, Capt., was born 3 Aug. 1869, eldest son of the late Lieut.-Colonel Cooper-King, R.M.A., F.R.G.S. He entered the Manchester Regt. as Second Lieutenant, from the Militia, 12 March, 1892; became Lieutenant 28 July, 1895, and Captain 18 March, 1899. He served with the 2nd Battn. Manchester Regt. in South Africa, 1900–2, performing the duties of Railway Staff Officer, 25 Feb. to 31 May, 1902; operations in the Orange Free State, April, 1900; operations in the Transvaal, east of Pretoria, Aug. to Sept. and Nov. 1900; operations in Orange River Colony, May to 29 Nov. 1900, including actions at Biddulphsberg and Wittebergen; operations in Cape Colony, south of Orange River, April 1900; operations in the Transvaal, July, 1901; operations in Orange River Colony 30 Nov. 1900, to 31 May, 1902. He was mentioned in Despatches [London Gazette, 10 Sept. 1901]; received the Queen's Medal with three clasps, the King's Medal with two clasps, and was created a Companion of the Distinguished Service Order [London Gazette, 27 Sept. 1901]: "George Courtenay Cooper-King, Capt., Manchester Regt. In recognition of services during the operations in South Africa." He was invested by the King 24 Oct. 1902. Capt. Cooper-King was unmarried. He was killed on the railway 27 Jan. 1909, and an obituary notice of him appeared in the "Times" of 29 Jan. 1909.

NEWBIGGING, WILLIAM PATRICK ERIC, Capt., was born 31 May, 1871, son of Lieut.-Colonel Newbigging, late Manchester Regt., of 124, Lexham Gardens, W. He was gazetted to the Manchester Regt. 23 March, 1892; became Lieutenant 28 July, 1895, and was Adjutant, Manchester Regt., 2 Nov. 1898, to 1 Nov. 1902, becoming Captain 18 March, 1899. He served in the South African War, 1899–1902, as Adjutant, 1st Battn. Manchester Regt.; was present at the operations in Natal, 1899, including action at Elandslaagte (severely wounded). He was employed with Mounted Infantry, and was present at the Relief of Ladysmith, including operations on Tugela Heights (14 to 27 Feb. 1900), and action at Pieter's Hill; operations in Natal, March to June, 1900; operations in the Transvaal, 1902. He was mentioned in Despatches [London Gazette, 10 Sept. 1901, and 29 July, 1902]; received the Queen's Medal with five clasps, the King's Medal with two clasps, and was created a Companion of the Distinguished Service Order [London Gazette, 27 Sept. 1901]: "William Patrick Eric Newbigging, Capt., Manchester Regt. In recognition of services during the operations in South Africa." He was invested by the King 18 Dec. 1902. Capt. Newbigging was Adjutant, Volunteers, 15 Dec. 1902, to 31 July, 1908; was promoted to Major 22 April, 1911; was Instructor, School of Signalling, 3 July, 1912, to 4 Aug. 1914. He served in the European War, 1914–18, as Deputy Director of Army Signalling, B.E.F., British Armies in France, 6 Feb. 1916, to 15 May, 1918; as Chief Signalling Officer, British Armies in France, 16 May, 1918, to 8 April, 1919; as Signalling Officer-in-Chief, British Army of the Rhine, 9 April, 1919. He was six times mentioned in Despatches, and was given the Brevets of Lieut.-Colonel (18 Feb. 1915) and Colonel (1 Jan. 1918); was created a C.M.G. in 1917, and a C.B. in 1918, and received the 1914 Star.

MACDONALD, KENNETH, Capt., was born 14 Aug. 1873, son of Lieut.-Colonel C. E. Macdonald, late R.M.L.I., and entered the Army in 1891; served in the Sudan Campaign, 1898 (Medal and Egyptian Medal); on the West Coast of Africa, 1898–99 (Medal with clasp); became Captain, 1899. Capt. Macdonald served in the South African War, 1899–1902; was mentioned in Despatches, and created a Companion of the Distinguished Service Order [London Gazette, 27 Sept. 1901]: "Kenneth Macdonald, Capt., Army Service Corps. In recognition of services during the operations in South Africa."

COATES, REGINALD CARLYON, Capt., was born 13 Oct. 1869, son of the Rev. G. A. A. Coates, Earls Croome, Worcester. He entered the R.A. 15 Feb. 1889, becoming Lieutenant 15 Feb. 1892, and Captain 25 May, 1899. He served in the South African War, 1899–1902, and was present at the Relief of Ladysmith, including operations of 17 to 24 Jan. 1900, and action at Spion Kop; operations of 5 to 7 Feb. 1900, and action at Vaal Kranz; operations on Tugela Heights (14 to 27 Feb. 1900), and action at Pieter's Hill; operations in Natal (March to June, 1900), including action at Laing's Nek (6 to 9 June); operations in the Transvaal, east of Pretoria, 1 July to 29 Nov. 1900, including actions at Belfast (26 and 27 Aug.) and Lydenburg (5 to 8 Sept.); operations in the Transvaal and Orange River Colony 30 Nov. 1900, to 31 May, 1902. He was mentioned in Despatches [London Gazette, 10 Sept. 1901]; received the Queen's Medal with six clasps, the King's Medal with two clasps, and was created a Companion of the Distinguished Service Order [London Gazette, 27 Sept. 1901]: "Reginald Carlyon Coates, Capt., Royal Horse and Royal Field Artillery. In recognition of services during the operations in South Africa." He was promoted to Major 1 Nov. 1904. Major Coates served in the European War from 1914, and was wounded; he became Lieut.-Colonel 30 Oct. 1914; was Temporary Brigadier-General, R.A., 61st Division, Central Force, Home Defence, British Armies in France, 19 April, 1916, to 21 April, 1917. Lieut.-Colonel R. C. Coates married, in 1903, Alice Maud, daughter of the late General Sir Henry Daly.

DAWNAY, THE HON. JOHN, Capt., was born in London 23 May, 1872, eldest son and heir of the 8th Viscount Downe and Viscountess Downe. He was educated at Eton, and was gazetted to the 10th Hussars 5 Dec. 1891; was Adjutant, 10th Hussars, 30 May, 1898, to 1901; became Captain 14 June, 1899. Capt. the Hon. J. Dawnay served in the South African War, 1900–1, as Adjutant, 10th Hussars, to 13 May, 1901; Acting Brigade Major 14 May to July, 1901. He was present at the Relief of Kimberley; operations in the Orange Free State, Feb. to May, 1900, including operations at Paardeberg (17 to 26 Feb.); actions at Poplar Grove, Dreifontein, Vet River (5 and 6 May) and Zand River; operations in the Transvaal in May and June, 1900, including actions near Johannesburg, Pretoria and Diamond Hill (11 and 12 June); operations in the Transvaal, west of Pretoria, Aug. to 29 Nov. 1900; operations in Orange River Colony, June to Aug. 1900, including actions at Wittebergen (1 to 17 July); operations in Cape Colony, south of Orange River, 1899–1900, including actions at Colesberg (1 Jan. to 5 Feb.); operations in the Transvaal 30 Nov. 1900, to July, 1901; operations in Cape Colony, July to Sept. 1901. He was mentioned in Despatches [London Gazette, 10 Sept. 1901]; received the Queen's Medal with seven clasps, and was created a Companion of the Distinguished Service Order [London Gazette, 27 Sept. 1901]: "The Honourable John Dawnay, Capt., 10th Hussars. In recognition of services during the operations in South Africa." The Insignia were presented to him by the King 24 Oct. 1901. He retired from the 10th Hussars 3 Aug. 1904, subsequently becoming Major of the King's Own Norfolk Imperial Yeomanry. When the European War broke out, Major Dawnay went to France as A.D.C., in 1915, to Sir John French, becoming Lord French's A.D.C. when the latter was appointed Commander-in-Chief in England in 1916, and later Military Secretary to Lord French in Ireland, with the temporary rank of Lieut.-Colonel. He was created a C.M.G. in 1915, and made a Chevalier of the Legion of Honour and given the Brevet of Lieut.-Colonel. He is Deputy Lieutenant and Justice of the Peace, C.C., North Riding of Yorkshire, also Justice of the Peace, Northants. He married, 24 July, 1902, at Hillington, Norfolk, Dorothy, only child of the late Sir W. ffolkes, 3rd Baronet, and they have two sons, Richard and George William ffolkes, and one daughter, Ruth Mary.

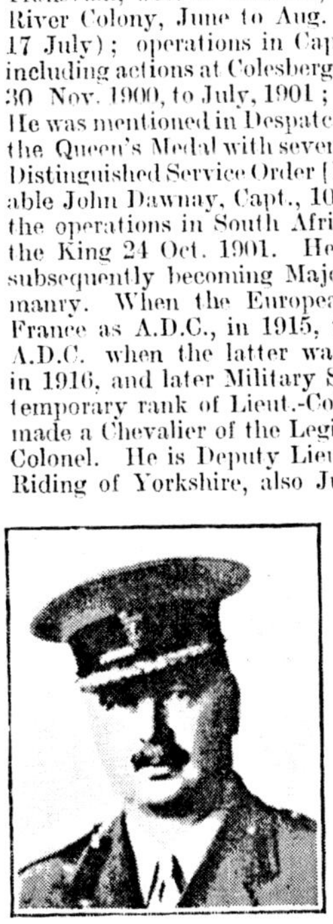

Richard Rolls Gubbins.

GUBBINS, RICHARD ROLLS, Capt., was born 14 Dec. 1868, eldest son of the late Rev. Richard Shard Gubbins, Rector of Upham, Hants, and of Ellen Rolls, sister of the 1st Baron Llangattock. He was gazetted to the Shropshire Light Infantry 1 March, 1890, becoming Lieutenant 21 Dec. 1891, and Captain 24 June, 1899. He served in the South African War, 1899–1902, and was present at operations in the Orange Free State, Feb. to May, 1900, including operations at Paardeberg, 17 to 26 Feb. (slightly wounded); actions at Houtnek (Thoba Mountain), Vet River (5 and 6 May) and Zand River; operations in the Transvaal in May and June, 1900, including actions near Johannesburg and Pretoria; operations in the Transvaal, east of Pretoria, July to 29 Nov. 1900; operations in the Transvaal, west of Pretoria, July to 29 Nov. 1900, including actions at Elands River (4 to 16 Aug.); operations in Orange River Colony, May to 29 Nov. 1900, including action at Rhenoster River; operations in Cape Colony, south of Orange River, 1899–1900. He served as Adjutant, 2nd Battn. Shropshire Light Infantry, 11 to 31 May, 1902; operations in the Transvaal 30 Nov. 1900, to Aug. 1901, and Jan to 31 May, 1902. He was mentioned in Despatches [London Gazette, 10 Sept. 1901]; received the Queen's Medal with three clasps, the King's Medal with two clasps, and was created a Companion of the Distinguished Service Order [London Gazette, 27 Sept. 1901]: "Richard Rolls Gubbins, Capt., Shropshire Light Infantry. In recognition of services during the operations in South Africa." The Insignia were presented by the King 29 Oct. 1901. Capt. Gubbins was Adjutant, Shropshire Light Infantry, 1 April, 1902, to 31 March, 1905, and Adjutant, Militia, 28 Sept. 1905, to 31 March, 1908, and was promoted to Major 17 June, 1908. He retired 6 March, 1912, and entered the Reserve of Officers. Major Gubbins served in the European War from 1914 as Temporary Lieut.-Colonel and Temporary Colonel, and was mentioned in Despatches. A newspaper report says: "Official news has been received at Old Hall, Rockliffe, that Colonel R. R. Gubbins, D.S.O., is missing. Colonel Gubbins, who held a Staff appointment abroad, was recently returning to duty, and the vessel on which he was travelling was sunk. One of the officers on board was not saved, and as Colonel Gubbins is reported missing there is grave reason to fear that he is the officer who has lost his life. Colonel Gubbins, who is 49 years of age, is the eldest son of the late Rev. Richard Shard Gubbins, Rector of Upham, Hampshire, and his mother was the sister of the 1st Baron Llangattock. In 1902, he married Agnes Edith, eldest daughter of the late Mr. G. W. Mounsey-Heysham, of Castletown, and there are two sons. Since his retirement from the Army he has lived at the Old Hall, Rockliffe. He was a very capable man of business, and took an active part in the management of the Castletown estates. His military career was spent in the Shropshire Light Infantry, in which he received his commission in 1890, the late Capt. R. C. Mounsey-Heysham being a brother officer. He served in the Boer War, in which he gained the D.S.O., and held the Queen's Medal with three clasps, and the King's Medal with two clasps. He retired from the Army with the rank of Major in 1912, and was placed in the Reserve of Officers. When the present war broke out he rejoined the Army, and was for a time employed on transport duty at Newcastle, subsequently receiving an appointment on the Staff. He was appointed a magistrate for Cumberland in 1913." The report of Colonel Gubbins's death proved to be true. It occurred on 24 Jan. 1918.

LOWTHER, HENRY CECIL, Capt., was born 27 Jan. 1869, youngest son of the late Hon. William Lowther. He entered the Scots Guards 20 Dec. 1888; became Lieutenant 13 April, 1892; was Adjutant, Scots Guards, 17 Feb. 1896, to 19 July, 1901, and Captain 24 June, 1899. He served in the South African War, 1899–1902, as Adjutant, 1st Battn. Scots Guards (Dec. 1900, to July, 1901), and afterwards on the Staff. He was present in the advance on Kimberley, including actions at Belmont, Enslin, Modder River and Magersfontein; operations in the Orange Free State, Feb. to May, 1900, including actions at Poplar Grove, Dreifontein, Vet River (5 and 6 May) and Zand River; operations in the Transvaal in May and June, 1900, including actions near Johannesburg, Pretoria and Diamond Hill (11 and 12 June); operations in the Transvaal, east of Pretoria, July to 29 Nov. 1900, including action of Belfast (26 and 27 Aug.); operations in the Transvaal, Dec. 1900, to March, 1902; operations in Orange River Colony, March to May, 1902; operations in Cape Colony in Dec. 1900. He was mentioned in Despatches [London Gazette, 10 Sept. 1901, and 29 July, 1902]; was placed on the list of officers considered qualified for Staff employment in consequence of service on the Staff in the Field; received the Queen's Medal with six clasps, the King's Medal with two clasps, and was created a Companion of the Distinguished Service Order [London Gazette, 27 Sept. 1901]: "Henry Cecil Lowther, Capt., Scots Guards. In recognition of services during the operations in South Africa." He was invested by the King 24 Oct. 1902. Capt. Lowther was Brigade Major, 1st Brigade, 1st Army Corps, 3 Dec. 1902, to 8 Oct. 1903; Staff Captain (Intelligence), H.Q. of Army, 9 Oct. 1903, to 29 Sept. 1905; was promoted to Major 12 March, 1904; was Military Attaché, Paris, Madrid and Lisbon 30 Sept. 1905, to 30 Sept. 1909; was created a C.M.G. in 1911; was Military Secretary to H.R.H. the Governor-General, Canada, 6 Oct. 1911, to 8 Oct. 1913; was created a C.V.O. in 1913; became Lieut.-Colonel 9 Oct. 1913. He served in the European War from 1914, in command of the 1st Scots Guards, and then of the 1st Guards Brigade, B.E.F., 13 Sept. 1914, to 22 Aug. 1915; as Military Secretary, B.E.F., 6 Sept. to 18 Dec. 1915; as Brigadier-General, General Staff, Home Forces, 19 Dec. 1915, to 15 March, 1919. He became Colonel 9 Oct. 1917, and was Temporary Major-General from 4 Oct. 1917, to 15 March, 1919. He was three times mentioned in Despatches; wounded at Troyon; created a C.B. in 1915, and a K.C.M.G. in 1918; was given the Brevet of Colonel 18 Feb. 1915. Sir Henry Lowther has the Swedish Order of the Svaerd; is Commander of the Legion of Honour, and has the Spanish Order of Military Merit. He was M.P. (Unionist), Northern Division of Westmorland, 1915–18. He wrote "From Pillar to Post."

Henry Cecil Lowther.

FIELDEN, HAROLD, Capt., was born 4 April, 1868, son of the late Joshua Fielden, of Nutfield Priory, Redhill. He joined the 7th Hussars 28 June, 1890, becoming Lieutenant 26 June, 1893, and Captain 26 June, 1899. Capt. Fielden served in the South African War, 1899 to 1901, employed with the 1st Regt. Damant's Horse, and afterwards with the Prince of Wales's Light Horse. He was mentioned in Despatches [London Gazette, 10 Sept. 1901]; received the Queen's Medal with five clasps, and was created a Companion of the Distinguished Service Order [London Gazette, 27 Sept. 1901]: "Harold Fielden, Capt., 7th Hussars. In recognition of services during the operations in South Africa." The Insignia were presented to him by the King 29 Oct. 1901. Capt. Fielden retired 4 Feb. 1904.

EARLE, MAXWELL, Capt., was born 6 April, 1871, son of Capt. Charles William Earle and Maria Theresa Villiers. He was gazetted to the Grenadier Guards 4 March, 1891; served in the Matabele War, 1893 (Medal); became Lieutenant 23 Jan. 1896, and Captain 12 July, 1899. Capt. Earle served in the South African War 22 Oct. 1899, to 16 March, 1900, employed with the Military Police (graded Staff Captain), and took part in the advance on Kimberley, including the actions at Belmont, Enslin and Modder River; He was mentioned in Despatches [London Gazette, 10 Sept. 1901]; received the Queen's Medal with two clasps, and for the action at Belmont was created a Companion of the Distinguished Service Order [London Gazette, 27 Sept. 1901]: "Maxwell Earle, Capt., Grenadier Guards. In recognition of services during the operations in South Africa." The Insignia were presented to him by the King 29 Oct. 1901. He was Brigade Major, Brigade of Guards, and 9th Brigade, 4th Army Corps, 1 Jan. 1904, to 9 July, 1905; Brigade Major, 1st (Foot Guards) Brigade, Aldershot Army Corps, 10 July, 1905, to 31 Dec. 1907; was promoted to Major 20 July, 1907; G.S.O.3, War Office, 1 April to 30 Dec. 1910; G.S.O.2, War Office, 31 Dec. 1910, to 31 March, 1914; employed with Canadian Forces 3 June to 8 July, 1914. He was given the Brevet of Lieut.-Colonel 5 Aug. 1914, and served in the European War in 1914 and 1915; was promoted to Lieut.-Colonel 11 Sept. 1914; wounded and mentioned in Despatches, and taken prisoner. He was created a C.M.G. in 1918; became Colonel 5 Aug. 1918; is a G.S.O., 1st Grade; has the 3rd Class Order of the Red Eagle of Prussia, and the Silver Medal of the Society for Saving Life from Fire. Colonel Earle married the Hon. Edith Elizabeth Loch, daughter of the 1st Baron Loch and Elizabeth, daughter of the Hon. E. E. Villiers and niece of the 4th Earl of Clarendon, and they had three children, of whom a daughter, Margaret, and a son, Charles (born in 1914), survive. Another daughter, Evelyn, was born in 1905 and died in 1917. A newspaper cutting says: "A very sad side-issue of the war comes to us in the announcement of the death of Evelyn, the twelve-year-old daughter of Colonel Max Earle, D.S.O., a son of that charming old lady, Mrs. Earle, whose books—especially 'Pot-Pourri from a Surrey Garden'—have been a source of delight to so many people. Colonel Earle married his first cousin, the eldest daughter of the late Lord Loch, and much sympathy is felt for him and his wife in this distressing bereavement. Colonel Max Earle was taken prisoner early in the war, and endured a long spell of captivity in Germany."

DINGWALL, KENNETH, Capt., was born at Caterham, Surrey, 17 July, 1869, son of Charles Dingwall, J.P., and Julie Blanche Dingwall. He was educated mainly on the Continent, and was gazetted to the 3rd Highland Light Infantry in 1888, and to the Gordon Highlanders 10 Oct. 1891, becoming Lieutenant 21 Nov. 1894. He served in the operations in Chitral, 1895, with the Relief Force, and was present at the storming of the Malakand Pass (Medal with clasp). He again saw active service in 1897–98 on the North-West Frontier of India, with the Mohmand Field Force at the base, 1897, and with the Tirah Field Force, 1898; was present at the action of Dargai, where he was severely wounded, and he received the Medal with three clasps. He served in the South African War, 1899–1902, on the Staff. He received the Queen's Medal with five clasps, the King's Medal with two clasps, for regimental service in the field, and was created a Companion of the Distinguished Service Order [London Gazette, 27 Sept. 1901]: "Kenneth Dingwall, Capt., Gordon Highlanders. In recognition of services during the operations in South Africa." He was invested by the King 29 Oct. 1901. Capt. Dingwall retired (without rank) in 1904. He became Temporary Major, 10th Seaforth Highlanders, and served in the European War, 1914–17. He was promoted Lieut.-Colonel, Army Unemployed List. He has been Deputy Judge-Advocate on various occasions. Lieut.-Colonel Dingwall married, 22 June, 1917, in Dunfermline, Fife, Caroline Annie McJannett, daughter of Sir Thomas Fraser, M.P., and Lady Fraser, and they have one son, Patrick Fraser, born 11 May, 1919.

Kenneth Dingwall.

BRAITHWAITE, WILLIAM GARNETT, Capt., was born 21 Oct. 1870. He was educated at Marlborough, and at the Royal Military College, Sandhurst; was gazetted to the Royal Welsh Fusiliers 23 May, 1891, becoming Lieutenant 16 May, 1894. He was Adjutant, 1st Battn. Royal Welsh Fusiliers, 2 March, 1898, to 5 March, 1900, and became Captain 19 July, 1899, serving in the South African War from 1899 to 1902; served as Brigade Major 6 March, 1900, to 27 March, 1901, and as D.A.A.G. 28 March, 1901, to 4 Aug. 1902, and as Assistant Commander. He took part, while serving as Adjutant, Royal Welsh Fusiliers, in operations in Natal, 1899; Relief of Ladysmith, including action at Colenso; operations on Tugela Heights (14 to 27 Feb. 1900) and action at Pieter's Hill. While serving on the Staff and as Assistant Commissioner, he was present at operations in the Transvaal, May and June, 1900; operations in the Transvaal, west of Pretoria, July to 29 Nov. 1900, including actions at Frederickstad (17 to 25 Oct.); operations in Cape Colony, north of Orange River, including action at Ruidam (slightly wounded); operations in the Transvaal 30 Nov. 1900, to April, 1901; operations in Cape Colony, April, 1902, to 31 May, 1902. He was mentioned in Despatches (Sir R. H. Buller, 30 March, 19 June and 9 Nov. 1900) [London Gazette, 8 Feb. 1901]; was given the Brevet of Major; received the Queen's Medal with six clasps, the King's Medal with two clasps, and was created a Companion of the Distinguished Service Order [London Gazette, 27 Sept. 1901]: "William Garnett Braithwaite, Capt., Royal Welsh Fusiliers. In recognition of services during the operations in South Africa." The Insignia were presented to him by the King 27 Oct. 1901. He was Adjutant, Volunteers, 26 March, 1902, to 31 Dec. 1904; Officer, Company of Gentleman Cadets, Royal Military College, 31 Jan. 1906, to 6 Sept. 1907; Adjutant, Royal Military College, 7 Sept. 1907, to 21 Jan. 1910; promoted Major 4 May, 1910; G.S.O.3, New Zealand Military Forces, 25 May, 1911, to 24 May, 1914. He served in the European War from 1914; as G.S.O.1, New Zealand Division, Egypt, and was promoted to Lieut.-Colonel 21 Aug. 1915; commanding the 2nd New Zealand Infantry Brigade 21 Dec. 1915, to Jan. 1918. He was given the Brevet of Colonel 3 June, 1917; was Brigade Commander, General Staff, 16 Feb. to 14 Oct. 1918; Brigade Commander 19 Oct. 1918. He was created a C.M.G. in 1916, and C.B. in 1918. Colonel Braithwaite is a J.P. for Westmorland. He married, in 1901, Gwendolen Elizabeth, daughter of the late Lieut.-General E. O. Hewett, C.M.G., R.E., and they have son and two daughters.

COBBE, HENRY HERCULES, Capt., was born 26 Feb. 1869, son of the late Sir Alexander H. Cobbe, K.C.B. He was gazetted Second Lieutenant, Royal Artillery, 27 July, 1888; became Lieutenant, Indian Staff Corps, 11 July, 1891. He served in Burma, 1895–96. He became Captain, Indian Army, 27 July, 1899. Capt. Cobbe served in the South African War, 1899–1901, as Special Service Officer, 20 Jan. to 6 Feb. 1900; afterwards employed with Transport (graded D.A.A.G.) 7 Feb. 1900, to 23 Aug. 1902; also as Commandant, Durbanville, and employed with Peninsular Horse. He was mentioned in Despatches [London Gazette, 16 April, 1901]; received the Queen's Medal with three clasps, the King's Medal with two clasps, and was created a Companion of the Distinguished Service Order [London Gazette, 27 Sept. 1901]: "Henry Hercules Cobbe, Capt., Indian Staff Corps. In recognition of services during the operations in South Africa." The Insignia were presented by the King 24 Oct. 1902. He became Major 27 July, 1906; was D.A.A.G., India, 18 Nov. 1908, to 17 Nov. 1912; promoted Lieut.-Colonel 27 July, 1914. He served in the European War from 1914 to 1918; as A.A.Q.M.G., British Expeditionary Force and British Armies in France, from 14 Dec. 1914. He was mentioned in Despatches; given the Brevet of Colonel 3 June, 1918, and created a C.M.G. in 1917. Colonel Cobbe married, in 1907, Jeanne, only daughter of the late Colonel W. H. Boyd, I.M.S.

PRICE, BARTHOLOMEW GEORGE, Capt., was born 7 May, 1870. He was gazetted to the Royal Fusiliers 18 June, 1892, becoming Lieutenant 15 Sept. 1896, and Captain 2 Aug. 1899. Capt. Price served in the South African War, 1899–1902; was present at the Relief of Ladysmith, including the actions at Colenso; operations on Tugela Heights 14 to 27 Feb. 1900, and action at Pieter's Hill; operations in the Transvaal, May and June, 1900; operations in Natal, March and June, 1900; operations in the Transvaal, east of Pretoria, July to 29 Nov. 1900; operations in Cape Colony, north of Orange River, including action at Ruidam. He served as Adjutant, 2nd Battn. Royal Fusiliers, from Aug. 1901, to 31 May, 1902; operations in the Transvaal 30 Nov. 1900, to Feb. 1901; operations in Cape Colony, Feb. 1901, to May, 1902. He was mentioned in Despatches [London Gazette, 10 Sept. 1901]; received the Queen's Medal with five clasps, the King's Medal with two clasps, and was created a Companion of the Distinguished Service Order [London Gazette, 27 Sept. 1901]: "Bartholomew George Price, Capt., Royal Fusiliers. In recognition of services during the operations in South Africa." The Insignia weer presented by the King 18 Dec. 1902. He was Adjutant, Royal Fusiliers, from 17 May, 1901, to 16 May, 1904; Adjutant, Militia, 18 Aug. 1904, to 14 Aug. 1909; was promoted to Major 5 March, 1910. He served in the European War, 1914–18; commanded the 150th Infantry Brigade, British Expeditionary Force, British Armies in France, 4 Feb. 1916, to 24 Feb. 1918; was Brigade Commander, Northern Section, Plymouth Garrison, 12 April to 14 Dec. 1918; Area Commandant, British Armies in France, 15 Dec. 1918. He was mentioned in Despatches; given the Brevets of Lieut.-Colonel (18 Feb. 1915) and Colonel, 3 June, 1917, and created a C.M.G. in 1917, and C.B. in 1918.

FORTE, HERBERT AUGUSTUS NOURSE, Capt., was born at Clifton, 14 Dec. 1868, eldest son of Capt. N. Forte, late Norfolk Regt., and Edith, daughter of Thomas Nurse, Esq., M.D. He was educated at Eton and Sandhurst, and was gazetted to the East Yorkshire Regt. 9 Nov. 1889, becoming Lieutenant 6 Sept. 1893, and Captain 15 Aug. 1899. Capt. Forte served in the South African War, 1899–1901; was employed with Mounted Infantry in operations in the Orange Free State, Feb. to May, 1900; operations in the Transvaal, May and June, 1900, including actions near Johannesburg, Pretoria and Diamond Hill (11 and 12 June); operations in the Transvaal, west of Pretoria, July to 29 Nov. 1900; operations in Orange River Colony, May to 29 Nov. 1900, including actions at Wittebergen (1 to 29 July, 1900), Ladybrand (2 to 5 Sept.), Bothaville and Caledon River (27 to 29 Nov.); operations in Cape Colony, south of Orange River, 1899–1900; operations in Orange River Colony 30 Nov. 1900, to Jan. 1901. He was mentioned in Despatches [London Gazette, 11 Sept. 1901]: received the Queen's Medal with five clasps, and was created a Companion of the Distinguished Service Order [London Gazette, 27 Sept. 1901]: "Herbert Augustus Nourse Forte, Capt., Gordon Highlanders. In recognition of services during the operations in South Africa."

The Insignia were presented by the King 18 Dec. 1902. He retired 15 June, 1907. From 1914 to 1918 he served in the European War, and became Major, Reserve of Officers, 8 Jan. 1916. Major Forte married, in 1907, Hannah Wright, daughter of the late William Olive and widow of Cyril Murray, M.D., and they have one son and three daughters.

CRAUFORD, GEORGE STANDISH GAGE, Capt., was born 19 Nov. 1872, eldest son of Sir Charles William Frederick Crauford, 4th Bart. (son of the Rev. Sir Charles William Crauford and the Hon. Hester King, daughter of Peter, 7th Lord King, and sister of the 1st Earl Lovelace), and of the Hon. Isolda Caroline Vereker, daughter of the 4th Viscount Gort. He was educated at Wellington College, and Sandhurst, and was gazetted to the Gordon Highlanders 18 June, 1892. He served in the Chitral Campaign in 1895, with the Relief Force, being present at the storming of the Malakand Pass (Medal with clasp). He was promoted Lieutenant 20 May, 1896, and next saw active service with the Tirah Expeditionary Force. He was slightly wounded in the action of Dargai, and was present at the operations in the Maidan Waran and Bazar Valleys, and received two clasps. He became Captain 17 Aug. 1899, and served in the South African War, 1899–1902, taking part in the advance on Kimberley, including the action at Magersfontein; operations in the Orange Free State, Feb. to May, 1900, including operations at Paardeberg (17 to 26 Feb.); actions at Poplar Grove, Dreifontein, Houtnek (Thoba Mountain) and Vet River (5 to 6 May) and Zand River; operations in the Transvaal in May and June, 1900, including actions near Johannesburg and Pretoria; operations in the Transvaal, east of Pretoria, July to 29 Nov. 1900, including actions at Belfast (26 and 27 Aug.) and Lydenberg (5 to 8 Sept.); operations in the Transvaal, west of Pretoria, July to 29 Nov. 1900; operations in Cape Colony, south of Orange River, 1899–1900; operations in Cape Colony, north of Orange River. He was afterwards in command of Mounted Infantry Battn.: operations in Cape Colony, March, 1901; operations in Orange River Colony, April to June, 1901; operations in the Transvaal, June to Nov. 1901. He was mentioned in Despatches [London Gazette, 10 Sept. 1901]; received the Queen's Medal with five clasps, the King's Medal with two clasps, and was created a Companion of the Distinguished Service Order [London Gazette, 27 Sept. 1901]: "George Standish Gage Crauford, Capt., Gordon Highlanders. In recognition of services during the operations in South Africa." He was invested by the King 18 Dec. 1902. Capt. Crauford was A.D.C. to the G.O. Commanding-in-Chief, Southern Command, 20 July to 13 Oct. 1905; was employed with the West African Frontier Force 14 Oct. 1905, to 14 Oct. 1908; became Major 10 Aug. 1911; was specially employed under the Government of India 29 May, 1911, to 13 April, 1915, and was created a C.I.E. in 1913. Major Crauford served in the European War, 1914 to 1918; as G.S.O.2, Training Centre, Northern Command, 26 June to 7 Dec. 1915; was promoted to Lieut.-Colonel 14 March, 1915; commanded the 3rd Infantry Brigade, British Armies in France, 28 Nov. 1916, to 14 March, 1917, and the 18th Infantry Brigade, British Armies in France, 13 Sept. 1917, to 8 April, 1919. He was appointed A.D.C. to the King 3 June, 1918; became Colonel 14 March, 1919, and commanded the 1st Brigade, Midland Division, British Army of the Rhine, from 26 April, 1919. Colonel Crauford was created a C.M.G. in 1916, and a C.B. in 1919, and was given the Brevet of Colonel 3 June, 1918.

STEWART, ALGERNON BINGHAM ANSTRUTHER, Capt., was born 6 Dec. 1869, eldest son of Colonel C. E. Stewart, C.B. He was gazetted to the Seaforth Highlanders as Second Lieutenant 29 Nov. 1890, and became Lieutenant 1 June, 1893. In that year he served with the Chitral Relief Force; was present at the action at Mamagair (Medal with clasp). He was promoted Captain 30 Aug. 1899. He served in the South African War, 1899–1902, taking part in the Advance on Kimberley, including the action at Magersfontein; operations in the Orange Free State, Feb. to May, 1900, including operations at Paardeberg (17 to 26 Feb.); actions at Poplar Grove and Dreifontein; operations in Orange River Colony, May to 29 Nov. 1900, including actions at Wittebergen (1 to 29 July); operations in the Transvaal, March to Aug. 1901, and March to 31 May, 1902; operations in Orange River Colony 30 Nov. 1900, to Jan. 1901, and Jan. to March, 1902; operations in Cape Colony, Feb. to March, 1901, and Aug. 1901, to Jan. 1902. He was Commandant at Fauresmith. Capt. Stewart was mentioned in Despatches [London Gazette, 10 Sept. 1901]; received the Queen's Medal with five clasps, the King's Medal with two clasps, and was created a Companion of the Distinguished Service Order [London Gazette, 27 Sept. 1901]: "Algernon Bingham Anstruther Stewart, Capt., Seaforth Highlanders. In recognition of services during the operations in South Africa." The Insignia were presented to him by the King 18 Dec. 1912. He was Adjutant, Militia, 1 June, 1903, to 21 Feb. 1908; was promoted to Major 22 Feb. 1908. He served in the European War, and became G.S.O. 21 Nov. 1915. On 23 May, 1916, he was killed in action. In 1911, he married Edith Evelyn, daughter of Sir Arthur Vivian.

JORDAN, RICHARD PRICE, Capt., was born 2 Nov. 1869. He was gazetted to the Gloucestershire Regt. 8 June, 1889; became Lieutenant 20 Dec. 1890; was Adjutant, Indian Volunteers, 8 July, 1897, to 7 Sept. 1899; became Captain 13 Sept. 1899. Capt. Jordan served in the South African War, 1900–2; was present at the Relief of Kimberley; operations in the Orange Free State, Feb. to May, 1900, including operations at Paardeberg (17 to 26 Feb.); actions at Poplar Grove and Dreifontein (slightly wounded); operations in Orange River Colony, May to 29 Nov. 1900; operations in Cape Colony, north of Orange River; operations in the Transvaal, Orange River Colony and Cape Colony, 30 Nov. 1900, to May, 1902. He was mentioned in Despatches [London Gazette, 10 Sept. 1901]; received the Queen's Medal with four clasps, the King's Medal with two clasps, and was created a Companion of the Distinguished Service Order [London Gazette, 27 Sept. 1901]: "Richard Price Jordan, Capt., Gloucestershire Regt. In recognition of services during the operations in South Africa." The Insignia were presented by the King 2 June, 1902. He was Adjutant, Militia, 16 May, 1902, to 15 Nov. 1906. Major Jordan served in the European War from 1914 to 1918, and commanded the 7th Battn. Gloucestershire Regt. from 19 Aug. 1914; that gallant battalion which immortalized itself in Gallipoli by fighting on, on Chunak Bair Ridge, after all its officers had become casualties. Major Jordan was given the Brevet of Lieut.-Colonel 1 Jan. 1918, and became Lieut.-Colonel 11 May, 1919. He was created a C.M.G. in 1918.

DE SAUSMAREZ, CECIL, Capt., was born 29 Sept. 1870, son of the Rev. Havilland De Sausmarez and Anne Preaulx Walters. He was educated at Winchester, and at the Royal Military Academy, Woolwich, and entered the Royal Artillery 27 July, 1889, becoming Lieutenant 27 July, 1892, and Captain 13 Sept. 1899. He served in the South African War, 1900–2, as Special Service Officer 3 Jan. to 22 Jan. 1900; employed with Transport 23 Jan. 1900, to 21 Aug. 1902. Capt. De Sausmarez was present at operations in the Transvaal 30 Nov. 1900, to Jan. 1901; Feb. to Dec. 1901; operations in Orange River Colony, March and April, 1901; operations in Cape Colony, Jan. to Feb. 1901, and Dec. 1901, to 31 May, 1902. He was twice mentioned in Despatches [London Gazette, 10 Sept. 1901, and 29 July, 1902]; received the Queen's Medal with three clasps; the King's Medal with two clasps, and was created a Companion of the Distinguished Service Order [London Gazette, 27 Sept. 1901]: "Cecil De Sausmarez, Capt., Royal Garrison Artillery. In recognition of services during the operations in South Africa." The Insignia were presented by the King 24 Oct. 1902. From 1904 to 1909 he commanded the 22nd Derajat Mountain Battery. Capt. De Sausmarez served on the North-West Frontier of India in 1908, taking part in operations in the Zakka Khel country. He was mentioned in Despatches [London Gazette, 22 May, 1908], and was given the Brevet of Major 16 July, 1908. From 17 April, 1909, until 1910, he was D.A.A.G., Abbottabad Brigade, and he became Major 21 July, 1910, and from 1910 to 16 April, 1913, was G.S.O.2, 2nd (Rawalpindi) Division. He served in the European War from Feb. to Sept. 1914. He was mentioned in Despatches; given the Brevet of Lieutenant-Colonel 18 Feb. 1915, and was severely wounded while commanding the 108th Heavy Battery at the Aisne. He was specially employed at the War Office from 28 Jan. 1915, as D.A.A.G., from 23 March to 9 July, 1915; as A.A.G., 10 July, 1915, to 11 Feb. 1917; as Deputy Director of Mobilization 12 Dec. 1917, to 31 Jan. 1919; as Inspector of Demobilization, War Office, 1 Feb. 1919. He was three times mentioned in Despatches; given the Brevet of Colonel 1 Jan. 1919, and created a C.M.G. in 1918. He had been promoted Lieutenant-Colonel on 17 July, 1916, and Temporary Brigadier-General from 12 Dec. 1917. He married, in 1905, Mildred, eldest daughter of the Rev. J. P. Morgan, and they have two daughters.

PUCKLE, JOHN, Capt., was born 6 Oct. 1869, at Mussouri, India, son of the late Colonel Henry Puckle, Madras Staff Corps, of Worthing, Sussex, and of his wife, Cecilia, daughter of General Tod. He was educated at Westward Ho! Bedford Grammar School, Malvern College, Peterhouse, Cambridge, and the Royal Military College, Sandhurst, and joined the South Wales Borderers, as Second Lieutenant, 21 Jan. 1893; became Lieutenant, Army Service Corps, 29 Sept. 1895. He became Captain, Army Service Corps, 20 Sept. 1899; served in South Africa with the 7th Division under Lord Roberts, and subsequently as D.A.A.G., Deputy Assistant Director of Supplies, 25 Aug. 1900, to 24 Jan. 1901, at Army Headquarters. He was present at the operations in the Orange Free State, Feb. to May, 1900, including actions at Paardeberg, Poplar Grove, Karee Siding and Zand River; operations in the Transvaal, May and June, 1900, including actions near Johannesburg and Pretoria; was mentioned in Despatches [London Gazette, 10 Sept. 1901]; received the Queen's Medal, and was created a Companion of the Distinguished Service Order [London Gazette, 27 Sept. 1901]: "John Puckle, Capt., Army Service Corps. In recognition of services during the operations in South Africa." He was invested by the King 29 Oct. 1901. He was promoted to Major 12 Dec. 1906. Major Puckle was one of the first officers to land in France at the outbreak of the European War in Aug. 1914, prior to the arrival of the British Expeditionary Force. He was mentioned in Despatches in May, 1915, and became Lieutenant-Colonel 30 Oct. 1914. Lieut.-Colonel Puckle embarked for service in Egypt in the Transport Arcadian on 1 April, 1917. The ship was attacked by a German submarine, and sunk in the Eastern Mediterranean on 15 April. Colonel Puckle was Officer Commanding Troops on board. He remained until the last at his post on the bridge, and, together with the Captain of the vessel, sank with the ship. The Captain was saved, but Colonel Puckle was never seen again. Lieut.-Colonel Puckle—who was partnered by Capt. A. Berger—won two years in succession the Army Racquets Championship Doubles at Prince's Club, and also—with his same partner—the Army Lawn Tennis Championship Doubles. He was a fine billiard player, and was a member of the Royal and Ancient Club of St. Andrews. On the 3rd Dec. 1896, at St. Peter's, Eaton Square, London, S.W., he married Mary, daughter of the late Hon. James Fellows, Agent-General for New Brunswick.

John Puckle.

GROVE, ERNEST WILLIAM, Capt., was born 17 Feb. 1870, second son of the late W. R. Grove, Esq., M.D., of St. Ives, Huntingdonshire. He was gazetted to the Royal Artillery 27 July, 1889, becoming Lieutenant 27 July, 1892, and Captain 9 Oct 1899. Capt. Grove served in the South

African War, 1899–1902, taking part in operations in the Orange Free State, Feb. to May, 1900; operations in Orange River Colony, May to 29 Nov. 1900, including actions at Bethlehem (6 and 7 July); Wittebergen (1 to 29 July) and Caledon River (27 to 29 Nov.); operations in Cape Colony, south of Orange River, 1899–1900; operations in the Transvaal, Dec. 1901, to 31 May, 1902; operations in Cape Colony 30 Nov. 1900, to Dec. 1901. He was mentioned in Despatches [London Gazette, 10 Sept. 1901]; received the Queen's Medal with three clasps; the King's Medal with two clasps, and was created a Companion of the Distinguished Service Order [London Gazette, 27 Sept. 1901]: "Ernest William Grove, Capt., Royal Horse and Royal Field Artillery. In recognition of services during the operations in South Africa." He was invested by the King 15 Dec. 1902. He was promoted to Major 14 Nov. 1905, and Lieutenant-Colonel 30 Oct. 1914. Lieut.-Colonel Grove married, in 1906, Grace, youngest daughter of James Macdonald, Esq., of Bombay, and they have one daughter.

VENOUR, WILFRED JOHN, Capt., was born 2 May, 1870, son of the late Lieut.-General Venour, I.S.C. He entered the Army, Royal Dublin Fusiliers, 29 Oct. 1890; became Lieutenant 16 Dec. 1893. He was employed with the Egyptian Army 28 Dec. 1898, to 13 Oct. 1899. Capt. Venour served in the South African War, 1899–1900; was present at the Relief of Ladysmith, including operations of 5 to 7 Feb. 1900, and action at Vaal Kranz; operations on Tugela Heights (14 to 27 Feb. 1900) and action at Pieter's Hill; operations in the Transvaal in June, 1900; operations in Natal, March to June, 1900, including action at Laing's Nek (6 to 9 June); operations in Orange River Colony, June, 1900. He was mentioned in Despatches [London Gazette, 8 Feb. and 10 Sept. 1901]; received the Queen's Medal with six clasps, and was created a Companion of the Distinguished Service Order [London Gazette, 27 Sept. 1901]: "Wilfred John Venour, Capt., Royal Dublin Fusiliers. In recognition of services during the operations in South Africa." He was employed with the West African Frontier Force 1 May, 1901, to 15 May, 1904, serving in 1901–2 in Southern Nigeria, in the Aro Expedition, in command of a column; was slightly wounded, and mentioned in Despatches 12 Sept. 1902; received the Brevet of Major 17 April, 1902. In 1902 he served in Southern Nigeria in command of operations in the Nsit Country (clasp). He was Adjutant, Militia, and Adjutant, Special Reserve, from 13 Jan. 1906; became Major 17 Aug. 1908. Major Venour died 6 April, 1914.

MACONCHY, FREDERICK CAMPBELL, Capt., was born 22 Aug. 1868, fourth son of the late George Maconchy, of Rathmore, Longford. He was gazetted to the East Yorkshire Regt. 21 Dec. 1889, and became Lieutenant 27 Jan. 1891, and Captain 9 Oct. 1899. He served in the South African War, 1900–1, as Adjutant, 2nd Battn. East Yorks Regt. 10 May, 1900, to 31 Oct. 1901; in operations in the Orange Free State, including action at Houtnek (Thoba Mountain); operations in Orange River Colony 30 Nov. 1900, to Jan. 1902. He was mentioned in Despatches [London Gazette, 10 Sept. 1901]; received the Queen's Medal with three clasps, and was created a Companion of the Distinguished Service Order [London Gazette, 27 Sept. 1901]: "Frederick Campbell Maconchy, Capt., East Yorkshire Regt. In recognition of services during the operations in South Africa." He retired 8 Sept. 1906. Capt. Maconchy married (1st), in 1899, Maud Ellinor, daughter of G. A. Thompson, of Terrington Hall, Cork; and (2ndly), in 1901, Eleanor Mary, daughter of Major Robert Beaton, of Nydie, Fife.

TUSON, GEORGE EDWARD, Capt., was born 20 Jan. 1871. He was gazetted to the 16th Lancers 8 Oct. 1890; became Lieutenant 31 July, 1894, and served on the North-West Frontier of India, 1897–98 (Tochi), as Regimental Commandant and Transport Officer (9 July to Nov. 1897), receiving the Medal and clasp. He was promoted to Captain 9 Oct. 1899. Capt. Tuson served in the South African War, 1900–2, taking part in the advance on Kimberley and the Relief of Kimberley (wounded); operations in the Orange Free State, Feb. to May, 1900, including operations at Paardeberg (17 to 26 Feb.); actions at Poplar Grove, Karee Siding, Houtnek (Thoba Mountain) and Zand River; operations in the Transvaal in May and June, 1900, including actions near Johannesburg, Pretoria and Diamond Hill (11 and 12 June); operations in the Transvaal, west of Pretoria, Aug. to Sept. 1900; operations in Orange River Colony, July to 29 Nov. 1900), including actions at Bethlehem (7 July) and Wittebergen (1 to 20 July); operations in Orange River Colony 30 Nov. 1900, to Feb. 1901, and March to June, 1901; operations in Cape Colony, Feb. and March, 1901, and June, 1901. He received the Queen's Medal with five clasps; the King's Medal with two clasps, and was created a Companion of the Distinguished Service Order [London Gazette, 27 Sept. 1901]: "George Edward Tuson, Capt., 16th Lancers. In recognition of services during the operations in South Africa." He was promoted to Major 23 May, 1903, and retired 9 June, 1909. Major Tuson married, in 1912, Isabel, eldest daughter of S. Bright-Williams, of Broadstairs, and widow of James Lawe, and they have one son and one daughter.

SHEWAN, HUGH MACKENZIE, Capt., was born 27 Oct. 1870, son of the late Deputy Surgeon-General Alexander Shewan. He was gazetted to the Royal Dublin Fusiliers 19 Oct. 1892; became Lieutenant 26 July, 1895, and Captain 9 Oct. 1899. Capt. Shewan served in the South African War, 1899–1902, taking part in operations in Natal, 1899, including actions at Talana and Lombard's Kop. He was present at the Relief of Ladysmith, including the action at Colenso (severely wounded); operations of 17 to 24 Jan. 1900, and action at Spion Kop; operations of 5 to 7 Feb. 1900, and action at Vaal Kranz; operations on Tugela Heights 14 to 27 Feb. 1900, and action at Pieter's Hill; operations in the Orange Free State, Feb. to May, 1900; operations in the Transvaal, west of Pretoria, July to 29 Nov. 1900, including actions at Frederickstad 17 Sept. 1901. He was mentioned in Despatches [London Gazette, 8 Feb. and 10 Sept. 1901];

received the Queen's Medal with six clasps; the King's Medal with two clasps, and was created a Companion of the Distinguished Service Order [London Gazette, 27 Sept. 1901]: "Hugh Mackenzie Shewan, Capt., Royal Dublin Fusiliers. In recognition of services during the operations in South Africa." The Insignia were sent to the G.O.C., Transvaal, and presented by the G.O.C., Forces, South Africa, on 25 March, 1903, at Pretoria. He was employed with the South African Constabulary 1 Feb. 1902, to 20 Dec. 1903, and was promoted to Major 5 March, 1912. Major Shewan served in the European War from 1914.

HORE-RUTHVEN, THE HONOURABLE WALTER PATRICK (MASTER OF RUTHVEN), Capt., was born 6 June, 1870, eldest son of the 8th Baron Ruthven and Lady Caroline Gore, daughter of the 4th Earl of Arran. He was educated at Eton; entered the Scots Guards 25 July, 1891; became Lieutenant 12 Feb. 1896; Captain 11 Oct. 1899; was Regimental Adjutant, Scots Guards, 1 Jan. 1902, to 6 Nov. 1903; was promoted to Major 25 April, 1900; to Lieutenant-Colonel 28 Jan. 1915; to Colonel 28 Jan. 1919; was Temporary Brigadier-General from 7 March, 1916, to 1 Jan. 1917, and from 7 Oct. 1918. He was A.D.C. (Extra) to G.O.C., Aldershot, 1 Jan. to 31 July, 1898; A.D.C. to G.O.C., Aldershot, 1 Aug. to 8 Oct. 1898; Transport Officer, South Africa, 24 Jan. 1900, to 6 Aug. 1901; D.A.A. and Q.M.G., 2nd London Division, London District, 1 April, 1908, to 21 Jan. 1911; Brigade Major, Brigade of Guards, London District, 3 Feb. 1912, to 4 Aug. 1914; Brigade Major, 4th Infantry Brigade, B.E.F., 5 Aug. to 18 Nov. 1914; G.S.O.1, 47th Division, B.E.F., 2 June to 24 Aug. 1915; G.S.O.1, Guards Division, B.E.F., 25 Aug. 1915, to 6 March, 1916; Brigadier-General, G.S., 8th Army Corps, British Armies in France, 7 March, 1916, to 1 Jan. 1917; G.S.O.1, London District, 1 Jan. to 18 Sept. 1918; Brigade Commander, 117th Infantry Brigade, British Armies in France, 18 Oct. 1918, to 8 Feb. 1919; Brigade Commander, Brigade of Guards, London District, 9 Feb. 1919. He served in the South African War, 1899–1900; took part in the advance on Kimberley, including actions at Belmont, Enslin, Modder River and Magersfontein; on Staff; was present at the Relief of Kimberley; took part in the operations in the Orange Free State, Feb. to May, 1900, including those at Paardeberg (17 to 26 Feb.); actions at Poplar Grove, Dreifontein, Karee Siding, Houtnek (Thoba Mountain), Vet River (5 and 6 May) and Zand River; in the Transvaal in May and June, 1900, including actions near Johannesburg, Pretoria and Diamond Hill (11 and 12 June); in the Transvaal, east and west of Pretoria, July to 29 Nov. 1900, including action at Elands River (4 to 16 Aug.); also in Orange River Colony, May to 29 Nov. 1900, including action at Bethlehem (6 and 7 July) and Wittebergen (1 to 29 July). He was mentioned in Despatches [London Gazette, 26 Jan. and 16 March, 1900, and 10 Sept. 1901]; received the Queen's Medal with eight clasps, and King's Medal with two clasps, and was created a Companion of the Distinguished Service Order [London Gazette, 27 Sept. 1901]: "The Honourable Walter Patrick Hore-Ruthven (Master of Ruthven), Capt., Scots Guards. In recognition of services during the operations in South Africa." For his services in the European War he was seven times mentioned in Despatches; was created a C.M.G. in 1915; a C.B. in 1919; given the Brevet of Colonel 3 June, 1916, and promoted Colonel. He married Jean Leslie, only daughter of the late Norman Lampson, of The Farm House, Pont Street, S.W., and they have four daughters.

FINCH-HATTON, EDWARD HENEAGE, Capt., was born 4 Jan. 1868, fifth son of the late Rev. W. R. Finch-Hatton, and Agnes, sister of Sir Percy Oxenden, 10th Bart. He was educated at Haileybury, and gazetted to the East Kent Regt. 17 Jan. 1891, becoming Lieutenant 26 April, 1893, and Captain 21 Oct. 1899. He served in the South African War, 1899–1902; was present at the Relief of Kimberley; operations in the Orange Free State, Feb. to May, 1900, including operations at Paardeberg (17 to 26 Feb.); actions at Poplar Grove and Dreifontein; operations in the Transvaal, east of Pretoria, July to 29 Nov. 1900; operations in Orange River Colony, May and June, 1900; operations in the Transvaal 30 Nov. 1900, to May, 1902. He was mentioned in Despatches [London Gazette, 10 Sept. 1901]; received the Queen's Medal with four clasps, the King's Medal with two clasps, and was created a Companion of the Distinguished Service Order [London Gazette, 27 Sept. 1901]: "Edward Heneage Finch-Hatton, Capt., East Kent Regt. In recognition of services during the operations in South Africa." He was invested by the King 18 Dec. 1902. Capt. Finch-Hatton was Adjutant, Militia, 10 Oct. 1902, to 9 Oct. 1907, and was promoted to Major 4 July, 1908. He served in the European War, 1914–18; became Lieutenant-Colonel 27 April, 1915; commanded the 118th Infantry Brigade, British Armies in France, 13 July, 1916, to 24 Jan. 1917; and the Edinburgh Reserve Infantry Brigade, Home Forces, 25 Jan. 1917, to 1 Dec. 1918; was promoted to Colonel 27 April, 1919, and created a C.M.G. in 1916. He married, in 1912, Dagmar Gladys, daughter of Colonel Wiehe, of Littlebourne Lodge, Sandgate, and they have two daughters.

BAINBRIDGE, NORMAN BRUCE, Capt., was born 22 Oct. 1869, second son of the late Colonel Sir E. Bainbridge, K.C.B. He entered the West Riding Regt. 3 May, 1890, becoming Lieutenant 1 Dec. 1893, and Captain 21 Oct. 1899. Capt. Bainbridge served in the South African War, 1899–1901, employed with Mounted Infantry, and took part in the Siege of Kimberley; operations in the Orange Free State, Feb. to May, 1900, including operations at Paardeberg (21 to 26 Feb.); actions at Poplar Grove, Dreifontein, Vet River (5 and 6 May) and Zand River; operations in the Transvaal in May and June, 1900, including operations near Johannesburg, Pretoria and Diamond Hill (11 and 12 June); operations in the Transvaal, east of Pretoria, July to 29 Nov. 1900, including action at Reit Vlei; operations in Orange River Colony 30 Nov. to Dec. 1900; operations in Cape Colony Dec. 1900, to Jan. 1901. He was mentioned in Despatches [London Gazette, 10 Sept. 1901], received the Queen's Medal with six clasps, and was created a Companion of the Distinguished Service Order [London Gazette, 27 Sept. 1901]: "Norman Bruce Bainbridge, Capt., West Riding

Regt. In recognition of services during the operations in South Africa." The Insignia, Warrant, etc., were sent to the G.O.C. Transvaal, and presented by the G.O.C. Forces, South Africa, 25 March, 1903. He was Adjutant, Army Ordnance Corps, 1 Sept. 1901, to 30 April, 1903, and Ordnance Officer, 4th Class, 30 July, 1901, to 30 April, 1903; Ordnance Officer, 3rd Class, 1 April, 1907, to 23 Oct. 1911; was promoted to Major 30 Nov. 1908; was Ordnance Officer, 3rd Class, 24 Feb. 1911, to 7 Dec. 1914. He served in the European War; became Lieutenant-Colonel 8 Dec. 1914; was Ordnance Officer, 2nd Class, from 8 Dec. 1914, and Ordnance Officer, 1st Class (temporary), from 27 May, 1916, with the temporary rank of Colonel. He was created a C.M.G. in 1917, and a C.B. in 1919. He married, in 1902, Dorothea Olivia Louisa, only daughter of the Rev. B. Hale, of Wortham, and they have one son and two daughters.

GRESSON, THOMAS TINNING, Capt. and Adjutant, was born 29 April, 1870, son of Major W. H. Gresson. He entered the Army as Second Lieutenant, York and Lancaster Regt., 9 Nov. 1889; was promoted Lieutenant 30 Sept. 1891; was Adjutant 21 Dec. 1896, to 1 Nov. 1899, and became Captain 23 Oct. 1899. He served in the South African War, 1899–1902, as Special Service Officer, Disembarking Officer, and rejoined Battalion as Adjutant, 1st York and Lancaster Regt., from 5 Feb. 1900, to 24 May, 1901; took part in the Relief of Ladysmith, including operations of 5 to 7 Feb. 1900, and action at Vaal Kranz; operations on Tugela Heights 14 to 27 Feb. 1900, and action at Pieter's Hill; operations in Natal, March to June, 1900, including action at Laing's Nek 6 to 8 June; operations in the Transvaal, Nov. to Dec. 1900, and May, 1901; operations in Orange River Colony, May 1901 and 1902. He served with the Mounted Infantry; was mentioned in Despatches [London Gazette, 8 Feb. and 10 Sept. 1901]; received Queen's Medal with six clasps; King's Medal with two clasps, and was created a Companion of the Distinguished Service Order [London Gazette, 27 Sept. 1901]: "Thomas Tinning Gresson, Capt. and Adjutant, York and Lancaster Regt. In recognition of services during the recent operations in South Africa." Brigadier-General W. J. Kirkpatrick, C.B. (formerly commanding 1st York and Lancaster Regt.), says he recommended Capt. and Adjutant T. T. Gresson, 1st Battn. The York and Lancaster Regt., for continuous good service and devotion to duty during the South African campaign. He obtained his Majority 9 Sept. 1908; became Lieutenant-Colonel 1 May, 1915, and retired from the York and Lancaster Regt. 1 July, 1919.

DANIELL, EDWARD HENRY EDWIN, Capt., was born 5 June, 1868. He was gazetted to the Royal Irish Regt. 9 April, 1892; became Lieutenant 27 June, 1894, and served on the North-West Frontier of India, 1897–98, taking part in the operations on the Samana (Medal with two clasps). He became Captain 28 Oct. 1899, and served in the South African War, 1899–1902. He took part in operations in the Orange Free State, March to May, 1900; operations in the Transvaal, east of Pretoria, Aug. to 29 Nov. 1900, including actions at Belfast (26 and 27 Aug.), and Lydenberg (5 to 8 Sept.); operations in Orange River Colony, May to Aug. 1900, including actions at Bethlehem (6 and 7 July) and Wittebergen (1 to 29 July); operations in Capt Colony, south of Orange River, 1900, including actions at Colesberg (25 Jan. to 12 Feb.). He was Assistant Provost-Marshal 16 Oct. 1900, to 5 March, 1901, and was afterwards employed with Damant's Horse (formerly Rimington's Guides). He was present at operations in the Transvaal 30 Nov. 1900, to May, 1901, and March, 1902, to 31 May, 1902, and at operations in Orange River Colony, May, 1901, to March, 1902. Capt. Daniell was mentioned in Despatches [London Gazette, 10 Sept. 1901 and 29 July, 1902]; was placed on the list of Officers considered qualified for Staff employment in consequence of service on the Staff in the Field, received the Queen's Medal with three clasps, the King's Medal with two clasps, and was created a Companion of the Distinguished Service Order [London Gazette, 27 Sept. 1901]: "Edward Henry Edwin Daniell, Capt., Royal Irish Regt. In recognition of services during the operations in South Africa." The Insignia were presented to him by the King 29 Oct. 1901. He was Adjutant of the Royal Irish Regt. 1 June, 1902, to 30 May, 1903; appointed D.A.A.G., North China, 11 Aug. 1903, to 31 Oct. 1905; D.A.A. and Q.M.G., North China, 1 Nov. 1905, to 13 Aug. 1907; was promoted to Major 28 Aug. 1909; employed on General Staff (3rd Grade), Army Headquarters and War Office, 15 Oct. 1909, to 25 Nov. 1911; appointed G.S.O. (3rd Grade), Malta, 26 Nov. 1911. During the European War he proceeded to France with the battalion; was promoted to Temporary Lieutenant-Colonel from 26 Sept. 1914, and believed killed in action 19 Oct. 1914, at the capture of the village of Le Pilly by the regiment. (Despatches Sir John French 8 Oct. 1914). Married, in 1904, Winifred, only daughter of Percival Currey, and they had one son and one daughter. He was a nephew of Major Daniell (late Royal Munster Fusiliers), of the Royal Hospital, Chelsea.

Edward H. E. Daniell.

HAMILTON, KEITH RANDOLPH, Capt., was born 28 Feb. 1871, fourth son of Lieut.-General Henry Meade Hamilton, C.B., and was gazetted to the Oxfordshire Light Infantry 18 May, 1892; became Lieutenant 16 Oct. 1893; served in the operations on the North-West Frontier of India, 1897–98, with the Mohmand Field and Tirah Expeditionary Forces (Medal and two clasps). He was promoted Captain, Oxfordshire and Buckinghamshire Light Infantry, 4 Nov. 1899. Capt. Hamilton served in the South African War, 1899 to 1902, on the Staff. He served as Adjutant, 7th Mounted Infantry Regt., 12 Feb. to 1 April, 1900; and as Staff Officer to Mounted Infantry Corps 7 April, 1900, to 2 Dec. 1900; operations in the Orange Free State, Feb. to May, 1900, including operations at Paardeberg (17 to 26 Feb.); actions at Poplar Grove, Houtnek (Thoba Mountain), Vet River (5 and 6 May) and Zand River; operations in the Transvaal in May and June, 1900, including actions near Johannesburg, Pretoria and Diamond Hill (11 and 12 June); operations in the Orange River Colony (May to 29 Nov. 1900), including actions at Wittebergen (1 to 29 July) (severely wounded), Bothaville and Caledon River (27 to 29 Nov.); operations in the Transvaal 30 Nov. 1900, to 31 May, 1902. He was mentioned in Despatches [London Gazette, 16 April, 1901], received the Queen's Medal with five clasps, the King's Medal with two clasps, and was created a Companion of the Distinguished Service Order [London Gazette, 27 Sept. 1901]: "Keith Randolph Hamilton, Capt., Oxfordshire Light Infantry. In recognition of services during the operations in South Africa." The Insignia, Warrant and Statutes were sent to the G.O.C., Transvaal, and presented by the G.O.C. the Forces in South Africa, at Pretoria, 25 March, 1903. He was employed with the South African Constabulary 11 Dec. 1900, to 18 March, 1904; Adjutant, Volunteers, 9 July, 1907, to 31 March, 1908; Adjutant, Territorial Force, 1 April, 1908; employed with the West African Frontier Force 27 June, 1900, to 6 Sept. 1905. He was promoted to Major 19 Nov. 1910, and retired 3 Dec. 1913. He married, in 1895, Ella Marcella, daughter of the late Major John Finlay (late 78th Highlanders), of Castle Toward, Argyllshire, and they had one son. Major Hamilton died 7 Dec. 1918.

M'DOUALL, ROBERT, Capt., was born 3 Nov. 1871, son of the late John M'Douall, of Stranraer, Wigtownshire. He was educated at Felsted School, and at the Royal Military College, Sandhurst, and was gazetted to the East Kent Regt. 2 Jan. 1892; became Lieutenant 4 Oct. 1893; served with the Chitral Relief Force, 1895, and was present at the actions of Panjkora River and Mamagai (Medal and clasp), and became Captain 18 Nov. 1899. Capt. M'Douall served in the South African War, 1899–1902, employed with the South African Constabulary (23 Oct. 1900, to 22 Oct. 1905). He was present at the Relief of Kimberley; operations in the Orange Free State, Feb. to May, 1900, including operations at Paardeberg (17 to 26 Feb.); actions at Poplar Grove and Dreifontein; operations in the Transvaal and Orange River Colony 30 Nov. 1900, to 31 May, 1902. He was mentioned in Despatches [London Gazette, 8 Feb. and 10 Sept. 1901]; received the Queen's Medal with four clasps, the King's Medal with two clasps, and was created a Companion of the Distinguished Service Order [London Gazette, 27 Sept. 1901]: "Robert M'Douall, Capt., East Kent Regt. In recognition of services during the operations in South Africa." The Insignia were presented by the King 29 Oct. 1901. He was Adjutant, East Kent Regt., 1 Oct. 1906, to 30 Sept. 1909; was promoted to Major, 4 Aug. 1910; employed with the West African Frontier Force 8 Feb. 1911, to 29 Oct. 1913. Major M'Douall served in the European War from 1914, as Temporary Lieutenant-Colonel, East Kent Regt., 15 Dec. 1914, to 20 Dec. 1914, and 29 Feb. 1915, to 1 June, 1915. He was given the Brevet of Lieutenant-Colonel 3 June, 1915; commanded the 61st Infantry Brigade, British Armies in France, 13 March, 1917, to 14 Dec. 1917; commanded the 1st Training Reserve Brigade 23 Dec. 1917, to 27 Aug. 1918; commanded the 41st Infantry Brigade, British Armies in France, 3 Sept. 1918. Lieut.-Colonel R. M'Douall married, in 1902, Mabel Constance, daughter of General Sir C. R. Pennington, K.C.B., and they have one son and one daughter.

TROTTER, GERALD FREDERIC, Capt., was born 21 July, 1871, in London, second son of the late Major-General Sir H. Trotter, G.C.V.O. (Grenadier Guards, 1864 to 1898; Lieutenant-Colonel of the Regt.), and the Hon. Ena Gifford. He was educated in H.M.S. Britannia, and joined Grenadier Guards 1892. He received the Jubilee Medal, 1897, and was promoted Captain in 1899. He served in the South African War, 1899-1902 (severely wounded in March, 1900, and had his arm amputated), during advance on Kimberley, including actions at Belmont, Enslin, Modder River and Magersfontein; during Feb. to May, 1900, operations in the Orange Free State, including actions at Poplar Grove and Dreifontein; took part in the operations in the Transvaal and Cape Colony, May, 1902; was mentioned in Despatches [London Gazette, 10 Sept. 1901], received the Queen's Medal with five clasps, and the King's Medal with clasp, and was created a Companion of the Distinguished Service Order [London Gazette, 27 Sept. 1901]: "Gerald Frederic Trotter, Capt., Grenadier Guards. In recognition of services during recent operations in South Africa." The Insignia were presented by H.M. the King 29 Oct. 1901. He was created an M.V.O. in 1906; was promoted to Major 8 Aug. 1907, and retired 27 July, 1912, joining the Reserve of Officers of the Grenadier Guards. He was superintendent of Gymnasia. On the outbreak of the European War in 1914, he rejoined the Grenadier Guards as Major, and served with the 1st Battn. of that regiment in France from 1914 until 1916. In 1915 he was appointed Temporary Lieutenant-Colonel in command of 1st Battn. Grenadier Guards until 1916, when he was appointed Brigadier-General in command of Infantry Brigade, which appointment he held until June, 1917. In Oct. 1917, appointed Brigadier-General on the General Staff to command the British Military Mission (Training) to U.S.A. He was mentioned in Despatches, Jan. and June, 1916; created a C.M.G., 1916, and given the Brevet of Lieutenant-Colonel 1 Jan. 1916; was mentioned in Despatches in Jan. 1917, and June, 1917, and created a C.B., June, 1917, and a C.B.E., 1919. On 19 Dec. 1918, he was given the honorary rank of Brigadier-General.

Gerald Frederic Trotter.

ALDRIDGE, JOHN BARTTELOT, Capt., was born 8 Feb. 1871, youngest son of the late Colonel Aldridge, of St. Leonard's Forest, Horsham. He entered the Royal Artillery in July, 1889; was promoted Captain in July, 1899, and from 22 Feb. 1900, to 3 Jan. 1902, served as A.D.C. to the Brigadier-General of the Cavalry Brigade in South Africa. He was present at the Relief of Kimberley and the operations at Paardeberg, actions at Poplar Grove, and Dreifontein, Houtnek and the Zand River in the Orange Free State, and in the Transvaal he took a share in the operations near Johannesburg, Pretoria, Diamond Hill, as well as several other engagements. He was twice mentioned in Despatches [London Gazette, 4 May, 1900, and 10 Sept. 1901], and for his services he received the Queen's Medal with six clasps, and in Nov. 1900, was appointed to the Distinguished Service Order. In 1899 he married Margaret Jessie, daughter of the late J. Goddard, of the Manor House, Newton Harcourt. Major Aldridge was serving in 1909 with the Rocket Troop, Royal Artillery, in India. He died at Bangalore 19 Jan. 1909. His D.S.O. was gazetted 27 Sept. 1901: "John Barttelot Aldridge, Capt., Royal Artillery. In recognition of services in the recent operations in South Africa."

John B. Aldridge.

MARTON, RICHARD OLIVER, Capt., was born 19 Aug. 1872, son of Colonel George Blucher Heneage Marton, J.P., D.L., and the Hon. Caroline Gertrude, daughter of the 5th Viscount Ashbrook. He was gazetted to the Royal Artillery 23 Nov. 1891, becoming Lieutenant 23 Nov. 1894, and Captain in Dec. 1899. He served in the South African War on Special Service 3 Jan. 1900, to 19 Jan. 1900; employed with Transport 20 Jan. 1900, to 10 July, 1900, and was present at operations in the Orange Free State, Feb. to May, 1900, including actions at Vet River (5 and 6 May) and Zand River. Operations in the Transvaal, May and June, 1900, including actions near Johannesburg, Pretoria, and Diamond Hill (11 and 12 June); operations in the Transvaal, east of Pretoria, including action at Reit Vlei; operations in the Transvaal, May to Sept. 1901; operations on the Zululand frontier of Natal, Sept. and Oct. 1901; operations in Orange River Colony, Dec. 1901, to 21 May, 1902. He was mentioned in Despatches [London Gazette, 10 Sept. 1901]; received the Queen's Medal with four clasps; the King's Medal with two clasps, and was created a Companion of the Distinguished Service Order [London Gazette, 27 Sept. 1901]: "Richard Oliver Marton, Capt., Royal Garrison Artillery. In recognition of services during the operations in South Africa." He was invested by the King 29 Oct. 1901. Capt. Marton was 4th Assistant Superintendent of Experiments, School of Gunnery, 20 June, 1902, to 31 Jan. 1903; 3rd Assistant Superintendent of Experiments, School of Gunnery, 1 Feb. 1903, to 11 May, 1905; 2nd Assistant Superintendent of Experiments, School of Gunnery, 12 May, 1905, to 31 May, 1905; 1st Assistant Superintendent of Experiments, Experimental Staff, 1 June, 1905, to 31 Dec. 1905; Instructor, School of Gunnery, 1 April, 1910, to 31 March, 1913. He was promoted to Major 29 May, 1912; was Major-Instructor, School of Gunnery, 1 April, 1913, to 31 March, 1914; became Lieutenant-Colonel 1 May, 1917; Superintendent of Experiments, School of Instruction for R.H. and R.F.A., Chapperton Down Artillery School, 10 Nov. 1917. Lieut.-Colonel Marton served in the European War, and was created a C.M.G. in 1916. He married, in 1899, Margaret Isabel, daughter of Egerton Leigh, of Jodrel Hall, Cheshire, and they have two sons.

HAMILTON, JOHN GEORGE HARRY, Capt., was born 6 Aug. 1869, son of George Hamilton, Esq. (deceased), of Skene House, Aberdeenshire. He was educated at Cheltenham College, and Sandhurst, and entered the Army as Second Lieutenant, Royal Highlanders, 8 Oct. 1890; he was promoted Lieutenant 3 Nov. 1892, and became Captain 12 Dec. 1899. He served in the South African War, 1899–1902, as Adjutant to the 2nd Battn. Royal Highlanders (from Dec. 1899, to 18 Feb. 1900); was in the advance on Kimberley, including action at Magersfontein; during operations in the Orange Free State, Feb. to May, 1900; in operations at Paardeberg 17 to 26 Feb. (was slightly wounded); in actions at Poplar Grove, Dreifontein and Vet River; operations in Orange River Colony, including actions at Rhenoster River, Wittebergen and Witpoort; during operations in Cape Colony, south of Orange River, 1899; operations in the Transvaal, March to May, 1902; during operations in Orange River Colony, Nov. 1900, to Feb. 1902. He was mentioned in Despatches [London Gazette, 8 Feb. and 10 Sept. 1901]; received the Queen's Medal with five clasps; the King's Medal with two clasps, and was created a Companion of the Distinguished Service Order [London Gazette, 27 Sept. 1901]: "John George Harry Hamilton, Capt., Royal Highlanders. In recognition of services in the recent operations in South Africa." He was invested by the King 18 Dec. 1902. He was employed with the West African Forces 26 Sept. 1903, to 8 April, 1905; became Adjutant (Militia), Special Reserve, 16 April, 1906. He was promoted Major 29 Jan. 1909, and received the Durbar Medal in 1912. In the European War he served 1914 to 1915; was mentioned in Despatches and given the Brevet of Lieutenant-Colonel 3 June, 1916. He became Lieutenant-Colonel 15 Sept. 1916; commanded the 154th Infantry Brigade, British Armies in France, 17 Sept. 1916, to Sept. 1917; was Commandant, Base Depôt, from 24 Nov. 1918. He married, 15 Oct. 1912, at St. Margaret's, Westminster, London, Sybil, daughter of E. Montefiore Micholls, Esq., and they have a son, John George Alistair, born 6 Oct. 1913, and a daughter, Jean Mary.

POWELL, EDWARD WEYLAND MARTIN, Capt., was born 3 Dec. 1869, youngest son of Lieut.-Colonel W. Martin Powell, of Brooklands. He was gazetted to the Royal Artillery 27 July, 1889; became Lieutenant 27 July, 1892, and Captain, 18 Dec. 1899. Capt. Powell served in the South African War, 1899–1901, and was present at the Relief of Kimberley; operations in the Orange Free State, Feb. to May, 1900, including operations at Paardeberg, actions at Poplar Grove, Karee Siding, Houtnek (Thoba Mountain) and Zand River; operations in the Transvaal, west of Pretoria, July to Aug. 1900, including actions at Eland's River and Venterskroon; operations in Orange River Colony, July to Nov. 1900, including actions at Bethlehem and Wittebergen; operations in Cape Colony, south of Orange River, 1899–1900, including actions at Colesberg; operations in Cape Colony, Nov. 1900, to Oct. 1901. He was mentioned in Despatches [London Gazette, 10 Sept. 1901]; received the Queen's Medal with five clasps, and was created a Companion of the Distinguished Service Order [London Gazette, 27 Sept. 1901]: "Edward Weyland Martin Powell, Capt., Royal Horse and Royal Field Artillery. In recognition of services during the operations in South Africa." The Insignia were presented by the King 29 Oct. 1901. He was Adjutant, Royal Artillery, 5 May, 1905, to 12 Feb. 1906; became Major 11 Feb. 1906; retired 2 July, 1910, entering the Reserve of Officers. Major Powell served in the European War, 1914–18; was mentioned in Despatches; created a C.M.G. in 1918; a C.B. in 1919, and awarded the Legion of Honour. He was given the Brevet of Lieutenant-Colonel, Reserve of Officers, 1 Jan. 1917, and the honorary rank of Brigadier-General 26 Feb. 1919.

MAURICE, DAVID BLAKE, Capt., was born 24 Dec. 1866, eldest son of the late Oliver Calley Maurice, J.P., of London Street, Reading, and Manton Grange, Marlborough. He was educated at Uppingham, and was in the Eleven and in the Fifteen, and entered the Royal Berkshire Regt. 17 April, 1889, and became Lieutenant 1st Royal Berkshire Regt. 3 Feb. 1892. He was Adjutant, 1st Royal Berkshire Regt., 29 Dec. 1894, to 28 Dec. 1898, and became Captain 26 Dec. 1899. Capt. Maurice served in South Africa, 1899–1901, employed with Mounted Infantry, and as Railway Staff Officer 17 Nov. 1900, to 30 April, 1901, and 1 May, 1901, to 11 Feb. 1902. He was present at operations in the Orange Free State, Feb. to May, 1900, including actions at Houtnek (Thoba Mountain), Vet River (5 and 6 May) and Zand River; operations in the Transvaal in May and June, 1900, including actions near Johannesburg, Pretoria and Diamond Hill (11 and 12 June); operations in the Transvaal, west of Pretoria, July to 29 Nov. 1900, including actions at Frederickstad (17 to 25 Oct.); operations in Orange River Colony, May to 29 Nov. 1900, including actions at Bethlehem (6 and 7 July), Wittebergen (1 to 20 July), Ladybrand (2 to 5 Sept.), and Bothaville; operations in Orange River Colony, 30 Nov. 1900, to 1901. He was mentioned in Despatches [London Gazette, 10 Sept. 1901]; received the Queen's Medal with five clasps, and was created a Companion of the Distinguished Service Order [London Gazette 27 Sept. 1901]: "David Blake Maurice, Capt., Royal Berkshire Regt. In recognition of services during the operations in South Africa." The Insignia were presented by the King 12 March, 1902. Capt. Maurice was Recruiting Officer, South African Constabulary, 8 Sept. 1902, to 7 March, 1903; Adjutant, Q.V.B. West Yorkshire Regt., 17 March, 1903, to 1 April, 1906; was promoted to Major, 27 Aug. 1908; commanded Depôt, Royal Berkshire Regt., 1908–12. He was Brigade Major, 77th Infantry Brigade, New Armies, 3 Oct. 1914, to 22 Feb. 1915; G.S.O.3, 2/1st North Midland Division, Central Force, Home Defence, 12 March, 1915, to 16 May, 1915; G.S.O.2, Humber Garrison, 17 May, 1915 to 14 July, 1917; promoted to Lieutenant-Colonel 4 Sept. 1916; G.S.O.1, Humber Garrison, 15 July, 1917, to 10 Nov. 1918. Lieut.-Colonel Maurice married, in 1903, Cecilia Evelyn, eldest daughter of James Simonds, J.P., of Redlands, Reading.

WORMALD, FREDERICK WILLIAM, Capt., was born 21 June, 1869, son of John Wormald, of Dewsbury. He was educated at Harrow, and was gazetted to the 7th Hussars 29 April, 1891, becoming Lieutenant 24 Oct. 1894, and serving in Bechuanaland, 1896–97 (Medal and clasp); becoming Lieutenant 24 Oct. 1894. He served in the Nile Expedition, 1898; was present at the Battle of Khartum (Medal and Egyptian Medal with clasp). He was promoted Captain 30 Dec. 1899, and served in the South African War, 1899–1902, as A.D.C. to Major-General, Cavalry Brigade, 9 Oct. 1899, to 10 Feb. 1900; as A.D.C. to Brigadier-General, Cavalry Brigade, 11 Feb. 1900, to 31 Oct. 1900. During the South African War he took part in the advance on and Relief of Kimberley; operations in the Orange Free State, Feb. to May, 1900, including operations at Paardeberg (17 to 26 Feb.), actions at Poplar Grove, Karee Siding and Zand River; operations in the Transvaal in May and June, 1900, including actions near Johannesburg, Pretoria and Diamond Hill (11 and 12 June); operations in the Transvaal, east of Pretoria, July to 29 Nov. 1900, including action at Belfast (26 and 27 Aug.); operations in Orange River Colony, May to 26 Nov. 1900, including actions at Wittebergen (1 to 26 July). He served as Adjutant, 7th Hussars, from 20 Dec. 1901, to 22 Jan. 1902, and 22 April to 31 May, 1902; and was present at operations in Cape Colony, Dec. 1901, to Jan. 1902. He was mentioned in Despatches [London Gazette, 10 Sept. 1901]; received the Queen's Medal with eight clasps, and was created a Companion of the Distinguished Service Order [London Gazette, 27 Sept. 1901]: "Frederick William Wormald, Capt., 7th Hussars. In recognition of services during the operations in South Africa." He was invested by the King, 29 Oct. 1901. Capt. Wormald was Adjutant, 7th Hussars, until 31 Oct. 1904; became Major, 8th Hussars, 10 Feb. 1906; was Instructor, Cavalry School, 15 Dec. 1906, to 14 Dec. 1910. He was promoted to Lieutenant-Colonel, 1st Dragoons, 21 Dec. 1915. Lieut.-Colonel F. W. Wormald married, in 1909, Evelyn Christina, daughter of T. H. Cardwell, of Newnton House, Tetbury, and they have one daughter.

RANKIN, CHARLES HERBERT, Capt., was born 26 May, 1873, second son of Sir James Rankin, 1st Bart., and Annie Laura, second daughter of Christopher Bushell, J.P., of Hinderton, Cheshire. He was gazetted to the 7th Hussars 21 Oct. 1893, and was promoted to Lieutenant 1 July, 1896. He served in South Africa in 1896, and again saw active service in the South African War, as Special Service Officer in South Africa 23 Sept. 1899, to 31 Dec. 1901 (including service as Adjutant, Rimington's Guides, to

March, 1901, and as District Commandant). He became Captain 30 Dec. 1899. Capt. Rankin was in command of the Western Province Mounted Rifles from 22 June, 1901, to May, 1902, and took part in the advance on Kimberley, including actions at Belmont, Enslin, Modder River and Magersfontein. He was present at the Relief of Kimberley; and at the operations in the Orange Free State, Feb. to May, 1900, including operations at Paardeberg (17 to 26 Feb.), actions at Poplar Grove, Dreifontein, Vet River and Zand River. Operations in the Transvaal in May and June, 1900, including actions near Johannesburg, Pretoria and Diamond Hill (11 and 12 June); operations in Orange River Colony, May to 29 Nov. 1900, including actions at Lindley, Bethlehem, Wittebergen and Bothaville; operations in Cape Colony, 1899 to 1900, including actions at Colesburg (1 Jan. to 12 Feb.); operations in Cape Colony, March, 1901, to 31 May, 1902. He was mentioned in Despatches [London Gazette, 27 Sept. 1901]; received the Queen's Medal with eight clasps, the King's Medal with two clasps, and was created a Companion of the Distinguished Service Order [London Gazette, 27 Sept. 1901]: "Charles Herbert Rankin, Capt., 7th Hussars. In recognition of services during the operations in South Africa." He was invested by the King 18 Dec. 1902. Capt. Rankin was Adjutant, Imperial Yeomanry, 17 Oct. 1902, to 16 Oct. 1905, and was promoted to Major 26 June, 1911. Major Rankin served in the European War from 1914; as Temporary Lieutenant-Colonel, whilst commanding the 4th Hussars, 17 April, 1915, to 15 April, 1916. He was given the Brevet of Lieutenant-Colonel 1 Jan. 1916; commanded the 105th Infantry Brigade, B.E.F., 16 April, 1916, to 30 April, 1916; the Ambala Cavalry Brigade, British Armies in France, 1 May, 1916, to 5 March, 1918, and the 4th Cavalry Brigade, British Armies in France, from 9 April, 1918. He was given the Brevet of Colonel 3 June, 1918. He was twice mentioned in Despatches, and created a C.M.G. in 1916. He married, in 1908, Enid, daughter of the late Judge Williams, and they have one son and one daughter.

STANLEY, THE HONOURABLE FERDINAND CHARLES, Capt., was born 28 Jan. 1871, fourth son of the 16th Earl of Derby and Lady Constance Villiers, eldest daughter of the 4th Earl of Clarendon, K.G. He was educated at Wellington and Sandhurst; joined the King's Royal Rifle Corps 10 Oct. 1891; was A.D.C. (extra) to the Viceroy of Ireland 11 Feb. 1896, to 31 Dec. 1896; served in the Nile Expedition, 1898, taking part in the Battle of Khartum (received the Egyptian Medal with clasp and the Medal); became Lieutenant, Grenadier Guards, 30 July, 1897, and Captain. He served in the South African War, 1899 to 1902, with the 4th Battn. Imperial Yeomanry, and was on the Staff (as Camp Commandant) at Headquarters from 29 Nov. 1900. He was present at operations in the Transvaal in May and June, 1900, including the actions near Johannesburg and Pretoria; operations in the Transvaal 30 Nov. 1900, to 31 May, 1902. He was mentioned in Despatches [London Gazette, 10 Sept. 1901]; received the Queen's Medal with three clasps, the King's Medal with three clasps, and was created a Companion of the Distinguished Service Order [London Gazette, 27 Sept. 1901]: "The Honourable Ferdinand Charles Stanley, Capt., Grenadier Guards. In recognition of services during the operations in South Africa." The Insignia were presented to him by the King 24 Oct. 1902. Capt. Stanley retired from the Grenadier Guards and entered the Reserve of Officers. He served in the European War from 1914 to 1918; was given the Brevets of Major and Lieutenant-Colonel; was Temporary Brigadier-General, commanding the 89th Infantry Brigade. He was mentioned in Despatches; was created a C.M.G. in 1918, and made a Commander of the Legion of Honour. He is Vice-Chairman, Associated Portland Cement Company; Chairman, British Portland Cement Company; Director, Forestal Land Company; Director, Birmingham Carriage and Wagon Company; Member, National Hunt Steeplechase Association. He married, in 1904, the Honourable Alexandra Fellowes, daughter of the 2nd Baron de Ramsey and Lady Rosamond Jane Frances Spencer-Churchill, daughter of the 7th Duke of Marlborough, K.G., and they have three sons.

NICHOLL, DONALD FITZ ROY, Capt., was born in 1872, son of the late General Thomas Nicholl, Colonel Commandant, Royal Artillery. He entered the Royal Artillery 12 Feb. 1892, and was promoted to Lieutenant 12 Feb. 1895; he served in South Africa from 16 Dec. 1899, to 11 Jan. 1900; as Assistant Disembarkation Staff Officer from 12 Jan. 1900, to 4 July, 1900, and he became Captain 1 Jan. 1900. Capt. Nicholl was present at operations in the Transvaal in May and June, 1900, including actions near Johannesburg, Pretoria and Diamond Hill (11 and 12 June); operations in the Transvaal, west of Pretoria, July to 29 Nov. 1900, including actions at Frederickstad (17 to 25 Oct.). He was mentioned in Despatches [London Gazette, 10 Sept. 1901]; received the Queen's Medal with four clasps, and was created a Companion of the Distinguished Service Order [London Gazette, 27 Sept. 1901]: "Donald Fitz Roy Nicholl, Capt., Royal Garrison Artillery. In recognition of services during the operations in South Africa." The Insignia, Warrant and Statutes were sent to the G.O.C., Malta, 10 Feb. 1902, and presented on 21 Feb. 1902, by the Commander-in-Chief, Malta. He was Officer, Company of Gentleman Cadets, Royal Military Academy, 8 Feb. 1909, to 7 Feb. 1913; was promoted to Major, 9 Aug. 1912. He served in the European War from 1914; was D.A.A. and Q.M.G., Thames and Medway Defences, 28 Nov. 1914, to 30 June, 1916; commanded a Heavy Artillery Group, B.E.F., France, 1916–18; was promoted to Lieutenant-Colonel 1 May, 1917. Lieut.-Colonel D. F. Nicholl married, in 1906, Ethel, daughter of the Rev. Canon Branch, of Trinidad.

H. M. Shaw-Stewart.

SHAW-STEWART, HOUSTON MICHAEL, Capt., was born 3 Oct. 1871, in London, son of the late Sir Michael Robert Shaw-Stewart, 7th Bart., V.D., Lord Lieutenant of Renfrewshire, and Lady Octavia Grosvenor, fifth daughter of the 2nd Marquis of Westminster. He was educated at Eton, and Christ Church, Oxford, and was gazetted to the 17th Lancers 12 Dec. 1894, becoming Lieutenant 13 Nov. 1895, and Captain. He served in the South African War; received the Queen's Medal with clasps for (1) Cape Colony; (2) Johannesburg; (3) Diamond Hill; (4) Wittebergen, and was created a Companion of the Distinguished Service Order [London Gazette, 27 Sept. 1901]: "Houston Michael Shaw-Stewart, Capt., 17th Lancers. In recognition of services during the operations in South Africa." The Insignia, Warrant and Statutes were sent to his father, Sir M. R. Shaw-Stewart, of Ardgowan, Greenock, N.B. It is understood that the D.S.O. awarded to Capt. H. M. Shaw-Stewart was a decoration allotted to his Regiment, the 17th Lancers, to be awarded to a particularly deserving officer who had distinguished himself in the campaign. Capt. H. M. Shaw-Stewart was accidentally drowned returning on sick-leave from South Africa in 1901. The above is furnished by his eldest brother, Sir M. Hugh Shaw-Stewart, Bart., C.B., of Ardgowan and Greenock.

BARTHOLOMEW, HUGH JOHN, Capt., was born 29 Dec. 1871; he entered the Army 5 Dec. 1891, as Second Lieutenant, Royal Worcestershire Regt. He was promoted to Lieutenant 10 July, 1893, and Captain 10 Jan. 1900. He served in the South African War, 1899–1902, and was Commandant at Wolvehoek during operations in the Transvaal, March to May, 1901; operations in Orange River Colony, May, 1901, to 31 May, 1902. He was mentioned in Despatches [London Gazette, 10 Sept. 1901]; received the Queen's Medal with three clasps, the King's Medal with five clasps, and was created a Companion of the Distinguished Service Order [London Gazette, 27 Sept. 1901]: "John Hugh Bartholomew, Capt., Worcestershire Regt. In recognition of services during recent operations in South Africa." Capt. Bartholomew was pro-

Hugh J. Bartholomew.

moted Major 2 March, 1907. He served in the European War, 1914–18; as G.S.O.2, 23rd Division, New Armies, 18 Sept. 1914, to 26 Feb. 1915; D.A.Q.M.G., Marseilles Base, 6 March, 1915, to 1 May, 1915; was Temporary Lieutenant-Colonel 4 May, 1915, to 13 May, 1916; in command of the 10th Battn. West Riding Regt. 4 May, 1915, to 29 Aug. 1916; Commandant, Lines of Communication, British Armies in France, 19 Oct. 1916, to 5 May, 1917; A.A. and Q.M.G., Lines of Communication, British Armies in France, 19 Oct. 1916, to 6 May, 1917. He was four times mentioned in Despatches; promoted to Lieutenant-Colonel 14 Feb. 1916, and created a C.M.G. in 1919. Lieut.-Colonel Bartholomew married, in 1910, Gladys Ethel Allen, daughter of Leonard Allen Shuter, of Mattingley Lodge, Winchfield, Hants, and they have one daughter.

WODEHOUSE, ERNEST CHARLES FORBES, Capt., was born 5 Aug. 1871, at Hove, Brighton, son of Lieut.-Colonel Charles Wodehouse, C.I.E., Bombay Political Service, at one time Resident of Kolhapur, and of his wife, J. Forbes, daughter of George Forbes, of Springhill, Aberdeenshire. He was educated at Wellington College, and Oxford Military College, and joined the Worcestershire Regt., as Second Lieutenant, 19 Oct. 1892, and was promoted Lieutenant 26 Dec. 1895, and Captain 10 Jan. 1900. He served in the South African War, 1899–1902, as District Adjutant, Heilbron, and as Adjutant, 2nd Battn. Worcestershire Regt., 30 Nov. 1898, to 31 May, 1902; during operations in Orange River Colony, May to 29 Nov. 1900, including actions at Bethlehem (6 and 7 July) and Wittebergen (till 29 July); operations in the Transvaal, west of Pretoria, July to 29 Nov. 1900; in the operations in Cape Colony, south of Orange River, 1899–1900,

Ernest C. F. Wodehouse.

including actions at Colesberg 1 Jan. to 12 Feb.; operations in the Transvaal 30 Nov. 1900, to May, 1901; operations in Orange River Colony, May, 1901, to 31 May, 1902; was mentioned in Despatches [London Gazette, 16 Sept. 1901, and on another occasion]; received the Queen's Medal with clasps for (1) Wittebergen; (2) Transvaal and (3) Cape Colony, and the King's Medal with two clasps, and was created a Companion of the Distinguished Service Order [London Gazette, 27 Sept. 1901]: "Ernest Charles Forbes Wodehouse, Capt., Worcestershire Regt. In recognition of services during the recent operations in South Africa." He was invested by the King 24 Oct. 1902. His D.S.O. was given for good work in South Africa, being Adjutant of the 2nd Battn. from 15 April, 1899, to April, 1903; was Acting D.A.A.G., Bloemfontein District, from April, 1903, to July, 1903; Adjutant of 6th Battn. from 10 Aug. 1903, to 1907. He became Major 27 Nov. 1907. Major Wodehouse served in the European War, 1914–15, and commanded the 1st Battn., as Temporary Lieutenant-Colonel, from 1 Jan. to 12 March, 1915, when he was killed in action at Neuve Chapelle. He was mentioned in Despatches, dated 31 May, 1915, published 22 June, 1915, for gallant and distinguished service in the field. A newspaper says: "An official telegram has been received in Worcester announcing the death at the front of Major E. C. F. Wodehouse, who was reported a fortnight ago to be 'wounded and missing.' Letters received from other officers at the front caused his friends to entertain the gravest fears for his safety, and they were therefore not unprepared for the worst news. The widespread sympathy shown to Mrs. Wodehouse and her family in their terrible suspense will be again tendered to them on the announcement of the death of this distinguished soldier. He was in command of the 1st Battn. from 30 Dec. last. He was killed on 12 March, whilst leading an attack on a strong position north-east of Neuve Chapelle. The deceased officer, who was the son of the late Colonel Charles Wodehouse, C.I.E., Indian Army, and political agent at Kolhapur, joined the 2nd Battn. Worcestershire Regt. from the County Militia in 1892." Lieut.-Colonel Wodehouse had married, 18 April, 1906, at St. John's Church, Worcester, Amy Violet Isaac, daughter of the late J. S. Isaac, Esq., of Boughton Park, Worcester. He was very fond of cricket and a good shot.

PHILLPOTTS, LOUIS MURRAY, Capt., was born 3 June, 1870, second son of the Rev. H. J. Phillpotts and Mrs. H. J. Phillpotts, of Shadwell, Speldhurst, Kent. He passed out of Woolwich into the Royal Artillery

14 Feb. 1890, becoming Lieutenant 14 Feb. 1893. He served in the South African War, 1899–1901, in the early part of which he performed the duties of Acting Staff Officer to the Officer Commanding the Lines of Communication, North. Afterwards he was in the advance on Kimberley and fought in the action of Modder River. He took part in the operations in the Orange River Colony, Feb. to May, 1900, including operations at Paardeberg (17 to 26 Feb.), and was also in the actions near Johannesburg. He was present also at the operations in the Transvaal and Orange River Colony 30 Nov. 1900, to Nov. 1901; was mentioned in Despatches [London Gazette, 10 Sept. 1901], received the Queen's Medal with three clasps, and

Louis M. Phillpotts.

was created a Companion of the Distinguished Service Order [London Gazette, 27 Sept. 1901]: " Louis Murray Phillpotts, Capt., Royal Horse and Royal Field Artillery. In recognition of services during the operations in South Africa." The Insignia, Warrant and Statutes were sent 6 March, 1902, to Walkern Rectory, Stevenage. He was promoted to Captain 23 Jan. 1900. He was Divisional Adjutant, R.A., 10 June, 1900, to 31 March, 1901; Adjutant, R.A., 1 April, 1901, to 9 June, 1904, and became Major 3 July, 1907. He held a first-class certificate in gunnery. Major Phillpotts served in the European War, and was gazetted Lieutenant-Colonel in Oct. 1914, and in the following year was promoted to the Staff, with the rank of Brigadier-General. Serving with great distinction, he was mentioned in Despatches, and was made a Companion of St. Michael and St. George. Brigadier-General L. M. Phillpotts was killed in action 8 Sept. 1916, and a memoir of him appeared in the " Times " of 18 Sept. 1916. The " Morning Post " of 13 Sept. 1916, had the following notice : " Killed in action on the 8th Sept.—Brigadier-General Louis Murray Phillpotts, D.S.O., C.M.G., R.F.A., the beloved husband of Amy Phillpotts, of Russelstown Park, Carlow, and second son of the Rev. H. J. and Mrs. Phillpotts, of Shadwell, Speldhurst, Kent."

GRAHAM, JOHN MALISE ANNE, Capt., was born 19 July, 1869, son of the late General Sir S. James Graham, K.C.B. (who died 11 May, 1917), and Laura Christiana (who died in 1874), daughter of the late A. H. Williams, H.E.I.C.S. He was gazetted to the Royal Lancaster Regt. 9 Nov. 1889; became Lieutenant 19 Aug. 1891; was Adjutant, Royal Lancaster Regt. 12 July, 1895, to 31 Dec. 1896; was employed with the Egyptian Army from 1 Jan. 1897, serving in the Nile Expedition of 1897 (Despatches [London Gazette, 25 Jan. 1898], Egyptian Medal with clasp); in the Nile Expedition of 1898, when he took part in the Expedition to Shendy and the Battles of Atbara and Khartum (Despatches [London Gazette, 30 Sept. 1898]), in the Relief of Gedaref and the Expedition to Kaka (4th Class Medjidie ; Medal ; two clasps to Egyptian Medal); in the Nile Expedition of 1899, as A.D.C. to Lord Kitchener of Khartum, in the operations in the first advance against the Khalifa. He served in the South African War, 1899–1902 (was promoted to Captain 25 Jan. 1900), as Special Service Officer, and was present at operations in the Orange Free State, Feb. to May, 1900, including the action at Zand River ; operations in the Transvaal in May and June, 1900, including actions near Johannesburg (29 May), Pretoria (4 June) and Diamond Hill (11 and 12 June), when he was severely wounded ; operations in the Transvaal, east of Pretoria, July to 29 Nov. 1900 ; operations in the Transvaal, west of Pretoria, July to 29 Nov. 1900, including action at Zilikat's Nek ; operations in Cape Colony, south of Orange River, 1899–1900. He served as Adjutant to a Mounted Infantry Battalion, May and June, 1900 ; was mentioned in Despatches [London Gazette, 10 Sept. 1901], received the Queen's Medal with five clasps, the King's Medal with two clasps, and was created a Companion of the Distinguished Service Order [London Gazette, 27 Sept. 1901]: " John Malise Anne Graham, Capt., Royal Lancaster Regt. In recognition of services during the operations in South Africa." He was invested by the King 24 Oct. 1902. Capt. Graham retired from the Royal Lancaster Regt. 4 July, 1903. He served in the European War, 1914–18, as Lieutenant-Colonel ; was mentioned in Despatches and awarded a Bar to the Distinguished Service Order, and retired in 1918. He married, in 1903, Eva, daughter of the late J. T. Satow.

TROTTER, EDWARD HENRY, Capt., was born 1 Dec. 1872, son of the late Major-General Sir Henry Trotter, G.C.V.O., and the Honourable Ena, eldest daughter of the 2nd Baron Gifford. He entered the Grenadier Guards as Second Lieutenant 28 June, 1893, and was promoted Lieutenant 25 Aug. 1897. He served in the Nile Expedition, 1898; took part in the Battle of Khartum, and received the Egyptian Medal with clasp. He was promoted Captain 28 Jan. 1900. He served during the South African

War, 1900–1902, with the City of London Imperial Volunteers, on the Staff ; during operations in the Orange Free State, May, 1900, including action at Zand River ; during operations in the Transvaal, May and

June, 1900, including actions near Johannesburg, Pretoria and Diamond Hill (11 and 12 June) ; during operations in the Transvaal, west of Pretoria, Aug. 1900. He was employed with Mounted Infantry during operations in Cape Colony, 1901–2 ; was mentioned in Despatches [London Gazette, 10 Sept. 1901], received the Queen's Medal with four clasps, and was created a Companion of the Distinguished Service Order [London Gazette, 27 Sept. 1901]: " Edward Henry Trotter, Capt., Grenadier Guards. In recognition of services during the operations in South Africa." The Insignia were presented by the King 29 Oct. 1901. He became Major 26 Sept. 1908.

Edward Henry Trotter.

Major Trotter served in the European War from 1914, as Temporary Lieutenant-Colonel from 1 Sept. 1914, commanding the 18th Battn. Liverpool Regt. He was killed in action 8 July, 1916. The following is an extract from a newspaper : " A tribute to the benefits of sport was paid in his will by Lieut.-Colonel E. H. Trotter, D.S.O., Grenadier Guards, who was killed in France in July. He left £25,170, and bequeathed :—' To the Grenadier Guards the regimental cup which I won the first year I joined, in the hope that sport of all sorts will long flourish in the regiment, it having been my experience in all the wars I have been in that the best sportsman makes the best soldier, and I should like this fact to be inscribed on the cup.' "

CHAMPION DE CRESPIGNY, CLAUDE, Capt., was born 11 Sept. 1873, in London, third son of Major Sir Claude Champion de Crespigny, Bart., of Champion Lodge, Maldon, Essex, and Georgiana Margaret, second

daughter of the late Robert McKerrall, of Hillhouse. He was educated at Hawtrey's and Eton, and was commissioned in the 2nd Life Guards 3 July, 1895, becoming Lieutenant 5 Aug. 1896, and Captain 3 Feb. 1900. Capt. de Crespigny served in the South African War, 1899–1900, and was present at the Relief of Kimberley and operations in the Orange Free State, Feb. to May, 1900, including operations at Paardeberg and actions at Poplar Grove (severely wounded); operations in Cape Colony, south of Orange River, 1899–1900, including actions at Colesberg (1 Jan. to 12 Feb.). He was mentioned in Despatches [London Gazette, 4 May, 1900, and 10 Sept. 1901]; received the Queen's Medal with three clasps; was recommended for the Victoria Cross, and was created a Com-

C. Champion de Crespigny.

panion of the Distinguished Service Order [London Gazette, 27 Sept. 1901]: " Claude Champion de Crespigny, Capt., 2nd Life Guards. In recognition of services during the operations in South Africa." The Insignia were presented to him by the King 12 March, 1902. Sir Audley Nield reported on the act of gallantry at Rensburg for which Capt. de Crespigny was recommended for the Victoria Cross, and there was a leading article in the " Army and Navy Gazette " on the subject. From Dec. 1900, to Jan. 1902, he was A.D.C. to the Governor-General of India, and from 31 Jan. 1903, to 31 Aug. 1903 was employed with the West African Frontier Force in Southern Nigeria, taking part in the operations against the Chief Adukukaika of Igarra ; operations against the Uris and the people of Omonoha and Ebima. He was wounded, and received the Medal and clasp. He was killed 18 May, 1910.

JONES, LLEWELLYN MURRAY, Capt., was born 23 Nov. 1871, son of the late Major-General R. Godfrey Jones, Madras Cavalry. He was gazetted to the Liverpool Regt. 17 Jan. 1891; became Lieutenant 1 March, 1893; was Adjutant, Liverpool Regt., 20 March, 1898, to 26 Aug. 1902, and was promoted to Captain 5 Feb. 1900. He served in the South African War, 1899–1902, and took part in operations in Natal, 1899, including actions at Rietfontein and Lombard's Kop. He was present at the Defence of Ladysmith ; operations in Natal, March to June, 1900 ; operations in the Transvaal, east of Pretoria, including action at Belfast (26 and 27 Aug.). He served as Adjutant, 1st Battn. Liverpool Regt., and performed the duties of Commandant, Waterval Onder. He was mentioned in Despatches [London Gazette, 8 Feb. 1901 (Sir G. S. White, 23 March, 1900 ; Sir R. H. Buller, 9 Nov. 1900), and London Gazette, 10 Sept. 1901]; received the Queen's Medal with three clasps, the King's Medal with two clasps, and was created a Companion of the Distinguished Service Order [London Gazette, 27 Sept. 1901]: " Llewellyn Murray Jones, Capt., The Liverpool Regt. In recognition of services during the operations in South Africa." Capt. Jones was Adjutant, Volunteers, 4 March, 1903, to 8 July, 1906; became Major 18 Sept. 1909; was Staff Captain, No. 4 District, Western Command, 17 Nov. 1913, to 17 Nov. 1914; D.A.A.G., Western Command, 18 Nov. 1914, to 3 Jan. 1916; A.A. and Q.M.G., 2nd East African Division, East African Force, to 14 Feb. 1916; Base Commandant, East African Force, 15 May, 1916, to 20 May, 1917. He was A.A. and Q.M.G., Humber Garrison, 24 April to 25 July, 1918; A.A. and Q.M.G., 35th Division, British Armies in France, from 6 Sept. 1918. Lieut.-Colonel Jones was given the Brevet of Lieut.-Colonel 1 Jan. 1918, and was created a C.M.G. in 1919 for his services in the European

War. He married, in 1902, Ida St. George, fourth daughter of the late John W. Nicholson, of St. John, New Brunswick.

EVANS, EDWARD, Capt., was born 28 June, 1872, son of the late Lieut.-Colonel E. W. Evans and Emily Sophia, daughter of the late John Dudding, of Lincoln. He was educated at Sandhurst, and was gazetted to the Wiltshire Regt. 19 March, 1893; became Lieutenant 16 Oct. 1895; was Adjutant, Wiltshire Regt., 5 April, 1899, to 4 Oct. 1903, and was promoted to Captain 9 Feb. 1900. He served in the South African War, 1900–2, and was severely wounded; was Garrison Adjutant, Pietersburg; served as Adjutant, 2nd Battn. Wiltshire Regt., to 31 May, 1902; operations in Orange River Colony, including actions at Colesberg (25 Jan. to 12 Feb.); operations in the Transvaal 30 Nov. 1900, to Jan. 1901, and April, 1901, to 31 May, 1902; operations in Cape Colony, Jan. to April, 1901. He was mentioned in Despatches [London Gazette, 10 Sept. 1901]; received the Queen's Medal with three clasps, the King's Medal with two clasps, and was created a Companion of the Distinguished Service Order [London Gazette, 27 Sept. 1901]: "Edward Evans, Capt., Wiltshire Regt. In recognition of services during the operations in South Africa." He was invested by the King 24 Oct. 1902. Capt. Evans was Staff Captain, Home Counties Grouped Regimental District, 17 Aug. 1905, to 31 March, 1908, and D.A.A. and Q.M.G., Home Counties Division, Eastern Command, 1 April, 1908, to 16 Aug. 1909; was promoted to Major 19 March, 1910; was D.A.A. and Q.M.G., East Anglian Division; 54th Division, Eastern Command; Central Force, Home Defence; Mediterranean Expeditionary Force 4 Jan. 1912, to 10 Sept. 1915; A.A. and Q.M.G., 54th Division, Mediterranean Expeditionary Force; Egyptian Expeditionary Force 11 Sept. 1915, to 1 May, 1917; became Lieut.-Colonel 2 April, 1917, and Temporary Brigadier-General 2 Aug. 1917; D.A. and Q.M.G., 20th Army Corps, Egyptian Expeditionary Force, 2 Aug. 1917, to 26 Jan. 1918; Assistant to D.Q.M.G., G.H.Q., Egyptian Expeditionary Force, 27 Jan. 1918. He was appointed A.D.C. to the King 3 June, 1918; was given the Brevet of Lieut.-Colonel 1 Jan. 1916, and of Colonel 3 June, 1918; was created a C.M.G. in 1918, and a C.B. in 1919. He married, in 1907, Helen Beatrix, daughter of Edward Huth, Esq., J.P., D.L., of Wykehurst Park, Haywards Heath, and of Edith, fourth daughter of the late Rev. F. A. S. Marshall, Vicar of Great Easton, and they have two sons and one daughter.

STUDD, HERBERT WILLIAM, Capt., was born 26 Dec. 1870, son of the late Edward Studd, of Tidworth House, Wilts, and 2, Hyde Park Gardens, W. He was educated at Eton, and Trinity College, Cambridge, and entered the Coldstream Guards 25 July, 1891, becoming Lieutenant 2 Jan. 1897, and Captain 11 Feb. 1900. He served in the South African War, 1899–1902, taking part in the advance on Kimberley, including the actions at Belmont, Enslin, Modder River and Magersfontein; operations in the Orange Free State, Feb. to May, 1900, including actions at Poplar Grove, Dreifontein, Vet River and Zand River; operations in the Transvaal in May and June, 1900, including actions near Johannesburg, Pretoria and Diamond Hill; operations in the Transvaal, east of Pretoria, July to Oct. 1900, including action at Belfast; operations in the Transvaal, west of Pretoria, Nov. 1900; operations in Cape Colony, south of Orange River, 1900; operations in the Transvaal, Nov. 1900; operations in Cape Colony, Dec. 1900, to 31 May, 1902. He was mentioned in Despatches [London Gazette, 10 Sept. 1901]; received the Queen's Medal with six clasps, the King's Medal with two clasps, and was created a Companion of the Distinguished Service Order [London Gazette, 27 Sept. 1901]: "Herbert William Studd, Capt., Coldstream Guards. In recognition of services during the operations in South Africa." He was invested by the King 18 Dec. 1902. Capt. Studd was D.A.A.G., London District, 27 Nov. 1905, to 26 Nov. 1909; was promoted to Major 24 June, 1908; was G.S.O.2, War Office, 1 April, 1912, to 4 Aug. 1914. He served in the European War, 1914–18, as G.S.O.2, 1st Army Corps, B.E.F., 5 Aug. to 16 Sept. 1914; commanded the 19th Reserve Infantry Brigade, Home Forces, 23 Oct. 1915, to 2 Jan. 1916, and the 180th Infantry Brigade, Home Forces; British Armies in France 3 Jan. to 8 Nov. 1916; became Lieut.-Colonel 3 Sept. 1916; was Brigadier-General, General Staff, 11th Army Corps, British Armies in France, 9 Nov. 1916, to 4 Dec. 1917; was Brigadier-General, General Staff, Supreme War Council, Versailles, 3 Dec. 1917, to June, 1918. He was dangerously wounded, and for his services in the European War was mentioned in Despatches; given the Brevet of Colonel 3 June, 1917; created a C.M.G. in 1917, and a C.B. in 1918. He married, in 1894, Mary, daughter of the late Major Horace de Vere, of Curragh Chase, County Limerick, and of his wife, the late Mrs. Maxwell, of Isserclеran, County Galway, and they have two daughters.

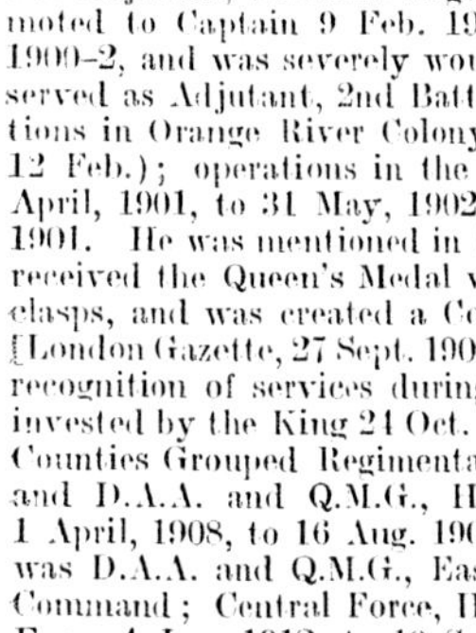
Herbert William Studd.

DOUGLAS, SHOLTO WILLIAM, Capt., was born 11 Oct. 1870, son of the late Major G. M. Douglas, 33rd Regt. He entered the Royal Artillery 25 July, 1890; became Lieutenant 25 July, 1893, and Captain 13 Feb. 1900. He served in the South African War, 1899–1900, and was present at operations in Natal in 1899, including actions at Elandslaagte, Rietfontein (slightly wounded and horse shot) and Lombard's Kop. He took part also in the Defence of Ladysmith, including the action of 6 Jan. 1900. Capt. Douglas was mentioned in Despatches [London Gazette, 8 Feb. and 10 Sept. 1901]; received the Queen's Medal with two clasps, and was created a Companion of the Distinguished Service Order [London Gazette, 27 Sept. 1901]: "Sholto William Douglas, Capt., Royal Horse and Royal Field Artillery. In recognition of services during the operations in South Africa." The Insignia were presented to him by the King 21 Oct. 1901. He passed the Staff College; was Orderly Officer, 4th Class, 31 March, 1903, to 14 April, 1904; Assistant Experimental Officer, Army Ordnance Department, 15 April, 1904, to 2 Feb. 1905; Army Ordnance Department, 3 Feb. to 21 Aug. 1905; Staff Captain, Headquarters of Army, 22 Aug. 1905, to 18 Feb. 1908; was promoted to Major 6 March, 1908; retired from the Royal Artillery 16 Dec. 1911. He was appointed Chief Constable, Metropolitan Police, 1910, and Chief Constable, The Lothians and Peeblesshire, in 1914. Major Douglas married, in 1901, Grace Catherine, daughter of Sir James Wolfe Murray, K.C.B., and Arabella (who died in 1900), daughter of W. Bray.

BLAKENEY, HERBERT NORWOOD, Capt., was born 30 April, 1871, son of the late Colonel Henry Blakeney. He entered the Middlesex Regt. 29 Nov. 1890, becoming Lieutenant 11 May, 1892, and Captain 17 Feb. 1900. He served in the South African War, 1899–1902, employed with Mounted Infantry and attached to the Army Service Corps, and was present at operations in the Orange Free State, Feb. to May, 1900, including actions at Houtnek (Thoba Mountain), Vet River (5 and 6 May) and Zand River; operations in the Transvaal in May and June, 1900, including operations near Pretoria, Johannesburg and Diamond Hill (11 and 12 June); operations in Orange River Colony (May to 29 Nov. 1900), including actions at Bethlehem (6 and 7 July), Wittebergen (1 to 29 July), Ladybrand (2 to 5 Sept.) and Bothaville; operations in Cape Colony, south of Orange River, 1899–1900; operations in Cape Colony, north of Orange River; operations in the Transvaal, July to Sept. 1901; operations in Orange River Colony, 30 Nov. 1900, to July, 1901; operations in Cape Colony, July, 1901, to 31 May, 1902. He was mentioned in Despatches [London Gazette, 10 Sept. 1901]; received the Queen's Medal with five clasps, the King's Medal with two clasps, and was created a Companion of the Distinguished Service Order [London Gazette, 27 Sept. 1901]: "Herbert Norwood Blakeney, Capt., Middlesex Regt. In recognition of services during the operations in South Africa." The Insignia, Warrant, etc., were sent to the G.O.C., Natal District, and presented by Colonel Dunlop at Newcastle, Natal, 28 Dec. 1902. He was promoted to Major 27 May, 1905. Major Blakeney served in the European War from 1914, as Temporary Lieut.-Colonel, Commanding Service Battn. Middlesex Regt., 5 Feb. to 29 Sept. 1916; became Lieut.-Colonel 28 Sept. 1916; in command, Service Battn. Middlesex Regt., 28 Sept. 1916. He was wounded, and was created a C.M.G. in 1918.

PERCIVAL, ARTHUR JEX BLAKE, Capt., was born 1 Dec. 1870, youngest son of the Right Reverend John Percival, Bishop of Hereford, and Louisa (who died in 1896), daughter of James Holland. He entered Marlborough College in 1885, but went on to Rugby in 1887, when his father was appointed Head Master of the school. He was in the XV. in 1889; was gazetted to the Northumberland Fusiliers 20 Feb. 1892, and was promoted Lieutenant 27 Oct. 1894. He served in the Nile Expedition of 1898, taking part in the Battle of Khartum (Medal and Egyptian Medal with clasp). He became Captain 17 Feb. 1900. Capt. Percival served in the South African War, 1899–1902, and was in the advance on Kimberley, including the actions at Belmont and Modder River. He was afterwards on the Staff 22 April, 1901, to 30 June, 1902; was mentioned in Despatches [London Gazette, 26 Jan. 1900, 10 Sept. 1901, and 18 July, 1902]; received the Queen's Medal with four clasps, the King's Medal with two clasps; was placed on the list of Officers considered qualified for Staff employment, in consequence of service on the Staff in the Field, and was created a Companion of the Distinguished Service Order [London Gazette, 27 Sept. 1901]: "Arthur Jex Blake Percival, Capt., Northumberland Fusiliers. In recognition of services during the operations in South Africa." The Insignia were presented by the King 24 Oct. 1902. He saw active service in the Egyptian Army, under Lord Kitchener, 1 Jan. 1903, to 12 Jan. 1908; was in command of the Camel Corps, and served in operations against Nigam-Nigam Tribes in the Bahr-el-Ghezal province, and at Talodi, in Southern Kordofan (two clasps and 4th Class Medjidie; Despatches 13 May, 1906). He was promoted Major 15 Aug. 1908, and later was employed on the Staff at the War Office and at the Staff College. He went to the Front at the beginning of the European War of 1914, as General Staff Officer to Major-General Monro, Commander of the 2nd Division and later of the 1st Army Corps; was mentioned in Despatches by Sir John French 8 Oct. 1914, and was one of the first English officers to receive the Cross of the Legion of Honour (Croix d'Officier). A week before his death it was decided that he was to be given a brigade immediately. He was told of this, but did not live long enough to be gazetted. Major (Temp. Lieut.-Colonel) Percival was killed on 31 Oct. 1914, by a shell, with four other officers of the Staff of the 1st and 2nd Divisions, who had met for a conference in the Château of La Hogue. General Lomax, who was present at this conference, was wounded, and subsequently died of his wounds. Field-Marshal Lord Methuen, G.C.B., G.C.V.O., C.M.G., wrote: "I had no officer serving under me in the South African War whose service as a regimental officer I valued more highly. He was a born leader of men, of splendid courage, and possessing a character which inspired all with whom he came in contact." General Gorringe, C.B., C.M.G., D.S.O., said: "He was the best Staff officer I have ever had. I don't say this only now. I have said so for some time, and had he been given, as he deserved, a command during the war, he would have won still higher honours." A brother officer wrote: "He and

Arthur J. B. Percival.

I were in the Egyptian Army together, and I learnt out there to admire his wonderful energy and great strength of character. I shall never forget the day he rode quietly into Wau, in the Bahr-el-Ghezal, on the date he said he would arrive, after a most extraordinary journey, in which his great qualities had had full play. His Arabs simply worshipped him. By his death we have lost one of the best officers in the army, and at a time when men of his type are priceless." Others spoke in these terms: "A very gallant soldier, loyal, straight, and the best of friends, with never an unkind word." "He was one of the few men I have ever met who apparently did not know fear." "The whole army knew of his splendid qualities. I always used to talk of him as the bravest man I have ever known. He simply knew no fear." The Sirdar, Mr. Asquith, Lord Lincolnshire, General von Donop, General Monro, General Belfield and many others sent telegrams and letters to Lieut.-Colonel Percival's family expressing their sorrow at his death. A letter from a private in his company sums up the general opinion of this gallant officer: "It is said that there are men who fear not death on the battlefield. Certainly no one could have faced death with more serene courage. His absolute indifference to danger was the theme of frequent discussion among the men. His infectious gaiety—no other word is applicable to his demeanour under fire—made a vivid impression upon us young soldiers." Capt. Percival married, in 1907, Cecil, daughter of Charles Henry Henland, and founder of the Princess Christian Hammersmith Day Nursery and of the National Society of Day Nurseries, and who has also published several children's books.

JEBB, JOSHUA HENRY MILES, Capt., was born 12 March, 1875, second son of the late J. G. Jebb, of Barnby Moor House, Notts. He was educated at Charterhouse, and was gazetted to the Manchester Regt. 28 Sept. 1895; became Lieutenant 19 Dec. 1896; was Adjutant, Manchester Regt., 1 Dec. 1899, to 30 Nov. 1903, and was promoted to Captain 27 Dec. 1899. Capt. Jebb served in the South African War, 1900–2, as Station Staff Officer; served as Adjutant, 2nd Battn. Manchester Regt.; operations in the Orange Free State, April, 1900; operations in the Transvaal, east of Pretoria, Aug. to Sept. and Nov. 1900; operations in Orange River Colony, May to 29 Nov. 1900, including actions at Biddulphsberg and Wittebergen; operations in Cape Colony, south of Orange River, April, 1900; operations in the Transvaal in July, 1901; operations in Orange River Colony 30 Nov. 1900, to 31 May, 1902. He was mentioned in Despatches [London Gazette, 10 Sept. 1901, and 29 July, 1902]; received the Queen's Medal with three clasps, the King's Medal with two clasps, and was created a Companion of the Distinguished Service Order [London Gazette, 27 Sept. 1901]: "Joshua Henry Miles Jebb, Capt., Manchester Regt. In recognition of services during the operations in South Africa." He was invested with the Insignia by the King 18 Dec. 1902. He became Major 8 May, 1912, and retired 20 July, 1912, and was Lieut.-Colonel Commanding the 4th Battn. Manchester Rifles, 1913 to 1919. He was mentioned in Despatches; was given the Brevet of Colonel, and promoted to Colonel, April, 1919.

EVANS, WILLIAM, Capt., was born 11 Feb. 1871, third son of V. W. Evans, M.D., of Clifton. He was gazetted to the Royal Artillery 24 July, 1891; became Lieutenant 24 July, 1894, and Captain 22 Feb. 1900. He served in the South African War, 1900–1, as Adjutant, 7th Brigade, Divisional Royal Field Artillery, 1 Nov. 1900, to 29 April, 1901. He was present at operations in the Transvaal, west of Pretoria, July to 29 Nov. 1900, including actions at Venterskroon (7 and 9 Aug.); operations in the Orange Free State, April to May, 1900; operations in Orange River Colony, May to 17 July, 1900, including the action at Lindley (1 June); operations in the Transvaal 30 Nov. 1900, to Jan. 1901, and Feb. and March, 1901; operations in Cape Colony, Jan. and Feb. 1901. He was mentioned in Despatches [London Gazette, 10 Sept. 1901]; received the Queen's Medal with four clasps, and was created a Companion of the Distinguished Service Order [London Gazette, 27 Sept. 1901]: "William Evans, Capt., Royal Horse and Royal Field Artillery. In recognition of services during the operations in South Africa." The Insignia were presented by the King 29 Oct. 1901. He was promoted to Major 19 April, 1909. Major Evans served in the European War from 1914 to 1918; became Lieut.-Colonel 12 May, 1915; was Brigadier-General, Royal Artillery, Guards Division, B.E.F.; British Armies in France 1 March, 1916, to 27 May, 1917, and Brigadier-General, Royal Artillery, 18th Division, British Armies in France, 1 July, 1917, to 10 Nov. 1918. He was six times mentioned in Despatches; was given the Brevet of Lieut.-Colonel 18 Feb. 1915, and created a C.M.G. in 1918. Lieut.-Colonel Williams married, in 1908, Dora Rosamund, daughter of James Young, of Bangalore, and they have one daughter.

CORY, GEORGE NORTON, Capt., was born 26 Dec. 1874, son of Charles D. Cory, of Halifax, Nova Scotia. He was gazetted to the Royal Dublin Fusiliers 28 Aug. 1895, becoming Lieutenant 5 Jan. 1897, and Captain 24 Feb. 1900. He served in the South African War, 1899–1902, as Adjutant, Composite Regt. of Mounted Infantry, from 12 June, 1900; operations in Natal, 1899, including actions at Talana and Lombard's Kop; Relief of Ladysmith, including action at Colenso; operations of 17 to 24 Jan. 1900, and action at Spion Kop; operations of 5 to 7 Feb. 1900, and action at Vaal Kranz; operations on Tugela Heights 14 to 27 Feb. 1900, and action at Pieter's Hill; operations in Natal, March to June, 1900, including action at Laing's Nek (6 to 9 June); operations in the Transvaal, east of Pretoria, July to 24 Nov. 1900; operations in the Transvaal 30 Nov. 1900, to Jan. 1902. He was mentioned in Despatches [London Gazette, 8 Feb. 1901 (Sir R. H. Buller, 30 March and 9 Nov. 1900) and London Gazette, 10 Sept. 1901]; received the Queen's Medal with seven clasps, the King's Medal with two clasps, and was created a Companion of the Distinguished Service Order [London Gazette, 27 Sept. 1901]: "George Norton Cory, Capt., Royal Dublin Fusiliers. In recognition of services during the operations in South Africa." The Insignia, Warrant and Statutes were sent to the Commander-in-Chief in India, and presented by the O.C. Aden Column, after Church Parade, 10 Jan. 1903, at Dehalla. He served in the Aden Hinterland in 1903, taking part in operations in the interior. Capt. Cory was Brigade Major, 7th Brigade, Southern Command, 2 April, 1911, to 30 Sept. 1913; was promoted to Major 19 Feb. 1913; was G.S.O., 3rd Grade, War Office, 1 Oct. 1913, to 4 Aug. 1914. He served in the European War, 1914–1918, as G.S.O.3, 3rd Division, B.E.F., 5 Aug. to 20 Aug. 1914; G.S.O.2, 3rd Division, B.E.F., 27 Aug. 1914, to 4 May, 1915; G.S.O.1, 51st Division, British Armies in France, 5 Aug. to 18 June, 1915; G.S.O.1, 27th Division, British Armies in France; Mediterranean Expeditionary Force 19 June to 17 Dec. 1915; Brigadier-General, General Staff, 16th Army Corps, Mediterranean Expeditionary Force; British Salonika Force 28 Dec. 1915, to 24 Aug. 1917; promoted to Major-General 1 Jan. 1919; Divisional Commander, British Salonika Force, 1919. He was twice mentioned in Despatches; given the Brevets of Lieut.-Colonel (18 Feb. 1915) and Colonel (1 Jan. 1917), and created a C.B. in 1918.

BRIERLEY, GEOFFREY TEALE, Capt., was born 14 July, 1873, at Presteign, Radnorshire, Wales, second son of the late Prebendary Joseph Henry Brierley and Mrs. Brierley, of Whitbourne, Herefordshire. He was educated at Rossall, and was gazetted to the Royal Artillery 1 April, 1893, becoming Lieutenant 1 April, 1896, and Captain 7 March, 1900. Capt. Brierley served in the European War, 1899–1902, with the Imperial Light Horse, and was severely wounded. He was present at operations in the Orange Free State, including actions at Vet River (5 and 6 May) and Zand River; operations in the Transvaal in May and June, 1900, including actions near Johannesburg, Pretoria and Diamond Hill (11 and 12 June); operations in the Transvaal, east of Pretoria, July to 29 Nov. 1900, including actions at Belfast (26 and 27 Aug.); operations in the Transvaal, west of Pretoria, 29 Nov. 1900, including actions near Frederickstad (17 to 25 Oct.); operations in the Transvaal and Orange River Colony 30 Nov. 1900, to 31 May, 1902. He was mentioned in Despatches [London Gazette, 9 July and 10 Sept. 1901, and 25 April, 1902]; received the Queen's Medal with four clasps, and was created a Companion of the Distinguished Service Order [London Gazette, 27 Sept. 1901]: "Geoffrey Teale Brierley, Capt., Royal Garrison Artillery. In recognition of services during the operations in South Africa." He was invested by the King 24 Oct. 1902. Capt. Brierley was Instructor, School of Gunnery, 12 Nov. 1902, to 5 July, 1905; Instructor (1st Class), School of Gunnery, 26 July to 11 Nov. 1905; Adjutant, R.A., 1 Nov. 1910, to 31 Oct. 1912. He was promoted to Major 1 April, 1914. Major Brierley served in France with the 1st Division, commanding 26th (Heavy) Battery, R.G.A. He took part in the Retreat and Advance on the Aisne; was present at Ypres, and was dangerously wounded 31 Oct. 1914; was D.A.A.G. in the disciplinary branch at the War Office, Aug. 1915, to Feb. 1918, when he became attached to the Royal Air Force, and was employed in similar work at the Air Ministry. He became Lieut.-Colonel 22 Nov. 1917, and was created a C.M.G. in 1919. He married, 10 May, 1916, Eily, only daughter of Inspector-General Coppinger, R.N.

Geoffrey Teale Brierley.

HINE-HAYCOCK, VAUGHAN RANDOLPH, Capt., was born 30 Oct. 1871. He entered the Royal Artillery 20 Nov. 1891, becoming Lieutenant 20 Nov. 1894, and Captain 10 March, 1900. He served in the South African War, 1899 to 1901, taking part in operations in the Orange Free State, Feb. to May, 1900, including the action at Zand River; operations in the Transvaal in May and June, 1900, including actions near Johannesburg, Pretoria and Diamond Hill (11 and 12 June); operations in the Transvaal, east of Pretoria, July to 29 Nov. 1900, including action at Belfast (26 and 27 Aug.); operations in Cape Colony, south of Orange River, 1900. He was mentioned in Despatches [London Gazette, 10 Sept. 1901]; received the Queen's Medal with five clasps, and was created a Companion of the Distinguished Service Order [London Gazette, 27 Sept. 1901]: "Vaughan Randolph Hine-Haycock, Capt., Royal Horse and Royal Field Artillery. In recognition of services during the operations in South Africa." The Insignia were presented by the King 29 Oct. 1901. Capt. Hine-Haycock retired 23 March, 1907, and became Deputy Assistant Director of Remounts in 1910. He served in the European War, 1914–18, and was created a C.M.G. He married, in 1902, Grace Mary, daughter of the late Major-General Charles Vaughan Arbuckle.

KINCAID-SMITH, KENNETH JOHN, Capt., was born 6 July, 1874, younger son of the late Major Kincaid-Smith, of Polmont, Falkirk, and the late Mrs. Kincaid-Smith, of Aldingbourne, Chichester. He entered the R.A. 23 Nov. 1891; was promoted to Lieutenant 23 Nov. 1894; was on special extra-regimental employment 29 April, 1895, to 6 Sept. 1896. He served in the South African War, 1899–1902; became Captain 15 March, 1900; was Assistant Provost-Marshal 30 May, 1900, to 12 Feb. 1901; was present at operations in Natal, 1899, including action at Lombard's Kop; Defence of Ladysmith; operations in the Transvaal 30 Nov. 1900, to Oct. 1901; operations on the Zululand Frontier of Natal in Sept. and Oct. 1901; operations in Cape Colony, Nov. 1901, to 31 May, 1902. He was afterwards on the Staff; as District and Station Commandant, and as Staff Officer to O.C.S., Western District. He was mentioned in Despatches [London Gazette, 8 Feb. and 10 Sept. 1901]; received the Queen's Medal with five clasps, the King's Medal with two clasps, and was created a Companion of the Distinguished Service Order [London Gazette, 27 Sept. 1901]: "Kenneth John Kincaid-Smith, Capt., Royal Horse and Royal Field Artillery. In recognition of services during the operations in South Africa." The Insignia, Warrant, etc., were sent to the G.O.C., Transvaal, and presented by Major-General Settle at Cape Town

1 May, 1903, or about that date. Capt. Kincaid-Smith was employed with the West African Frontier Force 28 Oct. 1905, to 5 Feb. 1907; became Major 5 June, 1909; was Assistant Military Secretary to the G.O. Commanding-in-Chief, Eastern Command, 5 May, 1908, to 3 April, 1912; was Assistant Military Secretary to the G.O. Commanding-in-Chief the Forces in Ireland 10 May, 1912, to 4 Aug. 1914. He served in the European War attached to the General Staff, 2nd Army Corps, B.E.F., 5 Aug. to 28 Dec. 1914; as Liaison Officer, B.E.F. and British Armies in France, 29 Dec. 1914, to 26 Oct. 1916; was promoted to Lieut.-Colonel 16 May, 1915; was Brigadier-General, Royal Artillery, 25th Division, British Armies in France, 27 Oct. 1916, to 8 April, 1919; was mentioned in Despatches; given the Brevet of Colonel 1 Jan. 1918; created a C.M.G. in 1916, and a C.B. in 1919.

JEFFCOAT, HENRY JAMESON POWELL, Capt., was born 17 Jan. 1872, son of Deputy-Surgeon-General J. H. Jeffcoat, of 12, Avenue Elmers, Surbiton. He was gazetted to the Royal Artillery 27 Jan. 1892; promoted to Lieutenant 27 Jan. 1895, and to Captain. He served in the South African War, and was created a Companion of the Distinguished Service Order [London Gazette, 27 Sept. 1901]: "Henry Jameson Powell Jeffcoat, Capt., Royal Horse and Royal Field Artillery. In recognition of services during the operations in South Africa." The Insignia, Warrant and Statutes were sent to the sole executor, Capt. A. C. Jeffcoat, D.S.O. (brother), 3 June, 1902, as Capt. H. J. P. Jeffcoat had died 20 Dec. 1901.

FERNYHOUGH, HUGH CLIFFORD, Capt., was born 22 Sept. 1872. He was gazetted to the Yorkshire Light Infantry 21 Oct. 1893, becoming Lieutenant 4 Dec. 1894, and serving on the N.W. Frontier of India, 1897–98, with the Tirah Expeditionary Force, when he was present at the affair at Shinkamar (Medal with two clasps). He served in the South African War, 1899–1902; became Captain 2 March, 1900; was Brigade Signalling Officer 14 May, to 7 Dec. 1900, and Signalling Officer 8 Dec. 1901, to 13 Nov. 1902. He took part in the advance on Kimberley, including the actions at Belmont and Enslin (wounded); operations in Orange River Colony (May to Aug. 1900), including actions at Lindley (26 June), Bethlehem (6 and 7 July) and Wittebergen (1 to 29 July); operations in the Transvaal, Aug. to 29 Nov. 1900; operations in the Transvaal 30 Nov. to Dec. 1900, and March, 1901, to 31 May, 1902; operations in Cape Colony, Jan. to March, 1901; was severely wounded. He was mentioned in Despatches [London Gazette, 10 Sept. 1901, and 11 April and 29 July, 1902]; received the Queen's Medal with three clasps, the King's Medal with two clasps, and was created a Companion of the Distinguished Service Order [London Gazette, 27 Sept. 1901]: "Hugh Clifford Fernyhough, Capt., Yorkshire Light Infantry. In recognition of services during the operations in South Africa." He was invested by the King 24 Oct. 1902. Capt. Fernyhough was transferred to the Army Ordnance Department in 1906; was Ordnance Officer, 4th Class, 1 Feb. 1906, to 31 Jan. 1913, and 1 Feb. to 22 May, 1913; was promoted to Major 23 May, 1913; was Chief Ordnance Officer, Sierra Leone; was Ordnance Officer, 3rd Class, 23 May, 1913. He served in the European War, 1914–18, as Ordnance Officer, 2nd Class (Temporary), 13 April, 1915; A.Q.M.G., G.H.Q., British Armies in France, 4 April, 1917, to 22 May, 1918; Ordnance Officer, 1st Class (acting), 23 May, 1918; Assistant Director of Ordnance Services. He was mentioned in Despatches twice, created a C.M.G. in 1917, and given the Brevets of Lieut.-Colonel 1 Jan. 1916, and Colonel 3 June, 1919. Colonel Fernyhough married, in 1903, Beatrice, daughter of the late H. A. James, of Suffolk Hall, Cheltenham.

WHEELER, HENRY LITTLETON, Capt., was born 8 May, 1863, at Bromwich House, Worcester, son of the late Hon. Canon T. Littleton Wheeler and Catherine, daughter of the late Capt. R. Bradshaw, R.N. He was educated privately, and joined the Worcestershire Militia in 1887 and entered the Hampshire Regt. 9 April, 1892; became Lieutenant 4 April, 1894, and Captain 24 March, 1900. He served in the South African War, 1900–2, taking part in operations in the Orange Free State, Feb. to May, 1900, including operations at Paardeberg (17 to 26 Feb.); actions at Poplar Grove, Karee Siding, Vet River (5 and 6 May) and Zand River; operations in the Transvaal in May and June, 1900, including actions near Johannesburg and Pretoria. He was attached to the A.S.C. from 26 July, 1901. Capt. Wheeler took part in operations in the Transvaal 30 Nov. 1900, to 31 May, 1902. He was mentioned in Despatches [London Gazette, 10 Sept. 1901, and 29 July, 1902, and on a third occasion]; received the Queen's Medal with three clasps, the King's Medal with two clasps, and was created a Companion of the Distinguished Service Order [London Gazette, 27 Sept. 1901]: "Henry Littleton Wheeler, Capt., Hants Regt. In recognition of services during operations in South Africa." He retired from the Hampshire Regt. 4 April, 1908, and became Secretary, Territorial Association, Staffordshire Regt., in 1908. He was created a C.B. in 1918, and became Major, Reserve of Officers, 28 April, 1914. Major Wheeler married, in Nov. 1903, at Portsmouth, Vera, youngest daughter of Colonel Gillum Webb, of Walton House, Ashchurch, and of his wife, Florence, only daughter of the late General E. Atlay, C.B., and they have one son, Richard Littleton Wheeler, born in 1906, and a daughter, Elizabeth Littleton Wheeler, born in 1904.

MOORES, CHARLES FREDERICK, Capt., was born 9 Sept. 1873, son of Colonel S. Moores, and brother of Colonel S. G. Moores, C.B., C.M.G. He was gazetted to the Royal Munster Fusiliers 26 April, 1893; became Lieutenant, Royal Munster Fusiliers, 27 Jan. 1896, and Army Service Corps 31 March, 1896, and Captain 1 April, 1900. He served in the South African War, 1899–1901, taking part in the advance on Kimberley, including actions at Belmont, Enslin, Modder River and Magersfontein; Relief of Kimberley; operations in the Orange Free State, Feb. to May, 1900, including operations at Paardeberg (17 to 26 Feb.); actions at Poplar Grove, Dreifontein and Karee Siding; actions at Houtnek (Thoba Mountain), Vet River (5 and 6 May) and Zand River; operations in the Transvaal in May and June, 1900, including actions near Johannesburg, Pretoria and Diamond Hill (11 and 12 June); operations in the Transvaal, east and west of Pretoria, July to 29 Nov. 1900, including action at Elands River (4–16 Aug.); operations in Orange River Colony, May to 29 Nov. 1900, including actions at Bethlehem (6 and 7 July) and Wittebergen (1 to 29 July). He was mentioned in Despatches [London Gazette, 10 Sept. 1901]; received the Queen's Medal with nine clasps, and was created a Companion of the Distinguished Service Order [London Gazette, 27 Sept. 1901]: "Charles Frederick Moores, Capt., Army Service Corps. In recognition of services during the operations in South Africa." He was D.A.A.G., Southern District, 8 Nov. 1903, to 31 May, 1905; D.A.A. and Q.M.G., Coastal Defences, Southern Command, 1 June, 1905, to 7 Nov. 1907; was promoted to Major 12 Jan. 1909; Deputy Assistant Director of Quartering, War Office, 20 April, 1911, to 6 Sept. 1915. He became Lieutenant-Colonel, R.A.S.C., 24 Feb. 1915; from 7 Sept. 1915, to 18 Dec. 1918, he was A.A. and Q.M.G., B.E.F. and British Armies in France, and from 19 Dec. 1918, he was A.A. and Q.M.G., British Armies in France. He was given the Brevet of Colonel 1 Jan. 1919.

MEIKLEJOHN, RONALD FORBES, Capt., was born 9 Oct. 1876, son of Capt. John F. Meiklejohn, late Royal Horse Artillery. He was educated at Rugby, and joined the Royal Warwickshire Regt. 5 Sept. 1896, becoming Lieutenant 6 April, 1898. He served in the Nile Expedition in 1898, taking part in the Battles of the Atbara and Khartum (Medal, and Egyptian Medal with clasps). He served in the South African War, 1899–1900, taking part in the Relief of Ladysmith; operations in Cape Colony, 1899. He was mentioned in Despatches [London Gazette, 8 Feb. and 10 Sept. 1901]; received the Queen's Medal with two clasps, and was created a Companion of the Distinguished Service Order [London Gazette, 27 Sept. 1901]: "Ronald Forbes Meiklejohn, Capt., Royal Warwickshire Regt. In recognition of services during the operations in South Africa." The Insignia were presented by the King 24 Oct. 1902. He had been promoted to Captain 1 April, 1900. Capt. Meiklejohn passed the Staff College; was Staff Captain, Naval Base, Cape Colony District, 18 June, 1901, to 1 May, 1906; Staff Captain, Coastal Defence, Eastern Command, 2 May, 1906, to 17 June, 1908; D.A.A. and Q.M.G., Coastal Defence, Scottish Command, 1 April, 1910, to 30 April, 1914; was promoted to Major 6 April 1914. He was employed under the Admiralty 5 April, 1918, to 20 Jan. 1919; was G.S.O., 2nd Grade, Northern Russia Expeditionary Force, 21 Jan. 1919. Major Meiklejohn married, in 1903, Kathleen Stella, daughter of the late Henry Myburgh, Imperial Ottoman Consul at Cape Town, and they have one son.

OLLIVANT, JOHN SPENCER, Capt., was born 31 July, 1872, son of Colonel E. A. Ollivant, of Nuthurst, Horsham. He was gazetted to the Royal Artillery 1 Oct. 1892, and became Lieutenant 1 Oct 1895, and Captain 7 April, 1900; was Divisional Adjutant, 5th Brigade, R.A., 16 Sept. 1900, to 31 March, 1901, and Adjutant, R.A., 1 April, 1901, to 21 Jan. 1904, serving in the South African War from 1899 to 1902. He was present at the Relief of Ladysmith, including operations of 5 to 7 Feb. 1900, and action at Vaal Kranz; operations in the Transvaal, June to 29 Nov. 1900; operations in Orange River Colony, Jan. to March, and May, 1902. He was mentioned in Despatches [London Gazette, 10 Sept. 1901]; received the Queen's Medal with five clasps, the King's Medal with two clasps, and was created a Companion of the Distinguished Service Order [London Gazette, 27 Sept. 1901]: "John Spencer Ollivant, Capt., Royal Artillery. In recognition of services during the operations in South Africa." He was invested by the King 24 Oct. 1902. Capt. Ollivant was Staff Captain, H.Q. of Army, 5 Nov. 1904, to 4 Nov. 1908; became Major 20 Oct. 1909. He served in the European War in France and Flanders, 1914–19; as Temporary Lieut.-Colonel, R.A., 21 Aug. to 13 Sept. 1915; became Lieut.-Colonel 14 Sept. 1915; was Brigadier-General, R.A., 3rd Division, British Armies in France, from 24 July, 1916. He was twice mentioned in Despatches; was given the Brevets of Lieut.-Colonel (18 Feb. 1915) and Colonel (1 Jan. 1918), and was created a C.M.G. in 1917, and a C.B. in 1919.

John Spencer Ollivant.

KNATCHBULL, REGINALD NORTON, Capt., was born 7 Feb. 1872, son of Colonel Norton Knatchbull, late Derbyshire Regt. He entered the Leicestershire Regt. 4 March, 1891, becoming Lieutenant 1 March, 1893, and Captain 9 April, 1900. He served in the South African War, 1899 to 1900, taking part in operations in Natal in 1899, including the actions at Talana and Lombard's Kop; Defence of Ladysmith, including action of 6 Jan. 1900; operations in Natal (March to June, 1900), including action at Laing's Nek (6 to 9 June); operations in the Transvaal, east of Pretoria, July to 29 Nov. 1900, including actions at Belfast (26 and 27 Aug.) and Lydenburg (5 to 8 Sept.). He was mentioned in Despatches [London Gazette, 10 Sept. 1901]; received the Queen's Medal with five clasps, and was created a Companion of the Distinguished Service Order [London Gazette, 27 Sept. 1901]: "Reginald Norton Knatchbull, Capt., Leicestershire Regt. In recognition of services during the operations in South Africa." The Insignia, Warrant, etc., were sent to the G.O.C. Troops, Cairo, 10 Feb. 1902, and presented by the O.C. Troops, Alexandria, 2 March, 1902. Capt. Knatchbull was Adjutant, Leicestershire Regt., 4 April, 1901, to 9 March, 1905. He was employed with the Ceylon Volunteers 10 March, 1905 to 14 March, 1908, and was promoted to Major 10 Sept. 1908. He married, in 1906, Winifred, daughter of W. F. Peel, and they had one daughter. Lieut.-Colonel Knatchbull died in Aug. 1917, on an Eastern front, from the effects of heat.

SAUNDERS, EDWARD ALDBOROUGH, Capt., was born 7 Jan. 1873, at Golden Fort, Stratford-on-Slaney, Ireland, son of Major Morley Caulfeild Saunders, 12th Suffolks, of Golden Fort, Stratford-on-Slaney.

Edward A. Saunders.

He was educated at The Old Hall School, Wellington, Shropshire, and at the R.M. Academy, Woolwich, and joined the Royal Artillery 1 Jan. 1894. He served in the South African War, 1899–1902: (1) as Special Service Officer, graded as Staff Captain, Lines of Communication, Headquarters, from 7 Aug. 1899, to 2 Jan. 1900; (2) took part in the advance on Kimberley, Jan. and Feb. 1900; (3) in the operations in the Orange Free State, April, 1900; became Captain 9 April, 1900; was A.D.C. to Major-General R. Pole-Carew, 1900; (4) operations in the Transvaal, west of Pretoria, July, 1900, to Jan. 1901, including Venterskroon (7 and 9 Aug. 1900); was A.D.C. to Major-General C. W. H. Douglas; (5) operations in the Orange River Colony, May and July, 1900, ncluding Lindley and Rhenoster River; (6) operations in Cape Colony, north of the Orange River, Feb. and March, 1900; (7) was employed as Staff Officer, Lines of Communication, and Cape Colony District, graded as D.A.A.G., March, 1901, to Dec. 1902. He was mentioned in Despatches [London Gazette, 10 Sept. 1901]; received the Queen's Medal with three clasps, the King's Medal with two clasps, and was created a Companion of the Distinguished Service Order [London Gazette, 27 Sept. 1901]: "Edward Aldborough Saunders, Capt., Royal Artillery. In recognition of services during operations in South Africa." There is no official account of any specific action for which Capt. Saunders's D.S.O. was awarded, but it was probably given in connection with an action against Christian De Wet at Rhenoster River 11 June, 1900, when seven Boers surrendered to him single-handed when he was on reconnaissance duty, and they were handed over by him personally, as prisoners of war, on the arrival of our troops. Capt. Saunders was at the time A.D.C. to Major-General C. W. H. Douglas. Capt. Saunders's subsequent services include: Staff Captain, R.A., South-Eastern District, 1904–5; Staff Officer for Defences and General Staff Officer, Newcastle-on-Tyne Coast Defences, 1905–8; Acting A.A.G., Headquarters, Army of Occupation in Egypt, July and Oct. 1908. He retired from the Army 5 April, 1911.

TOTTENHAM, CHARLES BOSVILE, Capt., was born 19 Oct. 1869, at 57, Belgrave Road, London, S.W., elder son of Colonel Charles George Tottenham, of Ballycurry, County Wicklow, late of the Scots Fusilier

Charles B. Tottenham.

Guards, and formerly Member of Parliament for New Ross, Wexford, and Catherine Elizabeth (who died in 1905), daughter of the Hon. and Rev. Sir F. Stapleton, 7th Bart., of Gray's Court, and granddaughter of the 22nd Lord Despencer. He was educated at Eton and Sandhurst, and joined the Scots Guards 29 Oct. 1890, and was transferred a few months later to the 14th Hussars (14 Jan. 1891). He became Lieutenant 23 Nov. 1892, and Captain 16 April, 1900. Capt. Tottenham served in the South African War, 1899–1902, and was present at the Relief of Ladysmith, including the operations of 5 to 7 Feb. 1900, and action at Vaal Kranz; operations on Tugela Heights 14 to 27 Feb. 1900, and action at Pieter's Hill; operations in the Orange Free State, Feb. to May, 1900, including actions at Houtnek (Thoba Mountain) and Zand River; operations in the Transvaal in May and June, 1900, including actions near Johannesburg, Pretoria and Diamond Hill (11 and 12 June); operations in the Transvaal, east of Pretoria, July to 29 Nov. 1900, including action at Belfast (26 and 27 Aug.); operations in the Transvaal 30 Nov. 1900, to Jan. 1901; operations in Orange River Colony, Feb. to 31 May, 1902; operations on the Zululand Frontier of Natal in Sept. and Oct. 1901. He was mentioned in Despatches [London Gazette, 10 Sept. 1901]; received the Queen's Medal with seven clasps, the King's Medal with two clasps, and was created a Companion of the Distinguished Service Order [London Gazette, 27 Sept. 1901]: "Charles Bosvile Tottenham, Capt., 14th Hussars. In recognition of services during the operations in South Africa." He was awarded the D.S.O. for his successful command of the rear-guard when the column was retreating from Geluk, Transvaal, on 13 Oct. 1900, when Colonel Brown-Synge Hutchinson (who is also in the 14th Hussars) won his V.C. He was promoted to Major 14 Jan. 1905. Major Tottenham was a noted rider, and won many regimental races. He married, in 1907, at Christ Church, Folkestone, Ruby, daughter of Mr. and Mrs. Piercy Benn. He left the Service in Oct. 1910, owing to ill-health, and died on the 11th Feb. 1911, at Mentone. (An obituary notice appeared in the "Times" of 14 Feb. 1911.)

GREEN, HENRY EDWARD, Capt., was born 9 March, 1876. He was educated at Beaumont and Sandhurst, and was gazetted to the Scottish Rifles 11 April, 1896, becoming Lieutenant 11 July, 1898. He served at Sierra Leone, 1898–99 (Medal with clasp). He again saw active service in the South African War, 1899–1902; became Captain in 1900, and was wounded. He was twice mentioned in Despatches; received the Queen's Medal with four clasps, the King's Medal with two clasps, and was created a

Companion of the Distinguished Service Order [London Gazette, 27 Sept. 1901]: "Henry Edward Green, Capt., Scottish Rifles. In recognition of services during the operations in South Africa." He was invested by the King 18 Dec. 1902. Lieut.-Colonel H. E. Green is married and has a daughter.

STEVENSON, EDWARD HALL, Capt., was born 21 July, 1872. He entered the Royal Artillery 18 Jan. 1893; became Lieutenant 18 Jan. 1896, and Captain 27 April, 1900. He served in the South African War, 1899–1902, and took part in the advance on Kimberley, including action at Magersfontein; operations in the Orange Free State, Feb. to May, 1900, including operations at Paardeberg; actions at Poplar Grove, Dreifontein, Karee Siding, Houtnek (Thoba Mountain) and Zand River; operations in the Transvaal in May and June, 1900, including actions near Johannesburg, Pretoria and Diamond Hill; operations in the Transvaal, west of Pretoria, July to 29 Nov. 1900. He was severely wounded. He was present in the operations in Orange River Colony in July, 1900, including actions at Wittebergen (1 to 29 July); operations in the Transvaal, Orange River Colony and Cape Colony, Feb. 1901, to Jan. 1902. He was Staff Captain (Intelligence) 28 March to 5 Aug. 1902. Capt. Stevenson was mentioned in Despatches [London Gazette, 10 Sept. 1901]; received the Queen's Medal with six clasps; the King's Medal with two clasps, and was created a Companion of the Distinguished Service Order [London Gazette, 27 Sept. 1901]: "Edward Hall Stevenson, Capt., Royal Horse and Royal Field Artillery. In recognition of services during the operations in South Africa." He was invested by the King 18 Dec. 1903. From 8 March, 1905, to 8 Sept. 1907, he was Adjutant, Royal Artillery; from 9 Sept. 1907, to 15 Jan. 1910, he was Garrison Adjutant, Eastern Command, and on 16 Jan. 1910, he was promoted to Major. Major Stevenson served in the European War, 1914–18; became Lieutenant-Colonel 9 Oct. 1915, and was Temporary Brigadier-General from 11 June, to Dec. 1917 (Brigadier-General, Royal Artillery, 30th Division, British Armies in France, 11 June, to 31 Aug. 1917; Brigadier-General, Royal Artillery, 29th Division, British Armies in France, 1 Sept. 1917). He was wounded; was mentioned in Despatches; was given the Brevets of Lieutenant-Colonel and Colonel (3 June, 1917), and created a C.M.G. in 1918. Colonel Stevenson married, in 1917, Ethel Vaughan, widow of Leopold Hudson, F.R.C.S.

COLLINS, ERNEST ROKEBY, Capt., was born 12 Oct. 1870, fourth son of Brigade Surgeon Francis Collins, late 5th Fusiliers, of Lyme Regis. He was gazetted to the East Lancashire Regt. 19 Nov. 1892; became Lieutenant 1 July, 1894, and Captain 4 June, 1900. He served in the South African War, 1900–2, employed with Mounted Infantry, and took part in operations in the Transvaal, Dec. 1900, to Jan. 1902, and April to 31 May, 1902; operations in Orange River Colony, July to Sept. 1901, and Jan. to Feb. 1902; operations in Cape Colony, May and Sept. 1901, and May, 1902. He was mentioned in Despatches [London Gazette, 10 Sept. and 15 Nov. 1901]; received the Queen's Medal with three clasps; the King's Medal with three clasps, and was created a Companion of the Distinguished Service Order [London Gazette, 27 Sept. 1901]: "Ernest Rokeby Collins, Capt., East Lancashire Regt. In recognition of services during operations in South Africa." Capt. Collins was invested by the King 18 Dec. 1902. He was promoted to Major 14 May, 1913, and served in the European War, 1914–18. Major Collins married Margaret Alice, second daughter of the Rev. E. W. Sotheron-Estcourt, M.A., of Estcourt, Tetbury, Gloucestershire, and of his wife, Eleanor Lucy, daughter of the Rev. W. J. Bucknall Estcourt.

AMOS, HERBERT GILBERT MACLACHLAN, Capt., was born in London 28 April, 1866, son of the Rev. James Amos, of St. Ibbs, Hitchin, Herts. He entered the West India Regt. 15 Oct. 1890; became Lieutenant, West India Regt., 29 April, 1892; Lieutenant, King's Own Scottish Borderers, 7 June, 1893; Adjutant, K.O.S.B., 25 July, 1898, and Captain, K.O.S.B., 24 Jan. 1900. He served in South Africa, 1900–1–2; operations in Orange Free State, Feb. to May, 1900; Paardeberg 16 to 26 Feb.; actions at Poplar Grove and Karee Siding, 29 March; actions at Vet River 5 and 6 May; Zand River 10 May; operations in Transvaal, May and June, 1900, including actions near Johannesburg and Pretoria; operations in Transvaal, east of Pretoria and west of Pretoria. He was created a Companion of the Distinguished Service Order [London Gazette, 27 Sept. 1901]: "Herbert Gilbert Maclachlan Amos, Capt., King's Own Scottish Borderers. In recognition of services during operations in South Africa." He was invested by the King 18 Dec. 1901, and was twice mentioned in Despatches [London Gazette, 10 Sept. 1901, and 29 July, 1902]. He retired, and became Hon. Major in the 3rd Battn. Norfolk Regt. (Special Reserve). Major Amos married, in 1893, Kate Isabella, daughter of General W. A. Stratton, and they have one son and one daughter.

RICHARDS, BERNARD OGILVIE, Capt., was born 20 July, 1874. He was gazetted to the Worcestershire Regt. 20 Feb. 1895; became Lieutenant 11 Aug. 1895, and Captain 20 June, 1900. Capt. Richards served in the South African War, 1899–1902, employed with Mounted Infantry. He was present at the Relief of Kimberley, and took part in operations in the Orange Free State, Feb. to May, 1900, including operations at Paardeberg (17 to 26 Feb.); actions at Poplar Grove and Dreifontein; operations in the Transvaal in May and June, 1900, including actions near Johannesburg, Pretoria and Diamond Hill (11 and 12 June); operations in the Transvaal, west of Pretoria, July to Nov. 1900, including action at Eland's River (16 Aug.); operations in Orange River Colony, May to 29 Nov. 1900, including actions at Wittebergen (8 to 16 July); operations in Cape Colony, south of Orange River, 1899–1900, including actions at Colesberg (14 Jan. to 5 Feb.); operations in the Transvaal 30 Nov. 1900, to Jan. 1902, and March to 31 May, 1902. He was mentioned in Despatches [London Gazette, 10 Sept. 1901]; received the Queen's Medal with six clasps; the King's Medal with two clasps, and was created a Companion of the Distinguished Service Order [London Gazette, 27 Sept. 1901]: "Bernard Ogilvie Richards, Capt., Worcestershire Regt. In recognition of services during the operations in South Africa." He was invested by the King 18 Dec. 1903. Capt. Richards was Adjutant, Militia, 20 Dec. 1902, to 19 Dec. 1907. He retired from the Worcestershire Regt. 2 April, 1910; became Captain, 3rd Battn. East Surrey Regt.; became Major, Reserve of Officers, 11 Sept. 1916. He served during the European War as Temporary Lieutenant-Colonel 9th Essex Regt.

LAMBTON, GEORGE CHARLES, Capt., was born 10 Nov. 1872, fourth son of Lieut.-Colonel Francis W. Lambton (third son of William Henry Lambton, youngest brother of the 1st Earl of Durham, and Henrietta Lambton, co-heiress of Cuthbert Ellison, Junior, of Durham), and Lady Victoria Alexandrina Elizabeth Campbell, daughter of the 2nd Earl Cawdor. He was educated at Wellington, and joined the Worcestershire Regt. 7 Dec. 1895, becoming Lieutenant 2 March, 1899, and Captain 23 June, 1900. Capt. Lambton served in the South African War, 1899–1902, employed with Mounted Infantry. He took part in operations in the Orange Free State, Feb. to May, 1900, including actions at Houtnek (Thoba Mountain), Vet River (5 and 6 May) and Zand River; operations in the Transvaal in May and June, 1900, including actions near Johannesburg, Pretoria and Diamond Hill (11 and 12 June); operations in Orange River Colony, May to 29 Nov. 1900, including actions at Wittebergen (1 to 29 July), Ladybrand (2 to 5 Sept.), Bothaville, Caledon River (27 to 29 Nov.); operations in the Orange River Colony 30 Nov. 1900, to March, 1902; operations in Cape Colony, Feb. to March, 1901, and Sept. to Oct. 1901. He was mentioned in Despatches [London Gazette, 10 Sept. 1901]; received the Queen's Medal with four clasps; the King's Medal with two clasps, and was created a Companion of the Distinguished Service Order [London Gazette, 27 Sept. 1901]: "George Charles Lambton, Capt., Worcestershire Regt. In recognition of services during the operations in South Africa." The Insignia, Warrant and Statutes were sent to the G.O.C., Transvaal and Orange Free State. He was Adjutant, Indian Volunteers, 16 Oct. 1909, to 25 July, 1912, and became Major 4 May, 1912. He served in the European War in 1914 and 1915; was Temporary Lieutenant-Colonel, Worcestershire Regt., 6 March, 1915, to 5 May, 1916; Temporary Lieutenant-Colonel, commanding Local Reserve Battn. Royal Fusiliers, 14 July, to 31 Aug. 1916; commanding Training Reserve Battn. 1 Sept. 1916, to 17 Jan. 1918; commanding Graduated Battn. 18 Jan. 1918; Acting Lieutenant-Colonel, Royal Welsh Fusiliers, Nov. 1918. For his services in the European War he was mentioned in Despatches, and given the Brevet of Lieutenant-Colonel 3 June, 1915.

LOCKETT, WILLIAM JEFFERY, Capt., was born 29 Nov. 1873, second son of the late Charles Harrison Lockett, of Redcliffe, New Brighton, Cheshire. He entered the 14th Hussars 11 March, 1893; became Lieutenant 10 Jan. 1894, and Captain, 1st Dragoon Guards, 4 July, 1900. Capt. Lockett served in the South African War, 1899–1902, and was present at the Relief of Kimberley; operations in the Orange Free State, Feb. to May, 1900, including operations at Paardeberg; actions at Poplar Grove, Dreifontein, Houtnek (Thoba Mountain), Vet River and Zand River; operations in the Transvaal in May and June, 1900, including actions near Johannesburg and Pretoria; operations in the Transvaal, east of Pretoria, including action at Belfast. He was afterwards employed with Imperial Yeomanry 1 Jan. to 2 May, 1902, and was Adjutant Imperial Yeomanry, 1 July, 1902, to 30 June, 1907. For his services in the South African War he was mentioned in Despatches [London Gazette, 10 Sept. 1901]: received the Queen's Medal with six clasps; the King's Medal with two clasps, and was created a Companion of the Distinguished Service Order [London Gazette, 27 Sept. 1901]: "William Jeffery Lockett, Capt., 5th Lancers. In recognition of services during the operations in South Africa." He was promoted to Major, 13th Hussars, 8 Jan. 1908, and was transferred to the 11th Hussars 4 Dec. 1909. Major Lockett served in the European War in 1914 and 1915, and was wounded. He was Instructor, Machine Gun Corps Training Centre, 9 Aug. to 3 Sept. 1916; was Temporary Lieutenant-Colonel, Machine Gun Corps, 1 Oct. 1916; Deputy Commander, Machine Gun Corps Training Centre, from 19 Dec. 1917, with the temporary rank of Colonel. He was given the Brevet of Lieutenant-Colonel 3 June, 1919. Lieut.-Colonel Lockett married, in 1908, Janetta, daughter of the late Major G. Paynter.

WOOD, ALEX. VAUGHAN LEIPSIC, Capt., was born 8 Sept. 1867, second son of the late Capt. C. Harcourt Wood and Mrs. Harcourt Wood, of Malshendre Glasbury-on-Wye, Breconshire. He was gazetted to the 5th Lancers 3 Oct. 1888; became Lieutenant 10 Sept. 1890; was A.D.C. to the G.O.C., Shorncliffe, 5 March, 1895, to 22 May, 1898; became Captain 16 June, 1900. He served in the South African War, 1899–1902; as Brigade Signalling Officer 23 March, to 31 July, 1900, and as A.D.C. to Brigadier-General 1 Jan. 1901, to 7 May, 1902. Capt. Wood was present in operations in Natal in 1899, including actions at Elandslaagte, Rietfontein and Lombard's Kop; Defence of Ladysmith, including sortie of 7 Dec. 1899, and action of 6 Jan. 1900; operations in Natal, March to June, 1900; operations in the Transvaal, east of Pretoria, July to 29 Nov. 1900, including actions at Belfast (26 and 27 Aug.) and Lydenberg (5 to 8 Sept.); operations in the Transvaal, Dec. 1900; operations in Cape Colony, May, 1902. He was mentioned in Despatches [London Gazette, 8 Feb. and 10 Sept. 1901]; received the Queen's Medal with five clasps; the King's Medal with two clasps, and was created a Companion of the Distinguished Service Order [London Gazette, 27 Sept. 1901]: "Alex. Vaughan Leipsic Wood, Capt., 5th Lancers. In recognition of services during the operations in South Africa." He was invested by the King 18 Dec. 1902. Capt. Wood was Adjutant, Militia, 18 June, 1902, to 10 Aug. 1905; became Major, 5th Lancers, 19 Oct. 1905. He retired in 1909; was recalled in Aug. 1914, and served in Ireland, France, Belgium and Germany, and later with Remounts in England. He married, in 1909, Marjorie Florence, daughter of the late William Henry Makins, 13th Hussars, and they have one son.

Edward Ussher.

USSHER, EDWARD, Capt., was born 26 Nov. 1869, eldest son of the late John Ussher, Esq., and Mrs. Ussher, of The Dene, Great Budworth, Cheshire. He was educated at Eton and at the Royal Military College, Sandhurst, and entered the 2nd Dragoons 29 March, 1890, and became Lieutenant 21 Sept. 1892, and Captain and Adjutant in 1900. He served in the South African War from Nov. 1899, to Feb. 1902; was mentioned in Despatches; received the Queen's and King's Medals, and was created a Companion of the Distinguished Service Order [London Gazette, 27 Sept. 1901]: "Edward Ussher, Capt., 2nd Dragoon Guards. In recognition of services during the operations in South Africa." Capt. Ussher died 28 Feb. 1902, from wounds received two days previously at Klippan, in the Transvaal. He had married, in 1897, Selina, daughter of John Bowen, Esq., of Burt House, County Donegal.

MACLEAN, HENRY DONALD NEIL, Capt., was born 24 June, 1872. He was gazetted to the King's Own Scottish Borderers 21 Jan. 1893, becoming Lieutenant 22 May, 1895, and taking part in operations on the North-West Frontier of India, 1897–98, with the Tirah Expeditionary Force (Medal with two clasps). He served in the South African War, 1899–1902; was promoted to Captain 9 June, 1900; was present at operations in the Orange Free State, Feb. to May, 1900, including operations at Paardeberg (17 to 26 Feb.); actions at Poplar Grove, Karee Siding, Vet River (5 and 6 May) and Zand River; operations in the Transvaal in May and June, 1900, including actions near Johannesburg and Pretoria; operations in the Transvaal, east of Pretoria, 1900; operations in the Transvaal, March, 1901, to 31 May, 1902. He was mentioned in Despatches [London Gazette, 10 Sept. 1901]; received the Queen's Medal with two clasps; the King's Medal with two clasps, and was created a Companion of the Distinguished Service Order [London Gazette, 27 Sept. 1901]: "Henry Donald Neil Maclean, Capt., King's Own Scottish Borderers. In recognition of services during the operations in South Africa." He was invested by the King 24 Oct. 1902. Major Maclean served in the European War from 19 Aug. 1914, to 9 May, 1918, as Temporary Lieutenant-Colonel, King's Own Scottish Borderers, and from 10 May, 1918, as Temporary Lieutenant-Colonel, commanding the King's Own Scottish Borderers. He was mentioned in Despatches, and was given the Brevet of Lieutenant-Colonel 1 Jan. 1916.

SKEFFINGTON, THE HONOURABLE ALGERNON WILLIAM JOHN CLOTWORTHY (VISCOUNT MASSEREENE AND FERRARD), Capt., was born 28 Nov. 1873, son of the 11th Viscount and Florence, only child of the late Major George John Whyte-Melville, the famous sporting poet and novelist, who was so much beloved and regretted. He was educated at Winchester and Sandhurst, and was gazetted to the 17th Lancers 20 Feb. 1895, becoming Lieutenant 13 Nov. 1895; Captain, 1900, and Adjutant, 17th Lancers, 1900. He served in the South African War, 1900–2, as Adjutant, 17th Lancers, 1 Nov. 1900, to 31 May, 1902, taking part in operations in the Orange Free State, Feb. to May, 1900, including actions at Vet River (5 and 6 May) and Zand River; operations in the Transvaal in May and June, 1900, including actions at Johannesburg, Pretoria and Diamond Hill (11 and 12 June); operations in Orange River Colony, May to 29 Nov.

Viscount Massereene.

1900, including action at Caledon River (27 to 29 Nov.); operations in Orange River Colony, 30 Nov. to Dec. 1900; Jan. to Feb. 1901, and April to June, 1901; operations in Cape Colony, Dec. 1900, to Jan. 1901; Feb. to April, 1901, and June, 1901, to 31 May, 1902. He was wounded; mentioned in Despatches [London Gazette, 10 Sept. 1901, and 29 July, 1902]; received the Queen's Medal with four clasps; the King's Medal with two clasps; was given the Brevet of Major, and created a Companion of the Distinguished Service Order [London Gazette, 27 Sept. 1901]: "The Hon. Algernon William John Clotworthy Skeffington, Capt., 17th Lancers. In recognition of services during the operations in South Africa." He was invested by the King 18 Dec. 1902. He was promoted to Major 29 Nov. 1904, and retired from the 17th Lancers 18 May, 1907, and entered the Special Cavalry Reserve. He served in the European War, 1914–15, with the North Irish Horse; and was twice mentioned in Despatches. He became D.A.A. and Q.M.G. He had succeeded his father in 1905 as (12th) Viscount Massereene and Ferrard (created 1660); Baron of Loughneagh (created 1660); Baron Oriel (created 1790); Viscount Ferrard (created 1797); Baron Oriel (U.K., created 1821). He owns about 16,000 acres, and amongst the treasures in his possession are a picture of Lord Oriel, the last Speaker of the Irish House of Commons, by Sir Thomas Lawrence, also solid silver-gilt mace, and Speaker's chair, and several pictures by Lely, Godfrey Kneller, Gainsborough, etc. He married, in 1905, Jean Barbara, eldest daughter of Sir John Stirling Ainsworth, Bart., M.P., and Margaret Catherine (who died in 1918), daughter of Robert Reid Macredie, and they have one son, the Honourable John Talbot Foster Whyte-Melville Clotworthy Skeffington, born 22 Oct. 1914, and one daughter. The late Major Whyte-Melville never met the late Adam Lindsay Gordon, whose fame was chiefly posthumous. Major Whyte-Melville at once recognized that Gordon was a real poet, and his letters were some of the few gleams of happiness that came to cheer Gordon's last years. They wrote to each other a good deal, but unfortunately Gordon's letters to Whyte-Melville are not extant, or, if they are, no one seems to know what has become of them. When Gordon wrote " Bush Ballads and Galloping Rhymes," he recognized the kindness and encouragement given to him by the better-known and more fortunate poet, and dedicated his " Bush Ballads and Galloping Rhymes " to " The Author of Holmby House " :

> " They are rhymes rudely strung with intent less
>   Of sound than of words,
> In lands where bright blossoms are scentless,
>   And songless bright birds ;
> Where, with fire and fierce drought on her tresses,
> Insatiable Summer oppresses
> Sere woodlands and sad wildernesses,
>   And faint flocks and herds.

> " Where in dreariest day, when all dews end,
>   And all winds are warm,
> Wild Winter's large flood-gates are loosen'd,
>   And floods freed by storm,
> From broken-up fountain-heads, dash on
> Dry deserts with long pent-up passion—
> Here rhyme was first framed without fashion,
>   Song shaped without form.

> " Whence gathered ?—The locust's glad chirrup
>   May furnish a stave ;
> The ring of a rowel and stirrup,
>   The wash of a wave,
> The chaunt of the marsh frog in rushes,
> That chimes through the pauses and hushes
> Of nightfall, the torrent that gushes,
>   The tempests that rave.

> " In the deep'ning of dawn when it dapples
>   The dusk of the sky,
> With streaks like the redd'ning of apples,
>   The ripening of rye.
> To eastward, when cluster by cluster,
> Dim stars and dull planets that muster,
> Wax wan in a world of white lustre
>   That spreads far and high.

> " In the gathering of night gloom o'erhead, in
>   The still, silent change,
> All fire-flush'd when forest-trees redden
>   On slopes of the range.
> When the gnarl'd, knotted trunks eucalyptian
> Seem carved, like weird columns Egyptian,
> With curious device—quaint inscription,
>   And hieroglyph strange.

> " In the Spring, when the wattle gold trembles
>   'Twixt shadow and shine,
> When each dew-laden air draught resembles
>   A long draught of wine ;
> When the sky-line's blue burnish'd resistance
> Makes deeper the dreamiest distance,
> Some song in all hearts hath existence,—
>   Such songs have been mine.

> " They came in all guises, some vivid
>   To clasp and to keep ;
> Some sudden and swift as the livid
>   Blue thunder-flame's leap.
> This swept through the first breath of clover
> With memories renewed to the rover—
> That flash'd while the black horse turn'd over
>   Before the long sleep.

> " To you (having cunning to colour
>   A page with your pen,
> That through dull days, and nights even duller,
>   Long years ago ten,
> Fair pictures in fever afforded)—
> I send these rude staves, roughly worded
> By one in whose brain stands recorded,
>   As clear now as then,

> " ' The great rush of grey Northern water,
>   The green ridge of bank,
> The " sorrel " with curved sweep of quarter
>   Curl'd close to clean flank,
> The Royalist saddlefast squarely,
> And, where the bright uplands stretch fairly,
> Behind, beyond pistol-shot barely,
>   The Roundheaded rank.

> " ' A long launch, with clinging of muscles,
>   And clenching of teeth !
> The loose doublet ripples and rustles !
>   The swirl shoots beneath ! '
> Enough. In return for your garland
> In lieu of the flowers from your far land——
> Take wild growth of dreamland or starland,
>   Take weeds for your wreath.

> " Yet rhyme had not fail'd me for reason,
>   Nor reason for rhyme ;
> Sweet Song ! had I sought you in season,
>   And found you in time,
> You beckon in your bright beauty yonder,
> And I, waxing fainter, yet fonder,
> Now weary too soon when I wander—
>   Now fall when I climb.

> " It matters but little in the long run :
>   The weak have some right—
> Some share in the race that the strong run,
>   The fight the strong fight.
> If words that are worthless go westward,
> Yet the worst word shall be as the best word,
> In the day when all riot sweeps restward
>   In darkness or light."

There is a beautiful monument to Lord Massereene's grandfather in the Guards' Chapel, and this is a beautiful monument too—made in Australia by one poet for another. And both of them have contributed to the music of two hemispheres, and their songs have found an abiding place in the hearts of many soldiers and sportsmen.

COODE, PERCIVAL, Capt., was born 1 Aug. 1871. He was gazetted Second Lieutenant in the West Riding Regt. 19 Nov. 1892 ; became Lieutenant 1 Jan. 1896, and in that year took part in the operations in South Africa, and was wounded. He was promoted to Captain, and served in the South African War of 1899–1902. For his services in this campaign he was created a Companion of the Distinguished Service Order [London Gazette, 27 Sept. 1901]: " Percival Coode, Capt., West Riding Regt. In recognition of services during the operations in South Africa." The Insignia, Warrant, etc., were sent to his brother, as Capt. Coode had died 8 April, 1902.

LAMBERT, ROBERT, Capt., was born at Weston Green, Thames Ditton, in 1873, son of the late Capt. Lambert, 43rd Light Infantry. He entered the 8th Hussars 29 May, 1895 ; was promoted to Lieutenant 2 Sept. 1896 ; was Adjutant, 8th Hussars, 14 Oct. 1900, to 3 Aug. 1904 ; became Captain 14 Oct. 1900. He served in the South African War, 1900–2 (as Adjutant, 8th Hussars, 14 Oct. 1900, to Feb. 1902) ; was present at operations in the Orange Free State, April and May, 1900, including actions at Houtnek (Thoba Mountain) and Zand River ; operations in the Transvaal in May and June, 1900, including actions near Johannesburg, Pretoria and Diamond Hill (11 and 12 June) ; operations in the Transvaal, east of Pretoria, July to Nov. 1900, including actions at Reit Vlei and Belfast (26 and 27 Aug.) ; operations in Cape Colony,

Robert Lambert.

south of Orange River, 1900 ; operations in the Transvaal and Orange River Colony 30 Nov. 1900, to Feb. 1902. He was mentioned in Despatches [London Gazette, 10 Sept. 1901] ; received the Queen's Medal with five clasps ; the King's Medal with two clasps, and was created a Companion of the Distinguished Service Order [London Gazette, 27 Sept. 1901]: " Robert Lambert, Capt., 8th Hussars. In recognition of services during the operations in South Africa." He was Adjutant, Montgomery Yeomanry, 1904–10, and retired from the 8th Hussars 2 Sept. 1910. From 1910 to 1914 he was Brigade Major, South Wales Mounted Brigade. He retired in 1916, with the honorary rank of Major, Special Reserve. Major Lambert married, in 1908, Henrietta Isabella, daughter of the late George Lowther, of Swillington, Yorkshire, and they have one daughter.

KELLER, RUDOLPH HENRY, Capt., was born 12 June, 1871. He was gazetted to the Derbyshire Regt. 21 Nov. 1896, and became Lieutenant 21 Nov. 1896. He served in the Tirah Campaign, 1897–98 ; was present at the capture of the Sampagha and Arhanga Passes, and at the operations in the Bazar Valley 25 to 30 Dec. 1897 (Medal with two clasps). He was Adjutant, Nottinghamshire and Derbyshire Regt., 1 Feb. 1900, to 31 Jan. 1904, and became Captain 11 June, 1900. Capt. Keller served in the South African War, 1899–1901, taking part in operations in the Orange Free State, Feb. to May, 1900, including actions at Houtnek (Thoba Mountain), Vet River and Zand River ; operations in the Transvaal, including actions near Johannesburg, Pretoria and Diamond Hill ; operations in the Transvaal, west of Pretoria ; operations in Orange River Colony ; operations in Cape Colony, south of Orange River. He served as Adjutant, 1st Battn. Nottinghamshire and Derbyshire Regt., taking part in operations in the Transvaal, Dec. 1900, to Sept. 1901 ; was severely wounded ; was present at operations in Cape Colony 30 Nov. to Dec. 1900. Capt. Keller was mentioned in Despatches [London Gazette, 10 Sept. 1901] ; received the Queen's Medal with five clasps, and was created a Companion of the Distinguished Service Order [London Gazette, 27 Sept. 1901]:

"Rudolph Henry Keller, Capt., Derbyshire Regt. In recognition of services during operations in South Africa." The Insignia were presented to him by the King 12 March, 1902. He retired from the Nottinghamshire and Derbyshire Regt. 2 March, 1910, entering the Reserve of Officers, and served in the European War, 1915 to 1918, as Commandant, Lines of Communication, from 1915. He became Major, Reserve of Officers, 26 June, 1916; was given the rank of Lieutenant-Colonel in the Army 7 Feb. 1919, and received the O.B.E. Lieut.-Colonel Keller married, in 1911, Florence Mary, only daughter of the late Peter Shaw, of Southampton.

COLLIS, ROBERT HENRY, Capt., was born 13 Jan. 1874. He entered the 6th Dragoon Guards 6 June, 1896; was promoted to Lieutenant 24 Feb. 1897, and to Captain 11 May, 1900. Capt. Collis served in the South African War, 1900–2, with the 6th Carabineers; was present at the Relief of Kimberley; at operations in the Orange Free State, Feb. to May, 1900, including operations at Paardeberg (17 to 26 Feb.); operations at Poplar Grove, Dreifontein (where he was dangerously wounded), Karee Siding and Zand River; operations in Cape Colony, south of Orange River, 1899–1900. He received the Queen's Medal with three clasps, and was created a Companion of the Distinguished Service Order [London Gazette, 27 Sept. 1901]: "Robert Henry Collis, Capt., 6th Dragoon Guards. In recognition of services during the operations in South Africa." He retired from the 6th Dragoon Guards 14 June, 1905; became a Major in the Pembrokeshire Yeomanry, and served during the European War as Temporary Lieutenant-Colonel in the Remount Service; was three times mentioned in Despatches, and created a C.M.G. in 1918.

WALTHALL, EDWARD CHARLES WALTHALL DELVES, Capt., was born 24 April, 1874, eldest son of the late Edward W. D. Walthall, of Wistaston Hall, and of his wife, Caroline Marion, youngest daughter of Charles Augustus Stewart, of West Hall, Cheshire. He was educated at Charterhouse and at the Royal Military Academy, Woolwich, and entered the Royal Artillery 1 April, 1894, becoming Lieutenant 1 April, 1897, and Captain 15 Oct. 1900. Capt. Walthall served in the South African War, 1899–1901, taking part in the advance on Kimberley, including the action at Magersfontein. He was present at the Relief of Kimberley; at the operations in the Orange Free State, Feb. to May, 1900, including operations at Paardeberg and Dreifontein; at operations in the Transvaal, including actions near Johannesburg and Diamond Hill. He served during the operations in the Transvaal 30 Nov. 1900, to Jan. 1901, and April to July, 1901; was mentioned in Despatches [London Gazette, 10 Sept. 1901]; received the Queen's Medal with six clasps, and was created a Companion of the Distinguished Service Order [London Gazette, 27 Sept. 1901]: "Edward Charles Walthall Delves Walthall, Capt., Royal Artillery. In recognition of services during the operations in South Africa." The Insignia were presented to him by the King 17 Dec. 1901. He was Adjutant, Royal Artillery, 29 June, 1906, to 4 July, 1909, and was promoted to Major 11 Feb. 1911. Major Walthall served in the European War, 1914–18, as Temporary Lieutenant-Colonel, Royal Artillery, 4 Oct. 1915, to 12 April, 1916; became Lieutenant-Colonel 13 April, 1916; was Brigadier-General, Royal Artillery, 34th Division, British Armies in France, from 10 May, 1917; was mentioned in Despatches; given the Brevets of Lieutenant-Colonel 3 June, 1915, and Colonel 3 June, 1919; was created a C.M.G. in 1918, and awarded the Order of Danilo, 3rd Class, 1917. Colonel Walthall married, in 1902, Isabel Sybil, daughter of Lieutenant-General Sir James Bevan Edwards, K.C.M.G.

ANLEY, BARNETT DYER LEMPRIERE GRAY, Capt., was born at Dalhousie, India, 22 Aug. 1873, eldest son of Colonel and Mrs. B. N. Anley. He entered the Army 10 Oct. 1894; became Lieutenant 14 Oct. 1897, and Captain 18 Oct. 1900; served in South Africa, 1899–1900, as Adjutant, 6th Battn. Mounted Infantry, De Lisle's Corps; was present at the Relief of Kimberley; operations in the Orange Free State, Feb. to May, 1900, including operations at Paardeberg (17 to 26 Feb.); actions at Poplar Grove, Karee Siding, Houtnek (Thoba Mountain), Vet River (5 and 6 May) and Zand River; operations in the Transvaal in May and June, 1900, including actions near Johannesburg, Pretoria and Diamond Hill (11 and 12 June); in the operations in the Transvaal, west of Pretoria; operations in Orange River Colony, including action at Wittebergen (1 to 29 July); operations in Cape Colony, south of Orange River 1899–1900, including actions at Colesberg (1 to 29 Jan.). He was mentioned in Despatches [London Gazette, 8 Feb. and 10 Sept. 1901], and created a Companion of the Distinguished Service Order [London Gazette, 27 Sept. 1901]: "Barnett Dyer Lempriere Gray Anley, Capt., Essex Regt." The Insignia were presented by the King 29 Oct. 1901. He passed the Staff College in 1908; G.S.O., 3rd Grade, Harwich Defences, 1909–12; G.S.O., 2nd Grade, War Office, 1912, to April, 1914; A.P.M. 5th Division, Aug. 1914, to 7 Jan. 1915; D.A.Q.M.G., 3rd Division, 8 Jan. to 30 Jan. 1915; commanded the 1st Manchester Regt. 31 Jan. to 31 March, 1915, including action of Neuve Chapelle 10–12 March, 1915; was present at all actions with the 5th Division, from Mons to action near La Bassée, Oct. 1915; was G.S.O., 1st Grade, Ripon Training Centre, June, 1915, to 14 Jan. 1916; G.S.O., 1st Grade, 41st Division, 14 Jan. 1916, to 3 May, 1917; was G.S.O.1., Headquarters, Home Forces, 4 May, 1917, to 14 Aug. 1918; commanded the 183rd Infantry Brigade, British Armies in France, 21 Sept. 1918, to 10 March, 1919; was G.S.O.1., Staff College, from 11 March, 1919. He has been five times mentioned in Despatches in the Great War, and has been given the Brevet of Lieutenant-Colonel 1 June, 1916, and Brevet of Colonel 3 June, 1918; became Chevalier de la Légion d'Honneur, May, 1917; was created a C.M.G. 4 June, 1917, and has the 1914 Star. He married, in 1902, Gwendolyn, eldest daughter of Major Leigh Gwatkin, J.P., and they have one daughter. His Distinguished Service Order was awarded "in recognition of services during the operations in South Africa."

Barnett D. L. G. Anley.

GIRDWOOD, AUSTIN CLAUDE, Capt., was born 24 April, 1875, son of John Girdwood, J.P., of Rose Bank, Binstead, Isle of Wight. He was commissioned in the Northumberland Fusiliers 6 June, 1896; was promoted to Lieutenant 22 April, 1898; served in the Nile Expedition, 1898, and was present at the Battle of Khartum (Medal and Egyptian Medal with clasp). He again saw active service in the South African War, 1899–1902, and was severely wounded. He took part in the advance on Kimberley, including the actions at Belmont, Enslin, Modder River and Magersfontein; operations in the Orange Free State, March to May, 1900; operations in the Transvaal, west of Pretoria, July to 29 Nov. 1900, including action at Venterskroon; operations in Orange River Colony, May to July, 1900, including action at Rhenoster River; operations in the Transvaal 30 Nov. 1900, to April, 1902; operations in Cape Colony, April to 31 May, 1902. He was mentioned in Despatches [London Gazette, 10 Sept. 1901, and 29 July, 1902]; received the Queen's Medal with four clasps; the King's Medal with two clasps, and was created a Companion of the Distinguished Service Order [London Gazette, 27 Sept. 1901]: "Austin Claude Girdwood, Capt., Northumberland Fusiliers. In recognition of services during the operations in South Africa." He was invested by the King 21 Oct. 1902. Capt. Girdwood passed the Staff College. He served on the North-West Frontier of India in 1908, in the Mohmand Expedition. He served throughout the European War; was G.S.O.3., 48th Division, Central Force, Home Defence, and British Expeditionary Force, 11 Jan. to 15 Sept. 1915; was promoted to Major 1 Sept. 1915; was G.S.O.2., New Armies, British Armies in France, 18 Sept. 1915, to 15 July, 1916; Temporary Lieutenant-Colonel, commanding Service Battn. Border Regt. 16 July, 1916, to 20 Aug. 1917; Temporary Brigadier-General from 21 Aug. 1917, commanding 96th Infantry Brigade, British Armies in France. He was given the Brevet of Lieutenant-Colonel 1 Jan. 1918; received the Croix de Guerre; was created a C.M.G. in 1919, and was awarded a Bar to the Distinguished Service Order. He married, in 1903, Constance, second daughter of Samuel Adshead, of Highfield, Upton, Macclesfield.

TEWKESBURY, LORD, GEOFFREY GEORGE GORDON (EARL OF MUNSTER), Major, was born 18 July, 1859, third son of the second Earl (who was a grandson of William IV. and Mrs. Jordan), by his wife, Wilhelmina, daughter of the Hon. John Kennedy Erskine, second son of the 12th Earl of Cassilis and 1st Marquis of Ailsa. In 1870 his elder brother, Viscount Fitzclarence, died. He entered the Army as a Subaltern of the 2nd Battn. King's Royal Rifle Corps (then the 60th Rifles); served in the Afghan War of 1879–80; was present at the engagements at Ahmed Kheyl and Uraes, near Ghaznee, and accompanied Lord Roberts in the march to Kandahar, and was present at the battle of that name. He also saw service with the 3rd Battn. of his regiment in the Boer War of 1881. He became Captain in 1888, and resigned his commission in the Regular Forces in 1895. After his retirement he joined the Militia Battn. of the Royal Scots, of which the late Marquis of Lothian was then Honorary Colonel, and after some years' service in command of a company was promoted to the rank of Major. When a battalion was embodied in Dec. 1899, Lord Tewkesbury, as he then was, joined, and has since served with it at home and in South Africa. For his services at the front he was mentioned in Despatches; received the Queen's South African Medal with clasps, and was created a Companion of the Distinguished Service Order [London Gazette, 27 Sept. 1901]: "Geoffrey George Gordon, Lord Tewkesbury (now Earl of Munster), Capt. and Honorary Major, 3rd Royal Scots. In recognition of services during the operations in South Africa." The Insignia were presented by the King 29 Oct. 1901. He succeeded to the title in April, 1901. Lord Munster was not married. He died from an accident at the Lace Mines on Sunday, 2 Feb. 1902, being then a Major in the 3rd (Militia) Battn. Royal Scots. He was succeeded in the title by his brother, the Hon. Aubrey Fitzclarence, a Gentleman Usher in Ordinary to the King, born June, 1862, and also unmarried. Another gallant soldier also descended from William IV. and Mrs. Jordan was the late Brigadier-General Charles Fitzclarence, V.C.

Lord Tewkesbury.

VIPAN, CHARLES, Capt., was born in 1849, second son of the late Thomas Curtis Vipan, of The Mansells, Harlington, Bedfordshire. He served in the South African War, 1899 to 1900, taking part in operations in the Orange Free State, March to May, 1900; operations in Orange River Colony, May to 29 Nov. 1900, including action at Lindley (26 June). He was mentioned in Despatches [London Gazette, 10 Sept. 1901]; received the Queen's Medal with two clasps, and was created a Companion of the Distinguished Service Order [London Gazette, 27 Sept. 1901]: "Charles Vipan, Capt., 3rd East Kent Regt. In recognition of services during the operations in South Africa." He was invested by the King 17 Feb. 1901. He is Honorary Captain in the Army, and retired in 1904. He has the rank of Major in the Militia. Major Vipan is a Fellow of the Linnean Society. He married Mary Frances, second daughter of the late Alfred Jones, of Needingworth, Hants, and sister and co-heiress to the late John Vipan Jones, also of Needingworth.

BEATTY, CHARLES HAROLD LONGFIELD, Capt., was born 16 Jan. 1870, eldest son of Capt. David Beatty, formerly in the 4th Hussars, of Borodale, County Wexford, who for many years lived at The Moat, Rugby. Capt. Beatty's other sons are Admiral Sir David Beatty, G.C.B., K.C.V.O., D.S.O., C.C. The Grand Fleet; Capt. Vandeleur Beatty, who now trains at Newmarket, and Capt. George Beatty, 1st Lancers, Indian Army (died in India in 1915). Charles Beatty was educated at Cheltenham, and at Trinity College, Stratford-on-Avon, and joined the 6th Battn. of the Warwickshire Regt. In 1892 he won his first steeplechase on a horse named Radical, owned by Mr. Ralli, in the Dunsmore Plate at Rugby. He won the Hunt Cup at Warwick. In one afternoon at Towcester, in 1894, he won four races, and was only beaten by a neck in a fifth. In 1895 Mr. Beatty steered Kestrel to victory in the Grand International Steeplechase at Sandown Park.

Charles Harold L. Beatty.

In the same year he won several races with the Nun, though he did not always ride the mare himself. In 1897 Mr. Beatty was second in the Grand National on Filbert, and in the following year he again had the mount of Filbert, and finished fourth. In 1898 Capt. Beatty gave up riding races, and went to Newmarket, where he superintended the training of horses owned by the late Colonel McCalmont. Shortly afterwards he left with his regiment for South Africa, and served in the Boer War of 1899–1902. He remained in South Africa for two years, serving in the Mounted Infantry and on the Staff of General Alderson; operations in the Transvaal in May and June, 1900; operations in Natal, March and April, 1900; operations in the Transvaal, west of Pretoria, July to 29 Nov. 1900, including actions at Frederickstad (17 to 25 Oct.); operations in Cape Colony, north of Orange River, including action at Ruidam. He served with mounted Infantry; operations in the Transvaal 30 Nov. to Dec. 1901; operations in the Orange River Colony, Jan. to March, 1902; operations in the Transvaal, March to 31 May, 1902 (Queen's Medal with three clasps; King's Medal with two clasps). For his services in this campaign Capt. Beatty was also twice mentioned in Despatches, and was created a Companion of the Distinguished Service Order [London Gazette, 27 Sept. 1901]: "Charles Harold Longfield Beatty, Capt., 6th Royal Warwickshire Regt. In recognition of services during the operations in South Africa." He was invested by the King 29 Oct. 1901. In 1901 Capt. Beatty returned to Newmarket, and in 1903, after the death of Colonel McCalmont, he took over the lease of the Stables and began to train on his own account. Shortly afterwards he took over the horses of Lord Howard de Walden. St. Maclou, who won the Lincolnshire Handicap in 1902, and beat Sceptre by a head, was trained by Capt. Beatty. In the same year St. Maclou won a Biennial at Newmarket; was beaten by a neck by Ballantrae, in the Cambridgeshire, to whom he was giving 31 lbs., and won the Manchester November Handicap. A year later he won the October Plate at Kempton Park, and the Select Stakes at Newmarket. In this same year, Zinfandel, also trained by Major Beatty, won five out of the six races in which he took part. His single glorious defeat was in the Cesarewitch, carrying 8 stones 4 lbs., and giving Grey Tick, the winner, three years and 23 lbs. The five races in which he came in first were the Manchester Cup, the Gold Vase at Ascot, the Gordon Stakes at Goodwood, the Brighton Cup and the Scarborough Stakes at Newmarket. In the following year Zinfandel again won five out of the six races in which he ran, in the last of which he took his revenge on Throwaway. As a five-year old Zinfandel ran twice; was beaten by Pretty Polly in the Coronation Cup, and won the Ascot Gold Cup. Capt. Beatty won the Jockey Club Stakes with Rising Glass. Major Beatty served in the European War from 1914–15, as A.D.C. to General Sir Edwin Alderson, while commanding the Canadian Expeditionary Force; was mentioned in Despatches [London Gazette, June, 1915]; while serving with Mounted Infantry was severely wounded at St. Eloi, April, 1916 (left arm amputated), and died of wounds 17 May, 1917. Major Beatty was buried at Atherstone with full military honours. The band of the Royal Warwickshire Regt., to which Major Beatty was attached, attended. Among the mourners were the widow and Major Vandeleur Beatty. Admiral Sir David Beatty was unable to be present. A memorial service was held at St. Agnes's Church, Newmarket, at the same time as the funeral at Atherstone. The Rev. — Colvil-Wallis, Rural Dean, officiated, and a number of racing folk were present. Capt. Beatty married, in 1905, Lucy Alice, eldest daughter of the late Edward Beck, Esq., of Gippsland, Victoria, widow of J. S. Langlands, Major, 43rd Oxfordshire Light Infantry, and there is one son, Charles Robert Longfield, born 24 Oct. 1910.

BAGGE, RICHARD LUDWIG, Capt., was born at Antwerp in 1872, son of Herbert Bagge, late of Gaywood Hall, King's Lynn, Norfolk, and of his wife, Maria Adelaide Rosalie, second daughter of Louis Duquesnoy, of Antwerp. He was educated at Charterhouse; was commissioned in the 3rd Norfolk Regt. in 1891; served in the South African War; was mentioned in Despatches; received the Queen's Medal with two clasps; the King's Medal with two clasps, and was created a Companion of the Distinguished Service Order [London Gazette, 27 Sept. 1901]: "Richard Ludwig Bagge, Capt., 3rd Norfolk Regt. In recognition of services during the operations in South Africa." The Insignia were presented to him by the King 29 Oct. 1901. He retired from the Militia, and rejoined in 1914, as Captain, Special List, attached Norfolk Regt. He was promoted to Major. Major Bagge is patron of three livings, and is Lord of the Manors of Gaywood, Islington, Haveless, Bawsey and Leziate. He married, 28 June, 1904, at St. Peter's, Cranley Gardens, Anna Victoria Wilmsdorff Mansergh, only daughter of the late Major W. G. Mansergh, of Roc Savage, County Cork, late of the 69th Regt., and they have five daughters Doreen Pleasance Anna; Nancy Adelaide; Sheila Clifford; Moira Mansergh and Rosaleen Margaret.

BULKELEY, HENRY CHARLES, Major, was born in 1860, only surviving son of the late Major Francis B. Bulkeley and Rosanna Marie daughter of the late Colonel W. W. J. Cockcraft. He served in the Sout African War, 1900–1; was mentioned in Despatches, and created a Companion of the Distinguished Service Order [London Gazette, 27 Sept. 1901] "Henry Charles Bulkeley, Capt. and Honarary Major, 4th West York shire Regt. In recognition of services during the operations in Sout Africa." The Insignia were presented to him by the King 29 Oct. 1901 Major Bulkeley retired from the Militia, but rejoined and served in th European War, 1914–18, as Temporary Lieutenant-Colonel, and wa created a C.M.G. in 1918. He married Gertrude Beatrice, daughter o the late Admiral Hudson, R.N., and they have two daughters.

NORMAN, MONTAGU COLLET, Capt., is the eldest son of the lat F. H. Norman, of Moor Place, Much Hadham, Herts. He was educate at Eton, and King's College, Cambridge, and served in the South Africa War, 1900–1; was mentioned in Despatches; received the Queen's Meda with four clasps, and was created a Companion of the Distinguished Servic Order [London Gazette, 27 Sept. 1901]: "Montagu Collet Norman Capt., 4th Bedfordshire Regt. In recognition of services during the operations in South Africa." He became Deputy Governor, Bank of Englan (1918), and Lieutenant, City of London.

ASPINALL, ROBERT LOWNDES, Capt., was born 3 March, 1869 elder son of the late Robert Augustus Aspinall, Esq., J.P., D.L. He wa educated at Eton and Sandhurst, and was gazetted to the 15th Hussar 10 Sept. 1888; was promoted Captain 10 July, 1895, and retired from th 15th Hussars 25 Jan. 1899. He went out to South Africa, 1900–2, wit the "Green Howards" (the Yorkshire Regt.), where he served on Sir Joh French's Staff as A.D.C., taking part in operations in the Transvaal, eas of Pretoria, July to 29 Nov. 1900, including actions at Reit Vlei and Belfast in the operations in the Transvaal 30 Nov. to Dec. 1900; operations i Orange River Colony, Dec. 1900, to March, 1901; operations in Cap Colony, March to May, 1902; was mentioned in Despatches [Londo Gazette, 10 Sept. 1901]; received the Queen's Medal with three clasps the King's Medal with two clasps, and was created a Companion of th Distinguished Service Order [London Gazette, 27 Sept. 1901]: "Rober Lowndes Aspinall, Capt., East Yorkshire Regt. In recognition of service during operations in South Africa." The Insignia were presented by th King 29 Oct. 1901. Colonel Aspinall commanded the 3rd Yorkshires a mobilization, and later commanded troops of the South Garrison, Redcar He then raised the 11th Yorkshires, a fine battalion, made up of Darlingto "Pals" and of men from Richmond, Pontefract and other North countr depôts. He said he would not have exchanged for a battalion of Guard if there had been any conceivable chance of leading the "Green Howards" in action, but when they became the New Army Reserve he transferre to the Cheshires and went with them to the Front. He was extremel well known in Darlington, and popular where the 11th Yorkshires wer assembled for training purposes. His men adored him, and did no attempt to conceal their chagrin when he transferred to the Cheshire Regt The battalion undoubtedly reached a magnificent state of efficiency unde his command, and his disappointment was very great when it was mad a Reserve Battalion, supplying drafts for the Dardanelles and for France Lieut.-Colonel Aspinall was killed in action on the 3rd July, 1916, nea Thiépval. He was a very well known writer on sporting subjects, an was a keen sportsman and a prominent figure in pre-war days at regimenta race-meetings. He won the Cavalry Brigade Cup at Aldershot in 1897.

HARBORD, EDWARD RALPH, Capt., was born 7 April, 1870, so of the late Honourable Ralph Harbord sixth son of the 2nd Baron Suffield. H served in the South African War, 1899–1901; was mentioned in Despatches received the Queen's Medal with thre clasps, and was created a Companion o the Distinguished Service Order [Londo Gazette, 27 Sept. 1901]: "Edward Ralp Harbord, Capt., 3rd Cheshire Regt. I recognition of services during the operations in South Africa." He was investe by the King 17 Dec. 1901. He becam Major, Special Reserve. Major Harbor served in the European War in 1914. H married, in 1906, Evelyn, eldest daughte of H. Riley-Smith, J.P., of Toulston, Tadcaster, Yorks, and they have two son and two daughters.

Edward Ralph Harbord.

PHILLIPS, HENRY JACOB VAUGHAN, Capt., served in the South African War, 1899–1902, as Acting Intelligence Officer. He also performed the duties of Transport Officer Capt. Jacob was present at the operations in the Orange Free State, Apri to May, 1900; operations in Orange River Colony, May to 29 Nov. 1900 operations in Cape Colony, 1900; operations in the Transvaal, May, 1901 to Jan. 1902; operations in the Orange River Colony from 30 Nov. 1900 to March, 1901; operations in Cape Colony, April to May, 1901, and Jan to Feb. 1902. He was mentioned in Despatches [London Gazette, 10 Sept. 1901]; received the Queen's Medal with three clasps; the King's Meda with two clasps, and was created a Companion of the Distinguished Servic Order [London Gazette, 27 Sept. 1901]: "Henry Jacob Vaughan Phillips Capt., 3rd South Wales Borderers. In recognition of services during th operations in South Africa." The Insignia were presented by the Kin 2 June, 1902. Major Phillips died 6 May, 1914.

BROMFIELD, HARRY HICKMAN, Capt., was born at Snitterfield, Warwickshire, 29 Jan. 1869, son of Henry Bromfield, of Newnham Hall (who died in 1888), and Mary Elizabeth, eldest daughter of the late John Colthurst, of Chew Court, Somersetshire. He was educated at Malvern College, and at Hertford College, Oxford, and served in the South African War, 1900–2, taking part in operations in the Orange Free State, Feb. to May, 1900, including actions at Karee Siding, Vet River (5 and 6 May) and Zand River; operations in the Transvaal in May and June, 1900, including action near Johannesburg; operations in the Transvaal, west of Pretoria, Aug. to 29 Nov. 1900; operations in Orange River Colony, June to Aug. 1900; operations in Cape Colony, south of Orange River, 1900; operations in the Transvaal 30 Nov. 1900, to Sept. 1901; operations in Orange River Colony; operations in Cape Colony, Sept. 1901, to Feb. 1902. He was mentioned in Despatches [London Gazette, 10 Sept. 1901]; received the Queen's Medal with three clasps, the King's Medal with two clasps, and was created a Companion of the Distinguished Service Order [London Gazette, 27 Sept. 1901]: "Harry Hickman Bromfield, Capt., 3rd South Wales Borderers. In recognition of services during the operations in South Africa." The Insignia were presented to him by the King 2 June, 1902. Major Bromfield was Chief Constable of Radnorshire. He married, 19 July, 1906, at St. John the Baptist's Church, Slebech, Pembrokeshire, Ethel Philippa, eldest daughter of Sir Charles Philipps, Bart., and Lady Philipps, of Picton Castle, Haverfordwest, Pembrokeshire, and their son is Charlie Henry Colthurst, born 17 July, 1907. He served in the European War as Major, 1st Battn. Welsh Guards, and was killed in action 10 Sept. 1916. An obituary notice of him appeared in the "Times" of 23 Sept. 1916.

Harry H. Bromfield.

BERNAL, GREVILLE HUGH WOODLEY, Capt., was created a Companion of the Distinguished Service Order [London Gazette, 27 Sept. 1901]: "Greville Hugh Woodley Bernal, Capt., 4th Derbyshire Regt. In recognition of services during the recent operations in South Africa."

GILLAM, WILLIAM ALBERT, Capt., was born 16 April, 1870, eldest son of the late F. A. Gillam, of London. He served in the South African War, 1900–2; was Commandant at Tulbagh; took part in operations in Cape Colony, south of Orange River, in 1900. He was mentioned in Despatches [London Gazette, 10 Sept. 1901]; received the Queen's Medal with clasp, the King's Medal with two clasps, and was created a Companion of the Distinguished Service Order [London Gazette, 27 Sept. 1901]: "William Albert Gillam, Capt., 6th Middlesex Regt. In recognition of services during the operations in South Africa." The Insignia were presented by the King 29 Oct. 1901. He joined the Royal Garrison Regt. as Captain, from the Militia, 16 Aug. 1902; became Captain, Manchester Regt., 26 Aug. 1905; was Adjutant, Militia, 7 Dec. 1906, to 6 Dec. 1911, and became Captain, 2nd Battn. Border Regt. 18 May, 1908. He served in the European War from 1914; was promoted to Major 18 May, 1915. Major Gillam married, in 1917, Beatrice Christian, daughter of A. E. Pullar, of Durn, Perth, and they have one daughter.

CLERKE, ALBERT WILLIAM, Capt., joined the 9th Battn. King's Royal Rifle Corps, and served in the South African War, 1900–1, as Commandant, Viljoen's Drift, taking part in operations in the Orange Free State, April to May, 1900; operations in Orange River Colony, May, 1900, to 29 Nov. 1900; operations in Cape Colony, south of Orange River, Feb. to April, 1900; operations in the Transvaal, May and June, 1901; operations in Orange River Colony 30 Nov. 1900, to May, 1901. He was mentioned in Despatches [London Gazette, 10 Sept. 1901]; received the Queen's Medal with four clasps, and was created a Companion of the Distinguished Service Order [London Gazette, 27 Sept. 1901]: "Albert William Clerke, Capt., King's Royal Rifle Corps. In recognition of services during the operations in South Africa." The Insignia were presented by the King 29 Oct. 1901. He retired from the 9th Battn. King's Royal Rifle Corps, and became Major, 3rd (Reserve) Battn. Royal Munster Fusiliers. Major Clerke married, in 1894, Emily Daly.

SOWERBY, HARRY JOHN, Major, was born in 1867, second son of the late Colonel George Sowerby, of Putteridge, Bury, Herts; Dalston Hall, Carlisle, and Dalton Hall, Richmond, Yorkshire. He was educated at Elstree and Harrow, and served in South Africa, 1900–1, as Commandant, Liewspruit, taking part in operations in the Orange Free State, April and May, 1900; operations in Orange River Colony, May to 29 Nov. 1900; operations in Cape Colony, south of Orange River, 1899–1900; operations in Orange River Colony 30 Nov. 1900, to May, 1901. He was mentioned in Despatches [London Gazette, 10 Sept. 1901]; received the Queen's Medal with three clasps, and was created a Companion of the Distinguished Service Order [London Gazette, 27 Sept. 1901]: "Harry John Sowerby, Capt. and Honorary Major, 3rd Durham Light Infantry. In recognition of services during the operations in South Africa." The Insignia were presented by the King 29 Oct. 1901. He became Lieut.-Colonel and Honorary Colonel and commanded the 3rd Battn. Durham Light Infantry, 1907–12. He received the Coronation Medal in 1911. Colonel Sowerby married, in 1912, Katharine Jane, daughter of the late Rev. Arthur Coles Haviland, M.A., Rector of Lilley, Herts, and they have two daughters.

LAYCOCK, JOSEPH FREDERICK, Capt., was born 12 June, 1867, only son of the late R. Laycock, M.P., and Annie, second daughter of Christian Allhusen, of Stoke Court, Bucks (she married, 2ndly, Lord D'Arcy Osborne, who died in 1895, brother of the 9th Duke of Leeds). He served in the South African War as A.D.C. to the G.O.C., Cavalry Division, and was present at operations in Natal in 1899, including actions at Elandslaagte, Rietfontein and Lombard's Kop. He took part in the advance on Kimberley, including the action at Magersfontein, and in the Relief of Kimberley; also in operations in the Orange Free State, Feb. to May, 1900, including operations at Paardeberg (17 to 26 Feb.); actions at Poplar Grove, Dreifontein, Houtnek (Thoba Mountain), Vet River (5 and 6 May) and Zand River; operations in the Transvaal in May and June, 1900, including actions near Johannesburg, Pretoria and Diamond Hill (11 and 12 June); operations in Cape Colony, south of Orange River, 1899 to 1900, including actions at Colesberg (1 Jan. to 12 Feb.). He was mentioned in Despatches [London Gazette, 4 May, 1900, and 10 Sept. 1901]; received the Queen's Medal with six clasps, and was created a Companion of the Distinguished Service Order [London Gazette, 27 Sept. 1901]: "Joseph Frederick Laycock, Capt., Nottinghamshire Yeomanry Cavalry. In recognition of services during the operations in South Africa." He was invested by the King 17 Dec. 1901. He served in the European War, 1914–18 (Nottinghamshire Horse Artillery, Territorial Force); was mentioned in Despatches; given the Brevet of Lieut.-Colonel; created a C.M.G. in 1917, and a K.C.M.G. in 1919. He is Honorary Captain in His Majesty's Army. Sir Joseph Laycock married, in 1902, Katherine M., third daughter of Hugh Henry Hare, and they have two sons and two daughters.

BALFOUR, JOHN EDMOND HEUGH, Major, was born 22 Jan. 1868, son of George Edmond Balfour. He was educated at Eton. He served in the South African War, 1899–1900, as A.D.C. to the G.O.C., Mounted Infantry Division, and took part in the advance on Kimberley and in the Relief of Kimberley; operations in the Orange Free State, Feb. to May, 1900, including operations at Paardeberg (17 to 26 Feb.); actions at Poplar Grove, Dreifontein, Houtnek (Thoba Mountain), Vet River (5 and 6 May) and Zand River; operations in the Transvaal in May and June, 1900, including actions near Johannesburg, Pretoria and Diamond Hill (11 and 12 June); operations in Orange River Colony, May to July, 1900, including actions at Bethlehem (6 and 7 July) and Wittebergen (1 to 29 July, 1900). He was mentioned in Despatches [London Gazette, 10 Sept. 1901]; was promoted to Major, Reserve of Officers; received the Queen's Medal with six clasps, and was created a Companion of the Distinguished Service Order [London Gazette, 27 Sept. 1901]: "John Edmond Heugh Balfour, Capt. and Honorary Major (Reserve of Officers), 1st Devon Yeomanry Cavalry. In recognition of services during the operations in South Africa." He served in the European War, 1914–18; was twice mentioned in Despatches, and created a C.M.G. in 1918; is Colonel, Royal 1st Devon Yeomanry Cavalry; Major, Reserve of Officers, late Captain, 11th Hussars. Colonel Balfour married, in 1910, Evelyn, daughter of the late Hon. R. J. Gerrard-Dicconson, and they have one daughter.

CARDIGAN, EARL OF, GEORGE WILLIAM CHANDOS (MARQUESS OF AILESBURY), Capt., was born 21 May, 1873, son of the Most Honourable Henry Augustus Brudenell-Bruce, 5th Marquess and a Baronet, and Sophia Maria, daughter of G. H. Pinckney, Esq., of Tawstock Court, Barnstaple. He was educated at Westminster, and joined the 3rd Battn. Argyll and Sutherland Highlanders, afterwards serving for some time with the Royal Wiltshire Yeomanry, with which members of his family have been identified ever since its formation more than a century ago. In Nov. 1899, Lord Cardigan went to India, and it was whilst he was engaged in big game shooting that the storm-cloud burst over South Africa. Lord Cardigan, who held a commission in the Royal Wiltshire Yeomanry and had been A.D.C. to Lord Wolseley in 1898, at once volunteered his military services, which were accepted. He was employed with the transport department of the Natal Field Force from 23 Oct. 1899, up to the Relief of Ladysmith, and underwent all the privations and hard fighting in connection with that memorable siege. After the Siege of Ladysmith had been raised, Lord Cardigan took an active part in the operations which followed; attached to the 3rd Battn. of Imperial Yeomanry (Sherwood Foresters) for a short time, under Colonel Younghusband. He was employed in March, 1900, in connection with the operations around Barkly West. He was next in charge of Major-General Smith-Dorrien's transport, in the advance from Kronstad to Pretoria (part of General Sir Ian Hamilton's force). Sir Ian Hamilton wrote to the Editors of this book about Lord Ailesbury: "As to Bester's Farm, he ought to know more about it than anyone. I remember well his cutting-out expeditions with his wood-cutters, and very gallant expeditions they were." He continued with General Smith-Dorrien until August. He also took part in the exciting operations which were organized under Lord Kitchener in pursuit of De Wet, and in the Relief of Colonel Hore's force at Elands River. For his services in this campaign, Lord Cardigan received the Queen's Medal with four clasps, and was mentioned in Despatches [London Gazette, 10 Sept. 1901], and, on the recommendation of the Field-Marshal Commanding-in-Chief in South Africa, was given a commission in the Regular Army, dated 29 Aug. 1900, in the 11th Hussars, which a former Lord Cardigan had led in the Charge of the Light Brigade at Balaklava. After being gazetted to the 11th Hussars, Lord Cardigan was temporarily attached to Paget's force, near Warmbaths, in Sept. 1901. He was created a Companion of the Distinguished Service Order [London Gazette, 27 Sept. 1901]: "George William Chandos, Earl of Cardigan, Capt., Royal Wiltshire Yeomanry Cavalry. In recognition of services during the operations in South Africa." The Insignia were presented to him by the King 29 Oct. 1901. He became Major in Wiltshire Yeomanry, 1903; A.D.C. to Sir A. Hunter, 1903; Major in the Middlesex Yeomanry from 1908; transferred to infantry end of 1914; trained a month with 2nd Irish Guards; posted to 8th Battn. Wiltshire Regt. (New Armies); was Second-in-Command to that battalion when it was formed into a depôt unit, when he transferred to A.S.C. From Nov. 1915, till the division was broken up in March, 1919 was "Second-in-

Command of Guards' Divisional Train, and O.C. Headquarters Coy. Since that date same job with Northern Divisional Train."

DARLEY, HENRY READ, Capt., was born 13 June, 1865, son of the late J. F. Darley, of Leeson Park, Dublin. He served in the South African War as A.D.C. to Lord Chesham. He was mentioned in Despatches; received the Queen's and King's Medals with five clasps, and was created a Companion of the Distinguished Service Order [London Gazette, 27 Sept. 1901]: "Henry Read Darley, Capt., Imperial Yeomanry, A.D.C. In recognition of services during the operations in South Africa." The Insignia were presented by the King 29 Oct. 1901. He became Major, Reserve of Officers (late Captain, 4th Dragoon Guards), and was awarded the O.B.E. Major Darley is a Barrister-at-Law, Inner Temple. He married, in 1893, Emily, daughter of the Honourable John Prendergast Vereker, and they have four sons.

MILLER, EDWARD DARLEY, Capt., was born in London 11 Feb. 1865, son of Edward Miller, of Hartsfield, Betchworth. He was educated at Harrow, and Trinity College, Cambridge, and was gazetted to the 17th Lancers in Oct. 1886, becoming Captain 26 Oct. 1892, in which year he retired, and entered the Reserve of Officers. He served in the South African War as Captain in Lancashire Hussars, Imperial Yeomanry, and as Brigade Major, Imperial Yeomanry. He was mentioned in Despatches [London Gazette, 10 Sept. 1901]; received the Queen's Medal with three clasps, and was created a Companion of the Distinguished Service Order [London Gazette, 27 Sept. 1901]: "Edward Darley Miller, Capt., Brigade Major, Imperial Yeomanry. In recognition of services during the operations in South Africa." The Insignia were presented by the King 29 Oct. 1901. He is Honorary Lieut.-Colonel, Pembrokeshire Yeomanry.

Edward Darley Miller.

He served in the European War, 1914–18; was mentioned in Despatches for services in France in 1914, and created a C.B.E. in 1919. Lieut.-Colonel E. D. Miller married, 25 April, 1899, Irene Langtry, daughter of the late Colonel Langtry, of the 8th Hussars, and they have two sons, Gordon and Desmond, both at Harrow, born 1900 and 1903 respectively. Lieut.-Colonel Miller is, of course, the famous polo player. Captain of Rugby team for 25 years, he also played in the winning team of the 17th Lancers in Inter-Regimental Tournaments in India, 1888 and 1889, and was in the winning team of the Championship Cup at Hurlingham on five occasions. He formerly managed at different times the polo at Hurlingham, Ranelagh, Roehampton, Rugby, Ostend, Cannes and Le Touquet Polo Clubs. He has written a book called, "Modern Polo and Horse Management in the Field."

GRAHAM-CLARKE, LIONEL ALTHAM, Capt., was born in 1867, son of Leonard John Graham-Clarke and Flora Eliza, daughter of Henry Brown. He was gazetted to the Royal Artillery; became Captain 18 May, 1898; retired and entered the Reserve of Officers. Capt. Graham-Clarke served in the South African War, 1900–1, and was present at operations in Orange River Colony, May to 29 Nov. 1900, including actions at Wittebergen (1 to 29 July), and operations in Orange River Colony 30 Nov. 1900, to Feb. 1901. He was mentioned in Despatches [London Gazette, 10 Sept. 1901]; received the Queen's Medal with three clasps, and created a Companion of the Distinguished Service Order [London Gazette, 27 Sept. 1901]: "Lionel Altham Graham-Clarke, Capt., 1st Battn. Imperial Yeomanry. In recognition of services during the operations in South Africa." The Insignia were presented by the King 29 Oct. 1901. He became Honorary Major, Royal Gloucestershire Hussars, Imperial Yeomanry. His home was Frocester Manor, Stonehouse. Major Graham-Clarke married, in 1893, Frances, daughter of C. E. Charlesworth, and they had one son. Major Graham-Clarke died 26 July, 1914, and an obituary notice appeared in the " Times " of 28 July, 1914.

BIRKIN, RICHARD LESLIE, Capt., was born 2 Feb. 1863, third son of Sir Thomas Isaac Birkin, Bart., and Harriet, daughter of Matthew Tebbutt, of Bluntisham. He was educated at Rugby. Capt. Birkin served in the South African War, 1900–2; was mentioned twice in Despatches, and created a Companion of the Distinguished Service Order [London Gazette, 27 Sept. 1901]: "Richard Leslie Birkin, Capt., 3rd Battn. Imperial Yeomanry. In recognition of services during the operations in South Africa." He was invested by the King 18 Dec. 1902. He retired from the Nottinghamshire Yeomanry as Major, and was given the Honorary rank of Lieut.-Colonel, Notts T.F.A., Imperial Yeomanry.

SEELY, JOHN EDWARD BERNARD, Capt., was born 31 May, 1868, youngest son of Sir Charles Seely, 1st Baronet, and Emily, daughter of William Evans and sister of Sir F. Evans, 1st Bart. He was educated at Harrow, and at Trinity College, Cambridge, and was called to the Bar, Inner Temple, in 1897. He served in the South African War, 1900, taking part in operations in Orange Free State, April and May, 1900; operations in Orange River Colony, May to 29 Nov. 1900, including actions at Biddulphsberg and Wittebergen (1 to 29 July); operations in Cape Colony, March, 1900. He was mentioned in Despatches [London Gazette, 10 Sept. 1901]; received the Queen's Medal with five clasps, and was created a Companion of the Distinguished Service Order [London Gazette, 27 Sept. 1901]: "John Edward Bernard Seely, Capt., 4th Battn. Imperial Yeomanry." The Insignia were presented by the King 29 Oct. 1901. He became Lieut.-Colonel Commanding the Hampshire Carabineers and retired. Colonel J. E. B. Seely served in the European War, 1914–18; was five times mentioned in Despatches; created a C.B. in 1916, and a

C.M.G. in 1918, and promoted Major-General in 1918. In 1891 he was awarded a gold medal by the French Government for saving life at sea. General Seely was M.P. for the Isle of Wight, 1900–6; M.P. (L.) Abercromby Division of Liverpool, 1906 to 1910; M.P. (L.), Ilkeston Division, Derby, from 1910; Under Secretary for the Colonies, 1908–10; was made a P.C. in 1909; Under Secretary of State for War, 1911; Secretary of State for War, 1912–14; Parliamentary Under Secretary, Ministry of Munitions and Deputy Minister of Munitions, 1918; Under Secretary of State for Air and President of Air Council, Jan. 1918. He married (1st), in 1895, Emily Florence (who died in 1913), daughter of Colonel the Hon. Sir H. G. L. Crichton, and they had two sons and four daughters. General Seely married (2ndly) The Hon. Mrs. Nicholson, youngest daughter of the 1st Viscount Elibank. His D.S.O. was awarded for services in South Africa.

COMPTON, LORD ALWYNE FREDERICK, Capt., was born 5 June, 1855, third son of the 4th Marquis of Northampton and the Marchioness of Northampton, Eliza, daughter of the late Hon. Sir G. Elliott, K.C.B.

Lord Alwyne Compton.

He was brother of the 5th Marquess and of Colonel Lord Douglas Compton, Countess Cowper and Lady Margaret Graham, wife of Sir Henry Graham, Clerk of Parliament. He was educated at Eton, and in 1874 he joined the Grenadier Guards, being transferred in 1879 to the 10th Hussars. With this regiment he saw service in the Sudan in 1884, and from 1885 to 1887, in which year he left, he was Adjutant. From 1882 to 1884 he had been A.D.C. to the Viceroy of India, Lord Ripon. He subsequently joined the Bedfordshire Yeomanry, of which regiment he was in command from 1905. At the time of the South African War he raised Compton's Horse, and took part in the operations in the Transvaal in 1900, including the actions near Pretoria and at Diamond Hill. For his services he was mentioned in Despatches; received the Queen's Medal with three clasps, and was created a Companion of the Distinguished Service Order [London Gazette, 27 Sept. 1901]: "Lord Alwyne Frederick Compton, Capt., 4th Battn. Imperial Yeomanry. For services during operations in South Africa." From 1895 to 1906 he represented the Biggleswade Division of Bedfordshire in the House of Commons, as a Unionist, having defeated Mr. G. W. E. Russell in the first-named year by a small majority. In 1900 he was returned unopposed, and at the General Election of 1906 was defeated in the same division. In Jan. and Dec. 1910, he was elected for the Brentford Division of Middlesex, but he subsequently resigned his seat on account of ill-health, and was succeeded by Mr. Joynson-Hicks. Lord Alwyne was a partner in the firm of Messrs. Panmure Gordon & Co., of the Stock Exchange, and Chairman of the West-End London Local Branch of the Royal Insurance Company He had also been a Director of the London Docks Company for many years, before the concern was taken over by the Port of London Authority. Lord Alwyne Compton died 16 Dec. 1911. Lord Alwyne had married, in 1886, Mary Evelyn, daughter of Mr. Robert Charles de Grey Vyner, of Gautby Hall, Lincolnshire, who survived him, and by whom he had two sons, Edward Robert Francis, at the time of his father's death a Lieutenant in the Bedfordshire Yeomanry, who was born in 1891, and for whom King Edward was sponsor, and Clare George, then a Naval Cadet, who was born in 1894.

BATES, CHARLES LOFTUS, Capt., was born 2 Aug. 1863, son of Thomas Bates, of Aydon, Northumberland. He was educated at Eton; joined the 1st Dragoon Guards; became Captain 18 June, 1890; retired, and joined the Reserve of Officers. He served in the South African War, 1899–1901, with the Imperial Yeomanry; was severely wounded; mentioned in Despatches [London Gazette, 10 Sept. 1901]; promoted to Major, Reserve of Officers; received the Queen's Medal with four clasps, and was created a Companion of the Distinguished Service Order [London Gazette, 27 Sept. 1901]: "Charles Loftus Bates, Capt., 5th Battn. Imperial Yeomanry. In recognition of services during the operations in South Africa." The Insignia were presented by the King 29 Oct. 1901. He served in the European War in Egypt, 1914–18, as Director of Remounts, 1915–19; four times mentioned in Despatches; created a C.M.G. in 1916; a C.B. in 1918, and a K.C.M.G. in 1919. He is Honorary Colonel, Yeomanry, and Honorary Brigadier-General retired. Sir C. L. Bates contested Hexham (Conservative) in 1910. He married, in 1892, Katharine, daughter of Edward Leadbitter, of The Spital, Northumberland, and they have one son.

MONEY, NOEL ERNEST, Capt., was born 17 March, 1867, eldest son of Capt. Albert William Money. He was educated at Radley College, and at Christ Church, Oxford, and served with the Shropshire Imperial Yeomanry in South Africa in 1900–1, and with the South African Constabulary in South Africa, 1901, to the end of the war, and was slightly wounded. He took part in operations in the Transvaal, west of Pretoria, July to 29 Nov. 1900, including action at Venterskroon (7 and 9 Aug.); operations in Orange River Colony, May to July, 1900, including action at Lindley (1 July) and Rhenoster River; operations in the Transvaal and Cape Colony 30 Nov. 1900, to 31 May, 1902. He was mentioned in Despatches [London Gazette, 10 Sept. 1901]; received the Queen's Medal with three clasps, the King's Medal with two clasps, and was created a Companion of the Distinguished Service Order [London Gazette, 27 Sept. 1901]: "Noel Ernest Money, Capt., 5th Battn. Imperial Yeomanry. In recognition of services during the operations in South Africa." He served in the European War, and commanded the 159th Infantry Brigade in the 53rd Welsh Division in Palestine; was wounded; mentioned in Despatches; created a C.M.G. in 1919 and awarded a Bar to the Distinguished Service Order. Brigadier-General N. E. Money married, in 1903, Maud Boileau, second daughter of Edward Wood, of Culmington Manor, Shropshire, and they have one son and one daughter.

DAVIDSON, PERCIVAL, Capt., was born 16 April, 1874, son of the late Percival Davidson. He took his M.B. degree; served in the South African War, 1900–1, as Medical Officer, with the Imperial Yeomanry, and was present at operations in the Orange River Colony, May to 29 Nov. 1900; operations in Cape Colony, north of Orange River; operations in the Transvaal 30 Nov. 1900, to March, 1901, and April to May, 1901; operations in Orange River Colony, March to April, 1901; operations in Cape Colony, Jan. 1901. He was mentioned in Despatches [London Gazette, 10 Sept. 1901]: received the Queen's Medal with four clasps, and was created a Companion of the Distinguished Service Order [London Gazette, 27 Sept. 1901]: "Percival Davidson, Capt. (Medical Officer), 4th Battn. Imperial Yeomanry. In recognition of services during the operations in South Africa." He was given the Honorary Freedom of the City of Newcastle-on-Tyne in 1901. He became Lieutenant, R.A.M.C., 1 Sept. 1902; Captain, 1 March, 1906, and Major 1 June, 1914. He served in the European War, 1914–18, as Temp. Lieut.-Colonel, R.A.M.C., 15 Jan. 1917, to 14 Jan. 1919, and was given the Brevet of Lieut.-Colonel 3 June, 1918; was Assistant Director of Medical Services, 1st Army, British Armies in France, 15 June, 1917, to 23 July, 1918; Assistant Director of Medical Services, G.H.Q., British Armies in France, 24 July, 1918, to 14 Jan. 1919; was three times mentioned in Despatches; created a C.M.G. in 1916; was given the Brevet of Lieut.-Colonel, and awarded the Military Order of Avis.

COATS, ANDREW, Capt., was born 27 May, 1862, at Ferguslie House, Paisley, son of the late Thomas Coats, Thread Manufacturer, of Ferguslie, Paisley, and Margaret, daughter of Thomas Glen, of Thornhill, Johnstone. He was educated at the Grammar School, Paisley, and at Glasgow University, and joined the Queen's Own Glasgow Yeomanry in 1888, and remained in it till the South African War, when he joined the Imperial Yeomanry 7 Feb. 1900, and served as Captain with the 6th Scottish Regt., Imperial Yeomanry, Feb. 1900, to May, 1901, during which time he trekked 4,500 miles. He served at Wittebergen and in the Transvaal and Cape Colony. He was mentioned in Despatches; received the Queen's Medal with four clasps, and was created a Companion of the Distinguished Service Order [London Gazette, 27 Sept. 1901]: "Andrew Coats, Capt., 6th Battn. Imperial Yeomanry. In recognition of services during the operations in South Africa." The Insignia were presented by the King 17 Dec. 1901. Major Coats married, in 1903, Isabella Alice, daughter of the late Capt. Lyon, R.N., of Kirkmichael, Dumfriesshire.

Andrew Coats.

MILLER, SIR JAMES PERCY, Capt., 2nd Bart., was born 22 Oct. 1864, son of the 1st Baronet and Mary Anne, daughter of the late J. F. Leith. He joined the 14th Hussars; was Captain, 1885–92, and Adjutant, 1888–92, and retired. Sir James Miller served in the South African War; was mentioned in Despatches, and created a Companion of the Distinguished Service Order [London Gazette, 27 Sept. 1901]: "Sir James Percy Miller, Bart., Capt., 6th Battn. Imperial Yeomanry. In recognition of services during the operations in South Africa." He was invested by the King 17 Dec. 1901. He became Major, Lothian and Berwickshire Yeomanry, and D.L. and J.P. He succeeded his father in 1887, and in 1893 married the Honourable Eveline Mary Curzon, third daughter of the 4th Baron Scarsdale. He died in 1906, and was succeeded by his brother, John Alexander. Sir John Miller died 16 Feb. 1918, the Baronetcy becoming extinct. Sir James Miller was Master of the Northumberland and Berwickshire Hounds, and he won the Derby in 1890 and 1903.

NAISMITH, WILLIAM JOHN, Capt., was born 8 Sept. 1847. He is M.D. Edinburgh, and F.R.C.S. Edinburgh, and served in South Africa, 1900–2, with the Imperial Yeomanry. He was present at operations in the Transvaal in May and June, 1900; operations in Orange River Colony, May to 29 Nov. 1900, including actions at Wittebergen, Witpoort, Bothaville and Caledon River; operations in Orange River Colony 30 Nov. 1900, to Feb. 1901, and March, 1901, to 31 May, 1902; operations in Cape Colony, Feb. to March, 1901, and Sept. 1901. He was mentioned in Despatches [London Gazette, 10 Sept. 1901]; received the Queen's Medal with three clasps, the King's Medal with two clasps, and was created a Companion of the Distinguished Service Order [London Gazette, 27 Sept. 1901]: "William John Naismith, Capt. (Medical Officer), 6th Battn. Imperial Yeomanry. In recognition of services during the operations in South Africa." He also received the Territorial Decoration in 1902. He became Surgeon-Lieut.-Colonel, Ayrshire Imperial Yeomanry, and Medical Officer, 6th Battn. Imperial Yeomanry. Lieut.-Colonel Naismith was appointed Surgeon, H.M. Prison of Ayr, Ayr Industrial Schools and Ayrshire County Constabulary. He married, in 1890, Edith Mary, youngest daughter of the late W. R. Sanders, M.D., F.R.C.P.E., Professor of Pathology in the University of Edinburgh, and they have one son and two daughters.

LEES, SIR ELLIOTT, 1st Bart., Capt., was born in Lancashire 23 Oct. 1860, son of the late T. Evans Lees, of Woodfield, Oldham, and Bernarda, daughter of Elliott Bay Turnbull. He was educated at Eton, and Christ Church, Oxford (M.A.). He married, in 1882, Florence, daughter of the late Patrick Keith, and they had three sons and five daughters. He was M.F.H., South Dorset Hunt, 1885–86, and winner of the House of Commons Point-to-Point, 1888–90. He contested Rochdale in 1885; was M.P. for Oldham, 1886–92; defeated Sir J. T. Hibbert in 1886, but was defeated by him in 1892. He contested Pontefract in 1893; was M.P. for Birkenhead, 1894–1900, and for some years subsequently, and was a Director of the "People" newspaper. He was created a Baronet in 1897. Sir Elliott Lees served in the South African War in 1900, in command of the 26th Dorsetshire Company, Imperial Yeomanry; was twice mentioned in Despatches; received the Queen's Medal with five clasps, and was created a Companion of the Distinguished Service Order [London Gazette, 27 Sept. 1901]: "Sir Elliott Lees, Bart., Capt., 7th Battn. Imperial Yeomanry. In recognition of services during the operations in South Africa." The Insignia were presented to him by the King 29 Oct. 1901. He became Honorary Lieut.-Colonel, Dorset (Queen's Own) Yeomanry. Sir Elliott Lees died 16 Oct. 1908, and was succeeded by his eldest son, Thomas Evans Keith Lees, who became the 2nd Baronet. He was educated at Eton, and Christ Church, Oxford (B.A.); became Second Lieutenant, 15th (The King's) Hussars (1902–12); extra A.D.C. to Lord Chelmsford, 1912. He married, in 1913, Benita Blanche, eldest daughter of Sir Harold Pelly, 4th Baronet. Sir Thomas Lees served in the European War, and was killed in action in 1915. He, in his turn, was succeeded by his brother, Capt. Sir John Victor Lees, 3rd Baronet, who entered the King's Royal Rifle Corps. He married, in 1915, Madeline, second daughter of Sir Harold Pelly, Bart., and has one daughter. He served in the European War; was twice wounded; won the Distinguished Service Order and the Military Cross.

HUNTINGTON, ARTHUR, Capt., was born 21 Feb. 1871. He served in the South African War, 1900–1; was mentioned in Despatches twice; received the Queen's Medal with three clasps, and was created a Companion of the Distinguished Service Order [London Gazette, 27 Sept. 1901]: "Arthur Huntington, Capt., 8th Battn. Imperial Yeomanry. In recognition of services during operations in South Africa." The Insignia were presented by the King 29 Oct. 1901. He became Major, Duke of Lancaster's Imperial Yeomanry, and resigned his commission He is Honorary Captain in the Army. Major Huntington married, in 1906, Gladys Blanche, daughter of the late C. W. Hazlehurst, of Moreton Court, Herefordshire.

PARRY, LLEWELLYN ENGLAND SIDNEY, Capt., was born in 1856, only son of the late Richard Parry, Royal Scots Greys, and Louisa, eldest daughter of the late Sir Richard England, G.C.B. He was educated at Rugby, and Trinity College, Oxford, and served in the South African War, 1899–1901; was mentioned in Despatches; received the Queen's Medal with three clasps, and was created a Companion of the Distinguished Service Order [London Gazette, 27 Sept. 1901]: "Llewellyn England Sidney Parry, Capt., 9th Battn. Imperial Yeomanry. In recognition of services during the operations in South Africa." The Insignia were presented by the King 17 Dec. 1901. He became Lieut.-Colonel and Honorary Colonel, Denbighshire Hussars, and was created a C.B.E. in 1919. Colonel Parry married, in 1880, Mary Sophia, second daughter of Sir Richard P. Puleston, 3rd Bart.

CROPPER, EDWARD DENMAN, Capt., served in the South African War, and was created a Companion of the Distinguished Service Order [London Gazette, 27 Sept. 1901]: "Edward Denman Cropper, Capt., 9th Battn. Imperial Yeomanry. In recognition of services during the operations in South Africa." He died before he could be invested with the Insignia of the Order.

BAILLIE, AUGUSTUS CHARLES, Capt., was born 25 March, 1861, second son of the late Evan P. Montagu Baillie. He was educated at Marlborough; joined the R.H.A., and retired as Lieutenant. He served in the South African War, 1900–2, commanding the 15th Battn. Imperial Yeomanry, from 14 April, 1901, to March, 1902; commanded a mobile column, March to 31 May, 1902. He was present at operations in the Transvaal, Jan. to March, 1900; in the advance on Kimberley, March to July, 1900; operations in the Transvaal, July to 29 Nov. 1900; operations in the Transvaal 30 Nov. 1900, to 31 May, 1902. He was mentioned in Despatches [London Gazette, 10 Sept. 1901]; received the Queen's Medal with three clasps, the King's Medal with two clasps, and was created a Companion of the Distinguished Service Order [London Gazette, 27 Sept. 1901]: "Augustus Charles Baillie, Capt., 10th Battn. Imperial Yeomanry. In recognition of services during the operations in South Africa." He was invested by the King 24 Oct. 1902. During the European War Lieut.-Colonel A. C. Baillie commanded the 2/2nd Lovat's Scouts, Sept. 1914, to Dec. 1916; served in France in charge of horses, Dec. 1916, to April, 1917; commanded 2/2nd Lovat's Scouts, May, 1917, to the end of the war. He was given the Brevet of Colonel. He married, in 1905, Meta, only daughter of the late Lieut.-General Sir Henry Trotter, G.C.V.O., and they have one son and one daughter.

MURRAY, EDWARD ROBERT, Capt. (Sir E. R. Murray, 13th Bart.), was born 22 June, 1875, eldest son of Sir William Murray, 12th Baronet, and Esther Elizabeth, daughter of J. Murray and widow of J. Rickard. He served in the South African War with the 10th Battn. Imperial Yeomanry; as Captain and Adjutant, 1st Regt. of 10th Imperial Yeomanry, and O.C., 2nd Regt. He was mentioned in Despatches [London Gazette, 10 Sept. 1901]; Queen's and King's Medals with five clasps, and was created a Companion of the Distinguished Service Order [London Gazette, 27 Sept. 1901]: "Edward Robert Murray, Capt., 10th Battn. Imperial Yeomanry. In recognition of services during the operations in South Africa." He succeeded his father in the Baronetcy in 1904. Lieut.-Colonel Sir E. R. Murray married, in 1904, Elsie Innes Macgeorge, eldest daughter of W. A. Brown.

POYNTER, ARTHUR VERNON, Capt., was born 9 Nov. 1871, only son of the late Lieut.-Colonel James Poynter, formerly 14th Hussars. He was educated at Radley College, joined the Scots Guards and retired;

served in the South African War, 1899–1901, with the Imperial Yeomanry ; was Commandant, Imperial Yeomanry Depôt. He took part in operations in the Transvaal ; was dangerously wounded ; was mentioned in Despatches [London Gazette, 10 Sept. 1901], and was created a Companion of the Distinguished Service Order [London Gazette, 27 Sept. 1901]: "Arthur Vernon Poynter, Capt., 10th Battn. Imperial Yeomanry. In recognition of services during the operations in South Africa." He was invested by the King 17 Dec. 1901. He was A.D.C. to the Viceroy of India, 1902–5 ; A.D.C. to the Governor-General of Canada, 1906–7 Major Poynter served in the European War, 1914–16, and was severely wounded. He married, in 1917, at Charlton Park Church, Malmesbury, Wiltshire, Lady Agnes Isabel Howard, third daughter of the 18th Earl of Suffolk.

MILLS, THE HONOURABLE EGREMONT JOHN, Capt., was born 4 Sept. 1866, third son of the 1st Baron Hillingdon. He served in the South African War, 1900–1, with the Imperial Yeomanry, taking part in operations in the Orange Free State, March to May, 1900 ; operations in Orange River Colony, May to 29 Nov. 1900, including action at Biddulphsberg ; operations in Orange River Colony, Dec. 1900. He was mentioned in Despatches [London Gazette, 10 Sept. 1901] ; received the Queen's Medal with four clasps, and was created a Companion of the Distinguished Service Order [London Gazette, 27 Sept. 1901]: "The Honourable Egremont John Mills, Capt., 11th Battn. Imperial Yeomanry. In recognition of services during the operations in South Africa." He was invested by the King 29 Oct. 1901. He was promoted to Major. He is a partner in the firm of Glynn, Mills, Currie and Co. In 1917 he married Florence, only daughter of A. Hozier.

GILLIAT, JOHN BABINGTON, Capt., was born 10 April, 1868, only son of the late J. S. Gilliat. He was called to the Bar, Inner Temple, in 1894 ; and served in the South African War, 1900–1, with the Imperial Yeomanry ; and took part in operations in the Transvaal 30 Nov. 1900, to Feb. 1901 ; was mentioned in Despatches [London Gazette, 10 Sept. 1901] ; received the Queen's Medal with four clasps, and was created a Companion of the Distinguished Service Order [London Gazette, 27 Sept. 1901]: "John Babington Gilliat, Capt., 12th Battn. Imperial Yeomanry. In recognition of services during the operations in South Africa." The Insignia were presented to him by the King 29 Oct. 1901. He became Major, Hertfordshire Yeomanry ; and Lieutenant-Colonel ; and Honorary Captain in the Army. Lieut.-Colonel Gilliat married, in 1908, Muriel, eldest daughter of G. Grinnell Milne, and they have two sons and one daughter.

CRANE, CHARLES PASTON, Capt., was born 12 Aug. 1857, son of the Rev. Canon Crane. He was educated at home, and at Exeter College, Oxford (B.A. ; Honours in Modern History, 1878 ; M.A., 1901). He joined the Royal Irish Constabulary as a Cadet in 1879, and served through the Land Agitation in Kerry, 1880–89 ; on special duty in Donegal and the South Eastern Province in 1889 and 1894 ; was Private Secretary to the Inspector-General, 1895 to 1897 ; Resident Magistrate in Donegal, 1897 to 1900 ; seconded in 1900 to serve as Captain and Adjutant of 12th Battn. Imperial Yeomanry, in the South African Campaign, to May, 1901 ; subsequently Adjutant, 12th Battn., to June, 1901 ; as Adjutant, Mounted Troops, Potchefstroom Column, 26 Aug. 1900, to 30 Jan. 1901 (Imperial Yeomanry). Operations in Cape Colony, south of Orange River, March to May, 1900 ; operations in Orange River Colony, May to Aug. 1900, including actions at Rhenoster River and Wittebergen (1 to 29 July) ; operations in the Transvaal, west of Pretoria, Aug. to 29 Nov. 1900 ; operations in the Transvaal, 30 Nov. 1900, to March, 1901 ; operations in Orange River Colony, March to April, 1901. He was mentioned in Despatches, received the Queen's Medal with four clasps, and was created a Companion of the Distinguished Service Order [London Gazette, 27 Sept. 1901]: "Charles Paston Crane, Capt., 12th Battn. Imperial Yeomanry. In recognition of services during the operations in South Africa." The Insignia were presented by the King 29 Oct. 1901. In Sept. 1914, he was seconded for service with the Army ; as Major, 11th (Service) Battn. Lancashire Fusiliers, Sept. 1914, to March, 1915 ; commanded the 2/4th (Hallamshire) Battn. York and Lancaster Regt., June, 1915, to July, 1916 ; and the 43rd Provisional Battn. July, 1916, to Oct. 1916 (Despatches). Lieut.-Colonel C. P. Crane wrote "Kerry" in the Little Guide Series. He married, in 1908, Mary Alice, Caroline second daughter of Colonel and Lady Mary Skrine, of Warleigh Manor, Somerset. He was awarded the O.B.E. in 1918.

Charles Paston Crane.

MARKS, CLAUD LAURIE, Capt., was born 11 Dec. 1863, son of the late Rev. P. W. Marks. He served in South Africa in 1880, 1881, 1884, 1889 and 1900 ; was mentioned in Despatches, received the Queen's Medal with two clasps, and was created a Companion of the Distinguished Service Order [London Gazette, 27 Sept. 1901]: "Claud Laurie Marks, Capt., 14th Battn. Imperial Yeomanry. In recognition of services during the operations in South Africa." The Insignia were presented by the King 29 Oct. 1901. He became Honorary Captain, 4th Battn. Highland Light Infantry. Major Marks married, in 1887, Caroline, daughter of A. Hoffnung, and they had two sons. He died 1 April, 1910, and an obituary notice of him appeared in the "Times" of 2 April, 1910.

SINCLAIR, SIR JOHN ROSE GEORGE, Capt., 8th Bart., was born at Slough 10 Aug. 1864,, eldest son of Colonel A. Y. Sinclair, 26th B.N.I. He succeeded his grandfather, the 7th Baronet, in 1873 ; was educated at the Military College, Oxford, and was Lieutenant, 4th Battn. Cheshire Regt.

1881–85 ; Lieutenant-Colonel Commandant, 1892–1900 ; Honorary Colonel, 1900, 1st Caithness Volunteer Artillery ; President, Caithness Territorial Force Association, 1908 ; has farmed since 1885 ; is a Justice of the Peace, and Deputy Lieutenant. Sir John Sinclair served in the South African War, 1900–1, with Imperial Yeomanry ; was mentioned in Despatches [London Gazette, 7 May and 10 Sept. 1901]: received the Queen's Medal with four clasps, and was created a Companion of the Distinguished Service Order [London Gazette, 27 Sept. 1901]: "Sir John Rose George Sinclair, Bart., Capt., 14th Battn. Imperial Yeomanry. In recognition of services during the operations in South Africa." The Insignia were presented by the King 29 Oct. 1901. He served in the European War, 1914–19, with the 14th Battn. King's Liverpool Regt. He married, in 1885, Edith, only daughter of Lieut.-Colonel W. M. Dunbar.

HOPKINSON, EMILIUS, Capt., was born in 1869, eldest son of Jonathan Hopkinson, of Frant, Sussex ; is M.A., M.B. (Oxon) ; M.R.C.S., L.R.C.P., F.Z.S. He served in the South African War, 1900–1 ; was mentioned in Despatches ; received the Queen's Medal with four clasps, and was created a Companion of the Distinguished Service Order [London Gazette, 27 Sept. 1901]: "E. Hopkinson, Capt. (Medical Officer), 15th Battn. Imperial Yeomanry. In recognition of services during the operations in South Africa." He was Protectorate Medical Officer, Gambia, West Africa, and later Travelling Commissioner, South Bank Province, Gambia. In 1912 Capt. Hopkinson published "A Vocabulary of the Mandingo Language."

CRADOCK, SHELDON WILLIAM KEITH, Capt., was born 1 Oct. 1858, eldest son of Christopher Cradock, of Hartforth, Yorkshire, and of his wife, Georgiana, third daughter of Major Duff. Another of their sons was Rear-Admiral Sir Christopher Cradock, who died so gloriously "with all conceivable odds" against him in the Battle of the Coronel, and was so gloriously avenged in the Battle of the Falkland Islands by Admiral Sir F. D. Sturdee, whom Lord Fisher despatched with all speed to make an end of Von Spee. Another of these gallant brothers is Lieut.-Colonel Montagu Cradock, C.B., C.M.G., who fought in the Afghan, South African and European Wars. Major Sheldon Cradock was formerly a Captain in the 5th Dragoon Guards. He served in the Egyptian Campaign of 1882, receiving the Medal with clasp and the Khedive's Star. For his services in the South African War of 1899–1902 he was mentioned in Despatches ; received the Queen's Medal with five clasps, and was created a Companion of the Distinguished Service Order [London Gazette, 27 Sept. 1901]: "Sheldon William Keith Cradock, Capt., 16th Battn. Imperial Yeomanry. In recognition of services during the operations in South Africa." Major Cradock served in the European War, 1914–16, with the 2nd King Edward's Horse, and was mentioned in Despatches.

Sheldon W. K. Cradock.

PERRY, ARTHUR CLYDE, Capt., was born 1 June, 1872, only son of the Rev. W. V. Perry, of Sandhurst, near Gloucester. He was educated at Marlborough, and served in the South African War ; was mentioned in Despatches, received the Queen's Medal with four clasps, and was created a Companion of the Distinguished Service Order [London Gazette, 27 Sept. 1901]: "Arthur Clyde Perry, Capt., 16th Battn. Imperial Yeomanry. In recognition of services during the operations in South Africa." He was invested by the King 17 Dec. 1901. Major Perry retired from the 4th Battn. the Manchester Regt. He served in the European War, 1914–17 ; served in the Machine Gun Corps. He married, in 1903, Margaret, youngest daughter of the late Capt. Thomas de Winton, R.H.A., of Wallsworth Hall, near Gloucester.

PEAKE, WALTER ANCELL, Capt., was born 22 March, 1853. He was educated at Marlborough, and Exeter College, Oxford, and served in the South African War of 1899–1902, being mentioned in Despatches [London Gazette, 10 Sept. 1901] ; received the Queen's Medal with four clasps, and was created a Companion of the Distinguished Service Order [London Gazette, 27 Sept. 1901]: "Walter A. Peake, Capt., 17th Battn. Imperial Yeomanry. In recognition of services during the operations in South Africa." He was invested by the King 29 Oct. 1901. He became Colonel, Leicestershire Yeomanry. Colonel Peake married, in 1878, Grace, daughter of the Rev. G. C. Fenwicke, of Stockerstone Hall, Uppingham, and they had one son and two daughters. He died in 1914.

CARDEN, HENRY CHARLES, Capt., was born 30 Jan. 1855, second son of Sir John C. Carden, 4th Bart., and of his second wife, Julia Isabella, daughter of Admiral Charles G. Robinson. He served in South Africa, 1899–1902 ; was mentioned in Despatches and created a Companion of the Distinguished Service Order [London Gazette, 27 Sept. 1901]: "Henry Charles Carden, Capt., 17th Battn. Imperial Yeomanry. In recognition of services during the operations in South Africa." The Insignia were presented by the King 29 Oct. 1901. He served in the European War, and was killed in action in France 26–27 Sept. 1915. Major Carden had married, in 1881, Blanche Katharine, daughter of Rear-Admiral J. Parry Jones-Parry, and they had two sons.

SCOTT, GEORGE JOHN, Capt., was born 7 May, 1858, and was educated at Marlborough. He joined the Shropshire Militia in 1875 ; became Sub-Lieutenant, 2nd Dragoon Guards, in 1879 ; served with the 7th Dragoon Guards in Egypt, 1882 (Medal, with clasp for Tel-el-Kebir, and Khedive's Star) ; exchanged into the 18th Hussars in 1885, and retired in 1889. He served in the South African War, 1900–1, with Imperial Yeomanry ; was present at operations in the Transvaal and Cape Colony, March to Nov.

1900; was mentioned in Despatches [London Gazette, 10 Sept. 1901]; received the Queen's Medal with two clasps, and was created a Companion of the Distinguished Service Order [London Gazette, 27 Sept. 1901]: "George John Scott, Capt., 19th Battn. Imperial Yeomanry. In recognition of services during the operations in South Africa." He was invested by the King 29 Oct. 1901. He served in the City of London Yeomanry, 1901–13; and in the 3rd Middlesex Yeomanry, 1915–16. Lieut.-Colonel G. J. Scott, married, in 1886, Mary Ethel (who died in 1906), daughter of J. F. Christy, J.P., of Upton, Alresford, Hants.

COLVIN, CECIL HODGSON, Capt., was born 30 April, 1858, at Pishopury, Sawbridgeworth, Herts, son of Beale Blackwell Colvin, of Pishopury, Herts, and Monkhams Hall, Essex, and Emma Elizabeth Colvin, daughter of Daniel Britten, of Kenswick, Worcester. He was educated at Marlborough College, and Trinity College, Cambridge, and joined the Army in Feb. 1883. He served throughout the Nile Expedition, attached to the 2nd Battn. Essex Regt., as Lieutenant, 1884–85 (Egyptian Medal and clasp for Nile, and Khedive's Star). He served from 1883 to 1903 in the 4th Battn. Essex Regt. (West Essex Militia), and was transferred to take command of the 3rd Battn. Essex Regt. He was seconded to serve with the 20th Battn. Imperial Yeomanry (Rough Riders) in the South African Campaign, from Feb. 1900, to June, 1901, taking part in operations in Cape Colony, May to June, 1900; operations in Orange River Colony, June to 29 Nov. 1900; operations

Cecil Hodgson Colvin.

in Orange River Colony and Cape Colony 30 Nov. 1900, to May, 1901. He was mentioned in Despatches [London Gazette, 10 Sept. 1901]; received the Queen's Medal and three clasps, and, for service with 76th Company, Imperial Yeomanry, around Bloemfontein and Ladybrand, 1900–1, was created a Companion of the Distinguished Service Order [London Gazette, 27 Sept. 1901]: "Cecil Hodgson Colvin, Capt., 20th Battn. Imperial Yeomanry. In recognition of services during the operations in South Africa." The Insignia were presented to him by the King 29 Oct. 1901. Colonel Colvin commanded the 3rd Battn. Essex Regt. from Feb. 1903, to 1 Jan. 1917, and was created a C.B. in 1916, and mentioned in Despatches on 26 Feb. 1917. He was appointed Commandant, Prisoner of War (Officers) Camp, Holyport, Maidenhead, April, 1917, to 1 Jan. 1920; was Deputy Lieutenant for the County of Essex, 1912. He married, 26 Jan. 1887, at St. Paul's Knightsbridge, Ida, daughter of the late Colonel Craigie Halkett, of Cramond, Midlothian, and their children are: Ivan Beale Colvin, Lieut., R.N., born 12 July, 1891, and Daphne Joan Ida, born 28 Feb. 1903.

HOLDEN, EDWARD CHARLES SHUTTLEWORTH, Capt., was born 7 Jan. 1865, only child of Charles Shuttleworth Holden. He served in South Africa, 1899–1900, with Imperial Yeomanry, attached to the Protectorate Regt., and took part in the defence of Mafeking, including actions of 26 Nov. 1899, and 12 May, 1900; operations in the Transvaal, east and west of Pretoria, May to Oct. 1900. He was mentioned in Despatches [London Gazette, 10 Sept. 1901]; received the Queen's Medal with three clasps, and was created a Companion of the Distinguished Service Order [London Gazette, 27 Sept. 1901]: "Edward Charles Shuttleworth Holden, Capt., Derbyshire Yeomanry Cavalry. In recognition of services during the operations in South Africa." The Insignia were presented by the King 29 Oct. 1901. He became Honorary Lieutenant-Colonel, Derbyshire Yeomanry Cavalry, and resigned in 1910. Lieut.-Colonel Holden married, in 1906, Aimée Marguerite (who died in 1913), youngest daughter of the late Vicomte de Labrosse and widow of William R. Cookson, of Binfield Park, Berkshire, and they had one son. He died 17 May, 1916.

GREEN, ALFRED LINGARD, Capt., was born 1 July, 1863, at Ballingdon, Essex, son of the late Rev. Thomas Lingard Green, Honorary Canon of Ely, late Rector of Sudbury, Suffolk, and afterwards Rector of Tingrith, Bedfordshire, and Louisa Letitia Lingard Green (née Stedman); and was educated at Ely Grammar School. He married, 27 Sept. 1888, Isabel, daughter of the late Robert Thorburn, Esq., of Vancouver, British Columbia, and they had three children: Arthur Adelbert, born 3 June, 1889; Frances Winifred, and Edgar Methuen, born 15 Sept. 1896. For his services in the South African War he was created a Companion of the Distinguished Service Order [London Gazette, 27 Sept. 1901]: "Alfred Lingard Green, Capt., Bedfordshire Regt. In recognition of services during the operations in South Africa."

Alfred Lingard Green.

The following is his Record of Service:
1880, Private in the West Suffolk Volunteers; 4 Jan. 1881, Second Lieutenant, the Bedfordshire Militia; 7 May, 1881, Lieutenant, Bedfordshire Militia; 8 May, 1882, passed Qualifying Examination of Militia Candidates for Commissions in the Army; March, 1885, Driver, Transport Service in the North-West Rebellion of Canada; 20 Feb. 1891, Second Lieutenant, 3rd Vol. Battn. Bedfordshire Regt.; 15 July, 1892, Lieutenant, Bedfordshire Regt., and Secretary, Bedfordshire Rifle Association; 20 Nov. 1895, Captain, Bedfordshire Regt., and Mess President; 1897, Captain,

and for short period Acting Adjutant; 14 Feb. 1900, Temporary Captain in the Army, whilst Commanding 1st Volunteer Active Service Company (South African War); 13 Feb. 1901, Major, 3rd Vol. Battn. Bedfordshire Regt.; 17 June, 1901, Honorary Captain in the Army; 17 Aug. 1901, Major, attached 10th Provisional Battn., Dover; July, 1902, Acting Second-in-Command; 5 Sept. 1902, Temporary in Command; 2 April, 1901, Mentioned in Despatches; 29 Oct. 1901, Invested with the D.S.O. and received the Queen's Medal with three clasps for South African War; 9 Aug. 1902, received Coronation Medal; 3 Dec. 1902, Lieutenant-Colonel, to command 3rd Vol. Battn. Bedfordshire Regt.; 31 March, 1903, Certificate of Proficiency for Field Officers attending School of Instruction, Chelsea Barracks; 1903, Hythe Certificate; 17 Dec. 1904, retired, with permission to retain rank and wear uniform; 1914, Lieutenant-Colonel Commanding Bloemfontein Civilian Training Association and Town Guard during South African Rebellion.

Lieut.-Colonel A. L. Green served in the European War from 1914, in South Africa, and afterwards in France; was in the 2nd Regt., 1st South African Infantry; was wounded at Delville Wood, and died of wounds received at Givenchy 16 July, 1915. An obituary notice of him appeared in the "Times."

REID, ALEXANDER, Capt., was born 2 Oct. 1863, son of Thomas Reid, of Hampstead. He served in the South African War in 1900; was mentioned in Despatches; received the Queen's Medal with four clasps, and was created a Companion of the Distinguished Service Order [London Gazette, 27 Sept. 1901]: "Alexander Reid, Capt., City Imperial Volunteers, 1st Volunteer Battn. Middlesex Regt. In recognition of services during the operations in South Africa." The Insignia were presented by the King, 28 Oct. 1901. Major Reid married, in 1906, Margaret Frederica, widow of the late Major Harry Chalmers Hudson, I.M.S., 16th Bengal Cavalry, and they have one son.

WATERLOW, JAMES FRANCIS, Capt., was born 25 April, 1869, son of the late J. Jameson Waterlow. He served in South Africa in 1900, with Mounted Infantry; was mentioned in Despatches, 10 Sept. 1901; received the Queen's Medal with six clasps, and was created a Companion of the Distinguished Service Order [London Gazette, 27 Sept. 1901]: "James Francis Waterlow, Capt., 2nd Volunteer Battn. Royal West Surrey Regt., City Imperial Volunteers. In recognition of services during the operations in South Africa." The Insignia were presented by the King 28 Oct. 1901. He became Major, 5th Battn. The Queen's Regt.

WRAY, KENNETH MACKENZIE, Capt., was born 7 June, 1855, son of the late George Cecil Gore Wray, of Ardnamona, County Donegal, and Dunseverick Castle, County Antrim. He served in the South African War, 1900–1, with the 6th Imperial Bushmen, taking part in operations in Rhodesia (17 to 25 May, 1900); operations in the Transvaal, west of Pretoria, July to Nov. 1900; operations in the Transvaal, Orange River Colony and Cape Colony, Nov. 1900, to June, 1901. He was mentioned in Despatches [London Gazette, 10 Sept. 1901]; received the Queen's Medal with five clasps; the King's Medal with two clasps, and was created a Companion of the Distinguished Service Order [London Gazette, 27 Sept. 1901]: "Kenneth Mackenzie Wray, Capt., New South Wales Imperial Bushmen. In recognition of services during the operations in South Africa." The Insignia were presented by Brigadier-General Finn, at Sydney, 26 April, 1902. He became Captain, 1st Australian Horse. Capt. Wray married, in 1882, Grace, fourth daughter of the late Benjamin Lloyd Edwards, of Molonglo, New South Wales, and they have two sons and four daughters.

McLEAN, ARCHIBALD ALEXANDER, Capt., was born in 1871. He served with the New South Wales Contingent in South Africa, 1900-2. He was present at the Relief of Kimberley; operations in the Orange Free State, Feb. to May, 1900, including operations at Paardeberg 17 to 26 Feb.; actions at Poplar Grove, Driefontein, Karee Siding, Houtnek (Thoba Mountain), Vet River (5 and 6 May) and Zand River; operations in the Transvaal in May and June, 1900, including actions near Johannesburg, Pretoria and Diamond Hill (11 and 12 June); operations in the Transvaal, west of Pretoria, July to Nov. 1900; operations in Orange River Colony (May to Nov. 1900), including actions at Wittebergen (1 to 29 July) and Bothaville; operations in the Transvaal and Orange River Colony, April, 1901, to April, 1902; Assistant Press Censor; was severely wounded; mentioned in Despatches [London Gazette, 16 April, 1901]; received the Queen's Medal with seven clasps, and was created a Companion of the Distinguished Service Order [London Gazette, 27 Sept. 1901]: "A. A. McLean, Capt., New South Wales Contingent. In recognition of services during the operations in South Africa." The Insignia were presented to him by Lord Tennyson, at Sydney, New South Wales, on 18 April, 1902. He became Honorary Major, Reserve of Officers.

BROWNE, HENRY HAMILTON, Capt., was born 20 June, 1863, son of the late James Hamilton Browne. He served in South Africa, 1900-2; was mentioned in Despatches, received the Queen's and King's Medals with six clasps, and was created a Companion of the Distinguished Service Order [London Gazette, 27 Sept. 1901]: "Henry Hamilton Browne, Capt., New South Wales Imperial Bushmen. In recognition of services during the operations in South Africa." The Insignia were presented to him by Major-General M. W. Willson, C.B. (the late Major-General Sir M. W. Willson, K.C.B.), at Bushey Kop, 1 June, 1902. Capt. Hamilton Browne was promoted to Major.

NORTON, ALFRED EDWARD MARSTON, Capt., was born 13 July, 1869, son of the late John Norton, of Golding Hall, Shropshire. He served in the South African War in 1900, taking part in operations in Orange River Colony and Cape Colony. He was mentioned in Despatches [London Gazette, 10 Sept. 1901]; received the Queen's Medal with two clasps, and was created a Companion of the Distinguished Service Order [London Gazette, 27 Sept. 1901]: "A. E. M. Norton, Capt., South Australian Contingent. In recognition of services during the operations in South Africa."

The Insignia were presented to him by Lord Tennyson, at Adelaide, 12 April, 1902. He became Major, Reserve of Officers, Unattached List, Australian Military Forces, 21 Aug. 1911. He served in the European War, and was given the Brevet of Lieutenant-Colonel. Lieut.-Colonel Norton married, in 1895, Fannie Margaret Stacy.

STAIRS, HENRY BERTRAM, Capt., was born 29 April, 1871, son of the late John Stairs, of Halifax, Nova Scotia. He became a Barrister, Supreme Court, Nova Scotia, in 1893, and a K.C. in 1910. He served in the South African War, 1899–1900, and was present at operations in the Orange Free State, Feb. to May, 1900, including operations at Paardeberg, 18 to 26 Feb.; actions at Poplar Grove, Dreifontein, Houtnek (Thoba Mountain) and Zand River; operations in the Transvaal in May and June, 1900, including actions near Johannesburg and Pretoria; operations in Orange River Colony, June, 1900; operations in Orange River Colony and Transvaal, east and west of Pretoria, July to Oct. 1900. He was mentioned in Despatches [London Gazette, 8 Feb. and 10 Sept. 1901]; was given the Brevet of Major; received the Queen's Medal with four clasps, and was created a Companion of the Distinguished Service Order [London Gazette, 27 Sept. 1901]: "Henry Bertram Stairs, Capt., Canadian Contingent. In recognition of services during the operations in South Africa." The Insignia of the D.S.O. were presented to him by the Governor at Halifax, 10 May, 1902. Major Stairs has the Colonial Auxiliary Forces Long Service Medal. He married, in 1903, Judith, daughter of the late George Henderson

MACDONELL, ARCHIBALD HAYES, Capt., was born at Toronto, Canada, 6 Feb. 1868, son of Angus Duncan Macdonell and Pauline Rosalie Macdonell (*née* De-la-Haye). He joined the Canadian Military Forces in Feb. 1886, and served with the 1st Canadian Contingent in South Africa, 1899–1900, taking part in operations in the Orange Free State, Feb. to May, 1900, including operations at Paardeberg, 17 to 20 May, 1900; actions at Poplar Grove and Dreifontein; operations in the Transvaal, July to 29 Nov. 1900; operations in Cape Colony, south of Orange River, 1899–1900. He served as a Battalion Adjutant (2nd Battn.), Royal Canadian Regt. of Infantry, Oct. to Dec. 1899; was mentioned in Despatches [London Gazette, 8 Feb. and 16 April, 1901]; was given the Brevet of Major; received the Queen's Medal with four clasps, and for work performed while commanding a Company of the Royal Canadian Regt. at Paardeberg on the surrender of General Cronje, was created a Companion of the Distinguished Service Order [London Gazette, 27 Sept. 1901]: "Archibald Hayes Macdonell, Capt., Canadian Military Forces. In recognition of services during the operations in South Africa." He served in Southern Nigeria in seven expeditions altogether: West Africa (Southern Nigeria), 1901–04: Aro Expedition (Medal with clasp); Ebeku Expedition (clasp, Despatches); Ibeku-Olokoro Expedition; also served in the Afikpo Expedition (clasp, Despatches); Mkpani Expedition (clasp); North Ibibio Expedition; operations at Obokum (clasp). He passed the Staff College; served in the European War, 1914–18; with the 1st Canadian Division from Sept. 1914, to Aug. 1915; appointed to command the Royal Canadian Regiment; took it to France; transferred to command of 5th Canadian Infantry Brigade; promoted to Brigadier-General 22 April, 1916; served in the 1st, 2nd and 3rd Canadian Divisions; was three times mentioned in Despatches, and created a C.M.G. in 1916. Brigadier-General Macdonell is a Chief of the Six Nations Indians (Onadagas), and is fond of big game shooting. He is unmarried.

BOWEN, HARRY JAMES AP-OWEN, Capt., was born 9 Feb. 1867, third son of the Rev. Arthur James Bowen, J.P., of Troedyraur, Cardiganshire. He is a solicitor, and is a steward of the Jockey Club of South Africa. He served in the South African War, 1899–1900; was severely wounded, mentioned in Despatches [London Gazette, 10 Sept. 1901]; received the Queen's Medal with two clasps, and was created a Companion of the Distinguished Service Order [London Gazette, 27 Sept. 1901]: "Harry James ap-Owen Bowen, Capt., Kimberley Light Horse. In recognition of services during the operations in South Africa." He married, in 1904, Amy Langford Pote.

PICKERING, WILLIAM, Capt., was born 25 Feb. 1856, son of the late Rev. E. Pickering. He served in Kreli-Gaika, in 1878; in the Zulu War in 1879; and in the South African War, 1899–1900, when he was created a Companion of the Distinguished Service Order [London Gazette, 27 Sept. 1901]: "William Pickering, Capt., Kimberley Town Guard. In recognition of services during the operations in South Africa." The Insignia of the D.S.O. were presented to Capt. Pickering at Port Elizabeth, by the Governor of Cape Colony, 5 April, 1905. He was Secretary to the De Beers Consolidated Mines, Limited, 1897 to 1917, and has been a Director since 1917. Capt. Pickering married, in 1890, Ethel Annie, daughter of the late George Wright, of Grahamstown.

JARDINE, JAMES BRUCE, Lieut., was born in Edinburgh 6 Jan. 1870, eldest son of M. L. P. Jardine, late 86th and 67th Regts. He was educated at Charterhouse and Sandhurst, and entered the 5th Lancers, as Second Lieutenant, 12 March, 1890, becoming Lieutenant 2 July, 1892. He served in the South African War, 1899–1902, taking part in operations in Natal in 1899, including actions at Elandslaagte, Rietfontein and Lombard's Kop; defence of Ladysmith, including sortie of 7 Dec. 1899, and action of 6 Jan. 1900; operations in Natal, March to June, 1900; operations in the Transvaal, east of Pretoria, July to 29 Nov. 1900. He received the Queen's Medal with five clasps, the King's Medal with two clasps, and was created a Companion of the Distinguished Service Order [London Gazette, 27 Sept. 1901]: "James Bruce Jardine, Lieut., 5th Lancers. In recognition of services during the operations in South Africa." The Insignia were presented to him by the King 24 Oct. 1902. He was promoted to Captain 5 Oct. 1901. During the latter part of the South African War he was Staff Officer to Colonel Callwell's Column, and he took part in General French's operations in the South-Eastern Transvaal and Cape Colony. Capt. Jardine was attached to the Japanese Army in Manchuria 30 April, 1904, to 6 July, 1905, during the Russo-Japanese War of 1904–5, and received the Japanes War Medal and the Order of the Sacred Treasure (4th Class). He becam Major 2 Oct. 1907. From 1914 to 1918 he served in the European War as Temporary Lieutenant-Colonel, 5th Lancers, 23 Sept. 1914, to 31 Au 1915; as Temporary Brigadier-General 1 Sept. 1915, to 2 March, 1917 commanding the 97th Infantry Brigade, New Armies, B.E.F., and Britis Armies in France, 1 Sept. 1915, to 2 March, 1917. He was promoted t Lieutenant-Colonel 16 Jan. 1917; commanded the 7th Cyclist Brigad Home Forces, in Great Britain, 12 June, 1917, to 29 April, 1919. He wa mentioned in Despatches four times; given the Brevet of Lieutenant Colonel 18 Feb. 1915,; created a C.M.G. in 1916, and made an Officer of th Legion of Honour. He married, in 1908, Agnes, eldest daughter of Sir A Hargreaves-Brown, 1st Bart., and Henrietta, daughter of C. R. Blandy, o Madeira, and they have two daughters.

OWEN-LEWIS, ARTHUR FRANCIS, Lieut., was born 6 Aug. 186 eldest son of the late Henry Owen-Lewis, D.L., of Inniskeen, Count Monaghan, M.P., County Carlow. He joined the Yorkshire Regt. 8 Jun 1889, becoming Lieutenant 28 July, 1892, and was Adjutant, 6th Battr Lancashire Fusiliers (Militia) from 1 July, 1898. He served in the Sout African War, 1900–2, as District Commandant; served as Adjutant, 6t Battn. Lancashire Fusiliers, 10 Feb. 1900, to 14 Oct. 1901. He took par in operations in Cape Colony, south of Orange River, Orange Free State an Transvaal, March to 29 Nov. 1900; operations in the Transvaal, Orang River Colony and Cape Colony, from 30 Nov. 1900. He was mentioned i Despatches [London Gazette, 10 Sept. 1901]; received the Queen's Med with three clasps, the King's Medal with two clasps, and was created Companion of the Distinguished Service Order [London Gazette, 27 Sep 1901]: "Arthur Francis Owen-Lewis, Lieut., Yorkshire Regt. In recog nition of services during the operations in South Africa." The Insign were presented by the King 29 Oct. 1901. He retired 25 July, 1907, an became Major, Reserve of Officers, 23 Jan. 1914. Major Owen-Lewis serve in the European War, 1914–18, as G.S.O., Irish Command and A.Q.M.G France; was mentioned in Despatches twice, and awarded the O.B.E. i 1918. He was appointed Inspector of Prisons for Ireland. In 1896 h married Kathleen, daughter of the late William Henry, of Tivoli, Count Dublin.

CARTER, AUBREY JOHN, Lieut., was born 18 Jan. 1872, son of th late T. A. Carter, Esq., of Shottery Hall, Stratford-on-Avon. He wa gazetted to the Loyal North Lancashire Regt. 9 Jan. 1892; was promote to Lieutenant 1 May, 1893; was Adjutant, North Lancashire Regt., 2 April to 17 May, 1898, and became Captain 20 Feb. 1901. He serve in the South African War, as a Railway Staff Officer from 6 Dec. 1899, t 2 March, 1900; and as a Brigade Signalling Officer from 7 Oct. 1900, to 2 March, 1901, and took part in the advance on Kimberley, including th actions at Belmont, Enslin, Modder River and Magersfontein; operatior in the Transvaal, west of Pretoria, July to 20 Nov. 1900; operations i Orange River Colony, including action at Lindley (26 June); operation in the Transvaal 30 Nov. 1900, to March, 1901. He was mentioned i Despatches [London Gazette, 10 Sept. 1901]; received the Queen's Med with five clasps, and was created a Companion of the Distinguished Servic Order [London Gazette, 27 Sept. 1901]: "Aubrey John Carter, Lieut North Lancashire Regt. In recognition of services during the operation in South Africa." The Insignia were presented by the King 29 Oct. 190 From 16 Dec. 1905, to Dec. 1909, he was an Instructor at the School c Musketry, where—with Lieut.-Colonel Norman McMahon—he was mainl responsible for the revolution in the musketry training of the Army, an in July, 1911, was appointed Commandant of the School of Musketr South Africa, with the temporary rank of Lieutenant-Colonel. He ha become Major in Feb. 1910. His services at the School of Musketry in Sout Africa were acknowledged in the following extract from a letter signed b Lord Gladstone: "In a special measure Ministers ask me to record thei grateful acknowledgment of the services rendered by Lieut.-Colonel Carte Commandant, School of Musketry, Tempe, and his Staff." He was late given charge of Musketry in the Irish Command, and eventually proceede to France to take command of the 1st Battn. Loyal North Lancashire Regt He led it in a charge thus described by a brother officer: "The men mean business this time. I looked into their faces and could see a sort of dul fierce look. After the many days of being cooped up in the trenches befor we ever arrived in this portion of the theatre of war, it was a real joy to then to be on the move and on the attack. They longed to get at them, an gradually, without a word of command being given, you could hear th click of the bayonet as each man fastened it to his rifle. Suddenly th cry arose: 'Come on, my lads, now for the trenches!' The cry wen along the line. Every one started yelling above the din of battle. W charged, yelling, shouting, screaming, rushing madly forward at the enemy How it looked from the German side I do not know; but it was granc simply magnificent, from our side. We crossed two hundred yards c root-field at a steady run under fire. We leapt into the enemy's trenche bayoneted those who were still living, and then rushed on to another lin of trenches in front. The whole of my battalion were in it. It was ou show." Lieut.-Colonel Carter fell in action near Ypres on 4 Nov. 191 "He was a tall, soldier-like figure, standing six feet four inches, and straigh as the proverbial pine. His was a soldier's end. He went out from th trenches to direct the machine-gun fire, but fell, shot dead, as the enem retired. He was a gallant commander, and a great leader, under whom i is an honour to have served." He had married, in 1906, Edith Mary daughter of the late Rev. G. H. Rigby and niece of the late Right Hon. Si John Rigby.

LEGGETT, EDWARD HUMPHREY MANISTY, Lieut., was bor 7 Dec. 1871, son of the late Major G. E. Leggett, 77th Regt. He was edu cated at Clifton College, and at the Royal Military Academy, Woolwic (Pollock Gold Medallist, 1900), and on the Staff of the London and Nort Western Railway. He was Board of Trade (British) Delegate to the Inte national Railway Congress, 1895. He became Second Lieutenant, Royal Engineers, 25 July, 1890; Lieutenant, 25 July, 1893; Railway Traffic Manager, Woolwich Arsenal, 15 Aug. 1895, to 6 Oct. 1899. He served in the South African War, as Deputy Assistant Director of Railways, 30 Oct. 1899, to 26 Nov. 1901; was Deputy Assistant Director of Railways, Headquarters, South Africa, 27 Nov. 1901, to 1 July, 1902, and Officer Commanding National Scouts and Orange River Colony Volunteers. He was present at operations in the Orange Free State; operations in the Transvaal in May and June, 1900, including actions near Johannesburg and Diamond Hill (11 and 12 June); operations in the Transvaal, east of Pretoria, July to Nov. 1900; operations in Orange River Colony, May to Nov. 1900; operations in Cape Colony, south of Orange River, 1899–1900; operations in the Transvaal and Orange River Colony 30 Nov. 1900, to 31 May, 1902. He was mentioned in Despatches [London Gazette, 10 Sept. 1901]; was given the Brevet of Major 26 June, 1902; received the Queen's Medal with four clasps, the King's Medal with two clasps, and was created a Companion of the Distinguished Service Order [London Gazette, 27 Sept. 1901]: "Edward Humphrey Manisty Leggett, Lieut., Royal Engineers. In recognition of services during the operations in South Africa." The Insignia, Warrant and Statutes were sent to the G.O.C., Transvaal, and presented by the G.O.C., Forces in South Africa, at Pretoria, 25 March, 1903. He was promoted to Captain 1 April, 1901, and was employed under the Civil Government in the Transvaal, 20 Oct. 1902, to 14 Feb. 1906; was employed in the East African Protectorate 1 Feb. 1907, to 1910, being lent to the Colonial Office for special duty under the Council of the British Cotton-Growing Association in East Africa and Uganda, 1907–10. Member of the Legislative Council of British East Africa, 1908–9; retired from the Army, with the rank of Major, 4 Feb. 1911. Major Leggett married, in 1907, Ada, daughter of John Dyson, of Merriott, Crewkerne, formerly Judicial Commissioner of Oudh.

WINWOOD, WILLIAM QUINTINE, Lieut., was born 24 Sept. 1873, son of the Rev. Henry Hoyt Winwood, M.A., F.R.G.S. He was gazetted to the 5th Dragoon Guards 15 March, 1893; became Lieutenant 21 Jan. 1894; was Adjutant, 5th Dragoon Guards, 16 July, 1899, to 15 July, 1903. He served in the South African War, 1899–1902, as Adjutant, 5th Dragoon Guards, to 23 Nov. 1902, taking part in operations in Natal in 1899, including action at Lombard's Kop; defence of Ladysmith, including sortie of 7 Dec. 1899, and action of 6 Jan. 1900; operations in the Transvaal in 1900; operations in Natal, 1900; operations in the Transvaal, east of Pretoria, 1900; operations in Orange River Colony, 1900; operations in the Transvaal 30 Nov. 1900, to Aug. 1901, and Nov. 1901, to March, 1902; operations in Orange River Colony, May, 1901; operations on the Zululand Frontier of Natal in Sept. and Oct. 1901. He was mentioned in Despatches [London Gazette, 8 Feb. 1901 (Sir G. S. White, 23 March, 1900; Sir R. H. Buller, 9 Nov. 1900), and London Gazette, 10 Sept. 1901]; received the Queen's Medal with three clasps; the King's Medal with two clasps, and was created a Companion of the Distinguished Service Order [London Gazette, 27 Sept. 1901]: "William Quintine Winwood, Lieut., 5th Dragoon Guards. In recognition of services during the operations in South Africa." The Insignia, Warrant and Statutes were sent to the Commander-in-Chief in India, and presented by the G.O.C., Oudh District, after Church Parade on 22 Feb. 1903. He was promoted to Captain 1 Feb. 1901, and to Major 10 March, 1901; was Assistant Military Secretary to the General Officer Commanding-in-Chief, South Africa, 1 June, 1907; became Lieutenant-Colonel 1 Sept. 1914. He served in the European War, 1914–18; was mentioned in Despatches; wounded; created a C.M.G., 1915, and awarded the O.B.E. in 1919, and the Belgian Croix de Guerre. He also received the Mons Star and was made a Commander of the Order of Leopold by the King of the Belgians in 1915. He commanded the 4th Reserve Regt. of Dragoons in France from April, 1919. Lieut.-Colonel Winwood married, in 1909, Gertrude, daughter of the Rev. Dolben Paul and widow of T. B. Hope.

BOWMAN-MANIFOLD, MICHAEL GRAHAM EGERTON, Lieut., was born 9 June, 1871, son of the late Surgeon-General Manifold. He entered the Royal Engineers 13 Feb. 1891; became Lieutenant 13 Feb. 1894; Captain 17 Oct. 1901; Major 13 Feb. 1911; Lieutenant-Colonel 24 Sept. 1918; Temporary Brigadier-General from 5 Feb. 1918. He was employed with the Egyptian Army 8 Nov. 1895, to 11 Jan. 1899; Staff Officer to Director of Railways, South Africa, 1 Jan. to 4 July, 1900; Telegraph Supt., South Africa, 5 July, 1900, to 12 Aug. 1901; G.S.O.3, Headquarters of Army, 9 June, 1909, to 20 Sept. 1912; G.S.O.2, War Office, 21 Sept. 1912, to 8 June, 1913; Director of Army Signals, Mediterranean Expeditionary Force; Egyptian Expeditionary Force, 20 March, 1915, to 4 Feb. 1918; Director of Army Signals, Egyptian Expeditionary Force, 5 Feb. 1918. He served with the Expedition to Dongola, 1896, as Staff Officer of Telegraphs; took part in the operations of 7 June (horse killed) and 19 Sept (Despatches [London Gazette, 3 Nov. 1896]; 4th Class Medjidie; Egyptian Medal with two clasps); served with the Nile Expedition, 1897, as Staff Officer of Telegraphs (clasp to Egyptian Medal); again with the Nile Expedition, 1898, as Staff Officer of Telegraphs, Headquarters Staff; was present at the battles of the Atbara and Khartoum (Despatches [London Gazette, 24 May, 1898]; 4th Class Osmanieh; two clasps to Egyptian Medal; Medal); served in the South African war, 1899–1901, on Staff (Despatches [London Gazette, 10 Sept. 1901]; Queen's Medal with three clasps). He was created a Companion of the Distinguished Service Order [London Gazette, 27 Sept. 1901]: "Michael Graham Egerton Bowman-Manifold, Lieut., Royal Engineers. For services during the recent operations in South Africa." The Insignia were presented by the King 29 Oct. 1901. For his services in the European War (Dardanelles, 1914–15) he was thrice mentioned in Despatches, and was created a C.B. in 1917; a C.M.G. in 1918, and a K.B.E. in 1919; was made Officer, Legion of Honour, and given the Brevets of Lieutenant-Colonel 18 Feb. 1915, and Colonel 8 Nov. 1915. Sir Michael Bowman-Manifold married Kathleen Cecilia, daughter of the late Admiral Sir T. Brandreth, K.C.B.

WOOD, JOHN LOCKHART, Lieut., was born 16 Dec. 1871, second son of the late Edward Herbert Wood, of Newbold Revel, Rugby, and Isle of Raasay, N.B. He was educated at Eton College; entered the 18th Hussars 12 March, 1892, becoming Lieutenant 12 June, 1894. He served in South Africa, 1899–1902; was mentioned in Despatches; received the Queen's Medal with five clasps, the King's Medal with two clasps, and was created a Companion of the Distinguished Service Order [London Gazette, 27 Sept. 1901]: "John Lockhart Wood, Lieut., 18th Hussars. In recognition of services during the operations in South Africa." He was invested by the King 18 Dec. 1902. Capt. Wood resigned from the Army. He was a J.P. for Hampshire. He served in the European War, and died on the 11th June, 1915, of wounds received in action 24 May, 1915, in Flanders. He had married in 1904, Mary Douglas, daughter of G. F. MacCorquodale, and they had one son.

FULTON, HARRY TOWNSEND, Lieut., was born 15 Aug. 1869, sixth son of the late Lieut.-General John Fulton, Royal Artillery. He entered the Argyll and Sutherland Highlanders, from the Local Military Forces in New Zealand, 9 April, 1892, becoming Lieutenant, Indian Staff Corps, 24 July, 1894. He served on the North-West Frontier of India, 1897–98; Malakand; operations in Bajaur (Medal and clasp); in the Tirah Campaign, 1897–98 (clasp). He served in South Africa, 1899–1901, employed with the New Zealand Mounted Rifles, taking part in operations in Rhodesia in May, 1900; operations in the Transvaal, west of Pretoria, 1900; operations in Cape Colony, north of Orange River, 1900. He was severely wounded; mentioned in Despatches [London Gazette, 10 Sept. 1901]; received the Queen's Medal with three clasps, and was created a Companion of the Distinguished Service Order [London Gazette, 27 Sept. 1901]: "Harry Townsend Fulton, Lieut., Indian Staff Corps. In recognition of services during the operations in South Africa." The Insignia, Warrant, etc., were sent to the Commander-in-Chief in India, and presented by the O.C. in Chitral 22 March, 1902. He was promoted to Captain 10 July, 1901. He married in 1905, Ada Hermina, second daughter of John James Dixon. Lieut.-Colonel H. T. Fulton was killed in action 29 March, 1918.

Harry Townsend Fulton.

READY, FELIX FORDATI, Lieut., was born 14 July, 1872, son of the late Colonel J. T. Ready, of Ellerslie, Hawkhurst, Kent. He entered the Army 5 Dec. 1891; became Lieutenant 28 July, 1894; was employed with the Egyptian Army 7 Jan. 1898, to 21 Jan. 1900. He served in the Nile Expedition in 1898, taking part in the battles of the Atbara and Khartum; was mentioned in Despatches [London Gazette, 30 Sept. 1898]; received the 4th Class of the Medjidie, the Medal, and the Egyptian Medal with two clasps. He served in the Nile Expedition in 1899, receiving a clasp to the Egyptian Medal. He next saw active service in South Africa in 1899 and 1900, and in 1902, taking part in operations in the Orange Free State, March to May, 1900; operations in the Transvaal, east of Pretoria, July to Oct. 1900; operations in the Transvaal, west of Pretoria, July and August, 1900, including action at Zilikat's Nek; operations in Orange River Colony, April to 31 May, 1902. He was mentioned in Despatches [London Gazette, 10 Sept. 1901]; received the Queen's Medal with four clasps, and was created a Companion of the Distinguished Service Order [London Gazette, 27 Sept. 1901]: "Felix Fordati Ready, Lieut., Royal Berkshire Regt. In recognition of services during the operations in South Africa." The Insignia were presented by the King 29 Oct. 1901. He became Captain 15 Jan. 1902; was D.A.Q.M.G., Gibraltar, 9 Sept. 1903, to 31 Oct. 1905; D.A.A. and Q.M.G., Gibraltar, 1 Nov. 1905 to 11 Sept. 1907; commanded a Company of Gentlemen Cadets (G.S.O., Royal Military College), 1 Aug. 1910, to 31 July, 1914; became Major 29 July, 1911; was D.A.A. and Q.M.G., 2nd Division, B.E.F., 19 Aug. 1914, to 1 June, 1915; A.A. and Q.M.G., 4th Division, B.E.F., 2 June, 1915, to 21 May, 1916; D.A.A. and Q.M.G., 1st Army Corps, British Armies in France, 22 May, 1916, to 4 Aug. 1916; D.A.A., Indian Expeditionary Force "D," 18 Aug. 1916, to 14 May, 1919; was promoted to Major-General 3 June, 1919. Major-General F. F. Ready served in the European War, 1914–18, and was mentioned in Despatches nine times. He was given the Brevets of Lieutenant-Colonel (3 June, 1915) and Colonel (1 Jan. 1917). He was created a C.M.G. in 1916; a C.B. in 1917; and a C.S.I. in 1919. He married, in 1900, Marguerite Violet, daughter of the late W. Cotterill, of Tongswood, Hawkhurst, Kent.

ABADIE, HARRY BERTRAND, Lieut., was born 20 June, 1872; he joined the 11th Hussars 5 Oct. 1892; became Lieutenant 20 Sept. 1894; was on Special Service, South Africa, 9 Oct. 1899. For his services in the South African War he was created a Companion of the Distinguished Service Order [London Gazette, 27 Sept. 1901]: "Harry Bertrand Abadie, Lieut., 11th Hussars. In recognition of services during the operations in South Africa." Lieut. Abadie died before he had been presented with the Insignia of the Order, so they were sent to his father, the late Major-General H. R. Abadie, C.B., 9th Lancers. One of General Abadie's sons, Major E. H. A. Abadie, D.S.O., was killed in action at Messines in Oct. 1914, and another, Capt. G. H. F. Abadie, C.M.G., died of fever at Kam, West Africa, in Feb. 1904.

SMITH, HORACE MACKENZIE, Lieut., was born 27 July, 1870, son of the late Henry Smith, of Ellingham Hall, Bungay, Suffolk, and of his second wife, Mary Grey, eldest daughter of James Dowse and widow of the Rev. H. P. Measor. He entered the Army 9 April, 1892; became Lieutenant 22 Dec. 1894, and was employed with the West African Frontier Force 3 July, 1898, to 13 Oct. 1899. He served in the South African War, 1899 to 1902 (employed with Mounted Infantry); took part in operations in the Orange Free State, Feb. to May, 1900, including the action at Poplar Grove (wounded); operations in the Transvaal 30 Nov. 1900, to 31 May, 1902. He was mentioned in Despatches [London Gazette, 10 Sept. 1901]; received the Queen's Medal with two clasps; the King's Medal with two clasps, and was created a Companion of the Distinguished Service Order [London Gazette, 27 Sept. 1901]: "Horace Mackenzie Smith, Lieut., Shropshire Light Infantry. In recognition of services during the operations in South Africa." The Insignia were presented by the King 13 Dec. 1902. He was promoted to Captain 9 March, 1901; to Major 6 March, 1912; was in command of a Service Battalion, Shropshire Light Infantry, 19 Aug. 1914, to 15 Aug. 1915; Temporary Lieutenant-Colonel commanding a Reserve Battn. Royal Fusiliers 24 May, to 26 July, 1916; Temporary Lieutenant-Colonel 28 July, 1916, to 14 March, 1917; in command Reserve Battn. Norfolk Regt. 28 July, 1916; in command Battn. Training Reserve 1 Sept. 1916, to 14 March, 1917; Temporary Lieutenant-Colonel commanding Service Battn. Shropshire Light Infantry 8 April, 1917, to 12 May, 1918. He was given the Brevet of Lieutenant-Colonel 2 March, 1918. Lieut.-Colonel H. M. Smith married, in 1904, Margaret Esther Hamilton, youngest daughter of the late Rear-Admiral H. Hamilton Beamish, C.B., and they have one son and two daughters.

PATERSON, EWING, Lieut., was born 8 June, 1873, second surviving son of the late John Paterson, of Kinburn and Langraw, St. Andrews, Fife. He was educated at St. Andrews, and in Germany, and joined the 3rd Militia Battn. Manchester Regt. in 1889, as Second Lieutenant, transferring to the 6th Dragoons 9 Sept. 1893; he was promoted to Lieutenant 1 Jan. 1895. He served in the South African War, 1899 to 1900, and was slightly wounded. He took part in operations in the Orange Free State, March to May, 1900, including actions at Karee Siding, Vet River (5 and 6 May) and Zand River; operations in the Transvaal in May and June, 1900, including actions near Johannesburg, Pretoria and Diamond Hill (11 and 12 June); operations in the Transvaal, east of Pretoria, including actions at Reit Vlei and Belfast (26 and 27 Aug.); operations in Orange River Colony, including action at Rhenoster River; operations in Cape Colony, south of Orange River, including action at Colesberg. There is a delightful book by Lieut.-Colonel J. Watkins Yardley, C.M.G., D.S.O., called "With the Inniskilling Dragoons." It has a heavenly red and green and yellow cover, with the regimental crest in gold, and the inside is still better. The following extracts are made without leave from him or Colonel Paterson. The book begins: "War! The regiment ordered to the front. Oh! the enthusiasm, the hopes and aspirations, the hustle-bustle of preparations, and the farewells! Mobilization was quickly followed by marching orders and embarkation. So hurried was the departure that the service kits from Pimlico had not reached the Curragh before the first squadron of the regiment entrained there for embarkation at Queenstown. Luckily, after being nearly lost, they arrived in the nick of time to be bundled on board. It was originally intended that on mobilization the Inniskilling Dragoons should be brigaded with the Royals and Scots Greys, in order to form again the old fighting Union Brigade—the cavalry of England, Scotland and Ireland. This, to our disappointment, fell through, owing to regiments, and even squadrons, being sent off to the front directly they landed, so urgent was the need for troops. Thus brigades were necessarily formed as the troops came to hand. The Inniskillings and Scots Greys were, however, brigaded together during the earlier stages of the war, but the Royals were separated, owing to their starting on the campaign from the Natal theatre of war. This was the first regiment of the brigade to land at Cape Town, but the immediate need of troops in Natal caused their re-embarkation for Durban, and so separation from the brigade. Later they worked with the Inniskillings when forming part of Colonel Pulteney's column. The 6th Inniskilling Dragoons, comprising 23 officers, 558 non-commissioned officers and men, with 496 horses, embarked at Queenstown in the S.S. Jamaican, S.S. Siberian and S.S. Persia on 23, 24 and 28 Oct. 1899, respectively." Lieut.-Colonel H. C. Page Henderson was commanding the regiment, and C Squadron was commanded by Major E. H. (now Lord) Allenby. It is said, by the way, that Lord Allenby was approached by various publishers who had views about a book on the Palestine Campaign. Their offers did not tempt Lord Allenby to follow the fashion among Field-Marshals. At last an American publisher came along. "Well," he said, "whatever anyone else has offered you to write a book, I'll *double* it. *And, what's more, I'll write the book myself!*" Prince Alexander of Teck and Lord Fincastle were attached to the Inniskilling Dragoons. Lieut. Ewing Paterson was with B Squadron on board the Jamaican. "From first to last," says Colonel Yardley, "the regiment was worked hard in the fighting line, without a single rest, and I doubt if any regiment experienced and accomplished so much without serious disaster of any kind. From beginning to end, commanded and led in turn by Colonels Page Henderson, Allenby, Rimington and Dauncey, its dash and gallantry were conspicuous." The first period comprises the work round Colesberg, the Relief of Kimberley, Paardeberg, and the occupation of Bloemfontein. On 11 Dec. Major Dauncey, with Lieut. Paterson and six men, set out on what proved to be a successful reconnaissance. Allenby and C Squadron did not arrive until 18 Dec. They had been unavoidably delayed by the wreck of their ship, the Persia. On 27 Feb. 1900: "B Squadron, Inniskilling Dragoons, under Lieut. Paterson, reconnoitred Rensburg. Finding it weakly held, they seized the position commanding it, drove off the Boer rearguard, and took the town—a very smart performance." On 3 March a patrol, under Lieut. Paterson made a successful reconnaissance. On 20 March, B Squadron, under Lieut. Paterson, took part in General Clements's march to Bloemfontein. Colonel Yardley tells us how General French boldly pushed into the Kalkheuval Pass late in the afternoon. During the fighting that ensued one of Colonel Yardley's troops, under Lieut. Paterson, "which was keeping communication between us and the 4th Brigade, found itself left alone and guarding the left flank, which the 4th Brigade had abandoned. Lucky, indeed, that it pluckily stuck to those heights, despite being fired on by our own men, otherwise the whole division might have experienced an awful disaster. The position appeared risky, but the enemy were pressed and retreated down the pass. We had now this one troop in occupation of the heights on our flank, with only a very rough road, and no spaces on each side to manœuvre, as they were all bush and rocks. The enemy in the bush on our flanks suddenly opened a heavy fire on the Carabinier troop in the road to the front; several (about seven) casualties at once occurred; two of the Carabinier troopers and several horses being shot dead in the road. Lieut. Rundle, with the advanced patrol of Carabiniers, had three horses shot under him, and Capt. Johnson one. General French and Staff, riding well ahead, had narrow escapes and had to retire. It was not reassuring to see our General and his Staff galloping back, but it was the best thing he could do, and, thank goodness, he ran the gauntlet of fire safely. The advanced guard, however, under Major Hamilton, behaved most gallantly, and, despite the sudden surprise and their heavy losses, held their ground. Major Allenby, who was next in advance with the Inniskillings, at once grasped the situation, and, although nearly overwhelmed by the horses galloping back on him from the front, he called loudly on the New South Wales Lancers and a Squadron of Inniskilling Dragoons, who at once dismounted, took up good positions on each side of the road, and poured in a heavy fire; this rallied all and prevented the panic which had appeared imminent. All credit for this must be given to Major Allenby, the New South Wales Lancers, under Major Lee, and the Inniskillings supporting the Carabiniers." Colonel Yardley goes on to speak of the literally "crowded" hour of glorious life spent by the division in the Pass. "Lieut. Paterson, who was in advance on the left front, inside the 4th Brigade, with a troop of Inniskillings, did good service by sticking to the heights when the 4th Brigade turned into the Pass, and was our only protection there. Gradually, however, a way was made, and the Mounted Infantry were got up from the rear to take up our positions." The release of the Waterval prisoners is later described, and the share in the fighting taken by Allenby and Paterson. Like the bridegroom at the fashionable wedding, Colonel Yardley just mentions that he himself "was there" on many of these occasions. He quotes a good description of the release of the Waterval prisoners, written by Barty Paterson, the Australian poet, who often appears in these pages. Colonel Yardley tells us how the Inniskillings, under Major Allenby, came upon the whole Boer army retreating with their guns on Middelburg. "Lieut. Paterson, with a small troop, opened fire on their main body at short range, causing the enemy to bring a Creusot gun into action and shell the ridge from which our small party were firing." It was sunset, and the Inniskillings' horses were done, and the Brigade had not pushed on rapidly to support them, so the Boer Army escaped in the dark. In the engagement at Roodehoogte, we read how "Lieut. Paterson, with his troop, galloped on to a big hill, and climbed the precipitous sides just in time to forestall the enemy and drive them back, giving us this commanding position. It was a fine piece of dash, and fairly surprised the Boers." In the fight at Tevreden, near Lake Chrissie, "Lieut. Paterson behaved with great dash, being slightly wounded as he galloped, unfortunately unarmed, alongside Commandant Smuts himself." After describing the gallantry of the Inniskillings, and the heroic death of Lieut. Swanston, Colonel Yardley says: "Lieut. Swanston and our other dead were buried at sunset at the foot of the Tevreden Hills, close by which I lay wounded, with Lieuts. Paterson and Harris. The sadness of it I shall never forget, with no feeling of victory to cheer the heart—only regret." And later: "Lieut. Paterson, shot through the thigh at Tevreden, pluckily returned to duty; but this inflamed his wound, and he was invalided home in consequence." It is rather the fashion to think that all wars before the Great War were mere picnics, and that decorations were handed out pretty freely to officers and men who had done nothing to deserve them. When people were given peerages in those days it was not necessary to recapitulate their good deeds, like Dorcas's (only *she* fell from her high estate), and to say how many music halls or cinemas they ran, or how many strikes they engineered. And after the South African War the London Gazette gave no details as to how decorations were won. It merely remarked that each officer's D.S.O. was "in recognition of services during the operations in South Africa." For this campaign Lieut. Paterson was mentioned in Despatches [London Gazette, 10 Sept. 1901]; received the Queen's Medal with five clasps, and was created a Companion of the Distinguished Service Order [London Gazette, 27 Sept. 1901]: "Ewing Paterson, Lieut., 6th Inniskilling Dragoons. In recognition of services during the operations in South Africa." The Insignia were presented by the King 29 Oct. 1901. He was Adjutant, Devon Yeomanry Brigade, 12 April, 1901, to 4 Aug. 1905; was promoted to Captain 10 July, 1901, and to Major 14 Oct. 1905. He served in the European War; commanded the Inniskilling Dragoons in France, 1915–18, and the 6th Cavalry Brigade 2 Sept. 1918, to the end of the War; became Lieutenant-Colonel 2 July, 1916, and was given the Brevet of Colonel 3 June, 1919. One has read of a charge of the Inniskilling Dragoons somewhere in France—near Cambrai, was it?—when the Doctor and his assistants and all the non-combatants, including the cooks, did not need to be pressed into the service. The casualties were very heavy. Colonel Paterson was Master, the Dundalk Harriers, 1896–97; North Devon Harriers, 1901; Barnstaple Staghounds, 1901–3. He married, in 1907, Jessy, widow of W. E. Rigden, and they have three daughters.

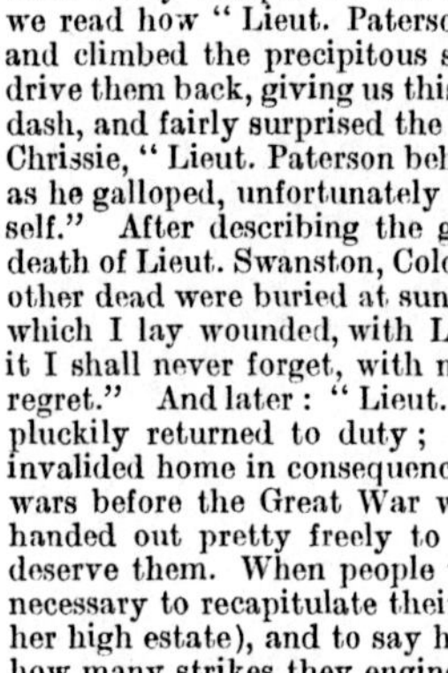

James Philip Moir.

MOIR, JAMES PHILIP, Lieut., was born 28 April, 1872, at Alloa, Scotland, son of James Moir, Banker, and Jane Williams Moir, *née* Mitchell. He was educated at Fettes College, Edinburgh, and joined the R.E. 12 Feb. 1892, becoming Lieutenant

12 Feb. 1895. He served in the Nile Expedition, 1898, taking part in the Battle of the Atbara, and received the Medal and the Egyptian Medal with clasp. He again saw active service in the South African War, 1899–1902, taking part in the advance on Kimberley, including actions of Belmont and Modder River; Relief of Kimberley; operations in the Orange Free State, Feb. to May, 1900, including operations at Paardeberg (17 to 26 Feb.); operations in the Transvaal in May and June, 1900, including actions near Johannesburg and Diamond Hill (11 and 12 June); operations in the Transvaal, east of Pretoria, July to 29 Nov. 1900, including action at Belfast (26 and 27 Aug.); operations in the Transvaal 30 Nov. 1900, to April, 1901; operations in Cape Colony, May to Aug. 1901; operations in Orange River Colony, Sept. 1901, to 31 May, 1902. He was mentioned in Despatches [London Gazette, 10 Sept. 1901]; received the Queen's Medal with seven clasps; the King's Medal with two clasps, and was created a Companion of the Distinguished Service Order [London Gazette, 27 Sept. 1901]: "James Philip Moir, Lieut., Royal Engineers. In recognition of services during the operations in South Africa." He was invested by the King 18 Dec. 1902. He was promoted to Captain 27 Oct. 1901; was employed in Southern Nigeria 21 Jan. 1905, to 31 Jan. 1908; became Major 12 Feb. 1912; was employed with the Egyptian Army 5 Sept. 1912. He served in the European War, 1914–17, and was given the Brevet of Lieutenant-Colonel 1 Jan. 1917. Lieut.-Colonel J. P. Moir was Director of Posts and Telegraphs, Egyptian Army, 1912–17. He has the Order of the Nile, 3rd Class. He married, 26 Oct. 1910, Ida Muriel, daughter of the Rev. H. A. Goodwin and Mrs. Goodwin, and they have two sons and one daughter.

VIGORS, RICHARD PERCY LITTLETON, Lieut., was born 25 Jan. 1873, second son of the late Rev. R. W. Vigors, M.A. He was educated at Marlborough, and entered the Army 20 May, 1893, becoming Lieutenant 29 May, 1895. He served in the South African War, 1899–1902, employed with Mounted Infantry; took part in the Relief of Kimberley; operations in the Orange Free State, Feb to May, 1900, including operations at Paardeberg (17 to 26 Feb.); actions at Poplar Grove and Dreifontein; operations in the Transvaal, May and June, 1900, including actions near Johannesburg Pretoria and Diamond Hill (11 and 12 June); operations in the Transvaal, east of Pretoria, July to 29 Nov. 1900, including action at Reit Vlei; operations in Cape Colony 30 Nov. 1900, to Feb. 1901; operations in Orange River Colony, Feb. 1901, to 31 May, 1902. He was mentioned in Despatches [London Gazette, 10 Sept. 1901]; received the Queen's Medal with five clasps, the King's Medal with two clasps, and was created a Companion of the Distinguished Service Order [London Gazette, 27 Sept. 1901]: "Richard Percy Littleton Vigors, Lieut., Connaught Rangers. In recognition of services during the operations in South Africa." The Insignia were presented by the King 13 Dec. 1902. Capt. Vigors resigned from the Army, 1906. He married, in 1911, Olive Muriel, youngest daughter of Col. H. J. O. Walker, late R.A., and they have two daughters.

Richard P. L. Vigors.

FARGUS, HAROLD, Lieut., was born 15 Oct. 1873, at Clifton, Bristol, son of the late Frederick John and Amy Fargus. He was educated at Clifton College, and was gazetted to the Duke of Cornwall's Light Infantry 25 March, 1893; became Lieutenant 1 July, 1895; was Adjutant, Duke of Cornwall's Light Infantry, 4 May, 1900, to 3 May, 1904, and was promoted to Captain 5 July, 1901. He served in the South African War, 1899–1902, serving as Adjutant, 2nd Duke of Cornwall's Light Infantry. He was present at the Relief of Kimberley; operations in the Orange Free State, Feb. to May, 1900, including operations at Paardeberg (17 to 26 Feb.); actions at Poplar Grove, Dreifontein, Houtnek (Thoba Mountain), Vet River (5 and 6 May) and Zand River; operations in Cape Colony, south of Orange River, 1899–1900, including actions at Colesberg (1 Jan. to 3 Feb.); operations in the Transvaal 30 Nov. 1900, to 31 May, 1902. He was mentioned in Lord Roberts's

Harold Fargus.

Despatches [London Gazette, 10 Sept. 1901]; received the Queen's South African Medal with four clasps; the King's South African Medal with two clasps, and was created a Companion of the Distinguished Service Order [London Gazette, 27 Sept. 1901]: "Harold Fargus, Lieut., The Duke of Cornwall's Light Infantry. In recognition of services during the operations in South Africa." The Insignia were presented to him by General Lyttelton, at Pretoria, 4 Jan. 1903. He was promoted to Major 1 March, 1912; was Brigade Major, Essex Infantry Brigade, Eastern Command, 11 March, 1912, to 4 Aug. 1914. He served in the European War; as Brigade Major, Essex Infantry Brigade, Central Force, Home Defence, and Brigade Major, 161st Infantry Brigade, Mediterranean Expeditionary Force, 5 Aug. 1914, to 24 April, 1916; became Lieutenant-Colonel 17 April, 1916; was G.S.O.2, 11th Division, Mediterranean Force, 25 April to 17 May, 1916; Brigade Commander, 125th Infantry Brigade, British Armies in France, 22 June, 1917. He was mentioned in Despatches; created a C.M.G. in 1916, and mentioned in Sir Douglas Haig's Despatch of New Year's Day, 1917, and

two other occasions; created a C.B. in 1919, and given the Brevet of Colonel 3 June, 1918. He married, 7 Oct. 1899, at Clifton, Bristol, Alice Gertrude Evans, daughter of J. L. Evans, Esq.

LE MOTTEE, EDWARD D'ALBRET, Lieut., was born 20 Oct. 1873, at Guernsey, Channel Islands, eldest son of Colonel John Edward Le Mottee, retired Army Officer, A.D.C. to King Edward VII. and King George V., and of Laura Lukin, daughter of Fred Lukin, of Guernsey. He was educated at Twyford School, Rugby, and the Royal Military College, Sandhurst, and joined the Army 21 Jan. 1893. He became Adjutant, 1898; was retained for a longer term in that appointment, during the South African War, 1899–1902, including the Relief of Kimberley, Paardeberg, Poplar Grove and Dreifontein; operations in Orange River Colony; operations in Transvaal (mentioned in Despatches twice; Queen's South African Medal and clasps); Relief of Kimberley, Paardeberg, Dreifontein and Transvaal (Queen's and King's Medals and six clasps, 1901–2), and was created a Companion of the Distinguished Service Order [London Gazette, 27 Sept. 1901]: "Edward D'Albret Le Mottee, Lieut., Gloucestershire Regt. In recognition of services during operations in South Africa." He became Captain 21 Jan. 1902; Major 8 Nov. 1914, and was appointed G.S.O.2, 9th Division, in the European War; was present at the Battle of Loos 27 Sept. 1915, since when he has been missing. He served in India and Aden after passing out of the Staff College in 1906, as D.A.A.G., Brigade Major and D.A.A. and Q.M.G.; joined the 1st Battn. Gloucestershire Regt. at home in 1912; commanded Company of Gentlemen Cadets (G.S.O., 2nd Grade), R.M.C., 1 Aug. 1914, to Jan. 1915; G.S.O., 2nd Grade, 9th Division, Jan. 1915; went to France 10 May, 1915; known to have very pluckily gone forward into trenches to rally the troops at Fosse 8, Battle of Loos, 27 Sept. 1915. The position was lost, and no more definite news has ever come through of him. He married, 20 Nov. 1912, at St. Mary's Church, Eastbourne, Charlotte Muriel Watts, second daughter of George Kempthorne Watts, and they had one daughter, Ethel Mary. The following are extracts from letters: "You will have heard by now that we are unable to trace the whereabouts of your husband. He very pluckily went forward on the morning of 27th Sept. to a place called Fosse 8, where there were very heavy casualties and fighting, and went into the trenches to rally the troops, and he did not return, and all inquiries failed to get any news of him. The position he went up to was retaken by the Germans, so there is a chance that he may have been slightly wounded and unable to get away, and that he is in their hands. I cannot say how sorry I am at this bad news. Your husband was a great friend of mine, and we are all very sad at his being unaccounted for. We can only hope he is in good hands and some news may come through of him soon.—With very sincere sympathy from us all." "I am most grieved at this distressing news. But you must not despair, in spite of all the anxiety you will feel, for until there is definite news hope cannot be gone. Any news I get, of course you shall have, but it is hard to get any. I am so very, very sorry for you, for your anxiety must be terrible, and my most heartfelt sympathy is with you. Your husband was such a help to me always, and I pray that better news may be forthcoming." "I was very sorry to hear the sad news. Your husband was a great friend of mine, and we worked together for all those months so happily. You know how much I grieve his loss, and how sincerely I sympathize with you." "I am sorry to say there is no more news, but I do not think we can expect any now unless it comes through from the German side. A message was received from your husband about 5.45, 27 Sept. 1915, saying he was coming back, and asking for a car to be sent to Vermelles (the limit for cars) to meet him. As the situation was an anxious one, General Thesiger went down to Vermelles in the car to meet your husband and hear the latest news from him of Fosse 8. After General Thesiger had started, affairs at Fosse 8 became very critical, and the General evidently went up there to try and re-establish the situation. Your husband must have gone with him, and has not been heard of since. I feel so much with you, and one cannot do anything to clear up the situation; but I don't despair, as I don't see any reason why he should not be in the hands of the Germans."

Edward D'A. Le Mottee.

STACPOOLE, GEORGE WILLIAM ROBERT, Lieut., was born at Eden Vale, Ennis, County Clare, Ireland, 27 May, 1872, son of Richard Stacpoole and of a daughter of John Massy Westropp, of Athyflin, County Limerick. He was educated at St. Columba's College, and Cheltenham College, and joined the Clare Artillery 1 April, 1890, and the South Staffordshire Regt. 19 Oct. 1892. He served in the South African War from Dec. 1899, to Aug. 1901, on the Staff; as Adjutant, Mounted Infantry, and Second-in-Command of Montmorency's Scouts. He served on the Staff (as Station and Railway Staff Officer, graded Staff Lieutenant) 10 Dec. 1899, to 4 March, 1900; as Station Staff Officer at De Aar 18 Nov. 1900, to Feb. 1901 (slightly wounded; horse shot). He was mentioned in Despatches [London Gazette, 10 Sept. 1901]; received the Queen's Medal with four clasps, and was created a Companion of the Distinguished Service Order [London Gazette, 27 Sept. 1901]: "George William Robert Stacpoole, Lieut., South Staffordshire Regt. In recognition of services during the operations in South Africa." The Insignia were presented by the King 29 Oct. 1901. He became Captain, Jan. 1901, and retired in Dec. 1907. In the European War he served as Assistant Provost-Marshal, No. 1 Base, on Mobilization; Assistant Provost-Marshal, 2nd Division, Feb. to Dec. 1915; Assistant Provost-Marshal, 5th Corps, to Oct. 1918; Deputy Provost-Marshal, Lines of Communication Area, to Demobilization, 20 April, 1919. Lieut.-Colonel Stacpoole has been four times mentioned in Despatches in the European War, and created a Chevalier de l'Ordre de Léopold by the King of Belgium, for services in the Ypres Salient; also received the Belgian Croix de Guerre; created O.B.E., New Year's Honours List, 1919. The Insignia were presented by the King 10 July, 1919.

HILL, CHARLES GLENCAIRN, Lieut., was born 22 Sept. 1872, son of the late Capt. Charles West Hill and his wife, Ellinor Jane Hill. He was educated at Haileybury and Sandhurst, and joined the 1st Royal Berkshire Regt. in Bermuda in 1893, being gazetted to that regiment on 20 May, 1893. He served in the South African War with the 1st Battn. Royal Scots Mounted Infantry; was slightly wounded; took part in operations in Orange Free State, including Defence of Wepener; operations in the Transvaal; operations in Orange River Colony, May to 29 Nov. 1900, including actions at Bethlehem (6 and 7 July) and Wittebergen (1 to 29 July); operations in Cape Colony, south of Orange River, 1899–1900; operations in the Transvaal 30 Nov. 1900, to Feb. 1901. He was mentioned in Despatches [London Gazette, 10 Sept. 1901]; received the Queen's Medal with five clasps, and was created a Companion of the Distinguished Service Order [London Gazette, 27 Sept. 1901]: "Charles Glencairn Hill, Lieut., Royal Berkshire Regt. In recognition of services during the operations in South Africa." The Insignia were presented by the King 17 Dec. 1901. He was killed in action 26 June, 1915, at Cuinchy, whilst commanding 1st Battn. Royal Berkshire Regt. He was mentioned in Despatches by Sir John French 31 May, 1915, for gallant and distinguished service in the field, and awarded the C.M.G. 3 June, 1915.

Charles Glencairn Hill.

BALFOUR, CHRISTOPHER EGERTON, Lieut., was born 14 Aug. 1872, son of Archibald Balfour, Esq., of 65, Pont Street, London, S.W. He was educated at Westminster, and at the Royal Military College, Sandhurst, and entered the King's Royal Rifle Corps 24 May, 1893, becoming Lieutenant 1 Jan. 1896. He went to India with his regiment, and they had just arrived in Calcutta when orders came for them to leave at once for South Africa. They stayed only long enough to change into another ship, and during part of the South African War of 1899 to 1902, Lieut. Balfour was Aide-de-Camp to Sir Neville Lyttelton. He was in Ladysmith during the Siege, and the starvation and hardships he then endured completely wrecked his constitution so that he never recovered, and he died 29 Aug. 1907. His D.S.O. was awarded [L.G. 27 Sept. 1901]: "Christopher Egerton Balfour, Lieut., K.R.R.C. For services in S. Africa." He married, in 1902, Dorothy Cecilia, eldest daughter of Gerald Paget, and they had two daughters, one of whom was born after her father's death.

Christopher E. Balfour.

HARE, ROBERT WILLIAM, Lieut., was born 14 Nov. 1872, only son of R. D. Hare, of Ballymore, Queenstown. He was educated at Harrow, and entered the Norfolk Regt. 19 Nov. 1892, becoming Lieutenant 7 March, 1896, and serving in South Africa, 1896, with Mounted Infantry (Mashonaland Medal). He served in the South African War, 1899–1902, as Special Service Officer (including service with Rhodesia Regt.) 15 July, 1899, to 22 July, 1900, and afterwards on the Staff (Staff Officer to Brigadier-General 3 July to 28 Aug. 1900, and D.A.A.G. 29 Aug. 1900, to 7 Aug. 1902). He was mentioned in Despatches [L. G., 10 Sept. 1901, and 29 July, 1902]; received the Queen's Medal with five clasps, the King's Medal with two clasps; was placed on the list of Officers considered qualified for Staff employment, in consequence of service in the field, and created a Companion of the Distinguished Service Order [London Gazette, 27 Sept. 1901]: "Robert

Robert William Hare.

William Hare, Lieut., Norfolk Regt. In recognition of services during the operations in South Africa." He became Captain 16 Feb. 1901, and was A.D.C. to the Lieut.-Governor, Orange River Colony, 15 Nov. 1902, to 22 Jan. 1905; Staff Captain, H.Q. of Army, 16 Jan. 1906, to 27 Sept. 1908; Brigade Major, 17th Brigade, Irish Command, 28 Sept. 1908, to 27 June, 1911. He was promoted to Major 13 March, 1912, and was G.S.O.2, War Office, 8 Oct. 1913, to 4 Aug. 1914. He served in the European War, 1914–18; as G.S.O.2, G.H.Q., B.E.F., 5 Aug. 1914, to 6 June, 1915; as G.S.O.1, 26th Division, New Armies, B.E.F.; Mediterranean Expeditionary Force 15 June, 1915, to 24 Jan. 1916. He was G.S.O.1, Staff School, Cambridge, 27 March, 1916, to 26 May, 1917; was promoted to Lieutenant-Colonel 12 Jan. 1917; Brigadier-General, General Staff, Northern Command, 15 Feb. 1919. He was twice mentioned in Despatches; was given the Brevet of Colonel 24 Jan. 1917,

and created a C.M.G. in 1919. In 1908 he married Helen Mary, only daughter of the late Lieut.-Colonel G. N. Atkinson, and they have one son and two daughters.

WOODWARD, FRANCIS WILLOUGHBY, Lieut., was born 5 Dec. 1872, son of Willoughby Woodward. He was educated at Shrewsbury School, and at the R.M.C., Sandhurst; was gazetted to the Loyal North Lancashire Regt. 21 Oct. 1893, and became Lieutenant 14 March, 1896. He served in the South African War, 1899 to 1902 (as Signalling Officer during the defence of Kimberley), and took part in the operations in the Orange Free State, April to May, 1900; operations in the Transvaal, west of Pretoria, July to 29 Nov. 1900; operations in the Orange River Colony, May to July, 1900, including actions at Lindley (1 June) and Rhenoster River; operations in Cape Colony, north and south of Orange River, 1899 to 1900. He served as Adjutant, 1st Battn. North Lancashire Regt., 5 June, 1901, to 31 May, 1902 (and after the South African War to 4 June, 1904), and was promoted to Captain 24 Dec. 1901. Capt. Woodward was present at operations in the Transvaal 30 Nov. 1900, to June, 1901; operations in Cape Colony, July, 1901, to May, 1902. He was mentioned in Despatches [London Gazette, 8 May, 1900, and 10 Sept. 1901]; received the Queen's Medal with three clasps, the King's Medal with two clasps, and was created a Companion of the Distinguished Service Order [London Gazette, 27 Sept. 1901]: "Frederick Willoughby Woodward, Lieut., Loyal North Lancashire Regt. In recognition of services during the operations in South Africa." He was invested by the King 24 Oct. 1902. From 23 March, 1906, to 22 March, 1916, he was employed with the Egyptian Army (3rd Class Medjidie and 3rd Class Order of the Nile). He was promoted to Major 12 Sept. 1914; was acting Lieut.-Colonel, commanding a service battalion Manchester Regt., 19 Feb. to 20 March, 1917, and 6 May, to 25 May, 1917; Temp. Lieut.-Colonel, commanding service battalion Manchester Regt., 26 May to 20 Dec. 1917; Temporary Colonel 21 Dec. 1917; promoted to Lieut.-Colonel 13 Sept. 1918. He was given the Brevet of Lieut.-Colonel 3 June, 1918. Lieut.-Colonel F. W. Woodward commands the 1st Loyal North Lancashire Regt. He has the Croix de Guerre and the Croce di Guerra.

BELLAMY, ROBERT, Lieut., was born 29 Nov. 1871, son of the late Colonel P. L. Bellamy, Border Regt. He was commissioned in the Royal Sussex Regt. 2 June, 1894, and became Lieutenant 8 April, 1896. He served in the South African War, 1900–2, as Adjutant, Royal Sussex Regt., 5 Oct. 1900 (and after the war to 4 Oct. 1904), and was present at operations in the Orange Free State, Feb. to May, 1900, including actions at Houtnek (Thoba Mountain), Vet River (5 and 6 May) and Zand River; operations in the Transvaal in May and June, 1900, including actions near Johannesburg, Pretoria and Diamond Hill (11 and 12 June); operations in Orange River Colony, May to 29 Nov. 1900, including actions at Wittebergen (1 to 29 July) and Ladybrand (2 to 5 Sept.). He was mentioned in Despatches [London Gazette, 10 Sept. 1901]; received the Queen's Medal with four clasps, the King's Medal with two clasps, and was created a Companion of the Distinguished Service Order [London Gazette, 27 Sept. 1901]: "Robert Bellamy, Lieut., Royal Sussex Regt. In recognition of services during the operations in South Africa." The Insignia, Warrant and Statutes were sent to the Commander-in-Chief in India, and the Insignia were presented by Major-General W. Meiklejohn at Ranikhet, India, 9 May, 1903. He became Captain 17 Sept. 1902; was Adjutant, Militia, and Adjutant, Special Reserve, 25 Oct. 1906, to 30 Sept. 1911; Brigade Major, South Lancashire Infantry Brigade, Western Command, 3 Oct. 1911, to 4 Aug. 1914; was promoted to Major 1 Nov. 1914; was Brigade Major, 1/1st South Lancashire Infantry Brigade, Central Force, Home Defence; Brigade Major, 172nd Infantry Brigade, Home Forces, 5 Aug. 1914, to 20 June, 1916; Temp. Lieut.-Colonel, commanding 13th Battn. Royal Sussex Regt., 31 July, to 5 Aug. 1916; Temp. Lieut.-Colonel, Royal Sussex Regt., 6 Aug. 1916, to 27 Aug. 1918, and 28 Aug. 1918. He married, in 1903, Constance Gwendoline, eldest daughter of the late Colonel Alfred Borton, Welsh Regt.

SKEFFINGTON SMYTH, GEOFFREY HENRY JULIAN, Lieut., was born at 42, Portman Square, London, W., 11 Dec. 1873, youngest son of the late E. Randal Skeffington Smyth, of Mount Henry, Portarlington, Ireland, Vice-Lieutenant for the Queen's County, late Lieutenant and Adjutant of the 28th Regt., in which he served and was wounded in the Crimean War. He was educated at the Rev. E. D. Stone's Preparatory School, at Stonehouse, Broadstairs, and at Eton College, and entered the 9th Lancers 29 May, 1895, becoming Lieutenant 4 July, 1896. He served in the South African War, 1899–1901, and was severely wounded. He took part in the advance on Kimberley, including the actions at Belmont, Enslin, Modder River and Magersfontein, and the Relief of Kimberley; operations in the Orange Free State, Feb. to May, 1900, including action at Karee Siding; operations in the Transvaal in May and June, 1900, including actions near Johannesburg, Pretoria and Diamond Hill; operations in the Transvaal, west of Pretoria, July to Nov. 1900; operations in Orange River Colony, May to Nov. 1900, including actions at Bethlehem and Wittebergen. It is believed that Lieut. Skeffington Smyth was recommended for the D.S.O. for acts of bravery in the field at the engagement at Quaggasfontein (Western Transvaal), when his troop of the 9th Lancers, together with a party of Kaffrarian Rifles, were heavily engaged, suffered severe losses, and were finally, at the end of the day, surrounded by the enemy, having run out of ammunition. No unwounded man was captured, however. Lieut. Skeffington Smyth received four wounds during the day, his leg being broken by the second one. He went back for and returned with ammunition under heavy fire (they were lying in the open within 600 yards of the enemy's position for some six hours or more), and he succoured the wounded under heavy fire. He says he doesn't know what he was mentioned in Despatches for, "unless it was for doing my duty as a 9th Lancer should." He was mentioned in Despatches [London Gazette, 10 Sept. 1901]; received the Queen's Medal with six clasps, and was created a Companion of the Distinguished Service Order [London Gazette, 27 Sept. 1901]: "Geoffrey Henry Julian Skeffington Smyth, Lieut., 9th Lancers. In recognition of services during the operations in South Africa." The Insignia were presented to him by the King 29 Oct. 1901. He was promoted to Captain 3 June, 1901, and retired 12 Dec. 1906. He became General Staff Officer, 1st Grade, and for his services during the European War was given the Brevet of Lieut.-Colonel 3 June, 1919. He was made Chevalier of the Legion of Honour by the French. "For the first 22 months of the present war," he says, "I was employed as G.S.O.3 and G.S.O.2 in the Military Operations (later Military Intelligence) Branch at the War Office. From June to Dec. I was on sick leave, and on 1 Feb. 1917, went to the Intelligence Staff, G.H.Q., British Armies in France. My pursuits before I received the wound, which broke my leg and prevented my riding to any extent, were those of hunting, shooting, polo and cricket, at none of which did I excel. I was a fair swordsman, and won second prize in the 'Sword v. Lance' competition at the Royal Military Tournament in 1896, a year after I joined the 9th Lancers. I owned my first motor-car in 1898." He married, in 1904, the Honourable Violet Frances Monckton, daughter of the 7th Viscount Galway, and Vere, Lady of Justice of the Order of St. John of Jerusalem, only daughter of Ellis Gosling, of Busbridge Hall, Godalming, Surrey, and they have three sons.

ORR, JOHN BOYD, Lieutenant, was born 16 Aug. 1871, only surviving son of the late Colonel Spencer Edward Orr, of Dullatur, Camberley, and of Mrs. Orr, now of Bellfield, Camberley. He entered the Norfolk Regt. 18 Oct. 1893, and became Lieutenant 29 Aug. 1896. He was awarded the Royal Humane Society's Medal in 1894, for saving from drowning a woman who had attempted suicide by throwing herself into the river at Bishop's Bridge, Norwich. Lieut. Orr served in the South African War; was A.D.C. to the Brigadier Commanding the Mounted Infantry Brigade, South Africa, from Nov. 1900, to Oct. 1901, and saw a great deal of service. He took part in the Relief of Kimberley, and among the actions in which he fought were those at Paardeberg, Poplar Grove, Dreifontein, Vet River, Zand River, Johannesburg, Pretoria and Diamond Hill. He was mentioned in Despatches [London Gazette, 10 Sept. 1901]: received the

John Boyd Orr.

Queen's Medal with five clasps, the King's Medal with two clasps, and was created a Companion of the Distinguished Service Order [London Gazette, 27 Sept. 1901]: "John Boyd Orr, Lieut., Norfolk Regt. In recognition of services during the operations in South Africa." He became Captain 25 Oct. 1901, and for two years from 1906 he was employed with the Transvaal Volunteers, and from May, 1910, to Dec. 1918, he was with the West African Frontier Force. He became Major in 1913. An obituary notice says: "A distinguished soldier is lost to the country in Major John Boyd Orr, D.S.O., 1st Battn. Norfolk Regt., who died on 24 Aug. 1914, from wounds received in action at the Battles of Mons."

GREENLY, WALTER HOWORTH, Lieut., was born 2 Jan. 1875, eldest son of Edward Howorth Greenly, of Titley Court, Titley, County Hereford, J.P. and D.L. He was educated at Eton and Sandhurst, and was gazetted to the 12th Lancers 20 Feb. 1895; became Lieutenant 1 Oct. 1896, and was Adjutant, 12th Lancers, 1 May, 1899, to 22 Aug. 1902. He served in the South African War, 1899 to 1902, as Adjutant, 12th Lancers, 1899, to June, 1901; Staff Officer to Officer Commanding Group of Columns, June, 1901, to 31 May, 1902. He took part in the advance on Kimberley, including action at Magersfontein; Relief of Kimberley; operations in the Orange Free State, Feb. to May, 1900, including operations at Paardeberg (17 to 26 Feb.); actions at Poplar Grove, Dreifontein, Karee Siding, Houtnek (Thoba Mountain), Vet River (5 and 6 May) and Zand River; operations in the Transvaal in May and June, 1900, including actions near Johannesburg, Pretoria and

Walter Howorth Greenly.

Diamond Hill (11 and 12 June); operations in the Transvaal, west of Pretoria, 1900, including action at Elands River; operations in Orange River Colony, July to 29 Nov. 1900, including actions at Lindley, Bethlehem and Wittebergen; operations in the Transvaal 30 Nov. 1900, to June, 1901; operations in Cape Colony, June, 1901, to 31 May, 1902. He was mentioned in Despatches [London Gazette, 10 Sept. 1901] and 29 July, 1902; was given the Brevet of Major 22 Aug. 1902; received the Queen's Medal with six clasps, the King's Medal with two clasps, and was created a Companion of the Distinguished Service Order [London Gazette, 27 Sept. 1901]: "Walter Howorth Greenly, Lieut., 12th Lancers. In recognition of services during the operations in South Africa." He was invested by the King 24 Oct. 1902. On 19 Jan. 1901, he was promoted to Captain; he was Staff Captain, H.Q. of Army, 15 Jan. to 24 Oct. 1906; Brigade Major, 1st Cavalry Brigade, Aldershot Army Corps, 25 Oct. 1906, to 31 March, 1909; became Major 25 March, 1908; was G.S.O.2, Staff College, 19 April, 1910, to 2 Jan. 1912; Lieut.-Colonel, 19th Hussars, 6 Jan. 1912. He served in the

European War, 1914–18; was G.S.O.1, 2nd Cavalry Division, B.E.F., 19 Sept. 1914, to 13 April, 1915; commanded the 9th Cavalry Brigade, B.E.F., 14 April, to 14 Nov. 1915; became Colonel 6 Jan. 1916; was Brigadier-General, General Staff; Brigadier-General, 13th Army Corps, B.E.F., and British Armies in France, 15 Nov. 1915, to 15 Nov. 1916; commanded 2nd Cavalry Division, British Armies in France, 16 Nov. 1916, to 5 April, 1918. He was given the Brevet of Colonel 3 June, 1915; was promoted to Major-General 1 Jan. 1917; became Colonel, 12th Lancers, 22 June, 1917; was created a C.M.G. in 1915, and a C.B. in 1919. Major-General Greenly is a J.P. for Herefordshire.

SPEDDING, CHARLES RODNEY, Lieut., was born 25 April, 1871, son of Benjamin H. Spedding, M.D., of Bangor, County Down. He was commissioned in the Royal Irish Rifles 23 Dec. 1893, becoming Lieutenant 6 Oct. 1896. He served in the South African War, 1899–1902, as Station Staff Officer; as Adjutant, 9th Battn. Mounted Infantry, 28 Dec. 1900, to 25 April, 1901; as Staff Officer to General Bruce Hamilton's Column of Mounted Infantry, 1901–2. He was present at operations in Orange Free State, March to May, 1900; operations in Orange River Colony, May to Nov. 1900; operations in Cape Colony, south of Orange River, 1899–1900; operations in the Transvaal, April, 1901, to 31 May, 1902; operations in Orange River Colony, 30 Nov. 1900, to April, 1901. He was mentioned in Despatches [London Gazette, 10 Sept. 1901, and 29 July, 1902]; received the Queen's Medal with three clasps, the King's Medal with two clasps, and was created a Companion of the Distinguished Service Order [London Gazette, 27 Sept. 1901]: "Charles Rodney Spedding, Lieut., Royal Irish Rifles. In recognition of services during the operations in South Africa." He was invested by the King 24 Oct. 1902. He was promoted to Captain 1 March, 1902; was A.D.C. to Major-General, Infantry Brigade, Malta, 16 June, 1906; commanded the 5th Regt. Mounted Infantry, Harrismith, South Africa, 1912. Major Spedding married, in 1907, Constance Mildred Edith, daughter of Lieut.-Colonel T. G. Cutbell, late 13th Hussars, and they had two daughters.

TRINGHAM, ARCHIBALD MONTGOMERY, Lieut., was born 16 Sept. 1869, son of the Rev. W. and Mrs. Tringham. He was educated at Charterhouse, and entered the Royal West Surrey Regt. 15 March, 1893, becoming Lieutenant 11 Nov. 1896. He took part in operations on the North-West Frontier of India, 1897–98, with the Malakand Field, Mohmand Field and Tirah Expeditionary Forces, and received the Medal with two clasps. He served in the South African War, 1899–1901, and was severely wounded. He was present in operations in Natal, 1899, including actions at Elandslaagte, Rietfontein and Lombard's Kop; Defence of Ladysmith, including sortie of 7 Dec. 1899; operations in Natal, March to June, 1900; operations in the Transvaal, east of Pretoria, July to 29 Nov. 1900, including actions at Belfast (26 and 27 Aug.) and Lydenberg (5 to 8 Sept.); operations in the Transvaal 30 Nov. 1900, to April, 1901. He was mentioned in Despatches [London

Archibald M. Tringham.

Gazette, 8 Feb. and 10 Sept. 1901]; received the Queen's Medal with four clasps, and was created a Companion of the Distinguished Service Order [London Gazette, 27 Sept. 1901]: "Archibald Montgomery Tringham, Lieut., Royal West Surrey Regt. In recognition of services during the operations in South Africa." The Insignia were presented to him by the King 29 Oct. 1901. He became Captain 22 Jan. 1902; was Brigade Major to the Inspector-General of Volunteers, India, 3 Sept. 1903, to 2 Feb. 1904; Adjutant, Special Reserve, 4 Dec. 1911, to 31 July, 1915. He served in the European War, 1914–18; was promoted to Major 19 May, 1915; was Temp. Lieut.-Colonel, commanding Service Battn. Royal West Surrey Regt. 31 Oct. 1915, to 1 Sept. 1918, and from 2 Sept. 1918. He was mentioned in Despatches, and given the Brevet of Lieut.-Colonel 3 June, 1917. Lieut.-Colonel A. M. Tringham married, in 1906, Mary, third daughter of B. W. Leader, R.A.

MARJORIBANKS, THE HON. DUDLEY CHURCHILL (LORD TWEEDMOUTH), Lieut., was born 2 March, 1874, only son of the 2nd Baron Tweedmouth and Lady F. O. L. Spencer Churchill, daughter of the 7th Duke of Marlborough. He was educated at Harrow; joined the Royal Horse Guards 3 July, 1895, and became Lieutenant 13 Jan. 1897, and served with a composite regiment of Household Cavalry in South Africa, 1899–1902; was present at the Relief of Kimberley; operations in the Orange Free State, Feb. to May, 1900, including operations at Paardeberg (17 to 26 Feb.); actions at Poplar Grove, Dreifontein, Houtnek (Thoba Mountain), Vet River (5 and 6 May) and Zand River; operations in the Transvaal in May and June, 1900, including actions near Johannesburg, Pretoria and Diamond Hill (11 and 12 June); operations in the Transvaal, west of Pretoria, in 1900, including actions at Elands River (4 to 16 Aug.); operations in Orange River Colony, May to Nov. 1900, including actions at Bethlehem (6 and 7 July) and Wittebergen (1 to 29 July); operations in Cape Colony, south of Orange River, 1899–1900, including actions at Colesberg (1 Jan. to 12 Feb.) He was mentioned in Despatches [London Gazette, 10 Sept. 1901]; received the Queen's Medal with six clasps, and was created a Companion of the Distinguished Service Order [London Gazette, 27 Sept. 1901]: "The Honourable Dudley Churchill Marjoribanks, Lieut., Royal Horse Guards. In recognition of services during the operations in South Africa." The Insignia were presented to him by the King. He was promoted to Captain 25 March, 1904; was Military Secretary to the High Commissioner in South Africa 29 April,

1905, to 31 March, 1908; was given the Brevet of Major 12 Aug. 1908; was D.A.A. and Q.M.G., West Lancashire Division, Western Command, 9 April, 1908, to 31 March, 1910. On the death of his father in 1909, he became the 3rd Baron Tweedmouth. Lord Tweedmouth served in the European War in 1914 and 1915; was Temp. Lieut.-Colonel, Royal Horse Guards, 7 Dec. 1914, to 6 Nov. 1918; served with the Guards' Machine Gun Regt. 10 May, 1918, to 4 March, 1919; was Temp. Lieut.-Colonel 10 May to 6 Nov. 1918; was Lieut.-Colonel, Household Cavalry, from 7 Nov. 1918. He was given the Brevet of Lieut.-Colonel 31 Jan. 1915, and created a C.M.G., 1915. He was Lord-in-Waiting to H.M. the King. Lord Tweedmouth married, in 1901, Muriel, eldest daughter of the 9th Viscount Midleton, and of Lady Hilda Charteris (who died in 1901), daughter of the 9th Earl of Wemyss, and they have two daughters.

RENNIE, GEORGE ARTHUR PAGET, Lieut., was born 6 Sept. 1872, in London, son of the late George Banks Rennie, of Denford, Hungerford. He was educated at Marlborough College, and joined the King's Royal Rifle Corps 18 Oct. 1893, becoming Lieutenant 30 Jan. 1897. He served in the South African War, 1899 to 1902, and was present at the Relief of Ladysmith, including the action at Colenso; operations of 17 to 24 Jan. 1900, and action at Spion Kop; operations of 5 to 7 Feb. 1900, and action at Vaal Kranz; operations on Tugela Heights (14 to 27 Feb. 1900), and action at Pieter's Hill; operations in Natal, March to June, 1900, including action at Laing's Nek (6 to 9 June); operations in the Transvaal 30 Nov. 1900, to 31 May, 1902; operations in Orange River Colony, May, June and Aug. to Sept. 1901. He was mentioned in Despatches [London Gazette, 8 Feb. and 10 Sept. 1901]; received the Queen's Medal with two clasps, and was created a Companion of the Distinguished Service Order [London Gazette, 27 Sept. 1901]: "George Arthur Paget Rennie, Lieut., King's Royal Rifle Corps. In recognition of services during the operations in South Africa." He was invested by the King 18 Dec. 1902. On 25 Feb. 1901, he was promoted to Captain; from 25 April, 1905, to 24 April, 1908, he was Adjutant, Militia, and he became Major 12 Aug. 1911. Major Rennie served in the European War, 1914 to 1918, as Temporary Lieutenant-Colonel, Commanding Special Reserve Battn. King's Royal Rifle Corps, 19 Aug. 1914, to 8 May, 1917, and as Temporary Brigadier-General 18 Oct. 1917, to 26 April, 1919; commanding the 146th Infantry Brigade, British Armies in France. He was given the Brevet of Lieutenant-Colonel, Honours List, 17 Feb. 1917, to date 1 Jan. 1917, and created a C.M.G. in 1918; was mentioned in Despatches in the New Year's Honours List, 1916; Birthday Honours List, 1916; New Year's Honours List 1917, and on two other occasions. He married, 4 March, 1894, in London, Florence Mary, daughter of the late Philip Wroughton, and they have three daughters: Winifred Ursula, Evelyn Julia and Angela Mary.

George Arthur P. Rennie.

ARCHER-SHEE, MARTIN, Lieut., was born 5 May, 1873, son of the late Martin Archer-Shee and Elizabeth Edith (*née* Dennistoun-Pell), of New York. He was educated at the Oratory School, H.M.S. Britannia, and at Sandhurst; served in the Royal Navy as Midshipman, 1888–90; entered the Army, 19th Hussars, 5 March, 1893; was Adjutant, 19th Hussars, 1 Jan. 1898, to 1901. He served in South Africa, 1899–1902, as Adjutant, 19th Hussars, to 31 Dec. 1901. He took part in operations in Natal in 1899, including actions at Rietfontein and Lombard's Kop; Defence of Ladysmith, including sortie of 7 Dec. 1899, and action of 6 Jan. 1900; operations in Natal (March to June, 1900), including action at Laing's Nek; operations in the Transvaal, east of Pretoria, July to 29 Nov. 1900, including actions at Belfast and Lydenburg; operations in Orange River Colony, May to 29 Nov. 1900; operations in the Transvaal 30 Nov. 1900, to 31 May, 1902; operations in Orange River Colony, May, 1902. He was severely wounded; was mentioned in Despatches [London Gazette, 8 Feb. and 10 Sept. 1901, and 25 April, 1902]; was given the Brevet of Major; received the Queen's Medal with four clasps, the King's Medal with two clasps, and was created a Companion of the Distinguished Service Order [London Gazette, 27 Sept. 1901]: "Martin Archer-Shee, Lieut., 19th Hussars. In recognition of services during the operations in South Africa." He was Assistant Adjutant, Cavalry School, 1904, and resigned, 1905. He became Major, Reserve of Officers, 19th Hussars He served in the European War; was Lieut.-Colonel, 12th Gloucesters, 1915–17; was wounded at Ypres 9 May, 1915; was mentioned in Despatches of 30 April, 1916 [London Gazette, 15 June, 1916], and 13 Nov. 1916 [London Gazette, 3 Jan. 1917]; appointed to command 2/4th York and Lancaster Regt. (B.E.F.), May, 1917, and invalided home, Nov. 1917. He later commanded the 10th Battn. King's Own Scottish Borderers (B.E.F.). Colonel Archer-Shee has been Unionist Member of Parliament for Central Finsbury since 1910. He married, in 1905, Frances, only daughter of the late Alfred Pell, of New York, and they have four sons and two daughters.

PEEBLES, ARTHUR STANSFIELD, Lieut., was born 16 Nov. 1872, second surviving son of the late Colonel Thomas Peebles, 11th Foot, of Haddo, Cheltenham. He was educated at Cheltenham College, and entered the Suffolk Regt. 12 Dec. 1894, becoming Lieutenant 17 Feb. 1897, and Capt. 4 Oct. 1901. He served in the South African War, 1899–1901, employed with Mounted Infantry, and took part in operations in the Orange Free State, April and June, 1900, including actions near Johannesburg and Pretoria; operations in the Transvaal, west of Pretoria, July to 29 Nov. 1900, including actions at Venterskroon (7 and 9 Aug.); operations in Orange River Colony, May to 29 Nov. 1900, including actions at Ladybrand (2 to 5 Sept.) and Bothaville (severely wounded); operations in Cape Colony, south of Orange River, 1899–1900, including actions at Colesberg (1 to 6 Jan.); operations in Orange River Colony 30 Nov. 1900, to Feb. 1901. He was mentioned in Despatches [London Gazette, 10 Sept. 1901]; received the Queen's Medal with four clasps, and was created a Companion of the Distinguished Service Order [London Gazette, 27 Sept. 1901]: "Arthur Stansfield Peebles, Lieut., Suffolk Regt. In recognition of services during the operations in South Africa." The Insignia were presented to him by the King 12 May, 1902. He was promoted to Captain 1 Oct. 1901; was Recruiting Staff Officer, London, 2 Feb. 1905, to 20 Feb. 1909; was promoted to Major 7 Jan. 1912. He served in the European War, 1914–17, and became Lieut.-Colonel 12 Sept. 1916. Lieut.-Colonel A. S. Peebles married, in 1905, Iris Mary Evelyn Woolley, and they have one son.

WHITE FREDERICK ALEXANDER, Lieut., was born 6 Aug. 1872. He entered the Suffolk Regt. 12 Dec. 1894, becoming Lieutenant 24 Feb. 1897. He served in the South African War, 1899–1902, on the Staff, taking part in operations in the Orange Free State, April and May, 1900; operations in the Transvaal in May and June, 1900, including action at Pretoria; operations in the Transvaal, west of Pretoria, July to 29 Nov. 1900, including actions at Venterskroon (7 and 9 Aug.); operations in Orange River Colony, May to 29 Nov. 1900, including actions at Ladybrand (5 Sept.) and Bothaville; operations in Cape Colony, south of Orange River, 1899–1900; operations in the Transvaal, Feb. 1901, to 31 May, 1902; operations in Cape Colony, Aug. to Sept. 1901, and May, 1902; operations in Orange River Colony 30 Nov. 1900, to Feb. 1901. He was mentioned in Despatches [London Gazette, 10 Sept. 1901]; received the Queen's Medal with three clasps; the King's Medal with two clasps, and was created a Companion of the Distinguished Service Order [London Gazette, 27 Sept. 1901]: "Frederick Alexander White, Lieut., Suffolk Regt. In recognition of services during the operations in South Africa." He was invested by the King 18 Dec. 1902. He was promoted to Captain 14 Oct. 1901; was Staff Captain, Mounted Infantry, 24 Jan. 1901, to 25 June, 1902; Adjutant, Volunteers, 30 June, 1907, to 31 March, 1908; Adjutant, Territorial Force, 1 April, 1908, to 28 June, 1912. He was Adjutant, Suffolk Regt., 1 Nov. 1903, to 31 Oct. 1906; became Major 11 Jan. 1914. Major White served in the European War from 1914, as Temporary Lieutenant-Colonel, Suffolk Regt., 29 June to 3 Oct. 1915. He died in 1918.

Frederick A. White.

CONRY, JAMES LIONEL JOYCE, Lieut., was born 16 Nov. 1873, son of Thomas Conry, Staff Surgeon, Royal Navy. He entered the Connaught Rangers 21 Oct. 1893; became Lieutenant 1 March, 1897. He served in the South African War, 1899–1902, taking part in the Relief of Ladysmith, including the action at Colenso; operations of 17 to 24 Jan. 1900, and action at Spion Kop; operations of 5 to 7 Feb. 1900, and action at Vaal Kranz; operations on Tugela Heights (14 to 27 Feb. 1900; slightly wounded), and action at Pieter's Hill; operations in the Orange Free State, May, 1900; operations in the Transvaal in May and June, 1900; operations in Natal, March and April, 1900; operations in the Transvaal, east of Pretoria, July to 29 Nov. 1900, including action at Reit Vlei; operations in Cape Colony, south of Orange River, April, 1900; operations in Cape Colony, north of Orange River, April and May, 1900; again in the Transvaal 30 Nov. to Dec. 1900; operations in Orange River Colony, Dec. 1900, to Oct. 1901, and Feb. to March, 1902; operations in Cape Colony, Dec. 1900, to Feb. 1901 and June, 1901, to 31 May, 1902. He was mentioned in Despatches [London Gazette, 8 Feb. and 10 Sept. 1901, and 29 July, 1902]; again slightly wounded (14 July, 1901). He received the Queen's Medal with five clasps; the King's Medal with two clasps, and was created a Companion of the Distinguished Service Order [London Gazette, 27 Sept. 1901]: "James Lionel Joyce Conry, Lieut., Connaught Rangers. In recognition of services during the operations in South Africa." He was invested by the King 21 Oct. 1902. He was promoted to Captain 21 May, 1901; was Adjutant, 1st Battn. Connaught Rangers, 18 Feb. 1903, to 17 Feb. 1906; was employed with the Egyptian Army 5 April, 1906; served in the Sudan in 1908 (Egyptian War Medal and clasp). He was promoted to Major. Major Conry died 3 March, 1914.

HILL, FRANK WILLIAM ROWLAND, Lieut., was born 19 Feb. 1875. He joined the Dorsetshire Regt. 20 Feb. 1895, becoming Lieutenant 14 June, 1897. He took part in operations on the North-West Frontier of India, 1897–98, with the Tirah Expeditionary Force, and received the Medal with two clasps. He served in the South African War, 1899–1901, taking part in operations in the Transvaal and Orange River Colony 30 Nov. 1900, to Aug. 1901; was mentioned in Despatches [London Gazette, 8 Feb. and 10 Sept. 1901]; received the Queen's Medal with four clasps, and was created a Companion of the Distinguished Service Order [London Gazette, 27 Sept. 1901]: "Frank William Rowland Hill, Lieut., Dorsetshire Regt. In recognition of services during the operations in South Africa." He was invested by the King 17 Dec. 1901. He was promoted to Captain 13 July, 1901; was Ordnance Officer, 4th Class (Temporary), 26 May, 1904, to 31 Dec. 1905; Ordnance Officer, 4th Class, 4 Feb. 1907, to 3 Feb. 1914; was promoted to Major 8 Dec. 1914; was Ordnance Officer, 3rd Class, from 8 Dec. 1914. He served in the European War, 1914–17; was Deputy Assistant Director, War Office, 2 Aug. 1915. He was mentioned in Despatches; given the Brevet of Lieutenant-Colonel 3 June, 1915; created a C.M.G. in 1917, and awarded an O.B.E. in 1919. Lieut.-

Colonel F. W. R. Hill married, in 1904, Susan, daughter of Colonel J. Moutray Read, of Oriel House, Folkestone.

STRONG, CHARLES POWLETT, Lieut., was born 9 Jan. 1875, son

Charles Powlett Strong.

of Lieut.-Colonel C. J. Strong. He was gazetted to the Bedfordshire Regt. on 6 March, 1895, and became Lieutenant 10 July, 1897. He served in the South African War, and was created a Companion of the Distinguished Service Order [London Gazette, 27 Sept. 1901]: "Charles Powlett Strong, Lieut., Bedfordshire Regt. (deceased)." Lieut. Strong was killed before his decoration was gazetted, and the Insignia, etc., were sent to his father.

WAY, ARTHUR STRACHAN, Lieut., was born on 5 March, 1876, son of the Rev. Bromley Way. He was educated at Marlborough College and the Royal Military College, Sandhurst, and joined the 2nd Battn. Durham Light Infantry, at Poona, in Jan. 1896. He served in South Africa from Jan. 1900, to 29 Jan. 1901, with the Mounted Infantry, and was killed in action on 29 Jan. 1901. He was created a Companion of the Distinguished Service Order [London Gazette, 27 Sept. 1901]: "Arthur Strachan Way, Lieut., Durham Light Infantry (deceased). In recognition of services during the operations in South Africa." The Insignia, Warrant and Statutes were sent to his father. His brother, Lieut.-Colonel Bromley Way, Sherwood Foresters, writes of Lieut. Way: "He went to South Africa with the Durham Light Infantry Company of the Burmah Mounted Infantry in Jan. 1900; was mentioned for gallantry at Sanna's Post and on subsequent occasions, and was killed in action 29 Jan. 1901."

CHARLES, JAMES RONALD EDMONDSTON, Lieut., was born 26 June, 1875, son of the late T. Edmondston Charles, M.D., Hon. Physician to His Majesty the King. He entered the Royal Engineers 17 Aug. 1894, becoming Lieutenant 17 Aug. 1897. He served in the South African War, 1899–1900, and was present at the Relief of Kimberley, including operations at Paardeberg (17 to 26 Feb.); actions at Poplar Grove, Dreifontein and Zand River; operations in the Transvaal in May and June, 1900, including actions near Johannesburg; operations in Cape Colony, south of Orange River, 1899–1900, including actions at Colesberg (Jan. to Feb.). He was mentioned in Despatches [London Gazette, 8 Feb. and 10 Sept. 1901]; received the Queen's Medal with four clasps, and was created a Companion of the Distinguished Service Order [London Gazette, 27 Sept. 1901]; "James Ronald Edmondston Charles, Lieut., Royal Engineers. In recognition of services during the operations in South Africa." The Insignia, Warrant and Statutes were sent to the Commander-in-Chief in India, and were presented by Colonel Des Vœux in India 5 April, 1902. He became Captain 1 April, 1901. Capt. Charles served on the North-West Frontier of India in 1908, taking part in operations in the Zakka Khel country; was mentioned in Despatches [London Gazette, 22 May, 1908]; also in operations in the Mohmand country; was mentioned in Despatches 14 Aug. 1908, and given the Brevet of Major 16 July, 1908. He was G.S.O.2, Headquarters, India, 26 Nov. 1910 to 29 Sept. 1914; served in the European War, 1914–18; was promoted to Major 17 Aug. 1914; was G.S.O.1, Lahore Division, British Expeditionary Force, 28 May to 31 July, 1915; Brigadier-General, General Staff, Indian Army Corps, British Expeditionary Force, 1 Aug. to 8 Dec. 1915; Brigadier-General, General Staff, 15th Army Corps, British Expeditionary Force, 17th Army Corps, British Armies in France, 9 Dec. 1915, to 15 July, 1918; Divisional Commander, 25th Division, British Armies in France, 4 Aug. 1918, to 5 March, 1919; Brigadier-General, General Staff, Staff College, 6 March, 1919. He was mentioned in Despatches five times; was created a C.B. in 1918, and a C.M.G. in 1919, and was made an Officer of the Legion of Honour by the French. He was given the Brevets of Lieutenant-Colonel 18 Feb. 1915, and Colonel 3 June, 1916. Major E. M. S. Charles, C.M.G., D.S.O., is Colonel Charles's brother.

LEIGH, CHANDOS, Lieut., was born in Aug. 1873, son of the Honourable Sir E. Chandos Leigh, K.C., of 45, Upper Grosvenor Street, W., and of Lady Leigh. He was educated at Harrow and Cambridge, and joined

Chandos Leigh.

the King's Own Scottish Borderers, through the Warwickshire Militia, 29 May, 1895, becoming Lieutenant 22 Sept. 1897. He served in the South African War, 1900–2, employed with Mounted Infantry, and took part in the Relief of Kimberley; operations in Orange Free State, 1900, including operations at Paardeberg; actions at Poplar Grove, Houtnek (Thoba Mountain), Vet River and Zand River; operations in the Transvaal in May and June, 1900, including actions near Johannesburg and Diamond Hill; operations in Orange River Colony in 1900, including actions at Wittebergen and Bothaville; operations in the Transvaal, Orange River Colony and Cape Colony 30 Nov. 1900, to 31 May, 1902. He was mentioned in Despatches [London Gazette, 10 Sept. 1901]; received the Queen's Medal with six clasps, and was created a Companion of the Distinguished Service Order [London Gazette, 27 Sept. 1901]: "Chandos Leigh, Lieut., King's Own Scottish Borderers. In

recognition of services during the operations in South Africa." The Insignia were presented to him by the King 29 Oct. 1901. He was promoted to Captain 1 April, 1901. Capt. Leigh then spent ten years in the Egyptian Army. He took part in the operations against the Nyam Nyam Tribes in the Bahr-el-Ghazal Province, and received the Orders of the Medjidie and Osmanieh, and the Bahr-el-Ghazal Medal and clasp. Major Leigh went to France with his regiment, and was reported missing on the 23rd Aug. 1914, at Mons. When last seen he was, though wounded, waving his men on, and telling them not to mind about him. Six months later returned wounded prisoners reported that he died in Aug. 1914, of wounds received in action at Mons. His only brother, Lieut. E. H. Leigh, 2nd Battn. Rifle Brigade, was killed on the Aubers Ridge in May, 1915, and their grief-stricken father died three days later. He called Harrovian to fall in the war. Major Leigh was a fine steeple-chase rider and polo player, as well as a keen cricketer and rider to hounds. He married Winifred, daughter of the late Right Honourable A. F. Jeffreys, M.P., of Buckham, Hampshire.

BAILEY, ARTHUR HAROLD, Lieut., was born 24 Aug. 1873, son of W. H. Bailey. He entered the South Lancashire Regt. 10 Oct. 1894, becoming Lieutenant 17 Oct. 1897. He served in South Africa in 1896, in Matabeleland, and was Adjutant, South Lancashire Regt., 24 April, 1899, to 23 April, 1903. He served in the South African War, 1899 to 1902, as Adjutant, 1st Battn. South Lancashire Regt., and was present at the Relief of Ladysmith, including operations of 17 to 24 Jan. 1900, and action at Spion Kop; operations of 5 to 7 Feb. 1900, and action at Vaal Kranz; operations on Tugela Heights 14 to 27 Feb. 1900; operations in the Transvaal 30 Nov. 1900, to 31 May, 1902; operations on the Zululand Frontier of Natal in Sept. and Oct. 1901. He was mentioned in Despatches [London Gazette, 8 Feb. and 10 Sept. 1901]; received the Queen's Medal with five clasps; the King's Medal with two clasps, and was created a Companion of the Distinguished Service Order [London Gazette, 27 Sept. 1901]: "Arthur Harold Bailey, Lieut., South Lancashire Regt. In recognition of services during the operations in South Africa." The Insignia, Warrant, etc., were sent to the Commander-in-Chief in India 12 June, 1903, and were presented at Jubbulpore 4 Aug. 1903. He became Captain 13 Dec. 1901. Captain Bailey was on half-pay from 18 Oct. 1913.

PATON, IAN VALENTINE, Lieut., was born 14 Feb. 1875, at Eaton Square, S.W., eldest son of Major-General George Paton, C.M.G., Colonel, South Wales Borderers, and Ethel (who died in 1885), daughter of the

Ian Valentine Paton.

late Major-General Edward Bagot. He was educated at Wellington College and Sandhurst, and joined the Royal Scots Fusiliers, Sept. 1895, becoming Lieutenant 6 Nov. 1897. He served in the South African War, 1899–1900, as A.D.C. to Lieutenant-General, Infantry Division, South Africa, 10 March, 1900, to 17 April, 1902, and was slightly wounded. He took part in the Relief of Ladysmith, including the action at Colenso; operations of 17 to 24 Jan. 1900, and 5 to 7 Feb. 1900; action at Vaal Kranz; operations on Tugela Heights (14 to 27 Feb.) and action at Pieter's Hill; operations in Cape Colony, north of Orange River, including action at Faber's Put. He was mentioned in Despatches [London Gazette, 8 Feb. 1901 (Sir R. H. Buller, 30 March, 1900; Sir C. Warren, 29 June, 1900), and (Lord Roberts) London Gazette, 10 Sept. 1901]; received the Queen's Medal with three clasps, and was created a Companion of the Distinguished Service Order [London Gazette, 27 Sept. 1901]: "Ian Valentine Paton, Lieut., Royal Scots Fusiliers. In recognition of services during the operations in South Africa." The Insignia were presented by the King 12 March, 1902. He was promoted to Captain 9 Dec. 1900, and was A.D.C. to the G.O.C., Thames District, 8 July, 1901, to 8 Dec. 1902. He retired 16 April, 1913. He rejoined in 1914; served in the European War; became Major, Reserve of Officers, 1 Sept. 1915, and was severely wounded at Herlies, Hohenzollern Redoubt, in 1916. Major Paton married, 19 June, 1915, at Noctorum, Cheshire, Catherine, only daughter of John Shutt, Esq., of The Grange, Noctorum.

MILLER, HUGH DE BURGH, Lieut., was born 4 June, 1873, son of Thomas de Burgh Miller. He entered the Royal Artillery 17 Nov. 1894, and became Lieutenant 17 Nov. 1897. He served in the South African War, 1899–1902; was present at the Relief of Ladysmith, including operations of 17 to 24 Jan. 1900, and action at Spion Kop; operations of 5 to 7 Feb. 1900, and action at Vaal Kranz; operations on Tugela Heights 14 to 27 Feb. 1900, and action at Pieter's Hill; operations in the Transvaal in May and June, 1900; operations in the Transvaal, east and west of Pretoria, July to 29 Nov. 1900; operations in Orange River Colony, May to 29 Nov. 1900; operations in Cape Colony, north of Orange River, including action at Ruidam; operations in the Transvaal 30 Nov. 1900, to Sept. 1901, and Nov. 1901, to May, 1902; operations in Orange River Colony, May, 1902; operations on the Zululand Frontier of Natal in Sept. and Oct. 1901. He was mentioned in Despatches [London Gazette, 10 Sept. 1901]; received the Queen's Medal with five clasps; the King's Medal with two clasps, and was created a Companion of the Distinguished Service Order [London Gazette, 27 Sept. 1901]: "Hugh de Burgh Miller, Lieut., Royal Horse and Royal Field Artillery. In recognition of services during the operations in South Africa." He was invested by the King 18 Dec. 1902. He was promoted to Captain 15 Jan. 1901, and to Major 9 Aug. 1911, was Officer in Charge of Danger Buildings, Woolwich, 21 Aug. 1911, to 26 April, 1913; 2nd Assistant Superintendent, Royal Laboratory, Woolwich, 27 April, 1913, to 17 June, 1914; Assistant Superintendent, Royal Laboratory, Woolwich, 18 June, 1914, to 2 Dec. 1915. He held a Special Appointment, Ministry of Munitions (graded A.A.G., War Office, 3 Dec, 1915, to 24 Sept. 1916 ; was promoted to Lieutenant-Colonel 24 April, 1916 ; held a Special Appointment, Ministry of Munitions, 25 Sept. 1916, to 31 March, 1919 ; was Deputy Director of Artillery, War Office, from 1 April, 1919. He was given the Brevets of Lieutenant-Colonel 29 Nov. 1915, and Colonel 1 Jan. 1917, and was created a C.B.E. in 1919. Colonel Miller married, in 1906, a daughter of Colonel A. W. Baird, C.S.I., F.R.S.

WILSON, FRANCIS ADRIAN, Lieut., was born 12 Oct. 1875, son of the late General Sir C. W. Wilson. He entered the Royal Artillery 17 Nov. 1894, and became Lieutenant 17 Nov. 1897. He served in the South African War, 1899–1902, taking part in operations in Natal, 1899, including actions at Talana and Lombard's Kop ; Defence of Ladysmith, including action of 6 Jan. 1903 ; operations in Natal, March to June, 1900, including action at Laing's Nek (6 to 9 June) ; operations in the Transvaal, east of Pretoria, July to 26 Nov. 1900 ; operations in the Transvaal, Orange River Colony and Cape Colony 30 Nov. to 31 May, 1902. He received the Queen's Medal with six clasps ; the King's Medal with two clasps, and was created a Companion of the Distinguished Service Order [London Gazette, 27 Sept. 1901] : " Frederick Adrian Wilson, Lieut., Royal Artillery. In recognition of services during the operations in South Africa." He was invested by the King 18 Dec. 1903. He became Captain 6 Feb. 1901 ; was Staff Captain, Royal Artillery, Scottish District, 11 June, 1904, to 24 Oct. 1905 ; Captain, Australian Commonwealth Military Forces, 25 Sept. 1908, to 21 Sept. 1912 ; was G.S.O.2, Australian Commonwealth Military Forces, 25 Sept. 1908, to 21 Sept. 1912 ; Major 1 Aug. 1911. He served in the European War from 1914, as Temporary Lieutenant-Colonel, Royal Artillery, 28 Oct. 1915, to 2 May, 1916 ; became Lieutenant-Colonel 3 May, 1916 ; was Brigadier-General, Royal Artillery, Guards Division, British Armies in France, 13 June, 1917. He was twice mentioned in Despatches ; wounded ; was given the Brevets of Lieutenant-Colonel 3 May, 1916, and Colonel 1 Jan. 1919 ; created a C.M.G. in 1917. Colonel Wilson married, in 1903, Mabel, daughter of Edward Wilson Crosfield.

ASHBURNER, LIONEL FORBES, Lieut., was born 18 Sept. 1874. He was educated at Cheltenham College, and entered the Army 16 Jan. 1895, as Second Lieutenant (unattached) ; joined the Indian Staff Corps 10 March, 1896, and the Durham Light Infantry 18 May, 1896. He became Lieutenant, Durham Light Infantry, 24 Nov. 1897. From 1899 to 1902 he served in the South African War, employed with Mounted Infantry, and he was present at operations in the Transvaal in July, 1901 ; operations in Orange River Colony, Nov. 1901, to April, 1902 ; operations in Cape Colony, Feb. and March, 1901. He was mentioned in Despatches [London Gazette, 8 Feb. ; 20 Aug. and 10 Sept. 1901] ; received the Queen's Medal with four clasps ; the King's Medal with two clasps, and was created a Companion of the Distinguished Service Order [London Gazette, 27 Sept. 1901] : " Lionel Forbes Ashburner, Lieut., Royal Fusiliers. In recognition of services during the operations in South Africa." He was invested by the King 18 Dec. 1902. He became Captain, Royal Fusiliers, 13 July, 1901 ; was Adjutant, Royal Fusiliers, 1 June, 1906, to 30 May, 1907 ; Brigade Major, India, 22 Nov. 1909, to 21 Nov. 1913. He served in the European War from 1914, as Brigade Major, 102nd Infantry Brigade, New Armies, 14 Dec. 1914, to 24 Feb. 1915 ; was promoted to Major 17 Dec. 1914 ; was Brigade Major, 34th Infantry Brigade, Mediterranean Expeditionary Force, 25 Feb. to 30 Sept. 1915 ; G.S.O.2, 1st Australian Division, Mediterranean Expeditionary Force, British Armies in France, 1 Oct. 1915, to 15 Aug. 1916 ; commanded the 96th Infantry Brigade, British Armies in France, 4 Dec. 1916, to 20 Aug. 1917 ; was Inspector of the Territorial Force (Temporary) 15 Oct. 1917, to 16 Oct. 1918 ; commanded 142nd Infantry Brigade, British Armies in France, 4 Dec. 1917. He was given the Brevet of Lieutenant-Colonel 1 Jan. 1916, and was five times mentioned in Despatches. He married, in 1907, Ethel Hermione, daughter of Sir Charles Bayley.

ARCHDALE, THEODORE MONTGOMERY, Lieut., was born 24 Sept. 1873, youngest son of the late Nicholas Montgomery Archdale, of Crock-na-Crieve, County Fermanagh. He entered the Royal Artillery 12 Dec. 1894, becoming Lieutenant 12 Dec. 1897, and Captain 12 March, 1901. He served in the South African War, 1899–1900, taking part in the Relief of Ladysmith, including operations of 17 to 24 Jan. 1900, and action at Spion Kop ; operations of 5 to 7 Feb. 1900, and action at Vaal Kranz ; operations on Tugela Heights (14 to 27 Feb.). He was mentioned in Despatches [London Gazette, 22 Feb. and 10 Sept. 1901] ; received the Queen's Medal with three clasps, and was created a Companion of the Distinguished Service Order [London Gazette, 27 Sept. 1901] : " Theodore Montgomery Archdale, Lieut., Royal Artillery. In recognition of services during the operations in South Africa." The Insignia were presented by the King 18 Dec. 1902. He was promoted to Captain 12 March, 1901, and was Adjutant, Militia, 28 Aug. 1901, to 27 Aug. 1904. Capt. Archdale married, in 1901, Helen Alexander, daughter of the late Alexander Russel. He was promoted to Major 16 Aug. 1911. He served in the European War from 1914 ; was wounded and mentioned in Despatches. He died 10 Oct. 1918.

DAWNAY, THE HONOURABLE HUGH, Lieut., was born on the 19th Sept. 1875, second son of Viscount Downe and Lady Cecilia Maria Charlotte Molyneux, V.A. (who died in 1910), daughter of the Earl of Sefton. He received his commission in the Rifle Brigade in Oct. 1895, and became Lieutenant in Jan. 1898, and took part in the Nile Expedition, being present at the Battle of Khartum, and being mentioned in Despatches [London Gazette, 30 Sept. 1898]. He received the Medal ; the 4th Class of the Order of the Medjidie, and the Egyptian Medal with clasp. From Feb. 1899, to Nov. 1900, he was Adjutant of his battalion, and in that capacity served in the South African War in 1899 and 1900, being present at operations in Natal, including actions at Lombard's Kop ; the Defence of Ladysmith, including sortie of the 10th Dec. 1899, and action of the 6th Jan. 1900. He was twice mentioned in Despatches [London Gazette, 8 Feb. and 10 Sept. 1901] ; received the Queen's Medal with clasp, and was created a Companion of the Distinguished Service Order [London Gazette, 27 Sept. 1901] : " The Honourable Hugh Dawnay, Lieut., The Rifle Brigade. In recognition of services during the operations in South Africa." The Insignia were presented by the King 29 Oct. 1901. He became Captain in the Rifle Brigade in March, 1901, and in Feb. of the same year was appointed A.D.C. to the Commander-in-Chief. Major Dawnay was transferred to the 2nd Life Guards, and served in the European War. He was killed in action on the 6th Nov. 1914. In 1902 he married Lady Susan Beresford, daughter of the 5th Marquess of Waterford, and they had four sons.

TYNDALL, WILLIAM ERNEST MARRIOTT, Lieut., was born 2 Feb. 1875. He entered the West Riding Regt., as Second Lieutenant, 6 March, 1895, becoming Lieutenant 29 Jan. 1899 ; was Adjutant, West Riding Regt., 29 Jan. 1899, to 27 Jan. 1903.

William E. M. Tyndall.

He served in the South African War, 1899–1902, Relief of Kimberley ; Orange Free State, including operations at Paardeberg (17 to 26 Feb.) ; actions at Poplar Grove and Dreifontein ; operations in the Transvaal, east of Pretoria, Aug. to 29 Nov. 1900, including actions at Rhenoster Kop ; operations in the Transvaal, west of Pretoria, Aug. to 29 Nov. 1900 ; operations in the Transvaal and Orange River Colony 30 Nov. 1900, to 31 May, 1902. He received the Queen's Medal with five clasps : the King's Medal with two clasps, and was created a Companion of the Distinguished Service Order [London Gazette, 27 Sept. 1901] : " William Ernest Marriott Tyndall, Lieut. West Riding Regt. In recognition of services during the operations in South Africa." He was invested by the King 18 Dec. 1902. He was promoted to Captain 22 Feb. 1901. Capt. Tyndall passed the Staff College. He was Officer, Company of Gentlemen Cadets. Royal Military College, Sandhurst, 28 Jan. 1903, to 21 Jan. 1906 ; Brigade Major, 15th Brigade, Irish Command, 19 April, 1908, to 27 Jan. 1912 ; D.A.A.G., Western Command, 13 May, to 17 Nov. 1914 ; D.A.A. and Q.M.G. 18 Nov. to 6 Dec. 1914 ; Temporary Lieutenant-Colonel, West Riding Regt., 6 Jan. to 4 April, 1915. He was given the Brevet of Lieutenant-Colonel 3 June, 1915. He died of wounds 1 Aug. 1916. Lieut.-Colonel Tyndall married, in 1908, Alice Lorna, daughter of the late Mr. Sedgwick, of Byfleet, Surrey.

FARQUHAR, FRANCIS DOUGLAS, Lieut., was born 17 Sept. 1874, son of Sir Henry Thomas Farquhar, 4th Bart., and the Honourable Alice Brand, daughter of the 1st Viscount Hampden. He joined the Coldstream Guards 29 April, 1896, and became Lieutenant 24 Jan. 1898. He served in the South African War, 1899–1900, on the Staff, and took part in the advance on Kimberley, including the action at Magersfontein ; operations in the Orange Free State, Feb. to May, 1900, including actions at Poplar Grove, Dreifontein, Vet River and Zand River ; operations in the Transvaal in May and June, 1900, including actions near Johannesburg, Pretoria and Diamond Hill ; operations in the Transvaal, east of Pretoria, July to Oct. 1900, including the action at Belfast. He was mentioned in Despatches [London Gazette, 10 Sept. 1901] ; received the Queen's Medal with five clasps, and was created a Companion of the Distinguished Service Order [London Gazette, 27 Sept. 1901] :

Francis D. Farquhar.

" Francis Douglas Farquhar, Lieut., Coldstream Guards. In recognition of services during the operations in South Africa." He was A.D.C. to Major-General, Infantry Brigade, South Africa, 11 April to 5 Dec. 1900 ; A.D.C. to Lieutenant-General, Infantry Division, South Africa, 10 April, 1900, to 6 Feb. 1901 ; was promoted to Captain, Coldstream Guards, 20 April, 1901 ; Chinese Royal Infantry, May, 1901, to June, 1902 ; on Special Service with the Somaliland Field Force 7 May, 1903, to 18 June, 1904, on the Staff (Medal with clasp). The late Maj. Farquhar married, in 1905, Lady Evelyn Hely-Hutchinson, sister of the 6th Earl of Donoughmore, and they had two daughters.

O'GORMAN, CHARLES JOHN, Lieut., was born 24 July, 1872. He was educated at Clongowes (is L.R.C.P.I. and L.R.C.S.I.), and entered the Royal Army Medical Corps 28 Jan. 1898. He served in the South African War, 1899 to 1902, and was present at the Defence of Kimberley ; operations in the Orange Free State, April to May, 1900 ; operations in the Transvaal, west of Pretoria, July to 29 Nov. 1900 ; operations in Orange River Colony, May to July, 1900, including actions at Lindley (1 June) and

Charles J. O'Gorman.

Rhenoster River; operations in Cape Colony, north and south of Orange River, 1899–1900; operations in the Transvaal 30 Nov. 1900, to 31 May, 1902. He was mentioned in Despatches [London Gazette, 8 May, 1900, and 16 April, 1901]; received the Queen's Medal with three clasps; the King's Medal with two clasps, and was created a Companion of the Distinguished Service Order [London Gazette, 27 Sept. 1901]: "Charles John O'Gorman, Lieut. Royal Army Medical Corps. In recognition of services during the operations in South Africa." The Insignia, Warrant, etc., were sent to South Africa, to the G.O.C., Transvaal, and were presented by General Lyttelton at Pretoria 14 Jan. 1903. He became Captain 28 Jan. 1901; was employed with the South African Constabulary 31 Dec. 1904, and was promoted to Major 28 Jan. 1910, and to Lieutenant-Colonel 1 Aug. 1915. He was Assistant Director of Medical Services, 2nd East African Division, East African Force, 23 Feb. to 31 March, 1916; Assistant Director of Medical Services, Lines of Communication, East African Force, 10 Dec. 1916, to 22 Feb. 1918; Assistant Director of Medical Services, General Headquarters, East African Force, 23 Feb. to 31 May, 1918; Assistant Director of Medical Services, 18th Division, British Armies in France, 18 Feb. 1919, and Acting Colonel.

JONES, FRANK AUBREY, Lieut., was born 4 Aug. 1873. He entered the Welsh Regt. 28 Sept. 1895; became Lieutenant 21 Feb. 1898, and served in Sierra Leone, 1898–99, on the Protectorate Expedition (wounded; Medal and clasp), and in South Africa, 1899–1902, when he was severely wounded; mentioned in Despatches; received the Queen's Medal with two clasps, and was created a Companion of the Distinguished Service Order [London Gazette, 27 Sept. 1901]: "Frank Aubrey Jones, Lieut., Welsh Regt. In recognition of services during the operations in South Africa." The Insignia, etc., were sent to the G.O.C., Transvaal and Orange River Colony, 15 Nov. 1902, and presented by General Lyttelton at Pretoria 14 Jan. 1903. Capt. Jones retired from the Welsh Regt. He served in the European War, and was killed in action 11 July, 1916.

CAMPBELL, JOHN VAUGHAN, Lieut., served in the South African War, and was created a Companion of the Distinguished Service Order [London Gazette, 27 Sept. 1901]: "John Vaughan Campbell, Lieut., Coldstream Guards. In recognition of services during the operations in South Africa." He was invested by the King 18 Dec. 1902. Lieut.-Colonel J. V. Campbell served in the European War, and was awarded the Victoria Cross in 1916, and created a C.M.G. in 1918.

DERRY, ARTHUR, Lieut., was born at Plymouth, 14 Oct. 1874, son of the late William Derry, of Houndiscombe. He was educated at Wellington College, and joined the 1st Battn. Welsh Regt. 7 Dec. 1895, having previously served in 3rd Battn. Duke of Cornwall's Light Infantry. He was promoted to Lieutenant, Welsh Regt. 22 April, 1898, and served in the South African War, 1899–1902, with 6th Mounted Infantry in command of a company. He was present at the Relief of Kimberley; operations in the Orange Free State, Feb. to May, 1900, including operations at Poplar Grove, Houtnek (Thoba Mountain), Vet River (5 and 6 May) and Zand River; Transvaal, May and June, 1900; actions near Johannesburg, Pretoria and Diamond Hill (11 and 12 June); operations in the Transvaal, west of Pretoria, July to Sept. 1900, including action at Venterskroon; operations in the Orange River Colony, May to 29 Nov. 1900, including action at Wittebergen (1 to 29 July) and Bothaville; operations in Cape Colony, south of Orange River, 1899–1900, including actions at Colesberg (14 Jan. to 1 Feb.); operations in Cape Colony 30 Nov. 1900, to Feb. 1901; operations in the Transvaal and Orange River Colony, Feb. 1901, to May, 1902. He was mentioned in Despatches [London Gazette, 10 Sept. 1901, and 29 July, 1902]; received the Queen's Medal with five clasps; the King's Medal with three clasps, and for gallantry at Diamond Hill he was created a Companion of the Distinguished Service Order [London Gazette, 27 Sept. 1901]: "Arthur Derry, Lieut., Welsh Regt. In recognition of services during the operations in South Africa." He was invested by the King 18 Dec. 1902. He was promoted to Captain 9 March, 1902; was Adjutant, 1st Welsh Regt., 11 March, 1907, to 10 March, 1910; D.A.A. and Q.M.G., Welsh Division, Western Command, 1 April, 1912, to 4 Aug. 1914. He served in the European War; became Major 1 Nov. 1914; was Temporary Lieutenant-Colonel and D.A.A. and Q.M.G., Welsh Division, 53rd Division, Mediterranean Expeditionary Force, 23 Nov. 1915, to 23 March, 1916; Brigade Major, 115th Infantry Brigade, British Armies in France, 11 July, 1916, to 1 April, 1917; G.S.O., 2nd Grade, 14th Army Corps, British Armies in France; Mesopotamia Expeditionary Force 1 Aug. 1917, to 24 March, 1918; G.S.O.2, 10th Army Corps, British Armies in France, 25 March, to 28 Aug. 1918; G.S.O.2, 27th Division, British Salonika Force, 29 Aug. to 21 Nov. 1918; D.A.A. and Q.M.G., Portsmouth Garrison, 15 May, 1919. He married, in 1902, Caroline Collette, eldest daughter of the Rev. W. Oxland, B.A., R.N., and has one daughter, Naomi Joan.

BATTYE, CLINTON WYNYARD, Lieut., was born 24 May, 1874, third son of the late Major Montagu Battye, His Majesty's Honourable Corps of Gentlemen-at-Arms. He was educated at Wellington College, and was gazetted to the Shropshire Light Infantry 7 March, 1894, becoming Lieutenant 8 June, 1898. He served in the South African War, 1899–1902, employed with Mounted Infantry, and was slightly wounded. He was present at operations in the Orange Free State, Feb. to May, 1900, including actions at Poplar Grove, Dreifontein, Vet River (5 and 6 May) and Zand River; operations in the Transvaal in May and June, 1900, including actions near Johannesburg, Pretoria and Diamond Hill (11 and 12 June); operations in the Transvaal, east of Pretoria, July to 29 Nov. 1900, including action at Reit Vlei; operations in Cape Colony, south of Orange River, 1899–1900; operations in the Transvaal, Orange River Colony and Cape Colony 30 Nov. 1900, to 31 May, 1902. He was mentioned in Despatches [London Gazette, 10 Sept. 1901]; received both S. A. Medals with six clasps, and was created a Companion of the Distinguished Service Order [London Gazette, 27 Sept. 1901]: "Clinton Wynyard Battye, Lieut., Shropshire Light Infantry. In recognition of services during the operations in South Africa." He was invested by the King 18 Dec. 1902. He was promoted to Captain 22 Jan. 1902. He took part in the Mohmand operations in 1908 (Medal and clasp). Capt Battye served in the European War; was promoted to Major 13 May, 1915, and subsequently to Lieutenant-Colonel. He was killed in action 25 Nov. 1917.

JEFFCOAT, ALGERNON CAUTLEY, Lieut., was born 14 Aug. 1877, youngest son of Deputy Surgeon-General J. H. Jeffcoat, of 12, Avenue Elmers, Surbiton. He was educated at Rugby and at the Royal Military College, Sandhurst, and entered the Royal Inniskilling Fusiliers 8 Sept. 1897, becoming Lieutenant 8 June, 1898. He served in the South African War, 1899–1902; was present at the Relief of Ladysmith, including action at Colenso; operations of 17 to 24 Jan. 1900, and action at Spion Kop; operations of 5 to 7 Feb. 1900, and action at Vaal Kranz; in the operations on Tugela Heights (14 to 27 Feb. 1900); operations in Natal, March to June, 1900; in the Transvaal, east of Pretoria, July to 29 Nov. 1900, including actions at Belfast (26 and 27 Aug.) and Lydenberg (5 to 8 Sept.); in the Transvaal 30 Nov. 1900, to Nov. 1901; during the operations in Orange River Colony, Nov. 1901, to March, 1902; performed duties of Assistant Provost-Marshal, and employed with Damant's Horse; Despatches [London Gazette, 8 Feb. and 10 Sept. 1901]; Queen's Medal with five clasps, and King's Medal with two clasps. He was created a Companion of the Distinguished Service Order [London Gazette, 27 Sept. 1901]: "Algernon Cautley Jeffcoat, Lieut., Royal Inniskilling Fusiliers. In recognition of services during the operations in South Africa." The Insignia were presented by the King 12 May, 1902. He was promoted to Captain, Royal Fusiliers, 14 Dec. 1901; was employed with the Egyptian Army 13 May, 1904, to 15 July, 1906. He served in the European War, as D.A.A.G., General Headquarters, British Expeditionary Force, 5 Aug. 1914, to 2 Oct. 1915; as D.A.A. and Q.M.G., 4th Army Corps, British Expeditionary Force, British Armies in France, 3 Oct. 1915, to 29 Aug. 1916; as A.A. and Q.M.G., 9th Division, British Armies in France, 30 Aug. 1916. He was given the Brevet of Lieutenant-Colonel 3 June, 1917. He was created a C.M.G. in 1916, and a C.B. in 1919; was five times mentioned in Despatches; received the Legion of Honour, Croix de Chevalier, and the Belgian Croix de Guerre. Lieut.-Colonel Jeffcoat's brother, Capt. H. J. P. Jeffcoat, D.S.O., was killed in action in the disaster at Tabelkop. Sir Arthur Conan Doyle tells us, on page 512 of "The Great Boer War," how "Damant was hit in four places, all of his staff were wounded, and hardly a man of the small body of Yeomanry was left standing. Nothing could exceed their gallantry. Gaussen, their Captain, fell at their head. On the ridge the men about the guns were nearly all killed or wounded. Of the gun detachment only two men remained, both of them hit, and Jeffcoat, their dying Captain, bequeathed them fifty pounds each in a will drawn upon the spot." Lieut.-Colonel Jeffcoat married (1st), in 1906, Mabel (who died in 1907), eldest daughter of the late William Burrows, and (2ndly), in 1910, Ethel, daughter of J. R. Temperley.

HIGGINS, JOHN FREDERICK ANDREWS, Lieut., was born 1 Sept. 1875, son of William Higgins, of The Chesnuts, Farnham. He entered the Royal Artillery 15 June, 1895, becoming Lieutenant 5 June, 1898. He served in the South African War, 1899–1902; took part in the operations in Natal, 1899, including actions at Reitfontein, and Lombard's Kop and Farquhar's Farm; was present at the Defence of Ladysmith, including action of 6 Jan. 1900 (severely wounded); in the Transvaal 30 Nov. 1900, to Dec. 1901; also during operations in Orange River Colony, Jan. to 31 May, 1902. He was mentioned in Despatches [London Gazette, 10 Sept. 1901]; received the Queen's Medal with four clasps, and King's Medal with two clasps. He was created a Companion of the Distinguished Service Order [London Gazette, 27 Sept. 1901]: "John Frederick Andrews Higgins, Lieut., Royal Horse and Royal Field Artillery. In recognition of services during the operations in South Africa." He was invested by the King 24 Oct. 1902. He was promoted to Captain 15 March, 1901, and Major, Royal Artillery, 30 Aug. 1911, and Royal Flying Corps 28 Oct. 1912, to 31 March, 1918. Capt. Higgins served in the European War from 1914, as Temporary Brigadier-General, commanding the 2nd Brigade, Royal Flying Corps, 25 Aug. 1915, to 31 March, 1918; employed under the Air Ministry from 1 April, 1918. He was mentioned in Despatches; was given the Brevets of Lieutenant-Colonel (18 Feb. 1915) and Colonel (1 Jan. 1918); was made an Officer of the Legion of Honour; created a C.B.; promoted to Major-General; Air Vice-Marshal; awarded the A.F.C.

John F. A. Higgins.

BIRCH, EDWARD MASSY, Lieut., was born 12 March, 1875, son of Lieut.-Colonel E. A. Birch, M.D. He was gazetted to the Royal Artillery 15 June, 1895, becoming Lieutenant 15 June, 1898. He served in the South African War, 1899–1902; took part in the operations in the Orange Free State, Feb. to May, 1900, including actions at Houtnek (Thoba Mountain), Vet River (5 and 6 May) and Zand River; was present during operations in the Transvaal in May and June, 1900, including actions near Johannesburg and Pretoria; in Cape Colony, south of Orange River, 1899–1900; served again in the Transvaal, Orange River Colony, on the Zululand Frontier of Natal in Sept. and Oct. 1901, and in Cape Colony, 1900–2. He was mentioned in Despatches [London Gazette, 10 Sept. 1901]; received the Queen's Medal with three clasps, and King's Medal with two clasps. He was created a Companion of the Distinguished Service Order [London Gazette, 27 Sept. 1901]: "Edward Massy Birch, Lieut., Royal Horse and Royal Field Artillery. In recognition of services during the opera-

tions in South Africa." He was invested by the King 24 Oct. 1902. He was promoted to Captain 2 March, 1901; was Remount Officer, South Africa, 17 Nov. 1903, to 21 Nov. 1904; G.S.O.2, Mauritius, 1 July, 1911, to 17 Dec. 1914; became Major 30 Sept. 1911. Major Birch served in the European War from 1915, as G.S.O.2, New Armies, British Expeditionary Force, 10 Jan. 1915, to 17 May, 1916; as G.S.O.1, 25th Division, British Armies in France, 18 May, 1916, to 11 Jan. 1917; was promoted to Lieutenant-Colonel 1 June, 1916; was G.S.O.1, 5th Army, British Armies in France, 12 Jan. to 18 May, 1917; G.S.O.1, 17th Division, British Armies in France. He was given the Brevet of Colonel 3 June, 1918; was created a C.M.G. in 1917, and a C.B. in 1919, and was made an Officer of the Legion of Honour by the French. Colonel Birch married, in 1917, Violet, widow of Alfred Evans Brown.

COLLEN, EDWARD HENRY ETHELBERT, Lieut., was born 6 May, 1875, son of the late Lieut.-General Sir E. H. Collen, G.C.I.E., C.B. He was educated at Cheltenham College, and was commissioned in the Royal

Edward H. E. Collen.

Artillery 15 June, 1895. He served on the North-West Frontier of India, 1897–98; Malakand; took part in the action at Landakai; served during operations in Bajaur and in the Mamund country; Buner; was present at the attack and capture of Tanga Pass (Medal with clasp); served at Tirah, 1897–98, as Orderly Officer to G.O.C., Oct. to 31 Dec. 1897; afterwards on Staff; in the actions of Chagru Kotal and Dargai; at the capture of the Sampagha and Arhanga Passes; reconnaissance of the Saran Sar and action of 9 Nov. 1897; took part in the operations at and around Dwatoi and action of 24 Nov. 1897; also in the Bazar Valley 25–30 Dec. 1897 (Despatches [London Gazette, 5 April, 1898]; clasp). He was promoted to Lieutenant 15 June, 1898, and again saw active service in the South African War, 1899–1900, as Special Service Officer; afterwards on Staff; took part in the operations in the Orange Free State, Feb. to May, 1900, including those at Paardeberg (17 to 26 Feb.); actions at Poplar Grove, Dreifontein, Houtnek (Thoba Mountain), Vet River (5 and 6 May) and Zand River; in the Transvaal in May and June, 1900, including actions near Johannesburg and Pretoria; in the Transvaal, east of Pretoria, July to 29 Nov. 1900; in the Transvaal, west of Pretoria, July to 29 Nov. 1900, including actions Zilikat's Nek and Elands River (4 to 16 Aug.) (Despatches [London Gazette, 10 Sept. 1901]: Queen's Medal with four clasps). He was created a Companion of the Distinguished Service Order [London Gazette, 27 Sept. 1901]: "Edward Henry Ethelbert Collen, Lieut., Royal Garrison Artillery. In recognition of services during the operations in South Africa." The Insignia were presented by the King 29 Oct. 1901. He was promoted to Captain 12 July, 1901, and to Major 19 Feb. 1910. He retired 12 Feb. 1913. Major Collen served in the European War from 1914; was mentioned in Despatches, and given the Brevet of Lieut.-Colonel 3 June, 1917. He was created a C.M.G. in 1919. Lieut.-Colonel Collen married, in 1906, Constance Mary, eldest daughter of C. J. Cater Scott.

BELCHER, HAROLD THOMAS, Lieut., was born 17 March, 1876, at Malvern, son of the Rev. Thomas Hayes Belcher, Vicar of Bramley, Basingstoke (late Head Master of Brighton College), and Annie, elder daughter of

Harold Thomas Belcher.

the late Frederick Neame, of Selling, Kent. He was educated at Brighton College, and the Royal Military Academy, Woolwich, where he won the long jump in 1894, and represented Woolwich against Sandhurst in that event. He was a fearless rider and keen on hunting and polo; later hunted with the Vyne Hunt, and often rode in the Royal Artillery Point-to-Point races. He joined the Royal Artillery 15 June, 1895, becoming Lieutenant 15 June, 1898. He served in the South African War, 1899–1900, throughout the campaign in Natal, including the Battles of Talana Hill and Nicholson's Nek, and was present at the actions of Dundee and Farquhar's Farm, and during the Siege of Ladysmith. The following is the record of his South African services taken from "Hart's Army List": "Belcher, Capt., H.T. (R. Art.).—Served in the South African War, 1899–1901.—Took part in the operations in Natal, 1899, including actions at Talana and Lombard's Kop (severely wounded). Was present at the Defence of Ladysmith. Operations in Natal, March to June, 1900, including action at Laing's Nek (6 to 9 June). Served during the operations in the Transvaal, east of Pretoria, July to 29 Nov. 1900. Again in the Transvaal 30 Nov. to 1901. Also took part in the operations on the Zululand Frontier of Natal, Sept. and Oct. 1901. (Despatches [London Gazette, 10 Sept. 1901]; Queen's Medal with six clasps; D.S.O.)." He was severely wounded at Lombard's Kop, and was created a Companion of the Distinguished Service Order [London Gazette, 27 Sept. 1901]: "Harold Thomas Belcher, Lieut., Royal Artillery. In recognition of services during the operations in South Africa." The Insignia, Warrant and Statutes were sent to the Commander-in-Chief in India, and presented at Mooltan, India, 13 March, 1902. He became Captain 14 May, 1901; was Adjutant, R.A., 3 Oct. 1904, to 5 Nov. 1907; served some years in India; commanded a company of Gentlemen Cadets at Woolwich, 1910–14; was promoted to

Major 15 Feb. 1912; held a 1st Class Certificate in Gunnery; was author of a book on Field Gunnery, and inventor of a special machine for instruction in ranging in use at the Royal Military Academy. He was promoted Temp. Lieut.-Colonel 13 Jan. 1916. He went to France at the beginning of the European War, Sept. 1914; served continuously since then with the exception of five weeks at home wounded, in the summer of 1915, till he was killed near Ypres, July, 1917. Lieut.-Colonel H. T. Belcher had the Russian Order of St. Anne (3rd Class with Swords). His two brothers, Capt. G. Belcher, M.C., Royal Berkshire Regt., and Major Raymond Douglas Belcher, M.C., R.F.A., were also killed in action in the Great War.

MAY, JOHN CYRIL, Lieut., was born 1 April, 1874, son of the late J. C. Frampton May, of Creech St. Michael, Taunton. He joined the East Surrey Regt. as Second Lieutenant, from the Militia, 29 May, 1895, and became Lieutenant 21 June, 1898. He served in the South African War, 1899–1902; was present at the Relief of Ladysmith, including action at Colenso; operations of 17 to 24 Jan. 1900, and action at Spion Kop; operations of 5 to 7 Feb. 1900, and action at Vaal Kranz; during the operations on Tugela Heights, and action at Pieter's Hill; in Natal, March to June, 1900, including action at Laing's Nek; in the Transvaal 30 Nov. 1900, to May, 1901; also in Orange River Colony, May, 1901 (Despatches [London Gazette, 8 Feb. 1901; Sir R. H. Buller, 30 March and 9 Nov. 1900; and London Gazette, 10 Sept. 1901]; Queen's Medal with five clasps, and King's Medal with two clasps). He was created a Companion of the Distinguished Service Order [London Gazette, 27 Sept. 1901]: "John Cyril May, Lieut., East Surrey Regt. In recognition of services during the operations in South Africa." The Insignia, Warrant and Statutes were sent to the Commander-in-Chief in India, and presented by the G.O.C., Oudh District, at church parade, 22 Feb. 1903. He was promoted to Captain 3 Oct. 1903; was Adjutant, Volunteers, 11 Sept. 1906, to 31 March, 1908, and Adjutant, Territorial Force, 1 April, 1908, to 30 Nov. 1909. He was Temp. Lieut.-Colonel, Royal Berkshire Regt. (attached), 11 Oct. 1915, to 22 May, 1916. He married, in 1907, Edith Margaret, youngest daughter of the late Colonel S. E. Maunsell, R.A.M.C., and they have one son.

BARNARDISTON, SAMUEL JOHN BARRINGTON, Lieut., was born 19 Aug. 1875, fifth son of the late Nathaniel Barnardiston, Esq. He was educated at Haileybury, and entered the Suffolk Regt. 24 March,

S. J. B. Barnardiston.

1897, becoming Lieutenant 13 Feb. 1894. In the South African War, 1899–1902, he served as Adjutant, 1st Battn. Suffolk Regt., from 30 Dec. 1900, to 31 May, 1902; was present during the operations in the Transvaal, east of Pretoria, July to 29 Nov. 1900; in the Orange River Colony, May to 29 Nov. 1900; also in the operations in Cape Colony, south of Orange River, 1899–1900; again in the Transvaal, Dec. 1900, to 31 May, 1902; again in Orange River Colony 30 Nov. to Dec. 1900; and again in Cape Colony, Dec. 1900 (Despatches [London Gazette, 10 Sept. 1901]; Queen's Medal with three clasps, and King's Medal with two clasps). He was created a Companion of the Distinguished Service Order [London Gazette, 27 Sept. 1901]: "Samuel John Barrington Barnardiston, Lieut., Suffolk Regt. In recognition of services in South Africa." He was invested by the King 18 Dec. 1902. He was Adjutant, Suffolk Regt., 30 Dec. 1900, to 29 Dec. 1904, and was promoted to Captain 18 April, 1903. Capt. Barnardiston was employed with the West African Frontier Force 3 April, 1909, to 31 Jan. 1914, and was promoted to Major 2 March, 1914. He served in the European War, 1914. Major Barnardiston married, in 1919, Mademoiselle von Riemsdyk.

GARVICE, CHUDLEIGH, Lieut., was born 12 Jan. 1875, at Cookham, Bucks, son of Charles and Elizabeth Garvice. His father was of course the famous novelist, of whom his friend, Mr. Douglas Sladen, writes as

Chudleigh Garvice.

follows: "The late Charles Garvice, father of this distinguished soldier, was the most popular novelist of his time, and a great figure in the literary world. He was Chairman of the Authors' Club, one of the most prominent members of the Garrick, and Chairman of the Committee of the new After Dinner Club, of which he was co-founder with Mrs. Baillie-Reynolds and Mr. Douglas Sladen. He was the life and soul of the clubs to which he belonged, for, in addition to his sociability and wit in the smoking-room, he was an admirable after-dinner speaker, and when it was necessary for the club to assert itself on any occasion, he was always willing to take the responsibility, although it might make enemies. He was fearless in the performance of a duty. His multifarious activities may best be judged by quoting the last biography of him which appeared in 'Who's Who':

"'GARVICE, Charles, F.R.S.L., novelist, dramatist and journalist; correspondent for several English and American papers; President of Institute of Lecturers; late President of Farmers' and Landowner's Association; C.C. for Northam, Devon; Conservator of Rivers. Publications—Poem: Eve. Novels: Nance, Her Heart's Desire, The Outcast of the Family, A Coronet of Shame, Just a Girl, In Cupid's Chains, Love Decides, Linked by Fate, Love the Tyrant, A Girl of Spirit, Diana and

Destiny, Where Love Leads, The Gold in the Gutter, In Wolf's Clothing, Queen Kate, The Scribbler's Club, Love in a Snare, Two Maids and a Man, The One Girl in the World, 1915. Plays: The Fisherman's Daughter, A Life's Mistake, part author of A Heritage of Hate, and Marigold comes to Town. Recreations: Riding, fishing, motoring, amateur farming.'

"His astonishing popularity as an author may be judged from the following facts: In the year 1913 alone 1,750,000 copies of his books were sold, and before the end of that year more than six million copies of his books had been sold.

"No literary man in England was more sincerely loved and respected: none had greater influence: none used it better. The secret of his extraordinary popularity as a writer was that his books were absolutely pure, absolutely sincere, extraordinarily sympathetic, and that he was a storyteller born. Charles Garvice was one of those men who do nothing but good wherever they go."

Chudleigh Garvice was educated at Blundell's School, Tiverton, and was gazetted to the Royal Dublin Fusiliers 9 Dec. 1896, and was promoted to Lieutenant 30 June, 1898. He served in the South African War from the commencement of hostilities until peace was signed, employed with Mounted Infantry, and was present at operations in Natal in 1899, including the action at Talana; operations in the Transvaal, east of Pretoria, July to 22 Nov. 1900; operations in Orange River Colony, May to July, 1900; operations in the Transvaal 30 Nov. 1900, to Jan. 1902. He was mentioned in Despatches [London Gazette, 10 Sept. 1901]: received the Queen's Medal with three clasps, the King's Medal with two clasps, and was created a Companion of the Distinguished Service Order [London Gazette, 27 Sept. 1901]: "Chudleigh Garvice, Lieut., Royal Dublin Fusiliers. In recognition of services during the operations in South Africa." He was promoted to Captain 28 May, 1902. In 1903 he served in the Aden Hinterland operations, and in the Sudan (Egyptian Army) from 1904 to 1912, in command of the Arab Battn. in various patrols, etc. (Sudan Medal, 1910); retired from the Royal Dublin Fusiliers 9 April, 1913, and became Major, Reserve of Officers, 31 Aug. 1914. In the Great War he served on the Western Front of Egypt in 1915-16, and later on the Staff in Egypt. Major Garvice was mentioned in the Despatches of General Maxwell, dated 1 March, 1916, and of General Allenby in the London Gazette, dated 15 Jan. 1918. He was awarded the O.B.E. in 1919, and has the 1914-15 Star, the General Service Medal, the Victory Medal, the 4th Class Osmanieh, 3rd Class Order of the Nile, 1st Class Order of the Redeemer (Greece). He married, 31 Jan. 1920, at Alexandria, Egypt, Isabel, daughter of Andrew Ormiston. He died 3 March, 1921.

BRYANT, HENRY GRENVILLE, Lieut., was born 5 June, 1872, eldest son of H. S. Bryant, of 2, Hesketh Crescent, Torquay. He was gazetted to the Bedfordshire Regt. 2 June, 1894, and the Shropshire Light Infantry 26 Sept. 1894, becoming Lieutenant, Shropshire Light Infantry, 3 July, 1898. He served in the South African War, 1899-1902, as Brigade Signalling Officer, 13 March to 9 June, 1900; 10 July to 2 Sept. 1900, and 16 Oct. 1900, to 23 July, 1901: on Staff (slightly wounded); took part in the operations in the Orange Free State, Feb. to May, 1900, including action at Paardeberg (17 to 26 Feb.); actions at Poplar Grove, Dreifontein, Houtnek (Thoba Mountain), Vet River (5 and 6 May) and Zand River; served during operations in the Transvaal in May and June, 1900, including actions near Johannesburg and Pretoria: in the Transvaal, east of Pretoria, July to 29 Nov. 1900; also in the Transvaal, west of Pretoria, July to 29 Nov. 1900, including actions at Elands

Henry Grenville Bryant.

River (4 to 16 Aug.); was present during the operations in Orange River Colony, May to 29 Nov. 1900, including action at Rhenoster River: in Cape Colony, south of Orange River, 1899-1900; also during the operations in the Transvaal 30 Nov. 1900, to 31 May, 1902 (Despatches [London Gazette, 10 Sept. 1901]; Queen's Medal with four clasps, and King's Medal with two clasps). He was created a Companion of the Distinguished Service Order [London Gazette, 27 Sept. 1901]: "Henry Grenville Bryant, Lieut., Shropshire Light Infantry. In recognition of services during the South African War." He was invested by the King 24 Oct. 1902. He was promoted to Captain 22 Jan. 1902. Capt. Bryant married, in 1904, Phyllis Mary, second daughter of the late J. R. W. Hildyard, of Horsley Hall, County Durham, and Hutton Bonfield Hall, Northallerton.

EMERSON, NORMAN ZEAL, Lieut., was born at Dartford, Kent, on 4 Oct. 1872, son of the late Ambrose Emerson and of Jessie Emerson, daughter of Orlando Stone. He was educated privately, and at Queenwood College, Hampshire, and was gazetted to the Devonshire Regt. 29 May, 1895, becoming Lieutenant 6 July, 1898. He took part in the operations on the North-West Frontier of India, 1897-98; with Tirah Expeditionary Force (Medal with two clasps). Lieut. Emerson served in the South African War, 1899-1902; took part in the operations in Natal, 1899, including actions at Elandslaagte, Rietfontein and Lombard's Kop; was present at the Defence of Ladysmith, including action of 6 Jan. 1900; in Natal, March

Norman Zeal Emerson.

to June, 1900; in the Transvaal, east of Pretoria, July to 29 Nov. 1900, including actions at Belfast (26 and 27 Aug.) and Lydenberg (5 to 8 Sept.); also during the operations in the Transvaal 30 Nov. 1900, to Dec. 1901 (Despatches [London Gazette, 8 Feb. 1901; Sir R. H. Buller, 13 Sept. and 9 Nov. 1900; and London Gazette, 10 Sept. 1901]; Queen's Medal with three clasps, and King's Medal with two clasps). He was created a Companion of the Distinguished Service Order [London Gazette, 27 Sept. 1901]: "Norman Zeal Emerson, Lieut., Devonshire Regt. For services during operations in South Africa." He was promoted to Captain 2 Dec. 1903, and retired 4 Nov. 1911, joining the Reserve of Officers. He rejoined the Army for service in the European War in Sept. 1914; was given the temporary rank of Major in Oct. 1914: served in France and Salonika, and was given the command of the 2nd Training Battn. Army Medical Corps in Sept. 1917. He was promoted to Major, Reserve of Officers, 1 Sept. 1915.

FUHR, ROBERT STRICKLAND HANNAY, Lieut., was born 27 Aug. 1871; became L.R.C.S.Edin., L.R.F.P.S.Glas. He entered the Army 27 July, 1898. He served in the South African War, 1899-1901; took part in the Relief of Ladysmith, including action at Colenso, operations 17 to 24 Jan. 1900, and action at Spion Kop; operations 5 to 7 Feb. 1900, and action at Vaal Kranz: operations on Tugela Heights 14 to 27 Feb. 1900, and action at Pieter's Hill; was present during operations in Orange Free State, April and May, 1900; also in the Transvaal, June and July, 1900 (Despatches [London Gazette, 16 April, 1901]; Queen's Medal with six clasps). He was created a Companion of the Distinguished Service Order [London Gazette, 27 Sept. 1901]: "Robert Strickland Hannay Fuhr, Lieut., Royal Army Medical Corps. In recognition of services during the operations in South Africa." He was invested by the King 17 Dec. 1901. He became Captain 27 July, 1901, and Major 28 Jan. 1910. He served in the European War from 1914; was twice mentioned in Despatches, and created a C.M.G. in 1917. Lieut.-Colonel Fuhr married, in 1896, Maud Lilian, daughter of H. H. Bottomley, and they had one son.

HOLT-WILSON, ERIC EDWARD BOKETON, Lieut., was born 26 Aug. 1875, eldest son of the late Rev. Thomas Holt-Wilson, of Redgrave, Suffolk, and Helen Emily, daughter of Sir E. Walter Greene, Bart., M.P.,

Eric E. B. Holt-Wilson.

of Nether Hall, Suffolk. He was educated at Harrow and Woolwich (Cricket Eleven; Football Eleven; Champion Revolver shot), and received his commission 3 Aug. 1895, in the Royal Engineers. He served in the South African War, 1899 to 1902, being present in the advance on Kimberley, including actions at Belmont, Enslin, Modder River and Magersfontein; operations in the Orange Free State, Feb. to May, 1900, including operations at Paardeberg; actions at Poplar Grove, Dreifontein, Houtnek (Thoba Mountain), Vet River and Zand River; operations in the Transvaal, May and June, 1900, including actions near Johannesburg and Pretoria; operations in the Transvaal, east of Pretoria, July to Nov. 1900; operations in the Transvaal, west of Pretoria, including action at Zilikat's Nek; operations in the Transvaal, Orange River Colony and Cape Colony, 1900-2. For his services he was mentioned in Despatches twice [London Gazette, 8 Feb. and 10 Sept. 1901]; received the Queen's Medal with five clasps, and the King's Medal with two clasps, and was created a Companion of the Distinguished Service Order [London Gazette, 27 Sept. 1901]: "Eric Edward Boketon Wilson, Lieut., Royal Engineers. In recognition of services during the operations in South Africa." He was invested by the King 17 Dec. 1901. He was an instructor at the School of Military Engineering from 1903 to 1906, becoming Captain in 1903; Commander of Field and Fortress Engineer Companies, 1907 to 1909, and Cadet Company Commander and Instructor in Military Engineering at the Royal Military Academy, Woolwich, 1909 to 1912, and retired to the Reserve of Officers, Royal Engineers, 21 Dec. 1912, in which he became Major 30 Oct. 1914. He joined the War Office Intelligence Department in 1912, and served with distinction in the European War (1914-19) on Special Intelligence Service in France, Egypt and Salonika, finally becoming Chief of the Police Commission in British Occupied Rhineland in 1919. He was given the Brevets of Major and Lieut.-Colonel; was mentioned in Despatches; created a C.M.G. in 1919, and awarded the Legion of Honour. He is the author of "Field Entrenchments, 1914." Lieut.-Colonel Holt-Wilson married, in 1903, Susannah Mary Shaw, and they have two sons and one daughter.

HUTCHINSON, HUGH MOORE, Lieut., was born 7 June, 1874, son of the late Rev. S. Hutchinson, M.A. He was educated at Cheltenham and Sandhurst; entered the Connaught Rangers as a Second Lieutenant 10 Oct. 1894. He was promoted Lieutenant 19 Oct. 1898, and was employed from Oct. 1898, for thirteen months with the West African Regt., serving in the Protectorate Expedition in Sierra Leone, for which he had the Medal and clasp. He next saw active service in South Africa, 1899 to 1901, taking part in the Relief of Ladysmith, including the action at Colenso; operations of 17 to 24 Jan. 1900, and action at Vaal Kranz; operations on Tugela Heights 14 to 24 Feb., in which he was dangerously wounded (with wounds in five places, 23 Feb.); operations in the Transvaal, east of Pretoria, Aug. to 29 Nov. 1900; operations in the Transvaal 30 Nov. to Dec. 1900; operations in the Orange River Colony, Dec. 1900, to June, 1901; operations in Cape Colony, Dec. 1900, to Feb. 1901, and June to July, 1901 (severely wounded in three places, 14 July). For his services in the South African War, Lieut. Hutchinson was mentioned in Despatches [London Gazette, 10 Sept. 1901]; was awarded the Queen's Medal with six clasps, and was created a Companion of the Distinguished Service Order [London Gazette, 27 Sept. 1901]: " Hugh Moore Hutchinson, Lieut., Connaught Rangers. In recognition of services during the operations in South Africa." The Insignia were presented by the King 29 Oct. 1901. Becoming Captain 12 April, 1902, he was employed until 10 April, 1912, with the Egyptian Army, and besides commanding the 1st Egyptian Battn. on Cholera Duty (4th Class Medjidieh), took part in three campaigns in the Soudan, viz.: Operations against the Nyam Nyam Tribes, in the Bahr-el-Ghazal Province, 1905 (Egyptian Medal with clasp); operations in Southern Kordofan at Talodi, 1906 (clasp to Egyptian Medal), and in Southern Kordofan, 1910 (Soudan Medal with clasp; 3rd Class Osmanieh). During this period he commanded the 12th Soudanese, 1906–12. He was promoted Major 3 June, 1914, and was Officer and Commander of a Company of Gentleman Cadets at Sandhurst from Dec. 1914, to April, 1915, and subsequently served in the European War as Temporary Lieut.-Colonel, and was created a C.M.G. in 1918. He became Temporary Lieut.-Colonel in command of the 3rd Battn. Royal Munster Fusiliers 21 Feb. 1919. Major Hutchinson married, in 1914, Eileen Millicent, youngest daughter of Minton Goode, and they have one son.

FORREST, CHARLES EVELYN, Lieut., was born 21 Aug. 1876, son of the late John Forrest, of Grymsdyke, Princes Risborough, Buckinghamshire. He joined the Oxfordshire Light Infantry, from the Militia, 1 Dec. 1897; was promoted Lieutenant 25 Oct. 1898. Lieut. Forrest served in the South African War, 1899 to 1902, employed with the Mounted Infantry, taking part in operations in the Orange Free State, Feb. to May, 1900, including actions at Vet River (5 and 6 May) and Zand River; operations in the Transvaal in May and June, 1900, including action near Johannesburg; operations in Cape Colony, south of Orange River, 1900; operations in the Transvaal, May to July, 1901, and Oct. 1901, to 31 May, 1902; operations in Orange River Colony, July to Oct. 1901. For his services he was mentioned in Despatches [London Gazette, 10 Sept. 1901]; had the Queen's Medal with three clasps and the King's Medal with two clasps, and was created a Companion of the Distinguished Service Order [London Gazette, 27 Sept. 1901]: " Charles Evelyn Forrest, Lieut., Oxfordshire Light Infantry. In recognition of services during the operations in South Africa." The Insignia were presented by the King 29 Oct. 1901. He received his Captaincy in the Oxfordshire and Buckinghamshire Light Infantry 22 Feb. 1903, and was from Oct. 1910, to July, 1911, a Territorial Adjutant. He was killed in action at Ctesiphon, Mesopotamia, in the evening of 22 Nov. 1915, aged 39. The ate Major Forrest married, in 1910, Ruth Mary, daughter of Lieut.-Colonel the Honourable Edward Holmes à Court, son of the 2nd Lord Heytesbury.

Charles Evelyn Forrest.

FOX, ARTHUR MAXWELL, Lieut., was born 1 July, 1875, son of the late C. D. Fox. He was commissioned 2 Nov. 1895, in the Royal Artillery. He served in South Africa from 1899 to 1902, taking part in the advance on Kimberley, including the actions at Belmont and Modder River; operations in the Orange Free State, Feb. to May, 1900, including operations at Paardeberg (17 to 26 Feb.); operations in the Transvaal, May and June, 1900, including the action near Johannesburg; operations in the Transvaal 30 Nov. 1900, to Jan. 1901; operations in Cape Colony, Feb. to March, 1901; operations in Orange River Colony, April, 1901, to 31 May, 1902. He was mentioned in Despatches [London Gazette, 10 Sept. 1901]; had the Queen's and King's Medals with six clasps, and was created a Companion of the Distinguished Service Order [London Gazette, 27 Sept. 1901]: " Arthur Maxwell Fox, Lieut., Royal Horse and Royal Field Artillery. In recognition of services during the operations in South Africa." He was invested by the King 18 Dec. 1902. He was promoted Captain 16 Nov. 1901, and holding this rank, joined the Reserve of Officers 27 Jan. 1902. Capt. A. M. Fox married, in 1913, Edith, youngest daughter of Colonel H. S. Tompson, of Alderminster Lodge, Bournemouth, and they have one daughter.

WILKINSON, WILLIAM THORNTON, Lieut., was born 10 June, 1877, son of the late Colonel W. H. Wilkinson, of North Deighton Manor, Wetherby, Yorkshire. He was educated at Uppingham and Sandhurst, and was commissioned as Second Lieutenant in the King's Own Scottish Borderers 8 Sept. 1897; was promoted Lieutenant 25 Nov. 1898. He served from 1900 to 1902 in the South African War, taking part in the operations in Orange Free State, Feb. to May, 1900, including operations at Paardeberg (17 to 26 Feb.); actions at Poplar Grove, Karee Siding, Vet River (5 and 6 May) and Zand River; operations in the Transvaal in May and June, 1900, including actions near Johannesburg and Pretoria; operations in the Transvaal, east of Pretoria, 1900; operations in the Transvaal, west of Pretoria, 1900, including action at Zilikat's Nek; operations in the Transvaal and Orange River Colony 30 Nov. 1900, to 31 May, 1902. He was mentioned in Despatches [London Gazette, 10 Sept. 1901]; had the Queen's Medal with three clasps and the King's Medal with two clasps, and was created a Companion of the Distinguished Service Order [London Gazette, 27 Sept. 1901]: " William Thornton Wilkinson, Lieut., King's Own Scottish Borderers. In recognition of services during the operations in South Africa." The Insignia were presented by the King 24 Oct. 1902. He was promoted Captain 4 Dec. 1903, and was employed with the West African Frontier Force 23 Feb. 1910, to 29 June, 1911, and served as a Territorial Adjutant from 10 March, 1913. He again saw active service in the European War; becoming Major 1 Sept. 1915, he was in command of a Territorial Battn. of the East Yorkshire Regt. from Sept. 1915, to Oct. 1918. He was made Brevet Lieut.-Colonel 1 Jan. 1918, and was awarded a Bar to the D.S.O. [London Gazette, 26 July, 1918]: " William Thornton Wilkinson, Major and Brevet Lieut.-Colonel, King's Own Scottish Borderers. Under difficult circumstances he extricated his battalion in good order, holding two rearguard positions to cover the withdrawal. On another occasion, with two battalions, he held on to some high ground from 9 a.m. to 5 p.m., although his right flank was in the air. Exposed to heavy machine-gun fire, he went up and down the line encouraging his men, being subsequently wounded in the head." From Oct. 1918, he was in command of a battalion of the King's Own Scottish Borderers. He was wounded and mentioned in Despatches. He married, in 1918, Evelyn Sybil, youngest daughter of the Rev. H. and Mrs. Ward, of The Vicarage, Amotherby, Malton.

STANSFELD, THOMAS WOLRICHE, Lieut., was born 30 June, 1877, youngest son of T. W. Stansfeld, Westwood Grove, Leeds. He was educated at Winchester, and joined Alexandra, Princess of Wales's Own Yorkshire Regt., from the Militia, 24 March, 1897; was promoted Lieut. 15 Dec. 1898. He saw active service in South Africa, employed with the Mounted Infantry, 1899 to 1902, being present at the Relief of Kimberley; operations in the Orange Free State, Feb. to May, 1900, including operations at Paardeberg (17 to 26 Feb.), and actions at Poplar Grove, Dreifontein, Vet River (5 and 6 May) and Zand River; operations in the Transvaal in May and June, 1900, including actions near Johannesburg, Pretoria and Diamond Hill (11 and 12 June); operations in the Transvaal, east of Pretoria, July to 29 Nov. 1900, including actions at Belfast (26 and 27 Aug.); operations in Cape Colony, and south of Orange River, 1899–1900, including actions at Colesberg (1 Jan. to 12 Feb.); operations in the Transvaal 30 Nov. 1900, to April, 1902. He was mentioned in Despatches [London Gazette, 10 Sept. 1901]; received the Queen's Medal with six clasps, the King's Medal with two clasps, and was created a Companion of the Distinguished Service Order [London Gazette, 27 Sept. 1901]: " Thomas Wolriche Stansfeld, Lieut., West Yorkshire Regt. In recognition of services during the operations in South Africa." The Insignia were presented by the King 2 June, 1902. He was transferred to the Royal Warwickshire Regt., becoming Captain 19 Feb. 1902, and served as an Adjutant of Mounted Infantry in South Africa from June, 1906, to June, 1909, rejoining the Yorkshire Regt. 8 Jan. 1908, and subsequently serving as a Special Reserve Adjutant, Oct. 1910, for three years. He was given his Majority 30 Oct. 1914. He saw active service in the European War, commanding battalions of the Yorkshire Regt. until June, 1916. He became Brevet Lieut.-Colonel 3 June, 1916, and in the following Oct. Temporary Colonel, retaining this position until appointed to the command of the 178th Infantry Brigade 6 April, 1917. For his services Brigadier-General Stansfeld was mentioned in Despatches; was made a C.M.G. in 1918, and was awarded the Legion of Honour and the French Croix de Guerre, with (3 June, 1919) the Brevet of Colonel. He has the 1914 Star. He married, in 1903, Ethel, daughter of the late William Hebden, of Scarborough, and they have two sons.

FRANCIS, SIDNEY GOODALL, Lieut., was born 24 Dec. 1874, son of the late Charles Francis, of Melbourne. He was commissioned Second Lieutenant (from the Local Military Forces of Victoria) in the West Yorkshire Regt. 28 Dec. 1895, and became Lieutenant 4 Jan. 1899. He served in the South African War from 1899 to 1902, taking part in operations in Natal, 1899; the Relief of Ladysmith, including action at Colenso, operations of 17 to 24 Jan. 1900, and action at Spion Kop; operations of 5 and 7 Feb. 1900, and action at Vaal Kranz; operations on Tugela Heights (14 to 27 Feb. 1900), and action at Pieter's Hill; operations in Natal, March to June, 1900, including action at Laing's Nek (6 and 9 June); operations in the Transvaal, east and west of Pretoria, July to 29 Nov. 1900; operations in the Transvaal 30 Nov. 1900, to 31 May, 1902. He was mentioned in Despatches [London Gazette, 8 Feb. and 10 Sept. 1901]; received the Queen's Medal with five clasps, the King's Medal with two clasps, and was created a Companion of the Distinguished Service Order [London Gazette, 27 Sept. 1901]: " Sidney Goodall Francis, Lieut., West Yorkshire Regt. In recognition of services during the operations in South Africa." The Insignia, Warrant and Statutes were sent to the G.O.C., Natal, 3 Feb. 1903; presented by the O.C., 4th Mounted Infantry, 29 March, 1903, at Middelburg. He became Captain 18 April, 1904, and was again on active service on the North-West Frontier of India in 1908, serving in the Mohmand Country, for which he had the Medal and clasp. He served in the European War from 1914 to 1918, attaining his Majority 1 Sept. 1915, and was employed with the 16th Division as G.S.O.3, Oct. 1915, to Feb. 1916; was Temporary Lieut.-Colonel Commanding 7th Battn. Royal Irish Rifles, Feb. 1916, to Oct. 1917, then becoming C.O. of the 111th Infantry Brigade. He was promoted Brevet Lieut.-Colonel 1 Jan. 1917, and was awarded a Bar to the Distinguished Service Order. He was made Brevet Colonel 1 Jan. 1919, and was mentioned in Despatches. Colonel Francis married, in 1916, Catherine Gwendoline, youngest daughter of W. B. Lowry, Leeon-the-Solent, and they have one son.

VILLIERS, EVELYN FOUNTAINE, Lieut., was born 4 May, 1875, youngest son of the late Rev. Charles Villiers, Rector of Croft, Yorkshire. He entered the Army as a Second Lieutenant in the Royal Sussex Regt. 7 Dec. 1895, being promoted Lieutenant 7 Jan. 1899. He served, 1900 to 1901, in the South African War; from 30 Sept. 1900, to 17 July, 1901, as Brigade Signalling Officer, and was present in operations in the Orange Free State, Feb. to May, 1900, including actions at Houtnek (Thoba Mountain), Vet River (5 and 6 May) and Zand River; operations in the Transvaal, May and June, 1900, including actions near Johannesburg, Pretoria and Diamond Hill (11 and 12 June); operations in Orange River Colony, May to 29 Nov. 1900, including actions at Wittebergen (1 to 29 July); operations in the Transvaal, Orange River Colony and Cape Colony 30 Nov. 1900, to May, 1901. For his services in the South African War he was mentioned in Despatches [London Gazette, 10 Sept. 1901];

received the Queen's Medal with four clasps, and was created a Companion of the Distinguished Service Order [London Gazette, 27 Sept. 1901]: "Evelyn Fountaine Villiers, Lieut., Royal Sussex Regt. In recognition of services during the operations in South Africa." The Insignia were presented by the King 2 June, 1902. He reached the rank of Captain 3 Sept. 1904, and from Feb. 1909, for five years was Adjutant of the Indian Volunteers. He saw active service in the European War from 1914 to 1916, receiving promotion to Major 1 Sept. 1915, and subsequently serving as Temporary Lieut.-Colonel. He was wounded; was five times mentioned in Despatches, and was created a C.M.G. in 1916. He became Commanding Officer of the 3rd Battn. Royal Sussex Regt. 9 May, 1919. Lieut.-Colonel Villiers married, in 1901, Muriel, third daughter of Colonel and Mrs. Wisden, of The Warren, Broadwater, near Worthing, and they have one son and three daughters.

KENSINGTON (HUGH EDWARDES), LORD, Lieut., was born 3 Sept. 1873, son of the 4th Baron and Grace, daughter of the late Robert Johnstone Douglas. He succeeded his brother in the title in 1900, as 6th Baron Kensington (created 1776), Baron Kensington (U.K.) (created 1886). He entered the Army as a Second Lieutenant in the 15th Hussars, and afterwards served in the South African War from 1899 to 1901, as A.D.C. to Lieut.-General Sir H. M. L. Rundle, for which he was mentioned in Despatches [London Gazette, 10 Sept. 1901]; had the Queen's Medal with two clasps, and was created a Companion of the Distinguished Service Order [London Gazette, 27 Sept. 1901]: "Hugh, Lord Kensington, Lieut., 15th Hussars. In recognition of services during the operations in South Africa." The Insignia were presented by the King 18 Feb. 1903. He became Lieut.-Colonel, Welsh Horse, in 1914. He again saw active service in the European War, taking part in the Dardanelles operations in 1915 (Despatches), in the Sinai and Jerusalem Campaigns, 1916 and 1917, and in 1918 with the British Expeditionary Force. He was again mentioned in Despatches, and created a C.M.G. in 1918. Lord Kensington owns property in Pembrokeshire. He married, in 1903, Mabel Carlisle, daughter of George Pilkington, of Stoneleigh, Woolton. His heir is the Honourable William Edwardes, and he has three other sons.

Lord Kensington.

WATSON, WILLIAM ERNEST, Lieut., was born 3 Sept. 1876, son of William Watson, of Bromborough, Cheshire. He entered the 6th Dragoon Guards 15 May, 1897, becoming Lieutenant 25 Jan 1899. He served in the South African War from 1899 to 1902, being from Jan. 1901, to May, 1902, Adjutant of the 1st Imperial Light Horse, and was present at the Relief of Kimberley; operations in the Orange Free State, Feb. to May, 1900, including operations at Paardeberg (17 to 26 Feb.); actions at Poplar Grove, Dreifontein, Karee Siding and Zand River; operations in the Transvaal in May and June, 1900, including actions near Johannesburg, Pretoria and Diamond Hill (11 and 12 June); operations in the Transvaal, east of Pretoria, July to 29 Nov. 1900, including actions at Reit Vlei and Belfast (26 and 27 Aug.); operations in Cape Colony, south of Orange River, 1899 to 1900, including the actions at Colesberg (1 Jan. to 12 Feb.). He was mentioned in Despatches [London Gazette, 10 Sept. 1901]; had the Queen's and King's Medals with eight clasps, and was created a Companion of the Distinguished Service Order [London Gazette, 27 Sept. 1901]: "William Ernest Watson, Lieut., 6th Dragoon Guards. In recognition of services during the operations in South Africa." The Insignia were presented by the King 18 Feb. 1903. He was promoted Captain 7 Dec. 1901, and was Adjutant of the 6th Dragoon Guards from 2 July, 1907, to 22 April, 1910; was promoted Major 23 April, 1910. He married, in 1905, Daisy, daughter of the Rev. T. Stanley Heanor, and left two daughters.

MACGREGOR, PHILIP ARTHUR, Lieut., was born 26 Feb. 1877. He entered the Army as Second Lieutenant, Coldstream Guards, 8 Sept. 1897, and was promoted Lieutenant 1 Feb. 1899. He served in the South African War from 1899–1900, taking part in the advance on Kimberley, including actions at Belmont, Enslin, Modder River and Magersfontein; during operations in the Orange Free State, Feb. to May, 1900, including actions at Poplar Grove, Dreifontein, Vet River (5 and 6 May) and Zand River; was present during the operations in the Transvaal in May and June, 1900, including actions near Johannesburg, Pretoria and Diamond Hill (11 and 12 June); during operations in the Transvaal, east of Pretoria, July to 29 Nov. 1900, including operations at Belfast (26 and 27 Aug.), and operations in the Orange River Colony, Nov. 1900. He was mentioned in Despatches [London Gazette, 10 Sept. 1901]; received the Queen's Medal with six clasps, and was created a Companion of the Distinguished Service Order [London Gazette, 27 Sept. 1901]: "Philip Arthur Macgregor, Lieut., Coldstream Guards. In recognition of services during operations in South Africa." The Insignia were presented by the King 18 Dec. 1902. He served during operations in West Africa, 1901 (Northern Nigeria), against the forces of Bida, taking part in the operations against the Emir of Gola, as Intelligence Officer. He was mentioned in Despatches [London Gazette, 18 April, 1902], and received Medal with clasp. He was promoted Captain 11 Nov. 1905, and became Major 29 Nov. 1913. He served during the European War, 1914 to 1919, and was given the Brevet of Lieut.-Colonel 1 Jan. 1916. He was twice mentioned in Despatches, and retired from the Army 4 April, 1919. Lieut.-Colonel Macgregor married, in 1904, Kathleen, daughter of Major-General Alexander C. U. Stewart, 2nd Life Guards.

NICHOLSON, OCTAVIUS HENRY LOTHIAN, Lieut., was born 23 July, 1877, sixth son of the late General Sir Lothian Nicholson, K.C.B. He was educated at St. Paul's School, and Sandhurst; passed into the Army 8 Sept. 1897, as Second Lieutenant, West Yorkshire Regt., and was promoted Lieutenant 15 Feb. 1899. He served during the South African War, 1899–1902, taking part in the operations in Natal, 1899; was present at the Relief of Ladysmith, including action at Colenso; during operations of 17 to 24 Jan. 1900, and action at Spion Kop; operations of 5 to 7 Feb. 1900, and action at Vaal Kranz; during operations on Tugela Heights 14 to 27 Feb. 1900, and action at Pieter's Hill; operations in Natal, March to April, 1900. He served as Adjutant, 2nd Battn. West Yorkshire Regt., from 1 Aug. 1901, to 31 May, 1902; operations in the Transvaal, Feb. 1901, to 31 May, 1902. He was mentioned in Despatches [London Gazette, 26 Jan. 1900, 8 Feb. and 10 Sept. 1901]; received the Queen's Medal with three clasps, the King's Medal with two clasps, and was created a Companion of the Distinguished Service Order [London Gazette, 27 Sept. 1901]: "Octavius Henry Lothian Nicholson, Lieut., West Yorkshire Regt. In recognition of services during the operations in South Africa." The Insignia were presented by the King 13 Dec. 1902. He was promoted Captain 17 Aug. 1904; was A.D.C. to G.O., Commanding-in-Chief, Bermuda, from 31 Oct. 1908, to 15 Dec. 1911. He served during the European War as D.A.Q.M.G. 5 Aug. 1914; was Brigade-Major, 3rd Infantry Brigade, B.E.F., 26 Nov. 1914, to 17 March, 1915; Brigade Major, 51st Infantry Brigade, New Armies, 10 June, 1915. He was given the Brevet of Major 18 Feb. 1915, and became Major 1 Sept. 1915. He was General Staff Officer, 2nd Grade, 8th Division, B.E.F., Oct. 1915, to 11 Jan. 1916; G.S.O. 2, 1st Army, 1916–17; General Staff Officer, 1st Grade, 5th Division, B.E.F., British Armies in France, 1917–1919; General Staff Officer, 1st Grade, War Office (Temporary), 27 March, 1919. He received the Brevet of Lieutenant-Colonel 3 June, 1917. He was mentioned eight times in Despatches, and created a C.M.G. in 1918; Chevalier of the Legion of Honour, and was awarded the Croix de Guerre avec Palme. Lieut.-Colonel Nicholson married, in 1911, Eileen May Montague, daughter of Major-General Montague Browne, of St. John's Point, Kellough, County Down, and they have one son and one daughter.

Octavius H. L. Nicholson.

HARDCASTLE, RICHARD NEWMAN, Lieut., was born 5 Nov. 1876. He entered the Army, from the Militia, 1 Dec. 1897, as Second Lieutenant, Manchester Regt., and was promoted Lieutenant 22 Feb. 1899. He served during the South African War, 1899–1902; during operations in Natal, 1899, including actions at Elandslaagte and Lombard's Kop, taking part in the Defence of Ladysmith, including action of the 6th Jan. 1900; during operations in Natal, March to June, 1900, and was present during operations in the Transvaal, east of Pretoria, July, 1900, and operations in 1901. He was mentioned in Despatches [London Gazette, 10 Sept. 1901]; received the Queen's Medal with three clasps, the King's Medal with two clasps, and was created a Companion of the Distinguished Service Order [London Gazette, 27 Sept. 1901]: "Richard Newman Hardcastle, Lieut., The Manchester Regt. In recognition of services during the operations in South Africa." The Insignia were presented by the King 28 Nov. 1902. He was promoted Captain 9 Jan. 1901. He served in the European War; was promoted Major 27 April, 1915; was Temporary Lieut.-Colonel from 18 May, 1916, to Jan. 1917. He was given the Brevet of Lieut.-Colonel 3 June, 1916, and was Brigade-Commander, 8th Infantry Brigade, Indian Expeditionary Force "D," 27 July to 2 Sept. 1916. He was wounded.

RILEY, RUPERT FARQUHAR, Lieut., was born 11 Oct. 1873. He entered the Army 9 Dec. 1896, as Second Lieutenant, Yorkshire Light Infantry. He was present during the operations on the North-West Frontier of India, 1897 to 1898, with the Tirah Expeditionary Force (Medal with clasp). He served during the South African War, 1899–1902; was employed with the Mounted Infantry, taking part in the advance on Kimberley, including actions at Belmont, Enslin, Modder River and Magersfontein; taking part during operations in the Orange Free State, Feb. to May, 1900, including actions at Dreifontein and Houtnek (Thoba Mountain), Vet River and Zand River; was present during operations in the Transvaal in May and June, 1900, including actions near Johannesburg, Pretoria and Diamond Hill (11 and 12 June); during operations in the Transvaal, east of Pretoria, July to 29 Nov. 1900; during operations in the Transvaal, west of Pretoria, including actions at Zilikat's Nek and Elands River (4 to 16 Aug.). He was present during operations in the Transvaal 30 Nov. 1900, to 31 May, 1902. He was mentioned in Despatches [London Gazette, 10 Sept. 1901]; received both S.A. Medals with seven clasps, and was created a Companion of the Distinguished Service Order [London Gazette, 27 Sept. 1901]: "Rupert Farquhar Riley, Lieut., Yorkshire Light Infantry. In recognition of services during the operations in South Africa." The Insignia were presented by the King 18 Dec. 1902. He was promoted Captain 15 April, 1901, and was Brigade Major, Nottinghamshire and Derbyshire Infantry Brigade, Northern Command, 1 Dec. 1910, to 4 July, 1911; Brigade Major, Essex Infantry Brigade, Eastern Command, 5 July, 1911, to 2 Jan. 1912, and Staff Captain, War Office, 3 Jan. 1912, to 17 March, 1915. He served during the European War; was promoted Major 1 Oct. 1914, and received the Brevet of Lieut.-Colonel 3 June, 1916, and was Deputy Assistant, War Office (Temp.), 18 March to 20 July, 1915; Assistant Director, War Office (Temp.), 21 July, 1915, to 15 April, 1917; was A.A.G.M., War Office, 16 April, 1917, to 11 March, 1918; A.A. and Q.M.G., Supreme War Council, Versailles, 12 March to 4

May, 1918, and Assistant Military Secretary, War Office (Temp.), 1 June, 1918. He was created a C.M.G. in 1917. Lieut.-Colonel Riley married, in 1903, Violet Louise, youngest daughter of the late Ernest St. G. Cobbold.

RYAN, GEORGE JULIAN, Lieut., was born 18 Sept. 1878, at Tenby, South Wales, son of the late Colonel George Ryan, R.A.M.C., of Ashby Cottage, Ryde, Isle of Wight, and of Mrs. Louisa C. Ryan. He was educated

George Julian Ryan.

at Elizabeth College, Guernsey, and at the United Service College, Westward Ho! He was gazetted to the 2nd Battn. The Royal Munster Fusiliers, as Second Lieutenant, 8 Sept. 1897, and became Lieutenant 11 March, 1899. He served during the South African War, 1899–1902, and was employed with the Mounted Infantry in the advance on Kimberley, including the actions at Belmont and Modder River; the operations in the Transvaal, June to 29 Nov. 1900; operations in Cape Colony; taking part in the operations in the Transvaal 30 Nov. 1900, to March, 1901; operations in Orange River Colony, March to June, 1901. He was mentioned in Despatches [London Gazette, 10 Sept. 1901]; received the Queen's Medal with five clasps, and was created a Companion of the Distinguished Service Order [London Gazette, 27 Sept. 1901]: "George Julian Ryan, Lieut., Royal Munster Fusiliers. In recognition of services during the operations in South Africa." The Insignia were presented by the King 24 Nov. 1902. He was promoted Captain 9 June, 1906. He was employed with the Egyptian Army 6 Feb. 1903, to 15 Feb. 1910. He served in the Soudan, 1905; during operations against the Nyam Nyam Tribes in the Bahr-el-Ghazal Province. He was mentioned in Despatches [London Gazette, 18 May, 1906], and received the Egyptian Medal with clasp. He took part in the operations in the Soudan, 1906, at Talodi, Southern Kordofan, and received clasp to Egyptian Medal. He took part during the operations in the Soudan, 1908, in the Blue Nile Province, with the force sent to punish the murderers of the Deputy Inspector and Police Commandant, who had been treacherously slain at Kam'lin (he was wounded). He received the Brevet of Major 7 Nov. 1908, and the Order of the Medjidie. He served during the European War in France and Flanders from 22 Aug. 1914, and was promoted Temporary Lieut.-Colonel 21 Jan. 1915. He was killed in action at Givenchy on 23 Jan. 1915, whilst in temporary command of the battalion (2nd Munsters), as he was returning across the danger-zone after inspecting his men. Lieut.-Colonel Ryan was mentioned in Field-Marshal Sir John (now Lord) French's Despatch of 22 June, 1915, and his mother received a telegram of sympathy from the King on the occasion of his death, and also from the late Lord Kitchener, saying what a loss he was to his country and to the army.

GREIG, RONALD HENRY, Lieut., was the eldest son of Lieut.-Colonel B. R. Greig, late Royal Artillery, and grandson of the late Sir T. O. Sibbald Scott. He was born on 4 April, 1876, and had his first commission 14 March, 1896, in the Royal Engineers, being promoted Lieutenant 14 March, 1899. He served in the South African War from 1899 to 1902, and was severely wounded. He was present in the advance on Kimberley, and actions at Belmont, Enslin and Modder River, and also took part in the operations in the Orange Free State; operations in the Transvaal, east of Pretoria, July to 29 Nov. 1900; operations in Orange River Colony, June and July, 1900; operations in Cape Colony, south of Orange River, 1899; operations in the Transvaal 30 Nov. 1900, to Sept. 1901, and operations in Orange River Colony, Sept. 1901, to 31 May, 1902. He was mentioned in Despatches [London Gazette, 10 Sept. 1901]; received the Queen's Medal with four clasps, the King's Medal with two clasps, and was created a Companion of the Distinguished Service Order [London Gazette, 27 Sept. 1901]: "Ronald Henry Greig, Lieut., Royal Engineers. In recognition of services during the operations in South Africa." The Insignia were presented by the King 24 Oct. 1902. He was promoted Captain 24 March, 1905; served as an Adjutant in the Territorial Force 28 Aug. 1909, to 17 May, 1912, and became Adjutant (Railway Companies and Depot), Royal Engineers, 31 Oct. 1913. He served in the Great War, in command of a Field Company, and was killed while superintending advanced trench work on the night of 27 Aug. 1914 (aged 40). Major Greig married Mary Hope, daughter of E. H. Clutterbuck, of Hardenhuish Park, Wiltshire, and left a son and two daughters. One obituary notice says that he was "a distinguished Engineer, who, in addition to service in the present war, was present right through the campaign in South Africa, 1899–1902." Another notice says that he had "a fine record of service in this war and in South Africa." The "Morning Post" notice of him reads as follows: "Major Ronald Henry Greig, D.S.O., Royal Engineers, in command of a Field Company (killed while superintending advanced trench work on the night of August 27), was born in 1876, and was son of Lieut.-Colonel B. R. Greig and Mrs. Greig, daughter of the late Sir J. D. Sibbald Scott. Major Greig married, in 1909, Mary Hope, daughter of Edmund H. Clutterbuck, of Hardenhuish Park, Wilts, and leaves one son and two daughters. Major Greig passed out of Woolwich into the Royal Engineers in March, 1896, and had promotion in March, 1899; he was Captain in 1905, and had his majority in October, 1914. He had served with distinction in the present war. In the South African War (1899–1902) he was severely wounded. He took part in the advance on Kimberley, including the actions at Belmont, Enslin and Modder River. Afterwards he served in many operations in the various Colonies. For these services he was mentioned in Despatches, made a Companion of the Distinguished Service Order, and received the Queen's and the King's Medals with six clasps."

CUNINGHAME, SIR THOMAS ANDREW ALEXANDER MONTGOMERY, Lieut., was born 30 March, 1877, elder son of Major Sir William James Montgomery Cuninghame, V.C. (late Rifle Brigade), and Elizabeth,

Sir Thomas Cuninghame.

youngest daughter of Edward Bouchier Hartopp, Esq., of Dalby Hall, near Melton Mowbray. He was educated at Eton and the Royal Military College, Sandhurst; was commissioned in the Rifle Brigade 17 Feb. 1897, and became Lieutenant 15 March, 1899. He served in South Africa, 1899–1902, as Brigade Signalling Officer 18 April to 31 July, 1900, and as Staff Captain (Intelligence) 1 Aug. 1900, to 5 Nov. 1903; at the Relief of Ladysmith, including action at Colenso; operations of 17 to 24 Jan. 1900; operations of 5 to 7 Feb. 1900, and action at Vaal Kranz (severely wounded); took part in the operations in Natal, March to June, 1900, including action at Laing's Nek (6 to 9 June); in the Transvaal, east of Pretoria, July to 29 Nov. 1900; afterwards on Staff. He was mentioned in Despatches [London Gazette, 8 Feb. and 10 Sept. 1901]; received the Queen's Medal with five clasps, the King's Medal with two clasps, and was created a Companion of the Distinguished Service Order [London Gazette, 27 Sept. 1901]: "Sir Thomas Andrew Alexander Montgomery Cuninghame, Lieut., Rifle Brigade. In recognition of services during the operations in South Africa." The Insignia, Warrant and Statutes were sent to the G.O.C. Transvaal, 3 Feb. 1903, and presented by the G.O.C. at Pretoria 25 March, 1903. He was promoted to Captain 18 Jan. 1902; was Staff Captain, 5th Division, Irish Command, 2 April, 1908, to 15 Jan. 1909; D.A.Q.M.G., 5th Division, Irish Command, 16 Jan. 1909, to 1 April, 1912; Military Attaché (G.S.O.), Vienna and Cettinje, 9 Aug. 1912, to 6 Sept. 1914. He served in the European War from 1914; was G.S.O.2, attached French Army, 7 Sept. to 7 Dec. 1914; G.S.O.2, 1st Army Corps, B.E.F., 8 Dec. 1914, to 17 Feb. 1915; Temp. Lieut.-Colonel and Military Attaché, Athens (temporary), 21 Feb. 1915, to 25 March, 1916; G.S.O.1, 68th Division, Home Forces, 17 May, 1916, to 22 Oct. 1917; G.S.O.1, School of Instruction, British Armies in France, 16 Oct. 1918; G.S.O.1, British Military Representative in Austria, 5 Dec. 1918. He was given the Brevet of Lieut.-Colonel 1 Jan. 1919. He succeeded his father in 1897, and is the 10th Baronet (created 1872) of Corsehill, Ayrshire, and Kirktonholm, in Lanarkshire. Sir Thomas Cuninghame married, in 1904, Alice Frances Denison, eldest daughter of Sir G. William Des Voeux, G.C.M.G., and granddaughter of the late Sir J. Pender, and they have one son, Alexander William Henry James, born 28 Oct. 1905, and one daughter.

WATSON, HAROLD FARNELL, Lieut., was born 25 July, 1876, son of W. Farnell Watson. He entered the Army in 1897, and saw service with the Tirah Expeditionary Force, 1897 to 1898, for which he had the

Harold Farnell Watson.

Medal and clasp; and in the South African War, 1899 to 1902, being employed as Adjutant of the 9th Mounted Infantry and afterwards of the 22nd Mounted Infantry. He took part in operations in Cape Colony, 1899 to 1900; operations in the Orange Free State, March to May, 1900; operations in Orange River Colony, May to Sept. 1900, and May, 1901, to 31 May, 1902. He was mentioned in Despatches [London Gazette, 10 Sept. 1901]; received the Queen's Medal with three clasps, the King's Medal with two clasps, and was created a Companion of the Distinguished Service Order [London Gazette, 27 Sept. 1901]: "Harold Farnell Watson, Lieut., Derbyshire Regt. In recognition of services during the operations in South Africa." He was promoted Captain in the Lancashire Fusiliers in 1902, and resigned his commission in 1903, the same year joining the 4th Battn. Lancashire Fusiliers, as Captain, in which he became Major in 1910. He became Lieut.-Colonel commanding the 11th Battn. Sherwood Foresters, June, 1915; was promoted Major (from the Special Reserve) 25 Aug. 1917, in the Regular Army, and commanded the 6th Royal Inniskilling Fusiliers from Jan. to Dec. 1918, then becoming Lieut.-Colonel to command the 53rd Battn. Liverpool Regt. Major Farnell married, in 1901, Georgina Barbara, daughter of George Allan.

ALLCARD, HERBERT, Lieut., was born 9 April, 1876, son of E. J. Allcard, Esq., of Holmsdale, Teddington. He became a Second Lieutenant in the Royal Artillery 21 March, 1896; Lieutenant 1 March, 1899, and Captain 22 Dec. 1901. He saw active service in the South African War from 1899 to 1902, being present in operations in Orange Free State, Feb. to May, 1900; operations in Transvaal, east of Pretoria, Oct. 1900; operations in Orange River Colony, May to 29 Nov. 1900, including actions at Biddulphsberg, Wittebergen (1 to 29 July) and Caledon River (27 to 29 Nov.); operations in Cape Colony, south of Orange River, 1899 to 1900; operations in Orange River Colony 30 Nov. 1900, to Feb. 1901, and March, 1901, to March, 1902; operations in Cape Colony, Dec. 1900, and Feb. 1901, to 31 May, 1902. He was mentioned in Despatches [London Gazette, 10 Sept. 1901]; received the Queen's Medal with three clasps, the King's Medal with two clasps, and was created a Companion of the Distinguished Service Order [London Gazette, 27 Sept. 1901]: "Herbert Allcard, Lieut.,

Royal Horse and Royal Field Artillery. In recognition of services during the operations in South Africa." He was invested by the King 18 Dec. 1902. He was promoted Major 29 July, 1912. He was Temporary Lieut.-Colonel, Royal Artillery, 23 Jan. to 20 Sept. 1916, when promoted to substantive rank. Lieut.-Colonel Alleard married, in 1905, Althea Beryl Molyneux, only daughter of the late H. Molyneux Carter, of Poulton Manor, near Bristol.

SMITH, LEONARD KIRKE, Lieut., was born 24 Jan. 1877, at Cliffe House, near Sheffield, son of Francis Patrick Smith, of Barnes Hall, near Sheffield, and Margaret Scott Smith, his wife (deceased). He was educated at Charterhouse, and joined the Army 20 Feb. 1897, as a Second Lieutenant in the Royal Scots, becoming Lieutenant 22 April, 1899. He served in South Africa with the Mounted Infantry, 1899 to 1902, and was present at the Relief of Kimberley; operations in the Orange Free State, Feb. to May, 1900, including operations at Paardeberg (17 to 26 Feb.); actions at Poplar Grove and Dreifontein; operations in Cape Colony, south of Orange River, 1899–1900, including actions at Colesberg (1 Jan. to 12, Feb.); operations in the Transvaal and Orange River Colony, April, 1901, to 31 May, 1902. He was mentioned in Despatches [London Gazette, 4 May, 1900, and 10 Sept. 1901]; received the Queen's Medal with four clasps, the King's Medal with two clasps, and was created a Companion of the Distinguished Service Order [London Gazette, 27 Sept. 1901]: "Leonard Kirke Smith, Lieut., The Royal Scots. In recognition of services during the operations in South Africa." The Insignia were sent to the Commander-in-Chief in India, and presented by the General Officer Commanding at Nagpore District at Full Parade, 4 April, 1903. He became Captain 9 May, 1903, and served as Adjutant, Royal Scots, 24 Nov. 1903, to 4 April, 1906, then being employed as Adjutant of Militia and of Special Reserve until 1 Jan. 1911. He served with the Egyptian Army from 23 March, 1911, onwards. Capt. Smith was, for a period in 1915, Temporary Major until promoted to substantive rank 1 Sept. 1915, and was Temporary Lieut.-Colonel from Sept. 1916, to June 1918. He was given the Brevet of Lieut.-Colonel 3 June, 1918. He has the 3rd Class Order of the Nile. He married, on 14 Aug. 1914, at Holy Trinity, Brompton, Vera, daughter of the late Capt. C. H. Hicks, Lancashire Fusiliers, and Mrs. Hicks, and granddaughter of the late Hicks Pasha, and they have two sons, Peter McKenzie, born 4 Aug. 1916, and Michael McKenzie, born 27 July, 1917.

ABADIE, EUSTACE HENRY EGREMONT, Lieut., was born 24 Jan. 1877, elder surviving son of the late Major-General Henry Richard Abadie, C.B., 9th Lancers, Lieut.-Governor of Jersey, 1900–4 (whose death occurred after that of his son), and of his first wife Kate (who died in 1883), daughter of G Sandeman. Eustace Abadie joined the 9th Lancers 11 Aug. 1897, becoming Lieutenant 3 May, 1899. He served with much distinction in the South African War, 1899–1902, and was present at the advance on Kimberley, including the actions at Belmont, Enslin and Magersfontein; Relief of Kimberley; took part in the operations in the Orange Free State, Feb. to May, 1900, including operations at Paardeberg (17 to 26 Feb.); actions at Poplar Grove, Dreifontein, Karee Siding, Houtnek (Thoba Mountain), Vet River (5 and 6 May) and Zand River; was present during the operations in the Transvaal in May and June, 1900, including actions near Johannesburg, Pretoria and Diamond Hill (11 and 12 June), again in the Transvaal, east of Pretoria, July to 29 Nov. 1900, including actions at Reit Vlei and Belfast; in the Transvaal, west of Pretoria, July to 29 Nov. 1900; operations in Cape Colony and the Transvaal 30 Nov. 1900, to 31 May, 1902. He was mentioned in Despatches [London Gazette, 10 Sept. 1901]; received the Queen's Medal with eight clasps, the King's Medal with two clasps, and was created a Companion of the Distinguished Service Order [London Gazette, 27 Sept. 1901]: "Eustace Henry Egremont Abadie, Lieut., 9th Lancers. In recognition of services during the operations in South Africa. The Insignia, Warrant, etc., were sent to the Commander-in-Chief in India, and presented by General Sir Bindon Blood at Full Garrison Parade at Rawal Pindi 8 April, 1903. It is said that no other officer received more than eight clasps to the Queen's Medal in the South African Campaign. He was promoted to Captain 15 March, 1904; was a Staff College Graduate; was Adjutant of his regiment from Feb. 1906, to Aug. 1907, and was promoted to Major in March, 1912. The names of members of this distinguished family appear first in most books of reference. The first name in "The Last Post," a book containing biographies of officers who lost their lives in the South African War, was that of a cavalry officer named Abadie, namely, Lieut. H. B. Abadie. D.S.O., Major E. H. E. Abadie's eldest brother. Another brother, Capt. G. H. F. Abadie, late 16th Lancers, died of fever in Feb. 1904, at Kam, West Africa, where he was serving as Resident, after having taken part in the Kam Sokoto Campaign, and been created a C.M.G. Major-General Abadie, their father, also had a most distinguished military career of 46 years, and, as has been said, survived the last of these three gallant sons only for a short time. For Major Eustace Abadie's services in the Great War he was mentioned in Sir John French's Despatch of 14 Jan. 1915. He was at first officially reported to be a prisoner of war; but as no official confirmation of his death was received, and as nothing was heard of or from him since, it was assumed that he had lost his life in action at Messines in Oct. 1914.

FISHER, HAROLD, Lieut., was born 3 March, 1877, at Fulham, S.W., son of the Rev. Frederic Horatio Fisher, M.A., Hon. Canon of St. Albans, of Church Croft, Hemel Hempstead, and Agnes Jeune, daughter of John Jackson, Bishop of London. He was educated at Haileybury, and entered the Manchester Regt., from the Suffolk Artillery Militia, 4 May, 1898, becoming Lieutenant 6 May, 1899. He served in the South African War, 1899–1902, and took part in the operations in Natal, 1899, including actions at Elandslaagte and Lombard's Kop; Defence of Ladysmith (severely wounded), including action of 6 Jan. 1900; in Natal, March to June, 1900; in the Transvaal, east of Pretoria, July to 29 Nov. 1900, including action at Belfast (26 and 27 Aug.); again in the Transvaal, 1901–2. He was mentioned in Despatches [London Gazette, 8 Feb. 1902 (Sir G. S. White, 2 Dec. 1899, and 23 March, 1900), and London Gazette, 10 Sept. 1901]; received the Queen's Medal with three clasps, the King's Medal with two clasps, and was created a Companion of the Distinguished Service Order 29 Nov. 1900 [London Gazette, 27 Sept. 1901]: "Harold Fisher, Lieut., Manchester Regt. In recognition of services during the operations in South Africa." The Insignia were presented by the King 12 May, 1902. He was promoted to Capt. 14 July, 1901. He was killed in in action 16 Dec. 1914, near La Bassée.

BOYALL, ALFRED MOREY, Lieut., was born 6 Oct. 1877, son of the late John Richard Boyall, of Ealing. He was educated at Harrow (The Park), 1891, and joined the Army as a Second Lieutenant in the West Yorkshire Regt. 16 Feb. 1898, becoming Lieutenant 28 May, 1899. He served in the South African War, taking part in the operations in Natal, 1899, and the Relief of Ladysmith with the action of Colenso; operations of 17 to 24 Jan. 1900; action at Spion Kop; operations of 5 to 7 Feb. 1900; action at Vaal Kranz; operations on Tugela Heights, and the action at Pieter's Hill, in which he was wounded; operations in Natal (including the action at Laing's Nek), March to June, 1900; operations east and west of Pretoria, in the Transvaal, July to 29 Nov. 1900, and in the Transvaal 30 Nov. 1900, to 31 May, 1902. He was twice mentioned in Despatches [London Gazette, 8 Feb. and 10 Sept. 1901]; received the Queen's and King's Medals with seven clasps, and was created a Companion of the Distinguished Service Order [London Gazette, 27 Sept. 1901]: "Alfred Morey Boyall, Lieut., West Yorkshire Regt. In recognition of services during the operations in South Africa." The Insignia were presented by the King 12 May, 1902. He had his captaincy 19 Jan. 1905, and between March, 1908, and March, 1912, was employed in the Militia, and in the Special Reserve as Adjutant. Capt. Boyall served again with distinction in the European War. After being employed as Staff Captain (March and April, 1915) and D.A.A.G. (April, 1915, to April, 1916) at the General Headquarters of the British Expeditionary Force, and becoming Brevet Major 1 Sept. 1915, he was Acting Lieut.-Colonel, West Yorkshire Regt., 1 Nov. 1916, to March, 1918. He was mentioned in Sir John French's Despatch of 15 Oct. 1915, dated War Office, 1 Jan. 1916. Mentioned in Sir Douglas Haig's Despatch, dated War Office, 15 June, 1916, and awarded a Bar to the Distinguished Service Order 4 Feb. 1918: "Alfred Morey Boyall, Acting Lieut.-Colonel, West Yorkshire Regt. When in command of an advanced guard battalion he pushed forward, after the capture of the first objective, and occupied a more advanced position, which was one of great importance, on his own initiative, His appreciation of the situation and display of bold initiative had considerable bearing on the success of the whole operations." He was given his Brevet Lieut.-Colonelcy 1 Jan. 1918. Lieut.-Colonel Boyall married, in 1905, Ida Mary Albina, daughter of Major-General Sykes.

LEGGETT, ARCHIBALD HERBERT, Lieut., was born in 1877, son of Major G. E. Leggett, late 77th Regiment of Foot. He was educated at Clifton College, and received his first commission in the Royal Scots Fusiliers 15 May, 1897. He served as Adjutant of the 2nd Battn. Royal Scots Fusiliers, 1899 to 1902, in the South African War, and was present at the Relief of Ladysmith, including the action at Colenso; operations of 17 to 24 Jan. 1900; operations of 5 to 7 Feb. 1900, and action at Vaal Kranz; operations on Tugela Heights (14 to 27 Feb.), and action at Pieter's Hill; operations in the Transvaal, May and June, 1900; operations in Natal, March and April, 1900; operations in the Transvaal, west of Pretoria, July to 29 Nov. 1900, including actions at Frederickstad (17 to 25 Oct.): operations in Cape Colony, north of Orange River; operations in the Transvaal 30 Nov. 1900, to 31 May, 1902; was promoted Captain 25 Sept. 1901, and was mentioned in Despatches [London Gazette, 10 Sept. 1901]; received the Queen's Medal with four clasps, the King's Medal with two clasps, and was created a Companion of the Distinguished Service Order [London Gazette, 27 Sept. 1901]: "Archibald Herbert Leggett, Lieut., West Yorkshire Regt. In recognition of services during the operations in South Africa." The Insignia were presented by the King 24 Oct. 1902. Capt. Leggett was Instructor, Royal Military Academy, from 1903 to 1907, and served from 1908 to 1910 in Japan, being attached to the British Embassy at Tokio, 1909 to 1910, serving for six months with the 29th Regiment of Infantry, Imperial Japanese Army, and passing as a 2nd Class Interpreter in Japanese. He was Brigade Major of the Hampshire Infantry Brigade from 1911 to 1913, when he retired from the Service (19 June). He served in the European War from 1915 to 1918, commanding the 5th (Territorial) Battn. Royal Scots Fusiliers from 1915 to 1917, and the 156th Infantry Brigade from 1917 to 1919. He was awarded a Bar to the Distinguished Service Order [London Gazette, 12 March, 1917]: "Archibald Herbert Leggett, D.S.O., Reserve of Officers, late Royal Scots Fusiliers. For conspicuous gallantry, coolness and resource when in command of an infantry battalion. He showed exceptional powers of leadership when attacked by the enemy, upon whom he inflicted a severe defeat." He was given the Brevets of Major 3 Jan. 1916, and of Lieut.-Colonel 1 Jan. 918; was created a C.M.G. in 1918; was four times mentioned in Despatches, and was awarded the Russian Order of St. Ann, 3rd Class, in 1916. On demobilization, 20 March, 1919, he was given the rank of Honorary Brigadier-General. Brigadier-General A. H. Leggett married, in 1903, Lilian Rose, eldest daughter of Major J. C. O'Neal, late Inniskilling Dragoons, and they have two sons and one daughter.

PRICE, CHARLES LEMPRIÈRE, Lieut., was the only child of Colonel Thomas Charles Price, of 8, Inverness Gardens, Kensington, W., late R.A., and his wife, Amy Earle, daughter of Charles Monteiro D'Almeida Lemprière, and grandson of Colonel Thomas Smith Price, H.E.I.C.S. (who received the Punjab Medal with clasps for Mooltan and Goojerat). He was born at Alderney, Channel Islands, 17 Sept. 1877. He was educated at St. Paul's School; privately, and the Royal Military College, Sandhurst; gazetted Second Lieutenant, Royal Scots, 8 Sept. 1897, and promoted Lieutenant

29 June, 1899, and Capt. 3 Nov. 1903. He served in the South African War, 1899–1902; took part in operations in Cape Colony, south of Orange River, 1899; operations in the Orange Free State, Feb. to May, 1900; operations in the Transvaal, east of Pretoria, July to 29 Nov. 1900 including actions at Belfast (26–27 Aug.) and Lydenberg (5–8 Sept.); operations in Orange River Colony, May to 29 Nov. 1900; operations in the Transvaal 30 Nov. 1900, to Dec. 1901, and Feb. to 31 May, 1902; operations in Orange River Colony, Dec. 1901, to Feb. 1902; was Acting Provost-Marshal, Komati Poort, and afterwards Station Staff Officer (twice mentioned in Despatches [London Gazette, 20 Aug. and 10 Sept. 1901]; Queen's Medal with three clasps, and King's Medal with two clasps; awarded D.S.O. "for gallantry in leading an attack on the Boer position at Bermondsey, East Transvaal, 16 May, 1901"). The award of his Distinguished Service Order was gazetted 27 Sept. 1901: "Charles Lemprière Price, Lieut., Royal Scots. In recognition of services during the operations in South Africa." He was invested by the King 24 Oct. 1902. He served in the European War with the Expeditionary Force in France and Flanders from — Aug.; was appointed Adjutant at the Front, and was killed in action at Vailly on 16 Sept. following, during the Battle of the Aisne, while in command of the regiment. A brother officer wrote: "I was present at the Battle of Mons with him and also at Le Cateau, and in the trying retreat almost as far as Paris, during the whole of which he was indefatigable, cheery, doing the work of ten men, full of resource, regardless of danger, the bravest and finest man I have ever known or wish to know; in losing him we have lost our best, a great sportsman and staunch friend. He will be mourned by the whole regiment, by whom he was respected and beloved"; and Private P. Clancy, in describing his experiences during this time, said ("Dundee Advertiser"): "We met the Germans on 23 Aug. On the 26th we were nearly annihilated at Cambray owing to the French reinforcements not coming up. About 7.30 o'clock that morning one of our airmen descended and reported that the French were advancing about 20 miles off, and would be able to reinforce us about midday. We waited anxiously, but 12 o'clock came and no French, and five o'clock and still no French. Half an hour later Major Butler gave the order, 'Retire, men, for God's sake; every man for himself.' Shells were flying thick about us, and it was an awful order to give. We got the order all right, but, with a few exceptions, it did not reach the Gordons, with disastrous results to them. So we began the never-to-be-forgotten retreat, with shells and bullets flying about everywhere. We got into Einecourt. When we got between a church and a farmhouse we came across two women and a child. Pipe-Major Duff said he would stay behind and look after them. This he did, and we saw no more of them. Our Adjutant, Capt. Price, who was one of the finest and most popular of the officers, and who was on horseback, said to us, 'Keep your heads, men. There are no marked men here. If the bullets are going to hit you they will hit you.' The Gordons, 18th Royal Irish and 2nd Royal Scots were all together on the retreat, falling back as fast as they could. The last fight on the retreat was at St. Quentin, and then we fell back to Hams, within 24 kilometres of Paris. We blew up all the bridges and the roads as we retreated except one bridge, and upon that solitary bridge and for five miles beyond it 150 guns of the outer defences of Paris were trained. On came the massed forces of the Germans and started to cross the bridge. Out blazed the guns and the bridge was blown to bits, along with the Germans who were approaching and crossing it. Their losses were awful. But for us it was a terrible retreat, and I shall never forget it. Then came the turning movement. We were seventeen days and nights in the trenches at the Aisne without being relieved. It was a time of artillery duels. Here we lost Capt. Price, who had saved thousands of men at Cambray. He lost his life trying to save another's. One of our N.C.O.'s was wounded and began to yell. Capt. Price was in his bomb-proof dug-out when he heard the shouting, and he called out to the man, 'All right, man, I will be with you in a few minutes.' Just as he got out of the trench he was hit by a bit of shell, and died a few hours afterwards. His loss was deeply regretted, because he was beloved by everybody." At Mons, when the troops were in full retreat, men of many regiments hurrying down the road, and getting hopelessly mixed and out of hand, under heavy shell fire, he noticed some guns on a ridge, and succeeded in rallying some of his men in all that ghastly confusion, and holding the ridge for over an hour, while the guns were removed. Capt. Price was mentioned in F.M. Sir John (now Lord) French's Despatch of 8 Oct. 1914, "for gallant and distinguished service in the field." He had the Coronation Medal and was Past Grand Sword Bearer of England. In a speech at the Annual Dinner of the Royal Scots, Edinburgh Association (29 March, 1902), Colonel Douglas described how, during the Boer War, Capt. Price was recommended for the V.C. They attacked the Boers, said Colonel Douglas, in a very strong position at Bermondsey, their flanks being protected by precipices. It was a difficult position to turn. He sent Lieut. Dalmahoy with E Company to the left, and they were round the Boer's right in no time. The guns were in action at 1,600 yards. But E Company made the Boers bolt. Major Moir and Lieut. Dalmahoy went after them. Then the Boers took up a rear-guard position, and it was here that Major Moir got hit in five places. He (Colonel Douglas) sent Lieut. Price with a message to the firing line. When he reached it Corpl. Paul was in command. Lieut. Dalmahoy, Private Sheddon and another man were lying wounded about 50 yards in front of the firing line, which was 400 yards from the Boers. Then men had two of the small entrenching implements with them, and with these each scraped up a littl earth in front of them. This was the only cover they had. Lieut. Pric ran out, picked up the nearest of the three wounded men, and carrie him in. He found it heavy work and called for three volunteers. Thre young L.-Corpls., M'Gill, Miller and Smith, at once responded. He mad them take off their equipment and coats, and did the same himself, an then unarmed and in shirt sleeves they ran out. Nevertheless, the Boer at once turned a heavy fire on them, and, in bringing in the wounded, on of the bearers was hit. Lieut. Dalmahoy was again hit in the head, an Private Sheddon was killed. Lord Kitchener promoted Corpl. Paul t Sergt. for his gallantry, and recommended Lieut. Price for the V.C., and th three young lance-corporals for Distinguished Conduct Medals.

Charles L. Price.

BERKELEY, CHRISTOPHER ROBERT, Lieut., was born 18 Jar 1877, son of the late Major Henry William Berkeley. He was educated a Oratory School, and at Sandhurst, and joined the Army as a Secon Lieutenant in the Welsh Regt. 8 Sept 1897, becoming Lieutenant 5 July, 189 He served in the South African War fron 1899 to 1902, and was present at the Relie of Kimberley; operations in the Orang Free State, Feb. to May, 1900, includin operations at Paardeberg, and the action at Poplar Grove, Dreifontein (severel wounded), Vet River and Zand River operations in the Transvaal, May and June 1900, including actions near Johannesburg Pretoria and Diamond Hill; operations i the Transvaal, east of Pretoria, July to 2 Nov. 1900, including action at Belfast operations in Cape Colony, south of Orang River, 1899–1900; operations in th Transvaal 30 Nov. 1900, to 31 May, 190 serving from 14 April, 1902, as Assistan Provost-Marshal. He was mentioned i Despatches [London Gazette, 8 Feb. and 10 Sept. 1901]; received th Queen's Medal with six clasps, the King's Medal with two clasps, and wa created a Companion of the Distinguished Service Order [London Gazette 27 Sept. 1901]: "Christopher Robert Berkeley, Lieut., Welsh Regt. I recognition of services during the operations in South Africa." He wa promoted Captain in the Welsh Regt. 13 May, 1904; was Adjutant fror 11 March, 1904, to 10 March, 1907, and Adjutant of Militia and in th Special Reserve from 27 Feb. 1908, to 26 Feb. 1912. Capt. Berkele served in the European War; was Brigade Major, 3rd Infantry Brigade B.E.F., 26 Feb. 1915, to 15 April, 1916, being promoted Major 1 Sept. 191 and Brevet Lieutenant-Colonel 1 Jan. 1916; was employed as D.A.A. an Q.M.G., 15th Division, France, 16 April to 27 Aug. 1916; as A.A. an Q.M.G., 15th Division, 28 Aug. 1916, to 25 Oct. 1918, then becomin A.Q.M.G., Q.M.G.'s Branch, G.H.Q., France. He was wounded; men tioned in Despatches six times; was created a C.M.G. in 1917 and a O.B.E. in 1919, and received the Legion of Honour and the Croix de Guerr avec Palme. Lieut.-Colonel Berkeley married, in 1919, Nest, younges daughter of Colonel J. A. Bradney, C.B., of Talycoed Court, Monmouth.

Christopher R. Berkeley.

DELAP, GEORGE GOSLETT, Lieut., was born at Dungrow Rectory County Donegal, 13 April, 1873, son of the late Canon Alexander Delaj of Valencia Island, County Kerry, and the late Mrs. Delap. He wa educated at Rathmines School, and at the Royal College of Surgeons Dublin (L.R.C.P.I., L.R.C.S.I.), and entered the Army as a Lieutenar in the Royal Army Medical Corps 27 July, 1899. He served in Sout Africa from 1899 to 1902, and was created a Companion of the Distir guished Service Order for attending wounded under fire at the Battle c Magersfontein [London Gazette, 27 Sept. 1901]: "George Goslett Delaj Lieut., Royal Army Medical Corps. In recognition of services durin the operations in South Africa." He was mentioned in Despatche by Lord Methuen after Magersfontein and by Lord Roberts afte Paardeberg, also serving in the actions at Karee Siding, Vet and Zan Rivers; operations in the Transvaal, including actions near Johar nesburg, Pretoria and Diamond Hill, and later in the action at Reit Vle and operations in Orange River Colony and Cape Colony. He receive the Queen's Medal with four clasps—for the Relief of Kimberley, Paard berg, Johannesburg and Diamond Hill—and the King's Medal with tw clasps. He became Captain 27 July, 1902, and was Assistant Instructo at the R.A.M.C. School of Instruction, June, 1908, to June, 1912, obtainin his Majority 27 April, 1914. Major Delap commanded the New Arm Training Centre, Llandrindod Wells, 9 Dec. 1914, to 9 Oct. 1915, an became Lieut.-Colonel 1 May, 1915. He served in the European W for three months at Salonika as D.A.D.M.S. and D.D.M.S., L. of C., 1 Nov. 1915, to 8 Jan. 1916; with Travelling War Office Board, in comman to 17 April, 1916; mobilized with the 33rd General Hospital; arrive at Basra, Mesopotamia, 11 June, 1916; in command of 33rd General Ho pital till 30 April, 1917; appointed A.D.M.S., Cavalry Division in Meso tamia, 29 April, 1917 (to 7 April, 1918); Temporary Colonel 13 May, 191 to 7 April, 1918; A.D.M.S., L. of C., Mesopotamia, from 27 Aug. 191 He has the Royal Humane Society's Bronze Medal for saving life. H married, in 1912, Mary Dorothy, youngest daughter of Surgeon-Gener W. J. Fawcett, C.B., A.M.S., and they have a son, Peter, born 11 Ma 1913, and a daughter, Kathleen Mary.

ENSOR, HOWARD, Lieut., was born 20 March, 1874, son of Edwa Ensor, M.A. He took his degrees, B.A. (1895), M.B., B.Ch. (1897), Durham University. He served with the 1st Battn. West African Fronti Force from Nov. 1897, to March, 1899, being Senior Medical Officer i the Lahai Expedition, June, 1898 (Medal and two clasps). Receivin his commission as Lieutenant in the Royal Army Medical Corps 2 July, 1899 he served in South Africa from 1899 to 1902 was prese at the genera actions of Magersfontein, Paardeberg, Poplar Grove and Dreifontein, and operations in the Transvaal. He was mentioned in Despatches [London Gazette, 16 April, 1901]; received the Queen's Medal with four clasps, the King's Medal with two clasps, and was created a Companion of the Distinguished Service Order [London Gazette, 27 Sept. 1901]: " Howard Ensor, Lieut., Royal Army Medical Corps. In recognition of services during the operations in South Africa." The Insignia, Warrant and Statutes were sent to the Commander-in-Chief in India; presented by the G.O.C., Bombay, at Poona, 10 Aug. 1902. He was promoted Captain 27 July, 1901, and was employed with the Egyptian Army from 2 May, 1902, to 1 May, 1912; seeing active service again in the South-Eastern Soudan, 1912, in operations against the Beir and Anuak tribes (Soudan Medal with clasps).

Howard Ensor.

He also received in 1910 the 4th Class Osmanieh, and in 1912 the 3rd Class Medjidie; became Major 28 Jan. 1911. He was restored to the establishment in 1912. Major Ensor served in the European War from 1914 to 1919. He was given the Brevet of Lieutenant-Colonel 18 Feb. 1915; Lieutenant-Colonel 1 March, 1915, and on 3 June, 1915, Brevet Colonel. He was A.D.M.S., 3rd Division, British Armies in France, 11 Aug. 1916, to 23 Aug. 1918, then becoming Commandant, Royal Army Medical Corps, School of Instruction, British Armies in France. For his services he was made a C.M.G. in 1918, and was six times mentioned in Despatches. Colonel Howard Ensor married, in 1912, Gladys Marian, youngest daughter of Colonel Maurice Tweedie, late Indian Army, and they have a son and a daughter.

LLOYD, LANGFORD NEWMAN, Lieut., was born 28 Dec. 1873, son of Colonel E. G. K. P. Lloyd. He entered the Army as a Lieutenant in the Royal Army Medical Corps 27 July, 1899, and served in South Africa from 1899 to 1901, receiving mention in Despatches twice [London Gazette, 8 Feb. and 10 Sept. 1901], and was created a Companion of the Distinguished Service Order [London Gazette, 27 Sept. 1901]: " Langford Lloyd, Lieut., Royal Army Medical Corps. In recognition of services during the operations in South Africa." The Insignia, Warrant and Statutes were sent to the G.O.C. Troops, Bermuda. Presented by General Geary 12 Feb. 1902. He also received the Queen's Medal with seven clasps. He became Captain 27 July, 1902; served as Adjutant of R.A.M.C., Volunteers, Nov. 1905, to March, 1908, and Adjutant, Territorial Force, April, 1908, to Oct. 1911; became Major 27 July, 1911. Serving in the European War, he was promoted Lieut.-

Langford Newman Lloyd.

Colonel 1 March, 1915; was employed as A.D.M.S., 4th Army, France, 15 June to 31 Oct. 1917; A.D.M.S., 11th Division, France, from 1 Nov. 1917, and Temporary Colonel from the same date. He was five times mentioned in Despatches for his war services, and was made a C.M.G. in 1916. Lieut.-Colonel Newman is an M.B.C.S. and L.R.C.P. He married Lilian May, daughter of Surgeon-General Sir W. R. Hooper, K.C.S.I.

ANDERSON, NELSON GRAHAM, Lieut., was born 14 Sept. 1875, youngest son of the late Major-General R. P. Anderson. He entered the Army, from the Militia, as a Second Lieutenant in the Royal Sussex Regt. 6 June, 1896. He was transferred to the Army Service Corps 2 Jan. 1899; became Lieutenant 20 Sept. 1900, and Captain 1 Jan. 1901. He served n the South African War from 1899 to 1902, and was present at the Relief of Ladysmith, including operations on Tugela Heights (14 to 27 Feb.); operations in the Transvaal, west of Pretoria, July to 29 Nov. 1900; operations in Cape Colony, north of Orange River; operations in the Transvaal 30 Nov. 1900, to March, 1902; operations in Cape Colony, March to 31 May, 1902; operations in Orange River Colony, March, 1902. He was mentioned in Despatches [London Gazette, 8 Feb. 1901]; received the Queen's Medal with five clasps, the King's Medal with two clasps, and was created a Companion of the Distinguished Service Order [London Gazette, 27 Sept. 1901]: " Nelson Graham Anderson, Lieut., Army Service Corps. In recognition of services during the operations in South Africa." The Insignia were sent to the G.O.C.-in-Chief in South Africa 2 March, 1902; invested by the King 18 Dec. 1902. He again saw active service on the North-West Frontier of India in the Zakka Khel Expedition, 1908 (Medal and clasp), and was specially employed in Somaliland 16 Dec. 1908, to 13 Jan. 1910; as Assistant Director of Supplies and Transport, receiving mention in Despatches [London Gazette, 17 June, 1910], and the Medal and clasp for the campaign in Somaliland, 1908 to 1910. He was promoted Major 23 Oct. 1912, and was employed from 16 Jan. 1913, until the outbreak of the European War, as D.A.Q.M.G., 5th Division, Irish Command. In the Great War he served as D.A.A. and Q.M.G., 5th Division, B.E.F., 5 to 26 Aug. 1914; A.A. and Q.M.G., 5th Division, 27 Aug. 1914, to 13 July, 1915; was promoted Brevet Lieut.-Colonel 18 Feb. 1915; A.Q.M.G., 7th Army Corps, 14 July, 1915, to 4 Aug. 1916; D.A. and Q.M.G., 1st Army Corps (Temporary Brigadier-General) 5 Aug. 1916, to 28 Feb. 1919. He became Brevet Lieutenant-Colonel 18 Feb. 1915; Lieut.-Colonel 16 April, 1917; Brevet Colonel 1 Jan.

1917. He was mentioned in Despatches six times; created a C.M.G. in 1916 and a C.B. in 1918. Brigadier-General Anderson married, in 1914, Fanny, youngest daughter of the late William Scott, of Hampden House, Ibrox, N.B., and widow of H. Herbert Harley.

DICK-CUNYNGHAM, JAMES KEITH, Lieut., was born 28 March, 1877, third son of the late Sir R. H. A. Dick-Cunyngham, 9th Bart., and Lady Dick-Cunyngham. He was educated at Cheltenham College, and was gazetted to the Gordon Highlanders 28 May, 1898, becoming Lieutenant 4 Oct. 1898. He served in the South African War, 1899–1902, and took part in the operations in Natal, 1899, including actions at Elandslaagte and Lombard's Kop; was present at the Defence of Ladysmith, including action of 6 Jan. 1900; during operations in Natal, March to June, 1900, including action at Laing's Nek (6 to 9 June); in the Transvaal, east of Pretoria, July to 29 Nov. 1900, including actions at Belfast (26 and 27 Aug.) and Lydenberg (5 to 8 Sept.); in the Transvaal, west of Pretoria, July to 29 Nov. 1900; and again in the Transvaal 30 Nov. 1900, to Dec. 1901. He was mentioned in Despatches [London Gazette, 10 Sept. 1901]; received the Queen's Medal with four clasps, the King's Medal with two clasps, and was created a Companion of the Distinguished Service Order [London Gazette, 27 Sept. 1901]: " James Keith Dick-Cunyngham, Lieut., Gordon Highlanders. In recognition of services during the operations in South Africa." The Insignia were presented by the King 2 June, 1902. He was promoted to Captain 24 Nov. 1902, and was Adjutant, Gordon Highlanders, 20 Aug. 1904, to 19 Aug. 1907. He served in the European War from 1914; as Assistant Provost-Marshal, 2nd Army Corps, B.E.F., 5 Aug. to 29 Sept. 1914; as Brigade Major, 14th Infantry Brigade, B.E.F., 30 Sept. 1914, to 3 Sept. 1915. He was promoted to Major 1 Sept. 1915; was G.S.O.2, 1st Army Corps, B.E.F., British Armies in France, 4 Sept. 1915, to 5 Aug. 1916; G.S.O.1, 51st Division, British Armies in France, 16 Nov. 1916, to 6 April, 1918; Temporary Brigadier-General 1 April to 11 June, 1918; commanding the 152nd Infantry Brigade, British Armies in France, 7 April to 11 June, 1918; A.A.G., War Office (Temporary), from 15 March, 1919. He was mentioned in Despatches, and was given the Brevets of Major 18 Feb. 1915, and Lieut.-Colonel 3 June, 1916, and created a C.M.G. in 1918. Lieut.-Colonel Dick-Cunyngham married, in 1905, Alice Daisy, youngest daughter of the late Sir Harold Deane, K.C.S.I., and they have two daughters.

HARRIS-ST. JOHN, CHARLES EDWARD, Lieut., was born 10 Nov. 1873, at Tilney Hall, Rotherwick, Hants, eldest son of Charles Edward Harris-St. John, J.P. (of Sheldons, Hook; Borough Court, Winchfield, Hants, and West Court, Finchampstead, Berks), and of Jessie St. John, daughter of Henry St. John, of West Court. He was educated at Eton, and was commissioned in the 5th Lancers 20 May, 1895, becoming Second Lieutenant, 16th Lancers, 25 Sept. 1895, and Lieutenant 9 Oct. 1899. He served in the South African War, 1900–2 (severely wounded); took part in the advance on Kimberley; was present at the relief of Kimberley; took part in the operations in the Orange Free State, Feb. to May, 1900, including those at Paardeberg (18 to 26 Feb.); actions at Poplar Grove, Karee Siding, Houtnek (Thoba Mountain), Vet River (5 and 6 May) and Zand River; in the transvaal in May and June, 1900, including actions near Johannesburg; in the Transvaal, west of Pretoria; in Orange River Colony, including actions at Bethlehem (7 July) and Wittebergen; again in Orange River Colony 30 Nov. 1900, to June, 1901; also in Cape Colony, June, 1901, to 31 May, 1902 [Despatches [London Gazette, 10 Sept. 1901]; Queen's Medal with five clasps and King's Medal with two clasps). He was created a Companion of the Distinguished Service Order [London Gazette, 27 Sept. 1901]: " Charles Edward St. John Harris, Lieut., 16th Lancers. In recognition of services during the operations in South Africa." The Insignia, Warrant and Statutes were sent to the G.O.C., Cape Colony District, and presented by Colonel E. Bethune at Middelburg, Cape Colony, 27 July, 1903. He was promoted to Captain 29 Jan. 1902; was Adjutant, 16th Lancers, 8 Aug. 1902, to 26 Jan. 1906; Major 19 Dec. 1910 and Lieutenant-Colonel 3 Dec. 1918. He served in the European War; with the 16th Lancers from July to May, 1915, when he was invalided. He was Assistant Military Secretary, British Armies in France, 17 July, 1916, to July, 1918, and was mentioned in Despatches in Jan. 1918. He was appointed to command the 16th Lancers, as from 19 Dec. 1918. Lieut.-Colonel Harris-St. John has the 1915 Star. He was awarded the Spanish Order of Military Merit in 1906. On 3 Oct. 1911, at Whitechurch, Salop, he married Winifred Rose, daughter of Charles Tertius Dugdale, Esq., of Terrick Hall, Whitechurch, Salop, and they have two sons : Edward Dugdale born 2 Aug. 1914; and Charles Dugdale, born 30 April, 1919; and two daughters : Anne and Rosamund Adela. His name was changed to Harris-St. John 12 April, 1907.

HAMILTON - TEMPLE - BLACKWOOD, LORD FREDERICK TEMPLE, Lieut., was born at Ottawa 26 Feb. 1875, fourth son of the 1st Marquess of Dufferin. He entered the 9th Lancers 11 Aug. 1897, as Second Lieutenant, from the Militia; became Lieutenant 9 Oct. 1899, and served in the South African War, 1899–1901; as Brigade Signalling Officer 15 Oct. 1900, to 14 Nov. 1900 (severely wounded); served in the advance on Kimberley, including actions at Belmont, Enslin, Modder River and Magersfontein; was present at the Relief of Kimberley; in the Orange Free State, Feb. to May, 1900, including operations at Paardeberg; in the actions at Poplar Grove and Karee Siding; served during the operations in the Transvaal in May and June, 1900, including actions near Johannesburg, Pretoria and Diamond Hill; in the Transvaal, west of Pretoria, July to Nov. 1900; also during operations in Orange River Colony, May to Nov. 1900, including actions at Bethlehem, Wittebergen and Caledon River; and in Cape Colony 30 Nov. to Dec. 1900 (Despatches [London Gazette, 8 Feb. and 10 Sept. 1901]; Queen's Medal with nine clasps). He was created a Companion of the Distinguished Service Order [London Gazette, 27 Sept. 1901]: " Lord Frederick Temple Hamilton-Temple-Blackwood, Lieut., 9th Lancers. In recognition of services during the operations in South Africa." The Insignia were presented by the King 29 Oct. 1901. He was promoted to Captain 10 Sept. 1910, and retired from the 9th Lancers 7 Sept. 1912. He was Military Secretary to the Governor-General of Australia in 1914. From 1914 he served in the European War, as Captain, Grenadier Guards. In 1908 the late Lord Frederick Blackwood married Brenda, eldest daughter of Robert Woodhouse, of Orford House, Bishop's Stortford, and they had one son and one daughter.

BAIRD, HENRY HUME CHISHOLM, Lieut., was born 13 April, 1878, son of Alexander Baird. He was educated at Cheltenham College, and was gazetted to the East Kent Regt., as Second Lieutenant, 8 Sept. 1897,

becoming Lieutenant 11 Oct. 1899. He served in the South African War, 1899–1902; as Brigade Signalling Officer 18 Jan. 1900, to 28 June, 1901; and as Staff Officer to Brigadier-General; was present at the Relief of Kimberley; in the Orange Free State, Feb. to May, 1900, and took part in the operations at Paardeberg (17 to 26 Feb.); in the actions at Poplar Grove and Dreifontein; served during the operations in the Transvaal, west of Pretoria, July to Nov. 1900; and in the operations in Orange River Colony (May to 29 Nov. 1900), including actions at Bothaville and Caledon River (27 to 29 Nov.); again in the operations in the Transvaal, May, 1902, and in Orange River Colony 30 Nov. 1900, to June, 1901 (Despatches [London Gazette,

Henry H. C. Baird.

10 Sept. 1901]; Queen's Medal with four clasps, and King's Medal with two clasps). He was created a Companion of the Distinguished Service Order [London Gazette, 27 Sept. 1901]: " Henry Hume Chisholm Baird, Lieut., East Kent Regt. In recognition of services during the operations in South Africa." The Insignia were presented by the King 29 Oct. 1901. He was promoted to Captain 15 Feb. 1901; was Adjutant, Volunteers, 28 April, 1905, to 31 Dec. 1907; retired in Nov. 1912. Capt. Baird rejoined in August, 1914, and was placed on the retired list in July, 1915, owing to ill-health caused by the War. He became Editor of the " Ex-Service Man." Capt. Baird married, in 1905, Margot, daughter of John Kerr (formerly M.P. for Preston) and Margaret, daughter of Thomas Melville, of Kersehill, Stirlingshire.

BARTON, CHARLES WALTER, Lieut., was born 15 Aug. 1876, son of W. C. Barton, M.I.C.E. He was educated at Harrow, and entered the Army 1 Dec. 1897, as Second Lieutenant, from the Militia. He became Lieutenant 18 Oct. 1899, and served in the South African War, 1899–1902; took part in the advance on Kimberley, including actions at Belmont (slightly wounded) and Magersfontein; was present during the operations in the Orange Free State, Feb. to May, 1900; served in the Transvaal, west of Pretoria, July to Nov. 1900, including actions at Venterskroon (7 and 9 Aug.); took part in the operations in Orange River Colony, including actions at Lindley (1 June) and Rhenoster River; also in the Transvaal 30 Nov. 1900, to 31 May, 1902 (Despatches [London Gazette, 10 Sept. 1901]; Queen's Medal with three clasps, and King's Medal with two clasps). He was created a Companion of the Distinguished Service Order [London Gazette, 27 Sept. 1901]: " Charles Walter Barton, Lieut., Northampton-shire Regt. In recognition of services during the operations in South Africa." He was invested by the King 24 Oct. 1902. He was employed with the King's African Rifles, 21 March, 1903, to 20 May, 1908, and served in East Africa in 1904, taking part in the operations in Somaliland, and was present at the action at Jidballi. He received the Medal with two clasps. He was promoted to Captain 23 Jan. 1905. Capt. Barton served in Nyassa-land in 1914, and was wounded; in German East Africa, 1918 (wounded); was employed with the 2nd King's African Rifles, 1903–8; with the Nyassa-land Volunteers Reserve from 14 June, 1913, to 1916; with the 1st King's African Rifles since 1917; was promoted to Major 2 June, 1915, and to Temporary Lieutenant-Colonel 22 Jan. 1917. He was created a C.M.G.

NEILSON, WALTER GORDON, Lieut., was born 1 Oct. 1876, son of the late Col. James Neilson, C.B. He was educated at Merchiston Castle School, and played for Scotland at Rugby football when still at school.

He was commissioned in the Argyll and Sutherland Highlanders 1 Dec. 1897; became Lieutenant 1 Oct. 1899. He served in the South African War, 1899–1902; took part in the advance on Kimberley, including action at Modder River (wounded), and Magersfontein; in the Orange Free State, Feb. to May, 1900, including operations at Paardeberg (17 to 26 Feb.); in the Transvaal, east of Pretoria, July to 29 Nov. 1900; in the Transvaal, west of Pretoria, July to 29 Nov. 1900, including action at Zilikat's Nek; in Orange River Colony, May to 29 Nov. 1900; served as Adjutant to 1st Battn. Argyll and Sutherland Highlanders, from 1 April to 31 May, 1902; also in Cape Colony May, 1902 (Despatches [London

Walter Gordon Neilson.

Gazette, 10 Sept. 1901, and 29 July, 1902]; Queen's Medal with three clasps, and King's Medal with two clasps). He was created a Companion of the Distinguished Service Order [London Gazette, 27 Sept. 1901]: " Walter Gordon Neilson, Lieut., Argyll and Sutherland Highlanders." In recognition of services during the operations in South Africa." The Insignia were presented by the King 24 Oct. 1902. He was Adjutant, Argyll and Sutherland Highlanders, 1 April, 1902, to 21

March, 1905; became Captain 16 July, 1907; was Brigade Major, Lothian Infantry Brigade, Scottish Command, 12 July, 1912, to 4 Aug. 1914. During the European War he was Brigade Major, 1/1st Lothian Infantry Brigade, Central Force, Home Defence, 5 Aug. 1914, to 19 March, 1915; Brigade Major, 139th Infantry Brigade, B.E.F., British Armies in France 1 June, 1915, to 21 July, 1916; was promoted to Major 1 Sept. 1915; was G.S.O.2, British Armies in France, 22 July, to 15 Aug. 1916; G.S.O.2, 34th Division, British Armies in France, 16 Aug. 1916, to 22 Feb. 1917; G.S.O.2, 15th Army Corps, British Armies in France, 23 Feb. to 17 Nov. 1917; Temporary Lieutenant-Colonel 18 Nov. 1917, to 2 June, 1918, and G.S.O.1, 63rd Division, British Armies in France, 18 Nov. 1917, to 21 July, 1918; G.S.O.1, 4th Army, British Armies in France, 22 July, 1918. He was five times mentioned in Despatches; was given the Brevet of Lieu-tenant-Colonel 3 June, 1918, and created a C.M.G. 1916. Lieut.-Colonel Neilson married, in 1908, Ida Lacon-Graham, of Duntrune, Forfarshire, only child of the late F. G. Lacon, and they have one daughter.

SIMS, REGINALD FRANK MANLEY, Lieut., was born 2 Aug. 1878, son of — Manley Sims, and Mrs. Manley Sims. He was gazetted to the King's Royal Rifle Corps, as Second Lieutenant, 23 Feb. 1898, and became Lieutenant 21 Oct. 1899. Lieut. Manley Sims served in the South African War, 1899–1902; took part in the Relief of Ladysmith, including action at Colenso; during the operations of 17 to 24 Jan. 1900, and action at Spion Kop; operations of 5 to 7 Feb. 1900, and action at Vaal Kranz (wounded); took part in the operations on Tugela Heights 14 to 27 Feb. 1900, and action at Pieter's Hill; in Natal, March to June, 1900, including action at Laing's Nek (6 to 9 June); afterwards on Staff (Despatches [London Gazette, 8 Feb. and 10 Sept. 1901]; Queen's Medal with five clasps, and King's Medal with two clasps). He was created a Companion of the Distinguished Service Order [London Gazette, 27 Sept. 1901]: " Reginald Frank Manley Sims, Lieut., King's Royal Rifle Corps. In recognition of services during the operations in South Africa." The Insignia, Warrant and Statutes were sent to the G.O.C., Transvaal and Orange Free State, for presentation. He retired from the King's Royal Rifle Corps, and has been attached to the Canadian Contingent since 1915. Colonel R. F. Manley Sims served in the European War from 1915; was Temporary Brigadier-General, and was created a C.M.G. in 1917.

FANE, CECIL, Lieut., was born at Biarritz, South of France, 15 Sept. 1876, son of the late Capt. F. A. Fane, Rifle Brigade. He was educated at Rugby, and was gazetted to the 12th (Prince of Wales's Royal) Lancers

9 June, 1897, and was promoted to Lieu-tenant 21 March, 1902. From 1899 to 1902 he served in the South African War, taking part in the advance on Kimberley, including action at Magersfontein; at the Relief of Kimberley; took part in the operations in the Orange Free State, Feb. to May, 1900, including those at Paarde-berg; actions at Poplar Grove, Dreifon-tein, Houtnek (Thoba Mountain) and Zand River; in the Transvaal in May and June, 1900, including actions near Johan-nesburg and Diamond Hill; in the Trans-vaal, west of Pretoria, July to 29 Nov. 1900; in the Orange River Colony, May to 29 Nov. 1900, including actions at Lindley, Bethlehem and Wittebergen; served as Adjutant, 12th Lancers, June, 1901, to 31 May, 1902; again served during opera-

Cecil Fane.

tions in the Transvaal 30 Nov. 1900, to July, 1901; also in Cape Colony, July, 1901, to 31 May, 1902 (Despatches [London Gazette, 8 Feb. and 10 Sept. 1901]; Queen's Medal with six clasps and King's Medal with two clasps). He was created a Companion of the Distinguished Service Order [London Gazette, 27 Sept. 1901]: " Cecil Fane, Lieut., 12th Lancers. In recognition of services during the operations in South Africa." The In-signia, Warrant and Statutes were sent to the Commander-in-Chief in India, and were presented by Major-General Creagh, at Umballa, at General Parade, 10 Feb. 1903. He was Adjutant, 12th Lancers, 23 Aug. 1902, to 31 Oct. 1903; was employed with the West African Frontier Force 2 April to 12 Nov. 1904; became Captain 21 May, 1904, and Major 28 Sept. 1912. He served in the European War from 1914 in France, and was twice wounded, three times mentioned in Despatches, and given the Brevet of Lieutenant-Colonel 18 Feb. 1915. He became Temporary Lieutenant-Colonel, commanding the 2/7th Territorial Force Battn. Nottinghamshire and Derbyshire Regt. (15 Feb. to 4 Oct. 1916), and was sent to Ire-land to quell the Rebellion. The 2/7th Sherwood Foresters were the leading Battalion in the thick of the two days' fighting. Lieut.-Colonel Fane was wounded the first day, but remained on duty both days. He was Acting Lieutenant-Colonel, 12th Lancers, 19 Oct. 1916, to 3 Sept. 1917, and was promoted to Lieutenant-Colonel 4 Sept. 1917. He was created a C.M.G. in 1916. Lieut.-Colonel C. Fane married, in 1918, Gladys Mac-george, daughter of Colonel Stanley Barry.

DE SALIS, EDWARD AUGUSTUS ALFRED, Lieut., was born 2 June, 1874, son of Lieut.-Colonel Edward J. de Salis, Naval Ordnance Depart-ment. He served in West Africa, 1897–98, in the Northern Terri-ories, Gold Coast (Medal with clasp), and was gazetted to the Royal Dublin Fusiliers 18 Jan. 1899, as Second Lieutenant, from the Militia, becoming Lieutenant on 24 Oct. of the same year. He served in the South African War, 1899–1901; was present at the Relief of Ladysmith, including action at Colenso; in the Transvaal, June, 1900; in Natal, March to June, 1900, including action at Laing's Nek (6 to 9 June); in the Transvaal, east of Pretoria, July, 1900; in Orange River Colony, June, 1900; again during the operations in the Transvaal 30 Nov. 1900, to March, 1901; also in Cape Colony, March to April, 1901 (Despatches [London Gazette, 8 Feb.

and 10 Sept. 1901]; Queen's Medal with seven clasps). He was created a Companion of the Distinguished Service Order [London Gazette, 27 Sept. 1901]: "Edward Augustus Alfred de Salis, Lieut., Royal Dublin Fusiliers. In recognition of services during the operations in South Africa." The Insignia were presented by the King 29 Oct. 1901. He was promoted to Captain, Worcestershire Regt., 2 Aug. 1902; was Adjutant, King's Own Malta Regt. of Militia, 24 Sept. 1907, to 23 Sept. 1912. He served in the European War, 1914–18; as Staff Captain, G.H.Q., B.E.F., 26 May, 1915, to 11 Nov. 1915; promoted to Major 13 June, 1915; was Staff Captain, G.H.Q., Mediterranean Expeditionary Force, 20 Nov. 1915, to 23 Jan. 1916; as acting Lieutenant-Colonel, commanding the 9th Battn. Worcestershire Regt. 29 Jan. 1916, to 5 April, 1916; as acting Lieutenant-Colonel, commanding a battalion of the Machine Gun Corps 1 Feb. 1917. Major de Salis married, in 1902, Emily Ethel, eldest daughter of the late Colonel A. D. Geddes, 27th Regt. (Royal Inniskilling Fusiliers).

WREFORD-BROWN, CLAUD WREFORD, Lieut., was born at Clifton, 17 Feb. 1876, fifth son of the late William Wreford-Brown and Clara Jane, daughter of Henry Clark, M.D. He was educated at Waynsflete, Durdham Down, Clifton; Wells House, Malvern Wells, and Charterhouse. He was commissioned from the Militia into the 1st Battn. 5th Northumberland Fusiliers 15 May, 1897. In 1898 he served in the Sudan Campaign; was present at the Battle of Omdurman and at the capture of Khartum (Medal and Egyptian Medal with clasp). He was employed in the Occupation of Crete in 1898; became Lieutenant 24 Nov. 1899, and served throughout the South African War of 1899–1902, taking part in the advance on Kimberley, including the

Claud W. Wreford-Brown.

actions at Belmont, Enslin, Modder River and Magersfontein; afterwards he took part in the operations in the Orange Free State (March to May, 1900), and in the Transvaal (July to Nov. 1900), including actions at Venterskroom and Rhenoster River. He was twice mentioned in Despatches [London Gazette, 9 July and 10 Sept. 1901]: received the Queen's Medal with four clasps; the King's Medal with three clasps, and was—for his services at Lichtenburg—created a Companion of the Distinguished Service Order [London Gazette, 27 Sept. 1901]: "Claud Wreford Wreford-Brown, Lieut., Northumberland Fusiliers. In recognition of services during the operations in South Africa." He was promoted to Captain 15 April, 1901. In 1908 he served on the North-West Frontier of India, during the operations in the Mohmand country, and was severely wounded, receiving the Medal and one clasp. Capt. Wreford-Brown served in the Great War, and was killed in action at the Dardanelles on 25 May, 1915.

BOYD-MOSS, ERNEST WILLIAM, Lieut., was born 26 Sept. 1876, youngest son of the late M. H. Moss, of Belsize, Worthing. He was educated at Tonbridge School, and entered the Worcestershire Regt. 1 Dec. 1897. He served in the South African War, 1900–2; as Acting A.S. Corps Officer; took part in the operations in Orange Free State, Feb. to May, 1900; in Orange River Colony, May to 29 Nov. 1900, including actions at Ladybrand 2 to 5 Sept.; in the Transvaal, Jan. to June, 1901, and again in Orange River Colony 30 Nov. 1900, to Jan. 1901, and June, 1901, to Feb. 1902 (Despatches [London Gazette, 10 Sept. 1901]; Queen's Medal with three clasps, and King's Medal with two clasps). He was created a Companion of the Distinguished Service Order [London Gazette, 27 Sept. 1901]: "Ernest William Moss, Lieut., Worcestershire Regt. In recognition of services during the operations in South Africa." He became Lieutenant 2 Jan. 1900, and Captain 6 Feb. 1901, and served with the West African Rifles 12 Nov. 1904, to 11 July, 1907 His name was changed to Boyd-Moss 10 June, 1914, by enrolled deed-poll. Capt. Boyd-Moss served in the Great War, and was killed in action at the Dardanelles on 10 Aug. 1915. He had married, in 1909, Mary Elizabeth Grace, only child of Frank M. Howard, and they had one son.

JOHNSON, HARRY CECIL, Lieut., was born 19 July, 1877, eldest son of the late Robert Henry Johnson, Lieut., 64th Foot. He entered the King's Royal Rifle Corps 17 March, 1897, and was promoted to Lieutenant 8 March, 1899. He served in the South African War, 1899–1902, and took part in the operations in Natal, 1899, including action at Lombard's Kop (severely wounded); was present at the Relief of Ladysmith, including action at Colenso; operations of 17 to 24 Jan. 1900, and action at Spion Kop; operations of 5 to 7 Feb. 1900, and on Tugela Heights (14 to 27 Feb. 1900), and action at Pieter's Hill; in Natal, March to June, 1900, including action at Laing's Nek (6 to 9 June); in the Transvaal, east of Pretoria, July to 29 Nov. 1900, including actions at Belfast (26 and 27 Aug.), and Lydenberg (5 to 8 Sept.); again in the Transvaal, Aug. 1901, to 31 May, 1902; Adjutant, 2nd Regt. Imperial Light Horse (from 3 Jan. 1901) (Despatches [London Gazette, 8 Feb. and 10 Sept. 1901]; Queen's Medal with six clasps, and King's Medal with two clasps). He was created a Companion of the Distinguished Service Order [London Gazette, 27 Sept. 1901]: "Harry Cecil Johnson, Lieut., King's Royal Rifle Corps. In recognition of Services during the operations in South Africa." He became Captain 7 Jan. 1902. Capt. Johnson served in East Africa in 1904, and took part in the operations in Somaliland (Medal with clasp). He served in the European War and died at Cambrai of wounds received in action on 26 Aug. 1914 ("Times," 16 Feb. 1915). Capt. Johnson had married, in 1911, Phyllis Dorothy, second daughter of Hugh G. Barclay, Esq., V.D., J.P., of Colney Hall, Norfolk, and Evelyn Louisa (who died in 1899), eldest daughter of Sir Stuart Hogg.

DORRIEN-SMITH, ARTHUR ALGERNON, Lieut., was born 28 Jan. 1876, eldest son of Thomas Algernon Smith Dorrien-Smith, J.P., D.L., and Edith Anna Maria (who died in 1892), daughter of Mr. and Lady Sophia Tower. He was gazetted to the Rifle Brigade 4 May, 1898; became Lieutenant, and served in South Africa, 1899–1902. He was mentioned in Despatches, received the Queen's Medal with four clasps; the King's Medal with two clasps, and was created a Companion of the Distinguished Service Order [London Gazette, 27 Sept. 1901]: "Arthur Algernon Dorrien-Smith. Lieut., Rifle Brigade. In recognition of services during the operations in South Africa." The Insignia were presented by the King 21 Oct. 1902. He was extra A.D.C., 1904–5, to Lord Northcote, Governor-General of Australia. He retired in 1906, and joined the Special Reserve of his Regiment. On the outbreak of the European War he was appointed to the Staff. Major Dorrien-Smith was twice

A. A. Dorrien-Smith.

mentioned in Despatches. He married, in 1909, Eleanor Salvin Bowlby, third daughter of the late Edward Salvin Bowlby, of Gilston Park, Harlow, and they have three sons: Algernon Robert Augustus, born in 1910; Thomas Mervyn, born in 1913, and Lionel Roger, born in 1918; and two daughters: Anne Elizabeth and Innis Mary.

DUNCOMBE SHAFTO, ARTHUR, Lieut., was born in London 8 April, 1880. He was the only surviving son of the late Charles Ottiwell and Mrs. C. Duncombe Shafto, of 9, South Bailey, Durham. He was educated at the Durham School, and the Royal Military College, Sandhurst, and obtained his commission in the Northumberland Fusiliers in Oct. 1899, becoming Captain in Dec. 1903. He served in the South African War, 1899–1900, and took part in the operations in the Orange Free State, Feb. to May, 1900; in the Transvaal, west of Pretoria, July to 29 Nov. 1900; in Orange River Colony, May to Nov. 1900; in Cape Colony, south of Orange River, 1899–1900; was present during the operations in the Transvaal, Dec. 1900, to Aug. 1901; also in Orange River Colony, Aug. 1901, to 31 May, 1902 (Despatches [London Gazette, 16 March, 1900, and 10 Sept. 1901]; Queen's Medal with three clasps, and King's Medal with two clasps). He was created a Companion of the Distin-

Arthur Duncombe Shafto.

guished Service Order [London Gazette, 27 Sept. 1901]: "Arthur Duncombe Shafto, Lieut., Northumberland Fusiliers. In recognition of services during the operations in South Africa." From 1905 to 1908 he was Staff Captain of the Border Grouped Regimental District and from 1908 to 1910, of No. 5 District. In May, 1908, he was transferred to the Royal Scots. He was serving with his battalion when he was killed in action at Audincourt on the 26th Aug. 1914. Capt. Duncombe Shafto had married Marguerite Cécile Catherine, daughter of the late Lieut.-Colonel Stapleton, 19th Hussars, and left two children, Mark, born in Aug. 1905, and Betty.

JENKINS, EDWARD VAUGHAN, Lieut., was born 14 Oct. 1879, son of the late Lieut.-Colonel Vaughan Jenkins. He was educated at Clifton; entered the West Riding Regt. 20 May, 1899, and served in the South African War, 1899–1902, being present at the Relief of Kimberley; in the Orange Free State, Feb. to May, 1900, including operations at Paardeberg (17 to 26 Feb.); actions at Poplar Grove and Dreifontein; in the Transvaal, east and west of Pretoria, Aug. to 29 Nov. 1900, including action at Rhenoster Kop; again in the Transvaal 30 Nov. 1900, to 31 May, 1902; was Railway Staff Officer (Despatches [London Gazette, 10 Sept. 1901]; Queen's Medal with four clasps, and King's Medal with two clasps). He was created a Companion of the Distinguished Service Order [London Gazette, 27 Sept. 1901]: "Edward Vaughan Jenkins, Lieut., West Riding Regt. In recognition of services during the operations in South Africa." He was promoted to Lieutenant 19 Feb. 1900; was employed with the King's African Rifles 22 April, 1902, to 21 April, 1912; became Captain 15 April, 1904; served in East Africa, 1905, in command of an expedition (Despatches [London Gazette, 13 March, 1908]; served at Nandi, 1905–6 (Medal with two clasps). He served in the European War from 1914; was promoted to Major 1 Sept. 1915, and was Assistant Embarkation Staff Officer, Southampton, from 5 Feb. 1919. Major Jenkins married, in 1904, Evelyn Marie, eldest daughter of the late Lieut.-Colonel Germon, J.P., Norfolk Regt.

SAUNDERS, ERNEST HOWIE, Lieut., was born 18 Nov. 1877, son of Colonel W. E. Saunders, C.B. He entered the Royal Irish Rifles 8 Sept. 1897, as Second Lieutenant, becoming Lieutenant in the Army 8 Dec. 1899, and in the Royal Irish Rifles 24 Feb. 1900. He served in the South African War, 1899–1902; employed with Mounted Infantry; took part in the operations in Orange Free State, March to April, 1900; in the Transvaal, June to Nov. 1900; also in Cape Colony, 1899 to 1900 (Despatches [London Gazette, 10 Sept. 1901]; Queen's Medal with three clasps, and King's Medal with two clasps). He was created a Companion of the Distinguished Service Order [London Gazette, 27 Sept. 1901]: "Ernest Howie Saunders, Lieut., Royal Irish Rifles. In recognition of services during the operations in South Africa." He was invested by the King 18 Dec. 1902. On 8 Sept. 1906, he was promoted to Captain in the Army, and on 24 Nov. 1908, was transferred to the Indian Army, in which he became Major 1 Sept. 1915. Major Saunders married, in 1906, Primrose Ellen, daughter of Carr Stephen.

CLEGG-HILL, THE HONOURABLE CHARLES ROWLAND, Lieut., son of the 3rd Viscount Hill, was born 5 May, 1876. He was gazetted to the Royal Welsh Fusiliers 9 Dec. 1896, and became Lieutenant 25 Feb. 1900. He served in the South African War, 1899–1902, employed with Mounted Infantry (slightly wounded). Served as Adjutant, 1st Battn. Royal Welsh Fusiliers (from 1 Feb. 1901); was present at the Relief of Kimberley; took part in the operations in the Orange Free State, Feb. to May, 1900, including those at Paardeberg 17 to 26 Feb.; actions at Poplar Grove, Dreifontein, Houtnek (Thoba Mountain) and Zand River; served during operations in the Transvaal in May and June, 1900, including actions near Johannesburg, Pretoria and Diamond Hill 11 and 12 June; in Orange River Colony, including actions at Wittebergen 1 to 29 July; in Cape Colony, south of Orange River, 1899–1900, including actions at Colesberg 1 Jan. to 8 Feb.; again in the Transvaal 30 Nov. 1900, to Sept. 1901; also in Orange River Colony, Sept. 1901, to 31 May, 1902 (Despatches [London Gazette, 4 May, 1900, and 10 Sept. 1901]; Queen's Medal with six clasps, and King's Medal with two clasps). He was created a Companion of the Distinguished Service Order [London Gazette, 27 Sept. 1901]: "The Honourable Charles Rowland Clegg-Hill, Lieut., Royal Welsh Fusiliers. In recognition of services during the operations in South Africa." (Invested by the King 18 Dec. 1902.) He was promoted to Captain 8 Feb. 1906, and was Adjutant, Militia, 1 Sept. 1904, to 9 July, 1908; and Adjutant, Territorial Force, from 10 July, 1908. He retired from the Royal Welsh Fusiliers 6 Nov. 1912. He became Major, Reserve of Officers, 3rd Battn. Royal Welsh Fusiliers 1 Sept. 1915, and was given the Brevet of Lieutenant-Colonel 3 June, 1919. He married, in 1903, Mildred, daughter of Thomas Bulteel, of Radford, South Devon, and they have two sons.

GRANT, ROBERT FRANCIS SIDNEY, Lieut., was born 18 Sept. 1877, son of the late Sir C. Grant, K.C.S.I., and Ellen, daughter of the Right Hon. Henry Baillie, of Redcastle, N.B. He was educated at Eton, and entered the Rifle Brigade 13 July, 1898, becoming Lieutenant 3 April, 1900. He was Adjutant, Rifle Brigade, 24 Dec. 1901, to 5 Jan. 1902. He served in the South African War, 1899–1902, and was present at the Relief of Ladysmith, including action at Colenso; operations of 17 to 24 Jan. 1900; operations of 5 to 7 Feb. 1900, and action at Vaal Kranz; in the operations on Tugela Heights (14 to 27 Feb. 1900), and action at Pieter's Hill; took part in the operations in Natal, March to June, 1900, including action at Laing's Nek (6 to 9 June); in the Transvaal, east of Pretoria, July to 29 Nov. 1900; in Orange River Colony, May, 1900; again in the Transvaal, 30 Nov. 1900, to April, 1902; again also in Orange River Colony, July and Aug. 1901 (Despatches [London Gazette, 10 Sept. 1901]; Queen's Medal with six clasps, and King's Medal with two clasps). He was created a Companion of the Distinguished Service Order [London Gazette, 27 Sept. 1901]: "Robert Francis Sidney Grant, Lieut., Royal Welsh Fusiliers. In recognition of services during the operations in South Africa." He was invested by the King 18 Dec. 1902. Lieut. Grant was A.D.C. to Major-General, North-Western District; A.D.C. to G.O. Commanding-in-Chief (acting), Western Command, 23 Jan. 1905, to 15 Dec. 1906; created an M.V.O., 1911; G.S.O.3, War Office, 1 May, 1914, to 28 Sept. 1914. He served in the European War, 1914–15; was promoted to Major 28 Nov. 1914; was mentioned in Despatches twice, and severely wounded, Feb. 1915. Major Grant married, in 1917, Vera, daughter of Lieut.-Colonel Walter Campbell, of The Ivy House, Hampton Court.

WEDD, LAWRENCE DUNKIN, Lieut., was born 9 Jan. 1878, and was gazetted to the Royal West Surrey Regt., as Second Lieutenant, 16 Feb. 1898. He was promoted to Lieutenant, and served in the South African War of 1899–1902; was created a Companion of the Distinguished Service Order [London Gazette, 27 Sept. 1901]: "Lawrence Dunkin Wedd, Lieut., Royal West Surrey Regt. In recognition of services during the operations in South Africa." The Insignia, Warrant and Statutes of the D.S.O. were sent to H. G. Wedd, Esq., Executor, as Lieut. Wedd had not survived to be decorated with the Order.

RUNDLE, WILLIAM JOHN SCOTT, Lieut., was born 26 March, 1876; was gazetted a Lieutenant in the 6th Dragoon Guards 11 Oct. 1899, from the local Military Forces in New South Wales, and became Lieutenant. He distinguished himself in the South African War, and was created a Companion of the Distinguished Service Order [London Gazette, 27 Sept. 1901]: "William John Scott Rundle, Lieut., 6th Dragoon Guards. In recognition of services during the operations in South Africa (since died of wounds)." The Insignia, Warrant and Statutes were sent to Mr. Nixon.

CAMERON, ALLAN, Lieut., was born 4 Nov. 1878, and entered the Gordon Highlanders from the Militia, becoming Lieutenant. He served, with distinction in the South African War, and was created a Companion of the Distinguished Service Order [London Gazette, 27 Sept. 1901]: "Allan Cameron, Lieut., Gordon Highlanders. In recognition of services during the operations in South Africa (since killed in action)." The Insignia, Warrant and Statutes were sent to his father.

WARDLE, ERNEST VIVIAN LIVESEY, Lieut., was born 28 June, 1878, son of Capt. T. Livesey Wardle. He was educated at Wellington, and entered the Army in 1897. He served in the South African War from 1899 to 1902, taking part in the Relief of Kimberley; operations in the Orange Free State, Feb. to May, 1900, including operations at Paardeberg, 17 to 26 Feb. (wounded, 23 Feb.); actions at Vet River and Zand River; operations in the Transvaal, May and June, 1900, including actions near Johannesburg and Pretoria, and Diamond Hill; operations in the Transvaal, east of Pretoria, including action at Belfast; operations in Cape Colony, south of Orange River, including the action at Colesberg; operations in the Transvaal 30 Nov. 1900, to 31 May, 1902. He was mentioned in Despatches [London Gazette, 10 Sept. 1901]; had the Queen's Medal with five clasps, and the King's Medal with two clasps, and was created a Companion of the Distinguished Service Order [London Gazette, 27 Sept. 1901]: "Ernest Vivian Livesey Wardle, Lieut., Yorkshire Regt. In recognition of services during the operations in South Africa." Capt. Wardle took part in the European War, serving from 1914 to 1917. He married, in 1908, Alice Kathleen, daughter of the late Edward Rennison.

KEARSEY, ALEXANDER HORACE CYRIL, Lieut., was born 17 Dec. 1877, son of the late Francis Kearsey, of Burstow Hall, Burstow, Horley, Sussex. He was educated at Rottingdean School, Clifton College, and the Royal Military College, Sandhurst, from which he was commissioned in the York and Lancaster Regt. 7 May, 1898. He was promoted Lieutenant 20 June, 1900, and took part in the South African War, 1899–1902, being present at the Relief of Ladysmith, including operations of 17 to 24 Jan. 1900 (severely wounded at Venters Spruit, 20 Jan.), and action at Spion Kop; operations of 5 to 7 Feb. 1900, and action at Vaal Kranz; operations on Tugela Heights (14 to 27 Feb. 1900), and action at Pieter's Hill; operations in Natal (March to June, 1900), including action at Laing's Nek (6 to 9 June); operations in the Transvaal, May to July, 1901; operations in Orange River Colony, Dec. 1901, to 31 May, 1902. He was mentioned in Despatches twice (30 March and 9 Nov. 1900), by Sir Redvers Buller, and in the London Gazette of 10 Sept. 1901; and was created a Companion of the Distinguished Service Order [London Gazette, 27 Sept. 1901]: "Alexander Horace Cyril Kearsey, Lieut., York and Lancaster Regt. In recognition of services during the operations in South Africa." The Insignia were presented by the King 14 March, 1902. He was promoted Captain 12 March, 1904, and was transferred to the 10th Hussars 22 Feb. 1905; was Adjutant in the Territorial Force, April, 1908, to March, 1911, and graduated at the Staff College, Camberley, at the end of 1914, being promoted Major 11 Nov. 1914. At the outbreak of the European War Major Kearsey was appointed to the Embarkation Staff at Southampton in Nov., and proceeded to Belgium, attached to the 1st Life Guards, 7th Cavalry Brigade, and was present at the First Battle of Ypres, and Neuve Chapelle. In 1915, he was attached to the Staff of the 7th Cavalry Brigade, and in Aug. of that year was appointed Brigade Major to 1/2nd South-Western Mounted Brigade, and served with them in Gallipoli. He commanded the 5th Dorset Regt. for five months, till May, 1916, and was then appointed G.S.O.1, with the 54th Division, Egyptian Expeditionary Force, and was present at the First and Second Battles of Gaza. He commanded the 1/5th King's Own Scottish Borderers, May to Nov. 1917, being wounded at the Battle of El Teb. For his services he was mentioned in Despatches thrice, and holds the Serbian Decoration, Karageorge. He commanded the Cadet Wing, Royal Air Force, and was appointed Staff Officer, 1st Grade, 28 Dec. 1918. Lieut.-Colonel A. H. C. Kearsey has published "The War Records of the York and Lancaster Regiment, South Africa, 1900–1902, 1903." He married, in 1907, the Honourable Frances Mitford, daughter of the 1st Lord Redesdale, and they have one son.

Alexander H. C. Kearsey.

DORRIEN-SMITH, EDWARD PENDARVES, Lieut., was born 26 Feb. 1879, son of Thomas Algernon Smith Dorrien-Smith and the late Edith Anna Maria, daughter of Mr. and Lady Sophia Tower. He joined the Army, from the Militia, as a Second Lieutenant in the King's Shropshire Light Infantry, 20 May, 1899, and was promoted Lieutenant 10 July, 1900. He served in the South African Campaign from 1899 to 1902, as Acting A.D.C. to the G.O.C., Infantry Brigade, and was present in operations in the Orange Free State, Feb. to May, 1900, including operations at Paardeberg (17 to 26 Feb.); actions at Poplar Grove, Dreifontein, Houtnek (Thoba Mountain), Vet River (5 and 6 May) and Zand River; operations in the Transvaal, May and June, 1900, including actions near Johannesburg and Pretoria; operations in the Transvaal, east of Pretoria, July to 29 Nov. 1900, including actions at Lydenberg (5 to 8 Sept.); operations in the Transvaal, west of Pretoria, July to 29 Nov. 1900, including actions at Elands River (4 to 16 Aug.); operations in Orange River Colony, May to 29 Nov. 1900; operations in Cape Colony, south of Orange River, 1899–1900; operations in the Transvaal 30 Nov. 1900, to July, 1901; operations in Orange River Colony, July to Aug. 1901, and Nov. 1901, to 31 May, 1902; operations on the Zululand Frontier of Natal in Sept. and Oct. 1901. For his services he was mentioned in Despatches [London Gazette, 10 Sept. 1901]; received the Queen's Medal and King's Medal with six clasps, and was created a Companion of the Distinguished Service Order [London Gazette, 27 Sept. 1901]: "Edward Pendarves Dorrien-Smith, Lieut., King's Shropshire Light Infantry. In recognition of services during the operations in South Africa." The Insignia were presented by the King 18 Dec. 1902. He became Captain 15 Feb. 1918, and from that date until 13 Feb. 1911, was Adjutant of the Shropshire Light Infantry. Capt. Dorrien-Smith served in the Great War as Assistant Embarkation Staff Officer, Aug. to Sept. 1914; Brigade-Major, 36th Infantry Brigade, New Armies, Sept. and Oct. 1914; Staff Captain, 9th Infantry Brigade, B.E.F., Dec. 1914, to March, 1915; Brigade-Major, 8th Infantry Brigade, B.E.F., March and April, 1915. He was given

E. P. Dorrien-Smith.

his Brevet Majority 3 June, 1915, and promoted substantive Major 1 Sept. 1915; was G.S.O.2, 41st Division, New Armies, Sept. 1915, to March, 1916; G.S.O.2, engaged in training duties in the U.S.A. April to Dec. 1918, and was afterwards specially employed at the War Office. He was mentioned in Despatches for services in the War. Major E. P. Dorrien-Smith married, in 1915, Frances Salvin, fourth daughter of Edward Salvin Bowlby, of Gilston Park, Harlow, and they have a son and a daughter.

PERCY-SMITH, DOUGLAS CYRIL, Lieut., was born 14 Nov. 1875, son of the late Major-General P. W. Percy-Smith. He was educated at Cheltenham College, and after serving in the 3rd Battn. Loyal North Lancashire Regt., the Indian Police (Bengal), and Lumsden's Horse, he received a commission as a Second Lieutenant in the Middlesex Regt. 4 April, 1900, becoming Lieutenant 4 Aug. 1900. He took part in the South African War from 1899 to 1902, serving in Lumsden's Horse and employed with the Mounted Infantry, and was present in operations in the Orange Free State, Feb. to May, 1900, including actions at Houtnek (Thoba Mountain), Vet River (5 and 6 May) and Zand River; operations in the Transvaal, May and June, 1900, including actions near Johannesburg, Pretoria and Diamond Hill (11 and 12 June); operations in the Transvaal, west of Pretoria, July to 29 Nov. 1900, including actions at Venterskroon (7 and 9 Aug.); operations in Orange River Colony, May to 29 Nov. 1900, including actions at Ladybrand (2 to 5 Sept.) and Bothaville (slightly wounded); operations in the Transvaal and Orange River Colony 30 Nov. 1900, to March, 1902. He was mentioned in Despatches [London Gazette, 10 Sept. 1901]; received the Queen's Medal with four clasps, and the King's Medal with two clasps, and was created a Companion of the Distinguished Service Order [London Gazette, 27 Sept. 1901]: "Douglas Cyril Percy-Smith, Lieut., Middlesex Regt. In recognition of services during the operations in South Africa." The Insignia were presented by the King 18 Dec. 1902. He became Captain 3 May, 1904, and was A.D.C. to Divisional Commander, India, 1 May, 1905, to 8 Jan. 1909, and since 24 March, 1911, has been employed with the Egyptian Army, becoming Major 1 Sept. 1915, and Temporary Lieutenant-Colonel 1 Aug. 1917. He was awarded the O.B.E.

JACKSON, GEORGE HANBURY NOBLE, Lieut., was born 20 Dec. 1876. He entered the Army, as a Second Lieutenant in the Border Regt. 20 Feb. 1897, becoming Lieutenant 8 Aug. 1900. He took part in the South African War, 1899 to 1902, serving in 1900 as Adjutant of Imperial Light Infantry, and was present at the Relief of Ladysmith, including operations of 17 to 24 Jan. 1900, and action at Spion Kop; operations of 5 to 7 Feb. 1900, and action at Vaal Kranz; operations on Tugela Heights (14 to 27 Feb. 1900) and action at Pieter's Hill; operations in the Transvaal, May and June, 1900; operations in Natal (March and June, 1900), including action at Laing's Nek (6 to 9 June); operations in the Transvaal and Orange River Colony 30 Nov. 1900, to 31 May, 1902. For his services he was mentioned in Despatches [London Gazette, 8 Feb. and 10 Sept. 1901]; received the Queen's Medal with six clasps, and the King's Medal with two clasps, and was created a Companion of the Distinguished Service Order [London Gazette, 27 Sept. 1901]: "George Hanbury Noble Jackson, Lieut., Border Regt. In recognition of services during the operations in South Africa." The Insignia, Warrant and Statutes were sent to the G.O.C., Transvaal; presented by the G.O.C., South Africa, at Pretoria, 25 March, 1903. He became Captain 15 March, 1907, and was Adjutant of the Border Regt. 1 Oct. 1907, to 30 Sept. 1910. Capt. Jackson served in the European War. After being employed for a period at home, he became G.S.O.3, 13th Division, New Armies, Mediterranean Expeditionary Force, 26 Jan. 1915; was promoted Major 18 May, 1915; became G.S.O.2, 2nd Australian Division, Sept. 1915, and G.S.O.1, of the same Division, Dec. 1915. He served with this Division in the Dardanelles and in France, and as G.S.O.1, 3rd Australian Division in France, from July, 1916, to Jan. 1918; was given the Brevet of Lieutenant-Colonel 3 June, 1916. On 20 Jan. 1918, he was given command of the 87th Infantry Brigade, and became Brevet Colonel 3 June, 1919. For his services in the Great War, Major Noble was mentioned in Despatches, and created a C.M.G. in 1917. He married, in 1917, Eileen, youngest daughter of Hume Dudgeon, Merville, Booterstown, Ireland.

George H. N. Jackson.

NEVILL, HUGH LEWIS, Lieut., was born 24 July, 1877, only son of the late Hugh Nevill, of the Ceylon Civil Service, and Mrs. Nevill, of 8, Cheyne Row, Chelsea. He had an entrance scholarship to Clifton College, and after passing direct into Woolwich, joined the Royal Artillery, as a Second Lieutenant, 1 Sept. 1897, becoming Lieutenant 1 Sept. 1900. He served in the South African War, 1899–1901, being present in operations in the Transvaal, east and west of Pretoria; operations in the Transvaal 30 Nov. 1900, to Jan. 1901; operations in Orange River Colony, Jan. 1901; operations in Cape Colony, Jan. to March, 1901. He was wounded at Noortgadacht; was mentioned in Despatches [London Gazette, 10 Sept. 1901]; received the Queen's Medal with four clasps, and was, on 2 Nov. 1900, created a Companion of the Distinguished Service Order [London Gazette, 27 Sept. 1901]: "Hugh Lewis Nevill, Lieut., Royal Artillery. In recognition of services during the operations in South Africa." The Insignia were presented by the King 29 Oct. 1901. Lieut. Nevill was promoted Captain 10 May, 1904, and was Adjutant from 20 July, 1909, to 21 Jan. 1912. He passed through the Staff College, Camberley, in Jan. 1914, and went to France as Captain in his Field Battery. He served through the Retreat from Mons and the Battle of the Aisne; was slightly wounded several times, but had to leave duty on one occasion, and was mentioned in Despatches by General French. He was promoted to Major 30 Oct. 1914. After serving in France for several months, he was given a Staff appointment in England in Feb. 1915, as D.A.Q.M.G. He went out to Gallipoli on 7 July, and was killed at the landing on 7 Aug. following. He was the author of "Campaigns on the North-West Frontier," with a preface of appreciation written by Lord Roberts. He left a widow, Dorothy Marion Nevill, and two sons.

TARBET, WILLIAM GODFREY, Lieut., is the eldest son of E. G. Tarbet, Solicitor, of Liverpool. He received his first commission 16 Feb. 1898, in the Yorkshire Regt., and served in the South African War with the Mounted Infantry, as Adjutant, 4th Battn., from 1900. He was twice wounded; was mentioned in Despatches; received the Queen's Medal with four clasps, and the King's Medal with two clasps; and was created a Companion of the Distinguished Service Order [London Gazette, 27 Sept. 1901]: "William Godfrey Tarbet, Lieut., Yorkshire Regt. In recognition of services during the operations in South Africa." The Insignia were presented by the King 18 Dec. 1902. He was promoted to a Captaincy in the Worcestershire Regt. in 1904, and died 20 April, 1911, at Jhansi, India, as a result of a fall from his horse.

SADLEIR-JACKSON, LIONEL WARREN DE VERE, Lieut., was born 31 Dec. 1876, son of the late Major Henry Sadleir-Jackson, of Ahanesk, Midleton, Cork. He entered the Army, from the Militia, as a Second Lieutenant in the 9th Lancers, 4 May, 1898, becoming Lieutenant 3 Oct. 1900. He took part in the South African War from 1899 to 1902, serving as A.D.C. to the Brigadier-General, South Africa, July to Sept. 1900, and as a Staff Officer; was present in the advance on Kimberley, including actions at Belmont, Enslin, Modder River and Magersfontein; the Relief of Kimberley; operations in the Orange Free State, Feb. to May, 1900, including operations at Paardeberg, and actions at Poplar Grove and Karee Siding; operations in the Transvaal, west of Pretoria, July to Nov. 1900; operations in Orange River Colony, May to Nov. 1900, including actions at Bethlehem, Wittebergen and Caledon River; operations in Orange River Colony 30 Nov. 1900, to June, 1901; operations in Cape Colony, June, 1901, to March, 1902. He was slightly wounded; thrice mentioned in Despatches [London Gazette, 8 Feb. and 10 Sept. 1901, and 17 Jan. 1902]; received the Queen's Medal with seven clasps, and the King's Medal with two clasps, and was created a Companion of the Distinguished Service Order [London Gazette, 27 Sept. 1901]: "Lionel Warren De Vere Sadleir-Jackson, Lieut., 9th Lancers. In recognition of services during the operations in South Africa." The Insignia, Warrant and Statutes were sent to the Commander-in-Chief in India, and presented by General Sir Bindon Blood at a full Garrison Parade at Rawal Pindi, India. He was promoted Captain 14 Dec. 1904, and resigned in 1909, but was reinstated in his original place in the Army in the same year, and was a Territorial Force Adjutant from July, 1909, to Sept. 1912, in which month he joined the Army Signal Service. He served in this branch of the Service in the European War until May, 1917, becoming Major, 9th Lancers, 1 March, 1915. From May, 1917, to Oct. he was in command of the 10th Battn. London Regt., and from Oct. 1917, to 1919, of the 54th Brigade, British Armies in France, receiving his Brevet of Lieutenant-Colonel 1 Jan. 1918. He took the Russian Relief Force to Archangel, and was in command of the 2nd Brigade, Russian Relief Force, 1918 to 1919. For his services in the European War and subsequent Russian Campaigns, he was twice mentioned in Despatches; was made a C.M.G. in 1915; was awarded a Bar to the Distinguished Service Order [London Gazette, 17 Sept. 1918]: "Lionel Warren De Vere Sadleir-Jackson, C.M.G., D.S.O., Major and Brevet Lieut.-Colonel (Temporary Brigadier-General), Lancers. For conspicuous gallantry and devotion to duty. Throughout recent operations he proved himself a bold leader of men, and under all conditions full of energy and fine fighting spirit. He personally organized and led most successful counter-attacks, in one of which he recaptured a village and took 150 prisoners and eleven machine guns. He did splendid work under very difficult conditions." He was created a C.B. in 1919, and also received the Legion of Honour and the Croix de Guerre with Star. Brigadier-General L. W. De V. Sadleir-Jackson is an F.R.G.S. His favourite pursuits are polo (he has published in collaboration with W. S. Buckmaster "Hints on Polo Combination"), big game shooting and hunting. He married, in 1912, Mrs. Marion Fulton.

WATSON, CHARLES FREDERICK, Lieut., was born 29 June, 1877, son of the late Colonel Fred Watson. He was educated at Wellington College, and entered the Army, from the Militia, as a Second Lieutenant in the Royal West Surrey Regt. 8 June, 1898, becoming Lieutenant 7 May, 1900. He served in South Africa from 1899 to 1902, and was present at the Relief of Ladysmith, including the action at Colenso; operations of 17 to 24 Jan. 1900, and action at Spion Kop; operations of 5 to 7 Feb. 1900, and action at Vaal Kranz; operations on Tugela Heights 14 to 27 Feb. 1900, and action at Pieter's Hill; operations in Natal (March to June, 1900), including action at Laing's Nek (6 to 9 June); operations in the Transvaal 30 Nov. 1900, to March, 1901, and May, 1901, to 31 May, 1902; operations in Orange River Colony, April and Aug. 1901; operations in Cape Colony, May, 1902. He was mentioned in Sir Redvers Buller's Despatches of 30 March and 9 Nov. 1900 [London Gazette, 8 Feb. and 10 Sept. 1901]; received the Queen's Medal with six clasps, and the King's Medal with two clasps, and was created a Companion of the Distinguished Service Order [London Gazette, 27 Sept. 1901]: "Charles Frederick Watson, Lieut., Royal West Surrey Regt.

Charles F. Watson.

In recognition of services during the operations in South Africa." The Insignia were presented by the King 24 Oct. 1902. He became Captain 7 June, 1903 ; passed through the Staff College, Camberley ; became Brevet Major 28 Sept. 1914. Major Watson saw active service in the European War ; was employed as G.S.O.3, with the 2nd Division, B.E.F., Nov. 1914, to Feb. 1915 ; as G.S.O.2, 23rd Division, Feb. 1915, to Feb. 1916, and as G.S.O.1, with the latter Division until Jan. 1917. In April and May, 1917, he commanded a Service Battn. of the Royal West Surrey Regt., and was G.S.O.1 at the General Headquarters of the Egyptian Expeditionary Force from July to Sept., becoming then Brigade Commander of the 139th Infantry Brigade, with this force. He was given his Brevet Lieutenant-Colonelcy Jan. 1918, and his Brevet Colonelcy 3 June, 1919. He was created a C.M.G. for his services in the war in 1916, and was three times mentioned in Despatches. Colonel Watson married, in 1906, Winifred, daughter of W. H. Woodruff, and they have two sons.

HART (now HART-SYNNOT), RONALD VICTOR OKES, Lieut., was born 24 July, 1876, son of the late Major-General Fitzroy Hart-Synnot, C.B., C.M.G. He was educated at King William's College, Sand-

hurst, and at the South-Eastern Agricultural College, Wye, and took the degree B.Sc. at London University. He joined his regiment, the East Surreys, in 1899. He served in South Africa, 1899 to 1902, taking part in the Battle of Colenso, and—as A.D.C. to Major-General Fitzoy Hart—in the actions of Spion Kop, Potgieter's Drift, Pieter's Hill, and the Relief of Ladysmith, for which he twice received mention in Despatches. He also saw fighting in the Orange River and Cape Colonies, 1901–2, and had the Queen's Medal with five clasps, and the King's Medal with two clasps, and was created a Companion of the Distinguished Service Order [London Gazette, 27 Sept. 1901] :

R. V. O. Hart-Synnot.

" Ronald Victor Okes Hart, Lieut., East Surrey Regt. In recognition of services during the operations in South Africa." He was invested by the King 18 Dec. 1902. He resigned his commission in 1904, and in 1909 was appointed Private Secretary to Sir Horace Plunkett, and Dean in the Faculty of Agriculture and Horticulture at University College, Reading. In 1915 he became Temporary Captain and A.D.C. to H.E. General Sir Reginald Hart in Guernsey, and in Feb. of the year following appointed to the Headquarters Staff, Southern Command, Salisbury. In 1918 he was promoted Temporary Major, also becoming Deputy Assistant Director of Labour. Major Hart-Synnot married, in 1912, Violet, eldest daughter of the Rev. Lord Theobald Butler and Annabella Beydon, daughter of the late Rev. Cosmo B. Gordon, D.D., and they have one son.

COULSON, GUSTAVUS HAMILTON BLENKINSOPP, Lieut., was created a Companion of the Distinguished Service Order [London Gazette, 27 Sept. 1901] : " Gustavus Hamilton Blenkinsopp Coulson, Lieut., King's Own Scottish Borderers (deceased). For services during the recent operations in South Africa." He was subsequently awarded the V.C. (See V.C. Volume.)

WICKHAM, CHARLES GEORGE, Lieut., was born 11 Sept. 1879, fourth son of W. W. Wickham, of Chestnut Grove, Boston Spa, Yorkshire. He was educated at Harrow (Head Master's, 1893), and entered the Army as a Second Lieutenant in the Norfolk Regt. 12 Aug. 1899, becoming Lieutenant 28 Aug. 1900. He served in the South African War from 1900 to 1902, employed with the Mounted Infantry and on the Staff (serving as Staff Lieutenant, Intelligence, 15 April to 10 July, 1902). He was slightly wounded ; was present in operations in the Transvaal, Orange River Colony and Cape Colony, Nov. 1900, to May, 1902, and for his services was awarded the Queen's Medal with five clasps ; the King's Medal with two clasps, and was created a Companion of the Distinguished Service Order [London Gazette, 27 Sept. 1901] : " Charles George Wickham, Lieut., Norfolk Regt. In recognition of services during the operations in South Africa." The Insignia, Warrant and Statutes were sent to the G.O.C., Transvaal and Orange River Colony, 15 Nov. 1902 ; presented by General Munro at Pochefstroom 11 Jan. 1903. He became Captain 16 Jan. 1906, and was employed with the Western Transvaal Volunteers from July, 1906, for five years, and from Dec. 1912, to Jan. 1914, was Adjutant in the Special Reserve. When the European War broke out he was serving as Staff Captain, Irish Command, becoming in Sept. 1914, Assistant Provost-Marshal, 7th Division, B.E.F. (until Oct.). He was promoted Brevet Major 3 June, 1915, and Substantive Major 1 Sept. 1915. He served as A.P.M., 7th Army Corps, B.E.F., July, 1915, to July, 1916 ; D.A.Q.M.G., Home Forces, 73rd Division, Nov. 1916, to Jan. 1917 ; D.A.Q.M.G., Aldershot Command, March to Oct. 1918. On 15 Oct. 1918, he became Temporary Lieutenant-Colonel, and accompanied the Military Mission, under General Knox, to Vladivostock, as A.Q.M.G., He was three times mentioned in Despatches. Lieut.-Colonel Wickham married, in 1916, Phyllis Amy, second daughter of Edward G. Rose, and they have one daughter.

GOODWYN, PERCY CHARLES WILDMAN, Lieut., was born 13 Oct. 1879. He entered the Army as a Second Lieutenant in the East Lancashire Regt. 18 Oct. 1899, becoming Lieutenant 7 June, 1900. He served in the South African War from 1900 to 1902, with the Mounted Infantry, being present in operations in the Orange Free State, including operations at Paardeberg (17 to 26 Feb.) ; actions at Vet River (5 and 6 May) and Zand River ; operations in the Transvaal, including actions near Johannesburg and Pretoria ; operations in the Transvaal, Dec. 1900, to Jan.

1902 ; operations in Orange River Colony, July, 1901, to Feb. 1902 ; operations in Cape Colony, May, 1901, Sept. 1901, and May, 1902. For his services he was mentioned in Despatches [London Gazette, 9 July and 10 Sept. 1901] ; had the Queen's Medal with three clasps ; the King's Medal with two clasps, and was created a Companion of the Distinguished Service Order [London Gazette, 27 Sept. 1901] : " Percy Charles Wildman Goodwyn, Lieut., East Lancashire Regt. In recognition of services during the operations in South Africa." He was invested by the King 18 Dec. 1902. He was promoted Captain 8 Feb. 1908, and served as Adjutant of Militia, and in the Special Reserve from Nov. 1907, to Nov. 1911. He again saw active service in the European War, being employed as Adjutant of the 7th Battn. Manchester Regt. Sept. 1914, to May, 1915. He became Major 28 May, 1915, and was Temporary Lieut.-Colonel, 7th Battn. East Lancashire Regt. Dec. 1915, to Oct. 1917 ; Temporary Lieutenant-Colonel, East Lancashire Regt. Oct. 1917, to March, 1918, and Temporary Lieutenant-Colonel, March, 1918, to March, 1919, when he was given the command of the 51st Battn. Manchester Regt. Lieut.-Colonel P. C. W. Goodwyn married, in 1908, Katharine Agnes, only daughter of the late R. W. J. Murray, of Edinburgh.

BOON, GEORGE, Lieut., was born in Norfolk 9 Sept. 1846, son of

Charles Boon, Farmer, and Elizabeth, his wife. He was educated at Great Yarmouth, and joined the Army 2 July, 1864. He saw service in the Perak Expedition, 1875–76, receiving the Medal and clasp. He was given a commission in the East Kent Regt. 24 June, 1891, and served in the South African War from 1899 to 1902, being employed from 18 Aug. 1900, with the Army Service Corps. He was present at the Relief of Kimberley ; operations in the Orange Free State, Feb. to May, 1900, including operations at Paardeberg (17 to 26 Feb.) ; actions at Poplar Grove and Dreifontein ; operations in the Transvaal, east of Pretoria, July to 29 Nov. 1900 ; operations in Orange River Colony, May and June, 1900 ; operations in the Transvaal 30 Nov. 1900, to Dec. 1901.

George Boon.

He was mentioned in Despatches [London Gazette, 10 Sept. 1901] ; received the Queen's Medal with four clasps ; the King's Medal with two clasps, and was appointed a Companion of the Distinguished Service Order [London Gazette, 27 Sept. 1901] : " George Boon, Quartermaster (Honorary Lieutenant), The Buffs, East Kent Regt. In recognition of services during the operations in South Africa." He retired from the East Kent Regt. 14 Dec. 1901, with the honorary rank of Captain (conferred 24 June, 1901). In 1871 he married Sarah Turgate Easter, and their children are : Ernest, born 5 Oct. 1875 ; Arthur, born 30 April, 1877 ; Edgar, born 3 Nov. 1879, and Charles, born 14 Aug. 1882.

LOWE, ARTHUR CECIL, Lieut., was born in 1868, son of Henry William Lowe, of Oakhill, Walton-on-Thames. He served in the South African War, with a Field Battery of the City of London Imperial Volunteers, taking part in operations in the Transvaal, east of Pretoria, Aug. and Sept. 1900 ; operations in the Transvaal, west of Pretoria, Aug. and Sept. 1900 ; operations in Orange River Colony, including actions at Lindley (26 June), Bethlehem (6 and 7 July) and Wittebergen (1 to 29 July). He was mentioned in Despatches [London Gazette, 10 Sept. 1901] ; received the Queen's Medal with three clasps, and was created a Companion of the Distinguished Service Order [London Gazette, 27 Sept. 1901] : " Arthur Cecil Lowe, Lieut., Honourable Artillery Company. In recognition of services during the operations in South Africa." He subsequently became Captain in the Honourable Artillery Company, and Major, and then Lieutenant-Colonel, Territorial Force. He was created a C.M.G., and was killed in action 24 Nov. 1917. An obituary notice says : " Brigadier-General Arthur Cecil Lowe, D.S.O., R.A., was killed on 24 Nov. Born in 1868, he was the son of Mr. Henry William Lowe, of Oakhill, Walton-on-Thames. Formerly he was Major in the 2nd City of London Horse Artillery, Military member of the City of London Territorial Force Association, and Temporary Lieutenant-Colonel, 2nd London Brigade, R.F.A. He served with the C.I.V. in the South African War, and was mentioned in Despatches and awarded the D.S.O. He married, in 1910, Amy Louisa, second daughter of the late Walter Samuel Partridge, of Tunbridge Wells."

PRIOR, JOHN HARVEY, Lieut., was born 14 Dec. 1871, son of E. H. Prior, of Bridgwater. He served in the South African War from 1899 to 1901, being employed as Station Staff Officer from 10 Feb. 1901, and was present in operations in Orange River Colony, May to 29 Nov. 1900 ; operations in Cape Colony, south of Orange River, 1899 to 1900, including the actions at Colesberg 1 Jan. to 12 Feb. 1900 ; operations in the Transvaal, May, 1901 ; operations in Orange River Colony 30 Nov. 1900, to May, 1901. For his services he was mentioned in Despatches [London Gazette, 10 Sept. 1901] ; was awarded the Queen's Medal with four clasps, and was created a Companion of the Distinguished Service Order [London Gazette, 27 Sept. 1901] : " John Harvey Prior, Lieut., Plymouth Division, Royal Engineers, Submarine Miners (Militia). In recognition of services during the operations in South Africa." The Insignia were presented by the King. Major (Temporary Lieut.-Colonel) J. H. Prior served in the European War. He was mentioned in Despatches, and was awarded a Bar to the Distinguished Service Order [London Gazette, 16 Sept. 1918] : " John Harvey Prior, D.S.O., Royal Engineers, Special Reserve. For conspicuous gallantry and devotion to duty in action, when he volunteered to attach himself and his company to a battalion which was threatened by an outflanking movement. By his personal courage and excellent handling of his company he was successful in holding the enemy and in assisting the battalion to withdraw at a very critical moment." He was also awarded the Legion of Honour. He married, in 1895, Emily Rose, widow of G. B. Long, J.P., of Wotton-under-Edge, Gloucestershire, and they have one daughter.

DE TRAFFORD, AUGUSTUS FRANCIS, Lieut., served in the South African War, and was created a Companion of the Distinguished Service Order [London Gazette, 27 Sept. 1901]: "Augustus Francis de Trafford, Lieut., 3rd South Staffordshire Regt. For services during the recent operations in South Africa." He died in hospital after a lingering illness on 1 June, 1904. When a memorial to Lieut. de Trafford was unveiled, Colonel Raitt said of him: "Here, among those who knew him, there is no need for me to say he was a well-loved comrade. You all know that his amiability of disposition, straightforwardness, modesty, and charm of manner would have been sure to endear him to those around him. But we also call him a most gallant comrade, and to show you these words also are used in all sincerity, I would like to give you two instances of his conduct in action. In June and July, 1900, he was with a wing of the battalion under my command at a place called Willow Grange, near Ficksburg, in the Orange Free State. The enemy's position was two or three miles in front of us. The intervening ground was a plateau running from our position up to theirs. One day we went out to cut barbed wire from the farm fences in front that we required to strengthen our defences. The Boers came out and shot at us, but did no harm. Apart from the incident I am about to relate, it was an insignificant affair. I left Augustus de Trafford with half a company on a little kopje to our right rear, in order to prevent the Boers working round under cover of the edge of the plateau, to enfilade us. When we had got all the wire we needed, I rode back to the kopje where I could get a better view, in order to see when I could safely retire the covering parties. It appears that the Boers had tried to get round our flank, and were under cover in some rocks at the edge of the plateau about 300 or 400 yards away. I did not know they were there, and those at the kopje, no doubt thinking I knew, never told me. I saw two soldiers lying alone a short distance in front away from their section. I asked what they were doing, and said they were to be ordered to rejoin it. I never meant Augustus de Trafford himself to go to them. The next thing I saw was he walking quietly up to them. The Boers opened fire on him, they had the exact range, and the bullets were striking the ground all round. Horrified at the result of my order, I shouted to him to run. He would not run, but walked quietly up to them, gave them their orders, and returned. Every moment I expected to see him drop. Well, I think a man might be brave enough, and yet have run without even waiting to be told to do so. At this time he was a subaltern in the 3rd (Militia) Battalion, and there was some difficulty about getting his commission in the line. I had an opportunity some time after of relating this incident to the General, who at once interested himself in the matter, and got his commission. I think, therefore, we may fairly say he gained his commission by his gallantry in action. The next incident was related to me by Major Williams, of our battalion, who was himself afterwards killed in action, and by Major Going, who is here to-day. It occurred with the Mounted Infantry near Vereeniging, in the Southern Transvaal, in July, 1901. They were being closely pressed by a very superior force of Boers; de Trafford's section, which was out in front, was ordered to fall back to a ridge, where the remainder of the regiment were. While they were doing so, he saw Major Williams' horse shot. He at once rode up to him and begged him to take his. Major Williams refused, and told him to go on after his section. He would not, and before Major Williams could persuade him to do so his horse also was shot. The Boers were right on to them, and they were surrounded and captured. Major Williams reported this incident, and it gained him the Distinguished Service Order."

Augustus F. de Trafford.

POORE, ROGER ALVIN, Lieut., was born 3 July, 1870, at Bath, son of Robert Poore, formerly Major, 6th Hussars, and Juliana Benita Poore, daughter of the late Rear-Admiral Sir Armar Lowry Corry, K.C.B., and Lady Corry (*née* Massy Dawson). Roger Alvin Poore, then a Lieutenant in the Royal Wiltshire Yeomanry, volunteered for the South African War, and was appointed to the Mounted Infantry Company of the Yorkshire Light Infantry (3rd Mounted Infantry) 17 Nov. 1899, and served with them in all engagements from Belmont 23 Nov., Graspan 25 Nov., Modder River 30 Nov., Magersfontein 11 Dec., the Relief of Kimberley, Paardeberg, etc., to the Battle of Diamond Hill on the 11th and 12th June, 1900. His horse was shot under him at Sanna's Post, and, in another engagement, a bullet passed through his helmet. Soon after Diamond Hill he was appointed District Magistrate, when, in the performance of his duties, "he was regarded as the soul of honour and uprightness, and a loyal, genuine friend," by both Boers and English. His Commanding Officer, Lieut.-Colonel Pilcher, wrote on 19 Dec. 1900: "I can think of no officer who has seen more, or as much, fighting as Lieut. Poore has done. I have on more than one occasion sent forward his name for honourable mention; I know no better patrol leader. He was on one occasion called out and thanked by Major-General Hutton for his good work. He is an excellent Mounted Infantry Officer." Lieut. Poore (then Captain) was mentioned in Lord Roberts's Supplementary Despatches 10 Sept. 1901. He was created a Companion of the Distinguished Service Order [London Gazette, 27 Sept. 1901]: "Roger Alvin Poore, Lieut., Royal Wiltshire Yeomanry. In recognition of services during the operations in South Africa." In 1911 Major Poore received the Coronation Medal. On the 11th Jan. 1915, he was appointed to the command of the 2/1st Royal Wiltshire Yeomanry, and, in the Supplement to the London Gazette, War Office, 24 Feb. 1917, the name of (Temporary) Lieut.-Colonel R. A. Poore is (with those of other officers) mentioned as having been brought before the Secretary of State for War "for valuable services rendered in connection with the war." In Feb. he was transferred to the 2nd Battn. Royal Welsh Fusiliers, and served with them till he was killed in action on 26 Sept. 1917. His Colonel, writing to Mrs. Poore, said: "There is one thing that you will hear with pride, and that is, that the battalion under your husband's command behaved most gallantly in the action and has covered itself with glory. Your husband has endeared himself to everybody in the battalion, and his loss will be most acutely felt. He had helped and supported me most loyally; indeed, I do not know how I will get on without his wise advice. He was one of the most gallant gentlemen I have ever met." Brigadier-General Mayne (of the 33rd Division) wrote, 2 Oct. 1917: "He" (Major Poore) "was so keen and enthusiastic about anything he did, and he set such a fine example by his devotion to duty and strength of character. The last time I saw him (25 Sept.) he was moving up with his battalion to the front line, full of enthusiasm and a splendid example to his officers and men." Major Poore was a splendid horseman, an excellent shot with both rifle and gun, and very keen on every kind of sport. At the Military Tournament at the Agricultural Hall in 1899, the only time he competed, he won First Prize for "Sabre *v.* Sabre." "The best of friends, the most gallant of men; an awful loss for all, and their name is legion, and for the country he served so well." He married, on 9 Dec. 1913, Lorne Margery, daughter of Major Richard James William Dennistoun and Mrs. Despard, of Hamilton, and their children were Lorne Heather Dennistoun, born 23 Dec. 1914 (died 22 Feb. 1915), and Roger Hamilton Poore, born 19 Aug. 1916.

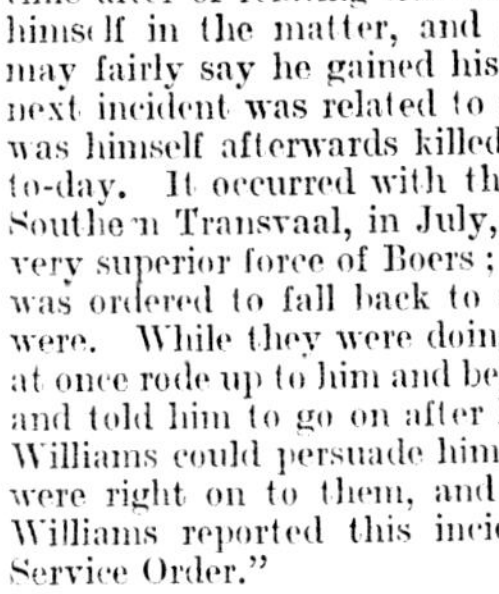

Roger Alvin Poore.

WILSON, CLIVE HENRY ADOLPHUS, Lieut., was born in 1876, and is the third son of the late Arthur Wilson, of Tranby Croft. He served in the South African War, 1900 to 1902, with the Imperial Yeomanry and Damant's Horse, and was severely wounded. He was mentioned in Despatches twice [London Gazette, 10 Sept. 1901, and 25 April, 1902]; received the Queen's and King's Medals with six clasps, and was created a Companion of the Distinguished Service Order [London Gazette, 27 Sept. 1901]: "Clive Wilson, Lieut., 12th Battn. Imperial Yeomanry. In recognition of services during the operations in South Africa." The Insignia were presented by the King 29 Oct. 1901. He retired from the East Riding of Yorkshire Yeomanry 6 Dec. 1902, and was given the honorary rank of Captain. He was a Director of Thomas Wilson and Company, Hull, the United Shipping Company, London, and of Story, Smithson and Company, Hull, and was Master of the Holderness Hounds. He married, in 1907, Elvira, daughter of the late Signor Magherim, of Florence.

THYNNE, ULRIC OLIVER, Lieut., was born in London 6 July, 1871, son of Lord Henry Frederick Thynne (son of the Marquis of Bath) and Lady Ulrica Thynne, daughter of the 12th Duke of Somerset. He was educated at Charterhouse and Sandhurst, and entered the Royal Wiltshire Yeomanry as a Second Lieutenant. He took part in the operations in Chitral with the Relief Force in 1895 (Medal with clasp), and served in South Africa in 1900 with the Imperial Yeomanry. In this campaign he was a Special Service Officer, and afterwards Brigade-Major, Rhodesian Field Force; was mentioned in Despatches [London Gazette, 10 Sept. 1901]; received the Queen's Medal with three clasps, and was created a Companion of the Distinguished Service Order [London Gazette, 27 Sept. 1901]: "Ulric Oliver Thynne, Lieut., Royal Wiltshire Yeomanry Cavalry (Rhodesian Field Force). In recognition of services during the operations in South Africa." The Insignia were presented by the King 2 June, 1902. Lieut.-Colonel U. O. Thynne served in the European War from 1914 to 1918, and was created a C.M.G. in 1918. He married, in London 16 May, 1899, Marjory, daughter of Edward Wormald, of 15, Berkeley Square, and they have four children: Oliver St. Maur, born 24 Oct. 1901; Edward Wormald, born 17 March, 1905; Brian Sheridan, born 29 Nov. 1907, and Ulrica Marjory, born 5 May, 1911.

DICKSON-POYNDER, SIR JOHN POYNDER (LORD ISLINGTON), Bart., Lieut., was born in 1866. He assumed the name of Poynder on succeeding to his maternal uncle's property in 1881, and succeeded his uncle as 6th Baronet (created 1802) in 1884. He was educated at Harrow and Christ Church, Oxford; was a Member of the London County Council for St. George's, Hanover Square, from 1898 to 1904, and Conservative Member of Parliament for the Chippenham Division of Wiltshire, 1892 to 1910. He joined the Royal Wiltshire Yeomanry, and served in the South African War with the Imperial Yeomanry, taking part in operations in the Transvaal, west of Pretoria, including actions at Zilikat's Nek, Elands River (4 to 6 Aug.) and Venterskroon (7 to 9 Aug.); operations in Orange River Colony, including actions at Lindley (1 to 26 June) and Rhenoster River. For his services he was mentioned in Despatches [London Gazette, 10 Sept. 1901]; received the Queen's Medal with three clasps, and was created a Companion of the Distinguished Service Order [London Gazette, 27 Sept. 1901]: "Sir John Poynder Dickson-Poynder, Bart., Lieut., 1st Battn. Imperial Yeomanry. In recognition of services during the operations in South Africa." The Insignia were presented by the King 29 Oct. 1901. He

retired from the Royal Scots, and subsequently from the Wiltshire Yeomanry. In 1910 he became 1st Baron Islington, and was Governor of New Zealand from 1910 to 1912, becoming Honorary Colonel of the 9th New Zealand Mounted Rifles, March, 1911; became a Privy Councillor and K.C.M.G. in 1911 and G.C.M.G. in 1913. Lord Islington was Under Secretary of State for the Colonies from 1914 to 1915, and Parliamentary Under Secretary for India from 1915 to 1918. He married, in 1896, Anne, daughter of R. H. D. Dundas and Catherine Anne, daughter of the 2nd Baron Napier of Magdala, and they have one daughter.

FLETCHER, WILLIAM ALFRED LITTLEDALE, Lieut., was born at Childwall 25 Aug. 1869, son of Alfred Fletcher, J.P., D.L. He was educated at Eton, and Christ Church, Oxford (Eton Eight, 1890; Oxford " Blue " for Rowing, 1890–1893); served in the South African War with the 2nd Battn. Imperial Yeomanry from 1899 to 1900. He was created a Companion of the Distinguished Service Order [London Gazette, 27 Sept. 1901]: " William Alfred Littledale Fletcher, Lieut., Imperial Yeomanry. In recognition of services during the operations in South Africa." The Insignia were presented by the King 29 Oct. 1901. He again saw service in the European War from 1914 to 1918, receiving for his services the Brevet of Major, three mentions in Despatches, and the Legion of Honour.

William A. L. Fletcher.

He died 14 Feb. 1919. The late Major Fletcher, besides being a great oarsman, went in for big game shooting, and had travelled considerably. He was world-famous as an oarsman, coach, umpire, and a member of important rowing committees. He gained the highest honours in rowing, first appearing at Henley in the Eton College Eight of 1888, which beat Radley, but went under to Pembroke College, Cambridge, in the semi-final of the Ladies' Plate. In the following year he was at 7 in the Christ Church, Oxford Crew, which won the Leander Plate and Thames Cup, and he rowed for the College in 1890 in the same two events unsuccessfully. In the next year he was at 6 in the powerful Leander Eight, stroked by C. W. Kent, which won the Grand Challenge Cup and beat record against London in the final, and was also in the final for the Goblets, being partnered by F. Wilkinson, and losing to Lord Ampthill and Guy Nickalls by a foot only. In 1892 he was again in the winning Leander Eight for the Grand, and won the Goblets with Vivian Nickalls. His record in the University Boat Race was the very brilliant one of four successive wins. He stroked the winning Oxford crew in 1890; was at 7 to Kent in 1891; at 6 to C. M. Pitman in 1892, and to M. C. Pilkington in 1893. In addition Colonel Fletcher has done splendid service for rowing in coaching, by umpiring at Henley, and by his work on the committee of management of Henley Regatta, and on the committee of the Amateur Rowing Association.

His death caused widespread regret, and some obituary notices of him read as follows:

" We regret to announce that Lieut.-Colonel William Alfred Littledale Fletcher, D.S.O., the Oxford Rowing Blue and coach, died of bronchopneumonia yesterday at Allerton, Liverpool, aged 49. The name of W. A. L. Fletcher is classical in the literature of rowing. There are many who would say that he was the finest of all heavy-weight oarsmen, and certainly among the welter-weights there are not half a dozen names that could possibly be classed with his. The eldest son of Mr. and Mrs. Alfred Fletcher, he was educated at Eton and Christ Church, Oxford. His prowess as an oarsman was not so remarkable at Eton as at Oxford, but he rowed in the Eton crew of 1888 for ' the Ladies.' In Jan. 1889, he went up to Oxford, and thenceforward developed very rapidly in weight and strength, besides improving out of knowledge as an oarsman. In the summer of 1889 he rowed ' 7 ' in the Christ Church eight, which won both the Ladies' Plate and the Thames Cup at Henley. This was followed by a remarkable success in the spring of 1890, when he stroked the Oxford crew, which beat Cambridge after four successive Cambridge victories. The tide of success in the University Boat Race had turned, and Oxford won for nine years consecutively, in the first four of which Mr. Fletcher was a mainstay of the Oxford crew. He rowed stroke in 1890 (at the record weight for the thwart of 13st.), ' 7 ' in 1891, and ' 6 ' in 1892 and 1893. As a ' 6 ' he was undoubtedly at his best. It is regarded by many as the most important position in the boat, and certainly a big man at ' 6,' who is also a superlatively good oar, can ' make ' a crew to an extent that is not possible even at stroke or ' 7.' Mr. Fletcher rowed in many very good crews and contributed greatly to their excellence. He also rowed in several college crews of fair standard that would have been of decidedly poor class without him. With Mr. Fletcher at ' 6 ' it would hardly have been possible for an eight, after a reasonable period of training, to be a bad one. His record of victories is not so remarkable as that of several oarsmen of less calibre, but they were nearly all victories of the very first class. A period of comparatively few years covers his rowing career, and during that period he never entered for more than two events in any one regatta at Henley. In the races for which he entered he was almost invariably victorious. He won ' the Grand ' on every occasion on which he rowed for it—namely, in the Leander crews of 1891, 1892 and 1893. In 1891 he was beaten in the final for ' the Goblets,' but in both the two following years, partnered by Mr. V. Nickalls, he won the event handsomely. This pair was probably the fastest that ever rowed at Henley. It may be added that the Leander eights of 1891 and 1893 were of exceptional excellence, and that the former won the final in record time. Subsequently, Mr. Fletcher became famous as a coach. He trained and coached many Cambridge as well as Oxford crews with conspicuous success. His oarsmanship was remarkable for its length and power, and in hardly less degree for its smooth and finished style. Added to a long reach and vast strength, Mr. Fletcher showed indomitable pluck and was possessed of great stamina. He was a man of strong and virile character, but, none the less, universally popular. Several years of his life were devoted to world-wide travel, which included an expedition into Tibet. In the South African War he won the D.S.O., and in the later stages of the present war he commanded the 2/6th (Rifles) King's Liverpool Regt. in France."

" The great oarsman and coach, Lieut.-Colonel W. A. L. Fletcher, D.S.O., died yesterday, a few hours after he had been elected chairman of the Henley Regatta Management Committee. He stroked the Oxford eight to victory against Cambridge in 1890, rowed ' 7 ' in the winning boat in 1891, and was ' 6 ' in the winning boats in 1892 and 1893."

" The rowing record of Colonel W. A. L. Fletcher, D.S.O., who died of pneumonia yesterday, is inscribed among the classics of sport. His other leading interest in life is less well known—he was an enthusiastic traveller. One of his journeys was an expedition into Tibet, in which he got within 43 miles of Lhassa. As might be expected, he made a fine soldier—his dauntless courage, his great power of physical endurance, and his determined character soon lifted him into the ranks of the first-class fighting men. He won his D.S.O. in the South African War for a splendid resistance put up by himself and a force reduced to 16 men, who barricaded themselves in a beleaguered house at Hamelfontein, and held out for the best part of a day and all night."

POWER, WILLIAM SAYER, Lieut., was born 2 Jan. 1859, son of the late William Power, of Bramcote. He served in the South African War, with the Imperial Yeomanry, from 1899 to 1900, and was present in operations in Orange River Colony, May to 29 Nov. 1900, including actions at Biddulphsberg, Lindley (1 June), Rhenoster River, Lindley (26 June), Bethlehem (6 and 7 July), Wittebergen (1 to 29 July) and Witpoort; operations in Cape Colony, south of Orange River, 1899 to 1900. He was wounded; mentioned in Despatches [London Gazette, 10 Sept. 1901]; received the Queen's Medal with two clasps, and was created a Companion of the Distinguished Service Order [London Gazette, 27 Sept. 1901]: " William Sayer Power, Lieut., 4th Battn. Imperial Yeomanry. In recognition of

William Sayer Power.

services during the operations in South Africa." The Insignia were presented by the King 29 Oct. 1901. He retired from the Derby Yeomanry 13 March, 1901, and is now Major, Territorial Force, Reserve of Officers. He married, in 1906, Jessy Isabel, eldest daughter of the late Vaughan Hanning Vaughan-Lee, J.P., D.L., of Dillington Park, Somerset, and widow of W. Boden, of Pastures, Derby.

VAUX, ERNEST, Lieut., was born in 1865, son of J. S. Vaux, of Sunderland. He saw service with the Durham Royal Garrison Artillery Volunteers, retiring 29 July, 1893. He served in South Africa with the Imperial Yeomanry, taking part in operations in the Transvaal, west of Pretoria, July to 29 Nov. 1900; operations in Orange River Colony, May to 29 Nov. 1900, including actions at Lindley (1 to 26 June) and Rhenoster River; operations in Cape Colony, north of Orange River, including action at Ruidam; operations in the Transvaal 30 Nov. 1900, to June, 1901. He was mentioned in Despatches [London Gazette, 10 Sept. 1901]; received the Queen's Medal with four clasps, and was created a Companion of the Distinguished Service Order [London Gazette, 27 Sept. 1901]: " Ernest Vaux, Lieut., 5th Battn. Imperial Yeomanry. In recognition of services during the operations in South Africa." The Insignia were presented by the King 29 Oct. 1901. He became Lieutenant-Colonel, 7th Battn. Durham Light Infantry. He served in the European War from 1914 to 1916. He was twice mentioned in Despatches; was created a C.M.G. in 1916, and has the Volunteer Decoration. Lieut.-Colonel E. Vaux married, in 1906, Emily L., daughter of H. Moon-Ord, and they have two sons.

WAUCHOPE, DAVID ALEXANDER, Lieut., was born 31 Jan. 1871, son of David Baird Wauchope, of Edinburgh. He was educated at Repton, and Trinity College, Cambridge, where he took his B.A. degree in 1892, and served in South Africa with the 6th Battn. (Lothians and Berwickshire) Imperial Yeomanry from 1899 to 1901. He was mentioned in Despatches [London Gazette, 10 Sept. 1901]; received the Queen's Medal with four clasps, and was created a Companion of the Distinguished Service Order [London Gazette, 27 Sept. 1901]: " David Alexander Wauchope, Lieut., 6th Battn. I.Y. For services in South Africa." He retired; was embodied with the Lothians and Border Horse in Aug. 1914, and went to France in 1915; commanded Divisional Mounted Troops in 1915, and Cape Mounted Troops in 1916. Lieut.-Colonel D. A. Wauchope has the Territorial Decoration and is a Member of the King's Body-Guard for Scotland, the Royal Company of Archers.

Edward John d'A. Cory

CORY, EDWARD JOHN D'ALMEIDA, Lieut., was born in 1861, son of the Rev. E. W. Cory, M.A., R.D., Vicar of Meldreth,

Cambridgeshire. He served in South Africa from 1900 to 1901. He was mentioned in Despatches, and created a Companion of the Distinguished Service Order [London Gazette, 27 Sept. 1901]: "Edward John Cory, Lieut., 7th Battn. Imperial Yeomanry. In recognition of services during the operations in South Africa." The Insignia were presented by the King 29 Oct. 1901. He retired from the 5th Battn. Royal Sussex Regt. 25 July, 1901. Capt. E. J. d'A. Cory (late Captain, 1st Cinque Port R.V.) married, in 1907, Rose Anna Georgina, daughter of the late W. Barrington d'Almeida, Barrister.

BROCKLEBANK, JOHN JASPER, Lieut., was born 5 Sept. 1875, second son of the late Sir Thomas Brocklebank, 2nd Baronet. He was educated at Eton and Cambridge. He served in South Africa, from 1900 to 1902, with the Imperial Yeomanry and the King's Dragoon Guards, being present in operations in the Transvaal, Orange River Colony and Cape Colony. He was mentioned in Despatches [London Gazette, 8 Feb. and 10 Sept. 1901]; awarded the Queen's Medal with three clasps, and was created a Companion of the Distinguished Service Order [London Gazette, 27 Sept. 1901]: "John Jasper Brocklebank, Lieut., 8th Battn. Imperial Yeomanry. For services in South Africa." The Insignia, Warrant and Statutes were sent to the G.O.C., Transvaal and Orange River Colony, 15 Nov. 1902. Major Brocklebank (Scottish Horse, late 1st Dragoon Guards) married, in 1914, Constance Mary, daughter of Sir R. Leonard Powell, and they have one son.

PALMER, ARTHUR PERCY, Lieut., served in the South African War with the Imperial Yeomanry and South African Constabulary. For his services he received the Queen's Medal with three clasps; the King's Medal with two clasps, and was created a Companion of the Distinguished Service Order [London Gazette, 27 Sept. 1901]: "Arthur Percy Palmer, Lieut., 11th Battn. Imperial Yeomanry. In recognition of services during the operations in South Africa." The Insignia, Warrant and Statutes were sent to the G.O.C., Transvaal, 3 Feb. 1903, and presented by the G.O.C., South Africa, at Pretoria, 25 March, 1903. He became Lieutenant, R. of O. and Capt. Reserve Cavalry. He was killed in action 27 Sept. 1915.

TOPPING, THOMAS EDWARD, Lieut., served in the South African War from 1900 to 1901, with the Imperial Yeomanry; was present in operations in the Orange River Colony, including actions at Lindley (1 June) and Rhenoster River; operations in the Transvaal, including actions at Elands River and Frederickstad; operations in Cape Colony, Orange River Colony and the Transvaal, 1901. He was mentioned in Despatches [London Gazette, 10 Sept. 1901], and was created a Companion of the Distinguished Service Order [London Gazette, 27 Sept. 1901]: "Thomas Edward Topping, Lieut., 15th Battn. Imperial Yeomanry. In recognition of services during the operations in South Africa." He was invested by the King 17 Dec. 1901. He also received the Queen's Medal with four clasps. He again saw active service in the European War from 1914 to 1918, and was made a C.M.G. in 1917, and a C.B. in 1919. He is Major and Temporary Lieutenant-Colonel, 2nd West Lancashire Brigade, Royal Field Artillery (Territorials); Honorary Captain in the Army.

SLATER, SYDNEY ARTHUR, Lieut., served in the South African War. He was created a Companion of the Distinguished Service Order [London Gazette, 27 Sept. 1901]: "Sydney Arthur Slater (since deceased), Lieut., 15th Battn. Imperial Yeomanry. In recognition of services during the operations in South Africa." The Insignia, Warrant and Statutes were sent to his executor, Colonel Slater.

THESIGER, THE HONOURABLE WILFRED GILBERT, Lieut., was born 25 March, 1871, son of the 2nd Baron Chelmsford and Adria Fanny, eldest daughter of Major-General Heath, Bombay Army. He was educated at Cheltenham, and was nominated Vice-Consul, Algiers, but did not proceed there, and was instead transferred to Taranto, Italy, in 1897. He served in South Africa with the Imperial Yeomanry from 1900 to 1901. He received mention in Despatches [London Gazette, 10 Sept. 1901]; received the Queen's Medal with four clasps, and was created a Companion of the Distinguished Service Order [London Gazette, 27 Sept. 1901]: "The Honourable Wilfred Gilbert Thesiger, Lieut., 15th Battn. Imperial Yeomanry. In recognition of services during the operations in South Africa." The Insignia were presented by the King 17 Dec. 1901. He retired as Honorary Captain 19 Dec. 1901; was appointed Vice-Consul at Belgrade in 1901; given the local rank of Second Secretary in the Diplomatic Service in 1902, and was in charge of the Legation at Belgrade from 1903 to 1906; was Consul for North and North-East Russia, 1906–7; H.B.M.'s Consul for Congo, 1907–8–9; Consul General, Abyssinia, 1909–14, with the local rank of Envoy Extraordinary and Minister Plenipotentiary. During the European War, 1914–19, Capt. the Honourable Wilfred Thesiger was on the General Staff of the War Office. He became Consul-General at New York in 1919. He married, in 1909, Kathleen, daughter of T. M. C. Vigors, of Burgage, County Carlow, and they had four sons.

MILNER, MARCUS HENRY, Lieut., was born 16 April, 1864, third son of H. B. W. Milner and Charlotte Beresford, daughter of the Archbishop of Armagh. He was educated at Wellington College, and at Trinity College, Cambridge. He served with the Imperial Yeomanry in the South African War, 1900–1, and was awarded the Queen's Medal with three clasps, and was created a Companion of the Distinguished Service Order [London Gazette, 27 Sept. 1901]: "Marcus Henry Milner, Lieut., 16th Battn. Imperial Yeomanry. In recognition of services during the operations in South Africa." The Insignia were presented by the King 29 Oct. 1901. Lieut. Milner was also created an M.V.O. in 1900. He retired from the 2nd County of London Imperial Yeomanry 7 Aug. 1907; was Honorary Assistant Private Secretary to the Under Secretary of State for War, and is now Controller to the Earl of Derby. Capt. Milner served in the European War as A.D.C. to the G.O.C., 55th Division, in France, and for his services was awarded the Croix de Guerre Belge. He has the 1915 Star. He married, in 1888, Caroline Agnes, Dowager Countess of Montrose, who died in 1894, and was the daughter of the 2nd Baron Decies.

LANGFORD, CHARLES, Lieut., was born in 1873, son of Capt. J. C. Langford, late 17th Foot. He served in the South African War from 1899 to 1901, with the Imperial Yeomanry. He was mentioned in Despatches; received the Queen's Medal with five clasps, and was created a Companion of the Distinguished Service Order [London Gazette, 27 Sept. 1901]: "Charles Langford, Lieut., 18th Battn. Imperial Yeomanry. In recognition of services during the operations in South Africa." The Insignia were presented by the King 29 Oct. 1901. He retired from the 8th King's Royal Irish Hussars. He served in the Great War, becoming Adjutant, Army Service Corps, in 1915, and Major in 1917, and was twice mentioned in Despatches. He married, in 1906, Agnes Sutherland, second daughter of the late Joseph Matterson, of Castle Tray House, Limerick, and they have one son.

PATTERSON, JOHN HENRY, Lieut., was born 10 Nov. 1867. He served in South Africa from 1900 to 1902. He was twice mentioned in Despatches [London Gazette, 9 July and 10 Sept. 1901], and was created a Companion of the Distinguished Service Order [London Gazette, 27 Sept. 1901]: "John Henry Patterson, Lieut., 20th Battn. Imperial Yeomanry. In recognition of services during the operations in South Africa." The Insignia were presented by the King 29 Oct. 1901. From Jan. to 31 May, 1902, he was in command of the 33rd Imperial Battn., and had the Queen's Medal with four clasps. He retired from the Essex Yeomanry 11 Feb. 1903. He served in the European War in Egypt, and in command of the Zion Mule Corps in Gallipoli in 1915, receiving mention in Despatches for this campaign. He was afterwards in command from July, 1916, to Jan. 1917, of the 4th Battn. Royal Irish Fusiliers; Jan. to Aug. 1917, and from 1917 in command of the 38th Battn. Royal Fusiliers, a Jewish battalion. Lieut.-Colonel Patterson has published "The Man-Eaters of Tsavo," 1907; "In the Grip of the Nyika," 1909; "With the Zionists in Gallipoli," 1916.

WYNNE, REGINALD, Lieut. and Quartermaster, was the son of the late Capt. Evan Wynne-Roberts, of Curzon Street, Mayfair, W. He was educated at Eton, and saw active service in South Africa from 1899 to 1901, with the Imperial Yeomanry. He was mentioned in Despatches, and was appointed a Companion of the Distinguished Service Order [London Gazette, 27 Sept. 1901]: "Reginald Wynne, Lieut. and Quartermaster, 20th Battn. Imperial Yeomanry. In recognition of services during the operations in South Africa." The Insignia were presented by the King 29 Oct. 1901. He afterwards served in South Africa as Major of the 2nd Company of Imperial Yeomanry, which he himself raised in 1901. He died suddenly of heart failure at Hôtel Maurice, Paris, 23 Sept. 1913, aged 56, and was buried at Cuxton, Rochester, and an obituary notice of him appeared in the "Times" of 25 Sept. 1913. Major Wynne married, in 1902, Hilda, daughter of the late J. Clifton Brown, of Rothwell Park, Yorkshire.

FORBES, HARRY, Lieut., was born 20 April, 1865, son of the late Harry Forbes, of Muirton of Barro, Oldmeldrum. He was educated at Aberdeen Academy, and joined the Army in 1881. He served in South Africa, 1899–1901, being employed from 26 Jan. 1901, onwards, as Station Staff Officer. Severely wounded in the campaign, he was present in operations in the Orange Free State, Feb. to May, 1900, including actions at Houtnek (Thoba Mountain), Vet River (5 and 6 May) and Zand River; operations in the Transvaal, May and June, 1900, including action near Johannesburg; operations in the Transvaal, east of Pretoria, July to 29 Nov. 1900, including actions at Belfast (26 and 27 Aug.) and Lydenberg (5 to 8 Sept.); operations in the Transvaal, west of Pretoria, July to 29 Nov. 1900; operations in Cape Colony, south of Orange River, 1899–1900. He was mentioned in Despatches [London Gazette, 10 Sept. 1901]; received the Queen's Medal with five clasps, and was created a Companion of the Distinguished Service Order [London Gazette, 27 Sept. 1901]: "Harry Forbes, Lieut., 4th Volunteer Battn. Gordon Highlanders. In recognition of services during the operations in South Africa." The Insignia were sent 25 April, 1901, to the G.O.C., Scottish District, and were presented by Colonel H. H. Matthias, C.B., A.D.C. He was promoted Lieutenant-Colonel, Nov. 1914, and served in France in the European War from March, 1917, to Jan. 1918. Lieut.-Colonel Forbes is a farmer and a breeder of Aberdeen-Angus cattle and Clydesdale horses. He has the Volunteer decoration. Lieut.-Colonel Forbes married, 27 April, 1904, in Aberdeen, E. E. Cook, of Carden House, Aberdeen, and they have a daughter, E. B. Forbes, born 10 Feb. 1905.

WILSON, THE HONOURABLE CHARLES HENRY WELLESLEY (LORD NUNBURNHOLME), Major, was born in 1875, son of the 1st Baron Nunburnholme, head of great shipping concerns, and for 30 years Liberal M.P. for Hull, and Florence, daughter of Colonel W. H. C. Wellesley. He was educated at Eton. He saw active service with the City Imperial Volunteers (Mounted Infantry) in South Africa in 1900, being present at the Relief of Kimberley; operations in the Orange Free State, Feb. to May, 1900, including actions at Karee Siding, Vet River (5 and 6 May) and Zand River; operations in the Transvaal, May and June, 1900, including actions near Johannesburg, Pretoria and Diamond Hill (11 June); operations in the Transvaal, west of Pretoria, July to 29 Nov. 1900, including actions at Zilikat's Nek and Elands River (4 to 16 Aug.); operations in Orange River Colony, July, 1900. For his services he was mentioned

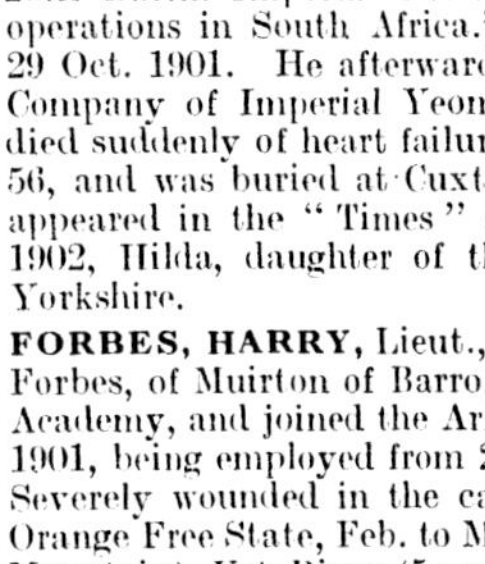

Lord Nunburnholme.

in Despatches [London Gazette, 10 Sept. 1901]; received the Queen's Medal with four clasps, and was created a Companion of the Distinguished Service Order [London Gazette, 27 Sept. 1901]: "The Honourable Charles Henry Wellesley Wilson, Lieut., City Imperial Volunteers (Major, 2nd Volunteer Battn. East Yorkshire Regt. In recognition of services during the operations in South Africa." The Insignia were presented by the King 29 Oct. 1901. He retired 1 Dec. 1900, and when his father was raised to the peerage succeeded him as Member for Hull, and so he remained until 1907. He is a large shipowner, and now H.M. Lieutenant for the East Riding of Yorkshire; he was created a C.B. in 1918. Lord Nunburnholme married, in 1901, Lady Marjorie Wynn Carrington, daughter of the 1st Marquess of Lincolnshire. His heir is the Honourable Charles John Wilson, born 25 April, 1904, and he has one other son and a daughter.

CONCANON, EDMOND GEORGE, Lieut., was born 24 June, 1875, in London, son of James Blake Concanon, Athenry, County Galway, Ireland. He was educated privately, and joined the 16th Middlesex Volunteers (London Irish Rifles), now the 18th Battn. London Irish Rifles. He served in South Africa with the City Imperial Volunteers, Mounted Infantry, and was present in operations in the Orange Free State, Feb. to May, 1900, including operations at Paardeberg (17 to 26 Feb.); action at Poplar Grove, Dreifontein, Karee Siding and Houtnek (Thoba Mountain); operations in the Transvaal in May and June, 1900, including actions near Johannesburg, Pretoria and Diamond Hill (11 and 12 June); operations in Orange River Colony, including actions at Belfast (26 and 27 Aug.), Lydenberg (5 to 8 Sept.) and Wittebergen (1 to 20 July). He was mentioned in Despatches [London Gazette, 10 Sept. 1901]; received the Queen's Medal with seven clasps, and was created a Companion of the Distinguished Service Order [London Gazette, 27 Sept. 1901]: "Edmond George Concanon, Lieut., C.I.V. (Capt., 16th Middlesex Volunteers, London Irish Rifles. In recognition of services during the operations in South Africa." He was invested by the King 29 Oct. 1901. He was gazetted Lieutenant-Colonel to command the 18th Battn. The London Regt. London Irish Rifles, in Nov. 1913, and in that year received the Territorial Decoration. He trained this regiment, and took it out to France in March, 1915; was invalided home in May, 1915, and afterwards commanded the 32nd Battn. The London Regt. Lieut.-Colonel Concanon was mentioned in Despatches for services rendered in the war in Feb. 1917. He married, 18 Oct. 1901, at Bray, Berkshire, Bertha Bekford Syvret, only daughter of T. Gosselin, of Bagot, Jersey, and their children are: Edmond James Blake, born 27 March, 1906, and Patrick Henry Gosselin, born in June, 1910.

BELL, HENRY STANLEY, Lieut., was born 6 June, 1874, son of the late Thomas Bell, J.P., D.C.L. He served in the South African War from 1899 to 1901, commanding the 1st Battery of the 1st Northumbrian Brigade, R.F.A. (T.F.), and was present in operations in the Transvaal, west of Pretoria, including the actions at Zilikat's Nek and Frederickstad (25 Oct.); operations in Orange River Colony, May to 29 Nov. 1900; operations in Cape Colony, south of Orange River. He was mentioned in Despatches [London Gazette, 10 Sept. 1901]; received the Queen's Medal with three clasps, and was created a Companion of the Distinguished Service Order [London Gazette, 27 Sept. 1901]: "Henry Stanley Bell, Lieut., Elswick Battery, 1st Northumberland Volunteer Artillery. In recognition of services during the operations in South Africa." The Insignia were presented by the King 29 Oct. 1901. He again saw active service in the European War; was made a C.M.G. in 1917, and was mentioned in Despatches. He has retired from the Territorial Force, R.F.A., having the Territorial Decoration. Lieut.-Colonel H. S. Bell is married, and has two sons and three daughters.

HORSFALL, ALFRED HERBERT, Lieut., was born 29 Jan. 1871, son of the late Jonas Horsfall, of Yorkshire and Melbourne, Victoria, Australia. He was educated at the Scotch College, Melbourne, and at Melbourne University (M.B. and Ch.B. 1893). He served in South Africa 1900–1, as Lieutenant, New South Wales Army Medical Corps, and as Medical Officer to the 1st Battn. Cameron Highlanders, and was present at the action near Bethune and march to Pretoria, Diamond Hill and at General Prinsloo's surrender. He received the Queen's Medal with clasps, and was created a Companion of the Distinguished Service Order [London Gazette, 27 Sept. 1901]: "Alfred Herbert Horsfall, Lieut., New South Wales Army Medical Corps. In recognition of services during the operations in South Africa." The Insignia were presented by the Governor-General of Canada at Government House, Ottawa. He was promoted Major; became M.O., Hamilton, 2nd Australian Commonwealth Military District, 1 July, 1912. In the European War he served as Major, R.A.M.C. (T.F.) in the Balkan States and Egypt, for which he was mentioned in Despatches; and as Surgeon, 2nd Northern General Hospital. He was formerly Resident Surgeon at Melbourne and Police Hospitals, Victoria, and Medical Superintendent at Newcastle, N.S.W., and practised at Newcastle as a surgeon. From 1915–1918 he was Unionist candidate, Pudsey Division, Yorkshire. He has done much travelling in America and the Far East; is a lecturer of the Royal Colonial Institute and the Social and Political Education League, and has published, among other works, "The Anglo-Saxon as an Empire Builder" and "Australia's Stake in the War." Major Horsfall married, in 1903, Gertrude Emily, daughter of the late Colonel C. F. Stokes, A.D.C., of Sydney, N.S.W., and they have one son and one daughter.

MORRISON, EDWARD WHIPPLE BANCROFT, Lieut., served in South Africa, 1899–1900, taking part in the operations in the Transvaal, east of Pretoria, July to 29 Nov. 1900, including actions at Belfast (26 and 27 Aug.); operations in Orange River Colony, May to Nov. 1900; operations in Cape Colony, south of Orange River, 1899–1900. He was mentioned in Despatches [London Gazette, 10 Sept. 1901]; was awarded the Brevet of Captain and was created a Companion of the Distinguished Service Order [London Gazette, 27 Sept. 1901]: "Edward Whipple Bancroft Morrison,

Lieut., Canadian Contingent. In recognition of services during the operations in South Africa." The Insignia were presented by the Governor-General of Canada. He commanded the 8th Artillery Brigade, Canadian Field Artillery, from 1909 to 1913; became Lieutenant Colonel 1 March, 1913; was Director of Artillery, Headquarters Staff, 1913 to 1914. Lieut.-Colonel Morrison had a distinguished record in the European War. He served as O.C., 1st Artillery Brigade, Canadian Expeditionary Force, 1914–15, being present at the Second Battle of Ypres, Festubert and Givenchy, and being promoted Brevet Colonel 1 Sept. 1915. In 1915 and 1916 he was G.O.C., 2nd Canadian Divisional Artillery, engaged at St. Eloi, the Third Battle of Ypres and the Somme; was G.O.C., Canadian Corps Artillery, 1916–19; in action at Vimy, Hill 70, Lens, Passchendaele, in 1917, and Amiens, Arras, Quéant–Drocourt Line, Canal du Nord, Bourlon Wood, capture of Cambrai, Valenciennes, Mons, 1918; in 1919 with the Army of Occupation in Germany. He was created a C.M.G. in 1917, C.B. in 1918, and K.C.M.G. 1919; was mentioned in Despatches, and on 31 July, 1918, became Major-General. In 1911 Major-General Sir E. W. B. Morrison married Mrs. Emma Fripp, of Ottawa.

MASON, JAMES COOPER, Lieut., was born in Toronto in 1875, eldest son of the late Brigadier-General the Honourable James Mason, Senator. He was educated at Toronto Collegiate Institute, and served as Lieutenant and Captain, Royal Canadian Regt., in South Africa from 1899 to 1900, being present in operations in the Orange Free State, including operations at Paardeberg (18 Feb.), during which he was slightly wounded; operations in Orange River Colony and Transvaal, west of Pretoria, Aug. 1900; operations in the Transvaal, east of Pretoria, July to 29 Nov. 1900. He was mentioned in Despatches [London Gazette, 10 Sept. 1901]; was given the Brevet of Major, the Queen's Medal with three clasps, and was created a Companion of the Distinguished Service Order [London Gazette, 27 Sept. 1901]: "James Cooper Mason, Lieut., Canadian Contingent. In recognition of services during the operations in South Africa." He became Major 1 Feb. 1902; was appointed Brigade Major of the 8th Canadian Infantry Brigade 9 Dec. 1909, and became Lieutenant-Colonel and Commanding Officer of his regiment, the 10th Royal Grenadiers Militia of Canada, 21 July, 1915. Lieut.-Colonel Mason is a Banker. He married, in 1904, Jean Florence, daughter of the late Alexander MacArthur.

DULY, CHARLES, Lieut., was born 1 Jan. 1870, son of the late Charles Duly, of Hastings. He served during the Matabele Rebellion of 1896, and in the South African War, 1899–1902; was mentioned in Despatches and created a Companion of the Distinguished Service Order [London Gazette, 27 Sept. 1901]: "Charles Duly, Lieut., Rhodesian Regt., Cyclist Section Rhodesian Volunteers. In recognition of services during the operations in South Africa." The Insignia, Warrant and Statutes were sent to South Africa, and presented by Lieut.-Colonel Chester Master 25 April, 1903. He served in East Africa in the European War, commanding the Mechanical Transport, British South African Police, under General Northey. Major Duly married, in 1901, Edith, daughter of William Harris, of Johannesburg.

MACKWORTH, HARRY LLEWELLYN, Second Lieut., was born 17 March, 1878, fourth son of the late Sir A. W. Mackworth, Bart., and Alice, daughter of Joseph Cubitt, C.E.; and brother of the 7th Baronet. He was educated at the Royal Military Academy, Woolwich, and entered the Army, as a Second Lieutenant in the Royal Engineers, 23 March, 1898, in which he became Lieutenant 14 Feb. 1901. He served in South Africa from 1899 to 1902, and was present at the Relief of Kimberley, operations in the Orange Free State, Feb. to May, 1900; operations in the Transvaal in May and June, 1900; operations in the Transvaal, east of Pretoria, July to 29 Nov. 1900; operations in the Transvaal 30 Nov. 1900, to Sept. 1901, and Nov. 1901, to 31 May, 1902; operations in Orange River Colony, Oct. and Nov. 1901; operations on the Zululand Frontier of Natal, Sept. and Oct. 1901. He was mentioned in Despatches [London Gazette, 4 May, 1900, and 10 Sept. 1901]; received the Queen's Medal with six clasps and the King's Medal with two clasps, and was created a Companion of the Distinguished Service Order [London Gazette, 27 Sept. 1901]: "Harry Llewellyn Mackworth, Second Lieut., Royal Engineers. In recognition of services during the operations in South Africa." He served in operations in Somaliland in 1903 and 1904, and was present at the action at Jidballi (Medal with two clasps); was employed with the Egyptian Army 20 Jan. 1905, to 24 Feb. 1909; became Captain 23 March, 1907; was employed with the Australian Commonwealth Military Forces from 29 March, 1912, becoming Director of Army Signals. Capt. Mackworth was promoted Captain 30 Oct. 1914. He served in the European War; took part in the Dardanelles Campaign, 1914–15 (Despatches), and served in Egypt, 1916–18. He was given the Brevet of Lieutenant-Colonel 3 June, 1916, after serving as Temporary and then Acting Lieutenant-Colonel, and was again mentioned in Despatches, and created a C.M.G. in 1918. Colonel H. L. Mackworth married, in 1913, Leonie, daughter of the late Professor Franklin Peterson.

WICKHAM, THOMAS EDMUND PALMER, Second Lieut., was born 30 Jan. 1879, eldest son of R. W. Wickham, of Ebley Court, Stroud. He was educated at Marlborough, and entered the Royal Artillery 23 June, 1898, as a Second Lieutenant; became Lieutenant 16 Feb. 1901. He served in South Africa from 1900 to 1902; was present at the Relief of Kimberley; operations in the Orange Free State, Feb. to May, 1900, including operations at Paardeberg (18 to 26 Feb.); actions at Poplar Grove, Dreifontein (wounded), Vet River (5 and 6 May) and Zand River; operations in the Transvaal, including actions near Pretoria and Diamond Hill (11 and 12 June); operations in Orange River Colony, including actions at Wittebergen (1 to 29 July); operations in Orange River Colony and Cape Colony 30 Nov. 1900, to May, 1902; operations in the Transvaal, May, 1902. He was mentioned in Despatches [London Gazette, 10 Sept. 1901]; received the Queen's Medal with six clasps, and the King's Medal with two clasps; and was created a Companion of the Distinguished Service Order [London Gazette, 27 Sept. 1901]: "Thomas Edmund Palmer Wickham, Second Lieut., Royal Horse and Royal Field Artillery. In recognition of services during the operations in South Africa." The Insignia, Warrant and Statutes were sent to the Commander-in-Chief in India, and presented at Meerut 1 March, 1903, at Church Parade, by the G.O.C., Bengal. He was promoted Captain 6 Jan. 1906; was Adjutant of Royal Artillery for two years, until Oct. 1911, and attained his Majority 30 Oct. 1914. He was given the Brevet of Major, and mentioned in Despatches for his services in the European War, and was wounded. He became Lieutenant-Colonel 2 Oct. 1918, after holding acting rank from Dec. 1916. He married, in 1908, Elsie, eldest daughter of N. W. Grieve, of Coyleigh, Groombridge, and they had two sons. Lieut.-Colonel T. E. P. Wickham died in July, 1917.

RYND, FRANCIS FLEETWOOD, Second Lieut., was born 19 Aug. 1877, son of the Rev. J. W. Rynd, Rector of Brasted, Kent. He had his first commission as a Second Lieutenant in the Royal Artillery 22 Dec. 1898, in which he was promoted Lieutenant 16 Feb. 1901. He saw active service in the South African War from 1899 to 1902, taking part in the defence of Kimberley, and in the operations in Cape Colony, north of Orange River. For his services in this campaign he received the Queen's Medal with two clasps, and was created a Companion of the Distinguished Service Order [London Gazette, 27 Sept. 1901]: "Thomas Fleetwood Rynd, Second Lieut., Royal Garrison Artillery. In recognition of services during the operations in South Africa." He was invested by the King 18 Dec. 1902. He was, from Oct. 1904, to Oct. 1907, employed as a Volunteer Adjutant, receiving his Captaincy 30 June, 1904, and was Garrison Adjutant, Cape Colony District, from Aug. 1909, to Aug. 1913; was promoted Major 30 Oct. 1913. He was Acting Lieutenant-Colonel for short periods in 1916 and 1917; was appointed Camp Commandant, Mesopotamian Expeditionary Force, 8 May, 1918

VENNING, GORDON RALPH, Second Lieut., was born 3 June, 1880, the eldest son of Alfred Reid Venning, of Straits Settlements, and 15, Springfield Place, Bath. He was gazetted to the Royal Artillery, as Second Lieutenant, 23 Dec. 1898, and served in the South African War. He was created a Companion of the Distinguished Service Order 29 Nov. 1900 [London Gazette, 27 Sept. 1901]: "Gordon Ralph Venning, Second Lieut., Royal Horse and Royal Field Artillery. In recognition of services during the operations in South Africa." He was killed in action 7 March, 1902, near Tweebosch, South Africa, on the occasion of Lord Methuen's capture by Delarey, aged 20. The rearguard of Methuen's force consisted of inexperienced irregular troopers, and these, when charged by a large body of Boers, took to flight. After this the handful of men who stood their ground were left in a hopeless position. The two guns of the 38th Battery were overwhelmed by the Boers, every man being killed or wounded, including Lieut. Nesham, "who acted up to the highest traditions of his corps." The infantry, however, though few in number, were seasoned troops, and they fought for some hours against overwhelming odds. "Two hundred of the Northumberland Fusiliers" (wrote Sir A. Conan Doyle) "lay round the wagons, and held the Boers off from their prey. With them were the two remaining guns, which were a mark for a thousand Boer riflemen. It was while encouraging by his presence and example the much-tried gunners of this section that the gallant Methuen was wounded by a bullet which broke the bone of his thigh. Lieut. Venning and all the detachment fell with their General round the guns."

SWAYNE, OSWALD ROCKE, Second Lieut., was born 25 Sept. 1879, sixth son of R. A. Swayne, of Tillington Court, near Hereford. He joined the Army, as a Second Lieutenant in the Royal Artillery, 20 May, 1899, and was promoted Lieutenant 16 Feb. 1901. He served in the South African War from 1899 to 1902, being present in operations in the Orange Free State, April to May, 1900, including actions at Vet River (5 and 6 May) and Zand River; operations in the Transvaal in May and June, 1900, including actions near Johannesburg, Pretoria and Diamond Hill (11 and 12 June); operations in Orange River Colony, June to 29 Nov. 1900, including action at Wittebergen (1 to 29 July); operations in Cape Colony, south of Orange River, 1900; operations in the Transvaal, July and Dec. 1901; operations in Orange River Colony 30 Nov. 1900, to 31 May, 1902. He was mentioned in Despatches [London Gazette, 10 Sept. 1901]; awarded the Queen's Medal with four clasps, and the King's Medal with two clasps, and was created a Companion of the Distinguished Service Order [London Gazette, 27 Sept. 1901]: "Oswald Roche Swayne, Second Lieut., Royal Garrison Artillery. In recognition of services during the operations in South Africa." He was invested by the King 24 Oct. 1902. He became Captain 15 March, 1906; was Adjutant, Royal Artillery, 1 June, 1911, to 31 May, 1914, and was promoted Major 30 Oct. 1914. He served in the European War, 1914–17 and 1918–19; was from July, 1917, to Aug. 1918, Major Instructor in the Gunnery School of Instruction for Siege and Heavy Artillery, Lydd. He was mentioned in Despatches, and was awarded the Brevet of Lieutenant-Colonel 1 Jan. 1919, and was wounded. Lieut.-Colonel Swayne married, in 1904, Brenda, youngest daughter of the late Arthur Butler, of Brooklyn, Chislehurst, Kent, and has four sons and one daughter.

CANNY, JAMES CLARE MACNAMARA, Second Lieut., was born 6 Dec. 1877, son of the late James Macnamara Canny. He was gazetted to the Royal Munster Fusiliers 20 May, 1899. He served in the South African War, 1899–1902, as Station Staff Officer, taking part in operations in the Transvaal, east of Pretoria, July to 29 Nov. 1900, including the action at Rhenoster Kop; operations in Orange River Colony, May to 29 Nov. 1900, including actions at Lindley (26 June), Bethlehem (6 and 7 July) and Wittebergen (1 to 29 July); operations in Cape Colony, north of Orange River; operations in the Transvaal 30 Nov. 1900, to July, 1901; operations in Orange River Colony, May, 1901; operations in Cape Colony, July, 1901, to 31 May, 1902. He was mentioned in Despatches [London Gazette, 10 Sept. 1901, and 25 April, 1902]; received the Queen's Medal with three clasps, the King's Medal with two clasps, and was created a Companion of the Distinguished Service Order [London Gazette, 27 Sept. 1901]: "James Clare Macnamara Canny, Second Lieut., Royal Munster Fusiliers. In recognition of services during the operations in South Africa." He was invested by the King 24 Oct. 1902. He was promoted to Lieutenant 7 July, 1901; was Adjutant, Royal Munster Fusiliers, 9 Feb. 1907, to 15 Sept. 1908; Captain, Royal Munster Fusiliers, 13 June, 1908, and Army Service Corps 23 Sept. 1908. He served in the European War, 1914–18 was promoted to Major, Royal Army Service Corps, 30 Oct. 1914; was Temporary Lieutenant-Colonel 8 April, 1915, to 31 Dec. 1917. He was mentioned in Despatches and given the Brevet of Lieutenant-Colonel 1 Jan. 1918; was Assistant Director of Transport, Mesopotamian Expeditionary Force from 19 March, 1918; was created a C.B.E. in 1919.

GOSCHEN, ARTHUR ALEC, Second Lieut., was born 6 Jan. 1880, third son of H. Goschen, of Heathfield, Surrey. He entered the Royal Artillery 25 June, 1899; served in South Africa, 1899–1901, taking part in operations in the Orange Free State, March to May, 1900; operations in Orange River Colony (May to 29 Nov. 1900), including action at Lady-brand; operations in Cape Colony Feb. 1900; operations in Orange River Colony 30 Nov. 1900, to April, 1901; operations in Cape Colony, April to Oct. 1901. He was mentioned in Despatches [London Gazette, 10 Sept. 1901]; received the Queen's Medal with five clasps, and was created a Companion of the Distinguished Service Order [London Gazette, 27 Sept. 1901]: "Arthur Alec Goschen, Second Lieut., Royal Horse and Royal Field Artillery. In recognition of services during the operations in South Africa." He was invested by the King 17 Dec. 1901. He was promoted to Lieutenant 16 Feb. 1901, and to Captain 4 Dec. 1907; was Adjutant, Royal Artillery, 2 Jan. 1908, to 22 March, 1910, and was promoted to Major 30 Oct. 1914. He served in the European War, 1914–1918, as Brigade Major, Royal Artillery, 19th Division, New Armies, B.E.F., 1 Feb. 1915, to 5 May, 1916; as Acting Lieutenant-Colonel, Royal Artillery, 19 Sept. 1916, to 9 Nov. 1916; Acting Lieutenant-Colonel, Royal Artillery, from 24 Nov. 1916. He was given the Brevet of Lieutenant-Colonel 1 Jan. 1918. Lieut.-Colonel A. A. Goschen married, in 1908, Marjorie Mary, daughter of the late Lieut.-Colonel W. Blacker, of Castle Martin, Newbridge, co. Kildare. He received two Bars to his D.S.O.

Arthur Alec Goschen.

FLANAGAN, EVELYN BRANSCOMBE, Second Lieut., was born 19 March, 1881. He served in the South African War from 1899 to 1901, for which he was mentioned in Despatches, received the Queen's Medal with four clasps, and was created a Companion of the Distinguished Service Order [London Gazette, 27 Sept. 1901]: "Evelyn Branscombe Flanagan, Second Lieut., 4th Cheshire Regt. In recognition of services during the operations in South Africa." He was invested by the King 17 Dec. 1901. He subsequently joined the 10th Gurkhas, Indian Army.

BUCHAN, ERNEST NORMAN, Second Lieut., was born in Hampshire 15 Feb. 1879, third son of the late Colonel H. P. Buchan, of Lockyer House, Plymouth, and of his wife, St. Clair, daughter of General Ireland, Governor of Singapore. Mrs. H. P. Buchan formerly lived in Jersey. Ernest Norman Buchan was educated at Mannamead School, Plymouth; joined the Militia (3rd East Lancashire Regt.), in which he served for one year and a hundred days; was gazetted as Second Lieut. to the Manchester Regt. from the Militia 4 May, 1901; was promoted to Lieut., Manchester Regt., 27 Nov. 1901, and to Capt., Manchester Regt., 1 Dec. 1912. Capt. Buchan served in the South African War from 1899 to 1902; as Acting Transport Officer from 20 April, 1900, taking part in the operations in the Orange Free State, Feb. to May, 1900, including the action at Karee Siding and the operations in the Transvaal and Orange River Colony. He was mentioned in Despatches [London Gazette, 10 Sept. 1901]; received the Queen's South African Medal with three clasps, the King's South African Medal with two clasps, and was created a Companion of the Distinguished Service Order [London Gazette, 27 Sept. 1901]: "Ernest Norman Buchan, Second Lieut., 3rd East Lancashire Regt. In recognition of services during the operations in South Africa." He was invested with the Insignia of the Distinguished Service Order by His Majesty King Edward VII. on the 24th of Oct. 1902. From 12 Sept. 1904, to 2 Dec. 1904, he was Garrison Adjutant, Straits Settlements, Singapore, and he was subsequently stationed at Secunderabad and in the Punjab. On the 25th of Sept. 1914, he proceeded to France, being appointed Brigade Major, 27th Brigade, 11th Division, in Aug. 1915. He was killed in action, during the Battle of Loos, at the Quarries, Hulloch, on the 25th of Sept. following. At first he was only said to be "missing," but was later "presumed to have been killed." Capt. Buchan was mentioned in Despatches by Field-Marshal Sir John (now Lord) French [London Gazette, 1 Jan. 1916], for gallant and distinguished service in the field. He married, at Singapore, Kythe Elizabeth Graeme, daughter of William Graeme St. Clair, of Singapore, and had two sons: Philip William, born 12 Aug. 1905, and Norman Ireland, born 24 April, 1907, both at Wellington, Nilgiri Hills, India.

London Gazette, 11 Oct. 1901.—"War Office, 11 Oct. 1901. The King has been graciously pleased to give orders for the following appointments to the Distinguished Service Order . . . in recognition of the services of the undermentioned Officers during the operations in South Africa."

ROWLEY, CECIL ALURED, Capt., was born 31 Oct. 1869, son of the late Thomas Rowley, of Bridgnorth, Shropshire. He was educated at Elizabeth College, Guernsey, and entered the Dorsetshire Regt. 10 Nov.

1888. He was promoted Lieutenant 21 June, 1890, and Captain 23 July, 1895. He served in the South African War, 1899–1902, employed with Mounted Infantry. Took part in the Relief of Ladysmith, including

operations of 17 to 24 Jan. 1900, and action at Spion Kop; operations of 5 to 7 Feb. 1900, and action at Vaal Kranz; during the operations on Tugela Heights (14 to 27 Feb. 1900), and action at Pieter's Hill; in the Transvaal in June, 1900; in Natal, March to June, 1900, including action at Laing's Nek (6 to 9 June); in Orange River Colony, June, 1900; in the Transvaal and Orange River Colony 30 Nov. 1900, to May, 1902; also during the operations on the Zululand Frontier of Natal in Sept. and Oct. 1901, including defence of Forts Itala and Prospect (in command of troops at Fort Prospect). He was mentioned in Despatches [London Gazette, 8 Feb. 1901 (Sir R. H. Buller, 19

Cecil Alured Rowley.

June and 9 Nov. 1900) and London Gazette, 10 Sept. and 11 Oct. 1901]; awarded the Brevet of Major 29 Nov. 1900; received the Queen's Medal with five clasps, and the King's Medal with two clasps, and was created a Companion of the Distinguished Service Order [London Gazette, 11 Oct. 1901]: " Cecil Alured Rowley, Capt., The Dorsetshire Regt. For gallantry in the defence of Forts Itala and Prospect, dated 26 Sept. 1901." After serving from April, 1902, as a Volunteer Adjutant, to 24 Oct. 1906, he was promoted Major 25 Oct. 1906, and retired with that rank from the Service 16 May, 1914. He is now Lieutenant-Colonel, in command of the 6th (Service) Battn. Dorset Regt. He married, in 1897, Agnes Ellen, eldest surviving daughter of the late John Lightbody, of Birchfield, Lancs, and has one son and one daughter.

PURCELL, JOHN FRANCIS, Capt., was born at Ballycuneen, Co. Clare, Ireland, 29 June, 1861, son of the late Thomas Purcell. He was educated at a private school, and joined the Cape Mounted Riflemen 28 Oct. 1880. He served in Basutoland, 1881 (Medal with clasp), and in the South African War from 1899 to 1902. He was promoted Captain 25 Oct. 1900; was present in operations in the Transvaal, west of Pretoria, July and Nov. 1900; operations in Orange River Colony, May and Nov. 1900; operations in Cape Colony, south of Orange River, 1899–1900; operations in Cape Colony, north of Orange River, 1900; operations in Orange River Colony, Nov. and Dec. 1900; operations in Cape Colony, Dec. 1900, to May, 1902. He was slightly wounded; was mentioned in Despatches [London Gazette, 9 July and 11 Oct. 1901], and was created a Companion of the Distinguished Service Order [London Gazette, 11 Oct. 1901]: " J. Purcell, Capt., Cape Mounted Rifles. For gallantry in capture of Lotter's Commando. Dated 5 Sept. 1901." He also received the Queen's Medal with three clasps and the King's Medal with two clasps; was promoted Brevet Major 1 Nov. 1901. He served in the Great War, and was mentioned in Despatches in Sept. 1916. He married, 21 July, 1909, at Umtata, Cape Province, South Africa, Frances, eldest daughter of W. T. Brownlee, Chief Magistrate, Native Territories, Cape Province, and they have two sons: John Francis Brownlee and Edward Stephen; and a daughter, Joan Brownlee.

LEFROY, BERTRAM PERCEVAL, Lieut., was born 18 May, 1878, in London, son of the late Thomas Charles Perceval Lefroy, of 11, Ashburn Place, S.W., and Isabella Napier, daughter of the late Alexander

Hastie, of Carnock, Fifeshire. He was educated at Harrow and Sandhurst, and joined the Royal Dublin Fusiliers 7 May, 1898; became Lieutenant 10 May, 1899. He served in the South African War, 1899–1901 (dangerously wounded); was present at the Relief of Ladysmith; took part in the operations in the Transvaal in June, 1900; in Natal, March to June, 1900, including action at Laing's Nek (6 to 9 June); in the Transvaal, east of Pretoria, July, 1900; in Orange River Colony, June, 1900; in the Transvaal, Dec. 1900, to Aug. 1901; also during the operations on the Zululand Frontier of Natal in Sept. 1901, including defence of Fort Itala. He was mentioned in Despatches 11 Oct. 1901; received the Queen's South African

Bertram P. Lefroy.

Medal with five clasps, and was created a Companion of the Distinguished Service Order [London Gazette, 11 Oct. 1901]: " Bertram Perceval Lefroy, Lieut., The Royal Dublin Fusiliers." The D.S.O. was awarded " for gallantry in the Defence of Forts Prospect and Itala." The defence of the two forts, though so few were engaged, was considered one of the most brilliant affairs in the war, the attacking force being about four times the number of the defenders, and the Boer loss larger in proportion than in almost any other action. Major Chapman was in command at Fort Itala. Lieut. Lefroy (with Lieut. Kane, South Lancashire Regt., who was killed) commanded about 90 of the Mounted Infantry at the outpost on the top of Itala Hill. He himself shot Potgieter, the enemy commander, and was very severely wounded. Lord Kitchener himself sent in Lieut. Lefroy's name for the D.S.O., and for his promotion, in getting which he was transferred to the 3rd Battn. The Royal Warwickshire Regt. The latter eventually proved in some ways unfortunate, as this battalion was one of those subsequently done away with, and caused Capt. Lefroy a serious loss of seniority. The following is an extract from a

letter written by Lieut. B. P. Lefroy while he was lying wounded after Itala (he had been wounded in four places, two of which just escaped being fatal): " When we heard that we were going to be attacked at Itala, I was sent right up to the top of the Itala Hill with about 90 men, to try and hold it, and prevent the Boers from attacking the camp from that direction. At about 2 a.m., 26 Sept., they attacked my post five or six hundred strong. It was fairly dark, and the ground was covered with little rocks, which made it very hard to distinguish people. We kept up a heavy fire on both sides. They worked right round our right, and then rushed the position. It was a very plucky rush, but as they were about five to one, we couldn't keep them out, and it ended in a sort of grand mêlée. I have a vivid recollection of popping off my revolver with Boers all round me, and then I got too full of lead to continue the operation. They took about 37 prisoners and held the position all day. We people with bullets in us had to lie all day on our backs in the sun, and we didn't get down again till 3 a.m. next morning, when the people in the camp, finding the Boers had cleared, sent up for us. It was bitterly cold during the night, and a damp mist. The camp held out splendidly all night and day, until the Boers didn't think it worth while losing any more men. There were about 1,500 Boers, and about 300 of us, so we didn't do so badly." He became Captain 2 Aug. 1902. After the Boer War, he served in England, Gibraltar, again in South Africa, returned to England, and went through the Staff College. At the outbreak of the Great War he was holding an appointment as General Staff Officer at the War Office. In Aug. 1914, he went out on the Staff of the First Division. After seven months he returned to England to serve on the Staff of the 26th Division at Warminster until July, 1915, when he went out to command the 2nd Battn. Warwickshire Regt. He was made Brevet Major in the King's Birthday Honours List, 1915; Major 8 Aug. and Lieut.-Colonel 1 Sept. 1915. Lieut.-Colonel Lefroy was fatally wounded at the Battle of Loos 25 Sept. 1915, and died in the Field Ambulance on the 27th. He was three times mentioned in Despatches during the War (17 Sept. 1914; 14 Jan. 1915 and 31 May, 1915); received the Cross of the Legion of Honour. He was much beloved by his men, and they would have followed him anywhere. The dying message he left for them was made a battalion order, and will not be forgotten by those of the old regiment who survive. It was: " Tell them my last thoughts are with them. I pray that their bravery in the hour of severe testing may win them through to success. Would to God I had been spared to serve and lead them a little longer. But as it is I trust that the men of the Warwickshire Regiment will pull together, work together and uphold the credit, the good name and the traditions that the Regiment has so nobly won. May God's blessing rest on them in their hour of danger or peace, and may the heroic self-sacrifice of their officers, non-commissioned officers and men who have fallen inspire them to deeds of unfaltering and unfailing bravery."

LICHTENBURG, JOHN WILLS, Lieut., was born 19 June, 1872, and joined the Army on 21 April, 1900, as a Second Lieutenant in the 18th Hussars; became Lieutenant 1 May, 1901. He served in the South African War, 1899–1902 (severely wounded). Took part in the operations in the Transvaal, Dec. 1900, to Sept. 1901, and Nov. 1901, to 31 May, 1902; in Orange River Colony, March and May, 1902; also during the operations on the Zululand Frontier of Natal in Sept. and Oct. 1901; was created a Companion of the Distinguished Service Order [London Gazette, 11 Oct. 1901]: " John Wills Lichtenburg, Lieut., 18th Hussars. For gallantry in action on Oliphant's River (Maseppa Drift) 30 June, 1901. Dated 30 July, 1901." The Insignia were presented by the King 24 Oct. 1902. He was promoted Captain on 29 Nov. 1904. Capt. Lichtenburg died 15 March, 1912.

CLEMENTI-SMITH, EUGENE, Lieut., was born 3 Dec. 1847, at the Rectory, Buckhurst Hill, Chigwell, Essex, eighth son of the Rev. John Smith, M.A., Rector of Buckhurst Hill, and Cecilia Susanna Clementi, daughter of Muzio Clementi. He was

educated at St. Paul's School, London, and joined the Winnipeg Field Battery in 1871, and in 1872 " undertook the reorganization of the Manitoba Rifle Association, and was elected the first vice-president and chief executive officer, in which capacity he served till he left Winnipeg for the North-West Territories in 1878. In 1874 he won the championship of his province, and in 1875 the Governor-General's (Lord Dufferin) silver medal and the gold medal of the D.A.G." (" Volunteer Record," 5 Oct. 1895.) Capt. Clementi-Smith was High Commissioner (H.M. Civil Service), and J.P. of Brandon, Manitoba, where, in 1882 he again organized a Rifle Associa-

Eugene Clementi-Smith.

tion, of which he was elected president, and in which he won grand aggregate medals in 1884 and 1885. In the latter year he was instrumental in assisting to raise the Manitoba Grenadier Regt. for active service, under General Middleton, in the Reil Rebellion, and in this regiment he held the commission of First Lieutenant, and served throughout the campaign, receiving the War Medal (N.W. Canada) in recognition of his services. He was mentioned in General Middleton's Despatches, 1887; returned to England, and in 1890 joined the Middlesex Yeomanry, having passed the Hythe School to qualify for the position of Instructor of Musketry to the corps. While connected with the regiment he took part in most of the National Rifle Association's meetings at Bisley, where for several years in succession he shot his way into the " Queen's Hundred." He also shot at Darnley, Altcar and Belfast, winning many cups and medals. He was champion of the South London Rifle Club in 1895, 1896, 1897 and 1898, and on the 30th April of the last-named year he made a record score in a friendly match on the Runnemede Range—the highest possible at 200, 500 and 600 yards, 21 bull's-eyes in all. As Hon. Secretary to the Middlesex Rifle Association for six years, his work should not be forgotten. From a state of bankruptcy he raised the Association to a sound financial position, with a large credit balance. During the last two years he freely bestowed his time and skill on the coaching of recruits, personally superintending the weekly "spoon shoots" at Bisley, which he organized in connection with the Association. On 27 Feb. 1901, he was gazetted as a Second Lieutenant in the Imperial Yeomanry, sailing for the front on 8 March, with the temporary rank of Captain and Adjutant. He was attached to the 8th Division (General Rundle), and remained on active service till his death. His work was so successful that on one occasion in June a complimentary message was heliographed from Lord Kitchener, and was followed by a personal interview with General Rundle, who said: "I have heard a great deal about your exploits and the keen interest you take in all your military duties. I have wanted to see you and thank you for your work at Bethlehem. I have consulted with Colonel Firman, and intend to give you a much freer hand in future, and you will have a party of Scouts, the selection being in your hands. I hope to increase your command in the near future." It was while leading "Clementi's Scouts" (nearly all Middlesex men) on trek from Bethlehem to Harrismith, and defending a position that was being attacked, that Capt. Clementi-Smith received, on 11 Sept., the severe wound in the right shoulder which afterwards proved fatal. He died 4 Oct. 1901, aged 54. In the London Gazette of 11 Oct. 1901, is the announcement of his creation to a Companionship of the Distinguished Service Order: "Eugene Clementi-Smith, Lieut., Imperial Yeomanry. For extreme gallantry in action at Harrismith (since died of wounds)." In Lord Kitchener's Despatch, published in the "Times" of Wednesday, 4 Dec., there is the following paragraph: "11th Imperial Yeomanry.—Lieut. E. Clementi-Smith (since died of wounds), on 11 Sept. 1901, in Harrismith district, advanced alone to occupy a position Boers were making or, and though wounded through right shoulder, continued to fire from left, keeping enemy off till he was reinforced. Awarded D.S.O. by War Office Telegram No. 9599, dated 9 Oct. 1901." His father was formerly Head Master of Mercers' School and Chaplain of the Company. Lieut. Clementi-Smith was educated at the Mercers' School, and his brother, the Rev. P. Clementi-Smith (Rector of St. Andrew's Church, Doctors' Commons, London, E.C.), as House Warden of the Mercers' Company, had the responsibility of arranging for the Memorial erected by the Mercers' Company in their Chapel to Lieut. Clementi-Smith, Lieut. J. S. Watney and Private F. J. Dubois. The N.R.A. have gold, silver and bronze medals which are shot for annually, as a memorial of Lieut. Clementi-Smith's work in the interests of rifle-shooting. He married, on 23 Nov. 1881, at St. Jude's Church, Southsea, Wilhelmina Maria Barnes, daughter of James Barnes, Esq., and their daughter is Lilian Clementi, born at Brandon, Manitoba, Canada, 28 Aug. 1883. She married Major A. M. Matthews, R.G.A.

London Gazette, 10 Dec. 1901.—"War Office, 10 Dec. 1901. The King has been graciously pleased to give orders for the following . . . appointments to the Distinguished Service Order . . . in recognition of the services of the undermentioned Officers during the operations in China. These rewards to bear the date of 29 Nov. 1900."

HOLMAN, HERBERT CAMPBELL, Capt., was born 3 May, 1869, son of the late William Laban Holman, of Murree, Punjab. He was educated at Dulwich and Sandhurst. He entered the Army 21 Sept. 1889, as a Second Lieutenant in the Devonshire Regt.; was promoted Lieutenant 25 March, 1891, and was transferred to the Indian Staff Corps 3 May, 1892. He served in Burma, 1891–2, with the Wuntho Expedition (slightly wounded). He was mentioned in Despatches [London Gazette, 9 Feb. 1892]; took part in the operations of the Irrawaddy Column, as Staff Officer (Medal with clasp). He became Captain 21 Sept. 1900. He served in China, 1900, as First Class Officer Interpreter and Special Service Officer, graded as D.A.A.G., and for his services was mentioned in Despatches [London Gazette, 13 Sept. 1905]; received the Medal, and was created a Companion of the Distinguished Service Order [London Gazette, 10 Dec. 1901]: "Herbert Campbell Holman, Capt., Indian Staff Corps. In recognition of services during operations in China." The Insignia, Warrant and Statutes were sent to His Excellency the Commander-in-Chief in India, and presented by him 23 April, 1902. He was Assistant Secretary, Military Department, Government of India, 27 May to 14 Aug. 1901; was Staff Captain, Intelligence Department, War Office, 29 Dec. 1902, to 20 Jan. 1904; D.A.Q.M.G., General Staff, 21 Jan. 1904, to 28 Dec. 1906; Attaché with the Russian Forces in Manchuria 17 June to 7 Nov. 1905 (Order of St. Stanislaus, 2nd Class with Swords, and Russian War Medal); was awarded the Humane Society's Medal, 1907; became Major 21 Sept. 1907; was G.S.O.2, Army Headquarters, India, 11 March to 21 Oct. 1910, and from 1 July, 1913; was given the Brevet of Lieutenant-Colonel 20 June, 1914. Lieut.-Colonel H. C. Holman served in the European War from 1914 to 1918. He held a special appointment with the Indian Army Corps, B.E.F., from 12 Oct. 1914, to 29 Jan. 1915; was A.Q.M.G., 1st Army, B.E.F., 30 Jan. to 3 Nov. 1915; was promoted Lieutenant-Colonel 21 Sept. 1915; Temporary Brigadier-General 4 Nov. 1915, to 12 Nov. 1916, while D.A. and Q.M.G. 11th Army Corps. He was given the Brevet of Colonel 1 Jan. 1916. From 13 Nov. 1916, he was Temporary Major-General (promoted to substantive rank 1 Jan. 1919), as D.A. and Q.M.G., 4th Army in France, until 15 May, 1919, and on 22 May, 1919, became Head of the British Military Mission in South Russia. He was mentioned in Despatches seven times; was awarded the Legion of Honour; was made a C.M.G. in 1915, and a C.B. in 1918, and was wounded. He married, in 1902, Annie Ethel Talbot, second daughter of Major-General W. Howey, and they have one son and one daughter.

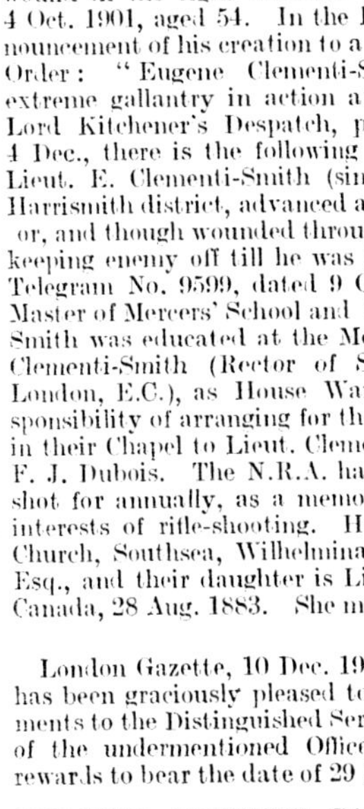

Herbert C. Holman.

LOCH, STEWART GORDON, Lieut., was born 13 April, 1873, at Ajmir, Rajputana, India, son of Capt. Robert Gordon Loch (deceased), late 20th Hussars and Indian Staff Corps. He was educated at Westward Ho!; Merchant Taylors' School, and the Royal Military Academy, Woolwich; joined the Royal Engineers, 10 Jan. 1893, as Second Lieutenant; was sent out to India in 1895, and served with the 2nd Q.V.O. Sappers and Miners until May, 1904. He became Lieutenant 10 Feb. 1896; served in the China Campaign of 1900–1, as Assistant to Field Engineer (Telegraphs); was present at the Relief of Pekin, and in the action at Peitsung. He received the Medal with clasp for the Relief of Pekin; was mentioned in General Gaselee's Despatch, dated 17 Jan. 1901 [London Gazette, 14 May, 1901], and for his services in this campaign was created a Companion of the Distinguished Service Order [London Gazette, 10 Dec. 1901]: "Stewart Gordon Loch, Lieut., Royal Engineers." He was invested by the King 17 Feb. 1901. He became Captain 10 Feb. 1904; passed through the Indian Staff College, 1905–7; served at Army Headquarters, Simla, as G.S.O., 2nd Grade, from July, 1907, to 30 Sept. 1911; was Brigade Major, Dehra Dun Brigade, 1 Oct. 1911, to 14 Sept. 1913; was given the Brevet of Major 21 Feb. 1912; became Major 10 Feb. 1913; was G.S.O., 2nd Grade, Bannu Brigade, from 15 Sept. 1913, until 18 Dec. 1914. He served in the European War; was Temporary Lieutenant-Colonel; G.S.O.1, Army Headquarters, India, from 9 Dec. 1914, until 6 July, 1916; was given the Brevet of Lieutenant-Colonel 1 Jan. 1917; was Temporary Brigadier-General, General Staff, Northern Army, India, from 17 July, 1916. He was given the Brevet of Colonel 17 Sept. 1917, and was created a C.S.I., 1919. He married, 1 July, 1902, at Sevenoaks, Kate Alice Muriel, only daughter of John Rathbone, of Highcroft, Sevenoaks, and they have three children: Ian Gordon Loch, born 15 April, 1903; Jean Muriel, and Douglas Gordon, born 9 Nov. 1911.

COWIE, HENRY EDWARD COLVIN, Lieut., was born 17 Dec. 1872, son of H. G. Cowie, of the Indian Finance Department, and Tiverton, Devonshire. He was educated at Shrewsbury, and the Royal Military Academy, Woolwich. He was in the Football XI. at Shrewsbury; in the Football XI. at the Royal Military Academy, Woolwich, and in the Royal Engineers Training Battn. Association Team, 1893–94. He entered the Army as a Second Lieutenant in the Royal Engineers 10 Feb. 1893. He was stationed at Chatham from 1893 to 1895, and in India from 1895 to 1900, in the Indian Public Works Department Railway Branch; was promoted Lieutenant 10 Feb. 1896. He served in China, 1900, as Assistant to Field Engineer (Railways); was present at the Relief of Pekin; was mentioned in Despatches [London Gazette, 13 Sept. 1901] (Medal with clasp). He was created a Companion of the Distinguished Service Order [London Gazette, 10 Dec. 1901]: "Henry Edward Colvin Cowie, Lieut., Royal Engineers. In recognition of services during the operations in China." The Insignia, Warrant and Statutes were sent to the G.O.C. Troops in China, and presented by Major-General Creagh. He was employed under the Chinese Government 10 Sept. 1902, to 28 Jan. 1903; was promoted Captain 1 March, 1904; Major 10 Feb. 1913; became Temporary Lieutenant-Colonel 18 May, 1916. He was created a C.B.E. in 1919. He married, in 1903, Mary Theodora, eldest daughter of the Rev. Daniel G. Thomas.

STIRLING, JAMES DAVID, Lieut., was born 17 Dec. 1873, son of the late William Stirling, of Tarduf, Stirlingshire. He entered the Argyll and Sutherland Highlanders, as a Second Lieutenant, 7 March, 1894, and was transferred to the King's Own Scottish Borderers on 18 April of the same year. He saw active service in Chitral with the Relief Force in 1895, and was at the storming of the Malakand Pass (Medal with clasp). He was promoted Lieutenant 21 July, 1897; was transferred again 29 July, 1897, to the Indian Staff Corps. Capt. Stirling served in China in 1900, and was mentioned in Despatches [London Gazette, 13 Sept. 1901]; received the Medal, and was created a Companion of the Distinguished Service Order [London Gazette, 10 Dec. 1901]: "James David Stirling, Lieut., Indian Staff Corps. In recognition of services during the operations in China." He was invested by the King 17 Dec. 1901. He was promoted Captain 7 March, 1903; served in the Bazar Valley Campaign, North-West Frontier of India in 1908 (Medal with clasp). In the spring of 1901 a band of about 1,400 Huang Houtzes (or Chunchuses) broke through the Great Wall and advanced via Yung Ping-fou towards the railway. The Chinese asked for help, and Major Browning and Lieut. Stirling, with 100 Rifles, 4th Punjab Infantry, left Shan-hai-kwan, Headquarters, 3rd Brigade, China Expeditionary Force, at daybreak on the 19th April, for Fooning, to restore confidence and ascertain the whereabouts of the brigands. The party detrained at a small station about 10 miles south of Fooning, where the night was spent. The Chinese informed Major Browning that the brigands had taken possession of the town of Tao-tai-ying, 10 miles further north. Major Browning left at daybreak with 80 men, and on approaching Tao-tai-ying, was fired on from a village. He, with some mounted men on mules, commenced a flanking attack, but they were fired on from another village on their flank, and the party was in danger of being

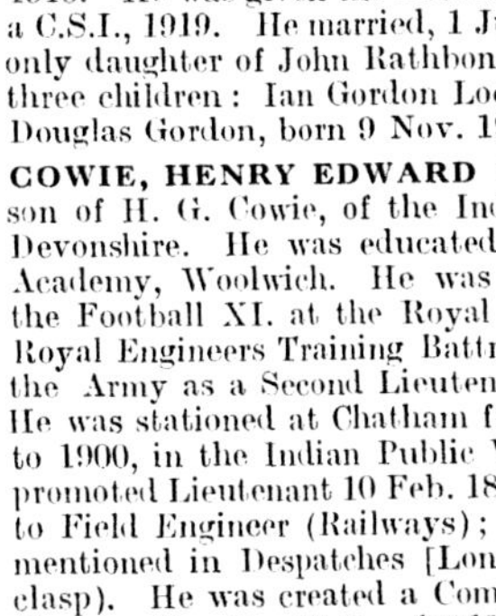

James David Stirling.

surrounded and their retreat cut off. Major Browning and three sepoys were killed immediately, and Lieut. Stirling, in command of the remainder, was also wounded through the neck and in the foot. Several men were also immediately hit, and, as firing was general from all sides, a retirement was begun. The Huang Houtzes pursued our men for 10 miles. Mounted as they were, they continually got round the small party of infantry. Again and again the Huang Houtzes closed round, and as often the men of the 4th Punjab Infantry kept them off until they reached the gates of Fooning, which were thereupon closed and barricaded. Not till next day was it known that the Huang Houtzes had lost 140 men, if not more, in the fight. Lieut. Stirling was recommended for the D.S.O. in recognition of the skill and judgment which he, though seriously wounded and hampered by casualties, extricated the party from a very difficult position after the death of Major Browning. The fact of his having been wounded did not transpire until the party at Fooning was relieved on the 21st April. Capt. Stirling was killed in action at Hayat Khan Kili, Bannu District, on 11 March, 1910, in what was described at the time as the most daring raid that had taken place on the North-West Frontier of India for many years. The Mullah Powindah of Waziristan despatched a band of 32 Mahsuds for the purpose of raiding the Government Treasury at Lakki, a town of considerable size, about 28 miles within the frontier. The raiders, having marched all night, arrived at dawn at a small hamlet named Hayat Khan Kili, about eight miles from Lakki. Here they were hospitably entertained by the headman of the village, who feigned friendship and installed them in the Weal Mosque. The headman promptly sent information to the police at Lakki, who in turn telegraphed to the military authorities at Bannu. Two squadrons of the 14th Cavalry and 180 men of the 57th Rifles were ordered to start at once. The police arrived from Lakki at about 2 o'clock, but being only about the same strength as those inside the mosque, all they could do was to keep up rifle fire on the mosque and await assistance from Bannu. The cavalry on their arrival at dusk formed a cordon round the mosque, and an advance party of 50 men of the infantry, under Capt. Stirling, reaching the scene of action an hour later, crept up to the surrounding wall and completely shut in the raiders, who took up a position on the roof and shot any man who attempted to get over the wall. Capt. Stirling, who was most zealous in creeping round and looking after his men, was killed while reconnoitring. Although additional troops had now arrived, nothing further could be done without guns, except with severe loss of life, and it was therefore decided to keep the mosque surrounded for the night and await the arrival in the morning of artillery. Firing was kept up on the only exit, but about nine o'clock the Mahsuds, knowing that they were trapped and that their only hope lay in escaping during the night (which was pitch dark), rushed out in a body, firing in all directions, and broke through the cordon. Besides Capt. Stirling, our casualties numbered 6 men and 12 wounded. Of the 32 raiders 15 were accounted for.

MACPHERSON, JAMES, Lieut., was born 20 June, 1876, son of Lieut.-Colonel R. N. Macpherson. He became Second Lieutenant, on the Unattached List, 22 Jan. 1896, and on 30 May, 1897, joined the Indian Staff Corps. He was promoted Lieutenant in the Indian Army 22 April, 1898. Serving in China in 1900, he was mentioned in Despatches [London Gazette, 14 May, 1901]; received the Medal, and was awarded the D.S.O. The following is a description taken from a newspaper of how he won his D.S.O.: "Lieut. Macpherson, whose deed of daring in China supplies the historian with the true record of a hair-breadth escape, had a town some eight miles from Peking as the scene of his adventure. Colonel Tulloch, whose detachment was fired upon by invisible assailants all using smokeless powder and modern guns, camped hear Koolying, where the rumour reached him of an intended Boxer attack from Dehhalying. The Colonel asked for reinforcements, and when these arrived in the shape of 50 men, under Lieut. Macpherson, an assault was made on the town. That was the Lieutenant's opportunity. He led a party with scaling ladders; was the first to reach the top of the wall, and to jump down upon the other side. His revolver accounted for five Chinese, and after that he drew his sword and defended himself until his men arrived just in time to save him from certain death." He was created a Companion of the Distinguished Service Order [London Gazette, 10 Dec. 1901]: "James Macpherson, Lieut., Indian Staff Corps. In recognition of services during the operations in China." The Insignia, Warrant and Statutes were sent to the O.C., India, 12 Feb. 1902, and presented by Major-General Burnett, commanding Poona District, India, 8 April, 1902. He was promoted Captain 22 Jan. 1905; served as Adjutant, Indian Volunteers, 19 Oct. 1908, to 18 Oct. 1913; was promoted Major 22 Jan. 1914. During the European War he was G.S.O.2, India, until 14 Oct. 1915, and A.Q.M.G., India, until 20 Feb. 1916; Acting Lieutenant-Colonel, Indian Army, 8 April to 17 Aug. 1917. He married, in 1907, Constance Margaret, fifth daughter of F. A. Primrose, and they have two sons.

WILLIAMS, HERBERT ARMSTRONG, Lieut., was born 11 Feb. 1875, son of H. M. Williams, J.P., of Williamston, Carvery, County Kildare. He entered the Indian Medical Service as a Lieutenant 27 Jan. 1900, and served in China from 1900 to 1901, for which he was mentioned in Despatches [London Gazette, 13 Sept. 1901]; received the Medal and was created a Companion of the Distinguished Service Order [London Gazette, 10 Dec. 1901]: "Herbert Armstrong Williams, Lieut., Indian Medical Service. In recognition of services during the operations in China." The Insignia, Warrant and Statutes were sent to His Excellency the Commander-in-Chief in India; presented by Colonel R. Oakes, R.G.A. He became Captain 27 Jan. 1903. He was Deputy Sanitary Commissioner in Burma in 1903; Plague Medical Officer, 1906; Superintendent, Rangoon Lunatic Asylum, 1907. Since 1907 he has been Superintendent of the Rangoon General Hospital. He was promoted Major 27 July, 1911, and was Temporary Lieutenant-Colonel from 17 Nov. 1917, to 5 March, 1919.

London Gazette, 28 Jan. 1902.—"The King has been graciously pleased to give orders for the following appointments to the Distinguished Service Order . . . in recognition of the services of the undermentioned Officers during the operations in South Africa. To be Companions of the Distinguished Service Order."

ROYSTON, JOHN ROBINSON, Lieut.-Colonel, was born 29 April, 1860, son of William Royston, of Bellair, Natal. He first saw active service in the Zulu Campaign of 1878–79 (Medal with clasp). He also served in the South African War of 1899 to 1902, and was present in operations in Natal in 1899, including the actions at Reitfontein and Lombard's Kop; the Defence of Ladysmith, including sortie of 7 Dec. 1899, and action of 6 Jan. 1900. Sir A. Conan Doyle thus describes the sortie from Ladysmith in "The Great Boer War," page 169: "December 7 was marked by a gallant exploit on the part of the beleaguered garrison. Not a whisper had transpired of the coming sortie, and a quarter of an hour before the start officers engaged had no idea of it. *O si sic omnia!* At ten o'clock a band of men slipped out of the town. There were six hundred of them, all irregulars, drawn from the Imperial Light Horse, the Natal Carabineers, and the Border Mounted Rifles, under the command of Hunter, youngest and most dashing of British generals. Edwardes and Royston were the sub-commanders. The men had no knowledge of where they were going or what they had to do, but they crept silently along under a drifting sky, with peeps of a quarter moon, over a mimosa-shadowed plain. At last in front of them there loomed a dark mass—it was Gun Hill, from which one of the great Creusots had plagued them. A strong support (four hundred men) was left at the base of the hill, and the others, one hundred Imperials, one hundred Borders and Carabineers, ten Sappers, crept upwards with Major Henderson as guide. A Dutch outpost challenged, but was satisfied by a Dutch-speaking Carabineer. Higher and higher the men crept, the silence broken only by the occasional slip of a stone or the rustle of their own breathing. Most of them had left their boots below. Even in the darkness they kept some formation, and the right wing curved forward to outflank the defence. Suddenly a Mauser crack and a spurt of flame—then another and another! 'Come on, boys! Fix bayonets!' yelled Karri Davies. There were no bayonets, but that was a detail. At the word the gunners were off, and there in the darkness in front of the storming party loomed the enormous gun, gigantic in that uncertain light. Out with the huge breech-block! Wrap the long, lean muzzle round with a collar of gun-cotton! Keep the guard upon the run until the work is done! Hunter stood by with a night-light in his hand until the charge was in position, and then, with a crash which brought both armies from their tents, the huge tube reared up on its mountings and toppled backwards into the pit. A howitzer lurked beside it, and this also was blown into ruin. The attendant Maxim was dragged back by the exultant captors, who reached the town amid shoutings and laughter with the first break of day. One man wounded, the gallant Henderson, is the cheap price for the best-planned and most dashing exploit of the war. Secrecy in conception, vigour in execution—they are the root ideas of the soldier's craft. So easily was the enterprise carried out, and so defective the Boer watch, that it is probable that if all the guns had been simultaneously attacked the Boers might have found themselves without a single piece of ordnance in the morning." He also took part in operations in Natal, March to June, 1900, including action at Laing's Nek; operations in the Transvaal, east of Pretoria, July to Oct. 1900, in command of the West Australian Mounted Infantry; operations in the Transvaal and Orange River Colony 30 Nov. 1900, to 31 May, 1902; operations on the Zululand Frontier of Natal in Sept. and Oct. 1901. He was mentioned in Despatches [London Gazette, 17 and 25 April, 1902, and 4 Dec. 1903]; received the Queen's Medal with four clasps; was created a C.M.G., and was also created a Companion of the Distinguished Service Order [London Gazette, 28 Jan. 1902]: "J. R. Royston, Lieut.-Colonel, West Australian Mounted Infantry. For ability and dash in the capture of laagers on 14 Dec. 1901, and 4 Jan. 1902, in Ermelo District." The Insignia were presented by H.R.H. The Prince of Wales, Horse Guards' Parade, 1 July, 1902. He was given the Brevet of Lieutenant-Colonel; became Major, Border Mounted Rifles, 3 Oct. 1904. In the Natal Native Rebellion of 1916 he raised and commanded "Royston's Horse;" was mentioned in Despatches [London Gazette, 25 June, 1907]; received the Medal and clasp, and was given the honorary rank of Lieutenant-Colonel in the Army 28 June, 1907. He retired with this rank. During the European War he became Honorary Brigadier-General; was awarded the Russian Order of St. Stanislaus, 3rd Class with Sword, in 1916.

SLOAN, JOHN MACFARLANE, Lieut., was born 22 July, 1872, son of Samuel Sloan, M.D., of Glasgow, and of Elizabeth Sloan (*née* Macfarlane). He was educated at Glasgow University (M.B., B.Ch.); entered the Army 28 Jan. 1899, as a Lieutenant in the Royal Army Medical Corps. He served in the South African War, 1899–1902; took part in the Defence of Ladysmith, including sorties of 7 and 10 Dec. 1899, and action of 6 Jan. 1900; took part in the operations in Natal (March to June, 1900); in the Transvaal, east of Pretoria, July to 29 Nov. 1900; again in the Transvaal 30 Nov. to June, 1901, and July, 1901, to April, 1902; also in Orange River Colony, June to July, 1901, and April to 31 May, 1902. He was mentioned in Despatches [London Gazette, 17 Jan. 1902]; received the Queen's Medal with four clasps; the King's Medal with two clasps, and was created a Companion of the Distinguished Service

John Macfarlane Sloan.

Order [London Gazette, 28 Jan. 1902]: "John Macfarlane Sloan, Lieut., Royal Army Medical Corps. For devotion to duty at Battle of Bakenlaagte 31 Oct. 1901." He became Captain 28 Jan. 1902, and Major 28 Oct. 1910; Brevet Lieutenant-Colonel 18 Feb. 1915; Lieutenant-Colonel (Substantive) 1 March, 1915; was mentioned in Despatches seven times; Brevet Colonel 1 Jan. 1916; D.A.D.M.S., Lahore Division, France and Mesopotamia, till May, 1916. A.D.M.S., Lahore Division, Mesopotamia, May, 1916, to Jan. 1917; D.D.M.S., 3rd Indian Army Corps, Jan. 1917, to Feb. 1919; C.M.G., Aug. 1917; 2nd Class St. Anne, with Swords.

BAIRD, ALEXANDER WALTER FREDERIC, Lieut., was born 2 Oct. 1876, son of Sir Alexander Baird, Bart., and the Hon. Annette Palk, daughter of the 1st Baron Haldon. He was educated at Eton (Cricket Eleven, 1894, 1895), and New College, Oxford, and joined the Army 15 May, 1897, as a Second Lieutenant in the Gordon Highlanders; was promoted Lieutenant 9 June, 1899. He served on the Staff during the South African War, 1899–1901; took part in operations in Natal, 1899, including actions at Lombard's Kop; was present at the Defence of Ladysmith, including sorties of 7 and 10 Dec. 1899, and action of 6 Jan. 1900; in Natal (March to June, 1900), including action at Laing's Nek (6 to 9 June); took part in the operations in the Transvaal, east of Pretoria, July to 29 Nov. 1900, including actions at Belfast (26 and 27 Aug.) and Lydenberg (5 to 8 Sept.); again in the Transvaal, Orange River Colony, and Cape Colony, 1900–2. He was mentioned in Despatches [London Gazette, 8 Feb. 1901 (Sir R. H. Buller, 13 Sept. and 9 Nov. 1900), and London Gazette, 10 Sept. 1901, and 28 Jan. 1902]; received the Queen's Medal with three clasps; the King's Medal with two clasps; the Brevet of Major 22 Aug. 1902, and was created a Companion of the Distinguished Service Order [London Gazette, 28 Jan. 1902]: "Alexander Walter Frederic Baird, Lieut., The Gordon Highlanders. For valuable services in the Intelligence Department." He was invested by the King 13 Oct. 1902. He was promoted Captain 22 June, 1902; became A.D.C. to 1st Class District Commander, India, 14 Nov. 1902; was Adjutant, Gordon Highlanders, 20 Aug. 1907, to 3 Oct. 1908. He served in the Mohmand Expedition, being employed as D.A.A.G. and Press Censor, Mohmand Field Force, 24 April to 5 June, 1908; G.S.O.2, Mauritius, 10 Oct. 1908, to 14 May, 1911; Staff Captain, War Office, 15 May, 1911, to 9 Oct. 1913; employed with the Egyptian Army from 15 July, 1914. He also served in the European War from 1914; was Temporary Lieutenant-Colonel, Gordon Highlanders, 2 Nov. 1914, to 7 April, 1915, and 23 April to 10 July, 1915. He was promoted Major 15 March, 1915; appointed G.S.O.2, B.E.F., 10 July, 1915; given his Brevet Lieutenant-Colonelcy 3 June, 1916; was Brigade Commander, 100th Infantry Brigade, 18 Feb. 1916, to 31 Jan. 1919; given the Brevet of Colonel, Jan. 1918. He was six times mentioned in Despatches; created a C.M.G., Feb. 1915; Commander of the Legion of Honour, 1916, and a C.B. 1919. Brigadier-General A. W. F. Baird became Military Attaché (British Military Representative), Sofia, 12 Feb. 1919. He married, in 1907, Maud Constance, daughter of the late Dr. Waylen, I.M.S., and they have one son, born in Jan. 1908.

Alexander W. F. Baird.

STIRLING, WALTER FRANCIS, Capt., was born 31 Jan. 1880, at Portsmouth, Hampshire, son of Capt. Francis Stirling, R.N. (deceased), and Mrs. Frances Stirling, of Hampton Court Palace. He was educated at Kelly College and at the Royal Military College, Sandhurst, and joined the 1st Royal Dublin Fusiliers as Second Lieutenant 11 Feb. 1899; became Lieutenant 16 Dec. 1899. He served with the Natal Field Force in South Africa with his regiment; with the 4th Division, Mounted Infantry, in Dundonald's Brigade; was afterwards appointed Adjutant, 14th Battn. Mounted Infantry. He took part in the Relief of Ladysmith; was present during operations in the Transvaal in June, 1900; operations in Natal (March to June, 1900), including action at Laing's Nek (6 to 9 June); in the Transvaal, east of Pretoria, July to 29 Nov. 1900, including action at Belfast (26 and 27 Aug.); in Orange River Colony (June, 1900), and again in the Transvaal, Dec. 1900, to May, 1902. He was mentioned in Despatches [London Gazette, 28 Jan. 1902]; received the Queen's Medal with five clasps, and the King's Medal with two clasps. The Distinguished Service Order was specially awarded in Army Orders [London Gazette, 28 Jan. 1902]: "Walter Francis Stirling, Lieut., The Royal Dublin Fusiliers. For skill and gallantry in action at Kaffirspruit 19 Dec. 1901." He was invested by the King 18 Dec. 1902. He joined the Egyptian Army 22 Aug. 1906; was promoted Captain 21 June, 1908, and retired from the Service 20 Jan. 1912; was Secretary of the Khedival Sporting Club, Cairo. At the outbreak of the European War Capt. Stirling was gazetted Observer in the Royal Flying Corps in Egypt. He afterwards rejoined the 1st Battn. Royal Dublin Fusiliers, 29th Division, in Gallipoli, as Second-in-Command, in April, 1915. He was appointed G.S.O.2, Intelligence, G.H.Q., Egypt, 1916, and afterwards G.S.O.2, to 52nd Lowland Division. He served on the General Staff until 1918; was promoted Major, Reserve of Officers, 18 Jan. 1917; became Deputy Chief Political Officer, Egypt and Syria. For his services in the European War Major Stirling was mentioned in Despatches, and was awarded the Military Cross and a Bar to the D.S.O.

COSTEKER, JOHN HENRY DIVES, Lieut., was born 28 March, 1879, son of William Costeker. He was educated at Harrow and Sandhurst, and entered the Army 3 Aug. 1898, as a Second Lieutenant in the Royal Warwickshire Regt., in which he was promoted Lieutenant 3 Feb. 1900.

He served in the South African War, 1901–2, as Adjutant, Mounted Infantry Battn., Sept. 1901, to 31 May, 1902; was present during operations in Cape Colony, Feb. to May, 1901; in Orange River Colony, May, 1901, to March, 1902; also in the Transvaal, March to 31 May, 1902. He was mentioned in Despatches [London Gazette, 17 Jan. 1902]; received the Queen's Medal with five clasps. He was created a Companion of the Distinguished Service Order [London Gazette, 28 Jan. 1902]: "John Henry Dives Costeker, Lieut., The Royal Warwickshire Regt. For the capture of Commandant Kolbe 11 Nov. 1901." He was invested by the King 19 Nov. 1902. He was promoted Captain 3 June, 1902; was Adjutant of the Royal Warwickshire Regt. 27 June, 1904, to 11 April, 1907; became Garrison Adjutant, Eastern Command, 1 June, 1907; Staff Captain, Irish Command, 1914. He was killed in action at the Dardanelles on 25 April, 1915, while serving as Brigade Major, 88th Infantry Brigade. He married, in 1914, Margaret, daughter of Percy C. Morris.

CLARKE, GOLAND VANHOLT, Lieut., was born 25 Nov. 1875, seventh son of the late Stephenson Clarke and Agnes Maria Clarke, of Brook House, West Hoathley, and Croydon Lodge, Croydon. He entered the 1st Dragoon Guards 25 March, 1896, and was transferred to the 18th Hussars 13 Jan. 1897. He served in the South African War, 1899–1902, taking part in the operations in Natal, 1899, including actions at Talana and Lombard's Kop; was present at the Defence of Ladysmith, including sorties of 7 Dec. 1899, and action of 6 Jan. 1900; was present during the operations in Natal, March to June, 1900, including action at Laing's Nek (6 and 9 June); in the Transvaal, east of Pretoria, July to 29 Nov. 1900, including actions at Belfast (26 to 27 Aug.) and Lydenberg (5 to 8 Sept.); again in the Transvaal 30 Nov. 1900, to Sept. 1901, and Nov. 1901, to 31 May, 1902; in Orange River Colony, March to May, 1902; also during the operations on the Zululand Frontier of Natal in Sept.

Goland Vanholt Clarke.

and Oct. 1901. He was mentioned in Despatches [London Gazette, 10 Sept. 1901, and 25 April, 1902]; was awarded the Queen's Medal with five clasps; the King's Medal with two clasps, and was created a Companion of the Distinguished Service Order [London Gazette, 28 Jan. 1902]: "Goland Vanholt Clarke, Lieut., 18th Hussars. For good service in Bruce Hamilton's operations in Ermelo District in Dec. 1901." He was invested by the King 24 Oct. 1902. He resigned from the 18th Hussars in 1907, and became Captain, City of London Yeomanry, Rough Riders, 1 Jan. 1910. He served in the European War from April, 1915, when he went out to Egypt with the Rough Riders. He was made Temporary Lieutenant-Colonel, June, 1915. He served with the Yeomanry in Gallipoli, and was present at the Charge of Chocolate Hill, Sept. 1915. He commanded a mobile column in the desert in 1916; was at Salonika in 1916 and 1917, and was given the Brevet of Lieutenant-Colonel for his services 1 Jan. 1917; was promoted Lieutenant-Colonel, Sept. 1917, and Brigadier-General, Dec. 1917; in Palestine, 1917 and 1918. Brigadier-General Clarke was mentioned in Sir Ian Hamilton's, Sir Archibald Murray's and Sir E. Allenby's Despatches, and in the New Year's Honours of 1917. He married (1stly), Mathilde, daughter of the late Colonel Key Hannigan, of New York (she died in 1912), and (2ndly), in Jan. 1918, Yvonne, only child of Monsieur Defrance, French Minister at Cairo.

MATURIN, REGINALD GEORGE, Lieut., was born 13 Nov. 1877, son of Colonel John Maturin. He joined the Royal Artillery 24 June, 1898, as a Second Lieutenant, and was promoted Lieutenant 16 Feb. 1901. He served in the South African War, 1900–2 (slightly wounded); took part in the operations in the Orange Free State, Feb. 1900; in Orange River Colony, May to Nov. 1900; in Cape Colony, Feb. 1900; in Orange River Colony and Cape Colony 30 Nov. 1900, to 31 May, 1902. He was mentioned in Despatches [London Gazette, 28 Jan. 1902]; received the Queen's Medal with two clasps, and King's Medal with two clasps. He was created a Companion of the Distinguished Service Order [London Gazette, 28 Jan. 1902]: "Reginald George Maturin, Lieut., Royal Artillery. For gallantry in Damant's action 20 Dec. 1901." He was invested by the King 24 Oct. 1902. He was employed with the West African Frontier Force 20 Dec. 1902, to 26 March, 1904, and saw active service in Northern Nigeria, 1903; took part in the operations against tribes on the direct route between Bauchi and Ibi. He became Captain 21 April, 1906, and was Adjutant of Royal Artillery 27 Feb. 1908, to 26 Feb. 1911; was promoted Major 30 Oct. 1914. Major Maturin again served with distinction in the European War, 1914–18, becoming Temporary Lieutenant-Colonel 13 April, 1916. He married, 21 Jan. 1917, at All Saints', Kingston-on-Thames, Ella, daughter of D. B. Maturin-Baird, of Newtownstewart, County Tyrone, and Kingston-on-Thames, and they have one daughter. For his services in the European War he was made Brevet Lieutenant-Colonel; mentioned in Despatches, and awarded a Bar to the D.S.O.

CLIFFORD, ERNEST STANLEY, Lieut.-Colonel, was born 25 Dec. 1873, son of S. La Poer Trench Clifford, Divisional Judge, India. He served in South Africa, 1899–1902, with the Imperial Light Horse; Lumsden's Horse, West Australians; 5th and 6th, and General Sir Walter Kitchener's Staff. He was mentioned in Despatches; received the Queen's Medal with clasps; the King's Medal with clasps, and was created a Companion of the Distinguished Service Order [London Gazette, 28 Jan. 1902]: "Ernest Stanley Clifford, Lieut., West Australian Mounted Infantry. For good service in Bruce Hamilton's operations in Ermelo District in Dec. 1901." In the European War Major Clifford went out with the 1st Canadian Division, Oct. 1914, on Headquarters Staff, as Assistant

R

Provost-Marshal, in 1915, with 1st Canadian Division. He was mentioned in Despatches, May, 1915, and 1917 ; promoted Lieutenant-Colonel 3 June, 1918. Lieut.-Colonel Clifford is married, and has one son.

London Gazette, 25 April, 1902.—" War Office, 25 April, 1902. The King has been pleased to give orders for the following appointments to the Distinguished Service Order and promotions in the Army, in recognition of the services of the undermentioned Officers during the operations in East and West Africa. To be Companions of the Distinguished Service Order."

KEMBALL, GEORGE VERO, Lieut.-Colonel, was born in Oct. 1859, son of the late Major-General John Shaw Kemball, of Fairseat, Wrotham. He was educated at Harrow, and entered the Royal Artillery, as Lieu-

George Vero Kemball.

tenant, 18 Dec. 1878. He served in Afghanistan, 1878–79 (Medal) ; became Captain 7 Sept. 1886 ; took part in the operations in Chitral, 1895, serving on the Staff, with the Relief Force. He was mentioned in Despatches [London Gazette, 15 Nov. 1895] ; was given the Brevet of Major 22 Jan. 1896, and received the Medal with clasp. He was promoted to Major 10 Sept. 1896, and served on he North-West Frontier of India in 1897, in the Tochi Expedition, on the Staff ; was mentioned in Despatches [London Gazette, 11 Feb. 1898], and received a clasp. In 1900 he served in West Africa, in Northern Nigeria, with the Kaduna Expedition (Medal and clasp). He was in command of the operations against the Forces of Bida and Kontagora ; was mentioned

n Despatches [London Gazette, 18 April, 1902]; received the Medal and clasp, and was created a Companion of the Distinguished Service Order [London Gazette, 25 April, 1902] : " George Vero Kemball, Lieut.-Colonel (Brigadier-General), Inspector General, West African Field Force. In recognition of services during the operations in West Africa (Kontagora and Bida Expeditions)." He was promoted to Lieutenant-Colonel 23 July, 1901. He commanded the Kano-Sokoto Expedition, 1903 (C.B. and clasp) ; was Director at the War Office, 1909–13, and commanded a brigade in India, 1914 ; was promoted to Major-General 8 April, 1914. Major-General Sir G. V. Kemball served in the Great War, 1915-16, in Mesopotamia, as Major-General, General Staff of the Expeditionary Force, and in command of the 28th Frontier Force Brigade. He was present at the actions and capture of Kurna, Battles of Kut and Ctesiphon, 1915, Battles of Sheik-Saad, the Wadi, Um-el-Hannah (2), Dujailah and Sannaiyat, 1916.

The following is an extract from a letter : " As regards Mesopotamia, it may be of interest to add : The 28th Frontier Force Brigade, consisting of the 2nd Leicestershire Regt. and 51st Sikhs, 53rd Sikhs and 56th Rifles (Frontier Force), lost, in the three months' fighting on the Tigris in the vain attempt to relieve Kut, well over 100 per cent. in killed and wounded. With a nominal establishment of some 3,100 of all ranks, the casualties from the enemy's fire, between 6 Jan. and 22 April, 1916, were over 3,800. The establishment of British officers was 75, and the casualties 121, of whom 39 were killed. At one time during that period less than half a dozen of the Regimental Staff and medical officers who had served in the Brigade remained untouched."

He was mentioned twice in Despatches ; was wounded at Sannaiyat, and created a K.C.M.G., June, 1916 ; commanded a division, India, 1917-19.

MORLAND, THOMAS LETHBRIDGE NAPIER, Brevet Lieut.-Colonel, was born in 1865. He entered the Army as a Lieutenant in the King's Royal Rifle Corps 23 Aug. 1884, and was promoted Captain 5 April, 1893. He was Aide-de-Camp to the Governor and Commander-in-Chief, Malta, 5 Feb. 1895, to 2 Feb. 1898. He was employed with the West African Frontier Force 5 Feb. 1898, to 3 May, 1904 ; served in West Africa 1897–98 ; took part in the operations on the Niger ; Lagos, employed in Hinterland. He was mentioned in Despatches [London Gazette, 23 May, 1899] ; received the Medal with clasp, and Brevet of Major 8 July, 1899 ; served in West Africa (N. Nigeria), 1900, with the Kaduna Expedition (in command) ; mentioned in Despatches [London Gazette, 16 April, 1901] (clasp). In West Africa, 1900 ; during the operations in Ashanti (Despatches [London Gazette, 4 Dec. 1900]) ; Brevet of Lieutenant-Colonel 29 Nov. 1900 ; in West Africa (Northern Nigeria), 1901 ; during the operations against the Emir of Yola ; in command (slightly wounded) (Despatches [London Gazette, 18 April, 1902] ; Medal with clasp). He was created a Companion of the Distinguished Service Order [London Gazette, 25 April, 1902] : " Thomas Lethbridge Napier Morland, Brevet Lieut.-Colonel, King's Royal Rifle Corps (Expedition against the Emir of Yola)." He was invested by the King 24 Oct. 1902. He was promoted Major 9 Oct. 1901. He subsequently served in Northern Nigeria, 1902, with the Bornu Expedition ; in command (Despatches [London Gazette, 24 April, 1903] ; clasp) ; in Northern Nigeria, 1903 ; during the Kano-Sokoto Campaign (Despatches [London Gazette, 31 July, 1903]) ; created a C.B. He was given the Brevet of Colonel 27 March, 1904 ; again employed with the West African Frontier Force 4 May to 21 June, 1904 ; Inspector-General, West African Frontier Force, 1 Sept. 1905, to 31 Aug. 1909 ; Substantive Colonel 1 Sept. 1905 ; Brigade Commander, 2nd Brigade, Aldershot Command, 1 June, 1910, to 29 June, 1913 ; Major-General 30 March, 1913. Major-General Morland served in the European War. He was Divisional Commander, 14th Division, New Armies, 5 to 31 Aug. 1914 ; Divisional Commander, 5th Division, B.E.F., 1 Sept. 1914, to 14 July, 1915 ; Temporary Lieutenant-General 15 July, 1915, until promoted Lieutenant-

General for distinguished service 1 Jan. 1918 ; Army Corps Commander 10th Army Corps, B.E.F. ; British Armies in France 15 July, 1915, to 1? April, 1918 ; Army Corps Commander, 13th Army Corps, British Armies in France, 16 April, 1918. He was mentioned in Despatches twice ; created a K.C.B. in 1915, and a K.C.M.G. in 1917. He was appointed Commander-in-Chief of the Army of the Rhine in 1920. Lieut.-General Sir T. L. N Morland married, in 1890, Mabel Eleanor Rowena, eldest daughter o Admiral Henry C. St. John, of Stokefield, Thornbury.

McCLINTOCK, AUGUSTUS, Capt. and Brevet Major, was born in 1866, fourth son of the late Colonel G. P. McClintock, D.L., of Seskinore, County Tyrone. He joined the Seaforth Highlanders 8 June, 1889, and was promoted Lieutenant 22 April, 1891. He served with his regiment in Ireland, England and in Crete. From Crete he was seconded for service with the Frontier Force, Northern Nigeria, 16 Feb. 1898, and took part in all the operations that followed the occupation of that colony, including the expedition to Egbon, Bida and Ilorin, in 1897, for which he received the Medal and clasp. He was promoted Captain 2 May, 1898. He also took part in the Munshi Expedition in 1900, when he was mentioned in Despatches [London Gazette, 16 April, 1901], and given the Brevet of Major. In 1901 he commanded the expedition against the Munshis, and was again mentioned in Despatches [London Gazette, 24 April, 1903. In the operations against the Emir of Yola he acted as Staff Officer, and was slightly wounded ; was again mentioned in Despatches [London Gazette, 18 April, 1902] ; received the Medal and clasp, and was created a Companion of the Distinguished Service Order [London Gazette, 25 April, 1902] : " Augustus McClintock, Brevet Major, Seaforth Highlanders." The Insignia, Warrant and Statutes were sent to the Colonial Office, and the Insignia presented by Brigadier-General Sir F. Lugard, at Zunguru, 21 April, 1903. In 1903 he commanded a battalion in the Kano-Sokoto Campaign, when he was again mentioned in Despatches [London Gazette, 31 July, 1903] (clasp). Since the settlement of Northern Nigeria, Major McClintock occupied the position of Resident Commissioner, having resigned his commission in the Army. Major McClintock died 24 June, 1912, at Marduguri, Northern Nigeria. The Colonial Secretary expressed his sincere condolence with Major McClintock's family, and his warm approval of his excellent work in the especially difficult and arduous operations attending the settlement of Northern Nigeria.

PHILLIPS, GEORGE EDWARD, Major, was born 28 Jan. 1865. He had a commission as Lieutenant in the Royal Engineers 5 July, 1884, and was promoted Captain 19 Dec. 1892. He was on Special Service from 7 Dec. 1895, to 26 March, 1896, in the Ashanti Expedition, for which he was honourably mentioned, and had the Ashanti Star. He again saw active service in the South African War, 1899–1900 ; was wounded and mentioned in Despatches. He was promoted Major in 1901. He was on special duty in Somaliland in 1902, being for his services there created a Companion of the Distinguished Service Order [London Gazette, 25 April, 1902] : " George Edward Phillips, Major, Royal Engineers. For services in the expedition against the Mullah in Somaliland." Major Phillips died in Oct. 1902.

PETRIE, CHARLES LOUIS ROWE, Major, was born 15 Dec. 1866.

He was educated at Marlborough, and entered the Manchester Regt., as a Second Lieutenant, 5 Feb. 1887 ; was promoted Lieutenant 10 April, 1899 ; Captain 13 July, 1896. He was employed in the Uganda Protectorate ; was promoted Major 21 Dec. 1901 ; served with the Uganda Rifles, 1901, and was mentioned in Despatches [London Gazette, 18 April and 12 Sept. 1902] ; received the Medal and clasp, and was created a Companion of the Distinguished Service Order [London Gazette, 25 April, 1902] : " Charles Louis Rowe Petrie, Major, Manchester Regt. (expedition into the Lango country)." The Insignia, Warrant and Statutes were sent to the Foreign Office 23 Jan. 1903. He was wounded in this campaign. He also served in operations in Somaliland, 1902–3, on the Staff, and as Staff Officer to the Inspector-General 16 July to 17 Aug. 1903. He was mentioned in Despatches [London Gazette, 2 Sept. 1904], and received the Medal and clasp. He retired 6 March, 1907. He served in the European War as Temporary Lieutenant-Colonel, commanding the 16th (Service) Battn. Manchester Regt. ; was given the rank of Lieutenant-Colonel in the Army 9 Jan. 1917. Lieut.-Colonel Petrie married, in 1912, Dorothy Frances, eldest daughter of the late Rev. E. P. Dew.

Charles Louis R. Petrie.

GORGES, EDMUND HOWARD, Major, was born 23 Nov. 1868, second son of the late Capt. Gorges, R.M.A. He was educated at the Royal Military College, Sandhurst, and entered the Army 14 Sept. 1887, as a Second Lieutenant in the Manchester Regt., in which he was promoted Lieutenant 3 July, 1889. He served with the 2nd Battn. in the East Indies, 1887–96 ; became Captain 6 Oct. 1896 ; served with the 1st Battn, Aldershot and Mediterranean, 1897–98 ; with the King's African Rifles. 1898–1908 ; saw active service in the Uganda Mutiny, 1897–98 (clasp) ; with the Maluka Expedition, British East Africa, 1898 (Medal with clasp). Capt. Gorges served in the South African War, 1900, as Special Service Officer. He was employed with the Mounted Infantry, and was present during operations in the Orange Free State, Feb. to May, 1900 (Queen's Medal with two clasps). He served again in Uganda in 1900, with the Nandi Expedition (Medal with clasp), and commanded the punitive force against the Suh Turkana and other hostile tribes in 1901. He became

Major 21 Dec. 1901; was mentioned in Despatches [London Gazette, 18 April, 1902], and was created a Companion of the Distinguished Service Order [London Gazette, 25 April, 1902]: "Edmund Howard Gorges, Major, Manchester Regt. (Turkana Punitive Expedition)." He was invested by the King 28 March, 1903. He was Commandant of the Camel Corps and Mounted Infantry in Somaliland, 1904; commanded the 1st Battn. King's African Rifles, 1905, and the Nandi Field Force, 1905 (Despatches [London Gazette, 18 Sept. 1906]; Brevet of Lieutenant-Colonel 26 March, 1906; clasp); served in East Africa, 1906 (Despatches). He was given the Brevet of Colonel 10 May, 1910; became Lieutenant-Colonel, West African Regt. 11 Jan. 1912, and was Commandant of the West African Regt. from 2 Jan. 1913, to 6 May, 1916. Brevet Colonel Gorges was the Commanding Officer of the British Contingent, Cameroon Expeditionary Force, from 1914 to 1916, and for his services was mentioned in Despatches twice; was made a C.B. in 1915, and Officer of the Legion of Honour. On 7 Sept. 1916, he became Temporary Brigadier-General to command the South Midland Brigade, Home Forces; was Brigade Commander, 200th Infantry Brigade, Home Forces, 17 April, 1917, to 24 Feb. 1918; was promoted Substantive Colonel 6 Dec. 1917; appointed Brigade Commander, 202nd Infantry Brigade, Home Forces, 25 Feb. 1918. He was made a C.B.E. in 1919. Brigadier-General E. H. Gorges is a Fellow of the Royal Geographical Society. He married, in 1900, Sylvia Rosalie, only daughter of Lieut.-Colonel H. F. Townshend, of Castle Townshend, Cork, and they have one daughter.

GODFREY, CHARLES, Capt., was born 16 Feb. 1872, son of Major-General Godfrey. He entered the North Lancashire Regt., as a Second Lieutenant, 2 May, 1891, and became Lieutenant in the Indian Staff Corps 26 June, 1892; was appointed Second-in-Command of the British Central Africa Rifles in May, 1898. He became Captain (26th Bombay Infantry). He served in Central Africa in 1902, and for his services was created a Companion of the Distinguished Service Order [London Gazette, 25 April, 1902]: "Charles Godfrey, Capt., Indian Staff Corps (for the Ashanti Expedition)." The Insignia, Warrant and Statutes were sent to his father, Major-General Godfrey, 13 Jan. 1903. Capt. Godfrey died 22 April, 1903.

London Gazette, 20 May, 1902.—"War Office, 20 May, 1902. The King has been graciously pleased to give orders for the following appointment to the Distinguished Service Order, in recognition of the services of the undermentioned Officer during the operations against the Mullah in Somaliland. To be a Companion of the Distinguished Service Order."

McNEILL, MALCOLM, Capt., was born 30 Jan. 1866, son of the late Lieut.-Colonel A. C. McNeill, C.S.I., Madras Army, of the family of McNeill, of Colonsay, and Annabella, daughter of General Sir John Campbell, K.C.S.I. He was educated at Cargilfield, Clifton, and Sandhurst, and entered the Army 7 Feb. 1885, with a commission in the Argyll and Sutherland Highlanders, in which he was promoted Captain 7 Nov. 1894. He saw a great deal of active service, including operations on the Indian North-West Frontier in Waziristan, 1894–95, as Assistant Superintendent of Signalling (Medal and clasp); in the Tochi Valley, 1897 (Medal and clasp); in Somaliland, 1901. For his services in the last campaign he was mentioned in Despatches 18 April, 1902; received the Medal and clasp, and was created a Companion of the Distinguished Service Order [London Gazette, 20 May, 1902]: "War Office, 20 May, 1902.—The King has been graciously pleased to give orders for the following appointment to the Distinguished Service Order, in recognition of the services of the under-mentioned Officer during the operations against the Mullah in Somaliland. To be a Companion of the Distinguished Service Order, Capt. Malcolm McNeill, Argyll and Sutherland Highlanders." He retired 21 Feb. 1906, after 21 years in the Army, joining the Reserve of Officers. When the European War broke out he at once returned to England. He was given the command of the 11th Argyll and Sutherland Highlanders in France, and was mentioned in Despatches, and created a C.M.G., 1916. He died, 3 June, 1917, at the Honourable Lady Murray's Hospital, at Tréport, France, suddenly, of heart failure after an attack of malaria. Capt. McNeill wrote "In Pursuit of the Mad Mullah." His favourite recreations were big game hunting and fishing. As a big game hunter he had a wide reputation, and his magnificent collection of trophies is kept in the museum attached to his house at Oban.

Malcolm McNeill.

London Gazette, 26 June, 1902.—"The King has been graciously pleased to give orders for the following appointments, in recognition of the services of the following Officers during the operations in South Africa. The whole to bear date 26 June, 1902, unless otherwise stated."

TUDWAY, ROBERT JOHN, Brevet Lieut.-Colonel, was born 19 Nov. 1859, son of the Rev. Henry Tudway, of Walton-in-Gordano, Somerset. He entered the Army as a Second Lieutenant in the 56th Foot 13 Aug. 1879, and became Lieutenant in the Essex Regt. 1 July, 1881. He served with the Soudan Expedition, 1884–

Robert John Tudway.

85, on the Nile; employed with Mounted Infantry; took part in the action of Abu Klea and reconnaissance of 17 Feb. He was mentioned in Despatches [London Gazette, 27 March and 25 Aug. 1885]; received the Medal with two clasps; Bronze Star. He became Captain 21 April, 1886; served in the Soudan, 1888, at Suakin; took part in the action of Gamaizah, in command of Mounted Infantry (Despatches [London Gazette, 11 Jan. 1889]; clasp; 4th Class Medjidie); accompanied the Expedition to Dongola, 1896, in command of Camel Corps; served during operations of 7 June and 19 Sept. (Despatches [London Gazette, 3 Nov. 1896]; Brevet of Major 18 Nov. 1896; Egyptian Medal with two clasps); served with the Nile Expedition, 1897 (Despatches [London Gazette, 25 Jan. 1898]; clasp to Egyptian Medal); with the Nile Expedition, 1898, in command of Camel Corps; at the Battle of Khartoum (Despatches [London Gazette, 30 Sept. 1898]; Brevet of Lieutenant-Colonel 16 Nov. 1898; clasp to Egyptian Medal, and Medal); served in the South African War, 1899–1902, on the Staff; at the Relief of Kimberley; took part in the operations in the Orange Free State, Feb. 1900, including operations at Paardeberg, 17 to 26 Feb. (severely wounded 18 Feb.); in the Transvaal, east of Pretoria, July, 1900; in Orange River Colony; also in Cape Colony, south of Orange River, 1899; again in Orange River Colony 30 Nov. 1900, to 31 May. 1902. He was promoted Major 15 Feb. 1900. For his services in South Africa he was mentioned in Despatches [London Gazette, 8 Feb. and 10 Sept. 1901]; received the Queen's Medal with four clasps; the King's Medal with two clasps, and was created a Companion of the Distinguished Service Order [London Gazette, 26 June, 1902]: "Robert John Tudway, Brevet Lieutenant-Colonel, Major, Essex Regt. In recognition of services during the operations in South Africa." The Insignia, Warrant and Statutes were sent to the G.O., Transvaal, and presented at Harrismith 16 March, 1903. He served as D.A.A.G., South Africa, 4 Nov. 1900, to 21 Sept. 1903; D.A.A.G., 5th Division, 2nd Army Corps, Southern Command, 22 Sept. 1903, to 7 March, 1905; was given the Brevet of Colonel 16 Nov. 1904; promoted Substantive Lieutenant-Colonel 16 May, 1906, to command the Essex Regt.; created a C.B. in 1909; Substantive Colonel 16 May, 1910; O.C., No. 3 District, Western Command, 5 Sept. 1911, to 30 Dec. 1914. He was promoted Temporary Brigadier-General 31 Dec. 1914, and commanded a Brigade until 20 June, 1915, serving in the Dardanelles. He became D.A. and Q.M.G. 21 June, 1915. For his services in the Dardanelles he was created a C.M.G. in 1916, and made an Officer of the Legion of Honour. He saw service in 1916 in France; was mentioned in Despatches, France, 1916; was placed on retired pay 18 Nov. 1916; received the honorary rank of Brigadier-General 11 April, 1917, and granted the Reward for Meritorious Service. Brigadier-General R. J. Tudway married, in 1906, Olive Winifred, daughter of E. W. Browne.

REID, ELLIS RAMSAY, Lieut.-Colonel, was born 23 Jan. 1859, son of Lestock Robert Reid, late Bombay Civil Service. He was educated at Harrow and Sandhurst, and joined the 108th Regt. as an Ensign in 1869; exchanged as Captain to the 44th Foot, 1878, and joined the Army Pay Department as Paymaster 11 March, 1881. He served in the Bechuanaland Expedition as District Paymaster of the Force, 1884–85, and was honourably mentioned. He became Honorary Major 11 March, 1886, and Staff Paymaster 31 Aug. 1893; Lieutenant-Colonel 16 Feb. 1899. He served in South Africa from Nov. 1899, to the end of the war; was mentioned in Despatches and created a Companion of the Distinguished Service Order [London Gazette, 26 June, 1902]: "Ellis Ramsay Reid, Lieut.-Colonel, Army Pay Department. In recognition of services during the operations in South Africa." The Insignia were presented by the King 18 Dec. 1902. He became Colonel 11 July, 1903; was created a C.B. in 1907, and retired 23 Jan. 1910; became Chief Paymaster, A.P.D. He died 14 Oct. 1918. Colonel Reid married, in 1901, Helena Kate Risley.

Ellis Ramsay Reid.

DORAN, WALTER ROBERT BUTLER, Major, Brevet Lieut.-Colonel, was born 15 Dec. 1861, son of the late General Sir John Doran, K.C.B. He joined the Royal Irish Rifles, as Lieutenant, 10 May, 1882. He served with the Egyptian Expedition, 1882; in the action at Kassassin, and Battle of Tel-el-Kebir (Medal with clasp; Bronze Star); served with the Soudan Expedition, 1884–85, on the Nile; served with native levies (clasp). He was Staff Captain, Egypt, 12 March to 21 Aug. 1885; Adjutant, Royal Irish Rifles, 1 Feb. 1887, to 31 March, 1891; was promoted Captain 26 Nov. 1888; served in the Hazara Expedition, 1888 (Medal with clasp). He passed the Staff College in 1894, and was employed with the Egyptian Army from 1 Jan. 1897, to 3 March, 1900; accompanied the Nile Expedition, 1897, and was mentioned in Despatches [London Gazette, 25 Jan. 1898], and received the Egyptian Medal with clasp; again accompanied the Nile Expedition, 1898, in charge of Store Depôt and hospital at Berber; at the battles of the Atbara and Khartoum, in command of an Egyptian battalion (Despatches [London Gazette, 4 Nov. 1898]; Brevet of Major 16 Nov. 1898; Medal); served with the Nile Expedition 1899; took part in the operations resulting in final defeat of Khalifa, in command of the 9th Sudanese (Despatches [London Gazette, 30 Jan. 1900]; Brevet of Lieutenant-Colonel 14 March, 1900). He served in the South African War, 1899–1902, on Special Service, 4 to 22 March, 1900; Brigade Major 23 April to 22 Nov. 1900; Staff Officer 23 Nov. 1900, to 2 July, 1902. He was promoted Major 19 Feb. 1901; took part in the operations in the Transvaal 30 Nov. 1900, to May, 1901; in Cape Colony, June, 1901, to 31 May, 1902, in command of a Flying Column,

Nov. 1901, to 31 May, 1902, and for his services he was mentioned in Despatches [London Gazette, 17 June, 1902]; received the Queen's Medal with three clasps; the King's Medal with two clasps, and was created a Companion of the Distinguished Service Order [London Gazette, 26 June, 1902]: "Walter Robert Butler Doran, Major, Brevet Lieut.-Colonel, Royal Irish Rifles. In recognition of services during the operations in South Africa." He was invested by the King 18 Dec. 1902. From 29 June, 1903, to 12 Aug. 1904, he was employed as D.A.A.G., 4th Army Corps. He became Lieutenant-Colonel 13 Aug. 1904; was given his Brevet Colonelcy 29 May, 1905; promoted Colonel 13 Aug. 1908; was created a C.B. in 1910; G.S.O.1, 5th Division, Irish Command, 22 July, 1909, to 7 April, 1912; Temporary Brigadier-General 8 April, 1912, to 10 March, 1915; Brigade Commander, 17th Brigade, Irish Command, 8 April, 1912, to 4 Aug. 1914; commanded the 2nd Battn. Prince of Wales's Leinster Regt. from 1914; He served in the European War; was Brigade Commander 5 Aug. 1914, to 10 March, 1915; Inspector of Infantry 12 April to 9 May, 1915; appointed Brigade Commander 10 May, 1915; Brigadier-General, General Staff, Aldershot Command, 25 Sept. 1915. He retired as an Honorary Brigadier-General 4 March, 1919. Brigadier-General Doran married, in 1911, Elsie, eldest daughter of Emile Teichmann, of Sitka, Chislehurst, and they have one son.

FLINTOFF, THOMAS, Lieut.-Colonel, was born 16 Nov. 1851, son of Thomas Flintoff. He was educated privately and at the New Veterinary College, Edinburgh, and entered the Royal Artillery 23 June, 1875, as Veterinary Surgeon. He was transferred to the 8th Hussars in 1878, and served with them through the Afghan War of 1879 to 1880, for which he received the Medal. He became 1st Class Veterinary Surgeon 23 June, 1885; was transferred as Veterinary Officer to the 2nd Life Guards 10 June, 1891, and became Veterinary Major 23 June, 1895; Veterinary Lieutenant-Colonel, 1901. He served in the Boer War of 1899–1902; received the Queen's Medal, and was created a Companion of the Distinguished Service Order [London Gazette, 26 June, 1902]: "Thomas Flintoff, Veterinary Lieutenant-Colonel, Army Veterinary Department. For services in South Africa." The Insignia, Warrant and Statutes were presented by the G.O.C., South Africa, 29 July, 1903. Lieut.-Colonel T. Flintoff retired from the Army in 1904. He died suddenly on 24 Aug. 1907, at Felixstowe, at the age of 55. He married, in 1885, Kate Hannah Frost (deceased), daughter of Isaac Frost, of High Street, Norwich.

McLAUGHLIN, HUBERT JAMES, Major, was born at Plymouth on 2 Dec. 1860, third son of the late Major-General E. McLaughlin and Mrs. McLaughlin (daughter of James Bromilow, of St. Helens, Lancashire), of the Lydiates, Brimfield, and grandson of the Rev. Prebendary McLaughlin and the Honourable Frederica Cotton. He was educated at Mr. Pipon's at Chester, and afterwards at Sandhurst. He obtained his commission in the 94th Foot in Aug. 1900, and in the following year went out to join his regiment, which was so cut up at Isandhlwana that there was nothing to join, and it was merged in the Connaught Rangers. He was besieged for 70 days at Standerton, and for his services in the Transvaal Campaign of 1881 was mentioned in Despatches. He transferred to the 19th Hussars in July, 1884, and took part in the Nile Expedition of 1884–85, for which he had the Medal with clasp and the Bronze Star. In May, 1888, he was promoted Captain, 5th Royal Irish Lancers; reached the rank of Major in 1893, and retired in 1899. He volunteered for the South African War, 1899–1902, and was employed with the Remount Department. He was promoted to Lieutenant-Colonel, in the Reserve of Officers, 18 Oct. 1902; received the Queen's Medal with three clasps; the King's Medal with two clasps; was mentioned in Despatches [London Gazette, 17 June, 1902], and was created a Companion of the Distinguished Service Order for showing extreme gallantry in going into Basutoland single-handed to get ponies [London Gazette, 26 June, 1902]: "Hubert James McLaughlin, Major, Reserve of Officers, late 5th Lancers. In recognition of services during the operations in South Africa." The Insignia, Warrant and Statutes were sent to the G.O.C., Transvaal, and presented by the G.O.C., South Africa, 18 May, 1903. After the South African War he had the entire charge of repatriating the Boers, and a long account of his work was in the "Times" at that time. At the time of his sudden death at Aldershot, 28 March, 1915, he was Commandant, Central Remount Depôt, Aldershot, and over 33,000 horses had passed through his hands. In 1915 he was offered the command of the 6th Reserve Cavalry, then at Dublin. Lieut.-Colonel McLaughlin married, in 1909, Winifred Hawthorne, only daughter of H. M. Hicks, of Brisbane, and left one son.

NICHOL, CHARLES EDWARD, Lieut.-Colonel, was born 31 May, 1859, son of the late T. Dale Nichol, of Jesmond, Newcastle-on-Tyne. He was educated at the Edinburgh Collegiate School and University (M.B. and C.M. 1881). He entered the Army Medical Service in 1882; served with the 3rd Brigade, Burma Field Force, 1885–87, and was present at several engagements around Ningyan and Jemethen (Medal with clasp). After 12 years' service he became Major, R.A.M.C., 4 Feb. 1894. He served in the South African War, 1899–1901; commanded the 19th Brigade Bearer Company. Took part in the operations in the Orange Free State, Feb. to May, 1900, including actions at Poplar Grove, Dreifontein, Houtnek (Thoba Mountain) and Vet River (5 and 6 May); in the Transvaal, east of Pretoria, July to 29 Nov. 1900, including actions at Lydenberg (5 to 8 Sept.); again in the Transvaal, west of Pretoria, July to 29 Nov. 1900, including action at Elands River (4 to 16 Aug.); also again in the Transvaal, Dec. 1900, to Aug. 1901 (Despatches [London Gazette, 16 April, 1901]; Queen's Medal with four clasps). He became Lieutenant-Colonel 4 Feb. 1902, and was created a Companion of the Distinguished Service Order [London Gazette, 26 June, 1902]: "Charles Edward Nichol, M.B., Lieut.-Colonel, Royal Army Medical Corps. In recognition of services during the operations in South Africa." Insignia, Warrant and Statutes sent to Commander-in-Chief in India; presented by the O.C. Roorkee, at a Review Parade at Roorkee, 21 Feb. 1903. Lieut.-Colonel Nichol was appointed Command-

ant, Royal Army Medical Corps School of Instruction, and O.C. Depôt, 5 Nov. 1906, and held this position until 31 Oct. 1909; was promoted Colonel and Principal Medical Officer, India, 9 March, 1912; became A.D.M.S., India. He served in the European War from 1914 to 1916, as D.D.M.S. of an Army Corps, and D.M.S. of an Army, and for his services was mentioned in Despatches and created a C.M.G. in 1916. He retired 26 Dec. 1917. Colonel Nichol married, in 1898, Emmeline Kingscote, daughter of the late Major T. Gordon, Indian Army.

ROLLESTON, LANCELOT, Lieut.-Colonel, was born 19 Aug. 1847, at Watnell Hall, Notts, son of Lancelot Rolleston, Esq., D.L., Colonel, Notts Militia, M.P. for South Nottinghamshire, and Eleanor Charlotte, daughter of the late Robert Fraser, of Torbreck. He was educated at Wellington College and Christ Church, Oxford, and joined the South Notts Hussars Yeomanry in Sept. 1868. In 1877 he was High Sheriff of Nottinghamshire. He became Lieutenant-Colonel in the South Notts Hussars 25 Nov. 1896, and commanded a squadron of his regiment in the South African War, from 1900 to 1901. He took part in several operations in Cape Colony, Orange River Colony and the Transvaal, and was severely wounded at Lindley on 1 June, 1900, in the attempt to rescue 500 prisoners taken by Piet de Wet. He was mentioned in Despatches

Lancelot Rolleston.

[London Gazette, 17 June, 1902]; received the Queen's Medal with four clasps, and was created a Companion of the Distinguished Service Order [London Gazette, 26 June, 1902]: "Lancelot Rolleston, Lieut.-Colonel, Imperial Yeomanry. For services during operations in South Africa." He commanded the South Notts Hussars from 1897 to 1907, and commanded the Notts and Derby Mounted Brigade from 1908. He was created a K.C.B., 1911; was Chairman of Quarter Sessions for Nottinghamshire, 1912; is D.L. and J.P. and Hon. Colonel, South Nottinghamshire Hussars. He was Master and Huntsman of the Christ Church Harriers at Oxford, 1869–72, and of the Rufford Foxhounds, 1889–1900. He was in command of the Yeomanry Brigade at the Coronation of King George V., and is County Commandant of the Nottinghamshire Volunteer Regt. Colonel Sir Lancelot Rolleston married, at Torquay, 25 Feb. 1882, Lady Charlotte Emma Maud Dalzell, C.B.E., daughter of Colonel the Honourable R. Dalzell and sister of the 12th Earl of Carnwath.

HARVEY, JOHN ROBERT, Lieut.-Colonel, was born 31 July, 1861, eldest son of the late Colonel John Edmund Harvey, 41st Regt., of Springfield, Taplow, Bucks, and Thorpe, Norfolk, and Octavia Lettice, daughter of the Rev. R. Stephens. He was educated at Rugby and at Trinity College, Cambridge, and served in the East Norfolk Militia, 16th Lancers and 5th Lancers; joined the 43rd Suffolk Hussars, as Captain, 15 Nov. 1899. He commanded the Suffolk Hussars and the 25th Battn. Imperial Yeomanry in South Africa, and served also as Staff Officer for Prisoners of War (graded as Staff Captain), Lines of Communication, from 1900 to 1902. He took part in the operations in the Orange Free State, Feb. to May, 1900; in the Transvaal, west of Pretoria, July to 29 Nov. 1900; in Orange River Colony, May to 29 Nov. 1900; in Cape Colony, south of Orange River, 1900; in the Transvaal, Feb. to 31 May, 1902; also during the operations in Cape Colony, Dec. 1901, to

John Robert Harvey.

Feb. 1902 (Despatches [London Gazette, 17 June, 1902]; Queen's Medal with three clasps, and King's Medal with two clasps). He was created a Companion of the Distinguished Service Order [London Gazette, 26 June, 1902]: "John Robert Harvey, Lieut.-Colonel, Imperial Yeomanry. In recognition of services during the operations in South Africa." The Insignia were presented by the King 24 Oct. 1902. He subsequently retired from the King's Own Norfolk Imperial Yeomanry. He is a Justice of the Peace and was Mayor of Norwich in 1902–3. In the European War he served with the 4th Battn. Norfolk Regt. in Gallipoli in 1915; became Brevet Colonel, 4th Battn. Norfolk Regt. He has written "Records of the Norfolk Yeomanry Cavalry, 1782 to 1908," "Hunting in Norfolk" and "Shannon and its Lakes." He is fond of hunting, polo, shooting, fishing and yachting. He married, 1stly, in 1888, Nora (died, 1889), second daughter of H. Adams, of Canon Hill, Bray; 2ndly, in 1890, Florence, daughter of F. W. Parsons, of Risley Hall, Derby, and has one son and two daughters.

MUNN, FREDERICK HENRY, Major, was born 13 May, 1857. He became a Sub-Lieutenant in the 89th Foot 11 Sept. 1876; Lieutenant, Royal Irish Fusiliers, 11 Sept. 1876; was Instructor of Musketry, Royal Irish Fusiliers, 27 May, 1881, to 26 May, 1886; Captain, 30 March, 1883. He saw active service in the Soudan Expedition in 1884, taking part in the battles of Teb and Tamai, the relief of Tokar and the affair at Tamanieb, and receiving the Medal and clasp and Bronze Star. He reached the rank of Major 1 July, 1888. He served with distinction in the South African War, and was created a Companion of the Distinguished Service Order [London Gazette, 26 June, 1902]: "Frederick Henry Munn, Major, Royal Irish Fusiliers (since deceased). In recognition of services during the operations in South Africa."

INGLEFIELD, NORMAN BRUCE, Major, was born 6 Dec. 1855, son of the late Rear-Admiral V. O. Inglefield. He was educated at the Royal Military Academy, Woolwich, and entered the Royal Artillery, as Lieutenant, 19 Aug. 1875. Lieut. Inglefield served in the Afghan War, 1878–79 (Medal). He was promoted Captain 27 Aug. 1884; served as Adjutant, Royal Artillery, 16 Nov. 1884, to 31 Jan. 1889, and attained his Majority 1 Oct. 1892. He was Brigade Major, School of Gunnery, 1 Jan. 1894 to 31 Dec. 1898, and qualified as Interpreter in French in Oct. 1897. He served in the South African War, 1899 to 1902, being employed from 15 June, 1901, to 8 July, 1902, as D.A.A.G., Field Force. Took part in the operations in the Orange Free State, April to May, 1900.; in the Transvaal, east of Pretoria, July, 1900; in the Transvaal, west of Pretoria, July to 29 Nov. 1900, including action at Zilikat's Nek; in Orange River Colony, May to July, 1900; also in Cape Colony, south of Orange River, 1900; again in the Transvaal 30 Nov. 1900, to June, 1901; again in Orange River Colony, June, 1901, to 31 May, 1902 (Despatches [London Gazette, 10 Sept. 1901]; Queen's Medal with three clasps, and King's Medal with two clasps). He was created a Companion of the Distinguished Service Order [London Gazette, 26 June, 1902]: "Norman Bruce Inglefield, Major, Royal Artillery. In recognition of services during the operations in South Africa." He became Lieutenant-Colonel 6 June, 1902; served as Chief Instructor, School of Gunnery, 15 Feb. 1904, to 14 Feb. 1908; was given the Brevet of Colonel 6 June, 1905, and became Colonel 13 July, 1907. In 1909 he became Brigadier-General in command of the South Irish Coast Defences, and was created a C.B. in 1910. Brigadier-General N. B. Inglefield died at Cork 7 Dec. 1912. He had married, in 1888, Catherine, daughter of W. F. Burnley, and left one daughter.

TRENCH, FREDERIC JOHN ARTHUR, Major, was born 2 Feb. 1857, son of the late Rev. J. E. Trench, M.A. He was educated at Geneva University, at the Royal Military Academy, Woolwich, and at the Staff College. He entered the Royal Artillery, as Lieutenant, 2 Feb. 1876. He served in the Zulu War of 1879, and was mentioned in Despatches [London Gazette, 21 Aug. 1879], "for conduct especially deserving of commendation at the Battle of Ulundi," receiving also the Medal and clasp. He was promoted Captain 4 Nov. 1884; was Adjutant, Royal Horse Artillery, 1883–84, and 1891–92; District Gunnery Instructor, 1889; became Major 19 Jan. 1893; D.A.A.G., Headquarters, Ireland, 18 Oct. 1895, to 11 Nov. 1898; Brigade Major, Royal Artillery, Western District, 10 April, 1899, to 27 Jan. 1901. He qualified as an Interpreter in French in 1899 (and in 1905 in German). Major Trench again saw active service in the South African War, being employed on the Staff as District Commandant 28 Jan. 1901, to 28 April, 1901; specially employed 29 April to 22 July, 1901; D.A.A.G. 23 July, 1901, to 1 March, 1902; Press Censor, Headquarters, South Africa, 2 March, to 2 July, 1902. He was present in operations in the Transvaal, July, 1901, to 31 May, 1902; in Orange River Colony, July, 1901; in Cape Colony, Jan. 1901, to July, 1901; was mentioned in Despatches [London Gazette, 17 June, 1902], and was created a Companion of the Distinguished Service Order [London Gazette, 26 June, 1902]: "Frederic John Arthur Trench, Major, Royal Artillery. In recognition of services during the operations in South Africa." The Insignia, Warrant and Statutes sent to the G.O.C., Gibraltar; presented at Gibraltar 24 Nov. 1903. He became Lieutenant-Colonel 1 Oct. 1902; was given the Brevet of Colonel 1 Oct. 1905; was attached to the German Forces in South-West Africa 13 May, 1905, to 21 March, 1906, from which he had the German Medal and three clasps; was mentioned in Despatches, and was made Commander of the Red Eagle with Swords and Diamonds, and was Military Attaché at Berlin 22 March, 1906, to 22 March, 1910. All his German decorations were returned in 1914, as a protest against German barbarities to women and wounded. He was a C.V.O. in 1906; became Colonel 2 Sept. 1908, and retired on 22 March, 1910, to work for Boy Scouts and National Service, in order to meet the German menace. Colonel Trench wrote a book called "Manœuvre Orders." He married, in 1900, Anne Somerville, daughter of John N. Craddock, of Tuscaloosa, U.S.A.

TURTON, WILLIAM HARRY, Major, was born 30 Dec. 1856, at Peshawar, India, son of Lieut.-Colonel and Brevet Colonel Joseph Turton, Bengal Artillery, and grandson of Zouch Turton, of Chepstow and Monmouth. He was educated at Clifton College (Schools' Gold Medal of the Royal Geographical Society), and at the Royal Military Academy, Woolwich (Pollock Medallist); and was gazetted to the Royal Engineers, as Lieutenant, 14 Aug. 1876. He became Captain 14 Aug. 1887, and Major 2 May, 1895. He served in the South African War, May, 1900, to May, 1902, chiefly in the Kimberley and Mafeking Districts, but arrived too late for the sieges. He was Commanding Royal Engineer, Western District, Transvaal, from 4 Oct. 1901 till the end of the war, and was engaged in constructing blockhouse lines along the railway, from Kimberley north as far as Gaberones, and a few across country. The greatest number of blockhouses erected in any one month was 375 (28 March to 28 April, 1902), perhaps a record. He was present in operations in the Transvaal, west of Pretoria, and in Orange River Colony, July to 29 Nov. 1900; operations in Cape Colony, north of Orange River, June to July, 1900; operations in the Transvaal 30 Nov. 1900, to March, 1901, and Oct. 1901, to 31 May, 1902; operations in Orange River Colony 30 Nov. 1900, to March, 1901; operations in Cape Colony, March to Oct. 1901. He was mentioned in Despatches 8 July, 1902 [London Gazette, 17 June, 1902], received the Queen's Medal with three clasps; the King's Medal with two clasps, and was created a Companion of the Distinguished Service Order [London Gazette, 26 June, 1902]: "William Harry Turton, Major, Royal Engineers. In recognition of services during the operations in South Africa." Lieut.-Colonel Turton says: "I was never officially informed as to why I was awarded the D.S.O. I do not think it was customary to do so in that war. But I have no doubt in my own mind that it was in consequence of my defence of Christiana, Transvaal, where I was in command from July, 1900, to March, 1901. At the request of the Editor, I wrote a short account of this for the 'Royal Engineers' Journal,' July 1901, but of course it had to be censored, and some of the most interesting parts were omitted." He became Lieutenant-Colonel 1 Oct. 1902, and retired from the Service 4 Oct. 1905. Lieut.-Colonel Turton is the author of a book called "The Truth of Christianity," now in its 40th thousand, which has been translated into Japanese, Italian, Chinese and Arabic. He is also the author of several hymns, one of which on the "Sacrament of Unity" has been included in the "Ancient and Modern," and at least a dozen other collections. He takes an interest in genealogy and conchology, and hopes to publish shortly a book on early European Genealogies, and possibly one on the Shells of Port Alfred, South Africa, where he has collected shells for many years.

William Harry Turton.

THOMPSON, HARRY NEVILLE, Major, was born 15 March, 1861, son of the late Rev. Mungo Neville Thompson, Rector of Clonmany, Donegal, and Charlotte Blake, of Castlegrove, Co. Galway. He was educated at Armagh Royal School and Trinity College, Dublin (B.A., M.B., B.Ch.), and joined the Army Medical Service 2 Aug. 1884; became Surgeon, 1884, and Major, Royal Army Medical Corps, 2 Aug. 1896. He served in the Nile Expedition, 1898 (Medal and Khedive's Medal), and throughout the South African War, attached 16th (The Queen's) Lancers (he is a member for life of the 16th Lancers' Mess, and of the 30th [East Lancashire] Mess); was present at the Relief of Kimberley; took part in the operations in the Orange Free State, Feb. to May, 1900, including operations at Paardeberg (17 to 26 Feb.); actions at Poplar Grove, Karee Siding, Vet River (5 and 6 May) and Zand River; in the Transvaal in May and June, 1900, including actions near Johannesburg, Pretoria and Diamond Hill (11 and 12 June); in Orange River Colony and Transvaal, west of Pretoria (May to 29 Nov. 1900), including actions at Wittebergen (1 to 29 July); also in Cape Colony, north of Orange River; again during operations in the Transvaal, Orange River Colony and Cape Colony 30 Nov. 1900, to Oct. 1901 (Despatches [London Gazette, 15 Nov. 1901]; Queen's Medal with five clasps and King's Medal with two clasps). He was created a Companion of the Distinguished Service Order [London Gazette, 26 June, 1902]: "Henry Neville Thompson, M.B., Major, Royal Army Medical Corps. In recognition of services during the operations in South Africa." The Insignia, Warrant and Statutes were sent to the Commander-in-Chief in India; presented at Delhi, on the Durbar Parade, 27 Dec. 1902. He received the Coronation and Delhi Durbar Medals, 1903; became Lieutenant-Colonel 2 Aug. 1904; received King George's Coronation Medal, 1911, and became Colonel 17 Nov. 1913, being then appointed D.D.M.S., Scottish Command. Colonel Thompson served in the European War. He became A.D.M.S., 2nd Division, B.E.F. 4 Aug. 1914; A.D.M.S., 48th Division, B.E.F. 5 May, 1915; D.D.M.S., 6th Army Corps, B.E.F., British Armies in France, 29 May, 1915; D.M.S., 1st Army, British Armies in France, 21 July, 1917, to April, 1919, becoming Surgeon-General 21 July, 1917, and Major-General 26 Dec. 1917. He was created a C.M.G. in 1916, a C.B., 1917, and a K.C.M.G. in 1918. He was mentioned five times in Despatches, and was awarded three foreign Orders, viz.: Grand Officer, Military Order of Avis (Portuguese); the French Croix de Guerre, and the American Distinguished Service Medal. Major-General Sir H. N. Thompson became, in April, 1919, D.M.S., British Army of the Rhine.

Harry Neville Thompson.

CARDEW, GEORGE HEREWARD, Major, was born 3 Jan. 1861, at Kingsclere, Woodlands, Hampshire, eldest son of the late Rev. George Cardew, of St. Minver, East Liss. He was educated at Haileybury College, and joined the Army, from the Militia, as a Lieutenant in the 18th Hussars 9 Aug. 1882; became Captain 7 July, 1886. He was Deputy Assistant Commissary-General, Commissariat and Transport Staff, 21 Oct. 1887, to 10 Dec. 1888; was attached to the Army Service Corps 11 Dec. 1888; transferred to the Army Service Corps 1 April, 1889, and promoted Major 17 April, 1898. He served in the South African War, 1900–2, on the Staff; took part in the operations in the Orange Free State, including actions at Vet River (5 and 6 May) and Zand River; served during the operations in the Transvaal in May and June, 1900, including actions near Johannesburgh, Pretoria, and Diamond Hill (11 and 12 June); was present during the operations in Orange River Colony, including actions at Wittebergen, July, 1900; also in Cape Colony, March, 1900; took part in the operations in the Transvaal, Dec. 1900, and May, 1902; in Orange River Colony 30 Nov. 1900, to Jan. 1902; also in Cape Colony, Feb. to March, 1901. He was mentioned in Despatches by Lord Kitchener [London Gazette, 17 June, 1902]; received the Queen's Medal with four clasps, and the King's Medal with two clasps, and was created a Companion of the Distinguished Service Order [London Gazette, 26 June, 1902]: "George Hereward Cardew, Major, Army Service Corps. In recognition of services during the operations in South Africa." The Insignia, Warrant and Statutes were sent to the G.O.C., Straits Settlements, 23 Jan. 1902; presented by Brigadier-General Dorward 17 April, 1903. He became Lieutenent-Colonel 1 Nov. 1905, and was given the Brevet of Colonel 1 Nov. 1908, and retired 23 April,

1911. Colonel Cardew served in the European War, rejoining in 1914, and holding the position of A.Q.M.G., Eastern Army, till 1916. Subsequently he became Group Commander of a Labour Corps for overseas service 13 Feb. 1917, and he served with the British Expeditionary Force in France in 1917 and 1918, being mentioned for valuable services. He was made a C.B.E. in 1919. He married, in 1888, Emmeline Marian, daughter of John Bolster Burchell, B.A. (T.C.D.), and they have one son.

ARMSTRONG, OLIVER CARLETON, Major, was born 16 Oct. 1859, son of Major W. C. Armstrong. He was commissioned Second Lieutenant in the 86th Foot 11 May, 1878; became Lieutenant 23 April, 1879, and was transferred to the Bengal Staff Corps 29 Jan. 1883. He served in Burma, in 1888 (Medal with clasp); became Captain, Indian Staff Corps, 11 May, 1889, and Major, Indian Army, 11 May, 1898. He served in the South African War, 1900–2, being first Financial Adviser to the Military Governor of Pretoria, and afterwards Financial Adviser to the General Commanding-in-Chief the Forces. For his services he was mentioned in Despatches 17 June, 1902, and was created a Companion of the Distinguished Service Order [London Gazette, 26 June, 1902]: " Oliver Carleton Armstrong, Major, Indian Staff Corps. In recognition of services during the operations in South Africa." The Insignia were presented by the King at Buckingham Palace 26 June, 1903, exactly a year after the decoration was gazetted. He received the Queen's Medal with three clasps, and the King's Medal with two clasps. He became Lieutenant-Colonel 11 May, 1904; was appointed A.A.G., Headquarters, India, 11 Jan. 1905; became Colonel 11 May, 1907. He retired from the Indian Army 11 May, 1910. Colonel Armstrong married, in 1909, Lilian Florence, daughter of Edward Madoc Jones, of Glentworth, Oswestry, and widow of Murray Greaves-Bagshawe, and they have one son.

NORIE, CHARLES EDWARD DE MANLEY, Brevet Major, was born 7 Aug. 1866. He is the son of the late Major-General Evelyn Medows Norie. He entered the Army, as a Lieutenant in the Yorkshire Light Infantry, 9 May, 1885, and was transferred to the Indian Staff Corps 31 July, 1887. In 1891 he was with the expedition to Manipur (Medal with clasp). He became Captain 9 May, 1896. He served on the North-West Frontier of India, 1897–98; took part in the operations on the Samana during Aug. and Sept. 1897; at the relief of Gulistan (Medal with two clasps); served at Tirah, 1897–98; took part in the actions of Chagru Kotal, Dargai and capture of the Sampagha and Arhanga Passes; took part in the operations in the Warran Valley and action of 16 Nov. 1897; during the operations at and around Dwatoi and action of 24 Nov. 1897; against the Khani Khel Chamkanis; also during operations in the Bara Valley 7 to 14 Dec. 1897 (severely wounded; Despatches [London Gazette, 1 March and 5 April, 1898]; given the Brevet of Major 20 May, 1898; clasp). He served in the South African War; was on Special Service, South Africa, 20 Jan. to 30 March, 1900 (including Staff Duty, under an Assistant Inspector-General); was Commandant 1 May to 21 Nov. 1900. He was mentioned in Despatches [London Gazette, 10 Sept. 1901]; received the Queen's Medal with two clasps, and was created a Companion of the Distinguished Service Order [London Gazette, 26 June, 1902]: " Charles Edward de Manley Norie, Brevet Major, Indian Staff Corps. For services during operations in South Africa." Insignia, Warrant and Statutes were presented by G.O.C., Lahore, at a full Garrison Parade at Dalhousie, 12 April, 1903. He was promoted Major 9 May, 1903; was D.A.A.G., India, 24 April, 1904, to 14 July, 1907; promoted Lieutenant-Colonel 2 April, 1911. Lieut.-Colonel Norie served in the European War from 1914 to 1917. He was G.S.O., Meerut Division, B.E.F., 6 Jan. to 15 July, 1915; was given the Brevet of Colonel 18 Feb. 1915; was temporary Brigadier-General 16 July, 1915, to 27 March, 1917; D.A. and Q.M.G., Indian Army Corps, B.E.F., 16 July to 13 Sept. 1915; Brigade Commander, Bareilly Brigade, B.E.F., and 21st Infantry Brigade, Indian Expeditionary Force " D," 11 Sept. 1915, to 27 March, 1917. He became Colonel 1 Jan. 1917. He served in the Mesopotamian Campaign, and was five times mentioned in Despatches, and created a C.B. in 1916, and a C.M.G. in 1917. His Regiment is the 2nd Goorkhas. He married, in 1899, Grace, daughter of the late W. H. Reynolds, and they have two daughters.

OTTLEY, GEORGE FREDERIC, Major, was born 15 July, 1860, son of the late George Lethbridge Ottley, Esq., late of the 44th Regt., and Lucy, daughter of John Isbell, Esq., M.D. He joined the Royal Wiltshire Militia 8 May, 1878, and was given a commission as Second Lieutenant, 105th Light Infantry, 17 April, 1880, becoming Lieutenant 10 Nov. 1880, and Captain, King's Own Yorkshire Light Infantry, 24 Oct. 1885. He served at home from 17 April, 1880, to 26 Dec. 1884; at Malta from 27 Dec. 1884, to 17 Feb. 1887, and in India 18 Feb. 1887, to 2 May, 1892. From 2 March, 1888 to 1 March, 1892, he was Adjutant, King's Own Yorkshire Light Infantry, serving with the 2nd Battn. with the Zhob and Ziderzai Expedition, and as Staff Officer of the Vihowa Column. He was again on home service 3 May, 1892, to 9 Dec. 1894, and then in India until 5 March, 1899, serving as Acting Adjutant 14 Feb. to 29 Oct. 1895, and Officiating Station Staff Officer, 1st Class, 25 Oct. 1896, to 12 July, 1897; was with the Tirah Expeditionary Force, and present at the action of Shin Kamar. He received the India Medal with two clasps. He was promoted Major 8 June, 1898; served in Mauritius 6 March to 3 Oct. 1899, and in the South African War from 4 Oct. 1899, to 17 March, 1900. He was present in the advance on Kimberley, and the battles of Belmont, Enslin and Modder River. At Modder River he was severely wounded (gun-

George Frederic Ottley.

shot wound, right wrist [Colles' fracture]; shell wound, head; multiple gun-shot wounds, left leg [leg amputated]). He received the Queen's South African Medal with two clasps; was mentioned in Despatches [London Gazette, 10 Sept. 1901], and was created a Companion of the Distinguished Service Order [London Gazette, 26 June, 1902]: " George Frederic Ottley, Major, Yorkshire Light Infantry. In recognition of services during the operations in South Africa." The Insignia were presented by the King 18 Dec. 1902. He was Recruiting Staff Officer, 2nd Class, London, 20 July, 1900, to 19 July, 1905; was promoted Lieutenant-Colonel 19 July, 1902. Lieut.-Colonel Ottley was compulsorily retired on appointment as Assistant to Officer in Command of Records 19 July, 1905, and held this post until 31 Aug. 1914. During the European War he was Supervisor of Infantry Record Office, War Office, 1 Sept. 1914, to 10 Aug. 1916; Officer in Charge of Infantry Records from 10 Aug. 1916, until replaced on account of illness 29 Dec. 1917. He was mentioned to the Secretary of State for War, for valuable services rendered during the European War, 24 Feb. 1917.

SARGENT, HARRY NEPTUNE, Major, was born 6 April, 1866, son of the late Major-General E. W. Sargent. He was educated in Ireland, and entered the Devonshire Regt. 10 Nov. 1886; was transferred to the Army

Harry Neptune Sargent.

Service Corps 15 May, 1890; became Captain 7 Jan. 1892; was Adjutant, Army Service Corps, 1 Jan. 1895, to 28 Feb. 1898. He served with the Nile Expedition in 1898, and was present at the Battle of Khartoum; was employed as Staff Officer to the Commandant, Assouan, for British Troops and Stores. He was mentioned in Despatches [London Gazette, 30 Sept. 1898]; was given the Brevet of Major 6 Nov. 1898; received the Medal with clasp, and the Khedive's Star. He became Major 1 April, 1900. Major Sargent served also in the South African War, as D.A.A.G. 13 Nov. 1899, to 8 July, 1902; took part in the Relief of Ladysmith, including operations of 17 to 24 Jan. 1900, and action at Spion Kop; operations of 5 to 7 Feb. 1900, and action at Vaal Kranz; during the operations on Tugela Heights (14 to 27 Feb. 1900), and action at Pieter's Hill; took part in the operations in Natal (March to June, 1900), including action at Laing's Nek (6 to 9 June); in the Transvaal, east of Pretoria, July to Oct. 1900; also during operations in Cape Colony, Nov. and Dec. 1899 (Despatches—Sir R. H. Buller, 30 March and 9 Nov. 1900 [London Gazette, 8 Feb. 1901]; Queen's Medal with six clasps, and King's Medal with two clasps). He was created a Companion of the Distinguished Service Order [London Gazette, 26 June, 1902]: " Harry Neptune Sargent, Major, Army Service Corps. In recognition of services during the operations in South Africa." Invested by the King 18 Dec. 1902. He was Assistant Director of Supplies and Transport, 3rd Army Corps, and Assistant Director of Supplies and Transport, Irish Command, 1 Oct. 1903, to 31 May, 1905, and Deputy A.D.S. and T. 1 June, 1905, to 30 Sept. 1906, and was promoted Lieutenant-Colonel 27 Oct. 1906. He commanded the Army Service Corps in Dublin, 1906–8, and the Service Companies, A.S.C., Aldershot, 1908–11, being given the Brevet of Colonel 27 Oct. 1909, and promoted Colonel 4 Oct. 1911. He was Colonel in Command, A.S.C. Records, Woolwich Dockyard, 1 Aug. 1912 to 14 Dec. 1913, and from 15 Dec. 1913, to the outbreak of the European War, A.D. of S. and T., Aldershot Command. He served in the European War as A.Q.M.G., 1st Corps, 5 Aug. to 26 Dec. 1914, and was in the retreat from Maubeuge, the Battles of the Marne and the Aisne and the First Battle of Ypres. From 27 Dec. 1914, to 21 May, 1916, he was D.A. and Q.M.G., 1st Corps, and Temporary Brigadier-General, and was present at the Battle of Loos, then becoming D.A. and Q.M.G., Reserve Army. This position he held until Oct., and from Oct. 1916, to 19 Dec. 1917, he was D.A. and Q.M.G. of the 5th Army (Temporary Major-General 7 July, 1916, to 19 Dec. 1917); was present at the Battles of the Somme, operations south of Arras, and the Third Battle of Ypres. He was Chief of the British Mission Headquarters, S.O.S. American Expeditionary Force, 18 April, 1918, to July, 1919. He was mentioned in Despatches eight times; received the 1914 Star with clasp, Victory and General Service Medals; was created a C.B. (Military) in 1915, and a C.B.E. in 1919; became Commander of the Legion of Honour, and received the American Distinguished Service Medal. He married (1st) Ethel, daughter of Daniel Twomey, of Kolor, Penshurst, Victoria, Australia, and (2ndly), Olive, daughter of Colonel N. Tufnell, of Lanleys, Chelmsford, Essex.

COLLINGS, GODFREY DISNEY, Major, was born 13 Nov. 1855, son of the Rev. P. B. Collings, M.A. He was educated at King's School, Canterbury, and entered the 91st Highlanders 28 Feb. 1874; became Lieutenant 28 Feb. 1876; served in the Zulu War in 1879, and was present at the Battle of Ginginhlovo and relief of Etstowe (Medal and clasp). He became Captain, Argyll and Sutherland Highlanders, 21 Feb. 1888; resigned 13 Aug. 1894, and joined the Army Pay Department, becoming Paymaster on that date. He was promoted to Honorary Major 13 Aug. 1894, and Substantive Major 13 Feb. 1899; became Staff Paymaster 23 April, 1899, and Lieutenant-Colonel. He served in the South African

Godfrey D. Collings.

War, 1900–2; operations in Cape Colony, April to June, 1900; operations in Orange River Colony, July, 1900; operations in the Transvaal, July to 29 Nov. 1900; operations in the Transvaal, 30 Nov. 1900, to 31 May, 1902. He was mentioned in Despatches [London Gazette, 17 June, 1902]; received the Queen's Medal with three clasps; the King's Medal with two clasps, and was created a Companion of the Distinguished Service Order [London Gazette, 26 June, 1902]: "Godfrey Disney Collings, Major, Army Pay Department. In recognition of services during the operations in South Africa." He was invested by the King 18 Dec. 1902. He was promoted to Lieutenant-Colonel 23 April, 1904, and became Colonel and Chief Paymaster, A.P.D., 13 Jan. 1908. Colonel Collings served in the European War, as Command Paymaster with the Forces in Egypt, and was mentioned in Sir John's Maxwell's Despatches. He retired 15 Nov. 1916. He married, in 1891, J. K., daughter of the late Honourable P. L. van der Byl, M.L.C., Cape Colony.

ELLIOT, WILLIAM HENRY WILSON, Major, was born 7 Oct. 1864, at Raipur, Central Provinces, India, son of William Charles Elliot, M.D., Medical Officer in Charge, 7th Madras Native Infantry. He was educated privately, and at the London University (M.B., F.L.S.), and joined the Army 31 March, 1887. He served in the Hazara Expedition, 1888 (Medal with clasp); in the Miranzai (1st) Expedition, 1891; in the Tochi Expedition, North-West Frontier of India (Medal with clasp "Punjab Frontier, 1897–98"). He was promoted to Major 31 March, 1899, and served in the South African War, 1899–1901, taking part in operations in Natal, including action at Lombard's Kop; defence of Ladysmith, including action of 6 Jan.; operations in Natal, March to June, 1900; operations in the Transvaal, east of Pretoria, Oct. 1900; operations in the Transvaal, 1901. He was mentioned in Despatches [London Gazette, 8 Feb. and 10 Sept. 1901]; received the Queen's Medal with three clasps, and was created a Companion of the Distinguished Service Order [London Gazette, 26 June, 1902]: "William Henry Wilson Elliot, M.B., Major, Indian Medical Service. In recognition of services during the operations in South Africa." He was invested by the King 24 Jan. 1902. Lieut.-Colonel W. H. W. Elliot was Secretary to the Principal Medical Officer, H.M. Forces in India, 1903 to 31 March, 1907, when he retired. He was re-employed during the European War, 1914–19, and was promoted to Colonel. He married, 29 Sept. 1891, at Sundridge, Kent, Charlotte Elizabeth, eldest daughter of the late Charles Furber, Esq., of 6, Upper Hamilton Terrace, London, N.W. She died 3 April, 1914. Their children are: William Grenfell Riversdale, born 17 April, 1892; Ian Frederick Lettsom, born 25 Oct. 1893; Charlotte Patricia Hazel, Heather Doris Noel and Evangeline Marguerite Ladys.

WALTER, JOHN MACNEILL, Major was born 10 June, 1861, at Meerut, son of the late General John MacNeill Walter, C.B., Colonel, Royal Sussex Regt. He was educated at Cheltenham College; was gazetted to the 12th Foot, 14 Jan. 1880, and was promoted to Lieutenant, Suffolk Regt., 26 Nov. 1880, and to Captain 21 April, 1886. He was Senior Staff Officer, India, 4 July, 1894, to 12 May, 1896; D.A.A.G., India, 13 May, 1896, to 12 July, 1899; served as D.A.A.G., 2nd Brigade, Tochi Field Force, 1897–8 (Medal with clasp); was promoted to Major 26 April, 1899. He served in the South African War, 1899–1902, and was present at the Relief of Ladysmith, including the action at Colenso. He was afterwards Commandant at Irene, and served on the Staff, including service as Chief Censor at Cape Town. He was mentioned in Despatches [London Gazette, 8 Feb. and 10 Sept. 1901]; received the Queen's Medal with four clasps, the King's Medal with two clasps, and was created a Companion of the Distinguished Service Order [London Gazette, 26 June, 1902]: "John MacNeill Walter, Major, Devonshire Regt. In recognition of services during the operations in South Africa." He was invested by the King 18 Dec. 1902. He became Lieutenant-Colonel 2 Oct. 1906; was given the Brevet of Colonel 2 Oct. 1909, and was promoted to Colonel 2 Oct. 1910; was A.A.G., Headquarters, India, 3 Oct. 1910, to 14 Sept. 1913; D.A.G., Headquarters, India (Temporary Brigadier-General), 15 Sept. 1913, to 24 Nov. 1915; Adjutant-General, India, 25 Nov. 1915, to 4 Feb. 1917; Major-General in charge of Administration, Northern Command, India, 1917; promoted to Major-General 16 June, 1918. He was created a C.B. in 1916, and a C.S.I. in 1918. Major-General Walter married Annie, daughter of the late Alfred Chenery, of Loyala and Delatite, Victoria, Australia.

CARLETON, GUY AUDOUIN, Major, was born 23 Nov. 1859, at Bangalore, India, son of Colonel George Carleton, R.A. He was educated at Rugby School; entered the Army 14 Jan. 1880; became Lieutenant, Royal Lancaster Regt., 1 July, 1881; Captain 21 May, 1888; was D.A.A.G., Intelligence, Headquarters of Army, 24 May, 1898, to 21 Oct. 1899, and was promoted to Major 25 Nov. 1899. Major Carleton served in the South African War, 1899–1902; was mentioned in Despatches; received the Queen's Medal with three clasps, and the King's Medal with two clasps, and was created a Companion of the Distinguished Service Order [London Gazette, 26 June, 1902]: "Guy Audouin Carleton, Major, The King's Own Royal Lancaster Regt. In recognition of services during the operations in South Africa." He was invested with the D.S.O. by the King 18 Dec. 1902. Major Carleton retired 23 Nov. 1907. In 1917 he married Adela Dorothy Webb, widow of Capt. C. W. Webb, The Prince of Wales's North Staffordshire Regt., of Elford House, near Tamworth, Staffordshire, and daughter of the late Colonel Arthur Blundell, The Buffs (East Kent Regt.).

WHIGHAM, ROBERT DUNDAS, Major, was born 5 Aug. 1865, son of the late David Dundas Whigham, of Prestwick, Ayrshire, N.B., and Ellen Murray, youngest daughter of the late James Campbell, of Craigie, Ayrshire. He was educated at Fettes College, Edinburgh, and at the Royal Military College, Sandhurst, and was gazetted to the 1st Battn. Royal Warwickshire Regt., as Lieutenant, 9 May, 1885; was Adjutant, Royal Warwickshire Regt., 18 Jan. 1892, to 17 Jan. 1896, and was promoted to Captain 3 March, 1892. He was employed with the Egyptian Army 29 Dec. 1897, to 20 Dec. 1898, and served in the Nile Expedition of 1898 with the 13th Sudanese Battn., and was present at the battles of the Atbara and Khartoum (Despatches [London Gazette, 30 Sept. 1898]; Egyptian Medal with two clasps; Medal). He served in the South African War, 1899–1902, first as A.D.C. to Major-General Sir Hector Macdonald, K.C.B., commanding the Highland Brigade (6 Feb. to 23 Dec. 1900), and afterwards as D.A.A.G. at Army Headquarters 24 Dec. 1900, to 16 Oct. 1902. He was promoted to Major 1 Aug. 1900. He took part in the operations in the Orange Free State, Feb. to May, 1900, including operations at Paardeberg (17 to 26 Feb.); actions at Poplar Grove, Dreifontein, and Vet River (5 and 6 May); in Orange River Colony (May to 29 Nov. 1900), including actions at Wittebergen (1 to 29 July) and Witpoort; in Cape Colony, south of Orange River, 1899–1900; again in Cape Colony, north of Orange River, 1900; in the Transvaal, Jan. 1901, to 31 May, 1902; also during further operations in Orange River Colony and Cape Colony, Dec. 1900 (Despatches [London Gazette, 10 Sept. 1901]; Queen's Medal with six clasps, and King's Medal with two clasps). He was created a Companion of the Distinguished Service Order [London Gazette, 26 June, 1902]: "Robert Dundas Whigham, Major, Royal Warwickshire Regt. In recognition of services during the operations in South Africa." He was invested by the King 24 Oct. 1902. Major Whigham was Brigade Major, 2nd Army Corps, 1 Nov. 1902, to 25 Oct. 1904; D.A.A.G., Headquarters of Army, 1 Oct. 1906, to 2 Feb. 1908, and 3 Feb. 1908, to 15 April, 1909; was promoted to Lieutenant-Colonel 3 Feb. 1908, and to Colonel 4 Oct. 1911; was G.S.O.1, War Office, 16 April, 1912, to 15 Sept. 1914. He served in the European War from 1914, as G.S.O.1,'2nd Division, B.E.F., 16 Sept. to 26 Dec. 1914; as Brigadier-General, General Staff, 1st Army Corps, B.E.F., 27 Dec. 1914, to 16 July, 1915; as Sub-Chief of the General Staff, B.E.F., 17 July to 22 Dec. 1915; Deputy Chief of the Imperial General Staff, War Office, 23 Dec. 1915, to 28 April, 1918; was promoted to Major-General 1 Jan. 1916; was Divisional Commander, 59th Division, B.E.F., 19 June to 26 Aug. 1918; Divisional Commander, 62nd Division, B.E.F., 27 Aug. 1918, to 31 March, 1919; Divisional Commander, Light Division, British Army of the Rhine, 2 April, 1919. He was twice mentioned in Despatches; created a C.B. in 1915; promoted to Major-General; wounded; created a K.C.M.G. in 1919, and was made a Commander of the Legion of Honour. Sir Robert Whigham has been a Member of the Army Council since 1918. He married, in 1899, Isabel Adeline, youngest daughter of the late F. A. Muntz, of Rossmore, Leamington.

MILNE, GEORGE FRANCIS, Major, was born 5 Nov. 1866, son of the late George Milne, of Westwood, Aberdeen. He entered the Royal Artillery, as Lieutenant, 16 Sept. 1885; became Captain, 4 July, 1895. He served in the Nile Expedition of 1898, and was present at the Battle of Khartum receiving the Medal and the Egyptian Medal with clasp. Capt. Milne served in the South African War, 1899–1902; was promoted to Major 1 Nov. 1899; served as D.A.A.G. 18 Feb. 1900, to 22 Aug. 1902, taking part in operations in the Orange Free State, Feb. to May, 1900, including operations at Paardeberg (17 to 26 Feb.); actions at Poplar Grove, Vet River (5 and 6 May) and Zand River; in the Transvaal in May and June, 1900, including actions near Johannesburg, Pretoria and Diamond Hill (11 June); in Cape Colony, south of Orange River, 1899–1900, including actions at Colesberg (18 Jan. to 8 Feb.); again in the Transvaal, 30 Nov. 1900, to 31 May, 1902 (Despatches [London Gazette, 16 April, 1901]; Brevet of Lieutenant-Colonel; Queen's Medal with four clasps, and King's Medal with two clasps). He was created a Companion of the Distinguished Service Order [London Gazette, 26 June, 1902]: "George Francis Milne, Major, Royal Artillery. In recognition of services during the operations in South Africa." He was invested by the King 24 Oct. 1902. He was given the Brevet of Lieutenant-Colonel 22 Aug. 1902, and was D.A.Q.M.G., Intelligence, Headquarters of Army, 26 Jan. 1903, to 25 Jan. 1907 He was G.S.O.2, Territorial Force, North Midland Division, Northern Command, 1 April, 1908, to 31 Oct. 1909; became Colonel 1 Nov. 1909; was G.S.O.1, 6th Division, Irish Command, from 1 Nov. 1909, to 30 Sept. 1913; created a C.B. (Military) 1912; Temporary Brigadier-Genreal, commanding Royal Artillery, 4th Division, Eastern Command, 1 Oct. 1913, to 4 Aug. 1914, and went out to the European War as such in Aug. 1914 (Despatches). He was promoted Major-General for services on the Field 18 Feb. 1915; promoted Temporary Lieutenant-General 14 Dec. 1915; commanded 16th Army Corps, 1915; went to Salonica in Jan. 1916, as Commander-in-Chief of the British Forces, and was later Commander-in-Chief of the Army of the Black Sea. He was promoted Lieutenant-General 1 Jan. 1917, and Temporary General 25 June, 1918; created a K.C.B. in 1918; a K.C.M.G. in 1919, and a G.C.M.G. in 1919. Sir George Milne received the 2nd Class Order of the Danebrog of Denmark (1905); the 3rd Class Star of Roumania (1906); the Grand Cross of the White Eagle of Serbia with Crossed Swords (1917); was made Grand Officer, Legion of Honour, France, 1917, and received the Grand Cross of the Legion of Honour, 1919. In 1917 he became Grand Officer of St. Maurice and St. Lazarus, Italy; in 1917 he was given the Grand Cross of the Order of the Redeemer, Greece; in 1919 the Grand Cross, Crown of Roumania; in 1918 the Croix de Guerre with Palm Leaves, and he also has the Greek Military Cross with Laurels. He married, in 1905, Claire Marjoribanks, daughter of Sir John Nisbet Maitland, 5th Bart., and they have one son and one daughter.

George Francis Milne.

There is a delightful book about the British Salonica Army, written by Mr. H. Collinson Owen. Its preface is written by General Sir George Milne, who says of the book : " It will help to lift the veil of mystery which hung over the doings of the Army, due to the lack of publicity given to those events in Macedonia which ultimately led to the defeat in the field of the Bulgarian Army, worn out by three years of constant and harassing warfare. The chapters dealing with the attacks on the Doiran position summarize the great difficulties which had to be surmounted by men whose strength was being slowly sapped by prolonged residence in the most unhealthy portion of Europe, but whose esprit de corps was of the highest and whose faith in ultimate victory never faltered. This book may help some to see in proper perspective how the crowning achievement of long and weary vigil in a secondary theatre of operations struck at the Achilles heel of the Central Powers, and materially aided in their rapid collapse during the dramatic autumn of 1918." In the book itself Mr. Owen wrote, on pages 76 and 77 : " There was one often to be met with up-country whom one cannot presume to include amongst one's friends, but who meant a great deal to the life of everyone in the B.S.F. Often on a lonely hill road one would see far ahead a car coming with something that fluttered on it. The driver would see it too, and unconsciously stiffen a little. Somebody on the roadside would see it, and stand very erect and ready. And then the car would flash past, with the Union Jack fluttering out. The British Commander-in-Chief was on his way up or down the line ; the man who held in his hand the thunders of Jove, or the kindly power to reward good work well done. It always gave a little thrill to meet the C.-in-C. on the road. One felt suddenly very much in touch with home, and England's power and all that she stands for. Here, in a sense, was the King himself ; or as near to him as we in Macedonia could hope to get. Many stories are told of encounters with the C.-in-C. on the road. Some are true, no doubt, and some only *ben trovato*. There are stories of swift and terrible lightnings ; other stories very kindly and gentle in demeanour, eminently satisfactory to all concerned. Stories of quite humble people being picked up and given a lift, and being able to air their views before Authority in a fashion they would never have dreamed of ; and other stories of people who fled wildly from the possibility of encounter. No doubt all Armies have similar stories about their Commanders-in-Chief. These things grow and expand, and take varying colours from the messes they pass through. And, as everybody knows, every good General has a nickname by which his troops know him. Unhappy the General who is only known by his proper rank and titles. Napoleon had his nickname. And our General was called ' Uncle George.' Perhaps he knew it, and perhaps he didn't, but there can be no doubt that it was a very good nickname to have." Mr. Owen tells us on page 153 how " After the victorious offensive in 1918, the Bishop of London, who was out visiting the Balkan Army, wrote a letter to the ' Times,' which, in the history of Salonica, may well rank with St. Paul's epistles to the Thessalonians. In it he asked eloquently for fairness to a gallant force, and in commenting on the letter, the ' Times ' put its finger right on the spot. ' Few of us at home,' it said, ' have any conception how much our praise, and, when necessary, our criticism, if only it is sympathetic, means for the Armies at the front—how much it sustains them in their trials and spurs them to fresh efforts to victory. . . . These men in our Eastern Armies have had the dust and toil, without the laurel, of the race to Victory.' As a matter of fact, the British troops in the Balkans were particularly good men. The four Divisions mainly concerned in the campaign were all of splendid quality. One might even call it a picked army. Average troops could certainly not have stuck the long campaign, and rallied so magnificently for the final desperate enterprise, as General Milne describes in his 1919 Despatch. But such was the fatality which pursued our Salonica Army that even when the great break-through occurred their names hardly figured in the general communiqué, which was issued from the French Command, and the people at home knew that there had been a great Balkan victory without knowing that our men had played a vital part in winning it. And while we are on this subject, it will be as well to give part of an interview which a French correspondent, M. Gaston Richard, had with one of the leading French commanders in the Balkans, and which was published in the ' Petit Parisien.' I took it from a Constantinople paper which had copied it. ' The Allied Armies were marvellously keyed up, and their high moral certainly dominated that of the Bulgars. No army endeavoured to act alone, and this harmony of forces counted for a great deal in the decision. Let us take, for example, the work of the Anglo-Greek Army, which operated on a front where the enemy was constantly expecting to be attacked, and where he had, in consequence, multiplied his defences, brought up great reserves, and placed in position an enormous quantity of artillery. Behind this thick curtain of defences, and in view of an offensive on their own part, the enemy had gathered formidable reserves of material. The mission of the Anglo-Greek Army was to pin the enemy to the ground and to oblige him to employ his reserves, in order to prevent him sending them to points menaced elsewhere. This rôle it filled marvellously, and if you had been able to be present at all that it accomplished, you would have been enthusiastic. And when later the Bulgars evacuated the Doiran Front, in order to fly towards Strumitza, the Anglo-Greek Army, in pressing the pursuit with energy, prevented any re-grouping of divisions and contributed to change the enemy retreat into an irremediable rout. This must be said for the honour of truth.' We ask for no more definite tribute to the part of the B.S.F. in the great victory which was the real and authentic beginning of the end. ' We knocked the props one by one from under him,' said Mr. Lloyd George. Doiran was the first prop." It is difficult to quote from General Milne's Despatches, because they are so interesting one does not know which part to choose. These are the concluding words of the Despatch of 22 Jan. 1919 : " I am glad to be in a position to report that our relations with our numerous Allies have been of a most cordial and intimate character, and that during the two-and-a-half years of my command I have received no complaint of serious injury to person or property against any one in the army, the dis-

cipline of which is of the highest. I desire to place on record the consideration I have always received from the Allied Commanders-in-Chief, General Guillaumat and General Franchet d'Esperey, and the complete harmony which has existed between the Allied Staffs. I cannot close this report without expressing my high appreciation of the splendid spirit and devotion to the service of their country shown by all ranks of this Army, the majority of whom will return to their homes with constitutions shattered by a prolonged stay in this malarious and inhospitable country."

Mr. Owen's book not only describes people, but places, so that we who have never been there might almost find our way about Salonica and recognize the people he describes : " During the long period when he reigned supreme, General Sarrail, Commander-in-Chief of the Allied Armies, was often to be seen about. Tall, handsome, white-haired and energetic, General Sarrail graced most functions with his presence. He loved to see and to be seen, and had the gift for mixing with men of all kinds. . . . But there was one whose presence also meant a great deal in Salonica, who was practically unknown to the Salonica public. I refer to General Sir George Milne, the British Army Commander. The two Generals were extraordinarily contrasted, and one avoided publicity as much as the other appreciated it. General Milne spent a very large part of his time up-country. During three years his journeys by motor-car averaged 75 miles a day, excluding great distances from point to point on horseback. One may say of our General that he was largely typical of his Army. Out of the limelight, saying little, doing much—this may stand fairly as the motto of the British Salonica Forces."

In " Salonica and After " one reads descriptions of the country and its drawbacks and its history—and its beauty, and he quotes from Capt. Owen Rutter's " Song of Tiadatha," which he calls " that little classic of the B.S.F." :

> " Very lovely is Kyoto
> In the days of cherry blossom ;
> Very lovely is the splendour
> Of the snow-capped Rocky Mountains ;
> Lovely are the coral islands
> Strung like jade in the Pacific ;
> And the palm trees of Malaya
> Black against an orange sunset.
> Lovely are the long white breakers
> On the beach at Honolulu,
> Even as the Thames Embankment
> On a misty day in Autumn.
> Gib. at dawn, Hong-Kong at evening,
> Lights of Rio in the darkness,
> And the golden gate of 'Frisco,
> All of these are very lovely ;
> Yet I know a sight still fairer :
> Doiran red and grey and yellow,
> Clustered on the Serbian hillside,
> Gleaming in the morning sunlight ;
> Ever gazing, like Narcissus,
> Down upon its own reflection
> In the lake that laps its houses."

But best of all is the story of the deathless glory won by men and battalions. Who can read unstirred the pages about the 12th Cheshires, when they climbed Jackson's Ravine, as it is told in the chapter on " Victory " ? : " Our men just melted away and lay on the parched brown grass of the slope up which they were labouring. Lieut.-Colonel the Hon. A. R. Clegg-Hill, D.S.O., fell, mortally wounded. In a few minutes the battalion had practically ceased to exist." Following hard on their heels came the 9th South Lancashires, and of them the historian of the B.S.F. writes : " Lieut.-Colonel B. F. Bishop, M.C., was killed there, and the battalion, as an official report said bluntly, was ' more or less annihilated.' " The story goes on : " The 8th K.S.L.I.'s pressed on behind the South Lancashires, and suffered very heavy casualties." On the right of the western half of the attack, the Welshmen of the 67th Brigade (Brigadier-General A. D. Macpherson) fought their way magnificently up the string of heights leading up to their main objective, Grand Couronné. Mr. Owen describes " the stern and bitter fighting " of the 11th Welsh Fusiliers, under Lieut.-Colonel A. H. Yatman. Following the Fusiliers, the 11th Welsh (Lieut.-Colonel L. H. Trist, M.C.) attacked from Shropshire Ravine. And then is the tale of the doings of the 7th South Wales Borderers, commanded by Lieut.-Colonel Dan Burges, D.S.O., who there won his Victoria Cross : " The last to leave those tragic slopes were the sole survivors of the South Wales Borderers—*eighteen unwounded men* and one wounded officer. Out of all the gallantry and horror and raging inferno of that early morning this was their reward— to come back, leaving all their comrades lying on the hot, bare rocks and in the sparse scrub above. True, the battalion only started a few hundreds strong. But is there anything in our history to surpass it ? Balaklava grows dim beside it. But it is unlikely that any Laureate will sing the story of Grand Couronné."

SECCOMBE, ARCHIBALD KENNEDY, Major, was born 22 March, 1868. He was commissioned in the Norfolk Regt. 30 Jan. 1889 ; served in the Nile Expedition, 1898 (4th Class Medjidie ; Medal ; Egyptian Medal), and transferred to the Army Service Corps 15 May, 1890, becoming Lieutenant 14 May, 1891, and Captain 18 April, 1894. He served in the South African War, 1899–1902, as D.A.A.G., 6 April, 1901, to 30 Oct. 1902. He took part in the operations in Natal, 1899, including actions at Reitfontein and Lombard's Kop ; at the Defence of Ladysmith, including sorties of 7 and 10 Dec. 1899, and action of 6 Jan. 1900 ; during the operations in the Orange Free State, Feb. to May, 1900 ; in Natal (March to June, 1900), including action at Laing's Nek (6 to 9 June) ; in the Transvaal, east of Pretoria, July to 29 Nov. 1900, including actions at Belfast (26 and 27 Aug.) and Lydenberg (5 to 8 Sept.); again in the Transvaal, Nov. 1900, to April 1901; afterwards on Staff; also in Cape Colony, April, to 31 May, 1902. He was mentioned in Despatches [London Gazette, 8 Feb. 1901 (Sir G. S. White, 23 March, 1900; Sir R. H. Buller, 9 Nov. 1900), and London Gazette, 10 Sept. 1901]; received the Queen's Medal with five clasps, and the King's Medal with two clasps. He was given the Brevet of Major, 29 Nov. 1900, and was created a Companion of the Distinguished Service Order [London Gazette, 26 June, 1902]: "Archibald Kennedy Seccombe, Major, Army Service Corps. In recognition of services during the operations in South Africa." He became Major 1 Jan. 1901; Lieutenant-Colonel 1 Aug. 1910, and Colonel 16 Dec. 1913. He served in the European War, 1914–18, as Deputy Director of Supplies, B.E.F., and British Armies in France from 13 May, 1915; as Temporary Brigadier-General from 5 April, 1918. He was created a C.M.G. in 1916, and a C.B. in 1919. Colonel Seccombe was married, and his wife, Mrs. Julia Seccombe, died in 1915.

KENNA, PAUL ALOYSIUS, V.C., Major, served in the South African War, and was created a Companion of the Distinguished Service Order [London Gazette, 26 June, 1902]: "Paul Aloysius Kenna, V.C., Major, 27th Lancers. In recognition of services during the operations in South Africa." An account of the late Brigadier-General P. A. Kenna's career is given in the Victoria Cross Volume of this work.

PRICHARD, CHARLES STEWART, Major, was born 20 Oct. 1861. He was educated at Marlborough, and joined the Northamptonshire Regt. as Lieutenant, 10 May, 1882, becoming Captain 2 Sept. 1889. He served in the South African War, 1899–1902; took part in the advance on Kimberley, including actions at Belmont, Enslin, Modder River and Magersfontein; in the Orange Free State, Feb. to May, 1900; in the Transvaal, west of Pretoria, July to Nov. 1900, including actions at Venterskroon (7 and 9 Aug.); in Orange River Colony, May to Nov. 1900, including actions at Lindley (1 June) and Rhenoster River; again during the operations in the Transvaal and Orange River Colony 30 Nov. 1900, to 31 May, 1902. He was mentioned in Despatches [London Gazette, 9 July and 3 Dec. 1901]; received the Queen's Medal with four clasps, and the King's Medal with two clasps. He was created a Companion of the Distinguished Service Order [London Gazette, 26 June, 1902]: "Charles Stewart Prichard, Major, Northamptonshire Regt. In recognition of services during the operations in South Africa." The Insignia, Warrant and Statutes were sent to the G.O.C., Transvaal, and presented by General Lyttelton at Pretoria 14 Jan. 1903. He was promoted to Major 30 Aug. 1901, and Lieutenant-Colonel 2 June, 1911. He served in the European War from 1914; became Colonel 15 Dec. 1914; was mentioned in Despatches, and created a C.B. in 1915. He retired from the Staff 7 Nov. 1918, with the honorary rank of Brigadier General.

BUCKLE, CHRISTOPHER REGINALD, Major, was born 18 Oct. 1862, at Norton House, near Chichester, son of Christopher Richard Buckle, of Norton House, and Caroline Cumberbatch, his wife. He was educated at Sherborne School and at the Royal Military Academy; entered the Royal Artillery, as Lieutenant, 14 Feb. 1883; was Adjutant, Midlothian Artillery (Volunteer), and subsequently Adjutant, Royal Artillery, Isle of Wight, 26 April, 1889, to 25 June, 1894; became Captain 1 Feb. 1892. He went to South Africa, as Divisional Adjutant, Royal Artillery, 16 Jan. to 9 Aug. 1900; was Transport Officer 10 Aug. 1900, to 31 Oct. 1901; Extra Staff Officer 1 Nov. 1901, to 5 April, 1902; D.A.A.G. 6 April to 25 Sept. 1902. He took part in the operations in Cape Colony, south of Orange River, Feb. to June, 1900; also in Cape Colony, north of Orange River, June, 1900; in the Transvaal, west of Pretoria, July to Sept. 1900; again in Cape Colony, Nov. 1900, to Dec. 1901; also again during operations in the Transvaal, Dec. 1901, to 31 May, 1902. He was mentioned in Despatches [London Gazette, 17 June, 1902]; received the Queen's Medal with three clasps, and the King's Medal with two clasps. Major Buckle was created a Companion of the Distinguished Service Order [London Gazette, 26 June, 1902]: "Christopher Reginald Buckle, Major, Royal Artillery. In recognition of services during the operations in South Africa." He was invested by the King 18 Dec. 1902. He became Major 2 Sept. 1901; was Assistant Military Secretary to Commander, Indian Army Corps; Assistant Military Secretary to Sir Evelyn Wood, G.O. Commanding-in-Chief, Southern Command, 18 Oct. 1902, to 30 Sept. 1905. When Sir E. Wood was in command of the 2nd Army Corps District, he says in "From Midshipman to Field Marshal": "I took my Senior Aide-de-Camp, who was also Assistant Military Secretary, without ever having seen him, from the recommendation of one of the best senior officers of Garrison Artillery in the district, Colonel W. W. Smith, writing to him, 'Will you please recommend me a Garrison Artillery Aide-de-Camp? He must be able to ride, and must have a good knowledge of, and be keen about his work.' He named Major C. Buckle, D.S.O." He became Brigade Major, R.A., Gibraltar, 10 Feb. 1908, to 10 Oct. 1911; was promoted to Lieutenant-Colonel 11 Oct. 1911; Lieutenant-Colonel Commanding Harwich Defences, 1913; Brigadier-General Commanding Harwich Fortress, Aug. 1914; reverted to Lieutenant-Colonel to command Howitzer Brigade, B.E.F., May, 1915; promoted to Colonel 11 Oct. 1915; Brigadier-General, R.A., No. 6 Group, Heavy Artillery Reserve, B.E.F., 26 Feb. to 4 April 1916; Brigadier-General, Heavy Artillery, 7th Army Corps, B.E.F., 5 April to 9 July, 1916; Brigadier-General, R.A., 17th Army Corps, British Armies in France, 10 July, 1916, to 6 July, 1917; Major General, R.A., 2nd Army, British Armies in France, 7 July to 16 Nov. 1917; Major-General, R.A., British Force in Italy, 12 Nov. 1917. He was promoted Major-General 1 Jan. 1919; was created a C.M.G. in 1916, and a C.B. in 1918. Major-General Buckle married, on 13 Dec. 1886, Elizabeth Braithwaite, daughter of Charles Colville Turner, and their children are: Christopher Galbraith, Doris Eden, Phillis Norton, Judith St. John and Christian.

Christopher R. Buckle.

AGNEW, QUINTIN GRAHAM KINNAIRD, Major, was born in London 8 Jan. 1861, son of the late Sir Andrew Agnew, 8th Baronet, of Lochnaw, and of the Lady Louisa (who died in 1892), daughter of the 1st Earl of Gainsborough. He was appointed to the Royal Ayr and Wigtownshire Militia, 1872, and granted a commission in the Royal Scots Fusiliers 28 April, 1886, for services on the Indian Frontier and in Upper Burma. He served 1 May to 25 July, 1886, as A.D.C. to the G.O.C., Upper Burma. He was mentioned in Despatches [London Gazette, 22 June, 1886, and 2 Sept. 1887] (Medal with clasp); operations on the North-West Frontier of India; A.D.C. and Persian Interpreter to General Sir George White, Commander-in-Chief in India, 1893–95; Tirah Expeditionary Force, as Orderly Officer to Sir William Lockhart; capture of Sampagha Pass; A.D.C. to General Sir George White, Commander-in-Chief in India, 1898–99 (Medal with two clasps). He served in the South African War, 1899–1902; operations in Natal; Relief of Ladysmith, including action at Colenso; operations of 17 to 24 Jan. 1900; operations of 6 to 7 Feb. 1900, and action at Vaal Kranz; operations on Tugela Heights 14 to 27 Feb. 1900, and action at Pieter's Hill; operations in Transvaal, west of Pretoria, July to 29 Nov. 1900, including action at Frederickstad 17 to 28 Oct. 1900; operations in Cape Colony, north of Orange River, including action at Ruidam; was afterwards on Staff; operations in the Transvaal 30 Nov. 1900, to Dec. 1901; operations in Cape Colony, Dec. 1901, to 31 May, 1902; was mentioned in Despatches [London Gazette, 10 Sept. 1901]; received the Queen's Medal with six clasps, and was created a Companion of the Distinguished Service Order [London Gazette, 26 June, 1902]: "Quintin Graham Kinnaird Agnew, Major, Manchester Regt. In recognition of services during the operations in South Africa." The Insignia, Warrant and Statutes were sent to the G.O.C., Gibraltar, 3 Jan. 1903, and the Insignia were presented at Gibraltar by Sir G. White 8 Jan. 1903. Capt. Agnew was promoted to Major 23 Oct. 1901; was Military Secretary to Sir G. White, Governor of Gibraltar, 1903–5; was created a C.V.O. in 1903, and retired 28 April, 1906, when he became a Member of His Majesty's Body Guard (Honourable Corps of Gentlemen-at-Arms). He has commanded the 3rd Battn. Royal Scots Fusiliers since 1910. Lieut.-Colonel Q. G. K. Agnew was on Special Service with the Mediterranean Expeditionary Force from June, 1915, to March, 1916, during which time he commanded the 1st King's Own Scottish Borderers; the 1st Inniskilling Fusiliers, the 87th Brigade, the 29th Brigade, and was Commandant of Mudros. He married (1st), in 1899, Evelyn Mary (who died in 1913), daughter of the late Capt. H. J. A. Alexander, and they had three sons. In 1916, he married (2ndly) Cicely Anne Churchill, daughter of the late James Inskip, of Clifton Park House, Bristol. Lieut.-Colonel Agnew is a J.P. and D.L. for Wigtownshire.

PERCEVAL, CLAUDE JOHN, Major, was born 28 Sept. 1864, third son of General John Maxwell Perceval, C.B. He entered the Royal Artillery, as Lieutenant, 28 July, 1883; was promoted to Captain 1 April, 1892, and was Adjutant, Royal Artillery, 17 Dec. 1897, to 2 Jan. 1899. He served in the South African War, 1899–1902; on Special Service 3 Jan. to 19 Jan. 1900; employed with Transport 20 Jan. 1900, to 1 Sept. 1901; as Extra Staff Officer for Transport 2 Sept. 1901, to 7 Sept. 1902. He took part in the operations in the Orange Free State, Feb. to May, 1900, including actions at Houtnek (Thoba Mountain), Vet River (5 and 6 May) and Zand River; in the Transvaal in May and June, 1900, including actions near Johannesburg, Pretoria and Diamond Hill (11 and 12 June); in Orange River Colony (May to 29 Nov. 1900), including actions at Wittebergen (1 to 29 July); also in Cape Colony, south of Orange River, 1899–1900, including actions at Colesberg (1 Jan. to 12 Feb.). He was mentioned in Despatches [London Gazette, 17 June, 1902]; received the Queen's Medal with four clasps, and the King's Medal with two clasps. He was created a Companion of the Distinguished Service Order [London Gazette, 26 June, 1902]: "Claude John Perceval, Major, Royal Artillery. In recognition of services during the operations in South Africa." He was invested by the King 24 Oct. 1902. On 30 Nov. 1901, he was promoted to Major; he was Brigade Major, Royal Artillery, South-Eastern District, Southern Command, 1 April to 17 Nov. 1903; G.S.O.2, Staff Officer for Defence, Southern Command, 18 Nov. 1903, to 31 May, 1905; G.S.O.2, Coast Defence, Southern Command, 1 June, 1905, to April, 1907; D.A.Q.M.G., India, 14 Nov. 1908, to 13 Nov. 1912. He became Lieutenant-Colonel 21 Oct. 1911. Lieut.-Colonel Perceval served in the European War from 1914, as A.A. and Q.M.G., 7th Division, B.E.F., 5 to 25 Oct. 1914; A.A. and Q.M.G., 29th Division, Mediterranean Expeditionary Force, 18 Jan. to 8 June, 1915; G.S.O.1, 29th Division, Mediterranean Expeditionary Force, 9 June to 16 Aug. 1915; Brigade Commander, 86th Infantry Brigade, Mediterranean Expeditionary Force, 17 Aug. to 20 Dec. 1915; was promoted to Colonel 21 Dec. 1915; was Brigadier-General, General Staff, 12th Army Corps, Mediterranean Expeditionary Force, 21 Dec. 1915, to 1916; A.Q.M.G., Scottish Command, 26 June to 28 July, 1916; G.S.O.1, G.H.Q., Home Forces, 29 July, 1916, to 30 April, 1917; Inspector, Royal Garrison Artillery, Home Forces in Great Britain, 21 Dec. 1917, and Temporary Brigadier-General. He was mentioned in Despatches three times; created a C.M.G. in 1915, and a C.B. in 1918. He married, in 1898, Isabel Gordon, only daughter of the late Colonel Morison, of Bognie, Aberdeen, N.B., and they have three daughters.

MILLER, ALFRED DOUGLAS, Major, was born 1 March, 1864, son of Lieut.-Colonel James Miller, of Shotover. He was educated at Eton, and was gazetted Lieutenant in the 2nd Dragoons 7 Feb. 1885;

became Captain 28 June, 1893; became Adjutant, 2nd Dragoons, 18 Jan. 1896, to 9 May, 1900. He served in the South African War, 1899–1902, as Adjutant, 2nd Dragoons, to 9 May, 1900; as Extra Staff Officer 10 July, 1900, to 23 Dec. 1901; D.A.A.G. to Sir John French 24 Dec. 1901, to 11 Sept. 1902. He took part in the Relief of Kimberley; in the Orange Free State, Feb. to May, 1900, including operations at Paardeberg; actions at Poplar Grove, Dreifontein and Karee Siding; in the Transvaal 30 Nov. 1900, to May, 1901; also during the operations in Cape Colony, May, 1901, to 31 May, 1902. He was mentioned in Despatches [London Gazette, 17 Jan. 1902]; received the Queen's Medal with four clasps, and the King's Medal with two clasps. He was placed on the list of

Alfred Douglas Miller.

officers considered qualified for Staff employment, in consequence of service on the Staff in the Field. He was created a Companion of the Distinguished Service Order [London Gazette, 26 June, 1902]: " Alfred Douglas Miller, Major, 2nd Dragoons. In recognition of services during the operations in South Africa." The Insignia, Warrant, etc., were sent to the G.O.C., Cape Colony, and presented by Major-General Settle, 2 April, 1903. He became Major 20 Feb. 1902; was D.A.A.G., North-Eastern District, from 6 Oct. 1903; was promoted to Lieutenant-Colonel 19 Aug. 1907, and to Colonel 30 Aug. 1911, and retired 18 March, 1914. He served in the European War in 1914 and 1915, as A.A.G. with the B.E.F., and in command of a Yeomanry Brigade; was mentioned in Despatches; given the honorary rank of Brigadier-General 22 March, 1918, and created a C.B.E. in 1919. He has the Mons Star, and is a Knight of St. Stanislaus of Russia. He is M.F.H., South Oxfordshire Hounds. He married, in 1899, Ella Geraldine, youngest daughter of John Fletcher, of Saltoun Hall, N.B., and they have three sons and two daughters.

CARLETON, LANCELOT RICHARD, Capt., was born 15 Sept. 1861, fourth son of Colonel G. Carleton, R.A. He was educated at Rugby School; Cheltenham College and Sandhurst; entered the Essex Regt. 10 May,

1882, as Lieutenant; was Adjutant, Essex Regt., 15 Sept. 1886, to 14 Sept. 1890, and became Captain 1 July, 1888. He was D.A.A.G., North-Western District, 14 Aug. 1897, to 17 Dec. 1899. Capt. Carleton served in the South African War, as Brigade Major, Infantry Brigade, 18 Dec. 1899, to 11 April, 1901; as D.A.A.G. 12 April, 1901, to 23 June, 1902; as D.A.A.G. 24 June, to 22 Oct. 1902. He took part in the operations in the Orange Free State, Feb. to May, 1900, including action at Karee Siding, Vet River (6 May) and Zand River; served during the operations in the Transvaal in May and June, 1900, including action near Johannesburg; again in the Transvaal 30 Nov. 1900, to

Lancelot R. Carleton.

31 May, 1902. He was mentioned in Despatches [London Gazette, 17 June, 1902]; received the Queen's Medal with three clasps, and the King's Medal with two clasps. He was created a Companion of the Distinguished Service Order [London Gazette, 26 June, 1902]: " Lancelot Richard Carleton, Capt., Essex Regt. In recognition of services during the operations in South Africa." He was invested by the King 18 Dec. 1902. He was promoted to Major 16 May, 1902; was Officer, Company of Gentleman Cadets, Royal Military College, 16 Aug. 1907, to 7 Aug. 1908; Commander, Company of Gentleman Cadets, Royal Military College, 27 Jan. 1904, to 17 April, 1906. He became Lieutenant-Colonel 16 May, 1910, and Colonel 16 Dec. 1913. He retired 15 Sept. 1918, with the honorary rank of Brigadier-General.

BIRCH, JAMES RICHARD KEMMIS, Capt., was born 19 May, 1859, son of the late J. S. Birch, of Birch Grove, Roscrea. He was gazetted Lieutenant,

in the East Surrey Regt., 22 Oct. 1881; served in the Sudan Expedition, 1885 (Suakin), with Mounted Infantry, taking part in the advance on Hasheen (severely wounded in Mardi). He was mentioned in Despatches [London Gazette, 25 Aug. 1885]; received the Medal with clasp, and the Bronze Star. He was promoted to Captain, Cheshire Regt., 15 Aug. 1888. From 4 July, 1892, to 16 Aug. 1897, he was Inspector of Army Signalling, Madras and Bombay. He served in the South African War, 1900–2; was mentioned in Despatches; received the Queen's Medal with five clasps; the King's Medal with two clasps, and was created a Companion of the Distinguished Service Order [London

James Richard K. Birch.

Gazette, 26 June, 1902]: " James Richard Kemmis Birch, Capt., Cheshire Regt. In recognition of services during the operations in South Africa."

He was invested by the King 18 Dec. 1902. Major Birch became Assistant Director of Signalling. He died 20 April, 1907, at Lichfield.

STOCKWELL, GEORGE CLIFTON INGLIS, Capt., was born 24 July, 1863, son of the late Major-General C. M. Stockwell, C.B. He was gazetted to the Wiltshire Regt. 9 Sept. 1882, as Lieutenant; was transferred to the Highland Light Infantry 21 Oct. 1882; was Adjutant, Highland Light Infantry, 18 Feb. 1885, to 17 Feb. 1890; was Brigade Major, Chitral Relief Force, 20 March to 21 Sept. 1895. He took part in the operations in Chitral, 1895, with the Relief Force (on Staff). He was mentioned in Despatches [London Gazette, 15 Nov. 1895 (Medal with clasp). From 3 Feb. to 30 Sept. 1900, he was on Special Service in South Africa; from 1 Oct. 1900, to 5 July, 1902, he was Brigade Major, South Africa. During the South African War he took part in the operations in the Orange Free State, Feb. to May, 1900; also in Orange River Colony (May to 29 Nov. 1900), including actions at Wittebergen and Witpoort; again in Orange River Colony 30 Nov. to Dec. 1900; also during operations in Cape Colony, Dec. 1900, to April, 1901 (Despatches, [London Gazette 17 June, 1902]; Queen's Medal with two clasps, and King's Medal with two clasps). He was created a Companion of the Distinguished Service Order [London Gazette, 26 June, 1902]: " George Clifton Inglis Stockwell, Capt., Highland Light Infantry. In recognition of services during the operations in South Africa." Capt. Stockwell was invested by the King 24 Oct. 1902. He was promoted to Major 9 Aug. 1902; passed the Staff College; was Brigade Major, 12th Brigade, Southern Command, 17 Oct. 1903, to 1 Dec. 1904. He became Lieutenant-Colonel 4 Nov. 1907, and Colonel 30 Aug. 1911. He served in the European War, as Brigade Commander up to 24 Jan. 1915; as Divisional Commander from 25 Jan. 1915. He retired 6 July, 1917; was created a C.M.G. in 1918, and given the honorary rank of Major-General 18 March, 1919. General Stockwell married, in 1900, Muriel Evelyn Maitland, youngest daughter of Richard Cochrane, of Calder Glen, County Lanark.

HARE, ROBERT HUGH, Capt., was born 14 Nov. 1872, only son of Edward Hare, C.S.I., Deputy Inspector-General of Hospitals, H.E.I.C.S. He was educated at Hermitage School, Bath; at the Royal Military Academy, Woolwich, and at the Staff College (1899), and was gazetted to the Royal Artillery, as Lieutenant, 24 July, 1886. He served in the Chitral Campaign, 1895, with the Relief Force; at the storming of the Malakand Pass; passage of the Swat River; action at Panjkora River, and at Mamagai (Medal with clasp). He became Captain 2 June, 1897. He served in South Africa, as A.D.C. to Lieutenant-General, Infantry Division, 9 Oct. 1899, to 3 March, 1900; as D.A.A.G., South Africa, 4 March, 1900, to 2 Oct. 1902; also performed the duties of an A.A.G., Lines of Communication; took part in the operations in the Orange Free State, Feb. to May, 1900; in Orange River Colony, May to 29 Nov. 1900; in the Transvaal, west of Pretoria, July to 29 Nov. 1900; again in the Transvaal 30 Nov. 1900, to 31 May, 1902. He was mentioned in Despatches [London Gazette, 17 June, 1902]; received the Queen's Medal with three clasps, and the King's Medal with two clasps. He was created a Companion of the Distinguished Service Order [London Gazette, 26 June, 1902]: " Robert Hugh Hare, Capt., Royal Artillery. In recognition of services during the operations in South Africa." He was invested by the King 24 Oct. 1902. He was Brigade Major, Royal Artillery, Malta, 20 Feb. 1904, to 23 Nov. 1905; was promoted to Major 6 Jan. 1905; was Assistant Military Secretary to the Governor and Commander-in-Chief, Malta, 24 Nov. 1905, to 2 May, 1907; created an M.V.O., 1907; G.S.O.2, Highland Division, Scottish Command, 1 April, 1908, to 31 March, 1912; Commander, Company of Gentleman Cadets, Royal Military College, 1 Jan. 1913, to 16 Nov. 1914. He served in the European War from 1914; was promoted to Lieutenant-Colonel 30 Oct. 1914; was Brigade Major, Royal Artillery, 27th Division, New Armies, British Expeditionary Force, 17 Nov. 1914, to 26 March, 1915; G.S.O.2, 5th Army Corps, British Expeditionary Force, British Armies in France, 27 March to 26 May, 1915; G.S.O.2, 28th Division, British Armies in France, 27 May, 1915, to 12 Nov. 1916; Temporary Brigadier-General from 13 Nov. 1916; commanding 83rd Infantry Brigade, British Salonika Force, 13 Nov. 1916. He was mentioned in Despatches; given the Brevet of Colonel 3 June, 1917; created a C.M.G. in 1916, and a C.B. in 1919. He married, in 1908, Lilian Louisa, eldest daughter of James Mellor, and they have two sons and one daughter.

PERKINS, JOHN CHARLES CAMPBELL, Colonel, was born in London 2 April, 1866, son of the late Surgeon-General R. H. Perkins, Indian Medical Service, Hon. East India Company's Service, and Anne

Bowden Campbell, of Inverneill and Ross; a direct descendant in eldest line of John Perkins, senior partner, Barclay & Perkins, Brewers. He was educated at Stamford Grammar School, and Rossall School; joined the Militia, 4th Battn. Shropshire Light Infantry; was commissioned in 1st Leinster Regt., 1887; joined 1st Battn, in India, 1888; joined Indian Staff Corps, 1890, 44th Gurkha Rifles; also served with 43rd Gurkha Rifles in Assam and Manipur; then for a short while with 10th Bengal Infantry. From 1900 to 1903 he held conjointly appointments of Controller of Military Accounts and Field Paymaster, Indian Contingent, and Officer Commanding Indian Details, South Africa Force. He

John Charles C. Perkins.

was mentioned in Despatches [London Gazette, 17 June, 1902], and created a Companion of the Distinguished Service Order [London Gazette, 26 June, 1902]: " John Charles Campbell

Perkins, Capt., Indian Staff Corps. In recognition of services during operations in South Africa." He was invested by the King 18 Feb. 1903.

The following is an extract from Divisional Orders by Major-General R. Lloyd-Payne, C.B., D.S.O., Commanding 5th (Mhow) Division, dated Mhow, the 1st March, 1916:

"ADMINISTRATION.

"130. Special. The General Officer commanding the Division regrets to announce the death of Lieut.-Colonel J. C. C. Perkins, D.S.O., Military Deputy Auditor-General, Southern Army. Lieut.-Colonel Perkins, in the course of his tour in the Division, came to Mhow with full military honours. Entering the Service on the 16th Nov. 1887, Lieut.-Colonel Perkins joined the Leinster Regt., and was transferred to the Indian Army on the 8th Jan. 1890. On the 15th Feb. 1894, he joined the Military Accounts Department, in which he served through the South African War, for his services in which he was mentioned in Despatches and received the D.S.O. On the reorganization of the Military Accounts Department, he was appointed Military Deputy Auditor-General, Southern Army, on 1 April, 1914, in which appointment he was serving at the time of his death. From the very beginning of the war, Colonel Perkins was called upon to undertake a mass of extra work of a very trying nature, and did not spare himself in the performance of his duty. The General Officer Commanding is assured that all will join with him in regretting the decease of this distinguished officer, whose decease was largely attributable, if not entirely due, to his unremitting labours in connection with the war."

Colonel Perkins was fond of cricket, football and racquets, and sport of all kinds. He married (1st) Emma Victoria Augusta, daughter of General Douglas Seafield Grant, I.S.C. (who died in 1912), and (2ndly), in 1913, Charlotte Mary, daughter of Harold Beauchamp.

SMITH, WILLIAM HUGH USHER, Capt., was born in Londonderry, Ireland, 26 May, 1869, son of the late Rev. Frank Smith, M.A., formerly Rector of Atherstone-on-Stour, Stratford-on-Avon. He was educated at Trinity College, Stratford-on-Avon, and at the Royal Military Academy, Woolwich, and became Second Lieutenant, Royal Artillery, 27 July, 1888, and Captain 23 Nov. 1898. He had become Ordnance Officer, 4th Class, 1 April, 1897. Capt. Smith served in the South African War, 1899–1902, and took part in the operations in Orange Free State, April to May, 1900; in Orange River Colony, May to 29 Nov. 1900; in Cape Colony, south of Orange River, 1899–1900; again in Orange River Colony 30 Nov. 1900, to Jan. 1902; also during operations in Cape Colony, Jan. to 31 May, 1902. He was mentioned in Despatches [London Gazette, 10 Sept. 1901]; received the Queen's Medal with two clasps, and the King's Medal with two clasps. He was created a Companion of the Distinguished Service Order [London Gazette, 26 June, 1902]: "William Hugh Usher Smith, Capt., Royal Artillery. In recognition of services during the operations in South Africa." The Insignia, Warrant and Statutes were sent to the C.O.C., Cape Colony District, 15 Nov. 1902, and presented at Cape Town 5 Jan. 1903. He was Ordnance Officer, 3rd Class, 1 April, 1902, to 8 April, 1907; was promoted to Major 1 April, 1904, and to Lieutenant-Colonel 29 Nov. 1907; was Ordnance Officer, 2nd Class, 14 Aug. 1907, to 7 Dec. 1914. He served in the European War, as Deputy Director of Ordnance Services, 1st Army; became Colonel; Ordnance Officer, 1st Class, 8 Dec. 1914; Temporary Brigadier-General from 20 Aug. 1917, and Director of Ordnance Services, British Salonika Force. He was created a C.B. in 1916, and a C.B.E. in 1919. He married, in 1897, Amy, eldest daughter of Lieut.-Colonel F. Hall, late 88th Connaught Rangers, and they have two sons and two daughters.

EASSIE, FITZPATRICK, Capt., was born 15 Oct. 1864, third son of the late W. Eassie, B.E. He joined the Army in 1889, and served with the Expedition to Manipur, 1891 (Medal with clasp); served in Burma, 1891–92–93–94; took part in the operations in the Chin Hills (Despatches, G.G.O. 733 of 1893; two clasps); served during operations in Chitral, 1895 (Medal with clasp). He became Captain, Army Veterinary Department, 11 Sept. 1899, and served in the South African War, 1899–1902; was present during operations in Cape Colony, south of Orange River, 1899–1900; in the Orange Free State, Feb. to May, 1900; in Orange River Colony, May to Nov. 1900; during the operations in the Transvaal, June, 1901; again in the Orange River Colony 30 Nov. 1900, to May, 1901, and June, 1901, to 31 May, 1902. He was mentioned in Despatches [London Gazette, 17 June, 1902]; received the Queen's Medal with three clasps, and the King's Medal with two clasps. He was created a Companion of the Distinguished Service Order [London Gazette, 26 June, 1902]: "Fitzpatrick Eassie, Veterinary Capt., Army Veterinary Department. In recognition of services during the operations in South Africa." The Insignia, etc., were sent to G.O.C., Transvaal and Orange River Colony, and presented at Bloemfontein 4 March, 1903. He was promoted to Lieutenant-Colonel, Army Veterinary Corps, 4 Oct. 1913, and appointed Inspecting Veterinary Officer in India. Lieut.-Colonel Eassie served in the European War from 1914, as Assistant Director of Veterinary Services, Lines of Communication, British Expeditionary Force, 8 Dec. 1914, to 4 Feb. 1915; Deputy Director of Veterinary Services, Indian Cavalry Corps, British Expeditionary Force, 5 Feb. to 5 Nov. 1915; Deputy Director of Veterinary Services, Salonika Army, British Salonika Force, 1 Dec. 1915, to 11 Oct. 1918. He was given the Brevet of Colonel, and promoted to Colonel, and became Director of Veterinary Services, British

Fitzpatrick Eassie.

Salonika Force, 12 Oct. 1918, with the temporary rank of Brigadier-General. He was created a C.M.G. in 1916, and a C.B. in 1919.

RADCLIFFE, NATHANIEL ROBERT, Capt., was born 22 June, 1870, in India, son of George Travis Radcliffe, General in the Indian Army (deceased) and Mrs. Radcliffe (née Cumberlege, daughter of General Cumberlege). He was educated at Overslade, near Rugby, and at Leamington College, and joined the 1st Battn. The Devonshire Regt. 17 Jan. 1891, from the Leicestershire Militia; served in Egypt and India with the 1st Battn. In the Chitral Campaign, 1895, he served as Signalling Officer, 2nd Brigade (30 March to 28 April, 1895); took part in actions at Malakand Pass and Panjkora River; received the Medal, and was mentioned in Despatches. He served in the South African Campaign of 1899–1902, with the 1st Mounted Infantry, and was at Stormberg, Sanna's Post, and Diamond Hill; served on the Staff as Brigade Major and D.A.A.G. for Mounted Infantry, on the General Staff; was Adjutant of the 4th (Militia) Battn. Devon Regt. He was present at operations in the Orange Free State, Feb. to May, 1900, including actions at Poplar Grove, Dreifontein, Vet River (5 and 6 May) and Zand River; operations in the Transvaal in May and June, 1900, including actions near Johannesburg, Pretoria and Diamond Hill (11 and 12 June); operations in the Transvaal, east of Pretoria, July to 29 Nov. 1900, including action at Reit Vlei; operations in Cape Colony, south of Orange River, 1899–1900. He was mentioned in Despatches (Earl Roberts and Lord Kitchener) [London Gazette, 17 June, 1902]; received the Queen's Medal with four clasps; the King's Medal with two clasps, and was created a Companion of the Distinguished Service Order [London Gazette, 26 June, 1902]: "Nathaniel Robert Radcliffe, Capt., Devonshire Regt. In recognition of services during the operations in South Africa." He was invested by the King 18 Dec. 1902. He retired 3 Feb. 1906; was appointed Brigade Major, Devon and Cornwall (T.F.) Infantry Brigade, for six years, in 1913; appointed to command the 6th Battn. Devon Regt. (T.F.). He took the battalion to India in Oct. 1914, and Mesopotamia, Dec. 1915. Colonel Radcliffe was created a C.I.E. in 1917. He married, 5 July, 1889, at Clyst St. Mary, near Exeter, Doreen Emily, daughter of the Rev. A. W. Hamilton-Gell, of Winslade, near Exeter, and their son is Robert Derwent Hamilton, born 14 May, 1903.

SCOTT, ROBERT KELLOCK, Capt., was born 29 Nov. 1871, at Perth, Ontario, Canada, third son of Colonel Thomas Scott, late Collector of Customs, Winnipeg, Canada. He was educated at the Royal Military College, Kingston, Canada, and served during the rising in the North-West Territories of Canada, 1885 (Medal). He joined the Royal Artillery as Second Lieutenant 16 July, 1891; was promoted to Lieutenant 16 July, 1894, and Captain 16 July, 1899. He was Ordnance Officer, 4th Class, 26 April, 1896, to 23 April, 1902. He served in the South African War, 1899–1902; appointed to act in a superior Departmental rank (A. Ord. Dept.); took part in the operations in Cape Colony, south of Orange River, 1899–1900; in Cape Colony, north of Orange River; in the Transvaal 30 Nov. 1900, to Feb. 1901; again in Cape Colony, March, 1901, to 31 May, 1902. He was mentioned in Despatches [London Gazette, 17 June and 29 July, 1902]; received the Queen's Medal with three clasps, and the King's Medal with two clasps. He was created a Companion of the Distinguished Service Order [London Gazette, 26 June, 1902]: "Robert Kellock Scott, Capt., Royal Artillery. For services during the operations in South Africa." The Insignia were presented by the King 12 June, 1903. Capt. Scott was also given the Brevet of Major 22 Aug. 1902. He was Ordnance Officer, 3rd Class, 24 April, 1902, to 25 April, 1903; 26 April, 1903, to 31 Jan. 1904; 1 Feb. 1904, to 31 March, 1907; was transferred to the Army Ordnance Department in 1903; was promoted to Major 1 Feb. 1904; to Lieutenant-Colonel 1 April, 1906; was seconded for service with the Canadian Militia in 1907; became Colonel 1 April, 1907; 2nd Class Ordnance Officer 1 April, 1907, to 7 Dec. 1914; was Principal Ordnance Officer, Canada, 1908; Chief Ordnance Officer, Bermuda, 1908–14. He became Assistant Director of Equipment and Ordnance Stores, War Office, 1 Aug. 1914; Colonel, ranking as Major-General, 8 Dec. 1914, and Ordnance Officer, 1st Class, 8 Dec. 1914. He served in the European War in France and Flanders; was appointed Director of Ordnance Services, East African Expeditionary Force, in Jan. 1916. He was created a C.M.G. in 1917, and a C.B. in 1919. General Scott married, 24 June, 1899, at Romsey, Hampshire, Edith Ferris Mortimer, second daughter of the late Major E. F. W. Mortimer, of Romsey, and they have two children: Edith Muriel Kellock, and John Mortimer Kellock, born 12 Oct. 1906.

MASSIE, JOHN HAMON, Capt., was born at Eaux Chaudes, Basses Pyrénées, France, 10 June, 1872, younger son of Edward Richard Massie, of Coddington, Cheshire, and Annefield, Gresford, North Wales, formerly

John Hamon Massie.

Lieutenant, 78th Highlanders, and his first wife, Baroness Olga Marie, daughter of Baron von Wessenberg-Ampringen, formerly Austrian Ambassador at St. James's. John Hamon Massie's paternal grandfather was Admiral Thomas Leche Massie, R.N. He was educated at Mr. Montagu Foster's School, Stubbington, Fareham, and at the Royal Military Academy, Woolwich, being gazetted to the Royal Artillery as Second Lieutenant 1 May, 1892, and became Lieutenant in May, 1895. He served in the Chitral Campaign in 1895, with the Relief Force, and received the Medal and clasp. In 1898 he passed the long course at Shoeburyness with first-class honours. He was promoted to Captain 19 Jan. 1900, and served in the South African War, 1900-2, in which, after landing at Cape Town, in Jan. 1900, he acted as Transport Officer with the 30th Remount Company, Army Service Corps, being graded as Deputy Assistant Adjutant-General. He was present at several actions and operations near De Wet's Dorp, the march to Pretoria and action at Zand River in May, 1900. He entered Pretoria with Lord Roberts on the 5th of June, 1900; took part in the actions at Diamond Hill and Heidelberg, and in the pursuit of De Wet from Bethlehem to the Transvaal; actions at Vredefort, and operations at Hekpoort Valley. He was then temporarily in command of a pom-pom section. In Nov. 1900, he was in the action near Schwartz Kopje. In Jan. 1902, he was appointed Staff Officer for Transport, a position which he held under various Generals Commanding, and he returned to England in Jan. 1902. He was mentioned in Despatches by Lord Kitchener. The following is the record of his services in South Africa as given in "Hart's Army List": "Capt. J. H. Massie, R.A., served in the South African War, 1900–2; took part in the operations in the Orange Free State, Feb. to May, 1900; in the Transvaal in May and June, 1900, including actions near Johannesburg and Diamond Hill; in the Orange River Colony, May to 29 Nov. 1900, including actions at Wittebergen; in the Transvaal 30 Nov. 1900, to March, 1902, and again in Orange River Colony, March to 31 May, 1902, as Special Service Officer; afterwards on Staff. Despatches [London Gazette, 17 Jan. 1902]; Queen's Medal with four clasps, and King's Medal with two clasps. D.S.O." He was created a Companion of the Distinguished Service Order [London Gazette, 26 June, 1902]: "John Hamon Massie, Capt., Royal Artillery. In recognition of services during the operations in South Africa." He was invested by the King 18 Dec. 1902. The clasps to the Queen's Medal were given to Capt. Massie for Cape Colony, Johannesburg, Wittebergen and Diamond Hill respectively. He was Instructor at the Royal Military Academy from 1 Jan. to 11 Sept. 1904; Commander of a Company of Gentleman Cadets there from 12 Sept. 1904, to 31 Dec. 1908, and Staff Captain, School of Gunnery, Shoeburyness, Nov. 1910, to Aug. 1914. He was promoted to Major 15 Feb. 1913. In the Great War he proceeded to France on the 24th Aug. 1914, for a week, to Havre, on Special Duty as Staff Officer to Brigadier-General Nicolls, R.A. On 1 Sept. 1914, he was gazetted as Staff Captain, Administrative Staff, and again went to Havre for duty with Heavy Artillery on the 9th Nov. He was kept at the base, St. Nazaire, till 1 Nov., when he left there to take command of the 26th Heavy Battery (sixty-pounders) at Ypres. On the 13th Nov. 1914, he was mortally wounded at Ypres, by a fragment of high explosive shell, while in command of the 26th Battery, and died in the Field Hospital on the 16th of that month. He was buried in Ypres Cemetery. Major Massie liked all games, and was good at most. He several times represented his regiment at billiards against the Royal Engineers, and he was for over three years Secretary and Treasurer of the Royal Artillery Games Fund. He married, at Southsea, on 3 Sept. 1903, Maria Margaret, elder daughter of Major-General Ernest Archibald Berger, late 10th (The Lincolnshire) Regt.

BONHAM, WALTER FLOYD, Capt., was born 3 Jan. 1869, eldest son of the late Edward Bonham. He was educated at Charterhouse, and at the Royal Military College, Sandhurst; graduated 1899, and was gazetted to the Essex Regt. 24 April, 1889, becoming Lieutenant 16 Sept. 1891. He served in South Africa, 1899–1902, and was on the Headquarter Staff from 1900 to the end of the campaign. He was mentioned in Despatches; received the South African Medals, and was created a Companion of the Distinguished Service Order [London Gazette, 26 June, 1902]: "Walter Floyd Bonham, Capt., Essex Regt. In recognition of services during the operations in South Africa." The Insignia were presented to Capt. Bonham by the King 18 Dec. 1902. He died 15 May, 1905.

SINGLETON, HENRY TOWNSEND CORBET, Capt., was born 27 Jan. 1874, son of Major L. C. Singleton, Gordon Highlanders, who died of wounds received at Majuba, and Emmeline Theodora, daughter of His Honour Judge de Moleyns, Q.C. He was educated at Wellington College and at Sandhurst, and joined the Highland Light Infantry as Second Lieutenant 6 March, 1895; was promoted to Lieutenant 5 March, 1898, and was employed in Crete, under the Foreign Office, as Chief of Police in the Malavezi District. He was on Special Service in South Africa 29 July, 1899, to 13 March, 1901, including service as Adjutant, Bechuanaland Protectorate Regt.; served in the Siege of Mafeking; was slightly wounded, and afterwards served as Station Staff Officer 14 March, 1901, to 22 Aug. 1902. He was mentioned in Despatches [London Gazette, 17 June, 1902]; received the Queen's Medal with three clasps; the King's Medal with two clasps, and was created a Companion of the Distinguished Service Order [London Gazette, 26 June, 1902]: "Henry Townsend Corbet Singleton, Capt., Highland Light Infantry. In recognition of services during the operations in South Africa." He was invested by the King 18 Dec. 1902. He was promoted to Captain 27 March, 1901; was Adjutant, Volunteers, 9 May, 1904, to 21 March, 1908; Adjutant, Territorial Force, 1 April, 1908, to 28 Feb. 1909; Adjutant, Indian Volunteers, 12 Sept. 1911, to 22 Aug. 1914. He served in the European War, as Brigade Major, 18th Reserve Brigade, New Armies, from 23 Dec. 1914; as D.A.A. and Q.M.G., 36th Division, New Armies, B.E.F., British Armies in France, 10 July, 1915, to 19 Sept. 1916; as A.A. and Q.M.G., 61st Division, British Armies in France, 20 Sept. 1916, to 14 Feb. 1919; as General Staff Officer, Headquarters, Military Governor, Occupied German Territory, 15 Feb. 1919. He became Major 22 March, 1915; was mentioned in Despatches; given the Brevet of Lieutenant-Colonel 3 June, 1917, and created a C.M.G. in 1919. He married, in 1902, Evelyn Elsie, daughter of General Philip Harris, C.B., and they have one son and one daughter.

BAILEY, PERCY JAMES, Capt., was born 2 Dec. 1873, eldest son of the late Sir James Bailey. He was gazetted to the 12th Lancers 11 Dec. 1895, and became Lieutenant 12 May, 1897. He served in the South African War, 1899–1902 (as Brigade Signalling Officer 13 Oct. 1900, to 25 June, 1903); took part in the advance on Kimberley, including action at Magersfontein; was present at the Relief of Kimberley; took part in the operations in the Orange Free State, Feb. to May, 1900, including those at Paardeberg, the actions at Poplar Grove (severely wounded), Dreifontein, Houtnek (Thoba Mountain) and Zand River; served during operations in the Transvaal, May and June, 1900, including actions near Johannesburg and Diamond Hill; again in the Transvaal, west of Pretoria, July to 29 Nov. 1900; in the Orange River Colony, May to 29 Nov. 1900, including actions at Lindley, Bethlehem and Wittebergen; served again in the Transvaal 30 Nov. 1900, to 31 May, 1902; afterwards on Staff (including service as Staff Officer to a Column). He was mentioned in Despatches [London Gazette, 17 June, 1902]; received the Queen's Medal with six clasps, and the King's Medal with two clasps. He was created a Companion of the Distinguished Service Order [London Gazette, 26 June, 1902]: "Percy James Bailey, Capt., 12th Lancers. In recognition of services during the operations in South Africa." He was invested by the King 24 Oct. 1902. He was promoted to Captain 17 April, 1901; was Adjutant and Quartermaster, Cavalry School, 14 Aug. 1905, to 13 Aug. 1909; became Major 22 Aug. 1908; was Assistant Commandant, Remount Service, Shirehampton, Southern Command, 3 Jan. to 5 April, 1919; Deputy Director of Remounts, G.H.Q., British Armies of the Rhine, 6 April, 1919. Major Bailey married, in 1907, Dorothy Jessica, daughter of Thomas Gibson Bowles, Esq., M.P., and of Jessica (who died in 1887), daughter of General Evans Gordon.

COOKE, AUBREY ST. JOHN, Capt., was born 5 Aug. 1872, son of the late Professor Samuel Cooke, M.A., B.E., F.I.C., etc. He joined the Royal Sussex Regt. on 18 May, 1892; became Lieutenant 24 Sept. 1894. He was transferred to the Indian Staff Corps, and served on the North-West Frontier of India, 1897–98 (Medal with two clasps). He again saw active service in the South African War, 1899–1902, as Special Service Officer 20 Jan. to 6 Feb. 1900; afterwards on Staff (as Staff Officer for Transport [graded Rate XIV., Scale B. Art. 115, Rl. Wt., 26 Oct. 1900], 7 Feb. to 15 Oct. 1900; Staff Capt. 16 Oct. 1901, to 23 Feb. 1902; D.A.A.G. from 24 Feb. 1902). He was mentioned in Despatches [London Gazette, 17 June, 1902]; received the Queen's Medal with three clasps, and the King's Medal with two clasps. He was created a Companion of the Distinguished Service Order [London Gazette, 26 June, 1902]: "Aubrey St. John Cooke, Capt., Indian Staff Corps. In recognition of services during the operations in South Africa." The Insignia, Warrant and Statutes were sent to the G.O.C., Transvaal, and presented at Pretoria 14 Jan. 1903. Capt. Cooke was Director of Transport, Repatriation Department, Transvaal, till Aug. 1904, and resigned his commission in 1904. He rejoined the Army 5 Aug. 1914; was Controller of Roads and Bridges (U.K.) for the War Office and Ministry of Munitions; Chairman, Road Stone Control Committee Controlling Quarries (U.K.); War Office Representative in Select Committee on Transport, 1918; Member, Road Transport Board (Board of Trade), 1918; resigned commission 29 Nov. 1918. He became Chairman, Vitkyk Collieries, Coke and Gas Ovens; Director, Egyptian Markets, Engine Development Company, and other companies. Lieut.-Colonel Cooke married, in 1889, Emmie Mathilde, daughter of the late Lorentz Tiden.

PRATT, MERVYN, Capt., was born 24 April, 1873, son of Joseph Pratt, Esq., J.P., D.L., and Madeline Charlotte, only daughter of James Hamilton, of Cornacassa, Monaghan. He was educated at Harrow, and entered the King's Royal Rifle Corps 26 June, 1895; became Lieutenant, K.R.R.C., 14 June, 1898, and Captain 24 Sept. 1901. He served in the South African War, 1899–1902, and was present at the Relief of Ladysmith, including action at Colenso; operations of 17 to 24 Jan. 1900, and action at Spion Kop; operations of 5 to 7 Feb. 1900, and action at Vaal Kranz; operations on Tugela Heights 14 to 27 Feb. 1900, and action at Pieter's Hill; operations in Natal, March to June, 1900, including action at Laing's Nek (6 to 9 June) (severely wounded); operations in the Transvaal 30 Nov. 1900, to 31 May, 1902; operations in Orange River Colony, 1901–2. He was mentioned in Despatches [London Gazette, 17 June, 1902]; received the Queen's Medal with six clasps; the King's Medal with two clasps, and was created a Companion of the Distinguished Service Order [London Gazette, 26 June, 1902]: "Mervyn Pratt, Capt., King's Royal Rifle Corps. In recognition of services during the operations in South Africa." He was invested by the King 15 Jan. 1903. Capt. Pratt retired 5 Aug. 1910; became Temporary Major, K.R.R.C., in 1914, and was promoted to Major, Reserve of Officers, 4 May, 1916.

Mervyn Pratt.

DILLON, CONSTANTINE THEOBALD FRANCIS, Capt., was born 9 Sept. 1873, eldest son of Lieutenant-Colonel H. B. C. Dillon, of Redhurst, Cranleigh. He was gazetted to the Worcestershire Regt. 19 July, 1899, and served in the South African War, 1900–1, employed with Mounted Infantry, and was dangerously wounded. He took part in the operations in the Orange Free State, Feb. to May, 1900; also in Orange River Colony, May to 29 Nov. 1900. He was mentioned in Despatches [London Gazette, 3 Dec. 1901]; received the Queen's Medal with three clasps, and was created a Companion of the Distinguished Service Order [London Gazette, 26 June, 1901]: "Constantine Theobald Francis Dillon, Capt., Worcestershire Regt. In recognition of services during the operations in South Africa." He was invested by the King 24 Oct. 1902. He was promoted to Captain in 1902, and retired from the 4th Battn. Worcestershire Regt.

TURNER, BINGHAM ALEXANDER, Capt., was born 30 May, 1877, son of the late General E. P. Bingham Turner and Helen, daughter of the late Sir Casimir Gzowski, A.D.C., K.C.M.G. He was educated at Wellington and Sandhurst, and was commissioned in the Rifle Brigade 22 Jan. 1898; served in the Nile Expedition, 1898, being present at the Battle of Khartoum; received the Medal and the Egyptian Medal with clasp. He became Lieutenant 11 Dec. 1899, and served in the South African War, 1899–1902, taking part in operations in Natal in 1899, including the action at Lombard's Kop. He took part in the defence of Ladysmith, including the sortie of 10 Dec. 1899, and action of 6 Jan. 1900; operations in Natal, March to June, 1900, including action at Laing's Nek (6 to 9 June); operations in the Transvaal, east of Pretoria, July to 29 Nov. 1900, including actions at Belfast (26 and 27 Aug.) (slightly wounded) and Lydenberg (5 to 8 Sept.). He was subsequently employed with Mounted Infantry; operations in the Transvaal 30 Nov. 1900, to 31 May, 1902. He was mentioned in Despatches [London Gazette, 25 April, 1902]; received the Queen's Medal with three clasps; the King's Medal with two clasps, and was created a Companion of the Distinguished Service Order [London Gazette, 26 June, 1902]: "Bingham Alexander Turner, Capt., The Rifle Brigade. In recognition of services during the operations in South Africa." He was invested by the King 24 Oct. 1902. In July, 1909, he retired from the Regular Army, and joined the 6th (Reserve) Battn. of his regiment, being attached to the 2nd Battn. K.R.R.C. for active service. He was killed in action 2 Nov. 1914. Capt. Turner had married, in 1906, Gladys, daughter of J. S. St. Vincent Jervis.

Bingham A. Turner.

JOHNSON, RAYMOND BAZLEY, Capt., was born 30 Jan. 1877, son of the late Capt. William Johnson, formerly 6th Dragoons, and Mrs. Johnson, of Oddington, Moreton-in-Marsh; and grandson of the late Sir William Arnott, 1st Bart. He was gazetted to the 1st Dragoons 4 May, 1898, and became Lieutenant 5 July, 1899, and subsequently Captain, 6th Inniskilling Dragoons. Lieut. R. B. Johnson embarked for South Africa, with B Squadron, 6th Inniskilling Dragoons, in S.S. Jamaican, at Queenstown, on 23 Oct. 1899. You come across him from time to time in "With the Inniskilling Dragoons" (Lieut.-Colonel J. Watkins Yardley, C.M.G., D.S.O.). On 9 Feb. 1900: "At dawn the Boers shelled Slingersfontein Camp for the first time, putting twenty-seven shells into it before our artillery silenced their guns.. Simultaneously the enemy in force attacked the windmill posts of Hobkirk's Farm and Bastard's Nek, occupied by the Victorian Mounted Rifles, driving them in, with the loss of one killed and three wounded. Lieut. Raymond Johnson, with his troop of Inniskilling Dragoons, who were inlying picket, and therefore ready saddled, at once galloped off to seize Hobkirk's Ridge before the enemy could reach it; he was just in time, but was attacked from right front and left rear, being almost surrounded. He dismounted the men, who fought splendidly. One Corporal was killed; another corporal was shot through the sleeve at close range by a young Boer of about fourteen years, whom he had to shoot in self-defence. Another man from one side of a bush poked a Boer in the stomach with the barrel of his unloaded carbine, loaded quickly, and shot the Boer. Five men were cut off, but hid in a kloof and rejoined later. Gallantly the little troop held on to the ridge until Major Dauncey, reinforced by the remainder of the Inniskillings and the South Australians, drove back the enemy, who remained all day sniping from Hobkirk's Farm." On Page 84 of Colonel Yardley's book, we are told how, from Dreifontein: "Lieut. Raymond Johnson, Inniskilling Dragoons, with six men, cleverly found his way, during the night, with General French's Despatches to Lord Roberts at Germiston. He had to elude several parties of the enemy, but returned safely, after a night full of adventures, his mission safely accomplished. He was accompanied by Mr. Paterson, the Australian poet and correspondent." On 30 Aug.: "President Kruger was reported to have been at Waterval Onder the previous day, and General French was anxious to obtain news. So B Squadron of the Inniskillings, under Major Dauncey, was ordered to descend to the town and bring away the prisoners we had taken, among whom was a wounded soldier of our own. The enemy, hidden in the rocky kloofs and bush beyond the town, completely commanded the drift and approaches, and also the town itself. The squadron gained the town, galloping over the exposed ground through a hail of bullets. Lieut. Lawlor, at the head of his troop, was mortally wounded, shot through the body. He was a fine officer and a great loss to the regiment, and died cheery and brave to the last. Major Dauncey himself, charging in advance of his squadron, with Lieuts. Lawlor and Johnson, was grazed by two bullets, but the town was reached. In it none could show without being shot, so cover was taken in the buildings and the prisoners were not brought away till darkness ensured a safe return." On 6 May, 1901, Colonel Yardley writes: "Lieut. Raymond Johnson and Second Lieuts. Dixon and Holland joined at Brakfontein with a draft, but Lieut. Raymond Johnson left next day to go upon Colonel Rimington's Staff as galloper to his column, which was forming at Standerton." On 23 Sept., when Colonel Rimington surprised the Boers between the Klip and Bilge Rivers, "Lieut. R. B. Johnson, Inniskillings (Provost-Marshal), with his police, came across a small laager of seventeen Boers, who were taken with all their wagons; two were killed and one wounded. It was a smart performance. For their gallant and dashing conduct Lieut. R. B. Johnson and Lieut. F. W. Moffitt, who was serving under him, were mentioned by Lord Kitchener in Despatches (8 Oct. 1901). On 1 June (1902) a telegram was received from the Commander-in-Chief that peace had been signed on the previous night, 31 May. This news was received by all our troops very quietly. On the breaking-up of the force, 20 June, the Inniskillings marched to Bloemfontein. A small contingent, under Capt. Raymond Johnson, proceeded to England early in June to represent the regiment at His Majesty's Coronation."

The record of Capt. Johnson's services in the South African War, as given in "Hart's Army List," is as follows: He served, 1899–1902; took part in the operations in the Orange Free State, March to May, 1900, including actions at Vet River and Zand River; in the Transvaal in May and June, 1900, including actions near Johannesburg, Pretoria, and Diamond Hill (11 and 12 June); in the Transvaal, east of Pretoria, July to 29 Nov. 1900, including actions at Reit Vlei and Belfast (26 and 27 Aug.); in Cape Colony, south of Orange River, including actions at Colesberg (1 Jan. to 12 Feb.); served as Adjutant, 6th Dragoons, 1 April to 31 May, 1902; again during operations in the Transvaal and Orange River Colony, 30 Nov. 1900, to 31 May, 1902. For his services in the South African War, Capt. Johnson was mentioned in Despatches [London Gazette, 10 Sept. and 3 Dec. 1901]; received the Queen's Medal with five clasps, the King's Medal with two clasps, and was created a Companion of the Distinguished Service Order [London Gazette, 26 June, 1902]: "Raymond Bazley Johnson, Capt., 6th Dragoons. In recognition of services during the operations in South Africa." He was invested by the King 24 Oct. 1902. Capt. Johnson retired from the Inniskilling Dragoons. He served in the European War, as Lieutenant-Commander, Royal Naval Armoured Cars, 1914–15; in the Cavalry Reserve, and as Commandant, School of Instruction, 1916–17; in the Royal Air Force, 1918. He married, in 1912, Lilian, youngest daughter of the late Herman Eckstein (of Johannesburg), and Mrs. R. P. Cobbold, of Welford Park, Newbury, Berkshire, and they have one son and two daughters.

GIBB, EVAN, Capt., was born 12 March, 1877, eldest son of the late William Gibb, of Craigton, Fintry. He joined the West India Regt. 16 Feb. 1898; was promoted to Lieutenant 16 Nov. 1898; served in the operations in Sierra Leone, 1898–99 (Medal with clasp); became Second Lieutenant, Army Service Corps, 2 Oct. 1899; Lieutenant, Army Service Corps, 2 Oct. 1900. He served in the South African War, 1899–1902; as Deputy Assistant Director of Supplies, South Africa, 7 Nov. 1900, to 31 March, 1902; as Staff Captain for Supply Duties, Headquarters, South Africa, 1 April to 11 Sept. 1902; took part in the operations in Natal, 1899; at the Relief of Ladysmith, including operations of 17 to 24 Jan. 1900, and action at Spion Kop; operations of 5 to 7 Feb. 1900, and action at Vaal Kranz; operations on Tugela Heights (14 to 27 Feb. 1900), and action at Pieter's Hill; took part in the operations in the Transvaal and Orange River Colony, 30 Nov. 1900, to 31 May, 1902 (Despatches [London Gazette, 8 Feb. 1901]; Queen's Medal with five clasps, and King's Medal with two clasps). He was created a Companion of the Distinguished Service Order [London Gazette, 26 June, 1902]: "Evan Gibb, Capt., Army Service Corps. In recognition of services during the operations in South Africa." He was invested by the King 24 Oct. 1902. He was promoted to Captain 1 April, 1902; was Adjutant, Army Service Corps, 10 Aug. to 26 Sept. 1902; and 19 March, 1905, to 31 Dec. 1906; was Staff Captain, Headquarters of Army, War Office, 1 Jan. 1907, to 31 Dec. 1909; Deputy Assistant Director, War Office, 1 Jan. to 31 Dec. 1910; was given the Brevet of Major 18 Jan. 1911; was Assistant Instructor, Army Service Corps Training Establishment, 1 Jan. 1911, to 4 Aug. 1914. He served in the European War from 1914; was promoted to Major 4 Aug. 1914; served as D.A.Q.M.G., Lines of Communication, British Expeditionary Force, 5 Aug. to 15 Dec. 1914; Assistant Director of Transport, British Expeditionary Force, 16 Dec. 1914, to 21 April, 1915; Temporary Lieutenant-Colonel 22 April, 1915, to 2 June, 1916; A.Q.M.G., British Expeditionary Force, British Armies in France, 22 April, 1915, to 3 Dec. 1916; Temp. Brigadier-General 4 Dec. 1916; Director of Labour, British Armies in France, 4 Dec. 1916, to 10 Feb. 1918; Controller of Salvage, British Armies in France, 11 Feb. 1918. He was mentioned in Despatches four times; was given the Brevets of Lieutenant-Colonel, 3 June, 1916, and Colonel, 1 Jan. 1918; was created a C.M.G. in 1915, and a C.B.E. in 1919. He married, in 1902, Beatrice Ramsay, only child of Major-General Henry Jardine Hallowes, and of Charlotte Elizabeth Ormonde (who died in 1916), daughter of the Hon. J. Hamilton Gray, D.C.L.

BALD, ALFRED CAMPBELL, Capt., entered the Army in 1882: served in the Sudan in 1884 (Medal and clasp; Khedive's Star); in the Nile Expedition, 1884–85, with the 1st Battn. Black Watch (clasp). He became Captain in 1888. Capt. Bald retired, and entered the Reserve of Officers. He served in the South African War, 1899–1900, with the 2nd Battn. Black Watch, and was created a Companion of the Distinguished Service Order [London Gazette, 26 June, 1902]: "Alfred Campbell Bald, Capt., Reserve of Officers. In recognition of services during the operations in South Africa." The Insignia, Warrant and Statutes were sent to the G.O.C., Transvaal, and presented at Pretoria 3 Feb. 1903. Capt. Bald died 4 April, 1905.

M'DONALD, ARCHIBALD WILLIAM, Capt., was born in 1869. He was educated at Edinburgh Academy; at Fort Augustus, and abroad; served in the Cameron Highlanders, as Second Lieutenant, and, on retiring, joined the 3rd Battn. (Inverness-shire Militia), becoming Captain 12 June, 1896. He served in South Africa as Captain and Adjutant, Lovat's Scouts, July, 1900, to Aug. 1901, taking part in operations in Orange River Colony, May to 29 Nov. 1900, including actions at Bethlehem (6 and 7 July), Wittebergen (1 to 29 July), Witpoort and Caledon River (27 to 29 Nov.); operations in Orange River Colony and Cape Colony, 30 Nov. 1900, to 31 May, 1902. He was mentioned in Despatches [London Gazette, 17 June, 1902]; received the Queen's Medal with three clasps, and was created a Companion of the Distinguished Service Order [London Gazette, 26 June, 1902]: "Archibald William M'Donald, Capt., Lovat's Scouts. In recognition of services during the operations in South Africa." He was invested by the King 18 Dec. 1902. He became Lieutenant-Colonel, Lovat's Scouts

Yeomanry, and Colonel, T.F., Inverness-shire T.F.A. Colonel M'Donald served with the 1st Lovat's Scouts in the Dardanelles in 1915 (Despatches); in Egypt, 1916, and in Salonika, 1916–17. He married, in 1904, Marion, eldest daughter of James Calder, of Ardargie, Perth, and widow of J. C. Berry, C.I.E., I.C.S.

WILLIAMS-WYNN, ROBERT WILLIAM HERBERT WATKIN,

R. W. Williams-Wynn.

Capt., was born 3 June, 1862, youngest son of the late Colonel Herbert Watkin Williams-Wynn, Royal Fusiliers, M.P., and of Mrs. Williams-Wynn, of Cefn, St. Asaph. He was educated at Wellington, and Christ Church, Oxford, and joined the Montgomeryshire Yeomanry in 1886. He served in the South African War, 1900–1, with the Montgomeryshire Yeomanry, and on Lord Chesham's Staff, taking part in operations in the Transvaal, east of Pretoria, Nov. 1900, including action at Rhenoster Kop; operations in the Transvaal, west of Pretoria; operations in Orange River Colony; operations in Cape Colony, south of Orange River; operations in the Transvaal 30 Nov. 1900, to June, 1901. He was mentioned in Despatches [London Gazette, 10 Sept.

1901]; received the Queen's Medal with four clasps, and was created a Companion of the Distinguished Service Order [London Gazette, 26 June, 1902]: " Robert William Herbert Watkin Williams-Wynn, Capt., Imperial Yeomanry (Major in Home Yeomanry). In recognition of services during the operations in South Africa." He was invested by the King 24 Oct. 1902. He was given the Brevet of Colonel, and commanded the Montgomeryshire Yeomanry, 1905–17; went out in command of the Montgomeryshire Yeomanry to Egypt in March, 1916; held District Commands in Egypt of Southern Section (over 200,000 square miles), and Sollum Section, 1917–19 (Despatches three times); was promoted Colonel. Colonel Williams-Wynn contested (C.) Montgomeryshire, 1894, 1895 and 1900. He married, in 1904, Elizabeth Ida, second daughter of the late George W. Lowther, of Swillington, and they have two sons: Owen Watkin, born 30 Nov. 1904 and Edward Watkin, born 20 Nov. 1908, and two daughters: Joyce and Margaret.

PHILLIPS, H. C. B., Capt., served with the Imperial Yeomanry in South Africa, 1900–2. He was mentioned in Despatches, received the Queen's Medal with three clasps, the King's Medal with two clasps, and was created a Companion of the Distinguished Service Order [London Gazette, 26 June, 1902]: " H. C. B. Phillips, Capt., Imperial Yeomanry. In recognition of services during the operations in South Africa." He served in Northern Nigeria in 1903, and received the Medal and clasp; was for some time Resident, Northern Nigeria, and died at Hadeija, Northern Nigeria, on 1 Sept. 1906. An obituary notice of him appeared in the " Times." Capt. Phillips had married, in 1885, H. E., daughter of Harwood Hoyle, of Lancashire.

SELL, EDGAR COLLINS, Capt., served in South Africa, 1900–2, and was created a Companion of the Distinguished Service Order [London Gazette, 26 June, 1902]: " Edgar Collins Sell, Capt., Imperial Yeomanry. In recognition of services during the operations in South Africa." The Insignia, etc., were sent to G.O.C., Transvaal; presented by G.O.C., at Pretoria, 29 July, 1903. Capt. Sell has retired from the Berkshire Imperial Yeomanry, and is an honorary Captain in the Army. He married, in 1910, Margaret, daughter of the late Robert Cochrane, of Loanhead, Ayrshire.

GRUBB, ALEXANDER HENRY WATKINS, Lieut., was born 18 April, 1873, son of Lieut.-Colonel Alexander Grubb, J.P., late Royal Artillery, of Elsfield House, Hollingbourne, Kent, and of Sarah Watkins Grubb. He

Alexander H. W. Grubb.

was educated at Wellington College, and at the Royal Military Academy, Woolwich (Pollock Gold Medal), and entered the Royal Engineers 12 Feb. 1892, becoming Lieutenant 12 Feb. 1895. He served with the Balloon Section at Aldershot, 1894–99. He served in the South African War, 1899–1902, taking part in the advance on Kimberley, including action at Magersfontein; at the Relief of Kimberley; took part in the operations in the Orange Free State, Feb. to May, 1900, including those at Paardeberg, and actions at Poplar Grove and Dreifontein; in the Transvaal in May and June, 1900, including actions near Johannesburg, Pretoria and Diamond Hill; in Orange River Colony, including actions at Wittebergen; in the Transvaal, Nov. 1900, to Jan. 1901, and March, 1901,

to 31 May, 1902; again during operations in Orange River Colony, Feb. to March, 1901, and July to Sept. 1901; took part in the operations on the Zululand Frontier of Natal in Oct. 1901; also in Cape Colony, Jan. to Feb. 1901 (Despatches [London Gazette, 16 March, 1900, and 17 June, 1902]; Queen's Medal with six clasps, and King's Medal with two clasps). He was created a Companion of the Distinguished Service Order [London Gazette, 26 June, 1902]: " Alexander Henry Watkins Grubb, Lieut., Royal Engineers. In recognition of services during the operations in South Africa." The Insignia, Warrant and Statutes were sent to the G.O.C., Transvaal, and Orange River Colony, 15 Nov. 1902, and were presented by Colonel Lyttelton at Pretoria 14 Jan. 1903. He was promoted to Captain, Royal Engineers, 12 Oct. 1902, and was on the Headquarters Staff at Pretoria

till 1904; specially employed, Headquarters of Army, 6 to 22 Feb 1909, and with the Signal Division, Aldershot, whence he was sent on active service in the European War. He became Major 1 Feb. 1912. He was Temporary Lieutenant-Colonel, Royal Engineers, 9 Jan. 1916, to 18 April, 1917; Temporary Colonel, 19 April, 1917, to 31 Dec. 1918; served in France, 1914–15; was Director of Army Signals, British Salonika Force, 19 April, 1917. He was six times mentioned in Despatches, and was given the Brevets of Lieutenant-Colonel 3 June, 1916, and Colonel 1 Jan. 1919. Colonel Grubb was created a C.M.G. in June, 1918. He has the Coronation Medal. In 1908 he married Frances Marie, daughter of the late J. Brent Cox, of Kentucky, U.S.A., and they have one son, Alexander James, born 25 July, 1909.

STIRLING, JOHN GORDON, Lieut., was born 28 May, 1874, son of the Right Hon. Sir James Stirling, LL.D., F.R.S., P.C., late Lord Justice of Appeal, and Aby, eldest daughter of John Thomson Renton, of Bradstone Brook, Shalford, Surrey. He joined the Lancers, as Second Lieutenant, from the Militia, 31 July, 1895, and became Lieutenant, 9th Lancers, July, 1896. He served in the South African War, and was created a Companion of the Distinguished Service Order [London Gazette, 26 June, 1902]: " John Gordon Stirling, Lieut., 9th Lancers (since deceased). In recognition of services during the operations in South Africa." The Insignia, Warrant and Statutes were sent to Lord Justice Stirling.

LAWRENCE, FREDERICK GEORGE, Lieut., was born 21 Aug. 1874, son of the late Hugh M. Lawrence. He was gazetted Second Lieutenant in the South Wales Borderers 10 Oct. 1894, and became Lieutenant 15 Nov. 1896. He served in South Africa, 1899–1902; as Railway Staff Officer 14 Jan. to 4 March, 1900, and 5 March, 1900, to 18 Aug. 1902, in Cape Colony, Orange River Colony and the Transvaal; was mentioned in Despatches [London Gazette, 10 Sept. 1901]; received the Queen's Medal with three clasps, the King's Medal with two clasps, and was created a Companion of the Distinguished Service Order [London Gazette, 26 June, 1902]: " Frederick George Lawrence, Lieut., South Wales Borderers. In recognition of services during the operations in South Africa." He was invested by the King 24 Oct. 1902. He was Adjutant, 3rd South Wales Borderers, Brecon, 1 Sept. 1902, to 13 Sept. 1905; was promoted to Captain 3 March, 1906; was Officer, Company of Gentleman Cadets, Royal Military College, 1 Feb. 1910 to, 31 Jan. 1914. He served in the European War; was promoted to Major 28 April, 1915; held a Special Appointment, G.H.Q., B.E.F., 23 Oct. 1915, to 31 March, 1916; Temporary Lieutenant-Colonel 1 April to 20 Aug. 1916; D.A.Q.M.G., 4th Army, British Armies in France, 19 Nov. 1916, to 28 Jan. 1917; A.Q.M.G., 15th Army Corps, British Armies in France, 29 Jan. to 15 Sept. 1917. He was A.Q.M.G., Southern Command, from 31 March, 1918, and Temporary Lieutenant-Colonel; G.S.O.3. He married, in 1902, Frances Mary, daughter of the late Osborne E. Mortimer, and they have one daughter.

LIVESAY, ROBERT O'HARA, Lieut., was born 27 June, 1876, only son of the late Colonel R. A. Livesay, R.E. He was gazetted to the Royal West Surrey Regt. 5 Sept. 1896, and became Lieutenant 18 May, 1898. He served in the South African War, 1899–1902, and took part in the Relief of Ladysmith, including action at Colenso; operations of 17 to 24 Jan. 1900, and actions at Spion Kop; operations of 5 to 7 Feb. 1900, and action at Vaal Kranz; in the operations on Tugela Heights (14 to 27 Feb. 1900), and action at Pieter's Hill; in Natal, March to June, 1900, including action at Laing's Nek (6 to 9 June); in the Transvaal and Orange River Colony 30 Nov. 1900, to Sept. 1901, and Nov. 1901, to 31 May, 1902; also during the operations on the Zululand Frontier of Natal in Sept. and Oct. 1901 (Despatches [London Gazette, 17 June, 1902]; Queen's Medal with five clasps, and King's Medal with two clasps). He was created a Companion of the Distinguished Service Order [London Gazette, 26 June, 1902]: " Robert O'Hara Livesay, Lieut., Royal West Surrey Regt. In recognition of services during the operations in South Africa." The Insignia, Warrant and Statutes were sent to the G.O.C., Transvaal, and presented at Bloemfontein, 4 March, 1903. He was promoted to Captain 1 Jan. 1903, and was Officer, Company of Gentleman Cadets, Royal Military College, 1 Aug. 1904, to 31 July, 1908; and Adjutant (attached General Staff), Officers' Training Corps, 21 June, 1909, to 21 Jan. 1911. Capt. Livesay went on retired pay 7 Jan. 1914, joining the Reserve of Officers, his previous full-pay service being from 5 Sept. 1896 to 6 Jan. 1914. He was recalled, and served 1 year and 58 days. Capt. Livesay served in the European War, 1914–18; from 5 Aug. 1914, to 12 May, 1916, as G.S.O.2, Central Force, Home Defence, 48th Division, B.E.F.; as G.S.O.2, 3rd Army, British Armies in France, 13 May to 12 July, 1916; as G.S.O.1, British Armies in France, 13 to 21 July, 1916; was Temporary Lieutenant-Colonel 13 July, 1916, to 2 June, 1917; was G.S.O.1, New Zealand Division, British Armies in France, 22 July, 1916, to 27 Oct. 1917. He was G.S.O.1, American Staff School, France, 28 Oct. 1917, to 15 March, 1918; G.S.O.1, 61st Division, British Armies in France, 16 March to 5 Sept. 1918; Temporary Brigadier-General from 6 Sept. 1918, commanding the 24th Infantry Brigade. He was mentioned in Despatches; was given the Brevets of Major, 3 June, 1916; Lieutenant-Colonel, 3 June, 1917, and Colonel, 3 June, 1918; and created a C.M.G. in 1919. He was also given the Legion of Honour by the French. In 1917 he married Margaret, only daughter of William Pretyman, of Five Ways, Torquay.

BINNY, STEUART SCOTT, Lieut., was born 1 July, 1871. He was commissioned in the 19th Hussars 2 June, 1894; became Lieutenant 22 Oct. 1898, and served in the South African War, 1899–1902, taking part in the operations in Natal, 1899, including actions at Rietfontein and Lombard's Kop; was present at the defence of Ladysmith, including sortie of 7 Dec. 1899, and action of 6 Jan. 1900; served during operations in the Transvaal, east of Pretoria, Oct. and Nov. 1900; served as Adjutant, 19th Hussars, 1 Jan. to 31 May, 1902; took part in the operations in Orange River Colony, March, 1902 (Despatches [London Gazette, 15 Nov. 1901]; Queen's Medal with two clasps, and King's Medal with two clasps). He was created a Companion of the Distinguished Service Order [London Gazette, 26 June, 1902]: "Steuart Scott Binny, Lieut., 19th Hussars. In recognition of services during the operations in South Africa." He was Adjutant, 19th Hussars, 1 Jan. 1902, to 31 Dec. 1904, and was promoted to Captain 1 April 1903; and to Major 9 July, 1910. Major Binny was killed in action in Flanders 3 March, 1916. He had married, in 1911, Marjorie, third daughter of Henry Champion, of Sibdon Castle, Salop.

FRASER, PERCY WILLIAM NORMAN, Lieut., was born 22 Jan. 1879, and was the eldest surviving son of the late Colonel G. L. Fraser, of Kirkside, Kincardineshire. He was educated at Wellington and Sandhurst, and was gazetted Second Lieutenant in the Queen's Own Cameron Highlanders 6 April, 1898; served in the Nile Expedition, 1898 (Egyptian Medal and Medal), and was promoted to Lieutenant 1 April, 1899. He served in the South African War, 1900–2; as A.D.C. to Major-General Sir Bruce Hamilton, K.C.B. 26 April, 1900, to 31 Oct. 1901; as Staff Lieutenant, Headquarters Staff, 1 Nov. 1901, to 22 June, 1902; took part in the operations in the Orange Free State, Feb. to May, 1900, including actions at Vet River (5 and 6 May) and Zand River; in the Transvaal in May and June, 1900, including actions near Johannesburg, Pretoria and Diamond Hill (11 and 12 June); in Orange River Colony May to 29 Nov. 1900, including action at Ladybrand (2 to 5 Sept.); in the Transvaal, Oct. 1901, to 31 May, 1902; again in Orange River Colony 30 Nov. 1900, to Sept. 1901; also during the operations on the Zululand Frontier of Natal in Sept. and Oct. 1901; and in Cape Colony, Feb. March and May, 1901 (Despatches [London Gazette, 10 Sept. 1901]; Queen's Medal with four clasps, and King's Medal with two clasps). He was created a Companion of the Distinguished Service Order [London Gazette, 26 June, 1902]: "Percy William Norman Fraser, Lieut., Cameron Highlanders. In recognition of services during the operations in South Africa." He was invested by the King, 18 Dec. 1902. He was promoted to Captain 21 April, 1902, and was on Special Service 7 Dec. 1903, to 5 Jan. 1904. Capt. Fraser served in East Africa, 1903–4; took part in the operations in Somaliland, on Staff (as Special Service Officer); action at Jidballi (Medal with two clasps). He became Major 5 April, 1909. He served in the European War, and was killed in action 23 Feb. 1915.

LISTER, THE HONOURABLE THOMAS, Lieut., was born in 1878, eldest son and heir to the 4th Lord Ribblesdale, and Charlotte Monckton (who died in 1911), daughter of Sir Charles Tennant, Bart., of The Glen, Peeblesshire. He was gazetted to the 10th Hussars 1 Dec. 1897, and was promoted to Lieutenant 5 Nov. 1899. He served throughout the South African War, at the Battles of Paardeberg, Poplar Grove, Dreifontein, Houtnek, Vet River, Diamond Hill, Wittebergen and the Relief of Kimberley, and was wounded once during this campaign. He was twice mentioned in Despatches, received both South African War Medals, and was created a Companion of the Distinguished Service Order [London Gazette, 26 June, 1902]: "The Honourable Thomas Lister, Lieut., 10th Hussars. For services during the operations in South Africa." In 1903 he was selected for special service in Somaliland, serving there as Remount Officer till Jan. 1904, when he was killed whilst carrying Despatches at the Battle of Jidballi, 10 Jan.

The Hon. Thomas Lister.

DUGDALE, JAMES GORDON, Lieut., was born at Burnley 27 July, 1874, second son of James Dugdale, of Ivy Bank, Burnley, and Sezincot, Moreton-in-Marsh, Gloucestershire, J.P. for Lancashire and Gloucestershire, by his wife, who was a daughter of the late John Brooks, of Sezincot, Moreton-in-Marsh, J.P. for Westmorland. He was educated at Marlborough, and Christ Church, Oxford, where he graduated B.A., 1895. He was gazetted Second Lieutenant, 18th Hussars, 1 Dec. 1897, and served with great distinction in the South African War, 1899–1902, taking part in operations in Natal, 1899, including actions at Elandslaagte, Rietfontein and Lombard's Kop; the defence of Ladysmith, including sortie of 7 Dec. 1899, and action of 6 Jan. 1900; operations in Natal, March to June, 1900, including action at Laing's Nek (6 to 9 June); operations in the Transvaal, east of Pretoria, July to 29 Nov. 1900, including actions at Belfast (26 and 27 Aug.) and Lydenberg (5 to 8 Sept.); operations in the Transvaal, 30 Nov. 1900, to Sept. 1901, and Nov. 1901 to 31 May, 1902; operations in Orange River Colony, March and May, 1902,; and operations on the Zululand Frontier of Natal in Sept. and Oct. 1901. For his services he was twice mentioned in Despatches [London Gazette, 10 Sept. 1901, and 25 April, 1902]; awarded the Queen's Medal with five clasps, the King's Medal with two clasps, and was created a Companion of the Distinguished Service Order [London Gazette, 26 June, 1902]: "James Gordon Dugdale, Lieut., 18th Hussars. In recognition of services during the operations in South Africa." He was promoted Lieutenant 24 Feb. 1900; Captain, Nov. 1904, and from 18 June, 1904, to 1907 was Adjutant to the West Somerset Imperial Yeomanry. He retired in 1908, and was placed on the Special Reserve of Officers. He held the appointment of Brigade Major, 2nd South Midland Mounted Brigade, 1909–10. He rejoined his regiment on the outbreak of war, and went to France, where he saw much hard fighting, and was twice mentioned in Despatches, viz., in Sir John French's Despatch of 14 Jan. 1916 [London Gazette, 17 Feb. 1916], and in Sir Douglas Haig's of 13 Nov. 1916 [London Gazette, 4 Jan. 1917]. He was appointed Assistant Provost-Marshal. He has had two French decorations conferred upon him, being a Chevalier de la Mérite agricole, and holding the Médaille d'honneur (silver, 2nd Class). He married, in 1903, Ellen Mabel, daughter of the late Major-General Compton-Turner, and has two sons: J. Frederick C., born 1904, and Nigel, born 1908; and a daughter, Pamela M.

GRANT, ARTHUR, Lieut., was born 14 Sept. 1879, eldest son of Sir Arthur Henry Grant, 9th Bart., J.P., D.L., and Mary, daughter of Capt. H. Sholto Douglas, late 42nd Highlanders. He was gazetted to the 12th Lancers 4 Jan. 1899, and served in the South African War, 1899–1902, taking part in the advance on Kimberley, including action at Magersfontein; at the Relief of Kimberley; was present during operations in the Orange Free State, Feb. to May, 1900, including those at Paardeberg; actions at Poplar Grove, Dreifontein, Houtnek (Thoba Mountain) and Zand River; in the Transvaal in May and June, 1900, including actions near Johannesburg; in the Transvaal, west of Pretoria, July to 29 Nov. 1900; in the Orange River Colony, May to 29 Nov. 1900, including actions at Lindley, Bethlehem, and Wittebergen; again in the Transvaal 30 Nov. 1900, to July, 1901; also in Cape Colony, July, 1901, to 31 May, 1902 (Despatches [London Gazette, 25 April, 1902]; Queen's Medal with five clasps, and King's Medal with two clasps). He was created a Companion of the Distinguished Service Order [London Gazette, 26 June, 1902]: "Arthur Grant, Lieut., 12th Lancers. In recognition of services during the operations in South Africa." The Insignia, Warrant and Statutes were sent to His Excellency the Commander-in-Chief in India, and presented by Colonel Penno at Umballa in Jan. 1903. He was promoted to Lieutenant 8 March, 1900, and to Captain 21 May, 1904, and retired 25 Sept. 1909. Lieut.-Colonel A. Grant served in the European War, and commanded the Gordon Highlanders till severely wounded in France in 1915. He was Commandant of a Camp from 1917 to 1918. In 1917 he succeeded his father as 10th Baronet, of Nova Scotia. Sir Arthur Grant is a J.P. and D.L. He married, in 1909, Evelyn, youngest daughter of the late Collingwood L. Wood, of Freeland, Perthshire, and they have two sons: Arthur Lindsay and Francis Cullen; and three daughters: Evelyn Mary Francis; Elspeth and Katherine Jean.

KIRKPATRICK, HEDLEY JOHN, Lieut., joined the Army in 1900, and served in South Africa, 1899–1902, at first with the South Australian Horse. He was mentioned in Despatches, received the Queen's Medal with five clasps; the King's Medal with two clasps, and was created a Companion of the Distinguished Service Order [London Gazette, 26 June, 1902]: "Hedley John Kirkpatrick, Lieut., 6th Dragoon Guards. In recognition of services during the operations in South Africa." The Insignia, Warrant, etc., were sent to the G.O.C., Transvaal, and presented at Pretoria 9 Dec. 1903. Lieut. Kirkpatrick resigned from the 6th Dragoon Guards in 1903.

HOBBS, REGINALD FRANCIS ARTHUR, Lieut., was born 30 Jan. 1878, at Fullwood, Manchester, son of Simpson Hockyett Hobbs, late Captain, 89th Foot, and Sarah Hobbs. He was educated at Wellington College, and at the Royal Military Academy, Woolwich, and joined the Royal Engineers 3 Jan. 1898, becoming Lieutenant 3 Jan. 1901. He served in the South African War, 1899–1900, and was given the D.S.O. for his services at Kleinfontein. On 23 Oct. 1901, at Kleinfontein, Transvaal, the rearguard of Von Donop's Column was cut off while passing through thick bush. The two guns of the 4th Battery, R.F.A., with the rearguard, were put out of action, the teams being shot down and the officer in charge and the gunners being killed or wounded. Lieut. Hobbs rode back, rallied the rearguard, got one of the guns into action, and fired it himself, and finally fetched a team of horses and helped to drive the two guns away to rejoin the main body, after the Boers had been driven off. The following is the official record of his services: Took part in the advance on Kimberley, including actions at Belmont, Enslin, and Modder River; was present during the operations in the Transvaal, west of Pretoria, July to 29 Nov. 1900; in Orange River Colony, May to Nov. 1900; in the Transvaal, 30 Nov. 1900, to Jan. 1901, and March, 1901, and April 1901, to 31 May, 1902; in Orange River Colony, March and April, 1901; also in Cape Colony, Jan. 1901 (Despatches [London Gazette, 17 Jan. 1902]; Queen's Medal with four clasps and King's Medal with two clasps). His D.S.O. was gazetted 26 June, 1902: "Reginald Francis Arthur Hobbs, Lieut., Royal Engineers. In recognition of services during the operations in South Africa." He was invested by the King 18 Dec. 1902. He served in East Africa in 1903; took part in the operations in Somaliland (Medal with clasp); was on Survey duty, Gold Coast, 24 Sept. 1904, to 14 Sept. 1905. He became Captain 3 Jan. 1907, and was Officer for Technical Duties at the School of Musketry, Hythe, 1 Nov. 1907, to 31 Dec. 1911. Serving in the European War, he was employed as D.A.A. and Q.M.G., 7th Division, B.E.F., 31 Aug. 1914, to 16 July, 1915, and was promoted Major 30 Oct. 1914. He was Temporary Lieutenant-Colonel, 17 July, 1915, and A.A. and Q.M.G., 5th Division, and held this post with the British Forces in France and afterwards in Italy until 26 Feb. 1918, being given the Brevet of Lieutenant-Colonel 3 June, 1917. He was appointed D.A. and Q.M.G. (Temporary Brigadier-General), 17th Army Corps, British Armies in France, 27 Feb. 1918; was given the Brevet of Colonel 3 June, 1919. In July, 1915, he was created a C.M.G., and he was three times mentioned in Despatches (1914, 1915 and 1916). His chief recreations are Rugby football and athletics. He married, 29 Aug. 1906, at Assington, near Colchester, Frances Graham, daughter of Sir William Stirling, K.C.B., and Lady Stirling. Their children are: Reginald Geoffrey Stirling, born 8 Aug. 1908; Peter Graham, born 19 March, 1911, and William Paul, born 6 April, 1914.

Reginald F. A. Hobbs.

HOLFORD, CHARLES FREDERICK, Lieut., was born 2 Sept. 1879, son of Thomas and Margaret Holford, of Castle Hill, Dorchester. He was educated

Charles F. Holford.

at Rugby, and commissioned 23 June, 1898, in the 14th Battery, Royal Field Artillery. He served in the South African War, 1899–1902, and was dangerously wounded. He was present at the Relief of Ladysmith, including the action at Colenso, and was a prisoner of war 15 Dec. 1899 (Colenso), till 5 June, 1900. He was mentioned in Despatches [London Gazette, 26 Jan. 1900, 9 July and 10 Sept. 1901]; received the Queen's Medal with four clasps, the King's Medal with two clasps, and was created a Companion of the Distinguished Service Order [London Gazette, 26 June, 1902]: " Charles Frederick Holford, Lieut., Royal Artillery. In recognition of services during the operations in South Africa." He was invested by the King 24 Oct. 1902. He became Lieutenant 16 Feb. 1901, and retired from the Royal Artillery 9 Oct. 1903. He married, in 1905, Ursula Isabel, daughter of R. Cecil Corbett, of Stableford, near Bridgnorth, and they have three sons and two daughters.

KARSLAKE, HENRY, Lieut., was born 10 Feb. 1879, son of the late Lewis Karslake. He was educated at Harrow, and at the Royal Military Academy, Woolwich, and joined the 83rd Field Battery 23 June, 1898. He served in the South African War, 1899–1902, and took part in the operations in the Orange Free State, Feb. to May, 1900, including actions at Poplar Grove, Dreifontein, Vet River (5 and 6 May) and Zand River; in the Transvaal in May and June, 1900, including actions near Johannesburg, Pretoria and Diamond Hill (11 and 12 June); in the Transvaal, east of Pretoria, July to 20 Aug. 1900; again in the Transvaal 30 Nov. 1900, to Jan. 1902, and March to 23 May, 1902; also during the operations in Orange River Colony, Jan. to March, 1902 (Despatches [London Gazette, 10 Sept. 1901, and 17 Jan. 1902]; Queen's Medal with four clasps, and King's Medal with clasps). He was created a Companion of the Distinguished Service Order [London Gazette, 26 June, 1902]: " Henry Karslake, Lieut., Royal Artillery. In recognition of services during the operations in South Africa." He was invested by the King 24 Oct. 1902. He was promoted to Lieutenant, 16 Feb. 1901; was posted to T Battery, R.H.A., 1901; and to Captain 20 Dec. 1905, and posted on promotion to the 100th Battery, R.F.A., 1906; was Officer, Company of Gentleman Cadets, Royal Military College, 20 Feb. 1907, to 19 Feb. 1911; posted to the 116th Battery, R.F.A., in 1911; was a Staff College student, 1912–13. He was posted to the 129th Howitzer Battery, 1914; served in the European War from 1914; became Major 30 Oct. 1914; was Brigade Major, R.A., 6th Division, B.E.F., 9 Dec. 1914, to 22 Feb. 1915; Brigade Major, R.A., 12th Division, New Armies, B.E.F., 6 March to 16 Aug. 1915; G.S.O.2, 3rd Army, B.E.F., British Armies in France, 17 Aug. 1915, to 26 June, 1916; G.S.O.1, 50th Division, British Armies in France, 27 June, 1916, to 15 Sept. 1917; G.S.O.1, 4th Division, British Armies in France, 16 Sept. 1917, to 4 Aug. 1918; G.S.O.1, Tank Corps, British Armies in France, 5 Aug. to 25 Oct. 1918; Brigade General, General Staff, Tank Corps, British Armies in France, 26 Oct. 1918, to 1 April, 1919; G.S.O.1, Southern Division, British Army of the Rhine. He was mentioned in Despatches; was given the Brevets of Lieutenant-Colonel, 1 Jan. 1917, and Colonel, 3 Jan. 1919; was created a C.M.G. in 1916, and was given the Légion d'Honneur. Colonel Karslake married, in 1905, Florence Cecil, daughter of Vice-Admiral E. Rooke, and they have two sons.

ANDERSON, JOHN, Lieut., was born in Morayshire, N.B., 17 Oct. 1852, son of John and Annie Anderson, of Forres, N.B. He was educated at Public School, Rafford, Forres. He served in the Royal Scots Greys for

John Anderson.

13½ years; exchanged to Army Service Corps 29 Aug. 1896, as Quartermaster, and served with it for 20 years. He served in the Matabele Rebellion, 1896, as Assistant Supply Officer (Medal); was Assistant Controller, B.S.A. Company, 1896–1900. He served in the South African War, 1899–1902, employed as Supply Officer, Rhodesian Regt., etc., Oct. 1899, to May, 1900; with the Rhodesian Field Force, May to Oct. 1900, and with the South African Constabulary, Oct. 1900, to May, 1902; was present in operations in the Transvaal, 1900–2. He was mentioned in Despatches [London Gazette, 10 Sept. 1901]; received the Queen's Medal and four clasps, and the King's Medal and two clasps, and was created a Companion of the Distinguished Service Order [London Gazette, 26 June, 1902]: " John Anderson, Honorary Lieut. and Quartermaster, Army Service Corps. In recognition of services during the operations in South Africa." The D.S.O. was presented by General Lyttelton 25 March, 1903. He was D.A.A.G., General Carrington's Rhodesian Field Force, May to Oct. 1900; joined the South African Constabulary 23 Oct. 1900, as Controller, with rank of Lieutenant-Colonel. Lieut.-Colonel Anderson retired from the Army in 1905, and in 1906 from his appointment as Controller, South African Constabulary. Lieut.-Colonel Anderson married, 19 Aug. 1878, at Dundalk, Philippa Charlotte Taylor, daughter of Henry Taylor, of Portsmouth, Their children are: John, born in 1882; William, born in 1885 (Lieutenant, 6th South African Infantry; killed in action 10 Aug. 1916, in German East Africa); Hannah and Violet.

SHEPPARD, SAMUEL GURNEY, Lieut., was born 23 March, 1865, at Walton-on-Thames, son of Samuel Gurney Sheppard, of Leggatt's, Potter's Bar, and of Mary Ann Sheppard. He was educated at Rottingdean,

Samuel G. Sheppard.

at Thorpe Mandeville, and at Eton, and afterwards travelled for a year, before going into the Stock Exchange. He served in the South African War of 1899–1901, with the Imperial Yeomanry. He took part in the several operations in the Transvaal, Orange River Colony and Cape Colony, April, 1901, to 31 May, 1902. He received the South African Medal, and was mentioned in Despatches [London Gazette, 3 Dec. 1901]: " 32nd Company, Imperial Yeomanry, Lieut. S. G. Sheppard, on 18 Sept. headed a party which swam to some islands on the Vaal River, held by armed Boers, and took them prisoners. On 19 Sept. rescued a man from drowning at great personal risk." He was created a Companion of the Distinguished Service Order [London Gazette, 26 June, 1902]: " Samuel Gurney Sheppard, Lieut., Imperial Yeomanry. In recognition of services during the operations in South Africa." (The D.S.O. was awarded for the former of the acts mentioned above.) He was invested by the King 24 Oct. 1902. He became Major in the Herts Yeomanry 20 Dec. 1905. He went to Egypt as Second-in-Command of the Hertfordshire Yeomanry 10 Sept. 1914; was promoted Temporary Lieutenant-Colonel in Jan. 1915; left for Gallipoli 14 Aug. 1915, and was killed in action in the advance on Chocolate Hill 21 Aug. 1915. The following is an extract from a letter written by a sergeant in the Hertfordshire Yeomanry: " Among the first to fall was our gallant leader, Lieut.-Colonel S. G. Sheppard. He was bravely marching at the head of the regiment, when he was terribly wounded by shrapnel, but as his men reached him he very gallantly sat up to urge them on. His last command : ' Go on, the Herts! Go on, the Herts ! ' will be remembered by all ranks for all time to come." He had married, 27 June, 1906, at Hayes, Kent, Eileen Mary Winchester, daughter of Winchester and Ellie Clowes, of Hitchin, Herts, and their children are : Kathleen Penelope; Daniel Gurney, born 21 Dec. 1908; Ellie Dorothea and Graham Hugh, born 3 April, 1913.

HUTH, PERCIVAL CUTHBERT, Second Lieut., was born 22 Feb. 1879, son of the late Percival Huth, of Freshford Manor, near Bath, and Marion, daughter of the Rev. — Dodd. He was educated at Malvern College, and at Oxford Military College, Cowley. He entered the Militia 3 May, 1900, and saw active service in the Ashanti Campaign of 1900, receiving the Medal. He served in the South African War, 1901–2, employed with Mounted Infantry (severely wounded); took part in the operations in the Transvaal, July, 1901; in Orange River Colony, May to June, 1901; July, 1901, to Jan. 1902, and Feb. 1902; also in Cape Colony, Jan. 1902 (Despatches [London Gazette, 25 April, 1902]; Queen's Medal with five clasps). He was commissioned Second Lieutenant in the Shropshire Light Infantry 23 April, 1902, and was created a Companion of the Distinguished Service Order [London Gazette, 26 June, 1902]: " Percival Cuthbert Huth, Second Lieut., Shropshire Light Infantry. In recognition of services during the operations in South Africa." The following is an official account of the services for which the D.S.O. was awarded : " Gallant defence of a position against heavy odds on one occasion ; carrying a wounded man back under a heavy and accurate fire on another occasion." The Insignia, Warrant and Statutes were sent to the Commander-in-Chief, India, 12 June, 1903; presented at Khaniket 21 July, 1903. He was promoted Lieutenant 1 Nov. 1906; Captain 6 Oct. 1914. He served in the European War, 1914–18; was given the Brevet of Major 18 Feb. 1915; was Brigade Major, 16th Reserve Infantry Brigade; 11th Reserve Infantry Brigade, 4 March to 6 Sept. 1915; Temporary Major, 6th Battn. Royal Warwickshire Regt., 14 April, 1916, to 2 July, 1917; became Major 23 April, 1917. He was twice wounded, and was mentioned in Despatches. He married, 27 June, 1912, at Ballynatray, Youghal, County Cork, Helena Anna Mary More, daughter of Colonel John Harry Graham Holroyd Smith, C.M.G., and Lady Harriet Holroyd Smith, daughter of the 5th Earl of Mount Cashell. They have one son, Percival Henry, born 5 Nov. 1915.

PATTERSON, NORMAN, Second Lieut., was born 17 April, 1879, at Long Benton, Northumberland, son of the Rev. Sutton Patterson, M.A., of Jesus College, Cambridge, Vicar of Madeley, Crewe. He was educated at

Norman Patterson.

Cambridge (Jesus College). He won two Scholarships at Cambridge, one at King's College, and the other at Jesus College, for Classics, the latter of which he accepted, and received his commission as an University Candidate. He won many prizes for athletics at Cambridge, and distinguished himself in Association Football. He was a great sportsman and shot much big game in India. He joined the Royal Horse Artillery, as a Second Lieutenant, 21 May, 1900. He served in the South African War, 1899–1900, under Lord Methuen. His military services were several times mentioned, and he was the youngest officer of his rank to receive the D.S.O. after the War. He took part in operations in the Transvaal and Cape Colony, July, 1901, to 31 May, 1902. He was mentioned in Despatches [London Gazette, 17 June, 1902]; received the Queen's Medal with five clasps, and was created a Companion of the Distinguished Service Order [London Gazette, 26 June, 1902]: "Norman Patterson, Second Lieut., Royal Artillery. In recognition of services during the operations in South Africa." He was invested by the King 24 Oct. 1902. He became Lieutenant 16 April, 1902. After the Boer War Lieut. Patterson served in India for several years. He passed the highest examinations for the Staff in India, and spoke Hindustani fluently. He was for some time Instructor in Signalling. Lieut. Patterson died at Bareilly, India, 2 May, 1909, from the effects of injuries caused by an accident to his horse.

WELCHMAN, EDWARD THEODORE, Second Lieut., was born 21 July, 1881, and joined the Army, as a Second Lieutenant in the West Yorkshire Regt. 11 July, 1900; was promoted Lieutenant 20 March, 1902. He served in the South African War, 1901–2; was present in operations in the Transvaal, April, 1901, to 31 May, 1902. He was mentioned in Despatches [London Gazette, 17 Jan. 1902]; received the Queen's Medal with three clasps, and was created a Companion of the Distinguished Service Order [London Gazette, 26 June, 1902]: "Edward Theodore Welchman, Second Lieut., West Yorkshire Regt. In recognition of services during the operations in South Africa." The Insignia, Warrant and Statutes were sent to the G.O.C., Natal District, 15 Nov. 1902. In 1908 he served in operations in the Mohmand Country, North-West Frontier of India, for which he received the Medal and clasp. He became Captain 7 March, 1910. He served in the European War, joining his battalion in France on 2 Oct. 1914. He was wounded in action near Lille on the 20th of the same month, and died of his wounds in the Base Hospital at Boulogne 25 Oct. 1914. He was buried at Boulogne. Capt. Welchman was formerly a Member of the York and Ainsty Hunt. His favourite recreations were polo and golf.

FORBES, DAVID, Capt., was born 13 Dec. 1864, son of David Forbes, of Athole, District of Ermelo, Transvaal (late of Perthshire, Scotland), and of Mrs. Forbes. He was educated privately, and started stock farming in the Transvaal and Mining in Swaziland; was a Member of the first Swaziland Government, formed under a Charter granted by the Swazi King, Umbandini, and at one time was Acting Chairman to that body. He served in the South African War, 1899–1902; was on General Sir John Dartnell's Staff for Intelligence; on General Bullock's Staff on the Mobile Column, Transvaal and Orange River Colony; General Spens' Staff, Transvaal and Orange River Colony; commanded the Lubounto Intelligence Scouts in the Southern Transvaal (Despatches by Lord Roberts, Lord Kitchener and General Sir John Dartnell); awarded South African Medals and clasps, and was created a Companion of the Distinguished Service Order [London Gazette, 26 June, 1902]: "David Forbes, Capt., Field Intelligence Department. In recognition of services during the operations in South Africa." The Insignia, Warrant and Statutes were sent to the Colonial Office, and presented at Ermelo 15 May, 1903. Capt. Forbes later became General Manager and Director of the Swazi Coal Mines, Limited, Swaziland.

David Forbes.

SHOTT, HENRY HAMMOND, Capt., was born at Dover 13 Oct. 1877, son of the late Chevalier Nils Schjott (Chevalier, Legion of Honour), of Dover. He was educated at Dulwich College, and joined Colonel Plumer's Matabeleland Relief Force, as a trooper, 1896; served throughout the Matabele War (Medal). He spent 1897 and 1898 in Rhodesia; went home in 1899; left England again the day war was declared, and joined Bethune's Mounted Infantry 15 Nov. 1899, as a trooper. He became Lance-Corporal in Jan.; Corporal, and Sergeant, and Lieutenant, in 1900. He served in the operations in Natal, 1899; at the Relief of Ladysmith, including action at Colenso; operations of 17 to 24 Jan. 1900, and action at Spion Kop; operations of 5 to 7 Feb. 1900, and action at Vaal Kranz; and during the operations on Tugela Heights 14 to 27 Feb. 1900; in Natal, March to June, 1900, including action at Laing's Nek (6 to 9 June); in the Transvaal, east of Pretoria, July to Nov. 1900; also in Orange River Colony, May, 1902. He became Captain; was transferred to the Royal Berkshire Regt. 8 Feb. 1902; was three times mentioned in Despatches [London Gazette, 8 Feb., and 16 April, 1901, and 17 June, 1902]; received the Queen's Medal with six clasps, and the King's Medal with two clasps, and was created a Companion of the Distinguished Service Order [London Gazette, 26 June, 1902]: "Henry Hammond Shott, Capt., Bethune's Mounted Infantry. (now Second Lieutenant, Royal Berkshire Regt.). In recognition of services during the operations in South Africa." The Insignia, Warrant, etc., were sent to the G.O.C., Egypt, and presented at Cairo, by O.C., 2nd Royal Berkshire Regt. He was promoted Lieutenant 15 Feb. 1905, and was employed with the West African Frontier Force from Oct. 1904, to July, 1909, including active service in Northern Nigeria in the Kano–Hadeiga Expedition, 1906 (Despatches [London Gazette, 2 July, 1907]; Medal and clasp); and was again employed with the West African Frontier Force from July, 1910, to July, 1913. He became Captain, Royal Berkshire Regt., 1911. He served in the European War. A sergeant of his battalion thus described the fight at Mons: "Capt. Shott. D.S.O., of our regiment, was, I think, the bravest man I ever met. On 23 Aug., when we were near and were lying in our trenches with shell fire constantly around us, he walked out into the open, and, with his cheery words, gave us good heart. He was puffing a cigarette, and he said: 'Lads, we will smoke!' He was an officer and a gentleman in every sense of the word, and when he was killed two days later it was a great blow to us." This incident was mentioned by a French writer (R. P.) in "Le Temps" of the 15th Sept. 1914, as an instance of "le sang froid britannique." Capt. Shott was reported in a War Office Communiqué of 19 Sept. 1914, as "believed to have been killed," and his name appeared in the monthly casualty list published in Oct. 1914, under the heading of "Casualties believed to have occurred" as "believed to have been killed in action," no place or date being mentioned. It was later ascertained that he was killed on the 25th Aug. 1914. After the conclusion of the War it was established that he was buried at Maroilles by French civilians. He had married at St. Mary Abbots, Kensington, 16 June, 1914, Hazel Morris Brown, of Yonkers, New York.

Henry Hammond Shott.

ROSS, H. F. C., Lieut., joined the Queen's Own Corps of Guides, Indian Army, and served in the South African War, 1900–1. He was mentioned in Despatches, and was created a Companion of the Distinguished Service Order [London Gazette, 26 June, 1902]: "H. F. C. Ross, Lieut., Corps of Guides. In recognition of services during the operations in South Africa." The Insignia, Warrant and Statutes were sent from the Colonial Office to Mrs. Ross, 3 March, 1904.

MAXWELL, DAVID LOCKHART, Capt., was born 16 Oct. 1872, son of Surgeon-Major Thomas Maxwell, of The Grange, Guildford. He served in the South African War, 1899–1902. He was mentioned in Despatches: received the Queen's Medal with five clasps; the King's Medal with two clasps, and was created a Companion of the Distinguished Service Order [London Gazette, 26 June, 1902]: "David Lockhart Maxwell, Capt., Imperial Light Horse. In recognition of services during the operations in South Africa." He was invested by H.R.H. the Prince of Wales, 1 July, 1902, on Horse Guards' Parade. He became Major, 3rd Scottish Horse, in 1914. Major Maxwell served in the European War, in the Dardanelles, 1915, and was mentioned in Despatches. He retired as Lieutenant-Colonel from the Scottish Horse Yeomanry. He married (1st), in 1905, Annie (died 1907), daughter of John Burns; (2ndly), in 1914, Alice, eldest daughter of James Kennedy, of Doonholm, Ayrshire, and they have one son.

MATHIAS, GEORGE MONTAGUE, Lieut., was born in Nov. 1865, son of the late George Mathias. He served in Matabeleland in 1896 (Despatches; Medal), and in the South African War of 1899–1902. He was twice mentioned in Despatches for his services in the Boer War; received the Medal with four clasps, and was created a Companion of the Distinguished Service Order [London Gazette, 26 June, 1902]: "G. Matthias, Lieut., Imperial Light Horse. In recognition of services during the operations in South Africa." The Insignia, Warrant and Statutes were sent to the Colonial Office, and presented at Johannesburg 7 June, 1903. He married, in 1895, Elsie, daughter of the Hon. P. Norton.

NICOL, ANDREW GEDDES BAIN, Capt., was born in the district of Albany, Cape Colony, in 1878, son of William Nicol, of Fife, Scotland, and A. S. Bain. He was educated at a County School in the district of Albany; was a Stock Farmer up to the age of 21; mining and managing electrical plant at Barberton. At the outbreak of the Transvaal War he joined Bethune's Mounted Infantry at Maritzburg as a Trooper; fought throughout Colenso, then in all fights up to the Relief of Ladysmith; then with Buller into the Transvaal; back to Vryheid. He served through Capt. Goff's disaster, and was one of the few who escaped. He was promoted Sergeant for this. He entered the Johannesburg Mounted Rifles as Lieutenant under Bruce Hamilton and Colonel Stewart; served with Hamilton's Column, and assisted in the capture of Cherry Emmett; captured the notorious Boer Goetser, Landrost of New Amsterdam, Transvaal; was awarded the D.S.O. for the latter. He was created a Companion of the Distinguished Service Order [London Gazette, 26 June, 1902]: "Andrew Geddes Bain Nicol, Capt., Johannesburg Mounted Rifles. In recognition of services during the operations in South Africa." Capt. Nicol recruited for the Johannesburg Mounted Rifles, and organized the Volunteer Movement in Johannesburg. He is a good game shot and rider.

WILSON, ALFRED ERNEST, Lieut.-Colonel, served in South Africa, 1900–2, with Kitchener's Fighting Scouts; was mentioned in Despatches; received the Queen's Medal with four clasps; the King's Medal with two clasps, and was created a Companion of the Distinguished Service Order [London Gazette, 26 June, 1902]: "Alfred Ernest Wilson, Lieut.-Colonel, Kitchener's Fighting Scouts. In recognition of services during the operations in South Africa." The Insignia, etc., were sent to the G.O.C., South Africa, and presented by Lord Milner 21 March, 1904.

MOSSOP, JOSEPH UPJOHN, Capt., was born at Greytown, Natal, 27 April, 1872, son of an Englishman who came to Natal in 1840. He was educated by a private tutor in Greytown, and was a burgher of the Transvaal and Despatch Rider to Generals C. L. Botha and Smuts during the early part of the war. He surrendered to General Buller, 1900; was caught and imprisoned by Boers; escaped and became guide to Generals Dartnell and Buller. He was made Intelligence Officer in Colonel Stewart's Column of Johannesburg Mounted Rifles; joined General Hamilton's Column; assisted in the capture of General C. E. Emmett. He was created a Companion of the Distinguished Service Order [London Gazette, 26 June, 1902]: "Joseph Mossop, Capt., Johannesburg Mounted Rifles. In recognition of services during the operations in South Africa." Capt. Mossop is a Farmer. He married, in 1904, Clarissa, daughter of Henry M. Meek, of Wakkerstroom District, Natal.

SILBURN, PERCY ARTHUR BAXTER, Capt., was born 10 May, 1876 son of A. Silburn, of Durban, Natal. He was educated privately, and joined the Cape Mounted Rifles in 1891; was present at the annexation of Pondoland, 1893; passed the School of Gunnery, 1898; returned to South Africa on the outbreak of the Boer War, and served with Gough's composite regiment in the Relief of Ladysmith. He served as Staff Officer to Generals Sir John Dartnell and General Hamilton in the Transvaal and Orange River Colony. For his services in this campaign he received the Queen's and King's Medals with seven clasps; was mentioned in Despatches, and created a Companion of the Distinguished Service Order [London Gazette, 26 June, 1902]: "Percy Arthur Baxter Silburn, Capt., Natal Volunteers. In recognition of services during the operations in South Africa." The Insignia, etc., were sent to the Commander-in-Chief, Natal District, South Africa, and presented by the Governor of Natal at Durban 19 March, 1903. He was Secretary of the Natal Defence Commission in 1903, and retired in 1904. Major Silburn was Chief Leader of the Militia Reserves in 1905. He was M.L.A. for Alfred County, Natal, from 1906 to 1909, and was Staff Officer and Gunnery Instructor, Colonial Forces, Natal. He has been Member for Durban in the first Union Parliament of South Africa since 1910. He has written "The Colonies and Imperial Defence," "The Governance of Empire" (1910), "The Evolution of Sea-Power" (1912). Major Silburn is a Fellow of the Royal Geographical Society, and was made a C.B.E. in 1918. He married, in 1901, Marie Antoinette, daughter of the late J. T. Riley Hartley, of Maritzburg, Natal, and they have three sons and one daughter.

LESLIE, G., Capt., served in South Africa, 1900, as Medical Officer to Roberts's Horse. He was created a Companion of the Distinguished Service Order [London Gazette, 26 June, 1902]: "G. Leslie, Medical Officer, Capt., Roberts's Horse. In recognition of services during the operations in South Africa." The Insignia, Warrant, etc., were sent to the Colonial Office, and presented privately 30 Nov. 1903.

MONTGOMERY, FRANCIS CHAMLEY, Lieut., was born 25 June, 1855, at Carnaveagh, Parish of Aughnamullen, County Monaghan, Ireland, son of Arthur Henry Montgomery, Esq., of Carnaveagh, County Monaghan Ireland, and Henrietta Francis Chamley, daughter of the Rev. Francis Chamley, Rector of Wicklow, Ireland. He was educated at Dr. Carrick's, Spring Hill, Southampton; joined the Transvaal Horse, and served as Sergeant-Major, and Lieutenant in the Transvaal Horse in 1881, in the Basuto War, under Commander Ferriera. He joined the Army in 1882, and served as a Trooper in the Life Guards through the Egyptian Campaign of 1882; was present at Kassassin and Tel-el-Kebir (Egyptian Medal, 1882, with one Bar for Tel-el-Kebir) (Khedive's Medal with Star, one Bar, 1882). He served as Sergeant-Major and Lieutenant with Roberts's Horse in the Boer War, South Africa, 1900. He was wounded 17 March, 1901, and died the following day at Lichtenberg. He would have received the Queen's Medal with six Bars (for Wittebergen, Diamond Hill, Johannesburg, Dreifontein, Paardeberg and the Relief of Kimberley). He was mentioned in Despatches, and created a Companion of the Distinguished Service Order [London Gazette, 26 June, 1902]: "Francis Chamley Montgomery, Lieut., late Sergt.-Major, Roberts's Horse (deceased). In recognition of services during the operations in South Africa."

Francis C. Montgomery.

MACKENZIE, IAN RUSSELL, Capt., served in the South African War, 1901–2. He was severely wounded; was mentioned in Despatches; received the King's Medal with two clasps, and was created a Companion of the Distinguished Service Order [London Gazette, 26 June, 1902]: "Ian Russell Mackenzie, Capt., Scottish Horse. In recognition of services during the operations in South Africa." He was invested by the King 18 Dec. 1902. He also served in Northern Nigeria in 1906.

STEINAECKER, BARON, FRANCIS CHRISTIAN LUDWIG, Major, was born in Berlin 28 Sept. 1854, son of Francis L. Baron von Steinaecker, Colonel, German Guards, and the Baroness von Steinaecker, (*née* Baroness von Thumen). He was educated in the Royal Cadet Corps at Waklstatt and Berlin, and entered the German Army (Leib Grenadiers) in the early seventies. He resigned his commission in 1879, and went to Bulgaria with Prince Alexander of Battenberg. During the Bulgarian Revolution of 1880 he had a command at Plevna, and he resigned about 1885. He led the expedition into the interior of German South-West Africa; returned in 1888, and came out to Pondoland in 1889. He settled in Natal in 1890; was President of the Political Association of this district; joined the British Forces (Colonial Scouts) on the outbreak of the South African War, 1899–1902, on 1 Nov. 1899, as a Trooper. He left Maritzburg at the beginning of March, 1900, to break, with a small patrol, the enemy's communication on the Delagoa Line; rode through Natal, Zululand, Tongaland and Swaziland; lost all his horses; smashed Malalene Bridge on the Delagoa Line on the 17th June, 1900, and took the Commandant of that line—Van Dam—prisoner. He recruited some British refugees from Portuguese territory, and, by activity of movement, drew considerable numbers of the enemy from the real theatre of war (Dalmanutha). In order to protect the railway between Campmunden and the border, he raised Steinaecker's Horse, in the enemy's country, without base to draw from, without transport or provisions. He landed stores and men at Koxi Bay from H.M. Gunboat (Capt. Gurney); was given command by Lord Kitchener of the Border and adjacent lowland country (Swaziland north to Letruba River). He received the Queen's Medal with four Bars, and the King's Medal with two; was mentioned in Despatches, and given the British decoration of the Distinguished Service Order [London Gazette, 26 June, 1902]: "Francis Christian Ludwig Steinaecker, Major, Steinaecker's Horse. In recognition of services during the operations in South Africa." The Insignia were presented publicly by General Lyttelton. Baron von Steinaecker was sent to Netley in April, 1902. He attended the Coronation of King Edward at the head of a contingent of his own regiment (Steinaecker's Horse) by direct orders from Lord Roberts, but could never get the Coronation Medal (in spite of official document in hand). He was pronounced medically unfit for further service by Medical Board, London, in July, 1902; "received honorary rank of Lieutenant-Colonel," he remarks, "probably *in lieu of pension*. Now destitute after . . . years of the most ghastly climate South Africa can produce." Baron von Steinaecker married, in 1881, the daughter of Geheimer Ober-Regierungs Rath Kegler, of Berlin.

Sir A Conan Doyle tells us in "The Great Boer War," in the chapter on "The Advance to Komatipoort," how "Colonel Steinaecker, an ex-officer of the German Imperial Army, with an irregular force of 600 men, had been operating upon the Boer line of communications in the same way as De Wet had on the British, though their operations were necessarily on a smaller scale. The whole romantic adventures of this small force, which passed through Zululand and Tongaland, and eventually made its way into Swaziland, after several times cutting the Boer railway and blowing up Malalene Bridge, are among the most curious and interesting incidents of the campaign. They captured the Boer officer in charge of the line of communication, and they gave work from first to last to a couple of thousand of the enemy, who had to guard the line from their constant descents. Some separate book will no doubt give a full account of the adventures of Steinaecker's Horse." Elsewhere, in describing how a small body of the South African Constabulary were outnumbered by the Boers, Sir A. Conan Doyle says: "Another small reverse occurred at a far distant point of the seat of war, for the irregular corps known as Steinaecker's Horse was driven from its position at Bremersdorp in Swaziland upon 24 July, and had to fall back sixteen miles, with a loss of ten casualties and thirty prisoners." Sir A. Conan Doyle also says: "After the conclusion of Blood's movement in July, several of his columns continued to clear the country, and to harass Viljeon in the Lydenburg and Dulstroom districts. Park, Kitchener, Spens, Beatson and Benson were all busy at this work, never succeeding in forcing more than a skirmish, but continually whittling away wagons, horses and men from that nucleus of resistance which the Boer leaders still held together. Though much hampered by the want of forage for their horses, the Boers were ever watchful for an opportunity to strike back, and the long list of minor successes gained by the British was occasionally interrupted by a petty reverse. Such a one befell the small body of South African Constabulary stationed near Vereeniging, who encountered, upon July 13, a strong force of Boers supposed to be the main commando of De Wet. The Constabulary behaved with great gallantry, but were hopelessly outnumbered, and lost their seven-pounder gun, four killed, six wounded and twenty-four prisoners . . . Thus in the heart of a native state the two great white races of South Africa were to be seen locked in a desperate conflict. However unavoidable, the sight was certainly one to be deplored."

DALLIMORE, P. JOSEPH, Capt., was born 24 March, 1871, son of Peter Dallimore. He served in the South African War of 1899–1902; was mentioned in Despatches, and created a Companion of the Distinguished Service Order [London Gazette, 26 June, 1902]: "Joseph Dallimore, Capt., 5th Victorian Mounted Rifles. In recognition of services during the operations in South Africa." The Insignia, Warrant, etc., were sent to the Colonial Office 10 Dec. 1902. He married, in 1899, Beatrice Mary, daughter of G. A. Wiggs.

PERCIVAL, HAROLD FRANZ PASSAWER, Lieut., was born in London 12 Feb. 1876, son of E. P. Percival, LL.D., and of Mrs. Percival. He was educated at Christ Church, Oxford, and became Second Lieutenant, in the Derbyshire Regt., 4 May, 1898, and Lieutenant 25 Feb. 1900. On 5 May, 1901, he was transferred as Second Lieutenant to the Army Service Corps, in which he became Lieutenant 1 May, 1901. Lieut. Percival took part in the South African War, with the Mounted Infantry, 1899 to 1902, and was present at operations in the Orange Free State, Feb. to May, 1900; operations in the Transvaal, east of Pretoria, July to 29 Nov. 1900, including the action at Belfast (26 and 27 Aug.); operations in Cape Colony, south of Orange River, 1899 to 1900; operations in the Transvaal 30 Nov. 1900, to 31 May, 1902. He was mentioned in Despatches [London Gazette, 17 June, 1902]; received the Queen's Medal with three clasps; the King's Medal with two clasps, and was created a Companion of the Distinguished Service Order [London Gazette, 26 June, 1902]: "Harold Franz Passawer Percival, Lieut., Army Service Corps. In recognition of services during the operations in South Africa." The Insignia were presented by the King 18 Dec. 1902. He became Captain, Army Service Corps, 18 Feb. 1904; was Staff Captain at the War Office 1 Jan. 1910, to 30 Sept. 1912, and D.A.Q.M.G., Staff College, 1 Oct. 1912, to 4 Aug. 1914. He became Major 7 Oct. 1914. He served in the European War, as D.A.Q.M.G., G.H.Q., British Expeditionary Force, 5 Aug. 1914, to 5 April, 1915; was Temporary Lieutenant-Colonel from 6 April, 1915, to 11 Dec. 1917, while holding the appointment of Assistant Director of Supplies at the War Office; Deputy Director of Supplies, War Office, 12 Dec. 1917, to 8 April, 1919. He was given his Brevet Lieutenant-Colonelcy 3 June, 1918. Lieut.-Colonel Percival was appointed 9 April, 1919, A.Q.M.G. in a Special Mission in connection with Russian prisoners of war in Germany. He was mentioned twice in Despatches; created a C.M.G. in 1917; has the 1914 Star, and was created an Officer of the Legion of Honour. He married, in 1904, Constance Lilian, daughter of J. Meyrick, and they have two daughters.

London Gazette, 2 Sept. 1902.—"War Office, 2 Sept. 1902. The King has been graciously pleased to give orders for the following appointments to the Distinguished Service Order, in recognition of the services of the undermentioned Officers during the Mahsud-Waziri operations and the capture of Nodiz Fort in Mekran, respectively."

MALCOLM, PULTENEY, Major, was born 16 Aug. 1861, son of the late General Sir George Malcolm, G.C.B., Bombay Army. He was educated at Summerfields, near Oxford; Burney's at Gosport; Wellington College and Sandhurst. He entered the Army 11 Aug. 1880, and joined the 2nd Battn. Royal Fusiliers, at Candahar, Afghanistan; was promoted Lieutenant 1 July, 1881. In 1886 he was transferred to the Indian Army, and was posted to the 2nd Battn. 4th Goorkhas then being raised. He received in 1887 the Albert Medal for attempting to save life on land. He served in the Chin Lushai Expeditionary Force, 1889–90 (Medal with clasp); was promoted Captain 11 Aug. 1891, and served with the Chitral Relief Force, 1895, being present at the storming of the Malakand Pass (Medal with clasp); in the North-West Frontier operations, 1897–98, as Provost-Marshal to the Relief Force, and subsequently as D.A.A.G., 1st Brigade, for which he was mentioned in Despatches

Pulteney Malcolm.

[London Gazette, 11 Feb. 1898] (clasp). He became Major 11 Aug. 1900; served as Chief Staff Officer, Malakand Field Force, 1900–1. He served in Waziristan, 1901–2, as Officiating A.A.G., Derajat District, and Chief Staff Officer to General Sir L. Dening, K.C.B., then in command of the district and of the operations in Waziristan. He was mentioned in Despatches twice; received a clasp to the Medal, and was created a Companion of the Distinguished Service Order [London Gazette, 2 Sept. 1902]: "Pulteney Malcolm, Major, Indian Staff Corps. In recognition of services during the Mahsud-Waziri operations." He was invested by King Edward VII. 18 Feb. 1903. Major Malcolm retired from the Indian Army 11 Aug. 1904. He was Head Constable of Kingston-on-Hull from 1904 to 1910. and has been Chief Constable of Cheshire since 1910. He was created an M.V.O. in 1913, and became Temporary Colonel during the European War, while employed as A.A. and Q.M.G. on the Divisional Staff of the New Armies (mentioned in Despatches). He was given the honorary rank of Lieutenant-Colonel 29 May, 1917. Lieut.-Colonel Malcolm married, in 1888, Emily, eldest daughter of T. R. Bowen. The only surviving child of the union—Capt. Pulteney Malcolm, who commanded the King's Company, Grenadier Guards—was killed in France on 25 Aug. 1918. He was a Scholar at Eton, and went up to Oxford with an Exhibition.

KIRKPATRICK, WILLIAM, Major, was born 2 Feb. 1863, at Bangalore, India, son of the late Deputy Surgeon-General James Kirkpatrick, and of Margaret Jane Proctor, daughter of Capt. William Proctor, late 21st Dragoons (now Lancers). He was educated at Blairlogie, Stirlingshire, and joined the Army 25 Aug. 1883. After becoming Lieutenant he served in the Burmese Expedition, 1885–87 (Medal and clasp; Despatches), and in the 1st Miranzai Expedition, 1891; with the Kurram Force, 1892–93. He became Captain 25 Aug. 1894, and served on the North-West Frontier of India, 1897–98, in Tochi; with the Gumatti Expedition, 1899 (Medal with clasp). He was promoted Major 25 Aug. 1901. Major W. Kirkpatrick took part in the Mahsud-Waziri operations in 1901 and 1902. He was mentioned in De-

William Kirkpatrick.

spatches [London Gazette, 8 Aug. 1902]: received the clasp, and was created a Companion of the Distinguished Service Order [London Gazette, 2 Sept. 1902]: "William Kirkpatrick, Major. Indian Staff Corps. For services during the Mahsud-Waziri operations." The D.S.O. was awarded for personal gallantry during a rearguard action. The Insignia, Warrant, etc., were sent to His Excellency the Commander-in-Chief, and presented at Delhi 27 Dec. 1902. He retired from the Indian Army with the rank of Major 1 Jan. 1905. Major Kirkpatrick married, in 1906, Lilias Elizabeth, daughter of Capt. Robert Stewart, D.L., of Westwood, Linlithgowshire.

SWANSTON, CHARLES OLIVER, Capt., was born at Cuddalore, Southern India, 8 April, 1865, elder son of the late Major-General William Oliver Swanston, Madras Staff Corps, who served as a Trooper in Havelock's Volunteer Cavalry in the Indian Mutiny. His grandfather was the late Capt. Charles (" Corygorm ") Swanston, who raised one thousand men for the Poona Auxiliary Horse; and he was great-grandnephew of Horatio Lord Nelson, his mother being a granddaughter of Mrs. Kitty Matcham. He was educated privately and at the Royal Military College, Sandhurst, and was gazetted to the Royal Irish Fusiliers, May, 1885. He was promoted to Lieutenant in 1887, and transferred to the 18th Bengal Lancers, Indian Army, in 1888. In 1896 and 1897 he was A.D.C. to Sir George White, Commander-in-Chief in India; was D.A.Q.M.G., Headquarters Staff of Tirah Expedition, 1897–98 (Despatches [London Gazette, 5 April, 1898]; Medal with two clasps).

Charles Oliver Swanston.

He was D.A.Q.M.G., Khyber Field Force, 1898–99; D.A.Q.M.G., Punjab Frontier Force, 1900–3; D.A.Q.M.G., Mahsud-Waziri operations, 1901–2. For his services in Waziristan he was mentioned in Despatches [London Gazette, 8 Aug. 1902], and was created a Companion of the Distinguished Service Order [London Gazette, 2 Sept. 1902]: "Charles Oliver Swanston, Capt., Indian Staff Corps. For services during the Mahsud-Waziri operations." In 1902 he took part in the operations against the Darwesh Khel Waziris, acting as Staff Officer to the General Officer Commanding, and was again mentioned in Despatches [London Gazette, 5 June, 1903]. He was on Headquarters Staff as D.A.Q.M.G. in the Somaliland Campaign of 1903–4, for which he received the Medal with two clasps, and was mentioned in Despatches [London Gazette, 2 Sept. 1904]. In 1905 Capt. Swanston passed the final examination of the Staff College, and in 1906 was promoted Major. In 1910 he was placed on the list of officers considered qualified for Staff employment for services in the field. In 1910 he became G.S.O., 2nd Grade, and in May, 1911, he reached the rank of Lieutenant-Colonel, being appointed Second-in-Command of the 34th Prince Albert Victor's Own Poona Horse from the Bengal Lancers in 1910, and, while serving on the General Staff, succeeded to the command of his regiment in the same year. Lieut.-Colonel Swanston was killed on the 2nd Nov. 1914, near Neuve Chapelle, while at the head of his regiment, which had been ordered up to the support of some of our trenches. He was a fine horseman, and won many flat races in India. Lieut.-Colonel Swanston married, 18 Jan. 1898, Miss Kathleen Bruce Johnston, daughter of the late R. Bruce Johnston, Esq., Writer to the Signet, of Edinburgh. His wife, however, predeceased him, and he left no family. His sister, Miss C. Olivia Swanston, writes: "I do not know if it is generally known that my brother's name was mentioned to serve on the Defence Committee by Lord Roberts in or about 1905 or 1906, but though he was not elected, as being younger and with less service qualifications than the officer who was chosen, it was a great source of gratification to my brother at the time."

McBARNET, ALEXANDER EDWARD, Capt., was born in Edinburgh 30 Sept. 1865, son of the late Capt. D. H. McBarnet, Cameron Highlanders. He became Second Lieutenant, in the Border Regt., 3 July, 1889, and became Lieutenant, Indian Staff Corps, 24 Aug. 1890. He served in the Manipur Expedition, 1891 (Medal with clasp). He became Captain 3 July, 1900, and took part in the Mahsud-Waziri operations, 1901–2. For his services he was mentioned in Despatches [London Gazette, 8 Aug. 1902]; received the Medal with clasp, and was created a Companion of the Distinguished Service Order [London Gazette, 2 Sept. 1902]: "Alexander Edward McBarnet, Capt., Indian Staff Corps. For services during the Mahsud-Waziri operations." He was invested by the King 24 Oct. 1902. He was created an M.V.O., 1904; was employed with the Egyptian Army 28 Dec. 1904, to 31 Oct. 1907, and became Major 3 July, 1907. He retired from the Indian Army 11 Oct. 1913. He served in the European War, in Gallipoli, 1915 (Mentioned in Despatches), as Lieutenant-Colonel, Scottish Horse, with the Egyptian Expeditionary Force, 1916, and in the Balkans, 1916–17. Lieut.-Colonel McBarnet married, in 1912, Ida Florence, daughter of the late Henry Sharman-Crawford, of Dublin.

COX, WALTER HULBERT, Capt., was born 9 Jan. 1875. He joined the Indian Medical Service 28 Jan. 1898, in which he became Captain 28 Jan. 1901. He served in the China Campaign, 1900–1 (Medal), and on the North-West Frontier of India, 1901–2, in the Mahsud-Waziristan Expedition, for which he was mentioned in Despatches [London Gazette, 8 Aug. 1902]; received the Medal with clasp, and was created a Companion of the Distinguished Service Order [London Gazette, 2 Sept. 1902]: "Walter Hulbert Cox, Capt., Indian Medical Service. For services during the Mahsud-Waziri operations." The Insignia, Warrant and Statutes were sent to His Excellency the Commander-in-Chief in India 30 Oct. 1902; presented in Turkish Arabia (Baghdad). He was promoted Major 28 Jan. 1910, and later held the position of Superintendent of the Burma Lunatic Asylum. Major Cox is an L.R.C.P. and L.R.C.S. Edinburgh; L.F.P.S. Glasgow, and holds the Medico-Psychological Certificate.

SHEPPARD, SEYMOUR HULBERT, Capt., was born 24 Dec. 1869, eldest surviving son of G. F. Sheppard, Esq., J.P. (retired I.C.S.), and Adeline Babington Sheppard. He was educated at Haileybury College, and the Royal Military Academy, Woolwich (Senior Under Officer, 1889, and Sword of Honour); joined the Royal Engineers, as Second Lieutenant, 14 Feb. 1890, and became Lieutenant 14 Feb. 1893. He served in the Waziristan Expedition, 1894–95 (Medal with clasp); on the North-West Frontier of India, 1897–98; in operations in the Mohmand country (Despatches [London Gazette, 11 Jan. 1898]; Medal with clasp); with the Tirah Expeditionary Force, 1897–98 (Despatches [London Gazette, 7 June, 1898]; clasp). He was promoted Captain 31 Dec. 1900, and served in the Mahsud-Waziri operations, 1902; as Staff Officer to a column, for which he was mentioned in Despatches [London Gazette, 8 Aug. 1902]; received

Seymour H. Sheppard.

a clasp, and was created a Companion of the Distinguished Service Order [London Gazette, 2 Sept. 1902]: "Seymour Hulbert Sheppard, Capt., Royal Engineers. For services during the Mahsud-Waziri operations." Capt. Sheppard served in the operations against the Kabul Khels, 1902, and in Tibet, 1903–4, being present in the action at Niani; the operations at and around Gyantse, and the march to Lhassa. He was mentioned in Despatches [London Gazette, 13 Dec. 1904]; received the Brevet of Major 10 Nov. 1904, and the Medal with clasp. In 1903 and 1906 he won the Army Rackets Single Championship, and in 1906 the Amateur Rackets Singles Championship. He passed the Staff College in 1907, and was D.A.A.G., Rawalpindi Division, India, then G.S.O., 2nd Grade, 9 July, 1908, to 9 July, 1912 ; was promoted Major 14 Feb. 1912 ; was G.S.O.., 2nd Grade, Staff College, Quetta, 21 Jan. 1913, to 15 Sept. 1914, becoming Brevet Lieutenant-Colonel 10 May, 1913. Brevet Lieut.-Colonel Sheppard served in the European War from 15 Sept, 1914 ; was with the East African Expeditionary Force from Oct. 1914, to Jan. 1916, as G.S.O.1 ; given the Brevet of Colonel 24 Aug. 1915, for distinguished service in the Field ; was Brigadier-General commanding 1st East African Brigade, Feb. 1916, to Feb. 1917 ; Brigadier-General, General Staff, East African Force, from Jan. 1917, to Dec. 1918 ; was promoted Colonel 18 March, 1918. He was four times mentioned in Despatches ; received the C.M.G. 1 Feb. 1917, and the C.B. 1 Jan. 1918, and was made a Major-General 1 Jan. 1919 ; commands No. 1 Division, Peshawar.

McVEAN, DONALD ARCHIBALD DUGALD, Capt., was born 22 July, 1870, and entered the Army as a Second Lieutenant in the Liverpool Regt 7 Nov. 1891. He was transferred to the Manchester Regt. 17 May, 1893, and became Lieutenant, Indian Staff Corps, 18 Feb. 1896. He served on the North-West Frontier of India, 1897–98, in the Malakand and Utman Khel operations (Medal with clasp). He was promoted to Captain in the Indian Army 10 July, 1901, and served in the campaign in Waziristan, 1901–2, in which he was severely wounded. For his services he was mentioned in Despatches [London Gazette, 8 Aug. 1902]; received the clasp, and was created a Companion of the Distinguished Service Order [London Gazette, 2 Sept. 1902]: " Donald Archibald Dugald McVean, Capt., Indian Staff Corps. For services during the Mahsud-Waziri operations." He was invested by the King 24 Oct. 1902. Capt. McVean took part in 1908 in the operations against the Zakka-Khels and in the Mohmand country, as Orderly Officer, Second Brigade (Medal with clasp) ; became Major 7 Nov. 1909. He became General Staff Officer, 2nd Grade, Derajat Brigade, in 1913, and held this position during the European War. He was promoted Lieutenant-Colonel 29 July, 1917. Lieut.-Colonel McVean is married.

ALEXANDER, EDWARD CURRIE, Lieut., was born 15 Sept. 1875, son of N. S. Alexander, late I.C.S., and of Mrs. Alexander. He was educated at Clifton College. He joined the Army 28 Sept. 1895, with a commission in the 1st Battn. Dorset Regt., and served on the North-West Frontier of India, 1897 (Medal with two clasps). taking part in the Tirah operations, including the actions of Chagru Kotai and Dargai and the capture of the Sampagha and Arhanga Passes ; the reconnaissance of the Saran Sar and the action of 9 Nov. 1897 ; operations in the Waran Valley and the action of 16 Nov. 1897 ; operations in the Bara Valley 7 to 14 Dec. 1897. For his services in the campaign in Waziristan of 1901–2, he was mentioned in Despatches [London Gazette, 8 Aug. 1902]; received a clasp to the Medal, and was created a Companion of the Distinguished Service Order [London Gazette, 2 Sept. 1902]; " Edward Currie Alexander, Lieut., Indian Staff Corps. For services during the capture of Nodiz Fort." The decoration was awarded for conspicuous gallantry in action on 25 Nov. 1901. The Insignia, Warrant and Statutes were sent to His Excellency the Commander-in-Chief in India 30 Oct. 1912, and sent to the O.C., 1st Punjab Infantry, Punjab Frontier Force. He was promoted Captain 28 Sept. 1904, and served in 1908 in the operations in the Mohmand country, being present at the engagement of Kargha (Medal and clasp). He was employed as Staff Captain, 1st Peshawar Division, India, 24 Jan. 1909, to 30 March, 1910 ; Brigade Major, Nowshara, India, 31 March, 1910, to 31 March, 1913 ; was promoted Major 28 Sept. 1913. He served in the European War, as Brigade Major, 30th Infantry Brigade, with the New Armies in the Mediterranean Expeditionary Force 2 Sept. 1914, to 3 Aug. 1915, as a First Grade General Staff Officer, Aden Field Force, 5 May, 1916, to 29 Oct. 1917 ; was given the Brevet of Lieutenant-Colonel 3 June, 1917. He became D.A.Q.M.G., Headquarters, Lines of Communication, Mesopotamian Expeditionary Force, 29 Oct. 1917 ; A.Q.M.G., Adv. Section, Lines of Communication, M.E.F., 12 Feb. 1918 ; became officiating D.Q.M.G., M.E.F., 1 June, 1919 ; G.S.O.1, 18th Division, 12 Dec. 1919. He was created a Companion of the Indian Empire [London Gazette, 4 March, 1919]. Lieut.-Colonel Alexander's Regiment is the 55th Coke's Rifles. In 1914 he married Isabella Katherine, daughter of the late Major G. O. Stoney, King's Own Scottish Borderers.

CORRY, JOHN BEAUMONT, Lieut., was born at Croydon 21 Aug. 1874, second son of John Corry, Esq., J.P., and Margaret Corry. He was educated at St. Paul's School, and at the Royal Military Academy, Woolwich (Pollock Medallist), and joined the Royal Engineers 27 Feb. 1894 ; became Lieutenant 27 Feb. 1897. He served on the North-West Frontier of India, 1897–98, and took part in operations on the Samara, and in the relief of Gulistan and in the Tirah Campaign, including the capture of the Sampagha and Arhanga Passes ; operations in the Waran and Bazar Valleys, and other engagements (Medal with two clasps). He again saw active service in the Mekran Expedition in 1901, including the capture of Nodiz Fort, where he was severely wounded. He was the leader of the attack, and killed the opposing leader, Mohammed Ali Khan (24 Dec. 1901). He was mentioned in Despatches ; received a clasp to the Medal, and was created a Companion of the Distinguished Service Order [London Gazette, 2 Sept. 1902]: " John Beau-

John Beaumont Corry.

mont Corry, Lieut., Royal Engineers. For services during the capture of Nodiz Fort." The Insignia, Warrant and Statutes were sent to His Excellency the Commander-in-Chief, India, and presented at Delhi 27 Dec. 1902. He was promoted Captain 1 April, 1904, and served with the 3rd Sappers and Miners until 1913. He received the Delhi Durbar Medal, and later was sent to Somaliland to strengthen the defences of Berbera. In 1912–13 he was employed in building roads and bridges in Assam ; came home on a year's leave in 1913–14, and was then appointed to Military Works, Bannu, North-West Province ; became Major, 1914. He received his orders for the front to the Great War in Aug. 1914 ; was delayed at Karachi and at the base ; rejoined the 3rd Sappers and Miners, and reached the fighting line only two days before he was killed by shell near Sailly-sur-la-Lys 4 Nov. 1914. He was a member of the Alpine Club, and climbed in Kashmir in 1911, making several new ascents.

GRANT, GEORGE PATRICK, Lieut., was born 22 Sept. 1876, and entered the Army on 5 Sept. 1896, as a Second Lieutenant in the Border Regt. He became Lieutenant 9 Oct. 1899, and was transferred to the Indian Army 27 Aug. 1901. He served in Mekran in 1901 ; in the attack and capture of Nodiz Fort. For his services on this occasion he was mentioned in Despatches [London Gazette, 8 Aug. 1902]. He was twice severely wounded, and was created a Companion of the Distinguished Service Order [London Gazette, 2 Sept. 1902]: " George Patrick Grant, Lieut., Indian Staff Corps. For services during the capture of Nodiz Fort." He was invested by the King 24 Oct. 1902. He was promoted to Captain 5 Sept. 1905 ; was Staff Captain, India, 1 Feb. to 3 June, 1910 ; G.S.O.3, Headquarters, India, 1 July, 1910, to 31 Oct. 1912 ; D.A.A. and Q.M.G., Indian Army, 1 Nov. 1912, to 31 Jan. 1914. He was promoted Major 5 Sept. 1914, and served at different periods during the European War as Acting Lieutenant-Colonel. He became a Second Grade General Staff Officer 20 Feb. 1917. His regiment is the 106th Hazara Pioneers. He married, in 1902, Gladys, only daughter of Macdonald Beaumont, Esq., of Hylands, Epsom, and they have two daughters.

London Gazette, 12 Sept. 1902.—" War Office, 12 Sept. 1902. The King has been graciously pleased to give orders for the following appointments to the Distinguished Service Order, in recognition of the services of the undermentioned Officers during operations in East and West Africa respectively."

HARMAN, GEORGE MALCOLM NIXON, Capt., was born in London 14 Nov. 1872, the eldest son of the late Lieut.-General Sir George B. Harman, K.C.B. He was educated at Marlborough, and entered the Army, as a Second Lieutenant in the Rifle Brigade, 7 Nov. 1891 ; became Lieutenant 11 Oct. 1893, and Captain 1 Jan. 1898. Capt. Harman was employed in the Uganda Protectorate and with the King's African Rifles from 19 Jan. 1900, to 9 Nov. 1904, and was on active service in Uganda in 1901 in the expedition into the Lango country. He was mentioned in Despatches 12 Sept. 1902 ; received the Medal with clasp, and was created a Companion of the Distinguished Service Order [London Gazette, 12 Sept. 1902]: " George Malcolm Nixon Harman, Capt., Rifle Brigade. For services during the operations in the Lango

George M. N. Harman.

District of Uganda." The Insignia, Warrant and Statutes were sent to the Foreign Office 23 Jan. 1903, and presented without formality about the 7th May, 1903, Latitude 1°, Longitude 31° 2', Anglo-German Boundary Commission. He served on the Anglo-German Boundary Commission, West of Victoria Nyanza, from 8 July, 1902, to 9 Nov. 1904 ; became Major 26 June, 1907. After East Africa he served in Malta and Alexandria with the 4th Battn., and, having obtained his Majority in June, 1907, he joined the 2nd Battn. in Calcutta. When war was declared the battalion was in Rawal Pindi, and was then ordered to France. Major Harman was killed by a shell at Laventie. He married, 21 Oct. 1913, at St. Mary Abbot's Church, Kensington, W., Mary, eldest daughter of Sir E. D. Jones, of Addison Road, W., and Pentower, Fishguard.

HODSON, GEORGE BENJAMIN, Major, was born 3 Oct. 1863. He entered the Army as a Lieutenant in the South Staffordshire Regt. 10 May, 1882 ; served in Egypt in 1882, including the reconnaissance of 5 Aug. 1882 (Medal ; Bronze Star) ; became Lieutenant, Oxfordshire Light Infantry, 2) Feb. 1884, and Indian Staff Corps 1 Sept. 1884. For his services in the Burmese Expedition of 1885–87, Lieut. Hodson was mentioned in Despatches [London Gazette, 2 Sept. 1887]; also receiving the Medal and clasp, and he had another clasp for Hazara in 1891. He became Captain 10 May, 1893 ; served in 1897–98 on the North-West Frontier of India—Malakand—in operations in Bajaur and the Mamund country, and Buner. He was twice mentioned in Despatches [London Gazette, 11 Jan. and 18 March, 1898, and received the Medal and clasp. He became Major 10 July, 1901, and in 1901 and 1902 again saw active service in Northern Nigeria in the Aro Expedition. He was mentioned in Despatches 12 Sept. 1902 ; received the Medal with clasp, and was created a Companion of the Distinguished Service Order [London Gazette, 12 Sept. 1902]: " George Benjamin Hodson, Major, Indian Staff Corps. For services during the Aro Expedition in Southern Nigeria." The Insignia, Warrant and Statutes were sent to the Commander-in-Chief in India 10 Jan. 1903, and presented by Major-General Sir C. Egerton at Mardan 28 Feb. 1903, at Ceremonial Parade. He was promoted Lieutenant-Colonel 13 Nov. 1905 ; was created a C.B. in 1911. Colonel G. B. Hodson was stationed for some time with his regiment, the 57th Wilde's Rifles, at Ferozepore in the Punjab. He served in the European War, and died of wounds at Malta 25 Jan. 1916. He married, in 1910, Dorothy Clara, daughter of Mr. Murray, of 42, Clanricarde Gardens, London, S.W.

HENEKER, WILLIAM CHARLES GIFFARD, Capt. and Brevet Major, was born 22 Aug. 1867, son of Richard William Heneker and of Elizabeth, daughter of Capt. E. Tuson, late of the Royal Navy. He was educated at Bishop's College School, Lennoxville, Canada, and the Royal Military College, Kingston, Canada, and entered the Army, as a Second Lieutenant in the Connaught Rangers, 5 Sept. 1888, and became Lieutenant 12 Feb. 1890; Captain 10 March, 1897. He was employed in the Niger Coast Protectorate from 19 June, 1897, to 31 Dec. 1899, and with the West African Frontier Force 1 April, 1900, to 31 July, 1903, serving in the Benin Territories Expedition as Intelligence and Survey Officer, 1899 (Despatches [London Gazette, 14 Sept. 1900]; Medal with clasp). He became Brevet Major 31 July, 1901. He served in Southern Nigeria, 1902, as Second-in-Command of the Southern Nigeria Regt., West African Frontier Force; commanded the Ulia and Ishan Expeditions, and various Columns in the Aro Expedition. He received the Medal with two clasps; was mentioned in Despatches [London Gazette, 18 April and 12 Sept. 1902], and was created a Companion of the Distinguished Service Order [London Gazette, 12 Sept. 1902]: "William Charles Giffard Heneker, Capt. and Brevet Major, Connaught Rangers. For services during the Aro Expedition in Southern Nigeria." He was invested by the King 18 Dec. 1903. He also commanded the operations in the Ibeku-Olokoro country, 1902 (clasp); the operations against the Chief Adukukaiku of Iggara (Despatches [London Gazette, 28 Oct. 1901]; Brevet of Lieutenant-Colonel 21 Aug. 1903; clasp), and the operations in the Afikpo country (clasp). He became Major 16 Feb. 1907, and was given the Brevet of Colonel 24 Oct. 1907; was D.A.A. and Q.M.G., Orange River Colony District, 21 April, 1906, to 20 April, 1910; Lieutenant-Colonel to command the 2nd Battn. North Staffordshire Regt. at Peshawar, India, 10 April, 1912; Temporary Brigade Commander, 1st Peshawar Infantry Brigade, 1912; Rawalpindi Infantry Brigade (temporary), 1913 and 1914; Commander, 1st Infantry Brigade, Quetta, Oct. 1914. He was one of the King's Aide-de-Camps from Oct. 1907, to June, 1917. He served in the European War as Temporary Brigadier-General commanding the 54th Infantry Brigade, British Expeditionary Force, 13 March to 14 Dec. 1915; was severely wounded; was promoted Colonel 10 April, 1916; commanded the 190th Infantry Brigade, Royal Naval Division, France, 29 Oct. to 8 Dec. 1916; became Major-General (substantive, 3 June, 1917), commanding the 8th British Division 9 Dec. 1916 (C.B., 1916); formed and commanded the Southern Division of the Rhine, holding a portion of the Bridgehead east of Cologne, March to Oct. 1919; commanded Independent Division, Rhine Army, Oct. 1919, to Feb. 1920; and the Rhine Garrison, Cologne, from March, 1920. He was made Commandeur of the Legion of Honour, 1918, and a K.C.B. in 1919. He is the author of "Bush Warfare," published in 1906. Major-General Sir W. C. G. Heneker married, in 1901, Clara Marion, daughter of the late E. Jones, of Velindre, Wales, and they have two sons: David William, born 31 March, 1906, and Patrick Allason Holden, born 1 Sept. 1908.

CARLETON, HUGH DUDLEY, Major, was born 24 Dec. 1865, son of the late General Henry Alexander Carleton, C.B. He joined the Army, as a Second Lieutenant, in the West India Regt., 6 March, 1889; was Garrison Adjutant, Sierra Leone, 10 April to 12 Aug. 1890; promoted Lieutenant 1 Nov. 1890; was again Garrison Adjutant, Sierra Leone, 26 Aug. 1891, to 3 Jan. 1892. He served in the Gambia Expedition in 1891-92, against the native chief, Fodey Kabba, receiving the Medal and clasp. From 18 Sept. 1893, to 17 Jan. 1894, he was A.D.C. to the Governor and Commander-in-Chief, Jamaica, and he became Garrison Adjutant, Jamaica, 7 Feb. 1895; was promoted Captain 29 July, 1896. He again saw active service, 1897-98, in Lagos, where he was employed in the Hinterland, and was mentioned in Despatches. He was promoted Major in 1901; served in 1902 in Ashanti (Provost-Marshal, Despatches; Medal with clasp for Relief of Kumasi). He received the D.S.O. for his services during the Aro Expedition in Southern Nigeria, where he served as Chief of the Staff; was mentioned in Despatches, and received the Medal and clasp. His Companionship of the Distinguished Service Order was gazetted 12 Sept. 1902: "Hugh Dudley Carleton, Major, West India Regt. In recognition of services during the Aro Expedition." He was invested by the King 24 Oct. 1902. He died 9 Aug. 1906. Major Carleton married, in 1904, Lady Jane Edith Seymour, youngest daughter of the 6th Marquess of Hertford.

GILLMAN, WEBB, Capt., was born 26 Oct. 1870, at Galle, Ceylon, youngest son of the late Herbert Webb Gillman, Esq., of Glouteadmore, Coachford, County Cork, Gentleman, and Annie Mackwood. He was educated at Dulwich, and the Royal Military Academy, Woolwich; was commissioned, Royal Field Artillery, 27 July, 1889, and became Lieutenant 27 July, 1892. He served in the South African War, 1899-1900, taking part in the advance on Kimberley; operations in the Orange Free State, Feb. to May, 1900, including operations at Paardeberg 17 to 26 Feb., and the actions at Poplar Grove and Dreifontein. He received the Queen's Medal and three clasps for the Relief of Kimberley, Paardeberg and Dreifontein. He became Captain 9 Oct. 1899; was Adjutant, Royal Horse Artillery, Aldershot, from 22 May, 1900, to 31 March, 1901; was employed in the Aro Expedition, Southern Nigeria, 30 Oct. 1901, to 10 May, 1902, as Staff Officer to various

Webb Gillman.

columns. He received the Medal and three clasps; was mentioned in Despatches 12 Sept. 1902, and for services during the Aro Expedition in Southern Nigeria was created a Companion of the Distinguished Service Order [London Gazette, 12 Sept. 1902]: "Webb Gillman, Capt., Royal Artillery." He was invested by the King 24 Oct. 1902. Capt. Gillman was promoted to Major 12 May, 1905; was G.S.O., 2nd Grade, Sierra Leone, 15 Dec. 1906, to 3 April, 1908; passed the Staff College, 1908; was A.M.S. to G.O. Commanding-in-Chief, Eastern Command, 4 April to 4 May, 1908; G.S.O., 2nd Grade, Portsmouth, 14 Aug. 1910, to 22 April, 1912. He was G.S.O., War Office, from 23 April, 1912, to 4 Aug. 1914; was given the Brevet of Lieutenant-Colonel 5 Aug. 1914, and served in the European War, first in France with the 114th Battery, 25th Brigade, R.F.A.; was G.S.O.2, G.H.Q., France, 26 Aug. 1914, to 6 Jan. 1915; was G.S.O.1, 13th Division, 11 Jan. to 9 Oct. 1915; was Temporary Brigadier-General, Royal Artillery, 9th Corps, 8 Oct. to 22 Nov. 1915; Brigadier-General, General Staff, Mediterranean Expeditionary Force, 23 Nov. 1915, to June, 1916; Special Liaison Officer, Feb. to May, 1915. He was given the Brevet of Colonel, 1916; promoted Temporary Major-General, May, 1916; Major-General, General Staff, Salonika, June, 1916, to 25 July, 1917; commanded the 17th Indian Division, July to 15 Nov. 1917; Major-General, General Staff (G.G.S.), Mesopotamia, Dec. 1917, to May, 1919. He was created a C.M.G., 1915; received the Order of St. Anne of Russia (2nd Class) with Swords, 1916; was created a C.B. in 1917; made Commandeur, Legion of Honour, 1917; received the Order of the White Eagle of Serbia (2nd Class) with Swords, 1917, and was made a Commander of the Order of St. Maurice and St. Lazarus of Italy, 1917; received the Order of the Redeemer of Greece (Higher Commander, 2nd Class), 1917, and was made a K.C.M.G. in 1919. He has been repeatedly mentioned in Despatches. Major-General Sir Webb Gillman married, at Eastbourne, 8 Feb. 1911, Caroline Grace Elizabeth, daughter of the late Charles Rube, Esq., of 17, Hill Street, London, W., and they have three children: Herbert Charles Rube, born 22 Jan. 1912; Catherine Rube, and Susan Elizabeth.

GRAHAME, JOHN CRUM, Capt., was born at Auldhouse, Renfrewshire, 2 Feb. 1870, son of James Grahame and Agnes Crum, daughter of John Crum, of Thornliebank; and great-grandson of Archibald Grahame, of Drumquhassle, Drymen, Stirlingshire. He was educated at Cargilfield, and Harrow; joined the 2nd Battn. Highland Light Infantry (from the Militia) 9 April, 1892; became Lieutenant 22 Nov. 1894. He served on the North-West Frontier of India, 1897-98, with the 2nd Battn. Highland Light Infantry, with Malakand and Buner Field Forces; in operations in Bajour and in the Mamund country; assault and capture of the Tanga Pass (India Medal and clasp "Punjab Frontier, 1897-98"). He took part in the operations in Ashanti, 1900—under Sir James Willcocks—attached to 1st Battn. West African Frontier Force, as Subaltern, and finally Captain (1 Aug. 1900), of F (Haussa) Company; was present at assault and capture of Kokofu; actions near Kumassi and Danassi, and the final defeat of the Ashantis near Obassi. He was mentioned in Despatches: "This officer did very good work" (Ashanti Medal, 1900, with clasp "Kumassi"). In the operations in Southern Nigeria, 1901-2, he was with the 3rd Battn. West African Frontier Force, as Captain, F (Yoruba) Company, and was appointed Local Major and to command a District. He was mentioned in Despatches by the Officer Commanding the Field Force: "After the capture of Aro Chuko, this officer was selected to disarm and subjugate a large extent of territory. So well was this duty carried out that I was enabled to bring hostilities to a close at least a month sooner than I anticipated, and before the rains set in." He took part in various engagements, was slightly wounded; received the African General Service Medal with clasp "Aro, 1901-2," and was appointed a Companion of the Distinguished Service Order [London Gazette, 12 Sept. 1902]: "John Crum Grahame, Capt., Highland Light Infantry. For services during the Aro Expedition in Southern Nigeria." He served with the Egyptian Army, 1903-7; attached Sudan Civil Administration, 1904-7; was promoted Major 18 Dec. 1908; commanded Detachment, 2nd Highland Light Infantry, which was on duty at the Coronation of H.M. King George V. (Coronation Medal). He commanded the Depôt of the Highland Light Infantry, 1911-12. In Aug. 1914, he was appointed to command the 10th (Service) Battn. Highland Light Infantry, which he raised, organized and trained. In May, 1915, he took this battalion to France, and served in the trenches near Festubert and Cambrai. He commanded the battalion at the Battle of Loos (severely gassed in action); was mentioned in Despatches (January, 1916), for "gallant and distinguished conduct in the field." He commanded the 10th Highland Light Infantry till 9 March, 1916, when he was invalided home; rejoined Expeditionary Force for the fourth time in Dec. 1916, and was in command in the trenches of the 10/11th Highland Light Infantry, and subsequently of the 12th Battn., and of the 9th Battn. (Glasgow Highlanders). On promotion to Substantive Lieutenant-Colonel (16 Dec. 1916), he took over command in the field of his old battalion, the 2nd Highland Light Infantry, with which he was serving when very severely wounded near Oppy during the Battle of Arras, April, 1917. Lieut.-Colonel Grahame had thus the honour of commanding in the Field Regular, Service and Territorial Units of the Highland Light Infantry. He has done a good deal of big game shooting on the Blue Nile, and has travelled considerably in Europe—Bosnia, Herzegovina, Croatia, Hungary and Galicia, and also in the Himalayas,

John Crum Grahame.

Lieut.-Colonel Grahame married, 27 July, 1905, at St. Giles Cathedral, Edinburgh, Alice Clara, younger daughter of John Purvis, of Kinaldy, Fife, and Wilhelmina, eldest daughter of William Berry, of Tayfield, Fife.

ROSE, THOMAS ALLEN, Capt., was born 17 Aug. 1874, son of Major T. C. Rose, Army Pay Department (formerly Royal Scots Fusiliers), and Augusta Decima Rose. He was educated at Shrewsbury, and entered the Army, from the Militia, as a Second Lieutenant in the Royal Scots Fusiliers, 7 Dec. 1895, in which he became Lieutenant 6 Feb. 1898. He was employed with the West African Frontier Force, Feb. 1899, to Nov. 1904; served in the Munshi Expedition, 1900, in Northern Nigeria (Medal with clasp). He was promoted Captain 16 Feb. 1901; served in Northern Nigeria, 1900–1, in the expedition against the Chief of Tawari, and in the operations against the Emir of Yola (Despatches [London Gazette, 18 April, 1902]; Medal with clasp). Capt. Rose was employed as a Staff Officer in Southern Nigeria, 1902, in the Aro Expedition. He was slightly wounded; mentioned in Despatches [London Gazette, 12 Sept. 1902], and created a Companion of the Distinguished Service Order [London Gazette, 12 Sept. 1902]: "Thomas Allen Rose, Capt., Royal Scots Fusiliers. For services during the Aro Expedition in Southern Nigeria." The Insignia, Warrant and Statutes were sent direct, 3 Jan. 1903. He served in Northern Nigeria, 1903–4, as Staff and Transport Officer in operations in the Bassa Province against the Okpotos (clasp), and was employed with the West African Frontier Force for a further period, March, 1907, to Nov. 1912; was Temporary Lieutenant-Colonel, commanding the 2nd Northern Nigerian Regt. from Nov. 1911, to Nov. 1912. He served in the European War, and was killed in action at Jemappes, near Mons, 23 Aug. 1914. He had married, in 1911, Elizabeth Mary, daughter of John Rearden, of Clonlea, Ballintemple, Cork.

Thomas Allen Rose.

MAYNE, CHARLES ROBERT GRAHAM, Capt., was born 10 Sept. 1874, in Edinburgh, son of Major Robert Graham Mayne, Indian Cavalry (died 1881), and Helen Carnegy, daughter of the late C. Forbes, Esq., of Kingairloch, Argyllshire. He was educated at Radley College, and joined the Highland Light Infantry 19 June, 1895. He served in Crete, 1898, during the International Occupation; and becoming Lieutenant 19 Jan. 1899, was employed with the West African Frontier Force, 17 June, 1899, to 19 Jan. 1903, fighting with the Ashanti Field Force and being present at the relief of Kumassi (mentioned in Despatches [London Gazette, 8 March, 1901]; Medal and clasp). He became Captain 27 March, 1901, and served in the operations against the Emir of Yola, 1901 (mentioned in Despatches, Jan. 1901; African General Service Medal and clasp). In 1901 and 1902 Capt. Mayne took part in the Aro Expedition, Southern Nigeria. He was mentioned in Despatches, May and Sept. 1902; received a clasp, and was created a Companion of the Distinguished Service Order [London Gazette, 12 Sept. 1902]: "Charles Robert Graham Mayne, Capt., Highland Light Infantry. For services during the Aro Expedition in Southern Nigeria." He was invested by the King 18 Dec. 1902. He was employed with the Egyptian Army, 1902 to 1913, serving in the operations on the Blue Nile, 1903 (Medal and clasp), and from 1908 to 1913 holding successively the appointments of A.A.G., G.S.O.2, and Military Secretary to the Sirdar and Governor-General of the Sudan, receiving the 3rd Class Medjidie and 4th Class Osmanieh. Capt. Mayne served in the European War, and was severely wounded in Nov. 1914, and May, 1915. He was promoted Major 1 Sept. 1915, and commanded the 20th Lancashire Fusiliers from Oct. 1915, to July, 1916, then becoming Brigade Commander, 19th Infantry Brigade, a position which he held until May, 1919. He was mentioned in Despatches, Feb. 1915, Jan., May and Dec. 1917, and Dec. 1918, and was made Brevet Lieutenant-Colonel 1 Jan. 1917, and Brevet Colonel 1 Jan. 1919. He became Assistant Military Secretary at the War Office 10 May, 1919, and was created a C.M.G. in Nov. 1919. Colonel Mayne married, 10 July, 1913, Elsie Bertha Huntington, youngest daughter of the late William B. Huntington, Esq., D.L., of 143, Piccadilly, and Blackmore Park, Worcestershire.

GOLDIE, MARK LEIGH, Capt., was born 13 June, 1875, son of Colonel M. H. G. Goldie, R.E., of Plymouth. He joined the Army 2 Nov. 1895, as a Second Lieutenant in the Royal Art'llery, in which he became Lieutenant 2 Nov. 1898, and Captain 16 Nov. 1901. He was created an M.V.O. He served in Southern Nigeria, 1901–2, taking part in the Aro Expedition, for which he was mentioned in Despatches [London Gazette, 12 Sept. 1902]; received the Medal with clasp, and was created a Companion of the Distinguished Service Order [London Gazette, 12 Sept. 1902]: "Mark Leigh Goldie, M.V.O., Capt., Royal Artillery. For services during the Aro Expedition in Southern Nigeria." He was invested by the King, 18 Dec. 1902. From 1907 Capt. Goldie was with B Battery, R.H.A., at Plymouth. He was promoted Major 10 May, 1912. He was accidentally killed in March, 1915.

KNOWLES, GEORGE, Lieut., was born 16 Oct. 1873, younger son of the late Colonel Fred Knowles, 2nd Bengal Cavalry, and Jane Barbara Knowles, of Tisbury Road, Hove. He was educated at Wellington College, and Sandhurst, and joined the Derbyshire Regt. 19 July, 1893. He became Lieutenant 10 June, 1896, and was transferred to the Indian Staff Corps 6 Aug. 1897. He served in Southern Nigeria in 1901, in operations in the Ishan and Ulia countries (Medal with clasp), and in the Aro Expedition, 1901–2, in which he was severely wounded, and for his services he was mentioned in Despatches [London Gazette, 12 Sept. 1902], and was created a Companion of the Distinguished Service Order [London Gazette, 12 Sept. 1902]: "George Knowles, Lieut., Indian Staff Corps. For services during the Aro Expedition in Southern Nigeria." The Insignia, Warrant and Statutes were sent to the Commander-in-Chief in India, and presented at Fyzabad 25 Oct. 1904. He joined the 2nd Lancers, Indian Army, becoming Captain 19 July, 1902, and served in East Africa, Somaliland, 1903–4, commanding the 6th Somali Camel Corps from 19 Aug. 1903. He was employed on Special Service with the Somaliland Field Force 14 Jan. 1903, to 16 Nov. 1914; served in Natal in the Zulu Rebellion, 1906, and was promoted Major 19 July, 1911. Major Knowles served in the European War from 1914 to 1918, in France, and was twice mentioned in Despatches, and received a Bar to the Distinguished Service Order, presented in London 9 Feb. 1918 [London Gazette, 4 Feb. 1918]: "George Knowles, D.S.O., Major, Indian Cavalry. He took command of the regiment when his Commanding Officer became a casualty, and remained in command though he was wounded. He made most skilful dispositions, and clung to his position with the greatest determination, though surrounded on all sides, until he was relieved. He showed great ability and courage." Major Knowles married, 29 Jan. 1918, at Christ Church, Mayfair, W., Florence Eugénie, only daughter of Colonel J. O. Goldie, Indian Army, of Hove, Sussex.

CAMPBELL, ARCHIBALD JOHN, Lieut., was born 15 Nov. 1872, son of the late Colonel J. H. Campbell. He was educated at Wellington, and joined the 19th (Queen Alexandra's Own Royal) Hussars, 23 Dec. 1893. He served in South Africa, 1899–1900, and was present at the operations in Natal, 1899, including the actions at Reitfontein and Lombard's Kop; the defence of Ladysmith, including the sortie of 7 Dec. 1899, and the action of 6 Jan. 1900 (Queen's Medal and clasp). He was in command of a Column in West Africa, 1901–2, in the Aro Expedition, and was severely wounded; received the Medal and clasp; was mentioned in Despatches [London Gazette, 12 Sept. 1902], and created a Companion of the Distinguished Service Order [London Gazette, 12 Sept. 1902]: "Archibald John Campbell, Lieut., 19th Hussars. For services during the Aro Expedition in Southern Nigeria." He was invested by the King; Warrant and Statutes were sent 8 Jan. 1903. He was in command of the Ibeku Expedition in 1902 (clasp). He became Captain 1 April, 1903, and joined the Reserve of Officers 10 Nov. 1909. He served in the European War as Staff Captain, 19th Hussars, 1914–15. Capt. Campbell married, in 1896, Ethel, third daughter of the late J. Gretton.

TOMPSON, REGINALD HENRY DALRYMPLE, Lieut., was born 25 March, 1879, son of the late Canon Reginald Tompson, Rector of St. Mary Stoke, Ipswich. He was educated at Winchester, and Merton College, Oxford (B.A., 1900; M.A. 1909), and entered the Army 26 May, 1900, with a commission in the Royal Artillery, in which he became Lieutenant 9 April, 1902. He was employed with the West African Frontier Force, 14 Dec. 1901, to 10 May, 1903, and served in the Aro Expedition, Southern Nigeria, 1901–2, for which he was mentioned in Despatches [London Gazette, 12 Sept. 1902]; received the Medal and clasp, and was created a Companion of the Distinguished Service Order [London Gazette, 12 Sept. 1902]: "Reginald Henry Dalrymple Tompson, Lieut., Royal Artillery. For services during the Aro Expedition in Southern Nigeria." He was invested by the King 13 June, 1903. He was also on active service in Southern Nigeria, 1902–3 (clasp). He became Captain 1 April, 1911, and was Adjutant from the 5th of Oct. 1912, to 18 Jan. 1914; was promoted Major 30 Oct. 1914. Major Tompson served in the European War, 1914–15, as Railway Transport Officer and Deputy Assistant Director of Railway Transport and D.A.Q.M.G. He was mentioned in Despatches, and was awarded the Brevet of Lieutenant-Colonel. Lieut.-Colonel Tompson married, in 1915, Bridget Dorothea, daughter of the Rev. F. N. Thicknesse, Rector of St. George's, Hanover Square, and Prebendary of St. Paul's, and Mary Sybilla Thicknesse.

London Gazette, 31 Oct. 1902.—"War Office, 31 Oct. 1902. The King has been graciously pleased to give orders for the following appointments to the Distinguished Service Order to the undermentioned Officers, in recognition of their services during the operations in South Africa."

BELFIELD, HERBERT EVERSLEY, Colonel, was born 25 Sept. 1857, son of the late Capt. Belfield, J.P., of Gloucestershire. He was educated at Wellington College, and joined the Army 26 Feb. 1876, as a Lieutenant in the Royal Munster Fusiliers, in which he became Captain 20 May, 1885; he passed the Staff College; was Brigade Major, Aldershot, 1 Aug. 1890, to 3 March, 1893; promoted Major 1 Feb. 1893; was D.A.A.G., Aldershot, 4 March, 1893, to 30 Sept. 1895. He served in Ashanti, 1895–96; as Chief Staff Officer; was honourably mentioned, and received the Brevet of Lieutenant-Colonel 25 March, 1896, and the Ashanti Star. He was promoted Lieutenant-Colonel, West Riding Regt., 28 July, 1897, and Colonel 18 Dec. 1899. Colonel Belfield took part in the South African War. He was A.A.G. 18 Dec. 1899, to 22 Jan. 1902; then Brigadier-General (Inspector-General, Imperial Yeomanry), 23 Jan. to 23 Oct. 1902, and was present in operations in the Orange Free State, Feb. to May, 1900; operations in the Transvaal, west of Pretoria, including the actions at Venterskroon (7 and 9 Aug.); operations in Orange River Colony, including the actions at Lindley (1 June) and Rhenoster River; operations in the Transvaal 30 Nov. 1900, to July, 1901, and Jan. to 31 May, 1902; operations in Orange River Colony, March and April, 1901; operations in Cape Colony, Jan. and Feb. 1901, and July, 1901, to Jan. 1902. He received the Queen's Medal with three clasps, and the King's Medal with two clasps; was mentioned in Despatches twice [London Gazettes, 16 April, 1901, and 29 July, 1902]; created a C.B., and was created a Companion of the Distinguished Service Order [London Gazette, 31 Oct. 1902]: "Herbert Eversley Belfield, C.B., Colonel, West Riding Regt. In recognition of services during the operations in South Africa." He was invested by the King 18 Dec. 1902. Colonel Belfield was A.A.G., 1st Army Corps, 11 Dec. 1902, to 7 Dec. 1903; commanded the 4th Infantry Brigade 8 Dec. 1903, to 28 Feb. 1907; became Major-General 1 Dec. 1906; commanded the 4th Division, Eastern Command, 12 May, 1907, to 1911, and became Colonel, The Duke of Wellington's (West Riding) Regt. 1909 ; became Lieutenant-General 10 Aug. 1912 ; was created a K.C.B. in 1914, and placed on the Retired List 12 May, 1914. Lieut.-General Sir H. E. Belfield, K.C.B., D.S.O., has been Director-General of Prisoners of War since 1914 ; was created a K.C.M.G. in 1918, and K.B.E., 1919. He married (1st), in 1882, Emily Mary, daughter of the late Right Rev. Herbert Binney, D.D., Bishop of Nova Scotia ; and (2ndly), Evelyn Mary, daughter of the late Albon Taylor, of Elm Grove, Barnes, and they have two daughters.

HENDERSON, DAVID, Capt. and Brevet Lieut.-Colonel, was born 11 Aug. 1862, son of the late David Henderson, of Glasgow. He joined the Argyll and Sutherland Highlanders, as Lieutenant, 25 Aug. 1883 ; became Captain 26 Feb. 1890. He was Staff Captain (Intelligence), Headquarters of Army, 1 Dec. 1897, to 12 July, 1898. He served with the Sudan Expeditionary Force, as A.D.C. to the Brigadier-General commanding the 2nd Brigade, British Division, 13 July to 8 Oct. 1898, and was present at the Battle of Khartoum. He was mentioned in Despatches [London Gazette, 30 Sept. 1898] ; was given the Brevet of Major 16 Nov. 1898, and the British and Khedive's Medals, with clasp. He was Staff Captain (Intelligence), Headquarters of Army, 18 Oct. 1898, to 31 March, 1899 ; D.A.Q.M.G., Headquarters of Army, 1 April to 30 June, 1899 ; D.A.A.G., Natal, 1 July, 1899, to 27 Oct. 1900. In the South African War he took part in operations in Natal, 1899, including the actions at Reitfontein and Lombard's Kop ; the defence of Ladysmith (temporarily in charge of the Field Intelligence Department), including sorties of 7 Dec. 1899 (wounded) and the action of 6 Jan. 1900. He was present in operations in Natal, March to June, 1900, including the action at Laing's Nek (6 to 9 June) ; operations in the Transvaal, east of Pretoria, July to 29 Nov. 1900, including actions at Belfast (26 and 27 Aug.) and Lydenberg (5 to 8 Sept) ; operations in the Transvaal 30 Nov. 1900, to 31 May, 1902. For his services in the Boer War he was mentioned in Despatches (Sir G. White, 2 Dec. 1899, and 23 March, 1900 ; Sir Redvers Buller, 19 June and 9 Nov. 1900) [London Gazettes, 8 Feb. 1901, and 29 July, 1902] ; received the Queen's Medal with four clasps, and the King's Medal with two clasps, and was given the Brevet of Lieutenant-Colonel 29 Nov. 1900, and created a Companion of the Distinguished Service Order [London Gazette, 31 Oct. 1902] : " David Henderson, Capt. and Brevet Lieut.-Colonel, Argyll and Sutherland Highlanders. In recognition of services during the operations in South Africa." The Insignia, etc., were sent to the G.O.C., Transvaal, and presented by the G.O.C., South Africa, 25 March, 1903. He became Major 12 Dec. 1903. Major Henderson was employed under the Civil Government in the Transvaal 20 Sept. 1902, to 30 April, 1903, was D.A.Q.M.G., 1st Army Corps, and D.A.Q.M.G., Aldershot Army Corps, 3 March, 1904, to 21 Nov. 1905 ; was given the Brevet of Colonel 22 Nov. 1905 ; was A.A.G., 1st Division, Aldershot Army Corps, 22 Nov. 1905, to 31st Dec. 1906 ; was G.S.O., 1st Grade, Aldershot Command, 1 Jan. to 20 Dec. 1907 ; became Lieutenant-Colonel 1 Jan. 1907, and Colonel 27 Nov. 1907 ; was Staff Officer (Brigadier-General, General Staff) to the Inspector-General of the Home Forces 21 Dec. 1907, to 29 Feb. 1912 ; Temporary Brigadier-General 4 April, 1908, to 25 Oct. 1914 ; Staff Officer to the Inspector-General of the Home Forces 1 March to 30 June, 1912 ; Director of Military Training, War Office, 1 July, 1912, to 31 Aug. 1913 ; Director-General of Military Aeronautics, 1 Sept. 1913, to 4 Aug. 1914. When the European War broke out he became Commander of the Royal Flying Corps, and held this position until 17 Oct. 1917. He was promoted Major-General 26 Oct. 1914, for distinguished service in the Field ; was Commanding Officer of the 1st Division, B.E.F., 21 and 22 Nov. and 20 Dec. 1914 ; was created a K.C.B. in 1914 ; was G.O.C., Royal Flying Corps, British Expeditionary Force, 21 Dec. 1914, to 17 Oct. 1917 ; Director-General of Military Aeronautics 22 Feb. 1916, to 17 Oct. 1917 ; promoted Lieutenant-General 1 Jan. 1917 ; Area Commandant, British Armies in France, 10 Aug. to 6 Oct. 1918 ; Military Counsellor, Paris, 7 Oct. 1918. He was made a K.C.V.O. in 1919 ; Commander of the Legion of Honour, 1915, and Grand Officer, 1919 ; is Grand Officer of the Order of the Crown of Belgium, and has the Orders Grand Crown of the Sacred Treasure of Japan, and of the White Eagle of Russia ; is Grand Officer of the Order of the Crown of Italy. He is the author of " The Art of Reconnaissance." Lieut.-General Sir David Henderson married, in 1899, Henrietta Caroline, daughter of Henry R. Dundas.

MILNER, GEORGE FRANCIS, Capt., was born 10 July, 1862, at the Deanery, Westminster, S.W., son of Henry B. W. Milner, second son of Sir W. Milner, 4th Bart., and Charlotte, daughter of the Right Rev. Marcus Beresford, Archbishop of Armagh. He was educated at Eton, and joined the 17th Lancers, as Lieutenant, from the Militia, 27 Jan. 1883 ; was promoted Captain into the 1st Life Guards 11 Jan. 1893. He served in the South African War from Dec. 1899, until June, 1902 ; as Captain in a Composite Regt. of Household Cavalry ; as Brigade Major to General Broadwood, 3rd Cavalry Brigade, and in command of the 12th Imperial Yeomanry, with the rank of Lieutenant-Colonel. He was present at the Relief of Kimberley ; operations in the Orange Free State, Feb. to May, 1900, including operations at Paardeberg (17 to 26 Feb.) ; actions at Poplar Grove, Dreifontein, Houtnek (Thoba Mountain), Vet River (5 and 6 May) and Zand River ; operations in the

George F. Milner.

Transvaal, May and June, 1900, including actions near Johannesburg, Pretoria and Diamond Hill (11 and 12 June) ; operations in Cape Colony, south

of Orange River, 1899 to 1900 ; operations in the Transvaal, July, 1901, and operations in Orange River Colony, April, 1901, to 31 May, 1902. He received the Queen's Medal with five clasps, and the King's Medal with two clasps ; was mentioned in Despatches [London Gazette, 29 July, 1902], and created a Companion of the Distinguished Service Order [London Gazette, 31 Oct. 1902] : " George Francis Milner, Capt., 1st Life Guards. In recognition of services during the operations in South Africa." He was invested by the King 18 Dec. 1902. He became Major 6 Dec. 1902 ; was given the Brevet of Lieutenant-Colonel 6 Dec. 1906 ; Lieutenant-Colonel, 5th Lancers, 16 Jan. 1909. He became Colonel, 19 July, 1911 ; was Brigade Commander, Lowland Mounted Brigade, Scottish Command, 31 Jan. 1913, to 26 June, 1914 ; was Colonel-in-Charge, Cavalry Records, York, 27 June to 9 Sept. 1914. He became Temporary Brigadier-General and Inspector of Cavalry (graded A.A.G.—temporary) 10 Sept. 1914 ; became Brigade Commander 19 April, 1915 ; commanded the 1st Reserve Cavalry Brigade until 3 May, 1918 ; became again Colonel-in-Charge of Cavalry Records at York 4 May, 1918. Brigadier-General G. F. Milner was mentioned in Despatches 20 Feb. 1917, for services in connection with the Great War, and again on 13 Feb. 1918, and was created a C.M.G. in 1918. He has the Order of the Crown of Prussia, 2nd Class. Brigadier-General G. F. Milner married, on 21 April, 1910, Phyllis Mary Lycett Green, daughter of Edward Lycett Green (eldest son of Sir Edward Green, Bart.), and Ethel Mary, second daughter of A. Wilson, of Tranby Croft, and they have two sons : George Edward Mordaunt, born 7 Feb. 1911, and Henry George, born 27 Oct. 1912.

WARD, THE HONOURABLE REGINALD, Capt., was born 11 June, 1874, at Dudley House, Park Lane, London, W., son of William Humble, Earl of Dudley. He was educated at Dr. Girdlestone's School at Sunningdale, and in Mr. Austin Leigh's House at Eton College, and entered the Royal Horse Guards, as a Second Lieutenant, 6 Feb. 1895 ; became Lieutenant 4 March, 1896. He took the Officers' Hythe Certificate 14 Dec. 1897, and received the Jubilee Medal ; was Assistant Adjutant 18 March, 1898, to 3 Dec. 1899 ; promoted Captain 24 Feb. 1900. He served in South Africa from 4 Dec. 1899, to 2 June, 1900, and from 2 Feb. 1901, to 11 July, 1902 (as A.D.C. to Lieut.-General J. D. P. French). He was mentioned in Despatches in 1901 ; was present at Paardeberg, Dreifontein and the Relief of Kimberley, and was created a Companion of the Distinguished Service Order, while serving as A.D.C. to Lieut.-General J. D. P. French [London Gazette, 31 Oct. 1902] : " The Honourable Reginald Ward, Capt., Royal Horse Guards. In recognition of services during the operations in South Africa." He was invested by the King 18 Dec. 1902. He received the Queen's South African Medal with four clasps, and the King's Medal with two clasps. Capt. the Honourable Reginald Ward died in London 7 March, 1904.

EASTWOOD, HUGH DE CRESPIGNY, Capt., was born 25 Jan. 1863, second son of the late T. S. B. Eastwood, J.P., Barrister-at-Law (of 28, Gloucester Terrace, London, W., and Lincoln's Inn), and of the late Rosalie Eastwood. He was educated at Eton, and joined the Royal Scots Greys, from the 1st Lanark Militia, 19 Aug. 1885 ; was transferred to the 1st King's Dragoon Guards, as Lieutenant, 29 Dec. 1886. He served in India, 1887–88 ; was Assistant Adjutant, Cavalry Depot, Canterbury, 1889–91 ; of the King's Dragoon Guards, 1891–94 ; was promoted Captain 4 June, 1894. He served in South Africa, 1901, and was present in operations in the Transvaal, Orange River Colony and Cape Colony. He was twice wounded (once severely) ; mentioned in Despatches [London Gazette, 17 Jan. 1902] ; received the Medal and four clasps, and was created a Companion of the Distinguished Service Order [London Gazette, 31 Oct. 1902] : " Hugh de Crespigny Eastwood, Capt., 1st Dragoon Guards. In recognition of services during the operations in South Africa." He was invested by the King 18 Dec. 1902. He became Major 20 June, 1903. He was Adjutant and Instructor, Imperial Yeomanry, Aldershot, 1902–4 ; retired 26 Feb. 1908. From 1910 to 1913 he was D.A.D.R., Aldershot Command ; D.R.O., 1913–14. He served in the Great War ; was promoted Lieutenant-Colonel, and was from 1915 to 1917 Commandant, Army Cyclist Training Centre. He was Inspector of Cyclist Units, 1916–18, and was promoted Colonel in 1916. He was mentioned in Despatches in 1919. Colonel Eastwood has the Order of the Iron Crown (Austria), 3rd Class. He married, 25 Jan. 1887, at Frimley, Surrey, Ellinor, youngest daughter of the late General John Hall Smyth, C.B., of Frimhurst, Frimley, Surrey, and they have three sons : Hugh Robert, Lieutenant-Commander, R.N., born Oct. 1888 ; Thomas Robert, D.S.O., M.C., Brevet Major, Rifle Brigade, born May, 1890 ; and Ronald de Crespigny, born Jan. 1903 ; and two daughters : Rosalie Joan, born 1892, and Violet, born 1895.

Hugh de C. Eastwood.

LE GRAVE, THE REVEREND WILLIAM, was born 5 Sept. 1843. He was educated at St. Edmund's College, Ware, and was ordained in 1867. He taught mathematics at St. Edmund's College, 1866–78 ; became a 4th class Chaplain to the Forces 18 Jan. 1878 ; was promoted

Rev. William Le Grave.

3rd class Chaplain 18 Jan. 1888; 2nd class, 18 Jan. 1893, and 1st class 18 Jan. 1898. He saw service in Malta and Bermuda, and was with the Ashanti Expedition in 1895 and 1896. He served as Senior Roman Catholic Chaplain in South Africa, 1900 to 1902, and was present in operations in Natal, Orange River Colony and the Transvaal, May to 29 Nov. 1900; operations in Orange River Colony and the Transvaal 30 Nov. 1900, to 31 May, 1902. He was mentioned in Despatches [London Gazette, 10 Sept. 1901, and 29 July, 1902]; received the Queen's Medal with three clasps, and the King's Medal with two clasps, and was created a Companion of the Distinguished Service Order [London Gazette, 31 Oct. 1902]: " The Reverend William Le Grave, Chaplain (1st Class). In recognition of services during the operations in South Africa." Invested by the King 18 Dec. 1902. He retired 11 Nov. 1903

McCRACKEN, FREDERICK WILLIAM NICHOLAS, Brevet Lieut.-Colonel, was born 18 Aug. 1859, youngest son of the late R. de Crez McCracken, of Blackheath, Kent, and of Elizabeth (Geary), his wife. He was educated at Sandhurst; joined the 49th Foot, as Second Lieutenant, 13 Aug. 1879, and became Lieutenant 28 July, 1880, in the Royal Berkshire Regt. He served in the Egyptian Campaign, 1882, and was present at the surrender of Kafr Dowar (Medal and Khedive's Star). He was Adjutant, 1st Berkshire Regt., 21 March, 1883, to 9 Oct. 1885; became Captain 15 Dec. 1884. He served in the Suakin Campaign, 1885; M'Neil's Zeriba; took part in the reconnaissance to Hasheen; actions at Hasheen and Tofrek; operations at and destruction of Tamai. He was mentioned in Despatches [London Gazette, 15 Aug. 1885]; received the Brevet of Major 14 Aug. 1885, and two clasps to the Medal. He served on the Egyptian Frontier, 1885–86, and was present at the action of Giniss; was D.A.A.G., Barbados, 1892 to 1897. He became Major 27 March, 1897, and served throughout the campaign in South Africa. He was in command of the 2nd Battn. Royal Berkshire Regt. from 12 Oct. 1901, to 5 May, 1902; was present in operations in the Orange Free State, March to May, 1900; operations in the Transvaal, east of Pretoria, July to 29 Nov. 1900; operations in the Transvaal, west of Pretoria, July and Aug. 1900, including actions at Zilikat's Nek; operations in Orange River Colony, May to July, 1900; operations in Cape Colony, south of Orange River, 1899, to 1900, including actions at Colesberg; operations in the Transvaal, Nov. 1900, to July, 1901; operations in Cape Colony, July, 1901, to 31 May, 1902; in command of a Column of mixed troops 21 June to 5 July, 1900. At the conclusion of the war he was in command of a section of the blockhouse line on the railway and across country in Cape Colony, garrisoned by four battalions. He was mentioned in Despatches twice [London Gazette, 4 May, 1900, and 29 July, 1902]; received the Brevet of Lieutenant-Colonel 29 Nov. 1900; the Queen's Medal with three clasps, and the King's Medal with two clasps, and was created a Companion of the Distinguished Service Order [London Gazette, 31 Oct. 1902]: " Frederick William Nicholas McCracken, Brevet Lieut.-Colonel, Royal Berkshire Regt. In recognition of services during the operations in South Africa." The Insignia, Warrant, etc., were sent direct, 10 Jan. 1903. He became Lieutenant-Colonel 30 April, 1903, and Brevet Colonel 13 Feb. 1905; A.A.G., India, and G.S.O.1, India, 2 Dec. 1907, to 16 March, 1911; was created a C.B. in 1910; was Brigadier-General, General Staff, Irish Command, 9 April, 1911, to 21 Oct. 1912; Brigadier-General Commanding the 7th Infantry Brigade, 3rd Division, 22 Oct. 1912, to 4 Aug. 1914. He served throughout the European War from 1914; was promoted Major-General for distinguished service in the Field 26 Oct. 1914; was Divisional Commander, 15th Division, New Armies and British Armies in France, 22 March, 1915, to 16 June, 1917; Temporary Lieutenant-General 17 June, 1917, to 31 Dec. 1918; commanding the 13th Army Corps, British Armies in France, 17 June, 1917, to 13 March, 1918; G.O.C.-in-Chief, Scottish Command, 5 May. 1918, to 8 June, 1919. He was seven times mentioned in Despatches; was created a K.C.B. in 1917, and promoted Lieutenant-General 1 Jan. 1919; appointed Commander of the Military Order of Savoy, Italy, 1917; Commander of the Order of Leopold (Belgium) in 1918, with Belgian War Cross; Commander of the Legion of Honour in 1919. In 1887 Lieut.-General Sir F. W. N. McCracken married Ann Liston, daughter of the late T. C. Glover, of Mount Grange, Edinburgh, and Earlsferry House, Elie, Fife, N.B., and they had one son, who died in 1914, aged 16, and have two daughters still living.

CAPPER, THOMPSON, Major and Brevet Lieut.-Colonel, was born 20 Oct. 1863, son of the late W. Copeland Capper, I.C.S. He joined the Army as a Lieutenant in the East Lancashire Regt. 9 Sept. 1882, and was promoted Captain 22 April, 1891, serving as Adjutant 29 Oct. 1890, to 28 Oct. 1894. He served during the operations in Chitral, 1895, with the Relief Force (Medal with clasp); was employed with the Egyptian Army 31 Dec. 1897, to 14 July, 1899; served with the Nile Expedition, 1898, with Egyptian Army; was present in the battles of the Atbara and Khartoum (Despatches [London Gazette, 30 Sept. 1898]; Brevet of Major 16 Nov. 1898; Egyptian Medal with two clasps; Medal). Served with the Nile Expedition, 1899 (clasp to Egyptian Medal). During the South African War he was Staff Captain (Intelligence), Headquarters of Army, 15 July to 12 Nov. 1899; D.A.A.G., 13 Nov. 1899, to 19 Oct. 1900; Staff Officer and A.A.G. 20 Oct. 1900, to 1 April, 1902. He became Major 5 Dec. 1901; was present at the Relief of Ladysmith, including operations of 17 to 24 Jan. 1900, and action at Spion Kop; in the operations of 5 to 7 Feb. 1900, and action at Vaal Kranz; and in the operations on Tugela Heights, 14 to 27 Feb. 1900, and action at Pieter's Hill; in Natal, March to June, 1900, including action at Laing's Nek (6 to 9 June); during the operations in Orange Free State and Transvaal; also in Cape Colony, Jan. 1901, to 31 May, 1902; in command of a Mobile Column (24 June, 1901, to end of operations) (Despatches—Sir R. H. Buller, 3 Feb., 30 March, 19 June and 9 Nov. 1900 [London Gazette, 8 Feb. 1901, and 29 July, 1902]; Brevet of Lieutenant-Colonel 29 Nov. 1900; Queen's Medal with six clasps, and King's Medal with two clasps). He was created a Companion of the Dis-

tinguished Service Order [London Gazette, 31 Oct. 1902]: " Thompson Capper, Major and Brevet Lieut.-Colonel, The East Lancashire Regt. In recognition of services during the operations in South Africa." He was Professor at the Staff College, 23 Dec. 1902, to 2 Feb. 1904, and D.A.A.G. at the Staff College 3 Feb. 1904, to 22 Dec. 1905. He was given his Brevet Colonelcy 11 Dec. 1904, and became Colonel 31 March, 1906, on taking up the appointment of Commandant at the Indian Staff College. He was created a C.B. in 1910; was given the command of the 13th Infantry Brigade, 1911; became Inspector-General of Infantry in 1914. He commanded the 7th Division in the European War; became Major-General 12 May, 1914 and was created a K.C.M.G. for his services. Major-General Sir Thompson Capper died 27 Sept. 1915, of wounds received the previous day. He had married, in 1908, the daughter of the Honourable R. Gerard, of Wrightington Hall, Lancashire.

COLE, ARTHUR WILLOUGHBY GEORGE LOWRY, Major and Brevet Lieut.-Colonel, was born 2) Nov. 1860, eldest son of the late Colonel A. L. Cole. He became a Second Lieutenant, 23rd Foot, 11 Aug. 1880, and Lieutenant, Royal Welsh Fusiliers, 1 July, 1881. He served with the Burmese Expedition, 1885–87 (Despatches [London Gazette, 2 Sept. 1887]; Medal with clasp). He became Captain 22 Jan. 1890, and was Adjutant, Royal Welsh Fusiliers, 23 April, 1894, to 30 Jan. 1898. Capt. Cole served in West Africa, 1897–98 (Borgu Medal with clasp). From 31 Jan. 1898, to 15 Feb. 1901, he was employed with the West African Frontier Force; was promoted Major 11 Jan. 1899. He served in West Africa (Northern Nigeria), 1900 (severely wounded); Munshi Expedition (in command), and Kaduna Expedition (Despatches [London Gazette, 16 April, 1901]; Brevet Lieutenant-Colonel 29 Nov. 1902; c asp). Again in West Africa (Northern Nigeria), 1900, with the Expedition against Chief of Tawari in command (Despatches [London Gazette, 18 April, 1902]; Medal with clasp). He served in the South African War, 1901–2; commanded Depôt Battn., Green Point; in command of 17th Mounted Infantry Mixed Column; afterwards Commandant, Vryburg Sub-District (Despatches [London Gazette, 29 July, 1902]; Queen's Medal with five clasps). He was created a Companion of the Distinguished Service Order [London Gazette, 31 Oct. 1902]: " Arthur Willoughby George Lowry Cole, Major and Brevet Lieut.-Colonel, The Royal Welsh Fusiliers. In recognition of services during the operations in South Africa." From 12 July to 6 Nov. 1903, he held a temporary appointment as A.A.G. in India, and was promoted Lieutenant-Colonel 24 Sept. 1904. He was again employed with the West African Frontier Force from 24 Sept. 1904, to 24 Sept. 1907; was given the Brevet of Colonel 27 Oct. 1905; was in command of the Sokoto Expedition in 1906, for which he was mentioned in Despatches [London Gazette, 2 July, 1907], and was created a C.B., 1907 (Medal and clasp). He was made Colonel 25 Sept. 1907, and on 29 Oct. 1907, became A.A.G., G.S.O.1, Peshawar Division, India. In 1912 he was appointed to the charge of Administration, Northern Command. He served in the European War, and died of wounds received in action in May, 1915. Brigadier-General A. W. G. L. Cole married, in 1908, Marion Gertrude, widow of Lieut.-Colonel C. H. Thorold.

SCOTT, ARTHUR BINNY, Major and Brevet Lieut.-Colonel, was born 3 Jan. 1862. He was educated at Cheltenham College, and at the Royal Military Academy, Woolwich, and entered the Army 23 Feb. 1881, as a Lieutenant in the Royal Artillery, in which he was promoted Captain 31 July, 1889, and Major 17 March, 1899. He served in the South African War, 1899–1902. Commanded 18th Battery, Royal Field Artillery, and P Battery, Royal Horse Artillery, and a Mobile Column. Took part in the advance on Kimberley, including actions at Belmont, Enslin, Modder River and Magersfontein; served during the operations in the Orange Free State, Feb. to May, 1900, including operations at Paardeberg, actions at Poplar Grove, Karee Siding, Vet River and Zand River; in the Transvaal in May and June, 1900, including actions near Johannesburg and Pretoria; in command of Mobile Column 26 Dec. 1901, to 18 Jan. 1902 (temporarily), and from 28 Jan. to 31 May, 1902; again in the Transvaal 30 Nov. 1900, to July, 1901, and Sept. 1901, to 31 May, 1902; in the Orange River Colony, July to Sept. 1901, and Jan. to March, 1902; also in Cape Colony, Sept. 1901, and May, 1902 (Despatches [London Gazette, 10 Sept. 1901, and 29 July, 1902]; Brevet of Lieutenant-Colonel 29 Nov. 1900; Queen's Medal with four clasps, and King's Medal with two clasps). He was created a Companion of the Distinguished Service Order [London Gazette, 31 Oct. 1902]: " Arthur Binny Scott, Major and Brevet Lieut.-Colonel, Royal Horse and Royal Field Artillery. In recognition of services during the operations in South Africa." He was given the Brevet of Colonel on becoming A.A.G., India, 22 Jan. 1906, and was promoted Lieutenant-Colonel 11 Feb. 1906; became Colonel 11 Feb. 1911, and from 22 Dec. 1911, to 1914 was in command of Royal Artillery in India. He was created a C.B. in 1914. Colonel Scott served in the European War. He was Brigadier-General, R.A., Meerut Division, British Expeditionary Force, 12 Oct. 1914, to 15 Feb. 1915; Brigadier-General, R.A., Indian Army Corps, B.E.F., 16 Feb. to 6 Sept. 1915; Major-General, R.A., 3rd Army, B.E.F., 3 Oct. 1915, to 25 April, 1918; promoted Major-General 1 Jan. 1916; Divisional Commander, 12th Division, B.E.F., and British Armies in France, 3 Oct. 1915, to 25 April, 1918. On 5 Aug. 1918, he became Divisional Commander, India. He was mentioned in Despatches, and was created a K.C.B. in 1918. Major-General Sir A. B. Scott married, in 1894, Aimée Byng, daughter of General Charles H. Hall.

KAVANAGH, CHARLES TOLER McMURROUGH, Major and Brevet Lieut.-Colonel, was born 25 March, 1864, son of the ate Right Hon. A. McMurrough Kavanagh, of Borris, County Carlow. He was educated at Harrow (Druri;'s), and entered the 3rd Dragoon Guards, as Lieutenant, 6 Feb. 1884. He was transferred to the 10th Hussars 20 Feb. 1884. From 7 March, 1889, to 21 April, 1891, he was A.D.C. to the Captain-General and Governor-in-Chief, Jamaica, being promoted to Captain 1 Feb. 1890, and from 1 July, 1895, to 1 Feb. 1900, Adjutant of Yeomanry. He became Major

6 Jan. 1900. He served in the South African War, 1899–1902 ; took part in the operations in the Orange Free State, Feb. to May, 1900, including actions at Poplar Grove, Dreifontein, Houtnek (Thoba Mountain), Vet River and Zand River. In the Transvaal in May and June, 1900, including actions near Johannesburg, Pretoria and Diamond Hill ; in the Transvaal, west of Pretoria, July to 29 Nov. 1900, including action at Elands River ; in Orange River Colony, May to 29 Nov. 1900, including action at Wittebergen ; again in the Transvaal 30 Nov. 1900, to July, 1901 ; also during the operations in Cape Colony, July, 1901, to 31 May, 1902 (in command of Mobile Column) ; in command, 10th Hussars, from 19 Oct. 1901 (Despatches [London Gazette, 10 Sept. 1901, and 29 July, 1902] ; Brevet of Lieutenant-Colonel 29 Nov. 1900 ; Queen's Medal with five clasps, and King's Medal with two clasps). He was created a Companion of the Distinguished Service Order [London Gazette, 31 Oct. 1902] : " Charles Toler McMurrough Kavanagh, Major and Brevet Lieut.-Colonel, 10th Hussars. In recognition of services during the operations in South Africa." He became Lieutenant-Colonel 7 May, 1904, taking command of the 10th Hussars, and in 1906 he was made an M.V.O. He was given the Brevet of Colonel 18 Aug. 1905 ; became Colonel 7 May, 1908, and was Temporary Brigadier-General 11 May, 1909, to 10 May, 1913, in command of the 1st Cavalry Brigade, Aldershot. He was made a C.B. and C.V.O. in 1909. From 5 Jan. 1914, to 17 Feb. 1915, he was again Temporary Brigadier-General, and was a Brigade Commander in India from 5 Jan. to 9 Sept. 1914. Brigadier-General Kavanagh served in the European War. He was Brigade Commander, 7th Cavalry Brigade, B.E.F., 10 Sept. 1914, to 14 April, 1915 ; was promoted Major-General 18 Feb. 1915 ; was Divisional Commander, 2nd Cavalry Division, B.E.F., 19 April to 14 July, 1915 ; Divisional Commander, 5th Division, B.E.F., 15 July, 1915, to 31 March, 1916 ; became Temporary Lieutenant-General 1 April, 1916 ; Army Corps Commander, 1st Army Corps, British Armies in France, 1 April to 3 Sept. 1916 ; Army Corps Commander, Cavalry Corps, British Armies in France, from 4 Sept. 1916. He was mentioned in Despatches, and was created a K.C.B. in 1917. Lieut.-General Sir C. T. McM. Kavanagh married, in 1895, May, second daughter of S. Perry, of Woodroof, County Tipperary. They have two daughters.

RAWNSLEY, CLAUDE, Lieut.-Colonel, was born 4 Aug. 1862, at Saltash, Cornwall, son of Lieut.-Colonel T. J. Rawnsley, A.O.D. (deceased), and Mrs. E. G. Rawnsley. He was educated at Queen Elizabeth's School, Cranbrook, and at the Royal Military Academy, Woolwich, and joined the Royal Artillery 22 Feb. 1882, as Lieutenant. He was transferred to the Army Service Corps, as Captain, April, 1889 ; promoted Major, April, 1896, and Lieutenant-Colonel, Jan. 1901. He served during the South African War, as D.A.A.G., and afterwards as A.A.G., Headquarters Staff, Lines of Communication. He was present at operations in Cape Colony, south of Orange River, Oct. 1899, to 29 Nov. 1900 ; operations in the Transvaal and Orange River Colony, July, 1901 ; operations in Cape Colony, 30 Nov. 1900, to June, 1901, and August,

Claude Rawnsley.

1901, to March, 1902. He was mentioned in Despatches [London Gazette, 29 July, 1902] ; received the Queen's Medal with three clasps, the King's Medal with two clasps, and was created a Companion of the Distinguished Service Order [London Gazette, 31 Oct. 1902] : " Claude Rawnsley, Lieut.-Colonel, Army Service Corps. In recognition of services during the operations in South Africa." He was given the Brevet of Colonel 10 Feb. 1904, and retired 14 March, 1906. Colonel Rawnsley was recalled to service 5 Aug. 1914, and served in the European War, 1914–18, in command of A.S.C. Section, General Headquarters, 3rd Echelon. He was three times mentioned in Despatches, created a C.M.G. and received the Bronze Star. He married, 29 Aug. 1887, at Woolwich, Lilian Maude Wood, younger daughter of the late Capt. Fred Augustus Wood, Royal Marines, and Receiver-General, Gold Coast, and they have one daughter, Vera Mary.

PRINGLE, ROBERT, Lieut.-Colonel, was born 25 Aug. 1855, son of Gilbert Pringle, of Stranraer. He joined the Army 5 Oct. 1878, and served in the Afghan War (Medal) ; in the Mahsud-Waziri Expedition, 1881 (mentioned in Despatches), and in the Zhob Valley Expedition in 1884. He was Principal Veterinary Officer, 3rd Army, 11 Dec. 1901, to 11 Feb. 1903. He served in the South African War, 1899–1902, as Senior Veterinary Officer, Lines of Communication ; operations in the Transvaal, Orange River Colony and Cape Colony, 30 Nov. 1900, to 31 May, 1902. He was mentioned in Despatches [London Gazette, 29 July, 1902] ; received the Queen's Medal with four clasps, and was created a Companion of the Distinguished Service Order [London Gazette, 31 Oct. 1902] : " Robert Pringle, Lieut.-Colonel, Army Veterinary Depart-

Robert Pringle.

ment. In recognition of services during the operations in South Africa." He became Principal Veterinary Officer and Lieutenant-Colonel 11 Dec. 1901 ; was Inspecting Veterinary Officer, India, 19 March, 1903, to 31 May, 1907 ; Principal Veterinary Officer, Aldershot Command, 5 Feb. 1908, to 14 Oct. 1910 ; created a C.B. in 1909. He was Director-General, A.V.S.,

15 Oct. 1910, to 1917. He was promoted to Colonel 15 Oct. 1910, and retired on that date with the honorary rank of Major-General. He was created a K.C.M.G. in 1917. Sir Robert Pringle married, in 1899, Sophie, eldest daughter of George Moir Byres, of Tonley.

ARMITAGE, THE REVEREND ROBERT, was born 5 March, 1857, eldest son of Arthur Armitage, Barrister-at-Law, of Bridstow, Herefordshire, and Isabel Jane Armitage, daughter of Dudley Perceval, Esq. He was educated at Marlborough, and at Magdalen College, Oxford ; was ordained Deacon in 1880, and Priest in 1882 ; was Curate of Llandingat, 1880–82 ; Chaplain, Oxford Military College, 1882–84 ; Curate of St. John Baptist, Leamington, 1884–86. He joined the Army in Oct. 1886, as Chaplain to the Forces, 3rd Class ; served at Aldershot, 1886–90 ; at Wellington Barracks, 1890–94 ; at Barbados, 1894–98 ; at Woolwich, 1898–99. He served in the South African War, 1899–1902 ; during the operations in the Orange Free State, Feb. to May, 1900, including actions at Vet River (5 and 6 May) and Zand River ; in the Transvaal, May and June, 1900, including operations near Johannesburg, Pretoria, and Diamond Hill (11 and 12 Jan.) ; again in the Transvaal, east of

The Rev. R. Armitage.

Pretoria, July to 29 Nov. 1900, including actions at Belfast (26 and 27 Aug.) ; in Cape Colony, south of Orange River, 1899–1900 ; a third time during operations in the Transvaal, 30 Nov. 1900, to 31 May, 1902 (Despatches [London Gazette, 16 April, 1901, and 29 July, 1902] ; Queen's Medal with five clasps, and King's Medal with two clasps). He was recommended for the D.S.O. by Lord Kitchener, and was created a Companion of the Distinguished Service Order [London Gazette, 31 Oct. 1902] : " The Rev. Robert Armitage, Chaplain to the Forces, 3rd Class. In recognition of services during the operations in South Africa." Mr. Armitage served at Woolwich, 1902–7 ; was C.F. at Cairo, 1907–11 ; at Plymouth, 1911–12 ; Vicar of St. Chad's, Tushingham, 1913–15 ; Vicar of Bunbury, Tarporley, from 1916.

HAMILTON-CAMPBELL, WILLIAM KENTIGERN, Lieut.-Colonel, was born at Cairnhill, Hurlford, Ayrshire, 30 Sept. 1865, eldest son of the late Charles Vereker Hamilton-Campbell and Mary, only daughter of Samuel Randall, of Orford, Suffolk. He was educated at Sedbergh School, Yorkshire, and joined the Ayrshire Yeomanry in Aug. 1888, and became Captain 5 June, 1891. He served in the South African War, 1899–1902, in command, Imperial Yeomanry Battn. (from 15 Sept. 1900, to 31 May, 1902) ; took part in the operations in the Transvaal in May and June, 1900 ; in Orange River Colony, May to 29 Nov. 1900, including actions at Wittebergen, Witpoort and Caledon River ; again in Orange River Colony, 30 Nov. 1900, to Feb. 1901, and March to Sept. 1901 ; also during the operations in Cape Colony, Feb. to March, 1901, Sept. 1901, April to 31 May, 1902. He was twice mentioned in Despatches : first by General Sir Charles Knox, for good work done while commanding the 6th Battn. Imperial Yeomanry during operations in pursuit of De Wet in Cape Colony, which ended in his force being broken up outside Hopetown, Cape Colony, on 25 Feb. 1901 ; again by Brigadier-General T. D. Pilcher, for operations carried out on the Oraaze River, just below Hopetown, when a party of 75 Yeomen defeated 300 Boers, commanded by Commandant Haasbroek, capturing 45 of them, 25 to 28 Feb. 1901. He received the Queen's Medal with three clasps, and the King's Medal with two clasps, and was created a Companion of the Distinguished Service Order for valuable services rendered during the period Jan. 1900, to June, 1902 [London Gazette, 31 Oct. 1902] : " William Kentigern Hamilton-Campbell, Lieut.-Colonel, 6th Battn. Imperial Yeomanry. In recognition of services during the operations in South Africa." He became Lieutenant Colonel, Ayrshire Yeomanry, and Honorary Lieutenant in the Army ; received the Territorial Decoration and King George's Coronation Medal. He was mentioned in Despatches for valuable services rendered during the European War 24 Feb. 1917. He died on 22 Nov. 1917. Lieut.-Colonel W. K. Hamilton-Campbell was a J.P. and D.L. for Ayrshire, and C.C. for Mauchline. He had married, 15 Oct. 1908, at Monkton Church, Ayrshire, Edith Agnes, daughter of Robert Angus, of Ladykirk, Monkton, Ayrshire, and left three children : Jean Mary ; Mungo Charles, born 19 March, 1912, and Margaret.

WIGHT-BOYCOTT, THOMAS ANDREW, Major, was born in 1872, son of Cathcart Boycott Wight-Boycott, of Rudge Hall, Salop, and Elizabeth Grazebrook. He was educated at Eton, and was an officer in the Staffordshire Yeomanry Cavalry from 1894, and previously held a commission in the North Staffordshire Militia. He was given command at Aldershot of 550 untrained men, whom he trained and formed into a regiment and took out to South Africa. He served in South Africa, 1900–1902, with the Imperial Yeomanry ; was twice mentioned in Despatches ; received the Queen's Medal with clasp, and was created a Companion of the Distinguished Service Order [London Gazette, 31 Oct. 1902] : " Thomas Andrew Wight-Boycott, Major, 4th Battn. Imperial Yeomanry (Lieut., Staffordshire Imperial Yeomanry). In recognition of services during the operations in South Africa." Lieut.-Colonel T. A. Wight-Boycott was given command of the Warwickshire Yeomanry in 1914, and in Feb. 1915, was made Temporary Brigadier-General of the 2nd South Midland Mounted Brigade. Brigadier-General Wight-Boycott was mentioned in Despatches by Sir Charles Monro. He died on 30 March, 1916, of disease contracted on active service at Gallipoli. He had married Anne Catherine, daughter of the late Rev. John Morgan, Rector of Llandudno, North Wales, and they had one daughter.

FISET, MARIE JOSEPH EUGENE, Lieut.-Colonel, was born 15 March, 1874, at Rimouski, Province of Quebec, Canada, son of Lieut.-Colonel the Honourable Senator Jean Baptiste Romuald Fiset, M.D., and Aimée Plamandon, daughter of the late Honoré Plamandon, of Quebec. He was educated at Rimouski College ; Laval University (M.B., 1896 ; M.D., C.M., 1898) ; specially qualified for treatment of ears, nose and throat, London and Paris, 1891. He entered the Volunteer Militia at the age of 16, and joined the 89th Regt. 11 July, 1890, as Provisional Second Lieutenant ; served during the South African War, 1899–1900 ; was present at the operations in Orange Free State, including operations at Paardeberg, actions at Poplar Grove, Dreifontein, Houtnek, Zand River ; operations in Orange River Colony, and Eastern and Western Transvaal ; was mentioned three times in Despatches ; received the Queen's Medal and four clasps ; was created a Companion of the Distinguished Service Order [London Gazette, 31 Oct. 1902], for bravery in the field : " Marie Joseph Eugène Fiset, Lieut.-Colonel, Canadian Army Medical Staff. In recognition of services during the operations in South Africa." He was Principal Medical Officer, Coronation Contingent, London, 1902 ; Director, General Medical Service, Canada, 1903–6 ; appointed Honorary Surgeon to His Excellency the Governor-General of Canada, 1905 ; Deputy Minister of the Department of Militia and Defence, 1906, and Vice-President of the Militia Council. Surgeon-General Fiset was created a C.M.G. in 1914. He married, 22 May, 1902, Stella Taschereau, daughter of the late Linière Taschereau, Esq., K.C., and Zoé Alleyn, and they have three daughters : Alleyn, Gabrielle and Allison.

LAWTON, T. E., Lieut.-Colonel, joined the Cape Garrison Artillery, and served in the South African War, 1899–1902. He was mentioned in Despatches [London Gazette, 29 July, 1902] ; received the Queen's Medal with a clasp, and the King's Medal with two clasps, and was created a Companion of the Distinguished Service Order [London Gazette, 31 Oct. 1902] : " T. E. Lawton, Lieut.-Colonel, Natal Garrison Artillery. In recognition of services during the operations in South Africa." He retired with the rank of Lieutenant-Colonel.

STANDFORD, WILLIAM, Lieut.-Colonel, served in the South African War of 1877–78, in the Gaika and Galeka campaigns (Medal with clasp) ; in the operations in the Transkei, 1880–81 (Medal with clasp) ; and in the South African War of 1899–1902, as Adjutant of the Duke of Connaught and Strathearn's Own Cape Town Highlanders, Oct. 1899, to 31 Dec. 1900 ; and in command of them 1 Jan. 1901, to 31 May, 1902. He was Assistant Staff Officer, Colonial Forces, and afterwards Staff Officer to the Commandant of the Cape Colonial Volunteers ; took part in operations in Cape Colony. Lieut.-Colonel Standford was mentioned in Despatches [London Gazette, 29 July, 1902] ; received the Queen's Medal with a clasp, and the King's Medal with two clasps, and was created a Companion of the Distinguished Service Order [London Gazette, 31 Oct. 1902] : " William Standford, Lieut.-Colonel, Cape Town Highlanders. In recognition of services during the operations in South Africa." In 1911 Colonel Standford was created an M.V.O.

CROMPTON, B., Lieut.-Colonel, served in the Zulu War, 1878–79 (Medal with clasp), and in the South African War of 1899–1902, with the Natal Volunteers, taking part in operations in Natal, 1899, including action at Reitfontein and Lombard's Kop ; the Defence of Ladysmith ; operations in Natal (March to June, 1900), including the action at Laing's Nek ; operations in the Transvaal, east of Pretoria, July to Oct. 1900. In command of Natal Volunteer Composite Regt., Jan. 1901, to May, 1902 ; operations in the Transvaal 30 Nov. 1900, to 31 May, 1902 ; operations on the Zululand Frontier of Natal, Sept. and Oct. 1901. He was mentioned in Despatches [London Gazette, 29 July, 1902] ; received the Queen's Medal with four clasps, and the King's Medal with two clasps, and was created a Companion of the Distinguished Service Order [London Gazette, 31 Oct. 1902] : " B. Crompton, Lieut.-Colonel, Natal Volunteers. In recognition of services during the operations in South Africa." He was placed on the Regimental Supernumerary List, Natal, in 1906 ; served in the Natal Native Rebellion, 1906 (Medal with clasp). Lieut.-Colonel Crompton has retired from the Natal Carabiniers.

BEALE, HENRY YELVERTON, Capt. and Adjutant, was born 13 Sept. 1860, son of Lieut.-Colonel H. G. Beale, Indian Staff Corps. He was commissioned Second Lieutenant in the 9th Foot 22 Jan. 1881 ; became Lieutenant, Norfolk Regt., 1 July, 1881, and Captain 29 Feb. 1888. Capt. Beale saw active service in the operations in the Northern Chin Hills, Burma, in 1892 and 1893, for which he was mentioned in Despatches (G.G.O. of 1893), and was given the Brevet of Major 29 Dec. 1903 (Medal and clasp). He became Adjutant of the 3rd Battn. Norfolk Regt. (Militia), 4 Feb. 1897 ; Major 8 July, 1899. Major Beale served in the South African War from 1900 to 1902, as Station Staff Officer ; in command of the 3rd Battn. Norfolk Regt. 20 June, 1901, to 20 March, 1902 ; and as Adjutant, 3rd Battn. Norfolk Regt. to 31 May, 1902. He was present in operations in Orange River Colony 30 Nov. 1900, to July, 1901 ; operations in Cape Colony, July, 1901, to March, 1902. He was mentioned in Despatches [London Gazette, 10 Sept. 1901, and 29 July, 1902] ; received the Queen's Medal with two clasps, and the King's Medal with one clasp, and was created a Companion of the Distinguished Service Order [London Gazette, 31 Oct. 1902] : " Henry Yelverton Beale, Capt. and Adjutant, Norfolk Regt. In recognition of services during the operations in South Africa." He retired from the Norfolk Regt. 15 Aug. 1903. At the outbreak of the European War he was re-employed, 5 Aug. 1914, as Major, Depôt, Norfolk Regt. He was appointed to command the Depôt of the Norfolk Regt., and was promoted to the temporary rank of Lieutenant-Colonel in Dec. 1916. Lieut.-Colonel Beale married, in 1900, Mary, daughter of the late Rev. T. Hayley.

BRERETON, EDWARD FITZGERALD, Major, was born 21 Jan. 1861, son of the late William Westropp Brereton, Q.C., of the Irish Bar. He was educated at Cheltenham College, and at Reading School, and entered the Army, as a Second Lieutenant in the 48th Foot, 11 Aug. 1880 ; became Lieutenant in the Northamptonshire Regt. 12 March, 1881, and was Adjutant 5 Aug. 1885, to 4 Aug. 1890, being promoted Captain 1 Sept. 1886. He served during operations on the North-West Frontier of India, 1897–98 ; took part in the operations on the Samana ; also with Tirah Expeditionary Force (Medal with three clasps). He was promoted Major 18 Jan. 1899. He served in the South African War, 1899–1902, as District Commandant ; afterwards Station Staff Officer, and as Assistant Provost-Marshal. Was present at the advance on Kimberley, including actions at Belmont, Enslin, Modder River and Magersfontein ; served in the Orange Free State, Feb. to May, 1900 ; also in Orange River Colony, May to Nov. 1900 ; in the Transvaal 30 Nov. to Dec. 1900, and March, 1901 and 31 May, 1902 ; also in Cape Colony, Dec. 1900, to March, 1901 (Despatches [London Gazette, 29 July, 1902] ; Queen's Medal with four clasps, and King's Medal with two clasps). He was created a Companion of the Distinguished Service Order [London Gazette, 31 Oct. 1902] : " Edward Fitzgerald Brereton, Major, Northamptonshire Regt. In recognition of services during the operations in South Africa." He was promoted Lieutenant-Colonel 2 June, 1907, and commanded the 2nd Northamptonshire Regt. until 1911 ; became Colonel 19 July, 1911, and was appointed to command the 2nd West Riding Brigade (T.F.) in 1912. He served in the European War from 1914 to 1918, and was created a C.B. in 1916. On 24 April, 1918, he retired with the rank of Brigadier-General. Brigadier-General Brereton married, in 1887, Fanny E., youngest child of the late Major-General E. Foster, late 12th Regt., and they have one daughter.

HOLT, MAURICE PERCY CUE, Major, was born 8 June, 1862. He was educated at King's College School and King's College Hospital (is M.R.C.S., L.S.A.), and joined the Royal Army Medical Corps, as Captain, 5 Feb. 1887. Capt. Holt was in Medical Charge of the Expedition to Sambana's and North Zululand, and received the thanks of the Colonial Office in 1895. He was promoted Major 5 Feb. 1899. He served in the South African War, 1900–1902 ; took part in the operations in Natal, 1899, including actions at Elandslaagte, Reitfontein and Lombard's Kop ; was present at the Defence of Ladysmith (Despatches [London Gazette, 29 July, 1902] ; Queen's Medal with three clasps, and King's Medal with two clasps). He was created a Companion of the Distinguished Service Order [London Gazette, 31 Oct. 1902] : " Maurice Percy Cue Holt, Major, Royal Army Medical Corps. In recognition of services during the operations in South Africa." He was promoted Lieutenant-Colonel 29 July, 1911, and was given the Brevet of Colonel 4 July, 1914. He served in the European War. He was A.D.M.S., 2nd Division, B.E.F., 16 Sept. 1914, to 21 Oct. 1915 ; was promoted Colonel 1 March, 1915 ; A.D.M.S., 22nd Division, British Expeditionary Force and Mediterranean Expeditionary Force, 22 Oct. 1915, to 23 Jan. 1916 ; D.D.M.S., 16th Army Corps, Mediterranean Expeditionary Force and British Salonika Force, 27 Jan. 1916, to 31 May, 1917 ; D.D.M.S., Lines of Communication, British Salonika Force, 1 June, to 20 Dec. 1917 ; was appointed D.D.M.S., British Salonika Force, 21 Dec. 1917. He was created a C.B. in 1915 ; a K.C.M.G. in 1917, and a K.C.B. in 1919. He was twice mentioned in Despatches, and was promoted to the rank of Major-General 15 April, 1918. Major-General Sir M. P. C. Holt is a specialist in operative surgery. He married, in 1887, Sarah Annie, daughter of the late Thomas M. Busteed, of Madras. They have a son and a daughter.

CROMPTON-ROBERTS, HENRY ROGER, Major, was born 18 May, 1863, eldest son of Charles Henry Crompton-Roberts, of Drybridge, Monmouthshire, and Mary, daughter and heiress of Roger Crompton, of Kearsley Lancashire. He entered the Army, as a Lieutenant in the 3rd Hussars, 6 Feb. 1884, and became Lieutenant in the Grenadier Guards 20 Feb. 1884 ; was promoted Captain 28 Oct. 1895, and Major, 3 May, 1899. He served in the South African War, from 1899 to 1901, and was present in the advance on Kimberley, including actions at Belmont, Enslin, Modder River and Magersfontein ; operations in the Orange Free State, Feb. to May, 1900, including actions at Poplar Grove, Dreifontein, Vet River (5 and 6 May) and Zand River ; operations in the Transvaal in May and June, 1900, including actions near Johannesburg, Pretoria and Diamond Hill (11 and 12 June) ; operations in the Transvaal, east of Pretoria, July to 29 Nov. 1900, including actions at Belfast (26 and 27 Aug.) ; operations in Orange River Colony, Dec. 1900 ; operations in Cape Colony, Dec. 1900, to 31 May, 1902. He was mentioned in Despatches [London Gazette, 10 Sept. 1901, and 29 July, 1902] ; received the Queen's Medal with six clasps, and the King's Medal with two clasps, and was created a Companion of the Distinguished Service Order [London Gazette, 31 Oct. 1902] : " Henry Roger Crompton-Roberts, Major, Grenadier Guards. In recognition of services during the operations in South Africa." He was promoted Lieutenant-Colonel 29 March, 1905, and retired from the Service with that rank 29 Aug. 1907. Lieut.-Colonel Crompton-Roberts married, in 1905, Blanche Alexandra, daughter of Lieut.-Colonel E. A. Hannay, of Ballylough, County Antrim, and they have one son and one daughter.

H. R. Crompton-Roberts.

MURRAY, WALTER GRAHAM, Major, was born 23 Oct. 1868, at Winkfield, near Windsor, eldest son of Major William Murray, of Ossemsley Manor, Christchurch, Hants. He was educated at Eton, and Oxford Military College, and entered the Army 30 Jan. 1889, as a Second Lieutenant in the 3rd Hussars, in which he was promoted Lieutenant 23 May, 1891, and Captain 23 May, 1896. He served in West Africa, 1897–98 (Northern Territories Gold Coast) ; with the expedition to Karaga

(Despatches [London Gazette, 7 March, 1899]; Medal with clasp; Brevet of Major 8 July, 1899). He was promoted Major 26 April, 1901. Major Murray served in the South African War, 1902; took part in the operations in the Transvaal and Orange River Colony, Jan. to 31 May, 1902. He was mentioned in Despatches [London Gazette, 29 July, 1902]: received the Queen's Medal with three clasps, and was created a Companion of the Distinguished Service Order [London Gazette, 31 Oct. 1902]: "Walter Graham Murray, Major, 3rd Hussars. In recognition of services during the operations in South Africa." He became Lieutenant-Colonel 14 July, 1910, and retired 2 April, 1913. Lieut.-Colonel W. G. Murray married, at Pretoria, on 20 April, 1911, Mary, daughter of E. F. Bourke, of Pretoria, and their children are: Dorothy Lillie; Elizabeth Mary and Patricia Evelyn Hamilton.

Walter Graham Murray.

KIRKPATRICK, HENRY POWNALL, Major, was born in 1862, eldest son of the late Edward Kirkpatrick, of Tyldesley, Lancs, and of Agnes, youngest daughter of the late James Pownall, of Pennington Hall, Leigh, Lancs. He was educated at Uppingham, and at Brasenose College, Oxford. He was gazetted to the 16th Lancers 5 Dec. 1883, as Lieutenant, and was promoted to Captain 2 Sept. 1890; was Adjutant, Yeomanry Cavalry, 4 Jan. 1896; and Major, 30 Aug. 1899. He served in the South African War, 1900–2. In command of the 16th Lancers, 11 Nov. 1900, to 4 March, 1902; operations in Cape Colony and Orange River Colony, 1900–2. He received the Queen's Medal with two clasps, the King's Medal with two clasps, and was created a Companion of the Distinguished Service Order [London Gazette, 31 Oct. 1902]: "Henry Pownall Kirkpatrick, Major, 16th Lancers. In recognition of services during the operations in South Africa." He was Second-in-Command of the 16th (Queen's) Lancers, and retired 23 May, 1903. He married, in 1898, Ruby, only daughter of Major W. B. Morris, 7th Hussars. Lieut.-Colonel H. P. Kirkpatrick died 30 Aug. 1919.

DAVIDSON, THOMAS ST. CLAIR, Major, was born 12 Sept. 1861, in Edinburgh, son of the late Colonel Sir David Davidson, K.C.B., of Edinburgh, and Margaret Buchanan. He was educated at Edinburgh Academy and Edinburgh University, and was gazetted to the Leinster Regt. 19 Dec. 1883, serving in Lushai in 1889, as a Transport Officer (clasp); and in Chin Lushai, 1889–90, as a Transport Officer (Medal and clasp). He became Captain 12 Jan. 1890; was Adjutant, Leinster Regt., 16 March, 1891, to 15 March, 1895; Adjutant, Volunteers, 1 Nov. 1895, to 30 April, 1901; and was promoted to Major 29 Nov. 1899. In South Africa Major Davidson served with the 1st Battn. Prince of Wales's Leinster Regt. (Royal Canadians), 1901–2, and took part in the operations in the Transvaal in June and July, 1901; also in the operations in Orange River Colony, June, 1901 to 31 May, 1902. He was mentioned in Despatches [London Gazette, 29 July, 1902]; received the Queen's Medal with five clasps, and was created a Companion of the Distinguished Service Order [London Gazette, 31 Oct. 1902]: "Thomas St. Clair Davidson, Major, The Leinster Regt. In recognition of services during the operations in South Africa." He was promoted to Lieutenant-Colonel 23 May, 1907, and retired 2 Sept. 1911. He served in the European War, from 3 Aug. 1914, as Censor in London; and from 25 Sept. 1914, to 19 April, 1916, as Lieutenant-Colonel, 9th (Service) Battn. The King's Own Royal Lancaster Regt. Lieut.-Colonel Davidson served in France and Salonika. He married (1st), on 2 Nov. 1892, at Bridgend, Agnes (died 1910), daughter of the late T. Davies, of Bryn Towy, Carmarthen, and they had four children: Dorothy Forster; Winefred Anne; Robert St. Clair (born 8 April, 1900), and Ileene Hanbury. On 16 Jan. 1912, at Reigate, Lieut.-Colonel Davidson married (2ndly) Flora Isabella, youngest daughter of the late James Farquhar, of Sunnyside, Reigate, and Hall Green, Kincardineshire, and they have one daughter, Diana Jean.

COX, EDWARD HENRY, Major, was born 21 May, 1863, son of the late Arthur Zachariah Cox, of Harwood Hall, Essex. He entered the Army 12 Nov. 1884; became Captain 15 March, 1892, and Major, 3 Feb. 1900. Major Cox served in the South African War, 1899–1902, on the Staff, and was present at the Relief of Ladysmith, including action at Colenso; took part in the operations on Tugela Heights 14 to 27 Feb. 1900, and action at Pieter's Hill; in the Transvaal in May and June, 1900; in Natal, March to June, 1900; in the Transvaal, west of Pretoria, July to 29 Nov. 1900, including actions at Frederickstad (17 to 25 Oct.); in Cape Colony, north of Orange River, including action at Ruidam; also during the operations in the Transvaal and Orange River Colony, Nov. 1900, to May, 1902 (Despatches [London Gazette, 10 Sept. 1901]; Queen's Medal with five clasps, and King's Medal with two clasps). He was created a Companion of the Distinguished Service Order [London Gazette, 31 Oct. 1902]: "Edward Henry Cox, Major, Royal Fusiliers. In recognition of services during the operations in South Africa." He was promoted to Lieutenant-Colonel 3 May, 1907, and retired 23 Aug. 1911

Cecil de C. Etheridge.

ETHERIDGE, CECIL DE COURCY, Major, was born at Littlehampton 21 Dec. 1859, son of Major-General H. T. Etheridge, C.S.I., Indian Army. He was educated at the Royal Military College, Sandhurst; was gazetted to the Royal Warwickshire Regt. 11 May, 1878, and first saw active service in the Afghan War, 1878–79–80, when he took part in the fighting in the Kurram Valley, and also was in the Zaimukt Expedition, receiving the Medal. He served in the Nile Expedition in 1898, and was present at the Battle of Khartum, receiving the Medal, the Egyptian Medal with clasp, and the 4th Class of the Osmanieh. He retired, as a Major, 23 Dec. 1898, having attained to that rank 16 Dec. 1896. Major Etheridge served in the South African War, from 1900 to 1902, as Remount Officer. He was mentioned in Despatches [London Gazette, 29 July, 1902]; received the Queen's Medal with three clasps, the King's Medal with two clasps; was promoted to Lieutenant-Colonel, in the Reserve of Officers, 18 Oct. 1902, and for good work during the campaign was created a Companion of the Distinguished Service Order [London Gazette, 31 Oct. 1902]: "Cecil de Courcy Etheridge, Major, Reserve of Officers. In recognition of services during the operations in South Africa." Lieut.-Colonel Etheridge served in the European War, 1914–1919, and was mentioned in Despatches, and created a C.B.E. in 1919. He is Secretary to the City of Edinburgh Territorial Force Association.

PORTAL, BERTRAM PERCY, Major, was born 10 Jan. 1866, third son of the late Sir Wyndham Spencer Portal, 1st Bart., and Lady Portal (who died in 1903), eldest daughter of William Hicks Beach, of Oakley, Hampshire. He was educated at Wellington College and Sandhurst, and was gazetted a Lieutenant in the 17th Lancers 29 Aug. 1885, and he became Captain 1 Jan. 1895. From 18 March, 1896, to 28 Feb. 1899, he was A.D.C. to the Governor of Madras, Sir Arthur Havelock. He served in the South African War, 1900–2, taking part in operations in the Orange Free State, Feb. to May, 1900, including actions at Vet River (5 and 6 May) and Zand River; operations in the Transvaal in May and June, 1900, including actions near Johannesburg and Pretoria; operations in Cape Colony, July, 1901, to 31 May, 1902. He was mentioned in Despatches [London Gazette, 29 July, 1902]; received the Queen's Medal with three clasps, the King's Medal with two clasps, and was created a Companion of the Distinguished Service Order [London Gazette, 31 Oct. 1902]: "Bertram Percy Portal, Major, 17th Lancers. In recognition of services during the operations in South Africa." He was promoted to Lieutenant-Colonel 30 Oct. 1903, and commanded the 17th Lancers from 1903 to 1907; was given the Brevet of Colonel 30 Oct. 1906, and retired 30 Oct. 1907. Colonel Portal served in the European War, as a Temporary Brigadier-General with the British Expeditionary Force in France, from June, 1916, to April, 1918. He was created a C.B. in 1917, for services in connection with the Irish Rebellion of 1916. He is Deputy Lieutenant and a Justice of the Peace for Hampshire. He married, in 1899, the Honourable Margaret Louisa Littleton, eldest daughter of the 3rd Baron Hatherton, and they have a son, Melville Edward Bertram, and five daughters.

FAIR, JAMES GEORGE, Major, was born 19 Nov. 1864, son of the late James Fair, of Hove. He entered the Army 29 Aug. 1885, as Lieutenant, 21st Hussars; served as Staff Officer to General Gatacre during the Atbara Campaign in 1898; was present at the Battles of the Atbara and Khartum; was mentioned in Despatches [London Gazette, 24 May, 1898]; received the 4th Class Medjidie; the Medal and the Egyptian Medal with clasp. He was Adjutant, 21st Hussars, 1 July, 1889, to 30 June, 1893; was promoted to Captain, 21st Lancers, 26 Oct. 1892; and Adjutant, Cavalry Depôt, from 30 May, 1899. In the South African War of 1899–1902, he served with the South African Constabulary from 14 May, 1901; Despatches; Queen's Medal with three clasps, and was created a Companion of the Distinguished Service Order [London Gazette, 31 Oct. 1902]: "James George Fair, Major (21st Lancers), South African Constabulary. In recognition of services during the operations in South Africa." From 1904 to 1908 he commanded a Division of the South African Constabulary in the Orange River Colony, retiring from the 21st Lancers 9 Dec. 1905. He became a Member of the Inter-Colonial Council of the Transvaal and Orange River Colony in 1906, and was Resident Commissioner and Commandant-General in Southern Rhodesia, 1908–11. Major J. G. Fair was Deputy Assistant Director of Remounts, 1911–15; became Lieutenant-Colonel, Reserve of Officers, 25 Feb. 1914; was Deputy Director of Remounts, Egypt, 1915–16; Deputy Assistant Director of Remounts, Southern Command. For his services in the Great War he was created a C.M.G. in 1916. Lieut.-Colonel J. G. Fair married, in 1901, Mary, daughter of the late Lieut.-General J. S. Sargent, C.B.

HOSKINS, ARTHUR REGINALD, Brevet Major, was born 30 May, 1871, son of Thomas Hoskins, of Belgrave Road, London, S.W. He was commissioned in the North Staffordshire Regt. 23 May, 1891; became Lieutenant 9 Jan. 1895, and was employed with the Egyptian Army 20 March, 1896, to 31 Jan. 1900. He accompanied the Expedition to Dongola, 1896 (Despatches [London Gazette, 3 Nov. 1896]; served with the Nile Expedition, 1897 (Despatches [London Gazette, 25 Jan. 1898]; served with the Nile Expedition, 1898; took part in the operations at Gedaref (Despatches [London Gazette, 30 Sept. 1898]; 4th Class of the Medjidie; Medal); with the Nile Expedition, 1899; was present during the operations resulting in final defeat of Khalifa. In command, Camel Transport, Flying Column (Despatches [London Gazette, 30 Jan. 1900]; Brevet of Major 21 March, 1900 (promoted to Captain 20 March, 1900). He served in the South African War, 1899–1902, on the Staff (Despatches [London Gazette, 29 July, 1902]; Queen's Medal with three clasps and King's Medal with two clasps, and was created a Companion of the Distinguished Service Order [London Gazette, 31 Oct. 1902]: "Arthur Reginald Hoskins, Brevet Major, North Staffordshire Regt. In recognition of services during the operations in South Africa." He was placed on the list of Officers considered qualified for Staff employment, in consequence of service on the Staff in the Field. He served in East Africa, 1902–3; took part in the operations in Somaliland, on the Staff (Despatches [London Gazette, 2 Sept. 1904]: Medal with clasp).

He was D.A.A.G., Egypt, 10 Feb. 1906, to 8 March, 1910; became Major 7 April, 1910; was G.S.O.2, Staff College, 23 April, 1910, to 14 Aug. 1913; was given the Brevet of Lieutenant-Colonel 18 Jan. 1911; was Inspector-General, King's African Rifles, 15 Aug. 1913, to 18 Sept. 1914. He served in the Great War; as G.S.O.1, 7th Division, B.E.F., 12 Nov. 1914, to 24 March, 1915; commanded the 8th Infantry Brigade, B.E.F., 25 March, 1915, to Feb. 1916; was promoted to Lieutenant-Colonel 10 April, 1916; commanded the 1st East African Division, East African Force, 1 April, 1916, to 27 July, 1917; became Major-General 1 Jan. 1917.

There is a book, "With the Nigerians in German East Africa," written by Capt. W. D. Downes, and published by Messrs. Methuen, of which it has been said: "This deeply interesting book begins with an account of the German East Africa Campaign before the arrival of the Nigerian Brigade. It then describes the doings of that Brigade. The operations and battles are narrated with great vividness, and the story ends with the passing of Von Lettow into Portuguese territory, at which moment Germany lost her last colony." General Hoskins, as Commander-in-Chief in East Africa in 1917, is, of course, mentioned from time to time in Major Downes's book, although it is mainly concerned with the doings of the Nigeria Regiment of the West African Frontier Force, which formed part of the Force which was in 1917 commanded by Sir Arthur Hoskins. Major Downes begins his book by saying that in British West African Colonies, "there are certain races and tribes that take to fighting as a duck takes to water. These are trained and led by officers and non-commissioned officers specially selected for service in the tropics, who are seconded for a certain period from their British regiments to the various battalions of the W.A.F.F. . . . . It is my hope that when the reader has finished this book, he will be as convinced as the writer that these soldiers from the borders of the sun-scorched Sahara, from the banks of the Niger and the Benue, from Yorubaland and Calabar, are second to none among the dark-skinned sons of the Empire as fighting men." Major Downes traces the history of the W.A.F.F. from June, 1863, when the first Hausas were trained as soldiers, thirty Hausa Police of the Lagos being armed and drilled that year. "This force went by the nickname of 'The Forty Thieves,' but why I do not know; nor have I any records of there being more than thirty all told." Commander, usually known as Captain, John Glover, R.N., Lieutenant-Governor of Lagos, wrote of this body of men: "They are very apt in their drill and are proud of being soldiers, and have shown on two recent occasions at Epe that they can fight faithfully and well." Glover by degrees increased the force by six hundred men, who were a sort of militia, while a hundred armed police were the permanent force. They were placed under his command, and Major Downes says: "Glover must therefore be looked upon as the father of the W.A.F.F.'s. Little did he know that in fifty years' time the force which he nurtured in its infancy would be called upon to fight a great and powerful European nation in three different theatres of war, namely, Togoland, the Cameroons, and German East Africa, and in each of these three theatres be victorious." As time went on the Hausa "Militia" became a force of the past, and a regular armed force, known at first as the Lagos Hausa Constabulary, was raised. This force saw much active service, both at home and overseas, taking a most active part, under Capt. Glover, in the Ashanti War of 1873–74. "The Hausa Constabulary, later the Lagos Battn. W.A.F.F., became the 2nd Southern Nigeria Regt. in 1905, the Southern Nigeria Regt. in 1911, and re-divided again in 1914 into the 3rd and 4th Nigeria Regt. In its ranks have served many famous black warriors, from the time of the native officer Yakubu, who was known in 1879 as the 'Father of the Hausas,' to Sergt.-Major Sumanu, with his five medals, both of our time. The Calabar Battn. of the Southern Nigeria Regt. descended from the forces of the Oil Rivers Protectorate, and part of the Royal Niger Constabulary, later known as the 3rd Nigeria Regt., prior to 1911 was known as the 1st Southern Nigeria Regt., but was amalgamated in that year with the 2nd Southern Nigeria Regt. into one regiment under the command of Lieut.-Colonel Cunliffe, who became Commandant of the Southern Nigeria Regt. On the 1st Jan. 1914, the battalion became the 3rd Nigeria Regt. The chief actions that the Southern Nigeria Regt. have taken part in since 1899 are: The Ashantee War of 1900; the Benin River Patrol; the Brass River Patrol; the Benin City Massacre Punitive Patrol; the Aro Expedition; the Onitsha Hinterland and Asaba Hinterland Expeditions; various Munshi Expeditions; the Ijebu Ode Expeditions; various Soukwala and other Pagan districts Expeditions and Patrols. The Northern Battn. of the Nigeria Regt. dates back to the days of the Oil Rivers Protectorate and the Niger Coast Protectorate. They were originally an irregular armed police, employed by the Royal Niger Company to protect their trade both by land and river. Later they became a disciplined regular force, known as the Royal Niger Constabulary." This body of men was later incorporated into the West African Field Force, and subsequently became the 1st and 2nd Nigeria Regts. In 1900 Sir Frederick Lugard sent and expeditionary force to represent Northern Nigeria in the Ashantee War. "There is no doubt that Sir James Willcocks, who commanded the troops in Ashantee, placed special reliance on the Northern Nigeria troops, to judge by the honours list of that campaign. Capt. Melliss was wounded no less than four times in three months, and was awarded the Victoria Cross, whilst Bugler Moma and Private Ojo Oyo both received the D.C.M." In the King's Speech at the opening of Parliament reference was made to the endurance and gallantry of the native troops of Nigeria, so ably commanded by Sir James Willcocks and led by British officers. On the 23rd of July, 1901, Sir James Willcocks resigned the appointment of Commandant of the Northern Nigeria Regt., and his place was taken by Colonel Morland. "In 1902 Northern troops were sent to assist the Southern Nigeria Regt. in the Aro Expedition, under command of Lieut.-Colonel Festing, D.S.O. In 1903 the towns of Kano and Sakoto were captured by Colonel Morland's Expedition, and formed the subject of mention in the King's Speech at the opening of Parliament on 17 Feb. 1903. Colonel Morland advanced on Zaria on 29 Jan. 1903, and in seven weeks had captured both these great towns, had fought four important engagements at Babeji, Kano, Sokoto, and again near Rawia against a Kano Army. The hardships during this expedition were very great, and many native soldiers and carriers died of cold and lack of water. During this year there first came into being the Mounted Infantry Battn., which was later known as the 5th Nigeria Regt. This year was a year of war for the W.A.F.F." which was engaged in many minor operations in addition to the Kano–Sokoto Expedition, the most important of these being the Bunni Expeditions, during which Major March and 12 natives were killed. In 1906 came the Sokoto outbreak, when Messrs. Hillary and Scott, together with Lieut. Blackwood and twenty-five rank and file of the Mounted Infantry Company, quartered at Sokoto, lost their lives. Major Goodwin, in command of six hundred troops, eventually quelled this rising. In 1906 and 1907 the W.A.F.F. took part in several minor operations, the best known of them being the cave fighting at Margki, under command of Lieuts. Chapman and Chaytor. "From 1900 up to the outbreak of the Great War in 1914, Nigerian troops, both North and South, have constantly been employed on patrols and other forms of military operations. No other forces of the Crown have seen so much fighting in the same fourteen years. . . . I hope that when my readers have read this account, poorly told as it is, by an amateur writer, they will in future respect the fighting black man of Africa, for he has at least proved himself a man. We in England owe our negro fellow-subject a great debt of gratitude for all he has done for our beloved Empire. Many a native of Nigeria has trekked his last trek and fought his last fight far away from his own land for the sake of the Empire. . . . The length of a man's life is not told in words, but in actions, irrespective of colour, race or creed; and until the 'Cease Fire' sounds on all fronts the W.A.F.F. will continue to sacrifice themselves willingly on the altar of duty, side by side with their different brothers of the Empire, for the sake of that Empire that has given them freedom, justice and all that makes life worth living. I personally feel it an honour to have served with such gallant troops, who at all times have been brave, chivalrous and cheerful, in spite of all they have been called upon to undergo. One realizes the truth in those four lines of Kipling after having served in action with these gallant fellows:

> "'Oh, East is East, and West is West, and never the twain shall meet,
> Till earth and sky stand presently at God's great judgment seat;
> But there is neither East nor West, Border nor Breed nor Birth,
> When two strong men stand face to face, tho' they come from the ends of the earth!'"

Major Downes gives an account of the foundation of the German Colony in East Africa in 1884, by Karl Peters & Co. He then tells us how from the outbreak of war in 1914 the first phase of the campaign against German East Africa lasted until the beginning of 1916. The second phase began when General Smuts assumed command of the forces in the field, and lasted to the crossing of the Rufiji by British troops. The third phase, from early January, 1917, till the Germans crossed into Portuguese territory. The fourth phase was the campaign continued in Portuguese East Africa. Major Downes describes the fighting up to the time when General Hoskins, who had been in command of a column, "took over the forces in East Africa on the 20th Jan. 1917. At this time the effective strength of the enemy's forces was put down at 1,100 Europeans and 7,300 Askaris, with 4 guns of 4-inch or 4.1 calibre, 16 smaller guns, and 73 machine guns. In the light of what took place later, I think these numbers were under-estimated. At one time it was hoped the supply question would be solved by using the Rufiji river for transport purposes, but this idea was very soon given up, for the river rose into a huge torrent with a speed of 20 miles an hour. At the end of January the situation of the Rufiji was most gloomy. The supply and transport situation was bad; there was no reserve of food in the advance depôt; the number of carriers was not nearly sufficient; pack animals died after a single journey, if not before; mechanical transport drivers far back on the lines of communication were so rapidly falling sick that hundreds of light cars stood for days without doing one journey. General Hoskins therefore withdrew from the river area all the troops he could." The following is an extract from General Hoskins's official Despatch, dated 30 May, 1917, but not published till 27 Dec. 1917: "All seemed to be going well when, on 25 Jan., heavy rain began to fall, ushering in the wettest season known in East Africa for many years. By the 27th the lines of communication from Mikesse to Kibambawe were interrupted by the washing away of bridges and the flooding of roads; and operations in all areas were henceforward seriously hampered by the untimely rain. It is perhaps hard to realize the difficulties which the rainy season in East Africa entailed for a force acting from such widely separated bases, with several different lines of communication running through every variety of difficult country, and necessitating in some cases as much as 130 miles of porter transport. In the Mgeta and Rufiji valleys, roads constructed with much skill and labour, over which motor transport ran continuously in January, were traversed with difficulty and much hardship by porters wading for miles in water above their waists. The Dodoma–Iringa line of communications crossed the great Ruaha in the dry weather by an easy ford; when the rain had really set in, supplies had to be transported not only over a flooded river, but also a swamp on each side of it six feet deep and as many miles wide. Considerable anxiety was caused by this extensive flooding across the Dodoma–Iringa communication, and every effort was made to cope with this. The Iringa Column was kept as small as possible, and special flat-bottomed boats were prepared, but eventually it became necessary to switch on to a new line along the road which runs south from the railway at Kilossa. The valley of the Rufiji and its various tributaries became a vast lake, in which the true courses of the streams were often only discernible with difficulty, if at all. Patrol work had to be carried out for some time in canoes, and the men found themselves making fast to the roofs of houses which had lately formed their quarters. The conditions of the Kilwa area were equally trying, as roads became impassable for motor transport, and animals died a few weeks after being landed. An even more serious factor, perhaps, was the sickness amongst the troops. The coastal belt and the valleys of the Mgeta and Rufiji even in dry weather are unhealthy for all but the indigenous African, and during the rains there is a great increase in malaria, while dysentery and pneumonia strike down even the African native. In 1916 many of our troops in East Africa spent the rain season in high and comparatively healthy localities. It was impossible to do this in 1917 without withdrawing from ground which had been hardly won and out of which the enemy would have to be driven again with equal difficulty, should he be allowed to reoccupy it. That the enemy had also to contend with sickness, and with sameness, if not with scarcity, of food, is certain ; but in a minor degree, since his white men were more acclimatized to German East Africa, and his native soldiers indigenous to the country. He had the advantage of falling back on interior lines ; of veteran troops from whose ranks nearly all waverers had by this time been eliminated ; and of his power of living on the country as he retired. This last was accentuated by the fact that whereas we are accustomed to take and pay for only what the villagers can spare, the Germans have no scruples about taking all. And after using men, women and children as porters, so far as they require, they send them back in a starving condition, thus increasing the difficulties of our advancing troops." Major Downes describes the operations during the rains, and the hardships suffered by both European and native troops are evident from an extract from General Hoskins's Despatch up to the 30th of May : " Meanwhile the feeding of the various columns was a source of much anxiety to me and to all my Column Commanders. As the rains increased in the Kilwa area, the animals died of fly, and light mechanical transport work became impossible ; porter transport had gradually to be adopted inland, and a system of dhows and boats up to riverhead on the Matandu river was instituted. Portions of the 1st Division located at Mohoro and subsequently at Utete were supplied by river transport up the Rufiji, under arrangements with the Navy, and the river became the main line of supplies for all troops in that area. The maintenance of the troops in the Iringa area by the Dodoma–Iringa line had become so precarious that in March the Kilossa–Iringa line had to be adopted, though it involved heavy casualties among porters and donkeys, and much sickness among the white personnel. It was not until May that weather conditions again permitted of the Dodoma–Iringa line being used. Difficulties of supply through the low-lying country between Kibambawe and the Uluguru uplands steadily increased, so that the troops were frequently on half rations. I therefore hastened the withdrawal of the remainder of General Beves' force to recuperate and refit. Sickness amongst Europeans and South African units had assumed such proportions as to necessitate their withdrawal to recuperate. I decided to send as many as possible to South Africa, and to recall them for offensive operations after the rains. The hardships of the campaign and the brunt of the fighting since 1914 had been borne by some Indian units, and by the King's African Rifles. These had also suffered severely from sickness, especially the Indians, but units were so weak as to make it impossible to withdraw any of the King's African Rifles, and only certain of the Indians were able to be sent to healthier ground to recuperate."

Major-General Hoskins commanded the 3rd Division, Mesopotamian Expeditionary Force, Egyptian Expeditionary Force, from 19 Aug. 1917. He was promoted to Lieutenant-General, and was created a K.C.B. in 1919. Sir Arthur Hoskins commanded the North Midlands Territorial Force from 1919.

DORLING, LIONEL, Major, was born 7 Aug. 1860, son of Henry Dorling, of Epsom. He was gazetted to the 105th Foot, as Second Lieutenant, 13 Aug. 1879, becoming Lieutenant, South Yorkshire Regt., 15 Nov. 1879 ; was Adjutant, South Yorkshire Regt., 20 May, 1882, to 20 Nov. 1887, and Captain, Yorkshire Light Infantry, 28 May, 1884 ; Adjutant, Militia, 1 July, 1889, to 31 March, 1889 ; Paymaster, A.P.D., 27 March, 1893, to 2 July, 1901 ; Major 27 March, 1900 ; Staff Paymaster, Army Pay Department, from 3 July, 1901. He served in the South African War, 1899–1902, employed as Field Paymaster, Natal Field Force ; was present at the Relief of Ladysmith, including action at Colenso ; in the operations on Tugela Heights (Despatches [London Gazette, 29 July, 1902]; Queen's Medal with five clasps, and King's Medal with two clasps). He was created a Companion of the Distinguished Service Order [London Gazette, 31 Oct. 1902]: " Lionel Dorling, Staff Paymaster, Army Pay Department. In recognition of services during the operations in South Africa." He became Accountant, Army Account Department, 1 May, 1905, and was promoted to Lieutenant-Colonel 3 July, 1906, and Colonel 12 Jan. 1911 ; was Command Paymaster, London District, 1 March, 1911, to 20 April, 1912 ; Malta, 29 April to 3 Aug. 1912 ; South Africa from 29 Sept. 1912. Colonel Dorling served in the Great War in 1915, in the Dardanelles (Despatches), and in Egypt in 1916, and became Paymaster, Eastern Command, 17 Dec. 1916. He was created a C.M.G. in 1919. Colonel Dorling married, in 1888, Constance, youngest daughter of W. H. Price, of Karachi.

ROUSE, HUBERT, Major, was born 22 Aug. 1864, son of H. J. Rouse, M.I.C.E., of Sussex Place, S.W., and Mrs. Rouse (née Saunders). He was gazetted to the Royal Artillery, as Lieutenant, 5 July, 1884, becoming Captain 4 Oct. 1893. He served on the North-West Frontier of India, 1897–98 (Malakand, Adjutant, Royal Artillery ; Buner, Adjutant, Royal Artillery) ; took part in the attack and capture of the Tanga Pass (Medal with clasp). Capt. Rouse served in the South African War, 1899–1902 ; at the Relief of Kimberley ; in the Orange Free State, Feb. to May, 1900, including operations at Paardeberg (17 to 26 Feb.), actions at Poplar Grove and Dreifontein ; in the Transvaal, east of Pretoria, July to 29 Nov. 1900, including action at Lydenberg (5 to 8 Sept.) ; in the Transvaal, west of Pretoria, July to 29 Nov. 1900, including action at Zilikat's Nek ; again in the Transvaal, 30 Nov. 1900, to 31 May, 1902 (Despatches [London Gazette, 10 Sept. 1901]; Queen's Medal with four clasps, and King's Medal with two clasps). He was created a Companion of the Distinguished Service Order [London Gazette, 31 Oct. 1902]: " Hubert Rouse, Major, Royal Artillery.

In recognition of services during the operations in South Africa." He was promoted to Major 5 May, 1900 ; to Lieutenant-Colonel 14 Sept. 1910, and to Colonel 15 June, 1914. Colonel Rouse served in the European War from 1914 ; was mentioned in Despatches and created a C.B. in 1916, and received the Mons Medal. He married, in 1893, Adeline Louisa, daughter of Charles N. Macnamara, F.R.S.S., of The Lodge, Chorley Wood, and they have one daughter, Eileen Mia, who married, in 1917, Charles F. Birley, of Bartle Hall, Preston.

TWYNAM, HUMPHREY MARTIN, Major, was born 16 March, 1858, youngest son of the late Thomas Twynam, of Fair Oak, Hampshire. He was educated at Sherborne School, and became Second Lieutenant, 33rd Foot, 11 May, 1878, and 59th Foot, 30 Oct. 1878. He served in the Afghan War, 1879–80 ; was present at the actions of Ahmed Khel and Urzoo ; was mentioned in Despatches [London Gazette, 30 July, 1889], and received the Medal with clasp. He was promoted to Captain 1 Oct. 1887 ; took part in the operations in Chitral, with the Relief Force in 1895 (Medal and clasp) ; was A.D.C. to Major-General, India, 13 May, 1896, to 5 March, 1899 ; served on the North-West Frontier of India, 1897–98, in the Tochi Expedition, on the Staff ; was mentioned in Despatches [London Gazette, 11 Feb. 1898], and received a clasp. He served in the South African War, 1899–1902, employed with the South African Constabulary, taking part in operations in the Transvaal ; was mentioned in Despatches [London Gazette, 29 July, 1902]; received the Queen's Medal with clasp, the King's Medal with two clasps, and was created a Companion of the Distinguished Service Order [London Gazette, 31 Oct. 1902]: " Humphrey Martin Twynam, Major, The East Lancashire Regt. (South African Constabulary). In recognition of services during the operations in South Africa." He was promoted to Major 24 May, 1900, and retired from the East Lancashire Regt. 16 March, 1906. He became Lieutenant-Colonel commanding the 5th Royal West Kent Regt., and died at his residence, 1, Hayes Road, Bromley, Kent, on 9 April, 1913. He had married Naomi (who died in 1911), daughter of the late George Leopold Seaward.

HENEAGE, THE HONOURABLE HENRY GRANVILLE, Major, was born 17 March, 1868, second son of the first Baron Heneage and Lady Eleanor Cecilia Hare. He was educated at Eton, joined the 3rd Lincolnshire (Militia) Regt. in 1885, and was gazetted to the 12th Lancers 16 May, 1888, becoming Captain 16 May, 1893. From 1895 to 1898 he was A.D.C. to the Governor of Bombay. He served in the South African War, 1899–1902, taking part in the advance on Kimberley, including the action at Magersfontein ; operations in the Orange Free State, Feb. to May, 1900, including operations at Paardeberg, actions at Poplar Grove, Dreifontein, Houtnek (Thoba Mountain) and Zand River ; operations in the Transvaal, May and June, 1900, including actions near Johannesburg and Diamond Hill ; operations in the Transvaal, west of Pretoria, July to 29 Nov. 1900 ; operations in Orange River Colony, May to 29 Nov. 1900, including actions at Lindley, Bethlehem and Wittebergen ; operations in the Transvaal 30 Nov. 1900, to July, 1901 ; operations in Cape Colony, July, 1901, to 31 May, 1902. He was mentioned in Despatches [London Gazette, 29 July, 1902]; received the Queen's Medal with six clasps, the King's Medal with two clasps, and was created a Companion of the Distinguished Service Order [London Gazette, 31 Oct. 1902]: " The Honourable Henry Granville Heneage, Major, 12th Lancers. In recognition of services during the operations in South Africa." He retired 29 Sept. 1905 ; is a J.P. for County Cork, and was Honorary Secretary to the Duhallow Hunt Club from 1909 to 1911. In 1904 he married Gladys Mary, third daughter of the late Sidney Cuthbert, of Beaufront Castle, Hexham.

POLLOK-MORRIS, WILLIAM POLLOK MORRIS, Major, was born 12 March, 1867, son of Colonel R. M. Pollok-Morris, of Kilmarnock, and Agnes Tennent, daughter of John Buchanan. He was educated at Harrow and at Trinity College, Cambridge ; became Lieutenant, 18th Hussars, 25 Aug. 1886 ; Captain 12 Feb. 1893. He served in the Chitral Expedition in 1895, with the Relief Force (Medal and clasp), and took part in operations on the North-West Frontier of India, 1897, with the Tirah Expeditionary Force, as Regimental Assistant to the Base Commissariat Officer (Oct. 1897, to April, 1898). He was mentioned in Despatches [London Gazette, 5 April, 1898], and received two clasps. He was Adjutant, 18th Hussars, 28 Aug. 1898, to 31 Aug. 1900 ; and was promoted to Major 1 Sept. 1900. He served in the South African War, 1899–1902, and was slightly wounded, being present at operations in Natal, 1899, including the action at Talana ; operations in the Transvaal, 30 Nov. 1900, to Sept. 1901, and Nov. 1901, to 31 May, 1902 ; operations in Orange River Colony, March and May, 1902 ; operations on the Zululand Frontier of Natal in Sept. and Oct. 1901. He was mentioned in Despatches [London Gazette, 29 July, 1902]; received the Queen's Medal with four clasps, and King's Medal with two clasps, and was created a Companion of the Distinguished Service Order [London Gazette, 31 Oct. 1002]: " William Pollok Morris Pollok-Morris, Major, 18th Hussars. In recognition of services during the operations in South Africa." He was Second-in-Command, Victoria Mary Princess of Wales's Hussars, in 1903 ; was Lieutenant-Colonel commanding the Regt. from 19 Feb. 1906, to 1910 ; was given the Brevet of Colonel 19 Feb. 1909, and retired with the rank of Colonel 4 June, 1913. He was created C.M.G. in 1918. Colonel Pollok-Morris is a D.L. and J.P. He married, in 1907, Jane Catherine, eldest daughter of Robert Jameson Torrie, of 1, Glenfinlas Street, Edinburgh, and they have one daughter, Ellison Janet.

WALKER, HAROLD BRIDGWOOD, Capt., was born 26 April, 1862, son of the late Rev. James H. Walker and of Mary Walker, of Fox Earth, Staffs. He was educated at Shrewsbury School, and at Jesus College, Cambridge ; joined the Army, from the Militia, as Second Lieutenant, The Duke of Cornwall's Light Infantry, 14 May, 1884. He served in the Nile Expedition, 1884–85, with the River Column (Medal with clasp ; Khedive's Star) ; on the Egyptian Frontier, 1885–86, with the Mounted Infantry Frontier Field Force, being present in the action at Giniss. He became Captain 16 Dec. 1891 ; served on the North-West Frontier of India,

1897–98, with the Tirah Field Force; was D.A.Q.M.G., Intelligence, India, 6 May, 1898, to 13 March, 1900 (Medal and two clasps). He served in South Africa, 1899–1902; as Special Service Officer in command of the 4th Regiment of Mounted Infantry 11 Nov. 1900, to 31 May, 1902. He was present at the operations in Orange Free State, Feb. to May, 1900, including actions at Vet River and Zand River; operations in the Transvaal, May and June, 1900, including the actions near Johannesburg, Pretoria and Diamond Hill (11 and 12 June); operations in the Transvaal, east of Pretoria, July to 29 Nov. 1900, including the action at Belfast (26 and 27 Aug.); operations in the Transvaal 30 Nov. 1900, to 31 May, 1902. He was mentioned in Despatches [London Gazette, 10 Sept. 1901, and 29 July, 1902]; received Queen's and King's Medals with seven clasps; the Brevet of Major 29 Nov. 1900, and was created a Companion of the Distinguished Service Order [London Gazette, 31 Oct. 1902]: "Harold Bridgwood Walker, Capt. and Brevet Major, The Duke of Cornwall's Light Infantry. In recognition of services during the operations in South Africa." He became Major 22 Nov. 1902; was transferred to the Border Regt. 2 July, 1904, as Second-in-Command; became Lieutenant-Colonel 1 July, 1908, and Colonel 7 March, 1912. Colonel Walker served in the European War. He became Brigadier-General 12 Dec. 1914, on the General Staff of the Australian and New Zealand Army Corps, and served with the Mediterranean Expeditionary Force from 1914 to 1916 at Gallipoli and at the landing of Anzac; became Brigade Commander of the 1st Australian Infantry Brigade 21 June, 1915, and Divisional Commander (Temporary Major-General), 1st Australian Division, 21 July, 1915. He afterwards commanded the 1st Australian Division in France, and on 4 July, 1918, was appointed to command the 48th Division of the British Army in Italy. He was present at the Battles on the Somme, 1916–17; advance on to the Hindenburg Line, 1917; operations round Ypres; Third Battle of Ypres and Passchendaele; operations in front of Amiens, April, 1918; operations in front of Hazebrouck 10 July, 1918; operations in Italy, July, 1918, to close of War and Armistice; on the Asiago Plateau, including the advance into Austria through the Val d'Assa, and occupation of the Trentino; on this occasion the 48th Division took 22,000 prisoners and captured over 600 guns of all calibres and innumerable machine guns. From 3 March to 10 June Major-General Walker commanded the troops in Italy, subsequently being sent on a mission into Austria. He was seven times mentioned in Despatches; twice wounded; created a C.B., 1915; promoted Major-General 1 Jan. 1916, and was created a K.C.B. 1 Jan. 1918, and a K.C.M.G., 1919. He is now in command of No. 4 Area and the South Midland T.F. Division. Major-General Sir H. B. Walker married, in 1887, Harriet Edith Coulthard, of Plymstock, and they have two sons: Capt. James Coulthard (Indian Cavalry), born March, 1889, and Lieut. Harold Thomas (Royal Navy), born March, 1891.

Harold B. Walker.

GILBERT, ARTHUR ROBERT, Major, was born 26 Jan. 1863, youngest son of the Rev. Clement Gilbert, of Strumpshaw Hall, Norfolk. He was educated at Cheltenham and Sandhurst, and entered the Royal Sussex Regt. 9 Sept. 1882, serving in the Hazara Expedition in 1888 (Medal with clasp); became Captain 9 Sept. 1892; served in the Tirah Campaign, 1897–98, and was present at the operations in the Bazar Valley 25 to 30 Dec. 1897 (Medal with two clasps). He served in the South African War, 1899–1902, and took part in the operations in the Orange Free State, Feb. to May, 1900, including actions at Houtnek (Thoba Mountain), Vet River (5 and 6 May) and Zand River; in the Transvaal in May and June, 1900, including actions near Johannesburg, Pretoria and Diamond Hill (11 and 12 June); in Orange River Colony, May to 29 Nov. 1900, including actions at Wittebergen (1 to 29 July) and Ladybrand (2 to 5 Sept.); again in Orange River Colony and Cape Colony, Jan. 1901, to Feb. 1902; also again in the Transvaal, Feb. to 31 May, 1902. He was mentioned in Despatches [London Gazette, 10 Sept. 1901, and 29 July, 1902]; received the Brevet of Major 29 Nov. 1900; the Queen's Medal with four clasps; the King's Medal with two clasps. He was created a Companion of the Distinguished Service Order [London Gazette, 31 Oct. 1902]: "Arthur Robert Gilbert, Major, The Royal Sussex Regt. In recognition of services during the operations in South Africa." He was promoted to Major 17 Sept. 1902; to Lieutenant-Colonel 12 Aug. 1907, and to Colonel 30 Aug. 1911. Colonel Gilbert served in the European War, as Temporary Brigadier-General, from 5 Aug. 1914. He commanded the Liverpool Brigade, Territorial Forces. He was created a C.B.E. in 1919. He became Senior Officer Commanding Troops, Jamaica. In 1903 Colonel Gilbert married Muriel, only daughter of H. Cook, of White House, Hanworth, Norfolk, and they have one son.

PRATT, ERNEST ST. GEORGE, Brevet Major, was born 3 Sept. 1863, youngest son of the late Spencer Pratt, of Stanwick House, Higham Ferrers. He was gazetted to the Durham Light Infantry 23 Aug. 1884; was Adjutant, Durham Light Infantry, 19 Nov. 1892, to 18 Nov. 1896, and became Captain 11 April, 1894. Capt. Pratt served in the South African War, 1899–1902, as Special Service Officer, and afterwards on the Staff, and in command of the Mounted Infantry Battn. He took part in the Relief of Ladysmith, including action at Colenso; operations of 17 to 24 Jan. 1900, and action at Spion Kop; operations of 5 to 7 Feb. 1900, and action at Vaal Kranz; during operations on Tugela Heights (14 to 27 Feb. 1900) and action at Pieter's Hill; in Natal, March to June, 1900, including action at Laing's Nek (6 to 9 June); in command of the 13th Battn. Mounted Infantry from 7 Nov. 1900, to 31 May, 1902; in the Transvaal, Dec. 1900, to July, 1901, and Nov. 1901, to 31 May, 1902; in Orange River Colony, July to Nov. 1901, aud May, 1902; during the operations on the Zululand Frontier of Natal, Sept. and Oct. 1901. He was mentioned in Despatches (Sir R. H. Buller, 30 March and 9 Nov. 1900) [London Gazette, 8 Feb. 1901, and 29 July, 1902]; received the Brevet of Major 29 Nov. 1900; the Queen's Medal with six clasps, and the King's Medal with two clasps. He was created a Companion of the Distinguished Service Order [London Gazette, 31 Oct. 1902]: "Ernest St. George Pratt, Capt. and Brevet Major, Durham Light Infantry. In recognition of services during the South African War." He was D.A.A.G. for Musketry, Eastern District, 2 Feb. 1903, to 31 May, 1905, and 1 June, 1905, to 31 May, 1906; was promoted to Major 7 May, 1903; was G.S.O.2, Lowland Division, Scottish Command, 1 April, 1908, to 17 Oct. 1909. He was given the Brevet of Lieutenant-Colonel 23 July, 1910, and became Lieutenant-Colonel 15 Aug. 1910; was Assistant Director, War Office, 28 July, 1913, to 20 July, 1915; became Colonel 16 Dec. 1913. During the European War he commanded a brigade from 21 July, 1915. He became Inspector of Infantry, and was created a C.B. in 1916. Brigadier-General E. St. G. Pratt died 24 Nov. 1918. He had married, in 1902, Edith, daughter of the late Capt. H. P. Andrew, 8th Hussars, and they have one daughter, Kathleen Marion.

KNIGHT, WYNDHAM CHARLES, Brevet Major, was born 30 Nov. 1863, son of Capt. William Brodnax Knight, late Queen's Bays, and grandson of Edward Knight, of Chawton, Hampshire. He was educated at Cheltenham College and Sandhurst, and was gazetted to the Worcestershire Regt., as Lieutenant, 25 Aug. 1883, and became Lieutenant, Indian Staff Corps, 29 April, 1885, and Captain, Indian Staff Corps, 25 Aug. 1894. He served on the North-West Frontier of India, 1897–98 (Mohmand), as Section Commandant (Sept. to 5 Oct. 1897). He was mentioned in Despatches [London Gazette, 11 Jan. 1898]; received the Medal with clasp. He served at Tirah, 1897–98, on the Staff; took part in the action of Dargai; at the capture of the Sampagha and Arhanga Passes; during the operations at and around Dwatoi, and action of 24 Nov. 1897 (Despatches [London Gazette, 5 April, 1898]; clasp). He served in the South African War, 1900–2, as Special Service Officer; afterwards on Staff; took part in the Relief of Kimberley; in the Orange Free State, Feb. to May, 1900, including operations at Paardeberg (17 to 26 Feb.); actions at Poplar Grove and Dreifontein; in Orange River Colony, May to 29 Nov. 1900, including actions at Wittebergen (1 to 29 July); in the Transvaal and Orange River Colony 30 Nov. 1900, to 31 May, 1902 (Despatches [London Gazette, 16 April, 1901, and 29 July, 1902]; Queen's Medal with five clasps, and King's Medal with two clasps). He was given the Brevet of Major 29 Nov. 1900, and was created a Companion of the Distinguished Service Order [London Gazette, 31 Oct. 1902]: "Wyndham Charles Knight, Capt. and Brevet Major, Indian Staff Corps. In recognition of services during the operations in South Africa." He was promoted to Major, Indian Army, 25 Aug. 1901; was D.A.A.G., Allahabad District, India, from 31 May, 1904, to 1908; Lieutenant-Colonel 25 Aug. 1909; was Commandant, 4th Indian Cavalry, 1910–12; was A.D.C. to the King from 19 March, 1912, to 30 Dec. 1917, and was given the Brevet of Colonel 19 March, 1912; was G.S.O.1, Headquarters, India, from 22 July, 1912. He commanded the Bombay Brigade, and was Embarkation Commandant from 10 Dec. 1915, to 1917, and was promoted to Major-General 1 Jan. 1917; created a C.B. in 1916; a C.S.I. in 1917, and a K.C.I.E. in 1919. Sir Wyndham Knight married, 23 June, 1896, Harriet Monica, daughter of the late Francis Johnstone, and they have two sons: Austen Bertram and Christopher Wyndham.

MARDEN, ARTHUR WILLIAM, Brevet Major, was born 21 Sept. 1868, son of the late Thomas Marden, of Weston Priory, Bath. He was gazetted to the Manchester Regt. 11 Feb. 1888; became Lieutenant 31 July, 1889; was Adjutant, Manchester Regt., 18 April, 1896, to 1 Nov. 1896, and was promoted to Captain 6 Oct. 1896. He served in the South African War, 1899–1902, as Adjutant, 1st Battn. Manchester Regt. (21 Oct. 1899, to 1 March, 1900, and 14 May to 29 Nov. 1900); took part in the operations in Natal, 1899, including actions at Elandslaagte and Lombard's Kop; Defence of Ladysmith, including action of 6 Jan. 1900 (slightly wounded); again in Natal (March to June, 1900); in the Transvaal, east of Pretoria, July to 29 Nov. 1900, including action at Belfast (26 and 27 Aug.), and again during operations in the Transvaal, 1901, as Staff Officer to Brigadier-General. He was mentioned in Despatches [London Gazette, 8 Feb. 1901 (Sir G. S. White, 2 Dec. 1899, and 23 March, 1900), and London Gazette, 10 Sept. 1901, and 29 July, 1902]; was given the Brevet of Major 1 June, 1902; received the Queen's Medal with three clasps, and the King's Medal with two clasps. He was created a Companion of the Distinguished Service Order [London Gazette, 31 Oct. 1902]: "Arthur William Marden, Capt. and Brevet Major, Manchester Regt. In recognition of services during the operations in South Africa." He became Major 29 Nov. 1900, retiring from the Manchester Regt. 22 April, 1911. He was given the Brevet of Lieutenant-Colonel, and was promoted to Colonel in the Army 19 Oct. 1917. Colonel Marden married, in 1903, Laura Elizabeth, daughter of the late Joseph Deakin, of Ellerhow, Grange-over-Sands.

VAUGHAN, CHARLES DAVIES, Capt., was born at Brynog, Cardiganshire, 22 Aug. 1868, son of the late Capt. Herbert Vaughan, late 68th Regt., and of Mrs. Vaughan, of Whittington, Worcester. Capt. Herbert Vaughan, himself a most delightful man, was one of the pupils, at Cheltenham College, of the late Capt. Adam Durnford Gordon,

Charles Davies Vaughan.

whom the late Colonel Cunliffe Martin described as "exactly like Colonel Newcome." On pages 139-140 of "Adam Lindsay Gordon and His Friends in England and Australia," published in 1912 by Messrs. Constable, and written by Edith Humphris and Douglas Sladen, we get some glimpses of Capt. Gordon and his pupil, Herbert Vaughan, as well as of Lindsay Gordon: "Capt. Herbert Vaughan was a pupil of Capt. A. D. Gordon's. He still keeps a silver pencil-case in his pocket which he says Capt. Gordon gave him, *not as a prize* but by way of encouragement to do better. Capt. Vaughan says that Capt. Gordon was a very charming man and tremendously clever, and was said to talk Hindustani like a native. He would not call him a disciplinarian or very cut out for a schoolmaster. He was a most thorough old gentleman, and tried to manage the boys by kindness and trusting them to do their work—which does not always answer with such creatures. They were all very fond of him. Inez Gordon used very often to come and fetch her father home from the College. Capt. Vaughan may have spoken to her, but he doesn't remember ever doing so. When asked if he thought her good-looking, he said, 'No; at any rate her good looks didn't appeal to us boys; she was very, very tall and lanky —like a yard of pump-water, in fact.' Gordon was never at the College when Capt. Vaughan was there, and he never remembers seeing him. But he has heard a good deal about him from friends who were actually at the College with Gordon. He says that, though Gordon was not formally expelled, he always understood that Capt. Gordon was told he had better remove Lindsay. Capt. Vaughan thinks this was because Gordon used to go off in school hours to ride in steeplechases, and that he did this not once but several times. He was a rather wild sort of boy, but with no real harm in him. He has heard that Gordon was far gone in consumption, practically dying, in fact, at the time he shot himself." Capt. and Mrs. Herbert Vaughan had six sons, all in the Navy or Army. Charles Davies Vaughan was educated at Cherbourg Naval College (May, 1880, to Aug. 1881), and at the U.S. College, Westward Ho! (Sept. 1881, to Dec. 1887). He was gazetted to the Border Regt. 8 June, 1889, as Second Lieutenant, and became Lieutenant 11 Nov. 1891. He served with the Waziristan Expedition, 1894-95 (Medal with clasp); served on the North-West Frontier of India, 1897-98 (Tochi), as Regimental Commandant; Transport Officer, 1st Brigade (28 Oct. to Nov. 1897) (Medal with clasp). He was promoted to Captain 11 Nov. 1898, and served in the South African War, 1899-1902; took part in the operations in Natal, 1899; at the Relief of Ladysmith, including operations of 17 to 24 Jan. 1900 (severely wounded 20 Jan.); during operations on Tugela Heights (14 to 27 Feb. 1900) and action at Pieter's Hill; in the Orange Free State, April and May, 1900; in the Transvaal in June, 1900; in the Transvaal, east of Pretoria, July, 1900; in the Transvaal, west of Pretoria, July to Nov. 1900; in Orange River Colony (May, 1900); in Cape Colony, south of Orange River, 1899; also during the operations in Cape Colony, north of Orange River, May, 1900; afterwards employed under Military Governor, Orange River Colony, from 5 Nov. 1900. He was mentioned in Despatches [London Gazette, 10 Sept. 1901, and 29 July, 1902]; received the Brevet of Major 29 Nov. 1900; the Queen's Medal with five clasps, and the King's Medal with two clasps. He was created a Companion of the Distinguished Service Order [London Gazette, 31 Oct. 1902]: "Charles Davies Vaughan, Capt. and Brevet Major, The Border Regt. (South African Constabulary). In recognition of services during the operations in South Africa." He was employed as a District Commissioner in Orange River Colony from Nov. 1900, to Feb. 1901, and with the S.A.C. from 1 March, 1901, to 28 Feb. 1906. He accompanied the 1st Battn. Border Regt., as Second-in-Command, to the Dardanelles, and was killed in action at the landing on 26 April, 1915. Major Vaughan had married, on 14 Aug. 1913, at Maymyo, Burma, Dorothy Jean, daughter of the late Ernest Ashley, Esq., and Mrs. Ashley, of Staines.

JOLY DE LOTBINIÈRE, HENRY GUSTAVE, Brevet Major, was born 10 March, 1868, son of the late Sir Henry de Lotbinière, grandson of Gaspard Joly, Seignior of Lotbinière, and of Louisa Josepha Gowan, and great-grandson of the last Marquis de Lotbinière. He was educated at Bishop's College School, Lennoxville, and at the Royal Military College, Kingston, Canada; was gazetted, as Second Lieutenant, to the Royal Engineers 28 June, 1888. He served for five months on Fortification Work at Gibraltar, 1890; became Lieutenant 28 June, 1891; proceeded to India early in 1891, and was employed on the Rawalpindi Water Supply, 1891-92; then on the Frontier at Gilgit for two years, opening up the country. After a year's furlough (1905) he returned to India. He was employed in Somaliland, as Resident Engineer, for nearly a year. In 1906 he transferred from Military Works to Public Works, and was employed at Nagpur, Central Provinces, as Executive Engineer, most of the time on Famine Relief Work. He served on the North-West Frontier of India, 1897-98, and took part in the operations on the Samana and in the Kurram Valley (Medal with two clasps); served at Tirah, 1897-98, in the action of Dargai; at the capture of the Sampagha Pass (clasp). He was employed at the War Office in 1899; became Captain 28 June, 1899; served in the South African War, 1899-1902, as Staff Officer to Sir Percy Girouard, 1900-1, on railways. He was transferred to Sir John Maxwell's Staff, to form a Native Refugee Department. During this campaign he took part in the advance on Kimberley. He was present during the operations in the Orange Free State, Feb. to May, 1900; in the Transvaal in June, 1900; in the Transvaal, east of Pretoria, July to 29 Nov. 1900, and in Cape Colony, south of Orange River, 1900. He was mentioned in Despatches [London Gazette, 10 Sept. 1901, and 29 July, 1902]; received the Brevet of Major 29 Nov. 1900; the Queen's Medal with three clasps, and the King's Medal with two clasps. He was created a Companion of the Distinguished Service Order [London Gazette, 31 Oct. 1902]: "Henry Gustave Joly de Lotbinière, Capt. and Brevet Major, Royal Engineers. In recognition of services during the operations in South Africa." He returned to England in 1903, and served in the Somaliland Campaign, 1903-4, in charge of a water-boring section (Medal with clasp). From 1906 to 1912 he served in Egypt in the Egyptian Survey Department (Osmanieh, 3rd Class). He served in England for three years, and was sent to France in July, 1915, where he served until Oct. 1918. For his services in the European War he was several times mentioned in Despatches; given the Brevet of Colonel 3 June, 1916, and received the Belgian Croix de Guerre. He became Lieutenant-Colonel 7 Oct. 1915 and Temporary Brigadier-General 15 Jan. 1917; returned to England in Oct 1918, and was employed as C.R.E., Cambridge District. He married, 31 March, 1902, at Newlands, Cape Town, South Africa, Mildred Louisa, daughter of Charles Seymour Grenfell and Elizabeth Grenfell (*née* Graham), and they have two sons: Edmond, born 17 March, 1903, and Seymour, born 21 Oct. 1905.

H. G. Joly de Lotbinière.

VAUGHAN, JOHN, Brevet Major, was born 31 July, 1871, at Nannau, Dolgelly, North Wales, son of John Vaughan, J.P., D.L., of Nannau, Dolgelly. He was educated at Eton and Sandhurst; was gazetted to the 7th Hussars 11 March, 1891; became Lieutenant 4 Sept. 1894 and served in Matabeleland, 1896, and Mashonaland, 1897, as Troop Commander in the 7th Hussars. He served with the Nile Expedition in 1898, as Troop Commander, 21st Lancers; was present at the Battle of Omdurman, and received the Medal and the Egyptian Medal with clasp. He was promoted to Captain 9 Oct. 1899, and served in the South African War, 1899-1902, on Staff (also acted as A.D.C. to G.O.C., Cavalry Division, and as D.A.A.G., Intelligence, Cavalry Division) (severely wounded); in command of a column 16 Jan. to 7 Feb. 1902; was present at the Relief of Kimberley; took part in the operations in the Orange Free State, Feb. to May, 1900; in the Transvaal in May and June, 1900; in the Transvaal, east of Pretoria; in Cape Colony, south of Orange River; in the Transvaal, March to 31 May, 1902; in Orange River Colony, Feb. to March, 1902; in Cape Colony, Dec. 1901, to Feb. 1902. Despatches; Brevet of Major 2 Nov. 1900; Queen's Medal with six clasps, and King's Medal with two clasps. He was created a Companion of the Distinguished Service Order [London Gazette, 31 Oct. 1902]: "John Vaughan, Brevet Major, 10th Hussars. For services during operations in South Africa." The services were as follows: On 1 April, 1902, near Springs, South Africa, when acting as Intelligence Officer to a Column, he led the Queen's Bays to capture some Boers in a deserted farm. After capturing some prisoners, this regiment was attacked at dawn by superior numbers, and fought a rear-guard action until the 7th Hussars came up and counter-attacked the enemy. Major Vaughan commanded one wing of the Bays during the retirement, after having been wounded before daylight, and subsequently advanced with a squadron of the 7th Hussars to assist them by his knowledge of the country. He continued fighting till he fainted.

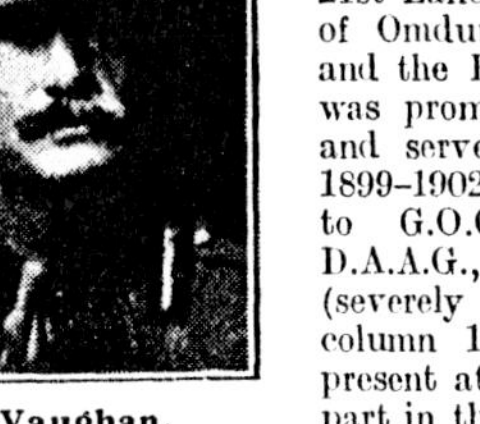

John Vaughan.

Sir A. Conan Doyle says on pages 522-523 of "The Great Boer War": "One of the consequences of the successful drives about to be described in the Orange River Colony was that a number of the Free Staters came north of the Vaal in order to get away from the extreme pressure upon the south. At the end of March a considerable number had reinforced the local commandos in that district to the east of Springs, no very great distance from Johannesburg, which had always been a storm centre. A cavalry force was stationed at this spot which consisted at that time of the 2nd Queen's Bays, the 7th Hussars, and some National Scouts, all under Colonel Lawley of the Hussars. After a series of minor engagements east of Springs, Lawley had possessed himself of Boschman's Kop, eighteen miles from that town, close to the district which was the chief scene of Boer activity. From this base he dispatched upon the morning of 1 April three squadrons of the Bays under Colonel Fanshawe, for the purpose of surprising a small force of the enemy which was reported at one of the farms. Fanshawe's strength was about three hundred men. The British cavalry found themselves, however, in the position of the hunter who, when he is out for a snipe, puts up a tiger. All went well with the expedition as far as Holspruit, the farm which they had started to search. Commandant Pretorius, to whom it belonged, was taken by the energy of Major Vaughan, who pursued and overtook his Cape cart. It was found, however, that Alberts's commando was camped at the farm, and that the Bays were in the presence of a very superior force of the enemy. The night was dark, and when firing began it was almost muzzle to muzzle, with the greatest possible difficulty in telling friend from foe. The three squadrons fell back upon some rising ground, keeping admirable order under most difficult circumstances. In spite of the darkness the attack was pressed fiercely home, and with their favourite tactics the burghers rapidly outflanked the position taken up by the cavalry. The British moved by alternate squadrons on to a higher rocky kopje on the east, which could be vaguely distinguished looming in the darkness against the sky-line. B squadron, the last to retire, was actually charged and ridden through by the brave assailants, firing from their saddles as they broke through the ranks. The British had hardly time to reach the kopje and to dismount and line its edge when the Boers, yelling loudly, charged with their horses

up the steep flanks. Twice they were beaten back, but the third time they seized one corner of the hill and opened a hot fire upon the rear of the line of men who were defending the other side. Dawn was now breaking, and the situation most serious, for the Boers were in very superior numbers and were pushing their pursuit with the utmost vigour and determination. A small party of officers and men whose horses had been shot covered the retreat of their comrades, and continued to fire until all of them, two officers and twenty-three men, wer e killed or wounded, the whole of their desperate defence being conducted within from thirty to fifty yards of the enemy. The remainder of the regiment was now retired to successive ridges, each of which was rapidly outflanked by the Boers, whose whole method of conducting their attack was extraordinarily skilful. Nothing but the excellent discipline of the overmatched troopers prevented the retreat from becoming a rout. Fortunately, before the pressure became intolerable, the 7th Hussars with some artillery came to the rescue and turned the tide. The Hussars galloped in with such dash that some of them actually got among the Boers with their swords, but the enemy rapidly fell back and disappeared. In this very sharp and sanguinary cavalry skirmish the Bays lost eighty killed and wounded out of a total force of 270. To stand such losses under such circumstances, and to preserve absolute discipline and order, is a fine test of soldierly virtue. The adjutant, the squadron leaders, and six out of ten officers were killed or wounded. The Boers lost equally heavily. Two Prinsloos, one of them a commandant, and three field-cornets were among the slain, with seventy other casualties. The force under General Alberts was a considerable one, not fewer than six hundred rifles, so that the action at Holspruit is one which adds another name of honour to the battle-roll of the Bays. It is pleasing to add that in this and the other actions which were fought at the end of the war our wounded met with kindness and consideration from the enemy."

His D.S.O. was gazetted 31 Oct. 1902: " John Vaughan, Capt. and Brevet Major, 7th Hussars. In recognition of services during the operations in South Africa." He was Brigade Major, 1st Cavalry Division, Aldershot Command, 31 Jan. to 10 Oct. 1904; was promoted to Major 14 May, 1904; to Lieutenant-Colonel 7 May, 1908; to Colonel 6 Dec. 1911, and was Commandant, Cavalry School, Netheravon, 30 Jan. 1911, to 4 Aug. 1914. He served in the European War from Aug. 1914, as G.S.O.1, 1st Cavalry Division, B.E.F., 5 Aug. to 14 Sept. 1914; G.O.C., 3rd Cavalry Brigade, B.E.F., 14 Oct. 1915; G.O.C., 3rd Cavalry Division, 15 Oct. 1915, to 14 Feb. 1918; Inspector of Q.M.G.'s Services, British Armies in France, 15 Feb. 1918, to 14 Feb. 1919; commanded Cavalry Brigade, Aldershot, from 28 March, 1919; was mentioned in Despatches; created a C.B. in 1915, and a C.M.G. in 1919, and made Commander, Légion d'Honneur. He married, 22 Oct. 1913, at St. Peter's, Eaton Square, S.W., Louisa Evelyn Wardell, daughter of Capt. Stewart, of Alltyroden, Cardiganshire, and widow of Harold P. Wardell, of Brynwern, Newbridge-on-Wye.

SMYTH, ROBERT NAPIER, Brevet Major, was born 26 June, 1868, son of the late General J. H. Smyth, C.B., of Frimhurst. He was educated at Wellington, and joined the 21st Hussars 12 Feb. 1890, as Second Lieutenant, becoming Lieutenant, 21st Lancers, 6 Nov. 1892. He served with the Nile Expedition, 1898; was present at the Battle of Khartoum, and was mentioned in Despatches [London Gazette, 30 Sept. 1898], receiving the Medal and the Egyptian Medal and clasp. He was A.D.C. to the G.O.C., Scottish District, 12 Aug. 1896, to 20 Jan. 1898, and was promoted to Captain 15 Sept. 1899. Capt. Smyth served in the South African War, 1899–1902, as D.A.A.G. (Intelligence), South Africa, 13 Nov. 1900, to 2 Oct. 1902. He was present at the Relief of Ladysmith, including the action at Colenso; operations of 17 to 24 Jan. 1900, and action at Spion Kop; operations of 5 to 7 Feb. 1900, and action at Vaal Kranz; during the operations on Tugela Heights (17 to 26 Feb.) and action at Pieter's Hill; in Natal, March to June, 1900, including action at Laing's Nek (6 to 9 June); in the Transvaal, east of Pretoria, July to 29 Nov. 1900, including actions at Reit Vlei, Belfast (26 and 27 Aug.), Lydenberg (5 to 8 Sept.) and Rhenoster Kop; again in the Transvaal and Orange River Colony 30 Nov. 1900, to 31 May, 1902. He was mentioned in Despatches [London Gazette, 8 Feb. 1901 (Sir R. H. Buller, 30 March and 9 Nov. 1900), and London Gazette, 10 Sept. 1901, and 29 July, 1902]. He was given the Brevet of Major 29 Nov. 1900; the Queen's Medal with four clasps; the King's Medal with two clasps, and was created a Companion of the Distinguished Service Order [London Gazette, 31 Oct. 1902]: " Robert Napier Smyth, Captain and Brevet Major, 21st Lancers. In recognition of services during the operations in South Africa." He was employed with the South African Constabulary 20 Dec. 1902, to 28 Feb. 1905; became Major 9 Dec. 1905; Lieutenant-Colonel 7 Sept. 1910, and Colonel 16 Dec. 1913. He served in the European War, as G.S.O.2, 2nd Cavalry Division, British Expeditionary Force, 19 Sept. to 9 Oct. 1914; was G.S.O.2, G.H.Q., B.E.F., 10 Oct. 1914, to 4 Jan. 1915; Commanded the North Midland Reserve Mounted Brigade, Home Forces, 12 Jan. 1915, to 10 Jan. 1917; commanded a Brigade 11 Jan. 1917, to 21 March, 1919; commanded the 7th Cyclist Brigade, Forces in Great Britain, 26 May, 1919. He was created a C.B.E. in 1919.

DU MAURIER, GUY LOUIS BUSSON, Major, was born 18 May, 1865, son of George du Maurier, and brother of Gerald du Maurier. He was educated at Marlborough (1879–1881, Cott.) and at Sandhurst, and was gazetted to the Royal Fusiliers, as Lieutenant, 17 Feb. 1885, becoming Captain 15 Sept. 1896. Capt. du Maurier served in the South African War, 1901–2, in command of the 20th Battn. Mounted Infantry, Aug. 1901, to 31 May, 1902; took part in the operations in the Transvaal, March to Dec. 1901; in Cape Colony and Orange River Colony, Dec. 1901, to 31 May, 1902. He was mentioned in Despatches [London Gazette, 29 July, 1902], and received the Queen's Medal with five clasps. He was created a Companion of the Distinguished Service Order [London Gazette, 31 Oct. 1902]: " Guy Louis Busson du Maurier, Major, The Royal Fusiliers, City

of London Regt. In recognition of services during the operations in South Africa." He was promoted to Major 12 Dec. 1900. From 29 June, 1906, he commanded a battalion of Mounted Infantry in South Africa. Lieut.-Colonel du Maurier became famous in 1909 as the author of " An Englishman's Home." He served in the European War, and was killed in action. In 1905 he married Gwendolen, eldest daughter of Edward Price, of Broadwater, Godalming.

FEILDEN, GRANVILLE CHOLMONDELEY, Major, was born 1[?] Feb. 1863, eldest son of the late Rev. J. P. Feilden, Hon. Canon of Norwich Cathedral, and of the Honourable Frances Blanche Ann Calthorpe (who

died 17 April, 1899), second daughter of the 4th Baron Calthorpe. He entered the Seaforth Highlanders 12 Nov. 1884, as Lieutenant, and became Captain 2 Sept. 1891. From 16 July, 1894, to 31 July, 1899, he was Adjutant, Militia. He served in the South African War, 1899–1902, taking part in the advance on Kimberley, including the action at Magersfontein. He was in command of the 2nd Battn. Seaforth Highlanders from 12 Dec. 1899, to 23 Jan. 1900; operations in the Orange Free State, Feb. to May, 1900, including operations at Paardeberg (severely wounded); operations in the Transvaal, March to Aug. 1901, and March to 31 May, 1902; operations in Orange River Colony, Jan. to March, 1902;

Granville C. Feilden.

operations in Cape Colony, Feb. and March, 1901, and Aug. 1901, to Jan. 1902. He received the Queen's Medal with three clasps; the King's Medal with two clasps, and was created a Companion of the Distinguished Service Order [London Gazette, 31 Oct. 1902]: " Granville Cholmondeley Feilden, Major, Seaforth Highlanders. In recognition of services during the operations in South Africa." He was promoted to Major 22 Dec. 1901, and retired 15 March, 1905. He became Adjutant, Corps of Commissionaires, commanding its London Division. Major Feilden married, in 1894, Edith Margaret Catherine Colquhoun, daughter of the late Sir H. C. MacAndrew, of Aisthorpe, Inverness, and they have four daughters and had a son, Granville John Henry, born 27 Aug. 1895. He joined the Seaforth Highlanders, and went to France in Sept. 1914. He was killed at St. Julien, Ypres, on Sunday, 25 April, 1915. Major Feilden's four daughters are : Frances Blanche Mary, Dorothy Robina Elliott, Millicent Edith, and Eugénie Cecilia Fiona.

ORR, MICHAEL HARRISON, Major, was born at Ballymena, County Antrim, on 23 Dec. 1859, son of the late William Orr, Solicitor, of Ballymena, and Mary Orr (née Harrison). He was educated at Trinity College, Stratford-on-Avon, and joined the 19th Regt. 14 Jan. 1880; served in the Egyptian War, 1884–86; Frontier Field Force in Egypt (Egyptian Medal and Khedive's Star). He served in the South African Campaign, 1899–1902; served in Lord Roberts's march from Bloemfontein to Pretoria; was present at the engagements of Brandfort, Vet River, Zand River, and the operations near Johannesburg and Pretoria, also Diamond Hill and Belfast; in the operations near Colesberg, under General Sir John French (dangerously wounded; Despatches). He was mentioned in Despatches 4 May, 1900, and 29 July, 1902; received the Queen's Medal with five clasps; the King's Medal with two clasps, and was created a Companion of the Distinguished Service Order [London Gazette, 31 Oct. 1902]: " Michael Harrison Orr, Major, Alexandra Princess of Wales's Own (Yorkshire) Regt. In recognition of services during the operations in South Africa." Major Orr retired from the 1st Battn. Yorkshire Regt. 23 Dec. 1907.

ROSS-JOHNSON, CYRIL MAXWELL, Major, was born at Hatherley Court, Cheltenham, 29 Jan. 1868, son of H. C. Ross-Johnson, F.R.G.S., Barrister-

at-Law. He was educated at Cheltenham College; entered the Royal Artillery 24 July, 1886, and was promoted to Captain 1 July, 1897, and to Major 24 Jan. 1902. He served in the South African War, 1900–2; took part in the Relief of Ladysmith, including operations of 5 to 7 Feb. 1900, and action at Vaal Kranz; and operations on Tugela Heights (14 to 27 Feb. 1900); served during operations in the Orange Free State, including action at Zand River; in the Transvaal in May and June, 1900, including actions near Johannesburg, Pretoria and Diamond Hill (11 and 12 June); in the Transvaal, east of Pretoria, July to 29 Nov. 1900, including actions at Reit Vlei and Belfast (26 and

Cyril M. Ross-Johnson.

27 Aug.); again in the Transvaal, Jan. to June, 1901, and in April, 1902; also during operations in Cape Colony, Aug. 1901, to March, 1902. He was mentioned in Despatches (London Gazette, 29 July, 1902); received the Queen's Medal with seven clasps, and the King's Medal with two clasps. He was created a Companion of the Distinguished Service Order [London Gazette, 31 Oct. 1902]: " Cyril Maxwell Ross-Johnson, Major, Royal Artillery. In recognition of services during the operations in South Africa." He became Lieutenant-Colonel 13 June, 1914; served in the European War, 1914–18; was mentioned in Despatches; given the Brevet of Colonel 1 Jan. 1917, and was created a C.M.G. in 1915 and a C.B. in 1918. He retired from the Staff with the honorary rank of Major-General 1 June, 1919.

SHARP, FRANK WILLIAM, Major, was born 6 Aug. 1858, and entered the Army 31 Dec. 1884. He served in the Sudan in 1885, in the Suakin Expedition, and received the Medal with clasp and the Bronze Star. He served in the South African War, 1899–1902, and took part in operations in Cape Colony, south of Orange River, 1899–1900 ; the Relief of Kimberley ; operations in the Transvaal, east and west of Pretoria, July to 29 Nov. 1900 ; operations in Orange River Colony, May to 29 Nov. 1900 ; operations in Cape Colony, Orange River Colony and the Transvaal 30 Nov. 1900, to 31 May, 1902. He was mentioned in Despatches [London Gazette, 29 July, 1902] ; received the Queen's Medal with three clasps ; the King's Medal with two clasps, and was created a Companion of the Distinguished Service Order [London Gazette, 31 Oct. 1902] : " Frank William Sharp, Major, Army Veterinary Department. In recognition of services during the operations in South Africa." Major Sharp retired 5 Jan. 1910.

WHITE, JOHN NICHOLAS, Major, was born 24 Dec. 1861, eldest son of John White, J.P., D.L., of Loughbrickland, County Down. He was educated at Stonyhurst College, and was gazetted to the Lancashire Fusiliers 10 Nov. 1886, as Lieutenant, from the Militia, and became Captain 31 March, 1895. He served in the Nile Expedition in 1898 ; was present at the Battle of Khartoum, and received the Medal and the Egyptian Medal with clasp. He was also present in 1898 at the occupation of Crete. He served in the South African War, 1899–1902 ; was severely wounded at Venter's Spruit, and so greatly distinguished himself that he was mentioned in Despatches five times, and created a Companion of the Distinguished Service Order [London Gazette, 31 Oct. 1902] : " John Nicholas White, Capt., Lancashire Fusiliers. In recognition of services during the operations in South Africa." He also received the Queen's Medal with five clasps, and the King's Medal with two clasps. Capt. White's favourite recreations were hunting, polo and shooting. He died 29 April, 1906, and an obituary notice of him appeared in the " Times " of 28 June, 1906.

WILSON-FARQUHARSON, DAVID LORRAINE, Major, was born 27 July, 1862, at Clifton, Bristol, son of James Wilson, Esq. (deceased), and Mrs. Wilson (deceased), and grandson of the late Robert Farquharson, of Allargue and Breda, Aberdeenshire. He was educated at Haileybury ; at Brasenose College, Oxford, and entered the Black Watch, as Lieutenant, from the Royal Military College, Sandhurst, 6 Feb. 1884. He served in the Nile Expedition, 1884–85 (Medal with two clasps, " The Nile, 1884–85," and " Kirbekan " ; Khedive's Bronze Star). He became Captain 29 Jan. 1891, and Major 24 Feb. 1902, and served in the South African War, 1900–2, taking part in operations in the Transvaal Nov. 1901 ; operations in Orange River Colony, Nov. 1900, to Sept. 1901, and Dec. 1901, to May, 1902 ; operations on the Zululand Frontier of Natal in Oct. 1901. He was mentioned in Despatches [London Gazette, 10 Sept. 1901, and 29 July, 1902] ; received the Queen's Medal with three clasps ; the King's Medal with two clasps, and was created a Companion of the Distinguished Service Order [London Gazette, 31 Oct. 1902] : " David Lorraine Wilson-Farquharson, Major, The Black Watch (Royal Highlanders). In recognition of services during the operations in South Africa." Major D. L. Wilson-Farquharson retired 13 June, 1908. He served in the European War ; was mentioned in Despatches 23 Feb. 1917, and promoted Lieutenant-Colonel, Reserve of Officers, 18 Jan. 1918. He married, 4 June, 1908, at Chislehurst, Alison Mary Sanderson, only daughter of the late John Sanderson, of Bullerswood, Chislehurst, and they have two daughters : Alice Jessie and Jean Alison.

REEVES, PAGET EDWARD STUART, Major, was born 10 Feb. 1862, eldest son of R. E. Reeves, of Capperd, Queen's County. He entered the Army, 1885 ; became Captain, 1891 ; Major, 1902 ; served in South Africa, 1900–2 ; was mentioned in Despatches ; received the Queen's and King's Medals, with five clasps, and was created a Companion of the Distinguished Service Order [London Gazette, 31 Oct. 1902] : " Paget Edward Stuart Reeves, Major, The Leinster Regt. In recognition of services during the operations in South Africa." He married Harriet, daughter of the Rev. R. R. Carey.

TONGE, WILLIAM CORRIE, Major, was born 14 April, 1862, son of William John Tonge, of Morants Court, Sevenoaks, Kent. He was educated at Brighton ; Tonbridge School and Cheltenham College, and entered the Royal Military College, Sandhurst, in 1881. He became Lieutenant, the Norfolk Regt., in 1882 ; served in South Africa, 1884–85, with Sir Charles Warren's Expedition to Bechuanaland. He became Captain in 1889. He served in the South African War, 1900–2 ; was mentioned in Despatches twice ; received the Queen's Medal with three clasps ; the King's Medal with two clasps, and was created a Companion of the Distinguished Service Order [London Gazette, 31 Oct. 1902] : " William Corrie Tonge, Major, Norfolk Regt. In recognition of services during the operations in South Africa." He became Major 23 July, 1902, and retired 29 March, 1905 ; was Lieutenant-Colonel commanding the 3rd Battn. in 1910. He served in the European War ; was mentioned in Despatches, and received the Brevet of Colonel. Colonel Tonge married, in 1898, Caroline Annie, daughter of Thomas Oliver, of Horsham, Sussex, and they have one son.

BEVERIDGE, WILFRED WILLIAM OGILVY, Major, was born in Edinburgh 16 Nov. 1864, son of J. S. Beveridge and Helen Ogilvy. He was educated in Kensington, and at Edinburgh University (is M.B., Ch.M. Edinburgh and D.P.H. Cambridge) ; joined the R.A.M.C. 29 July, 1890, and served in China, India, Bermuda, South Africa and Canada. He was on Special Service, Poona Plague Commission, in 1897. He was promoted to Major 29 Sept. 1902. Major Beveridge served in the South African War, 1900–2 ; took part in the operations in Natal, March to June, 1900 ; served during operations in the Transvaal, July to 29 Nov. 1900 ; again in the Transvaal and Orange River Colony 30 Nov. 1900, to 31 May, 1902. He was mentioned in Despatches [London Gazette, 29 July, 1902] ; received the Queen's Medal with three clasps, and the King's Medal with two clasps.

He was created a Companion of the Distinguished Service Order [London Gazette, 31 Oct. 1902] : " Wilfred William Ogilvy Beveridge, Major, Royal Army Medical Corps. In recognition of services during the operations in South Africa." He was promoted to Lieutenant-Colonel 18 Sept. 1912 ; was Professor, Royal Army Medical College, 1 Nov. 1912, to 4 Aug. 1914. He served on the Headquarters Staff in the European War, 1914–18 ; was twice mentioned in Despatches ; created a C.B. in 1915 and a C.B.E. in 1918. He became Colonel 26 Dec. 1917. Colonel Beveridge has the Légion d'Honneur, Croix de Chevalier and the Order of St. Stanislas. He is Master of Surgery, Fellow of the Chemical Society, Fellow of the Royal Sanitary Institute, Fellow of the Royal Entomological Society of London ; Analyst to the Army Medical Advisory Board, War Office ; Examiner in Public Health to the Royal College of Physicians and Surgeons, London. He has written " On a New Method of Extracting Gases from Liquids," " On the Use of Potassium Nitrate as a Food Preservative," " Experiments on Tinned Foods," on the determination of the amount of tin in tin-plate, " Factors in the Construction of Field Service and Expeditionary Rations," etc. He is joint author of " A Sanitary Officer's Handbook on Practical Hygiene." Colonel Beveridge married, in 1889, Mary, daughter of George Spencer Walker.

GLOVER, ROBERT FREDERICK BROUGHTON, Major, was born 22 June, 1859, son of the late Capt. Glover, King's Own Yorkshire Light Infantry. He was educated privately, and served in the Nile Expedition, 1884–85, and was present at the action of Kirbekan (Medal with two clasps ; Bronze Star). He became Lieutenant, South Staffordshire Regt., 26 March 1884 ; Captain 1 Nov. 1890, and Major 3 Aug. 1902. He served in the South African War, 1900–2, and took part in the operations in the Orange Free State, April to May, 1900 ; in Orange River Colony, May to 29 Nov. 1900, including actions at Wittebergen (1 to 29 July) ; in the Transvaal in July, 1901, and again in Orange River Colony 30 Nov. 1900, to 31 May, 1902. He was mentioned in Despatches [London Gazette, 10 Sept. 1901, and 29 July, 1902] ; received the Queen's

Robert F. B. Glover.

Medal with three clasps, and the King's Medal with two clasps, and was created a Companion of the Distinguished Service Order [London Gazette, 31 Oct. 1902] : " Robert Frederick Broughton Glover, Major, South Staffordshire Regt. In recognition of services during the operations in South Africa." He became Lieutenant-Colonel 22 June, 1907, and Lieutenant-Colonel, Middlesex Regt., 21 Feb. 1908. He commanded the 3rd Middlesex Regt. ; became Colonel 19 July, 1911, and retired 23 May, 1914. In the European War he served with the British Expeditionary Force, in command of the 12th Middlesex Regt., and was mentioned in Despatches. Colonel Glover married, in 1886, Frances Alice de Courcy, daughter of the late Colonel and the Honourable Mrs. Stretton, and they have one son.

SHELTON, WILLINGTON AUGUSTUS DAVID, Major, was born 14 May, 1849, eldest son of the late Colonel J. R. W. Shelton, of Bruree House, Limerick. He joined the 3rd Royal West Surrey Regt. ; served in the South African War, 1900–2 ; was mentioned in Despatches twice ; received the Queen's Medal with clasp ; the King's Medal with two clasps, and was created a Companion of the Distinguished Service Order [London Gazette, 31 Oct. 1902] : " Willington Augustus David Shelton, Major, 3rd Battn. Royal West Surrey Regt. In recognition of services during the operations in South Africa." Lieut.-Colonel W. A. D. Shelton married (1st), in 1877, May, daughter of Henry Goodlake ; (2ndly), Victoria, daughter of John Chancellor, and (3rdly), in 1889, Florence, daughter of Edward Campbell, of Stapleton, Gloucester. He died 14 June, 1909.

DOUGLAS, WILLIAM CHARLES, Major, was born on the 18th June, 1862, son of the late William Douglas, of Brigton, County Angus, and Ellen, daughter of the late John Thomas Rigge, of Hawkshead, Lancashire. Brigadier-General W. C. Douglas is eleventh in direct descent from father to son, from Archibald " Bell-the-Cat," fifth Earl of Angus, being descended from James, second son (eldest by his second wife) of Sir Archibald Douglas, of Glenbervie, Kincardineshire, the eldest son, Sir William, becoming ninth Earl of Angus. This Sir Archibald Douglas—who died in 1570—was the common ancestor of the present Duke of Hamilton ; of the present Earl of Home (on the female side), and of the extinct Earls of Forfar, the second and last of whom fell fighting under the Royal banner at Sheriffmuir, having received no fewer than sixteen broadsword wounds, besides a pistol shot in the knee.

William Charles Douglas.

James Douglas (born 1761)—great-grandson of the eleventh Earl of Angus, and first Marquis of Douglas—raised the Cameronians in 1689 (12 May)—he being their first Colonel—and was killed at their head, at Steinkirk, when but 21 years of age, 3 Aug. 1692. To this day the Cameronians carry as their badge the mullet (French, molette—the spur-rowel), the chief and ancient charge of the Douglas coat of arms, and they have—except for a short period—since 1881, worn the Douglas tartan. The time when they did not do so was when the militia regiments lost their distinct character as county battalions and matters were not quite fixed up as to the

T

uniform, when they first became third and fourth battalions of the line regiments. During this interregnum a "fancy" tartan was used for a short period by both line and militia regiments, after which the Douglas tartan was adopted by the Cameronians, doubtless in recognition of their origin, when, by the Marquis of Douglas, "1,200 men were enrolled in one day, without beat of drum and without levy money." Sir William Douglas, K.C.B. (General W. C. Douglas's great-uncle), commanded the Highland Brigade at Waterloo, while his brother, Graham Douglas, accompanied Sir John Moore in the famous retreat on Corunna, taking part in the "ceaseless rear-guard fighting which marked every step of the retreat." Such was Sir John Moore's opinion of William Douglas and others of his brothers that he made application to their father for "more of the breed" for his regiment, promising advantageous conditions of joining up, could they be provided. To this Sir William Douglas a monument was erected by his brother officers in the church at Forfar, as a tribute of "their respect and esteem for his distinguished services in the field" and of his "amiable qualities in private life." "He fell an early victim to the duties of his profession at Valenciennes, in France, on the 23rd Aug. 1818, aged 42 years, universally regretted by all who knew him." William Charles Douglas was educated at the Royal Naval School, New Cross, and at Cheltenham College; spent some years in the United States, and joined the Royal Lanark Militia, as Second Lieutenant, on 4 June, 1881, the year of the inauguration of the Territorial System, upon its adoption the 1st and 2nd Lanark Militia becoming the 3rd and 4th Battns. The Cameronians. He became Lieutenant, the 4th Scottish Rifles, on 1 July, 1881; Captain 26 Sept. 1885, and Major, 3rd Scottish Rifles, 25 Dec. 1895. As Senior Major he commanded a battalion at Aldershot, and was in charge of the detachment in London on the occasion of the Jubilee Celebration in 1897. He served during the South African War in 1901–2, as Commandant at Boshof, Orange River Colony, and in acting command of his battalion, the 3rd Cameronians, from June, 1901, to May, 1902, which had fifteen months' experience of the war; and took part in the operations in Cape Colony and the Orange River Colony. For his services in this campaign, Major Douglas was mentioned in Lord Kitchener's Despatches [London Gazette, 29 July, 1902]; was promoted to Lieutenant-Colonel 6 Dec. 1902; received the Queen's Medal and four clasps, and was created a Companion of the Distinguished Service Order [London Gazette, 31 Oct. 1902]: "William Charles Douglas, Major, the Cameronians (Scottish Rifles). In recognition of services during the recent operations in South Africa." The decoration was awarded for continuous good service during the war. He commanded the 3rd Battn. Scottish Rifles from 6 Dec. 1902, to 20 May, 1908, and was granted an extension of command for two years, but did not take advantage of it, and was granted the honorary rank of Colonel 27 April, 1908. He retired 20 May, 1908. In the European War Colonel Douglas commanded the 2/5th Black Watch (Royal Highlanders) from 27 Sept. 1914, to 15 Jan. 1915, and commanded the 194th Infantry Brigade from 15 Jan. 1915, to 17 March, 1916. For services in the war he was granted the honorary rank of Colonel in the Army [London Gazette, 12 April, 1917]; the honorary rank of Brigadier-General [London Gazette, 10 Aug. 1917]; was invested with the Insignia of Companion of the Most Honourable Order of the Bath (Military Division) 9 Feb. 1918, and has held the post of County Commandant Forfarshire Volunteer Regt. since 24 July, 1917. Brigadier-General Douglas's favourite recreations are shooting and fishing. He married, in Aug. 1892, Jeannette (who died 2 Dec. 1916), second daughter of the late P. Hutchison, Esq., Shipowner, of Glasgow, and they had four daughters.

BENNETT, ALFRED CHARLES, Lieut.-Colonel, the son of the late St. John Bennett, Barrister-at-Law, of Colewood Park, Sussex, and of 31, Cambridge Square, S.W. He was educated privately, and joined the Army on 19 July, 1876. He served in South Africa, 1899–1902; was mentioned in Despatches; received both Medals and one clasp, and was created a Companion of the Distinguished Service Order [London Gazette, 31 Oct. 1902]: "Alfred Charles Bennett, Major and Hon. Lieut.-Colonel, West Yorkshire Regt. In recognition of services during the operations in South Africa." He was Commandant of Boer Prisoners of War at Simon's Town; Commandant of Kimberley for part of the time the battalion was there, and Officer Commanding troops at Worcester, Cape Colony. He subsequently retired, and joined the Reserve of Officers. Directly war broke out in 1914 he applied for employment, and was appointed Recruiting Officer at Southend, which post he held until his death. He died 16 Jan. 1915, at Ardleigh Park, Colchester. He had married, in 1886, Emma Charlotte, daughter of Lieut. F. Vere-Hopegood, of Hadley (late of the 70th Regt.), and widow of Lieut. Wilmot Lambert, Rifle Brigade, of Banstead, Surrey.

Alfred Charles Bennett.

Cecil Wedgwood.

WEDGWOOD, CECIL, Major, was born 28 March, 1863, at Trentram, Staffs, son of Godfrey Wedgwood and May, his wife. He was educated at Clifton College and Geneva University, and joined the 4th Battn. North Staffordshire Regt. 1882; served in the South African War from

1900 to 1902, as Commandant, Dec. 1900, to June, 1901; then as Railway Staff Officer (graded as a Staff Captain), and subsequently as District-Commandant to July, 1901; Commandant, Carnarvon, July to Aug. 1901; Commandant, De Aar, April to May, 1902. He was mentioned in Despatches twice; received Medal with clasp; the King's Medal with two clasps, and was created a Companion of the Distinguished Service Order [London Gazette, 31 Oct. 1902]: "Cecil Wedgwood, Major, North Staffordshire Regt. In recognition of services during the operations in South Africa." Major Wedgwood retired from the Army, and joined the Reserve of Officers. He was a Director of Messrs. Josiah Wedgwood and Sons, and was the first Mayor of the Federated Borough of Stoke-on-Trent, 1910–12. He served in the European War from 1914, till he was killed in action on 3 July, 1916.

JOHNSTON, HORACE JAMES, Capt., was born at Brighton, Sussex, 30 Jan. 1866, son of Francis John Johnston, of Dunsdale, Westerham, Kent, and Caroline, daughter of Sir Hardman Earle, 1st Baronet. He was educated by Mr. Meyrick-Jones, at Yverdon House, Blackheath, S.E., and privately at Heidelberg and Paris, and joined the Militia Battalion of the Duke of Wellington's West Riding Regt., as a Sub-Lieutenant, in 1886. He served in the South African War, 1900–2, as Assistant Staff Officer to the O.C., Western District, from 2 June, 1901; operations in Cape Colony, south of Orange River, 1900; operations in Orange River Colony and Cape Colony, Dec. 1900, to April, 1902. He was mentioned twice in Despatches; received the Queen's and the King's Medals with four clasps, and

Horace J. Johnston.

was created a Companion of the Distinguished Service Order [London Gazette, 31 Oct. 1902]: "Horace James Johnston, Capt., Duke of Wellington's West Riding Regt. In recognition of services during the operations in South Africa." He became Captain, 1902, and Colonel, 1908. He served in the European War, commanding the 8th Battn. Duke of Wellington's West Riding Regt. from 1 Jan. 1915. Colonel Johnston was reported as "missing" in the action at Suvla Bay 9 to 11 Aug. 1915, and from private information received, there unfortunately appears to be no doubt that he fell in action on the 9 Aug. 1915. On 28 April, 1904, at Carlow, Ireland, he married Florence Hope, fourth daughter of William Brown Clayton, of Brown's Hill, County Carlow, and they had two sons: Francis William, born in 1905, and Patrick James, born in 1908, and a daughter, Hope Caroline.

SEGRAVE, O'NEAL, Major, of Cabra, was born 31 Dec. 1856, son of the late Capt. Henry Segrave, J.P., D.L., of Kiltymon, County Wicklow; Cabra, County Dublin, and Calla, County Galway. He was educated in Belgium, and joined the Colonial Forces in 1876. He served in South Africa, 1877–8–9 (Medal and clasp); the Basuto War, 1880–1 (Medal and clasp); the Transvaal War, 1900–2; was mentioned in Despatches; awarded the Queen's Medal with four clasps; the King's Medal with two clasps, and was created a Companion of the Distinguished Service Order [London Gazette, 31 Oct. 1902]: "O'Neal Segrave, Major, 18th Battn. Imperial Yeomanry. In recognition of services during the operations in South Africa." He served in the Great War, as Draft Conducting Officer, May, 1915, to June, 1917; as Town Major and

O'Neal Segrave.

Area Commandant at Brisleux-au-Mont, France, June, 1917, to Feb. 1918; as O.C., VI. Corps Employment Company and Commandant, VI. Corps. Troops, from 1 March, 1918. He received the Mons Star, Victory Medal and Allied Medal. He married, in 1882, Beatrix, elder daughter of the late Capt. W. J. J. Warneford, and has two sons: Capt. O'Neal Segrave, late Royal Irish Regt., and Capt. H. J. Segrave, Wiltshire Regt., attached R.A.F.

CHRISTOPHERS, EDGAR, Major, was born 6 March, 1860, son of the late Richard Rawe Christophers, of Trevithick, Cornwall. He was educated at Shrewsbury and abroad, and joined the East Kent Imperial Yeomanry in 1899, as Trooper, proceeding to South Africa in 1900. He was promoted to Corporal, Sergeant, Quartermaster-Sergeant and Sergeant-Major in 1900; to Lieutenant in 1900; Captain in 1901; Major, Second-in-Command, 12th Regt., Imperial Yeomanry, in 1902. He was mentioned in Despatches, and was created a Companion of the Distinguished Service Order [London Gazette, 31 Oct. 1902]: "Edgar Christophers, Major, 12th Battn. Imperial Yeomanry. In recognition of services during the operations in South Africa." Major Christophers returned home in command of Imperial Yeomanry details to represent the Imperial Yeomanry at the Coronation (postponed). He married, in 1889, Violet, only daughter of the late Richard Smyth Wallis, of Drishane Castle, Cork.

Henry Maitland Kersey.

KERSEY, HENRY MAITLAND, Major

son of the late S. Overbury Kersey, of Kersey, Suffolk. He was educated at Repton and abroad, and served in South Africa, 1900–2, first on the Staff of General St. George Henry, C.B.; afterwards with the 15th Battn. Imperial Yeomanry, and finally commanding the battalion; operations in the Transvaal, Nov. 1900, to Jan. 1901, and April to June, 1901; operations in Cape Colony, Jan. 1901, to May, 1902. He was mentioned in Despatches; received the King's Medal with two clasps, and was created a Companion of the Distinguished Service Order [London Gazette, 31 Oct. 1902]: "Henry Maitland Kersey, Major, 15th Battn. Imperial Yeomanry. In recognition of services during the operations in South Africa." He is Major, Hertfordshire Yeomanry, and Honorary Major in the Army.

HAUGHTON, HENRY WILFRED, Major, was born 12 Aug. 1862, son of Benjamin Haughton, of Carlow, and Westminster, S.W., Civil Engineer, and of Emma Isabella, daughter of John Kelly, J.P., of Lunestown, Westmeath, Ireland. He was educated at Dulwich College, and joined the 16th (The Queen's) Lancers. He was tranferred to permanent staff, Bucks Yeomanry, 1894; appointed R.S.M.; proceeded to South Africa, Feb. 1900, as R.S.M., 10th Battn. Imperial Yeomanry; Lieutenant 1 May, 1900; promoted Captain, April, 1901; Major, Nov. 1901; Second-in-Command, 2nd Battn. Imperial Yeomanry, and appointed to command composite regiment of Imperial Yeomanry. He was mentioned in Despatches; received the Queen's Medal with three clasps; the King's Medal with two clasps, and was created a Companion of the Distinguished Service Order [London Gazette, 31 Oct. 1902]: "Henry Wilfred Haughton, Major, 2nd Battn. Imperial Yeomanry. In recognition of services during the operations in South Africa." He became private secretary to Major-General Lord Chesham, K.C.B., I.G.I.Y., 1902. Major Haughton retired and was Adjutant, Gordon Boys' Home, 1904–14. In Sept. 1914, he joined the Royal Buckinghamshire Hussars (T.F.) as Adjutant, and was promoted Major, Squadron Leader, Oct. 1915. He was seconded 22 Dec. 1917, and appointed to command the Road-Quarry Troops Depôt, Royal Engineers, Bordon; Acting Lieutenant-Colonel 1 June, 1919, to command Railway Construction Troops, Royal Engineers, Longmoor. He was mentioned in Despatches, March, 1919; awarded O.B.E., May, 1919. In 1902 he married May, daughter of T. R. Seaton, J.P., of Aylesbury, Bucks.

CARINGTON, THE HONOURABLE RUPERT CLEMENT GEORGE, Lieut.-Colonel, born 18 Dec. 1852, is brother of the Marquess of Lincolnshire, and son of the second Lord Carington. He was educated at Eton, and entered the Grenadier Guards 28 Oct. 1871; contested Buckinghamshire in 1876; served in the Zulu War, 1879, and Boer War (Medal and clasp); was M.P. (L.) for Buckinghamshire, 1880–5; contested Wycombe, 1885; commanded the 3rd New South Wales Imperial Bushmen in South Africa, 1901–2, taking part in the operations in the Transvaal and Orange River Colony, 1901; operations in Cape Colony, 1901–2. He was mentioned in Despatches [London Gazette, 20 July, 1902]; received the Queen's Medal and five clasps, and was created a Companion of the Distinguished Service Order [London Gazette, 31 Oct. 1902]: "The Hon. Rupert Clement George Carington, Lieut.-Colonel, 3rd New South Wales Imperial Bushmen. In recognition of services during the operations in South Africa." He was promoted Colonel, and was created a C.V.O. in 1905. He married, in 1891, Edith (who died in 1908), daughter of John S. Horsfall, of Widgiewa, New South Wales, and they had one son, Rupert Victor John Carington, born in 1891 (married in 1916 the Hon. Sybil Marion, daughter of the second Viscount Colville, and they have one son and one daughter).

O'FARRELL, M., Major, was born in Oct. 1852. He served in the South African War, with the Victorian Mounted Rifles, 1900–2; with the Rhodesian Field Force, on the Staff, Western District, and as Staff Officer, No. 13 Martial Law Area, Cape Colony District; operations in Rhodesia, Transvaal and Orange River Colony. He was mentioned in Despatches [London Gazette, 29 July, 1902]; received the Queen's Medal with five clasps, the King's Medal with two clasps, and was created a Companion of the Distinguished Service Order [London Gazette, 31 Oct. 1902]: "M. O'Farrell, Major, Victorian Contingent. In recognition of services during the operations in South Africa." He was placed on the retired list, with the rank of Major, 1 Aug. 1908.

DEVINE, JAMES ARTHUR, Major, was born 9 Nov. 1869, son of Capt. Devine, late Deputy Surveyor-General, Ontario. He was educated at Cardinal Manning's College, West Kensington, London, W., and at Trinity College, Dublin (M.A., M.B., B.Ch., B.A.O., M.D.). He served in South Africa with the Canadian Contingents, the 1st Canadian Mounted Rifles and the 2nd Canadian Mounted Rifles; was mentioned in Despatches [London Gazette, 18 July, 1902, and on another occasion]; received the Queen's Medal with four clasps, and was created a Companion of the Distinguished Service Order [London Gazette, 31 Oct. 1902]: "James Arthur Devine, Surgeon-Major, 2nd Canadian Mounted Rifles. In recognition of services during the operations in South Africa." He became Temporary Major, Royal Army Medical Corps, 1902. Major Devine is on the Permanent Army Medical Staff (Canada); is Principal Medical Officer, Military Districts 10 and 11 (Manitoba, N.W.T., and British Columbia); Professor of Therapeutics and Clinical Medicine, Manitoba Medical College; Member of Council and Examiner in Materia Medica and Therapeutics and Clinical Medicine, University of Manitoba; Physician to Winnipeg General Hospital; Senior Physician to the Isolated Wards, St. Boniface Hospital. He served in the European War; became Temporary Major, Royal Army Medical Corps, 1915; served at various times as O.C. Troops' Hospital Ships, H.M.H. Ships St. George, Dover and Gloucester Castle. Altogether Major Devine had four years' overseas service. He married, in 1916, Mary Hilda, eldest daughter of the late Henry Miles.

ABBOTT, FREDERICK WILLIAM, Major, was born in Devonshire in 1865. He joined the New Zealand Volunteers, as Lieutenant, in 1898, and was promoted Captain in the same year; Major in 1901, and Lieutenant-Colonel in 1902. He served in South Africa, 1900–2, with the 5th, 7th and 9th New Zealand Contingents, taking part in operations in the Transvaal, west of Pretoria, Aug. to 29 Nov. 1900; operations in the Transvaal, 30 Nov. 1900, to July, 1901; Aug. to Dec. 1901, and April to 31 May, 1902; operations in the Orange River Colony, July to Aug. 1901, and Dec. 1901, to April, 1902; operations on the Zululand Frontier of Natal, Sept. and Oct. 1901. He was mentioned in Despatches [London Gazette, 29 July, 1902]; received the Queen's Medal with four clasps, the King's Medal with two clasps, and was created a Companion of the Distinguished Service Order [London Gazette, 31 Oct. 1902]: "Frederick William Abbott, Major, New Zealand Forces. In recognition of services during the operations in South Africa." He received the New Zealand Veterans' Medal. Lieut.-Colonel Abbott married Annie E., daughter of the late Patrick Grant Ritchie, of Wellington, New Zealand. He died about 1917.

BARTLETT, EDWIN, Major, served in South Africa, with the New Zealand Mounted Rifles, 1902. He was mentioned in Despatches; received Medal with five clasps, and was created a Companion of the Distinguished Service Order [London Gazette, 31 Oct. 1902]: "Edwin Bartlett, Major, New Zealand Forces. In recognition of services during the operations in South Africa."

TREMEER, CHARLES ARTHUR CLAUDE, Major, was born in London 25 Nov. 1856, son of Thomas Brockwell Tremeer, of Cornwall, and of Julie Chevret Tremeer. He was educated at Belgrave House School, London. He joined the Cape Frontier Mounted Police in June, 1875; served in the Native Rebellion, in the Transkei, and in the Gaika and Galeka wars. In 1880 he was in command of the King William's Town Artillery in Umtata, and for his brilliant defence of that town was presented with a Sword of Honour. Lieut.-Colonel Tremeer served in the South African War, from 1899–1902, with the Mounted Irregular Forces; was Field Staff Officer on the Staff of Lord Roberts, and also of Lord Kitchener. He was mentioned in Despatches [London Gazette, 29 July, 1902]; awarded the Queen's and King's Medals with two clasps, and was created a Companion of the Distinguished Service Order [London Gazette, 31 Oct. 1902]: "Charles Arthur Claude Tremeer, Major, South African Mounted Forces. In recognition of services during the operations in South Africa." During the European War Lieut.-Colonel Tremeer served as D.A.Q.M.G. in the German South-West African Campaign, and was mentioned in Despatches. In 1886 he retired as Major from the King William's Town Artillery, and founded the firm of Tremeer & Cummings in 1887—the first firm in Johannesburg, and was the first President of the Johannesburg Chamber of Commerce. From 1892–1915 he was on the staff of the Farrar–Anglo-French group. He was also the Imperial Trade correspondent to H.M. Board of Trade till the time of his death. On 2 Nov. 1918, Lieut.-Colonel Tremeer was knocked down by a motor-car in Johannesburg, and died a few hours later.

Charles A. C. Tremeer.

BROWNE, JOHN WILLIAM, Major, served in the South African War in 1902. He was mentioned in Despatches; created a Companion of the Distinguished Service Order [London Gazette, 31 Oct. 1902]: "John William Browne, Major, Cape Police. In recognition of services during the operations in South Africa." Major Browne was District Inspector, Cape Mounted Police. He died about 1914.

COWAN, BRYCE WALTER, Major, was born 17 Jan. 1866, at Wheatrig, Kilmaurs, Scotland, son of George Cowan, of Wheatrig, Kilmaurs, Scotland. He was educated at Kilmarnock Academy, and at the Glasgow Technical College, and travelled through Canada, the United States and South Africa in 1892; raised the Bechuanaland Rifles, and has commanded them since 1896. He served in the South African War, and served throughout the siege of Mafeking, including the actions of 26 Dec. 1899, and 12 May, 1900, and with Major-General Baden-Powell in the Transvaal, taking part in operations in the Transvaal in May and June, 1900; operations in the Transvaal, west of Pretoria, July to 29 Nov. 1900; operations in Cape Colony, north of Orange River. During part of this time he was serving under Major-General Douglas. He served eventually with Major-General Lord Methuen, when he had command of a special mobile column, Sept. 1901, to 31 May, 1902. He took part in operations in the Transvaal, Orange River Colony and Cape Colony; was mentioned in Despatches [London Gazette, 8 Feb. 1901; 16 April, 1901; 3 Dec. 1901 and 29 July, 1902]; received the Queen's Medal with three clasps, the King's Medal with two clasps, and was created a Companion of the Distinguished Service Order [London Gazette, 31 Oct. 1902]: "Bryce Walter Cowan, Major, Bechuanaland Rifles. In recognition of services during the operations in South Africa." The regiment was called out in Aug. 1914, to quell the Rebellion in South Africa. In Jan. 1915, the regiment was attached to the Eastern Force, which proceeded via Kuruman and Kalahari Desert to German South-West Africa, until the finish of the war there, and then Lieut.-Colonel Cowan proceeded to Europe and took over command of a battalion of the Royal Fusiliers (The City of London Regt.). He has the Volunteer Decoration. He married, 13 Oct. 1904, in Cape Town, South Africa, Marion Hamilton, youngest daughter of Robert Hamilton, of Langmuir, Kilmaurs, Ayrshire, and Breckonridge, Strathavon, Lanarkshire, and they have four children: Bryce George, born 17 Jan. 1906; Marion Elizabeth Young; Robert Hamilton, born 22 Jan. 1909, and John Girvan, born 14 April, 1913.

OWEN-LEWIS, CYRIL ALEXANDER, Major, joined the Cape Colony Cyclists' Corps, and served in the South African War of 1899–1902. He was created a Companion of the Distinguished Service Order [London Gazette, 31 Oct. 1902]: "P. A. Owen-Lewis, Major, Cape Colonial Cyclists' Corps. In recognition of services during the operations in South Africa." The London Gazette of 13 May, 1904, says that Major Owen-Lewis's initials were not "P. A.," but "C. A."—Cyril Alexander. Major Owen-Lewis was later Member for Beaufort West in the Cape Parliament. He died of pneumonia in London. His brother is Major A. F. Lewis, D.S.O.

BENTINCK, BARON WALTER GUY, Capt., was born on 5 Nov. 1864, son of the late Walter Bentinck (13th Baron, holding a Dutch title), 15th Hussars, and of Henrietta J. C. Bentinck, of Alton House, Alton, Hants. He was educated at Marlborough College, and the Royal Military College, Sandhurst, and became Lieutenant in the Rifle Brigade 9 May, 1885; Captain Nov. 1894, and Major 7 Nov. 1902; retired 6 Dec. 1905. Baron Bentinck served throughout the South African War of 1899–1902; Relief of Ladysmith, including action at Colenso; operations of 17 to 24 Jan. and 5 to 7 Feb. 1900, and action at Vaal Kranz; operations on Tugela Heights, 14 to 27 Feb. 1900 (he was wounded at Monte Cristo 18 Feb.); operations in Natal, March to June, 1900, including action at Laing's Nek; operations in Transvaal, east of Pretoria, July to Nov. 1900; Assistant District Commissioner, Vereeniging, from 18 Aug. 1900, to 1901 (mentioned in Despatches [London Gazette, 29 July, 1902]); operations in Transvaal, April, 1901, to March, 1902. He received the Queen's Medal with six clasps; King's Medal with two clasps, and was created a Companion of the Distinguished Service Order [London Gazette, 31 Oct. 1902]: "Walter Guy Bentinck, Capt., The Rifle Brigade. In recognition of services during the operations in South Africa." He was on Special Service, South African Peace Conference, 1902; Resident Magistrate, District of Wakkerstroon, Transvaal, 1901–7. He was Assistant Imperial Secretary to the High Commissioner, South Africa, 1907–11; received the Union of South Africa Medal in 1911; was created C.M.G. in 1912. Lieut.-Colonel Baron Bentinck served in the European War in 1914–15, in the B.E.F., with Directorate, Military Intelligence, War Office, 1916–17; War Office, 1918; in charge of No. 2 Infantry Record Office, Preston, 1918–19. He was promoted Temporary Lieutenant-Colonel 1915; Lieutenant-Colonel, Reserve of Officers, 1919. He was mentioned twice in Despatches. He is fond of travel, and a member of the Travellers' Club. He married, in 1904, Anne, youngest surviving daughter of the late Colonel Burnett-Ramsay, Rifle Brigade, of Banchory, N.B., and they have one son: Walter Thomas Bernhard Ramsay Bentinck, born on 30 Sept. 1905, now at Eton College.

BAKER, ROBERT JOSEPH, Capt., was born 28 April, 1857, in County Dublin, son of John Baker, Esq., and Mrs. Baker. He was educated privately. He served in the South African War, 1899–1902, as Acting Army Service Corps Officer, afterwards Supply Officer; was present at the operations in the Transvaal and Orange River Colony, and in the operations in Cape Colony. He was twice mentioned in Despatches; received the Queen's Medal with three clasps; the King's Medal with two clasps, and was created a Companion of the Distinguished Service Order [London Gazette, 31 Oct. 1902]: "Robert Joseph Baker, Capt., Royal Dublin Fusiliers. In recognition of services in the operations in South Africa." Major Baker retired from the Service in 1911. In the European War he was employed from 1914–19 in the Remount Service. He married, 24 Nov. 1880, Florence Mary Josephine, eldest daughter of the late J. B. Meerwald, Ceylon Civil Service, and they have three sons, born on 17 Sept. 1881; 23 July, 1884 and 9 June, 1885, and three daughters.

MAKINS, ERNEST, Major, was born 14 Oct. 1869, son of the late H. F. Makins, of 180, Queen's Gate, S.W. He was educated at Winchester, and Christ Church, Oxford; joined the 4th Battn. Essex Regt. in 1889, and was gazetted to the Royal Dragoons 23 Jan. 1892, becoming Lieutenant 31 Aug. 1893. He became Captain 2 Feb. 1898, and Major 3 Sept. 1902. He served in the South African War, 1899–1902; Relief of Ladysmith, including action at Colenso; operations of 17 to 24 Jan. 1900, and action at Spion Kop; operations of 5 to 7 Feb. 1900, and action at Vaal Kranz; operations on Tugela Heights, and action at Pieter's Hill; operations in Natal, March to June, 1900; operations in Orange River Colony, May to 29 Nov. 1900; operations in Transvaal, Jan. 1901; operations in Orange River Colony and Cape Colony, Dec. 1900 and Jan. 1901. He was mentioned in Despatches [London Gazette, 10 Sept. 1901, and 29 July, 1902]; received the Queen's Medal with six clasps; the King's Medal with two clasps, and was created a Companion of the Distinguished Service Order [London Gazette, 31 Oct. 1902]: "Ernest Makins, Major, Royal Dragoons. In recognition of services in the operations in South Africa." He was promoted Lieutenant-Colonel 2 Feb. 1910, and Colonel 2 June, 1913. Colonel Makins served in the European War, 1914–17, and retired 21 June, 1919, with the honorary rank of Brigadier-General. He was mentioned in Despatches; was created a C.B., and an Officer of the Italian Order of St. Maurice and Lazarus. He has the 2nd Class Order of the Crown of Prussia, and the 3rd Class Order of the Red Eagle. In 1903 Major Makins married Florence, daughter of Sir J. R. Mellor and Anne Jane, eldest daughter of Thomas Shaw, and they have three sons.

GARSIA, HERBERT GEORGE ANDERSON, Major, was born 5 Feb. 1871. He joined the East Surrey Regt. 9 Jan. 1892, becoming Lieutenant. East Surrey Regt., 11 May, 1893, and Lieutenant, Army Service Corps, 1 April, 1894. He was employed with the Egyptian Army 31 Dec. 1897, to 17 Aug. 1902; served in the Sudan in 1898, and received the British and Khedive's Medals. He was promoted Captain 25 Aug. 1898. He served in South Africa, 1899–1902, on the Staff; in the operations in Orange Free State, Feb. to May, 1900, including operations at Paardeberg (17 to 26 Feb.); actions at Poplar Grove and Dreifontein; operations in the Transvaal, May and June, 1900, including actions near Pretoria and Diamond Hill (11 and 12 June); operations in Orange River Colony, including actions at Wittebergen (1 to 27 July, 1900). He was mentioned in Despatches [London Gazette, 16 April, 1901, and 29 July, 1902]; awarded the Queen's Medal with five clasps; the King's Medal with two clasps, and was created a Companion of the Distinguished Service Order [London Gazette, 31 Oct. 1902]: "Herbert George Anderson Garsia, Major, Army Service Corps. In recognition of services in the operations in South Africa." He became Lieutenant-Colonel 2 Feb. 1914, and retired 2 Sept. 1914. Lieut.-Colonel H. G. A. Garsia served in the European War, as A.A.G., Egyptian Army.

HOME, ROBERT ELTON, Capt., was born 29 May, 1869, son of the late Colonel Robert Home, C.I.E., and of Elizabeth Georgiana, daughter of the late Major H. N. Elton, M.D., Indian Medical Service. He was educated at Cheltenham, and entered the Army 17 Feb. 1888, with a commission in the Royal Artillery. He served in the Waziristan Expedition, 1894–5 (Medal with clasps); in the Punjab, 1897–8 (Medal with two clasps); became Captain in Nov. 1898. He served in the South African War, 1899–1902, in command of the 57th Company, Royal Garrison Artillery; Relief of Ladysmith, including operations on Tugela Heights (17 to 24 Feb. 1900), and action at Pieter's Hill; operations in Natal, March to June, 1900, including action at Laing's Nek (6 to 9 June); operations in the Transvaal, east of Pretoria, July to 29 Nov. 1900; operations in the Transvaal, 30 Nov. 1900, to 31 May, 1902. He was mentioned in Despatches three times [London Gazette, 8 Feb. and 10 Sept. 1901, and 29 July, 1902]; awarded Queen's Medal with five clasps; King's Medal with two clasps, and was created a Companion of the Distinguished Service Order [London Gazette, 31 Oct. 1902]: "Robert Elton Home, Capt., Royal Garrison Artillery. In recognition of services during the operations in South Africa." He became Major 15 Dec. 1908, and Lieutenant-Colonel 6 Jan. 1916. Colonel Home was given the Brevet of Colonel on 1 Jan. 1917, for services in connection with the European War, as Commandant of the Ordnance College, Woolwich, and also created a C.B.E. 1 Jan. 1919. He married, in 1904, Delphine, youngest daughter of the late W. J. Etheridge, and they have two daughters: Margaret Home and Isobel Blanche.

POOLE, FREDERICK CUTHBERT, Capt., was born 3 Aug. 1869, son of the late Rev. R. H. Poole, Rector of Rainton, County Durham, and of Elizabeth Lawrence Poole (Pawlett). He was educated at Durham, and the Royal Military Academy, Woolwich, and joined the Army in Feb. 1889. He served in the Tirah Expedition, 1897–8 (Medal with two clasps); in the South African War of 1899–1902; operations in Natal, March to June, 1900, including action at Laing's Nek; operations in the Transvaal, east of Pretoria, including actions at Belfast and Lydenberg; operations in Cape Colony, south of Orange River, 1899–1900; operations in the Transvaal, Orange River Colony and Cape Colony. He was mentioned three times in Despatches [London Gazette, 8 Feb. and 10 Sept. 1901, and 29 July, 1902]; awarded the Queen's Medal with four clasps; the King's Medal with two clasps, and was created a Companion of the Distinguished Service Order [London Gazette, 31 Oct. 1902]: "Frederick Cuthbert Poole, Capt., Royal Garrison Artillery. In recognition of services in the operations in South Africa." He had become Captain in June, 1899; served in East Africa, 1903–4, in command of the 1st Somali Camel Corps; operations in Somaliland; Special Service Officer (Despatches; Medal with clasp); was promoted Major in June, 1909. He served in the European War, and for his services he was seven times mentioned in Despatches; promoted Lieutenant-Colonel June, 1915, and Brevet Colonel June, 1917, and created C.M.G. 1917; promoted Colonel June, 1919; created C.B. in 1918; created K.B.E. June, 1919; Officier de la Légion d'Honneur (France), 1915; Officer (1st Class) Order of St. Stanislaus, 1917; Officer (1st Class) Order of St. Anne, 1917; Officer (2nd Class) Order of St. Vladimir, 1918 (all Russian decorations); Grand Officer of the Crown of Roumania, 1917; Temporary Brigadier-General April, 1916; Temporary Major-General May, 1917. He married, in 1906, Alice Maude, only daughter of Sir C. A. Hanson, Bart. M.P., J.P., of Fowey Hall, Cornwall.

MAIRIS, GEOFFREY BROUNCKER DE MAIRIS, Capt., was born 16 April, 1870, son of the late General Geoffrey Mairis. He joined the Army 9 Sept. 1893, becoming Lieutenant 25 June, 1896, and Captain 21 Feb. 1900; and was Adjutant, East Kent Regt., 20 March, 1901, to 19 March, 1905. He served in the South African War, 1899–1902; as Adjutant of the 2nd Battn. East Kent Regt., 4 May, 1900, to May, 1902; operations in Natal, 1899; Relief of Ladysmith, including action at Colenso; operations of 17 to 24 Jan. 1900, and action at Spion Kop; operations of 5 to 7 Feb. 1900, and action at Vaal Kranz; operations on Tugela Heights (14 to 27 Feb. 1900), and action at Pieter's Hill; operations in Natal, March, 1900; operations in the Transvaal, east of Pretoria, July to 29 Nov. 1900; operations in Orange River Colony, May to June, 1900; operations in the Transvaal, 31 Nov. 1900, to 31 May, 1902. He was mentioned in Despatches [London Gazette, 10 Sept. 1901]; received the Queen's Medal with five clasps; the King's Medal with two clasps, and was created a Companion of the Distinguished Service Order [London Gazette, 31 Oct. 1902]: "Geoffrey Brouncker de Mairis Mairis, Capt., The Buffs (East Kent Regt.). In recognition of services during the operations in South Africa." He was Brigade-Major, Orange Free State, 1907–9. He was specially promoted to his Majority in the Yorkshire Regt. in 1911. In the European War, Major Mairis served as G.S.O.2, Bombay, 1915–16, and from 1916 to 1918 as Temporary Lieutenant-Colonel, in command of the 7th (Service) Battn. Yorkshire Regt. He was severely wounded; mentioned in Despatches; was given the Brevet of Lieutenant-Colonel 3 June, 1918; and became Lieutenant-Colonel 15 May, 1919, and was made a Chevalier of the Legion of Honour.

MOORE, WILLIAM HENRY, Capt., was born 6 Dec. 1873, son of Major-General C. A. Moore, late Bombay Cavalry. He was educated at the Bedford Grammar School, and entered the Royal Artillery 4 July, 1894, becoming Lieutenant 4 July, 1897. He served in the South African War, 1899–1902; operations in Natal, 1899, including action at Lombard's Kop;

operations in the Transvaal, June, 1900; operations in Orange River Colony, 1900, including actions at Wittebergen and Caledon River. He served as Adjutant, Royal Garrison Artillery, 28 Jan. to May, 1902; operations in the Transvaal, Oct. 1901, to Jan. 1902; operations in Orange River Colony, 30 Nov. to Dec. 1900, and April to Oct. 1901; operations in Cape Colony, Dec. 1900, to April, 1901. He was mentioned twice in Despatches; awarded the Queen's Medal and King's Medal with five clasps, and was created a Companion of the Distinguished Service Order [London Gazette, 31 Oct. 1902]: "William Henry Moore, Capt., Royal Garrison Artillery. In recognition of services in the operations in South Africa." He became Captain 9 May, 1900, and was Adjutant, Royal Artillery, 23 Nov. 1904, to 21 Jan. 1907. He was G.S.O.3, War Office, 20 April, 1910, to 19 April, 1914; was promoted to Major 30 Oct. 1914; Brevet Lieutenant-Colonel, 1915; was G.S.O.2, War Office, 1 Dec. 1914, to 29 Feb. 1916; G.S.O.2, 1st Division, British Armies in France, 15 April to 2 June, 1916; G.S.O.2, Harwich Garrison, 2 Dec. 1916, to 27 April, 1917; was promoted to Lieutenant-Colonel 17 Nov. 1918. In 1911 he married H. E., daughter of the late Lieut. A. W. Caldecott, R.A.

BAYARD, REGINALD, Major, was born 11 Sept. 1860, son of Robertson Bayard, B.L., of St. Louis, New Brunswick. He was educated privately; entered the 2nd Foot 23 April, 1881; became Lieutenant 1 July, 1881; was Adjutant, East Kent Regt., 11 April, 1885, to 10 April, 1890; became Captain 7 Jan. 1893; was Adjutant, Militia, 1 Feb. 1896, to 31 July, 1902. He served in South Africa, 1899–1902, as Garrison Adjutant and Station Staff Officer, Kroonstad, 26 June, 1901, to 10 Jan. 1902; in operations in Orange River Colony, May to 29 Nov. 1900, including action at Lindley (26 June). He was mentioned in Despatches twice [London Gazette, 17 June and 29 July, 1902]; received the Medal with two clasps, and was created a Companion of the Distinguished Service Order [London Gazette, 31 Oct. 1902]: "Reginald Bayard, Major, The Buffs (East Kent Regt.). In recognition of services during the operations in South Africa." Major Bayard served in the operations in the interior of Southern Arabia, 1903–4. He became Lieutenant-Colonel 7 Feb. 1907; was in command of the 2nd Battn. The Buffs, 1909–11; retired 23 Aug. 1911, as Colonel; served as Brigade Commander, Territorial Force (late The Buffs); was given the honorary rank of Brigadier-General 5 Jan. 1918. His favourite recreations are hunting, polo, cricket, golf and skating. Brigadier-General R. Bayard married Edith (died 1916), daughter of the late John Geain, J.P., County Dublin, and they had one daughter.

LEWIN, ARTHUR CORRIE, Capt., was born 26 July, 1874, son of Frederick T. Lewin, D.L., of Castlegrove, County Galway, and Cloghans, County Mayo, and of Lucy, daughter of William Byrom Corrie, of Cheltenham. He was educated at Cheltenham College, and at Trinity Hall, Cambridge; was gazetted to the King's Regt. 7 Dec. 1895; became Lieutenant, 4 Feb. 1899, and Captain 5 Dec. 1900. He served in the South African War, 1899–1902, with the 1st Mounted Infantry, taking part in the operations in the Orange Free State, Feb. to May, 1900, including operations at Paardeberg, actions at Poplar Grove, Dreifontein, Vet River and Zand River; operations in the Transvaal, June, 1900; operations in Orange River Colony, June to Nov. 1900, including actions at Rhenoster River and Wittebergen. He was mentioned in Despatches [London Gazette, 10 Sept. 1901, and 29 July, 1902]; awarded the Queen's Medal and five clasps; the King's Medal and two clasps, and was created a Companion of the Distinguished Service Order [London Gazette, 31 Oct. 1902]: "Arthur Corrie Lewin, Capt., The King's (Liverpool) Regt. In recognition of services during the operations in South Africa." In 1905 he was transferred to the 19th Hussars, and he retired from that regt. 25 Jan. 1908, and was appointed to the 3rd Battn. Connaught Rangers, in which he was promoted to Major in 1910, and of which he assumed the command in 1913. In the war of 1914–19 he served in the Dardanelles Campaign; was appointed to the command of the 5th (Service) Battn. Wiltshire Regt., Sept. 1915, and promoted Brigadier-General, 40th Infantry Brigade, Oct. 1915. On the evacuation of Suvla he was transferred to Helles, and took part in the final withdrawal from that place. From 1916 to 1919 Brigadier-General Lewin served in Mesopotamia. He took part in the operations with the Kut relieving force in 1916; the advance on Baghdad, and the subsequent fighting up to, and including, the final overthrow of the Turkish forces on the Tigris at the Battle of Shergat, Oct. 1918, during the latter fighting in command of the column operating against the Turkish right wing. He commanded Troops in North Persia, July to Sept. 1918. He was mentioned in Despatches six times; has the British and Allies' Medals, and the 1915 Star. He was created a C.M.G. 1916; C.B. 1916; was given the Brevet of Colonel in 1917; was appointed A.D.C. to the King 1918. He also has the Order of St. Anne of Russia. He relinquished his commission in 1919. He is a Magistrate for County Galway; was High Sheriff, County Mayo, 1912. In 1900 Brigadier-General Lewin married Norah Constance, daughter of the late William Higgin, of Rosganna, Carrickfergus, and they have two sons: Patrick William, born in 1903, and Thomas Chippindale Colquitt, born in 1907.

Arthur Corrie Lewin.

GOFF, CECIL WILLIE TREVOR THOMAS, Capt., was born 26 May, 1860, second son of Joseph Goff and Lady Adelaide Henrietta Louisa Hortense Knox, daughter of the 2nd Lord Ranfurley. He was educated at Radley, and entered the 59th Foot 14 Jan. 1880; became Lieutenant, East Lancashire Regt., 19 May, 1881; Captain 10 Aug. 1890; was Adjutant, Militia, from 19 March, 1895; promoted to Major in 1901. He served in the South African War of 1899–1902; as Adjutant of the 3rd Battn. East Lancashire Regt. 1900–1, and in 1902 with the 1st Battn.; received the Queen's and King's Medals with two clasps, and was created a Companion of the Distinguished Service Order [London Gazette, 31 Oct. 1902]: "Cecil Willie Trevor Thomas Goff, Capt., East Lancashire Regt. In recognition of services during the operations in South Africa." He died 4 Aug. 1907, of heart failure, at Folkestone.

SANDILANDS, JAMES WALTER, Capt., was born 6 Sept. 1874, second son of the late A. Sandilands. He was educated at Harrow, and entered the Gordon Highlanders, from the Militia, as Second Lieutenant, 24 March, 1897. He was transferred to the Cameron Highlanders 1 May, 1897, and served in the Sudan Campaign in 1898, being present at the battles of the Atbara and Khartum. He was mentioned in Despatches, and received the British Medal and Khedive's Medal with two clasps. He became Lieutenant 28 Sept. 1898, and Captain 29 May, 1901, and served in the South African War, 1900–1, with the Mounted Infantry, and took part in the operations in the Orange Free State, March to May, 1900; in the Transvaal, May and June, 1900, including the actions near Pretoria, and at Diamond Hill, and from July to 29 Nov. 1900, including the action at Eland's River, in the Orange River Colony, June to Nov. 1900, including the actions in the Wittebergen; Cape Colony, 1900; in the Transvaal, 30 Nov. 1900, to Jan. 1901. He was dangerously wounded at Noitgedacht on 13 Dec. 1900; mentioned in Despatches twice [London Gazette, 10 Sept. 1901, and 29 July, 1902]; awarded the Queen's Medal with five clasps, and was created a Companion of the Distinguished Service Order [London Gazette, 31 Oct. 1902]: "James Walter Sandilands, Capt., Cameron Hldrs. In recognition of services during the operations in South Africa." He became Captain 29 May, 1901; was Officer in Charge of Musketry Duties, Welsh and Midland Command; Captain attached to General Staff, Western Command, 23 Oct. 1905, to 1909; student at the Staff College, 1910–11. During the European War he served as D.A.A. and Q.M.G., Scottish Coast Defences, 5 Aug. to 1 Nov. 1914; commanded the London Scottish in 1914; was Brigade Major, 46th Infantry Brigade, New Armies, 24 Feb. to 22 April, 1915; was promoted to Major 16 Feb. 1915; was Temporary Lieutenant-Colonel, commanding the 7th Battn. Cameron Highlanders, 23 April, 1915, to 13 April, 1916; Brigade Commander, 104th Infantry Brigade, British Armies in France, from 14 April, 1916, and commanded it for three years, also the 1st Northern Brigade; 2nd Highland, and 20th Prov. Brigade, until 1 April, 1920. He was mentioned in Despatches six times; was given the Brevets of Lieutenant-Colonel 3 June, 1916, and Colonel 3 June, 1918; created a C.M.G. in 1916, and a C.B. in 1919.

MACLEAN, DONALD CHARLES HUGH, Capt., was born 13 July, 1875, at Hurst Lodge, Dalhousie, India, son of Major-General Charles Smith MacLean, C.B., C.I.E., and Mrs. C. S. MacLean. Of General and Mrs. MacLean's gallant sons, one was the late Lieut. Hector Lachlan Stewart MacLean, V.C., of the Guides. Their youngest son, the late Capt. Alastair FitzHugh MacLean, of the 33rd Punjabis, was killed at Gallipoli, while serving with the 14th Sikhs, after the landing at Suvla. He was mentioned in Despatches, 19 March, 1917. He was married. Capt. Colin Kenneth MacLean, C.B., D.S.O., R.N., happily still survives. He served on the Staff of Admiral Bacon at Dover, and served at Zeebrugge, and with the Destroyer Flotilla of Harwich Force. Donald MacLean was gazetted to the Royal Scots, as Second Lieutenant, 28 Sept. 1895, and became Lieutenant 4 Nov. 1896, and Captain 1 July, 1901. He served in the South African War, 1899–1902, attached to the Army Service Corps, and employed with Mounted Infantry, taking part in operations in the Orange Free State, Feb. to May, 1900; operations in the Transvaal, east of Pretoria, July to 29 Nov. 1900, including actions at Belfast (26 and 27 Aug.), and Lydenberg (5 to 8 Sept.); operations in Orange River Colony (May to 29 Nov. 1900); operations in Cape Colony, south of Orange River, 1899–1900; operations in the Transvaal, 30 Nov. 1900, to Oct. 1901; operations in Orange River Colony, Oct. 1901, to 31 May, 1902. He was mentioned in Despatches [London Gazette, 10 Sept. 1901, and 29 July, 1902]; received the Queen's Medal with three clasps; the King's Medal with two clasps, and was created a Companion of the Distinguished Service Order [London Gazette, 31 Oct. 1902]: "Donald Charles Hugh MacLean, Capt., The Royal Scots. In recognition of services during the operations in South Africa." He was Adjutant, Militia, 22 June, 1903, to 5 April, 1906, and Adjutant, Indian Volunteers, 29 April, 1907. He married, at Bombay, 26 Oct. 1907, Gwendoline Katherine Hope, and their son is Hector Charles Donald MacLean. Capt. MacLean died 20 April, 1909.

PAINE, ALBERT INGRAHAM, Capt., was born 12 Jan. 1874, son of the late Hammon Paine, Esq., and of Helen Paine. He was educated at Harrow and Sandhurst, and joined the King's Royal Rifle Corps 10 Dec. 1894. He served in the South African War, 1899–1902, with the 1st Battn. Mounted Infantry, of which he was Adjutant 1900–2; promoted Captain June, 1901. He was twice mentioned in Despatches, and for his services in the 1st Mounted Infantry during the South African War of 1899–1902 was created a Companion of the Distinguished Service Order [London Gazette, 31 Oct. 1902]: "Albert Ingraham Paine, Capt., King's Royal Rifle Corps. In recognition of services during the operations in South Africa." He resigned his commission April, 1905; rejoined 7 Sept. 1914, and was given command of the 12th (Service) Battn. King's Royal Rifles, 21 Oct. 1914, serving in the European War, 1914–18. He was twice mentioned in Despatches; created C.M.G. June, 1916. Lieut.-Colonel Paine married, 21 Feb. 1906, Elsie Caroline, fourth daughter of Philip Wykeham, Esq., of Tythrop House, Thame, Oxon, and they have two children: Susan, born 10 May, 1907, and Rosemary, born 19 Feb. 1917.

JACKSON, THOMAS DARE, Capt., was born 14 June, 1876, eldest son of the late Sir Thomas Jackson, 1st Bart., and Amelia Lydia Dare. He was educated at Cheltenham College, and joined the Royal Lancaster Regt. 1 Dec. 1897, becoming Lieutenant 16 Aug. 1899. He served in South

Africa, 1901–2, taking part in operations in Cape Colony, Orange River Colony and the Transvaal, March, 1901, to April, 1902. He was mentioned in Despatches [London Gazette, 17 Jan. 1902]; received the Queen's Medal with five clasps, and was created a Companion of the Distinguished Service Order [London Gazette, 31 Oct. 1902]: "Thomas Dare Jackson, Capt., King's Own Royal Lancaster Regt. In recognition of services during the operations in South Africa." He became Captain 7 Oct. 1901; was Adjutant, Royal Lancaster Regt. 11 Aug. 1902, to 10 Aug. 1905; was A.D.C. to Lieutenant-General, India; A.D.C. to G.O.C., Southern Army, India, 22 June, 1906, to 29 Oct. 1908. He was promoted Major 3 Sept. 1914. Major Jackson served in the European War, 1914–17. He was in command 1st Battn. King's Own Regt. for 1 year; in command 11th Battn. Manchester Regt. for 1 year; in command 55th Infantry Brigade for 1 year, and retired 6 Nov. 1919, with honorary rank of Brigadier-General. He was mentioned in Despatches; received the Brevet of Lieutenant-Colonel 1 Jan. 1916, and was awarded a Bar to the D.S.O. [London Gazette, 1 Jan. 1918]: "Major and Brevet Lieut.-Colonel Sir Thomas Dare Jackson, Bart., M.V.O., D.S.O., Royal Lancaster Regt." Lieut.-Colonel T. D. Jackson succeeded his father as 2nd Baronet in 1915. Sir Thomas Jackson married, 25 Jan. 1919, Mary Lilian Vera, eldest daughter of Brigadier-General S. E. Massy Lloyd, of Westwood House, Ipswich.

TWEEDIE, HENRY CARMICHAEL, Capt., was born 25 Jan. 1876, second son of the late Major-General Michael Tweedie, of Boveney, Folkestone, formerly of the Royal Artillery. He was educated privately, and at the Royal Military College, Sandhurst, and joined the North Staffordshire Regt. 6 Sept. 1896; became Lieutenant 24 Feb. 1899, and Captain 13 Nov. 1901. He served in South Africa, 1900–2, being employed throughout the war with the Mounted Infantry; took part in operations in the Orange Free State, Feb. to May, 1900, including operations at Paardeberg, 17 to 26 Feb.; action at Dreifontein; operations in the Transvaal, June to 29 Nov. 1900; operations in the Transvaal, 30 Nov. 1900, to Dec. 1901, and March to 31 May, 1902; operations in Orange River Colony, June to Sept. 1901, and Jan. to March, 1902; operations in Cape Colony, Sept. to Nov. 1901. He was mentioned in Despatches [London Gazette, 25 April, 1902]; awarded the Queen's Medal with four clasps; the King's Medal with two clasps, and was created a Companion of the Distinguished Service Order [London Gazette, 31 Oct. 1902]: "Henry Carmichael Tweedie, Capt., North Staffordshire Regt. In recognition of services during the operations in South Africa." He became Assistant Commandant, Mounted Infantry School, 1909; was promoted Major Dec. 1913. He served during the Mohmand disturbances, North-West Frontier of India, in 1914 and 1915; and in the European War, in France, attached to the South Staffordshire Regt. He was severely wounded, and subsequently became Commandant R.A.F. School, Henley-on-Thames. He was awarded the O.B.E. May, 1919. In 1914 he married Catherine (Katie) Lucy Minnie, daughter of Colonel A. W. Prior, of Lyncroft House, Lichfield, Staffordshire, and has two daughters.

SHUTER, REGINALD GAUNTLETT, Capt., was born 11 Jan. 1876, son of the late Charles Shuter, of Greendale, Victoria. He had a commission in the Local Military Forces of Victoria, 1894–6, and was gazetted to the 2nd Battn. Royal Irish Fusiliers, 28 Dec. 1895; became Lieutenant 5 April, 1899, and Captain, 23 Nov. 1901, in the Manchester Regt. He served during the first phase of the South African War with the Royal Irish Fusiliers, and during the last phase as Adjutant of Mounted Infantry, taking part in the Relief of Ladysmith, and the operations in Natal, March, 1900; the Transvaal, 30 Nov. 1900, to April, 1902, and Orange River Colony, March, 1902. He was twice mentioned in Despatches [London Gazette, 10 Sept. 1901, and 29 July, 1902]; received the Queen's South African Medal with five clasps and the King's South African Medal with two clasps, and was created a Companion of the Distinguished Service Order [London Gazette, 31 Oct. 1902]: "Reginald Gauntlett Shuter, Capt., Manchester Regt. In recognition of services during the operations in South Africa." He was Adjutant, Manchester Regt., 14 April, 1905, to 23 Jan. 1907; employed with the Egyptian Army, 24 Jan. 1907, to 23 Feb. 1908; and became Captain, Royal Irish Fusiliers, 8 Jan. 1908. He served in the European War; as Temporary Major, Royal Irish Fusiliers, 18 Sept. to 4 Oct. 1914; was promoted to Major, Royal Irish Fusiliers, 5 Oct. 1914; Brigade Major, 15th Reserve Infantry Brigade, New Armies, 5 Nov. 1915, to 25 Jan. 1916; Temporary Lieutenant-Colonel, Royal Irish Fusiliers, from 26 Jan. to 23 May, 1916; Temporary Brigadier-General, 109th Infantry Brigade, British Armies in France, 24 May, 1916, to 13 Jan. 1917; held a special appointment as Instructor, Senior Officers' School, Aldershot, 3 Jan. to 3 Aug. 1918. He was twice mentioned in Despatches, and received the Brevet of Lieutenant-Colonel 3 June, 1916. In 1915 he married Muriel Irene, daughter of George Ellis, and they have one son.

Wilfred C. N. Hastings.

HASTINGS, WILFRED CHARLES NORRINGTON, Capt., was born at Devonport 24 Dec. 1873, son of the Rev. Francis Henry Hastings, retired Captain, R.N. He was educated at Trinity College School, Stratford-on-Avon, and entered the 4th Battn. South Wales Borderers in 1892; was seconded for the Sierra Leone Frontier Force in 1898; served in the Hut Tax War, 1898–99 (wounded; Medal and clasp). On 24 June, 1899, he entered the Manchester Regt., and became Lieutenant 1 Dec. 1899, and Captain 25 Dec. 1901. He served in the South African War, 1900–2, taking part in operations in the Orange Free State, April, 1900; operations in the Transvaal, east of Pretoria, Aug. to Se t. and Nov. 1900 operations in

Orange River Colony, May to 29 Nov. 1900, including actions at Biddulphsberg and Wittebergen; operations in Cape Colony, south of Orange River, April, 1900; operations in the Transvaal, July, 1901; operations in Orange River Colony, 30 Nov. 1900, to 31 May, 1902. He was awarded the South African and King's Medals; mentioned in Despatches [London Gazette, 29 July, 1902], and was created a Companion of the Distinguished Service Order [London Gazette, 31 Oct. 1902]: "Wilfred Charles Norrington Hastings, Capt., Manchester Regt. In recognition of services during the operations in South Africa." He was employed with the West African Frontier Force, 28 March, 1903, and served with the 1st Battn. Northern Nigerian Regt. 1903; with the Munshi Expedition, 1906. He served in the European War, in France, 1914; became Temporary Lieutenant-Colonel 17 April, 1915, commanding the Sierra Leone Battn. West African Frontier Force, and took part in the Cameroon Campaign, 1915–16. His chief pastimes are shooting, fishing and boxing.

JEBB, GLADWYN DUNDAS, Capt., was born 27 March, 1877, son of the late Capt. J. G. Jebb, 54th Foot, of Barnby Moor House, Notts, and of the Honourable Mrs. Jebb, sister of the 5th Viscount Melville. He was educated at Charterhouse, and joined the Army 5 Sept. 1896, as a Second Lieutenant in the Bedfordshire Regt.; became Lieutenant 22 Jan. 1898, and Capt. 11 Jan. 1902. He served in the South African War, 1899–1902; was on Police Duty under Military Governor, Pretoria, 15 June to 4 Sept. 1900, and afterwards as a Signalling Officer from 11 Sept. 1900. He was employed with the Mounted Infantry; operations in the Orange Free State, Feb. to May, 1900; operations in the Transvaal, west of Pretoria, July to 29 Nov. 1900; operations in Orange River Colony, 29 Nov. 1900; operations in Cape Colony, south of Orange River, 1899 to 1900, including the actions at Colesberg, 1 Jan. to 12 Feb.; operations in Orange River Colony, 30 Nov. 1900, to May, 1902. He was mentioned in Despatches twice [London Gazette, 10 Sept. 1901, and 29 July, 1902]; awarded the Queen's Medal with three clasps; the King's Medal with two clasps, and was created a Companion of the Distinguished Service Order [London Gazette, 31 Oct. 1902]: "Gladwyn Dundas Jebb, Capt., Bedfordshire Regt. In recognition of services during the operations in South Africa." He passed the Staff College; served on the Staff there from May, 1908, to May, 1912, and held Staff appointments from Jan. 1913, throughout the European War. He was on active service in the European War (Temporary Brigadier-General, 1915), from Aug. 1914, till March, 1917. From 5 Aug. to 17 Sept. 1914, he was D.A.Q.M.G., G.H.Q., B.E.F.; from 18 Sept. 1914, to 6 Feb. 1915, D.A.A. and Q.M.G., 1st Cavalry Division, B.E.F.; from 7 Feb. to 13 July, 1915, he was A.A.Q.M.G., 2nd Division, B.E.F.; from 31 Dec. 1915, to 1 Dec. 1916, D.A.Q.M.G., 10th Army Corps, B.E.F.; from 2 Dec. 1916, to 15 March, 1917, D.A.Q.M.G., 15th Army Corps, B.E.F.; from 19 June, 1917, to 4 March, 1918, D.A.Q.M.G., Northern Army, Home Force; from 5 March, 1918, Brigadier-General in charge of Administration, Western Command. He was five times mentioned in Despatches, and was given the Brevet of Lieutenant-Colonel; created a C.M.G. June, 1916, and C.B.E. Dec. 1919. Brigadier-General Jebb married, at Farnborough, 2 Jan. 1912, Norah May, daughter of the late Lieut.-General S. H. Lomax and Mrs. Lomax, and they have two children: David Gladwyn, born 18 Dec. 1912, and Michael, born 18 June, 1918.

STEWART, WILLIAM EDMOND LOGAN, Capt., was born 8 Oct. 1873, at Rhosygilwin, Cilgerran, South Wales, son of the late Capt. James Stewart, of the Madras Horse Artillery, of Allyrodyn, Llandyssil, South

Wales, J.P. and D.L. for County Cardigan, and of Louisa Charlotte, daughter of William Butler, Madras Army. He was educated at Winchester, and was gazetted to the Welsh Regt. 29 May, 1895, becoming Lieutenant 3 Feb. 1898. He served throughout the South African Campaign, 1899–1902, with the 1st Mounted Infantry from Oct. 1899, to Dec. 1901, first in command of Maxim guns, and later in command of a company and Maxims. He was present at the Relief of Kimberley, Paardeberg, Dreifontein, Sanna's Post, and at the advances on Brandfort, Zand River, Vet River, Johannesburg and Diamond Hill; at the operations southeast of Pretoria; the advance on Middelburg (Transvaal); Belfast, and advance on Komati Poort.

William E. L. Stewart.

He was later with Colonel Williams' Column pursuing Kritzinger, De Wet and others in Cape Colony and Orange River Colony. After Jan. to the end of the war he was A.D.C. to General Sir E. A. H. Alderson, C.B., A.D.C., Commanding the Mounted Infantry in South Africa. He was mentioned three times in Despatches; received the Queen's Medal with six clasps; the King's Medal with two clasps, and was created a Companion of the Distinguished Service Order [London Gazette, 31 Oct. 1902]: "William Edmond Logan Stewart, Capt., The Welsh Regt. In recognition of services during the operations in South Africa." He was promoted to Captain 22 Jan. 1902. He left the Army 2 May, 1906, on retired pay, and joined the Pembrokeshire Yeomanry. Major Stewart mobilized with the Pembrokeshire Yeomanry at the beginning of the European War, but was invalided out owing to a badly broken skull 9 April, 1916. Major Stewart formerly hunted and played polo, but has had to give up these pursuits as his wounds prevent him from riding. He shoots and is fond of fishing. On 30 Jan. 1908, at Tilmanstone, Kent, he married Mary Adela Morland Rice, daughter of Major C. A. Rice, R.E., of Danefield House, Eastry, Kent, and their children are: John Logan, born 16 May, 1911, and Mary Elizabeth.

PAUL, JAMES ROBERT ALEXANDER HUNTER, Capt., was born 11 July, 1873, only surviving son of the late James Paul, of Drumcondra, Ireland. He joined the 2nd Battn. Leicestershire Regt. 9 Sept. 1893, becoming Lieutenant 3 Oct. 1896, and Captain 25 Jan. 1902. He served in the South African War, 1899–1902; operations in Natal, 1899, including actions at Talana and Lombard's Kop; Defence of Ladysmith; operations in Natal, March to June, 1900, including action at Laing's Nek (6 to 9 June); operations in Transvaal, east of Pretoria, including actions at Belfast (26 to 27 Aug.), and Lydenberg (5 to 8 Sept.). He served as Adjutant, 25th and 26th Mounted Infantry Battns., to 31 May, 1902; operations in the Transvaal 30 Nov. 1900, to 31 May, 1902. He was mentioned three times in Despatches; awarded the Queen's Medal with four clasps; the King's Medal with two clasps, and was created a Companion of the Distinguished Service Order [London Gazette, 31 Oct. 1902]: "James Robert Alexander Hunter Paul, Capt., Leicestershire Regt. In recognition of services during the operations in South Africa." He was employed with the Ceylon Volunteers from 30 Dec. 1907, to 11 Dec. 1912, and became Major, Leicestershire Regt., 10 Sept. 1912, and Major 1914. He became Adjutant, Mounted Rifles, Planters' Corps, and was Temporary Lieutenant-Colonel, 1st Battn. Cambridgeshire Regt., 2 Dec. 1916, to 22 March, 1918. Major Paul married, in 1903, Amy Elizabeth, daughter of George Sanderson, of Richmond, Surrey.

MANGLES, ROLAND HENRY, Capt., was born 9 Feb. 1874, son of the late Ross L. Mangles, V.C. (Bengal Civil Service), and of the late Henrietta Anne Mangles, daughter of James More-Molyneux, Esq., of Losley Park, Guildford. He was educated at Marlborough; joined the Royal West Surrey Regt. 12 Dec. 1894, becoming Lieutenant 21 Nov. 1896; was employed with the West African Frontier Force 5 March, 1898, to 15 Oct. 1899, and took part in operations on the Niger River and served in Borgu (Despatches; Medal with clasp). He was promoted to Captain 20 Feb. 1902. He served in the South African War, 1899–1902 (as Brigade Signalling Officer 24 Aug. 1900, to 30 June, 1902), and took part in the Relief of Ladysmith, including the action at Colenso; operations of 17 to 24 Jan. 1900, and action at Spion Kop; operations of 5 to 7 Feb., and action at Vaal Kranz; operations on Tugela Heights and action at Pieter's Hill; subsequently in the operations in Natal, March to June, 1900, including action at Laing's Nek, and finally on the Staff as a Brigade Signalling Officer, and took part in operations in the Transvaal and Orange River Colony. He was wounded in the attack on Monte Cristo; was mentioned in Despatches, and awarded the Queen's Medal with five clasps; the King's Medal with two clasps, and was created a Companion of the Distinguished Service Order [London Gazette, 31 Oct. 1902]: "Roland Henry Mangles, Capt., The Queen's Royal West Surrey Regt. In recognition of services during the operations in South Africa." He was specially employed at the War Office 21 March to 20 June, 1910; G.S.O.3, War Office, 15 Oct. 1910, to 8 March, 1912; Brigade Major, 16th Brigade, Irish Command, 9 March, 1912, to 4 Aug. 1914. He served in the European War, 1914–18, as Brigade Major, 16th Infantry Brigade, B.E.F., 5 Aug. 1914, to 19 Feb. 1915; G.S.O.2, 20th Division, New Armies, B.E.F., 1 March, 1915, to 8 Feb. 1916; G.S.O.1, 1st Grade, 34th Division, B.E.F., British Armies in France, 9 Feb. 1916, to 18 Feb. 1917; G.S.O.1, War Office, 19 Feb. to 5 Nov. 1917; G.S.O.1, 58th Division, British Armies in France, 16 July, 1918; Brigadier-General, General Staff, 5th Army Corps, British Armies in France, from 16 July, 1918; Brigadier-General, General Staff, 20th Army Corps, Egypt, from 18 May, 1919. He was mentioned in Despatches, (Feb. 1915; Jan. and June, 1916; Jan. and June, 1917; June, 1918; Jan. and June, 1919); awarded the Brevets of Major, Lieutenant-Colonel and Colonel, and was awarded the C.M.G. and Order of St. Ann with Cross Swords. Capt. Mangles married, in Dec. 1909, Sylvia Amy Rhys, daughter of the late Rev. W. Hand, and they have two sons: Ross Patrick and David Ross, born 19 March, 1912, and 22 Oct. 1916, respectively.

LONG, WALTER, Capt., was born 26 July, 1879, eldest son of the Right Honourable Walter Long, P.C., J.P., D.L., F.R.S., LL.D., M.P., First Lord of the Admiralty, and Lady Doreen, fourth daughter of the 9th Earl of Cork and Orrery. He was educated at Harrow (Moretons, March, 1893, to Feb. 1898); was commissioned in the Scots Greys, 20 May, 1899, from the Militia; became Lieutenant 10 July, 1900, and Captain 23 April, 1902. He served in the South African War, 1899–1902, and was severely wounded after the Relief of Kimberley, having taken part in the famous ride of Sir John French; part of the time he served as A.D.C. to Sir John French. He was present during the operations in the Transvaal, May, 1901, to May, 1902; on the Zululand Frontier of Natal in Sept. and Oct. 1901, also in Cape Colony in May, 1902. He was mentioned in Despatches [London Gazette, 29 Aug. 1902]; received the Queen's Medal with two clasps; the King's Medal with two clasps, and was created a Companion of the Distinguished Service Order [London Gazette, 31 Oct. 1902]: "Walter Long, Capt., 2nd Dragoons. In recognition of services during the operations in South Africa." He was A.D.C. to Major-General Scobell, 1st Cavalry Brigade, Aldershot, 1 April to 30 Sept. 1903, and 1 Oct. 1903, to 31 March, 1906; Adjutant, Scots Greys, 11 Oct. 1906, to 1909; A.D.C. to the Governor-General and Commander-in-Chief, Dominion of Canada, 6 Oct. 1911, to 5 Oct. 1913. He was for a time A.D.C. to Sir O'Moore Creagh, Commander-in-Chief in India; specially employed at the War Office 24 April to 31 May, 1912; Staff Captain, War Office, 1 June, 1912, to 25 Jan. 1915; D.A.A.G. 26 Jan. to 13 July, 1915; A.A.G. 14 July, 1915. He went to France in Aug. 1914, being then Captain in charge of a Squadron, and was shortly afterwards promoted Major (1 April, 1915), then Lieutenant-Colonel Commanding the 6th Battn. Wiltshire Regt. (from 14 Dec. 1915), and received the C.M.G. He was several times mentioned in Despatches, and promoted to Brigadier-General Commanding 56th Brigade, 19th Division, and made a Brevet Lieutenant-Colonel. He was killed in action when in the trenches at Hébuterne on 28 Jan. 1917.

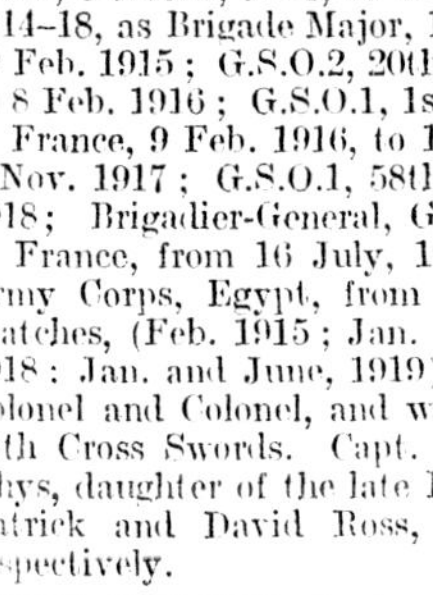

Walter Long.

His Majesty the King wrote: "The Queen and I are deeply grieved to hear that your son has been killed in action after such a distinguished career, and in the prime of youth. I regret that my Army has lost one of its promising young Generals."

H.R.H. the Duke of Connaught wrote: "In Toby the Army and the Scots Greys have lost a splendid officer, who has always set the finest example and whose name will long be remembered. His has been a glorious death, falling in action in command of his Brigade."

Field-Marshal Sir Douglas Haig wrote: "As the General under whom he was directly serving will have told you, his death deprives the Army of one of our best Brigadiers. As a soldier he was so practical, and thoroughly up to his work. I always felt he was sure to attain high rank, and, as a man, he was loved and admired by us all for his manly straightforward ways."

At a meeting held in furtherance of the War Loan in the City Town Hall, Mr. Walter Long was the chief speaker. "The Colonial Secretary, who had a very sympathetic reception, said it was no secret that an event which had occurred this week in his domestic circle would in ordinary circumstances have led him to choose seclusion rather than appearance on a public platform; but he felt that it was his duty to come to the meeting in order to spread the lesson that they must all put their backs into the war in order to bring it to a triumphal conclusion. He had this further incentive that his wife and daughter-in-law desired him to come in order to say that their one thought was that the people of this country should not hesitate to do their duty. A still stronger incentive was the knowledge that there had come to him from the son whose loss he should deplore as long as he lived a message, silently given, that nothing should prevent him doing his duty. Until we at home realized the issue of this war, depended on ourselves and on the sacrifices that we were prepared to make, we should not have the determination that was necessary to make our cause triumphant. It was pitiful and almost incredible that at a time like the present men should have to be searched for and dug out in order to obtain their services. It was not because they were not patriotic or ready to serve, but because of the widespread prevalence of the idea that everything that was necessary was being done. Since he had been at the Colonial Office he had been very much struck by the liberality and spontaneity of the contributions from various parts of the Empire where money was none too plentiful. Recently separate contributions of £800, £200 and £20 had been received from three native treasury chests in Northern Nigeria, accompanied by expressions of fervent hope for our victory over Germany. With such examples before us, surely we, who had taken real liberty and real freedom into the countries over which we ruled, would give our last penny in order that these priceless assets might not only remain with us, but might be handed down unimpaired to those who came after. We were profiting by what our forefathers had done. Let us take care that our children should profit by what we were doing to-day. It was the duty of all to give to the Government every penny they could possibly spare, in order that our sailors and soldiers might have the reward they so much desired, namely, the winning of this war speedily. In talking matters over with a dear old friend, he had come to the conclusion that he might help those whom he was addressing to realize what duty really was if he referred to the example of the son whom he had lost. He was a very true Knight, *sans peur et sans reproche;* he lived his whole life for one thing, and one thing alone—duty—and he died as he had lived. The General Officer Commanding his son's division had written of him: 'And now he is gone to join that gallant band to which we have all contributed, and will contribute without fear. They are never far from us out here—the gallant dead—they watch our progress keenly and cheer us by their memory and example.' A fine thought for all of us to-day! That as the gallant dead are not gone but are cheering on their comrades to victory, so must they be cheering us on here to still greater effort, not blaming us, not reproaching us, but telling us, in voices to which our ears cannot be deaf, that it is our bounden and sacred duty to do our utmost to help our country in her time of difficulty and trial."

Lieut.-Colonel Long was Champion Light Weight Boxer, and twice won the Middle Weight Boxing Championship of the British Army. He married, in 1910, the Hon. Sibell Johnstone, eldest daughter of Lord Derwent and Ethel (who died in 1901), eldest daughter of Capt. H. Strickland, late of the Life Guards, and there is one son.

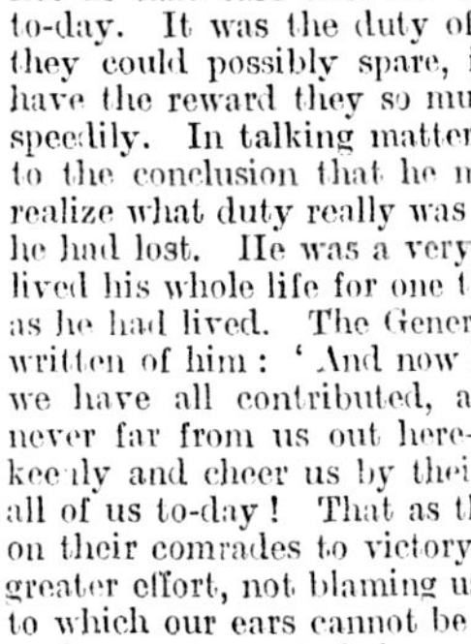

William Lynn Allen

ALLEN, WILLIAM LYNN, Capt., was born 8 May, 1871, at West Lynn, Altrincham, Cheshire, son of the late Bulkeley Allen, J.P., of West Lynn, Altrincham (son of John Allen, J.P., of Oldfield Hall, Altrincham), and Mary Emma Lynn, daughter of Dr. Edward Lynn. He was educated at Rugby; was gazetted to the 3rd (Militia) Battn. The King's Own Yorkshire Light Infantry in 1891, and to the Border Regt. 9 Sept. 1893. He was promoted Lieutenant 29 July, 1896; Captain 23 July, 1902, and Major in Oct. 1913. Throughout the whole of the South African

War he served in the 1st Battn., being Regimental Transport Officer in the earlier stages, and Adjutant in the latter part of the war; he continued to hold this position afterwards until 1904. He was present at the operations in Natal, 1899; at the Relief of Ladysmith, including the action at Colenso, and actions of Spion Kop and Vaal Kranz; operations on the Tugela Heights; action at Pieter's Hill; operations in the Orange Free State; in the Transvaal, east and west of Pretoria; in the Orange River Colony, and in Cape Colony, north and south of Orange River. For his services in this campaign he was twice mentioned in Despatches [London Gazette, 10 Sept. 1901, and 29 July, 1902]; received the Queen's Medal with five clasps; the King's Medal with two clasps, and was created a Companion of the Distinguished Service Order [London Gazette, 31 Oct. 1902]: "William Lynn Allen, Capt., The Border Regt. In recognition of services during the operations in South Africa." From Sept. 1905, to Sept. 1909, he was Adjutant of the Discharge Depôt, and he received his Majority in Oct. 1913, in the 2nd Battn., in which he had commanded a company. Early in Oct. 1914, he went to the front with the 7th Division, which defended the town of Ypres from 19 Oct. to 6 Nov. On the evening of 28 Oct. he was holding a point between the villages of Krusik and America, about 4⅓ miles from Ypres. For the previous seven days, Major Lynn Allen had been occupying with his men a salient point at the extreme left of his regiment, and his company were badly in need of reinforcements. On that particular night about 100 of the enemy made their way over trenches occupied by a neighbouring battalion, and appeared in the vicinity of a farmhouse in the rear of the Borders. After an interchange of firing, a considerable number were killed, and immediately afterwards the remainder signified their wish to surrender, asking for an English officer. In response Major Lynn Allen left his trench with two men, and had hardly advanced a step or more before the enemy treacherously opened fire, and he fell back mortally wounded. His C.O. in South Africa, Lieut.-Colonel Ovens, now Brigadier-General, states: "No officer of the battalion was more gallant and devoted, and it is doubtful if any other gave such valuable services as he did as Transport Officer and Adjutant." Major Bosanquet, the senior surviving officer of his battalion at Ypres, wrote of him as being "an exceptionally capable officer, and a very great loss to the regiment." On 8 June, 1898, at St. Peter's Church, Woking, Surrey, Major Allen married Adeline Miriam, second daughter of Isaac Garbutt Dickinson, and they have three children: Bulkeley Garbutt Lynn, born 20 July, 1899: Esmond Harcourt Lynn, born 22 Aug. 1903, and Sylvia Pomona Lynn, born 15 Oct. 1907.

MACKENZIE, THOMAS CAMPBELL, Capt., was born 26 July, 1879, son of James Mackenzie, of Kinsale, late Land Commissioner, Ireland. He is L.R.C.P.I. and L.R.C.S.I.; joined the Army 27 July, 1899, becoming Captain 27 July, 1902. He served in South Africa, 1899–1902, and was slightly wounded, taking part in the advance on Kimberley, including actions at Modder River and Magersfontein; operations in the Orange Free State, Feb. to May, 1900; operations in Orange River Colony, May to 29 Nov. 1900, including actions at Wittebergen 1 to 29 July, and at Witpoort; operations in Orange River Colony 30 Nov. 1900, to Feb. 1901; operations in Cape Colony, Feb. 1901, to 31 May, 1902. He was mentioned in Despatches twice [London Gazette, 10 Sept. 1901, and 20 July, 1902]; awarded the Queen's Medal and King's Medal with four clasps, and was created a Companion of the Distinguished Service Order [London Gazette, 31 Oct. 1902]: "Thomas Campbell Mackenzie, Capt., Royal Army Medical Corps. In recognition of services during the operations in South Africa." Capt. Mackenzie received the Stanhope Gold Medal, Royal Humane Society, 1904; the Silver Medal, Royal Humane Society; Lloyd's Meritorious Medal; the Arnott Memorial Medal (Ireland), 1904; the Gold Medal of the Ministère de la Marine, France. He was attached to the Egyptian Army from 1 March, 1906, to 28 Feb. 1913; served in the Nyma Expedition, Kordofan, 1908 (Despatches; Sudan Medal and clasp, and 4th Class Medjidie); became Major 27 July, 1911; was D.A.D. of Medical Services, Northern Division, Northern Command, from 5 Nov. 1913. He served in the European War in the Dardanelles, 1915 (Despatches); became Lieutenant-Colonel 1 March, 1915; served in Salonika, 1916 (Despatches); was Assistant Director of Medical Services, 24th Division, B.E.F., 7 Nov. 1917, to 19 April, 1918. He was given the Brevet of Colonel 3 June, 1919. He married, in 1912, Elsie Burgoyne, only daughter of the late C. Moyle-Borlase, of Penzance.

NUNN, THOMAS HENRY CLAYTON, Capt., was born 11 Aug. 1873, son of the Rev. John Bridges Nunn. He joined the Militia in 1891; entered the Royal West Kent Regt., as Second Lieutenant from the Militia, 2 June, 1894, becoming Lieutenant 16 May, 1896, and Captain 2 Aug. 1902. He served in South Africa, 1900–2, taking part in the operations in Orange Free State, Feb. to May, 1900; operations in the Orange River Colony, May to 29 Nov. 1900; operations in Cape Colony, south of Orange River, 1899 to 1900. He served as Adjutant, 27th Battn. Mounted Infantry, 27 Jan. to 31 March, 1902; operations in the Transvaal, Nov. 1901, to April, 1902; operations in Orange River Colony, March, 1902. He was mentioned in Despatches [London Gazette, 29 July, 1902]; awarded the Queen's Medal with five clasps, and was created a Companion of the Distinguished Service Order [London Gazette, 31 Oct. 1902]: "Thomas Henry Clayton Nunn, Capt., The Queen's Own Royal West Kent Regt. In recognition of services during the operations in South Africa." He served as Adjutant, Mounted Infantry, Egypt, 26 May, 1902, to 12 June, 1905, and Brigade Major, Southern Mounted Infantry Brigade, Southern Command, 2 Nov. 1911, to 4 Aug. 1914. He became Major 1 Sept. 1914. He was twice mentioned in Despatches, and given the Brevet of Lieutenant-Colonel. He served in the European War from 1914, as Brigade Major, Southern Mounted Infantry Brigade; Central Force, Home Defence, B.E.F.; 145th Infantry Brigade, B.E.F., 5 Aug. 1914, to 21 Nov. 1915; G.S.O.2, 46th Division, B.E.F., 22 Nov. 1915, to 18 March, 1916 G.S.O.1, G.H.Q., Home Forces, 27 June to 28 July, 1916; G.S.O.1, 58th Division, Home Forces; British Armies in France 5 Sept. 1916, to 19 March, 1917; G.S.O.1, Humber Garrison, 13 Nov. 1918. In 1902, he married Aileen Sybil, daughter of the late Major John Tatham, R.H.A.

HEATH, RONALD MACCLESFIELD, Capt., was born 5 March, 1876, son of Lieut.-Colonel J. M. Heath, C.M.G. He was educated at Marlborough; joined the York and Lancaster Regt. 15 May, 1897 becoming Lieutenant 29 July, 1899, and Captain, Middlesex Regt., 2 Aug. 1902. He served in South Africa, 1899–1902, employed with the Mounted Infantry, taking part in operations in the Orange Free State, Feb. to May, 1900, including operations at Paardeberg 12 to 26 Feb.; actions at Poplar Grove, Dreifontein, Houtnek (Thoba Mountain), Vet River (6 May) and Zand River; operations in the Transvaal in May and June, 1900, including actions near Johannesburg, Pretoria and Diamond Hill (11 and 12 June); operations in the Transvaal, west of Pretoria, including actions at Elands River (4 to 16 Aug.); operations in Orange River Colony, May to 29 Nov. 1900, including actions at Wittebergen (1 to 18 July); operations in Cape Colony, south of Orange River, 1899–1900; operations in the Transvaal and Orange River Colony 30 Nov. 1900, to 31 May, 1902; operations in Cape Colony, Aug. and Sept. 1901. He was mentioned in Despatches [London Gazette, 10 Sept. 1901, and 29 July, 1902]; awarded the Queen's Medal with six clasps; the King's Medal with two clasps, and was created a Companion of the Distinguished Service Order [London Gazette, 31 Oct. 1902]: "Ronald Macclesfield Heath, Capt., Middlesex Regt. In recognition of services during the operations in South Africa." He was employed with the Egyptian Army 4 June, 1905, to 3 June, 1913, and commanded the Camel Corps of the Egyptian Army in the Sudan from 1908 to 1912: took part in the operations in Southern Kordofan, 1908 (Egyptian Meda and clasp, and 4th Class Osmanieh), and in operations in Southern Kordofan, 1910; Sudan, 1910 (Medal and clasp, and 3rd Class Medjidie). He served with the Army Cyclists' Corps in the early part of the European War, and was promoted to Major 1 Sept. 1915; was Temporary Lieutenant-Colonel commanding the 10th Battn. Royal Warwickshire Regt. 19 Feb. to 2 July, 1916; Acting Lieutenant-Colonel commanding 10th Battn. Warwickshire Regt. 7 Sept. 1916, to 27 July, 1917; Temporary Lieutenant-Colonel commanding 10th Warwickshire Regt. 28 July, 1917, to 6 April, 1918; Temporary Brigadier-General commanding the 56th Infantry Brigade, British Armies in France, 7 April, 1918. He was mentioned in Despatches; given the Brevet of Lieutenant-Colonel 1 Jan. 1918; created a C.M.G. in 1919, and awarded the French Croix de Guerre.

APPLIN, REGINALD VINCENT KEMPENFELDT, Capt., was born 11 April, 1869, at Exeview, Alphington, near Exeter, eldest son of the late Capt. Vincent J. Applin, R.M.T. (Crimean and China Campaigns), and Mrs. W. J. Applin. He was educated at Sherborne School, and entered the British North Borneo Service as a Cadet in Dec. 1889; was Police Magistrate and J.P. for Crown Colony, Labuan, 1894; District Officer, Interior, 1897. He served through the Syed and Nat Salleh Rebellions, 1895–97 (Medal and clasp). He was twice thanked by Board of Directors, B.N.B., for services against the Tumnunam tribes. He became Captain, 6th Battn. Lancashire Fusiliers, 28 July, 1898; served through the South African War, 1899–1901; was District Commissioner from 1 June, 1900, at Bloemfontein; Staff Officer and Acting Provost-Marshal, O.R., 10 Oct. to 24 Nov. 1900; took part in operations in Cape Colony, south of Orange River, Orange Free State (against Hertzog), and Transvaal, March to 29 Nov. 1900, including action at Luckhoff, Nov. 1900; operations in Orange River Colony 30 Nov. to Dec. 1900; operations in Cape Colony (against De Wet), Dec. to Sept. 1900. He was mentioned in Despatches [London Gazette, 10 Sept. 1901, and 29 July, 1902]; awarded the Queen's Medal with four clasps, and was created a Companion of the Distinguished Service Order [London Gazette, 31 Oct. 1902]: "Reginald Applin, Capt., Lancashire Fusiliers. In recognition of services during the operations in South Africa." He became Captain, 14th (King's) Hussars, 19 July, 1905; was D.A.A.G. for Musketry, Malta, 26 Aug. 1905, to 3 Dec. 1906; Major, 14th Hussars, 3 June, 1911; Commandant, School of Musketry (temporary); became Temporary Lieutenant-Colonel 16 Oct. 1916. In the Great War Lieut.-Colonel Applin commanded the Machine Guns of the 2nd A.N.Z.A. Corps at the battles of Messines and Passchendaele, and the Third Battle of Ypres, 1916–17. He headed the British Machine-Gun Mission to the U.S.A., and received the thanks of the Secretary of State for War, U.S.A., 1918. In Jan. 1920, was offered O.B.E., but refused it with thanks. He was twice mentioned in Despatches, and was given the Brevet of Lieutenant-Colonel 1 Jan. 1919. He was appointed Lieutenant-Colonel in command of the 14th King's Hussars 22 Feb. 1919. Lieut.-Colonel Applin is the author of "Machine-Gun Tactics," the first book to deal exhaustively with this subject, published by Hugh Rees in 1907. His favourite recreations are hunting, shooting and fishing. He married, 17 April, 1902, at Plymouth, Beatrice, Caroline, eldest surviving daughter of the late George Bather, of Wroxeter Salop.

Reginald V. K. Applin.

EVANS, FISHER HENRY FREKE, Major, was born 21 April, 1868, only son of the late Capt. Richard Fisher Evans, and of Mary Helen Campbell von Dadelezen. He was educated at Rossall, and St. Peter's College, Cambridge (B.A., 1890); joined the 4th Battn. King's Own Royal Lancashire Regt. Militia in 1893, and served in South Africa, 1900 to 1901, taking part in operations in Orange Free State, April, 1900; operations in

Cape Colony, south of Orange River, Feb. to 29 Nov. 1900; operations in Cape Colony 30 Nov. 1900, to July, 1901. He was mentioned in Despatches [London Gazette, 29 July, 1902]; received the Medal with three clasps, and was created a Companion of the Distinguished Service Order [London Gazette, 31 Oct. 1902]: "Fisher Henry Freke Evans, Major, King's Own Royal Lancs. Regt. In recognition of services during the operations in South Africa." He was Major, Special Reserve, King's Own Royal Lancaster Regt., from 1902 to 1908, when he retired. He was attached to the Loyal North Lancashire Regt. 1914 to 1917. Major Evans is D.L. and Magistrate, County Donegal, and was High Sheriff of the County in 1911. He married, 1 June, 1892, Marie Louise Evans, eldest daughter of the late Major A. K. Haslett, R.E., and they have one surviving son, Patrick Harry Freke, born 5 June, 1905, the elder son, the late Capt. Fisher Arthur Haslett Freke Evans, The King's Own Royal Lancaster Regt., having been killed in action in Mesopotamia 12 Jan. 1917.

TURNER, FRANK CECIL, Capt., was born 16 Sept. 1868, son of the late Capt. Francis Charles Turner, Cameron Highlanders and Dorset Regt., and of Emma Gracioza Turner (*née* Doering), and grandson of Major-General William Turner, C.B., Bombay Army. He was educated at Edinburgh Academy and St. Andrews University, and joined the 4th Battn. the Cheshire Regt., Jan. 1900. He served in South Africa, 1900–2, with the 4th Battn. Cheshire Regt., commanding Mounted Infantry Company. He was present in operations in the Orange Free State, Feb. to May, 1900; operations in Orange River Colony, May to 29 Nov. 1900; operations in Cape Colony, south of Orange River, 1899–1900; operations in Orange River Colony and Cape Colony, Nov. 1901, to April, 1902. He was mentioned in Despatches [London Gazette, 10 Sept. 1901, and 29 July, 1902]; awarded the Queen's Medal with two clasps; the King's Medal with two clasps, and was created a Companion of the Distinguished Service Order [London Gazette, 31 Oct. 1902]: "Frank Cecil Turner, Capt., Cheshire Regt. In recognition of services during the operations in South Africa." (In particular for the capture of a Boer laager on the Caledon River, Orange Free State, 1901.) He became Major in the 31st Regt. (British Columbia Horse) 28 Nov. 1913, in which he commanded a squadron. He joined Lord Strathcona's Horse (R.C.) 2 Oct. 1914, and served in the European War with the British Expeditionary Force in France and Flanders, again in command of a squadron. He was demobilized 27 March, 1919

BOULTON, CHARLES PERCY, Capt., was born 1 Sept. 1868, at Cosgrove Priory, Northamptonshire, son of Charles G. Boulton, J.P., and Georgiana Nicholl. He was educated at Haileybury, and Magdalen College, Oxford (B.A., 1890); and was gazetted to the 4th Bedfordshire Militia 28 Jan. 1888. He served in the South African War from March, 1900, to June, 1902 (from Nov. 1900, to June, 1902, in command of the 4th Bedfordshire Regt.); was Camp Commandant at Mafeking. He was present in the operations in the Transvaal, west of Pretoria, to Sept. 1900; in Cape Colony, south of Orange River, 1901; in Cape Colony, north of the Orange River; in the Transvaal and Orange River Colony, Sept. 1901, to April, 1902. He was Temporarily Commander of Bloemhof Sub-District, and assisted in the operations in Cape Colony in Dec. 1900, to Sept. 1901. He was mentioned in Despatches [London Gazette, 29 July, 1902]; received the Queen's Medal with three clasps; the King's Medal with two clasps, and was created a Companion of the Distinguished Service Order [London Gazette, 31 Oct. 1902]: "Charles Percy Boulton, Capt., 4th Bedfordshire Regt. In recognition of services during the operations in South Africa." He was subsequently promoted Major; was invalided out of the Army in 1915, and through ill health was unable to take any part in the Great War. He died 24 Feb. 1916.

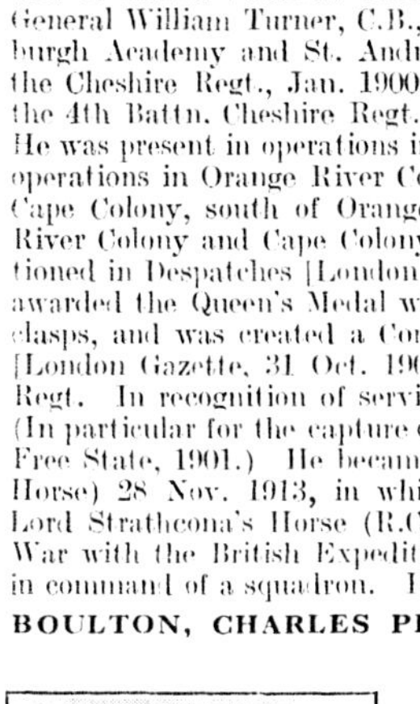

Charles Percy Boulton.

DE LA BERE, RICHARD NORMAN, Capt., was born in 1869, son of the late Major Charles R. de la Bere, R.M.L.I. He joined the 3rd Battn. King's Own Royal Lancaster Regt., and saw active service in South Africa, 1900–2; was Assistant Provost-Marshal; operations in Orange River Colony, May to 29 Nov. 1900; operations in Cape Colony, south of Orange River, March to May, 1900; operations in Orange River Colony 30 Nov. 1900, to Sept. 1901; operations in Cape Colony, Sept. 1901, to Jan. 1902. He was mentioned in Despatches twice [London Gazette, 10 Sept. 1901, and 29 July, 1902]; awarded the Queen's Medal with two clasps; the King's Medal with two clasps, and was created a Companion of the Distinguished Service Order [London Gazette, 31 Oct. 1902]: "Richard Norman de la Bere, Capt., King's Own Royal Lancaster Regt. In recognition of services during the operations in South Africa." He was promoted Captain, Reserve of Officers, 6 Feb. 1902, and became Major 14 May, 1904; has retired from the Reserve of Officers.

GRAVES, PERCIVAL HOPE, Capt., is the son of the late Capt. Alexander Hope Graves. He joined the 6th Battn. Middlesex Regt., and served in South Africa, 1899–1902, as Acting Adjutant and Quartermaster, Rest Camp, Stellenbosch, 5 Nov. 1900, to 6 Jan. 1901. He was present in operations in Cape Colony, south of Orange River, 1900; operations in Cape Colony 30 Nov. 1900, to Jan. 1902. He was mentioned in Despatches [London Gazette, 29 July, 1902]; received the Queen's Medal and clasp; the King's Medal and two clasps, and was created a Companion of the Distinguished Service Order [London Gazette, 31 Oct. 1902]: "Percival Hope Graves, Capt., Middlesex Regt. In recognition of services during the operations in South Africa." Capt. Graves afterwards served in the 3rd (Reserve) Battn. The Middlesex Regt.

PERKINS, ALFRED THRALE, Capt., was born at Kerrachi, India, 1869, only surviving son of Colonel Alfred Thrale Perkins, C.B., of East Court, Wells, Somerset, J.P., and of Mary Frances, daughter of Major-General A. V. Falls, R.A. He was educated at Cheltenham College, and joined the Army in July, 1887. He served in Matabeleland, 1893–94, with the Matabeleland Mounted Police and the Rhodesian Horse; in South Africa, 1899–1902; with the 3rd Battn. The Welsh Regt., and as Staff Officer for Supply and Transport, with the grade of D.A.A.G. He was mentioned in Despatches twice; awarded both Medals with clasps, and was created a Companion of the Distinguished Service Order [London Gazette, 31 Oct. 1902]: "Alfred Thrale Perkins, Capt., The Welsh Regt. In recognition of services during the operations in South Africa." He served in the war of 1914–18, with the Royal Warwickshire Regt. and the Worcestershire Regt., and was awarded the 1914–15 Star, the British War Medal and the Victory Medal. Major Perkins is a Justice of the Peace for the county of Somerset. In 1916 he married Naomi Kirwan, elder daughter of the late Dr. Kirwan Sylvester, of Trowbridge, Wiltshire.

WOOD, CHARLES PEEVOR BOILEAU, Capt., joined the Royal Scots Regt.; saw service in South Africa, 1900–2, being present in operations in the Orange Free State, Feb. to May, 1900; operations in the Transvaal, west of Pretoria, July to 29 Nov. 1900, including action at Venterskroon (9 Aug.), and operations in Orange River Colony, May to 29 Nov. 1900; operations in Cape Colony, south of Orange River, 1900; operations in Orange River Colony. He was mentioned in Despatches [London Gazette, 29 July, 1902]; awarded the Queen's Medal, and King's Medal with five clasps, and was created a Companion of the Distinguished Service Order [London Gazette, 31 Oct. 1902]: "Charles Peevor Boileau Wood, Capt., Royal Scots. In recognition of services during the operations in South Africa." He is Major and Honorary Lieutenant-Colonel, 3rd Battn. The Royal Scots. Lieut.-Colonel Wood contested the Wellington Division of Salop, 1910, as a Conservative.

COLE-HAMILTON, CLAUD GEORGE, Capt., was born 27 Jan. 1869, son of the late Capt. W. Cole-Hamilton, of Balitore, County Kildare, and Beltrim, County Tyrone, and of Caroline Elizabeth Josephine, daughter of the Honourable Andrew Godfrey Stuart. He was educated at Bedford and Ripon, and joined the 5th Battn. Royal Irish Rifles in March, 1900. He fought in the South African War, 1901–2, commanding a Mounted Infantry Company, and taking part in the operations in the Transvaal and Cape Colony, Nov. 1901, to 31 May, 1902; operations in Orange River Colony, April to Nov. 1901. He was promoted Captain in April, 1901. He was mentioned in Despatches [London Gazette, 29 July, 1902]; awarded the Queen's Medal with five clasps, and was created a Companion of the Distinguished Service Order [London Gazette, 31 Oct. 1902]: "Claud George Cole-Hamilton, Capt., The Royal Irish Rifles. In recognition of services during the operations in South Africa." Capt. Cole-Hamilton was transferred to the 6th Battn. Royal Irish Rifles, with which he served till the battalion was disbanded in 1907. He was then transferred to the 4th Special Reserve Battn. He served in the European War, joining the 12th Service Battn. Royal Irish Rifles 8 Feb. 1915, as Major and Second-in-Command. He became Temporary Lieutenant-Colonel 3 Aug. 1915, to command the 8th (Service) Battn. Royal Irish Rifles, and was given the command of the 15th (Service) Battn. 9 Sept. 1917. He was wounded at the Somme in 1916, and at Ypres in 1917; was created a C.M.G. in 1917, and was both wounded and gassed in the German offensive on 21 March, 1918. From 21 March to 14 Dec. 1918, he was a prisoner of war in Germany. He was three times mentioned in Despatches (June, 1917; April, 1918; March, 1919), and for his services on 21 March, 1918, was awarded a Bar to the Distinguished Service Order [London Gazette, 21 March, 1920]: "Claud George Cole-Hamilton, C.M.G., D.S.O., Reserve of Officers, late Royal Irish Rifles, Special Reserve." Lieut.-Colonel Cole-Hamilton is Chief Constable of Breconshire. He married, in April, 1893, Lucy, daughter of Reginald H. Thorold.

HUMBY, JAMES FREDERICK, Capt., was born 21 July, 1860, son of the late Fred Peter Humby, of Southbroom, Devizes, Wilts. He was educated in Paris. He joined the 3rd Battn. Royal Irish Rifles, as Second Lieutenant, in 1891, and became Captain in 1896. He served in the South African War, 1900–2; commanded the 54th (Ulster) Imperial Yeomanry from Feb. 1900. He took part in the operations in Orange Free State, Feb. to May, 1900; operations in the Transvaal, east of Pretoria, July to 29 Nov. 1900; operations in Orange River Colony and Cape Colony 30 Nov. 1900, to 31 May, 1902. He was taken prisoner at Lindley with the 13th Battn., but escaped 30 Aug. 1900. He became Major in 1901, and commanded the 74th (Dublin) Imperial Yeomanry from June, 1901; 8th Battn. Imperial Yeomanry from May, 1902. He was mentioned twice in Despatches; received the Queen's Medal with four clasps; the King's Medal with two clasps, and was created a Companion of the Distinguished Service Order [London Gazette, 31 Oct. 1902]: "James Frederick Humby, Capt., 8th Battn. Imperial Yeomanry; Major, 3rd Battn. The Royal Irish Rifles. In recognition of services during the operations in South Africa." Lieut.-Colonel J. F. Humby served in the European War from 1914 to 1916, and was created a C.M.G. in 1916 for his services. He married, in 1883, Bertha Elizabeth, youngest daughter of the late Rev. Canon Rich-Jones, of The Vicarage, Bradford-on-Avon.

GOWANS, JAMES, Major, was born 23 April, 1872. He was educated at Harrow (The Knoll), where he was in the School Cricket and Football Elevens; then at Clare College, Cambridge. He was in the Cambridge Rugby Fifteen, 1892–93, and was a Member of the Scotland Rugby Fifteen in 1893–94–95–96. He served in South Africa, 1900–1; in operations in Natal, March to June, 1900; operations on the Zululand Frontier of Natal in Sept. and Oct. 1901, including the defence of Forts Itala and Prospect; operations in Orange River Colony, Feb. to 31 May, 1902. He was mentioned in Despatches [London Gazette, 29 July, 1902]; was awarded the Queen's Medal with three clasps; the King's Medal with two clasps, and was created a Companion of the Distinguished Service Order [London Gazette, 31 Oct. 1902]: "James Gowans, Major, Durham Artillery (Militia). In recognition of services during the operations in South Africa." He retired as Captain, Durham Royal Field Reserve Artillery (Major and Honorary Lieutenant-Colonel, Reserve of Officers). He married, in 1902, Erin Laura Muriel, daughter of William Wheelright, of Durban, Natal, and they have one son and two daughters.

BLACKBURNE, CHARLES HAROLD, Capt., was born 20 May, 1876, son of the late C. E. Blackburne and of Mary Riley, now widow of W. Shadforth Boger. He was educated at Tonbridge; served in South Africa with the 11th Battn. Imperial Yeomanry, 1900–2. He was mentioned in Despatches [London Gazette, 29 July, 1902]; awarded the King's and Queen's Medals, and created a Companion of the Distinguished Service Order [London Gazette, 31 Oct. 1902]: "Charles Harold Blackburne, Capt., 11th Battn. Imperial Yeomanry. In recognition of services during the operations in South Africa." He was Assistant Secretary to the Transvaal Repatriation Department in 1902, and from 1902 to 1906 Manager of the Transvaal Government

Charles H. Blackburne.

Stud. He became Captain in the 5th Dragoons (from the Special Reserve) 5 Aug. 1914. He served in the European War. He was severely wounded at Ypres 13 May, 1915, and was given the Brevet of Major 3 June following. He served on the Headquarters Staff, Dublin, and was given the Brevet of Lieutenant-Colonel 1 Jan. 1917, in recognition of his services during the Irish Rebellion. He was appointed G.S.O.2, 25 Jan. 1917, and G.S.O.1, 19 April, 1918; was mentioned in Despatches. Lieut.-Colonel Blackburne was foully murdered, together with both his children, by the torpedoing of the Leinster 10 Oct. 1918. He married, in 1903, Emily Beatrice, daughter of the Rev. Canon H. D. Jones, and the two small children who went down with their father were: Charles Bertram, born 3 Sept. 1911, and Beatrice Audrey, born 24 June, 1907.

JENKINS, FREDERICK, Capt., served in South Africa, 1901–2; taking part in operations with the Imperial Yeomanry in Cape Colony, Orange River Colony and the Transvaal; was mentioned in Despatches [London Gazette, 29 July, 1902]; received the Queen's Medal with five clasps, and was created a Companion of the Distinguished Service Order [London Gazette, 31 Oct. 1902]: "Frederick Jenkins, Capt., Imperial Yeomanry. In recognition of services during the operations in South Africa." He has retired from the Second Cinque Ports, Royal Garrison Artillery.

BACKHOUSE, MILES ROLAND CHARLES, Capt., was born 24 Nov. 1878, at the Rookery, Middleton Nyas, Yorkshire, son of Sir Jonathan E. Backhouse, Bart., and Florence, daughter of Sir John S. Trelawny, 9th Baronet (all deceased). He was educated at Eton, and Trinity Hall, Cambridge, and became Second Lieutenant, Northumberland Hussars (Yeomanry Cavalry) in April, 1897. He was employed in the 14th Yeomanry Squadron, Imperial Yeomanry, South Africa, from Jan. to the end of the war, in which he served as Lieutenant from Jan. 1900, to April, 1901, and was then promoted Captain (Honorary), and given command of a squadron. He was severely wounded; mentioned in Despatches [London Gazette, 29 July, 1902]; received the Queen's Medal with three clasps; the King's Medal with two clasps, and was created a Companion of the Distinguished Service Order [London Gazette, 31 Oct. 1902]: "Miles Roland Charles Backhouse, Capt., 5th Battn. Imperial Yeomanry. In recognition of services during the operations in South Africa." He married, 3 Sept. 1904, at Dunston, Norwich, Olive, second daughter of Geoffrey Fowell Buxton and Mary, daughter of the Honourable and Rev. John Harbord, and they have three sons: Roger Trelawny, born 5 Sept. 1905; Jonathan, born 16 March, 1907; Wilfrid Jasper, born 28 July, 1913, and one daughter, Patricia, born 23 April, 1911. He was promoted Major, and retired from the Territorial Force 27 June, 1903. He served in the European War from 1914–19; went out with the Northumberland Hussars, as Second-in-Command, Oct. 1914; in command, Feb. to May, 1915; commanded the North Somerset Yeomanry, Sept. 1915 to March, 1917; commanded the 8th Battn. Yorkshire Regt. 1 Oct. 1917, to Jan. 1919. He is now Lieutenant-Colonel in the Territorial Force Reserve. He was mentioned in Despatches four times: June, 1915; Jan. 1917; June, 1918; March, 1919, and awarded a Bar to the Distinguished Service Order, for services in operations on the Piave, Italy, in Sept. and Oct. 1918 [London Gazette, 18 Nov. 1918].

ARDAGH, GEORGE HUTCHINGS, Capt., was born in 1863, eldest son of the late General Richard D. Ardagh, Indian Staff Corps. He was educated at Harrow (Church Hill) and Sandhurst, from which he was commissioned in the 58th Second Northampton Regt. He commanded the 31st Montgomeryshire Yeomanry in the Boer War of 1899–1902, under Sir Bruce Hamilton and Colonel Damant, C.B.; was mentioned in Despatches thrice; awarded the Queen's Medal with three clasps; the King's Medal, and was created a Companion of the Distinguished Service Order [London Gazette, 31 Oct. 1902]: "George Hutchings Ardagh, Capt., 9th Battn. Imperial Yeomanry. In recognition of services during the operations in South Africa." He joined the Reserve of Officers, with the rank of Captain, 18 July, 1903, and subsequently became Major, 13th Battn. Royal Fusiliers. He commanded this battalion in the European War until incapacitated through wounds. He was then attached to the Staff of the 2nd Army until Aug. 1917. He was twice mentioned in Despatches.

UNIACKE, ANDREW GORE, Capt., was born in 1874. He served with the Canadian North-West Police (including Yukon Force), 1894–98, and fought in the South African War, 1899–1902, with the Canadian Mounted Rifles and 21st Imperial Yeomanry. He was mentioned in Despatches [London Gazette, 29 July, 1902]; awarded the South African Medals and six clasps, and was created a Companion of the Distinguished Service Order [London Gazette, 31 Oct. 1902]: "Andrew Gore Uniacke, Capt., 21st Battn. Imperial Yeomanry. In recognition of services during the operations in South Africa." He was placed on the retired list with the honorary rank of Captain, Third County of London Yeomanry, 11 Sept. 1902. Capt. Uniacke served in West Africa (Northern Nigeria), 1903–4, taking part in the operations in the Bassa Province against the Okpotos, for which he received the West African General Service Medal. He is Commissioner of the Northern Nigeria Police.

BRODIE, IAN ASHLEY MORTON, Capt., was born 26 Sept. 1868, eldest son of the late Hugh Brodie of Brodie and Lady Eleanor Brodie, sister of the 3rd Earl of Ducie. He is Lord Lieutenant of Nairnshire and a landed proprietor there. He was educated at Eton and Cambridge, and joined the Scots Guards in 1890, serving in that regiment for about three years. He served in the South African War with Lord Lovat's Scouts, 1900–2, and took part in operations in the Transvaal, May and June, 1900, including actions near Johannesburg, Pretoria and Diamond Hill (11 and 12 June); operations in Orange River Colony, May to 29 Nov. 1900, including action at Wittebergen; operations in the Orange River Colony and Cape Colony 30 Nov. 1900, to 31 May, 1902. He was mentioned in Despatches [London Gazette, 29 July, 1902]; awarded the Queen's and King's South African Medals with six clasps, and was created a Companion of the Distinguished Service Order [London Gazette, 31 Oct. 1902]: "Ian Ashley Morton Brodie, Capt., Lovat's Scouts (Imperial Yeomanry). In recognition of services during the operations in South Africa." He became Major 30 March, 1903, and retired from the Service. Major Brodie of Brodie served in the European War, 1915, in the Dardanelles, Egypt and Palestine. For his services he received a mention in Despatches and was awarded the Military Cross. He married, in 1904, Violet, daughter of Colonel Montagu Hope, and they have one son.

THYNNE, ALGERNON CARTERET, Capt., was born 9 April, 1868, second son of the late Francis John Thynne, of Haynes Park, Bedfordshire, and of 67, Eaton Place, London, S.W., and grandson of the Rev. Lord John Thynne, D.D. His mother

Algernon C. Thynne.

was Edith Marcia Caroline, eldest daughter of Richard Brinsley Sheridan, of Frampton Court, Dorset. He was educated at Charterhouse, and subsequently became Captain in the Bedfordshire Regt. (3rd Battn.). He went out from Bath, as a Lieutenant, in the North Somerset Yeomanry, to serve in South Africa, and served throughout the campaign, first in that capacity, and afterwards as a Captain in the 7th Battn. Imperial Yeomanry. He took part in operations in the Orange Free State, Feb. to May, 1902, including operations at Vet River (5 and 6 May) and Zand River; operations in the Transvaal, May and June, 1900, including actions near Johannesburg, Pretoria and Diamond Hill (11 and 12 June); operations in the Transvaal 30 Nov. 1900, to 31 May, 1902. He was mentioned in Despatches [London Gazette, 10 Sept. 1901, and 29 July, 1902]; received the Queen's Medal with four clasps; the King's Medal with two clasps, and was created a Companion of the Distinguished Service Order [London Gazette, 31 Oct. 1902]: "Algernon Carteret Thynne, Capt., 7th Battn. Imperial Yeomanry. In recognition of services during the operations in South Africa." He became Honorary Captain in the Army in Aug. 1902, and was transferred in 1903 to the Royal North Devon Hussars. He served in the European War, 1914–17, in Gallipoli and Egypt, also in Palestine, as Lieutenant-Colonel in command of his regiment, until he fell mortally wounded at the Battle of Sheria 6 Nov. 1917. The late Colonel Thynne succeeded to the Grenville Estate, Cornwall, on the death of his father in 1910. He was an Alderman of Cornwall County Council, and a Magistrate for Cornwall, and at the outbreak of war was Master of the Tetcott Hounds. A Memorial Service for him and those who fell with him in Palestine was held in St. George's, Hanover Square, London (where Prebendary Thicknesse officiated); also in Stratton Church, Cornwall. He married, in 1904, Constance, daughter of the late Edward Bonham, of Bramling House, Kent, and widow of Francis Philips, of Lee Priory, Kent.

UPTON, EDWARD JAMES GOTT, Capt., was born 17 Oct. 1868, at Debdin Green, Loughton, Essex, son of the late Major R. D. Upton, 9th Lancers, and of Sophia Upton (née Turner). He was educated at Durham School. He served in South Africa, with the Imperial Yeomanry, 1900–2, receiving a commission as Lieutenant, March, 1901, and becoming Captain 25 May, 1901; was present in operations in the Orange Free State; in the engagements at Wittebergen. He was mentioned in Despatches; awarded the Queen's Medal with three clasps; the King's Medal with two clasps, and created a Companion of the Distinguished Service Order [London Gazette, 31 Oct. 1902]: "Edward James Gott Upton, Capt., 17th Battn. Imperial Yeomanry. In recognition of services during the operations in South Africa." He served with Brand's Horse in the suppression of the Boer Rebellion in 1914, and in the European War in 1915 in German South-West Africa, Otzimbingue and Otavifontein. Capt. Upton married, in 1914, Joanna, second daughter of Vice-Admiral William Wilson, of Clyffe Manor, Swindon, Wiltshire.

BURNABY, HUGO BEAUMONT, Capt., was born 5 May, 1874, youngest son of the Rev. Sherrard Beaumont Burnaby, late Vicar of Hampstead, N.W. He was educated at Uppingham, and was engaged in ranching in British Columbia from 1893 to 1899. He served in the South African War, 1900-2, first in the ranks, until commissioned in March, 1901; became Captain in June, 1901, in the 1st Battn. Imperial Yeomanry. He was mentioned in Despatches; received the Medal, and was created a Companion of the Distinguished Service Order [London Gazette, 31 Oct. 1902]: "Hugo Beaumont Burnaby, Capt., 1st Battn. Imperial Yeomanry. In recognition of services during the operations in South Africa." He married, in 1906, Evelyn Violet, youngest daughter of the late Major-General C. H. Smith, C.B., R.H.A., and they had one son and two daughters. He became a Game Farmer at Wendover, Buckinghamshire. Lieut.-Colonel H. B. Burnaby served in the European War. He was killed in action in Sept. 1916.

JOHNSON, ARTHUR EVANS, Capt., served in South Africa, 1899-1902. He was wounded; mentioned in Despatches [London Gazette, 3 Dec. 1901]; awarded the Queen's and King's Medals, and was created a Companion of the Distinguished Service Order [London Gazette, 31 Oct. 1902]: "Arthur Evans Johnson, Capt., 10th Battn. Imperial Yeomanry. In recognition of services during the operations in South Africa." He retired from the Army 10 Aug. 1902, with the honorary rank of Captain; joined the Reserve of Officers. He served in West Africa, 1906, receiving the African General Service Medal; subsequently became Inspector-General, Northern Nigeria Police (Colonial Civil Service). Lieut.-Colonel Johnson served in the European War, 1914-18, and in Russia, 1919.

HUGHES, ALFRED MAHONEY, Capt., took part in the South African War, 1899-1902, serving as Intelligence Officer. He was twice mentioned in Despatches [London Gazette, 10 Sept. 1901, and 29 July, 1902]; received the Queen's Medal with three clasps; the King's Medal with two clasps, and was created a Companion of the Distinguished Service Order [London Gazette, 31 Oct. 1902]: "Alfred Mahoney Hughes, Capt., Field Intelligence Department. In recognition of services during the operations in South Africa." He was afterwards Secretary of the Transvaal Repatriation Department and Inspector of Prisons in the Transvaal; retrenched from the Transvaal Civil Service in 1907; is now farming in Cape Colony. In 1918 he was created a C.B.E.

DICKSON, JOHN QUAYLE-, Capt., was born in 1860, son of the late Major-General E. J. Dickson, of Castletown, Isle of Man, and the late Lucy Mylrea, youngest daughter of the late John Quayle, of Braust, Isle of Man. He was educated at King William's College, Isle of Man. He served in South Africa, with the Field Intelligence Department; was mentioned in Despatches; awarded the Queen's and King's Medals, and was created a Companion of the Distinguished Service Order [London Gazette, 31 Oct. 1902]: "John Quayle-Dickson, Capt., Field Intelligence Department. In recognition of services during the operations in South Africa." Major Dickson was a Member of the South African Native Affairs Commission, 1903-5; Adviser in Native Affairs to Orange River Colony Government, 1903-9; Resident Commissioner, Gilbert and Ellice Islands Protectorate, 1909-13; Colonial Secretary of the Falkland Islands, 1913-14; Sub-Commandant, Alien's Detention Camp, Knockaloe, Isle of Man, 1915. He married, in 1888, Annie, daughter of William Hyde, of Grahamstown, and has two daughters. His only son, Capt. E. J. Quayle-Dickson, M.C., fell in action in the European War.

HOLMAN, RICHARD C., Capt., was born at Upwey 26 Sept. 1861, eldest son of F. Holman, of Biddenden, Kent, and grandson of the late Dr. Puckett, Medical Officer for Dorsetshire. He was educated at King's College, London. He served in the ranks of Methuen's Horse in the Bechuanaland Expedition of 1884-85; in the New South Wales Police Force, 1886-88. He went to South Africa with the 1st New South Wales Mounted Troops, as Regimental Sergeant-Major, 1899, and took part in the Relief of Kimberley; operations in Orange Free State, Feb. to May, 1900, including operations at Paardeberg, actions at Poplar Grove, Dreifontein, Karee Siding, Vet River (5 and 6 May) and Zand River; operations in the Transvaal in May and June, 1900, including actions near Johannesburg, Pretoria and Diamond Hill (11 and 12 June); operations in the Transvaal, west of Pretoria, July to Nov. 1900, including actions at Venterskroon and Elands River; operations in the Orange River Colony, May to Nov. 1900, including action at Wittebergen. He was promoted in the field to Captain and Adjutant of the New South Wales Mounted Rifles, and served with them in operations in the Transvaal from April, 1901, till the end of the war. He was awarded the Distinguished Conduct Medal; the Queen's Medal with six clasps, and was created a Companion of the Distinguished Service Order [London Gazette, 31 Oct. 1902]: "Richard Holman, Capt., New South Wales Mounted Rifles. In recognition of services during the operations in South Africa." Major Holman was appointed Brigade Major, 3rd Light Horse Brigade, on the Instructional Staff, Commonwealth Military Forces of Australia, 1 Oct. 1911. He subsequently became Commandant of the Concentration Camps, 2nd Military District, and for his services was given the Brevet of Lieutenant-Colonel 16 Sept. 1916. In 1890 Major Holman married Harriette Blanche, eldest daughter of R. Mills, of Sydney and Nova Scotia, and they have one son and three daughters.

MACDONALD, PETER, Capt., was born in 1869. He served in South Africa, with the New South Wales Contingent, and was created a Companion of the Distinguished Service Order [London Gazette, 31 Oct. 1902]: "Peter MacDonald, Capt., New South Wales Contingent. In recognition of services during the operations in South Africa." He was confirmed in the rank of Honorary Captain and Adjutant, 5th Australian Light Horse Regt., New South Wales, to date from 28 Feb. 1901, and placed on the retired list after the Boer War.

STEVENSON, ROBERT, Capt., was born in 1870. He served in South Africa with the New Zealand Contingent, 1900 to 1902, taking part in operations in the Orange Free State, April to May, 1900; operations in the Transvaal, May and June, 1900, including actions near Johannesburg and Pretoria; operations in the Transvaal, east of Pretoria, Oct. to 29 Nov. 1900, including the action at Rhenoster Kop; operations in Cape Colony, south of Orange River, March and April, 1900; operations in the Transvaal 30 Nov. 1900, to Feb. 1901; April to July, 1901; Oct. 1901, to 31 May, 1902; operations in the Orange River Colony, March, 1901; July, 1901, and Aug. to Oct. 1901. He was mentioned in Despatches [London Gazette, 7 May, 1901, and 29 July, 1902]; awarded the Queen's Medal with four clasps; the King's Medal with two clasps, and was created a Companion of the Distinguished Service Order [London Gazette, 31 Oct. 1902]: "Robert Stevenson, Capt., New Zealand Contingent. In recognition of services during the operations in South Africa."

DODDS, THOMAS HENRY, Capt., was born 11 Dec. 1873, son of Thomas Dodds, of Newcastle. He served in South Africa, as Adjutant of the 5th Contingent, Queensland Imperial Bushmen, 20 Feb. 1901, to 5 May, 1902, taking part in operations in the Transvaal and Orange River Colony, April 1901, to March, 1902; operations in Cape Colony, April, July, and Aug. 1901, and March, 1902. He was mentioned in Despatches [London Gazette, 29 July, 1902]; awarded the Queen's Medal with five clasps, and created a Companion of the Distinguished Service Order [London Gazette, 31 Oct. 1902]: "Thomas Henry Dodds, Capt., Queensland Contingent. In recognition of services during the operations in South Africa." He was promoted Major 1 Jan. 1913. He served in the European War, as A.A.G. and Director of Personnel (A.I.F.), Headquarters, and became Lieutenant-Colonel 1 Dec. 1915. He was created a C.M.G. in 1918. He married, in 1902, Elizabeth Jane, daughter of the late George Hancock, of Brisbane.

HUTCHENS, HAROLD JOHN, Surgeon-Capt., served in the South African War, with the Queensland Contingent, 1901-2; in operations in the Transvaal and Orange River Colony, April, 1901, to May, 1902; operations in Cape Colony, April, July and Aug. 1901. He was mentioned in Despatches [London Gazette, 29 July, 1902]; awarded the Queen's Medal with two clasps, and was created a Companion of the Distinguished Service Order [London Gazette, 31 Oct. 1902]: "Harold John Hutchens, Surgeon-Capt., Queensland Contingent. In recognition of services during the operations in South Africa." He became Professor of Comparative Pathology at Durham University. He is a Master of Arts, a Member of the Royal College of Surgeons, a Licentiate of the Royal College of Physicians, and holds the Oxford Diploma of Public Health. Capt. Hutchens married, in 1906, Ada Muriel, daughter of Charles Clay, M.R.C.S., of The Manor House, Dewsbury, and has one son.

WATT, JOHN ALEXANDER, Capt., was born in Aberdeenshire in 1856. He served in South Africa, with the South Australian Contingent, 1901-2, taking part in operations in the Transvaal and Orange River Colony. He was mentioned in Despatches [London Gazette, 15 Nov. 1901]; awarded the Queen's Medal with five clasps, and was created a Companion of the Distinguished Service Order [London Gazette, 31 Oct. 1902]: "John Alexander Watt, Capt., South Australian Contingent. In recognition of services during the operations in South Africa." Capt. Watt was transferred to the Reserve of Officers 10 Dec. 1907, as Captain, and on 1 July, 1913, was appointed an Area Officer, 4th Military District, Australian Commonwealth. He has served for over a quarter of a century, and has the Volunteer Decoration.

BELL, GEORGE JOHN, Lieut., was born 29 Nov. 1872. He served in South Africa, with the Victorian Contingent, 1899-1902; was present in operations in the Transvaal and Orange River Colony; operations in Cape Colony, south of Orange River, and was severely wounded. He was mentioned in Despatches twice; received two Medals and nine clasps, and was created a Companion of the Distinguished Service Order [London Gazette, 31 Oct. 1902]: "George John Bell, Lieut., Victorian Contingents. In recognition of services during the operations in South Africa." He became Honorary Captain, 10th Australian Light Horse, to date from 1 Jan. 1902, on retiring after the Boer War. Capt. Bell rejoined for service in the European War, and served in Egypt, 1915-1918, being created a C.M.G. in 1918, and rising to the rank of Lieutenant-Colonel

BRUCE-STEER, T., Capt., served in the South African War, 1899-1902. He was created a Companion of the Distinguished Service Order [London Gazette, 31 Oct. 1902]: "T. Bruce-Steer, Capt., Thorneycroft's Mounted Infantry. In recognition of services during the operations in South Africa."

CULLUM, G. C., Capt., served in the South African War, 1899-1902, with the Duke of Edinburgh's Own Volunteer Rifles (Cape of Good Hope). He was present in operations in Cape Colony, south of Orange River, Oct. 1899, to May, 1900; operations in Cape Colony, north of Orange River, May to 29 Nov. 1900; operations in Cape Colony, 30 Nov. 1900, to May, 1902. He was mentioned in Despatches twice [London Gazette, 7 May and 20 Aug. 1901]; received the Queen's Medal with a clasp, and the King's Medal with two clasps, and was created a Companion of the Distinguished Service Order [London Gazette, 31 Oct. 1902]: "G. C. Cullum, Capt., Duke of Edinburgh's Own Volunteer Rifles. In recognition of services during the operations in South Africa."

DENNISON, CHARLES GEORGE, Capt., was born 21 Nov. 1844, at Cradock, Cape Colony, son of George Dennison, Farmer, Cape Colony, and Mary Dennison (Webber). His father, who was a volunteer, died of wounds received in the Kaffir War of 1851, in Lower Albany, Cape Colony. He was educated at Graham's Town, and says: "I always, from my boyhood, had a desire to be a soldier. My forefathers have nearly all been in the Army or Navy; my grandfather served through the American War as a Colour-Sergeant in the 55th Regt., being wounded at Bunker Hill, and also in the Peninsular War. South African boys of my age were born and lived for years in an atmosphere of warfare and inured to danger and hardships, as also subsequently, which has made our South African lads what they are. I have commanded Regulars and troops from New Zealand and Australia, who are all fine and brave men, but none so adaptable, so mobile, as our South Africans, who have done many daring and gallant acts in our South African War. I allude to English and Dutch combined. I first saw active service when I fought at the age of 19 or 20 in the Free State War of 1865, with the Basutos, when I served as a trooper in the Bloemfontein Rangers (O.F.S. Republican Forces). I commanded the Rustenburg Rifles, a local corps raised in Rustenburg, Transvaal Republic, in 1876, with the late Thomas Burgher, the President of the Transvaal, in command of his bodyguard. I was Second-in-Command of the Border Horse, under Colonel Weatherley, under Colonel Sir E. Wood in Zululand in 1879, and when they were practically wiped out and both Colonel Weatherley and his son fell at Hlobane on 28 March, was promoted to the command, with the rank of Commandant and Colonel's pay (Zululand Medal); served under Sir Garnet Wolseley in Secocolm's Country (in the Boer War of 1891), as Commandant, commanding Border Horse; raised troops on two occasions in Bechuanaland; defeated the natives during the Rebellion of Mashonwing River, Bechuanaland; captured the rebel chief Golishwe—who caused the rising—in the Kalahan Desert, and thus stopped what might have been a prolonged and costly rising to the Cape Government (Bechuanaland Medal); raised Dennison's Scouts, and served with them as O.C., with the Irregular Mounted Forces in the Boer War of 1899–1902. I cannot give particulars as to which particular act gained me the D.S.O. Got the Column—known as the Kimberley Column—out of difficulties on different occasions during the Boer War." He received the Queen's Medal with five clasps, and the King's Medal with two clasps; was mentioned in Despatches, and created a Companion of the Distinguished Service Order [London Gazette, 31 Oct. 1902]: "Charles George Dennison, Capt., South African Mounted Irregular Forces. In recognition of services during the operations in South Africa." He rose to the rank of Major. Major Dennison had four grandsons fighting in the European War, two of whom were severely wounded. He is particularly fond of hunting. Most of this has been done in Mashonaland and Matabeleland. He often met the late Major F. C. Selous, D.S.O., the great hunter, and knew him well. He married, 29 Aug. 1867, at Aliwal North, Annie M. Hoffman, descendant on her mother's side of the De Villiers family of French Huguenots, and their children were: Alexander George, who fell in the Boer War; Lillie Elizabeth; Annie Mary; Clifford, who fell in the Boer War; Harold James; Emmie, and Frederick Weatherley.

Charles G. Dennison.

DONALDSON, JAMES, Capt., was born in London, 28 Feb. 1863. He served in South Africa with the Imperial Light Horse from 1899 to 1902; present in operations in Natal, 1899, including actions at Elandslaagte, Reitfontein and Lombard's Kop; defence of Ladysmith, including sortie of 7 Dec. 1899, and action of 6 Jan. 1900; Relief of Mafeking; operations in the Transvaal, east and west of Pretoria, July to Nov. 1900; operations in the Transvaal and Orange River Colony, Nov. 1900, to May, 1901. He was severely wounded; was mentioned in Despatches twice; received the Queen's Medal with five clasps, and the King's Medal with two clasps, and was created a Companion of the Distinguished Service Order [London Gazette, 31 Oct. 1902]; "J. Donaldson, Capt., 1st Imperial Light Horse. In recognition of services during the operations in South Africa." He joined the Reserve of Officers, Imperial Light Horse, 12 Dec. 1902, and was promoted Lieutenant-Colonel 1 July, 1907. He served in the European War, first in the South-West African campaign, and later commanding the 19th Royal Scots, British Expeditionary Force, France. Lieut.-Colonel Donaldson married, in 1903, Miss A. E. Newton, of New Zealand; they have one son.

GEDYE, JAMES BANFIELD, Capt., was born in Cape Colony, South Africa, in 1877, fifth son of the Rev. Edwin Gedye. He served in the Boer War, in Cape Colony, Orange River Colony and the Transvaal, 1899–1902. He served in Montmorency's Scouts, 1899–1900; 2nd Kitchener's Fighting Scouts, 1900 to 1902; was wounded on 27 Dec. 1901, in Orange River Colony. He received the Queen's Medal, 1899–1900, with three clasps; the King's Medal, 1900–1902, with clasps, and was created a Companion of the Distinguished Service Order [London Gazette, 31 Oct. 1902]: "James Banfield Gedye, Capt., British South African Police. In recognition of services during the operations in South Africa." He also received the Coronation Medal, June, 1902.

Charles Hugh Gilson.

GILSON, CHARLES HUGH, Major, was born 8 Nov. 1870, at Maritzburg, Natal, the son of Alexander Daniel Gilson, retired Civil Servant, and Miriam Jane Gilson, of The Croft, Greytown, Natal. He was educated at Maritzburg College; served as Clerk in the Civil Service in Natal and Zululand; received a commission in the Zululand Police, 1894, as Sub-Inspector; transferred to B.S.A. Police, as Inspector with local rank of Captain, in 1897; was transferred in 1902 to S.A. Constabulary, still with the rank of Captain. Capt. Gilson served in the South African War of 1899–1902; was twice mentioned in Despatches; received the Queen's Medal with a clasp; the King's Medal with two clasps, and was created a Companion of the Distinguished Service Order [London Gazette, 31 Oct. 1902]: "C. H. Gilson, Capt., British South African Police. In recognition of services during the operations in South Africa. (Especially for his services in suppressing a Native Rising in the north of Southern Rhodesia, during the rainy months in a fever-stricken district.)" When the Swaziland Police were formed in 1907 Major Gilson was given command. He has the Matabele Medal. Major Gilson married, 21 July, 1908, at Mbabane, Swaziland, Clytie Rowena, daughter of William Anderson Knight, C.M.G. Their children are: Ina Rowena, born 19 June, 1909; Helen Phyllis, born 6 Jan. 1911; Kenyon Tilden, born 14 March, 1912, and Jean Miriam, born 26 May, 1913.

JARDINE, W., Capt., served in South Africa with the Imperial Light Horse, from 1899 to 1902. He was present in operations in Natal, 1899, including the actions at Reitfontein and Lombard's Kop; the defence of Ladysmith, including the sortie of 7 Dec. 1899, and the action of 6 Jan. 1900; the Relief of Mafeking; operations in the Transvaal, east and west of Pretoria, July to 29 Nov. 1900, including action at Frederickstad (17 to 25 Oct.); operations in the Transvaal and Orange River Colony 30 Nov. 1900, to 31 May, 1902. He was mentioned in Despatches [London Gazette, 17 Jan. and 25 April, 1902]; received the Queen's Medal with three clasps, and the King's Medal with two clasps, and was created a Companion of the Distinguished Service Order [London Gazette, 31 Oct. 1902]: "W. Jardine, Capt., 1st Imperial Light Horse. In recognition of services during the operations in South Africa." He became Captain, Northern Mounted Rifles, Transvaal, 12 Dec. 1902, and Adjutant, 1 July, 1907. He took part in the quelling of the Natal Native Rebellion in 1906.

LAING, JOHN, Capt., was born in Wigtownshire 29 Jan. 1868. At fifteen he went to sea for three years as an apprentice sailor; lived for a period in Brazil and Argentina, settling in South Africa in 1889. He went on active service on 1 Oct. 1899, as a trooper in the Natal Carabineers; served with that regiment for a year and a half, and was then given a troop in the Johannesburg Mounted Rifles. He was three times mentioned in Despatches for his services in South Africa; received the Queen's Medal with three clasps, and the King's Medal with two clasps, and was created a Companion of the Distinguished Service Order [London Gazette, 31 Oct. 1902]: "John Laing, Capt., Johannesburg Mounted Rifles. In recognition of services during the operations in South Africa." Capt. Laing joined the Reserve of Officers. He married, in 1901, Agnes Augusta, daughter of William O'Mash, of Oxford. They have one daughter.

McLOUGHLIN, MARK WILSON, Capt., was born on 23 Sept. 1877, at Bradford, Yorkshire, son of Mark McLoughlin, of Cork, and of Jane McLoughlin (maiden name, Harrison, of Cork). He was educated at a private school, and joined the Army on 26 Dec. 1899. He served in South Africa with Roberts's Horse, the Western Light Horse, and Scott's Railway Guards, 1899 to 1902. He was mentioned in Despatches; awarded the Queen's and King's Medals with seven clasps, and was created a Companion of the Distinguished Service Order, for extricating a patrol from an ambush under difficult and hazardous circumstances [London Gazette, 31 Oct. 1902]: "Mark Wilson McLoughlin, Capt., Scott's Railway Guards. In recognition of services during the operations in South Africa." He rejoined the Army, with the rank of Major, 21 Dec. 1914, and was mentioned in Despatches for his services in connection with the German South-West African Campaign and the campaign in German East Africa. He was promoted Lieutenant-Colonel 1 July, 1917, and was awarded the O.B.E. in 1918.

MACMILLAN, ALEXANDER, Capt., was born 19 Nov. 1871, son of William MacMillan, of Vancouver, British Columbia, and of Mrs. MacMillan. He is married and has one son. He served in South Africa from 1899 to 1902, and commanded the Canadian Scouts from Feb. to May, 1902; took part in operations in the Orange Free State, Feb. to May, 1900, including actions at Vet River (5 and 6 May) and Zand River; operations in the Transvaal, May and June, 1900, including operations near Pretoria and Diamond Hill (11 and 12 June); operations in the Transvaal, east of Pretoria, July to 29 Nov. 1900, including actions at Reit Vlei and Belfast (26 and 27 Aug.); operations in the Transvaal, Jan. to April, 1901; operations in Orange River Colony, Jan. to 31 May, 1902. He was awarded the Queen's Medal with three clasps, and the King's Medal with two clasps, and created a Companion of the Distinguished Service Order [London Gazette, 31 Oct. 1902]: "Alexander MacMillan, Capt., Canadian Scouts. In recognition of services during the operations in South Africa." Capt. MacMillan also had the Medals for Queen Victoria's Diamond Jubilee and King Edward VII.'s Coronation. He was given the Brevet of Captain, Canadian Permanent Force, 24 Aug. 1908, and promoted Captain, Royal Canadian Dragoons, 21 Jan. 1911. He served in the European War from 1914 to 1918, and was Assistant Provost-Marshal in 1915. He was mentioned in Despatches, and awarded a Bar to the D.S.O.

MIDGLEY, STEPHEN, Capt., was born at M'Leay River, New South Wales, 29 May, 1871, fourth son of James Midgley, of Queensland, Australia. He was educated privately, and served in South Africa, 1900–1 and 1902; was promoted from Lieutenant to Captain in the Field, when serving with the Pietersburg Light Horse. He was mentioned in Despatches; awarded the Queen's and King's Medals, and created a Companion of the Distinguished Service Order [London Gazette, 31 Oct. 1902]: "Stephen Midgley, Capt., Pietersburg Light Infantry. In recognition of services during the operations in South Africa." He received a commission as Lieutenant with Royston's Horse; served during the Natal Rebellion of 1906 (Medal). In the European War Major Midgley was wounded, and for his services was mentioned in Despatches, and created a C.M.G. in 1916.

In the autumn of 1916 he was promoted Lieutenant-Colonel, and given the command of the 54th Battn. Australian Imperial Force. He was sent to Australia on account of ill-health in Dec. 1917. Colonel Midgley married, in 1916, Katharine Emily Mary, widow of Frank Evans, Junior, of Bredwardine, Hereford.

POLLARD, W. A., Capt., served in South Africa with Bethune's Mounted Infantry, 1900–2. He was mentioned in Despatches; awarded the King's Medal with two clasps, and was created a Companion of the Distinguished Service Order [London Gazette, 31 Oct. 1902]: "W. A. Pollard, Capt., Bethune's Mounted Infantry. In recognition of services during the operations in South Africa."

RAMSBOTHAM, J. B., Capt., served in the South African War, 1899–1902, with the Mounted Irregular Forces. He was mentioned in Despatches; received the Queen's Medal with three clasps; the King's Medal with two clasps, and was created a Companion of the Distinguished Service Order [London Gazette, 31 Oct. 1902]: "J. B. Ramsbotham, Capt., South African Mounted Irregular Forces. In recognition of services during the operations in South Africa."

RATTRAY, P. M., Capt., served in South Africa with the 1st Scottish Horse, 1899–1902. He was mentioned in Despatches, and was created a Companion of the Distinguished Service Order [London Gazette, 31 Oct. 1902]: "P. M. Rattray, Capt., 1st Scottish Horse. In recognition of services during the operations in South Africa."

SCOTT, W., Capt., served in South Africa with Damant's Horse, 1900–2. He received the Queen's Medal with six clasps; the King's Medal with two clasps, and was created a Companion of the Distinguished Service Order [London Gazette, 31 Oct. 1902]: "W. Scott, Capt., Damant's Horse. In recognition of services during the operations in South Africa."

SMITH, CHARLES FUTCHER, Capt., was born on 26 Feb. 1876. He served in South Africa with Driscoll's Scouts, 1899–1902, taking part in operations in Cape Colony and the Transvaal; operations in the Orange Free State, including the defence of Wepener; operations in Orange River Colony, including actions at Wittebergen. He was mentioned in Despatches [London Gazette, 29 July, 1902]; awarded the Queen's Medal with four clasps; the King's Medal with two clasps, and was created a Companion of the Distinguished Service Order [London Gazette, 31 Oct. 1902]: "Charles Futcher Smith, Capt., Driscoll's Scouts. In recognition of services during the operations in South Africa." Capt. Smith was placed on retired pay 30 July, 1909

WISHART, ROBERT, Capt., was born on 12 Sept. 1875, at Barry Reef, Victoria, Australia, son of Harry and Alena Wishart. He was educated at Allendale, Victoria, and joined the Army, as a private, in Nov. 1899. He served in South Africa, 1899–1900, with Bethune's Mounted Infantry; 1900–2, with the Johannesburg Mounted Rifles. He was three times mentioned in Despatches; awarded the Queen's Medal with five clasps, and the King's Medal with two clasps, and was created a Companion of the Distinguished Service Order—he believes, for going to the succour of Private Scott, of the Johannesburg Mounted Rifles, who was badly wounded (Capt. Wishart understood that he was recommended on that occasion for the Victoria Cross, by the O.C., Johannesburg Mounted Rifles). The award of the D.S.O. appeared in the London Gazette of 31 Oct. 1902: "Robert Wishart, Capt., Johannesburg Mounted Rifles. In recognition of services during the operations in South Africa." Capt. Wishart commanded the Johannsburg Mounted Rifles at the Coronation of King Edward VII., and received the Coronation Medal. He is now farming in the Transvaal. He married Edith Carr, and has three children: Basil, Robert Carr and Edith Joan.

FAIRWEATHER, JAMES McINTYRE, Capt., was born at Dundee, Scotland, 13 Oct. 1876, eldest son of Joseph Fairweather, Sculptor, of Dundee, and his wife, Jane, daughter of James McIntyre, Wood Merchant, of Dundee. He was educated at the Harris Academy, Dundee, and by private tutors, and originally intended for the legal profession, but in 1896 went to South Africa, and joined the Staff of the East London Harbour Board. At the outbreak of the South African War he was Assistant Town Clerk at East London, and volunteered for active service with the Kaffrarian Rifles, receiving a commission in that Corps, later being promoted Captain and Adjutant. He was present in operations in the Orange Free State, Feb. to May, 1900, including the defence of Wepener; operatoins in Orange River Colony (May to 29 Nov. 1900), including action at Wittebergen (1 to 29 July); operations in the Transvaal and Orange River Colony. He was three times wounded; was mentioned in Despatches in March, 1901, and March, 1902. Doing especially good service at the Relief of Wepener and at Quaggasfontein, he also commanded the troops which entered the town when Aliwal North was ceded by the rebels. He was created a Companion of the Distinguished Service Order [London Gazette, 31 Oct. 1902]: "James McIntyre Fairweather, Capt., Cape Colony Forces. In recognition of services during the operations in South Africa." At the conclusion of the war he was offered a commission in the Regular Army, but deciding to return to civil life, he accepted a position on the Headquarters Staff of the Central South African Railways, and at the time of his death held the post of Superintendent attached to the personal Staff of Sir William Hoy, General Manager of the South African Railways. At the time of the Union, he rendered valuable service as one of the special Committee who undertook the task of assimilating the general conditions of service for the administration of the entire staff (involving over 60,000 employees) of the Union Railways. He took a keen interest in military matters in South Africa, and after the Union became Commanding Officer of the Transvaal Motor and Cycle Corps, and later of the Rand Light Infantry. In 1913, during the July disturbances on the Rand, he was in military control of Bramfontein, and again during the strike in Jan. 1914, he rendered valuable services. In July, 1914, he was one of two South African officers who left for England on the invitation of the War Office to represent the Union Defence Department at the autumn army manœuvres. He arrived in England a few days after the declaration of war, and sought permission to proceed to the Western Front, but was instructed to return at once to South Africa. On the suppression of the Rebellion he proceeded to German West Africa with the Rand Light Infantry. A new regiment had to be formed in German West Africa to expedite the reconstruction of the destroyed railway line from Aus westward to Keetmanshoop, thence north to Windhuk, then south through Kalkfontein to meet the new railway line which was being built from Uppington, and all railway servants with combatant units were ordered to transfer to this. It was styled the Railway Regt., and Colonel Fairweather was given the command. He achieved splendid results under very difficult conditions, and was mentioned in Despatches in Aug. 1918, in this connection. On returning to the Transvaal several months later than the military contingent from German West Africa, he returned for a short time to his civil duties at Railway Headquarters, but later was given the command of the South African Motor Cyclist Corps, and was killed in action on 18 Feb. 1917, at Rupira, in the Livingstone Range, and is buried there. His brother, Major Joseph Fairweather, of the South Wales Borderers, was killed in action near Kut on 15 Jan. of the same year. Writing of Colonel Fairweather, Mr. H. E. M. Bourne, the Secretary of the Defence Department of South Africa, said: "The death of this officer will be a very great loss, not only to the Railway Administration, but to the Union generally, and especially to the Union Defence Forces, as he was one of the oldest and keenest of Citizen Force officers, and full of soldierly qualities. The example set by Colonel Fairweather was a very high one, and I trust and hope will long be followed by the more junior officers of the Active Citizen Force." Brigadier-General Sir Charles Crewe, K.C.M.G., C.B., M.L.A., writing of him, said: "A most gallant officer, and one for whom I have always had the greatest regard. . . . He again in West Africa showed the same gallantry and devotion to duty which was so noticeable in the 1900 campaign. He met his death, and we who all deplore his loss must also feel that he, like many others who have made the greatest sacrifice man can make, died as he would himself have chosen, in action serving the Empire." Colonel H. B. Cuming, C.B., who commanded the Kaffrarian Rifles during the South African War, wrote: "He was without doubt the most gallant fellow I ever worked with in the field. His complete indifference to shell fire and bullets amazed me. He was an excellent officer in every way, and his death is an irreparable loss to the Active Union Defence Force. In every detail of his work he was thorough and full of useful ideas," while a Railway correspondent writes of him: "The men who served under him were unanimous in their praise and liking of their Commander, whose chief anxiety at all times, even at great personal sacrifice, lay in promoting the welfare and comfort of the rank and file. . . . Quick to commend and reward good services, he was equally spontaneous in his denunciation of the bad. . . . He was a man of the most honourable and lofty principles, and the country generally, still more the Railway Administration and the military service, can ill spare him."

James M. Fairweather.

WHITEHEAD, ERNEST KILVE, Capt., was born in 1874. He served in South Africa with the Natal Volunteers, 1900–2. He was mentioned in Despatches; awarded the Queen's and King's Medals with six clasps, and was created a Companion of the Distinguished Service Order [London Gazette, 31 Oct. 1902]: "Ernest Kilve Whitehead, Capt., Natal Volunteers. In recognition of services during the operations in South Africa." He subsequently joined the Northern Mounted Rifles, Transvaal. Capt. Whitehead married, in 1907, Edith Henrietta, daughter of Lieut.-Colonel T. J. R. Mallock, of Doune Raph, Camberley, and they have one son.

COLLINS, (THE HONOURABLE) RICHARD HENN, Lieut., was born 2 April, 1873, eldest son of the late Lord Collins. He was educated at Winchester College, and joined the Army with a commission as Second Lieutenant in the Berkshire Regt. 13 Aug. 1892. He became Lieutenant 8 Jan. 1895, and passed through the Staff College. He served in the South African War, as A.D.C., and with the Mounted Infantry; operations in the Orange Free State, Feb. to May, 1900; operations in the Transvaal, east of Pretoria, July to Sept. 1900; operations in the Transvaal, west of Pretoria, July to 29 Nov. 1900, including action at Zilikat's Nek; operations in Orange River Colony, May to July, 1900, including action at Rhenoster River; operations in Cape Colony, south of Orange River, 1899; operations in the Transvaal, Nov. 1900, to March, 1902; operations in Cape Colony, March to 31 May, 1902. He was mentioned in Despatches [London Gazette, 29 July, 1902]; awarded the Queen's Medal with three clasps; the King's Medal with two clasps, and was created a Companion of the Distinguished Service Order [London Gazette, 31 Oct. 1902]: "Richard Henn Collins, Lieut., Princess Charlotte of Wales's Royal Berkshire Regt. In recognition of services during the operations in South Africa." He was promoted Captain 8 Sept. 1902; served as D.A.A. and Q.M.G., 3rd Division, Southern Command, March, 1910, to Oct. 1912; was employed with the New Zealand Military Forces, as G.S.O.3, Nov. 1912, to Jan. 1913, and as A.G., Feb. 1913, to 28 Aug. 1914; was promoted Major 14 March, 1914. He served in the European War in France and Belgium from Oct. 1914, to Aug. 1915, as D.A.A. and Q.M.G., 4th and 2nd Corps, and from that date until the Armistice as A.A. and Q.M.G., 3rd and 4th Divisions. He was mentioned in Despatches; given the Brevet of Lieutenant-Colonel, and created a C.M.G. (1917) for services in the War, and in 1917 was created a Chevalier of the Italian Order of

SS. Maurice and Lazarus. He became Lieutenant-Colonel 10 Jan. 1919. In 1909 the Hon. R. H. Collins married May Eveline, youngest daughter of the late H. G. Bainbridge, of Malvern Hall, Solihull, and they have three sons: Richard Henn, born 20 April, 1911; William Jonathan Henn, born 2 March, 1913, and Christopher Arthur Henn, born 5 June, 1915.

MEARES, AUBREY, Lieut., was born 12 Oct. 1873, son of Hugh Meares, of Ryde. He was educated at Burneys and the Royal Military Academy, Woolwich, and joined the Army 10 Feb. 1893, as a Second Lieutenant in the Royal Engineers. He served in South Africa, 1899–1902, taking part in the advance on Kimberley, including actions at Belmont, Enslin, Modder River and Magersfontein; operations in the Transvaal, west of Pretoria, July to 29 Nov. 1900, including actions at Venterskroon (7 and 9 Aug.); operations in Orange River Colony, May to 29 Nov. 1900, including actions at Lindley (1 June) and Rhenoster River. He was mentioned in Despatches twice [London Gazette, 10 Sept. 1901, and 29 July, 1902]; awarded the Queen's Medal with four clasps; the King's Medal with two clasps, and was created a Companion of the Distinguished Service Order [London Gazette, 31 Oct. 1902]: "Aubrey Meares, Lieut., Royal Engineers. In recognition of services during the operations in South Africa." He was promoted Captain 5 Jan. 1904, and retired with that rank from the Service 8 Dec. 1909. Capt. Meares returned to serve in the beginning of the European War, but had to leave on account of ill-health. Capt Meares married, in 1906, Edna Clara Amethyst, daughter of Capt. E. Wigley Burt, R.N., of Fernleigh, Ryde, and they have two sons.

BRADLEY, ROBERT WILLIAM, Lieut., was born 26 Jan. 1874, only child of Commander W. H. Bradley, R.N. He was educated at Harrow and Sandhurst, and joined the Army 7 March, 1894, as a Second Lieutenant in the South Wales Borderers. He was promoted Lieutenant 14 Nov. 1896. In the South African War he served as Station Staff Officer 10 June to 7 July, 1900, and afterwards as Garrison Adjutant, Klerksdorp, 8 July to 8 Aug. 1900; as Adjutant of the 2nd Battn. of his regiment 10 Jan. 1900, to 31 May, 1902; was present in operations in the Orange Free State, Feb. to May, 1900, including actions at Karee Siding, Vet River (5 and 6 May) and Zand River; operations in the Transvaal, May and June, 1900, including action near Johannesburg; operations in the Transvaal, west of Pretoria, Aug. to 29 Nov. 1900; operations in Orange River Colony, June to Aug. 1900; operations in the Transvaal 30 Nov. 1900, to 31 May, 1902. He was mentioned in Despatches [London Gazette, 10 Sept. 1901]; awarded the Medal with three clasps; the King's Medal with two clasps, and was created a Companion of the Distinguished Service Order [London Gazette, 31 Oct. 1902]: "Robert William Bradley, Lieut., South Wales Borderers. In recognition of services during the operations in South Africa." He became Captain 11 Dec. 1905; was Assistant Instructor, School of Musketry, Jan. 1903, to Jan. 1906. He was an Officer of a Company of Gentleman Cadets, Royal Military Academy, Woolwich, Jan, to Aug. 1913, and Commander of a Company, Aug. 1913, to Oct. 1914; became Major 27 Sept. 1914. Serving in the European War, 1915–18, he was Temporary Lieutenant-Colonel, Machine Gun Corps, from Sept. 1914, to July, 1917; graded as A.A.G., while employed on special duties, Machine Gun Corps Training Centre, July to Sept. 1916. He was given the Brevet of Lieutenant-Colonel for his services 1 Jan. 1917; was Temporary Lieutenant-Colonel, Tank Corps, July to Nov. 1917. His chief amusements are shooting, fishing, riding, cricket and golf. Lieut.-Colonel Bradley married (1st), in 1898, Dorothea Lilias (died 1908), only child of Lieut.-Colonel A. H. Bircham; (2ndly), in 1910, Eleonora Kathleen, daughter of the late Right Rev. John Lloyd, Bishop of Swansea.

MANCE, HARRY OSBORNE, Lieut., was born 2 Oct. 1875, at Karachi, India, son of Sir Henry Christopher Mance, Kt., C.I.E., LL.D. (the inventor of the heliograph), and Annie, daughter of John Sayer, of Yatton. He was educated at Bedford Grammar School and the Royal Military Academy, Woolwich; was gazetted Second Lieutenant, Royal Engineers, 15 March, 1895. He became Lieutenant 15 March, 1898, and served through the South African War, 1899–1901, as Staff Officer to the Assistant Director of Railways, and afterwards as Deputy Assistant Director of Railways, and D.A.D.R. of Armoured Trains, Kimberley Line, from 1 Jan. 1900, to 30 Sept. 1902, taking part in the operations in Cape Colony, north of the Orange River, in 1899. He was mentioned in Despatches [London Gazette, 29 July, 1902]; received the Queen's South African Medal and clasp for Belmont; the King's South African Medal with two clasps, and was created a Companion of the Distinguished Service Order [London Gazette, 31 Oct. 1902]: "Harry Osborne Mance, Lieut., Royal Engineers. In recognition of services during the operations in South Africa." He became Captain 1 April, 1904. From 4 July, 1908, to 9 Jan. 1912, Capt. Mance was employed in Northern Nigeria on the construction of the Baro-Kano Railway. Capt. Mance was Staff Captain at the War Office 2 Dec. 1912, to 23 Jan. 1915, and became Major 30 Oct. 1914. He was D.A. Director, War Office (temporary) 29 Jan. to 22 April, 1915; given the Brevet of Lieutenant-Colonel 1 April, 1915; Assistant Director of Railway Transport, War Office (temporary), 23 April, 1915 (Temporary Brigadier-General from 14 Aug. 1916) and Director of Railways, Light Railways and Roads, War Office, and Temporary Brigadier-General from 26 Sept. 1916. He was created a C.M.G. in 1917, and C.B. in 1918, and was mentioned in Despatches in 1917 and 1918 for distinguished services at the War Office. He acted as Transportation Adviser to the British Delegation at the Peace Conference, and as one of the British Delegates on the Ports, Waterways and Railways Commission, and on the commission for the revision of the treaties of 1839, and has also been President of the Communications Section of the Supreme Economic Council. He was Revolver Champion of the Army in 1914. He married, at St. Albans, 2 Nov. 1911, Elizabeth Hope, youngest daughter of the late Major-General W. Stenhouse, Indian Army, and their children are: Henry Stenhouse Mance, born 5 Feb. 1913; Herbert William, born 15 June, 1919, and Mary Hope Jeanne, born 20 Aug. 1916.

Harry Osborne Mance.

PLACE, CHARLES OTLEY, Lieut., was born 3 Oct. 1875. He entered the Army as a Second Lieutenant in the Royal Engineers 7 Aug. 1895, and was promoted Lieutenant 7 Aug. 1898. He served in the South African War, 1899 to 1902, taking part in the Relief of Ladysmith, including operations of 17 to 24 Jan. 1900; operations of 5 to 7 Feb. 1900, and action at Vaal Kranz; operations on Tugela Heights (14 to 27 Feb. 1900) and action at Pieter's Hill; operations in the Transvaal, June, 1900; operations in Natal, March to June, 1900, including action at Laing's Nek (6 to 9 June); operations in the Transvaal, east of Pretoria, July to 29 Nov. 1900. He was mentioned in Despatches [London Gazette, 29 July, 1902]; awarded the Queen's Medal with five clasps; the King's Medal with two clasps, and was created a Companion of the Distinguished Service Order [London Gazette, 31 Oct. 1902]: "Charles Otley Place, Lieut., Royal Engineers. In recognition of services during the operations in South Africa." He was promoted Captain, Royal Engineers, 7 Aug. 1904; was employed as Adjutant, Militia, and Adjutant, Special Reserve, May, 1905, to June, 1908; Officer of a Company of Gentleman Cadets, Royal Military Academy, Jan. to Sept. 1909, and Commander of a Company, Sept. 1909, to Jan. 1910; General Staff Officer, 3rd Grade, Western Command, April, 1912, to the outbreak of the European War. He was promoted Major 30 Oct. 1914. He served in the European War, holding the following appointments, viz.: G.S.O.2, First Army, Central Force, Home Defence, 5 Aug. to 4 Oct. 1914; G.S.O.3, Fourth Army, British Expeditionary Force, 5 Oct. 1914, to 9 Feb. 1915; G.S.O.2, 19th Division, New Armies, British Expeditionary Force, 15 Feb. 1915, to 4 April, 1916; Temporary Lieutenant-Colonel and G.S.O.1, 36th Division, British Armies in France, 5 April, 1916, to 26 May, 1918. He was mentioned in Despatches; given the Brevet of Lieutenant-Colonel 3 June, 1916, and created a C.M.G. in 1917. Lieut.-Colonel Place was specially employed at the War Office 4 Feb. to 31 March, 1919, and became G.S.O., War Office (temporary), 1 April, 1919.

Charles Otley Place.

KELLY, JAMES ALPHONSE MARI JOSEPH PATRICK, Lieut., was born 27 Aug. 1875, only son of His Honour Judge Kelly, K.C., and of Bertha, daughter of the Comtesse de Buisseret. He was educated at the Oratory School; entered the Army 16 Oct. 1895, as a Second Lieutenant, in the Royal Irish Regt., in which he became Lieutenant 8 Dec. 1898. He served in South Africa, 1899–1902, and was severely wounded. He was present in operations in the Orange Free State, March to May, 1900; operations in the Transvaal, east of Pretoria, Aug. to 29 Nov. 1900, including actions at Belfast (26 and 27 Aug.) and Lydenberg (5 to 8 Sept.); operations in Orange River Colony, May to Aug. 1900, including actions at Bethlehem (6 and 7 July) and Wittebergen (1 to 29 July); operations in Cape Colony, south of Orange River, 1900, including action at Colesberg (24 Jan. to 12 Feb.). He was mentioned in Despatches [London Gazette, 10 Sept. 1901, and 29 July, 1902]; received the Queen's Medal with three clasps; the King's Medal with two clasps, and was created a Companion of the Distinguished Service Order [London Gazette, 31 Oct. 1902]: "James Alphonse Mari Joseph Patrick Kelly, Lieut., The Royal Irish Regt. In recognition of services during the operations in South Africa." He was promoted Captain 9 April, 1903, and was Adjutant of Volunteers 11 April, 1906, to 8 June, 1908. He died at Agra 23 Oct. 1909. He had married, in 1905, the widow of E. Blake Price.

GRIMSHAW, CECIL THOMAS WRIGLEY, Lieut., was born 22 Oct. 1875, son of the late Thomas Wrigley Grimshaw, C.B., Registrar-General for Ireland. He was educated at Eastman's Royal Naval Academy and at Dublin University, where he took his B.A. degree, and joined the Royal Dublin Fusiliers, as a Second Lieutenant, 15 May, 1897, being promoted Lieutenant 28 Dec. 1898. He served in the South African War, 1899–1902 (employed with Mounted Infantry); took part in the operations in Natal, 1899, including action at Talana; in the Transvaal, east of Pretoria, July to 29 Nov. 1900; in Orange River Colony, May to 29 Nov. 1900; again in the Transvaal 30 Nov. 1900, to 31 May, 1902. He was mentioned in Despatches [London Gazette, 10 Sept. 1901, and 29 July, 1902]; received the Queen's Medal with three clasps, and the King's Medal with two clasps. He was created a Companion of the Distinguished Service Order [London Gazette, 31 Oct. 1902]: "Cecil Thomas Wrigley Grimshaw, Lieut., Royal Dublin Fusiliers. In recognition of services during the operations in South Africa." He served at Aden, 1903, during operations in the interior; was promoted Captain 14 July, 1904; became Adjutant, Royal Dublin Fusiliers, 28 Dec. 1911. He served in the European War, and was killed in action at the Dardanelles in 1915. He had married, in 1906, Agnes Violet, youngest daughter of George B. Alderson, of Alexandria, and left two sons.

KINGTON, WILLIAM MYLES, Lieut., was born at Cheltenham 25 April, 1876, son of the late Colonel M. Myles Nairne Kington, formerly of the 4th Hussars. He was educated at Glenalmond College and at Sandhurst, and joined the 1st Royal Welsh Fusiliers at Aden in Sept. 1896, and became Lieutenant in Jan. 1899. He served in the South African War of 1899–1902, on the Staff as Brigade Signalling Officer from Nov. 1899, to Dec. 1900. He was present at the Relief of Ladysmith and the Battle of Colenso; operations and action at Vaal Kranz; on the Tugela Heights and action at Pieter's Hill; in the Transvaal at the beginning and end of 1900, including the action at Frederickstad, and in Cape Colony, including the action at Ruidam. He was again in the Transvaal in 1901 and 1902, and in the Orange River Colony. He was four times mentioned in Despatches [London Gazette of 8 Feb., 9 July, and 10 Sept. 1901, and 29 July, 1902]; received the Queen's Medal with five clasps; the King's Medal with two clasps, and was created a Companion of the Distinguished Service Order [London Gazette, 31 Oct. 1902]: "William Myles Kington, Lieut., The Royal Welsh Fusiliers. In recognition of services during the operations in South Africa." From Feb. 1902, to May, 1904, he was employed with the South African Constabulary, and from April, 1906, in which month he received his company, to Sept. 1910, he was an Adjutant of Volunteers and of the Territorial Force. He served in the European War, and was killed by a shell in the First Battle of Ypres on 28 Oct. 1914. He was a very popular officer, and a man in the battalion who was present said in an account of the engagement: "For three days we remained in the trenches, firing and being fired at, without food or water. Lieut. Hoskyns, who commanded my platoon, was killed by a sniper, and about three hours later Capt. Kington, D.S.O., was killed. He was a very fine officer, and would crack a joke in the trenches which would set us all laughing our sides out. It made us all mad to avenge his death." He was a well-known cricketer, a member of the M.C.C., the I Zingari and the Free Foresters, and was an excellent shot. Capt. Kington was very artistic, and has been described as a "musical genius." He married Edith, only daughter of Mr. F. W. Soames, of Bryn Estyn, Wrexham, and left one son.

TROUSDALE, ROBERT CECIL, Lieut., was born 4 June, 1876, son of the Rev. H. Trousdale. He joined the Army, as a Second Lieutenant in the South Lancashire Regt., 24 March, 1897, and was promoted Lieutenant 25 Jan. 1899. He served in the South African War, 1899–1902 (employed with Mounted Infantry); was present at the Relief of Ladysmith, including operations of 17 to 24 Jan. 1900, and action at Spion Kop; operations of 5 to 7 Feb. 1900, and action at Vaal Kranz, and during the operations on Tugela Heights (14 to 27 Feb.); took part in the operations in the Transvaal 30 Nov. 1900, to 31 May, 1902; also during operations on the Zululand Frontier of Natal in Sept. and Oct. 1901, including the defence of Fort Itala. He was mentioned in Despatches [London Gazette, 10 Sept. 1901, and 17 Jan. 1902]; received the Queen's Medal with five clasps, and the King's Medal with two clasps. He was created a Companion of the Distinguished Service Order [London Gazette, 31 Oct. 1902]: "Robert Cecil Trousdale, Lieut., The Prince of Wales's Volunteers, South Lancashire Regt. In recognition of services during the operations in South Africa." He was promoted Captain 28 Feb. 1904; Officer of a Company of Gentleman Cadets R.M.C. 18 Sept. 1905, and retired from the Service 27 March, 1912. Major (R. of O.) 8 June, 1916.

CROSSMAN, GEORGE LYTTON, Lieut., was born 18 Feb. 1877, son of the late Edward Crossman, M.D. He was educated at Radley College and at Sandhurst, and joined the Army, as a Second Lieutenant in the West Yorkshire Regt., 20 Feb. 1897. He was promoted Lieutenant 4 Feb. 1899. He served in the South African War, 1899–1902, as Staff Officer to Commandant and Railway Staff Officer, Frederickstad; took part in the operations in Natal, 1899; was present at the Relief of Ladysmith, including action at Colenso; in the operations of 17 to 24 Jan. 1900, and action at Spion Kop; operations of 5 to 7 Feb. 1900, and action at Vaal Kranz; also during operations on Tugela Heights (14 to 27 Feb. 1900) and action at Pieter's Hill; in Natal, March to June, 1900, including action at Laing's Nek (6 to 9 June); in the Transvaal, east and west of Pretoria, July to 29 Nov. 1900; again in the Transvaal 30 Nov. 1900, to 31 May, 1902. He was mentioned in Despatches [London Gazette, 10 Sept. 1901, and 29 July, 1902]; received the Queen's Medal with five clasps, and the King's Medal with two clasps. He was created a Companion of the Distinguished Service Order [London Gazette, 31 Oct. 1902]: "George Lytton Crossman, Lieut., The Prince of Wales's Own (West Yorkshire Regt.). In recognition of services during the operations in South Africa." He became Captain 26 May, 1904; was Adjutant of the 2nd West Yorkshire Regt. from 1 Nov. 1904, to 31 Oct. 1907, and was Officer of a Company of Gentleman Cadets, Royal Military College, 26 Jan. 1908, to 25 Jan. 1912. Serving in the European War, Capt. Crossman held the following Staff appointments, viz.: Staff Captain, 21st Infantry Brigade, B.E.F., 13 Nov. 1914, to 15 April, 1915; Brigade Major, 21st Infantry Brigade, B.E.F., British Armies in France, 16 April, 1915, to 13 July, 1916 (promoted to Major 1 Sept. 1915); G.S.O.2, 30th Division, British Armies in France, 14 July, 1916, to 16 Feb. 1917; G.S.O.2, 7th Army Corps, British Armies in France, 17 Feb. to 10 Nov. 1917; G.S.O.1, Headquarters, Royal Flying Corps, British Armies in France, 11 Nov. 1917, to 31 March, 1918; employed under the Air Ministry 1 to 11 April, 1918; G.S.O.1, 59th Division, British Armies in France, 14 April to 20 Sept. 1918; G.S.O.1, 5th Army, British Armies in France, 21 Sept. to 13 Nov. 1918; G.S.O., No. 1 Tank Group, British Armies in France, 14 Nov. 1918, to 11 Feb. 1919; G.S.O., G.H.Q., British Armies in France, 12 to 27 Feb. 1919. He was created a C.M.G. in 1916, and given the Brevet of Lieutenant-Colonel 3 June, 1918. Lieut.-Colonel Crossman married, in 1914, Julia Mary Anne, eldest daughter of the late Rev. J. J. Tapson, Vicar of Hooe, South Devon.

BOND, CHARLES EARBERY, Lieut., was born 14 Oct. 1877. He was educated at Wellington, and entered the Royal Sussex Regt. 4 May, 1898; was promoted Lieutenant 2 April, 1899. He served in the South African War, 1900–2; took part in the operations in the Orange Free State, Feb. to May, 1900, including actions at Houtnek (Thoba Mountain), Vet River (5 and 6 May) and Zand River; was present during operations in the Transvaal in May and June, 1900, including actions near Johannesburg, Pretoria and Diamond Hill (11 and 12 June); in Orange River Colony, May to 29 Nov. 1900, including actions at Wittebergen (1 to 29 July); again in the Transvaal, Feb. to May, 1902, also in Orange River Colony and in Cape Colony, June, 1901, to Feb. 1902. He was mentioned in Despatches [London Gazette, 10 Sept. 1901, and 29 July, 1902]; received the Queen's Medal with four clasps, and the King's Medal with two clasps. He was created a Companion of the Distinguished Service Order [London Gazette, 31 Oct. 1902]: "Charles Earbery Bond, Lieut., Royal Sussex Regt. In recognition of services during the operations in South Africa." He was promoted Captain 2 Feb. 1907, and was Adjutant of the Royal Sussex Regt. 5 Oct. 1907, to 4 Oct. 1910. Capt. Bond served in the European War, 1914–18. He was promoted Major 1 Sept. 1915, and was Temporary Lieutenant-Colonel from 24 Nov. 1915, to 31 May, 1917, first with the Worcestershire Regt., and from Dec. 1915, commanding a Service battalion of the Border Regt. He was Brigade Commander, 51st Infantry Brigade, British Armies in France, 1 June, 1917, to 30 May, 1918, and on 1 July, 1918, became Brigade Commander, Chatham Reserve Infantry Brigade, Home Forces. He became Temporary Brigadier-General 1 June, 1917; was created a C.M.G. in 1916; was given the Brevet of Lieutenant-Colonel 1 Jan. 1918, and was five times mentioned in Despatches. He has the Mons Medal.

Charles Earbery Bond.

JOHNSON, CHARLES REGINALD, Lieut., was born 23 Dec. 1876, son of Lieut.-Colonel C. H. Johnson, M.P., of Thorngumbald, Yorkshire, and of Mrs. I. Johnson, of Hull, Yorkshire. He was educated at Clifton College, and entered the Army 29 July, 1896, in the Royal Engineers in which he was promoted Lieutenant 29 July, 1899. He served in South Africa, 1899–1902, taking part in the advance on Kimberley, including actions at Belmont, Enslin, Modder River and Magersfontein; operations in the Orange Free State, Feb. to May, 1900, including operations at Paardeberg, actions at Poplar Grove and Dreifontein; operations in the Transvaal, west of Pretoria, July to Nov. 1900, including action at Frederickstad; operations in Orange River Colony, May to July, 1900: operations in the Transvaal and Orange River Colony, 1900 to 1902. He was mentioned in Despatches [London Gazette, 29 July, 1902]; received the Queen's Medal with five clasps; the King's Medal with two clasps and was created a Companion of the Distinguished Service Order [London Gazette, 31 Oct. 1902]: "Charles Reginald Johnson, Lieut., Royal Engineers. In recognition of services during the operations in South Africa." He was employed as Instructor at the Royal Military Academy, Aug. 1903, to Sept. 1904, and as Assistant Adjutant, Royal Military Academy, Sept. 1904, to Sept. 1905. He was promoted Captain 29 July, 1905, and was from Sept. 1905, to the end of 1908, an officer of a Company of Gentleman Cadets at the Royal Military Academy. From 1909 to 1913 he commanded the 2nd Field Troop, Royal Engineers, which was stationed at Potchefstroom, South Africa. He was promoted Major 30 Oct. 1914. Major Johnson served in the European War, 1914–18. From Oct. 1914, to March, 1916, he commanded the 2nd Field Squadron Royal Engineers, of the 2nd Cavalry Division, and took part in the First and Second Battles of Ypres; from April, 1916, to Jan. 1917, he was employed at Aldershot; from Feb. 1917, to March, 1919, he was C.R.E. of the 4th Division, and took part in the final advance in Oct. and Nov. 1918. He was wounded twice; was mentioned in Despatches five times; was given the Brevet of Lieutenant-Colonel, and created a C.M.G. (1919) for his services. He also has the Order of St. Stanislas, 3rd Class. Lieut.-Colonel Johnson married, in 1904, Ida, daughter of F. A. Hutchinson, Esq., of Preston, Yorkshire, and they have two sons.

BAYFORD, EDMUND HESELTINE, Lieut., was born 16 March, 1873, son of Robert Augustus Bayford, Esq., K.C., and Emily Jane, daughter of the late John Deverell, of Purbrook, Hampshire. He was educated at Eton, and joined the Army, as a Second Lieutenant, in the 18th (Queen Mary's Own) Hussars, 10 Oct. 1894, becoming Lieutenant 5 Aug. 1899. He served in the South African War, 1899–1902; took part in the operations in Natal, 1899, including action at Talana (wounded) and Lombard's Kop; was present at the defence of Ladysmith, including sortie of 7 Dec. 1899: was present during operations in Natal, March to June, 1900, including action at Laing's Nek (6 to 9 June); in the Transvaal, east of Pretoria, July to 29 Nov. 1900, including actions at Belfast (26 and 27 Aug.) and Lydenberg (5 to 8 Sept.); again in the Transvaal 30 Nov, 1900, to April, 1901, and Dec. 1901, to 31 May, 1902; also in Orange River Colony, March and May, 1902. He was mentioned in Despatches [London Gazette, 10 Sept. 1901, and 29 July, 1902]; received the Queen's Medal with five clasps, and the King's Medal with two clasps. He was created a Companion of the Distinguished Service Order [London Gazette, 31 Oct. 1902]: "Edmund Heseltine Bayford, Lieut., 18th Hussars. In recognition of services during the operations in South Africa." From 1903 to 1906 he was A.D.C. to the Governor of Bombay. He was promoted Captain 20 March, 1906; was Adjutant of the 18th Hussars 20 March, 1906, to 18 June, 1909, and Adjutant in the Territorial Force 19 June, 1909, to 31 Dec. 1912. He served in the European War. He was Brigade Major, 1st South-Western Mounted Brigade, Central Force, Home Defence, 11 Aug. 1914, to 23 Feb. 1916; G.S.O.3, 24th Division, British Armies in France, 9 June to 22 Oct. 1916; Brigade Major, 14th Canadian Infantry Brigade, England, 7 Nov. 1916, to 17 Aug. 1917; Brigade Major, 48th

Infantry Brigade, British Armies in France, 24 Sept. 1917, to 2 Jan. 1918. He was promoted Major 17 June, 1918; Brigade Major, 201st Infantry Brigade, Forces in Great Britain, 18 Oct. 1918, to 3 March, 1919. He is Adjutant of the City of London Yeomanry (Rough Riders). Major Bayford married, in 1911, Muriel, only daughter of John Buller-Colthurst.

DEEDES, CHARLES PARKER, Lieut., was born 9 Aug. 1879, at Nether Broughton, near Melton Mowbray, son of the Rev. Philip Deedes, of Little Parndon, Essex, and Josephine, daughter of Joseph Parker, Esq., of Brettenham Park, Suffolk. He was educated at Winchester College, and at the Royal Military College, Sandhurst, and joined the Yorkshire Light Infantry, as Second Lieutenant, 11 Feb. 1899. He became Lieutenant 9 Oct. 1899. He served in the South African War, as Adjutant, 20th Battn. Mounted Infantry, from Dec. 1901, to 31 May, 1902, taking part in operations in the Transvaal, April to Dec. 1901, and April to 31 May, 1902; operations in Orange River Colony, Jan. to March, 1902; operations in Cape Colony, March, 1901. He was mentioned in Despatches [London Gazette, 29 July, 1902]; received the Queen's Medal with five clasps, and was created a Companion of the Distinguished Service Order [London Gazette, 31 Oct. 1902]: "Charles Parker Deedes, Lieut., The King's Own Yorkshire Light Infantry. In recognition of services during the operations in South Africa." He became Captain 21 March, 1903, and served as Adjutant, 1st Battn. King's Own Yorkshire Light Infantry, 6 April, 1905, to 5 April, 1908. Capt. Deedes passed the Staff College, 1911, and was General Staff Officer, 3rd Grade, Scottish Command, 1 April, 1912, to 4 May, 1913; G.S.O., 3rd Grade, War Office, 5 May to 4 Aug. 1914. During the European War he was G.S.O., 3rd Grade, at G.H.Q., France, 5 Aug. 1914, to 8 Feb. 1915; G.S.O., 2nd Grade, G.H.Q., 9 Feb. 1915, to 2 Jan. 1916; was promoted Major 15 Sept. 1915; was G.S.O.2, 14th Army Corps, British Expeditionary Force, 3 Jan. to 3 April, 1916; G.S.O.1, 2nd Division, British Armies in France, 14 April, 1916, to 6 May, 1917; G.S.O.1, War Office (temporary), 7 May, 1917, to 13 Jan. 1918; became Temporary Brigadier-General and Deputy Director of Staff Duties, War Office (temporary), 1 Feb. 1918. He was given three Brevets: that of Major 3 June, 1915; of Lieutenant-Colonel 1 Jan. 1917, and of Colonel 1 Jan. 1918. He was seven times mentioned in Despatches. Brevet Colonel Deedes was created a C.M.G., 1916, and a C.B., 1919; is a Chevalier of the Legion of Honour, and holds the American Distinguished Service Medal and the French Croix de Guerre. He is an excellent cricketer; besides playing in 1898 for the Royal Military College, Sandhurst, and captaining the Staff College Cricket Eleven, Camberley, in 1911, he has played for Hertfordshire, and is a Member of the M.C.C. and the Free Foresters. Capt. Deedes married, 4 July, 1906, at Brompton Oratory, London, Eve Mary, only daughter of Capt. Stanley Dean-Pitt, C.B., R.N., and they have two children: Charles Julius, born 18 Oct. 1913, and Mary Josephine, born 7 March, 1910.

Charles Parker Deedes.

ROMILLY, BERTRAM HENRY SAMUEL, Lieut., was born 6 Nov. 1878, eldest son of Samuel Henry Romilly, Esq., J.P., D.L., of Huntington Park, Herefordshire, and of Lady Arabella Charlotte (died 1897), eldest daughter of the 9th Earl of Southesk and sister of the 10th Earl. He entered the Army, 9 March, 1898, as a Second Lieutenant in the Scots Guards. He was promoted Lieutenant 1 Dec. 1899. Lieut. Romilly served in the South African War from 1899 to 1902. He took part in the advance on Kimberley; operations in the Orange Free State, Feb. to May, 1900, including actions at Poplar Grove, Dreifontein, Vet River (5 and 6 May), and Zand River; operations in the Transvaal, May and June, 1900, including actions near Johannesburg, Pretoria, and Diamond Hill (11 and 12 June); operations in the Transvaal, east of Pretoria, July to 29 Nov. 1900, including action at Belfast (26 and 27 Aug.); operations in the Transvaal, west of Pretoria, July to 29 Nov. 1900; operations in Orange River Colony, May to 29 Nov. 1900; operations in the Transvaal, Dec. 1900, to July, 1901; operations in Orange River Colony from July, 1901; operations in Cape Colony, Dec. 1900. He was mentioned twice in Despatches [London Gazette, 10 Sept. 1901, and 29 July, 1902]; received the Queen's Medal with five clasps, and was created a Companion of the Distinguished Service Order [London Gazette, 31 Oct. 1902]: "Bertram Henry Samuel Romilly, Lieut., Scots Guards. In recognition of services during the operations in South Africa." In 1903 he was attached to the Egyptian Camel Corps, and was employed with the Egyptian Army from Dec. 1903, to Aug. 1906, and again from Sept. 1907, being in the interval Adjutant of the Scots Guards. He was promoted Captain 7 March, 1904, and Major 16 Sept. 1914. He served in the European War, 1914 to 1915, and was wounded. He was mentioned in Despatches and given the Brevet of Lieutenant-Colonel 10 March, 1915. He was temporary Lieutenant-Colonel, Scots Guards, from April to Oct. 1917, and then became Temporary Lieutenant-Colonel of the Reserve Battn. Scots Guards. In 1919 Lieut.-Colonel Romilly was appointed Military Governor of the province of Tiberias, Palestine. He married, in 1915, Nellie, daughter of the late Colonel Sir Henry Hozier (brother of the late Lord Newlands), and of Lady Blanche Hozier, daughter of the 7th Earl of Airlie, and they have two sons.

CAMPBELL, WILLIAM ROBINSON, Lieut., was born 26 Nov. 1876, eldest son of Sir Charles Campbell, 10th Bart. On 11 Feb. 1899, he entered the Army as a Second Lieutenant in the 14th Hussars, in which he was promoted Lieutenant 13 Dec. 1899. He served in the South African War, 1899–1902; was present at the Relief of Ladysmith, including operations of 5 to 7 Feb. 1900, and action at Vaal Kranz; in the operations on Tugela Heights (14 to 27 Feb. 1900) and action at Pieter's Hill; took part in th operations in the Orange Free State, Feb. to May, 1900, including action at Houtnek (Thoba Mountain) and Zand River; in the Transvaal in Ma and June, 1900, including actions near Johannesburg, Pretoria and Diamon Hill (11 and 12 June); in the Transvaal, east of Pretoria, July to 29 Nov 1900, including actions at Belfast (26 and 27 Aug.); in operations in th Transvaal, 30 Nov. 1900, to June, 1901; in Orange River Colony, Feb. t 31 May, 1902; on the Zululand Frontier of Natal in Sept. 1901. He serve as Adjutant of the 14th Hussars from 12 Aug. 1901. He was mentioned i Despatches [London Gazette, 10 Sept. 1901 and 29 July, 1902]; receive the Queen's Medal with seven clasps, and the King's Medal with two clasps and was created a Companion of the Distinguished Service Order [Londo Gazette, 31 Oct. 1902]: "William Robinson Campbell, Lieut., 14th Hussars In recognition of services during the operations in South Africa." He wa employed as Adjutant of the 14th Hussars until 11 Aug. 1904; was promote Captain 30 May, 1904, and was Adjutant of Imperial Yeomanry 10 Sept 1906, to 31 March, 1908, and in the Territorial Force 1 April, 1908, to 2 March, 1911. He attained his Majority 22 Feb. 1911. Major Campbel served in the European War, and was killed in action in Flanders on 13 May 1915. He had married, in 1907, Maud Kathleen, youngest daughter o the late Capt. S. Y. H. Davenport, 47th Loyal North Lancashire Regt.

HOWARD, GEOFFREY WESTON, Lieut., was born 14 Dec. 1876 third son of Henry Howard, of Stone House, Worcester. He entered th Army as a Second Lieutenant in the Essex Regt. 1 Dec. 1897, and wa promoted Lieutenant 29 Jan. 1900. He was A.D.C. to Major-General South Africa, from 5 March, 1900, to 21 July, 1906, and served in the Sout African War, 1899–1902. He took part in the Relief of Kimberley; wa present during the operations in the Orange Free State, Feb. to May, 1900 including those at Paardeberg (17 to 26 Feb.); actions at Poplar Grove an Dreifontein; in the Transvaal in May and June, 1900, including action near Johannesburg, Pretoria and Diamond Hill (11 and 12 June); in the Transvaal, east of Pretoria, July to 29 Nov. 1900, including action at Belfast (26 and 27 Aug.); in Cape Colony, south of Orange River, 1899–1900 including actions at Colesberg (1 Jan. to 12 Feb.) (Despatches [London Gazette, 10 Sept. 1901, and 29 July, 1902]; Queen's Medal with six clasps and King's Medal with two clasps). He was created a Companion of the Distinguished Service Order [London Gazette, 31 Oct. 1902]: "Geoffrey Weston Howard, Lieut., Essex Regt. In recognition of services during the operations in South Africa." He became Captain 25 Dec. 1907, and wa appointed G.S.O.3, Malta, 25 April, 1914. Capt. Howard served in the European War from 1914 to 1918. He held the appointment of Brigade Major, 48th Infantry Brigade, New Armies, B.E.F., 22 April, 1915, to 5 Feb. 1916. He was promoted Major 1 Sept. 1915; was G.S.O.2, 2nd Army, B.E.F., British Armies in France, 6 Feb. to 11 Aug. 1916; G.S.O.2, 24th Division, British Armies in France, 12 Aug. to 14 Oct. 1916; was Temporary Lieutenant-Colonel from 15 Oct. 1916, until given the Brevet of Lieutenant-Colonel 3 June, 1917; and G.S.O.1, 7th Division, British Armies in France, British Force in Italy, 15 Oct. 1916, to 8 Oct. 1918; Temporary Brigadier-General, 9 Oct. 1918, to 3 March, 1919, while Brigade Commander of the 145th Infantry Brigade, British Force in Italy; was given the Brevet o Colonel 3 June, 1919. He was mentioned in Despatches seven times, and was made a C.M.G. in 1919. He married, in 1905, M ta Minnie Gregory.

WILLIS, EVELYN STUART CONSTANTINE, Lieut., was born 6 Oct. 1879, son of Richard A. Willis, M.A., formerly of The Hermitage, Woking, and of Marion Willis. He was educated at Harrow, and Heidelberg College, and entered the Devonshire Regt. 11 Feb. 1899. He was promoted Lieutenant 24 Feb. 1900, and served in South Africa, 1899–1902, taking part in the Relief of Ladysmith, including action at Colenso; operations of 17 to 24 Jan 1900, and action at Spion Kop; operations of 5 to 7 Feb. 1900, and action at Vaal Kranz; operations on Tugela Heights (14 to 27 Feb. 1900) and action at Pieter's Hill; operations in Natal, March to June, 1900; operations in the Transvaal, east of Pretoria, July to 24 Nov. 1900, including actions at Lydenberg (5 to 8 Sept.); operations in the Transvaal, 30 Nov. 1900, to Dec. 1901. He was mentioned in Despatches [London Gazette, 17 Jan. 1902]; received the Queen's and King's Medals with five clasps, and was created a Companion of the Distinguished Service Order [London Gazette, 31 Oct. 1902]: "Evelyn Stuart Constantine Willis, Lieut., The Devonshire Regt. In recognition of services during the operations in South Africa." He was transferred to the 58th Rifles, Frontier Force, Indian Army, 10 Dec. 1903, and became Captain 11 Feb. 1908, and Major on 1 Sept. 1915. He served in the European War in France from 1914 to March, 1917; in Mesopotamia, 1917; in Palestine, 1918, and in Cilicia, 1919, serving both as a regimental officer and on the Staff in each theatre; he was wounded 23 Nov. 1914; mentioned in Despatches in 1914, for gallantry in action at Festubert, and again in 1917, and was given the Brevet of Lieutenant-Colonel in 1919. Lieut.-Colonel Willis married, in 1915, Frances Fernande, daughter of G. Blanchard Fry, of Osterley Court, Middlesex.

Evelyn S. C. Willis.

MOORE, ATHELSTAN, Lieut., was born 9 July, 1879, and was the second son of the late Edward S. F. Moore, Barrister-at-Law, and Mrs. Moore. He joined the Royal Dublin Fusiliers from the 3rd Durham Light Infantry, 18 Oct. 1899, and proceeded to South Africa, where he took part in the Relief of Ladysmith and the action at Tugela Heights, after which he commanded a Mounted Infantry Company of the Royal Dublin Fusiliers until the termination of hostilities, taking part in the operations in the

Transvaal, Dec. 1900, to May, 1901; Aug. to Sept. 1901, and Jan. to May, 1902. He was mentioned in Despatches [London Gazette, 29 July, 1902]; received the King's and Queen's Medals with four clasps, and was created a Companion of the Distinguished Service Order [London Gazette, 31 Oct. 1902]: "Athelstan Moore, Lieut., Royal Dublin Fusiliers. In recognition of services during the operations in South Africa." He was seconded to the West African Field Force in Dec. 1902, and saw active service in 1903 in the Kano-Sokoto Campaign, Northern Nigeria (Medal and clasp); in Southern Nigeria, 1903 (clasp); Southern Nigeria, 1903–4 (Despatches [London Gazette, 25 Aug. 1905]; clasp); Southern Nigeria, 1904 (clasp); the Bende-Onitsha Hinterland Expedition, Southern Nigeria, 1905–6 (clasp). He became Captain 21 June, 1908. Capt. A. Moore was employed with the New Zealand Military Forces from 1 April, 1911, when he was appointed Instructor in Infantry duties of the Otago Military District, and Brigade Major of the Otago Infantry, with Headquarters at Dunedin. During the European War he commanded the 2nd Otago Regt. in the Suez Canal in 1914–15, landing in Gallipoli in April, 1915. In Nov. of the same year he was severely wounded. He rejoined the Otago Regt. in France in May, 1916, and was transferred to the command of the 2nd Royal Munster Fusiliers in Aug. 1916, and was engaged in the fighting on the Somme until Jan. He underwent an operation at home, returned to France, and assumed command of the 1st Royal Dublin Fusiliers in April, 1917. He died on 14 Oct. 1918, of wounds received the same day at Dadizeele, on the road to Courtrai, Belgium. In the Great War he was mentioned in Despatches, was given the Brevet of Lieutenant-Colonel, and wounded five times. He had married Norah Kathleen Moore, and left one son.

BENSON, CHARLES BINGLEY, Lieut., was born 21 Aug. 1876, son of the late J. R. Benson, M.D. He was educated at Radley, and joined the Army 4 Jan. 1899, as a Second Lieutenant in the Oxford and Buckinghamshire Light Infantry. He served in the South African War, 1901–2, with the Mounted Infantry, taking part in operations in Orange River Colony, March to Dec. 1901, and Jan. to May, 1902; operations in Cape Colony, Feb. to March, 1901, and Dec. 1901, to Jan. 1902. He was mentioned in Despatches [London Gazette, 29 July, 1902]; received the Queen's Medal with four clasps, and was created a Companion of the Distinguished Service Order [London Gazette, 31 Oct. 1902]: "Charles Bingley Benson, Lieut., Oxfordshire and Buckinghamshire Light Infantry. In recognition of services during the operations in South Africa." He was promoted Captain 4 May, 1905, and was placed on retired pay 14 March, 1914. He served in the European War in France, Belgium and Germany, 1917 to 1919. He was promoted Major in the Reserve of Officers in Sept. 1915, and subsequently became Lieutenant-Colonel. For his services he was mentioned in Despatches, and awarded a Bar to the Distinguished Service Order. He married, in 1904, Maud Margaret, only daughter of the late Colonel L. F. Heath, Indian Army, and they have one daughter.

Charles Bingley Benson.

STEPHEN, ALBERT ALEXANDER LESLIE, Lieut., was born 3 Feb. 1879, son of Major J. Z. Stephen and Augusta Henrietta Mary (*née* Ricketts). He was educated at Eton, and joined the Scots Guards 4 Jan. 1899, becoming Lieutenant 4 April, 1900. He served in the South African War, in which he was present at a large number of engagements. He took part in the advance on Kimberley, with the action at Belmont, and was present at Enslin, Modder River and Magersfontein, and also at the operations in the Orange Free State, Transvaal, Orange River Colony and Cape Colony, including actions at Poplar Grove, Dreifontein, Vet and Zand Rivers; the action near Johannesburg, those at Pretoria, Diamond Hill and Belfast. From Jan. 1901, he was Assistant Provost-Marshal to Pulteney's Column, and he was Intelligence Officer to Garrett's Column in 1902. He was twice mentioned in Despatches [London Gazette, 10 Sept. 1901, and 29 July, 1902]; received the Queen's Medal with six clasps; the King's Medal with two clasps, and was created a Companion of the Distinguished Service Order [London Gazette, 31 Oct. 1902]: "Albert Alexander Leslie Stephen, Lieut., Scots Guards. In recognition of services during the operations in South Africa." He was promoted Captain 10 April, 1904, and from April, 1906, to March, 1909, was employed with the Macedonian Gendarmerie under the Foreign Office; from March, 1909, to Jan. 1911, with the Turkish Gendarmerie. He was awarded the Order of the Medjidie, 3rd Class, and in 1911 the Coronation Medal. From Sept. 1910, to Sept. 1913, he was an Adjutant of the Territorial Force, and in April, 1914, was appointed Adjutant of the 1st Battn. of his own regiment. Capt. Stephen served in the European War, and was killed in action on the 31st of Oct. 1914, just 12 years to the day after his D.S.O. was gazetted.

CLAYHILLS, GEORGE, Lieut., was born at Darlington 24 July, 1878, fourth son of Thomas Clayhills, of Invergowrie, Forfarshire, and Thornton-le-Moor, Yorkshire, by his wife, Elizabeth, daughter of John Rob, of Catton, Yorkshire. He was educated at Cheltenham College, and Trinity Hall, Cambridge. He received his commission, and joined the 4th Battn. of the Cheshire Regt. 8 Sept. 1896, from which he was gazetted Second Lieutenant, 1st Battn. East Lancashire Regt., 4 Jan. 1899; and was promoted Lieutenant, 4 June, 1900, and Captain, 8 Feb. 1908; and was Adjutant of his regiment from April, 1906, to April, 1909. He went with his regiment to South Africa, and served with the 8th Mounted Infantry during the war, 1900–2, and took part in the operations at Paardeberg, and actions at Poplar Grove, Dreifontein, Karee Siding, Vet River and Zand River, and engagements near Johannesburg and Pretoria; operations in the Transvaal and Orange River Colony from Nov. 1900, to the end of the war. He was twice mentioned in Despatches (by Lords Roberts and Kitchener) [London Gazette, 10 Sept. 1901, and 17 Jan. 1902]; received the Queen's Medal with four clasps, and the King's Medal with two clasps, and was created a Companion of the Distinguished Service Order [London Gazette, 31 Oct. 1902]: "George Clayhills, Lieut., The East Lancashire Regt. In recognition of services during the operations in South Africa." He was Adjutant, East Lancashire Regt., from April, 1906, to April, 1909, and became Captain 8 Feb. 1908. On the outbreak of the European War he left with his regiment for the Front in Aug. 1914, and served in France and Flanders, taking part in the Retreat from Mons, the Battles of the Marne and the Aisne. Miss Clayhills writes: "George led an attack and cleared a wood in a very fine way, 31 Oct. . . . There is an account in Conan Doyle's book of a fight the 1st East Lancashire Regt. did well in, and Colonel Lawrence wrote that my brother led his company so well that day that he forwarded his name for mention in Despatches. It never appeared—I was told so many were killed about that time that the names of nearly all the fallen were cut out. The following is Conan Doyle's account: 'The British Campaign in France and Flanders, 1914' (page 229): 'La Bassée–Armentières operations on 21 Oct.—The Germans crossed the River Lys in considerable force, and upon the morning of the 22nd they succeeded in occupying the village of Le Gheir upon the western side, thus threatening to outflank the positions of the 2nd Cavalry Division to the north. In their advance in the early morning of the 22nd they stormed the trenches held by the 2nd Inniskilling Fusiliers, this regiment enduring considerable loss. The trenches on the right were held by the 1st Royal Lancasters and 2nd Lancashire Fusiliers. These two regiments were at once ordered by General Aulay of the 12th Brigade to initiate a counter-attack under the lead of Colonel Buller. Aulay himself, who is a hard-bitten soldier, moved forward his men, while General Hunter Weston, the indefatigable blower-up of railway lines in South Africa, supported the counter-attack with the Somerset Light Infantry and the 1st East Lancashire Regt. The latter regiment, under Colonel Lawrence, passed through a wood and reached such a position that they were able to enfilade the Germans in the open, causing them very heavy losses. The action was a brilliant success. The positions lost were reoccupied and the enemy severely punished; over a thousand Germans were killed and wounded, while 300 were taken prisoners. These belonged to the 104th and 179th Saxon Regts.'" Capt. Clayhills was killed in action at the First Battle of Ypres, 2 Nov. 1914, near Armentières, and was buried about three miles north of that town and one mile east of the Ploegsteert-le-Chair Road. Capt. Clayhills was a good all-round sportsman, a good rider, fond of hunting, shooting and cricket, and, in fact, all games and sport. Three of his great-uncles fought at Waterloo; his grandfather was in the Navy guarding the Channel at the time.

WILSON, (THE HONOURABLE) GUY GREVILLE, Lieut., was born 19 May, 1877, son of the 1st Baron Nunburnholme and Florence, daughter of Colonel W. H. C. Wellesley; and brother of the 2nd Baron Nunburnholme, who was also awarded the D.S.O. for services in the Boer War. He was educated at Eton, and joined the 11th Hussars 11 May, 1898. He served in South Africa in 1902, with Damant's Horse (formerly Rimington's Guides), taking part in operations in the Transvaal, Orange River Colony and Cape Colony. He was mentioned in Despatches [London Gazette, 29 July, 1902]; received the Queen's Medal with five clasps, and was created a Companion of the Distinguished Service Order [London Gazette, 31 Oct. 1902]: "Guy Greville Wilson, Lieut., 11th Hussars. In recognition of services during the operations in South Africa." He left the Army in 1903. He became M.P. for West Hull in 1907, and is Deputy Lieutenant for East Riding of Yorkshire and a Director of Thomas Wilson and Company Ltd., Shipowners, Hull, and of Earle's Shipbuilding and Engineering Company Ltd., Hull. He was Parliamentary Private Secretary to the First Lord of the Admiralty, 1915, and served from 1915 to 1918 in Egypt and Palestine. He was three times mentioned in Despatches for his services, and was created a C.M.G. in 1919. He is Lieutenant-Colonel in command of the East Riding of Yorkshire Imperial Yeomanry. His favourite recreations are shooting, golf and hunting. The Honourable G. G. Wilson married, (1stly), in 1904, Lady Isabel Innes-Ker (died 1905), third daughter of the 7th Duke of Roxburghe and Anne V. A., daughter of the 7th Duke of Marlborough, K.G.; and (2ndly), in 1911, Avery, third daughter of Geoffrey Buxton and Mary, daughter of the Honourable and Rev. John Harbord, and has three daughters: Oriel Susan; Malise Joy, and Alison Ann.

DAWNAY, GUY PAYAN, Lieut., was born 23 March, 1878, at St. James's Palace, London, S.W., son of Lieut.-Colonel the Honourable Lewis Payan Dawnay, second son of the 7th Viscount Downe and Lady Victoria Grey, sister of the 4th Earl Grey. He was educated at Eton College, and Magdalen College, Oxford, and joined the 1st Battn. Coldstream Guards at Gibraltar, July, 1899. He became Lieutenant 10 July, 1900. He served throughout the South African War of 1899–1902, taking part in the advance on Kimberley, including the actions at Belmont, Enslin, Modder River and Magersfontein; operations in the Orange Free State, Feb. to May, 1900 including the actions at Poplar Grove, Dreifontein, Vet River (5 and 6 May), and Zand River; operations in the Transvaal in May and June, 1900, including actions near Johannesburg, Pretoria and Diamond Hill (11 and 12 June); operations in the Transvaal, east of Pretoria, July to Nov. 1900, including the actions at Belfast (26 and 27 Aug.); operations in the Orange River Colony, Nov. 1900; operations in the Transvaal, Oct. 1901, to 31 May, 1902; operations in Cape Colony 30 Nov. 1900, to Oct. 1901. He carried out the duties of Railway Staff Officer, May to June, 1901, and was afterwards on the Staff. He was mentioned in Despatches [London Gazette, 29 July, 1902]; received the Queen's Medal with six clasps, and the King's Medal with two clasps, and was created a Companion of the Distinguished Service Order, particularly for his services when A.D.C. to General Sir Bruce Hamilton, K.C.B. [London Gazette, 31 Oct. 1902]: "Guy Payan Dawnay, Lieut., Coldstream Guards. In recognition of services during the operations in South Africa." Lieut. Dawnay was A.D.C. to the Major-General, 5th Brigade, 1st Army Corps, 9 April, 1903, to 29 Feb. 1904; A.D.C. to the Major-General, 2nd Division and 3rd Brigade, 1st Army Corps, 1 March to 1 May, 1904; A.D.C. to the Major-General, 2nd Division, 1st Army Corps, 2 May to 15 June, 1904. He was Adjutant of the Guards' Depôt from 5 Nov. 1904, to 4 Nov. 1906, and was made an M.V.O. in 1906. He was at the Staff College in 1908 and 1909; was promoted Captain 16 Feb. 1909, and joined the Committee of Imperial Defence in 1910. In the following year he left the Coldstream Guards with the rank of Captain, and joined the Reserve of Officers. Capt. Dawnay served in the European War from its outbreak to 30 April, 1919. He took part with distinction in the Dardanelles Campaign, March, 1915, to Jan. 1916; the fighting in Egypt and Sinai, 1916; in Palestine, until the taking of Jerusalem, 1917; in France, 1918 to 1919. He was mentioned in Despatches eleven times; created a C.B. and C.M.G. in 1918, and was given the Brevets of Major and Lieutenant-Colonel, and awarded the following foreign distinctions: the Legion of Honour (Officier); Order of St. Anne (Russia); Order of St. Maurice and St. Lazarus (Italy), and the Distinguished Service Medal (U.S.A.). He was promoted Lieutenant-Colonel 3 May, 1919, and retired with the rank of honorary Major-General. Major-General Dawnay married, 12 July, 1906, at Holy Trinity, Sloane Street, S.W., Cecil, youngest daughter of the late Francis W. Buxton, Esq., and the Hon. Mrs. Buxton, and their children are: Pamela; Christopher Payan (born 6 July, 1909), and Elizabeth Lavender.

POPHAM, ROBERT STEWART, Lieut., was born 27 July, 1876, son of Benjamin Popham, of Kinsale, Cork. He was educated at Trinity College, Dublin, and joined the Army 20 May, 1899, in the Derbyshire Regt. He became Lieutenant, Notts and Derbyshire Regt., 13 July, 1900. He served in South Africa, 1899–1902, being employed from 7 Oct. 1901, as Staff Officer and Assistant Provost-Marshal. He was present at operations in the Orange Free State, including the actions at Houtnek (Thoba Mountain), Vet River and Zand River; operations in the Transvaal, including actions near Johannesburg, Pretoria and Diamond Hill; operations in the Transvaal, west of Pretoria; operations in Orange River Colony, including action at Wittebergen; operations in Cape Colony, south of Orange River; operations in the Transvaal 30 Nov. 1900, to 31 May, 1902. He was mentioned in Despatches [London Gazette, 10 Sept. 1901]; received the Queen's Medal with four clasps, and the King's Medal with two clasps, and was created a Companion of the Distinguished Service Order [London Gazette, 31 Oct. 1902]: "Robert Stewart Popham, Lieut., The Derbyshire Regt. In recognition of services during the operations in South Africa." He served as Adjutant of his regiment, 1 Feb. 1904, to 31 Jan. 1907, and became Captain 22 Feb. 1906; was Adjutant, Special Reserve, 6 March, 1911, to 5 March, 1914. Serving in the European War, he was promoted Major 1 Sept. 1915; was Brigade Major, 104th Infantry Brigade, 96th Infantry Brigade, New Armies, B.E.F., and British Armies in France, 12 Jan. 1915, to 6 Sept. 1916; G.S.O.2, 55th Division, British Armies in France, 7 Sept. 1916, to 1 March, 1917; G.S.O.2, 8th Army Corps, British Armies in France, 2 May, 1917, to 6 Feb. 1918; G.S.O.2, Headquarters, British Salonika Force, 3 March to 18 May, 1918; was appointed G.S.O.1, G.H.Q., British Salonika Force, 19 May, 1918, and promoted Temporary Lieutenant-Colonel. He was mentioned in Despatches four times; awarded the Brevet of Lieutenant-Colonel 3 June, 1918, and created a C.M.G. in 1919, for his services in the Great War. In 1907 Colonel Popham married Mildred Mary Stewart, daughter of the late Major A. J. Roberts, 44th Regt., and they have one son: Robert Home Stewart, born on 4 May, 1909.

GRANT, ARCHIBALD SEAFIELD, Lieut., was born 17 Feb. 1878, eldest son of Major F. W. Seafield Grant, Oxfordshire Light Infantry, and Anne Seafield Grant, of 5, Third Avenue, Hove, Sussex. He was educated at Eton, and entered the Army 11 Jan. 1899, with a commission in the Royal Highlanders (The Black Watch). He served in the South African War, 1899–1902, taking part in the advance on Kimberley, including action at Magersfontein; operations in Cape Colony, south of Orange River, 1899; operations in Cape Colony, Nov. 1900, to May, 1902. He was employed on the Staff. He was mentioned in Despatches [London Gazette, 29 July, 1902]; received the Queen's Medal with three clasps; the King's Medal with two clasps, and was created a Companion of the Distinguished Service Order [London Gazette, 31 Oct. 1902]: "Archibald Seafield Grant, Lieut., The Black Watch (Royal Highlanders). In recognition of services during the operations in South Africa." He became Captain 15 Feb. 1906, and retired 4 Feb. 1914. Capt. Grant served in the European War, 1914–18, as Deputy Assistant Director of Railway Transport. He was mentioned in General French's Despatches of Dec. 1914. He became Major, Reserve of Officers, Royal Highlanders, 1 Sept. 1915

PITT-TAYLOR, WALTER WILLIAM, Lieut., was born 30 Aug. 1878, son of Charles Pitt-Taylor, Esq. He was educated at Eton, and became Second Lieutenant, Rifle Brigade, 18 Oct. 1899; Lieutenant 1 Aug. 1900. He served in the South African Campaign from Nov. 1899, to the end of the war with the 1st Battn. Rifle Brigade, being present at the Relief of Ladysmith, including action at Colenso; operations of 17 to 24 Jan. 1900; operations of 5 to 7 Feb. 1900, and action at Vaal Kranz; operations on Tugela Heights 14 to 27 Feb. 1900, and action at Pieter's Hill; operations in Natal, March to June, 1900; operations in the Transvaal, east of Pretoria, July to 29 Nov. 1900; operations in the Transvaal, Dec. 1900, to 31 May, 1902. He was mentioned in Despatches [London Gazette, 29 July, 1902]; received the Queen's and King's Medals with six clasps, and was created a Companion of the Distinguished Service Order [London Gazette, 31 Oct. 1902]: "Walter William Pitt-Taylor, Lieut., Rifle Brigade. In recognition of services during the operations in South Africa." He was Adjutant, Rifle Brigade, 17 July, 1903, to 16 July, 1906; became Captain 23 Jan. 1905; was on Special Service in Egypt 5 Oct. 1908, to 4 April, 1909, and 3 Sept. to 4 Oct. 1909. Capt. Pitt-Taylor served in the European War. He was G.S.O. 3rd Grade, 3rd Army Corps, 5 Aug. 1914, to 31 March, 1915; Brigade Major, 12th Infantry Brigade, B.E.F., from 1 April to 30 Sept. 1915; G.S.O., 2nd Grade, 37th Division, from 1 Oct. 1915, to 4 Feb. 1916; G.S.O.1, 4th Army, B.E.F., British Armies in France, 5 Feb. 1916, to 30 Oct. 1917; G.S.O.1, 14th Army Corps, British Armies in France, 31 Oct. to 9 Nov. 1917; G.S.O.1, British Mission with the Italian Army, 11 Nov. 1917, to 27 Aug. 1918; Temporary Brigadier-General 28 Aug. 1918, to 9 March, 1919; Brigade Commander, 145th Infantry Brigade, British Armies in France, 28 Aug. to 8 Oct. 1918; Brigadier-General, General Staff, 14th Army Corps, British Armies in France, 9 Oct. 1918, to 9 March, 1919. He was appointed Temporary Military Assistant (G.S.O.1), Imperial General Staff, 10 March, 1919. Colonel Pitt-Taylor was nine times mentioned in Despatches; was given the Brevet of Major 3 June, 1915; of Lieutenant-Colonel 1 Jan. 1917, and of Colonel 3 June, 1918; was created a C.M.G. in 1918, and C.B. in 1919. He is an Officer of the Legion of Honour; has the French and Italian War Crosses and also the Italian Silver Medal for Valour.

HORE-RUTHVEN, THE HONOURABLE CHRISTIAN MALISE, Lieut., was born 24 April, 1880, third son of the 8th Lord Ruthven and Lady Caroline Annesley-Gore (died 1915), daughter of the 4th Earl of Arran, K.P. He was educated at Wellington, and joined the 1st Battn. The Black Watch 3 June, 1899. He was promoted Lieutenant 21 Oct. 1900. He served in the South African War, 1899–1902, taking part in the advance on Kimberley, including actions at Magersfontein; operations in the Orange Free State, Feb. to May, 1900, including the action at Vet River; operations in Orange River Colony, including actions at Wittebergen and Witpoort; operations in Cape Colony, south of Orange River, 1899; operations in the Transvaal, Dec. 1900, to Jan. 1902, and April and May, 1902; operations in Orange River Colony, Nov. 1900, and Feb. and March, 1902. He was mentioned in Despatches three times [London Gazette, 16 March, 1900; 10 Sept. 1901, and 29 July, 1902]; received the Queen's Medal and King's Medal with five clasps, and was created a Companion of the Distinguished Service Order [London Gazette, 31 Oct. 1902]: "The Hon. Christian Malise Hore-Ruthven, Lieut., The Black Watch, Royal Highlanders. In recognition of services during the operations in South Africa." He was promoted Captain 1 May, 1906; was attached to the Egyptian Army from 7 May, 1906, to 29 July, 1908; was A.D.C. to the Viceroys of India and Ireland. Capt. C. M. Hore-Ruthven served in the Great War. He was G.S.O.3, Highland Division, Central Force, Home Defence, 5 to 17 Aug. 1914, and Staff Captain, Scottish Horse Brigade, Central Force, Home Defence, 18 Aug. to 21 Sept. 1914; was Brigade Major, 54th Infantry Brigade, New Armies, British Expeditionary Force, 10 Feb. 1915, to 18 Feb. 1916. He was promoted Major 1 Sept. 1915; was G.S.O.2, 2nd Canadian Division, British Expeditionary Force, British Armies in France, 19 Feb. 1916, to 17 Feb. 1917; G.S.O.1, 5th Canadian Division, England, 27 Feb. to 29 July, 1917; G.S.O.1, 3rd Canadian Division, British Armies in France, 5 Aug. 1917, to 5 Feb. 1919; G.S.O.1, 15th Division, British Armies in France, 6 Feb. to 31 March, 1919; became G.S.O.1, 59th Division, British Armies in France, British Troops in France and Flanders, 1 April, 1919. For his services he was mentioned in Despatches; given the Brevet of Lieutenant-Colonel 1 Jan. 1917, and was created a C.M.G. in 1918. His favourite recreation is hunting.

MACLACHLAN, ALEXANDER FRASER CAMPBELL, Lieut., was born at Newton Valence, Hampshire, 23 July, 1875, son of the late Rev. A. N. Campbell Maclachlan, Vicar and Patron of Newton Valence, Hampshire. He was educated at Cheam School, Eton, and Magdalen College Oxford (B.A., 1897), and entered the Army 18 Oct. 1899, as a Second Lieutenant in the King's Royal Rifle Corps, in which he was promoted Lieutenant 14 Nov. 1900. He served in the South African War, 1899–1902; was present at the Relief of Ladysmith, including action at Colenso; operations of 17 to 24 Jan. 1900, and action at Spion Kop; operations of 5 to 7 Feb. 1900, and action at Vaal Kranz; in the operations on Tugela Heights 14 to 22 Feb. 1900 (severely wounded); afterwards O.C., Rest Camp, Machadadorp. He was mentioned in Despatches [London Gazette, 8 Feb. and 10 Sept. 1901, and 29 July, 1902]; received the Queen's Medal with four clasps, and the King's Medal with two clasps. He was created a Companion of the Distinguished Service Order for gallantry at Pieter's Hill, South Africa [London Gazette, 31 Oct. 1902]: "Alexander Fraser Campbell Maclachlan, Lieut., King's Royal Rifle Corps. In recognition of services during the operations in South Africa." He was promoted Captain 25 Aug. 1906, and was Adjutant of the King's Royal Rifle Corps 10 Dec. 1907, to 30 Nov. 1910. He received the Durbar Medal for serving on the King's Staff during His Majesty's visit to India, 1911–12 as extra A.D.C. He served in the European War with the First Expeditionary Force; was present at the Retreat from Mons, and was severely wounded in Sept. 1914. He was promoted Major 1 Sept. 1915, and became Temporary Lieutenant-Colonel commanding the Manchester Regt., 1916, being mentioned in Despatches in the same year. He was created a C.M.G. Lieut.-Colonel Maclachlan was killed in action 22 March, 1918.

John Bayford Wells.

WELLS, JOHN BAYFORD, Lieut., was born 12 April, 1881, son of Charles A. E. Wells, of Heathfield, Albury, Guildford, Surrey, and of the late Annie Macdonald Susannah Wells (Burt). He was educated at Westminster, and entered the Army from the Militia, 20 May, 1899; was promoted Lieutenant 4 Jan. 1901. He served in South Africa, 1899–1902; was in the

advance on Kimberley, including actions at Belmont, Enslin, Modder River and Magersfontein; operations in the Orange Free State, April to May, 1900; operations in the Transvaal, west of Pretoria, July to 20 Nov. 1900; operations in the Orange River Colony, May to July, 1900, including actions at Lindley (1 June) and Rhenoster River; operations in Cape Colony, north and south of Orange River, 1899–1900; operations in the Transvaal 30 Nov. 1900, to April, 1902; operations in Orange River Colony, Aug. 1901; operations in Cape Colony, Sept. and Oct. 1901, and May, 1902. He was mentioned in Despatches twice [London Gazette, 20 Aug. 1901, and 29 July, 1902]; received the Queen's Medal and King's Medal with six clasps, and was created a Companion of the Distinguished Service Order [London Gazette, 31 Oct. 1902]: "John Bayford Wells, Lieut., The Loyal North Lancashire Regt. In recognition of services during the operations in South Africa." He was Adjutant of the 1st Battn. of his regiment, March, 1906, to March, 1909; was promoted Captain 5 May, 1906; at the Staff College, Camberley, 1910–11; Staff Captain at the War Office 1 June, 1912, to 25 Jan. 1915. He took part in the European War, serving in France, Gallipoli and Egypt. He was D.A.A.G., G.H.Q., France, and Mediterranean Expeditionary Force, 26 Jan. to 13 July, 1915 (Substantive Major 1 Sept. 1915); A.A.G., G.H.Q., Mediterranean Expeditionary Force and Egyptian Expeditionary Force, 14 July, 1915, to 16 April, 1916, and was employed at the War Office as A.A.G. 17 April, 1916, to 30 Nov. 1917, becoming Deputy Director of Organization, War Office, 1 Dec. 1917, and receiving the rank of Temporary Brigadier-General. He was given the Brevets of Major, April, 1915; Lieutenant-Colonel 3 June, 1917, and Colonel 3 June, 1919; was created a C.M.G. in 1918; was mentioned in Despatches twice, and also received the Legion of Honour (Chevalier) and the White Eagle of Serbia, 3rd Class, with Swords. He married, in 1916, Arabella, daughter of the late William Walter Wright, and they have one son, Theodore John Macdonald, born 11 Nov. 1918.

ASSER, VERNEY, Lieut., was born at Beadonwell, Kent, 28 Dec. 1873, third son of S. B. V. Asser, J.P., of Windlesham, Surrey. He was educated at Uppingham School, and joined the Yorkshire Artillery in 1893; served with the British South African Police in the Matabele War of 1898 (Medal). He was commissioned to the Royal Artillery 4 March, 1899; was promoted Lieutenant 16 Feb. 1901. He fought in the South African War from 1900 to 1902, with the 83rd Battery, Royal Artillery, taking part in operations in the Transvaal and Orange River Colony; operations on the Zululand Frontier of Natal in Sept. and Oct. 1901. For his services in the Boer War he was mentioned in Despatches [London Gazette, 29 July, 1902]; received the Queen's Medal with three clasps; the King's Medal and clasps, and was created a Companion of the Distinguished Service Order [London Gazette, 31 Oct. 1902]: "Verney Asser, Lieut., Royal Horse and Royal Field Artillery. In recognition of services during the operations in South Africa." He was Adjutant, 11th Brigade, 1 Oct. 1905, to 31 Jan. 1908; was promoted Captain 3 July, 1907; served in the operations on the Blue Nile, 1908 (Medal); was attached to the Egyptian Army 1 Feb. 1908, to 31 Jan. 1912; Officer of a Company and Commander of a Company of Gentleman Cadets at the Royal Military Academy, Woolwich, from 16 Sept. 1912, to 25 Aug. 1913; Adjutant, Royal Military Academy, 26 Aug. 1913, to 30 Sept. 1914; was promoted Major 30 Oct. 1914. Major V. Asser served in the European War from 1914 to 1918. He was employed as Staff Captain, Royal Artillery, 8th Division, British Expeditionary Force, 1 Oct. 1914, to 26 March, 1915; Brigade Major, Royal Artillery, 27th Division, British Expeditionary Force, Egyptian Expeditionary Force, 27 March, 1915, to 27 March, 1916; G.S.O.2, 26th Division, Salonika Army, 28 March to 19 Sept. 1916; became Acting Lieutenant-Colonel, Royal Artillery, 10 Oct. 1916; Brigadier-General, Royal Artillery, 27th Division, British Salonika Force, 4 Sept. 1918. He was mentioned in Despatches; received the Brevet of Lieutenant-Colonel 1 Jan. 1916, and was created a C.M.G. in 1919. He married, in 1911, Hyacinth, daughter of Henry Irwin, C.I.E., of Madras, and of Henrietta Helen, daughter of the Rev. Robert Irwin, and they have one daughter.

VICKERY, CHARLES EDWIN, Lieut., was born 6 July, 1880, son of T. G. Vickery, Assistant Solicitor, Corporation of London, and of Mrs. Vickery, of Foxway Rise, Fleet. He was educated at Felsted School Essex, and at Aerzen, near Hanover, Germany; obtained his first commission in the Royal Field Artillery 7 April, 1900, and was promoted Lieutenant 3 April, 1901. He served with the 42nd Battery in South Africa; was present in operations in Natal, March to June, 1900, including action at Laing's Nek (6 and 9 June); operations in the Transvaal, east of Pretoria, July to 29 Nov., including actions at Belfast (26 and 27 Aug.) and Lydenberg (5 to 8 Sept.); operations in the Transvaal 30 Nov. 1900, to Feb. 1902, and April to 31 May, 1902; operations in Orange River Colony, Feb. to April, 1902. He was mentioned in Despatches [London Gazette, 29 July, 1902]; received the Queen's and King's Medals with five clasps, and was created a Companion of the Distinguished Service Order [London Gazette, 31 Oct. 1902]: "Charles Edwin Vickery, Lieut., Royal Horse and Royal Field Artillery. In recognition of services during the operations in South Africa." Lieut. Vickery was employed with the West African Frontier Force 4 July, 1903, to 12 Aug. 1906, and with the South Nigerian Regt. 1903–4, in Southern Nigeria (wounded; Medal with clasp); Southern Nigeria, 1904 (clasp); Southern Nigeria, 1904–5; operations of the Ezza Patrol (Despatches); Southern Nigeria, 1905–6; the Bende-Onitsha Hinterland Expedition (Despatches; clasp). He was with the Egyptian Army 13 Oct. 1907, to 13 Feb. 1912; was engaged in the campaign in the Sudan in 1908, taking part in the operations in Jebul Nyima District in Southern Kordofan (Egyptian Medal with clasp); was promoted Captain 23 Sept. 1909; was again engaged in operations in Southern Kordofan in 1910 (Sudan Medal with clasp; 4th Class Medjidie). He served in England and India, 1912–13. He was reappointed to the Egyptian Army 8 March, 1913, and was with it until 23 May, 1915, receiving his Majority 30 Oct. 1914. Major Vickery, during the European War, took part in operations in the Sudan, 1914, for which he received another clasp to the Sudan Medal, and the Fourth Class Order of the Nile. He served in Gallipoli on the Staff of the 11th Division (including the evacuation of Suvla), and Egypt, 1915, and France, 1916. He was employed in a special mission to the King of the Hedjaz, Dec. 1916, to March, 1917, and returning to France in 1917, took part in the Battle of Arras, in command of a battery of the 3rd Division. He became Acting Lieutenant-Colonel 8 Aug. 1917, and was appointed to command a Brigade of Artillery in the Guards Division. With this brigade he took part in the battles of Flanders and Cambrai in 1917, and the German offensive and the British offensive in 1918, marching from Maubeuge to Cologne after the Armistice, and remaining with the brigade until it was broken up after the march through London in March, 1919. He was wounded; was seven times mentioned in Despatches; was given the Brevet of Lieutenant-Colonel 3 June, 1918; created a C.M.G. in 1919; awarded the Croix de Guerre and the Second Class Order of Nahda (conferred by the King of the Hedjaz), and was awarded a Bar to the Distinguished Service Order.

SMITH, GEOFFREY, Lieut., was the son of T. Hector Smith, of 33 Drumsheugh Gardens, Edinburgh. He was born 26 March, 1878, and entered the Royal Artillery, as a Second Lieutenant, 12 May, 1900; was promoted Lieutenant 1 Nov. 1901. He served with the Imperial Yeomanry in the South African War, 1900–2, and was severely wounded. He was present in operations in the Transvaal, east of Pretoria, Aug. and Sept. 1900; operations in the Transvaal, west of Pretoria, Oct. 1900, including actions at Frederickstad; operations in Orange River Colony, July, 1900; operations in Cape Colony, 1900; operations in the Transvaal, 1900, to 31 May, 1902. He was twice mentioned in Despatches [London Gazette, 20 Aug. 1901, and 18 July, 1902]; received the Queen's Medal with three clasps; the King's Medal with two clasps, and was created a Companion of the Distinguished Service Order [London Gazette, 31 Oct. 1902]: "Geoffrey Smith, Lieut., Royal Horse and Royal Field Artillery. In recognition of services during the operations in South Africa." Lieut. Smith died at Rawalpindi, Punjab, India, on 23 Nov. 1910, as the result of a gun accident.

KINSMAN, WILLIAM AUGUSTUS CECIL, Lieut., was born 15 April, 1878, son of the late Harold John Kinsman, Colonel, Royal Artillery, and Emily Anne, daughter of the late Rev. R. Fitzgerald, Ballydonaghue, of Tarbert, County Kerry. He joined the Royal Inniskilling Fusiliers, as a Second Lieutenant, 21 April, 1900, and was promoted Lieutenant 14 Dec. 1901. He served in the South African War, 1899–1902, and was dangerously wounded; took part in the operations in Natal, 1899, to May, 1900; in the Transvaal and Orange River Colony, Feb. to 31 May, 1902. He was mentioned in Despatches [London Gazette, 29 July, 1902]; received the Queen's Medal with three clasps, and the King's Medal with two clasps. He was created a Companion of the Distinguished Service Order [London Gazette, 31 Oct. 1902]: "William Augustus Cecil Kinsman, Lieut., Royal Inniskilling Fusiliers. In recognition of services during the operations in South Africa." He was an Adjutant of Volunteers and in the Territorial Force 9 Oct. 1906, to 8 Oct. 1911, receiving his Captaincy 13 Jan. 1907; and was Recruiting Staff Officer, Belfast Recruiting Area, 1 April, 1912, to 31 March, 1914. He served in the European War, being employed as Assistant Inspector of Recruiting, Irish Command, until 11 Dec. 1916, and afterwards as Assistant Inspector of Recruiting. He was Temporary Major from Oct. 1915, to Dec. 1918, and was given the Brevet of Major 1 Jan. 1919. Major Kinsman married, in 1909, Frances Elizabeth, daughter of R. J. Newell, of Monkstown, County Dublin, and they have one daughter.

BOYD, GERALD FARRELL, Lieut., was born 17 Oct. 1877, second son of the late Robert Boyd. He was educated at St. Paul's School, and enlisted in the Devonshire Regt. in 1895; became Sergeant 1899; was commissioned Second Lieutenant, East Yorkshire Regt., 5 May, 1900; became Lieutenant 26 April, 1902. He served in the South African War, 1899–1902, being employed with the Mounted Infantry; was present at the Relief of Ladysmith, including action at Colenso; took part in the operations in Orange River Colony, including actions at Wittebergen (1 to 29 July); served in the Transvaal, Feb. to March, 1901, and Aug. 1901, to March, 1902; was present during operations in Orange River Colony 30 Nov. 1900, to Aug. 1901, and March to 31 May, 1902; took part in the operations on the Zululand Frontier of Natal in Sept, and Oct. 1901, also in Cape Colony. He was mentioned in Despatches [London Gazette, 10 Sept. 1901; 25 April and 29 July, 1902]; received the Medal for distinguished conduct in the field; the Queen's Medal with three clasps, and the King's Medal with two clasps. He was created a Companion of the Distinguished Service Order [London Gazette, 31 Oct. 1902]: "Gerald Farrell Boyd, Lieut., East Yorkshire Regt. In recognition of services during the operations in South Africa." He became Captain in the Leinster Regt. 19 March, 1904, and was Brigade Major, 11th Infantry Brigade, Eastern Command, 21 Sept. 1912, to 4 Aug. 1914. He was also Brigade Major of the 11th Infantry Brigade, British Expeditionary Force, during the European War until 23 Feb. 1915. He was promoted Major, Royal Irish Regt., 18 March, 1915, and was given the Brevet of Lieutenant-Colonel 19 March, 1915; was employed as G.S.O.2, 1st Division, British Expeditionary Force, 3 March to 5 July, 1915; G.S.O.1, 6th Division, B.E.F., British Armies in France, 6 July, 1915, to 19 June, 1916. He was Temporary Brigadier-General from 20 June, 1916, to 4 Sept. 1918, employed as Brigadier-General, General Staff, 5th Army Corps, British Armies in France, 20 June, 1916, to 15 July, 1918, and Brigade Commander, 170th Infantry Brigade, British Armies in France, 16 July to 4 Sept. 1918. He was given the Brevet of Colonel 1 Jan. 1917. He was Temporary Major-General in command of the 46th Division, British Armies in France, 5 Sept. 1918, to 10 April, 1919, when he was appointed Brigadier-General, General Staff, G.H.Q., British Army of the Rhine, and was made a Major-General 3 June, 1919. For his services in the European War he was four times mentioned in Despatches, and was created a C.M.G. in 1918, and a

C.B. in 1919. Major-General G. F. Boyd married, in 1913, Grace Sophia, eldest daughter of Arthur Hugo Burdett, of Coolfin, Banagher, Ireland. He has two sons.

HERRING-COOPER, WILLIAM WELDON, Lieut., was born 19 March, 1873, second son of the late Herman Herring-Cooper, of Shrule Castle, Carlow, Ireland. He was educated at Corrig School, Ireland, and joined the Army on 3 Aug. 1901, as a Second Lieutenant, in the Army Service Corps, being promoted Lieutenant a year later. He served in South Africa, 1900–2, with the Imperial Yeomanry, taking part in operations in the Transvaal, March to April, 1901, and April to May, 1902; operations in Orange River Colony 30 Nov. 1900, to Feb. 1901, and Feb. to March, 1902. He was mentioned in Despatches [London Gazette, 29 July, 1902]; was awarded the King's and Queen's Medals with five clasps, and was created a Companion of the Distinguished Service Order [London Gazette, 31 Oct. 1902]: "William Weldon Herring-Cooper, Lieut., Army Service Corps. In recognition of services during the operations in South Africa." He became Captain 1 May, 1906, and from 6 Dec. 1913, to 26 Aug. 1916, was employed under the Sudan Government, becoming Major 30 Oct. 1914. Major Herring-Cooper served in the European War. He was Acting Lieutenant-Colonel from Oct. 1916, to Sept. 1917, and Assistant Director of Supplies and Transport, 21st Army Corps, Egyptian Expeditionary Force, 5 Sept. 1917, to 8 Feb. 1919. For his services he was given the Brevet of Lieutenant-Colonel 3 June, 1918, and was created an O.B.E.

SIDGWICK, CHARLES KATER DURY, Lieut., was born 12 July, 1873, third son of the late Edward Sidgwick and Lucy Matilda, third daughter of the Rev. Theodore Dury. He was educated at Rottingdean, and at Winchester College, and served his apprenticeship with the London and North Western Railway Company at Crewe, 1892–95; was private pupil of the Chief Mechanical Engineer, F. W. Webb, 1896–97, and on the Locomotive Running Staff of the London and North Western Railway Company, 1897–1901. He was in the Cheshire Volunteer Engineers, 1896–1902, and receiving a commission in the Royal Engineers, served in the Boer War of 1899 to 1902. He was created a Companion of the Distinguished Service Order [London Gazette, 31 Oct. 1902]: "Charles Kater Dury Sidgwick, Lieut., Royal Engineers (Volunteers). In recognition of services during the operations in South Africa." He subsequently resigned from the Army, and was District Locomotive Superintendent, Eastern and Northern Sections, Central South African Railway, 1901–4; Locomotive Superintendent of Orange River Colony at Bloemfontein, 1904–5, being then appointed District Locomotive and Carriage and Wagon Superintendent, Bombay, Baroda and Central India Railway, Bombay, Southern Division. He became Captain in the B.B. and C.I.R. Volunteer Rifles 26 Oct. 1906. His favourite recreations are golf, tennis, cricket and racquets. He married, in 1902, Gertrude Caroline Louisa, fourth daughter of John Henry Tod, and they have two sons.

HICKEY, DANIEL ALOYSIUS, Lieut., served in South Africa, 1900–2, taking part in operations in the Transvaal, west of Pretoria, Aug. 1900, and Oct. to 29 Nov. 1900; operations in the Transvaal, Dec. 1900, to July, 1901, and Aug. to Dec. 1901; operations in the Orange River Colony, July to Aug, 1901, and Dec. 1901, to Feb. 1902; operations on the Zululand Frontier of Natal, Sept and Oct. 1901. He was twice severely wounded; was mentioned in Despatches [London Gazette, 25 April, 1902]; was awarded the Queen's Medal with four clasps; the King's Medal with two clasps, and was created a Companion of the Distinguished Service Order [London Gazette, 31 Oct. 1902]: "Daniel Aloysius Hickey, Lieut., New Zealand Contingent. In recognition of services during the operations in South Africa." He was promoted Captain, New Zealand Staff Corps, 8 May, 1907, and became General Staff Officer, Otago Military District, 12 Aug. 1914. He was promoted Major 1 Jan. 1915, and became A.Q.M.G., Otago Military District, 19 Feb. 1916.

TOWNLEY, NORMAN VINCENT, Lieut., was born 4 March, 1872, at Rockhampton, Queensland, son of Capt. William Townley and of Gertrude Anne Townley (Burton). He was educated at the Brisbane Grammar School, and joined the Army in Feb. 1900. He served in South Africa, 1900–2, with the Queensland Contingents, the 3rd Queensland Mounted Infantry and 5th Queensland Bushmen, and also with Doyle's Australian Scouts. He took part in operations in Rhodesia, April to 25 May, 1900; the Relief of Mafeking; operations in the Transvaal, east of Pretoria, July to 29 Nov. 1900, including action at Rhenoster Kop; operations in the Transvaal, west of Pretoria, July to 29 Nov. 1900, including actions at Eland's River (4 to 16 Aug.); operations in the Transvaal 30 Nov. 1900, to May, 1902; operations in Orange River Colony, March, 1902; operations in Cape Colony, Feb. to March, 1901. He was awarded the Queen's Medal with five clasps; the King's Medal with two clasps, and was created a Companion of the Distinguished Service Order [London Gazette, 31 Oct. 1902]: N. V. Townley, Lieut., Queensland Contingent. In recognition of services during the operations in South Africa."

TUDOR, PIERS LLOYD, Lieut., served in South Africa with the New Zealand Contingent, 1901. He was mentioned in Despatches; received the Queen's Medal with three clasps, and was created a Companion of the Distinguished Service Order [London Gazette, 31 Oct. 1902]: "Piers Lloyd Tudor, Lieut., New Zealand. In recognition of services during the operations in South Africa." He died in 1913.

BOLAND, SINON B., Lieut., was born 12 July, 1875, son of Edmund Boland. He was educated at Roman Catholic and Public Schools. He served in South Africa with the Queensland Contingent, 1901–2, taking part in operations in the Transvaal and Orange River Colony, May, 1901, to May, 1902; operations on the Zululand Frontier of Natal, Sept. and Oct. 1901. He was slightly wounded; was mentioned in Despatches [London Gazette, 29 July, 1902]; received the Medal and two clasps, and was created a Comp. of the D.S.O. [L.G., 31 Oct. 1902]: "Sinon Boland, Lieut., Queensland Contingent. For services during operations in S. Africa." He was transferred to the Reserve of Officers as Captain, Unattached List, 10 De[c.] 1904. Capt. Boland served in Gallipoli in the European War, 1915, bu[t] was invalided home. He was formerly an Interstate and Internationa[l] footballer and an Interstate oarsman, and is a coach. His favourit[e] amusements are horse-racing and bridge. He is married, and has two son[s].

MACFARLANE, S. C., Lieut., served in the South African War, 1899–190[2]. He was awarded the King's Medal with two clasps, and created a Com[-]panion of the Distinguished Service Order [London Gazette, 31 Oct. 1902]: "S. C. MacFarlane, Lieut., South Australian Contingent. In recognitio[n] of services during the operations in South Africa." He was reported i[n] the "Times" as killed in action under Colonel Mackenzie against Zulu rebelling in Natal in June, 1906.

McCORMICK, JOHN, Lieut., was born in 1878. He served in Sout[h] Africa, 1899–1902, with the Tasmanian Imperial Bushmen, becoming Lieu[-]tenant 14 March, 1901. He was present in operations in the Orange Fre[e] State, 1900; operations in the Transvaal in May and June, 1900, includin[g] actions near Johannesburg and Diamond Hill; operations in the Transvaa[l] east of Pretoria, including the action at Belfast; operations in Cape Colony operations in Orange River Colony, Aug. to Sept. 1901; operations in Cap[e] Colony, April, 1901, to May, 1902. He was mentioned in Despatche[s] [London Gazette, 29 July, 1902]; received the Queen's Medal with fiv[e] clasps, and was created a Companion of the Distinguished Service Orde[r] [London Gazette, 31 Oct. 1902]: "John McCormick, Lieut., Tasmanian[s]. In recognition of services during the operations in South Africa." O[n] retiring after the South African War he was confirmed in his rank o[f] Honorary Lieutenant.

BESSELL-BROWNE, ALFRED JOSEPH, Lieut., was born 3 Sept[.] 1877, son of William H. Bessell-Browne, of Sydney. He served in Sout[h] Africa with the West Australian Contingent, 1899–1902, and took part i[n] operations in the Orange Free State, including actions at Vet River an[d] Zand River; operations in the Transvaal in May and June, 1900, includ[-]ing actions near Johannesburg, Pretoria and Diamond Hill; operations i[n] Natal; operations in Orange River Colony. He was mentioned in De[-]spatches [London Gazette, 29 Aug. 1901]; received the Queen's Medal wit[h] four clasps, and was created a Companion of the Distinguished Servic[e] Order [London Gazette, 31 Oct. 1902]: "A. J. Browne, Lieut., Wes[t] Australians. In recognition of services during the operations in Sout[h] Africa." (Warrant altered to A. J. Bessell-Browne.) He became Major 28 Aug. 1911, 13th Australian Field Artillery Brigade, 5th Military Distric[t] Major Bessell-Browne served in the European War from 1914 to 1918 He was appointed A.D.C. to His Excellency the Governor-General of Aus[-]tralia 1 April, 1917; became Temporary Brigadier-General, Australia[n] Imperial Force. For his services he was given the Brevet of Lieutenant Colonel 24 Sept. 1917; was made a C.M.G. in 1915, and a C.B. in 1918. H[e] has the Volunteer decoration. He married, in 1903, Muriel Maud, daughte[r] of Henry E. Manning.

DALY, PATRICK JOSEPH, Lieut., was born in 1872, son of Jame[s] Daly, of Alstonville, Richmond River, New South Wales, and Mrs. Daly He served in South Africa with the West Australian Contingent, 1901–2; became Lieutenant 18 Jan. 1902; was present in operations in the Trans[-]vaal and Orange River Colony. He was severely wounded; was five time[s] mentioned in Despatches; received the South African Medal with clasps and was created a Companion of the Distinguished Service Order [Londo[n] Gazette, 31 Oct. 1902]: "Patrick Joseph Daly, Lieut., Western Australia In recognition of services during the operations in South Africa." H[e] was confirmed in the rank of Lieutenant as honorary rank on retiring afte[r] the South African War. He became Lieutenant, 103rd Regt. of Canada 21 Feb. 1915, and served in the European War from 1915 to 1917, risin[g] to the rank of Lieutenant-Colonel. He was created a C.M.G. in 1917.

BAILLIE, JOHN ANDREW, Lieut., was born 22 Oct. 1876, son of th[e] late A. J. Baillie, R.N. He was educated at Douro House School. He wa[s] seconded for Service under the Foreign Office; was first in the India[n] Police, and then served with the South African Mounted Forces and Sout[h] African Constabulary, 1900–2, in the Boer War. He was mentioned i[n] Despatches, awarded the two Medals, and was created a Companion of th[e] Distinguished Service Order [London Gazette, 31 Oct. 1902]: "Joh[n] Andrew Baillie, Lieut., Steinacker's Horse. In recognition of services durin[g] the South African operations." Lieut. Baillie commanded a contingent o[f] his regiment at the Coronation of King Edward VII.; served in the Hamp[-]shire Royal Horse Artillery, and later with the Royal Horse Artillery He took part in the European War from 1914–18. He received promotio[n] to Major, Royal Horse Artillery, 1 June, 1916; was wounded, mentione[d] in Despatches. He is married.

HARE-BOWERS, DILLON ALDWORTH, Lieut., was born at March[-]wood, Hampshire, 26 Sept. 1870, son o[f] John Thomson Bowers, Capt., 6th War[-]wickshire Regt., and Cape Mounted Rifle[-]men, who served through the Mutiny, and also in the Basutoland Campaign of 1881, by his wife, Henrietta, daughter of the Honourable Henry Hare. He was educated at Dale College, King William's Town, Cape Province, South Africa, and joined the Cape Mounted Riflemen (now the 1st South African Mounted Riflemen), 26 Oct. 1886, as a Private. He served in the Bechuanaland Campaign, 1897 (Medal and clasp), taking part in the engagements of Gamaloos, Oliphant's Hoek, Puduhusche, Gamaseh I. and II.; and for his services was promoted to commissioned rank as Lieutenant 1 July, 1897

Dillon A. Hare-Bowers

He again saw active service in the Anglo-Boer War, from Dec. 1899, to the conclusion of hostilities. He was employed with the Field Intelligence Department, and was present in operations in the Orange Free State, March to May, 1900, including the defence of Wepener; operations in the Transvaal, west of Pretoria, Aug. to Nov. 1900; operations in Orange River Colony, May to Aug. 1900, including actions at Wittebergen (1 to 29 July); operations in Cape Colony, south of Orange River, 1899–1900; operations in the Transvaal, Dec. 1900; operations in Orange River Colony, Nov. 1900, to March, 1901; operations in Cape Colony, 1901–2. He was awarded the D.S.O. for conspicuous gallantry at the capture of Lotter's Commando, near Petersburg, in the Graaff-Reinet district; was mentioned in Despatches [London Gazette, 20 Aug. and 15 Nov. 1901], and was personally thanked for his services by General French, who on one occasion wired to him asking him to raise a detachment for active service at a time when the Boers were becoming particularly active in Cape Colony. Such a contingent was afterwards found to be unnecessary, but the fact that he was asked to raise it showed the high opinion General French had of him. He was thanked also by Colonel H. Scobell (later Major-General Sir H. Scobell, K.C.V.O., now deceased), under whom he served during the latter part of the war as Intelligence Officer, who wrote: "Will you please keep my field-glasses as a small offering from me to you? I had always intended getting you some and having an inscription put on them, but as you have mine, I believe, keep them, please. If I had had them inscribed I should have said: 'From Colonel Scobell to Lieut. Bowers, C.M.R. As a very small token of the regard, respect and admiration felt by Colonel Scobell towards one of the bravest officers and most thorough gentlemen it has ever been his good fortune to meet.'" Lieut. Hare-Bowers received the Queen's Medal with four clasps and the King's Medal with two clasps. He was created a Companion of the Distinguished Service Order [London Gazette, 31 Oct. 1902]: "Dillon Aldworth Hare-Bowers, Lieut., Cape Mounted Rifles. In recognition of services during the operations in South Africa." In Dec. 1904, he became Adjutant of Prince Albert's Guard, Port Elizabeth, a position which he held for two years, raising them during that time to a high state of efficiency. He was then offered promotion as Squadron Commander of his old regiment, the Cape Mounted Rifles, in Griqualand, and accepted it. He was promoted Captain 1 Dec. 1910. He carried out his military duties and those of police officer in a most efficient way, and was recommended for and obtained the position of District Officer under the Defence Scheme of 1911, the Resident Magistrate, Libode, South Africa (among many others) writing: "I have known this gallant officer all his life, and have watched his career, step by step, with great satisfaction. Capt. Bowers has served with me as Police Officer, and did excellent service in the recovery of stolen stock from the above District, and I cannot speak too highly of the services he rendered, which met with great favour from the public at the time. Capt. Bowers has a thorough knowledge of the languages, and I strongly recommend him for any position of trust." When the European War commenced Capt. Hare-Bowers saw active service once more in the German South-West African campaign, and in the Boer rebellion in 1914–15, and was awarded the Military Cross for distinguished service in the field in German South-West Africa. He commanded the 3rd Regt. South African Mounted Rifles for some months in German South-West Africa, including the rebellion of 1915, during the absence of the Commanding Officer, and was highly commended for his services by Major-General Sir H. T. Lukin, K.C.M.G., who commanded the Brigade. On the cessation of hostilities there Capt. Hare-Bowers volunteered for active service in the main theatre of war. He was attached to the Royal Fusiliers; was promoted Temporary Major 3 Feb. 1917, and served in France and Flanders in 1917 and 1918. He was promoted Major 1 Dec. 1918. Major Hare-Bowers had two brothers serving in the European War, one a Sergeant in the Cape Mounted Rifles, the other in the South African Constabulary. His favourite recreations are cricket, tennis, golf and polo. On 17 Oct. 1901, he married, at Umtata, Transvaal, South Africa, Alice, daughter of John and Alice Bishop, of Galbally, Tipperary, Ireland.

BRABANT, GUY ALFRED, Lieut., was born 6 Oct. 1873, at East London, South Africa, son of the late Major-General Sir Edward Yewd Brabant, K.C.B., C.M.G., and Lady Brabant. His father greatly distinguished himself in the Boer War, and was the head of Brabant's Horse. He was created a K.C.B., and was promoted Major-General for his services. Another son was killed during a cavalry reconnaissance from Ladysmith. G. A. Brabant joined the Army in Dec. 1900, and served in the South African War from then until 1902. He received the South African Medals with two clasps each; was promoted Captain, and created a Companion of the Distinguished Service Order [London Gazette, 31 Oct. 1902]: "Guy Alfred Brabant, Lieut., South African Mounted Irregular Forces. In recognition of services during the operations in South Africa." The decoration was awarded in particular for gallantry near Pearston, Cape Colony, 10 March, 1902. While with Colonel Price's Column, Lieut. Brabant attacked a very strong position held by six Boers. He himself, with Second Lieut. Francis and Sergts. Walsh and Metcalf, shot three of the six Boers and wounded one, and also captured six horses, saddles, etc. He was mentioned in Lord Kitchener's Despatch of 1 June, 1902. He retired from the Cape Colonial Forces, as Captain, 26 Sept. 1902, and became Lieutenant, Border Light Horse, Cape of Good Hope, 25 May, 1903. Capt. Brabant is now farming in Cape Colony. His favourite recreations are cricket, tennis and shooting. On 27 Dec. 1910, at Koungha, Cape Town, Capt. Brabant married Mary Ethel Austin Reaney, eldest daughter of C. T. Reaney, of Freetown, and they have a son, Richard Brabant, born 14 Nov. 1912.

DOBRÉE, GEORGE, Lieut., was born 10 May, 1873, at St. Andrew's Rectory, Guernsey, son of the Rev. Henry Lissignol Dobrée, B.A., late Rector of St. Andrew's, Guernsey, and of Amelia, daughter of the Rev. Peter Carey, M.A., sometime Rector of St. Saviour's, Guernsey. He was left an orphan at the age of six, and was educated at King William's College, Isle of Man, and at the Royal Military Academy, Woolwich, which he entered straight from school in 1900; but owing to circumstances he resigned his cadetship and went to the Continent to study modern languages. Returning to England in 1893, he entered Caius College, Cambridge, and obtained a third-class in the Modern Languages Tripos in 1896. Throughout his Cambridge career, 1893–96, he was a very keen and enthusiastic member of the Cambridge University Rifle Volunteers, and when Captain of C Troop raised it to a high state of efficiency. It was inspected by King Edward (then Prince of Wales) in May, 1896. After leaving Cambridge he studied for the Guernsey Bar at Caen University, and volunteered, while a student there, for the South African War. He joined Paget's Horse, Jan. 1900, as Corporal in the first section of the first company, and on arrival in South Africa was gazetted to Kitchener's Horse, as Lieutenant, 12 May, 1900, and took part in the engagements at Klipriversdorp, Six Mile Spruit and Diamond Hill. On 12 June, 1900, he was appointed A.D.C. to Lieut.-Colonel Legge, D.S.O., 6th Mounted Infantry Corps, and served in the operations in the Orange Free State against De Wet. Returning to the Transvaal, the Corps became attached to the Column under General Clements, and took part in the action at Doornkloof. On 13 Dec. 1900, at Nooitgedacht, the camp was surprised in the early morning by Delarey, and Colonel Legge and other officers killed and wounded. Lieut. Dobrée assisted Colonel Legge to reinforce the piquets under heavy fire continuously (this appears in the "Times History of the War," page 96), and helped materially in initiating and facilitating the safe retirement of the Column. It was for gallantry in this action that he received his D.S.O. [London Gazette, 31 Oct. 1902]: "George Dobrée, Lieut., South African Mounted Irregular Forces. In recognition of services during the operations in South Africa." He was invested by King Edward. After further service under General French he was recommended for leave, and returned to England in Jan. 1901. In addition to the D.S.O. he received mention in Lord Kitchener's Despatch of 9 March, 1901, published in the London Gazette of 7 May, 1901, and received the Queen's Medal with clasps for Wittebergen, Diamond Hill, Johannesburg and Cape Colony. During his residence in Guernsey he became an enthusiastic officer in the Guernsey Militia Artillery, obtaining the rank of Captain. He died in Guernsey 20 July, 1907. Capt. Dobrée was a keen sportsman and an accomplished musician. He played the violin, piano and organ, but his chief forte was as a conductor. He was conductor of the Guernsey Orchestral Society. He was one of the founders of the Stade Française, R.U.F.C., and arranged for their first visit to Cambridge in 1894.

FOXCROFT, M. C., Lieut., served in the South African War of 1899–1902. He was created a Companion of the Distinguished Service Order [London Gazette, 31 Oct. 1902]: "M. C. Foxcroft, Lieut., South African Mounted Irregular Forces. In recognition of services during the operations in South Africa."

KELLY, OLIVER W., Lieut., was born in 1878, youngest son of the late Lieut.-Colonel John Lionel Kelly. He was educated at Clongowes Wood School, Ireland. He served with the West Australian Mounted Infantry from 1900 to their disbandment; then joined the Scottish Horse as a Lieutenant, and served with them in South Africa, 1900–1. He was mentioned in Despatches; was severely wounded at Wagon Drift, and was created a Companion of the Distinguished Service Order [London Gazette, 31 Oct. 1902]: "Oliver W. Kelly, Lieut., 2nd Scottish Horse. In recognition of services during the operations in South Africa." He resigned at the end of the war.

LYLE, J. C. V., Lieut., served in the South African War, 1900–1902. He was awarded the Queen's Medal with three clasps, and created a Companion of the Distinguished Service Order [London Gazette, 31 Oct. 1902]: "J. C. V. Lyle, Lieut., 1st Kitchener's Fighting Scouts. In recognition of services during the operations in South Africa." He also took part in the Great War, and reached the rank of Lieutenant-Colonel (Labour Corps) 26 June, 1918. He was awarded the Military Cross and the O.B.E.

MALCOLM, JOHN ALEXANDER, Lieut., was born in 1872, son of J. F. Malcolm, of Victoria, Australia. He served in the South African War of 1899–1902. He was mentioned in Despatches; awarded the Medal, and created a Companion of the Distinguished Service Order [London Gazette, 31 Oct. 1902]: "J. A. Malcolm, Lieut., South African Constabulary. In recognition of services during the operations in South Africa." Capt. Malcolm married, in 1903, Mabel Jane, third daughter of Charles J. Oertel, Abraham's Kraal, Orange River Colony.

NICHOLSON, BERTRAM, Lieut., served in South Africa with the Imperial Light Horse, 1902. He was awarded the Medal, and created a Companion of the Distinguished Service Order [London Gazette, 31 Oct. 1902]: "Bertram Nicholson, Lieut., 2nd Imperial Light Horse. In recognition of services during the operations in South Africa." He was Sub-Native Commissioner, Hlatikulu, Swaziland, 1902–7; Assistant Resident Magistrate, 1904–7; Assistant Commissioner, 1907.

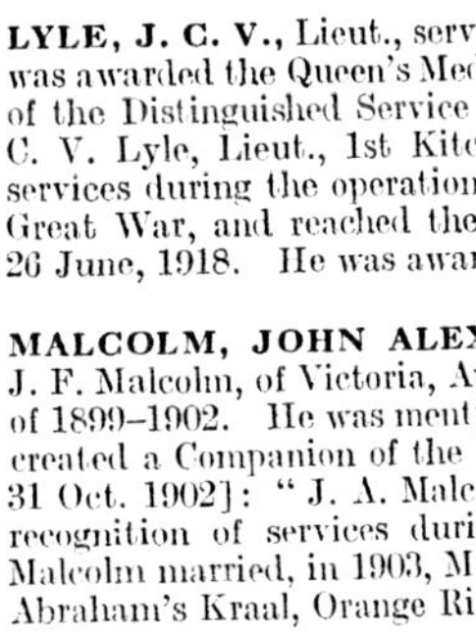

Bertram Nicholson.

OSWALD, WILLIAM DIGBY, Lieut., was born at Southampton 20 Jan. 1880, youngest son of Thomas Ridley Oswald and the only son of Wilhelmina Catherine, his second wife (*née* Russell), formerly of Southampton, and afterwards of Castle Hall, Milford Haven, and of Blackheath. He went to Rugby in 1895, and in 1898 he won the Wrigley Cup for his House by his own unaided efforts, winning four events—the Quarter Mile, High Jump, Weight, and Hurdles. He left the same year,

and in 1899 entered the Army, through the Militia, being gazetted to the 2nd Battn. Leicestershire Regt. He saw service in Egypt, and later in South Africa, as Lieutenant and Adjutant of the Railway Pioneer Regt. He was mentioned in Lord Kitchener's Despatches (8 March, 1902), and was created a Companion of the Distinguished Service Order [London Gazette, 31 Oct. 1902]: "William Digby Oswald, Lieut., 3rd Rly. Pnr. Regt. For services during operations in South Africa," viz.: the rescue of a Native Scout on 31 Jan., the enemy being close to him, and pursuing for some miles. So reticent was he in some matters pertaining to himself, that it is doubtful if even his most intimate friends ever knew for what special act of gallantry he was awarded this high distinction. After

William Digby Oswald.

the South African War he began mining in South Africa. He served also as Captain and Adjutant of Royston's Horse in the Natal Rebellion in 1906, and was wounded in fierce bush fighting in Zululand. He continued mining in Rhodesia until May, 1914, and lived at Bulawayo. On the outbreak of the European War he joined the 5th Dragoon Guards (Special Reserve), as Lieutenant, on 7 Aug. 1914, and a week later went to France with the 1st Cavalry Brigade. He was in the Retreat from Mons, and took part in the Battles of the Marne and the Aisne. He was wounded at Messines on 31 Oct. 1914, and was sent home. In May, 1915, eager to get to the front again, he was attached as Captain to the Royal Field Artillery, and was with the 3rd Division in the heavy fighting round Ypres. After serving on the Staff as A.D.C. to Major-General J. A. L. Haldane, and as Assistant Provost-Marshal (for which he was mentioned in Despatches), he was, in Dec. 1915, appointed Second-in-Command of the 12th Battn. West Yorkshire Regt., and in March, 1916, took over the command. He took part in much fighting at St. Eloi, and in the early stages of the Battle of the Somme. On 14 July, 1916, the 3rd Division took part in a highly successful attack on the ridge between Bazentin-le-Petit and Longueval, and Lieut.-Colonel Oswald (his promotion was gazetted posthumously [London Gazette, Oct. 12, 1916], and also mentioned in Despatches after his death), was struck in the chest by a misfire from an English gun (a tragic incident—he had seen that the gun was wrongly focussed during the day, and had sent orders to that effect), and, after seeming to make a good recovery, sank rapidly and died on 16 July, 1916. Major-General Haldane, commanding the 3rd Division, wrote: "His loss I feel much personally, but still more as Commanding Officer, for a man like him was worth a battalion of infantry." Another officer wrote: "I always thought it an extremely sporting thing to give up a pleasant post such as Assistant Provost-Marshal, and take on infantry work in the trenches." In dedicating a memorial tablet to his memory at Victoria, Rhodesia, Canon Ashworth told how junior officers vied with each other to serve under him, and how his servant three months after Colonel Oswald's death broke down completely in describing his life in the trenches with his men and the way in which he met his death. He had lived a life of movement and adventure; he was a very good horseman, a keen polo player, and loved big game shooting in Rhodesia, but, perhaps, the Great War brought out what was best in him.

"One who never turned his back, but marched breast forward,
　Never doubted clouds would break,
Never dreamed, though right were worsted, wrong would triumph.
Held we fall to rise, are baffled to fight better,
　Sleep to wake."

The officers of the 5th Dragoons and his friends in the 3rd Division intend to erect a memorial, in the form of a drinking fountain for animals, in Surrey or Dorset. Lieut. Oswald had married, on 7 March, 1905, at St. John's Church, Weymouth, Dorset, Catherine Mary, daughter of the Rev. J. Scott Yardley, of St. Chad's, Shrewsbury, and Mary Yardley (maiden name, Loxdale), and there are three daughters: Theodora Betty; Ambrosine Mary, and Patricia Catherine.

SOAMES, ALFRED, Lieut., was born 16 Sept. 1862, son of the late Rev. Charles Soames, M.A., of Mildenhall, Marlborough, Wiltshire.

He served in the South African War in 1901. He received the Queen's Medal with a clasp, and was created a Companion of the Distinguished Service Order [London Gazette, 31 Oct. 1902]: "Alfred Soames, Lieut., South African Mounted Irregular Forces. In recognition of services during the operations in South Africa." Lieut. Soames served in the Great War with the 6th Battn. East Kent Regt. (The Buffs), and was killed in action 13 Oct. 1915.

Alfred Soames.

STEEL, J. E., Lieut., served in the South African War in 1902. He was mentioned in Despatches; awarded the Queen's Medal with six clasps, and was created a Companion of the Distinguished Service Order

[London Gazette, 31 Oct. 1902]: "J. E. Steel, Lieut., South African Light Infantry. In recognition of services during the operations in South Africa."

J. E. Steel.

DALMAHOY, PATRICK CARFRAE, Second Lieut., was born 31 Oct. 1872, at Edinburgh, son of Major-General Patrick Carfrae Dalmahoy and Emily Jane Dalmahoy, daughter of Edward Wylly, Bengal Civil Service. His father fought in the Indian Mutiny, and was present at the siege and capture of Delhi. He was educated at Haileybury College, and Edinburgh University and passed as Writer to the Signet, Edinburgh, in 1896. He joined the Mounted Infantry, City Imperial Volunteers, as a Private, for service in the South African War, 18 Jan. 1899 and was employed with them until gazetted to a commission in 1900 in the 1st Battn. The Royal Scots, with whom he served to the end of the war. Major-General Dalmahoy writes: "I have not in my possession any written account of the deed that won for him the D.S.O., but I have been told on more than one occasion by Colonel Douglas (now General Sir William Douglas), who commanded the column that the success was in a great measure accomplished by the tactful and dashing action of the company, Royal Scots, under

Patrick C. Dalmahoy.

my son's command. The scene was the Battle of Bermondsey, in the Transvaal 1901, I think. By order of Colonel Douglas the company was detached to turn the Boer right, and this he fully effected. He was severely wounded. I am told that he was specially mentioned by Lord Kitchener. I may mention that my son never in any way alluded to his action, and it was only through Sir William Douglas that I heard of it." Second Lieut. Dalmahoy was twice wounded; was mentioned in Despatches, awarded the King's and Queen's Medals, and was created a Companion of the Distinguished Service Order [London Gazette, 31 Oct. 1902]: "Patrick Carfrae Dalmahoy, Second Lieut., The Royal Scots (Lothian) Regt. In recognition of services during the operations in South Africa." He resigned his commission at the end of the war, and was appointed to the Civil Service in South Africa. He was Assistant Resident Magistrate at Germiston, then Resident Magistrate at Benoni, Transvaal, and is now Resident Magistrate at Heidelberg, Transvaal. His favourite pastime is golf. He married, 25 Oct. 1911, at Edinburgh, Mabel Houston, daughter of the late W. Rogers, of Johannesburg and they have three children: Emily Muriel, born 18 Oct. 1912; Mabel Lilias Jane, born 4 Oct. 1914, and Frances Diana Maud, born 13 Oct. 1918.

RAW, RUPERT GEORGE, Second Lieut., was born 28 July, 1880 son of George Henry Raw. He was educated at Clifton College, and Brasenose College, Oxford. He served in South Africa, 1901-2, taking part in operations in the Transvaal, Nov. 1901, to March, 1902; operations in Cape Colony, Oct. to Nov. 1901; Jan. 1902, and March to 31 May, 1902. He was mentioned in Despatches [London Gazette, 29 July, 1902]; awarded the Queen's Medal with five clasps, and was created a Companion of the Distinguished Service Order [London Gazette, 31 Oct. 1902]: "Rupert George Raw, Second Lieut., The Northumberland Fusiliers. In recognition of services during the operations in South Africa." Lieut. R. G. Raw afterwards retired from the Service, and joined the Reserve of Officers He served in the European War; was promoted Captain, 8th Battn. Northumberland Fusiliers. He was killed in action, Aug. 1915, in Gallipoli was married, and left a son and a daughter.

HAMOND, PHILIP, Second Lieut., was born 1 May. 1883, son of C. A Hamond, of Twyford Hall, East Dereham. He served in South Africa with the Mounted Infantry from 1901 to June, 1902, taking part in operations in the Transvaal, June, 1901, to May, 1902; operations in the Orange River Colony, June, 1901; operations in Cape Colony, May to June, 1901 He was given a commission in the 2nd Battn. Norfolk Regt. 7 May, 1902 after serving with the 4th Battn. from May, 1900, to May, 1902. He was dangerously wounded at Rooival; was mentioned in Despatches; awarded the Medal, and created a Companion of the Distinguished Service Order [London Gazette, 31 Oct. 1902]: "Philip Hamond, Second Lieut., The Norfolk Regt. In recognition of services during the operations in South Africa." He was promoted Lieutenant 4 Jan. 1905, and retired from the Service 20 Feb. 1909. He was subsequently placed on half pay, but re joined for service in the European War, and was promoted Captain, Special Reserve, Norfolk Regt. 10 June, 1915. He took part in the European War from 1915 to 1918, and became a Major in the Tank Corps. He was awarded the Military Cross and a Bar to the D.S.O. In 1909 he married Rita Gladys Ethel, daughter of Charles Edward Hammond, of St. Fabian's, Newmarket

London Gazette, 8 May, 1903.—"The King has been graciously pleased to give orders for the following appointment to the Distinguished Service Order. To be a Companion of the Distinguished Service Order."

DICKINSON, NEVILLE HOPE CAMPBELL, Major, was born 11 Nov 1862, eldest son of the late T. W. Carr Dickinson, of Fairholme, Cheltenham; and grandson of the late Generals T. Dickinson and H. Dickinson H.E.I.C.S., his mother, Elizabeth Charlotte Dickinson, being second daughter of the latter. He was educated at Cheltenham College, and served as Lieutenant in the 3rd (South Regt.) Royal Guernsey Light Infantry Militia, 1881-5. He joined the Prince of Wales's Leinster Regt. (Royal Canadians) 23 May, 1885; served with the 44th Gurkha Light Infantry, B.S.C. in the Upper Burma Campaign, 1885-7 (Medal with clasp), and 1887-9 (clasp). He was Station Staff Officer, Kohima, Naga Hills,

Neville H. C. Dickinson.

Assam, and was brought to the notice of the Commander-in-Chief in India for his good service on detached duty by the General Officer Commanding Eastern Frontier, Bengal. He became Captain 12 Aug. 1891. He was in the Ordnance Store Department, 1891-3; D.A.C.G.O., 1893-6; Ordnance Officer, 4th Class, Army Ordnance Department, 1896-8. He served with the 1st Battn. Prince of Wales's Leinster Regt. (Royal Canadians) (100th), in the South African War, 1900-1, and was present at the action of Wittebergen (Queen's Medal and four clasps). He became Major 28 June, 1901. He served with the West African Frontier Force, 1st Battn. Northern Nigeria Regt., 1901-4; Acting Commandant and Brigade Major, Northern Nigeria Regt., West African Frontier Force. He was in command of the Kontagora Expedition, 1902, for which, in addition to mention in Despatches, he received the Medal and clasp, and was created a Companion of the Distinguished Service Order [London Gazette, 8 May, 1903]: "Major Neville Hope Campbell Dickinson, The Prince of Wales's Leinster Regt. (Royal Canadians). In recognition of services in effecting the capture of the ex-Emir of Kontagora." Major Dickinson retired from the Army 20 Dec. 1905. He was Military Resident, Province of Borgu, and J.P., Northern Nigeria, 1901 to 1904, and among the important appointments which he subsequently held was that of Mechanical Engineer of the Construction Company of the Central Uruguay Eastern Extension Railway, 1906. When the Great War began Major Dickinson became, on 6 Aug. 1914, a First Class Inspector of Mechanical Transport, Army Service Corps, and was employed in that position during the war until 8 Jan. 1918, serving in France in 1916, being brought to the notice of the Secretary of State for War for valuable services in 1917 and 1918. He has the British War Medal and the Allies' Medal. From 9 Jan. 1918, to 15 Oct. 1919, he was employed with the Army Ordnance Department and Royal Army Ordnance Corps, as Ordnance Officer, 4th and 3rd class. Major Dickinson married, in 1896, Elizabeth Frankland, second daughter of Isaac Garlbutt Dickinson, of Woking and Newcastle.

London Gazette, 26 June, 1903.—"The King has been graciously pleased to give orders for the following appointment to the Distinguished Service Order. To be a Companion of the Distinguished Service Order."

ALEXANDER, AUBREY DE VERE, Lieut.-Colonel and Brevet Colonel, was born 28 May, 1849, son of the late G. H. M. Alexander, I.C.S., and of Henrietta Ruth Maria Read. He was educated at Wellington College, and joined the Army 8 Dec. 1869. He served with the Khyber Field Force in the Afghan War of 1879-80 (Medal); became Captain 8 Dec. 1881, and Major 8 Dec. 1889; Lieutenant-Colonel 8 Dec. 1895; was given the Brevet of Colonel 8 Dec. 1899. For his services with the China Field Force in 1900-1, Colonel Alexander was mentioned in Despatches, and created a Companion of the Distinguished Service Order [London Gazette, 26 June, 1903]: "Aubrey de Vere Alexander, Lieut.-Colonel and Brevet Colonel, Indian Army. In recognition of services during the occupation of China by International Troops." Colonel A. de V. Alexander was later Officiating Colonel on the Staff, Rawal Pindi. He retired from the Indian Army 15 Feb. 1908, with the rank of Colonel in the Army. During the European War Colonel Alexander served in the Intelligence Department of the War Office from 3 Oct. 1914, to 23 July, 1919. He married, in 1875, Mary Georgina Carter, daughter of the late General Sir James Brind, G.C.B.

Aubrey de Vere Alexander.

London Gazette, 26 June, 1903.—"The King has been graciously pleased to give orders for the following appointments to the Distinguished Service Order. To be Companions of the Distinguished Service Order."

ROWAND, ALEXANDER, Commander, was born 22 Aug. 1868, son of the late Alexander Rowand, of Glasgow. He was educated at Stubbington House, Fareham, and joined the Indian Marine in March, 1899. He served in South Africa, 1899 to 1900, on the Naval Transport Staff, for which he was mentioned in Despatches and received the Medal; and in China, 1900 to 1902, for which he was again mentioned in Despatches, received the Medal, and was created a Companion of the Distinguished Service Order [London Gazette, 26 June, 1903]: "Alexander

Alexander Rowand.

Rowand, Commander, Royal Indian Marine. In recognition of services during the occupation of China by International Troops." He also received the Medal for service in Somaliland, 1902 to 1904. He took part in the European War from 1914 to June, 1919, as Temporary Commander, Royal Navy, including service with the Expeditionary Force in France. He was mentioned in Despatches by Lord French. He married, in 1914, Ann Helen Woods Ommanney.

HALL, PERCY BYNG, Lieut., was born 29 June, 1880, son of the late General C. H. Hall, B.S.C. He joined the Indian Army in 1899; served in China, 1900 (Medal); was promoted Lieutenant 25 April, 1901, in the 34th Sikh Pioneers. He was created a Companion of the Distinguished Service Order [London Gazette, 26 June, 1903]: " Percy Byng Hall, Lieut., Indian Army. For the capture of a band of brigands on 17 Dec. 1901, in the district of Chun-liang-Chang." He retired to the Reserve of Officers in 1906, and on 16 Sept. 1912, became Captain in the 88th Regt. (Victoria Fusiliers), British Columbia, in which he was promoted Major 25 April, 1914. He married, in 1905, Muriel, daughter of Sir Francis O'Callaghan, and they have two sons and one daughter.

London Gazette, 7 Aug. 1903.—" The King has been graciously pleased to give orders for the following appointment to the Distinguished Service Order. To be a Companion of the Distinguished Service Order."

FOSTER, WILFRID LIONEL, Capt., was born 2 Dec. 1874, at Great Malvern, son of the Rev. Henry Foster, of Malvern College, and Mrs. Henry Foster, and is a member of the well-known family of Worcestershire cricketers. He was educated at Malvern College, and joined the Royal Artillery in Nov. 1894. He served in the South African War, 1899 to 1902, and was in the advance on Kimberley, including the actions at Enslin, Modder River and Magersfontein, and the Relief of Kimberley; operations in the Orange Free State, Feb. to May, 1900, including operations at Paardeberg (17 to 26 Feb.); operations in Cape Colony, Feb. to April, 1901; operations in Orange River Colony and the Transvaal, May, 1901, to May, 1902. He received the Queen's Medal with four clasps; the King's Medal with two clasps, and was mentioned in Despatches [London Gazette, 10 Sept. 1901]. He served as a Special Service Officer on the Staff in the Somaliland Campaign of 1902-3; was mentioned in Despatches [London Gazette, 7 Aug. 1903, and 2 Sept. 1904]; received the Medal, and was created a Companion of the Distinguished Service Order [London Gazette, 7 Aug. 1903]: " Capt. Wilfrid Lionel Foster, Royal Artillery. In recognition of services with the Boer Contingent during the recent operations in Somaliland." He retired from the Army to the Reserve of Officers in 1908, and was promoted Major, Reserve of Officers, R.H. and R.F.A., 6 May, 1915. He was created a C.B.E. in 1919. Major Foster, with his brother H. K., won the Public School Racquets in 1892 and the Racquets Amateur Doubles Championship in 1898; also the latter again in 1907 with his brother B. S. He was a member of the Corinthian Football Club. As a cricketer he was a really great batsman, and with his brothers H. K. and R. E. was responsible for raising Worcestershire to the position of a first-class county. Major Foster married in London, in Oct. 1901, Evelyn Mary Cammell, daughter of Bernard E. Cammell, of Guildford, and they have two daughters, Nancy and Molly, and one son, Wilfrid, born in July, 1915.

Wilfrid Lionel Foster.

London Gazette, 3 July, 1903.—"The King has been graciously pleased to give orders for the following appointments to the Distinguished Service Order, in recognition of the services of the undermentioned Officers on the occasion of the capture of Gumatti Fort during the operations against the Darwesh Khel Waziris in November last. To be Companions of the Distinguished Service Order.

DAVIES, CHARLES HENRY, Capt., was born 20 Nov. 1867, at Dibrugarh, India, son of the late Major-General Frederick John Davies (died 1901), of Teignmouth. He was educated at the United Service Club, Westward Ho! and at Newton College, Newton Abbott, and joined the Army on 5 Feb. 1887, as a Second Lieutenant in the Cheshire Regt. He became Lieutenant in the Indian Staff Corps 1 Sept. 1889, and Captain in the Indian Army 5 Feb. 1898. He served on the North-West Frontier, 1897-8, taking part in operations on the Samana and in the Kurram Valley during August and Sept. 1897 (Medal with two clasps); and in the Tirah, 1897-8, including the action at Dargai and the capture of the Sampagha and Arhanga Passes, the reconnaissance of the Saran Sar and the action of 9 Nov. 1897; the operations against the Khani Khel Chamkanis; the operations in the Bazar Valley, 25 to 30 Dec. 1897 (clasp). He received a Medal for service in China, 1900, and served in 1902 in the operations against the Darwesh Khel Waziris, North-West Frontier. In this campaign he was wounded slightly, and for his services was mentioned in Despatches [London Gazette, 5 June, 1903], and created a Companion of the Distinguished Service Order [London Gazette, 3 July,

Charles Henry Davies.

Colleg

1903]: "Charles Henry Davies, Capt., Indian Army. For operations against the Darwesh Khel Waziris." He was promoted Major 5 Feb. 1905; served in the Zakka Khel Expedition in 1908; in the Mohmand Expedition, including the engagement at Kargha, 1908 (Despatches; Medal with two clasps). He became Lieutenant-Colonel 5 Feb. 1913. He served in the European War (in Mesopotamia), 1914–18. He was given the Brevet of Colonel 3 June, 1916; was promoted Temporary Brigadier-General on becoming Brigade Commander, 28th Infantry Brigade, Indian Expeditionary Force "D," Mesopotamian Expeditionary Force, 6 July, 1916. He was wounded; was created a C.M.G. in 1917 and a C.B. in 1919. Brigadier-General Davies married, 5 Sept. 1894, at Teignmouth, Devon, Beatrice Mary, fourth daughter of the late Christopher Sparrow, of Bitton, Teignmouth, and Urmston Lodge, near Manchester, and they have one son, Frederick Arthur Davies (Second Lieutenant, Queen's Own Corps of Guides).

BROWNE, CHARLES MICHAEL, Lieut., was born 26 Nov. 1878, son of the late Lieut.-Colonel Charles Michael Browne and of the late Sarah Josephine Browne. He was educated at the United Services College, Westward Ho! and joined the Army on 23 Dec. 1897, as a Second Lieutenant in the Royal Engineers, in which he was promoted Lieutenant 23 Dec. 1900. He served in Waziristan, 1901–2 (Medal and clasp), and for his services in the operations against the Darwesh Khels, 1902, was mentioned in Despatches [London Gazette, June, 1903], and created a Companion of the Distinguished Service Order for the same services [London Gazette, 3 July, 1903]: "Charles Michael Browne, Lieut., Royal Engineers. For operations against the Darwesh Khel Waziris." He was promoted Captain 23 Dec. 1906; Major 30 Oct. 1914. Major C. M. Browne served in the European War; he was Adjutant, Royal Engineers, 7 Nov. 1914, to 1915; Acting Lieutenant-Colonel, Sept. 1916, to May, 1917, and again 2 June, 1917. For his services he was four times mentioned in Despatches; given the Brevet of Lieutenant-Colonel 1 Jan. 1916; created a C.M.G., 1918, and made a Knight of the Legion of Honour by the French. Lieut.-Colonel Browne also served in the Russian Relief Force, 1919, and was awarded the Order of St. Anne, 2nd Class, by the Russians. He married, in 1905, Isabel (died 1916), daughter of the late Gilbert Lovell Nicolay, and has one son: Charles Gordon Knight, born 27 April, 1909.

Charles Michael Browne.

London Gazette, 4 Dec. 1903.—"The King has been graciously pleased to give directions for the following appointment to the Distinguished Service Order. To be a Companion of the Distinguished Service Order."

SANGMEISTER, F. A. W., Major, served in the South African War from 1899 to 1901. He was present in operations in Natal in 1899, including actions at Reitfontein and Lombard's Kop; the Defence of Ladysmith, including sortie of 7 Dec. 1899, and action of 6 Jan. 1900; operations in Natal, March to June, 1900, including the action at Laing's Nek. He was mentioned in Despatches [London Gazette, 4 Dec. 1903]; received the Queen's Medal with two clasps, and was created a Companion of the Distinguished Service Order [London Gazette, 4 Dec. 1903]: "Major F. A. W. Sangmeister, Border Mounted Rifles. In recognition of services during the operations in South Africa, 1899–1900, the reward to bear date 29 Nov. 1900." He was promoted Major 16 Nov. 1904, and was placed as Lieutenant-Colonel on the Regimental Supernumerary List, Natal, 6 March, 1906. He also served in the Natal Native Rebellion in 1906, for which he received the Medal and Clasp. He has the Volunteer Decoration.

London Gazette, 11 Sept. 1903.—"The King has been graciously pleased to give orders for the following appointments to the Distinguished Service Order, in recognition of their services with the Kano-Sokoto Expedition. To be Companions of the Distinguished Service Order."

CUBITT, THOMAS ASTLEY, Capt. and Brevet Major, was born 9 April, 1871, youngest son of Major F. Astley Cubitt, of Thorpe Hall, Norwich. He received his first commission in the Royal Artillery 13 Feb. 1891. He served on the Staff in West Africa in 1898, in the Expeditions to Lapai and Anam (Medal and clasp); was promoted Captain 13 Feb. 1900; served in the Munshi Expedition, Northern Nigeria, 1900 (Despatches [London Gazette, 16 April, 1901]; clasp); in Northern Nigeria, 1901, in the operations against the forces of Kontagora, and in the operations against those of Bida (Despatches [London Gazette, 18 April, 1902]; Medal with clasp; Brevet of Major); in 1902 in the Bornu Expedition, Northern Nigeria, as Staff Officer in command of operations in the Bassama and Wurkum countries (Despatches [London Gazette, 24 April, 1903]; clasp). For his services in Northern Nigeria in 1903, as Staff Officer to Colonel T. L. W. Morland in the Kano-Sokoto Campaign, Major Cubitt was mentioned in Despatches [London Gazette, 31 July, 1903]; received a clasp to the African Medal, and was created a Companion of the Distinguished Service Order [London Gazette, 11 Sept. 1903]: "Thomas Astley Cubitt, Capt. and Brevet Major, Royal Artillery (West African Frontier Force. In recognition of services with the Kano-Sokoto Expedition." He was promoted Substantive Major, Royal Artillery, 12 Sept. 1908; was employed as Brigade Major, 3rd Cavalry Brigade, Irish Command, Feb. 1908, to May, 1911, and on 29 July, 1914, was promoted Local Lieutenant-Colonel on taking up an appointment in Somaliland. He was employed in Somaliland during the Great War until 19 Jan. 1916, becoming Substantive Lieutenant-Colonel 1 April, 1915; was Brigade Commander of the 57th Infantry Brigade, British Armies in France, 6 April, 1917, to 22 May, 1918, and was Temporary Major-General Commanding the 38th Division, British Armies in France, from 23 May, 1918; confirmed in the rank of Major-General 3 June, 1919. Major-General Cubitt was given the Brevet of Colonel 1 Jan. 1918; was created a C.M.G. in 1916, and a C.B. in 1919.

DYER, STEWART BARTON BYTHESEA, Lieut. (Local Capt.), was born 26 Nov. 1875, in London, son of Capt. Stewart John Dyer, late The Buffs (youngest son of the late Sir Thomas Swinnerton Dyer, 9th Bart., of Westcroft Park, Chobham, Surrey). His parents came of old Wiltshire families; the Dyers held lands in Wilts (Heytesbury and Somerset) before 1400, most of which they lost fighting for Charles I., whose successor, Charles II., created the Baronetcy. The Dyers have been mostly soldiers, and have fought through the Peninsular and Crimean Wars and the Indian Mutiny. His mother belonged to the Bythesea family, which has owned the Weeke House estate since the time of James I. He was educated by a private tutor, and at Balliol College, Oxford, and joined the 4th Battn. Royal Munster Fusiliers (Kerry Militia) 9 Feb. 1894, and served during four trainings. He joined the 2nd Life Guards 5 Jan. 1899. In June, 1899, Lieut. Dyer was seconded for service in Northern Nigeria, where he took part in (1) the Kaduna Expedition, 1900 (Despatches; Medal and clasp); (2) the Bornu Expedition, and operations in the Wurkum Hills and Bassama country, 1902 (wounded; Despatches; Medal and clasp). The London Gazette of 24 April, 1903, contained Sir F. Lugard's Despatches, dated from Mureji, 16 Aug. 1902, with reference to the Expedition to Bornu, and the operations which resulted in the capture of the ex-Emir of Kontagora, as well as other expeditions in Northern Nigeria. The Expedition, under Colonel Morland, started from Ibi (which is three hundred miles up the Benue from Lokoja) at the end of January. After subjugating the Yerguins, a turbulent hill tribe, Colonel Morland was attacked beyond Bautshi on the 16th Feb. by a strong force of some seven hundred dervishes dressed in the "Jibbeh," followers of the Mallam Jibrella, who called himself the Mahdi, and had long been the firebrand of that part of the Protectorate, and hitherto invariably victorious. The enemy was defeated with great loss, and the pursuit resulted in the capture of the Mallam by Lieut. Dyer, who—as Colonel Morland relates—"rode seventy miles in seventeen hours, with ten men only, and was back at Gujba in forty-two hours; a remarkable performance indeed in a roadless country." In the difficult operations which followed the Bassama and the Wurkum and Djen tribes were defeated in several actions, until they sued for peace." Sir F. D. Lugard adds: "I concur in the selection of officers made by Colonel Morland for special mention, viz.: . . . . Lieut. Dyer, an officer who has always been distinguished for intrepidity and dash." For his services in this expedition Lieut. Dyer received the Medal and clasp. He was wounded. (3) He served in the Kano-Sokoto Expedition in 1903; wounded. The "Daily Mail" of 16 Feb. 1903, says: "The following telegram was received late on Friday night by the Colonial Office from the Governor, Sir F. D. Lugard: "Fifty miles from Zaria, 8 Feb. Kano occupied by Colonel Morland, 3 Feb. Lieut. S. B. B. Dyer, 2nd Life Guards, severely wounded, sword-cuts, wrists." Kano was occupied on 3 Feb., after considerable fighting, the enemy defending the walls, which were 15 feet high, and proof against millimetre shell. After a fruitless bombardment of the main gate, the British troops stormed a smaller gate a mile off. Lieut. Dyer (2nd Life Guards) led the storming party with great gallantry, and was twice wounded. The operations were entirely under Colonel Morland, and were brilliantly carried out. He mentioned the splendid work of the Mounted Infantry, under Lieuts. Porter and Wright, and especially commends Major McClintock, Major Cubitt, Lieut. Dyer and Mr. Wallace, the Deputy Commissioner. For his services in this expedition Lieut. Dyer received a clasp; was twice mentioned in Despatches, and was created a Companion of the Distinguished Service Order [London Gazette, 11 Sept. 1903]: "Lieut. (Local Capt.) Stewart Barton Bythesea Dyer, 2nd Life Guards, West African Frontier Force. In recognition of services with the Kano-Sokoto Expedition." (4) He was in command of the Dakakari Expedition, 1904 (Despatches and clasp). A report dated 18 April, 1904, by Capt. R. H. Goodwin, says: "Orderly Room, 1st Battn., Northern Nigeria Regt., West African Frontier Force. I have much pleasure in conveying to you H.E.'s congratulations and appreciation of the manner in which the operations recently performed by you in Dakakari were carried out." H.E. Colonel Sir Frederick Lugard, K.C.M.G., writes: "I should have liked to express my congratulations to Capt. Dyer (1) on the success of his expedition; (2) on its small cost; (3) on the maps and itineraries. A commander who succeeds in all these three points is ideal. The expedition seems to have been carried out in a very gallant, effective, and at the same time humane manner. I am particularly glad to see that my suggestions as to disarmament and as to giving towns sufficient warning to let women and non-combatants escape were given effect to, and also that the troops are remaining for a while in the country." Major Dyer retired in Jan. 1910, and joined the Special Reserve of Officers, the Wiltshire Militia. He was prospective Liberal candidate for Salisbury, 1912. He was Intelligence Officer on the Staff at Weymouth, 1914–15, and was awarded the War Badge, Sept. 1916, for services rendered. He was appointed Military Attaché, British Embassy at Madrid, in the autumn of 1915; but ill-health compelled him to relinquish the appointment for that of Honorary Attaché, having failed to satisfy the Medical Board. He retired from the Reserve of Officers, owing to ill-health, in Jan. 1917, and died 26 Jan. 1917, at his flat near the British Embassy, Madrid. He was buried in the English Cemetery outside the town. The expeditions in West Africa had undermined a naturally fine constitution, and he succumbed to the disease from which he

Stewart B. B. Dyer.

had been suffering for some time, but was able to continue his work at the Embassy up to within a fortnight of his death, continuing to play polo and fence to the last, and showing no apparent sign of ill-health. The inscription on his tomb, "Sans peur et sans reproche," well describes a very gallant officer who maintained throughout his life the tradition of a long line of brave men from whom he sprang. Major Dyer played football for the War Office v. Harrow in 1899; he took a first class for Musketry at Hythe, 1902; won the Thirty Guinea Challenge Cup and the Ten Guinea Silver Cup in the Epée v. Epée Competition during the Royal Military Tournament at Olympia in 1909, and won medals at the Fencing Tournaments (Epée v. Epée) at Ostende and Houlgate in 1909, and also many medals of the Epée Club at Ranelagh and Hurlingham. He was the winner of silver and bronze medals at the International Fencing Tournament at Prague in 1911. When he retired from the 2nd Life Guards he gave a cup to be annually competed for by teams of five non-commissioned officers and men of the regiment for sabre-fencing. He won a medal for pistol shooting at the International Tournament at Ostende in 1909. Major Dyer was also a good rider to hounds, and hunted with the Bicester and Garth Hunts. He gave a fine set of big game heads to the Cavalry Club. He played polo in H.M. the King of Spain's team in Madrid in 1916, where he won the Ladies' Nomination Cup given that season, and was also fond of big game shooting. Capt. Dyer married, on 11 June, 1906, at St. George's Church, Hanover Square, W., Mai, only child of the late Capt. S. L. Osborne, R.N., and their son is Thomas Musgrave Swinnerton Dyer, born 5 July, 1907.

London Gazette, 6 Sept. 1904.—"The King has been graciously pleased to give orders for the following appointments to the Distinguished Service Order, in recognition of the services of the undermentioned Officers during the operations in Somaliland."

HOOD, THE HONOURABLE HORACE LAMBERT, Capt., Royal Navy, was born at 20, South Street, Mayfair, W., 2 Oct. 1870. He was the second son of Francis Wheeler, Fourth Viscount Hood, and his wife, Edith, daughter of Arthur Wood, Esq., of Calverley Park, Tunbridge Wells. He came of an old Dorset family famous for its seamen and good fighters, being fifth in descent from the illustrious Admiral Sir Samuel Hood (afterwards Viscount Hood), who was second in command to Lord Rodney in his great victory off Domenica in 1782, when he defeated the superior French fleet commanded by the Comte de Grasse. Nelson said of this Lord Hood, who was his sea daddy and precursor, that he was "England's best naval commander." Viscount Bridport, who was this Lord Hood's brother, was second in command to Lord Howe on "the glorious first of June," and blockaded Brest from 1798. Lord Hood, on board the Zealous (a name since adopted for the family motto), first sighted the French fleet in Aboukir Bay, and took part in the Battle of the Nile. Another brother, Capt. Alexander Hood, died in the moment of victory aboard the Mars, in the famous duel with the French ship Hercule. Admiral Horace Hood was thus not the first of his family to be killed in action. Horace Hood was educated at Farnborough School until he entered H.M.S. Britannia. In 1883 he joined the Royal Navy as a Cadet at the age of 13. He served in the Temeraire in 1885, and was a Midshipman in H.M.S. Calliope when the indomitable courage of her commander, Capt. (later Vice-Admiral) Kane, saved that cruiser from destruction in the terrible hurricane in Samoa in March, 1889, when the United States cruisers and other vessels were driven ashore and were lost. In passing his examination for Lieutenant he obtained five first-class certificates with 4,398 marks out of a possible 4,600; this is the highest number of marks ever obtained by an officer at this examination. He was awarded the Beaufort Testimonial, a Goodenough Medal, and the Rider Memorial Prize. He was promoted Lieutenant in 1890, and specialized in gunnery. In 1898 he served with the gunboat flotilla employed during Kitchener's operations on the Nile, and was present at the battles of the Atbara and Omdurman. He was mentioned in Despatches by Sir Herbert Kitchener for his good service, and was promoted Commander. He also received the Egyptian Medal and the Fourth Class of the Turkish Order of the Medjidie. He was promoted Captain, R.N., in 1903, and commanded H.M.S. Hyacinth on the East India Station. He was Flag Captain to Rear-Admiral Atkinson Willes, and landed in command of a naval brigade which stormed and captured on the 21st April, 1904, the stronghold of Illig, in Somaliland, the headquarters of the "Mad Mullah." Capt. Hood's behaviour on that occasion is thus described in a contemporary record: "Capt. Hood, of H.M.S. Hyacinth, greatly distinguished himself in the close fighting which followed the British charge. With sword in one hand and revolver in the other he entered the caves from which the dervishes were firing and accounted for many of them. A Corpl. Flowers followed and despatched a dervish, who was in the act of spearing Capt. Hood from behind." For this exploit Capt. Hood was made a Companion of the Distinguished Service Order [London Gazette, 6 Sept. 1904]: "The Honourable Horace Lambert Hood, Capt., Royal Navy. In recognition of services during the operations in Somaliland." He received the General South African Medal with clasp for Somaliland (190--4). Capt. Hood was created a Member of the Royal Victorian Order in April, 1904. As Captain of H.M.S. Berwick he formed part of the escort which accompanied His Majesty the King to India. He was Naval Attaché at Washington, U.S.A., from Oct. 1907, to Nov. 1908. From Oct. 1910, to Jan. 1913, Capt. Hood was in command of the Royal Naval College, Osborne. He was created a C.B. on the Coronation of King George, and for a short time before attaining flag rank he was A.D.C. to His Majesty (July, 191- to May, 1913). He was promoted to the rank of Rear-Admiral 17 May, 1913, being only 41 years of age. In June, 1914, he was appointed Naval Secretary to the First Lord of the Admiralty, a post which he held till Oct. 1914, when he took command of the Dover Patrol. For some months he was in charge of this, with the flotilla of monitors and destroyers and other vessels which kept the Straits clear of the enemy, and engaged the flank of the German Army from the sea off the Belgian coast. He earned distinction also in land fighting, and was mentioned for gallant and distinguished service in the field by Field-Marshal Lord French in a Despatch dated 18 Feb. 1915, in connection with the part he took to prevent the Germans reaching the Channel Ports. With the guns from his ship he smashed a large portion of the German transport which was advancing by the coast road, and destroyed the bridging material with which they had hoped to cross the Yser. The delay which thus took place in the execution of the German plan had an important bearing on the ultimate defeat of the enemy. On relinquishing command of the Dover Patrol he took command of the Naval Patrol in Irish waters, and held this appointment until he was transferred to the Grand Fleet in command of the Third Battle Cruiser Squadron, H.M.S. Invincible being his flagship. On 31 May (the eve of the anniversary of Lord Howe's glorious first of June, in which Lord Bridport (a Hood) took such a leading part) was fought the Battle of Jutland. Rear-Admiral Hood was Second-in-Command of the Battle Cruiser Fleet, but having been detached with his 3rd Battle Cruiser Squadron, did not arrive on the scene of action till the afternoon, when he was just ahead of the battleships under Admiral Jellicoe. In the words of Admiral Beatty's Despatch: "Admiral Hood, without an instant's hesitation, and in a manner that excited the highest admiration of all who were privileged to witness it, placed his ships in line ahead of Admiral Beatty's squadron. No admiral ever crowned an all too short career more devotedly or in a manner more worthy of the name he bore." At first the 3rd Battle Cruiser Squadron took up its station in advance of the ships under Sir David Beatty, and at one time the Invincible closed to within short range of the enemy's guns. It was here that the Invincible was sunk by a purely chance explosion, only a quarter of an hour after she had come into action. In that short time, however, the descendant of Nelson's tutor had done deadly work. The leading ship of the enemy's line was shattered by salvoes of the Invincible and driven out of action, in fact, before the Grand Fleet came fully into action the van of the enemy was crumpled up, and his line was so disordered that light cruisers engaged his battleships, and the enemy never afterwards appeared as an organized force. With Admiral Hood perished the whole of his crew except two officers and four men. He was awarded posthumously the K.C.B., by Gazette dated 15 Sept. 1916. Admiral Beatty, writing to a friend, uses these words: "I have no regrets except for the gallant comrades who have gone—who died gloriously. It would have warmed your heart to see the gallant Hood leading his squadron into action." The death of this heroic member of a famous family could scarcely have taken place under more fitting circumstances, so well in keeping with the splendid traditions of his great family.

"Zealous he was in life, fearless in death."

The Hon. H. L. Hood.

On the 19th Jan. 1910, at Burlington, Iowa, U.S.A., he married Ellen, widow of George Nickerson, Esq., of Dedham, Mass., and daughter of A. F. Touzalin, Esq., of Boston, U.S.A. Their sons are: Samuel, born 15 Oct. 1910, and Alexander Lambert, born 11 March, 1914.

KENDALL, CHARLES JAMES COPE, Commander, Royal Indian Marine, was born in 1864, son of the late Surgeon-General H. Kendall, A.M.D., and Annie, daughter of General Sir James Brind, G.C.B. He was educated at Epsom, and entered the Royal Indian Marine in 1885; served in Burma, 1885–89 (Medal with two clasps); with the Marine Survey, India, 1889–97; in China, 1900 (Medal), and in Somaliland, 1904. For his services in the last-mentioned campaign he was created a Companion of the Distinguished Service Order [London Gazette, 6 Sept. 1904]: "Charles James Cope Kendall, Commander, Royal Indian Marine. In recognition of services during the operations in Somaliland." Capt. Kendall served in the European War. He was appointed Junior Marine Transport Officer at Suez 22 Aug. 1914, and held that post until transferred to Cairo, as Divisional Naval Transport Officer, 11 Feb. 1918, reverting to the Royal Indian Marine 12 June, 1919. He was created a C.I.E. in 1919, and was also given the 3rd Class Order of the Nile. He married, at St. Paul's, Knightsbridge, 26 June, 1901, Lilian Mary (died 1909), youngest daughter of the late Rev. William Maule, of Eyensbury, St. Neots, and has one son, Bryan Harold Maule, born 14 Feb. 1906.

ALLEN, ROBERT FRANKLIN, Major, was born 21 Feb. 1860, son of the late Major R. Austen Allen, M.D., A.M.S. He joined the Royal Engineers 6 April, 1879, as a Lieutenant, and became Captain 1 April, 1889. He served in the expedition to Manipur in 1891, as Field Engineer, Kohima Column, and C.R.E. of the Force (Despatches [London Gazette, 14 Aug. 1891]; Medal with clasp); was promoted Major 19 Dec. 1897; served in East Africa in 1903 and 1904; in operations in Somaliland and the action at Jidballi, serving as C.R.E. from 22 July, 1903. He was mentioned in Despatches [London Gazette, 2 Sept. 1904]; received the Medal with two clasps, and was created a Companion of the Distinguished Service Order [London Gazette, 6 Sept. 1904]: "Robert Franklin Allen, Major, Royal Engineers. In recognition of services

Robert Franklin Allen.

during the operations in Somaliland." He was promoted Lieutenant-Colonel 14 April, 1905, and was given the Brevet of Colonel 14 April, 1908; was placed on retired pay (Indian Pensions) 7 April, 1909. He died 20 Nov. 1916. He married, in 1886, Alice Gordon, daughter of the late Surgeon-General Inkson, and left one son.

APLIN, PHILIP JOHN HANHAM, Major, was born 18 Dec. 1858, son of Capt. P. H. P. Aplin and his wife, Jane, daughter of C. E. Hanham, Esq. He entered the Army as a Second Lieutenant in the 86th Foot 1 May, 1878, and was transferred 22 March, 1879, to the 15th Foot. He served in the Afghan War of 1879 and 1880 (receiving the Medal). He joined the Bombay Staff Corps 22 May, 1880; received the Medal with two clasps for the Burmese Expedition, 1885 to 1889; was promoted Captain 1 May, 1889, in the Indian Staff Corps, and became Major 1 May, 1898. Major Aplin took part in the Somaliland operations, East Africa, from 1902 to 1904, serving from 31 Oct. 1903, as Post Commandant, Lines of Communication. He received the Medal with clasp; was mentioned in Despatches [London Gazette, 2 Sept. 1904], and created a Companion of the Distinguished Service Order [London Gazette, 6 Sept. 1904]: "Philip John Hanham Aplin, Major, Indian Army. In recognition of services during the operations in Somaliland." He received promotion to Lieutenant-Colonel 1 May, 1904, and was given the Brevet of Colonel 1 May, 1907. In the European War Colonel P. J. H. Aplin commanded the 18th Middlesex Pioneers. He married, in 1905, Mary Bertha, daughter of Brigade-Surgeon C. F. Oldham, of The Lodge, Great Bealings, and they have a son and a daughter.

BRIDGES, GEORGE TOM MOLESWORTH, Capt. and Brevet Major, was born 20 Aug. 1871, son of Major T. W. Bridges, Royal (late Bengal) Artillery, and Mary Ann, daughter of F. T. Philippi, Esq., He was educated at Newton College; joined the Royal Artillery 19 Feb. 1892, and was promoted Lieutenant 19 Feb. 1895. He was employed with the Central African Rifles for a few months in 1899, and became Captain 5 April, 1900. He served in South Africa, 1899–1901, with the Imperial Light Horse, and as Commandant, Hanover Road, being present at the Relief of Ladysmith; operations in the Transvaal, April to July, 1901 (in command of the 5th and 6th West Australian Mounted Infantry, May to July 1901); operations in Orange River Colony, Aug. to Sept. 1901, and Oct. to Nov. 1901; operations on the Zululand Frontier of Natal in Sept. and Oct. 1901; operations in Cape Colony 30 Nov. 1900, to March, 1901. For his services in the Boer War he was given the Brevet of Major 22 Aug. 1902; was mentioned in Despatches [London Gazette 8 Feb. 1901, and 29 July, 1902], and received the Queen's Medal with six clasps. He served in Somaliland, as Special Service Officer, 1902–4; raised and commanded the Tribal Horse, and was severely wounded; took part in the action at Jidballi. He was specially mentioned in Despatches; received the Medal with two clasps, and was created a Companion of the Distinguished Service Order [London Gazette, 6 Sept. 1904]: "George Tom Molesworth Bridges, Capt. and Brevet Major, Royal Artillery. In recognition of services during the operations in Somaliland." He was Staff Captain, and later G.S.O.3, Headquarters of Army, from Feb. to Nov. 1907, and Instructor, Cavalry School, Dec. 1907, to June, 1908. He was promoted to Major, 4th Dragoon Guards, 19 Aug. 1908, and served as Military Attaché at The Hague, Brussels, Copenhagen and Christiania from March, 1910, to March, 1914; became Lieutenant-Colonel, 4th Hussars, 20 Sept. 1914. He had a very distinguished record in the European War, in which he served, in turn, as the Head of the Military Mission with the Belgian Field Army; in command of the 19th Division, from Dec. 1915, to Oct. 1917, except from April to June, 1917, when he was a Military Member of Mr. Balfour's Mission to U.S.A.; as Head of the British War Mission to U.S.A. in 1918; as Chief of the British Military Mission to the Army of the Orient 9 Jan. 1920. He was wounded three times; was given the Brevet of Colonel 1 Jan. 1916; was promoted Major-General for distinguished service 1 Jan. 1917, and Temporary Lieutenant-General, April to June, 1917, and again in Jan. 1919. He was created a C.M.G. in 1915, a C.B. in 1918, and a K.C.M.G. in 1919, and has the following foreign orders, viz.: Officer of Leopold, Grand Croix de la Couronne, Médaille de Guerre (Belgian), and Officer of the Legion of Honour and the Croix de Guerre with two Palms (French), and the American Distinguished Service Medal. Lieut.-General Sir G. T. M. Bridges is also a Fellow of the Royal Geographical Society. He married, in 1908, Janet Florence, widow of Major W. Marshall, Grenadier Guards, and daughter of the late G. Menzies, of Haliburton House, Perth.

EUSTACE, ALEXANDER HENRY, Major, was born 14 June, 1863, son of Colonel J. T. Eustace. He joined the East Surrey Regt., as Second Lieutenant, 6 May, 1885, and became Lieutenant, Indian Staff Corps, 13 July, 1887. He served in the Hazara Expedition of 1888 (Medal with clasp), and in the Hazara Expedition of 1891, as Field Intelligence Officer, 1st and 2nd Brigades (clasp); became Captain, Indian Army, 6 May, 1896, and Major 6 May, 1903. He served in East Africa, 1903–4; was mentioned in Despatches [London Gazette, 2 Sept. 1904]; received the Medal and clasp, and was created a Companion of the Distinguished Service Order [London Gazette, 6 Sept. 1904]: "Alexander Henry Eustace, Major, Indian Army. In recognition of services during the operations in Somaliland." Major Eustace was promoted to Lieutenant-Colonel 22 Sept. 1907, and Colonel, 52nd Sikhs, Frontier Force, 1 Dec. 1911. He served in the European War; was Temporary Brigadier-General 7 Dec. 1914, to 3 Dec. 1916; was promoted Major-General 1 Jan. 1917. He was created a C.B. in 1916, and a C.B.E. in 1919. In 1904 Major-General Eustace married Evelyn Mary, youngest daughter of the late Samuel Stonestreet, of Kimberley, and they have one son.

Alexander H. Eustace.

BERESFORD, THE HON. JOHN GRAHAM HOPE HORSLEY DE LA POER, Major, was born 5 Dec. 1866, son of the 3rd Baron Decies and Catharine Anne, daughter of William Dent, R.N., of Shortflatt Tower, Northumberland. He was educated at Eton, and entered the 7th Hussars 5 Feb. 1887. He was A.D.C. to Lord Connemara (then Governor of Madras), and Adjutant of the 7th Hussars, and served as A.D.C. to H.R.H. The Duke of Connaught, 1894–1900; served under General Plumer in the operations against the Matabele in 1896 (Despatches [London Gazette, 9 March, 1897]). Capt. the Hon. J. G. H. H. de la P. Beresford commanded the 37th Imperial Yeomanry in South Africa in 1902, with the rank of Lieutenant-Colonel (Medal). He became Major 26 June, 1903, and as Lieutenant-Colonel commanded the Tribal Horse in Somaliland, 1903–4, where he was also employed as a Special Service Officer; was present at the action of Jidballi. He was mentioned in Despatches [London Gazette, 2 Sept. 1904]; and was created a Companion of the Distinguished Service Order [London Gazette, 6 Sept. 1904]: "The Honourable John Graham Hope Horsley Beresford, Major, 7 Hussars. In recognition of services during the operations in Somaliland." He succeeded his brother as 5th Baron Decies (created 1912) in 1910, and on 12 Feb. 1910, retired from the 7th Hussars. Lord Decies became Lieutenant-Colonel Commanding the South Irish Horse in 1912. He is a Representative Peer for Ireland, and was appointed a Privy Councillor for Ireland in 1918. He belongs to the Military Order of Spain. His recreations are cricket, hunting, and polo and racing. In 1911, he married Helen Vivien, daughter of George Jay Gould and Edith M. Gould (*née* Kingdon), and they have one son, the Hon. Arthur George Marcus Douglas de la Poer Beresford, born 25 April, 1915, and two daughters.

SHAKERLEY, GEOFFREY CHARLES, Capt., was born 19 Nov. 1869, eldest son of the late Mr. Geoffrey J. Shakerley (who was also in the Artillery, and fought in the Crimean War), of Grove Park, Warwick. He entered the Army 29 Nov. 1890, as a Second Lieutenant in the King's Royal Rifle Corps; was promoted Lieutenant 9 Sept. 1893, and Captain 29 Dec. 1898; from Oct. 1895, to Oct. 1899, he was Adjutant of his regiment. He served with the Mounted Infantry in the South African War, 1899 to 1902, taking part in operations in Natal in 1899, including action at Reitfontein and Lombard's Kop; defence of Ladysmith, including action of 6 Jan. 1900; operations in Natal, March to June, 1900, including action at Laing's Nek; operations in Orange River Colony 30 Nov. 1900, to 31 May, 1902. He was mentioned in Despatches [London Gazette, 10 Sept. 1901], and received the Queen's Medal with five clasps. He served in Somaliland (with Mounted Infantry), 1902–4, being present in the action at Jidballi; was severely wounded; mentioned in Despatches [London Gazette, 7 Aug. 1903], and in Despatches of Brigadier-General Manning, 17 Aug. 1903, and Sir O. C. Egerton, 30 May, 1904 [London Gazette, 2 Sept. 1904]; received the Medal with two clasps, and was created a Companion of the Distinguished Service Order [London Gazette, 6 Sept. 1904]: "Geoffrey Charles Shakerley, Capt., King's Royal Rifle Corps. In recognition of services during the operations in Somaliland." Capt. Shakerley served as Adjutant of Militia from April, 1905, to Dec. 1907, and was promoted Major 18 Dec. 1907. He served in the European War, and was killed in action in France 15 May, 1915. His brother, Lieut. Arthur Cecil Shakerley, R.F.A., the fourth and only surviving son of the late Mr. Geoffrey Shakerley, was killed in action on 22 April, 1917. Major Geoffrey Shakerley had married, in 1905, Marjory, youngest daughter of Audley Harvey, of Ickwell Bury, Bedfordshire, and they had one son and one daughter.

HARRIS, CHARLES BERESFORD MAULE, Capt., was born 13 Jan. 1866. He was educated at King's College, London, and at the Royal Veterinary College, London (F.R.C.V.S.). He entered the Army on 27 Aug. 1890, with a commission in the Army Veterinary Corps, and served on the North-West Frontier of India, 1897–98 (Tochi), as Veterinary Officer, 2nd Brigade, and on the Staff (Medal with clasp). He served in South Africa, 1899 to 1902, and was present at operations in Natal in 1899, and the defence of Ladysmith; operations in Natal, March to June, 1900, including the action at Laing's Nek (6 to 9 June); operations in the Transvaal, east of Pretoria, July to 29 Nov. 1900, including actions at Belfast (26 and 27 Aug.) and Lydenberg (6 to 8 Sept.); operations in Cape Colony, Dec. 1900 (Queen's Medal with five clasps, and King's Medal with two clasps); was promoted Captain 27 Aug. 1900. He served in Somaliland, 1903 to 1904, as Inspecting Veterinary Officer from 28 May, 1903. He was mentioned in Despatches [London Gazette, 2 Sept. 1904]; received the Medal with clasp, and was created a Companion of the Distinguished Service Order [London Gazette, 6 Sept. 1904]: "Charles Beresford Maule Harris, Capt., Army Veterinary Department. In recognition of services during the operations in Somaliland." He was promoted Major 27 Aug. 1905, and retired from the Army Veterinary Corps 8 May, 1912. He became Lieutenant-Colonel, Reserve of Officers, Army Veterinary Corps, 13 Dec. 1915. He served in the European War with the 48th Division and 4th Army Corps, and was three times mentioned in Despatches. His favourite recreations are hunting and shooting. Lieut.-Colonel C. B. M. Harris married, in 1898, Mary Augusta, daughter of the late Major John Tatham.

Charles B. M. Harris.

HUDSON, CORRIE, Capt., was born 5 April, 1874, at Manilla Hall, Clifton, Bristol, son of Charles Thomas Hudson, M.A., LL.D. (Cantab.), F.R.S. (Head Master of Clifton Grammar School, and later of Manilla Hall, Clifton; Naturalist and Scientist), and Louisa Maria fiott Hudson (née Hammond).

Corrie Hudson.

He was educated at Manilla Hall School, Clifton, and Charing Cross Hospital, London (F.R.C.S.E., M.R.C.S., L.R.C.P., and joined the Indian Medical Service 28 Jan. 1899. He served in China in 1900 (Medal), and was from 1900 to 1903 Medical Officer, 2nd Q.V.O. Rajput Light Infantry, with the China Expeditionary Force under Sir O'Moore Creagh. He became Captain 28 Jan. 1902. On his return to India he went to the Delhi Durbar to an Indian General Hospital in 1903, and then joined the Somaliland Field Force, with which he served from 1903 to 1904 as Secretary to the P.M.O., and later in a Section of Field Ambulance. He was present at the action of Jidballi. He was mentioned in Despatches by Sir Charles Egerton [London Gazette, 2 Sept. 1904], there being a special notice "for particularly valuable work" in the London Gazette of 3 Sept. 1904, and was created a Companion of the Distinguished Service Order [London Gazette, 6 Sept. 1904]: "Corrie Hudson, Capt., I.M.S. For services in Somaliland." He received the Medal. He served as Staff Surgeon, Bangalore, from 1908 to 1912. He became Major 23 July, 1910; served as Officer Commanding No. 2 Bulgarian Red Cross Unit, with a British Red Cross Unit, in the Turco-Balkan War of 1912-13, and in 1913 served in the Persian Gulf, in Persia and Arabia in operations directed against gun-running by the Arabs (Red Cross Medal). Major Hudson served in France as D.A.D.M.S., 1st Indian Cavalry Division, from Oct. 1914, to June, 1916, in operations around Festubert, Neuve Chapelle, Ypres, Loos and the River Ancre, for which he was mentioned in Despatches in Jan. 1916. In 1917 he was D.A.D.M.S., 16th Indian Division, Burhan, and was Commandant, School of Instruction for Temporary I.M.S. Officers at Rawalpindi in 1918, becoming Lieutenant-Colonel 28 July, 1918. In 1919 he served as Commanding Officer of the 14th Indian General Hospital at Rawalpindi, and A.D.M.S., Lines of Communication, Waziristan Force. Lieut.-Colonel Hudson has the Mons Star, the British General Service Medal and the Victory Medal. On 23 July, 1904, at St. Mary Abbots, Kensington, London, W., he married Frances Edith Barratt, daughter of Alfred Barratt, late Education Department, Whitehall, London, S.W., and they have one daughter, Edith Joyce Corrie, born 20 Nov. 1905.

HAMERTON, ALBERT ERNEST, Capt., was born 9 Dec. 1873, at Stalybridge, Lancashire, son of the Rev. T. J. Hamerton, Vicar of St. Alban's, Leeds, and Elizabeth, daughter of the late Frederick Piggin, of Nottingham. He was educated at Leeds Grammar School, and at the School of Medicine, University of Leeds, and joined the Royal Army Medical Corps 25 April, 1900, becoming Captain 25 April, 1903. He served in the Somaliland Campaign, 1903-6, and was present at the action of Jidballi, 1904. He was mentioned in Despatches [London Gazette, 2 Sept. 1904]; received the Medal with two clasps, and was created a Companion of the Distinguished Service Order [London Gazette, 6 Sept. 1904]: "Albert Ernest Hamerton, Capt., Royal Army Medical Corps. In recognition of services during the operations in Somaliland." Capt. Hamerton was seconded for service with the Sleeping Sickness Commission, Royal Society, in Uganda (24 Sept. 1908, to 24 Dec. 1910), and Nyasaland (20 July, 1911, to 27 March, 1914), receiving promotion to Major 25 Jan. 1912. He served in France from the beginning of and continuously throughout the European War, in command of a Cavalry Field Ambulance (1914-16), and of a Casualty Clearing Station (1916-18); was present at the First Battle of Ypres in 1914, the Second Battle of Ypres in 1915, and other actions. He became Acting Lieutenant-Colonel 2 July, 1916, and was promoted to substantive rank 26 Dec. 1917. For his services in the European War he was mentioned in Despatches in April and on 3 June, 1918, and was created a C.M.G. in June, 1918. After the European War he was A.D.M.S., 25th Division, from Nov. 1918, until appointed O.C., No. 30 General Hospital, in March, 1919. His favourite pursuit is zoology. Lieut.-Colonel Hamerton married, 17 Sept. 1919, Amelia, widow of Morris Miller, and daughter of the late Alfred Jacob, of Bloemfontein, South Africa.

BREADING, GEORGE REMINGTON, Capt., was born 2 Oct. 1877; he was slightly wounded at Jidballi, and had the Medal with two clasps, and was created a Companion of the Distinguished Service Order [London Gazette, 6 Sept. 1904]: "Capt. George Remington Breading, The Worcestershire Regt. (employed with the King's African Rifles). In recognition of services during the operations in Somaliland." He served with the West African Frontier Force, 1906-10, and saw war service in Somaliland, 1908 to 1910 (clasp), becoming Temporary Major and Second-in-Command, King's African Rifles, 29 Sept. 1909. He retired from the Worcestershire Regt. as Captain; became Major 29 Jan. 1917, Reserve of Officers, Worcestershire Regt. (Temporary Lieutenant-Colonel in the Army); is Temporary Major, Somaliland Camel Corps.

HORTON, JAMES HENRY, Lieut., was born 27 Dec. 1871. He was educated at Guy's Hospital, and won the Arthur Durham Prize in 1891; was Member and held the Certificate of the Medical Psychological Association; became M.R.C.S. and L.R.C.P., London, in 1895, and was Home Physician at Bethlem Royal Hospital, and at Guy's Hospital in 1895; won the Marshall Webb Prize and Medal at Netley in 1902. He entered the Indian Medical Service 29 Jan. 1902, and served in East Africa, taking part in the operations in Somaliland, and being present at the action of Jidballi. He received the Medal and two clasps for this campaign (1902 to 1904); was mentioned in Despatches [London Gazette, 7 Aug. 1903], and was also created a Companion of the Distinguished Service Order [London Gazette, 6 Sept. 1904]: "James Henry Horton, Lieut., Indian Medical Service. In recognition of services during the operations in Somaliland." He became Captain 29 Jan. 1905. On the North-West Frontier of India in 1908 he accompanied the expedition into the Mohmand country (Medal with clasp). He also rendered service as a Special Medical Officer on plague duty in India, and was later Personal Assistant to the Surgeon-General with the Government of Bombay, at Poona, India. He served in the Balkan War in 1912, and was promoted to Major 29 July, 1913. He served in the European War with the Indian Expeditionary Force in Mesopotamia in 1914 and 1915. Brevet Colonel James Henry Horton died in July, 1917, in India. He held the Russian Order of St. Vladimir and St. George.

London Gazette, 11 Nov. 1904.—Special Memorandum (see below) relating to the undermentioned officer.

M'CORMICK, HAROLD BARRY, Lieut., was born 3 Sept. 1867, son of William H. M'Cormick, Solicitor, of Geelong, Victoria, and of Mrs. M'Cormick. He served in South Africa with the West Australian Contingent, and was promoted Lieutenant 14 March, 1901. He was mentioned in Despatches [London Gazette, 29 July, 1902], and was created a Companion of the Distinguished Service Order in recognition of services during the operations in South Africa. The award of the decoration to Lieut. H. B. M'Cormick was evidently confused with that to Lieut. John M'Cormick, of the Tasmanian Imperial Bushmen. Memorandum [London Gazette, 11 Nov. 1904]: "The notification which appeared in the London Gazette of 21 April, 1903, relating to Lieut. H. M'Cormick and the award to him of the Distinguished Service Order, is in addition to—and not in substitution of—those of the 29th July, 1902, and the 31st Oct. 1902, relating to Lieut. J. M'Cormick. The description of the first-named officer is Lieut. H. B. M'Cormick, 6th Contingent, West Australian Mounted Infantry." He retired with the rank of Lieutenant after the South African War. He became Captain, Special Reserve, East Lancashire Regt., 29 Aug. 1914. He served in the European War in 1914 and 1915, in Gallipoli (wounded) and in Mesopotamia. He was appointed Lieutenant-Colonel of a service battalion of the East Lancashire Regt. 15 May, 1917. Capt. M'Cormick was a pioneer in West Australian gold-mining, and was Secretary of the West Australian Chamber of Mines; explored and developed minerals in Lower Egypt and the Sudan. He is engaged in opening up the rubber industry in Burmah. His favourite recreations are golf and big game shooting. He rowed No. 5 in the Victoria Interstate Eight. He married, in 1904, and has a son and a daughter.

London Gazette, 16 Dec. 1904.—"The King has been graciously pleased to give orders for the following appointments to the Distinguished Service Order, in recognition of the services of the following Officers with the Tibet Mission Escort."

MULLALY, ALEXANDER, Major, was born 26 July, 1866. He joined the Middlesex Regt. 30 Jan. 1886, becoming Lieutenant, Indian Staff Corps, 16 April, 1887; took part in the operations in Chitral, 1895, with the Relief Force (Medal with clasp); promoted Captain 30 Jan. 1897; served at Tirah, 1897-98, as Brigade Commandant Officer, 1st Brigade, 1st Division (3 Oct. 1897, to 6 April, 1898). He was mentioned in Despatches [London Gazette, 5 April, 1898]; awarded two clasps. He served on the West Frontier of India, Waziristan, 1901-2, as Supply and Transport Officer (Despatches [London Gazette, 8 Aug. 1902]; Brevet of Major 5 June, 1902; clasp). He was promoted Major 30 Jan. 1904. Major Mullaly served in Tibet in 1903 and 1904, as Chief Supply and Transport Officer. He was mentioned in Despatches [London Gazette, 13 Dec. 1904]; received the Medal, and was created a Companion of the Distinguished Service Order [London Gazette, 16 Dec. 1904]: "Alexander Mullaly, Major, Indian Army. In recognition of services with the Tibet Mission Escort." He served on the North-West Frontier of India, 1908, as Divisional Transport Officer; took part in the operations in the Zakka Khel country (Despatches [London Gazette, 22 May, 1908]; Brevet of Lieutenant-Colonel 16 July, 1908). Lieut.-Colonel A. Mullaly died in 1913. He had married Mary Harriet, eldest daughter of the late Major-General Doveton, Madras Staff Corps.

MURRAY, FRANK, Major, was born 10 June, 1864, and received his commission in the Devon Regt. 7 Feb. 1885.

Frank Murray.

In the following year he transferred to the Indian Staff Corps. He saw service with the Burmese Expedition of 1885-89 (Medal with two clasps), and the Waziristan Expedition, 1894-95 (clasp); became Captain 7 Feb. 1896, and Major 7 Feb. 1903. Major Murray took part in the Campaign in Tibet in 1903 and 1904, including the operations at and around Gyantse and the march to Lhassa. He was mentioned in Despatches [London Gazette, 13 Dec. 1904]; received the Medal and clasp, and was created a Companion of the Distinguished Service Order [London Gazette, 16 Dec. 1904]: "Frank Murray, Major, Indian Army. In recognition of services with the Tibet Mission Escort." He became Lieutenant-Colonel 5 June, 1909. He served in the operations in the Abor country, 1911-12 (Despatches [London Gazette, 16 July, 1912]; Brevet of Colonel; Medal with clasp); became Colonel (8th Gurkha Rifles) 22 Oct. 1913, and was appointed Temporary Brigadier-

General 24 Sept. 1914. Brigadier-General F. Murray served in the European War. He died at sea on service 18 April, 1917, aged 52 years.

LYE, ROBERT COBB, Major, was born 27 Nov. 1865, and entered the

Robert Cobb Lye.

Hampshire Regt. as Lieutenant 7 Feb. 1885, from which he was transferred to the Indian Staff Corps 26 Jan. 1888. He had a record of very distinguished service, which included the Burmese Expedition of 1885–87 (slightly wounded); Despatches [London Gazette, 2 Sept. 1887]; Medal with clasp); the First Miranzai Expedition of 1891, and service with the Chitral Relief Force, 1895 (Medal with clasp). He was promoted to Captain in the Indian Army 7 Feb. 1896, and served on the North-West Frontier, 1897–98, in the Malakand operations, as Assistant to the C.C.O. (6 Aug. to Oct. 1897); in operations in Bajour and in the Mamund country, Utman Khel and Buner, as Assistant to the C.C.O.; in the attack and capture of the Tanga Pass (clasp). He was promoted Major 7 Feb. 1903. He was with the Tibet Mission Escort in 1903 and 1904, including the action at Niani and the operations at and near Gyantse. He was severely wounded; mentioned in Despatches [London Gazette, 3 Dec. 1904]; received the Medal and clasp, and was created a Companion of the Distinguished Service Order [London Gazette, 16 Dec. 1904]: "Robert Cobb Lye, Major, Indian Army. In recognition of services with the Tibet Mission Escort." He also served in operations in the Zakka Khel country in 1908, for which he received the Medal with clasp; became Lieutenant-Colonel 8 Oct. 1909. He was appointed Commandant, Line of Communications (graded as D.A.A.G., War Office), 17 Nov. 1914, and served in the Great War in this position until 24 Jan. 1916. Colonel R. C. Lye, 23rd and 34th Sikh Pioneers, died at Sialkot, while on active service, 28 June, 1917.

RAY, MACCARTHY REAGH EMMET, Major, was born at Allahabad, India, 17 Nov. 1867, son of Thomas Britt Ray, Assistant Commissioner of Inland Customs, North-West Provinces and Oudh, India, and Emily

MacCarthy R. E. Ray.

Julia Ray (née Ashe). He was educated at St. Michael's College, Bayswater, London, W; Bedford Grammar School, and Sandhurst; was gazetted to the 1st Battn. Norfolk Regt. 29 Aug. 1885. He transferred to the Indian Army in 1889, and served in the Burma Campaign of 1889, commanding the Mounted Infantry, 33rd Bengal Infantry, in the operations in Magwe, from July to Sept. He received the Medal and clasp, and a letter of appreciation from Brigadier-General W. Penn Symons, dated 9 Aug. 1889. In the Chin Lushai Expedition of 1891–92, under Major-General Graham, he commanded the Zandwin Column of the 7th Bengal Infantry, operating in the Chin Bok country, South Chin Hills. He received the Medal and a Letter of Appreciation from Lord Roberts, Commander-in-Chief in India, dated 21 June, 1892. He served in Hong Kong from 1892 to 1897, and was awarded the Macgregor Memorial Medal in 1902. In the China Campaign he served as Field Intelligence Officer (June and July, 1900), and then as D.A.A.G., Lines of Communication. In the actions near Tientsin, Aug. 1900, he was D.A.A.G. to the International Expedition to Tulin, and Staff Officer to the G.O.C., International Force, and both to Brigadier-General A. R. F. Doward, C.B., D.S.O. In the Paoting Fu Expedition he was D.A.A.G. to Lieut.-General Sir Alfred Gaselee, K.C.B., and Special Service Officer under Major-General O'Moore Creagh, V.C. In 1901 he was D.A.A.G., Lines of Communication, until Aug., and went as Special Service Officer to Shanghai until Nov. (Medal with clasp; Despatches [London Gazette, 14 May, 1901]; American Order of the Dragon, and a Letter from Major-General A. R. Chaffee, American Army, dated 13 May, 1901]. Returning to India, he was D.A.Q.M.G., I.B.Q.M.G.'s Department, May to July, 1902; D.A.Q.M.G. for the 1/3rd Infantry Division, Delhi Manœuvres, and 2nd Infantry Division, Durbar Troops, during the winter of 1902–3; D.A.Q.M.G. in March, 1903, and promoted Major 29 Aug. 1903. He served as D.A.Q.M.G. on the Staff of Brigadier-General J. R. L. Macdonald, C.B., R.E., in the Tibet Expedition of 1903–4; was twice mentioned in Despatches (Gyantse, 11 July, 1904: "Major Ray twice crossed the danger zone to bring information to the G.O.C. of progress of attack, and helped to carry up gun-cotton," and London Gazette, 13 Dec. 1904). For these services he was created a Companion of the Distinguished Service Order [London Gazette, 16 Dec. 1904]: "MacCarthy Reagh Emmet Ray, Major, Indian Army. In recognition of services with the Tibet Mission Escort." He was invested by the King at Buckingham Palace 10 Feb. 1905. Major Ray also received the Medal with clasp. In May, 1905, he was appointed Second-in-Command of the 1st Brahmans. He was invalided home from India in April, 1906, and died at St. Heliers, Jersey, 27 June, 1906. Major Ray was a good shot with the rifle. He travelled widely in the Far East, through China, via Siam, and through Manchuria. He also visited Japan, North America, and parts of Europe. He was an excellent linguist, and speaking French fluently, was appointed one of the Interpreters for the British Army in the China Expedition for the Relief of the Legations. He was acquainted with Russian, and had qualified in

Hindustani, Persian and Higher Pushtu. His mind was intellectual and refined, with a taste for both literature and art. Actuated by a high sense of duty, he served his country and generation faithfully, and gave them of his best. In memory of Major Ray, a MacCarthy Ray Memorial Prize has been founded for the Military Class of the Bedford Grammar School.

MOORE, CHARLES HESKETH GRANT, Capt., was born 5 July, 1868. He joined the Army 11 Feb. 1888, with a commission in the West Yorkshire Regt.; became Lieutenant 24 Sept. 1890, and joined the Indian Staff Corps 11 Sept. 1891. He served on the North-West Frontier of India, 1897–98, taking part in the Malakand operations as Assistant to the Base Commandant Officer (6 Aug. to Oct. 1897), and in the operations in Bajaur and in the Mohmand country. He was mentioned in Despatches [London Gazette, 18 March, 1898], and received the Medal and clasp. He became Captain 11 Feb. 1899. Capt. Moore took part with distinction in the operations in Tibet in 1903 and 1904; was present in the action at Niani; operations at and around Gyantse and the march to Lhassa. He was mentioned in Despatches [London Gazette, 13 Dec. 1904], and was created a Companion of the Distinguished Service Order [London Gazette, 16 Dec. 1904]: "Charles Hesketh Grant Moore, Capt., Indian Army. In recognition of services with the Tibet Mission Escort." He also received the Medal and clasp. He was promoted Major 11 Feb. 1906, and served in 1908 as Brigade Transport Officer, 1st Brigade, in operations in the Mohmand country, including the engagement at Kargha, for which he was mentioned in Despatches [London Gazette, 14 Aug. 1908], and awarded the Medal with clasp. He became Lieutenant-Colonel 11 Feb. 1914. He served in the European War from 1914–17; was Assistant Director of Supplies and Transport, Indian Cavalry Corps, British Expeditionary Force, 1 Feb. 1915, to 11 March, 1916. He was mentioned in Despatches, and was made a C.M.G. in 1915; became Temporary Colonel 18 Nov. 1918; holds the position of Deputy Director of Supplies and Transport, Southern Command, East Indies. He married, in 1899, Cecile Louisa, daughter of Major C. Murphy, R.A.

LUKE, THOMAS MAWE, Capt., was born 13 May, 1872, son of Colonel H. F. Luke, of Kensington, W., and of Frances Matilda Burke. He was educated at a private school, and joined the Royal Artillery 4 May, 1892; became Lieutenant 4 May, 1895. He served on the North-West Frontier of India, 1897–98, with the Tirah Expeditionary Force (Medal with clasp). He was promoted Captain 19 Jan. 1900. Capt. Luke served in Tibet, 1903–4, in the operations at and around Gyantse; was mentioned in Despatches [London Gazette, 13 Dec. 1904]; received the Medal with clasp, and was created a Companion of the Distinguished Service Order, "for marked ability in handling his guns and devotion to duty during a very trying campaign" [London Gazette, 16 Dec. 1904]: "Thomas Mawe Luke, Capt., Royal Artillery. In recognition of services with the Tibet Mission Escort." He served on the North-West Frontier of India (Mohmand), 1908 (Medal with clasp), and became Major 15 Feb. 1913. In the European War he served as D.A.A.G., A.A.G., D.A.G., and from Oct. 1916, to June, 1919, as Director of Administration, General Headquarters, India, with the rank of Brigadier-General. He was given the Brevet of Lieutenant-Colonel 29 Nov. 1915, and became Lieutenant-Colonel, May, 1917. Lieut.-Colonel Luke was C.R.A., Kohat Kurran Force, from June, to 31 Sept. 1919, in the last Afghan War. He was made an O.B.E. in 1918, and a C.B.E. in Sept. 1919, for his services in the war, and has the General Service and Victory Medals. He married, in 1901, Mary Elizabeth, daughter of J. Lamb, of Penrith, and they have one son, Stephen Elliot Vyvyan, born 26 Sept. 1905.

FISHER, JULIAN LAWRENCE, Capt., was born 1 May, 1877, son of the late Walter Fisher, of Amington Hall, Tamworth. He was educated at Harrow (The Park), and joined the 1st Battn. The Royal Fusiliers, as Second Lieutenant, 1 Dec. 1897; became Lieutenant 16 Nov. 1898, and Captain 13 July, 1901. Capt. Fisher was Adjutant, Royal Fusiliers, 2 July, 1902, to 7 April, 1905, and served in the Tibet Expedition, 1904, being present at the action at Niami; operations at and around Gyantse and the march to Lhassa (Medal with clasp); mentioned in Despatches [London Gazette, 13 Dec. 1904], and was created a Companion of the Distinguished Service Order [London Gazette, 16 Dec. 1904]: "Julian Lawrence Fisher, Capt., Royal Fusiliers. In recognition of services with the Tibet Mission Escort." Capt. Fisher was Adjutant, Mounted Infantry, in South Africa, 1 Dec. 1907, to 30 Nov. 1910. He was Adjutant, Special Reserve, 20 May, 1912, to 1915. He served in the European War, 1914–15, taking part in operations in the Dardanelles. He was mentioned in Sir Ian Hamilton's Despatch, dated War Office, 5 Aug. 1915, for services in the Dardanelles; was promoted to Major 11 March, 1915, and Temporary Lieutenant-Colonel, Royal Fusiliers, 16 July to 6 Aug. 1915. He was wounded; given the Brevet of Lieutenant-Colonel 3 June, 1917, and was

D. W. H. Humphreys

created a C.M.G. in 1919. He married, in 1913, Dora, youngest daughter of the late Sir W. Richmond-Brown, Bart., and they have two sons; Walter Julian, born, 1915; Gerald, born, 1918; and a daughter, Eileen, born, 1916.

HUMPHREYS, DASHWOOD WILLIAM HARRINGTON, Capt., was born 6 Feb. 1872, and was the last surviving son of the late T. W. D. Humphreys, of Donoughmore, Castlefin, Ireland, and joined the Army, Unattached List, 28 Nov. 1894, joining the Indian Staff Corps 18 Feb. 1896. He was promoted Lieutenant, Indian Army, 28 Feb. 1897, and Captain 28 Nov. 1903. He served in Tibet, 1903 and 1904, being present in the action at Niani, and in the operations at and around Gyantse and in the march to Lhassa. He was slightly wounded; received the Medal with clasp; was mentioned in Despatches [London Gazette, 13 Dec. 1904], and was created a Companion of the Distinguished Service Order [London Gazette, 16 Dec. 1904]: "Dashwood William Harrington Humphreys, Capt., Indian Army. In recognition of services with the Tibet Mission Escort." He became A.D.C. to the Political Resident at Aden 18 April, 1910. Major Humphreys served in the European War, and was killed in action 17 Feb. 1917.

HODGSON, GEORGE CECIL, Lieut., was born 10 July, 1876, son of the late Lieut.-Colonel George Robert Hodgson, Bombay Staff Corps. He was educated at the United Services College, Westward Ho! and entered the Army (Unattached List), 20 Jan. 1897; joined the Indian Staff Corps 26 March, 1898, and became Lieutenant, Indian Army, 20 April, 1899. He served in Waziristan, 1901–2 (Medal with clasp); and in Tibet, 1903–4, taking part in the action at Niani; operations at and around Gyantse (severely wounded) and the march to L'hassa. He was mentioned in Despatches [London Gazette, 13 Dec. 1904]; received the Medal and clasp, and was created a Companion of the Distinguished Service Order [London Gazette, 16 Dec. 1904]: "George Cecil Hodgson, Lieut., Indian Army. In recognition of services with the Tibet Mission Escort." He was promoted Captain 20 Jan. 1906; served in the Abor Expedition, 1911–12 (Medal with clasp); became Major, 32nd Sikh Pioneers, 25 Jan. 1915. He served in the European War; was employed as D.A.Q.M.G., India, until 12 Oct. 1916; Acting Lieutenant-Colonel, Dec. 1916, to Feb. 1918, and again in Dec. 1918.

London Gazette, 28 Oct. 1904.—"The King has been graciously pleased to give orders for the following appointments. To be Companions of the Distinguished Service Order."

PORTER, HERBERT ALFRED, Capt. and Brevet Major, was born 15 Jan. 1872. He joined the Army 2 June, 1894, as a Second Lieutenant in the 19th Hussars, and was promoted Lieutenant 2 Nov. 1898. Employed with the West African Frontier Force 5 Feb. 1898, to 29 Jan. 1900; served in West Africa (Borgu) in 1898 (Medal with clasp); in South Africa, 1900; employed with the West African Frontier Force 21 March, 1900, to 1 Feb. 1905; served in the operations against the forces of Bida (Despatches [London Gazette, 18 April, 1902]; Brevet of Major 2 April, 1903; Medal with clasp); was promoted Captain 1 April, 1903; served in the Kontagora Expedition, 1902 (Despatches [London Gazette, 24 April, 1903]), and in 1903 in the Kano-Sokoto operations. He was mentioned in Despatches [London Gazette, 31 July, 1902]; received a clasp to the Medal, and was created a Companion of the Distinguished Service Order [London Gazette, 28 Oct. 1904]: "Herbert Alfred Porter, Capt. and Brevet Major, 19th Hussars. In recognition of his services with the Kano-Sokoto Expedition." He was transferred to the Liverpool Regt. as Captain, 24 May, 1905, and became Major in the West African Regt. 21 Sept. 1907. Major Porter retired from the Service 25 June, 1910. In 1912 he married Rachel, daughter of the late Arthur Edwards, of Liverpool.

HOGG, IAN GRAHAM, Capt., was born 2 Feb. 1875, at Richmond Terrace, Whitehall, S.W., son of the late Quinton Hogg, Esq. (Partner in the West Indian Firm of Hogg, Curtis and Campbell), and of Mrs. Quinton Hogg, of 41, Cumberland Terrace, Bryanston Square, W. He was educated at Eton and Sandhurst, and entered the Army 15 Jan. 1896, as a Second Lieutenant in the King's Royal Rifle Corps; was transferred 12 Feb. 1896, to the 4th Hussars. He was employed in the Niger Coast Protectorate 23 Sept. to 31 Dec. 1899; became Captain 3 Nov. 1900; was employed with the West African Frontier Force 1 Jan. 1900, to 23 May, 1905. He served in the South African War, 1901; Commandant, Wellington, attached to Field Intelligence Department on Sir Bruce Hamilton's Staff; was present during operations in Cape Colony, Nov. to Dec. 1901; in the Transvaal, Oct. 1901; in the Orange River Colony, June to Oct. 1901 (Queen's Medal with four clasps); served in West Africa (Southern Nigeria), 1901, during the operations in the Ishan country (Medal with clasp); in West Africa (Southern Nigeria), 1902, with the Aro expedition (clasp); in West Africa (Southern Nigeria), 1902, during the operations in the Ibekwe country; in command (clasp); in West Africa, (Northern Nigeria), 1903, during the Kano-Sokoto Campaign (clasp); in West Africa (Southern Nigeria), 1903 (Despatches [London Gazette, 28 Oct. 1904]. He was created a Companion of the Distinguished Service Order [London Gazette, 28 Oct. 1904]: "Ian Graham Hogg, Capt., 4th Hussars. In recognition of his services during the operations in Southern Nigera, 1903." He served in West Africa (Southern Nigeria), 1903–4, with the expedition against the towns of Osea, Oriri and Ndoto; in command (clasp); in West Africa (Southern Nigeria), 1904; took part in the operations against the natives of Asaba Hinterland; in command; and in the Kwale country; in command (Despatches [London Gazette, 25 Aug. 1905]; Brevet of Major 7 July, 1904; clasp); and in West Africa (Southern Nigeria), 1904–5, during the operations of the Irua Patrol on the west of the Niger: in command. He became Adjutant of the 4th Hussars 19 June, 1905; was promoted Lieutenant-Colonel, May, 1913. Lieut.-Colonel Ian Hogg was killed in action at Haramont, France, 2 Sept. 1914, while acting in command of part of the rear-guard during the Retreat from Mons.

Ian Graham Hogg.

WARD, ARTHUR CLAUD, Lieut., was born at Rosslyn Hall, Jamaica, West Indies, 15 April, 1878, third son of the late Colonel the Honourable C. J. Ward, C.M.G., Member of the Legislative and Privy Councils of Jamaica, and of Mrs. Ward. On the maternal side his great-grandfather was J. Z. Holwell, Governor of Fort William, Calcutta, who so greatly distinguished himself by his bravery and leadership of the gallant defence of the Old Fort of Calcutta in June, 1756. He survived the tragedy of the Black Hole; erected a monument to those who perished, and died in London in 1798, aged 87 years. Arthur Ward was educated at Beaumont College, Old Windsor, and joined the 6th (Militia) Battn. of the Lancashire Fusiliers in 1899. He served in the South African War, 1900–1, and was present at operations in Cape Colony, for which he received the Queen's Medal with two clasps, and a direct commission in the 2nd Battn. Lancashire Fusiliers (Regulars), as Second Lieutenant, 21 April, 1900. He became Lieutenant 27 Feb. 1901, and in 1901 and 1903 was seconded for service under the Colonial Office, taking part in the Aro Expedition, 1901–2, in Southern Nigeria; in Southern Nigeria, 1902; in Southern Nigeria, 1902–3, in operations against the Chief Adukukaiku of Igarra; operations against the Uris and the people of Omonoha and Ebima, with the 3rd Southern Nigerian Frontier Force. For his services he was mentioned in Despatches [London Gazette, 28 Oct. 1904]; received the African General Service Medal with three clasps, and was created a Companion of the Distinguished Service Order [London Gazette, 28 Oct. 1904]: "Arthur Claud Ward, Lieut., Lancashire Fusiliers. In recognition of services during the operations in Southern Nigeria, 1903." He became Captain 15 March, 1910. Capt. Ward served in the European War. On the 26th Aug. 1914, forty-eight hours after landing in France, there was a sudden attack by an overwhelming force of the enemy near Cambrai at dawn on 12th Infantry Brigade, of which his battalion formed part, and it was smothered by machine-gun fire. The battalion held on most gallantly, but had scarcely any artillery to assist them, and had not time to dig themselves in. Capt. Ward was trying to assist wounded subalterns when he was killed instantaneously. He had married, in 1906, Ruby, daughter of Colonel R. W. Mansbridge, of Staines, and they had two daughters: Daphne and Audrey.

London Gazette, 24 Jan. 1905.—"War Office, 24 Jan. 1905. The King has been graciously pleased to give orders for the following appointments to the Distinguished Service Order, in recognition of the services of the undermentioned Officers during the Sokoto-Burmi operations, Northern Nigeria, 1903."

BARLOW, CHARLES WYNN, Capt. and Brevet Major, was born 21 July, 1868, and entered the Army (Essex Regt.) 24 April, 1889, becoming Lieutenant 15 Dec. 1891. He was promoted to Captain 29 Jan. 1900. Capt. Barlow served in the South African War, 1899–1902, taking part in operations in the Orange Free State, March to May, 1900, including actions at Poplar Grove, Dreifontein, Houtnek (Thoba Mountain), Vet River (5 and 6 May) and Zand River; operations in the Transvaal in May and June, 1900, including actions near Johannesburg, Pretoria and Diamond Hill (11 and 12 June); operations in Orange River Colony, June to 29 Nov. 1900, including actions at Wittebergen (1 to 29 July), Witpoort and Bothaville. He was slightly wounded; received the Queen's Medal with three clasps, and the King's Medal with two clasps; was given the Brevet of Major 22 Aug. 1902, and was mentioned in Despatches [London Gazette, 29 July, 1902]. Major Barlow was employed with the West African Frontier Force from Jan. 1903, to Aug. 1907, taking part in 1903 in the Sokoto-Burmi operations, for which he was mentioned in Despatches [London Gazette, 24 Jan. 1905]; received the Medal and clasp, and was created a Companion of the Distinguished Service Order [London Gazette, 24 Jan. 1905]: "Charles Wynn Barlow, Capt. and Brevet Major, The Essex Regt. (employed with the West African Frontier Force. In recognition of services during the Sokoto-Burmi operations, Northern Nigeria, 1903." He became Major, Essex Regt. 23 Feb. 1908. He again saw active service in the European War. He was attached to the General Staff (graded as G.S.O.2), Reserve Centre, 28 Sept. 1915, to 9 Oct. 1916, and was G.S.O.2, Northern District, Irish Command, 13 Oct. 1916, to 23 Sept. 1918, when he was appointed G.S.O.2, with the Egyptian Expeditionary Force. He was given the Brevet of Lieutenant-Colonel 3 June, 1917.

BROWNE, WALTER HAMILTON, Capt., was born 25 Jan. 1875, son of the late Walter J. Browne, Indian Telegraphs, and of Mrs. Browne. He joined the 4th Battn. Royal Fusiliers in 1895, and became Lieutenant, 6th Royal Fusiliers, 29 July, 1899; served with the West African Frontier Force, and in 1900 took part in the Munshi Expedition, Northern Nigeria (Medal with clasp). He became Captain 19 Oct. 1900. He served in the Burmi-Sokoto operations in 1903, in Northern Nigeria, and was severely wounded. He was mentioned in Despatches [London Gazette, 24 Jan. 1905]; received a Medal and clasp, and was created a Companion of the Distinguished Service Order [London Gazette, 24 Jan. 1905]: "Walter Hamilton Browne, Capt., 6th Battn. The Royal Fusiliers (City of London Regt.) (3rd Class Resident, Northern Nigeria). In recognition of services during the Sokoto-Burmi operations, Northern Nigeria, 1903." He retired from the Army with the rank of Captain; became Major, Special Reserve, 20 Aug. 1907, and subsequently retired from the Reserve. Major W. Hamilton Browne was transferred to the Provincial Administration, Northern Nigeria, 1904, and promoted 2nd Class Resident, 1909. He married, in 1900, Lilian Cecelia, daughter of the late J. H. Righton, Mus.Bac., of Bedford, and they have two daughters.

CHRISTY, STEPHEN HENRY, Lieut., was born 27 April, 1879, youngest son of the late Stephen Christy, of Highfield, Bramall, Cheshire. He was educated at Harrow (Mr. B. Smith's, 1893–97), and at Christ Church, Oxford, and joined the 20th Hussars in 1899; served in South Africa, 1901–2; was on the Staff as Signalling Officer from March to May, 1902, and was present at the operations in the Transvaal and in the Orange River Colony from Jan. to April, 1902 (Queen's Medal with four clasps). He served in West Africa in 1903 (Northern Nigeria), taking part in the Sokoto-Burmi operations, during which he was slightly wounded. He was mentioned in Despatches 2 Jan. 1905, and was created a Companion of the Distinguished Service Order [London Gazette, 24 Jan. 1905]: "Stephen Henry Christy, Lieut., 20th Hussars. In recognition of services during the Sokoto-Burmi operations, Northern Nigeria, 1903.". He retired from the Active List of the Army in 1906. He was fond of hunting and big game shooting. After his retirement he became Master of the South Shropshire Foxhounds. At the beginning of the European War he rejoined his regiment, with the rank of Captain, on the 16th Aug. 1914, and was killed in action at La Ferte-sous-Douane 27 Aug. 1914. The late Capt. Christy had married, in 1905, Violet, daughter of the late William Chapell-Hodge, of Pounds, South Devon.

London Gazette, 14 April, 1905.—"War Office, 14 April, 1905. The King has been graciously pleased to give orders for the following appointments to the Distinguished Service Order, in recognition of the services of the undermentioned Officers during the operations in connection with the protection of the Aden Boundary Commission 1903-4."

ENGLISH, FREDERICK PAUL, Lieut.-Colonel, was born 25 Oct. 1859, son of J. T. English, Esq., J.P., of Bradford Manor, Bradford, North Devon. He was educated at Cheltenham College, and the Royal Military College,

Frederick P. English.

Sandhurst, and entered the Army 22 July, 1879, with a commission in the Royal Dublin Fusiliers; became Lieutenant 12 Jan. 1881; was A.D.C. to Major-General Commanding Troops in Egypt, 1885-87; became Captain 1 July, 1887; and A.D.C. to Major-General Commanding Troops in Ceylon, 1887-88: promoted Major 6 Nov. 1894; was Adjutant of Volunteers 15 Jan. 1892, to 4 Jan. 1897. He served in South Africa, 1899-1902, taking part in operations in Natal, 1899, including actions at Talana and Lombard's Nek; Relief of Ladysmith, including operations of 17 to 24 Jan. 1900 (slightly wounded, 20 Jan.), and action at Spion Kop; operations of 5 to 7 Feb. 1900, and action at Vaal Kranz; operations on Tugela Heights 14 to 27 Feb. 1900, and action at Pieter's Hill; operations in the Orange Free State, Feb. to May, 1900; operations in the Transvaal, west of Pretoria, July, to 29 Nov. 1900 (slightly wounded, 31 July), including actions at Frederickstad; operations in the Transvaal, west of Pretoria, July to 29 Nov. 1900. He was mentioned in Despatches [London Gazette, 8 Feb. 1901]; received the Brevet of Lieutenant-Colonel 29 Nov. 1900; Queen's Medal with six clasps, and King's Medal with two clasps. Brevet Lieut.-Colonel English served with the Aden Boundary Commission, in command of a Column, 1903-4, becoming Lieutenant-Colonel 5 March, 1904. He was created a Companion of the Distinguished Service Order [London Gazette, 14 April, 1905]: "Frederick Paul English, Lieut.-Colonel, Royal Dublin Fusiliers. In recognition of services during the operations connected with the protection of the Aden Boundary Commission, 1903-4." He commanded the 2nd Battn. Royal Dublin Fusiliers, 1904-8; was given the Brevet of Colonel 17 July, 1905; became Colonel 5 March, 1908, and retired from the Service 21 July, 1909, being placed on the Reserve of Officers. He was recalled on 2 Aug. 1914, and served in the European War, as Temporary Brigadier-General (promoted 30 Nov. 1914). He was twice mentioned in Despatches, given the honorary rank of Brigadier-General 26 Jan. 1918, and was created a C.M.G. in 1917. Brigadier-General English married (1st), in 1887, Elizabeth (died 1915), daughter of the Hon. W. Telfair, of Bonair, Mauritius; and (2ndly), on 29 Sept. 1917, at All Saints', Sunderland, Winifred, daughter of the late John Crown and Elizabeth Crown, of Roker, Sunderland.

RAVENHILL, EDGAR EVELYN, Lieut.-Colonel, was born 8 Dec. 1859.

Edgar Evelyn Ravenhill.

He entered The Buffs (East Kent Regt.) 23 July, 1879; was promoted Lieutenant 1 July, 1881; was Adjutant of the East Kent Regt., May, 1885, to May, 1890; Captain 1 Sept. 1887; Adjutant of Volunteers, July, 1890, to July, 1895; Major 23 March, 1898. He served in operations on the North-West Frontier, 1897-98, with the Malakand Field Force in the expedition into the Mamund country; with the Utman Khel Column of the Malakand Field Force; also with the Buner Field Force; attack and capture of the Tanga Pass (Medal with clasp). He became Lieutenant-Colonel in 1904. He served at Aden, 1903-4 (Boundary Commission), and was created a Companion of the Distinguished Service Order [London Gazette, 14 April, 1905]: "Edgar Evelyn Ravenhill, Lieut.-Colonel, The Buffs, East Kent Regt. In recognition of services during the operations in connection with the protection of the Aden Boundary Commission." Lieut.-Colonel Ravenhill died 6 Feb. 1907, at Wynberg, South Africa.

DELAMAIN, WALTER SINCLAIR, Major, was born 18 Feb. 1862. He joined the Royal Berkshire Regt. 22 Oct. 1881, and was transferred to the Indian Staff Corps 1 Feb. 1885. He served in the Egyptian Expedition of 1882, and was present at the surrender of Kafr Dowar (Medal; Bronze Star); in the Burma Expedition, 1885-88 (Medal with two clasps); on the Somali Coast, 1890, with the Zaila Field Force, being

present at the affair at Hussein Zariba. He became Captain, I.S.C., 22 Oct. 1892, and Major, Indian Army, 10 July, 1901. For his services in China in 1900, he was mentioned in Despatches [London Gazette, 14 May, 1901], and received the Medal,

Walter S. Delamain.

and also a Medal and clasp for the Waziristan operations on the North-West Frontier of India in 1901. He was with the Aden Boundary Commission, 1903-4, for which he was mentioned in Despatches [London Gazette, 17 Feb. 1905], and was created a Companion of the Distinguished Service Order [London Gazette, 14 April, 1905]: "Walter Sinclair Delamain, Major, Indian Army. In recognition of services during the operations in connection with the protection of the Aden Boundary Commission, 1903-4." He was made Lieutenant-Colonel 12 Jan. 1905; was given the Brevet of Colonel 12 Jan. 1908, and became Colonel 1 Jan. 1911; was A.A.G. at Headquarters, India, from Nov. 1912, to 27 Sept. 1914, when he was promoted to Temporary Brigadier-General. He served in the European War as a Brigade Commander, and from 1916 to 1918 as A.A.G. in Mesopotamia; was promoted to Major-General 3 June, 1915. He was twice mentioned in Despatches and created a C.B. in 1914, and a K.C.M.G. in 1918. Major-General Sir W. S. Delamain married, in 1897, Gladys Frances, daughter of Thomas Russell, J.P.

SYMES, GEORGE STEWART, Lieut., was born 29 July, 1882, only son of the late Lieut.-Colonel W. A. Symes, 71st Highland Light Infantry, and the Honourable Mrs. Symes. He was educated at Malvern College,

George Stewart Symes.

and Sandhurst, from which latter he joined the Army 11 Aug. 1900, as a Second Lieutenant in the Hampshire Regt.; became Lieutenant 21 April, 1902. He served in the South African War, 1902, in operations in the Transvaal (Queen's Medal with two clasps). He saw active service again in the Aden Hinterland, 1903-4; was mentioned in Despatches [London Gazette, 17 Feb. 1905], and was created a Companion of the Distinguished Service Order [London Gazette, 14 April, 1905]: "George Stewart Symes, Lieut., The Hampshire Regt. In recognition of services during the operations in connection with the protection of the Aden Boundary Commission, 1903-4." He was employed with the Egyptian Army from 28 Dec. 1905, and from Oct. 1906, to May, 1908, was A.D.C. to the Sirdar; became Captain 9 May, 1907. He served in the Blue Nile Expedition, Sudan, 1908, for which he received the Egyptian Medal; was a G.S.O.3 from May, 1911, to Dec. 1913; received the 4th Class Osmanieh in 1912; was appointed Private Secretary to the Sirdar and Governor-General of the Sudan, Jan. 1914. He became Major, Hampshire Regt., 1 Sept. 1915. Major Symes served in the European War, on Special Service as G.S.O.1 on the Staff of the High Commissioner in Egypt, with the temporary rank of Lieutenant-Colonel, and was four times mentioned in Despatches. He received the 3rd Class Order of the Nile in 1915, and the C.M.G. in 1917, and was given the Brevet of Lieutenant-Colonel 3 June, 1917. Lieut.-Colonel Symes married, in 1913, Violet Colston, youngest daughter of the late J. Felix Brown, and they have a son and a daughter.

London Gazette, 25 Aug. 1905.—"War Office, 25 Aug. 1905. The King has been graciously pleased to give orders for the following appointments to the Distinguished Service Order, in recognition of the services of the undermentioned Officers during the operations in Northern Nigeria in 1903-4."

MERRICK, GEORGE CHARLTON, Capt., was born 26 April, 1872. He was educated at the United Services College, Westward Ho! and entered the Royal Artillery 24 July, 1891; became Lieutenant 24 July, 1894; took part in the operations on the North-West Frontier of India, 1897-98; in the operations on the Samana; also with the Tirah Expeditionary Force (Medal with three clasps); became Captain 7 Nov. 1899; served in West Africa, 1900, during the operations in Ashanti (Despatches [London Gazette, 4 Dec. 1900]; in West Africa (Northern Nigeria), 1901, during the operations against the forces of Kontagora; commanded Royal Artillery; also against the forces of Bida (Despatches [London Gazette, 18 April, 1902]; Medal with clasp); in West Africa (Northern Nigeria), 1902, during the operations of Argungu; in command (Despatches [London Gazette, 28 Oct. 1904]; clasp); in West Africa, 1903; during the Kano-Sokoto Campaign (Despatches [London Gazette, 31 July, 1903]; clasp); in West Africa (Northern Nigeria), 1903-4; took part in the operations in the Bassa Province against the Okpotos; in command (clasp); again in West Africa (Northern Nigeria), 1904, during the operations against the people of Semolika; in command (Despatches, 5 Sept. 1904, and 24 April, 1905 [London Gazette, 25 Aug. 1905]; clasp). He was created a Companion of the Distinguished Service Order [London Gazette, 25 Aug. 1905]: "George Charlton Merrick, Capt., Royal Artillery. For services during operations in Northern Nigeria." He qualified as an Interpreter in Hausa in July, 1906; served on the General Staff. Major Merrick died at Salisbury Plain 3 Oct. 1913.

WILLIAMS, EDWARD ERNEST, Capt., was born 4 Dec. 1875, son of the Honourable Sir Hartley Williams and Edith Ellen (died, 1885), daughter of Commissary-General Horne. He joined the Army 25 March, 1896, as a Second Lieutenant in the Northumberland Fusiliers, in which he was promoted Lieutenant 21 Jan. 1898, and Captain 1 July, 1900. He was employed with the West African Frontier Force from 8 April, 1899, to 16 Oct. 1904; served in West Africa (Northern Nigeria), 1900; with the Kaduna Expedition (Despatches [London Gazette, 16 April, 1901]; Medal with clasp); served in West Africa (Northern Nigeria), 1903; during the Kano-Sokoto Campaign (Despatches [London Gazette, 31 July, 1903]; Medal with clasp); served in West Africa (Northern Nigeria), 1903–4; during the operations in the Bassa Province against the Okpotos (Despatches [London Gazette, 25 Aug. 1905]; clasp). He was created a Companion of the Distinguished Service Order [London Gazette, 25 Aug. 1905]: " Edward Ernest Williams, Capt., The Northumberland Fusiliers. For services during operations in Northern Nigeria, 1903–4." Capt. Williams was employed again with the West African Frontier Force from 27 Oct. 1906, to 3 Oct. 1911, serving in command of the Sura Expedition, Northern Nigeria, 1907–8. He served in the European War; became Temporary Major 29 Oct. 1914. He was killed on 19 Aug. 1915, at the Dardanelles.

MAUD, CHARLES CARUS, Capt., born 15 Jan. 1875, youngest son of the late Lieut.-Colonel William Sheres Maud, R.E., and Mrs. W. S. Maud, of Milton House, Bournemouth. He was educated at Wellington, and received his commission in the Somerset Light Infantry from the Militia 6 Jan. 1896, and became Lieutenant 12 Jan. 1899. He served during the South African War, 1902, taking part in the operations in the Transvaal, March and April, 1902, and received the Queen's Medal with two clasps. He served in West Africa (Northern Nigeria), 1903; during the Kano-Sokoto Campaign, taking part in the operations in the district of the east of Zaria; received Medal with clasp. He was promoted Captain 3 Feb. 1904; took part in the Sokoto-Burmi operations; was mentioned in Despatches [London Gazette, 24 Jan. 1905], and was created a Companion of the Distinguished Service Order [London Gazette, 25 Aug. 1905]: " Charles Carus Maud, Capt., The Prince Albert's (Somerset Light Infantry). For services during operations in Northern Nigeria, 1903–4." In the Sudan, in 1908, Capt. Maud took part in the operations in the Jebal Nyima District of Southern Kordofan, and was awarded the Egyptian Medal with clasp, and the 4th Class Medjidie. He was also mentioned in Despatches. Capt. Maud was killed in action 19 Dec. 1914.

OLDMAN, RICHARD DEARE FURLEY, Capt., was born 31 July, 1877. He entered the Army as Second Lieutenant, Norfolk Regt., 20 Feb. 1897, and became Lieutenant 19 April, 1898. He served in West Africa (Northern Nigeria), 1903 to 1904; during operations in the Kabba Province, and took part in the operations in the Bassa Province against the Okpotos. He was promoted Captain 25 Feb. 1905, and for his services was mentioned in Despatches [London Gazette, 25 Aug. 1905], and was created a Companion of the Distinguished Service Order [London Gazette, 25 Aug. 1905]: " Richard Deare Furley Oldman, Capt. For services during the operations in Northern Nigeria, 1903–4." He again saw active service in West Africa in 1906, and was employed with the West African Frontier Force until 9 Aug. 1910. Capt. Oldman served during the European War, 1914 to 1917. He was D.A.A.G., G.H.Q., B.E.F., 24 Sept. 1914, to 1 March, 1915; was promoted Major 25 April, 1915; was Temporary Lieutenant-Colonel, Cheshire Regt., 18 Sept. 1915, to 14 April, 1916; Temporary Brigadier-General 15 April, 1916, to 14 April, 1919. He was Brigade Commander, 117th Infantry Brigade, British Armies in France, 15 April, 1916, to 4 March, 1917 ; Brigade Commander, Sheppey, Infantry Brigade, Home Forces, 20 March to 2 Nov. 1917 ; Brigade Commander, 15th Infantry Brigade, British Armies in France, 3 Nov. 1917, to 11 April, 1919 ; Acting Lieutenant-Colonel, 53rd Battn. Bedford and Herts Regt., 15 April to 31 July, 1919, and Brigade Commander, 2nd Brigade, Eastern Division, Northern Command, 1 Aug. 1919 ; he was mentioned in Despatches, and in 1917 was created C.M.G.; was given the Brevet of Lieutenant-Colonel 3 June, 1916, and of Colonel 1 Jan. 1919. Colonel Oldman married, in 1912, Helen Marie, daughter of Walter Pigot, Dundrum, and they have two sons.

GALLOWAY, LENNOX, Lieut., was born 23 Oct. 1880, eldest son of Lieut.-Colonel F. Galloway, of Norwood House, Leamington. He entered the Army as Second Lieutenant, Royal Artillery, 22 Nov. 1899, and was promoted Lieutenant 16 Feb. 1901. He served during the South African War, 1899–1901, in the operations in the Transvaal, Nov. 1900, to Jan. 1901, and Dec. 1901, taking part in the operations in the Orange River Colony, Jan. to Nov. 1901; in operations in Cape Colony, Dec. 1901. He was mentioned in Despatches [London Gazette, 10 Sept. 1901, and received the Queen's Medal with four clasps. He was employed with the West African Frontier Force from 14 March, 1902, to 18 June, 1907, and from 17 Oct. 1908, to 12 Jan. 1912. He took part in operations in Northern Nigeria, 1903, in the Kabba Province ; 1903–4, during operations in the Bassa Province against the Okpotos (Medal with clasp). He served in 1904 in Northern Nigeria, during operations against the people of Semolika ; was twice wounded ; was mentioned in Despatches [London Gazette, 5 Sept. and 24 April, 1905]. He received a clasp, and was created a Companion of the Distinguished Service Order [London Gazette, 25 Aug. 1905]: " Lennox Galloway, Lieut., Royal Artillery. For services during operations in Northern Nigeria." He was promoted Captain 7 Oct. 1907, and was Adjutant, Territorial Forces, 1 Jan. 1910, to 31 Dec. 1913. He served during the European War, 1914 to 1916 ; became Major 22 March, 1915, and was twice mentioned in Despatches. Major Galloway married, in 1916, Eileen, the only daughter of E. T. Reece, and they have one son.

London Gazette, 5 Sept. 1905.—" War Office, 5 Sept. 1905. The King has been graciously pleased to give orders for the following appointment to the Distinguished Service Order, in recognition of the services of the undermentioned Officer with the Tibet Mission Escort."

RYDER, CHARLES HENRY DUDLEY, Capt., was born 28 June, 1868, the seventh son of the late Lieut.-Colonel Spencer Charles Dudley Ryder and Julia, the eldest daughter of the Rev. W. Money. He was educated at Cheltenham College, and entered the Army as Second Lieutenant, Royal Engineers, 12 May, 1886, becoming Captain 31 Dec. 1896. He served with the China Field Force in 1900 ; was present at the Relief of Pekin, and during the actions of Peitsang and Yangtsun ; he was mentioned in Despatches [London Gazette, 14 May, 1901], and received Medal with clasp. He served with Tibet Mission, 1903 to 1904, as Survey Officer, during the action at Niani, taking part in the operations at and around Gyantse and march to Lhassa ; was mentioned in Despatches [London Gazette, 13 Dec. 1904] ; received Medal with clasp, and was created a Companion of the Distinguished Service Order [London Gazette, 5 Sept. 1905]: " Charles Henry Dudley Ryder, Capt., Royal Engineers. In recognition of services with the Tibet Mission Escort." He was promoted Major 29 March, 1905, and Lieutenant-Colonel 14 July, 1913. He served during the European War, and was created a C.I.E. in 1915. He was promoted Colonel 14 July, 1917 ; served with the Mesopotamian Field Force, 1917–18, and was Deputy Director of Surveys, Mesopotamian Expeditionary Force 1 May, 1918, to 14 Feb. 1919 ; was mentioned in Despatches. He has held the appointment as Surveyor-General of India since 1919. Colonel Ryder was awarded Patron's Gold Medal, Royal Geographical Society ; the Silver Medal Scottish R.G.S., and Gold Medal, French G.S., for explorations in China and Tibet. He married, in 1892, Ida Josephine, eldest daughter of the late Lieut.-Colonel E. E. Grigg, of Orchard Court, Stevenage, Herts, and they have three sons and three daughters.

London Gazette, 23 Feb. 1906.—" War Office, 23 Feb. 1906. The King has been graciously pleased to give orders for the following appointments to the Distinguished Service Order."

MOORHOUSE, HARRY CLAUDE, Capt., was born 30 Jan. 1872. He entered the Army, as Second Lieutenant, Royal Artillery, 4 Nov. 1891. He served in Uganda in 1898 (Medal) ; became Captain, 1899. He was employed with the West African Field Force, 1900, during the operations in Ashanti, and was mentioned in Despatches [London Gazette, 8 March, 1901]. He served in Southern Nigeria from 1901–2, during the Aro Expedition, as Chief Transport Officer ; was mentioned in Despatches [London Gazette, 12 Sept. 1902], and received the Brevet of Major 17 April, 1902 (Medal with clasp). He served in the Asaba Hinterland Expedition, in command, 1902 (clasp). He served in Northern Nigeria in 1903, during the Kano-Sokoto Campaign, and was mentioned in Despatches [London Gazette, 31 July, 1903] (clasp). He next saw active service in Southern Nigeria, 1904–5, during the Onitsha Hinterland Expedition, in command ; he was mentioned in Despatches [London Gazette, 23 Feb. 1906], and was created a Companion of the Distinguished Service Order [London Gazette, 23 Feb. 1906]: " Harry Claude Moorhouse, Capt. and Brevet Major, Royal Artillery. In recognition of his services in command of the Onitsha Hinterland Expedition, Southern Nigeria, Nov. 1904, to March, 1905." He retired 26 Sept. 1908, with the rank of Lieutenant-Colonel, Reserve of Officers. He was Chief Assistant to the Colonial Secretary, Southern Nigeria, 1908, and Provincial Commissioner, 1911. He served during the European War, in Nigeria, from 1914 to 1915, and was mentioned in Despatches, and in 1914 was created a C.M.G. ; was made an Officer of the Legion of Honour. Major Moorhouse has been Secretary, Southern Province, Nigeria, since 1914.

PALMER, CYRIL EUSTACE, Capt., was born 5 Sept. 1870, at Amritsar, Punjab, India, son of Colonel R. H. Palmer, Bengal Staff Corps. He was educated at Charterhouse and Westward Ho! and entered the Royal Artillery, as a Second Lieutenant, 25 July, 1890. He was promoted Lieutenant 25 July, 1893, and Captain 9 Feb. 1900. Capt. Palmer was employed with the West African Frontier Force 23 Nov. 1901, to 19 April, 1907 ; served in West Africa (Liberia), 1905, during the operations of the Kissi Field Force, in command. He was mentioned in Despatches [London Gazette, 23 Feb. 1906] ; received the Medal with clasp. He was created a Companion of the Distinguished Service Order [London Gazette, 23 Feb. 1906]: " Cyril Eustace Palmer, Capt., Royal Artillery. In recognition of his services in command of the

Cyril Eustace Palmer.

Kissi Field Force, Liberia, March to June, 1905." He became Major 4 March, 1908 ; was G.S.O.2, Sierra Leone, 20 June, 1908, to 19 June, 1911, and was employed with the Egyptian Army 9 May, 1912, to 16 July, 1916, serving as A.A.G., G.S.O.2, 10 Dec. 1912. Major Palmer served during the European War, 1914–1918. He was Commandant, Artillery, and Director of Ordnance 29 Dec. 1914, to 16 July, 1916 ; was promoted Lieutenant-Colonel 23 Jan. 1915 ; became Temporary Brigadier-General, 25 Dec. 1917, Royal Artillery, 49th Division, British Armies in France. He was created a C.M.G. in 1918, and a C.B. in 1919, and has the 2nd Class Order of the Nile. Brigadier-General Palmer married, 5 Aug. 1914, at Firle, Sussex, Nina Kathleen, daughter of Harry Scarlett, Esq., J.P., and they have one daughter, Clarissa Mary.

London Gazette, 18 Sept. 1906.—" War Office, 18 Sept. 1906. The King has been graciously pleased to give orders for the following appointments to the Distinguished Service Order, in recognition of the services of the undermentioned Officers during operations in Northern and Southern Nigeria."

TRENCHARD, HUGH MONTAGUE, Major, was born 3 Feb. 1873. He entered the Army as Second Lieutenant, Royal Scots Fusiliers, 9 Sept. 1893, being promoted Lieutenant 12 Aug. 1896, and Captain 28 Feb. 1900. He served during the South African War, 1899–1902, and was employed with the Imperial Yeomanry, Bushman Corps; afterwards with the Canadian Scouts. He was dangerously wounded; took part in the operations in the Transvaal, west of Pretoria, July to 29 Nov. 1900. He served with the Mounted Infantry during operations in the Transvaal, July, 1901, to Jan. 1902; during operations in Orange River Colony, April to May, 1902; during operations in Cape Colony, May, 1902. He was given the Brevet of Major 22 Aug. 1902; the Queen's Medal with three clasps, and the King's Medal with two clasps. Capt. Trenchard was employed with the West African Frontier Force 24 Oct. 1903, to 3 Nov. 1910. He served in West Africa (Southern Nigeria), 1904; during operations in the Omerri district, in command. He was mentioned in Despatches [London Gazette, 25 Aug. 1905], and received the Medal with clasp. He was also in command during the patrol through the unsettled portion of the Ibibio and Kwa country in 1904–5, and received a clasp. He again saw active service in West Africa, 1904 to 1905, taking part in the Bende-Onitsha Hinterland Expedition, in command. He received a clasp to the Medal, and was mentioned in Despatches; created a Companion of the Distinguished Service Order [London Gazette, 18 Sept. 1906]: " Hugh Montague Trenchard, Capt. and Brevet Major, Royal Scots Fusiliers. In recognition of services during the operations in the Bende-Onitsha Hinterland, Southern Nigeria, Nov. 1905, to April, 1906." He was Instructor (graded Squadron Commander), Central Flying School, Royal Flying Corps, 1 Oct. 1912, to 22 Sept. 1913, and Assistant Commandant (graded Squadron Commander), Royal Flying Corps, 23 Sept. 1913, to 6 Aug. 1914. He served during the European War, as Commander (temporary), R.F. Corps, M.W., 7 Aug. to 8 Nov. 1914, and Commander, R.F. Corps, British Expeditionary Force, 9 Nov. 1914, to 24 April, 1915. He was given the Brevet of Lieutenant-Colonel 18 Jan. 1915; was A.D.C. (extra) to the King 3 June, 1915, to 31 Dec. 1916; was given the Brevet of Colonel 3 June, 1915; was Brigade Commander, 1st Brigade, R.F. Corps., B.E.F., 25 Aug. 1915, to 23 March, 1916, and became Major-General 1 Jan. 1917; he was employed under the Air Ministry 3 Jan. 1918, as Chief of the Royal Air Staff, and promoted Air-Marshal, 1919. He was created C.B., 1914, and K.C.B., 1918, and made a Baronet, 1919; was made Commandant of the Legion of Honour; was given the Order of St. Anne (3rd Class with Swords), and the Order of King Leopold, and the American Distinguished Service Medal.

MAIR, GEORGE TAGORE, Capt., was born 28 April, 1873, in London, son of Robert Slater Mair and the late Mrs. R. S. Mair. He was educated at Epsom College, and at the Royal Military Academy, Woolwich (1891–93), and entering the Royal Artillery, as Second Lieutenant, 3 June, 1893, was promoted Lieutenant 30 June, 1896, and Captain 25 June, 1900. He served in the South African War, 1899–1900; took part in the operations in Orange River Colony, Sept. to Nov. 1900, including action at Bothaville (severely wounded) (Queen's Medal with three clasps). He was employed with the West African Frontier Force 15 Aug. 1903, to 11 Oct. 1908; served in West Africa (Southern Nigeria), 1903. He was mentioned in Despatches [London Gazette, 25 Aug. 1905]; received the Medal with clasp. He served in West Africa (Southern Nigeria), 1905–6, with the Bende-Onitsha Hinterland Expedition, in command of a Column (Despatches [London Gazette, 18 Sept. 1906]; clasp). He was created a Companion of the Distinguished Service Order [London Gazette, 18 Sept. 1906]: " George Tagore Mair, Capt., Royal Artillery. In recognition of his services during the operations in the Bende-Onitsha Hinterland, Southern Nigeria, Nov. 1905, to April, 1906." He was promoted Major 13 May, 1910, and was again employed with the West African Frontier Force, from 16 Feb. 1910, to 4 July, 1915. Major Mair served in the European War. He was promoted Lieutenant-Colonel 20 Dec. 1915; became Temporary Brigadier-General, Royal Artillery, 52nd Division, British Armies in France, 15 Oct. 1918. For his services he was created a C.M.G. in 1919, and was made Chevalier of the Legion of Honour.

George Tagore Mair.

SHORT, PERCY HAMILTON, Capt., was born 15 April, 1874, and was educated at Wellington College. He entered the Army, as a Second Lieutenant in the Gloucestershire Regt., 7 Dec. 1895, becoming Lieutenant 7 July, 1898. He served in the South African War, 1899–1900; took part in the operations in Natal, 1899, including actions at Rietfontein and Lombard's Kop (slightly wounded); afterwards on Staff, as Railway Staff Officer (Queen's Medal with three clasps). He was employed with the West African Frontier Force 2 Oct. 1901, to 28 Feb. 1907; served in West Africa (Northern Nigeria), 1903, during the Kano-Sokoto Campaign (Medal with clasp); served during the operations in district to the east of Zaria; in West Africa (Northern Nigeria), 1904; took part in the operations against the Pagan tribes who occupy the country north of Wase, in command He was mentioned in Despatches [London Gazette, 25 Aug. 1905]; awarded a clasp. He became Captain 13 Oct. 1905. He served again in West Africa (Northern Nigeria), 1906 [Despatches [London Gazette, 18 Sept. 1906]; clasp). He was created a Companion of the Distinguished Service Order [London Gazette, 18 Sept. 1906]: " Percy Hamilton Short, Capt., The Gloucestershire Regt. In recognition of his services during the operations in the Munshi country." He was employed with the West African Frontier Force again from 29 Feb. 1908, and on 27 Jan. 1912, retired from the Service. He was from 1914 to 1918 Acting District Commissioner, Bole, Gold Coast.

London Gazette, 28 June, 1907.—" War Office, 28 June, 1907. The King has been graciously pleased to give orders for the following appointments to the Distinguished Service Order, in recognition of the services of the undermentioned Officers during the Native Rebellion in Natal, 1906."

BRU-DE-WOLD, HILMAR THEODORE, Colonel, was born 25 Aug. 1842, son of Hans C. Bru-de-Wold, of Trondhjem, Norway. He was educated at the Naval College, Norway. He joined the Volunteer Forces, Natal, in 1873; served in the Zulu Campaign of 1878–79, with the Alexandra Mounted Rifles (Medal and clasp), and became Lieutenant, Alexandra Mounted Rifles, 7 Aug. 1882. He served in the Boer War, 1899–1902, as Chief Staff Officer, Natal Volunteer Force. He took part in operations in Natal, 1899, including the actions at Rietfontein and Lombard's Kop; defence of Ladysmith (severely wounded), including action of 6 Jan. 1900; operations in Natal, March to June, 1900, including action at Laing's Nek; operations in the Transvaal, east of Pretoria, July to Oct. 1900; operations on the Zululand Frontier of Natal, Sept. and Oct. 1901; in command of the Natal Volunteer Brigade 10 April to 31 May, 1902. He was mentioned in Despatches [London Gazette, 8 Feb. 1901 (Sir G. S. White, 2 Dec. 1899, and 23 March, 1900), and London Gazette, 16 April, 1901]; received the Queen's Medal with three clasps, and was created a C.M.G. He was promoted Colonel 1 July, 1905, and on the outbreak of the Natal Native Rebellion, as Commandant of the Natal Militia, he took command of all troops operating, and carried the campaign to a satisfactory end. He received the Natal Native Rebellion Medal and clasp, and was created a Companion of the Distinguished Service Order [London Gazette, 28 June, 1907]: " For services during the Native Rebellion in Natal, 1906: Hilmar Theodore Bru-de-Wold, C.M.G., Commandant, Local Forces, Natal." On 25 Aug. 1907, he retired to the Staff Supernumerary List at the age of 65. He had the Volunteer Decoration. Colonel Bru-de-Wold died 8 Sept. 1913. He married (1st), in 1871, Sarah (died 1892), eldest daughter of John Bazley, of Nil Desperandum, Ifofa, Natal, and their children were: Jane Bernardine, born 30 April, 1873 (married A. H. Borgnis, Lieutenant, 3rd S.A.M.R.), and Thorkill Walhan Brue-de-Wold, born 26 Jan. 1879 (Lieutenant, South African Infantry; killed at Delville Wood). He married (2ndly), in 1895, Helen Mary, daughter of J. D. Shuter, of Durban.

LEUCHARS, GEORGE, Lieut.-Colonel and Brevet Colonel, C.M.G., was born 16 April, 1868. He represented Umvoti County in the Natal Parliament, 1893–1906, and served in command of the Umvoti Mounted Rifles in the Boer War, 1899–1902. He was present in operations in Natal, 1899; the Relief of Ladysmith, including the operations on Tugela Heights; operations in Natal, March to June, 1900, including the action at Laing's Nek; operations in the Transvaal, east of Pretoria, July to Oct. 1900; operations on the Zululand Frontier of Natal, Sept. and Oct. 1901. He was mentioned in Despatches [London Gazette, 16 April, 1901]; received the Queen's Medal with four clasps, and the King's Medal with two clasps, and was created a C.M.G. From 1903–5 he was Minister of Native Affairs and Public Works. He also served in the Natal Native Rebellion; was given the Brevet of Colonel, and was Commanding Officer of the Troops in Natal. He received the Medal and clasp; was mentioned in Despatches [London Gazette, 25 June, 1907], and was created a Companion of the Distinguished Service Order [London Gazette, 28 June, 1907]: " For services during the Native Rebellion in Natal, 1906: George Leuchars, C.M.G., Lieut.-Colonel and Brevet Colonel, Umvoti Mounted Rifles." He became Colonel on the Regimental Supernumerary List 22 May, 1908. In 1910 he was returned for the Umvoti Division to the Union Parliament; was made a J.P.; was Minister of Commerce and Industries, Union of South Africa, 1911; Minister of Public Works, and Acting Minister of Posts and Telegraphs, 1912, in which year he resigned. In 1914 and 1915 he was Officer-in-Command of Troops in Natal, and was created a K.C.M.G. in 1915. Colonel the Honourable Sir George Leuchars married, in 1891, Marion, daughter of the late W. Mackenzie, M.A.

London Gazette, 2 July, 1907.—" War Office, 2 July, 1907. The King has been graciously pleased to give orders for the following appointments to the Distinguished Service Order, in recognition of the services of the undermentioned Officers employed with the West African Frontier Force during the operations near Sokoto, in Northern Nigeria, 1906."

MACDONELL, IAN HARRISON, Capt., was born 31 March, 1875, son of the late James Macdonell, of Glengarry, and Annie J. Harrison, of Springfield, Cheshire. He was educated at Abbotsholm, Rochester, and Victoria University, and was sent to East Africa by the Foreign Office in 1898, where he explored and made part of the survey through the Mau Mountains for the Uganda Railway. From Uganda he went to South Africa in 1900, and served as Lieutenant, 4th Yeomanry Regt., and as Captain commanding Leicester Squadron, 1901. He served till the end of the war, and received the Queen's Medal with five clasps. He joined the Mounted Infantry, Northern Nigeria Regt., in 1903, and saw service twice in that year. He took part in the operations in Sept. and Oct. 1903, and was in the Battle of Satiru (near Sokoto) in 1906; was wounded; mentioned in Despatches: " An officer of exceptional ability. His influence and example went far to establish the confidence of his company, which had been roughly handled in the fight of 14 Feb. Although wounded early in the day, he continued to lead his men with dash and gallantry, himself cutting down seven of the enemy." He received the African General Service Medal, and was created a Companion of the Distinguished Service Order, for services at the Battle of Satiru 10 March, 1906 [London Gazette, 2 July, 1907]: "Employed in the West African Frontier Force during the operations near Sokoto, in Northern Nigeria, 1906: Capt. (Hon. Captain in the Army) Ian H. Macdonell, City of London Rough Riders, Imperial Yeomanry." In the European War he served with the Nigeria Regt. in the Cameroons in 1914; was severely wounded at Tepe 24 Aug. 1914, and mentioned in Despatches. He was a pilot in the Royal Flying Corps in France in 1915; became Captain, Highland Light Infantry, 2 Dec. 1915, and went to Mesopotamia with them; was in the Kut Relief Force, and was severely wounded 18 April, 1916. He served in France in 1917; was Acting Major, Royal Inniskilling Fusiliers, and Acting Lieutenant-Colonel, Dorset Regt., for short periods, becoming Acting Major, H.L.I., Aug. 1907, and Acting Lieutenant-Colonel, June, 1918. He is a Fellow of the Royal Geographical Society. Major Macdonell's favourite recreations are big game shooting, polo and tennis. He married, in 1917, at Holy Trinity Church, Sloane Street, S.W., Ursula, daughter of Capt. A. Vaughan-Williams and Mrs. Vaughan-Williams, and niece of Viscountess Maitland.

GALLAGHER, ALBERT ERNEST, Capt., was born 2 Feb. 1872, son of the late Capt. J. Gallagher, I.M.S. He was educated privately. He served in the South African War, 1900; took part in the operations in Orange River Colony, July to 29 Nov. 1900; in Cape Colony, south of Orange River, July, 1900; in the Transvaal, 30 Nov. to Dec. 1900; also in Orange River Colony and Cape Colony, Dec. 1900 (Queen's Medal with two clasps); served in West Africa (Northern Nigeria), 1902; took part in the operations at Argunga. He was mentioned in Despatches [London Gazette, 28 Oct. 1904]; received the Medal with clasp; in West Africa (Northern Nigeria), 1903, during the Kano-Sokoto Campaign (clasp); again in West Africa (Northern Nigeria), 1906 (severely wounded; Despatches [London Gazette, 2 July 1907]; clasp). He was created a Companion of the Distinguished Service Order [London Gazette, 2 July, 1907]: "Employed with the West African Frontier Force during the operations near Sokoto in Northern Nigeria, 1906: Albert E. Gallagher, 9th Battn. King's Royal Rifle Corps." He was Company Commander, with the Northern Nigeria Regt., 1901–8; in the Political Department, Northern Nigeria, 1908–9; Local Commandant, Cyprus Military Police, from 1909, and Chief Commandant from 1915. He is Captain in the Reserve of Officers. His favourite recreations are cricket, hunting and polo. Capt. Gallagher married, in 1911, Marjorie, youngest daughter of the late S. C. Macaskie, K.C., Recorder of Sheffield, and they have one son and one daughter.

FENDALL, PERCY PAUL WENTWORTH, Lieut., was born 18 May, 1879. He entered the Army in 1901, and first saw active service in the South African War, 1899–1902, taking part in operations in the Transvaal from 30 Nov. 1900. He received the Queen's Medal with five clasps, and the King's Medal with two clasps. He served in Northern Nigeria in 1906; was wounded; mentioned in Despatches (Major Green, 12 March, and Major Goodwin, 15 March, 1906) [London Gazette, 2 July, 1907], and was created a Companion of the Distinguished Service Order [London Gazette, 2 July, 1907]: "Employed with the West African Frontier Force during the operations near Sokoto, in Northern Nigeria, 1906]: Percy Paul Wentworth Fendall, Lieut., The Border Regt." He died 14 Feb. 1910.

London Gazette, 9 Nov. 1907.—"War Office, 9 Nov. 1907. The King has been graciously pleased to give orders for the following appointments to the Distinguished Service Order, in recognition of the services of the undermentioned Officer in command of the Colonial Forces (consisting of Cape Rifleman), during the engagement with Morenga and his followers at Witpan, in the Kalahari Desert, on 21 Sept. 1907."

ELIOTT, FRANCIS AUGUSTUS HEATHFIELD, Major, was born 3 July, 1867, at Langley, Bucks, eldest son of Major George Augustus Eliott and his first wife, Helen Janet, daughter of W. Jardine Gallon. He was educated at the Oxford Military College, Cowley, and joined the Bechuanaland Border Police in 1892. On the annexation of the then Crown Colony to the Cape Colony, he was appointed Sub-Inspector in the C.M.P. He served during the Bechuanaland Campaign of 1896–97 (Cape of Good Hope General Service Medal and clasp), and in the South African War of 1899–1902, during which he took part in the defence of Kimberley and in operations in the Orange Free State. He was mentioned in Despatches [London Gazette, 8 May, 1900, and 16 April, 1901], and received the Queen's and King's Medals with two clasps each. He was created a Companion of the Distinguished Service Order [London Gazette, 9 Nov. 1907]: "Francis Augustus Heathfield Eliott, Commanding North-West Border Riflemen, Cape Colony." The decoration was awarded for services on the North-West Frontier of the Union of South Africa. He was twice mentioned in Despatches by the High Commissioner for South Africa, for conduct on the German Frontier (South-West Africa) in 1907, when he was operating in conjunction with the Imperial German Troops against Morenga. Besides the D.S.O., he received the 2nd Class Order of the Royal Crown of Prussia with Swords, and also (in 1905) the German War Medal, South-West Africa, with clasp for Kalahari. He became Major in the Cape Colonial Forces, and District Inspector in the Cape Mounted Police. He served in the European War, 1914–18. He took part in the campaign in South-West Africa, under General Botha, as Lieutenant-Colonel in command of the 3rd Regt., South African Mounted Riflemen. He also served under General Smuts in East Africa, with the 6th Mounted Brigade, in command of the 4th South African Horse, and with the 1st Mounted Brigade, and was mentioned in Despatches twice; was subsequently in Flanders on the Staff of the 5th Army until invalided with malaria. His favourite recreations are shooting, fishing and tennis. Lieut.-Colonel Eliott married, in 1896, Evelyn Georgina, daughter of R. W. MacDermott, and they have two sons and three daughters.

London Gazette, 13 March, 1908.—"War Office, 13 March, 1908. The King has been graciously pleased to give orders for the following appointments to the Distinguished Service Order, in recognition of the services of the undermentioned Officers during minor operations in East Africa, 1902–6, and in Northern and Southern Nigeria, 1906–7, respectively."

POPE-HENNESSY, LADISLAUS HERBERT RICHARD, Capt. and Brevet Major, was born in 1875, eldest son of the late Sir John Pope-Hennessy, K.C.M.G., M.P., of Rostellan Castle, County Cork, and Catherine, only daughter of Sir Hugh Low, G.C.M.G. He was educated at Beaumont College, and joined the Welsh Regt., as a Second Lieutenant, 28 Sept. 1895; became Lieutenant, Oxford Light Infantry, 5 Feb. 1898. He was employed with the West African Frontier Force 5 Feb. 1898, to 2 Sept. 1899, and in the British East Africa Protectorate with the King's African Rifles from 29 Sept. 1899, to 4 Aug. 1908. He served in West Africa, 1897–98 (Lagos); employed in Hinterland (Medal with clasp); served in British East Africa, 1901. He became Captain 11 Sept. 1902; took part in the operations against the Ogaden Somalis, in Jubaland (Medal with clasp); served in East Africa, 1903, during the operations in Somaliland (Despatches [London Gazette, 7 Aug. 1903]; clasp); served in East Africa, 1905, in command of the operations in Sotik. He was mentioned in Despatches [London Gazette, 13 March, 1908], and was created a Companion of the Distinguished Service Order [London Gazette, 13 March, 1908]: "For services during minor operations in East Africa, 1902–6: Ladislaus Herbert Richard Pope-Hennessy, The Oxfordshire Light Infantry (employed with the King's African Rifles." He served in the operations at Nandi, 1905–6 (Despatches [London Gazette, 18 Sept. 1906]; Brevet of Major 26 March, 1906; (clasp); in Somaliland, 1908 to 1910 (specially employed Jan. to Dec. 1909) (Despatches [London Gazette, 10 June, 1910]; (clasp). From May, 1912, to Aug. 1914, he was Brigade Major of the 1st West Riding Infantry Brigade, Northern Command, attaining his Majority 25 Oct. 1913. Serving in the European War, Major Pope-Hennessy held the following appointments: Brigade Major, 1st West Riding Infantry Brigade, Central Force, Home Defence, 5 Aug. 1914, to 14 March, 1915; G.S.O.3, Headquarters, R.F. Corps, B.E.F., 15 March to 14 July, 1915; G.S.O.2, Headquarters, R.F. Corps, B.E.F., 15 July to 19 Oct. 1915; Special Appointment, Home Forces, 18 Jan. to 28 Feb. 1916; G.S.O.2, 41st Division, New Armies, British Armies in France. He was Acting Lieutenant-Colonel from Oct. 1916, to Sept. 1917, and commanded the 1st Battn. Oxfordshire and Buckinghamshire Light Infantry in Mesopotamia in 1916 and 1917; was G.S.O.1, 3rd Division, Indian Expeditionary Force "D," Mesopotamian Expeditionary Force, 20 March to 23 July, 1917; G.S.O.1, M.E.F., 24 July to 4 Sept. 1917. From 5 Sept. 1917, to 16 April, 1919, he was Brigadier-General, General Staff, 1st Indian Army Corps, Mesopotamian Expeditionary Force. He was three times mentioned in Despatches; given the Brevet of Lieutenant-Colonel 1 Jan. 1918, and of Colonel 1 Jan. 1919, and was made a Chevalier of the Legion of Honour. He married, in 1910, Una, only daughter of the late Sir Arthur Birch, K.C.M.G., and they have two sons. His wife is the author of "Anna von Schurman," "Secret Societies and the French Revolution," "Madame Roland," "A Study in Revolutions," and other works, and also a contributor to the "Edinburgh Review" and other reviews.

MAYCOCK, FREDERIC WILLIAM ORBY, Lieut., was born 5 June, 1877, at 21, Claverton Street, S.W., son of Frederic Maycock, late Captain, 29th Regt., of 111, The Avenue, West Ealing, W., and Mrs. F. Maycock. He was educated at a private school at Eastbourne. He joined the Suffolk Regt 1 Dec. 1897; served in India for a few years with the 2nd Battn. of his regiment; became Lieutenant 25 Aug. 1899, and was then employed with the King's African Rifles from March, 1902, to Sept. 1907, where he held command of various columns (between 1902 and 1906) in punitive expeditions, viz.: East Africa, 1902, in command; East Africa, 1905; Nandi, 1905–6, in command of a column; East Africa, 1906, in command. He was twice mentioned in Despatches [London Gazettes of 18 Sept. 1906, and 13 March, 1908]; received the African General Service Medal and four clasps, and was created a Companion of the Distinguished Service Order [London Gazette, 13 March, 1908]: "Frederic Orby Maycock, Lieut., the Suffolk Regt. (employed with the King's African Rifles). In recognition of his services during the minor expeditions in East Africa in 1907." He became Captain 17 Sept. 1908. He was appointed, Sept. 1912, to the Staff of the Royal Military College, Sandhurst, as Instructor in Military History. He wrote several text books for the use of students of Military History, notably: "Napoleon's European Campaign and the Napoleonic Campaign of 1805." He became Major in March, 1915, and fell in the fighting near Ypres on 25 May, 1915. He was last seen standing on the parapet of an enemy trench leading his men in the attack. The details above are supplied by Major Maycock's cousin, Sir Willoughby Maycock, K.C.M.G.

Frederic W. O. Maycock.

RUDKIN, WILLIAM CHARLES ERIC, Capt., was born 22 Feb. 1875. He joined the Royal Artillery 15 June, 1895, and became Lieutenant 15 June, 1898. He served in the South African War, 1899–1901 (severely wounded). He took part in the operations in the Orange Free State, Feb. to May, 1900, including actions at Poplar Grove, Dreifontein, Vet River (5 and 6 May) and Zand River; in the Transvaal in May and June, 1900, including actions near Johannesburg, Pretoria and Diamond Hill (11 and 12 June) ; in the Transvaal, east of Pretoria, July to 29 Nov. 1900, including action at Belfast (26 and 27 Aug.) ;

William C. E. Rudkin.

also in Cape Colony, south of Orange River, 1900 (Queen's Medal with six clasps ; Despatches [London Gazette, 9 July, 1901]). He was promoted Captain 6 May, 1901 ; was Adjutant of Royal Artillery 27 April, 1904, to 26 Jan. 1906, and was employed with the West African Frontier Force 27 Jan. 1906, to 31 Jan. 1908 ; served in West Africa (Southern Nigeria), 1906, in command. He was mentioned in Despatches [London Gazette, 13 March, 1908], and received the Medal with clasp. He was created a Companion of the Distinguished Service Order [London Gazette, 13 March, 1908] : " William Charles Eric Rudkin, Capt., Royal Artillery (late employed with the West African Frontier Force). In recognition of his services with the Owa Column during operations in Southern Nigeria." He was promoted Major 29 Nov. 1911. Major Rudkin served in the European War. He was given the Brevet of Lieutenant-Colonel 3 June, 1915, and was Temporary Lieutenant-Colonel from Nov. 1915, until promoted to substantive rank 22 June, 1916 ; was promoted Temporary Brigadier-General to command the 57th Division, British Armies in France, 16 Aug. 1918 ; given the Brevet of Colonel 3 June, 1919. He was created a C.M.G. in 1918 ; became one of H.M. the King's Aide-de-Camps 3 June, 1919, and was mentioned in Despatches seven times.

CHAPMAN, PAUL, Lieut., was born 18 Oct. 1878, son of Sir Arthur Wakefield Chapman, Kt., and Agnes, daughter of the late Captain Mangles, of Poyle Park, Tongham, Surrey. He was educated at Eton, and entered the Royal Fusiliers as a Second Lieutenant 4 April, 1900, becoming Lieutenant 13 July, 1901. He served in South Africa, and was present in operations in the Transvaal, east of Pretoria, Aug. to 29 Nov. 1900 ; operations in Orange River Colony, May to Aug. 1900 ; operations in the Transvaal, Dec. 1900, to Jan. 1901 ; operations in Cape Colony, Jan. 1901, to May, 1902 (Queen's Medal with three clasps ; King's Medal with two clasps). From 15 Oct. 1904, he was employed with the West African Frontier Force. He again saw active service in 1906–7, in Northern Nigeria ; was mentioned in Despatches [London Gazette, 13 March, 1908] ; received the Medal and clasp, and was created a Companion of the Distinguished Service Order [London Gazette, 13 March, 1908] : " Paul Chapman, Lieut., The Royal Fusiliers (City of London Regt.) (employed with the West African Frontier Force). In recognition of his services with the Caibuk Expedition, Northern Nigeria." He became Captain 17 Aug. 1908, and retired in 1910. Capt. Chapman served during the European War in East Africa, 1914–16, and was mentioned in Despatches.

London Gazette, 14 Aug. 1908.—" War Office, 14 Aug. 1908. The King has been graciously pleased to give orders for the following appointments to the Distinguished Service Order of the undermentioned Officers, in recognition of their services in connection with the recent operations against the Zakka Khel and Mohmands. The whole to bear date 16 July, 1908."

BIRDWOOD, WILLIAM RIDDELL, Colonel, was born 13 Sept. 1865, eldest surviving son of the late H. M. Birdwood, Esq., C.S.I., J.P., LL.D., M.A. (Cantab.), I.C.S., and of Edith, eldest daughter of the late Surgeon-

William R. Birdwood.

Major Elijah Impey, Bombay Horse Artillery. He was educated at Clifton College and the Royal Military College, Sandhurst, and became Lieutenant, 4th Battn. Royal Scots Fusiliers, in March, 1883 ; was transferred to the 12th Lancers 9 May, 1885, and to the 11th Bengal Lancers 20 Dec. 1886. He served in Hazara in 1891 (Medal with clasp) ; in Isazai Campaign, 1892 ; was Adjutant, Viceroy's Bodyguard, 1893. He became Captain 9 May, 1896. Served on the North-West Frontier of India, 1897–98 ; took part in the operations on the Samana (Medal with two clasps) ; served at Tirah, 1897–98, as Orderly Officer, 2nd Division (13 Oct. to 17 Dec. 1897) ; afterwards on the Staff ; was present in the actions of Chagru Kotal and Dargai, and capture of the Sampagha and Arhanga Passes ; in the reconnaissance of the Saran Sar and action of 9 Nov. 1897 ; during the operations in the Waran Valley and action of 16 Nov. 1897 also at and around Dwatoi and action of 24 Nov. 1897 ; and in the Bara Valley 7 to 14 Dec. 1897 (Despatches [London Gazette, 7 June, 1898] ; clasp). He served in the South African War, 1899–1902 ; special service, South Africa, 8 Nov. 1899, to 9 Jan. 1900 ; Brigade Major, South Africa, 10 Jan. to 14 Oct. 1900 ; D.A.A.G., South Africa, 15 Oct. 1900, to 4 June, 1902 ; Military Secretary to the G.O.C.-in-C., Forces in South Africa (General Lord Kitchener), 5 June to 12 July, 1902 ; specially employed, Headquarters of Army, 13 July to 28 Oct. 1902. He took part in the operations in Natal, 1899 ; was present at the Relief of Ladysmith, including action at Colenso ; operations of 17 to 24 Jan. 1900, and action at Spion Kop ; in the operations of 5 to 7 Feb. 1900, and action at Vaal Kranz ; during operations on Tugela Heights (14 to 27 Feb. 1900) and action at Pieter's Hill ; served during operations in Natal (March to

June, 1900), including action at Laing's Nek (6 to 9 June) ; took part in the operations in the Transvaal, June, 1900 ; also in the Transvaal, east of Pretoria, July to 29 Nov. 1900 (severely wounded—horse killed), including actions at Belfast (26 and 27 Aug.) and Lydenberg (5 to 8 Sept. ; in Orange River Colony and Cape Colony, Nov. 1900 ; again in the Transvaal, Orange River Colony and Cape Colony 30 Nov. 1900, to 31 May, 1902 (Despatches [London Gazette, 8 Feb. 1901 (Sir R. H. Buller, 30 March, 19 June and 9 Nov. 1900), and London Gazette, 29 July, 1902] ; Brevets of Major, 29 Nov. 1900, and Lieutenant-Colonel, 26 June, 1902 ; (Queen's Medal with six clasps, and King's Medal with two clasps). From 28 Nov. 1902, to 31 Aug. 1904, he was Assistant Military Secretary and Persian Interpreter to the Commander-in-Chief, East Indies ; was promoted Major 9 May, 1903, and Lieutenant-Colonel 1 Sept. 1904 ; was A.A.G., H.Q., India, 1 Sept. 1904, to 21 Dec. 1905 ; became Colonel 26 June, 1905 ; Military Secretary to Commander-in-Chief, East Indies, 22 Dec. 1905, to 27 June, 1909 ; A.D.C. to the King 14 Feb. 1906. He was Chief Staff Officer, Mohmand Field Force, 10 May to 3 June, 1908, and took part in the operations in the Mohmand Country. He was mentioned in Despatches [London Gazette, 14 Aug. 1908] ; received the Medal and clasp, and was created a Companion of the Distinguished Service Order [London Gazette, 14 Aug. 1908] : " William Riddell Birdwood, Colonel, C.I.E., A.D.C., Indian Army. In recognition of . . . services in connection with the recent operations against the Zakka Khel and Mohmands (. . . to bear date 16 July, 1908)." He was created a C.I.E. in 1908, and a C.S.I. in 1910. He became Brigadier-General ; was Brigade Commander (Colonel on Staff), India, 28 June, 1909, to 31 May, 1911 ; Brigade Commander, India, 1 June, 1911, to 3 May, 1912, He was created a C.B. in 1911, and promoted Major-General 3 Oct. 1911 ; was Q.M.G., India, 4 May to 16 Nov. 1912 ; Secretary to the Government of India in the Army Department and Member of the Governor-General's Legislative Council 4 May, 1912, to 11 Dec. 1914. He was created a K.C.M.G. in 1914. Major-General Sir W. R. Birdwood served in the European War from 1914. He was Temporary Lieutenant-General 12 Dec. 1914, to 27 Oct. 1915, and was in command of the Australian and New Zealand Army Corps, Mediterranean Expeditionary Force, 12 Feb. 1914, to 18 Nov. 1915, being in command of the detached landing of the Australian and New Zealand Army Corps on Gallipoli above Gaba Tepe. He was made in 1915 a K.C.S.I., and on 18 Sept. 1915 was appointed by the Commonwealth Government G.O.C. of the Australian Imperial Force. He was G.O.C.-in-Chief, Mediterranean Expeditionary Force 17 to 26 Oct. 1915 ; was promoted Lieutenant-General 28 Oct. 1915 ; was Commander of the Dardanelles Army, Mediterranean Expeditionary Force, 19 Nov. 1915, to Jan. 1916 ; Army Corps Commander, Australian Army Corps, British Armies in France, from 1916 to 30 May, 1918. He became General 23 Oct. 1917, and was appointed A.D.C. General to the King 3 Nov. 1917. He became Commander of the 5th Army, British Armies in France, 31 May, 1918. He was wounded in the Great War, and for his services was mentioned in Despatches ; was created a K.C.B. in 1917, and a G.C.M.G. and a Baronet in 1919. He became Grand Officer of the Legion of Honour, and received the French Croix de Guerre ; was made Grand Officer of the Crown of Belgium, and received the Belgian Croix de Guerre. General Sir William Birdwood married, in 1894, Jeannette Hope Gonville, eldest daughter of Colonel Sir B. P. Bromhead, C.B., 4th Bart., of Thurlby Hall, Lincoln, and Annie (died, 1902), daughter of the Rev. J. Smith, and they have one son, Christopher Bromhead, and two daughters : Constance and Judith.

UNWIN, GASTON BOUVERIE, Lieut.-Colonel and Brevet Colonel, was born 9 July, 1859. He was educated at Wellington, and entered the 8th Foot as Second Lieutenant 25 May, 1878 ; was transferred to the 13th

Gaston Bouverie Unwin.

Foot 29 June, 1878 ; became Lieutenant, Bengal Staff Corps, 28 April, 1881, and Captain 25 May, 1889. He served with the Zhob Valley Expedition, 1890 ; served with the Waziristan Expedition, 1894–95 (Medal with clasp) ; served on the North-West Frontier of India, Tochi, 1897–98 (Medal with clasp). He became Major 25 May, 1898 ; served on the North-West Frontier of India, Waziristan, 1901–2 (clasp). He became Lieutenant-Colonel 25 May, 1904, and was given the Brevet of Colonel 15 Sept. 1907. He served in the Mohmand Expedition, 1908 ; received the Medal and clasp ; was mentioned in Despatches, and was created a Companion of the Distinguished Service Order [London Gazette, 14 Aug. 1908] : " Gaston Bouverie Unwin, Lieut.-Colonel and Brevet Colonel, Indian Army. In recognition of services in connection with the recent operations against the Zakka Khel and the Mohmands (to bear date 16 July, 1908)." He retired with the rank of Colonel in the Army 17 April, 1912. His regiment was the 21st Cavalry. Colonel Unwin married, in 1898, Katherine, eldest daughter of Sir Arthur Fanshawe, K.C.I.E., C.S.I., C.V.O., and Louisa, daughter of Captain Chase, and they have two daughters.

FULLER, RICHARD WOODFIELD, Major and Brevet Lieut.-Colonel, was born 28 Sept. 1861, son of the late Major A. R. Fuller, Royal (Bengal) Artillery. He was educated at Wellington College, and at the Royal Military Academy, Woolwich, and joined the Royal Artillery 27 July, 1880, as a Lieutenant, becoming Captain 14 Jan. 1889. He served during the operations in Chitral, 1895, with the Relief Force. He was promoted Major 14 Sept. 1898. Served in Tibet, 1903–4 ; took part in the action at Niani ; was present during the operations at and around Gyantse ; in the march to Lhassa (Despatches [London Gazette, 13 Dec. 1904]) ; Brevet of Lieutenant-Colonel 10 Nov. 1904. Served on the North-West Frontier of India, 1908 took part in the operations in the Mohmand country; engagement at Kargha. He was mentioned in Despatches, and was created a Companion of the Distinguished Service Order [London Gazette, 14 Aug. 1908]: " Richard Woodfield Fuller, Major and Brevet Lieut.-Colonel, Indian Army. In recognition of services in connection with the recent operations against the Zakka Khel and Mohmands (to bear date, 16 July, 1908)." He was promoted Lieutenant-Colonel 14 July, 1908; was given the Brevet of Colonel 11 Sept. 1909, and promoted Colonel 16 July, 1913. Colonel Fuller served in the European War in the Dardanelles, 1915 (Despatches), and in France, 1916. He was Temporary Brigadier-General 20 March, 1915, to 7 Feb. 1916, and from 26 Feb. 1916. He retired from the Service 25 Aug. 1916; became Honorary Brigadier-General 21 June, 1918. Brigadier-General Fuller married Adeline, daughter of the late P. W. Hewett, 1st Bombay Grenadiers.

Charles Astley Fowler.

FOWLER, CHARLES ASTLEY, Lieut.-Colonel, was born in the Punjab, India, 9 Nov. 1865, son of Surgeon-General Henry Day Fowler and Mary Caroline (née Oliver). He joined the Devonshire Regt., as Lieutenant, 7 Feb. 1885, and the Indian Staff Corps 16 Aug. 1886. He served on the North-West Frontier of India, 1891, in the 1st Miranzai Expedition. He became Captain 7 Feb. 1896; was D.A.A.G., India (temporary), 23 Aug. 1900; served on the North-West Frontier of India in the operations against the Darwesh Khel Waziris, 1902; became Major 7 Feb. 1903; became Lieutenant-Colonel 22 Sept. 1907. In 1908 Lieut.-Colonel C. A. Fowler served in the operations in the Mohmand country, and was present at the engagement of Kargha. He was mentioned in the Despatches of Sir James Willcocks on the Mohmand Expedition, 1908; received the Medal with clasp, and was created a Companion of the Distinguished Service Order [London Gazette, 14 Aug. 1908]: " In recognition of (his) services in connection with the recent operations against the Zakka Khel and Mohmands: Charles Astley Fowler, Lieut.-Colonel, Indian Army." He became Colonel, 22 Punjabis, 12 Nov. 1911; Temporary Brigadier-General 24 Aug. 1914, to 12 Feb. 1916, in command of the 37th Infantry Brigade; was mentioned in Sir John French's Despatches published Jan. 1916, and was created a C.B. for his services from 1914–1916 [London Gazette, Jan. 1916]. He held a special appointment in the Department of the Assistant Censor 21 Aug. 1916, to 24 May, 1917, and was Temporary Brigadier-General 6 July, 1917, to 5 April, 1918. On 6 April, 1918, he was promoted Major-General. Major-General C. A. Fowler married, in 1894, Florence Cicely, eldest daughter of the late James Tisdall Woodroffe, Advocate-General, Bengal; they have one son.

WESTMORLAND, PERCY THUILLIER, Major, was born 25 July, 1863, son of Colonel J. P. Westmorland, R.E. (retired), and the late Rose Julia, eldest daughter of the late General Sir Henry Thuillier, C.S.I., R.A.

Percy T. Westmorland.

He was educated at Wellington College and Sandhurst, and joined the Army 9 Sept. 1882, as a Second Lieutenant in the Bedfordshire Regt., in which he was promoted Captain 28 Aug. 1889. He was transferred to the West India Regt. 7 Dec. 1892, and was employed with the Army Pay Department 12 May, 1894, to 31 Dec. 1897. He served on the West Coast of Africa, 1894, with the Expedition to the Gambia against Fodey Silah (Despatches [London Gazette, 4 May, 1894]; Medal with clasp). Served with the Ashanti Expedition, 1895–96 (Star). He was promoted Major 22 Dec. 1897. Served in the South African War, 1899–1900; Staff Officer, Glencoe, and in command, St. Helena (Medal); served in West Africa, 1901; served with the Expedition up the Gambia (Medal with clasp). He served on the North-West Frontier of India, 1908, and took part in the operations in the Mohmand country, for which he was mentioned in Despatches, and was created a Companion of the Distinguished Service Order [London Gazette, 14 Aug. 1908]: " Percy Thuillier Westmorland, Major, Royal Warwickshire Regt. In recognition of (his) services in connection with the recent operations against the Zakka Khel and Mohmands (to bear date 16 July, 1908)." Major Westmorland retired from the Service 4 Dec. 1912. He served in the European War from 1914–1916, for which he was mentioned in Despatches and was created a C.M.G. in 1916. He was a Brigade Commander in 1916, and joined the Territorial Force Reserve in 1918, as Lieutenant-Colonel. He is one of the 134 descendants of the Rev. C. Cardew, D.D. (1747–1831), Rector of St. Erme, Cornwall, who served in the British forces in the Great War.

STANTON, FREDERICK WILLIAM STARKEY, Major, was born 2 Aug. 1863, son of the late Major-General F. S. Stanton, R.E. He was educated at Marlborough and Woolwich, and entered the Royal Artillery, as a Lieutenant, 14 Feb. 1883. He served with the Burmese Expedition, 1886–87; served with the Zhob Valley Expedition, 1890; became Captain 1 Feb. 1892; took part in the operations in Chitral, 1895, with the Relief Force; at the storming of the Malakand Pass, passage of the Swat River, action at Panjkora River (Medal with clasp); served at

Tirah, 1897–98; in the actions of Chagru Kotal and Dargai; at the capture of the Samphaga and Arhanga Passes; at the reconnaissance of the Saran Sar and action of 9 Nov. 1897; during the operations in the Waran Valley, and action of 16 Nov. 1897; also in the Bara Valley 7 to 14 Dec. 1897 (two clasps); became Major 2 Sept. 1901; served on the North-West Frontier of India, 1908, during the operations in the Mohmand country. Major Stanton was mentioned in Despatches, and was created a Companion of the Distinguished Service Order [London Gazette, 14 Aug. 1908]: " Frederick William Starkey Stanton, Major, Royal Artillery. In recognition of services during the recent operations against the Zakka Khel and Mohmands (to bear date 16 July, 1908)." He was promoted Lieutenant-Colonel 22 Nov. 1911. Lieut.-Colonel Stanton became Temporary Brigadier-General in 1915, and retired from the Service with the rank of Honorary Brigadier-General 5 Dec. 1918.

Frederick W. S. Stanton.

He married, in 1904, Louisa Maud, daughter of the late J. T. Stanton, J.P., of the Leaze, Stonehouse, Gloucestershire.

GILBERT, GERALD EDWIN LLOYD, Major, was born in 1864, son of the late E. L. Gilbert, Civil Engineer, Public Works Department, India. He was educated at the Royal Military College, Sandhurst, and entered the Dorsetshire Regt., as Lieutenant, 9 May, 1885; became Lieutenant, Indian Staff Corps, 8 July, 1886. He saw active service in the Hazara Expedition, 1888 (Medal with clasp); Isazai Expedition, 1892; operations in Chitral with the Relief Force, 1895 (Medal with clasp). He was promoted Captain, Indian Army, 9 May, 1896, and served in Tirah, 1897–98, including the operations in the Bara Valley 7 to 12 Dec. 1897 (two clasps); in China, 1900 (Medal); promoted Major, 9 May, 1903. He saw active service again on the North-West Frontier of India in 1908, in operations in the Mohmand country, commanding his regiment,

Gerald E. L. Gilbert.

the 34th Sikh Pioneers. He was mentioned in Despatches; received the Medal and clasp, and was created a Companion of the Distinguished Service Order [London Gazette, 14 Aug. 1908]: " In recognition of (his) services in connection with the recent operations against the Zakka Khel and Mohmands: Gerald Edward Lloyd Gilbert, Major, Indian Army (to bear date 16 July, 1908)." He was D.A.Q.M.G., India, 8 June, 1907, to 22 April, 1908. He became Lieutenant-Colonel 9 May, 1911, and retired from the Service 6 Sept. 1912. In the European War he commanded the 1st Entrenching Battn. He is the author of a book called " The Evolution of Tactics." He married, in 1891, Emily Sophia, daughter of the late Samuel Fenton, J.P., County Wicklow. They have a son and a daughter.

ALLEN, HUGH MORRIS, Major, was born 6 Oct. 1867. He entered the Army as a Second Lieutenant in the Welsh Regt. 14 Sept. 1887; became Lieutenant, Indian Staff Corps, 25 March, 1888, and Captain, Indian Army, 14 Sept. 1898. He served on the North-West Frontier of India, 1897–98, Malakand and Mohmand (Medal with clasp); again on the North-West Frontier of India, Waziristan, 1901–2 (clasp). He became Major 14 Sept. 1905; was Brigade Major, India, 27 Dec. 1904, to 23 Sept. 1905; and became D.A.A.G., India, 24 Sept. 1905. Major Allen served for the third time on the North-West Frontier of India, 1908; D.A.A.G., 2nd Brigade, operations in the Mohmand country. He was created a Companion of the Distinguished Service Order [London Gazette, 14 Aug. 1908]: " In recognition of (his) services in the recent operations against the Zakka Khel and Mohmands: Hugh Morris Allen, Major, Indian Army (to bear date 16 July, 1908)." He was promoted Lieutenant-Colonel 14 Sept. 1913, and retired from the Indian Army on 4 Oct. following. In the European War he commanded the 7th Battn. The Black Watch, serving from 1914–18. He was created a C.M.G. in 1916.

GRAY, FREDERICK WILLIAM BARTON, Major, was born 7 Feb. 1867, son of the Rev. Thomas T. Gray, of Carn Park, County Westmeath. He entered the Army as a Second Lieutenant in the Royal Berkshire Regt. 22 Aug. 1888, and became Lieutenant in the Indian Staff Corps 22 Jan. 1890. He accompanied the Waziristan Expedition, 1894–95 (Medal with clasp); became Captain 22 Aug. 1899; served in China, 1900 (Medal); became Major 22 Aug. 1906. Major Gray was mentioned in Despatches and created a Companion of the Distinguished Service Order [London Gazette, 14 Aug. 1908: " In recognition of (his) services in the recent operations against the Zakka Khel and Mohmands, on the North-West Frontier of India, in 1908: Frederick William Barton Gray, Major, Indian Army (to bear date 16 July, 1908)." He also received the Medal and clasp. He became Lieutenant-Colonel 8 March, 1914. He took part in the Great War from 1914 to 1918, serving with the Egyptian Expeditionary Force from 15 April, 1916, to 27 Nov. 1917, as Brigade Commander (Temporary Brigadier-General); also Temporary Brigadier-General from 13 May, 1918; was wounded, mentioned in Despatches, created a C.M.G. in 1915, and given the Brevet of Colonel, 1 Jan. 1918. He married, in 1907, Winifred Frances, daughter of James Stewart, of Tientsin, North China.

TARVER, ALEXANDER LEIGH, Capt., was born 30 Aug. 1871. He joined the Army as a Second Lieutenant in the Royal Welsh Fusiliers 29 Oct. 1890, and after receiving promotion in that regiment to Lieutenant 6 Aug. 1892, was transferred to the Indian Staff Corps 12 April, 1893. He served in East Africa, 1895–96, during the operations against the Mazrui Rebels (Medal) ; served at Tirah, 1897–98 (Medal with two clasps). He became Captain 10 July, 1901 ; was Brigade Major, India, 18 July, 1907, to 18 April, 1909 ; D.A.A.G., Bazar Valley Field Force, 14 Feb. to 1 March 1908 ; D.A.A.G., Mohmand Field Force, 19 April to 1 June, 1908. Served on the North-West Frontier of India, 1908 ; D.A.A.G., 1st Brigade ; took part in the operations in the Zakka Khel country (Despatches [London Gazette, 22 May, 1908]) ; also during operations in the Mohmand country. He was mentioned in Despatches and was created a Companion of the Distinguished Service Order [London Gazette, 14 Aug. 1908] : " In recognition of . . . services during the recent operations against the Zakka Khel and Mohmands : Alexander Leigh Tarver, Capt., Indian Army (to bear date 16 July, 1908.)" He was promoted Major 24 May, 1910 ; was G.S.O.2, India, from 19 April, 1909, to 18 April, 1911, and 12 March, 1913, to 30 Nov. 1915. He served in the European War, 1915–16 ; was Temporary Lieutenant-Colonel from 1 Dec. 1915, until given the Brevet of Lieutenant-Colonel 3 June, 1916 ; became Lieutenant-Colonel 29 Oct. 1916. On 3 June, 1918, he was given the Brevet of Colonel, and was made an A.D.C. to the King. He is now G.S.O.1 at Peshawar, India.

LANGHORNE, ALGERNON PHILIP YORKE, Lieut., was born 18 July, 1882, son of the late Rev. J. Langhorne. He was educated at Marlborough ; entered Royal Artillery 24 May, 1902 ; Lieutenant, Royal Artillery, 5 April, 1905. He was A.D.C. to the Divisional Commander, India, 2 Feb. 1908, to 5 Oct. 1910 ; A.D.C. to the G.O.C., Bazar Field Force, 13 Feb. to 1 March, 1908, and to the G.O.C., Mohmand Field Force, 24 April to 31 May, 1908. He served on the North-West Frontier of India, 1908 ; took part in the operations in the Zakka Khel country (Despatches [London Gazette, 22 May, 1908]) ; also during the operations in the Mohmand country (Despatches [London Gazette, 14 Aug. 1908]). He was created a Companion of the Distinguished Service Order [London Gazette, 14 Aug. 1908] : " In recognition of (his) services during the operations against the Zakka Khel and Mohmands : Algernon Philip Yorke Langhorne, Lieut., Royal Artillery (to bear date 16 July, 1908)." From 6 Oct. 1910, to 1 Feb. 1913, Lieut. Langhorne was A.D.C. to the G.O.C., Northern Army, India. He served in the European War, 1914–1918, holding the following appointments : A.D.C. to the G.O.C., Indian Army Corps, British Expeditionary Force, 30 Oct. to 28 Dec. 1914 (promoted Captain 30 Oct. 1914) ; Camp Commandant, Indian Army Corps, British Expeditionary Force, 29 Dec. 1914, to 31 July, 1915 ; Acting Major, Royal Artillery, 25 Sept. 1916, to 30 April, 1917 ; Brigade Major, Royal Artillery, Heavy Artillery, 15th Army Corps, British Armies in France, 11 Jan. to 27 Sept. 1917 (promoted Major 1 May, 1917) ; G.S.O.2, 6th Army Corps, British Armies in France, 28 Sept. to 26 Oct. 1917 ; G.S.O.2, 2nd Army Corps, British Armies in France, 27 Oct. 1917, to 26 July, 1918 ; G.S.O.2, Tactical School, Camberley, 7 Aug. 1918. He was mentioned in Despatches, awarded the Military Cross, and was given the Brevet of Lieutenant-Colonel 7 Aug. 1918.

London Gazette, 24 Nov. 1908.—" The King has been graciously pleased to give orders for the following appointments to the Distinguished Service Order, in recognition of the gallant conduct of the undermentioned Officers during the recent operations on the North-West Frontier of India against the Mohmands."

WATERWORTH, GERALD FRANCIS, Lieut., was born 15 April, 1879, son of Thomas Waterworth and Mary Ann Waterworth. He was educated at Blundell's School, and entered the Army on 19 Sept. 1900, as a Second Lieutenant in the Warwickshire Regt. ; became Lieutenant 8 Jan. 1902. He served on the North-West Frontier of India, 1908, in operations in the Mohmand country ; was present at the engagement at Matta ; was mentioned in Despatches [London Gazette, 14 Aug. 1908], and created a Companion of the Distinguished Service Order [London Gazette, 24 Nov. 1908] : " In recognition of services during the recent operations on the North-West Frontier against the Mohmands : Gerald Francis Waterworth, Lieut., Royal Warwickshire Regt." He became Captain 15 July, 1910 ; was Adjutant, Indian Volunteers, 26 May, 1912, to 1915. Capt. Waterworth served in the European War from 1914–17. He was Temporary Major of a Service Battn. of the Hampshire Regt. from Aug. 1915 ; was promoted Major 1 Sept. 1915 ; was Temporary Lieutenant-Colonel commanding a Territorial Force Battn. of the Middlesex Regt., April to Oct. 1917. In 1914 he married Annie Farquhar, daughter of the late Peter Baillie, of Inverness, and they have one daughter, Mary Geraldine Baillie.

PLATT, WILLIAM, Second Lieut., was born 14 June, 1885, son of John Platt, of Hyning, Carnforth ; and was educated at Marlborough (1898–1902). He entered the Northumberland Fusiliers 16 Aug. 1905. He served on the North-West Frontier of India in 1908, in the Mohmond country, being present at the engagement at Matta. He was mentioned in Despatches [London Gazette, 14 Aug. 1908], and was created a Companion of the Distinguished Service Order [London Gazette, 24 Nov. 1908] : " William Platt, Second Lieutenant, The Northumberland Fusiliers." He was promoted Lieutenant 19 June, 1909, and Captain 1 Nov. 1914. Capt. Platt served in the European War from 1914, to 1917. He became Captain 1 Nov. 1914 ; held the following Staff appointments : Brigade Major, 103rd Infantry Brigade, New Armies, British Armies in France, 8 Jan. 1915, to 21 Nov. 1916 ; G.S.O.2, British Armies in France, 22 Nov. to 6 Dec. 1916 ; G.S.O.2, 21st Division, British Armies in France, 7 Dec. 1916, to 4 July, 1917 ; G.S.O.2, 2nd Australian and New Zealand Army Corps, 22nd Army Corps, British Armies in France, 5 July, 1917, to 9 July, 1918 ; became Temporary Lieutenant-Colonel and G.S.O.1, 37th Division, British Armies in France, 10 July, 1918. He was given the Brevet of Major 1 Jan. 1917. His D.S.O. was awarded for services against the Mohmands.

London Gazette, 19 June, 1911.—" The King has been graciously pleased to give orders for the following appointment to the Distinguished Service Order, in recognition of the services of the undermentioned Officer during the operations at Dibai, in the Persian Gulf, in Dec. 1910."

Granville Mackay Heriot.

HERIOT, GRANVILLE MACKAY, Major, was born 3 Oct. 1871, son of Major-General Mackay A. H. J. Heriot, Royal Marine Light Infantry, and Rosa, daughter of Thomas Fisher, M.D., of Canterbury, New Zealand. He entered the Royal Marines as a Second Lieutenant 1 Sept. 1889 ; became Lieutenant 1 July, 1890 ; Captain 1 April, 1898 ; Major, 23 April, 1908. Major Heriot was created a Companion of the Distinguished Service Order [London Gazette, 19 June, 1911] : " Granville Mackay Heriot, Major, Royal Marine Light Infantry. In recognition of services during operations at Dibai, in the Persian Gulf, in Dec. 1910." He became Lieutenant-Colonel 14 July, 1915, and retired 25 Jan. 1916.

London Gazette, 23 Aug. 1912.—" The King has been graciously pleased to give orders for the following appointments to the Distinguished Service Order, in recognition of the services of the undermentioned Officers in connection with the recent operations against the Abors on the North-Eastern Frontier of India."

DAVIDSON, JAMES, Major, was born 27 Nov. 1865, at Yetholm, Roxburghshire, son of the late Rev. Adam Davidson, M.A., Minister of the Parish of Yetholm, Scotland. He was educated by private tuition, at Edinburgh Academy and Edinburgh University (M.A., 1886 ; M.B., C.M., 1891 ; M.D., 1902), and entered the Indian Medical Service on 29 July, 1893. He served with the Waziristan Expedition, 1894–5 (Indian Medal of 1894 with clasp for Waziristan) ; became Captain 29 July, 1896, Indian Medical Service, Bengal ; served in the Chitral Relief Force, Lines of Communication, 1895 (India Medal of 1895 with clasp for Chitral) ; with the Dongola Expedition, 1896 ; with the Indian Brigade at Suakin (Medal, Egyptian Medal) ; with the Tirah Expedition, 1897–98 (two clasps to the India Medal) ; with the Tibet Expedition, 1903–4, taking part in the action at Niani ; the operations in and around Gyantse, and the march to Lhassa (Medal with clasp for Gyantse). He became Interpreter in Russian in 1903 ; was promoted Major 30 Jan. 1905. Major Davidson served with the Abor Expeditionary Force, as A.D.M.S. in 1911 and 1912, for which he received the Medal and clasp. He was mentioned in Despatches [London Gazette, 16 July, 1912], and was created a Companion of the Distinguished Service Order [London Gazette, 23 Aug. 1912] : " James Davidson, M.D., Major, Indian Medical Service. In recognition of services in connection with the recent operations against the Abors on the North-Eastern Frontier." He also received the Medal with clasp. He became Lieutenant-Colonel 30 Jan. 1913, and was Medical Officer, 1st Battn. 2nd King Edward's Own Gurkha Rifles. He served in the European War as O.C., Hospital Ship Syria ; visited Egypt, Boulogne, Anzac and Basra.

James Davidson.

WILSON, JAMES ALBAN, Major, was born 12 Feb. 1865, son of the late James Buck Wilson, J.P., of Firbank. He was educated at Uppingham, and joined the 2nd Seaforth Highlanders, as Second Lieutenant, 16 Nov. 1887 ; became Lieutenant 4 Sept. 1889, and joined the Indian Staff Corps 1 Nov. 1889 ; became Lieutenant, 44th Light Infantry (now the 8th Gurkhas) 1898. He accompanied the Expedition to Manipur, 1891 (Medal with clasp) ; served on the North-Eastern Frontier of Assam, 1894, with the Abor Expedition ; served in Burma, 1895–96 ; served as Staff Officer in the Expedition to Kiaruma. He became Captain, Indian Army, 16 Nov. 1898 ; served on the North-West Frontier of India, Waziristan, 1901–2 ; served as D.A.A.G. of Punjab Frontier Force and Mahsud Blockade operations ; served as Staff Officer with Lieut.-Colonel V. C. Tonnochy's Column (Despatches [London Gazette, 8 Aug. 1902] ; Medal with clasp). Capt. Wilson was D.A.A.G., India, 15 April, 1901, to 14 April, 1906. He became Major 16 Nov. 1904. He took part in operations in the Abor country, 1911-12 (Medal and clasp ; Despatches [London Gazette, 16 July, 1912]). He was created a Companion of the Distinguished Service Order [London Gazette, 23 Aug. 1912] : " In recognition of services in connection with the recent operations against the Abors on the North-Eastern Frontier of India : James Alban Wilson, Major, Indian Army." In 1913 he commanded the Naga Hills Expedition ; Brevet of Lieutenant-Colonel 27 March, 1913. He became Lieutenant-Colonel 16 Nov. 1913. Lieut.-Colonel Wilson served in the European War, commanding the 1/8th Gurkhas in Mesopotamia, 1916–17 ; raising and commanding the 3/8th Gurkhas, 1917–18. He is a Knight of the Order of the Red Eagle of Prussia, and a Knight of the Order of Merit of Pyrmont-Waldeck. His favourite recreations are shooting and fishing. He married, in 1898, Carrie, daughter of the late General F. J. Priestley.

VAUGHAN, EDWARD GYLES, Major, was born 21 Nov. 1867, at Bath, son of Major Richard Vaughan, R.A., of Roscrea, County Tipperary, Ireland. He was educated at Wellington College, and entered the Bedfordshire Regt. 11 Feb. 1888, becoming Lieutenant, Indian Staff Corps, 26 July, 1889. He served with the Chin-Lushai Expedition, 1889-90 (Medal with clasp); in Burma, 1891; on the North-West Frontier of India, 1897-98; Malakand, Assistant to Base Commandant Officer (2 Aug. to Oct. 1907); Mohmand; Buner; Brigade Commandant Officer to a Column (Medal with clasp); in Uganda, 1898-99 (Medal with clasp). He became Captain 11 Feb. 1899, and served in British East Africa, 1901, during the operations against the Ogaden Somalis in Jubaland (Medal with clasp). He became Major 11 Feb. 1906; Major Vaughan served on the North-West Frontier of India, 1908; operations in the Zakka Khel country, and operations in the Mohmand country (Medal with clasp); in operations in the Abor country, 1911-12. He was mentioned in Despatches [London Gazette, 16 July, 1912], and was created a Companion of the Distinguished Service Order [London Gazette, 23 Aug. 1912]: "Edward Gyles Vaughan, Major, Indian Army. In recognition of . . . services in connection with the operations against the Abors on the North-Eastern Frontier of India." He was promoted Lieutenant-Colonel 11 Feb. 1914, and was for a year (1914-15) with the Indian Expeditionary Force, 2nd Indian Cavalry Division, Supply and Transport Corps, on the Western Front, returning to India in Oct. 1915. He became Assistant Director of Transport at Lucknow in 1915.

CULLEN, ERNEST HENRY SCOTT, Major, was born 16 Nov. 1869, and entered the Army as a Second Lieutenant in the West Yorkshire Regt. 1 March, 1890. He became Lieutenant 21 Jan. 1892, and was transferred to the Indian Staff Corps 2 July, 1892. Lieut. Cullen took part in the operations in Chitral, 1895, with the Relief Force (Medal with clasp); served on the North-West Frontier of India, 1897-98, Mohmand (clasp); in Tirah, 1897-98; took part in operations in the Bara Valley 7 to 14 Dec. 1897 (clasp). He was promoted Captain 1 March, 1901. He served again on the North-West Frontier of India, Waziristan, 1901-2 (clasp); in Tibet, 1903-4; action at Niani; during the operations at and around Gyantse; in the march to Lhassa (Despatches [London Gazette, 13 Dec. 1904]; Medal with clasp). He became Major 1 March, 1908; was created an M.V.O. 1911. In 1911-12 he took part in operations in the Abor country; was mentioned in Despatches [London Gazette, 16 July, 1912], and was created a Companion of the Distinguished Service Order [London Gazette, 23 Aug. 1912]: "In recognition of (his) services in connection with the recent operations against the Abors on the North-Eastern Frontier of India: Ernest Henry Scott Cullen, M.V.O., Major, Indian Army." He served in the European War, 1914-16, in Mesopotamia, and was created a C.M.G. in 1916. He became Lieutenant-Colonel 24 March, 1915. His regiment is the 32nd Pioneers.

KENNEDY, MYLES ARTHUR CLAUDE, Lieut., was born 12 Aug. 1885, only son of Colonel Claude Kennedy. He entered the Army, as Second Lieutenant, Unattached List, 5 Aug. 1905; was transferred 31 Nov. 1906, to the Indian Army, 8th Gurkha Rifles, and was promoted Lieutenant 5 Nov. 1907. He served in the Abor Expedition in 1912; was mentioned in Despatches; received the Medal with clasp, and was created a Companion of the Distinguished Service Order [London Gazette, 23 Aug. 1912]: "In recognition of . . . services in connection with the recent operations against the Abors on the North-Eastern Frontier of India: Myles Arthur Claude Kennedy, Lieut., Indian Army." Capt. M. A. C. Kennedy died 2 Nov. 1918. He had married, in 1913, Nora Constance Marion, daughter of the late William L. Mumford, M.D. They had one daughter.

London Gazette, 3 Sept. 1912.—"War Office, 3 Sept. 1912. The King has been graciously pleased to give orders for the following appointment to the Distinguished Service Order, in recognition of the services of the undermentioned Officer during the operations referred to in Sir F. R. Wingate's Despatch (operations in the South-Eastern Sudan against the Beir and Annak tribes, Jan. to March, 1912)."

LEVESON, CHARLES HENRY, Major, was born 18 Oct. 1868, son of the late Rev. C. Leveson. He entered the Army as a Second Lieutenant in the 18th Hussars, 23 Oct. 1889, becoming Lieutenant 29 July, 1891. He took part in the operations in Chitral, 1895, with the Relief Force (Medal with clasp); served during the operations on the North-West Frontier of India, 1897-98, with the Tirah Expeditionary Force (two clasps). From 5 June, 1899, to 20 Feb. 1901, he was employed with the West African Regt., and was present in operations in Ashanti (Medal with clasp). He became Captain 24 Feb. 1900. He served in the South African War, 1901-2 (severely wounded). He served in the operations in the Transvaal, April to Sept. 1901, and Nov. 1901, to 31 May, 1902; in Orange River Colony, March and May, 1902; also during the operations on the Zululand Frontier of Natal in Sept. and Oct. 1901 (Despatches [London Gazette, 29 July, 1902]; Queen's Medal with four clasps). Capt. Leveson was employed with the Egyptian Army 27 Feb. 1903, to 26 Feb. 1913, and was promoted Major 19 Feb. 1906. He served in the Sudan, 1906; took part in the operations at Talodi in Southern Kordofan (Egyptian Medal with clasp; 4th Class Osmanieh), and again in the Sudan in 1912. For this campaign he received the 3rd Class Medjidie and the Egyptian Medal with clasp; was mentioned in Despatches, and was created a Companion of the Distinguished Service Order [London Gazette, 3 Sept. 1912]: "For services during operations referred to in above Despatch (Sir F. R. Wingate's relative to operations in the South-Eastern Sudan against the Beir and Annak tribes, Jan. to March, 1912): Charles Henry Leveson, Major, 18th (Queen Mary's Own) Hussars, employed with the Egyptian Army." Major Leveson served in the European War in 1914, and was severely wounded. He was subsequently specially employed at the War Office, and was G.S.O.3, 2 and 1, War Office; was given the rank of Lieutenant-Colonel in the Army 15 Dec. 1917, and retired from the 18th Hussars 17 Aug. 1918. Lieut.-Colonel Leveson married Annie Marguerite, daughter of the late C. W. Lomer, of Perrott's Brook House, North Cerney, Cirencester, and they have two sons and one daughter.

London Gazette, 4 Aug. 1914.—"The King has been graciously pleased to give orders for the appointment of the undermentioned Officer to the Distinguished Service Order, in recognition of his services whilst in command of a party of 25 rank and file of the 3rd Battn. King's African Rifles on the occasion of a reconnaissance on 3 Sept. 1913, on the east shore of Lake Rudolph, East African Protectorate."

JONES, WILLIAM LLOYD, Lieut., was born on 13 Jan. 1886, and joined the Middlesex Regt., as a Second Lieutenant, 24 Jan. 1906. He was promoted to Lieutenant 10 Oct. 1908, and was employed with the King's African Rifles from 17 Aug. 1911, to 7 Aug. 1914. He served in the East African Protectorate in 1913, in command of the reconnaissance on the east shore of Lake Rudolph. He was severely wounded, and created a Companion of the Distinguished Service Order [London Gazette, 4 Aug. 1914]: "In recognition of his services whilst in command of a party of 25 rank and file of the 3rd Battn. King's African Rifles, on the occasion of a reconnaissance on the 3rd Sept. 1913, on the east shore of Lake Rudolph, East African Protectorate. To be a Companion of the Distinguished Service Order, William Lloyd Jones, Lieut., Middlesex Regt. The following Despatch, dated 12 June, 1914, relating to the engagement of the 3rd Sept. last, in which Lieut. W. Lloyd Jones, Middlesex Regt., was severely wounded, has been received in the Colonial Office from the Governor of the East African Protectorate: During a reconnaissance to the north of Loizangalani, on the east shore of Lake Rudolph, in the East African Protectorate, on the 3rd of Sept. 1913, Lieut. W. Lloyd Jones, who, with 25 rank and file of the 3rd Battn. King's African Rifles, was acting as escort to the Political Officer, came into touch with a party of Abyssinians at a water hole named Bwann (30° 17' N. and 36° 44' E.). The latter retired behind a dense thorn zariba eight feet high, containing one gate. Lieut. Lloyd Jones, after reconnoitring the zariba, advanced into the open within 25 yards of the enemy, and summoned them through his Abyssinian orderly to come out, at the same time assuring them that they would be granted their lives. The enemy replied that they would not come out, and immediately began to barricade the gate. Seeing this, Lieut. Lloyd Jones, though unaware of the numbers of the enemy, at once ordered his men to charge, and himself ran forward at their head. His Abyssinian orderlies heard those inside shout, 'Shoot the white man!' Almost immediately the bugler, who was just behind Lieut. Lloyd Jones, was hit by a bullet in the chest, and he himself, before he could reach the gate, received a shot in the left ankle which completely shattered the bone and brought him to the ground. The orderlies and a sergeant rushed on, and, breaking through the gate, shot down everyone inside the zariba. Lieut. Lloyd Jones, not knowing whether there were any more of the enemy in the vicinity, then had himself carried up to some high ground overlooking the water, and threw out a screen of scouts on the neighbouring hills. On the return of the Political Officer, who was surveying not far away, Lieut. Lloyd Jones was carried back to Loizangalani, where he arrived on the 7th Sept." Lieut. W. Lloyd Jones was the last officer to win the D.S.O. before the European War. At the outbreak of the European War he was given a special appointment (graded as G.S.O.3), Aug. 1914, to March, 1915. He was promoted Captain 8 Dec. 1914; was specially employed at the War Office 4 Oct. 1915.

London Gazette, 9 Nov. 1914.—"War Office, 9 Nov. 1914.—His Majesty the King has been graciously pleased to approve of the appointment of the undermentioned Officers to be Companions of the Distinguished Service Order, in recognition of their services with the Expeditionary Force, specified below."

BURNE, ALFRED HIGGINS, Lieut., was born 26 Sept. 1886, fifth son of Colonel Lambrooke Thomas Higgins Burne, V.D., J.P., of Loynton Hall, and Julia Susanna, daughter of the late Valentine Vickers, of Offley Grove, Staffordshire. He was educated at Winchester College, and joined the Army in July, 1906. He served in the European War, 1914-18. He was created a Companion of the Distinguished Service Order [London Gazette, 9 Nov. 1914]: "Alfred Higgins Burne, Lieut., J Battery, Royal Horse Artillery. For gallant handling of his section under heavy fire at Gibralter, France, on the 8th Sept. 1914." This was the first D.S.O. gazetted during the Great War. He was promoted Captain, 30 Oct. 1914, and Major 12 Feb. 1917, and was appointed to Brigade Major, R.A., 32nd Division, British Armies in France, 30 Aug. 1918. Capt. Burne was five times mentioned in Despatches, and was awarded a Bar to his D.S.O. [London Gazette, April, 1918].

Alfred Higgins Burne.

Algernon J. R. Lamb.

LAMB, ALGERNON JOSEPH RUTHERFURD, Lieut., was born 4 Oct. 1891, in Edinburgh, son of William Rutherfurd Lamb, Esq., of Ryton Hall, County Durham, and Goldsborough Hall, Knaresborough. He was educated at Eton College and Sandhurst; was gazetted to the Queen's Bays 4 Feb. 1911; joined his regiment 1 April, 1911, and became Lieutenant 13 Oct. 1911. He served in the European War from 1914. He was mentioned in Despatches, and was created a Companion of the Distinguished Service Order [London Gazette, 9 Nov. 1914]: "Algernon Joseph Rutherfurd Lamb, Lieut., 2nd Dragoon Guards (Queen's Bays). As Machine Gun Officer, by his coolness and promptitude the hostile gunfire was got under, and, mainly owing to the fire of his detachment, eight hostile guns were abandoned by the enemy." This was the second D.S.O. gazetted for the Great War. Capt. Lamb writes: "The decoration was awarded for service at the Battle of Nery, which took place near Compèigne during the Retreat from Mons on 1 Sept. 1914. This was the action during which L Battery, Royal Horse Artillery, was destroyed, after a most gallant fight. I was Machine Gun Officer of my regiment. Early on this morning the 1st Cavalry Brigade, who were bivouacking in and around the village of Nery, were attacked by a German Cavalry Division with 12 guns; eight of these had been brought up to within 700 yards of the village under cover of a dense mist. When the mist lifted at about 6 a.m., these guns revealed their presence by opening a heavy fire on L Battery and the horses of my regiment, which were feeding in the lines. I was shaving, and was in full view of the enemy when the mist cleared and the artillery fire began. The ensuing fight has so often been described in books and newspaper articles that it seems unnecessary to repeat it all. I collected all the available machine gunners of my two gun teams, amounting to seven in all (the remainder being in a different part of the village when the action began), and mounted the guns on the edge of a slightly sunk road in face of the German guns, whence I was able to bring a destructive fire to bear on the hostile gun teams. In about two hours or so, the enemy, having attempted repeatedly to withdraw their guns, which they failed to do owing to the missiles that were dropping around the gun positions, retired and abandoned the eight guns. A dismounted attack made by German cavalrymen towards the right of our position through standing crops failed to materialize." He also received the Croix de Chevalier (Légion d'Honneur). He became Captain, 2nd Dragoon Guards, 21 April, 1917, and was employed with the Egyptian Army to command the Sudanese Squadron of Cavalry and Mounted Infantry from 15 April, 1916, and later as D.A.A.G.

HARDINGE, THE HONOURABLE EDWARD CHARLES, Lieut. was born at Constantinople on 3 May, 1892, elder son of Charles, Baron Hardinge of Penshurst, K.G., P.C., G.C.B., G.C.S.I., G.C.M.G., G.C.I.E., G.C.V.O., I.S.O., late Viceroy and Governor-General of India, and of the Honourable Winifred Sturt (who died in 1914), daughter of the 1st Baron Alington. He was a nephew of Colonel Viscount Hardinge, A.D.C., and of Lord Alington; was educated at Wellington College, and while there was a Page of Honour to His late Majesty King Edward VII., and afterwards went to the Royal Military College, Sandhurst. He was gazetted to the 15th Hussars in Sept. 1911, and in Dec. of that year was Honorary A.D.C. to the Viceroy during the Durbar. In Jan. 1912, he joined his regiment in South Africa, and he was promoted to Lieutenant in Aug. 1914. In 1914 he rode remarkably well at the International Horse Show at Olympia, winning full marks in the London to Aldershot ride. He was a Member of the Cavalry Club, a very keen rider to hounds, a good polo player, and he won the Subalterns' Point-to-Point Race at the regimental races in Jan. 1914. He served with his regiment in the European War, and greatly distinguished himself before he died on the 18th Dec. 1914, from several severe wounds in both arms, which he had received on the 27 Aug., near Le Cateau, and the King himself sent a telegram to Lord Hardinge, saying: "I have had great pleasure in conferring the Distinguished Service Order on your son, for ability and gallantry in reconnaissance under great difficulty and machine-gun fire on three successive days, when he was severely wounded. Glad to say he is progressing satisfactorily."

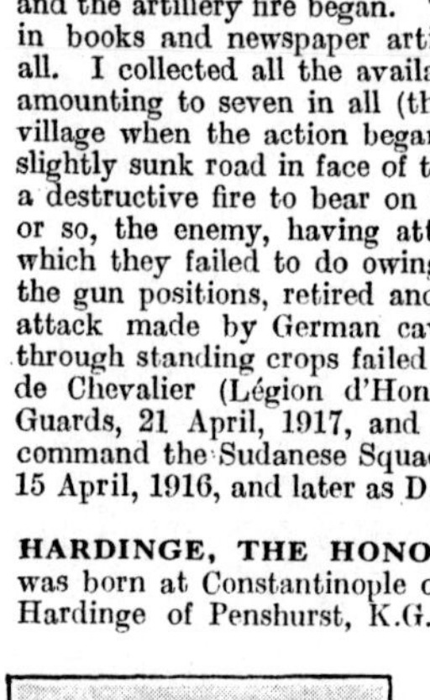

The Hon. E. C. Hardinge.

We quote accounts of two conspicuous acts of great gallantry by Lieut. the Honourable E. C. Hardinge; on the latter occasion he received the wound of which he unhappily died: "On 23 Aug., about 9.30 p.m., Lieut. Hardinge was sent out from Rouveroy on a most difficult and dangerous night reconnaissance towards Binche, to ascertain movements of the Germans, of which information was very urgently needed. He succeeded in reaching the village of Estinne Hud-Mont. Having avoided Uhlan patrols, and having hidden his small patrol in a stone electric machinery building, he climbed the church tower with a sergeant, and waited for dawn to break. Whilst waiting, a Uhlan patrol entered the village, and others came round it. He remained quietly in observation, and they failed to discover him or his patrol. In the early morning he was able to locate German batteries in position south-west of Binche, a brigade of cavalry moving due west from that place, and their infantry massing near a wood south of it. His difficulty was then to get away, being surrounded, but fortunately another patrol, under Lieut. Nicholson, 15th Hussars, seeing his predicament, came to his assistance by firing on the Uhlans, and then, by withdrawing, drew them off and so enabled Lieut. Hardinge to get through with his most valuable information. He was very highly complimented and noted for reward. (2.) On 27 Aug. two troops (Lieut. Hardinge's being one) were sent out at 4 a.m. from Oisy, on rear-guard work, his troop reconnoitring and observing on the right front, and right of the rear-guard position being held. German columns were reported advancing, and about 10.30 a.m. the patrols were driven in by German infantry. The attack gradually developed, and shortly before 1 p.m. became very heavy, and the flanking company of the Royal Munster Fusiliers, near Bergues, was in difficulties. Lieut. Hardinge, with his troop, was sent to their assistance, and came into action on their left opposite three machine guns, which he located and tried to silence. A fourth then came into action, outflanking him, and, causing some casualties forced him to retire. Realizing that the position of the Munsters was untenable (who had to hold on to prevent the rest of the battalion being cut off) unless this machine gun was put out of action, he led a few men up again most gallantly to try and capture it. Whilst trying to locate it exactly he had to stand up and use his glasses, and so became exposed to its fire. He was very severely wounded in both arms, one arm being badly shattered. After having it temporarily bound up, he told his men to hold on as long as they could, and to help the Munsters out, and then quite calmly walked back to where his horses were, and was then taken on to the ambulance."

Lord Ernest Hamilton says in "The First Seven Divisions" (pages 70–73): "The story of the rescue of the Munsters, by the 15th Hussars is one of which the latter regiment may well be proud. Two troops only of the 15th Hussars were engaged, and yet the number of honours that fell to them is remarkable. . . . The story of this affair is as follows: It was reported to the General Commanding that the Munster Fusiliers were in trouble, and the 15th Hussars, who were acting as divisional cavalry, were sent back to help. The country in the neighbourhood of Bergues is a difficult one, being traversed by numerous narrow byways cutting in all directions, and the 15th Hussars, not knowing just where the Munster Fusiliers were, separated into troops and beat the country northwards. Just south of Bergues, where the road from that place meets the main road to La Capelle, Mr. Nicholson's troop found 150 of the Munster Fusiliers in great difficulties with some Germans in pursuit not 200 yards distant. He at once dismounted the troop, and sending the horses off for shelter to a farmyard behind, lined the hedges on the side of the main road and opened fire on the Germans. These retired to a farm some 200 yards up the road, from which they presently brought a machine gun to bear on the hedges, and under cover of this they shortly afterwards emerged, driving a herd of cattle before them down the road. The Hussars, however, shot down both cattle and Germans, and sent the survivors scuttling back once more into the farm. In the meanwhile the Hon. E. Hardinge's troop, having heard the firing, arrived on the scene from another direction, and —also dismounting—crept up to a position from which they could command the farmyard, and opened fire on the Germans massed inside, doing tremendous execution at first, as it was a complete surprise. The Germans, however, quickly recovered themselves, and returned the fire with machine guns. Almost at the first discharge Mr. Hardinge fell mortally wounded, and Sergt. Papworth took over command of the troop. Bodies of the enemy were now seen advancing on all sides, and it was obvious that, if the little British force was to escape being surrounded, it was time to move. There is always a disposition on such occasions for very tired men to throw up the sponge and surrender. In the present instance, however, any such inclination was summarily checked by the energy and determination of Mr. Nicholson and Sergt. Papworth, who, taking prompt charge of the situation, brought the whole party—Munsters and all—safely out of the difficulty. They had to put in twenty-eight miles of steady marching before they finally caught up with their division."

For these services, as has been said, he was created a Companion of the Distinguished Service Order [London Gazette, 9 Nov. 1914]: "The Honourable Edward Charles Hardinge, Lieut., 15th (The King's) Hussars, 1st Divisional Cavalry. For ability and gallantry in reconnaissance under great difficulty and machine-gun fire, on 22–23 and 27 Aug., during which he was severely wounded." The details given in the quotations given above were confirmed by Major Pilkington, of the 15th Hussars, who was Lieut. Hardinge's Squadron leader, and endorsed by Major Courage, Second-in-Command of the Squadron at the time.

VALLENTIN, HENRY EDWARD, Major, was born 5 Jan. 1870, son of the late Sir James Vallentin. He entered the Royal Artillery 15 Feb. 1889 became Lieutenant 15 Feb. 1892; Captain 18 Sept. 1899; was Adjutant, R.A., 1 Jan. 1900, to 31 March, 1903, and was promoted to Major 13 Feb. 1905. He served in the European War from 1914, and was created a Companion of the Distinguished Service Order [London Gazette, 9 Nov. 1914]: "Henry Edward Vallentin, Major, 27th Battery, Royal Field Artillery. For bravery and devotion in withdrawing guns by hand under a heavy fire, near Ligny, France, on 26 Aug." He was promoted to Lieutenant-Colonel 30 Oct. 1914; was specially employed at the War Office 8 Oct. 1916, to 7 May, 1917; was A.A.G., War Office, from 8 May, 1917.

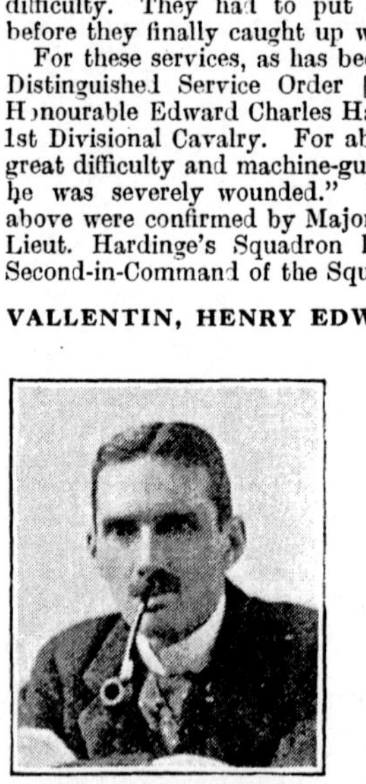

Henry E. Vallentin.

GOSSELIN, ALWYN BERTRAM ROBERT RAPHAEL, Capt., served in the European War, and for his services in 1914 was created a Companion of the Distinguished Service Order [London Gazette, 9 Nov. 1914]: "Alwyn Bertram Robert Raphael Gosselin, Capt., 2nd Battn. Grenadier Guards. Although wounded and in considerable pain, commanded his Company for two days in action, against the advice of the Medical Officer and until he could be relieved by another officer." The "Times" of 13 Feb. 1915, says: "Capt. A. B. R. R. Gosselin, D.S.O., of Blakesware, Herts, 2nd Battn. Grenadier Guards, was killed near Béthune on 7 Feb. Born on 17 Feb. 1883, he was the only surviving son of the late Sir Martin Gosselin, of Blakesware, British Minister at Lisbon, and of the Hon. Lady Gosselin, second daughter of the 1st Lord Gerard. He received his first appointment in Oct. 1901, and was promoted Lieutenant in 1905, and Captain in 1910." A solemn Requiem

Mass was celebrated on 18 Feb. 1915, for the soul of Capt. Gosselin, in the Roman Catholic Church in Farm Street.

BECKWITH-SMITH, MERTON, Second Lieut., was born 11 July, 1890, only son of Beckwith Smith, Esq., of Aberarder, Inverness-shire, N.B. He entered the Coldstream Guards 1 Aug. 1912. He served in the European War from 1914; was promoted Lieutenant 18 Dec. 1914; was Adjutant, Coldstream Guards, 15 March to 20 Aug. 1915; Staff Captain 27 Aug. 1915, to 3 July, 1916; became Captain 23 Feb. 1916; was Brigade Major 4 July, 1916, to 26 Aug. 1917; G.S.O.2, 27 Aug. 1917, to 2 April, 1919; he was three times mentioned in Despatches, and created a Companion of the Distinguished Service Order [London Gazette, 9 Nov. 1914]: "Merton Beckwith-Smith, Second Lieut., 1st Battn. Coldstream Guards. On the night of 4 Oct., near Vendresse, with a party of 50 men, he attacked and carried with the bayonet the advanced German trenches, disabling 20 of the enemy, and displayed great enterprise and coolness in this operation, in which he was wounded." Capt. Beckwith Smith was Brigade Major, 2nd Guards Brigade, Forces in Great Britain, 3 April, 1919. He was Adjutant, Coldstream Guards, March to Sept. 1915; was promoted to Captain, and served as Brigade Major, 1st Guards Brigade. He was awarded the Military Cross, and also received the Croix de Guerre. On 14 March, 1918, at St. Margaret's, Westminster, Capt. Beckwith-Smith married Honor, only daughter of Mr. John Blundell Leigh, of Stratton Audley, Bicester. Princess Marie Louise was present at the wedding.

MARTIN, CYRIL GORDON, Lieut., served in the European War, and was created a Companion of the Distinguished Service Order [London Gazette, 9 Nov. 1914]: "Cyril Gordon Martin, Lieut., 56th Company, Royal Engineers. At Le Cateau, on the 26th Aug., he held, with his section, a post from which infantry had been driven, and remained there under a very heavy fire until the infantry relieved him." His was one of the first decorations to be gazetted in the Great War, and he subsequently was awarded the Victoria Cross. (See Victoria Cross Volume.)

HEWITT, THE HONOURABLE ARCHIBALD RODNEY, Capt., was born 25 May, 1883, at Torquay, Devon, son of Viscount and Viscountess Lifford, of Court, Cronfall, Hants. He was educated at Eastman's; Bonn; Dulwich and Sandhurst, and was commissioned in the 1st Battn. East Surreys 22 Oct. 1902, and became Lieutenant 18 June, 1904, and Captain 17 May, 1910. He was Acting Adjutant to the 1st Battn. East Surreys in India, and Adjutant to the 2nd Battn. in Dublin in 1914. He served in the European War, and was twice mentioned in Despatches from France; was severely wounded at the Marne River Battle on the 9th Sept. 1914, and was created a Companion of the Distinguished Service Order [London Gazette, 9 Nov. 1914]: "The Honourable Archibald Rodney Hewitt, Capt., 1st Battn., The East Surrey Regt. For moving out of the trenches at Le Cateau, under heavy shell fire, and bringing back men who were dribbling to the rear." His D.S.O. was one of the first to be gazetted during the present war. Recovering from his wounds, he was appointed to the 3rd Battn. East Surrey Regt. 23 Feb. 1915, and was killed at the Second Battle of Ypres 25 April, 1915, while gallantly leading his company.

The Hon. A. R. Hewitt.

The following are extracts of letters referring to the late Capt. The Hon. A. R. Hewitt, D.S.O., East Surrey Regiment:

Letter from Colonel, 2nd Battn. East Surreys, dated 10 May, 1915: "He was one that could ill be spared; his influence was all for good, and his cheery and kindly disposition were invaluable on Service, as they were appreciated by all of us in peace time. His regiment has indeed suffered a severe loss. I know what they thought of him."

Letter from Colonel of 2nd Battn. East Surreys, dated 2 May, 1915: "Like everyone who knew him, I liked that dear good fellow from the first day I met him, and the liking grew stronger yearly, and was accompanied by a very high opinion of his character. He had done most gallant service all through the war, and showed the highest promise. It is very sad so valuable a life should be cut short."

Letter from Colonel, 1st Battn. East Surreys, dated 30 April, 1915: "Your son joined under my command in Dublin, and has ever been one of our best friends in the regiment, and until the day before his death was commanding my battalion; the Major under whom he was early last month was loud in his praises of his zeal and dependability. I can honestly assure you the regiment's loss is very, very great. Ever bright and cheery, even under the most adverse circumstances, he was an asset of the greatest value when troops were called upon to do their best."

Letter of the Major he was under in March, 1915, dated 28 April, 1915: "For your dear son I am not sorry; he lived like a man, and died like a man, the death we all hope for. He was the most gallant and faithful soul I ever knew."

BURNETT, JOHN CURTEIS, Capt., was born 5 March, 1882, son of the late Capt. Lindsay Robert Burnett, late of the Sherwood Foresters, and Agnes Henrietta Burnett, daughter of the late Rev. S. Curteis, of Sevenoaks, Kent. He joined the Army, as a Second Lieutenant, Un-

John Curteis Burnett.

John Chaplyn Burnett

attached, 8 Jan. 1901, and joined the 2nd Battn. The Duke of Wellington's West Riding Regt. in April, 1901. He became Lieutenant 6 April, 1904; was Adjutant, Territorial Force, 15 Aug. 1908, to 31 Oct. 1911; was promoted Captain 23 Dec. 1909. He served in the European War from 1914, and was created a Companion of the Distinguished Service Order [London Gazette, 9 Nov. 1914]: "John Curteis Burnett, Capt., 2nd Battn. The Duke of Wellington's (West Riding) Regt. He trained and commanded the 5th Divisional Cyclist Company, on the remarkable efficiency, disregard of risk in reconnaissance and vigilance of which the security of the 5th Division has often entirely depended." His decoration was gazetted in the first list published for the European War. He was wounded 11 Nov. 1914. He was Temporary Major, Army Cyclist Corps, 17 May, 1915, to 7 June, 1916, and became Major, West Riding Regt. 8 Jan. 1916, and Temporary Lieutenant-Colonel from Jan. 1917. He married, in Oct. 1908, Mary Isabelle, daughter of John Haddon, Esq., J.P., of Gloucestershire.

KAY, SIR WILLIAM ALGERNON IRELAND, BART., Major, was

William Algernon Kay.

born 21 March, 1876, son of Lt.-Col. William Algernon Kay, 5th Bart. (U.K., 1803), 68th Regt. (retired), and Emily, daughter of the late Thomas James Ireland, of Ousden Hall, Suffolk. He was educated at Harrow (The Knoll), and joined the Army in 1896. He served in Sierra Leone, 1898–99 (Medal with clasp). He served in the South African War, 1899–1902 (Despatches; Queen's Medal with four clasps, and King's Medal with two clasps). He became Captain, 1901; was Adjutant, Volunteers, 1906–8, and Territorials, 1908–9. He succeeded his father in 1914, as 6th Baronet. He became Major, 1914, and served in the European War. He was created a Companion of the Distinguished Service Order [London Gazette, 9 Nov. 1914]: "William Algernon Kay, Major, 2nd Battn. The King's Royal Rifle Corps. He made a personal reconnaissance of great value on 1 Oct., reaching a point within 100 yards of the enemy's outposts." This was one of the first D.S.O.'s gazetted during the European War. He was given the Brevet of Lieutenant-Colonel, and was promoted to Lieutenant-Colonel, 1915, and mentioned in Sir Douglas Haig's Despatch dated War Office, 15 June, 1916, and on five other occasions, and created a C.M.G. Brigadier-General Sir William Kay was killed in action 4 Oct. 1918.

BOSCAWEN, THE HONOURABLE GEORGE EDWARD, Lieut.,

The Hon. G. E. Boscawen.

was born 6 Dec. 1888, second son of the 7th Viscount Falmouth and Kathleen, daughter of the 2nd Lord Penrhyn. He entered the Army in Dec. 1907. He served in the European War from 1914; became Captain 30 Oct. 1914; was mentioned in Despatches, and was created a Companion of the Distinguished Service Order [London Gazette, 9 Nov. 1914]: "The Honourable George Edward Boscawen, Lieut., Royal Field Artillery. For gallantly fighting his section of guns in front of La Bassée on 13 Oct., when all his detachment except himself were wounded, and all infantry had fallen back from where the guns were." The award of his D.S.O. was published in the first list gazetted for the European War. He became Captain 30 Oct. 1914, and was given the Brevet of Major. He died of wounds 27 May, 1918.

HOWARD, GUY ROBERT, Lieut., was born 5 Feb. 1886, son of Colonel W. Howard. He joined the Essex Regt., and retired, entering the Special Reserve. He served in the European War; was wounded, mentioned in Despatches and created a Companion of the Distinguished Service Order [London Gazette, 9 Nov. 1914]: "Guy Robert Howard, Lieut., The Essex Regt. (Special Reserve). While in command of a patrol of the 2nd Battn. Essex Regt. on the 24th of Sept., to the south of Vregny, made a valuable reconnaissance through a thick wood, reaching a point 150 yards from the enemy's trenches." He joined the Royal Flying Corps, and became Temporary Major.

ARIS, CHARLES JOHN, Second Lieut., was born 1 Feb. 1874, son of John Aris, of Branksome, College Road, Norwich. He was commissioned in the 16th Lancers 1 Oct. 1914, and for his services in the European War was mentioned in Despatches, and created a Companion of the Distinguished Service Order [London Gazette, 9 Nov. 1914]: "Charles John Aris, Second Lieut., 16th (The Queen's) Lancers. For gallantry and determination when on patrol at Katsberg on the 12th of Oct., in charging and driving off a German patrol, and although twice wounded, persisted in sending in his report to his Squadron leader." His decoration was one of the first to be gazetted for the European War. He was A.D.C., 5th Aug. 1914, to 4 Jan. 1915, and Staff Captain from 5 Jan. 1915.

STANLEY-CREEK, ROBERT FORBES, Capt., was born at Cheltenham 8 Feb. 1878, son of Colonel Edward Stanley-Creek, late Royal Welsh Fusiliers. He was educated at Marlborough (92–93 B.2), and joined the Royal West Surrey Regt. 4 Jan. 1899, from the Militia. He became Lieutenant, 1 Aug. 1900, and Captain 2 Aug. 1910. He served in the European War from 1914; present at Gheluvelt, Pilkem Inn and Battle of the Aisne ; was mentioned in Despatches and created a Companion of the Distinguished Service Order [London Gazette, 9 Nov. 1914] : " Robert Forbes Stanley-Creek, Capt., 1st Battn. The Queen's (Royal West Surrey Regt.). For conspicuous gallantry and able leading in the attack on the Inn on the 23rd of Oct. This attack, made in conjunction with the 2nd Infantry Brigade, was so successful that many German prisoners were taken, and 70 of our men previously captured were released."

Robert F. Stanley-Creek.

Mrs. Stanley-Creek writes : " About the Battle of Pilkem Inn on 23 Oct., for which he got his D.S.O., my husband wrote to me : ' We had a great day on the 23rd. My company was in the firing line and captured a small village held by the Germans. We took about 40 prisoners and released 60 Cameron Highlanders who had been captured. After that I had to advance to a trench, which we held until dusk. After dark the Germans crept round our flank, and got right behind us, and I managed to lead the remainder of my company round to the left and to rejoin headquarters. We had about 60 casualties during the night. We were fighting from early morning, and did not get back until about 2 the next morning.' I am afraid my husband did not hear about his D.S.O. before his stand at the 31st Oct. (Battle of Gheluvelt), when only 40 men and two officers of his regiment got away. . . . He has been reported missing since 31 Oct. 1914, and so I am writing for him." (20th March, 1917) : " I think about the clearest information I have about the battle is from a man, Jaggers, in the regiment who was wounded and taken prisoner on that day, and later on escaped and got back to England. He said my husband would not surrender (I suppose he hoped for reinforcements), but went on firing his revolver when the German officer called on him to give up his sword, until two or three German soldiers crept up behind him and beat him on the head with their rifle-butts. As to sporting achievements, he was very fond of riding, and I quote from his father's letter : ' His good riding to hounds and between flags, Polo-team from the day he joined the Queen's. Third best average of winning mounts his last year in India.' He was the bravest man and the best of husbands, and I hope he may yet turn up again, although things look black." Mrs. Stanley-Creek wrote 29 April, 1917 : " My husband was wounded on the 14th Sept. 1914, at the Battle of the Aisne, but never left the regiment ; in fact, had to take command of it for eight hours, everyone else being killed or wounded, until (then Capt.) Watson (now Major, I believe) came back to the regiment from the Staff to take the command." Capt. Stanley-Creek married, 26 Nov. 1908, at Camberley, Surrey, Marie T. Stanley-Creek, daughter of the late Sir David Masson, Bart., and Lady Masson, of Lahore, India, and they had a daughter, Braida Stanley-Creek.

RISING, ROBERT EDWARD, Capt., was born 23 May, 1871, son of Thomas Alfred and Kate Rising, of The Manor House, Ormesby, Norfolk. He was educated at Charterhouse, where he was in the Football XV. and

Robert Edward Rising.

in the Cadet Corps, and at Trinity College, Cambridge. He passed into the Royal Military College, Sandhurst, sixth on the list, and passed out twelfth with Honours. In Nov. 1892, he was gazetted to the 1st Battn. The Gloucestershire Regt. In 1898 he obtained the " extra " certificate in Musketry. He became Captain, Feb. 1900, and served in the South African War of 1899–1900, being present at the Relief of Kimberley and at the operations in the Orange Free State, including actions at Paardeberg, Poplar Grove and Dreifontein, and also in Natal (Queen's Medal and four clasps). In Nov. 1902, he passed the examination for promotion, attaining the higher standard of proficiency, carrying a special certificate. In April, 1906, he passed the Signalling Course, also with a special certificate. Capt. Rising served in the European War, from 1914, and for gallant conduct at the defence of Langemarck on the 23rd of Oct. 1914, was created a Companion of the Distinguished Service Order [London Gazette, 9 Nov. 1914] : " Robert Edward Rising, Capt., 1st Battn. The Gloucester Regt. Went up with supports and conspicuously controlled the defence of the battalion's trenches against a determined attack by the enemy. But for this stout defence the line must have been penetrated." His D.S.O. was one of the first to be gazetted during the European War. He became Major, Nov. 1914, and the promotion was not gazetted until after his death. Major Rising died of wounds received in action at the first Battle of Ypres 7 Nov. 1914. He was mentioned in Sir John French's Despatch of the 14 Jan. 1915. In 1896 he married Amy Worship, who died the following year ; and in 1901 he married Constance Elizabeth, youngest daughter of Colonel R. W. Edis, C.B., of The Old Hall, Ormesby, Norfolk, and they had two children : Robert Edis, born in Aug. 1905, and Elsie Mary Elizabeth, born in July, 1909.

REES, HUBERT CONWAY, Capt., was born 26 March, 1882, at Conway, North Wales, son of the Rev. Canon Henry Rees, M.A., Hon. Canon and Precentor, Bangor Cathedral, and formerly Vicar of Conway, North Wales. He was educated at Charterhouse ; was commissioned in the 3rd (Militia) Battn. East Surrey Regt. in Dec. 1900, and served in the South African

War, 1901–2, taking part in the operations in Cape Colony and Orange River Colony in July, 1901 ; also in Cape Colony, July, 1901, to 31 May, 1902, receiving the Queen's Medal with clasp. He was gazetted to the Welsh Regt., as Second Lieutenant, 28 Jan.

Hubert Conway Rees.

1903 ; became Lieutenant 9 Sept. 1906, and Captain 12 June, 1912. Capt. Rees served in the European War with the 2nd Battn. The Welsh Regt. ; landed in France 12 Aug. 1914, and took part in the following actions : the Retreat, Marne, Aisne, Langemarck, First Battle of Ypres, Festubert (21 Dec. 1914), Givenchy (25 Jan. 1915) and the Somme. He was created a Companion of the Distinguished Service Order [London Gazette, 9 Nov. 1914], this being one of the first D.S.O.'s awarded for the European War : " Hubert Conway Rees, Capt., The Welsh Regt. In the course of the action on 21 Oct., by his particularly skilful reconnaissances and by gallant leading, successfully supported the advanced line with a company under a heavy fire, relieving the pressure on the South Wales Borderers." He commanded the 2nd Battn. Welsh Regt. during the latter half of the First Battle of Ypres (Givenchy). He was mentioned in Despatches 17 Feb. 1915 ; was given the Brevet of Major 18 Feb. 1915 ; was Officer, Company of Gentleman Cadets, Royal Military College, 15 March to 20 April, 1915 ; G.S.O.2, 43rd (afterwards 38th) Division, New Armies, British Armies in France, 1 July to 7 Dec. 1916 ; commanded the 94th Infantry Brigade, which attacked Serre 1 July, 1916 (15 to 30 June, 1916) ; commanded the 11th Infantry Brigade (1 July to 7 Dec. 1916), in succession to Brigadier-General Prowse (who had been killed in action). He took part in actions in front of Le Transloy in Oct. 1916 ; commanded the 13th Reserve Brigade, Home Forces, 8 Dec. 1916, to 7 March, 1917 ; was given the Brevet of Lieutenant-Colonel 1 Jan. 1917 ; commanded the 149th Infantry Brigade, British Armies in France, 8 March to 16 Sept. 1917, and the 150th Infantry Brigade, British Armies in France, 27 Feb. to 27 July, 1918. During the Great War he was five times mentioned in Despatches, and he was created a C.M.G. in 1918. He married, 20 Nov. 1914, at St. Andrew's by the Wardrobe, London, Katharine Adelaide Loring, daughter of John Loring, Esq., and they have a daughter, Mary Katharine, born 26 April, 1916.

The London Gazette of the 20th Oct. 1914, and the London Gazette of the 23rd Oct. 1914, contain naval Despatches, from which extracts are given below in the biographies of the officers awarded the Distinguished Service Order in recognition of services described in the Despatches.

London Gazette, 23 Oct. 1914.—" Admiralty, 21 Oct. 1914. The King has been graciously pleased to give orders for the following appointments to the Distinguished Service Order . . . in respect of the undermentioned Officers in recognition of their services mentioned in the foregoing Despatches."

BLUNT, WILLIAM FREDERICK, Capt., was born 3 March, 1870, third son of F. W. Blunt, of Culcheth Hall, Teddington. He entered the Royal Navy ; was Midshipman of H.M.S. Garnet during the blockade of

William Frederick Blunt.

the Zanzibar Coast, 1888–89. He was Lieutenant in command of H.M.S. Dragon during the operations at Crete in 1897–98 ; Lieutenant in Command of H.M.S. Esk in China, 1900–1 (Medal). He was in command of H.M.S. Fearless at the action in Heligoland Bight 28 Aug. 1914. Capt. Blunt was mentioned in Rear-Admiral A. H. Christian's Despatches, dated 28 Sept. 1914 [London Gazette, 23 Oct. 1914] : " Commodore Reginald Y. Tyrwhitt was in charge of the Destroyer Flotillas, and his report is enclosed herewith. His attack was delivered with great skill and gallantry, and he was most ably seconded by Capt. William F. Blunt, in the Fearless, and the officers in command of the Destroyers, who handled their vessels in a manner worthy of the best traditions of the British Navy." Commodore Reginald Tyrwhitt said in his Despatch dated 26 Sept. 1914 [London Gazette, 23 Oct. (Admiralty 21 Oct.), 1914] : " I beg again to call attention to the services rendered by Capt. W. F. Blunt, of H.M.S. Fearless, and the Commanding Officers of the 1st and 3rd Flotillas, whose gallant attacks on the German Cruisers at critical moments undoubtedly saved the Arethusa from more severe punishment and possible capture." In recognition of his services on this occasion, Capt. Blunt was created a Companion of the Distinguished Service Order [London Gazette, 23 Oct. 1914] : " William Frederick Blunt, Capt., Royal Navy." Capt. Blunt took part in the Cuxhaven Raid, Christmas Day, 1914. He was Captain of H.M.S. Gloucester at the Battle of Jutland 31 May, 1916, and was mentioned in Despatches 15 Sept. 1916, and specially commended for his services on that occasion. A newspaper paragraph, entitled " The Glory of the Gloucester," says : " Arrangements have been made for the white ensign flown by His Majesty's Ship Gloucester in the Jutland Battle to be deposited in Gloucester Cathedral on 17 Oct. Capt. Blunt, D.S.O., who was in command of the cruiser, in a letter to the Mayor of Gloucester, says : ' It may interest the citizens of Gloucester to know that, though their name-ship was fortunate enough to escape both injuries and casualties, she was able to give a very good account of herself, and provided the finishing touches which sank a German light cruiser of the Elbing class. The bearing and conduct of officers and men were all that could be desired. I have the greatest pleasure in thus testifying to the citizens of Gloucester that nothing but the utmost credit is due to the ship named after their illustrious city.'" He became Captain in command of H.M.S. Berwick, and late of H.M.S. Archilles. He married, in 1896, Laura, only daughter of the late Major-General Henry Way Mawbey, R.F.A., and they have two sons.

MEADE, THE HONOURABLE HERBERT, Commander, R.N., was born 3 Nov. 1875, son of the 4th Earl of Clanwilliam and Elizabeth, daughter of Sir A. E. Kennedy, G.C.M.G., Governor of Queensland; and brother of the 5th Earl of Clanwilliam. He served in the European War, from 1914; was present at the engagement off Heligoland, Friday, 28 Aug. 1914. He was mentioned in Commodore Tyrwhitt's Despatch, dated 26 Sept. 1914 [London Gazette, 23 Oct. (Admiralty 21 Oct.), 1914]: "H.M.S. Goshawk, Commander the Honourable Herbert Meade, who took his division into action with great coolness and nerve, and was instrumental in sinking the German Destroyer V.187, with the boats of his division saved the survivors in a most chivalrous manner." In recognition of the services recorded above he was created a Companion of the Distinguished Service Order [London Gazette, 23 Oct. 1914]: "The Honourable Herbert Meade, Commander, Royal Navy." He became Captain in 1915; was present in the action off the Dogger Bank in 1915, and in the Battle of Jutland, 1916, and was mentioned in Despatches [London Gazette, 15 Sept. 1916]. He was later employed on Naval Mobilization. He married, in 1911, Margaret Glyn, daughter of the Right Rev. The Honourable E. C. Glyn, Bishop of Peterborough, and Lady Mary Emma Campbell, daughter of the 8th Duke of Argyll, and they have one son and two daughters.

ROSE, FRANK FORRESTER, Commander, Royal Navy, was born in 1878, youngest son of the late William Rose. He was educated at Stubbington House, Fareham; entered the Royal Navy in 1892, and became Lieutenant in 1901. He was promoted to be Commander in 1913, and served in the European War from 1914. He commanded H.M.S. Laurel in the action off Heligoland 28 Aug. 1914; was wounded, and mentioned in Commodore R. Y. Tyrwhitt's Despatch, dated 26 Sept. 1914 [London Gazette, 23 Oct. 1914]: "H.M.S. Laurel, Commander Frank F. Rose, who most ably commanded his vessel throughout the early part of the action, and after having been wounded in both legs, remained on the bridge until 6 p.m., displaying great devotion to duty." For his services on this occasion he was created a Companion of the Distinguished Service Order [London Gazette, 23 Oct. (Admiralty, 21 Oct.), 1914:] "Frank Forrester Rose, Commander, Royal Navy." He was promoted to Captain in 1918. He married in 1911, Breda Edith, only daughter of Walter Alwynne Gordon, and they have one son.

SAMSON, CHARLES RUMNEY, Commander, Royal Navy, was born at Crumpsall, Lancashire, 8 July, 1883, second son of Charles Leopold Samson, of Grundy, Kershaw, Samson & Co., Solicitors, and N. A. Samson (deceased). He was educated at Lockers Park, Hemel Hempstead; at The Limes, Greenwich, and in the Britannia, and entered the Royal Navy in July, 1883. He served in Pomone, Somaliland, 1903–4 (Medal and clasp); became Lieutenant in 1904; was First Lieutenant, Philomel, during the operations in the Persian Gulf, 1909–10 (Medal and clasp); took his certificate as Air Pilot in 1911, and carried out the first seaplane experiments and the first cross-country night flights; made the first ascent from the deck of a man-of-war while steaming, 1912. He served in the European War from 1914, in France and Flanders, 1914–15; in the Dardanelles (during the whole of the operations); in Egypt, Palestine and the Red Sea. He was present at the Siege of Antwerp; the First Battle of Ypres; commanded a Brigade of French Territorials, etc., at the Battle of Orchies; received a letter of thanks from the French General, and was made a Chevalier of the Legion of Honour and given the Croix de Guerre. He was promoted Commander, and was mentioned in a memorandum by the Director of the Air Department, Admiralty, dated 11 Oct. 1914 [London Gazette, 23 Oct. (Admiralty, 21 Oct.), 1914]: "Commander Charles R. Samson, R.N., was in command of the Aeroplane and Armoured Motor Support of the Royal Naval Air Service, between the dates of 1 Sept. to 5 Oct. During this period several notable air reconnaissances were made, and skirmishes took place. Of these particular mention may be made of the aeroplane attack on the 4th Sept. on four enemy cars and 40 men, on which occasion several bombs were dropped, and of the successful skirmishes at Cassel on 4 Sept.; Savy on 12 Sept.; Aniche on 22 Sept.; Orchies on 23 Sept." For these services he was created a Companion of the Distinguished Service Order [London Gazette, 23 Oct. (Admiralty, 21 Oct.), 1914]: 'Charles Rumney Samson, Commander, Royal Navy." Commander Samson was mentioned in Despatches six times, and awarded a Bar to his D.S.O. [London Gazette, 23 Jan. 1917]: "Charles Rumney Samson, Commander, Royal Navy. For continual gallantry and service as an aeroplane pilot." He commanded the Ben-my-Chree on the Syrian Coast: "H.M. Seaplane Carrier Ben-my-Chree (Wing-Commander C. R. Samson, D.S.O.) was sunk by gun-fire in Kastelorizo Harbour (Asia Minor) on 11 Jan. 1916. The only casualties were one officer and four men wounded. The Ben-my-Chree, which before the war was well-known to holiday-makers who visited the Isle of Man, was a vessel of 2,550 tons. She was built at Barrow by Messrs. Vickers in 1908, and formerly belonged to the Isle of Man Steam Packet Company." He was promoted to Wing-Captain, R.N.A.S., in Jan. 1918; Lieutenant-Colonel and Temporary Colonel, R.A.F., in command of a group, 1 April, 1918; created a C.M.G. in 1918. He is a Chevalier, Legion of Honour, and was given the Croix de Guerre (with Palm) for cutting through the Germans surrounding Douai and making a passage for the French troops surrounded in that town. In 1907 Commander Samson won the Middle Weight Officers' Boxing Championship, Royal Navy and Marines. Commander Samson married in Ceylon, 7 April, 1917, Honor Oakdene Patrickson, only daughter of Herbert L. Storey, of Ballrigg, Lancashire, and they have a daughter, Margaret Diana Rumney Samson.

Charles Rumney Samson.

HORTON, MAX KENNEDY, Commander, is the son of R. J. Horton, of Minster, Thanet. He joined the Royal Navy, and in 1911 was awarded the Silver Medal for saving life on the occasion of the loss of the Delhi, off Cape Spartel. He served in the European War from 1914 to 1918, and was mentioned in a Despatch (dated 17 Oct. 1914) of Commodore Roger J. B. Keyes, C.B., M.V.O., for his services in the action of Heligoland on Friday, 28 Aug. 1914: "On the 13th Sept. E9 (Lieut.-Commander Max K. Horton) torpedoed and sank the German light cruiser Hela six miles south of Heligoland. A number of destroyers were evidently called to the scene after E9 had delivered her attack, and these hunted her for several hours. On the 14th Sept., in accordance with his orders, Lieut.-Commander Horton examined the outer anchorage of Heligoland, a service attended by considerable risk. . . . On the 6th Oct., E9 (Lieut.-Commander Max K. Horton), when patrolling off the Ems, torpedoed and sank the enemy's destroyer S126. The enemy's torpedo craft pursued tactics, which, in connection with their shallow draft, make them exceedingly difficult to attack with torpedo, and Lieut.-Commander Horton's success was the result of much patient and skilful zeal. He is a most enterprising submarine officer, and I beg to submit his name for favourable consideration." Commander Horton was—for those services—created a Companion of the Distinguished Service Order [London Gazette, 23 Oct. 1914]: "Max Kennedy Horton, Commander, Royal Navy." At the same time he was noted for early promotion. He was promoted to Commander 31 Dec. 1914. In July, 1916, Commander Horton sank the German battleship Pommern in the Baltic. He has sunk two other destroyers, besides two transports and several merchant ships, and was made a Chevalier of the Legion of Honour and given the 4th Class Order of St. Vladimir with Swords, and the 2nd Class Order of St. Anne with Swords and Diamonds. He was awarded a Bar to the Distinguished Service Order.

"Deeds that Thrill the Empire" (pages 401–408) says: "As the pioneer of our submarine successes in the great war, the name of Lieut.-Commander Max Kennedy Horton will always be remembered with honour. This young officer had had a good deal of experience in the submarine service before the war broke out, and, in command of E9, he was present at the Battle of the Heligoland Bight on 28 Aug. 1914, though on that occasion none of our submarines was able to get in a blow at an enemy ship. He was also favourably mentioned in Despatches for having, on 14 Sept. 1914, 'examined the outer anchorage of Heligoland, a service attended by considerable risk;' but he is best remembered by the ships he has sunk. Since the earliest hours of the war British submarines have maintained a close and unceasing watch off the German coast. Owing to the great extent of the mine-fields laid by the enemy and the precautions taken whenever their ships put to sea, the number of victims that have fallen to them is necessarily small—and Horton's distinction is thereby the greater. The Germans considered it a great feat for one of their submarines to sink a British merchantman, though more than twenty thousand such vessels are to be found ploughing the seven seas. How much greater, therefore, must be the honour due to a British submarine which managed to find a German warship at sea and sink it, seeing that the sea was the last place a German warship thought of visiting? On the morning of Sunday, 13 Sept. 1914, two of our submarines, of which E9 was one, were stealthily cruising about in the neighbourhood of Heligoland. That was their station; and they were there not so much for the purpose of sinking ships —the opportunities for doing so were likely to be so rare—but rather to gather what information they could regarding what was going on in the naval fastnesses of the enemy. When, therefore, a small German cruiser was seen approaching from the direction of Wilhelmshaven there was a good deal of excitement on board the submarines—it was so unusual, even within a few miles of the German coast, to see a German warship. To decide to attack the ship was the work of a moment. She was, in fact, the light cruiser Hela—a two-thousand-ton vessel that had seen better days, for she was launched in 1895; but only a few years before the war began she had been practically rebuilt, and was attached to the High Sea Fleet as a despatch vessel. With their periscopes a few feet above the water our submarines warily watched the enemy's approach. As she came nearer, they dived altogether, and then, after a brief interval, the E9 poked her periscope gingerly above the surface again and looked about her. There was the Hela, within easy range, and no sign that the presence of a submarine was suspected. Doubtless the people on board the cruiser would have jeered at anyone who might have suggested the possibility of a British submarine prowling around within six miles of Heligoland. Precisely at half-past six on that Sunday morning there came the disillusionment. With his eye glued to the mirror of the periscope, Horton watched the cruiser closely for a minute or two while he took his bearings. Then, in quick succession, came the orders to dive and to release the two bow torpedoes. One can almost—but not quite—imagine the scene on board the submarine at such a moment. Every man is at his station, for the safety of the ship depends upon each one watching over the section of the complicated machinery that is allotted to him. Nevertheless, every man, calm enough at his own job, must be on the tiptoe of excitement as he waits for the muffled report that shall tell him the torpedo has struck home—or for the continued silence that tells of a miss. In the E9 the men waited just thirty-five seconds. Then there came to them the subdued boom, followed by a slight disturbance of the water, which told them

of success. One torpedo at least had got home. To have come to the surface at once would have been to court disaster, for unless the cruiser was mortally injured her men would be at their action stations with all the guns ready to open fire at once. So the E9 waited in patience for fifteen minutes, and when she came to surface it was plain enough that the Hela was doomed. She had a heavy list to starboard, and a number of vessels had already arrived to take off her crew and hunt for her assailant. Therefore the submarine promptly dived again, and when, after another short interval, she rose to the surface a second time, the Hela had disappeared. Round about, however, were a large number of destroyers sent out from Heligoland, armed with the most cunning devices for snaring and destroying submarines; but the E9 eluded them for many hours, and ultimately arrived safely at Harwich. Less than a month later—on 6 Oct.—Horton and the E9 scored their second success. This time the submarine was operating almost in the mouth of the River Ems, outside the important naval and mercantile port of Emden, and evidently her presence had become known, for a flotilla of destroyers, equipped for a regular submarine hunt, came steaming down the river. These hunts are usually a serious business for the submarine, as the German Navy has good cause to know; but thanks to luck and the capable handling of her skipper, the E9 suffered no harm, though it was an extremely anxious time for all on board. Down on the bed of the sea she waited, listening to the noise of the destroyers' engines and the rattling of their snaring implements, never knowing when she might be canted up on end or blown to eternity. Presently the almost intolerable strain passed, and cautiously Horton began to edge his boat towards the surface. The periscope nosed into the air, and, swinging it round to scan the waters, Commander Horton espied two destroyers within six hundred yards of him. One was moving fairly fast, the other was proceeding dead slow. A short word of command, and the submarine was heading bows on to the laggard. Another, and the deadly torpedo was on its way. The submarine dived, but there was no mistake about the explosion. The torpedo struck the destroyer square amidships. She was broken clean in two, and when the submarine came up again to see what had happened nothing was visible of her but the forward end of her bows pointing vertically into the air. The E9's second victim was the destroyer S126, a vessel of 413 tons, launched in 1903, and carrying a crew of about eighty officers and men—of whom very few were saved. For these services and for sinking S126 he was given the Distinguished Service Order, and was noted for early promotion—he was, in fact, made a Commander on 31 Dec. 1914. These two successes, however, seem small in comparison with another which he achieved in the summer of 1915. He was one of the first British submarine officers to take his boat into the Baltic to help our Russian Allies against the heavy naval odds which confronted them; and, as might have been expected from such an officer, he was by no means the least successful. The Germans, from their vast superiority over the Russians at sea, imagined themselves to be undisputed masters of the Baltic; but on 2 July, 1915, when a small German fleet was cruising off the Gulf of Danzig, Commander Horton happened to be on the spot, with the result that the Germans lost one of their best pre-Dreadnought battleships. The whole of the operations in the Baltic were under the direction of the Russian Admiralty, whose reports regarding the work of our submarines in those waters have been exceedingly meagre; but although details are lacking, it is at least known that on the date mentioned Commander Horton torpedoed and sank a German battleship of the Pommern class. The battleship was a vessel of 13,040 tons, launched in 1905, and built at a cost of £1,214,000, and carrying a crew of 736 officers and men. Commander Horton received a high honour from the Emperor of Russia for this great feat, but the strictest secrecy was preserved as to the manner in which it was accomplished."

WILLIAMS-FREEMAN, FREDERICK ARTHUR PEERE, Lieut., joined the Royal Navy. He served in the European War from 1914; was in Submarine E6 during the action in the Heligoland Bight, on Friday, 28 Aug. 1914, and, having fouled a mine, he managed to clear it without exploding it. "After half an hour's patient work this was effected by Lieut. Frederick A. P. Williams-Freeman and Able Seaman Ernest Randall Cremer, Official Number 21425, and the released mine descended to its original depth." (Despatch, dated 17 Oct. 1914, of Commodore Roger J. B. Keyes, C.B., M.V.O. [London Gazette, 23 Oct. (Admiralty, 21 Oct.), 1914]). He was created a Companion of the Distinguished Service Order [London Gazette, 23 Oct. (Admiralty, 21 Oct.), 1914]: "Frederick Arthur Peere Williams-Freeman, Lieut., Royal Navy. In recognition of services mentioned in the foregoing Despatches."

GREY, MANDER SPENCER DOUGLAS ADAIR, Squadron Commander, was born 10 Feb. 1889, son of the late Douglas Grey. He joined the Royal Navy, and served in the European War from 1914–18; was mentioned in a Memorandum by the Director of the Air Department, Admiralty, dated 11 Oct. 1914 [London Gazette, 23 Oct. (Admiralty, 21 Oct.) 1914]: "Squadron Commander Spencer Grey, whilst in charge of a flight of naval aeroplanes at Antwerp, penetrated as far as Cologne on the 8th Oct. He circled the city under fire at 600 feet, and discharged his bombs on the military railway station. Considerable damage was done." In recognition of this exploit he was created a Companion of the Distinguished Service Order [London Gazette, 23 Oct. (Admiralty, 21 Oct.), 1914]: "Spencer Douglas Adair Grey, Squadron Commander, Royal Naval Air Service." He was promoted to Wing Commander. Wing Commander S. D. A. Grey married, in 1915, Dorothy, daughter of the late Lionel Ashton Dering, and they have a daughter.

MARIX, REGINALD LENNOX GEORGE, Flight Lieut., R.N., was born 17 Aug. 1889, the son of James Marix and Amy Marix. He was educated at Radley College. He entered the R.N.V.R. in 1909, and was appointed to H.M.S. Actaeon 1 Nov. 1912, as Sub-Lieutenant for aviation duties, since when he served continuously in the Naval Wing of the Royal Flying Corps, being appointed Flight Lieutenant, R.N., 1 July, 1914. He served in the European War, joining the Naval Aeroplane Squadron at Antwerp in Sept. 1914; took part in the first two air raids into Germany, and was mentioned in a Memorandum by the Director of the Air Department, Admiralty, dated 11 Oct. 1914 [London Gazette, 23 Oct. (Admiralty, 21 Oct.), 1914]: "Flight-Lieut. Marix, acting under the orders of Squadron Commander Spencer Grey, carried out a successful attack on the Düsseldorf airship shed during the afternoon of the 8th Oct. From a height of 600 feet he dropped two bombs on the shed, and flames 500 feet high were seen within 30 seconds. The roof of the shed was also observed to collapse. Lieut. Marix's machine was under heavy fire from rifles and mitrailleuses, and was five times hit whilst making the attack." For his services on this occasion he was created a Companion of the Distinguished Service Order [London Gazette, 23 Oct. 1914]: "Reginald Lennox George Marix, Flight Lieut., Royal Navy." After the evacuation of Antwerp he served under Commander Samson, D.S.O., R.N., in the naval armoured cars, taking part in the First Battle of Ypres. Later he was stationed at Dunkirk, and took part in the early air raids on the Belgian Coast. He was promoted Flight Commander, R.N., 1 Jan. 1915; proceeded in Feb. 1915, with his Wing, to the Dardanelles, and took part in the aerial operations during the landings at Cape Helles, Anzac and Suvla Bay; was mentioned in Despatches by the Admiral Commanding; in Oct. 1915, he returned home, and formed a Canadian squadron; was promoted to Squadron Commander, R.N., 1 Jan. 1916. In Oct. 1916, he was severely injured whilst flying in France. In 1917 was created a Chevalier of the Order of the Crown of Belgium. On 1 April, 1918, he was transferred from the Royal Naval Air Service to the Royal Air Force as Major. He is married, and has a son.

Reginald L. G. Marix.

COLLET, CHARLES HERBERT, Lieut., was born 4 Feb. 1888, second son of James Francis Herbert Collet, of Milbrook, Southampton, late of the Public Works Department of the Government of India, Engineer, and his wife, Teresa, daughter of Francis and Teresa Pilley. He was educated at Elizabeth College, Guernsey, and Dulwich College, London, S.E.; joined the Royal Marine Artillery 1 Sept. 1905, and was promoted to Lieutenant 1 July, 1906, and was transferred to the Naval Wing of the Royal Flying Corps in 1915. He was regarded as one of the best naval airmen, and first attracted attention by his flying in the big biplane bought by the Admiralty from the Deutsche Flugzeug Werks of Leipzig, in 1913. Early in 1914 he had this machine equipped with a big petrol tank in place of the passenger's seat, and started from Plymouth on a non-stop flight to John o'Groats. He was brought down by engine trouble at Grimsby, but the flight stood as a British "record" for distance across country. While stationed at the Royal Naval Flying School at Eastchurch, Collet was the first officer in the Naval Air Service to loop the loop He held several trophies for boxing and shooting, and was a winner of the Navy and Marine Light-Weight Boxing Championship, and was in the final for the Army and Navy Light-Weight Championships. On the outbreak of the European War he served on the Western Front, and took part in the defence of Antwerp until the evacuation. On the 23rd Sept. 1914, British aeroplanes of the Naval Wing delivered an attack on the Zeppelin sheds at Düsseldorf. Conditions were very difficult on account of the misty weather, but Flight Lieut. Collet, flying a Sopwith tractor biplane, made a long flight, and succeeded in dropping three bombs on the Zeppelin shed, approaching within 400 feet. His machine was struck by one projectile, but he returned safely. The Director of the Air Department of the Admiralty, in a Memorandum dated 11 Oct. [London Gazette, 21 Oct. (Supplement, 23 Oct.) 1914], described the feat as "notable—gliding down from 6,000 feet, the last 1,500 in mist, he finally coming in sight of the air-ship shed, when at a height of 400 feet, and when only a quarter of a mile distant. . . . The importance of this incident lies in the fact that in the event of further bombs being dropped into Antwerp or other Belgian towns measures of reprisals can certainly be adopted, if desired, to almost any extent." For this—the pioneer exploit of its kind—Lieut. Collet was created a Companion of the Distinguished Service Order [London Gazette, 23 Oct. (Admiralty, 21 Oct.), 1914]: "Charles Herbert Collet, Lieut., Royal Marine Artillery, and Flight Lieut., Royal Naval Air Service." He was mentioned in Despatches by the Admiralty [London Gazette, 21 Oct. 1914], and again by F.M. Sir John French [London Gazette, 17 Feb. 1915]. He was twice brought down in France, but managed to escape. The first time he was forced to alight between the firing lines. On the second occasion his engine was damaged by shrapnel when he was over the German lines, and he had to volplane, just managing to reach the Belgian lines and coming under fire from both sides, as the Belgians mistook him for a German and seized him as a prisoner. He was gazetted Flight Commander 23 Feb. 1915; served in the Dardanelles, and took part in the landing on the Gallipoli Peninsula 25 April, 1915, and was engaged in several fights with hostile aeroplanes. He lost his life in the Eastern Mediterranean, while on patrol duty, by an accident to his aeroplane resulting from engine failure, 19 Aug. 1915. Michael Sullivan Keogh Chief Petty Officer, H.M.S. Ark Royal, was awarded the Albert Meda (2nd Class) for his gallantry in endeavouring to rescue Capt. Collet. The official record in the London Gazette of 14 Jan. 1916, is as follows: "On 19 Aug. 1915, an aeroplane, piloted by the late Capt. C. H. Collet, D.S.O., R.M.A., was ascending from Imbros aerodrome, and had reached a height of 150 feet, when the engine stopped. The machine was upset by the powerful air currents from the cliffs, and fell vertically to the ground, while the petrol carried burst into flames, which immediately enveloped the aeroplane and pilot. Chief Petty Officer Keogh, upon arriving at the scene of the accident, at once made an attempt to save Capt. Collet by dashing into the midst of the wreckage, which was a mass of flames. He had succeeded in dragging the fatally injured officer nearly clear of the flames when he himself was overcome by the burns which he had received from the blazing petrol." A General Officer with whom he served for a time on observation duty in the Dardanelles wrote of him to his father in the highest terms.

London Gazette, 11 Nov. 1914.—" His Majesty the King has been graciously pleased to approve of the appointment of the undermentioned Officers to be Companions of the Distinguished Service Order, in recognition of their services with the Expeditionary Force, specified below."

WALFORD, JOHN COLQUHOUN, Capt., was born 22 May, 1882. He was gazetted to the Royal Artillery, as Second Lieutenant, 23 July, 1901 ; became Lieutenant 23 July, 1904 ; was Adjutant, R.A., 2 Jan. 1911, to 4 Oct. 1912, and was promoted to Captain 23 July, 1914. He served in the European War from 1914 ; was wounded ; mentioned in Despatches, and created a Companion of the Distinguished Service Order [London Gazette, 11 Nov. 1914] : " John Colquhoun Walford, Capt., 119th Battery, Royal Field Artillery. For gallant conduct at Eloges, on 24 Aug., where he was wounded in two places, and at Le Cateau, on 26 Aug., where, in spite of pain from his wounds, he showed a fine example in bringing limbers and teams up under a heavy fire." He became Major 9 Nov. 1915 ; was Brigade Major, R.A., 63rd Division, British Armies in France, 7 Oct. 1917, to 4 Nov. 1918, and Acting Lieutenant-Colonel, R.A., from 6 Nov. 1918. He married, in 1909, Honoria Cecilia, daughter of the Rev. C. W. Hunt-Holly.

JARDINE, COLIN ARTHUR, Second Lieut., was born in Paris 24

Colin Arthur Jardine.

Sept. 1892, one of the six sons of Sir John Jardine, Bart., K.C.I.E., M.P., LL.D., Indian Civil Service (retired), and Minnie, daughter of J. Hogg, M.R.C.S. He was educated at Charterhouse, and at the Royal Military Academy, Woolwich, and joined the Army 19 July, 1912. He served in the European War ; went with the 4th Division to France in Aug. 1914 ; was four times mentioned in Despatches, and three times wounded, and created a Companion of the Distinguished Service Order London Gazette, 11 Nov. 1914] : " Colin Arthur Jardine, Second Lieut., Royal Field Artillery. For his fearlessness and enterprise in giving information from the firing line, both on the Aisne and on 21 Oct., when he was severely wounded." He was promoted to Lieutenant 9 June, 1915, and to Captain 8 Aug. 1916, and was Acting Major from 26 Nov. 1916. He was also awarded a Bar to the Distinguished Service Order. He was awarded the Military Cross [London Gazette, in Sept. 1916]. Capt. Jardine married, in 1919, Jean Evelyn Livesay, daughter of Major-General W. A. Liddell, C.B.

SMYTH, GERALD BRICE FERGUSON, Lieut., was born 7 Sept. 1885. He entered the Royal Engineers 29 July, 1905 ; became Lieutenant 3 Feb. 1908, and Captain 30 Oct. 1914. Capt. Smyth served in the European War from 1914, and was created a Companion of the Distinguished Service Order [London Gazette, 11 Nov. 1914] : " Gerald Brice Ferguson Smyth, 17th Company, Royal Engineers. For consistent skill, daring and hard work in reconnaissance and defensive preparations by night and day throughout the campaign, and especially during the Battle of the Aisne and in the trenches at Givenchy, until wounded on 25 Oct. by a shell, entailing the loss of his left arm." He was given the Brevet of Major 3 June, 1916 ; was acting Lieutenant-Colonel, commanding a Service Battn. King's Own Scottish Borderers, 2 Dec. 1916, to 2 May, 1917, and 4 Nov. 1917, to 23 March, 1918 ; Temporary Lieutenant-Colonel, commanding a Service Battn. King's Own Scottish Borderers, 10 May to 2 Oct. 1918 ; Temporary Brigadier-General, commanding the 93rd Infantry Brigade, British Armies in France, 3 Oct. 1918. He was severely wounded ; was given the Brevet of Lieutenant-Colonel 3 June, 1919 ; was four times mentioned in Despatches and awarded a Bar to the Distinguished Service Order.

BUCKLEY, WILLIAM PERCY, Lieut., was born 13 Sept. 1887 ; entered

William Percy Buckley.

the Army, 1907 ; became Captain, 1915, and Major, 1918. He served in the European War, 1914–15 ; was mentioned in Despatches, and created a Companion of the Distinguished Service Order [London Gazette, 11 Nov. 1914] : " William Percy Buckley, Lieut., 1st Battn. The Duke of Cornwall's Light Infantry. For great gallantry at Beauputts on the night of the 18th Oct., when the enemy's fire had set alight two ricks, in endeavouring to extinguish (under a heavy fire of machine guns) the flames, which were already showing clearly to the enemy the position of the battalion's trenches."

KENTISH REGINALD JOHN, Capt., was born 20 Dec. 1876, son of George Kentish, of 12, Courtfield Gardens, London, S.W., and Caroline Kentish, of Bungay,

Suffolk. He was educated at St. Albans, Malvern and Sandhurst ; joined the 1st Battn. The Royal Irish Fusiliers 8 Aug. 1897. He served in the South African War from 1899–1902 ; was Special Service Officer for Mounted Infantry from 15 Feb. to 1 April, 1901 (Queen's Medal with four clasps, and King's Medal with two clasps). He became Lieutenant 1 Dec. 1899, and Captain 1 Aug. 1902, and was Adjutant, 1st Battn. The Royal Irish Fusiliers, from 31 Dec. 1904, to 30 Dec. 1907. Capt. Kentish was A.D.C. to the G.O.C., 2nd Division, Aldershot Command, from 1 Feb. 1910, to 31 March, 1911 ; Brigade Major, 6th London Infantry Brigade, from 24 Feb. 1913, to 6 Sept. 1914. He served in the

Reginald John Kentish.

European War from 1914, beginning with the rank of Captain ; was present at the Battles of the Aisne, Meteren, Armentières, First Battle of Ypres, Second Battle of Ypres, the Somme, including Montauban, Longueval, Delville Wood, Guillemont, Maltzhorn and Maurepas, Cambrai, the Lys, including the defence of Givenchy, with the 55th Division, the advance in 1918, and the occupation of La Bassée : the successive crossings of the Haute Beule, Scheldt and the Dendre Rivers, and the final march to Tournai, Leuze and Brussels, all with the 55th Division, in which he commanded the 166th Infantry Brigade. He was mentioned in Despatches six times, and was created a Companion of the Distinguished Service Order (Immediate Reward) [London Gazette, 11 Nov. 1914] : " Reginald John Kentish, Capt., Royal Irish Fusiliers. On 17 Oct., near Houplines, Capt. Kentish set fire to a farm building occupied by some Germans, who had killed and wounded many of the attacking party. It was then found that some of the wounded lying close to the door were suffering from burning debris. He organized a rescue party, and himself, at a range of a few feet, tried by firing down the passage to keep down the fire of the occupants whilst the wounded were being removed." Capt. Kentish was also made an Officer of the Legion of Honour in 1917, and a Companion of St. Michael and St. George in 1918. He was Temporary Major 5 Oct. to 17 Dec. 1914 ; became Major 18 Dec. 1914 ; was Temporary Lieutenant-Colonel whilst commanding 1st Battn. East Lancashire Regt. 18 May to 24 Sept. 1915, and whilst commanding the 1st Battn. Royal Irish Fusiliers 25 Sept. to Nov. 1915 ; he was promoted a Brevet Lieutenant-Colonel 1 Jan. 1916, and appointed Temporary Brigadier-General 24 March, 1916, a rank he held continuously until Aug. 1919, and during which period he successively commanded the 76th Infantry Brigade in the 3rd Division, the Senior Officers' School, Aldershot, and the 166th Infantry Brigade in the 55th Division. On the 3rd June, 1919, he was promoted to the rank of Brevet Colonel for services he had rendered during the time he was at the head of the Senior Officers' School. He originated the first of the Big Army Infantry Schools, viz. : the 3rd Army School, at Flixécourt in France, of which he was Commandant. This school and the system of training evolved by Brigadier-General R. J. Kentish subsequently became the model on which was based the whole of the school and training system for the Armies in the United Kingdom and Overseas. Included in that system was the Theory, Demonstration, Practice System of Teaching, which produced the most remarkable results in the shortest possible time. Other far-reaching and urgent reforms affecting deeply the whole of the moral of the British Army were originated by this officer whilst at the head of these big training establishments, and especially when Commandant of the Senior Officers' School at Aldershot, a school which lives to-day and which has become a part of the post-war Army and on the lines he suggested. Prior to the war he originated the policy of placing the soldier on his honour, which led to the abolition of picquets in the Aldershot Command, and subsequently in the whole Army. He was also the originator of the scheme for providing adequate recreation grounds throughout every garrison and station in the United Kingdom, and, in 1913, was officially appointed by the Army Council to report on the whole question. The scheme arrived at provided every regiment with two football grounds, one cricket ground, one running track, and four tennis courts. This scheme was brought to completion in the Aldershot Command, and was in process of completion in every station in the United Kingdom when the Great War broke out. Brigadier-General Kentish has since the Armistice been again appointed to carry on the work which he originated in 1909, and is at the present moment engaged on that work, not only for the Regular Army but also for the Territorial Army which is in process of being raised. Brigadier-General R. J. Kentish has been Honorary Secretary, Army Football Association, since 1913 ; is on the Committee of the Army Rifle Association ; on the Committee of the Army Fencing Union ; a Councillor of the Football Association, and also a Member of the British Olympic Council. He is the author of many books and papers on matters affecting the training and welfare of the soldier. He is a Member of the Army and Navy Club, Pall Mall, S.W. ; the Junior United Service Club, Charles Street, S.W. ; the Sports Club, St. James's Square, S.W., and the National Sporting Club, Covent Garden, W.C.

London Gazette, Tuesday, 1 Dec. 1914.—" War Office, 1 Dec. 1914. His Majesty the King has been graciously pleased to approve of the appointment of the undermentioned Officers to be Companions of the Distinguished Service Order, in recognition of their Services with the Expeditionary Force, specified below."

ANDERSON, ERIC LITCHFIELD BROOKE, Lieut., was born 10 Sept. 1889, son of Colonel E. B. Anderson, Indian Army. He was educated at Clifton College, and at the Royal Military Academy, Woolwich, and entered the Royal Artillery 22 July, 1909, becoming Lieutenant 23 July, 1912.

He served in the European War from 1914, and was created a Companion of the Distinguished Service Order [London Gazette, 1 Dec. 1914]: " Eric Litchfield Brooke Anderson, Lieut., Royal Field Artillery. On 26 Sept. displayed conspicuous bravery with his gun in the infantry firing line, bringing it out of its emplacement to meet the enemy's infantry attack. The gun was struck by a shell, and he and three of the detachment were wounded." He was Staff Captain 1 Feb. to 6 Dec. 1915 ; became Captain 23 July, 1915 ; was Acting Major, R.A., 25 Sept. 1916, to 30 July, 1917 ; Temporary Lieutenant-Colonel 11 March to 14 Sept. 1918 ; Captain Instructor in Gunnery, School of Instruction for R.H. and R.F.A., 15 Sept. to 24 Oct. 1918 ; Acting Major 25 Oct. 1918, to 5 May, 1919 ; Major Instructor in Gunnery, School of Instruction for R.H. and R.F.A., 25 Oct. 1918, to 5 May, 1919 ; Staff Captain, War Office, 6 April, 1919. Capt. Anderson has the Order of Danilo.

ATKINSON, HENRY NOEL, Second Lieut., was born at Audlem Vicarage, Cheshire, 25 Dec. 1888, son of Arthur Atkinson (deceased), Clerk in Holy Orders, Hon. Canon of Chester Cathedral, and Ursula Mary Atkin-

Henry Noel Atkinson.

son ; and grandson of the late Bishop Cotton, of Calcutta. He was educated at Moorland House, Heswall, Cheshire ; at Charterhouse, and St. John's College, Cambridge, and was gazetted to the 3rd Battn. (Special Reserve) of the Cheshire Regt. 12 March, 1913. He joined the 1st Battn. for training at Londonderry 1 Nov. 1913. On mobilization Lieut. H. N. Atkinson was immediately attached to the 1st Battn. of the Cheshire Regt., then stationed at Londonderry, and embarked with his regiment on 14 Aug. 1914, for France, where they formed part of the 15th Brigade of the 5th Division. He served unscathed all through the fighting and Retreat of Mons, Le Cateau, the Aisne, etc., until 22 Oct. 1914, when, at Violaines, near La Bassée, he won his D.S.O., but was subsequently officially reported as " Missing," and was believed to have been captured. He is known to have been wounded, and was subsequently reported (unofficially) to have been taken to, and seen in, a French Hospital at Douai, which fell into the hands of the Germans. He was created a Companion of the Distinguished Service Order [London Gazette, 1 Dec. 1914]: " Henry Noel Atkinson, Second Lieut., 3rd Battn. The Cheshire Regt. For conspicuous gallantry under heavy fire from both flanks, by collecting a few men and checking the enemy, thereby facilitating the retirement of his comrades." He was mentioned in Sir John French's Despatch of 14 Jan. 1915 [London Gazette, 17 Feb. 1915]: " For gallant and distinguished service in the Field." He was promoted to Lieutenant 2 Feb. 1915 (3rd Battn. Special Reserve, Cheshire Regt.). His pursuit was farming ; his favourite recreations were hunting, shooting, cricket, billiards and golf (Welsh Amateur Golf Champion, 1913). He was the winner of the Carnarvon Golf Challenge Bowl, 1913.

BAINES, CUTHBERT SAVILE, Lieut., was born 25 May, 1890, son of Lieut.-Colonel Cuthbert Johnson Baines,

Cuthbert Savile Baines.

J.P., of The Lawn, Shirehampton, Gloucestershire, and Ada Cornelia, daughter of Colonel H. B. O. Savile, C.B., J.P. He was educated at Winchester and Sandhurst ; was gazetted to the Oxfordshire and Buckinghamshire Light Infantry 14 May, 1910, and became Lieutenant 8 Oct. 1913. He served in the European War from 1914 ; was twice wounded, three times mentioned in Despatches, and created a Companion of the Distinguished Service Order [London Gazette, 1 Dec. 1914]: " Cuthbert Savile Baines, Lieut., 2nd Battn. The Oxfordshire and Buckinghamshire Light Infantry. Did good work in attack on 21 Oct., pushing on when all his company officers were killed or wounded ; also good work in repelling attacks on 22 and 23 Oct." He was Staff Captain, Ministry of Munitions, 18 Aug. 1915, to 22 June, 1916 ; Temporary Captain, Oxfordshire and Buckinghamshire Light Infantry, 1 Sept. to 17 Oct. 1915 ; was promoted to Captain 18 Oct. 1915 ; was Temporary Major, Territorial Force Battn. Royal Warwickshire Regt., 23 June to 27 Aug. 1916 ; Acting Major, Oxfordshire and

Frederick H. Blackwood.

Buckinghamshire Light Infantry, 29 Aug. 1916, to 9 Sept. 1917 ; Temporary Lieutenant-Colonel, commanding Territorial Force Battn. Liverpool Regt., 10 Sept. 1917. He served in the North Russian Campaign in 1919, and was wounded. Capt. Baines was awarded a Bar to the Distinguished Service Order.

BLACKWOOD, FREDERICK HERBERT, Lieut., was born 9 Nov. 1885, at Stobo, Peeblesshire, N.B., son of Alexander Blackwood, Esq., and Geraldine Blackwood. He joined the Militia, 3rd Battn. Lincolnshire Regt., in Dec. 1903 ; joined the Lincolnshire Regt. at Tidworth, his commission being dated 23 May, 1906 ; was transferred to India, 1908 to 1912 ;

to the Depôt, Lincoln, in 1913 ; became Lieutenant 10 May, 1911. He rejoined the 1st Battn. Lincolnshire Regt. in France, Aug. 1914, as Machine Gun Officer, until appointed Adjutant on the death of Capt. R. E. Drake. He was twice mentioned in Despatches, and created a Companion of the Distinguished Service Order [London Gazette, 1 Dec. 1914]: " Frederick Herbert Blackwood, Lieut., Acting Adjutant, 1st Battn. Lincolnshire Regt. On 1 Nov. at Wytschaete, during an attack on the village, rallied and kept men in their places after every company commander had been killed or wounded, showing great gallantry and coolness under heavy fire." This attack took place at night, when two battalions of the Northumberland Fusiliers and the Lincolns respectively were ordered up to the support of the cavalry." He was invalided home and appointed Adjutant at the Depôt, Lincoln, until convalescent. He was promoted to Captain 24 Nov. 1914. He was transferred to the 13th Sudanese, Egyptian Army, in Jan. 1916, and took part in the Darfur Expedition in 1916. Capt. Blackwood was appointed Commandant of the Military School, Khartoum, 1916. His favourite pursuits are hunting and shooting. He married, 9 Feb. 1915, at St. Jude's, Southsea, Nora, younger daughter of Dr. Ponsonby Widdup (late British Guiana Government Service) and Mrs. Ponsonby Widdup, and they have a daughter, Patricia Mary, and a son, Michael Frederick Ponsonby.

BLEWITT, RALPH, Lieut., was born 24 Aug. 1890, second son of Major-General William Edward Blewitt, C.B., C.M.G., and Harriett Agnes, daughter of the late J. Rigby, of Moss House, West Derby, and widow of R. A. Fitzgerald. He was educated at Harrow ; entered the Royal Field Artillery 23 July, 1910, and became Lieutenant 23rd July, 1913. He served in the European War from 1914. He was mentioned in Despatches, and created a Companion of the Distinguished Service Order [London Gazette, 1 Dec. 1914]: " Ralph Blewitt, Lieut., Royal Field Artillery. For gallant and skilful handling of a single gun in support of infantry on the road to Gheluvelt on 31 Oct., being all the time under heavy fire. This action was of greatest use to the infantry." He was Temporary Captain from 11 Aug. 1915, and was promoted Captain 23 July, 1916 ; was Acting Major, R.A., 25 Sept. 1916, to 14 Feb. 1917, and 18 Feb. to 24 March, 1918. Captain-Instructor in Gunnery, School of Instruction for R.H. and R.F.A., 11 May, 1918. Capt. Blewitt married, in 1915, Denys Beatrix, second daughter of James Henderson, of 86, Eaton Place, S.W., and they have one son.

BRABAZON, THE HONOURABLE ERNEST WILLIAM MAITLAND MOLYNEUX, Capt., was born 22 March, 1884, at The Mansion, Richmond, Surrey, son of the Earl and Countess of Meath (née Lady Jane

Hon. E. W. M. M. Brabazon.

Maitland, only surviving daughter of the 11th Earl of Lauderdale). He was educated at Dover College, and joined the Coldstream Guards, 9 Jan. 1904 ; was promoted Lieutenant 5 Sept. 1906, and Captain 4 April, 1912. Capt. the Hon. W. M. M. Brabazon served in the European War. He was mentioned in Field-Marshal Sir John French's Despatch [London Gazette, 1 Dec. 1914], and on another occasion, and was created a Companion of the Distinguished Service Order [London Gazette, 1 Dec. 1914]: " The Honourable Ernest William Maitland Molyneux Brabazon, Capt., 3rd Battn. Coldstream Guards. Has shown conspicuous efficiency in Staff duties, and in keeping a long line of front, composed of many units, where communication was often difficult. He has carried and delivered messages under fire with promptitude and despatch." He was killed in action near La Bassée on 17 June, 1915, and was buried in Cambrin Cemetery, near where he fell. Lord Cavan, commanding the Guards Brigade, wrote : " We simply *loved* him. I can never tell you what he was to me, not only as a Staff Officer but as a friend. He was priceless, invaluable and never wearying in his work for the Brigade." And Colonel J. R. Drummond Hay, commanding the Coldstream Guards : " By his death the Army, as well as the regiment, has lost heavily." He was keen on musketry and sport, and a good shot. His three brothers also served in the Great War : Brigadier-General Lord Ardee, C.B., C.B.E., commanded the 1st Battn. Irish Guards ; and the 4th Guards Brigade, from Feb. 1918, and was wounded ; Capt. the Honourable Arthur Brabazon was on special service in Egypt, and Major the Honourable Claude Brabazon, O.B.E., Irish Guards, served in the Royal Air Force. Capt. the Honourable Ernest W. M. M. Brabazon married, 29 Oct. 1912, at the Guards' Chapel, Wellington Barracks, Dorothy Mary, youngest daughter of Colonel Horace Ricardo, C.V.O.

CATOR, ALBEMARLE BERTIE EDWARD, Major, was born 12 April, 1877, second surviving son of the late Albemarle Cator, D.L., of Woodbastwick Hall, Norfolk, and Mary Molesworth Cardelia, third daughter of C. A. Molesworth Harris, of Hayne, Devon. He was gazetted to the Scots Guards, as Second Lieutenant, from the Militia, 9 June, 1897, and became Lieutenant, 17 May, 1899 ; served in the South African War from 1899 to 1902, and was present at the advance on Kimberley, including actions at Belmont, Enslin, Modder River and Magersfontein ; took part in the operations in the Orange Free State, Feb. to May, 1900, including actions at Poplar Grove, Dreifontein, Vet River (5 and 6 May) and Zand River ; served during the operations in the Transvaal in May and June, 1900, including actions near Johannesburg, Pretoria and Diamond Hill (11 and 12 June) ; in the Transvaal, east of Pretoria, July to 29 Nov. 1900, including action at Belfast (26 and 27 Aug.) ; in the Transvaal, west of Pretoria, July to 29 Nov. 1900 ; also during operations in Orange River Colony, May to 29 Nov. 1900 ; served in the Transvaal, Dec. 1900, to July, 1901 :

in Orange River Colony, July, 1901, to May, 1902; also in Cape Colony, Dec. 1900. He was mentioned in Despatches [London Gazette, 10 Sept. 1901]; was awarded the Queen's Medal with six clasps, and the King's Medal with two clasps. He was promoted to Captain 3 Nov. 1903. From 1 May, 1908, to 30 April, 1911, he was Commandant, School of Instruction for Volunteer Infantry Officers, and for Officers of the Territorial Force, at Chelsea Barracks. He was Adjutant, Scots Guards, from 1 Oct. 1912, to 8 Oct. 1913; was promoted to Major 9 Oct. 1913. Major Cator served in the European War from 1914; as Brigade Major, 20th Infantry Brigade, B.E.F., 5 Aug. 1914, to 4 April, 1915; in command of the 37th Infantry Brigade, B.E.F., 13 Feb. 1916, to 5 Oct. 1917. He was Temporary Major-General, commanding the 58th Division, British Armies in France, 6 Oct. 1917, to May, 1918. He was mentioned in Despatches five times; was given the Brevets of Lieutenant-Colonel 3 June, 1916, and Colonel 3 June, 1917. He was created a Companion of the Distinguished Service Order [London Gazette, 1 Dec. 1914]: "Albemarle Bertie Edward Cator, Major, Scots Guards. He commanded the 20th Brigade in action for five days after the Brigadier was wounded, and has shown an example of cheerfulness and optimism which has helped materially to pull it together." Major Cator was Temporary Lieutenant-Colonel 4 April, 1915, to 12 Feb. 1916, and was Temporary Brigadier-General from 13 Feb. 1916; promoted to Colonel 2 June, 1919. He commanded the Young Soldiers' Brigade, Forces in Great Britain, 5 Feb. to 1 April, 1919. In 1903 he married Violet Eveleen, daughter of Francis R. H. S. Sutton and Lady Susan Sutton.

CONGREVE, CHARLES RALPH, Lieut., was born 14 May, 1886, in Argentina, South America, second son of Walter Congreve, Esq. (deceased), and of Mary, daughter of William Gordon Rich. He was educated at Cheltenham College; joined the 2nd Battn. Durham Light Infantry 28 Jan. 1905, and became Lieutenant 19 Sept. 1908. Lieut. Congreve served in the European War. He was created a Companion of the Distinguished Service Order [London Gazette, 1 Dec. 1914]: "Charles Ralph Congreve, Lieut., 2nd Battn. The Durham Light Infantry. On 28 Oct. saved the life of Captain Wallace by bringing him, when wounded, into cover under heavy fire." His name appeared in the first list of awards of the D.S.O. for the European War. He was Temporary Captain 15 Nov. 1914, to April, 1915, and Captain 2 April, 1915; Staff Captain, 18th Infantry Brigade, B.E.F., 22 July to 22 Oct. 1915; Brigade Major, 43rd Infantry Brigade, B.E.F., British Armies in France, 23 Oct. 1915, to 23 Feb. 1917. He was G.S.O.2, 34th Division, British Armies in France, 24 Feb. 1917, to 16 Sept. 1918; G.S.O.2, 13th Army Corps, British Armies in France, 30 Oct. 1917, to 16 Sept. 1918; G.S.O.2, 7th Army Corps, British Armies in France, 8 Feb. to 18 March, 1919; Brigade Major, Aldershot Command, 19 March, 1919. He was given a Brevet Majority in the Honours List of 1 Jan. 1917, and was five times mentioned in Despatches. On the 20th Jan. 1914, at Holy Trinity Church, Brompton Road, S.W., he married Phillida Mary, only daughter of Colonel (Temporary Major-General) Robert Wanless-O'Gowan, C.B., and they have a son, Walter Richard, born 4 Nov. 1914.

Richard Banastre Crosse.

CROSSE, RICHARD BANASTRE, Lieut., was born 17 April, 1888, at Snelson House, Chelford, Cheshire, elder son of Capt. Robert Legh Crosse, 52nd Light Infantry (now deceased), and Mary his wife. He was educated at Bilton Grange, Rugby; at Rugby School, and at the Royal Military College, Camberley; was commissioned into the 52nd (2nd Oxfordshire and Buckinghamshire Light Infantry) Foot 29 Aug. 1906, and joined the regiment 5 Oct. 1906. He became Lieutenant 22 April, 1909, and was Adjutant, Oxfordshire and Buckinghamshire Light Infantry, 1 March, 1913, to 29 Feb. 1916. Lieut. Crosse served in the European War from 13 Aug. 1914, to 1918. He was created a Companion of the Distinguished Service Order [London Gazette, 1 Dec. 1914]: "Richard Banastre Crosse, Lieut., 2nd Battn. The Oxfordshire and Buckinghamshire Light Infantry. As Adjutant, for consistent good work during the campaign." He was promoted to Captain 17 May, 1915, and became Acting Major 1 March, 1916; was Temporary Lieutenant-Colonel 8 July, 1916, to 23 Aug. 1918. Lieut.-Colonel R. B. Crosse has served with the 52nd Light Infantry continuously from the date of his first appointment. He was given the Brevet of Major 3 June, 1916, and was mentioned in Despatches four times. He was given the Croix de Chevalier of the Legion of Honour (France) in 1917, and was awarded a Bar to the Distinguished Service Order.

DENT, JOSEPH LESLIE, Lieut., served in the European War, and was created a Companion of the Distinguished Service Order [London Gazette, 1 Dec. 1914]: "Joseph Leslie Dent, Lieut., 2nd Battn. South Staffordshire Regt. On 7 Oct. he located an enemy's trench by daring scouting at night, subsequently rushing it with two sections and driving the enemy away." He was killed in action 11 April, 1917.

DENT, LEONARD EDWARD MAURICE, Second Lieut., was born 18 June, 1888, in London, son of Edward Dent, Esq., J.P., M.A., and Mabel Penelope, daughter of G. L. Phipps Eyre, Esq. He was educated at Eton, and Trinity College, Cambridge; joined the 1st Royal Dragoons

Leonard E. M. Dent.

in 1911, and retired in 1913. He joined the Special Reserve, and became Secretary and A.D.C. to Sir West Ridgeway in 1913, and accompanied him to North Borneo and China. He served in the European War from 1914, and was created a Companion of the Distinguished Service Order [London Gazette, 1 Dec. 1914]: "Leonard Edward Maurice Dent, Second Lieut., 6th Dragoon Guards (Carabiniers), Special Reserve. For gallantry during the operations between 27 Oct. and 1 Nov. 1914, in volunteering whenever a difficult piece of work had to be done." He was wounded; mentioned in Despatches, Feb. 1915; became Lieutenant in 1916; Temporary Captain, 1917, and was appointed A.D.C. to General Edward Perceval in Aug. 1915, and G.S.O.3, of the 49th Division, 12 June, 1916, to 14 July, 1917. He was gazetted Captain in the Oxfordshire and Buckinghamshire Light Infantry 11 June, 1917; acted as Brigade Major, 148th Brigade, 15 July, 1917, to 28 March, 1918; was G.S.O.2 29 March, 1918, to 19 March, 1919, and Temporary Major 29 March, 1918, to 9 April, 1919; was selected for the Junior Staff Course at Cambridge in 1918; was G.S.O.2, 2nd Army Corps, British Armies in France, 20 March to 9 April, 1919; Brigade Major, 1st Brigade, British Army of the Rhine, 10 April, 1919. Capt. Dent was wounded in the European War, and mentioned in Despatches.

DUNNE, JAMES STUART, Capt., was born 2 Nov. 1877. He is F.R.C.S.I., L.R.C.P.I., L.M.; Gold Medallist, Operative Surgery; Silver Medallist, Midwifery; was Specialist Advanced Operative Surgery, R.A.M.C., July, 1911; became Lieutenant, R.A.M.C., 31 July, 1905, and Captain 31 Jan. 1909. He served in the European War, and was twice mentioned in Despatches, and created a Companion of the Distinguished Service Order [London Gazette, 1 Dec. 1914]: "James Stuart Dunne, Capt., Royal Army Medical Corps. During a German attack on the night of 31 Oct., near Messines, he established a dressing station just behind the trenches, and was the means of saving many lives, he himself going several times into the trenches to attend to wounded men who could not be moved."

DURAND, HENRY MARION, Major, was born 23 Feb. 1876, son of the Right Hon. Sir (Henry) Mortimer Durand, G.C.M.G., K.C.S.I., K.C.I.E., P.C., and Ella (who died in 1913), daughter of T. Sanlys. He entered the Royal Artillery 13 May, 1896; became Lieutenant 12 March, 1898, and Major 15 March, 1908. Major Durand served in the European War; was three times mentioned in Despatches, and was created a Companion of the Distinguished Service Order [London Gazette, 1 Dec. 1914]: "Henry Marion Durand, 9th Lancers, Brigade Major, 4th Cavalry Brigade. During a night attack by Germans near Messines, on 31 Oct–1 Nov., he volunteered to go to the support trenches to ascertain the situation, and brought back information, displaying coolness and nerve." He was given the Brevet of Lieutenant-Colonel 1 Jan. 1919. Lieut. Colonel Durand retired from the Staff 11 March, 1919.

FEILDING, VISCOUNT RUDOLPH EDMUND ALOYSIUS, Lieut., was born 12 Oct. 1885, eldest son of the 9th Earl of Denbigh and the Honourable Cecilia Mary Clifford, daughter of the 8th Baron Clifford of Chudleigh. He was educated at the Oratory School, Edgbaston, and at Christ Church, Oxford, and entered the Army 29 Aug. 1906, becoming Lieutenant 16 Feb. 1909. He retired, and entered the Special Reserve, serving in the European War, and was created a Companion of the Distinguished Service Order [London Gazette, 1 Dec. 1914]: "Rudolph Edmund Aloysius, Viscount Feilding, Lieut., Coldstream Guards (Special Reserve), attached 3rd Battn. For conspicuous gallantry in leading a platoon during an attack on 21 Oct. He handled it with skill, and held an advanced post for two days under heavy shell fire. He has done other good work in preparing defensive positions." Lord Feilding was also given the Brevet of Major; was mentioned in Despatches, and created a C.M.G. in 1918. He married, in 1911, Imelda, daughter of Francis Egerton Harding, and they have two sons.

FORMAN, ARTHUR BARON, Major, was born 26 Sept. 1873. He joined the Royal Artillery 14 March, 1894; became Lieutenant 14 March, 1897, and Captain 15 Sept. 1900. He served in the South African War in 1902, and took part in the operations in Cape Colony in Jan. 1902, and also in the Transvaal and Orange River Colony, Feb. to 31 May, 1902. He received the Queen's Medal with three clasps. He was Adjutant, R.A., 29 April, 1906, to 28 April, 1909, and was promoted to Major 24 Dec. 1910. From 14 Aug. 1913, to 31 March, 1918, he was Major, Royal Flying Corps Reserve. He served in the European War from 1914, and was created a Companion of the Distinguished Service Order [London Gazette, 1 Dec. 1914]: "Arthur Baron Forman, Major, Royal Horse Artillery. For exceptionally good work during the operations of 23 Oct. to 4 Nov., near Messines, during which time he did splendid work." He was Temporary Lieutenant-Colonel, R.A., 21 Oct. 1915, to 13 March, 1916; was promoted to Lieutenant-Colonel 14 March, 1916; was Brigadier-General, R.A., 49th Division, British Armies in France, from 18 July, 1917. He was mentioned in Despatches, and created a C.M.G. in 1918.

FOX, CHARLES VINCENT, Capt., was born 31 Dec. 1877, son of the late Capt. Henry Charles Fox, King's Dragoon Guards, and of Mary Rebecca Fox, daughter of the late Capt. A. Coakley, Ceylon Rifles. He was educated at Clongowes and Oxford University, and was gazetted into the Scots Guards 21 April, 1900; was employed with the West African Frontier Force 16 Nov. 1901, to 24 Sept. 1907; served in West Africa, 1901–2, in the Aro Expedi-

Charles Vincent Fox.

tion; was wounded; mentioned in Despatches, and received the Medal and clasp. He served again in West Africa (Southern Nigeria), 1902 (clasp). He was promoted to Lieutenant 23 April, 1902; took part in the operations in the Northern Ibibio District, in command of a column (clasp); again in West Africa, 1904–5, in the Onitsha Hinterland Expedition. He was mentioned in Despatches [London Gazette, 23 Feb. 1900], and served again in 1905–6, in the Bende-Onitsha Hinterland Expedition, when he was again mentioned in Despatches [London Gazette, 18 Sept. 1906], and received a clasp. He was promoted to Captain 28 April, 1906, and was employed with the Egyptian Army 11 Sept. 1908, to 27 April, 1914; was Political Inspector, Mongolia Province, Sudan, 1912–14; took part in the Annak and Beir Patrol Expedition (Medal and clasp). He successfully conducted the Elephant Poacher Hunt in 1913; was taken prisoner. Subsequently decorated with the Order of the Medjidieh. Capt. Fox was Special War Correspondent in the Balkans, with the Turkish Army, in 1913. He served in the European War in 1914, covering the retirement of the German Army from Antwerp; was present at the First Battle of Ypres; was twice mentioned in Despatches, and was created a Companion of the Distinguished Service Order [London Gazette, 1 Dec. 1914]: "Charles Vincent Fox, Capt., 2nd Battn. Scots Guards. For conspicuous gallantry at Kruseik, in which action he captured five officers and 200 prisoners." He was thrice wounded, and was later taken prisoner by the Germans at Kruseik 26 Oct. 1914, and was interned in the following Prison Camps: Crefeld, Werl, Legarden, Brandenburg and Schwarmstedt. He escaped from Crefeld and was recaptured; escaped from the Berlin Express and was recaptured, and escaped from Schwarmstedt in 1917. He arrived in England 6 July, 1917; was received by the King, and was elected President of the Escapers. A Majority was conferred on him, dating from 1 Sept. 1915, and he was employed under the Ministry of Munitions from 1 April, 1918. He has been mentioned in Despatches eight times, and has the 1914 Star. Major Fox is a record holder, Championship of Great Britain (Wingfield Sculls), 1900; record holder, Oxford University Sculls, 1899. He won the Diamond Sculls in 1901; the Championship of France, and the Championship of Ireland. He was runner-up, Army Boxing Championship (Middle-Weight) in 1900. Among his recreations are yachting, football, cricket and big game hunting.

GIBBONS, EDWARD STEPHEN, Capt., entered the Army 6 Dec. 1902; was promoted to Lieutenant 6 Dec. 1904, and to Captain. He served in the European War, and was created a Companion of the Distinguished Service Order [London Gazette, 1 Dec. 1914]: "Edward Stephen Gibbons, Capt., 1st Battn. Middlesex Regt. He displayed great coolness and zeal in the action at Le Maisnil on 21 Oct. in a serious emergency."

GUNNER, FRANK HUGH, Lieut., was born 8 Dec. 1887, at Southsea, son of William Henry Ridge Gunner, Lieut.-Colonel. He was educated at Twyford School, near Winchester, and at Haileybury College, where he was in the Cricket Eleven in 1905 and 1906, and in the Racquet Pair in 1906. He joined the 2nd Battn. South Staffordshire Regt., at Pretoria 15 May, 1908, remaining with his regiment in South Africa until Jan. 1911. He was promoted to Lieutenant 22 April, 1909. From Jan. 1911, until Sept. 1913, he was stationed at Lichfield, and from Sept. 1913, to Aug. 1914, all the time with the 2nd Battn. South Staffordshire Regt. He served in the European War from Aug. 1914, being Battalion Machine Gun Officer until Dec. 1914. He was mentioned in Despatches 1 Dec. 1914, and was created a Companion of the Distinguished Service Order [London Gazette, 1 Dec. 1914]: "Frank Hugh Gunner, Lieut., 2nd Battn. South Staffordshire Regt. For conspicuous and consistent good work in charge of Machine Gun Section 12 Sept. to 4 Nov.—almost continually in action; he displayed the greatest courage, coolness and judgment in dangerous and difficult situations." He was Temporary Company Commander from Dec. 1914, to July, 1915, and was mentioned in Despatches, Feb. 1915. He became Captain 1 March, 1915; was Brigade Machine Gun Officer from July to Dec. 1915; Staff Captain from Dec. 1915, to May, 1916; Brigade Major from May to Sept. 1916; was wounded 17 Sept. 1916. He was given the Brevet of Major 1 Jan. 1917, and mentioned in Despatches 1 Jan. 1917. From 5 April, 1917, to 1918 he was Brigade Major at home; from 25 Feb. 1915, D.A.Q.M.G., Eastern Command. On 10 July, 1916, at Highfield Church, Southampton, Capt. Gunner married Aimée, widow of Annesley C. Denham.

Frank Hugh Gunner.

HAMILTON, LORD CLAUD NIGEL, Lieut., was born 10 Nov. 1889, seventh son of the second Duke of Abercorn. He was educated at Wellington; entered the Grenadier Guards 1 Feb. 1911, and became Lieutenant 24 Aug. 1912. He served throughout the European War from 1914; was twice mentioned in Despatches, and created a Companion of the Distinguished Service Order [London Gazette, 1 Dec. 1914]: "Lord Claud Nigel Hamilton, Lieut., 1st Battn. Grenadier Guards. He commanded a machine gun for five days and nights in forward trenches without relief, with great effect, under severe fire." He was A.D.C. 5 Jan. 1915, to 2 March,

Lord Claud N. Hamilton.

1919; was promoted to Captain 3 July, 1915, and was appointed Equerry-Ordinary to the Prince of Wales 3 March, 1919. The following is taken from "The First Seven Divisions" (pages 217–218), by permission of Lord Ernest Hamilton: "While four of the Guards' battalions were . . . pushing their way through the Polygon Wood, near Reutel, the two Guards' battalions in the 20th Brigade were enacting a small drama of their own at the village of Kruseik, south of the Menin Road. Here two companies of the Scots Guards and the King's Company 1st Grenadiers had been posted in some advance trenches east of the village, in the direction of the country road running from the village of Vieux Chien to Werwick. About 8.30 at night these advance trenches were attempted by peculiarly German methods. Through the intense darkness that reigned that night, and through the torrential rain, the enemy crept up close to our lines with the aid of every device known to modern warfare. Some said they had come to surrender, others said they were the South Staffords, and others again called appealingly for Capt. Paynter, who was, in actual fact, in command of the right wing of the two Scots Guards' companies. That officer's response, however, took the form of a well-directed fire, and the friendly inquirers departed with some haste. Lord Claud Hamilton (1st Grenadiers), who was in charge of the Machine Gun Section, was also undeceived by the friendliness of the visitors, and his Maxims contributed to the haste of their departure. This officer had now been seven days and nights unrelieved in the machine-gun trenches, and the coolness and resource which he displayed during that period gained for him the D.S.O. He was relieved early on the morning following this night attack by an officer of the Scots Guards, who was killed the same day."

HANBURY-SPARROW, ARTHUR ALAN, Lieut., was born 1 April, 1892, at The Uplands, Tettenhall, near Wolverhampton, son of Alan Bertram Hanbury-Sparrow, Esq., of Hillside, Church Stetton, Salop. He was educated at Lockers Park, Hemel Hempstead, Winchester College, and the Royal Military College, Sandhurst; joined the Royal Berkshire Regt., as Second Lieutenant, 20 Sept. 1911, and became Lieutenant 4 March, 1914. He served in the European War from 1914. He was twice severely wounded; mentioned in Despatches, March, 1915, and was created a Companion of the Distinguished Service Order [London Gazette, 1 Dec. 1914]: "Arthur Alan Hanbury-Sparrow, Lieut., 1st Battn. Princess Charlotte of Wales' Regt. (Royal Berkshire Regt.). He has done good work throughout the campaign; was severely wounded during an attack on a German position at Passchendaele-Becelaire Road, which resulted in taking the enemy's trenches and seventy prisoners." He was Temporary Captain, Royal Berkshire Regt., from 10 June to 28 July, 1915, and became Adjutant 23 July, 1915, and Captain 28 July, 1915. He was again mentioned in Despatches. From 22 March to 3 July, 1916, he was G.S.O.3; was awarded the Military Cross; became Temporary Lieutenant-Colonel, and was awarded a Bar to his D.S.O. [London Gazette, 26 Sept. 1917]: "Arthur Alan Hanbury-Sparrow, D.S.O., M.C., Acting Lieut.-Colonel, Royal Berkshire Regt."

A. A. Hanbury-Sparrow.

HANCOCK, RALPH ESCOTT, Lieut., was born at Llandaff, South Wales, 20 Dec. 1887, son of Frank Hancock, of Ford, Wiveliscombe, Somerset, and Mrs. Hancock. He was educated at Connaught House Preparatory School, Portmore, Weymouth, and at Rugby, where he played for the 1st Cricket Eleven in 1905 and 1906, and from which he passed direct into the Royal Military College, Sandhurst, in Aug. 1906. In Jan. 1908, he was gazetted to the 2nd Battn. Devonshire Regt., then stationed at Devonport. He became Lieutenant in Feb. 1911, and served with his regiment at Crete, Malta and Alexandria from 1909 to 1912. He was then at the Depôt, Exeter, for two years, and on the 30th Aug. 1914, left with a draft to reinforce the First Battalion in France. Lieutenant Hancock was killed in action on the 28th Oct. 1914. He was created a Companion of the Distinguished Service Order [London Gazette, 1 Dec. 1914]: "Ralph Escott Hancock, Lieut., 1st Battn. Devonshire Regt. (since killed in action). On 23 Oct. he displayed conspicuous gallantry in leaving his trench under very heavy fire and going back some sixty yards to pick up Corpl. Warwick, who had fallen whilst coming up with a party of reinforcements. Lieut. Hancock conveyed this non-commissioned officer to the cover of a haystack and then returned to his trench." He was mentioned in Sir John French's Despatch of the 14th Jan. 1915. Lieut. Hancock was a good athlete and rider. At Malta he played in the polo team that won the regimental cup, and captained the Army Polo Team v. the Navy. He played cricket and football for the county of Somerset. He won the East Devon Hunt Heavy-Weight Point-to-Point in 1913 and 1914, on horses trained by himself, and was a well-known follower of the West Somerset and Devon Fox Hounds. He also won several prizes for shooting. On 17 Sept. 1913, at Milverton, Somerset, Lieut. Hancock married Mary Hamilton, younger daughter of

Ralph Escott Hancock.

the Rev. P. P. and Mrs. Broadmean, of Olands, Milverton, Somerset, and they had one son, Patrick Frank, born 23 June, 1914.

HUGGINS, HENRY WILLIAM, Second Lieut., was born 26 Oct. 1891, son of Henry Huggins, of Leamington Spa. He was educated at Rugby and at Trinity College, Cambridge, and was gazetted to the Royal Artillery 19 July, 1912. He served in the European War, 1914–18; was thrice mentioned in Despatches, and created a Companion of the Distinguished Service Order [London Gazette, 1 Dec. 1914]: "Henry William Huggins, Second Lieut., R.F.A. For consistent gallantry in going forward to a cottage between the German trenches and our own, so as to be better able to direct his battery's fire. He remained there for three days under heavy rifle fire, directing with success by telephone, directing and observing fire, day after day from a very exposed position." He became Lieutenant 9 June, 1915; Captain 8 Aug. 1916, and was given the Brevet of Major 3 June, 1919.

INNES-KER, LORD ALASTAIR ROBERT, Capt., was born 2 Nov. 1880, son of the 7th Duke of Roxburghe and Lady Anne Emily V. A., daughter of the 7th Duke of Marlborough. He was educated at Sandhurst, and was gazetted to the 1st Dragoons, as Second Lieutenant, 21 Feb. 1900. He served in the South African War, 1900–2 (both Medals with five clasps). He was promoted to Lieutenant 1 Jan. 1901, and became Lieutenant, Royal Horse Guards, 24 June, 1905, and Captain 10 May, 1909. Lord A. R. Innes-Ker served in the European War from 1914, as Captain, Royal Flying Corps, from 24 May, 1916, to 31 March, 1918; Temporary Major 21 Dec. 1916, to 18 Aug. 1917; Temporary Lieutenant-Colonel and Commandant, School of Military Aeronautics, Royal Flying Corps, 19 Aug. 1917, to 31 March, 1918; employed under the Air Ministry from 1 April, 1918. He was mentioned in Despatches, and created a Companion of the Distinguished Service Order [London Gazette, 1 Dec. 1914]: "Lord Alastair Robert Innes-Ker, Capt., Royal Horse Guards. During a critical situation at Kruseik on Oct. 26 the regiment was sent to relieve pressure of determined attack. The operation was entirely successful. Captain Innes-Ker showed conspicuous courage with the advance squadron, bringing wounded men out of action under very heavy fire." He married Anne, daughter of the late W. L. Breese, and they have three children.

ISAAC, JOHN EDMUND VALENTINE, Capt., was born 14 Feb. 1880, at Powyke Court, Worcestershire, son of John Swinton Isaac, D.L., of Boughton Park, Worcester, Banker, and Amelia Alicia Anne, daughter of Major-General R. H. Crofton, Royal Artillery. He was educated at Wixenford and Harrow, and was gazetted to the 5th Northumberland Fusiliers at York 9 May, 1900. He joined his regiment in South Africa, on active service, leaving England on 28 June, 1900. He was dangerously wounded at Nooitgedacht (General Clements' action on the Mahaliesburg 13 Dec. 1900); and, after two years' sick leave, went back to duty. He had been gazetted Lieutenant 28 Nov. 1900, and became Captain 1 April, 1905. On the disbandment of his battalion he was gazetted to the Rifle Brigade 24 June, 1908, and subsequently served in Malta and Egypt. In the autumn of 1911 he sent in his papers, and went to Vancouver, British Columbia. On rumours of war he at once returned to England, and joined the Rifle Brigade, Reserve of Officers, 1 Sept. 1914. Capt. J. E. V. Isaac was appointed A.D.C. to Major-General Sir Thompson Capper, Commanding the 7th Division, and went to Flanders on his Staff in Oct. 1914. He was present at the First Battle of Ypres, where he was badly wounded in the left arm. For his services at that time he was mentioned in Despatches, and created a Companion of the Distinguished Service Order [London Gazette, 1 Dec. 1914]: "John Edmund Valentine Isaac, Capt., Reserve of Officers, The Rifle Brigade (The Prince Consort's Own). He has shown conspicuous gallantry on all occasions, and has always obtained reliable and valuable information when required. On 24 Oct. he guided a unit to a critical point with great skill, which resulted in checking the enemy. He was wounded in the engagement." With his arm still rather useless, he returned to duty on 19 Dec. 1914, and obtained leave to rejoin his regiment, 2nd Battn. Rifle Brigade 5 May, 1915. Four days later he was killed, leading his men, on the Fromelles Ridge. The "Athletic News" of 6 Sept. 1915, says: "Capt. J. E. V. Isaac (Rifle Brigade), unofficially reported killed, was a member of the well-known Worcestershire cricketing family. Since 1903 he had been a member of the M.C.C. In Nov. last he received the D.S.O." Capt. Isaac was a good cricketer; played for his county and his regiment. He was a member of I Zingari and the Free Foresters' Club. He won the Cairo Grand National in 1911, while with his regiment in Egypt. He was a keen huntsman and hunted with the Worcestershire, Pytchley, York and Ainsty, etc., etc.

John Edmund V. Isaac.

John Peake Knight.

KNIGHT, JOHN PEAKE, Lieut., was born 3 Aug. 1890, at Brighton, eldest son of James Percy Knight, of Sundridge Park, Bromley, Kent, and Ellen Knight; and grandson of the late Mr. J. P. Knight, for many years General Manager of the London, Brighton and South Coast Railway. He entered the Royal Military

Academy, Woolwich, in Sept. 1909, and was gazetted to the Royal Field Artillery on 23 Dec. 1910. He received his jacket as Subaltern; went to France with the 2nd Division 18 Aug. 1914, and was in the following battles: Mons, the Retreat, the Marne, the Aisne, First Battle of Ypres, Neuve Chapelle, Festubert, Loos and Vermelles, and the First Battle of the Somme. He was mentioned in Despatches, 19 Oct. 1914, and created a Companion of the Distinguished Service Order [London Gazette, 1 Dec. 1914]: "John Peake Knight, Lieut., Royal Field Artillery. For conspicuous and consistent gallantry in assisting infantry, especially on 10 Nov. Has shown himself full of enterprise and initiative. His work has much encouraged the infantry." King George gave him his D.S.O. on 3 Dec. 1914, at Hazebroucke Station. He was again mentioned in Despatches 17 Feb. 1915; promoted to Captain in Oct. 1915. After having fought with distinction in the Great War, Capt. J. Peake Knight was killed in action whilst commanding the 35th Battery, Royal Field Artillery, during the First Battle of the Somme, 31 Aug. 1916. On 21 Nov. 1914, at St. John's, Bromley, Kent, he had married Phyllis Olivia Knight, eldest daughter of Mr. and Mrs. Gray-Knight, of Brighton, and they had one daughter, Anne Peake Knight.

KREYER, HUBERT STANLEY, Lieut., was born 4 July, 1890, son of Frederick Arthur Christian Kreyer, Lieut.-Colonel, Indian Army (retired in 1910). He was educated at Victoria College, Jersey, Channel Islands. 1906–8; was at the Royal Military College, Sandhurst, from Sept. 1909, to Dec. 1910, and played for the Royal Military College and Royal Military Academy at Association football and hockey. He joined the 2nd Battn. Prince of Wales's Own Yorkshire Regt. 25 March, 1911, and proceeded to France with the 7th Division 4 Oct. 1914; landed at Zeebrugge on 5 Oct. 1914; was present at the First Battle of Ypres. He was created a Companion of the Distinguished Service Order [London Gazette, 1 Dec. 1914]: "Hubert Stanley Kreyer, Lieut., 2nd Battn. Alexandra, Princess of Wales's Own (Yorkshire Regt.). Has shown conspicuous gallantry on several occasions in conveying messages along the trenches under heavy fire. His Commanding Officer considers that it was largely due to the services rendered by this Officer that the battalion was extricated from a difficult position." He was mentioned in Despatches in Jan. 1915; was present at the Battle of Neuve Chapelle; was wounded 13 March, and invalided home; rejoined the B.E.F., France, 1 Oct. 1915. and was invalided home through an injury to his knee 20 March, 1916. He was promoted Captain 16 April, 1916. Capt. Kreyer acted as Brigade Major, 192nd Rifle Brigade, Home Forces, 10 Aug. 1917, to 14 May, 1918; as Brigade Major, 185th Infantry Brigade, British Armies in France, 15 July, 1918, to 13 April, 1919; as G.S.O.3, G.H.Q., British Army of the Rhine, 14 April to 13 June, 1919; as Brigade Major 14 June, 1919. He was given the Brevet of Major 3 June, 1919. In 1918 he married Alice Leonie, second daughter of the late Capt. J. S. Berkeley, 85th Regt.

Hubert Stanley Kreyer.

LAMB, CAMERON, Capt., was born 25 May, 1879, at Old Charlton, Kent, son of the late Sir John Cameron Lamb, C.B., C.M.G., and of Bella, daughter of the late John Farquharson. One of his brothers is Capt. B. Lamb, R.G.A., late of the Egyptian Army, and A.D.C. to the Governor of Barbadoes. He was educated at Blackheath School, Exeter College, Oxford, and Guy's Hospital Medical School; was gazetted to the 4th Battn. Durham Light Infantry in Aug. 1900, and joined Lovat's Scouts (Imperial Yeomanry) in June, 1901. He served in the South African Campaign, 1899–1901, and took part in the operations in Cape Colony and the Orange River Colony during the South African War, for which he received the Queen's Medal with four clasps. He was gazetted to the Border Regt. in Jan. 1903, and served with it in South Africa, India and Burma. He was fond of rowing, boxing and hockey, and had many trophies of his big-game expeditions in Central Africa. He travelled across Canada from east to west, on foot for most of the way. He spent some time in studying the Franco-Belgian Frontier before the war with Germany broke out, for he had a strong belief that the British would be called upon to operate there in his lifetime. His belief was justified, and he served in the European War; was promoted Captain in 1914, and created a Companion of the Distinguished Service Order [London Gazette, 1 Dec. 1914]: "Cameron Lamb, Capt., 2nd Battn. The Border Regt. For repeated gallantry and exceptionally good work, scouting daily in and amongst the enemy's lines." He was decorated by the King while His Majesty was in Belgium. We are told that "Lieut. Lamb went out on an average every morning and night searching the farm for snipers, trying to discover the enemy's positions, and rounding up the enemy's patrols. He went out one morning with two men, and put four of the enemy out of action. He went to the place to see the result, and found another officer wounded. He insisted on bringing the officer away, and, under German fire, carried the wounded officer three-quarters of a mile. The firing, however, became too hot for him, and he left the man at a farm, and at night sent the stretcher-

Cameron Lamb.

bearers to bring him in." An account of another incident reads : " When the front trenches were taken, all that remained to hold the position were the headquarters and scouts. Lieut. Lamb stood on the top of the trench and shouted : ' Now, come on, boys, and give it to them ! Show them what the Scouts are made of ! ' Our fire proved very effective, and some of the enemy had to retire, but they found that we were numerically weak, and came on again. We had made such a bold show that Mr. Lamb remarked that he could die smiling because he knew that the Scouts had done their work." Capt. Lamb was hit in the left arm and left leg while leading A Company of the 2nd Border Regt. in an attack on the German trenches near Fromelles, five or six miles west of Lille, on the night of the 19th Dec. 1914. An officer of the Artists' Rifles wrote : " I have just heard that my old friend Lamb, of the Borderers, has died of wounds. He was one of the best people I have ever met. He died a magnificent death. When they carried him out of the trenches, horribly wounded, he was whistling the whole time, and refused to pay any attention to his wounds. He died in hospital before they could get him back to England." Capt. Lamb died on the 29th Dec. at the British Hospital, Hôtel Ballerive, Wimereux, near Boulogne, and was buried in the cemetery there. The Colonel of his battalion had written of Capt. Lamb in Nov. : " I must just write you a line to say how well your son—my Scout Officer—has done during the war. He is one of the bravest young officers I know, and absolutely fearless. He has been invaluable to me, and you will, I know, be proud of him. He did so well on that Monday, 26 Oct., when my old regiment lost so many officers and men, and he was the last to come away with me when we withdrew at dusk. I only hope, when I return, I may have him with us again." And after his death he wrote : " The old battalion has lost, by his death, a very gallant officer, and we shall all deeply mourn his loss. He was so brave and full of spirit all the time, even when things looked blackest, and, as you know, he was beloved by all—officers, non-commissioned officers and men, and on the field admired by all." An obituary notice of Capt. Lamb appeared in the " Times " of 4 Jan. 1915.

LLOYD, HUMPHREY WILLIS CHETWODE, Lieut., was born 19 Feb. 1892. He entered the 1st Battn. Wiltshire Regt. 19 Jan. 1912 ; became Lieutenant 25 Oct. 1914 ; Captain 1 Oct. 1915 ; was G.S.O.3 from 16 May, 1918. For his services in the European War, 1914–18, he was twice mentioned in Despatches, and created a Companion of the Distinguished Service Order [London Gazette, 1 Dec. 1914] : " Humphrey Willis Chetwode Lloyd, Lieut., Wiltshire Regt. On 19 Oct. led an attack and effected an important lodgment in enemy's lines, from which he was subsequently withdrawn as general advance was checked. Has acted for Adjutant for a month, and has always volunteered and performed good work with information patrols."

McCONNEL, JAMES KENNETH, Lieut., was educated at Winchester, and was gazetted to the 20th Hussars in 1912 ; entered the Special Reserve ; was seconded, serving with the M.G.C., prior to his appointment as Assistant Instructor, notified in the Gazette of 9 June, 1916. He served in the European War from 1914 ; was twice mentioned in Despatches, and created a Companion of the Distinguished Service Order [London Gazette, 1 Dec. 1914] : " James Kenneth McConnel, Lieut., 20th Hussars. For coolness, gallantry and exceptionally good work during the operations of 23 Oct. to 4 Nov. near Messines, and for exceptionally good service in covering with his machine guns the retirement of his regiment from the trenches with great skill and gallantry on 1 Nov. near Messines."

MAITLAND-DOUGALL, WILMOT EDWARD, Second Lieut., was born 1 Dec. 1890, youngest son of the late Capt. W. Maitland-Dougall. He entered the R.A. 23 July, 1910 ; became Lieutenant 23 July, 1913 ; Captain 23 July, 1916 ; was mentioned in Despatches ; given the Brevet of Major 1 Jan. 1919 ; awarded the Military Cross, and created a Companion of the Distinguished Service Order [London Gazette, 1 Dec. 1914] : " Wilmot Edward Maitland-Dougall, Second Lieut., R.A. For conspicuous enterprise in spotting the shield of an enemy's gun only 600 yards away, getting up a gun into the firing line, successfully knocking enemy's gun out, and also checking the enemy's infantry advance."

W. E. Maitland-Dougall.

John Kevin Martin.

MARTIN, KEVIN JOHN, Lieut., was born 3 July, 1890, at Ootacamund, Nilgerri Hills, India, son of Lieut.-Colonel Patrick Richard Martin and Isabella Maria Martin, daughter of Lieut. W. Carr Hamond, R.E. He was educated at Beaumont College, Old Windsor, and joined the Royal Engineers, as Second Lieutenant, 23rd July, 1910. Lieut. Martin served in the European War from 1914 ; was present at all battles in France and Flanders in 1916, 1917 and 1918. He was created a Companion of the Distinguished Service Order [London Gazette, 1 Dec. 1914] : " Kevin John Martin, Lieut., Royal Engineers. For conspicuous gallantry in taking his section across heavily swept ground to prepare a house with loopholes from which our infantry hoped to be able to overcome the enemy, who were fortified in some other neighbouring buildings. He successfully placed

a machine gun in position, and helped the infantry for the rest of the day. Again on 12 Nov. did good work, and was wounded." He was Officer of a Company of Gentleman Cadets, Class A., Royal Military Academy (temporary), from 23 March to 23 July, 1915. He became Adjutant. R.E., 9 Aug. 1915, and Temporary Captain 23 Sept. 1915. He was mentioned in Despatches five times, and given a Brevet Majority 1 Jan. 1918. He was G.S.O.3, 26th Division, B.E.F. 7 March to 27 April, 1916 ; G.S.O.3, 3rd Army, British Armies in France, 11 May to 14 July, 1916 ; Brigade Major, 32nd Infantry Brigade, British Armies in France, 15 July, 1916, to 3 Nov. 1917 ; G.S.O.2, 6th Division, British Armies in France, 18 Nov. 1917, to 19 March, 1918 ; G.S.O.2, 15th Army Corps, British Armies in France, 28 April to 4 May, 1918 ; G.S.O.2, attached Headquarters, Commander-in-Chief, Allied Forces, near Nancy, 5 May, 1918, to 21 Feb. 1919. He was previously for a time Officier de Liaison with the Italian Army. On 29 July, 1915, at Louth, Lincolnshire, he married Hilda, youngest daughter of C. W. Burkenshaw, of Cotes Grange, Louth.

MENZIES, STEWART GRAHAM, Capt., was born 30 Jan. 1890, son of the late J. Graham Menzies and Susannah West (now Lady Holford), daughter of the late Arthur Wilson, of Tranby Croft. He was educated at Eton, and joined the 2nd Life Guards 8 June, 1910. He served in the European War, 1914–18, was mentioned in Despatches, received the Legion of Honour and the Crown of Belgium ; was given the Brevet of Major, awarded the Military Cross and created a Companion of the Distinguished Service Order [London Gazette, 1 Dec. 1914] : " Stewart Graham Menzies, Capt., 2nd Life Guards. Showed great coolness during the attack on German position led by Major the Honourable A. F. Stanley, 1st Life Guards, on the 7th Nov., in support of the right flank of the 4th Guards Brigade, and again on the evening of that day." Major Menzies married, in 1918, Lady Avice Sackville, daughter of the late Earl de la Warr.

MONTAGU-DOUGLAS-SCOTT, LORD FRANCIS GEORGE, Capt., was born at Dalkeith, Scotland, 1 Nov. 1879, sixth son of the 6th Duke of Buccleuch and Lady Louisa Jane Hamilton (died 1912), Mistress of the Robes to the Queen, third daughter of the 1st Duke of Abercorn. He was educated at Eton (Cricket Eleven, 1898), and Christ Church, Oxford, and joined the 3rd Battn. The Royal Scots, in 1898, and the 2nd Battn. Grenadier Guards 29 Nov. 1899. He served in the South African War from April, 1900, to July, 1902, with the 2nd Battn. Grenadier Guards, and took part in the operations in the Orange Free State, April to May, 1900 ; in Orange River Colony, May to 29 Nov. 1900, including actions at Biddulphsberg and Wittebergen (1 to 29 July) ; in the Transvaal, Feb. to March, 1901 ; and again during operations in Orange River Colony, Dec. 1900, to Feb. 1901, and March, 1901, to 31 May, 1902 (Queen's Medal with three clasps, and King's Medal with two clasps). He became Lieutenant 17 Sept. 1901 ; was A.D.C. to the Viceroy of India 18 Nov. 1905, to 22 Nov. 1910, and became Captain 22 Jan. 1908. He served in the European War from 1914 to 1918, and was created a Companion of the Distinguished Service Order [London Gazette, 1 Dec. 1914] : " Lord Francis George Montagu-Douglas-Scott, Capt., Grenadier Guards (attached Irish Guards). For persistent and gallant efforts to rally the battalion when much shaken by heavy losses, and by helping to restore steadiness by his good example." The D.S.O. was awarded whilst attached to the 1st Battn. Irish Guards, from 18 Sept. to 31 Oct. 1914, serving on the Aisne and in the First Battle of Ypres. The account in official Despatch was not accurate, as it was described as rallying men after heavy losses, whereas such occasion never occurred. It is believed that the real reason was for running across the open to give orders to a subaltern under heavy fire from the enemy, and being wounded severely in so doing. He was mentioned in Despatches, Jan. 1915. He was promoted to Major 11 Nov. 1914 ; became Temporary Lieutenant-Colonel 4 Dec. 1916 ; was in command of a Service Battn. Royal Fusiliers, 1 Sept. to 4 Nov. 1915 ; was mentioned in Despatches, and was given the Brevet of Lieutenant-Colonel 3 June, 1918. His favourite recreations are hunting, shooting, cricket, polo and golf. Capt. Lord Francis Scott married, 11 Feb. 1915, Lady Eileen Elliott, daughter of the 4th Earl of Minto, late Governor-General of Canada and Viceroy of India, and Mary, daughter of the Honourable Charles Grey, and they have two daughters.

MONTGOMERY, BERNARD LAW, Captain, was born 19 Sept. 1887, at St. Mark's Vicarage, Kennington Oval, son of the Right Rev. Bishop Henry Hutchinson Montgomery, D.D., D.C.L., sometime Bishop of Tasmania, and Maud, daughter of the late Dean Farrar. He was educated at St. Paul's School and Sandhurst, and was gazetted to the Royal Warwickshire Regt. 19 Sept. 1908, and joined the 1st Battn. in India in Nov. 1908. He became Lieutenant 1 April, 1910, and was Temporary Captain 14 Sept. to 13 Oct. 1914, and Captain 14 Oct. 1914. He served in the European War from 1914, and was mentioned in Despatches in Nov. 1914, and created a Companion of the Distinguished Service Order [London Gazette, 1 Dec. 1914] : " Bernard Law Montgomery, Capt., The Royal Warwickshire Regt. For conspicuous gallant leading on 13 Oct., when he turned the enemy out of their trenches with the bayonet. He was severely wounded." The incident described in the Gazette took place during the attack of the 4th Division on Meteren 13 Oct. 1914, in the Ypres-Armentières Battle. He became Brigade Major 12 Feb. 1915. He was again mentioned in Despatches, Jan. 1917 ; appointed G.S.O., 2nd Grade, 22 Jan. 1917, and given the Brevet of Major

Bernard L. Montgomery.

3 June, 1918; appointed G.S.O., 1st Grade, with temporary rank of Lieutenant-Colonel, 16 July, 1918.

NICHOLSON, LAWRENCE CAIL, Lieut., was born 30 Aug. 1882, fourth son of Frederick W. Nicholson, of Shiplake, late of Maidenhead. He was educated at Uppingham; joined the 14th (King's) Hussars in March, 1902, and served in the Boer War. He became Lieutenant in Jan. 1905; retired from the active list in 1907, and was appointed Lieutenant in the 3rd Battn. Royal Berkshire Regt., July, 1910. He served in the European War. He was created a Companion of the Distinguished Service Order [London Gazette, 1 Dec. 1914]: "Lawrence Cail Nicholson, Lieut., 14th Hussars, 3rd (attached 1st) Battn. (Princess Charlotte of Wales's) Royal Berkshire Regt. Led and commanded his platoon admirably during an attack on the German position, Passchendaele–Becelaere Road, which resulted in the taking of the enemy's trenches and seventy prisoners. (Has since died of his wounds)." Lieut. Nicholson died 2 Nov. 1914, of wounds received in action near Ypres on 23 Oct.

ORR-EWING, SIR NORMAN ARCHIBALD, BART., Capt., was born 23 Nov. 1880, son of Sir Archibald Ernest Orr-Ewing, of Ballikinrain, Stirlingshire, N.B., 3rd Bart., and the Hon. Mabel Addington, youngest daughter of the 3rd Viscount Sidmouth and Georgina, daughter of the Hon. and Very Rev. George Pellew, D.D., late Dean of Norwich. He was educated at Eton, and joined the Militia in 1899. He served in it for 281 days; became Second Lieutenant (from Militia) Scots Guards 12 Sept. 1900; served in South Africa, 1899–1901; was present at operations in Orange River Colony, 1900 (Queen's Medal and two clasps). He became Lieutenant 1 April, 1903; Captain 5 June, 1907; invalided home with enteric; was employed with the Egyptian Army 5 Feb. 1907; served with Camel Corps until 1 Aug. 1910; was Adjutant, Scots Guards, 2 Aug. 1910, to 30 Sept. 1912. He served in the European War; was present at the Aisne, First Battle of Ypres, Givenchy and Quinchy (1914), Loos, the Somme and Passchendaele Ridge; also Cambrai (Nov. 1917), German Attack (1918), operations at Buzancy and the Vesle, Hulloch (1918), The Advance (1918). He was twice wounded; mentioned five times in Despatches, and created a Companion of the Distinguished Service Order [London Gazette, 1 Dec. 1914]: "Norman Archibald Orr-Ewing, Capt., Scots Guards (attached Irish Guards). For persistent and gallant efforts to rally the battalion when much shaken after its heavy losses, and by his good example helping to restore it to its usual steadiness." He was again wounded at Loos, and mentioned in Despatches; was promoted Major 1 Sept. 1915, and Temporary Lieutenant-Colonel 27 Dec. 1915, commanding 3rd Reserve Battn. Scots Guards and 2nd Battn. Scots Guards, B.E.F., from Sept. 1916, to May, 1918. He was awarded the Cavalier Military Order of Savoy, May, 1917; the Croix de Guerre, Nov. 1917; became Temporary Brigadier-General, commanding 45th Infantry Brigade, May, 1918; was given the Brevet of Lieutenant-Colonel 1 Jan. 1919; awarded the Légion d'Honneur, Croix d'Officier, Aug. 1918. He succeeded his father in 1919. Sir Norman Orr-Ewing married, 24 July, 1911, Laura Louisa, fourth daughter of Abraham John Robarts, D.L., and the Hon. Mrs. Robarts, of Tile House, Lillingstone Dayrell, Bucks, and they have two sons: Ronald Archibald, born 14 May, 1912, and Alan Lindsay, born 13 Jan. 1915, and one daughter, Jean Marjorie.

Norman A. Orr-Ewing.

OSBORNE, EDMUND ARCHIBALD, Capt., was born 26 July, 1885. He entered the Royal Engineers 1 Oct. 1904, becoming Lieutenant 23 June, 1907, and Captain 30 Oct. 1914. Capt. Osborne served in the European War from 1914, as G.S.O.3, 9th Division, British Expeditionary Force, 8 Oct. 1915, to 2 Jan. 1916; Brigade Major, 28th Infantry Brigade, British Expeditionary Force, 3 Jan. to 7 May, 1916; Brigade Major, 101st Infantry Brigade, British Armies in France, 8 May, 1916, to 10 Jan. 1917; G.S.O.2, G.H.Q., British Armies in France, 3 Feb. to 24 July, 1918; G.S.O.1, 33rd Division, British Armies in France, 23 July, 1918. He was mentioned in Despatches, was given the Brevet of Major 1 Jan. 1916, and was created a Companion of the Distinguished Service Order [London Gazette, 1 Dec. 1914]: "Edmund Archibald Osborne, Capt., Royal Engineers. Repeated gallantry and coolness in action on 31 Oct. He recovered a cable wagon which had been abandoned by the enemy. Has frequently shown great capacity for command."

PARDOE, FRANK LIONEL, Capt., was born 26 Feb. 1880, at Biarritz, France, son of the late Rev. John Pardoe, of Leyton, Essex, and Graveley, Herts, and of Mrs. Pardoe. He was educated at Eton and Sandhurst; entered the Army 10 March, 1900, and joined the 60th Rifles about the 20th March, 1900. He served in the South African War, 1899 to 1902, and was present at the operations in Natal (March to June, 1900); in the Transvaal, east of Pretoria, July to 29 Nov. 1900 (slightly wounded); in the Transvaal, 30 Nov. 1900, to July, 1901; also during the operations in Cape Colony, March to 31 May, 1902. He was wounded, and received the Queen's Medal with two clasps, and the King's Medal with two clasps. He was promoted to Lieutenant 15 April, 1901, and Captain 23 Oct. 1908. He proceeded to France 12 Aug. 1914; served in the European War, as Brigade M.G. Officer, 6th Brigade, from 1914, and was present in the Retreat from Mons, and in the Battles of the Marne, Aisne, and the First Battle of Ypres, for his services in which engagement he was mentioned in Despatches, and created a Companion of the Distinguished Service Order [London Gazette, 1 Dec. 1914]: "Frank Lionel Pardoe, Capt., 1st Battn. The King's Royal Rifle Corps. On 30 Sept. and previous days this Officer carried messages under rifle and shell fire. He was knocked down by a shell, but did not relinquish his duty." The date given in the Gazette as 30 Sept. should have read 20 Oct. He was wounded, and mentioned in Despatches 18 Feb. 1915. He was present at Neuve Chapelle (Givenchy operations) and Festubert; and was again wounded, and mentioned in Despatches 31 May, 1915. He left France 20 May, 1915 (wounded). He became Major 1 Sept. 1915, and embarked for Egypt 5 Aug. 1916; was employed as Machine Gun Instructor at the Imperial School of Instruction, Zeitoun, Cairo, from Aug. 1915, to March, 1917, being mentioned in Despatches for the fourth time on 21 June, 1916; was appointed G.S.O.2, for Machine Guns, at G.H.Q., E.E.F., in March, 1917, becoming G.S.O.1, for Machine Guns, and Temporary Lieutenant-Colonel in March, 1918. He served on the Staff of G.H.Q., Palestine, throughout the operations which commenced with the capture of Beersheba and Gaza, and ended in the occupation of that theatre of war, and was mentioned in Despatches for the fifth time on 14 June, 1918. On 12 Dec. 1911, in London, Capt. Pardoe married Sybil Margaret, widow of the late Lieut. C. D. Eyre, 60th Rifles, and daughter of Capt. Clayton Mitchell, R.N., of West Highlands, Winchester, and they have a son, John, born 27 Oct. 1912, and a daughter, Felicity.

PAYNTER, GEORGE CAMBORNE BEAUCLERK, Capt., was born at Eaton Square, London, S.W., 2 Aug. 1880, son of George Paynter, Major, King's Dragoons Guards, and of Frances Janetta Paynter, daughter of the late Lord and Lady Augustus Beauclerk. He joined the 2nd Battn. Scots Guards, as Second Lieutenant, from the Militia, 18 Oct. 1899. He served in South Africa, 1900–2; was all the time with the 8th Division. He took part in the operations in Orange River Colony, May to 29 Nov. 1900, including actions at Biddulphsberg and Wittebergen (1 to 29 July); in the Transvaal and Orange River Colony, 30 Nov. 1900, to 31 May, 1902 (Queen's Medal with three clasps, and King's Medal with two clasps); became Lieutenant 16 March, 1901, and Captain 14 Dec. 1904. He served in the European War from 1914; was Major, commanding the Scots Guards, 26 Oct. 1914, to 12 March, 1915; was six times mentioned in Despatches; was Temporary Brigadier-General, 172nd Infantry Brigade, 57th Division, from 20 Aug. 1916, to 7 April, 1919; twice wounded; commanding 2nd Battn. Scots Guards from July, 1919. He was created a Companion of the Distinguished Service Order [London Gazette, 1 Dec. 1914]: "George Camborne Beauclerk Paynter, Capt., 2nd Battn. Scots Guards. On the night of 24 Oct., while in command of the battalion, fought his trenches all night against repeated attacks from front and rear." He was A.D.C. to the Commander-in-Chief, British Expeditionary Force; A.D.C. to Field-Marshal Commanding-in-Chief, Home Forces; was given the Brevet of Lieutenant-Colonel 1 Jan. 1918. He was mentioned in Despatches; created a C.M.G. (Sir D. Haig's last list); received the Croix de Guerre in Dec. 1919, and was awarded a Bar to the Distinguished Service Order in Sept. 1919.

We have quoted from Lord Ernest Hamilton's "First Seven Divisions" in the account of Lord C. Hamilton in this book where he describes the inhospitable reception which made the German night attack on two battalions of the Guards at the village of Kruseik "a distinct failure as far as Capt. Paynter's company was concerned. The left-hand trenches were less fortunate. It may be that they were more unsuspecting, or perhaps the British accent of the figures advancing through the darkness was purer on the left than on the right. In any event, a report reached the battalion headquarters in rear about nine o'clock that these trenches had been rushed and all the occupants killed. On receipt of this news the two reserve companies of the Scots Guards were sent up under Major the Hon. H. Fraser to investigate, and if necessary to retake the lost trenches. These two companies filed silently through the main street of Kruseik, keeping close under the shadow of the houses on either side. Not a light was burning, and not a shot was to be heard. At the far end of the village Major Fraser halted the column and went forward alone to try and get into touch with Capt. Paynter in the right-hand forward trenches, and find out from him what the truth of the matter really was. He managed after a time to find that officer, who assured him that not only were his trenches still uncaptured, but that he had every intention of keeping them so. As to the trenches on his left he knew nothing. With this information Major Fraser made his way back to the east end of the village where he had left his men. He decided to investigate for himself the truth as to the left-hand trenches, and accordingly, accompanied by Lieut. Holbeche in the capacity of guide, and forty men, he crept down the cinder track which led from the road to the trenches in question. The trenches were in absolute silence, and he was beginning to doubt the story of their occupation, when suddenly a flashlight was turned on to his party, a word of command rang out, and a volley broke the stillness of the night. Major Fraser gave the word to charge, and the little party dashed forward with fixed bayonets, but they were shot down before the trenches were reached. Major Fraser was killed and Lieut. Holbeche severely wounded, and of the whole party only four returned. In the meanwhile the rest of the two companies which had been waiting at the end of the village street noticed a light in a house standing by itself in the fields. Lord Dalrymple and Capt. Fox held a consultation, and decided to surround it. When this was done, Sergt. Mitchell, with great courage, went up to the door and knocked. It was flung open and he was at once shot dead. The house, however, was well surrounded, and all within it were taken prisoner. They numbered over two hundred, including seven officers, and they were promptly sent to the rear under escort. Further back, however, the prisoners were transferred to the custody of some of the 2nd Queen's, and the Scots Guards escort rejoined the two companies at the end of the village, whereupon the lost trenches were recaptured and connection once more established with Capt. Paynter. This was not effected without considerable further loss. In addition to those already mentioned, Lieuts. Gladwin and Dormer were killed, and Colonel Bolton, Lord Dalrymple, Capt. Fox, Lord G. Grosvenor and the Hon. J. Coke were all wounded, and in the darkness of the night fell into the enemy's hands. The 2nd Scots Guards in all lost nine officers during this night's fighting. On the following day the battalion was ordered to abandon the Kruseik trenches, and was taken back into reserve, mustering only 450. Capt. Paynter and Capt. Fox got the D.S.O. for this night's work."

He was promoted to Major 28 Jan. 1915 ; was extra A.D.C. 4 Sept. to 18 Dec. 1915.

PENDAVIS, HUGH VALENTINE, Second Lieut., was born 14 Feb. 1895, son of the Rev. Whylock Pendavis, Rector of Hethe. He served in the European War, and was mobilized in the Special Reserve 179 days, and joined the Oxfordshire and Buckinghamshire Light Infantry, from the Special Reserve, 31 Jan. 1915 ; was Second Lieutenant, Royal Flying Corps, 9 May, 1915, to 31 May, 1918, as Observer, and from 1916 as Pilot. He was promoted to Lieutenant 27 July, 1916. He was employed under the Air Ministry 1 April, 1918. For his services in the European War he was mentioned in Despatches, and was created a Companion of the Distinguished Service Order [London Gazette, 1 Dec. 1914]: " Hugh Valentine Pendavis, Second Lieut., 3rd Oxfordshire and Buckinghamshire Light Infantry, attached 2nd Battn. On 3 Nov. conspicuous good work in advancing from his trench and assisting in driving away the enemy, who were commencing to dig a new trench within thirty yards of his own. Thirty of the enemy were shot down on this occasion."

PEPYS, FRANCIS, Second Lieut., was born at Budleigh Salterton, Devonshire, 2 April, 1891, son of Colonel Arthur Pepys, late 60th Rifles. He was educated at Charterhouse, where he was in the Cricket Eleven, and he subsequently joined the Special Reserve, attached to the Devonshire Regt. He was gazetted to the 2nd Oxfordshire and Buckinghamshire Light Infantry, as Second Lieutenant, in May, 1913. He served in the European War, and was created a Companion of the Distinguished Service Order [London Gazette, 1 Dec. 1914]: " Francis Pepys, Second Lieut., 2nd Battn. The Oxfordshire and Buckinghamshire Light Infantry. On 3 Nov., for conspicuous good work in advancing from his trench and assisting in driving away a party of the enemy who were commencing to dig a new trench within 30 yards of his own ; 30 of the enemy were shot down on the occasion. (Since killed in action)." His Commanding Officer wrote : " He most thoroughly earned it for the splendid way he, with three others, turned 30 or 40 Germans out of a trench, and for his splendid leading on other occasions." He was killed on 12 Nov. 1914, while stepping out of his trench the morning after his battalion had materially contributed to the rout of the Prussian Guard. He was mentioned in Sir John French's Despatch of the 14th Jan. 1915. Second Lieut. F. Pepys was fond of shooting, steeplechasing, cricket, golf, fishing and ski-ing. He played cricket for the Aldershot Command in 1913 and 1914, and won the Officers' Race in the Vine Hunt Point-to-Point in 1914.

Francis Pepys.

RAIT-KERR, WILLIAM CHARLES, Lieut., was born 6 Aug. 1886, at Rathmoyle, Edenderry, Ireland, son of Sylvester Rait-Kerr, a Scotchman residing in Ireland, and Mary Isabel Rait-Kerr, an Englishwoman, third daughter of the late Major-General C. S. Hutchinson, C.B., R.E., for many years Government Inspector of Railways. He was educated at a Preparatory School, Arnold House, Llanddulas ; at Rugby, and at the Royal Military Academy, Woolwich, and obtained his commission in the Royal Field Artillery 28 July, 1907. He served at home till war broke out, and then went to France with the 1st Division, from Aldershot, under Sir Douglas Haig, in the 57th Battery, 43rd Brigade, Royal Field Artillery. He was gazetted Captain 4 Nov. 1914. Capt. Rait-Kerr was said to be specially useful all through the fighting, in the Retreat from Mons and during the Battle of Ypres, in directing the fire of his battery by telephone. For about 10 days before his death he was in command of an advanced gun—the rest of the battery having gone to the rear to rest and refit. During that time he did very good work, and on 8 Nov. received the congratulations of his Brigadier, who enclosed to him a letter of thanks from the Colonel of a French Zouave Regiment. He was on his way from the advanced trench to the gun when he was shot through the head by a German sniper (10 Nov. 1914). His body was recovered next day and buried beside the advanced gun, near Veldhoek, four miles east of Ypres. The following appeared in " Eye Witness's " account in the " Times " of 17 Nov. 1914, and is an exact description of the work done by Capt. Rait-Kerr : " On our extreme left, one of our Howitzer Batteries, whose fire was being most effectively directed, selected, as its first target, a farm from which a machine gun was harassing our infantry. It scored a hit at the first round and knocked out the machine gun. The second target was a house occupied by snipers. This was set alight by a shell, and when the occupants bolted they came under the rapid fire of our infantry. The third target was another building, from which the Germans were driven and then caught in the open by shrapnel." Capt. Rait-Kerr was mentioned in Sir John French's Despatch, dated 14 Jan. 1915, and was created a Companion of the Distinguished Service Order [London Gazette, 1 Dec. 1914]: " William Charles Rait-Kerr, Lieut., Royal Field Artillery. For gallant conduct in bringing up a gun to within

William C. Rait-Kerr.

250 yards of the enemy in a wood, blowing down a house in which the enem were working a machine gun. (Since killed in action)."

RUSSELL, JAMES REGINALD, Second Lieut., was born 9 Oct. 189; at Westbury, Pembridge, Herefordshir son of Henry Freeman Russell, J.P., Southfield, Leominster, Herefordshire, a Martha Mary Russell. He was educate at Bromsgrove and Sandhurst; gazett to the West Kents in July, 1914 ; join the Queen's Own Royal West Kent Reg 8 Aug. 1914, and served in the Europe: War ; was present at the Battle of tl Marne, being for some weeks at Misse; the Battle of the Aisne, and Neu Chapelle. It was here that Lieut. Russ was one of the two officers left out of 1 It was left to them to fight the regime and bring it out of action, and for whic they were personally congratulated b General Smith-Dorrien. He served as Seco Lieutenant till 27 Oct. 1914, and was pr moted Lieutenant 28 Oct. 1914. Lieu J. R. Russell was mentioned in Despatches in Jan. 1915, and created Companion of the Distinguished Service Order [London Gazette, 1 De 1914], being one of the D.S.O.'s first gazetted during the European Wa " James Reginald Russell, Second Lieut., 1st Battn. The Queen's Ov (Royal West Kent Regt.). For exceptional grit and gallantry in tl trenches near Neuve Chapelle between 23 and 29 Oct." He was promote to Captain. In 1919 Capt. Russell married Gwendolen Edith, daughter the Rev. G. W. Lawson.

James R. Russell.

SAMPSON, GEORGE ELLIS, Lieut., was born 27 July, 1887, son Capt. George Dennis Sampson, J.P., of Scarriff, County Clare, and Fann Catherine (who died in 1915), daughter of W. E. Wall. He was gazett to the Royal Inniskilling Fusiliers 4 May, 1907 ; became Lieutenant, Roy Inniskilling Fusiliers, 21 May, 1910, and Army Signal Service 2 Sept. 191 He served in the European War from 1914 ; was promoted to Capta 1 Feb. 1915 ; was Acting Major 28 Sept. 1917, to 10 Nov. 1918, and Actin Lieutenant-Colonel from 11 Nov. 1918. He was mentioned in Despatch four times, and created a Companion of the Distinguished Service Ord [London Gazette, 1 Dec. 1914]: " George Ellis Sampson, Lieut., The Roy Inniskilling Fusiliers (Army Signal Service). On 30 Sept. and previo days this Officer carried messages under rifle and shell fire. He was knocke down by shell fire, but did not relinquish his duty." He became Captai Royal Inniskilling Fusiliers, 1 Feb. 1915, and was given the Brevet of Majo 3 June, 1917.

SAMPSON, PATRICK, Capt., was born 4 Jan. 1881, son of M. Sampson entered the Army 30 Jan. 1906 ; became Captain 30 July, 1909 ; Majo 30 Jan. 1918 ; served in the European War, 1914–17 ; was wounded twice mentioned in Despatches, and created a Companion of the Dis tinguished Service Order [London Gazette, 1 Dec. 1914]: " Patrick Samp son, Capt., R.A.M.C. Has shown frequent and conspicuous gallantr throughout the campaign, especially on 21 and 22 Oct., attending wounde men under very heavy shell fire." He married, in 1917, Dorothea, daught of Commander D. H. Kirwan, R.N.

SCHREIBER, EDMUND CHARLES ACTON, Lieut., was born : April, 1890, son of Colonel (Temporary Brigadier-General) Acton Lemu: Schreiber, C.B., D.S.O., A.D.C., and Evelyn May, daughter of Lieut Colonel Edmund Darcy Hunt. He was gazetted to the Royal Artiller 23 Dec. 1909, and became Lieutenant 23 Dec. 1912. Lieut. Schreibe served in the European War from 1914 ; was promoted to Captain 23 De 1915, and Staff Captain, 1st Army, British Armies in France, 17 June t 2 Nov. 1916. He was mentioned in Despatches ; was given the Brevet c Major 1 Jan. 1918, and created a Companion of the Distinguished Servic Order [London Gazette, 1 Dec. 1914]: " Edmund Charles Acton Schreibe Lieut., Royal Field Artillery. For very gallant conduct on 14 Sept. i saving horses which had become entangled in a blocked road, and mai handling guns away from a position which had become untenable from very heavy shell fire, continuing to work, although wounded." He wa Temporary Captain from 29 May to 22 Dec. 1915, and became Captain 2 Dec. 1915. Capt. Schreiber married, in 1916, Phyllis, only daughter c the late Major Barchard, and they have one daughter.

SPENCER, AUBREY VERE, Lieut., was born 4 April, 1886, at Kensing ton, London, only son of Aubrey J Spencer, Esq., M.A., J.P., Barrister-a Law, of Wheatfield Park, Oxfordshire, an Florence Mary Spencer, daughter of th late Frederick H. Janson, Esq. He wa educated at Marlborough (1900–4 B 1 and joined the 3rd Battn. Oxfordshire an Buckinghamshire Light Infantry 28 Jar 1907 ; became Lieutenant 5 March, 1910 Captain 2 Feb. 1915, and Temporary Majo 27 June, 1918. He proceeded to Franc with the 2nd Battn. Oxfordshire an Buckinghamshire Light Infantry, in th Expeditionary Force, 13 Aug. 1914, an took part in the battles of the Marne, th Aisne and Ypres, 1914. He was mentione in Despatches, and created a Companio of the Distinguished Service Order [Londo Gazette, 1 Dec. 1914]: " Aubrey Vere Spencer, Lieut., 3rd Battn. Th Oxfordshire and Buckinghamshire Light Infantry. For good work in a

Aubrey Vere Spencer.

attack on 24 Oct., and in repelling night attacks on 21, 22 and 23 Oct." He was wounded on 26 Nov. 1914, and transferred to England 3 Dec. 1914. Capt. Spencer was again mentioned in Despatches 17 Feb. 1915; was Adjutant, 3rd Battn. Oxfordshire and Buckinghamshire Light Infantry, 27 Jan. 1916, to 7 Oct. 1917; promoted Temporary Major 27 June, 1918.

STANLEY, THE HONOURABLE ALGERNON FRANCIS, Major. was born 8 Jan. 1874, sixth son of the 16th Earl of Derby and Lady Constance Villiers, daughter of the 4th Earl of Clarendon. He was educated at Wellington College, and entered the Army in Oct. 1899, in the 1st Life Guards. He served in South Africa, 1899–1900, as Special Service Officer; took part in the operations in Cape Colony, south of Orange River, in 1900, and received the Queen's Medal with two clasps. He became Captain 4 April, 1906. He served in the European War from 1914 to 1918; became Major 5 Nov. 1914; was Temporary Lieutenant-Colonel, 1st Life Guards, 2 Dec. 1914, to 19 June, 1916; Temporary Colonel, commanding 14th Mounted Brigade, Home Forces, 6 April to 28 July, 1916; Temporary Colonel, Guards' Machine Gun Regt., 10 May, 1918, to 4 March, 1919. He was mentioned in Despatches, and created a Companion of the Distinguished Service Order [London Gazette, 1 Dec. 1914]: "The Hon. Algernon Francis Stanley, Major, 1st Life Guards. On 7 Nov. he led his regiment with great resolution and skill during an advance to support and protect the right flank of the 4th Guards Brigade, which had become uncovered by the retreat of a portion of the line. He held on to his position although out of touch on either flank, and thereby materially helped the 4th Guards Brigade to re-establish their line during the following night." He was given the Brevet of Lieutenant-Colonel in Jan. 1915, and promoted to Lieutenant-Colonel, July, 1916, to command 2nd Life Guards. He married, in April, 1918, Lady Mary Crichton, widow of Viscount Crichton, M.V.O., D.S.O., daughter of the late Duke of Westminster and the Dowager Duchess of Westminster.

STEWARD, SIDNEY JOHN, Capt., was born at Worcester, 1879, son of John A. Steward, J.P. He was educated at Cathedral King's School, Worcester; Downing College, Cambridge, and St. Thomas's Hospital, London. He served in the European War from 1914; was present at the Retreat from Mons; advance on the Marne and Aisne; Ypres, 1914; Loos, 1915 (with No. 1 Field Ambulance, 1 Division until March, 1916); Medical Officer, No. 5 Infantry Base Depôt, Rouen; Senior Medical Officer, Paris (March, 1917); Second-in-Command, 1/2nd East Lancashire Field Ambulance (June, 1917); Second-in-Command, 24th Field Ambulance (8th Division) (Oct. 1917), and with this unit (Acting Major, Jan. 1918) at Villers Bretonneux, March, 1918, and Retreat to the Marne, 1918; O.C., 31st Motor Ambulance Convoy (June, 1918),

Sidney John Steward.

and with this unit (8th Corps) in advance during Oct. 1918, reaching Mons on Armistice Day, 1918; also served as a combatant in the 1st Battn. Suffolk Regt., in the South African War, 1899 to 1901. He was mentioned in Despatches, and created a Companion of the Distinguished Service Order [London Gazette, 1 Dec. 1914]: "Sidney John Steward, Capt., Royal Army Medical Corps (Special Reserve). Went with a party of stretcher-bearers across ground swept by rifle and shell fire to Langemark village, and removed 11 wounded men."

STEWART, HERBERT WILLIAM VANSITTART, Lieut., was born 15 Aug. 1886, fourth son of Lieut.-General John Mackie Stewart, Bengal Infantry, and Florence, daughter of the late Henry Vansittart. He was educated at Fettes College, Edinburgh, and joined the Royal Scots Fusiliers from Sandhurst, as Second Lieutenant, 29 Aug. 1906; became Lieutenant 21 Jan. 1911. He served in the European War from 1914 to 1918; became Captain 24 Oct. 1914. He was mentioned in Despatches, and created a Companion of the Distinguished Service Order [London Gazette, 1 Dec. 1914]: "Herbert William Vansittart Stewart, Lieut., 2nd Battn. The Royal Scots Fusiliers. On 24 Oct., when two German machine guns were enfilading his trench at 200 yards' range, he went out and shot down two teams, one after the other, and silenced the guns." He held a Special Appointment commanding a Company of Gentleman Cadets 29 Sept. 1918. Capt. Stewart married, in 1919, Doreen Evelyn, youngest daughter of J. G. Ohlenschlager, of Ashurst, Fernhurst, Sussex.

Herbert W. V. Stewart.

Frederick C. Tanner.

TANNER, FREDERICK COURTNEY, Capt., was born 2 Dec. 1879, son of C. F. Tanner and Mrs. Tanner. He was educated at Marlborough (1893–97); joined the Lancashire Fusiliers, as Second Lieutenant, 12 Aug. 1899; became Lieutenant 16 May, 1900, and Captain 15 Feb. 1904, and was Adjutant from 1901–4; was transferred to the Royal Scots, 1908. He served in the

European War; was wounded; mentioned in Despatches, and created a Companion of the Distinguished Service Order [London Gazette, 1 Dec. 1914]: "Frederick Courtney Tanner, Capt., attached 2nd Battn. The Royal Scots (Lothian Regt.). By gallant leading, forced passage of canal north of Vieille Chapelle on 12 Oct., and was largely responsible for success of general operations. Has invariably done well." Capt. Tanner was invested with the decoration by the King 27 May, 1915. He was employed at the Royal Military College, Camberley, Feb. 1915, to April, 1916; on the General Staff, France, April, 1916, to April, 1917; as Instructor at the Staff Course, Cambridge, April to Dec. 1917; on the General Staff, Italy, Dec. 1917, to April, 1918, and in France from April, 1918. He was given the Brevet of Lieutenant-Colonel 3 June, 1918, and was created a C.M.G. in 1919; received the Croix de Guerre, and was made an Officer of the Order of the Crown of Italy, 1915.

TRAILL, THOMAS BALFOUR, Capt., was born 21 Nov. 1881, only son of the late Major-General George Traill, C.B. He joined the Army, as Second Lieutenant (Unattached), 28 July, 1900, and the Indian Staff Corps 9 Oct. 1901; became Lieutenant 28 Oct. 1902; Captain, Indian Army, 28 July, 1909, and Royal Scots Fusiliers 18 July, 1914. He served in the European War from 1914; was wounded; mentioned in Despatches, and created a Companion of the Distinguished Service Order [London Gazette, 1 Dec. 1914]: "Thomas Balfour Traill, Capt., 1st Battn. The Royal Scots Fusiliers. After being wounded in the knee, rode back under fire for reinforcements, returned and remained with his company during retirement (Aug. 23)." He became G.S.O., 3rd Grade, War Office (temporary), 26 July, 1915; was given the Brevet of Major 1 Jan. 1917, and retired with the rank of Major 24 April, 1919. He married, in 1918, Winifred Jean Bertha, daughter of Major W. A. Warren.

TURNBULL, DUDLEY RALPH, Second Lieut., was born 15 Oct. 1891, son of Colonel Charles F. A. and Evelyn Turnbull, of Whiteways, near Farnham, Surrey. He was educated at Wellington College and Sandhurst, and was gazetted to the Gordon Highlanders 13 March, 1912, and went with the regiment to France in Aug. 1914, with the original Expeditionary Force, and at the time of his death had served with great distinction throughout the war. He fought at Mons and Cambrai, and took part in the Grand Retreat. When his battalion was reformed he was placed in charge of the Machine Gun Section, and was for conspicuous gallantry awarded the Distinguished Service Order on 13 Oct. His decoration was gazetted 1 Dec. 1914: "Dudley Ralph Turnbull, Second Lieut., Gordon Highlanders. For conspicuous gallantry on 13 Oct., in serving his Maxim gun when detachment were all wounded, until he also was wounded in two places, and his gun damaged by a shell. He

Dudley R. Turnbull.

subsequently recovered the gun, bringing it away on his shoulder." He had become Lieutenant 30 Oct. 1914, and was sent home wounded, and on recovery returned to the front, serving in the trenches in the winter of 1914–15. He was sent home suffering from pneumonia, Jan. 1915, and shortly again returned to the front. He was promoted Temporary Captain 1 Feb. 1915, and appointed to the Staff. He became Captain 1 Oct. 1915. It was while on Staff duty that he received orders to proceed to the 2nd Battn. of his regiment, which was heavily engaged. His C.O. fell in this action, and Capt. Turnbull assumed command, which he held for some months. He was given his Brevet as Major, for distinguished service in the field, and next held several Staff appointments, and was on the Divisional Staff till he was given command of the 20th Battn. of the Manchesters. Lieut.-Colonel Turnbull, who had been three times mentioned in Despatches, was killed in action 1 Oct. 1917, when only 25 years of age, when attached to and in command of a battalion of the 20th Manchester Regt. He was a member of the London Scottish Rugby Fifteen, and Londoners will remember him as a member of the Scottish side that played Rugby football at Richmond. He also took a keen interest in the regimental team of the 1st Gordon Highlanders.

The Second-in-Command of the battalion writes: "Although with the battalion a comparatively short time, he won the respect and admiration of all by his thorough knowledge of his job, his soldierly bearing, and, above all, the care he showed for all ranks."

His Adjutant writes: "I have lost the best commanding officer I ever had, and also the best friend. We all loved him in the battalion, and the men would have gone anywhere with him—he was such a fine soldier."

In a letter dated 30 Sept. 1917, immediately before going into action, Lieut.-Colonel Dudley Ralph Turnbull, D.S.O., wrote: "I am very pleased with the efficiency of my battalion now, and am sure they will do well." His Second-in-Command writes: "The battalion he trained has done magnificently during the recent operations." In the middle of Sept. 1917, Lieut.-Colonel Dudley Ralph Turnbull, D.S.O., was commanding his brigade, in the temporary absence of his General.

The following telegram has been received:—

"Buckingham Palace.

"To Colonel C. F. A. Turnbull,
"Whiteways, Farnham, Surrey.

"The King and Queen deeply regret the loss you and the Army have sustained by the death of your son in the service of his country. Their Majesties have read with much interest the splendid record of your son's services, and much deplore the death of so gallant an officer.

"Keeper of the Privy Purse."

The General Commanding the Division in which Lieut.-Colonel Dudley Turnbull, D.S.O., was serving, writes with reference to him: "He fell in the great battle we are now fighting, just after his battalion had distinguished itself in beating off a German counter-attack. He was moving about amongst his men, and setting a magnificent example of courage and coolness. He had done so much for the battalion he commanded that I know he will be sadly missed, but I feel sure his gallant spirit will live in them, and that all the soldierlike qualities they learnt from him will help them to do their duty like men. No one in this Division had a finer record, and we all feel we have lost a brave comrade, whom we could ill spare."

The Signalling Officer writes: "I can say with all my heart that I never met a braver man nor an officer who took as much pains to look after and guide those serving under him. We have lost a very great soldier and a very great man. I feel the loss very greatly indeed, as Colonel Turnbull was not only my C.O., but, I am happy to say, my friend, as he was to all, indeed. On many occasions your son's coolness and bravery had helped us all to do our duty, and the men would have followed him anywhere."

The following are extracts from letters written by brother officers of the Gordon Highlanders since received: "I cannot tell how very, very keenly all his friends feel his death. I saw him and wished him good luck only a few hours before the end, and I am very glad I had the chance."

"We were all so proud of your son in the regiment, and proud of the way he had got on."

Another officer writes: "This supreme sacrifice will be felt in the regiment enormously, and I can picture to myself all the men and N.C.O.'s in both battalions talking it over and relating all the small as well as the big things that he used to do that made them all love him so. I have heard numerous men of all ranks talking about him up here, and at the same time a feeling of proudness that he was in the Gordons. If it is any consolation to you to know that, your dear son was *beloved* by all officers, N.C.O.'s and men, and they would have followed him anywhere."

A memorial service was held at Seale Parish Church on Monday, 15 Oct. 1917.

WEMYSS, HENRY COLVILLE BARCLAY, Lieut., was born 26 April, 1891, son of the late Alexander Wemyss and Louise Frances Amelia Wemyss, of Mauritius and Bedford. He was educated at Bedford and Woolwich, and joined the Royal Engineers, as Second Lieutenant, 23 Dec. 1910, and became Lieutenant 21 Dec. 1912; Captain 23 Dec. 1916, and Brevet Major 3 June, 1918; Acting Lieutenant-Colonel since 19 Sept. 1917. He served in the European War from 1914; was present at Mons, the Marne, the Aisne, the First Battle of Ypres, at the Suvla Bay landing and evacuation, at the Suez Canal Defence, in Salonika, in the Struma Valley, at the Third Battle of Gaza (1917), and in the Palestine and Syria Campaign, 1918. He was promoted to Captain 23 Dec. 1916; was G.S.O.3, British Salonika Force, Egyptian Expeditionary Force, 28 May to 16 Sept. 1917; was Acting Lieutenant-Colonel, R.E., from 19 Sept. 1917. He was given the Brevet of Major 19 Sept. 1917; was five times mentioned in Despatches, and created a Companion of the Distinguished Service Order [London Gazette, 1 Dec. 1914]: "Henry Colville Barclay Wemyss, Lieut., Royal Engineers. Has shown conspicuous efficiency in Staff duties, and in keeping up communication with a long line of front composed of many units, where communication was often difficult. He has carried and delivered messages under fire with promptness and despatch." Lieut. H. C. B. Wemyss was also awarded the Military Cross [London Gazette, June, 1916].

HAYDON WHITE, HENRY BASIL, Lieut., was born 15 Feb. 1892, at Nottingham, son of Charles Haydon White, M.R.C.S., L.R.C.P., and Ethel Gertrude Handley White. He was educated at Cheltenham, and at the Royal Military College, Sandhurst, and joined the Royal West Kent Regt. 13 March, 1912. He served in the European War; was Temporary Lieutenant 1 Sept. 1914, and Lieutenant 3 Sept. 1914. He was created a Companion of the Distinguished Service Order [London Gazette, 1 Dec. 1914]: "Henry Basil Haydon White, Lieut., 1st Battn. The Queen's Own (Royal West Kent Regt.). Near Neuve Chapelle, for bringing his battalion out of action after ten successive days in the trenches, during which time he showed great powers of leadership and determination of a high order." On the night of 26 Oct. the enemy were in possession of all the trenches on the north-east side of Neuve Chapelle, but on the south-east side the Wiltshire Regt., the Royal West Kents, the King's Own Yorkshire Light Infantry and the East Surreys were still holding their ground, in advance of the town, behind which the rest of the 3rd Division were thrown back. The Wiltshires had to retire by noon, and the Royal West Kents now had the enemy on three sides of them. They would not, however, retire. Major Buckle and Capt. Legard were killed, and Lieuts. Williams and Holloway wounded. All the company officers on the left flank were now down, but the formation was re-organized under the direction of Sergt.-Major Penney, and Sergt.-Major Crossley. In the evening our troops in rear of the town counter-attacked and drove the Germans back for the whole of that night, but their machine guns continued to work havoc in the ranks of the assailants, and early on the morning of the 28th the attacking force had to fall back and the Germans reoccupied the town. Lord Ernest Hamilton says in "The First Seven Divisions" (page 197): "The position of the Royal West Kents was now as bad as ever, and once more half the battalion had to face about to its left flank and rear. The execution of this movement again took its toll of officers, Capt. Battersby and Lieut. Gore being killed, and Lieut. Moulton-Barratt wounded. The battalion had now lost twelve out of the fourteen officers with which it had gone into the trenches; Second Lieut. White and Second Lieut. Russell alone being left, and on these two it now devolved to maintain the spirit of the corps." At this time practically the whole of Neuve Chapelle was in the hands of the Germans, except the south-east corner by the La Bassée road, which was still held by the Royal West Kents, while, on the other side of that road, the angle which it makes with the Richebourg Road was held by the King's Own Yorkshire Light Infantry. At 8 a.m. on the 28th a force of French and British, under the command of General McCracken, attacked the town after a bombardment by French Artillery. At 5 p.m., however, the Germans were still in possession of Neuve Chapelle with the exception of the small area held by the Royal West Kents and the King's Own Yorkshire Light Infantry. In the evening, however, the Germans vacated the town. "The heroes of the three days' fighting," says Lord Ernest Hamilton, "were, of course, the Royal West Kents, who immortalized themselves by a performance which in many ways must be unique. The two surviving officers, Second Lieuts. White and Russell, were each awarded the D.S.O., and were, in addition, the subjects of some particularly flattering remarks on the part of Sir Horace." Sergt.-Majors Penney and Crossley were given the D.C.M., as were Sergt. Stroud and Private Alison. When, on the 28th at 2 a.m., the battalion was relieved by the Seaforths, it had lost over 300 men in the trenches of Neuve Chapelle. Lieut. Haydon White was mentioned in Despatches in Jan. 1915; was promoted to Captain 1 Dec. 1915, and was employed with the Egyptian Army in the Sudan from 26 Feb. 1916. He married, 20 June, 1917, at Cowes, Isle of Wight, Miriam Olive, youngest daughter of Alfred Barrett, of Lammas, Cowes, Isle of Wight, and they have one son.

Henry B. Haydon White.

WILLIAMS, OSMOND TRAHAIRN DEUDRAETH, Second Lieut., was born 26 Feb. 1883, eldest surviving son of Sir Osmond Williams, Bart., of Castle Deudraeth, Lord Lieutenant of Merionethshire and formerly M.P. for that county. He was educated at Eton, and received his first commission in the 19th Hussars. He fought in the South African War. He had retired from the Army, but enlisted on the outbreak of the European War in the Scots Greys. He was promoted to Second Lieutenant for gallantry in the field. He was created a Companion of the Distinguished Service Order [London Gazette, 1 Dec. 1914]: "Osmond Williams, Second Lieut., 2nd Dragoons (Royal Scots Greys). For general gallant service near Messines in ascertaining under fire the progress of night operations, and especially, on the night of 31 Oct., for leading the 12th Lancers to position for counter-attack, in which he took part, accounting for 11 of the enemy himself." Subsequently he exchanged into the Welsh Guards. He was gazetted Captain in April, 1915, and died 30 Sept. 1915, of wounds received on 27 Sept. while leading No. 1 Company, Welsh Guards, into action at Loos. Obituary notices appeared in the "Times" for 2 Oct. 1915. He had married, in 1912, Lady Gladys Margaret Finch-Hatton, only daughter of Lord Winchilsea, and they had one son, Michael Osmond, born 22 April, 1914, and one daughter, Elizabeth Anne, born 28 Aug. 1915.

WOODMAN, JAMES EDWARD SOMERVILLE, Capt., was born at Clifton 26 July, 1870, son of Commander C. E. S. Woodman, R.N. He served in the European War from 1914, and was created a Companion of the Distinguished Service Order [London Gazette, 1 Dec. 1914]: "James Edward Somerville Woodman, Capt., 2nd Battn. The Lancashire Regt. Commanded three companies of his regiment in the attack at Le Touquet, and afterwards commanded the section of defence which included the village." He was decorated by the King 2 Dec. 1914, on the occasion of His Majesty's visit to the Expeditionary Force. Major Woodman was killed in action in France 25–27 Sept. 1915. The Officer Commanding the 12th Northumberland Fusiliers wrote: "Major Woodman was with us through the bad time the battalion had on Saturday, 25 Sept., and after orders were received to take the German trenches by assault on the morning of Sunday, 26 Sept., he came up the hill with us and encouraged the men in the charge. The men could not run up the hill the whole way without a rest to get their breath again, and it was then that Major Woodman sat up and put up his field-glasses to look at the enemy's position. He was immediately shot through the heart, and fell over on his side. He was a brave and gallant officer, and you have the satisfaction of knowing that he died at the head of the battalion, facing the foe. We suffered very badly; only seven of our officers remained with the battalion after the charge, and of these only two were unhit. We all deplore Major Woodman's loss, as he was a man of very wide experience, and was of the greatest help to us. One of the last things he did was to tell my servant to get back down the hill, as the boy had been wounded in the wrist, but still was going on."

James E. S. Woodman.

Extract from the "Morning Post," 18 Oct. 1915: "Major James Edward Somerville Woodman, D.S.O., Lancashire Fusiliers, attached 12th Battn. Northumberland Fusiliers (killed in action), was born in July, 1870, and entered the West India Regt. in Jan. 1891. Promotion came in 1893 and 1898 (Captain), and in 1900 he transferred to the Lancashire Fusiliers, being posted to the 2nd Battn. He was recently promoted and attached to the Northumberland Fusiliers. From March, 1903, to Feb. 1906, Major Woodman was employed with the West African Frontier Force, and from July, 1909, to March, 1912, he held the Adjutancy of the King's Own Malta Regt. of Militia. Major Woodman had fought with great distinction in the present war. He was twice mentioned in Despatches in the London Gazette in Dec., and was decorated with the D.S.O. Before this he had seen service

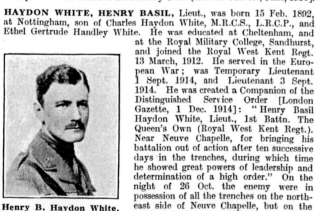

in Ashanti (1895-96), for which he received the Star; in the operations in Sierra Leone (1898-99), and in West Africa (Northern Nigeria—1903-4) (Medal with clasp)."

WYNDHAM, THE HONOURABLE EDWARD SCAWEN, Capt., was born 30 April, 1883, at Petworth House, Sussex, son of the 2nd Lord Leconfield. He joined the 1st Life Guards, as Second Lieutenant, in March, 1904, and became Lieutenant 21 Nov. 1904. He was promoted to Captain 10 May, 1911, and served in the European War from 1914, having gone to France in Aug. of that year as a Captain in the Expeditionary Force. He was mentioned in Despatches in Nov. 1914, and created a Companion of the Distinguished Service Order [London Gazette, 1 Dec. 1914]: "The Hon. Edward Scawen Wyndham, Capt., 1st Life Guards. Near Messines on 31 Oct.-1 Nov., during a night attack by the Germans, after some of his trenches had been taken and himself wounded, he counter-attacked, retook his trenches, and subsequently withdrew his squadron." "On 31 Oct.," says another account, "Capt. Wyndham, being already wounded in his lung, counter-attacked and retook his trenches." He was invested by the King at Buckingham Palace; returned to France in May, 1915; became Major 1 July, 1915; was Acting Lieutenant-Colonel 14 Dec. 1916, to 4 March, 1919, and Lieutenant-Colonel, 1st Life Guards, 1 July, 1919. He married, in 1907, Gladys Mary, daughter of Fitzroy W. J. Farquhar, brother of the 4th Baronet, and they have one son and one daughter.

London Gazette, 9 Dec. 1914.—"War Office, 9 Dec. 1914. His Majesty the King has been graciously pleased to approve of the appointment of the undermentioned Officers to be Companions of the Distinguished Service Order, in recognition of their services with the Expeditionary Force, specified below."

BEDINGFIELD, HENRY, Lieut., was born 10 Dec. 1889. He was educated at the Universities of Edinburgh (M.B., Ch.B., Honours), and London, and became House Surgeon, Queen's Hospital for Children, Hackney Road, E.; Assistant Medical Officer, Hackney Infirmary, and Clinical Assistant, City of London Chest Hospital. He entered the Army 24 Jan. 1913; served in the European War from 1914, and was created a Companion of the Distinguished Service Order [London Gazette, 9 Dec. 1914]: "Henry Bedingfield, M.B., Lieut., Royal Army Medical Corps. For coolness and daring in repeatedly superintending removal of wounded from the firing line under heavy fire." He became Captain 30 March, 1915. Capt. Bedingfield married, in 1915, Edith, fourth daughter of the late P. Grant, of Edinburgh.

BIRT, LIGHTLY HAROLD, Capt., was born 22 Oct. 1879, third surviving son of the late Sir William Birt, of Hatfield, and of Lady Birt, of Brickett Road, St. Albans. He got his commission from the Volunteers in 1900, and was promoted to Captain in 1910. He served in the European War from 1911. He was created a Companion of the Distinguished Service Order [London Gazette, 9 Dec. 1914]: "Harold Lightly Birt, Capt., 1st Battn. Royal Berkshire Regt. For skill and courage at Villers-Cotterets on 1 Sept. and at Metz Farm Valley 7 Sept. in holding his position." He was killed in action 5 Jan. 1915, aged 35 years. An obituary notice appeared in the "Times" of 11 Jan. 1915.

BURNETT-HITCHCOCK, BASIL FERGUSON, Capt., was born 3 March, 1877, at Chatham, son of the late Colonel T. Burnett-Hitchcock, of Week Manor, Winchester, Hants, and Amelia Burnett-Hitchcock. He was educated at Harrow and Sandhurst (Sword of Honour, Anson Memorial Sword, 1st passing out); joined the Sherwood Foresters 20 Feb. 1897; served in South Africa, 1899-1901, with the 1st Battn. Sherwood Foresters, Mounted Infantry, and on the Staff. Took part in the operations in the Orange Free State, Feb. to May, 1900; in Orange River Colony, May to 29 Nov. 1900; also in Cape Colony 1899-1900; again during operations in Orange River Colony and Cape Colony 30 Nov. 1900, to Feb. 1901 (Queen's Medal with three clasps). He became Captain 12 March, 1901; Staff College, 1903-4. He was Staff Captain, Eastern Command, 1905-9; General Staff Officer, 2nd Grade, Bermuda, 1910-12; D.A.A. and Q.M.G., 4th Division, Eastern Command, 1912.

B. F. Burnett-Hitchcock.

Capt. Burnett-Hitchcock served in the European War from 1914; was present at Le Cateau, the Marne, the Aisne, the First Battle of Ypres, Festubert (1915), Second Battle of Ypres, Loos and Battle of the Somme. He was mentioned in Despatches, 19 Oct. and 9 Dec. 1914, and was created a Companion of the Distinguished Service Order [London Gazette, 9 Dec. 1914]: "Basil Ferguson Burnett-Hitchcock, Capt., Sherwood Foresters (Nottinghamshire and Derbyshire Regt.). On 26 Aug. at Haucourt, France, for gallantry in rallying troops in disorder and leading them against the enemy, thereby ensuring an orderly evacuation of the village." He also received the 1914 Bronze Star. Capt. Hitchcock was again mentioned in Despatches 17 Feb. 1915, and was given the Brevet of Major 18 Feb. 1915; became Major 1 Sept. 1915; was mentioned in Despatches 1 Jan. 1916, and given the Brevet of Lieutenant-Colonel 3 June, 1916; was again mentioned in Despatches 15 June, 1916, 4 Jan. and 15 May, 1917; was given the Brevet of Colonel 1 Jan. 1917; was again mentioned in Despatches in Jan. 1918; was made a Chevalier of the Legion of Honour, 1914, and created a C.B., 1918. He was appointed Temporary Brigadier-General in France in 1916; Director of Mobilization at the War Office, with rank of Temporary Brigadier-General, 1917, and Director-General of Mobilization, with temporary rank of Major-General, 1918; was made an Officer of St. Maurice and St. Lazarus (Italy), 1918; Croix de Guerre (France), 1920;

promoted Major-General 3 June, 1919. On 22 Oct. 1902, at St. Margaret's, Westminster, Major-General Burnett-Hitchcock married Anne Austin, daughter of J. Robertson-Walker, of Gilgerran, Distington, Cumberland, and they have a son, Denys Austin, born 21 Sept. 1904.

BUTLER, SIDNEY GEORGE, Major, was born 18 May, 1874. He became Lieutenant, Royal Army Medical Corps 27 July, 1899; served in South Africa, 1899-1902. He was present at the Relief of Ladysmith, including action at Colenso; in the operations of 17 to 24 Jan. 1900, and action at Spion Kop; in the operations of 5 to 7 Feb. 1900, and action at Vaal Kranz; and the operations on Tugela Heights (14 to 27 Feb. 1900), and action at Pieter's Hill; served in the Transvaal in May and June, 1900; again in the Transvaal, west of Pretoria, 1900, including action at Frederickstad (17 to 25 Oct.); in Cape Colony, north of Orange River, including action at Ruidam; and again in the Transvaal, June to Oct. 1901, and Jan. to May, 1902 (Queen's Medal with five clasps, and King's Medal with two clasps). He was promoted to Major 27 April, 1911. Major S. G. Butler served in the European War, 1914-18, and was created a Companion of the Distinguished Service Order [London Gazette, 9 Dec. 1914]: "Sidney George Butler, Major, Royal Army Medical Corps. At Nissy, on 15 Sept. For coolness and courage in continuing all day to collect wounded under severe shell fire." He became Lieutenant-Colonel 1 March, 1915

CARLETON, CORNELIUS ASGILL SHAW, Capt., was born 18 May, 1883. He became Second Lieutenant, Welsh Regt., 22 Dec. 1906; Lieut. 25 May, 1910; and was employed with the West African Frontier Force, 1908-13. He served in the European War from 1914; 2nd Battn. (attached 6th Battn.) Welsh Regt.; became Captain 1 Nov. 1914; was created a Companion of the Distinguished Service Order [London Gazette, 9 Dec. 1914]: "Cornelius Asgill Carleton, Capt., 2nd Battn. The Welsh Regt. For daring and successful reconnaissances on several occasions, on the last of which, on 15 Sept., he was severely wounded." He was given the Brevet of Major 3 June, 1916, and was employed with the West African Frontier Force 16 April, 1919.

COTTRELL-DORMER, CHARLES MELVILLE, Second Lieut., was born at Bicester Hall, Bicester, 18 Feb. 1892, son of Capt. Cottrell-Dormer, of Rousham, Oxfordshire, and of Heath House and Stapleton Park, Gloucestershire, and Ursula Cottrell-Dormer, daughter of Thomas and Lady Elizabeth Leslie-Melville Cartwright. Through his mother, Lieut. Cottrell-Dormer was the great-grandson of David, 8th Earl of Leven and 7th Earl of Melville. He was educated at Mr. Lionel Helbert's, West Downs, and at Eton, and gazetted Second Lieutenant from the Special Reserve in June, 1915, to the 3rd Battn. Coldstream Guards, which is one of the best shooting units in the Service. Its officers and men have all fought with distinction, and the mentions range from Private Childer to Lieut.-Colonel Fielding. All Lieut. Cottrell-Dormer's men used to say that they thought he "had a charmed life." He had a wonderful eye, and hence was a good shot, and excellent at games. He

C. M. Cottrell-Dormer.

was deeply read in most subjects. After being twice mentioned in Despatches, Lieut. Cottrell-Dormer was created a Companion of the Distinguished Service Order [London Gazette, 9 Dec. 1914]: "Charles Melville Cottrell-Dormer, Second Lieut., 3rd Battn. Coldstream Guards. After all his men had been driven out of the trenches by enfilade fire, he remained to the last and got his wounded men away." He was promoted to Lieutenant; was invested by the King with the Order on 13 Jan. Lieut. Cottrell-Dormer was present at the end of Nov. 1914, at a Memorial Service held for his elder brother, the late Lieut. Clement Cottrell-Dormer, of the Scots Guards, and he had only recently returned to the front after sick leave (the last days and hours of which he spent visiting the wounded, and comforting bereaved widows and mothers), when he was mortally wounded during an attack on La Bassée on his late brother's 24th birthday, 6 Feb. He died on 8 Feb. 1915, aged 22, at Bethune, where he is buried, and a Memorial Service was held for him on his own 23rd birthday, so that the two brothers who were devoted to one another were not long divided by death.

Colonel J. A. C. Richardson Drummond-Hay, Coldstream Guards, wrote to Lieut. Cottrell-Dormer's parents as follows: "It is all the harder to bear when the son was such 'a very perfect gentil knight,' as poor Melville undoubtedly was, but it is a comfort to feel that his life that he laid down, though short, was such a beautiful one. I would have been terribly sorry if the regiment had not been represented (at the Memorial Service in Rousham Church), when your boy had done so much for its honour and glory. Two points that stand foremost in his death are these, that he was back with his beloved No. 3 Company, 3rd Battalion, Coldstream Guards, and that his devoted servant, Johnson, was by his side when he fell mortally wounded, and never left him till he passed peacefully away at 1 p.m. on Monday, 8 Feb., never having regained consciousness."

Capt. Vaughan (Coldstream Guards) wrote of him: "No words of mine can express the admiration, love and respect I had for your son. He was gallant, brave and a leader of men, and worshipped by the non-commissioned officers and men who came in contact with him, and if you could only have heard them talking of him, as I have done, in that very trying time in the early part of the war, when he was left alone to command No. 3 Company, you would know how we one and all will miss him."

Mrs. Monck, wife of General Monck, says: "Every officer in his regiment whom we have seen when they were at home for a few days' leave, have spoken so much of him and his great and wonderful bravery, and the Coldstream soldiers could not say enough of his great kindness to them as well as of his example of great courage."

Another extract from a letter reads : " I was his Company Sergeant-Major on the Aisne, and was with him throughout until he was invalided from St. Julien, near Ypres, just after the officer commanding the company was killed. He was then in temporary command of No. 3, and he carried that duty out excellently. The company thought such a great deal of him, as he was a brave and fearless leader, and his death is keenly felt by us all."

Sergt. W. Ward wrote : " May I offer you my deepest sympathy in your terrible loss (my boy commander). May God help you to bear it."

His servant wrote : " A braver man I have never known, and I shall miss him because I loved him."

ELLIOT, WILLIAM GRENFELL RIVERSDALE, Lieut., was born 17 April, 1892, at Muree, Punjab, India, son of William Henry Wilson Elliott, D.S.O., Lieut.-Colonel, I.M.S. (retired), and Charlotte E. P. (who died in 1914), eldest daughter of the late C. Furber. He was educated at Cheltenham, and at the Royal Military College, Sandhurst, and joined the Cheshire Regt., as Second Lieutenant, 11 Oct. 1911. He became Lieutenant 14 March, 1914, and served in the European War ; was wounded ; twice mentioned in Despatches, 19 Oct. and 9 Dec. 1914, and created a Companion of the Distinguished Service Order [London Gazette, 9 Dec. 1914] : " William Grenfell Riversdale Elliot, Lieut., 1st Battn. The Cheshire Regt. On 24 Aug. when, during a retirement, he ran back, picked up a wounded man, and carried him 100 yards to safety under a hot fire, being himself shot through both ankles." He became Captain 1 Oct. 1915. Capt. Elliott has the 1914 Star.

FLINT, ROBERT BRADFORD, Lieut., was born at Blackheath 30 Aug. 1891, son of James George Harry Flint, Elder Brother of Trinity House, and of Helen M. Flint. He was educated at Lindisfarne, Blackheath, and at Cheltenham College, and joined the Royal Engineers 20 July, 1911. He served in the European War from Aug. 1914 ; was four times mentioned in Despatches ; made a Chevalier of the Legion of Honour for gallantry during the operations between 21 and 30 Aug. 1914, and was created a Companion of the Distinguished Service Order [London Gazette, 9 Dec. 1914] : " Robert Bradford Flint, Lieut., Royal Engineers. At Missy, on 14 Sept., under a heavy shell fire, he assisted Capt. W. H. Johnston in working all day until 7 p.m., with their own hands, two rafts bringing back wounded and returning with ammunition, thus enabling the advanced brigade to maintain its position on the other side of the river." Lieut. Flint was mortally wounded on the night of the 22nd Jan. 1915, while at work in the trenches, and died a few hours afterwards, in the early hours of the 23rd. He was buried with full military honours in the graveyard at Dranôutre, Belgium.

Robert Bradford Flint.

FULLBROOK-LEGGATT, CHARLES ST. QUENTIN OUTEN, Lieut., was born 16 Aug. 1889. He was educated at Bath College, and at the Royal Military College, Sandhurst ; joined the Royal Berkshire Regt. 18 Sept. 1909, and became Lieutenant 17 Aug. 1911. He served in the European War from 1914 ; was Adjutant, Royal Berkshire Regt. 11 Sept. 1914, to 12 Feb. 1916 ; was promoted to Captain 10 May, 1915, and served on the Staff in France 30 March, 1916, to 7 May, 1919. Capt. Fullbrook-Leggatt was given the Brevet of Major 3 June, 1918. He was wounded ; mentioned in Despatches four times, and created a Companion of the Distinguished Service Order [London Gazette, 9 Dec. 1914] : " Charles St. Quentin Outen Fullbrook-Leggatt, Lieut., 1st Battn. Princess Charlotte of Wales's (Royal Berkshire) Regt. For gallant conduct during an attempt to regain a bridge over the Sambre, near Marnilles, on the night of the 25–26th Aug." He was also awarded the Military Cross. Capt. Fullbrook-Leggatt married, in 1917, Mary Katherine, daughter of Colonel C. H. Bittleston, R.A., of Ashleigh, Whitchurch, Devon.

GRIFFITH, ARTHUR LEFROY PRITCHARD, Lieut., was born 7 May, 1886, son of the Venerable Henry Wager Griffith (Vicar of Thorp Arch, Yorkshire, since 1905 ; late Archdeacon of Lahore) and Eleanor Eva, daughter of Lieut.-Colonel Pritchard, R.A. He was educated at Bilton Grange ; at Dover College, and at Clare College, Cambridge (B.A., 1908) ; entered the Royal Artillery 23 Dec. 1909, and became Lieutenant 23 Dec. 1912. He served in the European War from 1914 ; was mentioned in Despatches three times ; was wounded at the Battle of the Aisne, and twice at the Third Battle of Ypres, and created a Companion of the Distinguished Service Order [London Gazette, 9 Dec. 1914] : " Arthur Lefroy Pritchard Griffith, Lieut., 36th Brigade, Royal Field Artillery. On 14 Dec., after being wounded, he gallantly assisted in manhandling guns out of action until exhausted." He was Temporary Captain 29 May to 22 Dec. 1915 ; was promoted to Captain 28 Dec. 1915, and commanded the 459th Howitzer Battery, 118th Brigade, R.F.A. Capt. Griffith was awarded a Brevet Majority on 3 June, 1917, for distinguished conduct in the field at the Battle of the Somme. His favourite recreations

Arthur L. P. Griffith.

are hunting and Rugby football ; reserve (Rugby football) for England ; played for Rest of England, the North, Welsh Trials, Yorkshire, the Army, Blackheath and United Services teams.

LAWRENCE, WILLIAM LYTTLETON, Major, was born 4 Sept. 1873, son of Dr. and Mrs. Lawrence, of The Cedars, Chepstow. He was gazetted to the South Wales Borderers in July, 1893, becoming Lieutenant in Jan. 1896, and Captain in Sept. 1904. From the latter date to Sept. 1907, he was Adjutant of his battalion, and in Dec. 1907, was appointed A.D.C. to a Divisional Commander in India. Major Lawrence served in the European War. He was mentioned in Sir John French's Despatch of 8 Oct. 1914. He was killed in action on the 31st Oct. 1914. He was created a Companion of the Distinguished Service Order [London Gazette, 9 Dec. 1914] : " William Lyttleton Lawrence, Major, 2nd Battn. The South Wales Borderers (deceased). For gallantry and ability in repelling the enemy on 28 Sept."

LECKIE, MALCOLM, Capt., was born at Eltham, Kent, 18 April, 1880, son of James Blyth Leckie, of Crowborough, Sussex, and a descendant of the Leckie of the Barony of Leckie (Stirlingshire, 1352). One of his ancestors, Sir Walter Leckie, of the Bodyguard of King Charles VII. of France, commanded the Scottish troops at the Battle of Lagny on the 10th Aug. 1432—the last exploit of the Maid of Orleans—when these troops were instrumental in the utter defeat of the English under the Duke of Bedford. Sir John French, in his first Despatch, said that for the advance from the Marne his left wing rested on Lagny. Malcolm Leckie was educated at Blackheath Proprietary School, and privately abroad, and carried out his medical studies at Guy's Hospital, London. He was a

Malcolm Leckie.

member of the Blackheath Hockey Club, and used to play for the Army, and he was Captain of Guy's Hockey Club when at the hospital. He had also represented England against France, and played for the Blackheath Hockey Club. After having obtained his medical qualifications he joined the Royal Army Medical Corps in Feb. 1908, and was attached for four years to the Egyptian Army. Capt. Leckie served in the Sudan, up the Blue Nile and in Upper Egypt. Capt. Leckie served in the European War, and was attached for duty to the 1st Northumberland Fusiliers. He was appointed to the D.S.O., was wounded by shrapnel at Frameries, and died there from the effects of these wounds on the 28th Aug. 1914. He was created a Companion of the Distinguished Service Order [London Gazette, 9 Dec. 1914] : " Malcolm Leckie, Capt., Royal Army Medical Corps. For gallant conduct and exceptional devotion to duty in attending to wounded at Frameries, where he was himself wounded."

LIVEING, CHARLES HAWKER, Major, was born 1 April, 1872. He joined the Royal Artillery 12 Feb. 1892 ; became Lieutenant 12 Feb. 1895 ; was employed in Uganda Protectorate 9 Nov. 1899, to 21 April, 1901 ; became Captain 15 March, 1900 ; was Instructor, Ordnance College, 1 Jan. 1904, to 31 Dec. 1906 ; was promoted Major 8 June, 1909. He served in the European War from 1914 ; was twice mentioned in Despatches, and created a Companion of the Distinguished Service Order [London Gazette, 9 Dec. 1914] : " Charles Hawker Liveing, Major, 135th Battery, Royal Field Artillery. For bravery and devotion in withdrawing guns by hand under a heavy fire near Ligny, France, on 26 Aug. 1914." He was given the Legion of Honour, 4th Class, and became Lieutenant-Colonel 8 July, 1915.

LUCAS-TOOTH, DOUGLAS KEITH LUCAS, Capt., was born in Sydney, New South Wales, Australia, 10 Oct. 1880, son of the late Sir Robert Lucas Lucas-Tooth, Baronet, and Lady Lucas-Tooth. He was educated at Eton ; was given a Colonial Cadetship, and was commissioned in the New South Wales Mounted Infantry in March, 1899. He went with the first unit sent to South Africa, 1899 ; did very good service during that year, and was mentioned in Despatches by Colonel De Lisle. He was given his commission in the 9th Lancers in Dec., and joined the regiment in South Africa. He became Captain, 1908 ; served in the European War in 1914, and was created a Companion of the Distinguished Service Order [London Gazette, 9 Dec. 1914] : " Douglas Keith Lucas Lucas-Tooth, Capt., 9th (Queen's Royal) Lancers

D. K. L. Lucas-Tooth.

(deceased). For gallantry in action against unbroken infantry at Andrignies, Belgium, on 24 Aug." He led the charge at Andrignies, and skilfully rallied and took the squadrons out of action. He was killed near Vendresse on 13 Sept. 1914, by shrapnel.

MARGETTS, CECIL FRANCIS MOWBRAY, Lieut., was born 16 Dec. 1884. He was educated at Bedford Grammar School, and entered the Dorsetshire Regt. 20 May, 1905, becoming Lieutenant 24 Sept. 1908, and Captain 14 Oct. 1914. He served in the European War from 1914 ; was wounded ; twice mentioned in Despatches, and created a Companion of the Distinguished Service Order [London Gazette, 9 Dec. 1914] : " Cecil Francis Mowbray Margetts, Lieut., 1st Battn. Dorsetshire Regt. On 24 Aug. at Paturage, when the 1st Line Transport was ambushed, he rode forward and engaged the enemy, thus giving time for his vehicles to wheel about and escape with slight loss, he himself being wounded."

O'KELLY, HENRY KANE, Second Lieut., was born 6 June, 1894, son of William Henry O'Kelly, of Monkstown, County Dublin. He was educated at Clongowes, and entered the 3rd West Riding Regt. 24 Dec. 1914, becoming Lieutenant, A.S.C. in 1915, and Captain 24 Dec. 1917, and retired from the R.A.S.C. 28 Jan. 1919. He served in the European War, 1914–18 ; was twice mentioned in Despatches, and created a Companion of the Distinguished Service Order [London Gazette, 9 Dec. 1914] : " Henry Kane O'Kelly, Second Lieut., Army Service Corps. For coolness and gallantry at Le Cateau on 26 Aug., and for initiating at Crepy an attack on two motor-cars, which he and a small party captured under heavy musketry fire."

Henry Kane O'Kelly.

PENNYCUICK, JAMES ALEXANDER CHARLES, Lieut., was born 9 Jan. 1890. He joined the Royal Engineers 26 July, 1910, and became Lieutenant 21 Dec. 1912. He served in the European War from 1914. He was created a Companion of the Distinguished Service Order [London Gazette, 9 Dec. 1914] : " James Alexander Charles Pennycuick, Lieut., Royal Engineers. On learning that the bridge at Pontoise had not been destroyed, he went back with another officer and successfully blew it up during the Retreat." He became Captain 23 July, 1916 ; was G.S.O.3, 3 July, 1918, to 6 April, 1919, and Staff Officer to the Chief Engineer, 4th Army Corps, British Armies of the Rhine.

STAVELEY, ROBERT, Second Lieut., was born 28 Feb. 1892. He entered the Royal Artillery 23 Dec. 1911 ; became Lieutenant 23 Dec. 1914 ; Captain 8 Aug. 1916 ; was Acting Major, R.A., from 25 Sept. 1916. He served in the European War, 1914–18 ; was mentioned in Despatches five times, and created a Companion of the Distinguished Service Order [London Gazette, 9 Dec. 1914] : " Robert Staveley, Second Lieut., 121st Battery, Royal Field Artillery. At Ciry, on 16 Sept., under a very heavy shrapnel and high explosive shell fire went out and helped to carry into safety Gunner Davies, a telephone operator, who had been wounded and was unable to move."

WALKER, JOHN BARRY, Capt., was born at Lucknow 29 April, 1881, son of Francis Blennerhassett Walker (deceased), Civil Railway Engineer under Government of India, and Katherine Walker (née Spring). He was educated at Bath College, and at the Royal Military Academy, Woolwich, and joined the Royal Artillery, as Second Lieutenant, 6 Jan. 1900 ; became Lieutenant 3 April, 1901. He served in Malta from 1900 to 1902, and in India from 1902 to 1906. He was employed with the Canadian Forces 15 April, 1910, to 18 May, 1912, and became Captain 2 Jan. 1911. Capt. J. B. Walker served in the European War from about 17 Aug. 1914, with the 48th Heavy Battery, Royal Garrison Artillery, 3rd Division ; was present at Mons, Le Cateau, the Retreat to near Paris, the Advance to the Aisne, Neuve Chapelle (Nov. 1914), Kemmel in the winter of 1914 (all with the 3rd Division) ; as Brigade Major in the battles of Neuve Chapelle, Festubert and Loos (1915) ; as Staff Officer, Royal Artillery, 2nd Army, 1916 ; as Counter Battery Staff Officer in the Battle of Messines and the fighting on the Ypres front, 1917 ; on various fronts, 1918 ; the Advance to the Scheldt and the fighting connected with it on the Wytschaete and Menin fronts, 1918 ; the Advance into Germany, in Command of the 41st Heavy Artillery Brigade, 1918 ; with the Army of Occupation up to Aug. 1919. He was mentioned in Despatches 16 Oct. 1914, and created a Companion of the Distinguished Service Order [London Gazette, 9 Dec. 1914] : " John Barry Walker, Capt., Royal Garrison Artillery. At the Battle of the Aisne, on the 14th Sept., rescued a wounded gunner from under an ammunition wagon under heavy fire." He was again mentioned in Despatches 15 June, 1915 ; acted as Brigade Major of No. 1 Group, Heavy Artillery Reserve, from 1 March, 1915 ; Major 5 Aug. 1915 ; was mentioned in Despatches, 4 Jan. and 17 Dec. 1917, and became Acting Lieutenant-Colonel 12 Feb. 1917 ; Staff Officer, Royal Artillery (Army), June, 1916, to Feb. 1917 ; became Counter Battery Staff Officer, 10th Corps, on 12 Feb. 1917 ; commanded the 41st Brigade, Royal Garrison Artillery, from 17 Nov. 1918, to 16 April, 1919. He was mentioned in Despatches 20 Dec. 1918 ; awarded the French Croix de Guerre with Palms on 29 Jan. 1919; reverted from Acting Lieutenant-Colonel to Major 16 April, 1919. He married, 4 April, 1910, at Alrewas House, Ashbourne, Derbyshire, Sara Beatrice Bond, daughter of G. M. Bond, Esq., of Alrewas House, Ashbourne, Derbyshire, and of Sara Bond (née Warner), and their children are : Jeffery Francis, born 19 Jan. 1911 ; George Barry, born 2 Dec. 1912 ; Mary Beatrice, born 12 April, 1914, and Katherine Hope, born 20 March,1919.

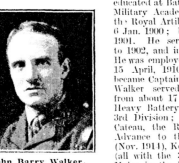
John Barry Walker.

WEST, ROGER ROLLESTON FICK, Second Lieut., was born 12 Jan. 1891, son

Roger R. F. West

of Samuel West, M.A., M.D.Oxon., F.R.C.P.London, and Margaret Nanny, daughter of Sir Edward Frankland, K.C.B., F.R.S., D.C.L., etc. He was educated at Rugby, and King's College, Cambridge (A.M.I.C.E., and B.A. Cantab.). He served in the European War, 1914–15 ; was twice mentioned in Despatches, and created a Companion of the Distinguished Service Order [London Gazette, 9 Dec. 1914] : " Roger Rolleston Fick West, Second Lieut., Intelligence Corps. For assisting Lieut. J. A. C. Pennycuick in the demolition of the bridge at Pontoise." He became Lieutenant.

London Gazette, 22 Dec. 1914.—" Admiralty, 22 Dec. 1914. The King has been graciously pleased to approve of the following appointment to the Distinguished Service Order, in respect of the undermentioned Officer, who was Second-in-Command of Submarine B11, which torpedoed the Turkish Battleship Messudiyeh, in the Dardanelles on the 13th Dec. 1914."

WINN, SYDNEY THORNHILL, Lieut., was born 29 Nov. 1888, at Boulogne-sur-Mer, France, son of Algernon William Winn, Surgeon, Royal Navy. He was educated at the Royal Naval College, Lee-on-Solent, and in H.M.S. Britannia ; joined the Royal Navy in May, 1904 ; served in H.M.S. Hindustan, 1904–6 ; in H.M.S. Glory, 1906–8 ; was Midshipman, Navigation School, 1908 ; Sub-Lieutenant, H.M.S. Hibernia, 1909–11 ; Lieutenant, H.M.S. Hampshire, 1911–12 ; H.M.S. Dolphin, for Submarines, 1912 ; H.M. Submarine C26 (1913) ; H.M. Submarine B11 (Mediterranean); H.M. Submarine B5 (Portsmouth); H.M. Submarine C1 (Sheerness) ; H.M. Submarine B7 (Venice). He served in the European War from 1914, in the Dardanelles Campaign, and was in Submarine B11 in her dash into the Dardanelles. He was created a Companion of the Distinguished Service Order [London Gazette, 22 Dec. 1914] : " Sydney Thornhill Winn, Lieut., Royal Navy." (See details above.) He was Instructional Officer and Senior Submarine Officer, Fort Blockhouse Submarine Depôt, Gosport, till April, 1918, when invalided out for eye-strain. He married, in 1919, Mary, eldest daughter of A. H. A. Knox, of Littlegarth House, Dorking.

Sydney Thornhill Winn.

London Gazette, 1 Jan. 1915.—" The King has been graciously pleased to approve of the following appointments to the Distinguished Service Order, in recognition of services with the Expeditionary Force, specified below."

ALEXANDER, THE HONOURABLE HERBRAND CHARLES, Capt., was born 28 Nov. 1888, son of the 5th Earl of Caledon and Lady Elizabeth Graham Toler, daughter of the 3rd Earl of Norbury. He was gazetted to the 5th Lancers 27 Jan. 1909 ; became Lieutenant 1 March, 1910, and Captain 11 Nov. 1914 ; was Acting Major, 25 April, to 29 Oct. 1918, and 4 Nov. to 14 Dec. 1918, and employed under the Air Ministry from 1 April, 1918. He was created a Companion of the Distinguished Service Order [London Gazette, 1 Jan. 1915] : " The Honourable Herbrand Charles Alexander, Capt., 5th (Royal Irish) Lancers. Has done exceedingly good work in action and in reconnaissance, since the commencement of the war." He married, in 1919, Millicent Valla, only daughter of Sir Henry Meredyth, Bart.

ARBUTHNOT, ALEXANDER GEORGE, Major, was born 30 Nov. 1873, at Woolwich, son of the late General Sir Charles Arbuthnot, G.C.B., Colonel Commandant, Royal Artillery, and Caroline, daughter of William Clarke, M.D. He was educated at Marlborough (1886–91, Cotton House), and the Royal Military Academy, Woolwich ; joined the Royal Field Artillery 21 Oct. 1893 ; served in England, India and Ireland ; became Lieutenant 21 Oct. 1896. He became Captain 8 Aug. 1900 ; was Adjutant, Royal Artillery, 16 April, 1904, to 15 April, 1907. He was promoted to Major 14 Nov. 1910, and served in the European War from 1914 ; was mentioned in Despatches in 1914, and twice in 1915, for services in France ; in 1916 (General Milne's Despatches), for services in Salonika, and again in Dec. 1917. He was created a Companion of the Distinguished Service Order [London Gazette, 1 Jan. 1915] : " Alexander George Arbuthnot, Major, 24th Battery, Royal Field Artillery. For very valuable work on several occasions between 19 Oct. and 23 Nov., in observing the fire of our batteries and furnishing valuable reports, though under very heavy shell fire from the enemy's guns, during the First Battle of Ypres-Armentières." He commanded the 24th Battery, R.F.A., in France, Sept. 1914, to Sept. 1915, and subsequently the 99th Brigade, R.F.A., in France and Salonika. He became Lieutenant-Colonel 3 March, 1916, and was created a C.M.G. in Jan. 1917, and awarded the Serbian Order of Karageorge with Swords. He later commanded a group of artillery in the 14th Corps during the Third Battle of Ypres in the autumn of 1917, and was severely wounded on 29 Nov. 1917. Capt. Arbuthnot married, 12 Sept. 1905, at Boldre, New Forest, Hampshire, Olive Mary May Burton, daughter of Colonel Burton, of Shirley Holmes, Lymington, Hampshire.

BOYD, JOHN DOPPING, Lieut., was born 14 Feb. 1886, eldest son of the late William Henry Boyd, Esq., J.P., D.L., Landowner, of Ballymacool, Letterkenny, County Donegal, Ireland, and of C. Agnes

John Dopping Boyd

Boyd, daughter of Colonel J. H. Dopping, of Ballymacool, Letterkenny. He entered the Queen's Royal West Surrey Regt. 6 July, 1907; became Lieutenant 10 Feb. 1911; Captain 10 Feb. 1915, and Brevet Major 1 Jan. 1917. He served in the European War from 1914 to 1918. He was mentioned in Despatches for the action on 31 Oct. 1914, and the First Battle of Ypres, and created a Companion of the Distinguished Service Order [London Gazette, 1 Jan. 1915]: "John Dopping Boyd, Lieut., 1st Battn. The Queen's (Royal West Surrey) Regt. For gallant leading of his men on the 31st Oct., and for consistently good work during the campaign." He was granted his Brevet Majority, and was mentioned in Despatches Jan. 1917; was also mentioned in Despatches in Dec. 1917, and awarded a Bar to the D.S.O. in Jan. 1918. He served with his battalion up to Jan. 1916, and subsequently as G.S.O.3, Brigade Major, and G.S.O.2. Major Boyd married, in Jan. 1916, Effie Harriet, daughter of H. D. Butterfield, Esq., of Durham, Bermuda, and they have a son, John Darrell Boyd, born 23 Sept. 1917.

CARY-BARNARD, CECIL DARCY VIVIEN, Capt., was born 11 Aug. 1876. He served in South Africa, 1900, with Lumsden's Horse, Feb. to Oct. 1900; took part in the operations in the Orange Free State, Feb. to

Cecil D. V. Cary-Barnard.

May, 1900, including actions at Karee Siding and Zand River; was present during operations in the Transvaal, May, 1900, including action near Johannesburg; also in Cape Colony, north of Orange River, 1900 (Queen's Medal with three clasps). He became Second Lieutenant, Wiltshire Regt., 27 Oct. 1900, and Lieutenant 13 Sept. 1902; was Lieutenant, West African Regt., 13 June, 1903, to 24 July, 1906; Captain 1 April, 1909, and Major 1 Sept. 1915. Major Cary-Barnard served in the European War from 1914. He was mentioned in Despatches, wounded, and created a Companion of the Distinguished Service Order [London Gazette, 1 Jan. 1915] "Cyril Darcy Vivien Cary-Barnard, Capt., 2nd Battn. Duke of Edinburgh's (Wiltshire Regt.). On the 11th Nov.

showed conspicuous gallantry and promptitude on his own initiative, in dislodging, with the aid of about 30 men, a company of Germans who had occupied a trench in our line." He was awarded a Bar to the Distinguished Service Order [London Gazette, 25 Aug. 1915]: "Cyril Darcy Vivien Cary-Barnard, D.S.O., Temporary Lieutenant-Colonel, Wiltshire Regt. For conspicuous gallantry and devotion to duty. He handled his battalion with conspicuous success and ability on numerous occasions, inspiring all ranks with confidence by his fearless example." He was given the Brevet of Lieutenant-Colonel 1 Jan. 1918; was Staff Captain, 51st Infantry Brigade, B.E.F., 17 Sept. to 29 Dec. 1915; commanded the 68th Infantry Brigade, British Armies in France, 14 Oct. 1917, to 31 Jan. 1919; was Base Commandant, Taranto, 11 Feb. 1919; Temporary Brigadier-General; was created a C.M.G. in 1919. In 1910 Lieut.-Colonel Cary-Barnard married Rita Persse, and they have one son and one daughter.

GRAHAM, FRANCIS, Second Lieut., was born 29 March, 1894, the only surviving son of Mr. and Mrs. Edward Graham, of Rendalls, Harrow, and Forston House, near Dorchester; and grandson of General Sir Robert

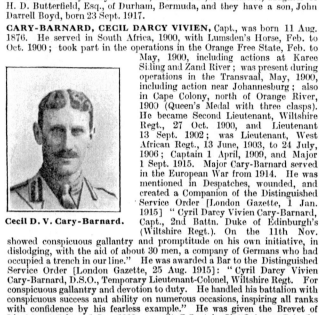

Francis Graham.

M. Stewart, G.C.B. He was educated at Harrow School, and the Royal Military Academy, Woolwich, and obtained his commission in the Royal Field Artillery in July, 1913. He served in France during the whole period of the war up to his death, taking part with the First Division in the Battles of Mons, the Marne, the Aisne, the First Battle of Ypres, Festubert, Richebourg and Loos; and with another Division in the chief battles of 1917. He was created a Companion of the Distinguished Service Order for an achievement in the First Battle of Ypres [London Gazette, 1 Jan. 1915]: "Francis Graham, Second Lieut., 51st Battery, Royal Field Artillery. When the officers of a part of the South Lancashire Regt. were disabled he took command and succeeded in holding an

important part of our trenches until relief arrived and drove out the enemy, who had effected a footing, the situation being thus saved by his prompt action." He was mentioned in Despatches in Feb. 1915; was promoted Lieutenant 9 June, 1915, and was given command of a battery, as First Lieutenant (Temporary Captain), in May, 1916. In Nov. of that year he was awarded the Military Cross [London Gazette, Nov. 1916]: "Francis Graham, Lieut., Temporary Capt., Royal Field Artillery. On one occasion he, with another officer, established his O.P. in a shell-hole on the outskirts of a village, and observed from thence under very heavy fire for the rest of the day. His coolness and gallantry are remarkable." He was gazetted Acting Major in Dec. 1916, and Captain in July, 1917. Major Graham was killed in action 28 March, 1918, by a shell which burst close to his battery.

GRENFELL, THE HONOURABLE JULIAN HENRY FRANCIS, Lieut., was born on 30 March, 1888, at 4, St. James's Square, London, S.W., eldest son of William Henry, 1st Baron Desborough, K.C.V.O., great-grandson of Pascoe Grenfell, M.P., of Taplow, and of Ethel Priscilla, daughter of the Honourable Julian Henry Charles Fane, and granddaughter of John, 11th Earl of Westmorland. He was educated at Summerfields,

Eton, and at Balliol College, Oxford. He rowed in the College boat, and in 1907 and 1908 was three in the Balliol Eight in the Ladies' Challenge Plate, and in the following year was bow in the Balliol Four which won the Wyfolds at Henley, and

Hon. J. H. F. Grenfell.

he also rowed for the O.U.B.C. coxswainless-fours. He was a fine boxer, and knocked out two professional pugilists in a boxing competition in the same week in which he wrote "Into Battle." At Johannesburg, in 1914, on Kangaroo, he made the record High Jump for South Africa—6 feet 5 inches. He was an excellent shot, and a good all-round sportsman. Of a fight in Johannesburg he wrote: "A member who was in training for the Amateur Championship said he would come and fight me. He was a fireman called Tye; he used to be a sailor, and he looked as hard as a hammer. I quaked in my shoes when I saw him, and quaked more when I heard he was 2 to 1 on favourite for the Championship, and quaked most when my trainer went to see him,

and returned with word that he had knocked out his men in a quarter of an hour. He went into the ring on the night, and he came straight at me like a tiger, and hit right; I stopped the left, but it knocked my guard aside, and he crashed his right clean on the point of my jaw. I was clean knocked out, but by the fluke of Heaven I recovered and came to and got on my feet again by the time they had counted six. I could hardly stand, and I could only see a white blur in front of me; but I just had the sense to keep my guard up, and hit hard at the blur whenever it came within range. He knocked me down twice more, but my head was clearing every moment, and I felt a strange sort of confidence that I was master of him. I put him down in the second round, with a right counter which shook him; he took a count of eight. In the third round I went in to him and beat his guard down, then crossed again with the right, and felt it go right home, with all my arm and body behind it. I knew it was the end, when I hit; and he never moved for twenty seconds. They said it was the best fight they had seen in Johannesburg, and my boxing men went clean off their heads and carried me twice round the hall. I was 11 stone 4 lbs., and he was 11 stone 3 lbs., and I think it was the best fight I shall ever have." Mrs. Meynell wrote in her "Memoir of Julian Grenfell": "When Julian left Summerfields for Eton at the age of thirteen he already had a serious conscious love of religion, such as was the tradition of his home. He was to have a life of wild physical activity, but he had a faith which could never be outstripped or left behind even from the boldest venture. He linked his belief to all physical activities that he so much loved. Faith has been carried among strange scenes and places by men in their enterprises, but faith has ridden her maddest rides with Julian, and with him on horseback made her wildest leaps into the air. All his life faith was the implicit companion of his energies. But now this thirteen-year-old belief was a very definite, straightforward thing, and had its expression in the simplest words. He was still at Summerfields. There had been a very bad thunderstorm. He said: 'I suddenly seemed to recognize God.' It was with him as with the poet who wrote: 'I saw eternity the other night.' In his after life he again referred more than ever to what he had experienced then. In his early years at Eton he began his love of Thomas à Kempis." Julian Grenfell passed into the Army first of all the University candidates. He was gazetted to the 1st Dragoons, as Second Lieutenant, on 15 Sept. 1909, and joined his regiment in India, whence he wrote: "The pig-sticking is beyond dreams. I can't tell you what it means to me. It is coursing with human greyhounds." And again: "The rains have come, but not real continuous rains; we go out on odd days to stick pigs in country blind with new bright grass, so that you gallop down a hidden well without any warning and without much surprise. I am afraid all other sports will fall flat after this." He became Lieutenant on 6 Oct. 1911, and in the winter of that year he went with his regiment to South Africa. He did not like Africa at first, but later he wrote: "I am getting fond of it in a way, almost against my better self," and at length he loved the veldt, with its "terrific greatness and greenness and dullness and bleakness." He had his greyhounds with him, and at this time wrote a poem "To a Black Greyhound," of which two verses are given:

> "Shining black in the shining light,
>   Inky black in the golden sun,
> Graceful as the swallows' flight,
>   Light as swallow, winged one,
> Swift as driven hurricane,
>   Double-sinewed stretch and spring,
> Muffled thud of flying feet—
>   See the black dog galloping,
>   Hear his wild hoof beat.
>
> "See him lie when day is dead,
>   Black curves curled on the broadest floor.
> Sleepy eyes, my sleepy head,
>   Eyes that were aflame before,
> Gentle now they turn no more,
>   Gentle now and softly warm,
> With the fire that made them bright.
>   Hidden as when after storm
>   Softly falls the night."

He wrote from South Africa: "My ponies are like Greek sculpture, only with a neater style of galloping; just think of how tired it would make you to play eight chukkers on horses which always had four legs in the air at once. The ground," he said, "is composed of holes and stones, thinly covered by a rough grass called Prativesticula. Thus for the horseman two alternatives lie open. Either you fall over the stone into the hole; when all that is to be done is to roll the stone on top of you and write the epitaph on it. Or, if you are careless enough to come down into the hole and fall on the stone, they have to lift your body, place it back in the hole, lift the stone, clean it, roll it on top of you, etc., which means 'more work for the undertaker.' I hope you follow me?" In July, 1914, he was looking forward to spending his leave in England when he heard the first rumours of the coming war, and wrote: "Don't you think it has been a wonderful and almost incredible rally to the Empire, with Redmond and the Hindus and Crooks and the Boers and the South Fiji Islanders all aching to come and throw stones at the Germans. It reinforces one's failing belief in the Old Flag and the Mother Country, and the Thin Red Line, and all the Imperial ideas, which get rather shadowy in peace time, don't you think? But this has proved to be a real enough thing." On 26 Sept. he reached England, and went straight with his regiment to Salisbury Plain. He had two days' leave at home, and on the night of 5 Oct. the regiment left for France. His sister had become a Probationer at the London Hospital, and his younger brother had been gazetted to the Rifle Brigade, as Second Lieutenant. Julian wrote from Flanders: "We have been fighting night and day; first rest to-day for four days. The worst of it is, no sleep practically. I cannot tell you how wonderful our men were, going straight for the first time into a fierce fire. They surpassed my utmost expectations. I have never been so fit or nearly so happy in my life before. I adore the fighting, and the continual interest which compensates for every disadvantage. I have longed to be able to say that I liked it, after all one has heard of being under fire for the first time. But it is beastly. I pretended for a bit to myself that I liked it, but it was no good, it only made one careless and unwatchful and self-absorbed; but when one acknowledged to oneself that it *was* beastly, one became all right again, and cool. After the firing had slackened we advanced again a bit into the next group of houses, which were the edge of the village proper. I cannot tell you how muddling it is. We did not know which was our front. We did not know whether our own troops had come round us on the flanks, or whether they had stopped behind and were firing into us. And besides, a lot of German snipers were left in the houses we had come through, and every now and then bullets came singing by from God knows where. Four of us were talking and laughing in the road, when about a dozen bullets came with a whistle. We all dived for the nearest door, and fell over each other, yelling with laughter, into a very dirty outhouse. James Leckie, the Old Old Man, said, 'I have a bullet through my best Sandon twillette breeches.' We looked, and he had. It had gone clean through. He did not tell us till two days afterwards that it had gone through him too. Here we are, in the burning centre of it all, and I would not be anywhere else for a million pounds and the Queen of Sheba. The only thing is that there's no job for the cavalry. So we have just become infantry, and man the trenches. I believe we're getting entrenching tools, which is good hearing. We want them. Colonel Burn is taking this, so I've only time to write one word of love. He's off. He tells me I was reported dead. But there's life in the old dog yet! Bless you both. I have not washed for a week, or had my boots off for a fortnight. But we cook good hot food in the dark in the morning before we start, and in the night when we get back to our horses; and we take our good cold rations with us in the daytime. It is all *the* best fun. I have never, never felt so well or so happy, or enjoyed anything so much. It just suits my stolid health, and stolid nerves, and barbaric disposition. The fighting excitement vitalizes everything, every sight and word and action. One loves one's fellow-man so much more when one is bent on killing him. And picnicking in the open day and night (we never see a roof now) is the real method of existence. There are loads of straw to bed-down on, and one sleeps like a log, and wakes up with the dew on one's face. The stolidity of my nerves surprises myself. I went to sleep the other day when we were lying in the trenches with the shrapnel bursting within fifty yards all the time, and a noise like nothing on earth. The noise is continual and indescribable. The Germans shell the trenches with shrapnel all day and all night; and the Reserves and ground in the rear with Jack Johnsons which, at last, one gets to love as old friends. You hear them coming for miles, and everyone imitates the noise; then they burst with a plump and make a great hole in the ground, doing no damage unless they happen to fall into your trench or on to your hat. They burst pretty nearly straight upwards. One landed within ten yards of me the other day, and only knocked me over and my horse. We both got up and looked at each other, and laughed. It did not even knock the cigarette out of my mouth. . . . We took a German officer and some men prisoners in a wood the other day. One felt hatred for them as one thought of our dead; and as the officer came by me I scowled at him, and the men were cursing him. The officer looked me in the face and saluted me as he passed, and I have never seen a man look so proud and resolute and smart and confident in his hour of bitterness. It made me feel terribly ashamed of myself. About the shells: after a day of them, one's nerves are really absolutely beaten down. I can understand now why our infantry have to retreat sometimes; a sight which came as a shock to me at first, after being brought up in the belief that the English infantry cannot retreat. . . . We had been worried by their snipers all along, and I had been always asking for leave to go out and have a try myself. Well, on Tuesday, the 16th, the day before yesterday, they gave me leave, only after great difficulty. They told me to take a section with me, and I said I would sooner cut my throat and have done with it. So they let me go alone. Off I crawled through sodden clay and trenches, going about a yard a minute, and listening and looking as I thought it was not possible to look and listen. I went out to the right of our lines, where the 10th were, and where the Germans were nearest. I took about thirty minutes to do thirty yards; then I saw the Hun trench, and I waited there a long time, but could see or hear nothing. It was about ten yards from me. Then I heard some Germans talking, and saw one put his head up over some bushes, about ten yards behind the trench. I could not get a shot at him; I was too low down, and of course I could not get up. So I crawled on again very slowly to the parapet of their trench. It was very exciting. I was not *sure* that there might not have been someone there, or a little further along the trench. I peeped through their loop-hole and saw nobody in the trench. Then the German behind put his head up again. He was laughing and talking; I saw his teeth glistening against my foresight, and I pulled the trigger very slowly. He just grunted and crumpled up. The others got up and whispered to each other. I do not know which were most frightened, them or me. I think there were four or five of them. They could not trace the shot; I was flat behind their parapet and hidden. I just had the nerve not to move a muscle and stay there. My heart was fairly hammering. They did not come forward and I could not see them, as they were behind some bushes and trees, so I crept back inch by inch. I went out again in the afternoon, in front of our bit of the line. About sixty yards off I found their trench again, empty again. I waited there for an hour, but saw nobody. Then I went back, because I did not want to get inside some of their patrols who might have been placed forward. I reported the trench empty. The next day, just before dawn, I crawled out there again and found it empty again. Then a single German came through the woods towards the trench. I saw him fifty yards off. He was coming along, upright and careless, making a great noise. I heard him before I saw him. I let him get within twenty-five yards, and shot him in the heart. He never made a sound. Nothing for ten minutes, and then there was a noise and talking, and a lot of them came along through the wood behind the trench about forty yards from me. I counted about twenty, and there were more coming. They halted in front, and I picked out the one I thought was the officer, or sergeant. He stood facing the other way, and I had a steady shot at him behind the shoulders. He went down, and that was all I saw. I went back at a sort of galloping crawl to our lines and sent a message to the 10th that the Germans were moving up their way in some numbers. Half an hour afterwards they attacked the 10th and our right in massed formation, advancing slowly to within ten yards of the trenches. We simply mowed them down. It was rather horrible. I was too far to the left. They did not attack our part of the line, but the 10th told me in the evening that they counted 200 dead in a little bit of the line, and the 10th and us only lost ten. They have made quite a ridiculous fuss about me stalking, and getting the message through. I believe they are going to send me up to our General, and all sorts. It was only up to someone to do it, instead of leaving it all to the Germans, and losing two officers a day through snipers. All our men have started it now. It is the popular amusement." A fine soldier, Lieut. Grenfell made a special study of reconnaissance work, and his remarkable physical strength, his fearlessness and courage were well known. On 20 Nov. 1914, he was mentioned in Despatches by Field-Marshal Lord French, and was created a Companion of the Distinguished Service Order [London Gazette, 1 Jan. 1915]: "The Honourable Julian Henry Francis Grenfell, Lieut., 1st (Royal) Dragoons. On the 15th of Nov. he succeeded in reaching a point behind the enemy's trenches and making an excellent reconnaissance, furnishing early information of an impending attack by the enemy." A friend thus described this reconnaissance in a letter written to Lord Desborough, dated 18 Nov. 1914: "We were in the trenches on a 48-hour tour of duty, and where we were, in a wood less than 100 yards from the German trenches, we were very much bothered by snipers who were doing a lot of damage. The day before yesterday Julian crept through the undergrowth right up to one of the German trenches and shot one of them dead through his loophole. Yesterday he crawled out in the same direction and found the trench evacuated, so he crept on some little way beyond. He put two more Germans in the bag and then came back with the most useful information that the Germans were advancing. Within half an hour they attacked the line very heavily and were repulsed with great loss. Both acts were not only extremely plucky, but showed great resource and presence of mind, not to say cunning. . . . So far he has shown that he is quite capable of taking care of himself, and more than a match for a whole lot of Germans." He was promoted Captain on 10 Dec. 1914, and was again mentioned, in Lord French's Despatches, 14 Jan. 1915. In April, 1915, Capt. Grenfell wrote the lines quoted below, of which a Professor of English literature wrote: "I don't know if you really know that Julian's poem is one of the swell things in English literature. It is safe for ever; I know it by heart, and I never learned it. It has that queer property which only the best poems have, that a good many of the lines have more meaning than there is any need for, so that new things keep turning up in it."

"INTO BATTLE.

"The naked earth is warm with spring,
And with green grass and bursting trees
Leans to the sun's gaze glorying,
And quivers in the sunny breeze;
And Life is Colour and Warmth and Light,
And a striving evermore for these;
And he is dead who will not fight;
And who dies fighting has increase.

"The fighting man shall from the sun
Take warmth, and life from the glowing earth;
Speed with the light-foot winds to run,
And with the trees to newer birth;
And find when fighting shall be done,
Great rest and fulness after death.

"All the bright company of Heaven
Hold him in their high comradeship,
The Dog Star, and the Sisters Seven,
Orion's Belt and Sworded Hip.

" The woodland trees that stand together,
    They stand to him each one a friend,
They gently speak in the windy weather,
    They guide to valley and ridges' end.

" The kestrel hovering by day
    And the little owls that call by night,
Bid him be swift and keen as they,
    As keen of ear, as swift of sight.

" The blackbird sings to him, ' Brother, brother,
    If this be the last song you shall sing,
Sing well, for you may not sing another ;
    Brother, sing.'

" In dreary, doubtful, wailing hours,
    Before the brazen frenzy starts,
The horses show him nobler powers ;
    O ! patient eyes, courageous hearts

" And when the burning moment breaks,
    And all things else are out of mind,
And only Joy of Battle takes
    Him by the throat, and makes him blind

" Through joy and blindness he shall know,
    Not caring much to know, that still
Nor lead nor steel shall reach him, so
    That it be not the Destined Will.

" The thundering line of battle stands,
    And in the air Death moans and sings ;
But Day shall clasp him with strong hands,
    And Night shall fold him in soft wings.

                           J. G.

" Flanders,
    " April, 1915."

These lines were sent to the " Times," but before they had appeared in print Capt. Grenfell was wounded in the head by shrapnel on 13 May, 1915. On the previous evening he was with his regiment about 500 yards behind the front line, near the Ypres–Menin Road, in support of an attack on the German trenches running south from Hooge Lake. The Royals were behind a small hill which Julian afterwards called the little hill of death. Early in the morning the Germans heavily bombarded this hill, and Julian Grenfell went to the look-out post and was knocked over by a shell which merely bruised him. He went down again and reported his observations, and then volunteered to get through with a message to the Somerset Yeomanry in the front line, which he successfully accomplished under very heavy fire. When he returned he went up the hill with his General and a shell burst four yards away, knocking them both down and wounding Julian Grenfell in the head. He said : " Go down, sir. Don't bother about me. I'm done." The General helped to carry him down, and was wounded while doing so. Julian said afterwards to a brother officer : " Do you know, I think I shall die," and when he was contradicted, remarked : " Well, you see if I don't." He was carried to the clearing station, and asked there whether he was going to die, adding : " I only want to know ; I am not in the least afraid." He was then taken to the hospital at Boulogne, and his sister came from Wimereux to nurse him, and his parents were both with him. When the surgeon asked him how long he had been unconscious after he was hit, Julian said : " I was up before the count." Mrs. Meynell says : " His strength and youth were fighting against the deadly poison of his wound. During all those eleven days when he lay there he prayed, probably unaware that he spoke aloud. Sometimes he prayed that he might be able to bear the pain. The psalms and the hymns of his childhood were said to him aloud ; that was what he liked, also George Herbert's poems." His brother arrived in France with his regiment and came to his bedside, and with those he loved around him Julian Grenfell died on the afternoon of 26 May. His younger brother wrote of him : " I love to think that he had attained that perfection for which he sought so untiringly. I seem to hear him cheering me on in the moments of stress here with even more vivid power. There is no one whose victory over the grave can be more complete." And he said also : " Death is such a frail barrier out here ; men cross it so smilingly and gallantly every day, one cannot feel it as a severing in any way. Pray that I may bear myself bravely when the burning moment breaks." On 30 July, his brother, the Hon. W. Grenfell, fell in action in a charge to take trenches near the Hooge Crater. He had gone 70 or 80 yards in the attempt, while leading his platoon, to cross the 250 yards of open ground under terrific fire. He just fell forward dead. Lieut.-Colonel Maclachlan had written to him : " Julian set an example of light-hearted courage which is famous all through the Army in France, and has stood out even above the lost lion-hearted." Julian's friend, Lord Lucas, who did not long survive him, wrote : " You know that I was fonder of Julian than of any living man, and never can anyone else be the same to me as he was. . . . I think of all the happy times we had, and of his spirits, his keenness, his skill, his intense enjoyment of everything that boy or man, sportsman or poet, loves."

                    " OUT OF BATTLE.

    " ' Sing well, for you may not sing another ;
        Brother, sing.'
                          " J. G."

" So let his life continue—born anew
    From depths of battle to became a star !
The soul of Adonais from afar
    Beacons, the Adonaides are not few.

" Sing, Blackbird Boy, the blackbird sang for you
    Unwitting ; her soft notes the parents are
To yon pure lay's melodious avatar
    That from shut mouth rings on unstopt and free.

" The blackbird's song !
    A wiser world shall listen,
While upon soldier eyes of strangers glisten
    The tears of praise, and your songs sung shall be
Things to make men like kings—nay ! better, make
    Men's hearts like birds' hearts
(For the blackbird's sake !).

                        " WILLIAM M. HARDINGE."

JULIAN GRENFELL.

" Because of you we will be glad and gay ;
    Remembering you we will be brave and strong ;
And hail the advent of each dangerous day,
    And meet the great adventure with a song.
And as you proudly gave your jewelled gift,
    We'll give our lesser offering with a smile,
Nor falter on that path where, all too swift,
    You led the way and leapt the golden stile.
Whether new seas, new heights to climb you find,
    Or gallop through the unfooted asphodel,
We know you know we shall not lag behind,
    Nor halt to waste a moment on a tear.
And you will speed us onward with a cheer,
    And know beyond the stars that all is well.

              British Expeditionary Force,
                        " France."

GUINNESS, THE REVEREND PERCY WYNDHAM, was born 18 May, 1875, son of the Rev. R. Wyndham Guinness, M.A., Rector of Rathdrum for 44 years, and Rural Dean, and Dora Sarah, daughter of the late Dr. William Boxwell, of Abbeyleix. He was educated at Monkton Comb School ; at Emmanuel College, and Ridley Hall, Cambridge ; was ordained in 1900 ; was Curate of Aston, Birmingham, 1900–11 ; joined the Army in Jan. 1911 ; Acting Chaplain to the Forces, Aldershot, 1911–12 ; Chaplain to the Forces, Curragh, 1912–14. He served in the European War from 1914. He was created a Companion of the Distinguished Service Order [London Gazette, 1 Jan. 1915] : " The Rev. Percy Wyndham Guinness, B.A., Chaplain to the Forces,

Rev. Percy W. Guinness.

3rd Cavalry Brigade. On the 5th Nov., at Kruistraal, when Major Dixon of the 16th Lancers was mortally wounded, he went on his own initiative into the trenches under heavy fire, and brought him to the ambulance, and on the afternoon of the same day, being the only individual in a shelled area, took a message under heavy fire from the 4th Hussars to the Headquarters of the 3rd Cavalry Brigade." He was mentioned in Despatches, 14 Jan. 1915, and also on 24 June, 1915. In the Retreat from Mons he rode twice alone through a fearfully shelled area to succour wounded men in a cave. He was Senior Chaplain to the East African Expedition, Jan. 1916, to 1919, and had to travel over 2,000 miles of communication. Major the Rev. P. W. Guinness was awarded the Military Cross.

LAMBART, RICHARD, Second Lieut., was born 26 June, 1875, son of the late Major Fred Lambart, Scots Fusiliers, and Catherine Gill, of Calderwood Castle. He was educated at Radley College, and entered the Army in Sept. 1914 ; served in the European War from 1914 ; was mentioned in Despatches, and created a Companion of the Distinguished Service Order [London Gazette, 1 Jan. 1915] : " Richard Lambart, Second Lieut., Intelligence Corps. For conspicuously gallant conduct in obtaining very valuable information, under most difficult and dangerous conditions." He became Lieutenant in 1914. Lieut. Lambart is said to have been the first actor to ever win the D.S.O.

LEWIS, DONALD SWAIN, Lieut. (Temporary Capt.), youngest son of Capt. E. Lewis, of Guildford. He was gazetted to the Royal Engineers in Dec. 1904. In Dec. 1913, he joined the Royal Flying Corps, and was promoted Captain in Oct. 1914. He served in the European War, and was created a Companion of the Distinguished Service Order [London Gazette, 1 Jan. 1915] : " Donald Swain Lewis, Lieut. (Temporary Capt.), Royal Engineers and Royal Flying Corps. For valuable information repeatedly furnished to the Royal Artillery with regard to the position of the enemy's guns. His direction of our artillery fire whilst flying has constantly led to direct hits on the enemy's batteries and the silencing of their guns." He was killed while flying 10 April, 1916.

Noel Y. Loftus Welman.

WELMAN, NOEL YVON LOFTUS, Capt., was born at the Barracks, Mullingar, Ireland, 8 Oct. 1889, son of Lieut.-Colonel Herbert Loftus Welman, late Royal Irish Rifles, and Annie Harriet Welman (deceased). He was educated at Charterhouse Preparatory School, Godalming; at the Grammar School, Wellingborough, and the Royal Military College, Sandhurst, and joined the Duke of Cambridge's Own Middlesex Regt., in Feb. 1909. He served in the European War from 1914; was promoted to Captain in Dec. 1914, and was created a Companion of the Distinguished Service Order [London Gazette, 1 Jan. 1915]: "Noel Yvon Loftus Welman, Capt., 1st Battn. The Duke of Cambridge's Own (Middlesex Regt). For gallant conduct on the 30th Oct. at La Boutillerie, when the heaviest attack was launched by the enemy on the platoon which he commanded. Eleven of the enemy were killed on the parapet and two others in front, Lieut. Welman accounting for three of the number himself." Capt. Welman was mentioned in Despatches 1 Jan. 1915, and was killed in action at Loos 25 Sept. 1915.

BUCKLAND, GERALD CHARLES BALFOUR, Capt., was born 18 May, 1884. He entered the Army 19 Aug. 1903; became Lieutenant, Indian Army, 19 Nov. 1905, and Captain 19 Aug. 1912. He served in the European War from 1914, as Staff Officer, Bareilly Infantry Brigade, B.E.F.; 21st Indian Infantry Brigade, Indian Expeditionary Force "D," 6 Nov. 1915, to 11 May, 1916; Brigade Major, 9th Infantry Brigade, Indian Expeditionary Force "D," 12 May, 1916, to 12 Aug. 1917; was promoted to Major 19 Aug. 1918. He was mentioned in Despatches; was wounded, and was created a Companion of the Distinguished Service Order [London Gazette, 1 Jan. 1915]: "Gerald Charles Buckland, Capt., 2nd Battn. 8th Gurkha Rifles. Near Festubert on 23 Nov. he displayed great gallantry in leading a counter-attack which led to decisive results. He then, although wounded, returned and brought up reinforcements." He was also awarded the Military Cross.

DILL, ROBERT FOSTER, Capt., was the second son of the Very Rev. Marcus Dill, D.D., ex-Moderator of the Church of Scotland, of Alloway Manse, Ayr, N.B. He was educated at Marlborough and Sandhurst; obtained a commission in the Indian Army 21 Jan. 1903; became Lieutenant 21 April, 1905, and Captain in 1912. At the outbreak of the war his regiment, the 129th Duke of Connaught's Own Baluchis, arrived in France with the Lahore Division. In Oct., when fighting in the trenches he was wounded, but after a few weeks he was able to return to duty. For his brilliant conduct on that occasion he was created a Companion of the Distinguished Service Order [London Gazette, 1 Jan. 1915]: "Robert Foster Dill, Capt., 129th Duke of Connaught's Own Baluchis, Indian Army. At Hollebeke, on 31 Oct., when wounded by a shell, he continued to fight his machine-gun section until one gun was put out of action and the whole detachment of the other gun was killed." He was killed in action 11 April, 1915, and an obituary notice appeared in the "Times" of 15 April, 1915. He had married, in 1913, Margaret Douglas, daughter of General Pengelle, R.M.A.

VERNON, LIONEL DOUGLAS, Capt., was born 25 Oct. 1878. He joined the Royal Artillery, as Second Lieutenant, from the Militia, 20 May, 1899. He became Lieutenant 16 Feb. 1901; Captain 21 Nov. 1907; was Adjutant, Royal Artillery, 11 Oct. 1909, to 10 Oct. 1912. He served in the European War from 1914; became Major 30 Oct. 1914; was Acting Lieutenant-Colonel, R.A., June, 1915, to May, 1918; was severely wounded, and mentioned in Despatches. He was created a Companion of the Distinguished Service Order [London Gazette, 1 Jan. 1915]: "Lionel Douglas Vernon, Capt., 37th Battery, Royal Field Artillery. Near Neuve Chapelle, 1 Nov., although severely wounded, laid a telephone wire to the forward trenches and continued to observe throughout the day, and by this act enabled the Battery Commander to range correctly on the enemy's trenches."

London Gazette, 1 Jan. 1915.—"Admiralty, 1 Jan. 1915. The King has been graciously pleased to give orders for the following appointments to the Distinguished Service Order in respect of the undermentioned Officers. To be Companions of the Distinguished Service Order."

FRENCH, ARTHUR HARWOOD, Major, was born 16 Oct. 1876, only child of General Arthur French, C.B., Royal Marine Artillery (retired), and Mary Julia Eveleigh, daughter of Capt. Belson, Royal Engineers. He joined the Royal Marines 1 Sept. 1894, and became Lieutenant 1 July, 1895. He served in the South African War, 1899–1900; was present at the operations in the Orange Free State, Feb. to May, 1900, including those at Paardeberg; actions at Poplar Grove, Dreifontein, Vet River and Zand River; in the Transvaal in May and June, 1900, including actions near Johannesburg, Pretoria and Diamond Hill (11 and 12 June); in the Transvaal, east of Pretoria, including action at Belfast; also during operations in Cape Colony (Despatches [London Gazette, 12 March, 1901]; Queen's Medal with six clasps). He became Captain 1 April, 1901. He was Instructor, Army Signalling School, 5 Sept. 1912, to 12 Aug. 1914, and became Major 3 Nov. 1913. He served in the European War from 1914; was present at the defence of Antwerp; was twice mentioned in Despatches, and was created a Companion of the Distinguished Service Order [London Gazette, 1 Jan. 1915]: "For services during operations round Antwerp. Arthur Harwood French, Major, Royal Marine Infantry, Royal Marine Brigade, Royal Naval Division." Major French afterwards served in Gallipoli. Lieut.-Col. French married, in 1912 Dorothy Maud, only daughter of Henry Nicoll, J.P., of Bullington Manor, Hants.

MEESON, EDWARD HICKMAN TUCKER, Engineer Lieut.-Commander, R.N., was born 20 Dec. 1877, son of Mr. Frederick Meeson, formerly of London, and Emily, daughter of Frederick Andrews. He was educated at Westminster School, and was trained at Keyham, 1894–99. For services in the Laurel, at the Battle of Heligoland Bight, he was promoted to Commander and created a Companion of the Distinguished Service Order [London Gazette, 1 Jan. 1915]: "Edward Hickman Tucker Meeson, Engineer Lieut.-Commander, His Majesty's Ship Laurel." He was present at the sinking of the Blücher, and at the evacuation of both Anzac and Cape Helles. He sank with his ship, the Defence, in the North Sea on 31 May, 1916, aged 38. Engineer-Commander E. Meeson had married Gladys, daughter of Mr. George Joy, and was survived by his widow and daughter, Margaret.

LOCKYER, EDMUND LAURENCE BRAITHWAITE, Lieut.-Commander, Royal Navy, was born 20 April, 1879, son of the late Colonel W. N. Lockyer, R.A. He was educated in H.M.S. Britannia, and joined the Royal Navy. He was Commander Instructor, Clyde Division, Royal Naval Volunteers Reserve, 1910–12; Executive and Gunnery Officer, H.M.S. Dublin, 1912–13, and retired as Lieutenant-Commander in 1913. He served in H.M.S. Carmania in the European War from 1914; was present off the coast of South America at the sinking of the German cruiser Cap Trafalgar, and for his services on that occasion was created a Companion of the Distinguished Service Order [London Gazette, 1 Jan. 1915]: "Edmund Laurence Braithwaite Lockyer, Lt.-Cdr., His Majesty's Ship Carmania." He commanded H.M.S. Monitor M.30 at the Dardanelles, 1915–16, which ship was sunk by hostile gun-fire in May, 1916. Commander Lockyer was on Special Service, 1916–17, and was awarded a Bar to his D.S.O. He married, in 1909, Kathleen Mary, daughter of the late Major T. F. P. Hamilton, R.A., and they have one son and two daughters.

Edward F. Briggs.

BRIGGS, EDWARD FETHERSTONE, Squadron Commander, R.N.A.S., was born 13 Feb. 1882, son of William Briggs and Florence Briggs, of Bristol. He entered the Navy in 1905; became Engineer Lieutenant-Commander. He served in the European War from 1914. He was made a Chevalier of the Legion of Honour, and created a Companion of the Distinguished Service Order [London Gazette, 1 Jan. 1915]: "Edward Fetherstone Briggs, Squadron Commander, R.N.A.S. For aerial attack on Zeppelin airship sheds and factory at Friedrichshafen." When leading the raid on Friedrichshafen in Nov. 1914, he was shot down and taken prisoner. He escaped from captivity in April, 1917. He became Colonel, R.A.F., on Headquarters Staff, North-Eastern Area, York. Colonel Briggs married, in 1918, Violet, only daughter of Ernest Long, of York.

BABINGTON, JOHN TREMAYNE, Flight-Comdr. R.N.A.S., was born 29 July, 1891, son of C. H. Babington, of Croan, Wadebridge. He served in the European War, 1914–15; was made Chevalier, Legion of Honour, and was created a Companion of the Distinguished Service Order [London Gazette, 1 Jan. 1915]: "John Tremayne Babington, Flight-Comdr. R.N.A.S. For aerial attack on three sheds and on the airship factory at Friedrichshafen." In 1916 he married Cecily, youngest daughter of Philip Beresford Hope, of Bedgebury, Kent.

Sidney Vincent Sippe.

SIPPE, SIDNEY VINCENT, Flight Lieut., Royal Naval Air Service, youngest son of C. H. Sippe, of Beckenham. He served in the European War from 1914; dropped bombs on the airship factory at Friedrichshafen, and was created a Companion of the Distinguished Service Order [London Gazette, 1 Jan. 1915]: "Sidney Vincent Sippe, Flight Lieut., R.N.A.S." He was also made a Chevalier of the Legion of Honour. He was promoted Flight Commander, and later became Major He was given the O.B.E. in 1919. He married, in 1915, Mabel Frances, only child of the late Gerald d'Arcy, and they have one son and one daughter.

London Gazette, 18 Feb. 1915.—"War Office, 18 Feb. 1915. The King has been graciously pleased to approve of the following appointments to the Distinguished Service Order of the undermentioned Officers, in recognition of gallantry and devotion to duty whilst serving with the Expeditionary Force."

BOND, RICHARD LAWRENCE, Lieut., was born 10 June, 1890, at Mussoori, India, son of Major-General F. G. Bond, late R.E., and A. M. Bond (née Vivian). He was educated at Cheltenham College, and at the Royal Military Academy, Woolwich, which he entered in Jan. 1909, and joined the Royal Engineers 23 July, 1910. He served in the European War, 1914–15, in the 23rd Field Company, Royal Engineers. He was mentioned in Despatches in Oct. 1914, and created a Companion of the Distinguished Service Order [London Gazette, 18 Feb. 1915]: "Richard Lawrence Bond, Lieut., 23rd Field Company, Royal Engineers. For gallantry on the 10th Jan. 1915, when leading the first party of Royal Engineers in the successful attack on the Railway Embankment at Cuinchy." He was again mentioned in Despatches in 1915. He was invalided home in June, 1915; returned to the B.E.F. in April, 1917; became Captain 23 July, 1916; Brigade Major 10 July, 1917, to 31 Jan. 1919; was mentioned in Despatches in May, 1918; D.A.A.G., Reinforcements, Havre, British Armies in France, 10 July, 1917, to 31 Jan. 1919, and was awarded the Military Cross [London Gazette, 26 July, 1918]. He married, 1 Aug. 1914, at St. George's Church, Camberley, Isabelle Helewise Raymond, daughter of the late Lieut.-Colonel T. J. R. Mallock, Royal Fusiliers, and Mrs. Mallock, and they have one daughter.

CAMPBELL, THE HONOURABLE JOHN BERESFORD, Capt., son of the Earl and Countess of Cawdor; served in the European War from 1914, and was created a Companion of the Distinguished Service Order [London Gazette, 18 Feb. 1915]: "The Hon. John Beresford Campbell, Capt., Reserve of Officers, 1st Battn. Coldstream Guards. For gallantry in the operations at Givenchy 21 to 23 Dec. 1914, when he handled his company with great efficiency."

COKE, THE HONOURABLE REGINALD, Capt., was born 20 Aug. 1876, fifth son of the 2nd Earl of Leicester and the Honourable Georgina Caroline Cavendish, eldest daughter of the 2nd Baron Chesham. He joined the Scots Guards, from which he retired, and joined the Reserve of Officers. He served in the 1st Battn. Scots Guards from the outbreak of the European War in 1914. He was mentioned in Despatches, and was created a Companion of the Distinguished Service Order [London Gazette, 18 Feb. 1915]: "The Honourable Reginald Coke, Capt., 1st Battn. The Scots Guards, formerly Captain, Reserve of Officers, Scots Guards. For gallantry and resource in the action at Cuinchy on the 1st Jan. 1915, when he led his company with great promptitude into the fight on the embankment at a critical moment." He married, in 1907, the Honourable Doreen O'Brien, youngest daughter of the 14th Baron Inchiquin, and they have two daughters.

DAVIDSON, DOUGLAS STEWART, Lieut., was born 12 Nov. 1892, at Strawberry Hill, Twickenham, Middlesex, son of Edward Chambers Davidson, Solicitor, and Frances Mary Vertue. He was educated at Rugby School and Sandhurst; was gazetted Second Lieutenant, 1st Royal Scots Fusiliers, 20 Sept. 1911, and promoted Lieutenant 10 Aug. 1912. He served with the British Expeditionary Force in France from Aug. to Nov. 1914, and was wounded at the First Battle of Ypres. He was created a Companion of the Distinguished Service Order [London Gazette, 18 Feb. 1915]: "Douglas Stewart Davidson, Lieut., 1st Battn. The Royal Scots Fusiliers. For conspicuous gallantry and ability on the 11th Nov. 1914, on the Ypres–Menin Road, in commanding his company with great success after his senior officers had been killed." He was pro-

Douglas S. Davidson.

moted Captain 1 Oct. 1915, and served in Egypt and Gallipoli, and subsequently in Mesopotamia, with 40th Infantry Brigade, 13th Division; afterwards on the Staff as D.A.Q.M.G. He was given the Brevet of Major 3 June, 1919; was awarded the Croix de Guerre 31 Aug. 1917, and the Military Cross [London Gazette, 27 Aug. 1917].

DOWDEN, CHARLES HENRY, Second Lieut., was born at Harmondsworth, Middlesex, 21 Oct. 1880, son of Charles and Jane Dowden. He was educated at Board Schools and Army Schools, and served in the Rifle Brigade in the ranks for 15 years. He served in the South African War, 1900–2, and received the Queen's Medal with five clasps. He served in the European War from 1914, and, having served through all ranks to Company Sergeant-Major, was promoted Second Lieutenant 24 Nov. 1914. He became Lieutenant 10 Feb. 1916; Captain 11 Oct. 1917; served as G.S.O., 3rd Grade, 19th Division, Sept. 1916, to Jan. 1917, and Brigade Major to 190th Brigade from Jan. 1917, to April, 1918; Temporary Major, May, 1918; served as G.S.O., 2nd Grade, 61st Division, to date. He was three times wounded; thrice mentioned in Despatches, Feb. 1915; about June, 1915, and Jan. 1918, and was created a Companion of the Distinguished Service Order [London Gazette, 18 Feb. 1915]: "Charles Henry Dowden, Second Lieut., 2nd Battn. King's Royal Rifle Corps. For conspicuous courage and marked ability on 9 Jan. 1915, and in reconnoitring near Cuinchy quite close to the enemy's position and obtaining valuable information. During the attack next day he was wounded in the head, but continued at his post until all his men were killed or wounded." He was awarded the Military Cross [London Gazette, 9 Sept. 1915], and a Bar to his D.S.O. in Jan. 1918. He married, 16 June, 1910, at Winchester, Hampshire, Elsie May, fourth daughter of the late A. Penton, of Winchester, and they have two daughters.

HARINGTON, FREDERICK JOHN, Lieut., was born 3 Aug. 1888, in Dublin, second son of Colonel Frederick William Harington, late commanding the 2nd Battn. the Prince of Wales's Own (West Yorks Regt.), and grandson of the late General Sir John Cox, K.C.B., who commanded the Somerset Light Infantry. He was educated at Bedford School, and joined the West Yorkshire Regt. at Lichfield, as Second Lieutenant, from the Territorial Forces, 13 Dec. 1912. He joined the 2nd Battn. in Malta, March, 1913, and became Lieutenant 1 Nov. 1913. He served in the European War, and was created a Companion of the Distinguished Service Order [London Gazette, 18 Feb. 1915]: "Frederick John Harington, Lieut., 2nd Battn. The Prince of Wales's Own (West Yorkshire Regt.). For conspicuous gallantry on the 18th Dec. 1914, when, accompanied by four men (all of whom were shot), he carried out a very successful attack on the enemy with bombs, under very heavy fire." He was Temporary Captain, West Yorkshire Regt., from 12 April to 9 Dec. 1915, and became

Captain 10 Dec. 1915; was Acting Major, West Yorkshire Regt., 4 Oct. 1918, to 14 March, 1919; G.S.O.3, 28 May, 1917, to 3 Oct. 1918. Capt. Harington married, 10 Aug. 1917, at All Saints', Fleet, Hants, Olive Isabel, only child of Commander Berkeley St. George Deane, R.N. (retired), J.P. for County Wicklow, and Mrs. Deane, of Concordia, Fleet, Hants, formerly of Glendaragh, Newtown, Mount Kennedy, Ireland.

LAFONE, CLAUDE ALEXANDER, Capt., was born at Hanworth, Middlesex, 24 Feb. 1877, elder son of Alfred William and Harriet Lafone, of Springfield, Walton-on-Thames, Surrey. He was educated at Harrow,

Claude A. Lafone

and joined the 1st Devonshire Regt., as Second Lieutenant, 1 Dec. 1897; became Lieutenant 9 March, 1899, and Captain 20 Dec. 1901. He served in the South African War; was present at the Relief of Ladysmith, including the action at Colenso; in operations of 17–24 Jan. 1900, and action at Vaal Kranz; in operations on Tugela Heights (14–27 Feb. 1900) and action at Pieter's Hill; in Natal, March to June, 1900, including action at Laing's Nek (6–9 June); in the Transvaal, 30 Nov. 1901, to 31 May, 1902. He was mentioned in Despatches [London Gazette, 10 Sept. 1901]; received the Queen's Medal with five clasps, and the King's Medal with two clasps. Capt. Lafone went to France 8 Nov. 1914. He was created a Companion of the Distinguished Service Order [London Gazette, 18 Feb. 1915]: "Claude Alexander Lafone, Capt., 2nd Battn. The Devonshire Regt. For conspicuous gallantry on the night of 18 Dec. 1914, near Neuve Chapelle, in capturing a trench from the enemy." He was killed in action at Neuve Chapelle 14 March, 1915. Capt. Lafone was a keen polo-player, fox hunter and rider in point-to-points.

OTTLEY, GEOFFREY CLAUDE LANGDALE, Lieut., was born at Southsea, on the 20th Jan. 1896, son of Rear-Admiral Sir Charles Langdale Ottley, K.C.M.G., C.B., M.V.O., and Lady Ottley, daughter of Colonel Alexander Stewart, R.A. He was edu-

Geoffrey C. L. Ottley.

cated at Harrow, from 1910–13, and passed into Sandhurst direct from Harrow in Feb. 1914, being the first of his batch of Guards' Cadets, gaining a Prize Cadetship. He served in the European War, and was appointed to the Distinguished Service Order, for conspicuous gallantry, but did not live to personally receive the decoration. Lieut. Ottley died in the Australian Hospital at Wimereux, Boulogne, 21 Dec. 1914, aged 18 years and 11 months, a few hours only before the arrival of his father and mother. It is believed Lieut. Ottley was one of the youngest, if not the youngest, officer to receive the D.S.O. He was mentioned in Sir John French's Despatch of 14 Jan. 1915, and was created a Companion of the Distinguished Service Order [London Gazette, 18 Feb. 1915]: "Geoffrey Claude Langdale Ottley, Lieut., late 2nd Battn. Scots Guards. For conspicuous gallantry in endeavouring to take a portion of the enemy's trenches after a previous effort had failed. In this attempt he was severely wounded, and has since died." Lieut. Ottley's body was brought to his beloved home, to be buried at Lochaber on Christmas Day, and at his funeral the pipers played "The Flowers of the Forest" and "Lochaber No More."

The "Oban Times" for 2 Jan. 1915, says: "Lieut. Geoffrey C. L. Ottley, of the 2nd Battn. Scots Guards, whose death at the Front we deeply regret to announce, was the only child of Rear-Admiral Sir Charles and Lady Ottley, of Coruanan Lodge, Fort William, and 17, Queen's Gate Gardens, London, S.W. Born on 20 Jan. 1896, he was educated at Harrow, and joined the Royal Military College at Sandhurst in Feb. 1914, passing in first of the batch of Guards' Cadets and obtaining a prize cadetship. During the brief summer vacation which he was spending in his Scottish home, the news of the impending outbreak of war arrived, and he rejoined Sandhurst immediately, looking forward with intense eagerness to the early prospect of seeing active service. His hopes received almost immediate fulfilment, for on 1 Oct. he was gazetted to a Second Lieutenancy in the Scots Guards. For five weeks thereafter he remained in England, taking part in the stately ceremonial drills and guard mountings at St. James's and Buckingham Palace, but to his great delight he received on 7 Nov. the long-expected order to leave with a draft of about 300 other officers and men to make good casualties in the 2nd Battn of his regiment in France. Letters since received from the Front indicate not merely his efficiency and the affection and respect which his blithe spirit and light-hearted courage inspired amongst his brother-officers and the men under his command, but his own letters amid jocular references to the hardships of the campaign, declared that he would not be elsewhere for anything in the world. 'If I were brought home by force,' he wrote recently, 'I should be absolutely wretched until I got back here again into the cold and wet.' In the six weeks of his campaigning experience, the gallant jocund schoolboy had developed in character, daily growing in the habit of command. Thus, on 9 Dec., he made a reconnaissance of the enemy's position in front of his own trenches, creeping forward across the muddy, fire-swept zone to within fifteen yards of the muzzles of the German rifles, and bringing back information so valuable as to invoke a special telegram of congratulation to Lieut. Ottley from the

General Officer Commanding. On the 10th Dec. he was gazetted Lieutenant, and ante-dated to 15 Nov. On 18 Dec. came the long-looked-for opportunity. An advance having been ordered, he led his men in attack against the enemy's position, and fell actually on the parapet of the German trenches, mortally wounded. He was brought back through the great gallantry of Corpl. Mitchell of the same corps, who, though himself wounded, insisted on staying with and assisting him, in spite of Lieut. Ottley's request that the Corporal should leave him and so secure his own life. Lieut. Ottley died in the Australian Hospital at Wimereux on 21 Dec., at 5 a.m., a few hours only before the arrival of his father and mother. During his brief sojourn in the beautifully-arranged hospital he had endeared himself to all, and the happy, calm, and peaceful end illustrated once again the time-honoured maxim that has been the guiding star of so many thousands of British officers— ' Dulce et decorum est pro patria mori.' To Sir Charles and Lady Ottley a pathetic tenderness will always attach to Christmas, for it was on that day that the body of their well-beloved son was brought from the scene of strife to be laid to rest amid the peace of Lochaber—a domain which had for the young officer a perfervid attachment. The special train which conveyed the funeral party to Fort William was met at the station by a contingent of the Argyll and Sutherland Highlanders, who shoulder-high bore the coffin, palled by the Union Jack and surmounted by the sword and cap of the deceased, to the Church of St. Andrew, where it was placed in the chancel. A pipe and drum band, playing the ' Flowers of the Forest,' led the van of the cortège, and there was a gripping sadness prevailing as the procession made its way through the main street. An impressive short service was conducted in the church, which was crowded, and on its conclusion the soldiers again carried the coffin to the graveside adjoining. When it had been lowered to the ground, the customary volleys were fired, between each of which a piper played ' Lochaber No More.' Thus passed a young life nobly and gladly laid down for King and Country. It might appropriately be said of him :

> " ' This was the happy warrior ; this was he
> Who every man in arms would wish to be ! '

" The chief mourners were Sir Charles and Lady Ottley, Mrs. Ottley, Major Stewart, and Mr. Edward Drummond Hay, R.N."

ROBERTS, FRANK CROWTHER, Lieut., served in the European War from 1914 ; was mentioned in Despatches, and created a Companion of the Distinguished Service Order [London Gazette, 18 Feb. 1915] : " Frank Crowther Roberts, Lieut., Worcestershire Regt. On the 3rd of Jan. 1915, Lieut. Roberts, with 25 men of the 1st Battn. Worcestershire Regt., attacked and captured by surprise, with complete success, a German sap-head situated about sixty yards in front of our lines near Neuve Chapelle." Major Roberts also received the Victoria Cross (see V.C. Volume) and the Military Cross.

WATSON, WILLIAM, Capt., was born 19 Jan. 1885, at Ruthven, Coldstream, Berwickshire, son of W. H. Watson, Esq., and Mrs. Watson. He was educated at Edinburgh Academy, and at the Royal Military College, Sandhurst (entered the Royal Military College, Sept. 1904) ; joined the 2nd Border Regt. in South Africa 22 Jan. 1906, and became Lieutenant 7 March, 1910. He was employed with the West African Frontier Force in Southern Nigeria, 4 Sept. 1912, to 21 May, 1914. He served in the European War from 1914 ; was in charge of Machine Gun Section in First Battle of Ypres in Oct. and Nov. 1914 ; was Temporary Captain 15 Nov. 1914, and Captain 30 Dec. 1914. He was evacuated to England (wounded) in Dec. 1914 ; rejoined 2nd Battn. as Adjutant, March, 1915 ; severely wounded and again invalided to England, May, 1916. He was created a Companion of the Distinguished Service Order [London Gazette, 18 Feb. 1915] : " William Watson, Capt., 2nd

William Watson.

Battn. Border Regt. For conspicuous gallantry on several occasions between the 18 and 24 Oct. 1914, in handling his machine guns under very heavy fire with great success. He was twice buried by shell-fire, and during the Battle of Ypres was twice wounded, but continued at his post." Capt. Watson was twice mentioned in Despatches during the European War. He was Adjutant, 3rd Reserve Battn., 17 Sept. to 20 Oct. 1916. He married, 28 Oct. 1916, at Christ Church, Mayfair, London, W., Theodora Stackhouse, widow of Capt. W. T. Stackhouse, Sherwood Foresters, and daughter of A. R. Norrington, Esq., of Plymouth, and Mrs. Norrington.

ROSS, ALAN CAMPBELL, Capt., was born 4 May, 1878. He joined the Royal Artillery, as Second Lieutenant, from the Militia, 4 March, 1899 ; became Lieutenant, Royal Artillery, 16 Feb. 1901 ; Indian Army, 21 May, 1908. He served in the European War from 1914 ; was mentioned in Despatches, and, for rescuing an Indian Officer under fire, was created a Companion of the Distinguished Service Order [London Gazette, 18 Feb. 1915] : " Alan Campbell Ross, Capt., 20th Deccan Horse, Indian Army. For conspicuous gallantry at Festubert on 21 Dec. 1914, during an attack on the enemy's position, in assisting to rescue a wounded Indian Officer under a most destructive fire." He was promoted to Major 1 Sept. 1915 ; served on the Staff in France to 4 March, 1918, and was given the Brevet of Lieutenant-Colonel 3 June, 1919.

HOLT, FELTON VESEY, Capt., was born 23 Feb. 1886, in London, son of Vesey G. M. Holt, Banker, 3, Whitehall Place, S.W., and of Mount Mascal, Bexley, and Mabel Mary Holt, eldest daughter of the late Walter Drummond. He was educated at Eton, and joined the Army in Sept. 1905 ; was promoted to Lieutenant 11 Jan. 1908 ; became

Felton Vesey Holt.

Lieutenant, Royal Flying Corps, 17 April, 1913, and Captain, Oxford and Bucks Light Infantry, 25 July, 1914. He served in the European War from 1914 ; was mentioned in Despatches, and was created a Companion of the Distinguished Service Order [London Gazette, 18 Feb. 1915] : " Felton Vesey Holt, Capt., The Oxfordshire and Buckinghamshire Light Infantry and Royal Flying Corps. For engaging single-handed a group of twelve German aeroplanes which were attacking the town of Dunkirk. He was subsequently joined by two of our own biplanes, which resulted in one of the German machines being brought down and its pilot and observer being captured." Capt. Holt's D.S.O. was an immediate award. He was several times mentioned in Despatches (once for the defence of London during air raids), and was also awarded the Brevet of Major for these services 1 Jan. 1917. He was Temporary Lieutenant-Colonel 20 March, 1916, to 31 March, 1918, and was employed under the Air Ministry 11 April, 1918. He was created a C.M.G. in 1919.

London Gazette, 19 Feb. 1915.—" Admiralty, 19 Feb. 1915. The King has been graciously pleased to give orders for the following appointment to the Distinguished Service Order . . . in respect of the undermentioned Officer, in recognition of services mentioned in Despatch by the Admiral Commanding the East Coast Mine Sweepers" (details below).

BOOTHBY, HUBERT, Lieut., R.N.R. "The following Memorandum [London Gazette, 19 Feb. 1915] has been furnished by the Admiral Commanding the East Coast Mine Sweepers, detailing the recent mine-sweeping operations off Scarborough :—From the 19th to the 31st Dec. sweeping operations were conducted by the East Coast Mine Sweepers with the object of clearing the minefield which had been laid by the enemy off Scarborough. At the beginning there was no indication of the position of the mines, although, owing to losses of passing merchant ships, it was known that a minefield had been laid. In order to ascertain how the mines lay, it was necessary to work at all times of tide, with a consequent large increase in the element of danger. The following officers are specially noticed for their services during the operations : Lieut. H. Boothby, R.N.R., H.M.S. Pekin. . . . When Trawler No. 99 (Orianda), in which he was serving, was blown up by a mine on the 19th Dec., Lieut. Boothby successfully got all his crew (except one who was killed) into safety. Lieut. Boothby was again blown up on 6 Jan. 1915, in Trawler No. 450 (The Banyers)." He was created a Companion of the Distinguished Service Order [London Gazette, 19 Feb. 1915] : " Lieut. H. Boothby, R.N.R."

London Gazette, 19 Feb. 1915.—" Admiralty, 19 Feb. 1915. The King has been graciously pleased to give orders for the following appointments to the Distinguished Service Order. To be Companions of the Distinguished Service Order . . . Capt. Cecil Francis Kilner, R.M.L.I. (Flight Commander) and Lieut. Charles Humphrey Kingsman Edmonds, R.N. (Flight Lieutenant).

Admiralty Memorandum on the combined operations by H.M. Ships and Naval Seaplanes on the 25th Dec. 1914. On the 25th Dec. 1914, an air reconnaissance of the Heligoland Bight, including Cuxhaven, Heligoland and Wilhelmshaven, was made by naval seaplanes, and the opportunity was taken at the same time of attacking with bombs points of military importance. The reconnaissance involved combined operations by light cruisers, destroyers and seaplane-carriers, under Commodore Reginald Y. Tyrwhitt, C.B., and submarines acting under the orders of Commodore Roger Keyes, C.B., M.V.O. The vessels detailed for the operations arrived at their rendezvous before daylight, and as soon as the light was sufficient the seaplanes were hoisted out and despatched. The following Air Service officers and observers took part in the reconnaissance. . . . At the beginning of the flight the weather was clear, but on nearing the land the seaplanes met with thick weather, and were compelled to fly low, thus becoming exposed to a heavy fire at short range from ships and shore batteries. Several machines were hit, but all remained in the air for over three hours, and succeeded in obtaining valuable information regarding the disposition of the enemy's ships and defences. Bombs were also dropped on military points. In the meanwhile German submarines, seaplanes and Zeppelins delivered a combined attack upon the light cruisers, destroyers and seaplane-carriers, but were driven off. Flight Commanders Kilner and Ross and Flight Lieutenant Edmonds regained their ships. . . . An expression of their Lordships' appreciation has been conveyed to Commodore Keyes (Commodore S.), Commodore Tyrwhitt (Commodore T.), and to Captain Sueter (Director of the Air Department), for their share in the combined operations which resulted in this successful reconnaissance.

KILNER, CECIL FRANCIS, Capt., was born 8 Oct. 1883, son of W. A. Kilner, of Kemsing, Kent. He joined the Royal Marines 1 Sept. 1902 ; became Lieutenant 1 July, 1903, and Captain 1 Sept. 1913. Capt. Kilner served in the European War from 1914, was mentioned in Despatches, and created a Companion of the Distinguished Service Order, as above mentioned. He was employed under the Admiralty 31 Oct. 1914, to 2 Jan. 1918 ; was Temporary Major from 1 Jan. 1916, to 30 Dec. 1917 ; was employed under the Air Ministry from 3 Jan. 1918. He was promoted to Wing Commander, and was awarded a Bar to the Distinguished Service Order.

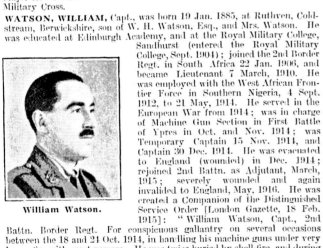

EDMONDS, CHARLES HUMPHREY KINGSMAN, Flight Lieut., Royal Naval Air Service, is the son of Mr. and Mrs. Charles Edmonds, of Lymington, Hants. He served in the Balkan War, 1911–13; was at the Central Flying School, 1912. He served in the European War from 1914, took part in the Cuxhaven Raid in Dec. 1914; was mentioned in Despatches, and created a Companion of the Distinguished Service Order, as above mentioned. He served in Gallipoli in 1915, and was mentioned in Despatches; was promoted to Wing Commander 31 Dec. 1917; received the French Croix de Guerre with Palm, 1918; became an Officer of the Crown of Italy, 1918. He married, in 1917, Lorna Karem Chadwick Osborn, daughter of Colonel George Osborn, R.N., and granddaughter of the late Robert Chadwick, J.P., of Sydney, New South Wales.

London Gazette, 18 Feb. 1915.—"War Office, 18 Feb. 1915. His Majesty the King has been graciously pleased to approve of the under-mentioned rewards for services rendered in connection with operations in the field. To be Companions of the Distinguished Service Order."

GATHORNE-HARDY, THE HONOURABLE JOHN FRANCIS, Major and Brevet Lieut.-Colonel, was born in London 14 Jan. 1874, second son of the Right Hon. John Stewart Gathorne-Hardy, 2nd Earl of Cranbrook, and the Countess of Cranbrook (Cicely Margaret Wilhelmina, daughter of the late Joseph Ridgway). He was educated at Cheam, Eton and Sandhurst (Sword of Honour at Sandhurst, 1894), and was gazetted to the Grenadier Guards 10 Oct. 1894, becoming Lieutenant 1 Jan. 1898. On 2 May, 1900, he was promoted to Captain; served in the South African War from 1900 to 1902; was Special Service Officer, including employment as Assistant Press Censor, Cape Town, and on the Staff. Took part in the operations in the Orange Free State, Feb. to May, 1900, including actions at Houtnek (Thoba Mountain), Vet River and Zand River; attached to Imperial Yeomanry; also in Cape Colony and Orange River Colony, July, 1901, to May, 1902. He was mentioned in Despatches [London Gazette, 10 Sept. 1901, and 29 July, 1902]; was given the Brevet of Major 22 Aug. 1902, and received the Queen's and King's Medals. He was Superintendent of Gymnasia, Home District, 22 Oct. 1902, to 7 March, 1904; was at the Staff College, 1905–6; Brigade Major, 1st Guards Brigade, 1 Jan. 1908, to 30 Sept. 1911; was promoted to Major 9 Oct. 1909; General Staff, War Office, 9 June, 1913, to 31 March, 1914; was given the Brevet of Lieutenant-Colonel 26 Nov. 1913. He served in the European War in France, as General Staff Officer, 2nd Grade, from 6 Aug. 1914, to 24 March, 1915, and as General Staff Officer, 1st Grade, from 25 March, 1915, to 2 Jan. 1916; was created a Companion of the Distinguished Service Order [London Gazette, 18 Feb. 1915]: "The Honourable John Francis Gathorne-Hardy, Major and Brevet Lieut.-Colonel, Grenadier Guards." He was promoted to Lieutenant-Colonel 15 July, 1915; was Temporary Brigadier-General, General Staff, 3rd Jan. 1916, to 8 Oct. 1918; was given the Brevet of Colonel 3 June, 1916; was four times mentioned in Despatches, and was promoted to Major-General 3 June, 1919; was Major-General, General Staff, British Forces in Italy, 9 Oct. 1918, to 20 Jan. 1919; was created a C.B. in 1918, and a C.M.G. in 1919. He married, in the Guards' Chapel, 10 Dec. 1898, Lady Isobel Stanley, daughter of the 16th Earl of Derby, and they have one daughter, Elizabeth His D.S.O. was awarded "for services in connection with operations in the field."

Hon. J. F. Gathorne-Hardy.

SAWYER, HENRY THOMAS, Lieut.-Colonel, was born 12 Aug. 1871. He joined the Army Veterinary Corps; served in Chitral, 1895, with the Relief Force (Medal and clasp); served in the South African War, 1899–1902; took part in the advance on Kimberley; was present during the operations in the Orange Free State, Feb. to May, 1900, including operations at Paardeberg (17 to 26 Feb.); actions at Poplar Grove, Dreifontein, Vet River and Zand River; in the Transvaal, May and June, 1900, including actions near Johannesburg and Pretoria; in the Transvaal, east of Pretoria, July to 29 Nov. 1900; in Cape Colony, south of Orange River, Nov. 1899, to Feb. 1900; again in the Transvaal 30 Nov. to 31 May, 1902. He was mentioned in Despatches [London Gazette, 8 Feb. 1901]; received the Queen's Medal with four clasps, and the King's Medal with two clasps, and was promoted Veterinary Captain 29 Nov. 1900. He became Major 7 Jan. 1906; was Assistant Director-General, Army Veterinary Service, 1 April, 1910, to 31 March, 1914; became Lieutenant-Colonel 25 April, 1914. He was Assistant Director of Veterinary Services, Northern Command, from 20 May to 4 Aug. 1914; became Assistant Director of Veterinary Services, Aldershot Command; Deputy Director of Veterinary Services 14 Dec. 1914, to 13 March, 1918, and 12 Dec. 1918. Lieut.-Colonel H. T. Sawyer served in the European War from 1914; was mentioned in Despatches, and created a Companion of the Distinguished Service Order [London Gazette, 18 Feb. 1915]: "Henry Thomas Sawyer, Lieut.-Colonel, Staff. For services in connection with operations in the field."

DE LA VOYE, ALEXANDER EDWIN, Lieut.-Colonel, was born 16 Nov. 1871. He was gazetted to the Suffolk Regt. 18 June, 1892; was transferred to the Army Service Corps 1 Oct. 1893, and became Lieutenant 30 Sept. 1894. He served in the Nile Expedition, 1898 (two Medals), and became Captain 6 Oct. 1898. Capt. De La Voye served in the South African War, 1899–1902, as D.A.A.G. (6 April, 1901, to 25 June, 1902); took part in the operations in the Orange Free State, Feb. to May, 1900, including those at Paardeberg (17 to 26 Feb.); actions at Poplar Grove, Dreifontein, Vet River (5 and 6 May) and Zand River; served during the operations in the Transvaal, east of Pretoria, July to 29 Nov. 1900, including actions at Belfast (26 and 27 Aug.); in the Transvaal 30 Nov. 1900, to Jan. 1902; also during the operations in Orange River Colony, Jan. to 31 May, 1902. He was mentioned in Despatches [London Gazette, 10 Sept. 1901]; was given the Brevet of Major 29 Nov. 1900, and received the Queen's Medal with four clasps, and the King's Medal with two clasps. On 3 Sept. 1905, he was promoted Major. From 1 Oct. 1910, to 4 Aug. 1914, Major De La Voye was Deputy Assistant Director of Supplies and Transport, Irish Command. He served in the European War from 1914; was D.A.Q.M.G. 5 Aug. 1914, to 4 Jan. 1915; A.A. and Q.M.G. 23 March, 1915, to 14 Feb. 1916, and D.A.Q.M.G., 1st Australian and New Zealand Army Corps, Mediterranean Expeditionary Force, British Armies in France, 15 Feb. 1916; Temporary Brigadier-General 15 Feb. 1916. He was six times mentioned in Despatches for his services in the Great War, and was created a Companion of the Distinguished Service Order [London Gazette, 18 Feb. 1915]: "Alexander Edwin De La Voye, Lieutenant-Colonel, Staff." He was created a C.M.G. in 1916, and a C.B. in 1918. He married, in 1902, Gladys Irene, daughter of the late John E. Stephens, and they have three daughters. The D.S.O. was given him "for services in connection with operations in the field."

BARTHOLOMEW, ARTHUR WOLLASTON, Major, was born 5 May, 1878, at Park House, Reading, son of Arthur Churchill Bartholomew, Esq., and of Clare St. George Wollaston. He was educated at Marlborough, and Trinity College, Oxford; joined the Royal Field Artillery, as Second Lieutenant, 26 May, 1900. He became Lieutenant 19 March, 1902; Captain 1 March, 1911, and Major 30 Oct. 1914. He was Adjutant, 15th Brigade, R.F.A. (originally 45th Brigade, R.F.A.), from March, 1910, to April, 1913; was Instructor, School of Army Signalling, Poona, 1911. He was on active service in the European War from 15 Aug. 1914; was Staff Capt., 5th Divisional Artillery, 5 to 26 Aug. 1914; Brigade Major, 5th Divisional Artillery, 26 Aug. 1914, to 11 Jan. 1916. He became D.A.A.G., R.A., 14th Corps, 12 Jan. 1916; G.S.O.2, R.A., 14th Corps, 28 Aug. 1917; G.S.O.1, R.A., G.H.A., Italy, 10 March, 1918, to 16 Feb. 1919; G.S.O.2, Aldershot Command, 17 Feb. 1919. He was given the Brevet of Lieutenant-Colonel in Jan. 1917, and created a C.M.G. in Jan. 1918; a C.B. in 1919, and was created a Companion of the Distinguished Service Order [London Gazette, 18 Feb. 1915]: "Arthur Wollaston Bartholomew, Major, Royal Field Artillery." On 7 July, 1906, at Bangalore, India, he married Helen May Ethel, elder daughter of the late Major-General W. W. Anderson. His D.S.O. was given "for services in connection with operations in the field."

GOSSET, FRANCIS WILLIAM, Major, was born at the House of Commons, London, 20 Oct. 1876, son of Francis Russell Gosset, Deputy Serjeant-at-Arms, House of Commons, and of Mary Snell Dalglish. He was educated at Marlborough College; the Royal Military Academy, Woolwich, and at the Staff College, Camberley. He joined the Army 2 Nov. 1895; served in the South African War from 1899–1902, on the Staff. He was present at the Relief of Ladysmith, including actions at Colenso, Spion Kop, Vaal Kranz and Pieter's Hill; in Natal, including action at Laing's Nek; in the Transvaal 30 Nov. 1900, to April, 1902, and May, 1902; in Orange River Colony, April and May, 1902; took part in the operations on the Zululand Frontier of Natal in Sept. and Oct. 1901. He was mentioned in Despatches [London Gazette, 20 Aug. 1901]; awarded the Queen's Medal with five clasps, and the King's Medal with two clasps. Lieut. Gossett became Captain 23 Aug. 1901; was Adjutant, R.H.A., from 1907–9; at the Staff College, 1909–11; became Major 15 Feb. 1912; was G.S.O., 3rd Grade, War Office, Jan. 1912, to Aug. 1914, and 2nd Grade from Aug. to Oct. 1914. He served in the European War, as G.S.O., 2nd Grade, with the British Expeditionary Force, from 5 Oct. until 31 Oct. 1914, when he was severely wounded at Ypres; was mentioned in Despatches 1 Jan. 1918, and created a Companion of the Distinguished Service Order [London Gazette, 18 Feb. 1915]: "Francis William Gosset, Major, Royal Artillery." From 27 Jan. to 29 June, 1915, he was G.S.O.2, War Office; from 30 June to 23 Aug. 1915, G.S.O.2, 32nd Division, New Armies; G.S.O.1, British Armies in France, 19 June to 12 July, 1916; G.S.O.1, 39th Division, British Armies in France, 13 July, 1916, to 10 Oct. 1918; became Lieutenant-Colonel 21 Aug. 1916; was G.S.O.1, 62nd Division, British Armies in France, 11 Oct. 1918. He was given the Order of Danilo, 3rd Class, Dec. 1916; was mentioned in Despatches 1 Jan. 1917; created a C.M.G.; mentioned in Despatches 1 Jan. 1918; given the Brevet of Colonel 1 Jan. 1919. Major Gosset married, 16 July, 1914, at St. Margaret's, Westminster, Mary Rokeby Maddock, only child of the late Mr. Frederick Trickett, and granddaughter of the late Sir Herbert Maddock, Deputy Governor of Bengal and President of the Council of India. His D.S.O. was awarded "for services in connection with operations in the field."

KEARSLEY, ROBERT HARVEY, Major, was born 28 March, 1880, son of Major Robert Wilson Kearsley, J.P., of 116, Eaton Square, London S.W. He was educated at Harrow, and at the Royal Military College, Sandhurst, and was gazetted to the 5th Dragoon Guards 11 Feb. 1899. He served in the South African War, 1899–1902, with his regiment in the Siege of Ladysmith, and later as A.D.C. to Major-General R. S. S. Baden-Powell 2 July to 22 Oct. 1900; was employed with the South African Constabulary 22 Oct. 1900, to 6 May, 1903; took part in the operations in Natal, 1899, including action at Lombard's Kop; was present at the defence of Ladysmith, including sortie of 7 Dec. 1899, and action of 6 Jan. 1900; in the Transvaal, 1900; in Natal, 1900; again in the Transvaal, west of Pretoria, 1900. He received the Queen's Medal with four clasps, and the King's Medal with two clasps. He became Lieutenant 27 June, 1900, and Captain 14 April, 1904, and was Adjutant, 5th Dragoon Guards, 16 July, 1906, to 15 July, 1909. He was promoted Major 6 March, 1912; graduated at the Staff College, Camberley, 1913; was Brigade Major, 3rd Cavalry Brigade, Irish Command, 4 Oct. 1913, to 4 Aug. 1914. He served in the European War from 1914; was Brigade Major 5 Aug. 1914, to 8

March, 1915. He was G.S.O., 2nd Grade, 9 March to 13 July, 1915; became Temporary Lieutenant-Colonel, and G.S.O., 1st Grade, 1st Canadian Division, 14 July, 1915. On 5 Aug. 1917, he became Brigadier-General, General Staff, and was appointed to the 6th Corps, British Armies in France. He has been several times mentioned in Despatches, and was created a Companion of the Distinguished Service Order [London Gazette, 18 Feb. 1915]: "Robert Harvey Kearsley, Major, 5th Dragoon Guards." He was given the Brevets of Lieutenant-Colonel 3 June, 1916, and Colonel 1 Jan. 1919; created an Officer of the Order of the Crown of Italy in 1917, and a Companion of the Order of St. Michael and St. George in Jan. 1918. From 1 March, 1919, he was Brigadier-General, General Staff, Staff College. Capt. Kearsley married, in 1908, Evelyn Molly, daughter of Samuel Arthur Peto, of Downs Court, Sandwich. His D.S.O. was awarded "for services in connection with operations in the field."

GREEN, JAMES EDWARD, Major, was born 11 Jan. 1874. He joined the 1st Battn. The East Lancashire Regt. 2 Dec. 1892, and became Lieutenant 18 June, 1895. He served in the South African War from 1899 to 1902; was promoted to Captain 5 June, 1900. He took part in the operations in Natal, 1899, including action at Rietfontein: at the defence of Ladysmith, including action of 6 Jan.; during the operations in Natal, March to June, 1900, including action at Laing's Nek (6 to 9 June); in the Transvaal 29 Nov. 1900, to Sept. 1901; in Orange River Colony, Sept. 1901, to April, 1902; also during the operations in Cape Colony, April to May, 1902; was Commandant at Kromellenburg and at Wolvehoek. He received the Queen's Medal with four clasps, and the King's Medal with two clasps. Capt. J. E. Green was Adjutant, Volunteers, from 1 Aug. 1902, to 31 July, 1907, and became Major 23 Sept. 1913. He served in the European War from 1914; was mentioned in Despatches, and created a Companion of the Distinguished Service Order [London Gazette, 18 Feb. 1915]: "James Edward Green, Major, on Staff." He was Temporary Lieutenant-Colonel 26 Sept. 1915, to 15 April, 1917; Acting Lieutenant-Colonel, East Lancashire Regt., 25 April to 5 June, 1917; Temporary Lieutenant-Colonel 4 Jan. to 22 June, 1918; Acting Lieutenant-Colonel, East Lancashire Regt., 26 June to 31 Dec. 1918; Temporary Lieutenant-Colonel, East Lancashire Regt., 1 Jan. 1919. His D.S.O. was awarded "for services in connection with operations in the field."

GRANT, CHARLES JOHN CECIL, Major, was born 16 Aug. 1877, son of the late Lieut.-Colonel Sir Robert Grant, G.C.B. He joined the Coldstream Guards 20 Feb. 1897; became Lieutenant 18 May, 1898; served in the South African War, 1899–1902; was present at the advance on Kimberley, including action at Belmont (wounded); took part in the operations in the Transvaal, east of Pretoria, July to 29 Nov. 1900, including action at Belfast (26 and 27 Aug.); in the Orange River Colony, Nov. 1900; in Orange River Colony, Jan. 1902; also in Cape Colony 30 Nov. 1900, to 31 May, 1902; Transport Officer to a Column and performed duties of Railway Staff Officer. He was wounded; received the Queen's Medal with three clasps, and the King's Medal with two clasps. He was Adjutant, Coldstream Guards, from 1 July, 1902, to 30 June, 1905, and became Captain 3 Oct. 1903. Capt. Grant passed the Staff College; was Brigade Major, Brigade of Guards, London District, 10 July, 1909, to 2 Feb. 1912; G.S.O., 3rd Grade, War Office, 3 Feb. 1912, to 28 July, 1913; was promoted Major 28 Oct. 1913. He served in the European War from 1914, and was created a Companion of the Distinguished Service Order [London Gazette, 18 Feb. 1915]: "Charles John Cecil Grant, Major, on Staff." He was also given the Brevet of Lieutenant-Colonel, and became Temporary Lieutenant-Colonel and G.S.O., 1st Grade, 12th Division, B.E.F., 4 Dec. 1915, to 14 Jan. 1917; G.S.O.1, 3rd Army, British Armies in France, 15 Jan. to 20 Oct. 1917; commanded 1st Infantry Brigade, British Armies in France, 21 Oct. 1917, to 30 March, 1918; Brigadier-General, General Staff, attached to G.H.Q., French Army, 31 March, 1918. He was given the Brevet of Colonel 1 Jan. 1919, and received the Legion of Honour in 1916. In 1905 he married Lady Sybil Myra Caroline Primrose (author of "Samphire," 1912, and "The Chequer Board," 1912), elder daughter of the 5th Earl of Rosebery, and they have one son. His D.S.O. was awarded "for services in connection with operations in the field."

DARELL, WILLIAM HARRY VERELST, Major, was born 23 Jan. 1878, second son of Sir Lionel Edward Darell, 5th Bart., of Richmond Hill, Surrey, and Helen Frances, only child of the late Edward Marsland, of Henbury Park, Cheshire. He was educated at Eton and Sandhurst; joined the Coldstream Guards 8 Sept. 1897; became Lieutenant 18 Jan. 1899. Lieut. Darell served in the South African War from 1899–1902, and took part in the advance on Kimberley, including actions at Belmont, Enslin, Modder River and Magersfontein; served during operations in the Orange Free State, Feb. to May, 1900, including actions at Poplar Grove, Dreifontein, Vet River and Zand River; in the Transvaal in May and June, 1900, including actions near Johannesburg, Pretoria and Diamond Hill; in the Transvaal, east of Pretoria, July to Oct. 1900; in the Transvaal, west of Pretoria, Nov. 1900; also in Cape Colony, south of Orange River, 1900; again during operations in the Transvaal, Nov. to Dec. 1900, and in Cape Colony, Nov. 1900, to 31 May, 1902. He received the Queen's Medal with five clasps, and the King's Medal with two clasps. He was promoted Captain 29 Nov. 1903. He became Major 29 Nov. 1913. Major Darell passed the Staff College; served in the European War from 1914, as D.A.A.G., 5 to 27 Aug. 1914, and D.A.Q.M.G. from 28 Aug. 1914, to 2 July, 1915; was mentioned in Despatches, and created a Companion of the Distinguished Service Order [London Gazette, 18 Feb. 1915]: "William Harry Verelst Darell, Major, on Staff." He was A.A. and Q.M.G., Guards Division, B.E.F., and British Armies in France and Temporary Lieutenant-Colonel, from 3 July, 1915, and Temporary Brigadier-General 24 Dec. 1916, to 8 April, 1919; D.A.A. and Q.M.G.; D.A.G., 4th Army Corps, British Armies in France, and was given the Brevet of Lieutenant-Colonel 1 Jan. 1919. He was created a C.M.G. in 1918. In 1907 they have one son and one daughter. His D.S.O. was awarded "for services in connection with operations in the field."

DANIELL, FRANCIS EDWARD LLOYD, Major, was the youngest son of Major F. F. Daniell, late Gordon Highlanders. He was born 19 Dec. 1874, and was educated at the Philberds, Maidenhead; at Malvern College, and the Royal Military College, Sandhurst. He obtained his commission in Sept. 1895, and was promoted Captain, March, 1901. Capt. Daniell served in the occupation of Crete in 1897, and in 1898 took part in the Sudan Expedition, when he was present at the Battle of Atbara, being mentioned in Despatches [London Gazette, 24 May, 1898], and receiving the British Medal and the Egyptian Medal with clasp. He served in the South African War, 1899–1901, as Special Service Officer, afterwards on Staff; took part in the operations in the Transvaal 30 Nov. 1900, to May, 1901; also in Cape Colony, May to Sept. 1901 (Queen's Medal with four clasps). In 1908 he saw service on the North-West Frontier of India, taking part in the operations in the Zakka Khel and the Mohmand countries, for which he received the Medal and clasp. He was Adjutant of the 1st Battn. Seaforth Highlanders, 1902 to 1906. He was promoted to Lieutenant-Colonel, Dec. 1913. Lieut.-Colonel Daniell served in the European War from 1914. He was twice mentioned in Despatches, and created a Companion of the Distinguished Service Order [London Gazette, 18 Feb. 1915]: "Francis Edward Lloyd Daniell, Major, 1st Battn. Seaforth Highlanders." He served as a G.S.O., 1st Grade. Lieut.-Colonel Daniell fell in action about 4 March, 1916. In 1907 he had married Maud Esmee, younger daughter of General H. W. Duperior, Royal Engineers, late Director-General of Military Works in India. His D.S.O. was awarded "for services in connection with operations in the field."

FISHER, BERTIE DREW, Major, was born 13 July, 1878. He was educated at Marlborough (1892–95), and was gazetted to the 17th Lancers 23 May, 1900. He served in the South African War from 1900 to 1902; was present at the operations in the Transvaal, east of Pretoria, July to 29 Nov. 1900; in the Orange River Colony, May to 29 Nov. 1900, including action at Caledon River (27 to 29 Nov.); again in Orange River Colony and Cape Colony 30 Nov. 1900, to 31 May, 1902. He received the Queen's Medal with three clasps, and the King's Medal with two clasps. He became Lieutenant 29 July, 1901, and was Adjutant, 17th Lancers, 1 Nov. 1904, to 31 Oct. 1907. He was promoted Captain 7 Sept. 1905; passed the Staff College, and was G.S.O., 3rd Grade, War Office, from 13 Oct. 1913, to 4 Aug. 1914. He became Major 7 Jan. 1914, and was G.S.O., 2nd Grade (temporary), War Office, from 5 Aug. to 15 Sept. 1914. He served in the European War from 1914; was Brigade Major, 6th Cavalry Brigade, 20 Sept. 1914, to 3 May, 1915. Major Fisher was mentioned three times in Despatches, and created a Companion of the Distinguished Service Order [London Gazette, 18 Feb. 1915]: "Bertie Drew Fisher, Major, on Staff." He was G.S.O., 2nd Grade, 4 May to 11 June, 1915; was Temporary Lieutenant-Colonel, Leicestershire Yeomanry, 7 July to 27 Aug. 1915; G.S.O., 1st Grade, and Temporary Lieutenant-Colonel, 28 Aug. 1915, to 17 Jan. 1918. He was given the Brevet of Lieutenant-Colonel 3 June, 1916; was Brigade Commander, 8th Infantry Brigade, British Armies in France, from 12 April, 1918; Lieutenant-Colonel, 17th Lancers, 24 Feb. 1919; was created a C.M.G. in 1919; received the Croix d'Officier, Legion of Honour, and a Bar to the Distinguished Service Order. His D.S.O. was awarded "for services in connection with operations in the field."

BROWN, EDWARD, Major, was born 22 Oct. 1876, at Bangor, County Down, Ireland, son of Henry Brown, of Cunningham, County Down, Ireland, and Zillah Brown. He was educated privately, and joined the Army Veterinary Department 9 Nov. 1898; served during the South African War of 1899–1902, as Senior Veterinary Officer, 11th Division; took part in the operations in Orange River Colony (May to 29 Nov. 1900), including actions at Biddulphsberg and Wittebergen (1 to 29 July); served during the operations in Cape Colony, south of the Orange River, Nov. 1899, to Feb. 1900; took part in the operations in the Transvaal, July, 1901, to May, 1902; in Orange River Colony, Dec. 1900; also during the operations on the Zululand Frontier of Natal, Sept. and Oct. 1901. He received the Queen's Medal with five clasps, and the King's Medal with two clasps. He became Captain 9 Nov. 1903, and Major 2 June, 1914. Major Brown served in the European War, as Assistant Director of Veterinary Services, 7th Division, B.E.F., 31 Aug. 1914, to 24 Feb. 1915; as Temporary Lieutenant-Colonel, R.A.V.C., 21 July, 1915. He was mentioned in Despatches twice; was given the Brevet of Lieutenant-Colonel 3 June, 1918, and created a Companion of the Distinguished Service Order [London Gazette, 18 Feb. 1915]: "Edward Brown, Major, Army Veterinary Corps." Lieut.-Colonel Brown married, in 1919, Mary Ethel, second daughter of the Very Rev. W. T. B. Hayter, M.A., Dean of Gibraltar, and of Maud, youngest daughter of Sir Thomas Proctor Beauchamp, Bart. His D.S.O. was awarded "for services in connection with operations in the field."

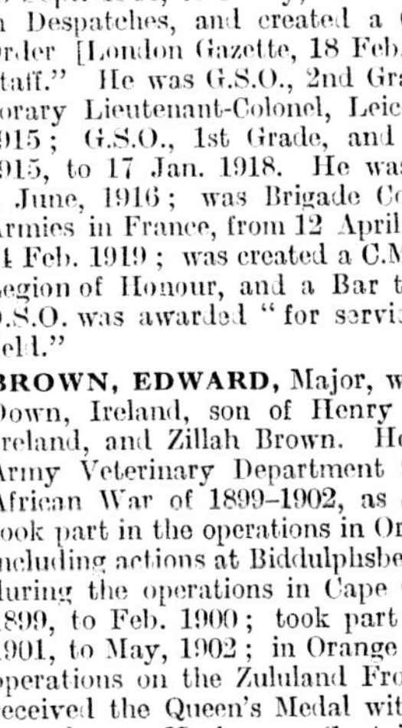

HOME, ARCHIBALD FRASER, Major (Temporary Colonel), was born 14 Sept. 1874, at Kasanti, India, eldest son of Colonel Frederick Jervis Home, C.S.I., late R.E., and Constance Stanley (who died in 1894), eldest daughter of J. S. M'Gowan. He was educated at Aldenham School, and joined the 11th Hussars 20 Feb. 1896, as Second Lieutenant, becoming Lieutenant 9 Oct. 1899. He became Captain 12 Nov. 1904; was Officer in Charge of Musketry Duties, Southern Command; Captain, attached General Staff mand, from 8 Sept. 1905, to 15 Jan. 1909; Brigade Major, 3rd Cavalry Brigade, Irish Command, 6 May, 1912, to 31 Sept. 1913; G.S.O., 2nd Grade, Staff College, 1 Oct. 1913, to 4 Aug. 1914; became Major 3 June, 1914. He served in the European War from 1914; G.S.O., 2nd Grade, 5 Aug. to 9 Oct. 1914. He was mentioned in Despatches 9 Dec. 1914, and 17 Feb. 1915, and was created a Companion of the Distinguished Service Order [London Gazette, 18 Feb. 1915]: "Archibald Fraser Home, Major (Temporary Colonel)." He was also mentioned in Despatches 22 June, 1915, and 1 Jan. 1916, and on another occasion; was given the Brevets of Lieutenant-Colonel 14 Jan. 1916, and of Colonel; was made a Commander of the Legion of Honour 6 Nov. 1916, and was mentioned a sixth time in Despatches 4 Jan. 1917; created a C.M.G. in 1918, and a C.B. in 1919. Brigadier-General A. F. Home retired in May, 1919. He married, in London, 17 Nov. 1900, Violet, daughter of the late W. K. D'Arcy, Esq., of Stanmore Hall, Stanmore, and their children are: Douglas, born 7 Aug. 1901, and Esther. His D.S.O. was awarded "for services in connection with operations in the field."

RAWLINS, STUART WILLIAM HUGHES, Major, was born 11 May, 1880, son of William Donaldson Rawlins, Esq., K.C., M.A., and Elizabeth Margaret, only daughter of the late Charles King. He was educated at Eton, and joined the Royal Marine Artillery 1 Jan. 1898, and the Royal Artillery 3 May, 1900, and became Lieutenant 3 April, 1901. He served in the South African War in 1902; was present at operations in the Orange River Colony and Cape Colony in May, 1902 (Queen's Medal with three clasps). He was employed with the King's African Rifles 3 Nov. 1903, to 2 Nov. 1908; was Adjutant, Royal Artillery, 6 Dec. 1909, to 5 Dec. 1912; became Captain 1 April, 1910. He passed the Staff College. Lieut.-Colonel Rawlins served in the European War from 1914; was Assistant Embarkation Staff Officer (graded Staff Captain) from 5 Aug. to 3 Sept. 1914; was Brigade Major 4 Sept. 1914, to 25 Aug. 1915; was promoted to Major 30 Oct. 1914. He was ten times mentioned in Despatches, and created a Companion of the Distinguished Service Order [London Gazette, 18 Feb. 1915]: "Stuart William Hughes Rawlins, Major, Staff." He was given the Brevet of Lieutenant-Colonel 1 Jan. 1916. Lieut.-Colonel Rawlins was D.A.A.G., 10 Nov. 1915, to 29 Feb. 1916; was G.S.O.2, 4th Army, B.E.F., 1 March to 7 June, 1916; G.S.O.2, 10 July, 1916, to 2 April, 1919; was given the Brevet of Colonel 1 Jan. 1919; received the 1914 Star, and the French and Belgian Croix de Guerre; is Chevalier of the Legion of Honour and Commandeur of the Order of Leopold, and was created a Companion of the Most Distinguished Order of St. Michael and St. George [London Gazette, 1 Jan. 1918. Lieut.-Colonel Rawlins married, in Nov. 1910, Dorothy Pepys, daughter of the late J. R. Cockerell, Madras Civil Service, and they have one son, Stuart Theodore Pepys. His D.S.O. was awarded "for services in connection with operations in the field."

SERGISON-BROOKE, BERTRAM NORMAN, Major, was born 20 July, 1880, in London, son of Arthur Basil Brooke (deceased), who was the third son of Sir Arthur Brooke, Bart., of Colebrooke, Brookeborough, Fermanagh. He was educated at Eton College, and joined the 3rd Battn. Grenadier Guards, as Second Lieutenant, 12 Aug. 1899. He served in South Africa, 1899–1902, and was present during operations in the Transvaal, east of Pretoria, July to 29 Nov. 1900, including actions at Belfast (26 and 27 Aug.); served during the operations in Orange River Colony and Cape Colony, Dec. 1900, to May, 1902. He received the Queen's Medal with three clasps, and the King's Medal with two clasps; became Lieutenant 14 Dec. 1900; was Adjutant, Grenadier Guards, 1 April, 1905 to 9 March, 1908; became Captain 10 Nov. 1907; was employed with the Egyptian Army 13 March, 1908, to 2 Nov. 1910. He passed the Staff College. Capt. Brooke served in the European War; was Assistant Embarkation Staff Officer (graded Staff Captain) 5 Aug. to 17 Sept. 1914; was Staff Captain 18 Sept. to 14 Nov. 1914; became Major 11 Nov. 1914, and went out with the 7th Division as Brigade Major, 1st Guards Brigade, 1 Nov. 1914, to 14 Nov. 1915. He was mentioned in Despatches, and created a Companion of the Distinguished Service Order [London Gazette, 18 Feb. 1915]: "Bertram Norman Brooke, Major, Grenadier Guards." He was Brigade Major, 2nd Guards Brigade, 18 Aug. to 25 Nov. 1915; G.S.O.2, 5th Corps, 26 Nov. 1915, to 26 Jan. 1916; Temporary Lieutenant-Colonel, Grenadier Guards, Jan. to 15 Sept. 1916, when he was wounded; Brigade Commander, 2nd Guards Brigade, British Armies in France, 22 Aug. 1917. He was given the Brevet of Lieutenant-Colonel 1 Jan. 1918. "Truth" said: "Major B. N. Sergison-Brooke, of the Grenadier Guards, steps into General Ponsonby's shoes, and becomes a Brigadier-General at the age of thirty-seven. He has been in the thick of many fights, and has had four mentions during the war, besides getting the D.S.O." He married, 8 July, 1915, at St. Margaret's, Westminster, Prudence, eldest daughter of the late Capt. C. Sergison, of Cuckfield Park, Sussex, and they have one daughter, Patience Ann. His D.S.O. was awarded "for services in connection with operations in the field."

MAXWELL-SCOTT, WALTER JOSEPH, Capt., was born 10 April, 1875, eldest son of the Honourable Joseph Constable-Maxwell (third son of Baron Herries of Terregles) and of the Honourable Mrs. Maxwell-Scott (Mary Monica, great-granddaughter of Sir Walter Scott, and daughter of the late J. R. Hope Scott, Q.C., and Charlotte Harriet Jane Lockhart, daughter of John Gibson Lockhart). He joined the Scottish Rifles, from the 3rd Royal Scots Militia, 24 March, 1897; served on the North-West Frontier of India, in the Tirah Campaign, 1897–98 (Medal with clasp). He became Lieutenant 28 Dec. 1898. He served in the South African War, 1899 to 1902; was present at the operations in Natal, 1899, including actions at Rietfontein and Lombard's Kop; at the defence of Ladysmith; during operations in the Transvaal, east of Pretoria, July to 29 Nov. 1900; again in the Transvaal 30 Nov. 1900, to 31 May, 1902; also during the operations on the Zululand Frontier of Natal in Sept. and Oct. 1901, including defence of Forts Itala and Prospect. He became Captain 22 June, 1901; received the Queen's South African Medal with two clasps, and the King's Medal with two clasps. He was Adjutant, Scottish Rifles, 29 Oct. 1902, to 28 Oct. 1905. Capt. Maxwell-Scott passed the Staff College in India; was G.S.O., 3rd Grade, War Office, 16 Oct. 1911, to 30 Nov. 1913; Brigade Major, 6th Infantry Brigade, Aldershot Command, 1 Dec. 1913, to 4 Aug. 1914. He served in the European War from 1914; was Brigade Major, 6th Infantry Brigade, 5 Aug. 1914, to 27 Feb. 1915. He was created a Companion of the Distinguished Service Order [London Gazette, 18 Feb. 1915]: "Walter Joseph Maxwell-Scott, Capt., Staff." He became G.S.O., 2nd Grade, 22nd Division, 3 March, 1915; was promoted Major, 11 March, 1915, and became Temporary Lieutenant-Colonel and G.S.O., 1st Grade, 22nd Division, 23 Oct. 1915. He was Brigadier-General, General Staff, 9th Army Corps, British Armies in France, 25 Dec. 1917, to 8 Nov. 1918; Brigadier-General, General Staff, 7th Army Corps, British Armies in France, 9 Nov. to 26 Dec. 1918; Brigadier-General, General Staff, 19th Army Corps, British Armies in France, 27 Dec. 1918. Lieut.-Colonel W. J. Maxwell-Scott received the Serbian Order of Kara Georg with Swords in 1916, and the Légion d'Honneur (Croix d'Officier), 1917. He was given the Brevet of Lieutenant-Colonel 3 June, 1916; the Brevet of Colonel 3 June, 1918; was five times mentioned in Despatches. He married, in 1918, Mairi Richmond, third daughter of the late Lieut.-Colonel Steuart Macdougall, of Lunga. His D.S.O. was awarded "for services in connection with operations in the field."

MOORE, CLAUDE DOUGLAS HAMILTON, Major, was born 9 Feb. 1875, son of Dr. Francis and Sophie S. Hamilton Moore. He is a Master of Arts of Cambridge (Trinity Hall), and has passed the Staff College. He joined the Royal Warwickshire Regt. 4 May, 1898; became Lieutenant 28 Dec. 1898, and Captain 16 Nov. 1901; was Adjutant, 2nd Battn. Royal Warwickshire Regt., 1 July, 1904, to 30 June, 1907. He was Garrison Adjutant (graded Staff Captain), Irish Command, 10 July, 1908, to 21 Jan. 1910; D.A.A. and Q.M.G., North China, from 14 Dec. 1912, to Aug. 1914. Capt. Hamilton Moore served in the European War from Aug. 1914; was Temporary Major, Royal Warwickshire Regt., from 25 Oct. to 18 Dec. 1914; promoted Major 19 Dec. 1914. He was D.A.Q.M.G. from 2 Feb. to 14 April, 1915; A.A. and Q.M.G. 15 April to 4 July, 1915; A.Q.M.G. 5 July, 1915, to 7 Feb. 1916; D.A. and Q.M.G., 9th Army Corps, 8 Feb. to 4 Oct. 1916; commanded 157th Infantry Brigade, Egyptian Expeditionary Force, 5 Oct. 1916. He was given the Brevet of Lieutenant-Colonel 3 June, 1916, and the Brevet of Colonel 1 Jan. 1917. He received the 5th Class of the Order of the Rising Sun of Japan, for war services at Tsingtau; the Legion of Honour (France), for operations in the Dardanelles; the 3rd Class of the Order of the Nile, for the fighting in Egypt and Palestine, and was created a Companion of the Distinguished Service Order [London Gazette, 18 Feb. 1915]: "Claude Douglas Hamilton Moore, Major, Royal Warwickshire Regt.," and a Companion of St. Michael and St. George, Jan. 1918. He was eight times mentioned in Despatches. His D.S.O. was awarded "for services in connection with operations in the field."

JAMES, ALFRED HENRY COTES, Capt., was born 30 Aug. 1873. He was educated at Sherborne, and at Merton College, Oxford, (B.A.), and entered the South Staffordshire Regt., as a Second Lieutenant, 15 May, 1897, becoming Lieutenant 15 Sept. 1899. He was Adjutant from 14 Aug. 1901, to 13 Aug. 1904. He served in the South African War, 1899–1902; took part in the operations in the Orange Free State, April to May, 1900; in Orange River Colony, May to 29 Nov. 1900, including actions at Wittebergen (1 to 29 July); in Cape Colony, south of Orange River, 1899–1900; served as Adjutant, 1st Battn. South Staffordshire Regt., from 14 Aug. 1901; also in the Transvaal in July, 1901; and again in Orange River Colony 30 Nov. 1900, to March, 1902, attached to the Army Service Corps (Despatches [London Gazette, 10 Sept. 1901, and 29 July, 1902]; Queen's Medal with three clasps, and King's Medal with two clasps). He became Captain 21 April, 1902; was Garrison Adjutant, Eastern Command, 1 April, 1908, to 31 March, 1912. Capt. James served in the European War, 1914–18. He was Assistant Provost-Marshal, 3rd Army Corps, B.E.F., 5 Aug. 1914, to 27 Oct. 1915; was created a Companion of the Distinguished Service Order [London Gazette, 18 Feb. 1915]: "Alfred Henry Cotes James, Capt., Staff." He became Major 26 May, 1915, and was Provost-Marshal, 3rd Army, B.E.F., British Armies in France, 28 Oct. 1915, to 2 Aug. 1918 (Temporary Lieutenant-Colonel, Dec. 1915, to June, 1918); became Provost-Marshal, Forces in Great Britain, 4 Aug. 1918, with the temporary rank of Brigadier-General. For his services he was twice mentioned in Despatches; was created M.V.O. in 1915, and was given the Brevet of Lieutenant-Colonel 3 June, 1918. He married in 1910, Edith Mary Bray, and has one son. His D.S.O. was awarded "for services in connection with operations in the field."

DRYSDALE, WILLIAM, Capt., was born 4 Nov. 1876, at Pitteadie, Kirkcaldy, N.B., youngest son of the late William Drysdale, Esq., of Kilrie, Fifeshire, and of Mrs. Drysdale (*née* Georgina Begbie). He was educated at Loretto, and worthily upheld the traditions of the school, both in work and sport, throughout his life. At the Royal Military College he won the First Prize for riding. He entered the Royal Scots 5 Sept. 1896; became Lieutenant 30 Aug. 1898, and Captain 19 Nov. 1902, and was Adjutant of Volunteers, Dec. 1903, to Dec. 1906. He was for many years in India and Burma, where he gained a reputation as a fine cricketer and polo player. When a Lieutenant in the Royal Scots, he was awarded a Medal for his plucky attempt to rescue a drowning comrade 24 Nov. 1902.

William Drysdale

At the Staff College in 1908–9, Capt. Drysdale had a distinguished career, being elected Captain of the cricket and hockey teams. He won the Staff College Point-to-Point, Golf and Tennis Tournaments. On leaving the Staff College he was appointed D.A.A. and Q.M.G. to the Wessex Division, Southern Command (May, 1910, to April, 1912), and from thence he went as Brigade Major to the 15th Infantry Brigade, Irish Command, at Belfast (April, 1912, to April, 1914). On the outbreak of war he went out as Brigade Major (Aug. 1914) to 21st Infantry Brigade, 7th Division, and served with great distinction. He became Major 27 Nov. 1914, and was created a Companion of the Distinguished Service Order [London Gazette, 18 Feb. 1915]: "William Drysdale, Capt., Staff." He received his decoration for gallant conduct throughout the terrible experience of the 7th Division in the First Battle of Ypres. Capt. Drysdale showed an unsurpassed example of fearlessness and cheerful courage, refusing to quit his brigade when wounded. After many months' hard fighting, he was made G.S.O.2 to the 16th and then to the 37th Division. On the 1st of Oct. 1915, he was given command of the 7th Battn. Leicestershire Regt., and was given his Brevet of Lieutenant-Colonel in the spring of 1916. He took part in, and was wounded at, the storming of Bazentin-le-Petit 14 July, 1916, and had only just returned to his battalion when he was killed in action on the 29th Sept. His General wrote: "He was a splendid officer, fearless and always cheery. He was the best man I knew for making other men fight." An officer of the battalion says: "Without exaggeration his loss is the biggest blow the battalion has yet received. He will never be forgotten by the regiment as long as there is any regiment left." Lieut.-Colonel Drysdale had married, 19 Jan. 1904, Mary Louisa, daughter of Sir J. Muir Mackenzie, K.C.S.I. His D.S.O. was awarded "for services in connection with operations in the field."

PAKENHAM, GEORGE DE LA POER BERESFORD, Capt., was born 4 Dec. 1875, in Armagh, Ireland, son of Major Charles Pakenham, late Adjutant, 3rd Battn. Royal Irish Fusiliers, and Blanche Harrison, of Singapore. He was educated at the United Services College, Westward Ho! and at the Royal Military College, Sandhurst; was gazetted to the Indian Staff Corps, as Second Lieutenant (unattached), 16 Jan. 1895, and joined the 17th Bengal Infantry 28 March, 1896; became Lieutenant 16 April, 1897, and was transferred to the 39th Garhwal Rifles in Oct. 1897; was promoted Captain 16 Jan. 1904, and exchanged into the Border Regt. 6 Dec. 1904. He passed through the Staff College (1907–8). He was Brigade Major, 14th Infantry Brigade, Irish Command, 30 May, 1909, to 29 May, 1913. On mobilization, 5 Aug. 1914, he became G.S.O., 3rd Grade, London District, and was employed in this capacity till 3 Sept. 1914. From 3 Sept. 1914, to 18 Feb. 1915, he was Brigade Major, 2nd Infantry Brigade, 1st Division, B.E.F.; was mentioned in Despatches, Feb. 1915, and created a Companion of the Distinguished Service Order [London Gazette, 18 Feb. 1915]: "George de la Poer Beresford Pakenham, Capt., Staff." He was G.S.O., 3rd Grade, 12th Division, B.E.F., from 5 March to 31 Oct. 1915; became Major, 1 May, 1915; was G.S.O., 2nd Grade, 33rd Division, B.E.F., from 1 Nov. 1915, to 27 Sept. 1916; was mentioned in Despatches in Jan. 1916; was G.S.O., 2nd Grade, 7th Corps., B.E.F., from 28 Sept. to 22 Oct. 1916; G.S.O., 1st Grade, 56th Division, 23 Dec. 1916, to 2 April, 1919, and Lieutenant-Colonel, whilst so employed. He was a third time mentioned in Despatches on 1 Jan. 1917. On 3 June, 1917, he was mentioned in Despatches, and given the Brevet of Lieutenant-Colonel; was mentioned in Despatches in Dec. following, and once more on 3 June, 1918, when he was created a C.M.G. From April to July, 1919, he was employed as G.S.O., 2nd Grade, Southern District, Ireland. He was appointed to the command of the 2nd Battn. The Border Regt. with effect from 18 May, 1919. Lieut.-Colonel Pakenham married, 23 Feb. 1905, at Old Charlton, Kent, Emilie Elsie, fourth daughter of the late W. Fowler, Esq., of Broadlands, Prince's Park, Liverpool, and their children are: Raymond Beresford, born 31 Dec. 1907, and William Antony Beresford, born 24 Nov. 1911. His D.S.O. was awarded "for services in connection with operations in the field."

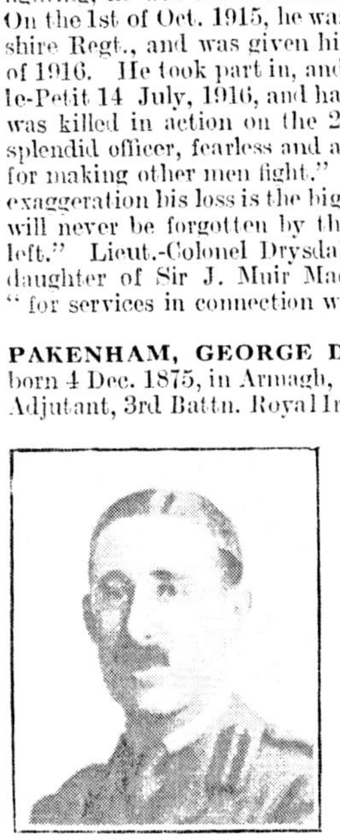

G. de la P. B. Pakenham.

THORPE, GERVASE, Capt., was born 10 Oct. 1877, son of the late Colonel James Thorpe, of Coddington Hall, Nottinghamshire, and Ardbrecknish, Argyll. He was educated at Eton, and joined the Army, as a Second Lieutenant in the Argyll and Sutherland Highlanders, 8 Sept. 1897; was promoted Lieutenant 16 July, 1899. He served in the South African War, 1899–1902, and was present in the advance on Kimberley, including actions at Modder River and Magersfontein; operations in the Orange Free State, Feb. to May, 1900, including operations at Paardeberg 17 to 26 Feb. (wounded); operations in the Transvaal, April, 1901, to 31 May, 1902; was Station Staff Officer (Queen's Medal with three clasps, and King's Medal with two clasps). He became Captain 5 Oct. 1904. Capt. Thorpe served in the European War; was D.A.Q.M.G., Military Landing Officer, British Expeditionary Force, 5 Aug. to 6 Sept. 1914; A.D.C. to the G.O.C., 3rd Division, B.E.F., 7 Sept. to 14 Oct. 1914; Adjutant, Argyll and Sutherland Highlanders, 1 Nov. 1914, to 10 Feb. 1915. He was created a Companion of the Distinguished Service Order [London Gazette, 18 Feb. 1915]: "Gervase Thorpe, Capt., Staff." He was Brigade Major, 5th Infantry Brigade, B.E.F., 11 Feb. to 8 Sept. 1915; was promoted Major 1 Sept. 1915; was G.S.O.2, G.H.Q., B.E.F., 9 Sept. 1915, to 18 March, 1916; G.S.O.1, 46th Division, 14 June, 1916, to 20 Oct. 1917; G.S.O.1, 3rd Army, British Armies in France, 21 Oct. 1917, to 6 June, 1918; Temporary Brigadier-General, Brigade Commander, 17th Infantry Brigade, British Armies in France, 7 June, 1918, to 16 Jan. 1919; became Temporary Lieutenant-Colonel, commanding the 3rd Battn. Royal Highlanders, 12 May, 1919. He was eight times mentioned in Despatches; was given the Brevet of Lieutenant-Colonel 1 Jan. 1917, and of Colonel 3 June, 1919, and was created a C.M.G. in 1918. He married, in 1917, Margaret, daughter of the late James Burt-Marshall, of Luncarty, Perthshire. His D.S.O. was awarded "for services in connection with operations in the field."

DILLON, ERIC FITZGERALD, Capt., was born 4 April, 1881, at 47, Oakley Street, Chelsea, S.W., son of the Honourable Conrad Adderly Dillon (younger son of Arthur, 16th Viscount Dillon), and of Ellen Louisa, daughter of Sir H. Dashwood, Bart., of Kirkington. He was educated at Rugby, and joined the King's Own Lancashire Militia, and then the Army Service Corps 1 July, 1900. He served in the South African War, 1900–1; was present in the operations in Cape Colony and Orange River Colony, Feb. to 29 Nov. 1900, including actions at Ladybrand (2 to 5 Sept.), Bothaville and Caledon River (27 to 29 Nov.); operations in Orange River Colony and Cape Colony 30 Nov. 1900, to Aug. 1901 (Queen's Medal with four clasps). He became Lieutenant 1 Nov. 1901, and Captain 1 Aug. 1905; passed through the Staff College, Camberley. Capt. Dillon was transferred to the Royal Munster Fusiliers 23 Sept. 1908; was specially employed at the War Office 9 May, 1912, to 12 May, 1913; was General Staff Officer, 3rd Grade, at the War Office, 19 May, 1912, to 4 Aug. 1914. Serving in the European War, he was G.S.O., 3rd Grade, 5th Division, 6 Aug. 1914, to 29 April, 1915, and was in the Retreat from Mons. He was created a Companion of the Distinguished Service Order [London Gazette, 18 Feb. 1915]: "Eric Fitzgerald Dillon, Capt., Staff." He was Brigade Major, 84th Infantry Brigade, B.E.F., 30 April to 12 June, 1915; was promoted Major 18 May, 1915; G.S.O.2, War Office, 19 July to 5 Aug. 1915; Brigade Major, 84th Infantry Brigade, British Expeditionary Force, 6 to 11 Aug. 1915; G.S.O.2, 7th Division, British Expeditionary Force, 12 Aug. 1915, to 14 April, 1916; G.S.O.2, 3rd Army, B.E.F., 15 April to 8 May, 1916; G.S.O.2, Liaison Officer with the French Army, 9 May to 27 Dec. 1916; G.S.O., British Mission to G.H.Q., French Army, 28 Dec. 1916, to 11 Aug. 1918; G.S.O., 32nd Division, British Armies in France, 3 Sept. to 30 Dec. 1918; G.S.O.1, G.H.Q., British Armies in France, 31 Dec. 1918, to 8 May, 1919; Private Secretary to the C.-in-C., British Army of the Rhine, 9 May, 1919. He was given the Brevet of Lieutenant-Colonel 1 Jan. 1917; is Chevalier and Officer of the Legion of Honour; Officier of the Order of Leopold, and has the French and Belgian Croix de Guerre. His chief recreation is hunting. Capt. Dillon married, 4 June, 1907, at Dewlish, Dorset, Norah Juanita Mabel, only child of Brigadier-General Charles Edward Beckett, C.B., late 3rd Hussars, and Louisa Augusta (died 1900), youngest daughter of the late Field-Marshal Sir J. Michel, G.C.B., of Dewlish, Dorset, and their children are: Michael Eric, born 13 Aug. 1911, and Pamela Louisa Elinor, born 15 Aug. 1915. His D.S.O. was awarded "for services in connection with operations in the field."

GRAHAM, CUTHBERT AUBREY LIONEL, Capt., was born 1 April, 1882, son of James Edward Duncan Graham. He was educated at King's School, Rochester, and at the Royal Military Academy, Woolwich, and joined the Royal Artillery 6 Jan. 1900; became Lieutenant 3 April, 1901, and Captain 1 April, 1908. He commanded the Malay States Guides, Mountain Battery, 16 June, 1908, to 16 Sept. 1910, and was Adjutant, Royal Artillery, 5 Feb. 1913, to 4 Aug. 1914. He served in the European War, as Staff Captain, 4th Divisional Artillery, British Expeditionary Force, 5 Aug. 1914, to 28 Feb. 1915, and was created a Companion of the Distinguished Service Order [London Gazette, 18 Feb. 1915]: "Cuthbert Aubrey Lionel Graham, Capt., Staff." He was Brigade Major, No. 2 Group, Heavy Artillery Reserve, B.E.F., 6 March, 1915, to 12 March, 1916; became Major 11 June, 1915; commanded the 18th Battery until May, 1916, when he was invalided. He was specially employed at the War Office in Oct. 1916; G.S.O.3, War Office, 1 Nov. 1916, to 27 June, 1917; D.A.A.G., War Office, 14 Nov, 1917, to 26 May, 1918, and D.A.A.G. 27 May to 23 Oct. 1918, proceeding to North Russia in June, 1918. He became Temporary Lieutenant-Colonel commanding a column, Oct. 1918, and Temporary Brigadier-General commanding the Dwina Force 30 Jan. 1919. He was mentioned in Despatches four times in France and two in North Russia; was given the Brevet of Lieutenant-Colonel 3 June, 1919, for services in North Russia, and also received the Croix de Guerre. He married, in 1911, Josephine Margaret, daughter of the late Sir Joseph Terry, of York, and they have one son, John, born 27 July, 1912. His D.S.O. was awarded "for services in connection with operations in the field."

GRAHAM, CHARLES PERCY, Capt., was born 12 July, 1881. He entered the Army, as a Second Lieutenant in the Unattached List, 28 July, 1900, and joined the Indian Army 17 Oct. 1901. He was promoted Lieutenant 1 June, 1903; Captain 28 July, 1909, and was transferred to the Welsh Regt. 22 Nov. 1913. Capt. Graham served in the European War, being employed from 5 Aug. 1914, to 27 May, 1915, as Assistant Provost-Marshal of the 1st Division, B.E.F. He was created a Companion of the Distinguished Service Order [London Gazette, 18 Feb. 1915]: "Charles Percy Graham, Captain, Staff." He served as A.P.M., 6th Army Corps, B.E.F., British Armies in France, 28 May, 1915, to 19 June, 1917, becoming Major 8 Jan. 1917; was A.P.M., Lines of Communication, British Forces in Italy, 4 Dec. 1917, to 15 May, 1918; Temporary Lieutenant-Colonel from June, 1917; Provost-Marshal, 3rd Army, British Armies in France, 3 Aug. 1918, to 2 April, 1919; became Deputy Provost-Marshal, Southern Command, 25 May, 1919. Major Graham was created a C.B.E. in 1919. He is married, and has one son. His D.S.O. was awarded "for services in connection with operations in the field."

REID, WALTER RICHARD, Capt., was born 11 April, 1880, son of Inspector-General Walter Reid, Royal Navy. He was gazetted to the Royal Artillery 26 May, 1900; became Lieutenant 15 Jan. 1903; was

Adjutant, Territorial Force, 22 June, 1908, to 31 Oct. 1911 ; was promoted to Captain 9 May, 1911, and was Adjutant, Royal Artillery, 8 Nov. 1913, to 4 Aug. 1914. Capt. Reid served in the European War, 1914 ; was employed as Staff Captain, R.A., 3rd Division, B.E.F., 5 Aug. 1914, to 14 Nov. 1915. He was promoted Major 30 Oct. 1914. He was created a Companion of the Distinguished Service Order [London Gazette, 18 Feb. 1915] : " Walter Richard Reid, Capt., Staff." He was D.A.A.G., 13th Army Corps, B.E.F., British Armies in France, 15 Nov. 1915, to 30 Oct. 1916, D.A.A.G., 4th Army Corps, British Armies in France, 1 April to 27 Aug. 1917 ; became G.S.O.2, 4th Army Corps, British Armies in France, 28 Aug. 1917. He was given the Brevet of Lieutenant-Colonel 3 June, 1918, and was twice mentioned in Despatches. His D.S.O. was awarded " for services in connection with operations in the field."

DAVIES, CLAUDE MARTIN, Capt., was born 23 Oct. 1881, son o Byam Martin Davies, Esq. He joined the Rifle Brigade 4 Dec. 1901 was promoted Lieutenant 1 July, 1905, and Captain 6 Oct. 1911 passed through the Staff College ; was Brigade Major, 12th Infantry Brigade, Eastern Command, 30 May, 1912, to 4 Aug. 1914. He served in the European War, 1914–18, in France, Gallipoli and Egypt ; was Brigade Major, 12th Infantry Brigade, B.E.F., 5 Aug. 1914, to 31 March, 1915, and was created a Companion of the Distinguished Service Order [London Gazette, 18 Feb. 1915] : " Claude Martin Davies, Capt., Staff." He subsequently held the following appointments : G.S.O.3, 3rd Army, Central Force, Home Defence, 12 April to 2 July, 1915 ; Special Appointment, Mediterranean Expeditionary Force in July, 1915 ; G.S.O.3, 8th Army Corps, Mediterranean Expeditionary Force, 5 July to 17 Aug. 1915 ; G.S.O.2, 52nd Division, Mediterranean Expeditionary Force, 18 Aug. 1915, to 20 April 1916 ; G.S.O.1, 52nd Division, Egyptian Expeditionary Force, 21 April to 7 Nov. 1916. He was given the Brevet of Major 3 June, 1916, and became Major 4 Dec. 1916 ; was G.S.O.1, with Frontier Force, Egyptian Expeditionary Force, 8 to 30 Nov. 1916 ; G.S.O.1, 73rd Division, Home Forces, to 31 Dec. 1917 ; G.S.O.1, 47th Division, British Armies in France, 20 Feb. to 15 July, 1918 ; became G.S.O.1, 58th Division, British Armies in France, 16 July, 1918. He was given the Brevet of Lieutenant-Colonel 1 Jan. 1919, and was three times mentioned in Despatches. His D.S.O. was awarded " for services in connection with opera-tions in the field."

BAIRD, JOHN LAWRENCE, Major, was born in London 27 April, 1874, eldest son of Sir Alexander Baird, Bart., of Urie, Lord Lieutenant of Kin-cardineshire, and the Hon. Annette Palk, daughter of Baron Haldon (who died in 1884). He joined the Diplomatic Service ; was Attaché at Vienna, 1896 ; Cairo, 1898 ; Abyssinia, 1899 ; Private Secretary to Sir William Garstin, Under-Secretary for Public Works in Egypt, 1900–2 ; Acting Agent and Consul-General in Abyssinia, 1902 ; Political Officer, British East Africa, and Abyssinian Frontier Survey, 1902–3. He served in the Somali Campaign, as Political Officer on Staff of Colonel Rochfort, with the Abyssinian Army, 1903–4 (C.M.G., 1904) ; Despatches ; Medal and clasp) ; Second Secretary, Paris, 1904–6 ; Buenos Ayres, 1906–8. He joined the 1/2nd Scottish Horse (Yeomanry) in 1906, and, on the outbreak of the European War, he went out with the Expeditionary Force to France 12 Aug. 1914, as Staff Captain in the Intelligence Corps. He was mentioned in Despatches [London Gazette, 18 Feb. 1915] ; received the Order of Leopold, and was created a Companion of the Distinguished Service Order [London Gazette, 18 Feb. 1915] : " John Lawrence Baird, C.M.G., Major, Scottish Horse Yeomanry." He was transferred to the War Office, Dec. 1915, as G.S.O., 3rd Grade, and became Parliamentary Member of the Air Board in May, 1916, and Parliamentary Secretary to the Air Board in 1917 ; Under Secretary of State for the Royal Air Force, 1918 ; Vice-President of Air Council, 1918. He is a J.P., D.L., and has been Unionist Member for the Rugby Division of Warwickshire since 1910. He married, in 1905, Lady Ethel Keith-Falconer, eldest daughter of the 10th Earl of Kintore, and they have two sons and two daughters. His D.S.O. was awarded " for services in connection with operations in the field."

BURKE, CHARLES JAMES, Capt. and Brevet Major (Temporary Lieut.-Colonel), was born 9 March, 1882, youngest son of the late Mr. C. C. Burke, of Ballinhone House, Armagh. He served in the South African War of 1899–1902 ; was present in operations in the Transvaal (Queen's Medal with two clasps). He joined the Royal Irish Regt., as Second Lieutenant from the Militia, 26 Sept. 1903 ; became Lieutenant 15 June, 1904 ; was employed with the West African Frontier Force 22 July, 1905, to 6 Dec. 1909 ; became Captain 22 Dec. 1909. He took up flying in 1910, and was employed in connection with the Aeroplanes and Balloon School 22 Nov. 1910, to 31 March, 1911, and flew the first aeroplane pur-chased by the British Government. He served with the Air Battn. Royal Engineers, Digits Formation, 1 April, 1911, to 12 May, 1912 ; joined the Royal Flying Corps 12 May, 1912. During these periods he was twice injured in aeroplane accidents 7 Jan. 1911, and 1 Aug. 1912. He was given the Brevet of Major 3 June, 1913. He served in the European War from 1914, and was mentioned in Despatches in Oct. of that year ; became Temporary Lieutenant-Colonel 9 Nov. 1914. He was mentioned in De-spatches in Jan. 1915, and created a Companion of the Distinguished Ser-vice Order [London Gazette, 18 Feb. 1915] : " Charles James Burke, Capt. and Brevet Major (Temporary Lieutenant-Colonel), Royal Irish Regt." He was appointed Commandant of the Central Flying School 1 Feb. 1916. Lieut.-Colonel C. J. Burke was killed in action 9 April, 1917, while com-manding a battalion of the East Lancashire Regt. He was a Member of the Royal United Service Institution and Meteorological Society, and an Associate Fellow of the Aeronautical Society. He married Beatrice Osborn, third daughter of W. Shakspeare, of 42 Prince's Gardens, S.W., and Yately, Hants. His D.S.O. was awarded " for services (R.F.C.) in connection with operations in the field."

SALMOND, JOHN MAITLAND, Capt. and Brevet Major, was borr 17 July, 1881, son of Major-General Sir William Salmond, K.C.B., and Emma Mary Hoyle, youngest daughter of William Fretwell Hoyle, of Hooton Levet Hall, Maltby, Yorkshire.

John M. Salmond.

He was educated at Wellington and Sand-hurst. He joined the Army 8 Jan. 1901, as Second Lieutenant (Unattached), and became Lieutenant, Royal Lancaster Regt., 9 March, 1901. He served in the South African War, 1901–2, and in the operations in the Transvaal, Jan. 1901, and Feb. to 31 May, 1902 (Queen's Medal with three clasps). He was employed with the West African Frontier Force 14 Nov. 1903, to 20 June, 1905 ; became Captain, Royal Lancaster Regt., 26 June, 1910, and Captain, Royal Flying Corps, 12 Nov. 1912. Capt. Salmond was In-structor (graded Flight Commander), Central Flying School, Royal Flying Corps, 12 Nov. 1912, to 20 May, 1913, and In-structor (graded Squadron Commander), Central Flying School, Royal Flying Corps, 31 May, 1913, to 20 April, 1914 ; was given the Brevet of Major 22 June, 1914. He served in the European War from 1914 to 1918, and was created a Companion of the Distinguished Service Order [London Gazette, 18 Feb. 1915] : " John Maitland Salmond, Capt. and Brevet Major, Royal Lancaster Regt., Royal Flying Corps." On 13 Feb. 1915, he was gazetted Temporary Lieutenant-Colonel (Wing Commander), and on the 23rd he took command of the Administrative Wing, R.F.C., South Farnborough. He became Major 8 Jan. 1916, and became Brigade Commander 1 Feb. 1916, then taking over the organization of the Training Brigade, Royal Flying Corps, Home Establishment, entirely reorganizing the system. He was promoted to the rank of Major-General 22 June, 1917, and four months later was appointed Director-General of Military Aeronautics at the War Office, becoming at the age of 36 a Member of the Army Council. On 11 Jan. 1918, he took command of the Royal Flying Corps, British Armies in France (vice Major-General H. M. Trenchard), and later on the Rhine, sub-sequently taking command of the Inland Area, Great Britain, with Head-quarters later at Uxbridge, Middlesex. Air Vice-Marshal Sir J. M. Salmond was created a C.M.G. in 1917, a C.V.O., 1918, and a K.C.B., 1919 ; was five times mentioned in Despatches ; is Officer of the Legion of Honour ; Commander of the Order of the Crown of Italy ; Commander of Order of Leopold (Belgium) ; belongs to the Order of the White Eagle (Russia), and has the American Distinguished Service Medal. He is a widower, and has one daughter.

The following telegrams were exchanged between the Air Ministry and General Salmond, G.H.Q., France :—

" The Air Council congratulate you and all ranks of R.N.A.S., R.F.C., and Australian Flying Corps on the splendid work carried out during this great battle. We are all following their great deeds, and know that they will keep it going.—Air Ministry."

" Very many thanks for Air Council's congratulations, which are much appreciated by all concerned. All ranks have their tails well up, and the superiority of British over enemy airmen has never been more marked.— General Salmond."

His D.S.O. was awarded " for services in connection with operations in the field."

MUSGRAVE, HERBERT, Capt. (Temporary Major), was born 11 May, 1876, youngest son of the late Sir Anthony Musgrave, G.C.M.G., and Jeanie Lucinda Field. He was educated at Harrow ; became Second

Herbert Musgrave.

Lieutenant, Royal Engineers, 1 March, 1898, and Lieutenant 1 March, 1899. He served in the South African War, 1899–1902 ; took part in the advance on Kimber-ley, including actions at Belmont, Enslin, Modder River and Magersfontein ; in the Orange Free State, Feb. 1900, including operations at Paardeberg ; in the Trans-vaal ; in Orange River Colony, June to Nov. 1900, including action at Witte-bergen ; in the Transvaal, June, 1901, to 31 May, 1902 ; again in Orange River Colony, Dec. 1900, to June, 1901 ; also during the operations in Cape Colony, Feb. to April, 1901 (Despatches [London Gazette, 8 Feb. and 10 Sept. 1901] ; Queen's Medal with five clasps, and King's Medal with two clasps) ; was employed with the South African Constabulary, 3 June, 1901, to 20 Sept. 1904 ; became Captain, Royal Engineers, 1 March, 1905, and Royal Flying Corps 30 April, 1913. He passed through the Staff College ; was D.A.A. and Q.M.G., Malta, 8 Aug. 1908, to 8 Aug. 1912. He was Deputy Assistant Director of Military Aeronautics, War Office (temporary), 5 Aug. to 14 Sept. 1914 ; was promoted Major, Royal Engineers, 30 Oct. 1914. He served in the European War from 1914, and was created a Companion of the Distinguished Service Order [London Gazette, 18 Feb. 1915] : " Herbert Musgrave, Capt., Temporary Major, Royal Engineers, attached Royal Flying Corps." He became D.A.Q.M.G. 4 March, 1915 ; was four times mentioned in Despatches, and was wounded. Major Musgrave returned to France 27 Dec. 1917, to the Staff of the 2nd Corps, and fell in action 3 June, 1918. In 1915 Major Musgrave married Georgeanna, only daughter of Mark Hopkins, of Pau, France, and they had one daughter, Jeanie Lucinda, and one son, Herbert William Dudley, born after his father's death. His D.S.O. was awarded "for services in connection with operations in the field."

MANSFIELD, WILLIAM HENRY CHARLES, Lieut. (Temporary Captain), was born 3 Oct. 1887, and was gazetted to the Shropshire Light Infantry 9 Oct. 1907, being promoted to Lieutenant 24 July, 1912. He served in the European War from 1914-17; became Lieutenant, Royal Flying Corps, 28 April, 1914, and was Temporary Captain from 7 Dec. 1914, to 9 June, 1915. Capt. Mansfield was mentioned in Despatches, and created a Companion of the Distinguished Service Order [London Gazette, 18 Feb. 1915]: "William Henry Charles Mansfield, Lieut. (Temporary Capt.), Shropshire Light Infantry, Royal Flying Corps." He became Captain 10 June, 1915; was Temporary Major, March, 1916, to Oct. 1917, and Temporary Lieutenant-Colonel, Oct. 1917, to March, 1918; was employed under the Air Ministry from 1 April, 1918; became Squadron Commander, Royal Flying Corps. His D.S.O. was awarded "for services in connection with operations in the field."

William H. C. Mansfield.

HARVEY-KELLY, HUBERT DUNSTERVILLE, Lieut., was born 9 Feb. 1891. He joined the Royal Irish Regt. 5 Oct. 1910; became Lieutenant 23 Oct. 1912, and Lieutenant, Royal Flying Corps Reserve, 14 Aug. 1913. He served in the European War from 1914 to 1918. He was mentioned in Despatches, and created a Companion of the Distinguished Service Order [London Gazette, 18 Feb. 1915]: "Hubert Dunsterville Harvey-Kelly, Lieut., Royal Irish Regt., Royal Flying Corps." He became Captain 23 May, 1915; Squadron Commander, Royal Flying Corps, and Temporary Major 30 Jan. 1916. His D.S.O. was awarded "for services in connection with operations in the field."

MAPPLEBECK, G. W., Lieut., served in the European War. He was mentioned in Despatches, and created a Companion of the Distinguished Service Order [London Gazette, 18 Feb. 1915]: "G. W. Mapplebeck, Lieut., The Liverpool Regt." His D.S.O. was awarded "for services in connection with operations in the field."

GURNEY, THOMAS CLAUD, Capt., was born 9 Aug. 1880, son of the late Charles Henry Gurney. He joined the 1st Dragoons 11 Aug. 1900, and was promoted Lieutenant 22 June, 1901. He served in the South African War, 1901-2 (as A.D.C. to Brigadier-General 5 May to 14 July, 1902, and as Adjutant, Imperial Yeomanry, 24 Oct. 1901, to 31 March, 1903); was present in the operations in the Transvaal, May to Aug. 1901, and March to 31 May, 1902; in Orange River Colony, Aug. 1901, to March, 1902; also in Cape Colony, May, 1902 (Queen's Medal with three clasps). He reverted to Second Lieutenant on joining the 2nd Life Guards 23 Jan. 1904; became Lieutenant 2 Sept. 1905; was Adjutant, Imperial Yeomanry, 24 Oct. 1907, to 31 March, 1908; Adjutant, Territorial Forces, 1 April, 1908, to 23 Oct. 1911, and was promoted Captain 6 March, 1909. Capt. Gurney served in the European War from 1914 to 1915. He was mentioned in Despatches, and created a Companion of the Distinguished Service Order [London Gazette, 18 Feb. 1915]: "Thomas Claud Gurney, Capt., 2nd Life Guards." He became Major 12 Jan. 1915, and was Temporary Lieutenant-Colonel 27 Aug. to 7 Sept. 1915. On 25 March, 1919, he retired from the Army with the rank of Lieutenant-Colonel. He married, in 1906, Muriel Frances, eldest daughter of the late Charles Percy Sykes, of West Ella Hall, Yorkshire. His D.S.O. was awarded "for services in connection with operations in the field."

HORNBY, CHARLES BECK, Capt., was born 7 Feb. 1883, son of the late Colonel John Frederick Hornby, 12th Lancers, and Mary Ellen Hornby, of Little Ness, Shrewsbury. He joined the 4th Dragoon Guards 8 May, 1901; became Lieutenant 14 Oct. 1903, and Captain 10 Oct. 1909. He was Adjutant, 4th Dragoon Guards, 21 Jan. 1911, to 20 Jan. 1914. Capt. Hornby served in the European War in 1914 and 1915. He was created a Companion of the Distinguished Service Order [London Gazette, 18 Feb. 1915]: "Charles Beck Hornby, Capt., 4th (Royal Irish) Dragoon Guards." He was promoted Major 5 Aug. 1915; was specially employed at the War Office 17 to 31 Oct. 1916; G.S.O.3, War Office, 1 Nov. 1916, to 22 May, 1917; specially employed, War Office, 23 May to 16 July, 1917. He was twice mentioned in Despatches, and

Charles Beck Hornby.

was awarded the Croix de Guerre, Jan. 1917. Major Hornby married, in 1914, Dorothy, daughter of the late C. W. C. Henderson, of The Riding, Hexham, and they have two daughters: Pamela Innocence, and Adriane Virginia Mary. His D.S.O. was awarded "for services in connection with operations in the field."

BALFOUR, EDWARD WILLIAM STURGIS, Capt., was born 6 Dec. 1884, second son of Edward Balfour, J.P., D.L., of Balbirnie, Markinch, N.B., and Isabella Weyman Hooper, of Boston, U.S.A. He was educated at Eton, and at the Royal Military Academy, Woolwich, and entered the Royal Artillery 29 July, 1904; was promoted Lieutenant 29 July, 1907, and was transferred to the 5th (Princess Charlotte of Wales's) Dragoon

Guards 11 March, 1908, becoming Captain 6 March, 1912. He was Adjutant of the 5th Dragoon Guards 16 July, 1912, to 10 May, 1915. Capt. Balfour served in the European War. He was created a Companion of the Distinguished Service Order [London Gazette, 18 Feb. 1915]: "Edward William Sturgis Balfour, Capt., 5th (Princess Charlotte of Wales's) Dragoon Guards." He subsequently held the following Staff appointments, viz.: Staff Captain, 7th Cavalry Brigade, B.E.F., 11 May to 8 July, 1915; Brigade Major, 7th Cavalry Brigade, B.E.F., British Armies in France, 9 July, 1915, to 31 March, 1917; G.S.O.2, 1st Cavalry Division, British Armies in France, 1 April, 1917, to 19 April, 1918; G.S.O.2, Irish Command, 1 June, 1918, to 16 Feb. 1919. He was awarded the Military Cross in 1917, and also received the O.B.E. Capt. Balfour married Ruth, daughter of the Right Hon. Gerald William Balfour, P.C., and of Lady Betty, daughter of the 1st Earl of Lytton, and they have one son and one daughter. His D.S.O. was awarded "for services in connection with operations in the field."

COMBE, HERBERT, Major, was born 30 March, 1878, seventh son of Charles Combe, J.P., D.L., of Cobham Park, Surrey, and Marianne (who died in 1900), only daughter of Capt. Inglis, R.N. He was educated at Wellington College, and joined the 3rd (King's Own) Hussars 10 Jan. 1899, as Second Lieutenant; became Lieutenant 21 March, 1900. He served in the South African War, taking part in operations in the Transvaal and Orange River Colony, Jan. to April, 1902 (Queen's Medal with three clasps). He became Captain 11 May, 1907. Capt. Combe was Adjutant, Territorial Yeomanry, Bedfordshire Yeomanry, from 13 March, 1910, to 12 March, 1913; became Major 3 Dec. 1913. He served in the European War from 1914; was wounded in Oct. 1914. He was mentioned in Despatches, and created a Companion of the Distinguished Service Order [London Gazette, 18 Feb. 1915]: "Herbert Combe, Major, 3rd (King's Own) Hussars." He became Acting Lieutenant-Colonel 3 June, 1916, commanding Leicestershire Yeomanry, and commanding the 15th Hussars 5 April, 1918. He was awarded a Bar to the D.S.O. [London Gazette, 26 Aug. 1915]. On 12 Aug. 1908, at Teignmouth, South Devon, he married Amy Kathleen, daughter of the late G. M. Rudkin, of Teignmouth, and they have one son, Patrick Heddon Harvey. His D.S.O. was awarded "for services in connection with operations in the field."

Herbert Combe.

FREEMAN-MITFORD, THE HONOURABLE CLEMENT BERTRAM OGILVY, Major, was born 14 Dec. 1876, at 100, Cheyne Walk, Chelsea, S.W., son of Algernon Bertram Freeman-Mitford, 1st Baron Redesdale, and Lady Clementine Gertrude Helen Ogilvy, daughter of the 7th Earl of Airlie. He was educated at Eton and Cambridge; joined the Army in Nov. 1899; was promoted Lieutenant 3 Oct. 1900, and served in the South African War with the 10 Hussars, 1899-1901. He took part in the operations in the Orange Free State, including actions at Houtnek (Thoba Mountain), Vet River and Zand River; in the Transvaal in May and June, 1900, including actions near Johannesburg, Pretoria and Diamond Hill; in the Transvaal, west of Pretoria, to 29 Nov. 1900, including action at Elands River; in Orange River Colony, including action at Wittebergen; again in the Transvaal 30 Nov. 1900, to July, 1901, and operations in Cape Colony, Aug. 1901 (twice wounded, slightly and severely; Queen's Medal with four clasps). He was Adjutant of the 10th Hussars from 14 May, 1904, to 13 May, 1907; was promoted Captain 10 Oct. 1904, and Major 7 Aug. 1912. Major the Hon. C. B. O. Freeman-Mitford served in the European War from 1914. He was mentioned in Despatches, and created a Companion of the Distinguished Service Order [London Gazette, 18 Feb. 1915]: "The Honourable Clement Bertram Ogilvy Freeman-Mitford, Major, 10th (Prince of Wales's Own Royal) Hussars." He was dangerously wounded in the First Battle of Ypres 23 Oct. 1914, and was killed in action 13 May, 1915, in the Second Battle of Ypres. On 25 Nov. 1909, at the Private Chapel, Cortachy Castle, Kirriemuir, he married Lady Helen Ogilvy, daughter of the 10th Earl of Airlie, and they had two daughters: Rosemary Anne Mitford, and Clementine Mabell Kitty Mitford. His D.S.O. was awarded "for services in connection with operations in the field."

MULHOLLAND, THE HONOURABLE CHARLES HENRY GEORGE, Capt., was born 19 Aug. 1886, at Strangford, County Down, Ireland, son of Lord Dunleath, D.L., J.P., County Down, R.E. (retired), and Norah, only daughter of the late Hon. Somerset R. H. Ward, and granddaughter of the 3rd Viscount Bangor. He was educated at Eton and Sandhurst, and was gazetted to the 11th Hussars 19 Sept. 1906; became Lieutenant 16 April, 1909; Adjutant, 11th Hussars, 1 Jan. 1914, and Capt. 14 Nov. 1914. He served in the European War, and was present at the battles of Mons, the Marne, the Aisne, and the First Battle of Ypres, being very severely wounded at Messines 31 Oct. 1914. He was twice mentioned in Despatches, and was created a Companion of the Distinguished Service Order [London Gazette,

Hon. C. H. G. Mulholland.

18 Feb. 1915]: " The Hon. Charles Henry George Mulholland, Capt., 11th (Prince Albert's Own) Hussars." He was Brigade Major, 3rd Cyclist Brigade, at Woodbridge, Suffolk, and Clanmorris, County Mayo, 15 June, 1917, to 3 April, 1919; was awarded the O.B.E., Dec. 1914; became Military Secretary to H.E. the Lord Lieutenant of Ireland 1 Aug. 1919. Capt. the Hon. C. H. G. Mulholland's polo handicap is 6, and he played for his regiment in 1913 and 1914. His D.S.O. was awarded " for services in connection with operations in the field."

HOBSON, GERALD WALTON, Major, was born 20 June, 1873, eldest son of the late Richard Hobson, D.L.,

Gerald Walton Hobson.

J.P., of The Marfords, Bromborough, Cheshire, and of Mary Eleanor, daughter of J. Chadwick, J.P., D.L., of Woodville, nr. Stockport. He was educated at Elstree and Harrow and Sandhurst, and joined the Army 5 Oct. 1892; became Lieutenant 9 Aug. 1893; Captain in 1900. He served in the South African War, 1899–1901. He was present in the advance on Kimberley, including the action at Magersfontein; operations in the Orange Free State, Feb. to May, 1900, including operations at Paardeberg, actions at Poplar Grove, Dreifontein and Karee Siding; actions at Houtnek (Thoba Mountain), Vet River and Zand River; operations in the Transvaal in May and June, 1900, including actions near Pretoria, Johannesburg and Diamond Hill; operations in the Transvaal, west of Pretoria, Aug. 1900, including action at Eland's River; operations in Orange River Colony, July, 1900, including action at Wittebergen; operations in the Transvaal, 30 Nov. 1900, to April, 1901. He was mentioned in Despatches [London Gazette, 10 Sept. 1901], and received the Queen's Medal with seven clasps. He became Major 7 April, 1906, and retired from the 12th Lancers 25 March, 1908. He served in the European War from 1914 to 1919; was created a Companion of the Distinguished Service Order [London Gazette, 18 Feb. 1915]: " Gerald Walton Hobson, Major (Reserve of Officers), 12th (Prince of Wales's Royal) Lancers." He became Temporary Lieutenant-Colonel in Jan. 1915, and Lieutenant-Colonel in Reserve of Officers Sept. 1919; was twice mentioned in Despatches, and was created a C.M.G. in 1919. Lieut.-Colonel Hobson married, in Oct. 1908, Winifred Hilda, daughter of the late J. Gardiner Muir, D.L., J.P., of Farmingwoods Hall, Thrapston, Northamptonshire. His D.S.O. was awarded " for services in connection with operations in the field."

BRYANT, CHARLES EDGAR, Capt., was born 6 April, 1885, and entered the Army (12th Prince of Wales's Royal Lancers) 28 Jan. 1905; became Lieutenant 30 May, 1907; Captain 27 July, 1914 (12th Lancers and 7th Hussars). Capt. Bryant served in the European War, 1914–17; was Adjutant of the 12th Lancers 27 July, 1914, to 3 June, 1916. He was created a Companion of the Distinguished Service Order [London Gazette, 18 Feb. 1915]: " Charles Edgar Bryant, Capt., 12th (Prince of Wales's Royal) Lancers." Capt. Bryant joined the Royal Flying Corps 13 Nov. 1916. He was awarded a Bar to the D.S.O. [London Gazette, 18 July, 1917]: " Charles Edgar Bryant, D.S.O., Capt., Lancers and Royal Flying Corps. For conspicuous gallantry and devotion to duty. He has displayed the utmost gallantry and skill in leading photographic reconnaissances. In spite of overwhelming opposition by hostile aircraft, he has never failed to carry out his difficult task." He was Temporary Major, Royal Flying Corps, from 9 July, 1917, to 31 March, 1918, and was employed under the Air Ministry from 1 April, 1918. He married, in 1919, Mrs. Lionel Platt. His D.S.O. was awarded " for services in connection with operations in the field."

PILKINGTON, FREDERICK CARLISLE, Major, was born 17 Feb. 1872, son of George Pilkington, of Stoneleigh, Woolton, Liverpool, and 64, Cadogan Place, London, S.W., and of Frances Ellen Carlisle. He was

Frederick C. Pilkington.

educated at St. David's, Reigate; Eton, where he was in the Eleven in 1890, and was the winner of school events for athletics; and at Trinity Hall, Cambridge. He was in the winning team in the Inter-Regimental Polo Tournament, India, in 1903. He joined the 15th Hussars, from the Militia, 12 Dec. 1894; became Lieutenant 6 Nov. 1895, and Captain 13 Dec. 1899. He was Adjutant, West Somerset Yeomanry, 14 Jan. to 31 March, 1908, and Adjutant, Territorial Force, 1 April, 1908, to 24 March, 1911, and was promoted to Major 25 March, 1911. He served in the European War from 16 Aug. 1914, to the end of the war; commanded Divisional Mounted Troops of the 1st Infantry Division. He was created a Companion of the Distinguished Service Order [London Gazette, 18 Feb. 1915]: " Frederick Carlisle Pilkington, Major, 15th (The King's) Hussars." He became Temporary Lieutenant-Colonel, commanding 15th Hussars, 11 May, 1915, and was Acting Lieutenant-Colonel, commanding Corps Mounted Troops in Italy from 14 Dec. 1917, to 18 March, 1918; was employed under the Air Ministry from 31 Aug. 1918, attached to the Royal Air Force, as Commandant, No. 9 (Observation) School of Aeronautics; became Substantive Lieutenant-Colonel 10 Oct. 1919. Lieut.-Colonel Pilkington was four times mentioned in Despatches (Oct. 1914, Feb. and Dec. 1915, and Nov. 1917). He married, 18 March, 1900, at Bom-

bay Cathedral, Ethel Hay, daughter of Henry Burrows, of Dee Park, Woolton, Liverpool, and they have one daughter, Joy Frances. Their only son, Eric Bryan, died in 1917. His D.S.O. was awarded " for services in connection with operations in the field."

NELSON, CHARLES, Capt., was born 28 Nov. 1877, son of the late Sir Montague Nelson and Mary Caroline, Lady Nelson, daughter of F. Wallis, Esq., F.R.C.S. He entered the Army 22 May, 1900, as a Second Lieutenant in the 15th Hussars, becoming Lieutenant 1 Feb. 1903. He served with the New Zealand Forces 5 Aug. 1907, to 31 Jan. 1909; became Captain, 15th Hussars, 1 Oct. 1908. He served in the European War from 1914 to 1916. He was wounded, twice mentioned in Despatches, and was created a Companion of the Distinguished Service Order [London Gazette, 18 Feb. 1915]: " Charles Nelson, Capt., 15th (The King's Hussars)." Capt. Nelson was G.S.O.3, 1st Army, British Armies in France, 25 June to 16 Aug. 1916; A.D.C. to the Commander-in-Chief, East Indies, 1 Oct. 1916, to 28 Aug. 1917. He married, in 1910, Meta, daughter of the late Louis Schuster, and they have one son. His D.S.O. was awarded " for services in connection with operations in the field."

ECCLES, CUTHBERT JOHN, Lieut.-Colonel, was born 2 Feb. 1870, at Southampton, son of Major-General Cuthbert Eccles and Amy Neat Eccles. He was educated privately; enlisted 10 July, 1890, and served in the ranks

Cuthbert John Eccles.

for four years. He became Second Lieutenant, 16th Lancers, 1 Aug. 1894; Lieutenant 4 Nov. 1896, and Captain 9 Nov. 1899. Capt. Eccles served in the South African War, 1900–2, as Assistant Provost-Marshal. He was slightly wounded; was present at the advance on Kimberley; at the Relief of Kimberley. He took part in the operations in the Orange Free State, Feb. to May, 1900, including those at Paardeberg (17 to 26 Feb.); actions at Poplar Grove, Houtnek (Thoba Mountain) and Zand River; operations in the Transvaal in May and June, 1900, including actions near Johannesburg; operations in the Transvaal, east of Pretoria, Aug. to Nov. 1900, including action at Belfast (26 and 27 Aug.); operations in Cape Colony, north of Orange River; operations in Orange River Colony, 30 Nov. 1900, to June, 1901; operations in Cape Colony, June, 1901, to 31 May, 1902 (Queen's Medal with four clasps, and the King's Medal with two clasps). He was promoted to Major 9 June, 1909. He served in the European War from 1914 to 1917. He was Temporary Lieutenant-Colonel, 16th Lancers, 24 Sept. to 10 Nov. 1914, and Lieutenant-Colonel 19 Dec. 1914. He was created a Companion of the Distinguished Service Order [London Gazette, 18 Feb. 1915]: " Cuthbert John Eccles, Lieut.-Colonel, 16th (The Queen's) Lancers." He was twice wounded and twice mentioned in Despatches. He retired from the Army 19 Dec. 1918. Lieut.-Colonel C. J. Eccles has the Spanish Order of Merit, presented to him by H.M. the King of Spain, on the occasion of His Majesty's wedding, Colonel Eccles being one of the mission of the 16th Lancers who went to Madrid to represent that regiment. His D.S.O. was awarded " for services in connection with operations in the field."

PARSONS, ALFRED WOODIS, Major, was born 17 June, 1878, at Oxford, son of the late John Parsons, of Tubney, Abingdon, Berks, and of The Old Bank, Oxford (profession, Banker), and of Mrs. Parsons. He was

Alfred Woodis Parsons.

educated at Rugby, and at the Royal Military College, Sandhurst, and joined the 19th (Queen Alexandra's Own) Hussars 7 May, 1898, as Second Lieutenant. He served with his regiment in South Africa (1899–1902), during the Siege of Ladysmith, and throughout the campaign. He took part in the operations in Natal, 1899, including actions at Rietfontein and Lombard's Kop; took part in the Defence of Ladysmith, including sortie of 7 Dec. 1899, and action of 6 Jan. 1900; in Natal (March to June, 1900), including action at Laing's Nek; in the Transvaal, east of Pretoria, July to 29 Nov. 1900, including actions at Belfast and Lydenberg; in Orange River Colony (May to 29 Nov. 1900); again in the Transvaal, 30 Nov. 1900, to 31 May, 1902; and again during operations in Orange River Colony, May, 1902 (Despatches [London Gazette, 10 Sept. 1901, and 29 July, 1902]; Queen's Medal with four clasps, and King's Medal with two clasps. He became Lieutenant 23 June, 1900; Captain 1 Jan. 1905; was Adjutant, 19th Hussars, 1 Jan. 1905, to 19 Feb. 1907; was promoted to Major 20 Jan. 1912; to Lieutenant-Colonel 9 Oct. 1918; was Adjutant, Territorial Force, 1 April, 1908, to 13 March, 1910. He served in the European War, 1914–18; was mentioned in Despatches five times; awarded the Légion d'Honneur (Croix de Chevalier); created a C.M.G., and created a Companion of the Distinguished Service Order [London Gazette, 18 Feb. 1915]: " Alfred Woodis Parsons, Major, 19th Hussars. In recognition of services in connection with operations in the field."

COOK, GEORGE TREVOR ROPER, Major, was born 11 Aug. 1877, son of George Ward Cook, of Hoylake. He was gazetted to the 3rd Dragoon Guards 8 Sept. 1897; became Lieutenant 28 May, 1898. Lieut. Cook served in the South African War, 1899–1902. He took part in the operations in the Transvaal, May and July, 1901; in Orange River Colony, Feb. to Aug. 1901 in Cape Colony, Feb. 1901 (Queen's Medal with three clasps).

He was promoted to Captain 18 Dec. 1900. He was Adjutant, Imperial Yeomanry, from 2 Feb. 1907, to 31 March, 1908, and Adjutant, Territorial Force, from 1 April, 1908, to 5 Sept. 1911 ; became Major, 3rd Dragoon Guards, 6 Sept. 1911, and was transferred to the 20th Hussars 18 Oct. 1913. Major Cook served in the European War from 1914. He was twice mentioned in Despatches, and was created a Companion of the Distinguished Service Order [London Gazette, 18 Feb. 1915] : " George Trevor Roper Cook, Major, 20th Hussars." He was promoted to Lieutenant-Colonel 9 Sept. 1915. Lieut.-Colonel G. T. R. Cook was killed in action 26 March, 1918. In 1902 he had married Alice, youngest daughter of A. J. Dorman, Esq., of Nunthorpe, Yorkshire, and they had one son and four daughters. His D.S.O. was awarded " for services in connection with operations in the field."

LITTLE, ARTHUR CAMPDEN, Major, was born 2 Feb. 1880, son of Frederick Campden Little, Esq. He was educated at Eton. He became Second Lieutenant, 20th Hussars, in Jan. 1901 ; served in the South African War, 1900 and 1901-2 ; was severely wounded. He took part in the operations in the Orange Free State, April to May, 1900 ; in Orange River Colony, May to June, 1900 ; also in Cape Colony, Jan. to March, and June to Aug. 1900 ; in the Transvaal and again in Orange River Colony, Jan. to May, 1902 (Queen's Medal with five clasps). He was promoted Lieutenant 23 Sept. 1902 ; was Adjutant, 20th Hussars, 7 May, 1907, to 6 May, 1910, and became Captain 13 March, 1911, from which date he was an Adjutant in the Territorials until 12 March, 1914. He served in the European War ; became Major 5 Sept. 1914. He was

Arthur Campden Little.

created a Companion of the Distinguished Service Order [London Gazette, 18 Feb. 1915] : " Arthur Campden Little, Major, 20th Hussars." He commanded his regiment, and was Acting Lieutenant-Colonel 10 April, 1918, to 8 April, 1919. He was four times mentioned in Despatches ; given the Brevet of Lieutenant-Colonel 3 June, 1919, and was awarded a Bar to the D.S.O. [London Gazette, Feb. 1918]. His D.S.O. was awarded " for services in connection with operations in the field."

SCLATER-BOOTH, THE HONOURABLE WALTER DASHWOOD, Lieut.-Colonel, was born 15 Feb. 1869, in London, son of the 1st Lord Basing (deceased). He was educated at Wellington College, and the Royal Military Academy, Woolwich, and joined the Royal Artillery 23 July, 1887, as Second Lieutenant ; became Lieutenant 23 July, 1890 ; Captain 23 Feb. 1898, and Major 4 April, 1903. He served in the European War, in command of L Battery, Royal Horse Artillery, during the Retreat from Mons ; became Lieutenant-Colonel 30 Oct. 1914. He was mentioned in Despatches in Nov. 1914, and was created a Companion of the Distinguished Service Order [London Gazette, 18 Feb. 1915] : " The Honourable Walter Dashwood Sclater-Booth, Lieut.-Colonel, Royal Horse Artillery (L Battery)." The decoration was awarded for action with L Battery near Andriegnes, 24 Aug. 1914, when attached to the 2nd Cavalry Brigade. He was wounded on 1 Sept. following this at Nery.

Hon. W. D. Sclater-Booth.

He became Commandant, School of Instruction for R.H. and R.F.A., Lynd, 18 May, 1915 ; Temporary Colonel 4 Feb. 1916 ; Temporary Brigadier-General 3 Oct. 1916 ; Colonel 30 Oct. 1918 ; retired with the honorary rank of Brigadier-General in Nov. 1919. He was created a C.B. in June, 1917, and a C.M.G. in Jan. 1918. His elder brother, the late Brigadier-General Lord Basing, C.B., was also a distinguished soldier, and his nephew, the present Lord Basing (the Honourable J. L. Sclater-Booth) is a Captain in the 1st Royal Dragoons. Brigadier-General the Hon. W. D. Sclater-Booth married, 24 June, 1913, at St. Peter's, Eaton Square, S.W., Miss Burdon, eldest daughter of Colonel Rowland Burdon, of Castle Eden, County Durham, and they have two daughters, Eleanor Mary and Nora Frances. His D.S.O. was awarded " for services in connection with operations in the field."

GILLSON, GODFREY, Lieut.-Colonel, was born 15 Dec. 1867. He entered the Royal Artillery 13 Nov. 1889, and was promoted Lieutenant 13 Nov. 1892. He served on the North-West Frontier of India, 1897-9 (Medal and clasp). He was employed with the Egyptian Army 14 Aug. 1899, to 3 Nov. 1907, and was with the Nile Expedition, 1899, in the first advance against the Khalifa (Egyptian Medal and clasp). He became Captain 17 Jan. 1900, and Major 22 Nov. 1906 ; Lieutenant-Colonel 30 Oct. 1914. Lieut.-Colonel G. Gillson served in the European War from 1914 to 1918. He was created a Companion of the Distinguished Service Order [London Gazette, 18 Feb. 1915] : " Godfrey Gillson, Lieut.-Colonel, Royal Horse Artillery." He was Brigadier-General, Royal Artillery Cavalry Corps, B.E.F., 9 Sept. 1915, to 11 March, 1916 ; Brigadier-General, Royal Artillery, 39th Division, B.E.F., British Armies in France, 22 March, 1916, to 10 Oct. 1917 ; Brigadier-General, Royal Artillery, 10th Army Corps, British Armies in France, 11 Oct. 1917, to 15 Sept. 1918 ; Brigadier-General, Royal Artillery, Southern Command, 30 Dec. 1918, to 12 April, 1919 ; became Deputy Director of Remounts 13 April, 1919. He was given the Brevet of Colonel 1 Jan. 1917 was created a C.M.G. in 1918 and received the 3rd

Class Order of Danilo. His D.S.O. was awarded " for services in connection with operations in the field."

JELF, WILFRID WYKEHAM, Major, was born at Halifax, Nova Scotia, 22 July, 1880, son of the late Colonel Richard Henry Jelf, C.M.G., R.E., formerly Governor, Royal Military Academy, and Margaret Jelf. He was educated at Cheam School and Eton, and joined the Army 25 Nov. 1899 ; was promoted Lieutenant 16 Feb. 1901. He served in the South African War, 1899–1902. He took part in the operations in the Orange Free State, Feb. to May, 1900, including actions near Grove, Dreifontein, Vet River (5 and 6 May) and Zand River ; in the Transvaal in May and June, 1900, including actions near Johannesburg, Pretoria and Diamond Hill (11 and 12 June) ; in the Transvaal, east of Pretoria, July to 29 Nov. 1900, including action at Belfast (26 and 27 Aug.) ; again in the Transvaal, 30 Nov. 1900, to Jan. 1901, and April, 1901, to 31 May, 1902 ; and in the operations in Orange River Colony, March and April, 1901

Wilfrid Wykeham Jelf.

(Despatches [London Gazette, 10 Sept. 1901 ; Queen's Medal with five clasps, and King's Medal with two clasps). He became Captain 1 April, 1908. He was Adjutant, Territorial Force, 20 Oct. 1908, to 19 Jan. 1912 ; became Major, 30 Oct. 1914. He served in the European War, being employed as Staff Captain, Royal Artillery, 1st Cavalry Division, B.E.F., 5 Aug. 1914, to 21 March, 1915. He was created a Companion of the Distinguished Service Order [London Gazette, 18 Feb. 1915] : " Wilfrid Wykeham Jelf, Major, Royal Horse Artillery." The decoration was awarded for services whilst Staff Officer to the Royal Horse Artillery, 1st Cavalry Division. He became Temporary Lieutenant-Colonel in Jan. 1917, and was given the Brevet of Lieutenant-Colonel 1 Jan. 1918. From 26 April to 20 July, 1918, he was Chief Instructor (General Staff Officer), Royal Military Academy (temporary), becoming Second-in-Command (temporary), 21 July, 1918. He was mentioned in Despatches five times, and was created a C.M.G. in 1919. He married, 26 July, 1906, Cicely Helen, daughter of the late John George Child and Helen Child, and sister of Sir Hill Child, Bart., D.S.O., M.V.O., and their children are : Richard Hill Jelf, born 2 July, 1910 ; Lilah Margaret Jelf, born 13 Oct. 1911, and Roderick Wilfrid Roylance Jelf, born 22 July, 1914. His D.S.O. was awarded " for services in connection with operations in the field."

HARRIS, OSCAR MARK, Major, was born 17 March, 1879, son of Henry Harris. He was educated at University College, London, and was gazetted to the Royal Artillery 22 Dec. 1898 ; became Lieutenant 16 Feb. 1901. He served in the South African War, 1900-2. He was present at the Relief of Kimberley ; took part in the operations in the Orange Free State, Feb. to May, 1900, including those at Paardeberg (17 to 26 Feb.) ; actions at Poplar Grove, Dreifontein, Houtnek (Thoba Mountain), Vet River (5 and 6 May), and Zand River ; served during the operations in the Transvaal in May and June, 1900, including actions near Johannesburg and Pretoria ; in the Transvaal, east of Pretoria, July to 29 Nov. 1900 ; in the Transvaal, west of Pretoria, July to 29 Nov. 1900 ; also in Orange River Colony, May to 29 Nov. 1900, including actions at Rhenoster River and Wittebergen (1 to 29 July) (Queen's Medal with five clasps, and King's Medal with two clasps). He was promoted to Captain 27 June, 1906. He was employed with the West African Frontier Force from 11 April, 1908. He served in the European War from 1914 ; became Major 30 Oct. 1914. Major Harris was created a Companion of the Distinguished Service Order [London Gazette, 18 Feb. 1915] : " Oscar Mark Harris, Major (N Battery), Royal Horse Artillery." He was Temporary Lieutenant-Colonel 26 April, 1916, to 24 May, 1917 ; Acting Lieutenant-Colonel 16 July, 1917, to 10 Oct. 1918. He was given the Brevet of Lieutenant-Colonel 1 Jan. 1918, and was mentioned in Despatches in 1915, 1916, 1917 (twice), 1918 and 1919. Lieut.-Colonel Harris married, on 20 Oct. 1910, the Honourable Marjorie Ruth Addington, second daughter of the 3rd Viscount Sidmouth. His D.S.O. was awarded " for services in connection with operations in the field."

STOCKDALE, HERBERT EDWARD, Lieut.-Colonel, was born 22 June, 1867, at Mears Ashby Hall, Northampton, son of Henry Minshull Stockdale, J.P., D.L., and Sarah Emily Stockdale. He was educated at Temple Grove, East Sheen ; Wellington College, Berkshire, and the Royal Military Academy, Woolwich (was in the Royal Military Academy Eleven and Fifteen), and joined the Royal Artillery 16 Feb. 1886, as Lieutenant ; became Captain 1 June, 1896 ; Major 16 March, 1901. He served in the South African War, 1899–1902 ; with the 9th and 11th Divisions, in the advance on Pretoria and Koomatie Poort. He was present at the actions of Poplar Grove, Dreifontein, Vet River, Johannesburg, Diamond Hill and Belfast, and served from March to Dec. 1901, with Sir H. Plumer's Column in the Eastern Transvaal and Orange River Colony. He was Divisional Adjutant, Royal Artillery, 10 Sept. 1900, to 15 March, 1901, and became Major 16 March, 1901. He was mentioned in Despatches [London Gazette, 10 Sept. 1901], and received the Queen's Medal with six clasps. He became Lieutenant-Colonel 17 Aug. 1913 ; served in the European War under Sir J. French up to Jan. 1915 ; was present in the Retreat from Mons, the battles of Le Cateau, the Marne and the Aisne, and the First Battle of Ypres. He was created a Companion of the Distinguished Service Order [London Gazette, 18 Feb. 1915] : " Herbert Edward Stockdale, Lieut.-Colonel, Royal Field Artillery." The decoration was awarded for general good service during operations in 1914, and not for any one particular action, Lieut.-Colonel Stockdale served under Sir Ian Hamilton until 28 Oct. 1915, and under Sir Charles Munro until 9 Jan. 1916 ; became Temporary Brigadier-General 3 Sept. 1915. In the

Gallipoli Campaign he was present at the landing at Helles, April, 1915 ; the operations at Helles, 1915, and the evacuation, 9 Jan. 1916. He was promoted Colonel 17 Aug. 1917 ; was under Sir William Marshall from Nov. 1917, to Nov. 1918 ; retired 18 April, 1919, and was granted the honorary rank of Brigadier-General. He was created a C.M.G. in 1916, and a C.B. in 1919, and was five times mentioned in Despatches. On 4 Feb. 1909, at the church of St. John the Divine, Kennington, S.E., Major Stockdale married Margaret Frances, elder daughter of the Rev. Canon J. T. Bartlet, Honorary Canon of Lincoln, and they have a daughter, Margaret Mary. His D.S.O. was awarded " for services in connection with operations in the field."

SANDERS, GEORGE HERBERT, Lieut.-Colonel, was born 14 Sept.

1868, at Binstead, Isle of Wight, son of Arthur Sanders, Barrister-at-Law, and Isabella Sanders (both deceased). He was educated at Harrow (The Grove, 1882) ; joined the Artillery 17 Feb. 1888, and became Lieutenant 17 Feb. 1891. He became Captain 18 May, 1898. He served in the South African War, 1899–1902, with the 19th Battery, R.F.A., and as Assistant Press Censor ; took part in the operations in the Transvaal, Nov. 1900, to March, 1901, and July to Dec. 1901 ; also in Orange River Colony, Jan. to May, 1902 (Despatches [London Gazette, 10 Sept. 1901] ; Queen's Medal with three clasps, and King's Medal with two clasps). He became Major 15 Nov. 1903. Major Sanders served in the European War, and com-

George Herbert Sanders.

manded 122nd Battery, R.F.A., from the beginning of the war ; became Lieutenant-Colonel 30 Oct. 1914, commanding the 28th Brigade, R.F.A. He was slightly wounded, Nov. 1914 ; was created a Companion of the Distinguished Service Order [London Gazette, 18 Feb. 1915] : " George Herbert Sanders, Lieut.-Colonel (28th Brigade), Royal Field Artillery." Lieut.-Colonel G. H. Sanders became Temporary Brigadier-General 14 Sept. 1915, and was C.R.A., 2nd Division, until the end of the war. He was mentioned in Sir Douglas Haig's Despatch, dated War Office, 13 June, 1916, and on five other occasions during the Great War ; became C.R.A., Light Division, Army of the Rhine. He was created a C.M.G. in 1917 ; was given the Brevet of Colonel 1 Jan. 1918 ; was created a C.B. in Jan. 1919, and was awarded the French Croix de Guerre in Dec. 1919. He married, at Caversham, Oxfordshire, 9 Sept. 1897, Vivien Lifford, eldest daughter of the late Honourable Arthur Plunket, and their sons are : Geoffrey Arthur Plunket Sanders, born 18 July, 1899, and Denis Coghill Sanders, born 5 Aug. 1903. His D.S.O. was awarded " for services in connection with operations in the field."

CARTWRIGHT, GARNIER NORTON, Lieut.-Colonel, was born 7 May, 1868, son of R. N. Cartwright, of Ixworth Abbey, Suffolk. He joined the Royal Artillery 17 Feb. 1888 ; became Lieutenant 17 Feb. 1891 ; Captain 1 July, 1898, and Major 9 Dec. 1903. Major Cartwright served in the European War from 1914 ; became Lieutenant-Colonel 30 Oct. 1914 ; was mentioned in Despatches, and created a Companion of the Distinguished Service Order [London Gazette, 18 Feb. 1915] : " Garnier Norton Cartwright, Lieut.-Colonel, 55th Battery, Royal Field Artillery." He was Temporary Brigadier-General, Royal Artillery, 1st Division, B.E.F., British Armies in France, from 15 Oct. 1915, to 19 Oct. 1917. He was created a C.M.G. in 1917. He married, in 1909, Isabel, daughter of the late T. J. Masters, of Llanelly Hall, Llantrisant. His D.S.O. was awarded " for services in connection with operations in the field."

PEEL, EDWARD JOHN RUSSELL, Lieut.-Colonel, was born 31 Aug. 1869, at The Gerwyn, Wrexham, North Wales, second son of Archibald Peel, J.P., D.L. (son of General the Right Honourable Jonathan Peel),

and Lady Georgiana Adelaide, daughter of the 1st Earl Russell. He was educated at Eton and Woolwich, and joined the Royal Artillery, as Second Lieutenant, 27 July, 1889, becoming Lieutenant 27 July, 1892, and Captain 13 Dec. 1899. He served in the South African War, 1899–1900 ; took part in the operations in Cape Colony, south of Orange River, 1899 ; in the Orange Free State, March to May, 1900, including actions at Vet River (5 and 6 May) and Zand River ; also in the Transvaal, May, 1900, including action near Johannesburg (Queen's Medal with three clasps). He was promoted to Major 11 Feb. 1906 ; served in the European War from 1914. Major Peel commanded the 54th Battery, R.F.A., from Mons to the Battle of Ypres, where he was wounded. He was mentioned

Edward John R. Peel.

in Despatches, and created a Companion of the Distinguished Service Order [London Gazette, 18 Feb. 1915] : " Edward John Russell Peel, Lieut.-Colonel (54th Battery), Royal Field Artillery." He was promoted Lieutenant-Colonel 30 Oct. 1914, and in the following spring went out with the 29th Division, in command of an Artillery Brigade, to Gallipoli, and served with that division until they evacuated the Peninsula on 8 Jan. 1916. He was again mentioned in Despatches, and promoted to Temporary Brigadier-General in April of that year, and posted to the 59th Division, as C.R.A. In Easter week he was sent with the division to Ireland, to quell the Sinn Fein Rebellion ; was transferred to the 58th Division, and proceeded to France in Jan. 1917. In Jan. 1918, he was created a C.M.G.,

and later relinquished his temporary appointment of Brigadier-General and was given the command of the 87th R.F.A. Brigade, in the 19th Division. Lieut.-Colonel Peel served with the 19th Division through the retreat of the 3rd Army in March, 1918 ; was awarded a Bar to the D.S.O., for gallantry and devotion to duty in action [London Gazette 16 Sept. 1918] : " This officer was in command of the brigade during ten days' operations. Although the enemy were close up to him in a village he kept his batteries in action under a ridge, handling them with consummate skill. It was owing to his personal influence with the brigade that the guns were saved, being withdrawn from under the nose of the enemy one by one as opportunity occurred by night. Throughout the operations he kept the men together and cheerful, and they fought splendidly." He was appointed C.R.A. (Temporary Brigadier-General) to 19th Division in Sept. 1918. Brigadier-General E. J. R. Peel played cricket and polo for the Royal Artillery ; won the Army Point-to-Point in Ireland in 1898, and in England in 1908, on both occasions riding his own horse ; has been a Steward of the Grand Military Meeting, and of the Royal Artillery Races. His favourite recreations are hunting, riding, steeplechasing, polo and cricket. On 13 June, 1901, in London, he married Mary Louisa Drummond, daughter of Edgar Atheling Drummond, of Cadland, Hampshire, and their children are : John, born in 1907 ; Peter, born in 1908, and Rosemary. His D.S.O. was awarded " for services in connection with operations in the field."

METCALFE, SYDNEY FORTESCUE, Lieut.-Colonel, was born 1 April, 1870, son of the late Fenwick Metcalfe and Mrs. Metcalfe, of Woodside, Albury, Guildford. He was educated at Bath College, and the Royal Military Academy, Woolwich. He joined the Royal Artillery 26 July, 1889 ; became Lieutenant 27 July, 1892. He served in the South African War, 1899–1900 ; was present at the Relief of Ladysmith, including operations of 17 to 24 Jan. 1900, and action at Spion Kop ; operations of 5 to 7 Feb. 1900, and action of Vaal Kranz ; operations on Tugela Heights (14 to 27 Feb. 1900) and action at Pieter's Hill ; operations in the Transvaal in May and June, 1900 ; operations in Cape Colony, south of Orange River, 1900 (Queen's Medal and four clasps). He became Captain 1 Jan. 1900, and Major 1 Aug. 1906 ; was Instructor (1st Class), School of Gunnery, 1 April, 1908, to 30 Sept. 1912. He served in the European War from 1914 (1914 Star), going to France with the 3rd Division in Aug. 1914. He was wounded in Oct. 1914, and sent home. He became Lieutenant-Colonel 30 Oct. 1914 ; was Major-Instructor in Gunnery, School of Gunnery (temporary), 13 Dec. 1914, to 14 March, 1915. He was Chief Instructor in Gunnery, School of Instruction for Royal Horse and Royal Field Artillery (temporary), 15 March to 18 April, 1915. He was posted to command the 83rd Brigade, R.F.A., 18th Division, with which he returned to France in July, 1915. He was created a Companion of the Distinguished Service Order [London Gazette, 18 Feb. 1915] : " Sydney Fortescue Metcalfe, Lieut.-Colonel, 23rd Brigade, Royal Field Artillery." He was Brigadier-General, R.A., 18th Division, British Armies in France, 31 May, 1916, to 6 July, 1917 ; Brigadier-General, R.A., 17th Army Corps, 7 July to Oct. 1917 ; was employed under the Ministry of Munitions 9 Jan. to 8 April, 1918 ; was Brigadier-General, R.A., 11th Army Corps, British Armies in France, 9 April to 18 Dec. 1918 ; G.O.C., R.A., Eastern Command, 1 Dec. 1918 ; C.R.A., 4th Division, Nov. 1919. He was given the Brevet of Colonel 1 Jan. 1917 ; created a C.M.G. 1 Jan. 1918, and was four times mentioned in Despatches. His D.S.O. was awarded " for services in connection with operations in the field."

PACKARD, HENRY NORRINGTON, Major, was born 12 March, 1870. He entered the Royal Artillery, as a Second Lieutenant, 25 July, 1890, and was promoted Lieutenant 25 July, 1893, and Captain 13 Feb. 1900. He was employed as D.A.A.G., R.A., India, 3 Jan. 1902, to 2 Jan. 1907 ; became Major 1 April, 1908, and was D.A.A. and Q.M.G., West Lancashire Division, Western Command, 1 April, 1910, to 31 March, 1914. Serving in the European War, Major Packard was mentioned in Despatches [London Gazette, 19 Oct. 1914], and was created a Companion of the Distinguished Service Order [London Gazette, 18 Feb. 1915] : " Henry Norrington Packard, Major, Royal Engineers." He fell in action 12 April, 1916. His D.S.O. was awarded " for services in connection with operations in the field."

LLOYD, HORACE GIESLER, Major, was born 26 Nov. 1872, at Highgate, son of Frederick Giesler Lloyd, Esq., and Elizabeth Lloyd (both deceased). He was educated at Clifton College, and the Royal Military Academy, Woolwich, and joined the Royal

Artillery, as Second Lieutenant, 12 Feb. 1892, becoming Lieutenant 12 Feb. 1895. He served in the Chitral Campaign in 1895, and received the Indian Frontier Medal with clasp ; became Captain 15 March, 1900. He was Divisional Adjutant, R.A., from 30 Aug. 1900, to 31 March, 1901, and Adjutant, R.A., from 1 April, 1901, to 29 Aug. 1904. He was promoted Major 8 June, 1909, and was Commanding Officer of a company of Gentlemen Cadets 1 Jan. 1908, to 31 Dec. 1911. Major Lloyd served in the European War continuously as Battery and Brigade Commander, and C.R.A., from the time when he landed in France on 23 Aug. 1914, to 23 March, 1918. He was present at Le Cateau, and for his services in that action

Horace Giesler Lloyd.

was mentioned in Despatches, Jan. 1915, and was created a Companion of the Distinguished Service Order [London Gazette, 18 Feb. 1915] : " Horace Giesler Lloyd, Major, 29th Brigade, Royal Field Artillery." He became Lieutenant-Colonel 16 May, 1915 ; was mentioned in Despatches in Jan. 1916; Jan. 1917, and Jan. 1918. He became a Temporary Brigadier-General 3 Jan. 1917 (C.R.A., 8th Division), and was transferred to the Home Forces, March, 1918; appointed C.R.A., 64th Division, 1 July, 1918. He returned to France 23 Oct. 1918, as C.R.A. 24th Division, remaining till the cessation of hostilities 11 Nov. 1918. He was created a C.M.G. 1 Jan. 1918. He married, 23 Sept. 1903, at Camberley, Annette Rose, daughter of Colonel C. H. Ewart, Indian Army, and they have a daughter, Annette Lena. His D.S.O. was awarded "for services in connection with operations in the field."

WILSON, LANCELOT MACHELL, Major, was born 23 July, 1873, at Bolton-by-Bowland, Clitheroe, Yorkshire, son of the Rev. Canon Wilson, J.P., of Taitlands, Stamforth, Yorkshire, and Catherine, daughter of Henry Remington, Esq., of Aynsome, Cartmel, Lancashire. He was educated at Sedbergh School, and at the Royal Academy, Woolwich, and joined the Royal Artillery 1 April, 1893; became Lieutenant 1 April, 1896, and Captain 28 May, 1900. He served at Tirah, 1897–98; took part in the operations in the Bara Valley 7 to 14 Dec. 1897 (Medal with two clasps); served in China, 1900; at the Relief of Pekin; in the actions of Peitsang and Yangtsun (Medal with clasp); served in the South African War, 1902; took part in the operations in Cape Colony (Queen's Medal with two clasps); was Adjutant, Royal Artillery, 12 Sept. 1905, to Sept. 1908, and became Major 23 April, 1910; was Instructor (1st Class), School of Gunnery, 20 Feb. 1912, to 31 March, 1913. He was Major Instructor, School of Gunnery, 1 April to 4 Aug. 1914. He served in the European War from 1914; was created a Companion of the Distinguished Service Order [London Gazette, 18 Feb. 1915]: "Lancelot Machell Wilson, Major, Royal Field Artillery (27th Brigade)." He was Major Instructor, School of Gunnery (temporary), 27 Feb. 1915, to 19 Feb. 1916; became Lieutenant-Colonel 15 Nov. 1915, and was Chief Instructor in Gunnery, School of Instruction for Royal Horse and Royal Field Artillery, 20 Feb. 1916, to 30 May, 1917. He served in France from May, 1917, to July, 1918, and was Deputy Director, Royal Artillery, War Office, 16 Aug. 1918, to 30 April, 1920. He was given the Brevet of Colonel 3 June, 1917; was three times mentioned in Despatches, and was created a C.M.G. in Jan. 1919. Colonel Wilson married, 20 Aug. 1914, at Newport, Isle of Wight, Lilian Stewart (who died in 1917), youngest daughter of the late Colonel J. Richardson, K.H.D., I.M.S. His D.S.O. was awarded "for services in connection with operations in the field."

ATLAY, HUGH WORDSWORTH, Major, was born 3 Jan. 1873, sixth son of James, sometime Bishop of Hereford, and brother of the late J. B. Atlay, the author. He was educated at Honiton and Cheltenham, and proceeded to the Royal Military Academy, Woolwich, in 1890; was gazetted Second Lieutenant 26 June, 1893; Lieutenant 26 June, 1896, and Captain 18 June, 1900. He served in the South African War, with the Natal Field Force, from Dec. 1899, to Dec. 1900; was A.D.C. to Major-General Commanding R.A. 24 May, 1900, to 16 Jan. 1901. He took part in the Relief of Ladysmith, being present at the action at Spion Kop, and also served in the actions at Vaal Kranz, Tugela Heights and Pieter's Hill (Queen's Medal with four clasps). He was Adjutant, Royal Artillery, 8 Oct. 1907, to 11 May, 1910; was promoted Major 12 May, 1910.

Hugh Wordsworth Atlay.

Major Atlay served in the European War from 1914, commanding the 54th Battery, Royal Field Artillery. He was mentioned in Despatches, and created a Companion of the Distinguished Service Order [London Gazette, 18 Feb. 1915]: "Hugh Wordsworth Atlay, Major, 15th Brigade, Royal Field Artillery. For services in connection with operations in the field." He was killed in France on 11 April, 1915, aged 42 years.

PATERSON, PHILIP JOSEPH, Major, was born 26 Sept. 1874. He joined the Royal Artillery 14 July, 1896; became Lieutenant 14 July, 1899. He served in the South African War, 1899–1901; took part in the advance on Kimberley, including actions at Belmont, Enslin, Modder River and Magersfontein; in the Orange Free State, Feb. to May, 1900, including operations at Paardeberg 17 to 27 Feb.; actions at Poplar Grove and Zand River; in the Transvaal in May and June, 1900, including action at Pretoria; in the Transvaal, east of Pretoria; in the Transvaal, west of Pretoria, including action at Zilikat's Nek; again during operations in the Transvaal 30 Nov. to Nov. 1901 (Queen's Medal with four clasps). He became Captain 28 Jan. 1902. Capt. Paterson was promoted to Major 16 Jan. 1913. He served in the European War from 1914–18. He was mentioned in Despatches, and created a Companion of the Distinguished Service Order [London Gazette, 18 Feb. 1915]: "Philip Joseph Paterson, Major (2nd Battery), Royal Field Artillery." He became Temporary Lieutenant-Colonel 31 Dec. 1915, and Lieutenant-Colonel 8 May, 1917; was created a C.M.G. in 1919. Lieut.-Colonel Paterson married, in 1905, Ethel Stawell, fourth daughter of Alexander Edward S. Heard, of Coolmain Castle, County Cork. His D.S.O. was awarded "for services in connection with operations in the field."

LIVINGSTONE-LEARMONTH, JOHN ERIC CHRISTIAN, Major, was born 25 Aug. 1876. He joined the Royal Field Artillery 21 Sept. 1896, and was promoted Lieutenant 21 Sept. 1899. He served in the South African War, 1899–1900; took part in the advance on Kimberley; in the Orange River Colony, Feb. to May, 1900; in the Transvaal, May and June, 1900, including actions near Pretoria (4 June) and Diamond Hill (11 and 12 June); also in operations in the Transvaal, east of Pretoria, July to Oct. 1900 (Queen's Medal with three clasps). He became Captain 1 Feb. 1902; was Adjutant, R.A., 29 April, 1905, to 8 March, 1908; became

Major 8 March, 1913. Major Livingstone-Learmonth served in the European War from 1914 to 1918. He was created a Companion of the Distinguished Service Order [London Gazette, 18 Feb. 1915]: "John Eric Christian Livingstone-Learmonth, Major (8th Brigade), Royal Field Artillery." He was D.A.A.G., G.H.Q., British Expeditionary Force, 5 Jan. 1915, to 2 Jan. 1916; A.A.G., G.H.Q., B.E.F., British Armies in France, 3 Jan. 1916, to 9 Nov. 1917; was promoted Lieutenant-Colonel 31 May, 1917; became Temporary Brigadier-General, A.G.'s Branch, A.G.'s and Q.M.G.'s Staff, British Armies in France, 10 Nov. 1917. He was also given the Brevet of Lieutenant-Colonel 1 Jan. 1917, and of Colonel 3 June, 1918; was created a Chevalier of the Legion of Honour in 1915, and in 1919 was created a C.M.G. He was six times mentioned in Despatches. He married, in Oct. 1901, Eleanor, second daughter of the late Capt. Villiers Sankey Morton. His D.S.O. was awarded "for services in connection with operations in the field."

ROCHFORT-BOYD, HENRY CHARLES, Major, was born at Birr, Queen's County, Ireland, 13 Oct. 1877. He was the only surviving son of Colonel Charles Augustus Rochfort-Boyd, C.M.G., late R.E., of Belvedere

House, Farnborough, Hants, by his first wife, Adeline, daughter of the late Mountifort Longfield, D.L., of Castle Mary, County Cork, and grandson of the late G. A. Rochfort-Boyd, D.L., of Middleton Park, Westmeath. He was educated at Summerfield; Wellington; Charterhouse and Woolwich, and passed out on the Artillery List from the Royal Military Academy, Woolwich, in 1897. He joined the Royal Artillery, as Second Lieutenant, 1 Sept. 1897; served with distinction in the South African War, 1899–1900; was present at the actions of Belmont, Enslin Siding, Modder River, Magersfontein and Paardeberg, and was twice mentioned in Despatches [London Gazette, 26 Jan. 1900, and 10 Sept. 1901]; received the Queen's Medal with three clasps. He became Lieutenant 1 Sept. 1900, and Captain 2 March, 1904. In Aug. 1914, he went with his battery to France in the 2nd Division; was wounded at Mons, narrowly escaped capture at Landrecies; rejoined his battery on the Aisne, and moved north with it to the First Battle of Ypres, where the support it gave to the Guards on the critical 21 and 23 Oct. earned the special thanks of the G.O.C. On 11 Nov., while observing in an advanced sap-head, he was passed on both sides by the Prussian Guards, advancing silently through the mist, but slipping behind them, succeeded in warning his brigade, with far-reaching consequences. He was again wounded in Jan. 1915, and for a third time severely in Feb., on the same day that he was awarded the D.S.O. He was appointed Major 10 Oct. 1914; mentioned in Despatches in Nov. 1914; Nov. 1916, and April and Nov. 1917. He was created a Companion of the Distinguished Service Order [London Gazette, 18 Feb. 1915]: "Henry Charles Rochfort-Boyd, Major, Royal Field Artillery (9th Battery)." When he recovered from his wound, Major Rochfort-Boyd returned to the front, and in Feb. 1916, was promoted Temporary Lieutenant-Colonel in the Royal Field Artillery, and saw much severe fighting. In Nov. 1916, he was transferred to command the Royal Horse Artillery of a Cavalry Division. Lieut.-Colonel Rochfort-Boyd died at Rouen 4 Dec. 1917, of wounds received in action, aged 40 years. Three days earlier, during the German attack on Cambrai, he had ridden forward to select an artillery position, and came under fire of a concealed machine gun at short range; his horse was killed, and he was taken prisoner, very severely wounded in three places, but succeeded in escaping after dark and reached the British outposts. He was a fine rider to hounds, and was for four seasons Master of the Royal Artillery Drag Hunt. Lieut.-Colonel Rochfort-Boyd had married, 1 June, 1908, Dorothy, daughter of Arthur Nicholson, Esq., of Brighton, and they had one son, Charles, born 9 April, 1912. His D.S.O. was awarded "for services in connection with operations in the field."

Henry C. Rochfort-Boyd.

CORNES, HUGH, Major, was born 23 Oct. 1879, at Teddington-on-Thames, son of Frederick Cornes, Esq., and of Alice Cornes (née Bull). He was educated at Clifton College, and at the Royal Military Academy, Woolwich, and joined the Royal Artillery, as Second Lieutenant, 23 Dec. 1898. He served in the South African War, as a Subaltern, 1900; was present in operations in Cape Colony and the Orange Free State, Jan. to May, 1900 (Queen's Medal with three clasps). He became Lieutenant 16 Feb. 1901, and Captain 5 April, 1907. He was Adjutant, Royal Artillery, (Territorial Force), 1 Oct. 1913, to 29 Oct. 1914. He served in the European War from 1914 to 1918. He was mentioned in Sir John French's Despatch 18 Oct. 1914; became Major 30 Oct. 1914, and was created a Companion of the Distinguished Service Order [London Gazette, 18 Feb. 1915]: "Hugh Cornes, Major (Divisional Ammunition Column), Royal Field Artillery." He was posted to home establishments, Jan. till July, 1915, and embarked again for France, July, 1915. Major Cornes was mentioned in Despatches by Sir Douglas Haig 3 Jan. 1917, and became Temporary Lieutenant-Colonel. He married, 17 Aug. 1910, at Teddington, Katherine Elizabeth, daughter of George H. Harding Weale, Esq. His D.S.O. was awarded "for services in connection with operations in the field."

RIDDELL, JOHN BALFOUR, Major, was born 20 May, 1890, son of the late Colonel R. V. Riddell, R.E. He was gazetted to the Royal Artillery 23 Dec. 1898; became Lieutenant 16 Feb. 1901, and Captain 27 May, 1907. He was Adjutant, Royal Artillery, 1 Sept. 1911, to 29 Oct. 1914. He served in the European War from 1914 to 1917; was promoted to Major 29 Oct. 1914. He was twice mentioned in Despatches and created a

Companion of the Distinguished Service Order [London Gazette, 18 Feb. 1915]: "John Balfour Riddell, Major, 42nd Brigade, Royal Field Artillery." Major Riddell was G.S.O.2 (Staff Officer to Major-General, Royal Artillery), 2nd Army, British Expeditionary Force, 21 Feb. to 3 June, 1916, and became Acting Lieutenant-Colonel, Royal Artillery, 7 July, 1916. He married, in 1908, Margaret, youngest daughter of the late J. W. Smith, and they have one son and two daughters. His D.S.O. was awarded "for services in connection with operations in the field."

FINLAYSON, ROBERT GORDON, Major, was born 15 April, 1881, son of the late David Finlayson, of 27, The Grove, Boltons, S.W. He joined the Royal Artillery, as Second Lieutenant, 17 March, 1900; became Lieutenant 3 March, 1901; was Lieutenant, Imperial Yeomanry, 3 April to 31 July, 1902; became Captain 20 Oct. 1908; was Adjutant, Royal Artillery, 22 Jan. to 29 Sept. 1910, and 22 July, 1912, to 29 Oct. 1914. He served in the European War from 1914 to 1918. He was promoted to Major 30 Oct. 1914; was Staff Captain, Royal Artillery, 7th Division, 14 Nov. 1914, to 26 Feb. 1915. He was created a Companion of the Distinguished Service Order [London Gazette, 18 Feb. 1915]: "Robert Gordon Finlayson, Major, Royal Field Artillery." He was Brigade Major, R.A., 3rd Division, B.E.F., 27 Feb. 1915, to 29 Feb. 1916; D.A.A.G., 1st Army Corps, B.E.F., British Armies in France, 1 March, 1916, to 17 Feb. 1917; was G.S.O.1, with the Special Mission to Russia, 19 March, 1917, to 20 Jan. 1918. He served as Deputy Commander of the North Russian Expeditionary Force 24 May, 1918, to 29 Jan. 1919 (temporary Brigadier-General). He was mentioned four times in Despatches; was given the Brevet of Lieutenant-Colonel 3 June, 1916, and was created a C.M.G. in 1918. He married, in 1912, Mary Leslie, daughter of James Richmond, of Kippenross, Dunblane, and they have two sons. His D.S.O. was awarded "for services in connection with operations in the field."

Robert G. Finlayson.

MUIRHEAD, MURRAY, Major, was born 1 Jan. 1878, son of John and Charlotte Jane Muirhead, of Dumfries. He was educated at Bedford Grammar School, and Pembroke College, Cambridge, and joined the Army 28 March, 1900, becoming Lieutenant 3 April, 1901. He served several years in India. He was Adjutant, Territorial Force, 20 May, 1908, to 7 Nov. 1910, and was promoted to Captain 19 April, 1909. Capt. Muirhead married, 9 June, 1900, at Otley, Yorkshire, Violet Edith Spence, only daughter of Albert Carter Spence, of Weston Manor, Otley, and they have a daughter, Masha Violet Otley. He was specially employed at the War Office from 12 Nov. 1912, to 11 Feb. 1913, and from that date to Feb. 1914, was in Russia, learning the language, of which he afterwards became an interpreter. Capt. Muirhead served in the European War from 1914 until its conclusion, in France, being in its early stages a Battery Commander in the 3rd Division, and receiving his Majority 30 Oct. 1914. He was mentioned in Despatches in Feb. 1915, and created a Companion of the Distinguished Service Order [London Gazette, 18 Feb. 1915]: "Murray Muirhead, Major, Brigade Ammunition Column, Royal Field Artillery." He was Brigade Major, 47th Division, 19 April, 1916, to 16 Jan. 1917; Staff Officer on the 18th Corps Staff 17 Jan. to 22 Nov. 1917, and afterwards served as Brigade Commander in the 9th Division, with which he went to the Rhine. He was mentioned in Despatches twice in 1917 and twice in 1918, and was given the Brevet of Lieutenant-Colonel 1 Jan. 1919; was made a Chevalier of the Legion of Honour, and was awarded a Bar to the D.S.O. (an immediate award in the field). His D.S.O. was awarded "for services in connection with operations in the field."

CARRUTHERS, JAMES, Major, M.V.O., was born 17 July, 1876, eldest son of the late Peter Carruthers, of Portrack, Dumfries. He was educated at Craigmount, Edinburgh, and Edinburgh University, and entered the Royal Artillery 12 May, 1900; became Lieutenant 12 Oct. 1901, and Captain 14 Nov. 1910; was created an M.V.O. in 1910; was A.D.C. to the Governor-General and Commander-in-Chief, Union of South Africa, 15 April, 1912, to 4 Aug. 1914. He served in the European War from 1914 to 1918; became Major 30 Oct. 1914. He was mentioned in Despatches, and was created a Companion of the Distinguished Service Order [London Gazette, 18 Feb. 1915]: "James Carruthers, M.V.O., Major, 134th Battery, Royal Artillery." Major Carruthers was Staff Captain, Ministry of Munitions, 20 July, 1916, to 30 Sept. 1917; Deputy Assistant Director of Artillery, G.H.Q., British Armies in France, 10 March, 1918, to 2 April, 1919. He married, in 1915, Violet Rosa, youngest daughter of the late Charles Markham, of Tapton House, Chesterfield. His D.S.O. was awarded "for services in connection with operations in the field."

NEWLAND, ARTHUR EDWARD, Major, was born 26 May, 1879, and was gazetted to the Royal Artillery 12 May, 1900. He served in the South African War, 1900–1; was Assistant Press Censor 19 April to 25 July, 1900; took part in the operations in Orange Free State, March to April, 1900; in Cape Colony, April to July, 1900; in the Transvaal, 30 Nov. 1900, to Nov. 1901; also during operations in the Orange River Colony, Jan. 1901 (Queen's Medal with three clasps). He became Lieutenant 7 Nov. 1901; served in Somaliland, 1908–9 (Despatches); with the King's African Rifles, 27 May, 1908, to 25 June, 1911; was promoted Captain 16 Nov. 1910. Capt. Newland served in the European War, 1914–15. He was promoted Major 30 Oct. 1914, and was created a Companion of the Distinguished Service Order [London Gazette, 18 Feb. 1915]: "Arthur Edward Newland, Major, Royal Field Artillery, 30th Brigade (Howitzer)." He became Brigade Major, Royal Artillery, 4th Canadian Division, 22 Nov. 1916; was acting Lieutenant-Colonel 28 Oct. 1917, to 4 July, 1918; Brigade Major, Royal Artillery, 69th Division, Forces in Great Britain, 5 July to 17 Oct. 1918; Acting Lieutenant-Colonel 18 Oct. 1918, to 28 Jan. 1919. He married, in 1911, Alice Mary, eldest daughter of Richard Burke, of Grove Fethard, County Tipperary, and they have one daughter. His D.S.O. was awarded for services in connection with operations in the field."

DAVIDSON, LESLIE EVAN OUTRAM, Capt., was born 23 Sept. 1882, son of the late Duncan Davidson, of Inchmarle. He was educated at Marlborough, and entered the Army, as a Second Lieutenant in the Royal Artillery, 24 May, 1902; was promoted Lieutenant 24 May, 1905. He served in the European War in 1914 and 1915; was promoted Captain 30 Oct. 1914; was mentioned in Despatches twice, and was created a Companion of the Distinguished Service Order [London Gazette, 18 Feb. 1915]: "Leslie Evan Outram Davidson, Capt., Royal Artillery." He became Adjutant, Royal Artillery, 17 Feb. 1915, and Major 23 Feb. 1916. Major Davidson married, in 1914, Matilda Rome, daughter of Lionel Maitland-Kirwan, R.N., of Collin, Castle Douglas. His D.S.O. was awarded "for services in connection with operations in the field."

EARLE, ERIC GREVILLE, Second Lieut., was born at Sangor, Central Provinces, India, 24 Feb. 1893, son of Lieut. Cecil Arthur Earle, R.F.A. (died at Sangor 27 July, 1897), and Mrs. C. A. Earle (formerly Lizzie Isabella (Betty) Scott), of Earles Court, Camberley, Surrey. He was educated at Lockers Park, Hemel Hempstead, Herts, 1902–5; at Wellington College, 1905–10, and at the Royal Military Academy, Woolwich. He left Wellington in Dec. 1910, where he was in the 1st Fifteen, 1910; in the 3rd Eleven, 1910, and a Colour-Sergeant in the Rifle Corps, with which he attended the funeral of King Edward VII. at Windsor. He passed direct into Woolwich in Feb. 1911, and passed out in July, 1912; was in the 2nd Fifteen, and ran for Woolwich against Sandhurst in the Mile in 1912 (the year that Sandhurst won every event). He was gazetted to the R.F.A. 19 July, 1912. He joined the 37th Battery, at Bulford, 9 Sept. 1912; moved to Kildare, Ireland, with them in Nov. 1912, and was stationed there until they sailed for France on 27 Aug. 1914. His pursuits in Ireland were hunting, cricket and football. He played for Monkstown Rugby Football Club, and for Kildare garrison team in the Army Cups; ran for the 8th Brigade, R.F.A. in the Irish Command Cross-country Championship, and in the Irish Command Athletic Meetings, 1911 and 1912. He landed in France 19 Aug. 1914; was present at Mons, 24 Aug., and Le Cateau, 26 Aug. At the latter place he was wounded three times, one wound causing the loss of the left eye. He was one of a party of volunteers who assisted the late Major (then Capt.) D. Reynolds, V.C., to save a gun under fire. Lord Ernest Hamilton says that "the work of the artillery all along the line was magnificent, and deeds of individual heroism were innumerable. The 37th Battery, for instance, kept up its shrapnel fire on the advancing line of Germans till they were within 300 yards of its position. Then Capt. Reynolds, with some volunteer drivers, galloped up with two teams and hitched them on to the two guns which had not been knocked out. Incredible as it may appear, in view of the hail of bullets directed at them, one of these guns was got safely away." ("The First Seven Divisions," page 68). For his share in this deed Second Lieut. E. C. Earle was created a Companion of the Distinguished Service Order [London Gazette, 18 Feb. 1915]: "Eric Greville Earle, Second Lieut., (8th Brigade) Royal Field Artillery." He was discharged from hospital in Dec. 1914, and joined a Division of the New Army; became Adjutant, R.A., Jan. 1915, and Staff Captain, R.A., 3 March, 1915, and accompanied the Division to France, July, 1915. He was promoted to Lieutenant in July, 1915; was present at the operations of 25 Sept. 1915; at the Third Battle of Ypres, June, 1916, and at the Battle of the Somme, Sept. and Nov. 1916. He became Captain in Nov. 1916, and returned to regimental duty at his own request, Jan. 1917. He was present at minor operations in the Somme area, Jan. and Feb. 1917, and was appointed Acting Major, Feb. 1917; commanded D/91 Battery, R.F.A. in the advance on the Somme front during March and April, 1917; also in the Fourth Battle of Ypres, July 31 to 18 Oct. (capture of Pilkem, Langemarck and Koekuit), Battles of Cambria, 20 and 30 Nov.; retreat from St. Quentin, 21 to 30 March, 1918; Battle of Lassigny (under the French), on 30 March, 1918, when he commanded a composite R.F.A. Brigade; Battle of Villers Bretonneux, 24 April, 1918, when he received two wounds, and was invalided home. In addition to receiving the D.S.O. he became Chevalier de l'Ordre de Léopold, Aug. 1917; received the Belgian Croix de Guerre, March, 1918, and has the 1914 Star; was mentioned in Despatches four times: Nov. 1914; Feb. 1915; Jan. 1916, and Jan. 1917. He married, on 17 Jan. 1918, Noel, youngest daughter of Edward Downes-Martin and the late Mrs. Helen Downes-Martin (Irwin), of Killoskehane Castle, County Tipperary. His D.S.O. was awarded "for services in connection with operations in the field."

Eric Greville Earle.

TYRRELL, GERALD ERNEST, Major, was born in India 31 Oct. 1871, son of Lieut.-General Francis Hardinge Tyrrell, Madras Infantry (retired), and Mary, daughter of General J. S. Halliday. Having passed through Woolwich, he entered the Royal Artillery 12 Feb. 1892, and served successively with the garrison, field and mountain batteries of the arm. He became Lieutenant 12 Feb. 1895, and saw a considerable amount of service on the North-West Frontier of India, with the Malakand Field Force, the Utman Khel Column, the Buner Field Force and the Tirah Expedition. He was present at the attack and capture of the Tanga Pass, and received the Medal and three clasps. He was promoted Captain 1 Jan. 1900. After the Tirah Campaign he became A.D.C. to Sir William Lockhart, then Commander-in-Chief in India, and after that General's death was given an appointment on the Viceregal Staff by Lord Curzon. Capt. Tyrrell was Vice-Consul at Van from 21 April, 1902, to 31 March, 1906; was employed at Drama, under the Murzteg programme, as British officer with the Macedonian Gendarmerie, 23 Aug. 1907, to 13 June, 1909, and received a gold medal for conspicuous bravery. In 1910 he was appointed Military Attaché (General Staff Officer) at Constantinople and Athens (4 Dec. 1909, to 14 Aug. 1911). He was Military Attaché (General Staff Officer), Constantinople, 15 Aug. 1911, to 3 Dec. 1913. While holding this appointment he went as British representative with the Turkish Headquarters Staff to the Balkans. He had qualified as a first-class interpreter in Turkish and French. He became Major 2 Sept. 1913. Major Tyrrell served in the European War from 1914. He was twice mentioned in Despatches for his services while commanding a heavy battery at the front, and was created a Companion of the Distinguished Service Order [London Gazette, 18 Feb. 1915]: "Gerald Ernest Tyrrell, Major, Royal Garrison Artillery (108th Heavy Battery)." He was invested by the King at Buckingham Palace, 6 July, 1915. He was Temporary Lieutenant-Colonel from 27 Jan. to 31 Dec. 1915, and was a Member of the British Military Mission at the General Headquarters of the Belgian Army, for which he was given the Brevet of Lieutenant-Colonel (1 Jan. 1916); was again mentioned in Despatches, and made an Officer of the Order of Leopold. He was transferred in Sept. 1915, to the General Headquarters Staff of the Mediterranean Expeditionary Force, Chief of the Intelligence Department, and served successively in Gallipoli, Egypt and Salonika, and was again mentioned in Despatches. In Sept. 1916, he was recalled to France, and there contracted the illness which proved fatal on 17 May, 1917. His D.S.O. was awarded "for services in connection with operations in the field."

HOLBROOKE, PHILIP LANCELOT, Major, was born 25 Nov. 1872, at Brighton, son of the late Rev. Frederick George Holbrooke, Rector of Kimpton, Hants, late Lieutenant in the Army. His grandfather was Bernard Holbrooke, Capt., 14th Light Dragoons, who was present at the landing in Egypt under Abercrombie; his great-grandfather was Capt. Bernard Holbrooke, who was present at the Siege of Belleisle, and his great-great-grandfather was Capt. Holbrooke, Royal Navy. He was educated at Felstead School, Essex, and joined the Army 25 May, 1892; became Lieutenant 25 May, 1895, and served in the South African War from Dec. 1899, to the end of the war, with a 5-inch Gun Battery, R.G.A. He was present at the Relief of Ladysmith, Tugela Heights, and in operations in the Transvaal, Orange River Colony and Cape Colony; was afterwards in command of D (1) Section, Pom-poms (two Medals with eight clasps). He became Captain 1 Feb. 1900. He was Adjutant at Plymouth, 1903–6; Instructor in Gunnery at Shoeburyness 16 May, 1908, to 15 May, 1912; commanded 100th Company, R.G.A., in Malta, 1912–14; became Major 6 Aug. 1913; Instructor in Gunnery 1 April, 1914, till the outbreak of war. Major Holbrooke served in the European War from 1914–18, in France. He was mentioned in Despatches, Feb. 1915, and created a Companion of the Distinguished Service Order [London Gazette, 18 Feb. 1915]: "Philip Lancelot Holbrooke, Major (4th Siege Battery), Royal Garrison Artillery." The decoration was awarded for good work while in command of the 4th Siege Battery, in the First Battle of Ypres, at the Aisne, and in Flanders. Major Holbrooke was brought home from France to train new Siege Batteries for six months, until Aug. 1915. He returned to France, Aug. 1915, and was Brigade-Major, 4th Heavy Artillery Reserve Group, Loos, Aug. to Nov. 1915. (Major Holbrooke has been a Siege Artillery Specialist for years.) He served as Staff Officer to the Major-General, R.A., Salonika Army, Nov. 1915, to Aug. 1916. He was again mentioned in Despatches in July, 1916, and was awarded the Russian Order of St. Stanislas, 3rd Class; commanded the 37th Heavy Artillery Group from Aug. 1916; was mentioned in Despatches, Jan. 1917, and given the Brevet of Lieutenant-Colonel, Jan. 1917. He became Lieutenant-Colonel 1 May, 1917, and was Temporary Brigadier-General, Royal Artillery, Heavy Artillery, British Salonika Force, 4 Oct. 1917, to 1 May, 1919. He was given the Brevet of Colonel 3 June, 1918, and was created a C.M.G. in 1919. He married, at Kimpton Church, 3 Oct. 1903, Eleanor Slade Gully, of Trevenan, Cornwall, Lady of the Manor of Trevenan, daughter of Capt. Slade Gully. His D.S.O. was awarded "for services in connection with operations in the field."

HILDEBRAND, ARTHUR BLOIS ROSS, Major, was born 6 April, 1870. He entered the Army, as a Second Lieutenant in the Royal Engineers, 14 Feb. 1890; was promoted Lieutenant 14 Feb. 1893; Captain 5 Dec. 1900. He served in the South African War, 1899–1902; took part in the operations in Natal, 1899; Defence of Ladysmith; operations in Natal (March to June, 1900); in the Transvaal, east of Pretoria, July to 29 Nov. 1900; in the Transvaal, west of Pretoria, July to 29 Nov. 1900 (Despatches [London Gazette, 9 July 1901]; Queen's Medal with five clasps, and King's Medal with two clasps). He was from 1 Aug. 1909, to 31 July, 1913, Chief Instructor at the Royal Military Academy, becoming Major 14 Feb. 1910. Major Hildebrand served in the European War, 1914–18; was created a Companion of the Distinguished Service Order [London Gazette, 18 Feb. 1915]: "Arthur Blois Ross Hildebrand, Major, Royal Engineers." He was given, in the same Gazette, the Brevet of Lieutenant-Colonel. He subsequently held the following Staff appointments: Deputy Director of Army Signals, 2nd Army, British Expeditionary Force, British Armies in France, 6 Feb. 1916, to 17 Nov. 1917; Deputy Director of Army Signals, British Forces in Italy, and 2nd Army, British Armies in France, 18 Nov. 1917, to 15 May, 1918 (promoted Lieutenant-Colonel 15 Jan. 1918); Chief Signal Officer, British Armies in France, 16 May to 11 Nov. 1918; Deputy Director of Army Signals, Forces in Great Britain (temporary Brigadier-General), 22 Nov. 1918. He was given the Brevet of Colonel 3 June, 1917; was created a C.M.G. in 1918, and a C.B. in 1919, and was twice mentioned in Despatches. His D.S.O. was awarded "for services in connection with operations in the field."

SINGER, CHARLES WILLIAM, Major, was born at Cheltenham, 3 July, 1870, son of Vice-Admiral Morgan Singer and of Fanny, daughter of General Robert Burn, R.A. He was educated at Felsted School; joined the Royal Engineers 14 Feb. 1890, and became Lieutenant 14 Feb. 1893. He served on the North-West Frontier of India, 1897–98 (Medal and two clasp); Tirah, 1897–8, including the actions of Chagru Kotal and Dargai (clasp). He became Captain 14 Feb. 1901; was Instructor, Royal Military Academy, 15 Sept. 1902, to 11 Sept. 1904, and Officer, Company of Gentleman Cadets (Class A), Royal Military Academy, 12 Sept. 1904, to 14 Sept. 1907. He became Major 14 Feb. 1910. Major Singer served in the European War from Aug. 1914, in France and Belgium. He commanded the 17th Field Company, Royal Engineers, 5th Division, until July, 1915. He was created a Companion of the Distinguished Service Order [London Gazette, 18 Feb. 1915]: "Charles William Singer, Major, Royal Engineers." He became Temporary Lieutenant-Colonel 16 July, 1915; was C.R.E., 50th Northumbrian Division, July, 1915, to April, 1917; became Temporary Brigadier-General 3 April, 1917; was Chief Engineer, 15th Corps, 3 April, 1917, to 11 Nov. 1918; then Chief Engineer, 10th Corps, until Sept. 1919, when he was appointed Engineer-in-Chief, British Army of the Rhine. He was given the Brevet of Lieutenant-Colonel 1 Jan. 1916; became Lieutenant-Colonel 15 March, 1918; was given the Brevet of Colonel 1 Jan. 1919; was created a C.M.G. in 1916, and was seven times mentioned in Despatches. He was also awarded the French Croix de Guerre and the Legion of Honour (Chevalier). He married, 28 July, 1898, Jessie Harriet Margaret, second daughter of Osmond de Haviland Stewart, of the family of Appin, Argyllshire, and their children are: Charles Morgan, born 10 Jan. 1900, and Jean Dorothea. His D.S.O. was awarded "for services in connection with operations in the field."

Charles William Singer.

HOWARD, FREDERICK GEORGE, Major, was born 19 Jan. 1872, son of Colonel Frederick Howard, Royal Artillery. He was educated at Haileybury, and Oxford Military College, and entered the Army, as a Second Lieutenant in the Royal Engineers, 12 Feb. 1892, becoming Lieutenant 12 Feb. 1895. Took part in the operations in Chitral, 1895, with the Relief Force; Assistant Field Engineer, Lines of Communication (12 May to Aug. 1895) (Medal with clasp). Served at Tirah, 1897–98; was present during operations in the Bazar Valley, 25 to 30 Dec. 1897 (two clasps). He was promoted Captain 23 Nov. 1902, and was A.M.S. and A.D.C. to the Governor and Commander-in-Chief, Malta, 4 Feb. 1911, to 11 Feb. 1912; was promoted Major 12 Feb. 1912; was created an M.V.O.; commanded the 57th Field Company, Royal Engineers. He served in the European War, and for his services was mentioned in Despatches by Sir John French, 19 Oct. 1914, and was created a Companion of the Distinguished Service Order [London Gazette, 18 Feb. 1915]: "Frederick George Howard, M.V.O., Major, Royal Engineers." He was killed in action in Flanders 19 Oct. 1915. His D.S.O. was awarded "for services in connection with operations in the field."

SANDYS, EDWARD SETON, Major, was born 17 Sept. 1872, at Tilbury Port, Essex, third son of Major E. W. Sandys, late R.A., of Fulford House, York. He was educated at Marlborough (1887–89, B1), and at the Royal Military Academy. He joined the Army 12 Feb. 1892; became Lieutenant 12 Feb. 1895; was A.D.C. to Lieutenant-General, India, 23 May, 1902, to 28 Oct. 1903. He was promoted Captain 17 Jan. 1903, and Major 12 Feb. 1912. He served from the commencement of the European War. He was mentioned in Despatches in Oct. 1914, and was created a Companion of the Distinguished Service Order [London Gazette, 18 Feb. 1915]: "Edward Seton Sandys, Major, Royal Engineers." He became Temporary Lieutenant-Colonel 4 Oct. 1915, and was mentioned in Despatches, Jan. and Dec. 1916, and Nov. 1917, and was given the Brevet of Lieutenant-Colonel on 1 Jan. 1918. His D.S.O. was awarded "for services in connection with operations in the field."

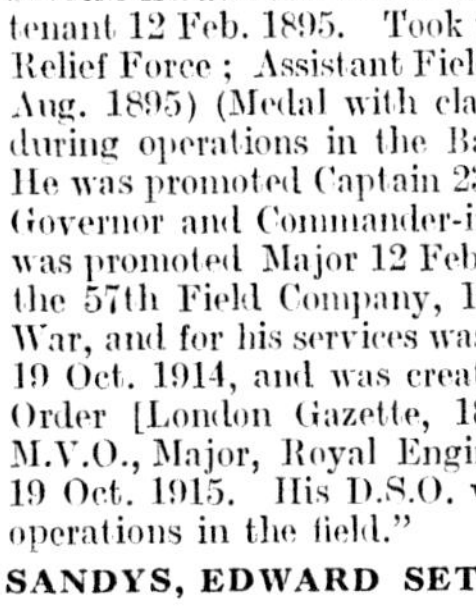

Edward Seton Sandys.

BROWNE, FREDERICK MACDONNELL, Major, was born 8 Aug. 1873, at Cananore, India, son of the late Ven. J. F. Browne, Archdeacon of Madras, and of Mrs. Browne, of 12, Park Street, Bath. He was educated at Newton College, Newton Abbot, Devon. He joined the Royal Engineers, 22 July, 1892; became Lieutenant 22 July, 1895. He served in China, was wounded at the Battle of Tientsin, 1900, and received the Medal for the Relief of Peking. He was promoted Captain 22 July, 1903, and Major 22 July, 1912. He acted as Instructor of Survey at the R.I.E. College, Cooper's Hill, after which he served for a time in India, and was sent to France in Sept. 1914. He served with the 38th Field Company, Royal Engineers, in the European War, and was mentioned in the Despatch from Field-Marshal Sir John French, dated 30 Nov. 1915, and published in the London Gazette dated 1 Jan. 1916, for "gallant and distinguished service in the field." He was created a Companion of the Distinguished Service Order [London Gazette, 18 Feb. 1915]: "Frederick MacDonnell Browne, Major, Royal Engineers." Major A. E. Sandbach wrote of Major Browne:

" I was his Chief Engineer in Ireland, and also in France, and saw him frequently, and admired his work and his character." Major Browne died of wounds at Chocques Military Hospital, 1 Oct. 1915. His D.S.O. was awarded " for services in connection with operations in the field."

MOORE, HERBERT TREGOSSE GWENNAP, Major, was born 12 March, 1875. He joined the Royal Engineers 17 Aug. 1894; became Lieutenant 17 Aug. 1897; served in the South African War, 1899–1902; was present at the Relief of Ladysmith, including action at Colenso; operations of 17 to 24 Jan. 1900, and action at Spion Kop; operations of 5 to 7 Feb. 1900, and action at Vaal Kranz; during the operations on Tugela Heights (14 to 27 Feb. 1900), and action at Pieter's Hill; in Natal, March to June, 1900, including action at Laing's Nek (6 to 9 June); also in the Transvaal 30 Nov. 1900, to 31 May, 1902 (Queen's Medal with six clasps and King's Medal with two clasps). He was promoted Captain 1 April, 1904. Capt. Moore was Assistant Commissioner, Yola-Cross River Boundary Commission, 17 Aug. 1907, to 6 Oct. 1909. He served in Southern Nigeria in 1908 (Despatches). He served in the European War from 1914 to 1918. He became Major 17 Aug. 1914, and was created a Companion of the Distinguished Service Order [London Gazette, 18 Feb. 1915]: " Herbert Tregosse Gwennap Moore, Major, Royal Engineers." He became Temporary Colonel 19 June, 1916, and was employed from then until 15 May, 1918, as Deputy Director of Army Signals, 1st Army, British Armies in France, becoming Chief Signal Officer, British Armies in France, 16 May, 1918. He was given the Brevet of Lieutenant-Colonel 1 Jan. 1918, and was created a C.M.G. in 1919. He married, in 1907, Hilda, daughter of the late Griffiths Phillips, of The Pines, Whitchurch. His D.S.O. was awarded " for services in connection with operations in the field."

DAY, HAROLD ERNEST, Capt., was born 16 Dec. 1880, son of Colonel F. J. Day, late Royal Engineers, and of Mrs. Day (formerly Randall). He joined the Royal Engineers 6 Jan. 1900. He served in the South African War, 1901–2; took part in the operations in the Transvaal, March to Nov. 1901; in Orange River Colony, Nov. 1901; also in Cape Colony, Nov. 1901, to March, 1902 (Queen's Medal with five clasps). He became Lieutenant 6 Jan. 1903, and Captain 6 Jan. 1909. He served in the European War from 1914 to 1918, and was created a Companion of the Distinguished Service Order [London Gazette, 18 Feb. 1915]: " Harold Ernest Day, Capt., Royal Engineers." He was created an M.V.O., 1915, and Chevalier de la Légion d'Honneur, 1916. He served as Temporary Major from Feb. 1916, until promoted to Substantive rank 2 Nov. 1916; was employed under the Air Ministry from 14 Oct. 1918; was mentioned in Despatches four times. Major Day married, in 1913, Dorothy Culling, daughter of F. C. Carr-Gomm, Esq., J.P., and they have one daughter, Elizabeth Culling. His D.S.O. was awarded " for services in connection with operations in the field."

Harold Ernest Day.

PRICKETT, CHARLES HENRY, Capt., was born 23 July, 1881, at his grandfather's house, The Avenue, Bridlington, son of Marmaduke Prickett, M.D. (retired) (born 14 April, 1844), of Cranbourne Lodge, Winkfield, Berkshire, and Alice, daughter of Charles Mortlock, Esq. He was educated at Mr. Baily's School, Limpsfield Common; at Marlborough (which he entered in 1895), and at the Royal Military Academy, Woolwich (which he entered in Jan. 1899), passing 12th in the examination for Woolwich. He passed third in the Woolwich Examination; was appointed Second Lieutenant in the Royal Engineers 2 May, 1900, and joined his corps at Chatham on 18 May, 1900. In Dec. 1901, he was ordered out to South Africa, to take part in the Boer War under General Plumer, and later under General William Kitchener. He received the Queen's Medal with four clasps. When peace was declared he was placed in charge of the R.E. Telegraph Section, then at Pretoria, and acted as Telegraph Officer for General Stephenson. He became Lieutenant 2 May, 1903. In Oct. 1906, he returned home, and was sent to Bulford Camp, Salisbury Plain. He became Captain 2 May, 1910. When the European War broke out Capt. Prickett was ordered to France. He went out to the Front 16 Aug. 1914; joined General Smith-Dorrien's Force, and took part in the Retreat from Mons. General Smith-Dorrien wrote to Lady Smith-Dorrien: " Charles Prickett is in splendid health, and doing magnificent work." On 19 Oct. 1914, Capt. Prickett's name was mentioned by General French in his Despatch, among officers specially commended for their services in the field. In Feb. 1915, he was again mentioned by General French in Despatches, and was created a Companion of the Distinguished Service Order [London Gazette, 18 Feb. 1915]: " Charles Henry Prickett, Capt., Royal Engineers." In Feb. 1915, he was summoned home, and appointed Divisional Signalling Camp Instructor in the New Army of Lord Kitchener, and was sent to several camps to give instruction, and lastly to the camp of Shefford, near Hitchin. On 14 Jan. 1916, he was sent to Salonika, and stationed at the Headquarters of the 16th Corps, on the hills overlooking the river Struma. He was mentioned thrice more in Despatches, and became Major 18 Oct. 1916, and Temporary Lieutenant-Colonel 6 Nov. 1916; was given the Brevet of Lieutenant-Colonel 3 June, 1918, and given the Serbian Order of the White Eagle, 4th Class, 1 Nov. 1918. Lieut.-Colonel Prickett is fond of all games, and a good rider. When he was stationed at Bulford Camp he won the Military Steeplechase there in April, 1909, for a silver cup given by Sir Ian Hamilton. He was married, by special license, at Amesbury, on 11 Aug. 1914, to Margaret Kemp, third daughter of the late James Kemp and of Mrs. Kemp, living at Oakhurst, Woodhay, Newbury. His D.S.O. was awarded for " services in connection with operations in the field."

LEATHAM, ROBERT EDWARD KENNARD, Capt., was born 23 Feb. 1885, only son of Arthur William Leatham and Mary Elise, only daughter of the late Henry Martyn Kennard, of Croft-y-Bwla, County Monmouth. He joined the Grenadier Guards 2 March, 1904; became Lieutenant 8 April, 1906, and Captain 22 March, 1913. Capt. Leatham served in the European War from 1914 to 1917. He was mentioned in Despatches, and created a Companion of the Distinguished Service Order [London Gazette, 18 Feb. 1915]: " Robert Edward Kennard Leatham, Capt., Grenadier Guards." He was promoted Major 9 July, 1916; was Acting Lieutenant-Colonel, Machine Gun Guards, April to May, 1918; became Temporary Lieutenant-Colonel, Guards' Machine Gun Regt., 10 May, 1918, and was given the Brevet of Lieutenant-Colonel 1 Jan. 1919. He married, in 1916, Menda, daughter of the late Ambrose Ralli, and widow of Lord Arthur Vincent Hay, and they have one son. His D.S.O. was awarded " for services in connection with operations in the field."

RASCH, GUY ELLAND CARNE, Capt., served in the European War, and was created a Companion of the Distinguished Service Order [London Gazette, 18 Feb. 1915]: " Guy Elland Carne Rasch, Capt., Grenadier Guards." His D.S.O. was awarded " for services in connection with operations in the field."

HEPBURN-STUART-FORBES-TREFUSIS, THE HONOURABLE JOHN FREDERICK, Major, was born 14 Jan. 1878, son of Lord and Lady Clinton. He served in the South African War as a Trooper in the Imperial Yeomanry. He was gazetted to the Irish Guards 10 July, 1901, becoming Lieutenant 2 Aug. 1902, and held many Staff appointments, viz.: A.D.C. to the Temporary Commander, 4th Army Corps; A.D.C. to the G.O.C.-in-C., Eastern Command, 6 June, 1904, to 31 Oct. 1907; A.D.C. to the G.O.C.-in-C., South Africa, 1 Nov. 1908, to 8 Oct. 1909; Adjutant, Irish Guards, 2 Dec. 1909, to 1 June, 1913 (promoted Captain 26 Oct. 1909); Officer of a Company of Gentleman Cadets, Royal Military College, 18 Sept. 1913, to 21 Jan. 1914; Adjutant, Royal Military College, 22 Jan. 1914. He served in the European War from 1914; was promoted Major 3 Sept. 1914, and in Dec. was gazetted Temporary Lieutenant Colonel of the Irish Guards. He was created a Companion of the Distinguished Service Order [London Gazette, 18 Feb. 1915]: " The Honourable J. F. Hepburn-Stuart-Forbes-Trefusis, Major, The Irish Guards." He was promoted Brigadier-General 16 Aug. 1915, and was killed in action on Sunday, 24 Oct. 1915. An appreciation of Brigadier-General the Hon. J. F. Trefusis was contributed to the " Times " of 29 Oct. 1915, by a brother officer in the Brigade of Guards: " ' Jack Tre,' to give him the name by which he was known in the Brigade of Guards, was probably one of the youngest of our Brigadier-Generals. Born in 1878, he first saw service as a Trooper of Yeomanry in the South African War, and in 1901 obtained a commission in the newly-formed Irish Guards. After some three years of regimental duty, he served as A.D.C. to Lord Methuen, who then commanded the 4th Army Corps, and subsequently accompanied his General to South Africa and Malta. In 1909 he returned to the regiment, and the same year was promoted Captain, and appointed Adjutant. After serving for four years in that capacity he was selected as a ' Company Officer ' at the Royal Military College, where, at the beginning of 1914, he took up the duties of Adjutant, a post which he held until the outbreak of the present war. His battalion, when he rejoined it upon the Aisne on 18 Sept. 1914, had already suffered heavily. During the retreat the Commanding Officer and the Second-in-Command had been killed, and the Adjutant being temporarily incapacitated by wounds, Trefusis was, on his arrival, immediately chosen to take his place. As Adjutant he took part in the withdrawal from the Aisne, and in the encounters which have been officially described as the First Battle of Ypres. So heavy had been the toll among the senior officers in these operations that, on 24 Nov. 1914, Trefusis, who had been gazetted Major in the previous Sept., found himself in command of the remnants of his sorely tried battalion. The condition of affairs when he assumed command was one which called for the exercise of those qualities which he possessed in an eminent degree. The battalion had lost heavily, both in officers and men, and was exhausted by a protracted struggle against overwhelming odds. Although the enemy's attacks had been driven off for the moment, there was little cause for elation in the military situation. The weather, moreover, was miserably wet and cold, and the general surroundings were depressing in the extreme. Those who served under him at this trying period would doubtless be the first to declare that it was mainly the example set by their Commanding Officer that enabled them so quickly to regain confidence, and to be ready once again to carry out whatever task might be set them. It was characteristic of his keenness and of his devotion to the Service that, on the occasion of his taking 72 hours' leave, he should spend one morning of his brief holiday among the cadets at Sandhurst, and another in visiting the reserve battalion of his regiment at Warley. In all the operations undertaken by the Guards Brigade during the winter campaign—and notably in the successful affair of 1 Feb. 1915—he commanded his battalion with marked distinction. On 17 May the Irish Guards were again in action, and again on this occasion suffered heavy losses. The brilliant qualities of their young Colonel had meanwhile not passed unnoticed. Early in the year he had been mentioned in Despatches, and had been awarded the D.S.O. Nor was further promotion long in coming. On 16 Aug. he bade farewell to his battalion, and took up the command of the 20th Brigade in the famous 7th Division. His leading of his brigade in the successful attack upon Loos still further enhanced his reputation. But this was the last operation of importance in which he was destined to participate. From the desperate fighting which marked the last days of Sept. he emerged scathless, only to fall on 24 Oct. in some affair the details of which are still unknown. In him the country has lost an officer of the highest merit and a most gallant gentleman." His D.S.O. was awarded " for services in connection with operations in the field."

DYSON, HARRY GO BERNARD, Major, was born 1 June, 1869, son of William H. Dyson. He joined the Royal Scots 9 Nov. 1889 ; became Lieutenant 16 Jan. 1893, and Captain 2 Jan. 1897. Capt. Dyson was D.A.A.G., India, 22 April, 1903, to 18 Sept. 1905, and from 19 Sept. 1905, to 4 Dec. 1907 ; promoted Major 27 March, 1907. Major Dyson served in the European War from 1914 ; was in command of the 11th Battn. Royal Scots, 19 Aug. to 9 Oct. 1914, and created a Companion of the Distinguished Service Order [London Gazette, 18 Feb. 1915] : " Harry H. Bernard Dyson, Major, the Royal Scots (Lothian Regt.)." He was attached General Staff (graded G.S.O., 2nd Grade), Reserve Centre, Western Command, 29 June, 1915, to 19 Jan. 1916, and became Temporary Lieutenant-Colonel 3 Feb. 1916, commanding the 2nd Battn. Royal Scots. He was promoted Lieutenant-Colonel 7 Aug. 1916. He was wounded ; twice mentioned in Despatches, and was awarded the O.B.E. He married, in 1910, Nora, second daughter of Alfred J. Whittell, of Woodside, Llandaff. His D.S.O. was awarded " for services in connection with operations in the field."

LONGBOURNE, FRANCIS CECIL, Capt., was born 20 June, 1883, son of Charles R. V. Longbourne (deceased) and Caroline E. A. Longbourne, of Highmead, Guildford. He served in the South African War, 1900-2 ; was present in operations with the Mounted Infantry in Cape Colony 30 Nov. 1900, to March, 1902 (Queen's Medal with three clasps). He joined the Queen's Regt., as Second Lieutenant, from the Militia, 30 April, 1902. He became Lieutenant 13 Aug. 1904 ; was employed with the Mounted Infantry in the West African Frontier Force 15 Nov. 1911, to 29 July, 1914 ; became Captain 2 March, 1913. Capt. Longbourne served in the European War from 12 Aug. 1914, to the conclusion of the war, and was created a Companion of the Distinguished Service Order [London Gazette, 18 Feb. 1915] : " Francis Cecil Longbourne, Capt., The Queen's Regt." Capt. Longbourne served for a month as Temporary Major, The Queen's Regt., and as Temporary Lieutenant-Colonel for 18 months. He was given the Brevet of Major 1 Jan. 1916, and promoted Major 4 Dec. 1916. He was given the Brevet of Lieutenant-Colonel 1 Jan. 1918, and held the temporary rank of Brigadier-General 23 Sept. 1917, to 30 Oct. 1918, while commanding the 171st Infantry Brigade, British Armies in France. He became a Chevalier of the Legion of Honour 22 May, 1917, and was created a C.M.G. in 1919. He was mentioned in Despatches eight times. His D.S.O. was awarded " for services in connection with operations in the field."

Francis Cecil Longbourne.

PARKER, ROBERT GABBETT, Major, was born 4 Dec. 1875, at Bally Valley, Killaloe, County Clare, Ireland, son of Robert Gabbett Parker, Esq., D.L., and Louisa Parker. He was educated at Clifton College and Sandhurst ; joined the King's Own Royal Lancaster Regt. 26 Feb. 1896, as Second Lieutenant, and became Lieutenant 10 June, 1897. He served in the South African War, 1899-1902 ; was present at the Relief of Ladysmith, including operations of 17 to 24 Jan. 1900, and action at Spion Kop ; operations of 5 to 7 Feb. 1900, and action at Vaal Kranz ; and during the operations on Tugela Heights 14 to 27 Feb. 1900 (wounded 22 Feb.) ; in the Transvaal in May and June, 1900 ; in Natal, March to June, 1900, including action at Laing's Nek ; in Orange River Colony, June, 1900 ; again in the Transvaal 30 Nov. 1900, to Jan. 1901 ; also during the operations on the Zululand Frontier of Natal in Sept. and Oct. 1901. He was twice mentioned in Despatches [London Gazette, 8 Feb. and 10 Sept. 1901] ; received the Queen's Medal with six clasps, and the King's Medal with two clasps. He was promoted Captain 27 Feb. 1900 ; was Adjutant, Militia, 30 Jan. 1902, to 29 Jan. 1905 ; passed the Staff College, 1908 ; attached General Staff (graded Brigade Major) 22 Aug. 1909, to 3 Sept. 1911 ; became Major 26 June, 1910 ; was Commander of a Company of Gentleman Cadets (G.S.O.), Royal Military College, 4 Sept. 1911, to 21 Aug. 1913. Major Parker served in the European War from 1914-18 ; was present at the Battle of Le Cateau 26 Aug. 1914 ; the Battle of the Marne (severely wounded 8 Sept. 1914). He was twice mentioned in Despatches, and created a Companion of the Distinguished Service Order [London Gazette, 18 Feb. 1915] : " Robert Gabbett Parker, Major, The King's Own (Royal Lancaster Regt.)." He became Lieutenant-Colonel 13 Oct. 1915 ; was G.S.O.1, Ripon Training Centre, 14 Jan. to 11 April, 1916 ; was specially employed at the War Office 28 April to 3 June, 1916 ; G.S.O.1. Thames and Medway Defences, 1 July, 1916, to 28 Feb. 1917 ; was G.S.O.1, 41st Division, British Armies in France, 3 May, 1917, to 28 Feb. 1918, and was present at the Battle of Messines 7 June, 1917 ; the Third Battle of Ypres, July to Sept. 1917 ; operations in Italy, Nov. 1917, to Feb. 1918. He became Brigadier-General, General Staff, 4th Army Corps, British Armies in France, 19 March, 1918 ; was present in operations in France round Bapaume 21 March to 5 April, 1918, and the advance into Belgium 21 Aug. to 11 Nov. 1918. He was three times more mentioned in Despatches ; was created a C.M.G. in 1918, and also awarded the French Croix de Guerre, and made an Officer of the Crown of Italy, 1918, and was made a C.B. in 1919. He became Colonel 13 Oct. 1919.

Robert Gabbett Parker.

His D.S.O. was awarded " for services in connection with operations in the field."

SOMERVILLE, WILLIAM ARTHUR TENNISON BELLINGHAM, Capt., was born 8 Aug. 1882, son of Bellingham Arthur Somerville and Margaret, youngest daughter of William Clinch. He joined the 1st Battn. The King's Own Royal Lancaster Regt. 8 May, 1901 ; became Lieutenant 7 April, 1904, and Captain 1 Feb. 1913. He served in the European War from 1914, and was Adjutant, Royal Lancaster Regt. 11 Aug. 1914, to 31 July, 1915. Capt. Somerville was twice mentioned in Despatches, and was created a Companion of the Distinguished Service Order [London Gazette, 18 Feb. 1915] : " William Arthur Tennison Bellingham Somerville, Capt., The King's Own (Royal Lancaster Regt.)." Capt. Somerville was G.S.O., 3rd Grade, 4th Division, B.E.F., 1 Aug. 1915, to 16 Jan. 1916, and Brigade Major, 11th Infantry Brigade, B.E.F., from 17 Jan. to 14 July, 1916. He was promoted Major 3 May, 1916 ; was G.S.O.2, 4th Division, British Armies in France, 15 July, 1916, to 11 May, 1917 ; Acting Lieutenant-Colonel, Royal Lancaster Regt., July to Dec. 1917 ; became Temporary Lieutenant-Colonel, Machine Gun Corps, Dec. 1917 ; was Temporary Colonel, July to Oct. 1918. He was given the Brevet of Lieutenant-Colonel 3 June, 1919, and was awarded a Bar to the D.S.O. His D.S.O. was awarded " for services in connection with operations in the field."

W. A. T. B. Somerville.

BOOTH, RAYMOND MITCHELL ST. JOHN, Capt., was born 31 Dec. 1879, youngest son of the late William C. Booth, of Oran, Catterick, N.B. He was educated at a private school, and entered the Army 4 Dec. 1901. He served in South Africa, 1901-2 ; took part in the operations in the Transvaal, June, 1901 ; served during operations in Orange River Colony, March to June, 1901, and April to 31 May, 1902 ; also in Cape Colony, March, 1901 (Queen's Medal with five clasps). He became Lieutenant 28 Aug. 1904 ; was employed with the King's African Rifles 24 Sept. 1908, to 23 Sept. 1913 ; became Captain 14 Sept. 1914. He served in the European War from 1914, being present in the Retreat from Mons ; the engagements up to 11 Nov. 1914, and from 13 to 31 May, 1915. He was twice wounded ; mentioned in Despatches, and created a Companion of the Distinguished Service Order [London Gazette, 18 Feb. 1915] : " Raymond Mitchell St. John Booth, Capt., The Northumberland Fusiliers." Capt. Booth was Brigade Major, 7th Provincial Infantry Brigade, Central Force, Home Defence, Home Forces, 30 Dec. 1915, to 24 June, 1916 ; Brigade Major, 10th Reserve Infantry Brigade, New Armies, 22 July, 1916, to 25 March, 1917 ; was promoted Major 8 May, 1916. He became Brigade Major, attached Headquarters Units. His D.S.O. was awarded " for services in connection with operations in the field."

BURNARD, CHARLES FRANCIS, Capt., was born 12 April, 1876, at Plymouth, second son of Robert Burnard, Esq., J.P., F.S.A., of Stoke Rectory, near Teignmouth. He was educated privately, and at Jesus College, Cambridge ; joined the 1st Battn. The Royal Warwickshire Regt. 18 April, 1900, and became Lieutenant 22 Jan. 1901. He served in the South African War with Mounted Infantry, 1901-2, being present during the several operations in the Transvaal and Orange River Colony, Dec. 1901, to May, 1902 (Queen's Medal with five clasps). Lieut. Burnard was employed with the West African Frontier Force 1 Dec. 1906, to 9 June, 1910, and was promoted Captain 23 March, 1910. He served in the European War, 1914-19. He was mentioned in Despatches, and created a Companion of the Distinguished Service Order, for work in the Retreat from Mons [London Gazette, 18 Feb. 1915] : " Charles Francis Burnard, Capt., Royal Warwickshire Regt." He was promoted Major 1 Sept. 1915, and joined the Labour Corps 6 March, 1918. His D.S.O. was awarded " for services in connection with operations in the field."

Charles Francis Burnard.

DONE, HERBERT RICHARD, Major, was born 23 Sept. 1876, youngest son of Richard Done and Louisa Doubeny. He was educated at Harrow and Sandhurst, and joined the Norfolk Regt. 5 Sept. 1896 ; became Lieutenant 5 Feb. 1898. He served in the South African War from 1900 to 1902, employed with Mounted Infantry ; took part in the operations in the Orange Free State, Feb. to May, 1900, including those at Paardeberg (17 to 26 Feb.) ; actions at Vet River (5 and 6 May) and Zand River ; during operations in the Transvaal, May and June, 1900, including action near Pretoria ; also in Orange River Colony, July, 1901, to 31 May, 1902 (Queen's Medal with three clasps, and King's Medal with two clasps). He became Captain 7 Dec. 1904 ; was Adjutant, Norfolk Regt., 7 Dec. 1904, to 6 Dec. 1907 ; was employed with the Egyptian Army 7 Jan. 1909, to 6 Jan. 1913 ; became Major 1 June, 1914. He served in the European War from 1914 ; was present at Mons and the Retreat, the First Battle of Ypres, the Somme, the Third Battle of Ypres, and the final attack against the Austrians and the advance into Austria. He was Temporary Lieutenant-Colonel from 23 Dec. 1914, to 14 Dec. 1915, and was created a Companion of the Distinguished Service Order [London Gazette, 18 Feb.

1915]: "Herbert Richard Done, Major, The Norfolk Regt." Lieut.-Colonel Done was Temporary Brigadier-General 15 Dec. 1915, to 2 April, 1919, and commanded the 145th Infantry Brigade, B.E.F., British Armies in France, 15 Dec. 1915, to 20 Nov. 1916; the Portsmouth Special Reserve Infantry Brigade, Home Forces, 30 Nov. 1916, to 7 March, 1917, and the 144th Infantry Brigade, British Armies in France; British Force in Italy 8 March, 1917, to 2 April, 1919. He was 10 times mentioned in Despatches; given the Brevet of Lieutenant-Colonel 3 June, 1915, and of Colonel 1 Jan. 1918; was created a C.M.G. in 1919, and was awarded a Bar to the D.S.O. [London Gazette, 20 Oct. 1916]. He married, in Nov. 1916, Elsie, daughter of the late Samuel Kingan, of Glenganagh, County Down. His D.S.O. was awarded "for services in connection with operations in the field," and the Bar to the D.S.O. "for conspicuous good service in action. He handled his brigade with great skill during two attacks, and showed great determination."

JOHNSTON, ROBERT HECTOR, Capt., was born 19 Dec. 1877, son of H. H. Johnston and J. M. Johnston (*née* Nelson). He was educated at Haileybury College, and joined the Lincolnshire Regt. 4 Jan. 1899; became Lieutenant 11 July, 1900; Captain 5 Nov. 1905, and was employed with the King's African Rifles 11 July, 1907, to 11 July, 1912, and served in Somaliland, 1908 to 1910 (Medal and clasp). He served in the European War from 1914–18, and was created a Companion of the Distinguished Service Order [London Gazette, 18 Feb. 1915]: "Robert Hector Johnston, Capt., The Lincolnshire Regt." He was promoted Major 1 Sept. 1915. Major Johnston was Temporary Lieutenant-Colonel, in command of a service battalion of the Lincolnshire Regt., 18 Nov. 1915, to 9 Dec. 1916; held a special appointment as Second-in-Command of an Officer Cadet Battalion 3 March to 14 Dec. 1917; was Brigade Major, British Honduras, 15 Dec. 1917, to 27 Dec. 1918; became Brigade Major, Milford Haven Garrison, 14 Feb. 1919. He married, 20 Dec. 1916, Kathleen Hariot, youngest daughter of the late W. F. Robinson, and they have one son, Robert Alan, born 15 April, 1918. His D.S.O. was awarded "for services in connection with operations in the field."

Robert Hector Johnston.

HOSKYNS, HENRY CHARLES WALTER, Capt., was born 28 June, 1875. He entered the Army, as a Second Lieutenant in the Lincolnshire Regt., 21 Sept. 1898, and became Lieutenant 11 June, 1900. He served in the South African War, 1900; took part in the operations in the Orange Free State, Feb. to May, 1900, including those at Paardeberg, actions at Poplar Grove, Karee Siding, Vet River and Zand River; also during the operations in the Transvaal in May and June, 1900, including actions near Johannesburg and Pretoria (Queen's Medal with three clasps). He was employed with the West African Frontier Force from 30 Nov. 1901, to 20 Dec. 1906, being promoted Captain 22 Dec. 1905. Capt. Hoskyns served in the European War. He was mentioned in Despatches [London Gazette, 19 Oct. 1914], and was created a Companion of the Distinguished Service Order [London Gazette, 18 Feb. 1915]: "Henry Charles Walter Hoskyns, Capt., Lincolnshire Regt. For services in connection with operations in the field." He was killed in action 25 Sept. 1915.

TATCHELL, EDWARD, Capt., was born 17 Aug. 1870, son of E. R. Tatchell, Esq., and Mrs. Tatchell. He was educated at Marlborough, and Trinity College, Cambridge; joined the Lincolnshire Regt. 9 Sept. 1893. He served in the Nile Expedition, 1898; was mentioned in Despatches; received the Queen's Medal with clasps for "Atbara" and "Khartum," and the Khedive's Medal. He served in the South African War, 1899–1900, employed with the Mounted Infantry; was present in operations in the Orange Free State, Feb. to May, 1900, including actions at Poplar Grove, Dreifontein, Houtnek (Thoba Mountain), Vet River (5 and 6 May) and Zand River; operations in the Transvaal in May and June, 1900, including actions near Johannesburg, Pretoria and Diamond Hill (11 and 12 June); operations in Orange River Colony (May to 18 Nov. 1900), including actions at Wittebergen (1 to 29 July). He was mentioned in Despatches [London Gazette, 10 Sept. 1901], and received the Queen's Medal with five clasps. He became Captain 2 Jan. 1903; retired 19 Sept. 1908, and joined the Reserve of Officers. Capt. Tatchell served in the European War from 1914 to 1917. He was mentioned in Despatches; severely wounded, and created a Companion of the Distinguished Service Order [London Gazette, 18 Feb. 1915]: "Edward Tatchell, Capt. (Reserve of Officers), The Lincolnshire Regt." He was subsequently promoted Temporary Lieutenant-Colonel. He married, 7 Aug. 1902, at Ootacamund, India, Helen, daughter of Henry Irwin, Esq., C.I.E., and Mrs. Irwin. His D.S.O. was awarded "for services in connection with operations in the field."

CLIFFORD, HENRY FREDERICK HUGH, Lieut.-Colonel, was born 13 Aug. 1867, second son of the late Major-General the Hon. Sir Henry Clifford, V.C. He entered the Suffolk Regt. 11 Feb. 1888; became Lieutenant 25 Feb. 1891; Captain 13 Oct. 1897. He served in the South African War of 1899, taking part in the operations in the Orange Free State, April and May, 1900; operations in the Transvaal in May and June, 1900, including action at Pretoria; operations in the Transvaal, east of Pretoria, July to 29 Nov. 1900; operations in Orange River Colony, May to 29 Nov. 1900; operations in Cape Colony, south of Orange River, 1899–1900, including actions at Colesberg (1 to 6 Jan.); operations in Cape Colony, north of Orange River; operations in the Transvaal, Dec. 1900, to 31 May, 1902; operations in Orange River Colony 30 Nov. to Dec. 1900 (Queen's Medal with three clasps, and King's Medal with two clasps). From Aug. 1902, to Jan. 1905, he was A.D.C. to Lieut.-General Sir William Butler, G.O.C. Western District, and he was promoted Major 7 June, 1910. Major Clifford served in the European War from 1914; was promoted to Lieutenant-Colonel 3 Sept. 1914. He was created a Companion of the Distinguished Service Order [London Gazette, 18 Feb. 1915]: "Henry Frederick Hugh Clifford, Lieut.-Colonel, The Suffolk Regt." In the following May he was reported wounded, and on 29 May was appointed to the command of a brigade. He fell in action on 11 Sept. 1916. Brigadier-General H. F. H. Clifford was a brother of Sir Hugh Clifford, Governor of the Gold Coast, whose only son, Lieut. H. G. F. Clifford, was reported "missing, believed killed," on 1 July, 1916. His D.S.O. was awarded "for services in connection with operations in the field."

DE LA PRYME, WILLIAM HENRY ASTLEY, Capt., was born 20 Feb. 1880, at 86, Gloucester Place, Portman Square, London, W., son of Charles de la Pryme, Esq., of Wistow Lodge, Huntingdon, and Mrs. de la Pryme (formerly Miss Cubitt, of Fritton House, Great Yarmouth). He was educated at Christ's College, Cambridge, and joined the Royal Warwickshire Regt., as Second Lieutenant, 4 May, 1901. He became Lieutenant, Royal Warwickshire Regt., 27 Dec. 1903, and West Yorkshire Regt. 5 Feb. 1908, and was promoted Captain 16 April, 1910. He was Adjutant, West Yorkshire Regt., 27 June, 1912, to 26 June, 1915. Capt. de la Pryme proceeded to France early in Sept. 1914, with the 6th Division, as Adjutant of the 1st Battn. (The Prince of Wales's Own) West Yorkshire Regt. He was mentioned in Despatches in Feb. 1915, and was created a Companion of the Distinguished Service Order [London Gazette, 18 Feb. 1915]: "William Henry Astley de la Pryme, Capt., The Prince of Wales's Own, West Yorkshire Regt." The decoration was awarded for services in the Battle of the Aisne and in the First Battle of Ypres. He was promoted Major 4 May, 1916; became Temporary Lieutenant-Colonel, to command the 9th Suffolks (Service Battalion), in France, 14 Nov. 1915, and commanded it until 14 May, 1916, on which date he received wounds in both legs, necessitating the amputation of the right one. He afterwards held the following Staff appointments at the War Office: Staff Captain 18 June, 1917, to 7 Feb. 1919; Deputy Assistant Military Secretary 8 Feb. to 23 March, 1919, when he was appointed D.A.A.G. His D.S.O. was awarded "for services in connection with operations in the field."

ANDERSON, DESMOND FRANCIS, Capt., was born 5 July, 1885, only son of the late Frank H. Anderson. He joined the Devon Regt. 28 Jan. 1905; was promoted Lieutenant 20 Aug. 1908; became Captain, East Yorkshire Regt., 28 Aug. 1910; Adjutant 30 July, 1912, to 29 May, 1915. He served in the European War, 1914–17, and was created a Companion of the Distinguished Service Order [London Gazette, 18 Feb. 1915]: "Desmond Francis Anderson, Capt., The East Yorkshire Regt." He was promoted Temporary Major 1 Sept. 1915. Major Anderson held the following Staff appointments: G.S.O.3, 5th Army Corps, B.E.F., 30 May, 1915, to 9 Feb. 1916; Brigade Major, 36th Infantry Brigade, B.E.F., British Armies in France, 10 Feb. 1916, to 14 Jan. 1917; G.S.O.2, 8th Division, British Armies in France, 15 Jan. to 18 July, 1917; G.S.O.2, War Office, 19 July, 1917, to 22 Feb. 1918; G.S.O.2, 5th Division, British Armies in France, 10 March to 29 June, 1918; G.S.O.2, 1st Army Corps, British Armies in France, 30 June to 5 Aug. 1918; G.S.O.1 (Temporary Lieutenant-Colonel), 25th Division, British Armies in France, 6 Aug. 1918, to 22 April, 1919; G.S.O.2, War Office, 23 April, 1919. He was given the Brevet of Major 1 Jan. 1917, and was created a C.M.G. in 1919. In 1915 he married Mary Hope Prisca, second daughter of the Rev. S. W. Wentworth Wilkin, C.F., of York, and they have one son. His D.S.O. was awarded "for services in connection with operations in the field."

BROWN, HENRY ROBERT SEGUIER, Capt., was born 6 July, 1872, at 1, Charles Street, Lowndes Square, London, S.W., son of Henry William Seguier Brown (deceased), H.M. Civil Service, and E. J. Edwards. He was educated at Charterhouse, and joined the East Yorkshire Regt. from the East Yorkshire Militia 5 Dec. 1895; became Lieutenant 11 May, 1898. He served in the South African War, 1900–2. He took part in the operations in the Orange Free State, including action at Houtnek (Thoba Mountain); served during operations in Orange River Colony, including actions at Biddulphsberg and Wittebergen (1 to 29 July); in the Transvaal, Feb. to March, 1901; again in Orange River Colony 30 Nov. 1900, to Feb. 1901, and March, 1901, to 31 May, 1902 (Queen's Medal with three clasps, and King's Medal with two clasps). He became Captain 16 Jan. 1902; retired 27 May, 1911, and joined the Reserve of Officers. He served in the European War from 1914, with the 1st Battn. The East Yorkshire Regt., until June, 1915, and afterwards commanded the Segregation Camp at Etaples for nearly two years. He was created a Companion of the Distinguished Service Order [London Gazette, 18 Feb. 1915]: "Henry Robert Seguier Brown, Capt., Reserve of Officers, East Yorkshire Regt. For services in connection with operations in the field." He became Major in the Reserve of Officers 1 Sept. 1915.

Henry R. S. Brown.

ALLASON, WALTER, Major, was born 18 March, 1875, in London, son of Mr. Alfred Allason, of 29, Randolph Crescent, W., and Elizabeth T. Allen. He was educated abroad and privately, and joined the 1st Bedfordshire Regt. 9 Dec. 1896, becoming Lieutenant 25 June, 1898. He served in South Africa, 1899–1900, and was present in the operations round Colesberg and in the Orange Free State; took part in the operations in Orange Free State, Feb. to May, 1900; also in the Orange River Colony, May to 29 Nov. 1900; served in Cape Colony, south of Orange River, 1899–

1900, including actions at Colesberg (1 Jan. to 12 Feb.) (Queen's Medal and two clasps). He became Captain 22 Jan. 1902, and Major 16 Oct. 1913. Major Allason served in the European War; was present at Mons, Le Cateau, the Marne, the Aisne, Givenchy (14 Oct.), Neuve Chapelle (Oct. 27), Ypres (Nov.), Hill 60 (April, 1915) and the Somme (1916). He was wounded four times; mentioned in Despatches four times, and created a Companion of the Distinguished Service Order [London Gazette, 18 Feb. 1915]: "Walter Allason, Major, Bedfordshire Regt." He was Brigade Major, 13th Reserve Infantry Brigade, New Armies, 24 Aug. 1915, to 14 April, 1916; G.S.O.2, Catterick Reserve Centre, 15 April to 21 June, 1916; became Acting Lieutenant-Colonel, Bedfordshire Regt. 17 July, 1916. He was awarded a Bar to his D.S.O. [London Gazette, 14 Nov. 1916]: "Walter Allason, D.S.O., Major (Temporary Lieutenant-Colonel), Bedfordshire Regt. He executed an attack with the greatest initiative and resource, thereby enabling a strong enemy position to be captured. He handled his battalion with great skill throughout the operations." He became Brigade Commander, 52nd Infantry Brigade, British Armies in France, 14 April, 1918; was given the Brevet of Colonel 1 Jan. 1919; was appointed to command the 51st Bedfordshire Regt. on the Rhine in April, 1919. Lieut.-Colonel Allason has won the Plunging Competition four times. He played Water Polo for Middlesex, and represented the South v. North of England. He won the "Officers' Cup" at Aldershot Rifle Meeting in 1911. On 18 Aug. 1908, at St. Peter's, Cranley Gardens, London, W., he married Katherine Hamilton Poland, of 4 Cresswell Gardens, South Kensington, S.W., and their children are: Dolores Celina, and James Harry, born 6 Sept. 1912. His D.S.O. was awarded "for services in connection with operations in the field."

FOSS, CHARLES CALVELEY, Capt., was created a Companion of the Distinguished Service Order [London Gazette, 18 Feb. 1915]: "Charles Calveley Foss, Capt., The Bedfordshire Regt. For services in connection with operations in the field." Since awarded the V.C. (See V.C. Volume.)

MACREADY, JOHN, Capt., was born 10 April, 1887, only surviving son of J. F. C. H. Macready, F.R.C.S. He was gazetted to the Bedfordshire Regt. 4 May, 1907; became Lieutenant 14 June, 1908; was Adjutant 18 April, 1912, to 7 June, 1915; became Captain 22 Jan. 1913. He served in the European War from 1914–18. He was twice mentioned in Despatches, and created a Companion of the Distinguished Service Order [London Gazette, 18 Feb. 1915]: "John Macready, Capt., The Bedfordshire Regt." Capt. Macready became Deputy A.M.S. (graded D.A.A.G.) 8 June, 1915. His D.S.O. was awarded "for services in connection with operations in the field."

John Macready.

GORDON, HERBERT, Lieut.-Colonel, was born 30 April, 1869. He entered the Army, as a Second Lieutenant in the Leicestershire Regt., becoming Lieutenant 1 April, 1891, and Captain 1 Jan. 1898. He was employed with the Egyptian Army 12 Nov. 1900, to 11 Nov. 1910, serving as A.A.G. from May, 1905, to 27 Dec. 1908. He served in the Soudan, 1900–2; was present at the re-occupation of the Bahr-el-Ghazal Province (Egyptian Medal with clasp); served in the Soudan, 1905; took part in the operations against the Nyam Nyam Tribes in the Bahr-el-Ghazal Province (Despatches [London Gazette, 18 May, 1906]; clasp to Egyptian Medal). He was promoted Major 26 June, 1907. He served in the European War, 1914–18; was Lieutenant-Colonel, Leicestershire Regt., 11 Nov. 1914, to 10 Nov. 1918; was created a Companion of the Distinguished Service Order [London Gazette, 18 Feb. 1915]: "Herbert Gordon, Lieut.-Colonel, Leicestershire Regt." On 8 Nov. 1915, he became Temporary Brigadier-General and Brigade Commander, 70th Infantry Brigade, B.E.F., British Armies in France. He was given the Brevet of Colonel 1 Jan. 1918, and promoted to substantive rank 11 Nov. 1918; was mentioned in Despatches; was created a C.M.G. in 1917, and a C.B. in 1919. His D.S.O. was awarded "for services in connection with operations in the field."

TIDSWELL, EDMUND SAMUEL WAITE, Capt., was born 24 Aug. 1881, only son of the late Rev. S. W. Tidswell, of Dover Court, Essex. He joined the 1st Battn. The Leicestershire Regt., as Second Lieutenant, 4 June, 1904; became Lieutenant 29 Dec. 1906, and Captain 14 Oct. 1912. He was Adjutant, Leicestershire Regt., 14 Oct. 1912, to 28 June, 1915. Capt. Tidswell served in the European War from 1914 to 1917. He was twice mentioned in Despatches, and created a Companion of the Distinguished Service Order [London Gazette, 18 Feb. 1915]: "Edmund Samuel Waite Tidswell, Capt., The Leicestershire Regt." Capt. Tidswell was Brigade Major, 81st Infantry Brigade, British Expeditionary Force, Egyptian Expeditionary Force, 29 June, 1915, to 20 Aug. 1916; G.S.O.2, 16th Army Corps, Egyptian Expeditionary Force, British Salonika Force, 21 Aug. 1916, to 12 Jan. 1918; became G.S.O.1, 26th Division, British Salonika Force, 13 Jan. 1918 (Temporary Lieutenant-Colonel). He was given the Brevet of Major 3 June, 1917, and was awarded the O.B.E. He married, in 1918, Patricia, only child of the late Lieut.-Colonel R. C. Pierce, 1st Battn. Royal Inniskilling Fusiliers. His D.S.O. was awarded "for services in connection with operations in the field."

MOSS-BLUNDELL, BRYAN SEYMOUR, Capt., was born 14 March, 1878, at Hessle, East Yorkshire, son of John Seymour Moss-Blundell, of Tranby Rise, Hessle. He was educated at Rugby and Dulwich College, and joined Alexandra, Princess of Wales's Own (Yorkshire) Regt., 29 Dec. 1900, becoming Lieutenant 29 May, 1903, and Captain 29 July, 1906. He was Adjutant, Territorial Force, 20 May, 1909, to 19 March, 1912.

Capt. Moss-Blundell served in the European War from 1914; was present at the First and Third Battles of Ypres and the Battle of Neuve Chapelle. He was mentioned in Despatches 5 Feb. 1915, and was created a Companion of the Distinguished Service Order [London Gazette, 18 Feb. 1915]: "Bryan Seymour Moss-Blundell, Capt., Alexandra, Princess of Wales Own (Yorkshire) Regt." He was promoted Major 29 Dec. 1915; was Brigade Major, 3rd Line Group, West Riding Division, Central Force, Home Defence, Home Forces, 7 Oct. 1915, to 11 July, 1916; D.A.A. and Q.M.G., D.A.A.G., 57th Division, Home Forces, British Armies in France, 12 June, 1916, to 5 Dec. 1918; A.A. and Q.M.G., 57th Division, British Armies in France, 6 Dec. 1918, to 4 April, 1919; became D.A.A. and Q.M.G., Headquarters Tank Group, British Army of the Rhine, 5 April, 1919. He was awarded the O.B.E. in 1918, and the Legion of Honour (Chevalier), March, 1920. On 17 July, 1907, at Wynberg, Cape Colony, Major Moss-Blundell married Kate Beatrice, daughter of Templar Horne, Surveyor-General, Cape Colony, and they have one son, John Seymour, born July, 1911. His D.S.O. was awarded "for services in connection with operations in the field."

GRIFFIN, CHRISTOPHER JOSEPH, Major, was born 24 Dec. 1874, fifth son of Patrick Griffin, of Woodhill Terrace, Tivoli, Cork. He joined the Army 28 Sept. 1895; became Lieutenant 6 April, 1898. He served in the South African War from 1899 to 1902; was present at the Relief of Ladysmith, including operations of 17 to 24 Jan. 1900, and action at Spion Kop (severely wounded); in the operations on Tugela Heights (14 to 27 Feb. 1900); in the Transvaal in May and June, 1900; in Natal, March to June, 1900, including action at Laing's Nek (6 to 9 June); in the Transvaal, east of Pretoria, July to 29 Nov. 1900; in Orange River Colony, May to 29 Nov. 1900; again in the Transvaal, Jan. 1901, to 31 May, 1902 (Queen's Medal with six clasps, and King's Medal with two clasps). He was promoted Captain 26 Jan. 1900, and Major 1 Sept. 1913. He served in the European War from 1914–18; became Temporary Lieutenant-Colonel 2 Jan. 1915, and was created a Companion of the Distinguished Service Order [London Gazette, 18 Feb. 1915]: "Christopher Joseph Griffin, Major, The Lancashire Fusiliers." He was given the Brevet of Lieutenant-Colonel 1 Jan. 1916; became Temporary Brigadier-General; commanded the 103rd Infantry Brigade, British Armies in France, 25 April to 28 Aug. 1917, and the 7th Infantry Brigade, British Armies in France, 29 Aug. 1917, to 1918. He was wounded; mentioned in Despatches; was created a C.M.G. in 1918, and was awarded a Bar to the D.S.O. He married, in 1919, Ruby, daughter of Capt. A. C. Ward, D.S.O. His D.S.O. was awarded "for services in connection with operations in the field."

SPOONER, ARTHUR HARDWICKE, Capt., was born in Liverpool 27 May, 1879, son of the Ven. Archdeacon George Hardwicke Spooner and Edith Spooner, daughter of the late Peter Swinton Boult, of Mossley Hall, Liverpool. He was educated at Haileybury College, and joined the 3rd South Lancashire Regt. (Militia) 30 Dec. 1899, and the Lancashire Fusiliers 21 April, 1900. He served in the South African War, 1899–1901, as Station Staff Officer and Railway Staff Officer; took part in the operations in Orange River Colony, May to 29 Nov. 1900; in Cape Colony, south of Orange River, Feb. to April, 1900, and again in Orange River Colony 30 Nov. 1900, to April 1901; operations in Cape Colony, April to July, 1901 (Queen's Medal with three clasps). He became Lieutenant 19 April, 1901; was Lieutenant, West African Regt., 27 Dec. 1904, to July, 1907. He became Captain 1 April, 1910, and Adjutant, Lancashire Fusiliers, 13 July, 1912. He served in the European War from 1914, and was made a Chevalier of the Legion of Honour, Dec. 1914. Capt. Spooner was created a Companion of the Distinguished Service Order [London Gazette, 18 Feb. 1915]: "Arthur Hardwicke Spooner, Capt., The Lancashire Fusiliers." He was created a C.M.G. in 1918. He was promoted Major 1 Sept. 1915, and Temporary Lieutenant-Colonel 3 Oct. 1915. He was given the Brevet of Lieutenant-Colonel 1 Jan. 1917, and was mentioned in Despatches 8 Dec. 1914; 17 Feb. 1915; 1 Jan. 1916; 4 Jan. and June, 1917; Jan. and June, 1918. He became a Temporary Brigadier-General 30 July, 1916, and was in command of the 183rd Infantry Brigade, British Armies in France, 30 July, 1916, to 29 Sept. 1918; in command of the 223rd Mixed Brigade and 191st Infantry Brigade, Forces in Great Britain, 1 Nov. 1918, to 20 March, 1919. He was awarded a Bar to his D.S.O. [London Gazette, June, 1918]: "R. H. Spooner, C.M.G., D.S.O., Major and Brevet Lieutenant-Colonel (Temporary Brigadier-General), Lancashire Fusiliers. He commanded his brigade in very difficult positions with consummate coolness and skill, and on every occasion displayed great initiative and resource. The clever handling of his brigade bettered the situation on the front of two divisions." He married (1st), on 16 Nov. 1907, Rosalie Augusta Pile (who died in 1908), youngest daughter of H. A. Pile, of Warleigh, Barbadoes; and (2ndly), on 24 Jan. 1912, Violet Hamilton Robarts, elder daughter of the late Lieut.-Colonel C. J. Robarts, late Indian Army, and of Mrs. Robarts, of Fleet, Hants, and they have four daughters: Marjorie Hilda, Veronica Joan, Patricia Margaret, and Lois Heather Barbara. His D.S.O. was awarded "for services in connection with operations in the field."

Arthur H. Spooner.

WILLIAMS, OLIVER DE LANCEY, Major, was born 5 Nov. 1875. He joined the 2nd Battn. The Royal Welsh Fusiliers, 10 Oct. 1894; became Lieutenant 9 Sept. 1896. He served in the South African War from 1889 to 1900; was present at the Relief of Ladysmith, including action at Colenso, and during operations on Tugela Heights (14 to 27 Feb. 1900);

in the Transvaal, west of Pretoria, July to 29 Nov. 1900 ; in Orange River Colony, May to Sept. 1900 ; also in Cape Colony, north of Orange River, including action at Ruidam (Queen's Medal with five clasps). He became Captain 4 Feb. 1903, and Major 19 April, 1913. He served in the European War from 1914 to 1917 ; became Temporary Lieutenant-Colonel 27 Nov. 1914 ; was mentioned in Despatches, and created a Companion of the Distinguished Service Order [London Gazette, 18 Feb. 1915] : " Oliver de Lancey Williams, Major, The Royal Welsh Fusiliers." Major Williams was given the Brevet of Lieutenant-Colonel 8 June, 1915 ; became Temporary Brigadier-General, 92nd Infantry Brigade, British Armies in France, 9 June, 1916. He was created a C.M.G. in 1917, and given the Brevet of Colonel 1 Jan. 1919. His D.S.O. was awarded " for services in connection with operations in the field."

CONNELL, JAMES CHARLES WALTER, Capt., was born 11 March, 1877. He entered the King's Own Scottish Borderers, as Second Lieutenant, 15 May, 1897. He served on the North-West Frontier of India, 1897–98, with the Tirah Expeditionary Force (Medal with clasp). He became Lieutenant 1 Jan. 1898, and again saw active service in the South African War in 1902 ; was present in operations in the Transvaal (Queen's Medal with two clasps). He became Captain 9 Oct. 1901. Capt. Connell was Adjutant, Volunteers, 23 Oct. 1903, to 28 Jan. 1905 ; Adjutant, Volunteers, 3 July, 1907, to 31 March, 1908 ; Adjutant, Territorial Force, 1 April, 1908, to 31 March, 1911, and Adjutant (attached General Staff), Officers' Training Corps, 8 July, 1913, to 4 Sept. 1914. He served in the European War from 1914 ; was Temporary Major, King's Own Scottish Borderers, from 11 Sept. to 10 Dec. 1914 ; became Major 11 Dec. 1914. He was mentioned in Despatches, and created a Companion of the Distinguished Service Order [London Gazette, 18 Feb. 1915] : " James Charles Walter Connell, Capt., The King's Own Scottish Borderers." Major Connell became Temporary Lieutenant-Colonel 11 Oct. 1915, commanding the 7th Battn. K.O.S.B., and from Dec. the 6th Battn. K.O.S.B., till invalided at the end of Oct. 1916. He was mentioned in Despatches, Dec. 1916, and was Second-in-Command of a Cadet Battalion from 20 Dec. 1917, to 6 Nov. 1918, when he was placed in command of the Young Soldiers' Battalion, Durham Light Infantry. He married (1st), in 1903, Mary Blanche (who died in 1904), daughter of E. W. Lake, of Westgate House, Bury St. Edmunds, and (2ndly), in 1910, Maude Kathleen, youngest daughter of the late Henry Scrymgour-Wedderburn, of Wedderburn. His D.S.O. was awarded " for services in connection with operations in the field."

BLAND, CHARLES ERNEST WILLIAM, Capt., was born at New Wandsworth, Surrey, 21 Aug. 1881, son of the late Capt. Horatio Bland, K.O.S.B., and Mrs. Bland, of Stretton House, near Alfreton, Derbyshire.

He was educated at Marlborough and Sandhurst, and joined the King's Own Scottish Borderers 20 Jan. 1900. He served in the Boer War, and was present at the actions at Vet River and Zand River ; those near Johannesburg and Pretoria, and at Zillikat's Nek, and in operations in the Transvaal, Nov. 1900, to July, 1901 ; in Orange River Colony, July, 1901, to May, 1902, and Cape Colony, 1902 (Queen's Medal with three clasps, and King's Medal with two clasps). He became Captain 9 March, 1908, and retired 10 April, 1910, being gazetted to the 3rd (Reserve) Battalion of his regiment. On the outbreak of the European War he rejoined ; was attached to the 2nd Battn., with which he went to the Front. He was twice mentioned in Despatches by Field-Marshal Sir John French, and was created a Companion of the Distinguished Service Order [London Gazette, 18 Feb. 1915] : " Charles Ernest William Bland, Capt., The King's Own Scottish Borderers." He was killed in the action around Ypres 23 April, 1915, and is believed to have been buried near Pilkem. How Capt. C. E. W. Bland obtained the D.S.O. is described in a letter written by his Major : " The actual event which gained him the D.S.O. was when we were holding trenches in front of Ypres in Nov. 1914. His trench was several times attacked by Prussian infantry, as well as being subjected to very heavy fire from Minenwerfer and artillery, but he stuck to it and defended his trench with great bravery." Capt. Bland was well known in the hunting field, and was frequently out with the Cottesmore and Belvoir packs. He had married, at Maynooth, 22 Oct. 1910, Isabella, daughter of William Brown-Lecky, Esq., of Ecclesville, County Tyrone, and had a daughter, Patricia, who was born 24 April, the day after her father was killed. His D.S.O. was awarded " for services in connection with operations in the field."

STORMONTH-DARLING, JOHN COLLIER, Capt., was born 9 Feb. 1878, at Kelso, Roxburghshire, son of Patrick Stormonth-Darling, of Lednathie, Forfarshire (deceased), and Mrs. Katharine Scott Stormonth-Darling, of Edenbank, Kelso. He joined the Militia Battalion of the King's Own Scottish Borderers in 1899, and obtained a commission as Second Lieutenant in the same year, in the 2nd Scottish Rifles, in which —and in Gough's Mounted Infantry—he served throughout the South African War of 1899–1902 with great distinction as Railway Staff Officer. He took part in the operations in the Transvaal, east of Pretoria, Nov. 1900 ; again in the Transvaal, 30 Nov. 1900, to June, 1901, and Nov. 1901, to April, 1902 ; in Orange River Colony, June to Sept. 1901, and Nov. 1901 ; also during the operations on the Zululand Frontier of Natal in Sept. and Oct. 1901. He was mentioned in Despatches [London Gazette, 17 Jan. 1902] ; received the Queen's Medal with three clasps, and the King's Medal with two clasps. He thereafter served in the 2nd Battn. in South Africa

and in this country and Malta, till his promotion to a Captaincy 12 March, 1912, when transferred to the 1st Cameronians, then in Glasgow. He served as Adjutant to both battalions. In the European War, Capt. Stormonth-Darling was in most of the heavy fighting during and after the Retreat from Mons. He was mentioned in Despatches, and created a Companion of the Distinguished Service Order [London Gazette, 18 Feb. 1915] : " John Collier Stormonth-Darling, Capt., The Cameronians (Scottish Rifles)." In the following Sept. he had his Majority, and in Dec. was given command of the 9th Battn. Highland Light Infantry (Glasgow Highlanders), and was killed, when taking his battalion into action, 1 Nov. 1916, and the news of his death was received in Kelso on the following Sunday. His two younger brothers, Capt. Robert Stormonth-Darling, Yeomanry, and Major P. Stormonth-Darling, Black Watch, also served in the European War. His D.S.O. was awarded " for services in connection with operations in the field."

RIDDELL-WEBSTER, THOMAS SHERIDAN, Capt., was born 12 Feb. 1886, son of the late J. Riddell-Webster, Esq., of Priors Gate, St. Andrews, Scotland, and Mrs. Riddell-Webster. He was educated at Harrow and Sandhurst, and joined the Cameronians (Scottish Rifles) 16 Aug. 1905 ; became Lieutenant 30 Sept. 1909, and Captain 24 Oct. 1913. He served in the European War from 1914–1917, proceeding to France 14 Aug. 1914, with the 1st Cameronians ; was Staff Captain in the 19th Infantry Brigade 3 Nov. 1914, to 16 July, 1915. He was mentioned in Despatches [London Gazette, 19 Nov. 1914, and 18 Feb. 1915], and was created a Companion of the Distinguished Service Order [London Gazette, 18 Feb. 1915] : " Thomas Sheridan Riddell-Webster, Capt., Scottish Rifles." He became D.A. and Q.M.G., 7th Division, 17 July, 1915 ; was given the Brevet of Major 1 Jan. 1916, and was appointed A.A. and Q.M.G., 41st Division, and Temporary Lieutenant-Colonel 9 July, 1917. He was further mentioned in Despatches [London Gazette, 1 Jan. 1916 ; 1 Jan. 1917 ; 1 Jan. and 3 June, 1918]. His D.S.O. was awarded " for services in connection with operations in the field."

STEWARD, GODFREY ROBERT VIVEASH, Capt., was born 2 Aug. 1881, at Manchester, son of Major-General Edward Harding Steward, C.M.G., R.E., and Mrs. Steward (née Jessie Baskerville). He was educated at Wellington College, Berkshire, and the Royal Military College, Sandhurst, and became Second Lieutenant, Royal Inniskilling Fusiliers, 6 Dec. 1899. He served in the South African War, 1899–1902 ; was present at Tugela Heights, the Relief of Ladysmith, and at the operations in Orange River Colony and Cape Colony (severely wounded ; Queen's South African Medal with four clasps ; King's South African Medal with two clasps). He became Lieutenant 15 March, 1901, and Captain 29 April, 1905. Capt. Steward served in the European War from Aug. 1914, as Company Commander, Royal Inniskilling Fusiliers ; was Adjutant, Royal Inniskilling Fusiliers, 1 Nov. 1914, to 3 Sept. 1915. He was very severely wounded 14 May, 1915 ; mentioned in Despatches in Jan. 1915, and recommended for the D.S.O. for the following acts : (1) Covering the straightening of the line south of Messines on 31 Oct. 1914 ; (2) Leading the counter-attacks which drove the enemy out of Ploegsteert Wood, where they had gained a footing, on 8 and 10 Nov. 1914. He was created a Companion of the Distinguished Service Order [London Gazette, 18 Feb. 1915] : " Godfrey Robert Viveash Steward, Capt., R. Inniskilling Fusiliers." Capt. Steward was promoted to Major 1 Sept. 1915, and became Temporary Lieutenant-Colonel, in command of a Service Battalion, Northumberland Fusiliers, 29 Sept. 1915. He was mentioned in Despatches, and given the Brevet of Lieutenant-Colonel 1 Jan. 1917. Lieut.-Colonel Steward subsequently held the following Staff appointments : Instructor, Senior Officers' School, Aldershot, 1 April to 6 July, 1917 ; Labour Commandant, 2nd Army Corps, British Armies in France, 1 Sept. 1918, to 6 March, 1919 ; Labour Commandant, 5th Army Corps, British Armies in France. He was created a C.B.E. in 1919. His D.S.O. was awarded " for services in connection with operations in the field."

BOWRING, EDWARD LANGLEY, Capt., was born 11 Sept. 1882, youngest son of the late Sir Charles Clement Bowring and Lady Bowring, of Park Grange, Derby. He entered the Army 5 Jan. 1901, as a Second Lieutenant in the Worcestershire Regt. ; became Lieutenant 21 Dec. 1901. He served in South Africa, 1901–2 ; was present in the operations in Orange River Colony, Aug. 1901, to 31 May, 1902 (Queen's Medal with five clasps). He became Captain 1 Oct. 1908. Capt. Bowring served in the European War from 1914 to 1916 ; was mentioned in Despatches, and created a Companion of the Distinguished Service Order [London Gazette, 18 Feb. 1915] : " Edward Langley Bowring, Capt., The Worcestershire Regt." He was employed as an A.P.M., 51st Division, B.E.F., British Armies in France, 24 June, 1915, to 17 Nov. 1916, attaining his

Edward L. Bowring.

Majority 26 Oct. 1915, and became A.P.M., Northern Command, 29 Nov. 1916 (Temporary Lieutenant-Colonel). He was awarded the O.B.E. Major Bowring married, in 1915, Laura Fraser, daughter of the late W. Fraser Biscoe, and they have one daughter. His D.S.O. was awarded " for services in connection with operations in the field."

CORNISH-BOWDEN, JAMES HUBERT THOMAS, Major, was born at Newton Abbot, Devon, 2 Aug. 1870, son of the late Admiral William Cornish-Bowden, of Laire, Newton Abbot, and Mrs. Cornish-Bowden, elder daughter and co-heiress of the late James Cornish, of Black Hall, Devon, sometime Member of Parliament for Totnes, and High Sheriff of Devon. James Cornish-Bowden was educated at Newton College, and became Second Lieutenant in the Duke of Cornwall's Light Infantry 22 March, 1892, and was promoted Lieutenant 5 Sept. 1893. Lieut. Cornish-Bowden accompanied the Tirah Expedition to the North-West Frontier of India (1897–98), and received the Medal with two clasps. He obtained his Captaincy 19 Feb. 1900, and was Adjutant to the Indian Volunteers from 15 Oct. 1900, to 14 Oct. 1905. He was promoted Major 19 Feb. 1908. Major Bowden served in the European War from 1914 to 1919. He was created a Companion of the Distinguished Service Order [London Gazette, 18 Feb. 1915]: " James Hubert Thomas Cornish-Bowden, Major, The Duke of York's Light Infantry." On 6 Feb. 1916, he became Staff Captain, G.H.Q., British Expeditionary Force; on 24 April, 1916, D.A.A.G., G.H.Q., B.E.F., British Armies in France, and on 7 June, 1917, Temporary Lieutenant-Colonel and A.A.G., G.H.Q., British Armies in France. He was given the Brevet of Lieutenant-Colonel 1 Jan. 1918, and was created a C.M.G. in 1919. He married, in Calcutta Cathedral, 12 June, 1915, Margaret E., youngest daughter of the late John Gaskoin, and they have a son and a daughter. His D.S.O. was awarded " for services in connection with operations in the field."

WOODHAM, CHARLES BURNETT, Capt., was born 14 Dec. 1874. He entered the Duke of Cornwall's Light Infantry, as a Second Lieutenant, 28 Sept. 1895, and was promoted Lieutenant 22 July, 1898, and Captain 12 Oct. 1901. He served in the South African War, 1899–1902, on the Staff; was Brigade Signalling Officer from 12 Feb. to 12 March, 1900; took part in the operations in the Orange Free State, Feb. to May, 1900, including operations at Paardeberg (17 to 26 Feb.); actions at Poplar Grove, Dreifontein, Houtnek (Thoba Mountain), Vet River (5 and 6 May) and Zand River; also in the Transvaal 30 Nov. 1900, to 31 May, 1902 (Queen's Medal with four clasps, and King's Medal with two clasps). He again saw active service in the European War. He was mentioned in Despatches by Sir John French [London Gazette, 19 Oct. 1914], and was created a Companion of the Distinguished Service Order [London Gazette, 18 Feb. 1915]: " Charles Burnett Woodham, Capt., The Duke of Cornwall's Light Infantry." His D.S.O. was awarded " for services in connection with operations in the field." He was killed in action 15 June, 1915.

UMFREVILLE, HARRY KIRWAN, Capt., was born 22 Sept. 1871, at Ingress Abbey, Greenhithe, Kent, son of S. E. Umfreville, of Ingress Abbey, Greenhithe, Kent, and of Emma Annette Maryon Umfreville (formerly Wilson). He was educated at Brighton College, and joined the Queen's Own Royal West Kent Regt. in April, 1892, and the Duke of Wellington's West Riding Regt. 7 Dec. 1895. He served in the South African War, 1899–1901, in the Mounted Infantry. He took part in the operations in Cape Colony, south of Orange River, Feb. 1900; in the Orange Free State, May, 1900, including actions at Houtnek (Thoba Mountain), Vet River (5 and 6 May) and Zand River; in the Transvaal, May and June, 1900, including actions near Johannesburg and Pretoria; in Orange River Colony, June to 29 Nov. 1900, including actions at Wittebergen (1 to 29 July), Witpoort and Bothaville; again in Orange River Colony 30 Nov. 1900, to Aug. 1901. He was mentioned in

Harry K. Umfreville.

Despatches twice: received the Queen's South African Medal with five clasps. He became Captain 1 Feb. 1902. Capt. Umfreville retired 15 July, 1911. He rejoined 6 Aug. 1914, and served in the 2nd Battn. of his regiment in the Expeditionary Force in the European War. He was on active service from 1914–17; was three times mentioned in Despatches, and, for commanding the 2nd Duke of Wellington's Regt. during the Battle of the Aisne and the First Battle of Ypres, was created a Companion of the Distinguished Service Order [London Gazette, 18 Feb. 1915]: " Harry Kirwan Umfreville, Capt. (Reserve of Officers), The Duke of Wellington's (West Riding Regt.)." " They never lost a trench or failed to regain one when lost by other units." He commanded the battalion from 13 Sept. 1914; was wounded, and commanded the 10th West Yorkshire Regt. from 29 March, 1915; became Temporary Lieutenant-Colonel; also commanded the 6th Lancashire Fusiliers and the 8th Somerset Light Infantry. He married, in Dec. 1902, at Clonevan, County Wexford, Ireland, Enid, daughter of Capt. R. D'Olier George, J.P., D.L., late 7th Dragoon Guards, of Cahore Gorey, County Wexford, Ireland, and they had two sons: Charles D'Olier, born in 1906; Michael, born in 1908, and a daughter, Enid. His D.S.O. was awarded for " services in connection with operations in the field." He was killed in action 15 June, 1915.

BARTON, BAPTIST JOHNSTON, Capt. (Temporary Lieutenant-Colonel), was born 21 Oct. 1876, son of the late Colonel Baptist Johnston Barton, D.L., A.D.C., of Greenfort; and Mrs. Barton, of Portsalon, County Donegal. He is a Deputy Lieutenant. He was educated at Foyle College and Sandhurst, and joined the Duke of Wellington's West Riding Regt. 5 Sept. 1896, becoming Lieutenant 20 Oct. 1899, and Captain 29 March, 1902. Capt. Barton retired from the Army 9 Sept. 1911. He served in the European War from 1914–18; was three times mentioned in Despatches, and created a Companion of the Distinguished Service Order [London Gazette, 18 Feb.

Baptist Johnston Barton.

1915]: " Baptist Johnston Barton, Capt., Reserve of Officers, The Duke of Wellington's West Riding Regt." He became Major, Reserve of Officers, Birthday Honours List, 3 June, 1915; was promoted Temporary Lieutenant-Colonel 18 May, 1917; commanded a Territorial Force Battalion of the Yorkshire Light Infantry; was awarded a Bar to the D.S.O. [London Gazette, Jan. 1916]. He married, in 1908, Kathleen Maude, daughter of Egbert de Hamel, of Middleton Hall, Warwickshire, and they have one daughter. His D.S.O. was awarded " for services in connection with operations in the field."

WARREN, GEORGE ERNEST, Major, was born 18 Jan. 1871, son of the late George K. Warren, formerly of British Guiana, and Fairlawn, Market Harborough. He was educated at St. John's College, Cambridge, and at Sandhurst, from which he was commissioned in The Border Regt. 19 Nov. 1892. He became Lieutenant 6 May, 1896, and Captain 21 June, 1902. He served in the South African War, 1899–1902, on the Staff, being employed as Assistant Provost-Marshal 7 March to 30 Oct. 1902, and was present at the Relief of Ladysmith, including operations of 17 to 24 Jan. 1900, and the action at Spion Kop; operations of 5 to 7 Feb. 1900, and the action at Vaal Kranz; operations on Tugela Heights (14 to 27 Feb. 1900) and action at Pieter's Hill; operations in the Orange Free State, April and May, 1900; operations in the Transvaal, June, 1900; operations in the Transvaal, east of Pretoria, July, 1900; operations in the Transvaal, west of Pretoria, July to Nov. 1900; operations in Orange River Colony, May, 1900; operations in Cape Colony, north of Orange River, May, 1900; operations in the Transvaal from 30 Nov. 1900. For his services he received the Queen's Medal with five clasps, and the King's Medal with two clasps. He served as Adjutant of Volunteers 8 May, 1903, to 31 May, 1908, and was promoted Major 29 Oct. 1914. Major Warren served in the European War, 1914–19, and was Temporary Lieutenant-Colonel, Border Regt., 29 Nov. to 18 Dec. 1914. He was created a Companion of the Distinguished Service Order [London Gazette, 18 Feb. 1915]: " George Ernest Warren, Major, The Border Regt." He was mentioned in Despatches. Major Warren married, in 1903, Norah Ingate, widow of H. G. T. Ingate Warren, and daughter of W. J. Roche, of Belfast, and they have one son, William Rollo George de W., born 30 Dec. 1907. His D.S.O. was awarded " for services in connection with operations in the field."

GREEN, EDGAR WALTER BUTLER, Lieut.-Colonel, was born 27 Aug. 1869. He entered the Royal Sussex Regt. 29 March, 1890; became Lieutenant 23 Dec. 1891; was Adjutant, Royal Sussex Regt., 24 Nov. 1897, to 4 Oct. 1900; was promoted to Captain 2 Feb. 1899. He served in the South African War, 1900–2, as Adjutant, 1st Battn. Royal Sussex Regt., to 4 Oct. 1900; took part in the operations in the Orange Free State, Feb. to May, 1900, including actions at Houtnek (Thoba Mountain), Vet River (5 and 6 May) and Zand River; in the Transvaal in May and June, 1900, including actions near Johannesburg, Pretoria and Diamond Hill (11 and 12 June); in Orange River Colony, May to 29 Nov. 1900, including actions at Wittebergen (1 to 29 July) and Ladybrand (2 to 5 Sept.); also during the operations in Orange River Colony and Cape Colony (Despatches [London Gazette 10 Sept. 1901]: Queen's Medal with four clasps and King's Medal with two clasps). From 10 July, 1902, to 11 March, 1903, he was Staff Officer, Orange River Colony, and he became Major 2 Feb. 1907. He served in the European War, 1914–18; was promoted to Lieutenant-Colonel 31 Oct. 1914; commanded the 45th Infantry Brigade, B.E.F., 12 Oct. 1915, to 12 April, 1916, and the Dover Special Reserve Infantry Brigade, Home Forces, 16 March, 1917, to 7 May, 1918; was mentioned in Despatches, and created a Companion of the Distinguished Service Order [London Gazette, 18 Feb. 1915]: " Edgar Walter Butler Green, Lieut.-Colonel, Royal Sussex Regt." He was appointed Officer in Charge of Records, No. 4 District, Shrewsbury, from 25 March, 1919. His D.S.O. was awarded " for services in connection with operations in the field."

PALK, THE HONOURABLE LAWRENCE CHARLES WALTER, Major, was born 28 Sept. 1870, second son of the late Lord Haldon and the Honourable Constance Mary Barrington, daughter of the 7th Viscount Barrington, of Palazzo Capomazza, Naples. He was educated at Wellington College, and enlisted in the 8th Hussars in 1890. After four years' service in the ranks, during which he rose to the rank of Sergeant, he obtained a commission in the Hampshire Regt. 4 July, 1894, in which he became Lieutenant 24 July, 1897, and Captain 11 Nov. 1900. He served in the South African War, 1901–2, as Station Commandant 10 to 24 May, 1901; in operations in the Transvaal, April, 1901, to Feb. 1902 (Queen's Medal with five clasps). He also saw service in India. When the European War broke out he went to the Front from India, with the 1st Battn. Hampshire Regt., and was awarded the Legion of Honour for gallantry in the Retreat from Mons. He was present

The Hon. L. C. W. Palk.

at Le Cateau, and was created a Companion of the Distinguished Service Order [London Gazette, 18 Feb. 1915]: " The Honourable Lawrence Charles Walter Palk, Major, The Hampshire Regt." The decoration was given for gallantry at the Battle of Le Cateau, and during the Retreat from Mons. Lieut.-Colonel the Hon. L. C. W. Palk was killed in action 1 July, 1916, while commanding his battalion at the Battle of the Somme during the attack on Beaumont Hamel. He was three times mentioned in Despatches. He was an extremely popular officer. On one occasion in the retreat he was asked whether he knew the song the men were singing, and answered: " No, how should I? " " Why, that's your tune—'We'll follow Charlie,'" was the reply. When leading his men he habitually carried nothing but a stick. He was a good horseman, a lover of sport and a keen student of military history. One who knew him well, wrote: "He invariably made it his business to befriend young officers on joining; he took his boys, as he called them, about with him anywhere, influencing them for good and keeping them from harm. He judged his fellow men shrewdly, and if he never suffered fools gladly, his nature led him always to take a charitable view of even the lamest of dogs he chanced to meet." His D.S.O. was awarded "for services in connection with operations in the field."

SAVAGE, MORRIS BOSCAWEN, Capt., was born 14 March, 1879, only son of Lieut.-Colonel H. B. Savage, R.M.A. (son of Colonel John Morris Savage, R.H.A., the latter being the son of Sir John Morris Boscawen Savage, Royal Marines), and E. M. Collyer, his wife. He followed in the steps of his ancestors, who had served in the Army since the Battle of the Boyne, by joining the Army 20 May, 1899, as a Second Lieutenant in the South Staffordshire Regt. He served for eight years in India, and for four years in South Africa; became Lieutenant 12 May, 1900; Captain 22 Jan. 1908; was Adjutant of the 2nd Battn. South Staffordshire Regt. 1 March, 1909, to 29 Feb. 1912; employed with the Egyptian Army 28 March, 1912, to 27 March, 1914. Capt. Savage served in the Great War, and took part in the Retreat from Mons; was present at the Battle of the Marne, the Aisne, and the First Battle of Ypres, where he was wounded 25 Oct. 1914. He was created a Companion of the Distinguished Service Order [London Gazette, 18 Feb. 1915]: "Morris Boscawen Savage, Capt., South Staffordshire Regt. For good handling of a company during the Retreat from Mons, the Battle of the Marne, the Aisne, and the First Battle of Ypres, and especially for the skilful handling of his company on 21 Sept. 1914, when he moved up to help the Wiltshire Regt., and assisted them to reoccupy their trenches at Chavonne." In March, 1915, he was appointed Staff Captain of the 110th Infantry Brigade, and proceeded again to France with his Brigade in July, 1915. He became Major 1 Sept. 1915; in Dec. 1915, he was appointed D.A.A and Q.M.G. of the 9th (Scottish) Division, and was present with that division during the operations on the Somme in 1916. In Feb. 1917, he was posted to the 19th Corps as D.A.A.G., and took part in the Battle of Arras and the Third Battle of Ypres. In Aug. 1917, he was appointed A.A. and Q.M.G. of the 6th Division, and was present with that Division at the Battle of Cambrai. He was five times mentioned in Despatches (1914, 1915, 1917, and twice in 1918); was given the Brevet of Lieutenant-Colonel for services in the field 3 June, 1918, and was created a C.B.E. in 1919. Lieut.-Colonel Savage married, at Alverstoke, Hants, 26 June, 1915, Helen Elise Tovil, and they have one son, Patrick Morris Boscawen, born 21 Aug. 1916. His D.S.O. was awarded "for services in connection with operations in the field."

SAUNDERS, CYRIL, Major, was born 26 Feb. 1875, at Canterbury, Kent, son of Brigadier-General A. A. Saunders. He was educated at the Elizabeth College, Guernsey, and entered the Army 28 Sept. 1895, as a Second Lieutenant in the Dorsetshire Regt.; became Lieutenant 26 Feb. 1898. He served in the South African Campaign, as Railway Staff Officer, 27 June, 1900, to 3 Aug. 1902, and also with the Mounted Infantry. He was present at the Relief of Kimberley; operations in the Orange Free State, Feb. to May, 1900, including the operations at Paardeberg (17 to 27 Feb.); actions at Poplar Grove, Dreifontein, Houtnek (Thoba Mountain), Vet River (5 and 6 May) and Zand River; operations in the Transvaal, May and June, 1900, including the actions near Johannesburg, Pretoria and Diamond Hill (11 and 12 June); operations in Cape Colony, south of Orange River, 1899–1900, including the actions at Colesberg (1 Jan. to 12 Feb.); operations in the Transvaal 30 Nov. 1900, to 31 May, 1902; operations in Cape Colony and Orange River Colony, June, 1901. He was twice mentioned in Despatches [London Gazettes of 4 May, 1900, and 10 Sept. 1901]; received the Queen's Medal with four clasps, and the King's Medal with two clasps. He was promoted Captain 7 April, 1902; was an Adjutant in the Territorial Force 8 March, 1910, to 7 March, 1913; became Major 3 June, 1914. Major Saunders took part in the European War, serving with the 1st Battn. The Dorsetshire Regt. He was created a Companion of the Distinguished Service Order [London Gazette, 18 Feb. 1915]: "Cyril Saunders, Major, 1st Battn. The Dorsetshire Regt." He was Commandant, School of Instruction; Staff Officer, 1st Class, Royal Flying Corps (Temporary Lieutenant-Colonel), 28 Sept. 1916, to 22 April, 1917; was acting Lieutenant-Colonel, Rank Corps, 13 March to 20 May, 1918; was placed on half-pay 17 Jan. 1919. Lieut.-Colonel C. Saunders was twice mentioned in Despatches, and wounded twice. His D.S.O. was awarded "for services in connection with operations in the field."

LILLY, CHARLES OTTO, Lieut., was born 18 Jan. 1890, son of Charles Edward Lilly, of 1, Park Village West, Regent's Park, London, N.W.1. He was educated at St. Paul's School, and Jesus College, Cambridge, and entered the Dorset Regt. 19 Sept. 1911, in which he was promoted Lieutenant 10 Aug. 1912. He served in the European War from 1914 to 1918. He was wounded; mentioned in Despatches 12 Oct. 1914; 18 Feb. and 5 May, 1915, and created a Companion of the Distinguished Service Order [London Gazette, 18 Feb. 1915]: "Charles Otto Lilly, Lieut., 1st Battn. Dorsetshire Regt." He was promoted Captain 1 Oct. 1915; served from 6 Oct. 1915, to 13 April, 1916, as G.S.O., 3rd Grade; was with the Machine Gun Corps from 17 May, 1916, to 7 Aug. 1917; R.F.C. and R.A.F. 10 Aug. 1917, to 28 Aug. 1919. Won Public Schools Boxing Championships, Middle-Weights, 1907, 1908. His D.S.O. was awarded "for services in connection with operations in the field."

RITCHIE, WILLIAM BUCHANAN, Major, was born 16 Sept. 1877, and was commissioned from the Militia in the Prince of Wales's Volunteers (South Lancashire Regt.) 25 Feb. 1899; was promoted Lieutenant 26 May, 1900, and Captain 1 Dec. 1904. Capt. Ritchie first saw service in the Great War. After serving for a period as Temporary Major, he became Major 11 Dec. 1914, and was created a Companion of the Distinguished Service Order [London Gazette, 18 Feb. 1915]: "William Buchanan Ritchie, Major, South Lancashire Regt." He subsequently served as Temporary Lieutenant-Colonel, South Lancashire Regt., Sept. 1915, to March, 1916; Temporary Lieutenant-Colonel, Royal Lancaster Regt., April, 1916, to March, 1918, and Temporary Lieutenant-Colonel to May, 1918; became Temporary Lieutenant-Colonel, South Lancashire Regt., 24 June, 1918. He was mentioned in Despatches for his services in the war. He became Camp Commandant 14 March, 1919. His D.S.O. was awarded "for services in connection with operations in the field."

MURRAY, JAMES THOMAS CROKATT, Major, was born 25 July, 1873. He entered the Army as a Second Lieutenant in the Black Watch (Royal Highlanders) 21 Oct. 1893, in which he became Lieutenant 1 April, 1898, and Captain 16 Feb. 1901. He first saw active service in the South African War, taking part in operations in Orange River Colony, Dec. 1901, to May, 1902, for which he received the Queen's Medal with five clasps. In 1908 he was engaged in fighting on the North-West Frontier of India, in the Mohmand country, and received the Medal and clasp. He was from 28 Jan. 1910, to 15 Feb. 1911, Adjutant, Territorial Force. He was promoted Major 25 Feb. 1911. Major Murray served in the European War from 1914. He was mentioned in Despatches 19 Oct. 1914, and created a Companion of the Distinguished Service Order [London Gazette, 18 Feb. 1915]: "James Thomas Crokatt Murray, Major, Royal Highlanders." Major Murray was killed accidentally on 16 Feb. 1915, two days before the award of his D.S.O. was gazetted. His D.S.O. was awarded "for services in connection with operations in the field."

MOFFITT, FREDERICK WILLIAM, Capt., was born at Woolston, Southampton, 14 June, 1872, son of Surgeon-Major Andrew Moffitt, A.M.S., and H. C. Moffitt (*née* Gordon), his wife. He was educated at Haileybury College, and joined the Army 8 Oct. 1890, with a commission in the Essex Regt.; was promoted Lieutenant 20 Feb. 1895. He served with the 4th Brigade, with the Tirah Expeditionary Force, as Transport Officer (Medal and clasp), in 1898. He became Captain 11 May, 1900; saw active service in South Africa, 1900–2, acting as Company Commander in the 1st Essex Regt., in the advance on Pretoria and subsequent operations until Peace was declared. He was present at actions on the Vet River, Zand River, at Johannesburg, Diamond Hill, Belfast, Frederickstadt, also taking part in operations in the Eastern Transvaal and the Orange River Colony. He was twice mentioned in Despatches [London Gazette, 10 Sept. 1901, and 29 July, 1902]; was promoted Brevet Major 22 Aug. 1902; awarded the Queen's Medal with five clasps and the King's Medal with two clasps. He was Staff Captain, 5th Division, Irish Command, 16 Jan. 1909, to 1 April, 1912, and D.A.Q.M.G., 5th Division, Irish Command, 2 April, 1912, to 15 Jan. 1913. Major Moffitt again saw active service in the European War from 1914, serving with the 2nd Battn. Essex Regt. during the Retreat and subsequent advance. He was present at the actions at Le Cateau, Marne, passage of the Aisne, Meterin, taking part in the operations round Ploegsteert and Armentières. He was severely wounded when holding back the enemy with half a company when Le Gheer village was temporarily lost 21 Oct. 1914. He was created a Companion of the Distinguished Service Order [London Gazette, 18 Feb. 1915]: "Frederick William Moffitt, Capt., The Essex Regt." He was promoted Major 4 May, 1915, and was A.A.G., Southern Command, 20 Jan. 1915, to 1 July, 1916, and G.S.O.1, Australian Training Centre, Salisbury Plain, 2 July, 1916, to 7 Dec. 1917, for both of which appointments he held the temporary rank of Lieutenant-Colonel. He was given the Brevet of Lieutenant-Colonel 1 Jan. 1918. His D.S.O. was awarded "for services in connection with operations in the field."

Frederick W. Moffitt.

WILLIAMS-FREEMAN, FRANCIS CLAVERING PEERE, Capt., was born 22 Feb. 1876. He entered the Army 5 Sept. 1896, as a Second Lieutenant in the Royal Warwickshire Regt., and was promoted Captain 16 Nov. 1901. He served in South Africa, 1900–2, being employed as Adjutant, Mounted Infantry Battn., 21 Feb. to 31 Dec. 1901. He was present at the Relief of Kimberley; operations in the Orange Free State, Feb. to May, 1900, including operations at Paardeberg (17 to 26 Feb.); actions at Poplar Grove, Dreifontein, Vet River (5 and 6 May) and Zand River; operations in the Transvaal, May and June, 1900, including the actions near Johannesburg and Pretoria. He was mentioned in Despatches twice [London Gazette, 7 May and 10 Sept. 1901], and received the Queen's Medal with four clasps, and the King's Medal with two clasps. Capt. Williams-Freeman retired 8 Jan. 1913. He rejoined at the outbreak of hostilities in Europe. He was created a Companion of the Distinguished Service Order [London Gazette, 18 Feb. 1915]: "Francis Clavering Peere Williams-Freeman, Capt. (Reserve of Officers), The Northamptonshire Regt." Capt. Williams-Freeman subsequently became Major (Reserve of Officers). His D.S.O. was awarded "for services in connection with operations in the field."

FINCH, HERBERT MARSHALL, Major, was born at Sonning, Berkshire, 10 May, 1866, eldest son of the Rev. Thomas Ross Finch and Caroline Mary, third daughter of William Marshall. He was educated at Winchester, and joined the King's Own Shropshire Light Infantry (Militia) 31 Jan. 1885, being gazetted a Lieutenant in the Royal Berkshire Regt. 10 Nov. 1886, in which he was promoted Captain 25 Aug. 1897. He was Adjutant of the Royal Berkshire Regt. 5 Aug. 1899, to 4 Aug. 1903.

He served in the South African War, 1899–1902, as a Railway Staff Officer and as Adjutant, and was present in operations in the Orange Free State, April and May, 1900; operations in the Transvaal, east of Pretoria, July to Nov. 1900; operations in the Transvaal, west of Pretoria, July and Aug. 1900, including actions at Zilikat's Nek; operations in Orange River Colony, May to July, 1900; operations in Cape Colony, south of Orange River, 1899 to 1900; operations in the Transvaal, Nov. 1900, to July, 1901; operations in Cape Colony, July, 1901, to 31 May, 1902 (Brevet of Major, 29 Nov. 1900; Despatches [London Gazette, 10 Sept. 1901]; Queen's Medal with three clasps, and King's Medal with two clasps). He became Major 12 Sept. 1906; commanded the Depôt at Reading from 1907 to 1911, and when the war broke out in Aug. 1914, was Second-in-Command of the 1st Battn. He went to France with the Expeditionary Force 12 Aug. 1914; was slightly wounded during the First Battle of Ypres, and invalided home. He was mentioned in Despatches by Field-Marshal Sir John (now Lord) French for gallant and distinguished service in the field, and for gallantry at the First Battle of Ypres; was created a Companion of the Distinguished Service Order [London Gazette, 18 Feb. 1915]: "Herbert Marshall Finch, Major, Royal Berkshire Regt." He returned to the front 2 May, 1915, to command the Second Battn., being promoted Lieutenant-Colonel 30 April, 1915, and was killed in action at Fromelles on the 9th, while gallantly leading his battalion. He was buried there behind the British lines. Lieut.-Colonel Graham, C.B., 1st Royal Berkshires, wrote: "I can only tell you what you already know—that is, what an irreparable loss his will be to the Army, and to the regiment in particular. You have a great consolation in feeling that he fell as he would wish to, 'gallantly leading his battalion in attack,'" and Major G. P. Hunt: "This war has taken so many of our best, but I know there is no one who will be more missed than your husband. Everyone admired him so much." Second Lieut. N. West wrote: "The situation was so terrible, and, in fact, the whole affair that morning had arisen to such a parlous condition, some details may possibly have missed me. However, when the General sent for me and told me to take the front line on, and I started over that bullet-swept area, I did not notice the Colonel; but as I was crawling back to our own trenches, I saw him lying near our wire; he had certainly been hit, but told me his leg was numbed and that he was unable to use it. He was lying in a small hole in the ground where he was fairly safe, and I can see him now plucking the grass round him, and telling me he thought he had better endeavour to get in, as his wound was not painful, but he could not use his leg. I looked everywhere, and thought out everything; it would have been madness to try and pick him up and carry him into the old fire trench; the only possible thing to do was for him to wait where he was while I got a party to sap out to him (i.e., about eight to ten yards). This I told him, and then made for the fire trench as quickly as I could, and just managed to get in by the skin of my teeth; both my arms were out of action. I went to find the best place to start the sap and to get extra shovels, when, to my horror, his head suddenly appeared over the parapet, and before another second passed a bullet hit him in the head and killed him instantly." A friend also wrote: 'It is with great grief I write to sympathize with you in your terrible loss. Since the war began we have heard endless tales from everyone who was with him of his courage and calmness. The regiment can ill afford to lose such a brilliant soldier, and not only that, I am sure it will be a personal grief to every one who knew him—however slightly. Later on it may help you to know how universally admired and loved your husband was by all his men, as well as his brother officers." Private T. Barlow, 1st Royal Berkshires, in speaking of the action at Marseilles, said: "We lost a lot of men in this engagement, but we were told afterwards that the retaking of the bridge had saved a lot of lives. I shall never forget the coolness of Major Finch in this attack; he walked about in a perfect hail of bullets, giving his men confidence, and I can safely say it was he who saved the situation that night," and a friend wrote on his return to the front: "Finch is a fine man—out with his beloved Berkshires again, a splendid lot." He married, at Bermuda, 20 April, 1895, Florence Kathleen (Pierremont, South Farnborough), elder daughter of Lieut.-Colonel Edward Crozier Sibbald Moore, C.R.E., Bermuda, and had four children: Frank Marshall, born 15 Jan. 1899; Harold Du Pré, born 29 Aug. 1903; Edward Ross, born 25 Aug. 1911, and Florence Mary Earnshaw. His D.S.O. was awarded "for services in connection with operations in the field."

Herbert Marshall Finch.

TULLOCH, RICHARD MURRAY GREGORIE, Capt., was born 20 May, 1878, youngest son of Major-General Sir Alexander Bruce Tulloch, K.C.B., C.M.G., and of Arabella, daughter of the late Stephen Herlis. He joined the Army 8 Sept. 1897, as a Second Lieutenant in the Royal West Kent Regt., in which he was promoted Lieutenant 28 Jan. 1899. He served in the South African War from 1900 to 1902, taking part in operations in the Orange Free State, April to May, 1900; operations in the Orange River Colony, May to 29 Nov. 1900, including actions at Biddulphsberg and Wittebergen (1 to 29 July); operations in Cape Colony, south of Orange River, 1900; operations in the Transvaal, Sept. Oct. and Nov. 1901; operations in Orange River Colony 30 Nov. 1900, to Sept. 1901, and Nov. 1901, to April, 1902; operations on the Zululand Frontier of Natal, Sept. and Oct. 1901 (Queen's Medal with three clasps, and King's Medal with two clasps). He became Captain 20 Jan. 1904, and was Adjutant of the Royal West Kent Regt. from 16 Nov. 1907, to 13 Aug. 1909, and Adjutant of Special Reserve 31 Aug. 1910, to 21 Jan. 1912. Capt. Tulloch served in the European War from 1914. He was created a Companion of the Distinguished Service Order [London Gazette, 18 Feb. 1915]: "Richard Murray Gregorie Tulloch, Capt., Royal West Kent Regt." He was promoted Major 26 May, 1915, and was G.S.O.3 and G.S.O.2, Training Centre, Ripon, June, 1915, to April, 1916; G.S.O., 64th Division, Home Forces, Sept. 1916, to March, 1917; G.S.O.2, 11th Army Corps, British Armies in France, May to July, 1917; held a special appointment as Chief Instructor at the Instructional School, Berkhampsted, 7 May to 22 July, 1918; was appointed G.S.O.2, School for Training Instruction, Berkhampsted, 23 July, 1918. He was given the Brevet of Lieutenant-Colonel 3 June, 1919, and twice mentioned in Despatches. Major Tulloch married, in 1916, Eleanor Margaret, only child of W. Malcolm Corrie, of Biarritz, and they have one daughter. His D.S.O. was awarded "for services in connection with operations in the field."

BUCHANAN-DUNLOP, HENRY DONALD, Capt., was born 24 July, 1878, son of Lieut.-Colonel H. D. Buchanan-Dunlop, late Royal Artillery, and Sabina Woolston. He was educated at the Royal Military College, Sandhurst, and entered the Queen's Own Royal West Kent Regt. 16 Feb. 1898, in which he was promoted Lieutenant 8 March, 1900, and Captain 19 March, 1904. Capt. Buchanan-Dunlop served in the European War from 1914; was Adjutant, Royal West Kent Regt., from 2 Nov. 1914. He was created a Companion of the Distinguished Service Order [London Gazette, 18 Feb. 1915]: "Henry Donald Buchanan-Dunlop, Capt., Royal West Kent Regt." He was promoted Major 1 Sept. 1915; was Temporary Lieutenant-Colonel, Royal West Kent Regt., 13 Sept. 1915, to 11 Sept. 1916, and Acting Lieutenant-Colonel 5 Dec. 1916, to 29 May, 1917; was appointed Temporary Lieutenant-Colonel, Machine Gun Corps, 27 Dec. 1917. He was five times mentioned in Despatches (Feb. 1915, Jan. and July, 1916, June, 1917 and Jan. 1918); was given the Brevet of Lieutenant-Colonel 1 Jan. 1919, and was created a C.M.G. in 1919. His D.S.O. was awarded "for services in connection with operations in the field."

TREVOR, HERBERT EDWARD, Major, was born in London 16 Dec. 1871, eldest son of Colonel G. H. Trevor, C.S.I., and of Mrs. Trevor, daughter of Colonel E. K. Elliot, B.S.C. He was educated at Winchester College, and at the Royal Military College, Sandhurst; entered the Army 14 Sept. 1892, in the King's Own Yorkshire Light Infantry, in which he was promoted Lieutenant 26 March, 1894, and Captain 9 Oct. 1899. He was employed as D.A.A.G., Cork District, 1900–1, and as Adjutant, 1st Battn. King's Own Yorkshire Light Infantry, April, 1901, to April, 1905; Officer of a Company of Gentleman Cadets, Royal Military College, Camberley, Feb. 1906, to Jan. 1910; Brigade Major, Northumberland Infantry Brigade, Northern Command, April, 1911, to April, 1912; was promoted Major 14 June, 1912; was Brigade Major, 6th London Infantry Brigade, London District, April, 1912, to Feb. 1913. Major Trevor saw active service in the European War, with the 2nd Battn. King's Own Yorkshire Light Infantry, Aug. to Oct. 1914, and was present in action from Mons to the First Battle of Ypres; acted as Brigade Major, 142nd Infantry Brigade, from Nov. 1914, to Oct. 1915, with the Central Force, Home Defence, and with the British Expeditionary Force. He was created a Companion of the Distinguished Service Order [London Gazette, 18 Feb. 1915]: "Herbert Edward Trevor, Major, King's Own Yorkshire Light Infantry." He commanded a Service Battn. of his regiment from 30 Nov. 1915, to 2 July, 1916, and was Temporary Brigadier-General while commanding the 103rd Infantry Brigade in France, July, 1916, to April, 1917, and Aug. to Nov. 1917, and while commanding the East Anglian Reserve Brigade, Nov. 1917, to April, 1919. He was given the Brevet of Lieutenant-Colonel 1 Jan. 1917. He was mentioned in Despatches five times, and created a C.M.G. in 1918. Lieut.-Colonel H. E. Trevor married, at Limerick, 17 April, 1902, Aileen Ismenia, daughter of the late Robert Hardinge Massy. His D.S.O. was awarded "for services in connection with operations in the field."

HEATHCOTE, CHARLES EDENSOR, Major, was born 8 April, 1875, son of Lieut.-Colonel C. L. Heathcote, late Durham Light Infantry, and Eleanor, youngest daughter of S. P. Austin, of Sunderland. He was educated at Bedford School, and entered the Army 7 March, 1894, as a Second Lieutenant in the Yorkshire Light Infantry, in which he was promoted Lieutenant 30 Jan. 1898 and Captain 23 April, 1900. Capt. Heathcote served as Superintendent of Gymnasia, Malta, from Jan. 1900, to Aug. 1902, and was employed with the West African Frontier Force 18 June, 1904, to 1 Sept. 1909, serving in the Onitsha Hinterland Expedition, 1904–5; the Bende-Onitsha Hinterland Expedition, 1905–6 (Despatches [London Gazette, 18 Sept. 1906]; Medal with clasp); Southern Nigeria, 1906 (Despatches [London Gazette, 13 March, 1908]); Southern Nigeria, 1908, in command (Despatches [London Gazette, 21 Dec. 1909]; clasp). He was employed as Superintendent of Gymnasia, Eastern Command, 6 March, 1911, to 5 Aug. 1914, and was promoted Major 11 Nov. 1913. He took part in the European War, serving with the Second Battn. of his regiment, from August to 31 Oct. 1914, as a Company Commander, then as Second-in-Command, and finally in command, and was present at the Battles of Mons, Le Cateau, the Marne, the Aisne, and the First Battle of Ypres (dangerously wounded at Messines). He was created a Companion of the Distinguished Service Order [London Gazette, 18 Feb. 1915]: "Charles Edensor Heathcote, Major, The King's Own Yorkshire Light Infantry." On returning to the front, Major Heathcote was Second-in-Command of the 2nd King's Own Yorkshire Light Infantry, and at the Second Battle of Ypres in April, 1915, and in command

Charles E. Heathcote.

of the 1st Battn. in the same battle from May to Sept., when he became Commanding Officer of the 4th Lincolnshire Regt. He commanded them at Loos and the capture of the Hohenzollern Redoubt, and afterwards in Egypt at the Suez Canal Defences, and in France on the Vimy Ridge, until May, 1916. He was given the Brevet of Lieutenant-Colonel 3 June, 1916; was Temporary Brigadier-General commanding the 7th Infantry Brigade, May to Sept. 1916, taking part in operations on Vimy Ridge, May, 1916, and the First Battle of the Somme; commanded the 9th King's Own Yorkshire Light Infantry at the Somme, Sept. 1916 (invalided); commanded the 7th Leicestershire Regt., Jan. to May, 1917, in the Battle of Arras. In May, 1917, he was ordered to Egypt to command a Brigade, and on 1 Sept. took over the command of the 231st Infantry Brigade. With it he was in action at the battles of Beersheba and Sheria; operations west of Jerusalem; the capture of Jerusalem; operations astride the Nablus Road. The brigade then went to the Western Front, and was engaged in operations south of Merville, Aug. 1918; the Third Battle of the Somme and the attack on the Hindenburg Line, east of Ronssoy and Templeux-le-Guerard; the operations resulting in the reoccupation of Aubers Ridge and Lille, the capture of Tournai, and advance to the Dendre at Ath. He was six times mentioned in Despatches, awarded the Order of the Nile, 3rd Class, and was created a C.M.G. in 1918, and a C.B. in 1919. Lieut.-Colonel Heathcote married, in 1909, May, second daughter of the late Edmund Severne, of Wallop, Shropshire, and Thenford, Northants, and they have two sons: Gilbert Gresley, born 24 May, 1911, and John Severne, born 17 April, 1913. His D.S.O. was awarded " for services in connection with operations in the field."

LUARD, EDWARD BOURRYAU, Major, was born 20 Sept. 1870, son of Lieut.-General R. G. A. Luard, C.B. He was educated at Sherborne and Clifton Colleges, and at Sandhurst, and entered the Army, as a Second Lieutenant in the Shropshire Light Infantry 2 May, 1891; was promoted Lieutenant 11 Feb. 1894, and Captain 11 Aug. 1900. He served in South Africa, 1899–1902; on the Staff, being present in operations in the Transvaal from 1900 to 1902; as Signalling Officer 9 June to 4 Sept. 1901, (Queen's Medal with three clasps). He was promoted Major 11 Feb. 1910. Lieut.-Colonel Luard served in the European War; was present at the Marne, Sept. 1914; Armentières, 1914–15; Ypres, 1915–16. He was created a Companion of the Distinguished Service Order [London Gazette, 18 Feb. 1915]: " Edward Bourryau Luard, Major, Shropshire Light Infantry." He was Lieutenant-Colonel commanding the 1st King's Shropshire Light Infantry 6 Aug. 1915; was mentioned in Despatches 14 Jan. and 30 Nov. 1915, and 30 April, 1916. He died of wounds 24 April, 1916. Lieut.-Colonel Luard had been awarded the Gold Medal for services rendered during the plague at Hong-Kong in 1894. His D.S.O. was awarded " for services in connection with operations in the field."

OSBORNE, HENRY PERCY, Major, was born 3 Sept. 1877. He entered the Army, from the Militia, as a Second Lieutenant in the Middlesex Regt. 4 Jan. 1899, and became Lieutenant 14 March, 1900. He served in the South African War, 1899–1900, being present at the Relief of Ladysmith; operations of 17 to 29 Jan. 1900, and the action at Spion Kop; operations of 5 to 7 Feb. 1900; operations on Tugela Heights (14 to 27 Feb.); operations in Natal, March and April, 1900; operations in Cape Colony, south of Orange River, 1899 (Queen's Medal with four clasps). He became Captain 12 Oct. 1901; graduated at the Staff College, Camberley. He served in the European War from 1914; was promoted Major 8 Oct. 1914, and for his services was created a Companion of the Distinguished Service Order [London Gazette, 18 Feb. 1915]: " Henry Percy Osborne, Major, Middlesex Regt." He was Brigade Major, 55th Infantry Brigade, New Armies and British Expeditionary Force, 19 April to 19 Oct. 1915; Temporary Lieutenant-Colonel commanding the 12th Battn. Middlesex Regt. 20 Oct. 1915, to 21 June, 1916; G.S.O.3, Australian Training Centre, 25 June, 1916, to 14 Aug. 1917; G.S.O.2, 3rd British Division in France, 7 Oct. 1917, to 1 Jan. 1918; Lieut.-Colonel Osborne commanded the 9th Battn. Cheshire Regt. in the Army of Occupation in Germany. He was twice mentioned in Despatches. His D.S.O. was awarded " for services in connection with operations in the field."

Henry Percy Osborne.

PHILIPS, LEWIS FRANCIS, Major, was born 4 Oct. 1870, son of John William Philips, of Heybridge, Staffordshire, and of Olivia, daughter of the Rev. William Dodsworth, D.D. He was educated at Winchester, and entered the Army 9 July, 1890, as a Second Lieutenant in the King's Royal Rifle Corps; was promoted Lieutenant 15 Feb. 1893, and Captain 18 May, 1898. He served in the South African War, 1899 to 1902, on the Staff (as Assistant Provost-Marshal 15 April, 1901, to 4 Feb. 1902), and took part in the Relief of Ladysmith, including the action at Colenso; operations of 17 to 24 Jan. 1900, and the action at Spion Kop; operations of 5 to 7 Feb. 1900, and action at Vaal Kranz; operations on Tugela Heights (14 to 27 Feb. 1900), and the action at Pieter's Hill; operations in Natal, March to June, 1900, including the action at Laing's Nek (6 to 9 June). For

Lewis Francis Philips.

his services he was mentioned in Despatches [London Gazette, 10 Sept. 1901]; was given the Brevet of Major 22 Aug. 1902; received the Queen's Medal with six clasps, and the King's Medal with two clasps. He was G.S.O.2, Northumbrian Division, Northern Command, 30 April, 1908, to 30 April, 1910; G.S.O.2, Canadian Forces, 27 July, 1911, to 30 Nov. 1912. He again saw active service in the European War, serving as Temporary Lieutenant-Colonel 1 Nov. 1914, to 10 Sept. 1915. He was created a Companion of the Distinguished Service Order [London Gazette, 18 Feb. 1915], for services at the First Battle of Ypres in particular: " Lewis Francis Philips, Major, The King's Royal Rifle Corps." He became Temporary Brigadier-General 11 Sept. 1915; was promoted Lieutenant-Colonel 18 Dec. 1915; commanded the 70th Infantry Brigade 11 Sept. to 9 Nov. 1915; the 189th Infantry Brigade 26 May, 1916, to 31 Oct. 1917; was appointed Base Commandant, Rouen (graded as Brigadier-General), 31 Oct. 1917; appointed to command the 1st Battn. King's Royal Rifle Corps 1 Aug. 1919; placed on half-pay, with the rank of Colonel 18 Dec. 1919, and appointed to the command of the Hampshire Infantry Brigade 1 March, 1920. Brigadier-General Philips was mentioned in Despatches, and created a C.M.G. in 1917 and a C.B.E. in 1919. He married, in 1909, Margaret Aline, daughter of Lieut.-Colonel A. H. Macdonald-Moreton, late Coldstream Guards, and they have a son, Norman, born 24 March, 1916, and two daughters, Anne and Margaret. His D.S.O. was awarded " for services in connection with operations in the field."

JELF, RUDOLF GEORGE, Major, was born in Aldershot Camp 19 Aug. 1873, son of the late Colonel R. Jelf, C.M.G., of the Royal Engineers, and Mrs. Margaret Jelf, daughter of Professor Blunt, of St. John's College, Cambridge. He was educated at Eton, and at the Royal Military College, Sandhurst, and obtained his first commission in the 1st Battn. King's Royal Rifle Corps 4 Oct. 1893. He took part in the Relief of Chitral, 1895 (Medal and clasp); was promoted Lieutenant 28 March, 1896. He served in the South African War, 1899–1902, taking part in operations in Natal in 1899, including the actions at Talana and Lombard's Kop; the Defence of Ladysmith, including the action of 6 Jan. 1900; operations in the Transvaal, Jan. 1901, to 31 May, 1902 (Queen's Medal with three clasps; King's Medal with two clasps). He became Captain 13 Jan. 1901; was Adjutant of Volunteers 2 Sept. 1902, to 31 Aug. 1905; A.D.C. to the Viceroy of India 19 July, 1907, to 31 March, 1911; was promoted Major 4 Nov. 1910. Major Jelf again saw active service in the European War from 1914 to 1919 on the Western Front. He was created a Companion of the Distinguished Service Order [London Gazette, 18 Feb. 1915]: " Rudolf George Jelf, Major, King's Royal Rifle Corps." He was Temporary Lieutenant-Colonel, King's Royal Rifle Corps, 15 June to 25 Sept. 1915; Brigade Commander, 73rd Infantry Brigade, 26 Sept. 1915, to 24 Nov. 1916; Brigade Commander, 86th Infantry Brigade, 30 April, 1917 (both in France); Brigade Commander, 1st London Reserve Infantry Brigade, Home Forces, 6 March, 1918. For his services in the war he was five times mentioned in Despatches, was made Brevet Lieutenant-Colonel 1 Jan. 1916, and was created a C.M.G. in 1919. Lieutenant-Colonel R. G. Jelf married, in 1919, Kathleen, youngest daughter of W. Rowe Green. His favourite recreations are hunting, fishing, shooting and golf. His D.S.O. was awarded " for services in connection with operations in the field."

OPPENHEIM, AUGUSTUS CHARLES, Capt., was born 12 Jan. 1883, youngest son of the late Henry Maurice William Oppenheim, of 16, Bruton Street, W., and Mrs. Henry Oppenheim. Educated at Eton, and the Royal Military College, Sandhurst, he entered the King's Royal Rifles 22 Oct. 1902, and was promoted Lieutenant 4 June, 1907. He was appointed Adjutant of the 5th Battn. London Regt. (London Rifle Brigade) 1 Jan. 1913; was promoted Captain 25 Sept. 1914. Serving in France with the 5th Battn. London Regt. until severely wounded 13 May, 1915 he was twice mentioned in Despatches, and was created a Companion of the Distinguished Service Order [London Gazette, 18 Feb. 1915]: " Augustus Charles Oppenheim, Capt., 2nd Battn. King's Royal Rifle Corps." He returned to his regiment in Dec. 1915, and became Acting Major and Second-in-Command in Jan. 1916; was Brigade Major, 48th Infantry Brigade, British Armies in France, 26 June to 2 Aug. 1916; Officer of a Company of Gentleman Cadets, Royal Military College, 26 Sept. 1917, to 6 May, 1918; Commander of a Company 7 May, 1918; promoted Major 22 Oct. 1917. Major Oppenheim married, in 1913, Audrey Beatrix, daughter of Lieut.-Colonel A. H. M. Moreton, of Hill Grove, Bembridge; they have one son and two daughters. His D.S.O. was awarded " for services in connection with operations in the field."

ROWAN, PERCY STEWART, Capt., was born 16 Sept. 1882. He was gazetted to the Wiltshire Regt. 5 Jan. 1901; became Lieutenant 13 June, 1903, and Captain 15 April, 1909; was Adjutant, Wiltshire Regt., 20 Sept. 1911, to 2 March, 1915; was promoted to Major 1 Sept. 1915; was Temporary Lieutenant-Colonel 6 April, 1918, to 31 March, 1919; specially employed at the War Office 3 March to 2 July, 1915; G.S.O.3, 32nd Division, B.E.F., 21 Feb. to 15 July, 1616; G.S.O.2, 32nd Division, British Armies in France, 17 July, 1916, to 16 Jan. 1917; G.S.O.2, 5th Army Corps, British Armies in France, 17 Jan. to 25 July, 1917; G.S.O.2, G.H.Q., British Armies in France, 25 July, 1917, to 19 March, 1918; G.S.O.2, 14th Division, British Armies in France, 20 March to 5 April, 1918; G.S.O.1, 37th Division, British Armies in France, 6 April to 9 July, 1918; G.S.O.1, 64th Division, Forces in Great Britain, 18 July, 1918, to 31 March, 1919. He served in the European War from 1914; was mentioned in Despatches, and created a Companion of the Distinguished Service Order [London Gazette, 18 Feb. 1915]: " Percy Stewart Rowan, Capt., Wiltshire Regt. For services in connection with operations in the field."

EVANS, WILFRED KEITH, Capt., was born 28 July, 1878, son of Ernest Richard Evans, F.R.C.S. He was educated at Uppingham, and entered the Army 21 April, 1900, from the Militia, as a Second Lieutenant in the Manchester Regt. He served in the South African Campaign

Wilfred Keith Evans.

from 1900 to 1902, taking part in operations in the Orange Free State, Feb. to May, 1900; operations in Orange River Colony, May to 29 Nov. 1900; operations in Cape Colony, south of Orange River, 1900. He was employed with the Mounted Infantry. He received the Queen's Medal with three clasps, and the King's Medal with two clasps. He became Lieutenant 13 Feb. 1901; was Adjutant of the Manchester Regt. 3 May, 1906, to 2 May, 1909; was promoted Captain 18 Dec. 1907. Capt. W. K. Evans served in the European War with distinction. He was again Adjutant, Manchester Regt., 30 Oct. 1914, to 1 Aug. 1915. He was created a Companion of the Distinguished Service Order [London Gazette, 18 Feb. 1915]: "Wilfred Keith Evans, Capt., The Manchester Regt." Capt. Evans held a special appointment with the 2nd Army for a fortnight in July, 1915; was promoted Major 1 Sept. 1915; served as G.S.O. 3, 2nd Army, Aug. 1915, to July, 1916, and commanded a service battalion of the 11th Cheshire Regt. from July, 1916, to Sept. 1917. He was promoted Brevet Lieutenant-Colonel 3 June, 1917, and gained a Bar to his D.S.O. [London Gazette, 16 Aug. 1917]: "Wilfred Keith Evans, D.S.O., Temporary Lieut.-Colonel, Manchester Regt., commanding Battn. Cheshire Regt. For conspicuous gallantry and devotion to duty. He led his battalion with great dash and initiative to their objective, capturing many guns and prisoners. He also repulsed strong hostile counter-attacks, and showed great coolness and promptitude in rallying and reorganizing troops who had been driven back through his line. His fine personal example saved a critical situation." He was Brigade Commander, 182nd Infantry Brigade, France, 25 Sept. 1917, with the rank of Temporary Brigadier-General. He was mentioned in Despatches, and made an Officer of the Legion of Honour, and in 1919 was created a C.M.G. Lieut.-Colonel Evans married, in 1913, Gladys Irene, daughter of the Rev. J. G. Leonard, M.A., Vicar and Rural Dean of Dalton-in-Furness, and they have two sons: Michael Patrick Ernest and Nigel Keith, and one daughter, Delia Mary Katharine. His D.S.O. was awarded "for services in connection with operations in the field."

EWALD, FERDINAND CHARLES TRACY, Capt., was born 12 June, 1876. He entered the North Staffordshire Regt. 5 May, 1900; became Lieutenant 24 March, 1901; Captain 17 March, 1909, and Major 1 Sept. 1915; was employed with the West African Frontier Force 27 June, 1908, to 29 Nov. 1912; Adjutant, Special Reserve, from 9 Sept. 1915; attached General Staff 5 March to 14 April, 1916; Major, General Staff, 15 April to 4 Oct. 1916; G.S.O.3, Southern Command, 5 Oct. 1916, to 26 May, 1918; Brigade Major, 21st Indian Infantry Brigade, Egyptian Expeditionary Force, from 27 May, 1918; attached General Staff, Southern Command, for Musketry Duties. He served in the European War in 1914 and 1915; was mentioned in Despatches, and created a Companion of the Distinguished Service Order [London Gazette, 18 Feb. 1915]: "Ferdinand Charles Tracy Ewald, Capt., North Staffordshire Regt." Major Ewald married, in 1916, Eleanor Dulce, daughter of the late Major-General T. J. Maclachlan, R.H.A., and widow of Capt. A. de V. Maclean. His D.S.O. was awarded "for services in connection with operations in the field."

BAYLEY, GERALD EDWARD, Major, was born at Nuwara, Eluja, Ceylon, 6 March, 1874, fifth son of the late Capt. Francis Bayley, Agent P. and O. Company, Colombo, Ceylon, and his wife, Lucy Matilda, daughter of the late Surgeon-General Atkinson, of Crawley Rise, Camberley. He was educated at Totteridge Park, and at Rugby School, and joined the 2nd Battn. York and Lancaster Regt., from the 3rd Battn., 12 Dec. 1894; was promoted Lieutenant 10 Nov. 1897, and Captain 12 May, 1902. He was employed with the Ceylon Volunteers from 28 Nov. 1902, to 31 Jan. 1908, as Adjutant; was present at the Coronation of King George, gaining the Coronation Medal, and was promoted Major in the York and Lancaster Regt. 1 July, 1912. Major Bayley served in the European War from 1914. He was in France from 6 Sept. 1914, to 25 Oct. 1915, and for his services there he was created a Companion of the Distinguished Service Order [London Gazette, 18 Feb. 1915]:

Gerald Edward Bayley.

"Gerald Edward Bayley, Major, York and Lancaster Regt." He was promoted Temporary Lieutenant-Colonel to command the 1st York and Lancaster Regt. 17 May, 1915; went to Egypt in Nov. 1915, and in Dec. was transferred to Salonika, where he remained until May, 1918, serving from 18 Nov. 1916, as Temporary Brigadier-General in command of the 65th Brigade. He went through the campaign unwounded, but spent a fortnight in hospital with malaria in Sept. 1917. He came home on a tour of duty, and took over the command of the West Riding Reserve (T.F.) Brigade 23 May, 1918, a position which he held until 16 April, 1919, when the brigade was disbanded. He was then given command of the 2nd Battn. York and Lancaster Regt., and served in Mesopotamia. He was four times mentioned in Despatches (Jan. 1916 and 1916, Jan. and Dec. 1917); was promoted Brevet Lieutenant-Colonel 1 Jan. 1917; created a C.M.G. 1 Jan. 1917, and was made an Officer of the Order of St. Maurice and

St. Lazarus. He is also the holder of Royal Humane Society's Silver Medal, awarded for brave conduct after the wreck of R.I.M.S. Warren Hastings 14 Jan. 1897. Lieut.-Colonel Bayley married, at the Chapel Royal, Savoy, 23 Aug. 1917, Marjorie Singleton Powell, elder daughter of Mr. and Mrs. H. S. Powell, of Pocklington, Yorks, and they have a daughter, Geraldine Diana, born 22 Feb. 1919. His D.S.O. was awarded "for services in connection with operations in the field."

BLUNT, ALLAN ST. JOHN, Capt., was born 27 Oct. 1880, third son of the late Colonel Arthur Blunt. He joined the York and Lancaster Regt. 6 Dec. 1899, and became Lieutenant 29 July, 1901. He served in South Africa, 1899–1902; was present at the Relief of Ladysmith, including operations of 17 to 24 Jan. 1900, and the action at Spion Kop; operations of 5 to 7 Feb. 1900, and the action at Vaal Kranz, and operations on Tugela Heights (14 to 29 Feb.) and action at Pieter's Hill; operations in Natal (March to June, 1900), including the action at Laing's Nek (6 to 9 June); operations in the Transvaal, May to Dec. 1901; operations in Orange River Colony, Dec. 1901, to 31 May, 1902 (Queen's Medal with six clasps; King's Medal with two clasps). He was promoted Captain 9 Sept. 1908, and served as Adjutant of the York and Lancaster Regt. from 12 March, 1910, to 11 March, 1913. He served in the European War from 1914 to 1918. He was created a Companion of the Distinguished Service Order [London Gazette, 18 Feb. 1915]: "Allan St. John Blunt, Capt., York and Lancaster Regt." He was promoted Major 1 Sept. 1915; was given the Brevet of Lieutenant-Colonel 1 Jan. 1918, and retired from the Service 20 March, 1919. Lieut.-Colonel A. St. J. Blunt married, in 1914, Doris Elizabeth, daughter of the late John G. Stephen. His D.S.O. was awarded "for services in connection with operations in the field."

BAILLIE, HUGH FREDERICK, Capt., was born 30 March, 1879, son of the late General Duncan J. Baillie, of Loch Loy, and Anna, daughter of the Rev. C. A. Burnaby, of Somerby Hall, Leicestershire. He was

Hugh Frederick Baillie.

educated at Wellington College, and joined the Seaforth Highlanders (The Ross-shire Buffs) (The Duke of Albany's) 3 Aug. 1898, and became Lieutenant 24 Feb. 1900. He served with the 2nd Seaforth Highlanders in South Africa, 1899–1902; was present in the advance on Kimberley, including actions at Magersfontein (wounded); operations in the Orange Free State, Feb. to May, 1900, including the actions at Paardeberg, Poplar Grove and Dreifontein; operations in Orange River Colony, May to 29 Nov. 1900, including the actions at Wittebergen (1 to 29 July); operations in the Transvaal, March to Aug. 1901; operations in Orange River Colony 30 Nov. 1900, to Jan. 1901; operations in Cape Colony, Feb. to March, 1901, and Aug. 1901, to May, 1902. He was employed with Lovat Scouts (Imperial Yeomanry) from Oct. 1901, to May, 1902; was awarded the Queen's Medal with five clasps, and the King's Medal with two clasps. He was attached to the West African Frontier Force from 14 March, 1903, to 17 Dec. 1904, and again saw active service in Northern Nigeria, in operations in the Bassa Provinces, against the Okpotos (Medal with clasp); was promoted Captain 5 Aug. 1904; was D.A.A. and Q.M.G., Highland Division, Scottish Command, 6 June, 1909, to 5 June, 1913. Capt. Baillie served in the European War from 1914, with the 2nd Seaforth Highlanders, and took part in the Retreat from Mons and subsequent advance to the Aisne, also in operations in Flanders, Oct. 1914, when he was wounded (23 Oct.). He was mentioned in Despatches, and created a Companion of the Distinguished Service Order [London Gazette, 18 Feb. 1915]: "Hugh Frederick Baillie, Capt., Seaforth Highlanders." Subsequently Capt. Baillie held various Staff Appointments with the British Expeditionary Force in France. He was G.S.O.3, 15th Division, B.E.F., Feb. to Nov. 1915; was promoted Major 1 Sept. 1915, and was G.S.O.2, 13th Corps, Nov. 1915, to Jan. 1916; G.S.O.2, 51st Division, Jan. to June, 1916; G.S.O.2 (Supernumerary), June to Sept. 1916; G.S.O.2, 15th Division, Sept. 1916, to Feb. 1917; G.S.O.2, 3rd Corps, Feb. to May, 1917; G.S.O.1, 15th Division (Temporary Lieutenant-Colonel), May, 1917, to July, 1918. He was given the Brevet of Lieutenant-Colonel 1 Jan. 1918; served as G.S.O.1, British G.H.Q., France, July to Aug. 1918; Assistant Director of Staff Duties, G.H.Q. (Temporary Colonel), Aug. 1918, to April, 1919; was appointed G.S.O.1, Highland Division, British Army on the Rhine, 2 April, 1919. His D.S.O. was awarded "for services in connection with operations in the field."

GRANT, JOHN PATRICK, Major, was born 18 July, 1872. He joined the Army in 1892; became Captain, 1899, and retired in 1904. He entered the 3rd Reserve Battn. Seaforth Highlanders. He served in the Chitral Campaign in 1895 (Medal with clasp); in the South African War, 1899–1902; was twice mentioned in Despatches, and received the Queen's Medal with three clasps, and the King's Medal with two clasps. Major Grant served in the European War in 1914 and 1915; was mentioned in Despatches and created a Companion of the Distinguished Service Order [London Gazette, 18 Feb. 1915]: "John Patrick Grant, Major, 3rd Reserve Battn. Seaforth Highlanders. For services in connection with operations in the field."

CAMPBELL, THE HONOURABLE ERIC OCTAVIUS, Lieut. The "Times," of 15 June, 1918, says: "Lieut.-Colonel the Hon. Eric O. Campbell, D.S.O., Seaforth Highlanders, who died in hospital in London of cerebral hæmorrhage on 4 June, was the youngest son of the third Earl Cawdor, and uncle of the present peer. He was born in 1885, and after going to Eton, passed into the Army through the Militia, being gazetted to the Seaforth Highlanders on 20 Dec. 1905. At the outbreak of the war he went to France as Adjutant of the 2nd Battalion; was awarded the D.S.O. on 18 Feb. 1915, and was wounded at St. Julian on 25 April, 1915. He was employed as Brigade Major from 3 Jan. to 24 Sept. 1916, his services being rewarded with a Brevet Majority on 3 June, 1916. He was in hospital in France towards the end of 1916, and on return to duty in Nov. went to the 2nd Battn., but resumed the appointment of Brigade Major to the 44th Infantry Brigade on 22 Jan. 1917. He returned to regimental duty on 27 May, 1917, and for a short time commanded the 2nd Battn. On 20 Oct. 1917, he was given command of another battalion of the Seaforth Highlanders, which he retained till the middle of May, 1918, when a breakdown in health, due to nearly four years' active service, compelled him to go to hospital. He arrived home on 25 May, having been reported wounded, but returned to duty immediately, as he was only bruised by a fragment of a shell. In the Gazette of 24 May he was mentioned in Despatches for the third time, and a Bar to his D.S.O. was awarded in the Gazette of 3 June, the day before his death." The London Gazette notice (18 Feb. 1915) of his D.S.O. is: "The Honourable E. O. Campbell, Lieut., The Seaforth Highlanders. For services in connection with operations in the field."

Hon. Eric O. Campbell.

BURNETT, JAMES LAUDERDALE GILBERT, Capt., was born 1 April, 1880, at Rattray House, Peterhead, eldest son of Sir Thomas Burnett, 12th Baronet, of Leys. He was educated at Wellington, and at the Royal Military College, and joined the 2nd Gordon Highlanders in 1899. He proceeded to South Africa at once, where he served as R.T.O. 18 Oct. to 12 Nov. 1900, and 4 Jan. to 7 April, 1901; took part in the operations in the Transvaal, May and June, 1900, including actions near Johannesburg and Pretoria; operations in the Transvaal, east of Pretoria, July to 29 Nov. 1900, including action at Reit Vlei; operations in the Transvaal, April to Sept. 1901, and Oct. 1901, to May, 1902; operations on the Zululand Frontier of Natal in Sept. 1901. He became Lieutenant 31 Jan. 1901. He was mentioned in Despatches [London Gazette, 10 Sept. 1901, for "coolness and resource on occasion of a train being derailed and attacked by Boers near Naboomspruit, Aug. 1901," and was also awarded the Queen's Medal with two clasps, and the King's Medal with two clasps (Laing's Nek and Belfast). He was promoted Captain 22 Jan. 1906. He saw much active service in the European War from 1914, serving with the British Expeditionary Force in France and Belgium. He was severely wounded; mentioned in Despatches, and for services at the First Battle of Ypres was created a Companion of the Distinguished Service Order [London Gazette, 18 Feb. 1915]: "James Lauderdale Gilbert Burnett, Capt., Gordon Highlanders." He was promoted Major 1 Sept. 1915; was an Officer of and in command of a Company of Gentleman Cadets, Royal Military College, Sandhurst, May, 1915, to Oct. 1916, and was promoted Lieutenant-Colonel, 1st Gordon Highlanders, 8 Jan. 1917, and while commanding the battalion was again mentioned in Despatches, the following award being announced in a Supplement of the London Gazette, 17 Sept. 1917: "Bar to D.S.O.—Lieut.-Colonel James Lauderdale Gilbert Burnett, D.S.O., Gordon Highlanders. For conspicuous gallantry and devotion to duty in commanding his battalion during the attack and capture of a position. The success of the attack was greatly due to his leadership and the confidence with which he inspired his men." He was promoted Brevet Lieutenant-Colonel 1 Jan. 1918, and was Brigade Commander, 186th Infantry Brigade, in France 3 Dec. 1917, to 1919. He was created a C.M.G. and given the Brevet of Colonel in 1919, and was made an Officer of the Legion of Honour. He was appointed Instructor, Senior Officers' School, Woking, 1920. Colonel Burnett's favourite recreations are shooting and fishing. He married, in 1913, Sybil Aird, youngest daughter of the late William Crozier Smith, of Whitehill, St. Boswells, N.B. His D.S.O. was awarded "for services in connection with operations in the field."

CRAIG-BROWN, ERNEST, Major, was born 20 June, 1871, eldest son of T. Craig-Brown, of Selkirk, and Mrs. T. Craig-Brown. He was educated at Merchiston Castle School, Edinburgh, and was first commissioned 20 Feb. 1895, in the West India Regt., in which he was promoted Lieutenant 16 Aug. 1897. He served in Sierra Leone, 1898, in the Karene Expedition (Medal with clasp; severely wounded), and was transferred to the Cameron Highlanders 13 April, 1898. He was promoted Captain 27 Dec. 1899, and served in the South African War, 1900–2, taking part in the operations in the Orange Free State, Feb. to May, 1900, including actions at Vet River (5 and 6 May) and Zand River; operations in the Transvaal, May and June, 1900, including actions near Johannesburg and Pretoria; operations in Orange River Colony, May to 29 Nov. 1900, including action at Wittebergen (1 to 29 July); operations in the Transvaal, May, 1901, to 31 May, 1902; operations in Cape Colony, Nov. 1900, to May, 1901, and May, 1902. He served as Station Commandant, afterwards as Staff Officer to the Commandant, Matjiesfontein, and subsequently performed the duties of Commandant, Matjiesfontein, from 9 Nov. 1900, and received the Queen's Medal with three clasps, and the King's Medal with two clasps. He was specially employed at Army Headquarters, July to Sept. 1908, and served as G.S.O.3, Army Headquarters, and at the War Office till 13 July, 1912. He was specially employed 14 July to 31 Dec. 1912; was D.A.A.G., Guernsey and Alderney, 4 Feb. to 4 Aug. 1914. At the beginning of the European War (5 Aug. to 24 Sept. 1914) he was G.S.O.2, Guernsey Defences and of the 17th Division. He became Major 17 Sept. 1914, and was Temporary Lieutenant-Colonel of a battalion in his regiment 21 Jan. to 10 May, 1915. He was mentioned in Despatches, Feb. 1915; June, 1915; Jan. 1916; June, 1917, and June, 1918, and was created a Companion of the Distinguished Service Order [London Gazette, 18 Feb. 1915]: "Ernest Craig-Brown, Major, The Queen's Own Cameron Highlanders." From 25 June, 1915, to 24 March, 1916, he was D.A.Q.M.G., 47th Division; Temporary Lieutenant-Colonel, Cameron Highlanders, 26 March, 1916, to 31 Jan. 1917; Temporary Brigadier-General, 56th Infantry Brigade, 1 Feb. to 5 Sept. 1917, and for his services was given the Brevet of Lieutenant-Colonel 3 June, 1917. He was Temporary Lieutenant-Colonel 14 Nov. 1917, to 31 Oct. 1918, and on 1 Nov. 1918, became Temporary Colonel and Base Commandant of the British Salonika Force. Lieut.-Colonel Craig-Brown married, in 1903, Constance Ellen, youngest daughter of the late Henry Guinness, of Stillorgan, County Dublin, and they have one son, Alan Guinness, born 7 April, 1912, and two daughters: Jean Mary, born 14 Aug. 1904, and Bridget Constance, born 3 Oct. 1908. His D.S.O. was awarded "for services in connection with operations in the field."

HILL-DILLON, STEPHEN SEARLE, Lieut., was born 27 Nov. 1887, son of John Dillon, late of Lyncombe Rise, Bath, late Governor of H.M. Prison, Liverpool. He was educated at Sandhurst, and was commissioned in the Royal Irish Rifles 9 Oct. 1907, in which he was promoted Lieutenant 22 April, 1909. He was Adjutant, Royal Irish Rifles, 27 Nov. 1913, to 19 Oct. 1914. Lieut. Dillon saw active service in the European War, and was Temporary Captain, Royal Irish Rifles, 20 Dec. 1914, to 14 March, 1915. He was mentioned in Despatches, and created a Companion of the Distinguished Service Order [London Gazette, 18 Feb. 1915]: "Stephen Searle Dillon, Lieut., Royal Irish Rifles." He was promoted Captain 15 March, 1915, and subsequently held the following appointments: Special appointment as Special Service Officer 2 June, 1915, to 18 March, 1916; G.S.O.3, 5th Army Corps, April to Aug. 1916; G.S.O.2, 5th Army Corps, Aug. 1916, to Nov. 1917; G.S.O.2, American Staff College, France, Nov. 1917, to April, 1918; G.S.O.2, 6th Division, April to June, 1918; G.S.O.2, 2nd Army Corps, June to Sept. 1918; G.S.O.2, 4th Army Corps, Nov. 1918, to 5 Feb. 1919; G.S.O.2, Irish Command, 6 Feb. 1919. He was three times mentioned in Despatches, and was given the Brevet of Major 1 Jan. 1918. Major Hill-Dillon (additional name of Hill assumed in 1916) married, in 1916, Gladys Muriel, daughter of the late Frances Heslop Hill, of Redenham, Hants, and Shroton, Dorset, and they have one daughter. His D.S.O. was awarded "for services in connection with operations in the field."

ELKAN, CLARENCE JOHN, Capt., was born in London 15 May, 1877, son of John Elkan, M.V.O., Member of the Common Council of the City of London, of 40, Hanover Gate Mansions, Regent's Park, N.W., and of Harriet Elkan (died 19 April, 1915). He was educated at the City of London School, and enlisted in the Hampshire Regt. 24 July, 1893. He served in China, 1900, and was granted a commission as Second Lieutenant in the Royal Irish Fusiliers, for specially meritorious services there in May, 1902, also receiving a Medal. He served in West Africa, as Subaltern, Gold Coast Regt.; as Assistant Commandant, Northern Territories Constabulary; as District Commissioner, Gold Coast, and was promoted Captain 3 Aug. 1912. Lieut.-Colonel Elkan retired R. I. Fusiliers 18 Feb. 1914, but rejoined the same year as Captain, 87th Royal Irish Fusiliers, proceeding to France with the battalion, which was part of the 4th Division, and remaining with it until appointed to the Staff in July, 1915. He was commanding a double company of his battalion at the time that he received mention in Despatches, and was created a Companion of the Distinguished Service Order [London Gazette, 18 Feb. 1915]: "Clarence John Elkan, Capt., 87th Royal Irish Fusiliers." He was promoted Major, Reserve of Officers, 13 May, 1915, and served as Temporary Lieutenant-Colonel, employed as A.Q.M.G., General Headquarters, France, and A.Q.M.G., Headquarters, Lines of Communication, France. He was mentioned in Despatches in June, 1916, in Dec. 1917, and Jan. and June, 1919; was given the Brevet of Lieutenant-Colonel 1 Jan. 1918, and promoted Substantive Lieutenant-Colonel in the Reserve of Officers 1 May, 1919. He was also made Chevalier of the Legion of Honour, and in 1919 was awarded the O.B.E. His chief recreations are reading and golf. Lieut.-Colonel Elkan married, in London, 3 March, 1915, Gladys, daughter of William Dagnell, of Cape Town, South Africa. His D.S.O. was awarded "for services in connection with operations in the field."

ALEXANDER, WILLIAM NATHANIEL STUART, Major, was born at Tipperah, Bengal, 8 May, 1874, son of the late Nathaniel Stuart Alexander, Bengal Civil Service, of Aghadoey, Coleraine, County Londonderry, and of Dora, daughter of Edward Currie. He was educated at Rugby, and joined the Army 7 March, 1894, with a commission in the Connaught Rangers, in which he was promoted Lieutenant 31 May, 1897; was employed with the Egyptian Army 1 Aug. 1900, to 31 May, 1901; became Captain 9 Oct. 1901. He served in South Africa, 1902, taking part in the operations in Orange River Colony, Feb. 1902, and in Cape Colony, Feb. to 31 May, 1902, for which he received the Queen's Medal with three clasps. He became Major 4 March, 1914, and took part in the European War from 1914, with the British Expeditionary Force in France and Belgium, and, for his share in the campaign from the action of Mons to the end of the First Battle of Ypres, was mentioned in Despatches, and created a Companion of the Distinguished Service Order [London Gazette, 18 Feb. 1915]: "William Nathaniel Stuart Alexander, Major, Connaught Rangers." Major Alexander also served in France from March to May, 1915, and from July, 1915, to 24 Feb. 1917, was employed on the Staff. He was in Gallipoli, July, 1915, until Jan. 1916; in Egypt, from Jan. to March, 1916; in Mesopotamia, March to June, 1916, and went to France in Sept. 1916. He served there on the Staff until 24 Feb. 1917, when he was given the command of the 7th Border Regt., which he held until 22 Sept. 1918. He remained in France until Oct. 1917, and then commanded battalions of the Training Reserve until April, 1918. He served in France again from April to July, 1918, and returned to the Connaught Rangers 23 Dec. 1918; subsequently Major Alexander commanded the 2nd Battn. Somerset Light Infantry on the North-West Frontier of India. He was awarded a Bar to the Distinguished Service Order [London Gazette, 1 Jan. 1918 (New Year's Honours List)]. His D.S.O. was awarded "for services in connection with operations in the field."

PAYNE, ROBERT LESLIE, Capt., was born 7 May, 1880. He entered the Connaught Rangers, as Second Lieutenant, from the Militia, 18 Oct. 1899, in which he was promoted Lieutenant, 17 Feb. 1901. He served

Robert Leslie Payne.

in the South African War, 1899–1902, and was present at the Relief of Ladysmith, including actions at Colenso; operations of 17 to 24 Jan. 1900, and action at Spion Kop; operations of 5 to 7 Feb. 1900, and action at Vaal Kranz; operations on Tugela Heights (14 to 27 Feb. 1900), and action at Pieter's Hill; operations in Natal, March to April, 1900; operations in Cape Colony, south of Orange River, April, 1900; operations in Cape Colony, north of Orange River, April, 1900; operations in Orange River Colony, May to June, 1901, and Feb. to March, 1902; operations in Cape Colony, Feb. to May, 1901, and June, 1901, to 31 May, 1902 (Queen's Medal with four clasps, and King's Medal with two clasps). He became Lieutenant, Connaught Rangers, 17 Feb. 1901, and Captain 8 Feb. 1906.

Capt. Payne saw active service in the European War from 1914.. He was mentioned in Despatches, and created a Companion of the Distinguished Service Order [London Gazette, 18 Feb. 1915]: "Robert Leslie Payne, Capt., 1st Battn. The Connaught Rangers." He became Major 1 Sept. 1915, and was Staff Service Brigade Major, 3rd Line Group, North Midland Division, 10 Jan. to Sept. 1916; D.A.Q.M.G., 4th Division, France, 5 Oct. to 31 Dec. 1916. Major R. L. Payne married, in 1914, Lilian Mary, daughter of Thomas Duncan. His D.S.O. was awarded "for services in connection with operations in the field."

HYSLOP, HENRY HUGH GORDON, Major, was born 9 Oct. 1873, son of the late Colonel Maxwell Hyslop, 93rd Highlanders, and Elizabeth Lumsden, of Auchindoir, Aberdeenshire. He was educated at Monkton Combe College, near Bath, and at Sandhurst, from which he joined the 2nd Battn. Argyll and Sutherland Highlanders, 10 Oct. 1894. He was promoted Lieutenant 3 April, 1897, and served with the Tochi Field Force, 1897–98 (Medal with clasp). He became Captain 13 April, 1901; took part in the South African War, 1902, serving as Station Staff Officer, and taking part in operations in the Transvaal, Jan. to 31 May, 1902, with the 1st Battn. Argyll and Sutherland Highlanders (Queen's Medal with three clasps). He was appointed Superintendent of Gymnasia, India, 5 Oct. 1904, a position which he held for four years, accompanying the British Mission to Bhutan in 1907. Lieut.-Colonel Hyslop saw active service in the European War from Aug. 1914; was promoted Major 3 Nov. 1914, and for his services was created a Companion of the Distinguished Service Order [London Gazette, 18 Feb. 1915]: "Henry Hugh Gordon Hyslop, Major, 2nd Battn. Princess Louise's (Argyll and Sutherland Highlanders)." He took part in the Retreat from Mons, including actions at Mons, Le Cateau and Néry; was present at the Battles on the Marne and the Aisne, and afterwards in the advance on Armentières, fighting on the Aubers Ridge and in the First Battle of Ypres. He afterwards took part in the following operations: the Battle of Loos, Sept. 1915; the Battle of the Somme, 1916; the taking of Beaumont Hamel, Nov. 1916; Vimy Ridge, March, 1917; Arras, April and May, 1917; the Third Battle of Ypres, 1917; the Battle of Cambrai, Nov. 1917; the German attack of March and April, 1918, and the advance in Belgium, Oct. and Nov. 1918. He was Temporary Lieutenant-Colonel in command of a Territorial Force Battn. 9 Nov. 1915, to 25 Aug. 1917; was promoted Brevet Lieutenant-Colonel 3 June, 1917; was Temporary Brigadier-General 26 Aug. 1917, to 30 Aug. 1919, commanding the 59th Infantry Brigade in France, Aug. 1917, to April, 1918; the 2nd Reserve Training Brigade, Home Forces, April to Oct. 1918; the 26th Infantry Brigade, France, Oct. to Dec. 1918, and was Commandant of the Army Area in Germany, Dec. 1918, to Aug. 1919. He was four times mentioned in Despatches, and has the 1914 Star. His chief amusements are golf, tennis and rackets, in all of which he has represented his regiment; he has done a good deal of big game shooting in India and Thibet. Lieut.-Colonel Hyslop married, in 1904, Beryl, daughter of J. C. White, C.I.E., and they have two sons: Hugh John Maxwell, born on 12 May, 1905, and Gordon Maxwell, born on 19 March, 1909. His D.S.O. was awarded "for services in connection with operations in the field."

WATSON, RONALD MACGREGOR, Capt., was born 30 June, 1887, son of Colonel R. S. Watson, of Leigh Grove, Surbiton. He was commissioned in the 2nd Battn. The Royal Dublin Fusiliers 4 May, 1907; became Lieutenant 18 Dec. 1909; was Adjutant, Royal Dublin Fusiliers, 12 Feb. 1913, to 2 Jan. 1916; became Captain 5 Aug. 1914. He served in the European War, as Staff Captain, 10th Infantry Brigade, B.E.F., 3 Jan. to 31 March, 1916; as Brigade Major, 98th Infantry Brigade, B.E.F., British Armies in France, 1 April, 1916, to 5 July, 1917; as G.S.O.2, 21st Division, British Armies in France, 6 July, 1917, to 16 March, 1918; as G.S.O.2, 6th Army Corps, British Armies in France, from 17 March, 1918. He was mentioned in Despatches; given the Brevet of Major 1 Jan. 1917, and was created a Companion of the Distinguished Service Order [London Gazette, 18 Feb. 1915]: "Ronald Macgregor Watson, Capt., Royal Dublin Fusiliers." Major Watson married, in 1918, Irene Gertrude Hallett (who died in 1919), youngest daughter of George Wood, of Woodlands, Gravesend.

His D.S.O. was awarded "for services in connection with operations in the field."

SALMON, GEOFFREY NOWELL, Major, was born at Naples 26 Nov. 1871, son of the late Admiral of the Fleet Sir Nowell Salmon, V.C., G.C.B., and Emily Augusta, daughter of the late Erasmus Saunders, of West-

Geoffrey Nowell Salmon.

brook, Upwey, Dorset. He was educated at Sherborne, and joined the Army, from the Militia, 2 June, 1894, as a Second Lieutenant in the Rifle Brigade, in which he was promoted Lieutenant 26 May, 1897, and Captain 31 Aug. 1900. He served in the South African War, 1899–1902, with the 1st Mounted Infantry, from 23 Nov. 1900, to 31 Dec. 1901, as Assistant Provost-Marshal, and from 1 Jan. 1901, to 31 Aug. 1902, employed under the Director of Military Intelligence. He took part in the Relief of Kimberley; operations in the Orange Free State, Feb. to May, 1900, including operations at Paardeberg (17 to 26 Feb.), actions at Poplar Grove and Dreifontein; operations in the Orange River Colony, May to 29 Nov. 1900; operations in Cape Colony, Jan. 1901, to 31 May 1902. He was mentioned in Despatches [London Gazette, 29 July, 1902] and received the Queen's South African Medal with three clasps, and the King's Medal with two clasps. Capt. Salmon was employed as Adjutant and Commandant, Mounted Infantry, Malta, 12 Sept. 1904, to 1 Jan. 1906, and was Second-in-Command of the 5th Mounted Infantry Battn. in South Africa 13 Oct. 1906, to 12 Oct. 1910. He became Major 3 July, 1912, and subsequently commanded three battalions of Mounted Infantry at Longmoor successively. He saw active service in the European War, with the 1st Battn. Rifle Brigade, Aug. to Dec. 1914, and was created a Companion of the Distinguished Service Order [London Gazette, 18 Feb. 1915]: "Geoffrey Nowell Salmon, Major, Rifle Brigade." He was promoted Lieutenant-Colonel 28 Sept. 1915, and commanded the 4th Battn. Rifle Brigade in Salonika from Dec. 1915, to May, 1917. From Feb. 1918, to the Armistice he was attached to the American Expeditionary Force, receiving for his service the American Distinguished Service Medal. He was four times mentioned in Despatches, and was created a C.M.G. 1 Jan. 1918. Lieut.-Colonel Salmon married, at Malta, 3 March, 1917, Gwladys Mary, eldest daughter of Mrs. Francis Lawson, of Pietà, Malta. His D.S.O. was awarded "for services in connection with operations in the field."

HAIG, ROLAND CHARLES, Major, was born in Kensington, London, W., 1 Feb. 1873, only son of Charles Edward Haig, M.A., of Pen-Ithon, Radnorshire, and Janet Stein Haig, of Cameron House, Windygate, Fife,

Roland Charles Haig.

N.B. He was educated at Winchester College, and at Sandhurst, from which he joined the Army 14 Nov. 1894, with a commission in the 16th Lancers. He was promoted Captain, 7th Dragoon Guards, in 1900, and served in the South African War in 1900, taking part in operations in the Orange Free State, April to May, 1900, including the action at Zand River; operations in the Transvaal, May and June, 1900, including the actions near Johannesburg, Pretoria and Diamond Hill (11 and 12 June); operations in Cape Colony, south of Orange River, March, 1900. He was awarded the Queen's Medal with clasps for "Cape Colony," "Orange River Colony," "Johannesburg" and "Diamond Hill." He retired from the 7th Dragoon Guards 10 Oct. 1903, and was

appointed Captain, 7th Battn. Rifle Brigade, Special Reserve, April, 1907. Becoming Major, 6th Rifle Brigade, 5 Aug. 1914, he proceeded to France, and served right through the European War up to July, 1918, with the exception of Aug. to Oct. 1917, when he was home wounded. He was Second-in-Command, 2nd South Staffordshire Regt., 1 Jan. to April, 1915, He was Second-in-Command of the 2nd Battn. Rifle Brigade, April and May, 1915; O.C. a Division of Mounted troops, May, 1915, to May, 1916; Major commanding 3rd Corps, Cyclist Regt., June, 1916; Lieutenant-Colonel commanding the 2nd Battn. Berkshire Regt., July, 1916, to July, 1917. From Nov. 1917, to June, 1918, he was Temporary Brigadier-General in command of the 24th Infantry Brigade, and was gassed at Berry-au-Bac. He received the Brevet of Lieutenant-Colonel, and was mentioned in Despatches six times; is now Temporary Brigadier-General commanding No. 1 Sub-District, Midland District, Irish Command. He was created a Companion of the Distinguished Service Order [London Gazette, 18 Feb. 1915]: "Roland Charles Haig, Major, 6th Rifle Brigade, attached to 1st King's Royal Rifles." He was awarded a Bar to the Distinguished Service Order: Direct reward for services on 4 March, 1917. He was awarded a Second Bar to the Distinguished Service Order: Direct reward for services in Somme Retreat, March, 1918. His D.S.O. was awarded "for services in connection with operations in the field."

HARGREAVES, ALAN KNYVETON, Capt., entered the Rifle Brigade 11 Aug. 1900; became Lieutenant 15 Jan. 1902, and Captain 24 March, 1910. He served in the South African War, 1902: took part in the operations in Orange River Colony, Jan. to 31 May, 1902; also in Cape Colony, Jan. 1902 (Queen's Medal with three clasps). Capt. Hargreaves served in the European War from 1914, and was created a Companion of the Distinguished Service Order [London Gazette, 18 Feb. 1915]: "Alan Hargreaves, Capt.,

The Rifle Brigade (The Prince Consort's Own). For services in connection with operations in the field." He was killed in action 9 May, 1915.

LIDDELL, GEOFFREY WILLIAM, Capt., was born 23 Nov. 1884, only surviving son of the late Edward Henry Liddell. He was educated at Eton, and at the Royal Military College, Sandhurst, and was commissioned in the Rifle Brigade (The Prince Consort's Own) 4 June, 1904, in which he became Lieutenant 3 Oct. 1907, and Captain 21 Sept. 1913. He served as Adjutant of the Rifle Brigade from 17 July, 1912, to 16 July, 1915. Capt. Liddell saw active service in the European War from 1914. He was created a Companion of the Distinguished Service Order [London Gazette, 18 Feb. 1915]: "Geoffrey William Liddell, Capt., 1st Battn. The Rifle Brigade (The Prince Consort's Own)." He was G.S.O.3, 69th Division, Central Force, Home Defence, 29 Sept. to 10 Dec. 1915; Officer and Commander of a Company of Gentleman Cadets, Royal Military College, Sandhurst, 11 Dec. 1915, to 6 May, 1918; became Acting Major of a Service Battn. of the Rifle Brigade 8 June, 1918, and Temporary Lieutenant-Colonel, Rifle Brigade, 17 Sept. 1918. He was given the Brevet of Major 3 June, 1919. He married, in 1915, Mary Sophia, daughter of the late Charles Lyon Liddell, and they have one son and one daughter. His D.S.O. was awarded "for services in connection with operations in the field."

RILEY, HAMLET LEWTHWAITE, Capt., was born 20 Oct. 1882, son of Hamlet Riley and Anne, his wife, eldest daughter of the late William Lewthwaite. He was educated at Eton, and at Magdalen College, Oxford. He was commissioned in the Rifle Brigade (The Prince Consort's Own) 3 March, 1906, in which he was promoted Lieutenant 9 Feb. 1910, and served as Adjutant in India 21 Feb. 1910, to 20 Feb. 1914. He saw active service in the European War, being promoted Captain the day after the outbreak of war. He was created a Companion of the Distinguished Service Order [London Gazette, 18 Feb. 1915]: "Hamlet Lewthwaite Riley, Capt., The Rifle Brigade (The Prince Consort's Own)." He served as Staff Captain, 25th Infantry Brigade, in France, Sept. and Oct. 1915; was Temporary Major of the 12th (Service) Battn. of the Rifle Brigade, Oct. 1915, to June, 1916; and was awarded the Montenegrin Order of Danilo, 4th Class, in 1916, and promoted Brevet Major 2 June, 1916. He was Temporary Lieutenant-Colonel commanding the 12th Service Battn. of his regiment, June, 1916, to Dec. 1917, and was then appointed Temporary Lieutenant-Colonel in the Machine Gun Corps; commanded the 20th Battn. 1918–19. He was three times wounded, and five times mentioned in Despatches. His D.S.O. was awarded "for services in connection with operations in the field."

LONGMORE, JOHN CONSTANTINE GORDON, Lieut.-Colonel, was born 8 Aug. 1870, son of Surgeon-General Sir Thomas Longmore, C.B., and Lady Longmore. He was educated at Westward Ho! and was commissioned in the East Lancashire Regt., from the Militia, 9 April, 1892. He was promoted Lieutenant 23 Sept. 1893, and was transferred on 1 Oct. of that year to the Army Service Corps, in which he became Captain 1 April, 1898. Capt. Longmore served in the South African War, 1899–1901, on the Staff, being employed from 10 June, 1901, to 23 Feb. 1902, as D.A.A.G. He was present in the advance on Kimberley, including actions at Belmont and Modder River; operations in Orange River Colony, May to 29 Nov. 1900, and operations in Orange River Colony 30 Nov. 1900, to Dec. 1901, and received the Queen's Medal with five clasps. He was promoted Major 28 Oct. 1904; was employed as Deputy Assistant Director Supplies and Transport, Southern Command, 1 April, 1910, to 14 Feb. 1913, and became Lieutenant-Colonel 15 Feb. 1913. He served in the European War from Aug. 1914, continuously. He was with the 3rd Division until 9 Oct. 1914, and was A.A. and Q.M.G. of the Cavalry Corps from 10 Oct. 1914, to 30 Oct. 1915. He was mentioned in Despatches [London Gazette, 9 Dec. 1914], and created a Companion of the Distinguished Service Order [London Gazette, 18 Feb. 1915]: "John Constantine Gordon Longmore, Lieut.-Colonel, Army Service Corps." He was again mentioned in Despatches [London Gazette, 22 June, 1915], and from 30 Oct. 1915, to 8 March, 1916, was D.A.Q.M.G. (Temporary Brigadier-General), Cavalry Corps, receiving another mention in Despatches 1 Jan. 1916. He was D.A.Q.M.G., 8th Corps, 9 March to 3 Sept. 1916, and D.A. and Q.M.G., Cavalry Corps, 4 Sept. 1916, to 1 April, 1919. He was mentioned again in Despatches [London Gazette, 4 Jan. 1917], and created a C.M.G., 1915; was promoted Colonel, Feb. 1917; given the Gold Order of Merit of Montenegro, March, 1917, and created a C.B.E. in 1919. He married, in 1897, Nita, daughter of the late Thomas Davis. His D.S.O. was awarded "for services in connection with operations in the field."

MASTER, ARTHUR GILBERT, Lieut.-Colonel, was born in Inverness Terrace, London, W., 6 June, 1867, fourth son of Charles Gilbert Master, C.S.I. and Emma Caroline, eldest daughter of Thomas Onslow, Esq., Madras Civil Service. He was educated at Clifton College, and at Exeter College, Oxford, taking the degrees B.A. (1889) and M.A. (1906). He obtained his first commission in the West India Regt. 4 March, 1891; was promoted Lieutenant 5 April, 1893; transferred to the Army Service Corps 1 Oct. 1893, and became Captain 1 April, 1898. Capt. Master took part in the South African War, 1899 to 1902, serving as D.A.A.G. from 17 Jan. to 14 Dec. 1902. He was present in the advance on Kimberley, including action at Belmont, Enslin, Modder River and Magersfontein; operations in the Orange Free State, 1900; operations in the Transvaal, west of Pretoria, 1900, including action at Frederickstad (17 to 25 Oct.); operations in Orange River Colony, 1900, including actions at Wittebergen (1 to 29 July); operations in the Transvaal 30 Nov. 1900, to Jan. 1902; operations in the Orange River Colony, Jan. to 31 May, 1902, and for his services was awarded the Queen's Medal with four clasps, and the King's Medal with two clasps. He attained his Majority 21 Sept. 1904, and was promoted Lieutenant-Colonel 26 Sept. 1913. He saw active service in the European War from 1914 to 1918; was mentioned in Despatches in Oct. 1914, and Jan. 1918, and was created a Companion of the Distinguished Service Order [London Gazette, 18 Feb. 1915]: "Arthur Gilbert Master,

Lieut.-Colonel, Army Service Corps." He retired from the Service 6 May, 1919. He married, at Fulford, York, 7 Oct. 1897, Elizabeth, second daughter of Edward Hotham Newton, J.P., D.L., of Fulford Park, York, and they have one son, Edward Streynsham, born 29 Jan. 1900, and two daughters: Audrey Margaret, born 5 Oct. 1898, and Hilary Elizabeth, born 15 Aug. 1905. His D.S.O. was awarded "for services in connection with operations in the field."

BURRARD, HARRY GEORGE, Lieut.-Colonel, was born 18 April, 1871, fourth son of the late Sidney Burrard. He was commissioned in the Lancashire Fusiliers, from the Militia, 9 Sept. 1893, from which he transferred to the Army Service Corps 1 April, 1895. He became Lieutenant 29 March, 1896. He served in West Africa, 1897–98 [Medal with clasp), and was employed on the Gold Coast, 1898–99. He was promoted Captain 1 April, 1900, and served in the South African War, 1899–1902, taking part in operations in Natal in 1899; operations in the Transvaal, May and June, 1900; operations in the Transvaal and Orange River Colony, June, 1901, to May, 1902; operations on the Zululand Frontier of Natal, Sept. and Oct. 1901 (Despatches [London Gazette, 8 Feb. 1901]; Queen's Medal with three clasps, and King's Medal with two clasps). He became Major 26 Sept. 1908. Major Burrard again saw active service in the European War from 1914 to 1918, with the Army Service Corps in France. He was promoted Lieutenant-Colonel 12 Dec. 1914. For his services he was mentioned in Despatches, and created a Companion of the Distinguished Service Order [London Gazette, 18 Feb. 1915]: "Harry George Burrard, Lieut.-Colonel, Army Service Corps." He was given the Brevet of Colonel 3 June, 1918, and was appointed A.D.C. to His Majesty the King 3 June, 1918. His D.S.O. was awarded "for services in connection with operations in the field."

STEWART, HERBERT ARTHUR, Major, was born 18 May, 1878, son of Arthur Stewart, of Rusher Road, Horsham, and Ellen Margaret Emma Stewart. He was educated at Portsmouth Grammar School, and was commissioned from the Militia 4 Jan. 1899, in the Suffolk Regt., from which he was transferred to the Army Service Corps 12 Feb. 1900, and was promoted Lieutenant 12 Feb. 1901, and Captain, Army Service Corps, 27 Aug. 1902. Capt. Stewart served in the South African War, 1899–1902, and was present in operations in the Transvaal, Nov. 1900, to 31 May, 1902; operations in the Orange River Colony, May, 1901; operations in the Cape Colony, Aug. 1901, and May, 1902. He received the Queen's Medal with three clasps, and the King's Medal with two clasps. He was Adjutant, Territorial Force, 1 Aug. 1911, to 31 July, 1914. He again saw active service in the European War from Aug. 1914, to the conclusion of hostilities, becoming Major the day war broke out. He was one of the very few British officers who entered Mons on Sunday, 23 Aug. 1914. For his services with the 3rd Division during the First Battles of Neuve Chapelle and Ypres in Oct. and Nov. 1914, he was created a Companion of the Distinguished Service Order [London Gazette, 18 Feb. 1915]: "Herbert Arthur Stewart, Major, Army Service Corps." He was employed with the 1st Army as Deputy Assistant Director of Supplies from Feb. 1915, until 25 Feb. 1916, when he was promoted Temporary Lieutenant-Colonel, and was Assistant Director of Supplies, Lines of Communication, France, from 1916 to 1918. He was awarded the O.B.E. in 1919. He is the author of "From Mons to Loos" (1916). He was a Member of the Regimental Polo Team, and also represented his regiment in Association and Rugby Football, and was a keen rider to hounds. Major H. A. Stewart married, in 1907, Janet Bertha, daughter of F. M. Passow, and they have three sons. His D.S.O. was awarded "for services in connection with operations in the field."

HARDING, GEORGE, Major, was born 28 Aug. 1877, eldest son of the late Henry J. Harding, of Nore View, Mountrath, Ireland. He was educated privately, and was commissioned in the Leinster Regt., from the Militia, 21 April, 1900, from which he was transferred to the Army Service Corps 1 May, 1901, and became Lieutenant 1 May, 1902. He served in the South African War, 1899 to 1902, being appointed to the Staff and employed as Transport Officer from 11 April, 1900, to 30 April, 1902. He took part in operations in the Orange Free State, Feb. to May, 1900, including actions at Karee Siding, Vet River (5 and 6 May) and Zand River; operations in the Transvaal, May and June, 1900, including actions near Johannesburg, Pretoria and Diamond Hill (11 and 12 June); operations in the Transvaal, east of Pretoria, July to 29 Nov. 1900, including actions at Reit Vlei and Belfast (26 and 27 Aug.); operations in the Transvaal, west of Pretoria, July to 29 Nov. 1900, including actions at Frederickstad (17 to 25 Oct); operations in Orange River Colony (May to 29 Nov. 1900); operations in Cape Colony, south of Orange River, 1899–1900. For his services he was mentioned in Despatches [London Gazette, 10 Sept. 1901], and was awarded the Queen's Medal with four clasps, and the King's Medal with two clasps. He attained his Captaincy 1 Nov. 1905, and his Majority 30 Oct. 1914. Major Harding saw active service in the European War, with the 5th Division, from 1914 to 1916, and was present at the Retreat from Mons and the advance to the Aisne, including the Battle of the Marne. He then served in Flanders, including the battles at La Bassée, Festubert, Neuve Eglise, and the First and Second Battles of Ypres. In Oct. 1915, he proceeded with the First Military Mission to Italy and Sicily, and returned invalided to England in May, 1916. He was mentioned in Despatches, and created a Companion of the Distinguished Service Order [London Gazette, 18 Feb. 1915]. He held the temporary appointment of Deputy Assistant Director of Supplies and Transport, Aldershot Command, from 9 March, 1917, to 30 April, 1918, when he was promoted Acting Lieutenant-Colonel. He held the appointment of Assistant Director of Supplies and Transport, Scottish Command, from 4 Oct. 1918, to 9 Nov. 1919. He was awarded the 1914 (Mons) Star, the General Service Medal and the Allies Medal. His favourite recreations are shooting, fishing and golf. Major Harding married, in 1911, Hope, eldest daughter of Sir William Quartus Ewart, Bart., J.P. and D.L. of Glenmachan, Strandtown, Belfast, and they have two sons: George William Cecil, born July, 1916, and Henry Christian, born Dec. 1919. The London Gazette notice of his D.S.O. is: "George Harding, Major, Army Service Corps. For services in connection with operations in the field."

BEARNE, LEWIS COLLINGWOOD, Major, was born 5 April, 1878, son of the late Lieut.-Colonel L. E. and Mrs. Bearne. He was educated at Newton College, and served in the South African War, 1900–2, at first with Lumsden's Horse, then with a commission attached to the Regulars. Subsequently he became Second Lieutenant in the Duke of Cornwall's Light Infantry 27 July, 1901, and was transferred, 1 Oct. 1902, to the Army Service Corps, to which he had been attached up till Aug. 1901. He took part in operations in the Orange Free State, Feb. to May, 1900, including actions at Karee Siding, Vet River (5 and 6 May) and Zand River; operations in the Transvaal, May and June, 1900, including action near Johannesburg and Pretoria; operations in the Transvaal 30 Nov. 1900, to Feb. 1901, and Sept. 1901, to 31 May, 1902; operations in Cape Colony, Feb. to Aug. 1901. He received for his services the Queen's Medal with three clasps, and the King's Medal with two clasps, and was for a period a prisoner in the Boers' hands. He became Lieutenant, A.S.C., 27 July, 1904; Captain 1 Jan. 1911, and Major 30 Oct. 1914. Major Bearne again saw active service in the European War from 1914. He was created a Companion of the Distinguished Service Order [London Gazette, 18 Feb. 1915]: "Lewis Collingwood Bearne, Major, Army Service Corps." He was Temporary Lieutenant-Colonel from July to Nov. 1916. On 22 Oct. of that year he (with Private A. E. Usher) gained the Albert Medal in recognition of his gallantry in saving life. The official account reads: "On 22 Oct. 1916, a French motor lorry, loaded with 3,000 lbs. of aeroplane bombs, caught fire in the middle of a camp of the Serbian Army. Efforts to beat out the flames proved ineffectual, and after the fire had been burning for seven or eight minutes, and the bomb cases were already involved, Major Bearne and Usher ran up with extinguishers. Both immediately crawled underneath the lorry, and eventually succeeded in extinguishing the flames, thus averting a serious disaster at the risk of their own lives. Major Bearne was severely burnt about the head and arms." His D.S.O. was awarded "for services in connection with operations in the field."

BATEMAN, HERBERT RAYMOND, Major, was born 28 Oct. 1876, son of the late Colonel D. F. Bateman, I.M.S. He was educated at a private school; in H.M.S. Conway, and finally at St. Thomas's Hospital; entered the Army, 29 Nov. 1900, as a Lieutenant in the Royal Army Medical Corps, in which he became Captain 29 Nov. 1903. He served from 1908 to 1910 as a member of the Uganda Sleeping Sickness Commission of the Royal Society, and was promoted Major 29 Aug. 1912. He served in the European War from Aug. 1914, to the Armistice. He was created a Companion of the Distinguished Service Order [London Gazette, 18 Feb. 1915]: "Herbert Raymond Bateman, Major, Royal Army Medical Corps." He was Acting Lieutenant-Colonel, Royal Army Medical Corps, from 15 May, 1917, until promoted to substantive rank 10 Oct. 1918. After the war he became Acting Colonel and A.D.M.S., 38th Division in France, in Feb. 1919, and reverted to Lieutenant-Colonel on vacating the appointment in April, 1919. His D.S.O. was awarded "for services in connection with operations in the field."

EVANS, CHARLES ROBERT, Major, was born 14 March, 1873. He entered the Royal Army Medical Corps 4 Dec. 1899, and served in the South African War, taking part in the operations in the Orange Free State and Cape Colony, Feb. to April, 1900, and receiving the Queen's Medal with two clasps. He was promoted Captain 4 Dec. 1902, and Major 4 June, 1911. Major Evans again saw active service in the European War, 1914–16. He was Temporary Lieutenant-Colonel from 13 Oct. 1914, to 28 Feb. 1915. He was created a Companion of the Distinguished Service Order [London Gazette, 18 Feb. 1915]: "Charles Robert Evans, Major, Royal Army Medical Corps." He became Lieutenant-Colonel 1 March, 1915; promoted Acting Colonel, May, 1918, and Colonel 3 June, 1919. He was mentioned in Despatches. His D.S.O. was awarded "for services in connection with operations in the field."

GOODBODY, CECIL MAURICE, Major, was born 12 Nov. 1874, son of W. R. Goodbody, of Tullamore, King's County, and of Emily Davis, of Langport, Somerset. He was educated at Merchant Taylors'; Whitgift, and St. Thomas's Hospital, and joined the Indian Medical Service, as Lieutenant, 27 Jan. 1900, and served on the North-West Frontier of India in Waziristan, 1901 and 1902, receiving the Medal and clasp. He became Captain 27 Jan. 1903, and Major 27 July, 1911. He served in the European War from 1914 to 1918; was present with the Indian Corps, 1914 to 1915. He was created a Companion of the Distinguished Service Order [London Gazette, 18 Feb. 1915]: "Cecil Maurice Goodbody, Major, Indian Medical Service." He was employed as A.D.M.S., Advanced Section, Lines of Communication, Mesopotamian Expeditionary Force, until 4 Feb. 1919. He was given the Brevet of Lieutenant-Colonel 3 June, 1916, and of Colonel 1 Jan. 1919; was mentioned in Despatches, and in 1918 was made a C.I.E. Colonel C. M. Goodbody married, in Sept. 1902, Edith Isabel, daughter of the late Alexander Saunderson, of Oakhill Park, Liverpool. His D.S.O. was awarded "for services in connection with operations in the field."

HARRISON, LAWRENCE WHITAKER, Major, was born 2 April, 1876, youngest son of the late Jonathan A. Harrison, M.D., J.P., of Haslingden, Lancashire. He was educated at Manchester Grammar School and Glasgow University, graduating as M.B., Ch.B. in 1897, and entered

Lawrence W. Harrison.

the Royal Army Medical Corps, as Lieutenant, 17 Nov. 1899, and saw active service in the South African War, 1900–2, being present at the Relief of Ladysmith, including operations of 17 to 24 Jan. 1900, and the action at Spion Kop; operations of 5 to 7 Feb. 1900, and the action at Vaal Kranz; operations on Tugela Heights 14 to 27 Feb. 1900, and the action at Pieter's Hill; operations in Natal, March to June, 1900; operations in the Transvaal, east of Pretoria, July to 29 Nov. 1900, including actions at Belfast (26 and 27 Aug.); operations in the Transvaal, November, 1900, to 31 May, 1902. He was mentioned in Despatches [London Gazette, 29 July, 1902]; received the Queen's Medal with four clasps, and the King's Medal with two clasps. He became Captain 17 Nov. 1902, and Major 17 May, 1911. Colonel Harrison served in the European War from 1914 to 1918. He was created a Companion of the Distinguished Service Order [London Gazette, 18 Feb. 1915]: "Lawrence Whitaker Harrison, M.B., Major, Royal Army Medical Corps." He was promoted Lieutenant-Colonel 1 March, 1915, and was given the Brevet of Colonel 26 Dec. 1917, on becoming Honorary Physician to His Majesty the King. He was mentioned in Despatches, and has the Mons Star. Colonel Harrison is the author of articles on Surgery, Bacteriology and Hygiene. He has written 20 papers on subjects relating to the diagnosis and treatment of venereal diseases (1910–18); "The Diagnosis and Treatment of Venereal Diseases in General Practice" (1918); part author of "Gonococcal Infections;" "Manual of Venereal Diseases, by Officers of the Royal Army Medical Corps;" and "A System of Syphilis, by D'Arcy Power and J. Keogh Murphy" (papers on Microbiology, Serum Diagnosis and Treatment of Syphilis). He retired from the Army 17 Nov. 1919, and is now a Special Medical Officer in the Ministry of Health; Adviser in Venereal Diseases to the Ministry of Health, and Director of the Venereal Department, St. Thomas's Hospital, S.E.1. He married, 7 March, 1905, at St. Jude's Church, Kennington, S.E.1, Mabel Alice, youngest daughter of the late Colonel E. J. Fairland, A.M.S., and they have two sons: Gerald Fairland, born 4 Jan. 1906, and Douglas Edwin, born 16 Jan. 1910, and two daughters: Elizabeth Rosamund and Rosemary Julia Violet. His D.S.O. was awarded "for services in connection with operations in the field."

NORRINGTON, HENRY LAWRENCE WEEKES, Major, was born at Clifton, Bristol, 16 Aug. 1872, son of Frederick Norrington and Clara Terrell Weekes. He was educated at Clifton College, and became a Lieutenant in the Royal Army Medical Corps 28 July, 1897. He served in the Nile Expedition, 1898–99, receiving the Medal and the Egyptian Medal. He was promoted Captain 28 July, 1900, and Major 28 Jan. 1909; was present at the International Occupation of Scutari, Albania, in 1914. He served in the European War from 1914 to 1918, commanding No. 13 Stationary Hospital; No. 14 General Hospital, and with the 11th Division. He was mentioned in Despatches, and created a Companion of the Distinguished Service Order, for work as O.C., No. 13 Stationary Hospital at Boulogne, in 1914 and 1915 [London

Henry L. W. Norrington.

Gazette, 18 Feb. 1915]: "Henry Lawrence Weekes Norrington, Major, Royal Army Medical Corps." He was promoted Lieutenant-Colonel 1 March, 1915, and retired 16 April, 1919. Lieut.-Colonel H. L. W. Norrington married, in June, 1899, at Blacklands, Wiltshire, Ethel Victoria May, daughter of General James Morris Topping and Mrs. Topping, and their children are: Guy Stanley, R.N., born 3 May, 1900; Charles Patrick, born 31 Oct. 1901, and Sybil Beryl, born 18 Sept. 1902. His D.S.O. was awarded "for services in connection with operations in the field."

STEPHENS, FREDERICK ARCHER, Major, was born 5 Jan. 1872. He was educated at Sherborne, and King's College, London, for the medical profession. He joined the Royal Army Medical Corps, as a Lieutenant, 14 Nov. 1900, and served in the South African War as a Civil Surgeon. He was present in operations in Cape Colony, south of Orange River, July to 29 Nov. 1900; operations in the Transvaal, Dec. 1900, to 31 May, 1902; operations in Orange River Colony and Cape Colony, 30 Nov. 1900, to May, 1901. He received the Queen's Medal with three clasps, and the King's Medal with two clasps. Lieut. Stephens was promoted Captain 14 Nov. 1903; was a Territorial Adjutant 15 June, 1908, to 31 Oct. 1911; was promoted Major 14 Nov. 1912. He served in the European War with the original Expeditionary Force from 1914. He was mentioned in Despatches, and created a Companion of the Distinguished Service Order [London Gazette, 18 Feb. 1915]: "Frederick Archer Stephens, Major, Royal Army Medical Corps." He afterwards served with the Serbian and British Armies in Macedonia, and was Acting Lieutenant-Colonel from Sept. to Dec. 1918. His D.S.O. was awarded "for services in connection with operations in the field."

SYMONS, FRANK ALBERT, Major, was born in April, 1869, son of the late John Hughes Symons, of Halifax, Nova Scotia. He was educated for the medical profession; took the degrees of M.B., C.M.Edinburgh, 1891, and joined the Royal Army Medical Corps, as Captain, 30 Jan. 1896 (after three years' previous service). He served in the South African War from 1899 to 1900, and was present at the Relief of Ladysmith, including the action at Colenso; operations in the Orange Free State, Feb. to March, 1900; operations in Cape Colony, south of Orange River, 1899–1900 (Queen's Medal with three clasps). He became Major 30 Oct. 1904. Major Symons served in the European War from 1914 to 1917, leaving England for France as Commanding Officer of No. 1 Casualty Clearing Station. He was mentioned by Viscount French in his Despatches in Oct. 1914, and twice again later, and was created a Companion of the Distinguished Service Order [London Gazette, 18 Feb. 1915]: " Frank Albert Symons, Major, Royal Army Medical Corps." He was promoted Lieutenant-Colonel in March, 1915, and Temporary Colonel the following Nov. He was also created a C.M.G. Lieut.-Colonel Symons was subsequently appointed Assistant Director of Medical Services. He fell in action 30 April, 1917. He had married, in 1900, Dorothy, second daughter of the late Edmund Grove Bennett, of The Close, Salisbury. His D.S.O. was awarded " for services in connection with operations in the field."

CRAWFORD, VINCENT JAMES, Major, was born 28 March, 1877, third son of the late Sir Thomas Crawford, K.C.B., late Director-General, Army Medical Department, and Jane, daughter of Major-General Edwards, late 18th Royal Irish. He was educated at Guy's Hospital, and was commissioned Lieutenant in the Royal Army Medical Corps 27 July, 1899. He served in South Africa, 1900–2, taking part in operations in the Orange Free State, 1900 ; operations in Orange River Colony, 1900 ; operations in Cape Colony, south of Orange River (Queen's Medal and King's Medal with two clasps each). He was promoted Captain 27 July, 1902, and Major 28 Jan. 1911. He served in the European War from 1914 ; was mentioned in Despatches, and created a Companion of the Distinguished Service Order [London Gazette, 18 Feb. 1915]: " Vincent James Crawford, Major, Royal Army Medical Corps." He became Lieutenant-Colonel 1 March, 1915, and was again mentioned in Despatches 1 Jan. 1916. Lieut.-Colonel Crawford married (1st) on 8 Feb. 1903, Ethel Mercy (who died at sea 3 Jan. 1914), daughter of Mr. G. Beck, and (2ndly) 17 March, 1917, at Clones Parish Church, Eileen Kathleen, daughter of the late Samuel Kidd Jackson and Mrs. Jackson, of Cara, Clones, Ireland. His D.S.O. was awarded " for services in connection with operations in the field."

FOX, ARTHUR CLAUD, Major, was born 23 April, 1868, son of the late Lieut.-Colonel W. S. Fox, I.M.S., and Mrs. Fox, of 95, Dorset Road, Bexhill-on-Sea. He was educated at Hampstead, and studied at the London Hospital for the medical profession, gaining the degrees M.R.C.S. and L.R.C.P.London, 1891. He joined the Royal Army Medical Corps ; became Captain 29 Jan. 1897, and Major 29 Oct. 1905. He saw active service in the European War from 1914 ; was present at Ypres and Armentières. He was mentioned in Despatches, and created a Companion of the Distinguished Service Order [London Gazette, 18 Feb. 1915]: " Arthur Claud Fox, Major, Royal Army Medical Corps." He was gazetted Lieutenant-Colonel in March, 1915, and was reported missing, believed drowned, 15 April, 1917. His D.S.O. was awarded

Arthur Claud Fox.

" for services in connection with operations in the field."

ORMSBY, GILBERT JOHN ANTHONY, Major, was born 16 Sept. 1876, only son of Sir Lambert H. Ormsby, Kt., a well-known surgeon, and his wife, the late Anastatia, only daughter of John Dickenson. His father was Lieutenant-Colonel and Honorary Consulting Surgeon of the New Zealand Expeditionary Force. G. J. A. Ormsby received his first commission as Lieutenant in the Royal Army Medical Corps 28 Jan. 1899. He served in South Africa from 1899 to 1902 ; was present at the Relief of Ladysmith, including action at Colenso ; operations of 17 to 24 Jan. 1900, and action at Spion Kop ; operations of 5 to 7 Feb. 1900, and action at Vaal Kranz ; operations on Tugela Heights (14 to 27 Feb. 1900) and action at Pieter's Hill ; operations in Natal, March to June, 1900, including action at Laing's Nek (6 to 9 June) ; operations in the Transvaal, Nov. 1900, to May, 1902 (Queen's Medal with four clasps, and King's Medal with two clasps). He became Captain 28 Jan. 1902, and Major 28 Jan. 1911. He served in the European War, 1914–18. He was mentioned in Despatches, and created a Companion of the Distinguished Service Order [London Gazette, 18 Feb. 1915]: " Gilbert John Anthony Ormsby, M.D., Major, Royal Army Medical Corps." He became Lieutenant-Colonel 1 March, 1915, and was Temporary Colonel while serving as A.D.M.S. 12 July, 1917, to 30 May, 1918. He was given the Brevet of Colonel 3 June, 1918, and became A.D.M.S., 34th Division, British Armies in France (Acting Colonel), 13 Nov. 1918. Colonel Ormsby married, in 1904, Alice, daughter of George Pirie, and they have one son and one daughter. His D.S.O. was awarded " for services in connection with operations in the field."

RUTHERFORD, NATHANIEL JOHN. CRAWFORD, Major, was born 6 Nov. 1874. He was educated at Dublin ; entered the Royal Army Medical Corps 28 Jan. 1899, and served in South Africa, 1899–1902 ; was in the advance on Kimberley, including actions at Belmont, Enslin, Modder River and Magersfontein ; Relief of Kimberley ; operations in the Orange Free State, Feb. to May, 1900, including operations at Paardeberg (17 to 26 Feb.) ; actions at Poplar Grove, Dreifontein, Karee Siding, Vet River (5 and 6 May) and Zand River ; operations in the Transvaal, May and June, 1900, including action near Johannesburg ; operations in Orange River Colony, June and July, 1900, including action at Rhenoster River ; operations in the Transvaal 30 Nov. 1900, to June, 1901 ; operations in Cape Colony, June, 1901, to May, 1902 (Queen's Medal with six clasps, and King's Medal with two clasps). He became Captain 28 Jan. 1902, and Major 28 Jan. 1911. Major N. J. C. Rutherford served in the European War from 1914 to 1917. He was mentioned in Despatches, and created a Companion of the Distinguished Service Order [London Gazette, 18 Feb.

1915]: " Nathaniel John Crawford Rutherford, M.B., Major, Royal Army Medical Corps." He was promoted Lieutenant-Colonel 1 March, 1915, and was appointed D.A.D., Medical Service. His D.S.O. was awarded " for services in connection with operations in the field."

WILSON, HARRY THEODORE, Capt., was born 2 March, 1879, son of J. Minden Wilson. He was educated at Bedford School, and St. Bartholomew's Hospital ; joined the Royal Army Medical Corps, as Lieutenant, 30 July, 1904, and was promoted Captain 30 Jan. 1908. Capt. Wilson saw active service in the European War from 1914 to 1917 ; was mentioned in Despatches, and created a Companion of the Distinguished Service Order [London Gazette, 18 Feb. 1915]: " Harry Theodore Wilson, M.R.C.P., L.R.C.S., Capt., Royal Army Medical Corps." He was promoted Major 1 July, 1915 ; Temporary Lieutenant-Colonel 16 Nov. 1915 ; Acting Lieutenant-Colonel, Oct. 1915. He married, in 1906, Vivien, daughter of Colonel William Wylie Norman. His D.S.O. was awarded " for services in connection with operations in the field."

WALSHE, SARSFIELD JAMES AMBROSE HALL, Capt., was educated at Edinburgh University and Royal College of Surgeons for the medical profession, and took the degrees M.B. and Ch.B. When the European War broke out he was Captain in the R.A.M.C., Special Reserve. He was on active service from 1914 to 1915 ; was mentioned in Despatches, and also created a Companion of the Distinguished Service Order [London Gazette, 18 Feb. 1915]: " Sarsfield James Ambrose Hall Walshe, Capt., Royal Army Medical Corps." He became Captain in the R.A.M.C., Regular Army, 6 Feb. 1918. Capt. Walshe is the author of " The Effect on Mental State of Minor and Major Attacks in Epileptic Insanity " (1912). He held the appointment of House

Sarsfield J. A. H. Walshe.

Surgeon at Torbay Hospital. He is married, and has a son. His D.S.O. was awarded " for services in connection with operations in the field."

POTTS, EDMUND THURLOW, Capt., was born 8 June, 1878. He was educated at the University and Royal College of Surgeons, Edinburgh (M.D.), and was formerly Resident Medical Officer, Hospital for Sick Children, Newcastle ; Chalmers Hospital, Edinburgh, and the Infectious Diseases Hospital, Edinburgh. He entered the Army, as a Lieutenant in the Royal Army Medical Corps, 31 July, 1905 ; was promoted Captain 31 Jan. 1909. He served from 1914 to 1918 in the European War ; was mentioned in Despatches, and created a Companion of the Distinguished Service Order [London Gazette, 18 Feb. 1915]: " Edmund Thurlow Potts, M.D., Capt., Royal Army Medical Corps." Capt. Potts was promoted to Major 15 Oct. 1915, and was Temporary Lieutenant-Colonel 4 Nov. 1917, to 30 March, 1919, while employed as A.D.M.S., 4th Army, British Armies in France ; was created a C.M.G. in 1918. His D.S.O. was awarded " for services in connection with operations in the field."

SMITH, WILLIAM DUNLOP, Lieut.-Colonel, was born 14 Aug. 1865. He took part in the expedition to Dongola in 1896, as Special Service Officer, for which he was mentioned in Despatches [London Gazette, 3 Nov. 1896], and received the 4th Class Medjidieh and the Egyptian Medal ; also in the Nile Expedition of 1898, including the Battle of Khartoum, for which he was again mentioned in Despatches [London Gazette, 30 Sept. 1898], and received the Medal as well as a clasp to the Egyptian Medal. He served in the South African War from 1899 to 1902. He was a Special Service Officer (including service with the Bechuanaland Protectorate Regt.), and was present in operations in the Transvaal, June, 1900 ; operations in the Transvaal, east and west of Pretoria, July to 29 Nov. 1900, including action at

William Dunlop Smith.

Rhenoster Kop ; operations in Orange River Colony and Cape Colony ; operations in the Transvaal 30 Nov. 1900, to March, 1901 ; operations in the Orange River Colony, May, 1901, to 31 May, 1902 ; operations in Cape Colony, March to April, 1901. He was mentioned in Despatches [London Gazette, 10 Sept. 1901]; received the Queen's Medal with three clasps, and the King's Medal with two clasps, and for his services was promoted Veterinary Captain. He became Major 7 Jan. 1906 ; Lieutenant-Colonel 13 Oct. 1913 ; was A.D.V.S., Curragh, from 13 Oct. 1913, to 4 Aug. 1914. He served in the European War, as A.D.V.S., B.E.F., 5 Aug. 1914, to 5 Feb. 1915. For his services he was mentioned in Despatches, and created a Companion of the Distinguished Service Order [London Gazette, 18 Feb. 1915]: " William Dunlop Smith, Lieut.-Colonel, Royal Army Veterinary Corps." He was appointed A.D.V.S., 1st Army, B.E.F., 6 Feb. 1915 ; served as D.D.V.S., Lines of Communication, B.E.F., and British Armies in France, 29 Sept. 1915, to 13 Aug. 1916 ; became Temporary Colonel 4 Oct. 1916, on receiving the appointment of D.D.V.S., Indian Expeditionary Force " D " ; Temporary Brigadier-General, D.D.V.S., Mesopotamian Expeditionary Force, 5 Nov. 1917 ; Acting Colonel, D.D.V.S., 28 Sept. 1918. He was mentioned in Despatches, and was made a C.M.G. in 1917. His D.S.O. was awarded " for services in connection with operations in the field."

BURNS-LINDOW, ISAAC WILLIAM, Major, was born at Hazel Holme, Cumberland, 10 June, 1868, son of Jonas Lindow Burns-Lindow, Esq., J.P., D.L., of Irton Hall and Ehen Hall, Cumberland, and Mary (who died in 1904), eldest daughter of the late M. H. Quayle, of Crogga, Isle of Man. He was educated at Christ Church, Oxford, and received his first commission 9 Jan. 1892, in the 8th Hussars, in which he was promoted Captain 1 March, 1898. Capt. Burns-Lindow served in the South African War, 1900-1, and was severely wounded. He was present in operations in Cape Colony, 1900; operations in the Orange Free State, Feb. to May, 1900; operations in Orange River Colony, May, 1900; operations in the Transvaal, May to June, 1900, including actions near Johannesburg and Diamond Hill; operations in the Transvaal, including the action at Belfast (Queen's Medal with five clasps). He retired from the 8th Hussars 21 Dec. 1904, and in 1905 joined the South Irish Horse. He served in the European War from 1914 to 1916. He was mentioned in Despatches in Oct. 1914, and again when his Companionship of the Distinguished Service Order was gazetted, 18 Feb. 1915 : " I. W. Burns-Lindow, Major, South Irish Horse." He was also mentioned in Despatches in Feb. and June, 1916, and was promoted Temporary Lieutenant-Colonel, Cavalry Special Reserve. He is an M.F.H., South Union. He married, 11 Feb. 1896, at Ormesby, Norfolk, Madelaine Harriette Mary Theresa, daughter of Colonel George Wilson Boileau, of Old Catton, Norfolk, and Fanny E., daughter of General M. Kynnett. His D.S.O. was awarded " for services in connection with operations in the field."

KENNARD, WILLOUGHBY ARTHUR, Capt., was born 20 May, 1881. He joined the 13th Hussars 21 March, 1900, being promoted Lieutenant 22 Feb. 1902. He saw active service in South Africa from 1899 to 1902, during which he was present in operations in the Transvaal 30 Nov. 1900, to Sept. 1901; Oct. 1901, to April, 1902, and May, 1902; operations in Orange River Colony, April to May, 1902; operations on the Zululand Frontier of Natal in Sept. and Oct. 1901 (Queen's Medal with four clasps). He became Captain 13 Dec. 1906, and took an appointment as a Territorial Force Adjutant 9 April, 1912. Capt. Kennard served in the European War from 1914 to 1916. He was mentioned in Despatches, and created a Companion of the Distinguished Service Order [London Gazette, 18 Feb. 1915] : " Willoughby Arthur Kennard, Capt., 13th Hussars." He was severely wounded, and died in Oct. 1918. His D.S.O. was awarded " for services in connection with operations in the field."

WATT, ALEXANDER FITZGERALD, Major, was born 13 Nov. 1872, eldest son of the late Alexander Y. Watt and Georgina, his wife, of Cadogan Gardens, London, S.W. He was educated privately, and at Jesus College, Cambridge. He saw active service in the South African War in 1900, being present in operations in Orange River Colony, May to Aug. 1900, including actions at Wittebergen (1 to 29 July) (Queen's Medal with three clasps). He was A.D.C. to the Inspector-General of the Forces, 1907-12, and Private Secretary to the Chief of the Imperial General Staff, 1912-14. He served in the European War as A.D.C. to the Commander-in-Chief, British Armies in France; was twice mentioned in Despatches; enrolled as a Knight of the Legion of Honour, and was created a Companion of the Distinguished Service Order [London Gazette, 18 Feb.

Alexander Fitzgerald Watt.

1915] : " Alexander Fitzgerald Watt, Major, Staff A.D.C. to the Field-Marshal Commander in-Chief, British Armies in the Field." Major Watt was given the Brevet of Lieutenant-Colonel in Dec. 1915. He was employed as A.D.C. to the Commander-in-Chief, Home Forces, 1916-18, and was appointed Comptroller of the Household, Viceregal Lodge, Dublin, in 1918; appointed Hon. Attaché to His Britannic Majesty's Legation in Vienna, 1920. Lieut.-Colonel Watt's regiment is the Yorkshire Hussars (Yeomanry). His favourite recreations are hunting, shooting, fishing and motoring. He is patron of one living. He married, in Oct. 1903, Georgina, only child of the late Augustine Robert Whiteway, Barrister-at-Law, of Hemingford Grey, Hunts, and they have one daughter. His D.S.O. was awarded " for services in connection with operations in the field."

DUNDAS, PATRICK HENRY, Major, was born 17 Oct. 1871, in Calcutta, son of Donald William Dundas, of the Bengal Police. He was educated at Denstone, and joined the Army, as a Second Lieutenant on the Unattached List, 3 Sept. 1892, being appointed to the Indian Staff Corps 5 Jan. 1894. He was promoted Lieutenant 3 Dec. 1894; served on the North-West Frontier of India, Tochi, 1897-98 (Medal with clasp), and in China, 1900 (Medal). He was promoted Captain, India, 3 Sept. 1901; was Staff Captain, India, to 31 Jan. 1909; Brigade-Major, India, 1 Feb. 1909, to 8 June, 1911; was promoted Major 3 Sept. 1910. He served in the European War; was mentioned in Despatches, and created a Companion of the Distinguished Service Order [London Gazette, 18 Feb. 1915] : " Patrick Henry Dundas, Major, Indian Army." He was Brigade-Major, 47th Infantry Brigade, New Armies, British Expeditionary Force, 3 July, 1915, to 16 March, 1916. He was mentioned in Despatches in Feb. 1916; was given the Brevet of Lieutenant-Colonel 3 June, 1917; was Acting Lieutenant-Colonel from 11 July, 1917, to 2 Sept. 1918; promoted Lieutenant-Colonel 3 Sept. 1918; appointed Administrator Commandant, Euphrates Section, Lines of Communication, Mesopotamian Expeditionary Force, 24 Feb. 1918. His regiment is the 6th Jat Light Infantry. He was given an O.B.E. in 1919. His D.S.O. was awarded " for services in connection with operations in the field."

DAVIDSON-HOUSTON,

C. E. D. Davidson-Houston.

CHARLES ELRINGTON DUNCAN, Major, was born 21 Jan. 1873, son of the late Rev. B. C. Davidson-Houston, M.A., Rector of St. John's, Dublin. He was commissioned Second Lieutenant on the Unattached List 28 June, 1893, and joined the Indian Staff Corps 28 Sept. 1895. He served in three campaigns on the North-West Frontier of India, viz. : 1897-98 (Tochi) (Medal and clasp); 1901-2 (Waziristan) (clasp); 1902, operations against the Darwesh Khel Waziris, in which he was slightly wounded. He was promoted Captain, Indian Army, 28 June, 1902, and Major 28 June, 1911. He served in the European War, receiving the temporary rank of Lieutenant-Colonel 3 Nov. 1914. He was mentioned in Despatches, and created a Companion of the Distinguished Service Order [London Gazette, 18 Feb. 1915] : " Charles Elrington Duncan Davidson-Houston, Major, Indian Army." He fell in action 25 Sept. 1915, near Neuve Chapelle. His D.S.O. was awarded " for services in connection with operations in the field."

NORIE, FRANK HAY, Major, was born in Madras, India, 8 March, 1870, son of the late Major-General Evelyn Medows Norie, Indian Staff Corps, and Anne Katherine (Edwards), his wife. He was educated at Fettes College; joined the 1st Hampshire Regt. 4 March, 1891, and was transferred in 1895 to the 42nd Gurkhas. He first saw active service as Assistant Commandant of the Apa Tanang Expedition in 1896, being mentioned in Despatches. He became Captain, 6th Gurkhas, in 1901; served in the Zakka Khel Expedition in 1908, and in the Mohmund Expedition in the same year; was promoted Major 4 March, 1909, and retired from the Service 4 March, 1912. On the outbreak of the European War he volunteered for active service, and accompanied the British Expeditionary Force to France, where he was attached to the 2nd King

Frank Hay Norie.

Edward's Own Gurkhas. He was severely wounded at Neuve Chapelle 2 Nov. 1914, and for gallantry in this action was created a Companion of the Distinguished Service Order [London Gazette, 18 Feb. 1915] : " Frank Hay Norie, Major, attached 2nd King Edward's Own Gurkhas." Major Norie served throughout the European War. He married, at Edgbaston, 26 July, 1908, Rachel Eveline, daughter of John and Frederica Sanders, and they have one daughter, Kathleen Mary, born 18 Jan. 1910. His D.S.O. was awarded " for services in connection with operations in the field."

London Gazette, 10 March, 1915.—" War Office, 10 March, 1915. His Majesty the King has been graciously pleased to approve of the appointment of the undermentioned Officers to be Companions of the Distinguished Service Order, in recognition of their gallantry whilst serving with the Expeditionary Force."

MACNAGHTEN, ERNEST BRANDER, Major and Brevet Lieut.-Colonel, was born 11 Sept. 1872, son of the late Colonel W. H. Macnaghten, C.B., and Alice Ellen, daughter of Lieut.-General M. J. Brander, I.S.C.

Ernest B. Macnaghten.

He entered the Royal Artillery, as a Second Lieutenant, 9 Nov. 1892, and became Lieutenant 9 Nov. 1895. He was employed with the West African Frontier Force 16 Feb. 1898, to 21 March, 1900, serving with the expedition to Dama (Medal with clasp). He again saw active service in South Africa, 1899-1902. He became Captain 18 April, 1900, and was on Special Service with the Rhodesian Field Force 24 April, 1900, to 14 April, 1901; was present in operations in Rhodesia 11 Oct. 1899, to 25 April, 1900; operations in the Transvaal, west of Pretoria, July to 29 Nov. 1900; operations in the Transvaal and Orange River Colony 30 Nov. 1900, to 31 May, 1902 (Queen's Medal with four clasps, and King's Medal with two clasps). From 16 Jan. 1903, to 17 June, 1904, he was Transport Officer with the Somaliland Field Force, and commanded the 2nd Somali Camel Corps from 16 July, 1903, receiving for his services in the Somaliland operations mention in Despatches by Brigadier-General Manning 17 Aug. 1903; by Sir G. C. Egerton 30 May, 1904, and in the London Gazette of 2 Sept. 1904 (Medal and clasp). Serving in 1906 in Northern Nigeria, he was again mentioned in Despatches [London Gazette, 2 July, 1907]. Capt. Macnaghten was Brigade Major, Royal Artillery, India, 18 Dec. 1909; received promotion to Major 18 Dec. 1909; was employed as Instructor, School of Gunnery, 1 Oct. 1912, to 31 March, 1913, and Major Instructor, School of Gunnery, 1 April, 1913, to 4 Aug. 1914. He served with distinction in the European War, 1914-18. He was mentioned in Despatches; was given the Brevet of Lieutenant-Colonel

18 Feb. 1915, and was created a Companion of the Distinguished Service Order [London Gazette, 10 March, 1915]: "Ernest Brander Macnaghten, Major and Brevet Lieut.-Colonel, 30th Battn. Royal Field Artillery. For conspicuous gallantry and ability on 25 Jan. 1915, during the attack by Germans on the village of Givenchy. Whilst exposed to very heavy fire he obtained valuable information as to the enemy's position." From 27 Feb. to 3 April, 1915, he was Brigade Major, Royal Artillery, 1st Army, B.E.F.; from 4 April to 17 Aug. 1915, G.S.O.2 (Staff Officer to Major-General, Royal Artillery, 1st Army), British Armies in France. He was promoted Lieutenant-Colonel 5 Oct. 1915, and held the temporary rank of Brigadier-General 24 April, 1916, to 23 April, 1919, commanding Royal Artillery 15th Division, British Armies in France, 24 April, 1916, to 7 Oct. 1918, and the 12th Infantry Brigade, British Armies in France, 8 Oct. 1918, to 23 April, 1919. He was created a C.M.G. in 1917, and was given the Brevet of Colonel 1 Jan. 1918. He married, in 1906, Yvonne Marie, daughter of the late Surgeon Colonel J. A. Forester, Royal Horse Guards, and they have one son and four daughters.

W. H. Macalpine-Leny.

MACALPINE-LENY, WILLIAM HARLEY, Major, was born at Dalswinton 28 Nov. 1880, son of the late W. Macalpine-Leny, of Dalswinton, Dumfries, and Duror, Argyllshire, and his wife, daughter of Walter Long, of Preshaw, Hants. He was educated at Marlborough College, and at the Royal Military Academy, Woolwich, joining the Army 24 June, 1899, and receiving promotion 16 Feb. 1901. He took part in the operations in the Aden Hinterland, 1902–3, and was promoted Captain 13 May, 1904. From 1 Jan. 1906, to 12 Nov. 1908, he was Adjutant, Royal Artillery, and from 13 Nov. 1908, to 13 Nov. 1913, Adjutant in the Territorial Force, becoming Major 30 Oct. 1914. Major Macalpine-Leny was serving at Malta on the outbreak of the European War, whence he proceeded to France. He was created a Companion of the Distinguished Service Order [London Gazette, 10 March, 1915]: "William Harley Macalpine-Leny, Major, 115th Battery, Royal Garrison Artillery. For conspicuous ability and courage at Wulverghem on 24 and 27 Jan., when he succeeded in destroying houses occupied by the enemy by the fire of his battery, during which period he had to observe the firing of his guns from a very exposed position." He served as Acting Lieutenant-Colonel, and was given the Brevet of Lieutenant-Colonel 3 June, 1918. He was four times mentioned in Despatches. Lieut.-Colonel Macalpine-Leny is a member of the I.Z. and Free Foresters Cricket Clubs, and for several years played cricket for Dorsetshire and hockey for Dorset County and the West of England. Capt. Macalpine-Leny married, at St. Jude's Church, South Kensington, 16 June, 1908, Anna Felicia, daughter of the Rev. L. B. Weldon, D.D., Canon of Salisbury, and granddaughter of Sir Anthony Weldon, Baronet, of Rohinderry, Queen's County, and Kilmory, Kildare, Ireland, and also of Sir Crocker Barrington, Baronet, of Glenstal, Limerick, and they have one son, Kenneth Harley, born 20 Oct. 1909.

FOULKES, CHARLES HOWARD, Major, was born 1 Feb. 1875, son of the Rev. Thomas Foulkes and Tessie Fischer. He was educated at Warminster Grammar School and at Bedford Modern School, and entered the Royal Engineers, as a Second Lieutenant, 27 Feb. 1894, becoming Lieutenant 27 Feb. 1897. He served in the operations in Sierra Leone, 1898–99 (Medal with clasp), and in the South African War, on the Staff, employed as Intelligence Officer (graded as Staff Captain), 15 July to 9 Sept. 1900; operations in the Orange Free State, Feb. to May, 1900, including the operations at Paardeberg; actions at Poplar Grove, Dreifontein, Karee Siding, Houtnek (Thoba Mountain), Vet River and Zand River; operations in the Transvaal in May and June, 1900, including actions near Johannesburg, Pretoria and Diamond Hill; operations in the Transvaal, west of Pretoria, including action at Elands River; operations in Orange River Colony, including actions at Bethlehem, Wittebergen and Witpoort; operations in Cape Colony, south of Orange River, 1900, including action at Colesberg (Queen's Medal with six clasps). He was Assistant Commissioner, Anglo-French Boundary Commission, east of the Niger, 4 Oct. 1902, to 2 July, 1904, and took part in the Kano-Sokoto Campaign in Northern Nigeria in 1903 (Medal with clasp); became Captain 1 April, 1904, and Major 27 Feb. 1914. He saw active service for the fourth time in the European War from 1914–18. He was created a Companion of the Distinguished Service Order [London Gazette of 10 March, 1915]: "Charles Howard Foulkes, Major, Royal Engineers. For conspicuous gallantry in assisting to rescue a wounded man under heavy fire, and for very valuable services rendered at Cuinchy, in placing in a state of defence the position which was captured from the enemy on 6 Feb. 1915." He held a special appointment (G.S.O.1) at G.H.Q., British Expeditionary Force, 27 May, 1915, to 16 Jan. 1916; was Brigade Commander (graded as A.A.G.) of a Special Brigade, Royal Engineers, B.E.F., 17 Jan. to 19 May, 1916; and Brigade Commander (graded as Brigadier-General), Special Brigade, Royal Engineers, British Armies in France, 20 May, 1916, to 16 June, 1917, and was promoted Temporary Brigadier-General on receiving the appointment of Director of Gas Services, British Armies in France, 17 June, 1917. For his services in the European War, Brigadier-General Foulkes was given the Brevets of Lieutenant-Colonel (1 Jan. 1917) and Colonel (1 Jan. 1919); was mentioned in Despatches, and was created a C.M.G. in 1918. He had the 1914 Star, the Legion of Honour, the French Croix de Guerre (with Palm), the Belgian Ordre de la Couronne (Commandeur) and Croix de Guerre, and the American Distinguished

Service Medal. He has played in international hockey for Scotland. He married, in 1904, Dorothea Fanny, eldest daughter of Herbert Oakey, and they have three sons.

WINGATE, MALCOLM ROY, Lieut., was born 28 Aug. 1893, at Whitehill, Newton Abbot, second son of General Sir Francis Reginald Wingate, G.C.B., G.C.V.O., Sirdar of the Egyptian Army, High Commissioner of Egypt, and Catherine Leslie, his wife, daughter of the late Capt. Joseph Sparkhall Rundle, Royal Navy. He was educated at Locker's Park, Hemel Hempstead, and at Winchester, passing 17th into Woolwich from Winchester in 1911. He passed out 10th in Dec. 1912, obtaining a commission in the Royal Engineers as Second Lieutenant. He joined at Chatham in April, 1913, the School of Military Engineering. On mobilization at the commencement of the European War in 1914 he was appointed to the 26th Field Company, Royal Engineers (1st Division, Expeditionary Force, Border Camp, Major H. Pritchard). He proceeded to France on the 14th Aug.; was in the Retreat from Mons; took part in operations on the Marne and Aisne, and at Ypres, fighting with his Field Company in all the fierce actions of that period. He was mentioned in Despatches in Feb. and March, 1915; was awarded the Military Cross [London Gazette, 19 Feb. 1915], and was created a Companion of the Distinguished Service Order [London Gazette, 10 March, 1915]: "Malcolm Roy Wingate, Lieut., 26th Field Company, Royal Engineers. For conspicuous gallantry on numerous occasions under dangerous conditions, especially at Givenchy on 27 Jan. 1915, when he led a small party and blew in the head of the enemy's sap at the White House." In Aug. 1915, he was appointed to the Staff as Staff Captain to the Engineer-in-Chief at General Headquarters in France, where he remained until 1917. During that time he was awarded the Croix de Guerre. He considered, however, that his place was at the front, and he asked to be allowed to return to a field company, which was eventually permitted. He was again mentioned in Despatches in May and Dec. 1917, and was given the Brevet of Major on 1 Jan. 1918, after considerably less than five years' service. He was commanding the 459th Field Company when he fell in action 21 March, 1918, aged twenty-four, when leading his men forward to their battle positions during the enemy's attack. A correspondent writes: "His strength of character was concealed under a singularly quiet, courteous and unassuming manner. He was resolute of purpose, punctilious in the discharge of his duty and fearless in carrying it out."

Malcolm Roy Wingate.

LEIGH-BENNETT, ARTHUR, Capt., was born 25 Nov. 1885, and was educated at Winchester. He joined the Coldstream Guards, as a Second Lieutenant, 28 Jan. 1905, and was promoted Lieutenant 22 Jan. 1907. He took part in the European War; was promoted Temporary Captain 15 Nov. 1914; was mentioned in Despatches; gained the Military Cross, and was created a Companion of the Distinguished Service Order [London Gazette, 10 March, 1915]: "Arthur Leigh-Bennett, Capt., 2nd Battn. Coldstream Guards. For conspicuous gallantry at Cuinchy on 1 Feb. 1915. Leading his men with great ability against the enemy, he stopped their advance, and eventually captured their position." He was killed in action in France 3 Oct. 1915.

CAUTLEY, WILLIAM OXENHAM, Major, was born at Gosport 7 Oct. 1875, elder son of Capt. William Tompson Cautley and Emily Marian Oxenham. Major Cautley came of military stock, his grandfather being Major-General George Cautley, 8th Bengal Cavalry, who served through both of the Oudh Campaigns in the forties, and his father, a Captain in the 1st South Staffordshire Regt., died on active service in 1883, leaving his four orphan children to the care of their uncle, the Rev. Proby L. Cautley, Vicar of Quainton, Bucks. The subject of this notice was educated at Bradford College, and distinguished himself in athletics. He entered first the 3rd Hussars through the Militia (3rd Battn. Suffolk Regt.); he rejoined the Suffolks on the outbreak of the South African War. He volunteered for service abroad on the outbreak of the European War, and proceeded to France in Oct., and went up to Ypres. During the first month he was attached to the 1st Sussex Regt., and then for the remainder of the time to the 1st Northamptonshires. He was created a Companion of the Distinguished Service Order [London Gazette, 10 March, 1915]: "William Oxenham Cautley, Major, The Suffolk Regt., attached 1st Northamptonshire Regt. For conspicuous gallantry on 22 Dec. 1914, near La Quinque Rue, where he handled his men with great skill, under very critical circumstances." The Special Brigade Order issued by Brigadier-General C. B. Westmacott on Christmas Day, 1914, gives high praise to the Northamptons and to Major Cautley: "The Brigadier-General desires me to take this opportunity of congratulating D Company, 1st Battn. Northamptonshire Regt., on its gallant and steady behaviour during the action of 22 Dec. The manner in which, under the command of Major Cautley, of the 3rd Battn. Suffolk Regt., it resisted the German

William O. Cautley.

counter-attack, and the steadiness with which it finally withdrew in the face of superior numbers, and eventually occupied a position in the rear to cover a gap made in the line, was worthy of all praise, and adds fresh laurels to the fine record of the old 48th. The Brigadier-General has heard of numerous individual gallant exploits in this engagement, and congratulates himself on having such a fine body of men as the 1st Northants in his brigade. He desires that this order be read out to the battalion on parade." An officer of the Northants writes: "The Commander-in-Chief, Lord French, saw the 1st Battn. of the Northamptonshire Regt. on parade, and delivered an appreciative address to them. He congratulated all ranks on its splendid performances during the campaign, and said that he was proud to have such a fine body of men as the 1st Northants under his command. He wished to express to each man how much he appreciated their gallant conduct, behaviour and endurance." Major Cautley was again mentioned in Despatches on 23 June, 1915. He fell in action on 9 May, 1915, near Richbourg, while leading the 1st Northants Regt. against the German trenches. Wounded in the right arm, he had been already attended to when he was struck by another bullet, death being instantaneous. In Battalion Orders, issued by Lieut.-Colonel Massey Lloyd, 3rd Suffolks, 20 May, appears the following: "It is with deep regret that the Commanding Officer has to announce the death of Major W. O. Cautley, D.S.O., killed in action. Major Cautley, by the keen interest he always took in the welfare of the battalion, endeared himself to all ranks, and in the end brought a great distinction not only to himself, but to the battalion to which he was so devoted. The Commanding Officer has lost a personal friend, and the Suffolk Regt. a brilliant soldier." He had married, 10 April, 1901, at St. Catherine's, Blairgowrie, Scotland, Agnes, second daughter of Charles Hill-Whitson, late Scots Greys, of Park Hill, Blairgowrie, and they had three children: Beatrice Sylvia Aimée; Marian Agnes, and William Hill, born 1906.

SALMON, HUGH MAXWELL BROOME, Capt., was born 6 June, 1888, at St. Leonards-on-Sea, son of Mordaunt Broome Salmon, (late) 3rd Queen's Own Bombay Light Cavalry (who took part in the Battle of Maiwand and siege of Kandahar, and was recommended for the V.C. He was killed at polo at Neemuch, on 30 Dec. 1887, his rank at the time of his death being that of Captain), and his wife, Maud Ethel, daughter of Colonel G. Hancock, of the Bombay Staff Corps, now Mrs. Vicars, of Avondale, Eastbourne. Hugh Salmon was educated at Wellington College, where he was in the 1st XV., 1904–5, and in the Gym. Pair, 1905, and at Sandhurst (entered Jan. 1907), where he was in the 1st XV., 1907. He became Second Lieutenant, 1st Battn. The 24th Regt. (South Wales Borderers), 22 Feb. 1908, and Lieutenant 1 April, 1911. He served in the European War from 1914. At the First Battle of Ypres, "the bombardment of Givenchy-les-Bassée Spur commenced about 7.30 p.m. on the 25th Jan. 1915, and ceased at 8.30 a.m. The Germans attacked in waves five times. I was in support," says Capt. Salmon, "at Windy Corner, and took up my company as reinforcement during the bombardment. At about 10 a.m. the Welsh Regt. were broken through and suffered very severely. The enemy put up a barrage of high explosive over Givenchy village and the road from Windy Corner. I took up a party of Royal Welsh Fusiliers (T.) and posted them where required, and received a machine-gun bullet through the leg while doing it. A platoon of my company, assisted by a company of the Black Watch, retook the Welsh trenches. Givenchy Spur was held this day by the 3rd Brigade. It was never held by any previous attack." For these services Capt. Salmon was created a Companion of the Distinguished Service Order [London Gazette, 10 March, 1915]: "Hugh Maxwell Broome Salmon, Capt. (temporary), 1st Battn. King's Own Scottish Borderers. For conspicuous courage at Givenchy on 25th Jan. 1915. Although wounded, he brought up men from the local reserves under heavy fire on two occasions, and remained throughout the day with his company in action." He was made Captain 24 Jan. 1915; was wounded at the First Battle of Ypres, 2 Nov. 1914; at Givenchy-les-Bassée 25 Jan. 1915, and was mentioned in Despatches, Feb. 1915, for the First Battle of Ypres. On 28 Dec. 1916, at Tewkesbury Abbey, Capt. Salmon married Violet Lucy, daughter of James Shapland Sargeaunt, Esq., of Tewkesbury Park, Tewkesbury.

TRAVERS, HUGH MORTIMER, Capt., was born at Calcutta on 2 Sept. 1873, son of Lieut.-Colonel Joseph Oates Travers, Leicestershire Regt., Chevalier of the Legion of Honour, a distinction which he received for the Crimean Campaign. Capt. Travers came of a distinguished military family, his grandfathers having been General Sir Robert Travers, of the Rifle Brigade, and Major-General Sir Henry Marion Durand, R.E., K.C.S.I., C.B. Sir Robert Travers was one of six brothers, four of whom were in the Rifle Brigade and two in the Navy, and the six brothers had amongst them twenty-four sons, all of whom went into the Army. At one time Sir Robert and three of his brothers and two of Mrs. Travers' first cousins were in the Rifle Brigade. The Travers crest is a cockle-shell, showing that the family took part in the Crusades, and their name is carved at Battle Abbey, and is in Battle Abbey Roll. They are descended from Baron Robert de Travers, who, in 1067, married the heiress of Nateby, in Lancashire. Another ancestor, Admiral Sir Eaton Travers, was engaged with the enemy over one hundred times, and was eight times mentioned for his gallant conduct. Hugh Mortimer Travers was educated at Wellington College, and was gazetted in the 1st Leicestershire Regt. from the Militia in Dec. 1896, joining the battalion at the Cape in 1897, where he remained till 1902. He took part in the South African War; was promoted Lieutenant in Oct. 1899, and was present with his battalion at Talana Hill; in the retreat from Dundee; at the actions of Lombard's Kop; in the siege of Ladysmith; in Sir Redvers Buller's advance on Lydenberg, and under General Sir John French in the Eastern Transvaal. In the last thirteen months of the war he was on an armoured train. For his services in this campaign he received the thanks of Lord Kitchener, and the Queen's Medal with two clasps. He also held the Coronation Medal. He was promoted Captain, and was selected for the Egyptian Army, but retired in 1907, as he had contracted blackwater fever. He joined the 5th Battn. Royal Munster Fusiliers in Nov. of that year. When the European War broke out he was attached to a battalion of the Regular Army, and was present at the Battle of the Aisne; at La Bassée and Givenchy, at all of which he did exceedingly well. Capt. Travers was killed in action on 8 Nov. 1914, being shot through the head in a bayonet charge, in which he gallantly led his men, near Hooge, a small village near Ypres. For his conduct in this action he was created a Companion of the Distinguished Service Order [London Gazette, 10 March, 1915]: "Hugh Mortimer Travers, Capt., 5th (attached 3rd) Battn. Royal Munster Fusiliers. For conspicuous gallantry and ability on 8 Nov. near Ypres, in organizing an attack and recapturing a trench from the enemy, and subsequently for leading a second attack and capturing another position fifty yards nearer to the front. Capt. Travers was killed while maintaining his post on this occasion." The Adjutant of his battalion, in a letter, said that he "died the death of a soldier and a very gallant gentleman," and a sergeant described his deed as "the coolest deed I have ever seen. It was gloriously brave." Capt. Travers was engaged to Wilhelmina Annette, daughter of Surgeon-General Sir William Taylor, M.D., K.C.B., and Lady Taylor, and the marriage had been postponed because Capt. Travers had to leave for the front at twenty-four hours' notice.

LANG, ERIC CHRISTIAN, Lieut., was born 26 Sept. 1888. He was educated for the medical profession (M.B.), joining the Royal Army Medical Corps, as Lieutenant, 26 July, 1912. He served in the European War, 1914–18, attached to the 1st Battn. Leicestershire Regt. He was mentioned twice in Despatches, and created a Companion of the Distinguished Service Order [London Gazette, 10 March, 1915]: "Eric Christian Lang, Lieut., Royal Army Medical Corps, attached 1st Battn. The Leicestershire Regt., For conspicuous gallantry and devotion to duty on two occasions, especially on 9 Feb. 1915, at Rue du Bois, in rescuing a severely wounded officer under very difficult circumstances while in full view of the enemy." He became Captain 30 March, 1915; was Acting Major, Jan. to April, 1918, and Acting Lieutenant-Colonel, April, 1918, to March, 1919.

SHAW, EDWARD WINGFIELD, Lieut., was born at Anerley, London, S.E., 19 Feb. 1895, youngest son of Colonel George Jocelyn Shaw, Indian Army (retired), and great-grandson of the late Sir Frederick Shaw, 3rd Baronet, of Bushy Park, Dublin. He was educated at Lancing and Dulwich Colleges, and at the Royal Military College, Sandhurst, joining the Middlesex Regt. 26 Aug. 1914. He was sent to France as Lieutenant, 1st Middlesex Regt., and got his Temp.-Captaincy within a month. He was mentioned in Despatches, and was created a Companion of the Distinguished Service Order [London Gazette, 10 March, 1915]: "Edward Wingfield Shaw, Lieut. (Temporary Captain), 1st Battn. (The Duke of Cambridge's Own) Middlesex Regt. For conspicuous gallantry on 30 Oct. 1914, at La Boutillerie. In leading a part of his platoon to recover a lost trench he was wounded and compelled to retire, but collecting another party, he went forward again to the attack and entered the enemy's trench, being wounded a second time in so doing. As a result of the action the trench was recovered, 30 of the enemy being killed or wounded and the remainder taken prisoner." Subsequently, and on recovering from his wounds, which were slight, he rejoined the 3rd Battn. of his regiment in France in Feb. 1915, and took part in the various operations near Ypres, being again mentioned in Despatches 18 June, 1915. He came home to England on sick leave in Sept. 1915, and rejoined the 1st Battn. of his regiment in France in Feb. 1916. He served continuously with his units until he was wounded, 28 Oct. 1916, while leading his company in an attack on Les Bœufs. He was moved to the base hospital at Rouen, and died 7 Dec. 1916. He was buried in St. Sever Cemetery, Rouen.

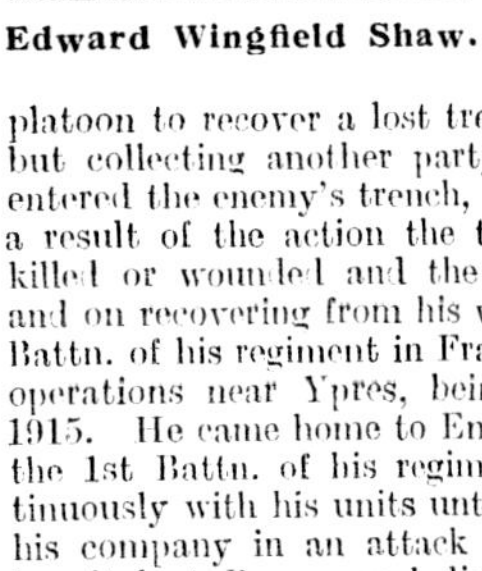

Edward Wingfield Shaw.

London Gazette, 3 March, 1915.—"Admiralty, 3 March, 1915. The King has been graciously pleased to give orders for the following appointment to the Distinguished Service Order to the undermentioned Officer, in recognition of services mentioned in Vice-Admiral Beatty's Despatch 3 March, 1915."

PETERS, FREDERIC THORNTON, Lieut., served in the European War, and took part in the action in the North Sea on Sunday, 24 Jan. 1915. He was on board H.M.S. Meteor during this engagement. He was created a Companion of the Distinguished Service Order [London Gazette, 3 March, 1915]: "Frederic Thornton Peters, Lieut., Royal Navy." Lieut. Peters was on active service from 1914–17. He died of wounds 7 Dec. 1916.

London Gazette, 16 March, 1915.—"War Office, 16 March, 1915. His Majesty the King has been graciously pleased to appoint the undermentioned Officer to be a Companion of the Distinguished Service Order."

JOHNSON, DUDLEY GRAHAM, Capt., served in the Great War at Tsingtau in 1914; was mentioned in Despatches, and created a Companion of the Distinguished Service Order [London Gazette, 16 March, 1915]: "Dudley Graham Johnson, Capt.,

Dudley Graham Johnson.

South Wales Borderers." He became Temporary Lieutenant-Colonel, and in 1919 was awarded the Victoria Cross (see Victoria Cross Volume). His D.S.O. was awarded "for conspicuous ability in the night of 5–6 Nov. 1914, during the operations against the German positions at Tsingtau, and for great gallantry in rescuing several wounded men whilst exposed to heavy fire."

London Gazette, 27 March, 1915.—"War Office, 27 March, 1915. His Majesty the King has been graciously pleased to approve of the appointment of the following Officers to be Companions of the Distinguished Service Order, in recognition of their gallantry and devotion to duty whilst serving with the Expeditionary Force."

BIRD, ARTHUR JAMES GLOVER, Capt., was born 4 Feb. 1883, at Jhelum, India, son of C. P. Bird, Esq., retired Indian Civil Service. He was educated at Cheltenham College, and obtained his first commission in the Royal Engineers 21 Dec. 1900; was promoted Lieutenant 21 Dec. 1903. He saw active service on the North-West Frontier of India, 1908, taking part in operations in the Zakka Khel country; operations in the Mohmand country, engagements at Matta and Kargha (Medal with clasp); was promoted Captain 21 Dec. 1910. Capt. Bird served in the European War from 1914 to 1918. For his services in France until Dec. 1915, he was twice mentioned in Despatches, and was created a Companion of the Distinguished Service Order

Arthur J. G. Bird.

[London Gazette, 27 March, 1915]: "Arthur James Glover Bird, Capt., Royal Engineers (No. 4 Company, 1st King George's Own Sappers and Miners), Indian Army. For conspicuous ability, gallantry and great initiative during the past four months. His great energy and zeal in organizing the work of barricade construction at all critical points immensely increased the power for resistance. His very effective work was most noticeable during the critical period in the firing line from 19 to 23 Dec. 1914." He was sent to Mesopotamia in 1915; was promoted Major 2 Nov. 1916; was mentioned in Despatches; given the Brevet of Lieutenant-Colonel 1 Jan. 1918; became acting Lieutenant-Colonel 27 May, 1918.

CARMICHAEL, GEORGE IVAN, Capt. (Temporary Major), was born 24 Aug. 1888. He entered the Royal Artillery 18 Dec. 1908, as a Second Lieutenant, and was promoted Lieutenant 18 Dec. 1911; joined the Royal Flying Corps 11 March, 1913, and became Temporary Captain 1 May, 1914. Capt. Carmichael served in the European War from 1914 to 1918 with the Royal Flying Corps. He became Captain (Royal Artillery) 18 Dec. 1914, and was created a Companion of the Distinguished Service Order [London Gazette, 27 March, 1915]: "George Ivan Carmichael, Capt., Royal Artillery and Royal Flying Corps. For conspicuous gallantry, daring and ability throughout the campaign. On 11th instant he destroyed the rails at Menin railway station by dropping a bomb weighing 100 lbs. thereon from a height of only 100 feet. On the return journey his engine was damaged by a bullet, which necessitated his flying at a height of less than 200 feet. Capt. Carmichael has also rendered valuable services in observing artillery fire." He was Temporary Major, March, 1915, to Feb. 1917; Temporary Lieutenant-Colonel, Feb. 1917, to March, 1918; was employed with the Royal Flying Corps until 31 March, 1918. He was employed from 1 April, 1918, under the Air Ministry, and was promoted Major, Royal Artillery, 20 May, 1918; was awarded the Air Force Cross in 1919. He married, in 1915, Kathleen Mary Foxon, youngest daughter of W. Casterton Smelt, of Braeside, Rosslyn Hill, N.W. They have one son.

MOORE, EDMUND HUGH, Lieut., was born at Horningsham, Wiltshire, 16 July, 1885, son of the Rev. William Moore (B.A. Oxon.), Rector of Mereworth, Kent. He was educated at Radley College, at Mareschal College, at Aberdeen University, and at London Hospital, and is an M.B. and B.Ch. He joined the Royal Army Medical Corps 9 Aug. 1914, and accompanied the British Expeditionary Force to France on 23 Aug. 1914, leaving a Base Hospital for the front within a fortnight. He served as Medical Officer to the Connaught Rangers, and later to the 2nd Leicestershire Regt. till wounded and sent back to England. He was mentioned in Despatches, and created a Companion of the Distinguished Service Order [London Gazette, 27 March, 1915]:

Edmund Hugh Moore.

"Edmund Hugh Moore, M.B., Lieut., Royal Army Medical Corps. For conspicuous gallantry on 23 Feb. 1915, near Richebourg l'Avoué, in going over with another officer and a stretcher-bearer to within 150 yards of the enemy and attending to a severely wounded soldier. The stretcher-bearer was then wounded, and Lieut. Moore remained in attendance on him, undoubtedly saving his life. On the next day this officer again went with the greatest gallantry to the assistance of a wounded man under the aimed fire of the enemy. He dressed the man's wounds and was immediately afterwards wounded himself." He was incapacitated for six months as the result of his wounds, and after a short spell of light duty in England went out to Gallipoli. After the evacuation of the Peninsula he was invalided home,

and returned to the Somme Front in Nov. 1916; served till 1917; subsequently became Captain, and in the course of the war was twice wounded and once gassed. His chief recreations are music and motoring.

POLLARD, GEORGE CHAMBERS, Major, first saw active service in the South African War, 1900–1, and was present in operations in the Orange Free State, May, 1900, including actions at Vet River (5 and 6 May), and Zand River; operations in the Transvaal in May and June, 1900, including actions near Johannesburg, Pretoria and Diamond Hill (11 and 12 June); operations in the Transvaal, east of Pretoria, including actions at Belfast 26 and 27 Aug.) (Queen's Medal with three clasps). He served with distinction in the European War, 1914–18; was created a Companion of the Distinguished Service Order [London Gazette, 27 March, 1915]: "George Chambers Pollard, Major, 1st (The Newcastle) Northumbrian Field Company, Royal Engineers. For conspicuous gallantry on the night of the 10th Feb. 1915, in assisting to carry a severely wounded officer into cover whilst exposed to continuous heavy fire. Major Pollard has been exposed almost daily to heavy rifle and shell fire in attending to his duties, and has shown a fine example of self-sacrifice and devotion to duty in all difficulties and dangers." Invested by the King 22 Sept. 1916. He was wounded; five times mentioned in Despatches, and was created a C.M.G. in 1918.

PRETYMAN, GEORGE FREDERICK, Lieut., was born 8 Sept. 1891, son of Maj.-Gen. Sir G. T. Pretyman, K.C.M.G., C.B. Educated at Wellington College; gazetted to the Somerset L.I. 25 March, 1911; Lieutenant 5 Aug. 1914; Captain 25 March, 1917. He became Wing Commander and Lieut.-Col. R.A.F.; mentioned in Despatches; given the Brevet of Major 1 Jan. 1918, and the O.B.E. 1919, and created a Companion of the Distinguished Service Order [London Gazette, 27 March, 1915]: "George Frederick Pretyman, Lieut., T. Capt., Somerset Light Infantry and R.F.C. For great gallantry, ability and initiative on numerous occasions, especially on the 12th inst. The clouds being low he had to fly very low for a considerable period all along the German positions to ascertain their movements, being exposed the whole time to a very heavy fire. On the 13th inst. he blew up the centre of a train at Don Station, damaged a building outside which a battalion of the enemy were forming up and drove off a German aeroplane." He married Maureen, daughter of Colonel E. S. Heard.

London Gazette, 10 April, 1915.—"Admiralty, 10 April, 1915. The King has been graciously pleased to give orders for the following appointments to the Distinguished Service Order of the undermentioned Officers, in recognition of their services as mentioned."

NUNN, WILFRID, Capt., served on the Staff, Royal Naval War College, 1911–12; War Staff Officer, 1912. He served in the European War, 1914–16, receiving a decoration for each of three years of service. He was created a Companion of the Distinguished Service Order [London Gazette, 27 March, 1915]: "Wilfrid Nunn, Commander (now Capt.), Royal Navy" (for services during the operations in the Shatt-el-Arab, Dec. 1914, resulting in the capture of Qurnah). For services at Amara he was mentioned in Despatches, and he received the Naval General Service Medal, Persian Gulf clasp, 1914. He subsequently served in Mesopotamia, as Commander of the Tigris Flotilla, and was made a C.M.G. in 1916, and a C.B. in 1917, for his work on the Tigris. He was several times mentioned in Despatches, Sir Percy Lake mentioning him as follows: (M.P. 14 Oct. 1916): "Nunn . . . and other officers of the Royal Navy have afforded us the able assistance which we have become accustomed to receive from them." He commanded H.M. Ships Aurora and Curlew in the Harwich Force, July, 1917, to April, 1919; the C.S.I. was given him in 1919. He has the 1914–15 Star.

DAVIES, RICHARD BELL, Squadron Commander, Royal Naval Air Service, served in the European War, and was created a Companion of the Distinguished Service Order [London Gazette, 10 April, 1915]: "Richard Bell Davies, Squadron Commander, Royal Naval Air Service. For services rendered in the aerial attack on Dunkirk." For his later services Wing Commander R. B. Davies was awarded the Victoria Cross (see Victoria Cross Volume).

PEIRSE, RICHARD EDMUND CHARLES, Flight Lieutenant, was born in 1892, only son of Admiral Sir Richard Peirse, Naval Member of the Central Committee, Board of Invention and Research (1914–18), and of Blanche, his wife, daughter of the Rev. E. J. Wemyss Whittaker. He was educated at Monkton Combe School, and King's College, London. He served in the European War from 1914 to 1918; was created a Companion of the Distinguished Service Order [London Gazette, 10 April, 1915]: "Richard Edmund Charles Peirse, Flight Lieutenant, Royal Naval Air Service. He repeatedly attacked the German submarine station at Ostend and Zeebrugge, being subjected on each occasion to heavy and accurate fire." He became Lieutenant-Colonel,

Richard E. C. Peirse.

Royal Air Force; was awarded the Air Force Cross; was appointed Senior Air Officer, Atlantic and Home Fleet. Lieut.-Colonel R. E. C. Peirse married, in 1915, Joyce, youngest daughter of Armitage Ledgard, of Manor House Thorner, Yorkshire. They have one daughter.

PALMES, GEORGE BRYAN, Lieut.-Commander, served in the European War, 1914–15. He was mentioned in Despatches, and created a Companion of the Distinguished Service Order, for services in command of the torpedo boat O 43, during the operations on the Suez Canal, Feb. 1915 [London Gazette, 10 April, 1915]: "George Bryan Palmes, Lieut.-Commander, Royal Navy." He was promoted Commander in 1917.

London Gazette, 15 April, 1915.—"War Office, 15 April, 1915. His Majesty the King has been graciously pleased to approve of the appointments of the undermentioned Officers to be Companions of the Distinguished Service Order, in recognition of their gallantry and devotion to duty whilst serving with the Expeditionary Force."

NEWCOME, HENRY WILLIAM, Major, was born 14 July, 1875. He was educated at Marlborough (1888–92, C 3 House), and entered the Army 14 June, 1895, as a Second Lieutenant in the Royal Artillery, and was promoted Lieutenant 15 June, 1898. He served in the South African War, 1899–1900, being employed as A.D.C. to the Major-General Commanding Royal Artillery, Natal, 20 March to 23 May, 1900. He was present at the Relief of Ladysmith, including the action at Colenso; operations of 17 to 24 Jan. 1900, and the action at Spion Kop; operations of 5 to 7 Feb. 1900, and the action at Vaal Kranz; operations on Tugela Heights (14 to 27 Feb.), and the action at Pieter's Hill; operations in Natal, March to June, 1900, including the action at Laing's Nek (6 to 9 June); operations in the Transvaal, east of Pretoria, July to Nov. 1900, including actions at Belfast (26 and 27 Aug.), and Lydenberg (5 to 8 Sept.). He was mentioned in Despatches [London Gazette, 8 Feb. 1901), and received the Queen's Medal with six clasps. He became Captain 14 March, 1901; was Adjutant, Royal Artillery, 7 Jan. 1902, to 6 Jan. 1905; Instructor, Ordnance College, 26 Feb. 1909, to 27 Oct. 1912; was promoted Major 21 Aug. 1911, and was Major Instructor, School of Gunnery, 1 April to 3 Aug. 1914. Major Newcome served in the European War, and was created a Companion of the Distinguished Service Order for distinguished work in reports and especially at Givenchy [London Gazette, 15 April, 1915]: "Henry William Newcome, Major, 47th Battery, Royal Field Artillery." From 18 Aug. 1915, to 9 Feb. 1916, he was G.S.O.2 (Staff Officer to Major-General, Royal Artillery), 1st Army, B.E.F. (wounded twice; Despatches, three times); from 10 Feb. to 9 July, 1916, G.S.O.1 (Staff Officer to Major-General, Royal Artillery), G.H.Q., B.E.F. and British Armies in France; was promoted Lieutenant-Colonel 1 June, 1916. He served also in 1916, as Lieutenant-Colonel Instructor, Gunnery School, Salisbury Plain (Despatches); became Temporary Brigadier-General 13 May, 1917, Royal Artillery, 21st Division, British Armies in France, which appointment he held until 4 Nov. 1918; on 5 Nov. 1918, was appointed Commandant, Chapperton Down Artillery School. He was given the Brevet of Colonel 1 Jan. 1918, and was created a C.M.G. in 1919.

GAULT, ANDREW HAMILTON, Major, was born in England 18 Aug. 1882, son of the late A. F. Gault, of Montreal, and Louisa S. Gault (Harman), his wife. He was educated at the Bishop's College School, Lennoxville, and at the McGill University. He took part in the Boer War of 1899–1902, as a Subaltern in the 2nd Canadian Mounted Rifles, serving in operations in the Transvaal and Cape Colony (Queen's Medal with three clasps). He became Captain Corps Reserve, Royal Highlanders of Canada, 14 Oct. 1905. He was Consul-General for Sweden in Canada, 1909–11, and a member of the Council of the Montreal Board of Trade, 1911–13; a Director of the Montreal Cottons, Ltd.; the Trent Valley Woollen Mills; the Crescent Company; Van Allen Co. Ltd.; Gordons Ltd., and other companies. He is president of Gault Bros. Co. and Gault Realties Ltd. Major Gault raised and equipped Princess Patricia's Canadian Light Infantry for active service in the European War (1914–16). He was wounded, was mentioned in Despatches, and was created a Companion of the Distinguished Service Order [London Gazette, 15 April, 1915]: "Andrew Hamilton Gault, Major, Princess Patricia's Canadian Light Infantry. For conspicuous gallantry at St. Eloi on 27 Feb. 1915, in reconnoitring quite close to the enemy's position, obtaining information of great value for our attack, which was carried out next day. On 28 Feb. Major Gault assisted in the rescue of the wounded under most difficult circumstances, while exposed to heavy fire." In 1919 he was given an O.B.E. Lieut.-Colonel Gault's favourite recreations are hunting, polo, shooting and fishing. He married, in 1904, Marguerite, daughter of the Honourable G. W. Stephens.

CROZIER, BAPTIST BARTON, Major, was born 17 July, 1878, son of the Archbishop of Armagh and Primate of All Ireland, the Most Reverend Dr. Crozier. He entered the Army, with a commission in the Royal Arlery, 22 Dec. 1898, and was promoted Captain 16 Feb. 1901. He served in the South African War, 1900–1, and was present in operations in Cape Colony, south of Orange River, 1899–1900; operations in Orange River Colony (Queen's Medal with three clasps). He was promoted Captain 18 Sept. 1907; was a Territorial Force Adjutant 18 May, 1908, to 17 May, 1911; became Major 30 Oct. 1914. Major Crozier served in the European War, and was created a Companion of the Distinguished Service Order [London Gazette, 15 April, 1915]: "Baptist Barton Crozier, Major, Royal Field Artillery. Rendered valuable service in observing our artillery fire during the actions of 10 and 11 March, 1915, at Givenchy, whilst exposed to the enemy's heavy rifle fire and our own shrapnel. Has been conspicuous for gallantry and coolness throughout the campaign." Major Crozier subsequently held the following appointments, viz.: Brigade Major, R.A., 3rd Australian Division, 10 July to 6 Aug. 1916; Brigade Major, R.A., 24th Division, British Armies in France, 9 Sept. to 30 Oct. 1916; D.A.A.G. (Staff Officer to G.O.C., Royal Artillery), 13th Army Corps, British Armies in France, 31 Oct. 1916, to 11 Feb. 1917; D.A.A.G. (Staff Officer to G.O.C., Royal Artillery), 2nd Army, British Armies in France, 12 Feb. to 27 Aug. 1917; G.S.O.1, 2nd Army, British Armies in France, 28 Aug. to 16 Nov. 1917; G.S.O.1, British Forces in Italy, 11 Nov. 1917; afterwards G.S.O.1, 2nd Army, British Armies in France, until 25 Nov. 1918; G.S.O.1, Staff College, 1 March, 1919. He was given the Brevet of Lieutenant-Colonel 3 June, 1917; was mentioned in Despatches, and in 1918 was made a C.M.G. In 1917 he became an Officer of the Crown of Italy, and in 1918 Chevalier of the Legion of Honour. He married Ethel Elizabeth, eldest daughter of W. Humphrys, J.P., of Ballyhaise House, County Cavan. They have one son and one daughter.

DENNE, WILLIAM HENRY, Major, was born 15 July, 1876, son of the late Rev. R. H. Denne and Mrs. Denne, of Brimpsfield, Gloucestershire. He was educated at Cheltenham College. He was in the Eleven for two years, and afterwards played cricket and hockey for the Bedfordshire Regt. He entered the Army, as a Second Lieutenant, 1 Dec. 1897; was promoted Lieutenant 18 April, 1899. He served in the South African War, employed with the Mounted Infantry, and was present in operations in the Orange Free State, Feb. to May, 1900; operations in the Orange River Colony, March to 29 Nov. 1900, including the actions at Wittebergen (1 to 29 July) and Witpoort; operations in Cape Colony, south of Orange River, 1899–1900, including actions at Colesberg (1 Jan. to 12 Feb.); operations in the Transvaal, Jan. 1901, to May, 1902; operations in Orange River Colony, 30 Nov. to Dec. 1900. He was mentioned in Despatches [London Gazette, 25 April, 1902]; received the Queen's Medal with three clasps, and the King's Medal with two clasps. Lieut. Denne was Adjutant of the Bedfordshire Regt. 6 Dec. 1905, to 5 Dec. 1908; was promoted Captain 22 July, 1906, and was Staff Captain, No. 9 District, Eastern Command, 1 April, 1912, to 4 Oct. 1914; became Major 31 Oct. 1914. He again saw active service in the European War. He became Major in the third month of the war, and rejoined his regiment in Nov., after serving for a few weeks in France as Staff Captain. He served as Temporary Lieutenant-Colonel from 19 Dec. 1914, to 12 Jan. 1915, and was mentioned in Despatches in Dec. 1914. He was wounded at Neuve Chapelle, and was created a Companion of the Distinguished Service Order for his services there [London Gazette, 15 April, 1915]: "William Henry Denne, Major, 2nd Battn. The Bedfordshire Regt. For conspicuous gallantry at Neuve Chapelle on 12 March, 1915, when he led a party of twenty men in a counter-attack under the most severe fire. All the twenty men were shot down, and he himself was seriously wounded." The G.C.O. said he desired to express his appreciation of the steady conduct of the 2nd Battn. The Bedfordshire Regt., and particularly of the gallant action of Major Denne and his small party, who had made a devoted counter-attack on the enemy in order to assist a neighbouring battalion. Major Denne was invested by the King at Queen Alexandra's Hospital for Officers, Highgate, N. 5 June, 1916. He never recovered from his wounds, and died in this hospital 21 Feb. 1917. He had married, on 12 July, 1912, at All Saints' Church, Glazebury, Lancashire, Ethel Fleetwood, second daughter of the Rev. George Feather, Vicar of Glazebury.

NICOL, WILFRED EDWARD, Capt., was born 16 Oct. 1882. He was educated at Winchester, and entered the Grenadier Guards, as a Second Lieutenant, 11 Aug. 1900. He served in operations in Cape Colony, Jan. to 31 May, 1902, receiving the Queen's South African Medal with two clasps. He was promoted Lieutenant 12 April, 1904; was employed from 10 Aug. 1907, to 14 March, 1909, with the Macedonian Gendarmerie; became Captain 11 July, 1908, and was employed with the Turkish Gendarmerie 15 March, 1909, to 10 July, 1911. Capt. Nicol served in the European War. He was mentioned in Despatches, and was created a Companion of the Distinguished Service Order [London Gazette, 15 April, 1915]: "Wilfred Edward Nicol, Capt., Grenadier Guards. For gallantry and ability at Neuve Chapelle, from 10 to 14 March, 1915, when he was largely instrumental in the capture of the great number of prisoners by reason of his able handling of the hand grenade company." He was subsequently promoted Major, and died 1 Oct. 1915, of wounds received on 29 Sept. 1915.

SAUNDERS-KNOX-GORE, WILLIAM ARTHUR CECIL, Capt., was born 26 May, 1888, at Bangalore, India, son of Colonel W. A. G. Saunders-Knox-Gore, of Belleek Manor, Ballina, D.L. County Mayo, J.P. Counties Mayo and Sligo, late Royal Artillery, serving during the European War in the Royal Field Artillery. He was educated at Harrow, shooting in the Harrow Eight in 1905, when the School won the Ashburton Shield and rapid-firing match at Bisley; and at the Royal Military College, Sandhurst, from which he received a commission as Second Lieutenant in the King's Royal Rifle Corps, 29 Aug. 1906; became Lieutenant 23 Dec. 1908. He won the Silver Jewel of the Army Championship at Bisley in 1913, and the Bronze Jewel in 1914. He served in the European War, 1914–18. He was created a Companion of the Distinguished Service Order [London Gazette, 15 April, 1915]: "William Arthur Cecil Saunders-Knox-Gore, Capt., 1st Battn. King's Royal Rifle Corps. For gallantry and conspicuous ability throughout the campaign. On 27 Feb. 1915, he photographed the enemy's position at Givenchy and made an important reconnaissance, the enemy's snipers being only 150 yards distant." He was mentioned in Despatches, 31 May, 1915; received the French Croix de Guerre, and was given the Brevets of Major 3 June, 1917, and Lieutenant-Colonel 1 Jan. 1919. Lieut.-Colonel Saunders-Knox-Gore held the following Staff appointments during the war: Brigade Major, Rhodesia and Nyassaland Force, 4 Dec. 1915, to 2 April, 1917; G.S.O.1, East African Force, 25 July, 1917, to 17 Aug. 1918; G.S.O.2, 59th Division, British Armies in France, 19 Nov. 1918. He married, in 1919, Monica, youngest daughter of the late R. J. Lawrence, of the Inner Temple.

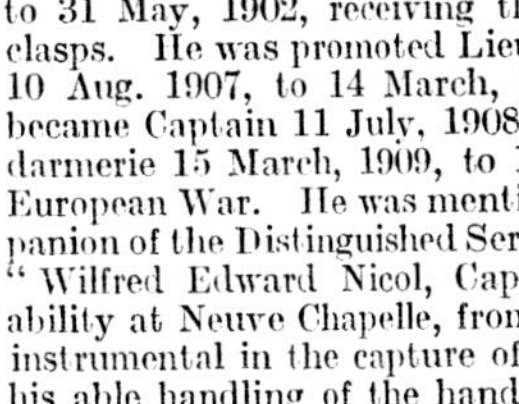

W.A.Saunders-Knox-Gore.

PORTEOUS, DICK MACDONALD, Capt., was born 15 June, 1883, in Dublin, son of Lieut.-Colonel J. J. Porteous, C.M.G. (late Royal Artillery) and Nelly, only daughter of Percy Morris, of The Hall, Uttoxeter.

He was educated at Wellington and Sandhurst, and was gazetted to the Argyll and Sutherland Highlanders 22 Oct. 1902, and was promoted to Lieutenant 19 Oct. 1907, and to Captain 13 Sept. 1913. He served in both battalions in South Africa, England and India, whence he proceeded with the 1st Battn. to France in Nov. 1914. On 24 Feb. 1915, Capt. Porteous's distinguished conduct in the field was reported to the Major-General Commanding the 27th Division; and again his gallant conduct on several occasions was mentioned in March, 1915, and was brought to the notice of higher authority. On one occasion Capt. Porteous called in at a German trench, and finding his involuntary host, a soldier, asleep, brought back his helmet as a souvenir; and on 22 Feb.

Dick M. Porteous.

1915, the following was written from the Army Corps Headquarters:

" To 27th Division.
" Reference your G.S. 444, dated 21 Feb. 1915, the Corps Commander has read the report on the reconnaissance carried out by Capt. D. M. Porteous, 1st Argyll and Sutherland Highlanders, and appreciates the very good work done by this officer.

(Signed) " W. Robertson, Major, G.S.,
" 21 Feb. 1915. " 5th Corps.

2

" Headquarters, 81st Infantry Brigade.
" For communication.

" H. L. Reed, Lieut.-Colonel, G.S.,
" 22 Feb. 1915." " 27th Division.

A letter forwarded to the O.C., 1st Argyll and Sutherland Highlanders, for his information and communication to Capt. D. M. Porteous by the G.O.C., 81st Infantry Brigade, reads as follows:

" To G.O.C., 81st Infantry Brigade.
" The G.O.C. wishes to convey through you to Capt. D. M. Porteous, 1st Battn. Argyll and Sutherland Highlanders, his appreciation of the excellent report (and sketch) of German trenches forwarded under your No. 81/148 of the 20th instant. The report contains matter of great value and importance. The G.O.C. is well aware of the difficulties and dangers which must have been overcome by Capt. Porteous in order to give such valuable information.

" H. L. Reed, Lieut.-Colonel, G.S.,
" 21 Feb. 1915." " 27th Division.

His utter contempt of danger was described in a letter from a brother officer, who said of him during a fight: " I saw him up there, *enjoying himself*." The same officer wrote: " A braver man I never expect to meet." He was created a Companion of the Distinguished Service Order [London Gazette, 15 April, 1915]: " Dick Macdonald Porteous, Capt., 1st Battn. Princess Louise's Argyll and Sutherland Highlanders. For conspicuous gallantry on many occasions throughout the campaign. His very great daring and total disregard of danger on reconnaissance duty, especially at St. Eloi on 19 Feb. 1915, were noticeable." Capt. Porteous was killed in action, being shot through the head in the trenches near Ypres 10 May, 1915. He was again mentioned in Field-Marshal Sir John (now Lord) French's Despatch of 31 May [London Gazette, 22 June, 1915], for Distinguished service in the field.

Major-General H. L. Reed, V.C., C.B., C.M.G., writes: " He was continually working out at night, prowling about No Man's Land in those very awful nights—winter, 1914–15—and in such mud as I have never seen since. He would come back with a rough plan drawn, and describe generally details of German trenches and how they ran, which without the greatest risk to life could not be obtained. He was well known by the Headquarters Staff of the Division on account of his daring and skill in reconnaissance. He realized the value of bombs—if one could call them

Gerald Arthur Cammell.

bombs, those old jam jars, more dangerous to friend than foe. He encouraged his men to use them, and I find that on the night of 26 Feb. 1915, ' Capt. Porteous displayed great activity and ability in leading bomb-throwers of his battalion, who stopped a German working party sapping towards our first line.' I only wish I had the ability to express clearly and justly one's great admiration for that brave, zealous young soldier, who put his duty before all things. Had he been spared he would have been very high up now."

CAMMELL, GERALD ARTHUR, Lieut., was born 11 Jan. 1889, only surviving son of the late Archibald Allen Cammell, of Brookfield Manor, Derbyshire.

He entered the Army, as a Second Lieutenant in the Royal Artillery, 23 Dec. 1909, and was promoted Lieutenant 23 Dec. 1912. He served in the European War from 1914 to 1917. He was twice mentioned in Despatches, and was created a Companion of the Distinguished Service Order for gallant services at the Battle of Neuve Chapelle [London Gazette, 15 April, 1915]: " Gerald Arthur Cammell, Lieut., 44th Battery, Royal Field Artillery. For conspicuous gallantry at Neuve Chapelle. When employed as Observing Officer he saw that the second line of the 1st Battn. 39th Garhwal Rifles had lost their British officers, and at once proceeded to lead the men. He went forward in the attack with four men under very heavy fire, but was wounded after going 20 yards, as were three of his four men." Invested by the King 27 May, 1915. He was Temporary Captain from June, 1915, until promoted to substantive rank 23 Dec. 1915, and Acting Major from April to Aug. 1917.

GREENLEES, JAMES ROBERTSON CAMPBELL, Lieut., was born 14 Dec. 1878, son of Matthew Greenlees, of Langdale, Dowanhill, Glasgow. Educated at Loretto, and at Cambridge and Glasgow Universities (M.B., B.C. Cantab.); Out-patient Physician, Western Infirmary, Glasgow, and Out-patient Physician, Royal Hospital for Sick Children, Glasgow. He joined the Royal Army Medical Corps, as a Lieutenant, 12 Aug. 1914, and was appointed to the 22nd Field Ambulance 14 Sept. 1914. He served in the European War, and was created a Companion of the Distinguished Service Order for his services at Neuve Chapelle [London Gazette, 15 April, 1915]: " James Robertson Campbell Greenlees, M.B., Temporary Lieutenant, 22nd Field Ambulance, Royal Army Medical Corps. For his great gallantry and devotion to duty at Neuve Chapelle from 10 to 14 March, 1915, in attending on the wounded under very heavy fire. Lieut. Greenlees has been twice previously brought to notice." He became Captain 12 Aug. 1915; became Commanding Officer of the 98th Field Ambulance, Aug. 1915; and was awarded a Bar to the Distinguished Service Order. He was also made a Chevalier of the Legion of Honour. He has retired from the Royal Army Medical Corps.

London Gazette, 28 April, 1915.—" War Office, 28 April, 1915. His Majesty the King has been graciously pleased to approve of the appointment of the undermentioned Officers to be Companions of the Distinguished Service Order, in recognition of their gallantry and devotion to duty whilst serving with the Expeditionary Force."

ARDEN, JOHN HENRY MORRIS, Capt., was born 2 Feb. 1875, son of the late Rev. A. H. Arden. He entered the Army 15 May, 1897, in the Worcestershire Regt., being promoted Captain 29 Dec. 1900. He served in the South African War from 1899 to 1902, and was present in operations in Cape Colony, south of Orange River, 1899–1900; operations in Cape Colony, Orange River Colony and the Transvaal, 30 Nov. 1900, to 31 May, 1902 (Queen's Medal with three clasps; King's Medal with two clasps); also saw active service in 1912, against the Beir and Annah Tribes, in South-Eastern Soudan, receiving the Soudan Medal with clasp, and the second class Osmanieh, and retired from the Service 11 Sept. 1912. He rejoined for service in the European War, 1914–18; was created a Companion of the Distinguished Service Order [London Gazette, 28 April, 1915]: " John Henry Morris Arden, Capt., Worcestershire Regt." He was twice mentioned in Despatches, and was given the Brevet of Lieutenant-Colonel; became Commandant, No. 2 Royal Flying Corps Cadet Wing. He died 23 July, 1918. His D.S.O. was awarded " for conspicuous gallantry and ability at Neuve Chapelle on 12 March, 1915. When the battalion on his right was driven from their trenches he formed his company under a heavy fire to a flank, counter-attacked the German right with great determination, and thereby enabled the battalion to reoccupy their trenches."

BASTARD, REGINALD, Capt., was born 2 Oct. 1880, only son of the late John Anderson Bastard. He entered the Lincolnshire Regt. 18 April, 1900; became Lieutenant 26 April, 1902; Captain 6 Jan. 1912; Major 1 Sept. 1915, and was Temporary Lieutenant-Colonel, Lincolnshire Regt., 11 March, 1916, to 30 July, 1917, and Acting Lieutenant-Colonel, Lincolnshire Regt., 9 April to 27 May, 1918. He held a special appointment (graded D.A.A.G.) as Instructor, Senior Officers' School, Aldershot, 7 Oct. 1917, to 8 April, 1918. He served in the South African War, 1899–1902; took part in the operations in the Orange Free State, April to May, 1900, including actions at Vet River and Zand River; served during operations in the Transvaal in May and June, 1900, including actions near Johannesburg and Pretoria; again in the Transvaal, Nov. 1900, to Aug. 1901 (Queen's Medal with two clasps, and King's Medal with two clasps.) He served in the European War, 1914–18, and for Neuve Chapelle was created a Companion of the Distinguished Service Order [London Gazette, 28 April, 1915]: " Reginald Bastard, Capt., 2nd Battn. The Lincolnshire Regt. For conspicuous gallantry at Neuve Chapelle on 10 March, 1915. In the attack on the German position he entered their trenches ahead of his company, having had to force his way through the entanglements." He became Major 1 Sept. 1915.

CARTER-CAMPBELL, GEORGE TUPPER CAMPBELL, Major, was born 2 April, 1869. He entered the Army, as Second Lieutenant in the Scottish Rifles, 23 Oct. 1889, becoming Lieutenant 29 April, 1892, and Captain 2 Nov. 1897. He served in the South African War from 1899–1902, serving as Adjutant, Scottish Rifles, 20 Nov. 1899 to 31 May, 1902, and afterwards to 21 July, 1903. He was present at the Relief of Ladysmith, including action at Colenso; took part in the operations of 17 to 24 Jan. 1900, and action at Spion Kop; operations of 5 to 7 Feb. 1900, and action at Vaal Kranz; operations on Tugela Heights, 14 to 27 Feb. 1900, and action at Pieter's Hill; served during operations in Natal (March to June, 1900), including action at Laing's Nek (6 to 9 June); in the Transvaal, east of Pretoria, July to 29 Nov. 1900; again in the Transvaal, 30 Nov. 1900, to Aug. 1901, and Nov. 1901, to 31 May, 1902; also during the operations on the Zululand Frontier of Natal in Sept. and Oct. 1901 (Despatches [London

Gazette, 8 Feb. 1901 (Sir R. H. Buller, 30 March and 9 Nov. 1900), and London Gazette, 10 Sept. 1901]; was given the Brevet of Major 29 Nov. 1900, and received the Queen's Medal with four clasps, and the King's Medal with two clasps.) On his return from Africa he became Adjutant to the Volunteers, 1904 to 1907; was promoted Major 3 May, 1907. On the outbreak of the European War in Aug. 1914, he went with the Expeditionary Force to serve on the Western Front, with the 2nd Battn. Cameronians. He was present at the Battle of Neuve Chapelle, and for his services was mentioned in Despatches, and created a Companion of the Distinguished Service Order [London Gazette, 28 April, 1915]: "George Tupper Campbell, Major, 2nd Battn. The Cameronians (Scottish Rifles). For conspicuous gallantry and ability at Neuve Chapelle, from 10 to 12 March, 1915. He took over command of the battalion on the 10th of March, and, although wounded, maintained with great determination the position which had been gained. He had only one surviving officer to assist him. For his conduct on this occasion he was also promoted Brevet Lieutenant-Colonel and Brevet Colonel." From 22 Sept. 1915, to 29 Jan. 1918, he commanded the 94th Infantry Brigade, B.E.F., British Armies in France; and from 16 March, 1918, was Temporary Major-General, commanding the 51st Division, British Armies in France. He was promoted Colonel 2 June, 1919. The Brevets of Lieutenant-Colonel and Colonel were given to him on 3 June, 1916 and 3 June, 1917 respectively, and he was created a C.B. in 1919. In 1908 he married Frances Elizabeth, daughter of Colonel David Ward, R.E., and they have one son and one daughter.

HARINGTON, HENRY DOUGLAS, Capt., was born 24 May, 1886, son of Colonel Frederick William Harington, late commanding 14th Regimental District, and 1st West Yorkshire Regt. He was educated at the Bedford Grammar School and Royal Military College, Sandhurst, obtaining his first commission in the West Yorkshire Regt. 7 Nov. 1906. He was promoted Lieutenant 24 April, 1909, and Captain 14 March, 1914. Capt. Harington served in France in the European War from 4 Nov. 1914, until Jan. 1917. He was mentioned in Despatches 28 April, 1915, 22 June, 1915, and 14 Nov. 1916, and was created a Companion of the Distinguished Service Order [London Gazette, 28 April, 1915]: "Henry Douglas Harington, Capt., 2nd Battn. The Prince of Wales's Own (West Yorkshire Regt.). For the ability and gallantry displayed on the 12th March, 1915, at Neuve Chapelle. After the enemy had gained temporary possession of a portion of our trenches he brought on flank fire to bear on them, which saved the situation." He was Brigade Major, 4th Canadian Infantry Brigade, B.E.F., British Armies in France, 10 Dec. 1915, to 12 Feb. 1917; was awarded the Military Cross: "For conspicuous gallantry and consistent good work. Regardless of personal safety he was frequently in a fire-swept area, encouraging all ranks. He was a splendid example. (Operations on the Somme)." Capt. Harington was Staff Captain, War Office, from 1 Sept. 1917, and was given the Brevet of Major 1 Jan. 1919.

OLDFIELD, LEOPOLD CHARLES LOUIS, Major, was born 3 Feb. 1872, and was gazetted to the Royal Artillery 1 April, 1892; became Lieutenant 1 April, 1895, and Captain 5 April, 1900. He was Adjutant, Volunteers, Oct. 1902, to Oct. 1905; Adjutant, R.A., 1 Aug. 1906, to 8 Oct. 1909, and was promoted to Major 2 Oct. 1909, and to Lieutenant-Colonel 3 Sept. 1915. Major Oldfield served in the European War, 1914–18, as Brigadier-General, R.A., 51st Division, British Armies in France, 2 July, 1918. He was mentioned in Despatches twice; was given the Brevet of Colonel 1 Jan. 1918; was created a C.B. in 1918, and a C.M.G. in 1919. He was created a Companion of the Distinguished Service Order [London Gazette, 28 April, 1915]: "Leopold Charles Louis Oldfield, Major, 33rd Battery, Royal Field Artillery. For conspicuous ability and gallantry at Neuve Chapelle on 10 March, 1915, in command of his battery in action, and for successful service in cutting wire entanglements. He took one of his guns to within 700 yards of the enemy, and so greatly facilitated the advance of our infantry."

WINNINGTON, JOHN FRANCIS SARTORIUS, Major, was born at Charlton Kings, Gloucestershire, 17 Sept. 1876, son of the late Capt. John Taylor Winnington, Dragoon Guards. He was educated at Worcester Park, Surrey, and at the Oxford Military College, Oxford, and was commissioned in the 1st Battn. Worcestershire Regt. 15 March, 1897. He served in the South African War from 1899 to 1900, with the 2nd Battn. Royal Dublin Fusiliers up to the Relief of Ladysmith, and later with the 2nd Battn. Worcestershire Regt. in the Orange River Colony. He was present at the Relief of Ladysmith, including action at Colenso; operations of 17 to 24 Jan. 1900, and action at Spion Kop; operations of 5 to 7 Feb. 1900, and action at Vaal Kranz; during the operations on Tugela Heights (14 to 27 Feb.) and action at Pieter's Hill; in the Orange Free State, Feb. to May, 1900; in the Orange River Colony, May to 29 Nov. 1900; also in Cape Colony, south of Orange River, 1899–1900 (Queen's Medal with four clasps: Relief of Ladysmith, Tugela Heights, Cape Colony and Orange Free State). He was promoted Captain 2 Jan. 1901, and served as Adjutant to the 5th Worcestershire Regt. from 1906 to 1910. He was appointed Adjutant to the 1st Battn. in 1912, and became Major in 1914. Major Winnington served in the European War; was mentioned in Sir John French's Despatch, 5 April, 1915, and was created a Companion of the Distinguished Service Order [London Gazette, 28 April, 1915]: "John Francis Sartorius Winnington, Major, 1st Battn. The Worcestershire Regt. For conspicuous gallantry and ability from 10 to 12 March, at Neuve Chapelle, when he commanded the two leading companies in several attacks, and subsequently commanded the battalion, showing great foresight in correctly anticipating the desires of the Brigade Commander in regard to the advance of other troops, at a time when orders could not be conveyed to them." He was given the Brevet of Lieutenant-Colonel for distinguished service in the Field while in command of the 4th Battn. The Worcestershire Regt., Gallipoli [London Gazette, 14 June, 1915]. Lieut.-Colonel Winnington was again mentioned in Despatches by Sir Ian Hamilton, Commanding the Mediterranean Expeditionary Force. He was subsequently appointed A.I.R., Headquarters, Western Command, Chester.

John F. S. Winnington.

London Gazette, 8 May, 1915.—"War Office, 8 May, 1915. His Majesty the King has been graciously pleased to approve of the appointment of the undermentioned Officers to be Companions of the Distinguished Service Order, in recognition of their gallantry and devotion to duty whilst serving with the Expeditionary Force."

COLLINS, LIONEL PETER, Capt., was born 27 Nov. 1878, seventh son of the late Henry Collins, Leopold House, Reading. He was educated at Marlborough, joined the Worcestershire Regt. 5 Jan. 1901, and became Lieutenant, Worcestershire Regt. 21 Dec. 1901; Lieutenant, Indian Army, 14 Nov. 1902; Captain 5 Jan. 1910, and Major, 1916. He was Acting Lieutenant-Colonel, Indian Army, 5 July, 1917, to 20 March, 1918 and 21 March to 19 May, 1918; was wounded three times; mentioned in Despatches; given the Brevet of Major 3 June, 1916, and created a Companion of the Distinguished Service Order [London Gazette, 8 May, 1915]: "Lionel Peter Collins, Capt., 1st Battn. 4th Gurkha Rifles. For conspicuous gallantry throughout the campaign, especially on 12 March, 1915, when he took the initiative with his company in the attack at Bois de Biez, and captured a German trench, took 100 prisoners, killing or wounding a considerable number of the remainder of the occupants." Major Collins married, in 1910, Gladys Lysaght, daughter of H. T. Rutherford, M.D., of Taunton, and they have one son.

CUTHBERT, THOMAS WILKINSON, Major, served in the European War, 1914–16; was mentioned in Despatches; created a C.M.G., 1916; promoted to Honorary Lieutenant-Colonel, and created a Companion of the Distinguished Service Order [London Gazette, 8 May, 1915]: "Thomas Wilkinson Cuthbert, Major, 4th (Ross Highland) Battn. Seaforth Highlanders (Ross-shire Buffs, The Duke of Albany's), Territorial Force. For conspicuous gallantry during the operations round Neuve Chapelle. After his Colonel had been wounded he commanded the battalion with great ability, although himself wounded in the head."

DIGBY, ARTHUR KENELM, Capt., was born 19 May, 1879, son of the late Sir K. E. Digby, G.C.B., P.C. He was educated at Harrow, and at Corpus Christi College, Oxford, and entered the Royal Artillery 25 April, 1902, from the Imperial Yeomanry, becoming Lieutenant 24 May, 1905; Captain 30 Oct. 1914, and Major 13 March, 1916. He was Acting Lieutenant-Colonel, R.A., from 3 Jan. 1919. He served in the South African War, 1901–2, with the Imperial Yeomanry; took part in the operations in the Transvaal, March to May, 1902; in the Orange River Colony, April, 1901, to 31 May, 1902; also in Cape Colony, April to May, 1901 (Queen's Medal with three clasps). In 1911 Major Digby married Violet, daughter of Sherbrooke Keatinge, late Indian State Railways. He served in the European War, and was created a Companion of the Distinguished Service Order [London Gazette, 8 May, 1915]: "Arthur Kenelm Digby, Capt., R.A. For conspicuous ability and gallantry during the campaign. He has been at the observing station on almost every occasion when his battalion was in action, and by his coolness and resource greatly contributed to the success attained. He was severely wounded at Neuve Chapelle on 10 March, 1915."

HAWKER, LANOE GEORGE, Lieut., served in the European War, and was awarded the Victoria Cross (see Victoria Cross Volume). He was created a Companion of the Distinguished Service Order [London Gazette, 8 May, 1915]: "Lanoe George Hawker, Lieut., Royal Engineers and Royal Flying Corps. For conspicuous gallantry on 19 April, 1915, when he succeeded in dropping bombs on the German airship shed at Gontrode from a height of only 200 feet under circumstances of the greatest risk. Lieut. Hawker displayed remarkable ingenuity in utilizing an unoccupied German captive balloon to shield him from fire while manœuvring to drop the bombs."

HUNTER, CHARLES GEORGE WOODBURN, Major, was born 21 Dec. 1871. He entered the Royal Engineers 25 July, 1890; became Lieutenant 25 July, 1893; Captain 21 May, 1901; Major 25 July, 1910; Lieutenant-Colonel 24 Sept. 1918, and was Temporary Brigadier-General 25 Dec. 1917, to 13 Jan. 1919. He was on Special Service, China Expedition, from 24 Sept. 1900; on Special Service, Somaliland Field Force, 8 Oct. 1903, to 4 June, 1904; Staff Captain, Headquarters of Army, 2 Aug. 1904, to 15 Dec. 1909; Chief Engineer, 12th Army Corps, British Salonika Force, 25 Dec. 1917, to 13 Jan. 1919; C.R.E., 26th Division. He served in the Tirah Campaign, 1897–98; Assistant Field Engineer (24 Feb. to April, 1898) (Medal with clasp). Served in China, 1900 (Despatches [London Gazette, 13 Sept. 1901]; Medal). Served in East Africa, 1903–4; took part in the operations in Somaliland; on Staff; in the action at Jidballi (Medal with two clasps). For his services in the European War he was mentioned in Despatches three times; was given the Brevets of Lieutenant-Colonel 1 Jan. 1916, and Colonel 1 Jan. 1919; created a C.M.G., 1918, and for Neuve Chapelle was created a Companion of the Distinguished Service Order [London Gazette, 8 May, 1915]: "Charles George Woodburn Hunter, Major, Royal Engineers. For conspicuous ability and gallantry on many occasions, especially on the 10 to 14 March, 1915, at Neuve Chapelle. He was in command of two companies, and succeeded in establishing a strong breastwork line under very difficult circumstances, whilst exposed to heavy shell and rifle fire." In 1911, Major Hunter married Gladys, daughter of C. H. Hutton.

LODWICK, JOHN THORNTON, Capt., was born at Fairlands, Sutton, Surrey, 8 Sept. 1882, son of Robert William Lodwick, late Indian Civil Service, and Justice of the Peace for Surrey, and of Florence, his wife, second daughter of the late Rev. W. Thornton, Rector of North Bovey, Devon. He served through the Boer War, as a Subaltern in the Royal Lancaster Regt. He was awarded the King's and Queen's Medals. He accompanied his regiment to Calcutta, where he received his appointment to the 3rd Gurkhas, being shortly afterwards appointed Military Instructor at Palhmalie, Central Provinces, subsequently holding the same position at Istaria, in the Bombay Presidency, where, by a strange coincidence, his grandfather, General Lodwick, had formerly served as British Resident at the Rajah's Court. When the European War broke out, the Gurkhas formed part of the Indian Force sent to Europe, and Captain Lodwick was appointed Brigade Machine Gun Officer, in which capacity he served at the Battle of Neuve Chapelle. He was created a Companion of the Distinguished Service Order [London Gazette, 8 May, 1915]: "John Thornton Lodwick, Capt., 2nd Battn. 3rd (Queen Alexandra's Own) Gurkhas. For conspicuous ability and gallantry as Brigade Machine Gun Officer from 10 to 13 March, 1915, at Neuve Chapelle. He reconnoitred the captured positions from end to end, and brought 20 machine guns into position, which caused an immense number of casualties to the enemy when they attacked on the 12th of March." He was appointed Musketry Instructor. Capt. Lodwick applied for permission to rejoin his regiment, and it was for this purpose that he was travelling in the Persia when it was torpedoed in the Mediterranean, 30 Dec. 1916. He met his death standing on the deck of the sinking ship, flinging chains and other things to the women and men struggling in the waters in an endeavour to save their lives. Being an excellent swimmer, he could easily have saved his own life by plunging into the sea, but he gave it for others without hesitation in one supreme choice. The Government of Bombay have presented a tablet recording his services, which is to be attached to the memorial to his grandfather, General Lodwick, at "Lodwick Point," in the Mahableshwar Sanitorium of the Bombay Presidency, a place which owes its origin and prosperity to the testimony of General Lodwick, in 1824, when British Resident in the Bombay Presidency, who brought to notice the salubrity of its climate. The following is an extract from a letter from Colonel Ormsby, dated 18 Jan. 1916: "His loss as a regimental officer is incalculable. In the course of thirty years' service, after intimate knowledge of many hundreds of officers, I have not come across half a dozen of his equals, and it is a melancholy pleasure to be able to remember that during the six years I have commanded the battalions, the terms I have used in my annual reports on him are such as I have seldom been able to use in their entirety to any other officer. He possessed a peculiar knack of getting the best and most willing work out of his men, and there was no man I would sooner have had with me in a tight place than him. I am perfectly certain that he died as he lived—calm and collected, and doing his best for those around him." The deceased officer was a fine horseman and polo player, a good shot and big game sportsman, and a splendid swimmer. Capt. Lodwick married, at Cheltenham Roman Catholic Church, 1 April, 1915, Kathleen, third daughter of the Hon. H. Crump, C.S.I., Indian Civil Service, Deputy Commissioner, Central Provinces; they had one son, John Alan, who was born at Cheltenham on 2 March, 1916, after his father's death.

John Thornton Lodwick.

ROMILLY, FRANCIS HENRY, Capt., was born 1 Oct. 1878, at Bangalore, South India, son of the late Capt. F. J. Romilly, R.E., who was killed in action in the Sudan, and Mary de Berdt Romilly (*née* Hovell). He was educated at Cheltenham College; was gazetted to the Welsh Regt. 4 Jan. 1899; became Lieutenant in March, 1908, and Captain 9 Feb. 1910. He served in the South African War, 1899–1902; took part in the Relief of Kimberley; in the Orange Free State, Feb. to May, 1900, including operations at Paardeberg (17 to 26 Feb.); actions at Poplar Grove, Dreifontein, Vet River (5 and 6 May) and Zand River; in the Transvaal in May and June, 1900, including actions near Johannesburg, Pretoria and Diamond Hill (11 and 12 June); in the Transvaal, east of Pretoria, July to 29 Nov. 1900, including action at Belfast (26 and 27 Aug.); in Cape Colony, south of Orange River, 1899–1900, including actions at Colesberg (14 Jan. to 1 Feb.); again in the Transvaal 30 Nov. 1900, to 31 May, 1902 (Queen's Medal with six clasps, and King's Medal with two clasps); served in West Africa (Northern Nigeria), 1903; during the Kano-Sokoto Campaign (Medal with clasp). He exchanged into the Leicestershire Regt. in 1910. Capt. Romilly served in the European War. He was created a Companion of the Distinguished Service Order [London Gazette, 8 May, 1915]: "Francis Henry Romilly, Capt., 2nd Battn. Leicestershire Regt. For conspicuous gallantry and enterprise and great daring at Neuve Chapelle 10 March, 1915. He led a small party with bombs against the German dug-outs and captured about 100 yards of their trenches, the occupants being all either killed or wounded by himself and his men." Capt. Romilly was constantly in action up to the day of his death. He was wounded in Feb. 1915, but never left the firing line, and fell in action 25 Sept. 1915. His death in the war was greatly mourned, not only by his regiment but by the whole division, where he was held in the highest esteem for his great courage and manly qualities. A brother officer wrote: "His name was a byword in the whole division for his extraordinary bravery. All his men loved him and followed him anywhere. He was the bravest of the brave."

TORRIE, CLAUD JAMESON, Capt., was born 20 March, 1879, son of the late Colonel L. J. Torrie, Indian Army. He was educated at Cheltenham College and at Sandhurst; was commissioned in the Royal Warwickshire Regt. 11 Feb. 1899; became Lieutenant, Royal Warwickshire Regt., 21 March, 1900, and was transferred to the Indian Army 14 Aug. 1900. He was promoted Captain, Indian Army, 11 Feb. 1908, and Major 1 Sept. 1915. Capt. Torrie was Inspector of Army Signalling in India 1 April to 6 Nov. 1912. He served in the European War, 1914–16; was mentioned in Despatches twice, and was created a Companion of the Distinguished Service Order [London Gazette, 8 May, 1915]: "Claud Jameson Torrie, Capt., 30th Punjabis, Commanding No. 35 Signal Company. For marked ability during the campaign, especially at Neuve Chapelle during the operations from 10 to 14 March, 1915, when the successful work of the division was to a very great extent dependent on the efficiency of the communication established and maintained by him under very heavy fire."

WATT, DONALD MUNRO, Major, was born 18 June. 1871, and entered the Gordon Highlanders 7 Nov. 1891; became Lieutenant 14 Feb. 1895. He was promoted Captain, Indian Army, 10 July, 1901; Major 7 Nov. 1909, and Lieutenant-Colonel 7 Nov. 1917. From 28 May to 27 Nov. 1916, he was Temporary Lieutenant-Colonel, Territorial Force Battn. West Riding Regt., and from 28 Nov. 1916, to 31 Aug. 1918, Temporary Brigadier-General. He was on Special Service with the Somaliland Field Force from 29 April, 1904; Adjutant, Indian Volunteers, 1905–6; Brigade Major, India, 6 Aug. 1908, to 5 Aug. 1912; G.S.O.2, 13th Division, British Armies in France, 19 Sept. to 11 Nov. 1914; G.S.O.2, Colchester Training Centre, 17 to 25 May, 1915; G.S.O.1, 25th Division, New Armies, B.E.F., 26 May, 1915, to 17 May, 1916; Brigade Commander, 145th Division, British Armies in France, 28 Nov. 1916, to 31 Aug. 1918. He took part in the operations in Chitral, 1895, with the Relief Force; at the storming of the Malakand Pass (slightly wounded; Medal with clasp); served at Tirah, 1897–98; was present at the capture of the Sampagha and Arhanga Passes; during operations in the Waran Valley and action of 16 Nov. 1897; during operations at and around Dwatoi and action of 24 Nov. 1897; against the Khani Khel Chamkanis; also in the Bara Valley 7 to 14 Dec. 1897 (two clasps); served in East Africa, 1904, during the operations in Somaliland, as Special Service Officer (Medal with clasp). For his services in the European War he was mentioned twice in Despatches; given the Brevet of Lieutenant-Colonel 3 June, 1916, and was created a Companion of the Distinguished Service Order [London Gazette, 8 May, 1915]: "Donald Munro Watt, Major, 2nd Battn. 2nd King Edward's Own Gurkha Rifles (Sirmoor Rifles). For conspicuous gallantry on 10 March, 1915, when he led his company with great ability in the attack on the Bois de Biez. On the next day he continued to lead his company, after being wounded, till he could go no further."

WICKS, HENRY WILLIAM CAIRNS, Capt., was born 21 Dec. 1881. He was gazetted to the Seaforth Highlanders 20 Jan, 1900; became Lieutenant 21 Jan. 1901; Captain 4 March, 1906; was Adjutant, Seaforth Highlanders, 1 May, 1909, to 30 April, 1912; was promoted to Major 1 Sept. 1915; was Temporary Lieutenant-Colonel 9 May to 8 Oct. 1916; Acting Lieutenant-Colonel 8 Jan. 1818. He was specially employed at the War Office 14 Oct. 1915, to 27 Feb. 1916; G.S.O.3, G.H.Q., Home Forces, 22 Feb. to 5 May, 1916; Brigade Major (Staff Officer, Rouen Base) 1 March, 1917, to 5 Jan. 1918; Commandant, School of Instruction, British Armies in France, 8 Jan. 1918. He served on the North-West Frontier of India, 1908 (Medal with clasp). In the European War, 1914–17, he was twice wounded. He was mentioned in Despatches twice, and was created a Companion of the Distinguished Service Order [London Gazette, 8 May, 1915]: "Henry William Cairns Wicks, Capt., Seaforth Highlanders (Ross-shire Buffs, The Duke of Albany's). For marked ability in the presence of the enemy on many occasions. He was wounded on 10 March, 1915, at Neuve Chapelle, while directing his company in the attack on the trenches."

London Gazette, 5 May, 1915.—"His Majesty the King has been pleased to approve of the following reward for distinguished service in the field, in connection with the successful operations against Dervish Forces at Shimber Berris, Somaliland, during the months of Nov. 1914, and Feb. 1915. To be a Companion of the Distinguished Service Order."

CARTON DE WIART, ADRIAN, Capt., served in the European War, 1914–15; was eight times wounded; was awarded the Victoria Cross (see Victoria Cross Volume); the C.B., the C.M.G., Croix d'Officier de l'Ordre de la Couronne and the Croix de Guerre (Belgian decorations). Brigadier-General Carton de Wiart was also created a Companion of the Distinguished Service Order [London Gazette, 5 May, 1915]: "Adrian Carton de Wiart, Capt., 4th (Royal Irish) Dragoon Guards. For distinguished service in the field in connection with the operations against Dervish Forces at Shimber Berris, Somaliland, during the months of Nov. 1914, and Feb. 1915." He married the Countess Frederica, eldest daughter of Prince Fugger Babenhausen, and Nora, Princess Hohenlohe, and they have two daughters.

London Gazette, 3 June, 1915.—"Admiralty, 3 June, 1915. The King has been graciously pleased to give orders for the appointment to the Distinguished Service Order in respect of the undermentioned Officers, in recognition of their services with the Mediterranean Expeditionary Force."

CAMPBELL, VICTOR LINDSEY ARBUTHNOT, Commander, was born 20 Aug. 1875, son of the late Capt. Hugh Campbell, Royal Navy. He was in the Antarctic Expedition in 1913, and was specially promoted to Commander, Royal Navy. He served in the European War, with the Mediterranean Expeditionary Force, taking part in the Dardanelles Expedition. He was mentioned in Despatches, and created a Companion of the Distinguished Service Order [London Gazette, 3 June, 1915]: "Victor Lindsey Arbuthnot Campbell, Commander, Royal Navy, commanding

Drake Battn., Royal Naval Division. In recognition of his services with the Mediterranean Expeditionary Force." He was awarded a Bar to his D.S.O. in June, 1917. In 1902 he married Lilian Mary, daughter of Lieut.-General Sir H. H. Settle, K.C.B. For services see p. 409 [L. G. 3 July, 1915].

FREYBERG, BERNARD CECIL, Lieut.-Commander, was born in 1890. He served in the European War, with the Mediterranean Expeditionary Force, and was wounded seven times; given the Brevets of Major and of Lieutenant-Colonel; awarded the Victoria Cross; created a C.M.G. in 1919, and was created a Companion of the Distinguished Service Order [London Gazette, 3 June, 1915]: "Bernard Cecil Freyberg, Lieut.-Commander, Royal Naval Volunteer Reserve, Hood Battn. Royal Naval Division. In recognition of his services with the Mediterranean Expeditionary Force." (See Victoria Cross Volume.) For services see p. 409 [L. G. 3 July, 1915].

London Gazette, 3 June, 1915.—"War Office, 3 June, 1915. The King has been graciously pleased to give orders for the following rewards for gallantry and devotion to duty in connection with the operations at the Dardanelles (Mediterranean Expeditionary Force). To be Companions of the Distinguished Service Order."

McNICOLL, WALTER RAMSAY, Lieut.-Colonel, was born 27 May, 1877, at South Melbourne, Victoria, Australia, son of William Walter Alexander McNicoll and Helen McNicoll (*née* Ramsay), his wife. He was educated at the Victorian State Schools; the Training College Melbourne, and at Melbourne University. He was commissioned in the Australian Cadet Forces 5 March, 1895, being transferred to the 5th Australian Infantry Regt. on the 29th Nov. 1905. On the outbreak of the European War, Major McNicoll joined the Australian Imperial Force 15 Aug. 1914, as Major, Second-in-Command of 7th Battn. He was promoted Lieutenant-Colonel to command the 6th Battn. 3 April, 1915; was mentioned twice in Despatches during his service in Gallipoli—by General Sir Ian Hamilton and General Sir W. Birdwood, and created a Companion of the Distinguished Service Order [London Gazette, 3 June, 1915]: "Walter Ramsay McNicoll, Lieut.-Colonel, Australian Imperial Force. For gallantry and devotion to duty in connection with the operations at the Dardanelles (Mediterranean Expeditionary Force)." He was wounded during an attack on Krithia 8 May, 1915, and returned to Australia on the 24th of the following Dec. Two months later (10 Feb. 1916) he was appointed Temporary Brigadier-General, and promoted Colonel in the same year. Brigadier-General McNicoll was sent to France in Nov. 1916, and was twice again mentioned in Despatches. He was created a C.B. in 1919, and a C.M.G. in 1918. For services see p. 409 [L. G. 3 July, 1915].

Walter R. McNicoll.

WHITE, CYRIL BRUDENELL BINGHAM, Lieut.-Colonel, served in the South African War in 1902, and received the Queen's Medal with three clasps. He passed the Staff College. On the outbreak of the European war he was appointed Director of Military operations of the Australian Military Forces. He also became a Member of the War Railway Council and a Member of the Headquarters Mobilization Committee. He was twice mentioned in Despatches; was appointed A.D.C. to the King, 1917; was created a K.C.M.G. in 1919; a C.B. in 1916; a C.M.G. in 1918, and was created a Companion of the Distinguished Service Order [London Gazette, 3 June, 1915]: "Cyril Brudenell Bingham White, Lieut.-Colonel, Royal Australian Garrison Artillery. For gallantry and devotion to duty in connection with the operations at the Dardanelles (Mediterranean Expeditionary Force)." He married, in 1905, Ethel, daughter of Walter Davidson, of Colibran Park, Victoria. For services see p. 409 [L. G. 3 July, 1915].

BECKWITH, ARTHUR THACKERAY, Major, was born 28 Oct. 1875, eldest son of the Rev. G. Beckwith, of Winchester Cathedral. He was educated at Radley College, and joined the Hants Regt 28 Sept 1895, becoming Lieutenant 19 Nov. 1897; Captain 28 Jan. 1903; was Adjutant, Hants Regt., 23 Oct. 1903, to 22 Oct, 1906; was promoted to Major 29 Dec. 1912; to Lieutenant-Colonel 1 Oct. 1915, and was Temporary Brigadier-General 2 Aug. 1917, to 12 July, 1918. He was Adjutant, Volunteers, 26 Jan. 1907, to 31 March, 1908; Adjutant, Territorial Force, 1 April, 1908, to 25 Jan. 1911; commanded the 153rd Infantry Brigade, British Armies in France, 10 Aug. to 20 Sept. 1918; commanded the 35th Infantry Brigade, British Armies in France, 10 Aug. to 20 Sept. 1918; commanded the 13th Infantry Brigade, British Armies in France, 21 Sept. 1918. He served with the South Lancashire Regt. in the South African War, 1899–1900; was present at the Relief of Ladysmith, including operations of 17 to 24 Jan. 1900, and action at Spion Kop; operations of 5 to 7 Feb. 1900, and action at Vaal Kranz, and in the operations on Tugela Heights (14 to 27 Feb. 1900) (Despatches [London Gazette, 8 Feb. and 10 Sept. 1901]; Queen's Medal with five clasps). He served at Aden, 1903–4; took part in the operations in the interior; served as Adjutant, 1st Battn. Hampshire Regt., 27 Oct. 1903, to 29 Feb. 1904. He served in the European War, at the Dardanelles, in command of the 2nd Hampshire Regt., in 1915, and elsewhere, 1916–18, commanding brigades in the 51st Highland Division, 12th Division and 5th Division, 1917–18. He was wounded; was created a C.B. in 1919; a C.M.G. in 1918, and was created a Companion of the Distinguished Service Order [London Gazette, 3 June, 1915]: "Arthur Thackeray Beckwith, Major, The Hampshire Regt. For gallantry and devotion to duty in connection with the operations at the Dardanelles (Mediterranean Expeditionary Force)." He married, in 1904, Dorothy, daughter of J. B. Thomson, I.C.S., and they have one son and one daughter. For services see p. 409 [L. G. 3 July, 1915].

BRAND, CHARLES HENRY, Capt., was born 4 Sept. 1873, son of the late Charles Hayman Brand, of Topsham, Exeter. He served for 18 years in the Education Department, Queensland, and for 10 years on the Administrative and Instructional Staff of the Australian Forces. He served in the South African War, 1900–1, and received the Queen's Medal with five clasps. He again saw active service in the European War, with the Mediterranean Expeditionary Force, taking part in the Dardanelles Campaign, 1914–15, and on the Western Front, 1914–17. He was promoted to Major 1 Jan. 1916; was six times mentioned in Despatches; given the Brevets of Major and of Lieutenant-Colonel; created a C.B. in 1918; a C.M.G. in 1916; promoted to Brigadier-General, commanding the 4th Infantry Brigade, Australian Imperial Forces, and was created a Companion of the Distinguished Service Order [London Gazette, 3 June, 1915]: "Charles Henry Brand, Capt., 3rd Infantry Brigade, Australian Imperial Forces. For gallantry and devotion to duty in connection with the operations at the Dardanelles (Mediterranean Expeditionary Force)." Brigadier-General C. H. Brand married Ella Arline, daughter of Charles Armstrong, of Charters Towers, Queensland, and they have two daughters. For services see p. 409 [L. G. 3 July, 1915].

DENTON, JAMES SAMUEL, Major, was born 1875. He joined the Australian Military Forces, and served in the European War, 1914–18, at the Dardanelles, and was created a Companion of the Distinguished Service Order [London Gazette, 3 June, 1915]: "James Samuel Denton, Major, 11th Australian Infantry Brigade. For gallantry and devotion to duty in connection with the operations at the Dardanelles (Mediterranean Expeditionary Force)." He married, in 1890, Eleanor Anne, daughter of John Henbry. For services see p. 409 [L. G. 3 July, 1915].

HART, HERBERT ERNEST, Major, was born at Wairarapa, 13 Oct. 1882, son of the late William Hart, Farmer, of Carterton, New Zealand. He was educated at Wellington, for the Law, entering the profession in civil life of Barrister and Solicitor. He served in the South African War, 1901–2, with the New Zealand Forces, and received the Queen's Medal with two clasps. Capt. Hart joined the 17th (Ruahine) Regt. New Zealand Forces 29 Oct. 1907, and became Major 14 Sept. 1912. He served in the European War; was mentioned in Despatches towards the end of May, 1915, and again in Jan. 1917, and was created a Companion of the Distinguished Service Order [London Gazette, 3 June, 1915]: "Herbert Ernest Hart, Major, 17th (Ruahine) Regt. New Zealand Forces. For gallantry and devotion to duty in connection with the operations at the Dardanelles (Mediterranean Expeditionary Force)." He was created a C.B. in 1919, and a C.M.G. in 1918; was promoted to Lieutenant-Colonel in 1915, and became Brigadier-General. He married, in 1903, Minnie Eleanor, second daughter of Roger Z. Renall, of Wairarapa, New Zealand, and they have one son and one daughter. For services see p. 409 [L. G. 3 July, 1915].

HEANE, JAMES, Major, joined the 9th Light Horse, Australian Military Forces; became Captain 27 June, 1911, and Major. He served in the European War; was mentioned twice in Despatches, and was created a Companion of the Distinguished Service Order [London Gazette, 3 June, 1915]: "James Heane, Major, 4th Australian Infantry Battn. (New South Wales). For gallantry and devotion to duty in connection with the operations at the Dardanelles (Mediterranean Expeditionary Force)." He was promoted Lieutenant-Colonel; was created a C.M.G. in 1917 and a C.B. in 1918. For services see p. 409 [L. G. 3 July, 1915].

MANSBRIDGE, WILLIAM OWEN, Major, was born 13 Jan. 1872, son of William Henry Mansbridge. He was educated for the Civil Service, privately, both in India and Australia, and became a Civil Servant in Western Australia. He was subsequently appointed Mining Warden, Registrar and Clerk of Petty Sessions, at the Kimberley, Murchison and Coolgardie Goldfields. He served in the European War, 1914–16, commanding the 44th Battn. 11th Infantry Brigade, 3rd Division, Australian Forces; was mentioned in Despatches, and was created a Companion of the Distinguished Service Order [London Gazette, 3 June, 1915]: "William Owen Mansbridge, Major, 16th Australian Infantry Battn. (South-Western Australia). For gallantry and devotion to duty in connection with the operations at the Dardanelles (Mediterranean Expeditionary Force)." He published a work on "Scheme for Training the Aboriginal Natives of Australia in the Use of Arms." He married Annie Caroline Jones, of Victoria, and they have five children. For services see p. 409 [L. G. 3 July, 1915].

William O. Mansbridge.

O'NEILL, EUGENE JOSEPH, Major, was born at Dunedin, New Zealand, in 1875. He was educated at the Christian Brothers' School, Dunedin, and at Otago University, and took his degrees of M.B. and F.R.C.S.; was Senior House Surgeon at Dunedin Hospital, 1899–1900; Resident Surgeon, Lock Hospital, London. He joined the New Zealand Medical Corps, and served in the South African War from 1901–2; was mentioned in Despatches, and received the Queen's Medal with five clasps. He became Major, New Zealand Medical Corps, attached to B (Howitzer) Battery, Dunedin, in Sept. 1903. Major O'Neill served in the European War, 1914–17, at the Dardanelles, in Egypt and in France; was mentioned in Despatches, and was created a Companion of the Distinguished Service Order [London Gazette, 3 June, 1915]: "Eugene Joseph O'Neill, Major, New Zealand Medical Corps. For gallantry and devotion to duty in connection with the operations at the Dardanelles (Mediterranean Expeditionary Force)." Promoted Lt.-Col. and created a C.M.G. He married Josephine Monaghan, of London. For services see p. 409 [L. G. 3 July, 1915].

RANKINE, ROBERT, Major, served in the European War, 1914–15, and was created a Companion of the Distinguished Service Order [London Gazette, 3 June, 1915]: "Robert Rankine, Major, 14th Australian Infantry Battn. (Victoria). For gallantry and devotion to duty in connection with the operations at the Dardanelles (Mediterranean Expeditionary Force)." For services see p. 409 [L. G. 3 July, 1915].

WAITE, FREDERICK, Major, entered the New Zealand Forces, and served in the European War from 1914, in Egypt and the Dardanelles. He was created a Companion of the Distinguished Service Order [London Gazette, 3 June, 1915]: "Frederick Waite, Major, New Zealand Engineers, Territorial Force. For gallantry and devotion to duty in connection with the operations at the Dardanelles (Mediterranean Expeditionary Force)." Major Waite was Chief Instructor of Engineers, New Zealand Expeditionary Force Training Camps, 1917–18. He married, in 1912, Ada Philipson Taylor. For services see p. 409 [L. G. 3 July, 1915].

ATKINSON, EDWARD WILLIAM, Capt., was born 12 Aug. 1873, eldest son of Edward Atkinson, of Ashfield, Moynalty, Kells, County Meath. He was educated at Trinity College, Dublin (B.A.); served in the 3rd Battn. Royal Inniskilling Fusiliers (Fermanagh Militia), 1893–96; entered the Army in 1896; became Captain in 1902, and Major, 1915. He was Adjutant, 6th Battn. Notts and Derby Regt., 1906–11; Hythe (Extra), 1898; was Signalling Certified Instructor, 1906; Provisional Course, 1911. He served in South Africa, 1900–2 (Queen's Medal with three clasps; King's Medal with two clasps). He served in the European War, 1914–15; was mentioned in Despatches, and created a Companion of the Distinguished Service Order [London Gazette, 3 June, 1915]: "Edward William Atkinson, Capt., 1st Battn. The Royal Inniskilling Fusiliers. For gallantry and devotion to duty in connection with the operations at the Dardanelles (Mediterranean Expeditionary Force)." He married Louise H. S. Oliver. For services see p. 409 [L. G. 3 July, 1915].

BUTLER, ARTHUR GRAHAM, Capt., joined the Australian Army Medical Corps, and served in the European War, with the 1st Australian Division, A.I.F.; was present at the Dardanelles Campaign, attached to the 9th Australian Infantry Battn. He was created a Companion of the Distinguished Service Order [London Gazette, 3 June, 1915]: "Arthur Graham Butler, Capt., Australian Army Medical Corps. For gallantry and devotion to duty in connection with the operations at the Dardanelles (Mediterranean Expeditionary Force)." He was promoted to Colonel. For services see p. 409 [L. G. 3 July, 1915].

CRITCHLEY-SALMONSON, ARTHUR CUNLIFFE BERNARD, Capt., was born 27 April 1886, son of Godfrey Critchley-Salmonson, of Torquay. He was educated at Eastman's Royal Naval Academy, Northwood Park, Winchester, and at the Royal Military Academy, Woolwich, and was gazetted to the Royal Munster Fusiliers 8 Oct. 1906, becoming Lieutenant 16 Sept. 1909, and Captain 28 Nov. 1914. He was employed with the New Zealand Military Forces 21 Dec. 1911, to 20 Dec. 1915, and was Adjutant, Canterbury Battn. New Zealand Expeditionary Force from its formation till 6 Aug. 1915; employed with the Egyptian Army 18 March, 1916; served in the Suez Canal engagement and at the Dardanelles during the European War, 1914–15; was twice wounded, mentioned in Despatches, and created a Companion of the Distinguished Service Order [London Gazette, 3 June, 1915]: "Arthur Bernard Critchley-Salmonson, Capt., Royal Munster Fusiliers, attached New Zealand Military Forces. For gallantry and devotion to duty in connection with the operations at the Dardanelles (Mediterranean Expeditionary Force)." For services see p. 409 [L. G. 3 July, 1915].

A. C. Critchley-Salmonson.

GEDDES, GUY WESTLAND, Capt., was born 8 Aug. 1880. He joined the New Zealand Contingent, and was gazetted to the Royal Munster Fusiliers 19 May, 1900, becoming Lieutenant 17 April, 1902; Captain 1 March, 1910; Major 1 Sept. 1915, and Temporary Lieutenant-Colonel, Royal Munster Fusiliers, 1 Sept. 1915, to 15 April, 1919. He was Brigade Major, 171st Infantry Brigade, Home Forces, British Armies in France, 13 June, 1916, to 18 July, 1917; G.S.O.2, 8th Division, British Armies in France, 19 to 20 July, 1917; Brigade Major, 47th Infantry Brigade, British Armies in France, 21 July to 3 Sept. 1917; Brigade Major, 1st Yeomanry Cyclist Brigade, Home Forces, 4 Oct. 1917, to 12 April, 1918; Brigade Major, 3rd Australian Training Reserve Brigade, England, 17 April, 1918, to 1919; Brigade Major, Special Reserve Brigade Forces in Great Britain, 14 April, 1919. He served in the South African War, 1899–1902, in the ranks, New Zealand Contingent; took part in the operations in Rhodesia, March, 1900; also in the Transvaal, west of Pretoria, July to 29 Nov. 1900; in Orange River Colony and Cape Colony, 30 Nov. 1900, to March, 1901; in the Transvaal, April to July, 1901; in Orange River Colony, Sept. 1901, to 31 May, 1902; also during operations in Cape Colony, July to Sept. 1901 (Despatches [London Gazette, 20 Aug. 1901]; Queen's Medal with four clasps, and King's Medal with two clasps). He served in the European War, 1914–16; was mentioned in Despatches and created a Companion of the D.S.O. [London Gazette, 3 June, 1915]: "Guy Westland Geddes, Capt., Royal Munster Fusiliers. For gallantry and devotion to duty in connection with the operations at the Dardanelles (Mediterranean Expeditionary Force)." For services see p. 409 [L. G. 3 July, 1915].

RIDINGS, CECIL, Capt., was born 9 July, 1876. He was gazetted to the Royal Inniskilling Fusiliers 20 May, 1899; became Lieutenant 20 June, 1900; Captain 27 Jan. 1904 and Major 1 Sept. 1915. From 1910 to 1913 he was employed with the Egyptian Army; from Dec. 1915, to June, 1916, he held a special appointment; from June, 1916, to March, 1918, was Brigade Major, B Group, Reserve Brigade, Home Counties Division, Home Forces; from 27 May, 1918, he was Brigade Major at Cape Town. He served in the European War, 1914–15, at the Dardanelles, and for the operations south of Krithia was mentioned in Despatches and created a Companion of the D.S.O. [London Gazette, 3 June, 1915]: "Cecil Ridings, Capt., 1st Battn. R. Inniskilling Fusiliers. For gallantry and devotion to duty in connection with the operations at the Dardanelles (Mediterranean Expeditionary Force)." For services see p. 409 [L. G. 3 July, 1915].

HAWORTH, RICHARD, Capt., was born at Cheadle, Cheshire, 25 Aug. 1882, son of Frederic Haworth, Honorary Colonel, 7th Battn. Lancashire Fusiliers (Territorial Force), Deputy Lieutenant and Justice of the Peace, Westmorland. He was educated at Horton Hall, Northamptonshire, and Charterhouse School, and at the Royal Military College, Sandhurst. He was commissioned in the 1st Battn. Lancashire Fusiliers, 28 Feb. 1902; became Lieutenant 23 Jan. 1905, and Captain 27 Nov. 1914, and served continuously with that battalion until 25 April, 1915, in Malta, Gibraltar, Egypt, India, Aden and in Gallipoli. He saw active service on the North-West Frontier of India, 1908, assisting in operations against the Mohmunds (attached 1st Battn. Prince of Wales's Own West Yorkshire Regt., and was awarded the Medal with clasp. He served during the European War, taking part in the landing on "W" Beach (Lancashire Landing), 25 April, in command of A Company, 1st Battn. Lancashire Fusiliers. Capt. Haworth, with 50 men, was told off to capture a very strongly-held redoubt, surrounded by formidable wire entanglements. Although wounded, he refused to be removed until more troops arrived, and continued to command with a bullet through his back. He was mentioned in General Sir Ian Hamilton's Despatch 12 June, 1915, and created a Companion of the Distinguished Service Order [London Gazette, 3 June, 1915]: "Richard Haworth, Capt., 1st Battn. The Lancashire Fusiliers. For gallantry and devotion to duty in connection with the operations at the Dardanelles." He was promoted to Major 18 Jan. 1917; was Officer, Company of Gentleman Cadets, Royal Military College, Sandhurst, March to Sept. 1917; Commander, Company of Gentleman Cadets at the R.M.C. Sandhurst. For services see p. 409 [L. G. 3 July, 1915].

O'HARA, HENRY DESMOND, Lieut., was born at Ballyduff, Thomastown, County Kilkenny, 21 May, 1892, son of W. J. O'Hara, Resident Magistrate, Ballincollig, County Cork, and Cecilia, seventh and youngest daughter of the late Peter Connellan, of Colmore, County Kilkenny, J.P. and D.L.; and grandson of the late Rev. James Dunn O'Hara, of O'Hara Brook and the Castle, Portstewart, County Antrim. He was educated at Dunchurch Hall; Rugby; Charterhouse, and the Royal Military College, Sandhurst, and was gazetted to the Royal Dublin Fusiliers 4 Sept. 1912, becoming Lieutenant 29 April, 1914. He went to the Dardanelles 7 March, 1915; took part in the heavy fighting following the landing there, and died on the Hospital Ship Arcadian 29 Aug. 1915, of wounds received in action on the 12th. He was buried in the Military Cemetery at Gibraltar. Lieut. O'Hara was mentioned in Sir Ian Hamilton's Despatch of 20 May [London Gazette, 5 Aug. 1915], for his conduct during and after the landing of the 29th Division on 25 April. He was created a Companion of the Distinguished Service Order for gallantry and resource on the 25th April, 1915, at Sedd-el-Bahr, where he took command of his battalion when all the other officers had been killed or wounded. At night when the enemy broke through the line he displayed great initiative and resource in organizing a successful counter-attack, restoring the line and causing great loss to the enemy [London Gazette, 3 June, 1915]: "Henry Desmond O'Hara, Lieut., 1st Battn. The Royal Dublin Fusiliers. For gallantry and devotion to duty in connection with the operations at the Dardanelles." For services see p. 409 [L. G. 3 July, 1915].

London Gazette, 23 June, 1915.—"War Office, 23 June, 1915. His Majesty the King has been graciously pleased to approve of the undermentioned Honours and Rewards for distinguished service in the field, with effect from 3 June, 1915, inclusive. To be Companions of the Distinguished Service Order."

ALEXANDER, HENRY LETHBRIDGE, Major, was born 9 March, 1878. He was gazetted to the Dorsetshire Regt. 24 March, 1897; became Lieutenant 11 Oct. 1899; Captain 1 April, 1904; Major 25 Oct. 1914; Colonel 1 Jan. 1918; was Temporary Brigadier-General 7 May, 1917, to 8 Oct. 1918. He was employed with the Transvaal Volunteers 8 July, 1902, to 31 March, 1903; Staff Captain, Eastern Command, 10 Nov. 1911, to 18 Sept. 1914; D.A.A. and Q.M.G., 8th Division, B.E.F., 19 Sept. 1914, to 30 May, 1915; D.A.A. and Q.M.G., B.E.F., 6th Army Corps, 31 May to 18 July, 1915; A.A. and Q.M.G., Junior Staff School, British Armies in France, 15 Oct. 1916, to 1 May, 1917; A.A. and Q.M.G., 18th Division, British Armies in France, 2 to 6 May, 1917; D.A. and Q.M.G., 14th Army Corps, British Armies in France, British Force in Italy, 7 May to 8 Oct. 1917; D.A. and Q.M.G., G.H.Q., British Force in Italy, 8 Oct. 1918, to 20 Jan. 1919; Director of Quartering, War Office, 1 March, 1919. He served in the South African War, 1901–2, employed with the South African Light Horse; operations in the Transvaal, March to 31 May, 1902; took part in the operations in Orange River Colony, March, 1902 (Queen's Medal with five clasps). He served in the European War, 1914–18; was mentioned in Despatches, given the Brevets of Lieutenant-Colonel 3 June, 1916, and Colonel 1 Jan. 1918; created a C.B. in 1919; a C.M.G. in 1919, and created a Companion of the Distinguished Service Order [London

Henry L. Alexander.

Gazette, 23 June, 1915]: "Henry Lethbridge Alexander, Major, The Dorsetshire Regt. For distinguished service in the field."

BAIRD, HARRY BEAUCHAMP DOUGLAS, Major, was born in London 4 April, 1877, only surviving son of the late Colonel A. W. Baird, C.S.I., F.R.S., R.E., of Palmer's Cross, Elgin. He was educated at Clifton College, and at the Royal Military College, Sandhurst, subsequently passing the Staff College at Quetta. He entered the Army as Second Lieutenant (unattached) 20 Jan. 1897, and the Indian Staff Corps 8 March, 1898, and was promoted to Lieutenant, Indian Army, 20 April, 1899; Captain 20 Jan. 1906; Major, 20 Jan. 1915; was Temporary Lieutenant-Colonel, commanding a battalion (T.F.), 6 Oct. 1915, to 22 June, 1916; Temporary Brigadier-General 1 Dec. 1916, to 8 Feb. 1918. He was A.D.C. to the G.O. Commanding-in-Chief, Aldershot Command, 1 March, 1912, to 4 Aug. 1914; A.D.C. to G.O.C., 1st Army Corps, B.E.F., 5 Aug. to 8 Dec. 1914; G.S.O.2, Indian Cavalry Corps, B.E.F., 18 Dec. 1914, to 4 Sept. 1915; G.S.O.2, 51st Division, British Armies in France, 23 June to 3 Sept. 1916; G.S.O.2, Cavalry Corps, British Armies in France, 4 Sept. to 30 Nov. 1916; commanded the 75th Infantry Brigade, British Armies in France, 1 Dec. 1916, to 8 Feb. 1918; Brigadier-General, Baluchistan Force, May, 1919. He served in the Tirah Campaign, 1897–98; engaged in the operations in the Bara Valley 7 to 14 Dec. 1897 (Medal with two clasps). For his services in the European War he was four times mentioned in Despatches; received the Croix de Guerre avec Palme; was created a C.M.G., 1916; given the Brevet of Lieutenant-Colonel 1 Jan. 1917, and created a Companion of the Distinguished Service Order [London Gazette, 23 June, 1915]: "Harry Beauchamp Douglas Baird, Major, Indian Army. For distinguished service in the field." In 1915 he married Ethel Mary Frances, daughter of Capt. Andrew E. Caldecott, of Oxford, and they have one son and one daughter.

Harry B. D. Baird.

BLAKE, WILLIAM ALAN, Major, was born 8 Oct. 1878. He was educated at Charterhouse, joining the Liverpool Regt. (from the Militia), as Second Lieutenant, on the 4th Jan. 1899; transferred almost immediately to the Wiltshire Regt.; was promoted Captain, Wiltshire Regt. in Aug. 1905, and Major, 1915, and served on the Staff, 1914–18, in the European War. He was mentioned in Despatches, and was created a Companion of the Distinguished Service Order [London Gazette, 23 June, 1915]: "W. A. Blake, Major, Wiltshire Regt. For distinguished service in the field." He was Temporary Lieutenant-Colonel from June, 1915, and subsequently became Brigadier-General. He was created a C.M.G. in 1918. In 1919 General Blake married Beryl, eldest daughter of the late John Harrison Packard, of Swafield Hall, North Walsham.

BRIND, JOHN EDWARD SPENCER, Major, was born 9 Feb. 1878. He entered the Royal Artillery 23 Dec. 1897; became Lieutenant, R.A., 23 Dec. 1900; Captain, R.A., 11 April, 1902; was Divisional Adjutant, R.A., 1 Feb. to 31 March, 1903; Adjutant, R.A., 1 April, 1903, to 13 March, 1906; was promoted to Major 30 Oct. 1914. He was D.A.Q.M.G., 2nd Division, B.E.F., 5 Aug. 1914, to 13 July, 1915; G.S.O.2, 10th Army Corps, British Expeditionary Force, 14 July, 1915, to 5 Feb. 1916; G.S.O.1, 56th Division, British Expeditionary Force, British Armies in France, 6 Feb. to 30 Oct. 1916; G.S.O.1, 1st Army, British Armies in France, 31 Oct. 1916, to 23 Nov. 1917; Brigadier-General, G.S., 11th Army Corps, British Armies in France, 27 Nov. 1917. He served in the South African War, 1899–1900; took part in the operations in the Orange Free State, April and May, 1900, including actions at Vet River (5 and 6 May) and Zand River (Queen's Medal with two clasps). For his services in the European War, 1914–18, he was mentioned in Despatches; given the Brevets of Lieutenant-Colonel 3 June, 1916, and Colonel 1 Jan. 1919; created a C.M.G. in 1918, and created a Companion of the Distinguished Service Order [London Gazette, 23 June, 1915]: "John Edward Spencer Brind, Major, Royal Artillery. For distinguished service in the field."

CADDELL, HENRY MORTIMER, Major, was born 20 Feb. 1875, son of Colonel Henry Caddell, of 27, Ailesbury Road, Dublin. He was gazetted to the Army Service Corps 2 May, 1900; became Lieutenant 1 June, 1901; Captain 1 Feb. 1905; was Adjutant, A.S.C., 1 Jan. 1911, to 30 Nov. 1913; was promoted to Major, R.A.S.C., 30 Oct. 1914; was Temporary Colonel 15 March to 9 May, 1919. He was Instructor, A.S.C., Training Establishment, 1 Jan. to 4 Aug. 1914; Deputy Assistant Director of Transport, B.E.F., 5 Aug. 1914, to 21 Jan. 1917; Assistant Director of Transport, B.E.F., British Armies in France, 13 May, 1915, to 21 Jan. 1917; Commandant, Army Service Corps Training Establishment, 27 Jan. 1917, to 24 June, 1918; Assistant Director of Transport, War Office, 25 June, 1918, to 14 March, 1919; Deputy Director of Transport, War Office, 10 May, 1919. He served in the South African War, 1899–1902; took part in the operations in the Transvaal, west of Pretoria, July to Oct. 1900, including action at Zilikat's Nek; in Orange River Colony, June and July, 1900, including actions at Wittebergen (1 to 29 July); also in Cape Colony, 1899–1900; was present during operations in the Transvaal, Jan. 1901, to March, 1902 (Despatches [London Gazette, 29 July, 1902]; Queen's Medal with three clasps, and King's Medal with two clasps). For his services in the European War he was three times mentioned in Despatches; was given the Brevet of Lieutenant-Colonel 3 June, 1918, and was created a Companion of the Distinguished Service Order [London Gazette, 23 June, 1915]: "Henry Mortimer Caddell, Major, Army Service Corps. For distinguished service in the field." Lieut.-Colonel H. M. Caddell married, in 1906, Margaret Caroline, daughter of the late Rev. Isaac Hughes-Jones.

CHARTERIS, JOHN, Major, was born 8 Jan. 1877, son of the late Professor Charteris, Glasgow University. He entered the Royal Engineers 21 March, 1896; became Lieutenant 21 March, 1899; Captain 21 March, 1905, and Major 30 Oct. 1914; was Temporary Brigadier-General 3 Jan. 1916, to 31 Aug. 1918. He was Staff Captain, Headquarters, India, 28 June, 1909, to 21 Oct. 1910; G.S.O.2, Headquarters, India, 22 Oct. 1910, to 29 Feb. 1912; A.M.S. to G.O. Commanding-in-Chief, Aldershot Command, 1 March, 1912, to 4 Aug. 1914; A.D.C. to G.O.C., 1st Army Corps, B.E.F., 5 Aug. to 16 Sept. 1914; G.S.O.2, 1st Army Corps, B.E.F., 18 Oct. 1914, to 2 Jan. 1916; Brigadier-General, G.S., G.H.Q., B.E.F., British Armies in France, 3 Jan. 1916, to 23 Jan. 1918; Deputy Director-General of Transportation, British Armies in France, 18 Feb. to 31 Aug. 1918. For his services in the European War he was mentioned in Despatches; created a C.M.G. in 1919; given the Brevets of Lieutenant-Colonel 24 Aug. 1915, and Colonel 1 Jan. 1917; the Legion of Honour; made Commander of the Order of the Couronne of Belgium; Rising Sun of Japan; Croix de Guerre; American Distinguished Service Cross, and created a Companion of the Distinguished Service Order [London Gazette, 23 June, 1915]: "John Charteris, Major, Royal Engineers. For distinguished service in the field." Colonel Charteris married Noel, daughter of C. D. Hodgson, and they have two sons.

CLIVE, GEORGE SIDNEY, Major, was born in London 16 July, 1874, eldest son of General Edward Henry Clive, Grenadier Guards (who died in March, 1916), and of Isabel, daughter of Daniel Hale Webb. He was educated at Harrow and Sandhurst, and entered the Grenadier Guards 21 Oct. 1893, becoming Lieutenant 26 Oct. 1897. He served with the Nile Expedition, 1898; was present at the Battle of Khartoum (Egyptian Medal with clasp; Medal). Served in the South African War, 1899–1900, as Special Service Officer; took part in the operations in the Orange Free State, April to May, 1900, including actions at Vet River (5 and 6 May) and Zand River; in the Transvaal in May and June, 1900, including actions near Johannesburg, Pretoria, and Diamond Hill (11 and 12 June); also in the Transvaal, east of Pretoria, July to 29 Nov. 1900, including actions at Belfast (26 and 27 Aug.) (Queen's Medal with five clasps). He was promoted to Captain 28 Jan. 1900, and to Major, 17 July, 1909. He passed the Staff College, and was G.S.O., 1905–9, and G.S.O.2, London District, 1 Oct. 1910, and G.S.O., London District, 1910–14. For his services in the European War, 1914–18, he was given the Brevet of Colonel, promoted to Major-General; created a C.B. in 1918; a C.M.G. in 1919; received the Order of St. Stanislaus, 1st Class (Russia); the Legion of Honour (Officier); the Order of the Crown (Commander), and the Croix de Guerre. He was created a Companion of the Distinguished Service Order [London Gazette, 23 June, 1915]: "George Sidney Clive, Major, Grenadier Guards. For distinguished service in the field." Major-General G. S. Clive became Military Governor at Cologne in 1919. On 24 March, 1901, at Holy Trinity Church, Sloane Street, S.W., he married Madeline, second daughter of the late Francis William Buxton, M.P., and they have two sons living, Archie, born in 1903, and Edmond, born in 1909, and two daughters, Catherine and Mary. One son, Robert, was born in 1904 and died in 1908.

FLETCHER, ALAN FRANCIS, Major, was born 23 April, 1876, only son of the late C. J. Fletcher. He entered the Army 1 Dec. 1897; was promoted to Lieutenant 14 Feb. 1900; to Captain 13 June, 1904; was Adjutant, Cheshire Yeomanry, from 6 April, 1908; became Major 15 May, 1912; Lieutenant-Colonel, Army, 19 Dec. 1915; retired 1 June, 1919. He served in the South African War, 1900; took part in the Orange Free State, Feb. to May, 1900, including actions at Vet River (5 and 6 May) and Zand River; in the Transvaal in May and June, 1900; also during operations in Orange River Colony 30 Nov. to Dec. 1900 (Queen's Medal with two clasps). For his services in the European War he was twice mentioned in Despatches; was created an M.V.O., 1917, and was created a Companion of the Distinguished Service Order [London Gazette, 23 June, 1915]: "Alan Francis Fletcher, Major, 17th Lancers. For distinguished service in the field." Lieut.-Colonel Fletcher married, in 1908, Lady Theresa Wentworth-Fitzwilliam, and they have one daughter.

FRASER, HENRY FRANCIS, Major, was born 20 Nov. 1872. He was gazetted to the 5th Lancers 7 Dec. 1895; was extra A.D.C. to the Viceroy of India, 1897; became Lieutenant 9 Oct. 1899; Captain, 21st Lancers, 29 May, 1901; Major 27 April, 1907, and Lieutenant-Colonel 6 Sept. 1915. He was employed with the Aro Expedition, Southern Nigeria, 30 Oct. 1901, to 27 April, 1902; Assistant Military Secretary to the G.O. Commanding-in-Chief, Eastern Command, 4 April, 1912, to 4 Aug. 1914; A.D.C. to the G.O.C., 2nd Army Corps, B.E.F., 5 Aug. to 4 Sept. 1914; A.P.M., Cavalry Corps, B.E.F., 10 Oct. 1914, to 12 July, 1915; P.M., 3rd Army, B.E.F., 13 July to 27 Oct. 1915; Specially employed, War Office, 9 March to 26 April, 1916; A.A.G., Southern Command, 2 July, 1916, to 7 March, 1917; A.A.G., War Office, 8 March to 24 Nov. 1917. He served in the South African War, 1899–1900; took part in the operations in Natal, 1899, including action at Elandslaagte, Rietfontein and Lombard's Kop; at the defence of Ladysmith, including sorties of 7 and 10 Dec. 1899, and action of 6 Jan. 1900 (Queen's Medal with two clasps). In the Aro Expedition he was slightly wounded, and was mentioned in Despatches [London Gazette, 12 Sept. 1902]; Medal with clasp. He was mentioned in Despatches for his services in the European War, 1914–17; was created a C.M.G., 1917, and created a

Henry Francis Fraser.

Companion of the Distinguished Service Order [London Gazette, 23 June, 1915]: "Henry Francis Fraser, Major, 21st Lancers. For distinguished service in the field."

GAME, PHILIP WOOLCOTT, Major, was born 30 March, 1876, son of George Beale Game, of Barn House, Broadway, Worcestershire. He was educated at Charterhouse and Woolwich, and has passed the Staff College, where he won the Light-Weight Point-to-Point in 1909. He entered the Royal Artillery 2 Nov. 1895, becoming Lieutenant 2 Nov. 1898, and Captain 3 June, 1901. He was Adjutant, R.A., 1 July, 1902, to 11 Sept. 1905; Major, 15 Feb. 1912; Lieutenant-Colonel 9 Aug. 1917. From 31 Dec. 1910, to 6 Sept. 1913, he was G.S.O.3, War Office, and also from 7 Sept. 1913, to 29 Nov. 1914. He was G.S.O.2, 4th Army Corps, B.E.F., 30 Nov. 1914, to 17 July, 1915; G.S.O.1, 46th Division, B.E.F., 18 July, 1915, to 18 March, 1916; G.S.O.1, Royal Flying Corps, B.E.F., British Armies in France, 19 March to 15 Oct. 1916; Brigadier-General, G.S., R.F.C., British Armies in France, 16 Oct. 1916, to 31 March, 1918; employed under the Air Ministry 1 April, 1918; acting Major-General, attached R.F.C. He served in the South African War, 1901–2, and took part in the operations in the Transvaal, Sept. to Dec. 1901; also in Orange River Colony, Jan to May, 1902 (Despatches [London Gazette, 29 July, 1902]; Queen's Medal with five clasps). He served in the European War, 1914–18; was given the Brevets of Lieutenant-Colonel, 1 Jan. 1915; Colonel 3 June, 1917; was six times mentioned in Despatches; received the Order of the Crown of Italy; was made Officer, Legion of Honour; created a C.B. in 1919, and created a Companion of the Distinguished Service Order [London Gazette, 23 June, 1915]: "Philip Woolcott Game, Major, Royal Artillery. For distinguished service in the field." He married on 11 Aug. 1908, Gwendolen, daughter of the late F. Hughes-Gibb and Mrs. Hughes-Gibb, of Gunville Manor House, Blandford, Dorset, and they have two sons: Philip, born 1 June, 1911, and David, born 16 June, 1914, and a daughter.

GOLDNEY, GEORGE FRANCIS BENNETT, Major, was born 12 April, 1879, son of the late George Goldney, of Chippenham House, Exmouth. He was commissioned in the Royal Engineers 23 June, 1898; became Lieutenant 14 Feb. 1901; Captain 2; June, 1907; was Adjutant (Training Battn.), R.E., 1 June, 1911, to 31 May, 1914; Adjutant, R.E., 18 Sept. 1914; was promoted to Major 30 Oct. 1914. He was specially employed, Headquarters of Army, 23 Feb. to 31 March, 1909; Staff Captain, War Office, 1 April, 1909, to 31 May, 1911. He served in the South African War, 1899–1901; took part in the operations in the Orange Free State, April and May, 1900; in Orange River Colony, May to 29 Nov. 1900, including actions at Biddulphsberg and Wittebergen (1 to 29 July); again in Orange River Colony 30 Nov. 1900, to Jan. 1901 (Queen's Medal with two clasps). For his services in the European War he was four times mentioned in Despatches; was given the Brevet of Lieutenant-Colonel 1 Jan. 1918; was created a C.M.G. in 1919; was made Chevalier, Legion of Honour, and created a Companion of the Distinguished Service Order [London Gazette, 23 June, 1915]: "George Francis Bennett Goldney, Major, Royal Engineers. For distinguished service in the field." He married, in 1914, Hilda Margaret, youngest daughter of the late Major-General H. Edmeades, of Nurstead Court, Meopham, Kent.

RIFFITH, DAVID MAITLAND, Major, was born 17 Oct. 1871, youngest son of the late Lieut.-Colonel J. G. T. Griffith, R.E., of Bombay. He was educated at the United Service College, Westward Ho! and at the Royal Military Academy, Woolwich, and entered the Royal Engineers 27 July, 1889, becoming Lieutenant 27 July, 1892; Captain 1 April, 1900; Major 20 Feb. 1909, and Lieutenant-Colonel 1 Jan. 1917. He took part in the operations on the North-West Frontier of India, 1897–98, with the Malakand Field Force; was present during operations in Bajaur and the Mohmand country, also with the Buner Field Force; at the attack and capture of the Tanga Pass (Medal with clasp). He served in the European War; was wounded, mentioned in Despatches, and created a Companion of the Distinguished Service Order [London Gazette, 23 June, 1915]: "David Maitland Griffith, Major, Royal Engineers. For distinguished service in the field." He took part in the operations on the Western Frontier of Egypt, and in the occupation of Sollum, as C.R.E., and was again mentioned in Despatches. Lieut.-Colonel Griffith married, in 1918, Kathleen Venetia, daughter of the late Wingfield Digby, M.P., and widow of Major Reginald Walker, R.E., and they have one son.

David M. Griffith.

HAYTER, ROSS JOHN FINNIS, Major, was born 28 Feb. 1875, eldest son of Ross W. Hayter, late of Toronto, Canada, and grandson of John Hayter, Court Painter to Queen Victoria. He was educated at Dover College and Upper Canada College, Toronto; at the Royal Military College, Kingston, Canada, and entered the Cheshire Regt. 28 Aug. 1895, becoming Lieutenant 6 April, 1898; Captain 15 Nov. 1901; Major 26 June, 1914. He was A.D.C. to Lieutenant-General, South Africa, 7 Nov. 1900, to 24 Sept. 1901; D.A.A. and Q.M.G., Malta, 10 Feb. 1906, to 15 March, 1912; G.S.O.2, Canadian Forces, 16 June, 1911, to 28 Sept. 1914; Brigade-Major, 1st Canadian Infantry Brigade, England, B.E.F., 20 Sept. 1914, to 12 Sept. 1915; G.S.O.2, Canadian Army Corps, British Expeditionary Force, 13 Sept. 1915, to 16 Jan. 1916; G.S.O.1, 3rd Canadian Division, B.E.F., British Armies in France, 17 Jan. 1916, to 3 Dec. 1917; Brigade Commander, 10th Canadian Infantry Brigade, British Armies in France, 4 Dec. 1917, to 27 Oct. 1918; Brigadier-General, G.S., Canadian Army Corps, British Armies in France, 28 Oct. 1918. He served in the South African War, 1899–1902, employed with Mounted Infantry, and on Staff; took part in the operations in the Orange Free State, including actions at Poplar Grove, Dreifontein, Houtnek (Thoba Mountain) and Zand River; in the Transvaal in May and June, 1900, including actions near Johannesburg, Pretoria, and Diamond Hill (11 and 12 June); in Orange River Colony, including actions at Wittebergen (1 to 29 July), Ladybrand (2 to 5 Sept.), and Bothaville (Queen's Medal with five clasps, and King's Medal with two clasps). He was seven times mentioned in Despatches for his services in the European War, 1914–18, when he served continuously with the Canadian Forces as Brigade Major; was given the Brevet of Lieutenant-Colonel 3 June, 1916; was created a C.B. in 1919; a C.M.G. in 1917, and was created a Companion of the Distinguished Service Order [London Gazette, 23 June, 1915]: "Ross John Finnis Hayter, Major, Cheshire Regt. For distinguished service in the field." In 1900 he married Edith, only daughter of Colonel E. Lawrie, Indian Medical Service.

HILL, HUGH, Major, was born 16 May, 1875, the only son of the late James Eardley Hill, Barrister-at-Law, and Mrs. Gerald Shepperson, of 45, Argyll Road, Kensington, W., and Beaconsfield, Buckinghamshire; and grandson of the late Sir Hugh Hill, Judge of the High Court, He was educated at Lockers Park, Rugby, and at Sandhurst. On passing out of Sandhurst he was gazetted to the Royal Welsh Fusiliers. He served in the South African War from 1899 to 1900, and was rewarded for his services in this campaign with the Queen's Medal with two clasps. He was promoted Captain in 1903, and was Adjutant of his regiment from 1904 to 1907. In 1905 he was appointed an honorary Aide-de-Camp to the Prince of Wales during his tour in India, and was afterwards made an M.V.O. In 1906 he was Aide-de-Camp (extra) to Lord Minto, in connection with the visit to Agra of the Amir of Afghanistan. He passed the Staff College, Quetta, in 1909. As extra Aide-de-Camp, he was on the Staff of the King for the Durbar and the subsequent tour. He was promoted Major in 1913, and as Brigade Major to the Jullundur Brigade accompanied the Indian contingent to France at the outbreak of the European War. He subsequently became D.A.A. and Q.M.G., and later A.Q.M.G., with temporary rank of Lieutenant-Colonel. In 1915 he was created a Companion of the Distinguished Service Order [London Gazette, 23 June, 1915]: "Hugh Hill, M.V.O., Major, Royal Welsh Fusiliers. For distinguished service in the field." He was appointed G.S.O. (1st grade) in 1915, and given the Brevet of Lieutenant-Colonel in May, 1916. During the war Lieutenant-Colonel Hill was mentioned three times in Despatches. He fell in action 10 Sept. 1916. "He did not know what fear was. The men, too, recognized what a fine character his was, and the words of a Scottish sergeant, who was the first to go to him after he was hit, were: 'A fine soldier, sir.'" A touching memorial service for Colonel Hill was held at Christ Church, Lancaster Gate, W., among those present being Major-General Sir Francis Lloyd (Commanding the Home District), Colonel of the Royal Welsh Fusiliers, attended by Lieut. the Earl of Stamford; General Hudson, to whose division Colonel Hill was Senior Staff Officer, and several officers of the Royal Welsh Fusiliers. He was a Fellow of the Royal Geographical Society.

HUTCHISON, ROBERT, Major, was born 5 Sept. 1873. He was gazetted to the 7th Dragoon Guards 10 Feb. 1900; became Lieutenant 3 Oct. 1900; served with the Imperial Yeomanry 25 Nov. 1901, to 11 May, 1902; was promoted to Captain, 11th Hussars, 2 Dec. 1905; to Major, 4th Dragoon Guards, 25 Nov. 1913; to Colonel 2 June, 1919; was Temporary Brigadier-General 27 April, 1916, to 30 April, 1917; Temporary Major-General 1 May, 1917. He was G.S.O.3, War Office, 3 Jan. 1912, to 31 March, 1914; Brigade Major, 1st Cavalry Brigade, B.E.F., 4 Sept. to 8 Nov. 1914; G.S.O.2, Cavalry Corps, B.E.F., 9 Nov. 1914, to 10 Feb. 1915; G.S.O.2, G.H.Q., B.E.F., 11 Feb. to 27 July, 1915; G.S.O.2, G.H.Q., B.E.F., 11 Feb. to 27 July, 1915; G.S.O.1, G.H.Q., B.E.F., 28 July, 1915, to 4 Feb. 1916; G.S.O.1, War Office, 5 Feb. to 26 April, 1916; Brigadier-General, G.S., Irish Command, 27 April, 1916, to 30 April, 1917; Director of Organization, War Office, 1 May, 1917, to 12 June, 1919; D.A.G. 13 June, 1919. He served in the South African War, 1900–2; as Adjutant, 12th Battn. Imperial Yeomanry, 30 Oct. 1901, to 3 May, 1902; took part in the operations in the Transvaal, east of Pretoria, July to 29 Nov. 1900; in the Transvaal, Dec. 1900; in Orange River Colony, Feb. 1901, to 31 May, 1902; in the operations on the Zululand Frontier of Natal in Oct. 1901; also during operations in Cape Colony, Dec. 1900, to Feb. 1901 (Queen's Medal with three clasps, and King's Medal with two clasps). For his services in the European War he was mentioned in Despatches, was given the Brevets of Lieutenant-Colonel 1 Jan. 1916, and Colonel 3 June, 1916, and created a C.B. in 1918. He was created a Companion of the Distinguished Service Order [London Gazette, 23 June, 1915]: "Robert Hutchison, Major, 4th Dragoon Guards. For distinguished service in the field." Colonel Hutchison married, in 1905, Agnes Begbie, only daughter of the late William Drysdale, of Kilrie, Fife.

IRONSIDE, WILLIAM EDMUND, Major, was born 6 May, 1880. He entered the Royal Artillery 25 June, 1899; became Lieutenant 16 Feb. 1901; Captain 18 Feb. 1908; Major 30 Oct. 1914; Temporary Major-General 17 Nov. 1918. He was Staff Captain, South Africa, 26 Sept. 1908, to 1 June, 1909; Brigade Major, South Africa, 2 June, 1909, to 25 Sept. 1912; Staff Captain, No. 3 Base, B.E.F., 5 Aug. to 28 Oct. 1914; G.S.O.2, 6th Division, B.E.F., 17 Feb. 1915, to 29 Feb. 1916; Staff Officer, 1st grade, 4th Canadian Division, England, British Armies in France, 3 March, 1916, to 6 Jan. 1918; Commandant, G.H.Q., Small Arms School, British Armies in France, 7 Jan. to 26 March, 1918; commanded the 99th Infantry Brigade, British Armies in France, 27 March to 19 Sept. 1918; Brigadier-General, G.S., 20 Sept. to 16 Nov. 1918; Commander, Archangel, North Russian Expeditionary Force, 17 Nov. 1918. He served in the South African War, 1899–1902; took part in the operations in the Transvaal, west of Pretoria, Sept. and Oct. 1900; in Orange River Colony (Oct. and Nov. 1900); in Cape Colony, south of Orange River, 1899–1900, including action at Kheis; in the Transvaal, Sept. to Oct. 1901; in Orange River Colony, Oct. 1901; also in Cape Colony, Feb. 1900, to Sept. 1901, and Oct. 1901, to May, 1902. (Despatches

[London Gazette, 10 Sept. 1901]; Queen's Medal with three clasps, and King's Medal with two clasps). For his services in the European War, 1914–19, he was mentioned in Despatches; was given the Brevets of Lieutenant-Colonel 3 June, 1916, and Colonel 1 Jan. 1919; created a Companion of the Distinguished Service Order [London Gazette, 23 June, 1915]: "William Edmund Ironside, Major, Royal Artillery. For distinguished service in the field." He was created a C.M.G., 1918; a K.B.E., 1919; received the Croix de Guerre avec Palme, the 2nd Class Order of St. Vladimir and the Croix d'Officier de la Légion d'Honneur. Sir William Ironside married, in 1915, Mariot Ysobel, daughter of Charles Cheyne, and they have one daughter.

IRVINE, FRANCIS STEPHEN, Major, was born 26 Dec. 1873. He entered the R.A.M.C. as Lieutenant 17 Nov. 1899; became Captain 17 Nov. 1902; Major 17 Aug. 1911; Lieutenant-Colonel 29 Sept. 1916. He was employed with the Transvaal Volunteers 13 Oct. 1906, to 12 Oct. 1909, and was Commandant and O.C. Depôt, R.A.M.C., Training Establishment, 4 Oct. 1918. He served in the South African War, 1899–1902; was present at the Relief of Ladysmith, including operations of 24 Jan. 1900, and action at Spion Kop; operations of 5 to 7 Feb. 1900, and action at Vaal Kranz; and in the operations on Tugela Heights (14 to 27 Feb. 1900); in the Transvaal, June to Dec. 1901, and Jan. to May, 1902; in Orange River Colony, March, 1902; also during the operations on the Zululand Frontier of Natal in Sept. and Oct. 1901 (Queen's Medal with four clasps, and King's Medal with two clasps). For his services in the European War, 1914–18, Lieutenant-Colonel Irvine was mentioned in Despatches; created a C.M.G. in 1918, and created a Companion of the Distinguished Service Order [London Gazette, 23 June, 1915]: "Francis Stephen Irvine, M.B., Major, R.A.M.C. For distinguished service in the field."

JOHNSON, RAYMOND HENRY, Major, was born 23 Jan. 1882. He entered the Royal Artillery 2 May, 1900; became Lieutenant 3 April, 1901; Captain 15 Oct. 1909; was Adjutant, R.A., 1 June, 1910, to 31 May, 1913; was promoted to Major 30 Oct. 1914. He was Assistant Embarkation Staff Officer 5 Aug. to 29 Sept. 1914; Brigade Major, R.A., 8th Division, B.E.F., 30 Sept. 1914, to 14 Nov. 1915; D.A.A.G., 2nd Army Corps, B.E.F., 15 Nov. 1915, to 16 June, 1916; G.S.O.2, 3rd Army, British Armies in France, 28 Aug. 1917, to 1 Aug. 1918; G.S.O.1, 62nd Division, British Armies in France, 30 Sept. to 11 Oct. 1918. For his services in the European War, 1914–18, he was given the Brevet of Lieutenant-Colonel 1 Jan. 1918; three times mentioned in Despatches; made Chevalier, Légion d'Honneur, and created a Companion of the Distinguished Service Order [London Gazette, 23 June, 1915]: "Raymond Henry Johnson, Major, Royal Artillery. For distinguished service in the field."

LAMBARDE, FRANCIS FANE, Major, was born 24 Dec. 1868, son of Francis Lambarde, of Sevenoaks, Kent. He entered the Army 17 Feb. 1888; was promoted to Major, Reserve of Officers, 1 May, 1907; retired 21 Feb. 1910. He served in South Africa, 1901–2 (Queen's Medal with four clasps). For his services in the European War, 1914–19, he was mentioned in Despatches; created a C.M.G. in 1919; became Chevalier de la Légion d'Honneur; received the Croix de Guerre of France and Belgium, and was created a Companion of the Distinguished Service Order [London Gazette, 23 June, 1915]: "Francis Fane Lambarde, Major, Reserve of Officers, 1st Canadian Division Staff. For distinguished service in the field." Brigadier General F. F. Lambarde married Marian Ethel, third daughter of Joseph Hinks, J.P., of Bournemouth.

LUKIN, ROBERT CLARENCE WELLESLEY, Major, was born 22 Dec. 1870. He was gazetted to the Yorkshire Light Infantry 3 May, 1890; became Lieutenant, Yorkshire Light Infantry, 11 May, 1892; Lieutenant, Indian Staff Corps, 16 June, 1892; Captain, Indian Army, 3 May, 1901; was Captain, Imperial Yeomanry, 3 Jan. to 3 Sept. 1902; was promoted to Major 3 Jan. 1908, and to Lieutenant-Colonel 3 May, 1916, and was Temporary Brigadier-General from 25 Sept. 1918. He was on Special Service, South Africa, 20 Dec. 1901, to 2 Jan. 1902; D.A.A.G., India, 25 March, 1913, to 25 Sept. 1914; D.A.A.G. 26 Sept. 1914, to 21 Sept. 1915; A.Q.M.G. 22 Sept. 1915, to 25 July, 1916. He took part in the operations in Chitral, 1895, with the Relief Force (Medal with clasp). Served at Tirah, 1897–98, during the operations in tha Bara Valley 7 to 14 Dec. 1897 (two clasps). Served in the South African War, 1901–2, employed with the Imperial Yeomanry; took part in the operations in the Transvaal and Orange River Colony 30 Nov. 1900, to 31 May, 1902 (Queen's Medal with five clasps). For his services in the European War, 1914–16, he was mentioned in Despatches and created a Companion of the Distinguished Service Order [London Gazette, 23 June, 1915]: "Robert Clarence Wellesley Lukin, Major, Indian Army. For distinguished service in the field." His regiment is the 9th Hodson's Horse.

LYNCH-STAUNTON, REGINALD KIRKPATRICK, Major, was born in London 9 April, 1880, son of Capt. G. S. Lynch-Staunton, of Purbrook House, Hants, and nephew of the late Sir George Thomas Staunton, Bart., M.P., of Leigh House, Hants. He was educated at Cheltenham College; joined the Hants and Isle of Wight Artillery in March, 1898, and was gazetted to the Royal Artillery 20 May, 1899. He served in the South African War in 1900, and received the Queen's Medal with three clasps. He became Lieutenant 16 Feb. 1901; was attached to the Royal Horse Artillery from 1903 to 1907, and was promoted to Captain 14 Oct. 1907. From 1907 to 1911 he was employed with the Egyptian Army, and was in command of an Egyptian Battery, taking part in operations in Southern Kordofan (Medal with clasp). From 1912 to 1914 he commanded U Battery, Royal Horse Artillery. He was subsequently Adjutant, R.H.A. Brigade, Meerut, and in 1914 was Secretary to the Meerut Tent Club. On the outbreak of the European War Major Lynch-Staunton mobilized as Second-in-Command, R.A., 7th (Meerut) Division, R.A., 11 Aug. 1914, and accompanied the Division to France in Oct. 1915, as Brigade Major. He was mentioned in Despatches and created a Companion of the Distinguished Service Order [London Gazette, 23 June, 1915]: "Reginald Kirkpatrick Lynch-Staunton, Major, Royal Artillery. For distinguished service in the field." He left France in Dec. 1915, for Mesopotamia, and served as Brigade Major, R.A., Tigris Corps, until 15 Aug. 1916. He was slightly wounded 7 Jan. 1916, but was able to take part the same month in operations at Hanneh, and Sanniyat, etc., in March and April, 1916. He was Acting Lieutenant-Colonel from 16 Aug. 1916, commanding the 13th Brigade, R.F.A., and commanded this Brigade during the operations of Dec. 1916, on the Hai, the Shumrar crossing, in the advance and capture of Baghdad, also in operations on the Dialah River and River Adheim, April, 1917. He was given the Brevet of Lieutenant-Colonel 3 June, 1916 [London Gazette, 22 Dec. 1916], and in 1917 was awarded the Order of St. Anne, 3rd Class, with Swords. Lieut.-Colonel R. K. Lynch-Staunton died 7 Nov. 1918.

R. K. Lynch-Staunton.

MACLEOD, CHARLES WILLIAM, Major, was born 25 May, 1881. He entered the Army Service Corps 21 Feb. 1900; became Lieutenant 1 April, 1901; Captain 1 Oct. 1904; was Adjutant, A.S.C., 1 Dec. 1913, to 4 Aug. 1914; was promoted to Major, R.A.S.C., 15 Oct. 1914; was Temporary Lieutenant-Colonel 13 Oct. 1915, to 18 Nov. 1917. He was D.A.Q.M.G., Lines of Communication, B.E.F., 5 Aug. 1914, to 26 April, 1915; D.A.D. of Transport 4 June to 12 Oct. 1915; A.D. of Transport, B.E.F., British Armies in France, 15 Oct. 1915, to 18 Nov. 1917; D.D. of Transport, Transport Directorate, British Armies in France, 19 Nov. 1917; Temporary Colonel 19 Nov. 1917. He served in the South African War, 1900–2; took part in the operations in Orange River Colony, Nov. 1900, to Dec. 1901; also in Cape Colony, Jan. to 31 May, 1902 (Queen's Medal with two clasps, and King's Medal with two clasps). For his services in the European War, 1914–18, he was given the Brevet of Lieutenant-Colonel 1 Jan. 1918; was created a C.M.G. in 1919, and created a Companion of the Distinguished Service Order [London Gazette, 23 June, 1915]: "Charles William MacLeod, Major, Army Service Corps. For distinguished service in the field." Lieut.-Colonel C. W. MacLeod married, in 1914, Jean Hewat, daughter of the late Dr. Loraine, of Hawick, and they have one daughter.

MOWBRAY, JOHN LESLIE, Major, was born 19 July, 1875. He entered the Army 28 July, 1900; became Lieutenant 28 July, 1903; was Staff Captain, India, from 4 April, 1909. He served in the European War; was promoted to Major 17 Dec. 1914; was created a Companion of the Distinguished Service Order [London Gazette, 23 June, 1915]: "John Leslie Mowbray, Major, Royal Artillery. For distinguished service in the field." Major Mowbray fell in action 24 July, 1916.

PALEY, ALAN THOMAS, Major, was born 1 May, 1876. He was commissioned in the Rifle Brigade 17 March, 1897; became Lieutenant 2 Aug. 1899; Captain 18 Jan. 1902; was Adjutant, Rifle Brigade, 7 March, 1905, to 14 Sept. 1907, and was promoted to Major 1 Nov. 1914. He was Temporary Lieutenant-Colonel 7 March to 2 June, 1916, and Temporary Colonel 18 Oct. 1917, to 31 Dec. 1918. From 15 Sept. 1907, to 21 Jan. 1911, he was Officer, Company of Gentlemen Cadets, Royal Military College; from 8 Sept. 1913, to 4 Aug. 1914, he was G.S.O.3, War Office. During the European War he was G.S.O.3, 6th Division, B.E.F., 5 Aug. to 28 Oct. 1914; Brigade Major, 18th Infantry Brigade, B.E.F., 29 Oct. 1914, to 13 July, 1915; G.S.O.2, 7th Army Corps, B.E.F., 14 July, 1915, to 6 March, 1916; G.S.O.1, 21st Division, British Armies in France, 7 March, 1916, to 16 Oct. 1917; Assistant Commandant, Royal Military College (temporary), 18 Oct. 1917, to 31 Dec. 1918. He served with the Nile Expedition, 1898; at the Battle of Khartoum (Egyptian Medal with clasp; Medal); served in the South African War, 1899–1900; took part in the defence of Ladysmith, including sortie of 10 Dec. 1899 (dangerously wounded) (Despatches [London Gazette, 8 Feb. and 10 Sept. 1901]; Queen's Medal with clasp). For his services in the European War, 1914–18, he was mentioned in Despatches five times; was given the Brevets of Lieutenant-Colonel 3 June, 1916, and of Colonel 1 Jan. 1919; created a C.M.G. in 1918, and created a Companion of the Distinguished Service Order [London Gazette, 23 June, 1915]: "Alan Thomas Paley, Major, The Rifle Brigade. For distinguished service in the field."

SCARLETT, JAMES ALEXANDER, Major, was born 16 June, 1877. He was commissioned in the Royal Artillery 17 Feb. 1900; became Lieutenant 3 April, 1901; Captain 1 Sept. 1908; was Adjutant, R.A., 1 Feb. 1913, to 29 Oct. 1914; was promoted to Major 30 Oct. 1914; was Acting Lieutenant-Colonel 18 Aug. 1917, to 29 April, 1918, and 13 June, 1918, to 10 March, 1919. He was Brigade Major, 12th Army Corps, Mediterranean Expeditionary Force, 21 Dec. 1915, to 1 Jan. 1916. For his services in the European War from 1914, he was mentioned in Despatches; given the Brevet of Lieutenant-Colonel 3 June, 1919, and created a Companion of the Distinguished Service Order [London Gazette, 23 June, 1915]: "James Alexander Scarlett, Major, Royal Artillery. For distinguished service in the field."

SMITH, HUBERT CLEMENTI, Major, was born 12 Aug. 1878. He entered the Royal Engineers 23 June, 1898; became Lieutenant 14 Feb. 1901; Captain 23 June, 1907; Major 30 Oct. 1914; was Temporary Lieutenant-Colonel, R.E., from 6 Feb. 1916. He was Assistant Director of Army Signals, 1st Division, Aldershot Command, 28 July, 1910, to 23 Nov. 1911; Instructor, Army Signal School, 1 Feb. 1913, to 4 Aug. 1914; G.S.O.1, Signal Service Training Centre, Home Forces, 2 Oct. 1917, to 30 March 1918 Deputy Director of Signals 2nd Army, British Armies in

France, 12 Nov. 1918, to 28 Feb. 1919; G.S.O.1, Staff College, 1 March, 1919. He served in the South African War, 1900–2, and took part in the operations in the Orange Free State, Feb. to May, 1900, including operations at Paardeberg; actions at Dreifontein; in Orange River Colony, May to Aug. 1900; also in the Transvaal 30 Nov. to 31 May, 1902 (Queen's Medal with four clasps, and King's Medal with two clasps). For his services in the European War, 1914–18, he was mentioned in Despatches four times; was given the Brevet of Lieutenant-Colonel 1 Jan. 1919; was made Officier, Légion d'Honneur, and awarded the Croix de Guerre, and was created a Companion of the Distinguished Service Order [London Gazette, 23 June, 1915]: "Hubert Clementi Smith, Major, R.E. For distinguished service in the field." Lieut.-Colonel H. Clementi Smith married, in 1909, Kathleen Margaret, only child of Sir Harry S. C. Clarke-Jervoise, 5th Bart., and they have one son and three daughters.

STEWART, IAN, Major, was born 2 Nov. 1874. He was gazetted to the Scottish Rifles 6 March, 1895; was promoted to Lieutenant 10 Oct. 1897; to Captain 10 April, 1900; to Major 11 March, 1915; was Temporary Lieutenant-Colonel 19 June, 1915, to 2 June, 1916; Temporary Brigadier-General 16 Nov. 1916. He was G.S.O.3, South Africa, 18 May, 1911, to 26 Sept. 1912; G.S.O.2, South Africa, 27 Sept. 1912, to 21 Sept. 1914; G.S.O.2, 7th Division, B.E.F., 22 Sept. 1914, to 18 June, 1915; G.S.O.1, 51st Division, B.E.F., British Armies in France, 19 June, 1915, to 15 Nov. 1916; Brigadier-General, G.S., 13th Army Corps, British Armies in France, 16 Nov. 1916. He served in the South African War, 1899–1902; took part in the operations in the Transvaal, east of Pretoria, July to 29 Nov. 1900; also in the Transvaal and Orange River Colony 30 Nov. 1900, to 31 May, 1902; during the operations on the Zululand Frontier of Natal in Sept. and Oct. 1901 (Despatches [London Gazette, 20 Aug. 1901; Brevet of Major 22 Aug. 1902; Queen's Medal with two clasps, and King's Medal with two clasps). He served in the European War, 1914–1918; was four times mentioned in Despatches; was given the Brevets of Lieutenant-Colonel 3 June, 1916, and of Colonel 1 Jan. 1918; was created a C.M.G. in 1919, and created a Companion of the Distinguished Service Order [London Gazette, 23 June, 1915]: "Ian Stewart, Major, Scottish Rifles. For distinguished service in the field." Colonel Stewart married Myra, daughter of James Kennedy, of Doonholm, Ayr, and they have one son and two daughters.

STEWART, JOHN HENRY KEITH, Major, was born in 1872, eldest son of Lieut.-General John Mackie Stewart, Bengal Infantry, and Florence, daughter of the late Henry Vansittart. He entered the Army, as Second Lieutenant, Unattached, 3 Sept. 1892, and the Indian Staff Corps 28 Dec. 1893; became Lieutenant, Indian Staff Corps, 3 Dec. 1894; Captain, Indian Army, 3 Sept. 1901; Major 3 Sept. 1910; Temporary Lieutenant-Colonel 4 Aug. 1916, to 2 June, 1916; Lieutenant-Colonel 1 July, 1916; Temporary Brigadier-General 13 March to 4 Sept. 1917, and again from 3 Oct. 1918; Commandant, 1st Battn. 39th Garhwal Rifles. He was D.A.A.G., Southern Army, India, 6 Feb. 1908, to 5 Feb. 1912; Brigade Major, Garhwal Brigade, B.E.F., 17 Dec. 1914, to 3 Aug. 1915; G.S.O.1, Lahore Division, B.E.F., Indian Expeditionary Force "D," 4 Aug. 1915, to 12 March, 1917; Brigadier-General, G.S., 1st Indian Army Corps, Mesopotamian Expeditionary Force, 13 March to 4 Sept. 1917; Brigadier-General, G.S., 3rd Indian Army Corps, Mesopotamian Expeditionary Force "D," 3 Oct. 1918. He served on the North-West Frontier of India, 1897–98 (Mohmand; Malakand); during the operations in Bajaur (Medal with clasp); served at Tirah, 1897–98 (clasp). For his services in the European War, 1914–18, he was mentioned in Despatches; was given the Brevets of Lieutenant-Colonel 3 June, 1916, and of Colonel 10 March, 1917, and created a Companion of the Distinguished Service Order [London Gazette, 23 June, 1915]: "John Henry Keith Stewart, Major, Indian Army. For distinguished service in the field." Colonel Stewart married, in 1898, Frances Jane, daughter of the late Hon. G. A. Hobart Hampden, I.C.S., and they have one daughter.

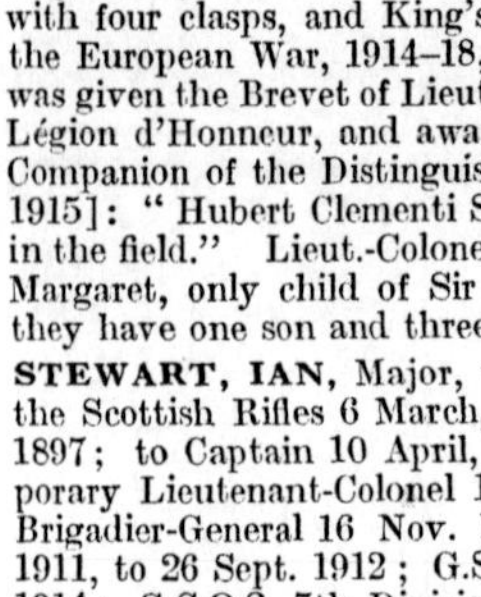

John Henry K. Stewart.

STOBART, GEORGE HERBERT, Major, was born 18 Feb. 1873, son of William Culley Stobart and Frances Dorothea, daughter of the Rev. George P. Wilkinson. He entered the Army 16 March, 1894; was promoted Lieutenant 16 March, 1897; Captain 17 Sept. 1900; Major 15 Jan. 1911; retired from the Royal Artillery 8 Feb. 1911. He served in the South African War, 1899–1900; took part in the operations in Natal, 1899, including actions at Reitfontein (slightly wounded) and Lombard's Kop; at the defence of Ladysmith, including action of 6 Jan. 1900 (Queen's Medal with clasp). For his services in the European War, 1914–18, he was mentioned in Despatches; was given the Brevet of Lieutenant-Colonel 1 Jan. 1918; created a C.B.E. in 1919, and was created a Companion of the Distinguished Service Order [London Gazette, 23 June, 1915]: "George Herbert Stobart, Major, Reserve of Officers, Royal Artillery. For distinguished service in the field." Lieut.-Colonel H. G. Stobart married, in 1900, Mary, daughter of the late Rev. H. G. Kinnear.

TREVOR, WILLIAM HERBERT, Major, was born 22 Jan. 1872, son of Colonel S. T. Trevor. He was educated at Marlborough and Sandhurst, and was gazetted to the East Kent Regt. 13 July, 1892, becoming Lieutenant 13 June, 1894, and Captain 13 Nov. 1899; was Adjutant, East Kent Regt., 20 March to 3 Aug. 1908; was promoted to Major 7 Feb. 1911; was Temporary Lieutenant-Colonel 29 Dec. 1915, to 2 June, 1917. He was Assistant Superintendent of Signalling, Malakand Field Force, 10 Aug. to 21 Nov. 1897, and 6 Dec. 1897 to 6 Jan. 1898; Assistant Superintendent of Signalling, Buner Field Force, 7 Jan. to 21 Jan. 1898; Assistant to Staff Officer for Prisoners of War, South Africa (graded Staff Captain), 13 June to 30 Nov. 1900; Assistant to Staff Officer for Prisoners of War (graded D.A.A.G.) 1 Dec. 1900, to 27 Nov. 1901. He was Adjutant, Volunteers, 1 Jan. 1902, to 31 Dec. 1904; Officer, Company of Gentleman Cadets, Royal Military College, 16 Sept. 1908, to 15 Sept. 1912; Garrison Adjutant, Belfast, 9 March to 19 Sept. 1914; Assistant Provost-Marshal (graded Staff Captain), G.H.Q., B.E.F., 20 to 29 Sept. 1914; A.P.M. (graded D.A.A.G.), 2nd Army Corps, B.E.F., 30 Sept. 1914, to 8 Feb. 1915; Provost-Marshal, B.E.F., British Armies in France, 9 Feb. 1915, to 13 Nov. 1917; P.M., 5th Army, British Armies in France, 23 May to 3 June, 1918; G.S.O.2, War Office, 20 June to 31 Dec. 1918; Assistant Commandant, G.S.O., Royal Military College, 1 Jan. 1919. He took part in the operations in Chitral, 1895, with the Relief Force; action of Mamagai (Medal with clasp); served on the North-West Frontier of India, 1897–98 (Malakand), on Staff; took part in the operations in Bajaur and in the Mamund country; Utman Khel, Signalling Officer; Buner, on Staff; was present at the attack and capture of the Tanga Pass (clasp); served in the South African War, 1899–1901, on Staff (severely wounded; Queen's Medal with three clasps). For his services in the European War he was given the Brevet of Lieutenant-Colonel 3 June, 1917, and was created a Companion of the Distinguished Service Order [London Gazette, 23 June, 1915]: "William Herbert Trevor, Major, East Kent Regt. For distinguished service in the field." Lieut.-Colonel W. H. Trevor married, in 1899, Evelyn Gordon Pirrie, and they have one son.

VAUGHAN, LOUIS RIDLEY, Major, was born 7 Aug. 1875, second son of the late Cedric Vaughan, J.P., of Leyfield House, Millom, Cumberland. He was educated at Uppingham, and at the Royal Military College, Sandhurst, and entered the Army, as Second Lieutenant, Unattached, 14 Aug. 1895, and the Indian Staff Corps 11 Dec. 1896. He was promoted to Lieutenant, Indian Army, 14 Nov. 1897; to Captain 14 Aug. 1904, and to Major 14 Aug. 1913; was Temporary Lieutenant-Colonel 24 Feb. 1915, to 11 April, 1916; Temporary Brigadier-General 12 April, 1916, to 20 May, 1917; was Temporary Major-General 21 May, 1917, to 31 Dec. 1918, and Major-General 1 Jan. 1919. He was G.S.O.3, Headquarters, India, 9 June, 1910, to 31 Jan. 1912; G.S.O.3, War Office, 1 Feb. 1912, to 4 Aug. 1914; G.S.O.2, War Office, 5 Aug. to 2 Nov. 1914; G.S.O.2, 2nd Division, B.E.F., 3 Nov. 1914, to 21 Feb. 1915; G.S.O.1, 2nd Division, B.E.F., 22 Feb. 1915, to 11 April, 1916; Brigadier-General, G.S., 15th Army Corps, British Armies in France, 12 April to 11 Oct. 1916; Major-General, G.S., 3rd Army Corps, British Armies in France, 21 May, 1917; Commandant, Staff College, Quetta, 1919. For his services in the European War, 1914–18, he was mentioned in Despatches; was given the Brevets of Lieutenant-Colonel 3 June, 1916, and of Colonel 1 Jan. 1917; promoted to Major-General; received the 1914 Star, and was created a C.B. in 1918, and a Companion of the Distinguished Service Order [London Gazette, 23 June, 1915]: "Louis Ridley Vaughan, Major (Temporary Lieutenant-Colonel), Indian Army. For distinguished service in the field." Sir Philip Gibbs says in "The Realities of War" (page 397): "I saw General Louis Vaughan . . . That charming man, with his professional manner, sweetness of speech, gentleness of voice and gesture, like an Oxford Don analysing the war correspondence of Xenophon."

WALKER, HENRY ALEXANDER, Major, was born 20 Oct. 1874. He was gazetted to the Royal Fusiliers 12 Dec. 1894; became Lieutenant 24 Nov. 1897; Captain 27 Jan. 1900; Major 3 Sept. 1910; was Temporary Lieutenant-Colonel 25 Oct. 1915, to 31 Dec. 1916, and Temporary Brigadier-General 26 Oct. 1917, to 2 Dec. 1918. He was employed with the Central African Rifles; with the King's African Rifles 8 July, 1901, to 15 May, 1910; Brigade Major, India, 15 Sept. 1913, to 11 Oct. 1914; Brigade Major, Dehra Dun Brigade, B.E.F., 12 Oct. 1914, to 14 June, 1915; G.S.O.2, 8th Division, B.E.F., 15 June to 21 Oct. 1915; G.S.O., New Armies, British Armies in France, 25 Oct. 1915, to 15 April, 1917; G.S.O.1, 65th Division, Home Forces, 21 April to 8 Oct. 1917; Brigade Commander, 16th Infantry Brigade, British Armies in France, 26 Oct. 1917, to 2 Dec. 1918. He served in East Africa, 1902–4; took part in the operations in Somaliland; in the action at Jidballi (Medal with two clasps); served at Nandi, 1905–6, in command of a column (Despatches [London Gazette, 18 Sept. 1906]; Brevet of Major 26 March, 1906; clasp). For his services in the European War, 1914–18, he was mentioned in Despatches four times; given the Brevet of Lieutenant-Colonel 1 Jan. 1917; created a C.M.G., 1918, and created a Companion of the Distinguished Service Order [London Gazette, 23 June, 1915]: "Henry Alexander Walker, Major, Royal Fusiliers. For distinguished service in the field."

WEATHERBY, JAMES THORPE, Brevet Major, was born 21 April, 1877, son of the late Edward Weatherby, of 6, Old Burlington Street, W. He was gazetted to the Oxford and Bucks Light Infantry 8 Feb. 1899; became Lieutenant 30 July, 1900; Captain 30 Dec. 1905; Major 1 Sept. 1915; was Temporary Lieutenant-Colonel 15 June, 1916, to 18 Nov. 1917; Temporary Lieutenant-Colonel 10 Dec. 1917. He was A.D.C. to the Commander-in-Chief, East Indies, 15 March to 27 Nov. 1902; on Special Service, Somaliland Field Force, from 3 Sept. 1903, to 12 June, 1904; G.S.O.3, War Office, from 23 Sept. 1912, to 30 April, 1914; Brigade Major, 15th Brigade, Irish Command, from 1 May, 1914, to 4 Aug. 1914; Brigade Major, 15th Infantry Brigade, B.E.F., 5 Aug. 1914, to 2 May, 1915; G.S.O.2, 5th Division, B.E.F., 3 May, 1915, to 14 June, 1916; G.S.O.1, 47th Division, British Armies in France, 15 June to 31 Oct. 1916; G.S.O.1, War Office, 28 Nov. 1916, to 18 Nov. 1917; G.S.O.1, 61st Division, British Armies in France, 10 Dec. 1917, to 16 March, 1918; G.S.O.1, G.H.Q., British Armies in France, 1 April to 2 June, 1918; Assistant Military Secretary, G.H.Q., British Armies in France, 3 June, 1918. For his services in East Africa during the operations in Somaliland, as Special Service Officer, he received the Medal with clasp. He served in the European War, 1914–16; was three times mentioned in Despatches; received the

Brevet of Major 18 Feb. 1915, and was created a Companion of the Distinguished Service Order [London Gazette, 23 June, 1915]: "James Thorpe Weatherby, Brevet Major, Oxfordshire and Buckinghamshire Light Infantry. For distinguished service in the field." He married Giana Dorothea, daughter of Howard Gilliat, of Abbots Ripton Hall, Hants, and they have one son.

WEIR, GEORGE ALEXANDER, Major, was born 1 Dec. 1876, son of the late Archibald Weir, M.D., of Malvern. He was educated at Harrow and Trinity College, Cambridge, and became Captain, 3rd Dragoon Guards, 11 Jan. 1902; Major 2 July, 1912, and Temporary Lieutenant-Colonel, Royal Irish Rifles, 24 June to 12 Oct. 1915; Temporary Brigadier-General 13 Oct. 1915. He was Senior Tactical Instructor, Cavalry School, 29 June to 4 Aug. 1914; Staff Captain, 4th Cavalry Brigade, B.E.F., 5 Aug. to 9 Oct. 1914; G.S.O.2, 2nd Cavalry Division, B.E.F., 14 Oct. 1914, to 23 June, 1915; commanded the 84th Infantry Brigade, B.E.F., Salonika Army, British Salonika Force, 13 Oct. 1915, to 21 March, 1918; commanded the 19th Infantry Brigade, Egyptian Expeditionary Force, 3 April to 6 Oct. 1918; commanded the 13th Cavalry Brigade, Egyptian Expeditionary Force, 7 Oct. 1918. He served in the South African War, 1899–1901, with the Imperial Yeomanry; took part in the various operations in the Transvaal, Orange River Colony and Cape Colony, 30 Nov. 1900, to Aug. 1901 (Despatches [London Gazette, 10 Sept. 1901, and 29 July, 1902]; Queen's Medal with four clasps). He served in the European War, 1914–18; was wounded; mentioned in Despatches; was given the Brevets of Lieutenant-Colonel 1 Jan. 1917, and Colonel 1 Jan. 1918; was made Officer of St. Maurice and St. Lazarus, and was created a Companion of the Distinguished Service Order [London Gazette, 23 June, 1915]: "George Alexander Weir, Major, 3rd Dragoon Guards. For distinguished service in the field." Colonel Weir married, in 1917, Margaret Irene, daughter of Robert More, of Woodsgate Place, Bexhill.

COX, EDGAR WILLIAM, Capt., was born in May, 1882, and educated at Christ's Hospital. He entered the Royal Engineers 21 Dec. 1900, and spent several years in Africa, where he was engaged in boundary and survey work. He was with the Sierra Leone and Liberia Boundary Commission from 1902 to 1903, and with the Anglo-Portuguese Boundary Commission from 1904 to 1906. He also did survey work in the East African Protectorate, 1906–9. He was promoted to Lieutenant 21 Dec. 1903, and to Captain in 1910; and was employed at the War Office as G.S.O. from 1912 to 1914. Capt. Cox served in the European War, and became G.S.O.1 and Temporary Brigadier-General (Intelligence) on the Headquarters Staff in France. He was mentioned in Despatches; given the Brevets of Major and Lieutenant-Colonel; was made Chevalier Legion of Honour, 1915, and created a Companion of the Distinguished Service Order [London Gazette, 23 June, 1915]; "Edgar William Cox, Capt., Royal Engineers. For distinguished service in the field." Colonel Edgar William Cox died 26 Aug. 1918.

Edgar William Cox.

DILL, JOHN GREER, Capt., was born 25 Dec. 1881. He was gazetted Second Lieutenant, Leinster Regt., 8 May, 1901; became Lieutenant 27 May, 1903; was Adjutant 15 Aug. 1906, to 14 Aug. 1909; was promoted to Captain 12 July, 1911; to Major 8 May, 1916; was Temporary Brigadier-General from 27 March, 1918. He was Brigade Major, 25th Infantry Brigade, New Armies, B.E.F., 5 Oct. 1914, to 2 Jan. 1916; G.S.O.2, B.E.F., British Armies in France, 3 Jan. to 11 July, 1916; G.S.O.2, Canadian Army Corps, British Armies in France, 3 Jan. to 11 July, 1916; G.S.O.1, 37th Division, British Armies in France, 1 Feb. to 28 Oct. 1917; G.S.O.1, G.H.Q., British Armies in France, 29 Oct. 1917, to 28 March, 1918; Brigadier-General, G.S., G.H.Q., British Armies in France, 27 March, 1918, to 28 Feb. 1919; Brigadier-General, G.S., Staff College, 1 March, 1919. He served in the South African War, 1901–2; took part in the operations in the Transvaal, Nov. 1901; in Orange River Colony, Oct. 1901, to 31 May, 1902; also in Cape Colony, Oct. 1901 (Queen's Medal with five clasps). For his services in the European War, 1914–18, he was given the Brevets of Lieutenant-Colonel 1 Jan. 1917, and Colonel 3 June, 1919; was created a C.M.G. in 1918, and created a Companion of the Distinguished Service Order [London Gazette, 23 June, 1915]: "John Greer Dill, Capt., The Leinster Regt. For distinguished service in the field."

DUGAN, WINSTON JOSEPH, Capt., was born 8 May, 1877, at Birr, son of Charles Winston Dugan (deceased) and Esther Dugan, of Oxmantown Mall, Birr. He was educated at Lurgan College, and Wimbledon, Surrey, and was commissioned in the 2nd Lincolnshire Regt. 8 April, 1896; was Adjutant, Lincolnshire Regt., 28 June, 1901, to 15 Nov. 1904. He served in the South African War, 1899–1902; served as Adjutant, 2nd Battn. Lincolnshire Regt., 20 June, 1901, to 31 May, 1902; was present during operations in the Transvaal, Jan. 1901, to May, 1902 (Queen's Medal with three clasps, and King's Medal with two clasps). He was promoted to Lieutenant 1 Nov. 1901, and Captain, Worcestershire Regt., 16 Nov. 1904, and was Adjutant, Worcestershire Regt., 23 Nov. 1907, to 22 Nov. 1909; Temporary Major, Royal Irish Regt., 18 to 31 Aug. 1915; promoted to Major 1 Sept. 1915; was Temporary Lieutenant-Colonel, Worcestershire Regt., 1 Sept. 1915; Temporary Brigadier-General 30 July to 25 Sept. 1916. He was appointed Garrison Adjutant (graded Staff Captain, Irish Command), Jan. 1910, to Jan. 1914; on Staff, East Anglian Division, Aug. to Oct. 1914; Provost-Marshal, B.E.F. (graded D.A.A.G.), Oct. 1914, to July, 1915; commanded 2nd Battn. Royal Irish Regt. 18 Aug. 1915, to 31 Aug. 1915, including the Somme Battle; Brigade Commander, Aug. 1916, till wounded in Sept. 1916, and again appointed to command a Brigade, Dec. 1916, to 15 July, 1918; Assistant Inspector of Training, British Armies in France, 16 July, 1918. On 17 Jan. 1912, at Holy Trinity Church, Brompton, he married Ruby Lilian, daughter of the late Charles Abbott and Mrs. Applewhaite Abbott, of 11, Cumberland Terrace, Regent's Park, N.W. He was created a Companion of the Distinguished Service Order [London Gazette, 23 June, 1915]: "Winston Joseph Dugan, Capt., Worcestershire Regt. For distinguished service in the field."

HAINING, ROBERT HADDEN, Capt., was born 28 July, 1882. He entered the Royal Artillery 23 July, 1901; became Lieutenant 23 July, 1904; Captain 23 July, 1914; Major 29 Oct. 1915. He was Staff Captain, R.A., 2nd Division, B.E.F., 1 Nov. 1914, to 9 June, 1915; Brigade Major, R.A., 6th Division, B.E.F., 10 June, 1915, to 12 March, 1916; D.A.A.G., R.A., 8th Army Corps, B.E.F., British Armies in France, 13 March to 18 Oct. 1916; D.A.A.G., G.H.Q., British Armies in France, 19 Oct. 1916, to 7 May, 1917; D.A.A.G., 5th Army Corps, British Armies in France, 8 May to 27 Aug. 1917; G.S.O.2, 5th Army Corps, British Armies in France, 28 July, 1917, to 8 Aug. 1918; G.S.O.1, Tactical School, Camberley, 7 Aug. 1918, to 7 March, 1919; G.S.O.2, R.A., 11th Army Corps, British Armies in France, British Troops in France and Flanders, 8 March, 1919. For his services in the European War he was mentioned in Despatches; was given the Brevet of Lieutenant-Colonel 3 June, 1918, and created a Companion of the Distinguished Service Order [London Gazette, 23 June, 1915]: "Robert Hadden Haining, Capt., Royal Artillery. For distinguished service in the field." Lieut.-Colonel R. H. Haining is married, and has one son.

HEADLAM, HUGH ROGER, Major, was born 15 July, 1877, fourth son of the late F. J. Headlam. He was educated at Wellington College, and the Royal Military College, Sandhurst, and was gazetted to the York and Lancaster Regt. 8 Sept. 1897, becoming Lieutenant 2 Nov. 1899; Captain 2 April, 1903; Major 25 April, 1915; Temporary Lieutenant-Colonel, commanding the 1 5th Battn. West Riding Regt. 1 Sept. 1915, to 11 June, 1916; Temporary Brigadier-General 12 June, 1916. He served in the South African War, 1899–1902, on the Staff; was present at the Relief of Ladysmith, including operations of 17 to 24 Jan. 1900; operations of 5 to 7 Feb. 1900, and action at Vaal Kranz; in the operations on Tugela Heights (14 to 27 Feb. 1900), and action at Pieter's Hill; took part in the operations in Natal, March to June, 1900, including action at Laing's Nek (6 to 9 June); in the Transvaal, 30 Nov. 1900, to Jan. 1901; also during operations on the Zululand Frontier of Natal in Sept. 1901 (Queen's Medal with six clasps, and King's Medal with two clasps). Served in the Soudan, 1905; took part in the operations against the Nyam Nyam Tribes in the Bahr-el-Ghazal Province (Egyptian Medal with clasp). He served in the European War, 1914–18; was wounded; mentioned in Despatches; given the Brevets of Lieutenant-Colonel 1 Jan. 1917, and Colonel 1 Jan. 1919; was created a C.M.G. in 1918, and created a Companion of the Distinguished Service Order [London Gazette, 23 June, 1915]: "Hugh Roger Headlam, Major, The York and Lancaster Regt. For distinguished service in the field." He married, in 1914, Maria Teresa, daughter of the late Right Hon. Sir Julian Goldsmid.

HILDYARD, REGINALD JOHN THOROTON, Major, was born 11 Dec. 1876, third son of the late General Sir H. J. T. Hildyard. He was commissioned in the Royal West Kent Regt. 5 Sept. 1896; became Lieutenant 9 Jan. 1899; Captain 4 Jan. 1904; Major 19 April, 1915; was Temporary Lieutenant-Colonel 10 Oct. to 31 Dec. 1915, and Temporary Brigadier-General 12 Sept. 1917, to 8 Feb. 1919. He was employed with the South African Constabulary, 22 Nov. 1900, to 21 Nov. 1903; was A.D.C. to Lieutenant-General, South Africa, 19 March, 1904, to 31 Oct. 1905; A.D.C. to G.O. Commanding-in-Chief in South Africa, 1 Nov. 1905, to 18 March, 1908; G.S.O.3, War Office, 1 Oct. 1911, to 30 Sept. 1913; Brigade Major, 7th Brigade, Southern Command, B.E.F., 1 Oct. 1913, to 25 Feb. 1915; G.S.O.2, 13th Division, New Armies, Mediterranean Expeditionary Force, 26 Feb. to 9 Oct. 1915; G.S.O.1, 13th Division, Mediterranean Expeditionary Force; Indian Expeditionary Force "D," Mesopotamian Expeditionary Force, 10 Oct. 1915, to 10 Sept. 1917; Brigade Commander, 51st Infantry Brigade, Mesopotamian Expeditionary Force, 12 Sept. 1917, to 8 Feb. 1919. He served in the South African War, 1899–1902, on duty under the Military Governor of Pretoria (Queen's Medal with four clasps; King's Medal with two clasps). For his services in the Great War, from 1914, he was twice mentioned in Despatches; was given the Brevets of Lieutenant-Colonel 1 Jan. 1916, and Colonel 1 Jan. 1919; was created a C.M.G. in 1917 (for Mesopotamia, 1916–17), and created a Companion of the Distinguished Service Order [London Gazette, 23 June, 1915]: "Reginald John Thoroton Hildyard, Major, Royal West Kent Regt. For distinguished service in the field." Colonel Hildyard married, in 1911, Muriel, daughter of H. Cosmo Bonsor, D.L.

HOLLAND, LANCELOT, Major, was born 17 July, 1876. He was educated at Merchiston Castle School, Edinburgh, and entered the Seaforth Highlanders 5 Sept. 1896; became Lieutenant 9 Oct. 1899; Captain 31 Oct. 1901; Major 27 May, 1915; was Temporary Lieutenant-Colonel 28 May to 31 Dec. 1917, and was promoted to Lieutenant-Colonel 10 Jan. 1919. He was Adjutant, Volunteers, 3 March, 1904, to 22 March, 1907; Brigade Major, 5th Brigade, Aldershot Command, 1 April, 1912, to 31 July, 1913; G.S.O.3, Northern Command, 1 Aug. 1913, to Sept. 1914; Brigade Major, 81st Infantry Brigade, New Armies, B.E.F., 3 Nov. 1914, to 14 June, 1915; G.S.O.2, 30th Division, New Armies, British Armies in France, 8 Sept. 1915, to 13 July, 1916; G.S.O.2, 72nd Division, Home Forces, 8 to 23 Nov. 1916; G.S.O.2, 28th Division, British Salonika Force, 7 Dec. 1916, to 27 May, 1917; G.S.O.1, 27th Division, British Salonika Force, 28 May, 1917, to 17 Oct. 1918; G.S.O.1, G.H.Q., British Salonika Force, 18 Oct. 1918, to 11 Jan. 1919; employed with the Malay States Guides 23 Jan. 1899, to 27 Sept. 1910; Adjutant, Militia, 10 March, 1903, to 9

March, 1908; Adjutant, Indian Volunteers, 16 April, 1910, to 15 April, 1914. He served with the Nile Expedition in 1898, and was present at the Battles of the Atbara and Khartum. He served in the South African War, 1901–2; was mentioned in Despatches [London Gazette, 29 July, 1902], and received the Queen's Medal with five clasps. For his services in the European War, 1914–18, he was mentioned in Despatches; was given the Brevet of Lieutenant-Colonel 1 Jan. 1918, and created a Companion of the Distinguished Service Order [London Gazette, 23 June, 1915]: "Lancelot Holland, Major, Seaforth Highlanders. For distinguished service in the field."

HOWARD-VYSE, RICHARD GRANVILLE HYLTON, Capt., was born 27 June, 1883, eldest son of Howard Henry Howard-Vyse, J.P., D.L., and Mabel Diana, only daughter of the late Rev. G. Granville Sykes Howard-Vyse; and a grandson of the 1st Lord Hilton. He entered the Royal Horse Guards 10 Dec. 1902; became Lieutenant 6 April, 1904; was Adjutant 25 Sept. 1907, to 24 Sept. 1910; Captain 4 April, 1908; Major 5 June, 1919; Temporary Brigadier-General 17 Aug. 1917, to 20 Sept. 1918, and from 7 Dec. 1918. He was employed with the Canadian Forces 6 June, to 8 July, 1913; Brigade Major, 5th Cavalry Brigade, Northern Command, British Expeditionary Force, 4 May, 1914, to 11 June, 1915; G.S.O.2, 1st Cavalry Division, B.E.F., 12 June, 1915, to 4 Feb. 1916; G.S.O.2, Cavalry Corps, B.E.F., 5 Feb. to 21 May, 1916; G.S.O.2, Reserve Corps, B.E.F., 12 March to 21 May, 1916; G.S.O.1, 3rd Cavalry Division, British Armies in France, 22 March to 26 May, 1916; G.S.O.1, 2nd Indian Division, British Armies in France, 27 May, 1916, to 1 Aug. 1917; Brigadier-General, G.S., Egyptian Expeditionary Force, 17 Aug. 1917, to 16 July, 1918; in Palestine, as Chief Staff Officer, Desert Mounted Corps, and G.O.C., 10th Cavalry Brigade, Egyptian Expeditionary Force, 17 July to 20 Sept. 1918; Commandant, 7 Dec. 1918. He was mentioned in Despatches; given the Brevets of Major 3 June, 1916, and Lieutenant-Colonel 3 June, 1917; created a C.M.G. in 1918, and created a Companion of the Distinguished Service Order [London Gazette, 23 June, 1915]: "Richard Granville Hylton Howard-Vyse, Capt., Royal Horse Guards. For distinguished service in the field."

LIDDELL, CLIVE GERARD, Capt., was born 1 May, 1883. He entered the Leicestershire Regt. 13 May, 1905; was Adjutant, Leicestershire Regt. 23 March, 1908, to 22 March, 1911; was promoted to Captain 17 Oct. 1908, and to Major 22 Oct. 1917. He was Staff Captain, No. 6 District, Northern Command, 1 April, 1912, to 15 Oct. 1914; D.A.A. and Q.M.G., 55th Division, 1st Army Corps, B.E.F., British Armies in France, 3 Jan. to 7 Dec. 1916; specially employed, War Office, 7 Feb. 1917, to 28 Feb. 1919; Instructor, Staff College, 1 March, 1919. For his services in the European War, 1914–18, he was three times mentioned in Despatches; created a C.M.G. in 1918; a C.B.E. in 1919; was given the Brevet of Lieutenant-Colonel 23 Oct. 1917, and created a Companion of the Distinguished Service Order [London Gazette, 23 June, 1915]: "Clive Gerard Liddell, Capt., The Leicestershire Regt. For distinguished service in the field." Lieut.-Colonel Liddell married (1st), in 1914, Clare Lambert Roberts (who died in 1917); and (2ndly), in 1918, Hilda Jessie Bisset, widow of Lieut. Maurice Cane, and they have three children.

MANSEL-JONES, CONWYN, Capt. (see Victoria Cross Volume), was created a Companion of the Distinguished Service Order [London Gazette, 23 June, 1915]: "Conwyn Mansel-Jones, V.C., Capt., Reserve of Officers, West Yorkshire Regt. For distinguished service in the field."

NORTH, OLIVER HENRY, Capt., was born 28 April, 1874, fifth son of the late North North, of Newton Hall, Lancashire. He was gazetted to the Lancashire Fusiliers 19 May, 1900; became Lieutenant 26 June, 1901; Captain 24 June, 1910; Major 1 Sept. 1915; was Temporary Lieutenant-Colonel, 1916 to 1918. He was Assistant Superintendent of Gymnasia, Eastern Command, 9 Jan. 1907, to 8 Jan. 1911; Staff Captain, 12th Infantry Brigade, B.E.F., 5 Aug. 1914, to 25 July, 1915; A.P.M., 7th Division, B.E.F., 26 July to 4 Aug. 1915; A.P.M., 6th Division, B.E.F., 5 Aug. to 10 Oct. 1915. He served in the South African War, 1899–1902, with Bethune's Mounted Infantry; was present at the Relief of Ladysmith, including operations of 17 to 24 Jan. 1900, and action at Spion Kop; operations of 5 to 7 Feb. 1900, and action at Vaal Kranz; and the operations on Tugela Heights (14 to 27 Feb. 1900); in Natal (March to June, 1900), including action at Laing's Nek (6 to 9 June); in the Transvaal, east of Pretoria, July to Aug. 1900; employed with Mounted Infantry; in the Transvaal, April, 1901, to Jan, 1902, and March to 31 May, 1902; in Orange River Colony, April, 1901, and Jan. to March, 1902; also during operations in Cape Colony, April, 1901, and May, 1902 (Queen's Medal with six clasps, and King's Medal with two clasps). For his services in the European War, 1914–19, he was three times mentioned in Despatches; received the 1914 Star; was given the Brevet of Lieutenant-Colonel 3 June, 1919, and created a Companion of the Distinguished Service Order [London Gazette, 23 June, 1915]: "Oliver Henry North, Capt., Lancs. Fusiliers. For distinguished service in the field." Lieut.-Colonel O. H. North married, in 1908, Edith Monica, only child of W. A. Smith Masters, and they have three sons.

Oliver Henry North.

OGSTON, CHARLES, Capt., was born 14 Sept. 1887, second son of Alexander Milne Ogston, D.L., of Ardoe, Kincardineshire. He was gazetted to the Gordon Highlanders 17 Nov. 1897; became Lieutenant 21 June, 1899; Captain 22 Jan. 1902; was Adjutant, Gordon Highlanders, 21 Jan. 1906, to 21 Jan. 1909; Major 1 Sept. 1915; was Temporary Brigadier-General 9 Oct. 1918, to 5 March, 1919; and from 26 March, 1919. He was D.A.A. and Q.M.G., Malta, 3 Aug. 1912, to 1914; D.A.A. and Q.M.G., 6th Division, B.E.F., 7 Nov. 1914, to 2 Jan. 1916; A.Q.M.G., 14th Army Corps, B.E.F., British Armies in France; British Force in Italy, 3 Jan. 1916, to 8 Oct. 1918; D.A. and Q.M.G., 14th Army Corps, British Force in Italy; D.A. and Q.M.G., Constantinople, 26 Nov. 1919; A.Q.M.G. He took part in the operations on the North-West Frontier of India, 1897–98, with the latter part of the Tirah Expedition (Medal with clasp). Served in the South African War, 1899–1902; took part in the advance on Kimberley, including action at Magersfontein; in the Orange Free State, Feb. to May, 1900, including operations at Paardeberg (17 to 26 Feb.), Houtnek (Thoba Mountain), Vet River (5 and 6 May) and Zand River; in the Transvaal in May and June, 1900, including actions near Johannesburg and Pretoria; in the Transvaal, east of Pretoria, July to 29 Nov. 1900, including actions at Belfast (26 and 27 Aug.) and Lydenberg (5 to 8 Sept.); in the Transvaal, west of Pretoria, July to 29 Nov. 1900; in Cape Colony, south of Orange River, 1899–1900; also in Cape Colony, north of Orange River; again in the Transvaal, 30 Nov. 1900, to 31 May, 1902; Intelligence Officer (Queen's Medal with four clasps, and King's Medal with two clasps). For his services in the European War he was mentioned in Despatches; was given the Brevet of Lieutenant-Colonel 1 Jan. 1917; was created a C.M.G. in 1918, and was created a Companion of the Distinguished Service Order [London Gazette, 23 June, 1915]: "Charles Ogston, Capt., Gordon Highlanders. For distinguished service in the field."

PHILLIPS, GEOFFREY FRANCIS, Capt., was born 3 May, 1880, son of J. H. Phillips. He was gazetted to the Duke of Cornwall's Light Infantry 30 May, 1900; became Lieutenant 19 Feb. 1904; Captain 20 Sept. 1910; Major 1 Sept. 1915, and was Temporary Lieutenant-Colonel 7 Nov. to 31 Dec. 1916; Temporary Colonel 6 Aug. 1917. He was employed with the King's African Rifles 2 Aug. 1906, to 29 Dec. 1912; Staff Captain, 14th Infantry Brigade, B.E.F., 3 Sept. to 3 Dec. 1915; G.S.O.2, H.Q., East African Force, 7 Dec. 1915, to 6 Nov. 1916; G.S.O.1, G.H.Q., East African Force, 7 Nov. 1916, to 28 July, 1917; employed with the King's African Rifles from 1 Jan. 1917; A.A.G., 20 July to 5 Aug. 1917; Assistant Commandant 6 Aug. 1917. For his services in East Africa he was given the Medal with clasp, and for the European War (1914–17), in which he was twice wounded, he was mentioned in Despatches; given the Brevet of Lieutenant-Colonel 1 Jan. 1917; created a C.B.E., and created a Companion of the Distinguished Service Order [London Gazette, 23 June, 1915]: "Geoffrey Francis Phillips, Capt., Duke of Cornwall's Light Infantry. For distinguished service in the field."

RENNY, LEWIS FREDERICK, Major, was born 4 July, 1877, son of William Renny, Registrar, County Court, Portsmouth, and Priscilla Renny (*née* Brotherhood). He was educated at Brighton College and Sandhurst, and entered the Army 8 Sept. 1897; became Lieutenant 28 Dec. 1898; Captain 16 July, 1904; Major 28 April, 1915; was Temporary Brigadier-General from 30 May, 1918. He was A.D.C. to Major-General, South Africa, 28 March, 1900, to 26 May, 1902; employed with the West African Frontier Force 2 April, 1904, to 29 June, 1908; Brigade Major, Infantry Brigade, Malta, 10 Jan. 1912, to 21 Sept. 1914; Brigade Major, 23rd Infantry Brigade, B.E.F., 22 Sept. 1914, to 4 Aug. 1915; G.S.O.2, 4th Division, B.E.F., 5 Aug. 1915, to 19 June, 1916; G.S.O.1, 6th Division, British Armies in France, 20 June, 1916, to 23 March, 1917; G.S.O.1, Machine Gun Corps, Training Centre, 15 April, 1917, to 29 May, 1918; Brigade Commander, 28th Training Reserve Brigade, Forces in Great Britain, 30 May to 22 Oct. 1918; Inspector of Machine Gun Units, G.H.Q., British Armies in France, from 23 Oct. 1918. He served in the South African War, 1899–1902, on Staff; took part in the operations in the Transvaal 30 Nov. 1900, to Jan. 1902 (Despatches [London Gazette, 8 Feb. 1901]; Queen's Medal with four clasps, and King's Medal with two clasps). For his services in the European War, 1914–18 he was mentioned in Despatches seven times; given the Brevets of Lieutenant-Colonel 1 Jan. 1917, and of Colonel 3 June, 1919; created a C.M.G. in 1918, and created a Companion of the Distinguished Service Order [London Gazette, 23 June, 1915]: "Lewis Frederick Renny, Major, Royal Dublin Fusiliers. For distinguished service in the field." He married Maud, second daughter of the Rev. Treasurer Nicholson, M.A., Rector of St. Nicholas Church, Cork, and Canon of St. Patrick's and of Cork Cathedral.

TAPLEY, JAMES JOHN BONIFANT, Capt., was born 14 Nov. 1877, son of S. G. Tapley. He entered the Army Veterinary Corps 16 May, 1903; became Captain 16 May, 1908; Major 10 July, 1915; was employed with the Egyptian Army 9 Nov. 1911, to 4 Aug. 1914; and from 11 Sept. 1915; P.V.O. He served in the South African War, 1901–2; took part in the operations in Cape Colony, Sept. 1901, to 31 May, 1902 (Queen's Medal with four clasps). For his services in the European War, 1914–17, he was given the Brevet of Lieutenant-Colonel 1 Jan. 1917, and created a Companion of the Distinguished Service Order [London Gazette, 23 June, 1915]: "James John Bonifant Tapley, Capt., Army Veterinary Corps. For distinguished service in the field."

THURLOW, EDWARD GUY LETHBRIDGE, Capt., was born 6 Nov. 1881, son of Lieut.-Colonel Hugh Thurlow (late Somerset Light Infantry). He was educated at Wellington College, and at Sandhurst, and entered the Somerset Light Infantry 11 Aug. 1900; became Lieutenant 21 Aug. 1903; Captain 1 Sept. 1911; Major, 1 Sept. 1915, and was Temporary Lieutenant-Colonel 30 June, 1916, to 2 June, 1917. He was Railway Staff Officer 19 Dec. 1901, to 16 Jan. 1903; employed with the West African Frontier Force 14 May, 1904, to 12 Oct. 1906; Railway Transport Officer 9 Aug. to 8 Oct. 1914; Brigade Major, 6th London Infantry Brigade, Central Force, Home Defence, 9 Oct. to 25 Nov. 1914; Brigade Major, 22nd Infantry Brigade, B.E.F., 20 Dec. 1914, to 20 Oct. 1915; D.A.A. and Q.M.G., 27th Division, B.E.F., Egyptian Expeditionary Force, 28 Oct. 1915, to 29 June, 1916; A.A. and Q.M.G., Salonika Army, British Salonika

Force, 30 June, 1916, to 16 March, 1918; G.S.O.1, Thames and Medway Garrison, 17 April to 29 Oct. 1918; G.S.O.2, War Office (temporary), 15 April, 1919. He served in the South African War, 1899–1902, on Staff; took part in the operations in Orange River Colony, Nov. 1900; in Cape Colony, north of Orange River, Oct. to Nov. 1900; in the Transvaal, April, 1901, to 31 May, 1902; also in Orange River Colony, 30 Nov. 1900, to April, 1901 (Queen's Medal with three clasps, and King's Medal with two clasps). Served in West Africa, (Northern Nigeria), 1906. For his services in the Great War, 1914–18, he was mentioned in Despatches seven times; was given the Brevet of Lieutenant-Colonel 3 June, 1917; was made Officer, Star of Roumania, and was created a Companion of the Distinguished Service Order [London Gazette, 23 June, 1915]: "Edward Guy Lethbridge Thurlow, Capt., Somerset Light Infantry. For distinguished service in the field." Lieut.-Colonel Thurlow married, in 1912, Margaret Merry, daughter of Lieut.-Colonel E. H. Vaughan, of Kenton, Devon, and they have two daughters.

VILLIERS-STUART, JOHN PATRICK, Capt., was born 1 March, 1879, youngest son of the late Lieut.-Colonel Villiers-Stuart, of Castlane, Carrick-on-Suir. He entered the Army 26 Jan. 1899, as Second Lieutenant (unattached), and was gazetted to the Indian Staff Corps 14 April, 1900, becoming Lieutenant, Indian Army, 25 April, 1901; Captain 25 Jan. 1908; Major 1 Sept. 1915, and was Temporary Lieutenant-Colonel 28 Oct. 1916, to 25 July, 1917, and 1 Nov. to 31 Dec. 1917. He was D.A.A.G., G.H.Q., British Expeditionary Force, 14 Oct. 1914, to 21 Aug. 1915; D.A.A. and Q.M.G., 2nd Army Corps, B.E.F., British Armies in France, 22 Aug. 1915, to 27 Oct. 1916; A.A. and Q.M.G., 2nd Division, British Armies in France, 28 Oct. 1916, to 25 July, 1917. He served in China, 1900 (Medal). Served on the North-West Frontier of India, Waziristan, 1901–2 (Medal with clasp). Served in East Africa, 1903–4, during operations in Somaliland; in the action at Jidballi (Medal with two clasps). Served on the North-West Frontier of India, 1908; Orderly Officer to O.C. and Brigadier; took part in the operations in the Zakka Khel country (Despatches [London Gazette, 22 May, 1908]). For his services in the European War he was mentioned in Despatches twice; was given the Brevet of Lieutenant-Colonel 1 Jan. 1918; the Legion of Honour, and was created a Companion of the Distinguished Service Order [London Gazette, 23 June, 1915]: "John Patrick Villiers-Stuart, Capt., Indian Army. For distinguished service in the field." Lieut.-Colonel J. P. Villiers-Stuart married, in 1914, Phyllis Mary, daughter of the late James Read, and they have two daughters.

WALCOT, BASIL, Capt., entered the Royal Engineers 6 Jan. 1900; became Lieutenant 19 Dec. 1902, and Captain 6 Jan. 1909. He served in the South African War, 1902; took part in the operations in the Transvaal, April to May, 1902; also in Cape Colony, May, 1902 (Queen's Medal with four clasps). For his services in the European War he was created a Companion of the Distinguished Service Order [London Gazette, 23 June, 1915]: "Basil Walcot, Capt., Royal Engineers. For distinguished service in the field." Major Walcot died 14 Sept. 1918.

PARES, BASIL, Surgeon-Major, was born 24 April, 1869, son of the late John Pares and Katherine, daughter of John Birch. He was educated at Lancing College; Emmanuel College, Cambridge, and St. Mary's Hospital, London, and became Surgeon-Major, Royal Horse Guards (The Blues), 17 Feb. 1906. He served in the South African War, 1899–1901, as a Civil Surgeon; took part in the Relief of Kimberley; was present during operations in the Orange Free State, Feb. to May, 1900, including operations at Paardeberg (17 to 26 Feb.), actions at Poplar Grove, Dreifontein, Vet River (5 and 6 May) and Zand River; also in Cape Colony, south of Orange River, 1899–1900 (Queen's Medal with five clasps). For his services in the European War in 1914 and 1915 he was created a C.M.G. in 1916, and a Companion of the Distinguished Service Order [London Gazette, 23 June, 1915]: "Basil Pares, Surgeon-Major, Royal Horse Guards. For distinguished service in the field." He married, in 1902, Evelyn Whistler, daughter of G. L. Whistler, and they have three sons, Martin (Royal Naval College, Osborne), Stephen and Basil; and three daughters, Ethel, Evelyn and Constance.

SEWELL, HORACE SOMERVILLE, Major, was born 10 Feb. 1881, son of Henry Sewell. He was educated at Harrow, and Trinity College, Cambridge, and was gazetted to the 4th Dragoon Guards 23 May, 1900; was promoted to Lieutenant 19 Feb. 1902; to Captain 25 Sept. 1907, and to Major 3 Sept. 1914. He was Temporary Lieutenant-Colonel, 4th Dragoon Guards, 13 March to 13 May, 1915, and 3 Dec. 1915, to 27 Sept. 1916; Acting Lieutenant-Colonel, 4th Dragoon Guards, 6 Dec. 1916; Temporary Brigadier-General 17 April, 1918, to 21 April, 1919. He was employed in Nigeria with the West African Frontier Force 8 June, 1907, to 20 Nov. 1910: in the Expedition in 1907–8; Northern Hinterland Patrol, 1908–9. He served with the 4th Dragoon Guards in the European War, 1914–18, including Mons, the First Battle of Ypres (1914); Second Battle of Ypres (1915); Somme Battle; Arras Battle (1917) He was wounded (1) at Bourg, on the Aisne, 13 Sept. 1914; (2) at Potige, during the Second Battle of Ypres, 13 May, 1915; (3) accidentally in billets, 3 Aug. 1915. Lieut.-Colonel Sewell commanded the 1st Cavalry Brigade, British Armies in France, 17 April, 1918, to 21 April, 1919. For his services in the European War he was mentioned in Despatches by Sir John French, 17 Feb. and 30 May, 1915; given the Brevet of Lieutenant-Colonel 1 Jan. 1918: was made Chevalier, Legion of Honour; was created a C.M.G. in 1919, and was created a Companion of the Distinguished Service Order [London Gazette, 23 June, 1915]: "Horace Somerville Sewell, Major, 4th (Royal Irish) Dragoon Guards. For distinguished service in the field." The decoration was awarded for various actions during the First Battle of Ypres, Oct. and Nov. 1914. He was awarded a Bar to the Distinguished Service Order. Lieut.-Colonel H. S. Sewell married, in 1916, Emma Whitlock, daughter of the late J. Berre King, of New York, and they have one son, David William Berre, and one daughter.

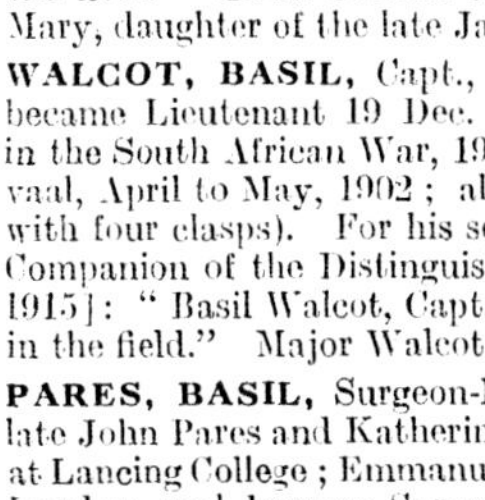

Horace S. Sewell.

HODGKIN, HARRY SIDNEY, Capt., was born 13 June, 1879. He served for a year and 43 days in the ranks of the Imperial Yeomanry, and was commissioned for 117 days, and then was gazetted to the Cheshire Regt. 26 June, 1901; was Second Lieutenant, West African Regt., 25 July, 1903, to 1 Oct. 1906; Lieutenant, Cheshire Regt., 1 Sept. 1904; Captain, Cheshire Regt., 21 April, 1908; 4th Dragoon Guards, 14 Sept. 1914; Reserve Regt. of Cavalry 15 Sept. to 4 Nov. 1914; Temporary Major, whilst commanding a Battalion, Cheshire Regt., 22 Dec. 1914, to 22 Feb. 1915; Lieutenant-Colonel, Territorial Force Battn. 6th Notts and Derby Regt., 15 April, 1916, to 11 Feb. 1919. He was Adjutant, Territorial Force, 11 April to 14 Sept. 1914. He served in the South African War, 1900–2, with the Imperial Yeomanry; took part in the operations in the Orange Free State, 21 April to May, 1900; in Orange River Colony, May to 6 Nov. 1900, including action at Wittebergen; in the Transvaal, March, 1901, to 31 May, 1902; again in Orange River Colony, 30 Nov. 1900, to Feb. 1901 (Queen's Medal with two clasps, and King's Medal with three clasps). For his services in the European War, 1914–18, he was mentioned in Despatches three times; was given the Brevet of Major 1 Jan. 1918, and was created a Companion of the Distinguished Service Order [London Gazette, 23 June, 1915]: "Harry Sidney Hodgkin, Capt., 1st Cheshire Regt. For distinguished service in the field." He married, in 1912, Elsie, daughter of R. J. McMordie, M.A., M.P., and they have two daughters.

LAKIN, MICHAEL LAURENCE, Capt., was born 24 Nov. 1881; entered the Army 26 Sept. 1900; became Lieutenant 18 June, 1901; Captain 3 Dec. 1908, and retired from the 11th Hussars 2 Nov. 1911. He served in the South African War in 1900. Served in the Mediterranean (Medals). He served in the European War, 1914–18, as Captain, Cavalry Special Reserve, and as Acting Major, Tank Corps, and was twice mentioned in Despatches; created a Companion of the Distinguished Service Order [London Gazette, 23 June, 1915]: "Michael Laurence Lakin, Capt., Special Reserve, 11th Hussars. For distinguished service in the field." He was also awarded the Military Cross. Capt. Lakin married, in 1914, Kathleen, youngest daughter of the late Lord Maurice FitzGerald, second son of the 4th Duke of Leinster and Lady Adelaide Forbes, eldest daughter of the 7th Earl of Granard, and they have one son.

STEWART, NOEL ST. VINCENT RAMSAY, Major, was born 4 Dec. 1870. He was commissioned in the 18th Hussars 10 Oct. 1891; became Lieutenant 25 April, 1894; Captain 3 June, 1901, and Major 19 Feb. 1914. He served in the South African War, 1899–1902; as A.D.C. to Lieut.-General Sir N. Lyttelton, K.C.B. 29 Nov. 1900, to 16 Sept. 1902. He took part in the operations in Natal, 1899, including actions at Talana and Lombard's Kop; at the Defence of Ladysmith, including action of 6 Jan. 1900; during operations in Natal, March to June, 1900, including action at Laing's Nek (6 to 9 June); in the Transvaal, east of Pretoria, July to 29 Nov. 1900, including actions at Belfast (26 and 27 Aug.) and Lydenberg (5 to 8 Sept.); in the Transvaal 30 Nov. 1900, to Feb. 1901, and Nov. 1901, to 31 May, 1902; in Orange River Colony, Feb. to April, 1901, and Nov. 1901, to 31 May, 1902; during the operations on the Zululand Frontier of Natal in Sept. and Oct. 1901; also in Cape Colony, Feb. to April, 1901 (Queen's Medal with six clasps, and King's Medal with two clasps). For his services in the European War from 1914 he was mentioned in Despatches, and created a Companion of the Distinguished Service Order [London Gazette, 23 June, 1915]: "Noel St. Vincent Ramsay Stewart, Major, 18th Hussars. For distinguished service in the field." Major Stewart married, in 1903, Mary Evelyn, daughter of C. B. E. Wright.

CALVERT, CHARLES ARCHIBALD, Major, was born 25 Oct. 1873, second son of the late Colonel A. M. Calvert, of Ockley Court. He entered the Army in 1894; became Captain, 1901, and retired from the 1st Dragoons 1 April, 1908. He served in South Africa, 1899–1902; was mentioned in Despatches; received the Queen's Medal with six clasps, and the King's Medal with two clasps. For his services in the European War he was given the Brevet of Lieutenant-Colonel, and was created a Companion of the Distinguished Service Order [London Gazette, 23 June, 1915]: "Charles Archibald Calvert, Major, Sussex Yeomanry. For distinguished service in the field." He served as Temporary Lieutenant-Colonel, Machine Gun Corps. Lieut.-Colonel Calvert married Winifred, daughter of the late Sir Hugh Cholmeley, Bart.

BARTON, PATTERSON, Major, was born 27 June, 1874, son of the late Major-General C. J. Barton, R.A. He entered the Royal Artillery 17 Nov. 1894; became Lieutenant 17 Nov. 1897; Captain 30 Jan. 1901; was Adjutant, R.A., from 16 Jan. 1899; was promoted to Major 21 July, 1911, and to Lieutenant-Colonel 24 April, 1916. He served in the European War, 1914–18; was given the Croix de Guerre, and created a Companion of the Distinguished Service Order [London Gazette, 23 June, 1915]: "Patterson Barton, Major, Royal Artillery. For distinguished service in the field." Lieut.-Colonel Barton married, in 1898, Frances Mary, daughter of the late Robert Sutton, of Blackrock.

BETHELL, ALFRED BRYAN, Major, was born 25 April, 1875, son of Alfred Bethell. He was educated at Cheltenham College and the Royal Military Academy, and was commissioned in the Royal Artillery 15 June, 1895; became Lieutenant 15 June, 1898; Captain 25 April, 1901; Major 1 Nov. 1911, and Lieutenant-Colonel 16 June, 1916. He was employed with the Egyptian Army 16 Aug. 1901, to 15 Aug. 1911. He served in the South African War, 1900–1; took part in the operations in the Orange River Colony, April, 1900; in Cape Colony, north of Orange River, April

to May, 1900, including action at Ruidam; served during the operations in the Transvaal in May and June, 1900; in the Transvaal, east and west of Pretoria, July to Nov. 1900, including action at Zilikat's Nek; also during operations in Cape Colony, Nov. 1900, to April, 1901 (Despatches [London Gazette, 10 Sept. 1901]; Queen's Medal with four clasps). He served in the Soudan, 1905; was present during operations against the Nyam Nyam Tribes in the Bahr-el-Ghazal Province (Despatches [London Gazette, 18 May, 1906]; Egyptian Medal with clasp). He served in the European War, 1914–18; from Aug. 1914, to Sept. with the 3rd Division, as Battery Commander; was mentioned in Despatches, June, 1915, and created a Companion of the Distinguished Service Order [London Gazette, 23 June, 1915]: "Alfred Bryan Bethell, Major, Royal Artillery. For distinguished service in the field." From Oct. 1915, he served with the Guards' Divisional Artillery as Brigade Commander, and was mentioned in Despatches in Jan. 1917. He was given the Legion of Honour and was created a C.M.G. in 1918. Lieut.-Colonel Bethell married, in 1913, Patience Wilson.

BUCHANAN-DUNLOP, COLIN NAPIER, Major, was born 14 April, 1877, at Aldershot, son of Lieut.-Colonel Henry Donald Buchanan-Dunlop, late Royal Artillery. He was educated at the Royal Military Academy, Woolwich, and entered the Army 21 Sept. 1896, becoming Lieutenant 21 Sept. 1899; Capt. 27 Feb. 1902; Major in 1913. From 1903 to 1905 he was Professor at the Royal Military College of Canada. He passed into the Staff College, Camberley, in 1911, and was employed with the Egyptian Army in 1913–14. He saw active service in South Africa, 1899–1902, and took part in the advance on Kimberley, including actions at Belmont, Enslin, Modder River (wounded) and Magersfontein; served during the operations in the Orange Free State, including operations at Paardeberg, actions at Poplar Grove, Karee Siding and Zand River; in the Transvaal, in May and June, 1900, including actions near Johannesburg, Pretoria and Diamond Hill (11 and 12 June); in the Transvaal, east of Pretoria, July, 1900; also in the Transvaal, west of Pretoria, Aug. to 29 Nov. 1900, including action at Zilikat's Nek; again in the Transvaal 30 Nov. 1900, to Jan. 1902, and March to 31 May, 1902; and in Orange River Colony, Jan. to March, 1902 (Despatches [London Gazette, 10 Sept. 1901]; Brevet of Major 28 Feb. 1902; Queen's Medal with five clasps, and King's Medal with two clasps). He went out to Flanders in Oct. 1914, and took part in the Battles of Ypres, Neuve Chapelle, Festubert, Givenchy, Loos, and the taking of the Hohenzollern Redoubt. He was killed by a shell on 14 Oct. 1915, at Vermelles. He was created a Companion of the Distinguished Service Order [London Gazette, 23 June, 1915]: "Colin Napier Buchanan-Dunlop, Major, Royal Artillery. For distinguished service in the field." Major C. N. Buchanan-Dunlop married Hilda, second daughter of Harrison Benn, J.P., of Holcombe Hall, Dawlish.

STANLEY-CLARKE, HENRY CALVERT, Major, was born 6 Dec. 1872, eldest son of the late Major-General Willoughby Charles Stanley-Clarke, Indian Army. He was educated at Bedford Grammar School, and entered the Royal Artillery 30 May, 1893; became Lieutenant 30 May, 1896; Captain 18 June, 1900; was Captain, Imperial Yeomanry, 18 Feb. 1902, to 6 Feb. 1903; was promoted to Major 23 April, 1910; to Lieutenant-Colonel 16 Nov. 1915; was Temporary Brigadier-General 10 Oct. 1916, to 26 Feb. 1919. From 18 Feb. 1905, to 16 July, 1909, he was employed with the West African Frontier Force, and from 10 Oct. 1916, to 26 Feb. 1919, he was Brigadier-General, R.A., 7th Division, British Armies in France. From 1914 to 1918 he served in the European War, and was given the Brevet of Colonel 3 June, 1918; created a C.B. in 1919; a C.M.G. in 1917, and a Companion of the Distinguished Service Order [London Gazette, 23 June, 1915]: "Henry Calvert Stanley-Clarke, Major, Royal Artillery. For distinguished service in the field." Colonel Stanley-Clarke married, in 1913, Alice, only daughter of Colonel Harvey Morris Stanley-Clarke, and they have two daughters.

COTTON, ARTHUR STEDMAN, Major, was born 18 Aug. 1873. He entered the Royal Artillery 1 Sept. 1893; became Lieutenant 1 Sept. 1896; Captain 26 July, 1900, and Major 24 Sept. 1910. Major Cotton served in the European War, as Temporary Lieutenant-Colonel, R.A., 13 Oct. 1915, to 28 Feb. 1916. He was promoted to Lieutenant-Colonel 29 Feb. 1916, and was Temporary Brigadier-General, R.A., 41st Division, British Armies in France, 12 Oct. 1917, to 14 April, 1919. He was created a Companion of the Distinguished Service Order [London Gazette, 23 June, 1915]: "Arthur Stedman Cotton, Major, Royal Artillery. For distinguished service in the field." He was given the Brevet of Colonel 3 June, 1919, and was created a C.M.G.

ELLERSHAW, ARTHUR, Major, was born 27 Feb. 1869, son of the Rev. John Ellershaw, M.A. He was educated at Westminster School, and at the Royal Military Academy, Woolwich, entering the Army 27 July, 1888; becoming Lieutenant 27 July, 1891; Captain 1 March, 1899, and was Divisional Adjutant, R.A., 28 June, 1899, to 16 March, 1900, and Adjutant, R.A., 7 Jan. to 11 July, 1901. He took part in operations on the North-West Frontier of India from 1897 to 1898, with the Malakand Field Force, and was present at the action of Landakai (Medal with clasp). He served in the South African War, and was present at the operations in Natal (March to June, 1900), including action at Laing's Nek (6 to 9 June); also in the Transvaal, east of Pretoria, July to Aug. 1900 (severely wounded; Queen's Medal with four clasps). Served in Aden, 1903–4, during operations in the interior. Capt. Ellershaw was Adjutant, R.A., 14 April, 1908, to 9 March, 1909, and was promoted to Major 8 May, 1909. He again saw active service in the European War; was promoted to Lieutenant-Colonel 9 April, 1916; was Brigadier-General, R.A., Heavy Artillery, 1st Army Corps, British Armies in France, 21 Feb. 1917, to 13 Feb. 1918; Brigadier-General, R.A., Heavy Artillery, 8th Army Corps, British Armies in France, 14 Feb. to 24 June, 1918; Brigadier-General, R.A., Heavy Artillery, 6th Army Corps, British Armies in France, from 25 June, 1918. He was five times mentioned in Despatches; was created a C.M.G. in 1918; was created a Companion of the Distinguished Service Order [London Gazette, 23 June,

1915]: "Arthur Ellershaw, Major, Royal Artillery. For distinguished service in the field." He was created a C.B. in 1919.

HARDING NEWMAN, EDWARD, Major, was born 30 July, 1872, son of B. Harding Newman, Esq., late of Nelms, Hornchurch, Essex. He was educated at Cheltenham College, and entered the Royal Artillery 1 Feb. 1893; was promoted Lieutenant 1 Feb. 1896; Captain 21 May, 1900; Major 13 Feb. 1910, and Lieutenant-Colonel 27 Oct. 1915. He was aide-de-camp to Major-General, India, 1899–1902, and was Staff Captain, Irish Command, 1905–9, and A.M.S. to the General Officer Commanding, Northern Command, 1911–14. He served in the European War, as Brigadier, R.A., 14th Division, British Armies in France, 8 Feb. 1917; was five times mentioned in Despatches, and created a Companion of the Distinguished Service Order [London Gazette, 23 June, 1915]: Edward Harding Newman, Major, R.A. For distinguished service in the field." He was created a C.M.G. [London Gazette, 1 Jan. 1918], and was given the Brevet of Colonel 1 Jan. 1919. He holds the Russian Order of St. Stanislas.

HAYWOOD, AUSTIN HUBERT WIGHTWICK, Major, was born 7

Austin H. W. Haywood.

March, 1878, youngest son of Lieut.-Colonel and Mrs. Wightwick Haywood. He was educated abroad, and at the Royal Military Academy, Woolwich, passing into the Royal Artillery 23 Dec. 1897. He was promoted Lieutenant 23 Dec. 1900, and Captain 19 April, 1902. He served in India, the Mediterranean and in West Africa; accompanied the West African Frontier Force, on the Staff, 1903–7, taking part in the Kwale-Ishan operations, Southern Nigeria, from 1905 to 1906. From 19 Dec. 1908, to 30 Aug. 1910, he was Adjutant, Royal Artillery. He was promoted Major 30 Oct. 1910, and was employed in West Africa from 31 Aug. 1910, to 14 June, 1916; as Temporary Lieutenant-Colonel from 8 Dec. 1913, to 14 June, 1916. In the Great War he took part in the operations in the Cameroon Mountains, in command of a Field Column. From 7 July to 3 Oct. 1917, he was Acting Lieutenant-Colonel, R.A., and again from 13 Jan. to 24 March, 1918, and from 9 Aug. 1918, to 10 March, 1919. He was mentioned in Despatches, and created a Companion of the Distinguished Service Order [London Gazette, 23 June, 1915]: "Austin Hubert Wightwick Haywood, Major (Temporary Lieutenant-Colonel), Royal Artillery. For distinguished service in the field." On 1 Jan. 1918, he was given the Brevet of Lieutenant-Colonel. He was also awarded the Croix de Guerre. Major Haywood was a Fellow of the Royal Geographical Society, and has published "English Hausa Vocabulary of 1,000 Words in Everyday Use" and "Through Timbuctoo and across the Great Sahara." He married, in 1915, Isabella Rosamond, only daughter of the Rev. Henry Walters.

HAYMES, ROBERT LEYCESTER, Major, was born at Hopesay Rectory, Aston-on-Clun, Shropshire, 31 Dec. 1870, son of the late Rev. Robert Evered Haymes, formerly of Great Glen, Leicestershire, and of Jane

Robert L. Haymes.

Henrietta Martha, his wife, daughter of the late General T. L. Green. He was educated at the Bedford Modern School, Oxford Military College, and the Royal Military Academy; joined the Army 24 July, 1891. Lieut. Haymes served in the Tirah Campaign, on the North-West Frontier of India, with No. 5 Bombay Mountain Battery (Indian General Service Medal with clasp, 1897). He was promoted Captain in Nov. 1899; was appointed Instructor in Gunnery at Bombay, which post he held from 1905 to 1909; and Adjutant, 1909 to 1911; was promoted Major in Oct. 1911. From 1911 to 1914 Major Haymes served as Second-in-Command of the Malay States Guides. He went out to France, in command of the 6th Siege Battery, Sept. 1914; took part in the Battle of Ypres in Oct. and of Neuve Chapelle, 10 March, 1915. He was one of the first to get O.P. in Neuve Chapelle and communications through. After this battle he was recommended by Major-General A. E. A. Holland, C.B., M.V.O., D.S.O. (then Brigadier-General, 8th Division) in Despatches, and in June, 1915, was created a Companion of the Distinguished Service Order [London Gazette, 23 June, 1915]: "Robert Leycester Haymes, Major, Royal Artillery. For distinguished service in the field." Major Haymes was severely wounded 16 May, 1915, at Festubert, while observing. He was twice mentioned in Despatches. On the 18th of Aug. 1897, Major Haymes married, at Addlestone, Surrey, Minnie Kathleen, youngest daughter of the late Major Wilmot Ellis, R.A., and they have three sons: Maxwell Freeland Leycester, born 11 Nov. 1907; Hamilton Alfred Leycester, born 4 Nov. 1909, and Richard Arthur Leycester, born 11 June, 1915, and two daughters: Dorothy Evelyn Leycester and Marjorie Eileen Leycester.

HOPE, JOHN WILLIAM, Major, was born 29 Jan. 1876, at Madras, India, son of the late James Hope, Indian Civil Service, and of the late Isabella Cunningham (née Mitchell). He was educated at the Edinburgh Academy, Bedford Grammar School and the Royal Military Academy. He obtained his first commission in the Royal Field Artillery 24 March, 1896, and until the outbreak of the European War his service was entirely in India, excepting the two years—1909–10—when he passed through the

Staff College, Camberley. He was promoted Captain in 1902, being employed as Adjutant from 1905 to 1908. He was promoted Major in 1912, serving on the Staff as Brigade Major, Jhansi Brigade, from Aug. 1911, to Oct. 1914. On the outbreak of the European War in Aug. 1914, he brought the 103rd Battery, R.F.A., home from India, taking it to France with the 28th Division in Jan. 1915. He took part in operations in front of Ypres; was wounded and sent to hospital at Nice, returning to his Battery on the 3rd April, 1915, in front of Ypres, and taking part in the Second Battle of Ypres from 22 April to 28 May. He was mentioned in Despatches, and created a Companion of the Distinguished Service Order [London Gazette, 23 June, 1915]: "John William Hope, Major, The Royal Artillery. For distinguished service in the field." In the same month Major Hope was appointed D.A.Q.M.G., 28th Division, serving in that capacity in France up to Oct. He was then sent to Alexandria and Salonika, where he was appointed A.Q.M.G., 16th Corps, March, 1916, with temporary rank of Lieutenant-Colonel. He was appointed to command the 67th Brigade, R.F.A., 10th Division, May, 1916, attaining the substantive rank of Lieutenant-Colonel 13 Nov. 1916. He was mentioned in Salonika Despatches, Nov. 1917. Proceeded to Palestine with the 10th Division in Sept. 1917, and on 20 Oct. 1917, was appointed Brigadier-General, R.A., 53rd Division, taking part in the capture of Beersheba. On 5 Nov. he was taken into hospital sick, and went to Cairo. On the 24th Dec. 1917, he was appointed to command the 302nd Brigade, R.F.A., 60th Division, and took part in operations round Jerusalem and in the Jordan Valley. In April, 1918, he was transferred to France, in temporary command of the 52nd Divisional Ammunition Column, and in May, 1918, assumed command of the 38th (Army) Brigade, R.F.A., taking part in operations round Kemmel, during which he temporarily commanded the 21st Infantry Brigade, 30th Division, for three weeks in Sept.; operations with the Belgian Army on 28 and 29 Sept., then on the Scheldt, etc. Finally he marched in command of the 38th (Army) Brigade, R.F.A., attached to the 29th Division, across Belgium to Cologne. He was awarded the Belgian Croix de Guerre [London Gazette, Sept. 1919]. On his return to England in June, 1919, he served temporarily as D.A.Q.M.G., Southern Command, for five months, and on 23 March, 1920, was appointed G.S.O.2, Lowland Territorial Division. He married, 1 Aug. 1906, in London, Ethel Obré Hope, daughter of the late Lieut.-Colonel A. Wintle, Royal Horse Artillery, and they have one son, James, born 6 May, 1907, and one daughter, Doreen, born 5 Feb. 1909.

HOWELL, HERBERT GWYNNE, Major, was born at The Strand, Builth, Wales, 15 Nov. 1879, son of Major M. Gwynne Howell, of Llanelwedd Hall, Radnorshire (a family who can trace their descent for some 1,200 years). He was educated privately. He took part in the Bechuanaland Expedition, 1897; at the Le Fleur Rebellion, 1898, and was with the Colonial Division in the early stages of the South African War (General Service Medal with clasp "Bechuanaland," 1897). He joined the Royal Field Artillery in May, 1900, and served in the South African War; was present at Stormberg, and in the advance to the Orange Free State; went through the siege of Wepener, when some 1,700 Colonial troops held at bay 12,000 Boers for over three weeks; in the De Wet hunt, under Lord Methuen; in the Relief of Klip River and drive to Mafeking; operations in the Brandwater Basin, and numerous drives in the Orange Free State and Western Transvaal; commanded the only guns on General Kekewich's famous long-distance drives, and was with the Advance Guard the whole time. He was twice mentioned in Despatches—June and Aug. 1902; awarded the Queen's Medal with four clasps, and the King's Medal with two clasps. Lieut. (Temporary Captain) Gwynne Howell served in Northern Nigeria, both as gunner and General Staff Officer, taking part in the successful Dakkakeri Campaign in 1908 as Chief Staff Officer. He was promoted Captain in June, 1911, and Major 14 Oct. 1914. He served in the European War; was employed as Head of the Intelligence Department (French–British) during the first phase of the Cameroon Campaign. He acted as G.S.O. to the British Contingent during the final stage of operations and the advance to Jaunde, when the Germans were driven out of the Cameroons and into Spanish Muni. He was twice mentioned in Despatches (June, 1915, and May, 1916), and was created a Companion of the Distinguished Service Order [London Gazette, 23 June, 1915]: "Herbert Gwynne Howell, Major, Royal Field Artillery. For distinguished service in the field." He commanded a group of Artillery at Pirbright in Oct. 1916, and then went to Egypt in Nov. of the same year. Commanded the 265th Brigade, R.F.A., during the First Battle of Gaza, and served throughout the Palestine operations, 1916–17. His Battery were the first British guns to march through Jerusalem. Served a short period with Headquarters, 20th Corps, then invalided to Egypt. Was Commandant Prisoners of War Camps, Cairo, until the termination of hostilities. He was mentioned in Despatches in Jan. 1919, and awarded the O.B.E. Major Gwynne Howell married, 12 Aug. 1919, Annable Martin, daughter of Capt. R. Martin, late The Buffs, of 25, Longford Terrace, Monkstown, Ireland. His pastimes are big game shooting, fishing, shooting and polo.

Herbert Gwynne Howell.

KINSMAN, GERALD RICHARD VIVIAN, Major, was born 18 May 1876, son of the late Colonel H. J. Kinsman, R.A., of Antron Hill, Penryn, Cornwall, and of Emily Anne Kinsman (*née* FitzGerald). He was educated at Bedford and the Royal Academy, Woolwich, and entered the Royal Artillery in March, 1896. He served with the West African Frontier Force from 1901 to 1903; was promoted Captain in 1902, and was employed as Adjutant to the Territorial Force from 1909 to 1912. He was promoted Major in Dec. 1912. Major Kinsman served in the European War; was present at Le Cateau, Aug. 1914; Ypres, 1915 and 1916; Bapaume and Ecouste, 1917. He was three times mentioned in Despatches, and was created a Companion of the Distinguished Service Order [London Gazette, 23 June, 1915]: "Gerald Richard Vivian Kinsman, Major, Royal Field Artillery. For distinguished service in the field." He was promoted Lieutenant-Colonel, Jan. 1917 (Temporary Lieutenant-Colonel from Dec. 1915). He was Chief Instructor of Gunnery, Shoeburyness, 1917–19; Commanding the 25th Brigade, R.F.A., from July, 1919. He was created a Companion of the Order of St. Michael and St. George, Jan. 1919. Lieut.-Colonel Kinsman married, in Jan. 1916, Dorothy, daughter of Arthur Whitaker, and there is one daughter, Dorothy Sheila, born Oct. 1916.

Gerald R. V. Kinsman.

LEGGETT, ERIC HENRY GOODWIN, Major, was born 31 Dec. 1880, son of Lieut.-Colonel F. O. and Mrs. Leggett, of Underhill House, Shorncliffe, and of High Grange, Hythe. He was educated at the Oxford Preparatory School (Mr. Lynam's), and was an Exhibitioner at Wellington College, Berks, 1894–7; was commissioned in June, 1899, in the Royal Artillery. He became Lieutenant in 1901, and Captain in 1907. He gained a first-class certificate for gunnery, and held various Staff appointments, commencing his Staff career with the Malay States Guides (May, 1905, to July, 1908); Staff Captain, Woolwich, 4th Division, and later Brigade Major. He was promoted Major in Oct. 1914. He served in the European War; was present at Mons, the Marne, the Aisne, the Lys, and Ypres; General Staff Officer, 2nd Grade. He was three times mentioned in Despatches, and created a Companion of the Distinguished Service Order [London Gazette, 23 June, 1915]: "Eric Henry Goodwin Leggett, Major, Royal Field Artillery. For distinguished service in the field." He died in hospital at St. Omer 30 July, 1916. He had married, in 1911, Mary, daughter of Colonel Howe, York and Lancaster Regt., and they had one son, born 8 Sept. 1912. His eldest brother, Major W. N. Leggett, R.G.A., and his youngest brother, Lieut. A. R. A. Leggett, North Staffordshire Regt., both lost their lives on the field, on 14 July, 1916, and 31 Oct. 1914, respectively.

MACKEY, HUGH JAMES ALEXANDER, Major, was born in Jamaica, 19 March, 1876, son of the late Hugh Allen Mackey, Capt., R.A. He was educated at Rottingdean; at Winchester, and at the Royal Military Academy, Woolwich; was gazetted to the Royal Artillery 21 March, 1896, and was promoted to Lieutenant 21 March, 1899, and to Captain 10 Jan. 1902; was Adjutant, R.A., 25 May, 1907, to 25 Aug. 1909. Capt. Mackey commanded the Gun Team at Osborne at the funeral of H.M. Queen Victoria, and was created a Member of the Victorian Order, 5th Class. He was Adjutant, Royal Military Academy, from 1909 to 1913, and became Major 5 Oct. 1912. He served in the European War; went to France in command of the 60th Battery, Royal Field Artillery, and was present at the battles of Mons and Ypres, also in operations on the Aisne. He was mentioned in Despatches in Oct. 1914, and was created a Companion of the Distinguished Service Order [London Gazette, 23 June, 1915]: "Hugh James Alexander Mackey, M.V.O., Major, Royal Field Artillery. For distinguished service in the field." He was also created a C.M.G. in 1915. In Nov. 1915, he was appointed to the command of the 13th Brigade, Royal Field Artillery, leaving France for Mesopotamia in Dec. to take part in operations for the Relief of Kut. He was Colonel, R.A., 14th Division, Mesopotamia, 12 May, 1916, to 6 April, 1919, and took part in the battles of Hai and Shumran Bend, and in the crossing of the Tigris; present at operations at Baghdad and Shatt-el-Adhaim. He was again mentioned in Despatches in Jan. 1916; was promoted Lieutenant-Colonel 3 Jan. 1917, and was Temporary Brigadier-General 12 May, 1916, to 6 April, 1919. He married, 16 April, 1904, at St. Stephen's Church, Gloucester Road, S.W., Violet Alice Edgar, eldest daughter of H. E. Rodwell, and they have two daughters: Eileen and Patricia.

MACLAVERTY, CHARLES FORBES SHAW, Major, was born 19 Feb. 1878, son of the Rev. A. Maclaverty, Vicar of Llangattock, Monmouth. He was at Christ Church, Oxford, when the Boer War broke out. He immediately volunteered, and joined the Army 25 July, 1900, serving till 1902. He took part in operations in Orange Free State, April and May, 1900; in Orange River Colony, May to 29 Nov. 1900, including action at Caledon River (27 to 29 Nov.); in Orange River Colony, Nov. 1900, to Feb. 1901, and March, 1901, to 31 May, 1902; in Cape Colony, Feb. to March, 1901 (Despatches [London Gazette, 10 Sept. 1901]; Queen's Medal with three clasps, and King's Medal with two clasps). On the 11th of June, 1904, he was seconded for service under the Colonial Office, and went to Nigeria, where he was employed with the West African Frontier Force 28 May, 1904, to 24 May, 1909, and 15 June, 1910, to 17 March, 1916. He became Captain 21 Aug. 1911, and Major 17 Dec. 1914. He served in the Great War; first in the Cameroons; was dangerously wounded; mentioned in Despatches and created a Companion of the Distinguished Service Order [London Gazette, 23 June, 1915]: "Charles Forbes Shaw Maclaverty, Major, Royal Artillery. For distinguished service in the field." In May, 1916, being recovered from his wound, he joined the 114th Battery, 1st Division, in France; was Acting Lieutenant-Colonel, R.A. (T.F.), 1 Feb. to 12 March, 1918, and was twice more mentioned in Despatches.

NAPIER, VERNON MONRO COLQUHOUN, Major, was born 9 Oct. 1881. He entered the Royal Artillery 2 May, 1900; became Lieutenant 3 April, 1901. He served in the South African War in 1902; took part in

the operations in the Transvaal and Orange River Colony, Jan. to 31 May, 1902; received the Queen's Medal with three clasps. He was promoted Captain 1 Feb. 1910; was Adjutant, R.A., 1 Nov. 1910, to 31 Jan. 1913. He served in the European War, 1914–18; was promoted Major 30 Oct. 1914; was D.A.A.G., Lines of Communication, B.E.F., 5 Aug. to 18 Nov. 1914; Brigade Major, R.A., 18th Division, B.E.F., 25 March to 20 Nov. 1915; D.A.A.G., Staff Officer to G.O.C., R.A., 6th Army Corps, B.E.F., British Armies in France, 21 Nov. 1915, to 27 Sept. 1917; G.S.O.1, 4th Army, B.E.F., 28 Sept. 1917, to 12 July, 1918; G.S.O.1, G.H.Q., British Armies in France, 13 to 17 July, 1918; Assistant Director of Staff Duties, British Armies in France, 18 July, 1918, and Temporary Colonel. For his services in the European War he was mentioned in Despatches, given the Brevet of Lieutenant-Colonel 1 Jan. 1918; created a C.M.G. in 1919, and was created a Companion of the Distinguished Service Order [London Gazette, 23 June, 1915]: "Vernon Monro Colquhoun Napier, Major, Royal Artillery. For distinguished service in the field."

RAMSDEN, JOSSLYN VERE, Major, was born 1 Dec. 1876, son of John C. F. Ramsden, grandson of Sir J. Ramsden, 4th Bart. He was educated at Eton, and New College, Oxford (M.A.), and entered the Royal Artillery 5 May, 1900, becoming Lieutenant 20 Aug. 1901; Captain 13 July, 1910. He was Adjutant, 1910–11; was promoted to Major 30 Oct. 1914; retired from the Staff 18 April, 1919. He was A.D.C. to Divisional Commander, India, 1908–9. For his services in the European War 1914–18, he was twice mentioned in Despatches; was given the Brevet of Lieutenant-Colonel 1 Jan. 1918; created a C.M.G. in 1919, and created a Companion of the Distinguished Service Order [London Gazette, 23 June, 1915]: "Josslyn Vere Ramsden, Major, Royal Artillery. For distinguished service in the field." In 1909 he married Olive Clotilde Bouhier, only daughter of F. W. Imbert Terry, of Aston, Herts, and they have one son.

Josslyn Vere Ramsden.

RIDDELL, EDWARD VANSITTART DICK, Major, was born 30 March, 1873, son of the late Colonel Robert Vansittart Riddell, R.E., and Louisa Flora, his wife, daughter of General Dick, and great grandson of the 2nd Baronet of Riddell. He was educated at Cheltenham College, and the Royal Military Academy, Woolwich. He joined the Royal Garrison Artillery, May, 1893; was promoted Captain, March, 1900. He served in the South African War from Jan. 1900, to July, 1902, being on the Staff from Sept. 1900, to the end of the war. He was awarded the Queen's Medal with two clasps, and the King's Medal with two clasps. He was given the rank of Brevet Major. He was appointed Adjutant in the Militia, 1903 to 1906; passed the Staff College in 1909, and was D.A.A.G. in Jersey from 1911 to 1914. He was promoted Substantive Major, April, 1914; was G.S.O., 2nd Grade, Aug. to Oct. 1914. He served in the European War; went to France in command of the 26th Heavy Battery, R.G.A., 1st Division, in Nov. 1914; was D.A.A. and Q.M.G., 25th Division, March to May, 1915, and was A.A. and Q.M.G., 18th Division, from 1915 to Nov. 1916. He was mentioned in Despatches [London Gazette, 1 June, 1915], and created a Companion of the Distinguished Service Order [London Gazette, 23 June, 1915]: "Edward Vansittart Dick Riddell, Major, 26th Heavy Battery, Royal Garrison Artillery. For distinguished service in the field." He was mentioned in Despatches, June, 1916, and promoted Brevet Lieutenant-Colonel. He took part in the Battle of the Somme 1 July, 1916, and subsequently was present at the Battle of Thiépval, Sept. 1916, and the attack on Serre, commanding the 111th Heavy Battery, Royal Garrison Artillery, from Nov. to Dec. 1916. In Dec. 1916, Lieut.-Colonel Riddell was appointed Chief Instructor in Tactics and Military History, and Second-in-Command of the Royal Military Academy, Woolwich. He was A.A. and Q.M.G., 24th Division, Dec. 1917, to April, 1918, and took part in the battle of 21 March, and retreat during the following days. In April, 1918, he was appointed D.A. and Q.M.G., 8th Corps, with the temporary rank of Brigadier-General, which he held till the Corps was disbanded in June, 1918. He was mentioned in Despatches in June, 1918, and Jan. 1919. In Aug. 1918, he was appointed to command the base in Italy, with the temporary rank of Colonel, and remained there till Jan. 1920. He was mentioned in Despatches in June, 1919, and in Jan. 1920, was created a Commander of the Order of the British Empire. He was promoted Substantive Lieutenant-Colonel in April, 1918. In April, 1920, he was appointed A.A. and Q.M.G. in the Eastern Command in England. In Feb. 1902, Major Riddell married, at Wynberg, near Cape Town, Edith Mary, daughter of Major-General E. P. Bingham Turner, R.A. (she died in July, 1914), and they had one son, E. A. B. Riddell, born in Feb. 1903.

STEEL, EDWARD ANTHONY, Major, was born at Ajmere, India, 12 Dec. 1880, son of Colonel J. P. Steel, late of the Royal Engineers, of 31 Nevern Square, London, S.W. He was commissioned in the Royal Artillery 6 Jan. 1900; became Lieutenant 3 April, 1901, and served with the Royal Horse Artillery from 1901 to 1904 in India. He took part in operations in Nigeria with the West African Frontier Force, 1904–5; was mentioned in Despatches twice, and received the African General Service Medal with clasp. He took part in the second expedition, 1905–6, again being mentioned in Despatches, and received a second clasp to his Medal. He was promoted Captain 4 April, 1908. In 1909 Capt. Steel passed the Ordnance College, and in the following year passed the London School of Economics. From 6 Jan. 1912, to 4 Aug. 1914, he was employed as Chief British Commissioner on the Rhodesian-Congo (Anglo-Belgian) Boundary

Commission. He became Major 30 Oct. 1914, and was Acting Lieutenant-Colonel, Royal Artillery, 9 Dec. 1918, to 10 Jan. 1919. He served in the European War, and was wounded in May, 1915. He was created a Companion of the Distinguished Service Order [London Gazette, 23 June, 1915]: "Edward Anthony Steel, Major, Royal Field Artillery. For distinguished service in the field." Major Steel was again severely wounded in Sept. 1916, temporarily losing the use of his right arm. He was again mentioned in Despatches. He served in Mesopotamia in 1918, and in Siberia in 1919.

TURNER, ARTHUR JERVOIS, Major (Temporary Lieut.-Colonel), was born 10 June, 1878. He was educated for the military profession, ultimately passing the Staff College, and he entered the Royal Artillery 23 Dec. 1897, becoming Lieutenant 23 Dec. 1900. He served in South Africa from 1899 to 1900, and again in 1902. He was present at operations in Natal, 1899; at the Relief of Ladysmith, including actions at Spion Kop and Vaal Kranz; during operations on Tugela Heights and action at Pieter's Hill; in the Transvaal, west of Pretoria, May to July, 1900; in Cape Colony, north of Orange River, including action at Ruidam; again in the Transvaal and Orange River Colony, April to 31 May, 1902 (Despatches [London Gazette, 10 Sept. 1901]; Brevet of Major 31 Jan. 1905; Queen's Medal with five clasps, and King's Medal with clasp; was severely wounded). He served with the West African Frontier Force from 1903 to 1904 (Medal with clasp). He was promoted Captain 30 Jan. 1905; was employed at the War Office from 1911 to 1913; became Substantive Major 30 Oct. 1914. From 22 Aug. 1913, to 22 Dec. 1915, he was Staff Officer to the Inspector-General, East African Rifles; from 23 Feb. to 5 May, 1916, G.S.O.2, 24th Division, British Expeditionary Force; from 6 May to 5 Nov. 1916, G.S.O.1, 2nd Army, British Armies in France; from 6 Nov. 1916, to 19 Feb. 1918, G.S.O.1, 47th Division, British Armies in France; from 20 Feb. to 21 April, 1918, G.S.O.1, American Staff School, British Armies in France. From 22 April, 1918, he commanded the 105th Infantry Brigade, British Armies in France. He was created a Companion of the Distinguished Service Order [London Gazette, 23 June, 1915]: "Arthur Jervois Turner, Major (Temporary Lieut.-Colonel), Royal Artillery. For distinguished service in the field." He was mentioned in General Dobell's Despatches 31 May, 1918, and was given the Brevets of Lieutenant-Colonel 1 Jan. 1917, and of Colonel 3 June, 1919. He married, in 1912, Maude (who died in 1913), only child of the late Michael Walton.

TWEEDIE, DAVID KELTIE, Major, was born 29 Nov. 1878. He was gazetted to the Royal Artillery 18 July, 1900; became Lieutenant 18 May, 1905; was Adjutant, Territorial Force, 25 May, 1908, to 31 Aug. 1911; was promoted to Captain 28 June, 1911; to Major 14 Nov. 1914, and was Acting Lieutenant-Colonel, Royal Artillery, from 16 Dec. 1918. He served in the European War, 1914–17; was twice mentioned in Despatches, and created a Companion of the Distinguished Service Order [London Gazette, 23 June, 1915]: "David Keltie Tweedie, Major, Royal Artillery. For distinguished service in the field."

WARD, HARRY, Major, was born 14 March, 1876. He entered the Royal Artillery, as Second Lieutenant, 21 March, 1896; was promoted Lieutenant 21 March, 1899, and Captain 4 Dec. 1901; was Adjutant, Royal Artillery, from 28 Feb. 1905, to 14 July, 1907, and became Major 26 July, 1912. Major Ward served in the European War, as Temporary Lieutenant-Colonel, R.A., 22 Oct. 1915, to 10 Sept. 1916, and became Lieutenant-Colonel 11 Sept. 1916. He was mentioned twice in Despatches, and created a Companion of the Distinguished Service Order [London Gazette, 23 June, 1915]: "Harry Ward, Major, Royal Artillery. For distinguished service in the field." He was created a C.M.G. in 1919, and was made a Knight of the Legion of Honour.

Harry Ward.

WILKINSON, ARTHUR CLEMENT, Major, was born 20 Nov. 1870. He was commissioned in the Royal Artillery 25 July, 1890; became Lieutenant 25 July, 1893; Captain 9 Oct. 1899; Major 7 May, 1911, and Lieutenant-Colonel 1 May, 1917. He served at Bermuda, Halifax, and with Mounted Artillery in India (Medal and clasp, 1897–98). In the European War he commanded the 35th Heavy Battery, R.G.A., B.E.F., from Aug. 1914. He served in France, 1914–18; received the Mons Star; was created a C.M.G. in 1918, and was created a Companion of the Distinguished Service Order [London Gazette, 23 June, 1915]: "Arthur Clement Wilkinson, Major, Royal Garrison Artillery. For distinguished service in the field." Lieut.-Colonel A. C. Wilkinson married, in 1909, Florence Camilla, daughter of Arthur Ellershaw, and they have two sons.

Arthur C. Wilkinson.

WILMER, ERIC RANDAL GORDON, Major, was born at Mussoori, India, 24 May, 1882, son of Colonel John Randal Wilmer, late Indian Staff Corps, Survey of India and late R.A., and Helen Florence Wilmer (née Gordon). He was educated at Stanley House, Bridge-of-Allan; St. Paul's School, and the Royal Military Academy, Woolwich. He joined the Royal Field Artillery 18 Aug. 1900. From Sept. 1900, to Sept. 1902, he served in the 137th Battery, Royal Field Artillery (Home); was posted in Oct. 1902, to the 33rd Battery in India; accompanied the battery home in Dec. 1906, and remained with it until March, 1909, when he took up the appointment of Adjutant, 4th Home Counties Brigade (Royal Field Artillery, Territorial Force), which position he held from March, 1909, to Jan. 1913. He was promoted Captain 11 Nov. 1911. In Feb. 1913, Capt. Wilmer returned to India, as Adjutant to the 9th Brigade, Royal Field Artillery, where he remained until the outbreak of the European War. He arrived in France 26 Sept. 1914, and took part in operations with the Meerut Division at Festubert, Neuve Chapelle, Richebourg, north of Loos and La Bassée. He was promoted Major 5 Jan. 1915, and was posted to the command of the 28th Battery, Royal Field Artillery. He was mentioned in Despatches in May, 1915, and created a Companion of the Distinguished Service Order [London Gazette, 23 June, 1915]: "Eric Randal Gordon Wilmer, Major, Royal Field Artillery. For distinguished service in the field." Major Wilmer was sent with his battery to Mesopotamia, and commanded it until the 15th March, 1916, when he was appointed Brigade Major, Royal Artillery, to the M.G.R.A., General Headquarters of the Mesopotamian Expeditionary Force. He was slightly wounded 7 Jan. 1916; mentioned in Despatches by Sir Percy Lake in Dec. 1916, and by Sir Stanley Maude 16 Aug. 1917, and in 1918. He received the Order of the Légion d'Honneur (Chevalier), and the Brevet of Lieutenant-Colonel 3 June, 1917. Lieut.-Colonel Wilmer has always been fond of open-air sports. At St. Paul's School he was in the Rowing Eight and First Fifteen (Rugby); at the Royal Military Academy, Woolwich, which he entered in Sept. 1899, he again was in the First Fifteen. He married, 16 July, 1910, at Ticehurst, Marjory Louisa, daughter of the late Major-General Richard Worsley, late Indian Staff Corps, and Mrs. Edith M. Worsley (*née* Staniland), and they have two sons and one daughter: David, born 6 Oct. 1913; Frederick Clive, born 6 Aug. 1916, and Thea, born 9 Dec. 1919.

WYNTER, HENRY WALTER, Major, was born 14 April, 1882. He entered the Royal Artillery, as Second Lieutenant, 18 Aug. 1900; was promoted Lieutenant 18 Aug. 1903; Captain 22 Jan. 1912, and Major 26 Jan. 1915. He served in the European War, as Brigade Major, R.A., 7th Division, B.E.F., British Armies in France, 26 Aug. 1915, to 7 June, 1916; D.A.A.G., 10th Army Corps, British Armies in France, 8 June, 1916, to 27 Aug. 1917; G.S.O.2, 10th Army Corps, British Armies in France, 28 Aug. 1917, to 1 April, 1918; G.S.O.1, G.H.Q., British Armies in France, from 2 April, 1918. He was twice mentioned in Despatches; was given the Brevet of Lieutenant-Colonel 1 Jan. 1918, and created a Companion of the Distinguished Service Order [London Gazette, 23 June, 1915]: "Henry Walter Wynter, Major, Royal Artillery. For distinguished service in the field."

YOUNG, HUGH GREVILLE, Major, was born 4 Nov. 1882, son of the late Rev. Henry S. Young. He entered the Royal Artillery 18 Aug. 1900; became Lieutenant 18 Aug. 1903; was Adjutant, Royal Artillery, from 21 Feb. 1907, to 19 Feb. 1910, and 9 Sept. 1911, to 22 July, 1915; became Captain 1 Nov. 1911, and Major 7 Jan. 1915. Major Young served in the European War, as Brigade Major, R.A., 1st Division, B.E.F., 23 July to 28 Oct. 1915; Acting Lieutenant-Colonel 10 March to 27 July, 1918. He was twice wounded; twice mentioned in Despatches; was given the Brevet of Major, and created a Companion of the Distinguished Service Order [London Gazette, 23 June, 1915]: "Hugh Greville Young, Major, Royal Artillery. For distinguished service in the field." Major Young married, in 1919, Constance, daughter of the late Brigadier-General N. D. Findlay, C.B., R.A., of Alphington, Frimley.

BURKE, HUBERT FRANCIS, Capt., was born 8 Oct. 1880, son of the late Lieut.-Colonel W. St. G. Burke, R.E. He entered the Royal Artillery 6 Jan. 1900, becoming Lieutenant 3 April, 1901. He served in Aden from 1903 to 1904; was promoted to Captain 2 Jan. 1911; to Major 5 Aug. 1915; was Staff Captain, War Office, 1 Oct. 1917, to 31 March, 1919; Deputy Assistant Director, War Office, 1 April, 1919. He served in the European War from 1914, and was twice mentioned in Despatches, and was created a Companion of the Distinguished Service Order [London Gazette, 23 June, 1915]: "Hubert Francis Burke, Capt., Royal Garrison Artillery. For distinguished service in the field." He was given the Brevet of Lieutenant-Colonel 3 June, 1919, and the Legion of Honour. Major Burke married, in 1916, Jane, only child of C. A. Denton, and they have one son.

ADDISON, GEORGE HENRY, Major, was born 13 May, 1876, son of Lieut.-Colonel G. W. Addison, late R.E. He was educated at Wellington, and at the Royal Military Academy, Woolwich. He entered the Army 1 Oct. 1895; became Lieutenant 1 Oct. 1898, and served in South Africa, 1899–1902; was present at the Relief of Kimberley; took part in the operations in the Orange Free State, Feb. to May, 1900, including action at Zand River; was in the Transvaal in May and June, 1900; again in the Transvaal, east of Pretoria, July to 29 Nov. 1900; in Cape Colony, south of Orange River, 1900; a third time in the Transvaal 30 Nov. 1900, to Sept. 1901, and Nov. 1901, to 31 May, 1902; took part in the operations on the Zululand Frontier of Natal in Sept. and Oct. 1901, including the defence of Forts Itala and Prospect (Queen's Medal with three clasps, and King's Medal with two clasps). He became Captain 1 Oct. 1904; was Instructor, R.M.A., 3 Aug. to 1 Sept. 1904; Officer, Company of Gentleman Cadets, R.M.A., 1 Jan. to 2 Aug. 1909. He served in the European War from 1914; was Adjutant, Royal Engineers, from 3 Nov. 1914, and was promoted to Major 30 Oct. 1914. He was given the Brevet of Lieutenant-Colonel 3 June, 1916, and was created a Companion of the Distinguished Service Order [London Gazette, 23 June, 1915]: "George Henry Addison, Major, Royal Engineers. For distinguished service in the field." He was created a C.M.G. in 1918, and received the 3rd Class Order of Anne of Russia with Swords (Sept. 1916). He was Assistant to Engineer-in-Chief 20 July to 14 Nov. 1918. Lieut.-Colonel G. H. Addison married, in 1905, Margaret, daughter of R. Henderson, and they have one son and one daughter.

BETTY, PAGET KEMMIS, Major, was born 12 May, 1876, son of the late Colonel Joshua F. Kemmis Betty. He entered the Royal Engineers 21 Sept. 1895; became Lieutenant 24 Sept. 1898. He served in the South African War, 1900–2; was present at the Relief of Kimberley; served during operations in the Orange Free State, Feb. to May, 1900, including those at Paardeberg; actions at Poplar Grove and Dreifontein; in Orange River Colony, May to 29 Nov. 1900; also in Cape Colony, south of Orange River, 1900; again in Orange River Colony 30 Nov. 1900, to 31 May, 1902 (Queen's Medal with four clasps, and King's Medal with two clasps). He became Captain 24 Sept. 1904; was Adjutant, Volunteers, 28 Sept. 1905, to 31 March, 1908; Adjutant, Territorial Forces, 1 April, 1908. He served in the European War from 1914; was promoted to Major 30 Oct. 1914; was Temporary Lieutenant-Colonel from 24 June, 1916. He was given the Brevet of Lieutenant-Colonel 3 June, 1917, and created a Companion of the Distinguished Service Order [London Gazette, 23 June, 1915]: "Paget Kemmis Betty, Major, Royal Engineers. For distinguished service in the field." He was created a C.M.G. in 1919. From 1919 he was Staff Officer, R.E., Western Command. Lieut.-Colonel Betty married, in 1910, Frances Enid Gwenllian, daughter of Judge John Bishop, of Dolygarreg.

BLANDY, LYSTER FETTIPLACE, Major, was born 21 Sept. 1874, son of the late Adam F. Blandy, of The Warren, Abingdon. He was educated at Haileybury and Woolwich; entered the Royal Engineers 26 March, 1895; became Lieutenant 26 March, 1898, and Captain 1 April, 1904. Capt. Blandy was employed with the Canadian Forces in 1906; was Inspector, Royal Engineers' Stores, 1911–13, and was promoted to Major 30 Oct. 1914. He served in the European War, 1814–19, as Temporary Lieutenant-Colonel, R.E., from 6 Feb. 1916, to 8 July, 1917; as Chief Experimental Officer, Signals Experimental Establishment, 10 July, 1917, to 17 April, 1918. He was employed under the Air Ministry from 18 April, 1918. He received the Belgian Medal (St. Leopold), and was created a Companion of the Distinguished Service Order [London Gazette, 23 June, 1915]: "Lyster Fettiplace Blandy, Major, Royal Engineers. For distinguished service in the field." He was given the Brevet of Lieutenant-Colonel 1 Jan. 1917. He married, in 1905, Violet Mary, daughter of Charles Vernon, of British Columbia.

BOILEAU, GUY HAMILTON, Major, was born 27 Sept. 1870, at Camberley, Surrey, son of the late Major C. H. Boileau, 61st Foot, Gloucestershire Regt. He was educated at Christ's Hospital, and the Royal Military Academy, Woolwich; entered the Royal Engineers 14 Feb. 1890, and served in West Africa in 1891, taking part in the Tamba Ra Expedition. He was mentioned in Despatches, and thanked by the Commander-in-Chief. In 1892 he accompanied the Gambia Expedition, assisting in the capture of Toniataba, being again mentioned in Despatches. He was promoted to Lieutenant 14 Feb. 1893. He was ordered to India and appointed Field Engineer to the Chitral Expeditionary Force, 1895. In 1900 he was sent to China in command of a Field Company of Sappers and Miners, and was present at the action at Tientsin on the 16th Aug. (clasp, "Relief of Pekin"). He was mentioned in Despatches, and received the thanks of the Government of India for his valuable services. He became Captain 14 Feb. 1901. In 1902 he was presented with the Coronation Medal and Delhi Durbar Medal, also receiving a second medal in the Delhi Durbar held in 1911. He was promoted to Major 14 Feb. 1910. Major Boileau served in the European War, as Major, Field Engineers, Lahore Division, from Sept. 1914, to Sept. 1915; Temporary Lieutenant-Colonel, Royal Engineers, 17 Sept. 1915, to 15 Nov. 1917. He was present at the Battle of Givenchy in Dec. 1914; Neuve Chapelle, 1915, and the Second Battle of Ypres in April, 1915. He was mentioned in Despatches five times, and was created a Companion of the Distinguished Service Order [London Gazette, 23 June, 1915]: "Guy Hamilton Boileau, Major, Royal Engineers. For distinguished service in the field." He was created a C.M.G. in 1918, and a C.B. in 1919 and was given the Brevet of Lieutenant-Colonel 3 June, 1916, and holds the Order of Danilo, 3rd Class. On 1 April, 1918, he was promoted to Lieutenant-Colonel. Lieut.-Colonel Boileau married, 17 Feb. 1909, at Umballa, India, Violet Mary Irene, daughter of Colonel W. J. Smyth Ferguson, late King's Dragoon Guards, and they have two daughters: Diana, born 31 Jan. 1910, and Susanna, born 9 Jan. 1915.

Guy Hamilton Boileau.

BROUGH, ALAN, Major, was born 20 March, 1876. He entered the Army 15 March, 1895; became Lieutenant 15 March, 1898; Captain 1 April, 1904, and Major 30 Oct. 1914. He served in the European War from 1914, as Temporary Lieutenant-Colonel, Royal Engineers, 1 Nov. 1915, to 9 July, 1917; as Deputy Director-General of Transportation, British Armies in France, and Temporary Brigadier-General 10 July, 1917, to 26 May, 1918; Deputy Director-General of Transportation, British Armies in France, 27 May to 25 Sept. 1918; Deputy Director-General of Transportation, Mesopotamian Expeditionary Force, from 26 Sept. 1918. He was created a Companion of the Distinguished Service Order [London Gazette, 23 June, 1915]: "Alan Brough, Major, Royal Engineers. For distinguished service in the field." He was also given the Brevet of Lieutenant-Colonel 3 June, 1916, and was created a C.M.G. in 1918.

EARLE, ROBERT GILMOUR, Major, was born 1 July, 1874. He entered the Army 21 Oct. 1894, becoming Lieutenant 24 Oct. 1897. He served in the South African War from 1899 to 1902 ; was present at the advance on Kimberley, including action at Magersfontein ; in the Orange Free State, including actions at Vet River (5 and 6 May) ; in the Transvaal in May and June, 1900, including actions near Johannesburg and Diamond Hill (11 and 12 June) ; again during the operations in the Transvaal, east of Pretoria, including action at Reit Vlei (Despatches [London Gazette, 29 July, 1902] ; Queen's Medal with four clasps, and King's Medal with two clasps). He was promoted Captain 1 April, 1904. He served in the European War ; was promoted Major 24 Oct. 1914, and was created a Companion of the Distinguished Service Order [London Gazette, 23 June, 1915] : " Robert Gilmour Earle, Major, Royal Engineers. For distinguished service in the field." He was Deputy Director of Army Signals, 4th Army, B.E.F., British Armies in France, 6 Feb. 1916, to 15 May, 1918 ; Chief Signalling Officer, British Armies in France, from 16 May, 1918. He was given the Brevet of Lieutenant-Colonel 3 June, 1917, and was created a C.M.G. in 1919.

SANKEY, CROFTON EDWARD PYM, Major, was born 17 May, 1877, son of Capt. M. H. P. R. Sankey, C.B., Director and Consulting Engineer to Marconi's Wireless Telegraph Co. Ltd., and other companies, and E. M. Sankey, daughter of General E. L. Pym, R.M.L.I. He was educated at Wellington College, and the Royal Military Academy, Woolwich, and entered the Royal Engineers 26 Dec. 1896, becoming Lieutenant 26 Dec. 1899. He served in the South African War from 1899 to 1900, and was present at the Relief of Kimberley ; was present during operations in the Orange Free State, Feb. to May, 1900, including operations at Paardeberg ; actions at Poplar Grove and Dreifontein ; also in Cape Colony, south of Orange River, 1900 (Queen's Medal with three clasps). He was promoted Captain 26 Dec. 1905, and was employed as First Assistant Instructor, School of Military Engineering, from 1908 to 1912, becoming Instructor in 1914. He served in the European War ; became Major 30 Oct. 1914 ; was Temporary Lieutenant-Colonel 14 Jan. 1916, to 2 June, 1917, and Assistant to Engineer-in-Chief, B.E.F. ; Acting Lieutenant-Colonel 21 Feb. 1918. He was mentioned in Despatches ; given a Brevet Lieutenant-Colonelcy 3 June, 1917 ; was awarded the Croix de Guerre avec Palme, and was created a Companion of the Distinguished Service Order [London Gazette, 23 June, 1915] : " Crofton Edward Pym Sankey, Major, Royal Engineers. For distinguished service in the field."

Crofton E. P. Sankey.

SYMONS, CHARLES BERTIE OWEN, Major, was born 29 Nov. 1874, eldest son of the late Colonel C. E. H. Symons, of Colombo. He was educated at Trent College, Derbyshire, and entered the Royal Engineers 16 Oct. 1894 ; was promoted to Lieutenant 16 Oct. 1897, and to Captain 1 April, 1904, having been Professor of the Royal Military College, Canada, 1899–1904. He was on Survey Duty, Gold Coast, 1905–7. Capt. Symons served in the European War ; was promoted to Major 16 Oct. 1914 ; was Acting Lieutenant-Colonel, R.E., from 19 March, 1917. He was wounded ; was created a Companion of the Distinguished Service Order [London Gazette, 23 June, 1915] : " Charles Bertie Owen Symons, Major, Royal Engineers. For distinguished service in the field." He was given the Brevet of Lieutenant-Colonel 1 Jan. 1918, and was created a C.M.G. in 1919. Lieut.-Colonel C. B. O. Symons married, in 1918, Sylvia, second daughter of the late Charles Lenox-Simpson, Senior Commissioner in China.

DOHERTY-HOLWELL, R. V., Capt., was gazetted to the Royal Engineers 4 Feb. 1901, becoming Lieutenant 4 Feb. 1904. He served in the European War, and was created a Companion of the Distinguished Service Order [London Gazette, 23 June, 1915] : " R. V. Doherty-Holwell, Capt., Royal Engineers. For distinguished service in the field." Lieut.-Colonel R. V. Doherty-Holwell was killed in action 9 Jan. 1917.

GANDY, HENRY GEORGE, Capt., was born 27 Nov. 1879, at Barndale House, Alnwick, Northumberland, son of Capt. Charles Gandy (deceased), 1st King's Dragoon Guards, and Mrs. Dorothy Jane Gandy. He was educated at Seabank School, Alnmouth, and Sedbergh School, Yorks, and at the Royal Military Academy, Woolwich, and entered the Royal Engineers 14 March, 1899 ; became Lieutenant 25 July, 1901 ; served in the South African War, 1901–2 ; took part in the several operations in the Transvaal, Orange River Colony and Cape Colony, Dec. 1901, to 31 May, 1902 (Queen's Medal with five clasps). He served in East Africa, 1903–4 ; was present during operations in Somaliland ; in the action at Jidballi (Medal with two clasps). He was Adjutant, Volunteers, 8 June, 1906, to 31 March, 1908 ; Adjutant, T.F., 1 April, 1908, to 13 Jan. 1909 ; was promoted to Captain 14 March, 1908 ; was employed with the Egyptian Army 21 Jan. 1909, to 21 Oct. 1912. He served in the European War from its outbreak until 1915, when he was invalided ; and he was mentioned in Despatches in Oct. 1914, and June, 1915, and for work with the 2nd Corps, R.E., from Aug. 1914, to April, 1915, was

Henry George Gandy.

created a Companion of the Distinguished Service Order [London Gazette, 23 June, 1915] : " Henry George Gandy, Capt., Royal Engineers. For distinguished service in the field." He was promoted to Major 12 Aug. 1915, and was Brigade Major and Secretary, School of Military Engineering, 1 Jan. 1916, to 9 Oct. 1918. Major Gandy was awarded the O.B.E. in June, 1918.

HAMILTON, GILBERT CLAUD, Major, was born 21 April, 1879, only son of the Right Hon. Lord Claud Hamilton, P.C., and Carolina (who died in 1911), daughter of the late Edward Chandos Pole, of Radbourne Hall, Derby, and Lady Anna Chandos Pole. He was gazetted to the Grenadier Guards 7 May, 1898 ; became Lieutenant 28 Oct. 1899, and was employed with the South African Constabulary 28 Nov. 1900, to 24 Sept. 1901, serving in the South African War, 1899–1902. He took part in the advance on Kimberley, including actions at Belmont, Enslin and Modder River ; was present during operations in the Orange Free State, Feb. to May, 1900, including actions at Vet River (5 and 6 May) and Zand River ; in the Transvaal in May and June, 1900, including actions near Johannesburg, Pretoria and Diamond Hill (11 and 12 June) ; in the Transvaal, east of Pretoria, July to 29 Nov. 1900, including actions at Belfast (26 and 27 Aug.) ; also during the operations in Orange River Colony and Cape Colony, Dec. 1900, to May, 1902 (Despatches [London Gazette, 29 July, 1902] ; Queen's Medal with six clasps, and King's Medal with two clasps). From 12 April, 1904, to 16 May, 1906, he was employed with the Macedonian Gendarmerie ; he was promoted to Captain 23 Jan. 1905 ; was Adjutant, Grenadier Guards, 1 July to 31 Dec. 1906 ; A.D.C. to the Governor of New Zealand 9 July, 1910, to 6 Jan. 1911 ; employed with the New Zealand Military Forces 7 Jan. 1911, to 30 July, 1913 ; promoted to Major 25 July, 1914. He served in the European War, as Temporary Lieutenant-Colonel, Grenadier Guards, from 14 Aug. to 27 Sept. 1915, and from 8 Feb. 1916, to 28 Aug. 1917 ; was Instructor, Senior Officers' School, 1 April to 28 Aug. 1917. He was three times mentioned in Despatches ; was created a C.M.G. in 1919, and a Companion of the Distinguished Service Order [London Gazette, 23 June, 1915] : " Gilbert Claud Hamilton, Major, Grenadier Guards. For distinguished service in the field." He married (1st), in 1911, Enid Awa (who died in 1916), daughter of Charles Elgar, of New Zealand ; and (2ndly), in 1916, Mary, daughter of J. A. Blair, of New York.

GREGGE-HOPWOOD, EDWARD BYNG GEORGE, Capt., was born 24 Dec. 1880, in Norfolk Street, Park Lane, W., son of Colonel and Mrs. Hopwood, of Hopwood Hall, Middleton, Lancashire. He was educated at Eton, joined the Militia in 1898, and served in the South African War, and was later commissioned in the Coldstream Guards. For his services in the European War he was twice mentioned in Despatches, and was created a Companion of the Distinguished Service Order [London Gazette, 23 June, 1915] : " Edward Byng George Gregge-Hopwood, Capt., Coldstream Guards. For distinguished service in the field." Lieut.-Colonel E. B. G. G. Hopwood was commanding the 1st Battn. Coldstream Guards when he fell in action, 20 July, 1917. Lieut.-Colonel Hopwood went with the 1st Division to France in Aug. 1914, at the commencement of the war. He was in all the battles the Coldstreams were engaged in, and in the Retreat from Mons. He was dangerously wounded in 1915, and again wounded in 1916. He received the D.S.O. for conspicuous valour and devotion to duty, and was twice mentioned in Despatches. He commanded the 1st Battn. from Oct. 1914, to the date of his death on 20 July, 1917. Lieut.-Colonel Hopwood was a fine all-round sportsman. At Eton he was a good cricketer and football player. He was a straight and hard rider to hounds, hunting in Cheshire and well known with the Meynell and the Melton packs. He was Master of the Windsor Garrison Draghounds. He rode in all the regimental races, and rode and won the Brigade of Guards' Point-to-Point Steeplechase in 1913. He was a fine shot. At polo he was seen at his best, and his Coldstream team had many victories to their credit. His example, courage and cheerfulness throughout the three years of the war were, as testified to by the General of the Division, the Colonel of the Coldstreams and other officers, beyond praise.

GROVES-RAINES, RALPH GORE DEVEREUX, Capt., was born 14 Aug. 1877. He entered the East Kent Regt. 4 May, 1898 ; became Lieutenant 13 Nov. 1899 ; Captain 14 Feb. 1903 ; was Adjutant, T.F., 1 Jan. 1911, to 20 Feb. 1913 ; served in the European War, 1914–16 ; was promoted to Major 1 Sept. 1915 ; was Officer, Company of Gentlemen Cadets, Royal Military College, 7 Oct. to 12 Dec. 1915 ; commanded a Company of Gentlemen Cadets, Royal Military College, 13 Dec. 1915, to 25 Sept. 1917 ; was Acting Lieutenant-Colonel, London Regt., 16 Nov. to 14 Dec. 1917. He was created a Companion of the Distinguished Service Order [London Gazette, 23 June, 1915] : " Ralph Gore Devereux Groves-Raines, Capt., East Kent Regt. For distinguished service in the field."

BORRETT, OSWALD CUTHBERT, Major, was born 4 March, 1878, fifth son of the late Major-General H. C. Borrett, C.B. He was educated at Wellington College, and entered the Royal Lancaster Regt. 7 May, 1898, becoming Lieutenant 5 Feb. 1900. He served in the South African War, 1899–1902, on the Staff, and took part in the operations in the Transvaal, Aug. to Oct. 1900 ; also in Orange River Colony, Nov. 1900 ; again in the Transvaal, March to June, 1901, and Feb. to 31 May, 1902 ; also again in Orange River Colony 30 Nov. 1900, to March, 1901 ; July, 1901, and Oct. 1901, to Feb. 1902 ; was present during operations in Cape Colony, Aug. and Sept. 1901 (Queen's Medal with three clasps, and King's Medal with two clasps). He was promoted to Captain 22 Jan. 1902 ; was Adjutant, Royal Lancaster Regt., 11 Aug. 1905, to 10 Aug. 1908, and Adjutant, Indian Volunteers, 1911–14. He served in the European War, 1914–19 ; became Major, 22 Oct. 1914 ; commanded the 197th Infantry Brigade, British Armies in France, 13 July, 1917, to 2 April, 1918 ; the 54th Infantry Brigade, British Armies in France, 11 Oct. 1917, to 18 Nov. 1918 ; the 55th Infantry Brigade, British Armies in France, from 19 Nov. 1918. He was appointed A.D.C. to the King 3 June, 1919 ; was given the Brevets of Lieutenant-Colonel

3 June, 1916, and Colonel 3 June, 1919; was created a C.M.G. in 1918, and a Companion of the Distinguished Service Order [London Gazette, 23 June, 1915]: "Oswald Cuthbert Borrett, Major, The King's Own Royal Lancaster Regt. For distinguished service in the field." He was awarded a Bar to the Distinguished Service Order. Colonel Borrett married Blanche, daughter of Colonel A. Murray.

MOULTON-BARRETT, EDWARD MAURICE, Major, was born 7 May, 1871. He was gazetted to the Northumberland Fusiliers 18 June, 1892; became Lieutenant 3 April, 1895. He served with the Nile Expedition, 1898, and was present at the Battle of Khartum (Egyptian Medal with clasp; Medal). He was promoted Captain 17 Feb. 1900; was Adjutant, Northumberland Fusiliers 27 June, 1900, to 26 June, 1904; was promoted to Major 23 Nov. 1909; was Temporary Lieutenant-Colonel, Northumberland Fusiliers, 19 March to 16 April, 1915; Acting Lieutenant-Colonel, commanding a Service Battn. Northumberland Fusiliers, 9 Dec. 1916, to 6 April, 1917; Temporary Lieutenant-Colonel, commanding a Service Battn. Northumberland Fusiliers, 7 April, 1917, to 2 Jan. 1918; Temporary Lieutenant-Colonel, Northumberland Fusiliers, 3 Jan. to 28 March, 1918; was promoted to Lieutenant-Colonel, Northumberland Fusiliers, 14 Oct. 1918. For his services in the European War, 1914-18, he was mentioned in Despatches, and was created a Companion of the Distinguished Service Order [London Gazette, 23 June, 1915]: "Edward Maurice Moulton-Barrett, Major, The Northumberland Fusiliers. For distinguished service in the field." He was awarded a Bar to the Distinguished Service Order.

HELY-HUTCHINSON, RICHARD GEORGE, Major, was born 3 March, 1871. He was commissioned in the Royal Fusiliers 13 May, 1891, becoming Lieutenant 25 Nov. 1892; Captain 20 July, 1898; was Superintendent of Gymnasia, Dublin District, 18 March, 1899, to 25 Sept. 1902; was promoted to Major 5 May, 1907; was Superintendent of Gymnasia, Mediterranean, 10 Dec. 1907, to 20 Nov. 1908; Superintendent of Gymnasia, Northern Command, 21 Nov. 1908, to 9 Dec. 1911. He served in the European War, 1914-15; as Temporary Lieutenant-Colonel, Royal Fusiliers, 22 Feb. to 16 June, 1915; became Lieutenant-Colonel 29 April, 1916; was Commandant, Reinforcement Camp, 3rd Army Corps, British Armies in France, 5 Nov. 1917, to 22 March, 1918; Administrative Commandant, British Armies in France, 19 Nov. 1918. Lieut.-Colonel Hely-Hutchinson was mentioned in Despatches, and created a Companion of the Distinguished Service Order [London Gazette, 23 June, 1915]: "Richard George Hely-Hutchinson, Major, The Royal Fusiliers (City of London Regt.). For distinguished service in the field."

BOXER, HUGH EDWARD RICHARD, Lieut.-Colonel, was born at Norbiton, Surrey, 8 Jan. 1871, second and only surviving son of Lieut. Edward William Frederick Boxer, R.N., and Edith Graham (who married, secondly, Colonel Frederick Swaine Le Grice, Royal Artillery), daughter of Coutts Stone. He was a grandson of Major-General Edward Mournier Boxer, R.A., F.R.S., and a great-grandson of Rear-Admiral Sir Edward Boxer, K.C.B. Lieut.-Colonel H. E. R. Boxer's father, Lieut. E. W. F. Boxer, R.N., was one of the officers lost in H.M.S. Captain, when she foundered off Cape Finisterre 7 Sept. 1870, as described in the Victoria Cross Volume of this book, in the biography of Capt. Hugh Talbot Burgoyne, V.C., R.N. Hugh Boxer was educated at the Royal Naval School, Stubbington; at Kelly College, and the Royal Military College, Sandhurst (Queen's Cadet); was gazetted to the Lincolnshire Regt. 27 Jan. 1892, and promoted to Lieutenant, 14 Aug. 1893; to Captain 7 April, 1900; to Major 25 March, 1911, and to Lieutenant-Colonel 27 May, 1915. He first saw active service in the Nile Expedition of 1898, when he was present at the Battle of the Atbara, where he was severely wounded, mentioned in Despatches [London Gazette, 24 May, 1898], and received the Medal, the Egyptian Medal and clasp. He was Adjutant of the Militia Battn. and Special Reserve of his Regt. 1 Sept. 1903, to 31 Aug. 1908; served in Malta, Egypt, India, Gibraltar and Bermuda; came home with his regiment and joined the British Expeditionary Force in France in Nov. 1914; was Second-in-Command of the 1st Battn. in the fighting around Ypres, and was afterwards transferred to the 2nd Battn. He took part in the engagements at Festubert, and then took over the command of the 1st Battn. at Hooge on the 27th of May, and was killed in action there 16 June, 1915, leading the regiment in the advance that day. He was mentioned in Despatches [London Gazette, 22 June, 1915], by Field-Marshal Sir John (now Lord) French, and was created a Companion of the Distinguished Service Order [London Gazette, 23 June, 1915]: "Hugh Edward Richard Boxer, Lieut.-Colonel, The Lincolnshire Regt. For distinguished service in the field." Lieut.-Colonel Boxer had married, at St. Columba's Church, Pont Street, S.W., on 22 Sept. 1897, Jane, daughter of Myles Patterson, and they had three children: Hugh Myles (Lieutenant, Lincolnshire Regt., who has been awarded the Military Cross), born 10 July, 1898; Charles Ralph, born 8 March, 1904, and Beryl Alice.

Hugh E. R. Boxer.

KINO, ALGERNON RODERICK, Capt., was born 17 June, 1880. He entered the Army 21 Feb. 1900; became Lieutenant 26 May, 1900; Captain 6 July, 1910, and Major 1 Sept. 1919. Capt. Kino served in the European War, 1914-18; was mentioned in Despatches, and created a Companion of the Distinguished Service Order [London Gazette, 23 June, 1915]: "Algernon Roderick Kino, Capt., The East Yorkshire Regt. For distinguished service in the field." He retired from the East Yorkshire Regt. 24 July, 1918

Cleland B. Cumberlege.

CUMBERLEGE, CLELAND BULSTRODE, Capt., was born 5 June, 1875, at Nagpore, India, son of Colonel. A. B. Cumberlege (Indian Army) and of E. F. Broadwood. He was educated at Eastbourne College, and joined the Imperial Yeomanry in Nov. 1899, for service in the South African War, 1900-1902. He served as Trooper in the Imperial Yeomanry, employed with Mounted Infantry; took part in the operations in the Transvaal, west of Pretoria, July to 29 Nov. 1900, including action at Elands River (4 to 16 Aug.); in Cape Colony, north of Orange River, including action at Fabers Put; in the Transvaal 30 Nov. 1900, to June, 1901; also in Orange River Colony, Sept. 1901, to May, 1902 (Queen's Medal with three clasps, and King's Medal with two clasps). He was given a commission in the Bedfordshire Regt. 27 July, 1901; became Lieutenant 23 March, 1904; Captain 1 April, 1910; was Adjutant, Militia, 22 Nov. 1911, to 30 Oct. 1914. He served in the European War, and was promoted Major 12 Nov. 1915; was Temporary Lieutenant-Colonel 5 Nov. 1916, to 13 July, 1917. He was recommended for good work at the Battle of Neuve Chapelle in March, 1915, when he was severely wounded. He was mentioned in Despatches, and created a Companion of the Distinguished Service Order [London Gazette, 23 June, 1915]: "Cleland Bulstrode Cumberlege, Capt., The Bedfordshire Regt. For distinguished service in the field." During the years 1895-99, and again in 1903-5, Major Cumberlege was an amateur steeplechase rider in the south of England and at military meetings. Major Cumberlege married, 19 Dec. 1905, at Wimbledon, Leila Macdonald, daughter of the late Simon Martin, Bengal Civil Service, East India Company, and they have a son, Cleland Cumberlege, born 14 Sept. 1906.

SMITH, HERBERT STONEY, Major, entered the Army 17 Jan. 1891; became Lieutenant 1 Jan. 1893; Captain 6 Feb. 1900, and Major 4 Sept. 1908. He served in the European War, and was created a Companion of the Distinguished Service Order [London Gazette, 23 June, 1915]: "Herbert Stoney Smith, Major, The Leicestershire Regt. For distinguished service in the field."

LEATHAM, BERTRAM HENRY, Capt., was gazetted to the Yorkshire Regt. 11 Aug. 1900; became Lieutenant 26 April, 1902, and Captain 21 July, 1906, and was Adjutant, Yorkshire Regt., from 16 Jan. 1908. He served in the European War, and was created a Companion of the Distinguished Service Order [London Gazette, 23 June, 1915]: "Bertram Henry Leatham, Capt., Alexandra, Princess of Wales's Own (Yorkshire Regt.). For distinguished service in the field."

DICK, DIGHTON HAY ABERCROMBY, Major, was born 26 Jan. 1869, son of Capt. Alfred Abercromby Dick, 11th Bengal Lancers (Probyn's Horse), and Fanny, daughter of Elliot Macnaghten, of Ovingdean, Sussex. He was educated at Wellington and Sandhurst, and entered the Army 11 April, 1888. He served on the North-West Frontier of India, 1897-98 (Medal; two clasps); in the Tirah Campaign, 1897-98 (clasp); in South Africa, 1899-1900 (severely wounded; Despatches; Queen's Medal with four clasps); was promoted Major 18 May, 1910; retired Royal Scots Fusiliers 9 July, 1910. He served in the European War, 1914-17, as Temporary Lieutenant-Colonel in 1915; was promoted to Lieutenant-Colonel, Special Reserve, in 1917; was twice mentioned in Despatches; made Officier de l'Ordre de Léopold, Belgium, 1917; given the Belgian Croix de Guerre, 1918, and created a Companion of the Distinguished Service Order [London Gazette, 23 June, 1915]: "Dighton Hay Abercromby Dick, Major, The Royal Scots Fusiliers (Special Reserve). For distinguished service in the field." He married, in 1902, Lilian, daughter of Francis Ricardo, J.P., D.L., of The Friary, Old Windsor, and they have one son and one daughter.

OWEN, CHARLES SAMUEL, Capt., was born 23 Jan. 1879, son of the late G. H. Owen, of Ynwich, Carnarvonshire. He entered the Royal Welsh Fusiliers 11 Feb. 1899; became Lieutenant 6 Oct. 1900; Captain 17 Nov. 1906; was Adjutant, R.W.F., 19 Oct. 1913, to 16 Dec. 1915; Major 1 Sept. 1915; Temporary Brigadier-General, commanding 36th Infantry Brigade, British Armies in France, 28 Nov. 1916. He served in China in 1900, and was present at the Relief of Tientsin; at the Relief of Pekin; also in the actions of Pietsang and Yangtsun (Medal with clasp). He served in the European War, 1914-18; was twice mentioned in Despatches; given the Brevet of Lieutenant-Colonel 1 Jan. 1917; created a C.M.G. 1918, and created a Companion of the Distinguished Service Order [London Gazette, 23 June, 1915]: "Charles Samuel Owen, Capt., The Royal Welsh Fusiliers. For distinguished service in the field." He was given temporary command of 6th Battn. Queen's Own Royal West Kent Regt. He married, in 1918, Viola Eva, daughter of the late Capt. George Carson Fenwick, Royal Welsh Fusiliers, of Plas Ffron, Wrexham.

STEWART, PATRICK ALEXANDER VANSITTART, Major, was born 29 June, 1875, second son of Lieut.-General John Mackie Stewart, J.P., of Carruchan, Dumfries, and Florence, daughter of the late Henry Vansittart. He was gazetted to the King's Own Scottish Borderers 18 July, 1896; became Lieutenant 31 Dec. 1897; Captain 24 June, 1901; was Adjutant, K.O.S.B., 31 March, 1908, to 22 Jan. 1911; was promoted to Major in Dec. 1914; was Temporary Lieutenant-Colonel 25 Feb. to 31 Dec. 1916. He was Commander, Company of Gentlemen Cadets (G.S.O.), Royal Military College), 1 Sept. 1913, to 16 Nov. 1914; Brigade Major, 80th Infantry Brigade, New Armies, B.E.F., 17 Nov. 1914, to 14 July, 1915; G.S.O., 2nd Grade, 4th Army Corps, British Expeditionary Force,

15 July, 1915, to 24 Feb. 1916; G.S.O.1, British Expeditionary Force, British Armies in France, 25 Feb. 1916, to Dec. 1917; G.S.O.1 (Liaison Officer, Ireland), 20 May to 5 Nov. 1918; G.S.O.1, Irish Command, 6 Nov. 1918. He took part in the operations on the North-West Frontier of India, 1897–98, with the Tirah Expeditionary Force (Medal with two clasps); served in the South African War, 1900–2; took part in the operations in the Transvaal (Queen's Medal with two clasps). He served in the European War, 1914–17; was given the Brevet of Lieutenant-Colonel 1 Jan. 1917; received the Belgian Croix de Guerre; was created a C.B.E. in 1919, and a Companion of the Distinguished Service Order [London Gazette, 23 June, 1915]: "Patrick Alexander Vansittart Stewart, Major, King's Own Scottish Borderers. For distinguished service in the field." Lieut.-Colonel P. A. V. Stewart married, in 1911, Mildred Annie Ferrers Young, daughter of the late T. Ferrers Guy, and widow of Capt. J. F. H. Young, R.A., and they have one son.

CHAPLIN, JAMES GRAHAM, Major, was born 1 July, 1873. He was gazetted to the Scottish Rifles 12 Dec. 1894; became Lieutenant 24 June, 1896; was Adjutant, Scottish Rifles, 29 Oct. 1898, to 28 Oct. 1902; was promoted to Major 24 Oct. 1913, and to Lieutenant-Colonel 2 June, 1919; was Temporary Brigadier-General from 20 Nov. 1917; was Adjutant, Special Reserve, 21 April, 1909, to 20 April, 1912; Brigade Commander, 103rd Infantry Brigade, British Armies in France, 20 Nov. 1917, to 31 Aug. 1918; Brigade Commander, 2nd Cyclist Brigade, Home Forces, from 10 Oct. 1918. He served in the European War, 1914–17; was given the Brevets of Lieutenant-Colonel 3 June, 1916, and of Colonel 1 Jan. 1919, and was created a Companion of the Distinguished Service Order [London Gazette, 23 June, 1915]: "James Graham Chaplin, Major, The Cameronians (Scottish Rifles). For distinguished service in the field." He married, in 1914, Lily Dora, daughter of the late Thomas Alexander, of Brentham Park, Stirling, and they have two sons and one daughter.

FERRERS, EDMUND BROMFIELD, Capt., was born 3 March, 1878. He was educated at Bath College, and at Gonville and Caius College, Cambridge, and entered the Scottish Rifles 18 Oct. 1899, becoming Lieutenant 1 Aug. 1900; Captain 14 April, 1909; Major 1 Sept. 1915. He was Temporary Lieutenant-Colonel 26 March, 1917, to 20 Feb. 1919. He served in the South African War, 1899–1902; was present at the Relief of Ladysmith, including operations of 5 to 7 Feb. 1900, and action at Vaal Kranz (severely wounded); afterwards attached to Army Service Corps from 22 July, 1901; took part in the operations in the Transvaal 30 Nov. 1900, to 31 May, 1902 (Queen's Medal with two clasps, and King's Medal with two clasps). From 1914 to 1916 he served in the European War; was mentioned in Despatches, and created a Companion of the Distinguished Service Order [London Gazette, 23 June, 1915]: "Edmund Bromfield Ferrers, Capt., The Cameronians (Scottish Rifles). For distinguished service in the field."

SCOTT, CHARLES BALIOL, Capt., son of Benjamin John Scott, of St. Katherine's, Weybridge. He was educated at Charterhouse, and in France, and served in the South African War, 1900–2, taking part in the operations in the Orange Free State, May, 1900, including actions at Vet River (5 and 6 May) and Zand River; in the Transvaal in May and June, 1900, including actions near Johannesburg and Pretoria; again in the Transvaal 30 Nov. 1900, to Feb. 1902 (Queen's Medal with three clasps, and King's Medal with two clasps). Capt. Scott served in the European War, 1914–17; was mentioned in Despatches, and created a Companion of the Distinguished Service Order [London Gazette, 23 June, 1915]: "Charles Baliol Scott, Capt., The Duke of Cornwall's Light Infantry. For distinguished service in the field."

TERRY, ROBERT JOSEPH ATKINSON, Major, entered the Army 13 July, 1892; became Lieutenant 28 Oct. 1896; Captain 18 Jan. 1908; was Commandant, Corps of Military Police, and Provost-Marshal from 8 Nov. 1910. He first saw active service in the operations on the North-West Frontier of India, 1897–8, with the Malakand Field, Mohmand Field, and Tirah Expeditionary Forces (Medal with two clasps). Served in the South African War, 1899–1902; took part in the several operations in the Transvaal, Orange River Colony and Cape Colony; Special Service Officer (for Mounted Infantry); afterwards employed as Adjutant, Driscoll's Scouts, from 17 April, 1901 (twice wounded, severely and slightly; Despatches [London Gazette, 29 July, 1902]; Brevet of Major, 22 Aug. 1902; Queen's Medal with five clasps, and King's Medal with two clasps.) He was created an M.V.O. Major Terry served in the European War, and was created a Companion of the Distinguished Service Order [London Gazette, 23 June, 1915]: "Robert Joseph Atkinson Terry, M.V.O., Major, The Royal Sussex Regt. For distinguished service in the field."

BECKETT, JOHN DOUGLAS MORTIMER, Capt., entered the Army 8 Jan. 1901; became Lieutenant 2 Sept. 1903, and Captain 9 May, 1907. He served in the South African War, 1901–2; took part in the operations in the Transvaal, May, 1901, to 31 May, 1902, and received the Queen's Medal with five clasps. Capt. Beckett served in the European War, and was created a Companion of the Distinguished Service Order [London Gazette, 23 June, 1915]: "John Douglas Mortimer Beckett, Capt., The Hampshire Regt. For distinguished service in the field."

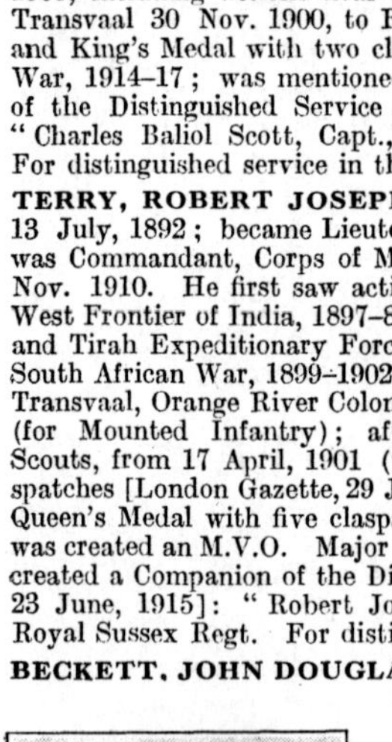

John D. M. Beckett.

SAVAGE-ARMSTRONG, FRANCIS SAVAGE NESBIT, Capt., entered the Army 19 Sept. 1900; became Lieutenant 9 Feb. 1904, and Captain 19 Oct. 1909. He served in the South African War, 1900–2; took part in the operations in Orange River Colony, May to 29 Nov. 1900, including action at Wittebergen; again in Orange River Colony, 30 Nov. 1900, to 31 May, 1902 (Queen's Medal with three clasps, and King's Medal with two clasps). Capt. Savage-Armstrong served in the European War, and was created a Companion of the Distinguished Service Order [London Gazette, 23 June, 1915]: "Francis Savage Nesbit Savage-Armstrong, Capt., The South Staffordshire Regt. For distinguished service in the field."

SUTHERLAND, HENRY HOMES, Major, was born 9 Nov. 1871. He entered the Royal Highlanders 15 March, 1893; was promoted to Lieutenant 7 April, 1897; to Captain 13 Nov. 1900; to Major 2 Dec. 1910, and to Lieutenant-Colonel 2 June, 1919. He was Adjutant, Militia, 16 April, 1901, to 15 April, 1906. He took part in the operations on the North-West Frontier of India, 1897-98, with the Malakand Field Force (Medal with clasp). He served in the European War, 1914–17; was Lieutenant-Colonel, 10th Battn. Gloucestershire Regt. from 1915. He was created a Companion of the Distinguished Service Order [London Gazette, 23 June, 1915]: "Henry Homes Sutherland, Major, The Black Watch (Royal Highlanders). For distinguished service in the field." Lieut.-Colonel Sutherland is married, and has one daughter.

DILLON, HENRY MOUNTIFORD, Capt., entered the Army 18 April, 1900; became Lieutenant 3 Oct. 1904, and Captain 19 Nov. 1910. He served in the South African War in 1900; also served in the Mediterranean (Medal). In 1906 he served in West Africa, in Northern Nigeria (Medal with clasp). Capt. Dillon served in the European War, and was created a Companion of the Distinguished Service Order [London Gazette, 23 June, 1915]: "Henry Mountiford Dillon, Capt., Oxfordshire and Buckinghamshire Light Infantry. For distinguished service in the field."

JONES, LUMLEY OWEN WILLIAMS, Capt., entered the Army 1 Dec. 1897; became Lieutenant 20 Jan. 1900, and Capt. 26 Sept. 1905. He served in the South African War, 1901–2; took part in the operations in the Transvaal, Dec. 1901; also in Orange River Colony, Dec. 1901, to 31 May, 1902 (Queen's Medal with four clasps). Served in West Africa (Southern Nigeria), 1905–6, during operations in the Kwale-Ishan District; served in West Africa (Southern Nigeria), 1906 (Medal with clasp). Capt. Jones served in the European War, and was created a Companion of the Distinguished Service Order [London Gazette, 23 June, 1915]: "Lumley Owen Williams Jones, Capt., The Essex Regt. For distinguished service in the field."

MORTIMORE, CHARLES REYNOLDS, Major, was born 27 June, 1872. He was gazetted to the Derbyshire Regt. 19 Nov. 1892; became Lieutenant 13 July, 1894; was Adjutant, Notts and Derby Regt., 2 Jan. 1900, to 1 Jan. 1904; was promoted to Captain 15 Feb. 1900, and to Major 11 Feb. 1912. From 6 March, 1906, to 5 March, 1911, he was Adjutant, Militia, and Adjutant, Special Reserve. He served at Tirah, 1897–8, in the action of Dargai; at the capture of the Sampagha and Arhanga Passes, and during the operations in the Bazar Valley, 25 to 30 Dec. 1897 (Medal with two clasps). Major Mortimore served in the European War, 1914–15; was Temporary Lieutenant-Colonel, Notts and Derby Regt., 21 Feb. to 11 March, 1915; was severely wounded, and created a Companion of the Distinguished Service Order [London Gazette, 23 June, 1915]: "Charles Reynolds Mortimore, Major, The Sherwood Foresters (Nottinghamshire and Derbyshire Regt.). For distinguished service in the field."

THORNTON, WILLIAM BROOKE, Major, was born 30 Oct. 1875. He entered the Royal Berkshire Regt. 25 March, 1896; became Lieutenant 1 May, 1899; Captain 8 May, 1904; Major 10 May, 1915; was Temporary Colonel 14 March to 2 April, 1918; was Adjutant, Militia, 15 Feb. 1905, to 14 Feb. 1908; employed with the Egyptian Army 19 June to 14 Nov. 1915; Brigade Commander, 1st Infantry Brigade, British Armies in France, 3 April to 21 Sept. 1918; Brigade Commander, Irish Reserve Brigade, Home Forces, 22 Sept. 1918. He served in the South African War, 1899–1902, employed with Mounted Infantry; took part in the operations in the Orange Free State, March to May, 1900; in Orange River Colony, May to Nov. 1900, including action at Rhenoster River; in Cape Colony, south of Orange River, 1899–1900; again during operations in Orange River Colony, Nov. 1900, to 31 May, 1902 (Despatches [London Gazette, 10 Sept. 1901, and 29 July, 1902]; Queen's Medal with three clasps, and King's Medal with two clasps). For his services in the European War, 1914–18, he was mentioned in Despatches; given the Brevet of Lieutenant-Colonel 1 Jan. 1918, and created a Companion of the Distinguished Service Order [London Gazette, 23 June, 1915]: "William Brooke Thornton, Major, Royal Berkshire Regt. For distinguished service in the field."

HARRIS, ARTHUR ELLIS FOWKE, Capt., was born 17 May, 1878. He entered the Royal Berkshire Regt. 4 May, 1898; became Lieutenant 13 July, 1900; Captain 27 Jan. 1909, and Major 1 Sept. 1915. He was Brigade Major, 10th Reserve Infantry Brigade, New Armies, 13 Jan. to 21 March, 1916; Brigade Major, 184th Infantry Brigade, Home Forces, 22 March to 19 April, 1916. He served in the South African War, 1899–1902; took part in the operations in the Orange Free State, April and May, 1900; in the Transvaal, east of Pretoria, July to Nov. 1900; in the Transvaal, west of Pretoria, July and Aug. 1900, including action at Zilikat's Nek; in Orange River Colony, May to July, 1900; in Cape Colony, south of Orange River, 1899–1900; again in the Transvaal, Nov. 1900, to July, 1901; and again during the operations in Cape Colony, July, 1901, to 31 May, 1902 (Queen's Medal with three clasps, and King's Medal with two clasps). For his services in the European War he was created a Companion of the Distinguished Service Order [London Gazette, 23 June, 1915]: "Arthur Ellis Fowke Harris, Capt., Royal Berkshire Regt. For distinguished service in the field."

BROOKE, CHRISTOPHER ROBERT INGHAM, Major, was born 4 July, 1869. He entered the Yorkshire Light Infantry 28 June, 1890; was promoted to Lieutenant 17 June, 1892; to Captain 26 March, 1899; commanded a Mounted Infantry Battn. in South Africa, 8 Jan. 1907, to 7 Jan.

1911; became Major 14 June, 1908; was in command of the 6th Battn. Yorkshire Light Infantry, 12 Aug. to 30 Nov. 1914; Temporary Lieutenant-Colonel, Yorkshire Light Infantry, 1 Dec. 1914, to 8 May, 1915, and 26 Aug. 1915, to 13 June, 1916; Lieutenant-Colonel 14 June, 1916; in command, Grad. Battn. 14 Nov. 1917, to 19 Sept. 1918; commanding the 82nd Infantry Brigade, Egyptian Expeditionary Force, 1 April to 29 Nov. 1916. He served in the South African War, 1899–1902, in command of the 2nd Battn. Mounted Infantry, 5 March, 1901, to 31 May, 1902; was present at the Relief of Kimberley; took part in the operations in the Orange Free State, Feb. to May, 1900, including operations at Paardeberg (17 to 26 Feb.), actions at Poplar Grove, Dreifontein, Houtnek (Thoba Mountain), Vet River (5 and 6 May), and Zand River; was present during operations in the Transvaal in May and June, 1900, including actions near Johannesburg and Pretoria; again in the Transvaal, west of Pretoria, Oct. to 29 Nov. 1900; in Cape Colony, south of Orange River, 1899–1900 (including actions at Colesberg (1 to 29 Jan.); again in the Transvaal, 30 Nov. 1900, to July, 1901, Oct. 1901, to Jan. 1902, and March to 31 May, 1902; also in Orange River Colony, Feb. and March, 1901, and July to Sept. 1901 (Despatches [London Gazette, 20 Aug. and 10 Sept. 1901]; Brevet of Major; Queen's Medal with four clasps, and King's Medal with two clasps). For his services in the European War he was created a C.M.G. and created a Companion of the Distinguished Service Order [London Gazette, 23 June, 1915]: "Christopher Robert Ingham Brooke, Major, Yorkshire Light Infantry. For distinguished service in the field."

STRICK, JOHN ARKWRIGHT, Major, was born 11 May, 1870, son of the late Colonel J. Strick, C.B., of Bar Hill, Madeley. He was gazetted to the Shropshire Light Infantry 1 March, 1890; became Lieutenant 1 Jan. 1892; was Adjutant, Shropshire Light Infantry, 23 July, 1895, to 4 March, 1899; was promoted to Captain 4 Dec. 1899; to Major 17 Nov. 1908; to Lieutenant-Colonel 19 Aug. 1917, and to Colonel 2 June, 1919. He was Adjutant, Indian Volunteers, 5 March, 1899, to 21 Oct. 1902; Adjutant, Militia, 23 April, 1903, to 22 April, 1906; Staff Captain, No. 4 District, Western Command, 1 April, 1908, to 24 Oct. 1909; D.A.A. and Q.M.G., Welsh Division, Western Command, 25 Oct. 1909, to 31 March, 1912; A.A. and Q.M.G., B.E.F., British Armies in France, 6 Aug. 1915, to 1 May, 1917; Commandant, Lines of Communication, British Armies in France, British Forces in Italy, 2 May, 1917, to 3 July, 1918; Inspector-General of Communications, British Forces in Italy, 4 July, 1918; Temporary Major-General. He took part in the operations on the North-West Frontier of India, 1897–98, with the Tirah Expeditionary Force, from 29 Dec. to the end of the Campaign (Medal with two clasps). For his services in the European War, 1914–18, he was mentioned in Despatches; was given the Brevets of Lieutenant-Colonel 1 Jan. 1917, and Colonel 3 June, 1918; was made a Chevalier, Légion d'Honneur; created a C.B. in 1919, and a Companion of the Distinguished Service Order [London Gazette, 23 June, 1915]: "John Arkwright Strick, Major, Shropshire Light Infantry. For distinguished service in the field." In 1914 he married Iris Gwendolen, daughter of the late George Cammell, of Brookfield Manor, Hathersage, and they have one son.

ATCHISON, C. E., Major, joined the Shropshire Light Infantry, and served in the South African War, 1899–1902 (slightly wounded). He took part in the operations in the Orange Free State, Feb. to May, 1900, including operations at Paardeberg (17 to 26 Feb.); present during the operations in Cape Colony, south of Orange River, 1899–1900; served in the Transvaal, Sept. 1901, to 31 May, 1902 (Queen's Medal with three clasps, and King's Medal with two clasps). He became Captain 11 Feb. 1902; was promoted to Major; served in the European War, and was created a Companion of the Distinguished Service Order [London Gazette, 23 June, 1915]: "C. E. Atchison, Major, Shropshire Light Infantry. For distinguished service in the field." He was killed in action 24 Aug. 1917.

BIRCHAM, HUMPHREY FRANCIS WILLIAM, Major, entered the Army 12 Feb. 1896; became Lieutenant 14 Sept. 1898; Captain 25 Oct. 1901, and Major 14 Feb. 1914. Major Bircham served in the European War, and was created a Companion of the Distinguished Service Order [London Gazette, 23 June, 1915]: "Humphrey Francis William Bircham, Major, King's Royal Rifle Corps. For distinguished service in the field." He died of wounds 23 July, 1916.

PARKER-JERVIS, WILLIAM SWYNFEN WHITEHALL, Capt., was born 27 Aug. 1879, eldest son of the late W. R. Parker-Jervis and Ethel Mary, daughter of the Rev. C. H. Mainwaring, Rector of Whitmore, Staffs. He was gazetted to the King's Royal Rifle Corps 25 Oct. 1899; became Lieutenant 1 Jan. 1901; Captain 10 Feb. 1907; Major 1 Sept. 1915; was Temporary Lieutenant-Colonel, commanding Special Reserve Battn. King's Royal Rifle Corps, 28 June, 1918. He served in the South African War, 1899–1902; took part in the Relief of Ladysmith, including action at Colenso; operations of 17 to 24 Jan. 1900, and action at Spion Kop; operations of 5 to 7 Feb. 1900, and action at Vaal Kranz; during the operations on Tugela Heights (14 to 27 Feb. 1900), and action at Pieter's Hill; in Natal, March to June, 1900, including action at Laing's Nek (6 to 9 June); in the Transvaal, east of Pretoria, July to 29 Nov. 1900, including actions at Belfast (26 and 27 Aug.) and Lydenberg (5 to 8 Sept.); again in the Transvaal, 30 Nov. 1900, to April, 1901; also during operations in Cape Colony, May, 1902 (Queen's Medal with six clasps, and King's Medal with two clasps). He served in the European War, 1914–16; was mentioned in Despatches, and was created a Companion of the Distinguished Service Order [London Gazette, 23 June, 1915]: "William Swynfen Whitehall Parker-Jervis, Capt., King's Royal Rifle Corps. For distinguished service in the field." Major Parker-Jervis was also given the Brevet of Lieutenant-Colonel 3 June, 1919.

WILLAN, FRANK GODFREY, Capt., was born 16 Sept. 1878, son of Colonel Frank Willan (late Colonel, 3rd Oxfordshire Light Infantry) and Louisa Marguerite Anne, daughter of the late Capt. Charles Robert George Douglas, late of the 32nd Bengal Light Infantry. He was gazetted to the King's Royal Rifle Corps 20 May, 1899; became Lieutenant 28 March, 1900; Captain 2 Feb. 1906; Major 1 Sept. 1915; Temporary Lieutenant-Colonel, commanding the 5th Battn. Royal Berkshire Regt., 11 Feb. 1916, to 20 July, 1917; Acting Lieutenant-Colonel, King's Royal Rifle Corps, 21 July to 5 Sept. 1917. He was Brigade Major, 54th Infantry Brigade, B.E.F., 9 Sept. to Oct. 1915; Brigade Major, 36th Infantry Brigade, B.E.F., 5 Nov. 1915, to 9 Feb. 1916; commanded the 56th Infantry Brigade, British Armies in France, 6 Sept. 1917, to 18 April, 1918; commanded 122nd Infantry Brigade, British Armies in France, 19 April to 11 May, 1918; commanded 6th Infantry Brigade, British Armies in France, 12 May, 1918. Capt. Willan served in the South African War, 1899–1900; was present at the Defence of Ladysmith, including action of 6 Jan. 1900; took part in the operations in Natal (March to June, 1900), including action at Laing's Nek (6 to 9 June) (Queen's Medal with three clasps). He served in the European War, 1914–18; was four times mentioned in Despatches; given the Brevet of Lieutenant-Colonel 1 Jan. 1918; created a C.M.G., and created a Companion of the Distinguished Service Order [London Gazette, 23 June, 1915]: "Frank Godfrey Willan, Capt., King's Royal Rifle Corps. For distinguished service in the field."

MAKIN, ERNEST LLEWELLYN, Capt., was born 9 Aug. 1877. He entered the Manchester Regt. 17 Feb. 1900; became Lieutenant 15 Aug. 1900; Captain 17 Feb. 1894; was transferred to the Wiltshire Regt. 29 Dec. 1906; was promoted to Major 1 Sept. 1915; was Temporary Lieutenant-Colonel 29 Oct. 1917, to 19 April, 1918. He was G.S.O.3, 33rd Division, New Armies, B.E.F., 22 July, 1915, to 2 June, 1916; G.S.O.2, 1st Division, British Armies in France, 3 June to 2 July, 1916; G.S.O.2, 35th Division, British Armies in France, 2 April to 28 Oct. 1917; G.S.O.1, 37th Division, British Armies in France, 29 Oct. 1917, to 3 March, 1918; G.S.O.2, Training Duties in U.S.A., 20 April to 18 Dec. 1918; G.S.O.2, Portsmouth Garrison, 16 April, 1919. For his services in the European War, 1914–16, he was mentioned in Despatches twice, and created a Companion of the Distinguished Service Order [London Gazette, 23 June, 1915]: "Ernest Llewellyn Makin, Capt., The Wiltshire Regt. For distinguished service in the field."

CLEMSON, WILLIAM FLETCHER, Lieut.-Colonel, was born 31 March, 1866. He was gazetted to the York and Lancaster Regt. 16 Nov. 1887; became Lieutenant 12 Feb. 1890; Captain 10 May, 1899; Adjutant, 1900–4; was promoted to Major 3 Oct. 1906; Lieutenant-Colonel 25 April, 1915, and Colonel 25 April, 1919; was Temporary Brigadier-General from 4 Nov. 1916, commanding 124th Infantry Brigade, New Armies, British Armies in France, 29 Sept. 1915, to 20 June, 1918; Inspector of Infantry 10 July, 1918. Colonel Clemson served in the European War, 1914–18; was wounded; given the Brevet of Colonel 1 Jan. 1918, and created a Companion of the Distinguished Service Order [London Gazette, 23 June, 1915]: "William Fletcher Clemson, Lieut.-Colonel, York and Lancaster Regt. For distinguished service in the field." He was awarded a Bar to the Distinguished Service Order.

JARRETT, AYLMER VIVIAN, Capt., was born in Calcutta 11 July, 1879, fourth son of Colonel Henry Sullivan Jarrett, of South Lodge, East Grinstead, and Agnes Delacour, daughter of the late Francis Beaufort, Bengal Civil Service. He was educated at Stonyhurst College, and was gazetted to the York and Lancaster Regt. 12 Aug. 1899; promoted to Lieutenant 14 Dec. 1900; to Captain 1 Jan. 1906; was Adjutant, 2nd Battn., 1 Dec. 1904, to 3 Nov. 1907, and from 29 Aug. 1908, to 19 Oct. 1911, was attached to the West African Regt. He served with the Expeditionary Force in France and Flanders; was mentioned in Despatches by Field-Marshal Sir John (now Lord) French [London Gazette, 22 June, 1915], for gallant and distinguished service in the field, and, his name having been sent up four times for special recognition, was created a Companion of the Distinguished Service Order [London Gazette, 23 June, 1915]: "Aylmer Vivian Jarrett, Capt., York and Lancaster Regt. For distinguished service in the field." Capt Jarrett died 22 June, 1915, at Vlamertinghe, of wounds received in action the same day near Ypres, and was buried near Vlamertinghe. His elder brother, Major Charles Harry Brownlow Jarrett, 1st Battn. Royal Munster Fusiliers, served in the South African War and in the Great War, and was killed at the landing at V Beach, Gallipoli, 25 April, 1915.

Aylmer Vivian Jarrett.

SOLTAU-SYMONS, LIONEL CULME, Capt., was born 22 June, 1876, youngest son of the late G. W. C. Soltau-Symons, J.P., D.L., of Chaddlewood, Devonshire. He was educated at Eton, and was gazetted to the Durham Light Infantry 9 Dec. 1896, becoming Lieutenant 1 Sept. 1898; Captain, Royal Warwickshire Regt., 19 Oct. 1902, and Major, Durham Light Infantry, 1 Sept. 1915. He was A.D.C. to the Governor and Commander-in-Chief, Bermuda, 8 April, 1903, to 28 April, 1904; and Adjutant, T.F., 24 Sept. 1911, to 29 Oct. 1915. He served in the South African War, 1899–1902, employed with Mounted Infantry; took part in the Relief of Ladysmith, including action at Colenso; operations of 17 to 24 Jan. 1900; operations of 5 to 7 Feb. 1900, and action at Vaal Kranz; during the operations on Tugela Heights (14 to 27 Feb. 1900), and action at Pieter's Hill; in Natal, March to June, 1900, including action at Laing's Nek (6 to 9 June) (Despatches [London Gazette, 10 Sept. 1901]; Queen's Medal with five clasps, and King's Medal with two clasps). Major Soltau-Symons served in the European War, 1914–17; was mentioned in Despatches, and created a Companion of the Distinguished Service Order [London Gazette, 23 June,

1915]: "Lionel Culme Soltau-Symons, Capt., Durham Light Infantry. For distinguished service in the field." He married, in 1907, the Hon. Lucy Jessie Lyon, only daughter of the 2nd Baron Playfair.

BURN, HENRY PELHAM, Capt., was born 1 May, 1882. He was gazetted to the Gordon Highlanders 4 Jan. 1901; was promoted to Lieutenant 30 May, 1904; to Captain 6 July, 1910. He was Adjutant, Gordon Highlanders, 9 Nov. 1914, to 20 Feb. 1915, and became Major 5 Jan. 1916. He was Adjutant, T.F., 18 Aug. 1913, to 29 Oct. 1914; Staff Captain, 8th Infantry Brigade, B.E.F., 21 Feb. to 13 April, 1915; Brigade Major, 8th Infantry Brigade, 76th Infantry Brigade, B.E.F., 14 April to 9 Dec. 1915; Temporary Brigadier-General from 16 July, 1916. He commanded the 152nd Brigade, British Armies in France, 16 July, 1916, to 6 April, 1918; commanded 3rd London Reserve Infantry Brigade, Forces in Great Britain, 8 May, 1918, to 13 Jan. 1919; commanded the Highland Reserve Infantry Brigade, Forces in Great Britain, 14 Jan. 1919. He served in the South African War, 1901–2; took part in operations in the Transvaal and Orange River Colony, May to Dec. 1901, and received the Queen's Medal with five clasps. For his services in the European War, 1914–18, he received the Brevet of Lieutenant-Colonel; was five times mentioned in Despatches; created a C.M.G. in 1918, and created a Companion of the Distinguished Service Order [London Gazette, 23 June, 1915]: "Henry Pelham Burn, Capt., Gordon Highlanders. For distinguished service in the field."

GORDON, LEWIS, Capt., was born at Banchory, Kincardineshire, 26 Feb. 1883, eldest son of Major Duncan Forbes Gordon, M.V.O., D.L., of 19, Queen's Road, Aberdeen, and his wife Elizabeth, daughter of the late Admiral John Leith. He was educated at Marlborough, and the Royal Military College, Sandhurst, and was gazetted to the Gordon Highlanders 8 May, 1901, becoming Lieutenant 10 March, 1905, and Captain 6 Aug. 1910. He served on the North-West Frontier of India, 1908 (Medal and clasp). He was employed with the Egyptian Army 9 March, 1911, to 18 Nov. 1914. Capt. Gordon went to France in Jan. 1915, and proceeded to Gallipoli on 19 Sept., when he was appointed Brigade Major of the 128th Infantry Brigade. He was created a Companion of the Distinguished Service Order [London Gazette, 23 June, 1915]: "Lewis Gordon, Capt., Gordon Highlanders. For distinguished service in the field." He died at Gallipoli 18 Oct. 1915, from wounds received in action, and was buried at Gully Beach, Gallipoli.

Lewis Gordon.

GOULD, PHILIP, Major, was born at Southsea 22 Aug. 1870, son of Capt. L. P. Gould and Louisa Gould. He was educated at Shrewsbury School and the Royal Military College, Sandhurst. He was gazetted to the Royal Irish Fusiliers 8 April, 1891; became Lieutenant 26 April, 1894, and Captain 24 Feb. 1900. He was Adjutant, Royal Irish Fusiliers, 31 Dec. 1900, to 30 Dec. 1904, and was promoted to Major 16 July, 1910. From 30 Aug. 1916, to 16 May, 1918, he was Temporary Lieutenant-Colonel, in command of the 4th Battn. Connaught Rangers. He served in the South African War, 1899–1902, as Adjutant to the 1st Battn. Royal Irish Fusiliers (from 31 Dec. 1900, to 31 May, 1902); took part in the operations in Natal, 1899, including actions at Talana and Lombard's Kop; at the Defence of Ladysmith, including action of 6 Jan. 1900; during the operations in Natal (March to June, 1900); in the Transvaal, east of Pretoria, July, 1900; in Orange River Colony (Sept. to 29 Nov. 1900); again in Orange River Colony, 30 Nov. 1900, to 31 May, 1902 (Despatches [London Gazette, 29 July, 1902]; Queen's Medal with five clasps, and King's Medal with two clasps; Brevet of Major, 22 Aug. 1902). For his services in the Great War, 1914–15, Major Gould was created a Companion of the Distinguished Service Order [London Gazette, 23 June, 1915]: "Philip Gould, Major, Royal Irish Fusiliers. For distinguished service in the field." The decoration was awarded for the action at St. Eloi. He married, at Willingdon, Sussex, 29 Nov. 1914, M. A. Stewart.

BULLEN-SMITH, GEORGE MOULTRIE, Major, was born 5 Feb. 1870. He was gazetted to the Royal Highlanders 17 June, 1891; became Lieutenant, Royal Highlanders, 15 April, 1894, and Leinster Regt. 20 June, 1894. On 24 Aug. 1898, he was promoted to Captain, and on 20 March, 1909, to Major. He was Temporary Lieutenant-Colonel, Leinster Regt., 20 Dec. 1914, to 2 June, 1915; and Temporary Lieutenant-Colonel, Leinster Regt., 21 Aug. to 28 Sept. 1915; became Lieutenant-Colonel 29 Sept. 1915, and was Temporary Brigadier-General 1 May, 1916, to 31 Oct. 1918. He was Adjutant, Volunteers, 8 Jan. 1900, to 7 Jan. 1905; commanded the 5th Infantry Brigade, British Armies in France, 15 May, 1916, to 4 April, 1918; commanded the Wessex Reserve Brigade, Forces in Great Britain, 24 April to 23 Oct. 1918. He served in the European War, 1914–18; was given the Brevet of Colonel 3 June, 1918; created a C.M.G., 1917, and a Companion of the Distinguished Service Order [London Gazette, 23 June, 1915]: "George Moultrie Bullen-Smith, Major, The Leinster Regt. For distinguished service in the field."

HARINGTON, JOHN, Major, was born 10 April, 1873, fifth son of the late Sir Richard Harington, 11th Bart. He entered the Rifle Brigade 19 June, 1895; became Lieutenant 15 Oct. 1897; Captain 6 March, 1901, and Major 24 March, 1914. From 30 Sept. 1903, to 28 May, 1907, he was employed with the King's African Rifles, and from 19 May, 1909, to 17 Nov. 1912, he was Adjutant, T.F. Major Harington was Brigade Major, 22nd Reserve Infantry Brigade, Home Forces, 28 Oct. 1915, to 28 Feb. 1916; and Temporary Brigadier-General, commanding the 139th Infantry Brigade British Armies in France, 24 July, 1918, to 9 April, 1919. He served with the Nile Expedition, 1898, at the Battle of Khartoum (Egyptian Medal with clasp; Medal). Served in the South African War, 1899–1902; took part in the operations in Natal, 1899, including action at Lombard's Kop; at the defence of Ladysmith, including sortie of 10 Dec. 1899, and action of 6 Jan. 1900; in Natal, March to June, 1900, including action at Laing's Nek (6 to 9 June); in the Transvaal, east of Pretoria, July to 29 Nov. 1900, including actions at Belfast (26 and 27 Aug.), and Lydenberg (5 to 8 Sept.); again in the Transvaal, 30 Nov. 1900, to 31 May, 1902, Station Commandant (Queen's Medal with three clasps, and King's Medal with two clasps). Served in East Africa, 1904; took part in the operations in Somaliland, in the action at Jidballi (Medal with two clasps); served at Nandi, 1905–6 (clasp). In the Great War he was wounded three times; was given the Brevet of Lieutenant-Colonel 1 Jan. 1916; was created a C.M.G. in 1919, and a Companion of the Distinguished Service Order [London Gazette, 23 June, 1915]: "John Harington, Major, The Rifle Brigade. For distinguished service in the field." In 1908 he married Lady (Frances) Aline Gore-Langton, fourth daughter of the 4th Earl Temple, of Stowe, and they have one son and one daughter.

BULLER, HERBERT CECIL, Capt. (Temporary Lieut.-Colonel), entered the Rifle Brigade 11 Aug. 1900; became Lieutenant 1 Aug. 1902, and Captain 22 Jan. 1910. He served in the European War; was created a Companion of the Distinguished Service Order [London Gazette, 23 June, 1915]: "Herbert Cecil Buller, Capt. (Temporary Lieut.-Colonel), The Rifle Brigade. For distinguished service in the field." He was killed in action 3 June, 1916.

POE, JOHN, Lieut.-Colonel, was born 24 Sept. 1873. He entered the R.A.M.C. 28 July, 1897; became Captain 28 July, 1900; Major 28 April, 1909; Lieutenant-Colonel 1 March, 1915, and Colonel 7 Feb. 1918. He was Assistant Director of Medical Services, 29th Division, British Armies in France, 3 May, 1917, to April, 1919; Assistant Director of Medical Services, 2nd Army Corps, British Armies in France, from 4 Feb. 1919. He served in the Great War, 1914–18; was mentioned in Despatches; given the Brevet of Colonel 1 Jan. 1918; created a C.M.G., 1919, and a Companion of the Distinguished Service Order [London Gazette, 23 June, 1915]: "John Poe, M.B., Lieut.-Colonel, R.A.M.C. For distinguished service in the field." Colonel Poe married, in 1889, Katharine (who died in 1918), daughter of R. J. Goff, of Piercetown, Newbridge, County Kildare.

COWEY, REGINALD VIONNÉE, Major, was born 14 June, 1873. He entered the R.A.M.C. 29 Jan. 1901; became Captain 29 Jan. 1904, and Major 29 Oct. 1912; was Acting Lieutenant-Colonel, R.A.M.C., Oct. 1917, to April, 1918; Temporary Lieutenant-Colonel April to May, 1918; Temporary Colonel, May, 1918, to March, 1919. He served in the European War, 1914–18; was twice mentioned in Despatches, and created a Companion of the Distinguished Service Order [London Gazette, 23 June, 1915]: "Reginald Vionnée Cowey, Major, Royal Army Medical Corps. For distinguished service in the field."

FIELDING, THOMAS EVELYN, Major, was born 27 July, 1873. He is B.A., T.C.D., M.B., B.Ch., B.A.O., University, Dublin, L.M.R. He became Lieutenant, R.A.M.C., 25 April, 1900; Captain 25 April, 1903; Major 25 Oct. 1911, and Lieutenant-Colonel 20 Dec. 1917. He was Adjutant, T.F., 2 April, 1910, to 30 March, 1913; and Assistant Director of Medical Services, 28th Division, British Salonika Force, 11 June, 1918. He served in the European War, 1914–18; was three times mentioned in Despatches, and created a Companion of the Distinguished Service Order [London Gazette, 23 June, 1915]: "Thomas Evelyn Fielding, M.B., Major, R.A.M.C. For distinguished service in the field." Colonel Fielding married Isabel Orpen, eldest daughter of Dr. B. A. Palmer, of Newry, County Down.

BROWNE, CUTHBERT GARRARD, Capt., was born 3 March, 1883. He entered the R.A.M.C. 31 July, 1905; became Captain 31 Jan. 1909, and Major 15 Oct. 1915. He served in the European War, 1914–18; was created a C.M.G. in 1919, and a Companion of the Distinguished Service Order [London Gazette, 23 June, 1915]: "Cuthbert Garrard Browne, Capt., R.A.M.C. For distinguished service in the field." He was given the Brevet of Lieutenant-Colonel 3 June, 1918.

CARTER, HERBERT ST. MAUR, Capt., was born 7 May, 1878. He was educated at Trinity College, Dublin, and entered the R.A.M.C. 30 July, 1904; became Captain 30 Jan. 1908; Major 1 July, 1915, and was Temporary Lieutenant-Colonel, R.A.M.C., 1 July, 1915, to 2 Jan. 1916. He served in the Balkan Campaign, 1912–13; was British Red Cross Commissioner with the Serbian Forces. He served in the European War, 1914–18; received the Order of St. Sava, 3rd Class, and was created a Companion of the Distinguished Service Order [London Gazette, 23 June, 1915]: "Herbert St. Maur Carter, M.D., Capt., R.A.M.C. For distinguished service in the field."

CREAN, THOMAS JOSEPH, Capt., served in the European War, 1914–15; was mentioned in Despatches, and was created a Companion of the Distinguished Service Order [London Gazette, 23 June, 1915]: "Thomas Joseph Crean, V.C., Capt., Reserve of Officers, R.A.M.C. For distinguished service in the field." (See Victoria Cross Volume.)

GALE, ROBERT, Capt., was born 16 Aug. 1887. He entered the R.A.M.C. 31 July, 1909; became Captain 31 Jan. 1913; was Acting Major, R.A.M.C., from 25 Feb. 1918. From 15 Nov. 1911, to 3 Sept. 1914, he was in civil employment in Egypt. He served in the European War, 1914–18; was twice mentioned in Despatches; given the Brevet of Major 3 June, 1919, and created a Companion of the Distinguished Service Order [London Gazette, 23 June, 1915]: "Robert Gale, M.B., Capt., Royal Army Medical Corps. For distinguished service in the field."

LLOYD-JONES, P. A., Capt., entered the R.A.M.C.; served in the European War, and was created a Companion of the Distinguished Service Order [London Gazette, 23 June, 1915]: "P. A. Lloyd-Jones, M.B., Capt., R.A.M.C. For distinguished service in the field."

McSHEEHY, OSWALD WILLIAM, Capt., was born 27 Nov. 1884, youngest son of Surgeon-Major E. L. McSheehy, J.P. He was educated at St. Edmund's College, and entered the R.A.M.C. 30 Jan. 1909, becoming Captain 30 July, 1912. He was Acting Major, R.A.M.C., 25 Feb. to 26 Oct. 1918; and Acting Lieutenant-Colonel from 26 Nov. 1918. He served in the European War, 1914–17; was mentioned in Despatches, and created a Companion of the Distinguished Service Order [London Gazette, 23 June, 1915]: "Oswald William McSheehy, M.B., Capt., R.A.M.C. For distinguished service in the field." Capt. McSheehy married, in 1911, Carrie, eldest daughter of the late Colonel H. Paterson, I.A., and they have one son and two daughters.

RICHARDS, OWEN, Temporary Capt., was born 30 Sept. 1873, son of the Rev. H. W. P. Richards, Prebendary of St. Paul's. He was educated at Eton (King's Scholar, 1887–92); New College, Oxford (Wykeham Prize Fellow, 1898–1905); Guy's Hospital (is M.D., M.Ch. (Oxford), F.R.C.S.), and became Professor of Clinical Surgery, Egyptian Government School of Medicine. He served in South Africa (Queen's Medal and three clasps), and in the European War in France, 1914–18, when he was twice mentioned in Despatches; created a C.M.G. in 1919, and created a Companion of the Distinguished Service Order [London Gazette, 23 June, 1915]: "Owen Richards, M.D., F.R.C.S., F.R.C.P., Temporary Capt., R.A.M.C. For distinguished service in the field." He married Catherine Cressall, and they have one daughter.

BURTON, GERARD WILLIAM, Capt., was born at Murree, India, 23 Aug. 1879, only son of the late Colonel Gerard Septimus Burton, Norfolk Regt., and Elizabeth, daughter of W. T. K. Perry-Keene. Capt. Burton's grandfather was the late Edmund Singer Burton, of Churchill House, Northamptonshire. He was educated at Weymouth College, and the Royal Military College, Sandhurst, and was gazetted to the 1st Battn. Norfolk Regt. 3 Aug. 1898, becoming Lieutenant 23 Oct. 1899. He transferred to the Indian Army 22 Aug. 1900, and after serving with the 1st Madras Infantry for a year, was appointed to the 39th Garhwal Rifles; was for four years Adjutant, and was promoted Captain 3 Aug. 1907. Capt. Burton left India with his regiment for active service in France, 22 Sept. 1914; was mentioned in Despatches by F.M. Sir John (now Lord) French [London Gazette, 22 June, 1915], and was created a Companion of the Distinguished Service Order [London Gazette, 23 June, 1915]: "Gerard William Burton, Capt., Indian Army. For distinguished service in the field." The decoration was especially awarded for great gallantry at Neuve Chapelle on 10 March. Capt. Burton was gazetted Major on 6 April, 1917, to rank as from 1 Sept. 1915; but this was a posthumous promotion, for he had been killed in action, near Givenchy, 12 Oct. 1915. He was buried in Gorre Château Cemetery, near Béthune. He had married, 3 Aug. 1910, at Norton Subcourse, Norwich, Blanche Ellen Beatrice, only daughter of the Rev. Arthur Thackeray, Vicar of Norton Subcourse.

Gerard William Burton.

CRUDDAS, H. W., Lieut.-Colonel, entered the Indian Army. He served in the European War, and was created a Companion of the Distinguished Service Order [London Gazette, 23 June, 1915]: "H. W. Cruddas, Lieut.-Colonel, Indian Army. For distinguished service in the field." He died of wounds in France 20 Jan. 1916.

WILLANS, THOMAS JAMES, Major, was born 2 Sept. 1872. He was gazetted to the Royal Irish Regt. 21 Oct. 1893; became Lieutenant, Royal Irish Regt., 10 July, 1896, and Lieutenant, Indian Staff Corps, 2 Sept. 1897; Captain, Indian Army, 21 Oct. 1902, and Major 21 Oct. 1911. He served on the North-West Frontier of India, 1897–98 (Medal with clasp), and again saw active service in the European War, 1914–17; was mentioned in Despatches, and created a Companion of the Distinguished Service Order [London Gazette, 23 June, 1915]: "Thomas James Willans, Major, 57th Wilde's Rifles, Frontier Force. For distinguished service in the field." He became Lieutenant-Colonel 8 March, 1918.

THOMSON, ALEXANDER GUTHRIE, Major, was born 11 Feb. 1873, son of the late A. W. Thomson, M.D., of Brechin, Forfarshire. He was educated at Cargilfield, and Fettes College, Edinburgh, and at Sandhurst, and was gazetted to the Northants Regt. 21 Oct. 1893; became Lieutenant, Northants Regt., 16 Sept. 1896; Lieutenant, I.S.C., 6 May, 1897; Captain, Indian Army, 21 Oct. 1902; Major 21 Oct. 1911, and was Temporary Lieutenant Colonel 30 March to 2 June, 1918. He passed the Staff College; was Staff Captain, India, 17 Sept. 1909, to 7 Aug. 1910; G.S.O.3, Headquarters, India, 8 Aug. 1910, to 26 Nov. 1911; G.S.O.2, Headquarters, India, 27 Nov. 1911, to 16 Sept. 1913; Brigade Major, 121st Brigade, New Armies, British Armies in France, 29 Sept. 1915, to 6 Sept. 1916; G.S.O.2, 40th Division, British Armies in France, 7 Sept. 1916, to 18 Feb. 1917; G.S.O.2, 13th Army Corps, British Armies in France, 19 Feb. to 2 July, 1917; G.S.O.2, 18th Army Corps, British Armies in France, 9 Aug. to 28 Oct. 1917; G.S.O.2, American Staff College, British Armies in France, 29 Oct. 1917, to 29 March, 1918; G.S.O., 36th Division, British Armies in France, 30 March to 16 Nov. 1918; G.S.O.1, 52nd Division, British Armies in France, 17 Nov. 1918. He was three times mentioned in Despatches; was given the Brevet of Lieutenant-Colonel 3 June, 1918; was created a C.M.G. in 1919, and a Companion of the Distinguished Service Order [London Gazette, 23 June, 1915]: "Alexander Guthrie Thomson, Major, 38th Vaughan's Rifles, Frontier Force. For distinguished service in the field." Lieut.-Colonel A. G. Thomson married, in 1907, Annie Wilhelmina, daughter of W. A. Finlay, M.D., F.R.C.S.Edinburgh, and they have one son and three daughters.

SHERINGHAM, ARTHUR THOMAS, Capt., was born 19 Aug. 1881, son of Colonel A. W. Sheringham, of Caston, Norfolk. He was gazetted to the West India Regt., as Second Lieutenant, from the Militia, 28 Jan. 1903; became Lieutenant, West India Regt., 22 Oct. 1904, and Indian Army, 11 Aug. 1905; Captain, Indian Army, 9 March, 1910, and Major 19 Dec. 1915. He passed 1st Class Interpreter in Persian, and passed High Proficiency in Hindustani. He served in the South African War, 1900–2 (Queen's Medal with three clasps, and King's Medal with two clasps). For his services in the European War, 1914–15, he was created a Companion of the Distinguished Service Order [London Gazette, 23 June, 1915]: "Arthur Thomas Sheringham, Capt., 121st Pioneers, Indian Army. For distinguished service in the field."

CRAMER-ROBERTS, MARMADUKE TORIN, Capt., was born 14 Dec. 1880, at Worleston Cottage, Worleston, near Nantwich, Cheshire, son of Mr. and Mrs. H. T. Cramer-Roberts, of the Gables, Neston, Cheshire; and grandson of Marmaduke Coghill Cramer-Roberts, D.L., of Sallymount, County Kildare, and of Henry Justice, D.L., of Kinstock Hall, Shropshire. He was educated at Mostyn House School, Parkgate, Cheshire, and at the Lycée de Marrac, Bayonne, France. He entered the Army, and became Lieutenant 14 Jan. 1905, and Captain 1 April, 1910, and Major 1 April, 1916. He served in the South African War, 1900–2, and took part in the operations in the Transvaal, Feb. 1902; also in Orange River Colony and Cape Colony, Nov. 1901, to April, 1902 (Queen's Medal with five clasps). He served in the European War, 1914–16; was mentioned in Despatches, and created a Companion of the Distinguished Service Order [London Gazette, 23 June, 1915]: "Marmaduke Torin Cramer-Roberts, Capt., 4th Gurkha Rifles. For distinguished service in the field."

The following are extracts from a Report by the Officer who commanded the attack on the German trenches on the night of the 19th–20th of Dec. 1914, in front of Festubert: "The first line, led by Major Nicolay, 1/4th Gurkha Rifles, and Lieut. Anderson, Highland Light Infantry, made a rush over the parapet, followed shortly after by the second line, under Capt. Pringle, Highland Light Infantry, accompanied by Major Brodhurst, 1/4th Gurkha Rifles, who had volunteered to join the force. . . . After an interval the third line was sent forward, under Capt. Cramer-Roberts, 1/4th Gurkha Rifles (wounded), and Lieut. Kerr, 1st Highland Light Infantry (killed). About now Major Brodhurst came back, saying no more troops could be accommodated in the trenches captured, and so the fourth line remained in the 1/4th Gurkha trenches. . . . There they remained with what wounded they could collect, under Major Nicolay, 1/4th Gurkha Rifles, until night fell, when he successfully withdrew them to our trench without loss. . . . During the afternoon, when we were still uncertain of the whereabouts of our own men in advance, a very plucky attempt to bring us news was made by Capt. Cramer-Roberts and a native Gurkha officer of the 1/4th Gurkha Rifles to rush across the open to us. They were both shot down, Capt. Cramer-Roberts being very severely wounded, but eventually crawled towards our parapet, and was fetched in and able to inform me on the situation in front. After dark Major Nicolay managed to bring away all the party confined in the sap without loss, remaining to the last himself. . . . I much regret the heavy loss entailed, but would like to bring the following names of officers to the favourable consideration of the G.O.C. for the excellent work they did, and the way in which the whole of the little force under my command fought that night. Capt. David Inglis, 1/4th Gurkha Rifles (killed). He guided the force to the right trench and then joined the first line in the rush on the German trench, when he was shot down. Major M. L. Brodhurst, 1/4th Gurkha Rifles, for bringing back important information with regard to the situation at the front, and again returning under heavy fire. Major Nicolay, 1/4th Gurkha Rifles, for leading the first line and . . . returning successfully with all the wounded he could collect on the night of the 19th, after holding the sap all day. Capt. M. T. Cramer-Roberts (severely wounded), for bringing in news of the situation, when he was shot down. Native Officer, Gurkha Rifles.—Refer to Capt. Cramer-Roberts. . . . These few extracts from my Report . . . of the events of the night attack on the 19th Dec. will, I think, interest you, and I bitterly regret that for some reason or other I fancy they were never forwarded to higher authorities. Some day perhaps it will be known why, but I am glad to let you know that my appreciation of all you fellows did was duly reported. It is meagre, I acknowledge, but I was sent for on the night of the 22nd . . . to write on the spur of the moment an account, as Headquarters were urgently calling for it. Had I had time to submit it in proper form I would have endeavoured to make it fuller. But, wet, tired, and fairly beat after fighting from the 19th to the 22nd, it was the best I could do."

During the fighting described in the above extracts Capt. Cramer-Roberts had some sixty yards to cross, and fell quite close to the parapet of our front-line trenches, by which he managed to crawl, and was pulled in. His right arm, close to the shoulder, and his right hip-joint were smashed, and he had a flesh wound in the lower part of his left leg. Major Cramer-Roberts married, in 1915, Gertrude, youngest daughter of Colonel Reginald Oakes, R.F.A., of Bealings, Suffolk.

HEYLAND, ARTHUR KYFFIN, Major, was born 22 April, 1874, son of the late Colonel A. R. Heyland, 31st Lancers. He entered the Army 30 Aug. 1893, as Second Lieutenant (unattached), and was gazetted to the Indian Staff Corps 24 Jan. 1895, becoming Lieutenant, I.S.C., 6 Oct. 1896; Captain, Indian Army, 30 Aug. 1902, and Major 30 Aug. 1911. He served in British East Africa, 1901; took part in the operations against the Ogaden Somalis in Jubaland (Medal with clasp). Served in Aden, 1903–4, during the operations in the interior. Major Heyland joined the Supply and Transport Corps. He served in the European War in France, 1914–15, and was created a Companion of the Distinguished Service Order [London Gazette, 23 June, 1915]: "Arthur Kyffin Heyland, Major, Supply and Transport

Corps. For distinguished service in the field." He subsequently served in Mesopotamia. He married Constance Ll., youngest daughter of General W. S. M. Price, and they have three sons.

TAYLOR, JOHN, Capt., was born 14 Feb. 1884. He is M.D. and D.P.H. He entered the I.M.S. 1 Sept. 1906; became Captain 1 Sept. 1909, and Major 1 March, 1918. In 1908 he served on the North-West Frontier of India (Medal with clasp). For his services in the European War, from 1914, he was created a Companion of the Distinguished Service Order [London Gazette, 23 June, 1915]. "John Taylor, M.B., Capt., Indian Medical Service. For distinguished service in the field." Major Taylor married Katherine, eldest daughter of the late Alexander Monro, C.I.E., and they have one son and two daughters.

BROOKE-POPHAM, HENRY ROBERT MOORE, Brevet Major (Temporary Lieut.-Colonel), was born 18 Sept. 1878, at Wetheringsett Manor, Suffolk, son of Henry Brooke (deceased), who served in the 42nd Highlanders, and Dulcibella, daughter of the late Rev. Robert Moore. He was educated at Haileybury and Sandhurst, and at the Staff College, and was gazetted to the Oxfordshire Light Infantry 7 May, 1898, becoming Lieutenant 24 Nov. 1899; Captain 9 Nov. 1904. He was D.A.A. and Q.M.G., Royal Flying Corps, B.E.F., 5 Aug. to 19 Nov. 1914; G.S.O.1, Royal Flying Corps, B.E.F., 26 May, 1915, to 11 March, 1916; D.A. and Q.M.G., Royal Flying Corps, British Armies in France, 12 March, 1916, to 8 Oct. 1917; D.Q.M.G., Royal Flying Corps, British Armies in France, 9 Oct. 1917, to 31 March, 1918; employed under the Air Ministry 1 April, 1918 (Temporary Brigadier-General). He was given the Brevet of Major 3 Sept.

H. R. M. Brooke-Popham.

1913. For his services in the European War, 1914–18, he was several times mentioned in Despatches; was given the Brevets of Lieutenant-Colonel 3 June, 1916, and Colonel 3 June, 1918; awarded the Legion of Honour (Officier); the Order of St. Stanislaus, and the Air Force Cross; created a C.B., a C.M.G. and a Companion of the Distinguished Service Order [London Gazette, 23 June, 1915]: "Henry Robert Moore Brooke-Popham, Brevet Major (Temporary Lieut.-Colonel), Oxfordshire and Buckinghamshire Light Infantry, and Royal Flying Corps. For distinguished service in the field." In 1904, by Royal Licence, he assumed the additional surname of Popham.

CARTHEW, THOMAS WALTER COLBY, Capt., was born 1 July, 1880. He entered the Northumberland Fusiliers in 1901 and retired in 1909. He served in South Africa, 1899–1902 (Queen's Medal with three clasps; King's Medal with two clasps). He served in the European War in 1914 and 1915, and was created a Companion of the Distinguished Service Order [London Gazette, 23 June, 1915]: "Thomas Walter Colby Carthew, Capt., Bedfordshire Regt. and Royal Flying Corps. For distinguished service in the field." He was called to the Bar in 1909, and contested South-West Ham (U.), in 1910.

WARD, ALBERT LAMBERT, Major, was born 7 Nov. 1876, only son of A. B. Ward, J.P. He was educated at St. Paul's School, in Paris, and at Darmstadt, and was commissioned in the Honourable Artillery Company in 1902, becoming Lieutenant in 1904; Captain in 1912; Major in 1914, and Lieutenant-Colonel in 1916; Second-in-Command in 1915. He served in the European War, with the Expeditionary Force in Flanders, 1914–15; was present at the operations on the Aisne; Ypres in 1914; Neuve Chapelle in 1914, and Ypres in 1915; was wounded twice, mentioned in Despatches twice, and created a Companion of the Distinguished Service Order [London Gazette, 23 June, 1915]: "Albert Lambert Ward, Major, Honourable Artillery Company. For distinguished service in the field." He commanded the 2nd Battn. H.A.C., during the operations on the Aisne, and during the advance of 1915; was wounded, and mentioned in Despatches. Lieut.-Colonel A. L. Ward contested West Hull (C.), Dec. 1910; was Conservative candidate for Burnley, 1912–13; was elected M.P. (C.U.) for Kingston-on-Hull in 1918. He is joint author of the "H.A.C. History of the European War, 1914–1918."

ARTHUR, JOHN MAURICE, Major, joined the Territorial Forces, and served in the European War. He was created a Companion of the Distinguished Service Order [London Gazette, 23 June, 1915]: "John Maurice Arthur, Major, 1st Lowland Field Artillery, Territorial Force. For distinguished service in the field." He was promoted to Lieutenant-Colonel, and was created a C.M.G. in 1918.

VARWELL, EDWARD HERON, Major, was born 18 Sept. 1879, son of Hawkins B. Varwell, of Chagford, Devon. He served in the European War, 1914–19; was mentioned in Despatches, and created a Companion of the Distinguished Service Order [London Gazette, 23 June, 1915]: "Edward Heron Varwell, Major, Wessex Divisional Signal Company, Royal Engineers, Territorial Force. For distinguished service in the field." Major Varwell married, in 1910, Winifred Janet, daughter of George S. Vinen, and they have two daughters.

GEMMILL, WILLIAM, Major, was born 4 Sept. 1878, son of William Gemmill, of Greendykes, East Lothian, and Elizabeth Cuninghame, daughter of the late David Cuninghame, of Chapleton, Ayrshire. He was educated at Watson's College, Edinburgh, and joined the Lothians and Berwickshire Imperial Yeomanry in Dec. 1899, serving in South Africa, 1899–1901 (Queen's Medal with four clasps). He joined the 8th Battn. the Royal Scots (formerly 7th Volunteer Battn. Royal

Scots), as Lieutenant, in April, 1904; became Captain, 1910; and proceeded to France in Nov. 1914, as Second-in-Command of the 1/8th Royal Scots (Temporary Major), and was Temporary Lieutenant-Colonel from 19 May, 1915. He was mentioned in Despatches [London Gazette, 31 May, 1915, and 1 Jan. 1916], and was created a Companion of the Distinguished Service Order [London Gazette, 23 June, 1915]: "William Gemmill, Major, 8th Battn. Royal Scots (T.F.). For distinguished service in the field."

William Gemmill.

Lieut.-Colonel Gemmill wrote about L.-Corpl. Angus, V.C.: "Angus was one of 120 men of the 8th Battn. Highland Light Infantry attached and posted to the 8th Royal Scots for the duration of the war; in fact, they were transferred to this battalion, but not at the time Angus was awarded the V.C. The 8th Highland Light Infantry did not volunteer for foreign service as a unit, and these men were sent to this battalion to complete its establishment when it was ordered to France at the end of Oct. 1914. My point is that I consider that Angus' V.C. should be included in the list of Honours awarded to the Royal Scots. I was in command of the battn. at the time, and sent in the official account of the act."

Lieut.-Colonel Gemmill is a Justice of the Peace for the County of East Lothian, and a member of the Territorial Force County Association.

FARGUS, NIGEL HARRY SKINNER, Capt., was born 2 July, 1881, son of Henry Robert Fargus. He was educated at Rugby and Sandhurst, and was gazetted to the Royal Scots 20 Jan. 1900, becoming Lieutenant 1 Sept. 1901; Captain 9 Sept. 1908; Major 1 Sept. 1915; Temporary Lieutenant-Colonel, commanding the 12th Battn. Royal Scots, 15 July, 1916, to 10 April, 1917. He was G.S.O.3, 3rd Division, New Armies, B.E.F., 11 June, 1915, to 6 March, 1916; Brigade Major, 74th Infantry Brigade, B.E.F., British Armies in France, 7 March to 21 July, 1916; D.A.A.G., 7th Army Corps, British Armies in France, 10 Dec. 1913, to 9 March, 1919; D.A.A.G., 2nd Army Corps, British Armies in France, 10 March, 1919. He served in South Africa, 1899–1902; took part in the operations in the Orange Free State, Feb. to May, 1900; in the Transvaal, east of Pretoria, July to 29 Nov. 1900, including actions at Belfast (26 and 27 Aug.) and Lydenberg (5 to 8 Sept.); in Orange River Colony, May to 29 Nov. 1900; in Cape Colony, south of Orange River, 1899–1900; also again during the operations in the Transvaal, 30 Nov. 1900, to April, 1902 (Queen's Medal with three clasps, and King's Medal with two clasps). For his services in the European War he was mentioned in Despatches, and created a Companion of the Distinguished Service Order [London Gazette, 23 June, 1915]: "Nigel Harry Skinner Fargus, Capt., 8th Battn. Royal Scots. For distinguished service in the field." Major Fargus married, in 1915, Lottie, daughter of Wilfred Trimmer, and they have one son.

REDDIE, ANTHONY JULIAN, Major, was born at Stonehaven 27 Aug. 1873, son of Capt. J. G. Reddie (deceased), of Redhouse, Fife, and Isabella Louisa Reddie (née Murray). He was educated at Cargilfield, Fettes College, and Sandhurst; was in the Football Fifteen at Fettes, 1889–90, and in the Sandhurst Fifteen, 1890–91–92. He was in the regimental polo team, 1st South Wales Borderers, 1893–1909; won the Infantry Cup in Egypt, 1893–94; Gibraltar, 1895–96; the Infantry Cup, India, 1898, and several smaller tournaments. He won the Medal at Gibraltar, 1896–97, for best man-at-arms, and has done a lot of big game shooting in the Central Provinces, Himalayas and Kashmir, also fishing. He entered the South Wales Borderers 19 Nov. 1892; became Lieutenant 1 July, 1895; was Adjutant, South Wales Borderers, 2 Sept. 1901, to 1 Sept. 1904; was promoted to Captain 22 Sept. 1901; was Temporary Lieutenant-Colonel, South Wales Borderers, 1 Dec. 1914, to 20 Aug. 1915; Temporary Brigadier-General from 23 Aug. 1915. He was Adjutant, T.F., 17 Nov. 1909, to 16 March, 1913; commanded the 1st Infantry Brigade, British Expeditionary Force, British Armies in France, 23 Aug. 1915, to 9 Nov. 1917; commanded the Welsh Reserve Infantry Brigade, Home Forces, 10 Nov. 1917, to 2 April, 1918; commanded the 187th Infantry Brigade, British Armies in France, 3 April, 1918. He went to France in Aug. 1914, as Senior Major, 1st South Wales Borderers, and took over temporary command from 1 Nov. 1914, to 21 Aug. 1915. He was with the 1st Division throughout the War, and in all their operations. For his services in the European War, 1914–19, he was six times mentioned in Despatches; was given the Brevet of Lieutenant-Colonel 1 Jan. 1916; was created a C.M.G. in 1919, and created a Companion of the Distinguished Service Order [London Gazette, 23 June, 1915]: "Anthony Julian Reddie, Major, South Wales Borderers. For distinguished service in the field." He also received the Légion d'Honneur pour Officier, and the Order of St. Stanislas, 3rd Class. Lieut.-Colonel A. J. Reddie married, 5 Jan. 1906, in Lucknow, Rose Robertson Murray, eldest daughter of Colonel R. D. Murray, late I.M.S.

MACLEAR, HARRY, Major, was gazetted to the East Lancashire Regt. 18 March, 1891; became Lieutenant 3 April, 1892; Captain 11 May, 1900, and Major 9 March, 1910. He served in the Chitral Campaign in 1895, with the Relief Force (Medal with clasp). Served on the North-West Frontier of India, 1897–98 (Malakand; clasp). Served in East Africa, 1903–4; commanded the 9th Somali Camel Corps from 20 Dec. 1903. Took part in the operations in Somaliland; Special Service Officer, Assistant to Base Supply and Transport Officer, Berbera (from Nov. 1903) (Medal with clasp). Major Maclear served in the European War, and was created a Companion of the Distinguished Service Order [London Gazette, 23 June,

1915]: "Harry Maclear, Major, East Lancashire Regt. For distinguished service in the field." He was killed in action in France 7 March, 1916.

CAMPBELL, C. H., Capt., served in the European War, and was created a Companion of the Distinguished Service Order [London Gazette, 23 June, 1915]: "C. H. Campbell, Capt., Canadian Highlanders. For distinguished service in the field." Capt. Campbell was invested by the King at Windsor Castle on 6 July, 1915. He was killed in action in France 14 March, 1916.

BATES, ARTHUR SYDNEY, Major, was born 18 June, 1879, son of S. E. Bates, of Manydown Park, Basingstoke, and Elizabeth J., daughter of Lieut.-Colonel G. G. Malet, 3rd Queen's Own Bombay Light Infantry. He was educated at Winchester College; served in the European War, 1914-18, as Temporary Lieutenant-Colonel, 1915, and was promoted to Lieutenant-Colonel, 1917. He commanded the London Rifle Brigade 17 months, and the 3/5th Battn. Loyal North Lancashire Regt. (T.F.) for 10 months; in France he commanded the 4th (Reserve) Battn. Loyal North Lancashire Fusiliers (T.F.), till disbandment. He was mentioned four times in Despatches; received the French Croix de Guerre with Palm, and was created a Companion of the Distinguished Service Order [London Gazette, 23 June, 1915]: "Arthur Sydney Bates, Major, 5th City of London Regt., London Rifle Brigade, Territorial Force. For distinguished service in the field." He is a Fellow of the Royal Philatelic Society, London. Lieut.-Colonel Bates married, in 1905, Mary da Costa, daughter of Lieut.-Colonel Charles Robert Crosse, C.M.G., M.V.O., and Catherine, only daughter of the late Major-General Whitworth Porter, R.E., and they have one daughter.

PAGE, FRANK, Major, joined the 1st Battn. Hertfordshire Regt.;

Frank Page.

became Lieutenant 9 July, 1904; was promoted to Captain and to Major. He served in the European War, and was created a Companion of the Distinguished Service Order [London Gazette, 23 June, 1915]: "Frank Page, Major, The Hertfordshire Regt. (T.F.). For distinguished service in the field." Lieut.-Colonel Page was killed in action in Aug. 1917, leaving a widow and three children. A Bar to his D.S.O. was awarded for his work on the Ancre. He served with great efficiency through the South African War.

INGLEFIELD, LIONEL DALTON, Major, was born 15 Sept. 1881. He entered the Royal Garrison Regt. 28 Jan. 1903; became Second Lieutenant, A.S.C., 9 Oct. 1905; Lieutenant 9 Oct. 1906; Captain 22 Dec. 1911; Major, R.A.S.C., 30 Oct. 1914; was Temporary Lieutenant-Colonel 20 Nov. 1917, to 31 Dec. 1918. He was D.A.D. of Transport, B.E.F., British Armies in France, 24 Feb. 1915, to 19 Nov. 1917; Assistant Director of Transport, British Armies in France, 20 Nov. 1917. He served in the South African War, 1899-1902; took part in the operations in the Orange Free State, Feb. to May, 1900; in Orange River Colony, May to 29 Nov. 1900, including actions at Lindley 26 June, Bethlehem, 6 and 7 July, and Wittebergen 1 to 29 July; was present during the operations in Cape Colony and Orange River Colony 30 Nov. 1900, to 31 May, 1902 (Queen's Medal with two clasps, and King's Medal with two clasps). For his services in the Great War, from 1914, he was mentioned in Despatches; was given the Brevet of Lieutenant-Colonel 1 Jan. 1919, and created a Companion of the Distinguished Service Order [London Gazette, 23 June, 1915]: "Lionel Dalton Inglefield, Major, A.S.C. For distinguished service in the field."

BLADES, WALTER WILLIAM, Major, was born 14 April, 1863, son of the late Lieut.-Colonel Joel Blades, R.A. He was commissioned in the Army 1 April, 1901, and became Deputy Commissary of Ordnance and Hon. Captain 4 Feb. 1909; Major 31 Jan. 1915, and Commissary of Ordnance, and retired 1 May, 1919. He served in the South African War, 1899-1901; took part in the operations in Cape Colony south of Orange River, Oct. 1899, to 29 Nov. 1900; again in Cape Colony 30 Nov. 1900, to Dec. 1901 (Despatches [London Gazette, 10 Sept. 1901]; Queen's Medal with two clasps). For his services in the European War he was created a Companion of the Distinguished Service Order [London Gazette, 23 June, 1915]: "Walter William Blades, Honorary Major, Army Ordnance Department. For distinguished service in the field." Major Blades married Janet Stoddart in 1914.

DANIELL, JOHN ACHESON STAINES, Capt., was born 7 May, 1882, son of Colonel W. S. Daniell, 105th Yorkshire Light Infantry. He was gazetted to the Yorkshire Light Infantry 8 May, 1901; became Lieutenant 20 June, 1904, and was transferred to the Indian Army 22 Dec. 1905, becoming Captain 8 May, 1910; Temporary Major, 6th Battn. Yorkshire Regt., 29 Oct. 1914, to 31 July, 1915; Acting Major, Indian Army, 1-2 Aug. 1915; Major 8 May, 1916. He served in the European War, 1914-15; was twice mentioned in Despatches, and created a Companion of the Distinguished Service Order [London Gazette, 23 June, 1915]: "John Acheson Staines Daniell, Capt., 14th King George's Own Ferozepore Sikhs, Indian Army. For distinguished service in the field." Major Daniell married, in 1916, Ellen Mary, only daughter of S. Taylor, and they have two daughters.

HANNYNGTON, JOHN ARTHUR, Major, entered the Army 8 June, 1889; became Lieutenant 17 Dec. 1891; Captain 8 June, 1900, and Major 8 June, 1907. He served in East Africa, 1895-96, during operations against the Mazrui Rebels (Medal). Served in Uganda, 1897-98 (severely wounded; Medal with clasp). Major Hannyngton served in the European War, and was created a Companion of the Distinguished Service Order [London Gazette, 23 June, 1915]: "John Arthur Hannyngton, C.M.G., Major,

129th Duke of Connaught's Own Baluchis, Indian Army. For distinguished service in the field." Brigadier-General J. A. Hannyngton died 21 Aug. 1918.

BURLAND, WILLIAM WATT, Lieut.-Colonel, was born 9 Sept. 1877, son of the late Lieut.-Colonel William Benjamin Burland, M.D., C.M. He became Lieutenant, Canadian Military Forces, 1895; Captain, 1903; Major, 1910, and Lieutenant-Colonel 12 Sept. 1912. He served in the European War, 1914-15; was mentioned in Despatches, and created a Companion of the Distinguished Service Order [London Gazette, 23 June, 1915]: "William Watt Burland, Lieut.-Colonel, 14th Canadian Battn. For distinguished service in the field."

William Watt Burland.

HUGHES, GARNET BURK, Lieut.-Colonel, was born 22 April, 1880, only son of Lieut.-General the Hon. Sir Sam Hughes, K.C.B., and Mary, daughter of H. W. Burk. He was educated at the Royal Military College of Canada, and joined the Military Forces, serving on the 1st Division Staff; as Brigade Major, 3rd Infantry Brigade, 1st Canadian Division; as G.S.O.2, 2nd Canadian Division, 1915. He served in the European War, 1914-17; was four times mentioned in Despatches, and created a Companion of the Distinguished Service Order [London Gazette, 23 June, 1915]: "Garnet Burk Hughes, Lieut.-Colonel, 1st Canadian Division, Staff. For distinguished service in the field." He was created a C.M.G. in 1917, and a C.B. in 1918, and was Temporary Brigadier-General in command of the 1st Infantry Brigade, 1st Canadian Division, Nov. 1915, to Feb. 1917. He is married, and has one son.

BETTY, HUBERT KEMMIS, Lieut.-Colonel, was born 27 Nov. 1872. He joined the Canadian Militia in 1896; became Lieutenant, Permanent Forces, 1899; Captain, 1905, and Major, 1910; Lieutenant-Colonel, 1st Division Staff. He served in the European War, 1914-18; as Brigade Major, 2nd Canadian Infantry Brigade; Officer in charge of Records, and Director of Personal Services, and was mentioned in Despatches, and created a Companion of the Distinguished Service Order [London Gazette, 23 June, 1915]: "Hubert Kemmis Betty, Lieut.-Colonel, 1st Canadian Division, Staff. For distinguished service in the field." Lieut.-Colonel H. Kemmis Betty married, in 1907, Ethel Antoinette, daughter of the late C. W. P. Watts, I.C.S., and they have one son.

LOOMIS, FREDERICK OSCAR WARREN, Lieut.-Colonel, joined the Canadian Military Forces. He served in the European War, 1914-18; commanded the 13th Canadian Infantry Battn., Royal Highlanders of Canada, and afterwards the 7th Canadian Infantry Brigade; the 2nd Canadian Infantry Brigade, and the 3rd Canadian Division. He was six times mentioned in Despatches; was created a C.M.G. in 1917; a C.B., 1918; a K.C.B., 1919; received the Légion d'Honneur, Croix d'Officier; the Order of Leopold (Commandeur); the Auxiliary Forces Officers' Decoration, and was created a Companion of the Distinguished Service Order [London Gazette, 23 June, 1915]: "Frederick Oscar Warren Loomis, Lieut.-Colonel, 13th Canadian Battn. For distinguished service in the field." He was awarded a Bar to the D.S.O., and was promoted to Major-General.

BALLANTINE, JAMES, Major, was born at Georgetown, Ontario, Canada, 3 Sept. 1876, son of John and Margaret M'Nab Ballantine. He was educated at Georgetown, and joined the Canadian Military Forces 21 Oct. 1891. He served in the European War, 1914-16, and was created a Companion of the Distinguished Service Order [London Gazette, 23 June, 1915]: "James Ballantine, Major, 4th Canadian Battn. For distinguished service in the field." He later was promoted to Lieutenant-Colonel, and commanded the 76th Battn. Canadian Expeditionary Force. Lieut.-Colonel Ballantine married, in 1905, Minnie E. Barber.

James Ballantine.

GODSON-GODSON, GILBERT, Major was born 13 Aug. 1872, son of the late Major Godson-Godson, of Redhill, Surrey. He was educated at Whitgift and in H.M.S. Worcester, and served in the South African War, 1898-1902, including the Siege of Ladysmith; was wounded, and received the Queen's Medal with four clasps and the King's Medal with two clasps. In 1906 he served during the Natal Native Rebellion, and received a Medal. He joined the Canadian Military Forces, and served in the European War, 1914-15, and was created a Companion of the Distinguished Service Order [London Gazette, 23 June, 1915]: "Gilbert Godson-Godson, Major, 16th Canadian Battn. For distinguished service in the field." Major Godson-Godson married, in 1891, Alice Maud Burchall, of Maritzburg, Natal, and they have one son and one daughter.

Gilbert Godson-Godson.

KING, WILLIAM BIRCHALL MACAULAY, Major, joined the Canadian Military Forces. He served in C Battery, R.C.F.A. in the South African War in 1900, and in the South African Constabulary, 1901–2 (Queen's Medal and four clasps ; King's Medal and two clasps). For his services in the European War, 1914–18, he was mentioned in Despatches ; was made Officier de l'Ordre de la Couronne, Belgium ; received the Croix de Guerre ; the Colonial Long Service Officers' Decoration ; was created a C.M.G. in 1918, and a Companion of the Distinguished Service Order [London Gazette, 23 June, 1915] : "William Birchall Macaulay King, Major, 10th Battery, 3rd Canadian Artillery Brigade. For distinguished service in the field." He became Brigadier-General, C.R.A., 4th Canadian Divisional Artillery.

LISTER, FREDERICK ALEXANDER, Major, was born 17 Sept. 1873, son of the late J. F. Lister, Judge of Court of Appeal, Toronto. He served in the European War, 1914–17 ; was mentioned in Despatches, and created a Companion of the Distinguished Service Order [London Gazette, 23 June, 1915] : "Frederick Alexander Lister, Major, Canadian Divisional Signal Company. For distinguished service in the field." Major Lister married, in 1905, Annie Hutton, eldest daughter of the late John Watson, of Saltcoats.

MARSHALL, W. R., Major, served in the European War. He was created a Companion of the Distinguished Service Order [London Gazette, 23 June, 1915] : "W. R. Marshall, Major, 15th Canadian Battn. For distinguished service in the field." He was killed in action 20 May, 1916.

MATTHEWS, H. H., Major, served in the European War, and was created a Companion of the Distinguished Service Order [London Gazette, 23 June, 1915] : "H. H. Matthews, Major, 8th Canadian Battn. For distinguished service in the field."

PRAGNELL, G. S. T., Major, was born in 1880, son of G. W. Pragnell. He entered the Sherwood Foresters, retired, and joined the Canadian Forces. He served in the South African War, 1901–2. For his services in the European War, 1914–16, he was mentioned in Despatches and was created a Companion of the Distinguished Service Order [London Gazette, 23 June, 1915] : "G. S. T. Pragnell, Major, 5th Canadian Battn. For distinguished service in the field." Major Pragnell married, in 1912, M. E. Tyler, of Cossington Hall, Leicester.

ARTHUR, CHRISTOPHER GEOFFREY, Capt., was born 27 Jan. 1882. He served in the European War, 1914–18 ; was mentioned in Despatches, and created a Companion of the Distinguished Service Order [London Gazette, 23 June, 1915] : "Christopher Geoffrey Arthur, Capt., 10th Canadian Battn. For distinguished service in the field." Major Arthur married, in 1917, Eirene Primrose Dodd, of The Grange, Buxton, and they have one daughter.

CHISHOLM, HUGH ALEXANDER, Capt. (Temporary Major), was born 8 Feb. 1883, son of Duncan Chisholm, of Tynwood, Nova Scotia. He served in the European War, 1914–17 (as A.D.M.S., Canadian Division, from 1916). He was mentioned in Despatches, and created a Companion of the Distinguished Service Order [London Gazette, 23 June, 1915] : "Hugh Alexander Chisholm, Capt. (Temporary Major), Canadian Army Medical Corps. For distinguished service in the field." He was created a C.M.G. in 1919. Colonel Chisholm married, in 1910, Mary Eulalia, daughter of the Hon. Peter Smyth.

MACBRIEN, JAMES HOWDEN, Capt. (Temporary Lieut.-Colonel), was born 30 June, 1878. He served in the South African War, 1900–2, and received the Queen's Medal with five clasps. In 1907 he married Nellie Louise, daughter of William Ross, and they have three sons and one daughter. For his services in the European War, 1914–18, he was promoted to Brigadier-General ; was mentioned in Despatches ; created a C.B., 1919 ; a C.M.G., 1918 ; was created a Companion of the Distinguished Service Order [London Gazette, 23 June, 1915] : "James Howden MacBrien, Capt. (Temporary Lieutenant-Colonel), 1st Canadian Division, Staff. For distinguished service in the field." He was awarded a Bar to the D.S.O., and was promoted to Major-General.

James Howden MacBrien.

MACPHAIL, ALEXANDER, Capt., was born in 1870, son of the late William Macphail and Catherine Macphail (née Moore Smith). He was appointed Professor of Engineering at Queen's University, Kingston, Canada. From 1914 to 1918 he served in the European War, as Officer Commanding the 1st Canadian Division Engineers, B.E.F. ; was mentioned in Despatches, and created a Companion of the Distinguished Service Order [London Gazette, 23 June, 1915] : "Alexander Macphail, Capt., 1st Field Company, Canadian Engineers. For distinguished service in the field." He was created a C.M.G. in 1919. Lieut.-Colonel Macphail married Agnes Mary, daughter of the late Ven. J. Macmorine, Archdeacon of Ontario, and they have one son.

M'KILLIP, THOMAS HENRY, Capt., was born 20 July, 1887. He served in the European War, 1914–17 ; was mentioned in Despatches, and created a Companion of the Distinguished Service Order [London Gazette, 23 June, 1915] : "Thomas Henry M'Killip, Capt., Canadian Army Medical Corps. For distinguished service in the field."

PARKS, JOHN HEGAN, Capt., served in the South African War, 1900–2. He served in the European War, 1914–15, and was created a Companion of the Distinguished Service Order [London Gazette, 23 June, 1915] : "John Hegan Parks, Capt., 1st Canadian Battn. For distinguished service in the field." Capt. Parks was awarded the Order of the White Eagle (Serbia), 4th Class, in 1917.

London Gazette, 29 June, 1915.—"War Office, 29 June, 1915. His Majesty the King has been graciously pleased to approve of the appointment of the undermentioned Officers to be Companions of the Distinguished Service Order, in recognition of their gallantry and devotion to duty in the field."

McCUAIG, DOUGLAS RYKERT, Major, was born 25 April, 1883, and is of British (Canadian) parentage. He is the son of Clarence J. McCuaig, of Montreal. He was educated at McGill College, Montreal, and is by profession a Stockbroker. He married Nora Balfe, and they have one son. From 1914 to 1916 he served in the European War ; was mentioned in Despatches ; was severely wounded, and captured at the Second Battle of Ypres, and (for Ypres) was created a Companion of the Distinguished Service Order [London Gazette, 29 June, 1915] : "Douglas Rykert McCuaig, Major, 13th Canadian Battn. In recognition of gallantry and devotion to duty in the field."

WRIGHT, GORDON BROOKS, Major, served in the European War, and was created a Companion of the Distinguished Service Order [London Gazette, 29 June, 1915] : "Gordon Brooks Wright, Major, 3rd Field Company, Canadian Engineers. In recognition of gallantry and devotion to duty in the field." He was killed in action 23 June, 1915.

MALLINSON, HENRY, Capt., was born 26 July, 1879. He was gazetted to the Yorkshire Light Infantry 20 May, 1899 ; became Lieutenant 17 Feb. 1900 ; Captain 1 Feb. 1906 ; Major 1 Sept. 1915, and was Temporary Lieutenant-Colonel, Yorkshire Light Infantry, from 2 April, 1916. He served in the South African War, 1899–1902, and took part in the advance on Kimberley, including actions at Belmont, Enslin, Modder River and Magersfontein ; in the Transvaal, west of Pretoria, Aug. to 29 Nov. 1900 ; in Orange River Colony, May to Aug. 1900, including actions at Lindley (26 June), Bethlehem (6 and 7 July) and Wittebergen (1 to 29 July) ; again in the Transvaal 30 Nov. 1900, to 31 May, 1902. He was mentioned in Despatches [London Gazette, 10 Sept. 1901] ; received the Queen's Medal with four clasps, and the King's Medal with two clasps. For his services in the European War, 1914–17, he was mentioned in Despatches twice ; was given the Brevet of Lieutenant-Colonel 1 Jan. 1917, and created a Companion of the Distinguished Service Order [London Gazette, 29 June, 1915] : "Henry Mallinson, Capt., Yorkshire Light Infantry. In recognition of gallantry and devotion to duty in the field."

London Gazette, 30 June, 1915.—"Admiralty, S.W., 30 June, 1915. The King has been graciously pleased to give orders for the following appointment to the Distinguished Service Order of the undermentioned Officer, in recognition of his services as mentioned. To be a Companion of the Distinguished Service Order."

KERR, CHARLES LESTER, Lieut.-Commander, Royal Navy, was born in 1886, only son of Capt. Schomberg Kerr, Rifle Brigade. He entered the Royal Navy. In 1908 he married Innes, daughter of the late Colonel Archer Chapman, R.F.A., and they have one son. From 1914 to 1918 he served in the European War. He was created a Companion of the Distinguished Service Order [London Gazette, 30 June, 1915] : "Charles Lester Kerr, Lieut.-Commander, Royal Navy. He was in command of a picket-boat which reconnoitred the position of the Austrian monitors on the Danube in April, 1915, and torpedoed one of them under heavy fire, the enterprise being boldly and skilfully conducted." He was mentioned in Despatches ; received the Order of Kara-George (Serbia) with Swords, 1915 ; the Order of the White Eagle (Serbia), 1916 ; the Croix de Guerre, 1917 ; was made Cavalier of the Order of the Crown of Italy in 1919.

Charles Lester Kerr.

London Gazette, 3 July, 1915 —"War Office, 3 July, 1915. His Majesty the King has been pleased to approve of the appointment of the undermentioned Officers to be Companions of the Distinguished Service Order, in recognition of their gallantry and devotion to duty whilst serving with the Expeditionary Force."

BORTON, AMYAS EDEN, Capt., was born 20 Sept. 1886, son of Lieut.-Colonel Arthur C. Borton, J.P., of Cheveney ; and grandson of the late Sir Arthur Borton, G.C.B., G.C.M.G. He is a brother of Lieut.-Colonel A. D. Borton, V.C., C.M.G., D.S.O., and a nephew of Colonel C. E. Borton, C.B. He entered the Royal Highlanders 23 May, 1906 ; became Lieutenant 23 Nov. 1907 ; was Lieutenant, Royal Flying Corps, 28 April, 1914, to 31 March, 1918 ; Temporary Captain, Royal Highlanders, 29 Sept. to 28 Nov. 1914 ; was promoted to Captain 29 Nov. 1914 ; was Temporary Major 27 Oct. 1915, to 31 July, 1916 ; Temporary Lieutenant-Colonel 1 Aug. 1916, to 20 Nov. 1917 ; Temporary Colonel 21 Nov. 1917, to 27 Jan. 1918 ; Temporary Brigadier-General 28 Jan.to 31 March, 1918. He held a Special Appointment, Royal Flying Corps, M.W., 21 Nov. 1917, to 27 Jan. 1918 ; was Brigade Commander, Palestine Brigade, Royal Flying Corps, Egyptian Expeditionary Force, 28 Jan. to 31 March, 1918 ; was employed under the Air Ministry from 1 April, 1918. In 1918 he flew from England to Calcutta in a Handley-Page aeroplane. He served in the European War, 1914–18 ; was severely wounded ; was given the Brevet of Lieutenant-Colonel ; received the 3rd Class Order of St. Stanislas (with Swords) ; the 3rd Class Order of the Nile ; was created a C.M.G., 1919 ; was awarded the D.F.C., and was created a Companion of the Distinguished Service Order [London Gazette, 3 July, 1915] : "Amyas Eden Borton, Capt.,

(The Black Watch) Royal Highlanders, attached Royal Flying Corps. When on flying reconnaissance over the neighbourhood of Staden on 7 June, 1915, Capt. Borton was wounded in the head and neck by a bullet fired from a hostile aeroplane, and although suffering severely from loss of blood, he continued, with the assistance of the Observer, Capt. Marshall, to bandage his wounds, and completed the reconnaissance on the prescribed course. His injuries are such that he is not yet out of danger. Capt. Marshall continued his observations after rendering all possible aid to the Pilot, who was gradually losing consciousness, notwithstanding that the German aeroplane was persistently attacking. The valuable report supplied by this Officer is as detailed and complete for the last as it is for the first part of the reconnaissance."

MARSHALL, ANTHONY, Capt., was born 4 April, 1882, son of Lieut.-Colonel Anthony Marshall (late of the 3rd Northumberland Fusiliers), of Amstead, Chatbill. He was educated at Edinburgh Academy and Sandhurst; entered the Northumberland Fusiliers 18 Jan. 1902, and became Lieutenant, Indian Army, 10 May, 1904; Captain, 18 Jan. 1911; was Adjutant, Royal Flying Corps, 12 Aug. to 31 Nov. 1915, was promoted to Major, Indian Army, 18 Jan. 1917. He was Temporary G.S.O.2, India. He served in the South African War in 1902, and received the Queen's Medal with three clasps. He served in the European War, 1914–17; was wounded while on a flying reconnaissance; was mentioned in Despatches, and created a Companion of the Distinguished Servce Order [London Gazette, 3 July, 1915]: "Anthony Marshall, Capt., 28th Light Cavalry, Indian Army, attached Royal Flying Corps. When on flying reconnaissance over the neighbourhood of Staden on 7 June, 1915, Capt. Borton was wounded in the head and neck by a bullet fired from a hostile aeroplane, and although suffering severely from loss of blood he continued, with the assistance of the Observer, Capt. Marshall, to bandage his wounds, and completed the reconnaissance on the prescribed course. His injuries are such that he is not yet out of danger. Capt. Marshall continued his observations after rendering all possible aid to the Pilot, who was gradually losing consciousness, notwithstanding that the German aeroplane was persistently attacking. The valuable report supplied by this Officer is as detailed and complete for the last as it is for the first part of the reconnaissance."

George Harold A. Ing.

ING, GEORGE HAROLD ABSELL, Major, was born 24 April, 1880, eldest son of George Ing. He was gazetted to the 2nd Dragoon Guards 5 Sept. 1900; became Lieutenant 22 Feb. 1901; Captain 10 Feb. 1904; Major 5 Aug. 1911, and Lieutenant-Colonel 1 April, 1919. He served in the South African War, 1900–2; was wounded, and received the Queen's Medal with five clasps. In the European War he served from 1911 to 1918, commanding the North Somerset Yeomanry from March, 1917, to March, 1918; was wounded twice; four times mentioned in Despatches; created a C.M.G., and created a Companion of the Distinguished Service Order [London Gazette, 3 July, 1915]: "George Harold Absell Ing, Major, 2nd Dragoon Guards (Queen's Bays). At Ypres, on 13 May, 1915, when the line was broken beyond the right flank of his regiment, he came out of his trench in the front line, stood on the road in the open under heavy shell fire, stopped the retirement of 40 men of another unit, and turned them into his section of the defence. The good results of this gallant action were far reaching." He was awarded a Bar to the Distinguished Service Order.

MASON, PHILIP GRANVILLE, Major, entered the Army 29 May, 1895; became Lieutenant 11 Oct. 1899, and Captain 29 July, 1906. He served in the South African War, 1901–2, and took part in the operations in the Transvaal, Feb. and April to May, 1902; also in Orange River Colony, Jan. to April and May, 1902 (Queen's Medal with four clasps). Major Mason served in the European War, and was killed in action near Loos 26 Sept. 1915. He was created a Companion of the Distinguished Service Order [London Gazette, 3 July, 1915]: "Philip Granville Mason, Major, 3rd (Prince of Wales's) Dragoon Guards. Whilst in command of Hooge Fort and the adjoining trenches, he showed conspicuous gallantry and ability in holding the village and defence line allotted to him, notwithstanding a terrific bombardment for several hours every day from 30 May till 2 June, 1915, in which practically all his trenches and dug-outs were blown in."

ARCHDALE-PORTER, JOHN GREY, Capt., was born 9 June, 1886, at Magheracross, County Fermanagh, Ireland, son of John Porter Porter, J.P., D.L., and Josephine Porter. He was educated at Harrow; entered the Army 29 Aug. 1906, and became Lieutenant 22 Jan. 1910. Capt. Archdale-Porter served in the European War; was mentioned in Despatches 24 June, 1915, and created a Companion of the Distinguished Service Order [London Gazette, 3 July, 1915]: "John Grey Porter, Capt., 9th (Queen's Royal) Lancers. On 10 May, 1915, when a very heavy attack was made on the front line near Hooge, Capt. Porter went up to the infantry line there and brought back very valuable information regarding the situation. On the 13th May he rendered the greatest possible assistance in

John G. Archdale-Porter.

taking messages under terrific shell fire to various parts of the line and reporting on various local situations. He set an example of coolness and total disregard of danger that was beyond all praise. He has been twice wounded previously in this campaign." Capt. Archdale-Porter died of wounds 22 Nov. 1917. He married, 6 Dec. 1915, Enid, only daughter of the late George William Duff-Assheton-Smith, of Vaynol, Carnarvonshire.

CRICHTON, CHARLES WILLIAM HARRY, Lieut.-Colonel, was born 7 July, 1872, son of Colonel the Hon. Sir H. G. L. Crichton, K.C.B., third son of the 3rd Earl of Erne, and of his first wife, a daughter of Major A. W. Cole-Hamilton. He entered the 10th Hussars 7 Dec. 1895; became Lieutenant 25 June, 1897, Captain 18 Sept. 1901, Major 4 May, 1907, and Lieut.-Colonel 15 May, 1915. He served in the South African War, 1899–1900, and received the Queen's Medal with three clasps. Lieut.-Colonel Crichton served in the European War, 1914–15; was twice wounded, twice mentioned in Despatches, and created a Companion of the Distinguished Service Order [London Gazette, 3 July, 1915]: "Charles William Harry Crichton, Lieut.-Colonel, 10th (Prince of Wales's Own Royal) Hussars. Near Ypres, on 13 May, 1915, showed conspicuous gallantry and ability in collecting and rallying men who were retiring under heavy shell fire through the 10th Hussars' position. In our counter-attack he continued to direct operations, giving great encouragement to his men whilst he lay in the open under heavy shell fire with his leg shattered." Lieut.-Colonel Crichton married, in 1912, Dorothy Maud, daughter of the Hon. Eustace Dawnay, and they have two sons.

COLVILLE, JOHN ROSS, Major, was born 12 April, 1878, son of John Colville, of Polmont Park, Stirlingshire. He was educated at Rugby School and at Magdalen College, Oxford; entered the Royal Artillery 24 June, 1898; became Lieutenant 18 Feb. 1901, Captain 17 April, 1906, Major 30 Oct. 1914, and Lieut.-Colonel 2 Oct. 1918. He served in the South African War, 1900–2, and took part in the operations in Natal, April to June, 1900; in the Transvaal, east of Pretoria, July to Nov. 1900, including actions at Belfast (26 and 27 Aug.) and Lydenberg (5 to 8 Sept.). Lieut.-Colonel J. R. Colville married, in 1906, Kathleen, daughter of the late Surgeon-Major James Good, A.M.S. He served in the European War; was wounded; mentioned in Despatches five times; was given the Brevet of Lieut.-Colonel 1 Jan. 1917; was awarded the Italian Croce de Guerra; received the 1914 Star, and was created a Companion of the Distinguished Service Order [London Gazette, 3 July, 1915] "John Ross Colville, Major, 55th Battery, Royal Field Artillery. Commanded his battery with great gallantry during the operations 9 and 10 May, 1915, near Rouges Bancs, observing fire from an isolated tree close behind the trenches, which were being heavily shelled. This officer has been previously brought to notice for valuable work at Neuve Chapelle, when he observed fire from the ruined houses, and sent excellent information for 36 hours under continuous shell and rifle fire."

John Ross Colville.

RUSSELL, THE HON. BERTRAND JOSEPH, Capt., was born 12 Aug. 1876. He entered the Royal Artillery 21 Sept. 1896; became Lieutenant 21 Sept. 1899, and Captain 7 March, 1902; Major, Reserve of Officers, 16 Nov. 1915; Lieut.-Colonel, Army, 21 June, 1919; retired Royal Artillery 26 Feb. 1910. He served in the South African War in 1900; took part in the operations in the Transvaal, west of Pretoria, July to 29 Nov. 1900, including the action at Zilikat's Nek (Queen's Medal with three clasps). He served in the European War, 1914–18; was thrice wounded; mentioned in Despatches, and created a Companion of the Distinguished Service Order [London Gazette, 3 July, 1915]: "The Honourable Bertrand Joseph Russell, Capt. (Reserve of Officers), 104th Battery, Royal Field Artillery. On 9 May, 1915, near Rue Petillon (Fromelles), this officer commanded a section in the trenches, greatly helping the infantry. He was heavily shelled all day, the parapet in front of one gun being destroyed. They kept on firing, however, and the success was greatly due to the courage displayed by Capt. Russell, who was twice wounded early in the day." Lieut.-Colonel the Hon. B. J. Russell married, in 1902, Dorothy, daughter of the late John George Leeming.

MAXWELL, WILLIAM FREDERICK, Major, was born 11 April, 1878, son of Staff Capt. W. F. Maxwell, R.N. (deceased), and Mrs. M. A. Maxwell. He was educated at Appuldurcombe College, Isle of Wight; entered the Royal Engineers 23 Sept. 1897; became Lieutenant 23 Sept. 1900, Captain 23 Sept. 1906, and Major 30 Oct. 1914. He served in Aden, 1903–4, during the operations in the interior. For his services in the European War he was twice mentioned in Despatches in June, 1915, and was created a Companion of the Distinguished Service Order [London Gazette, 3 July, 1915]: "William Frederick Maxwell, Major, Royal Engineers (attached Lahore Divisional Signal Company). Near Ypres, during the operations from 24 April to 4 May, 1915, he rendered excellent service when responsible for maintaining the signalling communications of the division, under most trying circumstances. The work was very heavy, and he also had to direct the constant repair of lines cut by the continuous heavy fire. This officer has done consistently well throughout the campaign." Major Maxwell married Janet, daughter of A. Sanders and widow of Colonel J. H. Bowes-Wilson, West Riding Regt.

BEALL, EDWARD METCALFE, Major, was born in 1874. He was educated at Beaumont College, and served in South Africa, 1900–4, and during the war he was from 1900–2 employed with Mounted Infantry; took part in the operations in the Transvaal, March to 31 May, 1902; was present during the operations in Cape Colony, Feb. to March, 1902 (Queen's Medal with three clasps). He served in the European War, 1914–18; was created a C.M.G. in 1918, and a Companion of the Distinguished Service Order [London Gazette, 3 July, 1915]: "Edward Metcalfe Beall, Major, 4th Battn. The King's (Liverpool Regt.). For excellent work throughout the operations near Ypres from 24 April to 4 May, 1915, especially during the attack on 27 April, when he was with the leading company in the front line. He returned to Battalion Headquarters for reinforcements, and took them forward with him to the front line. He was also conspicuous in the attack on 1 May."

BONNER, SINGLETON, Capt., entered the Army 21 April, 1900; became Lieutenant 12 Oct. 1901, and Captain 1 April, 1908. He served in the South African War, 1899–1902; took part in the operations in Orange River Colony, Sept. to 29 Nov. 1900; in the Transvaal, and again in the Orange River Colony 30 Nov. 1900, to May, 1901, and Nov. 1901, to 31 May, 1902 (Queen's Medal with two clasps, and King's Medal with two clasps). Capt. Bonner served in the European War, and was created a Companion of the Distinguished Service Order [London Gazette, 3 July, 1915]: "Singleton Bonner, Capt., 1st Battn. The South Staffordshire Regt. For particularly good and gallant services rendered at Festubert from 16 to 18 May, 1915, when he showed a fine example in coolness, bravery and power of command." He died of wounds 23 April, 1917.

STREET, EDMUND ROCHFORT, Capt., was born 20 May, 1876, at London, Ontario, Canada, son of the

Edmund Rochfort Street.

Hon. William Purvis Rochfort Street, Justice of the Supreme Court of Judicature, Ontario (who died in 1906), and Eleanor, youngest daughter of the late Thomas Sheppard Smyth, of London, Ontario. He was educated at Upper Canada College, Toronto, and at the University of Toronto. On leaving Toronto University, he entered the 10th Royal Grenadiers (Canadian Militia), from which he was given a commission in the 1st Battn. Hampshire Regt. in Dec. 1897. He served on the North-West Frontier of India for two years, and subsequently exchanged into the 2nd Battn., joining it in the field in South Africa. Here he obtained the South African (Queen's) Medal with three clasps. After the South African War he was employed on garrison duty at Malta and Bermuda. He retired on grounds of health with the rank of Captain in 1906. On the outbreak of the European War in 1914, he offered his services to the War Office, and was given a commission in the 3rd Battn. Sherwood Foresters (Nottinghamshire and Derbyshire Regt.). He was subsequently attached to the 2nd Battn. in France in Jan. 1915. He was several times mentioned in Despatches, and in June, 1915, he was awarded the Distinguished Service Order for conspicuous good work under heavy fire, and for assisting in the rescue of men from a gassed mine. He was promoted Temporary Major at the end of 1915, and in the spring of 1916 he was in command of the battalion for three months. He was mortally wounded in action on the Somme on Sunday, 15 Oct. 1916, and died of his wounds the same day. He lies buried in the British Military Cemetery at Méaulte, near Albert. His Distinguished Service Order was gazetted 3 July, 1915: "Edmund Rochfort Street, Capt., 3rd Battn. The Sherwood Foresters (Nottinghamshire and Derbyshire Regt.). For conspicuous good work under heavy fire between 13 and 16 May, 1915, near Le Touquet, and for going down a gassed mine to assist in the rescue of men."

WOOD, PERCY, Capt., served in the European War, 1915–18, and was created a Companion of the Distinguished Service Order [London Gazette, 3 July, 1915]: "Percy Wood, Capt., 5th Battn. The Durham Light Infantry, Territorial Force. For conspicuous gallantry displayed in rallying troops under heavy bomb and hand-grenade fire, and for holding an advanced trench partly occupied by the enemy for four hours, until ordered to retire to a new line. He greatly impeded the enemy by building obstacles and entanglements in the trench down which the retirement took place." Capt. Wood is married, and has one son.

BURT-MARSHALL, DAVID BANNERMAN, Capt., was born 14 July, 1887, and was educated at Rugby and Sandhurst. He entered the Seaforth Highlanders 19 Sept. 1908; became Lieutenant, Seaforth Highlanders, 12 Oct. 1911; Army Signal Service 10 Sept. 1914, to 8 Jan. 1916; was promoted to Captain 26 April, 1915. He was G.S.O.3, 48th Division, B.E.F., 9 Jan. to 17 April, 1916; Brigade Major, 3rd Infantry Brigade, B.E.F., British Armies in France, 18 April, 1916, to 22 March, 1917; Brigade Major, 223rd Infantry Brigade, Home Forces, 16 June, 1917, to 13 April, 1918; G.S.O.2, G.H.Q., British Salonika Force, 14 April to 6 May, 1918; G.S.O.2, 22nd Division, British Salonika Force, 7 May, 1918. For his services in the European War he was four times mentioned in Despatches; was given the Brevet of Major 3 June, 1917; awarded the O.B.E., and created a Companion of the Distinguished Service Order [London Gazette, 3 July, 1915]: "David Bannerman Burt-Marshall, Capt., Seaforth Highlanders (Ross-shire Buffs, The Duke of Albany's), Signal Service. During the heavy fighting and gassing east of Ypres, early on the morning of 24 May, 1915, he was sent forward to get in touch with the front line and to remain there, keeping his Brigadier-General informed of the progress of events. This he did with conspicuous success, continually travelling over fire-swept ground to establish communication. Every Commanding Officer has brought his name to notice for the good work done on that day. His reports were valuable and always perfectly clear. He was wounded in the shoulder about midday, but continued to carry on his duties, not even waiting to have the wound dressed."

INGHAM, JOHN PATRICK MICHAEL, Capt., was born in 1884,

John P. M. Ingham.

eldest son of the late Joseph D. Ingham, of Drumany Montagh, Belturbet, and Dublin; and grandson of John Stannus Ingham, Solicitor, of Lisnamaine, County Cavan. He was educated at Belvedere College (S.J.), Dublin, and joined the Royal Munster Fusiliers from the Special Reserve 2 Oct. 1915; was Acting Major, Service Battn. Lancashire Fusiliers, 12 Sept. 1917; Temporary Major, Service Battn. Lancashire Fusiliers, 28 Aug. 1918; Acting Lieut.-Colonel, Service Battn. Lancashire Fusiliers, 6 Feb. to 11 Feb. 1919, and 27 Feb. 1919. Capt. Ingham served in the European War, 1914–18; was wounded, twice mentioned in Despatches, and created a Companion of the Distinguished Service Order [London Gazette, 3 July, 1915]: "John Patrick Michae Ingham, Capt., 4th Battn. The Connaught Rangers. On 26 April, 1915, in the action near Ypres, displayed great gallantry in leading his men forward beyond the last piece of cover, and when the few men who had reached him were finally stopped by very heavy close-range fire (most of them being wounded), exposed himself time after time in reorganizing them, and later in the afternoon in assisting in bringing under cover those who were helpless from their wounds. When night fell he was indefatigable in assisting to organize the defence of the line held. This officer has been brought to notice before for the excellence of his work since Oct. 1914."

CHRISTIE, GEORGE JAMES, Major, served in the European War, 1914–15, and was created a Companion of the Distinguished Service Order [London Gazette, 3 July, 1915]: "George James Christie, Major, 9th (The Dumbartonshire) Battn. Princess Louise's (Argyll and Sutherland Highlanders), Territorial Force. Showed conspicuous bravery in rallying his men near Wieltje on 24 May, 1915, and leading about 50 of them up to the front line through the gas and heavy shell fire. It is understood that this officer did excellent work on 10 May when attached to another brigade, but owing to his colonel being killed on that day his good work was not mentioned."

PLEYDELL-RAILSTON, HENRY GEORGE MORETON, Captain, was born at Hamilton, N.B., 27 Nov. 1895, son of Colonel Henry Edward Railston, late Cameronians, and of 23, Queen's Gate, London,

H. G. M. Pleydell-Railston.

S.W., and his wife, Magdalen, daughter of the Rev. C. E. and Lady Georgina Oakley, and granddaughter of the 2nd Earl of Ducie. He was educated at Wellington and Sandhurst; was gazetted to the Rifle Brigade as Second Lieutenant 13 Aug. 1904; became Lieutenant 24 April, 1908; was Adjutant, Special Reserve, 10 March, 1913, to 5 Feb. 1915, and was promoted to Captain 4 Oct. 1913. His record of active service is as follows: Served in France with 4th Division (1st Rifle Brigade), Feb. to July, 1915; Macedonia, Jan. 1916, to Dec. 1918, as Acting Staff Captain to Mounted Brigade; Staff Captain, 84th Infantry Brigade; Brigade Major, 30th Brigade, 10th Division (Irish); commanded Scottish Horse (13th Battn. Black Watch), April, 1917, to June, 1918; commanded 4th Battn. Rifle Brigade, June to Dec. 1918. His awards were: The Distinguished Service Order, Immediate Award, France, 1915; Brevet of Major 3 June, 1917; Brevet of Lieut.-Colonel 3 June, 1918; Croix de Guerre avec Palme, Sept. 1919; mentioned in Despatches 3 July, 1915, 1st Jan. 1916, 29 March, 1917, and 21 July, 1917. His Distinguished Service Order was gazetted 3 July, 1915: "Henry George Moreton Railston, Capt., 1st Battn. The Rifle Brigade (The Prince Consort's Own). For great gallantry at Hannebeck on 3 May, 1915. He was in command of a section of the front-line trench 200 yards long. The trench and all the traverses were smashed by shell fire, and all the garrison except three men killed or wounded. Capt. Railston had been slightly wounded and had been buried by a shell, but he continued to defend the trench, and displayed the greatest coolness throughout, keeping back the enemy with rapid fire. He held the trench with his small party for several hours, until it was impossible to reinforce him, and when the question of retirement was mooted he refused to entertain the suggestion." There is a very interesting account of Capt. Railston's gallantry on this occasion in "Deeds that thrill the Empire," published by Messrs. Hutchinson. Lieut.-Colonel Railston's younger brother, Lieut. Spencer Railston, of the 18th (King George's Own) Lancers, was at home on leave from India when war was declared, and succeeded in getting attached to the 4th Dragoon Guards, and went with them to France on 14 Aug. 1914. On 1 Nov. 1914, he lost his life in a most gallant attempt to rescue a wounded peasant woman, who in very heavy village fighting had got between the British and the German lines. Lieut. Railston left his cover to do this, and was almost immediately riddled with bullets from a machine gun. This heroic young officer, who joined the Army in 1907, was one of the many good all-round sportsmen who have given their lives for their country, a very fine horseman, a good polo player and big-game shot, and at one time champion light-weight boxer of India. Lieut.-Colonel Railston married, 22 April, 1919, at Brompton Parish Church, Vivien, eldest daughter of the late Lieut.-Colonel Mansel-Pleydell, 12th Lancers, and Mrs. Mansel-Pleydell, of Whatcombe, Dorset.

BOWEN, ALFRED JOHN HAMILTON, Capt., became Captain The Monmouthshire Regt. 1 July, 1910. He served in the European War, and was created a Companion of the Distinguished Service Order [London Gazette, 3 July, 1915]: "Alfred John Hamilton Bowen, Capt., 2nd Battn. The Monmouthshire Regt. (Territorial Force). On the 13th May, 1915, east of Ypres, though wounded in two places in the head before dawn, he refused to leave his company, and continued to command it with conspicuous ability. After the action was over and the battalion returned to La Brique, he was found to be suffering from two other wounds in the body. He was then sent to hospital." He was killed in action 2 March, 1917.

CLARK, WILLIAM GEORGE, Capt., was born 17 June, 1889, in London, son of Mr. and Mrs. W. H. Clark, of Roselawn, Bromley, Kent. He entered the 4th Battn. Royal Fusiliers; became Captain in 1914, and subsequently Major; served in the European War; was mentioned in Despatches in Oct. 1915, and created a Companion of the Distinguished Service Order [London Gazette, 3 July, 1915]: "William George Clark, Capt., 4th (City of London) Battn. The London Regt. (Royal Fusiliers), Territorial Force. Near Ypres, on 27 May, 1915, while under very heavy shell and rifle fire, he collected men of his own and other companies, gallantly led them forward and held the position he gained until ordered to retire after dark." Major Clark married, in 1914, Jessica, eldest daughter of Marcus A. Pettitt.

KIMBER, EDMUND GIBBS, Capt., was born 6 Aug. 1870, son of Edmund and Marion Kimber. He was educated at University College, London, and was called to the Bar at Lincoln's Inn in 1892; is a Member of the South-Eastern Circuit and South London and Surrey Sessions. He was commissioned in Dec. 1896, in the 18th Middlesex Rifle Volunteers, serving continuously from that date in the Volunteers and Territorials to 31 March, 1920; from 1896 to 1908 in the 18th Middlesex Rifle Volunteers; from 1908 to 1912 in the 10th London Regt. (Paddington Rifles), and from 1912 to 1920 in the 13th London Regt. (Princess Louise's Kensington Battn.). He was promoted Captain in 1899; Major 1 June, 1916, and Lieutenant-Colonel 13 July, 1917. He served in the European War with the original British Expeditionary Force from 2 Nov. 1914, to 9 May, 1915; was present at the Battle of Neuve Chapelle, and was wounded at the Battle of Fromelles 9 May, 1915 (for further particulars of the part taken by his regiment—the 13th London—see Buchan's "History of the War"). He was created a Companion of the Distinguished Service Order [London Gazette, 3 July, 1915]: "Edmund Gibbs Kimber, Capt., 1/13th (County of London) Princess Louise's Kensington Battn. The London Regt., Territorial Force. For conspicuous ability and coolness in leading his company and getting it into position under a heavy fire south of Farm Delangre on 9 May, 1915. He held on to his position for six hours with heavy casualties, until nearly surrounded by the enemy, and then extricated the remnants of his company." He was Prosecutor and Judge-Advocate, Courts-Martial, Irish Rebellion, 1916; Staff Captain, War Office, 1917; D.A.A.G., War Office, 1918; A.A.G., War Office, 1919. He was twice mentioned in Despatches; twice or three times mentioned otherwise, and was awarded the C.B.E. 3 June, 1919, for services at the War Office. He has the Territorial Decoration. Lieut.-Colonel Kimber married, at Hampstead, N.W., on 9 May, 1913, Maud, daughter of William B. Wilson.

FIGG, DONALD WHITELY, Capt., served in the European War, and was created a Companion of the Distinguished Service Order [London Gazette, 3 July, 1915]: "Donald Whitely Figg, Capt., 24th (County of London) Battn. The London Regt. (The Queen's), Territorial Force. For conspicuous and continuous gallantry on the night of 25–26 May, 1915, and following day at Givenchy, when, after taking part in an assault on a trench, he led repeated rushes with bombs into a German work, and when most of the bombers were killed continued the attack single-handed. His extraordinary bravery and disregard of danger enabled the dangerous flank he commanded to hold its own against constant assaults by the German bombers and riflemen. On the 26th May, when his line was enfiladed by rifle and very heavy shell fire, his determination held his men to their ground until relieved four hours later. For seventeen hours his conduct was a brilliant example to the hard-pressed men around him, and more than anyone in the battalion he contributed to the successful retention of the position won." He died of wounds 5 March 1917.

Donald Whitely Figg.

London Gazette, 3 July, 1915.—"War Office, 3 July, 1915. With reference to the notification in the London Gazette of the 3rd June, 1915, the acts of gallantry and distinguished services at the Dardanelles for which the rewards of the Distinguished Service Order were granted by His Majesty the King, are as follows:—Lieut.-Colonel Walter Ramsey McNicoll, 6th Australian Infantry Battn. (Victoria). On the night of 25–26 April, 1915, during operations near Gaba Tepe, for repeatedly exhibiting great gallantry and skill in the command of his battalion.—Lieut.-Colonel Cyril Brudenell Bingham White, Royal Australian Garrison Artillery, Staff. During the operations near Gaba Tepe on 25 April, 1915, and subsequently for his distinguished service in co-ordinating staff work, and in reorganization after the inevitable dislocation and confusion arising from the first landing operations. He displayed exceptional ability. —Major Arthur Thackeray Beckwith, The Hampshire Regt. On 26 April, 1915, at Sedd-el-Bahr, for brilliant and gallant leading of troops in the attack on the fort and town. Showed exceptional coolness and efficiency. —Major Charles Henry Brand, 3rd Infantry Brigade (Australian Forces). On 25 April, 1915, during operations in the neighbourhood of Gaba Tepe, for conspicuous gallantry and ability in organizing stragglers under heavy fire, and for organizing and leading an attack resulting in the disablement of three of the enemy's guns. Major Brand conveyed messages himself on many occasions under fire during emergencies.—Major James Samuel Denton, 11th Australian Infantry Battn. (West Australia). During the operations in the neighbourhood of Gaba Tepe on 25 April, 1915, for valuable services in obtaining and transmitting information to ships' guns and mountain batteries, and subsequently for holding a trench, with about 20 men, for over six days, repulsing several determined attacks.—Major Herbert Hart, Wellington Battn. 17th (Ruahine) Regt., New Zealand Forces. On 26 April, 1915, during operations near Gaba Tepe, for distinguished service in rallying men and digging into an important forward position in the face of an extremely severe fire. The country was wooded and difficult, and unreconnoitred, and his force was subject to constant surprise attacks.—Major James Heane, 4th Australian Infantry Battn. (New South Wales). On 1 May, 1915, during the operations near Gaba Tepe, for displaying conspicuous gallantry in leading his company to the support of a small force which, in an isolated trench, was without means of reinforcement, replenishment, or retreat. He attained his object at a heavy sacrifice.—Major William Owen Mansbridge, 16th Australian Infantry Battn. On 25 April, 1915, during operations near Gaba Tepe, for exceptional gallantry and resource during the first assault, and again on the 2nd and 3rd May during an assault on a difficult position.—Major Eugene Joseph O'Neill, F.R.C.S., New Zealand Medical Corps. On 25 and 26 April, 1915, during operations near Gaba Tepe, for exceptionally good service, and exhibiting initiative and resource in command of a bearer subdivision.—Major Robert Rankine, 14th Australian Infantry Battn. (Victoria). On the night of 26–27 April, 1915, during operations in the neighbourhood of Gaba Tepe, for gallantly leading an assault resulting in the capture of a most important post, and subsequently for holding that position against repeated attacks for five days without relief.—Major Frederick Waite, New Zealand Engineers, Territorial Force. On the night of 2–3 May, 1915, during operations in the neighbourhood of Gaba Tepe, for gallantry and resource in rallying his men and leading them forward at critical moments.—Capt. Edward William Atkinson, 1st Battn. The Royal Inniskilling Fusiliers. On 2 May, 1915, during operations south of Krithia, for gallantly leading a counter-attack, capturing a Turkish trench 300 yards to his front, and for the efficient command of his battalion, all the senior officers having become casualties.—Capt. Arthur Graham Butler, Australian Army Medical Corps (attached 9th Australian Infantry Battn.). During operations in the neighbourhood of Gaba Tepe on 25 April, 1915, and subsequent dates, for conspicuous gallantry and devotion to duty in attending wounded under heavy fire, continuously displaying courage of a high order.—Capt. Arthur Cunliffe Bernard Critchley-Salmonson, The Royal Munster Fusiliers (attached New Zealand Forces). During operations in the neighbourhood of Gaba Tepe on 25 April, 1915, for great gallantry and resource in command of a small party, and saving a difficult situation. Again, on the night of 2–3 May, he successfully led a small party to an advanced trench under great difficulties.—Capt. Guy Westland Geddes, 1st Battn. The Royal Munster Fusiliers. On 25 April, 1915, at Sedd-el-Bahr, for gallantly leading his men into lighters and then swimming ashore under heavy fire. He continued doing duty till nightfall, although wounded early in the day.—Capt. Richard Haworth, The Lancashire Fusiliers. On 25 April, 1915, at Sedd-el-Bahr, for gallantly leading 50 men to the wire entanglements of a strongly held redoubt. Although wounded, he refused to be removed until more troops arrived, and continued to command with a bullet through his back.—Capt. Cecil Ridings, 1st Battn. The Royal Inniskilling Fusiliers. On 28 April, 1915, during operations south of Krithia, for exceptionally gallant and capable leading under difficult conditions, maintaining a forward position in spite of heavy losses at a critical moment, although unsupported on either flank, and being himself severely wounded.—Lieut. Henry Desmond O'Hara, 1st Battn. The Royal Dublin Fusiliers. On 25 April, 1915, at Sedd-el-Bahr, took command of his battalion when all other officers had been killed or wounded. At night, when the enemy broke through the line, he displayed great initiative and resource in organizing a successful counter-attack, restoring the line and causing great loss to the enemy."

London Gazette, 3 July, 1915.—"Admiralty, 3 July, 1915. With reference to the list of awards to Officers and Men of the R.N.D. in recognition of their services with the Mediterranean Expeditionary Force, which appeared in the London Gazette of 3 June, the following are statements of the services of the Officers therein mentioned:—Commander Victor Lindsay Arbuthnot Campbell, R.N. Displayed conspicuous ability and initiative during the operations between 5 and 10 May, near Krithia, Cape Helles; owing to his skill as Officer Commanding the forward line, losses, though heavy, were less severe than they would otherwise have been.—Lieut.-Commander Bernard Cecil Freyburg, R.N.V.R. Displayed conspicuous gallantry on 25 April during the landing operations in the Gulf of Xeros. He swam with flares, and, although alone, reconnoitred the enemy's position and swam back; he was over two hours in the water."

London Gazette, 24 July, 1915.—"War Office, 24 July, 1915. The King has been graciously pleased to approve of the following rewards for gallantry and devotion to duty in the field. To be Companions of the Distinguished Service Order."

WILSON, JAMES THOMSON RANKINE, Lieut.-Colonel, was born 27 June, 1875. He was educated at Edinburgh Academy, and served in the European War, 1914–15. He was created a Companion of the Distinguished Service Order [London Gazette, 24 July, 1915]: "James

Thomas Rankine Wilson, Lieut.-Colonel, 1/5th Battn. Royal Scots (Queen's Edinburgh Rifles), Territorial Force. For conspicuous ability and resource on 19 June, 1915, during operations in the neighbourhood of Krithia,

James T. R. Wilson.

Dardanelles, where he reorganized and carried out the recapture of a Turkish trench from which the troops of another division had been forced back. The success gained was due to Lieut.-Colonel Wilson's skilful and bold leading, and his prompt assumption of responsibility." He married, in 1897, Dora Florence, daughter of Thomas Hall, and they have five sons and two daughters.

ARMITAGE, CHARLES LEATHLEY, Capt., was born 6 March, 1871, at Breckenbrough, Cheltenham, son of the Rev. Arthur Armitage, of St. John's Church, Cheltenham. He was educated at Winchester College, and joined the King's (Liverpool) Regt. 12 March, 1892. He retired in March, 1907; was Chief Constable of Southport to 14 Aug. 1914. On the outbreak of war Capt. Armitage was appointed to Preston Record Office, and was transferred to the Worcestershire Regt. in Oct. 1914. He disembarked in France, 1 Oct. 1914; served continuously in France in various parts of the line from Bailleux to Vermelles till 26 Oct. 1915, when he was wounded in an assault at Loos. He disembarked in England 1 Nov. 1915. For his services in the field on 19 Sept. 1915, he was awarded the rank of Brevet Major; was twice mentioned in Despatches, and was created a Companion of the Distinguished Service Order [London Gazette, 24 July, 1915]: "Charles Leathley Armitage, Capt., 6th Battn Worcestershire Regt. (attached 2nd Battn.). For conspicuous coolness and gallantry in an assault on the German lines at Richebourg on the night of 15 May, 1915. He led the assault in the face of a very heavy rifle and machine-gun fire, and after his assault had been forced back he skilfully withdrew and reorganized the attack behind our breastworks. He also showed conspicuous ability in organizing the rescue of the wounded under heavy fire throughout the night." Major Armitage is Chief Constable of Southport. He married, 15 Jan. 1901, Esther Armitage, daughter of Richard Armitage, of Highfield, Ben Rhydding, Leeds.

Charles L. Armitage.

BROCK, ALEC WALTER SAUMAREZ, Capt., was born 1 Aug. 1878. He was gazetted to the Leicestershire Regt. 21 April, 1900; became Lieutenant 23 Oct. 1901; Captain 29 April, 1907; was Adjutant, Leicestershire Regt. 13 Nov. 1908, to 29 Jan. 1911; was promoted to Major 1 Sept. 1915; was Acting Lieutenant-Colonel, Leicestershire Regt., 31 July, 1916, to 5 July, 1917; Acting Lieutenant-Colonel, commanding Territorial Force Battn. Dorsetshire Regt. 6 July to 11 Aug. 1917; Acting Lieut.-Colonel, Leicestershire Regt., 12 Aug. 1917, to 31 Dec. 1918; Temporary Lieutenant-Colonel, Leicestershire Regt. 1 Jan. 1919. He served in the South African War, 1899–1902; took part in the operations in the Transvaal, west of Pretoria; was present during operations in Orange River Colony; also in Cape Colony, south of Orange River (Queen's Medal with three clasps). For his services in the European War, 1914–18, he was given the Brevet of Lieutenant-Colonel 3 June, 1917; created a C.M.G., 1919, and created a Companion of the Distinguished Service Order [London Gazette, 24 July, 1915]: "Alec Walter Saumarez Brock, Capt., 2nd Battn.Leicestershire Regt. For conspicuous gallantry near Neuve Chapelle on 1 May, 1915, when in command of a company containing 50 per cent. of reinforcements who had not previously been under fire. His trench was heavily bombarded, and several casualties occurred, while he himself was knocked down and badly bruised by the explosion of a big shell. It was owing to his coolness and skill in getting his men under cover that the casualties were not much heavier, and that his company was ready to receive and repulse an infantry attack made later by the enemy. Capt. Brock displayed the highest qualities of a company commander under very trying circumstances."

BROWN, HAROLD, Capt., was born at Weetwood, near Leeds, 4 Jan. 1879, son of G. W. Brown, Esq., of Belsize Park Gardens, N.W., and Weetwood, Leeds. He was educated at Loretto, and at Jesus College, Cambridge, and was a member of the Cambridge University Rifle Volunteers from 1899–1902. He received a commission in the 5th Yorkshire Regt. in April, 1914. He served in the European War. He was created a Companion of the Distinguished Service Order [London Gazette, 24 July, 1915]: "Harold Brown, Capt., 5th Battn. Yorkshire Regt. (T.F.). For conspicuous gallantry and ability on several occasions, notably near Hooge, on the night of 11 June, 1915, when he made a very successful reconnaissance of the German trenches. He remained out close to the German barbed wire for one and a

Harold Brown

Hugh Barrington Brown

quarter hours, although fired at several times. Both before and since this occasion Capt. Brown has made similar daring and successful reconnaissances." Capt. Brown was awarded the Military Cross in 1916, for his services in a raid. He was cut off from his party in a German trench, but succeeded in clearing the trench, killing seven of the enemy and taking one prisoner. He also received the French Croix de Guerre, for organizing and carrying out a successful raid on an enemy consolidated crater. He was mentioned in Despatches in 1915, 1916 and 1917, and was given the Brevet of Major in the New Year's Honours List in 1917. He was killed in action in April, 1918. Major Brown married, 29 Nov. 1904, Dorothy J. Ellison, daughter of the late William Carr Ellison and Mrs. Carr Ellison, of Sheffield and Scarborough, and they had four children: John Ellison, born 13 March, 1907; Elizabeth Ayrton, born 12 Dec. 1910; Dorothea Ellison, born 12 Sept. 1912, and Lynette Ellison, born 1 Aug. 1915.

ESCOMBE, WILLIAM MALCOLM LINGARD, Capt., was born at Bromley, Kent, 25 Dec. 1891, son of R. L. Escombe. He was educated at Bradfield College, and joined the Army (T.F.) in March, 1911. He served in the European War in France from March to Sept. 1915. He was mentioned in Despatches, and was created a Companion of the Distinguished Service Order for services rendered at Givenchy at the end of May, 1915. The award appeared in the London Gazette of 24 July, 1915: "William Malcolm Lingard Escombe, Capt., 20th Battn. London Regt. (Blackheath and Woolwich), T.F. For conspicuous gallantry and skill in establishing himself on the crest of the Givenchy bluff on 28 May, 1915, under very heavy fire, and from there directing bomb-throwers with great success for an hour. His prompt action not only repelled a hostile attack, but secured fresh ground, which was consolidated." Capt. Escombe was wounded at the Battle of Loos 25 Sept. 1915. In Dec. 1916, he was appointed Assistant Instructor at the 2nd Army Central School, British Expeditionary Force. He describes his principal pursuit as "making both ends meet," and his sporting achievements as "getting married on his Army pay." He married Eileen, youngest daughter of Dr. W. Love.

EVANS, LEWIS PUGH, Capt., was awarded the V.C. (see Victoria Cross Volume). He was created a Companion of the Distinguished Service Order [London Gazette, 24 July, 1915]: "Lewis Pugh Evans, Capt., Royal Highlanders. For conspicuous gallantry and devotion to duty on 16 June, 1915, at Hooge, when, after troops had become much mixed up, he continually moved up and down the firing line under heavy fire from 10 a.m. till midnight reorganizing units and bringing back their reports."

LEE-WARNER, HARRY GRANVILLE, Capt., was born 1 Jan. 1882, only son of the late John Lee-Warner, I.C.S. He was commissioned in the Royal Artillery 31 July, 1901, becoming Lieutenant 31 July, 1905, and Captain 30 Oct. 1914. He served in the European War from 1914–17, and was created a Companion of the Distinguished Service Order [London Gazette, 24 July, 1915]: "Harry Granville Lee-Warner, Capt., 9th Battn. Royal Field Artillery. For conspicuous gallantry and devotion to duty during the operations near Rue du Bois from 9 to 19 May, 1915. Although wounded on the 9th, he remained in command of his battery till forced to give in on the 19th, and during this period he was indefatigable in reconnoitring and reporting on the situation. He was twice shelled out of his observation stations, and did excellent work under heavy shell fire." He was awarded the Military Cross in 1916; was promoted Major 13 April, 1916; was Acting Lieutenant-Colonel from Nov. 1916, to Aug. 1917; Brigade Major, Royal Artillery, 8th Division, British Armies in France, 3 Sept. 1917, to 27 Aug. 1918. He was wounded five times, and was twice mentioned in Despatches. Major Lee-Warner married Audrey, daughter of Rwholl Dare, of Newtownbarry, County Wexford.

RADFORD, MAURICE CLIVE, Capt., was born 5 April, 1884. He was gazetted to the Royal Berkshire Regt. 16 Aug. 1905, and was promoted Lieutenant 5 April, 1909. He served in the European War. He was created a Companion of the Distinguished Service Order [London Gazette, 24 July, 1915]: "Maurice Clive Radford, Capt., 1st Battn. Royal Berkshire Regt. For conspicuous gallantry and devotion to duty at Cuinchy on the night of 21 June, 1915, when the Germans pumped gas into a mine in which four of our men were on listening-post. Under direction of Capt. Radford, who displayed great gallantry and resource, the efforts of two N.C.O.'s and two men, who bravely went down the mine, were successful in getting the men out. At about 4.15 a.m., on 22 June, following their gas attack, the Germans exploded a mine in front of our own, in which were a sergeant and about eight of our men, but owing to the gallant efforts of Capt. Radford, another officer and a few men, who repeatedly went down among the fumes, all the men were rescued, although the rescuers suffered considerably." He was killed in action in France 28 Sept. 1915.

ROE, CHARLES DOUGLAS, Capt., was born 26 April, 1882, son of Capt. R. G. Roe, R.N. He entered the Royal Irish Regt. 18 Jan. 1902, and was promoted Lieutenant 3 June, 1904; was transferred to the Indian Army 18 Aug. 1904, and became Captain 18 Jan. 1911. Capt. Roe served in the European War, 1914–15. He was twice mentioned in Despatches, and was created a Companion of the Distinguished Service Order [London Gazette, 24 July, 1915]: "Charles Douglas Roe, Capt., 1/4th Gurkha Rifles. For conspicuous gallantry and resource near the Bois de Biez on 2 and 4 July, 1915, when reconnoitring the enemy's positions by day. He collected information of great value, and on one occasion, though opposed by overwhelming numbers, he kept them at bay by bombs and rifle fire, and brought back his party with only one wounded, after inflicting considerable loss on the enemy." He was promoted Major 18 Jan. 1917. Major C. D. Roe married, in 1904, Daisy Blanche Marion, eldest daughter of the late Major H. J. W. Mackenzie-Kennedy, Norfolk Regt., and they have one son.

SCOTT, JAMES MORISON, Capt., entered the Army (Territorial Force) in 1905. He served in the European War from 1914–18. He was created a Companion of the Distinguished Service Order [London Gazette, 24 July, 1915]: "James Morison Scott, Capt., 7th Battn. Argyll and Sutherland Highlanders, Territorial Force. For conspicuous gallantry and resource on many occasions. He was the only officer left with his battalion at the end of the day on 24 May, 1915, near Wieltje, where his conduct when in charge of machine guns was marked by the highest ability and bravery." He became Acting Lieutenant-Colonel commanding the 5th Seaforth Highlanders. He received the Belgian Order of Leopold.

STURGES, CHARLES HERBERT MANSFIELD, Capt., was born 6 April, 1884, son of the Rev. Herbert Court Sturges, M.A. (deceased). He was educated at Haileybury College, and the Royal Military Academy, Woolwich, and was commissioned in the Royal Artillery 24 Dec. 1902. He was promoted Lieutenant 24 Dec. 1905, and was employed with the West African Frontier Force from 3 July, 1909, to 12 Sept. 1913, serving in the operations in the Ogwashi Oku country, Southern Nigeria, 1909–10 (Medal and clasp). Capt. Sturges served in the European War from 17 Sept. 1914, to 17 Nov. 1915, and 24 May, 1916 onwards. He was promoted Captain 30 Oct. 1914. He was mentioned in Despatches, and created a Companion of the Distinguished Service Order [London Gazette, 24 July, 1915]: "Charles Herbert Mansfield Sturges, Capt., 1st Siege Battery, Royal Garrison Artillery. For conspicuous gallantry and general good work as an Observing Officer and throughout the campaign, notably during the attack at the Rue du Bois on 9 May, and during attacks on 15 and 16 May. During these last attacks he was shelled out of two houses in succession, but proceeded to a third, where, although blown down the ladder by the force of a shell, he still continued to observe and correct the fire of his battery." Capt. Sturges was again mentioned in Despatches 1 Jan. 1916, and attained his Majority 2 Aug. 1917. He also received the Order of Leopold and the Croix de Guerre. His battery is the 96th Siege Battery, Royal Garrison Artillery.

Charles H. M. Sturges.

WOODGATE, AUSTIN BRADFORD, Capt., was born 12 Sept. 1884, only son of the late Alfred Henry Augustus Woodgate. He was educated at St. Edward's School, Oxford. He served with the 3rd Battn. (Militia) of the King's Own Regt., 1904–7, then resigned his commission, and served in the South African Mounted Police. He rejoined the Army after the declaration of war: was gazetted Lieutenant to the 3rd Battn. The King's Own Royal Lancaster Regt. (attached 1st Battn.) in Sept. 1914; became Captain in Feb. 1915; Captain, 1st Battn. East Lancashire Regt. 2 Oct. 1915. Capt. Woodgate served in the European War from 1914 to 1916. He was thrice wounded; was awarded the Military Cross, and was created a Companion of the Distinguished Service Order [London Gazette, 24 July, 1915]: "Austin Bradford Woodgate, Capt., 3rd Battn. Royal Lancaster Regt. (attached 1st Battn.). For conspicuous gallantry on 24 May, 1915, when, after the Germans had captured the trenches held by the battalion on his right, he, with another officer and three men, held up the enemy from working along the trench. Although the enemy was in force and with an unlimited supply of hand-grenades, he not only held them up, but succeeded under a heavy shell fire in capturing two traverses and a German flag, which had been put up to mark their position. Capt. Woodgate also rendered invaluable service throughout the winter, especially during the underground fight in the mine gallery at Le Touquet." He was attached to the Machine Gun Corps 18 Dec. 1915, and became Temporary Major 16 Feb. 1918. Capt. Woodgate's favourite recreations are hockey and lawn tennis.

Austin B. Woodgate.

London Gazette, 7 Aug. 1915.—"Admiralty, 7 Aug. 1915. The King has been graciously pleased to give orders for the following appointments to the Distinguished Service Order of the undermentioned Officers, in recognition of their services in the patrol cruisers since the outbreak of war."

HEARD, HUGH LINDSAY PATRICK, Capt., was born 2 Aug. 1869, at Bangalore, Madras Presidency, son of Samuel Thomas Heard, D.L., and Katherine, daughter of William Bradley, M.L.C., of Goulburn, New South Wales. He was educated at Dedham (Essex); Stubbington, and in H.M.S. Britannia, and entered the Navy 15 Jan. 1885, becoming Lieutenant, 1892; Commander, 1903; Captain, 1910, and Commodore in May, 1918. In the European War Capt. Heard served from 2 Aug. to Nov. 1914, in H.M.S. Grafton, and from Nov. 1914, to July, 1915, in H.M.S. Columbella, both in the 10th Cruiser Squadron. He was created a Companion of the Distinguished Service Order [London Gazette, 7 Aug. 1915]: "Hugh Lindsay Patrick Heard, Capt., Royal Navy. In recognition of services in the patrol cruisers since the outbreak of war." He was in H.M.S. Duncan from 1 July, 1915, to April, 1917, in the British Adriatic Squadron and the British Eastern Mediterranean Squadron, and from March 1917, to Jan. 1919, Senior Naval Officer at Berehaven Auxiliary Patrol Base. He

was mentioned in Despatches, and was appointed Commander of the Crown of Italy.

TREWBY, GEORGE, Capt., was born in Essex 19 Oct. 1874, son of the late George Careless Trewby, M.I.C.E., Civil Engineer. He was educated privately, and in H.M.S. Britannia, which he entered in Oct. 1887. He was promoted Captain 31 June, 1913. He served in the European War from 1914 to 1917. He was created a Companion of the Distinguished Service Order for services in the Blockade Squadron (10th Cruiser Squadron), in command of H.M. Ships Crescent and Alsatian, and as Flag Captain to Admiral Sir D. R. De Chair from the outbreak of War [London Gazette, 7 Aug. 1915]: "George Trewby, Capt., Royal Navy. In recognition of services in the patrol cruisers since the outbreak of war." Capt. Trewby married, 28 Aug. 1916, at Capetown, South Africa, Dorothea, only daughter of Dr. and Mrs. A. de W. Allan, of Port Nolloth, Namaqualand, and they have one son.

EDWARDS, HUGH, Capt., Royal Navy, served in the European War from 1914. He was created a Companion of the Distinguished Service Order [London Gazette, 7 Aug. 1915] "Hugh Edwards, Capt., Royal Navy. In recognition of services in the patrol cruisers since the outbreak of war." Capt. Hugh Edwards died 5 Dec. 1916, of wounds.

OUTRAM, EDMUND, Commander, served in the European War in H.M.S. Alsatian, 1914–15. He was created a Companion of the Distinguished Service Order [London Gazette, 7 Aug. 1915]: "Edmund Outram, Commander, Royal Naval Reserve. In recognition of services in the patrol cruisers since the outbreak of war."

MAIN, FRANK MORGAN, Lieut.-Commander, served in the European War from 1914–17, on patrol duty. He was mentioned in Despatches, and was created a Companion of the Distinguished Service Order [London Gazette, 7 Aug. 1915]: "Frank Morgan Main, R.D., Lieut.-Commander, Royal Naval Reserve. In recognition of services in the patrol cruisers since the outbreak of war."

SMITH, HENRY PHILIP BASDEN, Lieut.-Commander, served in the European War on patrol duty. He was mentioned in Despatches, and was created a Companion of the Distinguished Service Order [London Gazette, 7 Aug. 1915]: "Henry Philip Basden Smith, R.D., Lieut.-Commander, Royal Naval Reserve. In recognition of services in the patrol cruisers since the outbreak of war."

BACON, SIDNEY KENRICK, Lieut.-Commander, was born 29 March, 1871, son of Capt. K. V. Bacon, late 29th Worcester Regt. He entered the Navy in 1901, becoming Lieutenant, 1903; Lieutenant-Commander, 1913; Commander, 1917. He saw active service in South Africa, 1901–2; was in the Egyptian Government Service from 1912–14. He served in the European War, 1914–15, on patrol duty; was mentioned in Despatches, and was created a Companion of the Distinguished Service Order [London Gazette, 7 Aug. 1915]: "Sidney Kenrick Bacon, Lieut.-Commander, Royal Naval Reserve. In recognition of services in the patrol cruisers since the outbreak of war."

WILSON, ROBERT, Chief Engineer, served in the European War, 1914–17. He was mentioned in Despatches, and was created a Companion of the Distinguished Service Order [London Gazette, 7 Aug. 1915]: "Robert Wilson, Chief Engineer, Royal Naval Reserve. In recognition of services in the patrol cruisers since the outbreak of war."

ROWE, WILLIAM, Chief Engineer, served in the European War, 1914–15. He was mentioned in Despatches for services in patrol work, and was created a Companion of the Distinguished Service Order [London Gazette, 7 Aug. 1915]: "William Rowe, R.D., Chief Engineer, Royal Naval Reserve. In recognition of services in the patrol cruisers since the outbreak of war."

DIXON, ELIAS STEPHENSON, Chief Engineer, served in the European War, 1914–18, engaged on patrol duties. He was created a Companion of the Distinguished Service Order [London Gazette, 7 Aug. 1915]: "Elias Stephenson Dixon, Chief Engineer, Royal Naval Reserve. In recognition of services in the patrol cruisers since the outbreak of war."

London Gazette, 7 Aug. 1915.—"Admiralty, 7 Aug. 1915. The King has further been pleased to give orders for the appointment to the Distinguished Service Order of the following Officer."

EDWARDS, HARRINGTON DOUTY, Lieut.-Commander, was born 22 Dec. 1885, at Tyrrel's House, Antigua, West Indies, son of Charles R. Edwards, M.R.C.S., and Ella Edwards. He was educated at St. Faith's, Cambridge, and at Chigwell School, and became a Midshipman in the Royal Navy 30 May, 1902. He entered the Submarine Branch of the Service in 1907. He served in the European War, and was created a Companion of the Distinguished Service Order [London Gazette, 7 Aug. 1915]: "Harrington Douty Edwards, Lieut.-Commander, Royal Navy." The decoration was awarded for some special service; no official account was published. Lieut.-Commander H. D. Edwards was lost in his submarine with all hands 11 March, 1916.

London Gazette, 16 Aug. 1915.—"Admiralty, 16 Aug. 1915. The King has been graciously pleased to give orders for the following appointments to the Distinguished Service Order of the undermentioned Officers, in recognition of their services as mentioned in the Despatch from Vice-Admiral de Robeck reporting the landing of the Army on the Gallipoli Peninsula 25–26 April, 1915."

JANVRIN, RALPH BENEST, Lieut.-Commander, is the son of the Rev. William Langston Benest Janvrin, M.A., Rector of Cradley, Malvern, and Prebendary in Hereford Cathedral. He served in the European War in the Dardanelles in 1914–15, being present at the landing of the Expeditionary Force on Gallipoli 25–26 April, 1915. Vice-Admiral Sir John de Robeck, in his Despatch reporting the landing, specially recommended him as follows : " Lieut.-Commander Ralph B. Janvrin conducted the trawlers into Morto Bay, for the landing at ' De Totts ' with much skill. This officer showed great judgment and coolness under fire, and carried out a difficult task with great success." For his services he was created a Companion of the Distinguished Service Order [London Gazette, 16 Aug. 1915] : " Ralph Benest Janvrin, Lieut.-Commander, Royal Navy. In recognition of services as mentioned in the foregoing Despatch." In 1916 he was employed in the North Sea, and was again mentioned in Despatches.

KEYES, ADRIAN ST. VINCENT, Lieut.-Commander, is the son of the late Sir Charles Keyes. He served in the European War in the Dardanelles from 1914–18. He was created a Companion of the Distinguished Service Order [London Gazette, 16 Aug. 1915] : " In recognition of services as mentioned in the foregoing Despatch, Adrian St. Vincent Keyes, Lieut.-Commander, Royal Navy." The Despatch referred to was that of Vice-Admiral Sir John de Robeck, describing the landing of the Army on the Gallipoli Peninsula 25 to 26 April, 1915, in which he received the following special recommendation : " General Sir Ian Hamilton reports as follows : ' Lieut.-Commander Keyes showed great coolness, gallantry and ability. The success of the landing on " Y " Beach was largely due to his good service. When circumstances compelled the force landed there to re-embark, this officer showed exceptional resource and leadership in successfully conducting that difficult operation.' I entirely concur in General Hamilton's opinion of this officer's services on 25–26 April." Lieut.-Commander Keyes has retired. He was made a C.B.E. in 1919. He married, in 1916, Eleanor, daughter of Lieut.-Colonel Walter Campbell, The Ivy House, Hampton Court.

MORSE, JOHN ANTHONY VERE, Lieut., was born 16 Oct. 1892, son of Mr. and Mrs. Sydney Morse, of 14, Airlie Gardens, Campden Hill, W. He was educated at Osborne ; entered the Royal Navy in 1905 ; became Lieutenant in 1914. He served in the European War in the Dardanelles in 1914 and 1915. Vice-Admiral Sir John de Robeck, in his Despatch regarding the landing of the Expeditionary Force on Gallipoli on 25–26 April, 1915, specially recommended him as follows : " Lieut. John A. V. Morse, R.N., assisted to secure the lighters at the bows of the River Clyde under a heavy fire, and was very active throughout the 25th and 26th at ' V ' Beach." He was created a Companion of the Distinguished Service Order [London Gazette, 16 Aug. 1915] : " John Anthony Vere Morse, Lieut., Royal Navy. In recognition of (his) services as mentioned in the foregoing Despatch." He was again mentioned in Despatches ; is in command of H.M.S. Unity. Lieut. Morse married, at St. John's, Westminster, S.W., on 5 April, 1917, Mary Faith, eldest daughter of the Rev. W. Howard Lees, C.F., and Mrs. Lees, of Little Nutcombe, Hindhead, and 11, Aubrey Walk, Campden Hill, W. They have two children, Jane Antonia Unity and Clyde Anthony Leeds.

John Anthony Vere Morse.

KELLY, PETER BURROWES, Surgeon, was born 23 Sept. 1888, son of Gilbert Graves Kelly. He was educated in Dublin and London. He served in the European War in 1914 and 1915, and was present at the landing of the Expeditionary Force on Gallipoli 25 and 26 April. He was mentioned in the Despatch of Vice-Admiral Sir John de Robeck, reporting on these operations, as follows : " Surgeon P. B. Kelly, R.N., attached to the R.N.A.S., was wounded in the foot on the morning of the 25th in the River Clyde. He remained in River Clyde until the morning of 27th, during which time he attended 750 wounded men, although in great pain and unable to walk during the last 24 hours." He was created a Companion of the Distinguished Service Order [London Gazette, 16 Aug. 1915] : " Peter Burrowes Kelly, Surgeon, Royal Navy. In recognition of (his) services as mentioned in the foregoing Despatch." Surgeon P. Burrowes Kelly was appointed Lieut.-Surgeon at the Royal Naval College, Osborne, Isle of Wight. His chief recreations are Rugby football, cricket and shooting. He is married and has one daughter.

London Gazette, 16 Aug. 1915.—" Admiralty, 16 Aug. 1915. The following awards have been made in recognition of services during the operations in the vicinity of the Dardanelles prior to 25–26 April. The King has been graciously pleased to give orders for the following appointments to the Distinguished Service Order of the undermentioned Officers, in recognition of their services as mentioned."

MELLOR, WILLIAM, Commander, was born 20 Aug. 1874, at Walton, Liverpool, son of the late John Mellor, of Rutland House, Blundellsands, and Mary Elizabeth, daughter of the late W. B. Kewley, of Waterloo, Liverpool. He was educated at the Merchant Taylors' School, Great Crosby, Liverpool, and in H.M.S. Britannia, which he entered in June, 1887. He became Midshipman 15 Aug. 1889 ; Sub-Lieutenant 20 Aug. 1893 ; Lieutenant, Royal Navy, 20 Aug. 1894, and Commander 30 June, 1906 ; commanded H.M.S. Odin in the Persian Gulf, Feb. 1912, to March, 1914 (Naval General Service Medal and clasp for prevention of gun-running). Commander Mellor served in the European War. He was in charge of the mine-sweeping operations in the Dardanelles, Jan. to May, 1915. He was created a Companion of the Distinguished Service Order [London Gazette, 16 Aug. 1915] : " William Mellor, Commander, R.N. Commander Mellor was in charge of the Trawler Mine-sweepers, and took part in all the mine-sweeping operations under fire prior to and including

the 18th March. He displayed conspicuous gallantry, always being to the fore in a picket-boat, in the most exposed positions, encouraging his sweepers and setting a fine example." He was present throughout the whole of the Gallipoli Campaign in command of H.M. Kite Balloon Ships Manica and Canning, and was subsequently D.N.T.O. at Salonika and Port Convoy Officer at Taranto and Marseilles.

MIDDLETON, JOHN RICKARDS, Lieut.-Commander (now Commander), was born 10 Oct. 1880, son of the late R. W. E. Middleton. He served in the South African War, landing as a Midshipman with the Naval Brigade for the defence of Ladysmith, 1900 (Despatches). He served in the European War, 1914–17, including the Dardanelles ; was mentioned in Despatches by Vice-Admiral Sir John de Robeck, and was created a Companion of the Distinguished Service Order [London Gazette, 16 Aug. 1915] : " John Rickards Middleton, Lieut.-Commander (now Commander), Royal Navy Lieut.-Commander Middleton on three occasions entered the mine-fields under heavy fire, where he organized and successfully carried out attacks—by means of explosive creeps—on the cables and jack-stays." Commander Middleton married, in 1910, Sara Towle.

SANDFORD, FRANCIS HUGH, Lieut., was born at Cornwood, Devon, 10 Oct. 1887, son of Ernest Grey Sandford, Archdeacon of Exeter (died in 1910), and Ethel R., daughter of Gabriel Poole. He was educated at Clifton College, and joined H.M.S. Britannia at Dartmouth in the summer of 1902 ; was promoted Sub-Lieutenant 3 Aug. 1907. He served in the European War in the Dardanelles in 1915 ; was severely wounded ; mentioned in Despatches of Vice-Admiral Sir John de Robeck, and created a Companion of the Distinguished Service Order [London Gazette, 16 Aug. 1915] : " Francis Hugh Sandford, Lieut., Royal Navy. Lieut. Sandford was specially recommended for his good work in connection with the attacks on the mine-fields, which he entered on several occasions, including night of 13–14 March. He invariably displayed great determination when under fire. Lieut. Sandford also rendered good service in the demolition of Fort Seddul Bahr." He received his promotion to Commander and the French Croix de Guerre avec Palme in 1918, for his services in the raids which closed the harbours at Zeebrugge and Ostend.

Francis Hugh Sandford.

COX, BERNARD THOMAS, A/Lieut., was born 22 June, 1884, at Atherstone-on-Stour, son of Rev. Cecil Walker Cox, Rector of North Kilworth, and Louisa Florence Cox (formerly Bridges). He was educated at St. Cuthbert's College, Worksop (1896–98), and in the Conway (1898–1900). He served in the European War, and was severely wounded at the Dardanelles. He was mentioned in Despatches by Vice-Admiral Sir John de Robeck, and was created a Companion of the Distinguished Service Order [London Gazette, 16 Aug. 1915] : " Bernard Thomas Cox, A/Lieut., Royal Naval Reserve. Lieut. Cox behaved in a most gallant manner when a volunteer in Trawler No. 318, during the attack on the mine-field on 13–14 March. Though severely wounded, he refused to quit his bridge until out of action. His vessel suffered serious damage and severe casualties." He was promoted Lieutenant 2 Sept. 1915 Lieut. Cox married Katherine Audrey, second daughter of the Rev. C. E. and Mrs. Couchman.

METCALFE, CHRISTOPHER POWELL, Capt., was born 25 March, 1873. He served in the European War ; was mentioned in Despatches by Vice-Admiral Sir John de Robeck, and created a Companion of the Distinguished Service Order [London Gazette, 16 Aug. 1915] : " Christopher Powell Metcalfe, Capt., Royal Navy. On the 18th March, after H.M.S. Irresistible struck a mine, Capt. Metcalfe took H.M.S. Wear alongside her, and rescued nearly the whole of her crew under a very heavy fire, which caused several casualties—a very fine display of seamanship." Capt. C. P. Metcalfe married Annie Duddell, daughter of George Minza.

ACHESON, THE HONOURABLE PATRICK GEORGE EDWARD CAVENDISH, M.V.O., Lieut.-Commander, was born 30 June, 1883, second son of the 4th Earl of Gosford and the Countess of Gosford. He was educated at the Naval College ; was created an M.V.O. in 1914. He served in the European War, 1914–15, and was in H.M.S. Inflexible in the Falkland Islands Battle, the Dardanelles, and the Battle of Jutland. He was mentioned in Despatches by Vice-Admiral Sir John de Robeck, and was created a Companion of the Distinguished Service Order [London Gazette, 16 Aug. 1915] : " The Honourable Patrick George Edward Cavendish Acheson, Lieut.-Commander (now Commander), Royal Navy. Lieut.-Commander Acheson, with Acting Sub-Lieut. Alfred E. B. Giles, Chief Engine Room Artificer, Second Class, Robert Snowdon, O.N. 270564, and Stoker, First Class, Thomas Davidson, O.N. K.147538, went down into the fore magazine and shell-room of H.M.S. Inflexible, when the parties working in these places had been driven out by fumes, caused by the explosion of a mine under the ship ; they closed valves and water-tight doors, lights being out. the shell-room having two feet of water in it, rising quickly, and the magazine flooding slowly. The fumes were beginning to take effect on Acting Sub-Lieut. Giles, but neither he nor the others left until ordered to do so by Lieut.-Commander Acheson, who was the last to leave the shell-room." Commander Acheson also has the Order of St. Stanislas, Second Class with Swords, He married, 24 Dec. 1915, at St. George's, Hanover Square, London, W., Norah, daughter of Alfred E. Jones, of Halifax, Nova Scotia, Canada ; they have one son, Nicholas Archibald Edward Patrick, born 23 May, 1917.

GILES, ALFRED EDWARD BOSCAWEN, Acting Sub-Lieut. (now Sub-Lieut.), served in the European War, 1914–15, in the Dardanelles; was in H.M.S. Inflexible when she was struck by a mine.

Alfred E. B. Giles.

He was mentioned in Despatches by Vice-Admiral Sir John de Robeck, and was created a Companion of the Distinguished Service Order [London Gazette, 16 Aug. 1915]: "Alfred Edward Boscawen Giles, Acting Sub-Lieut. (now Sub-Lieut.), Royal Navy. Lieut.-Commander Acheson, with Acting Sub-Lieut. Alfred E. B. Giles, Chief Engine Room Artificer, 2nd Class, Robert Snowdon, O.N. 270564, and Stoker, First Class, Thomas Davidson, O.N. K.147538, went down into the fore magazine and shell-room of H.M.S. Inflexible, when the parties working in these places had been driven out by fumes, caused by the explosion of a mine under the ship; they closed valves and water-tight doors, lights being out, the shell-room having two feet of water in it, rising quickly, and the magazine flooding slowly. The fumes were beginning to take effect on Acting Sub-Lieut. Giles, but neither he nor the others left until ordered to do so by Lieut.-Commander Acheson, who was the last to leave the shell-room." Sub-Lieut. A. E. B. Giles was accidentally drowned 25 Oct. 1917.

LASHMORE, HARRY, Engineer-Commander, was born at Southampton 16 Nov. 1868, son of Henry Lashmore, Journalist, and Helen Lashmore (deceased). He was educated at Southampton Boys' College and High School, and was afterwards an Engineer Student in H.M. Ship Marlborough at Portsmouth, and at the Royal Naval College at Devonport. He became Assistant Engineer, Royal Navy, 1 Aug. 1890; was promoted Engineer-Lieutenant 1 Feb. 1895. He was an officer of H.M.S. Ormele when the Pioneer collided with that vessel in Corfu Bay early in 1903, and was complimented by two courts-martial; was promoted to Engineer-Commander for Special Service, 1907. He was appointed to the Inflexible 8 Jan. 1914, and served in her at the Dardanelles in charge of the engine room. He was created a C.B. (Military Division), King's Birthday Honours, June, 1915, and was created a Companion of the Distinguished Service Order [London Gazette, 16 Aug. 1915]: "Harry Lashmore, C.B., Engineer-Commander, Royal Navy. During the time H.M.S. Inflexible was steaming to Tenedos—after having struck a mine—the engine-room being in semi-darkness and great heat, the ship in possible danger of sinking on passage, a high standard of discipline was called for in the Engineer Department, a call which was more than met. Engineer-Commander Harry Lashmore, responsible for the discipline of the engine-room department, was in the starboard engine-room throughout the passage, and set a fine example to his men." He was also mentioned in Despatches by Vice-Admiral Sir John de Robeck. He subsequently served for about two and a half years on the Staff at Port Said, and was then appointed to represent the Admiralty on the International Control Board. He became Engineer-Captain in 1917. His ship is H.M.S. Euryalus. Engineer-Captain Lashmore is a Member of the Institute of Naval Architects. He married, at Llanelly, 15 Aug. 1900, Beatrice, daughter of the late John Evans and Mrs. Evans, of Cardiff.

LESTER, ARTHUR ELLIS, Engineer-Lieut.-Commander, served in the European War, 1914–18, in H.M.S. Inflexible. He was present at the Battle of the Falkland Islands and at the Dardanelles. He was mentioned in Despatches by Vice-Admiral Sir John de Robeck, and was created a Companion of the Distinguished Service Order [London Gazette, 16 Aug. 1915]: "Arthur Ellis Lester, Engineer-Lieut.-Commander, Royal Navy. During the time H.M.S. Inflexible was steaming to Tenedos—after having struck a mine—the engine-room being in semi-darkness and great heat, the ship in possible danger of sinking on passage, a high standard of discipline was called for in the Engineer Department, a call which was more than met. Engineer-Commander Harry Lashmore, responsible for the discipline of the engine-room department, was in the starboard engine-room throughout the passage, and set a fine example to his men. Engineer-Lieut.-Commander Lester was in the port engine-room, carrying out the same duties as Engineer-Commander Lashmore did in the starboard engine-room." Engineer Lieut.-Commander Lester was present at the Battle of Jutland 29 May, 1916, and was specially commended and promoted Engineer-Commander.

PARRY, RAY GRIFFITH, Engineer-Lieut., served in the European War in the Dardanelles, 1914–15, and was on board H.M.S. Inflexible when she was struck by a mine. He was mentioned in Vice-Admiral Sir John de Robeck's Despatches, and was created a Companion of the Distinguished Service Order [London Gazette, 16 Aug. 1915]: "Ray Griffith Parry, Engineer-Lieut., Royal Navy. During the time H.M.S. Inflexible was steaming to Tenedos—after having struck a mine—the engine-room being in semi-darkness and great heat, the ship in possible danger of sinking on passage, a high standard of discipline was called for in the Engineer Department, a call which was more than met. Engineer-Lieut. Parry went twice through the thick fumes to the refrigerator flat to see if the doors and valves were closed; he also closed the escape hatch from the submerged flat, fumes and vapour coming up the trunk at the time."

LANGFORD, MARTYN HENRY, Surgeon, served in the European War. He was at the Dardanelles, 1914–15, and was in H.M.S. Inflexible when she was mined. He was created a Companion of the Distinguished Service Order [London Gazette, 16 Aug. 1915]: "Martyn Henry Langford, Surgeon, Royal Navy. During the time H.M.S. Inflexible was steaming to Tenedos—after having struck a mine—the engine-room being in semi-darkness and great heat, the ship in possible danger of sinking on passage,

a high standard of discipline was called for in the Engineer Department, a call which was more than met. Surgeon Langford brought up the wounded from the fore distributing station in the dark. Fumes permeated the place, rendering five men unconscious. Surgeon Langford, though partially overcome by the fumes, continued his work." He was also mentioned in Despatches by Vice-Admiral Sir John de Robeck. Surgeon Langford died 15 Dec. 1918.

GODWIN, CLAUD HERBERT, Lieut., is the youngest son of the Rev. H. Godwin, of Ivy Lodge, Ightham. He served in the European War in the Dardanelles in 1914–15; was mentioned in Despatches by Vice-Admiral Sir John de Robeck, and was created a Companion of the Distinguished Service Order [London Gazette, 16 Aug. 1915]: "Claud Herbert Godwin, Lieut., Royal Navy. Lieut. Godwin commanded H.M.S. Majestic's picket boat, and was responsible for the successful shot by which the Submarine E15 was destroyed after running aground." Lieut.-Commander C. H. Godwin married, in 1918, Jean, daughter of the late George Torraster, of Leith.

London Gazette, 25 Aug. 1915.—"War Office, 25 Aug. 1915. His Majesty the King has been graciously pleased to approve of the appointment of the following Officers to be Companions of the Distinguished Service Order, in recognition of their gallantry and distinguished service in the field."

NIGHTINGALE, MANNERS RALPH WILMOT, Major, was born at Sidmouth, Devonshire, on the 15th April, 1871, son of Percy Nightingale, Inspecting Commissioner, Cape Civil Service, and grandson of Sir Charles Nightingale, 11th Baronet, of Kneesworth, Cambridgeshire. From Cape Colony he took a Scholarship to the Royal Military College, Sandhurst, and was commissioned 1 March, 1890, 1st Battn. Cheshire Regt.; subsequently he was attached to the 22nd Madras Infantry at Thayetmyo.

Manners R. W. Nightingale.

He commanded Mounted Infantry during the rising in Karenni headed by Minlaung, and was at the capture of the rebel Minlaung's stockade at Dawdkeoo in West Karenni 7 June, 1892, and the action at Loikau Bridge in Eastern Karenni 25 June, 1892, on which latter occasion he was mentioned by the General Officer Commanding, Burma District, for "gallant conduct, very commendable and deserving of great praise," and the Commander-in-Chief in India recorded his appreciation. On the 18th Feb. 1894, he joined the 2nd Battn. 5th Gurkha Rifles. He served with the Gurkha Scouts during the Tirah Expedition of 1897–98 (Indian Medal, 1895, and one clasp). He served with the China Field Force as Assistant to the Brigade Commissariat and Transport Officer, 2nd Brigade, British Contingent, China Field Force, 1900–1 (Medal); was promoted Captain 1 March, 1901. He became an Interpreter in Russian. On his return to India, much of his time was spent with his regiment, and in July, 1907, he became 4th Double Company Commander, 1st Battn. 5th Gurkha Rifles, and became Major 1 March, 1908. He was Recruiting Staff Officer at Gorakhpur from 10 June, 1910, to 10 June, 1914, and then rejoined his regiment. In Nov. 1914, he left Bombay with the 1st Battn. 5th G.R.F.F., and saw service with the Canal Defence Force, Egypt. On the 3rd June, 1915, the 1/5th G.R.F.F. disembarked at Beach "V," Gallipoli Peninsula, about 3 a.m. Lieut.-Colonel Nightingale led No. 2 Double Company in the Third Battle of Krithia on the 4th June, 1915, and was awarded the Distinguished Service Order for his action in this battle [London Gazette, 25 Aug. 1915]: "Manners Ralph Wilmot Nightingale, Major, 1st Battn. 5th Gurkha Rifles. For most conspicuous gallantry on 4 June, 1915, during operations in the neighbourhood of Krithia, Dardanelles, in leading an attack up a difficult spur after he had been wounded. He reached the crest and was again wounded, but coming back a few yards rallied his men and again led them on. He was then wounded a third time, but still endeavoured to advance till he fainted." The G.O.C.'s Order (List No. 8, issued with General Routine Orders, dated 15 July, 1915) concluded: "Were it not for the unprecedented crop of gallant deeds produced by the battles of the Dardanelles, the General Commanding would have put forward this officer's name for the Victoria Cross." After being so very severely wounded, Lieut.-Colonel Nightingale returned to England, and on rejoining the 1/5th G.R.F.F. at Peshawar on the 29th March, 1916, became Temporary Commandant. He was promoted Lieut.-Colonel 1 March, 1916. On the 12th March, 1917, he left Abbottabad at the head of a young battalion, 1/5th G.R.F.F., for service in Mesopotamia. He became Temporary Brigadier-General 20 Dec. 1917, to command the 54th Infantry Brigade, Mesopotamian Expeditionary Force; was made a C.M.G. in 1918, and given the Brevet of Colonel 1 Jan. 1919. He married Anna Forestier, fifth daughter of Arthur George Walker, I.C.S. They have two children.

ABBOTT, FRANK BERKELEY, Capt., was born 2 Aug. 1885. He was commissioned on the Unattached List 13 Aug. 1904, and joined the Indian Army 30 Oct. 1905; was promoted Lieutenant 13 Nov. 1906, and Captain 13 Aug. 1913; employed with the King's African Rifles 19 April, 1910, to 18 April, 1913. Capt. Abbott served in the European War. He was created a Companion of the Distinguished Service Order [London Gazette, 25 Aug. 1915]: "Frank Berkeley Abbott, Capt., 1st Battn. 6th Gurkha Rifles. For gallant and distinguished conduct on 28 and 29 June, 1915, during operations on the Gallipoli Peninsula. He showed great skill in organizing bombing attacks, which resulted in regaining a portion of the trench which had been captured by the enemy. Advancing single-handed, he cleared the enemy out of one-third of the trench. He was wounded for the third time during the war when leading a bayonet charge, after the bombs were exhausted. He showed exceptionally fine leadership, dash and resource." He became Acting Major 26 Nov. 1917.

ANDERSON, STANLEY JOHN, Capt., was born 8 July, 1878, at Milngavie, Scotland, son of George Murray Anderson, and Jean, second daughter of Alexander Williamson. He was educated in Glasgow; served with the Glasgow Highlanders, 1895–1901, and the London Scottish, 1907–8; was commissioned in the 60th Rifles of Canada (Militia) in April, 1911. He served in the European War on the Western Front, becoming Captain, Aug. 1914. He was created a Companion of the Distinguished Service Order [London Gazette, 25 Aug. 1915]: "Stanley John Anderson, Capt., 5th Battn. (Western Cavalry) Canadian Expeditionary Force Unit. For conspicuous gallantry at Festubert on 20 May, 1915, when he refused to go on the ambulance after being wounded until his tour of duty was completed. Capt. Anderson was again wounded in the head on 24 May, but remained the whole day and night gallantly leading his men in the attacks." He was mentioned in Despatches by Sir John French in Dec. 1915; was appointed Staff Captain, 5th Training Brigade, Shorncliffe, 1 May, 1916; returned to Canada as General Staff Officer, 3rd Grade, 12 May, 1916; promoted Major 22 June, 1916; promoted General Staff Officer, 2nd Grade, 1 Sept. 1916; detailed for special duty at Militia Headquarters, Canada, 11 Nov. 1916, as Acting Director-General of Musketry and Acting Director of Military Training. Major Anderson married Margaret H. R., younger daughter of William Samuel.

FOWLER, HUGH GRIFFITH COKE, Capt., South Wales Borderers, was born 12 Jan. 1882, son of the late John Bacon Fowler. He was educated at Mr. Wilkinson's School, Southfield, and Tonbridge, and joined the Army in 1901. He served in South Africa, 1902–4 (Queen's Medal with four clasps), and later qualified as a First Class Interpreter in Russian, 1912. He was promoted Captain 1 Feb. 1913, and at the outbreak of war was employed with the 3rd Battn. of his regiment at Brecon. He played cricket and Rugby football for his regiment, and he reached the semi-final in the Officers' Middle-Weight Class of the Army and Navy Boxing Competition. He has a special certificate for signalling, and a special certificate for gymnastics. He proceeded to France in Dec. 1914, and was mentioned in Despatches for his services, and wounded at Festubert 21 Dec. 1914. In 1915 he proceeded to Gallipoli, and was created a Companion of the Distinguished Service Order [London Gazette, 25 Aug. 1915]: "Hugh Griffith Coke Fowler, Capt., 12th Battn. South Wales Borderers. For great gallantry on 18 and 19 June, on the Gallipoli Peninsula. In a counter-attack on a Turkish trench he led the party which eventually cleared it. This officer himself threw some 30 bombs, some of which were enemy bombs, which he picked up and threw back at great personal risk." After an attack on the trench had failed, he, the Sergt.-Major of the Inniskillings and two privates of the South Wales Borderers, volunteered to bomb the trench, working from traverse to traverse. He and the sergeant-major threw the bombs, and when it was cleared, Capt. Fowler was left to hold it alone till relief came. Afterwards 96 dead Turks were counted in this trench, in addition to which 15 prisoners were taken. He was G.S.O.3, 68th Division, Central Force, Home Defence, 16 Sept. to 16 Dec. 1915; became Adjutant, Special Reserve, 21 April, 1916; was Acting Lieut.-Colonel, 1st Battn. South Wales Borderers, 25 Nov. to 21 Dec. 1917; served in France, 1917–18; held a special appointment, Intelligence Corps, North Russia, from 1 Nov. 1918, until the evacuation in Sept. 1919. He married Muriel Powys Aveline, only daughter of the late Henry Oxenford Aveline Maybery, and has four children.

Hugh G. C. Fowler.

LUCKOCK, RUSSELL MORTIMER, Capt., was born in 1877, son of the late Very Rev. H. M. Luckock, Dean of Lichfield. He was educated at Harrow and Cambridge University, and was commissioned in the King's Own (Royal Lancaster Regt.) 17 Feb. 1900; became Lieutenant 21 July, 1900; served in the South African War, 1899–1902; took part in the operations in the Transvaal in June, 1900; in Natal, June, 1900, including action at Laing's Nek; again in the Transvaal 30 Nov. 1900, to March, 1901; also during the operations in Orange River Colony, May to June, 1901 (Queen's Medal with three clasps, and King's Medal with two clasps). He was promoted Captain 22 Jan. 1907; was Assistant Instructor, School of Musketry, Hythe, 28 Dec. 1907, to 27 Dec. 1911. Capt. Luckock served in the European War, 1914–18. He was Staff Captain (Assistant Military Landing Officer), British Expeditionary Force, 5 Aug. 1914, to 7 Jan. 1915; Brigade Major, 24th Infantry Brigade, British Expeditionary Force, 8 Jan. to 23 Nov. 1915. He was created a Companion of the Distinguished Service Order [London Gazette, 25 Aug. 1915]: "Russell Mortimer Luckock, Capt., King's Own (Royal Lancaster Regt.). For gallantry during the fighting at Neuve Chapelle from 10 to 14 March, 1915, when he performed excellent work as Brigade Major, showing marked ability as a Staff Officer." He was promoted Major 1 Sept. 1915; was G.S.O.2, 17th Division, British Expeditionary Force, 24 Nov. 1915, to 4 Feb. 1916; G.S.O.2, H.Q., 4th Army, British Expeditionary Force, British Armies in France, 5 Feb. 1916, to 30 Jan. 1917; G.S.O.1, 4th Army and 2nd Army, British Armies in France, 31 Jan. 1917, to 28 Feb. 1919; became G.S.O.1, Staff College, 1 March, 1919. He was given the Brevet of Lieut.-Colonel 1 Jan. 1917; created a C.M.G. in 1918; mentioned in Despatches, and awarded the Legion of Honour. Lieut.-Colonel Luckock married, in 1903, Mabel Thorne, daughter of the late S. L. Seckham.

MORISON, FRANK, Capt., received his Captaincy in the 91st Regt. Canadian Highlanders 19 May, 1913. He served in the European War, and was created a Companion of the Distinguished Service Order [London Gazette, 25 Aug. 1915]: "Frank Morison, Capt., 16th Canadian Infantry Battn. For conspicuous gallantry and ability on 20 May, 1915, when he commanded the leading company in the attack on the orchard at La Quinque Rue. Capt. Morison captured the enemy's position, which was of primary importance, under heavy shrapnel, rifle and machine-gun fire."

NASH, JOHN FOSTER PATON, Capt., served in the South African War, 1899–1902. He was present in operations in Natal, March to June, 1900; operations in the Transvaal, east of Pretoria, July to 29 Nov. 1900, including actions at Belfast (26 and 27 Aug.) and Lydenberg (5 to 8 Sept.); operations in the Transvaal, west of Pretoria, July to 29 Nov. 1900, including action at Frederickstad (17 to 25 Oct.); operations in Orange River Colony (May to Nov. 1900), including action at Caledon River (27 to 29 Nov.); operations in the Orange River Colony between 30 Nov. 1900, and 31 May, 1902 (Queen's Medal with four clasps). He became Captain, 31st Regt. (British Columbia Horse), 8 Dec. 1911. He served in the European War, and was created a Companion of the Distinguished Service Order [London Gazette, 25 Aug. 1915]: "John Foster Paton Nash, Capt., 5th Canadian Infantry Battn. For conspicuous gallantry throughout the action at Festubert 22–24 May, 1915. He repaired the telephone wires personally under very heavy fire. Capt. Nash was again brought to notice for excellent work performed under fire at Fleurbaix and at Gravelstafen."

RAWSON, CRESWELL DUFFIELD, Capt., was born 22 Oct. 1883, son of the late Edward Creswell Rawson, Indian Civil Service, and Marion Emma Rawson (née Duffield). He was educated at The Grange, Eastbourne; Malvern College, and the Royal Military Academy, Woolwich, and entered the Royal Artillery 24 Dec. 1902, becoming Lieutenant 24 Dec. 1905, and Captain 30 Oct. 1914. Capt. Rawson served in the European War, serving in operations at the Suez Canal, Feb. 1915 (Despatches [London Gazette, 22 June, 1916], and in Gallipoli. He was mentioned in Despatches, and created a Companion of the Distinguished Service Order [London Gazette, 25 Aug. 1915]: "Creswell Duffield Rawson, Capt., Royal Artillery, 21st Kohat Mountain Battery (Frontier Force), Indian Army. For gallant conduct and distinguished service on 14 May, during operations in the neighbourhood of Gaba Tepe, Dardanelles. Having discovered that the enemy had constructed an emplacement enfilading an important position, he constructed a position for one gun in the firing line, facing the enemy's guns at a range of 650 yards. He then arranged with neighbouring Field Artillery to occupy the attention of other enemy guns, while he knocked down the parapet in front of his own gun and engaged the enemy by direct fire, and without cover, and succeeded in destroying the new emplacement he had observed. He distinguished himself by unceasing good work from 26 April to 26 June, on which latter day he was wounded." He became Staff Captain, Royal Artillery, India, 7 May, 1916; served in Mesopotamia, and was promoted Major 30 July, 1917; was again mentioned in Despatches. Major Rawson married Gladys, youngest daughter of Arthur Niblett.

Creswell D. Rawson.

RYAN, DENIS GEORGE JOCELYN, Capt., was born in 1885, son of the late Capt. C. A. Ryan, R.A., and Thomasine Caroline, daughter of Major-General George Shaw, C.B. He was educated at Stonyhurst, and was commissioned in the Royal Sussex Regt. 28 Jan. 1905, becoming Lieutenant in the Indian Army 11 July, 1907, and Captain 28 Jan. 1914. He served in the European War; was created a Companion of the Distinguished Service Order [London Gazette, 25 Aug. 1915]: "Denis George Jocelyn Ryan, Capt., 1st Battn. 6th Gurkha Rifles. On 13 May, 1915, during operations near Krithia, Dardanelles, for carrying out a daring and well-executed reconnaissance on the enemy's position. The success of the subsequent attack, leading to the capture of the Turkish position, was due in a great measure to this officer's work. He was again brought to notice for gallant work on 28 and 29 June." Capt. Ryan was given the Brevet of Major 1 Jan. 1919. He was twice mentioned in Despatches.

SMITH, STANLEY ALWYN, Capt., was born 12 Nov. 1882, son of Lieut.-Colonel T. J. Smith, V.D. He was educated at Repton School and Edinburgh University (M.B., Ch.B., 1905); is M.D., M.Ch., F.R.C.S., Edinburgh, and Fellow of the American College of Surgeons. He was at one time private assistant to Surgeon-General Sir Robert Jones, Director of British Military Orthopædics; latterly doing consulting orthopædic work in Winnipeg, Canada; Orthopædic Surgeon, Winnipeg General Hospital and Children's Hospital. He became Captain, Canadian Army Medical Service, 21 Dec. 1913. Capt. Smith served in the European War, 1914–16; was thrice mentioned in Despatches, and was created a Companion of the Distinguished Service Order [London Gazette, 25 Aug. 1915]: "Stanley Alwyn Smith, Capt., No. 3 Field Ambulance, Canadian Army Medical Corps. For conspicuous gallantry and devotion to duty at Festubert on the night of 20 May, 1915. Capt. Smith, with a party of eight men, went out voluntarily to remove the wounded from an orchard whilst under heavy fire, and eventually succeeded in bringing all into safety. Four of the eight men of the rescue party were wounded, and two of these have since died." He afterwards became Surgeon-in-Chief, Granville Canadian Special Hospital, Ramsgate, and then Orthopædic Surgeon-in-Chief, Welsh

Metropolitan War Hospital, near Cardiff. He has written monographs on surgical subjects. Major Smith married Pearl Evangeline, daughter of N. D. Bradley, and they have two sons.

STONEY, GEORGE BUTLER, Capt. (Temporary Major), was born 13 Aug. 1877. He was commissioned in the King's Own Scottish Borderers 8 Sept. 1897; promoted Lieutenant 20 April, 1899, and Capt. 21 Sept. 1904; was employed with the Egyptian Army from 23 April, 1908. He saw active service on the North-West Frontier of India, 1897–98, with the Tirah Expeditionary Force (Medal with two clasps). He served in the European War; was created a Companion of the Distinguished Service Order [London Gazette, 25 Aug. 1915]: "George Butler Stoney, Capt. (Temporary Major, Egyptian Army), 1st Battn. King's Own Scottish Borderers. For conspicuous gallantry and ability during operations south-west of Krithia, Dardanelles, from 4 to 7 June, 1915. He showed great coolness and good leading, holding together in a most praiseworthy manner the battalion, which had suffered greatly. He had been previously brought to notice for gallant conduct during the operations up to May 5th." He was killed in action in Gallipoli on 15 Oct. 1915.

George Butler Stoney.

THOM, JOHN HERBERT, Capt., was born 10 Nov. 1882. He entered the Royal Artillery 4 Dec. 1901; was promoted Lieutenant 30 June, 1904, and Captain 30 Oct. 1914. Capt. Thom was created a Companion of the Distinguished Service Order for services in the Gallipoli Campaign [London Gazette, 25 Aug. 1915]: "John Herbert Thom, Capt., Royal Artillery, 21st Kohat Mountain Battery (Frontier Force), Indian Army. For exceptionally gallant conduct on 21 June, 1915, near Gaba Tepe, Dardanelles. He engaged two of the enemy's guns at a range of 450 yards with one 10 pr. b.l. gun, which he had concealed in a tunnelled emplacement in the firing-line parapet, and put them out of action. During this duel, which lasted about an hour, he was knocked down by a high-explosive shell from other guns. Recovering, he continued to direct the fire of his gun, and, having won the fight, withdrew it undamaged and without casualty. Again, on 26 June, he was in an observation station with another officer and gunner. Both officers were wounded and the gunner killed by a shell, but Capt. Thom remained at duty until the following day, when a large piece of metal was removed from his head." He became Major 1 May, 1917; served with the Mesopotamian Expeditionary Force; was Brigade Major, Royal Artillery, Heavy Artillery, 1st Army Corps, M.E.F., 16 Jan. to 14 May, 1918; Brigade Major, Royal Artillery, Heavy Artillery, Army Troops, M.E.F., 15 May to 11 Nov. 1918; G.S.O.2, to Major-General Royal Artillery, General Headquarters, M.E.F., 12 Nov. 1918, to 3 April, 1919.

DOWNES, OSCAR CLAYTON, Capt., was born in 1884, only son of Sir A. H. Downes, Kt., and his first wife, Evelyn, daughter of James Downes and niece of Sir Oscar Clayton. He was commissioned in the Northumberland Fusiliers 4 June, 1904, becoming Lieutenant 1 June, 1907, joining the Rifle Brigade 24 June, 1908, in which he was promoted Captain 1 Feb. 1913. Capt. Downes was Assistant Superintendent of Gymnasia, Irish Command, 3 July, 1913, to 4 Aug. 1914. Serving in the European War, 1914–18, he was employed as Assistant Embarkation Staff Officer, Belfast, 5 Aug. to 8 Dec. 1914; was Temporary Major, Rifle Brigade, Feb. to July, 1915. He was mentioned in Despatches, and was created a Companion of the Distinguished Service Order [London Gazette, 25 Aug. 1915]: "Oscar Clayton Downes, Capt., 1st Battn. The Rifle Brigade (The Prince Consort's Own). For conspicuous gallantry and ability when organizing and leading the assault on the enemy's trenches south of Pilkem on 6 July, 1915. He carried out his duties with great bravery and efficiency until he was wounded." He was G.S.O.3, 2nd Army, British Expeditionary Force, 31 Oct. 1915, to 8 April, 1916; Brigade Major, 100th Infantry Brigade, British Expeditionary Force, British Armies in France, 9 April to 22 Dec. 1916; Brigade Major, 10th Training Reserve Brigade, 26 March, 1917, to 10 Jan. 1918; G.S.O.2, 1st Army Corps, British Armies in France, 24 March, 1918. Capt. Downes married Mary, daughter of the late Capt. Villiers Morton.

London Gazette, 6 Sept. 1915.—"War Office, 6 Sept. 1915. His Majesty the King has been graciously pleased to approve of the appointment of the undermentioned Officers to be Companions of the Distinguished Service Order, in recognition of their gallantry and devotion to duty in the field."

HESKETH, JAMES ARTHUR, Major, was born in 1863. He was educated at the Royal Military College, Canada; joined the Military Forces; served in the European War, and was created a Companion of the Distinguished Service Order [London Gazette, 6 Sept. 1915]: "James Arthur Hesketh, Major, Lord Strathcona's Horse (Royal Canadians). For conspicuous gallantry and devotion to duty on 1 Aug. 1915, near Messines, when a magazine in a farm containing much small-arm ammunition and many bombs and grenades was set on fire by the enemy's shells. One box of ammunition began to burn, and the cartridges were exploding in all directions, when Major Hesketh left his dug-out, entered the farm, still under heavy shell fire, put out the fire, and removed all the ammunition. The risk was very great, and but for his gallant action the reserve ammunition would have been destroyed." He was promoted to Lieutenant-Colonel, and was created a C.M.G. in 1917.

PRATT, GEORGE McDONALD, Capt., was born 14 Oct. 1871. He joined Roberts's Horse, and entered the York and Lancaster Regt. 19 May, 1900, becoming Lieutenant 10 Nov. 1901; Captain 17 April, 1909, and Major 1 Sept. 1915; was Temporary Lieutenant-Colonel commanding 11th Battn. Northumberland Fusiliers 27 Oct. 1916, to 16 March, 1917. He served in the South African War, 1899–190; served with Mounted Infantry; took part in the Relief of Kimberley; in the Orange Free State, Feb. to May, 1900, including operations at Paardeberg (17 to 26 Feb.); actions at Poplar Grove, Dreifontein, Houtnek (Thoba Mountain), Vet River (5 and 6 May) and Zand River; in the Transvaal in May and June, 1900, including actions near Johannesburg, Pretoria and Diamond Hill (11 and 12 June); in the Transvaal, west of Pretoria, 1900, including actions at Elands River (4 to 16 Aug.); in Orange River Colony (May to 29 Nov. 1900), including actions at Bethlehem (6 and 7 J ly) and Wittebergen (7 to 16 July); again in the Transvaal and Orange River Colony, Feb. 1901, to 31 May, 1902 (Queen's Medal with six clasps, and King's Medal with two clasps). For his services in the European War he was given the Brevet of Major 3 June, 1915, and was created a Companion of the Distinguished Service Order [London Gazette, 6 Sept. 1915]: "George McDonald Pratt, Capt., The York and Lancaster Regt. For conspicuous gallantry during an attack on Hooge on 9 and 10 Aug. 1915. He was first into the enemy's position, and rendered his Commanding Officer great assistance in the front-line fighting."

BEAUMAN, ARCHIBALD BENTLEY, Capt., is the son of Bentley Martin Beauman. He was educated at Malvern College and Sandhurst, and entered the 2nd South Staffordshire Regt. 22 Feb. 1908, becoming Lieutenant 8 Jan. 1909, and Captain 1 March, 1915; was Temporary Brigadier-General 31 May, 1918, to 5 April, 1919. He was Staff Captain 22nd Infantry Brigade, British Expeditionary Force, 22 Sept. 1915, to 5 May, 1916; D.A.A. and Q.M.G., 35th Division, British Armies in France, 6 May to 22 Sept. 1916; Brigade Commander, 69th Infantry Brigade, British Armies in France, British Force in Italy, 31 May, 1918, to 5 April, 1919. He landed in France with the original Expeditionary Force; was invalided home in Nov. 1914; rejoined in France in Jan. 1915; served continuously on active service from that time; was five times mentioned in Despatches; received the Italian Silver Medal and the Italian Croce de Guerra; was given the Brevets of Major 3 June, 1917, and Lieutenant-Colonel 1 Jan. 1919, and was created a Companion of the Distinguished Service Order [London Gazette, 6 Sept. 1915]: "Archibald Bentley Beauman, Capt., 1st Battn. The South Staffordshire Regt. For conspicuous gallantry and ability at Festubert on 16 May, 1915, when commanding the leading company of his battalion in the attack. He handled his men with great skill, clearing the trenches to his right with his company and bombers, and, after reaching the line allotted to the battalion, entrenching himself and held on under heavy artillery fire during the 16th, 17th and 18th May." He was awarded a Bar to the Distinguished Service Order.

BROWN, HUGH BARRINGTON, Capt., was born 24 July, 1886. He entered the Leicestershire Regt. 31 May, 1909; became Lieutenant 18 Sept. 1911, and Captain 18 Dec. 1914. He was Staff Captain, 16th Infantry Brigade, B.E.F., 16 Aug. 1915, to 4 April, 1916; Brigade Major, 59th Infantry Brigade, B.E.F., British Armies in France, 5 April, 1916, to 22 Aug. 1918; was given the Brevet of Major 3 June, 1918, and was created a Companion of the Distinguished Service Order [London Gazette, 6 Sept. 1915]: "Hugh Barrington Brown, Capt., 1st Battn. The Leicestershire Regt. For conspicuous gallantry and good service in the trenches at Hooge between 2 and 5 Aug. 1915, when in charge of a brigade bombing party. He got his party up to the trenches by day under shell fire, and remained in them three days during a heavy bombardment. All his bombs were exploded by shell fire, and his party was several times buried and had to be dug out. He has brought his battalion bombers to a high state of efficiency." Portrait page 410.

FORSTER, ALFRED LEONARD, Capt., son of the Rev. Bennet Forster, late Rector of Sevington, Kent. He was educated at Blackheath School, and entered the R.M.A. 1 Sept. 1903, becoming Lieutenant 1 July, 1904, and Captain 1 Sept. 1914. He served in the European War; was mentioned in Despatches twice; given the Brevet of Major 3 June, 1918, and was created a Companion of the Distinguished Service Order [London Gazette, 6 Sept. 1915]: "Alfred Leonard Forster, Capt., Royal Marine Artillery. For conspicuous gallantry on 16 June, 1915, near Zillebeke. During an attack, when two companies of an infantry regiment were crossing some open ground, heavy shrapnel fire was opened on them, three being killed and ten wounded. Capt. Forster, with Corpl. Stone, of the Royal Marine Artillery, who volunteered, went out under heavy shrapnel fire, and brought the wounded into shelter. Capt. Forster has on many occasions showed the highest qualities of an officer when fearlessness and good judgment were essential to success." Major Forster married Gladys, only daughter of R. F. Godfrey-Faussett.

HANBURY, PHILIP LEWIS, Major, was born 1 May, 1879. He was educated at Eastbourne College, and entered the Shropshire Light Infantry 18 Oct. 1899; became Lieutenant 22 Jan. 1901; was Adjutant, Shropshire Light Infantry, 1 April, 1905, to 14 Feb. 1908; was promoted to Capt. 6 March, 1909, and Major 1 Sept. 1915; was Temporary Lieut.-Colonel 29 Oct. 1916, to 2 June, 1917. He was Brigade Major, 82nd Infantry Brigade, New Armies, Mediterranean Expeditionary Force; D.A.A.G. and Q.M.G., 16th Army Corps, Mediterranean Expeditionary Force, Egyptian Expeditionary Force, 25 Jan. to 29 Aug. 1916; G.S.O.2, 27th Division, Egyptian Expeditionary Force, 1 Sept. to 28 Oct. 1916; G.S.O.1, 26th Division, British Salonika Force, 29 Oct. 1916, to 12 Jan. 1918; G.S.O.1, G.H.Q., British Salonika Force, 13 Jan. 1918. He served in the South African War, 1899–1902, and took part in the operations in the Orange Free State, Feb. to May, 1900, including those at Paardeberg (17 to 26 Feb.); actions at Poplar Grove, Dreifontein, Houtnek (Thoba Mountain), Vet River (5 and 6 May) and Zand River; in the Transvaal in May and June, 1900, including actions near Johannesburg and Pretoria; in the Transvaal, east of Pretoria, July to 29 Nov. 1900; in the Transvaal, west of Pretoria, July to 29 Nov. 1900, including actions at Elands River (4 to 16 Aug.); in Orange River Colony, May to 29 Nov. 1900, including action at Rhenoster River; also in Cape Colony, south of Orange River, 1899–1900; again in the Transvaal 30 Nov. 1900, to 31 May, 1902 (Queen's Medal with four clasps, and King's Medal with two clasps). For his services in the European War, 1914–16, he was mentioned in Despatches; was given the Brevet of Lieut.-Colonel 3 June, 1917; received the Order of SS. Maurice and Lazarus, Italy, and was created a Companion of the Distinguished Service Order [London Gazette, 6 Sept. 1915]: " Philip Leonard Hanbury, Major, The King's (Shropshire Light Infantry). For consistent good work as Brigade Major during the first four months of 1915, notably at St. Eloi, during the attacks of 14 and 15 Feb. and 14 and 15 March." He married Jess, daughter of W. G. Allan.

HEPBURN, WILLIAM CLAY, Capt., was born 25 June, 1877, son of the late James S. Hepburn and the late Ellen Gertrude Hepburn (née Clay). He was educated at Amersham Hall, Caversham, at New College, Eastbourne, and is a Graduate of the School of Mines, Camborne, Cornwall. He was mining for four years in British Columbia, and later in the Transvaal; obtained an English Colliery Manager's Certificate in 1905; was Manager in 1907, and subsequently Agent to the Oakdale Navigation Collieries, Ltd. He joined the 1st Monmouth Regt. as Second Lieutenant in 1908, Captain in 1913, and was mobilized 5 Aug. 1914. He commanded the 172nd Coy., Royal Engineers, in 1915; was mentioned in Despatches twice, and created a Companion of the Distinguished Service Order [London Gazette, 6 Sept. 1915]: " William Clay Hepburn, Capt., 1st Battn. Monmouthshire Regt., Territorial Force, attached 172nd Coy., Royal Engineers. For conspicuous energy and good work near Ypres on 12 July, 1915. After the enemy had exploded a mine just short of our parapet, a gallery was driven out to protect the trench, and the enemy's mine was struck. It was found to contain a charge of about 1,350 lbs. of explosive, some detonators, and part of the main electric firing lead. These were successfully withdrawn by the united efforts of Capt. Hepburn and two officers and four men working under him." Major Hepburn has retired. He married, in 1906, Helen, daughter of David Hannah, and they have two sons and one daughter.

JONES, KINGSMILL WILLIAMS, Capt., served in the European War, and was created a Companion of the Distinguished Service Order [London Gazette, 6 Sept. 1915]: " Kingsmill Williams Jones, M.D., Capt., Royal Army Medical Corps (Special Reserve), attached 1st Battn. East Kent Regt. For conspicuous gallantry and devotion to duty at Hooge. During the entire night of 9–10 Aug. 1915, and the whole of the following day and night, he was attending to and evacuating wounded from the front trenches, time after time exposing himself to shell and rifle fire. He was twice slightly wounded, but stuck to his work with unflagging energy. It was entirely owing to Capt. Jones that the crater was successfully evacuated of wounded."

Kingsmill W. Jones.

PHILBY, HAROLD PAYNE, Capt., was born 22 July, 1887, third son of the late Harry Montague Philby, of Cocoawatte and Galoola Estates, Ceylon, and of May Beatrice Philby. He was educated at Streete Court, Westgate, and at Aldenham School; entered the Royal Military College 13 Sept. 1906; gazetted as Second Lieutenant, The York and Lancaster Regt. 19 Sept. 1908; promoted Lieutenant 1 April, 1910; seconded with W.A.F.F. 4 Oct. 1911, to 3 Aug. 1914; rejoined 2nd Battn. The York and Lancaster Regt. 4 Aug. 1914, on outbreak of war, and went with them to France (6th Division), Sept. 1914; appointed Temporary Captain, York and Lancaster Regt. 15 Nov. to 28 Nov. 1914; promoted Captain 29 Nov. 1914; appointed Adjutant, The York and Lancaster Regt. 15 Dec. 1914; appointed Temporary Major 6 Feb. 1916; appointed to the command of 2nd Battn. The York and Lancaster Regt., April, 1916; killed in action 17 May, 1916. He was mentioned in Despatches [London Gazette, 6 Sept. 1915, and 1 Jan. 1916], and awarded the Distinguished Service Order [London Gazette, 6 Sept. 1915]: " Harold Payne Philby, Capt., 2nd Battn. The York and Lancaster Regt. For conspicuous and consistent good service throughout the campaign, notably during the fighting at Hooge on the 9th Aug. 1915, when with the greatest coolness and energy he frequently visited all portions of the firing line under heavy shell fire, and personally supervised the despatch of reinforcements, bombs, etc." Major Philby was a very fine soldier, and was beloved and admired by all who knew him.

SHEEPSHANKS, ARTHUR CHARLES, Temporary Capt., served in the European War, and was created a Companion of the Distinguished Service Order [London Gazette, 6 Sept. 1915]: " Arthur Charles Sheepshanks, Temporary Capt., The Rifle Brigade (The Prince Consort's Own). For conspicuous gallantry in a counter-attack on 30 July, 1915, when he continued to advance with his company, till only he and six riflemen were left standing. He then checked a bomb attack by the enemy, and held on to his trench till late in the evening. He was wounded in the head early in the day, but returned to duty with his company after the wound had been dressed."

STOCKWELL, CLIFTON INGLIS, Capt., was born 27 Sept. 1879, son of Colonel C. de N. Stockwell, Lincolnshire Regt., and Emily Stockwell. He was educated at Haileybury, and at Sandhurst in 1898, and was appointed to the 2nd Battn. Royal Welsh Fusiliers 11 Feb. 1899; served with them in China and India; promoted to Captain in 1st Battn. at Aldershot, 1907; served with 1st Battn. in England and Ireland;

appointed to Depôt at Wrexham, 1912; joined the 2nd Battn. as 1st Reinforcement the first day of the Battle of the Aisne, 1914; commanded A Coy., 2nd Battn., till March, 1915; mentioned in Despatches in Nov. 1914; transferred to the 1st Battn. R.W.F.; commanded A Coy., 1st R.W.F.; attacked and captured Canadian Orchard at Battle of Festubert 16 May, 1915; at the end of the day was senior surviving officer; awarded the D.S.O.; mentioned in Despatches; was Brigade Major, 59th Infantry Brigade, in Sept. 1915; promoted Major 15 Sept. 1915; mentioned in Despatches 1 Jan. 1916; given command 1st Battn. R.W.F. in Feb. 1916; commanded the battalion during the actions of 1 July, 1916 (attack on Fricourt); 4 July (night attack on the Triangle Trench); 14 July (attack on Bazentin-le-Petit); 27 Aug. (attack on Delville Wood, and Ale, Hop and Beer Alleys), and 3 Sept. (attack on Guinchy).

Clifton Inglis Stockwell.

He was mentioned in Despatches, in July, 1916; appointed to command the 164th Infantry Brigade, 55th Division, 18 Sept. 1916; commanded the 164th Infantry Brigade during the attack on the Gord Line and Gueudecourt 27 Sept. 1916; given the Brevet of Lieutenant-Colonel, and mentioned in Despatches in Jan. 1917; attack of 31 July, 1917 (Third Battle of Ypres) (mentioned in Despatches); attack of 20 Sept. 1917 (Third Battle of Ypres); attack of 20 Nov. in support to the Battle of Cambrai; counter-attack of 30 Nov. to enemy attack at Cambrai; awarded the C.M.G., and mentioned in Despatches in Jan. 1918. On 9 April, 1918, held Givenchy with the 164th Infantry Brigade, and successfully repulsed heavy attack, taking 700 prisoners; mentioned in Despatches in July, 1918; on 20 Sept. captured the enemy position at Givenchy by surprise attack; pursuit of the enemy from La Bassée to Tournai, including the forcing of the Haute Dendre Canal, Marque River; on 9 Nov. commanded mobile column (Stockwell's Force) which reached a point a mile from Enghien on the day of the Armistice, having forced the Dendre at 5 a.m. that day; billeted in Brussels with the 164th Infantry Brigade for Christmas; awarded the C.B., and mentioned in Despatches in Jan. 1919; Staff College in April, 1919; granted a p.s.c., and posted to the 2nd Battn. in Limerick in Jan. 1920; awarded the French Croix de Guerre in March, 1920. His Distinguished Service Order was gazetted 6 Sept. 1915: " Clifton Inglis Stockwell, Capt., Royal Welsh Fusiliers. For conspicuous gallantry and ability at Festubert on 16 May, 1915, when he led his company in an attack on the German trenches. After his company had lost heavily, he reorganized it, and collected men of other units and made two further successful advances. It was largely due to his gallant and capable leading that the troops succeeded in establishing the line so far forward." He married Hilda Rose, daughter of Colonel T. P. Westmorland, late Royal Engineers.

TURNER, ARNOLD GEOFFREY, Capt., was born 17 May, 1880. He entered the Royal Engineers 6 Jan. 1900; became Lieutenant 6 Jan. 1903; Captain 6 Jan. 1909; Major 2 Nov. 1916; was Acting Lieutenant-Colonel, Royal Engineers, from 1 May, 1918. He was 2nd Assistant Instructor, School of Military Engineering, 1 Feb. 1910, to 13 April, 1912; on Special Service in Egypt from Oct. 1910, to April, 1911; and 14 Oct. 1911, to 20 March, 1912; 1st Assistant Instructor, School of Military Engineering, 14 April, 1912, to 31 Jan. 1913; employed on Rhodesia and Angola Boundary Commission 1 Feb. 1913, to 26 April, 1915. For his services in the European War he was given the Brevet of Lieutenant-Colonel 3 June, 1919, and was created a Companion of the Distinguished Service Order [London Gazette, 6 Sept. 1915]: " Arnold Geoffrey Turner, Capt., Royal Engineers. For conspicuous gallantry and devotion to duty during the attack on Hooge on 9 Aug. 1915. After leading two sections and six blocking parties of his company through the first line under heavy artillery and machine-gun fire, he immediately put out wire in front of the captured position. When the Senior Infantry Officers were killed or wounded, Capt. Turner assumed command of the whole party in his vicinity, and proceeded to consolidate his position, continuing to do so after being wounded till incapacitated by loss of blood."

London Gazette, 15 Sept. 1915.—" War Office, 15 Sept. 1915. His Majesty the King has been graciously pleased to approve of the appointment of the undermentioned Officers to be Companions of the Distinguished Service Order, in recognition of their gallantry and devotion to duty in the field."

BECHER, JOHN PICKARD, Capt., was born 20 July, 1880, son of the late John Henry Becher, of Hill House, Southwell, Notts. He joined the Nottinghamshire and Derbyshire Territorials 1 Nov. 1906, becoming Lieutenant 15 July, 1907, and Captain 9 May, 1910, and was created a Companion of the Distinguished Service Order [London Gazette, 15 Sept. 1915]: " John Pickard Becher, Capt. (Temporary Major), 8th Battn. The Sherwood Foresters (Nottinghamshire and Derbyshire Regt.), T.F. For conspicuous gallantry and good service on several occasions. On 24 April, 1915, at Kemmel, when part of his trench was blown in, he organized the defence of the breach under heavy fire, and personally assisted in repairing the parapet, digging out seven buried men. On 15 June, at Kemmel, when part of his trench was blown in by mines, shells and trench mortars, he displayed great gallantry and coolness in reorganizing the defence. On 30 July and subsequent days, at Ypres, he displayed great coolness, cheerfulness and resource under trying circumstances, when in temporary command of a battalion." He died on 1 Jan. 1916, of wounds received on 14 Oct. 1915.

MONTEITH, HUGH GLENCAIRN, Capt., was born 11 May, 1883, son of the Rev. John Monteith, of Moniave-Glenluiart, Dumfriesshire. He was educated at Fettes College, and Pembroke College, Cambridge, for the medical profession, and joined the Royal Army Medical Corps in July, 1910, as Lieutenant, becoming Captain in Jan. 1914. He served in the European War; was at one time attached to the 2nd Duke of Cornwall's Light Infantry; was present at Ypres, Yser, the Marne, etc. He held various Staff and other appointments; was mentioned in Despatches four times; received the O.B.E., and was created a Companion of the Distinguished Service Order [London Gazette, 15 Sept. 1915]: "Hugh Glencairn Monteith, Capt., Royal Army Medical Corps (attached 2nd Battn. The Duke of Cornwall's Light Infantry). For conspicuous gallantry and devotion to duty in picking up and attending to the wounded under heavy fire in the actions near St. Jean and Wieltje, east of Ypres, between 23 and 27 April, 1915, when the casualties in the battalion to which he was attached were very heavy." He played Rugby for Cambridge and for Scotland, and also for the London Hospital (where he was trained). Capt. Monteith married, in 1915, Dorothy Huntly, eldest daughter of Owen R. Dunell, of Garboldisham Manor, Norfolk, and they have one son and one daughter.

POWELL, HENRY GEORGE, Capt., was born 17 Feb. 1867. He joined the Army 5 Feb. 1887, and became Captain 3 Dec. 1894, and retired from the North Lancashire Regt. 8 July, 1903. On the outbreak of the European War, Capt. Powell took part in the campaign on the Western Front. He was given the Brevet of Major, Reserve of Officers, 3 June, 1916, and was created a Companion of the Distinguished Service Order [London Gazette, 15 Sept. 1915]: "Henry George Powell, Capt. (Temporary Lieut.-Colonel), Reserve of Officers, The Loyal North Lancashire Regt. For conspicuous gallantry on 23 Oct. 1914, near Bixschoote, when he led his company in the attack, and by his fine and courageous example contributed greatly to the success achieved. He was wounded in the action."

SACKVILLE, LIONEL CHARLES STOPFORD, Capt., was born 30 April, 1891, son of the late Colonel Lionel Stopford Sackville (who commanded the 4th Battn. Rifle Brigade, and died in 1905), and of Evelyn Stopford Sackville, daughter of Major A. Gosling. He was educated at Eton and Sandhurst, and was commissioned in the Rifle Brigade 17 Dec. 1910. He served in Egypt in 1911, and in the Soudan in 1912, in which year he was promoted Lieutenant, and he was sent to India in 1913, where he remained until 1914. He served in the European War in France and Flanders, 1914–15, and on 29 Dec. 1915, he went to Salonika, remaining there till 1918. He became Captain 20 March, 1915; was Staff Officer, 80th Infantry Brigade, British Salonika Force, 26 Nov. 1916, to 1 Aug. 1917; Brigade

L. C. Stopford Sackville.

Major, 65th Infantry Brigade, British Salonika Force, 2 Aug. 1917, to 3 Nov. 1918. Capt. Stopford Sackville was mentioned in Despatches in June, 1915; was given the Brevet of Major 1 Jan. 1919; received the Croix de Guerre avec Palme, and created a Companion of the Distinguished Service Order [London Gazette, 15 Sept. 1915]: "Lionel Charles Stopford Sackville, Capt., 4th Battn. The Rifle Brigade (The Prince Consort's Own). For conspicuous gallantry and ability since he obtained command of a company in Feb. 1915. Near Ypres, from 8 to 15 May, he did excellent work in the trenches, keeping up his men's spirits under very heavy bombardments. He took command of another company in addition to his own when it had lost all its officers. On the night of the 14th–15th March, near St. Eloi, he took a barricade with half his company, went forward by himself to reconnoitre, and then, returning for his company, led them back and cleared the houses on the road."

London Gazette, 13 Sept. 1915.—"Admiralty, 13 Sept. 1915. The King has been graciously pleased to give orders for the appointment of the following Officers to the Distinguished Service Order, in recognition of the services mentioned."

TALBOT, CECIL PONSONBY, Commander, Royal Navy, served in the European War, and was created a Companion of the Distinguished Service Order [London Gazette, 13 Sept. 1915]: "Cecil Ponsonby Talbot, Commander, Royal Navy. For his services in sinking a German torpedo-boat destroyer off the enemy's coast on the 26th July, 1915, whilst on patrol duty in his submarine."

WATERLOW, JOHN BEAUCHAMP, Lieut.-Commander (now Commander), Royal Navy, served in the European War, and was created a Companion of the Distinguished Service Order [London Gazette, 13 Sept. 1915]: "John Beauchamp Waterlow, Lieut.-Commander (now Commander), Royal Navy. For his services in the mine-sweeping operations in the Dardanelles between the 19th Feb. and 17th March, 1915. Lieut.-Commander Waterlow took part in these operations on several occasions under a heavy fire, notably on the night of 13–14 March, when he carried the attack through an area illuminated by six powerful searchlights and covered by the fire of four forts, as well as numerous light guns." He was killed in action 31 May, 1916.

COOKSON, EDGAR CHRISTOPHER, Lieut.-Commander, Royal Navy, served in the European War, and was created a Companion of the Distinguished Service Order [London Gazette, 13 Sept. 1915]: "Edgar Christopher Cookson, Lieut.-Commander, Royal Navy. For services during the operations in the Shatt-el-Arab. Lieut.-Commander Cookson was concluding a reconnaissance up a creek of the Euphrates, west of Gurnah, in the armed launch Shushan, on the 9th May, 1915, when he was heavily attacked by Arabs concealed in the reeds. Although severely wounded early in the action, he resumed command after his wound had been temporarily dressed, and succeeded in most ably extricating the vessel from a perilous position under heavy rifle fire." He was subsequently awarded the Victoria Cross (see Victoria Cross Volume).

Edgar C. Cookson.

HERBERT, GODFREY, Lieut.-Commander, Royal Navy, was born in 1884. He served in the European War, and was present at the Battle of Heligoland Bight, in the Submarine D5, which he subsequently commanded. He was promoted to Commander in 1917, and was created a Companion of the Distinguished Service Order [London Gazette, 13 Sept. 1915]: "Godfrey Herbert, Lieut.-Commander, Royal Navy (with Claude Congreve Dobson, Lieut.-Commander, Royal Navy, and Archibald Douglas Cochrane, Lieut.-Commander, Royal Navy). For services in a submarine in the Sea of Marmora, where they did great damage to enemy shipping, and after blocking the railway line near Kava Burnu by bombarding it from the sea, shelled a troop train and blew up three ammunition cars attached to it." Commander Herbert married, in 1916, the widow of Major Francis Arthur Nelson, Royal Marine Light Infantry, and they have one daughter.

DOBSON, CLAUDE CONGREVE, Lieut.-Commander, Royal Navy, served in the European War, and was created a Companion of the Distinguished Service Order [London Gazette, 13 Sept. 1915]: "Claude Congreve Dobson, Lieut.-Commander, Royal Navy (with Godfrey Herbert, Lieut.-Commander, Royal Navy, and Archibald Douglas Cochrane, Lieut.-Commander, Royal Navy). For services in a submarine in the Sea of Marmora, where they did great damage to enemy shipping, and after blocking the railway line near Kava Burnu by bombarding it from the sea, shelled a troop train and blew up three ammunition cars attached to it."

COCHRANE, THE HON. ARCHIBALD DOUGLAS, Lieut.-Commander, was born 8 Jan. 1885, second son of the 1st Baron Cochrane (son of the 11th Earl of Dundonald), and Lady Gertrude Boyle, daughter of the 6th Earl of Glasgow. He served in the European War, 1914–18; was present at the Battle of Heligoland Bight; was mentioned in Despatches, and was created a Companion of the Distinguished Service Order [London Gazette, 13 Sept. 1915]: "Archibald Douglas Cochrane, Lieut.-Commander, Royal Navy (with Godfrey Herbert, Lieut.-Commander, Royal Navy, and Claude Congreve Dobson, Lieut.-Commander, Royal Navy). For services in a submarine in the Sea of Marmora, where they did great damage to enemy shipping, and after blocking the railway line near Kava Burnu by bombarding it from the sea, shelled a troop train and blew up three ammunition cars attached to it."

SKETCHLEY, ERNEST FREDERICK POWYS, Capt., was born 6 Aug. 1881, at West Kensington, W., son of the Rev. E. Powys Sketchley, of Ballater, Bromley, Kent, Assistant Secretary of the Society for the Propagation of the Gospel, and Mrs. Powys Sketchley. He was educated at Dulwich College, and joined the Royal Marine Light Infantry as a Second Lieutenant 1 Jan. 1900. From 1905 to 1908 he was A.D.C. and Secretary to His Excellency Sir F. G. D. Bedford, G.C.B., the Governor of Western Australia. He became Lieutenant 1 Jan. 1901, Captain in 1911, and Major in Sept. 1914, when he was also made a G.S.O.2. From 1914 he was on the Staff of the Royal Naval Division: served at Ostend and Antwerp; went to Gallipoli, and for his services there was twice mentioned in Despatches, and was created a Companion of the Distinguished Service Order [London Gazette, 13 Sept. 1915]: "Ernest Frederick Powys Sketchley, T./Major, Portsmouth Division, Royal Marine Light Infantry. For services in the Gallipoli Peninsula 3 July, 1915, during operations south of Achi Baba, where a retreat began and rapidly developed, which might have had very serious consequences. Major Sketchley, who was in the supports, assisted by L.-Corpl. J. G. Way, prevented some of the men from retiring further. He then gathered together about forty of them, reorganized them, and, leading them forward, reoccupied some of the trenches. He returned twice to gather more men, and, collecting in all about a hundred, retook further trenches, captured forty prisoners and secured the position. He exhibited great courage, presence of mind, and powers of personal leadership in a moment of crisis." He married Phyllis F. M., daughter of J. F. Campbell, Esq., Deputy Master of the Royal Mint, Perth, Western Australia. Major Sketchley died of wounds received in action 12 Oct. 1916.

SINGLETON, MARK, Lieut., Royal Navy, served in the Great War, and was created a Companion of the Distinguished Service Order [London Gazette, 13 Sept. 1915]: "Mark Singleton, Lieut., Royal Navy. For his services during the advance from Qurnah and capture of Amara at the beginning of June, 1915. Lieut. Singleton was in command of the armed launch Shaitan, and displayed great skill and energy in pursuit of the enemy gunboat Marmariss and other craft. He went ahead of the main force through Amara in a gallant manner, and performed the remarkable

D D

feat in his small armed tug of bringing to surrender a body of about 11 officers and 250 men of the Turkish troops, whom he had intercepted, and causing a large number to retire, thus largely contributing to the surrender of the town."

BIGSWORTH, ARTHUR WELLESLEY, Wing-Commander, was born 27 March, 1885, son of Arthur Wellesley (and Kate) Bigsworth. He was educated at a naval crammer's, by a tutor, and in H.M.S. Worcester. He

first went to sea in 1901, and served several years in the Mercantile Marine as an officer; joined the Royal Naval Reserve in 1904; was promoted to Sub-Lieutenant in Jan. 1911, and shortly after taking his certificate, was appointed to the Naval Flying School at Eastchurch as a flying officer. He was subsequently transferred to the Royal Naval Air Station at Calshot, and when the Naval Air Service was organized, he graded as a Flight Commander 1 July, 1914. He is described as being "very modest and levelheaded, a man who would keep steady in a tight corner." He served in the European War, first in France with No. 1 Naval Aeroplane Wing; at Antwerp, Lille, Ostend, etc. On 17 May, 1915, he succeeded in destroying, single-handed, a

Arthur W. Bigsworth.

Zeppelin that had raided Ramsgate, dropping four bombs, which set one of the compartments on fire. This feat is recorded by the Admiralty in a statement issued 17 May: " . . . The Zeppelin that attacked Ramsgate early this morning was chased off by Eastgate and Westgate machines as far as the West Hinder Lightship. When off Nieuport she was attacked by eight naval machines from Dunkirk. Three machines were able to attack her at close range by fire. Flight-Commander Bigsworth dropped four bombs from 200 feet above the airship. A large column of smoke was seen to come out of one of her compartments. The Zeppelin then rose to a great height, 11,000 feet, with her tail down, and is believed to be severely damaged. All our machines were exposed to a heavy fire from the Zeppelin." The Admiralty report makes it evident that in fighting the enemy air machine Flight-Commander Bigsworth ran great risk from anti-aircraft fire and machine-gun fire from four machine guns on the Zeppelin. In recognition of this gallant exploit he was mentioned in Despatches, and appointed Wing-Commander, Royal Naval Air Service. This was the first Zeppelin to be attacked during the war, and it is believed that it was destroyed. In Aug. of the same year Wing-Commander Bigsworth was created a Companion of the Distinguished Service Order [London Gazette, 13 Sept. 1915]: "Arthur Wellesley Bigsworth, Wing-Commander, Royal Naval Air Service. For his services in destroying, single-handed, a German submarine on the morning of 26 Aug. 1915, by bombs dropped from an aeroplane. Squadron-Commander Bigsworth was under heavy fire from the shore batteries and from the submarine whilst manœuvring for position. Nevertheless, displaying great coolness, he descended to 500 feet, and after several attempts was able to get a good time for dropping the bombs with effect." The Insignia of the Distinguished Service Order were presented to Commander Bigsworth by the King at Buckingham Palace 14 Oct. 1915. At one time he was ordered to the Dardanelles, but at the last moment was told to remain in France, where he had been doing good work consistently at the front. On 1 Oct. 1917, he received a Bar to his D.S.O.

PLAYNE, BASIL ALFRED, Surgeon, Royal Navy, served in the Great War, and was created a Companion of the Distinguished Service Order [London Gazette, 13 Sept. 1915]: "Basil Alfred Playne, Surgeon, Royal Navy, Royal Naval Division. For gallantry and good service during operations near Gaba Tepe from 28 April to 1 May, 1915. On several occasions he rushed across the open (the communication trench being incomplete) into the fire trenches, and attended the seriously wounded, regardless of the severity of the enemy's fire; on one occasion he carried a wounded officer on his back from the fire trench to the communication trench under heavy fire. His conspicuous bravery not only inspired the stretcher-bearers to perform fine work, but gave confidence and spirit to all ranks. He was again several times brought to notice for gallant deeds when attending wounded on May 3rd and 4th."

London Gazette, 24 Sept. 1915.—"Admiralty, 24 Sept. 1915. The King has been graciously pleased to give orders for the appointment of the undermentioned Officer to be a Companion of the Distinguished Service Order."

HAMILTON, LOUIS HENRY KEPPEL, Lieut., Royal Navy, was born 31 Dec. 1890, son of the late Admiral Sir Frederick Tower Hamilton, G.C.V.O., K.C.B. He joined the Royal Naval College, Osborne, as a Naval Cadet in Sept. 1903. He served in the European War, serving in the Cameroons in charge of a river flotilla, and was present at the Battle of Jutland, for which he received the Order of St. Stanislas. He was created a Companion of the Distinguished Service Order [London Gazette, 24 Sept. 1915]: "Louis Henry Keppel Hamilton, Lieut., Royal Navy. For his services in the operations in the Cameroons. Lieut. Hamilton was in charge of a river flotilla which drove the Germans out of Dehane at the end of Dec. 1914. He was later in command of the detachment which transported a naval gun 160 miles up the lower reaches of the Niger River, thence 480 miles up the Benue River, and 60 miles by land, and thus contributed in large measure to the success of the operations which culminated in the surrender of Garua on the 10th June, 1915." Commander Hamilton was subsequently employed on special duty in the War Office. He has published various small works on signalling. He married Margaret, youngest daughter of B. P. Blockley, and they have one daughter.

London Gazette, 8 Oct. 1915.—"Admiralty, 8 Oct. 1915. The King has been graciously pleased to approve of the appointment of the undermentioned Officer to be a Companion of the Distinguished Service Order."

DOYLEY-HUGHES, GUY, Lieut., Royal Navy, served in the European War. He was created a Companion of the Distinguished Service Order [London Gazette, 8 Oct. 1915]: "Guy Doyley-Hughes, Lieut., R.N.D.S.C. For his services on the 21st Aug. 1915, when he voluntarily swam to the shore alone from a submarine, and blew up a low brickwork support to the Ismid railway line, in spite of the presence of an armed guard within 150 yards of him. After a running fight of about a mile, he dived into the sea, and was finally pulled on board the submarine utterly exhausted, having had to swim nearly a mile in his clothes."

London Gazette, 15 Oct. 1915.—"His Majesty the King has been graciously pleased to confer the undermentioned rewards for distinguished service in the field. To be Companions of the Distinguished Service Order."

MOLESWORTH, EDWIN ALGERNON, Major, was born 9 May, 1875, son of the late Colonel St. Aubyn Molesworth, R.H.A. He was gazetted to the Royal Dublin Fusiliers 9 Dec. 1896; became Lieutenant 25 June, 1898; Captain 26 Oct. 1901, and Major 5 Dec. 1914. Major Molesworth served in the European War, and was created a Companion of the Distinguished Service Order [London Gazette, 15 Oct. 1915]: "Edwin Algernon Molesworth, Major, Royal Dublin Fusiliers. For distinguished service in the field." In 1916, Major Molesworth married Ruth, daughter of Leslie Creery.

FARMAR, HAROLD MYNORS, Major, was born at Southampton 15 June, 1878, son of the late Major-General William Roberts Farmar and Ellinor Louisa, his wife, daughter of Lewis Girardot. He was educated at the Isle of Wight College, and at the Royal Military College, Sandhurst, passing into the Lancashire Fusiliers 7 June, 1898. He accompanied the Nile Expedition; was present at the Battle of Khartoum, and received the Khedive's Egyptian Medal with clasp, and the Medal. He served during the Insurrection in Crete, 1898, and with the Mounted Infantry in the South African War from 1899 to 1900, being present at the operations in the Orange Free State, Feb. to May, 1900, including actions at Vet River (5 and 6 May) and Zand River; in the Transvaal, including actions near Johannesburg, Pretoria and Diamond Hill (11 and 12 June); in the Transvaal, east of Pretoria, including action at Reit Vlei; also during operations in the Transvaal, west of Pretoria, including action at Zilikat's Nek. He was mentioned in Despatches [London Gazette, 10 Sept. 1901]; and received the Queen's Medal with four clasps. He became Captain, Lancashire Fusiliers, 1901, and accompanied the North China Field Force, 1901. He was Adjutant, Lancashire Fusiliers, from 1904 to 1907, and was on the Staff, Royal Military Academy, Woolwich, 1907–11. Capt. Farmar served in the European War from 1914, first as Staff Captain with the Aden Mobile Column. He took part in the celebrated Lancashire Landing on the Gallipoli Peninsula. This landing was accomplished in the morning of the 25th April, 1915, with the 1st Battn. (Lancashire Fusiliers). The fighting was terrific; the Brigadier-General was wounded, and the Brigade Major killed, leaving Capt. Farmar in command of the Brigade from early morning until the afternoon, when fresh troops landed and captured the Turkish Redoubts. In this battle the 86th Brigade suffered casualties at the rate of 50 per cent. Capt. Farmar now became Brigade Major, and on 28 April led the successful attack of the 86th Brigade on the Krithia Wood, after the 88th Brigade had been compelled to fall back. He was created a Companion of the Distinguished Service Order [London Gazette, 15 Oct. 1915]: "Harold Mynors Farmar, Major, The Lancashire Fusiliers. For distinguished service in the field." In July, 1915, he was wounded. He was passed fit for duty in Nov., and appointed D.A.A. and Q.M.G.; was A.A. and Q.M.G., and Temporary Lieutenant-Colonel 10 July, 1916, to 3 Sept. 1917, with the 3rd Australian Division; A.A. and Q.M.G., 35th Division, British Armies in France, 4 Sept. 1917, to 5 Sept. 1918; A.Q.M.G., American Staff College, British Armies in France, 6 Sept. to 26 Oct. 1918; A.Q.M.G., 9th Army Corps, British Armies in France, 27 Oct. 1918, to Jan. 1919; A.M.S., Western Command, 25 April, 1919. He was given the Brevet of Lieutenant-Colonel 3 June, 1917, and created a C.B. in 1919. He played cricket and hockey for Sandhurst in 1897, and polo for his regimental team. Lieut.-Colonel Farmar married Violet, youngest daughter of Sir William Dalby, and they have one son and two daughters.

MOORE, FRANCIS, Major, was born at Bury, Lancashire, 22 Dec.

1879, eldest son of the late Colonel Francis Moore, Royal Munster Fusiliers, and Cara Eliza, daughter of Thomas Cummins, Esq., of Coolaha, County Cork; and grandson of the late Capt. Francis Moore, Royal Dragoons. He was educated at the Elizabeth College, Guernsey, and at Blundell's School, Tiverton, passing into the Royal Fusiliers, as Second Lieutenant, 4 Jan. 1899, from the 1st Regt. Royal Guernsey Light Infantry. He became Lieutenant 31 Jan. 1900. He served in the South African War from 1899 to 1902, with the Royal Fusiliers Mounted Infantry Company, and was slightly wounded; took part in the operations in the Transvaal, April to Dec. 1901, and March to May, 1902; in Orange River Colony, Jan. to March, 1902; also in Cape Colony,

Francis Moore.

May, 1902 (Queen's Medal with five clasps). He was wounded 6 July, 1901; was promoted to Captain 19 Oct. 1904, and was employed as Chief Instructor of the School of Musketry, South Africa, with the temporary rank of Major, from 1909 to 1913, becoming Major 1 Sept. 1915. During the

European War he was present with the 2nd Battn. Royal Fusiliers (29th Division) at the first landing on the Gallipoli Peninsula 25 April, 1915. During the subsequent operations he was twice slightly and once severely wounded. He was Acting Lieutenant-Colonel, Machine Gun Corps, 26 Nov. 1916, and was Deputy Inspector of Machine Gun Units, Allied Forces, Archangel, 1918–19. He was mentioned in Despatches in 1915, and was created a Companion of the Distinguished Service Order [London Gazette, 15 Oct. 1915]: "Francis Moore, Major, The Royal Fusiliers (City of London Regt.). For distinguished service in the field." He was awarded the O.B.E. in 1919. He married Anne Early, youngest daughter of the late William Van Wyck, Esq., of New York, U.S.A., and they have one daughter.

WOOD, ALGERNON GEORGE NEWCOME, Major, was born at Warley, Essex, 19 May, 1879, son of Lieut.-Colonel George Wilding Wood, of Nithsdale, Ingatestone, Essex (late 56th Regt., Pompadours), and Anna Maria, his wife, daughter of the Rev. James Morton, of Little Island, Clonmel. He was educated at Haileybury College, obtaining his first commission in the Essex Regt. 11 Feb. 1899, and became First Lieutenant 11 March, 1900; Captain 14 March, 1905, and Adjutant, 1st Battn. Essex Regt. from Nov. 1912. Lieut. Wood went right through the South African War, from 1899–1902, on the Staff, employed with the Mounted Infantry. He took part in the Relief of Kimberley, and was engaged in many of the chief actions of the war; took part in the operations in the Orange Free State, including operations at Paardeberg (17 to 26 Feb.); actions at Poplar Grove, Dreifontein, Vet River (5 and 6 May) and Zand River; in the Transvaal in May and June, 1900, including actions near Johannesburg, Pretoria and Diamond Hill (11 and 12 June); in the Transvaal, east of Pretoria, including action at Belfast (26 and 27 Aug.); again in the Transvaal, west of Pretoria, including action at Frederickstad (17 to 25 Oct.); in Cape Colony, south of Orange River, 1899–1900, including actions at Colesberg (1 to 29 Jan.); again during operations in the Transvaal and Cape Colony 30 Nov. 1900, to 31 May, 1902. He received the Queen's Medal with six clasps, and the King's Medal with two clasps. He served in the European War, in the Eastern Area, landing with the 1st Essex Regt. in the 88th Brigade, 29th Division, in Gallipoli, 25 April, 1915, and was one of the few surviving original officers left when the battle was over. He was created a Companion of the Distinguished Service Order [London Gazette, 15 Oct. 1915]: "Algernon George Newcome Wood, Major, The Essex Regt. For distinguished service in the field." Major Wood was shot in the trenches 30 Oct. of the same year, the term of his Adjutancy expiring on the day he was killed. He was awarded the Serbian Order of the Eagle.

Algernon G. N. Wood.

M'LAGAN, DOUGLAS CRAIG, Capt., was born in Edinburgh, 12 March, 1880, son of Thomas Thomson M'Lagan, M.A., Royal High School, Edinburgh, and of Margaret Cunningham Campbell (or M'Lagan), daughter of Murdoch Campbell. He was educated at the Royal High School, and at Edinburgh University, eventually becoming a Solicitor. He joined the Volunteers (Q.R.V.B.R.S.) in April, 1900; became Second Lieutenant 22 Nov. 1902, and Captain in Oct. 1906. On the outbreak of the European War in Aug. 1914, he mobilized with the 5th Royal Scots, and formed the 2/5th Royal Scots (Sept. 1914). He returned to the 1/5th in Nov. 1914, and went to Gallipoli, where he landed on the memorable 25 April, 1915; commanded the 1/5th from 28 April until 18 May. He was mentioned in Despatches, and created a Companion of the Distinguished Service Order [London Gazette, 15 Oct. 1915]: "Douglas Craig M'Lagan, Capt., 1/5th Battn. The Royal Scots. For distinguished service in the field." Capt. M'Lagan was wounded during these operations, and invalided home. From Sept. to Nov. 1915, he was employed in a Staff Office in Edinburgh, and from Dec. to Jan. 1916, was Second-in-Command, 3/5th Royal Scots, with the rank of Major. In the spring of 1916, Major M'Lagan rejoined the 1/5th Royal Scots in France, taking over the command, with the rank of Lieutenant-Colonel, on 15 April, and was invalided home in Feb. 1917, remaining on home service until demobilized on 19 Feb. 1919.

TURNBULL, WILLIAM McGREGOR, Major, served in the European War, and was created a Companion of the Distinguished Service Order [London Gazette, 15 Oct. 1915]: "William McGregor Turnbull, Major, New Zealand Staff Corps. For distinguished service in the field."

SMITH, GEOFFREY SAMUEL, Major, served in the European War, and was created a Companion of the Distinguished Service Order [London Gazette, 15 Oct. 1915]: "Geoffrey Samuel Smith, Major, 14th (South Otago) Regt. For distinguished service in the field."

London Gazette, 28 Oct. 1915.—"War Office, 28 Oct. 1915. His Majesty the King has been pleased to confer the undermentioned reward for distinguished service in the field, in connection with the recent military operations in Togoland. To be a Companion of the Distinguished Service Order."

POTTER, HARMAN BARNES, Capt., was born 9 April, 1882. He joined the Army, as Second Lieutenant, 8 Jan. 1901, and was attached to the East Kent Regt. in the following March; became Lieutenant 9 July, 1904, and was Adjutant, East Kent Regt. 4 Aug. 1908, to 3 Aug. 1911. He was promoted Captain 24 July, 1912, and Major 8 Jan. 1916, and was employed with the West African Frontier Force 8 May, 1912, to 13 Jan. 1915, and 21 Feb. 1917, to 7 April, 1919. He was Local Lieutenant-Colonel 13 March, 1917, to 31 Oct. 1918, and 1 Nov. 1918, to 1 Feb. 1919. He was given the Brevet of Lieutenant-Colonel 3 June, 1919, and was created a Companion of the Distinguished Service Order [London Gazette, 28 Oct. 1915]: "Harman Barnes Potter, Capt., East Kent Regt. For distinguished service in the field."

London Gazette, 29 Oct. 1915.—"War Office, 29 Oct. 1915. His Majesty the King has been graciously pleased to confer the undermentioned rewards for distinguished service in the field."

HAMILTON, ANTHONY, Commander, Royal Indian Marine, was born 12 March, 1872, son of Capt. Andrew Hamilton, late 31st Regt. He was educated at Brentwood, and joined the Royal Indian Marine in 1892, becoming Lieutenant in 1897, and Commander in 1909. He served in Somaliland, 1902–4 (Medal), and commanded various ships of the R.I.M. He made a survey of the river Tigris from Basra to Baghdad in 1906, jointly with Commander Charles Gardner, R.I.M., which became the standard map of the river during the war. From 1909 to 1912 he was Port Officer and Collector of Customs at Bassein, Burma. Commander Hamilton served in the Great War in 1914–15, as Principal Marine Transport Officer, Mesopotamia. He was subsequently on Special Duty at the War Office. He was mentioned in Despatches four times, and created a Companion of the Distinguished Service Order [London Gazette, 29 Oct. 1915]: "Anthony Hamilton, Commander, Royal Indian Marine. For distinguished service in the field." In 1911, he married Margaret, youngest daughter of B. P. Brockley, and they have one daughter.

BRANSBURY, HENRY ARTHUR, Major, was born 2 Oct. 1877, son of Henry Bransbury, late of Southsea, and now of Redhill, Surrey. He was educated privately, and at St. George's Hospital, London, and joined the Royal Army Medical Corps 29 Jan. 1901, becoming Captain 29 Jan. 1904; Major 29 July, 1912, and Lieutenant-Colonel 30 May, 1918. He served in the European War, and was present at Mesopotamia, 1914 to July, 1916, and with the Egyptian Expeditionary Force, Aug. 1917, until the Armistice. He was created a Companion of the Distinguished Service Order [London Gazette, 29 Oct. 1915]: "Henry Arthur Bransbury, Major, Royal Army Medical Corps. For distinguished service in the field." The Insignia were presented to him 4 Nov. 1916.

DUNCAN, HENRY CLARE, Major, was born 12 July, 1876. He was gazetted to the Durham Light Infantry 20 Feb. 1897; became Lieutenant, Indian Army, 2 Nov. 1900; Captain 20 Feb. 1906; Major 20 Feb. 1915, and was Temporary Lieutenant-Colonel 11 Jan. to 16 Nov. 1918. He was D.A.A. and Q.M.G., India, 1 Feb. to 28 Oct. 1914; D.A.Q.M.G., India, 29 Oct. to 23 Dec. 1914; Brigade Major from 24 Dec. 1914; Brigade Major, India, 6 March, 1916, to 22 March, 1917; A.Q.M.G., Dunsterforce, Mesopotamian Expeditionary Force, 11 Jan. to 21 Oct. 1918; A.A. and Q.M.G., 14th (Indian) Division, Mesopotamian Expeditionary Force, 22 Oct. to 16 Nov. 1918. He was given the Brevet of Lieutenant-Colonel 1 Jan. 1919, and was created a Companion of the Distinguished Service Order [London Gazette, 29 Oct. 1915]: "Henry Clare Duncan, Major, 9th Gurkha Regt., Indian Army. For distinguished service in the field." He married Edith Irene (who died in 1918), eldest daughter of the late R. Byng Campbell, C.B.

KNOX, ROBERT WELLAND, Major, was born 6 Sept. 1873, son of Sir George Edward Knox, C.S.I., I.S.O., LL.D., and Katherine Anne Louise, daughter of the late Major W. Loch, 1st Bombay Lancers. He was educated at Westminster, and at Edinburgh University, and became Lieutenant, Indian Medical Service, 28 Sept. 1897; Captain 28 July, 1900; Major 28 Jan. 1909, and Lieutenant-Colonel 28 Jan. 1917. From 23 Nov. 1918, he was Assistant Director of Medical Services, 60th Division, Egyptian Expeditionary Force. For his services in the Great War (Dardanelles), 1915–16, he was mentioned in Despatches; received the Serbian Order of the White Eagle, and was created a Companion of the Distinguished Service Order [London Gazette, 29 Oct. 1915]: "Robert Welland Knox, M.B., Major, Indian Medical Service. For distinguished service in the field." He married in 1900, Lilian Margaret, daughter of the late Colonel J. L. Loch.

LANGHORNE, JAMES ARCHIBALD DUNBOYNE, Major, was born 24 Feb. 1879, son of the Rev. J. Langhorne, M.A.Camb., Vicar of Lamberhurst, Kent. He was educated at Tonbridge School. He was commissioned in the Royal Artillery 23 June, 1898; was promoted Lieutenant 16 Feb. 1901; Captain 1 Feb. 1904, and Major 30 Oct. 1914. He was Adjutant, Royal Artillery, 27 July, 1907, to 26 July, 1911, also Adjutant, Royal Artillery, 2 April, 1912, to 25 April, 1914. Major Langhorne served in the European War, and was present at the Turkish attack on the Suez Canal and operations on the Canal, 1914–15; the Battle of the Somme, 1916 (wounded); the Third Battle of Ypres, 1917, and operations round Hazebrouck and advance, 1918, to Armistice. He was D.A.Q.M.G. 14 Jan. 1915, to 6 Jan. 1916; A.Q.M.G., 10th Indian Division, Mediterranean Expeditionary Force; Egyptian Expeditionary Force, and Temporary Lieutenant-Colonel 7 Jan. to 29 Feb. 1916; A.Q.M.G., 15th Army Corps, 1 March to 15 April, 1916; Acting Lieutenant-Colonel from 26 March, 1917. He was given the Brevet of Lieutenant-Colonel in March, 1920, and was created a Companion of the Distinguished Service Order [London Gazette, 29 Oct. 1915]: "James Archibald Dunboyne Langhorne, Major, Royal Garrison Artillery. For distinguished service in the field."

MACMULLEN, CYRIL NORMAN, Major, was born 13 Dec. 1877. He entered the Army, as Second Lieutenant, Unattached, 4 Aug. 1897; became Lieutenant, Indian Staff Corps, 29 Nov. 1898; Lieutenant, Indian Army, 4 Nov. 1899; Captain 4 Aug. 1906; Major 4 Aug. 1915, and was Temporary Brigadier-General 7 Feb. to 18 June, 1916, and 26 Sept. 1917, to 29 Nov. 1918. He was G.S.O.3, Headquarters, India, 7 Jan to 3 Dec. 1913; G.S.O.2, Headquarters, India, 4 Dec. 1913, to 11 Nov. 1914; Staff Captain, 2nd Expeditionary Force, 12 Nov. 1914, to 6 May, 1915; G.S.O.2, 8th Army Corps, Mediterranean Expeditionary Force, 5 June to 3 Oct. 1915; G.S.O.1, 2nd Mounted Division, Mediterranean Expeditionary Force, 4 Oct. 1915, to 6 Feb. 1916; Brigadier-General, G.S., 15th Army Corps, Mediterranean Expeditionary Force, 7 Feb. to 18 June, 1916; G.S.O.1,

British Armies in France, 19 to 30 June, 1916 ; G.S.O.1, Reserve Army, 5th Army, British Armies in France, 1 July, 1916, to 11 Jan. 1917 ; G.S.O.1, G.H.Q., British Armies in France, 12 Jan. to 25 Sept. 1917 ; Brigadier-General, G.S., 19th Army Corps, British Armies in France, 26 Sept. 1917, to 29 Nov. 1918. He was given the Brevets of Lieutenant-Colonel 1 Jan. 1916, and of Colonel 1 Jan. 1918 ; was created a C.M.G., and was created a Companion of the Distinguished Service Order [London Gazette, 29 Oct. 1915] : " Cyril Norman Macmullen, Major, Indian Army. For distinguished service in the field."

MOBERLY, BERTRAND RICHARD, Major, was born 15 Oct. 1877. He entered the Army 4 Aug. 1897, as Second Lieutenant, Unattached ; became Lieutenant, I.S.C., 7 Nov. 1898 ; Lieutenant, I.A., 4 Nov. 1899, Captain 4 Aug. 1906, Major 4 Aug. 1915, and was Temporary Lieut.-Colonel 2 July, 1916, to 2 June, 1918. He was Staff Officer, Base and Lines of Communication, Somaliland Field Force, 5 March to 16 April, 1903 ; Staff Captain, H.Q., India, 7 Jan. to 27 June, 1909 ; D.A.Q.M.G., H.Q., India, 28 June, 1909, to 6 Jan. 1913 ; G.S.O.2, 13 Aug. to 20 Sept. 1914 ; Staff Captain, Indian Expeditionary Force, 21 Sept. to 23 Dec. 1914 ; D.A.A. and Q.M.G. 24 Dec. 1914, to 4 June, 1915 ; G.S.O.2, 29th Division, Mediterranean Expeditionary Force, 5 June to 18 June, 1915 ; G.S.O.2, G.H.Q., Mediterranean Expeditionary Force, 13 Aug. 1915, to 24 Jan. 1916 ; G.S.O.2, 16th Army Corps, Mediterranean Expeditionary Force, 25 Jan. to 9 Feb. 1916. He was given the Brevet of Lieut.-Colonel 3 June, 1918, and was created a Companion of the Distinguished Service Order [London Gazette, 29 Oct. 1915] : " Bertrand Richard Moberly, Major, 56th Punjabi Rifles (Frontier Force), Indian Army. For distinguished service in the field."

QUERIPEL, LESLIE HERBERT, Major, was born 14 July, 1881, son of Col. A. E. Queripel, C.B., and Mary Queripel (née Watson). Educated privately, and at the Royal Military Academy, Woolwich ; entered the Royal Artillery 22 Nov. 1899 ; became Lieutenant 16 Feb. 1901, Captain 17 March, 1908, and Major 30 Oct. 1914 ; was Temporary Lieut.-Colonel 1 April, 1915, to 17 Aug. 1916 ; Temporary Colonel 28 Sept. to 28 Oct. 1917 ; Acting Lieut.-Colonel, Royal Artillery, 29 June, 1918. He was Deputy Director of Army Signals, Indian Expeditionary Force " D," 1 April, 1915, to 23 May, 1916 ; Director of Army Signals and Telegraphs, Indian Expeditionary Force " D," Mediterranean Expeditionary Force, 24 May, 1916, to 28 Oct. 1917. He served in China in 1900 (Medal with clasp). For his services in the Great War, 1914–18, he was given the Brevet of Lieut.-Colonel 3 June, 1916 ; was created a C.M.G. in 1918, and was created a Companion of the Distinguished Service Order [London Gazette, 29 Oct. 1915] : " Leslie Herbert Queripel, Major, Royal Artillery. For distinguished service in the field." He married, 1st, in 1914, Margaret Kidner (who died in 1914), and 2ndly, in 1918, Sybil, daughter of John Kidner, of Dodhill House, Taunton, and they have one daughter.

RUSSELL, REGINALD EDMUND MAGHLIN, Major, was born 2 Sept. 1879, son of E. M. Russell, of Milford House, Limerick. He was educated at Cheltenham College, and the Royal Military Academy, Woolwich ; was gazetted to the Royal Engineers 23 June, 1898 ; became Lieut. 9 March, 1901, Captain 23 June, 1907, and Major 30 Oct. 1914 ; was Temporary Lieut.-Colonel 7 Feb. 1916, to 28 Feb. 1917 ; Temporary Brigadier-General 1 March to 1 Aug. 1917 ; Acting Lieut.-Colonel, Royal Engineers, 2 Aug. 1917. He was employed with the Egyptian Army 2 April, 1905, to 1 April, 1915 ; was G.S.O.2, Mediterranean Expeditionary Force, 13 June, 1915, to 6 Feb. 1916 ; G.S.O.1, Forces in Egypt, 7 Feb. to 31 March, 1916 ; G.S.O.1, West Frontier Force, Egyptian Expeditionary Force, 1 April to

Reginald E. M. Russell.

5 Nov. 1916 ; G.S.O.1, 52nd Division, Egyptian Expeditionary Force, 6 Nov. 1916, to 28 Feb. 1917 ; Chief Engineer, Desert Column, Egyptian Expeditionary Force, 1 March to 1 Aug. 1917 ; employed under the Air Ministry 23 April, 1918. He served in the Annak Expedition (Sudan) in 1912 (Medal and clasp and 4th Class Medjidie). He again saw active service in the South African War, 1901–2 ; took part in the operations in the Transvaal, March to April, 1901 ; in Orange River Colony, April to Nov. 1901 ; also in Cape Colony, April, 1901, to April, 1902 (Despatches [London Gazette, 29 July, 1902] ; Queen's Medal with five clasps). He served in the European War, with the British Expeditionary Force in Egypt and Palestine, and took part in operations on the Suez Canal in 1915, Senussi Campaign in 1916, Sinai in 1916–17, and Jerusalem in 1917. He was four times mentioned in Despatches ; was given the Italian Order of St. Maurice and St. Lazarus, and the 4th Class Order of the Nile ; was given the Brevet of Lieut.-Colonel 1 Jan. 1918 ; was created a C.B.E. in 1919, and was created a Companion of the Distinguished Service Order [London Gazette, 29 Oct. 1915] : " Reginald Edmund Maghlin Russell, Major, Royal Engineers. For distinguished service in the field." Lieut.-Colonel Russell married, in 1918, Dorothy B., twin daughter of Major E. B. Crake Rifle Brigade, and they have one daughter.

SCOTT, GERALD BASSETT, Major, was born 27 Oct. 1875, son of the late Lieut.-Colonel H. B. Scott ; entered the Army 22 Jan. 1896 ; Indian Staff Corps 1 April, 1897 ; Lieutenant, Indian Army, 22 April, 1898 ; Captain 22 Jan. 1905 ; Major 22 Jan. 1914 ; served Waziristan, 1901–2 (Despatches) ; Somaliland, 1903–4 (Medal and two clasps ; mentioned in Despatches) ; European War, and was created a Companion of the Distinguished Service Order [London Gazette, 29 Oct. 1915] : " Gerald Bassett Scott, Major, 27th Punjabis, Indian Army. For distinguished service in the field."

SKEEN, OLIVER ST. JOHN, Major, was born at Meerut, India, 2 Nov. 1874, son of the late Surgeon-General William Skeen and Mary Keen Skeen. He was educated at the Aberdeen Grammar School, and at Sandhurst, passing into the Army 16 Jan. 1895. He became Lieutenant 16 April, 1897, and Captain 16 Jan. 1904. He served in the South African War, employed on Special Service ; served with the Mounted Infantry, 1902, and took part in the operations in the Transvaal and Cape Colony, May, 1902 ; also in Orange River Colony, Jan. to March, 1902 (Queen's Medal with four clasps). He served in Tibet, 1903–4 ; took part in the action at Niani, during the operations at and around Gyantse, and the march to Lhassa (Medal with clasp). He

Oliver St. John Skeen.

served in the European War with the 62nd Punjabis, and was created a Companion of the Distinguished Service Order [London Gazette, 29 Oct. 1915] : " Oliver St. John Skeen, Major, 62nd Punjabis. For distinguished service in the field." The following record of Major Skeen's gallantry is taken from General A. Wilson's Despatch : " Major O. St. J. Skeen displayed great promptitude and courage in charging the enemy, when disembarking from their pontoons. His skilful leading in the attack of 4 Feb. was instrumental in causing the surrender of the enemy, upon whose trenches he brought to bear an effective enfilading fire." Major Skeen fell in action at the Persian Gulf 21 Jan. 1916. He married, 29 Dec. 1905, at Bombay, India, Mabel, daughter of the late Henry A. Hawkins, and they had one son, Oliver St. John, born 10 April, 1907, and Kathleen Mary. He was a keen fisherman and good shot (small game).

CHOPE, ARTHUR JOHN HERBERT, Capt., was educated at Sandhurst, and was commissioned in the West Riding Regt. (Duke of Wellington's). He passed into the Indian Army in 1906 ; served in the Abor Expedition, 1911–12 ; was Adjutant of the 2nd King Edward's Own Gurkhas (The Sirmoor Rifles). He served in the European War from 1914 ; was mentioned in Despatches, and created a Companion of the Distinguished Service Order [London Gazette, 29 Oct. 1915] : " Arthur John Herbert Chope, Capt., 2nd King Edward's Own Gurkha Rifles (The Sirmoor Rifles) (attached Bikanir Camel Corps). For distinguished service in the field." He also received the Order of the Nile, 4th Class. Captain Chope married Elizabeth Susanna Winifred, widow of Major H. C. Nicolay.

MORGAN, MOUNTIFORD HICKMAN LLEWELLYN, Major, served in the European War. He was created a Companion of the Distinguished Service Order [London Gazette, 29 Oct. 1915] : " Mountiford Hickman Llewellyn Morgan, Major, 62nd Punjabis. For distinguished service in the field."

PEPYS, GERALD LESLIE, Major, served in the South African War, 1900–2, as Railway Staff Officer ; in the Transvaal 30 Nov. to Dec. 1900, and March, 1901, to 31 May, 1902 ; also during operations in Cape Colony, Dec. 1900, to March, 1901 (Queen's Medal with three clasps, and King's Medal with two clasps). He served in the European War, and was created a Companion of the Distinguished Service Order [London Gazette, 29 Oct. 1915] : " Gerald Leslie Pepys, Major, 57th Wilde's Rifles (Frontier Force), Indian Army. For distinguished service in the field."

SCOTT, HENRY ST. GEORGE STEWART, Capt., served in the South African War, 1901–2 ; took part in the operations in the Transvaal, March, 1901, to Jan. 1902 (Queen's Medal with three clasps). He served in the European War, and was created a Companion of the Distinguished Service Order [London Gazette, 29 Oct. 1915] : " Henry St. George Stewart Scott, Capt., 4th Gurkha Rifles. For distinguished service in the field." He was also awarded a Bar to his D.S.O.

WILLIS, GERALD CHARLES WALE, Capt., was educated at Cheltenham College. He served in the European War, and was created a Companion of the Distinguished Service Order [London Gazette, 29 Oct. 1915] : " Gerald Charles Wale Willis, Capt. 31st Duke of Connaught's Own Lancers, Indian Army. For distinguished service in the field."

SHEEPSHANKS, RICHARD HASELL, Lieut., was born at Park Place, Harrogate, 19 Feb. 1885, son of the Rev. T. Sheepshanks, M.A., and Mrs. Sheepshanks, daughter of Andrew Grieve, W.S., of Edinburgh.

He was educated at Harrow, and Trinity College, Cambridge, becoming Second Lieutenant, Royal 1st Devon Yeomanry, in 1904. He joined the 12th Cavalry, Indian Army, 19 Jan. 1907, as Lieutenant. He saw active service in the European War in Mesopotamia near Awaz. He was mentioned in Despatches 25 June, 1915. The following is the record of his service in General Sir A. Barrett's Mention : " Lieut. R. H. Sheepshanks, 12th Cavalry, attached 33rd Cavalry, was conspicuous for his gallantry and skilful handling of a small body of cavalry 3 March. Reforming his troop, he repeatedly charged the foremost lines of the enemy and inflicted heavy losses on them." The late Cavalry Brigade Commander wrote : " There was no one with that force, cavalry or

Richard H. Sheepshanks.

infantry, who did better. His skilful leading, energy and dash were talked of by everyone." Another wrote : " Sheepshanks has been doing wonders on the other side of the Tigris with 22 men of the 33rd Cavalry ; his last effort was when the Arab Horse got into the guns. He charged with eleven men, buckled his sword in an Arab, took a heavy toss, picked himself up although much hurt, and killed fourteen men with his rifle and saved a wounded gunner. Thirty-three men of a British regiment stood, and all the guns were saved, except one. The tales of Sheepshanks' prowess are like fairy-tales, only true." He was created a Companion of the Distinguished Service Order [London Gazette, 29 Oct. 1915]: "Richard Hasell Sheepshanks, Lieut., 12th Cavalry, I.A. For distinguished service in the field." He was promoted Captain, and was appointed A.D.C. to the Viceroy of India in 1916, whose third daughter, the Hon. Bridget Thesiger, he married, 25 June, 1919. Capt. Sheepshanks was subsequently invalided home suffering from severe attacks of fever and neuralgia, the result of the Mesopotamian Campaign.

London Gazette, 29 Oct. 1915.—"War Office, 29 Oct. 1915. His Majesty the King has been graciously pleased to approve of the appointment of the undermentioned Officers to be Companions of the Distinguished Service Order, in recognition of their gallantry and devotion to duty in the field."

HARVEY, JOHN, Lieut.-Colonel, served in the South African War, 1899-1901 ; took part in the operations in the Transvaal, east of Pretoria, July to 29 Nov. 1900, including action at Belfast (26 and 27 Aug.) ; also during the operations on the Zululand Frontier of Natal in Sept. 1901 (Queen's Medal with three clasps, and King's Medal with two clasps). He served in the European War, and was created a Companion of the Distinguished Service Order [London Gazette, 29 Oct. 1915]: "John Harvey, Lieut.-Colonel, 8th City of London Battn. London Regt. (P.O. Rifles), Territorial Force. For conspicuous ability, coolness and devotion to duty in the command of his unit during the attack on the German trenches at Festubert on 25 and 26 May, 1915. His gallant example greatly aided the successful attack." He was mentioned in Sir John French's Despatch of 15 Oct. 1915, dated War Office, 1 Jan. 1916.

BAYLEY, HADRIAN, Major, served in the European War, and was created a Companion of the Distinguished Service Order [London Gazette, 29 Oct. 1915]: "Hadrian Bayley, Major, 15th County of London Battery, Royal Field Artillery, Territorial Force. For conspicuous gallantry and ability from 12 to 26 May, 1915, at Le Plantin, when his battery rendered excellent service by its effective fire. He was heavily shelled by the enemy in his observation stations, but throughout the operations he sent back prompt and reliable information."

CLARK, WILLIAM ELLIS, Major, son of the late John William Hyne Clark, Barrister-at-Law, and Mrs. Akenhead, of Riseholme, The Mount, York. He was educated at Dulwich, and at the Royal Military Academy, Woolwich ; was commissioned in the Royal Artillery 21 Sept. 1896 ; became Lieut. 21 Sept. 1899, and Capt. 9 March, 1902 ; Adjutant 16 Aug. 1908, to 4 Aug. 1911. He served in the South African Campaign, 1899-1902 ; was present during operations in Orange Free State, Feb. to May, 1900 ; operations in the Orange River Colony, May to Oct. 1900, including actions at Wittebergen ; operations in the Transvaal, west of Pretoria, Oct. and Nov. 1900 ; during operations in Cape Colony, south of Orange River, 1899-1900, including operations in the Transvaal and Orange River Colony, 1900-02. He received the Queen's Medal with three clasps, and King's Medal with two clasps. He served in the European War, and was mentioned in Despatches, and created a Companion of the Distinguished Service Order [London Gazette, 29 Oct. 1915]: "William Ellis Clark, Major, Royal Artillery. For conspicuous gallantry and good work during operations between 9 and 19 May, 1915, near Rue-du-Bois, especially when under heavy shell fire at the observation station of his battery. His reports and observations on the course of events were of great value." He was promoted Lt.-Col. 1917 and created a C.M.G.

LEES, RODERICK LIVINGSTONE, Major, served in the European War, and was created a Companion of the Distinguished Service Order [London Gazette, 29 Oct. 1915]: "Roderick Livingstone Lees, Major, 1/6th Battn. The Lancashire Fusiliers, Territorial Force. For most conspicuous gallantry and determination during an attack near Krithia, Gallipoli Peninsula, on 8 Aug. 1915. He commanded the defence of a position against heavy odds with great skill and tenacity, and showed absolute disregard of personal danger in leading and encouraging his men."

STANDISH, IVON TATHAM, Major, served in the European War, in Gallipoli, 1915, with No. 3 Battery, Royal New Zealand Artillery. He was mentioned in Despatches, and was created a Companion of the Distinguished Service Order [London Gazette, 29 Oct. 1915]: "Ivon Tatham Standish, Major, No. 3 Battery, Royal New Zealand Artillery. For conspicuous gallantry in the Gallipoli Peninsula on 27-28 Aug. 1915. He was controlling the fire of a very exposed section of guns, performing this duty on a flank under heavy fire, when one of his guns was put out of action, and a fire broke out round his ammunition pit. He at once left his observing station, ran to the pit, and personally assisted in extinguishing the fire." He was created a C.M.G. in 1917.

BLAIR, RICHARD CURWEN RICHMOND, Capt., served in the South African War, 1899-1901 ; performed duties of Station Staff Officer ; was present during the operations in the Orange Free State, Feb. to May, 1900 ; took part in the operations in the Transvaal, west of Pretoria, July to 29 Nov. 1900 ; served during the operations in Orange River Colony, May, to 29 Nov. 1900, including action at Rhenoster River ; also in Cape Colony, south of Orange River, 1899-1900 (Queen's medal with four clasps). He served in Aden, 1903-4, during operations in the interior. He served in the European War, and was created a Companion of the Distinguished Service Order [London Gazette, 29 Oct. 1915]: "Richard Curwen Richmond Blair, Capt., 1/5th (Cumberland) Battn. The Border Regt., Territorial Force. For conspicuous gallantry on the night of 27 Sept. 1915, at Armentières. He went out with a party of ten to bomb

the enemy's trenches. Finding conditions unfavourable, the party lay down and waited about 50 yards from the enemy's wire. Soon afterwards a party of 14 Germans were seen advancing towards them. Capt. Blair held his fire till they were ten yards away, when he shot four of them with his revolver. His party accounted for all the remainder except two, and returned unscathed. Capt. Blair was constantly taking part in arduous and enterprising night work." Capt. Blair was killed in Oct. 1916.

CALLAGHAN, CECIL ARTHUR, Capt., served in the European War' and was created a Companion of the Distinguished Service Order [London Gazette, 29 Oct. 1915]: "Cecil Arthur Callaghan, Capt., 2nd Battery, Field Artillery, Australian Imperial Force. For conspicuous gallantry and ability on 12 July, 1915, during an action on the Gallipoli Peninsula. As Forward Observing Officer, he advanced with the first line of infantry, and established telephone communication with his battery from captured hostile trenches. During the day he continued to advance under heavy fire, sending back accurate reports, valuable not only to the guns but also to the Corps Staff."

DOUIE, FRANCIS McCRONE, Capt., was born 20 March, 1886. He entered the Royal Engineers 5 Aug. 1906 ; became Lieutenant 22 Nov. 1908, and Captain 30 Oct. 1914. He served in the European War, and was created a Companion of the Distinguished Service Order [London Gazette, 29 Oct. 1915]: "Francis McCrone Douie, Capt., Royal Engineers, No. 3 Coy., 1st King George's Own Sappers and Miners, Indian Army. For conspicuous gallantry on 22 May, 1915, west of Ferme-du-Bois. In broad daylight, accompanied by his orderly, Sapper Jiwa Khan, he got over the parapet, and went within 80 yards of the German trenches, which were being shelled by our guns, and brought back to safety a wounded man. He also assisted to bring in another wounded man on a stretcher. The Germans were

Francis McCrone Douie.

alert at the time, and opened fire at once."
He was given the Brevet of Major 3 June, 1917, and was awarded the Military Cross. Major Douie is the eldest son of Sir James McC. Douie, K.C.S.I.

FINN, BERTRAM SIBBALD, Capt., served in the European War, and was created a Companion of the Distinguished Service Order [London Gazette, 29 Oct. 1915]: "Bertram Sibbald Finn, Capt., New Zealand Medical Corps. For conspicuous devotion to duty in the Gallipoli Peninsula during operations from 6 to 9 Aug. 1915, when he worked day and night with unceasing zeal and without rest evacuating the wounded. His work was carried out under continuous fire, on one occasion the dressing station being heavily shelled for an hour, and many assistants and wounded being hit. Owing to Capt. Finn's efforts the wounded lying in the more exposed positions were got into a place of greater safety."

GARDINER, HARRY, Capt., served in the European War, and was created a Companion of the Distinguished Service Order [London Gazette, 29 Oct. 1915]: "Harry Gardiner, Capt., 2nd Battn. The Duke of Wellington's (West Riding Regt.), attached 8th Battn. For conspicuous gallantry and determination during operations at Suvla Bay, Gallipoli Peninsula, on the 8th Aug. 1915. He continued to lead his men forward after being twice wounded, and only gave up after being wounded a third time."

GREANY, JOHN WINGATE, Capt., was born in 1892, son of Surgeon-General J. P. Greany, I.M.S. He served in the European War, and was created a Companion of the Distinguished Service Order [London Gazette, 29 Oct. 1915]: "John Wingate Greany, Capt., 5th Battn. The Duke of Edinburgh's (Wiltshire Regt.). For conspicuous gallantry in the Gallipoli Peninsula. On 10 Aug. 1915, his battalion suffered severely in the Salzi Beit Valley and on the 25th Aug. two men arrived in an exhausted condition, bringing word that five others were still alive at the upper end of the valley, having lived for 14 days among the dead and wounded. Capt. Greany formed a rescue party of volunteers from his regiment, and although it was found impossible, owing to bright moonlight, rifle fire and meeting a Turkish patrol, to complete the search on the night of the 25th-26th Aug., yet on the following night he found and brought in the five men under heavy fire. Capt. Greany also brought back valuable information regarding the country and the enemy's movements." He was killed in action on 9 April, 1916.

John Wingate Greany.

Cecil Duncan Sasse.

SASSE, CECIL DUNCAN, Capt., was born in Kensington, in 1891, son of F. C. Sasse. He was educated at Eastbourne and Sandhurst, passing into the 1st Battn. The East Yorkshire Regt. in 1911. Owing to an accident to his knee he resigned in 1913, and went to Australia ; but when the European War broke out, he joined the Australian Imperial Force, and served in Egypt and Gallipoli. He was created a Companion of the Distinguished Service Order [London Gazette, 29 Oct. 1915]: " Cecil Duncan Sasse, Capt., 1st Battn. (New South Wales) Australian Imperial Force. For conspicuous gallantry and determination during the attack on Lone Pine, Gallipoli Peninsula, on the 6th-7th Aug. 1915, when he led several bayonet charges on trenches occupied by the enemy, resulting in substantial gains. Capt. Sasse was three times wounded, but remained on duty." He was sent with his regiment to France, being promoted Major. He played cricket for Blue Mantles and Yorkshire Gentlemen, and football for his regiment, Ealing and Eastbourne.

SCOTT, ALLAN HUMPHREY, Capt., was born at Tumut, New South Wales, Australia, 3 April, 1891, son of D. H. Scott, of Edgmond, Wahroonga, New South Wales. He was educated at the Sydney Grammar School, and entered the 1st Battn. New South Wales Scottish Rifles in 1911. In Aug. 1914, he was gazetted Captain, 1st Contingent of the Australian Imperial Force. He accompanied this force to Gallipoli, serving in that theatre of war from the landing to the evacuation in 1915. He was created a Companion of the Distinguished Service Order [London Gazette, 29 Oct. 1915]: " Allan Humphrey Scott, Capt., 1st Contingent, Australian Imperial Force. For conspicuous gallantry in the attack on Lone Pine on 6-7 Aug. 1915. He held on to a very exposed position till all the wounded had been removed. Later, after a heavy bombing attack by superior forces had compelled him to retire, he led a bayonet charge which retook and held a position, in face of the enemy's enfilading machine-gun fire. This position was of great importance as linking up the positions captured on either flank." He was killed in action on 30 Sept. 1917.

WILLIAMS, GUY CHARLES, Brevet Major, was born at Bangalore, India, 10 Sept. 1881, son of the late Lieut.-Colonel Richard Francis Williams. He was educated at Sherborne School, passing into the Army 2 May, 1900. He was stationed at Bermuda from 1901 to 1904 ; returned home to proceed to Colchester, where he remained until 1908. From 1909 to 1914 he was employed in East Africa on survey duty under the Colonial Office ; became Captain 2 May, 1910, and was promoted Director of Surveys in 1912. Capt. Williams served in the European War, and was mentioned five times in Despatches, and created a C.M.G. ; also awarded the Order of St. Stanislaus, 3rd Class, with Sword, and was promoted Brevet Major 18 May, 1915. He was created a Companion of the Distinguished Service Order [London Gazette, 29 Oct. 1915]: " Guy Charles Williams, Captain and Brevet Major, 173rd (Tunnelling) Coy., Royal Engineers. For conspicuous gallantry and initiative in France. He pushed his advanced galleries through those of the enemy, thereby successfully carrying out mining operations. From the commencement of this dangerous and difficult operation Major Williams directed and controlled the work with great forethought and daring, which alone enabled an almost unique result to be obtained." Capt. Williams attained his substantive Majority, becoming Temporary Lieut.-Colonel in 1915, and was employed as Controller of Mines, 1st Army.

London Gazette, 4 Nov. 1915.—" War Office, 4 Nov. 1915. His Majesty the King has been graciously pleased to approve of the appointment of the undermentioned Officers to be Companions of the Distinguished Service Order, in recognition of their gallantry and devotion to duty in the field."

ALLANSON, CECIL JOHN LYONS, Major, was born at Carnarvon, North Wales, 2 April, 1877, son of John B. Allanson, of Bath, and of Constance Lyons, his wife, of Brookhill, County Antrim. He was educated at Bedford Grammar School, and Woolwich, passing into the Royal Artillery in 1897. From 1899 to 1902 he was employed as A.D.C. to the Lieut.-Governor of Bengal, and was transferred into the Indian Army. He was promoted Adjutant in 1903, and passed the Staff College in 1907 ; was Brigade Major in 1908 ; was employed as Private Secretary to the Lieut.-Governor of Bengal from 1909 to 1910. In 1910 he was appointed Tutor Guardian to the Maharaja of Hathwa, and served during the Imperial Delhi Durbar. From 1912 to 1915 he acted as Military Secretary to the Governor of Madras. He was pro-

Cecil John L. Allanson.

moted Major in March, 1915. Major Allanson was appointed to command the 1st Battn. 6th Gurkha Rifles in Gallipoli. He was three times wounded ; was mentioned in Despatches twice, and was created a Companion of the Distinguished Service Order [London Gazette, 4 Nov. 1915]: " Cecil John Lyons Allanson, Major, 1st Battn. 6th Gurkha Rifles. For most conspicuous gallantry and marked ability on 9 Aug. 1915, in leading his battalion to the attack on the Chunuk Bair Ridge, Gallipoli. Major Allanson, with two companies, reached the summit of the ridge under a very destructive fire from the enemy, where he was wounded by a bayonet thrust. When it was obvious that no supports could reach him, he skilfully withdrew his men, and notwithstanding the pain from his wound, remained with his battalion throughout the whole day, being the only British officer left." Major Allanson was recommended for the Victoria Cross by his Brigade and Divisional Commander, and was referred to in Sir Ian Hamilton's Despatch of the 7th Jan. 1916, as " that fine leader of men." Major Allanson was made a Companion of the Indian Empire, and was placed on the General Staff in 1916. He married, 12 Sept. 1916, Ethel, widow of Edward Temple Patterson, at St. Martin-in-the-Fields, London, W.C., the ceremony being performed by the Rev. Herbert

Davies, his brother-in-law. He was awarded the Croix de Guerre (avec Palme) in 1918, and created a C.M.G. in 1919.

DUTTON, THE HON. JAMES HUNTLY (now Baron Sherborne), Temporary Major, was born 5 March, 1873, eldest son of the late Colonel the Hon. Charles Dutton, and May Arbuthnot, his wife, daughter of the late George Noble Taylor. He was educated at Wellington College. He served in the European War with the 12th Royal Scots, and took part in operations at Loos. He also served in the South African War from 1899-1902, with the 2nd Battn. Scottish Rifles. He was created a Companion of the Distinguished Service Order [London Gazette, 4 Nov. 1915]: " James Huntly Dutton, Temporary Major, 12th Battn. The Royal Scots (Lothian Regt.). For conspicuous gallantry, resource and determination at ' Fosse 8,' from 26 to 28 Sept. 1915, as Officer Commanding the Battalion. He repeatedly organized the defence of his line against German counter-attacks, and maintained his position till relieved." He married, 27 Feb. 1908, Ethel Mary, eldest daughter of William Baird, late Lieut.-Colonel and Honorary Colonel Commanding the Fife Royal Garrison Artillery (Militia), and they have two sons : Charles, born on 13 May, 1911, and George Edward, born 23 Sept. 1912, and two daughters.

GORDON, ADRIAN CHARLES, Major, was born at Enfield 4 July, 1891, son of Charles Wood Gordon, Shipowner, and Florence Gordon, his wife. He was educated at Bishop's Stortford School, joining the Volunteers when in his teens. He was employed in shipping. He served during the European War, and early in 1915 went to France as Major. He was mentioned in Despatches, and was created a Companion of the Distinguished Service Order [London Gazette, 4 Nov. 1915]: " Adrian Charles Gordon, Major, 16th County of London Battery, 6th London Brigade, Royal Field Artillery, Territorial Force. For conspicuous gallantry, ability and resource at Maroc 25 Sept. 1915, when he got close up to the German lines to reconnoitre, and although under heavy fire, captured 12 Germans, after shooting one man with a revolver. On the afternoon of the same day he again went up to reconnoitre the enemy's second line under very heavy fire. On the following day Major Gordon

Adrian Charles Gordon.

rendered valuable service at Loos by reorganizing men who had become detached and taking them to the firing line." The following record is taken from " Truth," 10 Nov. 1915 : " Of all the brave deeds done at the Battles of Loos, one of the bravest was that of Major Adrian Charles Gordon, Commanding the 16th County of London Territorial Force, who while reconnoitring on 25 Sept., close up to the German lines, cut off 12 German soldiers, who were holding a trench, and after shooting one of them, ordered the others to hold up their hands and file past him as his prisoners. If ever a D.S.O. was well earned, it was by Major Gordon." He was gazetted Lieut.-Colonel in 1916. Lieut.-Colonel Gordon fell in action 12 Dec. 1917. The Chaplain of the Brigade wrote as follows to his widow : " He was one of the finest commanding officers that any brigade could have. He had all the qualities which go to make the ideal leader of men, and they would have followed him anywhere. He died just after the accomplishment of the greatest achievement in his military career, after having done something with his brigade which it will be given to few artillery officers to be able to do. His name has been on everybody's lips in this division, and not in this division alone. Further honours would certainly have come to him in the near future."

HUGHES, GEOFFREY WALLACE GRAINGER, Major, was born 2 Sept. 1880, son of Colonel Emilius Hughes, C.B., C.M.G. He was educated at King's College London, being appointed House Surgeon, King's College Hospital, in 1902. Dr. Hughes joined the R.A.M.C. io 1903, and served with the Egyptian Army from 1904 to 1911, gaining the 4th Class Medjidie in 1911. He became Captain in 1906. In 1913 he became a Specialist in Ophthalmology, and became Major in 1914. He served during the European War with the Royal Army Medical Corps ; was twice mentioned in Despatches, and created a Companion of the Distinguished Service Order [London Gazette, 4 Nov. 1915]: " Geoffrey Wallace Grainger Hughes, Major, 6th Cavalry Field Ambulance, Royal Army Medical Corps. For conspicuous ability and good work in arranging for the care and evacuation of the wounded at Loos on 26 and 27 Sept. 1915 A large number of wounded infantry were tended and evacuated by the two cavalry field ambulances, in addition to wounded cavalrymen. During the greater part of the time Loos was under heavy bombardment." He married, in 1911, Rosamond, daughter of the late Rev. Henry Goodwin, and they have one son and one daughter. Lawn tennis and golf are his favourite recreations.

LEWIS, FREDERICK, Major, was born 19 Jan. 1870. He joined the Army in 1889, serving in the ranks until Feb. 1896, when he received a commission as Second Lieutenant in the Leicestershire Regt. He became Lieutenant 28 May, 1898, and Captain 26 April, 1902. From 1903 to 1907 he was employed with the West African Frontier Force. He served during the South African War, 1899 to 1902 ; took part in the operations in Natal, 1899, including actions at Talana and Lombard's Kop ; at the Defence of Ladysmith, including sortie of 7 Dec. 1899 ; in Natal, March to June, 1900, including action at Laing's Nek (6 to 9 June) ; in the Transvaal, east of Pretoria, including actions at Belfast (26 and 27 Aug.) and Lydenberg (5 to 8 Sept.) ; again in the Transvaal, Nov. 1900, to 31 May, 1902 ; also during operations in Orange River Colony, April to May, 1902 (Queen's Medal with five clasps, and King's Medal with two clasps). He served in West Africa (Northern Nigeria) in 1903 ; took part in the operations in the

Kabba Province ; during operations against tribes on the direct route between Bauchi and Ibi ; Sokoto-Burni operations ; was slightly wounded (Medal with clasp). Major Lewis served on the Western Front, and was created a Companion of the Distinguished Service Order [London Gazette, 4 Nov. 1915]: " Frederick Lewis, Major, Leicestershire Regt. For conspicuous gallantry and ability during the action near Pietre Farm on 25 Sept. 1915, when, as second-in-command, he directed the assault with the utmost coolness. At an early stage he was wounded by shrapnel in the neck, but refused to leave his post for three hours, and then returned immediately after his wound was dressed. He set a fine example to those around him. About 3.30 p.m. he took command of his battalion, his senior officer being wounded. He has previously been brought to notice for gallant conduct." He was promoted to the rank of Major, Sept. 1915.

LOWE, SIDNEY JOSEPH, Major, was born 29 Aug. 1880. He joined the Royal Fusiliers in Aug. 1899 ; became Lieutenant in June, 1900, and was employed as Railway Staff Officer from March to Oct. 1901. He became Captain in 1905, and was appointed Adjutant to the Volunteers in Sept. 1906. He was transferred as Adjutant to the Territorial Force in 1908. Major Lowe served during the European War, and from Aug. 1914, to the following Oct. he was employed as Embarkation Staff Officer (graded as Staff Captain), and was promoted to Major in Sept. 1915. He was created a Companion of the Distinguished Service Order [London Gazette, 4 Nov. 1915]: " Sidney Joseph Lowe, Major, R.F., City of London Regt. For conspicuous gallantry and coolness at Maroc and Loos on 25 and 26 Sept. 1915, when he visited captured German lines under heavy fire and reported on the situation. On 26 Sept., again under heavy fire, he collected and reorganized men who were retiring and directed them back to their positions."

McLEAN, CHARLES WESLEY WELDON, Major, was born at St. John, New Brunswick, 26 Aug. 1882, son of Major-General Hugh Havelock McLean, K.C., M.P., and of Jennie M. McLean (née Porteous), deceased. He entered the Royal Artillery as Second Lieutenant from Local Military Forces, Canada, 7 March, 1900 ; became Lieutenant 3 April, 1901, Captain 12 Sept. 1908, and Major 29 Oct. 1914 ; was Acting Lieut.-Colonel, Royal Artillery, 21 July, 1917, to 21 March, 1918, and 3 July to 11 Nov. 1918 ; seconded as M.P. 28 Dec. 1918. From 28 Feb. to 7 Oct. 1916, he was Brigade Major, Royal Artillery, 59th Division, Home Forces. He was educated at the Royal Military College, Kingston, and served in the South African War, 1899–1900, taking part in the advance on Kimberley ; was present during operations in the Orange Free State, Feb. to May, 1900, including those at Paardeberg (17 to 26 Feb.) ; actions at Poplar Grove and Dreifontein ; in Orange River Colony, May to Aug. 1900 ; also during operations in Cape Colony, south of Orange River, 1899–1900 (Queen's Medal with three clasps). He served in the European War, and since 1918 has been M.P. (C.U.) for the Brigg Division of Lindsey, Lincolnshire. For his services in the war, when he commanded the 52nd Brigade, Royal Artillery, 9th Division, he was mentioned in Despatches ; created a C.M.G. in 1919 ; promoted to Colonel, and was created a Companion of the Distinguished Service Order [London Gazette, 4 Nov. 1915]: " Charles Wesley Weldon McLean, Major, 52nd Brigade, Royal Field Artillery. For conspicuous gallantry and ability on many occasions between May and Sept. 1915, notably the following : On 21 Sept. 1915, when, although stunned when his observation station was hit, he remained at his post and continued to observe the fire of his guns. On 25 Sept., when he brought forward his battery with great dash over the open in close support of the infantry near Hohenzollern Redoubt, and ran a wire at once, under heavy fire, to the Battalion Headquarters. He observed fire from a very exposed position till after dark, when he was wounded after rejoining his battery. He refused to leave his battery, and brought it out of action himself from a most critical situation." He was awarded two Bars to his Distinguished Service Order.

POPHAM, GILBERT LEYBOURNE, Major, was born 14 May, 1881. He was educated at Cheltenham College, and entered the Royal Artillery 6 Jan. 1900 ; became Lieutenant 3 April, 1901 ; Captain 10 Aug. 1908 ; was Adjutant, Royal Artillery, 1 Sept. 1908, to 31 Aug. 1911 ; was promoted to Major 30 Oct. 1914. He was Adjutant, Territorial Force, 1 Sept. 1913, to 18 July, 1916. He served in the European War, and was created a Companion of the Distinguished Service Order [London Gazette, 4 Nov. 1915]: " Gilbert Leybourne Popham, Major, 26th Brigade, Royal Field Artillery. For conspicuous gallantry on 10 Sept. 1915, at Vermelles. While giving instruction to a battery, a shell set fire to the covering of a gun emplacement, in which were some high-explosive shells. Major Popham removed these shells himself, thereby probably saving a very serious explosion. He also did excellent work during the operations from 21 Sept. till he was severely wounded on 25 Sept."

ROSS, HUGH ALEXANDER, Capt. (Temporary Major), was born at Glasgow, 19 Feb. 1880, son of the late John McDonald Ross, of Ledgowan, Achnasheen, Ross-shire, and of Robine, eldest daughter of the late Alexander Gilroy, of Craigie, Fifeshire. He was educated at Loretto School, and entered the Gordon Highlanders 5 Jan. 1901 ; became Lieutenant 6 Feb. 1904, and Captain 3 June, 1910. He served in the South African War, 1901–2, and received the Queen's Medal with five clasps. He served in the European War ; was thrice mentioned in Despatches, and was created a Companion of the Distinguished Service Order [London Gazette, 4 Nov. 1915]: " Hugh Alexander Ross, Capt. (Temporary Major), 2nd Battn.

Hugh Alexander Ross

The Gordon Highlanders. For conspicuous gallantry and devotion to duty on 25 Sept. 1915, near Hulluch. When his Commanding Officer was wounded early in the morning, he took command, and led his battalion with great judgment. He held on to an advanced and exposed position all day, after his battalion had suffered heavy casualties, and he himself was badly gassed. Capt. Ross remained with the battalion till it came back into support, and then only left it on being ordered to go to hospital." He also received the Order of Danilo of Montenegro.

ADAMSON, JAMES EDGAR, Temporary Capt., served in the European War, and was created a Companion of the Distinguished Service Order [London Gazette, 4 Nov. 1915]: " James Edgar Adamson, Temporary Capt., 8th Battn. The Gordon Highlanders. For conspicuous gallantry at Haisnes 25 Sept. 1915. After leading his company across the open under heavy shell and rifle fire, and across the lines of wire, where he was exposed to heavy machine-gun fire, he pressed on with great determination into the village of Haisnes, far in advance of any other detachment, and held on there from 8 a.m. until 5 p.m., causing heavy losses to the attacking Germans. Finally, when completely isolated and exposed to bombs and artillery and rifle fire on three sides, he brought back what remained of his company in good order. He exhibited throughout the greatest coolness and courage."

BELL, WHITEFORD JOHN EDWARD, Capt., was born 26 Jan. 1881, son of the late Colonel Whiteford John Bell, 93rd Sutherland Highlanders, of Troqueer Moat, Dumfries. He was educated at Wellington College, and at Edinburgh University, and entered the Royal Army Medical Corps 30 July, 1906 ; became Captain 30 Jan. 1910 ; was Temporary Major, R.A.M.C., 16 March, 1916, to 29 July, 1918 ; Acting Lieutenant-Colonel, R.A.M.C., 22 Aug. 1916 ; was promoted to Major 30 July, 1918. For his services in the European War he was thrice mentioned in Despatches, and created a Companion of the Distinguished Service Order [London Gazette, 4 Nov. 1915]: " Whiteford John Edward Bell, M.B., Capt., No. 2 Field Ambulance, Royal Army Medical Corps. For conspicuous gallantry and devotion to duty on all occasions, notably near Loos between 28 Sept. and 1 Oct. 1915, when he visited the advanced bearer post day and night under continuous shell fire, and personally supervised the arrangements for collecting and evacuating the wounded in that area. Capt. Bell has commanded a bearer division since Aug. 1914." He married, in 1919, Vyvian Lydia Winifred, A.R.R.C., daughter of Harington Bird, A.R.C.A.

BIRD, JOHN WILFRED, Major, was born 28 March, 1872, at Toronto, Canada, son of the late Lieut. John Sealy Bird, 67th Regt. He was educated privately, and at Guy's Hospital, London ; served in the Royal Navy as Surgeon from 1897 to 1905 ; joined the Territorial Force in 1908, and was gazetted Captain in the 6th London Field Ambulance, Royal Army Medical Corps (T.F.) ; served four years, and then went into the Territorial Force Reserve. On the outbreak of war in Aug. 1914, he rejoined the Ambulance ; was promoted Major (temporary) 10 Sept. 1914 ; later landed in France in March, 1915, and served in the 47th Division (T.F.), and was present at many engagements, amongst which were Richebourg, Festubert, Givenchy, Maroc and Loos. In April, 1916, he was recalled by the War Office, and given Command of the 2/6th London Field Ambulance, 60th (London) Division (T.F.) ; temporary rank of Major was made substantive dating 10 Sept. 1914 ; promoted Lieutenant-Colonel (temporary) 13 May, 1916. He went abroad with the unit, and joined the British Expeditionary Force in France in June, 1916. In Dec. 1916, the division was transferred to the Salonika Army. He was created a Companion of the Distinguished Service Order [London Gazette, 4 Nov. 1915]: " John Wilfred Bird, Major, 6th London Field Ambulance, Royal Army Medical Corps (Territorial Force). For conspicuous devotion to duty during operations at Maroc and Loos, between 25 and 30 Sept. 1915, in dealing with casualties. On one occasion he worked for 23 hours without any cessation, in dressing and tending the wounded. He set a fine example, which had far-reaching results." He was mentioned in Despatches 1 Jan. 1917. Major Bird married, 2 March, 1903, Marjorie Jane, daughter of Edwin Byrne, of Shanghai, and they have two children : John Alan Geoffrey, born 20 May, 1906, and Madeline Mary, born 7 Sept. 1904.

John Wilfred Bird.

BLOGG, EDWARD BASIL, Capt., (Temporary Major), became Second Lieutenant, Royal Engineers (T.F.), 14 May, 1909. He served in the European War, and was created a Companion of the Distinguished Service Order [London Gazette, 4 Nov. 1915]: " Edward Basil Blogg, Capt. (Temporary Major), 4th London Field Coy., Royal Engineers (Territorial Force). For conspicuous gallantry and ability from 27 Aug. to 25 Sept. 1915, near Loos and Hill 70, when he pushed forward the construction of front-line trenches with great energy. His area came under heavy fire, but he carried on his work, displaying great bravery and coolness. After the assault he personally directed the consolidation of the captured positions. In Loos, he himself unloaded the mines under the church tower, carrying out this dangerous work under heavy shell fire." Major Blogg was killed in action in France in 1916.

BURRARD, GERALD, Major, was born 17 Jan. 1888, son of Sir Sidney Gerald Burrard, K.C.S.I., R.E., F.R.S., and Gertrude, daughter of Major-General C. Haig. He was educated at Cheltenham College, and at the Royal Military Academy, Woolwich ; entered the Royal Artillery 23 July,

1909; became Lieutenant 23 July, 1912; Captain 23 July, 1915, and Major 19 Sept. 1918. He served in India until the outbreak of the European War, and then went to France with the Indian Expeditionary Force in Nov. 1914. He was present at the actions of Givenchy, Neuve Chapelle, Ypres, Festubert, Loos and the Somme. He was mentioned in Despatches, and was created a Companion of the Distinguished Service Order [London Gazette, 4 Nov. 1915]: "Gerald Burrard, Major, 52nd Brigade, Royal Field Artillery. For conspicuous gallantry on many occasions, notably the following: On 25 Sept. 1915, when, as Brigade Adjutant, he guided his brigade across the open under continuous shell and rifle fire to the close support of the infantry near Hohenzollern Redoubt, and pointed out their positions to the batteries. On the night of 27 Sept., when he arranged and assisted in laying wires under a heavy shell and rifle fire. Major Burrard has been continuously on active service since Nov. 1914, and his name was brought to notice for gallantry after actions at Givenchy, Ypres and Festubert." He was severely wounded at the Somme in Aug. 1916, when his right leg was amputated. In consequence he was retired from the Army in Oct. 1919. He was then appointed to the staff of the "Field." Major Burrard is an F.R.G.S. He married Hilda Elizabeth, youngest daughter of Mr. and Mrs. R. J. Mumm.

Gerald Burrard.

DAWSON, JAMES, Capt. (Temporary Major), was created a Companion of the Distinguished Service Order [London Gazette, 4 Nov. 1915]: "James Dawson, Capt. (Temporary Major), 6th (Banff and Donside) Battn. The Gordon Highlanders (Territorial Force). For conspicuous gallantry and ability near Hulluch on 25 Sept. 1915, when he materially assisted his Commanding Officer to organize an advanced position, and took command of the battalion when the latter was killed. All through the day and up to midnight he held on to this position, and displayed great coolness and judgment."

James Dawson.

DENNIS, MICHAEL FREDERICK BEAUCHAMP, Temporary Capt., was born 3 Sept. 1880. He joined the 4th Battn. Royal Munster Fusiliers, and retired from the Service in March, 1904. Lieut. Dennis rejoined at the beginning of the European War, and went to the Western Front. He was created a Companion of the Distinguished Service Order [London Gazette, 4 Nov. 1915]: "Michael Frederick Beauchamp Dennis, Temporary Capt., 7th Battn. The King's Own Scottish Borderers. For conspicuous gallantry and devotion to duty near Loos, and Hill 70 on 25 Sept. 1915. He was wounded in the trenches immediately before the assault, but after his wound was bandaged, he advanced with his company, cheering and encouraging his men till he was again wounded. He was carried back to the dressing station, from which he disappeared after his wound was dressed. Later he was seen catching up his company, and again cheering them on till he was wounded a third time." He was killed in action 19 May, 1918.

GWYNN, KINGSMILL DOUGLAS HOSEASON, Temporary Capt., served in the European War, and was created a Companion of the Distinguished Service Order [London Gazette, 4 Nov. 1915]: "Kingsmill Douglas Hoseason Gwynn, Temporary Capt., 8th Battn. The Devonshire Regt. For conspicuous gallantry near Hulluch on 25 Sept. 1915. At 7.15 a.m., when all the other officers of his battalion, except one Second Lieutenant, had been killed or wounded, he took command, led the men on, and captured four German guns. He was in command all day, and with great coolness and energy held on to the positions captured in the morning. He was wounded by a bomb at about 7.30 p.m."

HAMILTON, CHARLES STEWART PARNELL, T. Capt., was born 14 Sept. 1891, son of Henry Thomas Hamilton, L.R.C.P.I. He was educated at Charing Cross Hospital, London (M.R.C.S., L.R.C.P.Lond., 1914), and was gazetted to the Royal Army Medical Corps as a Temporary Lieutenant 7 Aug. 1914, to 6 Aug. 1915, and was a Temporary Captain 7 Aug. 1915, to 31 May, 1918. He was Capt., R.A.M.C., 7 Feb. to 1 June, 1918; served in the European War, 1915–18; was mentioned in Despatches, and created a Companion of the Distinguished Service Order [London Gazette, 4 Nov. 1915]: Charles Stewart Parnell Hamilton, Temporary Capt., Royal Army Medical Corps, attached 2nd Battn. The Buffs (East Kent Regt.). For conspicuous gallantry and devotion to duty from 27 to 30 Sept. 1915, in France. He dressed the wounded in the firing line, being for hours together under heavy shell fire, and went to points of great danger, often to where bombers were actually fighting."

Charles S. P. Hamilton.

KEARSLEY, EDWARD REGINALD, Major, was born 27 Aug. 1883. He was educated at Harrow, and joined the Royal Welsh Fusiliers as Second Lieutenant 10 Oct. 1903; became Lieutenant 12 Jan. 1907; Captain 18 Dec. 1918, and Major 10 Oct. 1918. From April, 1913, to Nov. 1914, Major Kearsley was employed with the Egyptian Army, but on the outbreak of the European War he accompanied the British Expeditionary Force to the Western Front. He was created a Companion of the Distinguished Service Order [London Gazette, 4 Nov. 1915]: "Edward Reginald Kearsley, Major, 1st Battn. The Royal Welsh Fusiliers. For conspicuous gallantry and devotion to duty during the attack in the German trench near Hulluch on 25 Sept. 1915. He was in command of the battalion, and, although severely wounded, rallied his men, and continued to advance under heavy fire until finally disabled by no less than seven wounds. His personal good leading and determination resulted in the capture of several lines of German trenches."

KERR, FRANK ROBISON, Capt., was born in Melbourne, Australia, 3 April, 1889, son of John H. Kerr, Paymaster, Treasury, Melbourne. He was educated at Wesley College, Melbourne; at the University of Melbourne (M.B., Ch.B. Melbourne); was Rhodes Scholar, Victoria, 1913; proceeded to Oxford (University College), and there studied physiology. He is a Triple Blue (Melbourne) in cricket, football and athletics; five-mile cross-country champion, Victoria, 1910, etc. He served in the European War, 1914–17; was mentioned in Despatches, and created a Companion of the Distinguished Service Order [London Gazette, 4 Nov. 1915]: "Frank Robison Kerr, M.B., Capt., Royal Army Medical Corps, Special Reserve. For conspicuous gallantry and splendid devotion to duty at Cuinchy 25 Sept. 1915. After an unsuccessful attack on the enemy's trenches, this officer crawled over our parapet and brought in a wounded man from about a dozen yards outside, in full view of the enemy, at a range of only 70 yards. He then went out again for 30 yards, and rescued a man whose thigh had been broken, being fired at the whole time. During the night of 25 Sept. Capt. Kerr was out attending to the wounded for two hours under constant machine-gun and rifle fire, and on the night of 27–28 Sept. he went within 25 yards of the enemy's position to rescue a man reported wounded, but found that he was dead." Capt. Kerr married, in 1916, Myrtle, daughter of John M'Meekin, of Mortlake, Victoria, and they have one son and one daughter.

Frank Robison Kerr.

LOW, CLAUD JOHN, Capt., was born 3 May, 1883, son of Thomas Vacher Low, of Holt House, Redhill, Surrey. He was educated at St. John's, School, Leatherhead, and served in the European War, being present at the capture of Givenchy, Les La Bassée, 23 Dec. 1914. Cambrin 23 Jan. 1915; Aubers Ridge attack 9 May, 1915; Loos 25 Sept. and 13 Oct. 1915; Gommecourt 1 July, 1916; Wancourt Ridge 3 May, 1917; Passchendaele Ridge, Ypres, Aug. 1917; Cambrai, Nov. 1917; Vimy Ridge, March, 1918 (German offensive), and Bullecourt 2 Sept. 1918. He was created a Companion of the Distinguished Service Order [London Gazette, 4 Nov. 1915]: "Claud John Low, Capt., 1/14th (County of London) Battn. The London Regt. (London Scottish), Territorial Force. For conspicuous gallantry and ability on 25 Sept. 1915, near Hulluch. He led his company with great skill during the attack, and when hung up by German wire, maintained his position in spite of heavy machine-gun fire from both flanks. By this action he largely induced the German surrender, after which he at once marched forward and occupied their third line."

Claud John Low.

MACGREGOR, WALTER WILLIAM, Capt., was born 27 April, 1877. He was educated at Eton, and entered the Gordon Highlanders 24 March, 1897; became Lieutenant 28 May, 1899, and Captain 15 Jan. 1902; retired from the Gordon Highlanders 5 Feb. 1913, and entered the Reserve of Officers. He was promoted to Lieutenant-Colonel in the Army. He served in the South African War, 1899–1902, and took part in the operations in Natal, 1899, including actions at Elandslaagte and Lombard's Kop; at the defence of Ladysmith, including action of 6 Jan. 1900 (severely wounded); in the Transvaal, Dec. 1900, to Dec. 1901, also during operations in Orange River Colony, Dec. 1900; received the Queen's Medal with five clasps, and the King's Medal with two clasps. In 1908 he served on the North-West Frontier of India, in the Mohmand Expedition. He served in the European War, 1914–17; was thrice mentioned in Despatches, and for gallantry at Loos was created a Companion of the Distinguished Service Order [London

Walter W. MacGregor.

Gazette, 4 Nov. 1915: "Walter William MacGregor, Capt. (Temporary Major), Reserve of Officers, The Gordon Highlanders, attached 9th (Pioneer) Battn. For conspicuous gallantry during the action at Loos on 26 Sept. 1915. He received an order to retire, but, after retiring to the German front-line trenches, he became doubtful of the authenticity of the order, and, although large numbers of men were retiring, he called on two companies and led them back to Loos under heavy shell fire. He reoccupied his defensive position, and held on from 5 to 8 p.m., when he received reinforcements, which enabled him to remain in position all night. His prompt action helped to prevent the Germans turning our flank."

McLEOD, DAVID, Capt., was born 5 Jan. 1869; entered the Army 14 July, 1900, and became Captain 16 Aug. 1905: retired from the Gordon Highlanders 5 Jan. 1914. He served in the Dongola Expedition, 1896, in the action of Firket (Egyptian Medal with clasp); with the Nile Expedition, 1897 (clasp to Egyptian Medal); with the Nile Expedition, 1898; took part in the battles of Atbara and Khartoum (two clasps to Egyptian Medal; Medal; Despatches [London Gazette, 30 Sept. 1898; Medal for distinguished conduct in the field); again with the Nile Expedition, 1899, during the operations in first advances against the Khalifa, and subsequent operations resulting in final defeat of Khalifa (two clasps to Egyptian Medal); served in the South African War, 1900–2 (Medals and clasps). He served in the European War; was Temporary Lieutenant-Colonel, Service Battn. Gordon Highlanders, and was created a Companion of the Distinguished Service Order [London Gazette, 4 Nov. 1915]: "David McLeod, Capt. (Temporary Major), Reserve of Officers, The Gordon Highlanders, attached 8th Battn. For conspicuous gallantry and devotion to duty on 25 Sept. 1915. In the attack on the Hohenzollern Redoubt, although wounded three times, he continued to lead his company forward till he fell from exhaustion."

MENZIES, ARTHUR JOHN ALEXANDER, Capt., was born 21 May, 1886, son of the late Alexander Menzies, of Lankat Estate, Sumatra. He was educated for the medical profession, and took his degree M.B., Ch.B., and subsequently joined the Royal Army Medical Corps in Feb. 1914. Lieut.-Colonel Menzies served in the European War, and landed in France with the 3rd Cavalry Division 8 Oct. 1914; was present at the First and Second Battles of Ypres and Loos, 1915; the Somme, 1916; Cambrai, 1917, and the Fifth Army Retreat, 1918; served in France till killed 9 Aug. 1918, commanding the 3rd Cavalry Field Ambulance; promoted to Captain in Feb. 1915, and Lieut.-Colonel in Feb. 1918. He was created a Companion of the Distinguished Service Order [London Gazette, 4 Nov. 1915]: "Arthur John Alexander Menzies, M.B., Capt., Royal Army Medical Corps, attached 1st (Royal) Dragoons. For conspicuous gallantry and devotion to duty from 26 to 29 Sept. 1915, in Loos. Capt. Menzies was unremitting in his attention for the wounded of all units. He was twice seen carrying wounded on a stretcher under rifle fire, and for 55 hours he was continually exposing himself to heavy shell fire while carrying out his duties." Capt. Menzies married Ethel Fanny Whitelock, youngest daughter of Mrs. D. L. Boyes. He was killed in action 9 Aug. 1918.

Arthur J. A. Menzies.

PULLMAN, ALFRED HOPEWELL, Capt., entered the Army 5 Jan. 1901; became Lieutenant 23 July, 1907, and Captain 1 Aug. 1909. Major Pullman has retired from the Royal West Kent Regt. He served in the South African War, 1901–2; took part in the operations in the Transvaal in Sept. 1901, and Oct. to Nov. 1901; in Orange River Colony, April to Sept. 1901, and Nov. 1901, to 31 May, 1902; also during the operations on the Zululand Frontier of Natal in Sept. and Oct. 1901, and in Cape Colony in April, 1901; received the Queen's Medal with five clasps. For his services in the European War he was created a Companion of the Distinguished Service Order [London Gazette, 4 Nov. 1915]: "Alfred Hopewell Pullman, Capt. and Temporary Major (Reserve of Officers), The Queen's Own (Royal West Kent Regt.), attached 8th Battn. For conspicuous gallantry near Hulluch on 26 Sept. 1915, when he commanded his company with skill during the retirement, although wounded, and collected men to cover the movement until it was completed. This was accomplished under heavy machine-gun fire from the enemy at close range." Major Pullman married Emilie Louisa Outram Marshall, and they have one son and one daughter.

RONALD, JOHN JAMES, Major, was born 19 Sept. 1874. He joined the Army 6 March, 1895; became Captain 16 Feb. 1901: retired 23 Sept. 1911; promoted Major, Reserve of Officers, 1 Sept. 1915. He served at Kandia, 1898, in the affair of 6 Sept.; served in the South African War, 1899–1902, as Commandant, Jamestown; took part in the operations in the Orange Free State, Feb. to May, 1900; in Orange River Colony, May to 29 Nov. 1900, including actions at Wittebergen (1 to 29 July) and Witpoort; again in Orange River Colony 30 Nov. 1900, to Feb. 1901; also during operations in Cape Colony, Feb. 1901, to May, 1902; received the Queen's Medal with two clasps, and the King's Medal with two clasps. He was created a Companion of the Distinguished Service Order [London Gazette, 4 Nov. 1915]: "John James Ronald, Capt. (Temporary Major), Reserve of Officers, The Highland Light Infantry, attached 11th Battn. For conspicuous gallantry and devotion to duty in the attack on 25 Sept. 1915, at a point where a sap was being pushed forward. A serious block stopped his company, which was moving to take up its assault position, but he at once jumped in to the top of the trench, completely exposed to artillery and machine-gun fire, cleared away the obstruction, and remained exposed until he had received several wounds."

STUART, HERBERT CRAVEN, Major, was born at Cuddapah, Madras, 29 Oct. 1872, son of the late Colonel C. J. Stuart, I.S.C., and a daughter of Bishop Sargent. He was educated at King's School, Canterbury; joined the South Lancashire Militia, 1892, and the 2nd Leinster Regt. 7 Dec. 1895 (Lieutenant 27 July, 1898), with which regiment he served in the South African War in 1902. He became Captain, 4th Royal Warwickshire Regt., in 1902, until it was disbanded in 1907, when he went on half-pay until he was posted to the 2nd Highland Light Infantry 26 Aug. 1908. He retired on a pension 12 June, 1912, and settled in Jamaica as a Banana Planter until 1914, when war broke out, and he was called up for service with the 10th Highland Light Infantry, 28th Infantry Brigade, 9th Division, formed in Aug. 1914. He went to France in May, 1915; was promoted to Major, Reserve of Officers, 1 Sept. 1915, and was Temporary Colonel, Labour Commandant, commanding the 10th Highland Light Infantry, 1915; the 7th Loyal North Lancashire Regt. 1917; was Chief Instructor, 2nd Army School, 1916–17; was transferred to a Labour Corps in 1918; was Officer Commanding, 20th Labour Group, Dieppe; Officer Commanding, 75th Labour Group, Marquise; Labour Commandant, 3rd Corps, 1918–19, during the operations on the Lille front which led to the cessation of hostilities. He was present at the Battle of Loos. Though he was gassed he reorganized what was left of his battalion near Cambrin. Major Stuart was mentioned in Despatches four times, and created a Companion of the Distinguished Service Order [London Gazette, 4 Nov. 1915]: "Herbert Craven Stuart, Major, Reserve of Officers, The Highland Light Infantry, attached 10th Battn. For conspicuous gallantry and ability near Cambrin on 25 Sept. 1915, when he led his company forward to the attack, and later, although himself gassed, reorganized what remained of his battalion, restored confidence and commanded it with marked skill." He married, in 1901, Julia McKenzie, daughter of Sir John Pringle, K.C.M.G., and Amy Zillah, daughter of the late Hon. J. Levy, and they have one son and one daughter.

SYKES, CHARLES HENRY, Capt., served in the European War, and was created a Companion of the Distinguished Service Order [London Gazette, 4 Nov. 1915]: "Charles Henry Sykes, Capt., 6th Battn. The Royal Fusiliers (City of London Regt.), attached 3rd Battn. For conspicuous gallantry near Vermelles on 29 Sept. 1915. When some troops on his left were bombed out of their position he led a charge with about a dozen men, drove out the Germans, and retook the lost portion of the trench. He even penetrated further, and only fell back later, owing to want of support. He saved a serious situation by his gallantry and initiative. Later on the same day, when under heavy shell fire, he supported a company which was being driven back by superior numbers, and succeeded in regaining all the lost ground. He displayed throughout great bravery and coolness. He was wounded in the morning of 30 Sept."

WILLIAMS, SIR RHYS, Capt., Bart., was born 20 Oct. 1865, son of Gwilym Williams, of Miskin Manor, Llantrisant, Glamorgan, and Mrs. Emma E. Williams. He was educated at Eton, and Oriel College, Oxford; joined the Grenadier Guards 5 Aug. 1914; served in France, Nov. 1914, to Sept. 1915; transferred to the Welsh Guards in Feb. 1915. He served in the European War, and took part in the Battle of Loos in Sept. 1915, when serving with the Welsh Guards. He subsequently served as Military Attaché, Teheran, Dec. 1915, to Dec. 1916; Assistant Director-General, Movements and Railways, War Office, 1917–1918; Deputy Director, Training and Staff Duties Division, Admiralty, 1918, to Dec. 1919. He was created a Companion of the Distinguished Service Order [London Gazette, 4 Nov. 1915]: "Rhys Williams, Capt., 1st Battn. Welsh Guards. For conspicuous gallantry and great determination on the night of 27–28 Sept. 1915, during the attack on Hill 70. Capt. Williams was in command of the Welsh Guards' Machine Guns, and performed very effective work until wounded. He then obtained a dressing for his wound, and returned to the guns, which he continued to control until midnight, having had to lie on his back for the purpose, owing to the nature of his injuries." He was promoted Captain in April, 1915; Temporary Major in April, 1917; Temporary Lieutenant-Colonel in July, 1917; Substantive Major in July, 1919; placed on Reserve with the rank of Lieutenant-Colonel in April, 1920.

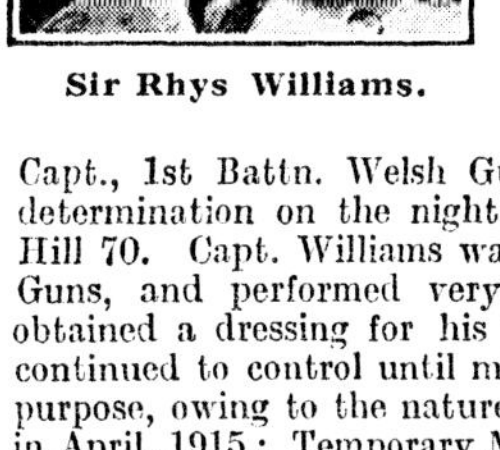

Sir Rhys Williams.

WILSON, WALTER CARANDINI, Capt., was born 22 June, 1885. He joined the Leicestershire Regt. as Second Lieutenant (from the Militia) in Jan. 1907, and became Lieutenant in Nov. 1903. From June, 1911, to Feb. 1914, he was employed with the West African Frontier Force, being promoted to Captain 1 Nov. 1913, and given the Brevet of Major 3 June, 1916. He was given the O.B.E., and awarded the Military Cross for services in the European War, as Staff Captain, 70th Infantry Brigade, B.E.F., 24 May, 1916, to 13 Feb. 1917; Brigade Major, 70th Infantry Brigade, British Armies in France, 24 May, 1916, to 18 Feb. 1917; G.S.O.2, 2nd Division, British Armies in France, 19 Feb. 1917, to 3 Jan. 1918; G.S.O.2, 2nd Army Corps, British Armies in France, 4 Jan. to March, 1918; G.S.O.1, British Military Mission to America, 9 April, 1918, to 3 March, 1919; G.S.O.1, 68th Division, Forces in Great Britain, 4 March, 1919, to 18 May, 1919. He was created a Companion of the Distinguished Service Order [London Gazette, 4 Nov. 1915]: "Walter Carandini Wilson, Capt., 2nd Battn. The Leicestershire Regt. For conspicuous gallantry and devotion to duty during an attack near Pietre Farm on 25 Sept. 1915. When giving final directions to his men he was severely wounded in the stomach, but he stuck to his work and went forward, encouraging his men till he could see through the smoke that they were on the German parapet. He was then helped back in an exhausted state. Capt. Wilson's name has several times been brought forward for gallantry and determination."

CRUIKSHANK, GUY LINDSEY, Lieut. (Temporary Capt.), entered the Gordon Highlanders 1 Dec. 1908. He served in the European War, and was created a Companion of the Distinguished Service Order [London Gazette, 4 Nov. 1915]: "Guy Lindsey .Cruikshank, Lieut. (Temporary Capt.), Gordon Highlanders and Royal Flying Corps. For conspicuous gallantry in France on 29 Sept. 1915, when he successfully carried out a special mission, involving very great risk." He was killed in action 15 Sept. 1916.

EVANS, FAITHFUL SIDNEY, Lieut. (Temporary Major), served in the Great War, and was created a Companion of the Distinguished Service Order [London Gazette, 4 Nov. 1915]: "Faithful Sidney Evans, Lieut., 1/9th Battn. King's (Liverpool Regt.), T.F. For conspicuous gallantry on 25 Sept. 1915, in the attack near Le Rutoire. He commanded his company with great skill and dash, and his cheerfulness and absolute disregard of danger had a marked effect on his men, who were attacking for the first time over open ground. He was wounded in the attack." Major Evans has retired.

LAWRENCE, GEORGE AUBREY KENNEDY, Lieut. (Temporary Capt. and Flight-Commander), was born at Tunbridge Wells 15 Sept. 1891. He comes of a good military stock, his father being Major-General William Alexander Lawrence, Honorary Colonel of the 17th Cavalry, Indian Army, and eldest son of Lieut.-General R. C. Lawrence, C.B., the youngest of the five brothers of Indian fame, and who received the Medals for the Indian Mutiny and the Sutlej Campaign. Major-General Lawrence's grandfather was the distinguished Colonel Alexander Lawrence, who took part in the storming of Seringapatam, where he was seriously wounded. George Lawrence was educated at The Grange, Folkestone (Mr. Jelf's); at Wellington College, Berks; at Mr. Cobbold's, West Wratting, and at the Royal Military Academy, Woolwich, passing into the Army 23 Dec. 1911. He served with the 112th Battery in Ireland from 1912 to 1914.

George A. K. Lawrence.

At the outbreak of the European War in 1914, he at once joined the Royal Flying Corps as Second Lieutenant, and proceeded to France in Sept. 1915, where he speedily distinguished himself. Sir John French, in his Despatch dated Headquarters, British Army in France, 15 Oct. 1915, refers to Lieut. Lawrence's work as follows: "On one occasion an officer of the Royal Flying Corps engaged four enemy machines and drove them off, proceeding on his reconnaissance." Again he writes: "As evidence of the dangers our flying officers are called upon to face, I may state that on one occasion a machine was hit in no fewer than 300 places soon after crossing the enemy's lines, and yet the officer successfully carried out his mission." And further on in the same Despatch: "The Royal Flying Corps has on several occasions carried out a continuous bombing of the enemy's communications, descending to 500 feet and under, in order to hit moving trains on the railway." The following extract from "London Opinion" in Oct. 1915, speaks of the 300 bullet-holes in his machine: "An officer, in a letter home, writing of the Royal Flying Corps, says: 'The record for bullet-holes in one's machine is much prized. It is held by a Capt. L., who returned from one flight with over 300 holes in his machine, the previous record having been 240 odd.'" In Nov. 1915, he was created a Companion of the Distinguished Service Order [London Gazette, 4 Nov. 1915]: "George Aubrey Kennedy Lawrence, Lieut. (Temporary Capt. and Flight-Commander), Royal Flying Corps. For conspicuous and repeated acts of gallantry in France, notably the following: On 21 Sept. 1915, he completed a reconnaissance to points 60 miles inside the German lines, although repeatedly attacked by a hostile machine. On 25 Sept. he attacked and hit a moving train near Lille, descending to 600 feet. On 26 Sept. he attacked and drove off a hostile aeroplane which was interfering with our bombing machines. On 30 Sept. he carried out a three-hour reconnaissance in very bad weather. Although his machine was hit in 70 places by anti-aircraft guns in crossing the German lines on his way out, he carried on and completed his work." He was received by the King at Buckingham Palace 9 Dec. 1915, and was invested with the Insignia of the Companionship of the Distinguished Service Order. From 16 Feb. to 26 June, 1916, he was employed as Squadron Commander in England, when he took a squadron of Sopwith machines to France, remaining there till the end of Dec. 1916, when he received the appointment of Assistant Commandant of the Central Flying School, Upavon, and Wing Commander and Temporary Lieut.-Colonel, Royal Flying Corps from 1 Jan. 1917, to date of his death. He was killed in England when testing an aeroplane 28 Jan. 1917, and was buried at Brooklands Cemetery. Lieut.-Colonel Lawrence was 25 years old and unmarried. The following is an extract from a letter received from Major-General Trenchard, D.S.O., C.B., Royal Flying Corps: "Headquarters, Royal Flying Corps, 10 March, 1915.—I always had an extremely high opinion of your son, and was greatly distressed to hear of his death. His example was excellent, not only by the thoroughness with which he carried out his duties, but by his courage and skill as a pilot. His squadron, which was under my immediate command during the Battle of the Somme, had heavy fighting and many

casualties, but the tone never deteriorated. This I attribute in no small degree to your son's personal example and cheerfulness under all conditions. His death was a real loss to the Royal Flying Corps." Lieut.-General Sir David Henderson, K.C.B., D.S.O., wrote: "London, 6 Feb. 1917.—I knew your son personally and by report as one of our best officers, and his death is a great loss to the corps. He was a brave boy and a good soldier." The Officer Commanding No. 70 Squadron, Royal Flying Corps, also recorded his high esteem for Lieut.-Colonel Lawrence in the following words: "Both officers and men feel Lieut.-Colonel Lawrence's death as a personal loss, and have asked me to express the great respect and confidence in which they held him during the time he was in command of No. 70 Squadron, Royal Flying Corps.—1 Feb. 1917." Lieut.-Colonel Lawrence was good at games and a fine ski-er.

PARK, MAITLAND ELPHINSTONE, Lieut., was born 12 Sept. 1894, son of Sir Maitland Hall Park, and Alice, daughter of Peter Baillie, of Inverness. He entered the Royal Highlanders 2 Sept. 1913, becoming Lieutenant 30 Sept. 1914, and Captain 2 March, 1916. He served in the Great War, was twice wounded, mentioned in Despatches, and created a Companion of the Distinguished Service Order [London Gazette, 4 Nov. 1915]: "Maitland Elphinstone Park, Lieut. (Temporary Capt.), 2nd Battn. Royal Highlanders (The Black Watch). For conspicuous gallantry at Mauquissart on 25 Sept. 1915, when leading his company and directing bombing parties in continuous close fighting from 6 a.m. to 10 a.m. During this time he drove the enemy back some 400 yards along two lines of trenches, and established three blocks, which he held until relieved. At Givenchy, on 8 Oct., the enemy exploded two mines about 20 yards from the parapet along which his company was posted. Although half-buried by the first explosion, he hurried along his fire trench, but was again half-buried and slightly wounded by the second. Six of his men were killed and many injured, but he rapidly replaced them from his supports, and was soon ready to meet any attack."

BUCHAN, JAMES IVORY, 2nd Lieut., served in the Great War, and was created a Companion of the Distinguished Service Order [London Gazette, 4 Nov. 1915]: "James Ivory Buchan, 2nd Lieut. (Temporary Capt.), 2nd Battn. Black Watch. For conspicuous gallantry at Mauquissart on 25 Sept. 1915, when rallying and leading his company after both he himself and many men had suffered from the effects of gas. He led his men over three lines of German trenches, his company being the first to enter their reserve line near the Moulin. He only gave the order to retire when the troops on both flanks had been forced back by the enemy's counter-attack and he himself had been wounded."

PUSCH, FREDERICK LEOPOLD, 2nd Lieut. (Temporary Lieut.), served in the Great War, and was created a Companion of the Distinguished Service Order [London Gazette, 4 Nov. 1915]: "Frederick Leopold Pusch, 2nd Lieut. (Temporary Lieut.), 19th (County of London) Battn. The London Regt. (St. Pancras), T.F. For conspicuous gallantry, marked ability and resource at Loos on 25 and 27 Sept. 1915. During the advance through Loos he led a party of bombers, and going alone into a house, captured seven Germans, although badly shot in the face by one of them. Notwithstanding his serious injury, this very gallant officer continued clearing the enemy out of the cellars in the town. Lieut. Pusch organized the bombing attack of Grenadiers on 27 Sept., operating from the Chalk Pit against the Copse, at great personal risk, and helped materially in its capture." The Insignia were presented by the King at Darley Barracks, Brentwood, 17 March, 1916. He was killed in action.

London Gazette, 8 Nov. 1915.—"War Office, 8 Nov. 1915. His Majesty the King has been graciously pleased to confer the undermentioned rewards for distinguished service in the field during the operations at the Dardanelles. To be Companions of the Distinguished Service Order."

BARLOW, CHARLES LESLIE, Major, entered the Army 18 Oct. 1899; became Lieutenant 24 Aug. 1901, and Captain 8 Feb. 1910. He served in the South African War, 1899–1901; was present at the Relief of Ladysmith, including action at Colenso; operations of 17 to 24 Jan. 1900 (wounded 21 Jan.) and action at Spion Kop; took part in the operations in Natal (March to June, 1900), including action at Laing's Nek (6 to 9 June); served in the Transvaal, east and west of Pretoria, July to 29 Nov. 1900; again in the Transvaal 30 Nov. 1900, to April, 1901 (Queen's Medal with four clasps). He served in East Africa, 1905. For his services in the European War he was created a Companion of the Distinguished Service Order [London Gazette, 8 Nov. 1915]: "Charles Leslie Barlow, Major, The Prince of Wales's Own (West Yorkshire Regt.), attached Essex Regt. For distinguished service in the field during the operations at the Dardanelles." He was killed in action.

BROWNING, JOHN COWAN, Major, youngest son of William Browning, J.P. He was educated at Cheltenham College. He became Lieutenant, 5th Lancashire Battery, Royal Field Artillery (T.F.), 22 June, 1910; was promoted to Major and retired. He served in the European War, 1914–18, was mentioned in Despatches, and created a Companion of the Distinguished Service Order [London Gazette, 8 Nov. 1915]: "John Cowan Browning, Major, 5th Lancashire Battery, Royal Field Artillery (T.F.). For distinguished service in the field during the operations at the Dardanelles." Major Browning married, in 1916, Beatrice, daughter of J. T. Kenyon, and they have one son.

CURLING, BRYAN JAMES, Major, was born 21 Sept. 1877. He entered the King's Royal Rifle Corps 29 Nov. 1899; became Lieutenant 19 Feb. 1901, Captain 22 Jan. 1908, and Major 1 Sept. 1915; Temporary Lieut.-Colonel 20 Dec. 1915, to 18 Aug. 1916; 25 Sept. 1916, to 20 April, 1917, and 8 June, 1917, to 28 Jan. 1918; Temporary Lieut.-Colonel Commanding 8th Battn. The King's Royal Rifle Corps, 30 Jan. to 2 Sept. 1918; Temporary Brigadier-General 3 Sept. 1918. He was Staff Captain, 5th

Division, Irish Command, 2 April, 1912, to 31 Dec. 1913; Staff Captain, War Office, 4 Jan. 1914, to 17 Jan. 1915; D.A.A. and Q.M.G., 29th Division, New Armies, Mediterranean Expeditionary Force, 18 Jan. to 1 June, 1915; G.S.O.2, 29th Division, Mediterranean Expeditionary Force, 19 June to 19 Dec. 1915; G.S.O.1, 26th Division, Mediterranean Expeditionary Force, Egyptian Expeditionary Force, 20 Dec. 1915, to 18 Aug. 1916; G.S.O.1, 65th Division, Home Forces, 25 Sept. to April, 1916; G.S.O.1, 12nd Division, British Armies in France, June 1917; Brigade Commander, 180th Infantry Brigade, British Armies in France, 3 Sept. 1918. He served in the South African War, 1899–1902; was present at the Relief of Ladysmith, including operations of 17 to 24 Jan. 1900, and action at Spion Kop; operations of 5 to 7 Feb. 1900, and action at Vaal Kranz; and the operations on Tugela Heights (14 to 27 Feb. 1900) and action at Pieter's Hill; in Natal, March to June, 1900, including action at Laing's Nek (6 to 9 June); in the Transvaal, east of Pretoria, July to 29 Nov. 1900; in the Transvaal 30 Nov. 1900, to Jan. 1901; in Orange River Colony, March, 1901, to 31 May, 1902; also during the operations in Cape Colony, Jan. to Feb. 1901 (Queen's Medal with six clasps, and King's Medal with two clasps). For his services in the European War he was given the Brevet of Lieutenant-Colonel 3 June, 1919, and was created a Companion of the Distinguished Service Order [London Gazette, 8 Nov. 1915]: " Bryan James Curling, Major, The King's Royal Rifle Corps. For distinguished service in the field during the operations at the Dardanelles."

GOING, JOHN, Major, son of the late John Going, private gentleman, Cragg, Birdhill, Limerick, and Eliza, daughter of the Rev. C. Mayne; was born 13 March, 1866. He was educated at The Abbey, Tipperary, Ireland; joined the 4th Gloucester Militia in 1886. He entered the South Wales Borderers 16 Nov. 1887; became Lieutenant 31 July, 1889, Captain 18 Nov. 1895, and Major 11 Dec. 1905 (Temporary Lieut.-Colonel South Wales Borderers 25 Aug. to 24 Sept. 1915). He became Lieut.-Colonel 29 Nov. 1915 (in command of Training Reserve Battn. 27 Aug. 1917, to 15 Jan. 1918). He was Adjutant, Volunteers, 28 April, 1898, to 7 April, 1903. He served with the Burmese Expedition, 1887–89 (Medal with clasp). He served in the European War; took part in the capture of Tsingtau in 1914, and was

John Going.

present at the landing at Gallipoli in 1915. He was mentioned in Despatches, and was created a Companion of the Distinguished Service Order [London Gazette, 8 Nov. 1915]: " John Going, Major, The South Wales Borderers. For distinguished service in the field during the operations at the Dardanelles." He married, at St. James's, Piccadilly, W., 30 Oct. 1894, Ethel Mary, the only daughter of the late Benjamin Bridges, of Manor House, Mitcham; they have one daughter, Joan Mary Mayne.

KIRKBY, HAROLD ALEC, Major, was born 27 Sept. 1874. He entered the Lancashire Fusiliers 5 May, 1900; became Lieutenant 19 April, 1901, Captain 14 June, 1910, and Major 1 Sept. 1915; Temporary Lieut.-Colonel, The Lancashire Fusiliers, 21 Oct. 1915, to 4 Feb. 1916; Acting Lieut.-Colonel, Lancashire Fusiliers, 3 June to 31 Dec. 1918; Temporary Lieut.-Colonel, Lancashire Fusiliers, 1 Jan. 1919; employed with West African Frontier Force 10 July, 1901, to 27 Aug. 1906. He was Adjutant, Territorial Force, 6 July, 1914, to 20 Oct. 1915; Special Appointment (graded Brigade Major) Commanding Officer Cadet Company, 1 Nov. 1916, to 4 Sept. 1917. He served in the South African War, 1899–1900; took part in the operations in the Orange Free State, May, 1900, including action at Zand River; in the Transvaal in May and June, 1900, including action near Johannesburg (Queen's Medal with three clasps); in West Africa (Southern Nigeria), 1901–2, with the Aro Expedition (Medal with clasp); in West Africa (Southern Nigeria), 1903 (clasp); in West Africa (Southern Nigeria) 1904, during the operations in the Northern Ibibio district (Despatches [London Gazette, 25 Aug. 1905]; clasp); in West Africa (Southern Nigeria), 1904–5, during the operations of the Ezza Patrol (Despatches [London Gazette, 23 Feb. 1906]); in West Africa (Southern Nigeria), 1905–6, with the Bende-Onitsha Hinterland Expedition (clasp). He served in the European War, and was created a Companion of the Distinguished Service Order [London Gazette, 8 Nov. 1915]: " Harold Alec Kirkby, Major, The Lancashire Fusiliers (attached 8th Battn. Territorial Force). For distinguished service in the field during the operations at the Dardanelles."

SINCLAIR-THOMSON, ANGUS ERIC METHVEN, Major, son of the late W. Sinclair-Thomson, M.D., was born 24 May, 1880. He was educated at Epsom College, and in France and Germany; joined the 1st Essex Regt., from the Militia, 15 Nov. 1899; became Lieutenant 18 April, 1900. He served in the South African War, 1899–1902; took part in the Relief of Kimberley; in the Orange Free State, Feb. to May, 1900, including operations at Paardeberg (17 to 26 Feb.; slightly wounded 18 Feb.); in Cape Colony, south of Orange River, 1899–1900, including actions at Colesberg (1 to 29 Jan.); also in the Transvaal and Cape Colony 30 Nov. 1900, to 31 May, 1902 (Queen's Medal with three clasps, and King's Medal with two clasps). He was promoted to Captain 7 May, 1909; was Adjutant, The Essex Regt., 1 Nov. 1909, to 31 Oct. 1912, in which year he married Rachel, daughter of Walter Ingram, of Broads, Lewes, and they have one son and one daughter. At the beginning of the European War he was employed as Staff Captain at the War Office for several months. He was then sent to Gallipoli as Staff Captain and Brigade Major, 29th Division, Gallipoli, and was there throughout the whole of that campaign, taking part in the landing on the River Clyde, and in the

evacuation of the Allied troops at Suvla and Helles. He was promoted to Major 1 Sept. 1915, and was created a Companion of the Distinguished Service Order [London Gazette, 8 Nov. 1915]: " Angus Eric Methven Sinclair-Thomson, Major, The Essex Regt. For distinguished service in the field during the operations at the Dardanelles." Major Sinclair-Thomson then accompanied his regiment to Egypt and Palestine. He was G.S.O., 1st Grade, 53rd Division, Egyptian Expeditionary Force, 15 Sept. 1916, to 30 June, 1919, and G.S.O.1, Scottish Command, 7 July, 1918, to 30 June, 1919. He was twice mentioned in Despatches, given the Brevet of Lieut.-Colonel 3 June, 1917, and made Chevalier Légion d'Honneur.

SYKES, FRANCIS BERNARD, Major (Temporary Lieut.-Colonel), son of T. G. Sykes, B.A., late Principal La Martinière College, Lucknow, India. He was educated at Gray's Inn, becoming a Barrister-at-Law, and joining the R.F.A. 23 May, 1900, to take part in the South African War, 1900–1. He served with the New Zealand Contingent; afterwards employed with Imperial Yeomanry; took part in the operations in Orange Free State, May, 1900, including actions at Vet River (5 and 6 May) and Zand River; in the Transvaal in May and June, 1900, including actions near Johannesburg and Pretoria; in Cape Colony, south of Orange River, 1899–1900; also in Orange River Colony, May, 1902; again during operations in Cape Colony, Feb. to March, 1901 (Queen's Medal with five clasps). In 1906 he was transferred to the Royal Horse

Francis Bernard Sykes.

Artillery, being gazetted Captain 1 Jan. 1911, and Major 30 Oct. 1914; was Adjutant, Territorial Force, 1 March, 1912, to 9 July, 1914. Major Sykes again saw active service in the European War, being employed with the New Zealand Force from 10 July, 1914, to 13 March, 1918, taking part in operations in Egypt, Gallipoli and France. He was mentioned five times in Despatches, and in Nov. 1915, was created a Companion of the Distinguished Service Order [London Gazette, 8 Nov. 1915]: " Francis Bernard Sykes, Major (Temporary Lieut.-Colonel), Royal Artillery (attached New Zealand Imperial Force). For distinguished service in the field during the operations at the Dardanelles." He was appointed Temporary Lieut.-Colonel in 1915, and subsequently appointed Inspector of Artillery, New Zealand Defence Forces, and placed in command of the 2nd New Zealand Field Artillery Brigade. Lieut.-Colonel Sykes married, in 1911, Alice Augusta, daughter of the Rev. H. C. Watson, M.A., Vicar of Gainford, County Durham, and they have one daughter.

WINTER, ORMONDE DE L'EPÉE, Major, son of W. H. and Fanny Cheney Winter, late of Sutton Court Lodge, Chiswick, W., was born 15 Jan. 1875. He was educated at Cheltenham College and at the Royal Military Academy, Woolwich, and was commissioned in the Royal Artillery 17 Nov. 1894, becoming Lieutenant 17 Nov. 1897; Captain 1 Feb. 1901; Major 24 July, 1911, and Lieutenant-Colonel 28 April, 1916. He was G.S.O.2, 13th Division, Mediterranean Expeditionary Force, 12 Oct. to 28 Dec. 1915; Brigadier-General, Royal Artillery, 11th Division, British Armies in France, 25 Dec. 1917. He was mentioned in Despatches six times, and was created a Companion of the Distinguished Service Order [London Gazette, 8 Nov. 1915]: " Ormonde de l'Epée Winter, Major, Royal Artillery. For distinguished ser-

Ormonde de L'E. Winter.

vice in the field during the operations at the Dardanelles." Major Winter was created a C.M.G. in 1917; a C.B. in 1919, and was also awarded a Bar to his Distinguished Service Order. Racing is his favourite recreation.

WOOD, GEORGE BENSON GLEN, Major, was born 11 Nov. 1881. He entered the Lancashire Fusiliers 11 Aug. 1900; became Lieutenant 19 March, 1902, and Captain 15 Jan. 1912; Temporary Major 17 Aug. to 31 Aug. 1915; Major 1 Sept. 1915 (Temporary Lieut.-Colonel 1 Sept. to 6 Sept. 1915; Temporary Lieut.-Colonel Commanding Territorial Force Battn. The Leicestershire Regt. 14 Jan. 1917); Adjutant, Territorial Force, 15 Jan. 1912, to 27 Nov. 1916; Brigade Major, 177th Infantry Brigade, Home Forces, 17 Feb. to 27 July, 1916. He served in the European War; was given the Brevet of Lieut.-Colonel 1 Jan. 1918, and was created a Companion of the Distinguished Service Order [London Gazette, 8 Nov. 1915]: " George Benson Glen Wood, Major, The Lancashire Fusiliers (Adjutant, 5th Battn. Territorial Force). For distinguished service in the field during the operations at the Dardanelles."

WYMER, HUBERT JULIAN DE CRESPIGNY, Major, second son of the late Major George Bannatyne Wymer, R.A.; was born at Sheerness 19 Nov. 1878. He was educated at Stubbington and at the Royal Military College, Sandhurst, passing into the West India Regt. 3 Aug. 1898; became Lieutenant 19 Oct. 1899. In 1901 he took part in operations with the Gambia Expedition from Jan. to May, and on 16 March, 1907, was gazetted Captain, 1st Battn. The Hampshire Regt. He saw active service in the European War, taking part in the landing at Gallipoli with the 29th Division in 1915, and was promoted to Major 1 Sept. 1915. He was wounded, mentioned in Despatches, and created a Companion of the Distinguished Service Order [London Gazette, 8 Nov. 1915]: " Hubert Julian de Crespigny Wymer, Major, The Hampshire Regt. For distinguished service in the field during the operations at the Dardanelles." He held a Special Appointment (graded Brigade Major) 29 Jan. 1918, to 14 Jan. 1919 ; was Officer Commanding Company of Gentleman Cadets, Royal Military College, from 15 Jan. 1919. Major Wymer married, on the 31st Dec. 1917, Dorothy May Joan Stockley, and they have one son.

ALEXANDER, HEBER MAITLAND, Major, second son of Major C. A. Alexander, late 4th Gloucestershire Regt. ; was born 1 Feb. 1881. He was educated at Clifton, and was gazetted to the Somerset Light Infantry 11 Aug. 1900, becoming Lieutenant 15 Sept. 1903 ; Capt., Indian Army, 19 June, 1911, and Major 1 Sept. 1915 ; was Temporary Lieut.-Colonel. On the outbreak of war in Europe was sent to France (Sept. 1914), in command of the 9th Mule Corps, Indian Army. He saw active service in Gallipoli with the Australian and New Zealand Army Corps from April to Nov. 1915, in command of the Mule Transport, being present at the first landing in Gallipoli and at the Battle of Suvla Bay (6–10 Aug.).

Heber M. Alexander.

He received the thanks of the Army Corps Commander in Orders, for services between 25 April and 5 May ; was mentioned in Sir Ian Hamilton's Despatch 8 Nov. 1915, and was created a Companion of the Distinguished Service Order [London Gazette, 8 Nov. 1915]: " Heber Maitland Alexander, Major, Supply and Transport Corps. For distinguished service in the field during the operations at the Dardanelles." He has published a book on the war, " On Two Fronts " (Heinemann, 1917). Major Alexander married, 13 Oct. 1909, at Hobart, Tasmania, Mary Brenda (died 15 March, 1914), daughter of the late J. H. B. Walch, of Hobart, Tasmania ; they had no children.

CREAGH, PETER HUBERT, Capt., was born 17 Aug. 1882. He entered the Leicestershire Regt. 22 Oct. 1902 ; became Lieutenant 10 July, 1905, and Captain 13 Nov. 1908 (Temporary Major, Leicestershire Regt., 3 July to 29 July, 1916 ; Acting Major, Leicestershire Regt. 22 Aug. 1916, to 21 Oct. 1917) ; Major, Leicestershire Regt., 22 Oct. 1917 ; Adjutant, Territorial Force, 12 June, 1911, to 9 Sept. 1916. He served in the European War, and was created a Companion of the Distinguished Service Order [London Gazette, 8 Nov. 1915]: " Peter Hubert Creagh, Capt., The Leicestershire Regt. (Adjutant, 7th Battn. The Manchester Regt. Territorial Force). For distinguished service in the field during the operations at the Dardanelles."

Peter Hubert Creagh.

D'APICE, JOHN EDMUND FRANCIS, Capt., was born in Sydney 7 July, 1877, son of the late Chevalier Charles D'Apice, K.S.S., formerly of Naples. He was educated at Riverview College, Sydney, and at Sydney University, and represented the University of Sydney and College in rowing (Blue, 1899), Rugby football, tennis and rifle shooting. He entered the Royal Artillery (from Local Military Forces, New South Wales) 23 May, 1900 ; became Lieutenant in Royal Artillery 13 Aug. 1901 ; Captain 23 May, 1913, and promoted Major 30 Dec. 1915 (Temporary Lieut.-Colonel 26 April to 2 June, 1919). He was Adjutant, Volunteers, 22 Jan.

John E. F. D'Apice.

1907, to 31 March, 1908 ; Adjutant, Territorial Force, 1 April, 1908, to 22 March, 1910, and 26 March, 1914, to 31 Jan. 1915 ; Staff Captain, Royal Artillery, 29th Division, New Armies, Mediterranean Expeditionary Force, 1 Feb. to 25 April, 1915 ; Brigade Major, Royal Artillery, 29th Division, Mediterranean Expeditionary Force, 26 April to 31 May, 1915 ; Staff Captain, Royal Artillery, 29th Division, Mediterranean Expeditionary Force, 1 June to 25 Aug. 1915 ; D.A.A. and Q.M.G., 52nd Division, Mediterranean Expeditionary Force, 26 Aug. to 29 Nov. 1915 ; D.A.A., 8th Army Corps, Mediterranean Expeditionary Force, and Q.M.G., 9th Army Corps, Mediterranean Expeditionary Force, 30 Nov. 1915 ; D.A.A. and Q.M.G., Northern District, Ireland, 28 Sept. 1916, to 25 May, 1917 ; D.A.A.G. (Temporary), 27 May, 1917, to 25 April, 1919 ; A.A. and Q.M.G., Thames and Medway Garrison, 26 April, 1919. He served with the New South Wales Mounted Rifles, and later with the Royal Artillery, in the South African War, 1899–1902 ; took part in the operations in the Orange Free State, including actions at Poplar Grove, Dreifontein, Karee Siding, Vet River and Zand River ; in the Transvaal ; in Orange River Colony, including action at Bethlehem and Wittebergen ; in Cape Colony, south of Orange River ; also during the operations in the Transvaal and Orange River Colony 30 Nov. 1900, to 31 May, 1902 (Queen's Medal with four clasps, and King's Medal with two clasps). He took the Gunnery Staff Course, 1912-13 ; served in the European War on the Staff

of the 29th Division for the original landing at Gallipoli, and on the Staff of the 8th Army Corps for the final evacuation in 1916. He commanded a heavy battery in the Battle of the Somme in 1916. He was twice wounded during the Great War, was twice mentioned in Despatches, given the Brevet of Lieut.-Colonel 3 June, 1919, and was created a Companion of the Distinguished Service Order [London Gazette, 8 Nov. 1915]: " John Edmund Francis d'Apice, Capt., Royal Artillery. For distinguished service in the field during the operations at the Dardanelles." Major d'Apice married, in 1904, Mary Holroyd, only daughter of Lieut.-Colonel J. J. L. Ratton, late I.M.S., and they have one son.

HOWELL-JONES, JOHN HYNDMAN, Capt., (Temporary Major), was born 13 Dec. 1877. He entered the Royal Marine Artillery 1 Sept. 1896, becoming Lieutenant 1 July, 1897, Captain 19 April, 1902, and Major 24 Nov. 1915. He was Ordnance Officer, 4th Class, from 30 April, 1909 ; Ordnance Officer, 3rd Class (Temporary), 12 Dec. 1914, to 23 Nov. 1915 ; Ordnance Officer, 3rd Class, from 23 Nov. 1915, and Ordnance Officer, 2nd Class, from 5 April, 1916. He took part in operations in Gallipoli, in the European War, in connection with the Army Ordnance Department, and was created a Companion of the Distinguished Service Order [London Gazette, 8 Nov. 1915]: " John Hyndman Howell-Jones, Capt. (Temporary Major), Army Ordnance Department. For distinguished service in the field during the operations at the Dardanelles." He was created a C.I.E., and was also given the Brevets of Major 3 June, 1916, and Lieut.-Colonel 1 Jan. 1918.

ROLLING, BERNARD ISMAY, Capt. (Temporary Major), son of George Miller Rolling, The Grove, Penistone, near Sheffield ; was born 31 May, 1883. He was educated as an Engineer in Leeds, becoming successively Assistant Engineer, Newcastle Electric Supply Company ; Chief Assistant Engineer, Motherwell Corporation ; Engineer and Manager for Scotland for Igranic Electric Company. He served in the European War with the 2nd Lowland Divisional Royal Engineers, Territorial Force, and took part in operations at the Dardanelles ; was mentioned four times in Despatches ; awarded the O.B.E. in 1919 ; given the Brevet of Major, and created a Companion of the Distinguished Service Order [London Gazette, 8 Nov. 1915]: " Bernard Ismay Rolling, Capt. (Temporary Major), 2nd Lowland Field Coy., Royal Engineers, Territorial

Bernard Ismay Rolling.

Force. For distinguished service in the field during the operations at the Dardanelles." He was promoted to Lieutenant-Colonel.

KANE, ROMNEY ROBERT GODRED, Capt., son of the late Judge R. R. Kane, 4, Fitzwilliam Place, Dublin, and Glendree, County Clare ; was born 11 Oct. 1888. He was educated at the Oratory School, Edgbaston, and at Sandhurst, passing into the Army 19 Sept. 1908. He became Lieutenant, Royal Munster Fusiliers, 14 March, 1910, and served in India and Burma until the outbreak of hostilities in Europe in Aug. 1914. He saw active service on the Staff in Gallipoli from the first landing till 13 July, 1915. From 1915 to 1916 Capt. Kane saw further service on the Staff in France. He was twice wounded, mentioned in Despatches, made a Chevalier of the Legion of Honour, and was created a Companion of the Distinguished Service Order [London Gazette, 8 Nov. 1915]: " Romney Robert Godred Kane, Capt., The Royal Munster Fusiliers. For distinguished service in the field during the operations at the Dardanelles."

EBELING, GUS, Major, served in the Great War, and was created a Companion of the Distinguished Service Order [London Gazette, 8 Nov. 1915]: " Gus Ebeling, Major, 8th Battn. (Victoria) Australian Imperial Force. For distinguished service in the field during the operations at the Dardanelles."

LLOYD, HERBERT WILLIAM, Major, son of William Lloyd, late of County Roscommon ; was born 24 Nov. 1883. He was educated at Wesley College, Melbourne ; joined the Australian Military Forces ; was Captain and Adjutant, Victoria Field Artillery, 1908-9 ; on the Administrative and Instructional Staff, 1910 ; served with the 2nd Battery, Royal Australian Field Artillery, up to 1917 ; was Adjutant, 1st Field Artillery Brigade, 1st Australian Division, Australian Imperial Force, 1914 ; landed at Anzac as Adjutant, and was promoted to command the 1st Australian (Regular) Battery at Helles, Gallipoli, in May, 1915. He was created a C.M.G. in 1917 ; appointed Brigade Major, 2nd Australian Divisional Artillery, Dec. 1915 ; mentioned in Despatches, given the Brevet of Lieut.-Colonel in 1918, created a C.B. in 1919, and created a Companion of the Distinguished Service Order [London Gazette, 8 Nov. 1915]: " Herbert William Lloyd, Major, 1st Field Artillery Brigade, A.I.F. For distinguished service in the field during the operations at the Dardanelles." Colonel Lloyd married, in 1914, Meredith, daughter of Colonel W. B. Pleasants, of Victoria, and they have one daughter.

LORENZO, FRANCIS MAXWELL DE FRAZER, Major, served in the Great War, and was created a Companion of the Distinguished Service Order [London Gazette, 8 Nov. 1915]: " Francis Maxwell de Frazer Lorenzo, Major, 10th Battn. (South Australia) Australian Imperial Force. For distinguished service in the field duirng the operations at the Dardanelles."

STEVENS, ARTHUR BORLASE, Major, served in the Great War, and was created a Companion of the Distinguished Service Order [London

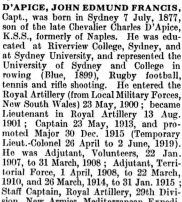

Gazette, 8 Nov. 1915] : " Arthur Borlase Stevens, Major, 2nd Battn. (New South Wales) Australian Imperial Force. For distinguished service in the field during the operations at the Dardanelles."

TILNEY, LESLIE EDWARD, Major (Temporary Lieut.-Colonel), served in the Great War, and was created a Companion of the Distinguished Service Order [London Gazette, 8 Nov. 1915] : " Leslie Edward Tilney, Major (Temporary Lieut.-Colonel), 16th Battn. Australian Imperial Force. For distinguished service in the field during the operations at the Dardanelles."

BROWN, CHARLES HENRY JEFFRIES, Major (Temporary Lieut.-Colonel), served in the Great War, and was created a Companion of the Distinguished Service Order [London Gazette, 8 Nov. 1915] : " Charles Henry Jeffries Brown, Major (Temporary Lieut.-Colonel), Canterbury Battn. New Zealand Infantry. For distinguished service in the field during the operations at the Dardanelles." He was killed about 8 June, 1917.

WHYTE, JAMES HENRY, Major, son of James Whyte, of Glasgow, and Jane Johnstone Whyte (*née* Birkenhead) : was born at Woodlands, Auckland, New Zealand, 17 Dec. 1878. He was educated at Auckland, New Zealand, joining the Army in 1897. During the South African War he saw active service as Sergt.-Major with the New Zealand Contingent, and gained the Distinguished Conduct Medal, the Queen's South African Medal with four clasps (Kimberley, Dreifontein, Johannesburg and Diamond Hill) and the King's South African Medal. Major Whyte again saw active service in the European War, and greatly distinguished himself at the operations in the attack on Hill 60, Gallipoli, 27 Aug. 1915. He was mentioned five times in Despatches, and was created a Companion of the Distinguished Service Order [London Gazette, 8 Nov. 1915] : " James Henry Whyte, Major, Wellington Mounted Rifle Regt. For distinguished service in the field during the operations at the Dardanelles." He was promoted to Lieut.-Colonel. On the 4th of April, 1916, in The Pines, Ghezireh, Cairo, Lieut.-Colonel Whyte married Dorothy Ann, daughter of the late Henry Rose, of Dunedin, New Zealand, and Grace Edith Rose, of Christchurch, New Zealand. He was awarded a Bar to the Distinguished Service Order.

YOUNG, ROBERT, Major, served in the Great War with the Wellington Battn. New Zealand Force, taking part in operations in Gallipoli. He was mentioned in Despatches, and in Nov. 1915, was created a Companion of the Distinguished Service Order [London Gazette, 8 Nov. 1915] : " Robert Young, Major, Wellington Battn. New Zealand Infantry. For distinguished service in the field during the operations at the Dardanelles." He was promoted to Lieut.-Colonel ; was created a C.B. in 1919, a C.M.G. in 1916, and was made Officer, Legion of Honour.

BECK, WILLIAM THOMAS, Honorary Capt., served in the Great War, and was created a Companion of the Distinguished Service Order [London Gazette, 8 Nov. 1915] : " William Thomas Beck, Honorary Capt., New Zealand Ordnance Corps. For distinguished service in the field during the operations at the Dardanelles."

London Gazette, 8 Nov. 1915.—" Admiralty, 7 Nov. 1915. The King has been graciously pleased to give orders for the appointment of the undermentioned Officers of the Royal Naval Division to be Companions of the Distinguished Service Order, in recognition of their services in the Gallipoli Peninsula."

MITCHELL, FRANCIS HERBERT, Capt., joined the Royal Navy. He took part in the European War, and was created a Companion of the Distinguished Service Order [London Gazette, 8 Nov. 1915] : " Francis Herbert Mitchell, Capt., Royal Navy. In recognition of services in the Gallipoli Peninsula."

KENNEDY-CRAUFURD-STUART, CHARLES, Capt. (Temporary Lieut.-Colonel), was born in London 29 Aug. 1879. He comes of a distinguished race, and is the senior male representative of the ancient Ayrshire families of Kennedy, of Ardmillan, and Craufurd, of Baidland and Ardmillan. He is the son of Robert Stuart, of Rye, Sussex, and Margaret Elizabeth Stuart, his wife, the third daughter of Clifford Craufurd, of Ardmillan. His grandfather was the Rev. Charles Stuart, B.A., of Rye, Sussex. Charles Kennedy-Craufurd-Stuart was educated at Merchant Taylors' School, London, and entered the Militia in 1899. On the 4th April, 1900, he was gazetted from the 3rd Battn. The South Lancashire Regt. to the 1st Battn. The Manchester Regt., with which latter regiment he saw active service in the South African War, 1900-2 ; took part in the operations in Natal, June, 1900 ; in Orange River Colony, May to 29 Nov. 1900 ; in Cape Colony, south of Orange River, Feb. to April, 1900 ; also during the operations in the Transvaal 30 Nov. 1900, to 31 May, 1902 (Queen's Medal with three clasps, and King's Medal with two clasps). On 8 Aug. 1903, he was transferred to the 1st Punjab Cavalry. Capt. Kennedy-Craufurd-Stuart served with the Burma Military Police from 1907 to 1914, exchanging into the 127th Baluchistan Light Infantry in 1913. He was promoted to Captain, Indian Army, 27 Jan. 1909, and to Major, Indian Army, 1 Sept. 1915 ; was Temporary Major, Royal Marines, 1914-15, and Temporary Lieut.-Colonel, Royal Marines, 10 May, 1915, to 19 Feb. 1916. He again saw active service in the European War, being sent with the Royal Naval Brigade to Gallipoli, as Lieut.-Colonel Commanding the Hood Battn., and in Nov. 1915, he was mentioned in Despatches [London Gazette, 5 Nov. 1915], for great gallantry in leading the Hood Battn. into the Turkish trenches, where he was wounded 4 June, 1915, and was created a Companion of the Distinguished Service Order [London Gazette, 8 Nov. 1915] : " Charles Kennedy-Craufurd-Stuart, Temporary Lieut.-Colonel, Royal Marines. In recognition of services in the Gallipoli Peninsula." His wounds proved very severe, including a shattered jaw. From Feb. 1916, to Oct. 1917, Major Stuart was sent to Egypt as Special Service Officer attached to the Sudan Government. He received the

thanks of the Sudan Government for successful action against Chief Ashwol in Bahr-el-Ghezal Province. He was in the United States, Jan. 1918, to May, 1919, as Private Secretary to the Earl of Reading, High Commissioner and Ambassador. Major Stuart has published two songs, " At Gloaming Tide " and " Make-Believe Land " ; he has also exhibited at the London Salon of Photography. He is a Fellow of the Royal Horticultural Society and a Fellow of the Zoological Society.

KING, HENRY DOUGLAS, Lieut.-Commander, Royal Naval Volunteer Reserve, was born 1 June, 1877, son of the late Capt. Henry Welchman King. He was educated in the Training Ship Conway, Liverpool, and afterwards in sailing ships until 1897, when he joined the P. and O. Service. In 1899 he left the sea, and took up farming. He afterwards studied Law, and was called to the Bar at the Middle Temple in 1905. He was adopted as the Unionist candidate for the Northern Division of Norfolk in 1909, and contested both General Elections in 1910. He was elected M.P. (Independent) for North Norfolk in 1918. He became Midshipman, Royal Naval Reserve, in 1893 ; served until 1902 ; served two years in the Inns of Court Rifle Volunteers ; was commissioned in the Royal Naval Volunteer Reserve, London Division, in 1904 ; appointed to Drake Battn. on the formation of the Royal Naval Division, and commanded it from June, 1915, to July, 1916 ; served at the Siege of Antwerp in Oct. 1914. On 26 April, 1915, he landed at Gallipoli Peninsula, and served there until the evacuation 9 Jan. 1916. He served afloat, and later with the Royal Naval Siege Guns in Flanders (Croix de Guerre and special promotion for distinguished war service). He was wounded, was three times mentioned in Despatches, and was created a Companion of the Distinguished Service Order [London Gazette, 8 Nov. 1915] : " Henry Douglas King, V.D., Lieut.-Commander (Temporary Commander), Royal Naval Volunteer Reserve. In recognition of services in the Gallipoli Peninsula." Commander King married, in 1900, Margaret Elizabeth, only daughter of the late William Robert Swan, of South Australia, and they have one son and four daughters.

WEDGWOOD, JOSIAH CLEMENT, Lieut.-Commander, Royal Naval Volunteer Reserve, the second son of C. F. Wedgwood, of Barlaston and Etruria (Staffordshire), and Emily C. Rendel, sister of the first Lord Rendel ; was born in 1872. He was educated at Clifton College, and at the Royal Naval College, Greenwich (Scholar, 1892). From 1895 to 1896 he was employed as Assistant Constructor, Portsmouth Dockyard, and from 1896 to 1900 he was Naval Architect to the Elswick Shipyard. In 1900 he proceeded to South Africa with the Elswick Battery as Captain, and served in the South African War, gaining the Medal with three clasps, and from 1902 to 1904 he acted as Resident Magistrate in Ermelo, Transvaal. In 1906 he became Member of Parliament (Liberal) for Newcastle-under-Lyme, and County Councillor

Josiah C. Wedgwood.

(Staffordshire) in 1910. He was appointed Honorary Secretary of the William Salt Archæological Society, and at one time acted as President of the English League for the Taxation of Land Values. He served in the European War, taking part in operations in Antwerp, France, Dardanelles and East Africa. He was wounded, twice mentioned in Despatches, and in Nov. 1915, was created a Companion of the Distinguished Service Order [London Gazette, 8 Nov. 1915] : " Josiah Wedgwood, Lieut.-Commander, Royal Naval Volunteer Reserve, M.P. In recognition of services in the Gallipoli Peninsula." He sat on the Mesopotamian Commission in July, 1916 ; was Assistant Director, Trench Warfare, 1917 ; on the Mission to Siberia with temporary rank as Colonel, 1918. Colonel Wedgwood has published a book on " Staffordshire Pottery and its History," and several pamphlets on the " Taxation of Land Values," and he wrote, in collaboration with Mrs. Wedgwood, " The Road to Freedom."

LAWS, HENRY WILLIAM, Lieut., Royal Naval Volunteer Reserve, served in the Great War, and was created a Companion of the Distinguished Service Order [London Gazette, 8 Nov. 1915] : " Henry William Laws, Lieut., Royal Naval Volunteer Reserve. In recognition of services in the Gallipoli Peninsula."

London Gazette, 16 Nov. 1915.—" War Office, 16 Nov. 1915. His Majesty the King has been graciously pleased to approve of the appointment of the undermentioned Officer to be a Companion of the Distinguished Service Order, in recognition of his gallantry and devotion to duty in the field."

SAYER, ARTHUR PENRICE, Capt., son of William Feetham Sayer and Edith A. Sayer (*née* Bell), was born 5 Nov. 1885. He was educated at Cholmeley School, Highgate, N., and at Woolwich, S.E., and entered the Royal Engineers 25 July, 1906 ; became Lieutenant 22 Nov. 1908, and was sent to Gosport in the same year. He was stationed at Gibraltar, 1909 to 1914 ; was promoted Captain 30 Oct. 1914, and was stationed at Weymouth from 1914 to 1915. He was Temporary Major 4 Oct. to 31 Dec. 1918. From 17 March, 1916, to 4 June, 1917, he was Officer, Company of Gentleman Cadets, Royal Military Academy, Woolwich, and from 5 June,

Arthur Penrice Sayer.

1917, he was Commander, Company of Gentleman Cadets, Royal Military Academy, Woolwich. Capt. Sayer saw active service in the European War ; he was wounded at the Battle of Loos, and for his services in this action he was created a Companion of the Distinguished Service Order [London Gazette, 16 Nov. 1915] : " Arthur Penrice Sayer, Capt., 91st Field Coy., Royal Engineers. For conspicuous gallantry near Loos on the morning of 26 Sept. 1915. He rallied men of various units, who were retiring from Hill 70, and led them up the hill again. It was largely due to his cool action at a critical moment that the troops in his locality were able to hold their ground. Later he rendered great services in collecting stragglers to fill the old German trenches, and continued doing this until he was overcome by gas." He was wounded, and was given the Brevet of Major 1 Jan. 1919. He represented the Royal Military Academy, Woolwich, against the Royal Military College, Sandhurst, in cricket. In 1916, Major Sayer married Blanche Mary, youngest daughter of the late Dr. J. W. Leacroft and widow of Capt. David S. Dodgson, R.A.

London Gazette, 19 Nov. 1915.—" Admiralty, 19 Nov. 1915. The King has been graciously pleased to give orders for the appointment of the undermentioned Officers to be Companions of the Distinguished Service Order."

BOYLE, PATRICK JAMES (VISCOUNT KELBURN), Commander, Royal Navy, son of the 7th Earl of Glasgow, and Dorothea, daughter of Sir Edward Hunter-Blair, 4th Baronet, was born 18 July, 1874. He entered the Royal Navy ; became Lieutenant in 1897, and Commander in 1909. Lord Kelburn served in the European War, 1914–19 ; he commanded H.M.S. Pyramus at the capture of the German Colony of Samoa, and took part in operations at the surrender of Apia in 1914. He also assisted in the Allied landing in the Persian Gulf in 1915, and for this special service he was created a Companion of the Distinguished Service Order [London Gazette, 19 Nov. 1915] : " Patrick James Boyle, Viscount Kelburn, Commander, Royal Navy. For his services during landing operations in the Persian Gulf in Aug. 1915." He succeeded his father in 1915, and is the 8th Earl of Glasgow (created in 1703). He is Deputy-Lieutenant, County Ayr ; owns about 5,000 acres. Lord Glasgow married, in 1906, Hyacinthe Mary, daughter of W. A. Bell, of Pendell Court, Bletchingley, and they have two sons (the elder being Viscount Kelburn, born 24 July, 1910), and two daughters.

Viscount Kelburn.

HALAHAN, HENRY CROSBY, Commander, Royal Navy, son of the late Colonel S. H. Halahan, of Chiddingfold. He entered the Navy in 1896, becoming Lieutenant in 1900. Lieut. Halahan was made a Member of the Victorian Order in 1907. He served in the European War, and in Nov. 1915, was created a Companion of the Distinguished Service Order [London Gazette, 19 Nov. 1915] : " Henry Crosby Halahan, Commander, Royal Navy. For his services in command of the Naval Heavy Batteries attached to the Belgian Army since 1 Jan. 1915. In the operations on the Belgian front, from 25 Sept. onwards, he displayed a gallantry and devotion to duty worthy of the best traditions of the Royal Navy." He was promoted Wing Captain, Royal Naval Air Service, in 1917, and was killed in action 23 March, 1918.

STOCKS, DAVID DE BEAUVOIR, Lieut.-Commander, Royal Navy, only son of John W. Stocks (Captain, C.B.L. Horse), of Babool Bonah, Beckenham, S.E., was born in 1885. He served in the European War, and in Nov. 1915, was created a Companion of the Distinguished Service Order [London Gazette, 19 Nov. 1915] : " David de Beauvoir Stocks, Lieut.-Commander, Royal Navy. For his services in command of a submarine in the Sea of Marmora, where he made a prolonged cruise, in spite of adverse conditions, and succeeded in inflicting much damage on the enemy." He was also made Chevalier, Legion of Honour. He was drowned at sea 31 Jan. 1918. Commander Stocks married Cheridah, youngest daughter of the late Capt. Ernst, Deputy Lieutenant and Justice of the Peace, of Westcombe, Evercreech S.O., Somerset.

David de Beauvoir Stocks.

WILMOT-SMITH, ANDREW, Lieut.-Commander, Royal Navy, second son of John Crosbie Wilmot-Smith, of Ballynanty, County Limerick, and of Killuran, County Clare, and Jane Grant, his wife, eldest daughter of the late Andrew Sherlock Lawson, of Boroughbridge Hall, Yorkshire. He was educated at Banstead and in H.M.S. Britannia, entering the Navy in 1900. He served in the European War from 1914, and was created a Companion of the Distinguished Service Order [London Gazette, 19 Nov. 1915] : " Andrew Wilmot-Smith, Lieut.-Commander, Royal Navy."

SEYMOUR, ARTHUR GEORGE, Lieut.-Commander, Royal Navy, third and youngest son of Lord Ernest (James) Seymour (third son of the 5th Marquess of Hertford and Lady Emily Murray, daughter of the 3rd Earl of Mansfield), and Lady Georgiana Seymour Fortescue (who died in 1915), daughter of the 3rd Earl Fortescue. He was edu-

cated in H.M.S. Britannia, at Dartmouth, and joined the Royal Navy. He served in the European War, as First Lieutenant, H.M.S. Espiègle, and in command of the armed launch Shushan in Mesopotamia. He was created a Companion of the Distinguished Service Order [London Gazette, 19 Nov. 1915] : " Arthur George Seymour, Lieut.-Commander, Royal Navy. For excellent work throughout operations in Mesopotamia. During the attack on Nasiriyeh on July 24th, 1915, Lieut.-Commander Seymour, who was in command of the armed launch ' Shushan,' fired the gun himself under very difficult conditions, and sank an armed Turkish patrol boat." He was promoted to Commander in 1919.

Arthur George Seymour.

ELLIOT, BERTRAM NOWELL, Capt. (Temporary Major), served in the European War, and was created a Companion of the Distinguished Service Order [London Gazette, 19 Nov. 1915] : " Bertram Nowell Elliot, Capt. (Temporary Major), Royal Marine Light Infantry. For his services in laying mines and in charge of minefields in the Serbian rivers for several months. This work has very many times been carried on under the fire of the enemy's patrols, and always with a fine courage and much skill in organization." He was killed in action on 23 April, 1918.

DACRE, GEORGE BENTLEY, Flight Lieutenant, Royal Navy, was born 22 March, 1891, son of John Dacre, M.R.C.S., L.R.C.P. He was educated at Clifton College, and at the University of Bristol (Pilot Aviator's Certificate, No. 162, 1911). In 1911 he was given an appointment on the experimental staff of the British and Colonial Aeroplane Co. Ltd., and in Aug. 1914, was gazetted Probationary Flight Sub-Lieutenant, Royal Naval Air Service, becoming Flight Lieutenant 31 Dec. 1914 ; Flight Commander in June, 1916 ; Captain, Royal Air Force, in April, 1918. He served in the European War (Gallipoli), 1915–16 ; (Egypt), 1916. He was created a Companion of the Distinguished Service Order [London Gazette, 19 Nov. 1915] : " George Bentley Dacre, Flight Lieutenant, Royal Navy. For his services in the Dardanelles when he flew over the Gallipoli Peninsula, and in spite of serious trouble with his machine, succeeded in carrying out a difficult operation, and afterwards returned safely to his base. Great nerve and courage were displayed in prosecuting an attack under very adverse conditions." In June, 1916, he was promoted Flight-Commander, and on 26 Aug. 1916, was reported to be a prisoner in Turkey, where he remained until Nov. 1918.

George Bentley Dacre.

London Gazette, 24 Nov. 1915.—" Admiralty, 24 Nov. 1915. The King has been graciously pleased to give orders for the appointment of the undermentioned Officer to be a Companion of the Distinguished Service Order, in recognition of the service described below."

SMYTH-PIGOTT, JOSEPH RUSCOMBE WADHAM, Flight Lieut., Royal Navy, was born in 1889, youngest son of the late Cecil Hugh Smyth-Pigott, of Brockley Court, Somerset. He was educated at the Oratory School, Edgbaston, and entered the Royal Navy, serving in the European War. He was mentioned in Despatches, and was created a Companion of the Distinguished Service Order [London Gazette, 24 Nov. 1915] : " Joseph Ruscombe Wadham Smyth-Pigott, Flight Lieut., R.N. On the night of 13–14 Nov. Flight Commander Smyth-Pigott volunteered to attack the railway bridge at Kuleli Burgas. He was able to locate the bridge by the moonlight shining on the river, and descended to within 300 feet of it before releasing his bombs. He was heavily fired on from several places, and in spite of trouble with his engine, which commenced before he reached the bridge, he returned safely to his base after a night flight which had lasted over four hours." He was also awarded a Bar to the D.S.O.

London Gazette, 8 Dec. 1915.—" Admiralty, 8 Dec. 1915. From Commander-in-Chief, Cape of Good Hope Station. Challenger, 15 July, 1915.—At 4.15 a.m., on the 6th July, H.M.S. Severn (Capt. Eric J. A. Fullerton), and H.M.S. Mersey (Commander Robert A. Wilson), weighed and proceeded across the bar into the Kikunja branch of the Rufiji river, which they entered about 5.20 a.m. The operations on the 6th July, though not a complete and final success, were creditable. A further attack was made to complete the destruction of the Königsberg on the 11th July, which was completely wrecked, having suffered from shell fire and explosions. His Majesty the King has been graciously pleased to give orders for the appointment of the following Officers to the Distinguished Service Order, in recognition of their services as mentioned, on the occasion of the operations against the Königsberg."

FULLERTON, ERIC JOHN ARTHUR, Capt., Royal Navy, son of Admiral Sir J. R. T. Fullerton, was born in 1878. He took part in the European War, and gained distinction in the two attacks on the Königsberg, as it lay in the Rufiji River. Two monitors were engaged in these operations, the Severn, under Capt. Fullerton, and the Mersey, under Commander Robert Ancotts Wilson, both under the orders of Capt. Fullerton. On 6 July, 1915, the two vessels proceeded across the bar into the Kikunja branch of the Rufiji River. Although subjected to very heavy and accurate fire, the two vessels did much damage to the enemy ship. A second attack was made to complete the destruction of the Königsberg 11 July, 1915, and on this occasion it was reduced to a complete wreck. For his services in the operations against the Königsberg, Capt. Fullerton was mentioned in the Despatch of Vice-Admiral H. King Hall, Commander-in-Chief, Cape of Good Hope Station, dated from the Challenger, 15 July, 1915, and was created a Companion of the Distinguished Service Order [London Gazette, 8 Dec. 1915]: " Eric John Arthur Fullerton, Capt., Royal Navy. Was in charge of the two monitors, and conducted the operations in the river with complete success. He, with Commander Robert Ancotts Wilson, had to deal with a very difficult task, entering a river of which very imperfect information was obtainable, against an unknown and invisible defence, which might well have been very serious, and there is no doubt that the monitors were most fortunate in not being more seriously handled by the enemy." He was mentioned in Despatches for subsequent operations on the coast of German East Africa ; commanded the battleship Orion, Grand Fleet, 1916-18. Capt. Fullerton was subsequently in charge of Naval Officers undergoing instruction at Cambridge University. He married, in 1908, the Hon. Dorothy Sybil, second daughter of Admiral of the Fleet Lord Fisher, of Kilverstone, O.M., G.C.B., G.C.V.O., and Frances (who died in 1918), daughter of the Rev. T. Delves Broughton.

WILSON, ROBERT ANCOTTS, Commander, Royal Navy, served in

Robert Ancotts Wilson.

the European War, and was given his Distinguished Service Order for the two attacks on the Königsberg, on the 6th and 11th July, as the vessel lay in the Rufiji River. Two monitors were engaged in these operations, the Severn, under Capt. Eric Fullerton, and the Mersey, under Commander Robert Ancotts Wilson. On the 6th July the two vessels proceeded across the bar into the Kikunja branch of the Rufiji River. Although subject to very heavy and accurate fire, the two monitors did much damage to the enemy ship. A second attack was made to complete the destruction of the Königsberg 11 July, 1915, and on this occasion it was reduced to a complete wreck. For his services in these operations, Commander Wilson was mentioned in the Despatch of Vice-Admiral H. King Hall, Commander-in-Chief, Cape of Good Hope Station, dated from the Challenger, 15 July, 1916, and was created a Companion of the Distinguished Service Order [London Gazette, 8 Dec. 1915]: " Robert Ancotts Wilson, Commander, Royal Navy. These two officers (Capt. Eric J. A. Fullerton) had to deal with a very difficult task, entering a river of which very imperfect information was obtainable, against an unknown and invisible defence, which might well have been very serious, and there is no doubt that the monitors were most fortunate in not being more severely handled by the enemy." Commander Wilson married Gladys (who died in 1918), granddaughter of W. Gillilan, of 6, Palace Gate, W.

GORDON, ROBERT, Squadron Commander, Royal Naval Air Service (Temporary Major, Royal Marines), eldest son of Robert Gordon, M.I.C.E., and Gertrude Mary Gordon, was born in Burma in 1882. He was educated at Fettes College, Edinburgh, and joined the Royal Marines in 1900. He served in the European War, and was Squadron Commander in command of the Air Squadron during the operations to encompass the destruction of the Königsberg, as it lay in the Rufiji River. For his services on the two occasions of attack, 6 and 11 July, 1915, he was mentioned in the Despatch of Vice-Admiral H. King Hall, Commander-in-Chief, Cape of Good Hope Station, dated from the Challenger, 15 July, 1915, and was created a Companion of the Distinguished Service Order [London Gazette, 8 Dec. 1915]: " Robert Gordon, Squadron Commander, Royal Naval Air Service (Temporary Major, Royal Marines), was in command of the Air Squadron. He was indefatigable in his work, and ran great risk in spotting and reconnoitring." He was in Mesopotamia with General Townshend's Force, and afterwards with the force attempting to relieve Kut. He was promoted to Wing Commander and to Temporary Lieutenant-Colonel.

CULL, JOHN TULLOCH, Flight Commander, R.N.A.S. (Lieut., R.N.), entered the Royal Navy, and became Lieutenant-Commander 15 March, 1909, and Squadron Commander, Royal Naval Air Service, 1 Jan. 1916. He served in the European War, and was mentioned in Vice-Admiral H. King Hall's Despatch of 15 July, 1915, and created a Companion of the Distinguished Service Order [London Gazette, 8 Dec. 1915]: " John Tulloch Cull, Flight Commander, R.N.A.S. (Lieut., R.N.). Flight Com- Commander Cull and Flight Sub-Lieut. Arnold were spotting on the 11th July, under fire, in a biplane, when the enemy's fire damaged it so that it descended in a quarter of an hour from 3,200 feet to 2,000 feet. During this time no attempt was made to return to Headquarters at Mafia, although it was obvious that this could not be done unless a start was made at once. Flight Sub-Lieut. Arnold continued to send his spotting signals the whole time, and when, a quarter of an hour later, the machine was again hit and forced to descend, Flight Commander Cull controlled the machine, and Flight Sub-Lieut. Arnold continued to send spotting corrections to the last, after warning the monitors that they were coming down and would endeavour to land near them. The aeroplane finally came down in the river, turning over and over. Flight Commander Cull was nearly drowned, but was assisted by Flight Sub-Lieut. Arnold, and both were rescued by a boat from the Mersey."

ARNOLD, HARWOOD JAMES, Flight Sub-Lieut., Royal Naval Air Service, served in the European War, and took part in the destruction of the Königsberg as it lay in the Rufiji River. For his services on the two occasions of attack, 6 and 11 July, 1915, he was mentioned in the Despatch of Vice-Admiral H. King Hall, Commander-in-Chief, Cape of Good Hope Station, and was created a Companion of the Distinguished Service Order [London Gazette, 8 Dec. 1915]: " Flight Commander Cull and Flight Sub-Lieut. Arnold were spotting on the 11th July, under fire in a biplane, when the enemy's fire damaged it, so that it descended in a quarter of an hour from 3,200 feet to 2,000 feet. During this time no attempt was made to return to Headquarters at Mafia, although it was obvious that this could not be done unless a start was made at once. Flight Sub-Lieut. Arnold continued to send his spotting signals the whole time, and when, a quarter of an hour later, the machine was again hit and forced to descend, Flight-Commander Cull controlled the machine, and Flight Sub-Lieut. Arnold continued to send spotting corrections to the last, after warning the monitors that they were coming down and would endeavour to land near them. The aeroplane finally came down in the river, turning over and over. Flight Commander Cull was nearly drowned, but was assisted by Flight Sub-Lieut. Arnold, and both were rescued by a boat from the Mersey." Vice-Admiral King Hall, in his Despatch [London Gazette, 8 Dec. 1915], writes: " Most serious risks have been run by the officers and men who have flown in this climate, where the effect of the atmosphere and the extreme heat of the sun are quite unknown to those whose flying experience is limited to moderate climates. ' Bumps ' of 250 feet have been experienced several times, and the temperature varies from extreme cold when flying at a height to a great heat, with burning, tropical sun, when on land. In the operations against the Königsberg, on the 6th July, both the personnel and material of the Royal Naval Air Service were worked to the extreme limit of endurance. The total distance covered by the two available aeroplanes on that date was no less than 950 miles, and the time in the air, working watch and watch, was 13 hours." Flight Sub-Lieut. Arnold was accidentally drowned 20 March, 1918.

London Gazette, 23 Dec. 1915.—" War Office, 23 Dec. 1915. His Majesty the King has been graciously pleased to approve of the appointment of the undermentioned Officers to be Companions of the Distinguished Service Order, in recognition of their gallantry and devotion to duty in the field."

ODLUM, VICTOR WENTWORTH, Lieut.-Colonel, son of Professor E. Odlum, M.A., B.Sc., and Mary Odlum (née Powell), was born at Cobourg, Ontario, 21 Oct. 1880. He was educated at Toronto University ; was Editor of the Vancouver " Daily World," and is a Director of Clapp-Anderson & Odlum, Ltd. When the South African War commenced he served for the British with the 1st Canadian Contingent (2nd Royal Canadian Rifles), and afterwards in the 3rd Canadian Mounted Rifles, gaining the South African Medal with three clasps. He was associated continuously for 22 years with the Canadian Militia (Colonial Long Service Medal), becoming Major and Second-in-Command, 11th Irish Fusiliers of Canada, allied with the Royal Irish Fusiliers. Major Odlum again saw active service in the European War, 1914-18. He was seven times mentioned in Despatches ; was created a C.M.G. in 1917 ; a C.B. in 1919, and awarded the Order of Danilo, 3rd Class. He became Brigadier-General, com- manding the 11th Infantry Brigade, 4th Canadian Division, and was created a Companion of the Distinguished Service Order [London Gazette, 23 Dec. 1915]: " Victor Wentworth Odlum, Lieut.-Colonel, 7th Canadian Infantry Battn. (1st British Columbia Regt.), Canadian Expeditionary Force. For conspicuous ability and energy. He personally superintended all arrangements for a bombing attack made by his battalion on the night of 16-17 Nov. 1915, near Messines, and by his coolness and determination was largely instrumental in bringing about the success of the exploit." He was awarded a Bar to the Distinguished Service Order. Capt. Odlum married, in 1904, Sada Eugenie Tressa, daughter of Isaac and Margaret Rogerson, and they have three sons and one daughter.

WARREN, WILLIAM ROBINSON, Major, was born 5 May, 1882. He

William R. Warren.

entered the Royal Artillery 2 May, 1900 ; became Lieutenant 3 April, 1901 ; Captain 24 Feb. 1910 ; Major 30 Oct. 1914 ; was Acting Lieutenant-Colonel, Royal Artillery, 13 Oct. 1917, to 30 March, 1918, and 9 Oct. 1918. He served in the European War, 1914-15 ; was wounded ; thrice mentioned in Despatches ; given the Brevet of Lieutenant-Colonel 1 Jan. 1919, and created a Companion of the Distinguished Service Order [London Gazette, 23 Dec. 1915]: " William Robinson Warren, Major, Royal Field Artillery. For conspicuous gallantry near Croix Barbée on 16 Sept. 1915. When one of his battery wagons had been set on fire by a shell, and both wagon body and one cartridge were blazing, he removed the remainder of the ammunition at great personal risk. The enemy at the time were directing a heavy and accurate fire on the battery."

COSTIGAN, CHARLES TELFORD, Capt., son of Thomas John Costigan and Jeannie Costigan (née Telford), of Ireland, was born 5 Sept. 1880, in Surrey. He was educated at Halbrake College. On the outbreak of the Euro- pean War, Charles Costigan immediately joined the 1st Canadian Division (4 Aug. 1914), proceeding to Europe with his regiment ; he was employed as Field Cashier, and in 1915 was transferred as Captain to the 10th Battn. Can- adian 1st Division. Capt. Costigan took part in a successful surprise attack on the German trenches at Messines. He was mentioned in Despatches, and in Dec. 1915, was created a Companion of the Distinguished Service Order [London Gazette, 23 Dec. 1915]: "Charles Telford Costigan, Capt., 10th Canadian Infantry Battn. For conspicuous gallantry near Messines on the night of 16–17 Nov. 1915. He led a bombing party into the German trench, shot the first three Germans he met with his revolver, and then led his bombers along the trench, which was filled with the enemy." In June, 1916, Capt. Costigan added to his honours by being again mentioned in Despatches, and was awarded the Military Cross. He was wounded and sent to a London hospital. Capt. Costigan died in Nov. 1918.

BARNES, CHARLES ROPER GORELL-, Lieut., was born at 29, Sloane Gardens, London, S.W., 1st July, 1896, eldest son of Sir Frederick Gorell-Barnes, D.L., J.P. (formerly Member of Parliament for North-East Kent), and of Caroline Anne Roper, only daughter of Sir Roper Lethbridge, K.C.I.E., and Eliza, daughter of W. Finlay. He was educated at Stubbington House, Fareham; at the Royal Naval College, Osborne; at Dartmouth, and at Pembroke College, Cambridge (History Scholar). He joined the 8th Battn. Rifle Brigade (Lord Kitchener's 1st Army) as Second Lieutenant in Sept. 1914, and proceeded to France with the 14th Division in May, 1915. He was promoted Lieutenant 30 July, 1915 [London Gazette, 16 Sept. 1915]; appointed Adjutant 31 July, 1915, and created a Companion of the Dis-

Charles R. Gorell-Barnes.

tinguished Service Order [London Gazette, 23 Dec. 1915]: "Charles Roper Gorell-Barnes, Adjutant, 8th Battn. The Rifle Brigade (The Prince Consort's Own). For conspicuous gallantry near Ypres on 23 Nov. 1915. A wounded officer was lying out in front of the German lines. After three attempts at rescue had failed and an officer and four men had been wounded, Lieut. Gorell-Barnes formed one of a fourth party to make the attempt. Although there was bright moonlight and a German covering party was heard quite close, they crawled out to the wounded officer, and succeeded with great difficulty in dragging him back under heavy rifle and machine-gun fire, thus undoubtedly saving his life." Lieut. Gorell-Barnes was mentioned in Sir John French's Despatch of 30 Nov. 1915 [London Gazette, 1 Jan. 1916]. In the same year he was awarded the Military Cross for distinguished service in the field [London Gazette, 14 Jan. 1916]; was mentioned in Sir Douglas Haig's Despatch of 30 April, 1916 [London Gazette, 15 June, 1916]. He was promoted Captain in the following Sept. Capt. Gorell-Barnes was appointed a General Staff Officer, 3rd Grade, in June, 1917.

HOLMES, WILLIAM DUMBLETON, Lieut., son of William Cuthbert Holmes (retired Indian Civil Service) and Clara Eveline, daughter of the late Henry Dumbleton, of Hall Grove, Bagshot, Surrey, and of Rocklands, Victoria, British Columbia; was born at Mangalore, Madras Presidency, India, 10 June, 1893. He was privately educated in France and Germany, and in British Columbia; was in the ranks of the 88th Victoria Fusiliers in 1913, and was given a commission. Lieut. Holmes saw active service in the European War, where he greatly distinguished himself. At Festubert, on the night of the 21st May, 1915, "the Canadians made a fine attack, in which they advanced our line several hundred yards," says Mr. John Buchan, in his "History of the War" (Volume VII., page 107). In this attack Lieut. W. D. Holmes was in command on the extreme right. Almost immediately after the

William D. Holmes.

attack began, all but two of his men were killed or wounded. Lieut. Holmes was himself wounded in the side by a shell, which threw him into a sort of stream, which he crossed, holding on to a couple of planks, and was followed by his remaining two men, who crawled over the planks. "We three," wrote Lieut. Holmes, "went on to a good planking position, where we could put up a rapid fire on the enemy, who were bombing our centre." Lieut. Holmes was again wounded, and a few minutes after that some reinforcements who had lost their officers crawled up. Our centre was somewhat advancing, and a lull in the firing giving opportunity, Lieut. Holmes and his men charged, roaring, "Canada, Canada! Forward, Canada!" "The Germans did not wait for us to run off in the dark," adds Lieut. Holmes. For his conduct in this affair he was recommended for the Victoria Cross, and it is believed that it is for his conduct at Festubert that he received the Military Cross. Lieut. Holmes was sent to England invalided for some months. On returning to the front he was attached to the famous 7th Canadian Infantry Battn., and some time afterwards, on the night of the 16–17th Nov. 1915, took a prominent part in the Messines affair. The River Douve lay in No Man's Land, between the German lines and ours. Lieut. Holmes and his scouts secretly cut three lanes through the German wire entanglements, laying three plank bridges (2 feet by 20 feet) across the Douve. Over these bridges and through the lanes they led a bombing party, which made a surprise and successful attack on the German trench. Lieut. Holmes was mentioned in F.M. Sir John French's Despatch of 30 Nov. 1915, and in the following

month he was created a Companion of the Distinguished Service Order [London Gazette, 23 Dec. 1915]: "William Dumbleton Holmes, Lieut., 7th Battn. 1st British Columbia Regt. For conspicuous gallantry and resource near Messines on 16–17 Nov. 1915, when in charge of the scouts during a bombing attack. He superintended the cutting of the German wire, and the laying of a bridge over the Douve, 16 yards from a heavily-manned German trench. His gallant conduct at Festubert was brought to notice in May last." Lieut. Holmes was promoted to Captain 12 Jan. 1916. He was again mentioned in Despatches by General Sir Douglas Haig. Capt. Holmes fell in action 13 June in the same year at the Third Battle of Ypres. The King caused a letter to be sent from the War Office, expressing his high appreciation of Capt. W. D. Holmes's services.

McILREE, JOHN RAYMOND, Lieut., son of J. H. McIlree, I.S.O., and C. E., daughter of the late J. Winter Humphreys, was born 19 Jan. 1893, at Regina, Saskatchewan, Canada. Educated at Trinity College School, Port Hope, Ontario, he joined the 88th Victoria Fusiliers in 1913, and when the European War broke out he served in France and Flanders, working himself up to the rank of Colour Sergeant-Major; was present at the battles of St. Julien (or Ypres) in April, 1915, and at Festubert. He was given a commission as Lieutenant in 1915, and was in charge of the first surprise attack on the German trenches at Messines, made on the night of 16–17 Nov. 1915, by the 7th Battn. (Canadians), under Lieut.-Colonel Odlum, who was awarded the Distinguished Service Order for planning this enterprise, which was completely successful. Lieut. McIlree was mentioned in Sir Douglas Haig's first Despatch, and was created a Companion of the Distinguished Service Order [London Gazette, 23 Dec. 1915]: "John Raymond McIlree, Lieut., 7th Canadian Infantry Battn. For conspicuous gallantry near Messines on the night of 16–17 Nov. 1915. He led a bombing party into the German trench, threw down the first German he met, and felled the second with a rifle. He was then joined by his bombing party, and led them along the trench, which was heavily manned by the enemy." The following is Lord Beaverbrook's account of this "surprise attack": "A small party of bombers crawled at night across the 'No-Man's-Land' separating the lines, climbed over the top of the parapet into the enemy's trench, remained there about a quarter of an hour, and then returned with a dozen prisoners. . . . Never can there have been a more exciting scene. . . . The noise was indescribable . . . while the whole picture was lit up by the flares that were being sent up by the dozen. Germans aroused from their sleep came lumbering out of their dug-outs, to be immediately collared by a stranger in khaki, and before they were wide-awake found themselves inside the British trench. . . . Lieut. McIlree, on emerging round the traverse (with emptied rifle), came right on top of a German who was standing on the firing platform. . . . Quick as lightning, the officer, an old Rugby football player, threw himself at the legs of his adversary, and pulled him to the bottom of the trench, where he sat on his chest, urging him to surrender. At the critical moment another German appeared round the corner, but the officer, seizing the rifle which had fallen from the hands of his first opponent, swung it round, and knocked the new-comer head over heels." He was promoted to Captain in 1916.

London Gazette, 7 Dec. 1915.—"War Office, 7 Dec. 1915. His Majesty the King has been graciously pleased to approve of the appointment of the undermentioned Officers to be Companions of the Distinguished Service Order, in recognition of their gallantry and devotion to duty in the field."

PAGAN, ALEXANDER WILLIAM, Major (Temporary Lieut.-Colonel), was born 23 Feb. 1878. He was gazetted to the Gloucestershire Regt. 11 Feb. 1899; became Lieutenant 24 Feb. 1900; Captain 29 Sept. 1906; was Adjutant, Gloucestershire Regt., 12 July, 1908, to 11 July, 1911; Major 1 Sept. 1915; Temporary Lieutenant-Colonel, Gloucestershire Regt., 1 Sept. 1915, to 7 Sept. 1916; Acting Lieutenant-Colonel, Gloucestershire Regt., 12 Nov. 1916, to 27 March, 1918; Temporary Brigadier-General from 28 March, 1918. He was Adjutant, Special Reserve, 16 Nov. 1911, to 2 Jan. 1915; Brigade Commander, 184th Infantry Brigade, British Armies in France, 28 March to 16 Oct. 1918. For his services in the European War he was mentioned in Despatches; was given the Brevet of Lieutenant-Colonel 1 Jan. 1917, and was created a Companion of the Distinguished Service Order [London Gazette, 7 Dec. 1915]: "Alexander William Pagan, Major (Temporary Lieut.-Colonel), 1st. Battn. The Gloucestershire Regt. For conspicuous good work when in command of his battalion, near Loos, on 8 Oct. 1915, during a heavy bombardment of four and a half hours, followed by a heavy infantry attack. He had already been brought to notice for good work done on 9 May and 25 Sept. 1915."

MARTIN, NORMAN, Second Lieut., eldest son of Lieut.-Colonel M. Martin (late R.E.) and Edith Martin, and grandson of Sir Ronald Martin, was born 5 March, 1897; was educated at the Inverness College and at Fettes. He offered his services to Lochiel, who was then raising the 5th Battn. of the Cameron Highlanders, but was ordered to await his 18th birthday, when he was commissioned in the 3rd Battn. Queen's Own Cameron Highlanders, and posted to his Corps at Invergordon. On the 30th Sept. 1915, he was ordered to France, and was posted to the 1st Battn. Camerons. On the 20th Oct. he was appointed Bomb Officer, and was complimented by the Commanding Officer in October for his conduct in fierce trench fighting in the following words: "You did darned good work, sir, darned good work." He was mentioned in Despatches by F.M. Sir John French, Commander-in-Chief in France, and in Dec. 1915, he was created a Companion of the Distinguished Service Order [London Gazette, 7 Dec. 1915]: "Norman Martin, Second Lieut., 3rd Battn. (attached 1st Battn.) Queen's Own Cameron Highlanders. For conspicuous gallantry and determination near Hulloch, on 13 Oct. 1915. During a bombing attack in a German communication trench one officer of the company was killed, another wounded, and three parties of bombers were all either killed or wounded.

Second Lieut. Martin then commenced throwing bombs himself, after which he expended all the rounds in his revolver, and continued to fire with a rifle. It was largely due to his coolness and courage that the barricade was held till more bombers had been obtained." He returned to active service, and, on the night of 22–23 July was killed by a single bullet while scouting near Martinpuich, probably the most advanced man of our forces at the moment of the occurrence. Colonel Craig-Brown, D.S.O., Commanding 1st Cameron Highlanders, writes : "The Camerons have lost an officer of more than ordinary promise, but he died a gallant death, and we are all proud of him."

WATSON, GILBERT FRANCE, Second Lieut., was created a Companion of the Distinguished Service Order [London Gazette, 7 Dec. 1915] : "Gilbert France Watson, Second Lieut., Welsh Field Company, Welsh Divisional Engineers, Royal Engineers, Territorial Force. For conspicuous gallantry and determination near Hooge. On the night of 24–25 Sept. 1915, he made an excellent reconnaissance of the enemy's wire, and on the 25th crawled out with two men, and successfully cut it before the assault. During the assault, with a party of 12 sappers and 25 infantry, he dug 80 yards of a communication trench in two hours under very heavy fire, by which nearly three-quarters of his men became casualties. He then reported for instructions, and took the remains of his party into the captured positions in order to consolidate them. When retirement was ordered he got back to our original trenches with one sergeant, who was killed almost at once, and three or four men, and, finding the trenches unoccupied, he collected about 25 men of the 4th Battn. Gordon Highlanders, and held on until relieved by another battalion after dark. Second Lieut. Watson set a fine example of bravery and devotion to duty."

NAMES OMITTED FROM CORRECT POSITIONS.

London Gazette, 27 Sept. 1901.—"War Office, 27 Sept. 1901. The King has been graciously pleased to give orders for the following appointment to the Distinguished Service Order to the undermentioned Officer, in recognition of services during the operations in South Africa. To bear date 29 Nov. 1900. To be a Companion of the Distinguished Service Order."

MALLOCK THOMAS RAYMOND, Lieut., was born 17 Sept.1869; entered the Royal Fusiliers 31 May, 1890; became Lieut., Royal Fusiliers, 2 July, 1894, Capt. 26 Oct. 1901, Major 28 Nov. 1905. He served in the South African War 1899–1902, taking part in operations in the Transvaal, east of Pretoria, July to 29 Nov. 1900; operations in Cape Colony, north of Orange River, including action at Ruidam ; employed with South African Light Horse ; afterwards in command of 2nd Battn. Imperial Yeomanry from 26 March, 1902, to end of operations ; operations in the Transvaal Oct. 1901 to Jan. 1902, and March to 31 May 1902 ; operations in Orange River Colony, June to Oct. 1901, and Jan. to March, 1902 ; operations in Cape Colo y, Jan. to June, 1901 ; mentioned in Despatches [London Gazette, 10 Sept. 1901] ; Queen's Medal with three clasps and King's Medal with two clasps. He was created a Companion of the Distinguished Service Order [London Gazette, 27 Sept. 1901] : "Thomas Raymond Mallock, Lieut., Royal Fusiliers. In recognition of services during the operations in South Africa." In the European War he was mentioned in Despatches [London Gazette, 19 Oct. 1914].

London Gazette, 23 June, 1915.—"War Office, 23 June, 1915. His Majesty the King has been graciously pleased to approve of the undermentioned honour for distinguished service in the field, with effect from 3 June, 1915, inclusive."

BRUCE, ARCHIBALD GORDON, Capt., was born 6 May, 1 77, son of Colonel E. A. Bruce, late Alexandra Princess of Wales's Yorkshire Regt. He was educated at Cheltenham College, and entered the Royal Scots Fusiliers 5 May, 1900, becoming Lieut. 22 Jan. 1902, Capt. 25 Oct. 1911 ; was Adjutant, West Surrey Regt., 22 Jan. 1912, to 7 Oct. 1913 ; promoted Major 1 Sept. 1915. He served in the South African War 1899–1902 (wounded ; Queen's Medal with four clasps and King's Medal with two clasps) ; in the European War from 1914 (Battles of Ypres, Armentières and Neuve Chapelle) ; was thrice wounded, twice mentioned in Despatches, and created a Companion of the Distinguished Service Order [London Gazette, 23 June, 1915] : "Archibald Gordon Bruce, Capt., Royal Scots Fusiliers. For distinguished service in the field." He married Aline Mary, daughter of E. Birch, late 2nd West India Regt., and they have one daughter.

PHOTOGRAPHS OMITTED FROM CORRECT POSITIONS.

| Col. W. R. Howell | Major E. H. Phillips | Col. G. Bridges | Col. Evan Gibb | Col. E. V. D. Riddell |
| (See Record p. 93–94). | (See Record p. 96). | (See Record p. 118). | (See Record p. 269). | (See Record p. 396). |

E 3

INDEX

INDEX

Printed in the United Kingdom
by Lightning Source UK Ltd.
109014UKS00001BA/1